LE MASQUE

STEINBERG

LE MASQUE

TEXTES PAR MICHEL BUTOR ET HAROLD ROSENBERG

PHOTOGRAPHIES D'INGE MORATH

MAEGHT EDITEUR

LE MASQUE

par Michel Butor

''Larvatus prodeo'' (Descartes)

Tout le monde se souvient d'un des plus anciens dessins de Saul Steinberg, repris en 1945 dans ''All in Line'' : une main qui dessine un bonhomme qui dessine un bonhomme qui dessine un bonhomme, etc. Dans un entretien publié à l'occasion de son ouvrage ''The New World'' (1965), il nous déclare :

''Ce livre est un recueil de dessins métaphysiques représentant des situations et des problèmes. Son épigraphe est ''Cogito ergo Cartesius est'' (je pense, donc Descartes existe)... Pour moi, cela veut dire que ce que je dessine c'est du dessin, que le dessin dérive du dessin. Ma ligne veut rappeler constamment qu'elle est faite d'encre. Je réclame la complicité de mon lecteur qui transformera cette ligne en signification, en utilisant notre fond commun de culture, d'histoire, de poésie. La contemporanéité en ce sens est complicité. Le lecteur, en suivant ma ligne avec ses yeux, devient un artiste. (Je regarde, donc Steinberg existe).''

L'œuvre de Steinberg se présente ainsi comme apparaissant, se produisant à l'intérieur d'un monde de dessin, elle est une réflexion du dessin sur lui-même et sur tout ce qui, dans notre monde, est de près ou de loin relié au dessin. Il suffit de la fréquenter pour prendre conscience du rôle immense de cette activité, presque aussi grand que celui du langage à qui elle est étroitement apparentée.

On comprend dès lors l'importance que prend de plus en plus chez lui la parodie, parodie de tout ce qui peut être fait avec une plume, un crayon, un pinceau, ou avec ce qui a été inventé pour relayer ces instruments : les modes d'impression quels qu'ils soient, parodie qui, lorsqu'elle s'attaque à des régions de ce monde du dessin étrangères aux beaux-arts et à leur prétendue gratuité, va jouer de la façon la plus plaisante

et la plus instructive avec la notion de " faux ", en particulier dans l'ouvrage nommé " The Passport ", bourré de faux diplômes, faux documents, faux papiers, fausses signatures, fausses écritures et faux tampons.

Mais la réflexion de Steinberg ne se contente pas d'emprunter à notre civilisation ses aspects " dessinés " pour les introduire dans un contexte qui les éclaire et qui les juge, elle procède à une analyse formelle de ces aspects, en extrait l'alphabet, isole un certain nombre de types de lignes qui vont être soumis à cette même investigation; d'où la remarquable animation d'éléments abstraits à l'intérieur de ce portrait de notre temps.

Dans le même entretien, l'artiste commente deux planches qui se font face, traitant toutes deux de la spirale :

" Ces dessins sont liés. Dans celui de gauche, la ligne d'horizon sur laquelle l'homme marche s'enroule derrière lui. C'est son passé; il est complètement périmé. Le futur contient toutes les illusions connues qu'il entretient à propos de sa vie. Il y a un arbre, un paysage, un château d'eau; mais le passé le mange.

Dans l'autre dessin le passé a plus de signification et le futur est en train d'engouffrer l'homme. Mais le futur est ce sur quoi il vit; c'est quelque chose qu'il fait lui-même. Cette ligne est son propre temps et espace — sa vie; en même temps, c'est sa destruction. Elle devient de plus en plus serrée. C'est un dessin effrayant. Ce pourrait être la vie de l'artiste qui vit par sa propre essence. Il devient la ligne elle-même, et finalement, quand la spirale est fermée, il devient la nature. "

Regardons, dans " Le Masque ", cet homme qui a entouré ses propres pieds du début d'une spirale, se juchant ainsi sur un piédestal, mais ne se rend pas compte qu'à chaque double spire c'est un nouveau barreau de cage qui l'enferme, le cache et finira par l'écraser.

Dans les pages qui entourent celle-ci, nous voyons la spirale, laquelle peut emprunter toutes sortes de styles et modulations, intégrer en son trajet la table, ce meuble

fondamental du dessinateur d'aujourd'hui, cet objet qui nous est à tous indispensable en tant que dessineurs et écriveurs. Ce sur quoi ces personnages dessinent, impliquait déjà le dessin, d'abord parce qu'il a fallu à un moment donné que quelqu'un le dessine pour qu'on le construise, mais surtout parce que la façon dont nous le percevons est profondément modifiée par le monde de dessin qui nous entoure et en particulier par le dessin que nous faisons. Ainsi la moindre ligne que je vais tracer sur ma table va se raccorder d'une façon ou d'une autre avec les bords de celle-ci et changer ma façon de la voir. Certains restent bien à l'écart de ce processus et l'observent, mais d'autres, tel cet artiste ''américain'' à coiffure d'indien, vont par leur dessin transformer non seulement ce qui est devant eux, mais tout ce qui est autour d'eux. La table devant laquelle ils se sont assis à l'origine, va, du fait de leur activité, se distribuer tout autour d'eux, elle sera véritablement leur sphère d'action et de perception.

Qu'ils soient hommes ou chats, mâles ou femelles. Le chat, qui hante depuis des années l'imagination de Steinberg, et dont il faudrait étudier les innombrables méta-morphoses, a adopté récemment pour lui un profil tout humain. Avec sa manie de sauter sur les tables, il figure l'artiste, ou sa femme, ou les autres artistes (voyez ce bataillon de peintres-chats-pompiers partant en guerre).

La table redressée devient le chevalet avec sa toile, et si l'artiste assis sur son pliant s'imagine y inscrire le paysage qu'il a devant les yeux, bien souvent la moindre touche qu'il va poser transformera pour lui le spectacle en entier, spectacle déjà trans-formé par tout le dessin qu'il a vu, qu'il a fait ou qu'il a subi.

Rendons la parole à Steinberg:

''Une belle femme est comme un arc-en-ciel, un coucher de soleil, la lune — tous ces trucs qu'il faut regarder mais pas peindre. Une belle femme ne peut être peinte que comme un totem — par comme une femme, mais comme une madone, une reine, un sphinx. C'est l'art des icônes — dont le seul vestige est dans la photographie de mode.

Ce qui fait qu'une femme moins belle est plus intéressante, c'est qu'elle a dans son visage et dans son corps l'empreinte de la société et du monde politique dont elle fait partie. Le visage a acquis un caractère qui représente toute sa vie, son passé et même son futur; il montre de l'ardeur ou de la terreur. C'est ça qui m'intéresse. J'éprouve les mêmes sentiments vis à vis de la nature. Je ne peux pas dessiner un paysage, mais je dessine des situations faites par l'homme: architectures, routes. En ce qui concerne la nature et tout ce qui n'est pas touché par les gens, j'utilise une série de clichés''.

Admirable dessinateur d'architectures, certes — qu'on pense à ces reportages parus dans ''All in Line'', ''The Passport'', ''The Labyrinth'', sur les maisons, les rues, les ponts et la façon dont les gens s'y promènent

(par ailleurs nous savons qu'il a été architecte, que la discipline de l'architecture a eu la plus grande influence sur lui ''combinaison de précision, d'habileté et de raison'', qu'il considère l'architecture comme ''la plus noble, la plus difficile et la plus philoso-sophique branche des arts'') —,

mais nous trouvons dans ''Le Masque'' toute une série de paysages, non point exécutés d'après nature, paysages ''philosophiques'', dans lesquels pourtant passe un remarquable ''sentiment de la nature'' et en particulier de cette nature sauvage, déserte, non touchée par les gens, les gens d'occident tout au moins, dans lesquels nous aurons l'agréable surprise de découvrir l'arc-en-ciel, la lune, et même le coucher du soleil.

C'est que la réflexion sur le dessin et le dessiné l'a amené à s'intéresser à la façon dont le paysage, la nature, apparaissait dans l'art, et en particulier aux schémas à travers lesquels les peintres devenaient capables de transformer notre vision du désert, des nuages ou des arbres. L'alphabet de clichés dont il se servait auparavant dans le seul souci de situer des constructions humaines, s'est ainsi considérablement augmenté, assoupli, nuancé (les trois arbres parodiant la fameuse série de Mondrian). A travers un paysage à l'européenne, il fait passer un décor de porcelaine chinoise, au

milieu d'une vision de la campagne aussi habituelle que possible dans sa quasi-puéri-lité, il creuse la fondrière, fait jaillir le geyser d'un paysage "abstrait".

Ce paysage primordial, ce désert, cette "wilderness" que l'alphabet des peintres nous permet de reconstituer, il se découvre au fin fond de notre imagination comme déjà peuplé d'habitants. C'est la première fois que Steinberg aborde le thème des Indiens, et de leur combat contre le sphinx américain près de sa pyramide inachevée qui orne le dos de chaque dollar, sphinx ou sphinge bientôt harpie.

Une autre grande nouveauté de ce recueil est la série des natures mortes. La réflexion sur la peinture en général et le paysage en particulier devait amener cette rencontre.

La table dont nous parlions tout à l'heure, voilà qu'elle devient paysage; loin d'être "rase" comme nous avions tendance à le croire, toute propre, se présentant comme une seule surface blanche toujours prête à recevoir un trait, elle se révèle couverte, encombrée de tout un matériel, de toute une sédimentation, de tout un désordre qu'il faudra débarrasser, dont il faudra au moins endiguer l'invasion pour pouvoir se mettre au travail: lettres, verres, bouteilles, étiquettes, assiettes, boîtes d'allumettes, tasses, tubes, ciseaux, carnets, médicaments, billets, compas, timbres, disques, journaux, papiers divers, billes, estampes. Seul un chat pourrait se mouvoir au milieu de cette accumulation sans provoquer d'écroulements.

Je n'ai identifié dans les recueils antérieurs qu'une seule nature morte. C'est dans "The Passport", et elle est la première esquisse de celles-ci: des objets sur une table, sur "la" table fondamentale, support du travail.

Il y a un verre, un pèse-lettres, une boîte de punaises, un paquet de Philipp Morris, quatre bouteilles d'encre de chine dont trois encore fermées dans leur support, la quatrième entrouverte, un bouchon supplémentaire, une boîte pharmaceutique avec l'inscription "curiously strong ALTOIDS peppermint oil", deux clés reliées par une

chaînette, et une boîte de café moulu '' Medaglia d'Oro '', dans une perspective volon-
tairement maladroite, avec des ombres hachurées.

Tous ces objets, comme les fragments de papier diversement imprimés,
dessinés, écrits dans un '' Merz '' de Schwitters, restituent puissamment l'atmosphère
d'un instant passé, mais ce qui se passe maintenant, c'est que Steinberg, au moment
où il va débarasser sa table pour se mettre à travailler, constate que tous ces papiers
accumulés constituent déjà quelque chose comme un Schwitters. Il va donc les coller
à plat, et pour faire tenir sur la table de son dessin les autres objets déplacés, il est
tout naturellement amené à adopter des solutions de perspective comparables à celles
des peintres cubistes. Il applique au paysage de sa table un alphabet de clichés pictu-
raux tout aussi varié que celui qu'il applique à la nature. Et ici le fait que l'objet
soit souvent déjà de l'imprimé ou du dessiné ou de l'écrit, qu'il le soit '' pour de vrai ''
ou qu'il soit du ''faux'', lui permet de nous montrer comment il réagit sur la perception
de ceux qui l'entourent. L'assiette chinoise projette un horizon chinois sur le bord de
la table. Les bords tricolores de l'enveloppe par avion se prolongent en itinéraires
labyrinthiques.

Les objets se mettent à parler; c'est un discours, en effet, qu'enclôt pour nous
l'enveloppe de la lettre ou la feuille pliée du journal. A ces textes imprimés ou
manuscrits, vont se superposer, grâce à la puissante convention de la ''bulle'' des
'' comic-books '', les représentations de leur sonorité, laquelle pourra inclure non
seulement d'autres fausses écritures mais d'autres dessins.

Au milieu de ces objets figurativement '' parlants '', voici l'objet vraiment parlant :
le disque, mais lui n'est point vraiment collé, ce n'est que sa représentation qui est
collée, c'est un disque de toute évidence, mais il n'est pas circulaire, ni même elliptique
comme dans une perspective classique, il est faussement elliptique, il se soulève en
quelque sorte hors de la table, relié pourtant aux éléments vraiment collés, les journaux

collés qui sont là pour représenter des journaux, par le fait que son étiquette est comme eux parfaitement "lisible", contrairement aux paroles ou aux écritures imitées.

Dans ces natures mortes nous avons toute une épaisseur de réflexion dont nous pouvons distinguer les niveaux :

1) les objets collés qui se représentent eux-mêmes; étiquettes, enveloppes, journaux, estampes,

2) les objets collés qui représentent autre chose qu'eux-mêmes : étiquettes qui deviennent des bouteilles ou des tiroirs,

3) les imitations d'objets collées : les disques,

4) les imitations d'objets dessinées à plat : enveloppes dessinées, étiquettes dessinées,

5) les imitations d'objets dessinées en perspective : verres à la Juan Gris,

6) les transpositions du "son" des objets : bulles à fausse écriture,

7) structures géométriques qui "émergent" de tout cela : cercles concentriques.

Ces cercles concentriques, eux aussi bien sûr allusions, entre autres choses, au style de quelques peintres contemporains, avaient déjà fait une discrète apparition dans "The New World", en particulier dans une planche que Steinberg décrit ainsi :

"Un homme qui va d'une technique à une autre, ou d'une signification à une autre : conflits ? espaces ? temps ? émotions ? Il part d'un dessin très simple, conventionnel, au sommet, descend par une échelle jusqu'à une représentation simplifiée du même dessin, prend un pont et va jusqu'à une série de cercles concentriques."

(Les deux premières stations représentent une petite maison auprès d'un arbre).

Ils sont ici l'extrémité abstraite de la nature morte qui équilibre l'extrémité vériste du collage. Dans un dessin de "The Labyrinth" on voyait un cube grossier rêver de sa perfection géométrique, ainsi que nous voyons le tampon du bureau de poste de la gare Montparnasse rêver de la circularité.

De même que les fausses écritures dans les ''bulles'' de ''comics'' sont la sonorité des écritures vraies ou fausses représentées à côté ou par ailleurs, de même ces purs cercles sont la sonorité rêvée de ces disques non-circulaires. Leur transparence et leur dynamisme interne, le fait qu'ils se diffusent comme des ondes, les fait jalonner en quelque sorte l'épaisseur temporelle et mentale de ces natures mortes, en émettre la signification vers nous. La ligne de petits cercles croissants qui aboutit à l'explosion du rêve ou de l'idée dans les ''comics'' et dans de nombreux dessins de Steinberg, trouve ici une perpendicularité idéale.

Ils sont par conséquent ce qui dans ces œuvres nous parle mais dépassera toujours notre déchiffrement.

Ainsi les objets s'y recomposent sous notre regard non seulement selon leur troisième dimension, mais selon tout un temps, temps de réflexion pleine d'humour sur l'art et sur l'industrie du dessin (l'écriture étant un cas particulier de celui-ci).

Mais comment appliquer de tels développements techniques à ce qui a toujours été le souci principal de notre auteur, le ''portrait'' (je mets le mot entre guillemets, parce que ce n'est jamais le portrait d'un ''modèle'' particulier); certes nous avons d'admirables exemples de personnages représentés dans leur style, tels qu'ils se voient ou s'imaginent, ce qui est encore plus frappant lorsqu'il y a plusieurs personnages côte à côte avec confrontation de styles, ainsi dans le trio monsieur, très net, très simple, qui ne s'embarrasse pas de complications, sans demi-teintes, noir et blanc, lumière et ombre, madame, ingresque, évanescente, et bébé, où nous voyons bien que cette triple représentation leur est commune, que c'est bien ainsi que chacun des trois est pour lui et pour les deux autres, donc qu'il y a entre ces trois styles des liens aussi étroits qu'entre les trois individus, que chacune de ces façons de dessiner dépend des deux autres, qu'il s'agit d'un complexe ou d'un groupe de styles,

mais comment arriver à traiter aussi le visage humain comme une matière brute,

à faire un équivalent du collage dans les natures mortes, pour déployer à son sujet tout le registre du dessin ?

Une première méthode est d'utiliser les photographies, car nous avons l'illusion que la photographie nous donne le visage tel que nous le voyons, et de l'intégrer à l'intérieur d'une interprétation dessinée; mais une photographie n'est jamais le visage même, et nous ne nous trouvons donc pas en présence d'un phénomène comparable à l'emploi des étiquettes ou des enveloppes pour se représenter elles-mêmes, mais déjà du collage d'une imitation de la chose, ce qui se passait pour les disques.

La solution la plus franche est donc de prendre des imitations de visages, des masques, lesquels seront faits d'un papier particulièrement apparenté à notre peau dans la civilisation américaine, non point apparemment mais fonctionnellement, celui de ces sacs bruns dans lesquels on nous emballe les produits que nous destinons à notre alimentation, que nous enfournerons dans le grand sac de notre peau, au sortir d'un supermarché.

Pour Steinberg nous portons tous des masques, notre visage est déjà un masque; la vérité du masque c'est que du moins il s'avoue comme tel, et qu'il nous force à interpréter comme un masque ce que nous prenions pour un visage :

''Un masque représente la façon dont les gens veulent apparaître, ce qu'ils veulent être. On pourrait diviser la vie de l'homme en deux parts : sa vie émotionnelle, physique, intime, et sa vie politique et mondaine, où il voit d'autres personnes et a constamment à apparaître dans une forme attendue. Vous devriez toujours porter le même visage et la même expression de façon à être rassurants pour les gens qui vous rencontrent. Les gens sont pris de panique si vous ne vous ressemblez plus ou si vous perdez du poids ou si vous grossissez.

Ce que les gens font, spécialement en Amérique, c'est de fabriquer pour eux-mêmes un masque de bonheur. Ils mettent sur leur visage un perpétuel sourire

rassurant; ça leur donne l'air gentil, aimable et en bonne santé et nous n'avons plus à nous préoccuper d'eux."

Or pendant des années Steinberg a fabriqué des masques de ce papier pour lui-même, en particulier pour répondre à cette imposition sournoise d'un masque inavoué que constitue la photographie officielle :

"Je devenais nerveux quand un photographe pointait son appareil vers moi. Aussi j'ai fait des masques de ma tête en sacs de papier. Je pouvais me détendre à l'intérieur des masques et montrer une image de moi-même constante à l'appareil... Ainsi j'ai utilisé la photographie d'une façon contraire à son propos..."

En se mettant un masque, Steinberg se sent devenir américain comme les autres. Mais voici les masques des autres, et peut-être le fait de les porter les fera-t-il devenir des américains comme eux-mêmes.

Regardez-les, ces masques, ce qu'ils prennent pour leurs visages, regardez-les ces visages détachés, appliqués sur cette lame de verre qu'est une feuille de papier pour les soumettre au spectroscope du dessin, regardez donc le commentaire que leur donnent ces vêtements, ces pieds, ces mains, ces bijoux, ces sculptures, ces meubles, ces pipes, ces tasses, ces automobiles, ces lampes, le commentaire qu'ils leur donnent, voyez comment l'aveu de leur dessin fait jaillir pour nous de la vie courante d'exquises inépuisables redoutables mélodieuses bulles de vérité.

L' "ART WORLD" DE STEINBERG

par Harold Rosenberg

Steinberg est de ces artistes Américains qui, profondément, marquèrent l'art pendant les années d'après-guerre en plaçant au centre de leur œuvre le problème de l'identité.

Dans ce mouvement, les immigrants — Arshile Gorky, Willem de Kooning, Mark Rothko, Hans Hoffmann, Steinberg (arrivé au début des années Quarante) — ont joué un rôle moteur. Avec eux, la question du "Qui suis-je ?" s'aiguisait d'un "Où suis-je ?".

L'art était un territoire ouvert où se réaliser; mais aussi, où se "faire un nom".

L'art dut assumer une fonction nouvelle : créer l'artiste, métaphysiquement, socialement.

Dans cette perspective, beaucoup du vieil attirail de la peinture — comme le dessin réaliste, la composition architectonique, l'harmonie des couleurs — devenait inutile, et pouvait être abandonné.

Durant ces vingt dernières années, peinture et sculpture, renchérissant sur la tendance des Dadaïstes et des Surréalistes, recoururent au "geste", au théâtre : là, on commence par la fiction dont on se délivre en jouant. "Les situations que je dessine *sont de l'homme,*" dit Steinberg, avec une admirable précision.

L'artiste se crée lui-même en créant un monde — ou, plus justement, un milieu.

Ce que nous appelons "nature" est, en réalité, la somme des styles qui coexistent en une période donnée : la nature est ornementale, "Naturaliste", abstraite, primitive... Cette vieille banalité que "la nature imite l'art" s'est vue investir, au Vingtième siècle, d'une puissance supérieure, par la surimpression toute physique dont ont marqué la terre et ses créatures les inventions humaines.

Dans l'idiome Steinbergien, la nature se compose de tampons, d'étiquettes, de papiers officiels (proclamations, diplômes, passeports), de photographies, d'architectures gouvernementales, de *paysages*, d'ornements typographiques. "Chiens et chats sont l'œuvre de l'homme", assure Steinberg. "Je pourrais dessiner des lions, tout aussi bien. Par l'allégorie et les armoiries, ils sont entrés dans la société."

Saisissant le mélange de la nature et de l'art, de l'artiste et du spectateur, Steinberg participe de la pensée artistique avancée de ce temps. Vingt ans avant le Pop Art, il en exposa les prémisses dans un grand nombre de dessins, non moins que dans la double relation qu'il entretient avec l'art commercial et le musée; et il a poussé les implications de son approche jusqu'en des régions que les autres ont encore à explorer.

Néanmoins, Steinberg offre un aspect plus profond que sa formulation personnelle des ambiguïtés de la vision. Il a su appliquer les possibilités de la comédie aux réalités de l'art, à la fois comme création de soi, et comme moyen de déterminer le visible.

De sa génération le dernier arrivé à New York, Steinberg fut le premier à devenir célèbre. Peut-être la réussite lui permit-elle de se laisser amuser par la tentation de "se faire un nom", substituée à la réalisation de l'individualité. Les éléments assis de la société ne sont pas les seuls à transformer la vie en une comédie de masques. L'artiste-héros est aussi ridicule que l'homme d'affaires ou la douairière.

Route vers l'être, l'art, Steinberg s'en aperçut, était parsemé de pièges.

Ce que l'esprit conçoit n'est pas le moi, mais un autre. "Je pense, donc Descartes est", déclare le petit homme du dessin.

Plus encore que la tête, la main est encline à échafauder la fiction : à peine la voit-on tenir une plume ou un pinceau, qu'elle commence à créer ce qui devrait être trouvé.

Au lieu d'un moi, l'artiste façonne un emblème qui rend le moi superflu. La plus profonde marque de son identité est son style. Mais le style est toujours, par sa nature même, un dérivé.

Dans son essence, l'art est ce que Steinberg appelle "politique", c'est-à-dire conscient du spectateur, à la fois qui regarde par-dessus l'épaule de l'artiste en la personne du maître, et qui attend dans l'entrée, éventuel admirateur et client.

L'art incite l'artiste à jouer la comédie, et à se transformer — en chevalier, en petit chat, en Indien, en sphinx. Celui qui n'est pas possédé par la passion du théâtre et de la renommée est fatalement privé d'énergie créatrice.

Ainsi l'art ne mène pas à la réalité, mais loin d'elle, à la mascarade. Sa plus haute récompense est la gloire — le personnage sur le piédestal. Mais la gloire, loin de solidifier le moi, réduit son détenteur, et l'enveloppe d'un amas d'abstractions.

Enfin l'artiste est une fiction parmi les fictions.

Non seulement la nature imite l'art, elle imite les artistes. Maintenant, elle a pris l'habitude de faire montre de sa mobilité.

La nature, elle-même, *joue les artistes*. Les gens, les animaux, les paysages passent leur temps à se donner l'air de quelque chose. Les arbres tentent de ressembler à des arbres, souvent en vain. Les chats s'illusionnent à se prétendre chats — chacun sait la vérité : ce sont des ressorts lovés, endormis dans un lait bleu.

Les montagnes forcent leur apparence de montagne. La nature s'emploie à revêtir des déguisements, — Shakespearienne est ici la sensibilité de Steinberg, — qui constituent la réalité même.

En somme, la nature est un artiste, et, comme tous les artistes, elle est sous l'empire des clichés. Qu'on la copie fidèlement, comme dans les dessins d'après modèle qui font partie de ce choix, et l'on verra paraître un véritable patron

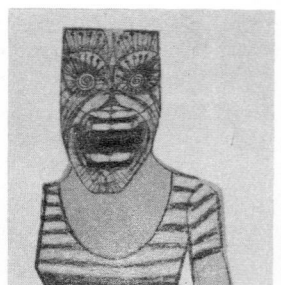

d'après lequel un monstre peut être composé.

Un dessin réaliste ou une photo sont des masques, au moins autant qu'une abstraction ou un dessin humoristique, et Steinberg n'hésite pas à les combiner.

Les corps, nus ou vêtus, sont des masques : on s'en rend compte dans le passage du torse réel à la tête en sac de papier, dans la suite des photos.

Etant donné les figures humaines qui se présentent journellement, il serait intéressant de savoir jusqu'où peut aller l'artiste sans que le masque cesse d'être plausible comme visage. La triste vérité, c'est qu'importe peu la gravité de la déformation, qui sera vite admise comme étant la réalité.

Où la nature diffère des autres artistes, c'est qu'elle ne craint pas de mêler les styles — les nuages baroques aux abstractions biomorphiques et mathématiques — ni de donner dans l'arbitraire. L'art de Steinberg s'identifie avec l'éclectisme de la nature, contre la manie d'unité de ses contemporains.

Il ne s'oppose ni au mélange, ni à l'impulsif pur et simple : les modes d'interprétation de beaucoup de ses dessins restent inépuisables, même pour Steinberg. Le dessin de l'Oncle Sam en sphinx armé, défendant la pyramide du *Novus Ordo Seclorum* contre un maigre Indien est aussi rempli de mystères que la "Bohémienne Endormie" du Douanier.

L'image d'art passe à l'objet qu'elle représente, qui est aussi un masque.

Les masques jouent leur rôle. Le théâtre Steinbergien, comme la société de La Rochefoucauld, est régi par *l'amour-propre*.

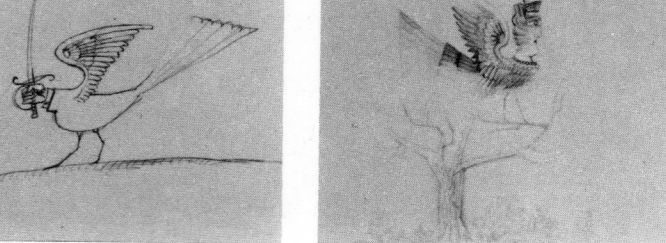

De pair avec la vanité va le sexe. Des figures dessinées deviennent érotiques à cause, précisément, des conventions du dessin.

Des lettres de l'alphabet s'humanisent en faisant l'amour à d'autres lettres dont l'anatomie s'y prête.

Chez Steinberg, l'univers de la personnification obéit à une logique de l'érotisme, de l'illusion et de la confusion d'identité, équivalente à celle du rêve. Il serait difficile de trouver un autre artiste qui passe aussi aisément de l'objet perçu à son écorce de métaphore.

"Je sens que je suis sur une frontière", a déclaré Steinberg. La bande de territoire mental qu'il occupe longe simultanément la lisière du nouveau monde et de l'ancien, du visuel et du verbal, du sérieux et du détraqué.

Des expériences-limites réclament des formes-limites. Sans doute les ambiguités éprouvées du sujet et de l'objet sont-elles à la racine de l'anti-traditionalisme de l'art moderne.

L'art de ce siècle n'a pas hésité à altérer la peinture au moyen de reliefs, et la sculpture au moyen d'objets trouvés.

Et pourtant, même créant sur ce bord où l'art se mêle à l'existence, les artistes n'ont pas été capables de se purger de l'ambition du chef-d'œuvre. Reniant l'Art, ils se sont désespérément efforcés d'assurer à leurs productions un avenir de trésors de musées.

Ce mélange des motivations a fait de l'art un jeu d'audace, où des œuvres maladroites sont défendues au nom de la vérité, et des œuvres vides au nom de l'histoire de l'art.

Au contraire, Steinberg, dès le départ, a suivi sans réserve la voie de la séparation d'avec les saints fétiches de l'art. Parmi les premiers à reconnaître que le magazine populaire et le musée d'art contemporain sont engagés dans des entreprises apparentées de culture des masses, il contourna le marécage moral de l'artiste-héros-de-la-culture, en se lançant ouvertement dans l'art destiné à la reproduction.

Dans l'humble dessin satirique, il trouva un moyen susceptible de se transformer en un alphabet aussi souple que celui des mots, mais pourvu de la dimension supplémentaire du signe visuel. Le potentiel intellectuel du dessin de magazine réside précisément en ce qu'il est un moyen *modeste,* ne répondant qu'au désir d'expression directe de l'artiste.

Tout en conservant comme noyau le dessin humoristique, Steinberg l'a considérablement accru, d'inventions dérivées des usages de l'art au vingtième siècle :

dessin automatique ('' le gribouillage est la songerie de la main ''), art enfantin, graffitti, facsimilés, parodies de maîtres modernes.

La métamorphose Steinbergienne du dessin humoristique en instrument de la méditation sur les litiges de l'art et du moi, constitue un développement des ressources de la composition en aplat comparable à celui que fut le collage. (Ses propres collages restituent le sens original de cette forme, par l'insistance mise sur les reproductions (disques, tableaux, étiquettes), et les moyens de communication (journaux, lettres, etc.).

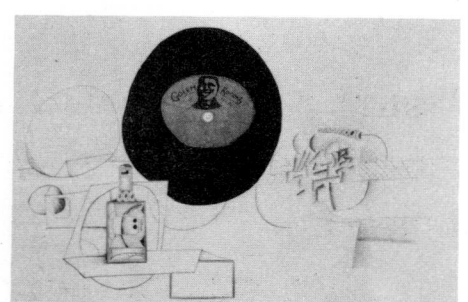

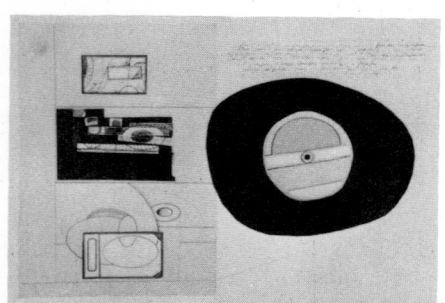

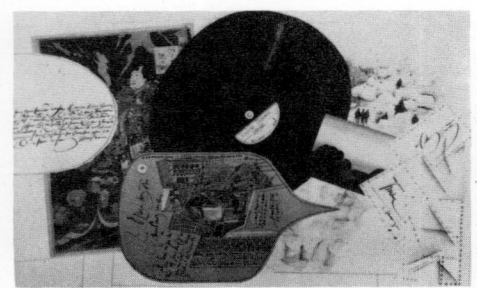

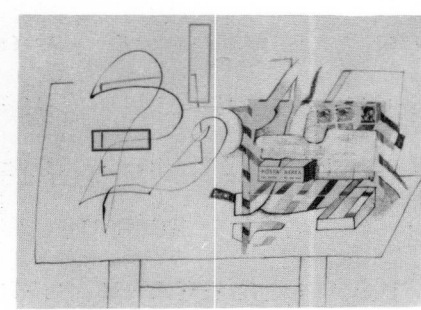

Par des formes étrangères à la tradition du musée, mais présentes depuis les origines de l'expression humaine, il a pu forger un moyen pour animer les cellules de l'esprit en dehors des aires chloroformées par '' Les Grandes Œuvres ''.

Le fond populaire des dessins de Steinberg leur confère une pente inhérente
vers la comédie, l'art qui touche de près au monde souterrain de l'esprit. La comédie
de Steinberg va du burlesque

au lyrique,

de la satire  à l'hallucination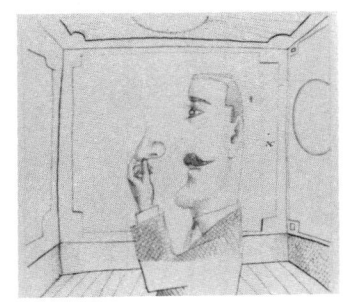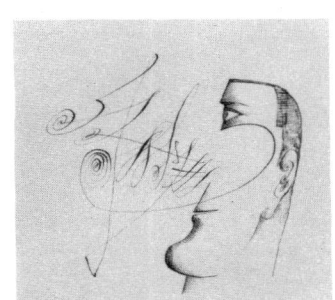

Son rire s'électrise, entre deux pôles d'angoisse : celui du masque immuable
qui falsifie la vie, et celui de la suppression du masque et de l'exposition du néant.

Avec les années, Steinberg est devenu de plus en plus philosophe. Remarquable
est l'aptitude du langage formé par ses signes à s'étendre en même temps que sa
pensée. Cet idiome appartient à une famille d'exceptions : c'est le capital poétique
redistribué, pour servir les besoins précis de cet esprit unique.

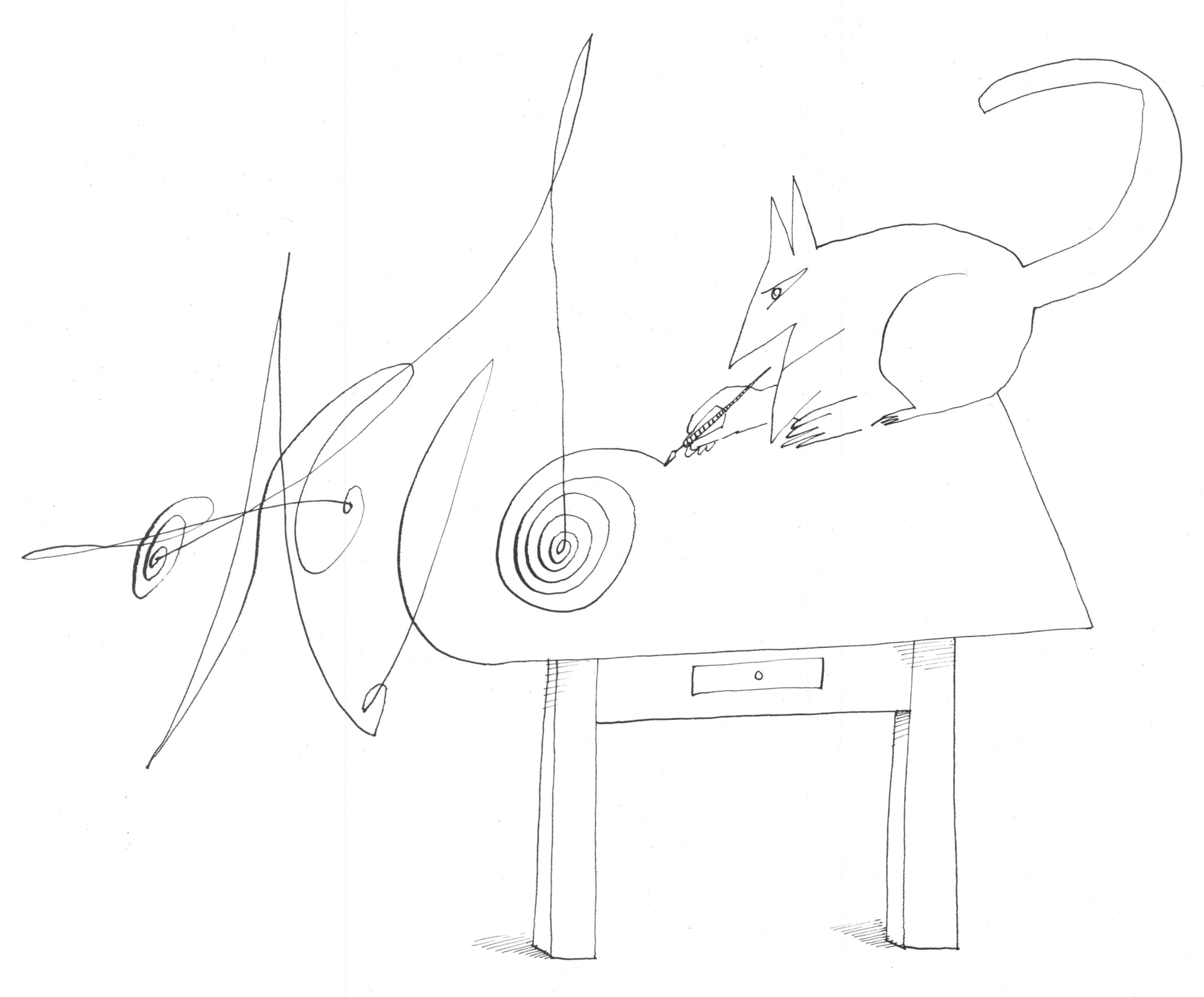

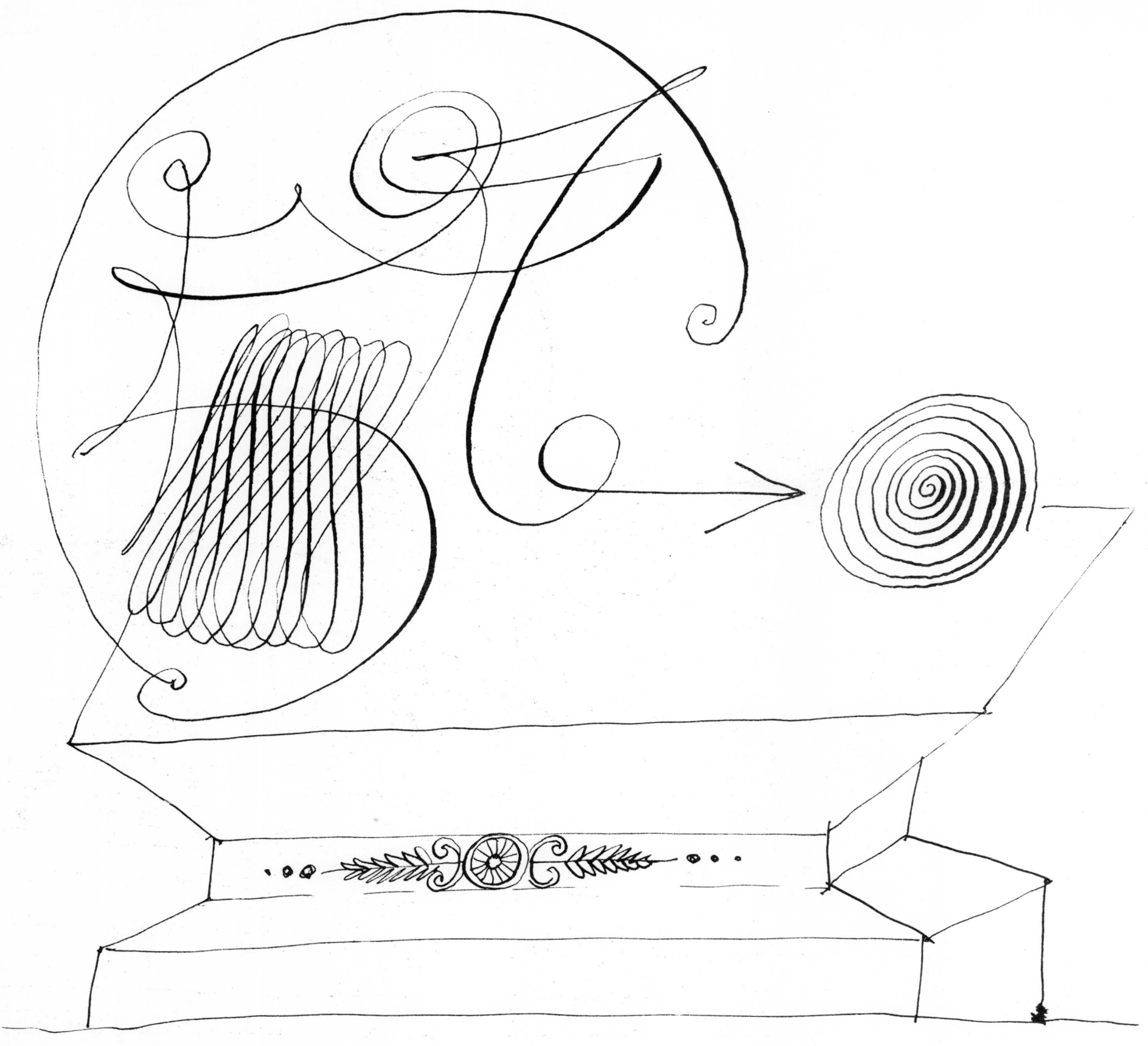

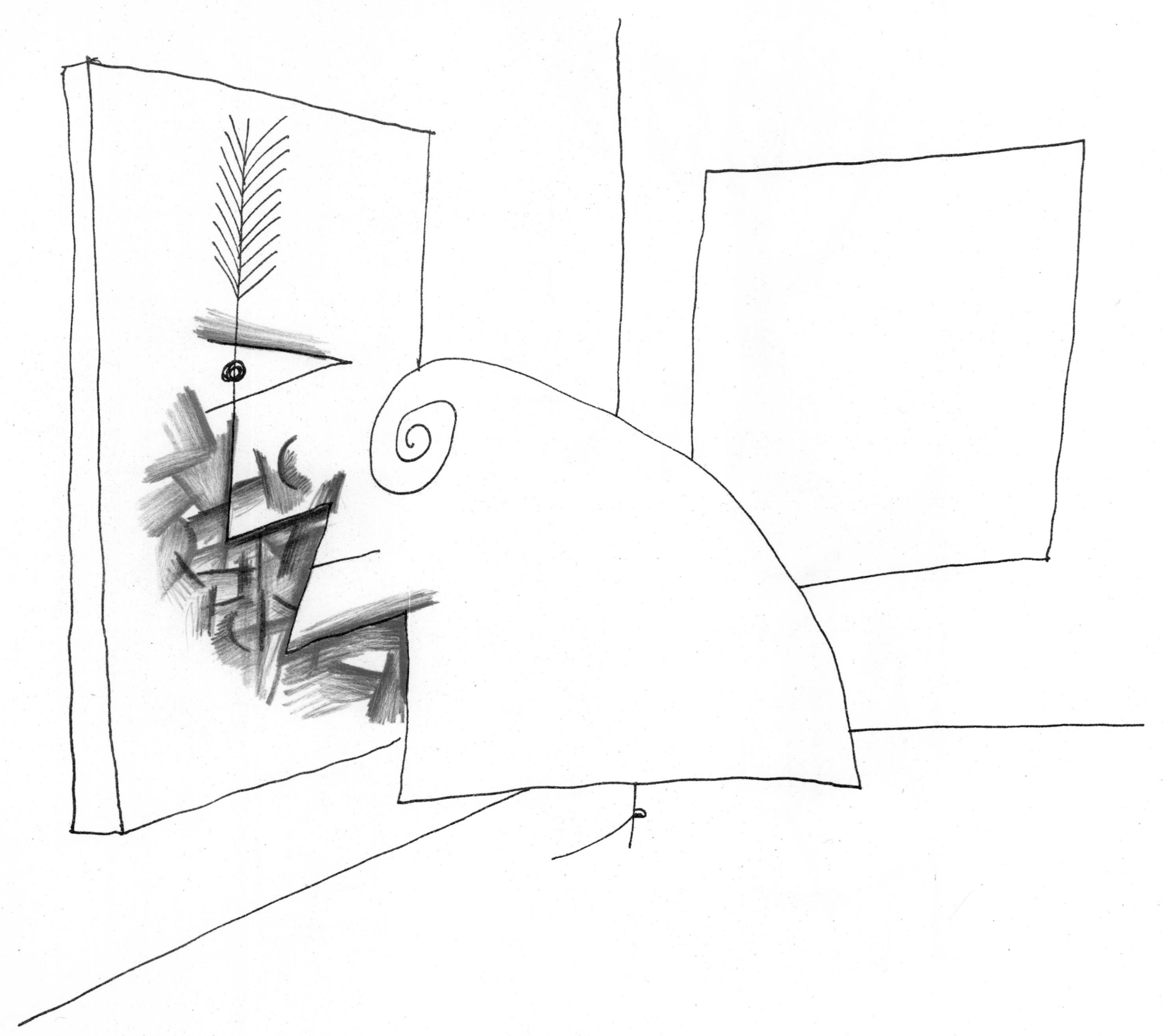

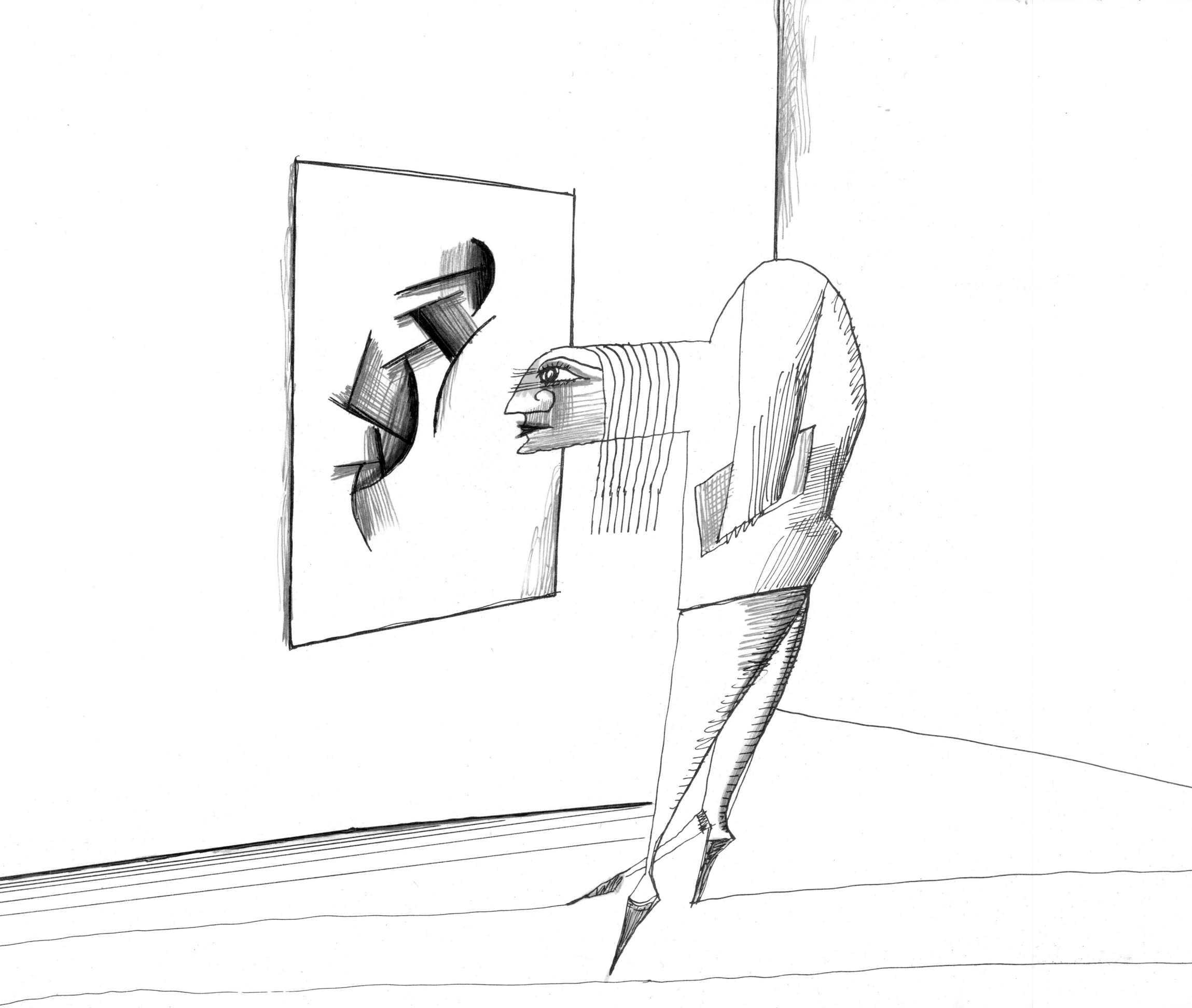

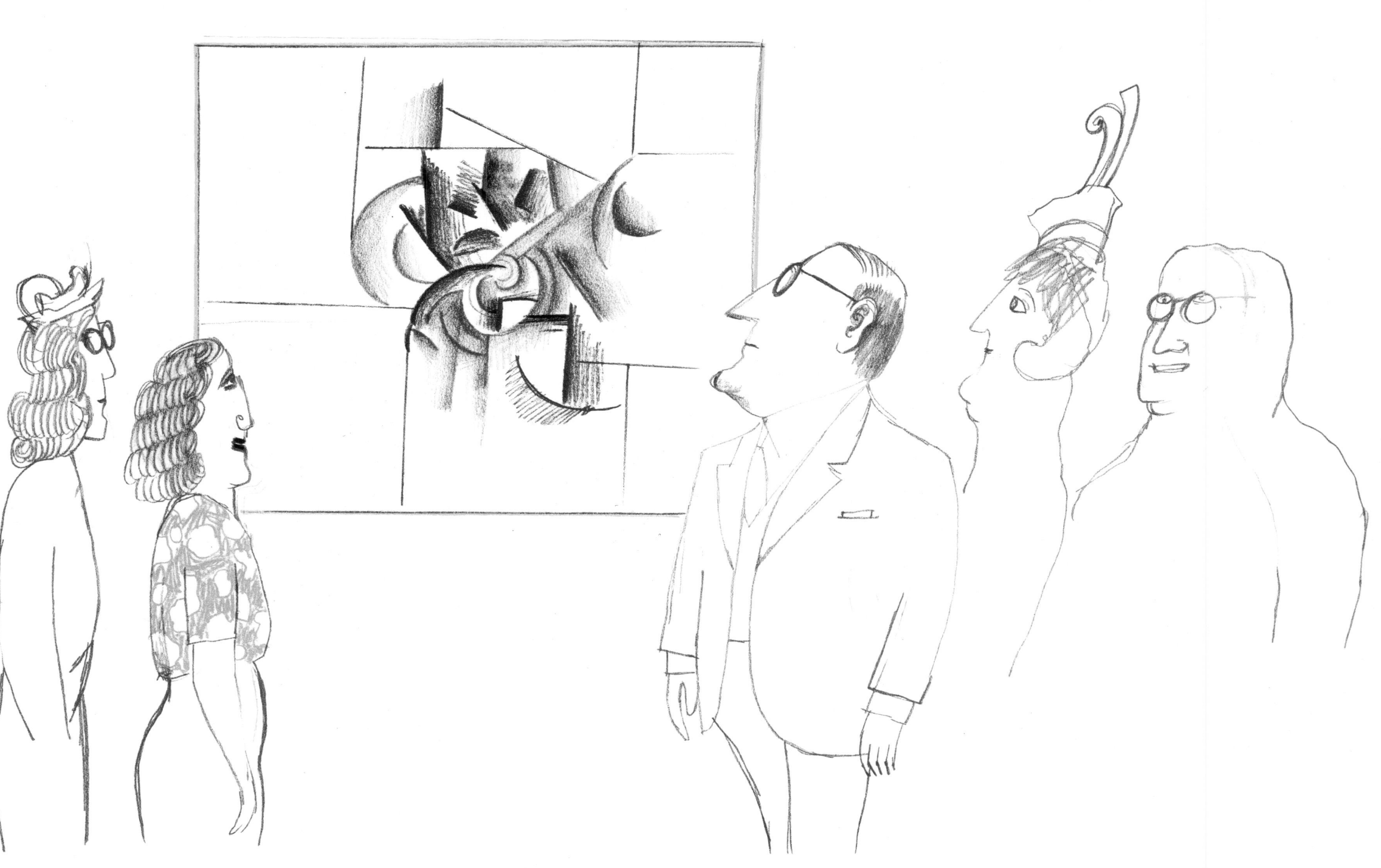

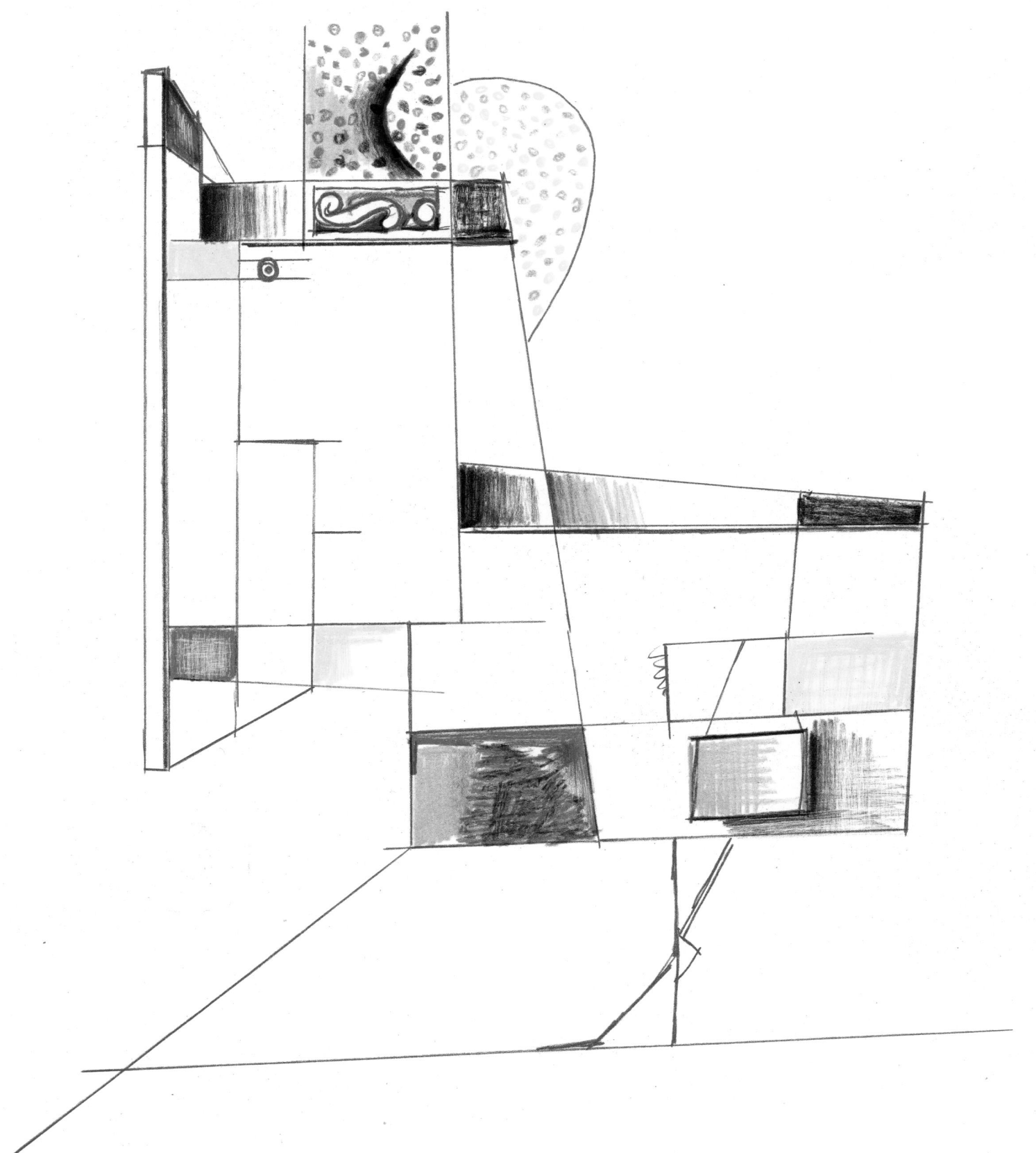

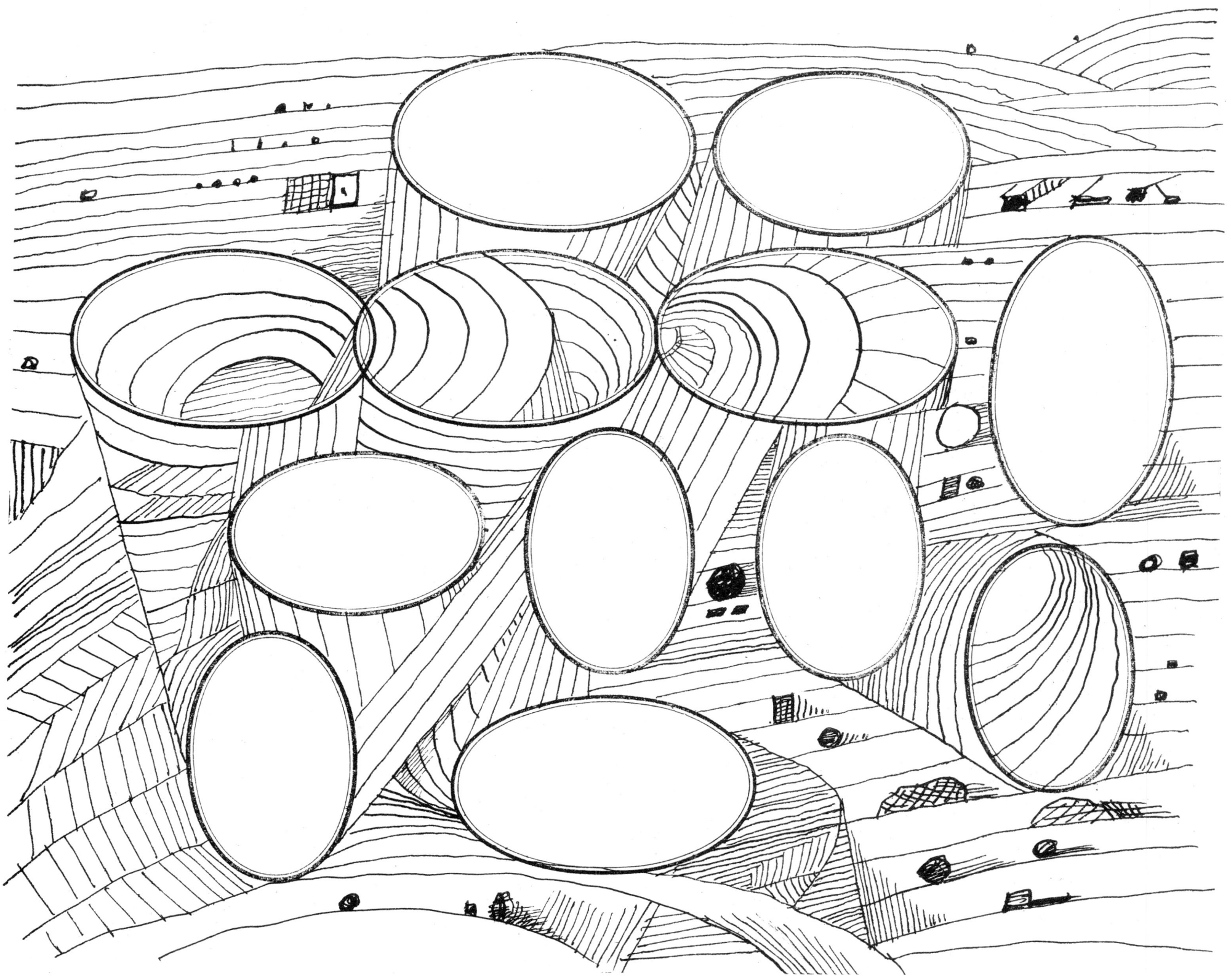

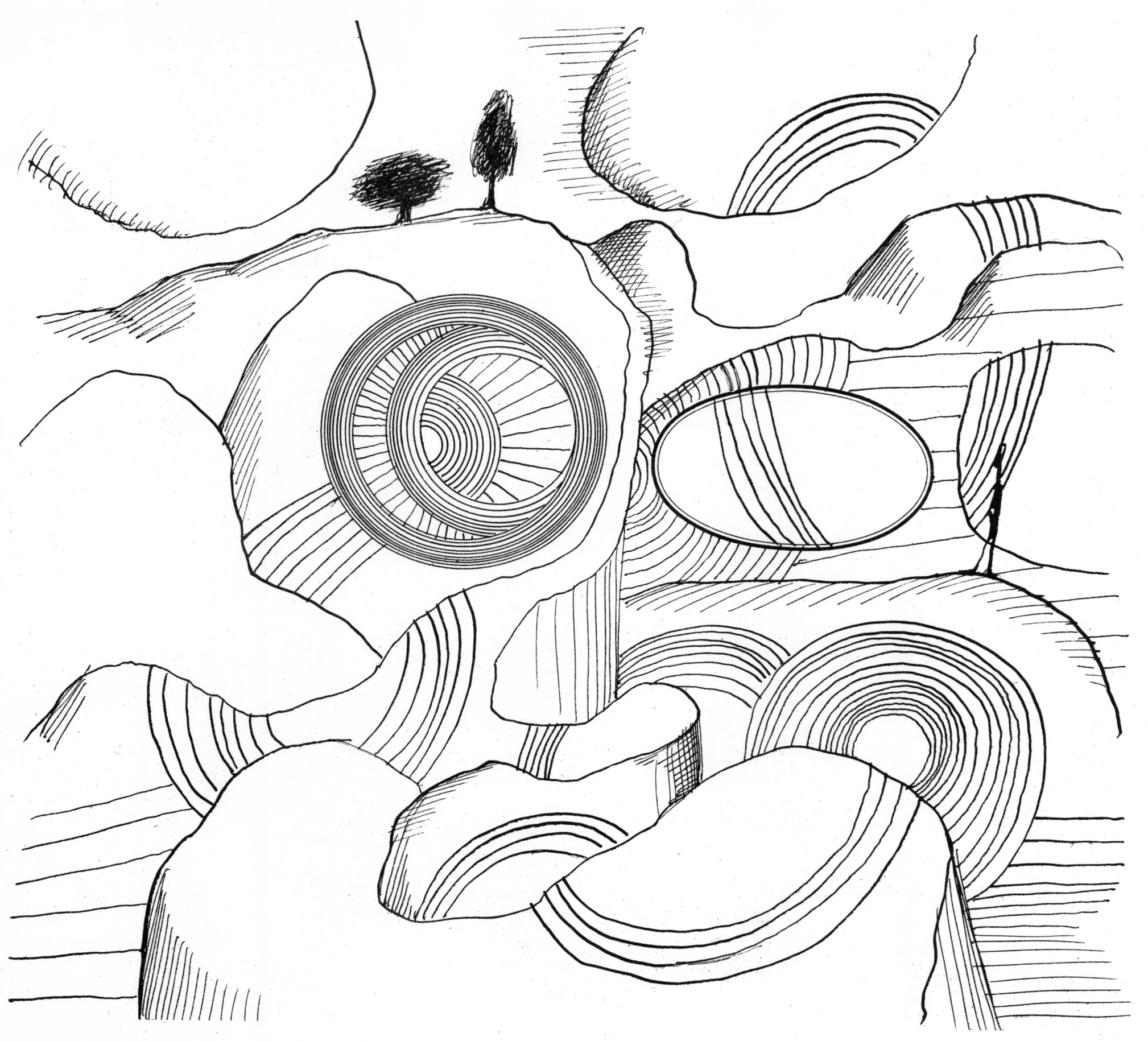

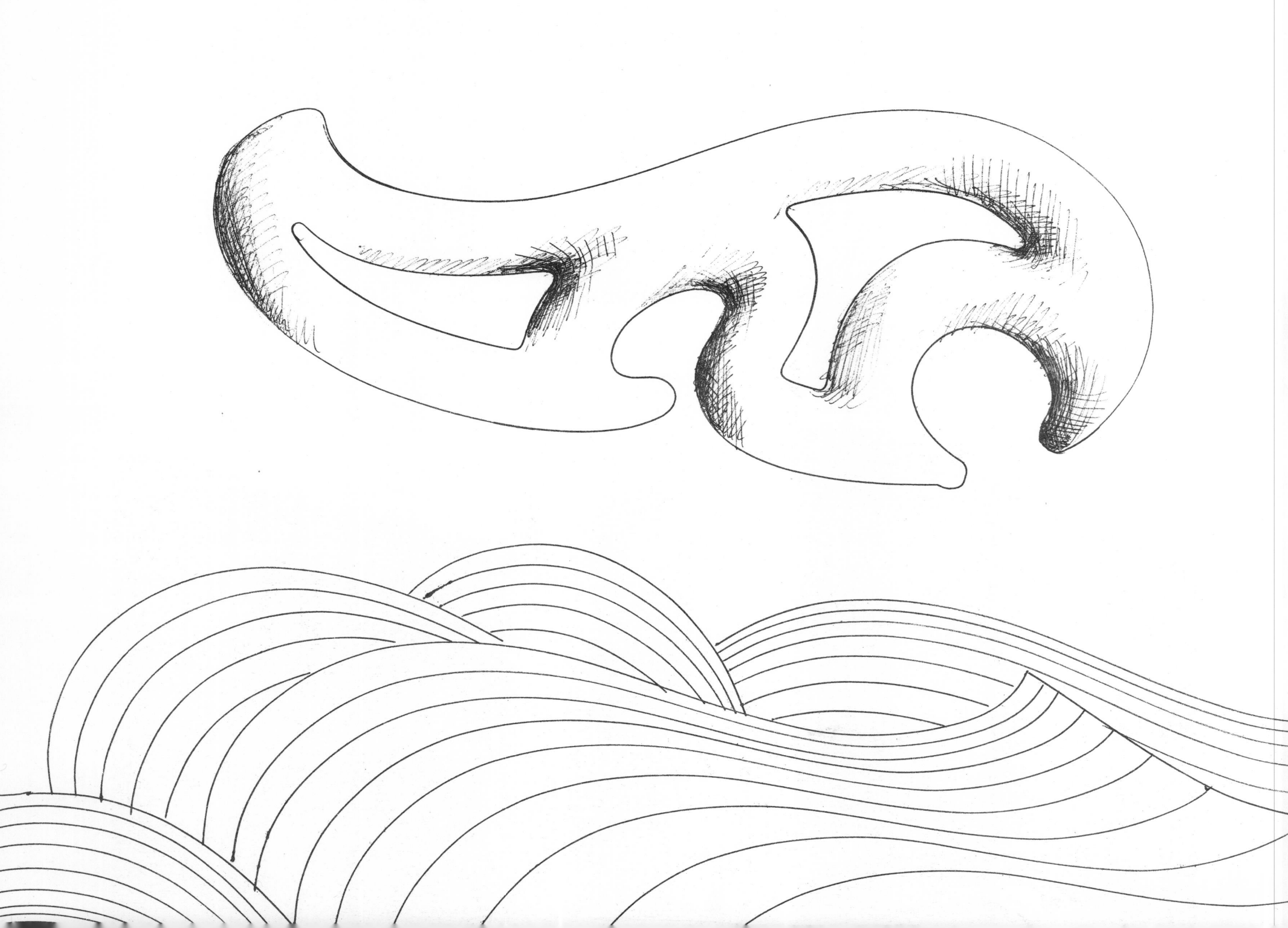

STEINBERG

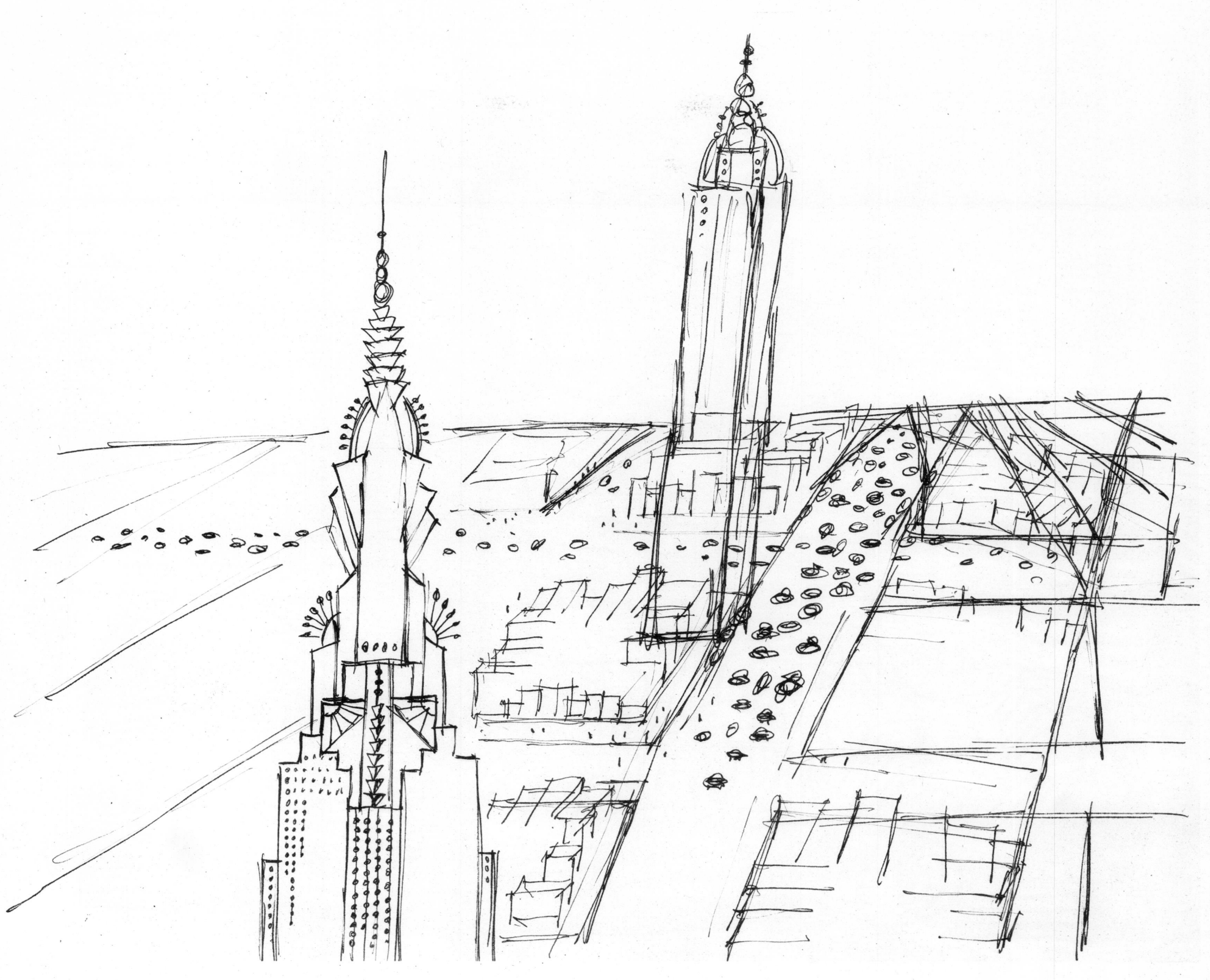

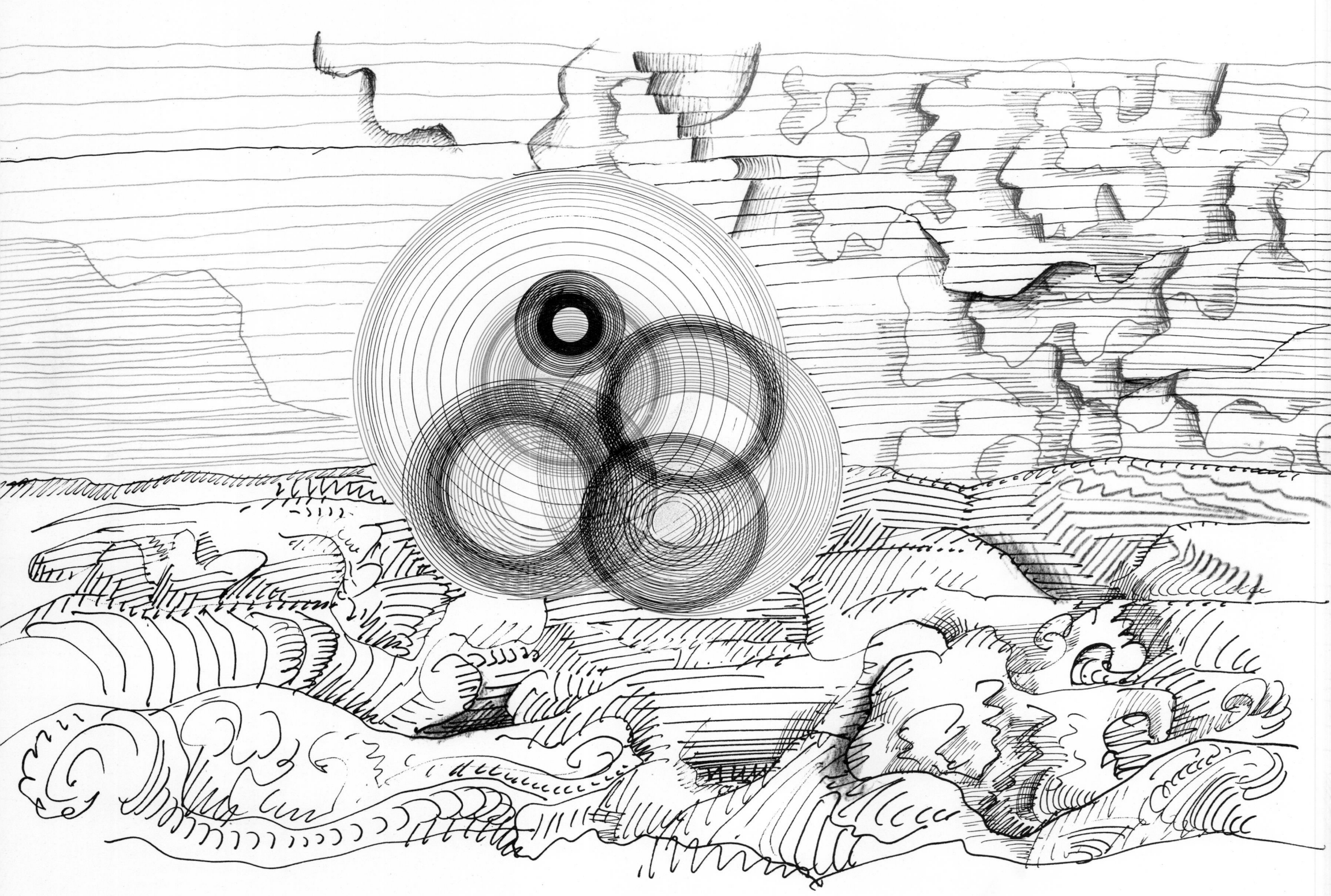

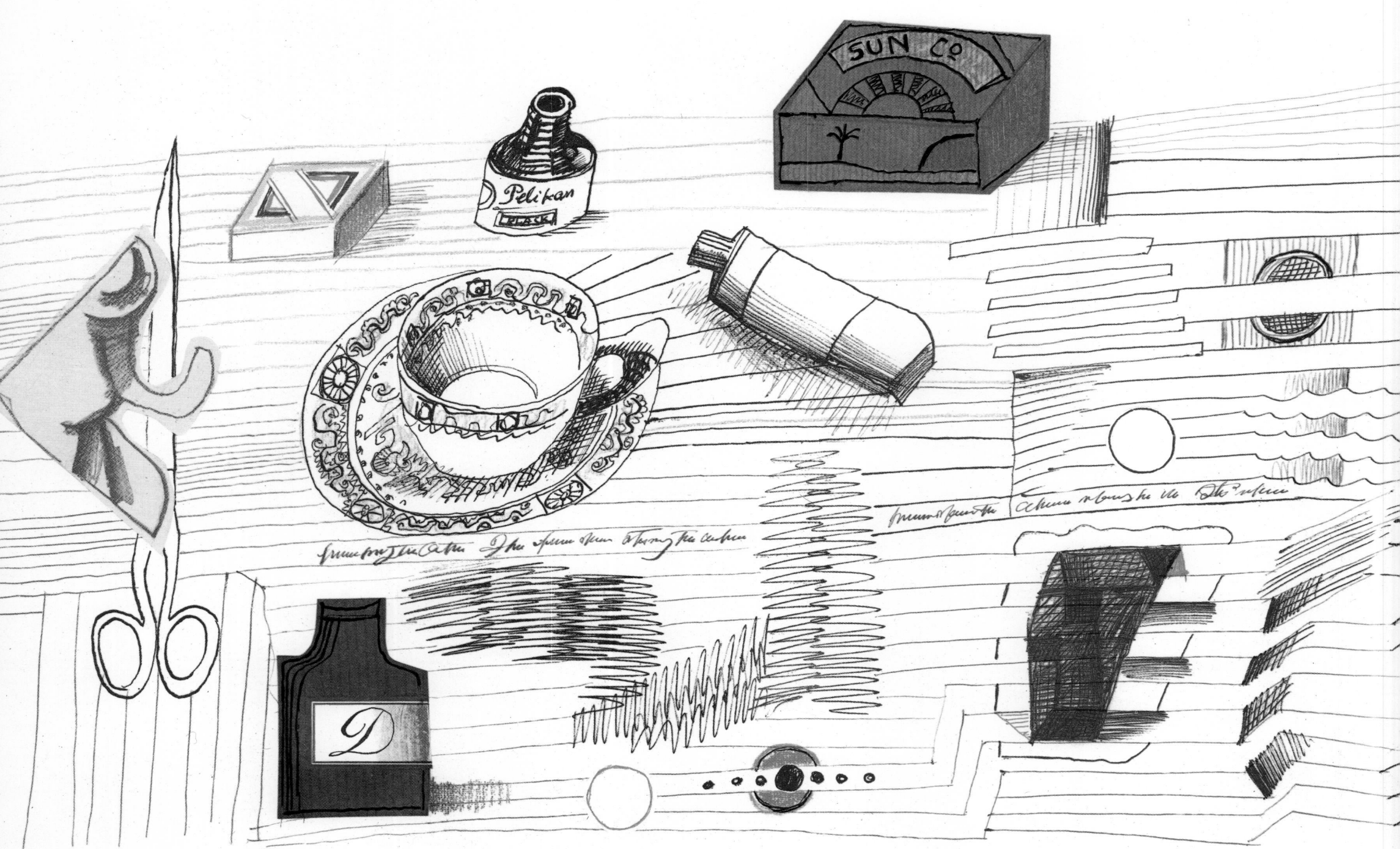

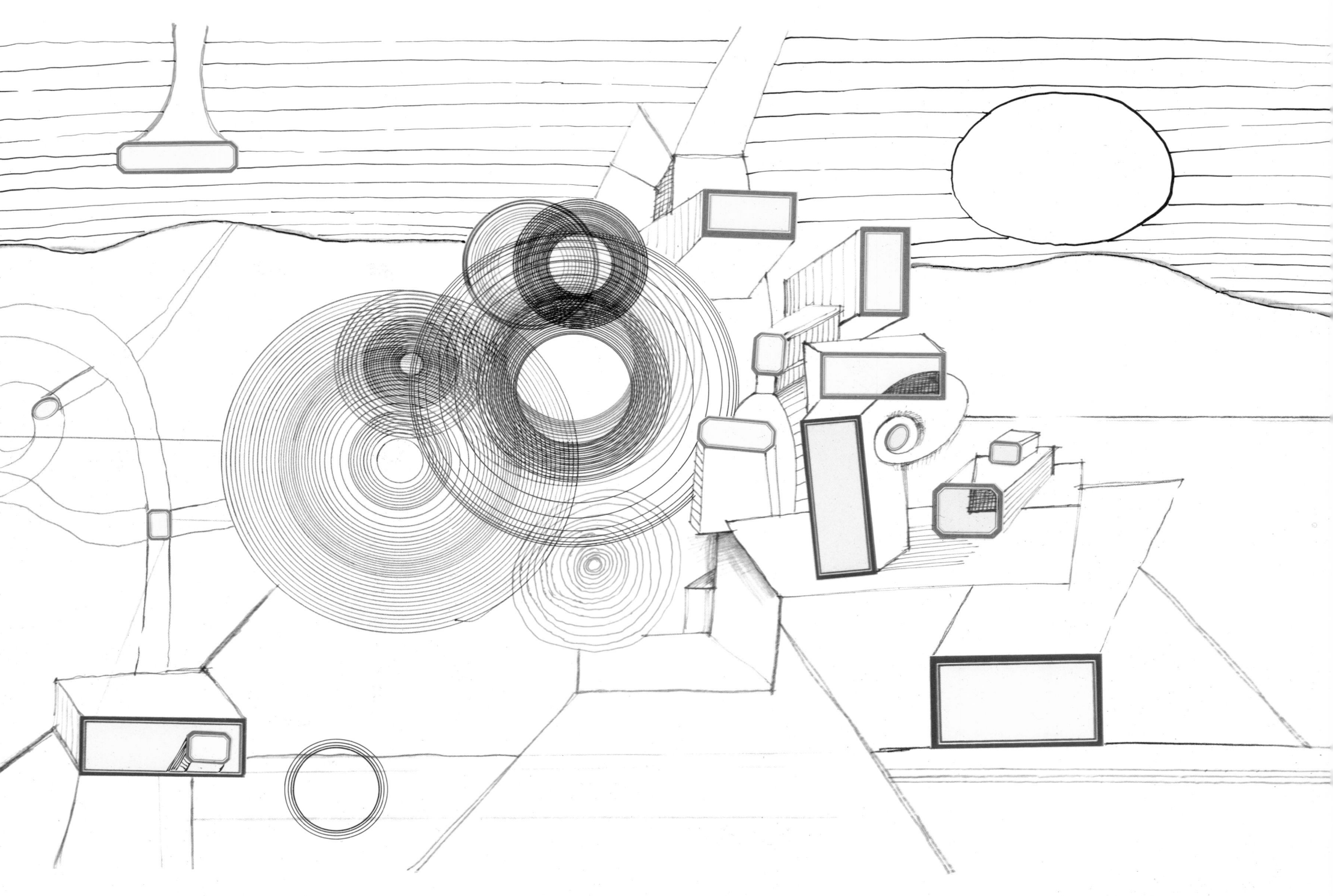

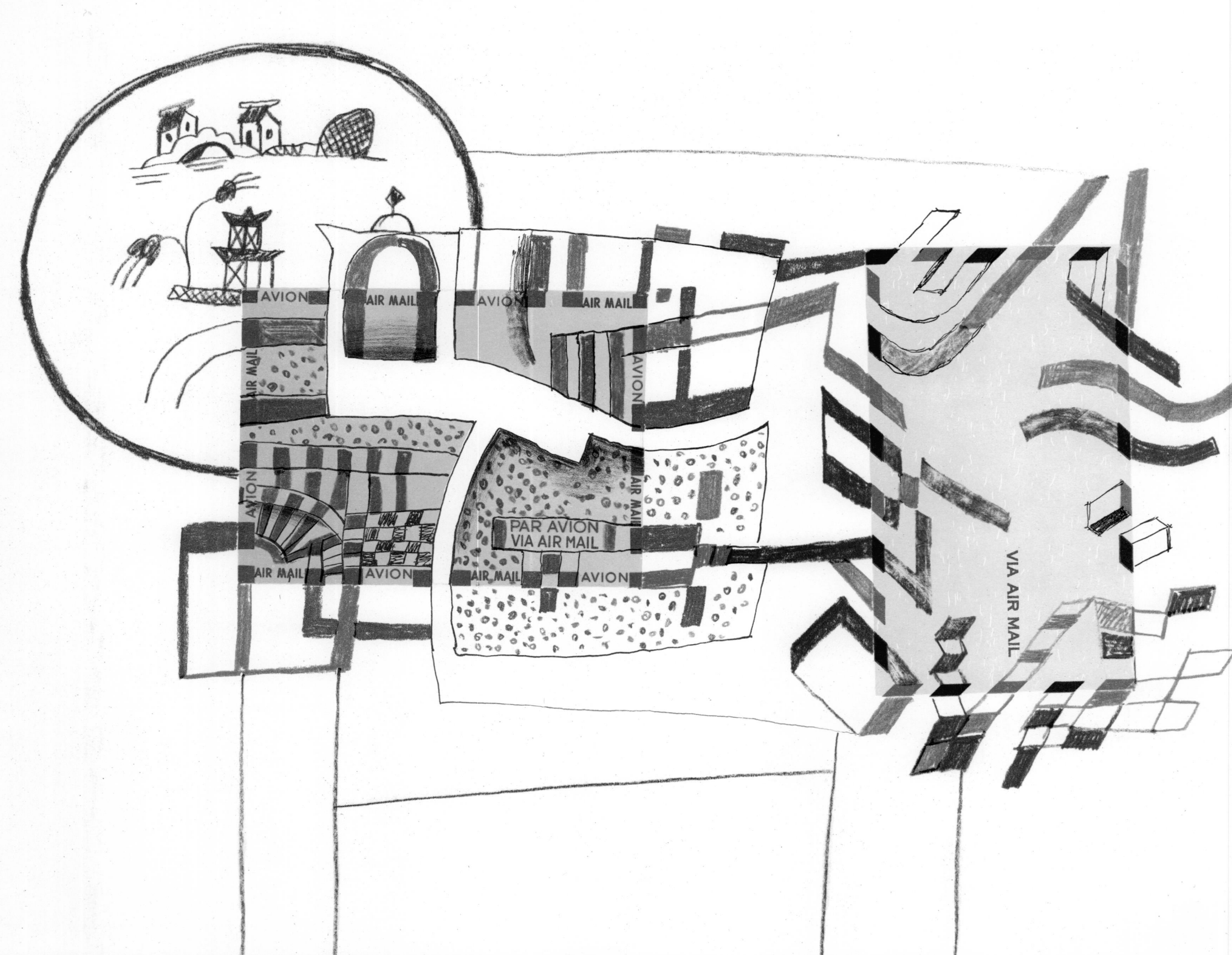

CHINA

VIA AIR MAIL

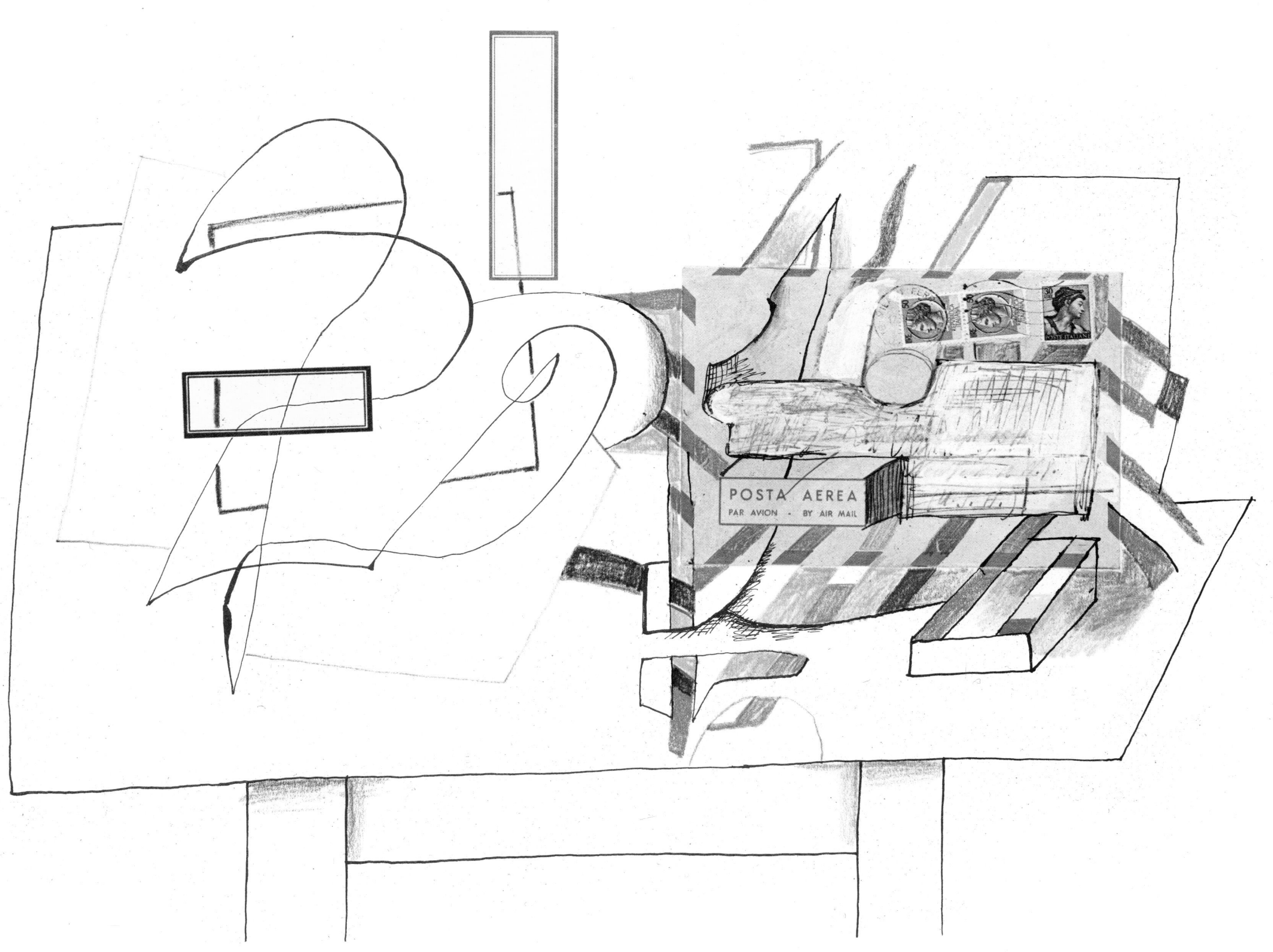

POSTA AEREA
PAR AVION · BY AIR MAIL

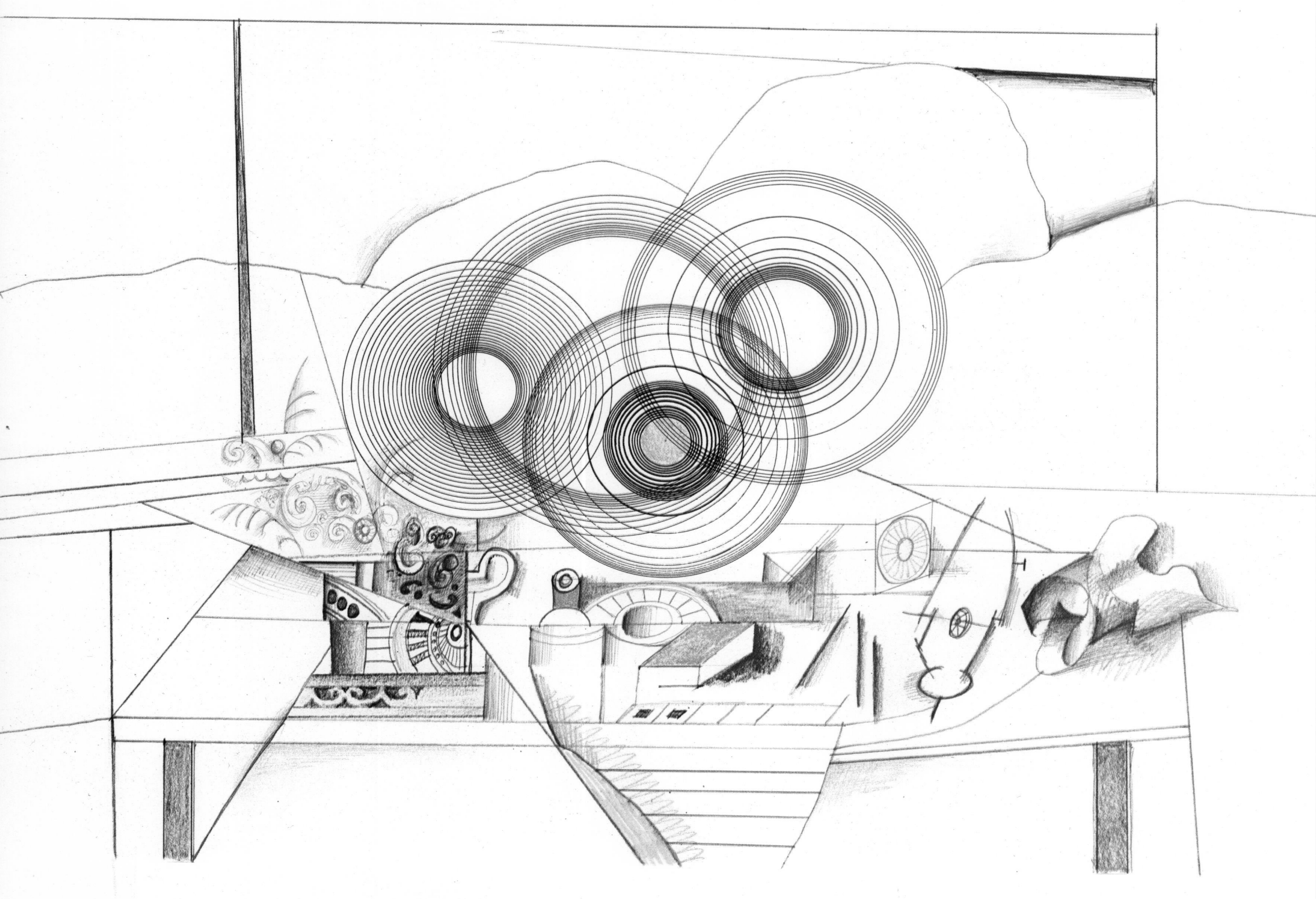

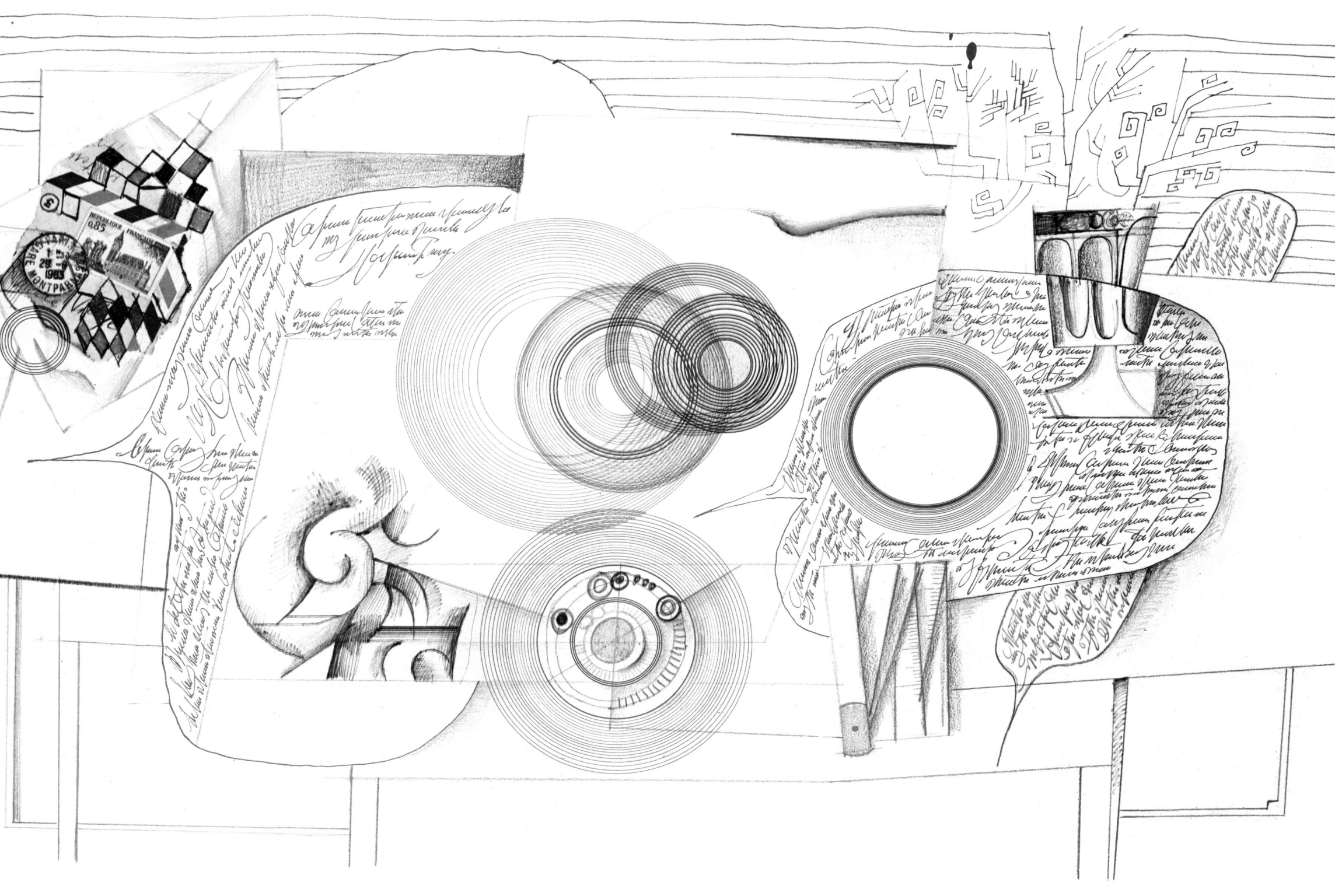

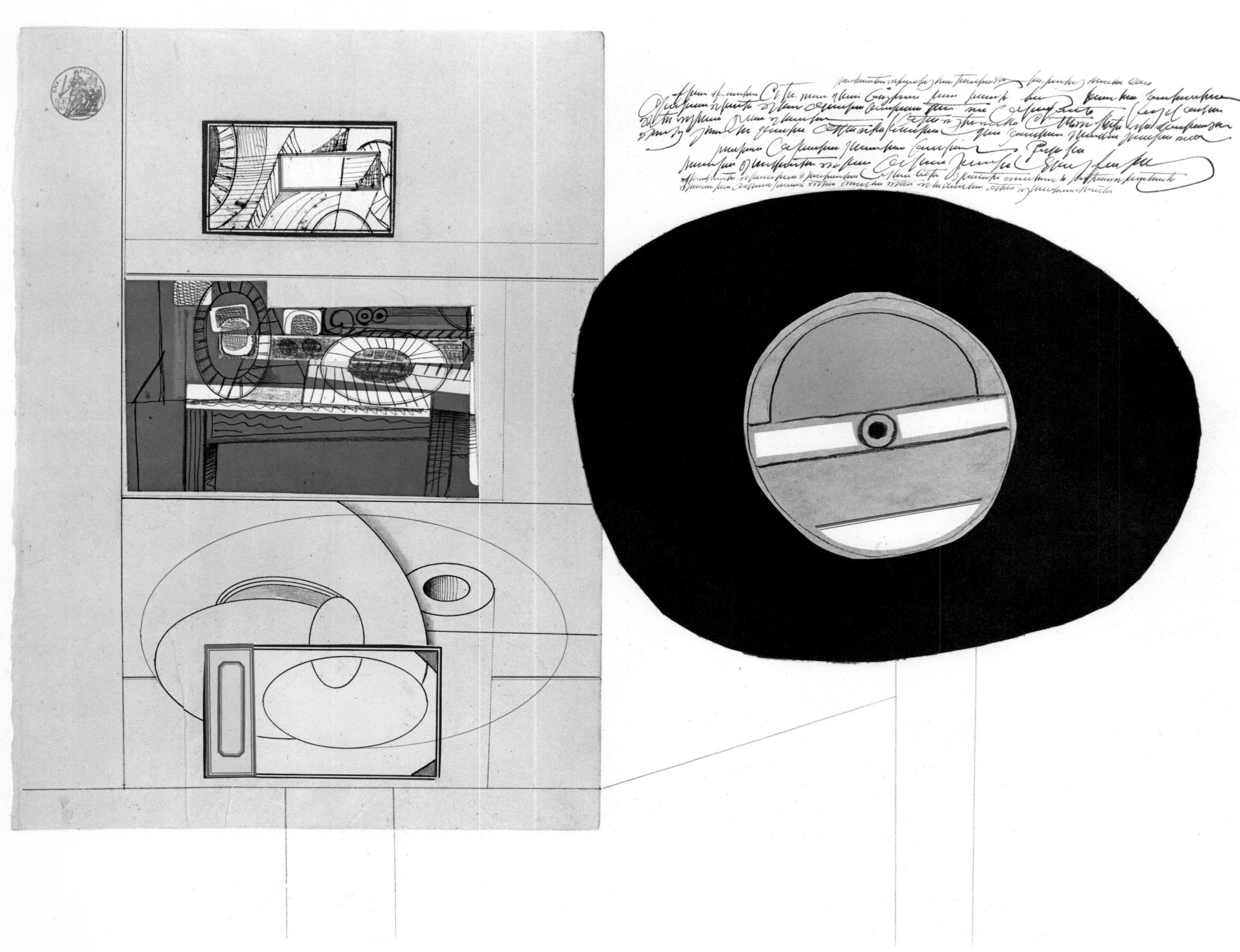

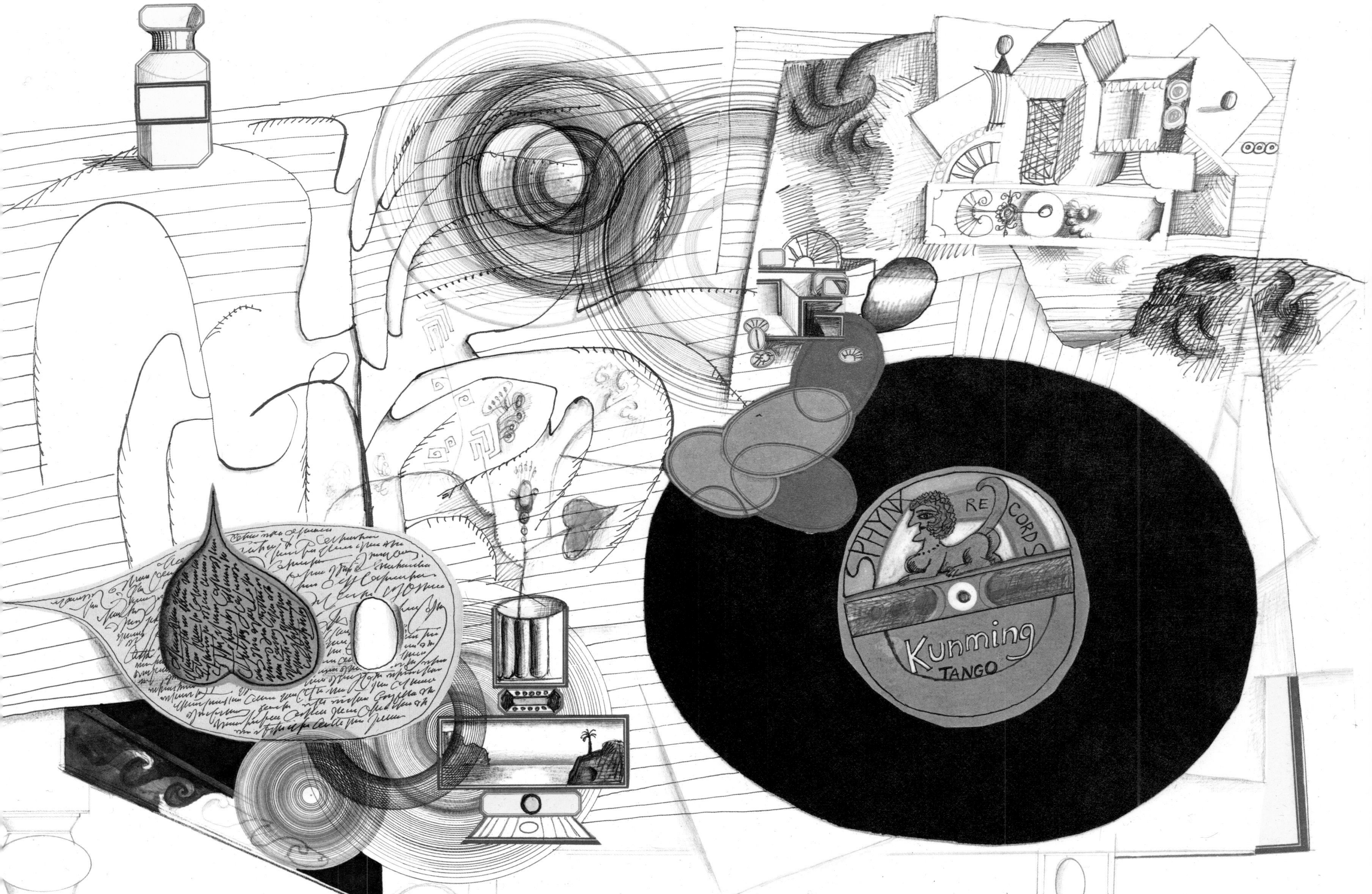
SPHYNX
RE
CORDS
Kunming
TANGO

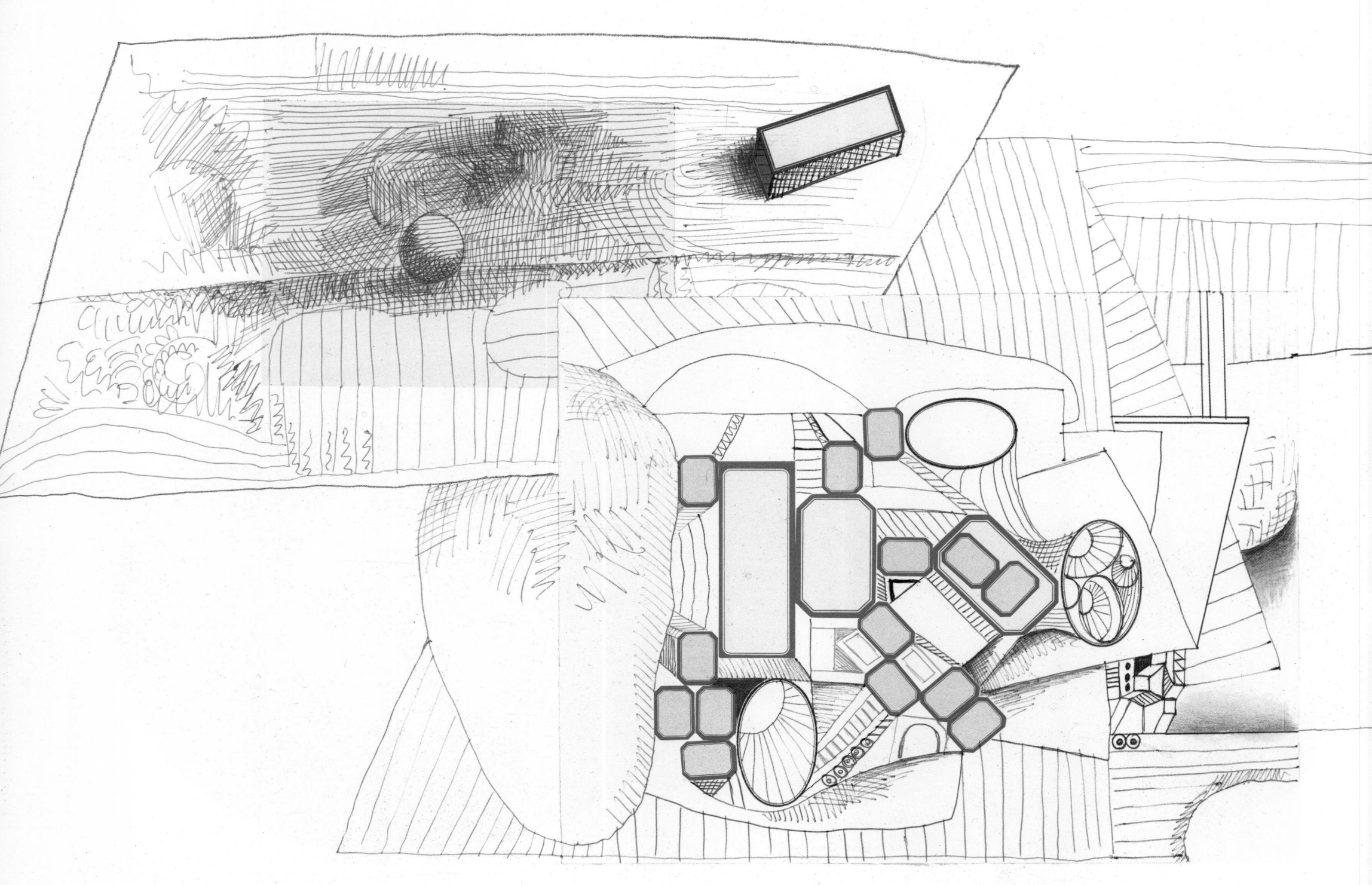

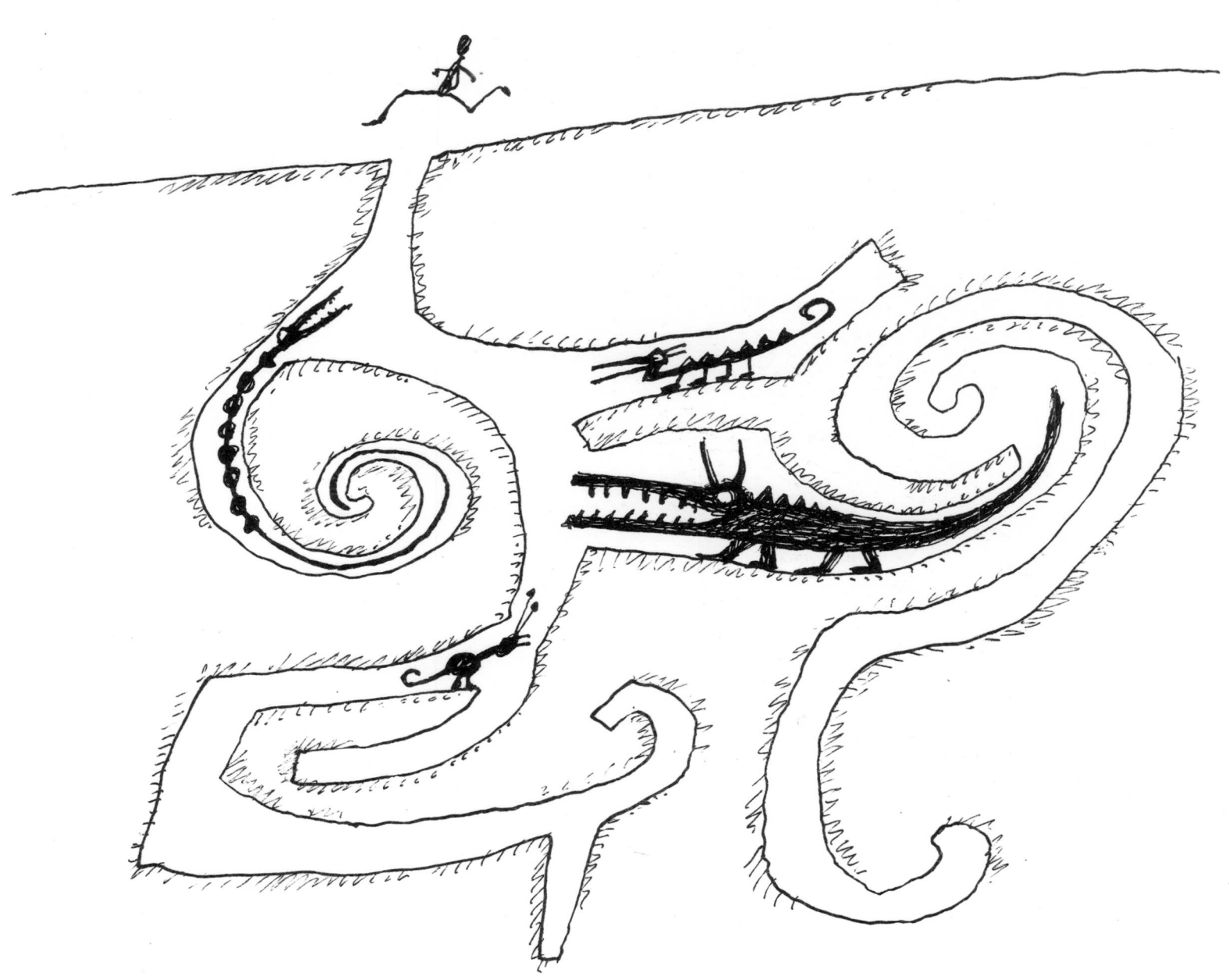

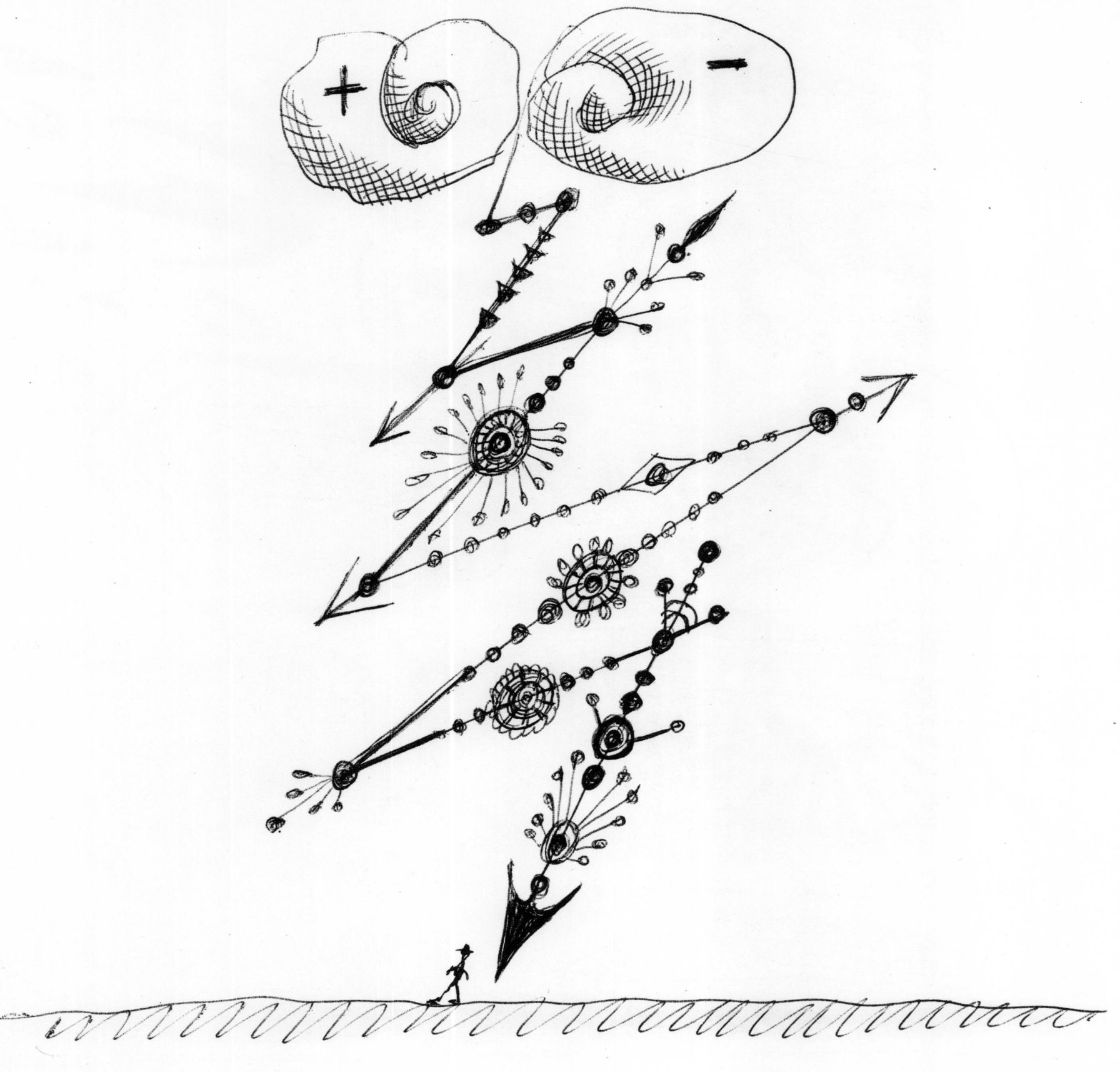

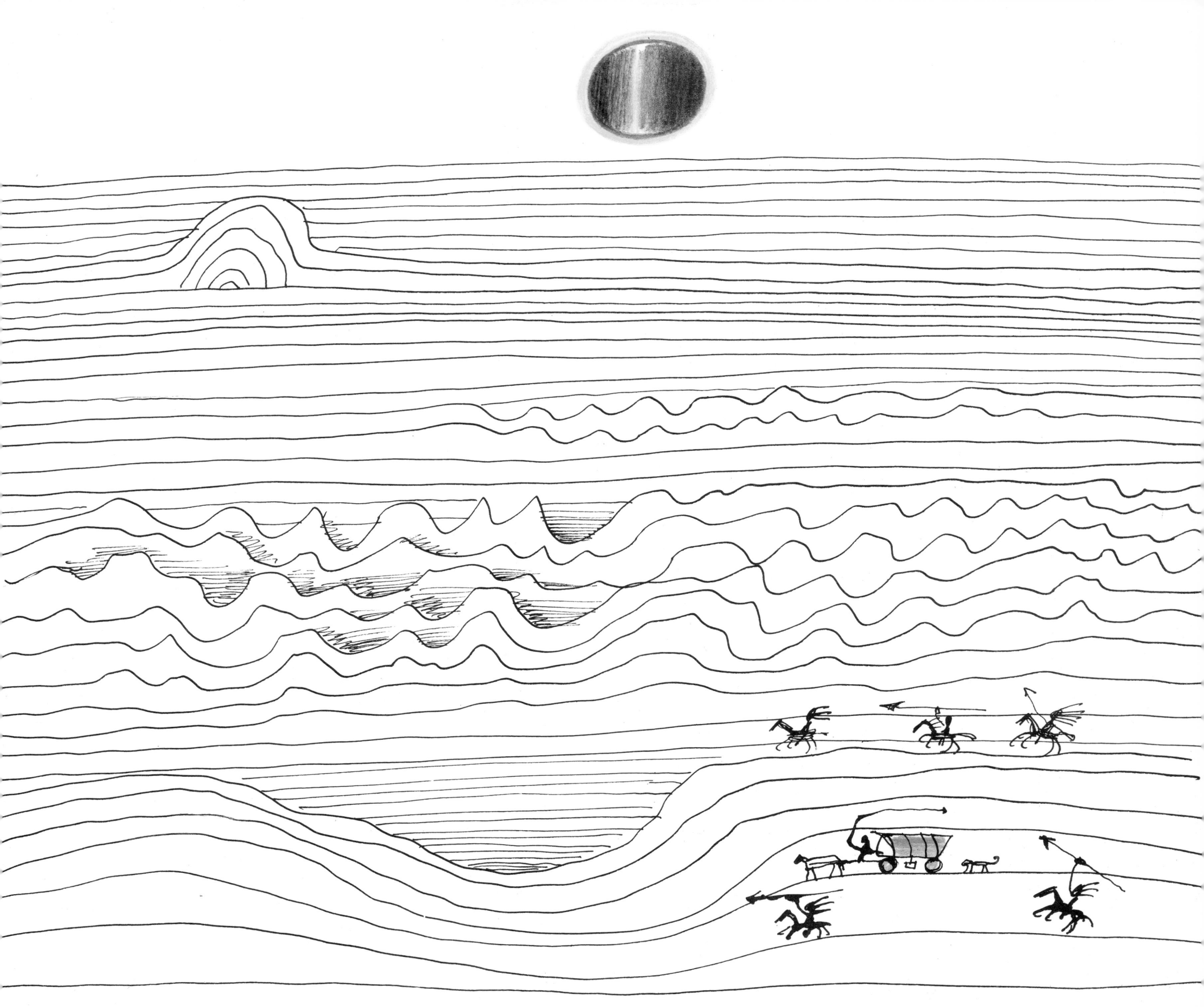

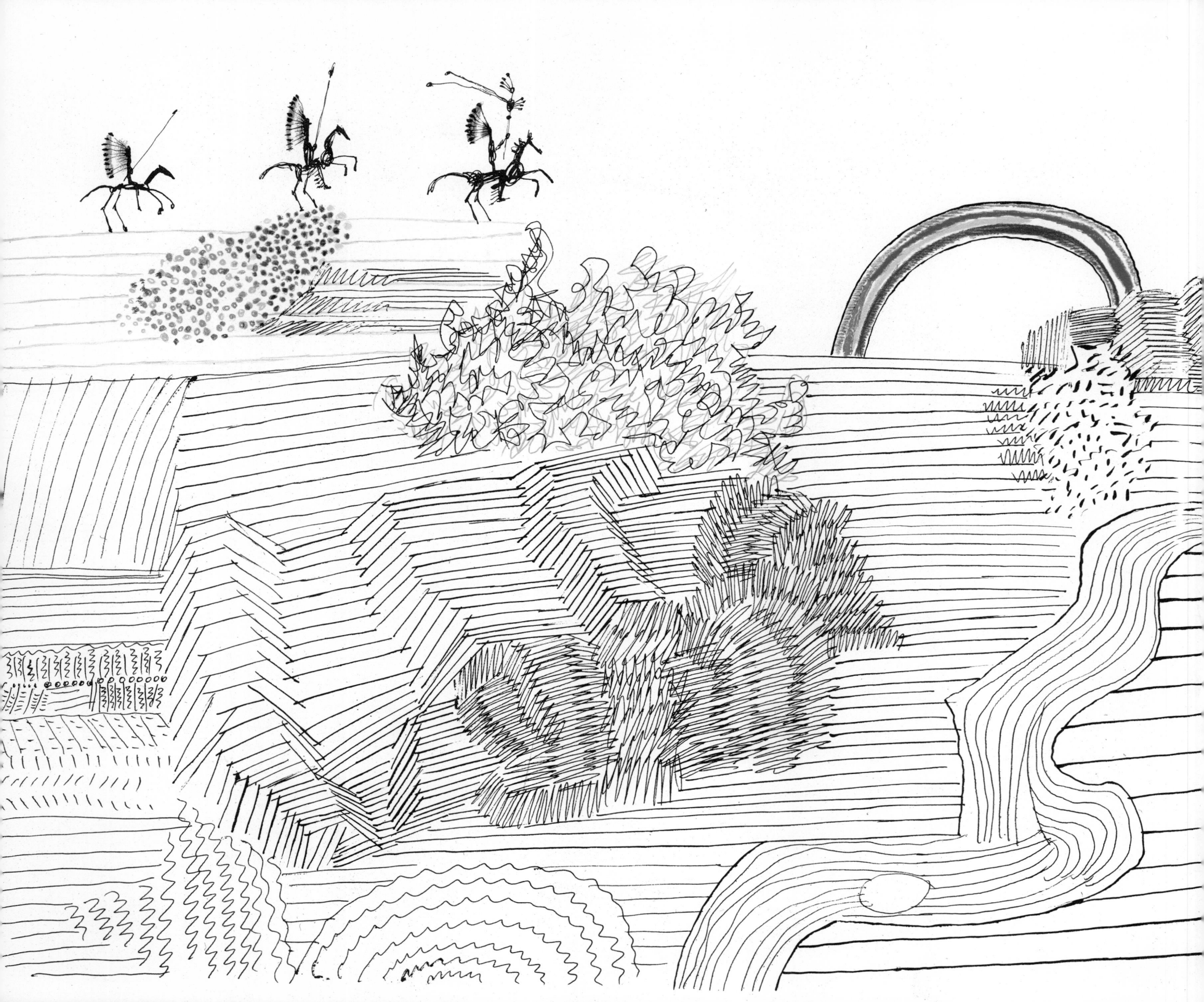

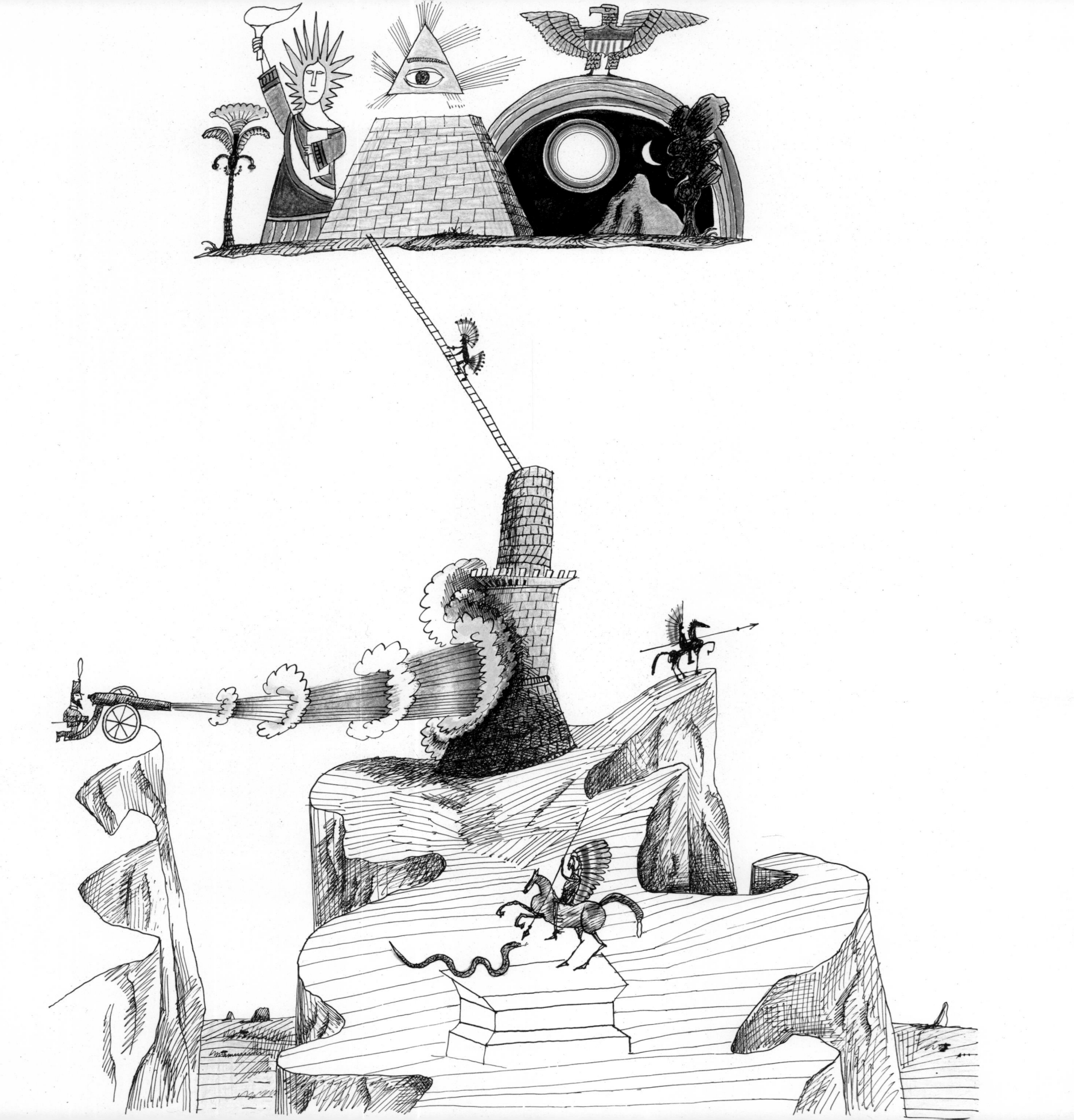

STEINBERG

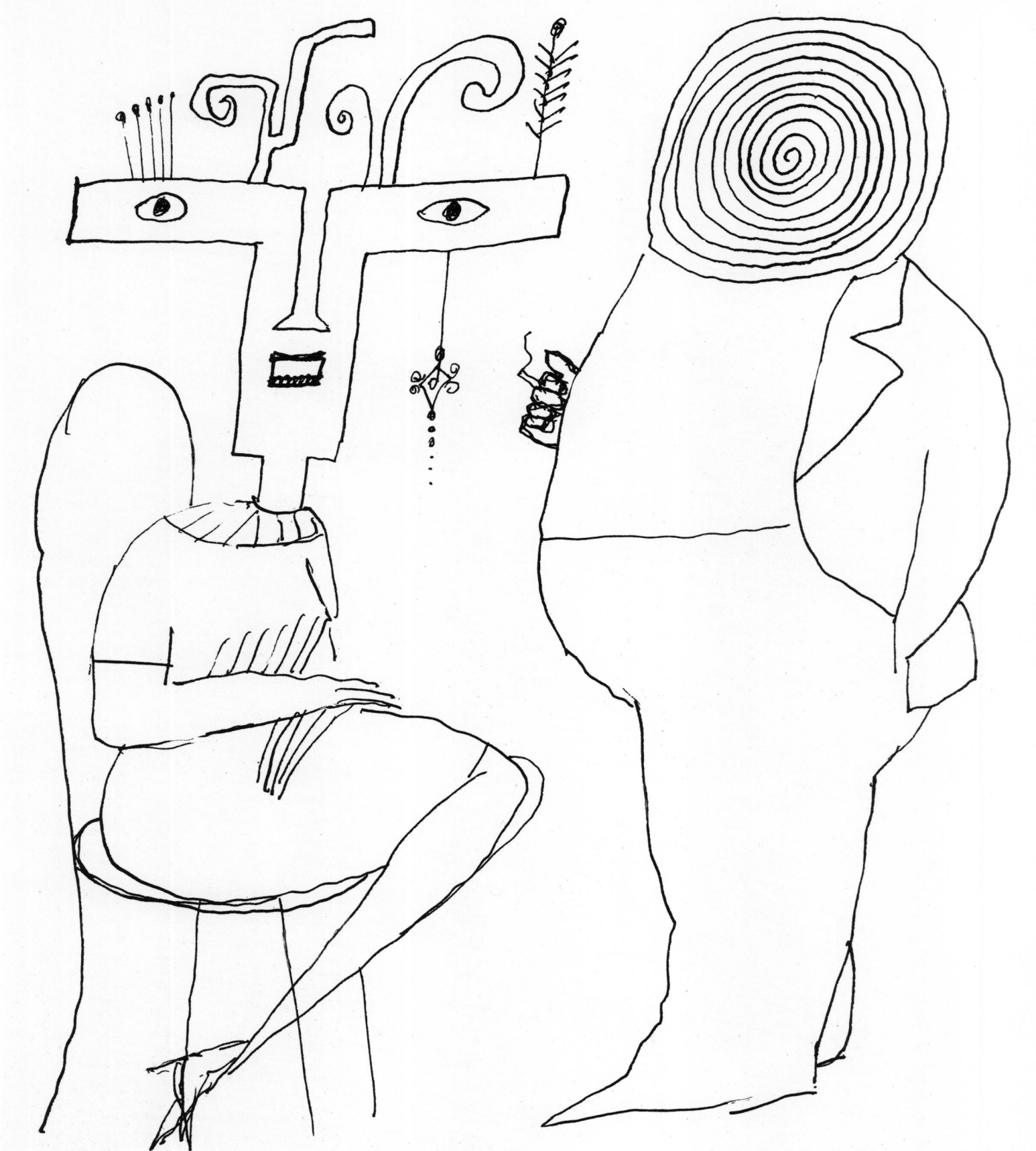

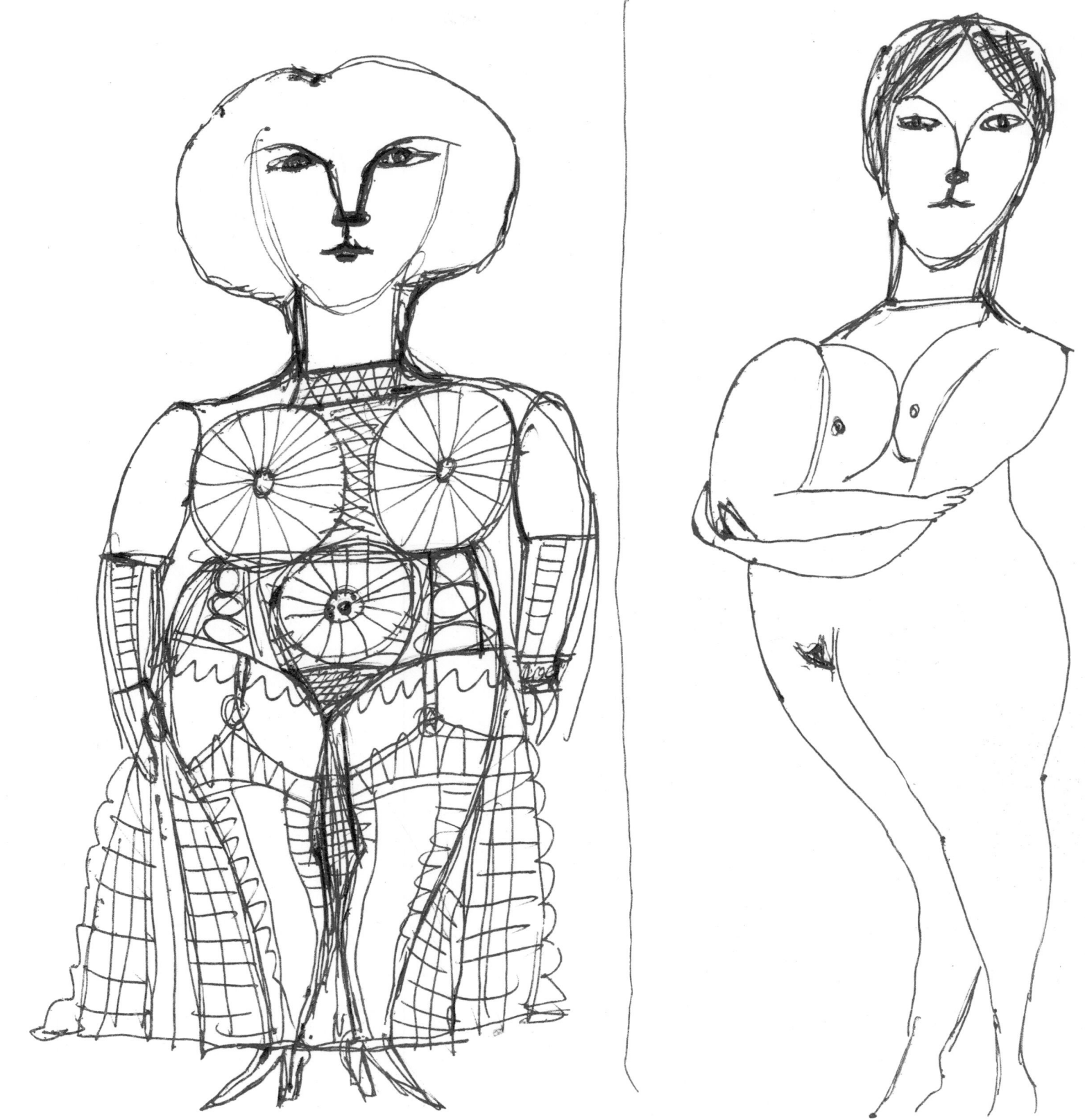

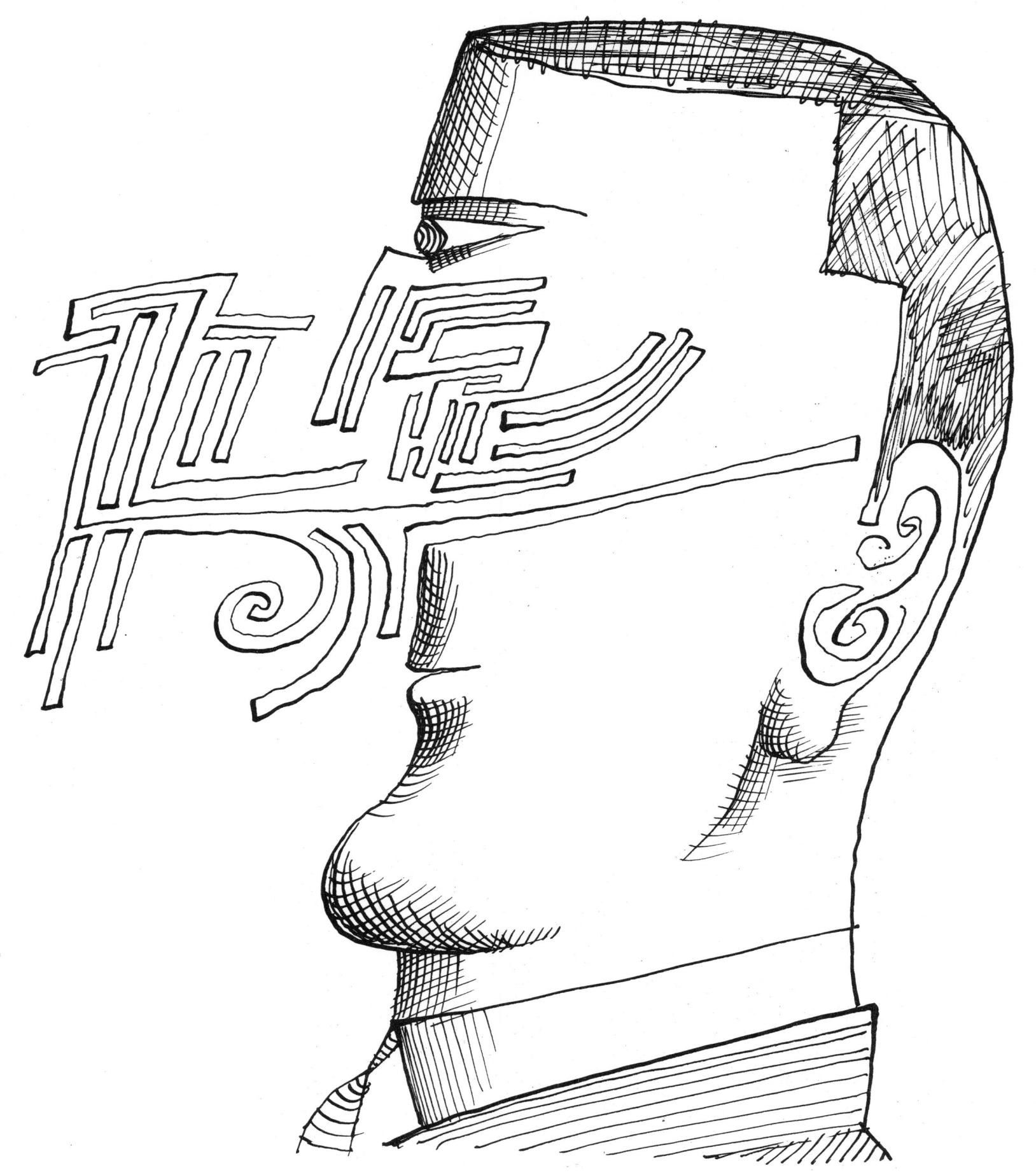

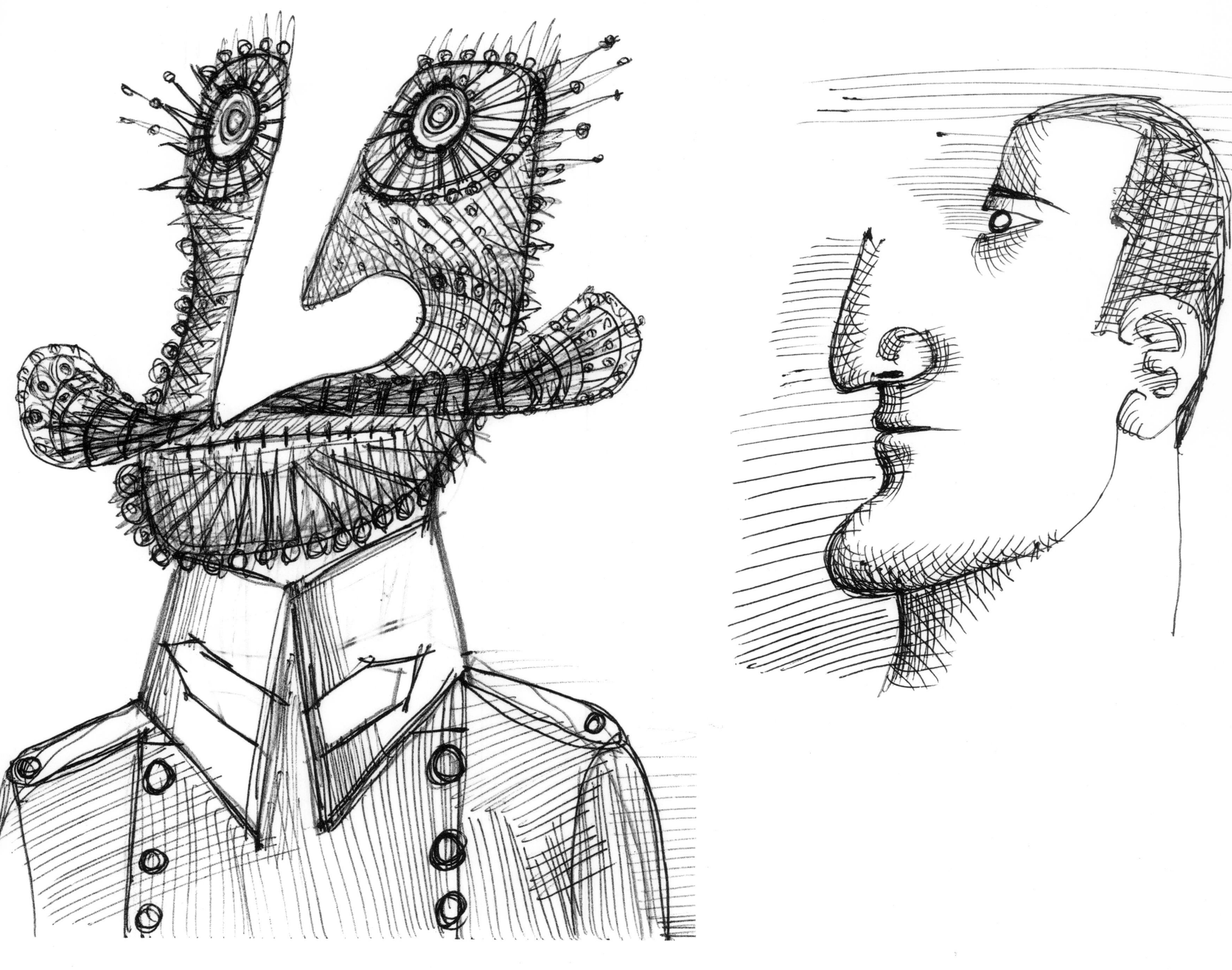

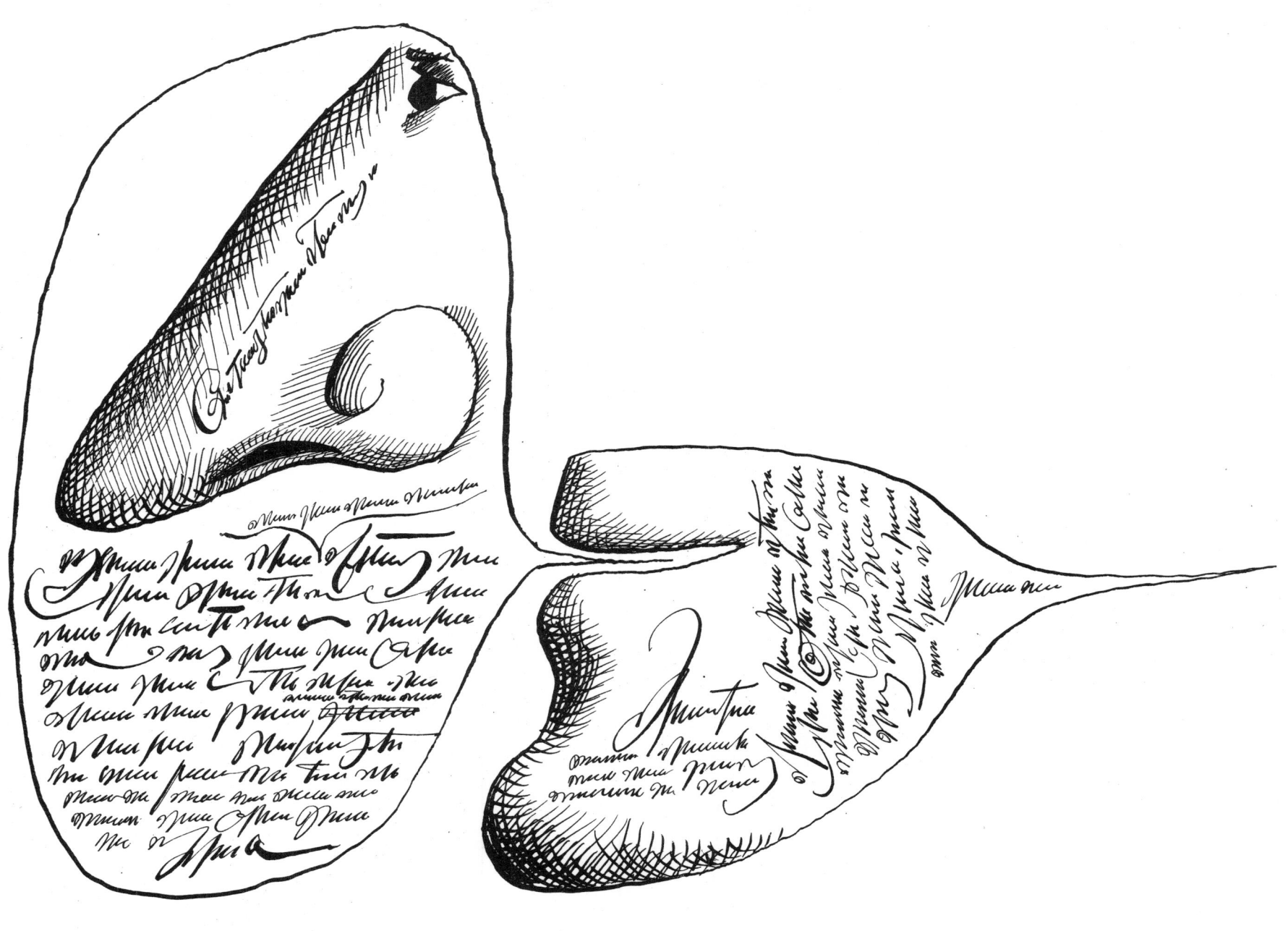

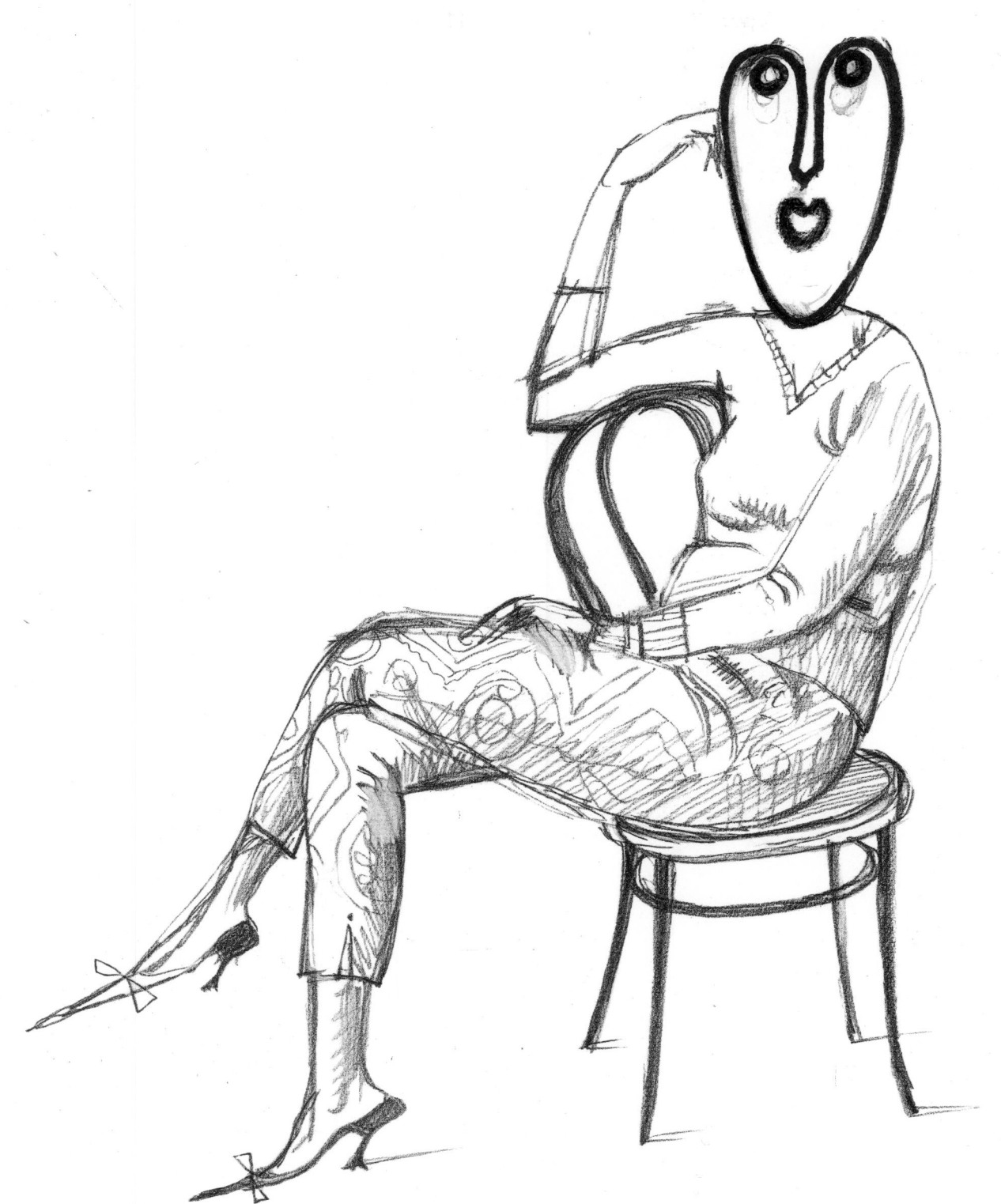

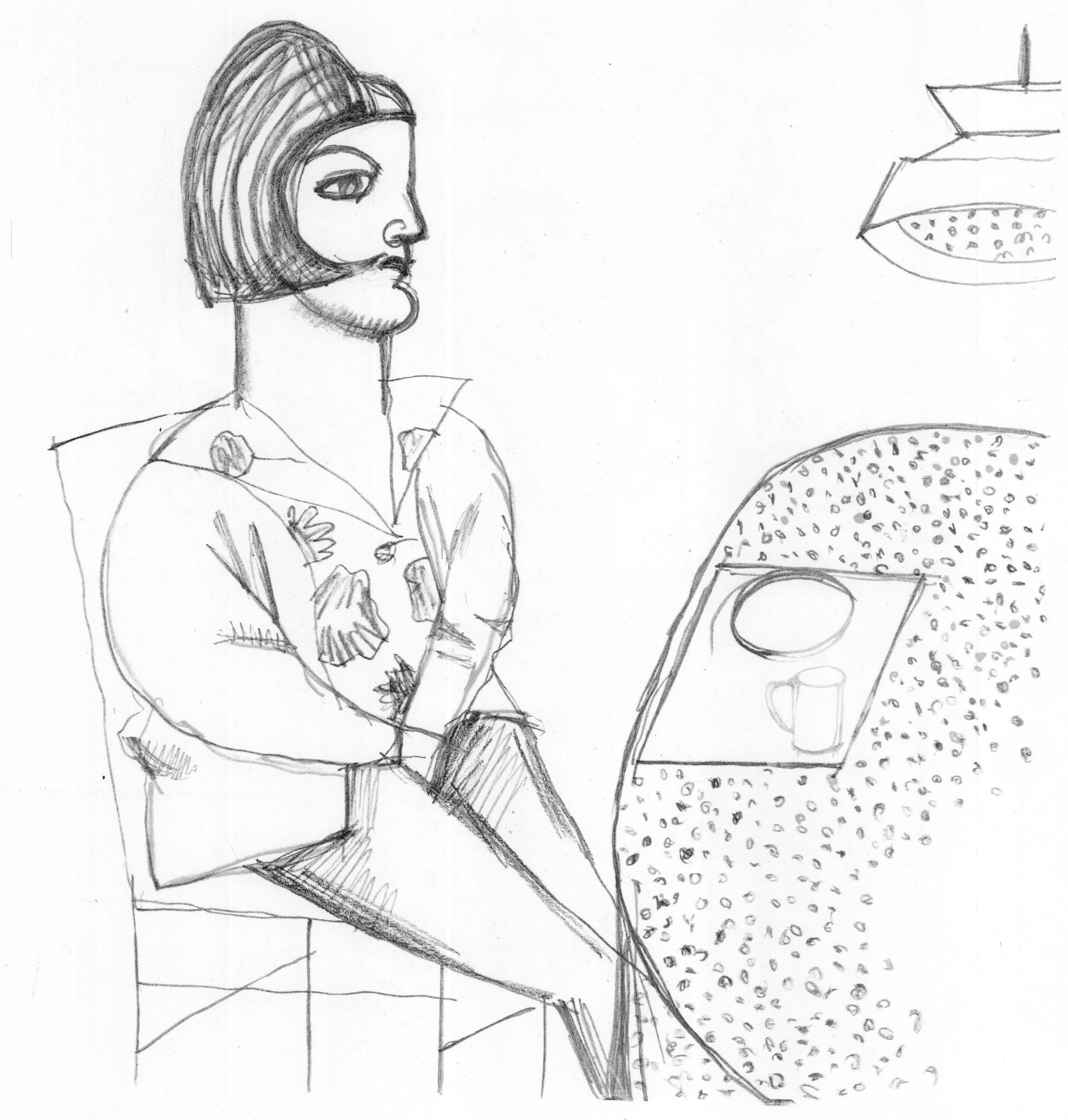

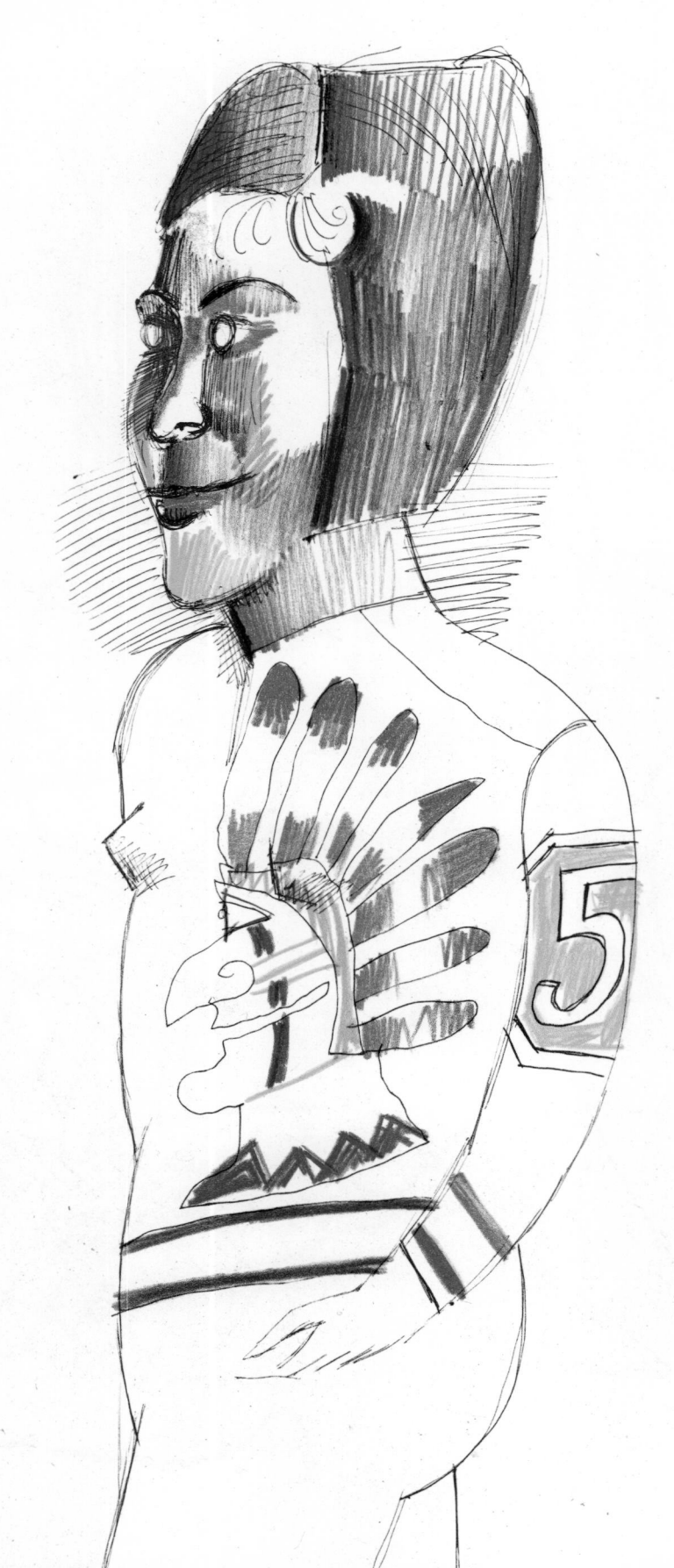

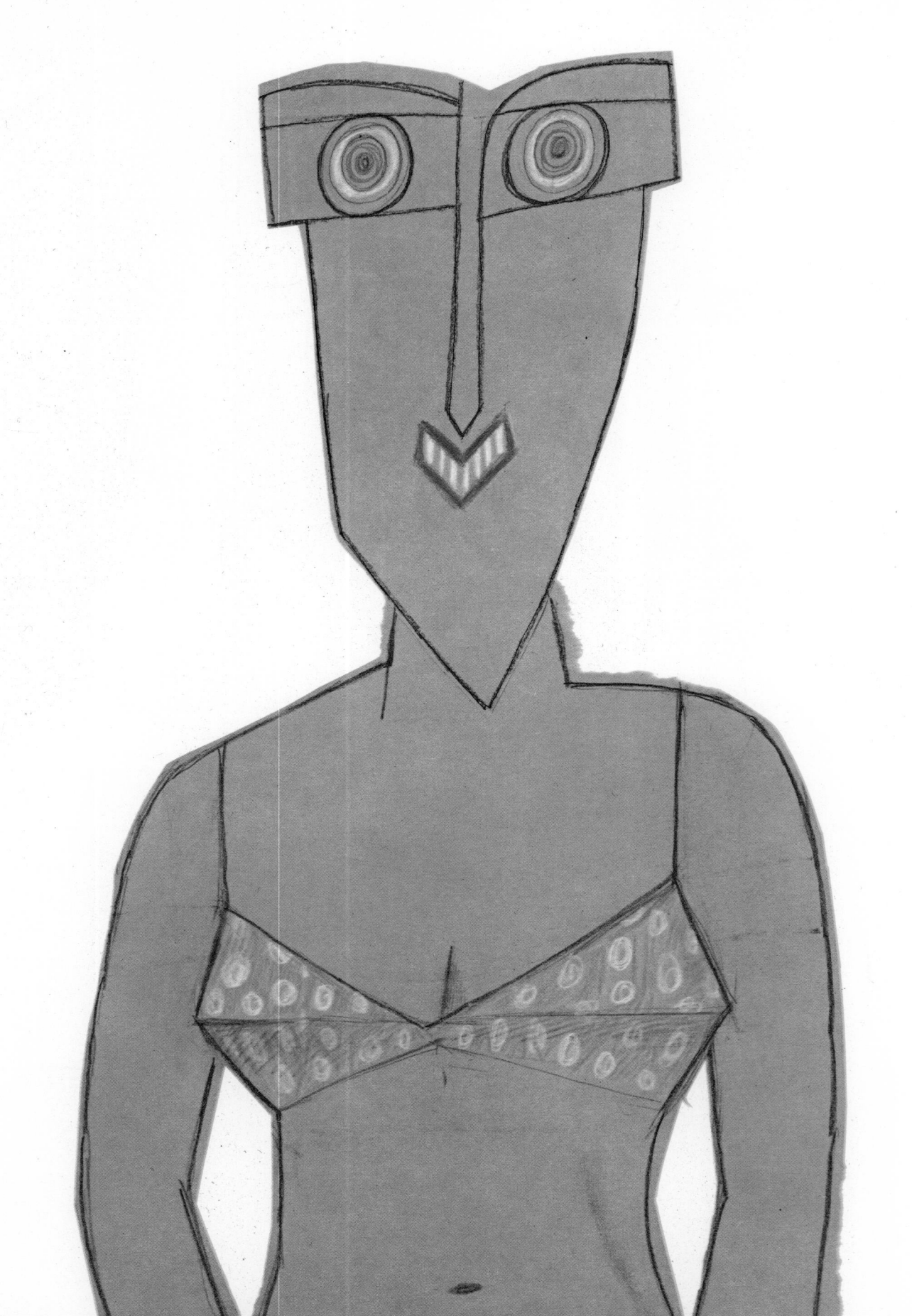

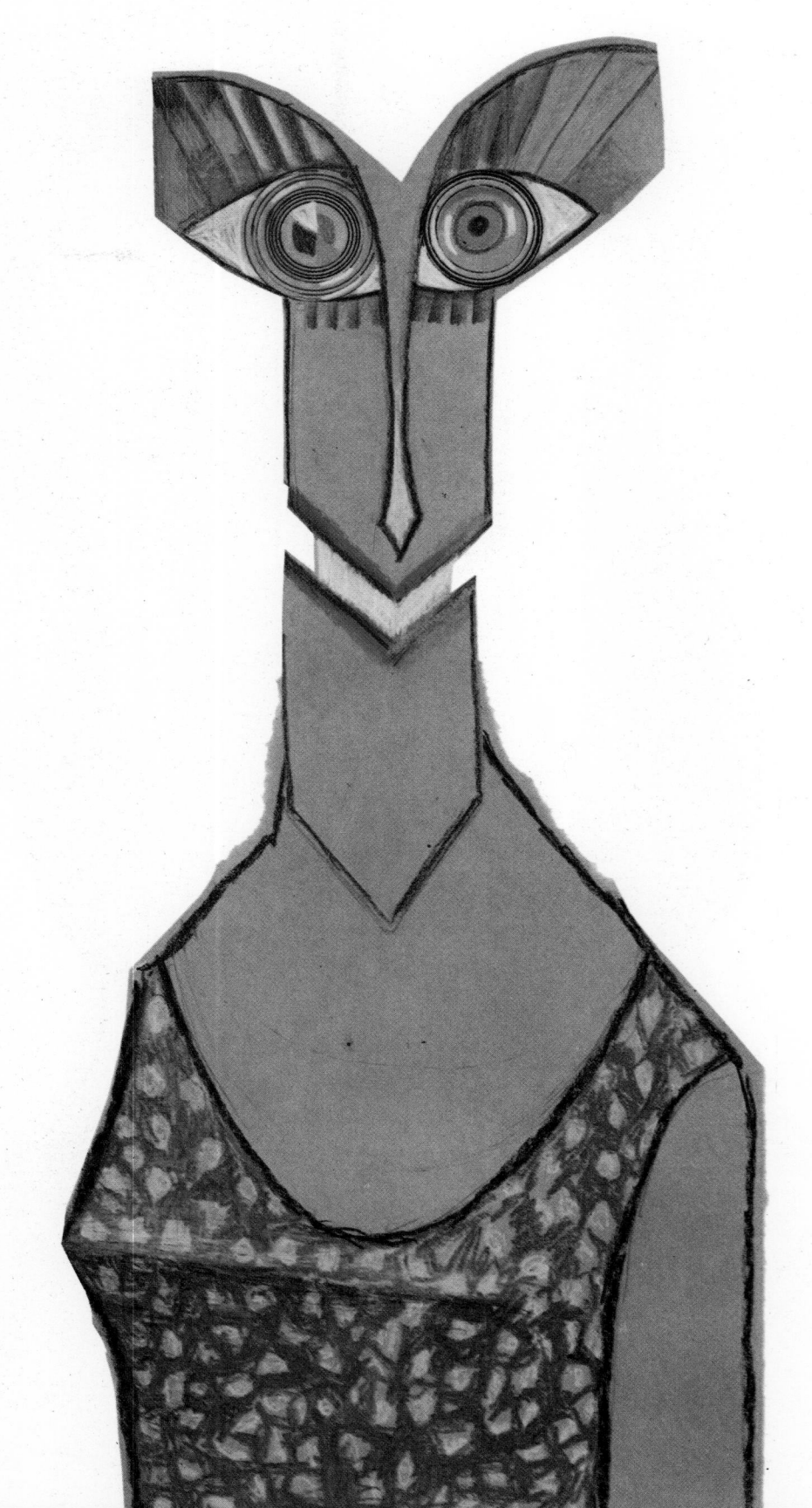

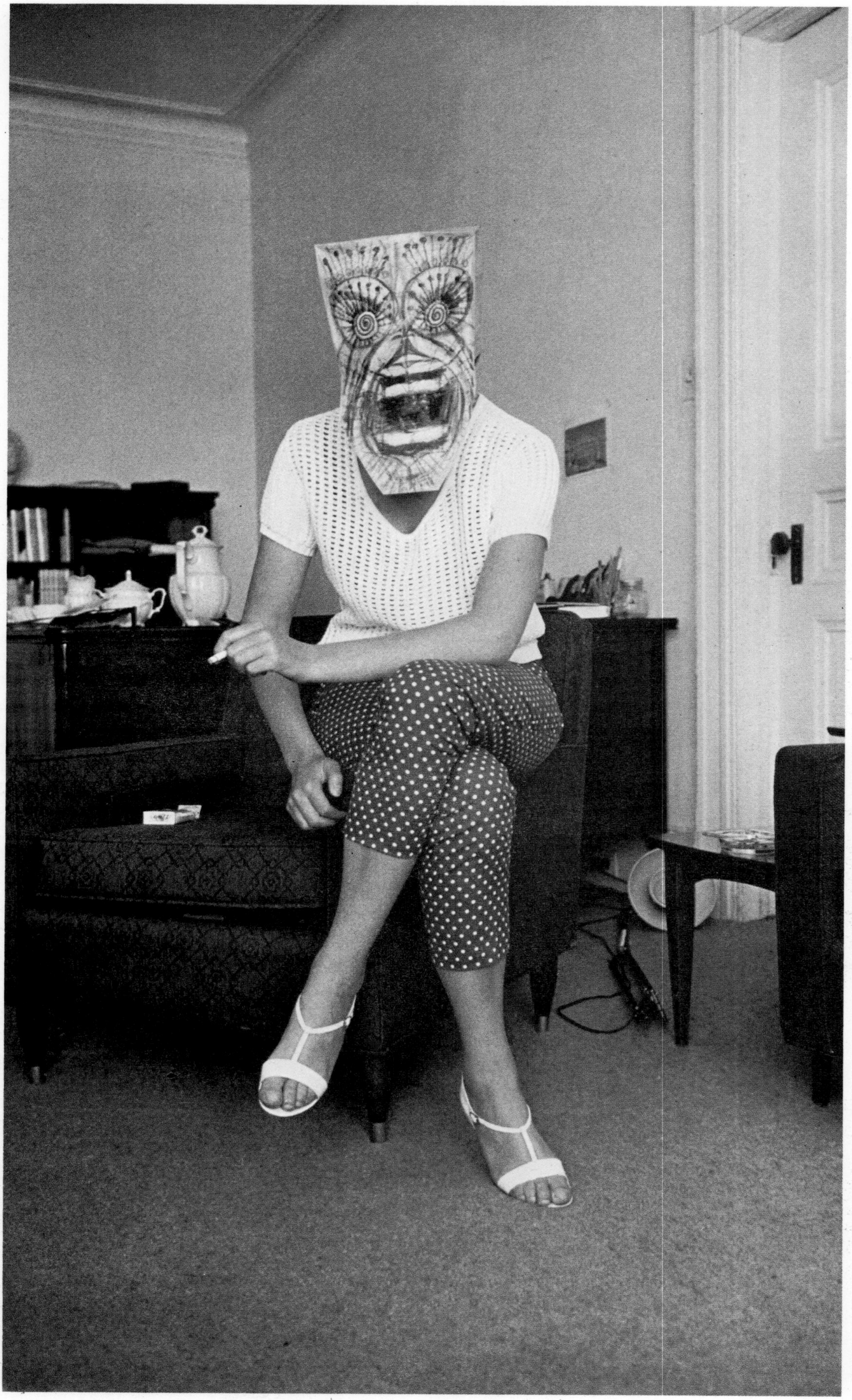
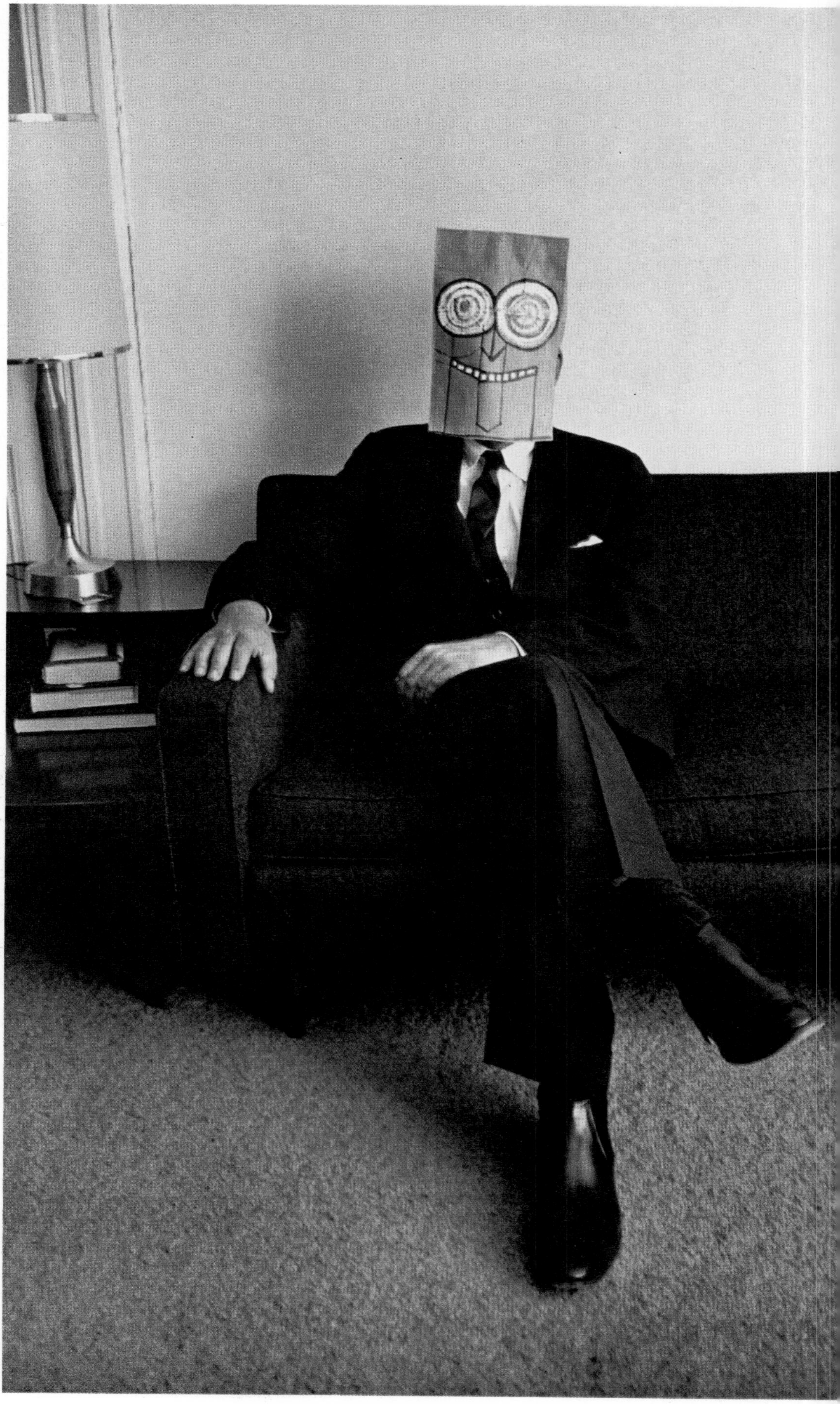

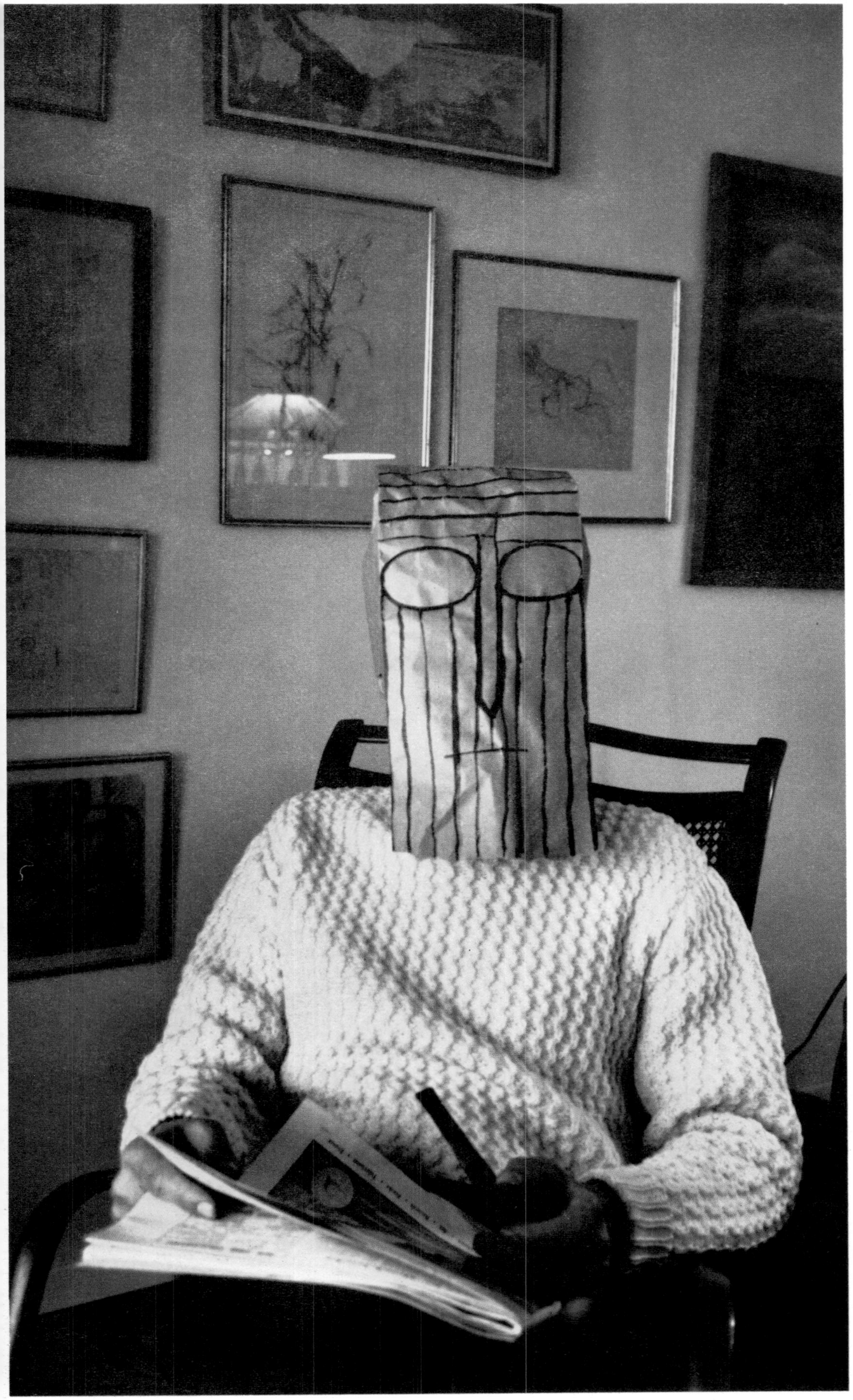

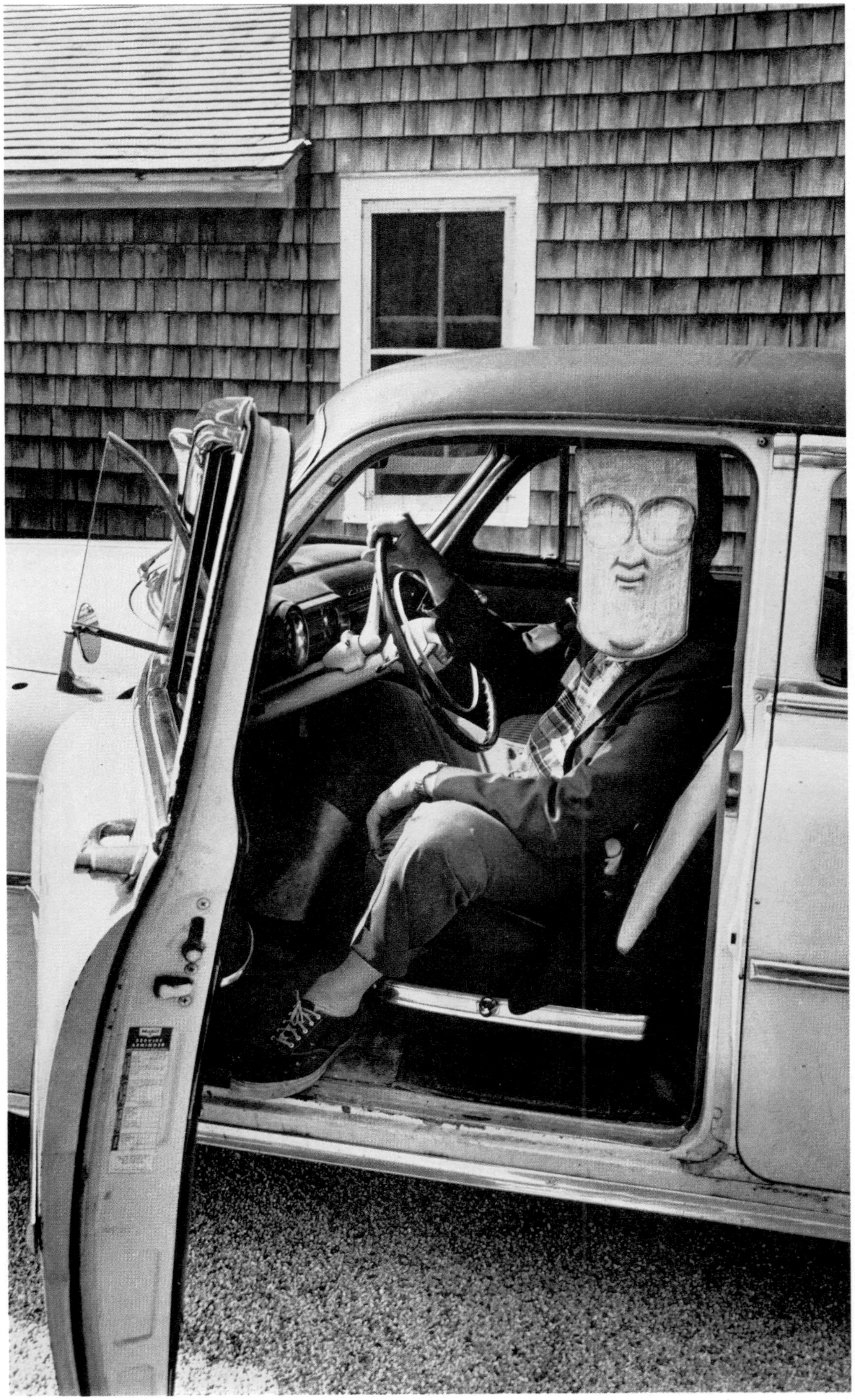

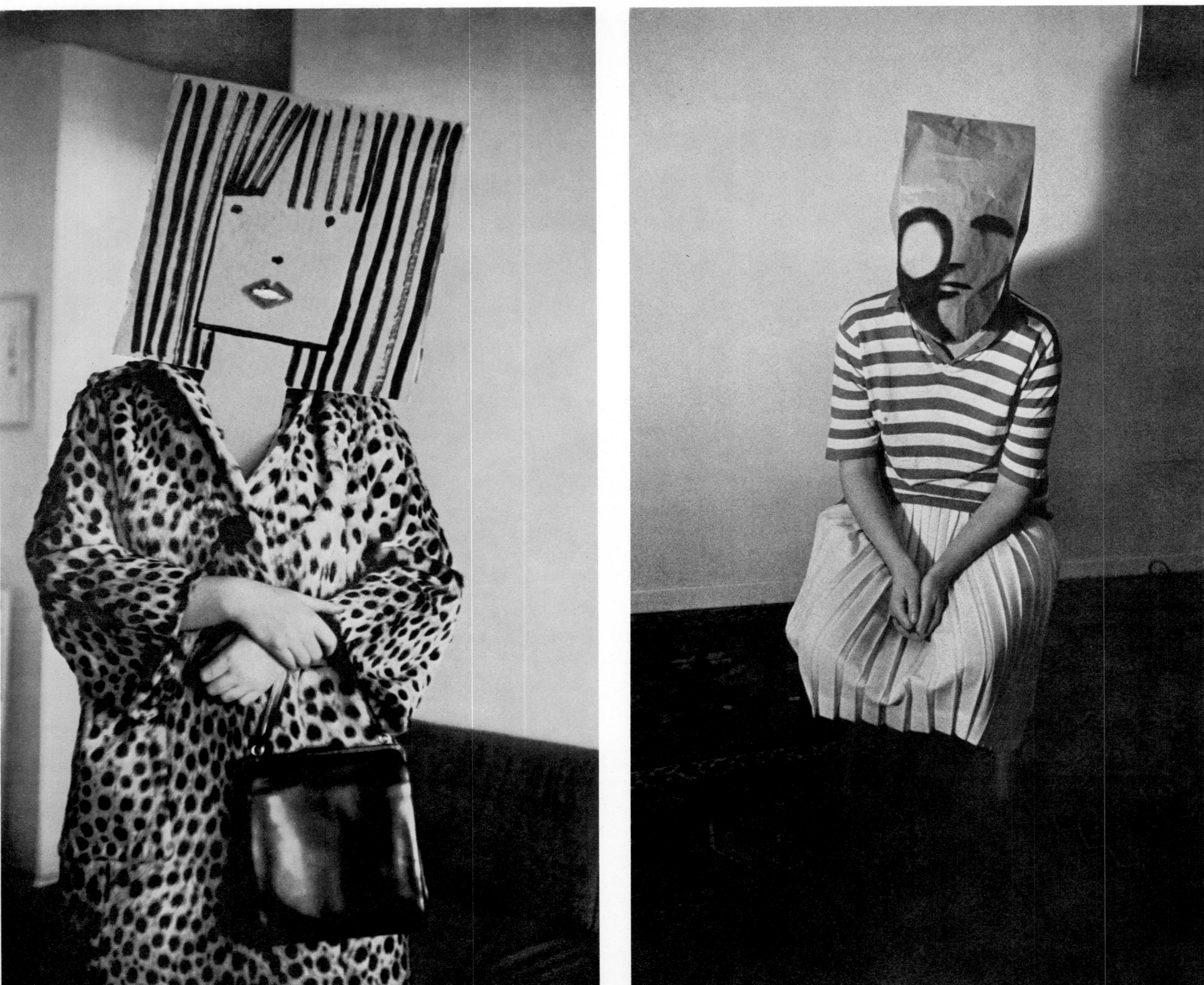

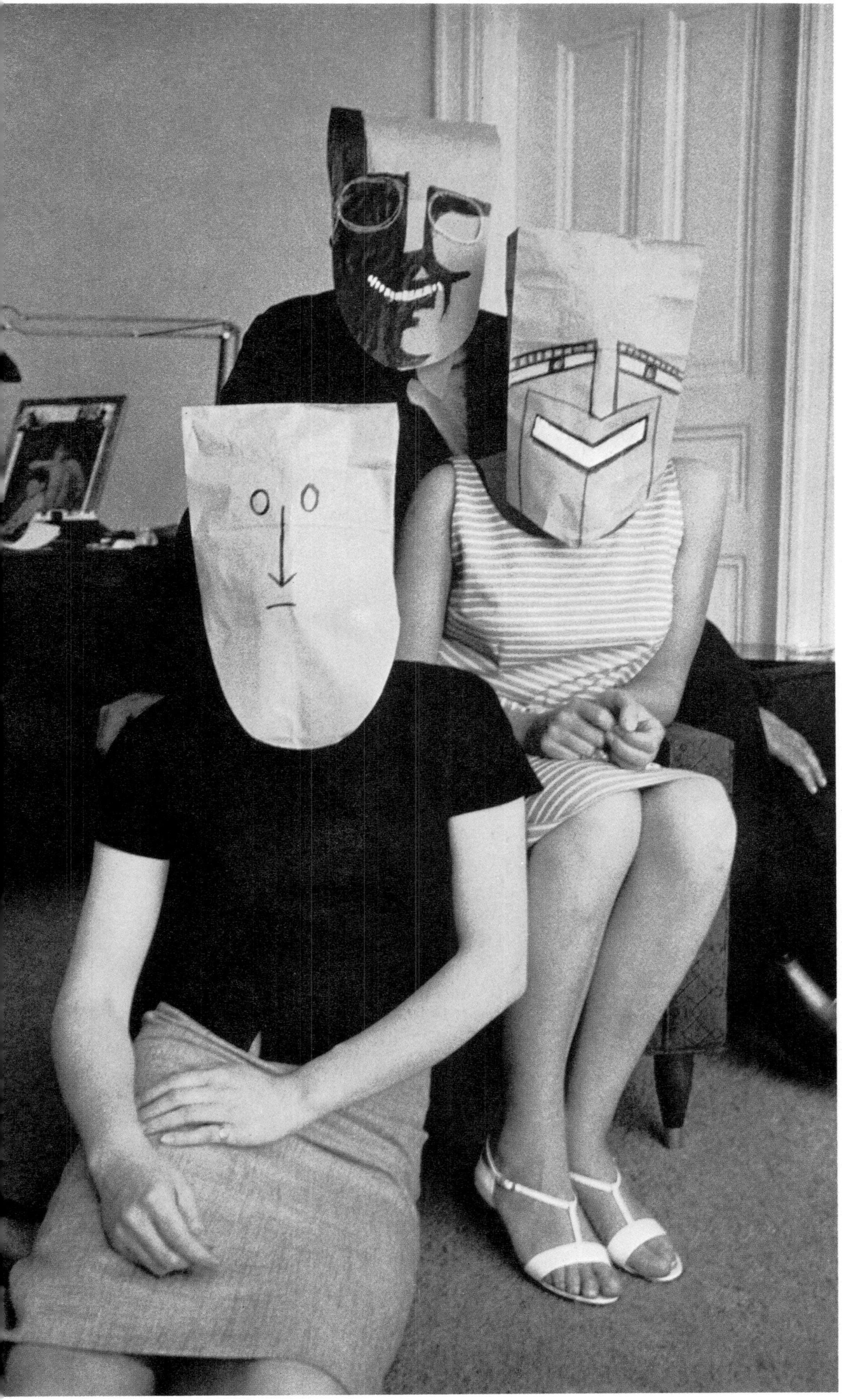

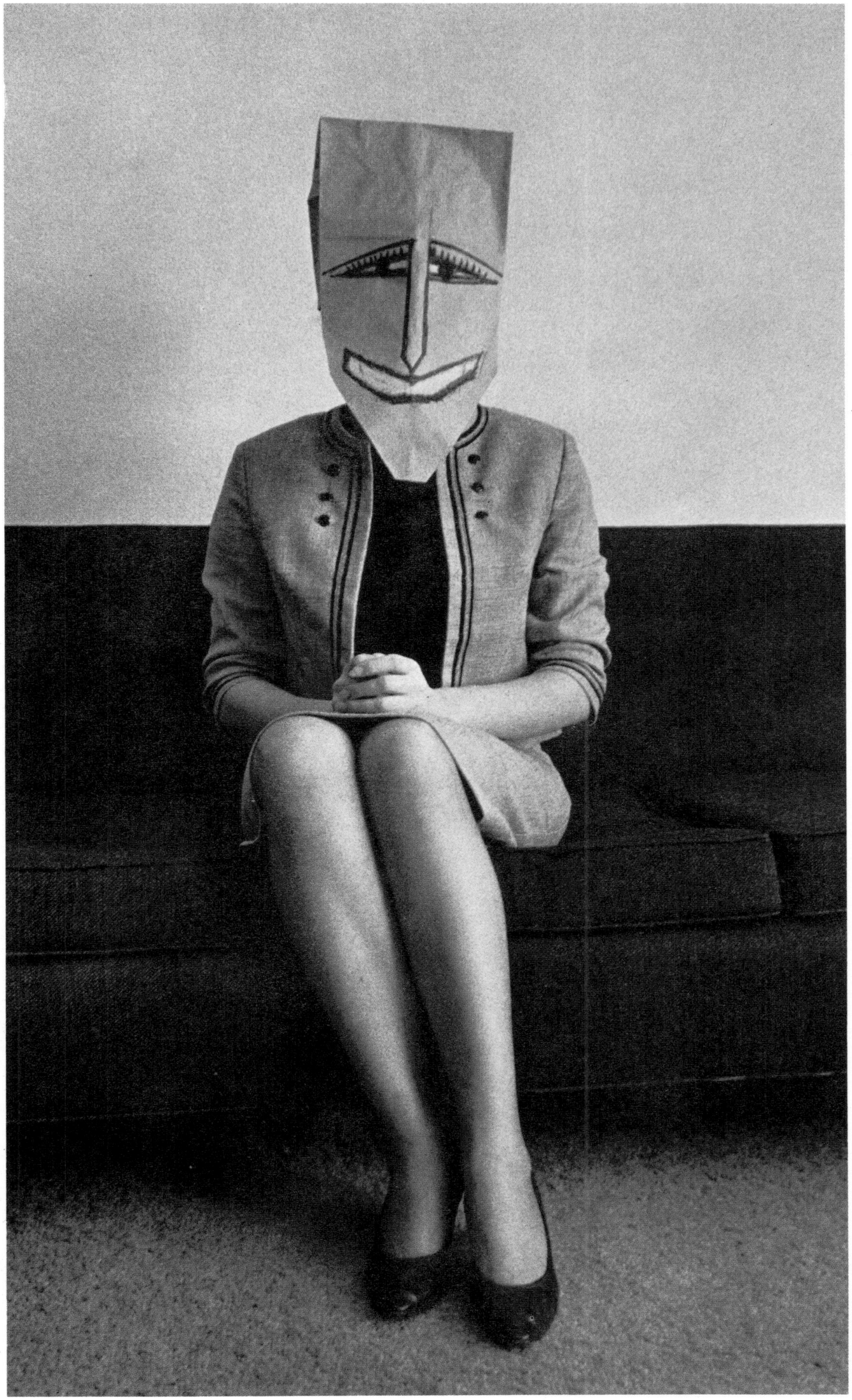

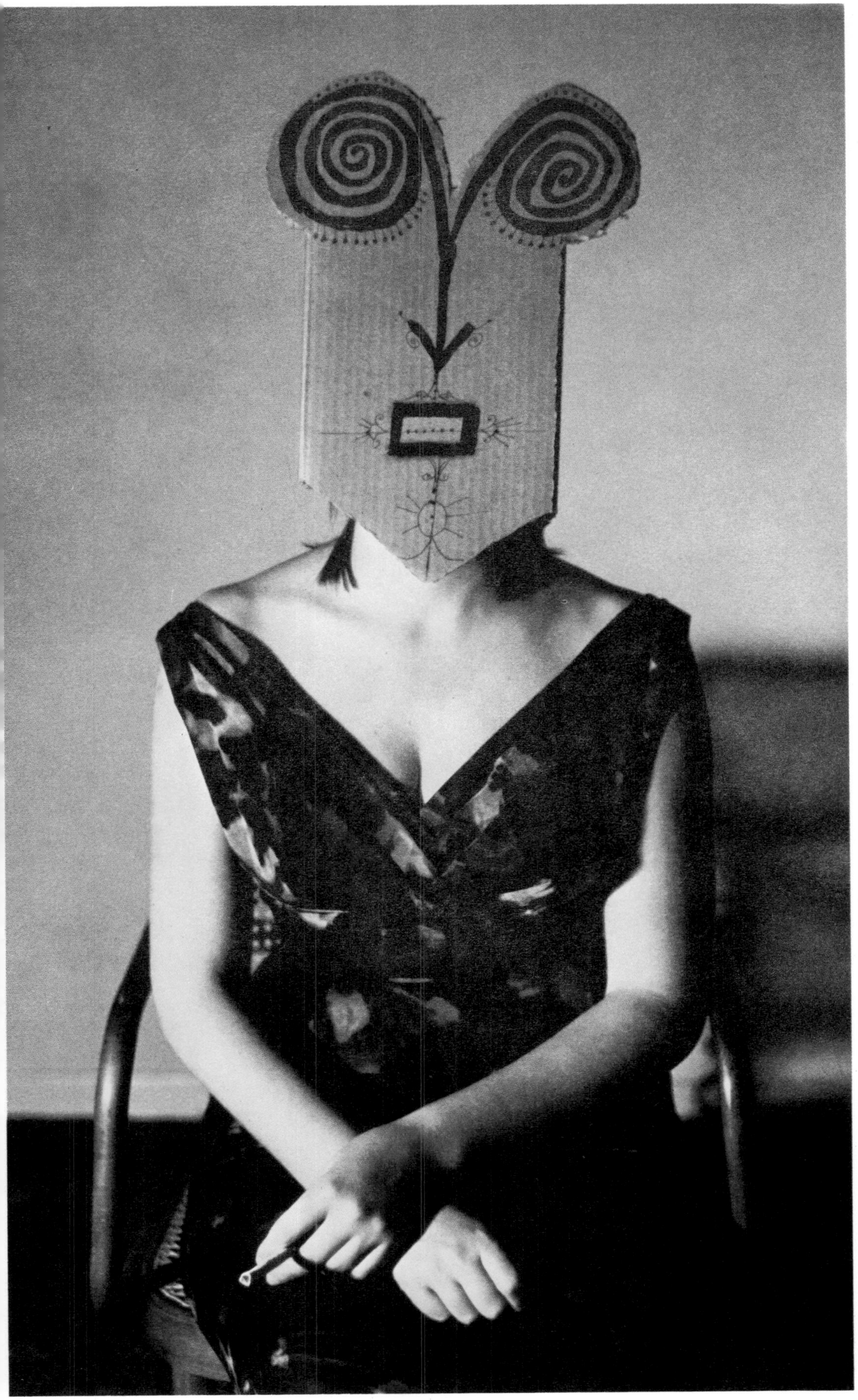

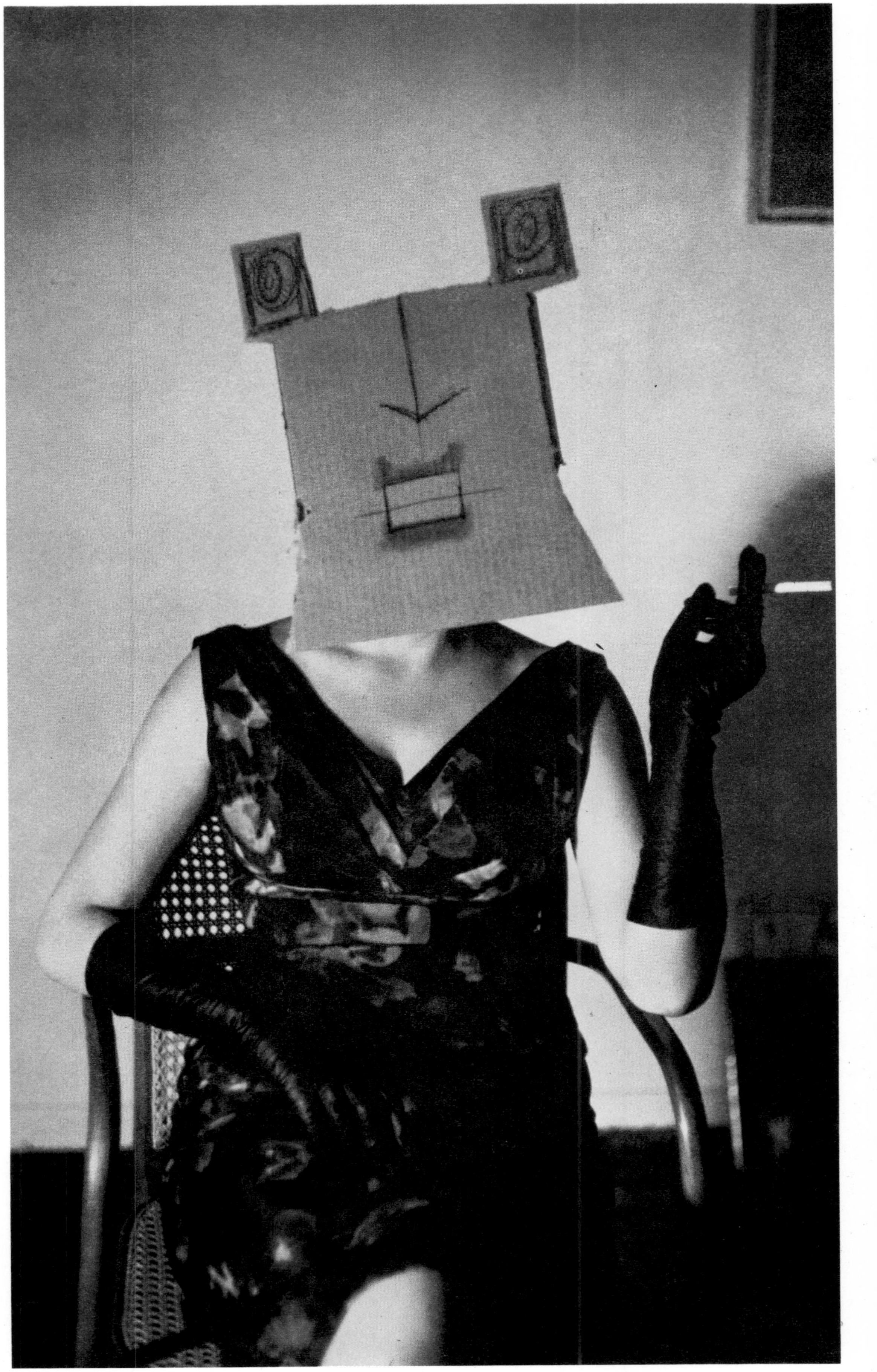

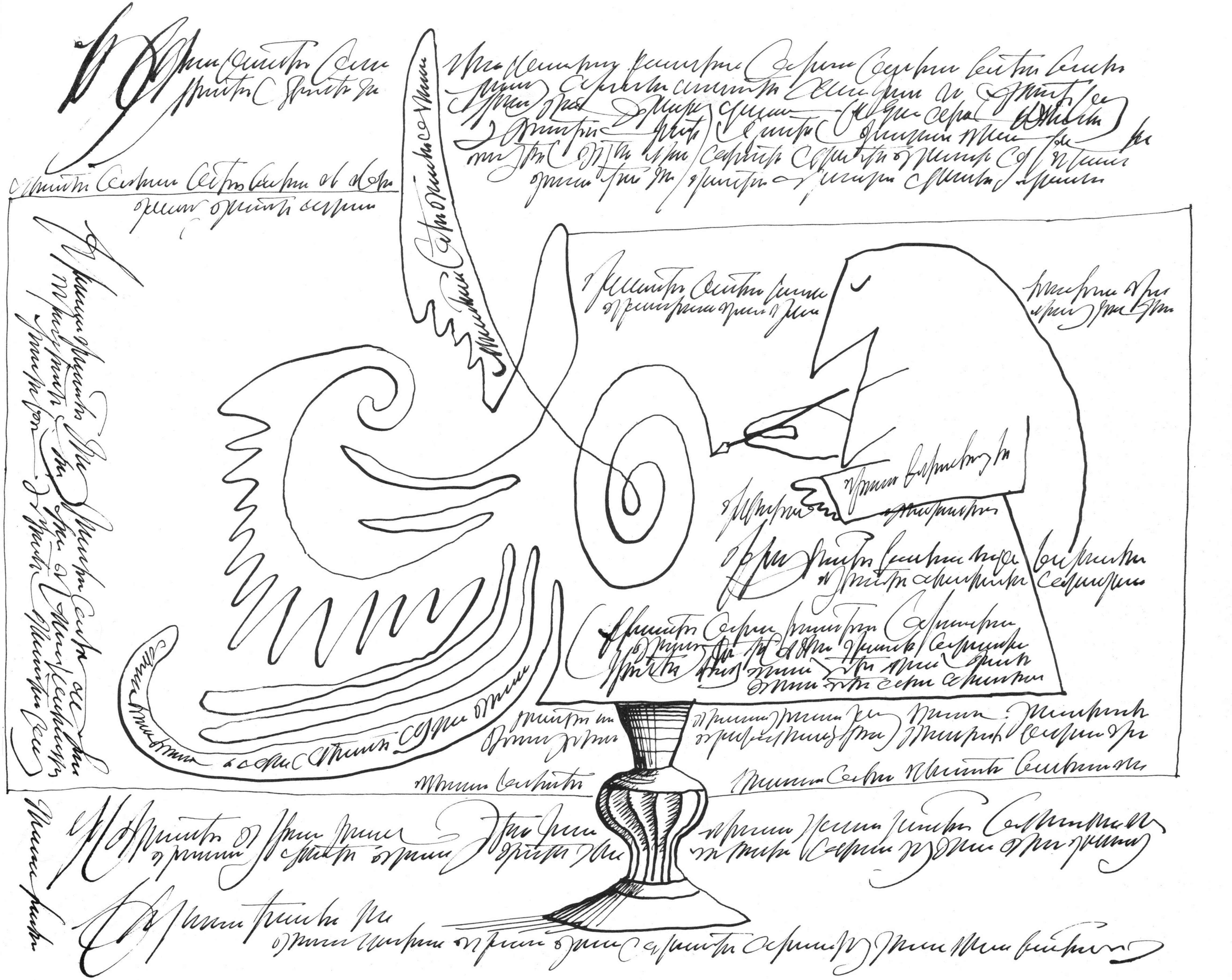

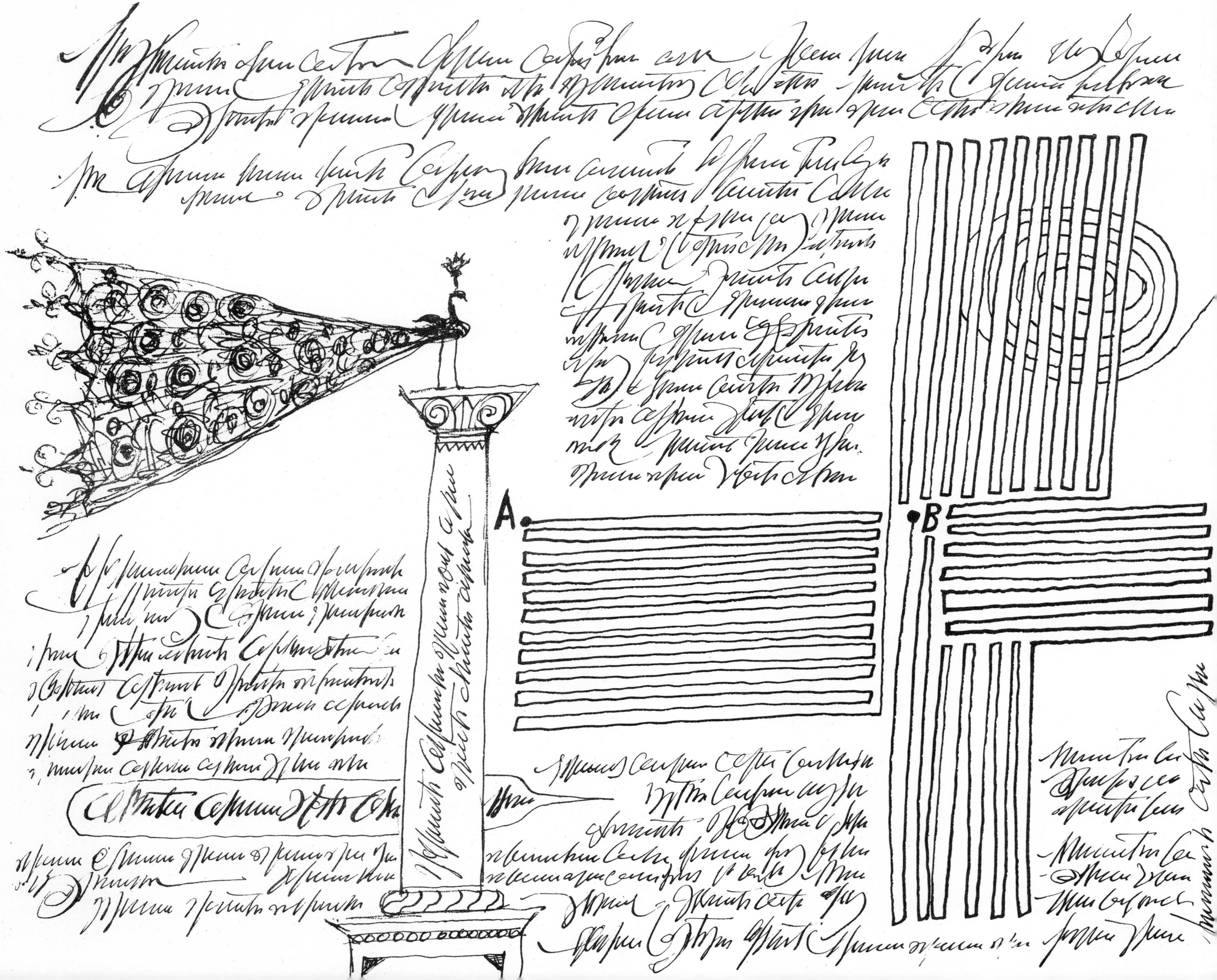
A
B

De cette édition originale du Masque, il a été tiré 300 exemplaires de tête numérotés de 1 à 300 comprenant une lithographie originale de Saul Steinberg justifiée et signée par l'artiste.

Les photographies sont de Inge Morath-Magnum. Michel Robic a traduit le texte de Harold Rosenberg.

Ce livre a été tiré sur les presses de Arte à Paris. Les clichés sont de Schwitter à Bâle, la reliure a été exécutée par Engel à Paris et la maquette est de Max Weber.

Achevé d'imprimer le 4 mars 1966 sur les presses de Arte à Paris.

MAP PAGES

106

**EUROPE AND
COUNTRY INDEX
ENDPAPER**

RUSSIA

DEN
FINLAND
ESTONIA
LATVIA
HUNGARY MOLDOVA
ATIA ROMANIA
SERBIA
BANIA BULG
GREECE

108

KAZAKHSTAN

110

MONGOLIA

166

104
TURKEY
GEORGIA
ARM. AZER.
TURKMENISTAN UZBEKISTAN
KYRGYZSTAN
TAJIK.

114

112

NORTH
KOREA

JAPAN

128
SYRIA
130
IRAQ
JORDAN

122
AFGHAN.
124
PAKISTAN

CHINA

SOUTH
KOREA

IRAN

KUWAIT
QATAR
U.A.E.
OMAN

NEPAL

126

INDIA

BANGLA-
DESH

BURMA

116

TAIWAN

Tropic of Cancer

137
EGYPT

BYA

SAUDI
ARABIA

120
LAOS

**PACIFIC
OCEAN**

156

CHAD
SUDAN
ERITREA
YEMEN
DJIBOUTI

SRI
LANKA

118
THAILAND
CAMB. VIETNAM

PHILIPPINES

CENTRAL
AFRICAN
REP.

SOUTH
SUDAN

ETHIOPIA

SOMALIA

131

121

142
UGANDA KENYA
GO
RWANDA
BURUNDI

CONGO
(DEM. REP OF THE)

TANZANIA

141

121

121 MALAYSIA

INDONESIA

Equator

154

GOLA

141

ZAMBIA MALAWI

141

MOZAMBIQUE

ZIMBABWE

MIBIA

BOTSWANA

MADAGASCAR

141

**INDIAN
OCEAN**

146

119

E. TIMOR

PAPUA
NEW GUINEA

148

150

150

AUSTRALIA

Tropic of Capricorn

SWAZILAND

SOUTH
AFRICA

LESOTHO

152

154

NEW
ZEALAND

MAP SYMBOLS

ADMINISTRATION			PHYSICAL FEATURES	
—— International boundaries	·········· Internal boundaries	**PERU** Country names	⌇ Perennial streams	Intermittent lakes	▲ 8848 Elevations in meters
– – International boundaries (undefined or disputed)	National parks	KENT Administrative area names	– · – Intermittent streams	Swamps and marshes	▼ 8500 Sea depths in meters
International boundaries show the *de facto* situation where there are rival claims to territory			Sand deserts	Permanent ice and glaciers	*1134* Height of lake surface above sea level in meters

OXFORD

NEW CONCISE

WORLD
ATLAS

OXFORD

NEW CONCISE
WORLD
ATLAS

FOURTH EDITION

THE EDITORS would like to thank **Richard Chiles** and the staff at
NPA Satellite Mapping, Edenbridge, Kent, UK (www.npa.cgg.com)
for sourcing and processing the satellite imagery that appears in the atlas.

Philip's,
a division of Octopus Publishing Group Limited,
Endeavour House, 189 Shaftesbury Avenue, London WC2H 8JY
An Hachette UK Company

Cartography by Philip's

Published in North America by
Oxford University Press
198 Madison Avenue
New York, NY 10016

www.oup.com/us

OXFORD
UNIVERSITY PRESS   Oxford is a registered trademark of Oxford University Press

Library of Congress Cataloging-in-Publication Data available

ISBN 978-0-19-982981-1

Printing (last digit): 9 8 7 6 5 4 3 2 1

Printed in Singapore

USER GUIDE

The reference maps which form the main body of this atlas have been prepared in accordance with the highest standards of international cartography to provide an accurate and detailed representation of the Earth. The scales and projections used have been carefully chosen to give balanced coverage of the world, while emphasizing the most densely populated and economically significant regions. A hallmark of Philip's mapping is the use of hill shading and relief coloring to create a graphic impression of landforms: this makes the maps exceptionally easy to read. However, knowledge of the key features employed in the construction and presentation of the maps will enable the reader to derive the fullest benefit from the atlas.

MAP SEQUENCE

The atlas covers the Earth continent by continent: first Europe; then its land neighbor Asia (mapped north before south, in a clockwise sequence), then Africa, Australia and Oceania, North America, and South America. This is the classic arrangement adopted by most cartographers since the 16th century. For each continent, there are maps at a variety of scales. First, physical relief

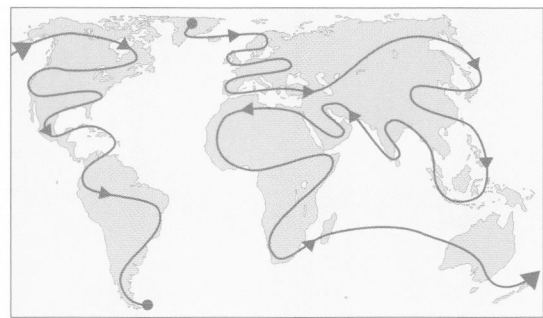

and political maps of the whole continent; then a series of larger-scale maps of the regions within the continent, each followed, where required, by still larger-scale maps of the most important or densely populated areas. The governing principle is that by turning the pages of the atlas, the reader moves steadily from north to south through each continent, with each map overlapping its neighbors.

MAP PRESENTATION

With very few exceptions (for example, for the Arctic and Antarctica), the maps are drawn with north at the top, regardless of whether they are presented upright or sideways on the page. In the borders will be found the map title; a locator diagram showing the area covered; continuation arrows showing the page numbers for maps of adjacent areas; the scale; the projection used; the degrees of latitude and longitude; and the letters and figures used in the index for locating place names and geographical features. Physical relief maps also have a height reference panel identifying the colors used for each layer of contouring.

MAP SYMBOLS

Each map contains a vast amount of detail which can only be conveyed clearly and accurately by the use of symbols. Points and circles of varying sizes locate and identify the relative importance of towns and cities; different styles of type are employed for administrative, geographical, and regional place names to aid identification. A variety of pictorial symbols denote landforms such as glaciers, marshes, and coral reefs, and man-made structures including roads, railroads, airports, and canals. International borders are shown by red lines. Where neighboring countries are in dispute, for example in parts of the Middle East, the maps show the *de facto* boundary between nations, regardless of the legal or historical situation. The symbols are explained on the front endpaper of the atlas.

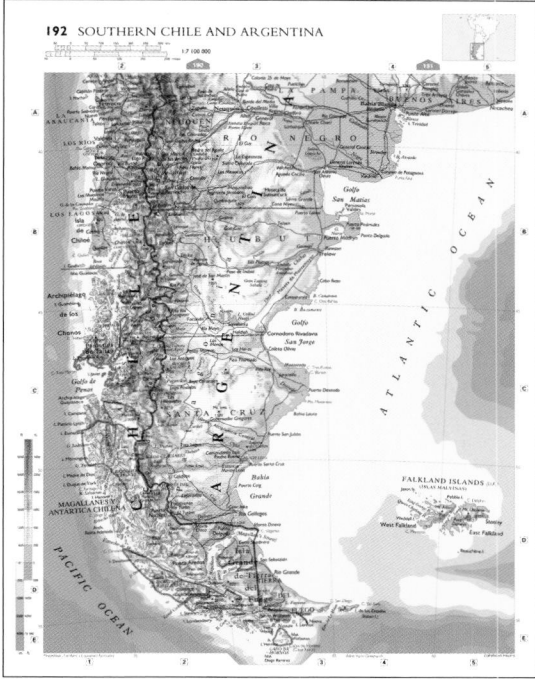

MAP SCALES

1:16 000 000
1 inch = 252 statute miles

The scale of each map is given in the numerical form known as the "representative fraction." The first figure is always one, signifying one unit of distance on the map; the second figure, usually in millions, is the number by which the map unit must be multiplied to give the equivalent distance on the Earth's surface. Calculations can easily be made in centimeters and kilometers, by dividing the Earth units figure by 100 000 (i.e. deleting the last five 0s). Thus 1:1 000 000 means 1 cm = 10 km. The calculation for inches and miles is more laborious, but 1 000 000 divided by 63 360 (the number of inches in a mile) shows that 1:1 000 000 means approximately 1 inch = 16 miles. The table below provides distance equivalents for scales down to 1:50 000 000.

LARGE SCALE		
1:1 000 000	1 cm = 10 km	1 inch = 16 miles
1:2 500 000	1 cm = 25 km	1 inch = 39.5 miles
1:5 000 000	1 cm = 50 km	1 inch = 79 miles
1:6 000 000	1 cm = 60 km	1 inch = 95 miles
1:8 000 000	1 cm = 80 km	1 inch = 126 miles
1:10 000 000	1 cm = 100 km	1 inch = 158 miles
1:15 000 000	1 cm = 150 km	1 inch = 237 miles
1:20 000 000	1 cm = 200 km	1 inch = 316 miles
1:50 000 000	1 cm = 500 km	1 inch = 790 miles
SMALL SCALE		

MEASURING DISTANCES

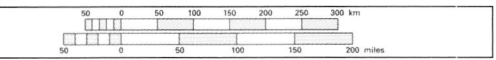

Although each map is accompanied by a scale bar, distances cannot always be measured with confidence because of the distortions involved in portraying the curved surface of the Earth on a flat page. As a general rule, the larger the map scale (that is, the lower the number of Earth units in the representative fraction), the more accurate and reliable will be the distance measured. On small-scale maps such as those of the world and of entire continents, measurement may only be accurate

along the "standard parallels," or central axes, and should not be attempted without considering the map projection.

MAP PROJECTIONS

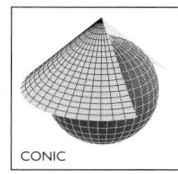  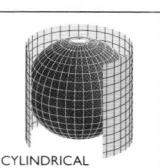

Unlike a globe, no flat map can give a true scale representation of the world in terms of area, shape, and position of every region. Each of the numerous systems that have been devised for projecting the curved surface of the Earth on to a flat page involves the sacrifice of accuracy in one or more of these elements. The variations in shape and position of land masses such as Alaska, Greenland, and Australia, for example, can be quite dramatic when different projections are compared. For this atlas, the guiding principle has been to select projections that involve the least distortion of size and distance. The projection used for each map is noted in the border. Most fall into one of three categories – conic, azimuthal, or cylindrical – whose basic concepts are shown above. Each involves plotting the forms of the Earth's surface on a grid of latitude and longitude lines, which may be shown as parallels, curves, or radiating spokes.

LATITUDE AND LONGITUDE

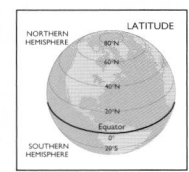 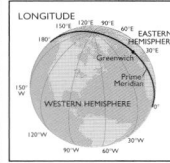 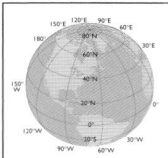

Accurate positioning of individual points on the Earth's surface is made possible by reference to the geometrical system of latitude and longitude. Latitude *parallels* are drawn west–east around the Earth and numbered by degrees north and south of the equator, which is designated 0° of latitude. Longitude *meridians* are drawn north–south and numbered by degrees east and west of the *prime meridian*, 0° of longitude, which passes through Greenwich in England. By referring to these coordinates and their subdivisions of minutes (1/60th of a degree) and seconds (1/60th of a minute), any place on Earth can be located to within a few hundred yards. Latitude and longitude are indicated by blue lines on the maps; they are straight or curved according to the projection employed. Reference to these lines is the easiest way of determining the relative positions of places on different maps, and for plotting compass directions.

NAME FORMS

For ease of reference, both English and local name forms appear in the atlas. Oceans, seas, and countries are shown in English throughout the atlas; country names may be abbreviated to their commonly accepted form (for example, Germany, not The Federal Republic of Germany). Conventional English forms are also used for place names on the smaller-scale maps of the continents. However, local name forms are used on all large-scale and regional maps, with the English form given in brackets only for important cities – the large-scale map of Russia and Northern Asia thus shows Moskva (Moscow). For countries which do not use a Roman script, place names have been transcribed according to the systems adopted by the British and US Geographic Names Authorities. For China, the Pin Yin system has been used, with some more widely known forms appearing in brackets, as with Beijing (Peking). Both English and local names appear in the index, the English form being cross-referenced to the local form.

CONTENTS

WORLD STATISTICS

COUNTRIES   8

CITIES   9

CLIMATE   10–11

PHYSICAL DIMENSIONS   12–13

IMAGES OF EARTH

LONDON, UNITED KINGDOM   16

AMSTERDAM, NETHERLANDS   17

ROME, ITALY   18

ISTANBUL, TURKEY   19

MUMBAI, INDIA   20

SINGAPORE CITY, SINGAPORE   21

BEIJING, CHINA   22

TOKYO, JAPAN   23

NOUAKCHOTT, MAURITANIA   24

CAIRO, EGYPT   25

JUBA, SOUTH SUDAN   26

CAPE TOWN, SOUTH AFRICA   27

SYDNEY, AUSTRALIA   28

CHRISTCHURCH, NEW ZEALAND   29

VANCOUVER, CANADA   30

QUÉBEC, CANADA   31

NEW YORK CITY, USA   32

CHICAGO, USA   33

SAN FRANCISCO, USA   34

LAS VEGAS, USA   35

MEXICO CITY, MEXICO   36

PANAMA CANAL, PANAMA   37

SANTIAGO, CHILE   38

RIO DE JANEIRO, BRAZIL   39

OCEAN SEAFLOORS

ARCTIC OCEAN SEAFLOOR   41

ATLANTIC OCEAN SEAFLOOR   42–43

PACIFIC OCEAN SEAFLOOR   44–45

INDIAN OCEAN SEAFLOOR   46

SOUTHERN OCEAN SEAFLOOR   47

WORLD MAPS

THE WORLD: PHYSICAL   50–51
1:84 000 000

THE WORLD: POLITICAL   52–53
1:84 000 000

ARCTIC OCEAN   54
1:31 100 000

ANTARCTICA   55
1:31 100 000

ATLANTIC OCEAN   56
1:45 000 000

GREENLAND   57
1:11 100 000

EUROPE

EUROPE: PHYSICAL   58
1:17 800 000

EUROPE: POLITICAL   59
1:17 800 000

SCANDINAVIA   60–61
1:5 300 000
Iceland 1:5 300 000
Færoe Islands 1:5 300 000

DENMARK AND SOUTHERN SWEDEN   62–63
1:2 200 000

IRELAND   64
1:1 800 000

SCOTLAND   65
1:1 800 000
Orkney Islands 1:1 800 000
Shetland Islands 1:1 800 000

ENGLAND AND WALES   66–67
1:1 800 000
Isles of Scilly 1:1 800 000

BRITISH ISLES   68
1:4 400 000

NETHERLANDS, BELGIUM
   AND LUXEMBOURG   69
1:2 200 000

NORTHERN FRANCE   70–71
1:2 200 000

SOUTHERN FRANCE   72–73
1:2 200 000

CENTRAL EUROPE   74–75
1:4 400 000

GERMANY AND SWITZERLAND   76–77
1:2 200 000

AUSTRIA, CZECH REPUBLIC
   AND SLOVAK REPUBLIC   78–79
1:2 200 000

HUNGARY, ROMANIA AND
   THE LOWER DANUBE   80–81
1:2 200 000

POLAND AND THE SOUTHERN BALTIC 82–83
1:2 200 000

BALTIC STATES, BELARUS
   AND UKRAINE   84–85
1:4 400 000

THE VOLGA BASIN AND
   THE CAUCASUS   86–87
1:4 400 000

WESTERN SPAIN AND PORTUGAL   88–89
1:2 200 000

EASTERN SPAIN   90–91
1:2 200 000
Menorca 1:2 200 000

NORTHERN ITALY, SLOVENIA
   AND CROATIA   92–93
1:2 200 000

SOUTHERN ITALY   94–95
1:2 200 000

THE BALKANS   96–97
1:2 200 000

SOUTHERN GREECE AND
   WESTERN TURKEY   98–99
1:2 200 000

THE BALEARICS, THE CANARIES
   AND MADEIRA   100
1:900 000 / 1:1 800 000

MALTA, CRETE, CORFU, RHODES
   AND CYPRUS   101
1:900 000 / 1:1 200 000

ASIA

ASIA: PHYSICAL   102
1:44 400 000

ASIA: POLITICAL   103
1:44 400 000

TURKEY AND TRANSCAUCASIA   104–105
1:4 400 000

RUSSIA AND NORTHERN ASIA   106–107
1:17 800 000

KAZAKHSTAN AND CENTRAL ASIA 108–109
1:8 900 000

CHINA AND THE FAR EAST   110–111
1:13 300 000
Hong Kong, Macau and Shenzhen 1:890 000

JAPAN   **112–113**
1:4 400 000
Ryukyu Islands 1:4 400 000

NORTHERN CHINA AND KOREA   **114–115**
1:5 300 000

SOUTHERN CHINA AND TAIWAN   **116–117**
1:5 300 000
Hainan 1:5 300 000

INDONESIA AND THE PHILIPPINES   **118–119**
1:11 100 000
Java and Madura 1:6 700 000
Bali 1:1 800 000

MAINLAND SOUTHEAST ASIA   **120–121**
1:5 300 000
Ko Phuket 1:900 000
Ko Samui 1:900 000
Pinang 1:900 000
Singapore 1:900 000

SOUTH ASIA   **122–123**
1:8 900 000

NORTHERN INDIA, PAKISTAN
   AND NEPAL   **124–125**
1:5 300 000
Jammu and Kashmir 1:5 300 000

SOUTHERN INDIA AND SRI LANKA   **126–127**
1:5 300 000
Lakshadweep Islands 1:5 300 000
Andaman and Nicobar Islands 1:5 300 000

THE MIDDLE EAST   **128–129**
1:6 200 000

THE NEAR EAST   **130**
1:2 200 000

ARABIA AND THE HORN OF AFRICA   **131**
1:13 300 000

AFRICA

AFRICA: PHYSICAL   **132**
1:37 300 000

AFRICA: POLITICAL   **133**
1:37 300 000

NORTHERN AFRICA   **134–135**
1:13 300 000
Azores 1:13 300 000
Cape Verde Islands 1:8 900 000

MOROCCO, ALGERIA AND TUNISIA   **136**
1:7 100 000

EGYPT   **137**
1:7 100 000

WEST AFRICA   **138–139**
1:7 100 000

CENTRAL AND SOUTHERN AFRICA   **140–141**
1:13 300 000
Seychelles 1:2 200 000
Réunion 1:2 200 000
Mauritius 1:2 200 000
Comoros 1:7 100 000
Madagascar 1:13 300 000

EAST AFRICA   **142–143**
1:7 100 000

SOUTHERN AFRICA   **144–145**
1:7 100 000

INDIAN OCEAN   **146**
1:45 000 000

AUSTRALIA AND OCEANIA

AUSTRALIA AND OCEANIA:
   PHYSICAL AND POLITICAL   **147**
1:44 400 000

WESTERN AUSTRALIA   **148–149**
1:7 100 000

EASTERN AUSTRALIA   **150–151**
1:7 100 000
Whitsunday Islands 1:2 200 000
Tasmania 1:7 100 000
Torres Strait 1:7 100 000

SOUTHEASTERN AUSTRALIA   **152–153**
1:3 500 000

NEW ZEALAND – NORTH ISLAND   **154**
1:3 100 000
Fiji 1:5 300 000

NEW ZEALAND – SOUTH ISLAND   **155**
1:3 100 000
Tahiti and Moorea 1:900 000
Chatham Islands 1:3 100 000

PACIFIC OCEAN   **156–157**
1:48 000 000

NORTH AMERICA

NORTH AMERICA: PHYSICAL   **158**
1:31 100 000

NORTH AMERICA: POLITICAL   **159**
1:31 100 000

CANADA   **160–161**
1:13 300 000
Northern Canada 1:13 300 000

WESTERN CANADA   **162–163**
1:6 200 000

EASTERN CANADA   **164–165**
1:6 200 000

UNITED STATES   **166–167**
1:13 300 000
Hawai'i 1:13 300 000
Alaska 1:13 300 000

UNITED STATES – WEST   **168–169**
1:6 250 000

CENTRAL AND SOUTHERN
   CALIFORNIA AND
   WESTERN WASHINGTON   **170–171**
1:2 200 000

UNITED STATES – MIDWEST
   AND NORTHEAST   **172–173**
1:6 250 000

NORTHEASTERN UNITED STATES   **174–175**
1:2 200 000

UNITED STATES – SOUTH   **176–177**
1:6 250 000

SOUTHEASTERN UNITED STATES   **178–179**
1:2 200 000

MEXICO   **180–181**
1:7 100 000

CENTRAL AMERICA AND
   THE WEST INDIES   **182–183**
1:7 100 000
Jamaica 1:2 700 000
Guadeloupe 1:1 800 000
Martinique 1:1 800 000
Puerto Rico 1:2 700 000
Virgin Islands 1:1 800 000
St Lucia 1:890 000
Barbados 1:890 000

SOUTH AMERICA

SOUTH AMERICA: PHYSICAL   **184**
1:31 100 000

SOUTH AMERICA: POLITICAL   **185**
1:31 100 000

SOUTH AMERICA – NORTH   **186–187**
1:14 200 000
Trinidad and Tobago 1:2 200 000

PERU AND THE CENTRAL ANDES   **188**
1:7 100 000

NORTHEASTERN BRAZIL   **189**
1:7 100 000

CENTRAL SOUTH AMERICA   **190–191**
1:7 100 000

SOUTHERN CHILE AND ARGENTINA   **192**
1:7 100 000

INDEX TO WORLD MAPS

    193–288

WORLD STATISTICS: COUNTRIES

This alphabetical list includes the principal countries and territories of the world. If a territory is not completely independent, the country it is associated with is named. The area figures give the total area of land, inland water, and ice. The population figures are 2012 estimates where available. The annual income is the Gross Domestic Product per capita in US dollars. The figures are the latest available, usually 2012 estimates.

Country/Territory	Area km^2 *Thousands*	Area $miles^2$ *Thousands*	Population *Thousands*	Capital	Annual Income US $
Afghanistan	652	252	30,420	Kabul	1,000
Albania	28.7	11.1	3,003	Tirana	8,000
Algeria	2,382	920	37,367	Algiers	7,500
American Samoa (US)	0.20	0.08	55	Pago Pago	8,000
Andorra	0.47	0.18	85	Andorra La Vella	37,200
Angola	1,247	481	18,056	Luanda	6,200
Anguilla (UK)	0.10	0.04	15	The Valley	12,200
Antigua & Barbuda	0.44	0.17	89	St John's	17,500
Argentina	2,780	1,074	42,192	Buenos Aires	18,200
Armenia	29.8	11.5	2,970	Yerevan	5,600
Aruba (Netherlands)	0.19	0.07	108	Oranjestad	21,800
Australia	7,741	2,989	22,016	Canberra	42,400
Austria	83.9	32.4	8,220	Vienna	42,500
Azerbaijan	86.6	33.4	9,494	Baku	10,700
Azores (Portugal)	2.2	0.86	236	Ponta Delgada	15,000
Bahamas	13.9	5.4	316	Nassau	31,300
Bahrain	0.69	0.27	1,248	Manama	28,200
Bangladesh	144	55.6	161,084	Dhaka	2,000
Barbados	0.43	0.17	288	Bridgetown	25,500
Belarus	208	80.2	9,644	Minsk	16,000
Belgium	30.5	11.8	10,438	Brussels	38,100
Belize	23.0	8.9	328	Belmopan	8,400
Benin	113	43.5	9,599	Porto-Novo	1,700
Bermuda (UK)	0.05	0.02	69	Hamilton	69,900
Bhutan	47.0	18.1	717	Thimphu	6,500
Bolivia	1,099	424	10,290	La Paz/Sucre	5,000
Bosnia-Herzegovina	51.2	19.8	3,879	Sarajevo	8,300
Botswana	582	225	2,098	Gaborone	16,800
Brazil	8,514	3,287	199,321	Brasília	12,000
Brunei	5.8	2.2	409	Bandar Seri Begawan	50,500
Bulgaria	111	42.8	7,038	Sofia	14,200
Burkina Faso	274	106	17,275	Ouagadougou	1,400
Burma (Myanmar)	677	261	54,585	Rangoon/Naypyidaw	1,400
Burundi	27.8	10.7	10,557	Bujumbura	600
Cambodia	181	69.9	14,953	Phnom Penh	2,400
Cameroon	475	184	20,130	Yaoundé	2,300
Canada	9,971	3,850	34,300	Ottawa	41,500
Canary Is. (Spain)	7.2	2.8	1,682	Las Palmas/Santa Cruz	19,900
Cape Verde Is.	4.0	1.6	524	Praia	4,100
Cayman Is. (UK)	0.26	0.10	53	George Town	43,800
Central African Republic	623	241	5,057	Bangui	800
Chad	1,284	496	10,976	Ndjaména	2,000
Chile	757	292	17,067	Santiago	18,400
China	9,597	3,705	1,343,240	Beijing	9,100
Colombia	1,139	440	45,239	Bogotá	10,700
Comoros	2.2	0.86	737	Moroni	1,300
Congo	342	132	4,366	Brazzaville	4,700
Congo (Dem. Rep. of the)	2,345	905	73,599	Kinshasa	400
Cook Is. (NZ)	0.24	0.09	11	Avarua	9,100
Costa Rica	51.1	19.7	4,636	San José	12,600
Croatia	56.5	21.8	4,480	Zagreb	18,100
Cuba	111	42.8	11,075	Havana	9,900
Curaçao (Netherlands)	0.44	0.17	146	Willemstad	15,000
Cyprus	9.3	3.6	1,138	Nicosia	26,900
Czech Republic	78.9	30.5	10,177	Prague	27,200
Denmark	43.1	16.6	5,543	Copenhagen	37,700
Djibouti	23.2	9.0	774	Djibouti	2,700
Dominica	0.75	0.29	73	Roseau	14,600
Dominican Republic	48.5	18.7	10,089	Santo Domingo	9,600
East Timor	14.9	5.7	1,144	Dili	9,500
Ecuador	284	109	15,224	Quito	8,800
Egypt	1,001	387	83,688	Cairo	6,600
El Salvador	21.0	8.1	6,091	San Salvador	7,700
Equatorial Guinea	28.1	10.8	685	Malabo	20,200
Eritrea	118	45.4	6,086	Asmara	800
Estonia	45.1	17.4	1,275	Tallinn	21,200
Ethiopia	1,104	426	91,196	Addis Ababa	1,200
Falkland Is. (UK)	12.2	4.7	3	Stanley	55,400
Faroe Is. (Denmark)	1.4	0.54	49	Tórshavn	30,500
Fiji	18.3	7.1	890	Suva	4,800
Finland	338	131	5,263	Helsinki	36,500
France	552	213	65,631	Paris	35,500
French Guiana (France)	90.0	34.7	203	Cayenne	8,300
French Polynesia (France)	4.0	1.5	275	Papeete	18,000
Gabon	268	103	1,608	Libreville	17,300
Gambia, The	11.3	4.4	1,840	Banjul	1,900
Georgia	69.7	26.9	4,571	Tbilisi	5,900
Germany	357	138	81,306	Berlin	39,100
Ghana	239	92.1	24,652	Accra	3,300
Gibraltar (UK)	0.006	0.002	29	Gibraltar Town	43,000
Greece	132	50.9	10,768	Athens	25,100
Greenland (Denmark)	2,176	840	58	Nuuk	38,400
Grenada	0.34	0.13	109	St George's	14,100
Guadeloupe (France)	1.7	0.66	453	Basse-Terre	7,900
Guam (US)	0.55	0.21	160	Agana	15,000
Guatemala	109	42.0	14,099	Guatemala City	5,200
Guinea	246	94.9	10,885	Conakry	1,100
Guinea-Bissau	36.1	13.9	1,629	Bissau	1,100
Guyana	215	83.0	742	Georgetown	8,000
Haiti	27.8	10.7	9,802	Port-au-Prince	1,300
Honduras	112	43.3	8,297	Tegucigalpa	4,600
Hungary	93.0	35.9	9,958	Budapest	19,800
Iceland	103	39.8	313	Reykjavik	39,400
India	3,287	1,269	1,205,074	New Delhi	3,900
Indonesia	1,905	735	248,645	Jakarta	5,000
Iran	1,648	636	78,869	Tehran	13,100
Iraq	438	169	31,129	Baghdad	4,600
Ireland	70.3	27.1	4,722	Dublin	41,700
Israel	20.6	8.0	7,591	Jerusalem	32,200
Italy	301	116	61,261	Rome	30,100
Ivory Coast (Côte d'Ivoire)	322	125	21,952	Yamoussoukro	1,700
Jamaica	11.0	4.2	2,889	Kingston	9,100
Japan	378	146	127,368	Tokyo	36,200
Jordan	89.3	34.5	6,509	Amman	6,000
Kazakhstan	2,725	1,052	17,522	Astana	13,900
Kenya	580	224	43,013	Nairobi	1,800
Kiribati	0.73	0.28	102	Tarawa	5,900
Korea, North	121	46.5	24,589	Pyŏngyang	1,800
Korea, South	99.3	38.3	48,861	Seoul	32,400
Kosovo	10.9	4.2	1,837	Pristina	7,400
Kuwait	17.8	6.9	2,646	Kuwait City	43,800
Kyrgyzstan	200	77.2	5,497	Bishkek	2,400

Country/Territory	Area km^2 *Thousands*	Area $miles^2$ *Thousands*	Population *Thousands*	Capital	Annual Income US $
Laos	237	91.4	6,586	Vientiane	3,000
Latvia	64.6	24.9	2,192	Riga	18,100
Lebanon	10.4	4.0	4,140	Beirut	15,900
Lesotho	30.4	11.7	1,930	Maseru	2,000
Liberia	111	43.0	3,888	Monrovia	700
Libya	1,760	679	5,613	Tripoli	13,300
Liechtenstein	0.16	0.06	37	Vaduz	89,400
Lithuania	65.2	25.2	3,526	Vilnius	20,100
Luxembourg	2.6	1.0	509	Luxembourg	80,700
Macedonia (FYROM)	25.7	9.9	2,082	Skopje	10,900
Madagascar	587	227	22,005	Antananarivo	1,000
Madeira (Portugal)	0.78	0.30	241	Funchal	25,800
Malawi	118	45.7	16,323	Lilongwe	900
Malaysia	330	127	29,180	Kuala Lumpur/Putrajaya	16,900
Maldives	0.30	0.12	394	Malé	8,700
Mali	1,240	479	15,494	Bamako	1,100
Malta	0.32	0.12	410	Valletta	26,100
Marshall Is.	0.18	0.07	68	Majuro	2,500
Martinique (France)	1.1	0.43	436	Fort-de-France	14,400
Mauritania	1,026	396	3,359	Nouakchott	2,100
Mauritius	2.0	0.79	1,313	Port Louis	15,600
Mayotte (France)	0.37	0.14	231	Mamoudzou	4,900
Mexico	1,958	756	114,975	Mexico City	15,300
Micronesia, Fed. States of	0.70	0.27	106	Palikir	2,200
Moldova	33.9	13.1	3,657	Kishinev	3,500
Monaco	0.001	0.0004	31	Monaco	63,400
Mongolia	1,567	605	3,180	Ulan Bator	5,400
Montenegro	14.0	5.4	657	Podgorica	11,700
Montserrat (UK)	0.10	0.39	5	Brades	8,500
Morocco	447	172	32,309	Rabat	5,300
Mozambique	802	309	23,516	Maputo	1,200
Namibia	824	318	2,166	Windhoek	7,800
Nauru	0.02	0.008	9	Yaren	5,000
Nepal	147	56.8	29,891	Katmandu	1,300
Netherlands	41.5	16.0	16,731	Amsterdam/The Hague	42,300
New Caledonia (France)	18.6	7.2	260	Nouméa	15,000
New Zealand	271	104	4,328	Wellington	28,800
Nicaragua	130	50.2	5,728	Managua	3,300
Niger	1,267	489	16,345	Niamey	900
Nigeria	924	357	170,124	Abuja	2,700
Northern Mariana Is. (US)	0.46	0.18	51	Saipan	12,500
Norway	324	125	4,707	Oslo	55,300
Oman	310	119	3,090	Muscat	28,500
Pakistan	796	307	190,291	Islamabad	2,900
Palau	0.46	0.18	21	Melekeok	8,100
Panama	75.5	29.2	3,510	Panamá	15,300
Papua New Guinea	463	179	6,310	Port Moresby	2,700
Paraguay	407	157	6,542	Asunción	6,100
Peru	1,285	496	29,550	Lima	10,700
Philippines	300	116	103,775	Manila	4,300
Poland	323	125	38,415	Warsaw	21,000
Portugal	88.8	34.3	10,781	Lisbon	23,000
Puerto Rico (US)	8.9	3.4	3,691	San Juan	16,300
Qatar	11.0	4.2	1,952	Doha	102,800
Réunion (France)	2.5	0.97	788	St-Denis	6,200
Romania	238	92.0	21,849	Bucharest	12,800
Russia	17,075	6,593	142,518	Moscow	17,700
Rwanda	26.3	10.2	11,690	Kigali	1,400
St Kitts & Nevis	0.26	0.10	51	Basseterre	15,500
St Lucia	0.54	0.21	162	Castries	13,300
St Vincent & Grenadines	0.39	0.15	104	Kingstown	11,900
Samoa	2.8	1.1	194	Apia	6,200
San Marino	0.06	0.02	32	San Marino	36,200
São Tomé & Príncipe	0.96	0.37	183	São Tomé	2,300
Saudi Arabia	2,150	830	26,535	Riyadh	25,700
Senegal	197	76.0	12,970	Dakar	1,900
Serbia	77.5	29.9	7,277	Belgrade	10,500
Seychelles	0.46	0.18	90	Victoria	26,200
Sierra Leone	71.7	27.7	5,486	Freetown	1,400
Singapore	0.68	0.26	5,353	Singapore City	60,900
Slovak Republic	49.0	18.9	5,483	Bratislava	24,300
Slovenia	20.3	7.8	1,997	Ljubljana	28,600
Solomon Is.	28.9	11.2	585	Honiara	3,400
Somalia	638	246	10,086	Mogadishu	600
South Africa	1,221	471	48,810	Cape Town/Pretoria	11,300
Spain	498	192	47,043	Madrid	30,400
Sri Lanka	65.6	25.3	21,481	Colombo	6,100
Sudan	1,886	728	34,207	Khartoum	2,400
Sudan, South	620	239	10,625	Juba	900
Suriname	163	63.0	560	Paramaribo	12,300
Swaziland	17.4	6.7	1,387	Mbabane	5,300
Sweden	450	174	9,104	Stockholm	41,700
Switzerland	41.3	15.9	7,926	Berne	45,300
Syria	185	71.5	22,531	Damascus	5,100
Taiwan	36.0	13.9	23,235	Taipei	38,500
Tajikistan	143	55.3	7,768	Dushanbe	2,200
Tanzania	945	365	46,913	Dodoma	1,700
Thailand	513	198	67,091	Bangkok	10,000
Togo	56.8	21.9	6,961	Lomé	1,100
Tonga	0.65	0.25	106	Nuku'alofa	7,500
Trinidad & Tobago	5.1	2.0	1,226	Port of Spain	20,400
Tunisia	164	63.2	10,733	Tunis	9,700
Turkey	775	299	79,749	Ankara	15,000
Turkmenistan	488	188	5,055	Ashkhabad	8,500
Turks & Caicos Is. (UK)	0.43	0.17	46	Cockburn Town	11,500
Tuvalu	0.03	0.01	11	Fongafale	3,300
Uganda	241	93.1	33,641	Kampala	1,400
Ukraine	604	233	44,854	Kiev	7,600
United Arab Emirates	83.6	32.3	5,314	Abu Dhabi	49,000
United Kingdom	242	93.4	63,047	London	36,700
United States of America	9,629	3,718	313,847	Washington, DC	49,800
Uruguay	175	67.6	3,316	Montevideo	15,800
Uzbekistan	447	173	28,394	Tashkent	3,500
Vanuatu	12.2	4.7	256	Port-Vila	4,900
Venezuela	912	352	28,048	Caracas	13,200
Vietnam	332	128	91,519	Hanoi	3,500
Virgin Is. (UK)	0.15	0.06	31	Road Town	38,500
Virgin Is. (US)	0.35	0.13	105	Charlotte Amalie	14,500
Wallis & Futuna Is. (France)	0.20	0.08	15	Mata-Utu	3,800
Yemen	528	204	24,772	Sana'	2,200
Zambia	753	291	13,817	Lusaka	1,700
Zimbabwe	391	151	12,620	Harare	500

WORLD STATISTICS: CITIES

This list shows the principal cities with more than 850,000 inhabitants. The figures are taken from the most recent census or estimate available, usually 2012, and as far as possible are the population of the metropolitan area or urban agglomeration. The list includes Metropolitan Statistical Areas from the United States 2010 Census. All the figures are in thousands. Local name forms have been used for the smaller cities (for example, Thessaloniki).

AFGHANISTAN	
Kabul	3,097
ALGERIA	
Algiers	2,916
ANGOLA	
Luanda	5,068
Huambo	1,098
ARGENTINA	
Buenos Aires	13,528
Córdoba	1,556
Rosario	1,283
Mendoza	1,072
San Miguel de Tucumán	868
ARMENIA	
Yerevan	1,116
AUSTRALIA	
Sydney	4,543
Melbourne	3,961
Brisbane	2,039
Perth	1,649
Adelaide	1,198
AUSTRIA	
Vienna	1,720
AZERBAIJAN	
Baku	2,123
BANGLADESH	
Dhaka	15,391
Chittagong	5,239
Khulna	1,781
Rajshahi	932
BELARUS	
Minsk	1,861
BELGIUM	
Brussels	1,949
Antwerpen	959
BENIN	
Cotonou	924
BOLIVIA	
Santa Cruz	1,719
La Paz	1,715
BRAZIL	
São Paulo	20,395
Rio de Janeiro	11,990
Belo Horizonte	5,910
Pôrto Alegre	4,115
Salvador	3,940
Recife	3,890
Fortaleza	3,740
Curitiba	3,490
Campinas	2,835
Brasília	2,330
Belém	2,205
Goiânia	2,155
Vitória	1,825
Santos	1,820
Manaus	1,802
Natal	1,315
São Luís	1,275
Guarulhos	1,222
Maceió	1,190
Joinville	1,065
Florianópolis	1,040
João Pessoa	1,010
Teresina	911
Duque de Caxias	855
BULGARIA	
Sofia	1,174
BURKINA FASO	
Ouagadougou	2,053
BURMA (MYANMAR)	
Rangoon	4,457
Mandalay	1,063
Naypyidaw	1,060
CAMBODIA	
Phnom Penh	1,550
CAMEROON	
Douala	2,449
Yaoundé	2,432
CANADA	
Toronto	5,573
Montréal	3,856
Vancouver	2,267
Calgary	1,216
Ottawa	1,208
Edmonton	1,142
CHAD	
Ndjamena	1,079
CHILE	
Santiago	6,355
Valparaíso	931
CHINA	
Shanghai	20,208
Beijing	15,594
Guangzhou, Guangdong	10,849
Shenzhen	10,630
Chongqing	9,977
Wuhan	9,158
Tianjin	8,744
Dongguan, Guangdong	7,280
Hong Kong	7,122
Chengdu	6,670
Foshan	6,486
Nanjing, Jiangsu	5,866
Harbin	5,687
Shenyang	5,568
Hangzhou	5,448
Xi'an, Shaanxi	4,975
Shantou	4,175
Zhengzhou	3,964
Qingdao	3,797
Jinan, Shandong	3,697
Changchun	3,694
Taiyuan, Shanxi	3,495
Kunming	3,472
Suzhou, Jiangsu	3,463
Wuxi, Jiangsu	3,366
Dalian	3,359
Changsha	3,335
Ürümqi	3,123
Hefei	3,012
Fuzhou, Fujian	2,897
Xiamen	2,880
Zhongshan	2,862
Shijiazhuang	2,841
Zibo	2,797
Ningbo	2,755
Wenzhou	2,733
Lanzhou	2,555
Guiyang	2,525
Nanchang	2,411
Changzhou, Jiangsu	2,405
Jinxi	2,268
Xuzhou	2,242
Nanning	2,136
Nanchong	2,046
Wanxian	1,963
Baotou	1,953
Jilin	1,942
Tangshan	1,927
Huzhou	1,856
Weifang	1,752
Anshan	1,694
Tianmen	1,676
Shangqiu	1,650
Lu'an	1,647
Haikou	1,624
Qiqihar	1,616
Daqing	1,603
Yangzhou	1,603
Xinghua	1,587
Luoyang	1,575
Pingxiang	1,562
Yantai	1,557
Xiantao	1,528
Hohhot	1,499
Linyi	1,454
Xianyang	1,450
Luzhou	1,447
Neijiang	1,441
Huainan	1,436
Changde	1,429
Suining, Sichuan	1,401
Datong	1,390
Liuzhou	1,390
Fushun	1,379
Xintai	1,334
Yancheng	1,330
Heze	1,318
Yiyang	1,318
Huai'an	1,316
Handan	1,306
Tai'an	1,276
Suqian	1,258
Jining, Shandong	1,246
Chifeng	1,238
Jingmen	1,228
Nanyang	1,227
Yuzhou	1,226
Xining	1,225
Zaozhuang	1,211
Zaoyang	1,210
Tianshui	1,199
Yueyang	1,184
Yongzhou	1,182
Baoding	1,177
Mudanjiang	1,171
Liupanshui	1,149
Anyang	1,144
Leshan	1,143
Hengyang	1,135
Jiangmen	1,130
Xiaoshan	1,130
Yixing	1,129
Yinchuan	1,119
Quanzhou	1,097
Zigong	1,087
Putian	1,084
Zhangjiakou	1,072
Jinzhou	1,070
Fuyu	1,068
Jixi	1,067
Yulin	1,060
Mianyang	1,052
Zhuzhou	1,047
Xinyang	1,045
Pingdingshan	1,041
Zhanjiang	1,041
Xinyi, Jiangsu	1,022
Lianyungang	1,017
Linqing	1,009
Jiamusi	1,006
Xiangfan	1,006
Huaibei	1,005
Guilin	992
Dongying	989
Benxi	980
Xiangtan	979
Puning	945
Xiangxiang	936
Zhangjiagang	936
Baoji	933
Xinyu	932
Yichun, Heilongjiang	916
Qinhuangdao	913
Yichun, Jiangxi	890
Zhaotong	879
Yuyao	876
Jinzhou	865
Anshun	864
Shaoguan	856
Xuanzhou	851
COLOMBIA	
Bogotá	8,743
Medellín	3,694
Cali	2,453
Barranquilla	1,900
Bucaramanga	1,120
Cartagena	988
CONGO	
Brazzaville	1,611
CONGO (DEM. REP. OF THE)	
Kinshasa	8,798
Lubumbashi	1,556
Mbuji-Mayi	1,504
Kananga	888
COSTA RICA	
San José	1,511
CROATIA	
Zagreb	1,067
CUBA	
Havana	2,116
CZECH REPUBLIC	
Prague	1,276
DENMARK	
Copenhagen	1,206
DOMINICAN REPUBLIC	
Santo Domingo	2,191
Santiago de los Caballeros	804
ECUADOR	
Guayaquil	2,287
Quito	1,622
EGYPT	
Cairo	11,169
Alexandria	4,494
Shubrâ el Kheima	937
EL SALVADOR	
San Salvador	1,605
ETHIOPIA	
Addis Ababa	2,979
FINLAND	
Helsinki	1,134
FRANCE	
Paris	10,620
Marseilles	1,489
Lyons	1,488
Lille	1,042
Nice	991
Toulouse	933
Bordeaux	852
GEORGIA	
Tbilisi	1,121
GERMANY	
Berlin	3,462
Hamburg	1,796
Munich	1,364
Cologne	1,006
GHANA	
Accra	2,573
Kumasi	2,019
GREECE	
Athens	3,414
Thessaloniki	883
GUATEMALA	
Guatemala City	1,168
GUINEA	
Conakry	1,786
HAITI	
Port-au-Prince	2,207
HONDURAS	
Tegucigalpa	1,088
HUNGARY	
Budapest	1,737
INDIA	
Delhi	22,654
Mumbai	19,744
Kolkata	14,402
Chennai	8,784
Bangalore	8,614
Hyderabad	7,837
Ahmedabad	6,425
Pune	5,100
Surat	4,661
Jaipur	3,102
Kanpur	2,928
Lucknow	2,926
Nagpur	2,511
Indore	2,188
Coimbatore	2,180
Patna	2,059
Bhopal	1,900
Vadodara	1,829
Agra	1,763
Vishakhapatnam	1,746
Ludhiana	1,622
Kochi	1,620
Nashik	1,579
Vijayawada	1,511
Madurai	1,472
Varanasi	1,443
Meerut	1,434
Rajkot	1,406
Jamshedpur	1,346
Faridabad	1,330
Srinagar	1,285
Ghaziabad	1,277
Jabalpur	1,273
Asansol	1,248
Allahabad	1,223
Aurangabad	1,201
Dhanbad	1,200
Amritsar	1,190
Solapur	1,155
Jodhpur	1,149
Raipur	1,140
Ranchi	1,137
Gwalior	1,111
Guwahati	1,075
Bhilainagar-Durg	1,069
Chandigarh	1,034
Thiruvananthapuram	1,030
Tiruchchirapalli	1,028
Kota	1,013
Trivandrum	1,010
Calicut	1,007
Mysore	991
Bareilly	990
Tiruppur	982
Hubli-Dharwad	950
Salem	925
Aligarh	919
Moradabad	900
Bhubaneswar	891
Jalandhar	880
Bhiwandi	859
Jammu	857
INDONESIA	
Jakarta	9,769
Surabaya	2,787
Bandung	2,429
Medan	2,118
Semarang	1,573
Palembang	1,455
Makassar	1,387
Batam	1,034
Bogor	978
Pekanbaru	955
Bandar Lampung	900
Denpasar	850
IRAN	
Tehran	7,304
Mashhad	2,713
Karaj	1,635
Esfahan	1,781
Tabriz	1,509
Shiraz	1,321
Ahvaz	1,082
Qom	1,065
Kermanshah	851
IRAQ	
Baghdad	6,036
Mosul	1,494
Irbil	1,039
Basra	942
As Sulaymaniyah	867
IRELAND	
Dublin	1,121
ISRAEL	
Tel Aviv-Yafo	3,381
Haifa	1,054
ITALY	
Rome	3,298
Milan	2,909
Naples	2,373
Turin	1,613
Palermo	915
IVORY COAST (CÔTE D'IVOIRE)	
Abidjan	4,288
Yamoussoukro	966
JAMAICA	
Kingston	875
JAPAN	
Tokyo	13,159
Yokohama	3,689
Osaka	2,665
Nagoya	2,264
Sapporo	1,916
Kobe	1,544
Kyoto	1,474
Fukuoka	1,463
Kawasaki	1,426
Saitama	1,222
Hiroshima	1,174
Kitakyushu	1,011
Sendai	1,008
Hamamatsu	1,000
Naha	970
Chiba	961
JORDAN	
Amman	1,179
KAZAKHSTAN	
Almaty	1,426
KENYA	
Nairobi	3,363
Mombasa	1,040
KOREA, NORTH	
Pyŏngyang	2,843
KOREA, SOUTH	
Seoul	9,888
Busan	3,372
Incheon	2,884
Daegu	2,447
Daejeon	1,538
Gwangju	1,503
Seognam	1,353
Suwon	1,159
Ulsan	1,100
Goyang	988
Bucheon	932
KUWAIT	
Kuwait City	2,406
LEBANON	
Beirut	2,022
LIBYA	
Tripoli	1,127
Benghazi	1,114
MADAGASCAR	
Antananarivo	1,987
MALAWI	
Lilongwe	870
Blantyre	860
MALAYSIA	
Kuala Lumpur	1,556
Klang	1,190
Johore Bharu	1,045
MALI	
Bamako	2,037
MEXICO	
Mexico City	20,446
Guadalajara	4,525
Monterrey	4,213
Puebla	2,335
Tijuana	1,820
Toluca	1,748
León	1,653
Ciudad Juárez	1,338
Torreón	1,242
Querétaro	1,143
San Luis Potosí	1,061
Mérida	1,040
Aguascalientes	957
Mexicali	957
Acapulco	883
Chihuahua	874
MONGOLIA	
Ulan Bator	1,184
MOROCCO	
Casablanca	3,046
Rabat	1,843
Fès	1,088
Marrakesh	939
MOZAMBIQUE	
Maputo	1,150
NEPAL	
Katmandu	1,015
NETHERLANDS	
Amsterdam	1,056
Rotterdam	1,014
NEW ZEALAND	
Auckland	1,452
NICARAGUA	
Managua	1,165
NIGER	
Niamey	1,297
NIGERIA	
Lagos	11,223
Kano	3,375
Ibadan	2,949
Abuja	2,153
Port Harcourt	1,894
Kaduna	1,524
Benin City	1,359
Ogbomosho	1,075
Aba	866
Maiduguri	851
NORWAY	
Oslo	915
PAKISTAN	
Karachi	13,876
Lahore	7,566
Faisalabad	3,038
Rawalpindi	2,026
Multan	1,775
Gujranwala	1,767
Hyderabad	1,701
Peshawar	1,523
Quetta	903
Islamabad	856
PANAMA	
Panamá	1,426
PARAGUAY	
Asunción	2,139
PERU	
Lima	9,130
PHILIPPINES	
Manila	11,862
Davao	1,565
Zamboanga	884
Cebu	855
POLAND	
Warsaw	1,723
Lódz	910
PORTUGAL	
Lisbon	2,843
Porto	1,367
PUERTO RICO	
San Juan	2,475
ROMANIA	
Bucharest	1,937
RUSSIA	
Moscow	11,621
St Petersburg	4,866
Novosibirsk	1,478
Yekaterinburg	1,355
Nizhniy Novgorod	1,245
Samara	1,166
Omsk	1,156
Kazan	1,147
Chelyabinsk	1,135
Rostov	1,092
Ufa	1,064
Volgograd	1,022
Perm	991
Krasnoyarsk	980
Voronezh	894
RWANDA	
Kigali	1,004
SAUDI ARABIA	
Riyadh	5,451
Jedda	3,578
Mecca	1,591
Medina	1,142
Dammam	941
SENEGAL	
Dakar	3,035
SERBIA	
Belgrade	1,135
SIERRA LEONE	
Freetown	1,007
SINGAPORE	
Singapore City	5,188
SOMALIA	
Mogadishu	1,554
SOUTH AFRICA	
Johannesburg	3,844
Cape Town	3,562
Durban	3,012
Pretoria	1,501
Vereeniging	1,200
Port Elizabeth	1,119
SPAIN	
Madrid	6,574
Barcelona	5,570
SRI LANKA	
Colombo	2,115
SUDAN	
Khartoum	4,632
SWEDEN	
Stockholm	1,385
SWITZERLAND	
Zürich	1,194
SYRIA	
Aleppo	3,164
Damascus	2,650
Homs	1,369
Hamah	933
TAIWAN	
Taipei	2,730
Kaohsiung	1,560
T'aichung	1,244
Tainan	1,205
TANZANIA	
Dar es Salaam	3,588
THAILAND	
Bangkok	8,426
Samut Prakan	1,212
TOGO	
Lomé	1,524
TUNISIA	
Tunis	2,385
TURKEY	
Istanbul	11,253
Ankara	4,194
Izmir	2,927
Bursa	1,713
Adana	1,468
Gaziantep	1,198
Konya	1,057
Antalya	907
UGANDA	
Kampala	1,659
UKRAINE	
Kiev	2,829
Kharkov	1,451
Dnepropetrovsk	1,100
Odessa	1,010
Donetsk	959
UNITED ARAB EMIRATES	
Dubai	1,978
Abu Dhabi	942
Sharjah	983
UNITED KINGDOM	
London	9,005
Birmingham	2,272
Manchester	2,213
Liverpool	1,519
Glasgow	1,137
Newcastle-upon-Tyne	874
UNITED STATES OF AMERICA	
New York	19,016
Los Angeles	12,945
Chicago	9,505
Dallas–Fort Worth	6,527
Houston	6,087
Philadelphia	5,992
Washington, DC	5,704
Miami	5,670
Atlanta	5,359
Boston	4,591
San Francisco	4,391
San Bernadino	4,305
Detroit	4,286
Phoenix–Mesa	4,263
Seattle	3,500
Minneapolis–St Paul	3,318
San Diego	3,140
Tampa–St Petersburg	2,825
St Louis	2,817
Baltimore	2,729
Denver	2,600
Pittsburgh	2,360
Portland	2,263
San Antonio	2,195
Sacramento	2,176
Orlando	2,171
Cincinnati	2,138
Cleveland	2,068
Kansas City	2,053
Las Vegas	1,970
San Jose	1,865
Columbus	1,858
Charlotte	1,795
Austin	1,784
Indianapolis	1,779
Norfolk–Virginia Beach	1,680
Nashville	1,617
Providence	1,600
Milwaukee	1,562
Jacksonville	1,360
Memphis	1,326
Louisville	1,295
Oklahoma	1,278
Richmond	1,269
Hartford	1,213
New Orleans	1,191
Raleigh	1,163
Salt Lake City	1,145
Buffalo	1,134
Birmingham	1,132
Rochester	1,055
Tucson	989
Honolulu	964
Tulsa	947
Fresno	943
Stamford	926
Albuquerque	899
Omaha	877
Albany	871
New Haven	861
URUGUAY	
Montevideo	1,672
UZBEKISTAN	
Tashkent	2,227
VENEZUELA	
Caracas	3,242
Maracaibo	2,310
Valencia	1,866
Barquisimeto	1,245
Maracay	1,115
VIETNAM	
Ho Chi Minh City	6,405
Hanoi	2,955
Can Tho	1,004
Haiphong	925
YEMEN	
Sana'	2,419
ZAMBIA	
Lusaka	1,802
ZIMBABWE	
Harare	1,542

WORLD STATISTICS: CLIMATE

Rainfall and temperature figures are provided for more than 70 cities around the world. As climate is affected by altitude, the height of each city is shown in meters beneath its name. For each location, the top row of figures shows the total rainfall or snow in millimeters, and the bottom row the average temperature in degrees Celsius; the total annual rainfall and average annual temperature are at the end of the rows. The map opposite shows the city locations.

CITY	JAN.	FEB.	MAR.	APR.	MAY	JUNE	JULY	AUG.	SEPT.	OCT.	NOV.	DEC.	YEAR
EUROPE													
Athens, Greece	62	37	37	23	23	14	6	7	15	51	56	71	402
107 m	10	10	12	16	20	25	28	28	24	20	15	11	18
Berlin, Germany	42	33	41	37	54	69	56	58	45	37	44	55	571
55 m	-1	0	4	9	14	17	19	18	15	9	5	1	9
Istanbul, Turkey	87	71	63	43	33	25	24	24	44	71	85	107	655
14 m	5	6	7	11	16	20	23	23	20	16	12	8	14
Lisbon, Portugal	111	110	69	54	44	16	3	4	33	62	93	103	702
77 m	11	12	14	16	17	20	22	23	21	18	14	12	17
London, UK	54	40	37	37	46	45	57	59	49	57	64	48	593
5 m	4	5	7	9	12	16	18	17	15	11	8	5	11
Málaga, Spain	61	51	62	46	26	5	1	3	29	64	64	62	474
33 m	12	13	16	17	19	29	25	26	23	20	16	13	18
Moscow, Russia	39	38	36	37	53	58	88	71	58	45	47	54	624
156 m	-13	-10	-4	6	13	16	18	17	12	6	-1	-7	4
Odessa, Ukraine	57	62	30	21	34	34	42	37	37	13	35	71	473
64 m	-3	-1	2	9	15	20	22	22	18	12	9	1	10
Paris, France	56	46	35	42	57	54	59	64	55	50	51	50	619
75 m	3	4	8	11	15	18	20	19	17	12	7	4	12
Rome, Italy	71	62	57	51	46	37	15	21	63	99	129	93	744
17 m	8	9	11	14	18	22	25	25	22	17	13	10	16
Shannon, Ireland	94	67	56	53	61	57	77	79	86	86	96	117	929
2 m	5	5	7	9	12	14	16	16	14	11	8	6	10
Stockholm, Sweden	43	30	25	31	34	45	61	76	60	48	53	48	554
44 m	-3	-3	-1	5	10	15	18	17	12	7	3	0	7
ASIA													
Bangkok, Thailand	8	20	36	58	198	160	160	175	305	206	66	5	1,397
2 m	26	28	29	30	29	29	28	28	28	28	26	25	28
Beirut, Lebanon	191	158	94	53	18	3	3	3	5	51	132	185	892
34 m	14	14	16	18	22	24	27	28	26	24	19	16	21
Colombo, Sri Lanka	89	69	147	231	371	224	135	109	160	348	315	147	2,365
7 m	26	26	27	28	28	27	27	27	27	27	26	26	27
Harbin, China	6	5	10	23	43	94	112	104	46	33	8	5	488
160 m	-18	-15	-5	6	13	19	22	21	14	4	-6	-16	3
Ho Chi Minh, Vietnam	15	3	13	43	221	330	315	269	335	269	114	56	1,984
9 m	26	27	29	30	29	28	28	28	27	27	27	26	28
Hong Kong, China	33	46	74	137	292	394	381	361	257	114	43	31	2,162
33 m	16	15	18	22	26	28	28	28	27	25	21	18	23
Jakarta, Indonesia	300	300	211	147	114	97	64	43	66	112	142	203	1,798
8 m	26	26	27	27	27	27	27	27	27	27	27	26	27

CITY	JAN.	FEB.	MAR.	APR.	MAY	JUNE	JULY	AUG.	SEPT.	OCT.	NOV.	DEC.	YEAR
ASIA (continued)													
Kabul, Afghanistan	34	60	68	72	23	1	6	2	2	4	19	22	313
1,815 m	-3	-1	6	13	18	22	25	24	20	14	7	3	12
Karachi, Pakistan	13	10	8	3	3	18	81	41	13	<3	3	5	196
4 m	19	20	24	28	30	31	30	29	28	28	24	20	26
Kolkata, India	10	31	36	43	140	297	325	328	252	114	20	5	1,600
6 m	20	22	27	30	30	30	29	29	29	28	23	19	26
Manama, Bahrain	8	18	13	8	3	0	0	0	0	0	18	18	81
5 m	17	18	21	25	29	32	33	34	31	28	24	19	26
Mumbai, India	3	3	3	3	18	485	617	340	264	64	13	3	1,809
11 m	24	24	26	28	30	29	27	27	27	28	27	26	27
New Delhi, India	23	18	13	8	13	74	180	172	117	10	3	10	640
218 m	14	17	23	28	33	34	31	30	29	26	20	15	25
Omsk, Russia	15	8	8	13	31	51	51	51	28	25	18	20	318
85 m	-22	-19	-12	-1	10	16	18	16	10	1	-11	-18	-1
Qazaly, Kazakhstan	10	10	13	13	15	5	5	8	8	10	13	15	125
63 m	-12	-11	-3	6	18	23	25	23	16	8	-1	-7	7
Shanghai, China	48	58	84	94	94	180	147	142	130	71	51	36	1,135
7 m	4	5	9	14	20	24	28	28	23	19	12	7	16
Singapore	252	173	193	188	173	173	170	196	178	208	254	257	2,413
10 m	26	27	28	28	28	28	28	27	27	27	27	27	27
Tehran, Iran	46	38	46	36	13	3	3	3	3	8	20	31	246
1,220 m	2	5	9	16	21	26	30	29	25	18	12	6	17
Tokyo, Japan	48	74	107	135	147	165	142	152	234	208	97	56	1,565
6 m	3	4	7	13	17	21	25	26	23	17	11	6	14
Ulan Bator, Mongolia	3	3	3	5	10	28	76	51	23	5	5	3	208
1,325 m	-26	-21	-13	-1	6	14	16	14	8	-1	-13	-22	-3
Verkhoyansk, Russia	5	5	3	5	8	23	28	25	13	8	8	5	134
100 m	-50	-45	-32	-15	0	12	14	9	2	-15	-38	-48	-17
AFRICA													
Addis Ababa, Ethiopia	3	3	25	135	213	201	206	239	102	28	3	0	1,151
2,450 m	19	20	20	20	19	18	18	19	21	22	21	20	20
Antananarivo, Madag.	300	279	178	53	18	8	8	10	18	61	135	287	1,356
1,372 m	21	21	21	19	18	15	14	15	17	19	21	21	19
Cairo, Egypt	5	4	4	1	1	0	0	0	0	1	4	6	26
116 m	13	15	18	21	25	28	28	28	26	24	20	15	22
Cape Town, S. Africa	15	8	18	48	79	84	89	66	43	31	18	10	508
17 m	21	21	20	17	14	13	12	13	14	16	18	19	17
Jo'burg, S. Africa	114	109	89	38	25	8	8	8	23	56	107	125	709
1,665 m	20	20	18	16	13	10	11	13	16	18	19	20	16

CITY	JAN.	FEB.	MAR.	APR.	MAY	JUNE	JULY	AUG.	SEPT.	OCT.	NOV.	DEC.	YEAR
AFRICA (continued)													
Khartoum, Sudan	3	3	3	3	3	8	53	71	18	5	3	0	158
390 m	24	25	28	31	33	34	32	31	32	32	28	25	29
Kinshasa, Congo (D.R.)	135	145	196	196	158	8	3	3	31	119	221	142	1,354
325 m	26	26	27	27	26	24	23	24	25	26	26	26	25
Lagos, Nigeria	28	46	102	150	269	460	279	64	140	206	69	25	1,836
3 m	27	28	29	28	28	26	26	25	26	26	28	28	27
Lusaka, Zambia	231	191	142	18	3	3	3	0	3	10	91	150	836
1,277 m	21	22	21	21	19	16	16	18	22	24	23	22	21
Monrovia, Liberia	31	56	97	216	516	973	996	373	744	772	236	130	5,138
23 m	26	26	27	27	26	25	24	25	25	25	26	26	26
Nairobi, Kenya	38	64	125	211	158	46	15	23	31	53	109	86	958
820 m	19	19	19	19	18	16	16	16	18	19	18	18	18
Timbuktu, Mali	1	0	0	1	4	16	54	74	29	4	0	0	183
301 m	22	24	28	32	34	35	32	30	32	31	28	23	29
Tunis, Tunisia	64	51	41	36	18	8	3	8	33	51	48	61	419
66 m	10	11	13	16	19	23	26	27	25	20	16	11	18
Walvis Bay, Namibia	3	5	8	3	3	3	3	3	3	3	3	3	23
7 m	19	19	19	18	17	16	15	14	14	15	17	18	18
AUSTRALIA, NEW ZEALAND AND ANTARCTICA													
Alice Springs, Aust.	43	33	28	10	15	13	8	8	8	18	31	38	252
579 m	29	28	25	20	15	12	12	14	18	23	26	28	21
Christchurch, NZ	56	43	48	48	66	66	69	48	46	43	48	56	638
10 m	16	16	14	12	9	6	6	7	9	12	14	16	11
Darwin, Australia	386	312	254	97	15	3	3	3	13	51	119	239	1,491
30 m	29	29	29	29	28	26	25	26	28	29	30	29	28
Mawson, Antarctica	11	30	20	10	44	180	4	40	3	20	0	0	362
14 m	0	−5	−10	−14	−15	−16	−18	−18	−19	−13	−5	−1	−11
Perth, Australia	8	10	20	43	130	180	170	149	86	56	20	13	881
60 m	23	23	22	19	16	14	13	13	15	16	19	22	18
Sydney, Australia	89	102	127	135	127	117	117	76	73	71	73	73	1,181
42 m	22	22	21	18	15	13	12	13	15	18	19	21	17
NORTH AMERICA													
Anchorage, USA	20	18	15	10	13	18	41	66	66	56	25	23	371
40 m	−11	−8	−5	2	7	12	14	13	9	2	−5	−11	2
Chicago, USA	51	51	66	71	86	89	84	81	79	66	61	51	836
251 m	−4	−3	2	9	14	20	23	22	19	12	5	−1	10
Churchill, Canada	15	13	18	23	32	44	46	58	51	43	39	21	402
13 m	−28	−26	−20	−10	−2	6	12	11	5	−2	−12	−22	−7
Edmonton, Canada	25	19	19	22	43	77	89	78	39	17	16	25	466
676 m	−15	−10	−5	4	11	15	17	16	11	6	−4	−10	3
Honolulu, USA	104	66	79	48	25	18	23	28	36	48	64	104	643
12 m	23	18	19	20	22	24	25	26	26	24	22	19	22
Houston, USA	89	76	84	91	119	117	99	99	104	94	89	109	1,171
12 m	12	13	17	21	24	27	28	29	26	22	16	12	21

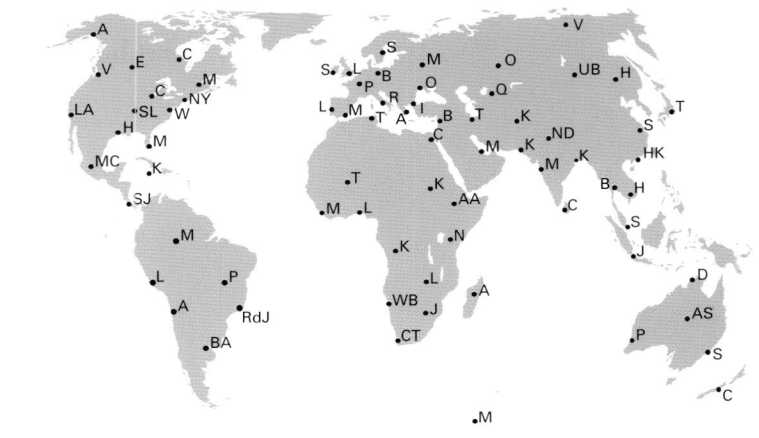

CITY	JAN.	FEB.	MAR.	APR.	MAY	JUNE	JULY	AUG.	SEPT.	OCT.	NOV.	DEC.	YEAR
NORTH AMERICA (continued)													
Kingston, Jamaica	23	15	23	31	102	89	38	91	99	180	74	36	800
34 m	25	25	25	26	26	28	28	28	27	27	26	26	26
Los Angeles, USA	79	76	71	25	10	3	3	3	5	15	31	66	381
95 m	13	14	14	16	17	19	21	22	21	18	16	14	17
Mexico City, Mexico	13	5	10	20	53	119	170	152	130	51	18	8	747
2,309 m	12	13	16	18	19	19	17	18	18	16	14	13	16
Miami, USA	71	53	64	81	173	178	155	160	203	234	71	51	1,516
8 m	20	20	22	23	25	27	28	28	27	25	22	21	24
Montréal, Canada	72	65	74	74	66	82	90	92	88	76	81	87	946
57 m	−10	−9	−3	−6	13	18	21	20	15	9	2	−7	6
New York City, USA	94	97	91	81	81	84	107	109	86	89	76	91	1,092
96 m	−1	−1	3	10	16	20	23	23	21	15	7	2	11
St Louis, USA	58	64	89	97	114	114	89	86	81	74	71	64	1,001
173 m	0	1	7	13	19	24	26	26	22	15	8	2	14
San José, Costa Rica	15	5	20	46	229	241	211	241	305	300	145	41	1,798
1,146 m	19	19	21	21	22	21	21	21	21	20	20	19	20
Vancouver, Canada	154	115	101	60	52	45	32	41	67	114	150	182	1,113
14 m	3	5	6	9	12	15	17	17	14	10	6	4	10
Washington, DC, USA	86	76	91	84	94	99	112	109	94	74	66	79	1,064
22 m	1	2	7	12	18	23	25	24	20	14	8	3	13
SOUTH AMERICA													
Antofagasta, Chile	0	0	0	3	3	3	5	3	3	3	3	0	13
94 m	21	21	20	18	16	15	14	14	15	16	18	19	17
Buenos Aires, Arg.	122	123	154	107	92	50	53	63	78	139	131	103	1,215
27 m	23	23	21	17	13	9	10	11	13	15	19	22	16
Lima, Peru	3	3	3	3	5	5	8	8	8	3	3	3	41
120 m	23	24	24	22	19	17	17	16	17	18	19	21	20
Manaus, Brazil	249	231	262	221	170	84	58	38	46	107	142	203	1,811
44 m	28	28	28	27	28	28	28	28	29	29	29	28	28
Paraná, Brazil	237	236	239	102	13	3	3	5	28	127	231	310	1,582
260 m	23	23	23	23	23	21	21	22	24	24	24	23	23
Rio de Janeiro, Brazil	125	122	130	107	79	53	41	43	66	79	104	137	1,082
61 m	26	26	25	24	22	21	21	21	21	22	23	25	23

WORLD STATISTICS: PHYSICAL DIMENSIONS

Each topic list is divided into continents and within a continent the items are listed in order of size. The bottom part of many of the lists is selective in order to give examples from as many different countries as possible. The order of the continents is as in the atlas, Europe through to South America. The world top ten are shown in square brackets; in the case of mountains this has not been done because the world top 30 are all in Asia. The figures are rounded as appropriate.

WORLD, CONTINENTS, OCEANS

THE WORLD

	km²	miles²	%
The World	509,450,000	196,672,000	–
Land	149,450,000	57,688,000	29.3
Water	360,000,000	138,984,000	70.7
Asia	44,500,000	17,177,000	29.8
Africa	30,302,000	11,697,000	20.3
North America	24,241,000	9,357,000	16.2
South America	17,793,000	6,868,000	11.9
Antarctica	14,100,000	5,443,000	9.4
Europe	9,957,000	3,843,000	6.7
Australia and Oceania	8,557,000	3,303,000	5.7
Pacific Ocean	155,557,000	60,061,000	46.4
Atlantic Ocean	76,762,000	29,638,000	22.9
Indian Ocean	68,556,000	26,470,000	20.4
Southern Ocean	20,327,000	7,848,000	6.1
Arctic Ocean	14,056,000	5,427,000	4.2

SEAS

PACIFIC

	km²	miles²
South China Sea	2,974,600	1,148,500
Bering Sea	2,268,000	875,000
Sea of Okhotsk	1,528,000	590,000
East China and Yellow Sea	1,249,000	482,000
Sea of Japan	1,008,000	389,000
Gulf of California	162,000	62,500
Bass Strait	75,000	29,000

ATLANTIC

	km²	miles²
Caribbean Sea	2,766,000	1,068,000
Mediterranean Sea	2,516,000	971,000
Gulf of Mexico	1,543,000	596,000
Hudson Bay	1,232,000	476,000
North Sea	575,000	223,000
Black Sea	462,000	178,000
Baltic Sea	422,170	163,000
Gulf of St Lawrence	238,000	92,000

INDIAN

	km²	miles²
Red Sea	438,000	169,000
Persian Gulf	239,000	92,000

MOUNTAINS

EUROPE

		m	ft
Elbrus	Russia	5,642	18,510
Dykh Tau	Russia	5,203	17,070
Shkhara	Russia/Georgia	5,201	17,064
Koshtan Tau	Russia	5,152	16,903
Kazbek	Russia/Georgia	5,047	16,558
Pushkin	Russia/Georgia	5,033	16,512
Katyn Tau	Russia/Georgia	4,979	16,335
Shota Rustaveli	Russia/Georgia	4,860	15,945
Mont Blanc	France/Italy	4,808	15,774
Monte Rosa	Italy/Switzerland	4,634	15,203
Dom	Switzerland	4,545	14,911
Liskamm	Switzerland	4,527	14,852
Weisshorn	Switzerland	4,505	14,780
Tebulos	Russia/Georgia	4,492	14,737
Taschorn	Switzerland	4,490	14,730
Matterhorn/Cervino	Italy/Switzerland	4,478	14,691
Mont Maudit	France/Italy	4,465	14,649
Bazar Dyuzi	Russia/Azerbaijan	4,462	14,639
Grandes Jorasses	France/Italy	4,208	13,806
Jungfrau	Switzerland	4,158	13,642
Barre des Ecrins	France	4,102	13,458
Gran Paradiso	Italy	4,061	13,323
Piz Bernina	Italy/Switzerland	4,049	13,284
Eiger	Switzerland	3,970	13,025
Grossglockner	Austria	3,797	12,457
Mulhacén	Spain	3,478	11,411
Etna	Italy	3,323	10,902
Zugspitze	Germany	2,962	9,718
Olympus	Greece	2,917	9,570
Galdhøpiggen	Norway	2,469	8,100
Ben Nevis	UK	1,344	4,408

ASIA

		m	ft
Everest	China/Nepal	8,850	29,035
K2 (Godwin Austen)	China/Kashmir	8,611	28,251
Kanchenjunga	India/Nepal	8,598	28,208
Lhotse	China/Nepal	8,516	27,939
Makalu	China/Nepal	8,481	27,824
Cho Oyu	China/Nepal	8,201	26,906
Dhaulagiri	Nepal	8,167	26,795
Manaslu	Nepal	8,156	26,758
Nanga Parbat	Kashmir	8,126	26,660
Annapurna	Nepal	8,078	26,502
Gasherbrum	China/Kashmir	8,068	26,469
Broad Peak	China/Kashmir	8,051	26,414
Xixabangma Feng	China	8,012	26,286
Gayachung Kang	Nepal	7,897	25,909
Himalchuli	Nepal	7,893	25,896
Disteghil Sar	Kashmir	7,885	25,869
Nuptse	Nepal	7,879	25,849
Kangbachen	Nepal	7,858	25,781
Khunyang Chhish	Kashmir	7,852	25,761
Masherbrum	Kashmir	7,821	25,659
Nanda Devi	India	7,817	25,646
Rakaposhi	Kashmir	7,788	25,551
Batura	Kashmir	7,785	25,541
Namche Barwa	China	7,782	25,531
Kamet	India	7,756	25,447
Soltoro Kangri	Pakistan	7,742	25,400
Gurla Mandhata	China	7,728	25,354
Trivor	Pakistan	7,720	25,328
Kongur Shan	China	7,719	25,324
Jannu	Nepal	7,710	25,295
Tirich Mir	Pakistan	7,690	25,229
K'ula Shan	Bhutan/China	7,543	24,747
Pik Imeni Ismail Samani	Tajikistan	7,495	24,590
Demavend	Iran	5,604	18,386
Ararat	Turkey	5,165	16,945
Gunong Kinabalu	Malaysia (Borneo)	4,101	13,455
Yu Shan	Taiwan	3,952	12,966
Fuji-San	Japan	3,776	12,388

AFRICA

		m	ft
Kilimanjaro	Tanzania	5,895	19,340
Mt Kenya	Kenya	5,199	17,057
Ruwenzori (Margherita)	Uganda/Congo (D.R.)	5,109	16,762
Meru	Tanzania	4,565	14,977
Ras Dashen	Ethiopia	4,533	14,872
Karisimbi	Rwanda/Congo (D.R.)	4,507	14,787
Mt Elgon	Kenya/Uganda	4,321	14,176
Batu	Ethiopia	4,307	14,130
Guna	Ethiopia	4,231	13,882
Toubkal	Morocco	4,165	13,665
Irhil Mgoun	Morocco	4,071	13,356
Mt Cameroun	Cameroon	4,070	13,353
Amba Ferit	Ethiopia	3,875	13,042
Pico del Teide	Spain (Tenerife)	3,718	12,198
Thabana Ntlenyana	Lesotho	3,482	11,424
Emi Koussi	Chad	3,415	11,204
Mt aux Sources	Lesotho/South Africa	3,282	10,768
Piton des Neiges	Réunion	3,069	10,069

OCEANIA

		m	ft
Puncak Jaya	Indonesia	4,884	16,024
Puncak Trikora	Indonesia	4,730	15,518
Puncak Mandala	Indonesia	4,702	15,427
Mt Wilhelm	Papua New Guinea	4,508	14,790
Mauna Kea	USA (Hawai'i)	4,205	13,796
Mauna Loa	USA (Hawai'i)	4,169	13,678
Aoraki Mt Cook	New Zealand	3,753	12,313
Mt Popomanaseu	Solomon Islands	2,439	8,002
Mt Orohena	French Polynesia (Tahiti)	2,241	7,352
Mt Kosciuszko	Australia	2,228	7,310

NORTH AMERICA

		m	ft
Mt McKinley (Denali)	USA (Alaska)	6,194	20,321
Mt Logan	Canada	5,959	19,551
Pico de Orizaba	Mexico	5,610	18,405
Mt St Elias	USA/Canada	5,489	18,008
Popocatépetl	Mexico	5,452	17,887

NORTH AMERICA (continued)

		m	ft
Mt Foraker	USA (Alaska)	5,304	17,401
Iztaccihuatl	Mexico	5,230	17,159
Mt Lucania	Canada	5,226	17,146
Mt Steele	Canada	5,073	16,644
Mt Bona	USA (Alaska)	5,005	16,420
Mt Blackburn	USA (Alaska)	4,996	16,391
Mt Sanford	USA (Alaska)	4,949	16,237
Mt Wood	Canada	4,840	15,880
Nevado de Toluca	Mexico	4,690	15,387
Mt Fairweather	USA (Alaska)	4,663	15,298
Mt Hunter	USA (Alaska)	4,442	14,573
Mt Whitney	USA	4,418	14,495
Mt Elbert	USA	4,399	14,432
Mt Harvard	USA	4,395	14,419
Mt Rainier	USA	4,392	14,409
Blanca Peak	USA	4,372	14,344
Longs Peak	USA	4,345	14,255
Tajumulco	Guatemala	4,220	13,845
Grand Teton	USA	4,197	13,770
Mt Waddington	Canada	4,019	13,186
Mt Robson	Canada	3,954	12,972
Chirripó Grande	Costa Rica	3,819	12,529
Pico Duarte	Dominican Rep.	3,175	10,417

SOUTH AMERICA

		m	ft
Aconcagua	Argentina	6,962	22,841
Ojos del Salado	Argentina/Chile	6,863	22,615
Monte Pissis	Argentina	6,793	22,287
Nevado Huascarán	Peru	6,768	22,205
Cerro Bonete	Argentina	6,759	22,175
Cerro Llullaillaco	Argentina/Chile	6,739	22,110
Cerro Mercedario	Argentina/Chile	6,720	22,047
Yerupaja	Peru	6,632	21,758
Nevado de Tres Cruces	Argentina/Chile	6,620	21,719
Tupungato	Argentina/Chile	6,570	21,555
Sajama	Bolivia	6,520	21,391
Coropuna	Peru	6,425	21,079
Illimani	Bolivia	6,402	21,004
Ausangate	Peru	6,384	20,945
Nevado de Cachi	Argentina	6,380	20,932
Cerro del Toro	Argentina	6,380	20,932
Siula Grande	Peru	6,356	20,853
Chimborazo	Ecuador	6,310	20,702
Incahuasi	Argentina/Chile	6,218	20,400
Alpamayo	Peru	5,947	19,511
Cerro Galan	Argentina	5,912	19,396
Cotapaxi	Ecuador	5,896	19,344
Pico Cristóbal Colón	Colombia	5,775	18,947
Pico Bolivar	Venezuela	4,981	16,342

ANTARCTICA

		m	ft
Vinson Massif		4,897	16,066
Mt Kirkpatrick		4,528	14,855
Mt Markham		4,349	14,268

OCEAN DEPTHS

ATLANTIC OCEAN

	m	ft	
Puerto Rico (Milwaukee) Deep	8,604	28,232	[7]
Cayman Trench	7,680	25,197	[10]
Gulf of Mexico	5,203	17,070	
Mediterranean Sea	5,121	16,801	
Black Sea	2,211	7,254	
North Sea	660	2,165	
Baltic Sea	463	1,519	
Hudson Bay	258	846	

INDIAN OCEAN

	m	ft
Java Trench	7,450	24,442
Red Sea	2,635	8,454
Persian Gulf	73	239

PACIFIC OCEAN

	m	ft	
Mariana Trench	11,022	36,161	[1]
Tonga Trench	10,882	35,702	[2]
Japan Trench	10,554	34,626	[3]
Kuril Trench	10,542	34,587	[4]
Mindanao Trench	10,497	34,439	[5]
Kermadec Trench	10,047	32,962	[6]

PACIFIC OCEAN (continued)		m	ft	
Peru–Chile Trench		8,050	26,410	[8]
Aleutian Trench		7,822	25,662	[9]

ARCTIC OCEAN		m	ft	
Molloy Deep		5,608	18,399	

SOUTHERN OCEAN		m	ft	
South Sandwich Trench		7,235	23,737	

LAND LOWS

		m	ft
Caspian Sea	Europe	−28	−92
Dead Sea	Asia	−422	−1,384
Lake Assal	Africa	−156	−512
Lake Eyre North	Oceania	−16	−52
Death Valley	North America	−86	−282
Laguna del Carbón	South America	−105	−344

RIVERS

EUROPE

		km	miles
Volga	Caspian Sea	3,700	2,300
Danube	Black Sea	2,850	1,770
Ural	Caspian Sea	2,535	1,575
Dnieper	Black Sea	2,285	1,420
Kama	Volga	2,030	1,260
Don	Black Sea	1,990	1,240
Pechora	Arctic Ocean	1,790	1,110
Oka	Volga	1,480	920
Belaya	Kama	1,420	880
Dniester	Black Sea	1,400	870
Vyatka	Kama	1,370	850
Rhine	North Sea	1,320	820
Northern Dvina	Arctic Ocean	1,290	800
Desna	Dnieper	1,190	740
Elbe	North Sea	1,145	710
Vistula	Baltic Sea	1,090	675
Loire	Atlantic Ocean	1,020	635

ASIA

		km	miles	
Yangtse	Pacific Ocean	6,380	3,960	[3]
Yenisey–Angara	Arctic Ocean	5,550	3,445	[5]
Huang Ho	Pacific Ocean	5,464	3,395	[6]
Ob–Irtysh	Arctic Ocean	5,410	3,360	[7]
Mekong	Pacific Ocean	4,500	2,800	[9]
Amur	Pacific Ocean	4,442	2,760	
Lena	Arctic Ocean	4,402	2,735	
Irtysh	Ob	4,250	2,640	
Yenisey	Arctic Ocean	4,090	2,540	
Ob	Arctic Ocean	3,680	2,285	
Indus	Indian Ocean	3,100	1,925	
Brahmaputra	Indian Ocean	2,900	1,800	
Syrdarya	Aral Sea	2,860	1,775	
Salween	Indian Ocean	2,800	1,740	
Euphrates	Indian Ocean	2,700	1,675	
Vilyuy	Lena	2,650	1,645	
Kolyma	Arctic Ocean	2,600	1,615	
Amudarya	Aral Sea	2,540	1,578	
Ural	Caspian Sea	2,535	1,575	
Ganges	Indian Ocean	2,510	1,560	
Si Kiang	Pacific Ocean	2,100	1,305	
Irrawaddy	Indian Ocean	2,010	1,250	
Tarim–Yarkand	Lop Nur	2,000	1,240	
Tigris	Indian Ocean	1,900	1,180	

AFRICA

		km	miles	
Nile	Mediterranean	6,695	4,160	[1]
Congo	Atlantic Ocean	4,670	2,900	[8]
Niger	Atlantic Ocean	4,180	2,595	
Zambezi	Indian Ocean	3,540	2,200	
Oubangi/Uele	Congo (D.R.)	2,250	1,400	
Kasai	Congo (D.R.)	1,950	1,210	
Shaballe	Indian Ocean	1,930	1,200	
Orange	Atlantic Ocean	1,860	1,155	
Cubango	Okavango Delta	1,800	1,120	
Limpopo	Indian Ocean	1,770	1,100	
Senegal	Atlantic Ocean	1,640	1,020	
Volta	Atlantic Ocean	1,500	930	

AUSTRALIA

		km	miles
Murray–Darling	Southern Ocean	3,750	2,330
Darling	Murray	3,070	1,905
Murray	Southern Ocean	2,575	1,600
Murrumbidgee	Murray	1,690	1,050

NORTH AMERICA

		km	miles	
Mississippi–Missouri	Gulf of Mexico	5,971	3,710	[4]
Mackenzie	Arctic Ocean	4,240	2,630	
Missouri	Mississippi	4,088	2,540	

NORTH AMERICA (continued)		km	miles	
Mississippi	Gulf of Mexico	3,782	2,350	
Yukon	Pacific Ocean	3,185	1,980	
Rio Grande	Gulf of Mexico	3,030	1,880	
Arkansas	Mississippi	2,340	1,450	
Colorado	Pacific Ocean	2,330	1,445	
Red	Mississippi	2,040	1,270	
Columbia	Pacific Ocean	1,950	1,210	
Saskatchewan	Lake Winnipeg	1,940	1,205	
Snake	Columbia	1,670	1,040	
Churchill	Hudson Bay	1,600	990	
Ohio	Mississippi	1,580	980	
Brazos	Gulf of Mexico	1,400	870	
St Lawrence	Atlantic Ocean	1,170	730	

SOUTH AMERICA

		km	miles	
Amazon	Atlantic Ocean	6,450	4,010	[2]
Paraná–Plate	Atlantic Ocean	4,500	2,800	[10]
Purus	Amazon	3,350	2,080	
Madeira	Amazon	3,200	1,990	
São Francisco	Atlantic Ocean	2,900	1,800	
Paraná	Plate	2,800	1,740	
Tocantins	Atlantic Ocean	2,750	1,710	
Orinoco	Atlantic Ocean	2,740	1,700	
Paraguay	Paraná	2,550	1,580	
Pilcomayo	Paraná	2,500	1,550	
Araguaia	Tocantins	2,250	1,400	
Juruá	Amazon	2,000	1,240	
Xingu	Amazon	1,980	1,230	
Ucayali	Amazon	1,900	1,180	
Uruguay	Plate	1,610	1,000	

LAKES

EUROPE

		km²	miles²
Lake Ladoga	Russia	17,700	6,800
Lake Onega	Russia	9,700	3,700
Saimaa system	Finland	8,000	3,100
Vänern	Sweden	5,500	2,100

ASIA

		km²	miles²	
Caspian Sea	Asia	371,000	143,000	[1]
Lake Baikal	Russia	30,500	11,780	[8]
Tonlé Sap	Cambodia	20,000	7,700	
Lake Balkhash	Kazakhstan	18,500	7,100	
Dongting Hu	China	12,000	4,600	
Aral Sea	Kazakhstan/Uzbekistan	6,800	2,620	
Issyk Kul	Kyrgyzstan	6,200	2,400	
Lake Urmia	Iran	5,900	2,300	
Koko Nur	China	5,700	2,200	
Poyang Hu	China	5,000	1,900	
Lake Khanka	China/Russia	4,400	1,700	
Lake Van	Turkey	3,500	1,400	

AFRICA

		km²	miles²	
Lake Victoria	East Africa	68,000	26,300	[3]
Lake Tanganyika	Central Africa	33,000	13,000	[6]
Lake Malawi/Nyasa	East Africa	29,600	11,430	[9]
Lake Chad	Central Africa	25,000	9,700	
Lake Bangweulu	Zambia	9,840	3,800	
Lake Turkana	Ethiopia/Kenya	8,500	3,290	
Lake Volta	Ghana	8,480	3,270	
Lake Kariba	Zambia/Zimbabwe	5,380	2,150	
Lake Albert	Uganda/Congo (D.R.)	5,300	2,050	
Lake Nasser	Egypt/Sudan	5,250	2,030	
Lake Mweru	Zambia/Congo (D.R.)	4,920	1,900	
Lake Kyoga	Uganda	4,430	1,710	
Lake Tana	Ethiopia	3,620	1,400	
Lake Cabora Bassa	Mozambique	2,750	1,070	
Lake Rukwa	Tanzania	2,600	1,000	
Lake Mai-Ndombe	Congo (D.R.)	2,300	890	

AUSTRALIA

		km²	miles²
Lake Eyre	Australia	8,900	3,400
Lake Torrens	Australia	5,800	2,200
Lake Gairdner	Australia	4,800	1,900

NORTH AMERICA

		km²	miles²	
Lake Superior	Canada/USA	82,350	31,800	[2]
Lake Huron	Canada/USA	59,600	23,010	[4]
Lake Michigan	USA	58,000	22,400	[5]
Great Bear Lake	Canada	31,800	12,280	[7]
Great Slave Lake	Canada	28,500	11,000	[10]
Lake Erie	Canada/USA	25,700	9,900	
Lake Winnipeg	Canada	24,400	9,400	
Lake Ontario	Canada/USA	19,500	7,500	
Lake Nicaragua	Nicaragua	8,200	3,200	
Lake Athabasca	Canada	8,100	3,100	
Smallwood Reservoir	Canada	6,530	2,520	
Reindeer Lake	Canada	6,400	2,500	
Nettilling Lake	Canada	5,500	2,100	

SOUTH AMERICA		km²	miles²
Lake Titicaca	Bolivia/Peru	8,300	3,200
Lake Poopo	Bolivia	2,800	1,100

ISLANDS

EUROPE

		km²	miles²	
Great Britain	UK	229,880	88,700	[8]
Iceland	Atlantic Ocean	103,000	39,800	
Ireland	Ireland/UK	84,400	32,600	
Novaya Zemlya (N.)	Russia	48,200	18,600	
Spitsbergen	Norway	39,000	15,100	
Novaya Zemlya (S.)	Russia	33,200	12,800	
Sicily	Italy	25,500	9,800	
Sardinia	Italy	24,000	9,300	
Nordaustlandet	Norway	15,000	5,600	
Corsica	France	8,700	3,400	
Crete	Greece	8,350	3,200	
Sjælland	Denmark	6,850	2,600	

ASIA

		km²	miles²	
Borneo	Southeast Asia	744,360	287,400	[3]
Sumatra	Indonesia	473,600	182,860	[6]
Honshu	Japan	230,500	88,980	[7]
Sulawesi (Celebes)	Indonesia	189,000	73,000	
Java	Indonesia	126,700	48,900	
Luzon	Philippines	104,700	40,400	
Mindanao	Philippines	101,500	39,200	
Hokkaido	Japan	78,400	30,300	
Sakhalin	Russia	74,060	28,600	
Sri Lanka	Indian Ocean	65,600	25,300	
Taiwan	Pacific Ocean	36,000	13,900	
Kyushu	Japan	35,700	13,800	
Hainan	China	34,000	13,100	
Timor	Southeast Asia	33,600	13,000	
Shikoku	Japan	18,800	7,300	
Halmahera	Indonesia	18,000	6,900	
Ceram	Indonesia	17,150	6,600	
Sumbawa	Indonesia	15,450	6,000	
Flores	Indonesia	15,200	5,900	
Samar	Philippines	13,100	5,100	
Negros	Philippines	12,700	4,900	
Bangka	Indonesia	12,000	4,600	
Palawan	Philippines	12,000	4,600	
Panay	Philippines	11,500	4,400	
Sumba	Indonesia	11,100	4,300	
Mindoro	Philippines	9,750	3,800	

AFRICA

		km²	miles²	
Madagascar	Indian Ocean	587,040	226,660	[4]
Socotra	Indian Ocean	3,600	1,400	
Réunion	Indian Ocean	2,500	965	
Tenerife	Atlantic Ocean	2,350	900	
Mauritius	Indian Ocean	1,865	720	

OCEANIA

		km²	miles²	
New Guinea	Indonesia/Papua NG	821,030	317,000	[2]
New Zealand (S.)	Pacific Ocean	150,500	58,100	
New Zealand (N.)	Pacific Ocean	114,700	44,300	
Tasmania	Australia	67,800	26,200	
New Britain	Papua New Guinea	37,800	14,600	
New Caledonia	Pacific Ocean	19,100	7,400	
Viti Levu	Fiji	10,500	4,100	
Hawai'i	Pacific Ocean	10,450	4,000	
Bougainville	Papua New Guinea	9,600	3,700	
Guadalcanal	Solomon Islands	6,500	2,500	
Vanua Levu	Fiji	5,550	2,100	
New Ireland	Papua New Guinea	3,200	1,200	

NORTH AMERICA

		km²	miles²	
Greenland	Atlantic Ocean	2,175,600	839,800	[1]
Baffin Island	Canada	508,000	196,100	[5]
Victoria Island	Canada	212,200	81,900	[9]
Ellesmere Island	Canada	212,000	81,800	[10]
Cuba	Caribbean Sea	110,860	42,800	
Newfoundland	Canada	110,680	42,700	
Hispaniola	Dominican Rep./Haiti	76,200	29,400	
Banks Island	Canada	67,000	25,900	
Devon Island	Canada	54,500	21,000	
Melville Island	Canada	42,400	16,400	
Vancouver Island	Canada	32,150	12,400	
Somerset Island	Canada	24,300	9,400	
Jamaica	Caribbean Sea	11,400	4,400	
Puerto Rico	Atlantic Ocean	8,900	3,400	
Cape Breton Island	Canada	4,000	1,500	

SOUTH AMERICA

		km²	miles²
Tierra del Fuego	Argentina/Chile	47,000	18,100
Falkland Islands (East)	Atlantic Ocean	6,800	2,600
South Georgia	Atlantic Ocean	4,200	1,600
Galapagos (Isabela)	Pacific Ocean	2,250	870

IMAGES
OF
EARTH

This image covers one of the most dynamic areas in the world, Hong Kong, with Shenzhen to its north. Hong Kong became a major port and international financial center during the period of British rule and retains a special status as a Special Administrative Region (SAR) with a high degree of economic autonomy, including the retention of the Hong Kong dollar. To its north Shenzhen was established by China as a Special Economic Zone (SEZ) in 1979, to attract foreign industry and investment. This has proved very successful and communications between the two have also improved, as can be seen by the sinuous Shenzhen Bay Bridge in the middle of the left-hand page. [Map page 117]
Source: RapidEye/NPA Satellite Mapping

The River Thames snakes from Chelsea Bridge in the west to Tower Bridge in the east in this image covering both the West End and the City of London. Despite having a population in excess of 8 million people, there are still many parks and open spaces around the city center. St James's Park and Green Park, together with Buckingham Palace and its gardens, can be seen at center left of the image, and, on the western edge, parts of Hyde Park and Regent's Park can also be seen. Just below the page title, at top center, the newly developing area around Kings Cross and St Pancras railroad stations can be seen. In addition, the low sun shows clearly the shadows of The Shard and the chimney of Tate Modern as well as the many high-rise buildings in the City. [Map page 67]
Source: GeoEye/NPA Satellite Mapping

As both the capital and the largest city in the Netherlands, with over 1 million inhabitants, Amsterdam is a major commercial and cultural center. Its name is derived from its position at the mouth of the River Amstel, flowing in from the south. The urban area is split by the Nordzeekanaal, which connects the Ijsselmeer to the North Sea. There is also the important Rijnkanaal, which links it with the major inland waterways of Europe via the River Rhine. The ancient core of the settlement is to the south, where the concentric rings of the famous canal system can be seen. This network is evidence of city planning to accommodate and service a fast-rising population in the 17th century. [Map page 69]
Source: RapidEye/NPA Satellite Mapping

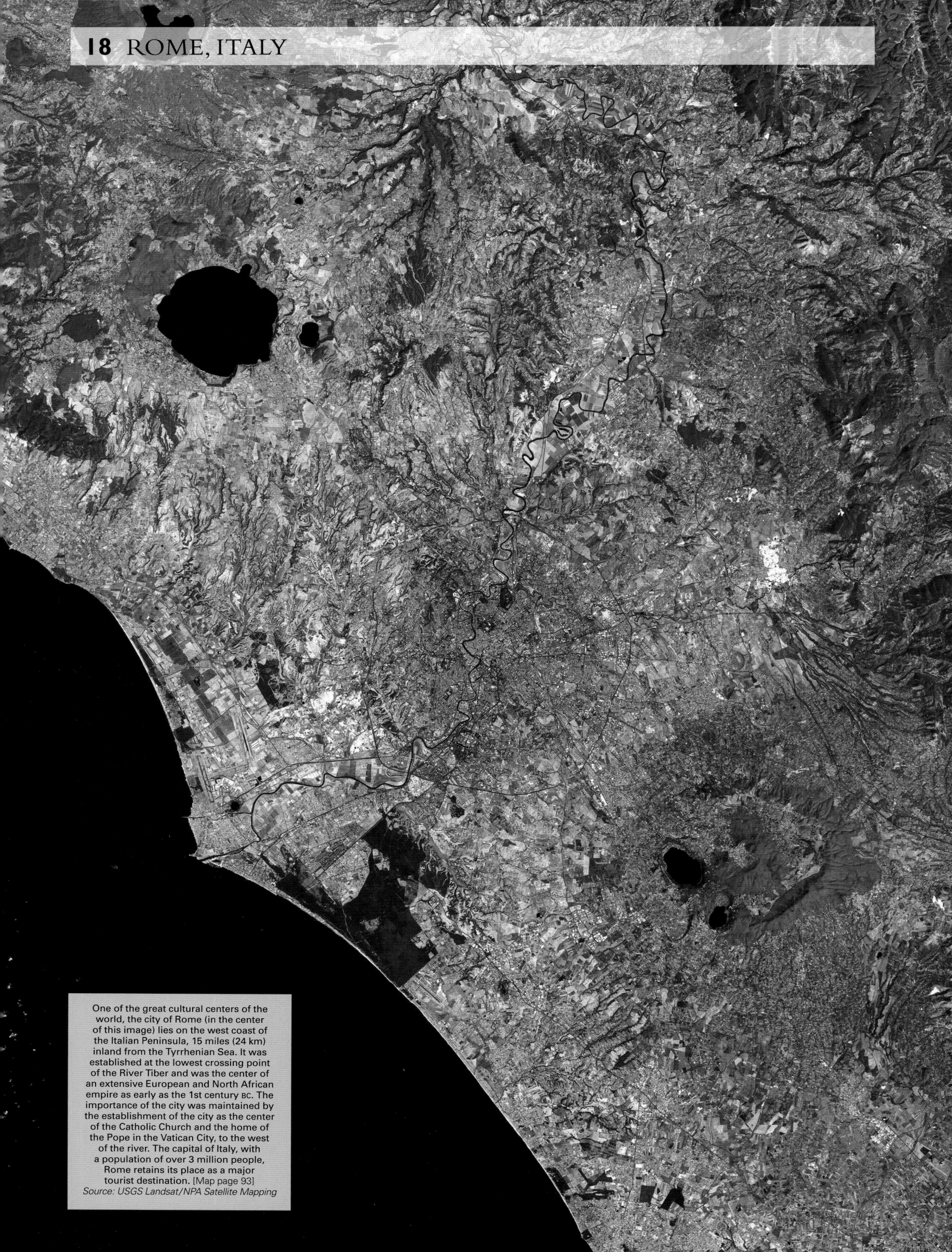

One of the great cultural centers of the world, the city of Rome (in the center of this image) lies on the west coast of the Italian Peninsula, 15 miles (24 km) inland from the Tyrrhenian Sea. It was established at the lowest crossing point of the River Tiber and was the center of an extensive European and North African empire as early as the 1st century BC. The importance of the city was maintained by the establishment of the city as the center of the Catholic Church and the home of the Pope in the Vatican City, to the west of the river. The capital of Italy, with a population of over 3 million people, Rome retains its place as a major tourist destination. [Map page 93]
Source: USGS Landsat/NPA Satellite Mapping

The city of Istanbul was formerly known as Constantinople and, before that, as Byzantium. It is split by the narrow stretch of water running from north to south called the Bosporus. This forms the continental boundary between Europe and Asia, connecting the Black Sea, to the north, to the Sea of Marmara, thence to the Mediterranean. It is because of this strategic position between the east–west (land) and north–south (sea) trade routes that the city has been important for such a long time. Under the Ottoman Empire it was the capital city of Turkey, but in 1923 this was moved to Ankara. Currently, over 11 million people live in Istanbul, the largest city in Turkey. [Map page 104]
Source: USGS Landsat/NPA Satellite Mapping

Also known as Bombay, Mumbai is the largest and most important commercial city in India, with a population of 20 million people. Its harbor is the best in the country, and the new port, built in 1989 and called Nhava Sheva (on the right-hand side of the image), handles 65% of the country's total container traffic. The growth of cotton weaving, and the opening of the Suez Canal in 1869, cemented its position as India's most important trading port. Diversifying into areas such as engineering and information technology, the city is also the center of the highly successful Hindi movie industry, or "Bollywood," which exports its products around the world. [Map page 126]
Source: RapidEye/NPA Satellite Mapping

Three countries can be seen in this image. At the top, partially covered by cloud, is the southern end of Malaysia; the large island just below is the independent city state of Singapore; and the islands at the bottom of the image are part of Indonesia. Singapore has developed a fast-growing economy based on being the focus of southeast Asian shipping routes and on the trans-shipment of goods between the Far East and the West. As a result, it is one of the world's major ports and much new development, by reclaiming land from the sea, can be seen in the south. The city state is one of the world's wealthiest countries, with a population of over 5 million people. [Map page 121]
Source: RapidEye/NPA Satellite Mapping

Beijing, also known as Peking, is the
capital and cultural center of China, with
a population of over 15 million people.
It is situated at the northern end of the
North China Plain and has a hot, dry
climate. Water supply is an ongoing
problem for such a large city, as too are
air pollution and dust storms. At the
center of the built-up area in this image
can be seen the small rectangle of the
Forbidden City, the palace compound
built from the 14th century onward.
The city is the terminus of several new
high-speed railroad lines, and Beijing
Capital International Airport, clearly
visible in this image to the northeast
of the city, is now the second busiest
airport in the world. [Map page 114]
Source: USGS Landsat/NPA Satellite Mapping

At the head of Tokyo Bay, the capital city forms the center of one of the world's most densely populated areas. With its satellites of Kawasaki and Yokohama, the population of over 34 million people makes this metropolitan area the world's largest "megacity." Owing to the shortage of space for expansion, much development takes place on areas reclaimed from the sea, such as Haneda International Airport, visible at the mouth of the Tama River, toward the southwest of the image. The area is prone to earthquakes, and in 1923 the Great Kanto Earthquake devastated the city, killing 143,000 people. Consequently, modern buildings are reinforced to withstand seismic activity. [Map page 113]
Source: RapidEye/NPA Satellite Mapping

Since being declared the capital of the newly independent state of Mauritania in 1960, Nouakchott, situated on the Atlantic coast of West Africa, has grown rapidly from a small fishing village. It now has a population of over 700,000 people, but with many more living in shanty towns around it. It is the largest town in the Sahara Desert and the shifting dunes almost engulf the settlement.

In such an arid area, it relies for its water supply on ancient subterranean reservoirs of water, or aquifers, trapped in underground porous rock structures.

There is a deep-water port through which Nouakchott imports most of its needs – over 95% of the goods handled are imports. [Map page 138]

Source: USGS Landsat/NPA Satellite Mapping

The largest city in Africa, with over 11 million inhabitants, Cairo evolved in a strategic location on the eastern bank of the River Nile just below its delta, 100 miles (165 km) from the Mediterranean Sea. This image clearly shows the differences between the arid desert areas to the southeast and southwest, the fertile lands of the Nile flood plain, and the urban area itself. Air pollution from vehicle emissions and industry is a major concern in this rapidly expanding metropolitan area. To ease congestion, three metro lines have been built. The shadows of the Pyramids on the Giza Plateau can be seen at the bottom left of the image, showing the modern city's links with Ancient Egypt. [Map page 137]
Source: RapidEye/NPA Satellite Mapping

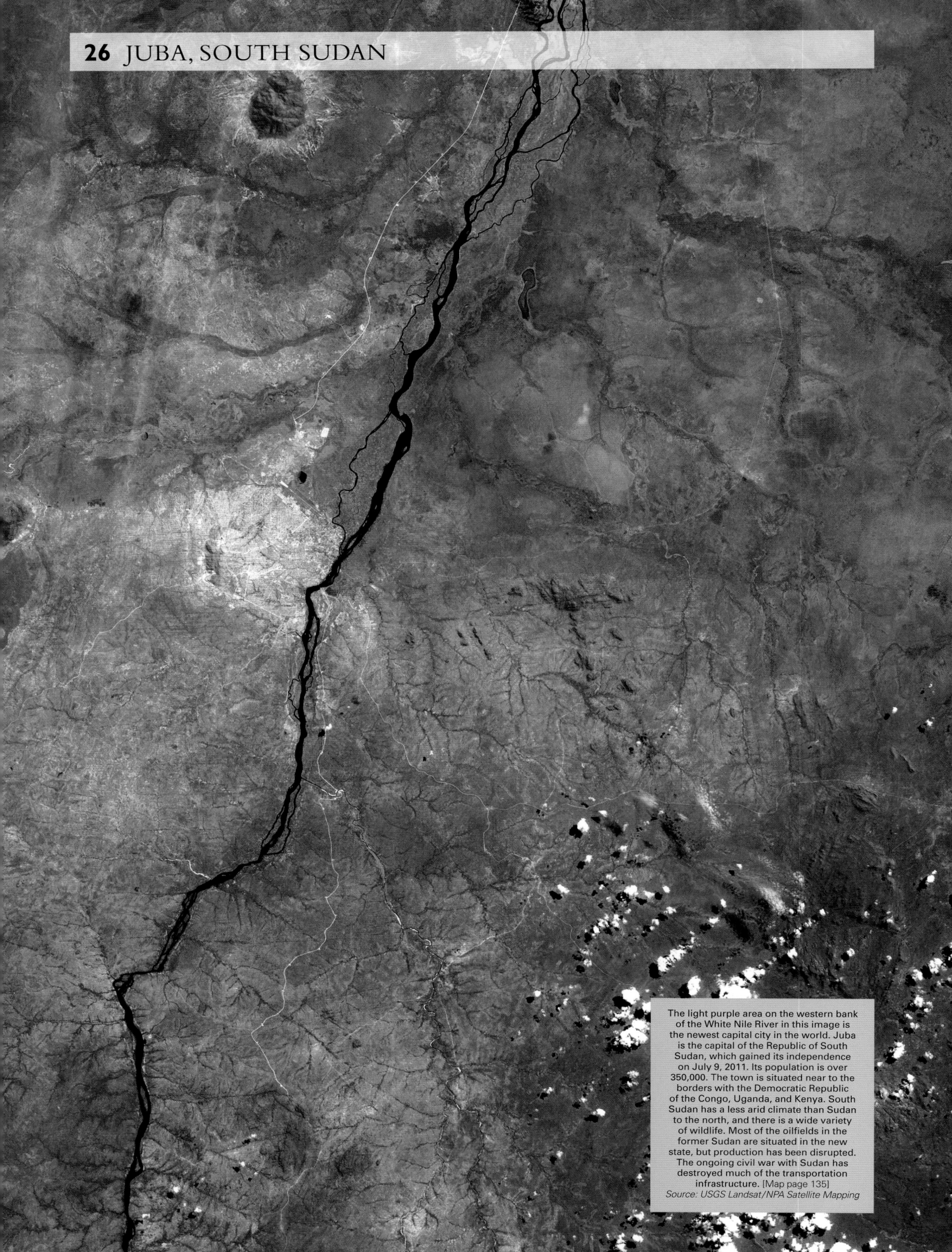

The light purple area on the western bank of the White Nile River in this image is the newest capital city in the world. Juba is the capital of the Republic of South Sudan, which gained its independence on July 9, 2011. Its population is over 350,000. The town is situated near to the borders with the Democratic Republic of the Congo, Uganda, and Kenya. South Sudan has a less arid climate than Sudan to the north, and there is a wide variety of wildlife. Most of the oilfields in the former Sudan are situated in the new state, but production has been disrupted. The ongoing civil war with Sudan has destroyed much of the transportation infrastructure. [Map page 135]
Source: USGS Landsat/NPA Satellite Mapping

The city of Cape Town sits at the northern end of the Cape Peninsula beneath Table Mountain – the port facilities are clearly visible in this image. It developed from the first settlement in the 17th century, founded by the Dutch East India Company, because of its safe north-facing harbor, looking across Table Bay toward Robben Island. The urban area now spreads to the east of the peninsula down to False Bay. As well as being the second largest city in South Africa, after Johannesburg, Cape Town is also the seat of the National Parliament and is the country's legislative capital. To the west of the port can be seen the oval shape of the Cape Town Stadium. [Map page 144]
Source: RapidEye/NPA Satellite Mapping

28 SYDNEY, AUSTRALIA

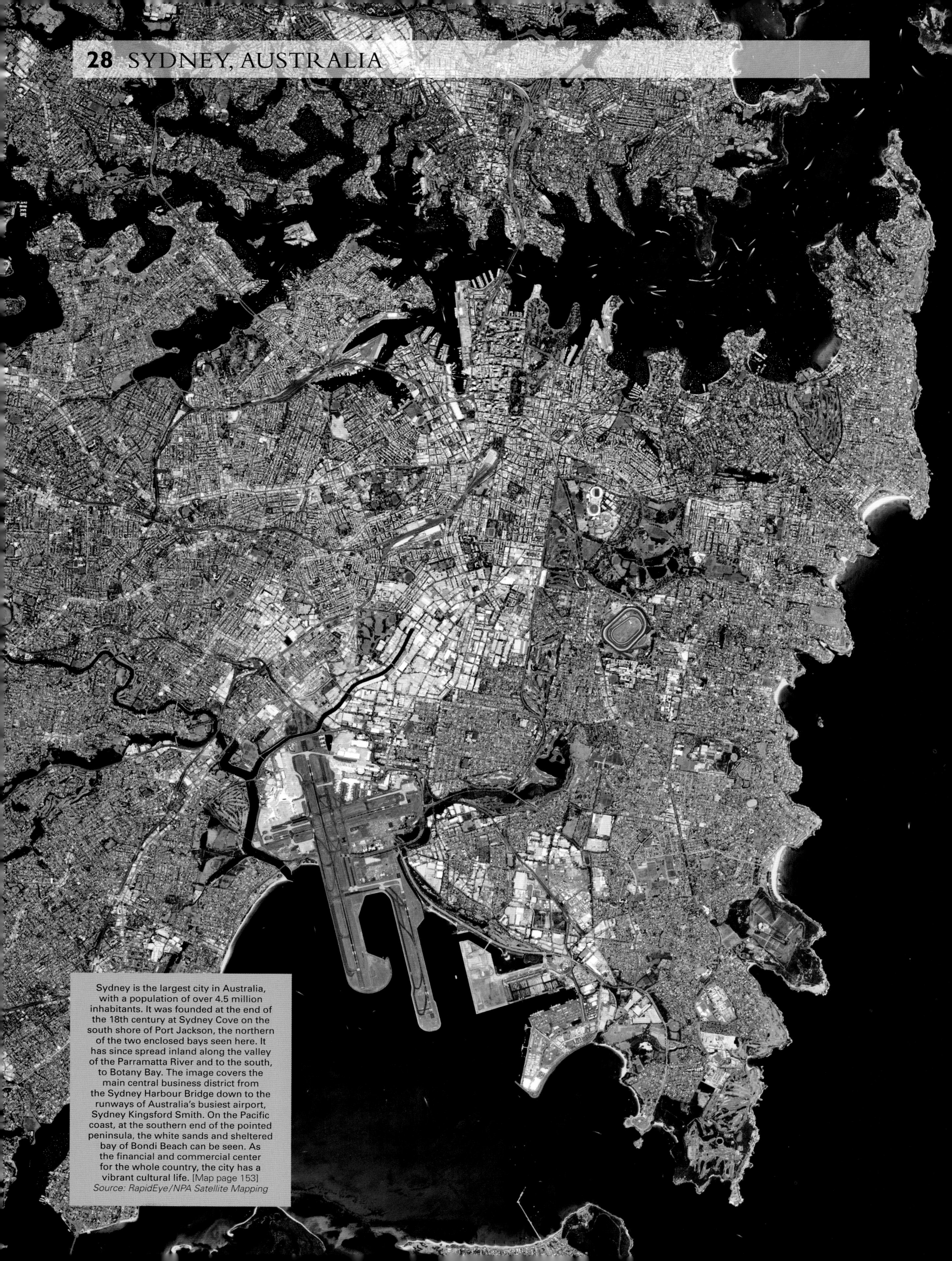

Sydney is the largest city in Australia, with a population of over 4.5 million inhabitants. It was founded at the end of the 18th century at Sydney Cove on the south shore of Port Jackson, the northern of the two enclosed bays seen here. It has since spread inland along the valley of the Parramatta River and to the south, to Botany Bay. The image covers the main central business district from the Sydney Harbour Bridge down to the runways of Australia's busiest airport, Sydney Kingsford Smith. On the Pacific coast, at the southern end of the pointed peninsula, the white sands and sheltered bay of Bondi Beach can be seen. As the financial and commercial center for the whole country, the city has a vibrant cultural life. [Map page 153]
Source: RapidEye/NPA Satellite Mapping

Situated on the east coast of South Island, the city of Christchurch, with almost 377,000 inhabitants, lies between the braided River Waimakiriri and the spectacular Banks Peninsula. The latter was formed by the erosion of two ancient volcanic cones by glaciers and their subsequent inundation by the sea, creating the indented coastline. This part of New Zealand is on the western edge of the Pacific tectonic plate, which is moving slowly toward and under the adjacent Australian plate. This resulted in the major earthquake of February 22, 2011, which, despite being only magnitude 6.3, caused extensive damage to the city center due to the relatively shallow depth of the epicenter. [Map page 155]
Source: USGS Landsat/NPA Satellite Mapping

On the north side of the Fraser River delta, the settlement grew up in the second half of the 19th century around its fine, natural harbor. It developed as the western railhead of the Canadian Pacific Railroad and is now the terminus of the Trans-Canada Highway, which crosses on the easternmost of the two road bridges visible here to the north. Vancouver is the largest cargo port in Canada. The larger metropolitan area of the city is home to over 2.25 million people. Downtown Vancouver is at the southern end of the peninsula which projects northward and separates Vancouver Harbour from Burrard Inlet. The wooded area at the northern end is Stanley Park, which is connected to West and North Vancouver via the Lions Gate Bridge. [Map page 162]
Source: RapidEye/NPA Satellite Mapping

Québec was founded as a trading post
in 1608, at the narrowest point of the
St Lawrence River, just to the southwest
of the Île d'Orléans, and is one of the
oldest cities in North America. Strategically,
the city controlled the movement of
shipping between the Atlantic Ocean
and the Great Lakes, and consequently
developed fortifications on the cliffs of
Cape Diamond, 320 ft (97 m) above the
river. The port is 850 miles (1,370 km)
from the Atlantic, 1,495 miles (2,404 km)
from Duluth, and 1,400 miles (2,252 km)
from Chicago. It has a population of
over 500,000 people and is the capital
city of the French-speaking province
of the same name. [Map page 165]
Source: RapidEye/NPA Satellite Mapping

This image covers parts of New York City (to the east) and Jersey City (to the west). Flowing from the north, the Hudson River divides them, and the elongated island of Manhattan with Central Park at its heart is clearly visible. It is the center of the most densely populated metropolitan area in the United States, with a population in excess of 19 million people. To the southeast is the end of Long Island, on which the suburbs of Brooklyn and Queens are situated. Southwest of Manhattan are two small islands: the first is Ellis Island, where the early immigrants first disembarked, and beyond that is Liberty Island, where the famous Statue of Liberty is located. [Map page 175]
Source: RapidEye/NPA Satellite Mapping

Situated on the southwestern shore of
Lake Michigan, Chicago is the center
of the third largest metropolitan area in
the United States, with a population of
over 9.5 million people. The central area
of the agglomeration, known by some as
"Chicagoland," can be seen on the lake
shore. It developed as a major transport
focus for the Midwest, with complex
road and rail networks radiating out to
its rich agricultural hinterland. It also
developed as a large port, trading these
commodities on a global scale. Chicago
boasts the fifth busiest airport in
the world, O'Hare International, which
handles over 66.6 million passengers
a year and which can be seen toward
the northwest of the city. [Map page 172]
Source: USGS Landsat/NPA Satellite Mapping

The northern end of the "Bay Area" is shown: hilly San Francisco is at the top end of the southern peninsula, with the Golden Gate Bridge connecting it to Sausalito to the north. Alcatraz Island, former home of the infamous prison, can be seen as a small island to the east of the bridge. On the opposite shore, connected by the double-decker Bay Bridge, are Oakland and Berkeley. Founded by the Spanish at the end of the 18th century, the town expanded rapidly with the Californian Gold Rush in the mid-19th century. Sitting close by the San Andreas Fault, the city was destroyed by an earthquake and subsequent fire in 1906, and there was further major earthquake damage in 1989. [Map page 170]
Source: RapidEye/NPA Satellite Mapping

The city is situated in a basin within the Mojave Desert in Nevada. Known worldwide for its night life and gambling, Las Vegas has also become a popular destination for retired people and families. The population of the metropolitan area is now almost 2 million people. To the east of the grid-pattern layout of the town lies the Hoover Dam, formerly known as Boulder Dam, which was built across the Colorado River in 1935. The lake behind the dam is known as Lake Mead, the largest man-made reservoir in the United States. It is used for flood control, irrigation, and hydroelectric-power generation in the region, but recent dry years have resulted in reduced water levels. [Map page 171]
Source: USGS Landsat/NPA Satellite Mapping

With a population of over 23 million people for the continuous metropolitan area visible here, Mexico City is one of North America's most important commercial centers. It was originally founded by the Aztecs in 1325, on an island in Lake Texcoco, which has dried up over time. The city sits in a valley some 7,350 ft (2,240 m) above sea level. The relentless growth of the urban area has resulted in both air pollution and water-supply problems. To the southeast of the city can be seen three towering snow-covered volcanic peaks. The southernmost of these is Popocatépetl, an active volcano 17,887 ft (5,452 m) high, which has two glaciers near its summit. [Map page 181]
Source: USGS Landsat/NPA Satellite Mapping

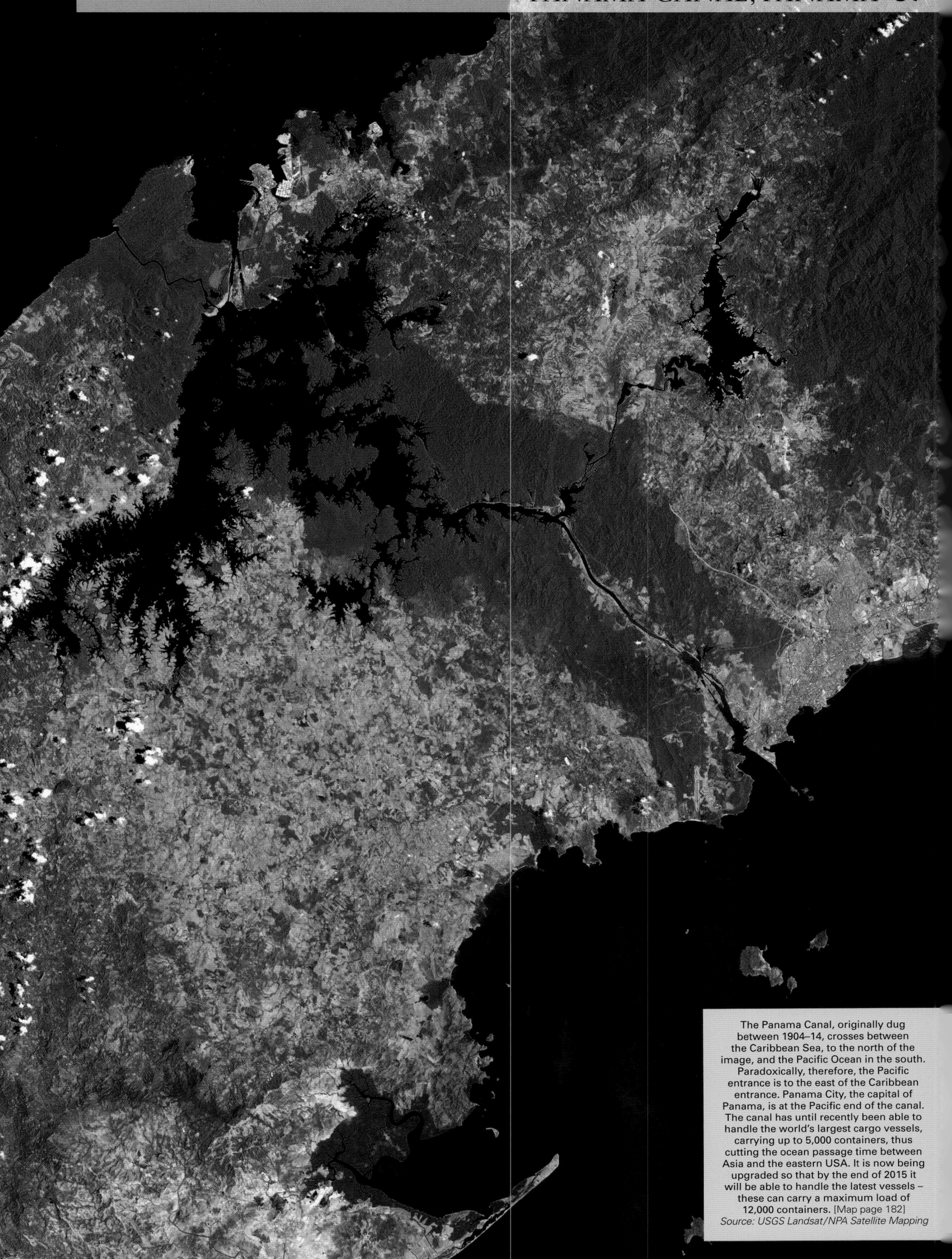

The Panama Canal, originally dug between 1904–14, crosses between the Caribbean Sea, to the north of the image, and the Pacific Ocean in the south. Paradoxically, therefore, the Pacific entrance is to the east of the Caribbean entrance. Panama City, the capital of Panama, is at the Pacific end of the canal. The canal has until recently been able to handle the world's largest cargo vessels, carrying up to 5,000 containers, thus cutting the ocean passage time between Asia and the eastern USA. It is now being upgraded so that by the end of 2015 it will be able to handle the latest vessels – these can carry a maximum load of 12,000 containers. [Map page 182]
Source: USGS Landsat/NPA Satellite Mapping

Santiago, the capital city of Chile, lies at the foot of the Andes in the country's fertile central valley at an altitude of 1,706 ft (520 m), some 37 miles (60 km) southeast of the main port of Valparaíso. To the east the mountains rise to over 20,000 ft (6,000 m). The boundary with Argentina runs north–south along the watershed some 46 miles (75 km) to the east. The city, which was founded as early as 1541, expanded rapidly to its current population of over 6 million inhabitants. This has resulted in some air pollution and smog problems, particularly during the winter months. The Mapocho River divides the city, flowing from the Andes to the Pacific Ocean. [Map page 190]
Source: USGS Landsat/NPA Satellite Mapping

Situated on the west side of the mouth of the Guanabara Bay, Rio de Janeiro is the most visited city in the southern hemisphere. It is famous for its beaches (Copacabana and Ipanema, both at the western entrance to the bay), its carnivals, the Sugar Loaf Mountain, and the famous Cristo Redentor (Christ the Redeemer) statue. It has a hot, humid climate with a mean daily temperature of 75°F (24°C), and was the capital city of Brazil until 1960, when the newly built capital Brasília superseded it. It is the second largest manufacturing center in Brazil, after São Paulo, and a major port. The metropolitan area has a population of almost 11 million people. [Map page 191]
Source: USGS Landsat/NPA Satellite Mapping

OCEAN
SEAFLOORS

– GREAT BARRIER REEF, AUSTRALIA –
First explored by Captain James Cook in
1770 and lying just off the east coast of
Queensland, the Great Barrier Reef is
composed of some 2,900 individual reefs
and over 900 islands, a few of which are
shown on this image. Designated a UNESCO
World Heritage Site and protected as
a Marine Park, this fragile environment
is home to over 1,500 species of fish and
400 species of coral, as well as turtles,
whales, and many species of birds.
[Map page 150]

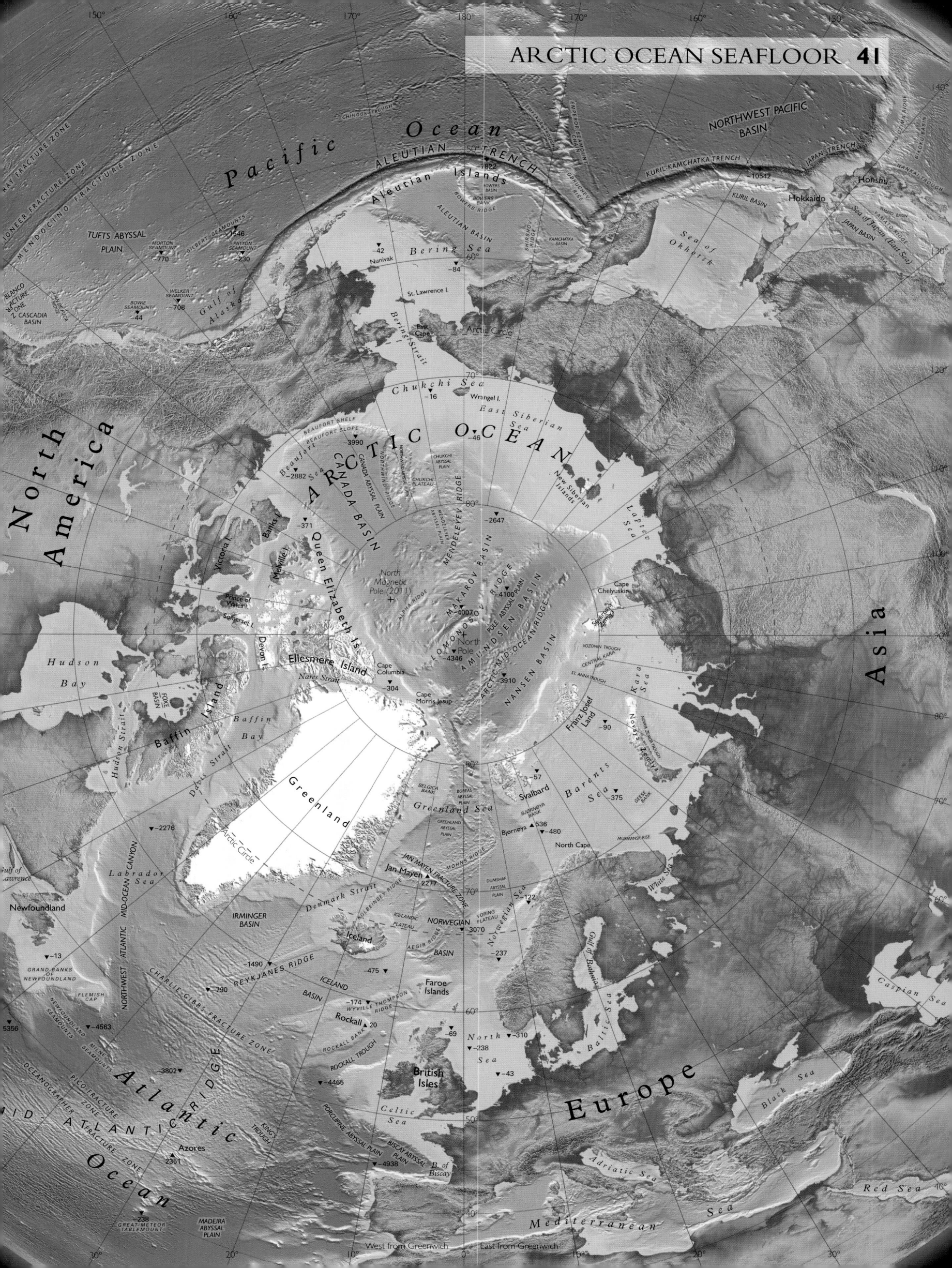

Pacific O c e a n

NORTHWEST PACIFIC
BASIN

RAY FRACTURE ZONE

PIONEER FRACTURE ZONE

MENDOCINO FRACTURE ZONE

BLANCO FRACTURE ZONE

Z. CASCADIA BASIN

TUFTS ABYSSAL PLAIN

MORTON SEAMOUNT −770

GILBERT SEAMOUNTS −646

PATTON SEAMOUNT −230

WELKER SEAMOUNT −708

BOWIE SEAMOUNT −44

Gulf of Alaska

CHINOOK TROUGH

ALEUTIAN TRENCH

50°

Aleutian Islands

BOWERS BANK

BOWERS BASIN

BOWERS RIDGE

ALEUTIAN BASIN

SHIRSHOV RIDGE

KAMCHATKA BASIN

OBRUTCHEV

EMPEROR SEAMOUNTS

KURIL-KAMCHATKA TRENCH

10542

Bering Sea

−42 Nunivak

St. Lawrence I.

−84 60°

East Cape

Arctic Circle

KURIL BASIN

Sea of Okhotsk

JAPAN TRENCH

Honshu

Hokkaido

Sea of Japan (East Sea)

JAPAN BASIN

YAMATO BASIN

NARKAII TROUGH

140°

130°

120°

Chukchi Sea
−16 Wrangel I.

East Siberian Sea
−46

New Siberian Islands

Laptev Sea

110°

BEAUFORT SHELF

BEAUFORT SLOPE

−3990

NORTHWIND RIDGE

CANADA ABYSSAL PLAIN

A R C T I C   O C E A N

NORTHWIND ESCARPMENT

CHUKCHI PLATEAU

CHUKCHI ABYSSAL PLAIN

MENDELEYEV RIDGE

MENDELEEV ABYSSAL PLAIN

−2647

Cape Chelyuskin

Severnaya Zemlya

N o r t h

A m e r i c a

Beaufort Sea
−2882

CANADA BASIN

Banks I.

Victoria I.

Melville I.

−371

A R C T I C

Queen Elizabeth Is.

ALPHA RIDGE

80°

MAKAROV BASIN
−40070

LOMONOSOV RIDGE

North Pole −4346

ARCTIC MID-OCEAN RIDGE

AMUNDSEN BASIN

NANSEN BASIN

−3910

NORTH POLE ABYSSAL PLAIN
−4100 PLAIN

VORONIN TROUGH

CENTRAL KARA RISE

ST. ANNA TROUGH

Kara Sea

A s i a

Prince of Wales I.

Somerset I.

Devon I.

North Magnetic Pole (2011) +

Ellesmere Island

Cape Columbia −304

Cape Morris Jesup

Franz Josef Land −90

Novaya Zemlya

90°

NORTH ZEMLYA TROUGH

Hudson Bay

FOXE BASIN

Hudson Strait

Baffin Island

Baffin Bay

Nares Strait

Greenland

VOZONIN TROUGH

80°

Barents Sea
−57

Svalbard

−375

GEESE BANK

MURMANSK RISE

BJØRNØYA BANK

Bjørnøya −536 −480

North Cape

Arctic Circle

BELGICA BANK

BOREAS ABYSSAL PLAIN

GREENLAND ABYSSAL PLAIN

Greenland Sea

MOHNS RIDGE

70°

−2276

LABRADOR SEA

Lincoln Sea

Devis Strait

NORTHWEST ATLANTIC MID-OCEAN

Newfoundland

−13

GRAND BANKS OF NEWFOUNDLAND

FLEMISH CAP

NEWFOUNDLAND SEAMOUNTS

5356

−4563

CHARLIE-GIBBS FRACTURE ZONE

MID ATLANTIC RIDGE

−3802

PICO FRACTURE ZONE

OCEANOGRAPHER FRACTURE ZONE

A t l a n t i c

O c e a n

Azores 2351

KING'S TROUGH

−238 GREAT METEOR TABLEMOUNT

MADEIRA ABYSSAL PLAIN

Gulf of Lawrence

−1490

REYKJANES RIDGE

−790

ICELAND BASIN

−475

Iceland

IRMINGER BASIN

Denmark Strait

KOLBEINSEY RIDGE

ICELANDIC PLATEAU

AEGIR RIDGE

−174 WYVILLE THOMPSON RIDGE

Rockall 20

ROCKALL BANK

ROCKALL TROUGH

PORCUPINE ABYSSAL PLAIN

JAN MAYEN FRACTURE ZONE

Jan Mayen 2271

NORWEGIAN BASIN

−3070

VØRING PLATEAU

−237

DUMSHAF ABYSSAL PLAIN

−122

Norwegian Sea

White Sea

Gulf of Bothnia

60°

−69

North Sea
−310

−238

−43

Baltic Sea

E u r o p e

Faroe Islands

British Isles

Celtic Sea

−4938

BISCAY ABYSSAL PLAIN

B. of Biscay

−4465

Caspian Sea

Black Sea

Adriatic Sea

M e d i t e r r a n e a n   S e a

Red Sea

West from Greenwich   East from Greenwich

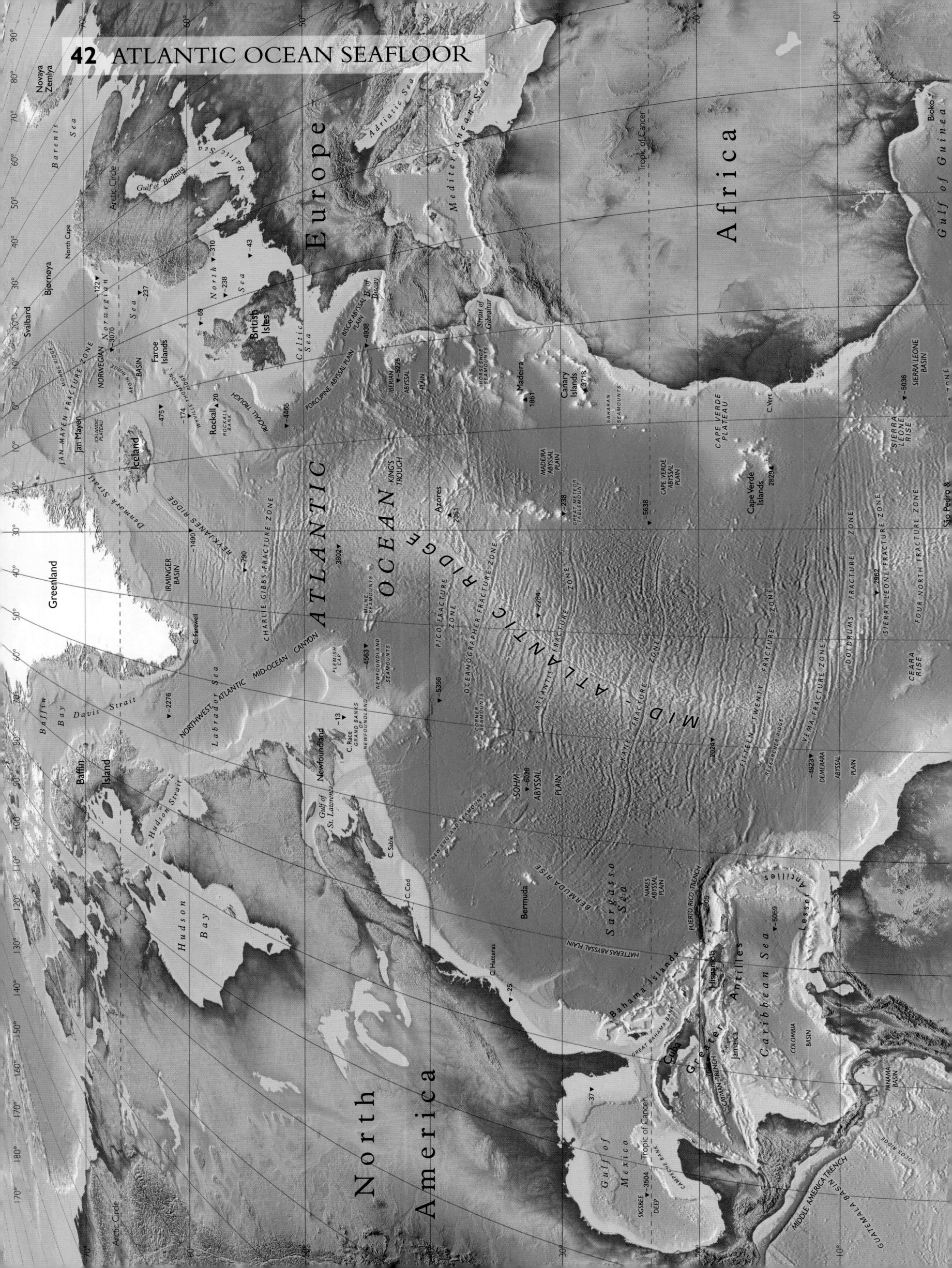

Europe

Africa

North America

Greenland

ATLANTIC OCEAN

MID ATLANTIC RIDGE

Sargasso Sea

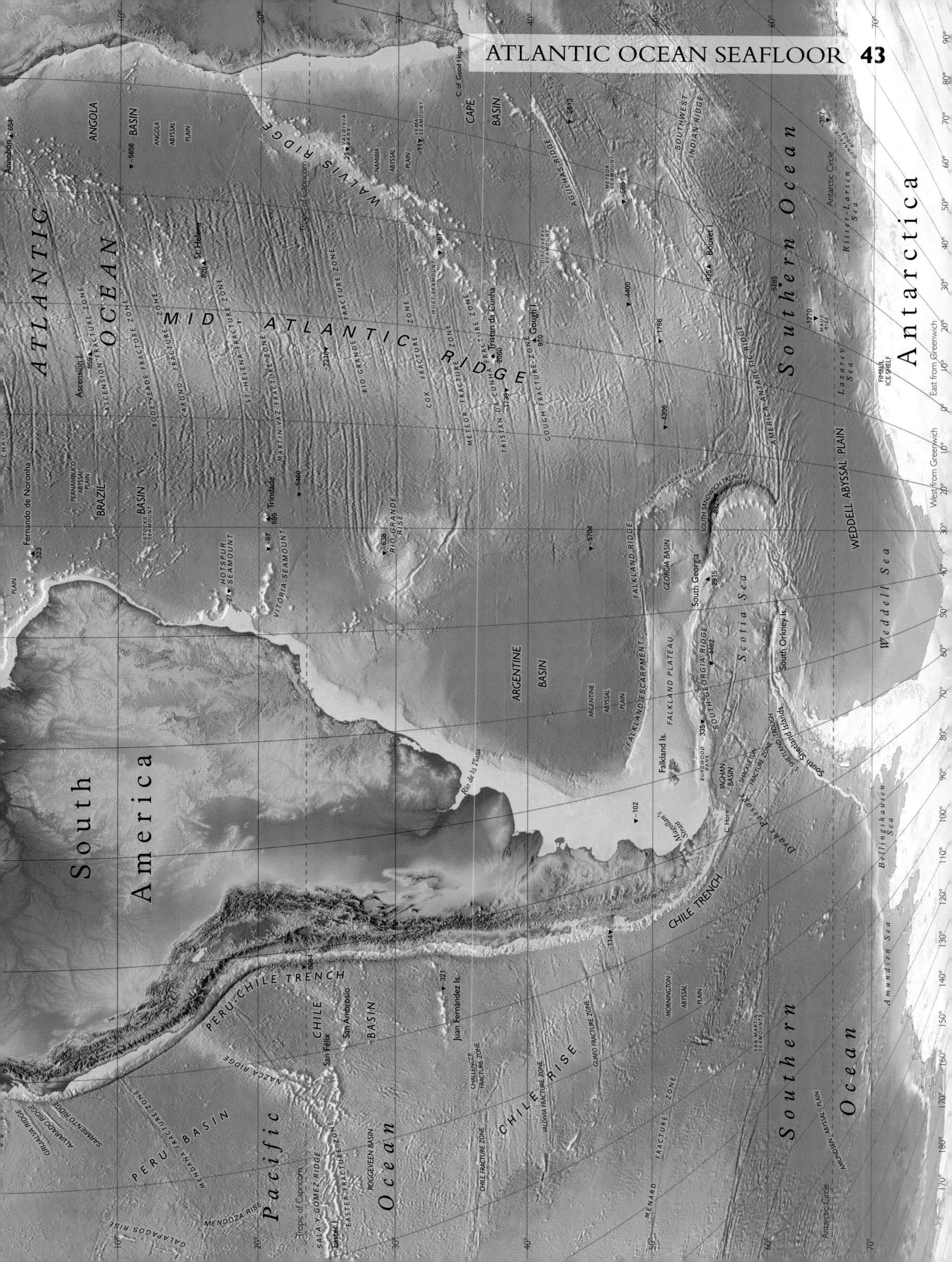

ATLANTIC

ANGOLA

ANGOLA BASIN

Annobón ▲ 654

▼-5656

ANGOLA ABYSSAL PLAIN

C. of Good Hope

CAPE BASIN

▲ 5613

▼-11

NAMIBIA ABYSSAL PLAIN

VEMA SEAMOUNT

SOUTHWEST INDIAN RIDGE

OCEAN

VALDIVIA BANK

▲ 23

Southern Ocean

AGULHAS RIDGE

▲ 357

DISCOVERY SEAMOUNT

METEOR SEAMOUNT

▼-566

Antarctica

MID ATLANTIC RIDGE

St. Helena

820 ▲

Ascension I.

▼-887

▼-4400

▲ 895

Bouvet I.

Risser-Larsen Sea

Ascension Fracture Zone

859 ▲

BODE VERDE FRACTURE ZONE

CARDNO FRACTURE ZONE

ST. HELENA FRACTURE ZONE

MARTIN VAZ FRACTURE ZONE

COX FRACTURE ZONE

WUST SEAMOUNT

METEOR FRACTURE ZONE

GOUGH FRACTURE ZONE

Tristan da Cunha 2060

Gough I. 910

▼-1799

▼-4306

MAUD RISE

▼-1270

Antarctic Circle

FIMBUL ICE SHELF

Lazarev Sea

East from Greenwich

West from Greenwich

RIO GRANDE FRACTURE ZONE

TRISTAN DA CUNHA FRACTURE ZONE

-5285

WEDDELL ABYSSAL PLAIN

▼-2210

BRAZIL

Fernando de Noronha

PERNAMBUCO ABYSSAL PLAIN

STOCKS SEAMOUNT

BRAZIL BASIN

▼-5460

Trindade

▲ 595 ▼-838

RIO GRANDE RISE

FALKLAND RIDGE

GEORGIA BASIN

South Georgia 2915

ISLAS ORCADAS RISE

SOUTH SANDWICH TRENCH

Weddell Sea

▼-5704

323 ▲

PLAIN

HOTSPUR SEAMOUNT

▲ 87

▲ 21

VITORIA SEAMOUNT

ARGENTINE BASIN

ARGENTINE ABYSSAL PLAIN

FALKLAND ESCARPMENT

FALKLAND PLATEAU

SOUTH GEORGIA RIDGE

▲ 4462

Scotia Sea

South Orkney Is.

South

Rio de la Plata

Falkland Is.

BURDWOOD BANK ▼-335

YAGHAN BASIN

SHACKLETON FRACTURE ZONE

South Shetland Islands

South Sandwich Islands

▼-102

Magellan Strait

C. Horn

Drake Passage

America

▼-114

CHILE TRENCH

Bellingshausen Sea

PERU-CHILE TRENCH

5064 ▼

Juan Fernández Is.

San Ambrosio

▲ 321

MORNINGTON ABYSSAL PLAIN

SAN MARTIN SEAMOUNTS

Amundsen Sea

Pacific

CHILE

San Félix

Easter I.

NAZCA RIDGE

SALA Y GÓMEZ RIDGE

CHILE BASIN

CHILENO FRACTURE ZONE

GUAFO FRACTURE ZONE

CHILE RISE

VALDIVIA FRACTURE ZONE

MENARD FRACTURE ZONE

ALVARADO RIDGE

GUALLAVA RIDGE

SARMIENTO RIDGE

Tropic of Capricorn

PERU BASIN

MENDANA FRACTURE ZONE

ROGGEVEEN BASIN

EASTER FRACTURE ZONE

MENDOZA RISE

GALÁPAGOS RISE

Ocean

Antarctic Circle

AMUNDSEN ABYSSAL PLAIN

Southern Ocean

WALVIS RIDGE

Tropic of Capricorn

Asia

Arctic Circle

St. Lawrence I.

Bering
Sea

Nuniva

Sea of
Okhotsk

−1000

Kamchatka

ALEUTIAN
BASIN

BOWERS RIDGE

BOWERS
BASIN

Aleutian   Islands

7822

ALEUTIAN   TRENCH

OBRUCHEV RISE

CHINOOK TROUGH

KURIL KAMCHATKA TRENCH

KURIL BASIN

Hokkaido

−10542

PACIFIC

NORTHWEST   BASIN

EMPEROR SEAMOUNT CHAIN

EMPEROR TROUGH

HESS RISE

NORTHWEST HAWAIIAN RIDGE

Sea of Japan
(East Sea)

YAMATO
RIDGE
BAND MON

Yellow
Sea

Honshu

−8412

JAPAN TRENCH

NANKAI TROUGH

NEW TRENCH

IZU OGASAWARA TRENCH

SHATSKY RISE

−2450

MID-PACIFIC SEAMOUNTS

MAPMAKERS
SEAMOUNTS

Midway Is.   13

HAWAIIAN

East
China
Sea

OKINAWA TROUGH

NANSEI SHOTO RIDGE
DAITO RIDGE

OKI DAITO RIDGE

PALAU KYUSHU RIDGE

WEST
MARIANA
BASIN

MARIANA RIDGE

MARIANA TROUGH

EAST MARIANA
BASIN

MARSHALL SEAMOUNTS

MAGELLAN SEAMOUNTS

CENTRAL
PACIFIC
BASIN

Tropic of Cancer

Taiwan

Gulf of
Tonkin

Hainan

Luzon

PHILIPPINE

Philippine
Sea

KYUSHU PALAU RIDGE

CHALLENGER
DEEP
−11022

MARIANA   TRENCH

Micronesia

CAROLINE SEAMOUNTS

791

Marshall
Is.

PACIFIC

Bay of
Bengal

Maudin Sun

Andaman Is.   732

Andaman
Sea

South
China
Sea

SOUTH CHINA BASIN

Philippine
Islands

BASIN

−10057

PHILIPPINE   TRENCH

Philippine
Basin

Palau
Is.

PALAU TRENCH

YAP TRENCH

EAURIPIK RISE

CAROLINE SEAMOUNTS

Pohnpei

CENTRAL
PACIFIC
BASIN

Ceylon

ANDAMAN
BASIN
−4267

Nicobar Is.   642

Gulf of
Thailand

−22

Sulu
Sea

PALAWAN TROUGH

SULU
BASIN

Mindanao

Celebes Sea
CELEBES
BASIN

WEST
CAROLINE
BASIN

EAST
CAROLINE
BASIN

MELANESIAN
BASIN

PACIFIC

Dondra Head

Equator

CEYLON PLAIN

−1550

COCOS
BASIN

Str. of Malacca

MENTAWAI BASIN

Sumatra

SUNDA SHELF

Borneo

Celebes

MACASSAR STRAIT

SOUTH
MAKASSAR
BASIN

NORTH BANDA
BASIN

Seram Sea

ONTONG
JAVA
PLATEAU

Phoenix Is.

AFANASY
NIKITINI
SEAMOUNT

Cocos Is.

NINETYEAST   RIDGE

INVESTIGATOR RIDGE

SUNDA TRENCH (JAVA TRENCH)

SUNDA TROUGH

Java Sea

Sunda Str.

Java

Flores Sea

SOUTH BANDA
BASIN

Banda Sea

Timor

Arafura
Sea

New Guinea

Bismarck
Sea

New
Britain

−8940

SOLOMON RISE

Solomon
Sea

Melanesia

MID-INDIAN

OCEAN

Christmas I.   361

−7125

ROO
RISE

−6204

NORTH
AUSTRALIAN
BASIN

Timor
Sea

ARAFURA
SHELF

Torres Str.

Papua
Plateau

POCKLINGTON TROUGH

−8322

NEW BRITAIN TRENCH
NEW IRELAND REACH

NORTH SOLOMON TRENCH

SOUTH SOLOMON TRENCH

−9165

GILBERT RIDGE

WEST

Samoa I.

BASIN

GASCOGNE
PLAIN

SANUL TROUGH

Timor
Shelf

Gulf of
Carpentaria

CORAL
SEA
BASIN

Espiritu
Santo

FIJI

Fiji Is.

Niue   88

Indian

Ocean

OSBORN
PLATEAU

WHARTON

BASIN

EXMOUTH
PLATEAU

WALLABY
PLATEAU

North West C.
CUVIER
BASIN

Coral
Sea

Queensland
PLATEAU

Great Barrier Reef

New
Caledonia

−570

LORD HOWE RISE

NEW CALEDONIA RIDGE

NORFOLK RIDGE

SOUTH NEW HEBRIDES TRENCH

LAU RIDGE

LAU BASIN

COLVILLE RIDGE

HAWKE TROUGH

TONGA TRENCH

SOUTH
FIJI
BASIN

Tropic of Capricorn

−10822

LOUISVIL

Tropic of Capricorn

−2067

EAST DIAMANTINA RIDGE

BATAVIA
KNOLL

GULDEN
DRAAK
KNOLL

BROKEN RIDGE

NATURALISTE FRACTURE ZONE

DIAMANTINA FRACTURE ZONE

CUVIER
PLATEAU

C. Inscription

PERTH

BASIN

BROUWER
SEAMOUNT
−5748

NATURALISTE
PLATEAU
C. Leeuwin

−8602

Australia

SOUTH AUSTRALIAN BASIN

AUSTRALIAN
ANTARCTIC
BASIN

Bass Str.

TASMAN ABYSSAL
PLAIN

Norfolk I.   319

Tasman
Sea

CHALLENGER
PLATEAU

New Zealand

KERMADEC TRENCH

North I.

Amsterdam I.   881

St. Paul Is.   284

SOUTHEAST   INDIAN   RIDGE

AUSTRALIAN ANTARCTIC DISCORDANCE

SOUTH TASMAN RISE

EAST
TASMAN
PLATEAU

TASMAN

BASIN

South I.

CHATHAM RISE

Chatham Is.

EL CANO
RISE

Crozet Is.

−1090   −4590

Kerguelen
Is.   3850

−274

Heard I.   2745

KERGUELEN PLATEAU

ELAN BANK

Tasmania

Tasmania

Bounty Is.
−60

Antipodes I.

BOUNTY
PLATEAU

BOUNTY TROUGH

Campbell I.
−272

HJORT TRENCH

−6240

BOLLONS
SEAMOUNT

LENA
SEAMOUNT
CONRAD RISE

−6739

VALDIVIA
ABYSSAL
PLAIN

AMERY
BASIN

ENDERBY ABYSSAL   PLAIN

Southern

−5325

C. Borley

PRINCESS
ELIZABETH
TROUGH

Davis
Sea

AUSTRALIAN-
ANTARCTIC
BASIN

SOUTH INDIAN
−4650
ABYSSAL PLAIN

Dumont d'Urville Sea

Vincennes
Bay

Paulding
Bay

Porpoise
Bay

Ocean

Macquarie I.

Auckland Is.
CAMPBELL
PLATEAU

Antarctic Circle

Prydz
Bay

Balleny Is.

Scott I.   50

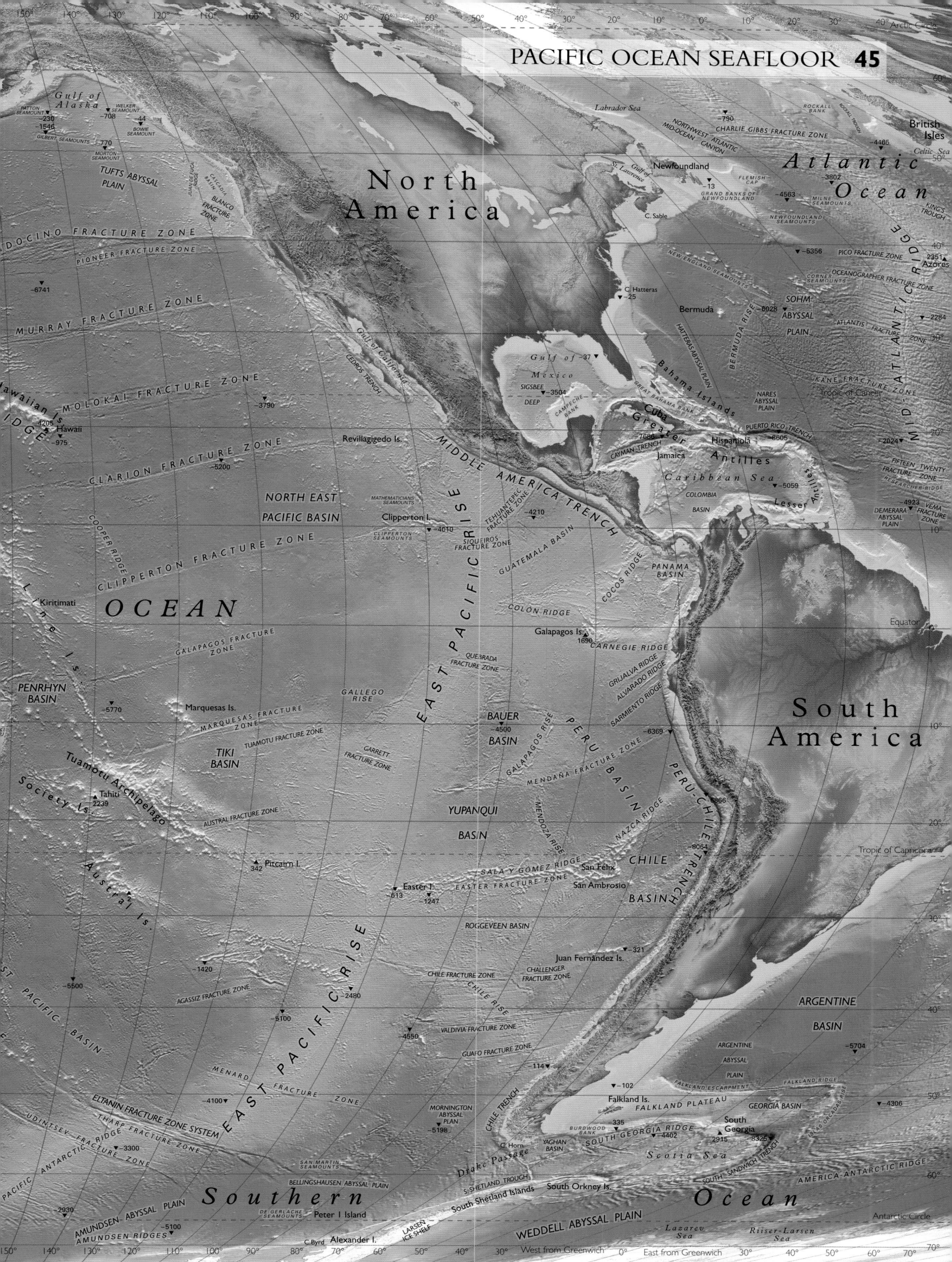

North
America

South
America

*Atlantic
Ocean*

OCEAN

Southern   Ocean

*Gulf of
Alaska*

Labrador Sea

British
Isles

Celtic Sea

TUFTS ABYSSAL
PLAIN

ROCKALL
BANK

NORTHWEST ATLANTIC
MID-OCEAN CANYON

CHARLIE GIBBS FRACTURE ZONE

Newfoundland

GRAND BANKS OF
NEWFOUNDLAND

C. Sable

PICO FRACTURE ZONE

Azores

OCEANOGRAPHER FRACTURE ZONE

ATLANTIS FRACTURE ZONE

KING'S
TROUGH

*Gulf of
Lawrence*

C. Hatteras

New England Seamounts

CORNER
SEAMOUNTS

Bermuda

SOHM
ABYSSAL
PLAIN

BERMUDA RISE

KANE FRACTURE ZONE

Tropic of Cancer

*Gulf of
Mexico*

SIGSBEE
DEEP

CAMPECHE
BANK

GREAT BAHAMA BANK

Bahama Islands

HATTERAS ABYSSAL PLAIN

NARES
ABYSSAL
PLAIN

Cuba

Greater

PUERTO RICO TRENCH

Antilles

FIFTEEN TWENTY
FRACTURE ZONE

RESEARCHER RIDGE

CAYMAN TRENCH

Jamaica

Hispaniola

Caribbean Sea

COLOMBIA
BASIN

Lesser

Antilles

DEMERARA
ABYSSAL
PLAIN

VEMA
FRACTURE ZONE

Revillagigedo Is.

MIDDLE AMERICA TRENCH

MATHEMATICIANS
SEAMOUNTS

TEHUANTEPEC
FRACTURE ZONE

NORTH EAST
PACIFIC BASIN

Clipperton I.

CLIPPERTON
SEAMOUNTS

SIQUEIROS
FRACTURE ZONE

GUATEMALA BASIN

PANAMA
BASIN

COCOS RIDGE

COLON RIDGE

Galapagos Is.

CARNEGIE RIDGE

Equator

GRIJALVA RIDGE

ALVARADO RIDGE

SARMIENTO RIDGE

GALAPAGOS FRACTURE
ZONE

EAST PACIFIC RISE

QUEBRADA
FRACTURE ZONE

GALAPAGOS RISE

PERU BASIN

PENRHYN
BASIN

Kiritimati

Line Is.

Marquesas Is.

GALLEGO
RISE

BAUER

BASIN

PERU-CHILE TRENCH

MARQUESAS FRACTURE
ZONE

NAZCA RIDGE

TIKI
BASIN

TUAMOTU FRACTURE ZONE

GARRETT
FRACTURE ZONE

MENDAÑA FRACTURE ZONE

MENDOZA RISE

Tuamotu Archipelago

Tahiti

Society Is.

YUPANQUI

BASIN

AUSTRAL FRACTURE ZONE

Austral Is.

Pitcairn I.

SALA Y GÓMEZ RIDGE

San Félix

CHILE

BASIN

Tropic of Capricorn

Easter I.

EASTER FRACTURE ZONE

San Ambrosio

ROGGEVEEN BASIN

Juan Fernández Is.

CHILE FRACTURE ZONE

CHALLENGER
FRACTURE ZONE

ARGENTINE

BASIN

EAST PACIFIC RISE

AGASSIZ FRACTURE ZONE

CHILE RISE

VALDIVIA FRACTURE ZONE

ARGENTINE

ABYSSAL

PLAIN

GUAFO FRACTURE ZONE

WEST PACIFIC BASIN

MENARD FRACTURE ZONE

FALKLAND ESCARPMENT

FALKLAND RIDGE

ELTANIN FRACTURE ZONE SYSTEM

THARP FRACTURE ZONE

MORNINGTON
ABYSSAL
PLAIN

CHILE TRENCH

Falkland Is.

FALKLAND PLATEAU

GEORGIA BASIN

UDINTSEV FRACTURE ZONE

PACIFIC-ANTARCTIC RIDGE

SAN MARTIN
SEAMOUNTS

C. Horn

YAGHAN
BASIN

BURDWOOD
BANK

South
Georgia

SOUTH GEORGIA RIDGE

Scotia Sea

SOUTH SANDWICH TRENCH

SOUTH ORKNEY RIDGE

AMUNDSEN ABYSSAL PLAIN

BELLINGSHAUSEN ABYSSAL PLAIN

Drake Passage

S. SHETLAND TROUGH

South Shetland Islands

South Orkney Is.

AMERICA-ANTARCTIC RIDGE

AMUNDSEN BRIDGES

DE GERLACHE
SEAMOUNTS

Peter I Island

C. Byrd   Alexander I.

LARSEN
ICE SHELF

WEDDELL ABYSSAL PLAIN

*Lazarev
Sea*

*Riiser-Larsen
Sea*

Antarctic Circle

Mediterranean Sea

Asia

Tropic of Cancer

Red Sea
−2211

Persian Gulf
▲ −60

Str. of Hormuz
Gulf of Oman
OMAN
BASIN

Gulf of Aden
E. SHEBA RIDGE
W. SHEBA RIDGE
CHAIN RIDGE
OWEN FRACTURE ZONE

*Arabian
Sea*

ARABIAN
BASIN

*Bay of
Bengal*

Maudin Sun

Andaman Is. ▲732
*Andaman
Sea*

Hainan

*South
China
Sea*

SADKO SEAMOUNT
−2758

Laccadive
Is.

ANDAMAN
BASIN
▼−4267

Gulf of
Thailand

SOUTH CHINA BA

Taiwan

Socotra
Ras Asir

CARLSBERG RIDGE

▼−5827

C. Comorin
Ceylon

Nicobar Is. ▲642

Dondra Head

SUNDA
SHELF

Africa

Equator

▼−2194

COCO-DE-MER
SEAMOUNTS

SEYCHELLES
BANK
Seychelles ▲905
−13
AMIRANTE TRENCH
−5273
FORTUNE
BANK

SOMALI
BASIN

MASCARENE PLATEAU

MAHABHISS FRACTURE ZONE
SEALARK FRACTURE ZONE
VITYAZ FRACTURE ZONE
−6402

YEMA FRACTURE ZONE

Maldives

Chagos
Arch.
CHAGOS
BANK
−5408

CHAGOS-LACCADIVE RIDGE

CEYLON PLAIN
−1550

AFANASY
NIKITIN
SEAMOUNT

MID-INDIAN

OCEAN

BASIN

COCOS
BASIN

NINETYEAST RIDGE

MENTAWAI IS.
MENTAWAI BASIN
SUNDA TRENCH
Sumatra

Borneo Equ

Java Sea
SUNDA TRENCH (JAVA TROUGH)
SUNDA
Java

Pemba
Zanzibar

−7 ▲

SAYA DE
MALHA
BANK

MASCARENE
BASIN
Tromelin

NAZARETH
BANK

ARGO FRACTURE ZONE

MARIE CELESTE FRACTURE ZONE

INDIAN

OCEAN

OSBORN
PLATEAU

Cocos Is. ▲

INVESTIGATOR RIDGE

Christmas I. ▲361

ROO
RISE

GASCOGNE
PLAIN

NORT
AUSTRA
BASIN

C. Delgado
Comoro Is.

Agalega Is.

MID-INDIAN RIDGE

WILSHAW RIDGE

CARGADOS
CARAJOS
BANK

Madagascar

−5194
MASCARENE
PLAIN
828 ▲
Réunion 3069

396 ▲ Rodrigues I.
RODRIGUES RIDGE
Mauritius

WHARTON

BASIN

EXMOUTH
PLATEAU

HORIZON RIDGE

EAST INDIAMAN RIDGE

BATAVIA
KNOLL

WALLABY
PLATEAU

North West C.
CUVIER
BASIN

Austr

Tropic of Capricorn

Bassas
da India
Europa

MOZAMBIQUE
BASIN

MOZAMBIQUE CHANNEL

MOZAMBIQUE ESCARPMENT

MADAGASCAR RIDGE

MADAGASCAR
BASIN

SOUTHEAST

−2067 ▼

BROKEN RIDGE

GULDEN
DRAAK
KNOLL

CUVIER
PLATEAU

C. Inscription

PERTH

BASIN

NATURALISTE FRACTURE ZONE

BROUWER
SEAMOUNT
−5746
NATURALISTE
PLATEAU
C. Leeuwin

Tropic of Capri

C. of
Good
Hope
C. Agulhas
AGULHAS
BANK
TRANSKEI
BASIN

NATAL VALLEY

SOUTHWEST INDIAN RIDGE

DISCOVERY II FRACTURE ZONE

INDOMED FRACTURE ZONE

GALLIENI FRACTURE ZONE

ATLANTIS FRACTURE ZONE

MELVILLE FRACTURE ZONE

CROZET

BASIN

Amsterdam I. ▲881
St. Paul Is. ▲284

INDIAN

RIDGE

8060

DIAMANTINA FRACTURE ZONE

−3902

AUSTRAL-ANTARCTIC
DISCORDANCE

−5371 ▼
AGULHAS
PLATEAU

AGULHAS
BASIN

PRINCE EDWARD FRACTURE ZONE

DEL CAÑO RISE

Prince Edward Is. ▲
1230

1090
Crozet Is. ▲
−4590

1850
Kerguelen Is. ▲

KERGUELEN PLATEAU

Heard I. ▲
2745

CONRAD RISE

LENA
SEAMOUNT

ELAN BANK

−6739

ENDERBY ABYSSAL PLAIN

Southern

AUSTRALIAN-
ANTARCTIC

BASIN

Ocean

SOUTH INDIAN

ABYSSAL PLAIN

−1270
MAUD
RISE

Antarctic Circle

*Lazarev
Sea*

Riiser-Larsen
Sea

Cosmonaut
Sea

C. Borley

VALDIVIA
ABYSSAL
PLAIN

AMERY
BASIN
PRINCESS ELIZABETH
TROUGH

Prydz
Bay

Vincennes
Bay

Paulding
Bay

Porpoise
Bay

Antarctic C

Antarctica

West from Greenwich
East from Greenwich

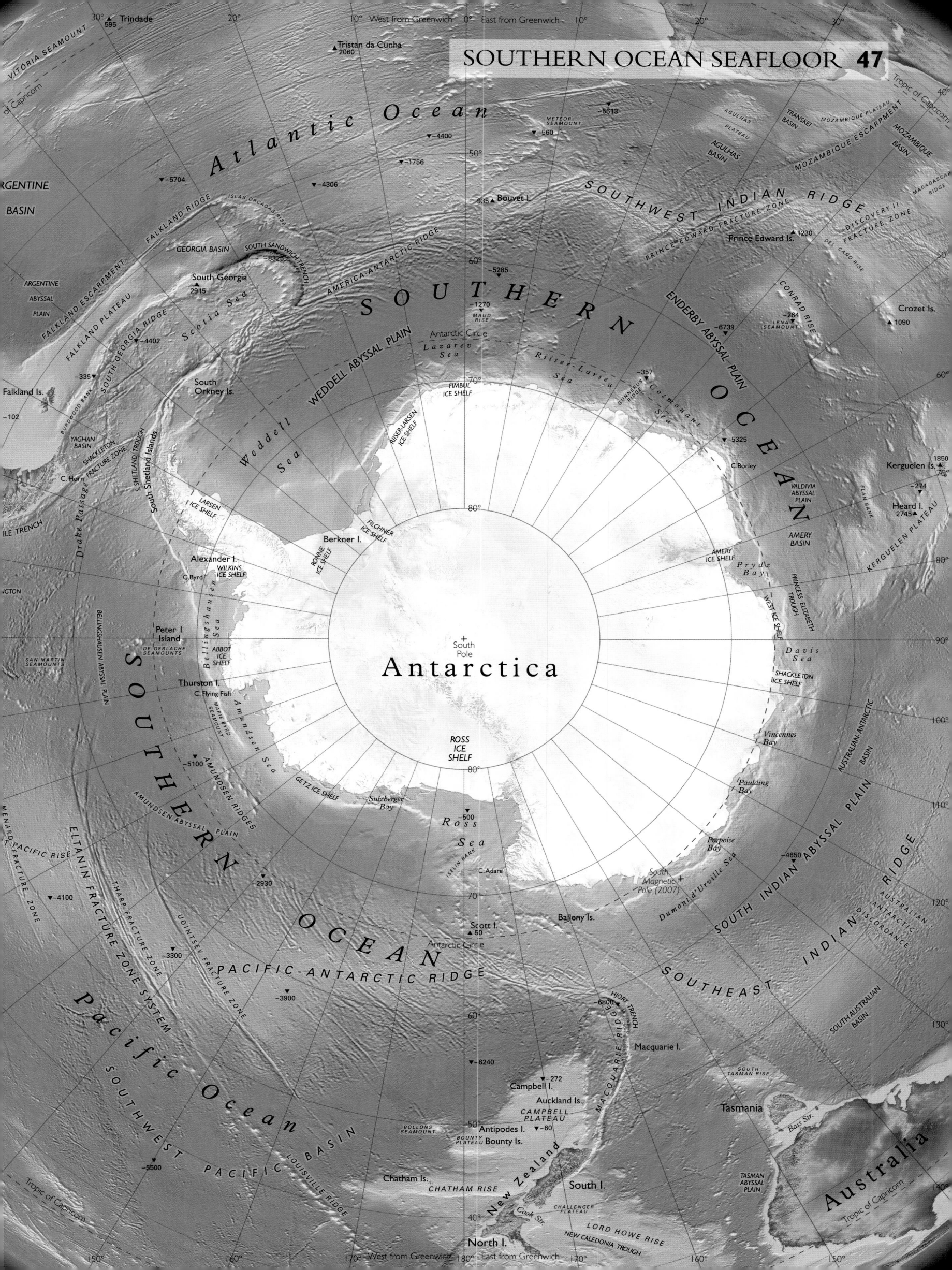

30° Trindade
595

▲ Tristan da Cunha
2060

Atlantic Ocean

VITORIA SEAMOUNT

of Capricorn

ARGENTINE
BASIN

ARGENTINE
ABYSSAL
PLAIN

Falkland Is.
−102

−335

−5704

−4306

−1756

▼ −4400

▼ −5613

▼ −560

935 ▲ Bouvet I.

GEORGIA BASIN

SOUTH SANDWICH TRENCH
−8325

South Georgia
2915

Scotia Sea

−4402

FALKLAND RIDGE

ISLAS ORCADAS RIDGE

FALKLAND ESCARPMENT

FALKLAND PLATEAU

SOUTH GEORGIA RIDGE

BURDWOOD BANK

YAGHAN
BASIN

C. Horn

SHACKLETON FRACTURE ZONE

South
Orkney Is.

South Shetland Islands

LARSEN
ICE SHELF

Drake Passage

ILE TRENCH

NGTON

SAN MARTIN
SEAMOUNTS

BELLINGSHAUSEN ABYSSAL PLAIN

Peter I
Island

DE GERLACHE
SEAMOUNTS

Thurston I.

C. Flying Fish

SOUTHERN

MENARD-PACIFIC RISE

MENARD FRACTURE ZONE

ELTANIN FRACTURE ZONE SYSTEM

THARP FRACTURE ZONE

−4100

−3300

−3900

−5100

UDINTSEV FRACTURE ZONE

−2930

Pacific Ocean

SOUTHWEST PACIFIC

LOUISVILLE RIDGE

−5500

Tropic of Capricorn

SOUTH WEST FROM GREENWICH 0° EAST FROM GREENWICH 10°

SOUTHERN

AMERICA-ANTARCTIC RIDGE

WEDDELL ABYSSAL PLAIN

Antarctic Circle

Lazarev
Sea

−1270
MAUD
RISE

−5285

O C E A N

SOUTHWEST INDIAN RIDGE

AGULHAS
PLATEAU

TRANSKEI
BASIN

MOZAMBIQUE PLATEAU

MOZAMBIQUE ESCARPMENT

MOZAMBIQUE
BASIN

AGULHAS
BASIN

PRINCE EDWARD FRACTURE ZONE

Prince Edward Is. ▲ 1230

DISCOVERY II
FRACTURE ZONE

DEL CANO RISE

MADAGASCAR
RIDGE

Crozet Is.
▲ 1090

264
LENA
SEAMOUNT

CONRAD RISE

ENDERBY ABYSSAL PLAIN

−6739
▼

−357

GUNNERUS RIDGE

COSMONAUT

Riiser-Larsen
Sea

FIMBUL
ICE SHELF

RIISER-LARSEN
ICE SHELF

Weddell
Sea

FILCHNER
ICE SHELF

Berkner I.

RONNE
ICE SHELF

Alexander I.

C. Byrd

WILKINS
ICE SHELF

ABBOT
ICE SHELF

Amundsen Sea

MARIE BYRD SEAMOUNT

GETZ ICE SHELF

Sulzberger
Bay

AMUNDSEN RIDGES

AMUNDSEN ABYSSAL PLAIN

Ross
Sea

−500

ISELIN BANK

C. Adare

Scott I.
▲ 50

Antarctic Circle

PACIFIC-ANTARCTIC RIDGE

−6240

BOLLONS
SEAMOUNT

BOUNTY
PLATEAU

Campbell I. ▲ 272

Auckland Is.

CAMPBELL
PLATEAU

Antipodes I. ▼ −60

Bounty Is.

Chatham Is.

CHATHAM RISE

New Zealand

South I.

Cook Str.

North I.

CHALLENGER
PLATEAU

NEW CALEDONIA TROUGH

LORD HOWE RISE

WEST FROM GREENWICH 180° EAST FROM GREENWICH

+
South
Pole

Antarctica

ROSS
ICE
SHELF

80°

70°

South
Magnetic +
Pole (2007)

Balleny Is.

Dumont d'Urville Sea

Porpoise
Bay

Paulding
Bay

Vincennes
Bay

Davis
Sea

SHACKLETON
ICE SHELF

Pryd\z
Bay

AMERY
ICE SHELF

WEST ICE SHELF

PRINCESS ELIZABETH TROUGH

AMERY
BASIN

VALDIVIA
ABYSSAL
PLAIN

C. Borley

−5325
▼

Kerguelen Is.
1850

−274

Heard I.
2745

ELAN BANK

KERGUELEN PLATEAU

AUSTRALIAN-ANTARCTIC BASIN

SOUTH INDIAN ABYSSAL PLAIN

−4650

SOUTHEAST INDIAN RIDGE

AUSTRALIAN ANTARCTIC DISCORDANCE

SOUTH AUSTRALIAN
BASIN

HJORT TRENCH
−6800

MACQUARIE RIDGE

Macquarie I.

SOUTH
TASMAN RISE

Tasmania

Bass Str.

TASMAN
ABYSSAL
PLAIN

Australia

Tropic of Capricorn

WORLD
MAPS

A   B   C   D   E   F   G   H

1   2   3   4   5   6   7   8   9

North Magnetic Pole
Queen Elizabeth Islands
Ellesmere I.
Greenland
Greenland Sea
Jan Mayen
Norwegian Sea
Beaufort Sea
Pt. Barrow
Banks I.
Parry Is.
Devon I.
Baffin Island
Arctic Circle
3693
Denmark Str.
Iceland
Faroe Is.
Alaska
Mt. McKinley 6194 (Denali)
Yukon
Gr. Bear L.
Gr. Slave L.
Hudson Str.
Davis Str.
Nelson
Hudson Bay
C. Farewell
Labrador Sea
British Isles
3344
Nor Se
Bering Str.
Bering Sea
Kodiak I.
Gulf of Alaska
Haida Gwaii (Queen Charlotte Is.)
Aleutian Is.
Vancouver I.
L. Winnipeg
Great Lakes
Laurentian Plateau
St. Lawrence
Newfoundland
C. Race
Nova Scotia
B. of Biscay
Pic d'A...
Iberian Pen.

North America
Great Plains
Rocky Mountains
Cascade Range
Coast Ranges
Columbia
Great Basin
C. Mendocino
Mt. Elbert 4399
Arkansas
Olsa
Mississippi
Mt. Mitchell 2037
Appalachian Mts.
C. Cod
C. Hatteras
Bermuda
Azores
ATLANTIC
OCEAN
Madeira
Canary Is.
3718
J. Toubkal
Maghre
Tropic of Cancer
S
A f...

Mt. Whitney 4418
Sierra Nevada
Death Valley
Colorado
Rio Grande
Lower California
C. San Lucas
Gulf of California
Sargasso Sea
Florida
Gulf of Mexico
Florida Str.
Bahamas
Cuba
Greater Antilles
Jamaica
Hispaniola
3175
Milwaukee Deep 8605
Puerto Rico
Lesser Antilles

Hawaiian Is.
Mauna Kea 4205
Revilla Gigedo Is.
Popocatepetl 5452
Pico de Orizaba 5610
Yucatan
4093
5779
Central America
Isthmus of Panama
Caribbean Sea
Trinidad
Orinoco
Guiana Highlands
Mt. Roraima 2810
2964
Negro

PACIFIC
OCEAN
Polynesia
Line Is.
Kiritimati
Galapagos Is.
Chimborazo 6310
Maranon
Japura
Amazon
Purus
Madeira
Xingu
Tapajos
Negro
South America
Selvas
Plateau of Mato Grosso
C. de São Roque
Ascension
Equator
Gulf of Guin...

Marquesas Is.
6768
St. Helena
Society Is.
Tahiti
Tuamotu Is.
Cook Is.
6402
Tubuai Is.
Pitcairn I.
Easter I.
Chile Trench 8050
Cerro Ojos del Salado 6863
L. Titicaca
Bolivian Plateau
Gran Chaco
Parana
Tocantins
São Francisco
Brazilian Highlands
2890
C. Frio
Trindade
Tropic of Capricorn
ATLANTIC
OCEAN

Arch. de Juan Fernandez
Cerro Aconcagua 6960
Pampas
Negro
R. de la Plata
Tristan da Cunha
OCEAN

Andes
Patagonia
4058
-40
-105
Magellan's Str.
C. Horn
Tierra del Fuego
Falkland Is.
2937
S. Georgia
Scotia Sea
South Sandwich Is.
South Orkney Is.
South Shetland Is.
Drake Passage
Antarctic Peninsula
Weddell Sea
Antarctic Circle

Bellingshausen Sea
Amundsen Sea
Thurston I.
Alexander I.
Palmer Land
Ellsworth Land
Vinson Massif 4897
Ronne Ice Shelf
Berkner I.
Caird Coast
Coats Land
Marie Byrd Land
Roosevelt I.
Ross Sea

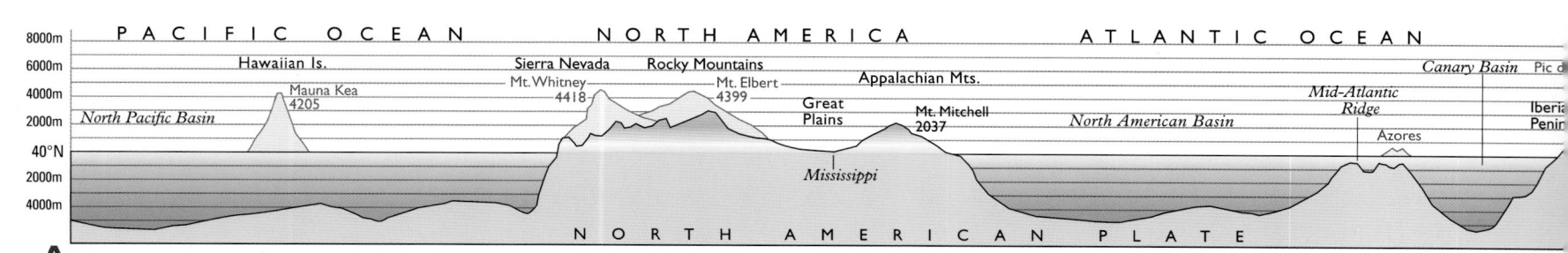

PACIFIC OCEAN   NORTH AMERICA   ATLANTIC OCEAN
Hawaiian Is.
Sierra Nevada
Rocky Mountains
Canary Basin   Pic
Mauna Kea 4205
Mt. Whitney 4418
Mt. Elbert 4399
Appalachian Mts.
Mid-Atlantic Ridge
Iberia
North Pacific Basin
Great Plains
Mt. Mitchell 2037
North American Basin
Azores
Penin
Mississippi
NORTH AMERICAN PLATE

8000m 6000m 4000m 2000m 40°N 2000m 4000m

A

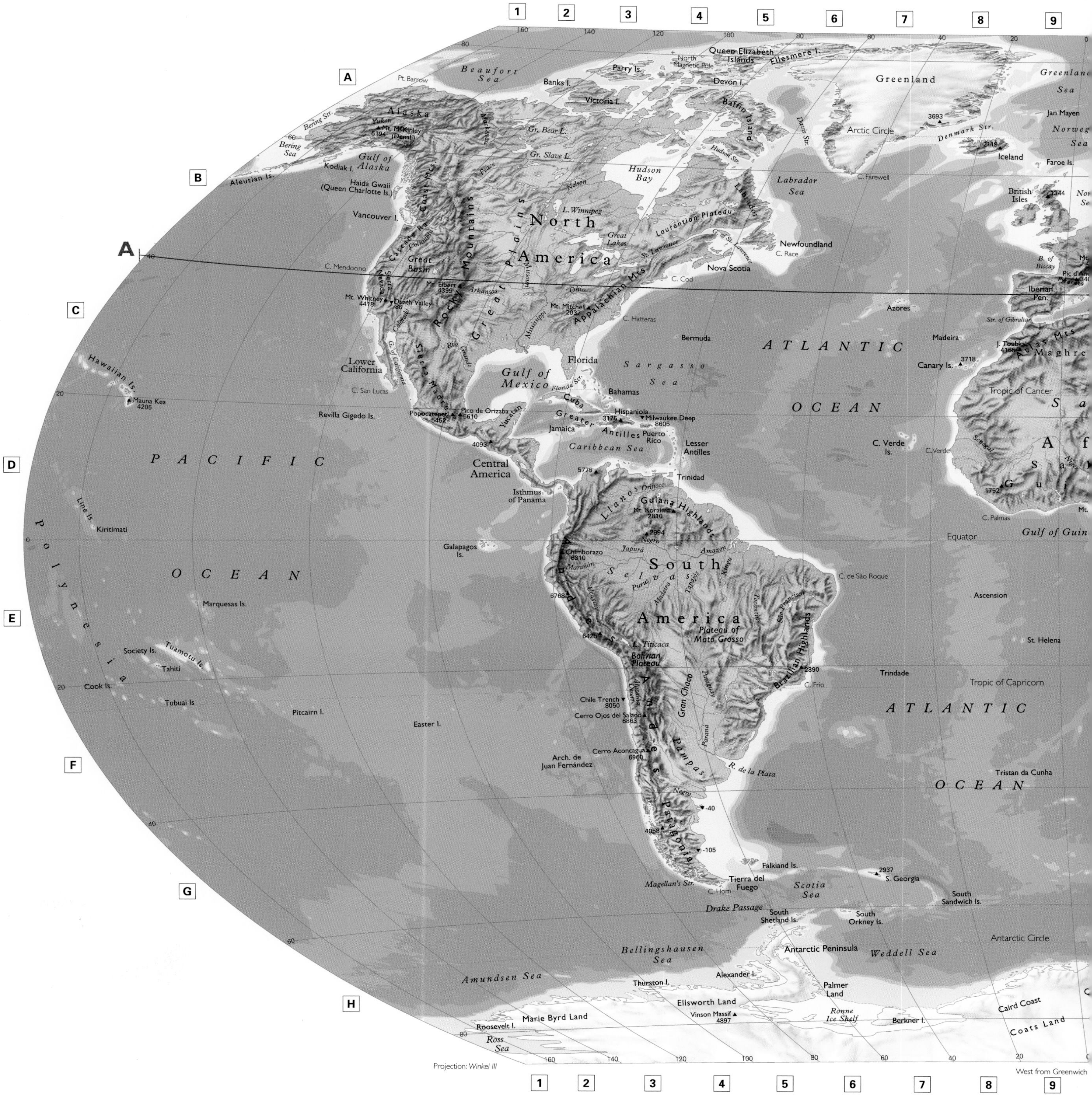

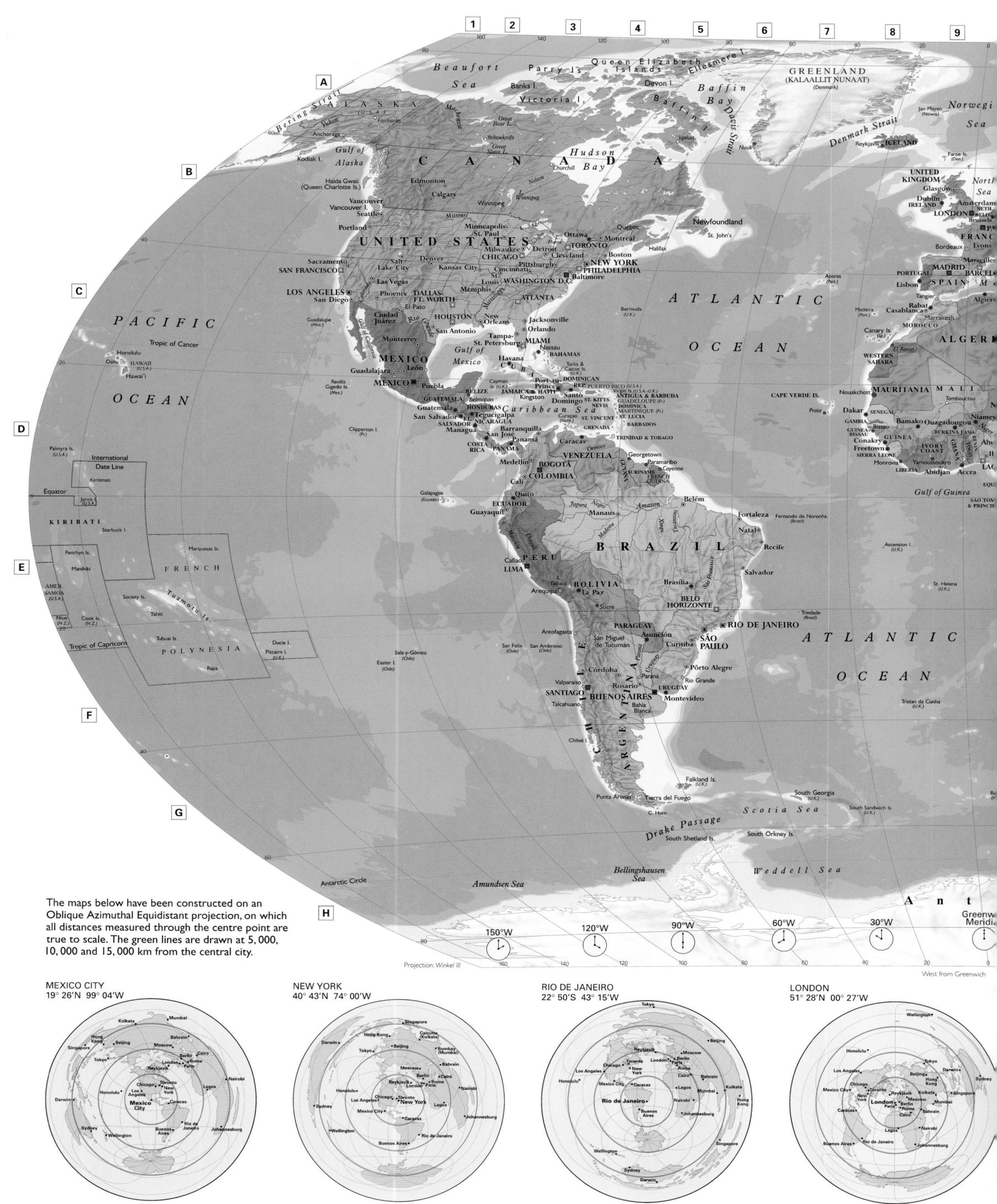

The maps below have been constructed on an Oblique Azimuthal Equidistant projection, on which all distances measured through the centre point are true to scale. The green lines are drawn at 5,000, 10,000 and 15,000 km from the central city.

Projection: Winkel III

West from Greenwich

MEXICO CITY
19° 26′N 99° 04′W

NEW YORK
40° 43′N 74° 00′W

RIO DE JANEIRO
22° 50′S 43° 15′W

LONDON
51° 28′N 00° 27′W

1:31 100 000

Projection : Zenithal Equidistant

COPYRIGHT PHILIP'S

Maximum extent of sea ice

Minimum extent of sea ice (September 2011)

Ice caps and permanent ice shelf

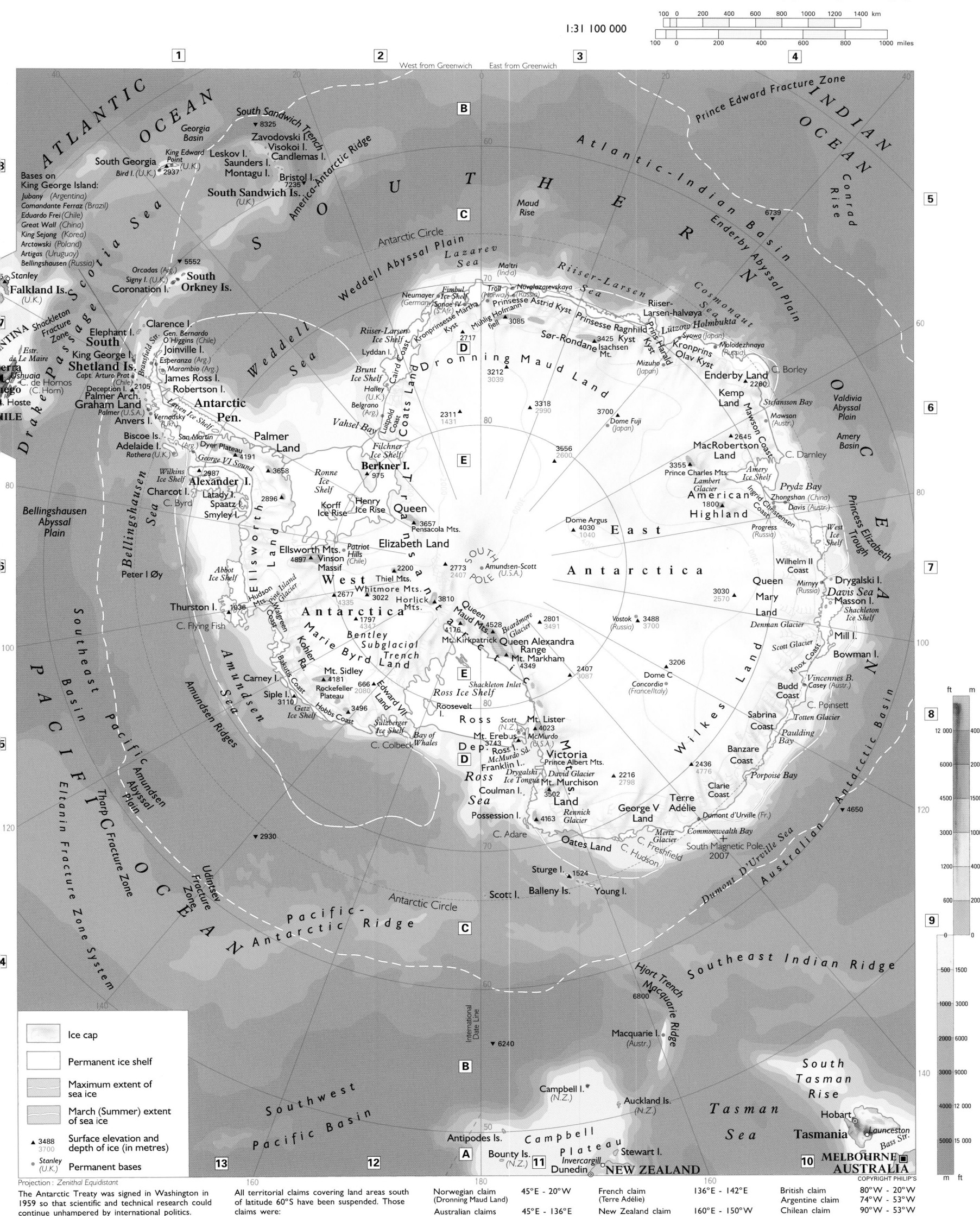

1:31 100 000

	Ice cap
	Permanent ice shelf
	Maximum extent of sea ice
	March (Summer) extent of sea ice
▲ 3488 ▼ 3700	Surface elevation and depth of ice (in metres)
• Stanley (U.K.)	Permanent bases

Projection : Zenithal Equidistant

The Antarctic Treaty was signed in Washington in 1959 so that scientific and technical research could continue unhampered by international politics.

All territorial claims covering land areas south of latitude 60°S have been suspended. Those claims were:

Norwegian claim (Dronning Maud Land)	45°E - 20°W	French claim (Terre Adélie)	136°E - 142°E	British claim	80°W - 20°W
Australian claims	45°E - 136°E	New Zealand claim (Ross Dependency)	160°E - 150°W	Argentine claim	74°W - 53°W
	142°E - 160°E			Chilean claim	90°W - 53°W

COPYRIGHT PHILIP'S

Bases on King George Island:
Jubany (Argentina)
Comandante Ferraz (Brazil)
Eduardo Frei (Chile)
Great Wall (China)
King Sejong (Korea)
Arctowski (Poland)
Artigas (Uruguay)
Bellingshausen (Russia)

CANADA

Hudson Bay
Churchill
L. Winnipeg
Nelson
Regina
Winnipeg
Minneapolis
St. Paul
Chicago
Detroit
Omaha
Pittsburgh
St. Louis
UNITED STATES
Atlanta
Houston
Galveston
New Orleans
Jacksonville
Orlando
Miami
Gulf of Mexico
Sigsbee 3504
Deep
Tampico
Veracruz
G. de Campeche
MEXICO
GUATEMALA
Guatemala
BELIZE
HONDURAS
EL SALVADOR
NICARAGUA
COSTA RICA
PANAMA
Panamá
Cali
Bogotá
COLOMBIA
Quito
ECUADOR
Guayaquil
Trujillo
Lima
PERU
La Paz
BOLIVIA
Arica
Iquique
Antofagasta
CHILE
Santiago
Valparaíso
Concepción
ARGENTINA
Córdoba
Rosario
Santa Fe
Buenos Aires
Montevideo
URUGUAY
Bahía Blanca
Puerto Montt
I. de Chiloé
Arch. de los Chonos
Pen. de Taitao
Golfo San Jorge
G. San Matías
Pen. Valdés
Punta Arenas
Tierra del Fuego
C. de Hornos

PACIFIC OCEAN

BRAZIL
Manaus
Belém
São Luís
Fortaleza
Natal
Recife
Maceió
Salvador
Brasília
Goiânia
Belo Horizonte
São Paulo
Rio de Janeiro
Santos
Curitiba
Pôrto Alegre
Porto Alegre
PARAGUAY
Asunción

VENEZUELA
Caracas
Barranquilla
Georgetown
GUYANA
Paramaribo
SURINAME
Cayenne
FRENCH GUIANA

GREENLAND (Denmark)
Nuuk
Tasiilaq
ICELAND
Reykjavik
Denmark Strait
Davis Strait
Labrador Sea
Hudson Str.
Newfoundland
St. John's
Halifax
Boston
New York
Philadelphia
Baltimore
Washington D.C.
Montréal
Ottawa
Toronto
Québec
Gulf of St. Lawrence
Sargasso Sea
Bermuda
BAHAMAS
Nassau
La Habana
CUBA
HAITI
DOM. REP.
Santo Domingo
Kingston
JAMAICA
West Indies
Puerto Rico
PUERTO RICO (U.S.A.)
San Juan
Caribbean Sea
Leeward Is.
GUADELOUPE (Fr.)
DOMINICA
MARTINIQUE (Fr.)
ST. LUCIA
BARBADOS
ST. VINCENT
GRENADA
Windward Is.
TRINIDAD & TOBAGO
Port of Spain

ATLANTIC OCEAN
Mid-Atlantic Ridge
Azores-Biscay Rise
King's Trough
Açores (Port.)
Ponta Delgada
Tropic of Cancer
Nares Abyssal Plain
Corner Seamounts
Equator
Tropic of Capricorn

NORWAY
Oslo
Bergen
Trondheim
Stockholm
Göteborg
Malmö
København
DENMARK
North Sea
UNITED KINGDOM
Glasgow
Edinburgh
Liverpool
Dublin
IRELAND
London
Amsterdam
NETH.
BELG.
Brussel
Hamburg
Berlin
GERMANY
POLAND
Warszawa
Gdansk
Le Havre
Paris
FRANCE
Bordeaux
Marseille
Bay of Biscay
Biscay Abyssal Plain
A Coruña
Vigo
Porto
Lisboa
Madrid
SPAIN
PORTUGAL
Barcelona
Corse
Sardegna
Roma
Napoli
ITALY
Milano
Wien
AUSTRIA
CZECH REP.
SLOVAK REP.
HUNGARY
Zagreb
CROATIA
Mediterranean Sea
Tanger
Rabat
Casablanca
MOROCCO
Marrakech
Madeira (Port.)
Funchal
Is. Canarias (Sp.)
Las Palmas
El Aaiún
WESTERN SAHARA
ALGERIA
Sahara
MAURITANIA
Nouadhibou
Nouakchott
CAPE VERDE IS.
Praia
Dakar
SENEGAL
GAMBIA
Banjul
GUINEA-BISSAU
GUINEA
Conakry
Freetown
SIERRA LEONE
Monrovia
LIBERIA
IVORY COAST
Abidjan
GHANA
Accra
TOGO
BENIN
NIGERIA
Lagos
Niger
Kano
Ouagadougou
BURKINA FASO
Bamako
MALI
NIGER
Tombouctou
Gulf of Guinea
EQUATORIAL GUINEA
SÃO TOMÉ & PRÍNCIPE
GABON
Libreville
CAMEROON
Port Harcourt
Pointe Noire
ANGOLA
Luanda
Benguela
Namibe
NAMIBIA
Walvis Bay
Lüderitz
SOUTH AFRICA
Cape Town
C. of Good Hope
Port Nolloth

Brazil Basin
Argentine Basin
Argentine Abyssal Plain
Falkland Ridge
Falkland Is.
Stanley
Falkland Plateau
Georgia Basin
South Georgia (U.K.)
Grytviken
South Sandwich Trench
Bouvetøya (Nor.)
Gough I. (U.K.)
Tristan da Cunha (U.K.)
Inaccessible I. (U.K.)
St. Helena (U.K.)
Ascension I. (U.K.)
Cape Basin
Walvis Ridge
Nambia Abyssal Plain
Agulhas Ridge
Discovery Seamount

Ferdinand de Noronha (Brazil)
Atol das Rocas
Trindade (Brazil)
Martin Vaz
Fernando de Noronha

Projection: Mollweide
West from Greenwich
COPYRIGHT PHILIP'S

1:11 100 000

54

ARCTIC OCEAN

CANADA

Axel Heiberg I.
Meighen I.
Nansen Sound
Eureka
QUTTINIRPAAQ NAT. PARK
2616
Lake Hazen
Alert
Cape Columbia
3548
1626
Lincoln Sea
1920
Kap Morris Jesup
Oodaaq
Frederick E. Hyde Fjord

Ellesmere Island
Robeson Chan.
Hans I.
Kennedy Chan.
2457
Victoria Fjord
Nansen Land
Peary Land
Koch Fjord
Jørgen Brønlund Fjord
Independence Fjord
Station Nord
Nordostrundingen

Nyeboe Land
Wulff Land
Warming Land
Washington Land
Petermann Gletscher
Hall Land
Kronprins Frederik Land
Academy Gletscher
Mylius Erichsen Land
Kronprins Christian Land
Ingolf Fjord
Mallemukfjeld

Kane Basin
Smith Sound
Inglefield Land
Humboldt Gletscher
Sermersuaq
Kong Frederik VIII.s Land
Danmark Fjord

Nansen Basin
McKinley Sea
Nordaustlandet
Nordkapp
Kvitøya
2770
Kong Karls Land
Olgastredet
Prins Karls Forland
Newtontoppen 1717
Longyearbyen
Barentsøya
Edgeøya
Storfjorden
Svalbard (Spitsbergen) (Norway)
1431
Sørkapp

2170

Kane Basin
Coburg I.
Grise Fiord
Jones Sd.
Devon Island
Kap Atholl
Qeqertarsuaq
Qaanaaq (Thule)
Uummannaq (Dundas) (Thule Air Base)
Kap York
Knud Rasmussen Land
Lauge Koch Kyst

Hovgaard Ø
Nioghalvfjerdsfjorden
Norske Øer
Franske Øer
Île de France
Lambert Land
Germania Land
Danmarkshavn
Store Koldewey
Dove Bugt
Hochstetter Forland
Shannon Ø
Dronning Margrethe II Land

GREENLAND SEA

Melville Bugt
Baffin Bay
2469
Clyde River (Kangiqtugaapik)
Steenstrup Gletscher
QAASUITSUP
2935

GRØNLANDS NATIONALPARK

Wollaston Forland
Daneborg
Zackenberg
Clavering Ø
Ole Rømer Land
Walterhausen Gletscher
Andrée Land
2940
Petermann Bjerg
Ymer Ø
Geographical Society Ø
Traill Ø
Kejser Franz Joseph Fd.
2277
Beerenberg
Jan Mayen (Norway)

Mohns Ridge

Nuussuaq (Kraulshavn)
Upernavik
Kangersuatsiaq
Upernavik Kujalleq
Nunavik
Illorsuit
Maarmorilik
Uummannaq
2062
Saggaq
Ikerasak
3238

Kong Oscar Fjord
Mestersvig
Uunartoq Qeqertaq (Warming I.)
Stauning Alper
Renland
Jameson Land
Milne Land
Ittoqqortoormiit (Scoresbysund)
Ittaqqimmiut
Scoresby Sund
Kangikajik (Kap Brewster)
Uunarteq
Kap Dalton

Icelandic Plateau

Qeqertarsuaq (Disko)
Sullorsuaq
Qeqertarsuaq (Godhavn)
Kangerluk
Disko Bugt
Aasiaat (Egedesminde)
Ikamiut
Ilulissat (Jakobshavn)
Qasigiannguit (Christianshåb)

GREENLAND (KALAALLIT NUNAAT) (Denmark)

SERMERSOOQ
Gunnbjørn Fjeld 3693
Blosseville Kyst
Arctic Circle

C. Dyer
Nordre Strømfjord
Sisimiut (Holsteinsborg)
Kangerlussuaq (Søndre Strømfjord)
Itilleq
Søndre Strømfjord
Kangaamiut
Kong Frederik IX.s Land
QEQQATA
Maniitsoq (Sukkertoppen)

Kangerdlugssuaq

Denmark Strait

Mt. Forel 3360
Kap Gustav Holm

Ísafjörður
Húnaflói
Blönduós
Breiðafjörður
Horn
Eyjafjörður
Akureyri
Húsavík
Neskaupstaður
ICELAND
Vatnajökull 2119
Öræfajökull
Höfn

Nuuk (Godthåb)
Kapisillit
Dronning Ingrid Land
Kangerluarsoruseq (Færingehavn)
Qeqertarsuatsiaat (Fiskenæsset)
Paamiut (Frederikshåb)
Narsalik
2850
Gyldenløve Fjord
Kap Møsting
Kap Moltke
Kap Skjold
Helheim Gletscher
Kuummiut
Ikkatteq
Isortoq
Tasiilaq (Ammassalik)
Kulusuk

Faxaflói
Reykjavík
Vestmannaeyjar
Surtsey
Heimaey

Kangilinnguit (Grønnedal)
Arsuk
Ivittuut
Narsaq
Narsarsuaq
Kong Frederik VI.s Kyst
Timmiarmiut
Mogens Heinesen Fjord
ATLANTIC OCEAN
Qaqortoq (Julianehåb)
Alluitsup Paa (Sydprøven)
KUJALLEQ
Nanortalik
2045
Lindenow Fjord
Nalgmasortoq
Nunap Isua (Kap Farvel)
Prins Christian Sund

Labrador Sea

Baffin I.
Davis Strait

Reykjanes Ridge

Projection: Conic with two standard parallels
West from Greenwich
COPYRIGHT PHILIP'S

Underlined towns give their name to the administrative area in which they stand.

1:17 800 000

1:17 800 000

■ LONDON Capital Cities

Projection: Bonne

West from Greenwich   East from Greenwich

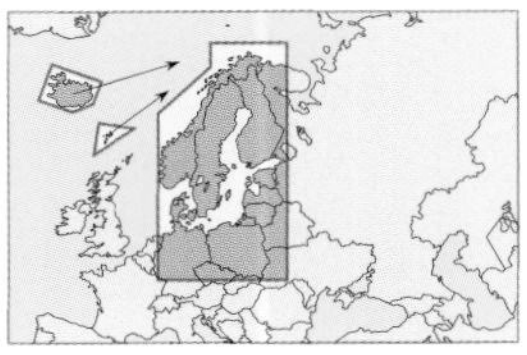

1:5 300 000

50 0 25 50 75 100 125 150 175 km
50 0 25 50 75 100 125 miles

ICELAND
on same scale

FÆROE
ISLANDS
on same scale

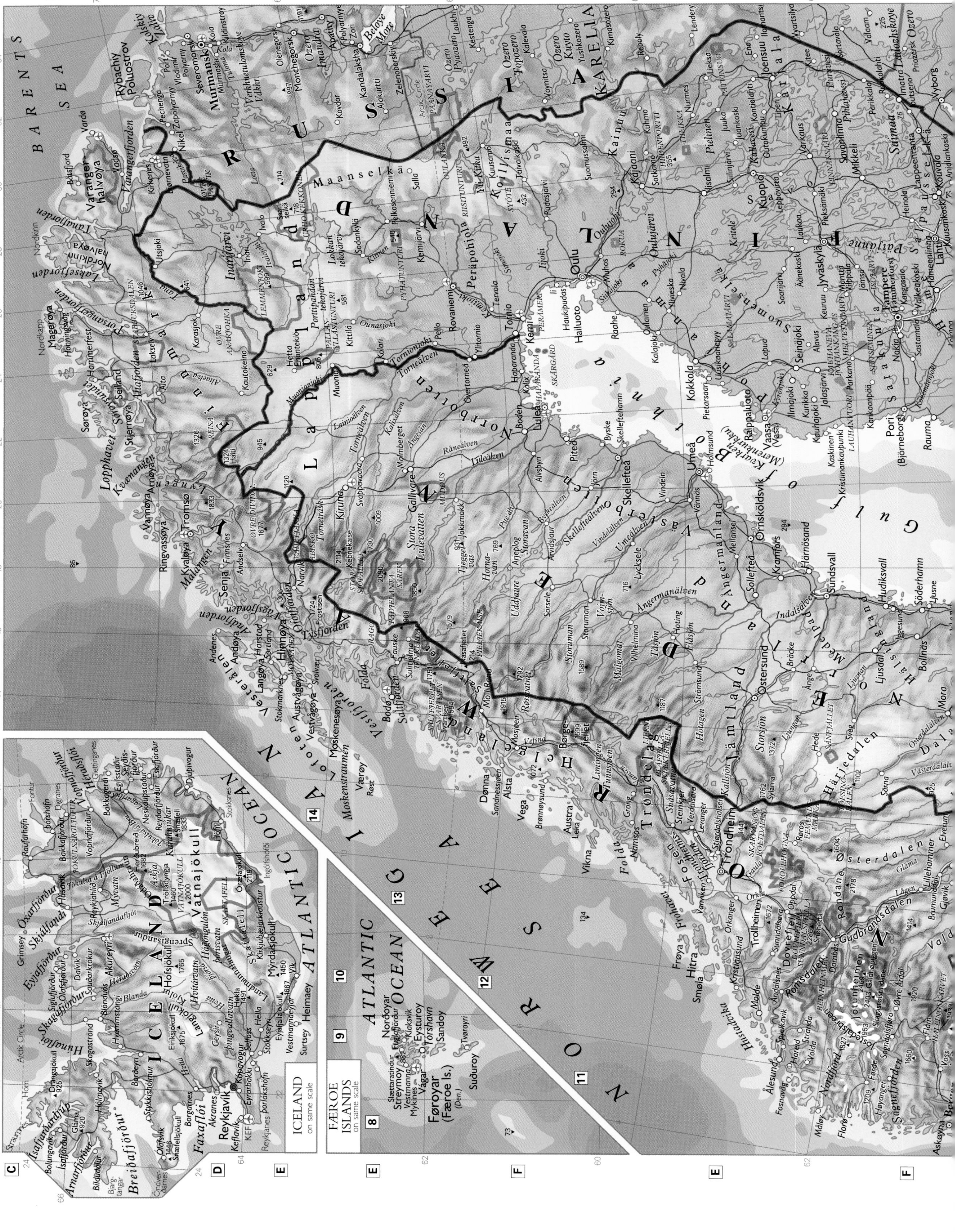

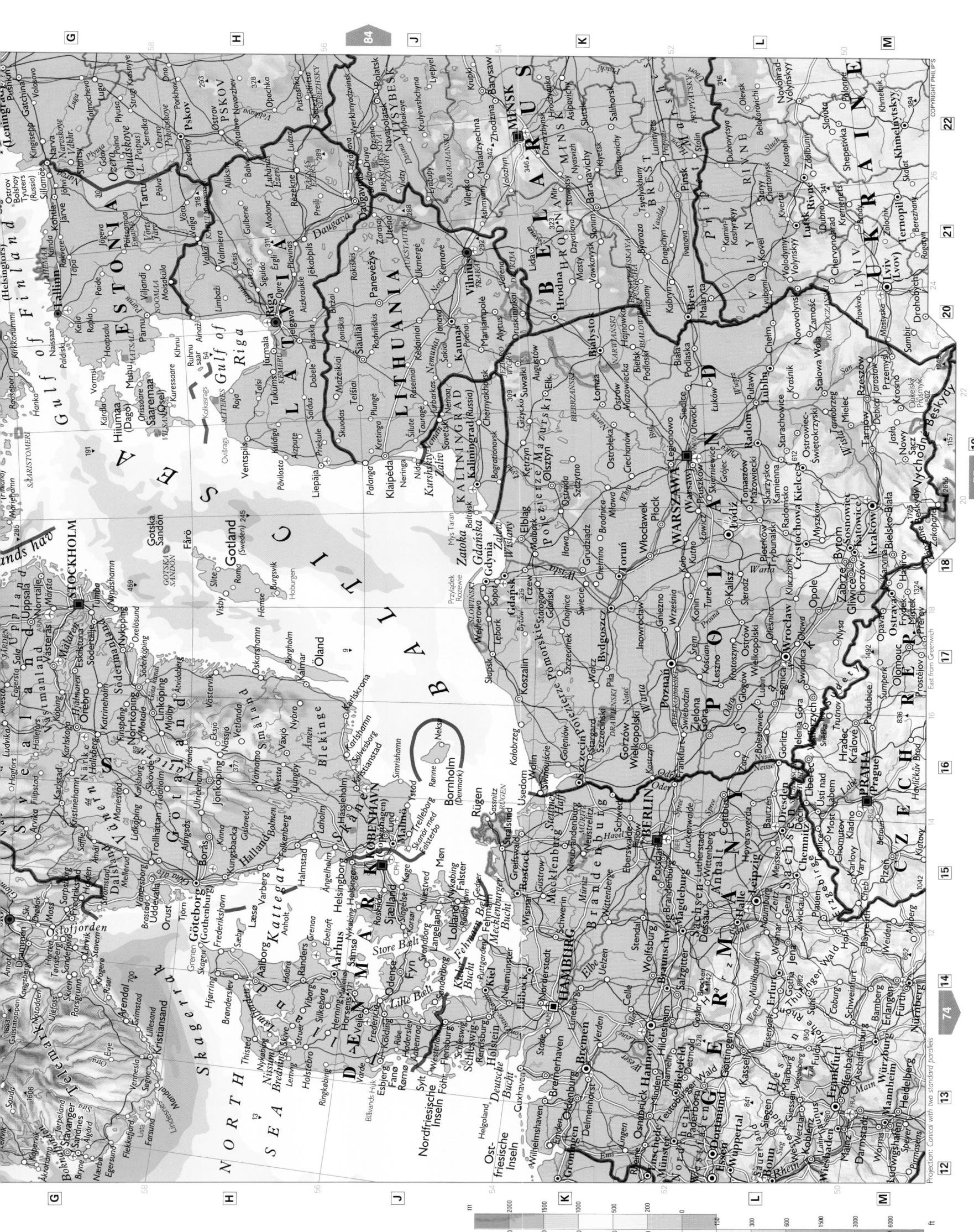

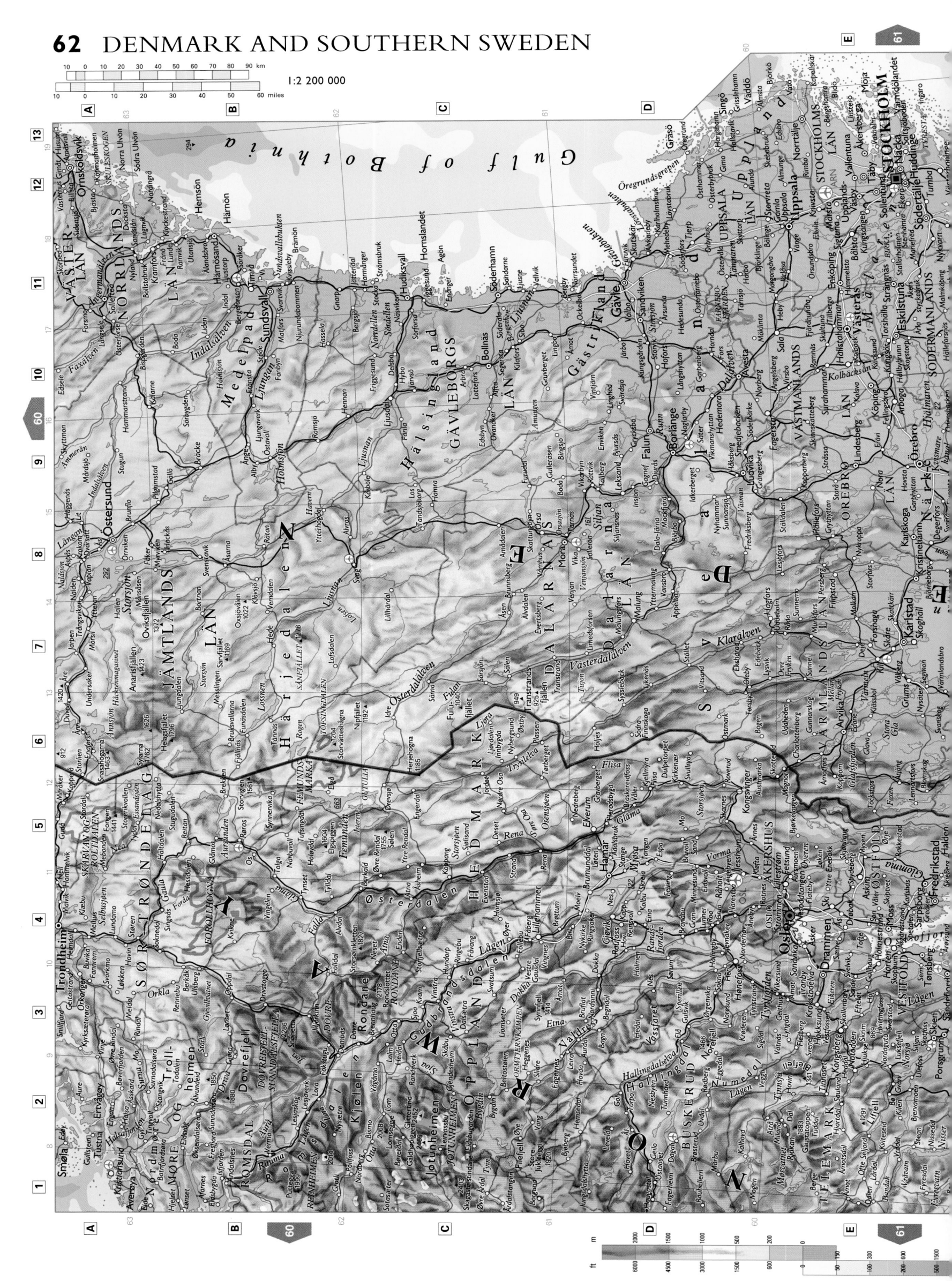

1:2 200 000

Gulf of Bothnia

Projection : Lambert's Conformal Conic

1:1 800 000

10 0 10 20 30 40 50 60 70 80 km
10 0 10 20 30 40 50 miles

SCOTLAND
Kintyre

ATLANTIC OCEAN

NORTHERN IRELAND

IRELAND

DUBLIN (Baile Átha Cliath)

Leinster

Munster

Connaught

CELTIC SEA

IRISH SEA

St. George's Channel

North Channel

WALES

Projection: Lambert's Conformal Conic

West from Greenwich

COPYRIGHT PHILIP'S

1:1 800 000

10 0 10 20 30 40 50 60 70 80 km
10 0 10 20 30 40 50 miles

Key to Scottish unitary authorities on map
1 CITY OF ABERDEEN
2 DUNDEE CITY
3 WEST DUNBARTONSHIRE
4 EAST DUNBARTONSHIRE
5 CITY OF GLASGOW
6 INVERCLYDE
7 RENFREWSHIRE
8 EAST RENFREWSHIRE
9 NORTH LANARKSHIRE
10 FALKIRK
11 CLACKMANNANSHIRE
12 WEST LOTHIAN
13 CITY OF EDINBURGH
14 MIDLOTHIAN

ORKNEY IS. on same scale

ORKNEY

North Ronaldsay
Papa Westray
Westray
Eday
Sanday
Rousay
Stronsay
Brough Hd.
Mainland
Stromness
Shapinsay
Kirkwall
481
Scapa Flow
Hoy
St. Mary's
Burray
South Ronaldsay
Burwick
Dunnet Hd.
Stroma
Duncansby Head
John o' Groats
Sinclair's Bay
Thurso
Pentland Firth

SHETLAND IS. on same scale

Muckle Flugga
Unst
Haroldswick
Yell
Fetlar
Esha Ness
453
Ulsta
Sullom Voe
Out Skerries
St. Magnus Bay
Whalsay
Papa Stour
Voe
Walls
Scalloway
Lerwick
Bressay
Foula
SHETLAND
West Burra
Boddam
Sumburgh Hd.

Butt of Lewis
Flannan Is.
Gallan Hd.
Broad Bay
Stornoway
Eye Peninsula
Lewis
EILEAN SIAR (WESTERN ISLES)
Taransay
Clisham 799
Harris
Toe Hd.
Tarbert
Sound of Harris
Pabbay
Berneray
North Uist
Lochmaddy
Baleshare
Grimsay
Benbecula
Ardivachar Pt.
Wiay
South Uist
Ben Mhor 620
Lochboisdale
Eriskay
Barra
Castlebay
Vatersay
Sandray
Barra Hd. 268

C. Wrath
Durness
L. Eriboll
Strathy Pt.
Dunnet Hd.
Stroma
Pentland Firth
Thurso
Scapa Flow
Hoy 481
Burwick
Noss Hd.
Wick
Halkirk
Caithness
Lybster
Ben Hope 927
Reay Forest
Tongue
Dounreay
Strathy
John o' Groats
Sinclair's Bay
Ord of Caithness
Helmsdale
Sutherland
Eddrachillis B.
Handa
L. Laxford
961
Helmdale
Brora
705
Golspie
Pt. of Stoer
Enard B.
L. Assynt
Ben More Assynt 998
Lochinver
Oykel
Laing
L. Shin
Dornoch
Bonar Bridge
Tain
Tarbat Ness
Dornoch Firth
Brora
Coigeach
Greenstone Pt.
Rubha Coigeach
Ullapool
L. Broom
1081
Ben Dearg
Cromarty
Invergordon
Alness
Moray Firth
Gruinard B.
L. Ewe
Gairloch
Rubha Hunish
L. Maree
1109
Ben Wyvis 1045
Dingwall
Strathpeffer
Fortrose
Nairn
Forres
Lossiemouth
Portknockie
Portsoy
Rosehearty
Kinnairds Hd.
Fraserburgh
Elgin
Buckie
Cullen
Banff
Macduff
Rattray Hd.
MORAY
Keith
Fochabers
Aberchirder
Turriff
Peterhead
Burghead
Rothes
Huntly
Buchan Ness
Cruden Bay
Charlestown of Aberlour
BUCHAN
Ellon
Oldmeldrum
Inverurie
Dufftown
Tomintoul
Grantown-on-Spey
ABERDEENSHIRE
Kintore
Dyce
Westhill
Aberdeen
Girdle Ness
Alford
Aboyne
Banchory
Peterculter
Stonehaven
Inverbervie
Dee
Braemar
Ballater
Lochnagar 1154
Forest of Atholl
ANGUS
Laurencekirk
Brechin
Montrose
Arbroath
Carnoustie
Monifieth
Firth of Tay
Dundee
St. Andrews
Fife Ness
Crail
Anstruther
Buckhaven
Leven
Glenrothes
Cowdenbeath
Kirkcaldy
Dunfermline
North Berwick
Dunbar
FIFE
KINROSS
Kinross
Cupar
Falkland
Auchtermuchty
Ochil Hills
Perth
Scone
Crieff
Auchterarder
PERTH AND KINROSS
Aberfeldy
Pitlochry
Blair Atholl
Ben Lawers 1214
Loch Tay
Killin
Blairgowrie
Alyth
Kirriemuir
Forfar
Dunkeld
Aberfoyle
Callander
Dunblane
Stirling
Alloa
Bannockburn
Grangemouth
Bo'ness
Falkirk
Denny
Kilsyth
Cumbernauld
Kirkintilloch
STIRLING
LOCH LOMOND AND THE TROSSACHS
Ben Lomond 973
Loch Lomond
Crianlarich
Ben More 1174
Ben Vorlich 983
Ben Cruachan 1126
Oban
ARGYLL AND BUTE
Lorn
Firth of Lorn
Inveraray
Lochgilphead
Helensburgh
Dumbarton
Alexandria
Clydebank
Greenock
Gourock
Port Glasgow
Dunoon
Rothesay
Bute
Largs
Paisley
GLASGOW
Hamilton
Motherwell
Airdrie
Coatbridge
East Kilbride
Wishaw
Carluke
Lanark
Edinburgh
Livingston
Musselburgh
Dalkeith
Bonnyrigg
Penicuik
Haddington
EAST LOTHIAN
Dunbar
Eyemouth
St. Abb's Head
Berwick-upon-Tweed
Lammermuir Hills
Duns
Coldstream
Kelso
Jedburgh
Galashiels
Melrose
Selkirk
Hawick
SCOTTISH BORDERS
Peebles
Biggar
Moffat
Broad Law 840
Moorfoot Hills
Pentland Hills
NORTH AYRSHIRE
Ardrossan
Saltcoats
Kilwinning
Irvine
Troon
Prestwick
Ayr
Kilmarnock
EAST AYRSHIRE
Cumnock
Dalmellington
Maybole
Girvan
SOUTH AYRSHIRE
Ailsa Craig
Arran
Goat Fell 874
Brodick
Kintyre
Campbeltown
Mull of Kintyre
Islay
Bowmore
Port Ellen
Jura
Colonsay
Oronsay
Scarba
Tiree
Coll
Mull
Tobermory
Iona
Staffa
Ulva
Morvern
Fort William
Ben Nevis 1344
Glen Coe
Ballachulish
Kinlochleven
Loch Linnhe
Rannoch Moor
Loch Rannoch
Loch Lochy
Loch Ness
Fort Augustus
Glen Affric
Cairn Eige 1182
Glen Moriston
L. Monar
Kyle of Lochalsh
Skye
Cuillin Hills 992
Portree
Dunvegan
Raasay
Scalpay
Rona
Applecross
L. Torridon
Gairloch
L. Carron
Strome Ferry
Mallaig
Arisaig
L. Morar
Eigg
Rùm (Rhum)
Canna
Muck
Pt. of Ardnamurchan
Sound of Mull
Inverness
HIGHLAND
WEST HIGHLANDS
NORTH WEST HIGHLANDS
Monadhliath Mts.
1141
Kingussie
Newtonmore
Carn Ban 1245
Aviemore
Cairn Gorm 1309
CAIRNGORMS
Ben Macdhui 1309
Cairngorm Mountains
Grampian Mountains
LOCHABER
Glen Spean 1148
Spean Bridge
Glen Garry

SCOTLAND

NORTH SEA
ATLANTIC OCEAN
Little Minch
North Minch
Sea of the Hebrides
Inner Hebrides
Outer Hebrides
Sound of Sleat
Kilbrannan Sd.
Firth of Clyde
Sound of Jura
Firth of Forth
Firth of Tay
North Channel
Solway Firth
Luce Bay
Wigtown B.
Loch Ryan

DUMFRIES & GALLOWAY
Dumfries
Lockerbie
Langholm
Annan
Gretna
Brampton
Sanquhar
New Galloway
Galloway
Gatehouse of Fleet
Castle Douglas
Dalbeattie
Kirkcudbright
Newton Stewart
Stranraer
Wigtown
Whithorn
Portpatrick
Cairnryan
Mull of Galloway
Burrow Hd.
Merrick 844

NORTHERN IRELAND
Larne
Carrickfergus
Bangor
Newtownards
Holywood
Belfast
Belfast L.
Donaghadee
Cushendall
Garron Pt.

ENGLAND
CUMBRIA
Carlisle
Wigton
Aspatria
Maryport
Workington
Cockermouth
Keswick
Whitehaven
St. Bees Hd.
Derwent Water
Ullswater
Penrith
Appleby-in-Westmorland
Skiddaw 931
Helvellyn 950
Scafell 977
NORTHUMBERLAND
Kielder Water
North Tyne
Haltwhistle
Hexham
Alston
Cross Fell 893
Newcastle-upon-Tyne
Blaydon
Gateshead
Stanley
Consett
DURHAM
Crook
Bishop Auckland
Barnard Castle
Morpeth
Amble
Alnwick
Alnmouth
Wooler
The Cheviot 816
Cheviot Hills
Flodden
Bamburgh
Farne Is.
Holy I.
NORTH YORK
CUMBRIA
Weardale

ft m
3000 1000
1500 500
600 200
300 100
0 0
50 150
200 600
500 1500
1000 3000
m ft

Projection : Lambert's Conformal Conic

West from Greenwich

COPYRIGHT PHILIP'S

1:1 800 000

10 0 10 20 30 40 50 60 70 80 km
10 0 10 20 30 40 50 miles

Key to English unitary authorities on map

25 HARTLEPOOL
26 DARLINGTON
27 STOCKTON-ON-TEES
28 MIDDLESBROUGH
29 REDCAR AND CLEVELAND
30 BLACKPOOL
31 BLACKBURN WITH DARWEN
32 HALTON
33 WARRINGTON
34 KINGSTON UPON HULL
35 NORTH EAST LINCOLNSHIRE
36 STOKE-ON-TRENT
37 TELFORD AND WREKIN
38 DERBY CITY
39 CITY OF NOTTINGHAM
40 LEICESTER CITY
41 RUTLAND
42 PETERBOROUGH
43 MILTON KEYNES
44 LUTON
45 NORTH SOMERSET
46 CITY OF BRISTOL
47 BATH AND NORTH EAST SOMERSET
48 SWINDON
49 READING
50 WOKINGHAM
51 WINDSOR AND MAIDENHEAD
52 SLOUGH
53 BRACKNELL FOREST
54 THURROCK
55 SOUTHEND-ON-SEA
56 MEDWAY
57 PLYMOUTH
58 TORBAY
59 POOLE
60 BOURNEMOUTH
61 SOUTHAMPTON
62 PORTSMOUTH
63 BRIGHTON AND HOVE
64 BEDFORD
65 CENTRAL BEDFORDSHIRE
66 CHESHIRE WEST AND CHESTER
67 CHESHIRE EAST

Key to Welsh unitary authorities on map

15 SWANSEA
16 NEATH PORT TALBOT
17 BRIDGEND
18 RHONDDA CYNON TAFF
19 MERTHYR TYDFIL
20 CAERPHILLY
21 BLAENAU GWENT
22 TORFAEN
23 CARDIFF
24 NEWPORT

NORTH SEA

IRISH SEA

NORTHERN IRELAND

SCOTLAND

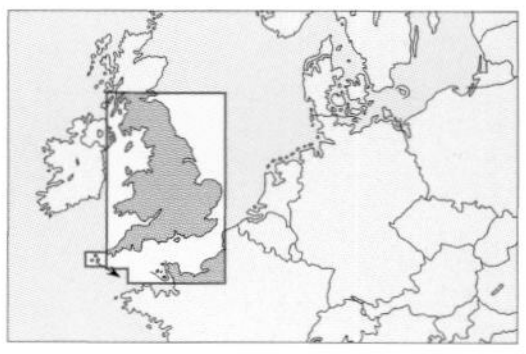

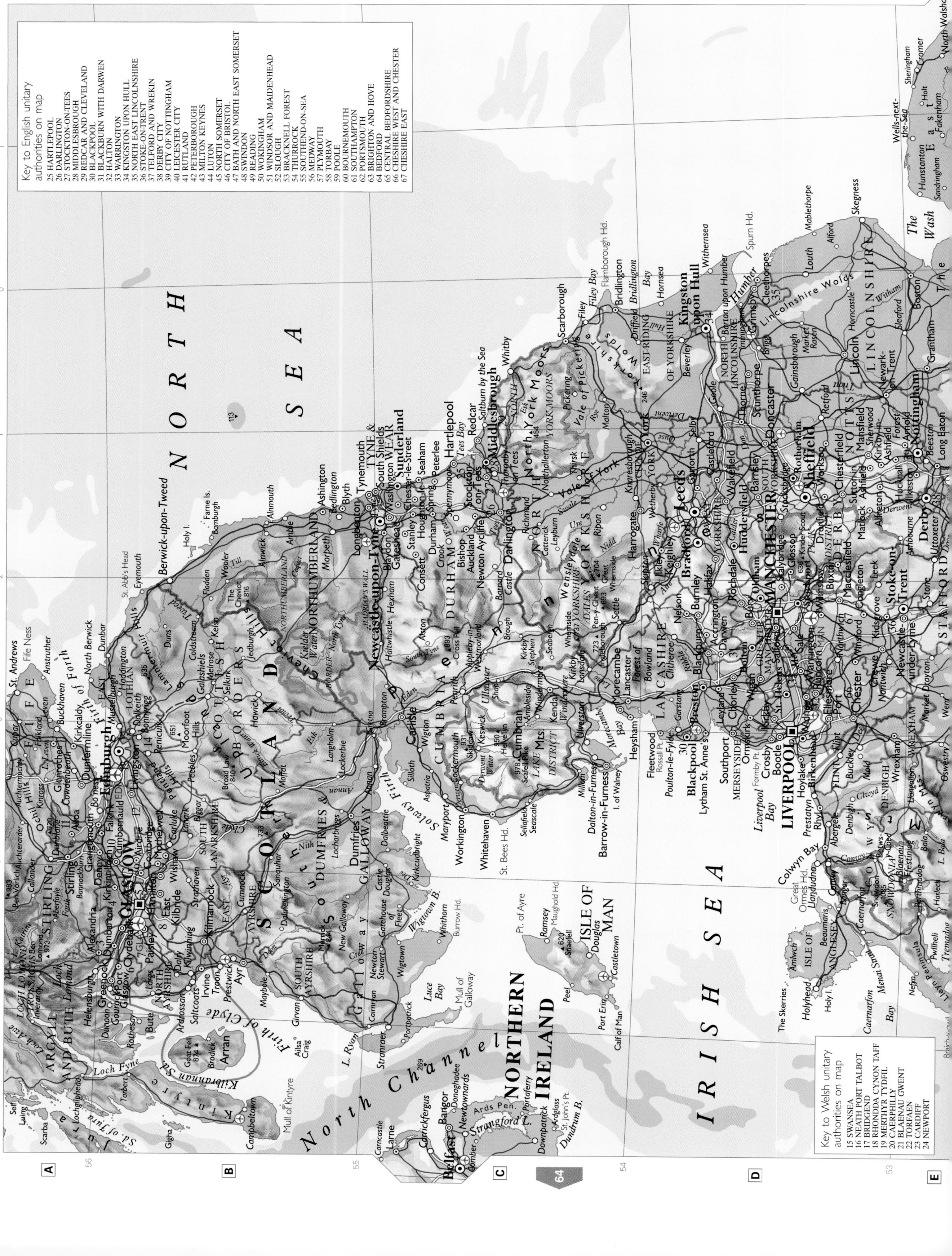

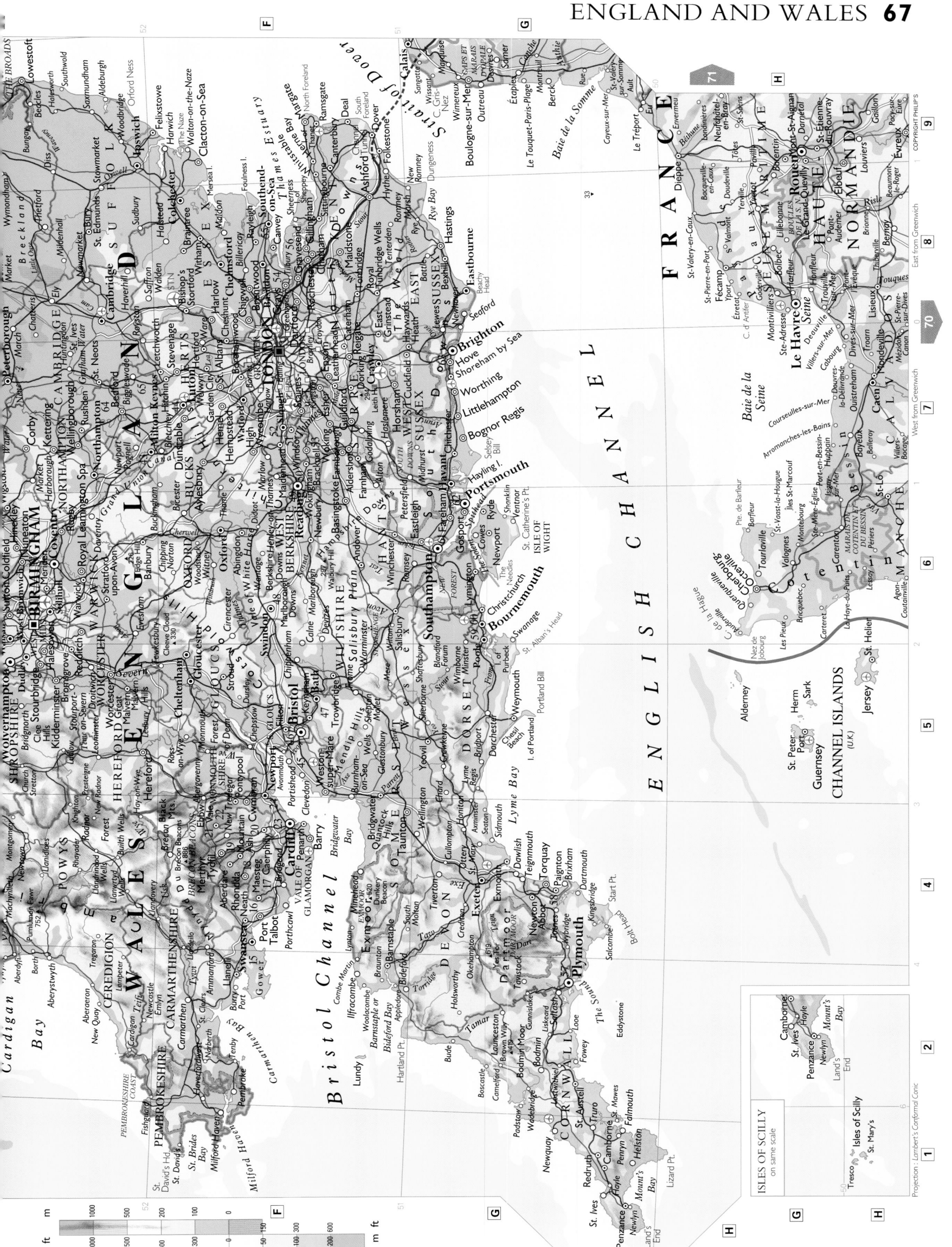

68 BRITISH ISLES

1:4 400 000

50 0 25 50 75 100 125 150 175 km
50 0 25 50 75 100 125 miles

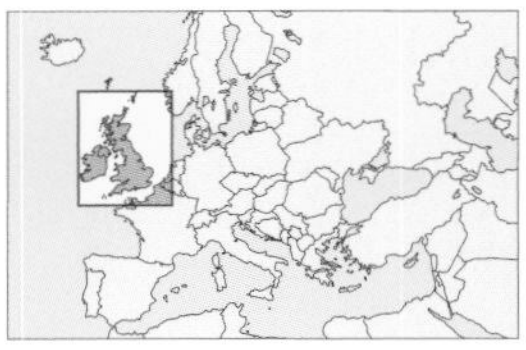

Projection: Conical with two standard parallels

ATLANTIC OCEAN

NORTH SEA

IRISH SEA

CELTIC SEA

English Channel

St. George's Channel

Bristol Channel

NORWAY

NETHERLANDS

BELGIUM

FRANCE

SCOTLAND

UNITED KINGDOM

IRELAND

ENGLAND

WALES

NORTHERN IRELAND

Shetland Is. (U.K.)
Orkney Is.
Outer Hebrides
Inner Hebrides

GLASGOW
Edinburgh
Aberdeen
Dundee
Inverness
Newcastle-upon-Tyne
Sunderland
Middlesbrough
Leeds
MANCHESTER
LIVERPOOL
Sheffield
Nottingham
BIRMINGHAM
Leicester
Norwich
Cambridge
LONDON
Bristol
Cardiff
Swansea
Southampton
Portsmouth
Plymouth
Exeter
Brighton
DUBLIN
Belfast
Cork
Limerick
Galway

East from Greenwich
COPYRIGHT PHILIP'S

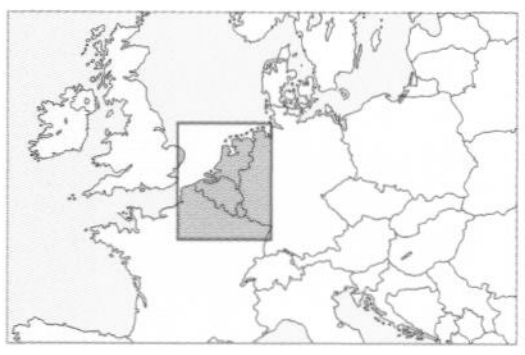

1:2 200 000

10 0 10 20 30 40 50 60 70 80 90 km

10 0 10 20 30 40 50 60 miles

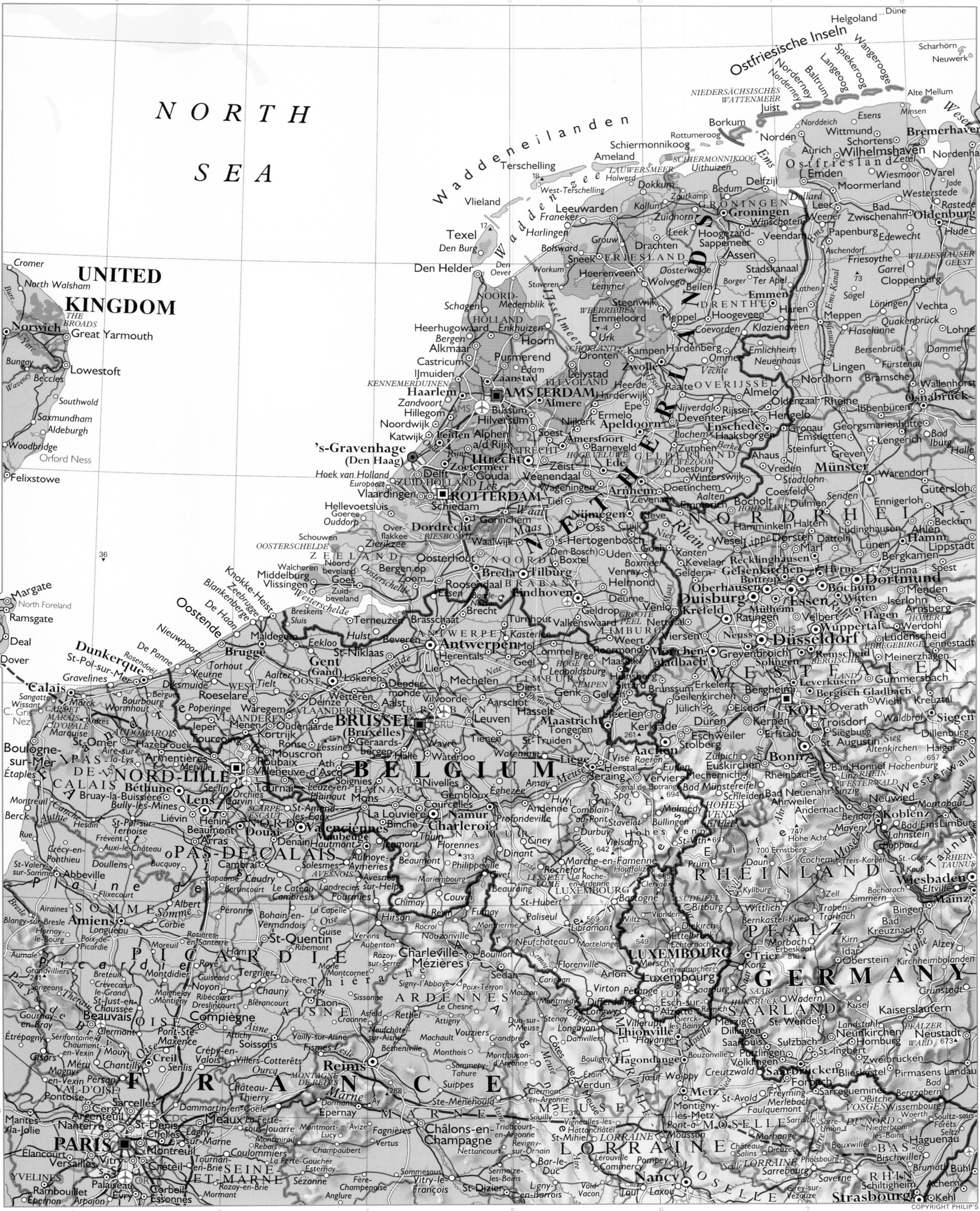

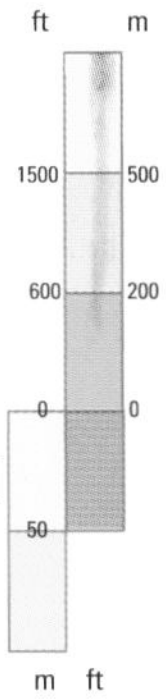

76

71

High-speed rail routes

Underlined towns give their name to the administrative area in which they stand.

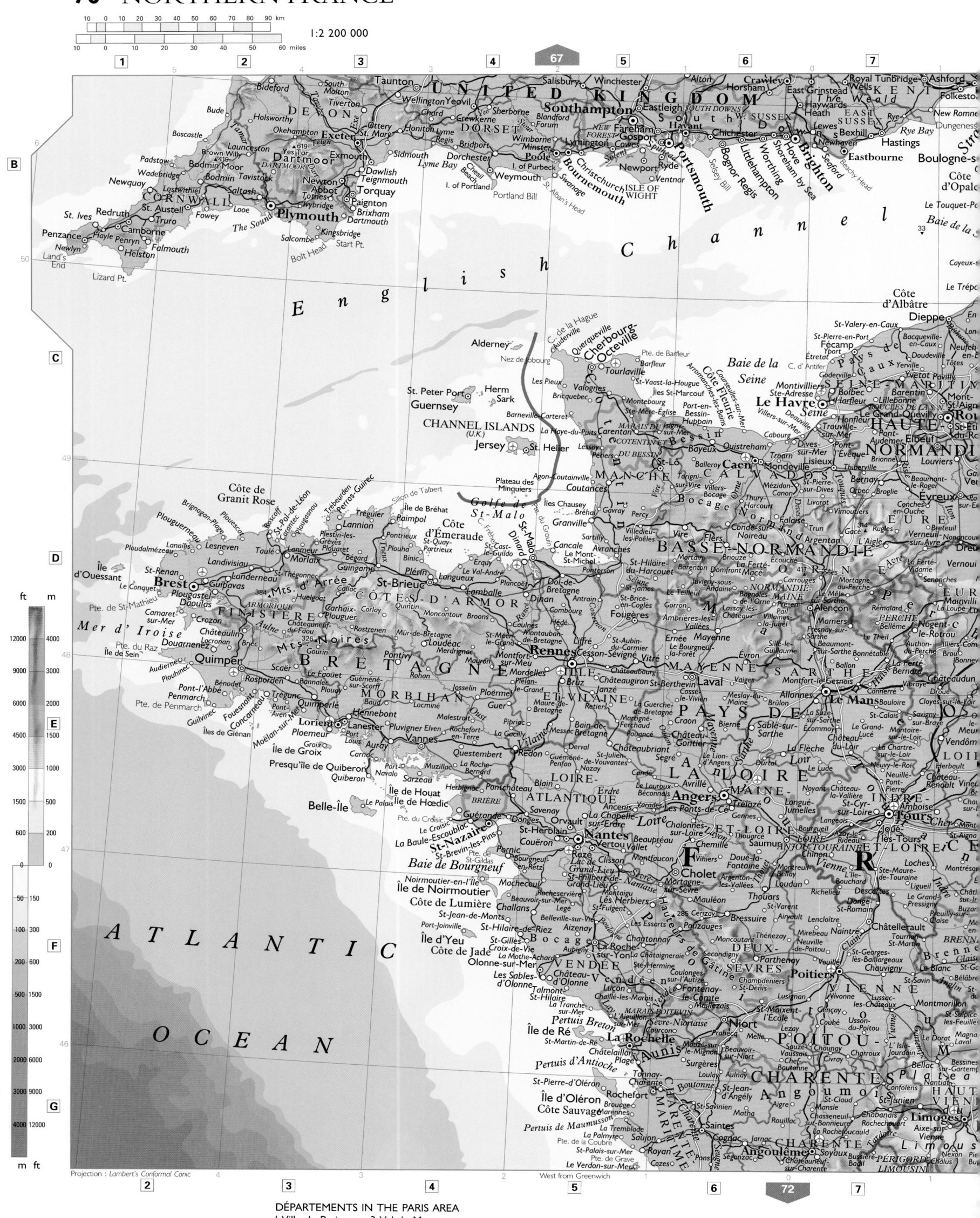

1:2 200 000

West from Greenwich

DÉPARTEMENTS IN THE PARIS AREA
1 Ville de Paris   3 Val-de-Marne
2 Seine-St-Denis   4 Hauts-de-Seine

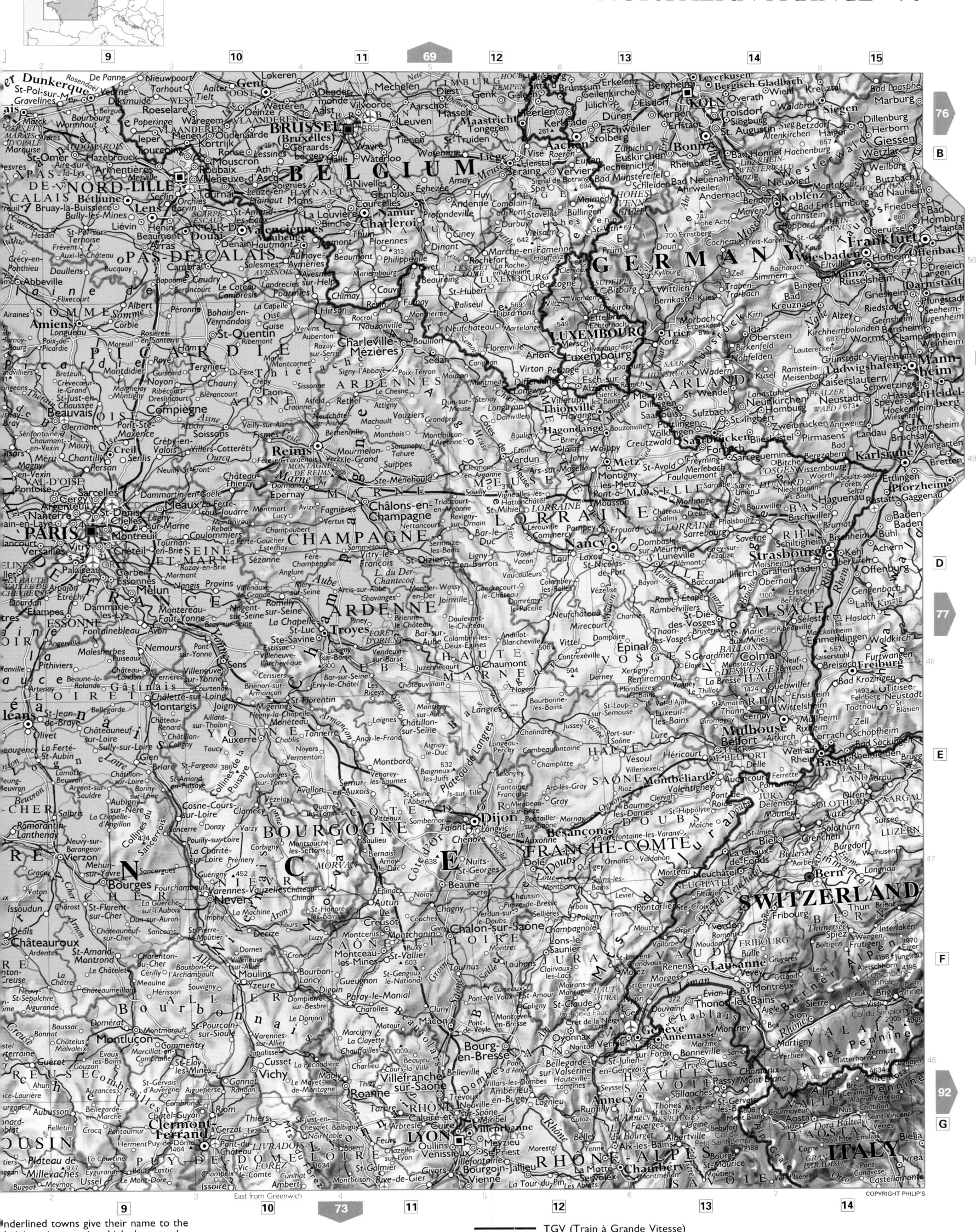

Underlined towns give their name to the administrative area in which they stand.

TGV (Train à Grande Vitesse)

COPYRIGHT PHILIP'S

East from Greenwich

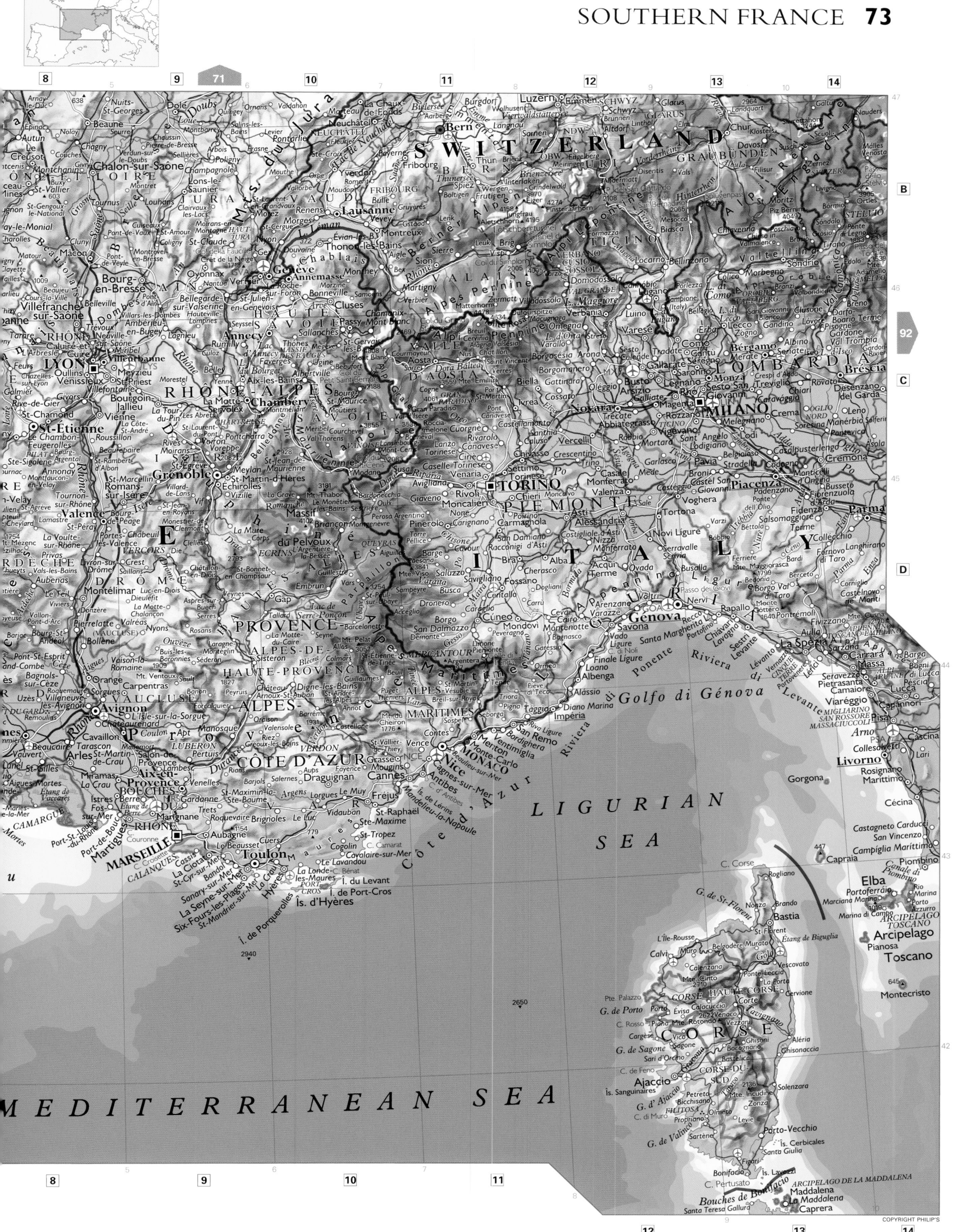

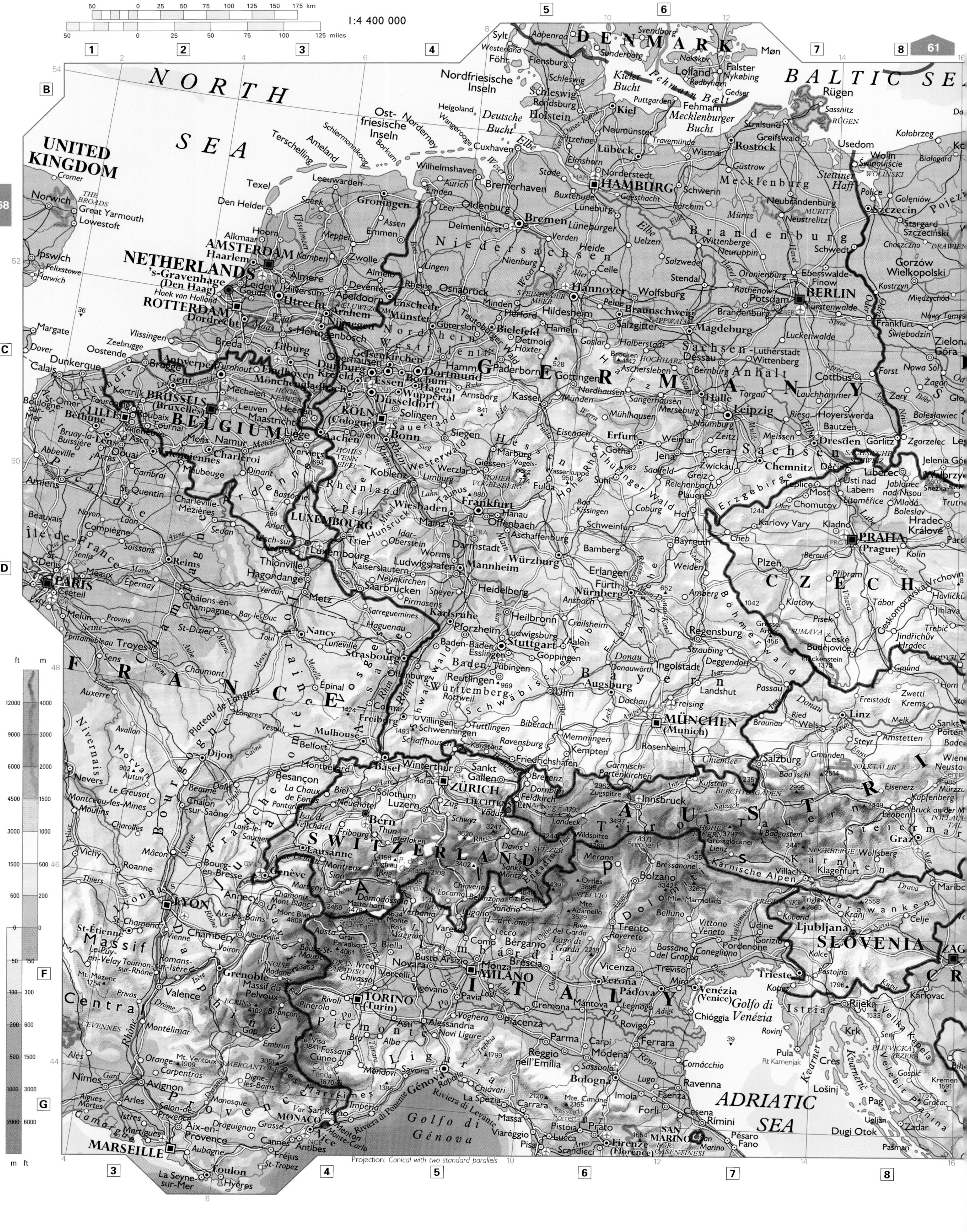

1:4 400 000
km
miles
NORTH SEA
BALTIC SEA
ADRIATIC SEA
UNITED KINGDOM
NETHERLANDS
BELGIUM
LUXEMBOURG
GERMANY
DENMARK
FRANCE
SWITZERLAND
LIECHTENSTEIN
AUSTRIA
CZECH
SLOVENIA
ITALY
MONACO
SAN MARINO
AMSTERDAM
's-Gravenhage (Den Haag)
ROTTERDAM
BRUSSELS (Bruxelles)
LUXEMBOURG
PARIS
BERLIN
HAMBURG
MÜNCHEN (Munich)
PRAHA (Prague)
ZÜRICH
Bern
LYON
MARSEILLE
TORINO (Turin)
MILANO
Ljubljana
Venézia (Venice)
Firenze (Florence)
Frankfurt
Köln (Cologne)
Stuttgart
Golfo di Venézia
Golfo di Génova
Deutsche Bucht
Kieler Bucht
Mecklenburger Bucht
Nordfriesische Inseln
Ost-friesische Inseln
Massif Central
Projection: Conical with two standard parallels

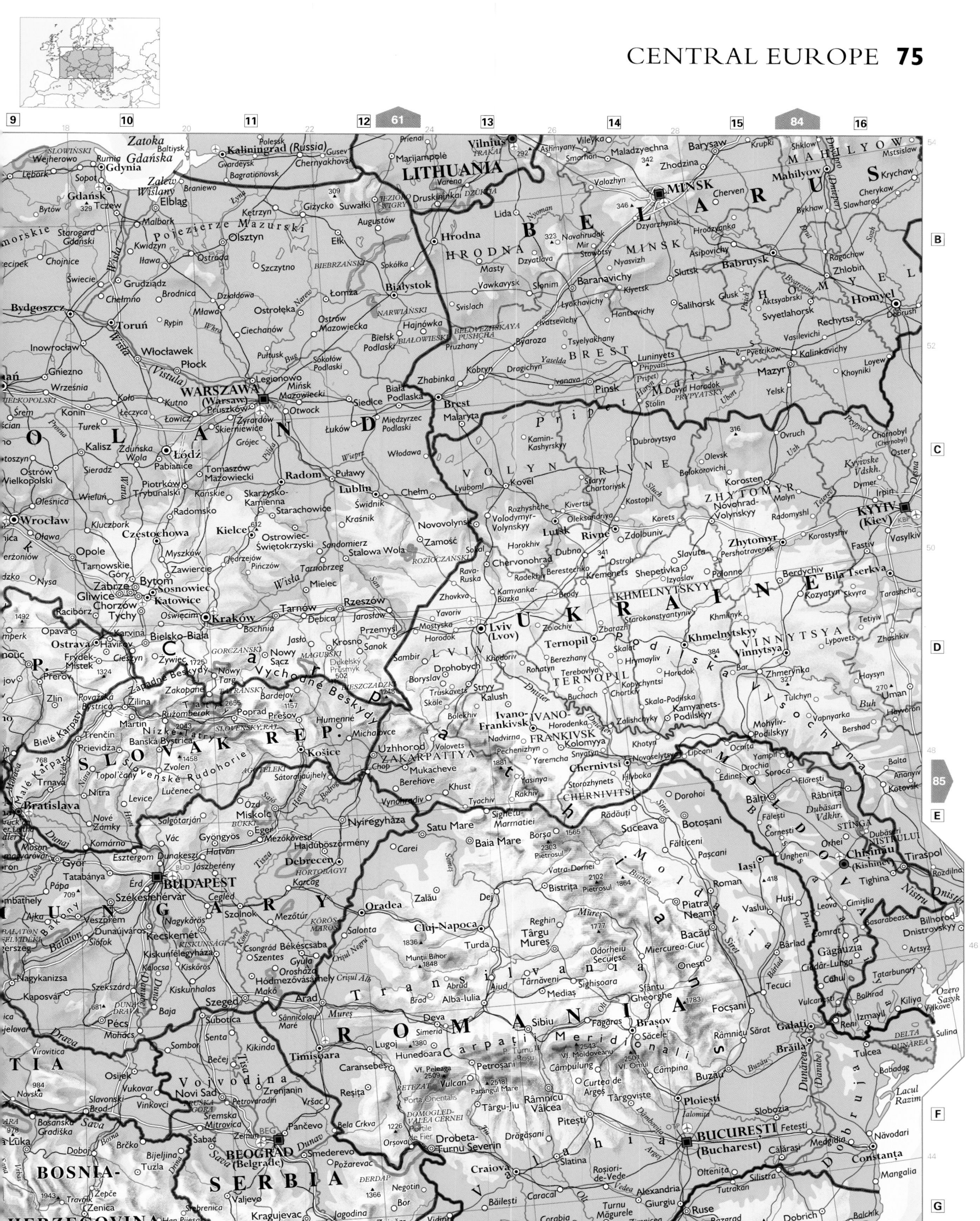

1:2 200 000

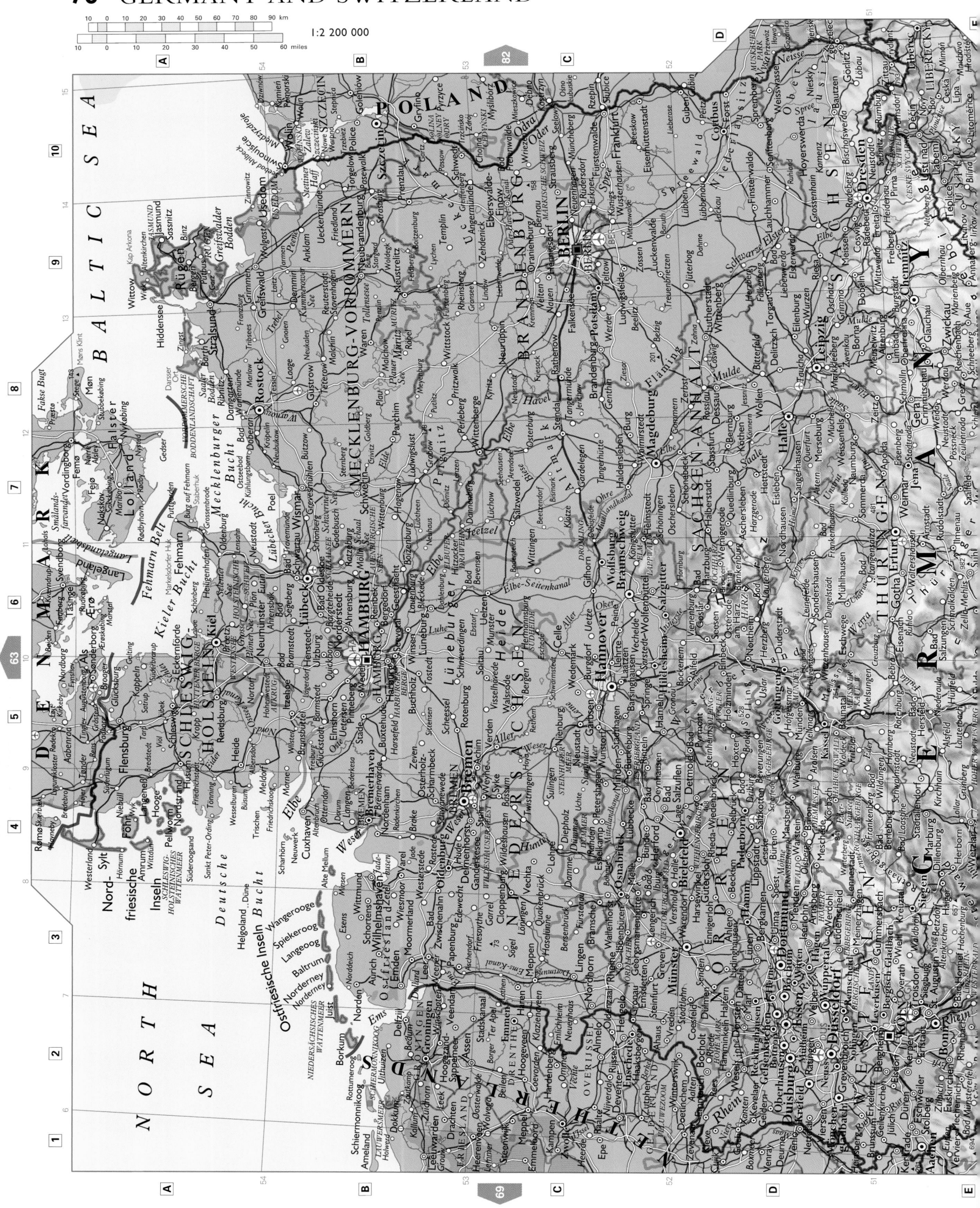

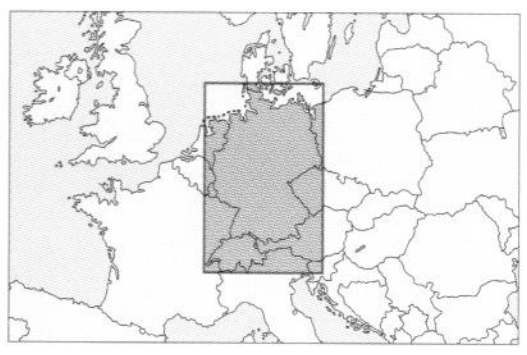

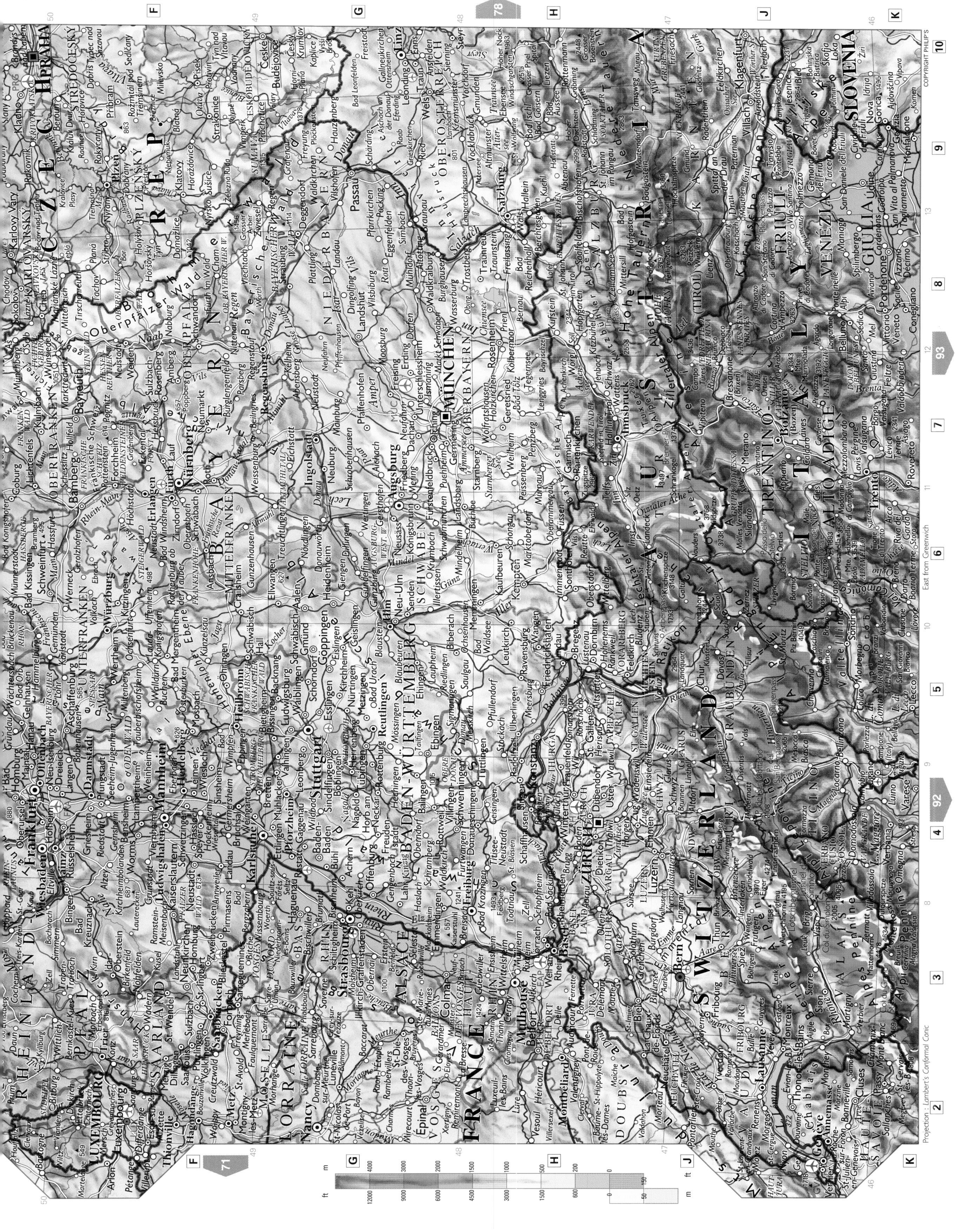

Projection: Lambert's Conformal Conic

East from Greenwich

COPYRIGHT PHILIP'S

——— High-speed rail routes

Underlined towns give their name to the administrative area in which they stand.

CZECH REP.

BAYERN

ÖBEROSTERREICH

NIEDERBAYERN

OBERPFALZ

OBERFRANKEN

MITTELFRANKEN

UNTERFRANKEN

SCHWABEN

OBERBAYERN

SALZBURG

TIROL

TRENTINO-ALTO ADIGE

VENEZIA GIULIA

FRIULI-

SLOVENIA

ITALY

SWITZERLAND

BADEN-WÜRTTEMBERG

RHEINLAND-PFALZ

SAARLAND

LUXEMBOURG

FRANCE

LORRAINE

ALSACE

GRAUBÜNDEN

Frankfurt · Darmstadt · Mannheim · Heidelberg · Karlsruhe · Stuttgart · Nürnberg · Würzburg · Bamberg · München · Augsburg · Regensburg · Passau · Linz · Salzburg · Innsbruck · Bozen · Trento · Strasbourg · Freiburg · Basel · Zürich · Luzern · Bern · Praha · Plzeň · Klagenfurt

ft m
4000
3000
2000
1500
1000
500
200
0

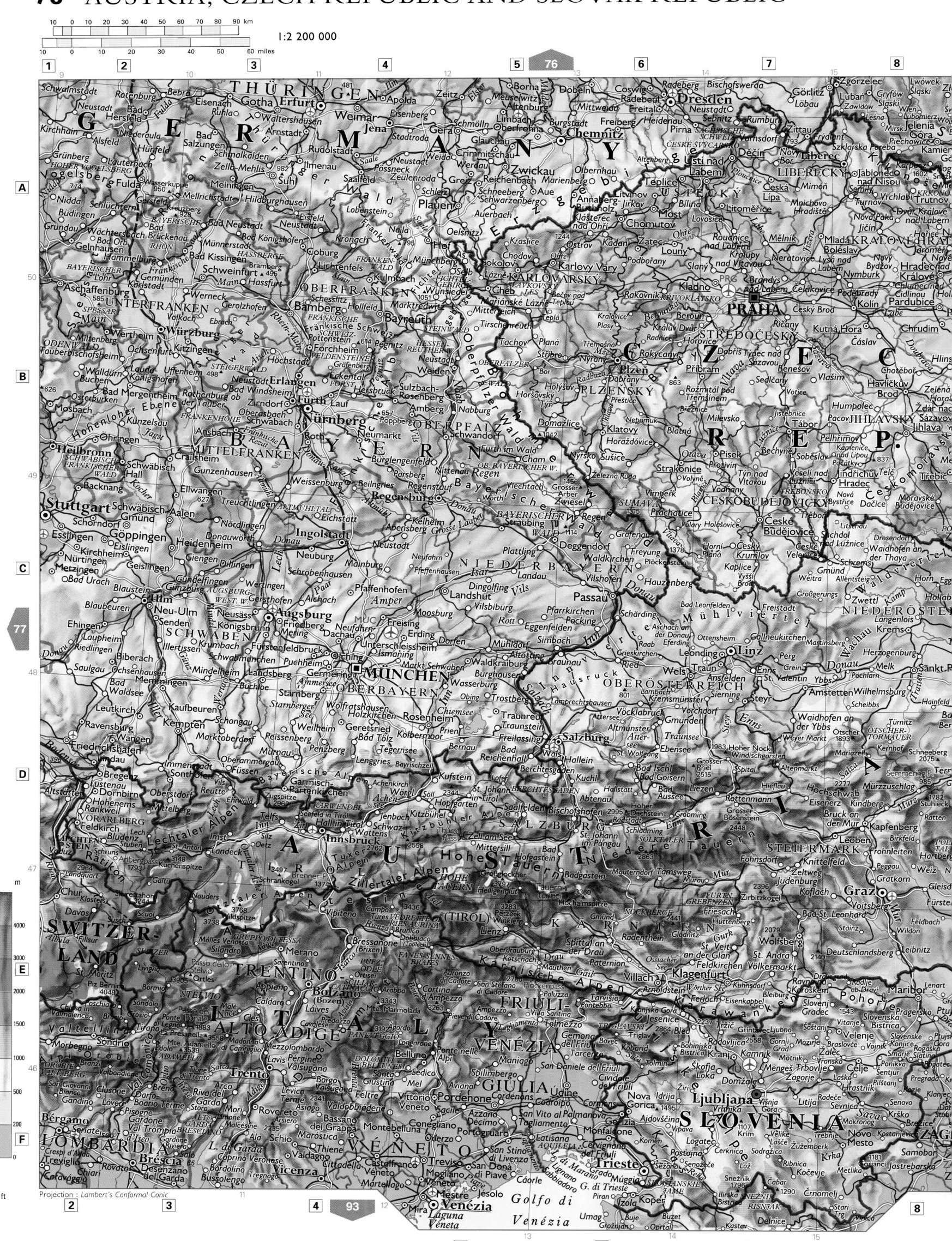

Underlined towns give their name to the administrative area in which they stand.

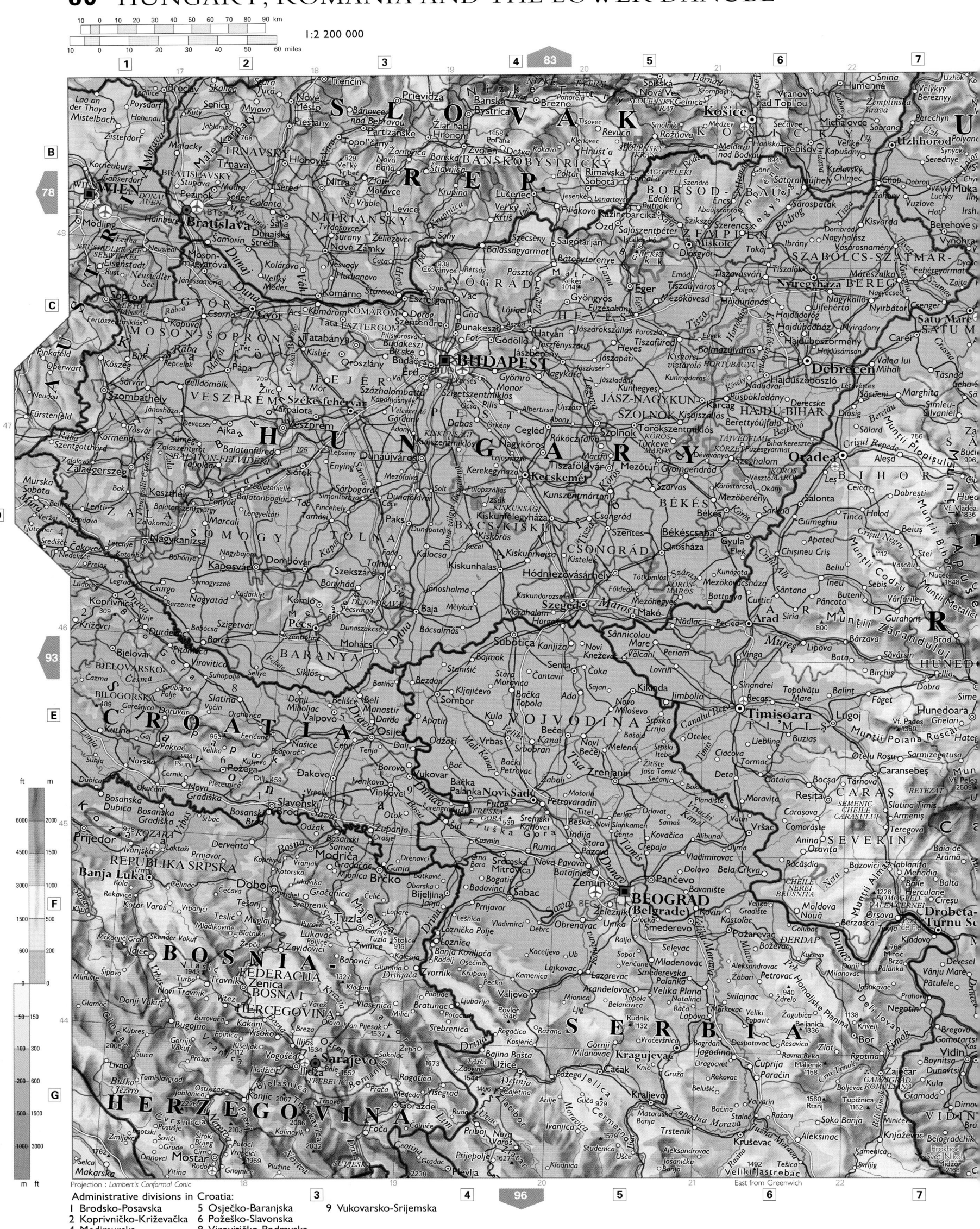

1:2 200 000

Projection : Lambert's Conformal Conic

East from Greenwich

Administrative divisions in Croatia:
1 Brodsko-Posavska   5 Osječko-Baranjska   9 Vukovarsko-Srijemska
2 Koprivničko-Križevačka   6 Požeško-Slavonska
4 Medimurska   8 Virovitičko-Podravska

Underlined towns give their name to the
administrative area in which they stand.

1:2 200 000

10 0 10 20 30 40 50 60 70 80 90 km
10 0 10 20 30 40 50 60 miles

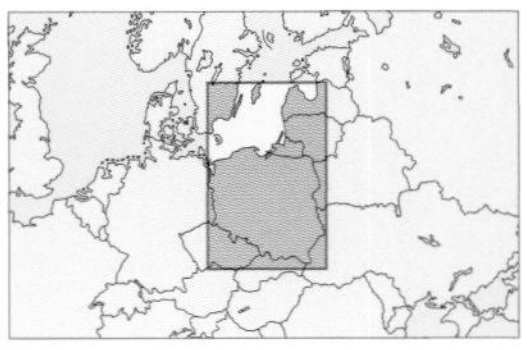

Major features

Gulf of Riga

Irbes saurums (Kura kurk)

SWEDEN

Gotland (Sweden)

Öland (Sweden)

Hanöbukten

Bornholm (Denmark)
BORNHOLMS AMT.

BALTIC SEA

LATVIA

LITHUANIA

KALININGRAD (Russia)

POLAND

Selected place names

Riga, Jūrmala, Jelgava, Bauska, Kaunas, Marijampolė, Hrodna

Ventspils, Liepāja, Klaipėda, Palanga, Nida, Neringa

Šiauliai, Telšiai, Plungė, Mažeikiai, Tauragė

Kaliningrad, Zelenodradsk, Sovetsk, Gusev, Chernyakhovsk

Gdańsk, Gdynia, Sopot, Gdańska, Zatoka Gdańska

Władysławowo, Hel, Puck, Wejherowo, Lębork, Słupsk, Ustka

Koszalin, Kołobrzeg, Darłowo, Białogard, Sławno

POMORSKIE, WARMIŃSKO-MAZURSKIE, ZACHODNIO-POMORSKIE

Curonian Spit (Kuršių Nerijos)

Nemunas (Neman)

Wisła

Gotland, GOTLANDS LÄN, Visby

KALMAR, Kalmar, ÖLANDS LÄN

JÖNKÖPINGS LÄN, Jönköping, Nässjö

BLEKINGE LÄN, Karlskrona, Karlshamn

SMÅLAND

Underlined towns give their name to the administrative area in which they stand.

COPYRIGHT PHILIP'S

Projection: Lambert's Conformal Conic

East from Greenwich

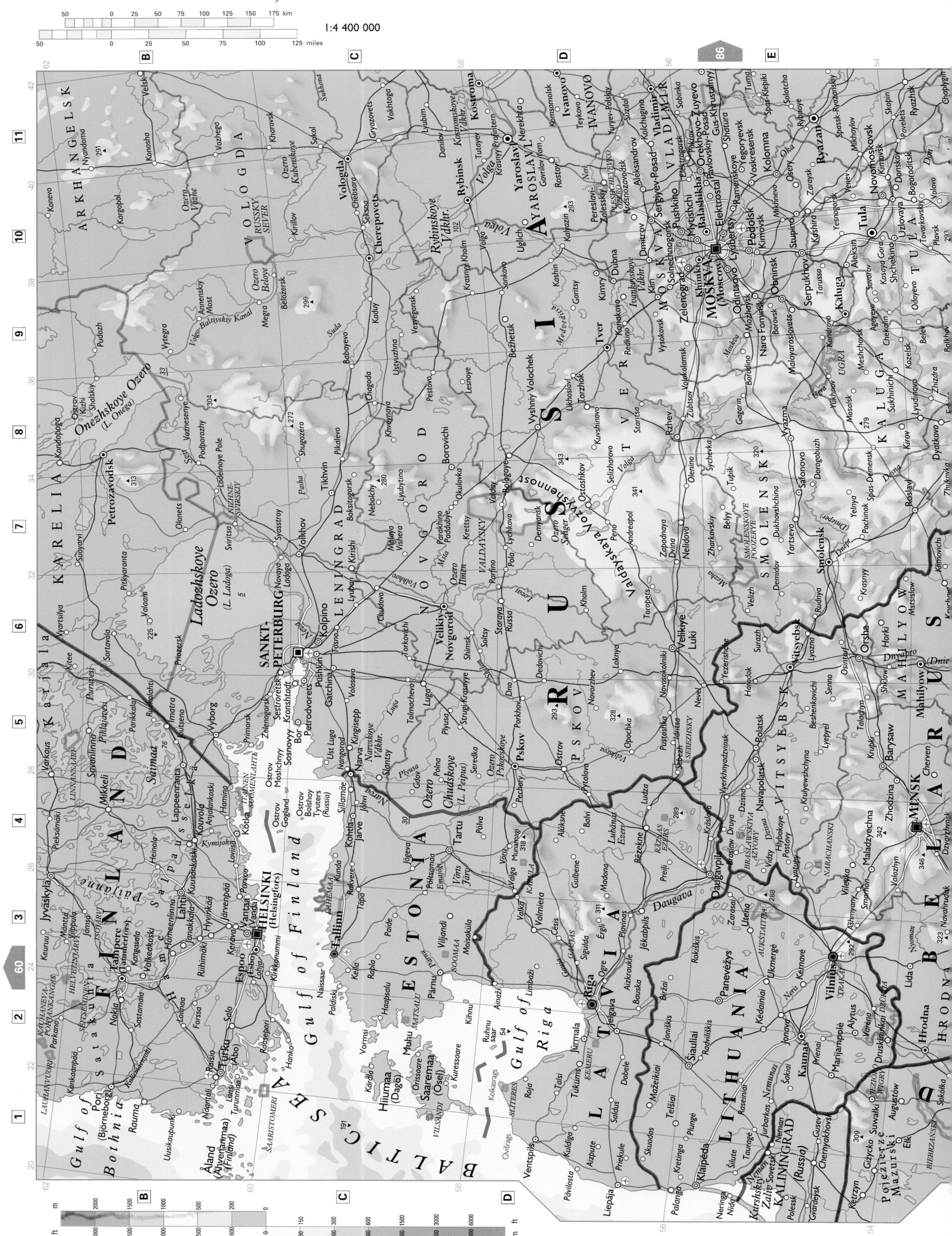

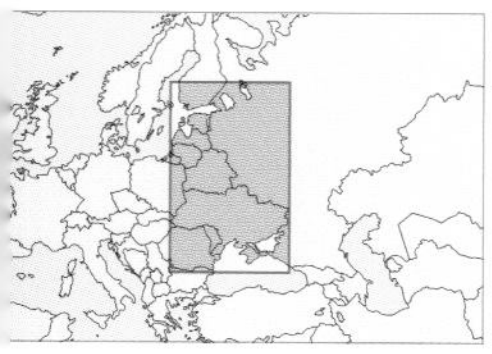

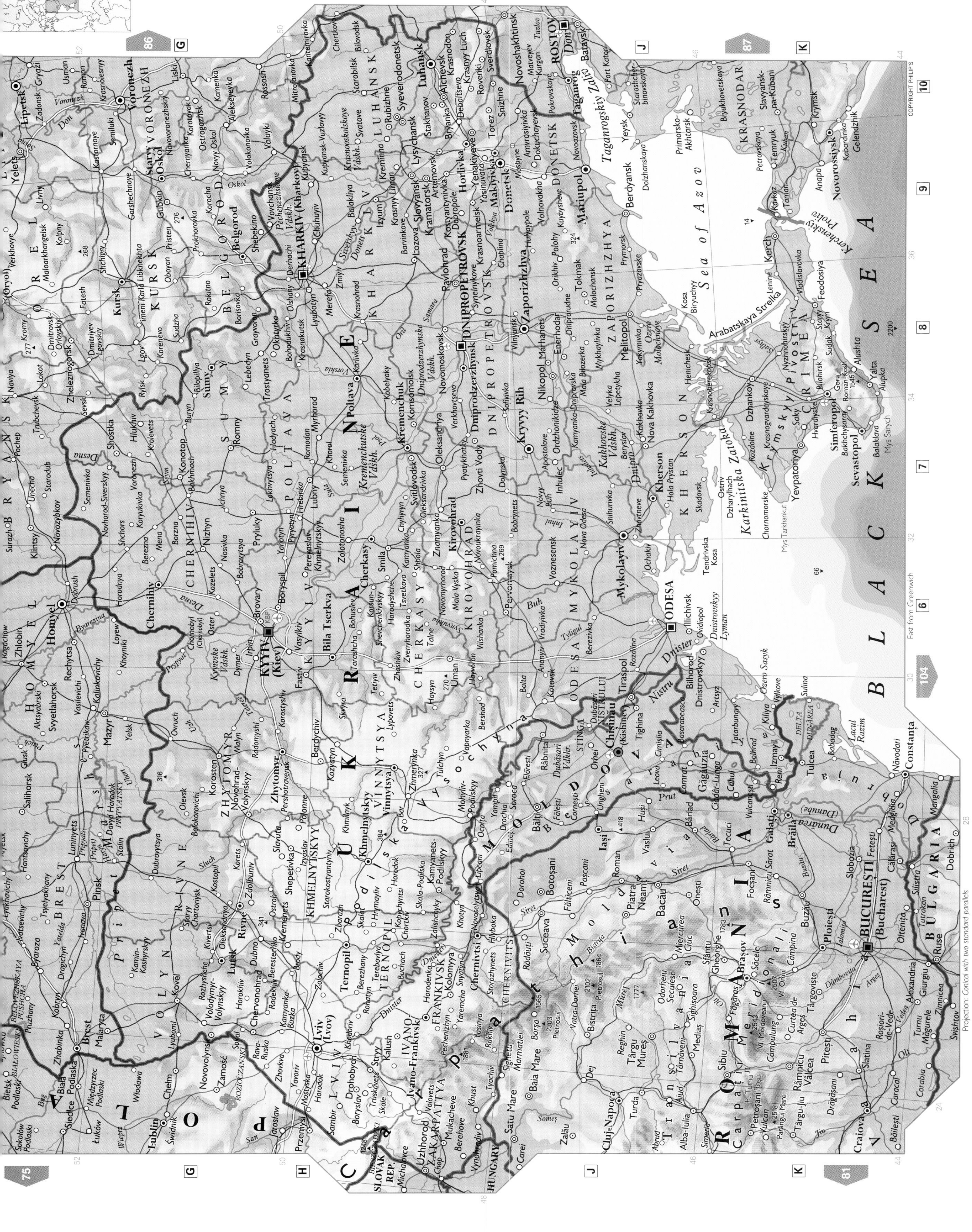

COPYRIGHT PHILIP'S

East from Greenwich

Projection: Conic with two standard parallels

RUSSIA

UKRAINE

MOLDOVA

ROMANIA

BULGARIA

HUNGARY

SLOVAK REP.

Sea of Azov

BLACK SEA

KYIV (Kiev)

KHARKIV (Kharkiv)

DNIPROPETROVSK

DONETSK

ODESA

MYKOLAYIV

KHERSON

CRIMEA

LUHANSK

ZAPORIZHZHYA

POLTAVA

SUMY

CHERNIHIV

KIROVOHRAD

CHERKASY

VINNYTSYA

KHMELNYTSKYY

TERNOPIL

LVIV (Lvov)

IVANO-FRANKIVSK

ZAKARPATTYA

VOLYN

RIVNE

ZHYTOMYR

BREST

HOMYEL

ROSTOV

KRASNODAR

VORONEZH

KURSK

BELGOROD

BRYANSK

CHERNIVTSI

Novorossiysk

Chişinău (Kishinev)

BUCUREŞTI (Bucharest)

Constanţa

Simferopol

Sevastopol

Yalta

Kerch

Mariupol

Taganrog

Dnister

Danube (Dunărea)

Prut

Siret

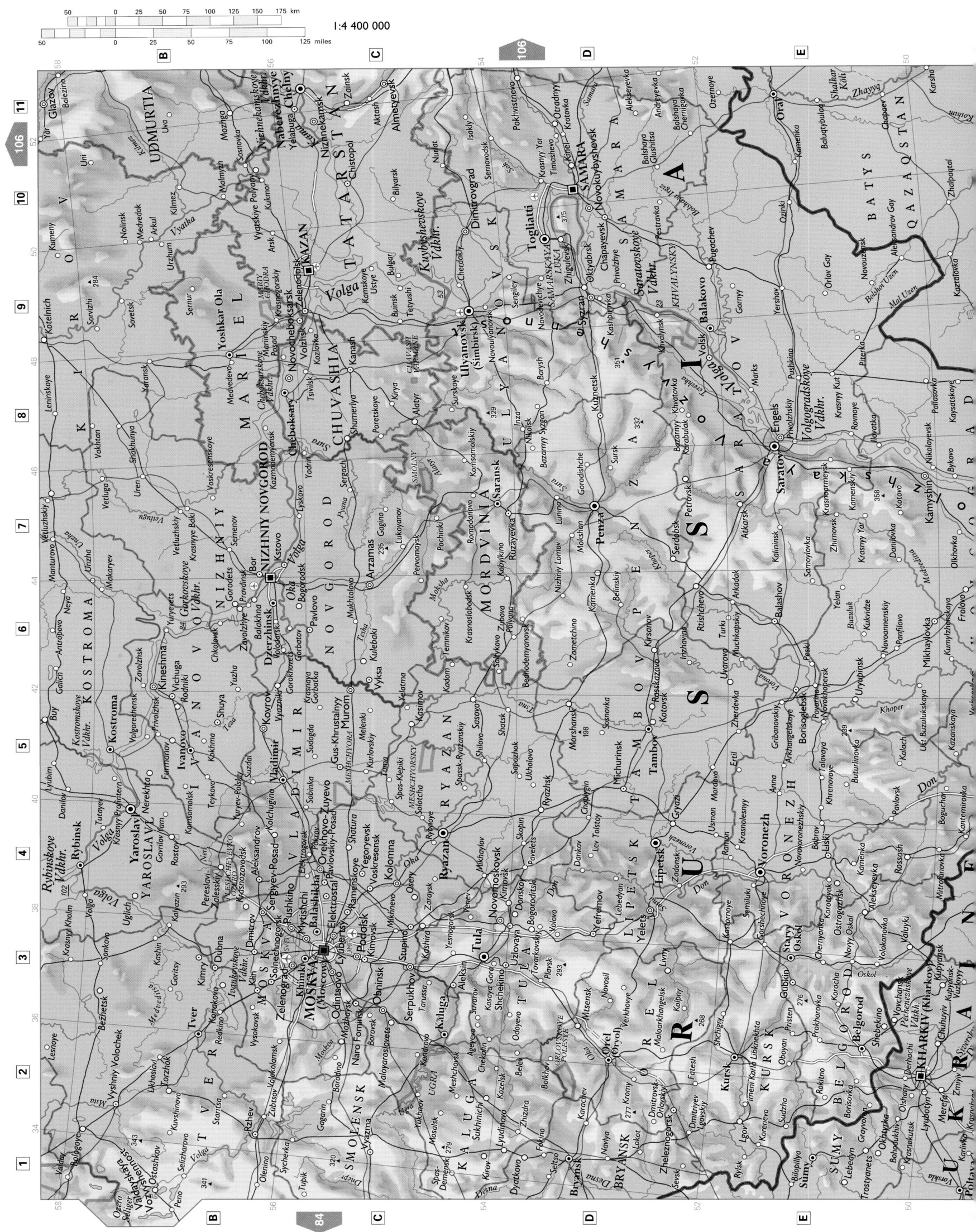

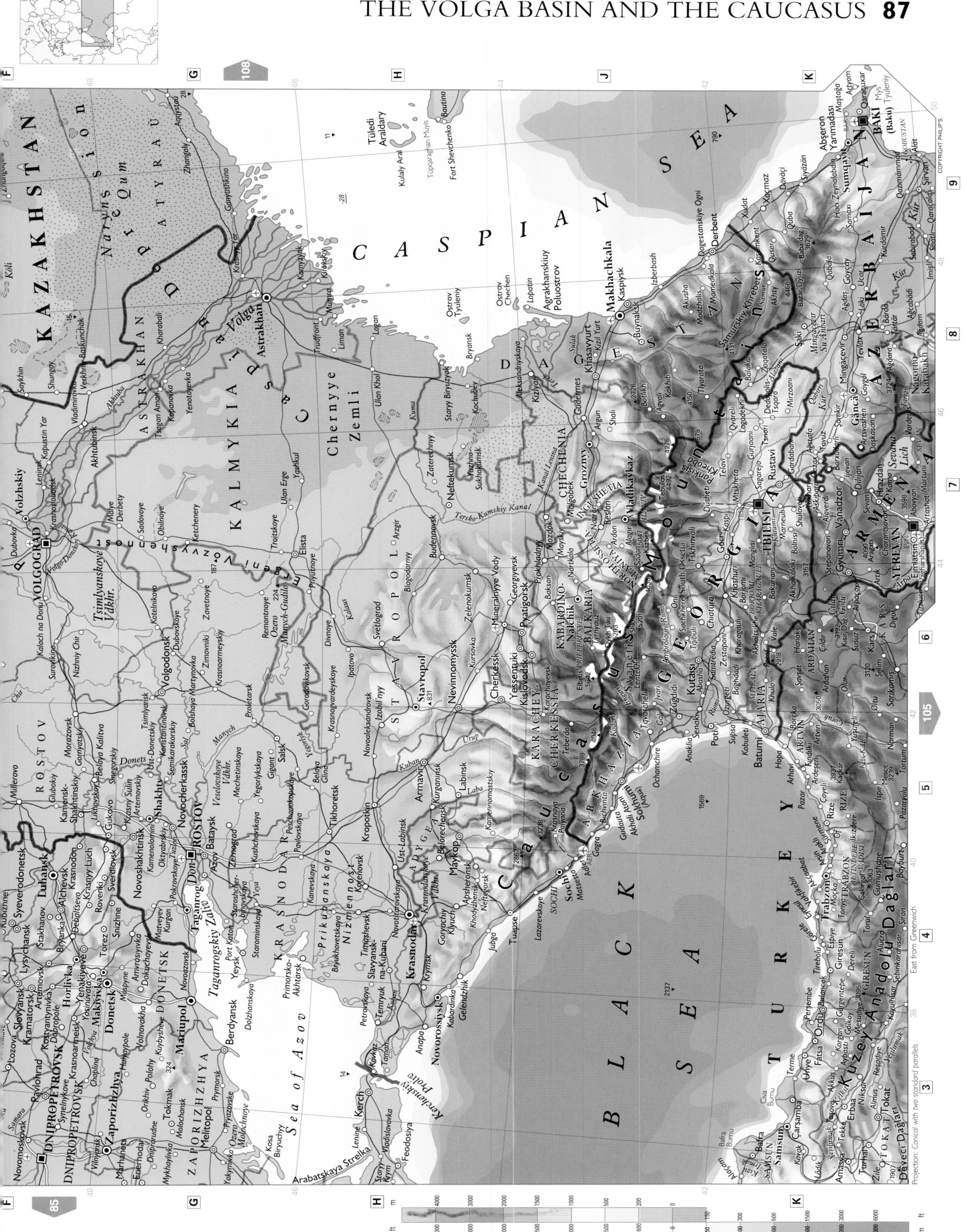

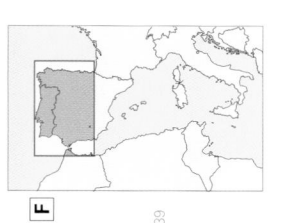

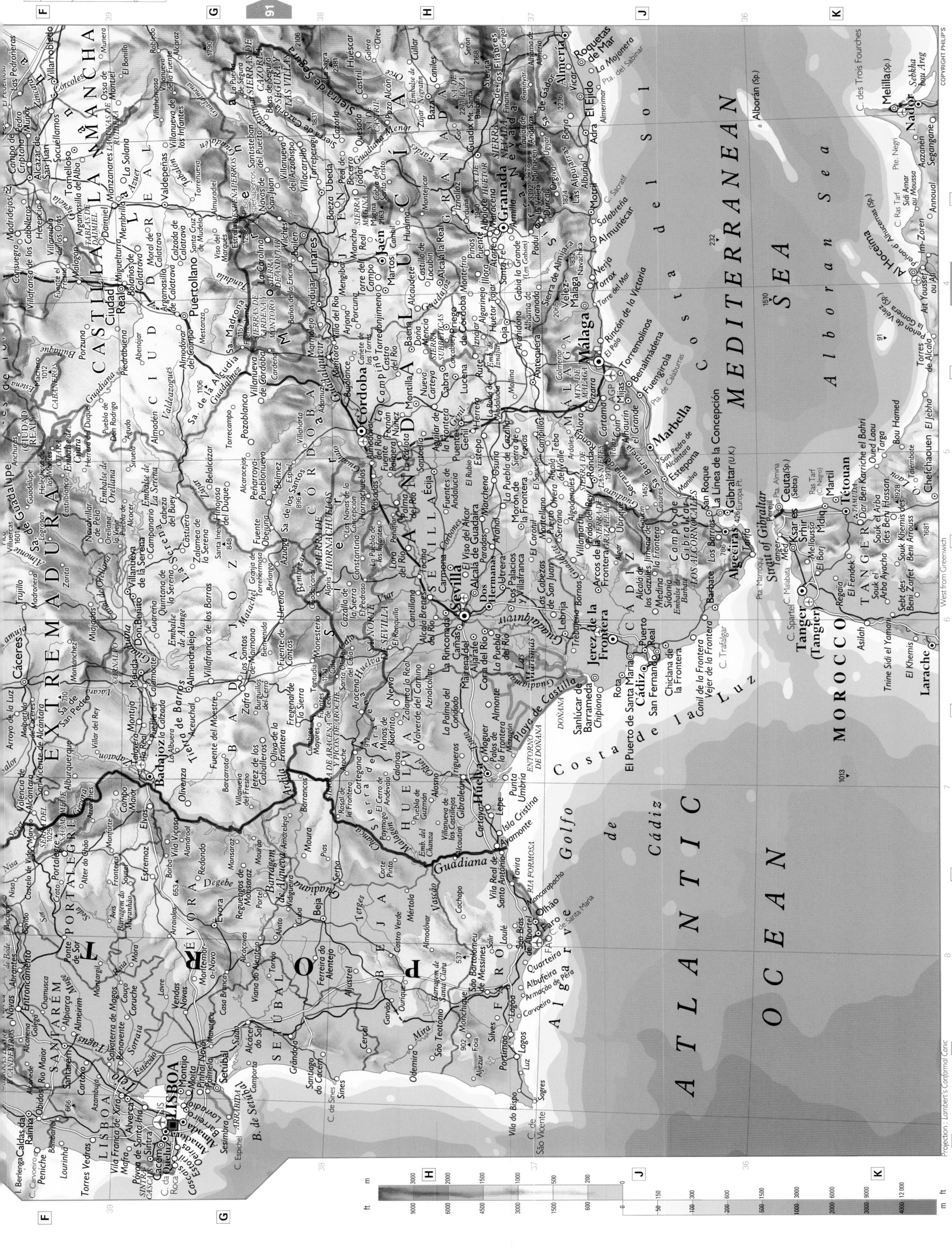

1:2 200 000

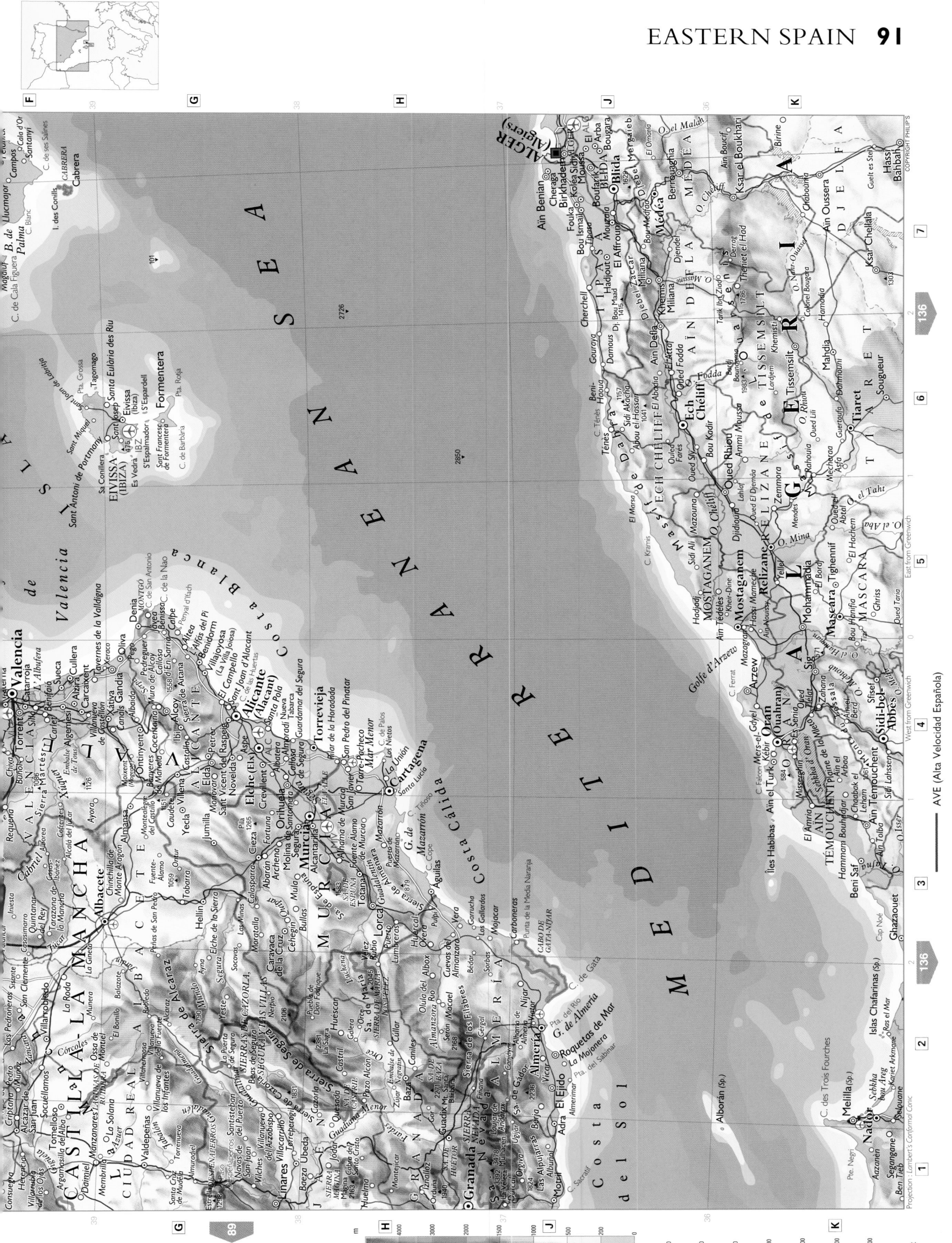

Projection: Lambert's Conformal Conic

AVE (Alta Velocidad Española)

1:2 200 000

Projection : Lambert's Conformal Conic

East from Greenwich

Underlined towns give their name to
administrative area in which they sta

nistrative divisions in Croatia:

dsko-Posavska	4 Medimurska	8 Viroviticko-Podravska
privnicko-Križevačka	6 Požeško-Slavonska	10 Zagreba čka
apinsko-Zagorska	7 Varaždinska	

—————— TAV (Treno Alta Velocità)

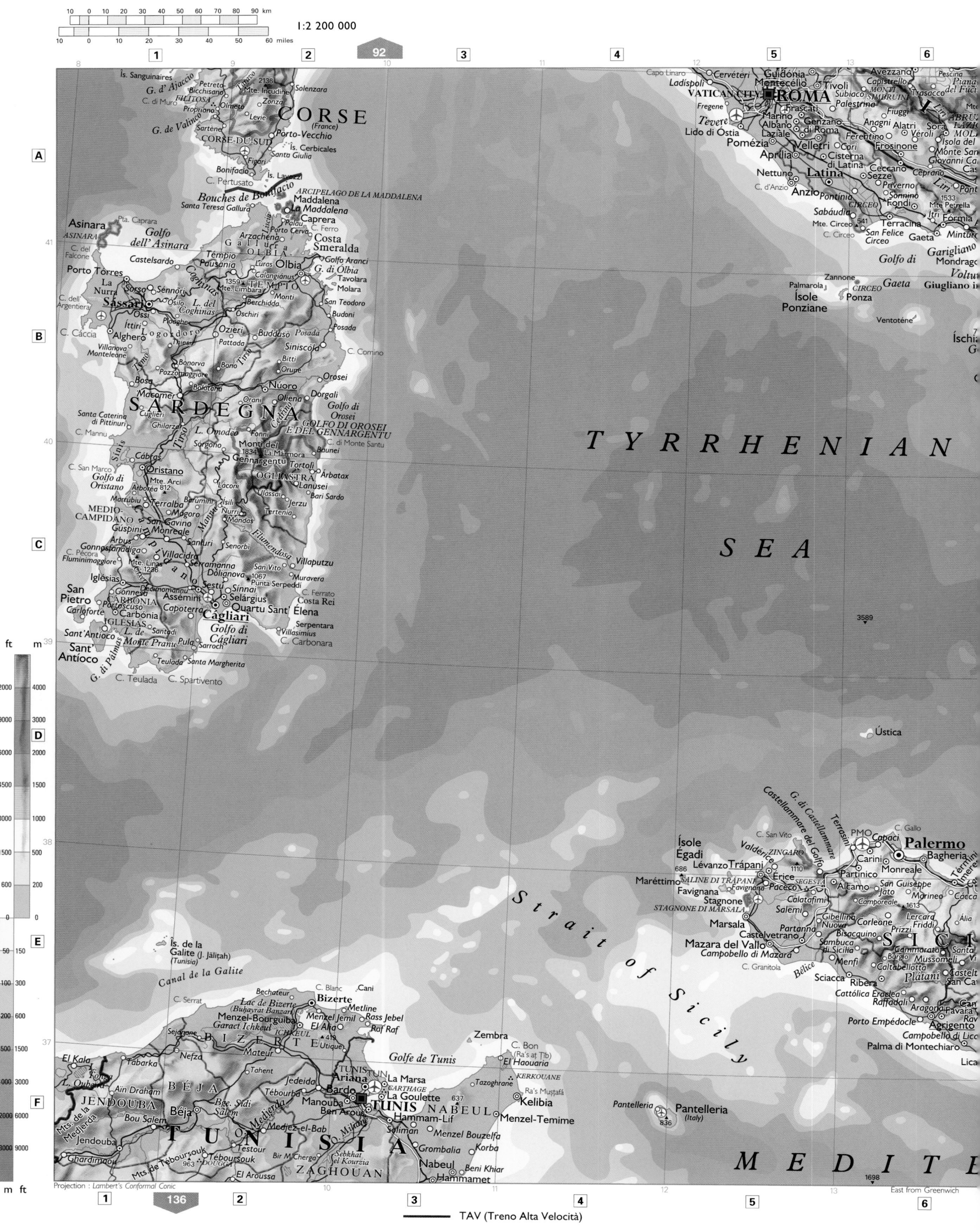

1:2 200 000

10 0 10 20 30 40 50 60 70 80 90 km

10 0 10 20 30 40 50 60 miles

ft m

12000 4000

9000 3000

6000 2000

4500 1500

3000 1000

1500 500

600 200

0 0

50 150

100 300

200 600

500 1500

1000 3000

2000 6000

3000 9000

m ft

Projection : Lambert's Conformal Conic

TAV (Treno Alta Velocità)

East from Greenwich

Underlined towns give their name to the administrative area in which they stand.

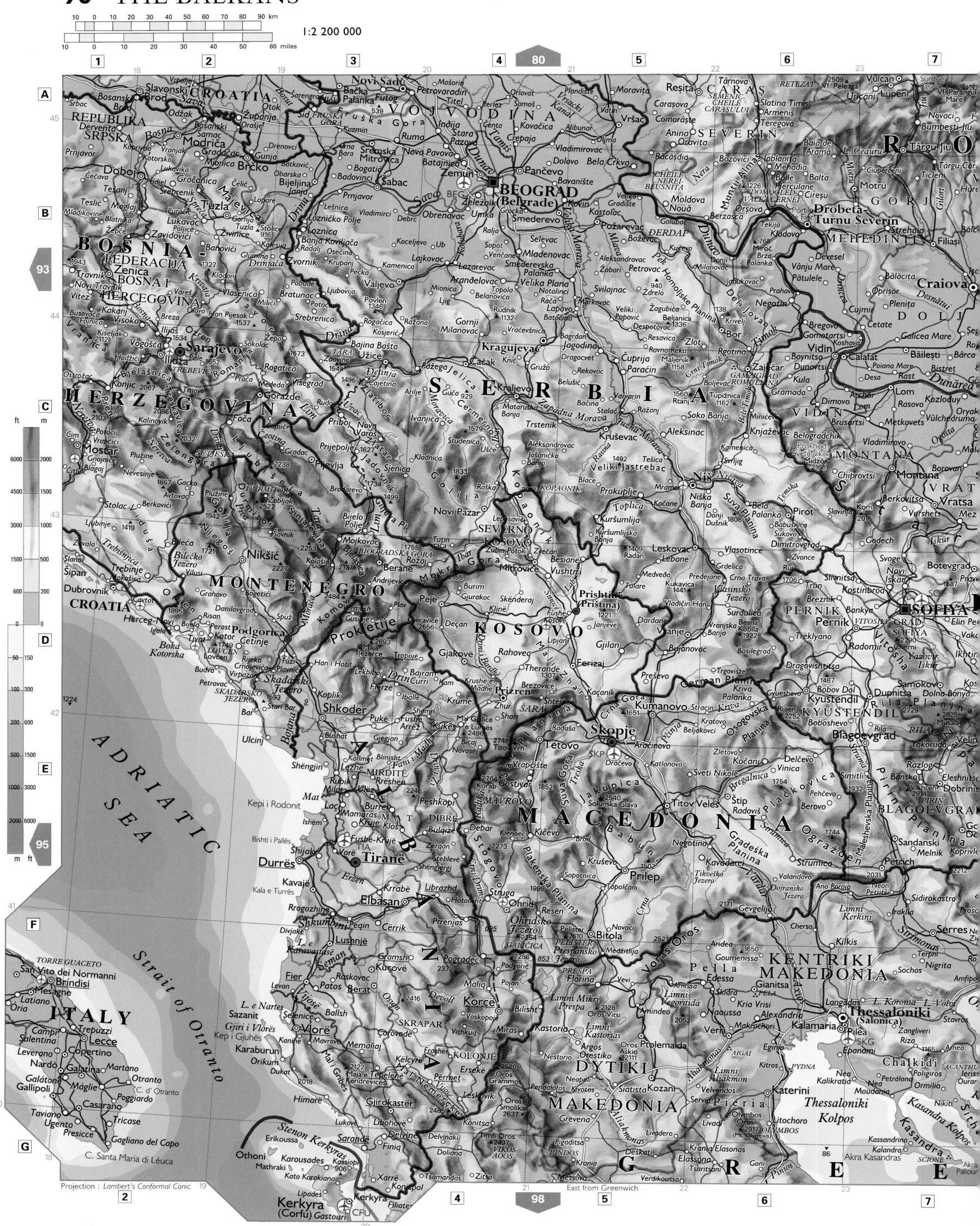

1:2 200 000

Projection : Lambert's Conformal Conic

East from Greenwich

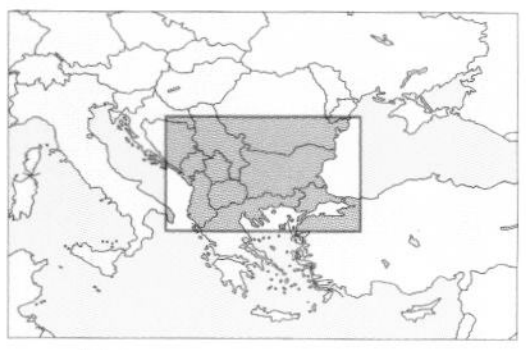

BLACK SEA

TURKEY

BULGARIA

Bucureşti (Bucharest)

Constanţa

Varna

Burgas

Burgaski Zaliv

İstanbul

Üsküdar

Bursa

Marmara Denizi (Sea of Marmara)

Sea of Thrace

DELTA DUNĂREA

Dunărea

Dunav (Danube)

CONSTANŢA

TULCEA

DOBRICH

SHUMEN

VARNA

RAZGRAD

SILISTRA

CĂLĂRAŞI

IALOMIŢA

BRĂILA

BUZĂU

PRAHOVA

DÂMBOVIŢA

GIURGIU

TELEORMAN

OLT

ARGEŞ

VELIKO TŬRNOVO

GABROVO

PLEVEN

PLOVDIV

STARA ZAGORA

SLIVEN

YAMBOL

BURGAS

KHASKOVO

KŬRDZHALI

EDİRNE

KIRKLARELİ

TEKİRDAĞ

ÇANAKKALE

KOCAELİ

ANATOLIKI MAKEDONIA

THRAKI

Galaţi

Brăila

Buzău

Ploieşti

Piteşti

Râmnicu Vâlcea

Târgovişte

Giurgiu

Ruse

Pleven

Gabrovo

Veliko Tŭrnovo

Shumen

Varna

Dobrich

Constanţa

Mangalia

Tulcea

Plovdiv

Pazardzhik

Asenovgrad

Stara Zagora

Sliven

Yambol

Burgas

Khaskovo

Kŭrdzhali

Smolyan

Edirne

Kırklareli

Lüleburgaz

Çorlu

Tekirdağ

İstanbul

Kartal

Gebze

Kocaeli (İzmit)

Gölcük

Yalova

Gemlik

Bandırma

Bursa

İnegöl

Çanakkale

Gökçeada (İmroz)

Bozcaada

Limnos

Thasos

Samothraki

Alexandroúpoli

Kavála

Komotiní

Xánthi

Gelibolu (Gallipoli)

Çanakkale Boğazı (Dardanelles)

İstanbul Boğazı (Bosporus)

Kaz Dağı

Uludağ 2543

COPYRIGHT PHILIP'S

Underlined towns give their name to the administrative area in which they stand.

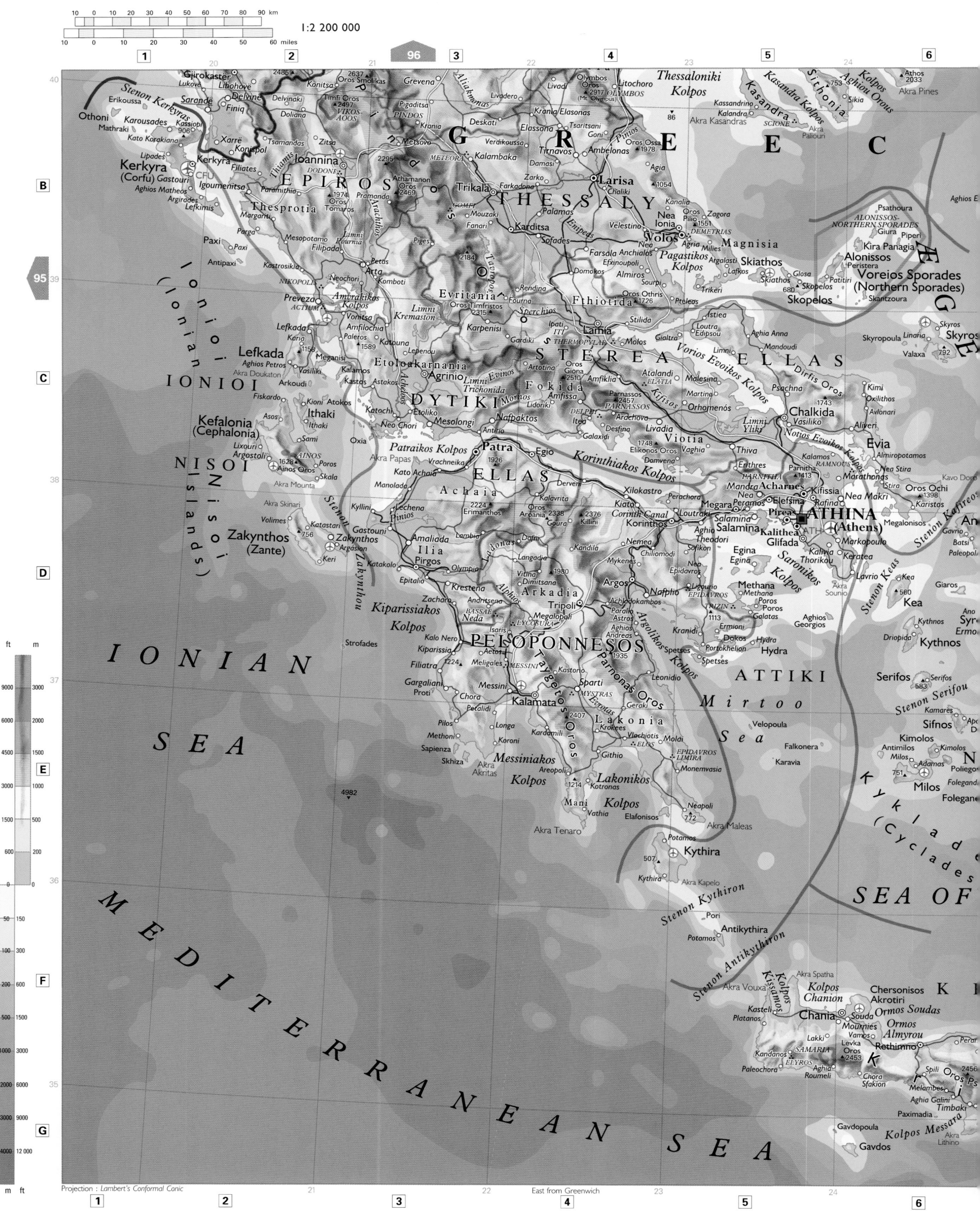

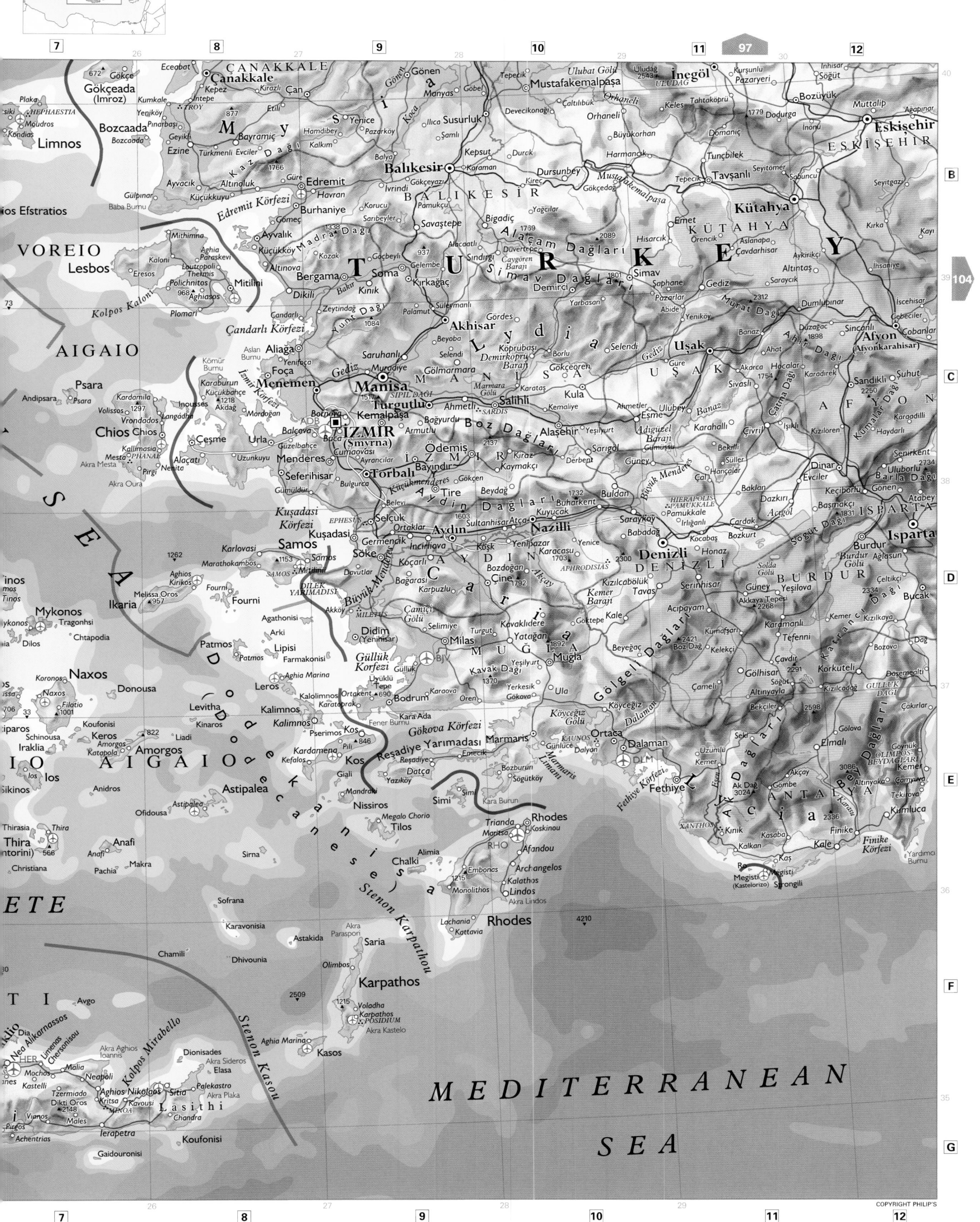

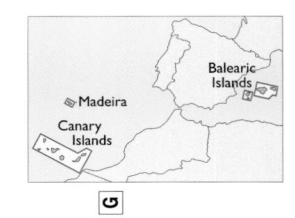

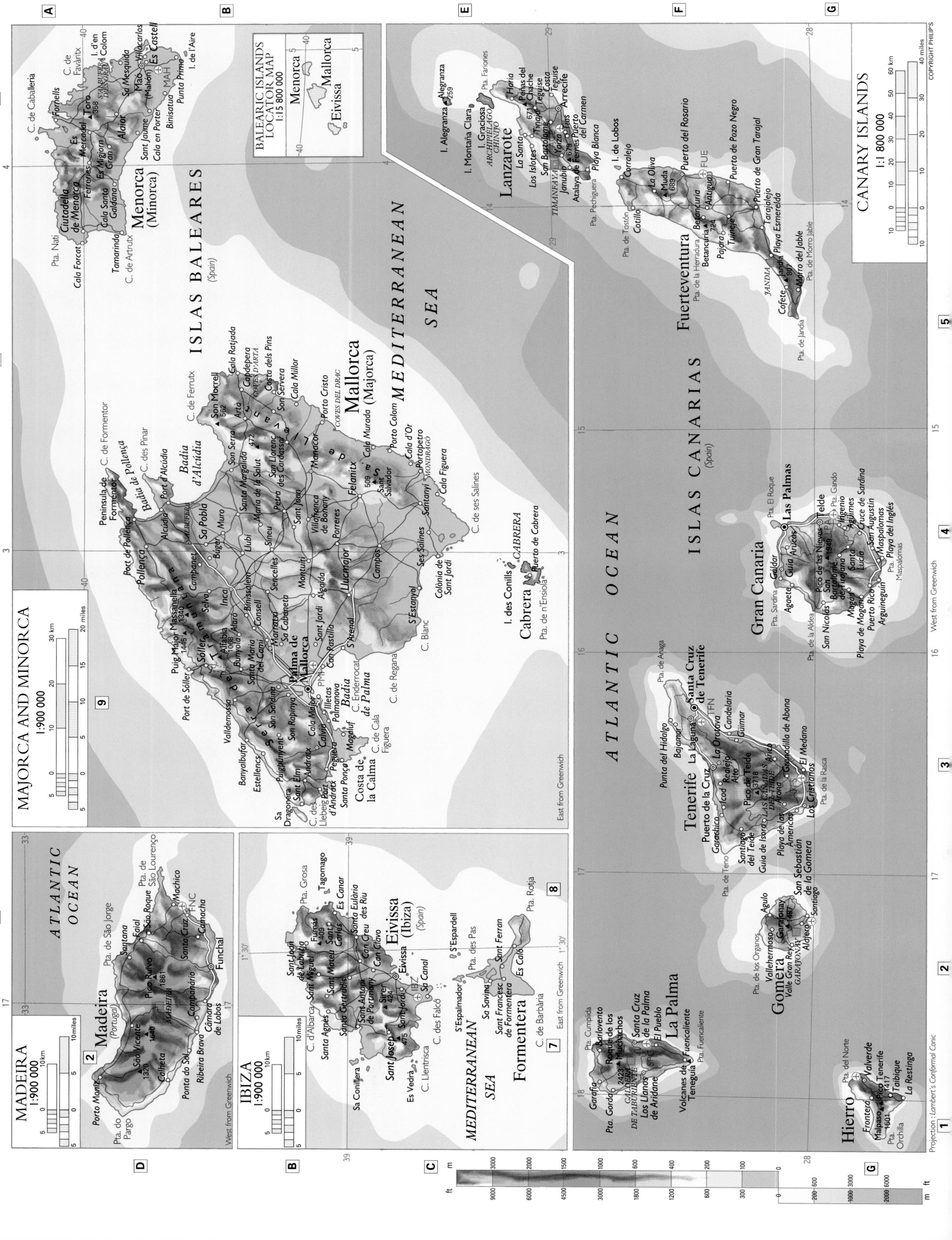

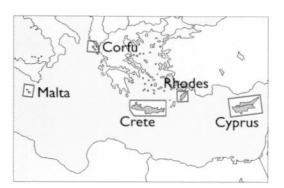

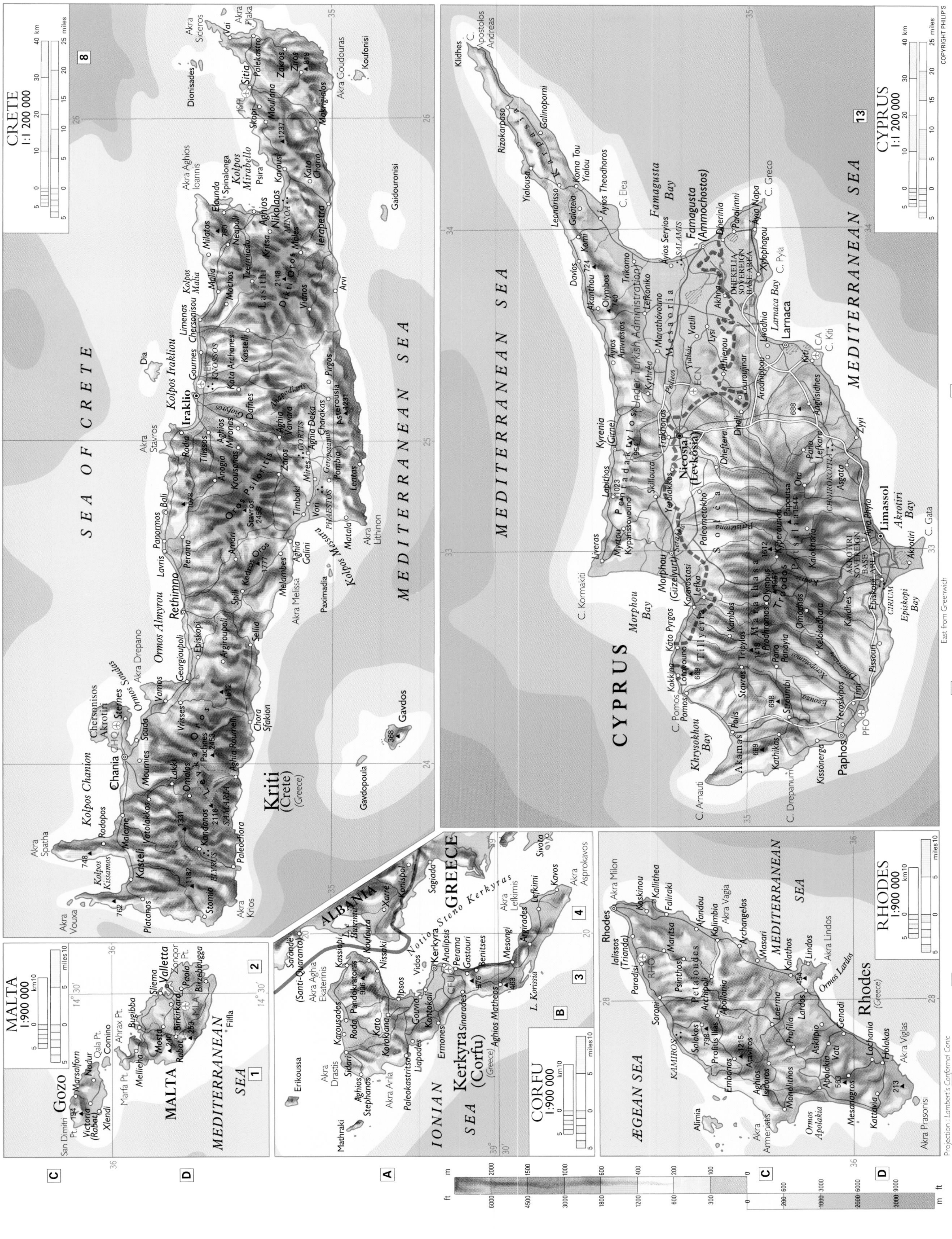

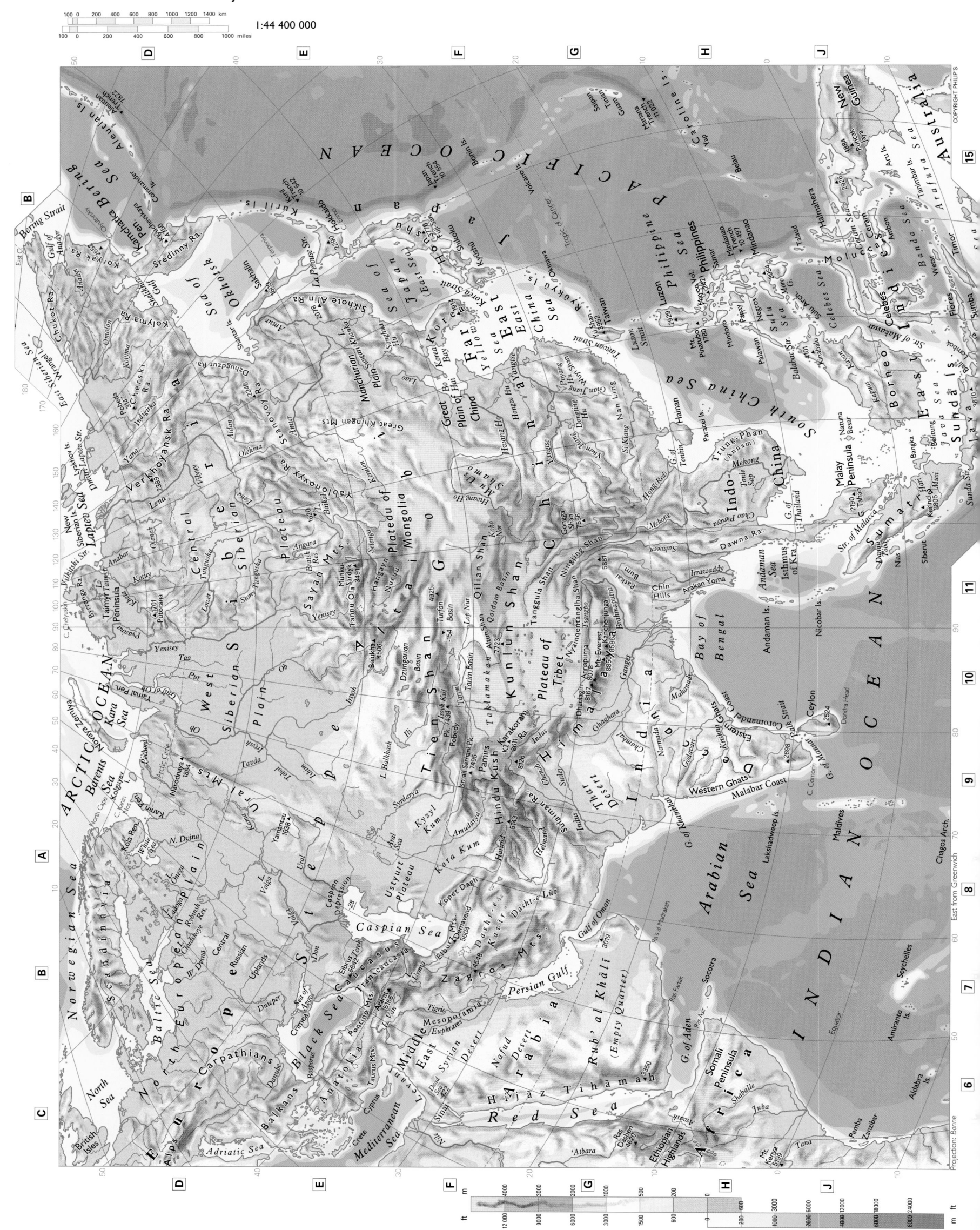

1:44 400 000

COPYRIGHT PHILIP'S

Projection: Bonne

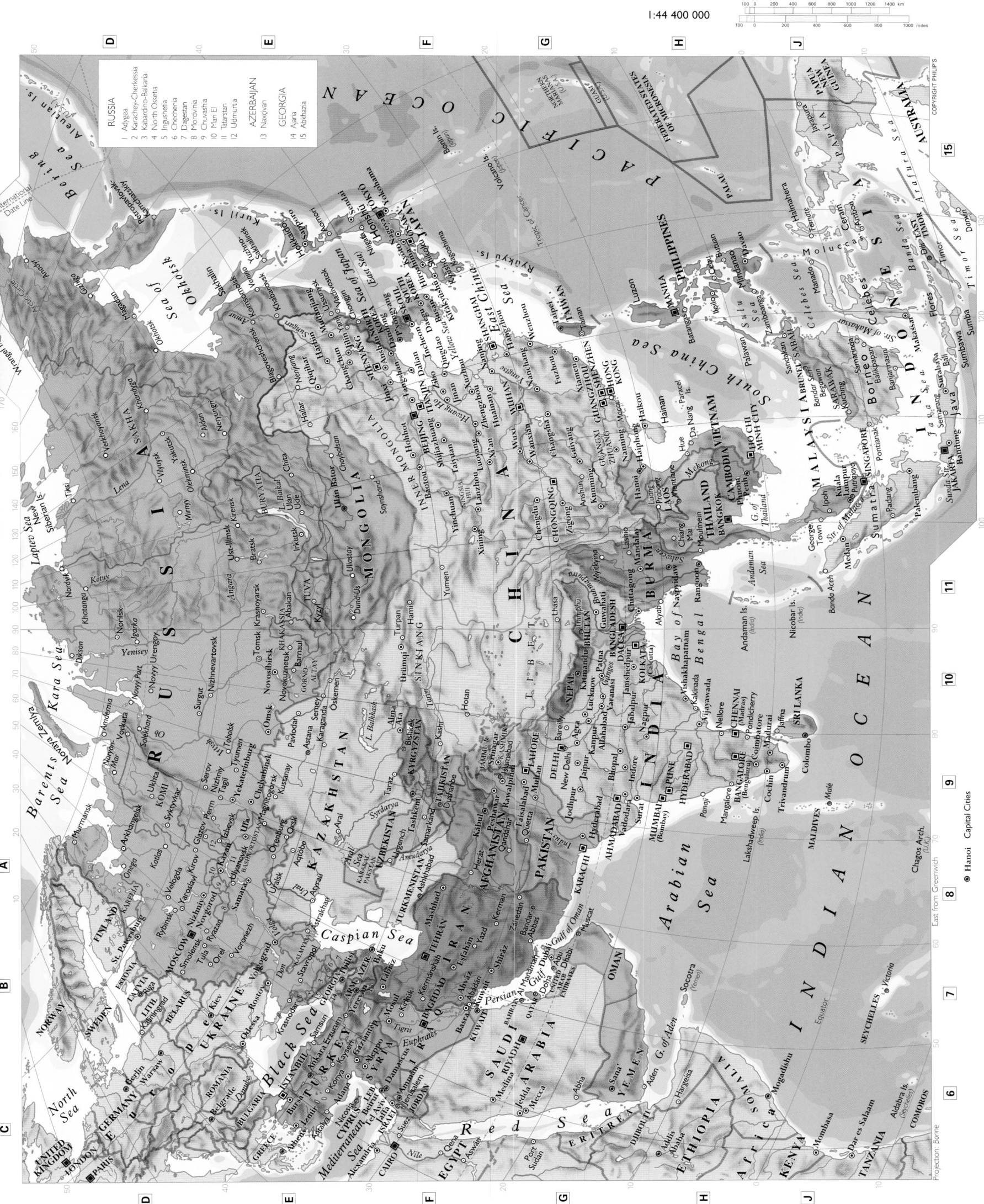

1:44 400 000

1: 4 400 000

Projection: Conical with two standard parallels

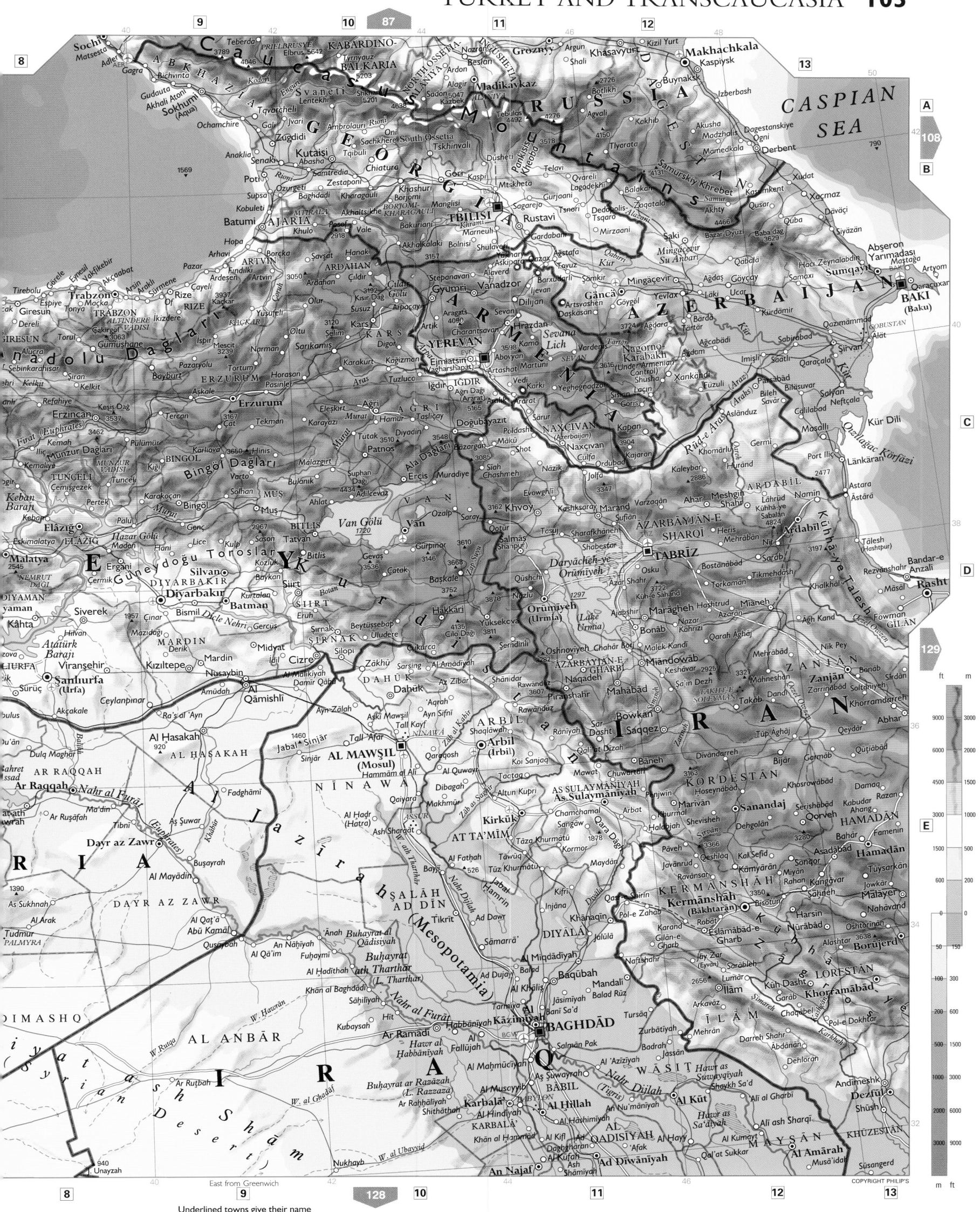

Underlined towns give their name
to the administrative area in which they stand

1:17 800 000

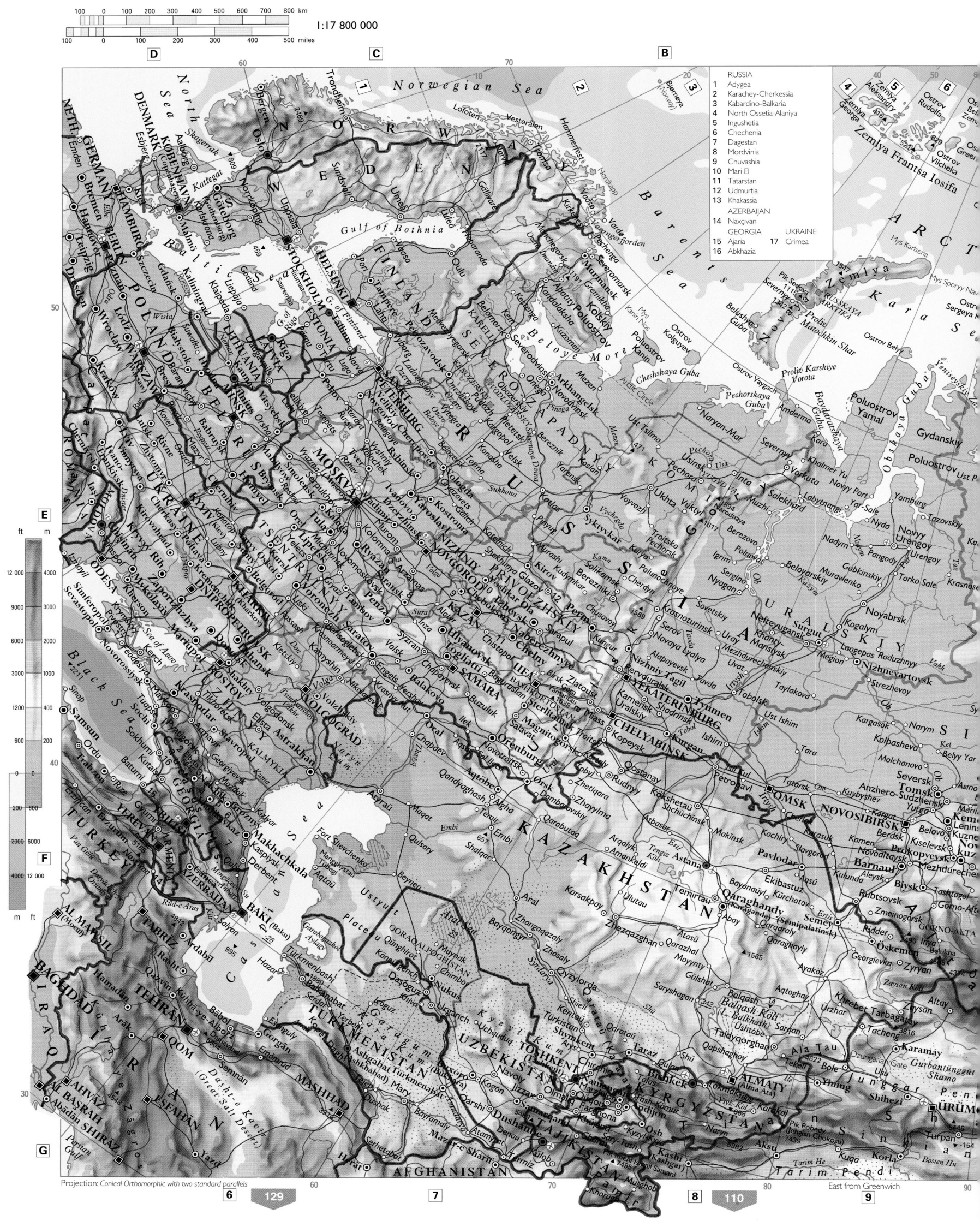

RUSSIA
1 Adygea
2 Karachey-Cherkessia
3 Kabardino-Balkaria
4 North Ossetia-Alaniya
5 Ingushetia
6 Chechenia
7 Dagestan
8 Mordvinia
9 Chuvashia
10 Mari El
11 Tatarstan
12 Udmurtia
13 Khakassia
AZERBAIJAN
14 Naxçivan
GEORGIA   UKRAINE
15 Ajaria   17 Crimea
16 Abkhazia

Projection: Conical Orthomorphic with two standard parallels

East from Greenwich

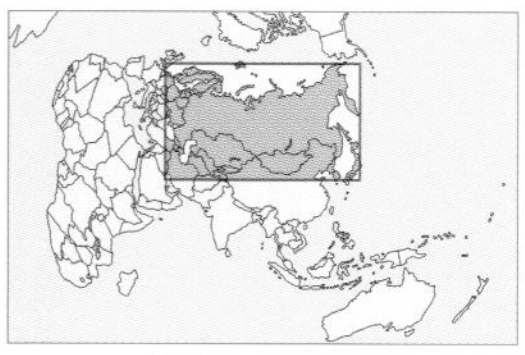

ARCTIC OCEAN

Severnaya Zemlya

Ostrov Shmidta

Ostrov Komsomolets

Ostrov Oktyabrskoy Revolyutsii

Ostrov Bolshevik

Laptev Sea

Novosibirskiye Ostrova

East Siberian Sea

Chukchi Sea

Bering Strait

Bering Sea

St. Lawrence I. (U.S.A.)

International Date Line

Poluostrov Taymyr

Gory Byrranga

Oz. Taymyr

Nordvik

Khatanga

Tiksi

Verkhoyansk

Khrebet Cherskogo

Verkhoyanskiy Khrebet

Kolymskoye Nagorye

Koryakskoye Nagorye

Poluostrov Kamchatka

Sredinnyy Khrebet

Kamchatka

Petropavlovsk-Kamchatskiy

Sea of Okhotsk

Kurilskiye Ostrova

Sakhalin

R U S S I A

DALNEVOSTOCHNYY

Yakutsk

Vilyuysk

Lena

Olekminsk

Aldan

Stanovoy Khrebet

Khrebet Dzhugdzur

Khrebet Sikhote Alin

Komsomolsk-na-Amur

Khabarovsk

Yuzhno-Sakhalinsk

Krasnoyarsk

Bratsk

Irkutsk

Ulan Ude

Chita

Blagoveshchensk

Amur

Svobodnyy

Birobidzhan

Vladivostok

Nakhodka

Hokkaidō

SAPPORO

Hakodate

Honshū

ULAANBAATAR

M O N G O L I A

Altay

Aerhtai Shan

Gobi

HARBIN

QIQIHAR

DAQING

JIAMUSI

MUDANJIANG

JILIN

CHANGCHUN

Manchuria (Dongbei)

SHENYANG

ANSHAN

FUSHUN

CHIFENG

NORTH KOREA

P'YONGYANG

Hamhŭng

Wŏnsan

Ch'ŏngjin

Sea of Japan (East Sea)

C H I N A

BEIJING

TANGSHAN

ZHANGJIAKOU

HOHHOT

BAOTOU

TIANJIN

DALIAN

DANDONG

SOUTH KOREA

SEOUL

INCHEON

DAEJEON

DAEGU

BUSAN

GWANGJU

JAPAN

KYOTO

ŌSAKA

KŌBE

COPYRIGHT PHILIP'S

50 0 100 200 300 400 km
1:8 900 000
50 0 50 100 150 200 250 miles

Projection: Modified Miller oblated stereographic

7 8 9 10 11 12 13

OMSK
Om
Tatarsk
NOVOSIBIRSK
Berdsk
Leninsk Belovo
Kuznetskiy
Kiselevsk Chernogorsk Minusinsk
Mamlyutka
Bülaevo
Petukhovo
Isil Kul
Kalachinsk
Novosibirskoye Vdkhr.
Iskitim
Cherepanovo
Prokopyevsk
Kemerovo
Abakan Shushenskoye
KRASNOYARSK Turan
Toora-Khem
Petropavl
Kishkeneköl
Cherlak
Karasuk
Kupino
Ozero
Chany
Kamen
Suzun
Novokuznetsk
Zarinsk
Tashtagol
SHUSHENSKY
BOR
Khrebet Akademika
Obrucheva

SOLTÜSTIK
QAZAQSTAN
Taymba
Köksheta
Rüzaevka
Makinsk
Stepnogorsk
PAVLODAR
Pavlodar
Aqsü
Ekibastuz
Mayqayyng
Bayanaül
Kürchatov
Semey
(Semipalatinsk)
Öskemen
Zyryan
Ridder
Belousovka
Shemonaikha
Zmeinogorsk
Gornyak
Rubtsovsk
Barnaul
Biysk
Ob
Mayma
Gorno-
Altaysk
GORNO-
ALTAY
ALTAI
Belukha 4506
TUVA
Tannu Ola
MONGOLIA

Astana
AQMOLA
Qorghalzhyn
Osakarovka
Atbasar
Esil (Ishim)
Tengiz
Köli
Shiderti
Bayanaül
Qazaqstan
Georgievka
Semey
SHYGHYS
QAZAQSTAN
Qotanqaraghay
Marqaköl
Zaysan Köli
(Oz. Zaysan)
Kürshim
Habahe
Altay
ALTAI
Ölgiy
Tolbo
Bogd Uul
Hyargas
Nuur
Har Us
Nuur
Hovd

Arqalyk
Qaraghandy
(Karaganda)
Abay
Qarqaraly
Qaraghayly
Shakhtinsk
Temirtaü
Sorang
USAQSHOGYLYGHY
Qaynar
SHYGHYS
QAZAQSTAN
Tarbagatay
Khrebet Zaysan
Ürzhar
Tacheng
(Qoqek)
Emin
Maqanshy
Toli
Karamay
Gurbantünggüt
Shamo
Junggar Pendi
HOVD

Sätbaev
Zhezqazghan
QARAGHANDY
Zhayrang
Aqadyr
Qarazhal
Atasü
Aqzhal
Moyynty
Balqash
Aqtoghay
Ayaköz
Barshatas
Sayaköli
Alaköl
(Ozero Alakol)
Üsharal
Dostyq
Bole
(Bortala)
Dzungarian
Ala Tau
Ebinur Hu
Kuytun
Usu
Shihezi
Changji
ÜRÜMQI
Miquan
Bogda Shan
Turpan

Ulutau
HSTAN
Betpaqdala
Saryshaghan
Balqash Köli
(L. Balkhash)
Ülken
Shyghanaq
Saryesik-Atyraü
Qumy
Üshtöbe
Molaly
Sarqan
Tekeli
ALMATY
Ala Tau
Taldyqorghan
Huocheng
Yining
(Gulja)
Qapqal
Gongliu
Borohoro Shan
Erbeng Shan
Toksun
Turpan Pendi
Aydingköl Hu

ONGTÜSTIK
QAZAQSTAN
ZHAMBYL
Sozaq
Moyynqum
Moyynkum
Balpyq Bi
Saryözek
ALTYN-EMEL
Zharkent
Köktal
Shonzhy
Tian
Shan
Kuruktag
Bosten
Hu
Bohu
Korla
Yuli
(Lop Nur)
Konqi He
Lop
Nur

Türkistan
Kentaü
Qarataü
Baltköl
Taraz
(Zhambyl)
Kighiz
Zhangatas
Qaratau
Sarykemer
Töle Bi
Shü
Qapshaghay
Shelek
Talghar
ALMATY
(Alma Ata)
Bishkek
(Frunze)
Kara-Balta
Tokmak
ILE-ALA-TAU
Küngey Ala Too
Cholpon-
Ata
Türp
Ysyk-Köl
Karakol
Pik Pobedy
(Jengish Chokusu) 7439
Pik Khan-Tengri
Baicheng
Kuqa
Xinhe
Kuqa
Xayar
Tarim He
Aksu

Shymkent
(Chimkent)
Qazyghurt
Lengea
Aqsü
Talas
Ala-Too
Toktogul
Kochkor
Song-Köl
Terskey Ala Too
YSYK-KÖL
Wensu
Aksu
Aksu He
Wushi
Taklamakan
Tarim Pendi
XINJIANG UYGUR ZIZHIQU
(SINKIANG)

TOSHKENT
(Tashkent)
Shardara
Angren
Namangan
Chust
Andijon
Osh
Gülchö
Sulaiman-Too
Kökand
Fergana
Farghona
Kara-Köl
Jalal-Abad
Baetov
Naryn
At-Bashy
KYRGYZSTAN
Karateki Shan
Torugart
Pass
Artux
Sugun
Bachu
Yarkand He
Markit
Shule
Shache
(Yarkand)
Shamo
Taklamakan
Ruoqiang
Altun Shan
Waxxari
Qiemo
Qemo

Jizzax
SIRDARYO
Bekobod
Istaravshan
Khujand
Samarqand
Turkeston Ra.
SUGHD
Batken
Sary
Tash
Kyzyl
Uluqqat
Wuqia
Kashi
(Kashgar)
Shule
Yengisar
Akta
Karakul
Kongur Shan
Muztagh-Ata
Zepu
Yecheng
Pishan
Moyu
Hotan
Qira
Keriya He
Yutian
Minfeng
Hadilik
Muz Tag
Ayakkum Hu

TAJIKISTAN
Dushanbe
Vahdat
KHATLON
Khrebet Gissarskiy
KÜHISTON
BADAKHSHON
(GORNO-
BADAKHSHAN)
Kalaikhum
Murghob
Pamir
Taxkorgan
Tajik
Zizhixian
Kokyar
Lop
Karatax Shan
Kunlun Shan
XIZANG ZIZHIQU
(TIBET)

Termiz
SURXON-
DARYO
Qürghonteppa
Kulob
Khorugh
Ishkoshim
Feyzabad
Talogan
Kondoz
BADAKHSHAN
Hindu Kush
Karakoram
Range
Rakaposhi
Gilgit
Baltistan
Nanga Parbat
Aksai
Chin
Kunlun Shan
Chagdo Kangri

Mazar-e
Sharif
Aybak
SAMANGAN
KABUL
PARVAN
Charikar
Jalalabad
NURISTAN
KHYBER
PAKHTUNKHWA
Chilas
JAMMU &
KASHMIR
PAKISTAN
Mardan
Abbottabad
SRINAGAR
Leh
Deosai
Mts
INDIA
Bangong Co
Rutog

70 75 80 85

Underlined towns give their name to the
administrative area in which they stand.

COPYRIGHT PHILIP'S

Projection: Bonne

East from Greenwich

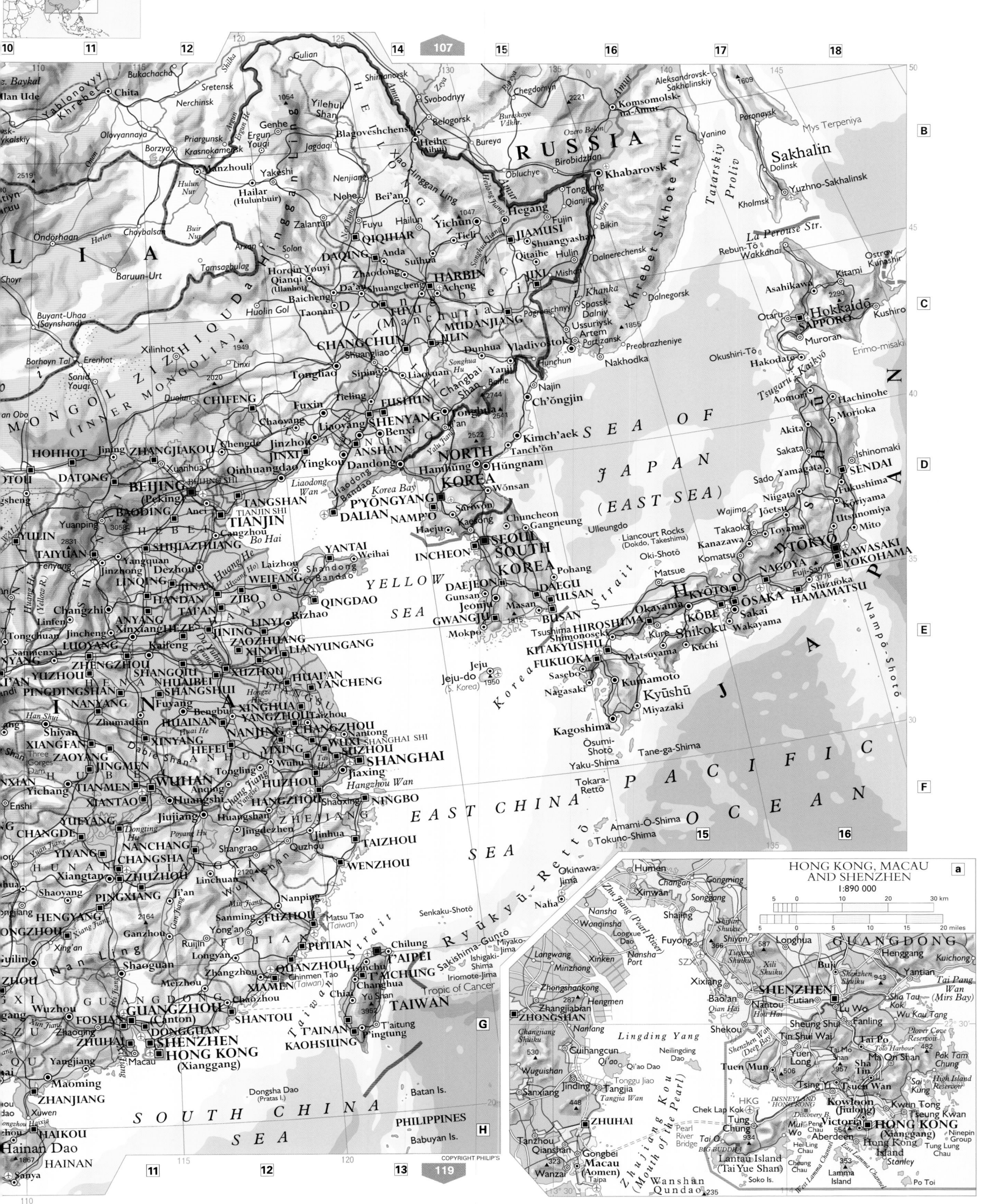

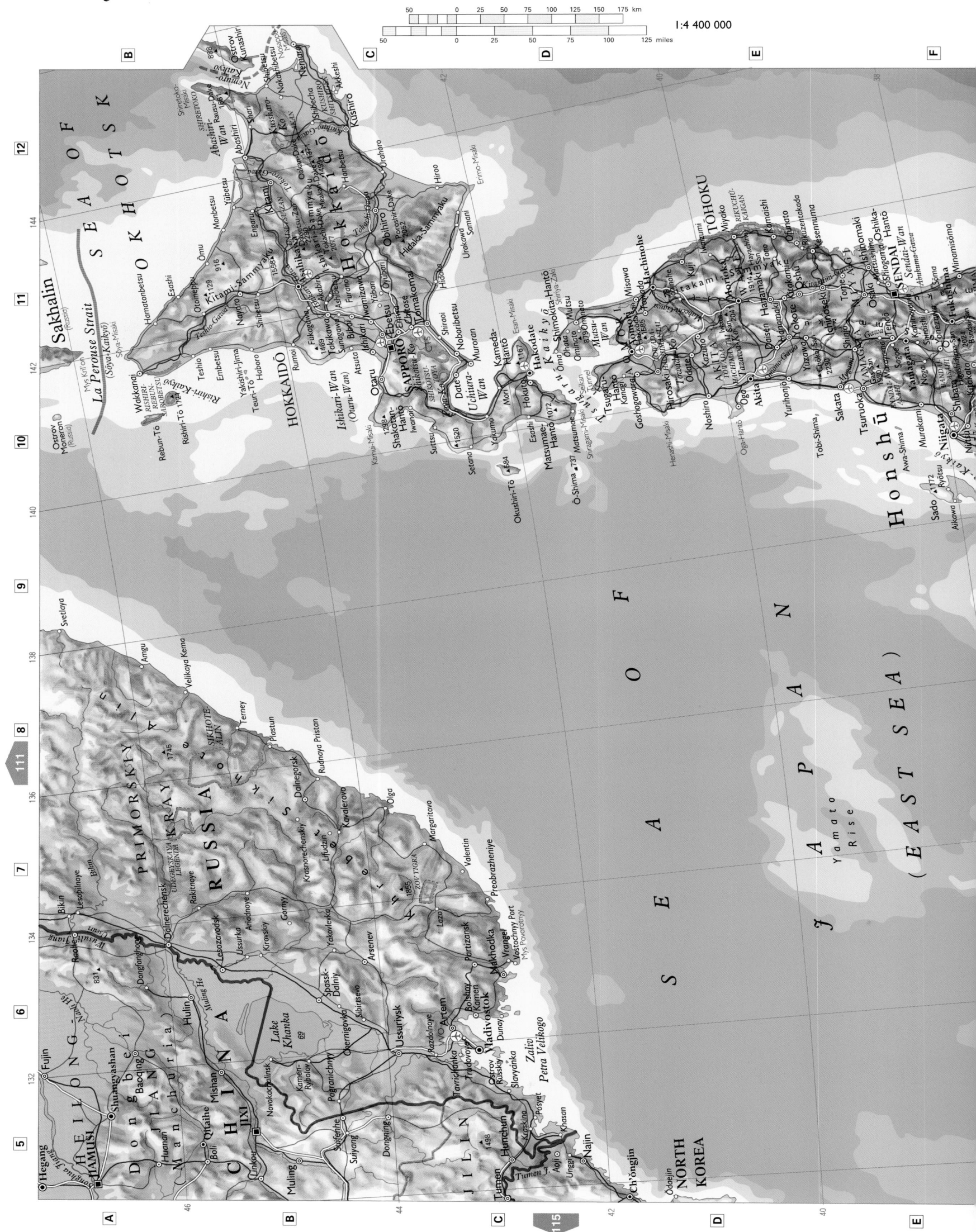

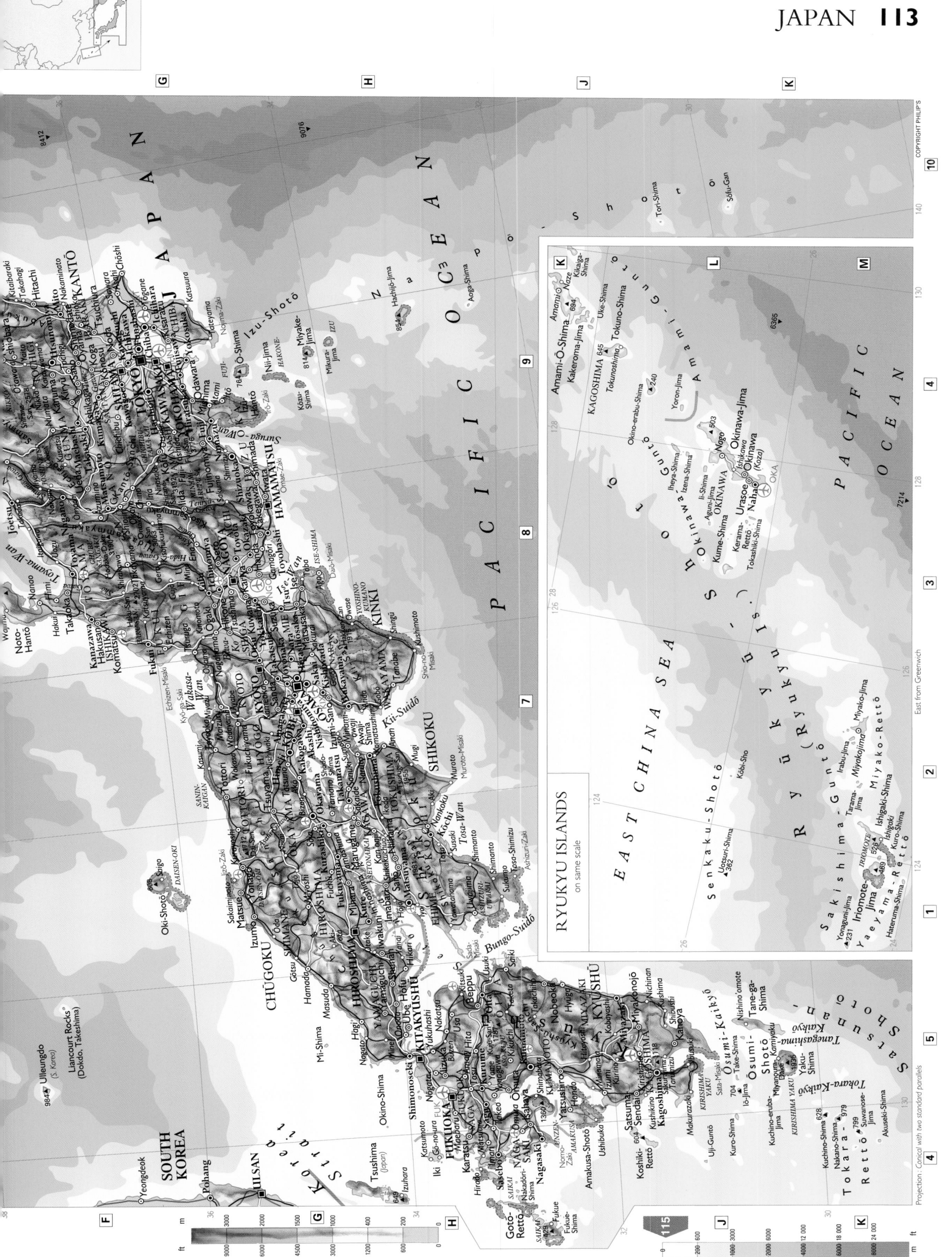

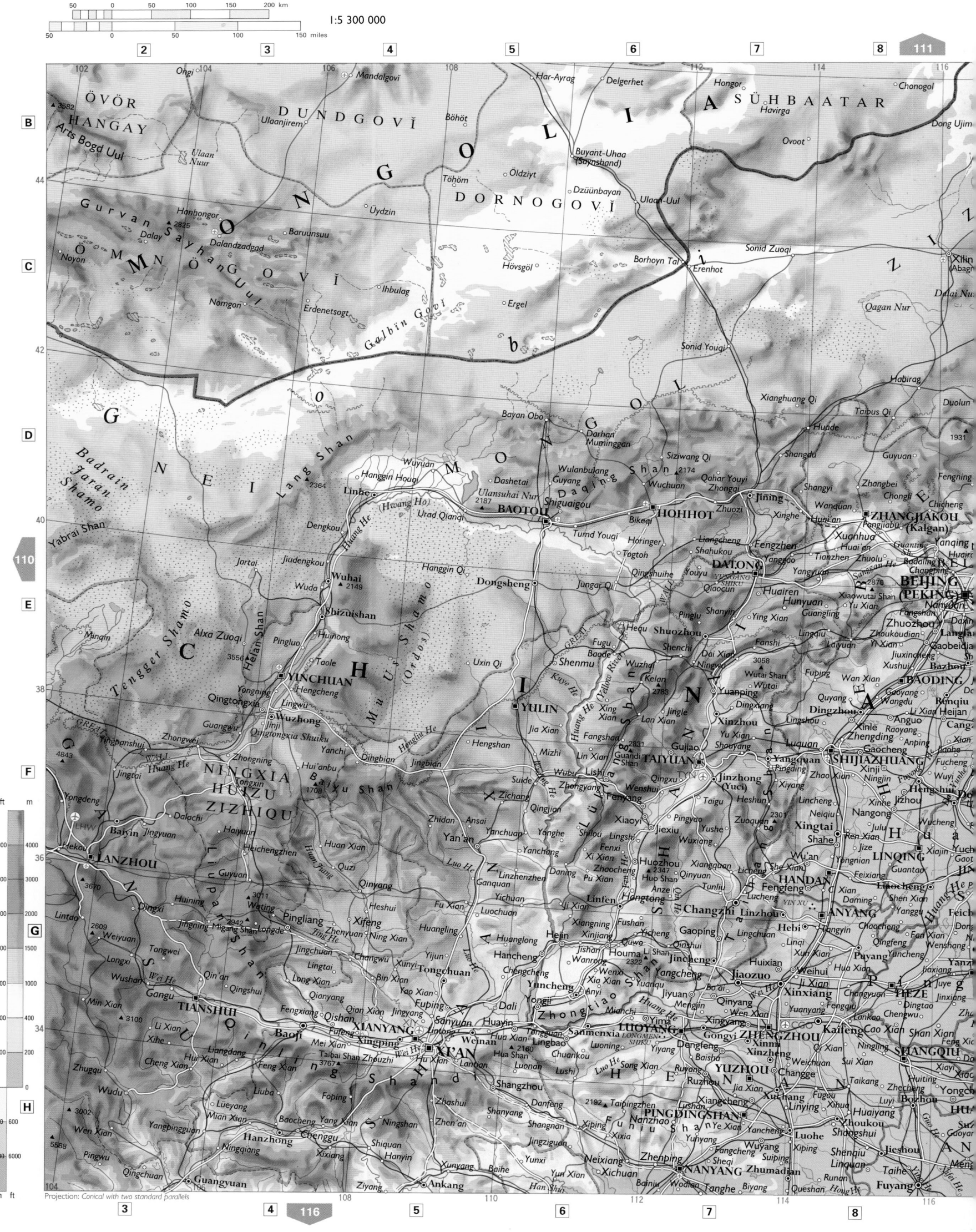

1:5 300 000

Projection: Conical with two standard parallels

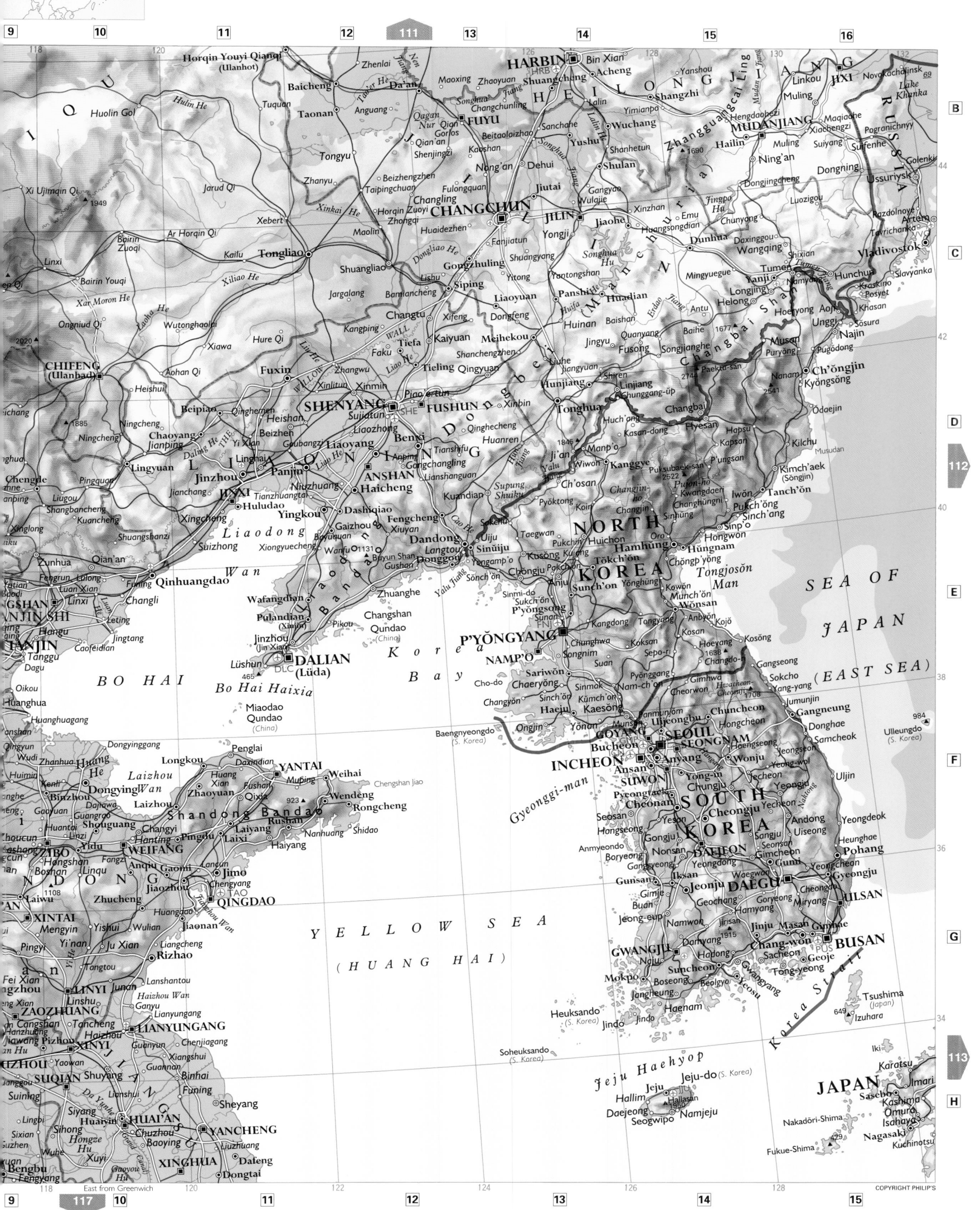

HEILONGJIANG

HARBIN
Bin Xian
Acheng
Shangzhi
Yanshou
Linkou
HXI
Novokachalinsk
Lake Khanka

Horqin Youyi Qianqi (Ulanhot)
Zhenlai
Shuangcheng
Changchunling
Zhangguangcailing
Maoxing
Zhaoyuan
Maqiaohe
Xiaochengzi
Hengdaobezi
Hailin
MUDANJIANG
Muling
Suiyang
Pogranichnyy
Suifenhe
RUSSIA
Golenki

Baicheng
Da'an
Songhua
Lalin
Yimianpo
Wuchang
Shanhetun
Yushu
Shulan
Ning'an
Muling
Dongjingcheng
Luozigou
Ussuriysk

Huolin Gol
Huanli
Hulin He
Tuquan
Taonan
Anguang
Nen
Qagan Nur Qian
Qian'an
Gorlos
Dehui
Nong'an
Dongning
Razdolnoye
Artem

IQU
Xi Ujimqin Qi
1949
Tongyu
Zhanyu
Beizhengzhen
Taipingchuan
Fulongquan
Changling
Jiutai
Gangyan
Wulajie
Jinchuan
Chunyang
Dangingou
Wangqing
Vladivostok
Slavyanka

Jarud Qi
Xebert
Xinkai He
Horqin Zuoyi Zhongqi
Maolin
Huaidezhen
CHANGCHUN
JILIN
Yitong
Yantongshan
Jiaohe
Emu
Xinzhan
Jingpo Hu
Mingyuegou
Yanji
Tumen
Namyang
Hunchun
Kraskino
Posyet

Ar Horqin Qi
Kailu
Tongliao
Shuangliao
Lishu
Siping
Gongzhuling
Panshihua
Huadian
Quanyang
Baishan
Antu
Helong
Longjing
Musan
Unggi
Aoji
Sosura
Najin

Bairin Zuoqi
Linxi
Lanhai He
Xiliao He
Jargalang
Bamiancheng
Liaoyuan
Xifeng
Dongfeng
Huifa
Jingyu
Fusong
Songjianghe
Baihe
1677
Erdao Jiang
Paektu-san
Hoeryong
Puryong
Pugodong

EP Qi
Bairin Youqi
Xar Moron He
Dongliao He
Changtu
Kangping
Meihekou
Shanchengzhen
Huinan
Hunjiang
Linjiang
Chunggang-ûp
2744
Changbai
Nanam
Ch'ongjin
Kyongsong

CHIFENG (Ulanhad)
Aohan Qi
Xiawa
WALL
Faku
Tiefa
Kaiyuan
Qingyuan
Tieling
Shiren
Jiangyuan
Huch'ang
Hyesan
Ödaejin
Kilchu
Musudan

2020
Ongniud Qi
Hure Qi
Zhangwu
Xinlitun
Liao He
Huch'ang
Kosan-dong
P'ungsan
Kapsan
Hapsu

1885
Ningcheng
Heishui
Fuxin
Xinmin
Piao'ertun
SHENYANG
FUSHUN
Xinbin
Tonghua
1845
Ji'an
Manp'o
Wiwon
Pukch'ang
Kilchu

Chengli
Ningcheng
Beipiao
Qinghemen
Heishan
Sujiatun
SHE
Qingshucheng
Huanren
Yalu
Kanggye
Pukchubaek-san
2522
Puk'ôn-ho
Kwangdae
Iwon
Tanch'on

Chaoyang
Jianping
Daling He
Beizhen
Liaoyang
Liaozhong
Benxi
Tianshifu
Kuandian
Ch'osan
Koin
2541
Changjin-ho
Changjin
Changhüngni
Pukch'ông
Sinch'ang

Chengde
Lingyuan
THE
Lingxi
Xi Xian
Anping
Gongchangling
Lianshanguan
Pyoktong
Changjin-ho
Puk'ôn
Hongwon

Jinzhou
Panjin
ANSHAN
Haicheng
LIAONING
DONG
Supung Shuiku
Hamhüng
Oro
Hongwon

Jianchang
Niuzhuang
Tianzhuangtai
HYXI
Dandong
Sakchu
Taegwan
Pukchin
Huichon
Chôngp'yông

Huludao
Xingcheng
Dashiqiao
Yingkou
Fengcheng
Xiuyan
Cao He
Uiju
Langtou
Ponggou
Sinuiju
Kusông
Kujang
NORTH
Tôkch'ôn
Yônghüng
Wônsan

Zunhua
Qian'an
Suizhong
Boyuquan
Xiongyuecheng
Gaizhou
Zhuanghe
Bryun Shan
Gushan
Yongamp'o
Chôngju
Pakch'ôn
KOREA
Kôwôn
Munch'ôn

Fengrun
Lulong
Funing
Qinhuangdao
Liaodong Wan
Wafangdian
Pulandian (Xinjin)
Changshan
Pikou
Zhuanghe
Sinmi-do
Sukch'ôn
Anju
P'yôngsong
Sunan
Chôngp'yông
Tongjosôn Man

GSHAN
Luan Xian
Linxi
Changli
Leting
Jintang
Jinzhou (Jin Xian)
Qundao (China)
Sunan
P'YONGYANG
Kangdong
Tongyang
Kosan
Kojô

NJIN SHI
Hangu
Tanggu
Dagu
LÜshun
465
DLC
DALIAN (Lüda)
NAMP'O
Chunghwa
Songnim
Suan
Sepo-ri
Hoeyang
1638
Changdo-ri
Gangseong

IANJIN
Caofeidian
BO HAI
Bo Hai Haixia
Miaodao Qundao (China)
Korea Bay
Cho-do
Sariwôn
Sinmak
Koksan
Nam-ch'ôn
Changdo-ri
Hwacheon
1708
Cheorwon
Sokcho
Yang-yang

Huanghua
Huanghuagang
Yalu Jiang
Sônch'ôn
Chaeryông
Sinch'ôn
Kûmch'ôn
Cheorwon
Cheongpyeong
Jumunjin

Yongqun
Dongyinggang
Longkou
Penglai
Changyôn
Haeju
Kaesông
Ongjin
Yônan
Panmunjom
Munsan
Uijeongbu
Chuncheon
Hongcheon
Gangneung
984

anshan
Huimin
Binzhou
Huang He
Laizhou Wan
Daxindian
YANTAI
Weihai
Baengnyeongdo (S. Korea)
GOYANG
SEOUL
Donghae
Samcheok
Ulleungdo (S. Korea)

Kenli
Zhanhua
Dajiwa
Huang Xian
Fushan
Muping
Chengshan Jiao
Bucheon
SEONGNAM
Haengseong
Jumunjin

Gaoqing
Dongying Wan
Laizhou
Zhaoyuan
Qixia
Wendeng
INCHEON
Anyang
Yong-in
Wonju
Yeong-wol
Uljin

Gaoyang
Boxing
Huantai
923
Rushan
Rongcheng
Ansan
Anseong
SUWON
Chungju
Yecheon
Andong

IBO
Hongshan
Linzi
Shouguang
Changyi
Laixi
Laiyang
Haiyang
Shidao
SOUTH
Pyeongtaek
Cheonan
Jecheon
Sangju
Uiseong
Heunghae

Boshan
Linqu
Anqiu
Gaomi
Pingdu
Jiaozhou
Nanhuang
Seosan
Cheongju
Goesan
Yeongju
Yeongdeok

 NDONG
Laiwu
WEIFANG
Jimo
Chengyang
TAO
QINGDAO
KOREA
Hongseong
Yeosan
Mungyeong
Gimcheon
Seonsan
Pohang

1108
Zhucheng
Jiaozhou Wan
Gongju
Nonsan
DAEJEON
Yeongdong
Gumi
Yeongcheon
Gyeongju

XINTAI
Yishui
Wulian
Liangcheng
Gunsan
Iksan
Waegwan
Hamyang
Cheongdo
ULSAN

Mengyin
Yi'nan
Haizhou Wan
Gimje
Jeonju
DAEGU
Goryeong
Miryang
Gimhae

Pingyi
Ju Xian
Rizhao
Buan
Namwon
Jirisan
1915
Jinju
Masan
Gimhae

Fei Xian
Junan
Linshu
Lanshantou
Jeong-eup
GWANGJU
Naju
Danyang
Hadong
Chang-won
PUS
BUSAN

agzhou
LINYI
Tangtou
Ganyu
Lianyungang
YELLOW SEA (HUANG HAI)
Naju
Suncheon
Gwangyang
Sacheon
Geoje
Tong-yeong

ZAOZHUANG
Cangshan
Tancheng
Haizhou
Mokpo
Boseong
Beolgyo
Yeosu
Korea Strait
Tsushima (Japan)
649

XINYI
Yaowan
Guannan
Xiangshui
Heuksando (S. Korea)
Jindo
Jindo
Haenam
Jangheung
Izuhara

IZHOU
Shuyang
Binhai
Soheuksando (S. Korea)
Iki
Karatsu

SUQIAN
Suining
Lianshui
Funing
Jeju Haehyop
JAPAN
Saeburo
Kashima
Imari

Lingbi
Siyang
Sihong
Hongze Hu
HUAI'AN
Chuzhou
Sheyang
Jeju
Jeju-do (S. Korea)
Nakadori-Shima
Omura
Isahaya

Sixian
Siyang
Baoying
Liuzhuang
Hallim
Hallasan
Namjeju
Nagasaki

Bengbu
Fengyang
XINGHUA
Dafeng
Dongtai
Daejeong
Seogwipo
Fukue-Shima
429
Kuchinotsu

1:5 300 000

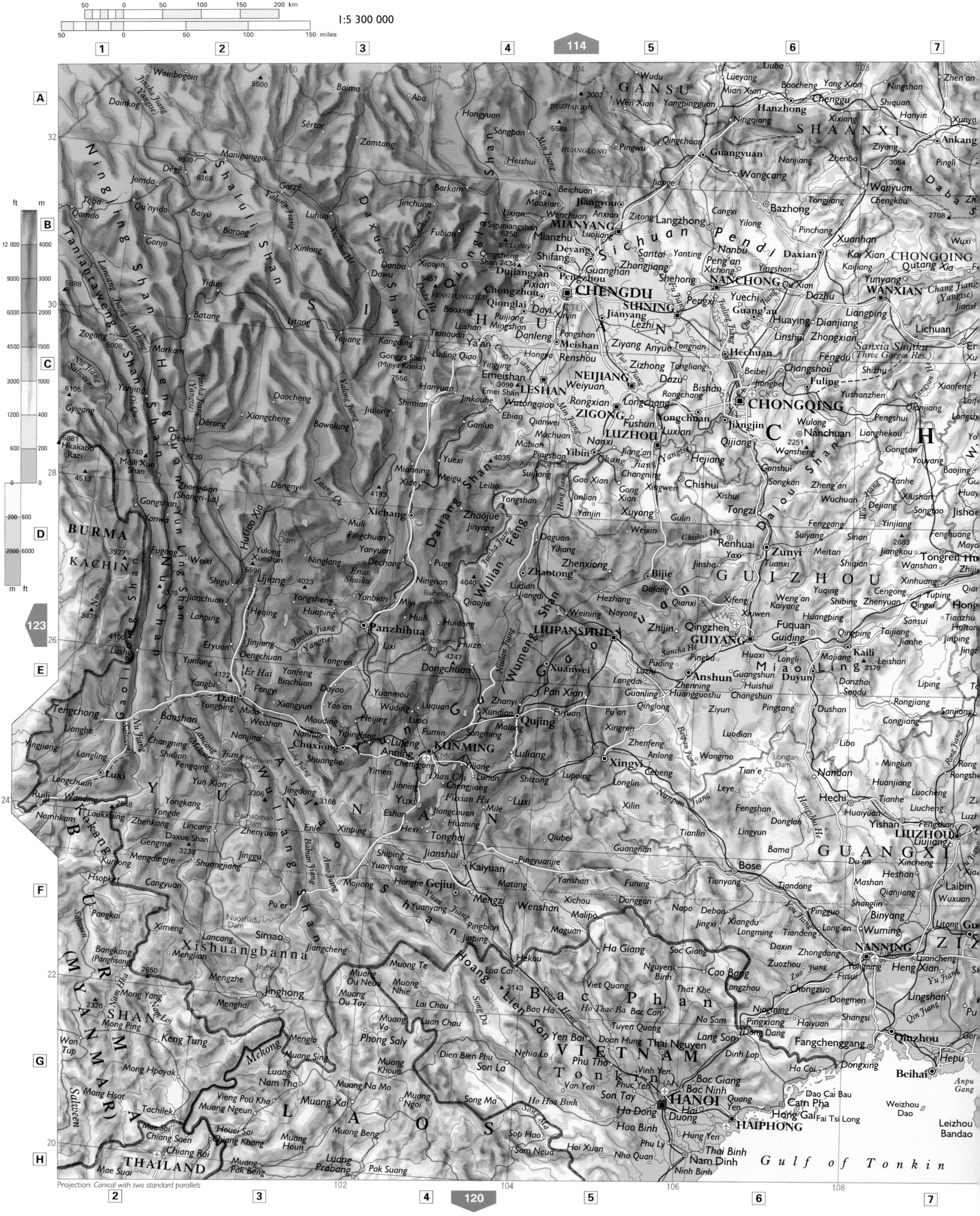

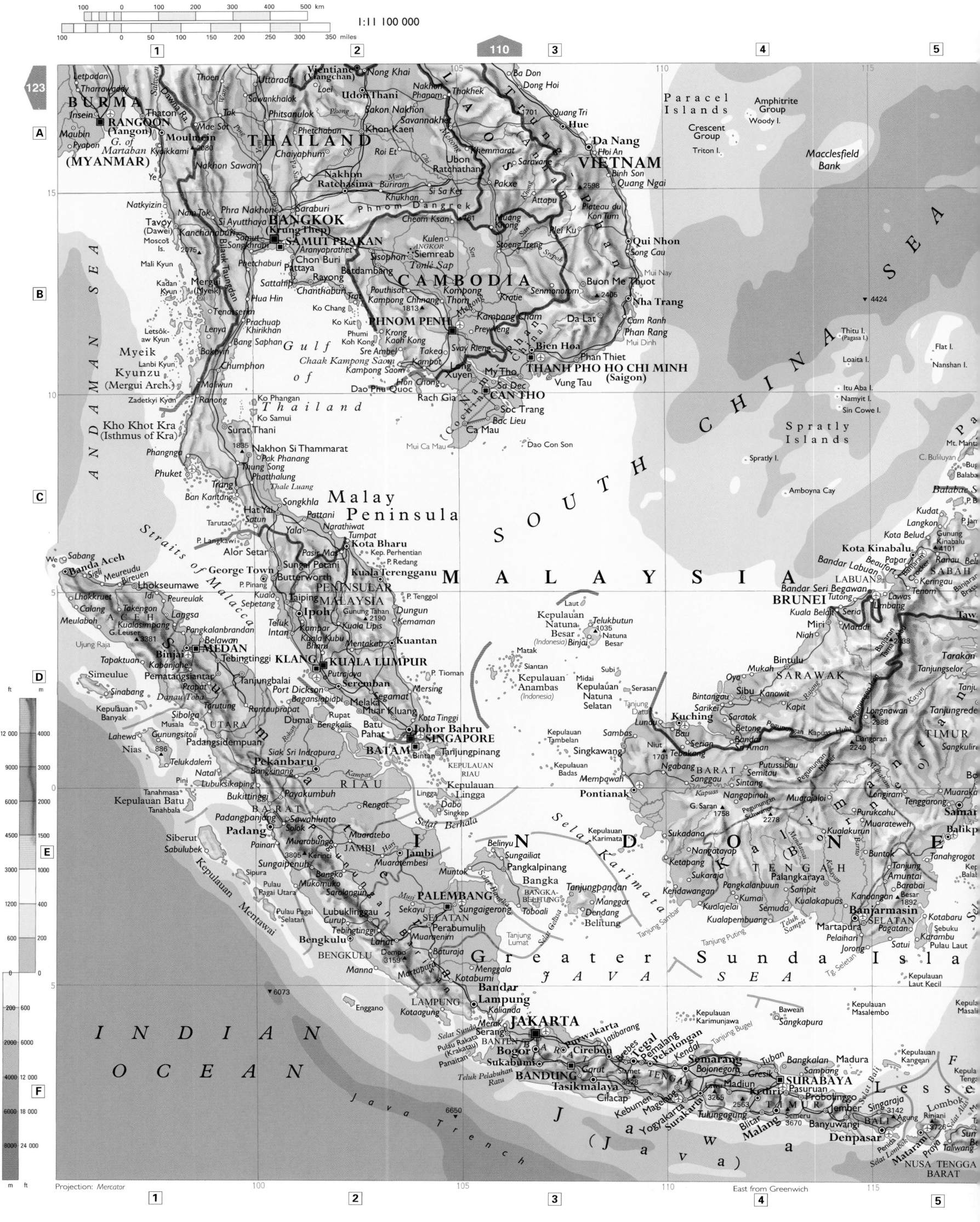

100 0 100 200 300 400 500 km

1:11 100 000

100 0 50 100 150 200 250 300 350 miles

A

Letpadan
Thoen
Vientiane (Vangchan)
Nong Khai
Ba Don
Dong Hoi
Tharrawaddy
Uttaradit
Loei
Udon Thani
Nakhon Phanom
Thakhek
Quang Tri
Hue
Insein
BURMA
RANGOON
(Yangon)
Tak
Mae Sot
Phitsanulok
Sakon Nakhon
Thoen
Da Nang
Hoi An
Maubin
Pyapon
Moulmein
Thaton
2080
THAILAND
Khon Kaen
Khemmarat
Saravane
VIETNAM
Kyaikkami
Chaiyaphum
Roi Et
Ye
G. of Martaban
Nakhon Sawan
Phetchabun
Nakhon Ratchasima
Buriram
Si Sa Ket
Ubon Ratchathani
Pakxe
2598
Binh Son
Quang Ngai

B

Tavoy (Dawei)
Moscos Is.
2075
Kanchanaburi
Si Ayutthaya
Phra Nakhon
Saraburi
Phnom Dangrek
Kulen
Cheom Ksan
Huang Hyong
Plei Ku
Plateau du Kon Tum
Qui Nhon
Song Cau
Mali Kyun
Phetchaburi
Songkhram
BANGKOK (Krung Thep)
SAMUT PRAKAN
Aranyaprathet
Siemreab
ANGKOR
Tonlé Sap
Stoeng Treng
Senmonorom
2405
Nha Trang
Kadan Kyun
Mergui (Myeik)
Hua Hin
Chon Buri
Pattaya
Batdambang
Pouthisat
1813
Kompong Thom
Kratie
Da-Lat
Cam Ranh
Tenasserim
Prachuap Khirikhan
Ko Chang
Chanthaburi
Sattahip
Rayong
Kampong Chhnang
Kompong Cham
Phan Rang
Letsôk-aw Kyun
Bang Saphan
PHNOM PENH
Krong Kaoh Kong
Sre Ambel
Preyveng
Bien Hoa
Mui Dinh
4424

Myeik Kyunzu (Mergui Arch.)
Lenya
Chumphon
Bokpyin
Phumi
Kampong Saom
Takeo
Kampot
Long Xuyen
My Tho
THANH PHO HO CHI MINH (Saigon)
Thitu I. (Pagasa I.)
Flat I.
Zadetkyi Kyun
Ranong
Malwun
Chaak Kampong Saom
Hon Chong
Rach Gia
Sa Dec
Vung Tau
Loaita I.
Nanshan I.
Gulf of Thailand
Dao Phu Quoc
CAN THO
Soc Trang
Itu Aba I.
Namyit I.
Sin Cowe I.

C

Kho Khot Kra (Isthmus of Kra)
Ko Phangan
Ko Samui
Surat Thani
Ca Mau
Bac Lieu
Spratly Islands
Phangnga
1835
Nakhon Si Thammarat
Mui Ca Mau
Dao Con Son
Phuket
Pak Phanang
Thung Song
Phatthalung
Thale Luang
Trang
Ban Kantang
Songkhla
Malay Peninsula
Spratly I.
Hat Yai
Pattani
Amboyna Cay
C. Buliluyan
Tarutao
Satun
Yala
Narathiwat
Tumpat
We
Sabang
P. Langkawi
Kota Bharu
Kep. Perhentian
P. Redang
SOUTH
Kudat
Langkon
Kota Belud
Banda Aceh
Sigli
Alor Setar
Pasir Mas
Sungai Patani
Kuala Terengganu
Gunung Kinabalu
4101
Kota Kinabalu

D

Meureudu
Bireuen
George Town
Butterworth
P. Pinang
M A L A Y S I A
Papar
Beaufort
Ranau
Lhokseumawe
Idi
Peureulak
Taiping
PENINSULAR
MALAYSIA
Dungon
Kemaman
SABAH
Keningau
Lhoksukon
Langsa
Ipoh
Kampar
Kuala Lipis
Kuantan
LABUAN
Tenom
Calang
Takengon
Kuala Kubu Bharu
Gunung Tahan
2190
Laut Natuna
Tambunan
Meulaboh
ACEH
Kualasimpang
Pangkalanbrandan
Sepetang
Teluk Intan
Mentakab
Matak
Kepulauan Natuna Besar (Indonesia)
1035
Natuna Besar
Telukbutun
BRUNEI
Miri
Niah
2438
G. Leuser
3381
Belawan
Kuala
Temerloh
Kuala Kubu
Marudi
Bandar Seri Begawan
Kuala Belait
Seria
Lawas
Ujung Raja
Tapaktuan
Binjai
MEDAN
Tebingtinggi
Tanjungbalai
P. Tioman
Subi
Siantan
Bintulu
Limbang
Tarakan
Simeulue
Pematangsiantar
Prapat
Danau Toba
KLANG
KUALA LUMPUR
Putrajaya
Mukah
Oya
Bintangor
Tanjungselor

E

Kuala
Sibolga
Musala
Tarutung
Seremban
Port Dickson
Mersing
Midai
Serasan
Kepulauan Anambas (Indonesia)
Kuching
Sibu
Kanowit
Kapit
Longnawan
2988
Tanjunggrede
Tanju
Sinabang
Rantauprapat
Bagansiapiapi
Melaka
Segamat
Muar
Kluang
Batu Tinggi
Niut
1701
Tebakang
Bau
Serian
Bandar
Sri Aman
Pegunungan Kapuas Hulu
Langpran
2240
TIMUR
Kepulauan Banyak
Dumai
Bengkalis
Johor Bahru
SINGAPORE
Kepulauan Tambelan
Sambas
Singkawang
Ngabang
Sanggau
Semitau
Sintang
Putussibau
Sangkulirap
Lahewa
Gunungsitoli
886
Pekanbaru
Bangkinang
Siak Sri Indrapura
BATAM
Bintan
Tanjungpinang
Kepulauan Riau
Kepulauan Badas
Mempawah
B A R A T
Nangapinoh
Muarajaloi
Muaratewen
Samar
Natal
Pini
Lubuksikaping
RIAU
Kampar
Lingga
Pontianak
Nangataman
Kapuas
Sintang
1758
G. Saran
2278
Purukcahu
Balikp

F

Tanahmasa
Bukittinggi
Payakumbuh
Rengat
Kepulauan Lingga
Dabo
Singkep
Sukadana
Nangataman
Ketapang
Pegunungan Schwaner
Longiram
Tenggarong
Muarak
Kepulauan Batu
Padangpanjang
Sawahlunto
B A R A T
Selat Berhala
Ketapang
Pangkalanbuun
Sampit
Buntok
Muarateweh
Tanahgrogot
Siberut
Padang
Solok
Muarabungo
Muaratembesi
Selat Karimata
Kumai
Kualakapuas
Kandangan
Sipura
Painan
3805
Kerinci
Sungaipenuh
Bangko
JAMBI
Muntok
Sungailiat
Belinyu
Pulau Pagai Utara
Sarolangun
Pangkalpinang
Bangka
Kualapembuang
Semuda
Besar
1892
Banjarmasin
Sebuku
Karamb
Pulau Laut
Pulau Pagai Selatan
Lubuklinggau
Curup
Tebingtinggi
Lahat
Muaraenim
Perabumulih
PALEMBANG
Sungaigerong
Toboali
Belitung
Tanjungpandan
Manggar
Dendang
Teluk Sampit
Martapura
Pelaihari
Jorong
Pagatan
Satui
Kotabaru
Kepulauan Mentawai
Enggano
Menggala
Baturaja
SELATAN
Tanjung Lumat
Tanjung Sambar
Tanjung Puting
Kepulauan
Bengkulu
Dempo
3159
Martapura
Kotabumi
G r e a t e r
S u n d a   I s l a
Kepulauan Laut Kecil
BENGKULU
Manna
6073
LAMPUNG
Kotaagung
Bandar Lampung
Kalianda
J a v a
Kepulauan Masalembo
Kepulauan Kangean
Kepula

INDIAN
6650
Merak
Serang
Panaitan
Pulau Rakata (Krakatau)
Selat Sunda
JAKARTA
Purwakarta
Jatibarang
Cirebon
Brebes
Tegal
Pemalang
Pekalongan
Kendal
Tuban
Bangkalan
Madura
Sangkapura
Bawean
Kepulauan Karimunjawa

OCEAN
Java Trench
Teluk Pelabuhan Ratu
Bogor
Sukabumi
BANDUNG
Garut
Tasikmalaya
Cilacap
Kebumen
Slamet
3428
Semarang
Magelang
Surakarta
Bojonegoro
Madiun
3265
Gresik
SURABAYA
Pasuruan
Probolinggo
Kediri
Blitar
Malang
3670
Tulungagung
Yogyakarta
Semeru
Jember
Situbondo
Sampong
Bondowoso
L e s s e
Singaraja
3142
Rinjani
3726
BALI
Agung
Banyuwangi
J a v a   (J a w a)
Blambangan
Selat Bali
Denpasar
Pendsa
Selat Lombok
Proja
Taliwang
Mataram
NUSA TENGGA
BARAT
Lombok
Sun
Be
Kepula

P a r a c e l   I s l a n d s
Amphitrite Group
Woody I.
Crescent Group
Triton I.
Macclesfield Bank

S O U T H   C H I N A   S E A

S A R A W A K

I N D O
K
(B)
N E

J a v a   S e a

Projection: Mercator

East from Greenwich

ft m

12 000 4000

9000 3000

6000 2000

4500 1500

3000 1000

1200 400

600 200

0 0

200 600

2000 6000

4000 12 000

6000 18 000

8000 24 000

m ft

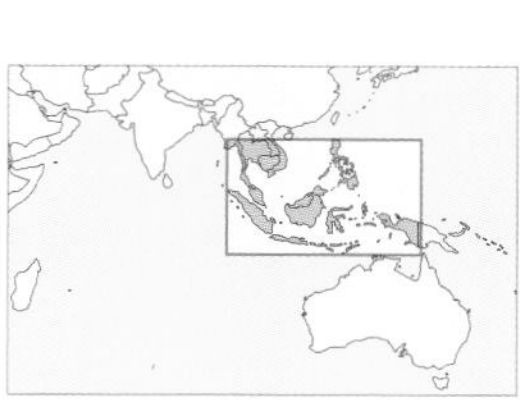

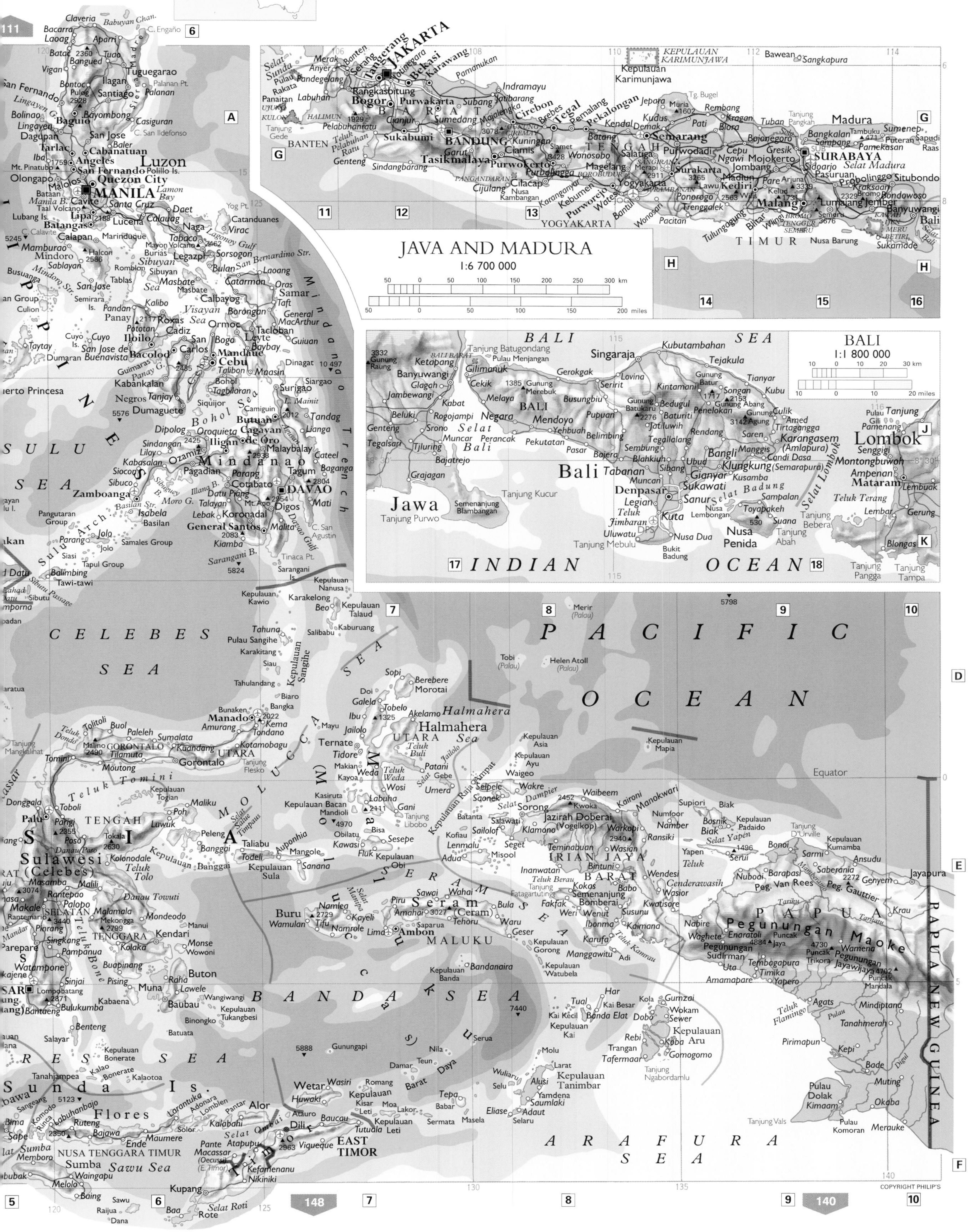

111

JAVA AND MADURA
1:6 700 000

50   0   50   100   150   200   250   300 km
50   0   100   200 miles

BALI
1:1 800 000
10   0   10   20   30 km
10   0   10   20 miles

PHILIPPINE SEA

CELEBES SEA

PACIFIC OCEAN

BALI SEA

INDIAN OCEAN

SULU SEA

MINDANAO

SULAWESI (Celebes)

MOLUCCA SEA

CERAM SEA

BANDA SEA

FLORES SEA

SAWU SEA

ARAFURA SEA

TIMOR SEA

JAKARTA
BANDUNG
SURABAYA
SEMARANG
Surakarta
Yogyakarta

MANILA
Quezon City
DAVAO
Cebu
Zamboanga
General Santos

Denpasar
Lombok
Mataram

Halmahera
Seram (Ceram)
Ambon
Buru
Buton
Sumba
Flores
Sumbawa

IRIAN JAYA
PAPUA NEW GUINEA
Jayapura
Pegunungan Maoke

EAST TIMOR

NUSA TENGGARA TIMUR

COPYRIGHT PHILIP'S

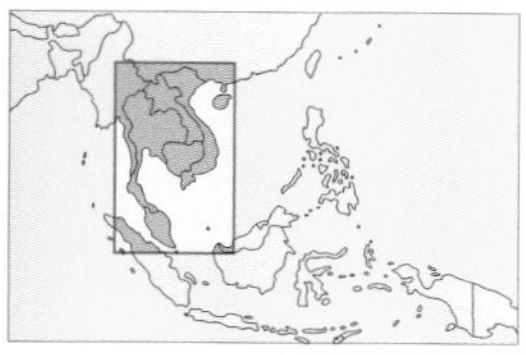

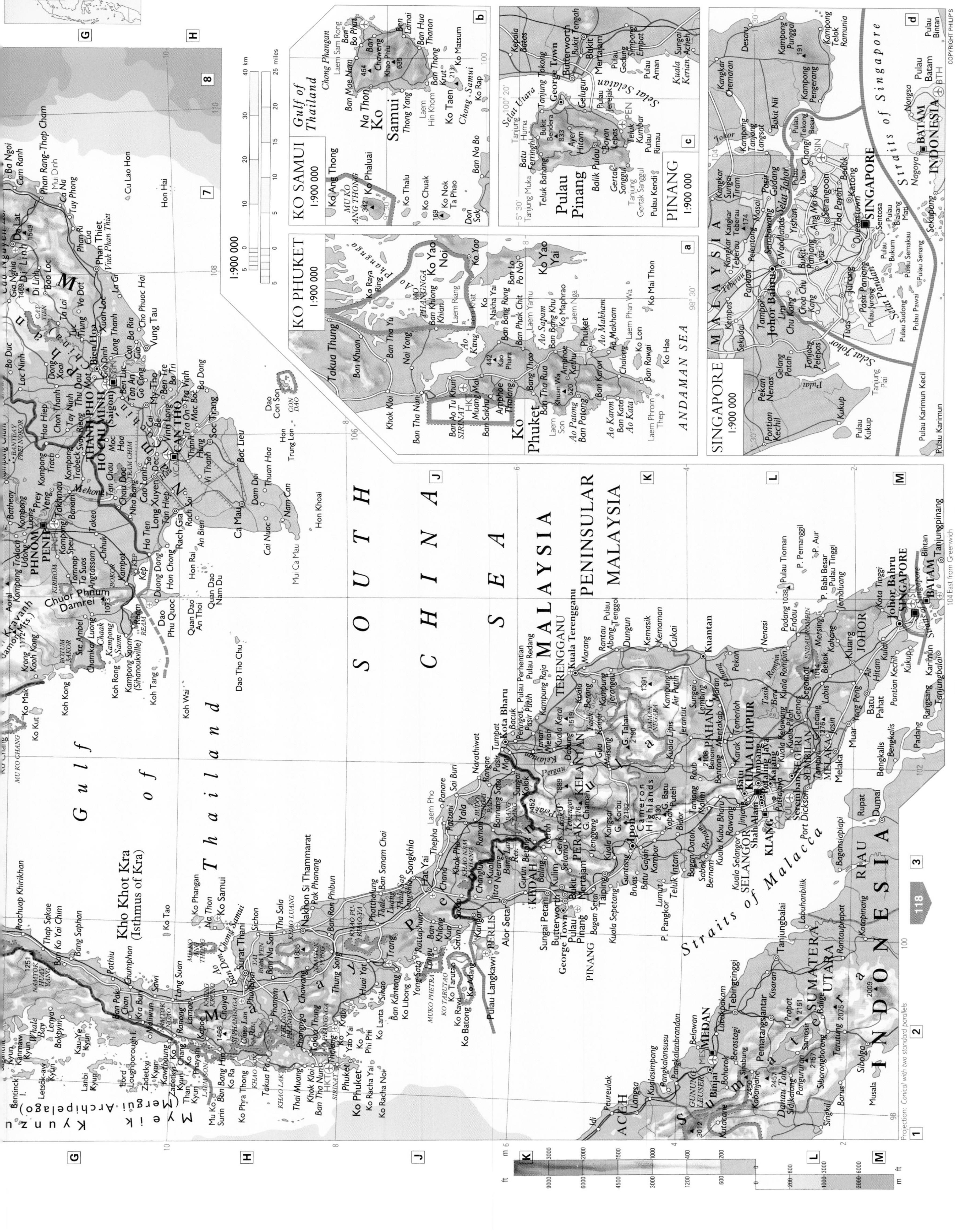

COPYRIGHT PHILIP'S

Inset maps

KO PHUKET 1:900 000

KO SAMUI 1:900 000

PINANG 1:900 000

SINGAPORE 1:900 000

Major labels

Gulf of Thailand

ANDAMAN SEA

SOUTH CHINA SEA

Gulf of Thailand

Straits of Malacca

Straits of Singapore

Selat Johor

Kho Khot Kra (Isthmus of Kra)

Mergui Archipelago (Myeik Kyunzu)

PENINSULAR MALAYSIA

MALAYSIA

SINGAPORE

INDONESIA

SUMATERA UTARA

ACEH

RIAU

Thailand

THANH PHO HO CHI MINH (Saigon)

PHNOM PENH

CAN THO

KUALA LUMPUR

JOHOR

PAHANG

TERENGGANU

KELANTAN

KEDAH

PERLIS

PERAK

SELANGOR

NEGERI SEMBILAN

MELAKA

PINANG

Projection: Conical with two standard parallels

East from Greenwich

1:8 900 000

50   0   100   200   300   400 km
50   0   50   100   150   200   250 miles

Projection: Conical with two standard parallels

continuation southwards
on same scale

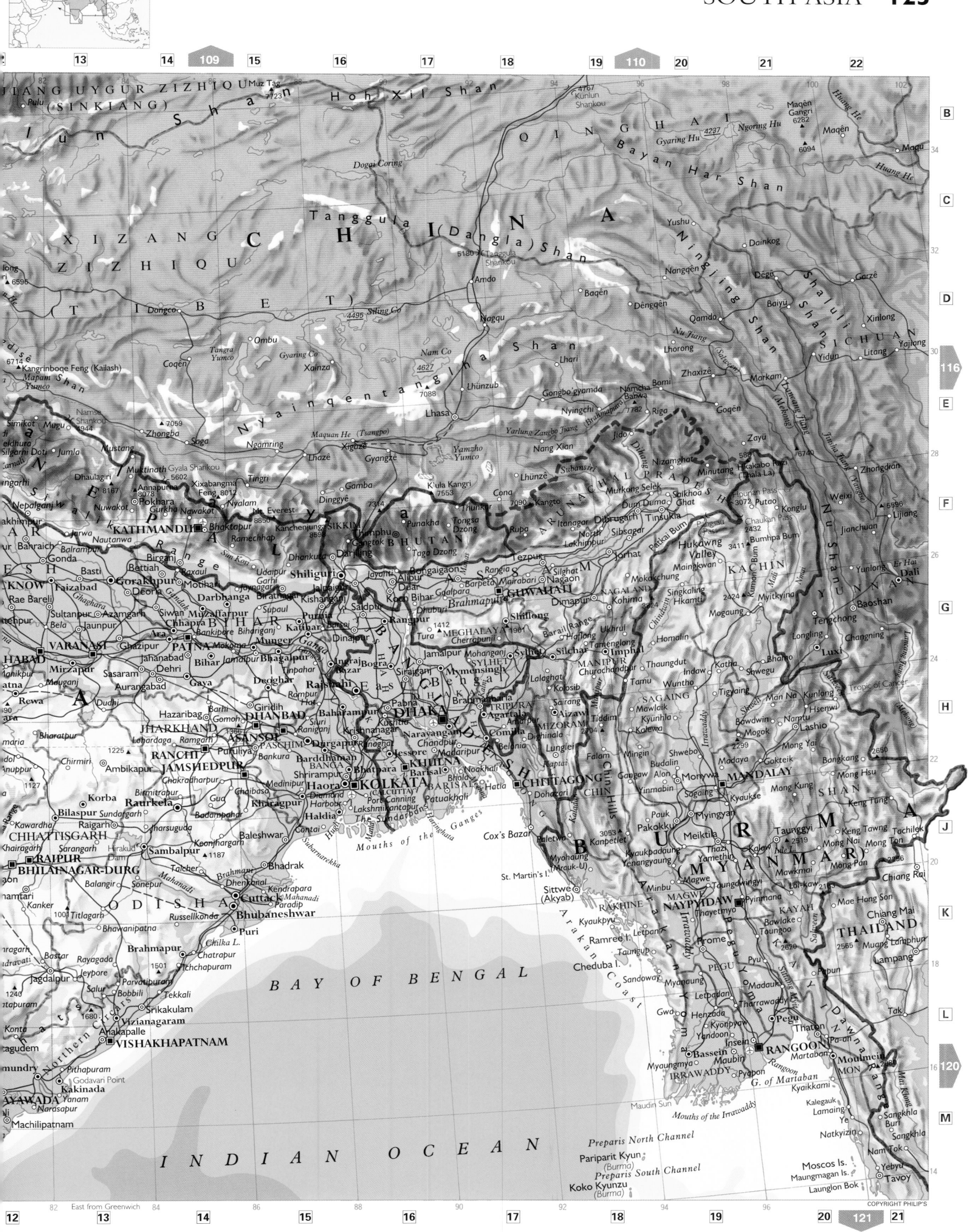

1:5 300 000

Projection: Conical with two standard parallels

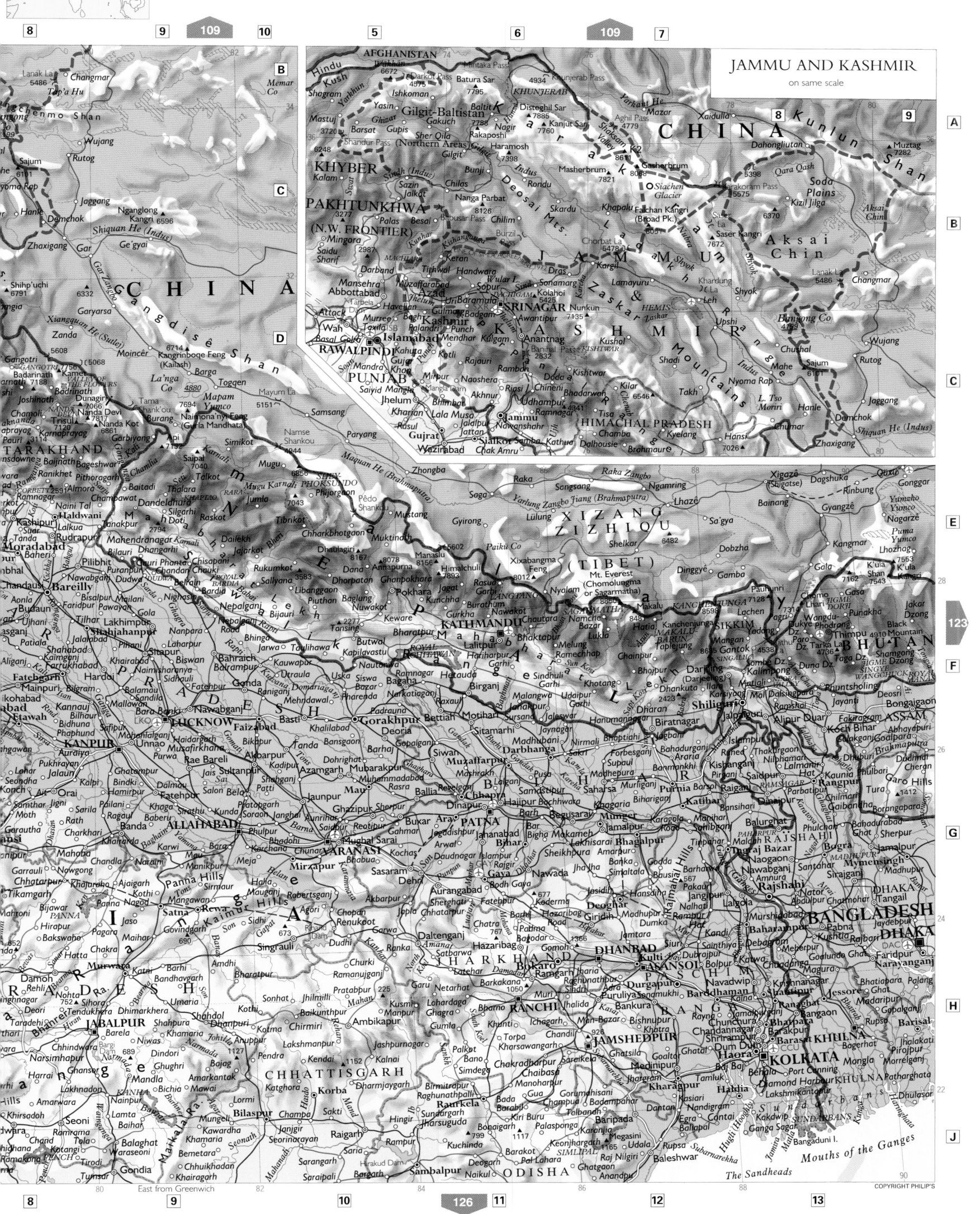

JAMMU AND KASHMIR
on same scale

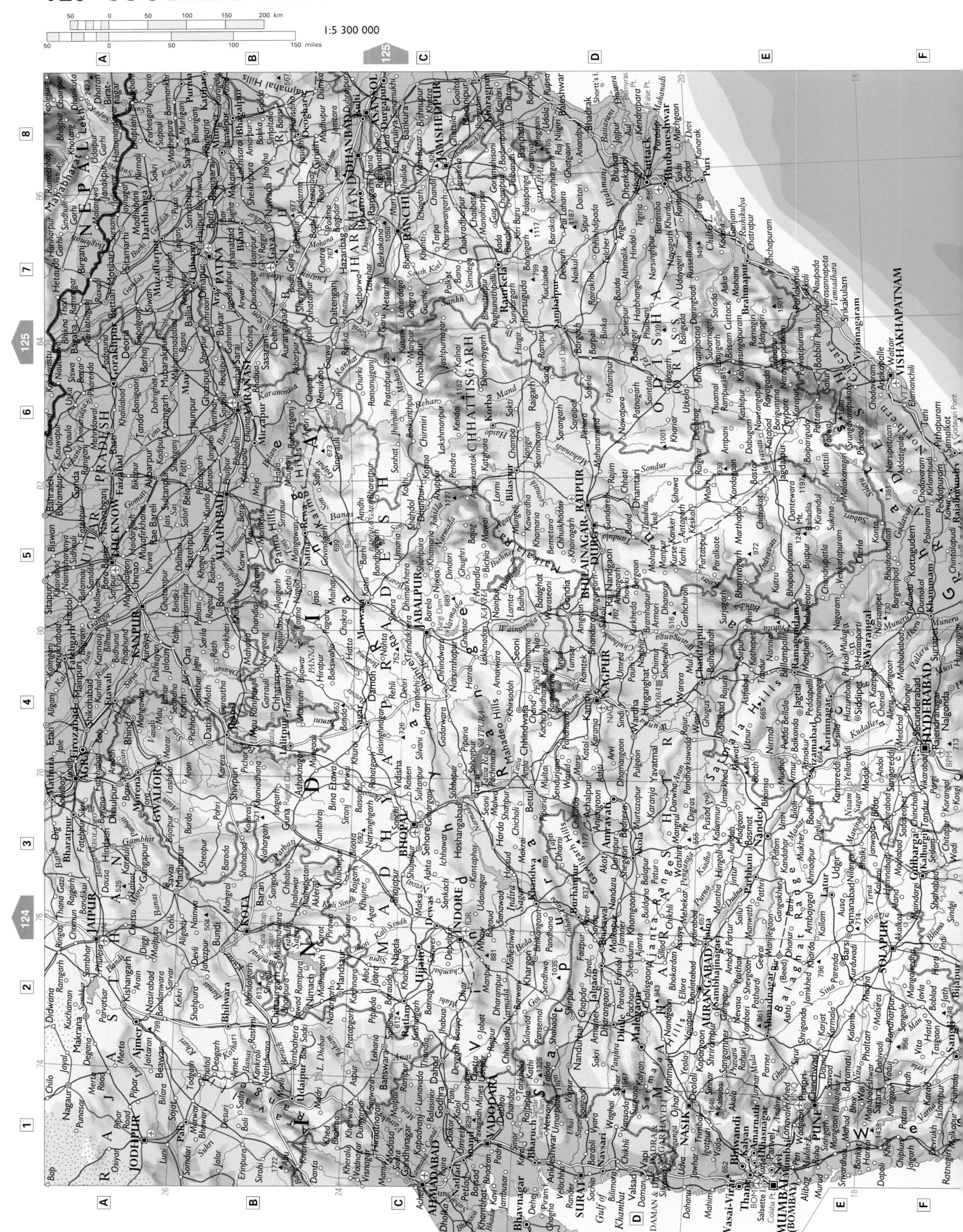

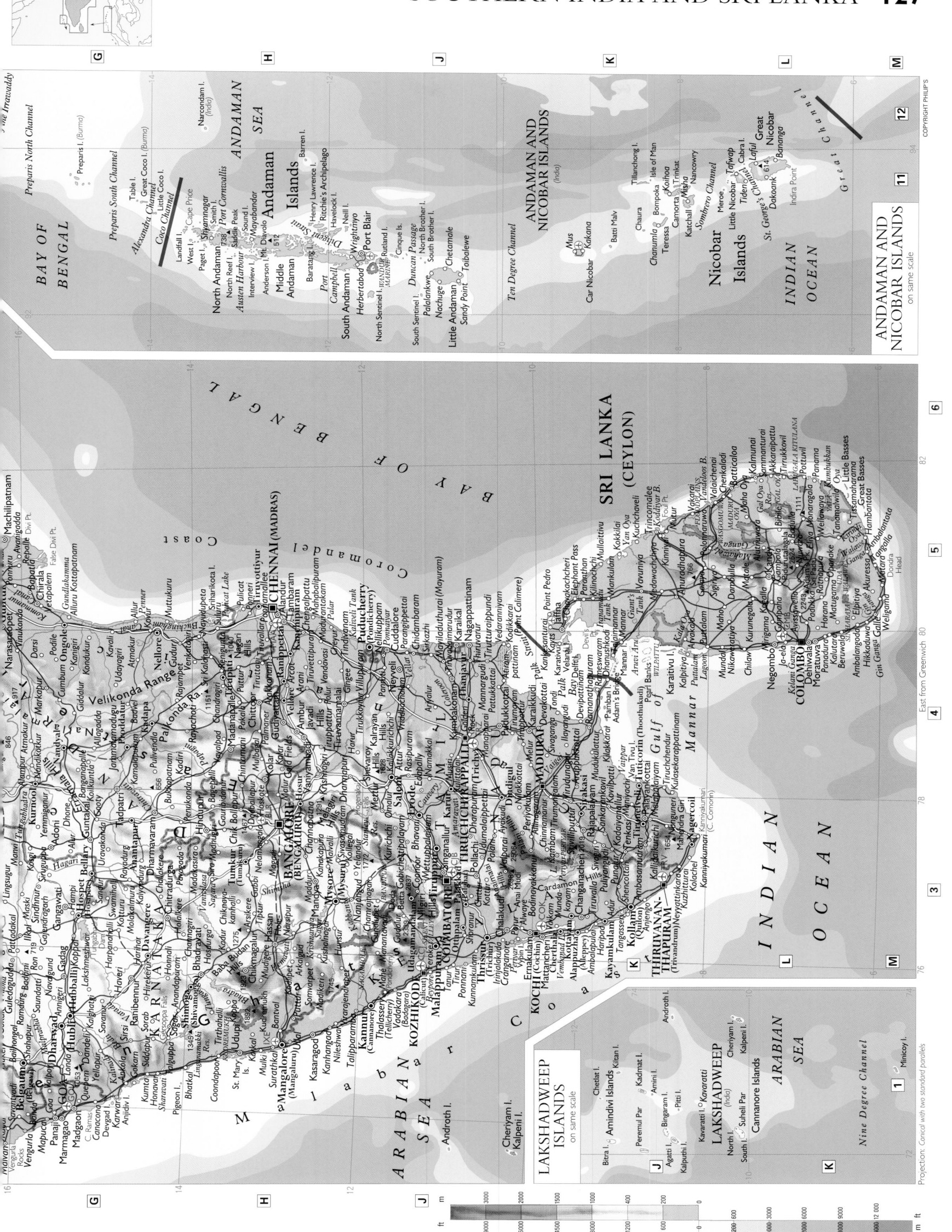

ANDAMAN AND
NICOBAR ISLANDS
on same scale

LAKSHADWEEP
ISLANDS
on same scale

Projection: Conical with two standard parallels

1:6 200 000

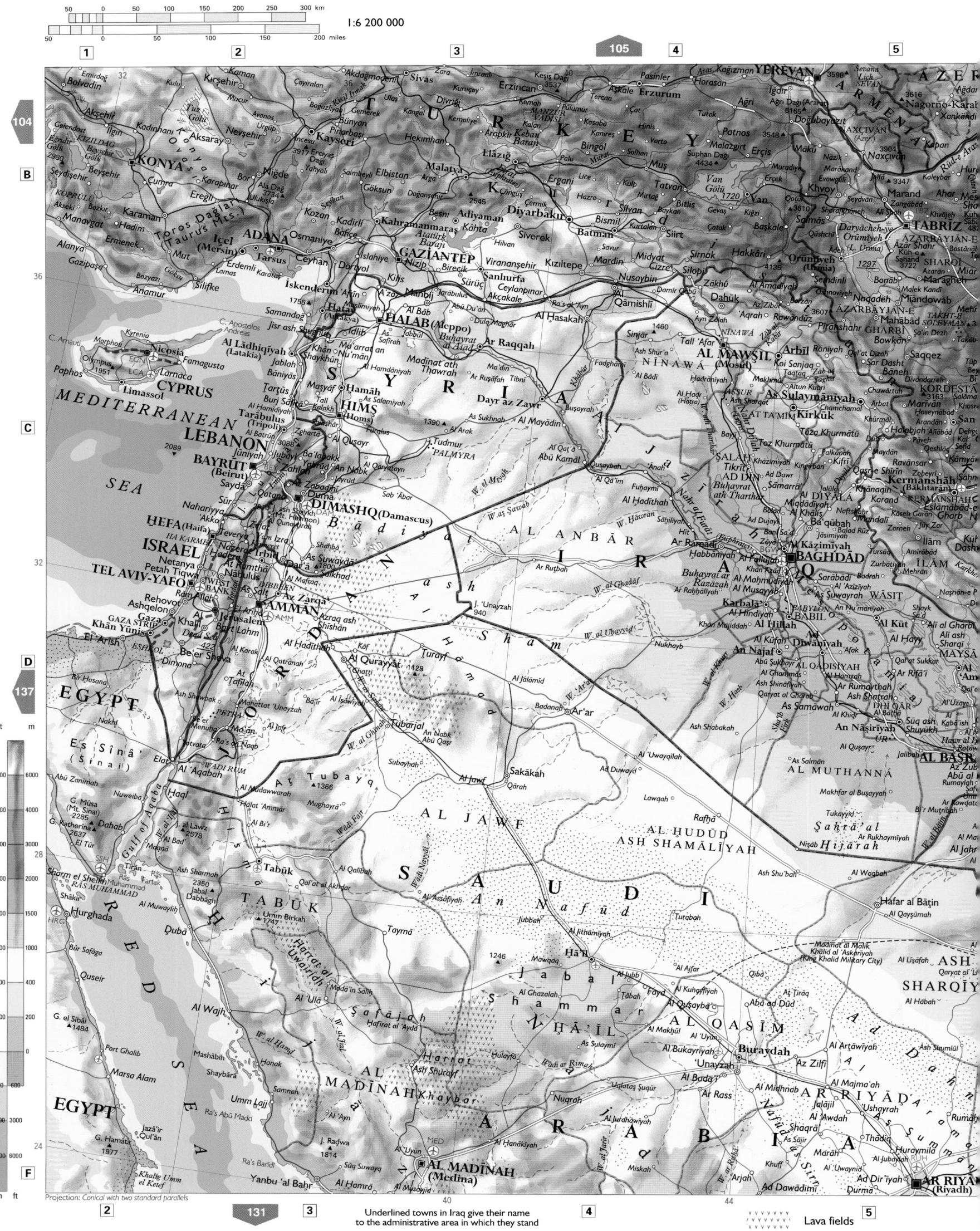

Underlined towns in Iraq give their name
to the administrative area in which they stand

v v v v v v
v v v v v v v   Lava fields
v v v v v v

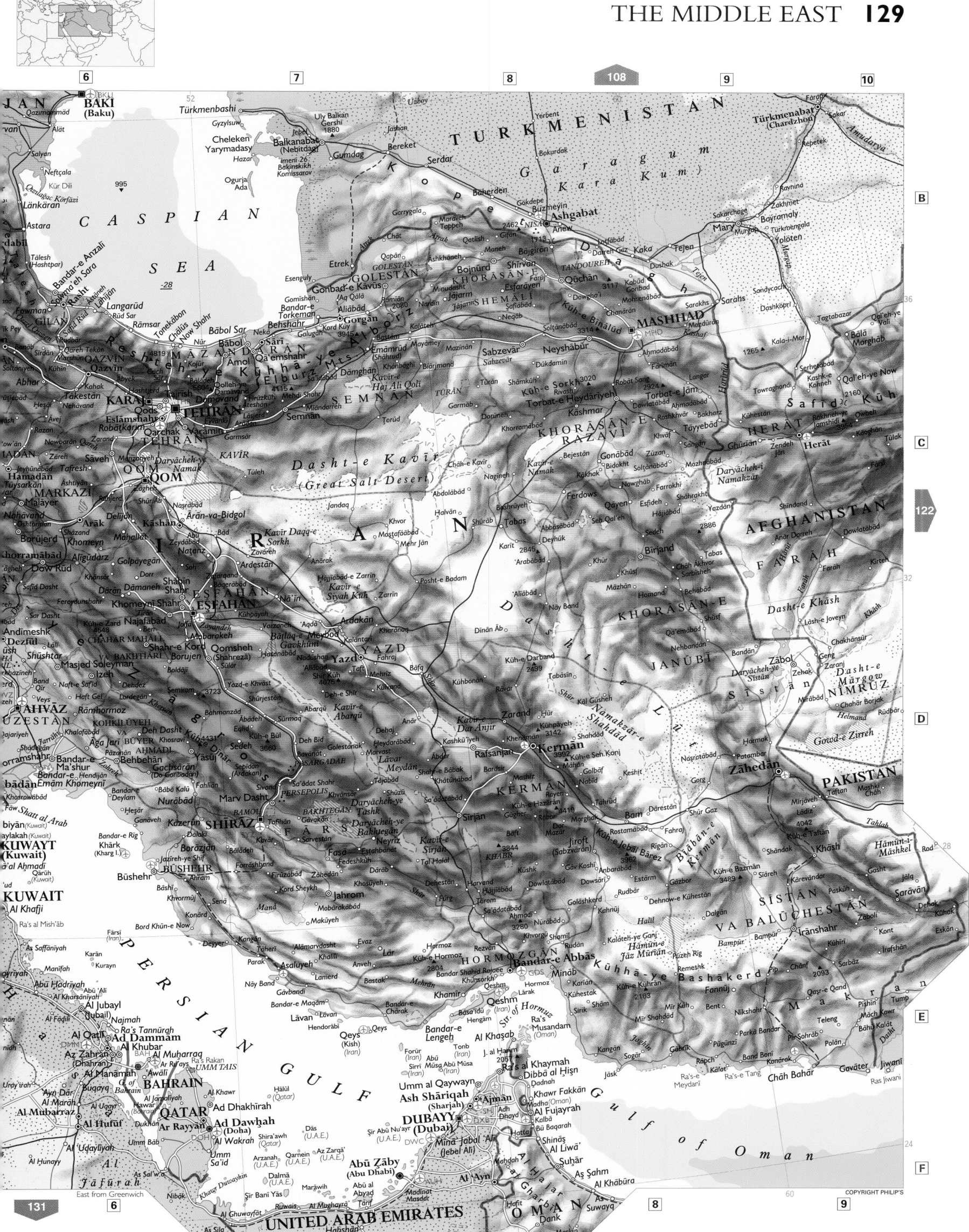

122
131

COPYRIGHT PHILIP'S

1:2 200 000

10 0 10 20 30 40 50 60 70 80 90 km
10 0 10 20 30 40 50 60 miles

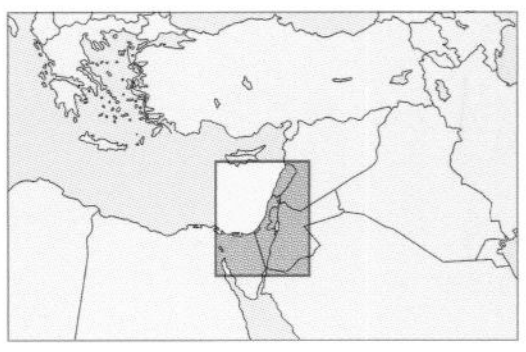

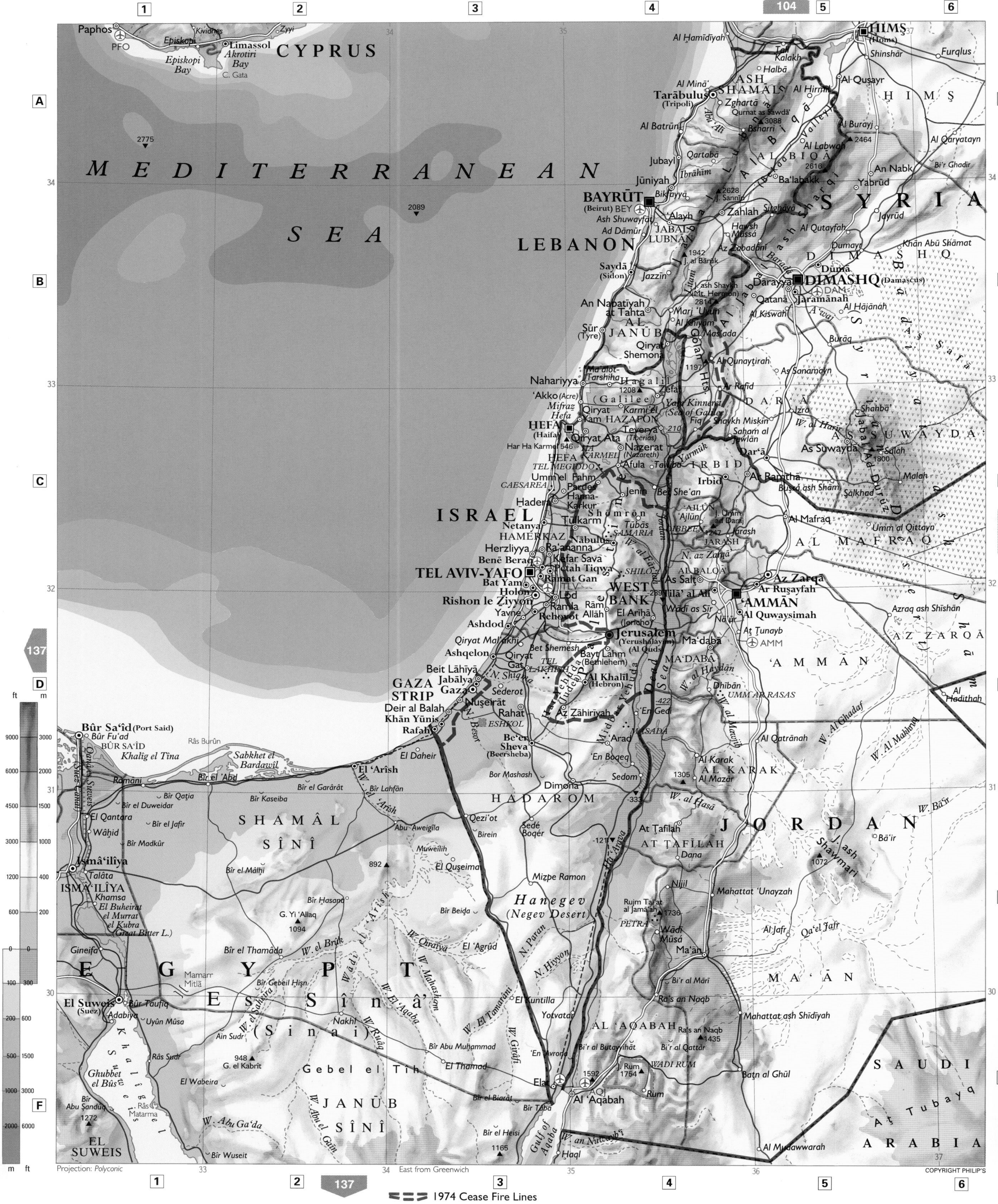

CYPRUS

MEDITERRANEAN SEA

LEBANON

SYRIA

ISRAEL

JORDAN

EGYPT

SAUDI ARABIA

BAYRŪT (Beirut) BEY
DIMASHQ (Damascus)
HIMŞ (Homs)
TEL AVIV-YAFO
Jerusalem (Yerushalayim) (Al Quds)
AMMĀN
GAZA STRIP
WEST BANK
HEFA (Haifa)

Bûr Sa'îd (Port Said)
El Suweis (Suez)
Ismâ'ilîya

SINAI (Sînî)
Hanegev (Negev Desert)
Gulf of Aqaba

Projection: Polyconic
East from Greenwich
COPYRIGHT PHILIP'S

◼◼◼ 1974 Cease Fire Lines

1:13 300 000

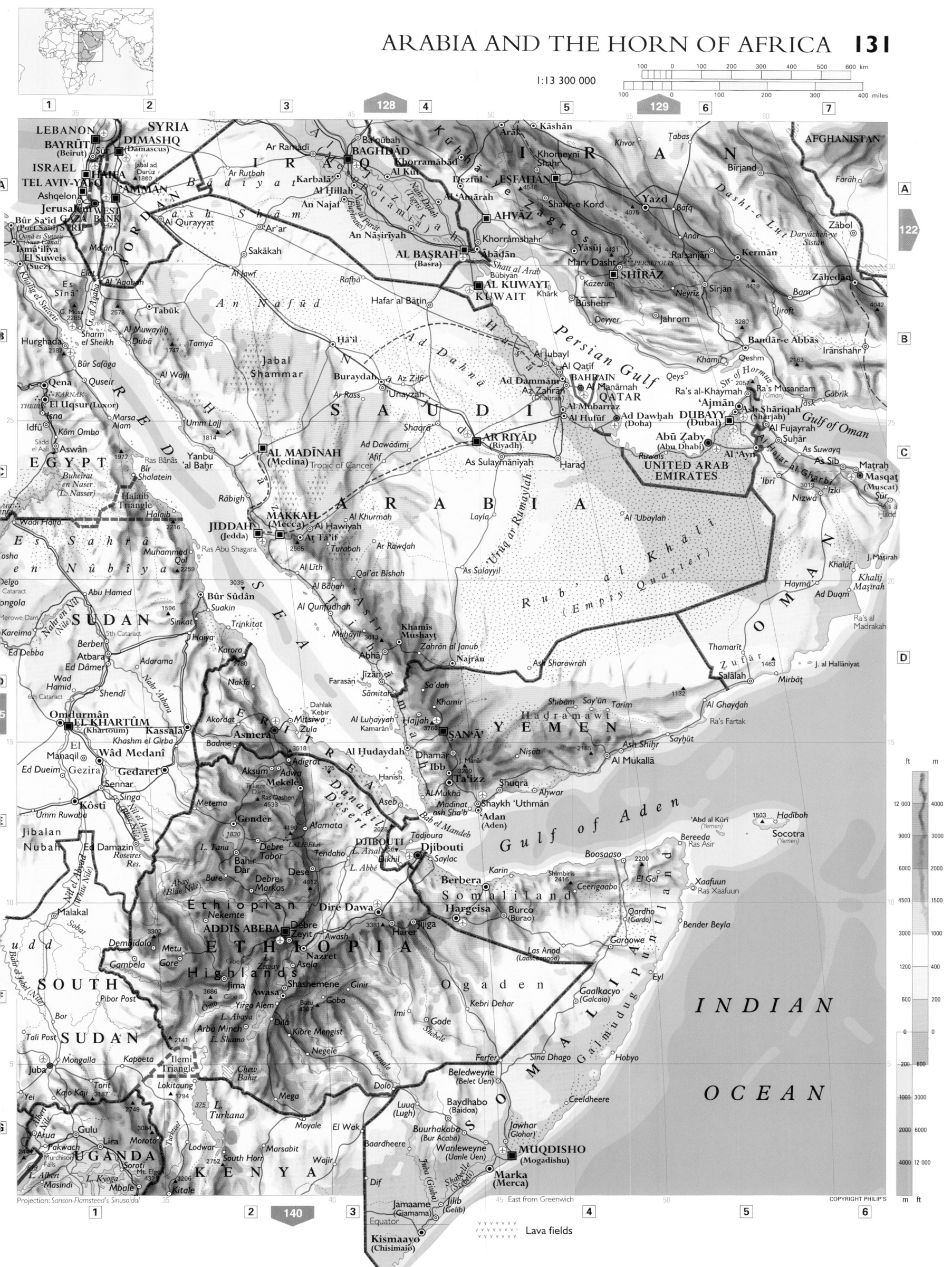

ft | m

12 000 — 4000
9000 — 3000
6000 — 2000
4500 — 1500
3000 — 1000
1200 — 400
600 — 200
0 — 0
200 — 600
1000 — 3000
2000 — 6000
4000 — 12 000

m ft

Lava fields

COPYRIGHT PHILIP'S

Projection: Sanson-Flamsteed's Sinusoidal   East from Greenwich

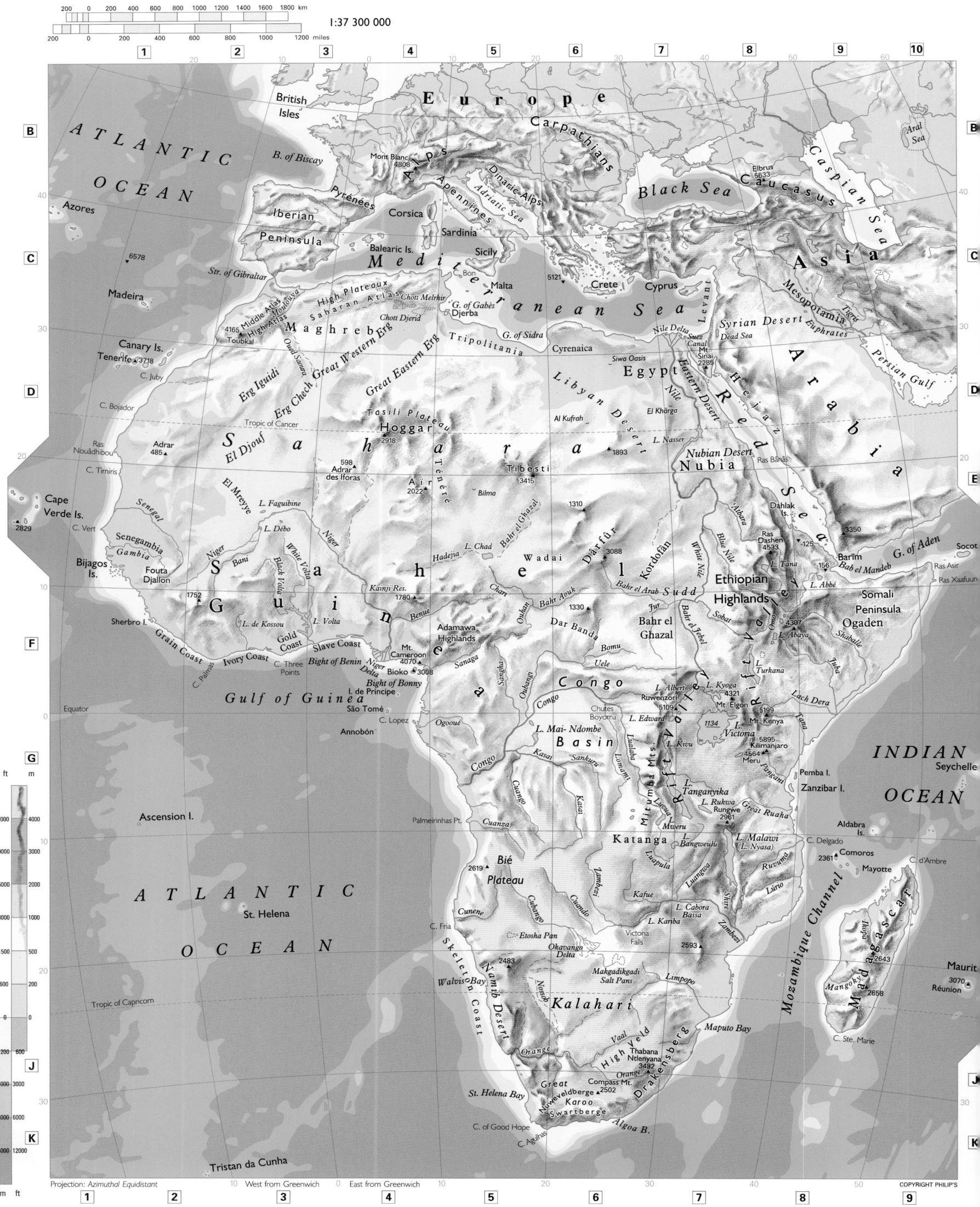

1:37 300 000

Projection: Azimuthal Equidistant

West from Greenwich   East from Greenwich

COPYRIGHT PHILIP'S

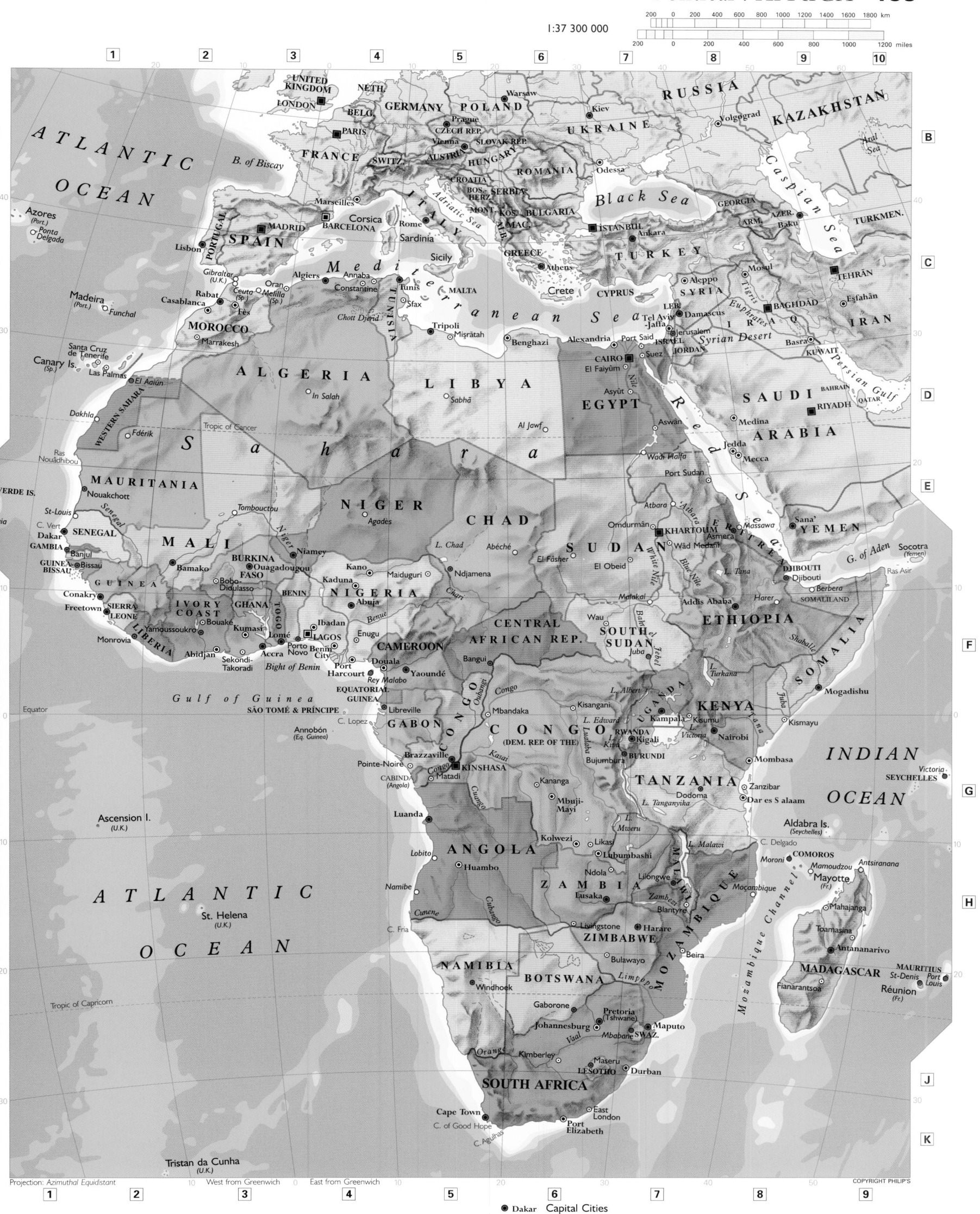

1:37 300 000

● Dakar Capital Cities

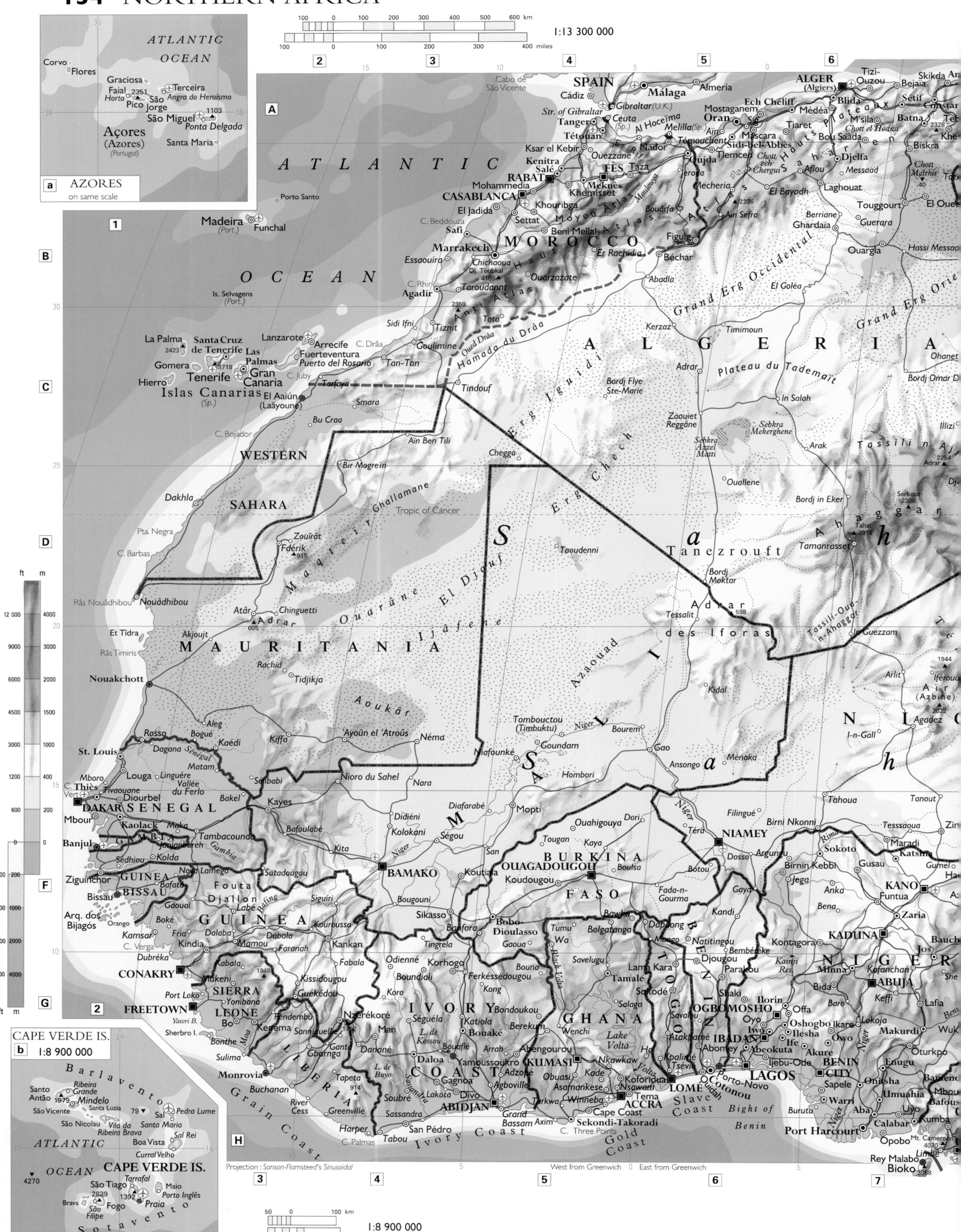

1:13 300 000

100   0   100   200   300   400   500   600 km
100   0   100   200   300   400 miles

a   AZORES
on same scale

ATLANTIC OCEAN

Corvo
Flores
Graciosa
Faial 2351 Terceira
Horta Pico Angra do Heroísmo
São Jorge
1103
São Miguel
Ponta Delgada
Santa Maria

Açores
(Azores)
(Portugal)

ATLANTIC OCEAN

SPAIN
Cabo de São Vicente
MÁLAGA Almería
Cádiz Gibraltar (U.K.)
Str. of Gibraltar
Tangér Ceuta (Sp.) Al Hoceima Melilla (Sp.)
Tétouan Nador
Ksar el Kebir Ouezzane
Kenitra Taza
Salé FES
RABAT Meknès Khemisset
Mohammedia Khouribga
CASABLANCA El Jadida Settat
Safi Beni Mellal
C. Beddouza
Essaouira Moyen Atlas
MARRAKECH MOROCCO
Chichaoua Dj. Toubkal 4165
Ouarzazate Er Rachidia
C. Rhir Taroudannt
Agadir Haut Atlas
Anti Atlas 2359
Sidi Ifni Tata
Tiznit Goulimine
Tan-Tan Hamada du Drâa
Tarfaya Oued Drâa
C. Juby Tindouf

ALGER (Algiers) Tizi-Ouzou
Skikda Annaba
Mostaganem Blida Bejaïa Sétif Constantine
Oran Médéa M'Sila Batna Guelma
Sidi-bel-Abbès Bou Saâda Biskra 2328
Tlemcen Chott ech Chergui Djelfa El Kantara
Aïn Messaad
Témouchent Aflou Touggourt El Oued
Oujda Laghouat Berriane Guerara
Jerada El Bayadh Ghardaïa Ouargla
Bouârfa Figuig El Goléa Hassi Messaoud
Abadla Grand Erg Occidental
Béchar Grand Erg Oriental
Kerzaz Timimoun Ohanet

ALGERIA
Adrar Plateau du Tademaït Bordj Omar
In Salah
Islas Canarias
La Palma Santa Cruz de Tenerife Las Palmas Lanzarote Arrecife
Gomera Tenerife Gran Canaria Fuerteventura
Hierro Puerto del Rosario
3718 2423
El Aaiún (Laâyoune) Smara Chegga
Bu Craa Aïn Ben Tili
C. Bojador Bir Mogrein
WESTERN SAHARA
Dakhla Zouîrât Taoudenni
Fdérik 915
C. Barbas 605 Bordj in Eker 2306
Adrar Tanezrouft Tamanrasset 2918 Tahat
Ras Nouâdhibou Nouâdhibou Atâr Chinguetti Tessalit Ahaggar
Et Tidra Akjoujt Adrar des Iforas In Guezzam
Râs Timiris Rachid Tropic of Cancer
MAURITANIA Tidjikja Kidal Arlit 1944
Nouakchott Aleg Tombouctou (Timbuktu) Gao Agadez 2022
Rosso Bogué Kaédi Niger Ansongo I-n-Gall
St. Louis Dagana Kiffa Néma Bourem Ménaka
Dakar Matam Gourma Tahoua Tanout
C. Vert Louga Vallée du Ferlo Mopti Niamey Birni Nkonni Tessaoua
Mbour Diourbel SENEGAL Nioro du Sahel Nara Diafarabé Tougan Téra Dosso Sokoto Maradi
Kaolack Kayes Didiéni Ségou Ouahigouya Dori Filingué Argungu Jega Gusau
GAMBIA Tambacounda Kolokani BAMAKO San Koutiala OUAGADOUGOU Fada-N'Gourma Gaya Birnin Kebbi Zaria KANO
Banjul Bafoulabé Kita BURKINA FASO Bawku Kandi Anka KADUNA
GUINEA-BISSAU Bissau MALI Bougouni Sikasso Koudougou Boulsa Djougou Parakou Kaïnji Res. Minna ABUJA NIGER
Ziguinchor Kolda Bobo-Dioulasso Tumu Bolgatanga Dapong BENIN Bida
Arq. dos Bijagós GUINEA Siguiri Banfora Wa Mango Natitingou Baro Kontagora
CONAKRY Kankan Odienné Korhogo Bouna Savelugu Lama Kara NIGERIA Lafia Jos
SIERRA LEONE Makeni Kissidougou Ferkéssédougou Kong Tamale Sokodé Ilorin Offa Oshogbo Keffi Makurdi
FREETOWN Kenema Séguéla Katiola Bouaké Salaga ABOMEY OGBOMOSHO Oyo Ife Akure Owo
LIBERIA Nzérékoré Bouaflé Yamoussoukro KUMASI GHANA IBADAN LAGOS BENIN CITY
Monrovia Man IVORY COAST Abengourou LOMÉ COTONOU Porto-Novo Warri
Buchanan Gagnoa Daloa ACCRA Cape Coast Sapele Onitsha
Greenville Divo Sekondi-Takoradi Port Harcourt Calabar
Harper San Pédro Abidjan Grand Bassam Bight of Benin Bioko 3088

b   CAPE VERDE IS.
1:8 900 000

Barlavento
Santo Antão Ribeira Grande Mindelo Sal Rei
São Vicente Santa Luzia Boa Vista
São Nicolau Vila da Ribeira Brava Sal Pedra Lume
ATLANTIC OCEAN Maio Porto Inglês
CAPE VERDE IS. São Tiago Tarrafal Praia
4270 Brava Fogo São Filipe Sotavento

Projection : Sanson-Flamsteed's Sinusoidal
West from Greenwich East from Greenwich

1:8 900 000
50   0   100 km
50   0   50 miles

Lava fields

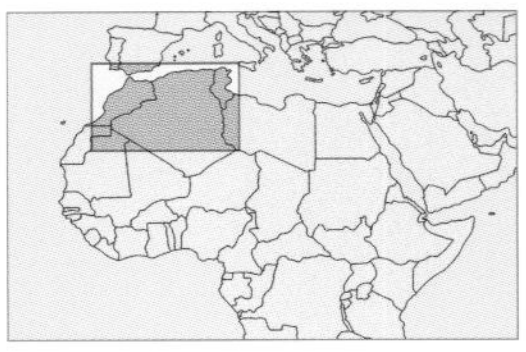

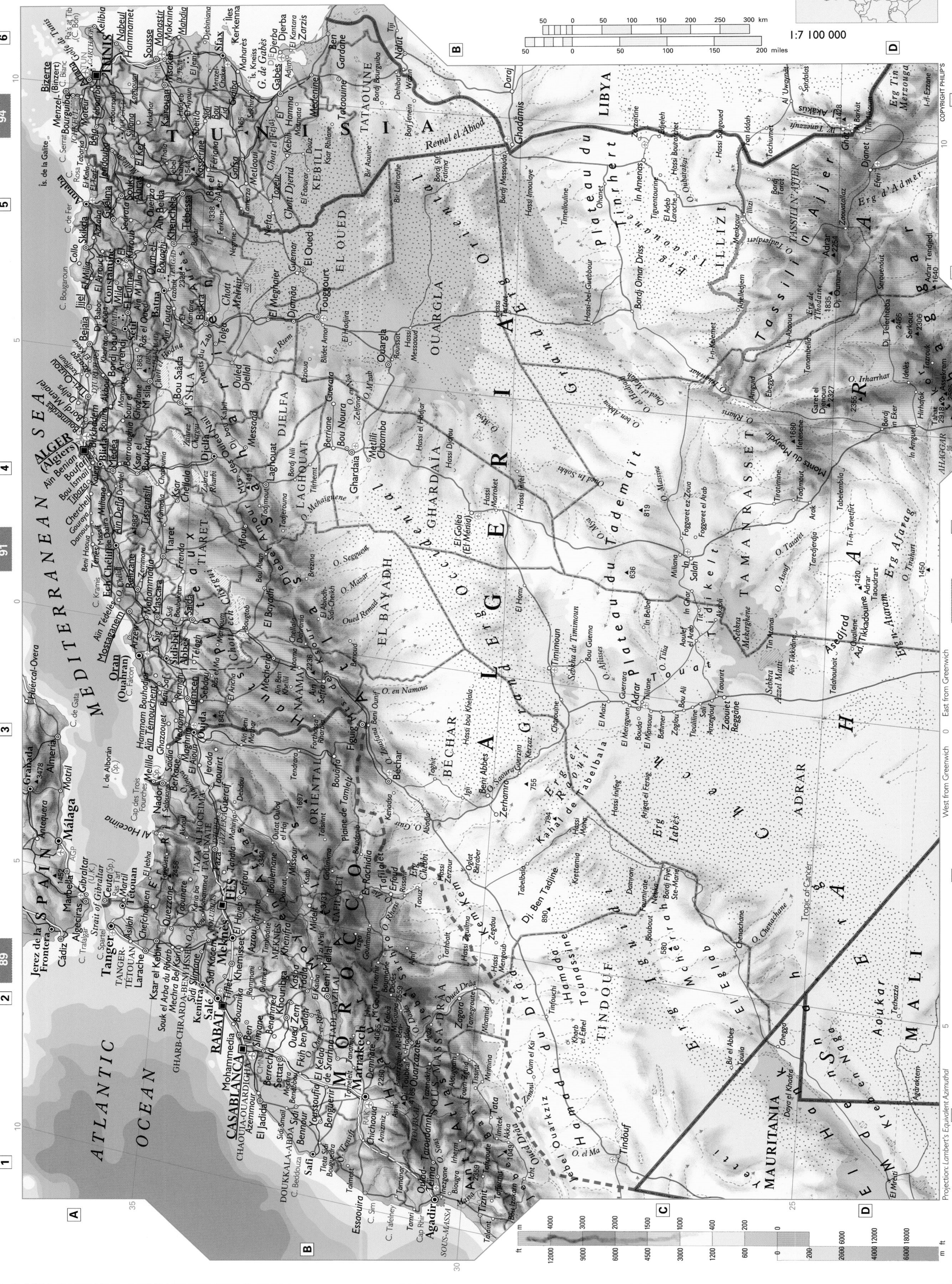
1:7 100 000
MEDITERRANEAN SEA
ATLANTIC OCEAN
MOROCCO
ALGERIA
TUNISIA
LIBYA
MAURITANIA
MALI
SPAIN
ALGER (Algiers)
TUNIS
RABAT
CASABLANCA
Marrakech
Oran (Ouahran)
Constantine
Tindouf
Projection: Lambert's Equivalent Azimuthal
COPYRIGHT PHILIP'S
West from Greenwich
East from Greenwich
Tropic of Cancer

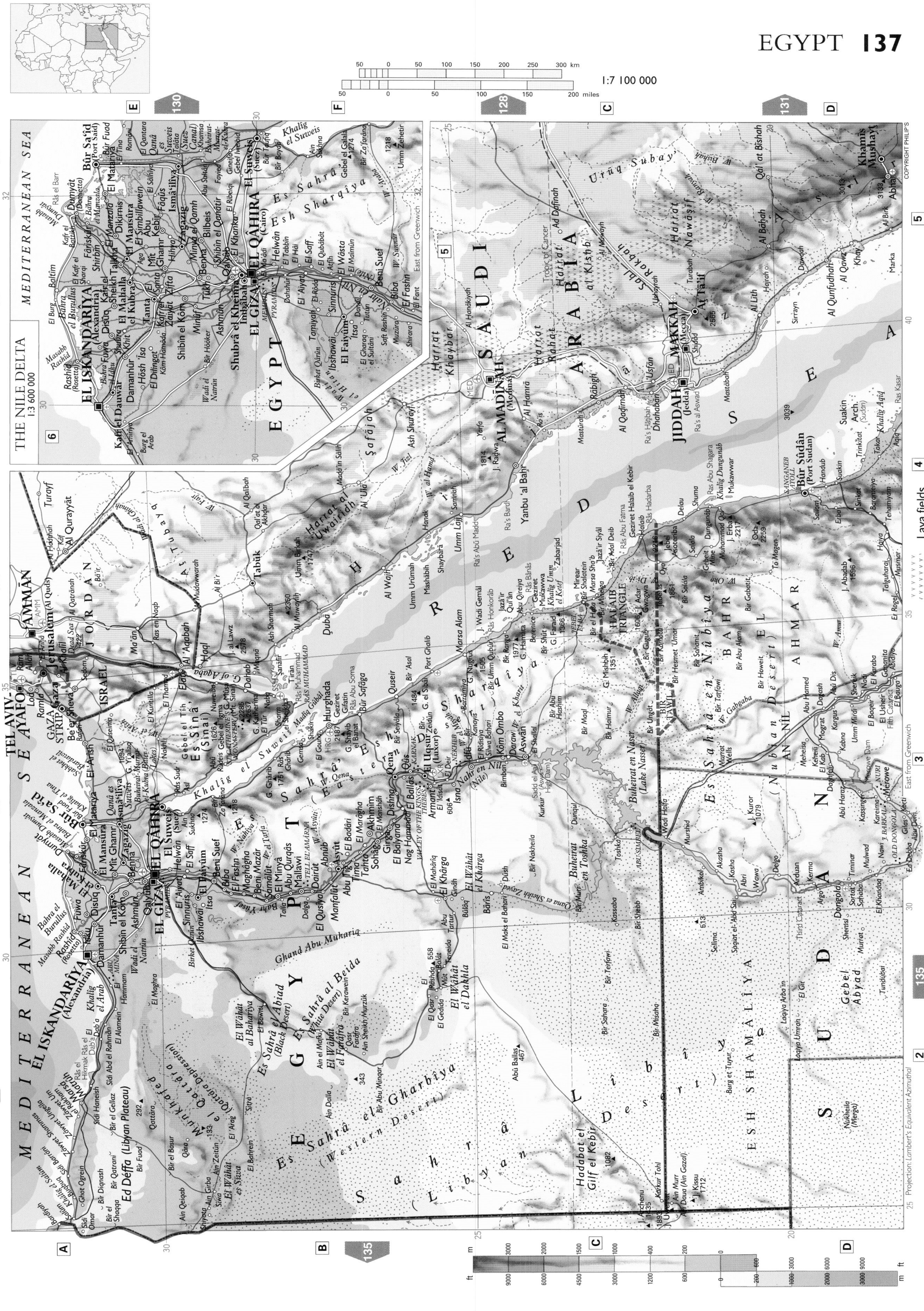

1:7 100 000

50   0   50   100   150   200   250   300 km
50   0   50   100   150   200 miles

THE NILE DELTA
1:3 600 000

MEDITERRANEAN SEA

EGYPT

Bûr Sa'îd (Port Said)
EL ISKANDARÎYA (Alexandria)
Rashîd (Rosetta)
Damanhûr
Dumyât (Damietta)
El Mansûra
Tanta
EL GIZA
EL QAHIRA (Cairo)
El Faiyûm
Beni Suef
Helwân

JORDAN
AMMÂN
ISRAEL
TEL AVIV-YAFO
Jerusalem (Al Quds)
GAZA STRIP
Be'er Sheva

SAUDI ARABIA
AL MADÎNAH (Medina)
MAKKAH (Mecca)
JIDDAH (Jedda)
At Tâ'if

Tropic of Cancer

RED SEA

Es Sahrâ esh Sharqîya (Eastern Desert)

Gebel Es Sînâ (Sinai)

Khalîg el Suweis (Gulf of Suez)

Gulf of Aqaba

G. Katherîna 2637

El Suweis (Suez)
Ismâ'ilîya
Suez Canal

El Minya
Asyût
Sohâg
Qena
THEBES
VALLEY OF THE KINGS
Luxor
Aswân
Lake Nasser (Buheirat en Nâsir)

Es Sahrâ el Gharbîya (Western Desert)
Libyan Desert (Sahrâ Lîbîya)

El Wâhât el Dâkhla
El Wâhât el Khârga
El Wâhât el Farâfra
El Wâhât el Baharîya

El Wâhât el Siwa

Munkhafed el Qattâra (Qattara Depression)

Libyan Plateau

Ghard Abu Muharik

Es Sahrâ al Beida (White Desert)
Es Sahrâ al Abiad (Black Desert)

SUDAN

Es Sahrâ en Nûbîya (Nubian Desert)

BAHR EL AHMAR

Bûr Sûdân (Port Sudan)

Wadi Halfa
Dongola
Merowe

HALAIB TRIANGLE
BIR TAWIL

Khamîs Mushayt

Lava fields

COPYRIGHT PHILIP'S

Projection: Lambert's Equivalent Azimuthal

East from Greenwich

ft m
9000 3000
6000 2000
4500 1500
3000 1200
1500 600
400 200
0
0 200-600
1000 3000
2000 6000
3000 9000
m ft

1:7 100 000

134

Underlined towns give their name to the
administrative area in which they stand.

Administrative divisions in Ivory Coast:
1 Dix-Huit Montagnes   4 Lagunes   7 Moyen-Comoé
2 Fromager   5 Marahoué   8 Sud-Bandama
3 Haut-Sassandra   6 Moyen-Cavally   9 Sud-Comoé

Projection : Lambert's Equivalent Azimuthal

West from Gr

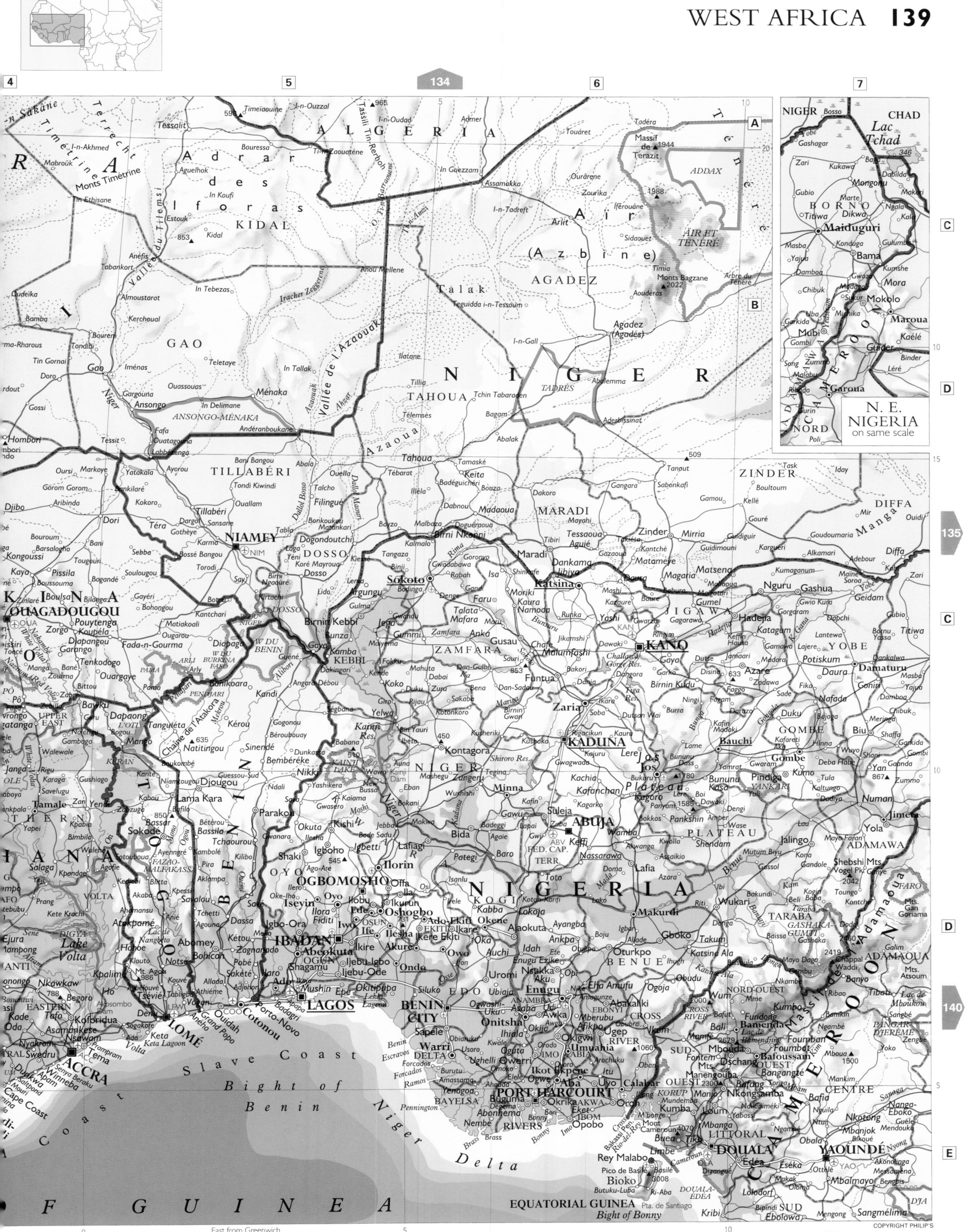

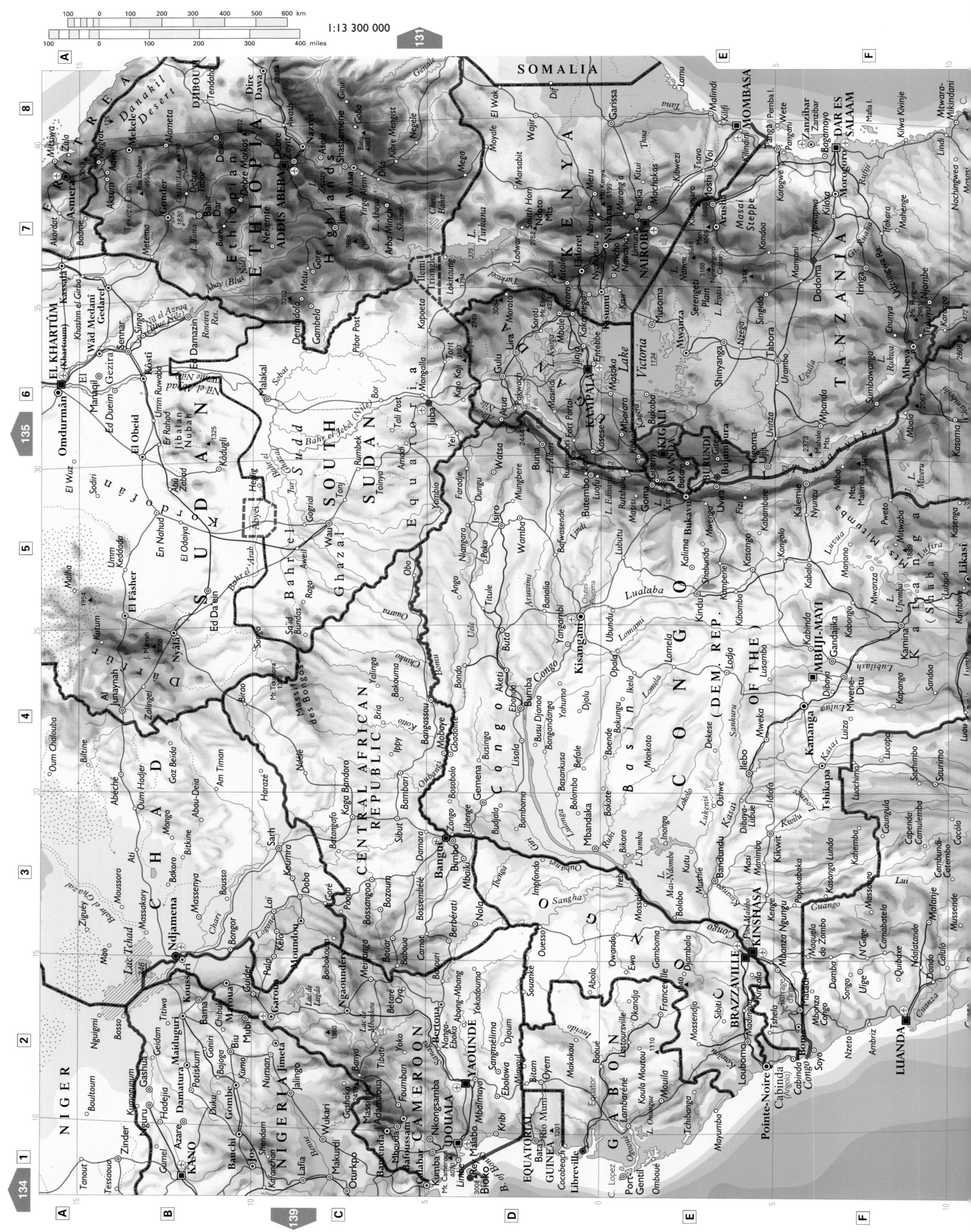

1:13 300 000

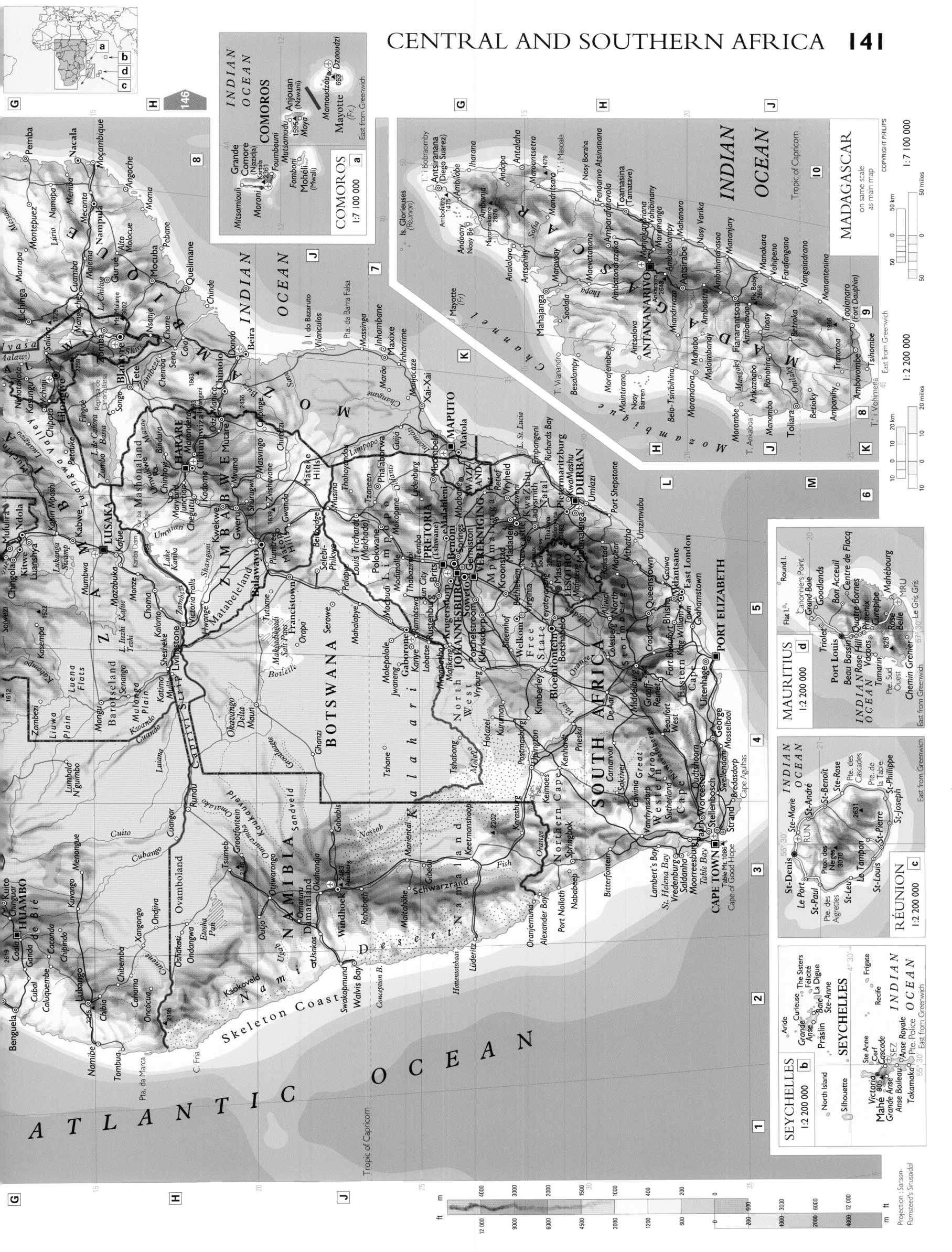

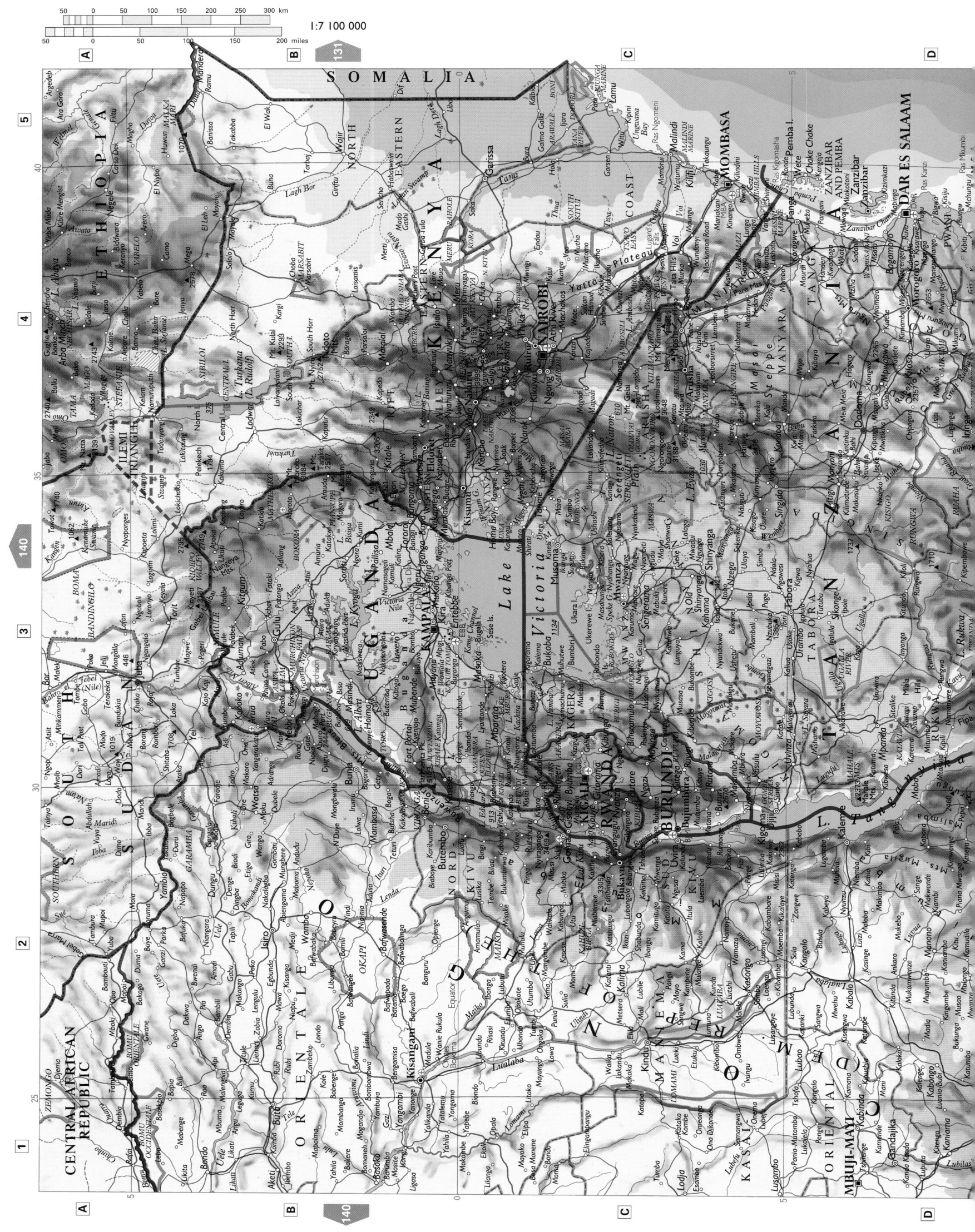

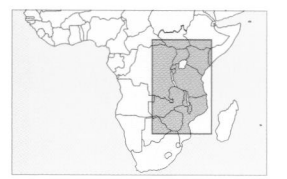

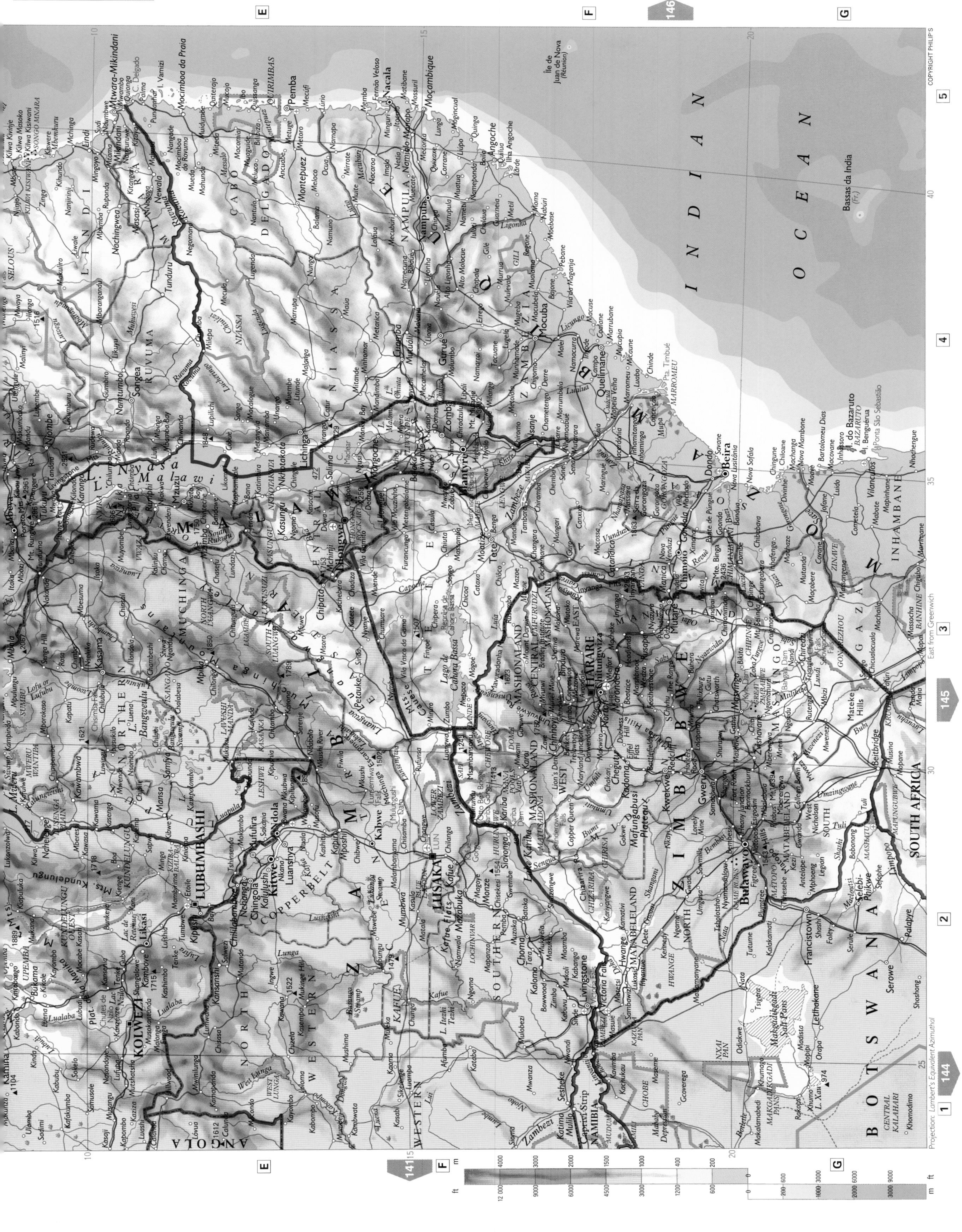

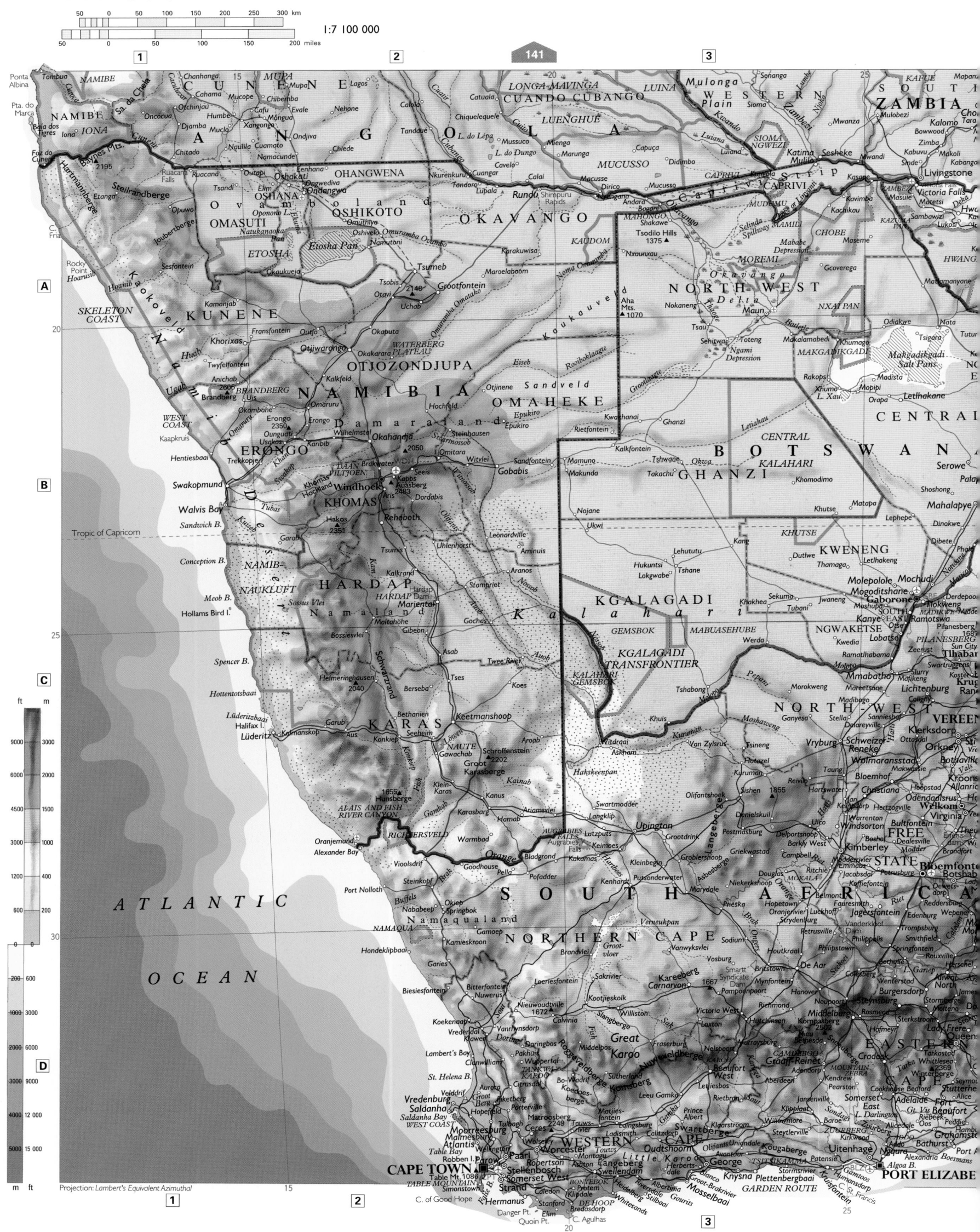

MOZAMBIQUE CHANNEL

INDIAN

OCEAN

Tropic of Capricorn

Bassas da India
(Fr.)

Île Europa
(Fr.)

Île de
Júan de Nova
(Fr.)

ZAMBEZIA

MALAWI

ZIMBABWE

MOZAMBIQUE

LIMPOPO

MPUMALANGA

SWAZILAND

KWAZULU NATAL

PRETORIA
(Tshwane)

JOHANNESBURG

HARARE
Chitungwiza

Beira

MAPUTO

DURBAN

Quelimane

Mocuba

Angoche

Equatorial Scale 1:45 000 000

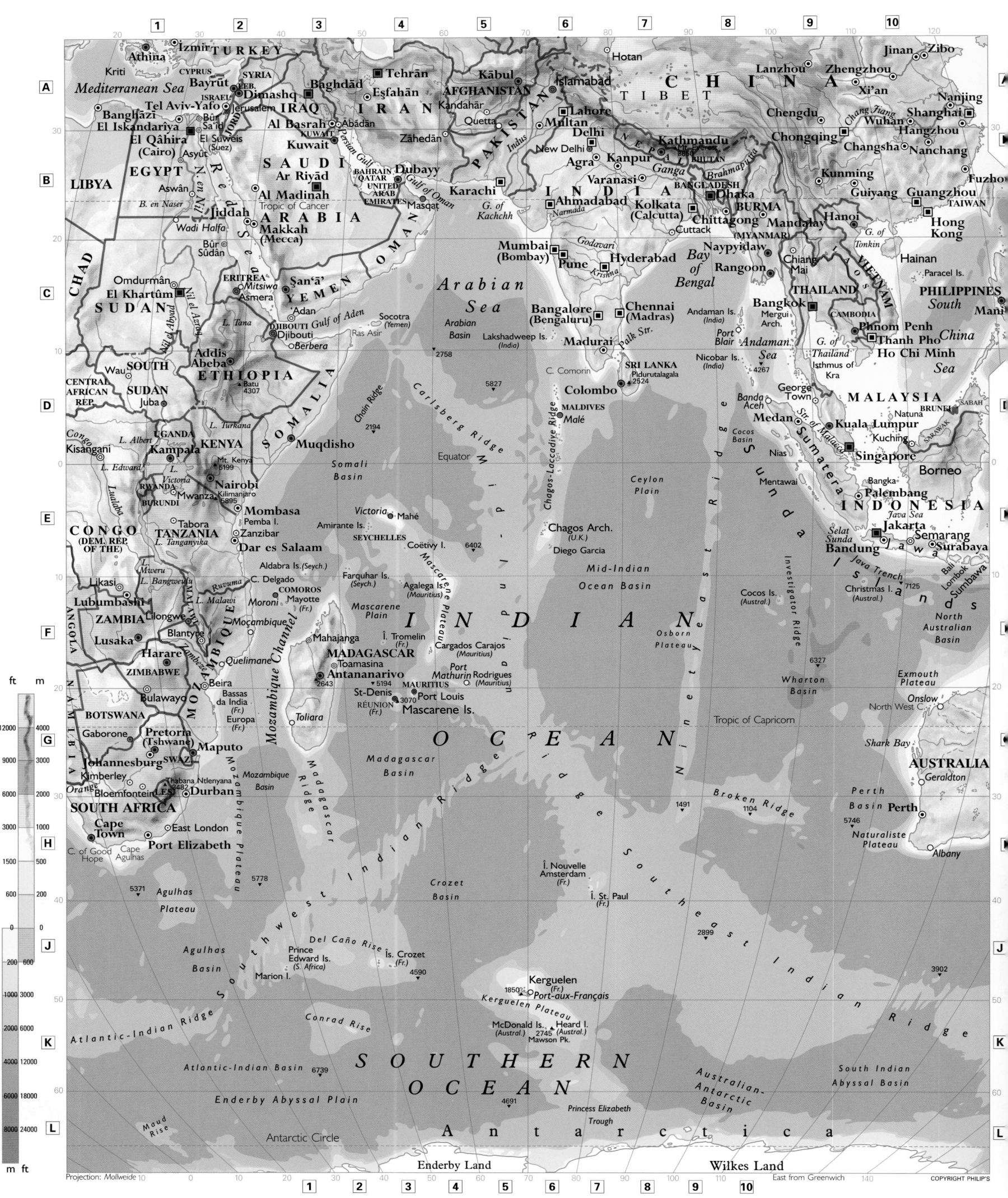

ft   m

12000   4000

9000   3000

6000   2000

3000   1000

1500   500

600   200

0   0

200   600

1000   3000

2000   6000

4000   12000

6000   18000

8000   24000

m ft

Projection: Mollweide

COPYRIGHT PHILIP'S

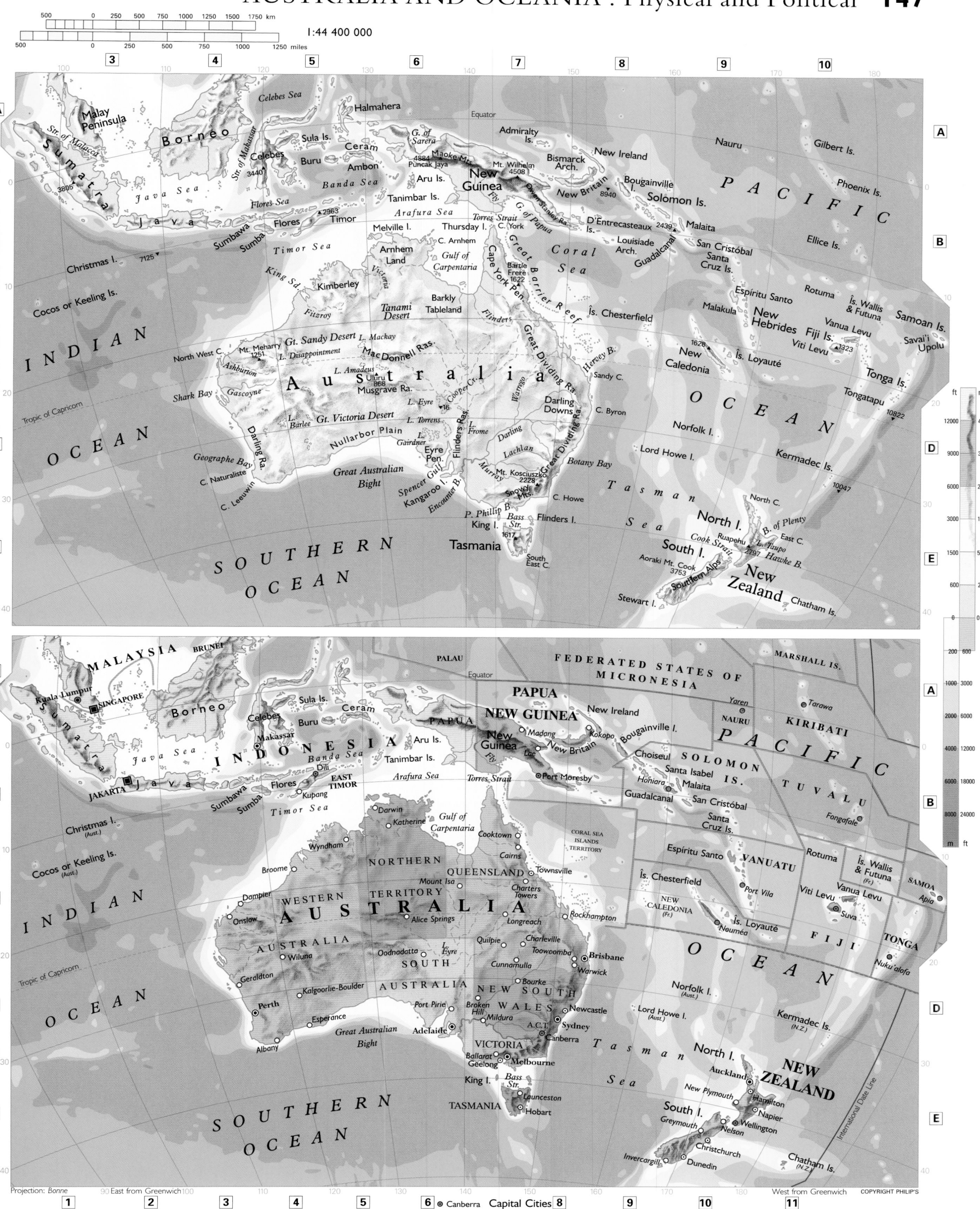

1:7 100 000

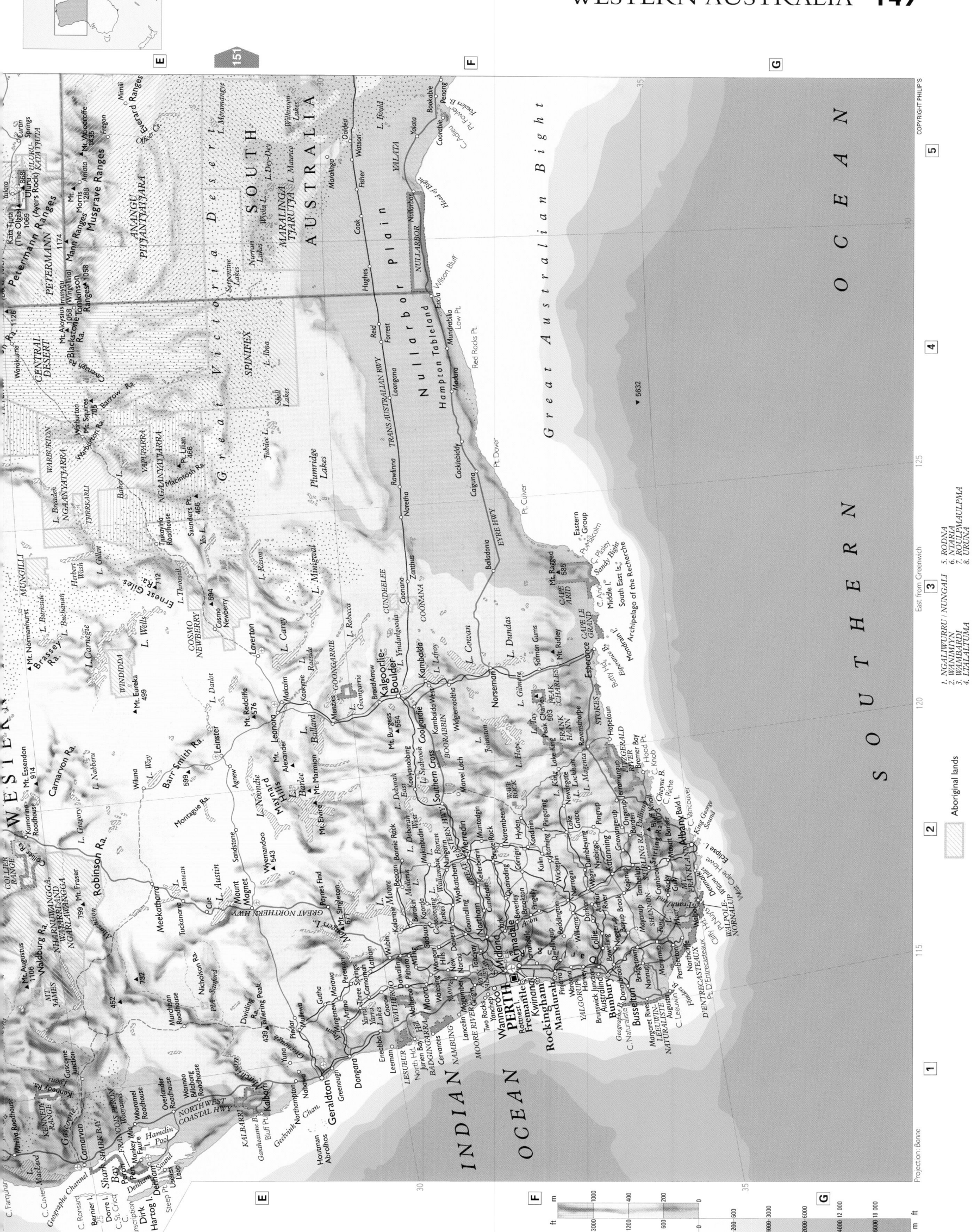

Aboriginal lands

1. NGALIYURRU / NUNGALI
2. WANJIIRRI
3. WAMBARDI
4. LIJALALTUMA
5. RODNA
6. NTHARA
7. ROULPMAULPMA
8. URUNA

Projection: Bonne

East from Greenwich

ft   m
3000 1000
      600
1200 400
      200
600   0
0
      -200 -600
2000 6000
4000 12 000
6000 18 000
m   ft

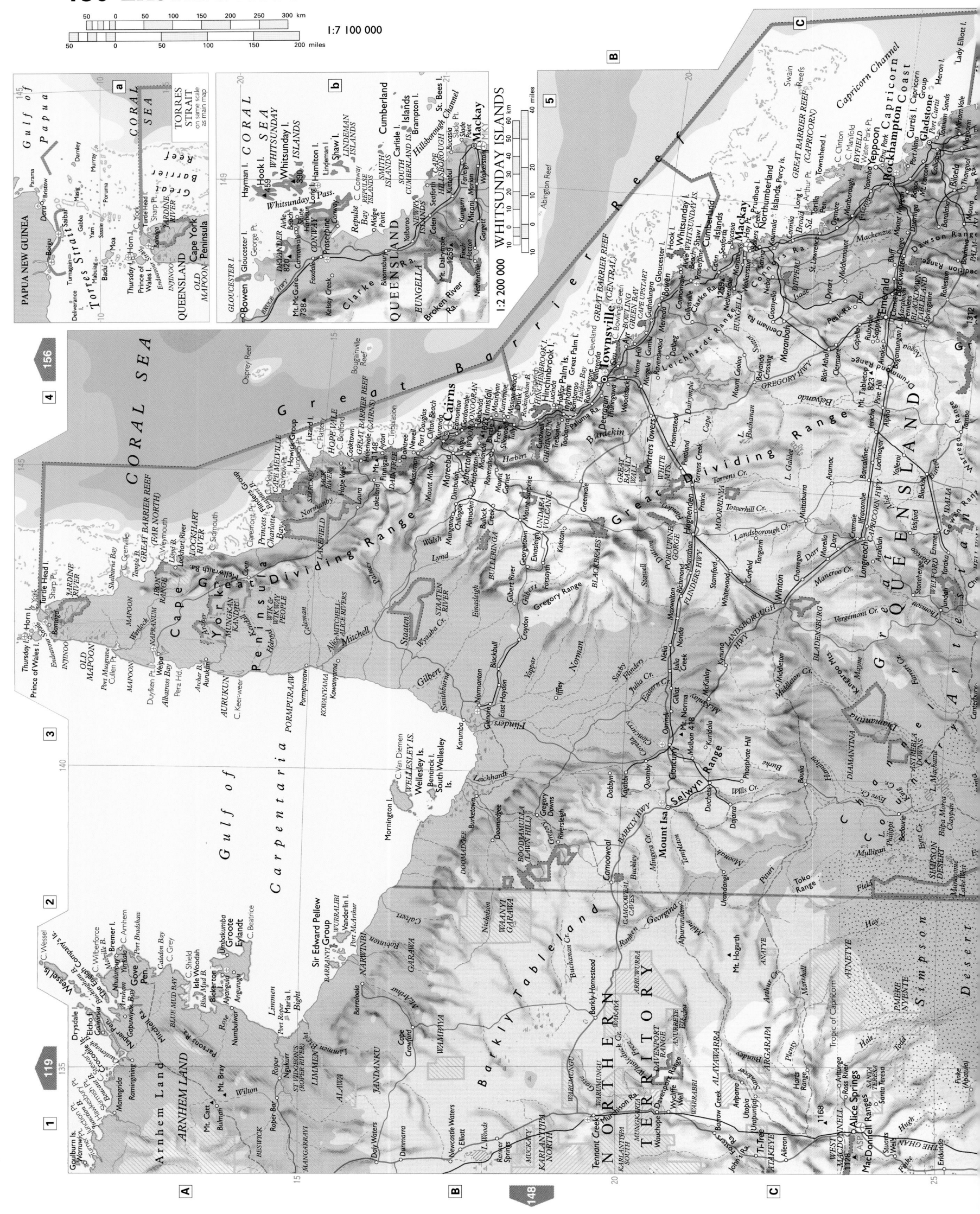

COPYRIGHT PHILIP'S

Aboriginal lands

on same scale

East from Greenwich

Projection: Bonne

1:3 500 000

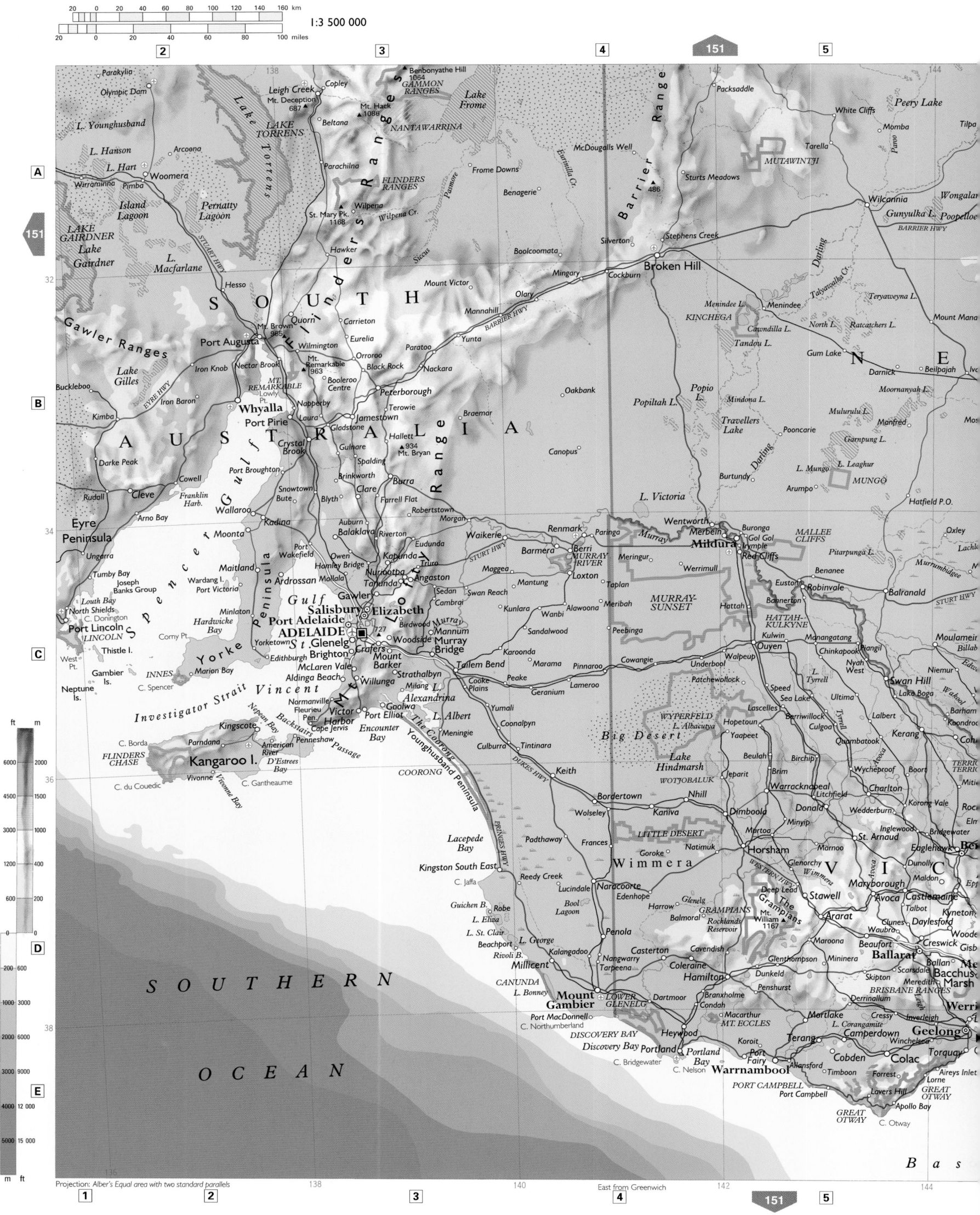

Projection: Alber's Equal area with two standard parallels

East from Greenwich

Aboriginal lands

10 0 20 40 60 80 100 120 140 km
1:3 100 000
10 0 20 40 60 80 100 miles

FIJI a
1:5 300 000
50 0 50 100 150 200 km
50 0 50 100 150 miles

FIJI inset

PACIFIC OCEAN

Great Sea Reef Kia Udu Pt. Ringgold Is.
Yaqaga Labasa Natewa Bay Rabi
Vanua Levu 1031 Buca Qamea
Yasawa Group Yadua Bua Taveuni 2323 UMA
Viwa Naviti Nacula Nabouwalu Namenalala Nasau Koro Vacata Kanacea Lomaloma Vanua Balavu
Waya Vomo Tavua Rakiraki Makogai Batiki Northern Lau Group Mago Vatu Vara
Bligh Water Tomaniivi Levuka Ovalau Nairai Vatu Mbau Cicia Tuvuca
Mamanuca Group KOROYANITU Korovou Yunidewa Sawakelo Gau Nayau Lakeba Passage Lakeba Tubou
Malolo Nadi Viti Levu Keiyasi Ndausori KORO SEA Vanua Vatu Oneata Moce
Sigatoka Korolevu Navua Suva FIJI Mago Southern Lau Group Kabara Namuka-i-Lau Yagasa Cluster
Vatulele Yanuca Beqa Kadavu Passage Moala Totoya Fulaga Ogea Levu
Kadavu Tavuki Vunisea Matuku Ono Ogea Driki

178 E 180 East from Greenwich West from Greenwich

North Island main map

C. Reinga North C.
Waitiki Landing Parengarenga Harbour
C. Maria van Diemen Houhora Heads
Ninety Mile Beach Awanui Rangaunu B.
Ahipara B. Kaitaia Mangonui Cavalli Is.
35 Kaeo C. Karikari Doubtless B.
Herekino Kerikeri Whangaroa Harb.
NORTHLAND 744 Okaihau Waitangi B. of Islands C. Brett
Kohukohu Raihia Russell Opua Whangaruru Harb.
Rawene Kaikohe Kawakawa Poor Knights Is.
Hokianga Harbour 781 Moerewa Hikurangi
Omapere Kamo Whangarei
Waipoua Forest Onerahi
Aranga Kirikopuni Whangarei Harb.
Dargaville Marsden Point Bream
Te Kopuru Waikiekie Paparoa Bream Hd.
36 Ruawai Waipu Bream Tail
Maungaturoto Maungtaniwha Needles Pt.
Wellsford Little Barrier Port Fitzroy
C. Rodney 722 627 Great Barrier I. Tryphena
Matakana C. Barrier
Helensville Snells Beach Coville Chan. Cuvier I.
Warkworth C. Colville 892 Port Charles
Whangaparaoa Pen. Coromandel Mercury Is.
C AUCKLAND Takapuna Ostend Waiheke I. Whitianga Mercury B.
AUCKLAND Otahuhu Coromandel Pen.
Muriwai Beach Piha Howick Tairua
Onehunga Mount Wellington 846 Pauanui
Papatoetoe Papakura Thames Ra. Whangamata
Manukau Harbour Manukau Thames Mayor I.
37 Waiuku Pukekohe Waihi Waihi Beach
Waikato Tuakau Mercer Katikati BAY OF
L. Waikare Te Kauwhata Paeroa Tauranga Harb. PLENTY
WAIKATO Huntly Waitoa Te Aroha Matakana I. Whakaari (White I.)
Glen Afton Ngaruawahia Morrinsville Mount Maunganui C. Runaway Hicks Bay
Glen Massey Matamata Te Puke Edgecumbe Whakatane Te Kaha Te Araroa
Raglan Harbour Hamilton Tauranga 1067 1753 East C.
Raglan Waharoa L. Rotorua Kawerau Ohiwa Harbour Hikurangi Waiapu
D Cambridge Karapiro Tirau L. Rotoiti Te Teko Opotiki Ruatoria
Aotea Harbour Leamington Arapuni Putaruru Taneatua Waipiro Bay
Kawhia Harbour Te Awamutu Kihikihi Rotorua Tokomaru Bay
Kawhia Otorohanga Ngongotaha 1111 Mt. Tarawera UREWERA
Albatross Pt. Waitomo Caves Tokoroa Mt. Tarawera Matawai Tolaga Bay
Tirua Pt. Te Kuiti Kinleith L. Tarawera GISBORNE
38 Mangakino Waiotapu Galatea Puha Te Karaka
TASMAN Aria 1185 Atiamuri Whakamaru Murupara Ngatapa Ormond
Herangi Ra. Ongarue Mokai Wairakei L. Waikareiti Gisborne
Mokau Ohura Hauhungaroa Ra. Manuoha Waikaremoana Tuaheni Pt.
SEA North Taranaki Bight Otahuhu Taupo 1392 Tuai Poverty B.
Pukearuhe Manunui 369 L. Taupo Taupo Rangitaiki Pututahi
Waitara Tahora Tokaanu Turangi 1383 Mohaka Frasertown
New Plymouth Owhango L. Rotoaira Waikaremoana Ra. Tarawera Nuhaka
39 TARANAKI Inglewood Whangamomona Mt. Tongariro 1968 Ahimanawa Ra. Wairoa Waikokopu
Okato Midhirst Huiroa Mt. Ngauruhoe 2280 Kaweka Ra. Table C.
Mt. Taranaki or Mt. Egmont Stratford 746 Ruapehu 2797 Putorino Mahia Pen.
C. Egmont 2518 Eltham Ohakune Rangataua Portland I. 403
EGMONT Rahotu Kaponga Normanby Raetihi 1726 Bay View Mahia
Opunake Kapuni Hawera Pipiriki Taradale Napier
Manaia South Taranaki Bight Waverley Turakina Waiouru Clive
Patea Maxwell Taihape WHANGANUI C. Kidnappers
Waitotara Mangaweka 1733 Hastings
Wanganui Hunterville Mangaweka Havelock North
40 Castlecliff Turakina Marton Apiti Waipawa
Bulls Halcombe Norsewood Waipukurau Hawke Bay
MANAWATU-WANGANUI Feilding Ormondville HAWKE'S BAY
112 Rangitikei Bunnythorpe Dannevirke Otane
Palmerston North Ashhurst Porangahau Tikokino
Rongotea Woodville Weber PACIFIC
Manawatu Foxton Pahiatua 803 Herbertville
Shannon Longburn Ekatahuna C. Turnagain
Levin Alfredton OCEAN
G Otaki Puketoi Ra.
Golden Bay Stephens I. Kapiti I. Tararua Ra. 1571 Mt. Mitre
Rangitoto ke te tonga (D'Urville I.) Mauriceville Castlepoint
Collingwood Separation Pt. French Pass Paraparaumu Tinui
Takaka Stephens I. Paekakariki Masterton
C. Farewell Farewell Spit Kahurangi Pt. Porirua Carterton WELLINGTON
ABEL TASMAN Tasman Paremata Upper Hutt Greytown
KAHURANGI Riwaka Pelorus Sd. Johnsonville Lower Hutt Featherston
Mts. Motueka Cook Strait Petone Martinborough
1780 Devil River Pk. NELSON 1203 Queen Charlotte Sd. Wellington L. Onoke 665 Flat Pt.
Karamea Riwaka Pelorus Havelock Terawhiti Wainuiomata Wairarapa
Brightwater Stoke Picton Eastbourne Palliser B.
H Wakefield Mt. Richmond 1756 Tuamarina Port Nicholson Ruamahanga C. Palliser
Mokihinui Belgrove Richmond Renwick Cloudy B. 981 Aorangi Mts.
1875 Tadmor Richmond Ra. Blenheim Surville Hd.
Lyell Glenhope Mt. Owen Wairau
Murchison TASMAN L. Rotoiti 2120 Seddon 3122
1780 Anatere Ward C. Campbell

Elevation scale
ft m
9000 3000
6000 2000
3000 1000
1500 400
600 200
0 0
200 600
1000 3000
1500 4500
3000 9000
m ft

Projection: Conical with two standard parallels East from Greenwich COPYRIGHT PHILIP'S

173 174 175 176 177 178 179

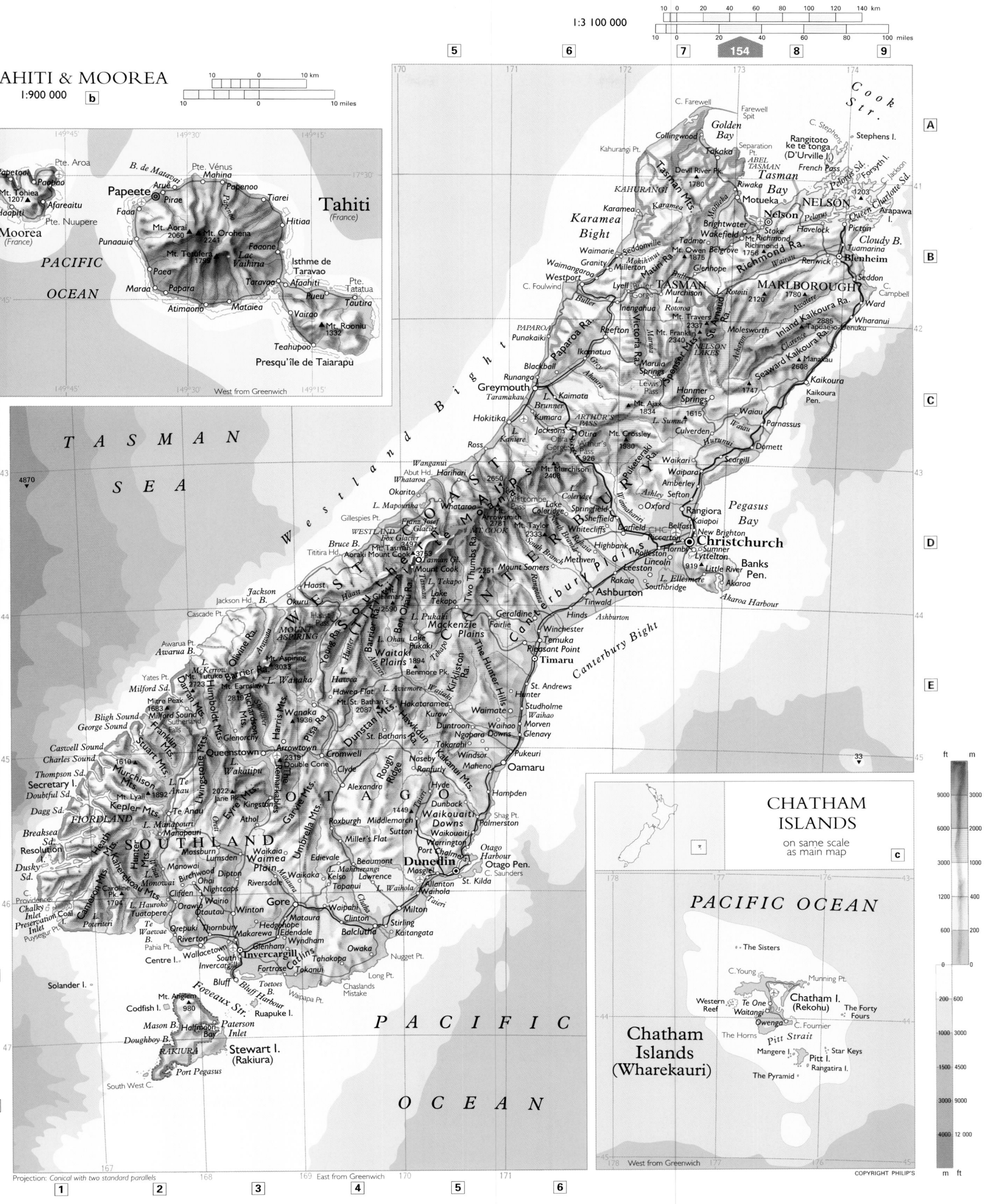

1:3 100 000

AHITI & MOOREA
1:900 000 b

TAHITI & MOOREA

Moorea (France)

PACIFIC OCEAN

Tahiti (France)

Presqu'île de Taiarapu

West from Greenwich

TASMAN SEA

PACIFIC OCEAN

CHATHAM ISLANDS
on same scale as main map c

PACIFIC OCEAN

Chatham Islands
(Wharekauri)

Chatham I. (Rekohu)

West from Greenwich

Projection: Conical with two standard parallels

COPYRIGHT PHILIP'S

RUSSIA

Moskva
Volga
Yekaterinburg
Tomsk
Novosibirsk
Astana (Aqmola)
Semey
Irkutsk
Oz. Baykal
Chita
Blagoveshchensk
Amur
Khabarovsk
Sakhalin
Okhotsk
Sea of Okhotsk
Poluostrov Kamchatka
Shirshov Ridge
Aleutian Basin
Komandorskiye Ostrova (Russia)
Near Is. (U.S.)
Andrea
Be

KAZAKHSTAN
Balqash Köl
Aral Sea
Almaty
Toshkent
KYRGYZSTAN
TAJIKISTAN
AFGHANISTAN
Kabul
Srinagar
PAKISTAN
Lahore
Delhi
Kanpur
Hyderabad

Ob
Lena
Ulaanbaatar
MONGOLIA
Altai
Changchun
Shenyang
Harbin
Vladivostok
Sapporo
Hakodate
Sea of Japan
La Pérouse Str.
Kurilskiye Ostrova (Russia)
Kuril-Kamchatka Trench
10,542
Petropavlovsk-Kamchatskiy
Aleuti
7822
Aleutian Trench

CHINA
Beijing
Tianjin
Taiyuan
Lanzhou
Xi'an
Nanjing
Qingdao
Dalian
NORTH KOREA
SOUTH KOREA
Seoul
Nagoya
Kyōto
Tōkyō
Yokohama
Sendai
JAPAN
Fuji-San 3776
Shikoku
Kyūshū
Kitakyūshū
Osaka
10,554
Japan Trench
Shatsky Rise
Pacific
Northwest
Emperor Seamount Chain
Chinook

Kunlun Shan
XIZANG
Lhasa
Himalaya
8850 Everest
NEPAL
Ganga
Brahmaputra
BANGLADESH
Kolkata (Calcutta)
Dhaka
INDIA
Chongqing
Wuhan
Hangzhou
Chang
Changsha
Shanghai
East China Sea
Okinawa
Ryūkyū-retto (Japan)
Iwo-Jima (Japan)
Kyūshū-Palau Ridge
Shitō Ozima Ridge
Ogasawara Gunto (Japan)
Minami-Tori-Shima (Japan)
Kazan-Rettō (Japan)
Midway Is. (U.S.A.)
Lisianski I. (U.S.A.)
Basin
Holo

Kunming
Guangzhou
Fuzhou
Taipei
Hong Kong
Macau
TAIWAN
Hainan
C. Engano
Paracel Is.
Luzon
Philippine Sea
West Mariana Basin
NORTHERN MARIANAS (U.S.A.)
Tinian
Saipan
East Mariana Basin
Wake I. (U.S.A.)
International Date Line
P A
PA
Mid-Pacific Moun

BURMA
Mandalay
Irrawaddy
Salween
Hanoi
LAOS
Rangoon
Bay of Bengal
THAILAND
Bangkok
Chennai (Madras)
Andaman Is. (India)
Mekong
VIETNAM
CAMBODIA
Phnom Penh
Manila
PHILIPPINES
Mindoro
Samar
10,497
Palawan
Sulu Sea
Mindanao
Davao
Melekeok
Yap
Challenger 11,022 Deep
GUAM (U.S.A.)
Mariana Trench
Caroline Is.
Chuuk
MARSHALL IS.
Bikini
Enewetak Atoll
Kwajalein
Ralik Chain
Ratak Chain
Majuro
Micronesia
Pohnpei
Jaluit I.
Cent

SRI LANKA
Colombo
Nicobar Is. (India)
G. of Thailand
Thanh Pho Ho Chi Minh
South China Sea
MALAYSIA
Celebes Sea
4101
Halmahera
Seram
PALAU
West Caroline Basin
Eauripik Rise
FED. STATES OF MICRONESIA
Palikir
East Caroline Basin
Melanesian Basin
Yaren
Butaritari
Tarawa
Gilbert Is.
Howland I.
Baker I.
Pac

Kuala Lumpur
PEN. MALAYSIA
Singapore
SARAWAK
BRUNEI
SABAH
Borneo
Sulawesi
Buru
Maluku
Puncak Jaya 4884 PAPUA
New Guinea
PAPUA NEW GUINEA
Admiralty Is.
Bismarck Arch.
New Ireland
NAURU
Banaba
Melanesia
Phoenix Is.
Abariri
Enderb
KI
O

Sumatera
Sunda East Ridge
Palembang
Jakarta
Makassar
Jawa Sea
Flores Sea
Banda Sea
7440
INDONESIA
Lae
Kokopo
8940
Bougainville
New Britain
SOLOMON IS.
Fongafale
TUVALU
'I Tarawa

Surabaya
Jawa
Bali
Sunda Islands
Java Trench
Flores
Sumbawa
Sumba
Dili
EAST TIMOR
Timor
Arafura Sea
Torres Strait
C. York
Port Moresby
Louisiade Arch.
Honiara
Guadalcanal
Santa Cruz Is.
9165
Rotuma
Îs. Wallis & Futuna (Fr.)
SAM
Tok

Cocos Is. (Austral.)
Christmas I. (Austral.)
C. Arnhem
Darwin
Gulf of Carpentaria
Coral Sea Basin
Coral Sea
VANUATU
Espíritu Santo
Port Vila
West Fiji Basin
Vanua Levu
Viti Levu
Suva
FIJI
Nuku'alofa

INDIAN
OCEAN
North Australian Basin
Exmouth Plateau
Broome
North West C.
Cairns
Townsville
Mount Isa
Great Barrier Reef
Great Dividing Ra.
Îs. Chesterfield
NEW CALEDONIA (Fr.)
Nouméa
Îs. Loyauté
7570
Middleton Basin
South Fiji Basin
10,822
Tonga Trough

Wharton Basin
AUSTRALIA
Alice Springs
Rockhampton
Brisbane
Lord Howe Rise
New Caledonia Ridge
Norfolk Ridge
Kermadec Is. (N.Z.)
Kermadec Trench 10,047

Broken Ridge
Geraldton
Perth Basin
Perth
Naturaliste Plateau
Albany
L. Eyre
Great Australian Bight
Adelaide
Canberra
Sydney
Murray
Mt. Kosciuszko 2228
Darling
Norfolk I. (Austral.)
Lord Howe I. (Austral.)
Middleton Basin
South Australian Basin
Tasman Sea
Auckland
NEW ZEALAND

Nouvelle Amsterdam (Fr.)
I. St. Paul (Fr.)
Melbourne
Bass Str.
Tasmania
Hobart
East Tasman Plateau
Tasman Basin
Aoraki Mt. Cook 3753
Wellington
Christchurch
Chath
Dunedin
Bounty Trough
Bounty Is. (N.Z.)

INDIAN
Mid-Indian Ridge
Kerguelen (Fr.)
SOUTHERN
South Tasman Rise
Invercargill
Antipodes Is. (N.Z.)
Campbell (N.Z.) Plateau
Campbell I. (N.Z.)
Macquarie I. (Austral.)

Heard I. (Austral.)
Îs. Crozet (Fr.)
OCEAN
Auckland Is. (N.Z.)

ft   m
12 000 4000
9000   3000
6000   2000
3000   1000
1500   500
600   200
0   0
200   600
1000   3000
2000   6000
4000   12 000
6000   18 000
8000   24 000
m ft

Arctic Circle

ALASKA
(U.S.A.)
Anchorage
5959
Bristol Bay
. (U.S.A.)
Gulf of Alaska
Juneau
Prince of Wales I.
(U.S.A.) Prince Rupert
Haida Gwaii
(Queen Charlotte Is.)
(Canada)
Tufts
Abyssal
Plain
Vancouver
Vancouver I.
Victoria
Seattle
Portland
Boise
Snake
Edmonton
Calgary
Regina
Winnipeg
L. Winnipeg
R O C K Y   M T S.
C A N A D A
Newfoundland
St. Lawrence
Québec
Montréal
Ottawa
St. John's
Minneapolis
Missouri
L. Superior
L. Huron
L. Michigan
Toronto
Detroit
Chicago
Pittsburgh
L. Ontario
L. Erie
Buffalo
Boston
New York
Philadelphia
Baltimore
Washington D.C.
B
50
C

Northeast
Mendocino Fracture Zone
C. Mendocino
Salt Lake
City
Denver
Colorado
4418
Kansas City
St. Louis
Cincinnati
UNITED STATES
Oklahoma City
Memphis
Appalachian Mts.
Atlanta
C. Hatteras
A T L A N T I C
Bermuda
(U.K.)
40
D

Sacramento
San Francisco
6741
Los Angeles
San Diego
Murray Fracture Zone
Pacific
Guadalupe
(Mex.)
Phoenix
Dallas
Houston
San Antonio
New
Orleans
Gulf of Mexico
Tampa
Miami
Jacksonville
Sargasso Sea
O C E A N
30
E

Tropic of Cancer
Basin
Molokai Fracture Zone
C. San Lucas
Monterrey
La Habana
Canal de Yucatán
BAHAMAS
West Indies

Honolulu
Maui
HAWAIIAN IS.
(U.S.A.)
Hilo
Hawaii
4205
Oahu
Kauai
Clarion Fracture Zone
Is. Revilla Gigedo
(Mex.)
Guadalajara
Mexico
5610
Puebla
Acapulco
Mérida
7680
CUBA
JAMAICA
HAITI
Kingston
8605
DOMINICAN REP.
PUERTO
RICO
(U.S.A.)
Leeward
Is.
F

P A C I F I C
Î. Clipperton
(Fr.)
Middle America Trench
6662
GUATEMALA
Guatemala
HONDURAS
San Salvador
EL SALVADOR
NICARAGUA
Managua
Guatemala
Basin
Caribbean Sea
BARBADOS
Windward Is.
Maracaibo
Barranquilla
San José
COSTA
RICA
Colón
PANAMA
Panamá
Caracas
VENEZUELA

Palmyra Is.
(U.S.A.)
Teraina
Tabuaeran
Kiritimati
Cooper Ridge
Clipperton Fracture Zone
Panama
Basin
I. del Coco
(Costa Rica)
Cocos Ridge
Medellín
I. de Malpelo
(Colombia)
Bogotá
Cali
COLOMBIA
G

Jarvis I.
(U.S.A.)
Line Islands
Christmas
West
Equator
Galápagos Fracture Zone
Galápagos
(Ecuador)
Carnegie Ridge
Quito
ECUADOR
0

Malden I.
Starbuck I.
Guayaquil
C. Paliñas
Iquitos
Amazonas
BRAZIL
H

K I R I B A T I
Penrhyn
(Tongareva)
Manihiki
Pukapuka
Manihiki
Plateau
Suwarrow Is.
Vostok I.
Caroline I.
(Millennium I.)
Flint I.
Nuku Hiva
Hiva Oa
Îs. Marquises
Marquesas Fracture Zone
Yupanqui
Basin
Mendaña
Galápagos
Fracture Zone
Trujillo
6369
PERU
Lima
Cusco
10
J

Îs. de la
Société
Bora Bora
Huahine
Raiatéa
Papeete
Tahiti
Rangiroa
Îs. Tuamotu
FRENCH POLYNESIA
Îs. Gambier
Mururoa
Peru Basin
Peru-
Chile
Arica
L. Titicaca
Nevado Ancohuma
6550
Arequipa
6866
La Paz
BOLIVIA
Nasca Ridge
East Pacific Ridge
20
K

Cook Is.
(N.Z.)
Aitutaki
Atiu
Rarotonga
Mangaia
Îs. Tubuai
Austral / Seamount Chain
Oeno I.
Henderson I.
Pitcairn I.
Ducie I.
(U.K.)
Rapa
Tropic of Capricorn
Easter Fracture Zone
Sala-y-Gómez
Sala-y-Gómez Ridge
I. de Pascua
(Chile)
San Félix
(Chile)
San Ambrosio
(Chile)
Iquique
Antofagasta
8050
Trench
PARAGUAY
Asunción
San Miguel
de Tucumán
Pôrto
Alegre

Southwest
Roggeveen
Basin
Arch. de
Juan Fernández
(Chile)
Córdoba
Aconcagua
6962
Rosario
URUGUAY
Montevideo
Río de la Plata
Buenos
Aires
Valparaíso
Santiago
Concepción
30
L

Pacific
Basin
Challenger Fracture Zone
Menard Fracture Zone
Chile Rise
Chile
ARGENTINA
ANDES
Patagonia
A N D E S
40
M

ATLANTIC
6212 OCEAN

Pacific - Antarctic Ridge
East
Punta Arenas
Est. de Magallanes
Tierra del Fuego
C. de Hornos
Drake Passage
Falkland Is.
(U.K.)
South Georgia
(U.K.)
50
N

Southeast
Pacific Basin

1:31 100 000

Projection: Bonne

West from Greenwich

COPYRIGHT PHILIP'S

1:31 100 000

100 0 200 400 600 800 1000 1200 1400 km

100 0 200 400 600 800 1000 miles

B | A | B

RUSSIA
Asia
St. Lawrence I.
Bering Strait

Bering Sea

ARCTIC OCEAN
International Date Line

Beaufort Sea

Queen Elizabeth Is.

Ellesmere I.

GREENLAND (Denmark)

Denmark Strait

ICELAND

Reykjavik

C

Baffin Bay

Davis Strait

Nuuk

D

ALASKA (USA)
Yukon
Porcupine
Anchorage
Fairbanks
Kodiak I.
Gulf of Alaska
Whitehorse
Juneau

NORTHWEST
Arctic Circle
YUKON TERRITORY
Mackenzie
Great Bear L.
Back
Dubawnt

TERRITORIES
Yellowknife
Liard
Great Slave L.

Victoria I.

NUNAVUT

Baffin Island

Hudson Strait
Iqaluit

Hudson Bay

D

CANADA

BRITISH COLUMBIA
Skeena
Fraser
Peace
Athabasca

ALBERTA
Edmonton
Calgary
Saskatchewan

SASKATCHEWAN
Athabasca
Regina

MANITOBA
Churchill
Nelson
L. Winnipeg

Eastmain

QUÉBEC

NEWFOUNDLAND & LABRADOR

St-Pierre et Miquelon (Fr.)
St. John's

E

Victoria
Vancouver
Olympia
Seattle
WASHINGTON
Portland
Salem

OREGON
Columbia
IDAHO
Boise
Snake

MONTANA
Helena
Missouri

Winnipeg

NORTH DAKOTA
Bismarck

SOUTH DAKOTA

MINNESOTA
St. Paul
Minneapolis

WISCONSIN
Madison
Milwaukee

L. Superior

ONTARIO

Ottawa
Montréal
Québec
Fredericton
NEW BRUNSWICK
PRINCE EDWARD
Charlottetown
NOVA SCOTIA
Halifax
MAINE
Augusta

40

Sacramento
Carson City
San Francisco
San Jose
NEVADA
CALIFORNIA
Salt Lake City
UTAH

WYOMING

NEBRASKA
Lincoln

IOWA

Chicago
L. Michigan
L. Huron
MICHIGAN
Lansing
Detroit
Toledo
Cleveland

TORONTO
L. Ontario
L. Erie
Buffalo
NEW YORK
Hartford
Pittsburgh
PA.
Providence
Boston
MASS.
VER.
Concord
N.H.

F

Las Vegas
LOS ANGELES
San Diego
Tijuana
Mexicali

Denver
COLORADO

KANSAS
Topeka
Kansas City

St. Louis
MISSOURI

ILLINOIS
Springfield
INDIANA
Indianapolis
Cincinnati
OHIO
Columbus

WASHINGTON D.C.
W.VA.
VIRGINIA
Richmond
Raleigh
NORTH CAROLINA
Charlotte

KENTUCKY
Nashville
TENNESSEE
Memphis

Baltimore
PHILADELPHIA
NEW YORK
MD.
DEL.
N.J.

Bermuda (U.K.)

Santa Fe
Albuquerque
NEW MEXICO
ARIZONA
Phoenix
Tucson

OKLAHOMA
Oklahoma City

ARKANSAS
Little Rock

Birmingham
ATLANTA
GEORGIA

SOUTH CAROLINA
Columbia
Charleston

G

El Paso
Ciudad Juárez

DALLAS-FT. WORTH

TEXAS
Austin
San Antonio

HOUSTON
Baton Rouge
LOUISIANA
New Orleans
MISSISSIPPI
Jackson
ALABAMA
Montgomery

Tallahassee
FLORIDA
Jacksonville
Orlando
Tampa-St. Petersburg
MIAMI

ATLANTIC OCEAN

PACIFIC OCEAN

Guadalupe (Mex.)

Hermosillo
Culiacán

Tropic of Cancer

MÉXICO
Torreón
Monterrey

Rio Grande

Gulf of Mexico
Florida Str.

Havana
CUBA
Nassau
BAHAMAS
Turks & Caicos Is. (U.K.)

20

Revilla Gigedo Is. (Mex.)

Guadalajara
León
Querétaro
San Luis Potosí

Mérida

MÉXICO
Toluca
Puebla
Acapulco

BELIZE
Belmopan

Cayman Is. (U.K.)

JAMAICA
Kingston

HAITI
Port-au-Prince
DOMINICAN REP.
Santo Domingo
San Juan
PUERTO RICO (U.S.A.)

H

GUATEMALA
Guatemala
San Salvador
EL SALVADOR
HONDURAS
Tegucigalpa
NICARAGUA
Managua
L. Nicaragua

Caribbean Sea

Maracaibo
Barranquilla
VENEZUELA

J

COSTA RICA
San José
PANAMÁ
Panamá
COLOMBIA
Medellín

South America

Projection: Bonne

West from Greenwich

COPYRIGHT PHILIP'S

7 | ■ MÉXICO Capital Cities | 8 | 9 | 10 | 11 | 12

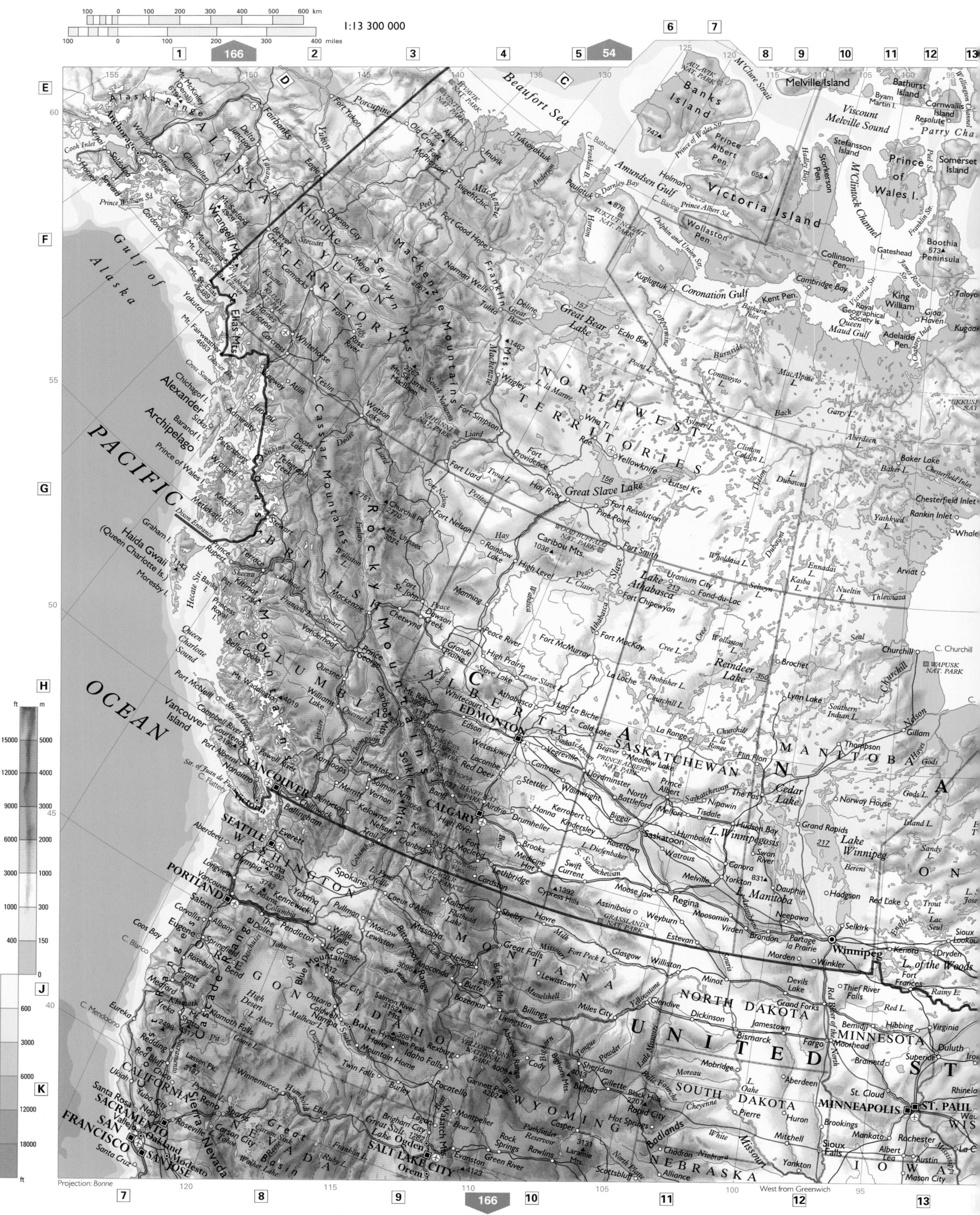

1:13 300 000

Projection: Bonne

West from Greenwich

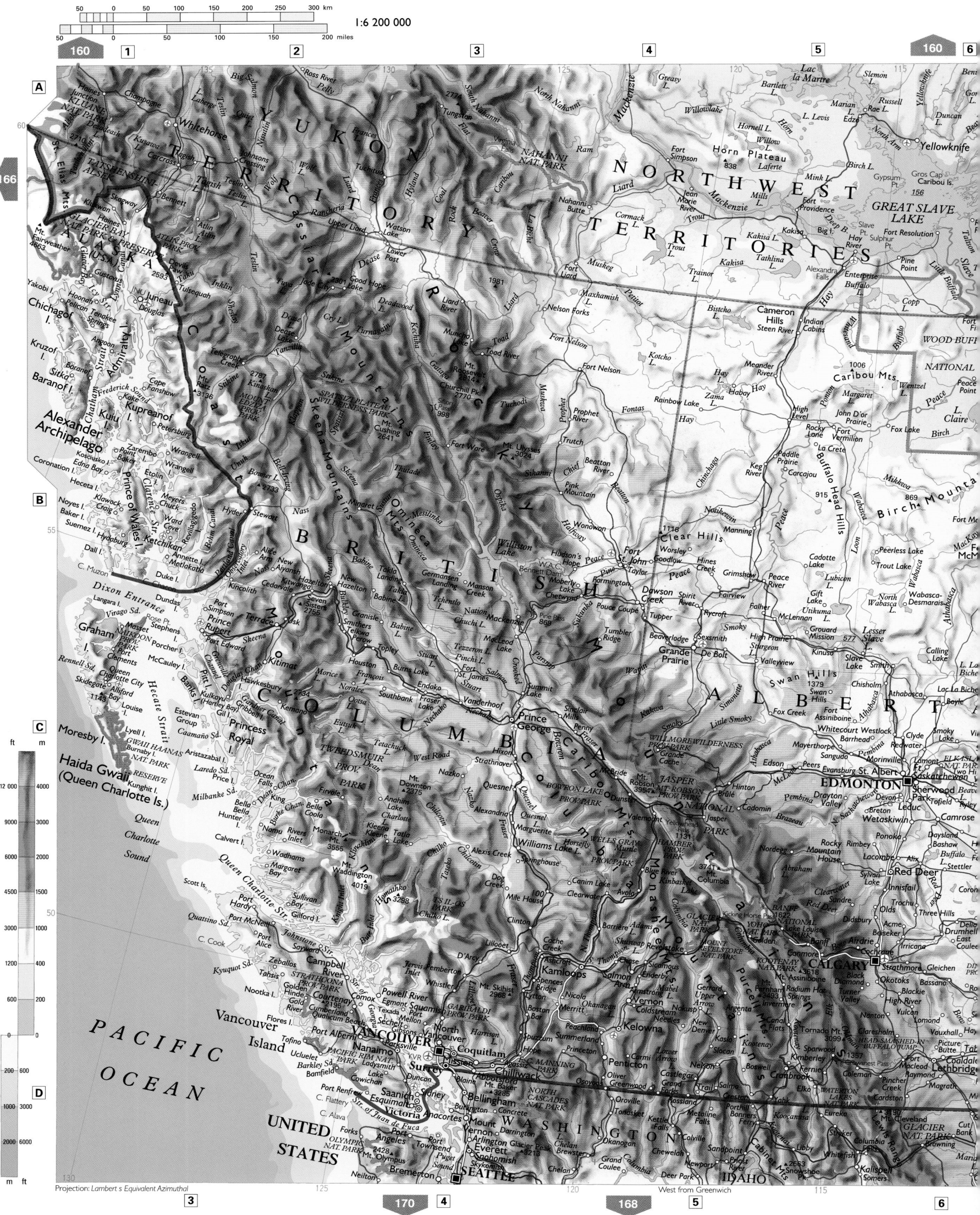

COPYRIGHT PHILIP S

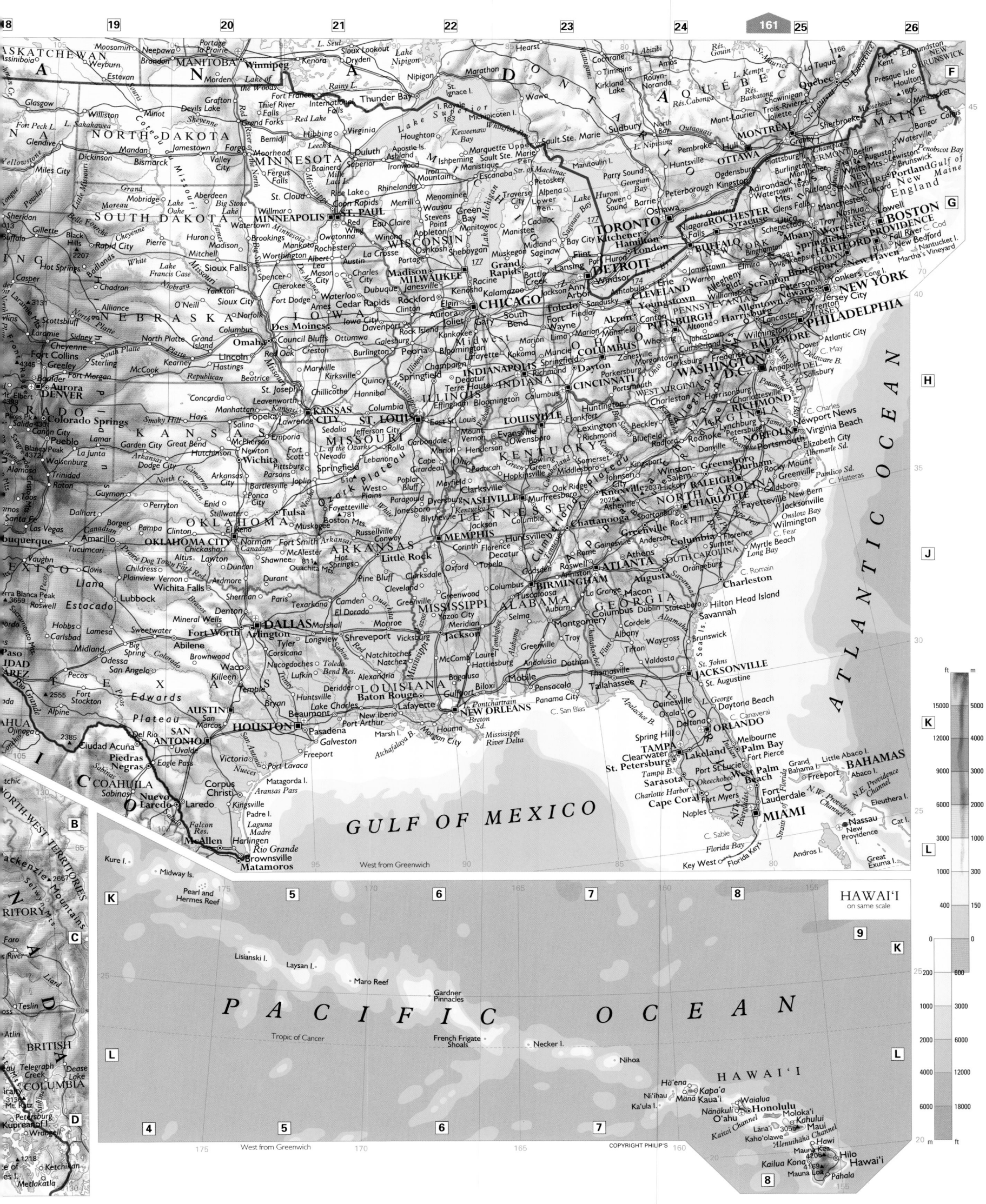

HAWAI'I
on same scale

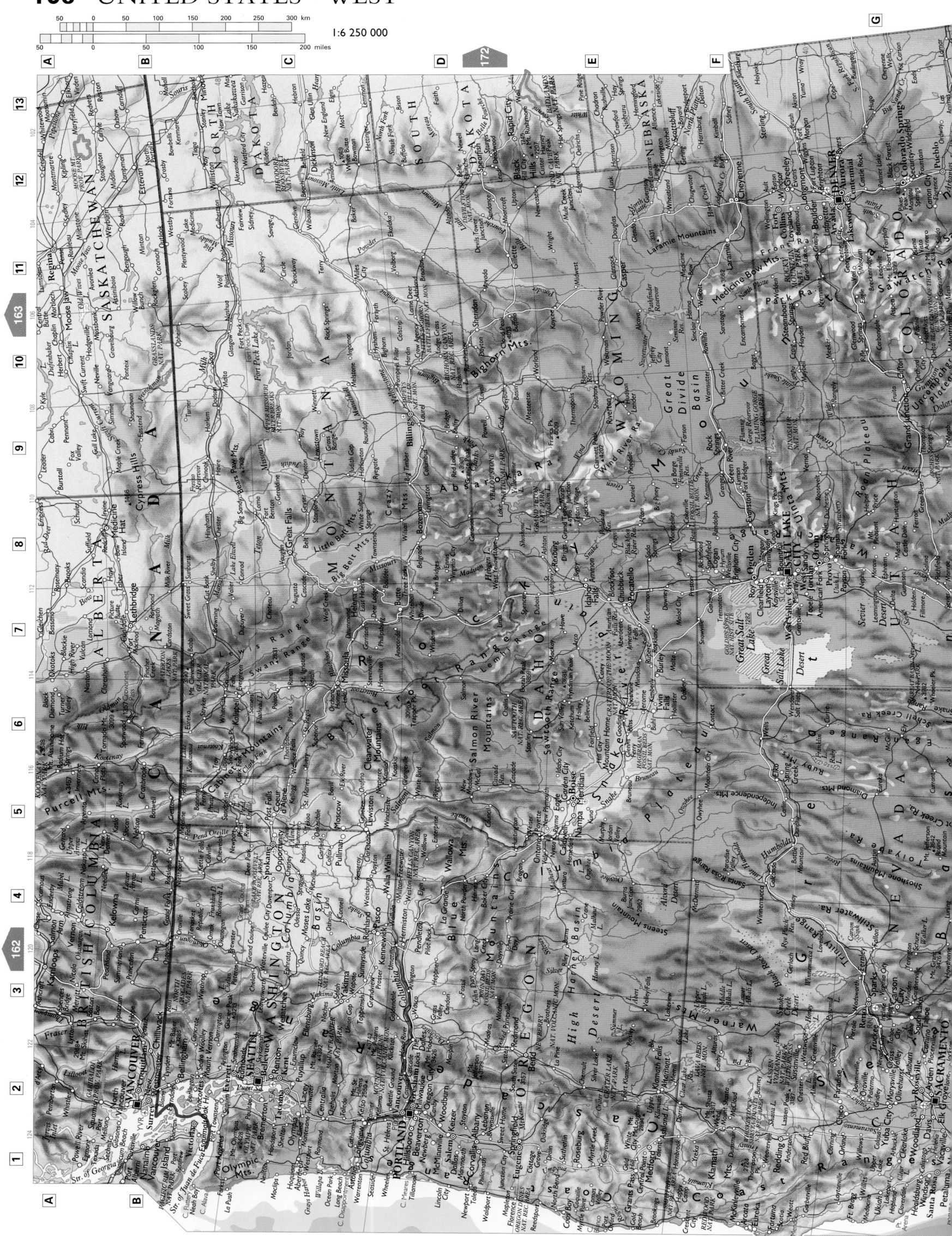

1:6 250 000

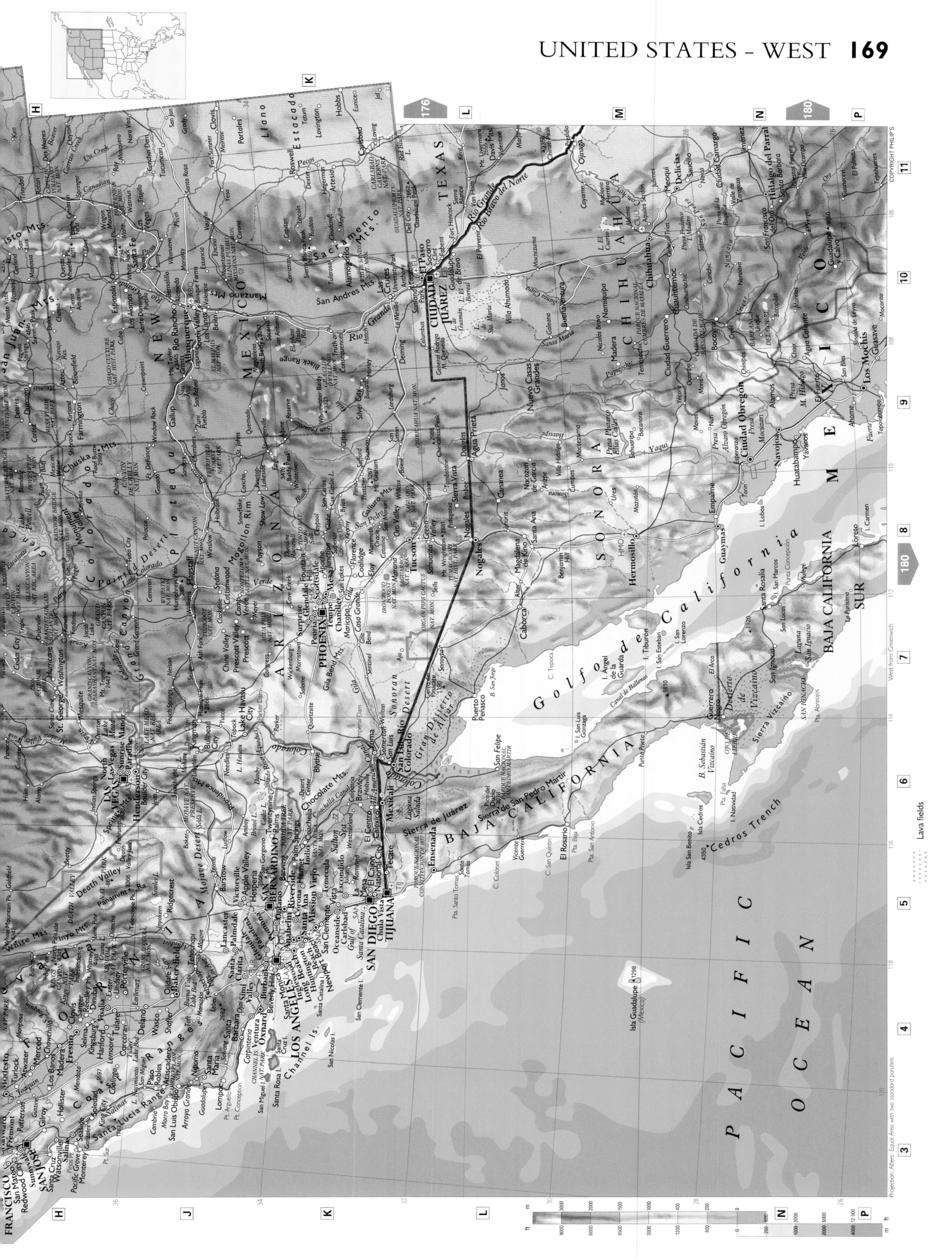

1:2 200 000

WESTERN WASHINGTON
REGION
on same scale

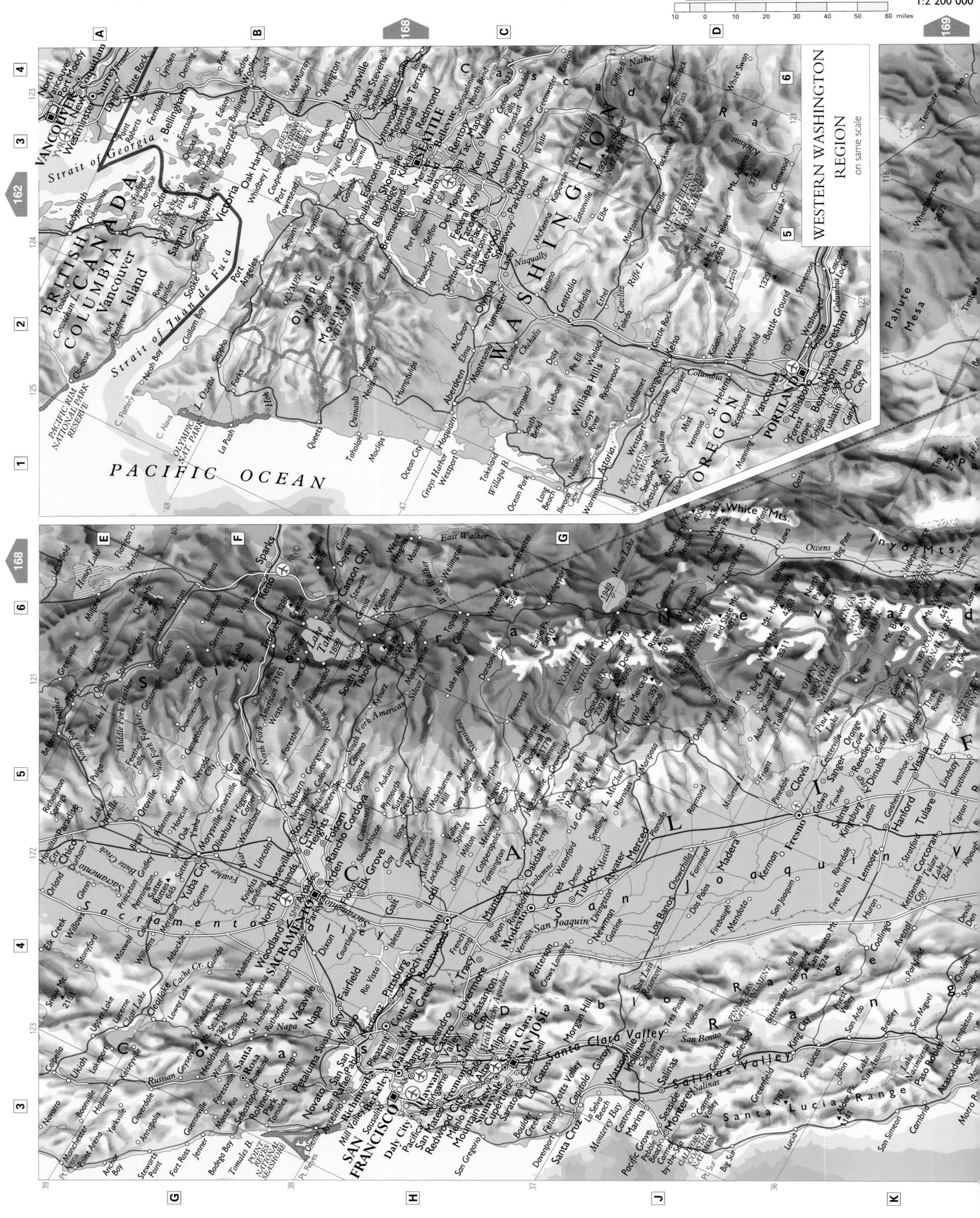

Lava fields

Projection: Bonne

COPYRIGHT PHILIP'S

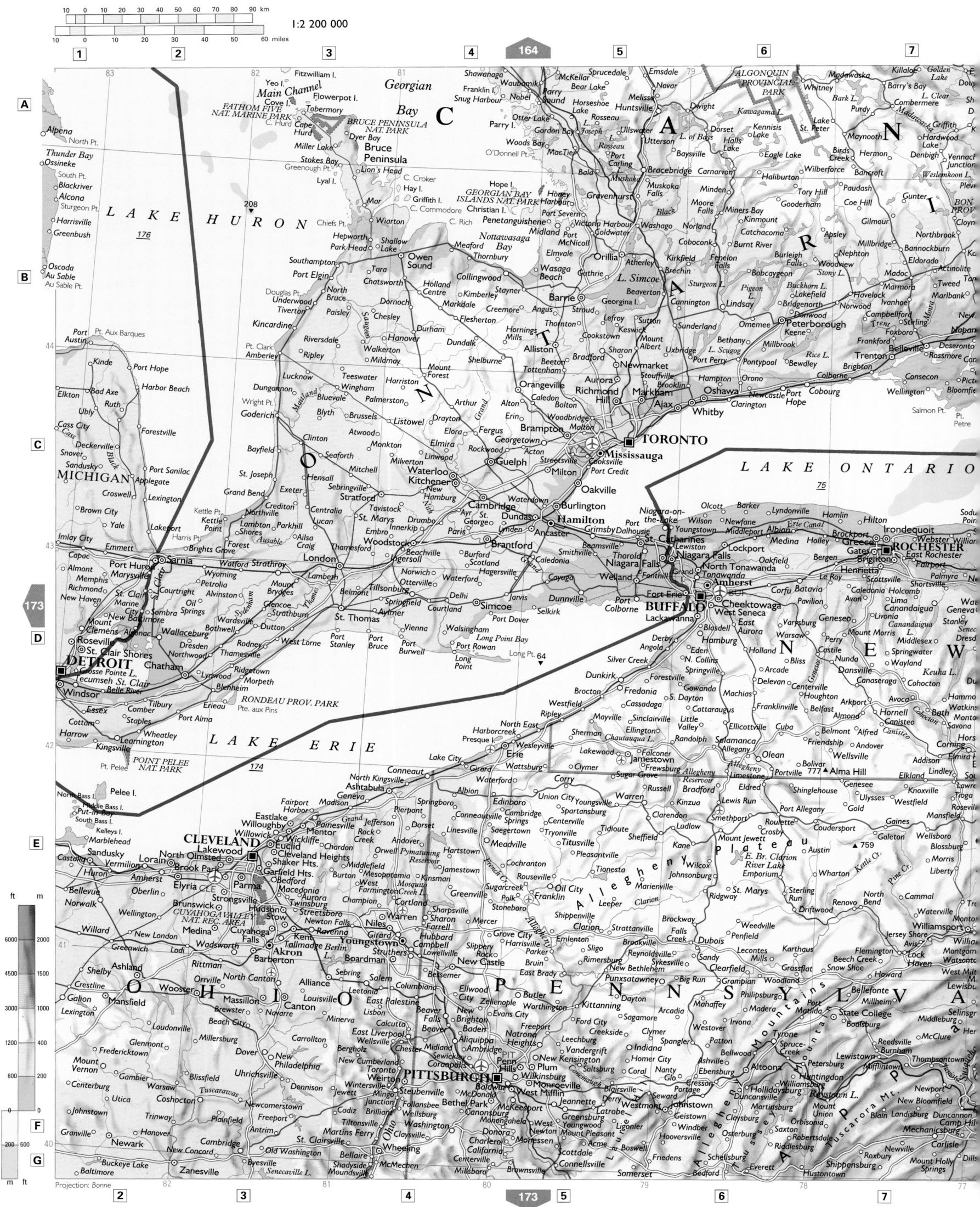

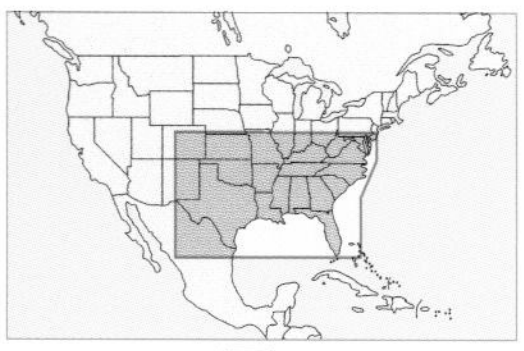

10 11 12 **173** 13 14 15 16 17

A

ILLINOIS INDIANA OHIO COLUMBUS PITTSBURGH PENNSYLVANIA PHILADELPHIA

B

INDIANAPOLIS CINCINNATI WEST VIRGINIA MARYLAND BALTIMORE WASHINGTON D.C. DELAWARE

C

LOUISVILLE KENTUCKY VIRGINIA RICHMOND NORFOLK Virginia Beach Chesapeake

D

NASHVILLE TENNESSEE NORTH CAROLINA CHARLOTTE RALEIGH Wilmington CAPE HATTERAS NAT. SEASHORE

MEMPHIS

E

BIRMINGHAM ATLANTA GEORGIA SOUTH CAROLINA Columbia Charleston

MISSISSIPPI ALABAMA

F

Jackson Montgomery Columbus Savannah Hilton Head Island

G

NEW ORLEANS FLORIDA JACKSONVILLE ATLANTIC OCEAN

GULF OF MEXICO

H

TAMPA ORLANDO Melbourne BAHAMAS Grand Bahama

St. Petersburg Lake Okeechobee West Palm Beach

J

MIAMI Fort Lauderdale Miami Beach New Providence Nassau

EVERGLADES NAT. PARK Florida Bay

1:2 200 000

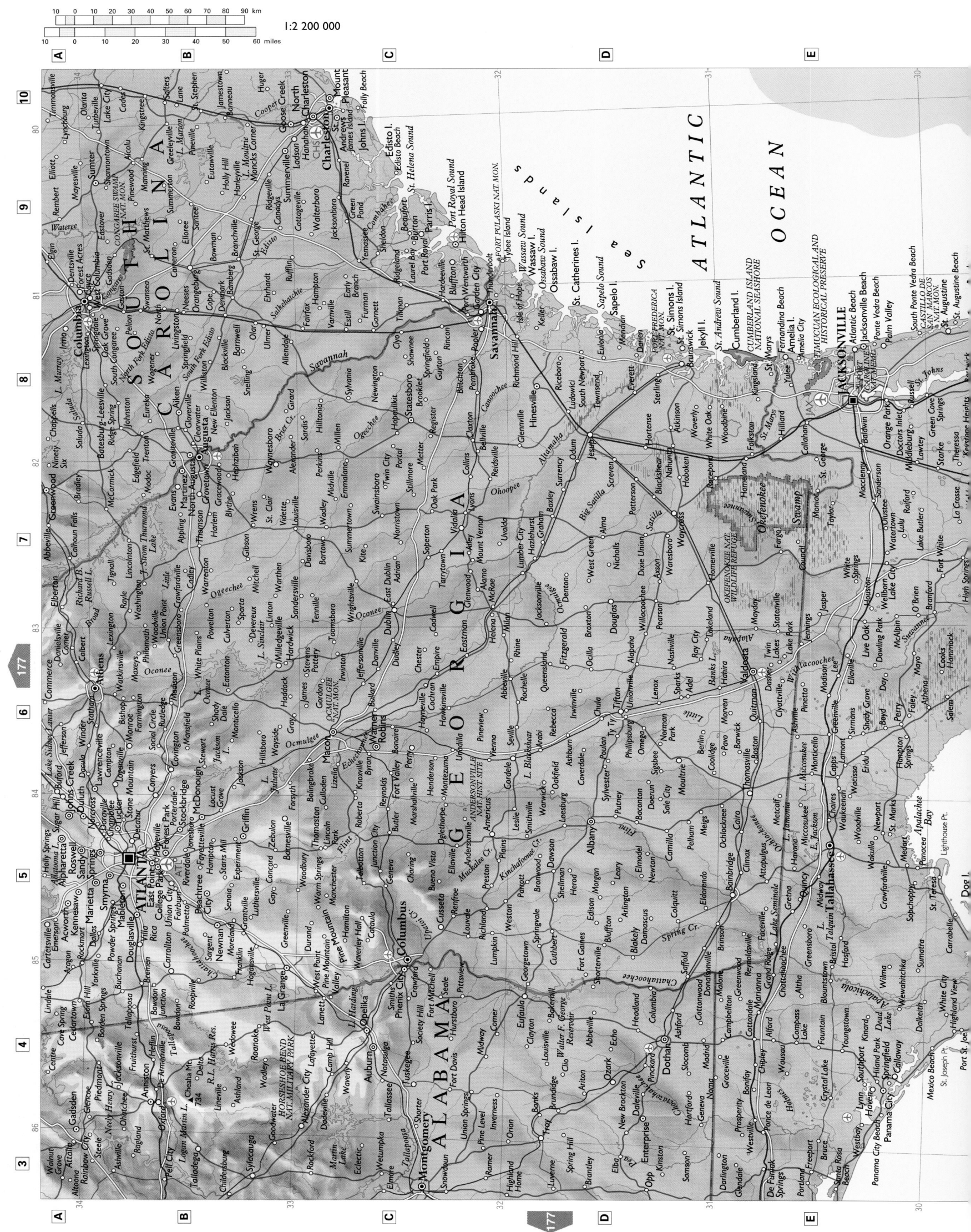

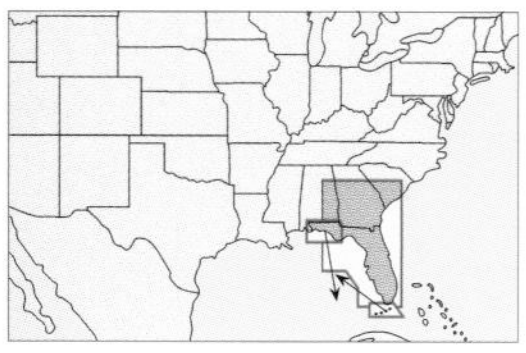

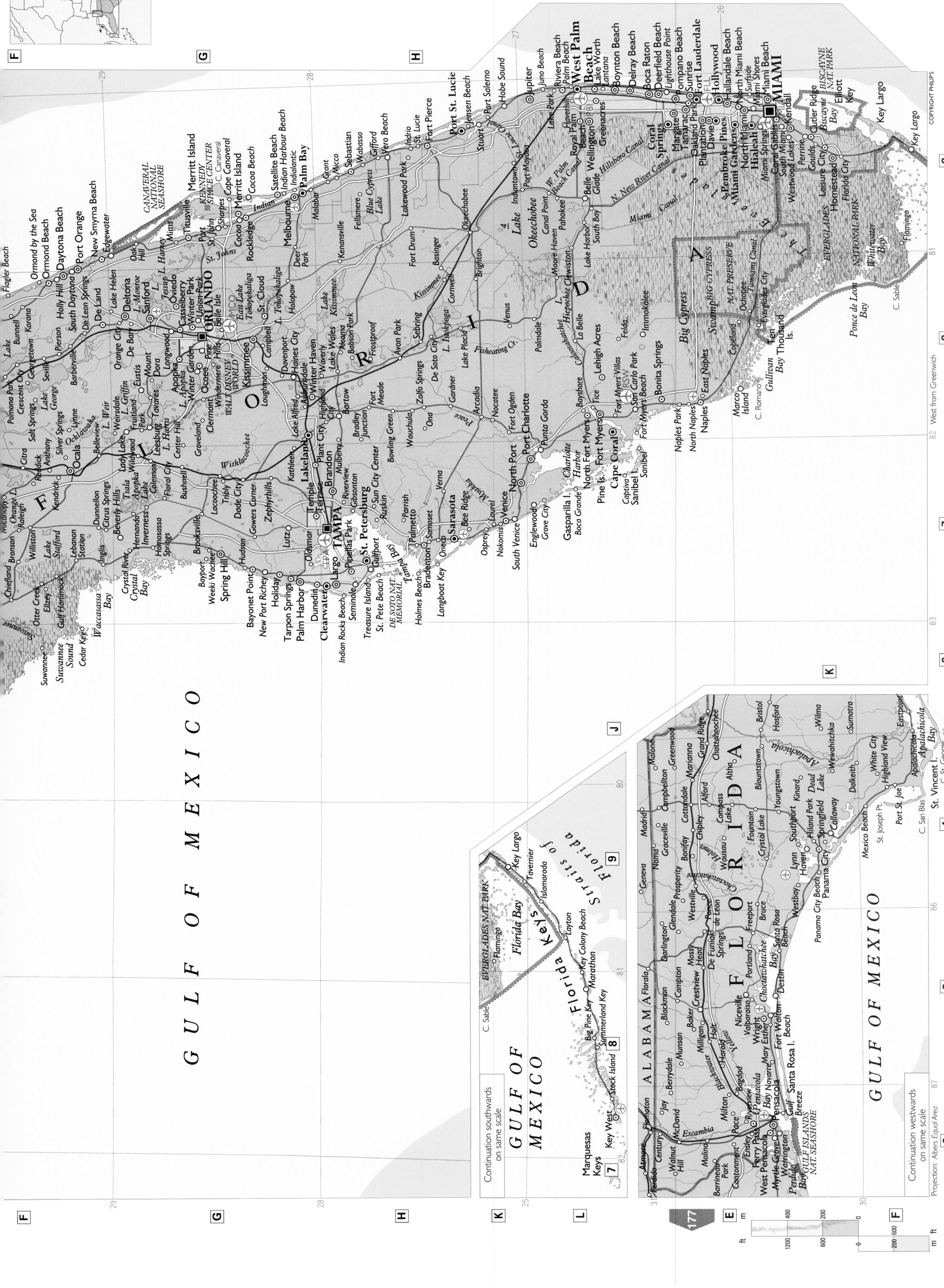

GULF OF MEXICO

F L O R I D A

COPYRIGHT PHILIPS

West from Greenwich

Projection: Albers Equal Area

CANAVERAL NATIONAL SEASHORE

KENNEDY SPACE CENTER

WALT DISNEY WORLD

ORLANDO

TAMPA

St. Petersburg

Clearwater

MIAMI

West Palm Beach

Fort Lauderdale

Hollywood

EVERGLADES NATIONAL PARK

BIG CYPRESS NAT. PRESERVE

BISCAYNE NAT. PARK

DE SOTO NAT. MEMORIAL

Lake Okeechobee

Straits of Florida

Florida Keys

Florida Bay

Key West

Key Largo

Marquesas Keys

ALABAMA

GULF ISLANDS NAT. SEASHORE

Pensacola

Panama City

Apalachicola

Apalachicola Bay

Continuation southwards on same scale

Continuation westwards on same scale

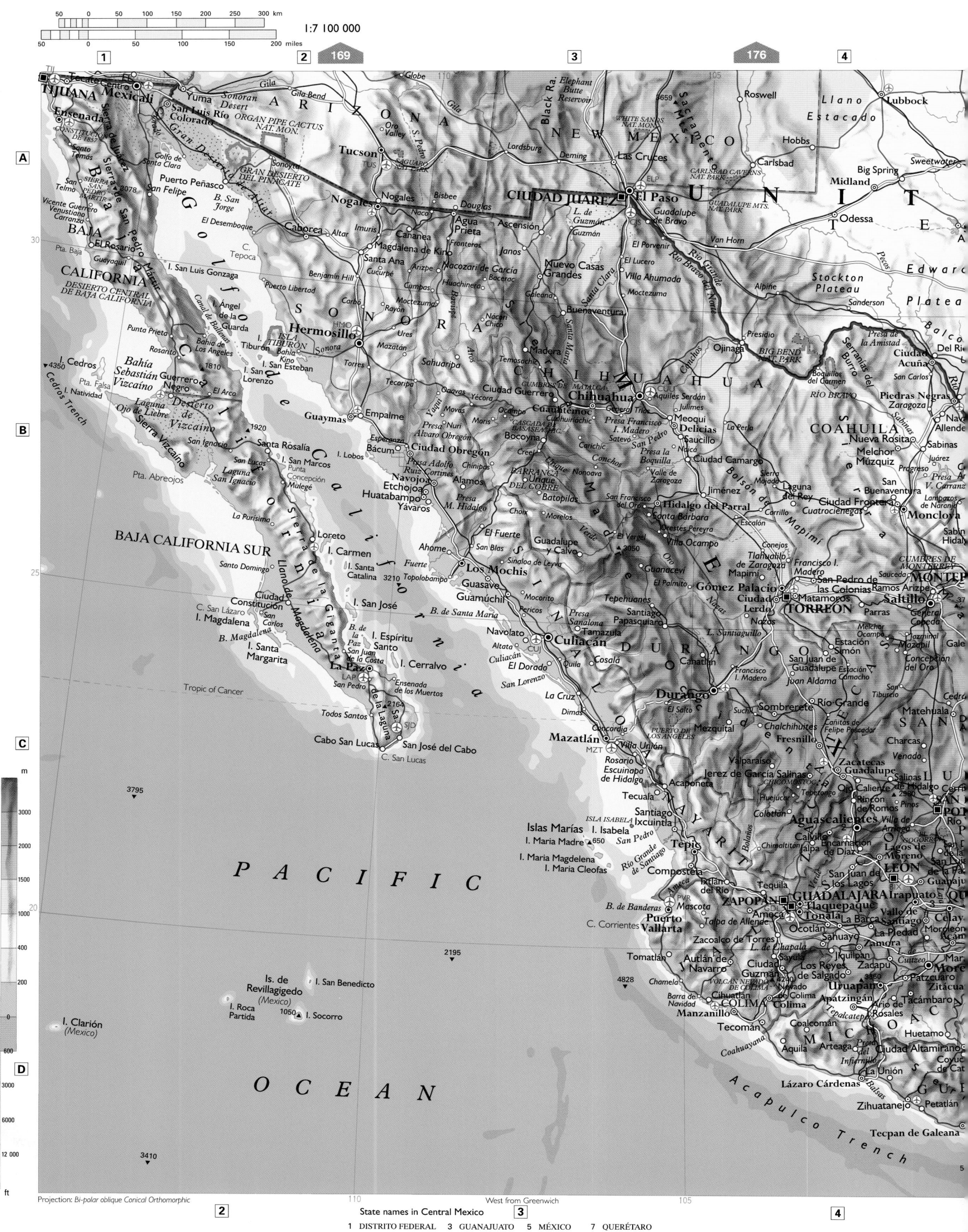

50 0 50 100 150 200 250 300 km
1:7 100 000
50 0 50 100 150 200 miles

169 176

ft   m
9000 3000
6000 2000
4500 1500
3000 1000
1200 400
600   200
0   0
200   600
1000 3000
2000 6000
4000 12 000
m   ft

Projection: Bi-polar oblique Conical Orthomorphic

West from Greenwich

State names in Central Mexico
1 DISTRITO FEDERAL   3 GUANAJUATO   5 MÉXICO   7 QUERÉTARO
2 AGUASCALIENTES   4 HIDALGO   6 MORELOS   8 TLAXCALA

COPYRIGHT PHILIP'S

1:7 10

50 0 50 100 150 200 250 300 km
0 50 100 150 200 miles

JAMAICA
1:2 700 000

10 0 10 20 30 40 50 km
10 0 10 20 30 miles

a

CARIBBEAN SEA

Montego Bay MBJ   Falmouth   Runaway Bay   St. Ann's Bay
Lucea   Ocho Rios   Galina Point
Negril   Wakefield   Port Maria
South Negril Pt.   Cambridge   Mount Denham   Moneague   Annotto Bay
Savanna-la-Mar   The Cockpit   985 ▲   Dry Harbour   Port Antonio
                   Country   Mountains
Maggotty   Don Figueueroa Mts.   Linstead   John Crow
Black River   Mandeville   Spanish   Blue Mountains   Mts.
             Santa Cruz   Town   2256 ▲ Blue Mountain
             Mts.   Peak
Great Pedro   May Pen   Portmore   Morant
Bluff   Alligator   Kingston   Point
             Pond   Port Morant
                     Portland   Morant
             Portland   Bight   Bay
             Point

1 I. Desterrada   **2**
I. Pérez
(Mexico)

B

Gulf of Mexico

Progreso   Dzilam   Rio Lagartos   C. Catoche
            de Bravo   El Cuyo   Isla Mujeres
MERIDA   Motul   Temax   Tizimín   Canal de Yucatán
DZIBILCHALTUN   Izamal   C. San Antonio
Maxcanú   YUCATAN   Espita   Cancún
CHICHEN   Puerto Morelos
Calkini   Sotuta   ITZA   Valladolid   Playa del Carmen
Tenabo   Ticul   MAYAPAN   Isla
Campeche   UXMAL   Peto   Cozumel
            Tekax   Cozumel
Champotón   Bolonchén   QUINTANA
            Hopelchén   ROO
Ciudad   Felipe Carrillo
del Carmen   San José Carpizo   Puerto   TULUM
I. de   MEXICO   Bacalar   B. de la Ascensión
Términos   Escárcega   SIAN KA'AN
PANTANOS   Chetumal   B. del Espíritu Santo
DE CENTLA   CAMPECHE   Orange Walk   B. de
Palizada   Balancán   CALAKMUL   Chetumal   Banco
            MIRADOR-RIO AZUL   Corozal   Chinchorro

Yucatan Basin

3 FLORIDA   L. Okeechobee   West Palm   West End   Little Abaco I.
Cape   U.S.A.   Beach   Boca   Free-   Grand   Hope Town
Coral   Fort Myers   Fort   Raton   port   Bahama   Abaco I.
A   Lauderdale   Northwest Providence Chan
Naples   The   FLL
         Everglades   Boca   Bimini Is.   Berry Is.
C. Romano   Hialeah   MIA   Nicolls   Nassau   New
EVERGLADES   MIAMI   Town   Eleuthera   Providence
NAT. PARK   Andros I.
C. Sable   Florida Bay   Andros   Exuma
Dry Tortugas   Key West   Island   Great
(U.S.A.)   Florida Keys   Guana Cay
              Straits of Florida   Cay Sal   Great
                                    Bank   Exum

LA HABANA   Guanabacoa   Santa Cruz del Norte   Canal Nicholas
(Havana)   Guanajay   Matanzas   Arch. de Sabana
Bahía Honda   San   Jovellanos   Sagua la Grande
La Esperanza   Antonio   Colón   Canal Viejo de Bahama
Pinar del Río   de los Baños   Batabanó   Santa   Caibarién   Arch. de
Guane   Jagüey   Clara   Placetas   Camagüey
San Luis   Pen. de   Grande   Morón   Cayo
La Fé   Zapata   CUBA   Romano
Nueva Gerona   Cienfuegos   Ciego   Nuevitas
Corrientes   I. de la   B. de   Trinidad   de Ávila   Puerto
             Juventud   Cochinos   Sancti Spíritus   Gibar
Arch. de los   Golfo de   Las Tunas
Canarreos   Júcaro   Santa Cruz   Holg
         Tunas   del Sur   Bayamo   Mto.
         de Zaza   Golfo de   Manzanillo
         Arch. de Jardines de la Reina   Guacanayabo   Sant
                                         DESEMBARCO   Sierra Maestra   de
                                         DEL GRANMA   Pico Turqu   1972

Cayman Islands   Cayman Brac
(U.K.)   Little Cayman
George Town   Montego   MBJ   St. Ann's Bay
Grand Cayman   Bay   Lucea   Falmouth   Port Maria
Misteriosa   7680   Negril   JAMAICA   Po
Bank   South Negril Pt.   Cambridge
Is. Santanilla   Savanna-la-Mar   Kingsto
(Swan Islands)   Black River   May   Spanish Town
(Honduras)   Mandeville   Pen
Rosalind   Pedro   Pedro Cays
Bank   Bank   (Jamaica)

Ciudad del Carmen   Banco   Chinchorro
Xenosique   Ambergris Cay
            San Pedro
Ocosingo   Uaxactún   Belize   Turneffe Is.
MIRADOR-RIO AZUL   City   Belize
SIERRA DE LACANDÓN   Belmopan   BELIZE   Barrier
Comitán de   San Ignacio   Middlesex   Reef
Dominguez   Flores   BLUE   Dangriga
MONTES   L. Petén Itzá   HOLE   Barrier
AZULES   CARACOL   Benque   Reef
LACANTÚN   TIKAL   Viejo   ▲1120
LAGUNA   San Luis   Maya Mts   Victoria Peak Reef
DE MONTE   San Antonio   Monkey River   Is. de
BELLO   Punta Gorda   Golfo de Honduras   la Bahía
L. de Izabal   Puerto   Roatán   Guanaja
GUATEMALA   RIO DULCE   Barrios   Utila   Roatán   Puerto
Culito   QUIRIGUA   Livingston   Castillo
3784 ▲   Puerto   C. Camarón
Cuchumatanes   Cortés   La Ceiba   Iriona
Vol. Tajumulco   Sierra de las Minas   Tela   Trujillo   Punta Patuca
4220   San Pedro   FIGO   Balfate
Huehuetenango   Sula   BONITO   Savá   Brus Laguna
Totonicapán   Zacapa   Choloma   Olanchito   Sico
Quezaltenango   Santa   El Progreso   Yoro   Auas   Laguna de Caratasca
María 3772   Barbara   Santa   SIERRA DE AGALTA   Puerto Lempira
Sololá   Chiquimula   Rosa   HONDURAS   C. Falso
Antigua   COPAN   de Copán   Juticalpa   C. Gracias a Dios
GUATEMALA   2849 ▲   Catacamas   Puerto Cabo
Jalapa   2730   Comayagua   Gracias á Dios
Amatitlán   La Esperanza   La Paz   Coco (Segovia)
Escuintla   El Jaral   TEGUCIGALPA   Leimus   Cayos Miskitos
San José   Yoro   Danlí   (Nicaragua)
Ahuachapán   Jocotán   Comayagua   Yuscarán   Pta. Gorda
Acajutla   Nacaome   Choluteca   Bonanza   Puerto Cabezas
Nueva San Salvador   Zacatecoluca   Catacamas   Rosita
SAN SALVADOR   San   Somoto   1963   Costa Isabela   I. de Providencia
EL   Miguel   Chinandega   Jalapa   SASLAYA   (Colombia)   Cayos Roncador
SALVADOR   La Unión   Estelí   Siuna   (Colombia)
G. de Fonseca   Corinto   Jinotega   Tuma   Tungla   San Andrés
         El Sauce   Matagalpa   San Pedro   I. de San Andrés
         1745   del Norte   (Colombia)
Chinandega   NICARAGUA   Muy Muy   La Barra
León   Managua   Boaco   Siquia   Cayos de
La Paz Centro   Tipitapa   Santo Domingo   Albuquerque
MANAGUA   Masaya   Juigalpa   Rama   (Colombia)
Diriamba   Granada   Bluefields   Punta de Perlas
Jinotepe   Lago de   Cord. de   Is. del
Rivas   Nicaragua   Yolaina   Maíz
San Juan del Sur   1610   Ometepe   El Bluff   (Nicaragua)
B. de Salinas   I. de   San Carlos   B. de
GUANACASTE   La Cruz   San Juan   San Juan
C. Santa Elena   Rincón de   Los   del Norte
SANTA ROSA   la Vieja   Chiles   San Juan del Norte
1196   COSTA
G. de Papagayo   Liberia   Volcán Irazú   TORTUGUERO
         G. de   3432   Volcán Poás
C. Velas   BALO   Cord.   2708   Isthmus
Santa Cruz   VERDE   Central   Siquirres   of   Panama
Nicoya   Alajuela   Limón
Carmona   SAN JOSÉ   Bribri   Mona
Puntarenas   Esparza   RICA   Bocas del   Changuinola   Pta.
Pen. de Nicoya   Cartago   Toro   Boquete   Manzanillo
C. Blanco   3875   Chiriquí   Nombre   Panama
Puerto   CORCOVADO   Buenos   Volcán   G. de los   de Dios   Canal
Quepos   Chirripó   Aires   Baru   Mosquitos   Portobelo   Colón
B. de   Ciudad   Volcán   Serranía de Tabasará   Balboa
Coronado   Cortés   Bajo   David   PANAMÁ
G. de Osa   San Vito   Boquete   La   Chorrera
Pen. de Osa   Golfito   Concepción   Penonomé   Chepo
G. Dulce   Remedios   Río Hato   Arch. de las
Puerto   Aguadulce   Perlas
Armuelles   Santiago   I. del
ISLA COIBA   Sona   Chitré   Rey   Golfo de Panamá
I. de Coiba   Pen. de   Las Tablas
Punta   Azuero   Pocrí   Pedasi
Mariato   Tonosí   CERRO HOYA   Jaqué

GUADELOUPE AND MARTINIQUE
1:1 800 000

10 0 10 20 30 40 50 60 km
10 0 10 20 30 40 miles

b
Pte. de la Grande Vigie
Port-Louis   Grande-
Petit-Canal   Terre
Ste-Rose   La   Le Moule   Désirade
Pointe-à-Pitre   Pointe des
Pointe-   Le Gosier   Châteaux
Noire   Ste-Anne   Îles de la
Basse-Terre   Petite Terre
Capesterre-
GUADELOUPE   Belle-Eau
Bouillante   (Fr.)   Îles de la
Soufrière   Marie-   Petite Terre
1467   Galante
Basse-   Trois-Rivières   St-Louis   204 ▲
Terre   Grand   Capesterre
Îles des Saintes   Bourg   Pte. des Basses

c
Cap St-Martin   Basse-Pointe
Le Prêcheur   1463   Ste-Marie
St-Pierre   Montagne   Presqu'île de
         Pelée   la Caravelle
         1397   La Trinité
Le Robert
Schœlcher   Le François
Fort-de-France   Le Lamentin   St-Esprit
EDF   Rivière-Salée   Le Marin
MARTINIQUE   Rivière-   Pte. d'Enfer
(Fr.)   Pilote

PACIFIC OCEAN

Guatemala Trench

Guadeloupe Trench

Cayman Trench

CARIBBEAN

CARI

C
D
E

4
3
2
1

PUERTO RICO **d**
1:2 700 000

VIRGIN ISLANDS **e**
1:1 800 000

ST. LUCIA **f**
1:890 000

BARBADOS **g**
1:890 000

ATLANTIC OCEAN

PUERTO RICO (U.S.A.)

Aguadilla Isabela Barceloneta SAN JUAN
Arecibo Manatí Vega Río Grande
San Sebastián Utuado Baja Bayamón Carolina Dewey
Mayagüez Adjuntas Cordillera Central Caguas Sierra de Fajardo Culebra
San German Cerro Luquillo Pta. Vieques
Yauco 1338 de Punta Cayey Humacao Puerca
San German Uroyan Mts. de Coamo Esperanza
Guánica Ponce Yabucoa
Pta. Aguila Guayama
Guánica I. Caja de Muertos

Virgin Islands (U.K.)

Virgin Is. (U.S.A.)
Jost Van Dyke I. Guana I. Great Camanoe Anegada The Settlement East Pt.
Hans Tortola 521 Virgin Gorda
Lollik I. Road Town Spanish Town
Charlotte Amalie Cruz Bay St. St. John I. Peter I.
Thomas I.

ST. LUCIA
Cap Point Pte. Hardy
Gros Islet Esperance Bay
Castries Marquis
Girard
Anse la Raye Millet Dennery
Canaries
Soufrière Mt. Gimie Trou Gras Pt.
Soufrière 750 950
Bay Petit Piton Micoud
Gros Piton Pt. 796 Vierge Pt.
Choiseul Gros Piton
Laborie Vieux Fort
C. Moule à Chique

BARBADOS
Crab Hill North Point
Spring Hall
Fustic Boscobelle
Portland 245 Belleplaine
Speightstown BARBADOS
Westmoreland Bathsheba Hillcrest
Alleynes Bay 840 Martin's Bay
Holetown Mt. Hillaby
Black Rock Bridgefield Massiah
Jackson Street Ragged Pt.
Bridgetown Ellerton Ivy Edey Six Cross Roads
Carlisle Bay Oistins The Crane
Worthing Bay St. Martins
Oistins Chancery Lane
South Point BGI

ATLANTIC OCEAN

ATLANTIC OCEAN

BAHAMAS

Nassau's Town
New Bight
Cat I.
Salvador I.
Conception I.
Rum Cay
Long I.
Clarence Town Samana Cay
Crooked I. Passage Crooked I.
Albert Town Plana Cays
Snug Corner Mayaguana I.
Acklins I. Mayaguana Passage
Mira por vos Cay Caicos Passage
Hogsty Reef Turks & Caicos Is. (U.K.)
Little Inagua I. Caicos Is.
Lake Rose Cockburn Town
INAGUA Turks Is.
Great Inagua I. Turks Island Passage
Matthew Town Mouchoir Bank
Silver Bank Passage
Silver Bank
Navidad Bank

ATLANTIC OCEAN

HAITI
Cap-Haïtien Monte Cristi LA ISABELA Santiago de los Caballeros
Port-de-Paix Puerto Plata
Fort Liberté San Francisco de Macorís Milwaukee Deep 8605
Î. de la Tortue La Vega Nagua Samana
Jean Rabel Gonaïves Hinche Cord. San José de Ocoa Sánchez
Cap-à-Foux St-Marc Cent. Pico Duarte Sabana de la Mar
Jérémie 3175 HAITÍ Hato Mayor
Dame G. de la Gonâve 2680 Higüey C. Engaño
PORT-AU-PRINCE San Juan San Pedro de Macorís
Î. de la Gonâve L. Enriquillo -40
Les Cayes Petit Goâve SANTO DOMINGO
Aquin Jacmel Azua La Romana
Î. à Vache Pedernales Barahona San Cristóbal I. Saona
Pointe-à-Gravois I. Beata C. Beata Isla Mona (U.S.A.)

DOMINICAN REP.

Puerto Rico Trench

Hispaniola

Antilles

CARIBBEAN SEA
Venezuelan Basin
Muertas Trough
5500
4530
Beata Ridge
COLOMBIAN BASIN
5420

Lesser Antilles

PUERTO RICO (U.S.A.)
Aguadilla Arecibo Bayamón SAN JUAN Carolina
Mayagüez Ponce Caguas Fajardo Virgin Gorda
Vieques Charlotte Amalie Virgin Is. (U.K.)
Guayama Virgin Is. (U.S.A.) Anegada
St. Thomas Sombrero (U.K.)
Christiansted Anguilla (U.K.)
St. Croix (U.S.A.) St. Eustatius St.-Martin (Fr.)
Frederiksted St. Kitts Saba (Neth.) St.-Barthélemy (Fr.)
Basseterre & Nevis St. Maarten (Neth.)
Redonda Nevis 1156 Barbuda
Montserrat Soufrière ANTIGUA & BARBUDA
(U.K.) 914 Hills St. John's Antigua
Ste-Rose Guadeloupe Passage Le Moule
GUADELOUPE 1467 Pointe-à-Pitre La Désirade
(Fr.) Basse-Terre Marie-Galante (Fr.)
I. des Saintes Grand-Bourg
(Fr.) Dominica Passage
Portsmouth 1447 DOMINICA
Morne Diablotin Roseau MORNE TROIS PITONS
Martinique Passage
Mt. Pelée Ste-Marie
1397 Le Robert
Fort-de- Rivière-Pilote
France FDF MARTINIQUE
St. Lucia Channel (Fr.)
Castries 950 ST. LUCIA
Soufrière UVF
St. Vincent Passage
Soufrière 1234 St. Vincent Speightstown
SVD 340 BGI
Kingstown Bridgetown
Bequia BARBADOS
Tobago
Canouan ST. VINCENT & THE GRENADINES
Carriacou The Grenadines Basin
840 GRENADA
St. George's GND

Leeward Islands

Anegada Passage

Windward Islands

Aves Ridge

Grenada Basin

ABC Islands
Oranjestad Curaçao Bonaire
Aruba (Neth.) Willemstad
AUA CUR
C. San Román ARC. LOS ROQUES
Pta. Gallinas Is. Las Aves (Ven.) I. Orchila (Ven.)
GUAJIRA Is. Los Roques (Ven.)
MACUIRA I. Blanquilla (Ven.)
Pen. de la Guajira Is. Los Hermanos (Ven.)
Pta. Espada I. La Tortuga (Ven.) Is. Los Testigos (Ven.)
Uribia NUEVA ESPARTA
COLOMBIA Pen. de Paraguaná I. de Margarita
Maicao Punto Fijo CERRO EL COPEY 920 Tobago
Ríohacha Punta Cardón La Asunción Scarborough
Santa Marta Golfo de Venezuela Porlamar Port of Spain
TAYRONA MÉDANOS DE CORO C. Codera Galera Point
Ciénaga Coro Puerto Cumarebo Pen. de Paria Trinidad
SOLEDAD La Vela Cumaná Carúpano Güiria Arima Río Claro
SA. NEVADA DE SANTA MARTA FALCON Carúpano POS TRINIDAD & TOBAGO
BARRANQUILLA Mene de Mauroa MARACAY Puerto Río Caribe SUCRE San Fernando
Fundación LARA Altagracia CARACAS La Cruz Caripito Serpent's Mouth
Calamar CERRO Vargas Río Chico MOCHIMA
Plato Barquisimeto Petare Barcelona Maturín
MAGDALENA SARACHICHE Los Teques 2640 MONAGAS
Zambrano MARACAIBO Valencia 2640 Caripe
CÉSAR Cabimas Villa de Cura Altagracia MARIUSA
Mompós Ciudad Ojeda VALENCIA San Juan de los Morros de Orituco DELTA
ZULIA Lago de Yaritagua Aragua de Tucupita
Magangué Maracaibo YURUBÍ Barcelona
El Banco TRUJILLO Acarigua Cantaura
Mene Grande El Sombrero Anaco
SIERRA DE PERIJÁ Betijoque Calabozo El Tigre
Majagual Trujillo PORTUGUESA Valle de
Valencia Valera COJEDES la Pascua AMACURO
El Banco San Carlos GUÁRICO Pariaguán
NORTE del Zulia ANZOÁTEGUI
SANTANDER MÉRIDA Santa María de Ipire
Machiques Guanare El Baúl
CATATUMBO-BARÍ MÉRIDA Calamar Ciudad Guayana
MÉRIDA SIERRA NEVADA Libertad El Pao
Ocaña Pico Bolívar Barinas Soledad
4981 BARINAS San Fernando Ciudad Bolívar
San Carlos Ciudad de Nutrias de Apure Sierra Imataca
Bolivia San Fernando SUCRE Los Barrancos
Cúcuta TÁCHIRA VENEZUELA Upata
Santa Barbara Apure El Callao
Achaguas Caicara Guasipati Tumeremo
Embalse de Guri
Orinoco

West from Greenwich

ft: 600 6000 12 000 18 000 24 000
m: 200 2000 4000 6000 8000
4000 3000 2000 1500 1000 600 400 200
12 000 9000 6000 4500 3000 1200 600

1:31 100 000

Projection: Lambert's Azimuthal Equal Area

COPYRIGHT PHILIP'S

1:31 100 000

100 0 200 400 600 800 1000 1200 1400 km
100 0 200 400 600 800 1000 miles

1   2   3   4   5   6   7

90   80   70   60   50   40

A

Tropic of Cancer

Havana
CUBA
BAHAMAS
Turks & Caicos Is.
(U.K.)

MEXICO
BELIZE
Cayman Is.
(U.K.)
HAITI
DOMINICAN REP.
Port-au-Prince
Santo Domingo
San Juan
PUERTO RICO
(U.S.A.)
Virgin Is. (U.S.A. - U.K.)
Anguilla (U.K.)
St. Martin (Fr. – Neth.)
ANTIGUA & BARBUDA
St. KITTS & NEVIS
Basse-Terre
GUADELOUPE (Fr.)

GUATEMALA
HONDURAS
Tegucigalpa
JAMAICA
Kingston
Caribbean Sea
DOMINICA
Fort-de-France
MARTINIQUE (Fr.)
B
ATLANTIC
OCEAN

Guatemala
San Salvador
EL SALVADOR
NICARAGUA
Managua
Castries
St. LUCIA
St. VINCENT
Kingstown
GRENADA
St. George's
BARBADOS
Bridgetown

COSTA RICA
San José
Panamá
PANAMA
ARUBA (Neth.)
Oranjestad
CURAÇAO (Neth.)
Willemstad
Port of Spain
TRINIDAD & TOBAGO

Barranquilla
Cartagena
Maracaibo
Caracas
Valencia
G. of Darién
Barquisimeto

I. del Coco
(Costa Rica)
Gulf of Panama
Cúcuta
San Cristóbal
Orinoco
Ciudad Guayana
10

Medellín
Bucaramanga
VENEZUELA
Georgetown
Paramaribo

I. de Malpelo
(Colombia)
Cali
BOGOTÁ
GUYANA
SURINAME
Cayenne
C. Orange
FRENCH GUIANA
C

COLOMBIA
Boa Vista
RORAIMA
Essequibo
Branco

Galapagos Is.
(Ecuador)
Quito
AMAPÁ
Macapá
Equator

ECUADOR
Guayaquil
G. of Guayaquil
Napo
Putumayo
Japurá
Amazon
Marajó I.
Belém
São Luís
Fortaleza

Iquitos
Marañón
Amazon
Manaus
Santarém

AMAZONAS
MARANHÃO
Teresina
CEARÁ
RIO G. DO NORTE
Natal

Chiclayo
Juruá
Purus
Madeira
Tapajós
Xingu
Imperatriz
PIAUÍ
Campina Grande
PARAÍBA
João Pessoa

Trujillo
Pôrto Velho
Parnaíba
PERNAMBUCO
Recife
D
Chimbote
ACRE
Rio Branco
RONDÔNIA
PARÁ
Palmas
TOCANTINS
ALAGOAS
Maceió
SERGIPE
Aracaju

PERU
Madre de Dios
Tocantins
Araguaia
BRAZIL
MATO GROSSO
São Francisco
BAHÍA
Salvador

Callao
LIMA
Cusco
Mamoré
Cuiabá
GOIÁS
DIS. FED.
Brasília

L. Titicaca
La Paz
BOLIVIA
Santa Cruz
Goiânia
MINAS GERAIS
E

Arequipa
Cochabamba
Sucre
MATO GROSSO DO SUL
Paraguay
Campo Grande
BELO HORIZONTE
Ribeirão Prêto
Juiz de Fora
ESPÍRITO SANTO
Vitória

Iquique
SÃO PAULO
Campinas
R. DE J.
Campos

PACIFIC
Antofagasta
PARAGUAY
Paraná
SÃO PAULO
RIO DE JANEIRO
Niterói
Santos

Salta
Pilcomayo
Asunción
PARANÁ
Curitiba
SANTA CATARINA

San Félix
(Chile)
San Ambroso
(Chile)
San Miguel de Tucumán
Resistencia
Corrientes
Uruguay
Florianópolis
F

OCEAN
Arch. de Juan Fernández
(Chile)
Robinson Crusoe
Córdoba
San Juan
Santa Fé
Paraná
RIO GRANDE DO SUL
Pôrto Alegre

Viña del Mar
Valparaíso
SANTIAGO
Mendoza
Rosario
URUGUAY
Pelotas

Talca
ARGENTINA
Buenos Aires
Montevideo

Concepción
La Plata
Río de la Plata
Mar del Plata

Neuquén
Bahía Blanca
G
Valdivia
Colorado
Negro
Viedma

Puerto Montt
Chubut
ATLANTIC
OCEAN

Comodoro Rivadavia
Gulf of San Jorge

Gulf of Penas
West Falkland
FALKLAND IS.
(U.K.)
Stanley
East Falkland
H

Punta Arenas
Magellan's Str.
Tierra del Fuego
C. Horn
South Georgia
(U.K.)

Projection: Lambert's Azimuthal Equal Area

COPYRIGHT PHILIP'S

90   80   70   60 West from Greenwich 50   40   30

1   2   3   4   5   6   7

■ LIMA   Capital Cities

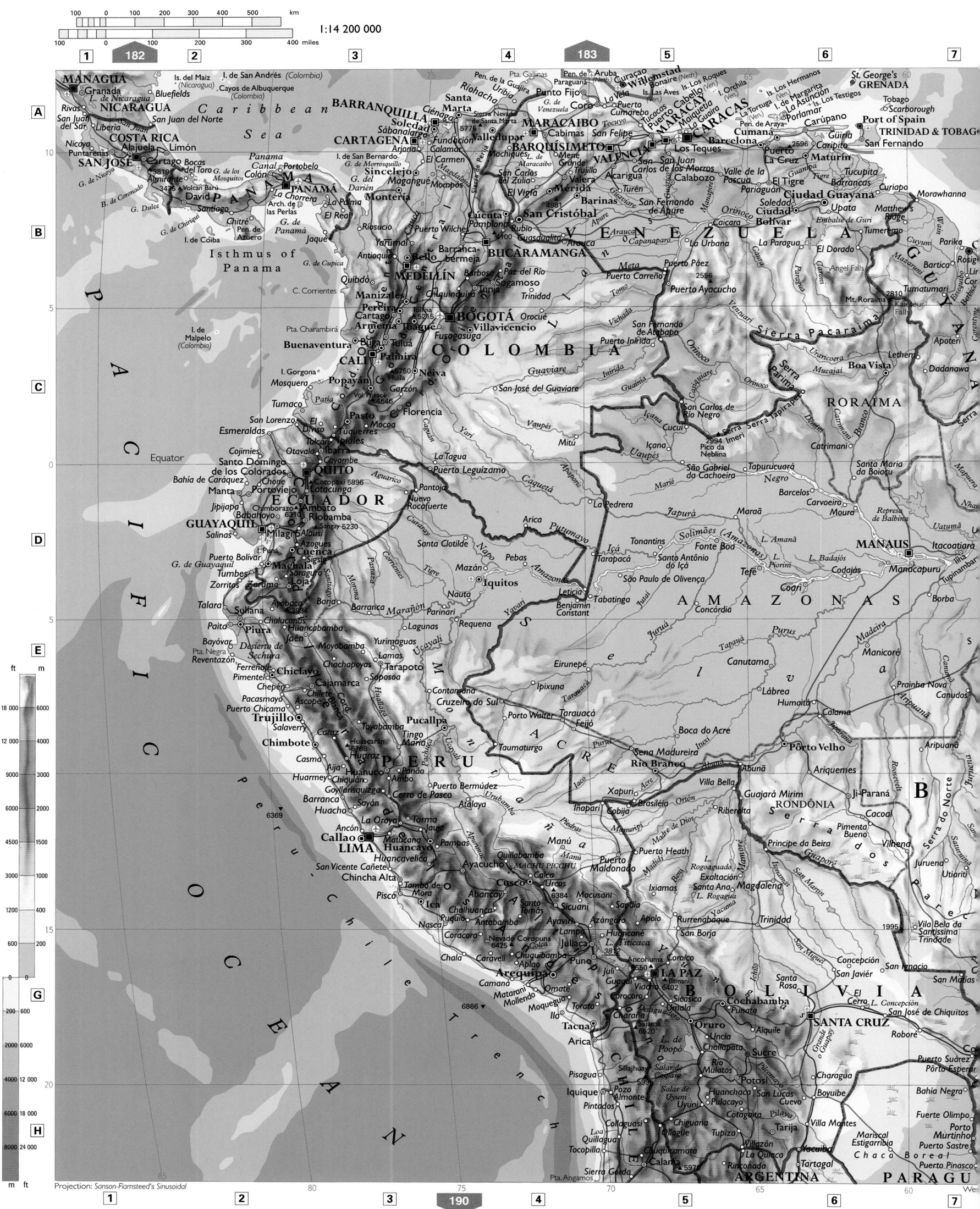

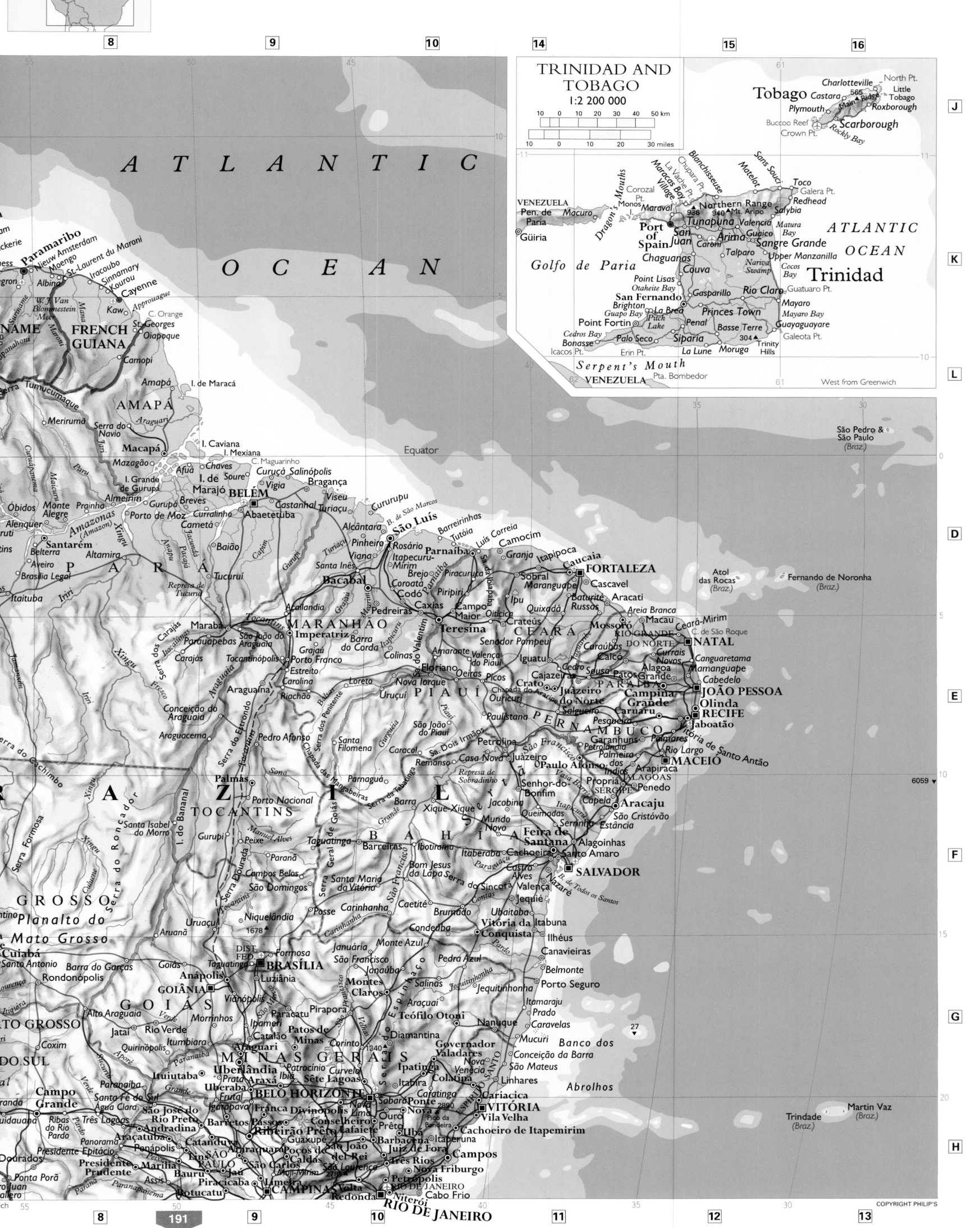

ATLANTIC

OCEAN

TRINIDAD AND TOBAGO
1:2 200 000

10 0 10 20 30 40 50 km
10 0 10 20 30 miles

Tobago
North Pt.
Charlotteville Castara 565 Little
Plymouth Main Ridge Tobago
Buccoo Reef Scarborough Roxborough
Crown Pt. Rockly Bay

Toco
Galera Pt.
Redhead
Salybia

ATLANTIC
OCEAN

VENEZUELA
Pen. de Paria
Maruro Güiria

Corozal Pt.
Monos I. Maraval
Port of Spain San Juan
Chaguanas
Couva

Blanchisseuse
La Vache Pt. Chupara Pt.
Marecas Bay Sans Souci
Maracas Bay Matelot
Northern Range
938 940 ▲Mt. Aripo
Tunapuna Valencia
Arima Guaico
Caroni Talparo Sangre Grande
Upper Manzanilla

Matura Bay

Point Lisas
Otaheite Bay Gasparillo Rio Claro
San Fernando
Brighton La Brea Penal Basse Terre
Guapo Bay Pitch 304 ▲
Point Fortin Lake
Cedros Bay Palo Seco Siparia La Lune Moruga

Nariva Swamp
Cocos Bay
Trinidad

Mayaro
Mayaro Bay
Guatuaro Pt.
Guayaguayare
Galeota Pt.

Golfo de Paria

Princes Town

Trinity Hills

Bonasse
Icacos Pt. Erin Pt. Pta. Bombedor
VENEZUELA

Serpent's Mouth

West from Greenwich

FRENCH GUIANA

Paramaribo
Nieuw Amsterdam
Moengo
St-Laurent du Maroni Iracoubo
Sinnamary
Albina Kourou
Cayenne
Kaw Approuague
C. Orange
St-Georges Oiapoque
Camopi

W. J. Van Blommestein Meer

SURINAME

AMAPÁ
Serra do Navio
Merirumã Araguari
Macapá Amapá
Mazagão I. de Maracá
I. Caviana
Afuá I. Mexiana
C. Maguarinho
I. Grande de Gurupá Chaves Salinópolis Curuçá
Almeirim I. de Soure Bragança
Porto de Moz Marajó Vigia
Monte Alegre Breves **BELÉM** Viseu
Prainha Curralinho Castanhal Turiaçu Cururupu
Óbidos Cametá Abaetetuba B. de São Marcos
Alenquer Gurupá **São Luís**
Santarém Baião Barreirinhas
Belterra Alcântara Pinheira Rosário Tutóia
Aveiro Capim Viana Parnaíba Luís Correia
Altamira Itapecuru- Camocim
Brasília Legal Mirim
Itaituba Tucuruí **Bacabal** Brejo Piracuruca Granja Itapipoca Caucaia
Represa de Codó Piripiri **FORTALEZA**
Tucuruí Caxias Campo Oiticica
Maior Sobral Cascavel
PARÁ Maranguape
Santa Inês Coroatá Ipu Baturité Aracati
Marabá Pedreiras Russas
Serra dos Carajás **MARANHÃO** Teresina **CEARÁ** Macau
São João do Senador Pompeu Caraúbas Ceará-Mirim
Parauapebas Araguaia **Imperatriz** Barra do Corda Amarante Mossoró C. de São Roque
Carajás Grajaú Crateús **RIO GRANDE** **NATAL**
Tocantinópolis Porto Franco Colinas Valença Iguatu DO NORTE Currais
do Piauí Cajazeiras Cedro Novos Canguaretama
Conceição do Estreito Floriano Picos Crato Sousa Mamanguape
Araguaia Carolina Loreto Oeiras Patos Cabedelo
Araguaína Riachão Juàzeiro **JOÃO PESSOA**
Araguacema Uruçuí **PIAUÍ** Paulistana do Norte Campina Olinda
São João Salgueiro Grande **RECIFE**
do Piauí Chapada do A. Caruaru Jaboatão
Pedro Afonso Santa Pesqueira
Filomena **PERNAMBUCO** Garanhuns
Palmas Caracol Remanso Petrolina Vitória de Santo Antão
Porto Nacional Parnaguá Casa Nova Juàzeiro Paulo Afonso Palmeira Rio Largo
TOCANTINS Senhor do Indios Arapiraca **MACEIÓ**
Xique-Xique Bonfim Propriá **ALAGOAS** Penedo
Taguatinga Barra Mundo Queimadas Capela SERGIPE
Novo **Aracaju**
Peixe Jacobina Serrinho São Cristóvão
Gurupi Paraná **BAHIA** Feira de Estância
Santa Maria Barreiras **Santana** Alagoinhas
Campos Belos da Vitória Itaberaba Cachoeira Santo Amaro
São Domingos Ibotitama **SALVADOR**
Caetité Castro Valença B. de Todos os Santos
Posse Carinhanha Alves Nazaré
Niquelândia Bom Jesus Jequié
Uruaçu da Lápa Serra do Sincorá
Aruanã Carinhanha Condeúba **Vitória da** Ilhéus
Formosa Brumado Ubaitaba
Goiás Januária **Conquista** Itabuna
DIST. Taguatinga São Francisco Pedra Azul Canavieiras
FED. **BRASÍLIA** Montes Salinas Belmonte
Anápolis Luziânia Claros Araçuaí Porto Seguro
GOIÂNIA Vianópolis Pirapora Jequitinhonha Itamaraju
Mornhinos Paracatu Teófilo Otoni Prado
GOIÁS Diamantina Nanuque Caravelas
Alto Araguaia Ipameri Patos de Governador Abrolhos
Jataí Catalão Minas Valadares Nova
Rio Verde Araguari Itabira Ipatinga Venécia São Mateus
Quirinópolis Itumbiara **MINAS GERAIS** Conceição da Barra
Uberlândia Curvelo Colatina
Uberaba Prata Sete Lagoas Itapira Cariacica
Frutal Araxá Sabará Ponte **VITÓRIA**
Franca **BELO HORIZONTE** Ouro Nova **Vila Velha**
Barretos Divinópolis Prêto Cachoeiro de Itapemirim
Ribeirão Prêto Conselheiro Ilha
São José Lafaiete Barbacena Itaperuna Campos
Andradina do Rio Prêto Poços de São João Juiz de Fora
Araçatuba Caldas del Rei Três Rios
Penápolis Amparo Mogi-Mirim Nova Friburgo
Presidente Jundiaí Petrópolis Cabo Frio
Prudente Marília Bauru Jaú **RIO DE JANEIRO**
Assis Piracicaba **CAMPINAS** Niterói
Botucatu Volta Redonda

BRAZIL

Serra do Cachimbo
Planalto do Mato Grosso
Serra Formosa
Serra do Roncador
I. do Bananal
Serra Dourada
Serra Geral de Goiás
Chapada das Mangabeiras
Represa de Sobradinho
Serra da Tabatinga

MATO GROSSO

MATO GROSSO DO SUL
Campo Grande
Coxim
Dourados
Ponta Porã
Presidente Epitácio

GOIÁS

ESPÍRITO SANTO

São Pedro & São Paulo (Braz.)

Fernando de Noronha (Braz.)

Atol das Rocas (Braz.)

6059 ▼

Banco dos Abrolhos

Martin Vaz (Braz.)
Trindade (Braz.)

27 ▼

COPYRIGHT PHILIP'S

Equator

50 0 50 100 150 200 250 300 km
50 0 50 100 150 200 miles

1:7 100 000

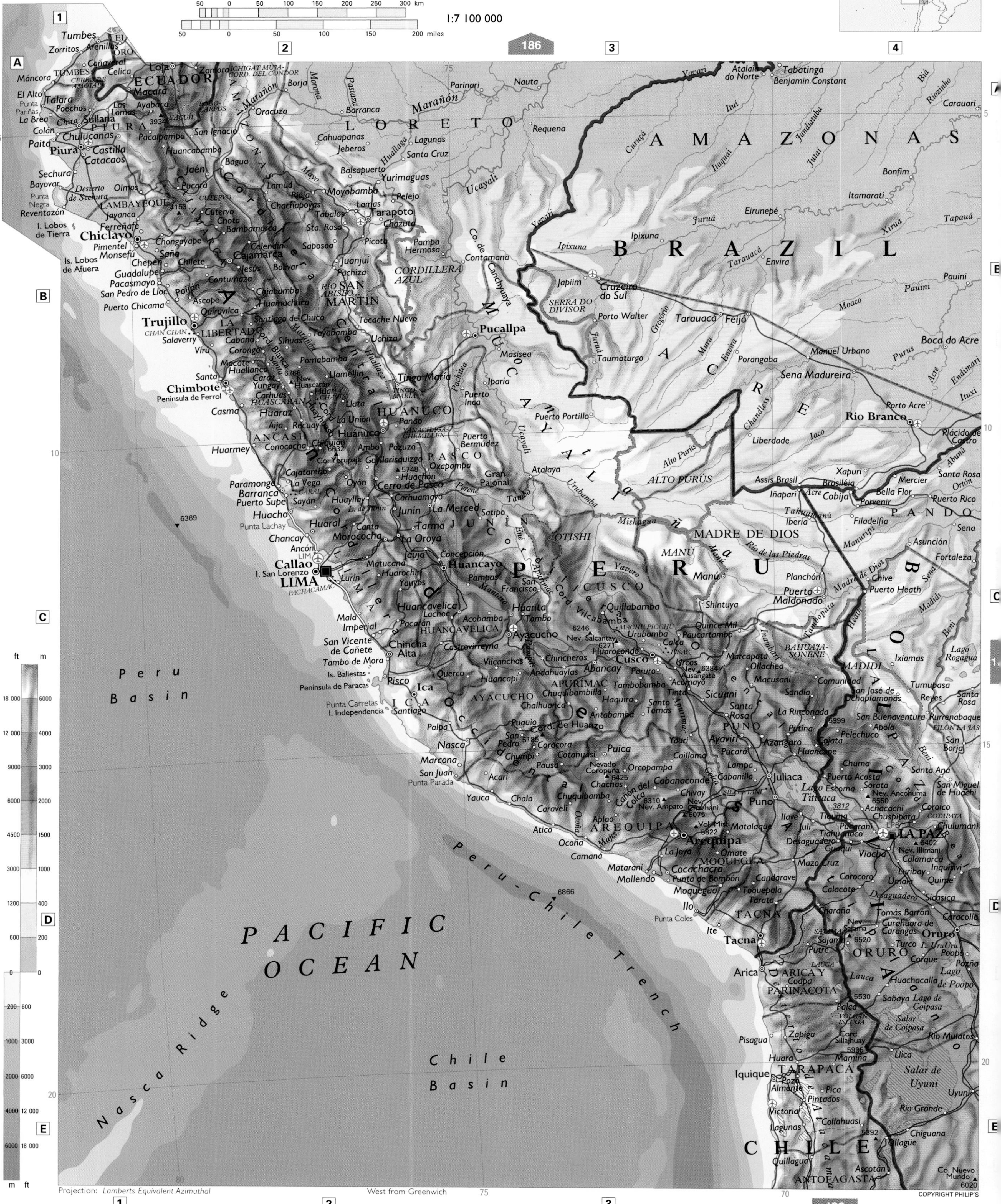

186

190

PACIFIC OCEAN

Peru Basin

Chile Basin

Nasca Ridge

Peru-Chile Trench

AMAZONAS

BRAZIL

PERU

BOLIVIA

CHILE

ECUADOR

LORETO

SAN MARTIN

CORDILLERA AZUL

HUANUCO

PASCO

JUNIN

LIMA

ICA

AYACUCHO

HUANCAVELICA

APURIMAC

CUSCO

MADRE DE DIOS

PUNO

AREQUIPA

MOQUEGUA

TACNA

TARAPACA

ORURO

ANCASH

LA LIBERTAD

LAMBAYEQUE

PIURA

TUMBES

EL ORO

ACRE

PANDO

LA PAZ

Lima
Callao
Trujillo
Chiclayo
Chimbote
Piura
Pucallpa
Cusco
Arequipa
Tacna
La Paz
Rio Branco

Tumbes
Zorritos
Talara
Paita
Sechura
Olmos
Cajamarca
Huancayo
Huánuco
Huaraz
Ica
Nasca
Juliaca
Puno
Oruro
Iquique
Antofagasta

Lago Titicaca

Lago de Poopó

Salar de Uyuni

Salar de Coipasa

Projection: Lamberts Equivalent Azimuthal

West from Greenwich

COPYRIGHT PHILIP'S

ft   m
18 000 6000
12 000 4000
9000   3000
6000   2000
4500   1500
3000   1000
1200   400
600   200
0   0
200   600
1000   3000
2000   6000
4000   12 000
6000   18 000
m   ft

187

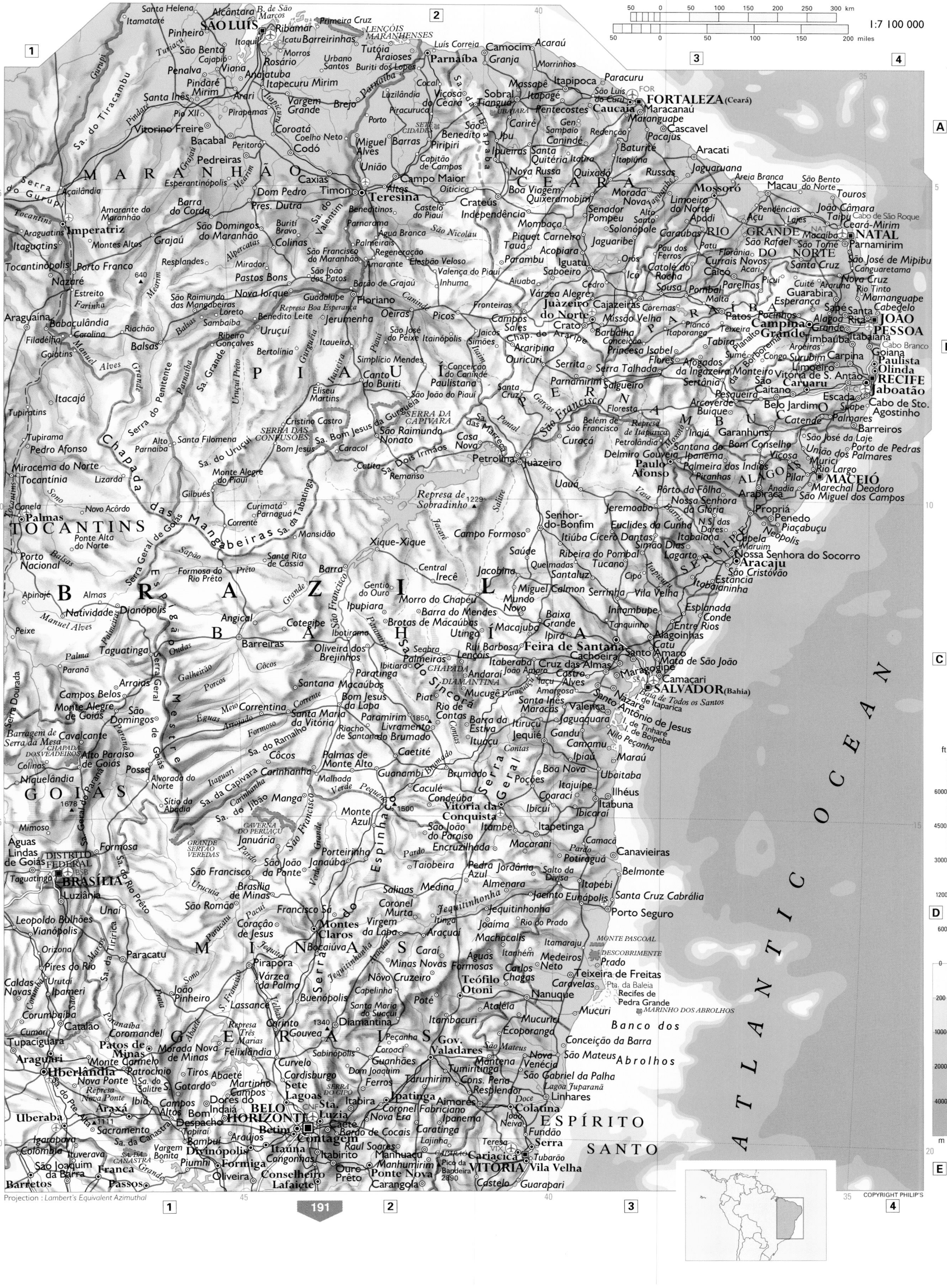

191

1:7 100 000

50 0 50 100 150 200 250 300 km
50 0 50 100 150 200 miles

Projection : Lambert's Equivalent Azimuthal

COPYRIGHT PHILIP'S

MARANHÃO

PIAUÍ

CEARÁ

RIO GRANDE DO NORTE

PARAÍBA

PERNAMBUCO

ALAGOAS

SERGIPE

BAHIA

TOCANTINS

GOIÁS

MINAS GERAIS

ESPÍRITO SANTO

B R A Z I L

ATLANTIC OCEAN

SÃO LUÍS
FORTALEZA (Ceará)
NATAL
JOÃO PESSOA
RECIFE
MACEIÓ
ARACAJU
SALVADOR (Bahia)
TERESINA
IMPERATRIZ
BRASÍLIA
DISTRITO FEDERAL
BELO HORIZONTE
VITÓRIA
Feira de Santana
Vitória da Conquista

ft m
6000 2000
4500 1500
3000 1000
1200 400
600 200
0
200 600
1000 3000
2000 6000
4000 12 000
m ft

50 0 50 100 150 200 250 300 km
1:7 100 000
50 0 50 100 150 200 miles

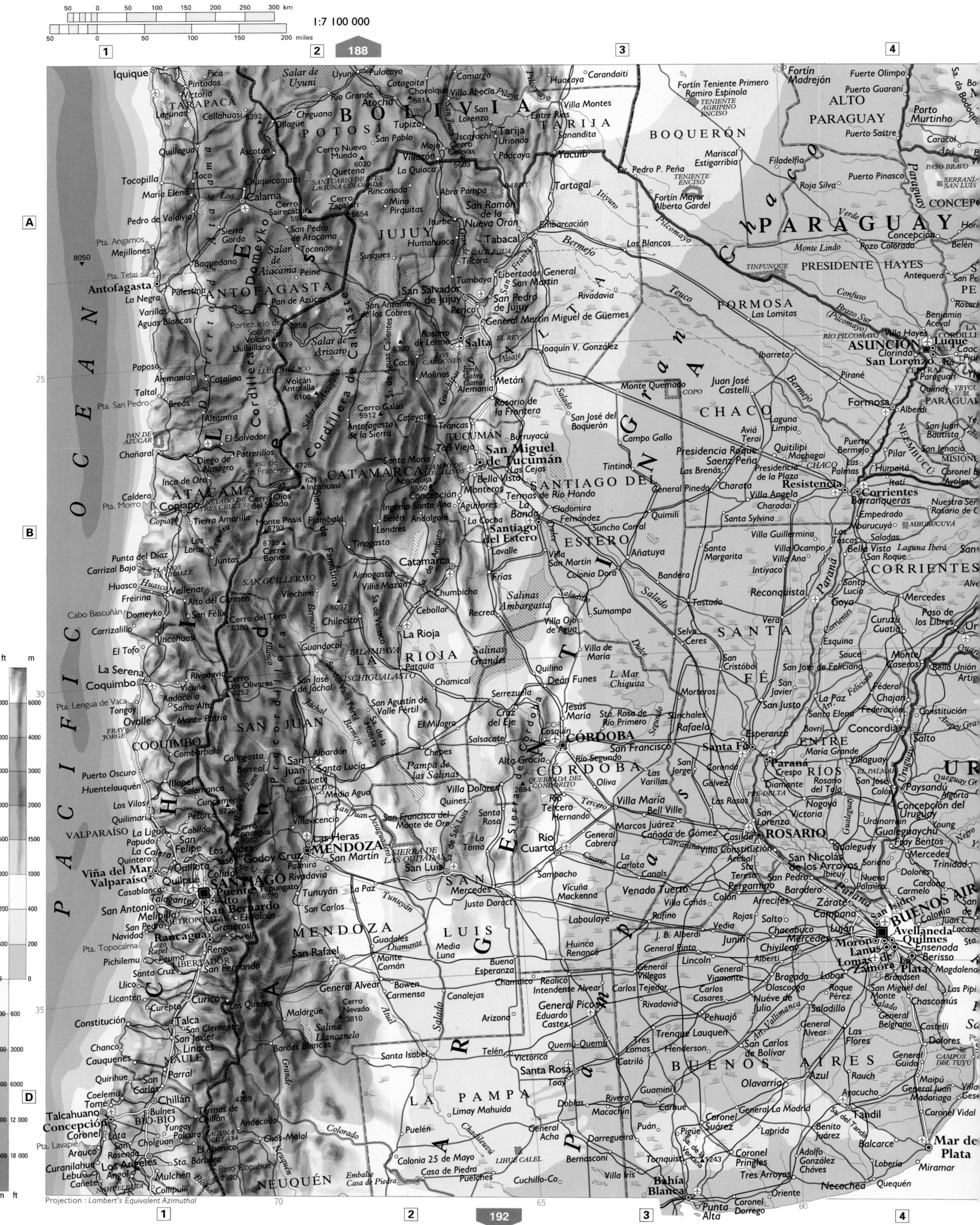

Projection : Lambert's Equivalent Azimuthal

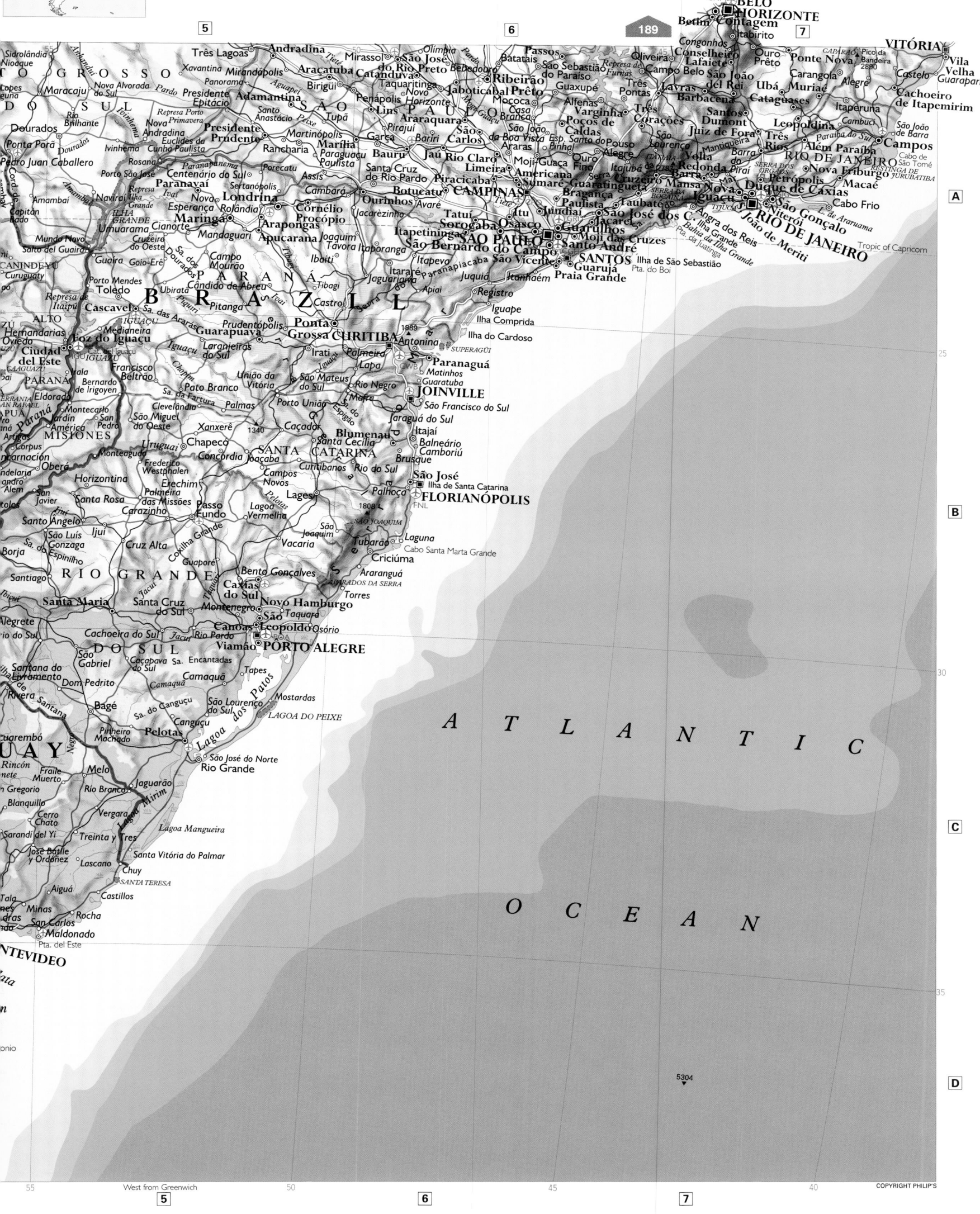

MATO GROSSO DO SUL

Três Lagoas
Andradina
Olímpia
São José do Rio Preto
Passos
Batatais
Oliveira
Conselheiro Lafaiete
Ouro Prêto
Ponte Nova
Pico da Bandeira 2880
VITÓRIA
Vila Velha

Sidrolândia
Nioaque
Xavantina
Mirandópolis
Panorama
Araçatuba
Catanduva
Ribeirão Prêto
São Sebastião do Paraíso
Campo Belo
São João del Rei
Ubá
Muriaé
Alegre
Castelo
Guarapari
Cachoeiro de Itapemirim

Maracaju
Presidente Epitácio
Adamantina
Birigüi
Penápolis
Novo Horizonte
Jaboticabal
Guaxupé
Mococa
Casa Branca
Santo Antonio do Pouso
Lavras
Barbacena
Cataguases
Itaperuna

Dourados
Nova Alvorada do Sul
Presidente Prudente
Nova Andradina
Euclides da Cunha Paulista
Rancharia
Marília
Tupã
Bauru
Garça
Bariri
São Carlos
Araraquara
São João da Boa Vista
Poços de Caldas
Varginha
Três Corações
Juiz de Fora
Leopoldina
Cambuci

Ponta Porã
Ivinhema
Martinópolis
Paraguaçu Paulista
Jaú
Rio Claro
Limeira
Americana
Itajubá
Pouso Alegre
São Lourenço
Além Paraíba
Campos
São João da Barra

Pedro Juan Caballero
Porto São José
Rosana
Paranapanema
Assis
Santa Cruz do Rio Pardo
Piracicaba
Sumaré
CAMPINAS
Bragança Paulista
São José dos C.
Volta Redonda
Petrópolis
Macaé
Cabo Frio

BRAZIL
PARANÁ
Maringá
Londrina
Rolândia
Apucarana
Botucatu
Tatuí
Sorocaba
Itapetininga
SÃO PAULO
Osasco
Guarulhos
Santo André
RIO DE JANEIRO
São Gonçalo
Tropic of Capricorn

Foz do Iguaçu
Cascavel
Guarapuava
Ponta Grossa
CURITIBA
Antonina
Paranaguá
Ilha do Cardoso

Ciudad del Este
Irati
Lapa
JOINVILLE
São Francisco do Sul

SANTA CATARINA
Blumenau
Itajaí
Balneário Camboriú
Brusque
São José
FLORIANÓPOLIS

RIO GRANDE DO SUL
Passo Fundo
Caxias do Sul
Criciúma
Cabo Santa Marta Grande

Santa Maria
Santa Cruz do Sul
Novo Hamburgo
Canoas
São Leopoldo
Osório
Torres

PORTO ALEGRE
Pelotas
Rio Grande

MONTEVIDEO

ATLANTIC OCEAN

1:7 100 000

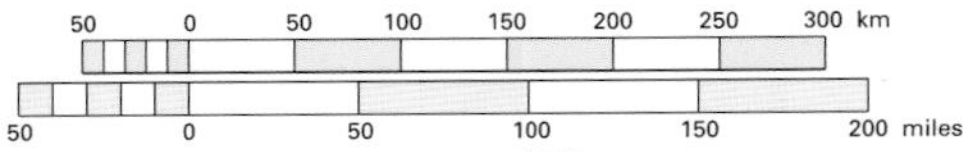

50 0 50 100 150 200 250 300 km
50 0 50 100 150 200 miles

Projection : Lambert's Equivalent Azimuthal

West from Greenwich

COPYRIGHT PHILIP'S

LA PAMPA

BUENOS AIRES

NEUQUÉN

RIO NEGRO

LA ARAUCANIA

LOS RÍOS

LOS LAGOS

CHUBUT

PATAGONIA

SANTA CRUZ

MAGALLANES Y ANTÁRTICA CHILENA

ATLANTIC OCEAN

PACIFIC OCEAN

SOUTHERN OCEAN

Golfo San Matías

Golfo San Jorge

Península Valdés

Temuco
Valdivia
Osorno
Puerto Montt
San Carlos de Bariloche
Neuquén
Roca
Viedma
Carmen de Patagones
Bahía Blanca
Puerto Madryn
Trelew
Rawson
Esquel
Comodoro Rivadavia
Sarmiento
Coihaique
Puerto Aisén
Balmaceda
Perito Moreno
Las Heras
Caleta Olivia
Puerto Deseado
Gobernador Gregores
Puerto San Julián
Puerto Santa Cruz
El Calafate
Río Gallegos
Puerto Natales
Punta Arenas
Porvenir
Río Grande
Ushuaia
Puerto Williams

Tierra del Fuego
Isla Grande de Tierra del Fuego

CABO DE HORNOS (Cape Horn)

Estrecho de Magallanes (Magellan's Strait)

Canal Beagle

I. de los Estados (Staten I.)

FALKLAND ISLANDS (U.K.)
(ISLAS MALVINAS)
West Falkland
East Falkland
Stanley
Port Darwin
Mt. Adam 700
Mt. Usborne 705
Pebble I.
Jason Is.
King George B.
Queen Charlotte B.
Weddell I.
C. Dolphin
C. Meredith
Beauchêne I.

Cerro Fitz Roy 3405
Cerro Murallón 3801
San Valentín 4058
San Lorenzo 3706
Paine Grande 3248

L. Buenos Aires (L. General Carrera)
L. Viedma
L. Argentino
Lago San Martín

ft m
9000 3000
6000 2000
4500 1500
3000 1000
1200 400
600 200
0 0
200 600
1000 3000
2000 6000
4000 12 000
m ft

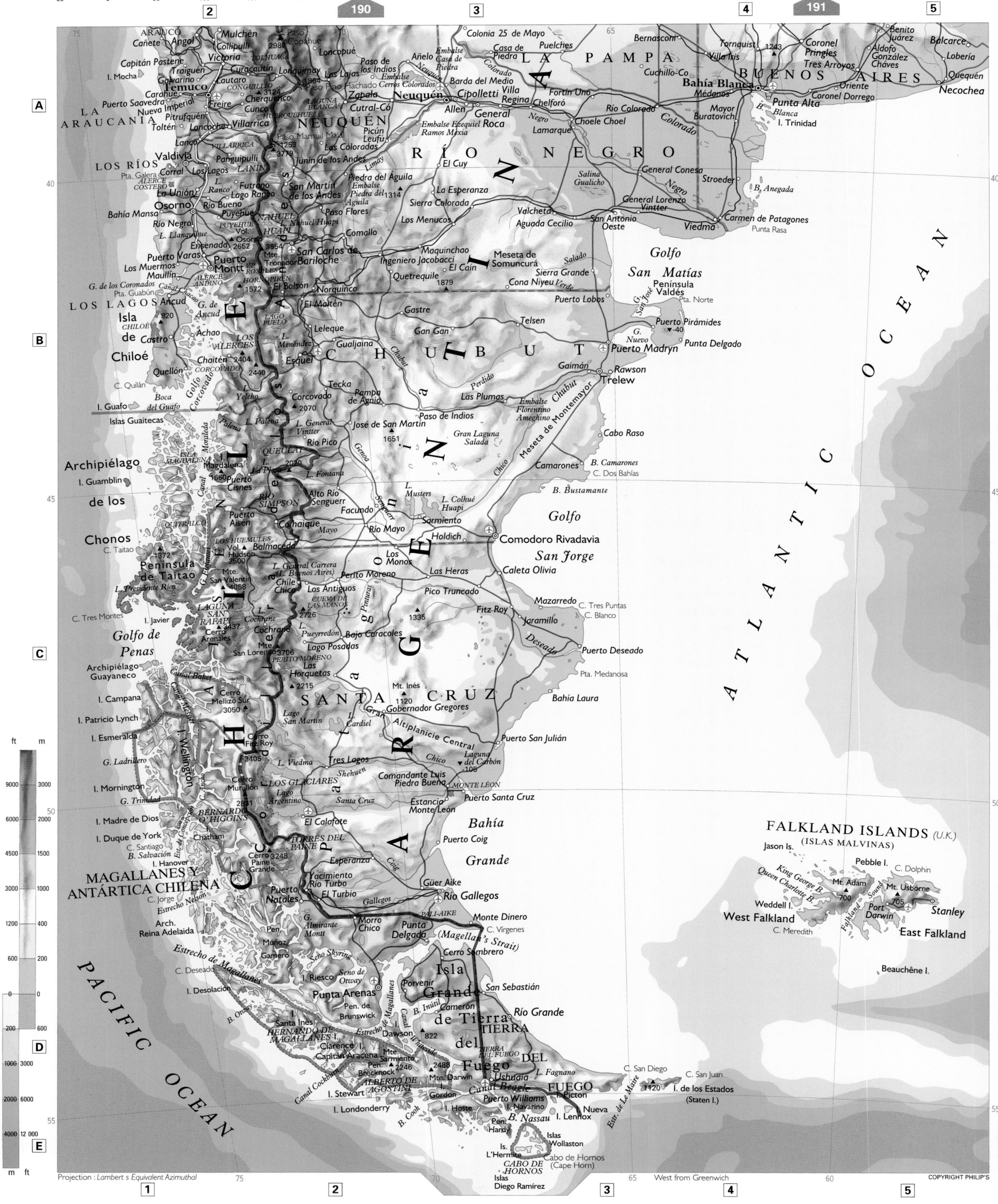

INDEX TO WORLD MAPS

HOW TO USE THE INDEX

The index contains the names of all the principal places and features shown on the World Maps. Each name is followed by an additional entry in italics giving the country or region within which it is located. The alphabetical order of names composed of two or more words is governed primarily by the first word, then by the second, and then by the country or region name that follows. This is an example of the rule:

Mir *Niger*	14°5N 11°59E	**139** C7
Mīr Kūh *Iran*	26°22N 58°55E	**129** E8
Mīr Shahdād *Iran*	26°15N 58°29E	**129** E8
Mira *Italy*	45°26N 12°8E	**93** C9

Physical features composed of a proper name (Erie) and a description (Lake) are positioned alphabetically by the proper name. The description is positioned after the proper name and is usually abbreviated:

| Erie, L. *N. Amer.* | 42°15N 81°0W | **174** D4 |

Where a description forms part of a settlement or administrative name, however, it is always written in full and put in its true alphabetical position:

| Mount Isa *Australia* | 20°42S 139°26E | **150** C2 |

Names beginning with M' and Mc are indexed as if they were spelled Mac. Names beginning St. are alphabetized under Saint, but Sankt, Sint, Sant', Santa and San are all spelt in full and alphabetized accordingly. If the same place name occurs two or more times in the index and all are in the same country, each is followed by the name of the administrative subdivision in which it is located.

The geographical co-ordinates which follow each name in the index give the latitude and longitude of each place. The first co-ordinate indicates latitude – the distance north or south of the Equator. The second co-ordinate indicates longitude – the distance east or west of the Greenwich Meridian. Both latitude and longitude are measured in degrees and minutes (there are 60 minutes in a degree).

The latitude is followed by N(orth) or S(outh) and the longitude by E(ast) or W(est).

The number in bold type which follows the geographical co-ordinates refers to the number of the map page where that feature or place will be found. This is usually the largest scale at which the place or feature appears.

The letter and figure that are immediately after the page number give the grid square on the map page, within which the feature is situated. The letter represents the latitude and the figure the longitude. A lower-case letter immediately after the page number refers to an inset map on that page.

In some cases the feature itself may fall within the specified square, while the name is outside. This is usually the case only with features that are larger than a grid square.

Rivers are indexed to their mouths or confluences, and carry the symbol ➔ after their names. The following symbols are also used in the index: ■ country, ☑ overseas territory or dependency, ▢ first-order administrative area, △ national park, ⌂ other park (provincial park, nature reserve or game reserve), ⊚ Australian Aborginal land, ✈ (LHR) principal airport (and location identifier).

HOW TO PRONOUNCE PLACE NAMES

English-speaking people usually have no difficulty in reading and pronouncing correctly English place names. However, foreign place name pronunciations may present many problems. Such problems can be minimized by following some simple rules. However, these rules cannot be applied to all situations, and there will be many exceptions.

1. In general, stress each syllable equally, unless your experience suggests otherwise.
2. Pronounce the letter 'a' as a broad 'a' as in 'arm'.
3. Pronounce the letter 'e' as a short 'e' as in 'elm'.
4. Pronounce the letter 'i' as a cross between a short 'i' and long 'e', as the two 'i's in 'California'.
5. Pronounce the letter 'o' as an intermediate 'o' as in 'soft'.
6. Pronounce the letter 'u' as an intermediate 'u' as in 'sure'.
7. Pronounce consonants hard, except in the Romance-language areas where 'g's are likely to be pronounced softly like 'j' in 'jam'; 'j' itself may be pronounced as 'y'; and 'x's may be pronounced as 'h'.
8. For names in mainland China, pronounce 'q' like the 'ch' in 'chin', 'x' like the 'sh' in 'she', 'zh' like the 'j' in 'jam', and 'z' as if it were spelled 'dz'. In general, pronounce 'a' as in 'father', 'e' as in 'but', 'i' as in 'keep', 'o' as in 'or', and 'u' as in 'rule'.

Moreover, English has no diacritical marks (accent and pronunciation signs), although some languages do. The following is a brief and general guide to the pronunciation of those most frequently used in the principal Western European languages.

		Pronunciation as in
French	é	day and shows that the 'e' is to be pronounced; e.g. Orléans.
	è	mare
	î	used over any vowel and does not affect pronunciation; shows contraction of the name, usually omission of 's' following a vowel.
	ç	's' before 'a', 'o' and 'u'.
	ë, ï, ü	over 'e', 'i' and 'u' when they are used with another vowel and shows that each is to be pronounced.
German	ä	fate
	ö	fur
	ü	no English equivalent; like French 'tu'.
Italian	à, é	over vowels and indicates stress.
Portuguese	ã, õ	vowels pronounced nasally.
	ç	boss
	á	shows stress.
	ô	shows that a vowel has an 'i' or 'u' sound combined with it.
Spanish	ñ	canyon
	ü	pronounced as 'w' and separately from adjoining vowels.
	á	usually indicates that this is a stressed vowel.

ABBREVIATIONS

A.C.T. – Australian Capital Territory
A.R. – Autonomous Region
Afghan. – Afghanistan
Afr. – Africa
Ala. – Alabama
Alta. – Alberta
Amer. – America(n)
Ant. – Antilles
Arch. – Archipelago
Ariz. – Arizona
Ark. – Arkansas
Atl. Oc. – Atlantic Ocean
B. – Baie, Bahía, Bay, Bucht, Bugt
B.C. – British Columbia
Bangla. – Bangladesh
Barr. – Barrage
Bos.-H. – Bosnia-Herzegovina
C. – Cabo, Cap, Cape, Coast
C.A.R. – Central African Republic
C. Prov. – Cape Province
Calif. – California
Cat. – Catarata
Cent. – Central
Chan. – Channel
Colo. – Colorado
Conn. – Connecticut
Cord. – Cordillera
Cr. – Creek
Czech. – Czech Republic
D.C. – District of Columbia
Del. – Delaware
Dem. – Democratic
Dep. – Dependency
Des. – Desert
Dét. – Détroit
Dist. – District
Dj. – Djebel
Dom. Rep. – Dominican Republic
E. – East

El Salv. – El Salvador
Eq. Guin. – Equatorial Guinea
Est. – Estrecho
Falk. Is. – Falkland Is.
Fd. – Fjord
Fla. – Florida
Fr. – French
G. – Golfe, Golfo, Gulf, Guba, Gebel
Ga. – Georgia
Gt. – Great, Greater
Guinea-Biss. – Guinea-Bissau
H.K. – Hong Kong
H.P. – Himachal Pradesh
Hants. – Hampshire
Harb. – Harbor, Harbour
Hd. – Head
Hts. – Heights
I.(s). – Île, Ilha, Insel, Isla, Island, Isle
Ill. – Illinois
Ind. – Indiana
Ind. Oc. – Indian Ocean
Ivory C. – Ivory Coast
J. – Jabal, Jebel
Jaz. – Jazīrah
Junc. – Junction
K. – Kap, Kapp
Kans. – Kansas
Kep. – Kepulauan
Ky. – Kentucky
L. – Lac, Lacul, Lago, Lagoa, Lake, Limni, Loch, Lough
La. – Louisiana
Ld. – Land
Liech. – Liechtenstein
Lux. – Luxembourg
Mad. P. – Madhya Pradesh
Madag. – Madagascar

Man. – Manitoba
Mass. – Massachusetts
Md. – Maryland
Me. – Maine
Medit. S. – Mediterranean Sea
Mich. – Michigan
Minn. – Minnesota
Miss. – Mississippi
Mo. – Missouri
Mont. – Montana
Mozam. – Mozambique
Mt.(s) – Mont, Montaña, Mountain
Mte. – Monte
Mti. – Monti
N. – Nord, Norte, North, Northern, Nouveau, Nahal, Nahr
N.B. – New Brunswick
N.C. – North Carolina
N. Cal. – New Caledonia
N. Dak. – North Dakota
N.H. – New Hampshire
N.I. – North Island
N.J. – New Jersey
N. Mex. – New Mexico
N.S. – Nova Scotia
N.S.W. – New South Wales
N.W.T. – North West Territory
N.Y. – New York
N.Z. – New Zealand
Nac. – Nacional
Nat. – National
Nebr. – Nebraska
Neths. – Netherlands
Nev. – Nevada
Nfld & L.. – Newfoundland and Labrador
Nic. – Nicaragua
O. – Oued, Ouadi
Occ. – Occidentale

Okla. – Oklahoma
Ont. – Ontario
Or. – Orientale
Oreg. – Oregon
Os. – Ostrov
Oz. – Ozero
P. – Pass, Passo, Pasul, Pulau
P.E.I. – Prince Edward Island
Pa. – Pennsylvania
Pac. Oc. – Pacific Ocean
Papua N.G. – Papua New Guinea
Pass. – Passage
Peg. – Pegunungan
Pen. – Peninsula, Péninsule
Phil. – Philippines
Pk. – Peak
Plat. – Plateau
Prov. – Province, Provincial
Pt. – Point
Pta. – Ponta, Punta
Pte. – Pointe
Qué. – Québec
Queens. – Queensland
R. – Rio, River
R.I. – Rhode Island
Ra. – Range
Raj. – Rajasthan
Recr. – Recreational, Récréatif
Reg. – Region
Rep. – Republic
Res. – Reserve, Reservoir
Rhld-Pfz. – Rheinland-Pfalz
S. – South, Southern, Sur
Si. Arabia – Saudi Arabia
S.C. – South Carolina
S. Dak. – South Dakota
S.I. – South Island
S. Leone – Sierra Leone
Sa. – Serra, Sierra

Sask. – Saskatchewan
Scot. – Scotland
Sd. – Sound
Sev. – Severnaya
Sib. – Siberia
Sprs. – Springs
St. – Saint
Sta. – Santa
Ste. – Sainte
Sto. – Santo
Str. – Strait, Stretto
Switz. – Switzerland
Tas. – Tasmania
Tenn. – Tennessee
Terr. – Territory, Territoire
Tex. – Texas
Tg. – Tanjung
Trin. & Tob. – Trinidad & Tobago
U.A.E. – United Arab Emirates
U.K. – United Kingdom
U.S.A. – United States of America
Univ. – University, Université, Universidad
Ut. P. – Uttar Pradesh
Va. – Virginia
Vdkhr. – Vodokhranilishche
Vdskh. – Vodoskhovyshche
Vf. – Vîrful
Vic. – Victoria
Vol. – Volcano
Vt. – Vermont
W. – Wadi, West
W. Va. – West Virginia
Wall. & F. Is. – Wallis and Futuna Is.
Wash. – Washington
Wis. – Wisconsin
Wlkp. – Wielkopolski
Wyo. – Wyoming
Yorks. – Yorkshire

A

A Baiuca *Spain* 43°19N 8°29W **88** B2
A Baña = San Vicenzo *Spain* 42°58N 8°46W **88** C2
A Cañiza *Spain* 42°13N 8°16W **88** C2
A Carballa *Spain* 43°13N 8°54W **88** B2
A Carreira *Spain* 43°21N 8°12W **88** B2
A Coruña *Spain* 43°20N 8°25W **88** B2
A Coruña □ *Spain* 43°10N 8°30W **88** B2
A Cruz do Incio *Spain* 42°39N 7°21W **88** C3
A Estrada *Spain* 42°43N 8°27W **88** C2
A Feira do Monte *Spain* 43°12N 7°34W **88** B3
A Fonsagrada *Spain* 43°8N 7°4W **88** B3
A Guarda *Spain* 41°56N 8°52W **88** D2
A Gudiña *Spain* 42°4N 7°8W **88** C3
A Pobre *Spain* 42°58N 7°3W **88** C3
A Ramallosa *Spain* 42°45N 8°30W **88** C2
A Rúa *Spain* 42°24N 7°6W **88** C3
A Serra de Outes *Spain* 42°52N 8°55W **88** C2
A Shau *Vietnam* 16°6N 107°22E **120** D6
Aabenraa *Denmark* 55°3N 9°25E **63** J3
Aabybro *Denmark* 57°10N 9°44E **63** G3
Aachen *Germany* 50°45N 6°6E **76** E2
Aalborg *Denmark* 57°2N 9°54E **63** G3
Aalborg Bugt *Denmark* 56°50N 10°35E **63** H4
Aalen *Germany* 48°51N 10°6E **77** G6
Aalestrup *Denmark* 56°42N 9°29E **63** H3
Aalst *Belgium* 50°56N 4°2E **69** D4
Aalten *Neths.* 51°56N 6°35E **69** C6
Aalter *Belgium* 51°5N 3°28E **69** C3
Äänekoski *Finland* 62°36N 25°44E **60** E21
Aarau *Switz.* 47°23N 8°4E **77** H4
Aarberg *Switz.* 47°2N 7°16E **77** H3
Aare → *Switz.* 47°33N 8°14E **77** H4
Aargau □ *Switz.* 47°26N 8°10E **77** H4
Aarhus *Denmark* 56°8N 10°11E **63** H4
Aars *Denmark* 56°48N 9°30E **63** H3
Aarschot *Belgium* 50°59N 4°49E **69** D4
Aasiaat *Greenland* 68°43N 52°56W **57** D5
Aba *China* 32°59N 101°42E **116** A3
Aba *Dem. Rep. of the Congo* 3°58N 30°17E **142** B3
Aba *Nigeria* 5°10N 7°19E **139** D6
Abaco I. *Bahamas* 26°25N 77°10W **182** A4
Abadab, J. *Sudan* 18°54N 35°56E **137** D4
Ābādān *Iran* 30°22N 48°20E **129** D6
Ābādeh *Iran* 31°8N 52°40E **129** D7
Abadín *Spain* 43°21N 7°29W **88** B3
Abadla *Algeria* 31°2N 2°45W **136** B3
Abaeté *Brazil* 19°9S 45°27W **189** D1
Abaeté → *Brazil* 18°2S 45°12W **189** D1
Abaetetuba *Brazil* 1°40S 48°50W **187** D9
Abagnar Qi = Xilinhot *China* 43°52N 116°2E **114** C9
Abah, Tanjung *Indonesia* 8°46S 115°38E **119** K18
Abai *Paraguay* 25°58S 55°54W **191** B4
Abakaliki *Nigeria* 6°22N 8°2E **139** D6
Abakan *Russia* 53°40N 91°10E **109** B12
Abala *Niger* 14°56N 3°22E **139** C5
Abalak *Niger* 15°22N 6°21E **139** B6
Abalemma *Niger* 16°12N 7°50E **139** B6
Abana *Turkey* 41°59N 34°1E **104** B6
Abancay *Peru* 13°35S 72°55W **188** C3
Abang, Gunung *Indonesia* 8°16S 115°25E **119** J18
Abano Terme *Italy* 45°22N 11°46E **93** C8
Abarán *Spain* 38°12N 1°23W **91** G3
Abariringa *Kiribati* 2°50S 171°40W **156** H10
Abarqū *Iran* 31°10N 53°20E **129** D7
Abasha *Georgia* 42°11N 42°13E **87** J6
Abashiri *Japan* 44°0N 144°15E **112** B12
Abashiri-Wan *Japan* 44°0N 144°30E **112** C12
Abaújszántó *Hungary* 48°16N 21°12E **80** B6
Abava → *Latvia* 57°6N 21°54E **82** A8
Ābay = Nîl el Azraq → *Sudan* 15°38N 32°31E **135** E12
Abay *Kazakhstan* 49°38N 72°53E **109** C8
Abaya, L. *Ethiopia* 6°30N 37°50E **131** F2
Abaza *Russia* 52°39N 90°6E **109** B12
Abbadia di Fiastra ⌂ *Italy* 43°12N 13°24E **93** E10
Abbadia San Salvatore *Italy* 42°53N 11°41E **93** F8
'Abbāsābād *Iran* 33°34N 58°23E **129** C8
Abbay = Nîl el Azraq → *Sudan* 15°38N 32°31E **135** E12
Abbaye, Pt. *U.S.A.* 46°58N 88°8W **172** B9
Abbé, L. *Ethiopia* 11°8N 41°47E **131** E3
Abbeville *France* 50°6N 1°49E **71** B8
Abbeville *Ala., U.S.A.* 31°34N 85°15W **178** D4
Abbeville *Ga., U.S.A.* 31°59N 83°18W **178** D6
Abbeville *La., U.S.A.* 29°58N 92°8W **176** G8
Abbeville *S.C., U.S.A.* 34°11N 82°23W **178** A7
Abbeyfeale *Ireland* 52°23N 9°18W **64** D2
Abbeyleix *Ireland* 52°54N 7°22W **64** D4
Abbiategrasso *Italy* 45°24N 8°54E **92** C5
Abbot Ice Shelf *Antarctica* 73°0S 92°0W **55** D16
Abbotsford *Canada* 49°5N 122°20W **162** D4
Abbottabad *Pakistan* 34°10N 73°15E **124** B5
Abbou, O. ben → *Algeria* 28°32N 5°14E **136** C5
ABC Islands *W. Indies* 12°15N 69°0W **183** D6
Abd al Kūrī *Yemen* 12°5N 52°20E **131** E5
Ābdānān *Iran* 32°56N 47°28E **105** F12
Ābdar *Iran* 30°16N 55°19E **129** D7
'Abdolābād *Iran* 34°12N 56°30E **129** C8
Abdulino *Russia* 53°42N 53°40E **108** B4
Abdulpur *Bangla.* 24°15N 88°59E **125** G13
Abéché *Chad* 13°50N 20°35E **135** F10
Abejar *Spain* 41°48N 2°47W **90** D2
Abel Tasman △ *N.Z.* 40°59S 173°3E **155** A8
Abengourou *Ivory C.* 6°42N 3°27W **138** D4
Abenójar *Spain* 38°53N 4°21W **89** G6
Åbenrå = Aabenraa *Denmark* 55°3N 9°25E **63** J3
Abensberg *Germany* 48°48N 11°51E **77** G7
Abeokuta *Nigeria* 7°3N 3°19E **139** D5
Aberaeron *U.K.* 52°15N 4°15W **67** E3
Aberayron = Aberaeron *U.K.* 52°15N 4°15W **67** E3
Aberchirder *U.K.* 57°34N 2°37W **65** D6
Abercorn *Australia* 25°12S 151°5E **151** D5
Abercrombie River △ *Australia* 34°5S 149°40E **153** C8
Aberdare *U.K.* 51°43N 3°27W **67** F4
Aberdare △ *Kenya* 0°22S 36°44E **142** C4
Aberdare Ra. *Kenya* 0°15S 36°50E **142** C4
Aberdaugleddau = Milford Haven *U.K.* 51°42N 5°7W **67** F2
Aberdeen *Australia* 32°9S 150°56E **153** B9
Aberdeen *Canada* 52°20N 106°8W **163** C7
Aberdeen *China* 22°14N 114°8E **111** a
Aberdeen *S. Africa* 32°28S 24°2E **144** D3
Aberdeen *U.K.* 57°9N 2°5W **65** D6
Aberdeen *Idaho, U.S.A.* 42°57N 112°50W **168** E7
Aberdeen *Md., U.S.A.* 39°31N 76°10W **173** F15
Aberdeen *Miss., U.S.A.* 33°49N 88°33W **177** E10
Aberdeen *S. Dak., U.S.A.* 45°28N 98°29W **172** C4
Aberdeen *Wash., U.S.A.* 46°59N 123°50W **170** D3
Aberdeen, City of □ *U.K.* 57°10N 2°10W **65** D6
Aberdeen L. *Canada* 64°30N 99°0W **160** E12
Aberdeenshire □ *U.K.* 57°17N 2°36W **65** D6
Aberdovey = Aberdyfi *U.K.* 52°33N 4°3W **67** E3
Aberdyfi *U.K.* 52°33N 4°3W **67** E3
Aberfeldy *U.K.* 56°37N 3°51W **65** E5
Aberfoyle *U.K.* 56°11N 4°23W **65** E4
Abergavenny *U.K.* 51°49N 3°1W **67** F4
Abergele *U.K.* 53°17N 3°35W **66** D4
Abergwaun = Fishguard *U.K.* 52°0N 4°58W **67** E3
Aberhonddu = Brecon *U.K.* 51°57N 3°23W **67** F4
Abermaw = Barmouth *U.K.* 52°44N 4°4W **66** E3
Abernathy *U.S.A.* 33°50N 101°51W **176** E4
Aberpennar = Mountain Ash *U.K.* 51°40N 3°23W **67** F4
Abert, L. *U.S.A.* 42°38N 120°14W **168** E3
Abertawe = Swansea *U.K.* 51°37N 3°57W **67** F4
Aberteifi = Cardigan *U.K.* 52°5N 4°40W **67** E3
Aberystwyth *U.K.* 52°25N 4°5W **67** E3
Abhā *Si. Arabia* 18°0N 42°34E **137** D5
Abhar *Iran* 36°9N 49°13E **105** D13
Abhayapuri *India* 26°24N 90°38E **125** F14
Abia □ *Nigeria* 5°30N 7°35E **139** D6
Abide *Turkey* 38°55N 29°20E **99** C11
Abidiya *Sudan* 18°18N 34°3E **137** D3
Abidjan *Ivory C.* 5°26N 3°58W **138** D4
Abilene *Kans., U.S.A.* 38°55N 97°13W **172** F5
Abilene *Tex., U.S.A.* 32°28N 99°43W **176** E5
Abingdon *U.K.* 51°40N 1°17W **67** F6
Abingdon *U.S.A.* 36°43N 81°59W **173** G13
Abington Reef *Australia* 18°0S 149°35E **150** B4
Abiod, Remel el *Tunisia* 31°45N 9°35E **136** B5
Abisko △ *Sweden* 68°18N 18°44E **60** B18
Abitau → *Canada* 59°53N 109°3W **163** B7
Abitibi → *Canada* 51°3N 80°55W **164** B3
Abitibi, L. *Canada* 48°40N 79°40W **164** C4
Abkhaz Republic = Abkhazia □ *Georgia* 43°12N 41°5E **87** J5
Abkhazia □ *Georgia* 43°12N 41°5E **87** J5
Abminga *Australia* 26°8S 134°51E **151** D1
Abnûb *Egypt* 27°18N 31°4E **137** B3
Åbo = Turku *Finland* 60°30N 22°19E **84** B2
Abohar *India* 30°10N 74°10E **124** D6
Aboisso *Ivory C.* 5°30N 3°5W **138** D4
Abomey *Benin* 7°10N 2°5E **139** D5
Abong-Mbang *Cameroon* 4°0N 13°8E **140** D2
Abonnema *Nigeria* 4°41N 6°49E **139** E6
Abony *Hungary* 47°12N 20°3E **80** C5
Aboso *Ghana* 5°23N 1°57W **138** D4
Abou-Deïa *Chad* 11°20N 19°20E **135** F9
Abovyan *Armenia* 40°16N 44°37E **87** K7
Aboyne *U.K.* 57°4N 2°47W **65** D6
Abra Pampa *Argentina* 22°43S 65°42W **190** A2
Abraham L. *Canada* 52°15N 116°35W **162** C5
Abrantes *Portugal* 39°24N 8°7W **89** F2
Abreojos, Pta. *Mexico* 26°50N 113°40W **180** B2
Abri *Sudan* 20°50N 30°27E **137** C3
Abrolhos, Banco dos *Brazil* 18°0S 38°0W **189** D3
Abrud *Romania* 46°19N 23°5E **80** D8
Abruzzo □ *Italy* 42°15N 14°0E **93** F10
Absaroka Range *U.S.A.* 44°45N 109°50W **168** D9
Abşeron Yarımadası *Azerbaijan* 40°28N 49°57E **87** K9
Abtenau *Austria* 47°33N 13°21E **78** D6
Abu *India* 24°41N 72°50E **124** G5
Abū al Abyad *U.A.E.* 24°11N 53°50E **129** E7
Abū al Khaşīb *Iraq* 30°25N 48°0E **128** D5
Abū 'Alī *Si. Arabia* 27°20N 49°27E **129** E6
Abū 'Alī → *Lebanon* 34°25N 35°50E **130** A4
Abū Ballas *Egypt* 24°26N 27°36E **137** C2
Abu Dhabi = Abū Ẓāby *U.A.E.* 24°28N 54°22E **129** E7
Abû Dis *Sudan* 19°12N 33°38E **137** D3
Abū Du'ān *Syria* 36°25N 38°15E **105** D8
Abu el Gaīn, W. → *Egypt* 29°35N 33°30E **130** F2
Abu Fatma, Ras *Sudan* 22°25N 36°25E **137** C4
Abu Ga'da, W. → *Egypt* 29°15N 32°53E **130** F1
Abū Ḩadrīyah *Si. Arabia* 27°20N 48°58E **129** E6
Abu Hamed *Sudan* 19°32N 33°13E **137** D3
Abu Haraz *Sudan* 19°8N 32°18E **137** D3
Abū Kamāl *Syria* 34°30N 41°0E **105** E9
Abu Kebîr *Egypt* 30°43N 31°40E **137** E7
Abū Madd, Ra's *Si. Arabia* 24°50N 37°7E **128** E3
Abu Mena = Abu Mina *Egypt* 30°51N 29°40E **137** E6
Abu Mina *Egypt* 30°51N 29°40E **137** E6
Abū Mūsā *U.A.E.* 25°52N 55°3E **129** E7
Abū Qaşr *Si. Arabia* 30°21N 38°34E **128** D3
Abu Qireiya *Egypt* 24°5N 35°28E **137** C4
Abu Qurqâs *Egypt* 28°1N 30°44E **137** F7
Abu Shagara, Ras *Sudan* 21°4N 37°19E **137** C4
Abu Simbel *Egypt* 22°18N 31°40E **137** C3
Abu Soma, Râs *Egypt* 26°51N 33°58E **137** B3
Abū Şukhayr *Iraq* 31°54N 44°30E **105** G11
Abu Sultân *Egypt* 30°24N 32°21E **137** E8
Abu Tig *Egypt* 27°4N 31°15E **137** B3
Abû Zabad *Sudan* 12°25N 29°10E **135** F11
Abū Ẓāby *U.A.E.* 24°28N 54°22E **129** E7
Abū Zeydābād *Iran* 33°54N 51°45E **129** C6
Abuja *Nigeria* 9°5N 7°32E **139** D6
Abukuma-Gawa → *Japan* 38°6N 140°52E **112** E10
Abukuma-Sammyaku *Japan* 37°30N 140°45E **112** F10
Abunã *Brazil* 9°40S 65°20W **186** E5
Abunã → *Brazil* 9°41S 65°20W **186** E5
Aburo *Dem. Rep. of the Congo* 2°4N 30°53E **142** B3
Abut Hd. *N.Z.* 43°7S 170°15E **155** D5
Åby *Sweden* 58°40N 16°10E **63** F10
Aby, Lagune *Ivory C.* 5°15N 3°14W **138** D4
Abyei □ *Sudan* 9°30N 28°30E **135** G11
Ābyek *Iran* 36°4N 50°33E **129** B6
Academy Gletscher *Greenland* 82°2N 34°0W **57** A7
Acadia △ *U.S.A.* 44°20N 68°13W **173** C19
Açailândia *Brazil* 4°57S 47°30W **189** A1
Acajutla *El Salv.* 13°36N 89°50W **182** D2
Acámbaro *Mexico* 20°2N 100°44W **180** D4
Acanthus *Greece* 40°27N 23°47E **96** F7
Acaponeta *Mexico* 22°30N 105°22W **180** C3
Acapulco *Mexico* 16°51N 99°55W **181** D5
Acaraí, Serra *Brazil* 1°50N 57°50W **186** C7
Acaraú *Brazil* 2°53S 40°7W **189** A2
Acari *Brazil* 6°31S 36°38W **189** B3
Acarí *Peru* 15°25S 74°36W **188** D3
Acarigua *Venezuela* 9°33N 69°12W **186** B5
Acatlán *Mexico* 18°12N 98°3W **181** D5
Acayucán *Mexico* 17°57N 94°55W **181** D6
Accéglio *Italy* 44°28N 7°0E **92** D4
Accomac *U.S.A.* 37°43N 75°40W **173** G16
Accous *France* 43°0N 0°36W **72** E3
Accra *Ghana* 5°35N 0°6W **139** D4
Accrington *U.K.* 53°45N 2°22W **66** D5
Acebal *Argentina* 33°20S 60°50W **190** C3
Aceh □ *Indonesia* 4°15N 97°30E **118** D1
Acerra *Italy* 40°57N 14°22E **95** B7
Aceuchal *Spain* 38°39N 6°30W **89** G4
Achacachi *Bolivia* 16°3S 68°43W **188** D4
Achaia *Greece* 38°5N 21°45E **98** C3
Achalpur *India* 21°22N 77°32E **126** D3
Achao *Chile* 42°28S 73°30W **192** B2
Acharnes *Greece* 38°5N 23°44E **98** C5
Acheloos → *Greece* 38°19N 21°7E **98** C3
Acheng *China* 45°30N 126°58E **115** B14
Achenkirch *Austria* 47°32N 11°45E **78** D4
Achensee *Austria* 47°26N 11°45E **78** D4
Achentrias *Greece* 34°59N 25°13E **99** G7
Acher *India* 23°10N 72°32E **124** H5
Achern *Germany* 48°37N 8°4E **77** G4
Acheron → *N.Z.* 42°16S 173°4E **155** C8
Achill Hd. *Ireland* 53°58N 10°15W **64** C1
Achill I. *Ireland* 53°58N 10°1W **64** C1
Achim *Germany* 53°1N 9°3E **76** B5
Achinsk *Russia* 56°20N 90°20E **107** D10
Achladokambos *Greece* 37°31N 22°35E **98** D4
Acıgöl *Turkey* 37°50N 29°50E **99** D11
Acıpayam *Turkey* 37°26N 29°22E **99** D11
Acireale *Italy* 37°37N 15°10E **95** E8
Ackerman *U.S.A.* 33°19N 89°11W **177** E10
Acklins I. *Bahamas* 22°30N 74°0W **183** B5
Acme *Canada* 51°33N 113°30W **162** C6
Acme *U.S.A.* 40°8N 79°26W **174** F5
Acobamba *Peru* 12°52S 74°35W **188** C3
Acomayo *Peru* 13°55S 71°38W **188** C3
Aconcagua, Cerro *Argentina* 32°39S 70°0W **190** C2
Aconquija, Mt. *Argentina* 27°0S 66°0W **190** B2
Acopiara *Brazil* 6°6S 39°27W **189** B3
Açores, Is. dos *Atl. Oc.* 38°0N 27°0W **134** a
Acornhoek *S. Africa* 24°37S 31°2E **145** B5
Acquapendente *Italy* 42°44N 11°52E **93** F8
Acquasanta Terme *Italy* 42°46N 13°24E **93** F10
Acquasparta *Italy* 42°41N 12°33E **93** F9
Acquaviva delle Fonti *Italy* 40°54N 16°50E **95** B9
Ácqui Terme *Italy* 44°41N 8°28E **92** D5
Acraman, L. *Australia* 32°2S 135°23E **151** E2
Acre = 'Akko *Israel* 32°55N 35°4E **130** C4
Acre □ *Brazil* 9°1S 71°0W **188** B3
Acre → *Brazil* 8°45S 67°22W **188** B4
Acri *Italy* 39°29N 16°23E **95** C9
Acs *Hungary* 47°42N 18°2E **80** C3
Actinolite *Canada* 44°32N 77°19W **174** B7
Actium *Greece* 38°57N 20°45E **98** C2
Acton *Canada* 43°38N 80°3W **174** C4
Açu *Brazil* 5°34S 36°54W **189** B3
Acworth *U.S.A.* 34°4N 84°41W **178** A5
Ad Dafinah *Si. Arabia* 23°18N 41°58E **137** C5
Ad Daghghāran *Iraq* 32°8N 44°55E **105** G11
Ad Dahnā *Si. Arabia* 24°30N 48°10E **131** C4
Ad Dammām *Si. Arabia* 26°20N 50°5E **129** E6
Ad Dāmūr *Lebanon* 33°43N 35°27E **130** B4
Ad Dawādimī *Si. Arabia* 24°35N 44°15E **128** E5
Ad Dawḩah *Qatar* 25°15N 51°35E **129** E6
Ad Dawr *Iraq* 34°27N 43°47E **105** E10
Ad Dhakhīrah *Qatar* 25°44N 51°33E **129** E6
Ad Dir'īyah *Si. Arabia* 24°44N 46°35E **128** E5
Ad Dīwānīyah *Iraq* 32°0N 45°0E **105** F11
Ad Dujayl *Iraq* 33°51N 44°14E **105** F11
Ad Duwayd *Si. Arabia* 30°15N 42°17E **128** D4
Ada *Ghana* 5°44N 0°40E **139** D5
Ada *Serbia* 45°49N 20°9E **80** E5
Ada *Minn., U.S.A.* 47°18N 96°31W **172** B5
Ada *Okla., U.S.A.* 34°46N 96°41W **176** D6
Adabiya *Egypt* 29°53N 32°28E **130** F1
Adair, C. *Canada* 71°30N 71°34W **161** C17
Adaja → *Spain* 41°32N 4°52W **88** D6
Adak *U.S.A.* 51°45N 176°45W **166** E4
Adak I. *U.S.A.* 51°45N 176°45W **166** E4
Adam, Mt. *Falk. Is.* 51°34S 60°4W **192** D4
Adamaoua □ *Cameroon* 6°30N 13°30E **139** D7
Adamaoua, Massif de l' *Cameroon* 7°20N 12°20E **139** D7
Adamawa □ *Nigeria* 9°20N 12°30E **139** D7
Adamawa Highlands = Adamaoua, Massif de l' *Cameroon* 7°20N 12°20E **139** D7
Adamello, Mte. *Italy* 46°9N 10°30E **92** B7
Adamello ⌂ *Italy* 46°4N 10°28E **92** B7
Adaminaby *Australia* 36°0S 148°45E **153** D8
Adams *Mass., U.S.A.* 42°38N 73°7W **175** D11
Adams *N.Y., U.S.A.* 43°49N 76°1W **175** C8
Adams *Wis., U.S.A.* 43°57N 89°49W **172** D9
Adams, Mt. *U.S.A.* 46°12N 121°30W **170** D5
Adam's Bridge *Sri Lanka* 9°15N 79°40E **127** K4
Adams L. *Canada* 51°10N 119°40W **162** C5
Adam's Peak *Sri Lanka* 6°48N 80°30E **127** L5
Adamuz *Spain* 38°2N 4°32W **89** G6
'Adan *Yemen* 12°45N 45°0E **131** E4
Adana *Turkey* 37°0N 35°16E **104** D6
Adana □ *Turkey* 37°0N 35°30E **104** D6
Adanero *Spain* 40°56N 4°36W **88** E6
Adang, Ko *Thailand* 6°33N 99°18E **121** J2
Adapazarı = Sakarya *Turkey* 40°48N 30°25E **104** B4
Adar Gwagwa, J. *Sudan* 22°15N 35°20E **137** C4
Adarama *Sudan* 17°10N 34°52E **135** E12
Adare *Ireland* 52°34N 8°47W **64** D3
Adare, C. *Antarctica* 71°0S 171°0E **55** D11
Adaut *Indonesia* 8°8S 131°7E **119** F8
Adavale *Australia* 25°52S 144°32E **151** D3
Adda → *Italy* 45°8N 9°53E **92** C6
Addatigala *India* 17°31N 82°3E **126** F6
Addis Ababa = Addis Abeba *Ethiopia* 9°2N 38°42E **131** F2
Addis Abeba *Ethiopia* 9°2N 38°42E **131** F2
Addison *U.S.A.* 42°1N 77°14W **174** D7
Addo *S. Africa* 33°32S 25°45E **144** D4
Addo △ *S. Africa* 33°30S 25°50E **144** D4
Adebour *Niger* 13°17N 11°50E **139** C7
Ādeh *Iran* 37°42N 45°11E **128** B5
Adel *U.S.A.* 31°8N 83°25W **178** D6
Adel Bagrou *Mauritania* 15°29N 6°57W **138** B3
Adelaide *Australia* 34°52S 138°30E **152** C3
Adelaide *S. Africa* 32°42S 26°20E **144** D4
Adelaide I. *Antarctica* 67°15S 68°30W **55** C17
Adelaide Pen. *Canada* 68°15N 97°30W **160** D12
Adelaide River *Australia* 13°15S 131°7E **148** B5
Adelaide Village *Bahamas* 25°0N 77°31W **182** A4
Adelanto *U.S.A.* 34°35N 117°22W **171** L9
Adele I. *Australia* 15°32S 123°9E **148** C3
Adélie, Terre *Antarctica* 68°0S 140°0E **55** C10
Adélie Land = Adélie, Terre *Antarctica* 68°0S 140°0E **55** C10
Adelong *Australia* 35°16S 148°4E **153** C8
Adelsk *Belarus* 53°24N 23°47E **82** E10
Ademuz *Spain* 40°5N 1°13W **90** E3
Aden = 'Adan *Yemen* 12°45N 45°0E **131** E4
Aden, G. of *Ind. Oc.* 12°30N 47°30E **131** E4
Adendorp *S. Africa* 32°15S 24°30E **144** D3
Aderbissinat *Niger* 15°34N 7°54E **139** B6
Adh Dhayd *U.A.E.* 25°17N 55°53E **129** E7
Adhoi *India* 23°26N 70°32E **124** H4
Adi *Indonesia* 4°15S 133°30E **119** E8
Adieu, C. *Australia* 32°0S 132°10E **149** F5
Adieu Pt. *Australia* 15°14S 124°35E **148** C3
Adige → *Italy* 45°9N 12°20E **93** C9
Adigrat *Ethiopia* 14°20N 39°26E **131** E2
Adıgüzel Barajı *Turkey* 38°13N 29°14E **99** C11
Adilabad *India* 19°33N 78°20E **126** E4
Adilcevaz *Turkey* 38°47N 42°43E **105** C10
Adirondack △ *U.S.A.* 44°0N 74°20W **175** D10
Adirondack Mts. *U.S.A.* 44°0N 74°0W **175** C10
Adis Abeba = Addis Abeba *Ethiopia* 9°2N 38°42E **131** F2
Adıyaman *Turkey* 37°45N 38°16E **105** D8
Adıyaman □ *Turkey* 37°30N 38°10E **105** D8
Adjim *Tunisia* 33°47N 10°50E **136** B6
Adjohon *Benin* 6°41N 2°32E **139** D5
Adjud *Romania* 46°7N 27°10E **81** D12
Adjumani *Uganda* 3°20N 31°50E **142** B3
Adjuntas *Puerto Rico* 18°10N 66°43W **183** d
Adlavik Is. *Canada* 55°0N 58°40W **165** B8
Adler *Russia* 43°28N 39°52E **87** J4
Admer *Algeria* 20°21N 5°27E **139** A6
Admer, Erg d' *Algeria* 24°0N 9°5E **136** D5
Admiralty G. *Australia* 14°20S 125°55E **148** B4
Admiralty Gulf ✪ *Australia* 14°16S 125°52E **148** B4
Admiralty I. *U.S.A.* 57°30N 134°30W **162** B2
Admiralty Inlet *Canada* 72°30N 86°0W **161** C14
Admiralty Is. *Papua N. G.* 2°0S 147°0E **147** B7
Adnan Menderes, İzmir ✕ (ADB) *Turkey* 38°23N 27°6E **99** C9
Ado *Nigeria* 6°36N 2°56E **139** D5
Ado-Ekiti *Nigeria* 7°38N 5°12E **139** D6
Adolfo González Chaves *Argentina* 38°2S 60°5W **190** D3
Adolfo Ruiz Cortines, Presa *Mexico* 27°15N 109°6W **180** B3
Adonara *Indonesia* 8°15S 123°5E **119** F6
Adoni *India* 15°33N 77°18E **127** G3
Adony *Hungary* 47°6N 18°52E **80** C3
Adour → *France* 43°32N 1°32W **72** E2
Adra *India* 23°30N 86°42E **125** H12
Adra *Spain* 36°43N 3°3W **89** J7
Adrano *Italy* 37°40N 14°50E **95** E7
Adrar *Algeria* 27°51N 0°19W **136** C3
Adrar *Mauritania* 20°30N 7°30W **134** D3
Adrar □ *Algeria* 25°45N 1°0E **136** C4
Adrar □ *Mauritania* 21°0N 10°0W **138** A3
Adrar des Iforas *Africa* 19°40N 1°40E **139** B5
Ádria *Italy* 45°3N 12°3E **93** C9
Adrian *Ga., U.S.A.* 32°33N 82°35W **178** C7
Adrian *Mich., U.S.A.* 41°54N 84°2W **173** E11
Adrian *Tex., U.S.A.* 35°16N 102°40W **176** D3
Adriatic Sea *Medit. S.* 43°0N 16°0E **58** G9
Adua *Indonesia* 1°45S 129°50E **119** E7
Adur *India* 9°8N 76°40E **127** K3
Adwa *Ethiopia* 14°15N 38°52E **131** E2
Adygea □ *Russia* 45°0N 40°0E **87** H5
Adzhar Republic = Ajaria □ *Georgia* 41°30N 42°0E **87** K6
Adzopé *Ivory C.* 6°7N 3°49W **138** D4
Aegae = Aigai *Greece* 40°28N 22°19E **96** F6
Ægean Sea *Medit. S.* 38°30N 25°0E **99** C7
Aerhtai Shan *Mongolia* 46°40N 92°45E **109** C12
Ærø *Denmark* 54°52N 10°25E **63** K4
Ærøskøbing *Denmark* 54°53N 10°24E **63** K4
Aetolia-Akarnania = Etoloakarnania *Greece* 38°45N 21°18E **98** C3
Aetos *Greece* 37°15N 21°50E **98** D3
Afaahiti *Tahiti* 17°45S 149°17W **155** b
'Afak *Iraq* 32°4N 45°15E **105** F11
Afandou *Greece* 36°18N 28°12E **101** C10
Afarag, Erg *Algeria* 23°50N 2°47E **136** D4
Afghanistan ■ *Asia* 33°0N 65°0E **122** C4
Afikpo *Nigeria* 5°53N 7°54E **139** D6
Aflisses, O. → *Algeria* 28°40N 0°50E **136** C4
Aflou *Algeria* 34°7N 2°3E **136** B4
Afogados da Ingàzeira *Brazil* 7°45S 37°39W **189** B3
Afognak I. *U.S.A.* 58°15N 152°30W **166** D9
Afragóla *Italy* 40°55N 14°18E **95** B7
Afram → *Ghana* 7°0N 0°52W **139** D4
Africa 10°0N 20°0E **132** E6
'Afrīn *Syria* 36°32N 36°50E **104** D7
Afşin *Turkey* 38°14N 36°55E **104** C7
Afton *N.Y., U.S.A.* 42°14N 75°32W **175** D9
Afton *Wyo., U.S.A.* 42°44N 110°56W **168** E8
Afuá *Brazil* 0°15S 50°20W **187** D8
'Afula *Israel* 32°37N 35°17E **130** C4
Afyon *Turkey* 38°45N 30°33E **99** C12
Afyon □ *Turkey* 38°25N 30°30E **99** C12
Afyonkarahisar = Afyon *Turkey* 38°45N 30°33E **99** C12
Aga *Egypt* 30°55N 31°10E **137** E7
Āgā Jarī *Iran* 30°42N 49°50E **129** D6
Agadés = Agadez *Niger* 16°58N 7°59E **139** B6
Agadez *Niger* 16°58N 7°59E **139** B6
Agadir *Morocco* 30°28N 9°55W **136** B2
Agaete *Canary Is.* 28°6N 15°43W **100** F4
Agaie *Nigeria* 9°1N 6°18E **139** D6
Agalega Is. *Mauritius* 11°0S 57°0E **146** F4
Ağapınar *Turkey* 39°48N 30°47E **99** B12
Agar *India* 23°40N 76°2E **124** H7
Agar → *India* 21°0N 82°57E **126** D6
Agartala *India* 23°50N 91°23E **123** H17
Ağaş *Romania* 46°28N 26°15E **81** D11
Agassiz *Canada* 49°14N 121°46W **162** D4
Agassiz Icecap *Canada* 80°15N 76°0W **161** A16
Agats *Indonesia* 5°33S 138°0E **119** F9
Agatti I. *India* 10°50N 72°12E **127** J1
Agattu I. *U.S.A.* 52°25N 173°35E **166** E2
Agawam *U.S.A.* 42°5N 72°37W **175** D12
Agbélouvé *Togo* 6°35N 1°14E **139** D5
Agboville *Ivory C.* 5°55N 4°15W **138** D4
Ağcabädi *Azerbaijan* 40°5N 47°27E **87** K8
Ağdam *Azerbaijan* 40°0N 46°58E **87** K8
Ağdara *Azerbaijan* 40°13N 46°49E **87** K8
Ağdaş *Azerbaijan* 40°44N 47°22E **87** K8
Agde *France* 43°19N 3°28E **72** E7
Agde, C. d' *France* 43°16N 3°28E **72** E7
Agdz *Morocco* 30°47N 6°30W **136** B2
Agdzhabedi = Ağcabädi *Azerbaijan* 40°5N 47°27E **87** K8
Agen *France* 44°12N 0°38E **72** D4
Agerbæk *Denmark* 55°36N 8°48E **63** J2
Agersø *Denmark* 55°13N 11°12E **63** J5
Ageyevo *Russia* 54°10N 36°27E **84** E9
Aggteleki △ *Hungary* 48°27N 20°36E **80** B5
Āgh Kand *Iran* 37°15N 48°4E **105** D13
Aghathonisi *Greece* 37°28N 27°0E **99** D8
Aghia Anna *Greece* 38°52N 23°24E **98** C5
Aghia Deka *Greece* 35°3N 24°58E **101** D6
Aghia Ekaterinis, Akra *Greece* 39°50N 19°50E **101** A3
Aghia Galini *Greece* 35°6N 24°41E **101** D6
Aghia Marina *Kasos, Greece* 35°27N 26°53E **99** F8
Aghia Marina *Leros, Greece* 37°11N 26°48E **99** D8
Aghia Paraskevi *Greece* 39°14N 26°21E **99** B8
Aghia Roumeli *Greece* 35°14N 23°58E **98** F5
Aghia Varvara *Greece* 35°8N 25°1E **101** D7
Aghiasos *Greece* 39°5N 26°23E **99** B8
Aghio Theodori *Greece* 37°55N 23°9E **98** D5
Aghion Oros □ *Greece* 40°25N 24°6E **97** F8
Aghios Andreas *Greece* 37°21N 22°45E **98** D4
Aghios Efstratios *Greece* 39°34N 24°58E **98** B6
Aghios Georgios *Greece* 37°28N 23°57E **98** D5
Aghios Ioannis, Akra *Greece* 35°20N 25°40E **101** D7
Aghios Isidoros *Greece* 36°9N 27°51E **101** C9
Aghios Kirikos *Greece* 37°34N 26°17E **99** D8
Aghios Matheos *Greece* 39°30N 19°47E **101** B3
Aghios Mironas *Greece* 35°15N 25°1E **99** F7
Aghios Nikolaos *Greece* 35°11N 25°41E **101** D7
Aghios Petros *Greece* 38°40N 20°36E **98** C2
Aghios Stephanos *Greece* 39°46N 19°39E **101** A3
Aghiou Orous, Kolpos *Greece* 40°6N 24°0E **96** F7
Aghireşu *Romania* 46°53N 23°15E **81** D8
Agia *Greece* 39°43N 22°45E **98** B4
Aginskoye *Russia* 51°6N 114°32E **107** D12
Agjert *Mauritania* 16°23N 9°17W **138** B3
Ağlasun *Turkey* 37°39N 30°31E **99** D12
Agly → *France* 42°46N 3°3E **72** F7
Agnéby □ *Ivory C.* 6°0N 4°15W **138** D4
Agnew *Australia* 28°1S 120°31E **149** E3
Agnibilékrou *Ivory C.* 7°10N 3°11W **138** D4
Agnita *Romania* 45°59N 24°40E **81** E9
Agnone *Italy* 41°48N 14°22E **93** G11
Ago-Are *Nigeria* 8°30N 3°25E **139** D5
Agofie *Ghana* 8°27N 0°15E **139** D5
Agogna → *Italy* 45°4N 8°54E **92** C5
Agoitz = Aoiz *Spain* 42°46N 1°22W **90** C3
Agön *Sweden* 61°34N 17°23E **62** C11
Agon-Coutainville *France* 49°2N 1°34W **70** C5
Ágordo *Italy* 46°18N 12°2E **93** B9
Agori *India* 24°33N 82°57E **125** G10
Agouna *Benin* 7°39N 1°47E **139** D5
Agout → *France* 43°47N 1°41E **72** E5
Agra *India* 27°17N 77°58E **124** F7
Agrakhanskiy Poluostrov *Russia* 43°42N 47°36E **87** J8
Agramunt *Spain* 41°48N 1°6E **90** D6
Ágreda *Spain* 41°51N 1°55W **90** D3
Ağri *Turkey* 39°44N 43°3E **105** C10
Ağri □ *Turkey* 39°45N 43°5E **105** C10
Agri → *Italy* 40°13N 16°44E **95** B9
Ağrı Dağı *Turkey* 39°50N 44°15E **105** C11
Ağri Karakose = Ağri *Turkey* 39°44N 43°3E **105** C10
Agria *Greece* 39°20N 23°1E **98** B5
Agrigento *Italy* 37°19N 13°34E **94** E6
Agrinio *Greece* 38°37N 21°27E **98** C3
Agrópoli *Italy* 40°21N 14°59E **95** B7
Ağstafa *Azerbaijan* 41°7N 45°27E **87** K7
Água Branca *Brazil* 5°50S 42°40W **189** B2
Agua Caliente *Mexico* 32°29N 116°59W **171** N10
Agua Caliente Springs *U.S.A.* 32°56N 116°19W **171** N10
Água Clara *Brazil* 20°25S 52°45W **187** H8
Agua Fria △ *U.S.A.* 34°14N 112°0W **169** J8
Agua Hechicera *Mexico* 32°28N 116°15W **171** N10
Agua Prieta *Mexico* 31°18N 109°34W **180** A3
Aguada Cecilio *Argentina* 40°51S 65°51W **192** B3
Aguadilla *Puerto Rico* 18°26N 67°10W **183** d
Aguadulce *Panama* 8°15N 80°32W **182** E3
Aguanga *U.S.A.* 33°27N 116°51W **171** M10
Aguanish *Canada* 50°14N 62°2W **165** B7
Aguanish → *Canada* 50°13N 62°5W **165** B7
Aguapey → *Argentina* 29°7S 56°36W **190** B4
Aguaray Guazú → *Paraguay* 24°47S 57°19W **190** A
Aguarico → *Ecuador* 0°59S 75°11W **186** D
Aguaro-Guariquito △ *Venezuela* 8°20N 66°35W **183** E
Aguas → *Spain* 41°20N 0°30W **90** D
Aguas Blancas *Chile* 24°15S 69°55W **190** A
Aguas Calientes, Sierra de *Argentina* 25°26S 66°40W **190** B
Águas Formosas *Brazil* 17°5S 40°57W **189** D
Águas Lindas de Goiás *Brazil* 15°46S 48°15W **189** D
Aguascalientes *Mexico* 21°53N 102°18W **180** C
Aguascalientes □ *Mexico* 22°0N 102°20W **180** C
Agudo *Spain* 38°59N 4°52W **89** G
Águeda *Portugal* 40°34N 8°27W **88** E
Agueda → *Spain* 41°2N 6°56W **88** D
Aguelhok *Mali* 19°29N 0°52E **139** B
Aguié *Niger* 13°31N 7°46E **139** C
Aguila, Punta *Puerto Rico* 17°57N 67°13W **183**
Aguilafuente *Spain* 41°13N 4°7W **88** D
Aguilar de Campóo *Spain* 42°47N 4°15W **88** C
Aguilar de la Frontera *Spain* 37°31N 4°40W **89** H
Aguilares *Argentina* 27°26S 65°35W **190** B
Águilas *Spain* 37°23N 1°35W **91** H
Agüimes *Canary Is.* 27°58N 15°27W **100** G
Aguja, C. de la *Colombia* 11°18N 74°12W **184** B
Agujereada, Pta. *Puerto Rico* 18°30N 67°8W **183**
Agulhas, C. *S. Africa* 34°52S 20°0E **144** D
Agulhas Ridge *Atl. Oc.* 42°0S 15°0E **56** L1
Agulo *Canary Is.* 28°11N 17°12W **100** F
Agung, Gunung *Indonesia* 8°20S 115°28E **118** F
Aguni-Jima *Japan* 26°30N 127°10E **113** L
Agur *Uganda* 2°28N 32°55E **142** B
Agusan → *Phil.* 9°0N 125°30E **119** C
Ağva *Turkey* 41°8N 29°51E **97** E1
Agvali *Russia* 42°36N 46°8E **87** J
Aha Mts. *Botswana* 19°45S 21°0E **144** A
Ahaggar *Algeria* 23°0N 6°30E **136** D
Ahaggar △ *Algeria* 23°0N 4°50E **136** D
Ahai Dam *China* 27°21N 100°30E **116** D
Ahal □ *Turkmenistan* 37°0N 57°0E **108** E
Ahamansu *Ghana* 7°38N 0°35E **139** D
Ahar *Iran* 38°35N 47°0E **105** C1
Ahat *Turkey* 38°39N 29°47E **99** C1
Ahaura → *N.Z.* 42°21S 171°34E **155** C
Ahaus *Germany* 52°4N 7°0E **76** C
Ahelledjem *Algeria* 26°37N 6°58E **136** C
Ahimanawa Ra. *N.Z.* 39°3S 176°30E **154** F
Ahipara B. *N.Z.* 35°5S 173°5E **154** B
Ahir Dağı *Turkey* 38°45N 30°10E **99** C1
Ahiri *India* 19°30N 80°0E **126** E
Ahlat *Turkey* 38°45N 42°29E **105** C1
Ahlen *Germany* 51°45N 7°53E **76** D
Ahmad Wal *Pakistan* 29°18N 65°58E **124** E
Ahmadabad *India* 23°0N 72°40E **124** H
Aḩmadābād *Khorāsān, Iran* 35°3N 60°50E **129** C
Aḩmadābād *Khorāsān, Iran* 35°49N 59°42E **129** C
Aḩmadī *Iran* 27°56N 56°42E **129** E
Ahmadnagar *India* 19°7N 74°46E **126** E
Ahmadpur *India* 18°40N 76°57E **126** E
Ahmadpur East *Pakistan* 29°12N 71°10E **124** E
Ahmadpur Lamma *Pakistan* 28°19N 70°3E **124** E
Ahmedabad = Ahmadabad *India* 23°0N 72°40E **124** H
Ahmednagar = Ahmadnagar *India* 19°7N 74°46E **126** E
Ahmetbey *Turkey* 41°26N 27°34E **97** E1
Ahmetler *Turkey* 38°28N 29°5E **99** C1
Ahmetli *Turkey* 38°32N 27°57E **99** C
Ahoada *Nigeria* 5°8N 6°36E **139** D
Ahome *Mexico* 25°55N 109°11W **180** B
Ahoskie *U.S.A.* 36°17N 76°59W **177** C1
Ahr → *Germany* 50°32N 7°16E **76** E
Ahram *Iran* 28°52N 51°16E **129** D
Ahrax Pt. *Malta* 36°0N 14°22E **101** D
Ahrensbök *Germany* 54°2N 10°35E **76** A
Ahrensburg *Germany* 53°40N 10°13E **76** B
Ahuachapán *El Salv.* 13°54N 89°52W **182** D
Ahun *France* 46°4N 2°5E **71** F
Ahuriri → *N.Z.* 44°31S 170°12E **155** E
Åhus *Sweden* 55°56N 14°18E **63** J
Ahvāz *Iran* 31°20N 48°40E **129** D
Ahvenanmaa = Åland *Finland* 60°15N 20°0E **61** F1
Aḩwar *Yemen* 13°30N 46°40E **131** E
Ahzar → *Mali* 15°30N 3°20E **139** B
Ai → *India* 26°26N 90°44E **125** F1
Ai-Ais *Namibia* 27°54S 17°59E **144** C
Ai-Ais and Fish River Canyon △ *Namibia* 24°45S 17°15E **144** B
Aichach *Germany* 48°27N 11°8E **77** G
Aichi □ *Japan* 35°0N 137°15E **113** G
Aigai *Greece* 40°28N 22°19E **96** F
Aigle *Switz.* 46°18N 6°58E **77** J
Aignay-le-Duc *France* 47°40N 4°43E **71** E1
Aigoual, Mt. *France* 44°8N 3°35E **72** D
Aigre *France* 45°54N 0°1E **72** C
Aigrettes, Pte. des *Réunion* 21°3S 55°13E **141** c
Aiguá *Uruguay* 34°13S 54°46W **191** C
Aigueperse *France* 46°3N 3°13E **71** F1
Aigues → *France* 44°7N 4°43E **73** D
Aigues-Mortes *France* 43°35N 4°12E **73** E
Aigues-Mortes, G. d' *France* 43°31N 4°3E **73** E
Aigües-Tortes i Estany de St. Maurici △ *Spain* 42°38N 0°31E **90** C
Aiguilles *France* 44°47N 6°51E **73** D10
Aiguillon *France* 44°18N 0°21E **72** D4
Aigurande *France* 46°27N 1°49E **71** F8
Aihui = Heihe *China* 50°10N 127°30E **111** A14
Aija *Peru* 9°50S 77°45W **188** B2
Aikawa *Japan* 38°2N 138°15E **112** E9
Aiken *U.S.A.* 33°34N 81°43W **178** B8
Ailao Shan *China* 24°0N 101°20E **116** F3
Aileron *Australia* 22°39S 133°20E **150** C1
Ailey *U.S.A.* 32°11N 82°34W **178** C7

Aillant-sur-Tholon
  France   47°52N 3°20E **71** E10
Aillik Canada   55°11N 59°18W **165** A8
Ailsa Craig Canada   43°8N 81°33W **174** C3
Ailsa Craig U.K.   55°15N 5°6W **65** F3
Aim Russia   59°0N 133°55E **107** D14
Aimogasta Argentina   28°33S 66°50W **190** B2
Aimorés Brazil   19°30S 41°4W **189** D2
Ain → France   46°5N 5°20E **71** F12
Ain □ France   45°45N 5°11E **73** C9
Aïn Beïda Algeria   35°50N 7°29E **136** A5
Aïn Ben Khellil Algeria   33°15N 0°49W **136** B3
Aïn Ben Tili Mauritania   25°59N 9°27W **134** C4
Aïn Beni Mathar Morocco   34°1N 2°0W **136** B3
Aïn Benian Algeria   36°48N 2°55E **136** A4
Aïn Dalla Egypt   27°20N 27°23E **137** B2
Aïn Defla Algeria   36°16N 1°58E **136** A4
Aïn Defla □ Algeria   36°10N 2°10E **136** A4
Aïn el Mafki Egypt   27°30N 28°15E **137** B2
Aïn Girba Egypt   29°20N 25°14E **137** B2
Aïn M'lila Algeria   36°2N 6°35E **136** A5
Aïn Murr Sudan   21°50N 25°9E **137** C2
Aïn Qeiqab Egypt   29°42N 24°55E **137** B1
Aïn Sefra Algeria   32°47N 0°37W **136** B3
Aïn Sheikh Murzûk
  Egypt   26°47N 27°45E **137** B2
Aïn Sudr Egypt   29°50N 33°6E **130** F2
Aïn Sukhna Egypt   29°32N 32°20E **137** F8
Aïn Tédelès Algeria   36°0N 0°21E **136** A4
Aïn Témouchent Algeria   35°16N 1°8W **136** A3
Aïn Témouchent □
  Algeria   35°20N 1°5W **136** A3
Aïn Tikkidine Algeria   25°33N 1°24E **136** C4
Aïn Touta Algeria   35°26N 5°54E **136** A5
Aïn Zeitûn Egypt   29°10N 25°48E **137** B2
Aïn Zorah Morocco   34°37N 3°32W **136** B3
Ainaži Latvia   57°50N 24°24E **84** D3
Ainsworth U.S.A.   42°33N 99°52W **172** D4
Aiquile Bolivia   18°10S 65°10W **186** G5
Aïr Niger   18°30N 8°0E **139** B6
Aïr et Ténéré △ Niger   17°30N 9°56E **139** B6
Airaines France   49°58N 1°55E **71** C8
Airdrie Canada   51°18N 114°2W **162** C6
Airdrie U.K.   55°52N 3°57W **65** F5
Aire → France   49°18N 4°49E **71** C11
Aire → U.K.   53°43N 0°55W **66** D7
Aire, I. de l' Spain   39°48N 4°16E **100** B11
Aire-sur-la-Lys France   50°37N 2°22E **71** B9
Aire-sur-l'Adour France   43°42N 0°15W **72** E3
Aireys Inlet Australia   38°29S 144°5E **152** F6
Airlie Beach Australia   20°16S 148°43E **150** b
Airvault France   46°50N 0°8W **70** F6
Aisch → Germany   49°49N 10°58E **77** F6
Aisén □ Chile   46°30S 73°0W **192** C2
Aisne □ France   49°42N 3°40E **71** C10
Aisne → France   49°26N 2°50E **71** C9
Aït India   25°54N 79°14E **125** G8
Aït Ben Haddou Morocco   31°3N 7°7W **136** B2
Aïtana, Sierra de Spain   38°35N 0°24W **91** G4
Aitkin U.S.A.   46°32N 93°42W **172** B7
Aitutaki Cook Is.   18°52S 159°45W **157** J12
Aiuaba Brazil   6°38S 40°7W **189** D2
Aiud Romania   46°19N 23°44E **81** D8
Aix-en-Provence France   43°32N 5°27E **73** E9
Aix-la-Chapelle = Aachen
  Germany   50°45N 6°6E **76** E2
Aix-les-Bains France   45°41N 5°53E **73** C9
Aix-sur-Vienne France   45°47N 1°9E **72** C5
Aïyina = Egina Greece   37°45N 23°26E **98** D5
Aïyion = Egina Greece   38°15N 22°5E **98** C4
Aizawl India   23°40N 92°44E **123** H18
Aizenay France   46°44N 1°38W **70** F5
Aizkraukle Latvia   56°36N 25°11E **84** D3
Aizpute Latvia   56°43N 21°40E **82** B8
Aizuwakamatsu Japan   37°30N 139°56E **112** F9
Ajabshir Iran   37°28N 45°54E **105** D11
Ajaccio France   41°55N 8°40E **73** G12
Ajaccio, G. d' France   41°52N 8°40E **73** G12
Ajai △ Uganda   2°52N 31°16E **142** B3
Ajaigarh India   24°52N 80°16E **125** G9
Ajalpan Mexico   18°22N 97°15W **181** D5
Ajanta India   20°30N 75°48E **126** D2
Ajanta Ra. India   20°28N 75°50E **126** D2
Ajaokuta Nigeria   7°28N 6°42E **139** D6
Ajari Rep. = Ajaria □
  Georgia   41°30N 42°0E **87** K6
Ajaria □ Georgia   41°30N 42°0E **87** K6
Ajax Canada   43°50N 79°1W **174** C5
Ajax, Mt. N.Z.   42°35S 172°56E **155** C7
Ajdābiyā Libya   30°54N 20°4E **135** B10
Ajdovščina Slovenia   45°54N 13°54E **93** C10
Ajka Hungary   47°4N 17°31E **80** C2
Ajlūn Jordan   32°18N 35°47E **130** C4
Ajlūn □ Jordan   32°18N 35°47E **130** C4
Ajman U.A.E.   25°25N 55°30E **129** E7
Ajmer India   26°28N 74°37E **124** F6
Ajnala India   31°50N 74°48E **124** D6
Ajo U.S.A.   32°22N 112°52W **169** K7
Ajo, C. de Spain   43°31N 3°35W **88** B7
Ak Dağ Turkey   36°30N 29°32E **99** E11
Ak Dağları Turkey   39°32N 36°12E **104** C7
Ak Dağları Turkey   36°30N 29°50E **99** E11
Ak-Dovurak Russia   51°11N 90°36E **109** B12
Akaba Togo   8°10N 1°2E **139** D5
Akabira Japan   43°33N 142°5E **112** C11
Akabli Algeria   51°1N 55°37E **108** B5
Akademika Obrucheva, Khrebet
  Russia   51°50N 96°0E **109** B13
Akagera △ Rwanda   1°31S 30°52E **142** C3
Akalkot India   17°32N 76°13E **126** D3
Akamas Cyprus   35°3N 32°18E **101** D11
Akan △ Japan   43°20N 144°20E **112** C12
Akarca Turkey   38°35N 29°59E **99** C11
Akaroa N.Z.   43°50S 172°55E **155** D7
Akasha Sudan   21°10N 30°32E **137** C3
Akashi Japan   34°45N 134°58E **113** G7
Akbarpur Bihar, India   24°39N 83°58E **125** G10
Akbarpur Ut. P., India   26°25N 82°32E **125** F10
Akbou Algeria   36°31N 4°31E **136** A4
Akbulak Russia   51°1N 55°37E **108** B5
Akçaabat Turkey   41°1N 39°34E **105** B8
Akçadağ Turkey   38°27N 37°43E **104** C7
Akçakale Turkey   36°41N 38°56E **105** D8
Akçakoca Turkey   41°5N 31°18E **104** B4
Akçaova Turkey   41°9N 29°57E **97** E13
Akçay Turkey   36°36N 29°45E **99** E11
Akçay → Turkey   37°50N 28°15E **99** D10

Akdağ Turkey   38°33N 26°30E **99** C8
Akdağmadeni Turkey   39°39N 35°53E **104** C6
Akdoğan = Lysi Cyprus   35°6N 33°41E **101** D12
Akelamo Indonesia   1°35N 129°40E **119** D7
Åkers styckebruk
  Sweden   59°15N 17°5E **62** E11
Åkersberga Sweden   59°29N 18°18E **62** E12
Akeru → India   17°25N 80°5E **126** F5
Aketi
  Dem. Rep. of the Congo   2°38N 23°47E **140** D4
Akhali Atoni Georgia   43°7N 40°50E **87** J5
Akhalkalaki Georgia   41°27N 43°25E **87** K6
Akhaltsikhe Georgia   41°40N 43°0E **87** K6
Akhisar Turkey   38°56N 27°48E **99** C9
Akhmīm Egypt   26°31N 31°47E **137** B3
Akhna Cyprus   35°3N 33°47E **101** D12
Akhnur India   32°52N 74°45E **125** C6
Akhtopol Bulgaria   42°6N 27°56E **97** D11
Akhtuba → Russia   47°41N 46°55E **87** F8
Akhtubinsk Russia   48°13N 46°7E **87** F8
Akhty Russia   41°30N 47°45E **87** K8
Akhtyrka = Okhtyrka
  Ukraine   50°25N 35°0E **85** G8
Aki Japan   33°30N 133°54E **113** H6
Akimiski I. Canada   52°50N 81°30W **164** B3
Akıncı Burnu Turkey   36°19N 35°46E **104** D6
Akıncılar = Louroujina
  Cyprus   35°0N 33°28E **101** E12
Akiōta Japan   34°36N 132°19E **113** G6
Åkirkeby Denmark   55°4N 14°55E **63** A8
Akita Japan   39°45N 140°7E **112** E10
Akita □ Japan   39°40N 140°30E **112** E10
Akjoujt Mauritania   19°45N 14°15W **138** B2
Aklavik Canada   68°12N 135°0W **160** D4
Aklera India   24°26N 76°32E **124** G7
Akmenė Lithuania   56°15N 22°45E **82** B9
Akmenrags Latvia   56°50N 21°4E **82** B8
Akmonte = Almonte
  Spain   37°13N 6°38W **89** H4
Aknoul Morocco   34°40N 3°55W **136** B3
Akō Japan   34°45N 134°24E **113** G7
Ako Nigeria   10°19N 10°48E **139** C7
Akola Maharashtra, India   20°42N 77°2E **126** D3
Akola Maharashtra, India   19°32N 74°23E **126** E2
Akonolinga Cameroon   3°50N 12°18E **139** E7
Akor Mali   14°59N 6°58W **138** C3
Akordat Eritrea   15°30N 37°40E **131** D2
Akot India   21°10N 77°10E **126** D3
Akoupé Ivory C.   6°23N 3°54W **138** D4
Akpatok I. Canada   60°25N 68°8W **161** E18
Åkrahamn Norway   59°15N 5°10E **61** G11
Akranes Iceland   64°19N 22°5W **60** D2
Akreïjit Mauritania   18°19N 9°11W **138** B3
Akritas, Ákra Greece   36°43N 21°54E **98** E3
Akron Colo., U.S.A.   40°10N 103°13W **168** F12
Akron Ohio, U.S.A.   41°5N 81°31W **174** E3
Akrotiri Cyprus   34°36N 32°57E **101** E11
Akrotiri, Ákra Greece   40°26N 25°27E **97** F9
Akrotiri Bay Cyprus   34°35N 33°10E **101** E12
Aksai Chin China   35°15N 79°55E **125** B8
Aksaray Turkey   38°25N 34°2E **104** C6
Aksaray □ Turkey   38°30N 33°45E **104** C5
Aksay = Aqsay
  Kazakhstan   51°11N 53°0E **108** B4
Akşehir Turkey   38°18N 31°30E **104** C4
Akşehir Gölü Turkey   38°30N 31°25E **104** C4
Akstafa = Ağstafa
  Azerbaijan   41°7N 45°27E **87** K7
Aksu China   41°5N 80°10E **109** D10
Aksu → Turkey   36°52N 30°57E **104** D4
Aksu He → China   40°26N 80°59E **109** D10
Aksum Ethiopia   14°5N 38°40E **131** E2
Aktash Russia   55°20N 52°3E **86** C11
Akto China   39°5N 75°59E **109** E9
Aktsyabrski Belarus   52°38N 28°53E **75** B15
Aktyubinsk = Aqtöbe
  Kazakhstan   50°17N 57°10E **108** B5
Aku Nigeria   6°40N 7°18E **139** D6
Akure Nigeria   7°15N 5°5E **139** D6
Akuressa Sri Lanka   6°5N 80°29E **127** L5
Akureyri Iceland   65°40N 18°6W **60** D4
Akuseki-Shima Japan   29°27N 129°37E **113** K4
Akusha Russia   42°18N 47°30E **87** J8
Akwa-Ibom □ Nigeria   4°30N 7°30E **139** E6
Akwanga Nigeria   8°55N 8°23E **139** D6
Akyab = Sittwe
  Burma   20°18N 92°45E **123** J18
Akyazı Turkey   40°40N 30°38E **104** B4
Al 'Adan = 'Adan
  Yemen   12°45N 45°0E **131** E4
Al Aḥsā = Hasa
  Si. Arabia   25°50N 49°0E **129** E6
Al Ajfar Si. Arabia   27°26N 43°0E **128** E4
Al Amādīyah Iraq   37°5N 43°30E **105** D10
Al 'Amārah Iraq   31°55N 47°15E **105** G12
Al Anbār □ Iraq   33°25N 42°0E **128** C4
Al 'Aqabah Jordan   29°31N 35°0E **130** F4
Al 'Aqabah □ Jordan   29°40N 35°0E **130** F4
Al Arak Syria   34°38N 38°35E **105** E8
Al 'Aramah Si. Arabia   25°30N 46°0E **128** E5
Al 'Arṭāwīyah
  Si. Arabia   26°31N 45°20E **128** E5
Al 'Āṣimah = 'Ammān □
  Jordan   31°40N 36°30E **130** D5
Al 'Awdah Si. Arabia   25°4N 38°59E **128** E3
Al 'Ayn U.A.E.   24°15N 55°45E **129** E7
Al 'Ayn Si. Arabia   25°30N 38°0E **128** E3
Al 'Azīzīyah Iraq   32°54N 45°4E **105** F11
Al Bāb Syria   36°23N 37°29E **104** C7
Al Bad' Si. Arabia   28°28N 35°1E **128** D2
Al Bada'i' Si. Arabia   23°55N 44°32E **128** E4
Al Bādī Iraq   35°56N 41°32E **128** C4
Al Baḥrah Kuwait   29°40N 47°52E **128** D5
Al Baḥral Mayyit = Dead Sea
  Asia   31°30N 35°30E **130** D4
Al Balqā' □ Jordan   32°5N 35°45E **130** C4
Al Bārūk, J. Lebanon   33°39N 35°40E **130** B4
Al Baṣrah Iraq   30°30N 47°50E **128** D5
Al Baṭḥā Iraq   31°6N 45°53E **128** D5

Al Batrūn Lebanon   34°15N 35°40E **130** A4
Al Baydā Libya   32°50N 21°44E **135** B10
Al Biqā Lebanon   34°10N 36°10E **130** A5
Al Bi'r Si. Arabia   28°51N 36°16E **128** D3
Al Bukayrīyah Si. Arabia   26°9N 43°40E **128** E4
Al Buraij Syria   33°36N 36°46E **130** A5
Al Faḍilī Si. Arabia   26°58N 49°10E **129** E6
Al Fallūjah Iraq   33°20N 43°55E **105** F10
Al Fatḥah Iraq   35°3N 43°33E **105** E10
Al Fāw Iraq   30°0N 48°30E **129** D6
Al Fujayrah U.A.E.   25°7N 56°18E **129** E8
Al Ghadaf, W. →
  Jordan   31°26N 36°43E **130** D5
Al Ghammās Iraq   31°45N 44°37E **128** D5
Al Ghazālah Si. Arabia   26°48N 41°19E **128** E4
Al Ghuwayfāt U.A.E.   24°10N 51°38E **129** E6
Al Ḥadīthah Iraq   34°0N 41°13E **105** E10
Al Ḥadīthah Si. Arabia   31°28N 37°8E **130** D6
Al Ḥadr Iraq   35°35N 42°44E **105** E10
Al Ḥājānah Syria   33°20N 36°33E **130** B5
Al Ḥajar al Gharbī
  Oman   24°10N 56°15E **129** E8
Al Ḥāmad Si. Arabia   31°30N 39°30E **128** D3
Al Ḥamdānīyah Si. Arabia   35°25N 36°50E **128** C3
Al Ḥamīdīyah Syria   34°42N 35°57E **130** A4
Al Ḥammār Iraq   30°57N 46°51E **128** D5
Al Ḥamrā' Si. Arabia   24°2N 38°55E **128** E3
Al Ḥamzah Iraq   31°43N 44°58E **128** D5
Al Ḥanākīyah
  Si. Arabia   24°51N 40°31E **128** E4
Al Ḥarūj al Aswad Libya   27°0N 17°10E **135** C9
Al Ḥasakah Si. Arabia   36°35N 40°45E **105** D9
Al Ḥasakah □ Syria   36°35N 40°45E **105** D9
Al Ḥāshimīyah Iraq   32°22N 44°39E **105** G11
Al Ḥayy Iraq   32°5N 46°5E **105** F12
Al Ḥijarah Asia   30°0N 44°0E **128** D4
Al Ḥillah Iraq   32°30N 44°25E **105** F11
Al Hindīyah Iraq   32°30N 44°10E **105** F11
Al Hirmil Lebanon   34°26N 36°24E **130** A5
Al Hoceïma Morocco   35°8N 3°58W **136** A3
Al Ḥudaydah Yemen   14°50N 43°0E **131** E3
Al Ḥudūd ash Shamālīyah □
  Si. Arabia   29°10N 42°30E **128** D4
Al Ḥufūf Si. Arabia   25°25N 49°45E **129** E6
Al Ḥumaydah
  Si. Arabia   29°14N 34°56E **128** D2
Al Ḥunayy Si. Arabia   25°58N 48°45E **129** E6
Al Ïsāwīyah Si. Arabia   30°43N 37°59E **128** D3
Al Jafr Jordan   30°18N 36°14E **130** E5
Al Jāfūrah Si. Arabia   25°0N 50°15E **129** E7
Al Jaghbūb Libya   29°42N 24°38E **135** C10
Al Jahrah Kuwait   29°25N 47°40E **128** D5
Al Jalāmīd Si. Arabia   31°20N 40°6E **128** D3
Al Janūb □ Lebanon   33°15N 35°21E **130** B4
Al Jawf Libya   24°10N 23°24E **135** D10
Al Jawf Si. Arabia   29°55N 39°40E **128** D3
Al Jazair = Algeria ■
  Africa   28°30N 2°0E **136** C4
Al Jazirah Iraq   33°30N 44°0E **105** E10
Al Jithāmīyah Si. Arabia   27°41N 41°43E **128** E4
Al Jubayl Si. Arabia   27°0N 49°50E **129** E6
Al Jubaylah Si. Arabia   24°55N 46°25E **128** E5
Al Jubb Si. Arabia   27°11N 42°17E **128** E4
Al Junaynah Sudan   13°27N 22°45E **135** F10
Al Kabā'ish Iraq   30°58N 47°0E **128** D5
Al Karak Jordan   31°11N 35°42E **130** D4
Al Karak □ Jordan   31°0N 36°0E **130** E5
Al Kāẓimīyah Iraq   33°22N 44°18E **105** F11
Al Khābūrah Oman   23°57N 57°5E **129** F8
Al Khafji Si. Arabia   28°24N 48°29E **129** E6
Al Khalīl West Bank   31°32N 35°6E **130** D4
Al Khāliṣ Iraq   33°49N 44°32E **105** F11
Al Kharsānīyah
  Si. Arabia   27°13N 49°18E **129** E6
Al Khaṣab Oman   26°14N 56°15E **129** E8
Al Khawr Qatar   25°41N 51°30E **129** E6
Al Khiḍr Iraq   31°12N 45°33E **128** D5
Al Khiyām Lebanon   33°20N 35°36E **130** B4
Al Khubar Si. Arabia   26°17N 50°12E **129** E6
Al Khums Libya   32°40N 14°17E **135** B8
Al Khurmah Si. Arabia   21°54N 42°3E **131** C3
Al Kifl Iraq   32°13N 44°22E **105** G11
Al Kiswah Syria   33°23N 36°14E **130** B5
Al Kūfah Iraq   32°2N 44°24E **105** F11
Al Kufrah Libya   24°17N 23°15E **135** D10
Al Kuhayfiyah Si. Arabia   27°12N 43°3E **128** E4
Al Kumayt Iraq   32°2N 46°2E **105** G12
Al Kūt Iraq   32°30N 46°0E **105** F11
Al Kuwayt Kuwait   29°30N 48°0E **128** D5
Al Labwah Lebanon   34°11N 36°20E **130** A5
Al Lādhiqīyah Syria   35°30N 35°45E **104** E6
Al Lādhiqīyah □ Syria   35°45N 36°0E **104** E6
Al Līth Si. Arabia   20°9N 40°15E **137** D5
Al Liwā' Oman   24°31N 56°36E **129** E8
Al Luḥayyah Yemen   15°45N 42°40E **131** D3
Al Madīnah Iraq   30°57N 47°16E **128** D5
Al Madīnah Si. Arabia   24°35N 39°52E **128** E3
Al Mafraq Jordan   32°17N 36°14E **130** C5
Al Mafraq □ Jordan   32°36N 32°0E **130** C5
Al Maghreb = Morocco ■
  N. Afr.   32°0N 5°50W **134** B4
Al Maḥmūdīyah Iraq   33°3N 44°21E **105** F11
Al Majma'ah Si. Arabia   25°57N 45°22E **128** E5
Al Makhruq, W. →
  Jordan   31°28N 37°0E **130** D6
Al Makḥūl Si. Arabia   26°37N 42°39E **128** E4
Al Mālikīyah Si. Arabia   35°25N 30°10E **105** D10
Al Manāmah Bahrain   26°10N 50°30E **129** E6
Al Maqwa' Kuwait   29°10N 47°50E **128** D5
Al Marāḥ Si. Arabia   25°0N 45°35E **128** E5
Al Marj Libya   32°25N 20°30E **135** B10
Al Maṣīrah = Masīrah □
  Si. Arabia   30°0N 41°0E **128** D4
Al Mawjil Iraq   36°15N 43°5E **105** D10
Al Mayādin Syria   35°1N 40°27E **105** E9
Al Mazar Iraq   35°3N 45°31E **105** D10
Al Midhnab Si. Arabia   25°50N 44°18E **128** E4
Al Minā' Lebanon   34°24N 35°49E **130** A4
Al Miqdādīyah Iraq   34°0N 45°0E **105** E11
Al Mubarras Si. Arabia   25°30N 49°40E **129** E6
Al Mudawwarah Jordan   29°19N 36°0E **130** F5
Al Mughayrā' U.A.E.   24°5N 53°32E **129** E7
Al Muḥarraq Bahrain   26°15N 50°40E **129** E6
Al Mukallā Yemen   14°33N 49°2E **131** E4
Al Mukhā Yemen   13°18N 43°15E **131** E3
Al Musayjīd Si. Arabia   24°5N 39°5E **128** E3
Al Musayyib Iraq   32°49N 44°20E **105** F11
Al Muthanná □ Iraq   31°30N 45°15E **128** D5
Al Muwayḥ Si. Arabia   22°41N 41°37E **137** C5
Al Muwayliḥ Si. Arabia   27°40N 35°30E **128** E2

Al Owuho = Otukpa
  Nigeria   7°9N 7°41E **139** D6
Al Qādisīyah □ Iraq   32°0N 45°0E **128** D5
Al Qā'im Iraq   34°21N 41°7E **105** E9
Al Qalībah Si. Arabia   28°24N 37°42E **128** D3
Al Qāmishlī Syria   37°2N 41°14E **105** D9
Al Qasim □ Si. Arabia   26°0N 43°0E **128** E4
Al Qaṭ'ā Syria   34°40N 40°48E **105** E9
Al Qaṭīf Si. Arabia   26°35N 50°0E **129** E6
Al Qaṭrānah Jordan   31°12N 36°6E **130** D5
Al Qaṭrūn Libya   24°56N 15°3E **135** D9
Al Qawz Si. Arabia   18°58N 41°26E **137** D5
Al Qayṣūmah Si. Arabia   28°20N 46°7E **128** D5
Al Quds = Jerusalem
  Israel/West Bank   31°47N 35°10E **130** D4
Al Qunayṭirah Syria   33°5N 35°45E **130** B4
Al Qunfudhah Si. Arabia   19°3N 41°4E **137** D5
Al Qurayyāt Si. Arabia   31°20N 37°20E **128** D3
Al Qurnah Iraq   31°1N 47°25E **128** D5
Al Quṣayr Iraq   30°39N 45°50E **128** D5
Al Quṣayr Syria   34°31N 36°34E **130** A5
Al Qutayfah Syria   33°44N 36°36E **130** B5
Al Quwayr Iraq   36°2N 43°29E **105** D10
Al Quwaysimah Jordan   31°55N 35°57E **130** D4
Al 'Ubaylah Si. Arabia   21°59N 50°57E **131** C5
Al 'Uḍaylīyah Si. Arabia   25°8N 49°18E **129** E6
Al 'Ulā Si. Arabia   26°35N 38°0E **128** E3
Al 'Uqayr Si. Arabia   25°40N 50°15E **129** E6
Al 'Uwaynid Si. Arabia   24°50N 46°0E **128** E5
Al 'Uwayqīlah
  Si. Arabia   30°30N 42°10E **128** D4
Al 'Uyūn Hijāz,
  Si. Arabia   24°33N 39°35E **128** E3
Al 'Uyūn Najd,
  Si. Arabia   26°30N 43°50E **128** E4
Al 'Uzayr Iraq   31°19N 47°25E **128** D5
Al Wajh Si. Arabia   26°10N 36°30E **128** E3
Al Wakrah Qatar   25°10N 51°40E **129** E6
Al Waqbah Si. Arabia   28°48N 45°33E **128** D5
Al Wari'āh Si. Arabia   27°51N 47°25E **128** E5
Al Yaman = Yemen ■
  Asia   15°0N 44°0E **131** E3
Ala Italy   45°45N 11°0E **92** C8
Ala Archa △
  Kyrgyzstan   42°32N 74°28E **109** D8
Ala Dağ Turkey   37°44N 35°9E **128** B2
Ala Dağları Turkey   39°15N 43°33E **105** C10
Ala Tau Asia   45°30N 80°40E **109** C10
Ala Tau Shankou = Dzungarian
  Gate Asia   45°10N 82°0E **109** C10
Alabama □ U.S.A.   33°0N 87°0W **177** E11
Alabama → U.S.A.   31°8N 87°57W **177** F11
Alabaster U.S.A.   33°15N 86°49W **177** E11
Alaca Turkey   40°10N 34°51E **104** B6
Alacam Turkey   41°36N 35°36E **104** B6
Alaçam Dağları Turkey   39°18N 28°49E **99** B10
Alacant = Alicante
  Spain   38°23N 0°30W **91** G4
Alaçatı Turkey   38°15N 26°22E **99** C8
Alachua U.S.A.   29°47N 82°30W **178** F7
Alaejos Spain   41°18N 5°13W **88** D5
Alagir Russia   43°3N 44°41E **87** J7
Alagna Valsésia Italy   45°51N 7°56E **92** C4
Alagoa Grande Brazil   7°3S 35°35W **189** D3
Alagoas □ Brazil   9°0S 36°0W **189** D3
Alagoinhas Brazil   12°7S 38°20W **189** E3
Alagón Spain   41°46N 1°12W **90** D3
Alagón → Spain   39°44N 6°53W **88** F4
Alahärmä
  Finland   63°12N 22°50E **60** E20
Alai Range Asia   39°45N 72°0E **108** D8
Alaior Spain   39°57N 4°8E **100** B11
Alajero Canary Is.   28°3N 17°13W **100** F2
Alajuela Costa Rica   10°2N 84°8W **182** D3
Alaknanda → India   30°8N 78°36E **125** D8
Alakol Kazakhstan   46°0N 81°5E **109** C10
Alakurtti Russia   66°58N 30°25E **60** C24
Alamarvdasht Iran   27°37N 52°59E **129** E7
Alameda Calif., U.S.A.   37°46N 122°15W **170** H4
Alameda N. Mex.,
  U.S.A.   35°11N 106°37W **169** J10
Alamo Ga., U.S.A.   32°9N 82°47W **178** E7
Alamo Nev., U.S.A.   37°22N 115°10W **171** H11
Alamogordo U.S.A.   32°54N 105°57W **169** K11
Alamos Mexico   27°1N 108°56W **180** B3
Alamosa U.S.A.   37°28N 105°52W **169** H11
Alampur India   15°55N 78°6E **126** F4
Åland Finland   60°15N 20°0E **61** F19
Åland Finland   17°36N 76°35E **126** F3
Alandroal Portugal   38°41N 7°24W **89** G3
Ålands hav Europe   60°0N 19°30E **61** F18
Ålandsbro Sweden   62°39N 17°51E **62** B11
Alandur India   13°0N 80°15E **127** H5
Alange, Embalse de Spain   38°45N 6°18W **89** G4
Alanís Spain   38°3N 5°43W **89** G5
Alaniya = North Ossetia-
  Alaniya □ Russia   43°30N 44°30E **87** J7
Alanya □ Russia   42°45N 44°30E **87** J7
Alanya Turkey   36°38N 32°0E **104** D5
Alapaha U.S.A.   31°23N 83°13W **178** D6
Alapayevsk Russia   57°52N 61°42E **106** D7
Alappuzha India   9°30N 76°28E **127** K3
Alar del Rey Spain   42°38N 4°20W **88** C6
Alaraz Spain   40°45N 5°17W **88** E5
Alarcón, Embalse de
  Spain   39°36N 2°10W **90** F2
Alaró Spain   39°42N 2°47E **100** B10
Alaşehir Turkey   38°23N 28°30E **99** C10
Alashtar Iran   33°51N 48°15E **105** F13
Alaska □ U.S.A.   64°0N 154°0W **166** C9
Alaska, G. of Pac. Oc.   58°0N 145°0W **160** F3
Alaska Peninsula
  U.S.A.   56°0N 159°0W **166** D8
Alaska Range U.S.A.   62°50N 151°0W **160** E1
Ālāt Azerbaijan   39°58N 49°25E **87** L9
Alatau Shan = Ala Tau
  Asia   45°30N 80°40E **109** C10
Alatri Italy   41°43N 13°21E **93** D5
Alatyr Russia   54°55N 46°35E **86** D8
Alatyr → Russia   54°52N 46°36E **86** C8
Alausi Ecuador   2°0S 78°50W **186** D3
Álava □ Spain   42°48N 2°28W **90** C2
Álava, C. U.S.A.   48°10N 124°44W **170** B2
Álava, Sierra de Spain   37°35N 5°10W **89** H5
Alaverdi Armenia   41°15N 44°37E **87** K7
Alavo = Alavus Finland   62°35N 23°36E **60** E20
Alavus Finland   62°35N 23°36E **60** E20
Alawa ♦ Australia   15°42S 134°39E **150** B1
Alawoona Australia   34°45S 140°30E **152** C3

Alayawarra ◇
  Australia   22°0S 134°30E **150** C1
'Alayh Lebanon   33°46N 35°33E **130** B4
Alayköy = Yerolakkos
  Cyprus   35°11N 33°15E **101** D12
Alazani → Azerbaijan   41°5N 46°40E **87** K8
Alba Italy   44°42N 8°2E **92** D5
Alba □ Romania   46°10N 23°30E **81** D8
Alba Adriática Italy   42°50N 13°56E **93** F10
Alba de Tormes Spain   40°50N 5°30W **88** E5
Alba-Iulia Romania   46°8N 23°39E **81** D8
Albac Romania   46°28N 22°58E **80** D7
Albacete Spain   39°0N 1°50W **91** F3
Albacete □ Spain   38°50N 2°0W **91** G3
Ålbæk Denmark   57°36N 10°25E **63** G4
Ålbæk Bugt Denmark   57°35N 10°40E **63** G4
Albaida Spain   38°51N 0°31W **91** G4
Albalate de las Nogueras
  Spain   40°22N 2°18W **90** E2
Albalate del Arzobispo
  Spain   41°6N 0°31W **90** D4
Alban France   43°53N 2°28E **72** E6
Albanel, L. Canada   50°55N 73°12W **164** B5
Albania ■ Europe   41°0N 20°0E **96** E4
Albano Laziale Italy   41°44N 12°39E **93** G9
Albany Australia   35°1S 117°58E **149** G2
Albany Ga., U.S.A.   31°35N 84°10W **178** D5
Albany N.Y., U.S.A.   42°39N 73°45W **175** D11
Albany Oreg., U.S.A.   44°38N 123°6W **168** D2
Albany Tex., U.S.A.   32°44N 99°18W **176** E5
Albany → Canada   52°17N 81°31W **164** B3
Albarca, C. d' Spain   39°4N 1°22E **100** B7
Albardón Argentina   31°20S 68°30W **190** C2
Albarracín Spain   40°25N 1°26W **90** E3
Albarracín, Sierra de
  Spain   40°30N 1°30W **90** E3
Albatera Spain   38°11N 0°52W **91** G4
Albâtre, Côte d' France   49°55N 0°50E **70** C7
Albatross B. Australia   12°45S 141°30E **150** A3
Albatross Pt. N.Z.   38°7S 174°46E **154** E3
Albegna → Italy   42°30N 11°11E **93** F8
Albemarle U.S.A.   35°21N 80°12W **177** D14
Albemarle Sd. U.S.A.   36°5N 76°0W **177** C16
Albenga Italy   44°3N 8°13E **92** D5
Alberche → Spain   39°58N 4°46W **88** F6
Alberdi Paraguay   26°14S 58°20W **190** B4
Albères, Mts. France   42°28N 2°56E **72** F6
Ålberga Sweden   58°44N 16°35E **63** F10
Albersdorf Germany   54°8N 9°17E **76** A5
Albert France   50°0N 2°38E **71** C9
Albert, L. Africa   1°30N 31°0E **142** B3
Albert, L. Australia   35°30S 139°10E **152** C3
Albert Edward Ra.
  Australia   18°17S 127°57E **148** C4
Albert Lea U.S.A.   43°39N 93°22W **172** D7
Albert Nile → Uganda   3°36N 32°2E **142** B3
Albert Town Bahamas   22°37N 74°33W **183** B5
Alberta □ Canada   54°40N 115°0W **162** C6
Alberti Argentina   35°1S 60°16W **190** D3
Albertina S. Africa   34°11S 21°34E **144** D3
Albertirsa Hungary   47°14N 19°37E **80** C4
Alberton Canada   46°50N 64°0W **165** C7
Albertville France   45°40N 6°22E **73** C10
Albertville U.S.A.   34°16N 86°13W **177** D11
Albi France   43°56N 2°9E **72** E6
Albia U.S.A.   41°2N 92°48W **172** E7
Albina Suriname   5°37N 54°15W **187** B8
Albina, Ponta Angola   15°52S 11°44E **144** A1
Albino Italy   45°46N 9°47E **92** C6
Albion Mich., U.S.A.   42°15N 84°45W **173** D11
Albion Nebr., U.S.A.   41°42N 98°0W **172** E4
Albion Pa., U.S.A.   41°53N 80°22W **174** E4
Albocàsser Spain   40°21N 0°1E **90** E5
Albolote Spain   37°14N 3°39W **89** H7
Alborán Medit. S.   35°57N 3°0W **89** K7
Alboran Sea Medit. S.   36°0N 3°0W **89** K7
Alborea Spain   39°17N 1°24W **91** F3
Ålborg = Aalborg Denmark   57°2N 9°54E **63** G3
Ålborg Bugt = Aalborg Bugt
  Denmark   56°50N 10°35E **63** H4
Alborz, Reshteh-ye Kūhhā-ye
  Iran   36°0N 52°0E **129** C7
Albox Spain   37°23N 2°8W **91** H2
Albreda Canada   52°35N 119°10W **162** C5
Albufeira Portugal   37°5N 8°15W **89** H2
Albula → Switz.   46°38N 9°28E **77** J5
Albuñol Spain   36°48N 3°11W **89** J7
Albuquerque U.S.A.   35°5N 106°39W **169** J10
Albuquerque, Cayos de
  Caribbean   12°10N 81°50W **182** D3
Alburno, Mte. Italy   40°33N 15°17E **95** B8
Alburquerque Spain   39°15N 6°59W **89** F4
Albury Australia   36°3S 146°56E **153** D7
Alby Sweden   62°30N 15°28E **62** B9
Alcácer do Sal Portugal   38°22N 8°33W **89** G2
Alcáçovas Portugal   38°23N 8°9W **89** G2
Alcalá de Guadaira
  Spain   37°20N 5°50W **89** H5
Alcalá de Henares Spain   40°28N 3°22W **90** E1
Alcalá de los Gazules
  Spain   36°29N 5°43W **89** J5
Alcalá de Xivert Spain   40°19N 0°13E **90** E5
Alcalá del Júcar Spain   39°8N 1°26W **91** F3
Alcalá del Río Spain   37°31N 5°59W **89** H5
Alcalá del Valle Spain   36°54N 5°10W **89** J5
Alcalá la Real Spain   37°27N 3°57W **89** H7
Álcamo Italy   37°59N 12°55E **94** E5
Alcanadre → Spain   41°43N 0°12W **90** D4
Alcanede Portugal   39°25N 8°49W **89** F2
Alcanena Portugal   39°25N 8°40W **89** F2
Alcañices Spain   41°41N 6°21W **88** D4
Alcañiz Spain   41°2N 0°8W **90** D4
Alcântara Brazil   2°20S 44°30W **189** C2
Alcántara Spain   39°41N 6°57W **88** F4
Alcántara, Embalse de
  Spain   39°44N 6°50W **88** F4
Alcantarilla Spain   37°59N 1°12W **91** H3
Alcaracejos Spain   38°24N 4°58W **89** G6
Alcaraz Spain   38°40N 2°29W **91** G2
Alcaraz, Sierra de Spain   38°40N 2°20W **91** G2
Alcaudete Spain   37°35N 4°5W **89** H6
Alcázar de San Juan
  Spain   39°24N 3°12W **91** F1
Alcchevsk Ukraine   48°30N 38°45E **85** H10
Alcira = Alzira Spain   39°9N 0°30W **91** F4

Alcobaça Portugal   39°32N 8°58W **89** F2
Alcobendas Spain   40°32N 3°38W **88** E7
Alcolea del Pinar Spain   41°2N 2°28W **90** D2
Alcoma U.S.A.   27°54N 81°29W **179** H8
Alcorcón Spain   40°20N 3°48W **88** E7
Alcoutim Portugal   37°25N 7°28W **89** H3
Alcoy Spain   38°43N 0°30W **91** G4
Alcubierre, Sierra de
  Spain   41°45N 0°22W **90** D4
Alcublas Spain   39°48N 0°43W **90** F4
Alcúdia Spain   39°51N 3°7E **100** B10
Alcúdia, B. d' Spain   39°47N 3°15E **100** B10
Alcúdia, Sierra de la
  Spain   38°34N 4°30W **89** G6
Aldabra Is. Seychelles   9°22S 46°28E **133** G8
Aldama Mexico   22°55N 98°4W **181** C5
Aldan Russia   58°40N 125°30E **107** D13
Aldan → Russia   63°28N 129°35E **107** C13
Aldea, Pta. de la
  Canary Is.   28°0N 15°50W **100** G4
Aldeburgh U.K.   52°10N 1°37E **67** E9
Alder Pk. U.S.A.   35°53N 121°22W **170** K5
Alderney U.K.   49°42N 2°11W **67** H5
Aldershot U.K.   51°15N 0°44W **67** F7
Aldinga Beach
  Australia   35°17S 138°27E **152** C3
Åled Sweden   56°44N 12°57E **63** H6
Aledo U.S.A.   41°12N 90°45W **172** E8
Aleg Mauritania   17°3N 13°55W **138** B2
Alegranza Canary Is.   29°23N 13°32W **100** E6
Alegranza, I. Canary Is.   29°23N 13°32W **100** E6
Alegre Brazil   20°50S 41°30W **191** A7
Alegrete Brazil   29°40S 56°0W **191** B4
Aleksandriya = Oleksandriya
  Kirovohrad, Ukraine   48°42N 33°3E **85** H7
Aleksandriya = Oleksandriya
  Rivne, Ukraine   50°37N 26°19E **75** C14
Aleksandriyskaya
  Russia   43°58N 47°14E **87** J8
Aleksandrov Russia   56°23N 38°44E **84** D10
Aleksandrov Gay Russia   50°9N 48°34E **86** E8
Aleksandrovac Serbia   43°28N 21°3E **96** C5
Aleksandrovka = Oleksandrivka
  Ukraine   48°55N 32°20E **85** H6
Aleksandrovo Bulgaria   43°14N 24°51E **97** C8
Aleksandrovsk-Sakhalinskiy
  Russia   50°50N 142°20E **111** A17
Aleksandrów Kujawski
  Poland   52°53N 18°43E **83** F5
Aleksandrów Łódzki
  Poland   51°49N 19°17E **83** G6
Alekseyevka Samara,
  Russia   52°35N 51°17E **86** D10
Alekseyevka Voronezh,
  Russia   50°43N 38°40E **85** G10
Aleksin Russia   54°31N 37°9E **84** E9
Aleksinac Serbia   43°31N 21°42E **96** C5
Além Paraíba Brazil   21°52S 42°41W **191** A7
Alemania Argentina   25°40S 65°30W **190** B2
Alemania Chile   25°10S 69°55W **190** B2
Alençon France   48°27N 0°4E **70** D7
Alenquer Brazil   1°56S 54°46W **187** D8
'Alenuihāhā Channel
  U.S.A.   20°30N 156°0W **167** L8
Alépé Ivory C.   5°29N 3°40W **138** D4
Aleppo = Ḥalab Syria   36°10N 37°15E **104** D7
Alerce Andino △ Chile   41°33S 72°39W **192** B2
Alerce Costero △ Chile   40°10S 73°30W **192** B2
Aléria France   42°5N 9°26E **73** F13
Alert Canada   83°2N 60°0W **161** A20
Aleru India   17°39N 79°3E **126** F4
Alès France   44°9N 4°5E **73** D8
Aleşd Romania   47°3N 22°22E **80** C7
Alessándria Italy   44°54N 8°37E **92** D5
Ålesund Norway   62°28N 6°12E **60** E12
Alet-les-Bains France   42°59N 2°14E **72** F6
Aletschhorn Switz.   46°28N 8°0E **77** J4
Aleutian Basin Pac. Oc.   57°0N 177°0E **156** B9
Aleutian Is. Pac. Oc.   52°0N 175°0W **156** B10
Aleutian Range U.S.A.   60°0N 154°0W **166** D8
Aleutian Trench
  Pac. Oc.   48°0N 180°0E **54** D17
Alexander U.S.A.   47°51N 103°39W **172** B2
Alexander, Mt.
  Australia   28°58S 120°16E **149** E3
Alexander Arch. U.S.A.   56°0N 136°0W **160** F4
Alexander Bay S. Africa   28°40S 16°30E **144** C2
Alexander City U.S.A.   32°56N 85°58W **177** E11
Alexander I. Antarctica   69°0S 70°0W **55** C17
Alexandra Australia   37°8S 145°40E **153** D6
Alexandra N.Z.   45°14S 169°25E **155** F4
Alexandra Channel
  Burma   14°7N 93°13E **127** G11
Alexandra Falls
  Canada   60°29N 116°18W **162** A5
Alexandria = El Iskandarîya
  Egypt   31°13N 29°58E **137** H6
Alexandria B.C.,
  Canada   52°35N 122°27W **162** C4
Alexandria Ont.,
  Canada   45°19N 74°38W **175** A10
Alexandria Romania   43°57N 25°24E **81** G10
Alexandria S. Africa   33°38S 26°28E **144** D4
Alexandria La., U.S.A.   31°18N 92°27W **176** F7
Alexandria Minn.,
  U.S.A.   45°53N 95°22W **172** C6
Alexandria S. Dak.,
  U.S.A.   43°39N 97°47W **172** D5
Alexandria Bay U.S.A.   44°20N 75°55W **175** B9
Alexandrina, L.
  Australia   35°25S 139°10E **152** C3
Alexandroupoli Greece   40°50N 25°54E **97** F9
Alexis → Canada   52°33N 56°8W **165** B8
Alexis Creek Canada   52°10N 123°20W **162** C4
Aley → Russia   52°40N 83°0E **108** A8
Aleysk Russia   52°40N 83°0E **108** A8
Alfabia Spain   39°44N 2°44E **100** B9
Alfambra → Spain   40°31N 1°5W **90** E3
Alfândega da Fé Portugal   41°20N 6°59W **88** D4
Alfaro Spain   42°10N 1°45W **90** C3
Alfatar Bulgaria   43°59N 27°13E **97** C11
Alfeld Germany   51°59N 9°50E **76** D5
Alfenas Brazil   21°20S 46°10W **191** A6

Alföld *Hungary* 46°30N 20°0E **80** D5
Alfonsine *Italy* 44°30N 12°3E **93** D9
Alford *Aberds., U.K.* 57°14N 2°41W **65** D6
Alford *Lincs., U.K.* 53°15N 0°10E **66** D8
Alford *U.S.A.* 30°42N 85°24W **178** E4
Alfred *Maine, U.S.A.* 43°29N 70°43W **175** C14
Alfred *N.Y., U.S.A.* 42°16N 77°48W **174** D7
Alfredton *N.Z.* 40°41S 175°54E **154** G4
Alfreton *U.K.* 53°6N 1°24W **66** D6
Alfta *Sweden* 61°21N 16°4E **62** C10
Algaida *Spain* 39°33N 2°53E **100** B9
Algar *Spain* 36°40N 5°39W **89** J5
Ålgård *Norway* 58°46N 5°53E **61** G11
Algarinejo *Spain* 37°19N 4°9W **89** H6
Algarve *Portugal* 36°58N 8°20W **89** J2
Algeciras *Spain* 36°9N 5°28W **89** J5
Algemesí *Spain* 39°11N 0°27W **91** F4
Alger *Algeria* 36°42N 3°8E **136** A4
Alger □ *Algeria* 36°45N 3°10E **91** J8
Alger ✕ (ALG) *Algeria* 36°39N 3°13E **91** J8
Algeria ■ *Africa* 28°30N 2°0E **136** C4
Algha *Kazakhstan* 49°53N 57°20E **108** C5
Alghero *Italy* 40°33N 8°19E **94** B1
Älghult *Sweden* 57°0N 15°35E **63** G9
Algiers = Alger *Algeria* 36°42N 3°8E **136** A4
Algoa B. *S. Africa* 33°50S 25°45E **144** D4
Algodonales *Spain* 36°54N 5°24W **89** J5
Algodor → *Spain* 39°55N 3°53W **88** F7
Algoma *U.S.A.* 44°36N 87°26W **172** C10
Algona *U.S.A.* 43°4N 94°14W **172** D6
Algonac *U.S.A.* 42°37N 82°32W **174** D2
Algonquin ⌓ *Canada* 45°50N 78°30W **164** C4
Algorta *Spain* 43°21N 2°59W **90** B2
Algorta *Uruguay* 32°25S 57°24W **190** C4
Alhama de Almería *Spain* 36°57N 2°34W **89** J8
Alhama de Aragón *Spain* 41°18N 1°54W **90** D3
Alhama de Granada *Spain* 37°0N 3°59W **89** H7
Alhama de Murcia *Spain* 37°51N 1°25W **91** H3
Alhambra *U.S.A.* 34°5N 118°7W **171** L8
Alhaurín el Grande *Spain* 36°39N 4°41W **89** J6
Alhucemas = Al Hoceïma *Morocco* 35°8N 3°58W **136** A3
'Alī al Gharbī *Iraq* 32°30N 46°45E **105** F12
'Alī ash Sharqī *Iraq* 32°7N 46°44E **105** F12
Āli Bayramlı = Şirvan *Azerbaijan* 39°59N 48°52E **87** L9
'Alī Khēl *Afghan.* 33°57N 69°43E **124** C3
Alī Shāh *Iran* 38°9N 45°50E **128** B5
Ália *Italy* 37°47N 13°43E **94** E6
'Alīābād *Golestān, Iran* 36°40N 54°33E **129** B7
'Alīābād *Khorāsān, Iran* 32°30N 57°30E **129** C8
'Alīābād *Kordestān, Iran* 35°4N 46°58E **128** C5
'Alīābād *Yazd, Iran* 31°41N 53°49E **129** D7
Aliade *Nigeria* 7°18N 8°29E **139** D6
Aliaga *Spain* 40°40N 0°42W **90** E4
Aliağa *Turkey* 38°47N 26°59E **99** C8
Aliakmonas → *Greece* 40°30N 22°36E **96** F6
Alibag *India* 18°38N 72°56E **126** E1
Alibori → *Benin* 11°56N 3°17E **139** C5
Alibunar *Serbia* 45°5N 20°57E **80** E5
Alicante *Spain* 38°23N 0°30W **91** G4
Alicante □ *Spain* 38°30N 0°37W **91** G4
Alicante ✕ (ALC) *Spain* 38°14N 0°36W **91** G4
Alice *S. Africa* 32°48S 26°55E **144** D4
Alice *U.S.A.* 27°45N 98°5W **176** H5
Alice → *Queens., Australia* 24°2S 144°50E **150** C3
Alice → *Queens., Australia* 15°35S 142°20E **150** B3
Alice, Punta *Italy* 39°24N 17°9E **95** C10
Alice Arm *Canada* 55°29N 129°31W **162** B3
Alice Springs *Australia* 23°40S 133°50E **150** C1
Alicedale *S. Africa* 33°15S 26°4E **144** D4
Aliceville *U.S.A.* 33°8N 88°9W **177** E10
Alicudi *Italy* 38°33N 14°20E **95** D7
Aliganj *India* 27°30N 79°10E **125** F8
Aligarh *Raj., India* 25°55N 76°15E **124** G7
Aligarh *Ut. P., India* 27°55N 78°10E **124** F8
Alīgūdarz *Iran* 33°25N 49°45E **129** C6
Alijó *Portugal* 41°16N 7°27W **88** D3
Alimia *Greece* 36°16N 27°43E **101** C9
Alingsås *Sweden* 57°56N 12°31E **63** G6
Alipur *Pakistan* 29°25N 70°55E **124** E4
Alipur Duar *India* 26°30N 89°35E **123** F16
Aliquippa *U.S.A.* 40°37N 80°15W **174** F4
Alishan *Taiwan* 23°31N 120°48E **117** F13
Aliste → *Spain* 41°34N 5°58W **88** D5
Alitus = Alytus *Lithuania* 54°24N 24°3E **84** E3
Aliveri *Greece* 38°24N 24°2E **98** C6
Aliwal North *S. Africa* 30°45S 26°45E **144** D4
Alix *Canada* 52°24N 113°11W **162** C6
Aljezur *Portugal* 37°18N 8°49W **89** H2
Aljustrel *Portugal* 37°55N 8°10W **89** H2
Alkamari *Niger* 13°27N 11°10E **139** C7
Alkhanay △ *Russia* 51°0N 113°30E **107** D12
Alkmaar *Neths.* 52°37N 4°45E **69** B4
All American Canal *U.S.A.* 32°45N 115°15W **171** N11
Allada *Benin* 6°41N 2°9E **139** D5
Allagadda *India* 15°8N 78°30E **127** G4
Allagash → *U.S.A.* 47°5N 69°3W **173** B19
Allah Dad *Pakistan* 25°38N 67°34E **124** G2
Allahabad *India* 25°25N 81°58E **125** G9
Allan *Canada* 51°53N 106°4W **163** C7
Allanche *France* 45°14N 2°57E **72** C6
Allanridge *S. Africa* 27°45S 26°40E **144** C4
Allansford *Australia* 38°26S 142°39E **152** E5
Allanton *N.Z.* 45°55S 170°15E **155** F5
Allaqi, Wadi → *Egypt* 23°7N 32°47E **137** C3
Allariz *Spain* 42°11N 7°50W **88** C3
Allassac *France* 45°15N 1°29E **72** C5
Allatoona L. *U.S.A.* 34°10N 84°44W **178** A5
Ålleberg *Sweden* 58°8N 13°36E **63** F7
Allegany *U.S.A.* 42°6N 78°30W **174** D6
Allegheny → *U.S.A.* 40°27N 80°1W **174** F5
Allegheny Mts. *U.S.A.* 38°15N 80°10W **173** F13
Allegheny Plateau *U.S.A.* 41°30N 78°30W **173** E14
Allegheny Res. *U.S.A.* 41°50N 79°0W **174** E6
Allègre *France* 45°12N 3°41E **72** C7
Allègre, Pte. *Guadeloupe* 16°22N 61°46W **182** b
Allen *Argentina* 38°58S 67°50W **192** A3
Allen, Bog of *Ireland* 53°15N 7°0W **64** C5
Allen, L. *Ireland* 54°8N 8°4W **64** B3
Allendale *U.S.A.* 33°1N 81°18W **178** B8
Allende *Mexico* 28°20N 100°51W **180** B4
Allentown *U.S.A.* 40°37N 75°29W **175** F9
Allentsteig *Austria* 48°41N 15°20E **78** C8
Alleppey = Alappuzha *India* 9°30N 76°28E **127** K3
Allepuz *Spain* 40°29N 0°44W **90** E4
Aller → *Germany* 52°56N 9°12E **76** C5
Alleynes B. *Barbados* 13°13N 59°39W **183** g
Alliance *Nebr., U.S.A.* 42°6N 102°52W **172** D2
Alliance *Ohio, U.S.A.* 40°55N 81°6W **174** F3
Allier □ *France* 46°25N 2°40E **71** F9
Allier → *France* 46°57N 3°4E **71** F10
Alliford Bay *Canada* 53°12N 131°58W **162** C2
Alligator Pond *Jamaica* 17°52N 77°34W **182** a
Allinagaram *India* 10°2N 77°30E **127** J3
Allinge *Denmark* 55°17N 14°50E **63** J8
Alliston *Canada* 44°9N 79°52W **174** B5
Alloa *U.K.* 56°7N 3°47W **65** E5
Allones *France* 48°20N 1°40E **70** D8
Allora *Australia* 28°2S 152°0E **151** D5
Allos *France* 44°15N 6°38E **73** D10
Alluitsup Paa *Greenland* 60°30N 45°35W **57** E6
Allur *India* 14°40N 80°4E **127** G5
Alluru Kottapatnam *India* 15°24N 80°7E **127** G5
Alma *Canada* 48°35N 71°40W **165** C5
Alma *Ga., U.S.A.* 31°33N 82°28W **178** D7
Alma *Kans., U.S.A.* 39°1N 96°17W **172** F5
Alma *Mich., U.S.A.* 43°23N 84°39W **173** D11
Alma *Nebr., U.S.A.* 40°6N 99°22W **172** E4
Alma *Wis., U.S.A.* 44°20N 91°55W **172** C8
Alma Ata = Almaty *Kazakhstan* 43°15N 76°57E **109** D9
Alma Hill *U.S.A.* 42°2N 78°0W **174** D7
Almacelles *Spain* 41°43N 0°27E **90** D5
Almada *Portugal* 38°41N 9°8W **89** G1
Almaden *Australia* 17°22S 144°40E **150** B3
Almadén *Spain* 38°49N 4°52W **89** G6
Almalyk = Olmaliq *Uzbekistan* 40°50N 69°35E **109** D7
Almanor, L. *U.S.A.* 40°14N 121°9W **168** F3
Almansa *Spain* 38°51N 1°5W **91** G3
Almanza *Spain* 42°39N 5°3W **88** C5
Almanzor, Pico *Spain* 40°15N 5°18W **88** E5
Almanzora → *Spain* 37°14N 1°46W **91** H3
Almas *Brazil* 11°33S 47°9W **189** C1
Almaş, Munţii *Romania* 44°49N 22°12E **80** F7
Almaty *Kazakhstan* 43°15N 76°57E **109** D9
Almaty □ *Kazakhstan* 44°30N 78°0E **109** D9
Almazán *Spain* 41°30N 2°30W **90** D2
Almazora *Spain* 39°57N 0°3W **90** F4
Almeirim *Brazil* 1°30S 52°34W **187** D8
Almeirim *Portugal* 39°12N 8°37W **89** F2
Almelo *Neths.* 52°22N 6°42E **69** B6
Almenar de Soria *Spain* 41°43N 2°12W **90** D2
Almenara *Brazil* 16°11S 40°42W **189** D2
Almenara *Spain* 39°46N 0°14W **90** F4
Almenara, Sierra de *Spain* 37°34N 1°32W **91** H3
Almendra, Embalse de *Spain* 41°10N 6°5W **88** D4
Almendralejo *Spain* 38°41N 6°26W **89** G4
Almere *Neths.* 52°20N 5°15E **69** B5
Almería *Spain* 36°52N 2°27W **89** J8
Almería □ *Spain* 37°20N 2°20W **91** H2
Almería, G. de *Spain* 36°41N 2°28W **91** J2
Almetyevsk *Russia* 54°53N 52°20E **86** C11
Älmhult *Sweden* 56°33N 14°8E **63** H8
Almirante *Panama* 9°10N 82°30W **182** E3
Almirante Montt, G. *Chile* 51°52S 72°50W **192** D2
Almiropotamos *Greece* 38°16N 24°11E **98** C6
Almiros *Greece* 39°11N 22°45E **98** B4
Almodôvar *Portugal* 37°31N 8°2W **89** H2
Almodóvar del Campo *Spain* 38°43N 4°10W **89** G6
Almodóvar del Río *Spain* 37°48N 5°1W **89** H5
Almond *U.S.A.* 42°19N 77°44W **174** D7
Almont *U.S.A.* 42°55N 83°3W **174** D1
Almonte *Canada* 45°14N 76°12W **175** A8
Almonte *Spain* 37°13N 6°38W **89** H4
Almora *India* 29°38N 79°40E **125** E8
Almoradí *Spain* 38°7N 0°46W **91** G4
Almorox *Spain* 40°14N 4°24W **88** E6
Almoustarat *Mali* 17°35N 0°8E **139** B5
Älmsta *Sweden* 59°58N 18°50E **62** E12
Almudévar *Spain* 42°3N 0°35W **90** C4
Almuñécar *Spain* 36°43N 3°41W **89** J7
Almunge *Sweden* 59°53N 18°3E **62** E12
Almuradiel *Spain* 38°32N 3°28W **89** G7
Almus *Turkey* 40°22N 36°54E **104** B7
Almvik *Sweden* 57°49N 16°30E **63** G10
Almyrou, Ormos *Greece* 35°23N 24°20E **101** D6
Alness *U.K.* 57°41N 4°16W **65** D4
Alnif *Morocco* 31°10N 5°8W **136** B2
Alnmouth *U.K.* 55°24N 1°37W **66** B6
Alnwick *U.K.* 55°24N 1°42W **66** B6
Aloi *Uganda* 2°16N 33°10E **142** B3
Alon *Burma* 22°12N 95°5E **123** H19
Alonissos *Greece* 39°12N 23°50E **98** B5
Alonissos-Northern Sporades △ *Greece* 39°15N 24°5E **98** B6
Alor *Indonesia* 8°15S 124°30E **119** F6
Alor Setar *Malaysia* 6°7N 100°22E **121** J3
Álora *Spain* 36°49N 4°46W **89** J6
Alosno *Spain* 37°33N 7°7W **89** H3
Alot *India* 23°56N 75°40E **124** H6
Alougoum *Morocco* 30°17N 6°56W **136** B2
Aloysius, Mt. *Australia* 26°0S 128°38E **149** E4
Alpaugh *U.S.A.* 35°53N 119°29W **170** K7
Alpe Apuane ⌓ *Italy* 44°4N 10°15E **92** D7
Alpedrinha *Portugal* 40°6N 7°27W **88** E3
Alpena *U.S.A.* 45°4N 83°27W **174** A1
Alpercatas → *Brazil* 6°2S 44°19W **189** B2
Alpes-de-Haute-Provence □ *France* 44°8N 6°10E **73** D10
Alpes-Maritimes □ *France* 43°55N 7°10E **73** E11
Alpha *Australia* 23°39S 146°37E **150** C4
Alpha Ridge *Arctic* 84°0N 118°0W **54** A2
Alpharetta *U.S.A.* 34°5N 84°18W **178** A5
Alphen aan den Rijn *Neths.* 52°7N 4°40E **69** B4
Alphios → *Greece* 37°40N 21°33E **98** D3
Alpiarça *Portugal* 39°15N 8°35W **89** F2
Alpine *Ariz., U.S.A.* 33°51N 109°9W **169** K9
Alpine *Calif., U.S.A.* 32°50N 116°46W **171** N10
Alpine *Tex., U.S.A.* 30°22N 103°40W **176** F3
Alpine △ *Australia* 36°56S 148°10E **153** D7
Alps *Europe* 46°30N 9°30E **74** E5
Alpu *Turkey* 39°46N 30°58E **104** C4
Alpurrurulam *Australia* 20°59S 137°50E **150** C2
Alqueta, Barragem do *Portugal* 38°20N 7°25W **89** G3
Alrø *Denmark* 55°52N 10°5E **63** J4
Als *Denmark* 54°59N 9°55E **63** K3
Alsace □ *France* 48°15N 7°25E **71** D14
Alsask *Canada* 51°21N 109°59W **163** C7
Alsasua *Spain* 42°54N 2°10W **90** C2
Alsek → *U.S.A.* 59°10N 138°12W **162** B1
Alsfeld *Germany* 50°44N 9°16E **76** E5
Alsta *Norway* 65°58N 12°40E **60** D15
Alsterbro *Sweden* 56°57N 15°55E **63** H9
Alstermo *Sweden* 56°58N 15°38E **63** H9
Alston *U.K.* 54°49N 2°25W **66** C5
Alta *Norway* 69°57N 23°10E **60** B20
Alta, Sierra *Spain* 40°31N 1°30W **90** E3
Alta Gracia *Argentina* 31°40S 64°30W **190** C3
Alta Murgia △ *Italy* 40°55N 16°30E **95** B9
Alta Sierra *U.S.A.* 35°42N 118°33W **171** K8
Altaelva → *Norway* 69°54N 23°17E **60** B20
Altafjorden *Norway* 70°5N 23°5E **60** A20
Altai = Aerhtai Shan *Mongolia* 46°40N 92°45E **109** C12
Altai = Gorno-Altay □ *Russia* 51°0N 86°0E **109** B11
Altai △ *Russia* 50°30N 85°30E **109** B11
Altamaha → *U.S.A.* 31°20N 81°20W **178** D8
Altamira *Brazil* 3°12S 52°10W **187** D8
Altamira *Chile* 25°47S 69°51W **190** B2
Altamira *Mexico* 22°24N 97°55W **181** C5
Altamira, Cuevas de *Spain* 43°20N 4°5W **88** B6
Altamont *U.S.A.* 42°42N 74°2W **175** D10
Altamura *Italy* 40°49N 16°33E **95** B9
Altanbulag *Mongolia* 50°16N 106°30E **110** A10
Altar *Mexico* 30°43N 111°44W **180** A2
Altar, Gran Desierto de *Mexico* 31°50N 114°10W **180** B2
Altata *Mexico* 24°40N 107°55W **180** C3
Altavista *U.S.A.* 37°6N 79°17W **173** G14
Altay *China* 47°48N 88°10E **109** C11
Altay *Mongolia* 46°22N 96°15E **110** B8
Altdorf *Switz.* 46°52N 8°36E **77** J4
Alte Mellum *Germany* 53°43N 8°10E **76** B4
Altea *Spain* 38°38N 0°2W **91** G4
Altenberg *Germany* 50°45N 13°45E **76** E9
Altenbruch *Germany* 53°49N 8°46E **76** B4
Altenburg *Germany* 50°59N 12°25E **76** E8
Altenkirchen *Mecklenburg-Vorpommern, Germany* 54°38N 13°22E **76** A9
Altenkirchen *Rhld-Pfz., Germany* 50°41N 7°39E **76** E3
Altenmarkt *Austria* 47°43N 14°39E **78** D7
Alter do Chão *Portugal* 39°12N 7°40W **89** F3
Altha *U.S.A.* 30°34N 85°8W **178** E4
Altınkaya Barajı *Turkey* 41°18N 35°30E **104** B6
Altınoluk *Turkey* 39°34N 26°45E **99** B8
Altınova *Turkey* 39°12N 26°47E **99** B8
Altıntaş *Turkey* 39°4N 30°7E **99** B12
Altınyaka *Turkey* 36°33N 30°20E **99** E12
Altınyayla *Turkey* 37°0N 29°33E **99** D11
Altiplano *Bolivia* 17°0S 68°0W **188** D4
Altkirch *France* 47°37N 7°15E **71** E14
Altmark *Germany* 52°45N 11°30E **76** C7
Altmühl → *Germany* 48°54N 11°52E **77** G7
Altmühltal ⌓ *Germany* 48°55N 11°15E **77** G7
Altmunster *Austria* 47°54N 13°45E **78** D6
Alto Adige = Trentino-Alto Adige □ *Italy* 46°30N 11°20E **93** B8
Alto Araguaia *Brazil* 17°15S 53°20W **187** G8
Alto Cuchumatanes = Cuchumatanes, Sierra de los *Guatemala* 15°35N 91°25W **182** C1
Alto del Carmen *Chile* 28°46S 70°30W **190** B1
Alto Douro *Portugal* 41°6N 7°47W **88** D3
Alto Garda Bresciano ⌓ *Italy* 45°42N 10°38E **92** C7
Alto Ligonha *Mozam.* 15°30S 38°11E **143** F4
Alto Molocue *Mozam.* 15°50S 37°35E **143** F4
Alto Paraguay □ *Paraguay* 21°0S 58°30W **190** A4
Alto Paraiso de Goiás *Brazil* 14°7S 47°31W **189** C1
Alto Paraná □ *Paraguay* 25°30S 54°50W **191** B5
Alto Parnaíba *Brazil* 9°6S 45°57W **189** B1
Alto Purús → *Peru* 9°12S 70°28W **188** B3
Alto Río Senguerr *Argentina* 45°2S 70°50W **192** C2
Alto Santo *Brazil* 5°31S 38°15W **189** B3
Alto Tajo ⌓ *Spain* 40°44N 2°30W **90** E2
Alton *Canada* 43°54N 80°5W **174** C4
Alton *U.K.* 51°9N 0°59W **67** F7
Alton *Ill., U.S.A.* 38°53N 90°11W **172** F8
Alton *N.H., U.S.A.* 43°27N 71°13W **175** C13
Altona *Canada* 49°6N 97°33W **163** D9
Altoona *Ala., U.S.A.* 34°2N 86°20W **178** A3
Altoona *Pa., U.S.A.* 40°31N 78°24W **174** F6
Altos *Brazil* 5°3S 42°28W **189** B2
Altötting *Germany* 48°12N 12°39E **77** G8
Altsasu = Alsasua *Spain* 42°54N 2°10W **90** C2
Altstätten *Switz.* 47°22N 9°33E **77** H5
Altun Kupri *Iraq* 35°45N 44°9E **105** E11
Altun Shan *China* 38°30N 88°0E **109** E11
Alturas *U.S.A.* 41°29N 120°32W **168** F3
Altus *U.S.A.* 34°38N 99°20W **176** D5
Altyn-Emel △ *Kazakhstan* 44°40N 78°26E **109** D9
Alucra *Turkey* 40°22N 38°47E **105** B8
Alūksne *Latvia* 57°24N 27°3E **84** D4
Alunda *Sweden* 60°4N 18°5E **62** D12
Alunite *U.S.A.* 35°59N 114°55W **171** K12
Alupka *Ukraine* 44°23N 34°2E **85** K8
Alur *India* 15°24N 77°15E **127** E3
Alushta *Ukraine* 44°40N 34°25E **85** K8
Alusi *Indonesia* 7°35S 131°40E **119** F8
Alustante *Spain* 40°36N 1°40W **90** E3
Alutgama *Sri Lanka* 6°26N 79°59E **127** L4
Alutnuwara *Sri Lanka* 7°19N 80°59E **127** L5
Aluva = Alwaye *India* 10°8N 76°24E **127** J3
Alva *U.S.A.* 36°48N 98°40W **176** C5
Alvaiázere *Portugal* 39°49N 8°23W **88** F2
Älvängen *Sweden* 57°58N 12°8E **63** G6
Alvão ⌓ *Portugal* 41°22N 7°48W **88** D3
Alvarado *Mexico* 18°46N 95°46W **181** D5
Alvarado *U.S.A.* 32°24N 97°13W **176** E6
Alvaro Obregón, Presa *Mexico* 27°52N 109°52W **180** B3
Älvdalen *Sweden* 61°13N 14°4E **62** C8
Alvear *Argentina* 29°5S 56°30W **190** B4
Alverca *Portugal* 38°56N 9°1W **89** G1
Alvesta *Sweden* 56°54N 14°35E **63** H8
Alvinston *Canada* 42°49N 81°52W **174** D3
Alvito *Portugal* 38°15N 7°58W **89** G3
Älvkarleby *Sweden* 60°34N 17°26E **62** D11
Alvord Desert *U.S.A.* 42°30N 118°25W **168** E4
Älvros *Sweden* 62°3N 14°38E **62** B8
Älvsbyn *Sweden* 65°40N 21°0E **60** D19
Alwar *India* 27°38N 76°34E **124** F7
Alwaye *India* 10°8N 76°24E **127** J3
Alxa Zuoqi *China* 38°50N 105°40E **114** E3
Alyangula *Australia* 13°55S 136°30E **150** A2
Alyata = Älät *Azerbaijan* 39°58N 49°25E **87** L9
Alyth *U.K.* 56°38N 3°13W **65** E5
Alytus *Lithuania* 54°24N 24°3E **84** E3
Alzada *U.S.A.* 45°2N 104°25W **168** D11
Alzamay *Russia* 55°33N 98°39E **107** D10
Alzey *Germany* 49°45N 8°7E **77** F4
Alzira *Spain* 39°9N 0°30W **91** F4
Am Timan *Chad* 11°0N 20°10E **135** F10
Amådalen *Sweden* 61°20N 14°44E **62** C8
Amadeus, L. *Australia* 24°54S 131°0E **149** D5
Amadi *Dem. Rep. of the Congo* 3°40N 26°40E **142** B2
Amadi *South Sudan* 5°29N 30°25E **135** G12
Amadjuak L. *Canada* 65°0N 71°8W **161** E17
Amadora *Portugal* 38°45N 9°13W **89** G1
Amagansett *U.S.A.* 40°59N 72°9W **175** F12
Amagasaki *Japan* 34°42N 135°23E **113** G7
Amager *Denmark* 55°36N 12°35E **63** J6
Amagi *Japan* 33°25N 130°39E **113** H5
Amagunze *Nigeria* 6°20N 7°40E **139** D6
Amahai *Indonesia* 3°20S 128°55E **119** E7
Amaiun-Maia *Spain* 43°12N 1°29W **90** B3
Amakusa = Hondo *Japan* 32°27N 130°12E **113** H5
Amakusa-Shotō *Japan* 32°15N 130°10E **113** H5
Åmål *Sweden* 59°3N 12°42E **62** E6
Amalapuram *India* 16°35N 81°55E **127** F5
Amalfi *Italy* 40°38N 14°36E **95** B7
Amaliada *Greece* 37°47N 21°22E **98** D3
Amalner *India* 21°5N 75°5E **126** D2
Amamapare *Indonesia* 4°53S 136°38E **119** E9
Amambaí *Brazil* 23°5S 55°13W **191** A4
Amambaí → *Brazil* 23°22S 53°56W **191** A5
Amambay □ *Paraguay* 23°0S 56°0W **191** A4
Amambay, Cordillera de *S. Amer.* 23°0S 55°45W **191** A4
Amami *Japan* 28°22N 129°27E **113** K4
Amami-Guntō *Japan* 27°16N 129°21E **113** L4
Amami-Ō-Shima *Japan* 28°16N 129°21E **113** K4
Aman, Pulau *Malaysia* 5°16N 100°24E **121** c
Amaná, L. *Brazil* 2°35S 64°40W **186** D6
Amanat → *India* 24°7N 84°4E **125** G11
Amanda Park *U.S.A.* 47°28N 123°55W **170** C3
Amankeldi *Kazakhstan* 50°10N 65°10E **108** B7
Amantea *Italy* 39°8N 16°4E **95** C9
Amapá *Brazil* 2°5N 50°50W **187** C8
Amapá □ *Brazil* 1°40N 52°0W **187** C8
Amarante *Brazil* 6°14S 42°50W **189** B2
Amarante *Portugal* 41°16N 8°5W **88** D2
Amarante do Maranhão *Brazil* 5°36S 46°45W **189** B1
Amaranth *Canada* 50°36N 98°43W **163** C9
Amaravati → *India* 11°0N 78°15E **127** J4
Amareleja *Portugal* 38°12N 7°13W **89** G3
Amargosa *Brazil* 13°2S 39°36W **189** C3
Amargosa → *U.S.A.* 36°14N 116°51W **171** J10
Amargosa Desert *U.S.A.* 36°40N 116°30W **171** J10
Amargosa Range *U.S.A.* 36°20N 116°45W **171** J10
Amari *Greece* 35°13N 24°40E **101** D6
Amarillo *U.S.A.* 35°13N 101°50W **176** D4
Amarkantak *India* 22°40N 81°45E **125** H9
'Amârna, Tell el *Egypt* 27°38N 30°52E **137** B3
Amarnath *India* 19°12N 73°22E **126** E1
Amaro, Mte. *Italy* 42°5N 14°5E **93** F11
Amarpur *India* 25°5N 87°0E **125** G12
Amarwara *India* 22°18N 79°10E **125** H8
Amasra *Turkey* 41°45N 32°23E **104** B5
Amassama *Nigeria* 5°1N 6°2E **139** D6
Amasya *Turkey* 40°40N 35°50E **104** B6
Amasya □ *Turkey* 40°40N 35°50E **104** B6
Amata *Australia* 26°9S 131°9E **149** E5
Amatikulu *S. Africa* 29°3S 31°33E **145** C5
Amatitlán *Guatemala* 14°29N 90°38W **182** D1
Amatrice *Italy* 42°38N 13°17E **93** F10
Amay *Belgium* 50°33N 5°19E **69** D5
Amazon = Amazonas → *S. Amer.* 0°5S 50°0W **187** D8
Amazonas □ *Brazil* 5°0S 65°0W **186** E6
Amazonas □ *Peru* 5°0S 78°0W **188** B2
Amazonas → *S. Amer.* 0°5S 50°0W **187** D8
Ambad *India* 19°38N 75°50E **126** E2
Ambagarh Chowki *India* 20°47N 80°43E **126** D5
Ambah *India* 26°43N 78°13E **124** F8
Ambajogal *India* 18°44N 76°23E **126** E3
Ambala *India* 30°23N 76°56E **124** D7
Ambalangoda *Sri Lanka* 6°15N 80°5E **127** L5
Ambalantota *Sri Lanka* 6°7N 81°1E **127** L5
Ambalapulai *India* 9°25N 76°25E **127** K3
Ambalavao *Madag.* 21°50S 46°56E **141** J9
Ambanja *Madag.* 13°40S 48°27E **141** G9
Ambarchik *Russia* 69°40N 162°20E **107** C17
Ambasamudram *India* 8°43N 77°25E **127** K3
Ambato *Ecuador* 1°5S 78°42W **186** D3
Ambato, Sierra de *Argentina* 28°25S 66°10W **190** B2
Ambatolampy *Madag.* 19°20S 47°35E **141** H9
Ambatondrazaka *Madag.* 17°55S 48°28E **141** H9
Ambelonas *Greece* 39°45N 22°22E **98** B4
Amberg *Germany* 49°26N 11°52E **77** F7
Ambergris Cay *Belize* 18°0N 87°55W **181** D7
Ambérieu-en-Bugey *France* 45°57N 5°20E **73** C9
Amberley *Canada* 44°2N 81°42W **174** B3
Amberley *N.Z.* 43°9S 172°44E **155** D7
Ambert *France* 45°33N 3°44E **72** C7
Ambidédi *Mali* 14°35N 11°47W **138** C2
Ambikapur *India* 23°15N 83°15E **125** H10
Ambikol *Sudan* 21°20N 30°50E **137** C3
Ambilobé *Madag.* 13°10S 49°3E **141** G9
Amble *U.K.* 55°20N 1°36W **66** B6
Ambleside *U.K.* 54°26N 2°58W **66** C5
Ambo *Peru* 10°5S 76°10W **188** C2
Ambohitra *Madag.* 12°30S 49°10E **141** G9
Amboise *France* 47°24N 1°2E **70** E8
Ambon *Indonesia* 3°43S 128°12E **119** E7
Amboseli, L. *Kenya* 2°40S 37°10E **142** C4
Amboseli △ *Kenya* 2°37S 37°13E **142** C4
Ambositra *Madag.* 20°31S 47°25E **141** J9
Ambovombe *Madag.* 25°11S 46°5E **141** K9
Amboy *U.S.A.* 34°33N 115°45W **171** L11
Amboyna Cay *S. China Sea* 7°50N 112°50E **118** C4
Ambridge *U.S.A.* 40°36N 80°14W **174** F4
Ambriz *Angola* 7°48S 13°8E **140** F2
Ambrolauri *Georgia* 42°31N 43°9E **105** A10
Ambur *India* 12°48N 78°43E **127** H4
Amchitka I. *U.S.A.* 51°32N 179°0E **166** E3
Amderma *Russia* 69°45N 61°30E **106** C7
Amdhi *India* 23°51N 81°27E **125** H9
Amdo *China* 32°20N 91°40E **110** E7
Ameca *Mexico* 20°33N 104°2W **180** C4
Ameca → *Mexico* 20°41N 105°18W **180** C3
Amecameca de Juárez *Mexico* 19°8N 98°46W **181** D5
Amed *Indonesia* 8°19S 115°39E **119** J18
Ameland *Neths.* 53°27N 5°45E **69** A5
Amélia *Italy* 42°33N 12°25E **93** F9
Amelia City *U.S.A.* 30°35N 81°28W **178** E8
Amelia I. *U.S.A.* 30°40N 81°25W **178** E8
Amendolara *Italy* 39°57N 16°35E **95** C9
Amenia *U.S.A.* 41°51N 73°33W **175** E11
America-Antarctica Ridge *S. Ocean* 59°0S 16°0W **55** B2
American Falls *U.S.A.* 42°47N 112°51W **168** E7
American Falls Res. *U.S.A.* 42°47N 112°52W **168** E7
American Fork *U.S.A.* 40°23N 111°48W **168** F8
American Highland *Antarctica* 73°0S 75°0E **55** D6
American River *Australia* 35°47S 137°46E **152** C2
American Samoa ☒ *Pac. Oc.* 14°20S 170°0W **157** J11
Americana *Brazil* 22°45S 47°20W **191** A6
Americus *U.S.A.* 32°4N 84°14W **178** C5
Amerigo Vespucci, Firenze ✕ (FLR) *Italy* 43°49N 11°13E **93** E8
Amersfoort *Neths.* 52°9N 5°23E **69** B5
Amersfoort *S. Africa* 26°59S 29°53E **145** C4
Amery Basin *S. Ocean* 68°15S 74°30E **55** C6
Amery Ice Shelf *Antarctica* 69°30S 72°0E **55** C6
Amerzgane *Morocco* 31°4N 7°14W **136** B2
Ames = Bertamirans *Spain* 42°54N 8°38W **88** C2
Ames *U.S.A.* 42°2N 93°37W **172** D7
Amesbury *U.S.A.* 42°51N 70°56W **175** D14
Amet *India* 25°18N 73°56E **124** G5
Amfiklia *Greece* 38°38N 22°35E **98** C4
Amfilochia *Greece* 38°52N 21°9E **98** C3
Amfipoli *Greece* 40°48N 23°52E **96** F7
Amfissa *Greece* 38°32N 22°22E **98** C4
Amga *Russia* 60°50N 132°0E **107** C14
Amga → *Russia* 62°38N 134°32E **107** C14
Amgaon *India* 21°22N 80°22E **126** D5
Amgu *Russia* 45°45N 137°15E **112** B8
Amguid *Algeria* 26°26N 5°22E **136** C5
Amgun → *Russia* 52°56N 139°38E **107** D14
Amherst *Canada* 45°48N 64°8W **165** C7
Amherst *Mass., U.S.A.* 42°23N 72°31W **175** D12
Amherst *N.Y., U.S.A.* 42°59N 78°48W **174** D6
Amherst *Ohio, U.S.A.* 41°24N 82°14W **174** E2
Amherst I. *Canada* 44°8N 76°43W **175** B8
Amherstburg *Canada* 42°6N 83°6W **164** D3
Amiata, Mte. *Italy* 42°53N 11°37E **93** F8
Amidon *U.S.A.* 46°29N 103°19W **172** B2
Amiens *France* 49°54N 2°16E **71** C9
Amindeo *Greece* 40°42N 21°42E **96** F5
Amindivi Is. *India* 11°23N 72°23E **127** J1
Amini I. *India* 11°6N 72°45E **127** J1
Aminuis *Namibia* 23°43S 19°21E **144** B2
Amīrābād *Iran* 33°20N 46°16E **128** C5
Amirante Is. *Seychelles* 6°0S 53°0E **102** J7
Amisk ⌓ *Canada* 56°43N 98°0W **163** B9
Amisk L. *Canada* 54°35N 102°15W **163** C8
Amistad, Presa de la *Mexico* 29°26N 101°3W **180** B4
Amistad ⌓ *U.S.A.* 29°32N 101°12W **176** G4
Amite *U.S.A.* 30°44N 90°30W **177** F9
Amizmiz *Morocco* 31°12N 8°15W **136** B2
Amla *India* 21°56N 78°7E **124** J8
Amlapura *Indonesia* 8°27S 115°37E **119** J18
Amlia I. *U.S.A.* 52°4N 173°30W **166** E5
Amlwch *U.K.* 53°24N 4°20W **66** D3
'Ammān *Jordan* 31°57N 35°52E **130** D4
'Ammān □ *Jordan* 31°40N 36°30E **130** D5
'Ammān ✕ (AMM) *Jordan* 31°45N 36°2E **130** D5
Ammanford *U.K.* 51°48N 3°59W **67** F4
Ammassalik = Tasiilaq *Greenland* 65°40N 37°20W **57** D7
Ammerån → *Sweden* 63°9N 16°13E **62** A10
Ammersee *Germany* 48°0N 11°7E **77** G7
Ammochostos = Famagusta *Cyprus* 35°8N 33°55E **101** D12
Ammon *U.S.A.* 43°28N 111°58W **168** E8
Amnat Charoen *Thailand* 15°51N 104°38E **120** E5
Amnura *Bangla.* 24°37N 88°25E **125** G13
Amo Jiang → *China* 23°0N 101°50E **116** F3
Āmol *Iran* 36°23N 52°20E **129** B7
Amorgos *Greece* 36°50N 25°57E **99** E7
Amory *U.S.A.* 33°59N 88°29W **177** E10
Amos *Canada* 48°35N 78°5W **164** C4
Åmot *Norway* 59°57N 9°54E **61** G13
Åmot *Sweden* 60°58N 16°27E **62** D10
Åmotfors *Sweden* 59°47N 12°22E **62** E6
Amour, Djebel *Algeria* 33°42N 1°37E **136** B4
Amoy = Xiamen *China* 24°25N 118°4E **117** E12
Ampang *Malaysia* 3°8N 101°45E **121** L3
Ampani *India* 19°35N 82°38E **126** E6
Ampanihy *Madag.* 24°40S 44°45E **141** J8
Ampato, Nevado *Peru* 15°40S 71°56W **188** D3
Ampenan *Indonesia* 8°34S 116°4E **119** K18
Amper *Nigeria* 9°25N 9°40E **139** D6
Amper → *Germany* 48°29N 11°55E **77** G7
Ampezzo *Italy* 46°25N 12°48E **93** B9
Amphitrite Group *S. China Sea* 16°50N 112°20E **118** A4
Amphoe Kathu *Thailand* 7°55N 98°21E **121** a
Amphoe Thalang *Thailand* 8°1N 98°20E **121** a
Amposta *Spain* 40°43N 0°34E **90** E5
Amqui *Canada* 48°28N 67°27W **165** C6
Amrabad *India* 16°23N 78°50E **127** F4
Amravati *India* 20°55N 77°45E **126** D3
Amreli *India* 21°35N 71°17E **124** J4
Amritsar *India* 31°35N 74°57E **124** D6
Amroha *India* 28°53N 78°30E **125** E8
Amrum *Germany* 54°38N 8°22E **76** A4
Amsterdam *Neths.* 52°23N 4°54E **69** B4
Amsterdam *U.S.A.* 42°56N 74°11W **175** D10
Amsterdam ✕ (AMS) *Neths.* 52°18N 4°45E **69** B4
Amsterdam I. = Nouvelle Amsterdam, Î. *Ind. Oc.* 38°30S 77°30E **146** H6
Amstetten *Austria* 48°7N 14°51E **78** C7
'Amūdah *Syria* 37°6N 40°55E **105** D9
Amudarya *Turkmenistan* 37°53N 65°15E **108** E7
Amudarya → *Uzbekistan* 43°58N 59°34E **108** D5
Amukta Pass *U.S.A.* 52°0N 171°0W **166** E5
Amund Ringnes I. *Canada* 78°20N 96°25W **161** B12
Amundsen Abyssal Plain *S. Ocean* 65°0S 125°0W **55** C14
Amundsen Basin *Arctic* 87°30N 80°0E **54** A
Amundsen Gulf *Canada* 71°0N 124°0W **160** C7
Amundsen Ridges *S. Ocean* 69°15S 123°0W **55** C14
Amundsen-Scott *Antarctica* 90°0S 166°0E **55** E
Amundsen Sea *Antarctica* 72°0S 115°0W **55** D15
Amungen *Sweden* 61°10N 15°40E **62** C9
Amuntai *Indonesia* 2°28S 115°25E **118** E5
Amur → *Russia* 52°56N 141°10E **107** D15
Amur, W. → *Sudan* 18°56N 33°34E **137** D3
Amurang *Indonesia* 1°5N 124°40E **119** D6
Amurrio *Spain* 43°3N 3°0W **90** B1
Amursk *Russia* 50°14N 136°54E **107** D14
Amusco *Spain* 42°10N 4°28W **88** C6
Amvrakikos Kolpos *Greece* 39°0N 20°55E **98** C2
Amvrosiyivka *Ukraine* 47°43N 38°30E **85** J10
Amyderya = Amudarya → *Uzbekistan* 43°58N 59°34E **108** D5
An Bang, Dao = Amboyna Cay *S. China Sea* 7°50N 112°50E **118** C4
An Bien *Vietnam* 9°45N 105°0E **121** H5
An Hoa *Vietnam* 15°40N 108°5E **120** E7
An Khe *Vietnam* 13°57N 108°51E **120** F7
An Nabatīyah at Tahta *Lebanon* 33°23N 35°27E **130** B4
An Nabk *Syria* 34°2N 36°44E **130** A5
An Nafūd *Si. Arabia* 28°15N 41°0E **128** D4
An Nāḩīyah *Iraq* 34°26N 41°33E **105** E9
An Najaf *Iraq* 32°3N 44°15E **105** G11
An Nāşirīyah *Iraq* 31°0N 46°15E **128** D5
An Nhon = Binh Dinh *Vietnam* 13°55N 109°7E **120** F7
An Nîl □ *Sudan* 19°30N 33°0E **137** D3
An Nu'ayrīyah *Si. Arabia* 27°30N 48°30E **129** E6
An Nu'mānīyah *Iraq* 32°32N 45°25E **105** F11
An Ros = Rush *Ireland* 53°31N 6°6W **64** C5
An Thoi, Quan Dao *Vietnam* 9°58N 104°0E **121** H5
Anabar → *Russia* 73°8N 113°36E **107** B12
Anaconda *U.S.A.* 46°8N 112°57W **168** C7
Anacortes *U.S.A.* 48°30N 122°37W **170** B4
Anadarko *U.S.A.* 35°4N 98°15W **176** D5
Anadia *Brazil* 9°42S 36°18W **189** B3
Anadia *Portugal* 40°26N 8°27W **88** E2
Anadolu *Turkey* 39°0N 30°0E **104** C5
Anadyr *Russia* 64°35N 177°20E **107** C18
Anadyr → *Russia* 64°55N 176°5E **107** C18
Anadyrskiy Zaliv *Russia* 64°0N 180°0E **107** C19
Anafi *Greece* 36°22N 25°48E **99** E7
Anaga, Pta. de *Canary Is.* 28°34N 16°9W **100** F3
Anagni *Italy* 41°44N 13°9E **93** G10
'Ānah *Iraq* 34°25N 42°0E **105** E10
Anaheim *U.S.A.* 33°50N 117°55W **171** M9
Anahim Lake *Canada* 52°28N 125°18W **162** C3
Anai Mudi *India* 10°12N 77°4E **127** J3
Anaimalai Hills *India* 10°20N 76°40E **127** J3
Anajatuba *Brazil* 3°16S 44°37W **189** A2
Anakapalle *India* 17°42N 83°6E **126** F6
Anakie *Australia* 23°32S 147°45E **150** C4
Anaklia *Georgia* 42°22N 41°35E **87** J5
Analalava *Madag.* 14°35S 48°0E **141** G9
Analipsis *Greece* 39°36N 19°55E **101** A3
Anambar → *Pakistan* 30°15N 68°50E **124** D3
Anambas, Kepulauan *Indonesia* 3°20N 106°30E **118** D3
Anambas Is. = Anambas, Kepulauan *Indonesia* 3°20N 106°30E **118** D3
Anambra □ *Nigeria* 6°20N 7°0E **139** D6
Anamosa *U.S.A.* 42°7N 91°17W **172** D8
Anamur *Turkey* 36°8N 32°58E **104** D5
Anamur Burnu *Turkey* 36°2N 32°47E **104** D5
Anan *Japan* 33°54N 134°40E **113** H7
Anand *India* 22°32N 72°59E **124** H5
Anandapuram *India* 14°5N 75°12E **127** G2
Anandpur *India* 21°16N 86°13E **126** D8
Ananes *Greece* 36°33N 24°9E **98** E6
Anangu Pitjantjatjara ◎ *Australia* 27°0S 132°0E **149** E5
Anantapur *India* 14°39N 77°42E **127** G3
Anantnag *India* 33°45N 75°10E **125** C6
Ananyiv *Ukraine* 47°44N 29°58E **81** C14
Anapa *Russia* 44°55N 37°25E **85** K9
Anapodiaris → *Greece* 34°59N 25°20E **101** E7
Anápolis *Brazil* 16°15S 48°50W **187** G9
Anapu → *Brazil* 1°53S 50°53W **187** D8
Anār *Iran* 30°55N 55°13E **129** D7
Anārak *Iran* 33°25N 53°40E **129** C7
Anarisfjällen *Sweden* 63°6N 13°10E **62** A7
Anas → *India* 23°26N 74°0E **124** H5
Anatolia = Anadolu *Turkey* 39°0N 30°0E **104** C5
Anatoliki Makedonia kai Thraki □ *Greece* 41°10N 24°30E **97** E8
Añatuya *Argentina* 28°20S 62°50W **190** B3
Anatye ◎ *Australia* 22°29S 137°3E **150** C2
Anaunethad L. *Canada* 60°55N 104°25W **163** A8
Anbyŏn *N. Korea* 39°1N 127°35E **115** E14

Ancares, Sierra dos Spain 42°51N 6°52W 88 C4
Ancares ⌓ Spain 42°50N 6°40W 88 C4
Ancash □ Peru 9°30S 77°45W 188 B2
Ancaster Canada 43°13N 79°59W 174 C5
Ancenis France 47°21N 1°10W 70 E5
Ancho, Canal Chile 50°0S 74°20W 192 D2
Anchor Bay U.S.A. 38°48N 123°34W 170 G3
Anchorage U.S.A. 61°13N 149°54W 160 E2
Anchuras Spain 39°29N 4°50W 89 F6
Anchuthengu India 8°40N 76°46E 127 K3
Anci China 39°20N 116°40E 114 E9
Ancohuma, Nevado Bolivia 16°0S 68°50W 188 D4
Ancón Peru 11°50S 77°10W 188 C2
Ancona Italy 43°38N 13°30E 93 E10
Ancud Chile 42°0S 73°50W 192 B2
Ancud, G. de Chile 42°0S 73°0W 192 B2
Ancy-le-Franc France 47°46N 4°10E 71 E11
Anda China 46°24N 125°19E 111 B14
Andacollo Argentina 37°10S 70°42W 190 D1
Andacollo Chile 30°14S 71°6W 190 C1
Andahuaylas Peru 13°40S 73°25W 188 C3
Andalgalá Argentina 27°40S 66°30W 190 B2
Åndalsnes Norway 62°35N 7°43E 60 E12
Andalucía □ Spain 37°35N 5°0W 89 H6
Andalusia = Andalucía □ Spain 37°35N 5°0W 89 H6
Andalusia U.S.A. 31°18N 86°29W 177 F11
Andaman & Nicobar Is. □ India 10°0N 93°0E 127 K11
Andaman Is. Ind. Oc. 12°30N 92°45E 127 H11
Andaman Sea Ind. Oc. 13°0N 96°0E 118 B1
Andamooka Australia 30°27S 137°9E 151 E2
Andapa Madag. 14°39S 49°39E 141 G9
Andara Namibia 18°2S 21°9E 144 A3
Andaraí Brazil 12°48S 41°20W 189 C2
Andelot-Blancheville France 48°15N 5°18E 71 D12
Andenes Norway 69°19N 16°18E 60 B17
Andenne Belgium 50°28N 5°5E 69 D5
Andéranboukane Mali 15°26N 3°2E 139 B5
Andermatt Switz. 46°38N 8°35E 77 J4
Andernach Germany 50°26N 7°24E 76 E3
Andernos-les-Bains France 44°44N 1°6W 72 D2
Anderslöv Sweden 55°26N 13°19E 63 J7
Anderson Australia 38°31S 145°26E 153 E6
Anderson Alaska, U.S.A. 64°25N 149°15W 166 C10
Anderson Calif., U.S.A. 40°27N 122°18W 168 F2
Anderson Ind., U.S.A. 40°10N 85°41W 173 E11
Anderson Mo., U.S.A. 36°39N 94°27W 172 G6
Anderson S.C., U.S.A. 34°31N 82°39W 177 D13
Anderson → Canada 69°42N 129°0W 160 D6
Anderson I. India 12°46N 92°43E 127 H11
Andersonville U.S.A. 32°12N 84°9W 178 C5
Andersonville ⌓ U.S.A. 32°12N 84°1W 178 C5
Anderstorp Sweden 57°19N 13°39E 63 G7
Andes U.S.A. 42°12N 74°47W 175 D10
Andes, Cord. de los S. Amer. 20°0S 68°0W 188 E4
Andfjorden Norway 69°10N 16°20E 60 B17
Andhra, L. India 18°54N 73°32E 126 E1
Andhra Pradesh □ India 18°0N 79°0E 126 F4
Andijon Uzbekistan 41°10N 72°15E 109 D8
Andijon □ Uzbekistan 40°45N 72°20E 109 D8
Andikithira = Antikythira Greece 35°52N 23°15E 98 F5
Andimeshk Iran 32°27N 48°21E 105 F13
Andimilos = Antimilos Greece 36°47N 24°12E 98 E6
Andiparos = Antiparos Greece 37°0N 25°3E 99 D7
Andipaxoi = Antipaxi Greece 39°9N 20°13E 98 B2
Andipsara Greece 38°30N 25°29E 99 C7
Andizhan = Andijon Uzbekistan 41°10N 72°15E 109 D8
Andkhvoy Afghan. 36°52N 65°8E 109 E7
Andoain Spain 43°13N 2°1W 90 B2
Andoany Madag. 13°25S 48°16E 141 G9
Andol India 17°51N 78°4E 126 F4
Andola India 16°57N 76°50E 126 F3
Andong S. Korea 36°40N 128°43E 115 F15
Andorra Spain 40°59N 0°28W 90 E4
Andorra ■ Europe 42°30N 1°30E 72 F5
Andorra La Vella Andorra 42°31N 1°32E 72 F5
Andover U.K. 51°12N 1°29W 67 F6
Andover Kans., U.S.A. 37°43N 97°7W 172 G5
Andover Maine, U.S.A. 44°38N 70°45W 175 B14
Andover Mass., U.S.A. 42°40N 71°8W 175 D13
Andover N.J., U.S.A. 40°59N 74°45W 175 F10
Andover N.Y., U.S.A. 42°10N 77°48W 174 D7
Andover Ohio, U.S.A. 41°36N 80°34W 174 E4
Andøya Norway 69°10N 15°50E 60 B16
Andradina Brazil 20°54S 51°23W 187 H8
Andratx Spain 39°39N 2°25E 100 B9
Andreanof Is. U.S.A. 51°30N 176°0W 166 E4
Andreapol Russia 56°40N 32°17E 84 D7
Andrée Land Greenland 73°40N 26°0W 57 C8
Andrews S.C., U.S.A. 33°27N 79°34W 177 E15
Andrews Tex., U.S.A. 32°19N 102°33W 176 E3
Andreyevka Russia 52°19N 51°55E 86 D10
Ándria Italy 41°13N 16°17E 95 A9
Andrijevica Montenegro 42°45N 19°48E 96 D3
Andritsena Greece 37°29N 21°52E 98 D3
Andros Greece 37°50N 24°57E 98 D6
Andros I. Bahamas 24°30N 78°0W 182 B4
Andros Town Bahamas 24°43N 77°47W 182 B4
Androscoggin → U.S.A. 43°58N 69°52W 175 C14
Androth I. India 10°50N 73°41E 127 J1
Andrychów Poland 49°51N 19°18E 83 J6
Andselv Norway 69°4N 18°34E 60 B18
Andújar Spain 38°3N 4°5W 89 G6
Andulo Angola 11°25S 16°45E 140 G3
Aneby Sweden 57°48N 14°49E 63 G8
Anéfis Mali 18°2N 0°36E 139 B5
Anegada Br. Virgin Is. 18°45N 64°20W 183 e
Anegada, B. Argentina 40°20S 62°20W 192 B4
Anegada Passage W. Indies 18°15N 63°45W 183 C7
Aného Togo 6°12N 1°34E 139 D5
Añelo Argentina 38°20S 68°45W 192 A3
Anenni-Noi Moldova 46°53N 29°15E 81 D14
Aneto, Pico de Spain 42°37N 0°40E 90 C5
Änew Turkmenistan 37°52N 58°31E 108 E5
Anfu China 27°21N 114°40E 117 D10
Ang Mo Kio Singapore 1°23N 103°50E 121 d
Ang Thong Thailand 14°35N 100°31E 120 E3
Ang Thong, Ko Thailand 9°37N 99°41E 121 b
Ang Thong, Mu Ko △ Thailand 9°40N 99°43E 121 b
Angamos, Punta Chile 23°1S 70°32W 190 A1
Angara → Russia 58°5N 94°20E 107 D10
Angara-Débou Benin 11°19N 3°34E 139 C5
Angarsk Russia 52°30N 104°0E 110 A9
Angas Hills Australia 23°0S 127°50E 148 D4
Angaston Australia 34°30S 139°8E 152 C3
Ånge Sweden 62°31N 15°35E 62 B9
Ángel, Salto = Angel Falls Venezuela 5°57N 62°30W 186 B6
Ángel de la Guarda, I. Mexico 29°20N 113°25W 180 B2
Angel Falls Venezuela 5°57N 62°30W 186 B6
Angeles Phil. 15°9N 120°33E 119 A6
Ängelholm Sweden 56°15N 12°50E 63 H6
Angels Camp U.S.A. 38°4N 120°32W 170 G6
Ängelsberg Sweden 59°58N 16°0E 62 E10
Ångermanälven → Sweden 63°0N 17°20E 62 A11
Ångermanland Sweden 63°36N 17°45E 60 E17
Angermünde Germany 53°0N 14°0E 76 B9
Angers Canada 45°31N 75°29W 175 A9
Angers France 47°30N 0°35W 70 E6
Angerville France 48°19N 2°0E 71 D9
Ängesån → Sweden 66°16N 22°47E 60 C20
Angical Brazil 12°0S 44°42W 189 C2
Angikuni L. Canada 62°12N 99°59W 163 A9
Angkor Cambodia 13°22N 103°50E 120 F4
Angledool Australia 29°5S 147°55E 151 D4
Anglem, Mt. N.Z. 46°45S 167°53E 155 G2
Anglès Spain 41°57N 2°38E 90 D7
Anglesey U.K. 53°17N 4°20W 66 D3
Anglesey, Isle of □ U.K. 53°16N 4°18W 66 D3
Anglet France 43°29N 1°31W 72 E2
Angleton U.S.A. 29°10N 95°26W 176 G7
Anglin → France 46°42N 0°52E 72 B4
Anglisidhes Cyprus 34°51N 33°27E 101 E12
Anglure France 48°35N 3°50E 71 D10
Angmagssalik = Tasiilaq Greenland 65°40N 37°20W 57 D7
Ango Dem. Rep. of the Congo 4°10N 26°5E 142 B2
Angoche Mozam. 16°8S 39°55E 143 F4
Angoche, I. Mozam. 16°20S 39°50E 143 F4
Angol Chile 37°56S 72°45W 190 D1
Angola Ind., U.S.A. 41°38N 85°0W 173 E11
Angola N.Y., U.S.A. 42°38N 79°2W 174 D5
Angola ■ Africa 12°0S 18°0E 141 G3
Angola Abyssal Plain Atl. Oc. 15°0S 2°0E 56 H12
Angola Basin Atl. Oc. 15°0S 3°0E 56 H12
Angoulême France 45°39N 0°10E 72 C4
Angoumois France 45°50N 0°25E 72 C4
Angra do Heroismo Azores 38°39N 27°13W 134 a
Angra dos Reis Brazil 23°0S 44°10W 191 A7
Angrapa → Russia 54°37N 21°54E 82 D8
Angren Uzbekistan 41°1N 70°12E 109 D8
Angtassom Cambodia 11°1N 104°41E 121 G5
Angu Dem. Rep. of the Congo 3°23N 24°30E 142 B1
Anguang China 45°15N 123°45E 115 B12
Anguilla ☒ W. Indies 18°14N 63°5W 183 C7
Angul India 20°51N 85°6E 126 D7
Anguo China 38°28N 115°15E 114 E8
Angurugu Australia 14°0S 136°25E 150 A2
Angus Canada 44°19N 79°53W 174 B5
Angus □ U.K. 56°46N 2°56W 65 E6
Angwa → Zimbabwe 16°0S 30°23E 145 A5
Anhanduí → Brazil 21°46S 52°9W 191 A5
Anholt Denmark 56°42N 11°33E 63 H5
Anhua China 28°23N 111°12E 117 C8
Anhui □ China 32°0N 117°0E 117 B11
Anhwei = Anhui □ China 32°0N 117°0E 117 B11
Anichab Namibia 21°0S 14°46E 144 B1
Anidros Greece 36°38N 25°43E 99 E7
Anié Togo 7°42N 1°8E 139 D5
Animas → U.S.A. 36°43N 108°13W 169 H9
Anin Burma 15°36N 97°50E 120 E1
Anina Romania 45°6N 21°51E 80 E6
Aninoasa Romania 44°47N 24°10E 81 F9
Anjalankoski Finland 60°45N 26°51E 84 B4
Anjangaon India 21°10N 77°20E 126 D3
Anjar = Hawsh Mūssá Lebanon 33°45N 35°55E 130 B4
Anjar India 23°6N 70°10E 124 H4
Anjengo = Anchuthengu India 8°40N 76°46E 127 K3
Anji China 30°46N 119°40E 117 B12
Anjidiv I. India 14°40N 74°10E 127 G2
Anjou France 47°20N 0°15W 70 E6
Anjouan Comoros Is. 12°15S 44°20E 141 a
Anju N. Korea 39°36N 125°40E 115 E13
Anka Nigeria 12°13N 5°58E 139 C6
Ankaboa, Tanjona Madag. 21°58S 43°20E 141 J8
Ankang China 32°40N 109°1E 114 H5
Ankara Turkey 39°57N 32°54E 104 C5
Ankara □ Turkey 39°55N 32°50E 104 C5
Ankaratra Madag. 19°25S 47°12E 141 H9
Ankarsrum Sweden 57°41N 16°20E 63 G10
Ankazoabo Madag. 22°18S 44°31E 141 J8
Ankeny U.S.A. 41°44N 93°36W 172 E7
Anklam Germany 53°51N 13°41E 76 B9
Ankleshwar India 21°38N 73°3E 126 D1
Ankola India 14°40N 74°18E 127 G2
Ankoro Dem. Rep. of the Congo 6°45S 26°55E 142 D2
Ankpa Nigeria 7°22N 7°38E 139 D6
Anlong China 25°2N 105°27E 116 E5
Anlong Veng Cambodia 14°14N 104°5E 120 E5
Anlu China 31°15N 113°45E 117 B9
Anmyeondo S. Korea 36°25N 126°25E 115 F14
Ånn Sweden 63°19N 12°33E 62 A6
Ann, C. U.S.A. 42°38N 70°35W 175 D14
Ann Arbor U.S.A. 42°17N 83°45W 173 D12
Anna Russia 51°28N 40°23E 86 E5
Anna U.S.A. 37°28N 89°15W 172 G9
Annaba Algeria 36°50N 7°46E 136 A5
Annaba □ Algeria 36°12N 7°45E 136 A5
Annaberg-Buchholz Germany 50°34N 13°0E 76 E9
Annalee → Ireland 54°2N 7°24W 64 B4
Annam = Trung-Phan Vietnam 17°0N 109°0E 120 D6
Annamitique, Chaîne Asia 17°0N 106°40E 120 D6
Annan U.K. 54°59N 3°16W 65 G5
Annan → U.K. 54°58N 3°16W 65 G5
Annapolis U.S.A. 38°59N 76°30W 173 F15
Annapolis Royal Canada 44°44N 65°32W 165 D6
Annapurna Nepal 28°34N 83°50E 125 E10
Annean, L. Australia 26°54S 118°14E 149 E2
Anneberg Sweden 57°44N 14°49E 63 G8
Annecy France 45°55N 6°8E 73 C10
Annecy, Lac d' France 45°52N 6°10E 73 C10
Annemasse France 46°12N 6°16E 71 F13
Annenskiy Most Russia 60°45N 37°10E 84 B9
Annette I. U.S.A. 55°9N 131°28W 162 B2
Annigeri India 15°26N 75°26E 127 G2
Anning China 24°55N 102°26E 116 E4
Anniston U.S.A. 33°39N 85°50W 178 B4
Annobón Atl. Oc. 1°25S 5°36E 133 G4
Annonay France 45°15N 4°40E 73 C8
Annot France 43°58N 6°38E 73 E10
Annotto B. Jamaica 18°17N 76°45W 182 a
Ånnsjön Sweden 63°19N 12°34E 62 A6
Annville U.S.A. 40°20N 76°31W 175 F8
Annweiler Germany 49°12N 7°57E 77 F3
Ano Poroia Greece 41°17N 23°2E 96 E7
Ano Siros Greece 37°29N 24°56E 98 D6
Anogia Greece 35°16N 24°52E 101 D6
Anou Mellene Mali 17°29N 0°33E 139 B5
Anoumaba Ivory C. 6°23N 4°38W 138 D4
Anping Hebei, China 38°15N 115°30E 114 E8
Anping Liaoning, China 41°5N 123°30E 115 D12
Anpu Gang China 21°25N 109°50E 116 G7
Anqing China 30°30N 117°3E 117 B11
Anqiu China 36°25N 119°10E 115 F10
Anren China 26°43N 113°18E 117 D9
Ansager Denmark 55°43N 8°45E 63 J2
Ansai China 36°50N 109°20E 114 F5
Ansan S. Korea 37°21N 126°52E 115 F14
Ansbach Germany 49°28N 10°34E 77 F6
Anse Boileau Seychelles 4°43S 55°29E 141 b
Anse la Raye St. Lucia 13°55N 61°3W 183 f
Anse Royale Seychelles 4°44S 55°31E 141 b
Ansfelden Austria 48°12N 14°17E 78 C7
Anshan China 41°5N 122°58E 115 D12
Anshun China 26°18N 105°57E 116 D5
Ansião Portugal 39°56N 8°27W 88 F2
Ansley U.S.A. 41°18N 99°23W 172 E4
Ansó Spain 42°51N 0°48W 90 C4
Ansoáin Spain 42°50N 1°38W 90 C3
Anson U.S.A. 32°45N 99°54W 176 E5
Anson B. Australia 13°20S 130°6E 148 B5
Ansongo Mali 15°25N 0°35E 139 B5
Ansongo-Ménaka ⌓ Mali 15°3N 1°37E 139 B5
Ansonia U.S.A. 41°21N 73°5W 175 E11
Anstruther U.K. 56°14N 2°41W 65 E6
Ansudu Indonesia 2°11S 139°22E 119 E9
Antabamba Peru 14°40S 73°0W 188 C3
Antagarh India 20°6N 81°9E 126 D5
Antakya = Hatay Turkey 36°14N 36°10E 104 D7
Antalaha Madag. 14°57S 50°20E 141 G10
Antalya Turkey 36°52N 30°45E 104 D4
Antalya □ Turkey 36°50N 30°45E 104 D4
Antalya Körfezi Turkey 36°15N 31°30E 104 D4
Antananarivo Madag. 18°55S 47°31E 141 H9
Antarctic Pen. Antarctica 67°0S 60°0W 55 C18
Antarctica 90°0S 0°0 55 E3
Antelope Zimbabwe 21°2S 28°31E 143 G2
Antep = Gaziantep Turkey 37°6N 37°23E 104 D7
Antequera Paraguay 24°8S 57°7W 190 A4
Antequera Spain 37°5N 4°33W 89 H6
Antero, Mt. U.S.A. 38°41N 106°15W 168 G10
Anthony Fla., U.S.A. 29°18N 82°7W 179 F7
Anthony Kans., U.S.A. 37°9N 98°2W 172 G4
Anthony N. Mex., U.S.A. 32°0N 106°36W 169 K10
Anti Atlas Morocco 30°0N 8°30W 136 C2
Anti-Lebanon = Sharqi, Al Jabal ash Lebanon 33°40N 36°10E 130 B5
Antibes France 43°34N 7°6E 73 E11
Antibes, C. d' France 43°31N 7°7E 73 E11
Anticosti, Î. d' Canada 49°30N 63°0W 165 C7
Antifer, C. d' France 49°41N 0°10E 70 C7
Antigo U.S.A. 45°9N 89°9W 172 C9
Antigonish Canada 45°38N 61°58W 165 C7
Antigua Canary Is. 28°24N 14°1W 100 F5
Antigua Guatemala 14°34N 90°41W 182 D1
Antigua W. Indies 17°0N 61°50W 183 C7
Antigua & Barbuda ■ W. Indies 17°20N 61°48W 183 C7
Antikythira Greece 35°52N 23°15E 98 F5
Antilla Cuba 20°40N 75°50W 182 B4
Antilles = West Indies Cent. Amer. 15°0N 65°0W 183 D7
Antimilos Greece 36°47N 24°12E 98 E6
Antioch U.S.A. 38°1N 121°48W 170 G5
Antioche, Pertuis d' France 46°6N 1°20W 72 B2
Antioquia Colombia 6°40N 75°55W 186 B3
Antiparos Greece 37°0N 25°3E 99 D7
Antipaxi Greece 39°9N 20°13E 98 B2
Antipodes Is. Pac. Oc. 49°45S 178°40E 156 M9
Antirio Greece 38°20N 21°46E 98 C3
Antlers U.S.A. 34°14N 95°37W 176 D7
Antofagasta Chile 23°50S 70°30W 190 A1
Antofagasta □ Chile 24°0S 69°0W 190 A2
Antofagasta de la Sierra Argentina 26°5S 67°20W 190 B2
Antofalla Argentina 25°30S 68°5W 190 B2
Antofalla, Salar de Argentina 25°40S 67°45W 190 B2
Anton U.S.A. 33°49N 102°10W 176 E3
Antonina Brazil 25°26S 48°42W 191 B6
Antrain France 48°28N 1°30W 70 D5
Antrim U.K. 54°43N 6°14W 64 B5
Antrim U.S.A. 40°7N 81°21W 174 F3
Antrim □ U.K. 54°56N 6°25W 64 B5
Antrim, Mts. of U.K. 55°3N 6°14W 64 A5
Antrim Plateau Australia 18°8S 128°20E 148 C4
Antrodoco Italy 42°25N 13°5E 93 F10
Antropovo Russia 58°24N 43°6E 86 A6
Antsalova Madag. 18°40S 44°37E 141 H8
Antsirabe Madag. 19°55S 47°2E 141 H9
Antsiranana Madag. 12°25S 49°20E 141 G9
Antsohihy Madag. 14°50S 47°59E 141 G9
Antu China 42°30N 128°20E 115 C15
Antwerp = Antwerpen Belgium 51°13N 4°25E 69 C4
Antwerp U.S.A. 44°12N 75°37W 175 B9
Antwerpen Belgium 51°13N 4°25E 69 C4
Antwerpen □ Belgium 51°15N 4°40E 69 C4
Anupgarh India 29°10N 73°10E 124 E5
Anuppur India 23°6N 81°41E 125 H9
Anuradhapura Sri Lanka 8°22N 80°28E 127 K5
Anurrete ✪ Australia 20°50S 135°38E 150 C2
Anveh Iran 27°23N 54°11E 129 E7
Anvers = Antwerpen Belgium 51°13N 4°25E 69 C4
Anvers I. Antarctica 64°30S 63°40W 55 C17
Anwen China 29°4N 120°26E 117 C13
Anxi Fujian, China 25°2N 118°12E 117 E12
Anxi Gansu, China 40°30N 95°43E 110 C8
Anxian China 31°40N 104°25E 116 B5
Anxiang China 29°27N 112°11E 117 C9
Anxious B. Australia 33°24S 134°45E 151 E1
Anyama Ivory C. 5°30N 4°3W 138 D4
Anyang China 36°5N 114°21E 114 F8
Anyang S. Korea 37°23N 126°55E 115 F14
Anyer Indonesia 6°4S 105°53E 119 G11
Anyi Jiangxi, China 28°49N 115°25E 117 C10
Anyi Shanxi, China 35°2N 111°2E 114 G6
Anyuan China 25°9N 115°21E 117 E10
Anyue China 30°9N 105°50E 116 B5
Anza U.S.A. 33°35N 116°39W 171 M10
Anze China 36°10N 112°12E 114 F7
Anzeglouf Algeria 26°50N 0°1E 136 C4
Anzhero-Sudzhensk Russia 56°10N 86°0E 106 D9
Ánzio Italy 41°27N 12°37E 94 A5
Ao Makham Thailand 7°50N 98°24E 121 a
Ao Phangnga △ Thailand 8°10N 98°32E 121 a
Aoga-Shima Japan 32°28N 139°46E 113 H9
Aohan Qi China 43°18N 119°43E 115 C10
Aoiz Spain 42°46N 1°22W 90 C3
Aoji N. Korea 42°31N 130°23E 115 C16
Aomen = Macau China 22°12N 113°33E 117 F9
Aomori Japan 40°45N 140°45E 112 D10
Aomori □ Japan 40°45N 140°40E 112 D10
tAonach, An = Nenagh Ireland 52°52N 8°11W 64 D3
Aonla India 28°16N 79°11E 125 E8
Aorai, Mt. Tahiti 17°34S 149°30W 155 b
Aoraki Mount Cook N.Z. 43°36S 170°9E 155 D5
Aoral, Phnum Cambodia 12°0N 104°15E 121 G5
Aorangi Ra. N.Z. 41°28S 175°22E 154 H4
Aosta Italy 45°45N 7°20E 92 C4
Aotea Harbour N.Z. 38°0S 174°50E 154 E3
Aotearoa = New Zealand ■ Oceania 40°0S 176°0E 154 G5
Aouderas Niger 17°45N 8°20E 139 B6
Aoukâr Mauritania 17°40N 10°0W 138 B3
Aoulef el Arab Algeria 26°55N 1°2E 136 C4
Aozou, Couloir d' Chad 22°0N 19°0E 135 D9
Apá → S. Amer. 22°6S 58°2W 190 A4
Apache U.S.A. 34°54N 98°22W 176 D5
Apache Junction U.S.A. 33°25N 111°33W 169 K8
Apalachee B. U.S.A. 30°0N 84°0W 178 E5
Apalachicola U.S.A. 29°43N 84°59W 178 F5
Apalachicola → U.S.A. 29°43N 84°58W 178 F5
Apalachicola B. U.S.A. 29°40N 85°0W 178 F3
Apam Ghana 5°19N 0°42W 139 D4
Apapa Nigeria 6°26N 3°21E 139 D5
Apaporis → Colombia 1°23S 69°25W 186 D5
Aparados da Serra △ Brazil 29°10S 50°8W 191 B5
Aparri Phil. 18°22N 121°38E 119 A6
Apateu Romania 46°36N 21°47E 80 D6
Apatin Serbia 45°40N 19°0E 80 E4
Apatity Russia 67°34N 33°22E 60 C25
Apatula = Finke Australia 25°34S 134°35E 150 D1
Apatzingán Mexico 19°5N 102°21W 180 D4
Apeldoorn Neths. 52°13N 5°57E 69 B5
Apen Germany 53°13N 7°48E 76 B3
Apennines = Appennini Italy 44°30N 10°0E 92 D7
Aphrodisias Turkey 37°42N 28°46E 99 D10
Api Nepal 30°0N 80°57E 110 F5
Apia Samoa 13°50S 171°50W 147 C11
Apiacás, Serra dos Brazil 9°50S 57°0W 186 E7
Apies → S. Africa 25°15S 28°8E 145 C4
Apinajé Brazil 11°31S 48°18W 189 C1
Apiti N.Z. 39°58S 175°54E 154 F4
Apizaco Mexico 19°25N 98°8W 181 D5
Aplao Peru 16°0S 72°40W 188 D3
Apo, Mt. Phil. 6°53N 125°14E 119 C7
Apodi Brazil 5°39S 37°48W 189 B3
Apolakia Greece 36°5N 27°48E 101 C9
Apolakia, Ormos Greece 36°5N 27°45E 101 C9
Apolda Germany 51°2N 11°32E 76 D7
Apollo Bay Australia 38°45S 143°40E 152 E5
Apollonia = Sūsah Libya 32°52N 21°59E 135 B10
Apollonia Greece 36°15N 27°58E 101 C9
Apolo Bolivia 14°30S 68°30W 188 C4
Apolonia Greece 36°58N 24°43E 98 E6
Apopa El Salv. 13°48N 89°10W 182 D2
Apopka U.S.A. 28°40N 81°31W 179 G8
Apopka, L. U.S.A. 28°37N 81°37W 179 G8
Aporé → Brazil 19°27S 50°57W 187 G8
Apostle Is. U.S.A. 47°0N 90°40W 172 B8
Apostle Islands ⌓ U.S.A. 46°55N 91°0W 172 B8
Apóstoles Argentina 28°0S 56°0W 191 B4
Apostolos Andreas, C. Cyprus 35°42N 34°35E 101 D13
Apostolovo Ukraine 47°39N 33°39E 85 J7
Apoteri Guyana 4°2N 58°32W 186 C7
Appalachian Mts. U.S.A. 38°0N 80°0W 173 G14
Äppelbo Sweden 60°29N 14°1E 62 D8
Appennino Lucano-Val d'Agri-Lagonegrese ⌓ Italy 40°5N 16°10E 95 B9
Appennino Tosco-Emiliano ⌓ Italy 44°10N 10°25E 92 D7
Appennini Italy 44°30N 10°0E 92 D7
Appennino Ligure Italy 44°30N 9°0E 92 D6
Appenzell-Ausser Rhoden □ Switz. 47°23N 9°23E 77 H5
Appenzell-Inner Rhoden □ Switz. 47°20N 9°25E 77 H5
Appiano Italy 46°28N 11°15E 93 B8
Apple Hill Canada 45°13N 74°46W 175 A10
Apple Valley U.S.A. 34°32N 117°14W 171 L9
Appleby-in-Westmorland U.K. 54°35N 2°29W 66 C5
Appledore U.K. 51°3N 4°13W 67 F3
Appleton U.S.A. 44°16N 88°25W 172 C9
Appling U.S.A. 33°33N 82°19W 178 B7
Approuague → Fr. Guiana 4°30N 51°57W 187 C8
Apricena Italy 41°47N 15°27E 93 G12
Aprília Italy 41°36N 12°39E 94 A5
Apsheronsk Russia 44°28N 39°42E 87 H4
Apsley Canada 44°45N 78°6W 174 B6
Apt France 43°53N 5°24E 73 E9
Apuane, Alpi Italy 44°7N 10°14E 92 D7
Apucarana Brazil 23°55S 51°33W 191 A5
Apulia = Púglia □ Italy 41°15N 16°15E 95 A9
Apure → Venezuela 7°37N 66°25W 186 B5
Apurímac □ Peru 14°0S 73°0W 188 C3
Apurímac → Peru 12°17S 73°56W 188 C3
Apuseni, Munţii Romania 46°30N 22°45E 80 D7
Āq Qālā Iran 37°10N 54°30E 129 B7
Aqaba = Al 'Aqabah Jordan 29°31N 35°0E 130 F4
Aqaba, G. of Red Sea 29°0N 34°40E 128 D2
'Aqabah, Khalīj al = Aqaba, G. of Red Sea 29°0N 34°40E 128 D2
Aqadyr Kazakhstan 48°17N 74°50E 109 C8
Āqchah Afghan. 36°56N 66°11E 109 E7
'Aqdā Iran 32°26N 53°37E 129 C7
Aqīq Sudan 18°14N 38°12E 137 D4
Aqīq, Khalīg Sudan 18°20N 38°10E 137 D4
Aqköl Kazakhstan 51°59N 70°56E 109 B8
Aqmola □ Kazakhstan 51°30N 70°0E 109 B8
'Aqrah Iraq 36°46N 43°45E 105 D10
Aqsay Kazakhstan 51°11N 53°0E 108 B4
Aqshataū Kazakhstan 47°59N 74°3E 109 C8
Aqsū Ongtüstik Qazaqstan, Kazakhstan 42°25N 69°50E 109 D7
Aqsū Pavlodar, Kazakhstan 52°2N 76°55E 109 B9
Aqsügek Kazakhstan 44°37N 74°30E 109 D8
Aqtaū Mangghystaū, Kazakhstan 43°39N 51°12E 108 D4
Aqtaū Qaraghandy, Kazakhstan 50°14N 73°3E 109 B8
Aqtöbe Kazakhstan 50°17N 57°10E 108 B5
Aqtoghay Kazakhstan 46°57N 79°40E 109 C9
Aqua = Sokhumi Georgia 43°0N 41°0E 87 J5
Aquidauana Brazil 20°30S 55°50W 187 H7
Aquila Mexico 18°36N 103°30W 180 D4
Aquileia Italy 45°46N 13°22E 93 C10
Aquiles Serdán Mexico 28°36N 105°53W 180 B3
Aquin Haiti 18°16N 73°24W 183 C5
Aquitaine □ France 44°25N 0°30W 72 D3
Ar Horqin Qi China 43°45N 120°0E 115 C11
Ar Rafīd Syria 32°57N 35°52E 130 C4
Ar Rahhālīyah Iraq 32°44N 43°23E 105 F10
Ar Ramādī Iraq 33°25N 43°20E 105 F10
Ar Ramthā Jordan 32°34N 36°0E 130 C5
Ar Raqqah Syria 35°59N 39°8E 105 E8
Ar Raqqah □ Syria 36°20N 39°10E 105 D8
Ar Rashidiya = Er Rachidia Morocco 31°58N 4°20W 136 B3
Ar Rass Si. Arabia 25°50N 43°40E 128 E4
Ar Rawdah Si. Arabia 21°16N 42°50E 131 C3
Ar Rayyan Qatar 25°17N 51°25E 129 E6
Ar Rifā'ī Iraq 31°50N 46°10E 128 D5
Ar Riyāḍ Si. Arabia 24°41N 46°42E 128 E5
Ar Ru'ays Qatar 26°8N 51°12E 129 E6
Ar Rukhaymīyah Iraq 29°22N 45°38E 128 D5
Ar Rumaythah Iraq 31°31N 45°12E 128 D5
Ar Ruṣāfah Syria 35°45N 38°49E 105 E8
Ar Rutbah Iraq 33°0N 40°15E 105 F9
Ara India 25°35N 84°32E 125 G11
Arab U.S.A. 34°19N 86°30W 177 D11
'Arab, Bahr el → South Sudan 9°0N 29°30E 135 G11
Arab, Khalîg el Egypt 30°55N 29°0E 137 E6
Arab, Shatt al → Asia 29°57N 48°34E 129 D6
'Araba, W. → Egypt 28°19N 33°31E 137 F8
'Arabābād Iran 33°2N 57°41E 129 C8
Araban Turkey 37°28N 37°44E 104 D7
Arabatskaya Strelka Ukraine 45°40N 35°0E 85 K8
Arabba Italy 46°30N 11°52E 93 B8
Arabi U.S.A. 31°50N 83°44W 178 D6
Arabia Asia 25°0N 45°0E 102 F6
Arabian Basin Ind. Oc. 11°30N 65°0E 146 C5
Arabian Desert = Es Sahrâ' Esh Sharqîya Egypt 27°30N 32°30E 137 B3
Arabian Gulf = Persian Gulf Asia 27°0N 50°0E 129 E6
Arabian Sea Ind. Oc. 16°0N 65°0E 102 G8
Araç Turkey 41°15N 33°21E 104 B5
Aracaju Brazil 10°55S 37°4W 189 C3
Aracati Brazil 4°30S 37°44W 189 A3
Araçatuba Brazil 21°10S 50°30W 191 A5
Aracena Spain 37°53N 6°38W 89 H4
Aracena, Sierra de Spain 37°50N 6°50W 89 H4
Arachova Greece 38°28N 22°35E 98 C4
Arachthos → Greece 39°20N 21°4E 98 B3
Aračinovo Macedonia 42°1N 21°34E 96 D5
Araçuaí Brazil 16°52S 42°4W 189 D2
Araçuaí → Brazil 16°46S 42°2W 189 D2
'Arad Israel 31°15N 35°12E 130 D4
Arad Romania 46°10N 21°20E 80 D6
Arad □ Romania 46°20N 22°0E 80 D6
Arādān Iran 35°21N 52°30E 129 C7
Aradhippou Cyprus 34°57N 33°36E 101 E12
Arafura Sea E. Indies 9°0S 135°0E 147 B6
Aragats Armenia 40°30N 44°15E 87 K7
Aragon U.S.A. 34°2N 85°3W 178 A4
Aragón □ Spain 41°25N 0°40W 90 D4
Aragón → Spain 42°13N 1°44W 90 C3
Aragona Italy 37°24N 13°37E 94 E6
Araguacema Brazil 8°50S 49°20W 187 E9
Araguaia → Brazil 5°21S 48°41W 187 E9
Araguaína Brazil 7°12S 48°12W 189 B1
Araguari Brazil 18°38S 48°11W 189 D1
Araguari → Brazil 1°15N 49°55W 187 C9
Araguatins Brazil 5°38S 48°7W 189 B1
Arahal Spain 37°15N 5°33W 89 H5
Arain India 26°27N 75°2E 124 F6
Araioses Brazil 2°53S 41°55W 189 A2
Arak Algeria 25°20N 3°45E 136 C4
Arāk Iran 34°0N 49°40E 129 C6
Arakan = Rakhine □ Burma 19°0N 94°15E 123 K18
Arakan Coast Burma 19°0N 94°0E 123 K19
Arakan Yoma Burma 20°0N 94°40E 123 K19
Arakkonam India 13°7N 79°43E 127 H4
Araklı Turkey 41°6N 40°2E 105 B9
Araks = Aras, Rūd-e → Asia 40°5N 48°29E 105 B13
Araks → Iran 39°10N 47°10E 108 E3
Aral Kazakhstan 46°41N 61°45E 108 C6
Aral Mangy Qaraqumy Kazakhstan 46°50N 63°10E 108 C6
Aral Sea Asia 45°0N 58°20E 108 C5
Aral Tengizi = Aral Sea Asia 45°0N 58°20E 108 C5
Aralık Turkey 39°52N 44°31E 105 C11
Aralkum Asia 44°30N 60°35E 108 D6
Aralsk = Aral Kazakhstan 46°41N 61°45E 108 C6
Aralskoye More = Aral Sea Asia 45°0N 58°20E 108 C5
Aralsor, Ozero = Aralsor Köli Kazakhstan 49°5N 48°12E 87 F9
Aralsor Köli Kazakhstan 49°5N 48°12E 87 F9
Aramac Australia 22°58S 145°14E 150 C4
Aran → India 19°55N 78°12E 126 E4
Aran, Val de Spain 42°50N 0°55E 90 C5
Aran I. = Arranmore Ireland 55°0N 8°30W 64 A3
Aran Is. Ireland 53°6N 9°38W 64 C2
Aranda de Duero Spain 41°39N 3°42W 88 D7
Arandān Iran 35°23N 46°55E 128 C5
Aranđelovac Serbia 44°18N 20°34E 96 B4
Aranga N.Z. 35°44S 173°40E 154 B2
Arani India 12°43N 79°19E 127 H4
Aranjuez Spain 40°1N 3°40W 88 E7
Aranos Namibia 24°9S 19°7E 144 B2
Aransas Pass U.S.A. 27°55N 97°9W 176 H6
Aranyaprathet Thailand 13°41N 102°30E 120 F4
Araouane Mali 18°55N 3°30W 138 B4
Arapahoe U.S.A. 40°18N 99°54W 172 E4
Arapawa I. N.Z. 41°11S 174°17E 155 B9
Arapey Grande → Uruguay 30°55S 57°49W 190 C4
Arapgir Turkey 39°5N 38°30E 105 C8
Arapiraca Brazil 9°45S 36°39W 189 B3
Arapis, Akra Greece 40°27N 24°0E 97 F8
Arapongas Brazil 23°29S 51°28W 191 A5
Arapuni N.Z. 38°4S 175°39E 154 E4
Ar'ar Si. Arabia 30°59N 41°2E 128 D4
Araranguá Brazil 29°0S 49°30W 191 B6
Araraquara Brazil 21°50S 48°0W 187 H9
Ararás, Serra das Brazil 25°0S 53°10W 191 B5
Ararat Armenia 39°48N 44°50E 105 C11
Ararat Australia 37°16S 142°58E 152 D5
Ararat, Mt. = Ağrı Dağı Turkey 39°50N 44°15E 105 C11
Arari Brazil 3°28S 44°47W 189 A2
Araria India 26°9N 87°33E 125 F12
Araripe, Chapada do Brazil 7°20S 40°0W 189 B3
Araripina Brazil 7°33S 40°34W 189 B2
Araruama, L. de Brazil 22°53S 42°12W 191 A7
Araruna Brazil 6°52S 35°44W 189 B3
Aras, Rūd-e → Asia 40°5N 48°29E 105 B13
Aratāne Mauritania 18°24N 8°32W 138 B3
Arauca Colombia 7°0N 70°40W 186 B4
Arauca → Venezuela 7°24N 66°35W 186 B5
Arauco Chile 37°16S 73°25W 190 D1
Araújos Brazil 19°56S 45°14W 189 D1
Aravalli Range India 25°0N 73°30E 124 G5
Arawale ⌓ Kenya 1°24S 40°9E 142 C5
Arawhata → N.Z. 44°0S 168°40E 155 E3
Araxá Brazil 19°35S 46°55W 189 D1
Araya, Pen. de Venezuela 10°40N 64°0W 186 A6
Arba Minch Ethiopia 6°0N 37°30E 131 F2
Arbat Iraq 35°25N 45°35E 105 E11
Árbatax Italy 39°56N 9°42E 94 C2
Arbīl Iraq 36°15N 44°5E 105 D11
Arbīl □ Iraq 36°20N 44°20E 105 D11
Arboga Sweden 59°24N 15°52E 62 E9
Arbois France 46°55N 5°46E 71 F12
Arboréa Italy 39°46N 8°35E 94 C1
Arborfield Canada 53°6N 103°39W 163 C8
Arborg Canada 50°54N 97°13W 163 C9
Arbre du Ténéré Niger 17°50N 10°4E 139 B7
Arbroath U.K. 56°34N 2°35W 65 E6
Arbuckle U.S.A. 39°1N 122°3W 170 F4
Arbus Italy 39°30N 8°33E 94 C1
Arc → France 45°34N 6°12E 73 C10
Arc-lès-Gray France 47°28N 5°34E 71 E12
Arcachon France 44°40N 1°10W 72 D2
Arcachon, Bassin d' France 44°42N 1°10W 72 D2
Arcade U.S.A. 42°32N 78°25W 174 D6
Arcadia = Arkadia Greece 37°30N 22°20E 98 D4
Arcadia Fla., U.S.A. 27°13N 81°52W 179 H8
Arcadia La., U.S.A. 32°33N 92°55W 176 E8
Arcadia Pa., U.S.A. 40°47N 78°51W 174 F6
Arcata U.S.A. 40°52N 124°5W 168 F1
Arcévia Italy 43°30N 12°56E 93 E9
Archanes Greece 35°16N 25°11E 99 F7
Archangel = Arkhangelsk Russia 64°38N 40°36E 106 C5
Archangelos Greece 36°13N 28°7E 101 C10
Archar Bulgaria 43°50N 22°54E 96 C6
Archbald U.S.A. 41°30N 75°32W 175 E9
Archena Spain 38°9N 1°16W 91 G3
Archer U.S.A. 29°32N 82°32W 179 F7
Archer → Australia 13°28S 141°41E 150 A3
Archer B. Australia 13°20S 141°30E 150 A3
Archer Bend = Mungkan Kandju △ Australia 13°35S 142°52E 150 A3
Archers Post Kenya 0°35N 37°35E 142 B4
Arches △ U.S.A. 38°45N 109°25W 168 G9
Archidona Spain 37°6N 4°22W 89 H6
Archipel-de-Mingan △ Canada 50°13N 63°10W 165 B7
Archipiélago Chinijo △ Canary Is. 29°20N 13°30W 100 E6
Archipiélago Los Roques △ Venezuela 11°50N 66°44W 183 D6
Arci, Mte. Italy 39°47N 8°45E 94 C1
Arcidosso Italy 42°52N 11°33E 93 F8
Arcila = Asilah Morocco 35°29N 6°0W 136 A2
Arcipelago de la Maddalena △ Italy 41°14N 9°24E 94 A2
Arcipelago Toscano △ Italy 42°45N 10°15E 92 F7
Arcis-sur-Aube France 48°32N 4°10E 71 D11

Arckaringa Cr. →
  Australia 28°10S 135°22E 151 D2
Arco Italy 45°55N 10°53E 92 C7
Arco U.S.A. 43°38N 113°18W 168 E7
Arcoona Australia 31°2S 137°1E 152 A2
Arcos de Jalón Spain 41°12N 2°16W 90 D2
Arcos de la Frontera
  Spain 36°45N 5°49W 89 J5
Arcos de Valdevez
  Portugal 41°55N 8°22W 88 D2
Arcot India 12°53N 79°20E 127 H4
Arcozelo Portugal 40°32N 7°47W 88 E3
Arctic Bay Canada 73°1N 85°7W 161 C14
Arctic Mid-Ocean Ridge
  Arctic 87°0N 90°0E 54 A
Arctic Ocean Arctic 78°0N 160°0W 54 B18
Arctic Red River = Tsiigehtchic
  Canada 67°15N 134°0W 160 D5
Arctowski Antarctica 62°30S 58°0W 5 C18
Arda → Bulgaria 41°40N 26°30E 97 E10
Arda → Italy 45°2N 10°2E 92 C7
Ardabīl Iran 38°15N 48°18E 105 C13
Ardabīl □ Iran 38°15N 48°20E 129 B6
Ardahan Turkey 41°7N 42°41E 105 B10
Ardahan □ Turkey 41°10N 42°50E 105 B10
Ardakān = Sepīdān Iran 30°20N 52°5E 129 D7
Ardakān Iran 32°19N 53°59E 129 C7
Ardala Sweden 58°22N 13°19E 63 F7
Ardales Spain 36°53N 4°51W 89 J6
Ardara Ireland 54°46N 8°25W 64 B3
Ardas → Greece 41°40N 26°30E 97 E10
Ardèche □ France 44°42N 4°16E 73 D8
Ardèche → France 44°16N 4°39E 73 D8
Ardee Ireland 53°52N 6°33W 64 C5
Arden Canada 44°43N 76°56W 174 B8
Arden Denmark 56°46N 9°52E 63 H3
Arden Calif., U.S.A. 38°36N 121°33W 170 G5
Arden Nev., U.S.A. 36°1N 115°14W 171 J11
Ardenne Belgium 49°50N 5°5E 69 E5
Ardennes = Ardenne
  Belgium 49°50N 5°5E 69 E5
Ardennes □ France 49°35N 4°40E 71 C11
Ardentes France 46°45N 1°50E 71 F8
Arderin Ireland 53°2N 7°39W 64 C4
Ardeşen Turkey 41°12N 41°2E 105 B9
Ardestān Iran 33°20N 52°25E 129 C7
Ardfert Ireland 52°20N 9°47W 64 D2
Ardglass U.K. 54°16N 5°36W 64 B6
Ardhéa = Aridea Greece 40°58N 22°3E 96 F6
Ardila → Portugal 38°12N 7°28W 89 G3
Ardino Bulgaria 41°34N 25°9E 97 E9
Ardivachar Pt. U.K. 57°23N 7°26W 65 D1
Ardlethan Australia 34°22S 146°53E 153 C7
Ardmore Pa., U.S.A. 40°1N 75°17W 175 F9
Ardmore Okla., U.S.A. 34°10N 97°8W 176 B6
Ardnamurchan, Pt. of
  U.K. 56°43N 6°14W 65 E2
Ardnave Pt. U.K. 55°53N 6°20W 65 F2
Ardon Russia 43°10N 44°18E 87 J7
Ardore Italy 38°11N 16°10E 95 D9
Ardres France 50°50N 1°59E 71 B8
Ardrossan Australia 34°26S 137°53E 152 C2
Ardrossan U.K. 55°39N 4°49W 65 F4
Ards Pen. U.K. 54°33N 5°34W 64 B6
Arduan Sudan 19°54N 30°20E 137 D3
Ardud Romania 47°37N 22°52E 80 C7
Åre Sweden 63°22N 13°15E 62 A7
Arecibo Puerto Rico 18°29N 66°43W 183 d
Areia Branca Brazil 5°0S 37°0W 189 A3
Arena, Pt. U.S.A. 38°57N 123°44W 170 G3
Arenal Honduras 15°21N 86°50W 182 C2
Arenales, Cerro Chile 47°5S 73°40W 192 C2
Arenas = Las Arenas
  Spain 43°17N 4°50W 88 B6
Arenas de San Pedro
  Spain 40°12N 5°5W 88 E5
Arendal Norway 58°28N 8°46E 61 G13
Arendsee Germany 52°52N 11°27E 76 C7
Arenys de Mar Spain 41°35N 2°33E 90 D7
Arenzano Italy 44°24N 8°41E 92 D5
Areópoli Greece 36°40N 22°22E 98 E4
Arequipa Peru 16°20S 71°30W 188 D3
Arequipa □ Peru 16°0S 72°0W 188 D3
Arès France 44°47N 1°8W 72 D2
Arévalo Spain 41°3N 4°43W 88 D6
Arezzo Italy 43°25N 11°53E 93 E8
Arga Turkey 38°21N 37°59E 128 B3
Arga → Spain 42°18N 1°47W 90 C3
Argalasti Greece 39°13N 23°13E 98 B5
Argamasilla de Alba Spain 39°8N 3°5W 89 F7
Argamasilla de Calatrava
  Spain 38°44N 4°4W 89 G6
Arganda del Rey Spain 40°19N 3°26W 88 E7
Arganil Portugal 40°13N 8°3W 88 E2
Argarapa → Australia 22°20S 134°58E 150 C1
Argelès-Gazost France 43°0N 0°6W 72 E3
Argelès-sur-Mer France 42°34N 3°1E 72 F7
Argens → France 43°24N 6°44E 73 E10
Argent, Côte d' France 44°15N 1°30W 72 D2
Argent-sur-Sauldre
  France 47°33N 2°25E 71 E9
Argenta Canada 50°11N 116°56W 162 C5
Argenta Italy 44°37N 11°50E 93 D8
Argentan France 48°45N 0°1W 70 D6
Argentário, Mte. Italy 42°24N 11°9E 93 F8
Argentat France 45°6N 1°56E 72 D5
Argentera Italy 44°12N 7°5E 92 D4
Argenteuil France 48°57N 2°14E 71 D9
Argentia Canada 47°18N 53°58E 165 C9
Argentina ■ S. Amer. 35°0S 66°0W 185 G4
Argentine Abyssal Plain
  Atl. Oc. 45°0S 45°0W 56 L1
Argentine Basin Atl. Oc. 45°0S 45°0W 56 L7
Argentino, L. Argentina 50°10S 73°0W 192 G2
Argenton-les-Vallées
  France 46°59N 0°27W 70 F6
Argenton-sur-Creuse
  France 46°36N 1°30E 71 F8
Argeș □ Romania 45°0N 24°45E 81 F9
Argeș → Romania 44°5N 26°38E 81 F11
Arghandab → Afghan. 31°30N 64°15E 124 D1
Argirades Greece 39°27N 19°58E 101 B3
Argiroupoli Greece 35°17N 24°20E 101 D6
Argo Sudan 19°28N 30°30E 137 D3
Argolikos Kolpos Greece 37°20N 22°52E 98 D4
Argos Greece 37°40N 22°43E 98 D4
Argos Orestiko Greece 40°27N 21°18E 96 F5
Argostoli Greece 38°11N 20°29E 98 C2

Arguedas Spain 42°11N 1°36W 90 C3
Arguello, Pt. U.S.A. 34°35N 120°39W 171 L6
Arguineguín
  Canary Is. 27°46N 15°41W 100 G4
Argun Russia 43°18N 45°52E 87 J7
Argun → Russia 53°20N 121°28E 111 A13
Argungu Nigeria 12°40N 4°31E 139 C5
Argus Pk. U.S.A. 35°52N 117°26W 171 K9
Argyle, L. Australia 16°20S 128°40E 148 C4
Argyll & Bute □ U.K. 56°13N 5°28W 65 E3
Århavi Turkey 41°21N 41°18E 105 B9
Århus = Aarhus Denmark 56°8N 10°11E 63 H4
Århus □ Denmark 56°15N 10°15E 63 H4
Ariadnoye Russia 45°8N 134°25E 112 B7
Ariamsvlei Namibia 28°9S 19°51E 144 C2
Ariana Tunisia 36°52N 10°12E 136 A6
Ariano Irpino Italy 41°9N 15°5E 95 A8
Ariano Tunisia 36°50N 9°52E 136 A5
Arica Chile 18°32S 70°20W 188 D4
Arica Colombia 2°0S 71°50W 186 D4
Arica y Parinacota □
  Chile 17°40S 69°50W 188 D4
Arico Canary Is. 28°9N 16°29W 100 F3
Arid, C. Australia 34°1S 123°10E 149 F3
Arida Japan 34°5N 135°8E 113 G7
Aride Seychelles 4°13S 55°40E 141 b
Aridea Greece 40°58N 22°3E 96 F6
Ariège □ France 42°56N 1°30E 72 F5
Ariège → France 43°30N 1°25E 72 E5
Ariet el Fersig Algeria 27°35N 2°7W 136 C3
Arīḥā Israel 31°51N 35°27E 130 E4
Arila, Akra Greece 39°43N 19°39E 101 A3
Arilje Serbia 43°44N 20°7E 96 C4
Arima Trin. & Tob. 10°38N 61°17W 183 D7
Arinos → Brazil 10°25S 58°20W 186 F7
Ario de Rosales
  Mexico 19°12N 101°43W 180 D4
Ariogala Lithuania 55°16N 23°28E 64 F8
Aripo, Mt. Trin. & Tob. 10°45N 61°15W 187 K15
Aripuanã Brazil 9°25S 60°30W 186 E6
Aripuanã → Brazil 5°7S 60°25W 186 E6
Ariquemes Brazil 9°55S 63°6W 186 E6
Arisaig U.K. 56°55N 5°51W 65 E3
Arīsh, W. el → Egypt 31°9N 33°49E 137 E8
Aristazabal I. Canada 52°40N 129°10W 162 C3
Ariton U.S.A. 31°36N 85°43W 178 D4
Ariyalur India 11°8N 79°8E 127 J4
Ariza Spain 41°19N 2°3W 90 D2
Arizaro, Salar de
  Argentina 24°40S 67°50W 190 A2
Arizona Argentina 35°45S 65°25W 190 D2
Arizona □ U.S.A. 34°0N 112°0W 169 J8
Arizpe Mexico 30°20N 110°10W 180 A2
'Arjah Si. Arabia 24°43N 44°17E 128 E5
Ärjäng Sweden 59°24N 12°8E 62 E6
Arjeplog Sweden 66°3N 17°54E 60 C17
Arjepluovve = Arjeplog
  Sweden 66°3N 17°54E 60 C17
Arjona Colombia 10°14N 75°22W 186 A3
Arjona Spain 37°56N 4°4W 89 H6
Arjuna Indonesia 7°49S 112°34E 119 G15
Arka Russia 60°15N 142°0E 107 C15
Arkadak Russia 51°58N 43°30E 86 E6
Arkadelphia U.S.A. 34°7N 93°4W 176 B7
Arkadia Greece 37°30N 22°20E 98 D4
Arkaig, L. U.K. 56°59N 5°10W 65 E3
Arkalgud India 12°46N 76°3E 127 H3
Arkalyk = Arqalyk
  Kazakhstan 50°13N 66°50E 109 B7
Arkansas □ U.S.A. 35°0N 92°30W 176 B8
Arkansas → U.S.A. 33°47N 91°4W 176 B9
Arkansas City U.S.A. 37°4N 97°2W 172 G5
Arkaroola Australia 30°20S 139°22E 151 E2
Arkavāz Iran 33°22N 46°35E 105 F12
Arkhangelsk Russia 64°38N 40°36E 106 C5
Arkhangelskoye Russia 51°32N 40°58E 86 E5
Arki Greece 31°9N 76°58E 124 D7
Arki India 31°9N 76°58E 124 D7
Arklow Ireland 52°48N 6°10W 64 D5
Arkona, Kap Germany 54°42N 13°26E 76 A9
Arkösund Sweden 58°29N 16°56E 63 F10
Arkoudi Greece 38°33N 20°43E 98 C2
Arkport U.S.A. 42°24N 77°42W 174 D7
Arkticheskiy, Mys
  Russia 81°10N 95°0E 107 A10
Arkul Russia 57°17N 50°3E 86 B10
Arkville U.S.A. 42°9N 74°37W 175 D10
Årla Sweden 59°17N 16°40E 62 E10
Arlanda, Stockholm × (ARN)
  Sweden 59°41N 17°56E 62 E11
Arlanza → Spain 42°6N 4°9W 88 C6
Arlanzón → Spain 42°3N 4°17W 88 C6
Arlbergpass Austria 47°9N 10°12E 78 D3
Arlbergtunnel Austria 47°9N 10°12E 78 D3
Arles France 43°41N 4°40E 73 E8
Arli Burkina Faso 11°35N 1°28E 139 C5
Arli → Burkina Faso 11°35N 1°28E 139 C5
Arlington S. Africa 28°1S 27°53E 145 C4
Arlington Ga., U.S.A. 31°26N 84°43W 178 D11
Arlington N.Y., U.S.A. 41°42N 73°54W 175 E11
Arlington Oreg.,
  U.S.A. 45°43N 120°12W 168 D3
Arlington S. Dak., U.S.A. 44°22N 97°8W 172 C5
Arlington Tex., U.S.A. 32°44N 97°6W 176 E6
Arlington Va., U.S.A. 38°53N 77°7W 173 F15
Arlington Vt., U.S.A. 43°5N 73°9W 175 C11
Arlington Wash.,
  U.S.A. 48°12N 122°8W 170 B4
Arlington Heights
  U.S.A. 42°5N 87°59W 172 D10
Arlit Niger 19°0N 7°38E 134 C7
Arlon Belgium 49°42N 5°49E 69 E5
Arlparra Australia 22°11S 134°30E 150 C1
Arltunga Australia 23°26S 134°41E 150 C1
Armação de Pêra Portugal 37°6N 8°22W 89 H2
Armadale Australia 32°9S 116°0E 149 F2
Armagh U.K. 54°21N 6°39W 64 B5
Armagh □ U.K. 54°18N 6°37W 64 B5
Armagnac France 43°50N 0°10E 72 E4
Armançon → France 47°59N 3°30E 71 E10
Armando Bermúdez △
  Dom. Rep. 19°3N 71°0W 183 C5
Armant Egypt 25°37N 32°32E 137 B3
Armatree Australia 31°26S 148°28E 153 B8
Armavir Armenia 45°2N 41°7E 87 H5
Armenia Colombia 4°35N 75°45W 186 C3
Armenia ■ Asia 40°20N 45°0E 87 K7
Armeniş Romania 45°13N 22°17E 80 D7
Armenistis, Akra Greece 36°8N 27°42E 101 C9

Armentières France 50°40N 2°50E 71 B9
Armidale Australia 30°30S 151°40E 153 A9
Armilla Spain 37°9N 3°37W 89 H7
Armori India 20°28N 79°59E 126 D7
Armorique △ France 48°22N 3°50W 70 D3
Armour U.S.A. 43°19N 98°21W 172 D4
Armstrong B.C.,
  Canada 50°25N 119°10W 162 C5
Armstrong Ont., Canada 50°18N 89°4W 164 B2
Armur India 18°48N 78°16E 126 E4
Armutlu Bursa, Turkey 40°31N 28°50E 97 F12
Armutlu İzmir, Turkey 38°24N 27°34E 99 C9
Arnarfjörður Iceland 65°48N 23°40W 60 D2
Arnaud → Canada 59°59N 69°46W 161 F18
Arnauti, C. Cyprus 35°6N 32°17E 101 D11
Arnay-le-Duc France 47°10N 4°27E 71 E11
Arnea Greece 40°30N 23°38E 96 F7
Arnedillo Spain 42°13N 2°14W 90 C2
Arnedo Spain 42°12N 2°5W 90 C2
Arnett U.S.A. 36°8N 99°46W 176 C5
Arnhem Neths. 51°58N 5°55E 69 C5
Arnhem, C. Australia 12°20S 137°30E 150 A2
Arnhem B. Australia 12°20S 136°10E 150 A2
Arnhem Land
  Australia 13°10S 134°30E 150 A1
Arnhem Land ◌ 12°50S 134°50E 150 A1
Arnissa Greece 40°47N 21°49E 96 F5
Arno → Italy 43°41N 10°17E 92 E7
Arno Bay Australia 33°54S 136°34E 152 B2
Arnold U.K. 53°1N 1°7W 66 D6
Arnold Calif., U.S.A. 38°15N 120°21W 170 G6
Arnold Md., U.S.A. 38°26N 90°23W 172 F8
Arnoldstein Austria 46°33N 13°43E 78 E6
Arnon → France 47°13N 2°1E 71 E9
Arnot Canada 55°56N 96°41W 163 B9
Arnøya Norway 70°9N 20°40E 60 A19
Arnprior Canada 45°26N 76°21W 175 A8
Arnsberg Germany 51°24N 8°5E 76 D4
Arnsberg Wald △
  Germany 51°25N 8°20E 76 D4
Arnstadt Germany 50°50N 10°56E 76 E6
Aroab Namibia 26°41S 19°39E 144 C2
Aroania Oros Greece 37°56S 22°12E 98 D4
Aroche Spain 37°56N 6°57W 89 H4
Arochuku Nigeria 5°21N 7°54E 139 D6
Aroeiras Brazil 7°31S 35°41W 189 B3
Arolsen Germany 51°23N 9°2E 76 D5
Aron India 25°57N 77°56E 124 G6
Aron → France 46°50N 3°28E 71 F10
Arona Canary Is. 28°6N 16°40W 100 F3
Arona Italy 45°46N 8°34E 92 C5
Aroona → Mexico 29°9N 107°57W 180 B3
Arosa, Ría de → Spain 42°28N 8°57W 88 C2
Arpa → Asia 39°28N 44°56E 105 C11
Arpaçay Turkey 40°50N 43°19E 105 B10
Arpajon France 48°36N 2°15E 71 D9
Arpajon-sur-Cère France 44°53N 2°28E 72 D6
Arpaşu de Jos Romania 45°47N 24°37E 81 E9
Arqalyk Kazakhstan 50°13N 66°50E 109 B7
Arrah = Ara India 25°35N 84°32E 125 G11
Arrah Ivory C. 6°40N 3°58E 84 H4
Arraias Brazil 12°56S 46°57W 189 C1
Arraiolos Portugal 38°44N 7°59W 89 G3
Arran U.K. 55°34N 5°12W 65 F3
Arranmore Ireland 55°0N 8°30W 64 A3
Arras France 50°17N 2°46E 71 B9
Arrasate Spain 43°4N 2°30W 90 A2
Arrats → France 44°6N 0°52E 72 D4
Arreau France 42°54N 0°22E 72 F4
Arrecife Canary Is. 28°57N 13°37W 100 F6
Arrecifes Argentina 34°6S 60°9W 190 C3
Arrée, Mts. d' France 48°26N 3°55W 70 D3
Arreso Denmark 55°58N 12°6E 63 d6
Arriaga Mexico 16°14N 93°54W 181 D6
Arribes del Duero △
  Spain 41°11N 6°39W 88 D4
Arrilalah Australia 23°43S 143°54E 150 C3
Arrino Australia 29°30S 115°40E 149 E2
Arriondas Spain 43°23N 5°11W 88 B5
Arrojado → Brazil 13°24S 44°20W 189 C2
Arromanches-les-Bains
  France 49°20N 0°38W 70 C6
Arronches Portugal 39°8N 7°16W 89 F3
Arros → France 43°40N 0°2W 72 E3
Arrow, L. Ireland 54°3N 8°19W 64 B3
Arrowsmith, Mt. N.Z. 43°40S 170°55E 155 D5
Arrowtown N.Z. 44°57S 168°50E 155 D3
Arroyo de la Luz Spain 39°30N 6°38W 89 F4
Arroyo Grande U.S.A. 35°7N 120°35W 171 K6
Ars Iran 37°9N 47°46E 128 B5
Ars-sur-Moselle France 49°5N 6°4E 71 C13
Arsenault L. Canada 55°6N 108°32W 163 B7
Arsenev Russia 44°10N 133°15E 112 B6
Arsiero Italy 45°48N 11°21E 93 C8
Arsikere India 13°15N 76°15E 127 H3
Arsin Turkey 41°8N 39°55E 105 B8
Arsk Russia 56°10N 49°50E 86 B9
Årsunda Sweden 60°31N 16°45E 62 D10
Arta Greece 39°8N 21°2E 98 B3
Artà Spain 39°41N 3°21E 100 B10
Artà, Coves d' Spain 39°40N 3°24E 100 B10
Artashat Armenia 40°0N 44°35E 105 C12
Arteaga Mexico 18°28N 102°25W 180 D4
Arteixo = A Baiuca
  Spain 43°19N 8°29W 88 B2
Artem Azerbaijan 40°28N 50°20E 87 K10
Artem Russia 43°22N 132°13E 112 C6
Artemovsk Russia 54°45N 93°35E 107 D10
Artemovsk Ukraine 48°35N 38°0E 85 H9
Artemovskiy Russia 47°45N 40°16E 87 G5
Artenay France 48°5N 1°50E 71 D8
Artern Germany 51°22N 11°18E 76 D7
Artesa de Segre Spain 41°54N 1°3E 90 D6
Artesia = Mosomane
  Botswana 24°2S 26°19E 144 B4
Artesia U.S.A. 32°51N 104°24W 169 K11
Arthington Liberia 6°35N 10°45W 138 D2
Arthur Canada 43°50N 80°32W 174 C4
Arthur → Australia 41°2N 144°40E 151 G3
Arthur Cr. →
  Australia 22°30S 136°25E 150 C2
Arthur Pt. Australia 22°7S 150°3E 150 C5
Arthur River Australia 33°20S 117°2E 149 F2
Arthur's Pass N.Z. 42°54S 171°35E 155 D5
Arthur's Pass △ N.Z. 42°56S 171°42E 155 D5
Arthur's Town
  Bahamas 24°38N 75°42W 183 B4
Artigas Antarctica 62°30S 58°0W 5 C18
Artigas Uruguay 30°20S 56°30W 190 C4

Artik Armenia 40°38N 43°58E 87 K6
Artillery L. Canada 63°9N 107°52W 163 A7
Artois France 50°20N 2°30E 71 B9
Artotina Greece 38°42N 22°2E 98 C4
Artova Turkey 40°5N 36°28E 104 B7
Artrutx, C. de Spain 39°55N 3°49E 100 B10
Arts Bogd Uul
  Mongolia 44°40N 102°20E 114 B2
Artsvashen Armenia 40°38N 45°30E 105 C11
Artsyz Ukraine 46°4N 29°26E 81 D14
Artux China 39°40N 76°10E 109 E9
Artvin Turkey 41°14N 41°44E 105 B9
Artvin □ Turkey 41°10N 41°50E 105 B9
Artyk Russia 64°12N 145°6E 107 C15
Artyom Azerbaijan 40°28N 50°20E 87 K10
Aru, Kepulauan
  Indonesia 6°0S 134°30E 119 F8
Aru Is. = Aru, Kepulauan
  Indonesia 6°0S 134°30E 119 F8
Arua Uganda 3°1N 30°58E 142 B3
Aruanã Brazil 14°54S 51°10W 187 F8
Aruba ☑ W. Indies 12°30N 70°0W 183 D6
Arucas Canary Is. 28°7N 15°32W 100 F4
Arud y France 43°7N 0°28W 72 E3
Arue Tahiti 17°31S 149°30W 155 b
Arumpo Australia 33°48S 142°55E 153 C3
Arun → Nepal 26°55N 87°10E 125 F12
Arun → U.K. 50°49N 0°33W 67 G7
Arunachal Pradesh □
  India 28°0N 95°0E 123 F19
Aruppukkottai India 9°31N 78°8E 127 K4
Arusha Tanzania 3°20S 36°40E 142 C4
Arusha □ Tanzania 3°20S 36°30E 142 C4
Arusha △ Tanzania 3°16S 36°47E 142 C4
Arusha Chini Tanzania 3°32S 37°20E 142 C4
Aruvi → Sri Lanka 8°48N 79°53E 127 K4
Aruwimi →
  Dem. Rep. of the Congo 1°13N 23°36E 142 B1
Arvada Colo., U.S.A. 39°48N 105°5W 168 G11
Arvada Wyo., U.S.A. 44°39N 106°8W 168 D10
Arvakalu Sri Lanka 8°20N 79°58E 127 K4
Arvayheer Mongolia 46°15N 102°48E 110 B9
Arve → France 46°11N 6°8E 71 F13
Arvi India 20°59N 78°16E 126 D6
Arviat Canada 61°6N 93°59W 163 A10
Arvidsjaur Sweden 65°35N 19°10E 60 D18
Arvika Sweden 59°40N 12°36E 62 E6
Arvin U.S.A. 35°12N 118°50W 171 K8
Arwal India 25°15N 84°41E 125 G11
Arxan China 47°11N 119°57E 111 B12
Åryd Sweden 56°49N 14°59E 63 H8
Arys Kazakhstan 42°26N 68°48E 109 D7
Arzachena Italy 41°5N 9°23E 94 A2
Arzamas Russia 55°27N 43°55E 86 C6
Arzanah U.A.E. 24°47N 52°34E 129 E7
Arzew Algeria 35°50N 0°23W 136 A3
Arzgir Russia 45°18N 44°23E 87 H7
Arzignano Italy 45°31N 11°20E 93 C8
Arzúa Spain 42°56N 8°9W 88 C2
Aš Czech Rep. 50°13N 12°12E 78 A5
As Pontes de García Rodríguez
  Spain 43°27N 7°50W 88 B3
As Ṣafā Syria 33°10N 37°0E 130 B6
As Saffānīyah Si. Arabia 27°55N 48°50E 128 E6
Aş Şafīrah Syria 36°5N 37°21E 104 D7
Aş Şahm Oman 24°10N 56°53E 129 E8
As Sājir Si. Arabia 25°11N 44°36E 128 E5
As Salamīyah Syria 35°1N 37°2E 104 E7
As Salmān Iraq 30°30N 44°32E 128 D5
As Salt Jordan 32°2N 35°43E 130 C4
As Sal'w'a Qatar 24°23N 50°50E 129 E6
As Samāwah Iraq 31°15N 45°15E 128 D5
As Sanamayn Syria 33°3N 36°10E 130 B5
As Sila' U.A.E. 24°4N 51°45E 129 E6
As Sukhnah Syria 34°52N 38°52E 105 E8
As Sulaymānīyah △ Iraq 35°35N 45°29E 105 E11
As Sulaymānīyah □
  Iraq 35°50N 45°30E 105 E11
As Sulaymī Si. Arabia 26°17N 41°21E 128 E4
As Sulayyil Si. Arabia 20°27N 45°34E 131 C4
As Summān Si. Arabia 25°0N 47°0E 128 E5
As Suwaydā' Syria 32°40N 36°30E 130 C5
As Suwaydā' □ Syria 32°45N 36°45E 130 C5
As Suwayrah Iraq 32°55N 45°0E 105 F11
Åsa Sweden 57°21N 12°8E 63 H6
Asab Namibia 25°30S 18°0E 144 C2
Asaba Nigeria 6°12N 6°38E 139 D6
Asad, Buḩayrat al Syria 36°0N 38°15E 105 D8
Asadābād Iran 34°47N 48°7E 105 C13
Asadā Ghana 6°20N 2°40W 138 D4
Asahi Japan 35°43N 140°39E 113 G10
Asahi-Gawa → Japan 34°36N 133°58E 113 G6
Asahigawa = Asahikawa
  Japan 43°46N 142°22E 112 C11
Asahikawa Japan 43°46N 142°22E 112 C11
Asamankese Ghana 5°50N 0°40W 139 D4
Asan → India 26°37N 78°24E 125 F8
Asansol India 23°40N 87°1E 125 H12
Åsarna Sweden 62°39N 14°22E 62 B8
Asbesberge S. Africa 29°0S 23°0E 144 C3
Asbestos Canada 45°47N 71°58W 165 C5
Asbury Park U.S.A. 40°13N 74°1W 175 F10
Åsby Sweden 57°14N 12°18E 63 H6
Ascea Italy 40°8N 15°11E 95 B8
Ascensión Mexico 31°6N 107°59W 180 A3
Ascensión, B. de la
  Mexico 19°40N 87°30W 181 D7
Ascension I. Atl. Oc. 7°57S 14°23W 133 G2
Aschach an der Donau
  Austria 48°22N 14°2E 78 C7
Aschaffenburg Germany 49°58N 9°6E 77 F5
Aschersleben Germany 51°45N 11°29E 76 D7
Asciano Italy 43°14N 11°33E 93 E8
Ascoli Piceno Italy 42°51N 13°34E 93 F10
Ascoli Satriano Italy 41°11N 15°32E 95 A8
Ascope Peru 7°46S 79°8W 186 E3
Ascotán Chile 21°45S 68°17W 190 A2
Aseb Eritrea 13°0N 42°40E 137 E5
Åseda Sweden 57°10N 15°20E 63 H9
Asedjrad Algeria 24°51N 1°29E 136 D6
Asela Ethiopia 8°0N 39°0E 131 F2
Åsen Sweden 63°37N 12°31E 62 A7
Asenovgrad Bulgaria 42°1N 24°51E 97 D8
Aseral Norway 58°37N 7°25E 63 d3
Asfeld France 49°28N 4°5E 71 C11
Asfûn el Matā'na Egypt 25°26N 32°30E 137 B3

Aşgabat = Ashgabat
  Turkmenistan 37°58N 58°24E 129 B8
Asgata Cyprus 34°46N 33°15E 101 E12
Ash Fork U.S.A. 35°13N 112°29W 169 J7
Ash Grove U.S.A. 37°19N 93°35W 172 G7
Ash Shabakah Iraq 30°49N 43°39E 128 D4
Ash Shāmāl □ Lebanon 34°25N 36°0E 130 A5
Ash Shāmīyah Iraq 31°55N 44°35E 105 F11
Ash Shāriqah U.A.E. 25°23N 55°26E 129 E7
Ash Sharmah Si. Arabia 28°1N 35°16E 128 D2
Ash Sharqāt Iraq 35°27N 43°16E 105 E10
Ash Sharqī, Jabal Lebanon 33°40N 36°10E 130 B5
Ash Shaṭrah Iraq 31°30N 46°10E 128 D5
Ash Shawbak Jordan 30°32N 35°34E 128 D2
Ash Shihr Yemen 14°45N 49°36E 131 E4
Ash Shināfīyah Iraq 31°35N 44°39E 128 D5
Ash Shu'bah Si. Arabia 28°54N 44°44E 128 D5
Ash Shumlūl Si. Arabia 26°31N 47°20E 128 E5
Ash Shūr'a Iraq 35°58N 43°13E 128 C4
Ash Shurayf Si. Arabia 25°43N 39°14E 128 E3
Ash Shuwayfāt
  Lebanon 33°45N 35°30E 130 B4
Asha Russia 55°0N 57°16E 108 D6
Ashanti □ Ghana 7°30N 1°30W 139 D4
Ashbourne U.K. 53°2N 1°43W 66 D6
Ashburn U.S.A. 31°43N 83°39W 178 D6
Ashburton N.Z. 43°53S 171°48E 155 D6
Ashburton →
  Australia 21°40S 114°56E 148 D1
Ashburton, North Branch →
  N.Z. 43°54S 171°44E 155 D6
Ashburton, South Branch →
  N.Z. 43°54S 171°44E 155 D6
Ashcroft Canada 50°40N 121°20W 162 C4
Ashdod Israel 31°49N 34°35E 130 D3
Ashdown U.S.A. 33°40N 94°8W 176 E7
Asheboro U.S.A. 35°43N 79°49W 177 D15
Asher Canada 51°11N 98°21E 163 C9
Asherton U.S.A. 28°27N 99°46W 176 G5
Asheville U.S.A. 35°36N 82°33W 177 D13
Asheweig → Canada 54°17N 87°12W 164 B2
Ashford Australia 29°15S 151°3E 153 D5
Ashford U.K. 51°8N 0°53E 67 F8
Ashgabat Turkmenistan 37°58N 58°24E 129 B8
Ashibetsu Japan 43°31N 142°11E 112 C11
Ashikaga Japan 36°28N 139°29E 113 F9
Ashington U.K. 55°11N 1°33W 66 B6
Ashizuri-Uwakai △
  Japan 32°56N 132°32E 113 H6
Ashizuri-Zaki Japan 32°44N 133°0E 113 H6
Ashkarkot Afghan. 33°3N 67°58E 124 C2
Ashkhabad = Ashgabat
  Turkmenistan 37°58N 58°24E 129 B8
Āshkhāneh Iran 37°26N 56°55E 129 B8
Ashland Ala., U.S.A. 33°16N 85°50W 178 D2
Ashland Kans., U.S.A. 37°11N 99°46W 172 G4
Ashland Ky., U.S.A. 38°28N 82°38W 173 F12
Ashland Maine, U.S.A. 46°38N 68°24W 173 B19
Ashland Mont.,
  U.S.A. 45°36N 106°16W 168 D10
Ashland Ohio, U.S.A. 40°52N 82°19W 174 E2
Ashland Oreg., U.S.A. 42°12N 122°43W 168 E2
Ashland Pa., U.S.A. 40°45N 76°20W 175 F8
Ashland Va., U.S.A. 37°46N 77°29W 173 G15
Ashland Wis., U.S.A. 46°35N 90°53W 172 B8
Ashley N. Dak., U.S.A. 46°2N 99°22W 172 B4
Ashley Pa., U.S.A. 41°12N 75°55W 175 E9
Ashley → N.Z. 43°15S 172°44E 155 D7
Ashmore and Cartier Is.
  Ind. Oc. 12°15S 123°0E 148 B3
Ashmore Reef Australia 12°14S 123°5E 148 B3
Ashmûn Egypt 30°18N 30°58E 137 E7
Ashmyany Belarus 54°26N 25°52E 75 A13
Ashokan Res. U.S.A. 41°56N 74°13W 175 E10
Ashoknagar India 24°34N 77°43E 126 B3
Ashqelon Israel 31°42N 34°35E 130 D3
Ashta India 23°1N 76°43E 124 H7
Ashtabula U.S.A. 41°52N 80°47W 174 E4
Ashti Maharashtra, India 18°50N 75°15E 126 E2
Ashti Maharashtra, India 19°43N 79°24E 126 E4
Āshtiyān Iran 34°31N 50°0E 129 C6
Ashton S. Africa 33°50S 20°5E 144 E3
Ashton U.S.A. 44°4N 111°27W 168 D8
Ashuanipi, L. Canada 52°45N 66°15W 165 D6
Ashuapmushuan →
  Canada 48°37N 72°20W 164 C5
Ashur = Assur Iraq 35°27N 43°15E 105 E10
Ashville Ala., U.S.A. 33°50N 86°15W 178 D3
Ashville Fla., U.S.A. 30°37N 83°39W 178 D6
Åsi = Orontes → Asia 35°49N 36°0E 130 A5
Asia 45°0N 75°0E 102 E9
Asia, Kepulauan
  Indonesia 1°0N 131°13E 119 D8
Asiago Italy 45°52N 11°30E 93 C8
Asifabad India 19°20N 79°24E 126 E4
Asilah Morocco 35°29N 6°0W 136 A3
Asinara Italy 41°4N 8°16E 94 A1
Asinara, G. dell' Italy 41°0N 8°30E 94 A1
Asino Russia 57°0N 86°0E 106 D9
Asipovichy Belarus 53°19N 28°33E 75 B15
'Asīr Si. Arabia 18°40N 42°30E 131 D3
Asir, Ras Somalia 11°55N 51°10E 131 E5
Aska India 19°2N 84°42E 126 E7
Aşkale Turkey 39°55N 40°41E 105 C9
Askersund Sweden 58°53N 14°55E 63 F9
Askham S. Africa 26°59S 20°47E 144 D3
Askī Mawşil Iraq 36°50N 42°55E 128 B4
Askim Norway 59°35N 11°10E 61 G14
Askio, Oros Greece 40°25N 21°35E 96 F5
Askja Iceland 65°3N 16°48W 60 D5
Asklipio Greece 36°1N 27°50E 101 C9
Askøyna Norway 60°29N 5°10E 60 F11
Asl Egypt 29°33N 32°44E 137 D3
Aslanapa Turkey 39°14N 29°52E 99 B11
Aslānduz Iran 39°26N 47°24E 105 C12
Asmara = Asmera
  Eritrea 15°19N 38°55E 131 E2
Asmera Eritrea 15°19N 38°55E 131 E2
Åsnæs Denmark 55°40N 11°0E 63 J4
Åsnen Sweden 56°40N 14°42E 63 H8
Asni Morocco 31°17N 7°58W 136 B3
Aso Kujū △ Japan 32°53N 131°6E 113 H5
Asola Italy 45°13N 10°24E 92 C7
Asos Greece 38°22N 20°33E 98 C2
Asoteriba, Jebel Sudan 21°51N 36°30E 137 C4
Asotin U.S.A. 46°20N 117°3W 168 C5
Aspatria U.K. 54°47N 3°19W 66 C4

Aspe Spain 38°20N 0°40W 91 G4
Aspen U.S.A. 39°11N 106°49W 168 G10
Aspendos Turkey 36°54N 31°7E 104 D4
Aspermont U.S.A. 33°8N 100°14W 176 E4
Aspet France 43°1N 0°48E 72 E4
Aspiring, Mt. N.Z. 44°23S 168°46E 155 E3
Aspres-sur-Buëch France 44°32N 5°44E 73 D9
Asprokavos, Akra
  Greece 39°21N 20°6E 101 B4
Aspromonte △ Italy 38°9N 15°58E 95 D8
Aspur India 23°58N 74°7E 124 H6
Asquith Canada 52°8N 107°13W 163 C7
Assab = Aseb Eritrea 13°0N 42°40E 131 E3
Assâba □ Mauritania 16°40N 11°40W 138 D2
Assâba, Massif de l'
  Mauritania 16°10N 11°45W 138 D2
Assagny △ Ivory C. 5°10N 4°48W 138 D4
Assaikio Nigeria 8°34N 9°55E 139 D6
Assal, L. Djibouti 11°40N 42°26E 131 E3
Assam □ India 26°0N 93°0E 123 G18
Assamakka Niger 19°21N 5°38E 139 B6
Assateague Island
  U.S.A. 38°15N 75°10W 173 F16
Assaye India 20°15N 75°53E 126 D2
Asse Belgium 50°24N 4°10E 69 D4
Assekrem Algeria 23°16N 5°49E 136 D5
Assémini Italy 39°17N 9°0E 94 C1
Assen Neths. 53°0N 6°35E 68 A6
Assens Denmark 55°16N 9°55E 63 J3
Assini Ivory C. 5°9N 3°17W 138 D4
Assiniboia Canada 49°40N 105°59W 163 D7
Assiniboine → Canada 49°53N 97°8W 163 D9
Assiniboine, Mt.
  Canada 50°52N 115°39W 162 C5
Assis Brazil 22°40S 50°20W 191 A5
Assis Brasil Brazil 10°55S 69°32W 188 C4
Assisi Italy 43°4N 12°37E 93 E9
Assur Iraq 35°27N 43°15E 105 E10
Assynt, L. U.K. 58°10N 5°3W 65 C3
Astaffort France 44°4N 0°42E 72 D4
Astakida Greece 35°53N 26°50E 99 F8
Astakos Greece 38°32N 21°0E 98 C3
Astana Kazakhstan 51°10N 71°30E 109 B8
Āstāneh Iran 37°17N 49°59E 129 B6
Astara Azerbaijan 38°30N 48°50E 105 C13
Āstārā Iran 38°20N 48°52E 105 C13
Asterousia Greece 34°59N 25°3E 101 E7
Asti Italy 44°54N 8°12E 92 D5
Astipalea Greece 36°32N 26°22E 99 E8
Astorga Spain 42°29N 6°8W 88 C4
Astoria U.S.A. 46°11N 123°50W 168 C2
Åstorp Sweden 56°9N 12°55E 63 H6
Astrakhan Russia 46°25N 48°5E 87 G9
Astrakhan = Hajdarabad Iran 47°45N 46°20E 87 H8
Astrebla Downs
  Australia 24°12S 140°34E 150 C3
Astudillo Spain 42°12N 4°22W 88 C6
Asturias □ Spain 43°15N 6°0W 88 B5
Asturias × (OVD) Spain 43°33N 6°3W 88 B4
Asunción Bolivia 11°46S 67°50W 188 C4
Asunción Paraguay 25°10S 57°30W 190 B4
Asunción Nochixtlán
  Mexico 17°28N 97°14W 181 D5
Åsunden Sweden 58°0N 15°51E 63 F9
Aswa → Uganda 3°43N 31°55E 142 B3
Aswa-Lolim △ Uganda 2°43N 31°35E 142 B3
Aswad, Ra's al Si. Arabia 21°20N 39°0E 137 C4
Aswân Egypt 24°4N 32°57E 137 C3
Aswân High Dam = Sadd el Aali
  Egypt 23°54N 32°54E 137 C3
Asyût Egypt 27°11N 31°4E 137 B3
Aszód Hungary 47°39N 19°28E 80 C5
Aszód Wadi → Egypt 27°11N 31°16E 137 B3
At-Bashy Kyrgyzstan 41°10N 75°48E 109 D9
At Ţafīlah Jordan 30°45N 35°30E 130 E4
Aţ Ţafīlah □ Jordan 30°45N 35°30E 130 E4
Aţ Ţā'if Si. Arabia 21°5N 40°27E 137 C4
Aţ Ta'mīm □ Iraq 35°30N 44°20E 128 C5
Aṭ Ţirāq Si. Arabia 27°19N 44°33E 128 E5
Aṭ Ţunayb Jordan 29°57N 35°57E 130 E4
Atabey Turkey 37°57N 30°39E 99 D12
Atacama □ Chile 27°30S 70°0W 190 B2
Atacama, Desierto de
  Chile 24°0S 69°20W 190 A2
Atacama, Salar de
  Chile 23°30S 68°20W 190 A2
Atakeye ☉ Australia 22°30S 133°45E 148 D5
Atakor Algeria 23°27N 5°31E 136 D6
Atakpamé Togo 7°31N 1°13E 139 D5
Atalandi Greece 38°39N 22°58E 98 C4
Atalaya Peru 10°45S 73°50W 188 C3
Atalaya de Femes
  Canary Is. 28°56N 13°47W 100 F6
Ataléia Brazil 18°3S 41°6W 189 C7
Atami Japan 35°5N 139°4E 113 G9
Atamyrat Turkmenistan 37°50N 65°12E 109 F7
Atapuerca, Cueva de
  Spain 42°22N 3°32W 88 C7
Atapupu Indonesia 9°0S 124°51E 119 F6
Atâr Mauritania 20°30N 13°5W 134 D3
Ataram, Erg n- Algeria 23°57N 2°0E 136 D6
Atarfe Spain 37°13N 3°40W 89 H7
Atari Pakistan 30°56N 74°2E 124 D6
Atascadero U.S.A. 35°29N 120°40W 170 K6
Atasū Kazakhstan 48°30N 71°0E 109 C8
Atatürk, İstanbul × (IST)
  Turkey 40°59N 28°49E 97 F12
Atatürk Barajı Turkey 37°28N 38°30E 105 D8
Atauro E. Timor 8°10S 125°30E 119 F7
Ataviros Greece 36°12N 27°50E 101 C9
Atbara Sudan 17°42N 33°59E 135 E12
'Atbara, Nahr →
  Sudan 17°40N 33°56E 137 D3
Atbasar Kazakhstan 51°48N 68°20E 109 B7
Atça Turkey 37°53N 28°13E 99 D10
Atchafalaya B. U.S.A. 29°25N 91°25W 179 H9
Atchison U.S.A. 39°34N 95°7W 172 F6
Atebubu Ghana 7°47N 1°0W 139 D4
Ateca Spain 41°20N 1°49W 90 D3
Aterno → Italy 42°11N 13°51E 93 F10
Atesine, Alpi Italy 46°55N 11°30E 93 B8
Atessa Italy 42°4N 14°27E 93 F11
Atfih Egypt 29°51N 31°17E 137 E7
Ath Belgium 50°38N 3°47E 69 D3
Athabasca Canada 54°45N 113°20W 162 C6

Athabasca → Canada 58°40'N 110°50W 163 B6
Athabasca, L. Canada 59°15N 109°15W 163 B7
Athabasca Sand Dunes △
  Canada 59°4N 108°43W 163 B7
Athagarh India 20°32N 85°37E 126 D7
Athamanon Oros Greece 39°30N 21°26E 98 B3
Athboy Ireland 53°36N 6°56W 64 C5
Athena U.S.A. 29°59N 83°30W 178 F6
Athenry Ireland 53°18N 8°44W 64 C3
Athens = Athina Greece 37°58N 23°43E 98 D5
Athens Ala., U.S.A. 34°48N 86°58W 177 D11
Athens Ga., U.S.A. 33°57N 83°23W 178 B6
Athens N.Y., U.S.A. 42°16N 73°49W 175 D11
Athens Ohio, U.S.A. 39°20N 82°6W 172 F6
Athens Tenn., U.S.A. 35°27N 84°36W 177 D12
Athens Tex., U.S.A. 32°12N 95°51W 176 E7
Atherley Canada 44°37N 79°20W 174 B5
Atherton Australia 17°17S 145°30E 150 B4
Athi River Kenya 1°28S 36°58E 142 C4
Athiéme Benin 6°37N 1°40E 139 D5
Athienou Cyprus 35°3N 33°32E 101 D12
Athina Greece 37°58N 23°43E 98 D5
Athina ✈ (ATH) Greece 37°56N 23°56E 98 D5
Athlone Ireland 53°25N 7°56W 64 C4
Athmallik India 20°43N 84°32E 126 D7
Athni India 16°44N 75°6E 126 F2
Athol N.Z. 45°30S 168°35E 155 F3
Athol U.S.A. 42°36N 72°14W 175 D12
Atholl, Forest of U.K. 56°51N 3°50W 65 E5
Atholl, Kap Greenland 76°25N 69°30W 57 B4
Atholville Canada 47°59N 66°43W 165 C6
Athos Greece 40°9N 24°22E 97 F8
Athy Ireland 53°0N 7°0W 64 C5
Ati Chad 13°13N 18°20E 135 F9
Atiak Uganda 3°12N 32°2E 142 B3
Atiamuri N.Z. 38°24S 176°5E 154 E5
Atico Peru 16°14S 73°40W 188 D3
Atienza Spain 41°12N 2°52W 90 D2
Atik L. Canada 55°15N 96°0W 163 B9
Atikaki △ Canada 51°30N 95°31W 163 C9
Atikameg → Canada 52°30N 82°46W 164 B3
Atikokan Canada 48°45N 91°37W 164 C1
Atikonak L. Canada 52°40N 64°32W 165 B7
Atimaono Tahiti 17°46S 149°28W 155 b
Atirampattinam India 10°28N 79°20E 127 J4
Atiu Cook Is. 20°0S 158°10W 157 J12
Atka Russia 60°50N 151°48E 107 C16
Atka I. U.S.A. 52°7N 174°30W 166 E5
Atkarsk Russia 51°55N 45°2E 86 E7
Atkinson Ga., U.S.A. 31°13N 81°47W 178 D8
Atkinson Nebr., U.S.A. 42°32N 98°59W 172 D4
Atlanta Ga., U.S.A. 33°45N 84°23W 178 B5
Atlanta Tex., U.S.A. 33°7N 94°10W 176 E7
Atlanta Hartsfield-Jackson Int. ✈
  (ATL) U.S.A. 33°38N 84°26W 178 B5
Atlantic U.S.A. 41°24N 95°1W 172 E6
Atlantic Beach U.S.A. 30°20N 81°24W 178 E8
Atlantic City U.S.A. 39°21N 74°27W 173 F16
Atlantic-Indian Basin
  Antarctica 60°0S 30°0E 55 B4
Atlantic Ocean 0°0 20°0W 56 F8
Atlantis S. Africa 33°34S 18°29E 144 D2
Atlas Mts. = Haut Atlas
  Morocco 32°30N 5°0W 136 B3
Atlin Canada 59°31N 133°41W 162 B2
Atlin, L. Canada 59°26N 133°45W 162 B2
Atlin → Canada 59°10N 134°30W 162 B2
Atmakur Andhra Pradesh,
  India 18°45N 78°39E 126 E4
Atmakur Andhra Pradesh,
  India 14°37N 79°40E 127 G4
Atmakur Andhra Pradesh,
  India 15°53N 78°35E 127 G4
Atmore U.S.A. 31°2N 87°29W 179 D2
Atoka U.S.A. 34°23N 96°8W 176 D6
Atokos Greece 38°28N 20°49E 98 C2
Atolia U.S.A. 35°19N 117°37W 171 K9
Atqasuk U.S.A. 70°28N 157°24W 166 A4
Atrai → Bangla. 24°7N 89°22E 125 G13
Atrak = Atrek →
  Turkmenistan 37°35N 53°58E 129 B8
Ätran Sweden 57°7N 12°57E 63 G6
Ätran → Sweden 56°53N 12°30E 63 H6
Atrauli India 28°2N 78°20E 124 E8
Atrek → Turkmenistan 37°35N 53°58E 129 B8
Atri Italy 42°35N 13°58E 93 F10
Atsiki Greece 39°56N 25°13E 99 B9
Atsoum, Mts. Cameroon 6°41N 12°57E 139 D7
Atsuta Japan 43°24N 141°26E 112 C4
Attalla U.S.A. 34°1N 86°6W 178 A3
Attapeu Laos 14°48N 106°50E 120 E6
Attapulgus U.S.A. 30°45N 84°29W 178 F5
Attawapiskat Canada 52°56N 82°24W 164 B3
Attawapiskat →
  Canada 52°57N 82°18W 164 B3
Attawapiskat L.
  Canada 52°18N 87°54W 164 B2
Attersee Austria 47°55N 13°32E 78 D6
Attica = Attiki □ Greece 37°33N 23°40E 98 D5
Attica Ind., U.S.A. 40°18N 87°15W 172 E10
Attica Ohio, U.S.A. 41°4N 82°53W 172 E4
Attichy France 49°25N 3°3E 71 C10
Attigny France 49°28N 4°35E 71 C11
Attikamagen L. Canada 55°0N 66°30W 165 B6
Attiki □ Greece 37°10N 23°40E 98 D5
Attleboro U.S.A. 41°57N 71°17W 175 E13
Attock Pakistan 33°52N 72°20E 124 C5
Attopeu = Attapeu
  Laos 14°48N 106°50E 120 E6
Attu I. U.S.A. 52°55N 172°55E 166 E2
Attunga Australia 30°55S 150°50E 153 A9
Attur India 11°35N 78°30E 127 J4
Atuel → Argentina 36°17S 66°50W 190 D2
Atura Uganda 2°7N 32°20E 142 B3
Åtvidaberg Sweden 58°12N 16°0E 63 F10
Atwater U.S.A. 37°21N 120°37W 170 H6
Atwood Canada 43°40N 81°1W 174 C3
Atwood U.S.A. 39°48N 101°3W 172 F3
Atyraū Kazakhstan 47°5N 52°0E 108 C4
Au Sable → U.S.A. 44°25N 83°20W 174 B1
Au Sable → U.S.A. 44°25N 83°20W 173 C12
Au Sable Forks
  U.S.A. 44°27N 73°41W 175 B11
Au Sable Pt. U.S.A. 44°20N 83°20W 174 B1
Auas Honduras 15°29N 84°20W 182 C3
Auasberg Namibia 22°37S 17°13E 144 B2
Aubagne France 43°17N 5°37E 73 E9
Aube □ France 48°15N 4°10E 71 D11
Aube → France 48°34N 3°43E 71 D10

Aubenas France 44°37N 4°24E 73 D8
Aubenton France 49°50N 4°12E 71 C11
Auberry U.S.A. 37°7N 119°29W 170 H7
Aubigny-sur-Nère France 47°30N 2°24E 71 E9
Aubin France 44°33N 2°15E 72 D6
Aubrac, Mts. d' France 44°40N 3°2E 72 D7
Auburn Ala., U.S.A. 32°36N 85°29W 178 B4
Auburn Calif., U.S.A. 38°54N 121°4W 170 G5
Auburn Ind., U.S.A. 41°22N 85°4W 173 E11
Auburn Maine, U.S.A. 44°6N 70°14W 173 C18
Auburn N.Y., U.S.A. 42°56N 76°34W 175 D8
Auburn Nebr., U.S.A. 40°23N 95°51W 172 E6
Auburn Pa., U.S.A. 40°36N 76°6W 175 F8
Auburn Wash., U.S.A. 47°18N 122°14W 170 C4
Auburndale U.S.A. 28°4N 81°48W 179 G8
Aubusson France 45°57N 2°11E 72 C6
Auce Latvia 56°28N 22°53E 82 B9
Auch France 43°39N 0°36E 72 E4
Auchi Nigeria 7°6N 6°13E 139 D6
Auchterarder U.K. 56°18N 3°41W 65 E5
Auchtermuchty U.K. 56°18N 3°13W 65 E5
Auckland N.Z. 36°52S 174°46E 154 D5
Auckland □ N.Z. 36°50S 175°0E 154 C3
Auckland Is. Pac. Oc. 50°40S 166°5E 156 N8
Aude □ France 43°8N 2°28E 72 E6
Aude → France 43°13N 3°14E 72 E7
Auden Canada 50°14N 87°53W 164 B2
Auderville France 49°43N 1°57W 70 C5
Audierne France 48°1N 4°34W 70 D2
Audincourt France 47°30N 6°50E 71 E13
Audomarois △ France 50°50N 2°30E 71 B9
Audubon U.S.A. 41°43N 94°56W 172 E6
Aue Germany 50°35N 12°41E 76 E8
Auerbach Germany 50°30N 12°24E 76 E8
Augathella Australia 25°48S 146°35E 151 D4
Aughnacloy U.K. 54°25N 6°59W 64 B5
Aughrim Ireland 53°18N 8°19W 64 C3
Augrabies Falls
  S. Africa 28°35S 20°20E 144 C3
Augrabies Falls △
  S. Africa 28°40S 20°22E 144 C3
Augsburg Germany 48°25N 10°52E 77 G6
Augsburg-Westliche Wälder △
  Germany 48°20N 10°45E 77 G6
Augusta Australia 34°19S 115°9E 149 F2
Augusta Italy 37°13N 15°13E 95 E8
Augusta Ark., U.S.A. 35°17N 91°22W 176 D9
Augusta Ga., U.S.A. 33°28N 81°58W 178 B8
Augusta Kans., U.S.A. 37°41N 96°59W 176 D6
Augusta Maine,
  U.S.A. 44°19N 69°47W 173 C19
Augusta Mont., U.S.A. 47°30N 112°24W 168 C7
Augustenborg Denmark 54°57N 9°53E 63 K3
Augustów Poland 53°51N 23°0E 82 E9
Augustus, Mt.
  Australia 24°20S 116°50E 149 D2
Augustus I. Australia 15°20S 124°30E 148 C3
Aujuittuq = Grise Fiord
  Canada 76°25N 82°57W 161 B15
Aukrug △ Germany 54°5N 9°45E 76 A5
Aukštaitija △ Lithuania 55°15N 26°0E 61 J22
Aukum U.S.A. 38°34N 120°43W 170 G6
Aul India 20°41N 86°39E 126 D8
Aulavik △ Canada 73°42N 119°55W 160 C8
Auld, L. Australia 22°25S 123°50E 148 D3
Ãülieköl Kazakhstan 52°32N 62°45E 108 B6
Aulifeltet Norway 60°30N 11°21E 62 D5
Aulla Italy 44°12N 9°58E 92 D6
Aulnay France 46°2N 0°22W 72 B3
Aulne → France 48°17N 4°16W 70 D2
Aulnoye-Aymeries
  France 50°12N 3°50E 71 B10
Ault France 50°8N 1°26E 70 B8
Ault U.S.A. 40°35N 104°44W 168 F11
Aulus-les-Bains France 42°49N 1°19E 72 F5
Aumale France 49°46N 1°46E 71 C8
Aumont-Aubrac France 44°43N 3°17E 72 D7
Auna Nigeria 10°9N 4°42E 139 C5
Aundah India 19°32N 77°3E 126 E3
Aundh India 18°32N 74°23E 126 F2
Auning Denmark 56°26N 10°23E 63 H4
Aunis France 46°5N 0°50W 72 B3
Auponhia Indonesia 1°58S 125°27E 119 E7
Aups France 43°37N 6°15E 73 E10
Aur, Pulau Malaysia 2°35N 104°10E 121 L5
Auraiya India 26°28N 79°33E 125 F8
Aurangabad Bihar,
  India 24°45N 84°18E 125 G11
Aurangabad Maharashtra,
  India 19°50N 75°23E 126 E2
Auray France 47°40N 2°59W 70 E4
Aurès Algeria 35°8N 6°30E 136 A5
Aurich Germany 53°28N 7°28E 76 B3
Aurillac France 44°55N 2°26E 72 D6
Auronzo di Cadore Italy 46°33N 12°26E 93 B9
Aurora Canada 44°0N 79°28W 174 C5
Aurora S. Africa 32°40S 18°29E 144 D2
Aurora Colo., U.S.A. 39°43N 104°49W 168 G11
Aurora Ill., U.S.A. 41°45N 88°19W 172 E9
Aurora Mo., U.S.A. 36°58N 93°43W 172 G7
Aurora N.Y., U.S.A. 42°45N 76°42W 175 D8
Aurora Ohio, U.S.A. 41°21N 81°20W 174 E3
Aurora Nebr., U.S.A. 40°52N 98°0W 172 E5
Aurukun Australia 13°20S 141°45E 150 A3
Aurukun © Australia 13°36S 141°48E 150 A3
Aus Namibia 26°35S 16°12E 144 C2
Ausa India 18°18N 76°30E 126 E3
Ausable → Canada 43°19N 81°46W 174 C3
Auschwitz = Oświęcim
  Poland 50°2N 19°11E 83 H6
Auski Roadhouse
  Australia 22°22S 118°41E 148 D2
Austen Harbour India 12°55N 92°45E 127 H11
Austerlitz = Slavkov u Brna
  Czech Rep. 49°10N 16°52E 79 B9
Austin Minn., U.S.A. 43°40N 92°58W 172 D7
Austin Nev., U.S.A. 39°30N 117°4W 168 G5
Austin Pa., U.S.A. 41°38N 78°6W 174 E6
Austin Tex., U.S.A. 30°17N 97°45W 176 F6
Austin, L. Australia 27°40S 118°0E 149 E2
Austin I. Canada 61°10N 94°0W 163 A10
Austra Norway 65°8N 11°55E 60 D14
Austral Is. = Tubuaï, Ís.
  French Polynesia 25°0S 150°0W 157 K13
Austral Seamount Chain
  Pac. Oc. 24°0S 150°0W 157 K13
Australia ■ Oceania 23°0S 135°0E 147 D6
Australian-Antarctic Basin
  S. Ocean 60°0S 120°0E 55 C9

Australian Capital Territory □
  Australia 35°30S 149°0E 153 C8
Australind Australia 33°17S 115°42E 149 F2
Austria ■ Europe 47°0N 14°0E 78 E7
Austvågøya Norway 68°20N 14°40E 60 B16
Autun France 46°58N 4°17E 71 F11
Auvergne □ France 45°20N 3°15E 72 C7
Auvergne, Mts. d' France 45°20N 2°55E 72 C6
Auvézère → France 45°12N 0°50E 72 C4
Auxerre France 47°48N 3°32E 71 E10
Auxi-le-Château France 50°15N 2°8E 71 B9
Auxonne France 47°10N 5°20E 71 E12
Auyuittuq △ Canada 67°30N 66°0W 161 D18
Auzances France 46°2N 2°30E 71 F9
Auzanguate, Nevado
  Peru 13°47S 71°13W 188 C3
Av-Dovurak Russia 51°17N 91°35E 107 D10
Ava U.S.A. 36°57N 92°40W 172 G7
Avachinskaya Sopka
  Russia 53°15N 158°50E 107 D16
Avallon France 47°30N 3°53E 71 E10
Avalon U.S.A. 33°21N 118°20W 171 M8
Avalon Pen. Canada 47°30N 53°20W 165 C9
Avanigadda India 16°0N 80°56E 127 G5
Avanos Turkey 38°43N 34°51E 104 C6
Avantas Greece 40°57N 25°56E 97 F9
Avaré Brazil 23°4S 48°58W 191 A6
Avawatz Mts. U.S.A. 35°40N 116°30W 171 K10
Avdan Dağı Turkey 40°23N 29°46E 97 F13
Aveiro Brazil 3°10S 55°5W 187 D7
Aveiro Portugal 40°37N 8°38W 88 E2
Aveiro □ Portugal 40°40N 8°35W 88 E2
Avej Iran 35°40N 49°15E 129 C6
Avellaneda Argentina 34°40S 58°22W 190 C4
Avellino Italy 40°54N 14°47E 95 B7
Avenal U.S.A. 36°0N 120°8W 170 K6
Aversa Italy 40°58N 14°12E 95 B7
Avery U.S.A. 47°15N 115°49W 168 C6
Aves, I. de W. Indies 15°45N 63°55W 183 C7
Aves, Is. las Venezuela 12°0N 67°30W 183 D6
Avesnes-sur-Helpe
  France 50°8N 3°55E 71 B10
Avesnois → France 50°10N 3°45E 71 B10
Avesta Sweden 60°9N 16°10E 62 D10
Aveyron □ France 44°22N 2°45E 72 D6
Aveyron → France 44°5N 1°16E 72 D5
Avezzano Italy 42°2N 13°25E 93 F10
Aviá Terai Argentina 26°45S 60°50W 190 B3
Aviano Italy 46°4N 12°36E 93 B9
Aviemore U.K. 57°12N 3°50W 65 D5
Aviemore, L. N.Z. 44°37S 170°18E 155 E3
Avigliana Italy 45°5N 7°23E 92 C4
Avigliano Italy 40°44N 15°43E 95 B8
Avignon France 43°57N 4°50E 73 E8
Ávila Spain 40°39N 4°43W 88 E6
Ávila □ Spain 40°30N 5°0W 88 E6
Ávila, Sierra de Spain 40°40N 5°15W 88 E5
Avila Beach U.S.A. 35°11N 120°44W 171 K6
Avilés Spain 43°35N 5°57W 88 B5
Aviño Spain 43°36N 8°8W 88 B2
Avintes Portugal 41°7N 8°33W 88 D2
Avis U.S.A. 41°11N 77°19W 174 E7
Avis Italy 46°6N 11°4E 92 B8
Avissawella Sri Lanka 6°56N 80°11E 127 L5
Aviz = Avis Portugal 39°4N 7°53W 89 F3
Avize France 48°59N 4°1E 71 D11
Avlonari Greece 38°31N 24°8E 98 C6
Avlum Denmark 56°16N 8°47E 63 H2
Avoca Australia 37°5S 143°26E 152 D5
Avoca U.S.A. 42°25N 77°25W 174 D7
Avoca → Australia 35°40S 143°43E 152 C5
Avoca → Ireland 52°48N 6°10W 64 D5
Avola Canada 51°45N 119°19W 162 C5
Avola Italy 36°56N 15°7E 95 F8
Avon → Australia 31°40S 116°7E 149 F2
Avon → Bristol, U.K. 51°29N 2°41W 67 F5
Avon → Dorset, U.K. 50°44N 1°46W 67 G6
Avon → Warks., U.K. 52°0N 2°8W 67 E5
Avon Park U.S.A. 27°36N 81°31W 179 H8
Avondale Zimbabwe 17°43S 30°58E 143 F3
Avonlea Canada 50°0N 105°0W 163 D8
Avonmore Canada 45°10N 74°58W 175 A10
Avonmouth U.K. 51°30N 2°42W 67 F5
Avranches France 48°40N 1°20W 70 D5
Avre → France 48°47N 1°20E 70 D8
Avrig Romania 45°43N 24°21E 81 E9
Avrillé France 47°30N 0°35W 70 E6
Avtovac Bos.-H. 43°9N 18°35E 96 C2
Awa-Shima Japan 38°27N 139°14E 112 E9
A'waj → Syria 33°23N 36°20E 130 B5
Awaji-Shima Japan 34°30N 134°50E 113 G7
'Awālī Bahrain 26°0N 50°30E 129 E6
Awantipur India 33°55N 75°3E 125 C6
Awanui N.Z. 35°4S 173°17E 154 B2
Awarja → India 17°5N 76°15E 126 F3
Awarua B. N.Z. 44°28S 168°4E 155 E3
Awarua Pt. N.Z. 44°15S 168°5E 155 E3
Awasa Ethiopia 7°2N 38°28E 131 F2
Awash Ethiopia 9°1N 40°10E 131 F3
Awaso Ghana 6°15N 2°22W 138 D4
Awat China 40°35N 80°22E 109 D10
Awatere → N.Z. 41°37S 174°10E 155 B9
Awbārī Libya 26°46N 12°57E 135 C8
Awbārī, Idehan Libya 27°10N 11°30E 135 C8
Awe, L. U.K. 56°17N 5°16W 65 E3
Awgu Nigeria 6°4N 7°24E 139 D6
Awjilah Libya 29°8N 21°7E 135 C10
Awka Nigeria 6°12N 7°5E 139 D6
Axat France 42°46N 2°13E 72 F6
Axe → U.K. 50°42N 3°4W 67 F5
Axel Heiberg I. Canada 80°0N 90°0W 161 B14
Axim Ghana 4°51N 2°15W 138 E4
Axintele Romania 44°37N 26°47E 81 F11
Axios → Greece 40°57N 22°35E 98 A4
Axminster U.K. 50°46N 3°0W 67 G4
Axson U.S.A. 31°17N 82°44W 178 D7
Ay France 49°3N 4°1E 71 C11
Ayabaca Peru 4°40S 79°53W 188 A2
Ayabe Japan 35°20N 135°20E 113 G7

Ayacucho Argentina 37°5S 58°20W 190 D4
Ayacucho Peru 13°0S 74°0W 188 C3
Ayacucho □ Peru 14°0S 74°0W 188 C3
Ayaguz = Ayaköz
  Kazakhstan 48°10N 80°10E 109 C10
Ayakkum Hu China 37°30N 89°20E 109 C11
Ayaköz Kazakhstan 48°10N 80°10E 109 C10
Ayaköz → Kazakhstan 46°40N 79°14E 109 C9
Ayakudi India 10°28N 77°56E 127 J3
Ayamé Ivory C. 5°39N 3°9W 138 D4
Ayamonte Spain 37°12N 7°24W 89 H3
Ayan Russia 56°30N 138°16E 107 D14
Ayancık Turkey 41°57N 34°35E 104 B6
Ayas Turkey 40°2N 32°21E 104 B5
Ayaviri Peru 14°50S 70°35W 188 C3
Äybak Afghan. 36°15N 68°5E 128 B4
Aybastı Turkey 40°41N 37°23E 104 B7
Aydarköl Uzbekistan 40°50N 67°10E 109 D7
Aydın Turkey 37°51N 27°51E 104 D2
Aydın □ Turkey 37°50N 28°0E 99 D10
Aydın Dağları Turkey 38°0N 28°0E 99 D10
Aydıngkol Hu China 42°40N 89°15E 109 C11
Ayenngré Togo 8°40N 1°1E 139 D5
Ayer U.S.A. 42°34N 71°35W 175 D13
Ayer Hitam Malaysia 5°24N 100°16E 121 c
Ayerbe Spain 42°17N 0°41W 90 C4
Ayer's Cliff Canada 45°10N 72°3W 175 A12
Ayers Rock = Uluru
  Australia 25°23S 131°5E 149 E5
Ayeyarwady = Irrawaddy →
  Burma 15°50N 95°6E 123 M19
Äyia Napa Cyprus 34°59N 34°0E 101 D13
Äyia Phyla Cyprus 34°43N 33°1E 101 E12
Äyios Amvrósios
  Cyprus 35°20N 33°35E 101 D12
Äyios Seryios Cyprus 35°12N 33°53E 101 D12
Äyios Theodhoros
  Cyprus 35°22N 34°1E 101 D13
Äyios Yeóryios = Aghios Georgios
  Greece 37°38N 23°57E 98 D5
Aykhal Russia 66°0N 111°30E 107 C12
Aykirikçi Turkey 39°8N 30°9E 99 B12
Aylesbury U.K. 51°49N 0°49W 67 F7
Aylmer Canada 42°46N 80°59W 174 D4
Aylmer, L. Canada 64°5N 108°30W 160 D10
'Ayn, Wādī al Oman 22°15N 55°28E 129 E7
Ayn Dār Si. Arabia 25°55N 49°10E 129 E7
Ayn Sifni Iraq 36°41N 43°20E 105 D10
Ayn Zālah Iraq 36°45N 42°35E 105 D10
Ayna Spain 38°34N 2°3W 91 G2
Ayolas Paraguay 27°10S 56°59W 190 B4
Ayon, Ostrov Russia 69°50N 169°0E 107 C17
Ayora Spain 39°3N 1°3W 91 G3
Ayorou Niger 14°53N 1°0E 139 C5
'Ayoûn el 'Atroûs
  Mauritania 16°38N 9°37W 138 B3
Ayr Australia 19°35S 147°25E 150 B4
Ayr Canada 43°17N 80°27W 174 C4
Ayr U.K. 55°28N 4°38W 65 F4
Ayr → U.K. 55°28N 4°38W 65 F4
Ayranci Turkey 37°21N 33°41E 104 D5
Ayrancılar Turkey 38°15N 27°18E 99 C9
Ayre, Pt. of I. of Man 54°25N 4°21W 66 C3
Ayribaba Turkmenistan 37°50N 66°34E 109 E7
Ayton Australia 15°56S 145°22E 150 B4
Aytos Bulgaria 42°42N 27°16E 97 D11
Ayu, Kepulauan
  Indonesia 0°35N 131°5E 119 D8
Ayutla Guatemala 14°40N 92°10W 182 D1
Ayutla de los Libres
  Mexico 16°54N 99°13W 181 D5
Ayutthaya = Phra Nakhon Si
  Ayutthaya Thailand 14°25N 100°30E 120 E3
Ayvacık Turkey 39°36N 26°24E 104 C2
Ayvalık Turkey 39°20N 26°46E 99 B8
Az Zabadānī Syria 33°43N 36°5E 130 B5
Az Zāhirīyah
  West Bank 31°25N 34°58E 130 D3
Az Zahrān Si. Arabia 26°10N 50°7E 129 E6
Az Zarqā' Jordan 32°5N 36°4E 130 C5
Az Zarqā' U.A.E. 24°53N 53°4E 129 E7
Az Zarqā □ Jordan 32°5N 36°4E 130 C5
Az Zāwiyah Libya 32°52N 12°56E 135 B8
Az Zībār Iraq 36°52N 44°4E 105 D11
Az Zilfī Si. Arabia 26°12N 44°52E 128 E5
Az Zubayr Iraq 30°26N 47°40E 128 D5
Azad Kashmir □
  Pakistan 33°50N 73°50E 125 C5
Azahar, Costa del Spain 40°0N 0°5E 90 F5
Azambuja Portugal 39°4N 8°51W 89 F2
Azamgarh India 26°5N 83°13E 125 F10
Azangaro Peru 14°55S 70°13W 188 C3
Azaouа Niger 15°50N 4°0E 139 B5
Azaouad Mali 19°0N 3°0W 138 B4
Azaouak → Mali 15°50N 3°20E 139 B5
Azaouak, Vallée de l'
  Mali 15°50N 3°20E 139 B5
Äzar Shahr Iran 37°45N 45°59E 105 D11
Azara Nigeria 8°22N 9°12E 139 D6
Azaran = Iran ■ Asia 33°0N 53°0E 128 C7
Äzarbāyjān = Azerbaijan ■
  Asia 40°20N 48°0E 87 K9
Äzarbāyjān-e Gharbī □
  Iran 37°0N 44°30E 128 B5
Äzarbāyjān-e Sharqī □
  Iran 37°0N 47°0E 128 B5
Azare Nigeria 11°55N 10°10E 139 C7
Azay-le-Rideau France 47°16N 0°30E 70 E7
A'zāz Syria 36°36N 37°4E 104 B7
Azazga Algeria 36°48N 4°22E 136 A4
Azbine = Aïr Niger 18°0N 8°0E 139 B6
Azeffoun Algeria 36°51N 4°26E 136 A4
Azemmour Morocco 33°20N 9°20W 136 B3
Azerbaijan ■ Asia 40°20N 48°0E 87 K9
Azkoien = Peralta Spain 42°20N 1°48W 90 C3
Aznalcóllar Spain 37°32N 6°17W 89 H4
Azogues Ecuador 2°35S 78°0W 186 D3
Azores = Açores, Is. dos
  Atl. Oc. 38°0N 27°0W 54 a
Azores-Biscay Rise
  Atl. Oc. 38°0N 28°0W 54 E6
Azov Russia 47°3N 39°25E 85 G4
Azov, Sea of Europe 46°0N 36°30E 85 J9
Azovskoye More = Azov, Sea of
  Europe 46°0N 36°30E 85 J9
Azpeitia Spain 43°12N 2°19W 90 C2
Azraq ash Shīshān
  Jordan 31°50N 36°49E 130 D5

Azrou Morocco 33°28N 5°19W 136 B2
Aztec U.S.A. 36°49N 107°59W 169 H10
Azua de Compostela
  Dom. Rep. 18°25N 70°44W 183 C5
Azuaga Spain 38°16N 5°39W 89 G5
Azuara Spain 41°15N 0°53W 90 D4
Azuer → Spain 39°8N 3°36W 91 F1
Azuero, Pen. de Panama 7°30N 80°30W 182 E3
Azul Argentina 36°42S 59°43W 190 D4
Azumino Japan 36°20N 137°50E 113 F8
Azur, Côte d' France 43°25N 7°10E 73 E11
Azusa U.S.A. 34°8N 117°52W 171 L9
Azzaba Algeria 36°48N 7°6E 136 A5
Azzano Décimo Italy 45°52N 12°56E 93 C9
Azzel Matti, Sebkra
  Algeria 26°10N 0°43E 136 C4

B

Ba Be △ Vietnam 22°25N 105°37E 120 A5
Ba Don Vietnam 17°45N 106°26E 120 D6
Ba Dong Vietnam 9°40N 106°33E 121 H6
Ba Ngoi Vietnam 11°54N 109°10E 121 G7
Ba Ria Vietnam 10°30N 107°10E 121 G6
Ba Tri Vietnam 10°2N 106°36E 121 G6
Ba Vi Vietnam 21°1N 105°22E 120 B5
Ba Xian = Bazhou
  China 39°8N 116°22E 114 E9
Baa Indonesia 10°50S 123°0E 148 B3
Baalbek = Ba'labakk
  Lebanon 34°0N 36°10E 130 B5
Baamonde Spain 43°7N 7°44W 88 B3
Baardheere Somalia 2°20N 42°27E 131 G3
Baarle-Nassau Belgium 51°27N 4°56E 69 C4
Bab el Mandeb Red Sea 12°35N 43°25E 131 E3
Baba Bulgaria 42°44N 23°59E 96 D7
Bābā, Koh-i- Afghan. 34°30N 67°0E 128 B4
Baba Budan Hills India 13°30N 75°44E 127 H2
Baba Burnu Turkey 39°29N 26°2E 99 B8
Baba dag Azerbaijan 41°0N 48°19E 87 K9
Bābā Kalū Iran 30°7N 50°49E 129 D6
Babaçulândia Brazil 7°13S 47°46W 189 B1
Babadag Romania 44°53N 28°44E 81 F13
Babadağ Turkey 37°49N 28°52E 99 D10
Babaeski Turkey 41°26N 27°6E 97 E11
Babahoyo Ecuador 1°40S 79°30W 186 D3
Babai = Bayi → Nepal 28°10N 82°21E 125 E10
Babana Nigeria 10°31N 3°46E 139 C5
Babar Algeria 35°10N 7°6E 136 A5
Babar Indonesia 8°0S 129°30E 119 F7
Babar Pakistan 31°7N 69°32E 124 D3
Babarkach Pakistan 29°45N 68°0E 124 E3
Babayevo Russia 59°24N 35°55E 84 C8
Babb U.S.A. 48°51N 113°27W 168 B7
Babenhausen Germany 49°57N 8°57E 77 F4
Băbeni Romania 44°59N 24°11E 81 F9
Babi Besar, Pulau
  Malaysia 2°25N 103°59E 121 L4
Babia Gora Europe 49°38N 19°38E 83 J6
Babian Jiang → China 22°52S 101°47E 116 F3
Bābil □ Iraq 32°30N 44°30E 128 C5
Babimost Poland 52°10N 15°49E 83 F2
Babinda Australia 17°20S 145°56E 150 B4
Babine Canada 55°22N 126°37W 162 B3
Babine → Canada 55°45N 127°44W 162 B3
Babine L. Canada 54°48N 126°0W 162 C3
Babiogórski △ Poland 49°38N 19°38E 83 J6
Babo Indonesia 2°30S 133°30E 119 E8
Babócsa Hungary 46°2N 17°21E 80 D2
Bābol Iran 36°40N 52°50E 129 B7
Bābol Sar Iran 36°45N 52°45E 129 B7
Babor, Dj. Algeria 36°31N 5°28E 136 A5
Baborów Poland 50°7N 18°1E 83 H5
Baboua C.A.R. 5°49N 14°58E 137 C8
Babruysk Belarus 53°10N 29°15E 75 B15
Babson Park U.S.A. 27°49N 81°32W 179 H8
Babuhri India 26°49N 69°43E 124 F3
Babuna Macedonia 41°30N 21°40E 96 E5
Babura Nigeria 12°51N 8°59E 139 C6
Babusar Pass Pakistan 35°12N 73°59E 125 B5
Bābušnica Serbia 43°7N 22°27E 96 C6
Babuyan Chan. Phil. 18°40N 121°30E 119 A6
Babylon Iraq 32°34N 44°22E 105 F11
Bač Serbia 45°29N 19°17E 80 E4
Bâc → Moldova 46°55N 29°26E 81 D16
Bac Can Vietnam 22°8N 105°49E 120 A5
Bac Giang Vietnam 21°16N 106°11E 116 G5
Bac Lieu Vietnam 9°17N 105°43E 121 H5
Bac Ninh Vietnam 21°13N 106°4E 116 G5
Bac Phan Vietnam 22°0N 105°0E 116 G5
Bacabal Brazil 4°15S 44°45W 189 A2
Bacalar Mexico 18°43N 88°27W 181 D7
Bacan, Kepulauan
  Indonesia 0°35S 127°30E 119 E7
Bacarra Phil. 18°15N 120°37E 119 A6
Bacău Romania 46°35N 26°55E 81 D11
Bacău □ Romania 46°30N 26°45E 81 D11
Baccarat France 48°28N 6°42E 71 D13
Bacchus Marsh
  Australia 37°43S 144°27E 152 D6
Bacerac Mexico 30°18N 108°50W 180 A3
Bach Long Vi, Dao
  Vietnam 20°10N 107°40E 116 G6
Bach Ma △ Vietnam 16°11N 107°49E 120 D6
Bacharach Germany 50°3N 7°46E 77 E3
Bachhwara India 25°35N 85°54E 125 G11
Bachu China 39°48N 78°33E 109 D9
Băcina Serbia 43°42N 21°3E 96 C5

Bād Iran 33°41N 52°1E 129 C7
Bad → U.S.A. 44°21N 100°22W 172 C3
Bad Aussee Austria 47°43N 13°45E 78 D6
Bad Axe U.S.A. 43°48N 83°0W 174 C2
Bad Bergzabern Germany 49°6N 7°59E 77 F3
Bad Berleburg Germany 51°2N 8°26E 76 D4
Bad Bevensen Germany 53°5N 10°35E 76 B6
Bad Bramstedt Germany 53°55N 9°53E 76 B5
Bad Brückenau Germany 50°18N 9°47E 77 E5
Bad Doberan Germany 54°6N 11°53E 76 A7
Bad Driburg Germany 51°43N 9°1E 76 D5
Bad Ems Germany 50°20N 7°43E 77 E3
Bad Frankenhausen
  Germany 51°21N 11°5E 76 D7
Bad Freienwalde
  Germany 52°46N 14°1E 76 C10
Bad Goisern Austria 47°38N 13°38E 78 D6
Bad Harzburg Germany 51°52N 10°34E 76 D6
Bad Hersfeld Germany 50°52N 9°42E 76 E5
Bad Hofgastein Austria 47°17N 13°6E 78 D6
Bad Homburg Germany 50°13N 8°38E 77 E4
Bad Honnef Germany 50°38N 7°13E 76 E3
Bad Iburg Germany 52°10N 8°3E 76 C4
Bad Ischl Austria 47°44N 13°38E 78 D6
Bad Kissingen Germany 50°11N 10°4E 77 E6
Bad Königshofen
  Germany 50°17N 10°28E 77 E6
Bad Kreuznach Germany 49°50N 7°51E 77 F3
Bad Krozingen Germany 47°54N 7°42E 77 H3
Bad Laasphe Germany 50°56N 8°25E 76 E4
Bad Langensalza
  Germany 51°5N 10°38E 76 D6
Bad Lauterberg Germany 51°38N 10°28E 76 D6
Bad Leonfelden Austria 48°31N 14°18E 78 C7
Bad Liebenwerda
  Germany 51°31N 13°24E 76 D9
Bad Mergentheim
  Germany 49°29N 9°46E 77 F5
Bad Münstereifel
  Germany 50°33N 6°46E 76 E2
Bad Nauheim Germany 50°21N 8°43E 77 E4
Bad Neuenahr-Ahrweiler
  Germany 50°32N 7°7E 76 E3
Bad Neustadt Germany 50°20N 10°13E 77 E6
Bad Oeynhausen
  Germany 52°12N 8°45E 76 C4
Bad Oldesloe Germany 53°48N 10°22E 76 B6
Bad Orb Germany 50°12N 9°21E 77 E5
Bad Pyrmont Germany 51°59N 9°16E 76 D5
Bad Reichenhall
  Germany 47°43N 12°54E 77 H8
Bad Säckingen Germany 47°33N 7°56E 77 H3
Bad Salzuflen Germany 52°5N 8°45E 76 C4
Bad Salzungen Germany 50°48N 10°14E 76 E6
Bad Sankt Leonhard
  Austria 46°58N 14°47E 78 E7
Bad Schwartau Germany 53°55N 10°41E 76 B6
Bad Segeberg Germany 53°56N 10°17E 76 B6
Bad Tölz Germany 47°45N 11°34E 77 H7
Bad Urach Germany 48°29N 9°23E 77 G5
Bad Vöslau Austria 47°58N 16°13E 78 D9
Bad Waldsee Germany 47°55N 9°45E 77 H5
Bad Wildungen Germany 51°6N 9°7E 76 D5
Bad Wimpfen Germany 49°13N 9°11E 77 F5
Bad Windsheim
  Germany 49°30N 10°25E 77 F6
Bad Zwischenahn
  Germany 53°12N 8°1E 76 B4
Bada Barabil India 22°7N 85°24E 125 H11
Badagara = Vadakara
  India 11°35N 75°40E 127 J2
Badagri Nigeria 6°25N 2°55E 139 D5
Badain Jaran Shamo
  China 40°23N 102°0E 110 C9
Badajós, L. Brazil 3°15S 62°50W 186 D6
Badajoz Spain 38°50N 6°59W 89 G4
Badajoz □ Spain 38°40N 6°30W 89 G4
Badakhshān □ Afghan. 36°30N 71°0E 109 E8
Badalona Spain 41°26N 2°15E 90 D7
Badalzai Afghan. 29°50N 65°35E 124 E1
Badami India 15°55N 75°41E 126 F2
Badampahar India 22°10N 86°10E 125 H12
Badanah Si. Arabia 30°58N 41°30E 128 D4
Badarinath India 30°45N 79°30E 125 D8
Badas, Kepulauan
  Indonesia 0°45N 107°5E 118 D3
Baddo → Pakistan 28°0N 64°20E 124 F2
Badeggi Nigeria 9°1N 6°8E 139 D6
Badghêri Niger 14°30S 13°9E 139 C9
Baden Austria 48°1N 16°13E 78 D9
Baden Switz. 47°28N 8°18E 79 A4
Baden U.S.A. 40°38N 80°14W 174 F4
Baden-Baden Germany 48°44N 8°13E 77 G4
Baden-Württemberg □
  Germany 48°20N 8°40E 77 G4
Badgam India 34°1N 74°45E 125 B6
Badgastein Austria 47°7N 13°9E 78 E6
Badger Canada 49°0N 56°4W 165 C8
Badger U.S.A. 36°38N 119°1W 170 J7
Bādghīs □ Afghan. 35°0N 63°0E 108 D9
Badgingarra △
  Australia 30°23S 115°22E 149 F2
Badia Polésine Italy 45°6N 11°30E 93 C8
Badiar △ Guinea 13°37N 13°11W 138 C2
Badin Pakistan 24°38N 68°54E 124 G3
Badinka → Mali 13°31N 9°28W 138 C3
Badlands U.S.A. 43°38N 102°30W 172 D2
Badlands △ U.S.A. 43°38N 102°0W 172 D2
Badme N. Afr. 14°43N 37°48E 131 E2
Badnera India 20°48N 77°44E 126 D3
Badogo Mali 11°2N 8°13W 138 C3
Badoumbé Mali 13°42N 10°5W 138 C2
Badrah Iraq 33°6N 45°58E 128 C5
Badrinath India 30°45N 79°30E 125 D8
Badu Australia 10°7S 142°11E 150 a
Badulla Sri Lanka 7°1N 81°7E 127 L5
Badung, Bukit
  Indonesia 8°49S 115°10E 119 K18
Badung, Selat
  Indonesia 8°40S 115°22E 119 K18
Badvel India 14°45N 79°3E 127 G4
Baena Spain 37°37N 4°20W 89 H6
Baengnyeongdo
  S. Korea 37°57N 124°40E 115 F13
Baerami Australia 32°27S 150°27E 153 B9
Baeza Spain 37°57N 3°25W 89 H7

Bafang Cameroon 5°9N 10°11E 139 D7
Bafatá Guinea-Biss. 12°8N 14°40W 138 C2
Baffin B. N. Amer. 72°0N 64°0W 158 B13
Baffin I. Canada 68°0N 75°0W 161 D17
Bafia Cameroon 4°40N 11°10E 139 E7
Bafilo Togo 9°22N 1°22E 139 D5
Bafing □ Ivory C. 8°20N 7°40W 138 D3
Bafing → Mali 13°49N 10°50W 138 C2
Bafing △ Mali 12°38N 10°28W 138 C2
Bafliyūn Syria 36°37N 36°59E 128 B3
Bafoulabé Mali 13°50N 10°55W 138 C2
Bafoussam Cameroon 5°28N 10°25E 139 D7
Bāfq Iran 31°40N 55°25E 129 D7
Bafra Turkey 41°34N 35°54E 104 B6
Bafra Burnu Turkey 41°45N 36°2E 104 B7
Bāft Iran 29°15N 56°38E 129 D8
Bafut Cameroon 6°6N 10°2E 139 D7
Bafwasende Dem. Rep. of the Congo 1°3N 27°5E 142 B2
Bagaha India 27°6N 84°5E 126 A7
Bagalkot India 16°10N 75°40E 127 F2
Bagam Niger 15°43N 6°35E 139 B6
Bagamoyo Tanzania 6°28S 38°55E 142 D4
Bagan Datoh Malaysia 3°59N 100°47E 121 L3
Bagan Serai Malaysia 5°1N 100°32E 121 K3
Baganga Phil. 7°34N 126°33E 119 C7
Bagani Namibia 18°7S 21°41E 144 A3
Bagansiapiapi Indonesia 2°12N 100°50E 118 D2
Bagasra India 21°30N 71°0E 124 J4
Bagaud India 22°19N 75°53E 124 H6
Bagdad Calif., U.S.A. 34°35N 115°53W 171 L11
Bagdad Fla., U.S.A. 30°36N 87°2W 179 E2
Bagdarin Russia 54°26N 113°36E 107 D12
Bagé Brazil 31°20S 54°15W 191 C5
Bagenalstown Ireland 52°42N 6°58W 64 D5
Bagepalli India 13°47N 77°47E 127 H3
Bageshwar India 29°51N 79°46E 125 E8
Bagevadi India 16°35N 75°58E 126 F2
Baggs U.S.A. 41°2N 107°39W 168 F10
Bagh Pakistan 33°59N 73°45E 125 C5
Baghain → India 25°32N 81°1E 125 G9
Baghdād Iraq 33°20N 44°23E 105 F11
Baghdadi Georgia 42°5N 42°49E 105 A10
Bagheria Italy 38°5N 13°30E 94 D6
Baghlān Afghan. 32°12N 68°46E 109 F7
Baghlān □ Afghan. 36°0N 68°30E 109 E7
Bagley U.S.A. 47°32N 95°24W 172 B6
Baglung Nepal 28°16N 83°36E 125 E10
Bagnara Cálabra Italy 38°17N 15°48E 95 D8
Bagnasco Italy 44°18N 8°2E 92 D5
Bagnères-de-Bigorre France 43°5N 0°9E 72 E4
Bagnères-de-Luchon France 42°47N 0°38E 72 F4
Bagni di Lucca Italy 44°1N 10°35E 92 D7
Bagno di Romagna Italy 43°50N 11°57E 93 E8
Bagnoles-de-l'Orne France 48°32N 0°25W 70 D6
Bagnols-sur-Cèze France 44°10N 4°36E 73 D8
Bagnorégio Italy 42°37N 12°5E 93 F9
Bago = Pegu Burma 17°20N 96°29E 123 L20
Bagodar India 24°5N 85°52E 125 G11
Bagrationovsk Russia 54°23N 20°39E 82 D7
Bagrdan Serbia 44°5N 21°11E 96 B5
Bagua Peru 5°35S 78°22W 188 B2
Baguio Phil. 16°26N 120°34E 119 A6
Bağyurdu Turkey 38°25N 27°41E 99 C9
Bagzane, Monts Niger 17°43N 8°45E 139 B6
Bahabón de Esgueva Spain 41°52N 3°43W 88 D7
Bahadurganj India 26°16N 87°49E 125 F12
Bahadurgarh India 28°40N 76°57E 124 E7
Bahama, Canal Viejo de W. Indies 22°10N 77°30W 182 B4
Bahamas ■ N. Amer. 24°0N 75°0W 183 B5
Bahār Iran 34°54N 48°26E 105 E13
Baharampur India 24°2N 88°27E 125 G13
Bahariya, El Wâhât al Egypt 28°0N 28°50E 137 F6
Baharu Pandan = Pandan Malaysia 1°32N 103°46E 121 d
Bahawalnagar Pakistan 30°0N 73°15E 124 E5
Bahawalpur Pakistan 29°24N 71°40E 124 E4
Bahçe Turkey 37°13N 36°34E 104 D7
Bahçecik Turkey 40°41N 29°44E 97 F13
Bäherden Turkmenistan 38°25N 57°26E 129 B8
Baheri India 28°45N 79°34E 125 E8
Bahgul → India 27°45N 79°36E 125 F8
Bahi Tanzania 5°58S 35°21E 142 D4
Bahi Swamp Tanzania 6°10S 35°0E 142 D4
Bahia = Salvador Brazil 13°0S 38°30W 189 C3
Bahia □ Brazil 12°0S 42°0W 189 C2
Bahía, Is. de la Honduras 16°45N 86°15W 182 C2
Bahía Blanca Argentina 38°35S 62°13W 190 D3
Bahía de Caráquez Ecuador 0°40S 80°27W 186 D2
Bahía de Los Angeles Mexico 28°56N 113°34W 180 B2
Bahía Honda Cuba 22°54N 83°10W 182 B3
Bahía Kino Mexico 28°47N 111°58W 180 B2
Bahía Laura Argentina 48°10S 66°30W 192 C3
Bahía Mansa Chile 40°33S 73°46W 192 B2
Bahía Negra Paraguay 20°5S 58°5W 186 H7
Bahir Dar Ethiopia 11°37N 37°10E 131 E2
Bahmanzād Iran 31°15N 51°47E 129 D6
Bahmer Algeria 27°32N 0°10W 136 C3
Bahr el Ahmar □ Sudan 20°0N 35°0E 137 D4
Bahraich India 27°38N 81°37E 125 F9
Bahrain ■ Asia 26°0N 50°35E 129 E6
Bahror India 27°51N 76°20E 124 F7
Bāhū Kalāt Iran 25°43N 61°25E 129 E9
Bai Mali 13°35N 3°28W 138 C4
Bai Bung, Mui = Ca Mau, Mui Vietnam 8°38N 104°44E 121 H5
Bai Thuong Vietnam 19°54N 105°23E 120 C5
Baia de Aramă Romania 45°0N 22°50E 80 E7
Baia Mare Romania 47°40N 23°35E 81 C8
Baia-Sprie Romania 47°41N 23°43E 81 C8
Baião Brazil 2°40S 49°40W 187 D9
Baïbokoum Chad 7°46N 15°43E 135 G9
Baicheng Jilin, China 45°38N 122°42E 115 B12
Baicheng Xinjiang Uygur, China 41°46N 81°52E 109 D10
Băicoi Romania 45°3N 25°52E 81 E10
Baidoa = Baydhabo Somalia 3°8N 43°30E 131 G3
Baie-Comeau Canada 49°12N 68°10W 165 C6
Baie-St-Paul Canada 47°28N 70°32W 165 C5
Baie Ste-Anne Seychelles 4°18S 55°45E 141 b
Baie-Trinité Canada 49°25N 67°20W 165 C6
Baie Verte Canada 49°55N 56°12W 165 C8
Baignes-Ste-Radegonde France 45°23N 0°25W 72 C3
Baigneux-les-Juifs France 47°31N 4°39E 71 E11
Baihar India 22°6N 80°33E 125 H9
Baihe Hubei, China 32°50N 110°5E 117 A8
Baihe Jilin, China 42°27N 128°9E 115 C15
Baihetan Dam China 27°11N 102°54E 116 D4
Ba'ījī Iraq 35°0N 43°30E 105 E10
Baijnath India 29°55N 79°37E 125 E8
Baikal, L. = Baykal, Oz. Russia 53°0N 108°0E 107 D11
Baikonur = Bayqonyr Kazakhstan 45°40N 63°20E 108 C6
Baikunthpur India 23°15N 82°33E 125 H10
Bailadila, Mt. India 18°43N 81°15E 126 E5
Baile Átha Cliath = Dublin Ireland 53°21N 6°15W 64 C5
Baile Átha Fhirdhia = Ardee Ireland 53°52N 6°33W 64 C5
Baile Átha Í = Athy Ireland 53°0N 7°0W 64 C5
Baile Átha Luain = Athlone Ireland 53°25N 7°56W 64 C4
Baile Átha Troim = Trim Ireland 53°33N 6°48W 64 C5
Baile Brigín = Balbriggan Ireland 53°37N 6°11W 64 C5
Băile Govora Romania 45°5N 24°11E 81 E9
Băile Herculane Romania 44°53N 22°26E 80 F7
Băile Olăneşti Romania 45°12N 24°14E 81 E9
Baile Sear = Baleshare U.K. 57°31N 7°22W 65 D1
Băile Tuşnad Romania 46°9N 25°51E 81 D10
Bailén Spain 38°8N 3°48W 89 G7
Băileşti Romania 44°1N 23°20E 81 F8
Bailhongal India 15°55N 74°53E 127 G2
Bailieborough Ireland 53°56N 6°59W 64 C5
Bailin China 33°0N 100°26E 116 A3
Bain-de-Bretagne France 47°50N 1°40W 70 E5
Bainbridge Ga., U.S.A. 30°55N 84°35W 178 E5
Bainbridge N.Y., U.S.A. 42°18N 75°29W 175 D9
Bainbridge Island U.S.A. 47°38N 122°32W 170 C4
Baine China 42°0N 128°0E 111 C14
Baing Indonesia 10°14S 120°34E 119 F6
Bainiu China 32°50N 112°15E 117 A9
Bā'ir Jordan 30°45N 36°55E 130 E5
Baiona Spain 42°6N 8°52W 88 C2
Baird Mts. U.S.A. 67°0N 160°0W 166 B8
Bairiki = Tarawa Kiribati 1°30N 173°0E 156 G9
Bairin Youqi China 43°30N 118°35E 115 C10
Bairin Zuoqi China 43°58N 119°15E 115 C10
Bairnsdale Australia 37°48S 147°36E 153 D7
Baisha China 34°20N 112°32E 114 G7
Baisha Li China 19°12N 109°20E 117 a
Baishan = Hunjiang China 41°54N 126°26E 115 D14
Baishan China 42°43N 127°14E 115 C14
Baissa Nigeria 7°14N 10°38E 139 D7
Baitadi Nepal 29°35N 80°25E 125 E9
Baitarani → India 20°45N 86°48E 126 D8
Baixa Grande Brazil 11°57S 40°11W 189 C2
Baixa Limia-Sierra do Xurés ⌂ Spain 41°59N 8°2W 88 D3
Baiyin China 36°45N 104°14E 114 F3
Baiyü China 31°16N 98°50E 116 B2
Baiyu Shan China 37°15N 107°30E 114 F4
Baj Baj India 22°30N 88°5E 125 H13
Baja Hungary 46°12N 18°59E 80 D3
Baja, Pta. Mexico 29°58N 115°49W 180 B1
Baja California Mexico 31°10N 115°12W 180 A1
Baja California □ Mexico 30°0N 115°0W 180 B2
Baja California Sur □ Mexico 25°50N 111°50W 180 B2
Bajag India 22°40N 81°21E 125 H9
Bajamar Canary Is. 28°33N 16°20W 100 F3
Bajana India 23°7N 71°49E 124 H4
Bajatrejo Indonesia 8°29S 114°19E 119 J17
Bajawa Indonesia 8°47S 120°59E 119 F6
Bajera Indonesia 8°31S 115°2E 119 J18
Bājgīrān Iran 37°36N 58°24E 129 B8
Bajimba, Mt. Australia 29°17S 152°6E 151 D5
Bajina Bašta Serbia 43°58N 19°35E 96 C3
Bajmok Serbia 45°57N 19°24E 80 E4
Bajo Boquete Panama 8°46N 82°27W 182 E3
Bajo Caracoles Argentina 47°27S 70°56W 192 C2
Bajo Nuevo Caribbean 15°40N 78°50W 182 C4
Bajoga Nigeria 10°57N 11°20E 139 C7
Bajool Australia 23°40S 150°35E 150 C5
Bak Hungary 46°43N 16°51E 80 D1
Bakala C.A.R. 6°15N 20°20E 140 C4
Bakassi Pen. Cameroon 4°42N 8°20E 139 E6
Bakel Senegal 14°56N 12°20W 138 C2
Baker Calif., U.S.A. 35°16N 116°4W 171 K10
Baker Fla., U.S.A. 30°48N 86°41W 179 E3
Baker Mont., U.S.A. 46°22N 104°17W 168 C11
Baker, Canal Chile 47°45S 74°45W 192 C2
Baker, L. Canada 64°0N 96°0W 160 E12
Baker, Mt. U.S.A. 48°50N 121°49W 168 B3
Baker City U.S.A. 44°47N 117°50W 168 D5
Baker I. Pac. Oc. 0°10N 176°35W 156 G10
Baker I. U.S.A. 55°20N 133°40W 162 B2
Baker L. Australia 26°54S 126°5E 149 E4
Baker Lake Canada 64°20N 96°3W 160 E12
Bakerhill U.S.A. 31°47N 85°18W 178 D4
Bakers Creek Australia 21°13S 149°7E 150 C4
Bakers Dozen Is. Canada 56°45N 78°45W 164 A4
Bakersfield Calif., U.S.A. 35°23N 119°1W 171 K8
Bakersfield Vt., U.S.A. 44°45N 72°48W 175 B12
Bakharden = Bäherden Turkmenistan 38°25N 57°26E 129 B8
Bakhchysaray Ukraine 44°40N 33°45E 85 K7
Bakhmach Ukraine 51°10N 32°45E 85 G7
Bākhtarān = Kermānshāh Iran 34°23N 47°0E 105 E12
Bākhtarān = Kermānshāh □ Iran 34°0N 46°30E 128 C5
Bakhtegān, Daryācheh-ye Iran 29°40N 53°50E 129 D7
Bakhtegān △ Iran 29°51N 53°40E 129 D7
Bakı Azerbaijan 40°29N 49°56E 87 K9
Bakır → Turkey 38°55N 27°0E 99 C9
Bakırdaği Turkey 38°13N 35°46E 104 C6
Bakkafjörður Iceland 66°2N 14°48W 60 C6
Bakkagerði Iceland 65°31N 13°49W 60 D7
Baklan Turkey 38°0N 29°36E 99 C11
Bako Ivory C. 9°8N 7°40W 138 D3
Bakony Hungary 47°10N 17°30E 80 C2
Bakony Forest = Bakony Hungary 47°10N 17°30E 80 C2
Bakori Nigeria 11°34N 7°25E 139 C6
Bakouma C.A.R. 5°40N 22°56E 140 C4
Baksan Russia 43°42N 43°32E 87 J6
Bakswaho India 24°15N 79°18E 125 G8
Baku = Bakı Azerbaijan 40°29N 49°56E 87 K9
Bakundi Nigeria 8°2N 10°45E 139 D7
Bakuriani Georgia 41°44N 43°31E 105 B10
Bakutis Coast Antarctica 74°0S 120°0W 55 D15
Baky = Bakı Azerbaijan 40°29N 49°56E 87 K9
Bala Canada 45°1N 79°37W 174 A5
Bala Senegal 14°1N 13°8W 138 C2
Balâ Turkey 39°32N 33°6E 104 C5
Bala U.K. 52°54N 3°36W 66 E4
Bala, L. U.K. 52°53N 3°37W 66 E4
Bālā Morghāb Afghan. 35°35N 63°20E 108 E6
Balabac I. Phil. 8°0N 117°0E 118 C5
Balabac Str. E. Indies 7°53N 117°5E 118 C5
Balabagh Afghan. 34°25N 70°12E 124 B4
Ba'labakk Lebanon 34°0N 36°10E 130 B5
Balabalangan, Kepulauan Indonesia 2°20S 117°30E 118 E5
Bălăciţa Romania 44°23N 23°8E 81 F8
Balad Iraq 34°0N 44°9E 105 F11
Balad Rūz Iraq 33°42N 45°5E 105 F11
Bālādeh Fārs, Iran 29°17N 51°56E 129 D6
Bālādeh Māzandaran, Iran 36°12N 51°48E 129 B6
Balaghat India 21°49N 80°12E 126 D5
Balaghat Ra. India 18°50N 76°30E 126 E3
Balaguer Spain 41°50N 0°50E 90 D5
Balakän Azerbaijan 41°43N 46°24E 87 K8
Balakhna Russia 56°25N 43°32E 86 B6
Balaklava Australia 34°7S 138°22E 152 C3
Balaklava Ukraine 44°30N 33°30E 85 K7
Balakliya Ukraine 49°28N 36°55E 85 H9
Balakovo Russia 52°4N 47°55E 86 D8
Balamau India 27°10N 80°21E 125 F9
Bălan Romania 46°39N 25°49E 81 D10
Balancán Mexico 17°48N 91°32W 181 D6
Balangir India 20°43N 83°35E 126 D6
Balapur India 20°40N 76°45E 126 D3
Balashikha Russia 55°48N 37°58E 84 E9
Balashov Russia 51°30N 43°10E 86 E6
Balasinor India 22°57N 73°23E 124 H5
Balasore = Baleshwar India 21°35N 87°3E 126 D8
Balassagyarmat Hungary 48°4N 19°15E 80 B4
Balât Egypt 25°36N 29°19E 137 B2
Balaton Hungary 46°50N 17°40E 80 D2
Balaton-Felvidéki △ Hungary 46°52N 17°30E 80 D2
Balatonboglár Hungary 46°46N 17°40E 80 D2
Balatonfüred Hungary 46°58N 17°54E 80 D2
Balatonszentgyörgy Hungary 46°41N 17°19E 80 D2
Balazote Spain 38°54N 2°9W 91 G2
Balbieriškis Lithuania 54°32N 23°53E 82 D10
Balbigny France 45°49N 4°11E 73 C8
Balbina, Represa de Brazil 2°0S 59°30W 186 D7
Balboa Panama 8°57N 79°34W 182 E4
Balbriggan Ireland 53°37N 6°11W 64 C5
Balcarce Argentina 38°0S 58°10W 190 D4
Balcarres Canada 50°50N 103°35W 163 C8
Bălceşti Romania 44°37N 23°57E 81 F8
Balchik Bulgaria 43°28N 28°11E 97 C12
Balclutha N.Z. 46°15S 169°45E 155 G4
Balcones Escarpment U.S.A. 29°30N 99°15W 176 G5
Balçova Turkey 38°22N 27°4E 99 C9
Bald I. Australia 34°57S 118°27E 149 F2
Bald Knob U.S.A. 35°19N 91°34W 176 D9
Baldock L. Canada 56°33N 97°57W 163 B9
Baldwin Fla., U.S.A. 30°18N 81°59W 178 E8
Baldwin Mich., U.S.A. 43°54N 85°51W 173 D11
Baldwin Pa., U.S.A. 40°21N 79°58W 174 F5
Baldwinsville U.S.A. 43°10N 76°20W 175 C8
Baldy Peak U.S.A. 33°54N 109°34W 169 K9
Bale Croatia 45°4N 13°46E 93 C10
Baleares, Is. Spain 39°30N 3°0E 100 B10
Balearic Is. = Baleares, Is. Spain 39°30N 3°0E 100 B10
Baleia, Pta. da Brazil 17°40S 39°7W 189 D3
Baleine → Canada 58°15N 67°40W 165 A6
Baleine, Petite R. de la → Canada 56°0N 76°45W 164 A4
Băleni Romania 45°48N 27°51E 81 E12
Baler Phil. 15°46N 121°34E 119 A6
Baleshare U.K. 57°31N 7°22W 65 D1
Baleshwar India 21°35N 87°3E 126 D8
Baley Russia 51°36N 116°37E 107 D12
Balezino Russia 58°2N 53°6E 86 B11
Balfate Honduras 15°48N 86°25W 182 C2
Balgo Australia 20°9S 127°58E 148 D4
Balharshah India 19°50N 79°23E 126 E4
Bali Cameroon 5°54N 10°0E 139 D7
Bali Greece 35°25N 24°47E 101 D6
Bali India 25°11N 73°17E 124 G5
Bali Indonesia 8°20S 115°0E 118 F4
Bali □ Indonesia 8°20S 115°0E 118 F5
Bali, Selat Indonesia 8°18S 114°25E 119 J17
Bali Barat △ Indonesia 8°12S 114°35E 119 J17
Bali Sea Indonesia 8°0S 115°0E 119 J17
Balia S. Leone 9°22N 11°1W 138 D2
Baliapal India 21°40N 87°17E 125 J12
Baligród Poland 49°20N 22°17E 83 J9
Baliguda India 20°12N 83°55E 126 D6
Balik Pulau Malaysia 5°21N 100°14E 121 c
Balıkeşir Turkey 39°39N 27°53E 99 B9
Balıkeşir □ Turkey 39°45N 28°0E 99 B9
Balīkh → Syria 35°52N 39°12E 105 E8
Balıklıçeşme Turkey 40°18N 27°5E 97 F11
Balikpapan Indonesia 1°10S 116°55E 118 E5
Balimbing Phil. 5°5N 119°58E 119 C5
Baling Malaysia 5°41N 100°55E 121 K3
Bälinge Sweden 59°57N 17°33E 62 E11
Balingen Germany 48°16N 8°51E 77 G4
Balinţ Romania 45°48N 21°54E 80 E6
Balkan □ Turkmenistan 40°0N 54°30E 108 D5
Balkan Mts. = Stara Planina Bulgaria 43°15N 23°0E 96 C7
Balkanabat Turkmenistan 39°30N 54°22E 129 B7
Balkh Afghan. 36°44N 66°47E 109 E7
Balkh □ Afghan. 36°50N 67°0E 109 E7
Balkhash = Balqash Kazakhstan 46°50N 74°50E 106 E8
Balkhash, Ozero = Balqash Köli Kazakhstan 46°0N 74°50E 109 C8
Balkonda India 18°52N 78°21E 126 E4
Ballachulish U.K. 56°41N 5°8W 65 E3
Balladonia Australia 32°27S 123°51E 149 F3
Ballaghaderreen Ireland 53°55N 8°34W 64 C3
Ballan Australia 37°35S 144°13E 152 D6
Ballarat Australia 37°33S 143°50E 152 D5
Ballard, L. Australia 29°20S 120°40E 149 E3
Ballater U.K. 57°3N 3°3W 65 D5
Ballé Mali 15°18N 8°33W 138 B3
Ballenas, Canal de Mexico 29°10N 113°29W 180 B2
Balleny Is. Antarctica 66°30S 163°0E 55 C11
Balleroy France 49°11N 0°50W 70 C6
Ballerup Denmark 55°43N 12°21E 63 J6
Ballestas, Is. Peru 13°44S 76°25W 188 C2
Ballı Turkey 40°50N 27°3E 97 F11
Ballia India 25°46N 84°12E 125 G11
Ballina Australia 28°50S 153°31E 151 D5
Ballina Ireland 54°7N 9°9W 64 B2
Ballinasloe Ireland 53°20N 8°13W 64 C3
Ballincollig Ireland 51°53N 8°33W 64 E3
Ballinger U.S.A. 31°45N 99°57W 176 F5
Ballinrobe Ireland 53°38N 9°13W 64 C2
Ballinskelligs B. Ireland 51°48N 10°13W 64 E1
Ballon France 48°10N 0°14E 70 D7
Ballons des Vosges ⌂ France 48°0N 7°0E 71 E14
Ballsh Albania 40°36N 19°44E 96 F3
Ballston Spa U.S.A. 43°0N 73°51W 175 D11
Ballyboghil Ireland 53°32N 6°16W 64 C5
Ballybunion Ireland 52°31N 9°40W 64 D2
Ballycanew Ireland 52°37N 6°19W 64 D5
Ballycastle U.K. 55°12N 6°15W 64 A5
Ballyclare U.K. 54°46N 6°0W 64 B5
Ballycroy △ Ireland 54°5N 9°50W 64 B2
Ballydehob Ireland 51°34N 9°28W 64 E2
Ballygawley U.K. 54°27N 7°2W 64 B4
Ballyhaunis Ireland 53°46N 8°46W 64 C3
Ballyheige Ireland 52°23N 9°49W 64 D2
Ballymena U.K. 54°52N 6°17W 64 B5
Ballymoney U.K. 55°5N 6°31W 64 A5
Ballymote Ireland 54°5N 8°31W 64 B3
Ballynahinch U.K. 54°24N 5°54W 64 B6
Ballyporeen Ireland 52°16N 8°6W 64 D3
Ballyquintin Pt. U.K. 54°20N 5°30W 64 B6
Ballyshannon Ireland 54°30N 8°11W 64 B3
Balmaceda Chile 46°0S 71°50W 192 C2
Balmaseda Spain 43°11N 3°12W 90 B1
Balmazújváros Hungary 47°37N 21°21E 80 C6
Balmertown Canada 51°4N 93°41W 163 C10
Balmoral Australia 37°15S 141°48E 152 D4
Balmorhea U.S.A. 30°59N 103°45W 176 F3
Balneário Camboriú Brazil 26°59S 48°38W 191 B6
Balochistan = Baluchistan □ Pakistan 27°30N 65°0E 122 F4
Balod India 20°44N 81°13E 126 D5
Balonne → Australia 28°47S 147°56E 151 D4
Balotra India 25°50N 72°14E 124 G5
Balpyq Bī Kazakhstan 44°52N 78°12E 109 D9
Balqash Kazakhstan 46°50N 74°50E 106 E8
Balqash Köli Kazakhstan 46°0N 74°50E 109 C8
Balrampur India 27°30N 82°20E 125 F10
Balranald Australia 34°38S 143°33E 152 C5
Balş Romania 44°22N 24°5E 81 F9
Balsapuerto Peru 5°48S 76°33W 188 B2
Balsas → Maranhão, Brazil 7°15S 44°35W 189 B2
Balsas → Tocantins, Brazil 9°58S 47°52W 189 B1
Balsas → Mexico 17°55N 102°10W 180 D4
Balsas del Norte Mexico 18°0N 99°46W 181 D5
Bålsta Sweden 59°35N 17°30E 62 E11
Balta Romania 44°54N 22°38E 80 F7
Balta Ukraine 47°56N 29°45E 81 C14
Baltakől Kazakhstan 43°47N 67°46E 109 D7
Baltanás Spain 41°56N 4°15W 88 D6
Bălţi Moldova 47°48N 27°58E 81 C12
Baltic Sea Europe 57°0N 19°0E 61 H18
Baltîm Egypt 31°35N 31°10E 137 E7
Baltimore Ireland 51°29N 9°22W 64 E2
Baltimore Md., U.S.A. 39°17N 76°36W 173 F15
Baltimore Ohio, U.S.A. 39°51N 82°36W 174 G2
Baltinglass Ireland 52°56N 6°43W 64 D5
Baltit Pakistan 36°15N 74°40E 125 A6
Baltiysk Russia 54°41N 19°58E 82 D6
Baltrum Germany 53°43N 7°24E 76 B3
Baluchistan □ Pakistan 27°30N 65°0E 122 F4
Baluqtybulaq Kazakhstan 50°51N 51°8E 86 E10
Balurghat India 25°15N 88°44E 125 G13
Balvi Latvia 57°8N 27°15E 84 D4
Balya Turkey 39°44N 27°35E 99 B9
Balykchy Kyrgyzstan 42°26N 76°12E 109 D9
Balyqshy Kazakhstan 47°4N 51°52E 108 C4
Bam Iran 29°7N 58°14E 129 D8
Bama China 24°8N 107°12E 116 E6
Bama Nigeria 11°33N 13°41E 139 C7
Bamaga Australia 10°50S 142°25E 150 A3
Bamaji L. Canada 51°9N 91°25W 164 B1
Bamako Mali 12°34N 7°55W 138 C3
Bamba Mali 17°5N 1°24W 139 B4
Bambamarca Peru 6°36S 78°32W 188 B2
Bambara Maoundé Mali 13°26N 4°3W 138 B4
Bambari C.A.R. 5°40N 20°35E 140 C4
Bambaroo Australia 18°50S 146°10E 150 B4
Bambaya Guinea 10°55N 13°38W 138 D2
Bamberg Germany 49°54N 10°54E 77 F6
Bamberg U.S.A. 33°18N 81°2W 178 B8
Bambey Senegal 14°42N 16°28W 138 C1
Bambili Dem. Rep. of the Congo 3°40N 26°0E 142 B2
Bamboi Ghana 8°13N 2°1W 138 D4
Bambuí Brazil 20°1S 45°58W 189 E1
Bamburgh U.K. 55°37N 1°43W 66 B6
Bamenda Cameroon 5°57N 10°11E 139 D7
Bamendjing, L. de Cameroon 5°50N 10°30E 139 D7
Bamfield Canada 48°45N 125°10W 162 D3
Bāmīān Afghan. 34°49N 67°49E 109 F7
Bāmīān □ Afghan. 35°0N 67°0E 122 B5
Bamiancheng China 43°15N 124°2E 115 C13
Bamkin Cameroon 6°3N 11°27E 139 D7
Bamou △ Iran 29°45N 52°35E 129 D7
Bampūr Iran 27°15N 60°21E 129 E9
Bampūr → Iran 27°24N 59°0E 129 E8
Ban Ao Tu Khun Thailand 8°9N 98°20E 121 a
Ban Ban Laos 19°31N 103°30E 120 C4
Ban Bang Hin Thailand 9°32N 98°35E 121 H2
Ban Bang Khu Thailand 7°57N 98°23E 121 a
Ban Bang Rong Thailand 8°3N 98°25E 121 a
Ban Bo Phut Thailand 9°33N 100°2E 121 b
Ban Chaweng Thailand 9°32N 100°3E 121 b
Ban Chiang Thailand 17°30N 103°10E 120 D4
Ban Chiang Klang Thailand 19°25N 100°55E 120 C3
Ban Choho Thailand 15°2N 102°9E 120 E4
Ban Dan Lan Hoi Thailand 17°0N 99°35E 120 D2
Ban Don = Surat Thani Thailand 9°6N 99°20E 121 H2
Ban Don Vietnam 12°53N 107°48E 120 F6
Ban Don, Ao → Thailand 9°20N 99°25E 121 H2
Ban Dong Thailand 19°30N 100°59E 120 C3
Ban Hong Thailand 18°18N 98°50E 120 C2
Ban Hua Thanon Thailand 9°26N 100°1E 121 b
Ban Kantang Thailand 7°25N 99°31E 121 J2
Ban Karon Thailand 7°51N 98°18E 121 a
Ban Kata Thailand 7°50N 98°18E 121 a
Ban Keun Laos 18°22N 102°35E 120 C4
Ban Khai Thailand 12°46N 101°18E 120 F3
Ban Kheun Laos 20°13N 101°7E 120 B3
Ban Khlong Khian Thailand 8°10N 98°26E 121 a
Ban Khlong Kua Thailand 6°57N 100°8E 121 J3
Ban Khuan Thailand 8°20N 98°25E 121 a
Ban Ko Yai Chim Thailand 11°17N 99°26E 121 G2
Ban Laem Thailand 13°13N 99°59E 120 F2
Ban Lamai Thailand 9°28N 100°3E 121 b
Ban Lao Ngam Laos 15°28N 106°10E 120 E6
Ban Le Kathe Thailand 15°49N 98°53E 120 E2
Ban Lo Po Noi Thailand 8°1N 98°34E 121 a
Ban Mae Chedi Thailand 19°11N 99°31E 120 C2
Ban Mae Nam Thailand 9°34N 100°0E 121 b
Ban Mae Sariang Thailand 18°10N 97°56E 120 C1
Ban Mê Thuôt = Buon Ma Thuot Vietnam 12°40N 108°3E 120 F7
Ban Mi Thailand 15°3N 100°32E 120 E3
Ban Muang Mo Laos 19°4N 103°58E 120 C4
Ban Na Bo Thailand 9°19N 99°41E 121 b
Ban Na San Thailand 8°53N 99°52E 121 H2
Ban Na Tong Laos 20°56N 101°47E 120 B3
Ban Nam Bac Laos 20°38N 102°20E 120 B4
Ban Nammi Laos 17°7N 105°40E 120 D5
Ban Nong Bok Laos 17°5N 104°48E 120 D5
Ban Nong Pling Thailand 15°40N 100°10E 120 E3
Ban Pak Chan Thailand 10°32N 98°51E 121 G2
Ban Patong Thailand 7°54N 98°18E 121 a
Ban Phai Thailand 16°4N 102°44E 120 D4
Ban Phak Chit Thailand 8°0N 98°24E 121 a
Ban Pong Thailand 13°50N 99°55E 120 F2
Ban Rawai Thailand 7°47N 98°20E 121 a
Ban Ron Phibun Thailand 8°9N 99°51E 121 H2
Ban Sakhu Thailand 8°4N 98°18E 121 a
Ban Sanam Chai Thailand 7°33N 100°25E 121 J3
Ban Tak Thailand 17°2N 99°4E 120 D2
Ban Tako Thailand 14°5N 102°40E 120 E4
Ban Tha Nun Thailand 8°12N 98°18E 121 a
Ban Tha Rua Thailand 7°59N 98°22E 121 a
Ban Tha Yu Thailand 8°17N 98°22E 121 a
Ban Thong Krut Thailand 9°25N 99°57E 121 b
Ban Xien Kok Laos 20°54N 100°39E 120 B3
Ban Yen Nhan Vietnam 20°57N 106°2E 120 B6
Banaba Kiribati 0°45S 169°50E 156 H8
Banagher Ireland 53°11N 7°59W 64 C3
Banalia Dem. Rep. of the Congo 1°32N 25°5E 142 B2
Banam Cambodia 11°20N 105°17E 121 G5
Banamba Mali 13°29N 7°22W 138 C3
Banana Is. S. Leone 8°7N 13°15W 138 D2
Bananal, I. do Brazil 11°30S 50°30W 187 F8
Bananga India 6°57N 93°54E 127 L11
Banaras = Varanasi India 25°22N 83°0E 125 G10
Banas → Gujarat, India 23°45N 71°25E 124 H4
Banas → Mad. P., India 24°15N 81°30E 125 G9
Bânâs, Ras Egypt 23°57N 35°59E 137 C4
Banaz Turkey 38°46N 29°46E 99 C11
Banaz → Turkey 38°12N 29°14E 99 C11
Banbridge U.K. 54°22N 6°16W 64 B5
Banbury U.K. 52°4N 1°20W 67 E6
Banchory U.K. 57°3N 2°29W 65 D6
Bancroft Canada 45°3N 77°51W 174 A7
Band Romania 46°30N 24°25E 81 D9
Band Bonī Iran 25°30N 59°33E 129 E8
Band Qīr Iran 31°39N 48°53E 129 D6
Banda Mad. P., India 24°3N 78°57E 125 G8
Banda Maharashtra, India 15°49N 73°52E 127 G1
Banda Ut. P., India 25°30N 80°26E 125 G9
Banda, Kepulauan Indonesia 4°37S 129°50E 119 E7
Banda Aceh Indonesia 5°35N 95°20E 118 C1
Banda Banda, Mt. Australia 31°10S 152°28E 153 A10
Banda Elat Indonesia 5°40S 133°5E 119 F8
Banda Is. = Banda, Kepulauan Indonesia 4°37S 129°50E 119 E7
Banda Sea Indonesia 6°0S 130°0E 119 F8
Bandai-Asahi △ Japan 37°38N 140°5E 112 F10
Bandai-San Japan 37°36N 140°4E 112 F10
Bandama → Ivory C. 6°32N 4°30W 138 D3
Bandama Blanc → Ivory C. 6°55N 5°30W 138 D4
Bandama Rouge → Ivory C. 6°55N 5°30W 138 D4
Bandān Iran 31°23N 60°44E 129 D9
Bandanaira Indonesia 4°32S 129°54E 119 E7
Bandanwara India 26°9N 74°38E 124 F6
Bandar = Machilipatnam India 16°12N 81°8E 127 F5
Bandar-e Abbās Iran 27°15N 56°15E 129 E8
Bandar-e Anzalī Iran 37°30N 49°30E 105 D13
Bandar-e Bushehr = Būshehr Iran 28°55N 50°55E 129 D6
Bandar-e Chārak Iran 26°45N 54°20E 129 E7
Bandar-e Deylam Iran 30°5N 50°10E 129 D6
Bandar-e Emām Khomeynī Iran 30°30N 49°5E 129 D6
Bandar-e Lengeh Iran 26°35N 54°58E 129 E7
Bandar-e Maqām Iran 26°56N 53°29E 129 E7
Bandar-e Ma'shur Iran 30°35N 49°10E 129 D6
Bandar-e Rīg Iran 29°29N 50°38E 129 D6
Bandar-e Torkeman Iran 37°0N 54°10E 129 B7
Bandar Labuan Malaysia 5°20N 115°14E 118 C5
Bandar Lampung Indonesia 5°20S 105°10E 118 F3
Bandar Maharani = Muar Malaysia 2°3N 102°34E 121 L4
Bandar Penggaram = Batu Pahat Malaysia 1°50N 102°56E 121 M4
Bandar Seri Begawan Brunei 4°52N 115°0E 118 D5
Bandar Shahid Rajaee Iran 27°7N 56°4E 129 E8
Bandar Sri Aman Malaysia 1°15N 111°32E 118 D4
Bandawe Malawi 11°58S 34°5E 143 E3
Bande Spain 42°3N 7°58W 88 C3
Bandeira, Pico da Brazil 20°26S 41°47W 189 E2
Bandera Argentina 28°55S 62°20W 190 B3
Banderas, B. de Mexico 20°40N 105°25W 180 C3
Bandhavgarh India 23°40N 81°2E 125 H9
Bandhavgarh △ India 23°45N 81°10E 126 C5
Bandi → India 26°12N 75°47E 124 F6
Bandia → India 19°2N 80°28E 126 E5
Bandiagara Mali 14°12N 3°29W 138 C4
Bandikui India 27°3N 76°34E 124 F7
Bandipur △ India 11°45N 76°30E 127 J3
Bandırma Turkey 40°20N 28°0E 97 F11
Bandjarmasin = Banjarmasin Indonesia 3°20S 114°35E 118 E4
Bandol France 43°8N 5°46E 73 E9
Bandon Ireland 51°44N 8°44W 64 E3
Bandon → Ireland 51°43N 8°37W 64 E3
Bandula Mozam. 19°0S 33°7E 143 F3
Bandundu Dem. Rep. of the Congo 3°15S 17°22E 140 E3
Bandung Indonesia 6°54S 107°36E 118 F3
Bané Burkina Faso 11°42N 0°15W 139 C4
Băneasa Romania 45°56N 27°55E 81 E12
Bāneh Iran 35°59N 45°53E 105 E11
Banes Cuba 21°0N 75°42W 183 B4
Banff Canada 51°10N 115°34W 162 C5
Banff U.K. 57°40N 2°33W 65 D6
Banff △ Canada 51°30N 116°15W 162 C5
Banfora Burkina Faso 10°40N 4°40W 138 C4
Bang Fai → Laos 16°57N 104°45E 120 D5
Bang Hieng → Laos 16°10N 105°10E 120 D5
Bang Krathum Thailand 16°34N 100°18E 120 D3
Bang Lamung Thailand 13°3N 100°56E 120 F3
Bang Lang △ Thailand 5°58N 101°19E 121 K3
Bang Lang Res. Thailand 6°6N 101°17E 121 J3
Bang Mun Nak Thailand 16°2N 100°23E 120 D3
Bang Pa In Thailand 14°14N 100°35E 120 E3
Bang Rakam Thailand 16°45N 100°7E 120 D3
Bang Saphan Thailand 11°14N 99°28E 121 G2
Bang Thao Thailand 7°59N 98°18E 121 a
Bangaduni I. India 21°34N 88°52E 125 J13
Bangala Dam Zimbabwe 21°7S 31°25E 143 G3
Bangalore India 12°59N 77°40E 127 H3
Banganapalle India 15°19N 78°14E 127 G4
Banganga → India 27°6N 77°25E 124 F6
Bangangté Cameroon 5°8N 10°32E 139 D7
Bangaon India 23°0N 88°47E 125 H13
Bangassou C.A.R. 4°55N 23°7E 140 D4
Banggai Indonesia 1°34S 123°30E 119 E6
Banggai, Kepulauan Indonesia 1°40S 123°30E 119 E6
Banggai Arch. = Banggai, Kepulauan Indonesia 1°40S 123°30E 119 E6
Banggi, Pulau Malaysia 7°17N 117°12E 118 C5
Banghāzī Libya 32°11N 20°3E 135 B10
Bangka Sulawesi, Indonesia 1°50N 125°5E 119 D7
Bangka Sumatera, Indonesia 2°0S 105°50E 118 E3
Bangka, Selat Indonesia 2°30S 105°30E 118 E3
Bangka-Belitung □ Indonesia 2°30S 107°0E 118 E3
Bangkalan Indonesia 7°2S 112°46E 119 G15
Bangkang Burma 22°4N 99°1E 116 F2
Bangkinang Indonesia 0°18N 101°5E 118 D2
Bangko Indonesia 2°5S 102°9E 118 E2
Bangkok Thailand 13°45N 100°35E 120 F3
Bangkok, Bight of Thailand 12°55N 100°30E 120 F3
Bangla = Paschimbanga □ India 23°0N 88°0E 125 H13
Bangladesh ■ Asia 24°0N 90°0E 123 H17
Bangli Indonesia 8°27S 115°21E 119 J18
Bangolo Ivory C. 7°1N 7°29W 138 D3
Bangong Co China 33°45N 78°43E 125 C8
Bangor Down, U.K. 54°40N 5°40W 64 B6
Bangor Gwynedd, U.K. 53°14N 4°8W 66 D3
Bangor Maine, U.S.A. 44°48N 68°46W 173 C19
Bangor Pa., U.S.A. 40°52N 75°13W 175 F9
Bangued Phil. 17°40N 120°37E 119 A6
Bangui C.A.R. 4°23N 18°35E 140 D3
Banguru Dem. Rep. of the Congo 0°30N 27°10E 142 B2
Bangweulu, L. Zambia 11°0S 30°0E 143 E3
Bangweulu Swamp Zambia 11°20S 30°15E 143 E3
Banhine △ Mozam. 22°49S 32°55E 145 B5
Bani Burkina Faso 13°43N 0°10W 139 C4
Baní Dom. Rep. 18°16N 70°22W 183 C5
Bani → Mali 14°30N 4°12W 138 C4
Bani, Jebel Morocco 29°16N 8°0W 136 C2
Bani Bangou Niger 15°3N 2°42E 139 B5
Banī Sa'd Iraq 33°34N 44°32E 105 F11
Bania Ivory C. 9°4N 3°6W 138 D4
Banihal Pass India 33°30N 75°12E 125 C6
Banikoara Benin 11°18N 2°26E 139 C5
Banissa Kenya 3°55N 40°19E 142 B4
Bāniyās Syria 35°10N 36°0E 104 E6
Banja Luka Bos.-H. 44°49N 17°11E 80 F2
Banjar India 31°38N 77°21E 124 D7
Banjar → India 22°36N 80°22E 125 H9
Banjarmasin Indonesia 3°20S 114°35E 118 E4
Banjul Gambia 13°28N 16°40W 138 C1
Banka India 24°53N 86°55E 125 G12
Bankas Mali 14°4N 3°31W 138 C4
Bankeryd Sweden 57°53N 14°6E 63 G8
Banket Zimbabwe 17°27S 30°19E 143 F3

Bankilaré Niger 14°35N 0°44E 139 C5
Bankipore India 25°35N 85°10E 123 G14
Bankot India 17°58N 73°2E 126 F1
Banks U.S.A. 31°49N 85°51W 178 D4
Banks I. = Moa
Australia 10°11S 142°16E 150 a
Banks I. B.C., Canada 53°20N 130°0W 162 C3
Banks I. N.W.T.,
Canada 73°15N 121°30W 160 C7
Banks L. U.S.A. 31°2N 83°6W 178 D6
Banks Pen. N.Z. 43°45S 173°15E 155 D8
Banks Str. Australia 40°40S 148°10E 151 G4
Bankura India 23°11N 87°18E 125 H12
Bankya Bulgaria 42°43N 23°8E 96 D7
Banmankhi India 25°53N 87°11E 125 G12
Bann → Armagh, U.K. 54°30N 6°31W 64 B5
Bann → L'derry., U.K. 55°8N 6°41W 64 A5
Bannalec France 47°57N 3°42W 70 E3
Bannang Sata Thailand 6°16N 101°16E 121 J3
Bannerton Australia 34°42S 142°50E 152 C5
Banning U.S.A. 33°56N 116°53W 171 M10
Bannockburn Canada 44°39N 77°33W 174 B7
Bannockburn U.K. 56°5N 3°55W 65 E5
Bannockburn
Zimbabwe 20°17S 29°48E 143 G2
Bannu Pakistan 33°0N 70°18E 122 C7
Bano India 22°40N 84°55E 125 H11
Bañolas = Banyoles Spain 42°16N 2°44E 90 C7
Banon France 44°2N 5°38E 73 D9
Baños de la Encina Spain 38°10N 3°46W 89 G7
Baños de Molgas Spain 42°15N 7°40W 88 C3
Bánovce nad Bebravou
Slovak Rep. 48°44N 18°16E 79 C11
Banovići Bos.-H. 44°25N 18°32E 80 F3
Bansagar Dam India 24°11N 81°17E 126 B5
Bansgaon India 26°33N 83°21E 125 F10
Banská Bystrica
Slovak Rep. 48°46N 19°14E 79 C12
Banská Štiavnica
Slovak Rep. 48°25N 18°55E 79 C11
Bansko Bulgaria 41°52N 23°28E 96 E7
Banskobystrický □
Slovak Rep. 48°20N 19°0E 79 C12
Banswara India 23°32N 74°24E 124 H6
Bantaeng Indonesia 5°32S 119°56E 119 F5
Bantaji → India 8°6N 10°5E 139 D7
Banteay Prei Nokor
Cambodia 11°56N 105°40E 121 G5
Banten ☐ Indonesia 6°30S 106°0E 119 G11
Bantry Ireland 51°41N 9°27W 64 E2
Bantry B. Ireland 51°37N 9°44W 64 E2
Bantva India 21°29N 70°12E 124 J4
Bantval India 12°55N 75°0E 127 G4
Banya Bulgaria 42°33N 24°50E 97 D8
Banya, Pta. de la Spain 40°33N 0°36E 90 E5
Banyak, Kepulauan
Indonesia 2°10N 97°10E 118 D1
Banyalbufar Spain 39°42N 2°31E 100 B9
Banyeres de Mariola
Spain 38°44N 0°38W 91 G4
Banyoles Spain 42°16N 2°44E 90 C7
Banyuls-sur-Mer France 42°28N 3°8E 72 F7
Banyuwangi Indonesia 8°13S 114°21E 119 J17
Banzare Coast Antarctica 68°0S 125°0E 55 C9
Bao Ha Vietnam 22°11N 104°21E 116 F5
Bao Lac Vietnam 22°57N 105°40E 120 A5
Bao Loc Vietnam 11°32N 107°48E 121 G6
Bao'an China 22°34N 113°52E 111 a
Baocheng China 33°12N 106°56E 116 A5
Baode China 39°1N 111°5E 114 E6
Baodi China 39°38N 117°20E 115 E9
Baoding China 38°50N 115°28E 114 E8
Baokang China 31°54N 111°12E 116 B7
Baoshan Shanghai,
China 31°24N 121°28E 117 B13
Baoshan Yunnan, China 25°10N 99°5E 116 E2
Baotou China 40°32N 110°2E 114 D6
Baoulé → Mali 12°36N 9°45W 138 C3
Baoxing China 30°24N 102°50E 116 B4
Baoying China 33°17N 119°20E 115 H10
Baoyou = Ledong China 18°41N 109°5E 117 a
Bap India 27°23N 72°18E 124 F5
Bapatla India 15°55N 80°30E 127 G5
Bapaume France 50°7N 2°50E 71 B9
Ba'qubah Iraq 33°2N 51°58E 129 C6
Baquedano Chile 23°20S 69°52W 190 A2
Bar Montenegro 42°8N 19°6E 96 D3
Bar Ukraine 49°4N 27°40E 75 D14
Bar Bigha India 25°21N 85°47E 125 G11
Bar Harbor U.S.A. 44°23N 68°13W 173 D19
Bar-le-Duc France 48°47N 5°10E 71 D12
Bar-sur-Aube France 48°14N 4°40E 71 D11
Bar-sur-Seine France 48°7N 4°20E 71 D11
Bara India 25°16N 81°43E 125 G9
Bâra Romania 47°2N 27°3E 81 C12
Bara Banki India 26°55N 81°12E 125 F9
Barabai Indonesia 2°32S 115°34E 118 E5
Baraboo U.S.A. 43°28N 89°45W 172 D9
Baracoa Cuba 20°20N 74°30W 183 B5
Baradá → Syria 33°33N 36°34E 130 B5
Baradero Argentina 33°52S 59°29W 190 C4
Baradine Australia 30°56S 149°4E 153 A8
Baraga U.S.A. 46°47N 88°30W 172 B9
Bărăganul Romania 44°49N 27°31E 81 F12
Baragoi Kenya 1°47N 36°47E 142 B4
Barah → India 25°29N 79°13E 125 G8
Barahona Dom. Rep. 18°13N 71°7W 183 C5
Barail Range India 25°15N 93°20E 123 G18
Barajas, Madrid ✈ (MAD)
Spain 40°26N 3°34W 88 E7
Barakaldo Spain 43°18N 2°59W 90 B2
Barakar → India 24°7N 86°14E 125 G12
Barakee △ Australia 31°37S 151°53E 153 A9
Barakot India 21°33N 84°59E 125 J11
Barakpur India 22°47N 88°21E 125 H13
Baralla Spain 24°13S 149°50E 150 C4
Baralzon L. Canada 60°0N 98°3W 163 B9
Baramati India 18°11N 74°33E 126 F2
Baramba India 20°25N 85°23E 126 D7
Barameiya Sudan 18°32N 36°38E 137 D4
Baramula Pakistan 34°15N 74°20E 126 B3
Baran India 25°9N 76°40E 124 G7
Baran → Pakistan 25°13N 68°17E 124 G3
Barāñain Spain 42°48N 1°40W 90 C3
Baranavichy Belarus 53°10N 26°0E 75 B14
Barani Burkina Faso 13°9N 3°51W 138 C4

Baranof U.S.A. 57°5N 134°50W 162 B2
Baranof I. U.S.A. 57°0N 135°0W 160 F4
Baranów Sandomierski
Poland 50°29N 21°30E 83 H8
Baranya □ Hungary 46°0N 18°15E 80 E3
Barão de Cocais Brazil 19°56S 43°28W 189 C2
Barão de Grajaú Brazil 6°45S 43°1W 189 B2
Baraolt Romania 46°5N 25°34E 81 D10
Baraona Spain 41°17N 2°39W 90 D2
Barapasi Indonesia 2°15S 137°5E 119 E9
Barasat India 22°46N 88°31E 125 H13
Barat Daya, Kepulauan
Indonesia 7°30S 128°0E 119 F7
Baratang I. India 12°13N 92°52E 127 H11
Barataria B. U.S.A. 29°20N 89°55W 177 G10
Barauda India 23°33N 75°15E 124 H6
Baraut India 29°13N 77°7E 124 E7
Barbacena Brazil 21°15S 43°56W 191 A7
Barbados ■ W. Indies 13°10N 59°30W 183 g
Barbalha Brazil 7°19S 39°17W 189 B3
Barban Croatia 45°5N 14°2E 93 C11
Barbária, C. de Spain 38°39N 1°24E 100 C7
Barbaros Turkey 40°54N 27°27E 97 F11
Barbas, C. W. Sahara 22°20N 16°42W 134 D2
Barbastro Spain 42°2N 0°5E 90 C5
Barbate Spain 36°13N 5°56W 89 J5
Barbeau Pk. Canada 81°54N 75°1W 161 A16
Barberino di Mugello
Italy 44°0N 11°15E 93 E8
Barberton S. Africa 25°42S 31°2E 145 C5
Barberton U.S.A. 41°1N 81°39W 174 E3
Barberville U.S.A. 29°11N 81°26W 179 F8
Barbezieux-St-Hilaire
France 45°28N 0°9W 72 C3
Barbosa Colombia 5°57N 73°37W 186 B4
Barbourville U.S.A. 36°52N 83°53W 173 G12
Barbuda W. Indies 17°30N 61°40W 183 C7
Bârca Romania 43°59N 23°36E 81 G8
Barcaldine Australia 23°43S 145°6E 150 C4
Barcarrota Spain 38°31N 6°51W 89 G4
Barcellona Pozzo di Gotto
Italy 38°9N 15°13E 95 D8
Barcelona Spain 41°22N 2°10E 90 D7
Barcelona Venezuela 10°10N 64°40W 186 A6
Barcelona □ Spain 41°30N 2°0E 90 D7
Barcelona ✈ (BCN) Spain 41°18N 2°5E 90 D7
Barceloneta Puerto Rico 18°27N 66°32W 183 d
Barcelonnette France 44°23N 6°40E 73 D10
Barcelos Brazil 1°0S 63°0W 186 D6
Barcin Poland 52°52N 17°55E 83 E9
Barclayville Liberia 4°48N 8°10W 138 E3
Barcoo → Australia 25°30S 142°50E 150 D3
Barcs Hungary 45°58N 17°28E 80 F2
Barczewo Poland 53°50N 20°42E 82 E7
Bârda Azerbaijan 40°25N 47°10E 87 K8
Barda del Medio
Argentina 38°45S 68°11W 192 A3
Bardaï Chad 21°27N 17°0E 135 D9
Bardas Blancas
Argentina 35°49S 69°45W 190 D2
Bardawîl, Sabkhet el
Egypt 31°10N 33°15E 130 D2
Barddhaman India 23°14N 87°39E 125 H12
Bardejov Slovak Rep. 49°18N 21°15E 79 B14
Bardera = Baardheere
Somalia 2°0N 42°27E 131 G3
Bardi Italy 44°38N 9°44E 92 D6
Bardīyah Libya 31°45N 25°5E 135 B10
Bardoli India 21°12N 73°5E 126 D1
Bardolino Italy 45°33N 10°43E 92 C7
Bardonécchia Italy 45°5N 6°42E 92 C3
Bardsey I. U.K. 52°45N 4°47W 66 E3
Bardstown U.S.A. 37°49N 85°28W 173 G11
Bareilly India 28°22N 79°27E 125 E8
Barela India 23°6N 80°3E 125 H9
Barellan Australia 34°16S 146°24E 153 E7
Barentin France 49°33N 0°58E 70 C7
Barenton France 48°38N 0°50W 70 D5
Barents Sea Arctic 73°0N 39°0E 54 B9
Barentsburg Svalbard 78°25N 21°20E 57 B13
Barfleur France 49°40N 1°17W 70 C5
Barfleur, Pte. de France 49°42N 1°16W 70 C5
Barga Italy 44°4N 10°29E 92 D7
Bargara Australia 24°50S 152°25E 150 C5
Bargarh India 21°20N 83°37E 126 D6
Bargas Spain 39°56N 4°3W 88 F6
Barge, La India 44°43N 7°20E 92 D4
Bargi Dam India 22°59N 80°0E 126 B7
Bargteheide Germany 53°44N 10°14E 76 B6
Barguzin Russia 53°37N 109°37E 107 D11
Barh India 25°29N 85°46E 125 G11
Barhaj India 26°18N 83°44E 125 F10
Barharwa India 24°52N 87°47E 125 G12
Barhi India 24°15N 85°25E 125 G11
Bari India 26°39N 77°39E 124 F7
Bari Italy 41°8N 16°51E 95 A9
Bari Doab Pakistan 30°20N 73°0E 124 D5
Bari Sadri India 24°28N 74°30E 124 G6
Baridi, Ra's Si. Arabia 24°17N 37°31E 128 E3
Barīm Yemen 12°39N 43°25E 132 E8
Barinas Venezuela 8°36N 70°15W 186 B4
Baring, C. Canada 70°0N 117°30W 160 D8
Baring, L. Kenya 0°47N 36°16E 142 B4
Barisal Bangla. 22°45N 90°20E 123 H17
Barisal □ Bangla. 22°45N 90°20E 123 H17
Barisan, Pegunungan
Indonesia 3°30S 102°15E 118 E2
Barito → Indonesia 4°0S 114°50E 118 E4
Baritú △ Argentina 23°43S 64°40W 190 A3
Barjac France 44°20N 4°22E 73 D8
Barjols France 43°34N 6°2E 73 E10
Barjūj, Wadi → Libya 25°26N 12°12E 135 C8
Bark L. Canada 45°27N 77°51W 174 A7
Barkakana India 23°37N 85°29E 125 H11
Barkal J. Sudan 18°32N 31°50E 137 D3
Barkam China 31°51N 102°28E 116 B4
Barker U.S.A. 43°20N 78°33W 174 C6
Barkley, L. U.S.A. 37°1N 88°14W 177 C10
Barkley Sound
Canada 48°50N 125°10W 162 D3
Barkly East S. Africa 30°58S 27°33E 144 D4
Barkly Homestead
Australia 19°52S 135°50E 150 B2
Barkly Tableland
Australia 17°50S 136°40E 150 B2
Barkly West S. Africa 28°5S 24°31E 144 C3

Barkol Kazak Zizhixian
China 43°37N 93°2E 110 C7
Bala Dağı Turkey 38°5N 30°40E 99 C12
Bârlad Romania 46°15N 27°38E 81 D12
Bârlad → Romania 45°38N 27°32E 81 E12
Barlee, L. Australia 29°15S 119°30E 149 E2
Barlee, Mt. Australia 24°38S 128°13E 149 D4
Barletta Italy 41°19N 16°17E 95 A9
Barlinek Poland 53°0N 15°15E 83 F2
Barlovento Canary Is. 28°48N 17°48W 100 F2
Barlovento C. Verde Is. 17°0N 25°0W 134 b
Barlow L. Canada 62°0N 103°0W 163 A8
Barmedman Australia 34°9S 147°21E 153 C7
Barmer India 25°45N 71°20E 124 G4
Barmera Australia 34°15S 140°28E 152 C4
Barmouth U.K. 52°44N 4°4W 66 E3
Barmstedt Germany 53°47N 9°46E 76 B5
Barna → India 25°21N 83°3E 125 G10
Barnagar India 23°7N 75°19E 124 H6
Barnala India 30°23N 75°33E 124 D6
Barnard → Australia 31°34S 151°25E 153 A9
Barnard Castle U.K. 54°33N 1°55W 66 C6
Barnato Australia 31°38S 145°0E 153 A6
Barnaul Russia 53°20N 83°40E 109 D10
Barnes Australia 36°2S 144°49E 152 D6
Barnesville Ga., U.S.A. 33°3N 84°9W 178 B5
Barnesville Minn.,
U.S.A. 46°43N 96°28W 172 B5
Barnet □ U.K. 51°38N 0°9W 67 F7
Barneveld Neths. 52°7N 5°36E 69 B5
Barneville-Cartevert
France 49°23N 1°46W 70 C5
Barnhart U.S.A. 31°8N 101°10W 176 F4
Barnsley U.K. 53°34N 1°27W 66 D6
Barnstable U.S.A. 41°42N 70°18W 173 E18
Barnstaple U.K. 51°5N 4°4W 67 F3
Barnstaple Bay = Bideford Bay
U.K. 51°5N 4°20W 67 F3
Barnwell U.S.A. 33°15N 81°23W 178 B6
Baro Nigeria 8°35N 6°18E 139 D6
Baroda = Vadodara
India 22°20N 73°10E 124 H5
Baroda India 25°29N 76°35E 124 G7
Baroe S. Africa 33°13S 24°33E 144 D3
Baron Ra. Australia 23°30S 127°45E 148 D4
Barong China 31°3N 99°20E 116 B2
Barotseland Zambia 15°0S 24°0E 141 H4
Barouéli Mali 13°4N 6°50W 138 C3
Barpali India 21°11N 83°35E 126 D6
Barpeta India 26°20N 91°10E 123 F17
Barqa Libya 27°0N 23°0E 135 C10
Barques, Pt. Aux U.S.A. 44°4N 82°58W 174 D2
Barquísimeto Venezuela 10°4N 69°19W 186 A5
Barr, Ras el Egypt 31°32N 31°50E 137 E7
Barr Smith Range
Australia 27°4S 120°20E 149 E3
Barra Brazil 11°5S 43°10W 189 C2
Barra Gambia 13°28N 16°32W 138 C1
Barra U.K. 57°0N 7°29W 65 E1
Barra, Sd. of U.K. 57°4N 7°25W 65 D1
Barra da Estiva Brazil 13°38S 41°19W 189 C2
Barra de Navidad
Mexico 19°12N 104°41W 180 D4
Barra do Corda Brazil 5°30S 45°10W 189 B1
Barra do Garças Brazil 15°54S 52°16W 187 G8
Barra do Mendes Brazil 11°43S 42°4W 189 C2
Barra do Pirai Brazil 22°30S 43°50W 191 A7
Barra Falsa, Pta. da
Mozam. 22°58S 35°37E 145 B6
Barra Hd. U.K. 56°47N 7°40W 65 E1
Barra Mansa Brazil 22°35S 44°12W 191 A7
Barraba Australia 30°21S 150°35E 153 A9
Barrackpur = Barakpur
India 22°47N 88°21E 125 H13
Barrafranca Italy 37°22N 14°12E 95 E7
Barrãmīya Egypt 25°3N 33°47E 137 B3
Barranca Lima, Peru 10°45S 77°50W 188 C2
Barranca Loreto, Peru 4°50S 76°50W 186 D3
Barrancabermeja
Colombia 7°0N 73°50W 186 B4
Barrancas Venezuela 8°55N 62°5W 186 B6
Barrancos Portugal 38°10N 6°58W 89 G3
Barranqueras Argentina 27°30S 59°0W 190 B4
Barranquilla Colombia 11°0N 74°50W 186 A4
Barras Brazil 4°15S 42°18W 189 B2
Barraute Canada 48°26N 77°38W 164 C4
Barre Mass., U.S.A. 42°25N 72°6W 175 D12
Barre Vt., U.S.A. 44°12N 72°30W 175 B12
Barreal Argentina 31°33S 69°28W 190 C2
Barreiras Brazil 12°8S 45°0W 189 C2
Barreirinhas Brazil 2°30S 42°50W 189 A2
Barreiro Portugal 38°39N 9°5W 89 G1
Barreiros Brazil 8°49S 35°12W 189 B3
Barrême France 43°57N 6°23E 73 E10
Barren, Nosy Madag. 18°25S 43°40E 141 H8
Barren I. India 12°16N 93°51E 127 H11
Barretos Brazil 20°30S 48°35W 189 E1
Barrhead Canada 54°10N 114°24W 162 C6
Barrie Canada 44°24N 79°40W 174 B5
Barrier, C. N.Z. 36°25S 175°32E 154 C4
Barrier Ra. Australia 31°0S 141°30E 152 A4
Barrier Ra. Otago, N.Z. 44°15S 169°32E 155 E4
Barrier Ra. W. Coast,
N.Z. 44°30S 168°30E 155 E3
Barrière Canada 51°12N 120°7W 162 C4
Barrineau Park U.S.A. 30°42N 87°26W 179 E2
Barrington U.S.A. 41°44N 71°18W 175 E13
Barrington L. Canada 56°55N 100°15W 163 B8
Barrington Tops
Australia 32°6S 151°28E 153 B9
Barrington Tops △
Australia 32°4S 151°25E 153 B9
Barringun Australia 29°1S 145°41E 151 D4
Barron U.S.A. 45°24N 91°51W 172 C8
Barrow → Ireland 52°25N 6°58W 64 D5
Barrow, Pt. U.S.A. 71°23N 156°29W 166 A4
Barrow Creek
Australia 21°30S 133°55E 150 C1
Barrow I. Australia 20°45S 115°20E 148 D2
Barrow-in-Furness U.K. 54°7N 3°14W 66 C4
Barrow Pt. Australia 14°20S 144°40E 150 A3
Barrow Ra. Australia 26°0S 127°40E 149 E4
Barrow Str. Canada 74°20N 95°0W 161 C10
Barry U.K. 51°24N 3°16W 67 F4
Barry's Bay Canada 45°29N 77°41W 174 A7

Barsalogho Burkina Faso 13°25N 1°3W 139 C4
Barsat Pakistan 36°10N 72°45E 125 A5
Barsham Syria 35°21N 40°33E 105 E9
Barshatas Kazakhstan 48°10N 78°39E 109 E9
Barsi India 18°10N 75°50E 126 E2
Barsinghausen Germany 52°18N 9°28E 76 C5
Barsoi India 25°48N 87°57E 123 G15
Barstow U.S.A. 34°54N 117°1N 171 L9
Barth Germany 54°22N 12°42E 76 A8
Bartica Guyana 6°25N 58°40W 186 B7
Bartin Turkey 41°38N 32°21E 104 B5
Bartle Frere Australia 17°27S 145°50E 150 B4
Bartlesville U.S.A. 36°45N 95°59W 176 C6
Bartlett Calif., U.S.A. 36°29N 118°2W 170 J8
Bartlett Tenn., U.S.A. 35°12N 89°52W 177 D10
Bartlett, L. Canada 63°5N 118°20W 162 A5
Bartolomeu Dias
Mozam. 21°10S 35°8E 143 G4
Barton U.S.A. 44°45N 72°11W 175 B12
Barton upon Humber
U.K. 53°41N 0°25W 66 D7
Bartoszyce Poland 54°15N 20°55E 82 D7
Bartow Fla., U.S.A. 27°54N 81°50W 179 H8
Bartow Ga., U.S.A. 32°53N 82°29W 178 C6
Barú, Volcan Panama 8°55N 82°35W 182 E3
Barumba
Dem. Rep. of the Congo 1°3N 23°37E 142 B1
Barúmini Italy 39°42N 8°59E 94 C1
Barung, Nusa
Indonesia 8°30S 113°30E 119 H15
Baruth Germany 52°4N 13°30E 76 C9
Baruun Urt Mongolia 46°46N 113°15E 111 B11
Baruunsuu Mongolia 43°43N 105°35E 114 C3
Barwani India 22°2N 74°57E 124 H6
Barwice Poland 53°44N 16°21E 82 E3
Barwick → Australia 30°0S 148°5E 153 A8
Barxudarlı Azerbaijan 41°0N 45°14E 105 B11
Barycz → Poland 51°42N 16°15E 83 G3
Barysaw Belarus 54°17N 28°28E 75 A15
Barysh Russia 53°39N 47°8E 86 D8
Barzán Iraq 36°55N 44°3E 128 B5
Bârzava Romania 46°7N 21°59E 80 D6
Bas-Rhin □ France 48°40N 7°30E 71 D14
Bas-Sassandra □ Ivory C. 5°30N 7°0W 138 D3
Bašaid Serbia 45°38N 20°25E 80 E5
Bāsa'idū Iran 26°35N 55°20E 129 E7
Basal Pakistan 33°33N 72°13E 124 C5
Basankusa
Dem. Rep. of the Congo 1°5N 19°50E 140 D3
Basarabeasca Moldova 46°21N 28°58E 81 D13
Basarabi Romania 44°10N 28°26E 81 F13
Basarabia = Bessarabia
Moldova 47°0N 28°10E 75 E15
Basauri Spain 43°13N 2°53W 90 B2
Basawa Afghan. 34°15N 70°50E 124 B4
Bascuñán, C. Chile 28°52S 71°35W 190 B1
Basel Switz. 47°35N 7°35E 77 H3
Basel Euroairport ✈ (EAP)
France 47°36N 7°33E 71 E14
Basel-Landschaft □
Switz. 47°26N 7°45E 77 H3
Basento → Italy 40°20N 16°49E 95 B9
Bashäkerd, Kühhä-ye
Iran 26°42N 58°35E 129 E8
Bashaw Canada 52°35N 112°58W 162 C6
Bāshī Iran 28°41N 51°4E 129 D6
Bashkir Republic =
Bashkortostan □
Russia 54°0N 57°0E 108 D9
Bashkiria △ Russia 52°58N 56°30E 108 D5
Bashkortostan □ Russia 54°0N 57°0E 108 D5
Bashtanivka Ukraine 45°46N 29°29E 81 E14
Basilan I. Phil. 6°35N 122°0E 119 C6
Basilan Str. Phil. 6°50N 122°0E 119 C6
Basildon U.K. 51°34N 0°28E 67 F8
Basilé Eq. Guin. 3°42N 8°48E 139 E6
Basilé, Pico de Eq. Guin. 3°36N 8°49E 139 E6
Basilicata □ Italy 40°30N 16°30E 95 B9
Basim = Washim India 20°3N 77°0E 126 D3
Basin U.S.A. 44°23N 108°2W 168 D9
Basinger U.S.A. 27°23N 81°2W 179 H8
Basingstoke U.K. 51°15N 1°5W 67 F6
Baška Croatia 44°58N 14°45E 93 D11
Baškale Turkey 38°28N 43°58E 95 B7
Baskatong, Rés.
Canada 46°46N 75°50W 164 C4
Basle = Basel Switz. 47°35N 7°35E 77 H3
Başmakçı Turkey 37°54N 30°1E 99 D12
Basmat India 19°15N 77°12E 126 E3
Basoda India 23°52N 77°54E 124 H7
Basoko
Dem. Rep. of the Congo 1°16N 23°40E 142 B1
Basque, Côte France 43°30N 2°0W 72 E2
Basque, Pays France 43°15N 1°20W 72 E2
Basque Provinces = País Vasco □
Spain 42°50N 2°45W 90 C2
Basra = Al Başrah Iraq 30°30N 47°50E 128 D5
Bass Str. Australia 39°15S 146°30E 151 F4
Bassano Greece 37°26N 21°53E 98 D3
Bassano Canada 50°48N 112°20W 162 C6
Bassano del Grappa
Italy 45°46N 11°44E 93 C8
Bassar Togo 9°19N 0°57E 139 D5
Bassas da India Ind. Oc. 22°0S 39°0E 143 G4
Basse-Normandie □
France 48°45N 0°30W 70 D6
Basse-Pointe Martinique 14°52N 61°8W 182 c
Basse Santa-Su
Gambia 13°13N 14°15W 138 C2
Basse-Terre Guadeloupe 16°0N 61°44W 182 b
Basse Terre Trin. & Tob. 10°7N 61°19W 187 K15
Bassein Burma 16°45N 94°30E 123 L19
Basses, Pte. des
Guadeloupe 15°52N 61°17W 182 b
Basseterre
St. Kitts & Nevis 17°17N 62°43W 183 C7
Bassett U.S.A. 42°35N 99°32W 172 D4
Bassi India 30°44N 76°21E 126 D7
Bassigny France 48°0N 5°10E 71 E12
Bassikounou Mauritania 15°55N 6°1W 138 C3
Bassila Benin 9°1N 1°46E 139 D5
Bassum Germany 52°50N 8°40E 76 C4
Bastak Iran 27°15N 54°25E 129 E7
Bastām Iran 36°29N 55°4E 129 B7
Bastar India 19°15N 81°40E 126 E5
Basti India 26°52N 82°55E 125 F10
Bastelica France 42°1N 9°3E 73 F13
Basti France 42°40N 9°30E 73 F13
Bastogne Belgium 50°1N 5°43E 69 D5
Bastrop La., U.S.A. 32°47N 91°55W 176 E9
Bastrop Tex., U.S.A. 30°7N 97°19W 176 F6
Basuo = Dongfang
China 18°50N 108°33E 117 a
Basuto
Dem. Rep. of the Congo 0°58N 26°33E 142 B2
Batamay Russia 63°30N 129°15E 107 C13
Batang China 30°1N 99°0E 116 B2
Batang Indonesia 6°55S 109°45E 119 G13
Batangafo C.A.R. 7°25N 18°20E 140 C3
Batangas Phil. 13°35N 121°10E 119 B6
Batanta Indonesia 0°55S 130°40E 119 E8
Bataais Brazil 20°54S 47°37W 191 A6
Batavia = Jakarta
Indonesia 6°9S 106°49E 119 G12
Batavia U.S.A. 43°0N 78°11W 174 D6
Bataysk Russia 47°3N 39°45E 85 J10
Batchelor Australia 13°4S 131°1E 148 B5
Batdambang Cambodia 13°7N 103°12E 120 F4
Batemans B. Australia 35°40S 150°12E 153 C9
Batemans Bay
Australia 35°44S 150°11E 153 C9
Batesburg-Leesville
U.S.A. 33°54N 81°33W 178 B6
Batesville Ark., U.S.A. 35°46N 91°39W 176 D9
Batesville Miss.,
U.S.A. 34°19N 89°57W 177 D10
Batesville Tex., U.S.A. 28°58N 99°37W 176 G5
Bath Canada 44°11N 76°47W 175 B8
Bath U.K. 51°23N 2°22W 67 F5
Bath Maine, U.S.A. 43°55N 69°49W 173 D19
Bath N.Y., U.S.A. 42°20N 77°19W 174 D7
Bath & North East Somerset □
U.K. 51°21N 2°27W 67 F5
Batheay Cambodia 11°59N 104°57E 121 G5
Bathsheba Barbados 13°13N 59°32W 183 g
Bathurst Australia 33°25S 149°31E 153 B8
Bathurst Canada 47°37N 65°43W 165 C6
Bathurst S. Africa 33°30S 26°50E 144 D4
Bathurst B. Australia 14°16S 144°25E 150 A3
Bathurst Harb.
Australia 43°15S 146°10E 151 G4
Bathurst I. Australia 11°30S 130°10E 148 B5
Bathurst I. Canada 76°0N 100°30W 161 B11
Bathurst Inlet Canada 66°50N 108°1W 160 D10
Batie Burkina Faso 9°53N 2°53W 138 D4
Batiki Fiji 17°48S 179°10E 154 a
Batken Kyrgyzstan 40°3N 70°50E 109 D8
Batken □ Kyrgyzstan 39°50N 71°0E 109 E8
Batlow Australia 35°31S 148°9E 153 C8
Batman Turkey 37°55N 41°5E 105 D9
Batn al Ghül Jordan 29°36N 35°56E 130 F4
Batna Algeria 35°34N 6°15E 136 A5
Batna □ Algeria 35°30N 5°55E 136 A5
Batočina Serbia 44°7N 21°5E 81 F10
Batoka Zambia 16°45S 27°15E 143 F2
Baton Rouge U.S.A. 30°27N 91°11W 176 F9
Batong, Ko Thailand 6°32N 99°12E 121 J2
Bátonyterenye Hungary 47°59N 19°50E 80 C4
Batopilas Mexico 27°1N 107°44W 180 B3
Batouri Cameroon 4°30N 14°25E 140 D2
Båtsfjord Norway 70°38N 29°39E 60 A23
Batsi Greece 37°52N 24°47E 98 D6
Battambang = Batdambang
Cambodia 13°7N 103°12E 120 F4
Batti Malv India 8°50N 92°51E 127 K11
Batticaloa Sri Lanka 7°43N 81°45E 127 L5
Battipáglia Italy 40°37N 14°58E 95 B7
Battle U.K. 50°55N 0°30E 67 G8
Battle → Canada 52°43N 108°15W 162 C7
Battle Creek U.S.A. 42°19N 85°11W 173 D11
Battle Ground U.S.A. 45°47N 122°32W 170 E4
Battle Harbour Canada 52°16N 55°35W 165 B8
Battle Lake U.S.A. 46°17N 95°43W 172 B6
Battle Mountain
U.S.A. 40°38N 116°56W 168 F5
Battlefields Zimbabwe 18°37S 29°47E 143 F2
Battleford Canada 52°45N 108°15W 163 C7
Battonya Hungary 46°16N 21°3E 80 D6
Batu Ethiopia 6°55N 39°45E 131 F2
Batu Malaysia 3°15N 101°40E 121 L3
Batu, Kepulauan
Indonesia 0°30S 98°25E 118 E1
Batu Ferringhi Malaysia 5°28N 100°15E 121 c
Batu Gajah Malaysia 4°28N 101°3E 121 K3
Batu Is. = Batu, Kepulauan
Indonesia 0°30S 98°25E 118 E1
Batu Pahat Malaysia 1°50N 102°56E 121 M4
Batu Puteh, Gunung
Malaysia 4°15N 101°31E 121 K3
Batuata Indonesia 6°12S 122°42E 119 F6
Batugondang, Tanjung
Indonesia 8°14S 115°23E 119 J17
Batukaru, Gunung
Indonesia 8°14S 115°23E 119 J17
Batumi Georgia 41°30N 41°44E 87 K5
Batur, Gunung
Indonesia 8°14S 115°22E 119 J18
Batura Sar Pakistan 36°30N 74°31E 125 A6
Baturaja Indonesia 4°11S 104°15E 118 E2
Baturité Brazil 4°28S 38°45W 189 A3
Batys Qazaqstan □
Kazakhstan 50°0N 50°0E 108 D4
Bau Malaysia 1°25N 110°9E 118 D4
Baubau Indonesia 5°25S 122°38E 119 F6
Baucau E. Timor 8°27S 126°27E 119 F7
Bauchi Nigeria 10°22N 9°48E 139 C6
Bauchi □ Nigeria 10°30N 10°0E 139 C6
Baud France 47°52N 3°1W 70 E3
Bauda India 20°50N 84°25E 126 D7
Baudette U.S.A. 48°43N 94°36W 172 A6
Bauer, C. Australia 32°44S 134°4E 151 E1
Bauhinia Australia 24°35S 149°18E 150 C4
Baukau = Baucau
E. Timor 8°27S 126°27E 119 F7
Bauld, C. Canada 51°38N 55°26W 165 B8

Baume-les-Dames
France 47°22N 6°22E 71 E13
Baunatal Germany 51°14N 9°24E 76 D5
Baunei Italy 40°2N 9°40E 94 B2
Baure Nigeria 12°52N 8°50E 139 C6
Bauru Brazil 22°10S 49°0W 191 A6
Bausi India 24°48N 87°1E 125 G12
Bauska Latvia 56°24N 24°15E 82 B11
Bautino Kazakhstan 44°35N 50°14E 87 H10
Bautzen Germany 51°10N 14°26E 76 D10
Bauya S. Leone 8°12N 12°38W 138 D2
Bavānāt Iran 30°28N 53°27E 129 D7
Bavānište Serbia 44°49N 20°55E 80 F5
Bavaria = Bayern □
Germany 48°50N 12°0E 77 G7
Båven Sweden 59°0N 16°56E 62 E10
Bavispe → Mexico 29°30N 109°11W 180 B3
Baw Baw △ Australia 37°50S 146°17E 153 D7
Bawdwin Burma 23°5N 97°20E 123 H20
Bawean Indonesia 5°46S 112°35E 118 F4
Bawku Ghana 11°3N 0°19W 139 C4
Bawlakhe Burma 19°11N 97°21E 123 K20
Bawolung China 28°50N 101°16E 116 C3
Baxley U.S.A. 31°47N 82°21W 178 D7
Baxter U.S.A. 46°21N 94°17W 172 B6
Baxter Springs U.S.A. 37°2N 94°44W 176 C7
Baxter State △ U.S.A. 46°5N 68°57W 173 B19
Bay City Mich., U.S.A. 43°36N 83°54W 173 D12
Bay City Tex., U.S.A. 28°59N 95°58E 176 G7
Bay Minette U.S.A. 30°53N 87°46W 177 F11
Bay of Plenty □ N.Z. 38°0S 177°10E 154 C5
Bay Roberts Canada 47°36S 53°16W 165 C9
Bay St. Louis U.S.A. 30°19N 89°20W 177 F10
Bay Springs U.S.A. 31°59N 89°17W 177 F10
Bay View N.Z. 39°25S 176°50E 154 C5
Baya
Dem. Rep. of the Congo 11°53S 27°25E 143 E2
Bayamo Cuba 20°20N 76°40W 182 B4
Bayamón Puerto Rico 18°24N 66°9W 183 d
Bayan Har Shan China 34°0N 98°0E 110 E8
Bayan Hot = Alxa Zuoqi
China 38°50N 105°40E 114 E3
Bayan Lepas Malaysia 5°17N 100°16E 121 c
Bayan Obo China 41°52N 109°59E 114 D5
Bayan-Ovoo = Erdenetsogt
Mongolia 42°55N 106°5E 114 C4
Bayana India 26°55N 77°18E 124 F7
Bayanaüyl Kazakhstan 50°45N 75°45E 109 B9
Bayanhongor Mongolia 46°8N 102°43E 110 B9
Bayard N. Mex., U.S.A. 32°46N 108°8W 169 K9
Bayard Nebr., U.S.A. 41°45N 103°20W 172 E2
Baybay Phil. 10°40N 124°55E 119 B6
Bayburt Turkey 40°15N 40°20E 105 B9
Bayburt □ Turkey 40°15N 40°20E 105 B9
Baydaratskaya Guba
Russia 69°0N 67°30E 106 C7
Baydhabo Somalia 3°8N 43°30E 131 G3
Bayelsa □ Nigeria 4°30N 6°0E 139 E6
Bayerische Alpen
Germany 47°35N 11°30E 77 H7
Bayerische Rhön △
Germany 50°15N 10°5E 77 E6
Bayerischer Spessart △
Germany 49°58N 10°15E 77 F6
Bayerischer Wald
Germany 48°56N 12°50E 77 G8
Bayern □ Germany 48°50N 12°0E 77 G7
Bayeux France 49°17N 0°42W 70 C6
Bayfield Canada 43°34N 81°42W 174 C3
Bayfield U.S.A. 46°49N 90°49W 172 B8
Bayındır Turkey 38°13N 27°39E 99 C9
Baykal, Oz. Russia 53°0N 108°0E 107 D11
Baykan Turkey 38°7N 41°44E 105 C9
Baymak Russia 52°36N 58°19E 108 D9
Baynes Mts. Namibia 17°15S 13°0E 144 A1
Bayombong Phil. 16°30N 121°10E 119 A6
Bayon France 48°30N 6°20E 71 D13
Bayona = Baiona Spain 42°6N 8°52W 88 C2
Bayonet Point U.S.A. 28°20N 82°41W 179 G7
Bayonne France 43°30N 1°28W 72 E2
Bayonne U.S.A. 40°40N 74°6W 175 F10
Bayovar Peru 5°50S 81°0W 188 B1
Bayport U.S.A. 28°32N 82°39W 179 G7
Bayqongyr Kazakhstan 45°40N 63°20E 108 C6
Bayram-Ali = Bayramaly
Turkmenistan 37°37N 62°10E 129 B9
Bayramaly
Turkmenistan 37°37N 62°10E 129 B9
Bayramiç Turkey 39°48N 26°36E 99 B8
Bayreuth Germany 49°56N 11°35E 77 F7
Bayrischzell Germany 47°41N 12°0E 77 H8
Bayrūt Lebanon 33°53N 35°31E 130 B4
Bays, L. of Canada 45°15N 79°4W 174 A5
Bayshore U.S.A. 26°43N 81°50W 179 J8
Baysville Canada 45°9N 79°7W 174 A5
Bayt Lahm West Bank 31°43N 35°12E 130 D4
Baytik Shan China 45°30N 90°50E 109 C12
Baytown U.S.A. 29°43N 94°59W 176 G7
Bayuquan China 40°16N 122°8E 115 D12
Bayzo Niger 13°52N 4°35E 139 C5
Baza Spain 37°30N 2°47W 89 H8
Bazar Dyuzi Russia 41°12N 47°50E 87 K8
Bazardüzü = Bazar Dyuzi
Russia 41°12N 47°50E 87 K8
Bāzārgān Iran 39°22N 44°26E 105 C11
Bazarny Karabulak
Russia 52°20N 46°29E 86 D8
Bazaruto, I. do Mozam. 21°40S 35°28E 145 B6
Bazaruto △ Mozam. 21°42S 35°26E 145 B6
Bazas France 44°27N 0°13W 72 D3
Bazhong China 31°52N 106°46E 116 B6
Bazmān, Kūh-e Iran 28°4N 60°1E 129 D9
Beach U.S.A. 46°58N 104°0W 172 B2
Beach City U.S.A. 40°39N 81°35W 174 F2
Beachport Australia 37°29S 140°0E 152 D3
Beachville Canada 43°5N 80°49W 174 C4
Beachy Hd. U.K. 50°44N 0°15E 67 G8
Beacon Australia 30°26S 117°52E 149 F2
Beacon U.S.A. 41°30N 73°58W 175 E11
Beaconsfield Australia 41°11S 146°48E 151 G4
Beagle, Canal S. Amer. 55°0S 68°30W 192 F3
Beagle Bay Australia 16°58S 122°40E 148 C3
Beagle Bay → Australia 14°33S 120°40E 148 C3
Beagle G. Australia 12°15S 130°25E 148 B5
Béal an Átha = Ballina
Ireland 54°7N 9°9W 64 B2

Béal Átha na Sluaighe =
  Ballinasloe Ireland 53°20N 8°13W 64 C3
Beals Cr. → U.S.A. 32°10N 100°51W 176 E4
Beamsville Canada 43°12N 79°28W 174 C5
Bear → Calif., U.S.A. 38°56N 121°36W 170 G5
Bear → Wash., U.S.A. 41°30N 112°8W 166 G17
Béar, C. France 42°31N 3°8E 72 F7
Bear I. Ireland 51°38N 9°50W 64 E2
Bear L. Canada 55°8N 96°0W 163 B9
Bear L. U.S.A. 41°59N 111°21W 168 F8
Bear Lake Canada 45°27N 79°35W 174 A5
Beardmore Canada 49°36N 87°57W 164 C2
Beardmore Glacier
  Antarctica 84°30S 170°0E 55 E11
Beardstown U.S.A. 40°1N 90°26W 172 E8
Bearma → India 24°20N 79°51E 125 G8
Béarn France 43°20N 0°30W 72 E3
Bearpaw Mts. U.S.A. 48°12N 109°30W 168 B9
Bearskin Lake Canada 53°58N 91°2W 164 B1
Beas → India 31°10N 74°59E 124 D6
Beas de Segura Spain 38°15N 2°53W 89 G8
Beasain Spain 43°3N 2°11W 90 B2
Beata, C. Dom. Rep. 17°40N 71°30W 183 C5
Beata, I. Dom. Rep. 17°34N 71°31W 183 C5
Beatrice Zimbabwe 18°15S 30°55E 143 F3
Beatrice U.S.A. 40°16N 96°45W 172 E5
Beatrice, C. Australia 14°20S 136°55E 150 A2
Beatton → Canada 56°15N 120°45W 162 B4
Beatton River Canada 57°26N 121°20W 162 B4
Beatty U.S.A. 36°54N 116°46W 170 J10
Beau Bassin Mauritius 20°13S 57°27E 141 d
Beaucaire France 43°48N 4°39E 73 E8
Beauce, Plaine de la
  France 48°10N 1°45E 71 D8
Beauceville Canada 46°13N 70°46W 165 C5
Beauchêne, I. Falk. Is. 52°55S 59°15W 192 D5
Beaudesert Australia 27°59S 153°0E 151 D5
Beaufort Australia 37°25S 143°25E 152 C5
Beaufort France 45°44N 6°34E 73 C10
Beaufort Malaysia 5°30N 115°40E 118 C5
Beaufort N.C., U.S.A. 34°43N 76°40W 177 D16
Beaufort S.C., U.S.A. 32°26N 80°40W 178 C9
Beaufort Sea Arctic 72°0N 140°0W 158 B5
Beaufort West S. Africa 32°18S 22°36E 144 D3
Beaugency France 47°47N 1°38E 71 E8
Beauharnois Canada 45°20N 73°52W 175 A11
Beaujeu France 46°10N 4°35E 71 F11
Beaujolais France 46°0N 4°22E 71 F11
Beaulieu → Canada 62°3N 113°11W 162 A6
Beaulieu-sur-Dordogne
  France 44°58N 1°50E 72 D5
Beaulieu-sur-Mer
  France 43°42N 7°20E 73 E11
Beauly U.K. 57°30N 4°28W 65 D4
Beauly → U.K. 57°29N 4°27W 65 D4
Beaumaris U.K. 53°16N 4°6W 66 D3
Beaumont Belgium 50°15N 4°14E 69 D4
Beaumont N.Z. 45°50S 169°33E 155 F4
Beaumont Calif.,
  U.S.A. 33°57N 116°59W 171 M9
Beaumont Tex., U.S.A. 30°5N 94°6W 176 F7
Beaumont-de-Lomagne
  France 43°53N 1°0E 72 E5
Beaumont-du-Périgord
  France 44°45N 0°46E 72 D4
Beaumont-le-Roger
  France 49°4N 0°47E 70 C7
Beaumont-sur-Sarthe
  France 48°13N 0°8E 70 D7
Beaune France 47°2N 4°50E 71 E11
Beaune-la-Rolande France 48°4N 2°25E 71 D9
Beaupré Canada 47°3N 70°54W 165 C5
Beaupréau France 47°12N 1°0W 70 E6
Beauraing Belgium 50°7N 4°57E 69 D4
Beaurepaire France 45°22N 5°1E 73 C9
Beausejour Canada 50°5N 96°35W 163 C9
Beauvais France 49°25N 2°8E 71 C9
Beauval Canada 55°9N 107°37W 163 B7
Beauvoir-sur-Mer France 46°55N 2°2W 70 F4
Beauvoir-sur-Niort
  France 46°12N 0°30W 72 B3
Beaver Okla., U.S.A. 36°49N 100°31W 176 C4
Beaver Pa., U.S.A. 40°42N 80°19W 174 F4
Beaver Utah, U.S.A. 38°17N 112°38W 168 G7
Beaver → B.C.,
  Canada 59°52N 124°20W 162 B4
Beaver → Ont., Canada 55°55N 87°48W 164 A2
Beaver → Sask.,
  Canada 55°26N 107°45W 163 B7
Beaver → U.S.A. 36°35N 99°30W 176 C5
Beaver City U.S.A. 40°8N 99°50W 172 E4
Beaver Creek Canada 63°0N 141°0W 160 E3
Beaver Dam U.S.A. 43°28N 88°50W 172 D9
Beaver Falls U.S.A. 40°46N 80°20W 174 F4
Beaver Hill L. Canada 54°5N 94°50W 163 C10
Beaver I. U.S.A. 45°40N 85°33W 173 C11
Beaverhill L. Canada 53°27N 112°32W 162 C6
Beaverlodge Canada 55°11N 119°29W 162 B5
Beaverstone →
  Canada 54°59N 89°25W 164 B2
Beaverton Canada 44°26N 79°9W 174 B5
Beaverton U.S.A. 45°29N 122°48W 174 D4
Beawar India 26°3N 74°18E 124 F6
Bebedouro Brazil 21°0S 48°25W 191 A6
Bebera, Tanjung
  Indonesia 8°44S 115°51E 119 K18
Bebra Germany 50°59N 9°48E 76 E5
Bécan Mexico 18°34N 89°31W 181 D7
Bécancour Canada 46°20N 72°26W 173 B17
Beccles U.K. 52°27N 1°35E 67 E9
Bečej Serbia 45°36N 20°3E 80 B5
Beceni Romania 45°23N 26°48E 81 D11
Becerreá Spain 42°51N 7°10W 88 C3
Béchar Algeria 31°38N 2°18W 136 B3
Becharof L. U.S.A. 30°15S 118°33E 166 D3 ?
Becharof L. U.S.A. 57°56N 156°23W 166 D18
Bedford Canada 45°7N 72°59W 175 A12

Becharre = Bsharri
  Lebanon 34°15N 36°0E 130 A5
Bechyně Czech Rep. 49°17N 14°29E 78 B7
Beckley U.S.A. 37°47N 81°11W 173 G13
Beckum Germany 51°45N 8°2E 76 D4
Beclean Romania 47°11N 24°11E 81 C9
Bečov nad Teplou
  Czech Rep. 50°5N 12°49E 78 A5
Bečva → Czech Rep. 49°31N 17°20E 79 B10
Bédar Spain 37°11N 1°59W 91 H3
Bédarieux France 43°37N 3°10E 72 E6
Beddouza, C. Morocco 32°33N 9°9W 136 B3
Bederkesa Germany 53°37N 8°50E 76 B4
Bedford Canada 45°7N 72°59W 175 A12

Bedford S. Africa 32°40S 26°10E 144 D4
Bedford U.K. 52°8N 0°28W 67 E7
Bedford Ind., U.S.A. 38°52N 86°29W 172 F10
Bedford Iowa, U.S.A. 40°40N 94°44W 172 E6
Bedford Ohio, U.S.A. 41°23N 81°32W 174 E3
Bedford Pa., U.S.A. 40°1N 78°30W 174 F6
Bedford Va., U.S.A. 37°20N 79°31W 173 G14
Bedford □ U.K. 52°4N 0°28W 67 E7
Bedford, C. Australia 15°14S 145°21E 150 B4
Bedków Poland 51°36N 19°44E 83 G6
Bednja → Croatia 46°20N 16°52E 93 B13
Bednodemyanovsk
  Russia 53°55N 43°15E 86 D6
Bedok Singapore 1°19N 103°56E 121 d
Bedónia Italy 44°30N 9°38E 92 D6
Bedourie Australia 24°30S 139°30E 150 C2
Bedti → India 14°50N 74°44E 127 M9
Bedugul Indonesia 8°17S 115°10E 119 J18
Bedum Neths. 53°18N 6°36E 69 A6
Będzin Poland 50°19N 19°7E 83 H6
Bee Ridge U.S.A. 27°17N 82°29W 179 H7
Beebe Plain Canada 45°1N 72°9W 175 A12
Beech Creek U.S.A. 41°5N 77°36W 174 E7
Beechworth Australia 36°22S 146°43E 153 D7
Beechy Canada 50°53N 107°24W 163 C7
Beef I. Br. Virgin Is. 18°26N 64°30W 183 e
Beelitz Germany 52°14N 12°58E 76 C8
Beenleigh Australia 27°43S 153°10E 151 D5
Be'er Menuha Israel 30°19N 35°8E 128 D2
Be'er Sheva Israel 31°15N 34°48E 130 D3
Beersheba = Be'er Sheva
  Israel 31°15N 34°48E 130 D3
Beeskow Germany 52°10N 14°15E 76 C10
Beesteekraal S. Africa 25°23S 27°38E 145 C4
Beeston U.K. 52°56N 1°14W 66 E6
Beeton Canada 44°5N 79°47W 174 B5
Beetzendorf Germany 52°42N 11°6E 76 C7
Beeville U.S.A. 28°24N 97°45W 176 G6
Befale
  Dem. Rep. of the Congo 0°25N 20°45E 140 D4
Bega Australia 36°41S 149°51E 153 D8
Bega, Canalul Romania 45°37N 20°46E 80 E5
Bégard France 48°38N 3°18W 70 D3
Beğendik Turkey 40°55N 26°34E 97 F10
Begoro Ghana 6°23N 0°23W 139 D4
Begusarai India 25°24N 86°9E 125 G12
Behābād Iran 32°24N 59°47E 129 C8
Behala India 22°30N 88°18E 125 H13
Behbehān Iran 30°30N 50°15E 129 D6
Behm Canal U.S.A. 55°10N 131°0W 162 B2
Behshahr Iran 36°45N 53°35E 129 B7
Bei Jiang → China 23°2N 112°58E 117 F9
Bei Shan China 41°30N 96°0E 110 C8
Bei'an China 48°10N 126°20E 111 B14
Beibei China 29°47N 106°22E 116 C6
Beichuan China 31°55N 104°39E 116 B5
Beihai China 21°28N 109°6E 116 G7
Beijing China 39°53N 116°21E 114 E9
Beijing □ China 39°55N 116°20E 114 E9
Beilen Neths. 52°52N 6°27E 69 B6
Beiliu China 22°41N 110°21E 117 F8
Beilngries Germany 49°2N 11°28E 77 F7
Beilpajah Australia 32°54S 143°52E 152 B5
Beinn na Faoghla = Benbecula
  U.K. 57°26N 7°21W 65 D1
Beipan Jiang → China 24°55N 106°5E 116 E6
Beipiao China 41°52N 120°32E 115 D11
Beira Mozam. 19°50S 34°52E 143 F3
Beirut = Bayrūt
  Lebanon 33°53N 35°31E 130 B4
Beiseker Canada 51°23N 113°32W 162 C6
Beit Lāḥiyā Gaza Strip 31°33N 34°30E 130 D3
Beit Lekhem = Bayt Lahm
  West Bank 31°43N 35°12E 130 D4
Beitaolaizhao China 44°58N 125°58E 115 B13
Beitbridge Zimbabwe 22°12S 30°0E 143 G3
Beiuș Romania 46°40N 22°21E 80 D7
Beizhen = Binzhou
  China 37°20N 118°2E 115 F10
Beizhen China 41°38N 121°54E 115 D11
Beizhengzhen China 44°31N 123°30E 115 B12
Beja Portugal 38°2N 7°53W 89 G3
Beja Tunisia 36°43N 9°12E 136 A5
Beja □ Portugal 37°55N 7°55W 89 H3
Bejaïa Algeria 36°42N 5°2E 136 A5
Bejaïa □ Algeria 36°40N 4°55E 136 A4
Béjar Spain 40°23N 5°46W 88 E5
Bejestán Iran 34°30N 58°5E 129 C8
Bekaa Valley = Al Biqā
  Lebanon 34°10N 36°10E 130 A5
Bekasi Indonesia 6°14S 106°59E 119 G12
Bekçiler Turkey 36°56N 29°44E 99 E11
Bekdash Turkmenistan 41°34N 52°32E 108 D4
Békés Hungary 46°47N 21°9E 80 D6
Békés □ Hungary 46°45N 21°0E 80 D6
Békéscsaba Hungary 46°40N 21°5E 80 D6
Bekili Turkey 38°17N 29°27E 99 C11
Bekok Malaysia 2°20N 103°7E 121 L4
Bekwai Ghana 6°30N 1°34W 139 D4
Bela India 25°50N 82°0E 125 G10
Bela Pakistan 26°12N 66°20E 124 F2
Bela S. Africa 24°51S 28°19E 145 B4
Bela Crkva Serbia 44°55N 21°27E 80 B6
Bela Palanka Serbia 43°13N 22°17E 96 C6
Bela Vista Brazil 22°12S 56°20W 190 A4
Bela Vista Mozam. 26°10S 32°44E 145 C5
Bélâbre France 46°34N 1°8E 72 B5
Belalcázar Spain 38°35N 5°10W 89 G5
Belan → India 24°2N 81°45E 125 G9
Belanovica Serbia 44°15N 20°23E 96 B4
Belarus ■ Europe 53°30N 27°0E 75 B14
Belau = Palau ■ Palau 7°30N 134°30E 156 G5
Belawan Indonesia 3°33N 98°32E 118 H1
Belaya → Russia 54°40N 56°0E 108 B5
Belaya Glina Russia 46°5N 40°48E 87 G5
Belaya Kalitva Russia 48°13N 40°50E 87 F5
Belaya Tserkov = Bila Tserkva
  Ukraine 49°45N 30°10E 75 D16
Belaya Zemlya, Ostrova
  Russia 81°36N 62°18E 106 A7
Belcești Romania 47°19N 27°7E 81 C12
Bełchatów Poland 51°21N 19°22E 83 G6
Belcher Is. Canada 56°15N 78°45W 164 A3
Belchite Spain 41°18N 0°43W 90 D5
Belcoo Canada 40°2N 121°17W 170 E5
Belebey Russia 54°7N 54°7E 108 B4
Beledweyne Somalia 4°30N 45°5E 135 G4
Belém Brazil 1°20S 48°30W 187 D9

Belém de São Francisco
  Brazil 8°46S 38°58W 189 B3
Belén Argentina 27°40S 67°5W 190 B2
Belén Paraguay 23°30S 57°6W 190 A4
Belen Turkey 36°31N 36°10E 104 D7
Belen U.S.A. 34°40N 106°46W 169 J10
Belene Bulgaria 43°39N 25°10E 97 C9
Bélesta France 42°55N 1°56E 72 F5
Belet Uen = Beledweyne
  Somalia 4°30N 45°5E 131 G4
Belev Russia 53°50N 36°5E 84 F9
Belevi Turkey 38°0N 27°28E 99 C9
Belfair U.S.A. 47°27N 122°50W 170 C4
Belfast = eMakhazeni
  S. Africa 25°42S 30°2E 145 C5
Belfast N.Z. 43°27S 172°39E 155 K4
Belfast U.K. 54°37N 5°56W 64 B6
Belfast Maine, U.S.A. 44°26N 69°1W 173 C19
Belfast N.Y., U.S.A. 42°21N 78°7W 174 D6
Belfast □ U.K. 54°40N 5°50W 64 B6
Belfield U.S.A. 46°53N 103°12W 172 B2
Belfort France 47°38N 6°50E 71 E13
Belfort, Territoire de □
  France 47°40N 6°55E 71 E13
Belfry U.S.A. 45°9N 109°1W 168 D9
Belgaum India 15°55N 74°35E 127 G2
Belgavi = Belgaum
  India 15°55N 74°35E 127 G2
Belgioioso Italy 45°10N 9°19E 92 C6
Belgium ■ Europe 50°30N 5°0E 69 D4
Belgodère France 42°35N 9°1E 73 F13
Belgorod Russia 50°35N 36°35E 85 G9
Belgorod □ Russia 50°45N 36°45E 85 G9
Belgorod-Dnestrovskiy =
  Bilhorod-Dnistrovskyy
  Ukraine 46°11N 30°23E 85 J6
Belgrade = Beograd
  Serbia 44°50N 20°37E 96 B4
Belgrade U.S.A. 45°47N 111°11W 168 D8
Belgrano Antarctica 77°52S 34°37W 55 D1
Belgrove N.Z. 41°27S 172°59E 155 K4
Belhaven U.S.A. 35°33N 76°37W 177 D16
Béli Guinea-Biss. 11°51N 13°56W 138 C2
Beli Drim → Europe 42°6N 20°25E 96 D4
Beli Manastir Croatia 45°45N 18°36E 80 E3
Beli Timok → Serbia 43°53N 22°14E 96 C6
Bélice → Italy 37°35N 12°55E 94 E5
Belimbing Indonesia 8°24S 115°2E 119 J18
Belinskiy Russia 53°0N 43°25E 86 D6
Belinyu Indonesia 1°35S 105°50E 118 E3
Beliton Is. = Belitung
  Indonesia 3°10S 107°50E 118 E3
Belitung Indonesia 3°10S 107°50E 118 E3
Beliu Romania 46°30N 22°0E 80 D6
Belize ■ Cent. Amer. 17°0N 88°30W 181 D7
Belize Barrier Reef Belize 17°9N 88°33W 181 D7
Belize City Belize 17°25N 88°10W 181 D7
Beljakovci Macedonia 42°6N 21°59E 96 D5
Beljanica Serbia 44°8N 21°43E 96 B5
Belkovskiy, Ostrov
  Russia 75°32N 135°44E 107 B14
Bell U.S.A. 29°45N 82°52W 178 F7
Bell → Canada 49°48N 77°38W 164 C4
Bell I. Canada 50°46N 55°35W 165 B8
Bell-Irving → Canada 56°12N 129°5W 162 B3
Bell Peninsula Canada 63°50N 82°0W 161 E15
Bell Ville Argentina 32°40S 62°40W 190 C3
Bella Italy 40°45N 15°33E 95 B8
Bella Bella Canada 52°10N 128°10W 162 C3
Bella Coola Canada 52°25N 126°40W 162 C3
Bella Flor Bolivia 11°9S 67°49W 188 C4
Bella Unión Uruguay 30°15S 57°40W 190 C4
Bella Vista Corrientes,
  Argentina 28°33S 59°0W 190 B4
Bella Vista Tucuman,
  Argentina 27°10S 65°25W 190 B2
Bella Vista U.S.A. 36°28N 94°16W 172 G6
Bellac France 46°7N 1°3E 72 B5
Bellágio Italy 45°59N 9°15E 92 C6
Bellaire U.S.A. 40°1N 80°45W 174 F4
Bellária Italy 44°9N 12°28E 93 D9
Bellary India 15°10N 76°56E 127 G3
Bellata Australia 29°53S 149°46E 151 D4
Belle Fourche → U.S.A. 44°40N 103°51W 172 C2
Belle Fourche →
  U.S.A. 44°26N 102°18W 172 C2
Belle Glade U.S.A. 26°41N 80°40W 179 J14
Belle-Île France 47°20N 3°10W 70 E3
Belle Isle Canada 51°57N 55°25W 165 B8
Belle Isle U.S.A. 28°27N 81°12W 179 G13
Belle Isle, Str. of
  Canada 51°30N 56°30W 165 B8
Belle Plaine U.S.A. 41°54N 92°17W 172 E7
Belle River Canada 42°18N 82°43W 174 D2
Belle Yella Liberia 7°24N 10°0W 138 D3
Belledonne France 45°20N 6°10E 73 C10
Bellefontaine U.S.A. 40°22N 83°46W 173 E12
Bellefonte U.S.A. 40°55N 77°47W 174 F7
Bellegarde France 47°59N 2°26E 71 E9
Bellegarde-en-Marche
  France 45°59N 2°18E 72 C6
Bellegarde-sur-Valserine
  France 46°4N 5°50E 71 F12
Bellême France 48°22N 0°34E 70 D7
Belleoram Canada 47°31N 55°25W 165 C8
Belleplaine Barbados 13°15N 59°34W 183 g
Belleview U.S.A. 29°4N 82°3W 179 G13
Belleville Canada 44°10N 77°23W 174 B7
Belleville France 46°7N 4°45E 71 F11
Belleville Ill., U.S.A. 38°31N 89°59W 172 F9
Belleville Kans., U.S.A. 39°50N 97°38W 172 F5
Belleville N.J., U.S.A. 40°47N 74°9W 175 F10
Belleville N.Y., U.S.A. 43°46N 76°10W 175 C8
Belleville-sur-Vie France 46°46N 1°25W 70 F5
Bellevue Canada 49°35N 114°22W 162 D6
Bellevue Idaho, U.S.A. 43°28N 114°16W 168 E6
Bellevue Nebr., U.S.A. 41°9N 95°54W 172 E6
Bellevue Ohio, U.S.A. 41°17N 82°51W 174 E2
Bellevue Wash.,
  U.S.A. 47°37N 122°12W 170 C4
Belley France 45°46N 5°41E 73 C9
Bellin = Kangirsuk
  Canada 60°0N 70°0W 161 F18
Bellinge Denmark 55°20N 10°20E 63 J4
Bellingen Australia 30°25S 152°50E 153 A10
Bellingham U.S.A. 48°46N 122°29W 170 B4
Bellingshausen Abyssal Plain
  S. Ocean 64°0S 90°0W 55 C16
Bellingshausen Sea
  Antarctica 66°0S 80°0W 55 C17
Bellinzona Switz. 46°11N 9°1E 77 J5

Bello Colombia 6°20N 75°33W 186 B3
Bellows Falls U.S.A. 43°8N 72°27W 175 C12
Bellpat Pakistan 29°0N 68°5E 124 E3
Bellpuig Spain 41°37N 1°1E 90 D6
Belluno Italy 46°9N 12°13E 93 B9
Bellville U.S.A. 32°9N 81°59W 178 D8
Bellwood U.S.A. 40°36N 78°20W 174 F6
Belmar U.S.A. 40°11N 74°2W 175 F10
Bélmez Spain 38°17N 5°17W 89 G5
Belmont S. Africa 33°4S 151°42E 153 B9
Belmont Canada 42°53N 81°5W 174 D3
Belmont S. Africa 29°28S 24°22E 144 C3
Belmont U.S.A. 42°14N 78°2W 174 D6
Belmonte Brazil 16°0S 39°0W 189 D3
Belmonte Portugal 40°21N 7°20W 88 E3
Belmonte Spain 39°34N 2°43E 91 F2
Belmopan Belize 17°18N 88°30W 181 D7
Belmullet Ireland 54°14N 9°58W 64 B2
Belo Horizonte Brazil 19°55S 43°56W 189 D2
Belo Jardim Brazil 8°20S 36°26W 189 B3
Belo-Tsiribihina Madag. 19°40S 44°30E 141 H8
Belogorsk = Bilohirsk
  Ukraine 45°3N 34°35E 85 K8
Belogorsk Russia 51°0N 128°20E 107 D13
Belogradchik Bulgaria 43°53N 22°42E 96 C6
Belogradets Bulgaria 43°22N 27°18E 97 C11
Beloha Madag. 25°10S 45°3E 141 F8
Beloit Kans., U.S.A. 39°28N 98°6W 172 F4
Beloit Wis., U.S.A. 42°31N 89°2W 172 D9
Belokorovichi Ukraine 51°7N 28°2E 75 C15
Belomorsk Russia 64°35N 34°54E 106 C4
Belonia India 23°15N 91°30E 123 H17
Belopolye = Bilopillya
  Ukraine 51°14N 34°20E 85 G8
Belorechensk Russia 44°46N 39°52E 87 H4
Belorussia = Belarus ■
  Europe 53°30N 27°0E 75 B14
Beloslav Bulgaria 43°11N 27°42E 97 C11
Belousovka Kazakhstan 50°8N 82°31E 109 D10
Belovezhskaya Pushcha =
  Białowieża △ Poland 52°43N 23°50E 83 F10
Belovo Bulgaria 42°13N 24°1E 97 D8
Belovo Russia 54°30N 86°0E 107 D10
Beloyarskiy Russia 63°42N 66°40E 106 C7
Beloye, Ozero Russia 60°10N 37°35E 84 B9
Beloye More Russia 66°30N 38°0E 58 B13
Belozem Bulgaria 42°12N 25°2E 97 D9
Belozersk Russia 60°1N 37°45E 84 B9
Belpasso Italy 37°35N 14°58E 95 E7
Belrain India 28°23N 80°55E 125 E9
Belt U.S.A. 47°23N 110°55W 168 C8
Beltana Australia 30°48S 138°25E 152 A3
Belterra Brazil 2°45S 55°0W 187 D8
Beltinci Slovenia 46°37N 16°20E 93 B13
Belton U.S.A. 31°3N 97°28W 176 F6
Beltsy = Bălți Moldova 47°48N 27°58E 81 C12
Belturbet Ireland 54°6N 7°26W 64 B4
Belukha Russia 49°50N 86°50E 109 C11
Beluran Malaysia 5°48N 117°35E 118 C5
Belušić Serbia 43°50N 21°10E 96 C5
Belvédere Maríttimo
  Italy 39°37N 15°52E 95 C8
Belvès France 44°46N 1°0E 72 D5
Belvidere Ill., U.S.A. 42°15N 88°50W 172 D9
Belvidere N.J., U.S.A. 40°50N 75°5W 175 F9
Belvis de la Jara Spain 39°45N 4°57W 88 F6
Belyando → Australia 21°38S 146°50E 150 C4
Belyando Crossing
  Australia 21°32S 146°51E 150 C4
Belyuen Australia 12°34S 130°42E 148 B5
Belyy Russia 55°49N 33°3E 84 F7
Belyy, Ostrov Russia 73°30N 71°0E 106 B8
Belyy Yar Russia 58°26N 84°39E 106 D9
Belyye Vody = Aqsū
  Kazakhstan 42°25N 69°50E 109 D7
Belz Ukraine 50°23N 24°1E 83 H11
Belzec Poland 50°23N 23°26E 83 H10
Belzig Germany 52°8N 12°35E 76 C8
Belzoni U.S.A. 33°11N 90°29W 177 E9
Bełżyce Poland 51°11N 22°17E 83 G9
Bembéréke Benin 10°11N 2°43E 139 C5
Bembesi Zimbabwe 20°0S 28°58E 143 G2
Bembesi → Zimbabwe 18°57S 27°47E 143 F2
Bembézar → Spain 42°37N 6°25W 88 C4
Bemboka Australia 36°35S 149°41E 153 D8
Bemetara India 21°42N 81°32E 125 J9
Bemidji U.S.A. 47°28N 94°53W 172 B6
Ben Iran 32°32N 50°45E 129 C6
Ben Boyd △ Australia 37°0S 149°55E 153 D8
Ben Cruachan U.K. 56°26N 5°8W 65 E3
Ben En △ Vietnam 19°37N 105°30E 120 C5
Ben Gardane Tunisia 33°11N 11°11E 136 B6
Ben Halls Gap △
  Australia 31°37S 151°1E 153 A9
Ben Hope U.K. 58°25N 4°36W 65 C4
Ben Lawers U.K. 56°32N 4°14W 65 E4
Ben Lomond N.S.W.,
  Australia 30°1S 151°43E 151 E5
Ben Lomond Tas.,
  Australia 41°38S 147°42E 151 G4
Ben Lomond U.K. 56°11N 4°38W 65 E4
Ben Lomond △
  Australia 41°33S 147°39E 151 G4
Ben Luc Vietnam 10°39N 106°29E 121 G6
Ben Macdhui U.K. 57°4N 3°40W 65 D5
Ben Mhor U.K. 57°15N 7°18W 65 D1
Ben More Argyll & Bute,
  U.K. 56°26N 6°1W 65 E2
Ben More Stirling, U.K. 56°23N 4°32W 65 E4
Ben More Assynt U.K. 58°8N 4°52W 65 C4
Ben Nevis U.K. 56°48N 5°1W 65 E3
Ben Ohau Ra. N.Z. 44°1S 170°4E 155 L3
Ben Quang Vietnam 17°3N 106°55E 120 D6
Ben Slimane Morocco 33°38N 7°7W 136 B4
Ben Tadjine, Djebel
  Algeria 29°10N 0°47W 136 C4
Ben Tre Vietnam 10°14N 106°22E 121 G6
Ben Wyvis U.K. 57°40N 4°35W 65 D4
Bena Nigeria 11°20N 5°50E 139 C6
Benaco = Garda, L. di
  Italy 45°40N 10°41E 92 C7
Benagerie Australia 31°25S 140°22E 152 A4
Benahmed Morocco 33°4N 7°9W 136 B4
Benalla Australia 36°30S 146°0E 153 D7
Benalmádena Spain 36°36N 4°34W 89 J6

Berau, Teluk Indonesia 2°30S 132°30E 119 E8
Berber Sudan 18°0N 34°0E 135 E12
Berbera Somalia 10°30N 45°2E 131 E4
Berbérati C.A.R. 4°15N 15°40E 140 D3
Berbice → Guyana 6°20N 57°32W 186 B7
Bénat, C. France 43°5N 6°22E 73 E10
Berchidda Italy 40°47N 9°10E 94 B2
Berchtesgaden Germany 47°38N 13°0E 77 H8
Berchtesgaden △
  Germany 47°34N 12°55E 77 H8
Berck France 50°25N 1°36E 71 B8
Berdichev = Berdychiv
  Ukraine 49°57N 28°30E 75 D15
Berdsk Russia 54°47N 83°2E 109 B10
Berdyansk Ukraine 46°45N 36°50E 85 J9
Berdychiv Ukraine 49°57N 28°30E 75 D15
Berea U.S.A. 37°34N 84°17W 173 G11
Berebere Indonesia 2°25N 128°45E 119 D7
Bereeda Somalia 11°45N 51°0E 131 E5
Berehomet Ukraine 48°10N 25°19E 81 D10
Berehove Ukraine 48°15N 22°35E 80 B7
Bereket Turkmenistan 39°16N 55°32E 129 B7
Berekum Ghana 7°29N 2°34W 138 D4
Berenice Egypt 24°2N 35°25E 137 C4
Berens → Canada 52°25N 97°2W 163 C9
Berens I. Canada 52°18N 97°18W 163 C9
Berens River Canada 52°25N 97°0W 163 C9
Beresford Canada 47°42N 65°42W 165 B6
Beresford U.S.A. 43°5N 96°47W 172 D5
Berestechko Ukraine 50°22N 25°5E 75 C13
Berestechko Ukraine 46°6N 27°50E 81 C12
Beretău → Romania 47°10N 21°50E 80 C6
Berettyó → Hungary 46°59N 21°7E 80 D6
Berettyóújfalu Hungary 47°13N 21°33E 80 C6
Bereza = Byaroza
  Belarus 52°31N 24°51E 75 B13
Berezhany Ukraine 49°26N 24°58E 75 D13
Berezina = Byarezina →
  Belarus 52°33N 30°14E 75 B16
Berezivka Ukraine 47°14N 30°55E 85 J6
Berezna Ukraine 51°35N 31°46E 85 G6
Bereznik Russia 62°51N 42°40E 106 C5
Berezniki Russia 59°24N 56°46E 106 D6
Berezovo Russia 64°0N 65°0E 106 C7
Berezyne Ukraine 46°14N 29°12E 81 D14
Berga Spain 42°6N 1°48E 90 C6
Berga Sweden 57°14N 16°3E 63 G10
Bérgama Turkey 39°8N 27°11E 99 B9
Bergamo Italy 45°41N 9°43E 92 C6
Bergantiños Spain 43°9N 2°8W 88 B2
Bergby Sweden 60°57N 17°2E 62 D11
Berge Norway 59°34N 8°10E 62 E2
Bergedorf Germany 53°28N 10°6E 76 B6
Bergeforsen Sweden 62°32N 17°23E 62 B11
Bergen Mecklenburg-Vorpommern,
  Germany 54°25N 13°25E 76 A9
Bergen Niedersachsen,
  Germany 52°49N 9°57E 76 C5
Bergen Neths. 52°40N 4°43E 69 B4
Bergen Norway 60°20N 5°20E 60 F11
Bergen op Zoom Neths. 51°28N 4°18E 69 C4
Bergerac France 44°51N 0°30E 72 D4
Bergheim Germany 50°57N 6°38E 76 E2
Bergholz U.S.A. 40°31N 80°53W 174 F4
Bergisch Gladbach
  Germany 50°59N 7°8E 76 E3
Bergisches Land △
  Germany 51°0N 7°30E 76 E3
Bergkamen Germany 51°37N 7°38E 76 D3
Bergkvara Sweden 56°23N 16°5E 63 H10
Bergshamra Sweden 59°38N 18°37E 62 E12
Bergsjö Sweden 61°59N 17°3E 62 C11
Bergstrasse-Odenwald △
  Germany 49°45N 5°55E 77 F1
Bergues France 50°58N 2°24E 71 B9
Bergviken Sweden 61°15N 16°40E 62 C10
Bergville S. Africa 28°52S 29°18E 145 C4
Berhala, Selat Indonesia 1°0S 104°15E 118 E2
Berhampore = Baharampur
  India 24°2N 88°27E 125 G13
Berhampur = Brahmapur
  India 19°15N 84°54E 126 F7
Berheci → Romania 45°58N 27°28E 81 E12
Bering Glacier
  U.S.A. 60°20N 143°30W 166 C11
Bering Sea Pac. Oc. 58°0N 171°0W 158 D2
Bering Strait Pac. Oc. 65°30N 169°0W 166 B6
Beringovskiy Russia 63°3N 179°19E 107 C18
Berisso Argentina 34°56S 57°50W 190 C4
Berja Spain 36°50N 2°56W 89 J8
Berkane Morocco 34°52N 2°20W 136 B3
Berkeley U.S.A. 37°51N 122°16W 170 H4
Berkner I. Antarctica 79°30S 50°0W 55 D18
Berkovitsa Bulgaria 43°16N 23°8E 96 C7
Berkshire U.S.A. 42°19N 76°11W 175 D8
Berkshire Downs U.K. 51°33N 1°29W 67 F6
Berlanga Spain 38°17N 5°50W 89 G5
Berlenga, I. Portugal 39°25N 9°30W 89 F1
Berlin Germany 52°31N 13°23E 76 C9
Berlin Ga., U.S.A. 31°4N 83°37W 178 D6
Berlin Md., U.S.A. 38°20N 75°13W 173 F16
Berlin N.H., U.S.A. 44°28N 71°11W 175 B13
Berlin N.Y., U.S.A. 42°42N 73°23W 175 D11
Berlin Wis., U.S.A. 43°58N 88°57W 172 D9
Berlin □ Germany 52°30N 13°25E 76 C9
Berlín Germany 52°30N 13°20E 76 C9
Bermagui Australia 36°25S 150°4E 153 D9
Bermeja, Sierra Spain 36°30N 5°11W 89 J5
Bermejo → Formosa,
  Argentina 26°51S 58°23W 190 B4
Bermejo → San Juan,
  Argentina 32°30S 67°30W 190 C2
Bermen, L. Canada 53°35N 68°55W 165 B6
Bermeo Spain 43°25N 2°47W 90 B2
Bermillo de Sayago Spain 41°22N 6°8W 88 D4
Bermuda ☑ Atl. Oc. 32°18N 64°45W 159 F13
Bermuda Rise Atl. Oc. 30°30N 65°0W 56 C5
Bern Switz. 46°57N 7°28E 77 J3
Bern □ Switz. 46°45N 7°40E 77 J3
Bernalda Italy 40°24N 16°44E 95 B9
Bernalillo U.S.A. 35°18N 106°33W 169 J10
Bernardo de Irigoyen
  Argentina 26°15S 53°40W 191 B5
Bernardo O'Higgins △
  Chile 48°50S 75°36W 192 C1
Bernardsville U.S.A. 40°43N 74°34W 175 F10
Bernasconi Argentina 37°55S 63°44W 190 D3

Bernau Bayern, Germany 47°47N 12°22E 77 H8
Bernau Brandenburg, Germany 52°40N 13°35E 76 C9
Bernay France 49°5N 0°35E 70 C7
Bernburg Germany 51°47N 11°44E 76 D7
Berndorf Austria 47°59N 16°1E 78 D9
Berne = Bern Switz. 46°57N 7°28E 77 J3
Berne = Bern □ Switz. 46°45N 7°40E 77 J3
Berner Alpen Switz. 46°27N 7°35E 77 J3
Berneray U.K. 57°43N 7°11W 65 D1
Bernier I. Australia 24°50S 113°12E 149 D1
Bernina, Piz Switz. 46°20N 9°54E 77 J5
Bernkastel-Kues Germany 49°55N 7°3E 77 F3
Béroubouay Benin 10°34N 2°46E 139 C5
Beroun Czech Rep. 49°57N 14°5E 78 B7
Berounka → Czech Rep. 50°0N 14°22E 78 B7
Berovo Macedonia 41°38N 22°51E 96 E6
Berre, Étang de France 43°27N 5°5E 73 E9
Berre-l'Étang France 43°27N 5°10E 73 E9
Berrechid Morocco 33°18N 7°36W 136 B2
Berri Australia 34°14S 140°35E 152 C4
Berriane Algeria 32°50N 3°46E 136 B4
Berridale Australia 36°22S 148°48E 153 D8
Berrigan Australia 35°38S 145°49E 153 C6
Berriwillock Australia 35°36S 142°59E 152 C5
Berrouaghia Algeria 36°10N 2°53E 136 A4
Berry Australia 34°46S 150°43E 153 C9
Berry France 46°50N 2°0E 71 F8
Berry Is. Bahamas 25°40N 77°50W 182 A4
Berrydale U.S.A. 30°53N 87°3W 179 E2
Berryessa, L. U.S.A. 38°31N 122°6W 170 G4
Berryville U.S.A. 36°22N 93°34W 176 C8
Berseba Namibia 26°0S 17°46E 144 C2
Bersenbrück Germany 52°34N 7°56E 76 C3
Bershad Ukraine 48°22N 29°31E 81 B14
Bertamirans Spain 42°54N 8°38W 88 C2
Berthold U.S.A. 48°19N 101°44W 172 A3
Berthoud U.S.A. 40°19N 105°5W 168 F11
Bertincourt France 50°5N 2°58E 71 B9
Bertolínia Brazil 7°38S 43°57W 189 B2
Bertoua Cameroon 4°30N 13°45E 140 D2
Bertraghboy B. Ireland 53°22N 9°54W 64 C2
Beruni Uzbekistan 41°41N 60°45E 108 D6
Beruwala Sri Lanka 6°30N 80°0E 127 L4
Berwick U.S.A. 41°3N 76°14W 175 E8
Berwick-upon-Tweed U.K. 55°46N 2°0W 66 B6
Berwyn Mts. U.K. 52°54N 3°26W 66 E4
Beryslav Ukraine 46°50N 33°30E 85 J7
Berzasca Romania 44°39N 21°58E 80 F6
Berzence Hungary 46°12N 17°11E 80 D2
Besal Pakistan 35°4N 73°56E 125 B5
Besalampy Madag. 16°43S 44°29E 141 H8
Besançon France 47°15N 6°2E 71 E13
Besar Indonesia 2°40S 116°0E 118 E5
Beshenkovichi Belarus 55°2N 29°29E 84 E5
Besianë Kosovo 42°54N 21°10E 96 D5
Beška Serbia 45°8N 20°6E 80 E5
Beslan Russia 43°15N 44°28E 87 J7
Besna Kobila Serbia 42°31N 22°10E 96 D6
Besnard L. Canada 55°25N 106°0W 163 B7
Besni Turkey 37°41N 37°52E 104 D7
Besor, N. → Egypt 31°28N 34°22E 130 D3
Bessarabiya Moldova 47°0N 28°10E 75 E15
Bessarabka = Basarabeasca Moldova 46°21N 28°58E 81 D13
Bessèges France 44°18N 4°8E 73 D8
Bessemer Ala., U.S.A. 33°24N 86°58W 177 E11
Bessemer Mich., U.S.A. 46°29N 90°3W 172 B8
Bessemer Pa., U.S.A. 40°59N 80°30W 174 F4
Bessin France 49°18N 1°0W 70 C6
Bessines-sur-Gartempe France 46°6N 1°22E 72 B5
Beswick Australia 14°34S 132°53E 148 B5
Beswick ✪ Australia 14°31S 132°51E 148 B5
Bet She'an Israel 32°30N 35°30E 130 C4
Bet Shemesh Israel 31°44N 35°0E 130 D4
Betancuria Canary Is. 28°25N 14°3W 100 F5
Betanzos Spain 43°15N 8°12W 88 B2
Bétaré Oya Cameroon 5°40N 14°5E 140 C2
Betera Spain 39°35N 0°28W 91 F4
Bétérou Benin 9°12N 2°16E 139 D5
Bethal S. Africa 26°27S 29°28E 145 C4
Bethanien Namibia 26°31S 17°8E 144 C2
Bethany Canada 44°11N 78°34W 174 B6
Bethany Mo., U.S.A. 40°16N 94°2W 172 E6
Bethany Okla., U.S.A. 35°31N 97°38W 176 D6
Bethel Alaska, U.S.A. 60°48N 161°45W 166 C7
Bethel Conn., U.S.A. 41°22N 73°25W 175 E11
Bethel Maine, U.S.A. 44°25N 70°47W 175 B14
Bethel Vt., U.S.A. 43°50N 72°38W 175 C12
Bethel Park U.S.A. 40°19N 80°2W 174 F4
Béthenville France 49°18N 4°23E 71 C11
Bethlehem = Bayt Lahm West Bank 31°43N 35°12E 130 D4
Bethlehem S. Africa 28°14S 28°18E 145 C4
Bethlehem U.S.A. 40°37N 75°23W 175 F9
Bethulie S. Africa 30°30S 25°59E 144 D4
Béthune France 50°30N 2°38E 71 B9
Béthune → France 49°53N 1°4E 70 C8
Bethungra Australia 34°45S 147°51E 153 C7
Betim Brazil 19°58S 44°13W 189 D2
Betioky Madag. 23°48S 44°20E 141 J8
Betong Malaysia 1°24N 111°31E 118 D4
Betong Thailand 5°45N 101°5E 121 K3
Betoota Australia 25°45S 140°42E 150 D3
Betpaqdala Kazakhstan 45°45N 70°30E 109 C8
Betroka Madag. 23°16S 46°0E 141 J9
Betsiamites Canada 48°56N 68°40W 165 C6
Betsiamites → Canada 48°56N 68°38W 165 C6
Bettendorf U.S.A. 41°32N 90°30W 172 E8
Bettiah India 26°48N 84°33E 125 F11
Bettna Sweden 58°55N 16°38E 63 F10
Bèttola Italy 44°47N 9°36E 92 D6
Betul India 21°58N 77°59E 126 D3
Betws-y-Coed U.K. 53°5N 3°48W 66 D4
Betxí Spain 39°56N 0°12W 90 F4
Betzdorf Germany 50°46N 7°52E 76 E3
Beuil France 44°6N 6°59E 73 D10
Beulah Australia 35°58S 142°29E 152 C5
Beulah Mich., U.S.A. 44°38N 86°6W 172 C10
Beulah N. Dak., U.S.A. 47°16N 101°47W 172 B3
Beuvron → France 47°29N 1°15E 70 E8
Beveren Belgium 51°12N 4°16E 69 C4
Beverley Australia 32°9S 116°56E 149 F2
Beverley U.K. 53°51N 0°26W 66 D7
Beverly U.S.A. 42°33N 70°53W 175 D14
Beverly Hills Calif., U.S.A. 34°5N 118°24W 171 L8
Beverly Hills Fla., U.S.A. 28°55N 82°28W 179 G7
Beverungen Germany 51°39N 9°22E 76 D5
Bewas → India 23°59N 79°21E 125 H8
Bewdley Canada 44°5N 78°19W 174 B6
Bex Switz. 46°15N 7°1E 77 J3
Bexhill U.K. 50°51N 0°29E 67 G8
Bey Dağları Turkey 36°38N 30°29E 99 E12
Beyānlū Iran 36°0N 47°51E 128 C5
Beyazköy Turkey 41°21N 27°42E 97 E11
Beyçayırı Turkey 40°15N 26°55E 97 F10
Beydağ Turkey 38°5N 28°13E 99 C10
Beyeğaç Turkey 37°14N 28°53E 99 D10
Beyin Ghana 5°1N 2°41W 138 D4
Beykoz Turkey 41°7N 29°7E 97 E13
Beyla Guinea 8°30N 8°38W 138 D3
Beynat France 45°8N 1°44E 72 C5
Beyneu Kazakhstan 45°18N 55°9E 108 C5
Beyoba Turkey 38°48N 27°47E 99 C9
Beyoğlu Turkey 41°1N 28°58E 97 E12
Beypazarı Turkey 40°10N 31°56E 104 B4
Beypore → India 11°10N 75°47E 127 J2
Beyşehir Turkey 37°41N 31°43E 104 D4
Beyşehir Gölü Turkey 37°41N 31°33E 104 D4
Beytüşşebap Turkey 37°35N 43°10E 105 D10
Bezdan Serbia 45°50N 18°57E 80 E3
Bezhetsk Russia 57°47N 36°39E 84 D9
Béziers France 43°20N 3°12E 72 E7
Bezwada = Vijayawada India 16°31N 80°39E 126 F5
Bhabua India 25°3N 83°37E 125 G10
Bhachau India 23°20N 70°16E 124 H4
Bhadar → Gujarat, India 22°17N 72°20E 124 H5
Bhadar → Gujarat, India 21°27N 69°47E 124 J3
Bhadarwah India 32°58N 75°46E 125 C6
Bhadgaon = Bhaktapur Nepal 27°38N 85°24E 125 F11
Bhadohi India 25°25N 82°34E 125 G10
Bhadra India 29°8N 75°14E 124 E6
Bhadra → India 14°0N 75°20E 127 H2
Bhadrachalam India 17°40N 80°53E 126 F5
Bhadrak India 21°10N 86°30E 126 D8
Bhadran India 22°19N 72°6E 124 H5
Bhadravati India 13°49N 75°40E 127 H2
Bhag Pakistan 29°2N 67°49E 124 E2
Bhagalpur India 25°10N 87°0E 125 G12
Bhagirathi → Paschimbanga, India 23°25N 88°23E 125 H13
Bhagirathi → Uttarakhand, India 30°8N 78°35E 125 D8
Bhainsa India 19°10N 77°58E 126 E3
Bhakkar Pakistan 31°40N 71°5E 124 D4
Bhakra Dam India 31°30N 76°45E 124 D7
Bhaktapur Nepal 27°38N 85°24E 125 F11
Bhalki India 18°2N 77°13E 126 E3
Bhamo Burma 24°15N 97°15E 123 G20
Bhamragarh India 19°30N 80°40E 126 E5
Bhandara India 21°5N 79°42E 126 D4
Bhanpura India 24°31N 75°44E 124 G6
Bhanrer Ra. India 23°40N 79°45E 125 H8
Bhaptiahi India 26°19N 86°44E 125 F12
Bharat = India ■ Asia 20°0N 78°0E 122 K11
Bharatpur Chhattisgarh, India 23°44N 81°46E 125 H9
Bharatpur Raj., India 27°15N 77°30E 124 F7
Bharatpur Nepal 27°34N 84°10E 125 F11
Bharno India 23°14N 84°53E 125 H11
Bharraig = Barra U.K. 57°0N 7°29W 65 E1
Bharraig, Caolas = Barra, Sd. of U.K. 57°4N 7°25W 65 D1
Bharuch India 21°47N 73°0E 126 D1
Bhatarsaigh = Vatersay U.K. 56°55N 7°32W 65 E1
Bhatghar L. India 18°10N 73°48E 126 E1
Bhatinda India 30°15N 74°57E 124 D6
Bhatkal India 13°58N 74°35E 127 H2
Bhatpara India 22°50N 88°25E 125 H13
Bhattu India 29°36N 75°19E 124 E6
Bhaun Pakistan 32°55N 72°40E 124 C5
Bhaunagar = Bhavnagar India 21°45N 72°10E 126 D1
Bhavani India 11°27N 77°43E 127 J3
Bhavnagar India 21°45N 72°10E 126 D1
Bhawanipatna India 19°55N 83°10E 126 E6
Bhawari India 25°42N 73°4E 124 G5
Bhayavadar India 21°51N 70°15E 124 J4
Bhearnaraigh = Berneray U.K. 57°43N 7°11W 65 D1
Bhera Pakistan 32°29N 72°57E 124 C5
Bheri → Nepal 28°47N 81°18E 125 E9
Bhikangaon India 21°52N 75°57E 124 J6
Bhilai = Bhilainagar-Durg India 21°13N 81°26E 126 D5
Bhilainagar-Durg India 21°13N 81°26E 126 D5
Bhilsa = Vidisha India 23°28N 77°53E 124 H7
Bhilwara India 25°25N 74°38E 124 G6
Bhima → India 16°25N 77°17E 126 F3
Bhimavaram India 16°30N 81°30E 127 F5
Bhimbar Pakistan 32°59N 74°3E 125 C6
Bhind India 26°30N 78°46E 125 F8
Bhinga India 27°43N 81°56E 125 F9
Bhinmal India 25°0N 72°15E 124 G5
Bhisho S. Africa 32°50S 27°23E 144 D4
Bhiwandi India 19°20N 73°0E 126 E1
Bhiwani India 28°50N 76°9E 124 E7
Bhogava → India 22°26N 72°20E 124 H5
Bhojpur Nepal 27°10N 87°3E 125 F12
Bhokardan India 20°16N 75°46E 126 D2
Bhola Bangla. 22°45N 90°35E 123 H17
Bholari Pakistan 25°19N 68°13E 124 G3
Bhongir India 17°30N 78°56E 126 F4
Bhopal India 23°20N 77°30E 124 H7
Bhopalpatnam India 18°52N 80°23E 126 E5
Bhor India 18°12N 73°53E 126 E1
Bhuban India 20°53N 85°50E 126 D7
Bhubaneshwar India 20°15N 85°50E 126 D7
Bhuj India 23°15N 69°49E 124 H3
Bhumiphol Res. Thailand 17°20N 98°40E 120 D2
Bhusawal India 21°3N 75°46E 126 D2
Bhutan ■ Asia 27°25N 90°30E 123 F17
Biafra, B. of = Bonny, Bight of Africa 3°30N 9°20E 139 E6
Biak Indonesia 1°10S 136°6E 119 E9
Biała Poland 50°24N 17°40E 83 H4
Biała → Poland 50°3N 20°55E 83 H7
Biała Piska Poland 53°37N 22°5E 82 E9
Biała Podlaska Poland 52°4N 23°6E 83 F10
Biała Rawska Poland 51°48N 20°29E 83 G7
Białobrzegi Poland 51°39N 20°57E 83 G7
Białogard Poland 54°2N 15°58E 82 D2
Białowieski △ Poland 52°43N 23°50E 83 F10
Białowieża Poland 52°41N 23°49E 83 F10
Biały Bór Poland 53°53N 16°51E 82 E3
Białystok Poland 53°10N 23°10E 83 E10
Biancavilla Italy 37°38N 14°52E 95 E7
Bianco Italy 38°5N 16°9E 95 D9
Biankouma Ivory C. 7°50N 7°40W 138 D3
Biaora India 23°56N 76°56E 124 H7
Bīārjmand Iran 36°6N 55°53E 129 B7
Biaro Indonesia 2°5N 125°26E 119 D7
Biarritz France 43°29N 1°33W 72 E2
Biasca Switz. 46°22N 8°58E 77 J4
Biba Egypt 28°55N 31°0E 137 F7
Bibai Japan 43°19N 141°52E 112 C10
Bibbiena Italy 43°42N 11°49E 93 E8
Bibby I. Canada 61°55N 93°0W 163 A10
Bibei → Spain 42°24N 7°13W 88 C3
Biberach Germany 48°5N 9°47E 77 G5
Bibiani Ghana 6°30N 2°8W 138 D4
Bible Sri Lanka 7°10N 81°25E 127 L5
Bibungwa Dem. Rep. of the Congo 2°40S 28°15E 142 C2
Bicaj Albania 41°58N 20°25E 96 E4
Bicaz Romania 46°53N 26°5E 81 D11
Bicazu Ardelean Romania 46°51N 25°56E 81 D10
Biccari Italy 41°23N 15°12E 95 A8
Bicester U.K. 51°54N 1°9W 67 F6
Bicheno Australia 41°52S 148°18E 151 G4
Bichia India 22°27N 80°42E 125 H9
Bichvinta Georgia 43°9N 40°21E 87 J5
Bickerton I. Australia 13°45S 136°10E 150 A2
Bicske Hungary 47°29N 18°38E 80 C3
Bid = Bir India 19°4N 75°46E 126 E2
Bida Nigeria 9°3N 5°58E 139 D6
Bidar India 17°55N 77°35E 126 F3
Biddeford U.S.A. 43°30N 70°28W 173 D18
Bideford U.K. 51°1N 4°13W 67 F3
Bideford Bay U.K. 51°5N 4°20W 67 F3
Bidhuna India 26°49N 79°31E 125 F8
Bidokht Iran 34°20N 58°46E 129 C8
Bidor Malaysia 4°6N 101°15E 121 K3
Bidyadanga Australia 18°45S 121°43E 148 C3
Bie Sweden 59°5N 16°12E 62 E10
Bié, Planalto de Angola 12°0S 16°0E 141 G3
Bieber U.S.A. 41°7N 121°8W 168 F3
Biebrza → Poland 53°13N 22°25E 83 E9
Biebrzański △ Poland 53°36N 22°45E 82 E9
Biecz Poland 49°44N 21°15E 83 J8
Biel Switz. 47°8N 7°14E 77 H3
Bielawa Poland 50°43N 16°37E 83 H3
Bielefeld Germany 52°1N 8°33E 76 C4
Bielersee Switz. 47°6N 7°5E 77 H3
Biella Italy 45°34N 8°3E 92 C5
Bielsk Podlaski Poland 52°47N 23°12E 83 F10
Bielsko-Biała Poland 49°50N 19°2E 83 J6
Bien Hoa Vietnam 10°57N 106°49E 121 G6
Bienne = Biel Switz. 47°8N 7°14E 77 H3
Bienvenida Spain 38°18N 6°12W 89 G4
Bienville, L. Canada 55°5N 72°40W 164 A5
Bierné France 47°48N 0°33W 70 E6
Bieruń Poland 50°6N 19°6E 83 H6
Bierutów Poland 51°7N 17°32E 83 G4
Biesbosch △ Neths. 51°45N 4°48E 69 C4
Biescas Spain 42°37N 0°20W 90 C4
Biese → Germany 52°53N 11°46E 76 C7
Biesiesfontein S. Africa 30°57S 17°58E 144 D2
Bieszczadzki △ Poland 49°5N 22°43E 83 J9
Bietigheim-Bissingen Germany 48°58N 9°8E 77 G5
Bieżuń Poland 52°58N 19°55E 83 F6
Biferno → Italy 41°59N 15°2E 93 G12
Big → Canada 54°50N 58°55W 165 B8
Big B. = Awarua B. N.Z. 44°28S 168°4E 155 E3
Big B. Canada 55°43N 60°35W 165 A7
Big Bear City U.S.A. 34°16N 116°51W 171 L10
Big Bear Lake U.S.A. 34°15N 116°56W 171 L10
Big Belt Mts. U.S.A. 46°30N 111°25W 168 C8
Big Bend Swaziland 26°50S 31°58E 145 C5
Big Bend △ U.S.A. 29°20N 103°5W 176 G3
Big Black → U.S.A. 32°3N 91°4W 177 E9
Big Blue → U.S.A. 39°35N 96°34W 172 F5
Big Buddha Hong Kong, China 22°15N 113°54E 111 a
Big Creek U.S.A. 37°11N 119°14W 170 H7
Big Cypress ⌓ U.S.A. 26°0N 81°10W 179 J8
Big Cypress Swamp U.S.A. 26°15N 81°30W 179 J8
Big Desert Australia 35°45S 141°10E 151 F3
Big Falls U.S.A. 48°12N 93°48W 172 A7
Big Fork → U.S.A. 48°31N 93°43W 172 A7
Big Horn Mts. = Bighorn Mts. U.S.A. 44°25N 107°0W 168 D10
Big I. Canada 61°7N 116°45W 162 A5
Big Lake U.S.A. 31°12N 101°28W 176 F4
Big Moose U.S.A. 43°49N 74°58W 175 C10
Big Muddy Cr. → U.S.A. 48°8N 104°36W 168 B11
Big Pine U.S.A. 37°10N 118°17W 170 H8
Big Pine Key U.S.A. 24°40N 81°21W 179 L8
Big Piney U.S.A. 42°32N 110°7W 168 E8
Big Quill L. Canada 51°55N 104°30W 163 C8
Big Rapids U.S.A. 43°42N 85°29W 173 D11
Big Rideau L. Canada 44°40N 76°15W 175 B8
Big River Canada 53°50N 107°0W 163 C7
Big Run U.S.A. 40°57N 78°55W 174 F6
Big Sable Pt. U.S.A. 44°3N 86°1W 172 C10
Big Salmon → Canada 61°52N 134°55W 162 A2
Big Sand L. Canada 57°45N 99°45W 163 B9
Big Sandy U.S.A. 48°11N 110°7W 168 B8
Big Sandy → U.S.A. 38°25N 82°36W 173 F12
Big Sandy Cr. = Sandy Cr. → U.S.A. 41°51N 109°47W 168 F9
Big Sandy Cr. → U.S.A. 38°7N 102°29W 168 G12
Big Satilla Cr. → U.S.A. 31°27N 82°3W 178 D7
Big Sioux → U.S.A. 42°29N 96°27W 172 D5
Big South Fork ⌓ U.S.A. 36°27N 84°47W 177 C12
Big Spring U.S.A. 32°15N 101°28W 176 E4
Big Stone City U.S.A. 45°18N 96°28W 172 C5
Big Stone Gap U.S.A. 36°52N 82°47W 173 G12
Big Stone L. U.S.A. 45°18N 96°27W 172 C5
Big Sur U.S.A. 36°15N 121°48W 170 J5
Big Timber U.S.A. 45°50N 109°57W 168 D9
Big Trout L. Canada 53°40N 90°0W 164 B2
Big Trout Lake Canada 53°45N 90°0W 164 B2
Biğa Turkey 40°13N 27°14E 97 F11
Biga → Turkey 40°20N 27°14E 97 F11
Bigadiç Turkey 39°22N 28°7E 99 B10
Biganos France 44°39N 0°59W 72 D3
Biggar Canada 52°4N 108°0W 163 C7
Biggar U.K. 55°38N 3°32W 65 F5
Bigge I. Australia 14°35S 125°10E 148 B4
Biggenden Australia 25°31S 152°4E 151 D5
Biggleswade U.K. 52°5N 0°14W 67 E7
Biggs U.S.A. 39°25N 121°43W 170 F5
Bighorn U.S.A. 46°10N 107°27W 168 C10
Bighorn → U.S.A. 46°10N 107°28W 168 C10
Bighorn Canyon ⌓ U.S.A. 45°10N 108°0W 168 D10
Bighorn L. U.S.A. 44°55N 108°15W 168 D9
Bighorn Mts. U.S.A. 44°25N 107°0W 168 D10
Bignona Senegal 12°52N 16°14W 138 C1
Bigorre France 43°10N 0°5E 72 E4
Bigstone L. Canada 53°42N 95°44W 163 C9
Biguglia, Étang de France 42°36N 9°29E 73 F13
Bigwa Tanzania 7°10S 39°10E 142 D4
Bihać Bos.-H. 44°49N 15°57E 93 D12
Bihar India 25°5N 85°40E 125 G11
Bihar □ India 25°0N 86°0E 125 G12
Biharamulo Tanzania 2°25S 31°25E 142 C3
Biharamulo ⌓ Tanzania 2°24S 31°26E 142 C3
Bihariganj India 25°44N 86°59E 125 G12
Biharkeresztes Hungary 47°8N 21°44E 80 C6
Bihor □ Romania 47°0N 22°10E 80 D7
Bihor, Munţii Romania 46°29N 22°47E 80 D7
Bijagós, Arquipélago dos Guinea-Biss. 11°15N 16°10W 138 C1
Bijaipur India 26°2N 77°20E 124 F7
Bijapur Chhattisgarh, India 18°50N 80°50E 126 E5
Bijapur Karnataka, India 16°50N 75°55E 126 F2
Bījār Iran 35°52N 47°35E 105 E12
Bijauri Nepal 28°6N 82°20E 125 E10
Bijawar India 24°38N 79°30E 125 G8
Bijela Montenegro 42°28N 18°39E 96 D2
Bijeljina Bos.-H. 44°46N 19°14E 80 F4
Bijelo Polje Montenegro 43°1N 19°45E 96 C3
Bijie China 27°20N 105°16E 116 D5
Bijnor India 29°27N 78°11E 124 E8
Bikaner India 28°2N 73°18E 124 E5
Bikapur India 26°30N 82°7E 125 F10
Bikeqi China 40°43N 111°20E 114 D6
Bikfayyā Lebanon 33°55N 35°41E 130 B4
Bikin Russia 46°50N 134°20E 112 A7
Bikin → Russia 46°51N 134°2E 112 A7
Bikini Atoll Marshall Is. 12°0N 167°30E 156 F8
Bikita Zimbabwe 20°6S 31°41E 145 B5
Bīkkū Bīttī Libya 22°0N 19°12E 135 D9
Bikoué Cameroon 3°55N 11°50E 139 E7
Bila Tserkva Ukraine 49°45N 30°10E 75 D16
Bilanga Burkina Faso 12°40N 0°1W 139 C4
Bilara India 26°14N 73°53E 124 F5
Bilaspur Chhattisgarh, India 22°2N 82°15E 125 H10
Bilaspur Punjab, India 31°19N 76°50E 124 D7
Biläsuvar Azerbaijan 39°27N 48°32E 105 C13
Bilauk Taungdan Thailand 13°0N 99°0E 120 F2
Bilauri Nepal 28°41N 80°21E 125 E9
Bilbao Spain 43°16N 2°56W 90 B2
Bilbao ✕ (BIO) Spain 43°18N 2°57W 90 B2
Bilbeis Egypt 30°25N 31°34E 137 E7
Bilbo = Bilbao Spain 43°16N 2°56W 90 B2
Bilbor Romania 47°6N 25°30E 81 C10
Bilche-Zolote Ukraine 48°47N 25°53E 81 B10
Bilciureşti Romania 44°44N 25°48E 81 F10
Bíldudalur Iceland 65°41N 23°36W 60 D2
Bílé Karpaty Europe 49°5N 18°0E 79 B11
Bileća Bos.-H. 42°53N 18°27E 96 D2
Bilecik Turkey 40°5N 30°5E 104 B4
Bilecik □ Turkey 40°0N 30°0E 104 B3
Bilećko Jezero Bos.-H. 42°48N 18°28E 96 D2
Bileh Savār Iran 39°21N 48°21E 105 C13
Bilgoraj Poland 50°33N 22°42E 83 H9
Bilgram India 27°11N 80°2E 125 F9
Bilhaur India 26°51N 80°5E 125 F9
Bilhorod-Dnistrovskyy Ukraine 46°11N 30°23E 85 J6
Bilibino Russia 68°3N 166°20E 107 C17
Bilibiza Mozam. 12°30S 40°20E 143 E5
Bilimora India 20°45N 72°57E 126 D1
Bilisht Albania 40°37N 21°2E 96 F5
Billabong Cr. → Australia 35°5S 144°2E 152 C6
Billdal Sweden 57°35N 11°57E 63 G5
Billiluna Australia 19°37S 127°41E 148 C4
Billings U.S.A. 45°47N 108°30W 168 D9
Billiton Is. = Belitung Indonesia 3°10S 107°50E 118 E3
Billsta Sweden 63°20N 18°28E 62 A12
Billund Denmark 55°44N 9°6E 63 J3
Bilma Niger 18°50N 13°30E 135 E8
Bilma, Grand Erg de Niger 18°30N 14°0E 135 E8
Bilo Gora Croatia 45°53N 17°15E 80 E2
Biloela Australia 24°24S 150°31E 150 C5
Bilohirsk Ukraine 45°3N 34°35E 85 K8
Biloli India 18°46N 77°44E 126 E3
Bilopillya Ukraine 51°14N 34°20E 85 G8
Bilovodsk Ukraine 49°13N 39°36E 85 H10
Biloxi U.S.A. 30°24N 88°53W 177 F10
Bilpa Morea Claypan Australia 25°0S 140°0E 150 D3
Biltine Chad 14°40N 20°50E 135 F10
Bilyarsk Russia 54°58N 50°22E 86 C10
Bim Son Vietnam 20°4N 105°51E 120 B5
Bima Indonesia 8°22S 118°49E 119 F5
Bimban Egypt 24°24N 32°54E 137 C3
Bimberi Pk. Australia 35°44S 148°51E 153 C8
Bimbila Ghana 8°54N 0°5E 139 D5
Bimbo C.A.R. 4°15N 18°33E 140 D3
Bimini Is. Bahamas 25°42N 79°25W 182 A4
Bin Xian Heilongjiang, China 45°42N 127°32E 115 B14
Bin Xian Shaanxi, China 35°2N 108°4E 114 G5
Bin Yauri Nigeria 10°46N 4°45E 139 C5
Bina-Etawah India 24°13N 78°14E 124 G8
Binalong Australia 34°40S 148°39E 153 C8
Bīnālūd, Kūh-e Iran 36°30N 58°30E 129 B8
Binatang = Bintangau Malaysia 2°10N 111°40E 118 D4
Binche Belgium 50°26N 4°10E 69 D4
Binchuan China 25°42N 100°38E 116 E3
Binder Chad 9°56N 14°27E 139 D7
Bindki India 26°2N 80°36E 125 F9
Bindslev Denmark 57°33N 10°11E 63 G4
Bindura Zimbabwe 17°18S 31°18E 143 F3
Binéfar Spain 41°51N 0°18E 90 D5
Bingara Australia 29°52S 150°36E 151 D5
Bingaram I. India 10°56N 72°17E 127 J1
Bingen Germany 49°57N 7°55E 77 F3
Bingerville Ivory C. 5°18N 3°49W 138 D4
Bingham U.S.A. 45°3N 69°53W 173 C19
Binghamton U.S.A. 42°6N 75°55W 175 D9
Bingöl Turkey 38°53N 40°29E 105 C9
Bingöl □ Turkey 38°55N 40°30E 105 C9
Bingöl Dağları Turkey 39°16N 41°9E 105 C9
Bingsjö Sweden 61°1N 15°39E 62 C9
Binh Dinh Vietnam 13°55N 109°7E 120 F7
Binh Son Vietnam 15°20N 108°40E 120 E7
Binhai China 34°2N 119°49E 115 G10
Binic France 48°46N 2°50W 70 D4
Binisatua Spain 39°50N 4°11E 100 B11
Binissalem Spain 39°41N 2°50E 100 B9
Binjai Indonesia 3°20N 98°30E 118 D3
Binji Nigeria 13°10N 4°55E 139 C5
Binka India 21°2N 83°48E 126 D6
Binnaway Australia 31°28S 149°24E 153 A8
Binongko Indonesia 5°57S 124°2E 119 F6
Binscarth Canada 50°37N 101°17W 163 C8
Bintan Indonesia 1°0N 104°0E 118 D2
Bintangau Malaysia 2°10N 111°40E 118 D4
Bintulu Malaysia 3°10N 113°0E 118 D4
Bintuni Indonesia 2°7S 133°32E 119 E8
Binyang China 23°12N 108°47E 116 F7
Binz Germany 54°24N 13°35E 76 A9
Binzert = Bizerte Tunisia 37°15N 9°50E 136 A5
Binzhou China 37°20N 118°2E 115 F10
Bio Bío □ Chile 37°35S 72°0W 190 D1
Biobío → Chile 36°49S 73°10W 190 D1
Biograd na Moru Croatia 43°56N 15°29E 93 E12
Biogradska Gora △ Montenegro 42°55N 19°40E 96 D3
Bioko Eq. Guin. 3°30N 8°40E 139 E6
Biokovo Croatia 43°23N 17°0E 93 E14
Biougra Morocco 30°15N 9°14W 136 B2
Bipindi Cameroon 3°6N 10°30E 139 E7
Bir India 19°4N 75°46E 126 E2
Bîr Abu Hashim Egypt 23°42N 34°6E 137 C3
Bîr Abu Minqar Egypt 26°33N 27°33E 137 B2
Bîr Abu Muḥammad Egypt 29°44N 34°14E 130 F3
Bîr Adal Deib Sudan 22°35N 36°10E 137 C4
Bi'r al Butayyihāt Jordan 29°47N 35°20E 130 F4
Bi'r al Mārī Jordan 30°4N 35°33E 130 E4
Bi'r al Qaţţār Jordan 29°47N 35°32E 130 F4
Bir Aouine Tunisia 32°25N 9°18E 136 B5
Bîr 'Asal Egypt 25°55N 34°20E 137 B3
Bir Atrun Sudan 18°15N 26°40E 137 D2
Bîr Beiḍa Egypt 30°25N 34°29E 130 E3
Bîr Diqnash Egypt 31°3N 25°23E 137 A2
Bir el Abbes Algeria 26°7N 6°9W 136 C2
Bîr el 'Abd Egypt 31°2N 33°0E 130 D2
Bir el Ater Algeria 34°46N 8°3E 136 B5
Bîr el Basur Egypt 29°51N 25°49E 137 B2
Bîr el Biarât Egypt 29°30N 34°43E 130 F3
Bîr el Duweidar Egypt 30°56N 32°32E 130 E1
Bîr el Garârât Egypt 31°3N 33°34E 130 D2
Bîr el Gellaz Egypt 30°50N 26°40E 137 A2
Bîr el Heisi Egypt 29°22N 34°36E 130 F3
Bîr el Jafir Egypt 30°50N 32°41E 130 E1
Bîr el Mâlḥi Egypt 30°38N 33°19E 130 E2
Bîr el Shaqqa Egypt 30°54N 25°1E 137 A2
Bîr el Thamâda Egypt 30°12N 33°27E 130 E2
Bîr Fuad Egypt 30°35N 26°28E 137 A2
Bîr Gebeil Ḥişn Egypt 30°2N 33°18E 130 E2
Bi'r Ghadīr Syria 34°6N 37°3E 130 A6
Bîr Haimur Egypt 22°45N 33°40E 137 C3
Bîr Ḥasana Egypt 30°29N 33°46E 130 E2
Bîr Hööker Egypt 30°22N 30°21E 137 E7
Bîr Kanayis Egypt 24°59N 33°15E 137 C3
Bîr Kaseiba Egypt 31°0N 33°17E 130 E2
Bîr Kerawein Egypt 27°10N 28°25E 137 B2
Bîr Lahfân Egypt 31°0N 33°51E 130 E2
Bir Lahrache Algeria 32°1N 8°12E 136 B5
Bîr Madkûr Egypt 30°44N 32°33E 130 E1
Bîr Maql Egypt 23°7N 33°40E 137 C3
Bîr Mîneiga Sudan 22°47N 35°12E 137 C4
Bîr Misaha Egypt 22°13N 27°59E 137 C2
Bir Mogreïn Mauritania 25°10N 11°25W 134 C3
Bîr Murr Egypt 23°28N 30°10E 137 C3
Bi'r Muţribah Kuwait 29°54N 47°17E 128 D5
Bîr Nakheila Egypt 24°1N 30°50E 137 C3
Bîr Qaţia Egypt 30°58N 32°45E 130 E1
Bîr Qatrani Egypt 30°55N 26°10E 137 A2
Bîr Ranga Egypt 24°25N 35°15E 137 C4
Bîr Sahara Egypt 22°54N 28°40E 137 C2
Bîr Seiyâla Egypt 26°10N 33°50E 137 B3
Bîr Shalatein Egypt 23°5N 35°25E 137 C4
Bîr Shebb Egypt 22°25N 29°40E 137 C2
Bîr Shût Egypt 23°50N 35°15E 137 C4
Bîr Terfawi Egypt 22°57N 28°55E 137 C2
Bîr Umm Qubûr Egypt 24°35N 34°2E 137 C3
Bîr Ungât Egypt 22°8N 33°48E 137 C3
Bîr Za'farâna Egypt 29°10N 32°40E 137 F8
Bîr Zeidûn Egypt 25°45N 33°40E 137 B3
Birāk Libya 27°31N 14°20E 135 C8
Biramféro Guinea 11°40N 9°10W 138 C3
Biratnagar Nepal 26°27N 87°17E 125 F12
Birawa Dem. Rep. of the Congo 2°20S 28°48E 142 C2
Birch → Canada 58°28N 112°17W 162 B6
Birch Hills Canada 52°59N 105°25W 163 C7
Birch I. Canada 52°26N 99°54W 163 C9
Birch L. N.W.T., Canada 62°4N 116°33W 162 A5
Birch L. Ont., Canada 51°23N 92°18W 164 B1
Birch Mts. Canada 57°30N 113°10W 162 B6
Birch River Canada 52°24N 101°6W 163 C8
Birchip Australia 35°56S 142°55E 152 C5
Birchiş Romania 45°58N 22°9E 80 E7
Birchwood N.Z. 45°55S 167°53E 155 F2
Bird Canada 56°30N 94°13W 163 B10
Bird I. = Aves, I. de W. Indies 15°45N 63°55W 183 C7
Bird I. S. Georgia 54°0S 38°3W 55 B1
Birds Creek Canada 45°6N 77°52W 174 A7
Birdsville Australia 25°51S 139°20E 150 D2
Birdum Cr. → Australia 15°14S 133°0E 148 C5
Birdwood Australia 34°51S 138°58E 152 C3
Birecik Turkey 37°2N 38°0E 105 D8
Birein Israel 30°50N 34°28E 130 E3
Bireuen Indonesia 5°14N 96°39E 118 C1
Birganj Nepal 27°1N 84°52E 125 F11
Birifo Gambia 13°30N 14°0W 138 C2
Birigüi Brazil 21°18S 50°16W 191 A5
Bīrjand Iran 32°53N 59°13E 129 C8
Birka Sweden 59°20N 17°32E 62 E11
Birkenfeld Germany 49°38N 7°9E 77 F3
Birkenhead U.K. 53°23N 3°2W 66 D4
Birkerød Denmark 55°50N 12°25E 63 J6
Birket Qârûn Egypt 29°30N 30°40E 137 F7
Birkfeld Austria 47°21N 15°45E 78 D8
Birkhadem Algeria 36°43N 3°3E 136 A4
Birlad = Bârlad Romania 46°15N 27°38E 81 D12
Birmingham U.K. 52°29N 1°52W 67 E6
Birmingham U.S.A. 33°31N 86°48W 177 E11
Birmingham Int. ✕ (BHX) U.K. 52°26N 1°45W 67 E6
Birmitrapur India 22°24N 84°46E 126 C7
Birni Ngaouré Niger 13°5N 2°51E 139 C5
Birni Nkonni Niger 13°55N 5°15E 139 C6
Birnin Gwari Nigeria 11°0N 6°45E 139 C6
Birnin Kebbi Nigeria 12°32N 4°12E 139 C5
Birnin Kudu Nigeria 11°30N 9°29E 139 C6
Birobidzhan Russia 48°50N 132°50E 111 B15
Birr Ireland 53°6N 7°54W 64 C4
Birrie → Australia 29°43S 146°37E 151 D4
Birsilpur India 28°11N 72°15E 124 E5
Birsk Russia 55°25N 55°30E 106 D6
Birtle Canada 50°30N 101°5W 163 C8
Birur India 13°30N 75°55E 122 N9
Biryuchiy Ukraine 46°10N 35°0E 85 J8
Biržai Lithuania 56°11N 24°45E 84 D3
Birzebbugga Malta 35°50N 14°32E 101 D2
Bisa Indonesia 1°15S 127°28E 119 E7
Bisáccia Italy 41°1N 15°22E 95 A8
Bisacquino Italy 37°42N 13°15E 94 E6
Bisalpur India 28°14N 79°48E 125 E8
Bisbee U.S.A. 31°27N 109°55W 169 L9
Biscarrosse France 44°22N 1°20W 72 D2
Biscarrosse et de Parentis, Étang de France 44°21N 1°10W 72 D2
Biscay, B. of Atl. Oc. 45°0N 2°0W 58 F5
Biscay Abyssal Plain Atl. Oc. 45°0N 8°0W 56 B11
Biscayne ⌓ U.S.A. 25°25N 80°12W 179 K9
Biscayne B. U.S.A. 25°40N 80°12W 179 K9
Biscéglie Italy 41°14N 16°30E 95 A9
Bischheim France 48°37N 7°46E 71 D14
Bischofshofen Austria 47°26N 13°14E 78 D6
Bischofswerda Germany 51°7N 14°10E 76 D10
Bischwiller France 48°46N 7°50E 71 D14
Biscoe Is. Antarctica 66°0S 67°0W 55 C17
Biscotasing Canada 47°18N 82°9W 164 C3
Biševo Croatia 42°57N 16°3E 93 F13
Bishah, W. → Si. Arabia 21°24N 43°26E 137 C5
Bishan China 29°33N 106°12E 116 C6
Bishkek Kyrgyzstan 42°54N 74°46E 109 D8
Bishnupur India 23°8N 87°20E 125 H12
Bisho = Bhisho S. Africa 32°50S 27°23E 144 D4
Bishop Calif., U.S.A. 37°22N 118°24W 170 H8
Bishop Ga., U.S.A. 33°49N 83°26W 178 B6
Bishop Tex., U.S.A. 27°35N 97°48W 176 H6
Bishop Auckland U.K. 54°39N 1°40W 66 C6
Bishop's Falls Canada 49°2N 55°30W 165 C8
Bishop's Stortford U.K. 51°52N 0°10E 67 F8
Bisignano Italy 39°31N 16°17E 95 C9
Bisina, L. Uganda 1°38N 33°56E 142 B3
Biskra Algeria 34°50N 5°44E 136 B5
Biskra □ Algeria 34°40N 5°25E 136 B5
Biskupiec Poland 53°53N 20°58E 82 E7
Bismarck U.S.A. 46°48N 100°47W 172 B3
Bismarck Arch. Papua N. G. 2°30S 150°0E 147 B7
Bismark Germany 52°40N 11°33E 76 C7
Bismil Turkey 37°51N 40°40E 105 D9
Biso Uganda 1°44N 31°26E 142 B3
Bison U.S.A. 45°31N 102°28W 172 C2
Bīsotūn Iran 34°23N 47°26E 105 E12
Bispgården Sweden 63°2N 16°40E 62 A10
Bissagos = Bijagós, Arquipélago dos Guinea-Biss. 11°15N 16°10W 138 C1
Bissam Cuttack India 19°31N 83°31E 126 E6
Bissau Guinea-Biss. 11°45N 15°45W 138 C1
Bissaula Nigeria 7°0N 10°27E 139 D7
Bissikrima Guinea 10°50N 10°58W 138 C2
Bissorã Guinea-Biss. 12°16N 15°35W 138 C1
Bistcho L. Canada 59°45N 118°50W 162 B5
Bistreţ Romania 43°54N 23°23E 81 G8
Bistrica = Ilirska-Bistrica Slovenia 45°34N 14°14E 93 C11
Bistriţa Romania 47°9N 24°35E 81 C9
Bistriţa → Romania 46°30N 26°57E 81 D11
Bistriţa Năsăud □ Romania 47°15N 24°30E 81 C9
Bistriţei, Munţii Romania 47°15N 25°40E 81 C10
Biswan India 27°29N 81°2E 125 F9
Bisztynek Poland 54°8N 20°53E 82 D7
Bitam Gabon 2°5N 11°25E 140 D2
Bitburg Germany 49°58N 6°31E 77 F2
Bitche France 49°2N 7°25E 71 C14
Bithynia Turkey 40°40N 31°0E 104 B4
Bitkine Chad 11°59N 18°13E 135 F9
Bitlis Turkey 38°20N 42°3E 105 C10
Bitlis □ Turkey 38°20N 42°5E 105 C10
Bitola Macedonia 41°1N 21°20E 96 E5
Bitolj = Bitola Macedonia 41°1N 21°20E 96 E5
Bitonto Italy 41°6N 16°41E 95 A9
Bitra I. India 11°33N 72°9E 127 J1
Bitter Creek U.S.A. 41°33N 108°33W 168 F9
Bitter L. = Buheirat-Murrat-el-Kubra Egypt 30°18N 32°26E 137 E8
Bitterfeld Germany 51°37N 12°20E 76 D8
Bitterfontein S. Africa 31°1S 18°32E 144 D2
Bitterroot → U.S.A. 46°52N 114°7W 168 C6
Bitterroot Range U.S.A. 46°0N 114°20W 168 D6
Bitterwater U.S.A. 36°23N 121°0W 170 J6
Bitti Italy 40°29N 9°23E 94 B2
Bittou Burkina Faso 11°17N 0°18W 139 C4
Biu Nigeria 10°40N 12°3E 139 C7
Bivolari Romania 47°31N 27°27E 81 C12
Bivolu, Vf. Romania 47°16N 25°58E 81 C10
Biwa-Ko Japan 35°15N 136°10E 113 G8
Biwabik U.S.A. 47°32N 92°21W 172 B7
Bixad Romania 47°56N 23°28E 81 C8
Bixby U.S.A. 35°57N 95°53W 176 D7
Biya → Russia 52°25N 85°0E 109 B11
Biyang China 32°38N 113°21E 117 A9
Biysk Russia 52°40N 85°0E 109 B11
Bizana S. Africa 30°50S 29°52E 145 D4
Bizen Japan 34°43N 134°8E 113 G7
Bizerte Tunisia 37°15N 9°50E 136 A5
Bizerte □ Tunisia 37°5N 9°35E 136 A5

Bjargtangar *Iceland* 65°30N 24°30W **60** D1
Bjärnum *Sweden* 56°17N 13°43E **63** H7
Bjästa *Sweden* 63°12N 18°29E **62** A12
Bjelasica *Montenegro* 42°50N 19°40E **96** D3
Bjelašnica *Bos.-H.* 43°43N 18°9E **80** G3
Bjelovar *Croatia* 45°56N 16°49E **93** C13
Bjerringbro *Denmark* 56°23N 9°39E **63** H3
Björbo *Sweden* 60°27N 14°44E **62** D8
Björklinge *Sweden* 60°2N 17°33E **62** D11
Björkö *Sweden* 59°52N 19°2E **62** E13
Björneborg = Pori
  Finland 61°29N 21°48E **84** B1
Björneborg *Sweden* 59°14N 14°16E **62** E8
Björnevatn *Norway* 69°40N 30°0E **60** B24
Bjørnøya *Arctic* 74°30N 19°0E **54** B8
Bjursås *Sweden* 60°25N 15°25E **62** D9
Bjuv *Sweden* 56°5N 12°55E **63** H6
Bla *Mali* 12°56N 5°47W **138** C3
Blå Jungfrun △ *Sweden* 57°16N 16°47E **63** G10
Blace *Serbia* 43°18N 21°17E **96** C5
Blachownia *Poland* 50°49N 18°56E **83** H5
Black → Da →
  Vietnam 21°15N 105°20E **116** G5
Black → *Canada* 44°42N 79°19W **174** B5
Black → *Ariz., U.S.A.* 33°44N 110°13W **169** K8
Black → *Ark., U.S.A.* 35°38N 91°20W **176** F9
Black → *La., U.S.A.* 31°16N 91°50W **176** F9
Black → *Mich., U.S.A.* 42°59N 82°27W **174** D2
Black → *N.Y., U.S.A.* 43°59N 76°4W **175** C8
Black → *Wis., U.S.A.* 43°57N 91°22W **172** D8
Black Bay Pen. *Canada* 48°38N 88°21W **164** C2
Black Birch L. *Canada* 56°53N 107°45W **163** B7
Black Canyon of the Gunnison △
  U.S.A. 38°40N 107°35W **168** G10
Black Diamond
  Canada 50°45N 114°14W **162** C6
Black Duck → *Canada* 56°51N 89°2W **164** A2
Black Forest = Schwarzwald
  Germany 48°30N 8°20E **77** G4
Black Forest *U.S.A.* 39°0N 104°43W **168** G11
Black Hd. *Ireland* 53°9N 9°16W **64** C2
Black Hills *U.S.A.* 44°0N 103°45W **172** D2
Black I. *Canada* 51°12N 96°30W **163** C9
Black L. *Canada* 59°12N 105°15W **163** B7
Black L. *Mich., U.S.A.* 45°28N 84°16W **173** C11
Black L. *N.Y., U.S.A.* 44°31N 75°36W **175** B9
Black Lake *Canada* 59°11N 105°20W **163** B7
Black Mesa *U.S.A.* 36°58N 102°58W **176** C3
Black Mountain
  Australia 30°18S 151°39E **153** A9
Black Mt. = Mynydd Du
  U.K. 51°52N 3°50W **67** F4
Black Mts. *U.K.* 51°55N 3°7W **67** F4
Black Range *U.S.A.* 33°15N 107°50W **169** K10
Black River *Jamaica* 18°0N 77°50W **182** a
Black River *U.S.A.* 44°0N 75°47W **175** C9
Black River Falls
  U.S.A. 44°18N 90°51W **172** C8
Black Rock *Australia* 32°50S 138°44E **152** B2
Black Rock *Barbados* 13°7N 59°37W **183** g
Black Rock Desert
  U.S.A. 41°10N 119°0W **168** F4
Black Sea *Eurasia* 43°30N 35°0E **58** G12
Black Tickle *Canada* 53°28N 55°45W **165** B8
Black Volta → *Africa* 8°41N 1°33W **138** D4
Black Warrior →
  U.S.A. 32°32N 87°51W **177** E11
Blackall *Australia* 24°25S 145°45E **150** C4
Blackball *N.Z.* 42°22S 171°26E **155** C6
Blackbraes △
  Australia 19°10S 144°10E **150** B3
Blackbull *Australia* 17°55S 141°45E **150** B3
Blackburn *U.K.* 53°45N 2°29W **66** D5
Blackburn, Mt.
  U.S.A. 61°44N 143°26W **166** C11
Blackburn with Darwen □
  U.K. 53°45N 2°29W **66** D5
Blackdown Tableland △
  Australia 23°52S 149°8E **150** C4
Blackfoot *U.S.A.* 43°11N 112°21W **168** E7
Blackfoot → *U.S.A.* 46°52N 113°53W **168** C7
Blackfoot Res. *U.S.A.* 42°57N 111°36E **168** E3
Blackman *U.S.A.* 30°56N 86°38W **179** E3
Blackpool *U.K.* 53°49N 3°3W **66** D4
Blackpool □ *U.K.* 53°49N 3°3W **66** D4
Blackriver *U.S.A.* 44°46N 83°17W **174** B1
Blacks Harbour *Canada* 45°3N 66°49W **165** C6
Blacksburg *U.S.A.* 37°14N 80°25W **173** G13
Blackshear *U.S.A.* 31°18N 82°14W **177** F13
Blackshear, L. *U.S.A.* 31°51N 83°56W **178** D6
Blacksod B. *Ireland* 54°6N 10°0W **64** B1
Blackstairs Mt. *Ireland* 52°33N 6°48W **64** D5
Blackstone *U.S.A.* 37°5N 78°0W **173** G14
Blackstone Ra.
  Australia 26°0S 128°30E **149** E4
Blackville *U.S.A.* 33°22N 81°18W **177** E14
Blackwater = West Road →
  Canada 53°18N 122°53W **162** C4
Blackwater *Australia* 23°35S 148°53E **150** C4
Blackwater → *Meath,*
  Ireland 53°39N 6°41W **64** C4
Blackwater → *Waterford,*
  Ireland 52°4N 7°52W **64** D4
Blackwater → *U.K.* 54°31N 6°35W **64** B5
Blackwater → *U.K.* 30°36N 87°2W **179** E2
Blackwell *U.S.A.* 36°48N 97°17W **176** C6
Blackwells Corner
  U.S.A. 35°37N 119°47W **171** K7
Bladensburg △
  Australia 22°30S 142°59E **150** C3
Blackville *U.S.A.* 46°17N 118°8W **168** C5
Blaenau Ffestiniog *U.K.* 53°0N 3°56W **66** E4
Blaenau Gwent □ *U.K.* 51°48N 3°12W **67** F4
Blåfjella-Skjœkerfjella △
  Norway 64°15N 13°8E **60** D15
Blagaj *Bos.-H.* 43°16N 17°55E **96** C1
Blagnac *France* 43°37N 1°23E **72** E5
Blagnac, Toulouse ✈ (TLS)
  France 43°37N 1°22E **72** E5
Blagodarnyy *Russia* 45°7N 43°37E **87** H6
Blagoevgrad *Bulgaria* 42°2N 23°5E **96** D7
Blagoevgrad □ *Bulgaria* 42°2N 23°5E **96** D7
Blagoveshchensk
  Russia 50°20N 127°30E **111** A14
Blahkiuh *Indonesia* 8°31S 115°12E **119** J18
Blain *France* 47°29N 1°45W **70** E5
Blain *U.S.A.* 40°20N 77°31W **174** F7
Blaine *Minn., U.S.A.* 45°10N 93°13W **172** C7
Blaine *Wash., U.S.A.* 48°59N 122°45W **170** B4
Blaine Lake *Canada* 52°51N 106°52W **163** C7
Blair *U.S.A.* 41°33N 96°8W **172** E5
Blair Athol *Australia* 22°42S 147°31E **150** C4

Blair Atholl *U.K.* 56°46N 3°50W **65** E5
Blairgowrie *U.K.* 56°35N 3°21W **65** E5
Blairsden *U.S.A.* 39°47N 120°37W **170** F6
Blairsville *U.S.A.* 40°26N 79°16W **174** F5
Blaj *Romania* 46°10N 23°57E **81** D8
Blakang Mati, Pulau
  Singapore 1°15N 103°50E **121** d
Blake Pt. *U.S.A.* 48°11N 88°25W **172** A9
Blakely *Ga., U.S.A.* 31°23N 84°56W **178** D5
Blakely *Pa., U.S.A.* 41°28N 75°37W **175** E9
Blambangan, Semenanjung
  Indonesia 8°42S 114°29E **119** K17
Blåmont *France* 48°35N 6°50E **71** D13
Blanc, C. *Spain* 39°21N 2°51E **100** B9
Blanc, C. *Tunisia* 37°15N 9°56E **136** A5
Blanc, Mont *Europe* 45°48N 6°50E **73** C10
Blanca, B. *Argentina* 39°10S 61°30W **190** D4
Blanca, Cord. *Peru* 9°10S 77°35W **186** E3
Blanca, Costa *Spain* 38°25N 0°10W **91** G4
Blanca Peak *U.S.A.* 37°35N 105°29W **169** H11
Blanche, C. *Australia* 33°1S 134°9E **151** E1
Blanche, L. *S. Austral.,*
  Australia 29°15S 139°40E **151** D2
Blanche, L. *W. Austral.,*
  Australia 22°25S 123°17E **148** D3
Blanchisseuse
  Trin. & Tob. 10°48N 61°18W **187** K15
Blanco *S. Africa* 33°55S 22°23E **144** D3
Blanco *U.S.A.* 30°6N 98°25W **176** F5
Blanco → *Argentina* 30°20S 68°42W **190** C2
Blanco, C. *Costa Rica* 9°34N 85°8W **182** E2
Blanco, C. *U.S.A.* 42°51N 124°34W **168** E1
Blanda → *Iceland* 65°37N 20°9W **60** D3
Blandford Forum *U.K.* 50°51N 2°9W **67** G5
Blanding *U.S.A.* 37°37N 109°29W **169** H9
Blanes *Spain* 41°40N 2°48E **90** D7
Blangy-sur-Bresle *France* 49°55N 1°37E **71** C8
Blanice → *Czech Rep.* 49°10N 14°5E **78** D7
Blankaholm *Sweden* 57°36N 16°31E **63** G10
Blankenberge *Belgium* 51°20N 3°9E **69** C3
Blankenburg *Germany* 51°47N 10°57E **76** D6
Blanquefort *France* 44°55N 0°38W **72** D3
Blanquilla, I. *Venezuela* 11°51N 64°37W **183** D7
Blanquillo *Uruguay* 32°53S 55°37W **191** C4
Blansko *Czech Rep.* 49°22N 16°40E **79** D9
Blantyre *Malawi* 15°45S 35°0E **143** F4
Blarney *Ireland* 51°56N 8°33W **64** E3
Blasdell *U.S.A.* 42°48N 78°50W **174** D6
Blaszki *Poland* 51°38N 18°30E **83** G5
Blato *Croatia* 42°56N 16°48E **93** F13
Blaubeuren *Germany* 48°24N 9°46E **77** G5
Blaustein *Germany* 48°25N 9°53E **77** G5
Blåvands Huk *Denmark* 55°33N 8°4E **63** J2
Blaydon *U.K.* 54°58N 1°42W **66** C6
Blaye *France* 45°8N 0°40W **72** C3
Blaye-les-Mines *France* 44°1N 2°8E **72** D6
Blayney *Australia* 33°32S 149°14E **153** E8
Blaze, Pt. *Australia* 12°56S 130°11E **148** B5
Blażowa *Poland* 49°53N 22°7E **83** D9
Bleckede *Germany* 53°17N 10°43E **76** B6
Bled *Slovenia* 46°27N 14°7E **93** B11
Bleiburg *Austria* 46°35N 14°49E **78** E7
Blejești *Romania* 44°19N 25°27E **81** F10
Blekinge *Sweden* 56°25N 15°20E **61** H16
Blekinge län □ *Sweden* 56°20N 15°20E **63** H9
Blenheim *Canada* 42°20N 82°0W **174** D3
Blenheim *N.Z.* 41°38S 173°57E **155** B8
Bléone → *France* 44°5N 6°0E **73** D10
Blérancourt *France* 49°31N 3°9E **71** C10
Bletchley *U.K.* 51°59N 0°44W **67** F7
Bleus, Monts
  Dem. Rep. of the Congo 1°30N 30°30E **142** B3
Blida *Algeria* 36°30N 2°49E **136** A6
Blida □ *Algeria* 36°35N 3°0E **136** A6
Blidet Amor *Algeria* 32°59N 5°58E **136** B5
Blidö *Sweden* 59°37N 18°53E **62** E12
Blidsberg *Sweden* 57°56N 13°30E **63** H9
Blieskastel *Germany* 49°14N 7°12E **77** F3
Bligh Sound *N.Z.* 44°47S 167°32E **155** E2
Bligh Water *Fiji* 17°0S 178°0E **154** a
Blind River *Canada* 46°10N 82°58W **164** C3
Blinisht *Albania* 41°52N 19°59E **96** E3
Bliss *Idaho, U.S.A.* 42°56N 114°57W **168** E6
Bliss *N.Y., U.S.A.* 42°34N 78°15W **174** D6
Blissfield *U.S.A.* 41°50N 83°58W **174** E1
Blitar *Indonesia* 8°5S 112°11E **119** H15
Blitchton *U.S.A.* 32°12N 81°26W **178** D8
Blitta *Togo* 8°23N 1°6E **139** D5
Block I. *U.S.A.* 41°11N 71°35W **175** E13
Block Island Sd.
  U.S.A. 41°15N 71°40W **175** E13
Bloemfontein *S. Africa* 29°6S 26°7E **144** C4
Bloemhof *S. Africa* 27°38S 25°32E **144** C4
Blois *France* 47°35N 1°20E **70** E8
Blomskog *Sweden* 59°16N 12°2E **62** E6
Blönduós *Iceland* 65°40N 20°12W **60** D3
Blongas *Indonesia* 8°53S 116°2E **119** K19
Blonie *Poland* 52°12N 20°37E **83** F7
Bloodvein → *Canada* 51°47N 96°43W **163** C9
Bloody Foreland *Ireland* 55°10N 8°17W **64** A3
Bloomer *U.S.A.* 45°6N 91°29W **172** C8
Bloomfield *Canada* 43°59N 77°14W **174** C7
Bloomfield *Iowa, U.S.A.* 40°45N 92°25W **172** E7
Bloomfield *N. Mex.,*
  U.S.A. 36°43N 107°59W **169** H10
Bloomfield *Nebr.,*
  U.S.A. 42°36N 97°39W **172** D5
Bloomington *Ill., U.S.A.* 40°28N 89°0W **172** E9
Bloomington *Ind.,*
  U.S.A. 39°10N 86°32W **172** F10
Bloomington *Minn.,*
  U.S.A. 44°50N 93°17W **172** C7
Bloomsburg *U.S.A.* 41°0N 76°27W **175** F8
Bloomsbury *Australia* 20°48S 148°38E **150** b
Blora *Indonesia* 6°57S 111°25E **119** G14
Blossburg *U.S.A.* 41°41N 77°4W **174** E7
Blosseville Kyst
  Greenland 68°50N 26°30W **57** D8
Blouberg *S. Africa* 23°8S 28°59E **145** B4
Blountstown *U.S.A.* 30°27N 85°3W **178** F4
Bludenz *Austria* 47°10N 9°50E **79** E5
Blue Cypress L. *U.S.A.* 27°44N 80°45W **179** H9
Blue Earth *U.S.A.* 43°38N 94°6W **172** D6
Blue Hole △ *Belize* 17°24N 87°30W **182** C2
Blue Lagoon △ *Zambia* 15°28S 27°26E **143** F2
Blue Mesa Res.
  U.S.A. 38°28N 107°20W **168** G10
Blue Mountain Lake
  U.S.A. 43°51N 74°27W **175** C10

Blue Mountain Pk.
  Jamaica 18°3N 76°36W **182** a
Blue Mt. *U.S.A.* 40°30N 76°30W **175** F8
Blue Mts. *Australia* 33°40S 150°15E **153** B9
Blue Mts. *Jamaica* 18°3N 76°36W **182** a
Blue Mts. *Maine,*
  U.S.A. 44°50N 70°35W **175** B14
Blue Mts. *Oreg., U.S.A.* 45°0N 118°20W **168** D4
Blue Mts. △ *Australia* 34°2S 150°15E **153** C9
Blue Mud B. *U.S.A.* 13°30S 136°0E **150** A2
Blue Mud Bay ◌
  Australia 13°25S 136°2E **150** A2
Blue Nile = Nîl el Azraq →
  Sudan 15°38N 32°31E **135** E12
Blue Rapids *U.S.A.* 39°41N 96°39W **172** F5
Blue Ridge *U.S.A.* 36°40N 80°50W **173** G13
Blue River *Canada* 52°6N 119°18W **162** C5
Bluefield *U.S.A.* 37°15N 81°17W **173** G13
Bluefields *Nic.* 12°20N 83°50W **182** D3
Bluevale *Canada* 43°51N 81°15W **174** C3
Bluff *Australia* 23°35S 149°4E **150** C4
Bluff *N.Z.* 46°37S 168°20E **155** G3
Bluff *U.S.A.* 37°17N 109°33W **169** H9
Bluff Harbour *N.Z.* 46°36S 168°21E **155** G3
Bluff Knoll *Australia* 34°24S 118°15E **149** F2
Bluff Pt. *Australia* 27°50S 114°5E **149** E1
Bluffton *Ind., U.S.A.* 31°3N 84°52W **178** D5
Bluffton *Ind., U.S.A.* 40°44N 85°11W **173** E11
Bluffton *S.C., U.S.A.* 32°14N 80°52W **178** D9
Blumenau *Brazil* 27°0S 49°0W **191** B6
Blunt *U.S.A.* 44°31N 99°59W **172** C4
Bly *U.S.A.* 42°24N 121°3W **168** E3
Blyde River Canyon △
  S. Africa 24°37S 31°2E **145** B5
Blyth *Australia* 33°49S 138°28E **152** B3
Blyth *Canada* 43°44N 81°26W **174** C3
Blyth → *U.K.* 55°8N 1°31W **66** B6
Blythe *Calif., U.S.A.* 33°37N 114°36W **171** M12
Blythe *Ga., U.S.A.* 33°17N 82°12W **178** D7
Blytheville *U.S.A.* 35°56N 89°55W **177** D10
Bo *S. Leone* 7°55N 11°50W **138** D2
Bo Duc *Vietnam* 11°58N 106°50E **120** G6
Bo Hai *China* 39°0N 119°0E **115** E10
Bo Hai Haixia *China* 38°25N 121°10E **115** E11
Bo Xian = Bozhou
  China 33°55N 115°41E **114** H8
Boa Esperança, Represa
  Brazil 6°50S 43°50W **189** B2
Boa Nova *Brazil* 14°22S 40°10W **189** C2
Boa Viagem *Brazil* 9°7S 39°44W **189** B3
Boa Vista *Brazil* 2°48N 60°30W **186** C6
Boa Vista *C. Verde Is.* 16°0N 22°49W **134** b
Boaco *Nic.* 12°29N 85°35W **182** D2
Bo'ai *China* 35°10N 113°3E **114** G7
Boal *Spain* 43°25N 6°49W **88** A4
Boalsburg *U.S.A.* 40°47N 77°49W **174** F7
Boane *Mozam.* 26°6S 32°19E **145** D5
Boao *China* 19°8N 110°34E **117** a
Boardman *U.S.A.* 41°2N 80°40W **174** E4
Boath *India* 19°20N 78°20E **126** E4
Bobadah *Australia* 32°19S 146°41E **153** B7
Bobai *China* 22°17N 109°59E **117** B9
Bobbili *India* 18°35N 83°30E **126** E6
Bobcaygeon *Canada* 44°33N 78°33W **174** B6
Boblad *India* 17°13N 75°26E **126** F2
Böblingen *Germany* 48°40N 9°1E **77** G5
Bobo-Dioulasso
  Burkina Faso 11°8N 4°13W **138** C4
Bobolice *Poland* 53°58N 16°37E **82** E3
Bobonong *Botswana* 21°58S 28°20E **145** B4
Bobov Dol *Bulgaria* 42°20N 23°0E **96** D7
Bóbr → *Poland* 52°4N 15°4E **83** F2
Bobraomby, Tanjon' i
  Madag. 12°40S 49°10E **141** G9
Bobrov *Russia* 51°5N 40°2E **86** E5
Bobrovytsya *Ukraine* 50°44N 31°23E **85** G6
Bobruysk = Babruysk
  Belarus 53°10N 29°15E **75** B15
Bobrynets *Ukraine* 48°4N 32°5E **85** H7
Boby, Pic *Madag.* 22°12S 46°55E **141** J9
Boca del Río *Mexico* 19°5N 96°4W **181** D5
Boca do Acre *Brazil* 8°50S 67°27W **188** B4
Boca Grande *U.S.A.* 26°45N 82°15W **179** J7
Boca Raton *U.S.A.* 26°21N 80°5W **179** J9
Bocaiúva *Brazil* 17°7S 43°49W **189** C2
Bocanda *Ivory C.* 7°5N 4°31W **138** D4
Bocas del Dragón = Dragon's
  Mouths *Trin. & Tob.* 10°N 61°50W **187** K15
Bocas del Toro *Panama* 9°15N 82°20W **182** E3
Boceguillas *Spain* 41°20N 3°39W **88** D7
Bochnia *Poland* 49°58N 20°27E **83** J7
Bocholt *Germany* 51°50N 6°36E **76** D2
Bochum = Senwabarana
  S. Africa 23°17S 29°7E **145** B4
Bochum *Germany* 51°28N 7°13E **76** D3
Bockenem *Germany* 52°1N 10°8E **76** C6
Boćki *Poland* 52°39N 23°3E **83** F10
Bocognano *France* 42°5N 9°4E **73** F13
Bocoyna *Mexico* 27°52N 107°35W **180** B3
Bocșa *Romania* 45°21N 21°47E **80** E6
Boda *Dalarna, Sweden* 61°1N 15°13E **62** C9
Böda *Kalmar, Sweden* 57°15N 17°3E **63** G11
Boda *Västernorrland,*
  Sweden 62°52N 16°39E **62** B10
Bodaybo *Russia* 57°50N 114°0E **107** D12
Boddam *U.K.* 59°56N 1°17W **65** B7
Boddington *Australia* 32°50S 116°30E **149** F2
Bode Sdn *Nigeria* 7°35N 4°30E **139** D5
Bodega Bay *U.S.A.* 38°20N 123°3W **170** G3
Boden *Sweden* 65°50N 21°42E **60** D19
Bodensee *Europe* 47°35N 9°25E **77** H5
Bodhan *India* 18°40N 77°44E **126** E3
Bodh Gaya *India* 24°41N 84°59E **125** G11
Bodinayakkanur *India* 10°2N 77°10E **128** G3
Bodinga *Nigeria* 12°58N 5°10E **139** C6
Bodmin *U.K.* 50°28N 4°43W **67** G3
Bodmin Moor *U.K.* 50°33N 4°36W **67** G3
Bodø *Norway* 67°17N 14°24E **60** C16
Bodrog → *Hungary* 48°11N 21°22E **80** B6
Bodrum *Turkey* 37°3N 27°30E **99** D9
Bódva → *Hungary* 48°19N 20°45E **80** B5
Boën *France* 45°44N 4°1E **73** C8
Boende
  Dem. Rep. of the Congo 0°24S 21°12E **140** E4
Boeotia = Viotía *Greece* 38°20N 23°0E **98** C5
Boerne *U.S.A.* 29°47N 98°44W **176** G5

Boesmans → *S. Africa* 33°42S 26°39E **144** D4
Boffa *Guinea* 10°16N 14°3W **138** C2
Bogalusa *U.S.A.* 30°47N 89°52W **177** F10
Bogan → *Australia* 30°20S 146°55E **153** A7
Bogan Gate *Australia* 33°7S 147°49E **153** B7
Bogandé *Burkina Faso* 12°58N 0°8W **139** C4
Bogantungan
  Australia 23°41S 147°17E **150** C4
Bogata *U.S.A.* 33°28N 95°13W **176** E7
Bogatić *Serbia* 44°51N 19°30E **96** B4
Boğazkale *Turkey* 40°2N 34°37E **104** B6
Boğazlıyan *Turkey* 39°11N 35°14E **104** C6
Bogda Shan *China* 43°35N 89°40E **109** D11
Bogen *Sweden* 60°4N 12°33E **62** D6
Bogense *Denmark* 55°34N 10°5E **63** J4
Boggabilla *Australia* 28°36S 150°24E **153** A9
Boggabri *Australia* 30°45S 150°5E **153** A9
Boggeragh Mts. *Ireland* 52°2N 8°55W **64** E3
Boglan = Solhan *Turkey* 38°57N 41°3E **105** C9
Bognor Regis *U.K.* 50°47N 0°40W **67** G7
Bogo *Phil.* 11°3N 124°0E **119** B6
Bogodukhov = Bohodukhiv
  Ukraine 50°9N 35°33E **85** G8
Bogong, Mt. *Australia* 36°47S 147°17E **153** D7
Bogor *Indonesia* 6°36S 106°48E **118** F3
Bogoroditsk *Russia* 53°47N 38°8E **84** F10
Bogorodsk *Russia* 56°4N 43°30E **86** B6
Bogoso *Ghana* 5°38N 2°3W **138** D4
Bogotá *Colombia* 4°34N 74°0W **186** C4
Bogotol *Russia* 56°15N 89°50E **106** D9
Bogou *Togo* 10°40N 0°12E **139** C5
Bogra *Bangla.* 24°51N 89°22E **123** G16
Boguchany *Russia* 58°40N 97°30E **107** D10
Boguchar *Russia* 49°55N 40°32E **86** F5
Bogué *Mauritania* 16°45N 14°10W **138** B2
Boguslav-Gorce *Poland* 50°45N 16°12E **83** H3
Bohain-en-Vermandois
  France 49°59N 3°28E **71** C10
Bohdan *Ukraine* 48°2N 24°22E **81** B9
Bohemian Forest = Böhmerwald
  Germany 49°8N 13°14E **77** F9
Bohena Cr. →
  Australia 30°17S 149°42E **153** A8
Böhmerwald *Germany* 49°8N 13°14E **77** F9
Bohmte *Germany* 52°22N 8°19E **76** C4
Bohodukhiv *Ukraine* 50°9N 35°33E **85** G8
Bohol □ *Phil.* 9°50N 124°10E **119** C6
Bohol Sea *Phil.* 9°0N 124°0E **119** C6
Bohongou *Burkina Faso* 12°30N 0°40E **139** C5
Böhönye *Hungary* 46°25N 17°28E **80** D2
Bohorodchany *Ukraine* 48°48N 24°32E **81** B9
Bohrok *Indonesia* 3°30N 98°12E **121** L2
Bohuslän *Sweden* 58°25N 12°0E **63** F5
Bohuslev *Ukraine* 49°33N 30°56E **85** H6
Boi *Nigeria* 9°35N 9°27E **139** D6
Boi, Pta. do *Brazil* 23°55S 45°15W **191** A6
Boiaçu *Brazil* 0°27S 61°46W **186** D6
Boigu *Australia* 9°16S 142°13E **150** a
Boileau, C. *Australia* 17°40S 122°7E **148** C3
Boipariguda *India* 18°46N 82°26E **126** E6
Boipeba, I. de *Brazil* 13°39S 38°55W **189** C3
Boiro *Spain* 42°39N 8°54W **88** C2
Boise *U.S.A.* 43°37N 116°13W **168** E5
Boise City *U.S.A.* 36°44N 102°31W **176** C3
Boissevain *Canada* 49°15N 100°5W **163** D8
Bóite → *Italy* 46°5N 12°5E **93** B9
Boitzenburg *Germany* 53°16N 13°35E **76** B8
Boizenburg *Germany* 53°23N 10°43E **76** B6
Bojador, C. *W. Sahara* 26°0N 14°30W **134** C2
Bojana → *Albania* 41°52N 19°22E **96** E3
Bojano *Italy* 41°29N 14°29E **95** A7
Bojanowo *Poland* 51°43N 16°42E **83** G3
Bøjden *Denmark* 55°6N 10°7E **63** J4
Bojnūrd *Iran* 37°30N 57°20E **129** B8
Boju *Nigeria* 7°22N 7°55E **139** D6
Boka *Serbia* 45°22N 20°52E **80** E5
Boka Kotorska
  Montenegro 42°23N 18°32E **96** C2
Bokala *Ivory C.* 8°31N 4°33W **138** D4
Bokani *Nigeria* 9°28N 5°10E **139** D6
Bokaro *India* 23°46N 85°55E **125** H11
Boké *Guinea* 10°56N 14°17W **138** C2
Bokhara → *Australia* 29°55S 146°42E **151** D4
Bokkos *Nigeria* 9°17N 9°1E **139** D6
Boknafjorden *Norway* 59°14N 5°40E **63** G11
Bokor △ *Cambodia* 10°50N 104°1E **121** G5
Bokora △ *Uganda* 2°12N 31°32E **142** B3
Bokoro *Chad* 12°25N 17°14E **135** F9
Bokpyin *Burma* 11°18N 98°42E **121** G2
Boksitogorsk *Russia* 59°22N 33°50E **84** C7
Bokungu
  Dem. Rep. of the Congo 0°35S 22°50E **140** E4
Bol *Croatia* 43°18N 16°38E **93** E13
Bol *Chad* 13°30N 15°30W **138** C1
Bolama *Guinea-Biss.* 11°30N 15°30W **138** C1
Bolan → *Pakistan* 28°38N 67°42E **124** E2
Bolan Pass *Pakistan* 29°50N 67°20E **122** E5
Bolaños → *Mexico* 21°12N 104°5W **180** C4
Bolaños de Calatrava
  Spain 38°54N 3°40W **89** G7
Bolayır *Turkey* 40°32N 26°45E **97** F10
Bolbec *France* 49°30N 0°30E **70** C7
Boldājī *Iran* 31°56N 51°3E **129** D6
Boldești-Scăeni *Romania* 45°3N 26°2E **81** E11
Bole *China* 44°55N 81°37E **109** C10
Bole *Ghana* 9°3N 2°23W **138** D4
Bolekhiv *Ukraine* 49°0N 23°57E **75** D12
Bolesławiec *Poland* 51°17N 15°37E **83** G2
Bolgatanga *Ghana* 10°44N 0°53W **139** C4
Bolgrad = Bolhrad
  Ukraine 45°40N 28°32E **81** E13
Bolhrad *Ukraine* 45°40N 28°32E **81** E13
Boli *China* 45°46N 130°31E **115** B16
Bolivar *Peru* 7°18S 77°48W **188** E3
Bolívar *Argentina* 36°15S 60°53W **190** D4
Bolivar *Mo., U.S.A.* 37°37N 93°25W **176** D7
Bolivar *N.Y., U.S.A.* 42°4N 78°10W **174** D6
Bolivar *Tenn., U.S.A.* 35°12N 89°0W **177** D10
Bolívar □ *Colombia* 9°0N 74°40W **186** B3
Bolívar, Pico *Venezuela* 8°32N 71°2W **183** E5
Bolivia ■ *S. Amer.* 17°6S 64°0W **186** G6
Bolivian Plateau = Altiplano
  Bolivia 17°0S 68°0W **188** G5
Boljevac *Serbia* 43°51N 21°58E **96** C5
Bolkhov *Russia* 53°25N 36°0E **84** F9
Bolków *Poland* 50°55N 16°6E **83** H3

Bollebygd *Sweden* 57°40N 12°35E **63** G6
Bollène *France* 44°18N 4°45E **73** D8
Bollnäs *Sweden* 61°21N 16°24E **62** D10
Bollon *Australia* 28°2S 147°29E **151** D4
Bollstabruk *Sweden* 62°59N 17°40E **62** B11
Bolmen *Sweden* 56°55N 13°40E **63** H7
Bolo
  Dem. Rep. of the Congo 2°6S 16°20E **140** E3
Bologna *Italy* 44°29N 11°20E **93** D8
Bologna ✈ (BLQ) *Italy* 44°34N 11°16E **93** D8
Bologoye *Russia* 57°55N 34°5E **84** D8
Bolomba
  Dem. Rep. of the Congo 0°35N 19°0E **140** D3
Bolonchén *Mexico* 20°1N 89°45W **181** D7
Bolótana *Italy* 40°20N 8°52E **94** B1
Bolsena *Italy* 42°39N 11°59E **93** F8
Bolsena, L. di *Italy* 42°36N 11°56E **93** F8
Bolshakovo *Russia* 54°53N 21°40E **82** D8
Bolshaya Chernigovka
  Russia 52°6N 50°52E **86** D10
Bolshaya Glushitsa
  Russia 52°28N 50°30E **86** D10
Bolshaya Martynovka
  Russia 47°19N 41°37E **87** G5
Bolshaya Vradiyevka
  Ukraine 47°50N 30°40E **85** J6
Bolshevik, Ostrov
  Russia 78°30N 102°0E **107** B11
Bolshoy Anyuy →
  Russia 68°30N 160°49E **107** C17
Bolshoy Begichev, Ostrov
  Russia 74°20N 112°30E **107** B12
Bolshoy Kamen *Russia* 43°7N 132°19E **112** C6
Bolshoy Kavkas = Caucasus
  Eurasia 42°50N 44°0E **87** J7
Bolshoy Lyakhovskiy, Ostrov
  Russia 73°35N 142°0E **107** B15
Bolshoy Tyuters, Ostrov
  Russia 59°51N 27°13E **84** C4
Bolsward *Neths.* 53°3N 5°32E **69** A5
Bolt Head *U.K.* 50°12N 3°48W **67** G4
Boltaña *Spain* 42°28N 0°4E **90** C5
Boltigen *Switz.* 46°38N 7°24E **77** J3
Bolton *Canada* 43°54N 79°45W **174** C5
Bolton *U.K.* 53°35N 2°26W **66** D5
Bolton Landing
  U.S.A. 43°32N 73°35W **175** C11
Bolu *Turkey* 40°45N 31°35E **104** B4
Bolu □ *Turkey* 40°40N 31°30E **104** B4
Boluo *China* 23°3N 114°21E **117** F10
Bolvadin *Turkey* 38°45N 31°4E **104** C4
Bolzano *Italy* 46°31N 11°22E **93** B8
Bom Conselho *Brazil* 9°10S 36°41W **189** B3
Bom Despacho *Brazil* 19°43S 45°15W **189** D1
Bom Jesus *Brazil* 9°4S 44°22W **189** B2
Bom Jesus da Gurguéia, Serra
  Brazil 9°0S 43°0W **189** B2
Bom Jesus da Lapa
  Brazil 13°15S 43°25W **189** C2
Boma
  Dem. Rep. of the Congo 5°50S 13°4E **140** F2
Bomaderry *Australia* 34°52S 150°37E **153** E9
Bombala *Australia* 36°56S 149°15E **153** D8
Bombarral *Portugal* 39°15N 9°9W **89** F1
Bombay = Mumbai
  India 18°56N 72°50E **126** E1
Bombay *U.S.A.* 44°56N 74°34W **175** B10
Bombedor, Pta.
  Venezuela 9°53N 61°37W **187** L15
Bomberai, Semenanjung
  Indonesia 3°0S 133°0E **119** E8
Bomboma
  Dem. Rep. of the Congo 2°25N 18°55E **140** D3
Bombombwa
  Dem. Rep. of the Congo 1°40N 25°40E **142** B2
Bomi *China* 29°50N 95°45E **110** F8
Bomi Hills *Liberia* 7°1N 10°38W **138** D2
Bomili
  Dem. Rep. of the Congo 1°45N 27°5E **142** B2
Bømlo *Norway* 59°37N 5°13E **61** G11
Bomokandi →
  Dem. Rep. of the Congo 3°39N 26°8E **142** B2
Bomu →
  C.A.R. 4°40N 22°30E **140** D4
Bon, C. = Ra's aţ Ṭīb
  Tunisia 37°1N 11°2E **136** A6
Bon Accueil *Mauritius* 20°10S 57°39E **141** d
Bon Echo △ *Canada* 44°55N 77°16W **174** B7
Bon Sar Pa *Vietnam* 12°24N 107°35E **120** F6
Bonāb *Āzarbājān-e Sharqī,*
  Iran 37°20N 46°4E **105** D12
Bonāb *Zanjān, Iran* 36°35N 48°41E **105** D13
Bonaigarh *India* 21°50N 84°57E **125** J11
Bonaire *W. Indies* 12°10N 68°15W **183** D6
Bonaire *W. Indies* 12°10N 68°15W **183** D6
Bonampak *Mexico* 16°44N 91°5W **182** D6
Bonang *Australia* 37°11S 148°41E **153** D8
Bonanza *Nic.* 13°54N 84°35W **182** D3
Bonaparte Arch.
  Australia 14°0S 124°30E **148** B3
Boñar *Spain* 42°52N 5°19W **88** C5
Bonar Bridge *U.K.* 57°54N 4°20W **65** D4
Bonasse *Trin. & Tob.* 10°5N 61°54W **187** L15
Bonaventure *Canada* 48°5N 65°32W **165** C6
Bonavista *Canada* 48°40N 53°5W **165** C9
Bonavista, C. *Canada* 48°42N 53°5W **165** C9
Bondeno *Italy* 44°53N 11°25E **93** D8
Bondo
  Dem. Rep. of the Congo 3°55N 23°53E **142** B1
Bondoukodi *Indonesia* 9°33S 119°0E **148** A2
Bondoukou *Ivory C.* 8°2N 2°47W **138** D4
Bondowoso *Indonesia* 7°55S 113°49E **119** G15
Bone, Teluk *Indonesia* 4°10S 120°50E **119** E6
Bonerate *Indonesia* 7°25S 121°5E **119** F6
Bonerate, Kepulauan
  Indonesia 6°30S 121°10E **119** F6
Bo'ness *U.K.* 56°1N 3°37W **65** E5
Bonete, Cerro
  Argentina 27°55S 68°40W **190** B3
Bong Son = Hoai Nhon
  Vietnam 14°28N 109°1E **120** E7
Bongabong *Phil.* 12°45N 121°28E **119** B4
Bongandanga
  Dem. Rep. of the Congo 1°24N 21°3E **140** D4
Bongor *Chad* 10°35N 15°20E **135** F9

Bongos, Massif des
  C.A.R. 8°40N 22°25E **140** C4
Bongouanou *Ivory C.* 6°42N 4°15W **138** D4
Bonham *U.S.A.* 33°35N 96°11W **176** E6
Boni *Mali* 15°3N 2°10W **138** B4
Boni → *Kenya* 1°35S 41°18E **142** C5
Bonifacio *France* 41°24N 9°10E **73** G13
Bonifacio, Bouches de
  Medit. S. 41°12N 9°15E **94** A2
Bonin Is. = Ogasawara Gunto
  Pac. Oc. 27°0N 142°0E **156** E6
Bonita Springs *U.S.A.* 26°21N 81°47W **179** J8
Bonkoukou *Niger* 14°0N 3°15E **139** C5
Bonn *Germany* 50°46N 7°6E **76** E3
Bonnat *France* 46°20N 1°54E **71** F8
Bonne Terre *U.S.A.* 37°55N 90°33W **176** E8
Bonneau *U.S.A.* 33°16N 79°58W **178** D8
Bonners Ferry *U.S.A.* 48°42N 116°19W **168** B5
Bonnétable *France* 48°11N 0°25E **70** D7
Bonneval *France* 48°11N 1°24E **70** D8
Bonneval-sur-Arc *France* 48°11N 1°24E **70** D8
Bonneville *France* 46°4N 6°24E **71** F13
Bonney, L. *Australia* 37°50S 140°20E **152** C2
Bonnie Doon *Australia* 37°2S 145°53E **153** D6
Bonnie Rock *Australia* 30°29S 118°22E **149** F2
Bonny *Nigeria* 4°25N 7°13E **139** E6
Bonny → *Nigeria* 4°20N 7°10E **139** E6
Bonny, Bight of *Africa* 3°30N 9°20E **139** E6
Bonny Hills *Australia* 31°36S 152°51E **153** A10
Bonny-sur-Loire *France* 47°33N 2°50E **71** E9
Bonnyrigg *U.K.* 55°53N 3°6W **65** F5
Bonnyville *Canada* 54°20N 110°45E **163** C6
Bono *Italy* 40°25N 9°2E **94** B2
Bonoi *Indonesia* 1°45S 137°41E **119** E9
Bonorva *Italy* 40°25N 8°46E **94** B1
Bonsall *U.S.A.* 33°16N 117°14W **171** M9
Bontang *Indonesia* 0°10N 117°30E **118** D5
Bontebok △ *S. Africa* 34°5S 20°28E **144** D3
Bonthe *S. Leone* 7°30N 12°33W **138** D2
Bontoc *Phil.* 17°7N 120°58E **119** A4
Bonyeri *Ghana* 5°1N 2°46W **138** D4
Bonyhád *Hungary* 46°18N 18°32E **80** D3
Bonython Ra.
  Australia 23°40S 128°45E **148** D4
Booderee △
  Australia 35°12S 150°42E **153** C9
Boodjamulla △
  Australia 18°15S 138°6E **150** B2
Bookabie *Australia* 31°50S 132°41E **149** F5
Booker *U.S.A.* 36°27N 100°32W **176** C4
Bool Lagoon *Australia* 37°7S 140°40E **152** C4
Boola *Guinea* 8°8N 8°41W **138** D3
Boolcoomata *Australia* 31°57S 140°33E **152** A4
Booligal *Australia* 33°58S 144°53E **153** B6
Boom Tsagaan Nuur
  Mongolia 45°35N 99°9E **110** B8
Boonah *Australia* 27°58S 152°41E **151** D5
Boone *Iowa, U.S.A.* 42°4N 93°53W **172** E7
Boone *N.C., U.S.A.* 36°13N 81°41W **177** C14
Booneville *Ark., U.S.A.* 35°8N 93°55W **176** D8
Booneville *Miss.,*
  U.S.A. 34°39N 88°34W **177** D10
Boonville *Calif., U.S.A.* 39°1N 123°22W **170** F3
Boonville *Ind., U.S.A.* 38°3N 87°16W **172** F10
Boonville *Mo., U.S.A.* 38°58N 92°44W **172** F7
Boonville *N.Y., U.S.A.* 43°29N 75°20W **175** C9
Boorabbin △ *Australia* 31°30S 120°10E **149** F3
Boorindal *Australia* 32°23S 146°11E **151** E4
Boorowa *Australia* 34°28S 148°44E **153** E8
Boort *Australia* 36°7S 143°46E **152** C3
Boosaaso *Somalia* 11°12N 49°18E **131** E4
Boothia, Gulf of *Canada* 71°0N 90°0W **160** C14
Boothia Pen. *Canada* 71°0N 94°0W **160** C13
Bootle *U.K.* 53°28N 3°1W **66** D4
Booué *Gabon* 0°5S 11°55E **140** E2
Boppard *Germany* 50°13N 7°35E **77** E3
Boquilla, Presa de la
  Mexico 27°31N 105°30W **180** B3
Boquillas del Carmen
  Mexico 29°11N 102°58W **180** B4
Bor *Czech Rep.* 49°41N 12°45E **78** D5
Bor *Russia* 56°28N 43°59E **86** B7
Bor *Serbia* 44°5N 22°7E **96** B6
Bor *South Sudan* 6°10N 31°40E **135** G12
Bor *Sweden* 57°9N 14°10E **63** H8
Bor *Turkey* 37°54N 34°32E **104** C6
Bor Mashash *Israel* 31°7N 34°50E **130** D3
Bora Bora
  French Polynesia 16°30S 151°45W **157** J12
Borah Peak *U.S.A.* 44°8N 113°47W **168** D7
Boraha, Nosy *Madag.* 16°50S 49°55E **141** H9
Borankul *Kazakhstan* 46°11N 54°25E **108** C4
Borås *Sweden* 57°43N 12°56E **63** G6
Borāzjān *Iran* 29°22N 51°10E **129** D6
Borba *Brazil* 4°12S 59°34W **186** D7
Borba *Portugal* 38°50N 7°26W **89** G3
Borborema, Planalto da
  Brazil 7°0S 37°0W **189** B3
Borcea *Romania* 44°20N 27°45E **81** F12
Borçka *Turkey* 41°25N 41°41E **105** B9
Bord Khūn-e Now *Iran* 28°3N 51°28E **129** D6
Borda, C. *Australia* 35°45S 136°34E **152** C2
Bordeaux *France* 44°50N 0°36W **72** D3
Bordeaux ✈ (BOD)
  France 44°50N 0°35W **72** D3
Borden *Australia* 34°3S 118°12E **149** F2
Borden-Carleton
  Canada 46°18N 63°47W **165** C7
Borden I. *Canada* 78°30N 111°30W **161** B9
Borden Pen. *Canada* 73°0N 83°0W **161** C15
Bordeño *Italy* 44°53N 11°25E **93** D8
Border Ranges △
  Australia 28°24S 152°56E **151** D5
Borders = Scottish Borders □
  U.K. 55°35N 2°50W **65** F6
Bordertown *Australia* 36°19S 140°45E **152** C4
Borðeyri *Iceland* 65°12N 21°6W **60** D3
Bordighera *Italy* 43°46N 7°39E **92** E4
Bordj bou Arreridj *Algeria* 36°4N 4°45E **136** A4
Bordj Bourguiba *Tunisia* 32°12N 10°12E **136** B4
Bordj Flye Ste-Marie
  Algeria 27°19N 2°32W **136** C5
Bordj in Eker *Algeria* 24°9N 5°3E **136** D6
Bordj Menaïel *Algeria* 36°46N 3°43E **136** A4
Bordj Messouda *Algeria* 30°12N 9°25E **136** B3
Bordj Mokhtar *Algeria* 21°20N 0°56E **136** D6
Bordj Nili *Algeria* 33°28N 3°2E **136** B6
Bordj Omar Driss
  Algeria 28°10N 6°40E **136** C6

Bordj Sif Fatima Algeria 31°6N 8°41E 136 B5
Bordj Tarat Algeria 25°55N 9°3E 136 C5
Borehamwood U.K. 51°40N 0°15W 67 F7
Borek Wielkopolski Poland 51°54N 17°11E 83 G4
Borensberg Sweden 58°34N 15°17E 63 F9
Borgå = Porvoo Finland 60°24N 25°40E 84 B3
Borgampad India 17°39N 80°52E 126 F5
Borgarnes Iceland 64°32N 21°55W 60 D3
Børgefjellet Norway 65°20N 13°45E 60 D15
Borger Neths. 52°54N 6°44E 69 B6
Borger U.S.A. 35°39N 101°24W 176 D4
Borgholm Sweden 56°52N 16°39E 63 H10
Bórgia Italy 38°49N 16°30E 95 D9
Borgo San Dalmazzo Italy 44°20N 7°30E 92 D4
Borgo San Lorenzo Italy 43°57N 11°23E 93 E8
Borgo Val di Taro Italy 44°29N 9°46E 92 D6
Borgo Valsugana Italy 46°3N 11°27E 93 B8
Borgomanero Italy 45°42N 8°28E 92 C5
Borgorose Italy 42°11N 13°13E 93 F10
Borgosésia Italy 45°43N 8°16E 92 C5
Borhoyn Tal Mongolia 43°50N 111°58E 114 C6
Bori Nigeria 4°42N 7°21E 139 E6
Borigumma India 19°3N 82°33E 126 E6
Borikhane Laos 18°33N 103°43E 120 C4
Borisoglebsk Russia 51°27N 42°5E 86 E6
Borisov = Barysaw Belarus 54°17N 28°28E 75 A15
Borisovka Russia 50°36N 36°1E 85 G9
Borj Jenein Tunisia 31°45N 10°9E 136 B6
Borja Peru 4°20S 77°40W 186 D3
Borja Spain 41°48N 1°34W 90 D3
Borjas Blancas = Les Borges Blanques Spain 41°31N 0°52E 90 D5
Borjomi Georgia 41°48N 43°28E 87 K6
Børkop Denmark 55°39N 9°39E 63 J3
Borkou Chad 18°15N 18°50E 135 E9
Borkum Germany 53°34N 6°40E 76 B2
Borlänge Sweden 60°29N 15°26E 62 D9
Borley, C. Antarctica 66°15S 52°30E 55 C5
Borlu Turkey 38°44N 28°27E 99 C10
Bormida → Italy 44°23N 8°13E 92 D5
Bórmio Italy 46°28N 10°22E 92 B7
Borna Germany 51°7N 12°29E 76 D8
Borne Sulinowo Poland 53°32N 16°36E 82 E3
Borneo E. Indies 1°0N 115°0E 118 D5
Bornholm Denmark 55°10N 15°0E 63 J8
Bornholmsgattet Europe 55°15N 14°20E 63 J8
Borno □ Nigeria 11°30N 13°0E 139 C7
Bornos Spain 36°48N 5°42W 89 J5
Bornova Turkey 38°27N 27°14E 99 C9
Bornu Yassa Nigeria 12°14N 12°25E 139 C7
Borobudur △ Indonesia 7°36S 110°12E 119 G14
Borodino Russia 55°31N 35°40E 84 E8
Borodino Ukraine 46°18N 29°15E 81 D14
Borogontsy Russia 62°42N 131°8E 107 C14
Borohoro Shan China 44°6N 83°10E 109 D10
Boromo Burkina Faso 11°45N 2°58W 138 C4
Boron U.S.A. 35°0N 117°39W 171 L9
Borongan Phil. 11°37N 125°26E 119 B7
Borotou Ivory C. 8°46N 7°30W 138 D3
Borovan Bulgaria 43°27N 23°45E 96 C7
Borovichi Russia 58°25N 33°55E 84 C7
Borovsk Russia 55°12N 36°24E 84 E9
Borovskoy Kazakhstan 53°48N 64°9E 108 B6
Borrby Sweden 55°27N 14°10E 63 J8
Borrego Springs U.S.A. 33°15N 116°23W 171 M10
Borriol Spain 40°4N 0°4W 90 E4
Borrisokane Ireland 53°0N 8°7W 64 D3
Borroloola Australia 16°4S 136°17E 150 B2
Borşa Cluj, Romania 46°56N 23°40E 81 D8
Borşa Maramureş, Romania 47°41N 24°50E 81 C9
Borsad India 22°25N 72°54E 124 H5
Borsec Romania 46°57N 25°34E 81 D10
Borshchiv Ukraine 48°48N 26°3E 81 B11
Borsod-Abaúj-Zemplén □ Hungary 48°20N 21°0E 80 B6
Bort-les-Orgues France 45°24N 2°29E 72 C6
Bortala = Bole China 44°55N 81°37E 109 C10
Borth U.K. 52°29N 4°2W 67 E3
Börtnan Sweden 62°45N 13°50E 62 B7
Borūjerd Iran 33°55N 48°50E 105 F13
Boryeong S. Korea 36°21N 126°36E 115 F14
Borynya Ukraine 49°4N 23°0E 83 J10
Boryslav Ukraine 49°18N 23°28E 83 J10
Boryspil Ukraine 50°21N 30°59E 85 G6
Borzhomi = Borjomi Georgia 41°48N 43°28E 87 K6
Borzna Ukraine 51°18N 32°26E 85 G7
Borzya Russia 50°24N 116°31E 111 A12
Bosa Italy 40°18N 8°30E 94 B1
Bosanska Dubica Bos.-H. 45°10N 16°50E 93 C13
Bosanska Gradiška Bos.-H. 45°10N 17°15E 80 E2
Bosanska Kostajnica Bos.-H. 45°11N 16°33E 93 C13
Bosanska Krupa Bos.-H. 44°53N 16°10E 93 D13
Bosanski Brod Bos.-H. 45°10N 18°0E 80 E2
Bosanski Novi Bos.-H. 45°2N 16°22E 93 C13
Bosanski Petrovac Bos.-H. 44°35N 16°21E 93 D13
Bosanski Šamac Bos.-H. 45°3N 18°29E 80 E3
Bosansko Grahovo Bos.-H. 44°12N 16°26E 93 D13
Boscastle U.K. 50°41N 4°42W 67 G3
Boscobelle Barbados 13°17N 59°35W 183 g
Bose China 23°53N 106°35E 116 F6
Boseong S. Korea 34°46N 127°5E 115 G14
Boshan China 36°28N 117°49E 115 F9
Boshof S. Africa 28°31S 25°13E 144 C4
Boshrūyeh Iran 33°50N 57°30E 129 C8
Bosilegrad Serbia 42°30N 22°27E 96 D6
Boskovice Czech Rep. 49°29N 16°40E 79 B9
Bosna → Bos.-H. 45°4N 18°29E 80 E3
Bosna i Hercegovina = Bosnia-Herzegovina ■ Europe 44°0N 18°0E 80 G2
Bosnia-Herzegovina ■ Europe 44°0N 18°0E 80 G2
Bosnik Indonesia 1°5S 136°10E 119 E9
Bosobolo Dem. Rep. of the Congo 4°15N 19°50E 140 D3
Bosporus = İstanbul Boğazı Turkey 41°5N 29°3E 97 E13
Bosque Farms U.S.A. 35°51N 106°42W 169 J10
Bosra = Buşra ash Shām Syria 32°30N 36°25E 130 C5
Bossangoa C.A.R. 6°35N 17°30E 140 C3
Bossé Bangou Niger 13°20N 1°18E 139 C5
Bossier City U.S.A. 32°31N 93°44W 176 E8
Bossiesvlei Namibia 25°1S 16°44E 144 C2
Bosso Niger 13°43N 13°19E 139 C7
Bosso, Dallol → Niger 12°25N 2°50E 139 C5
Bossol, Proliv Russia 46°30N 151°0E 107 E16
Bostan Pakistan 30°26N 67°2E 124 D2
Bostānābād Iran 37°50N 46°50E 105 D12
Bosten Hu China 41°55N 87°40E 109 D11
Boston U.K. 52°59N 0°2W 66 E7
Boston Ga., U.S.A. 30°47N 83°47W 178 E6
Boston Mass., U.S.A. 42°22N 71°3W 175 D13
Boston Bar Canada 49°52N 121°30W 162 D4
Boston Mts. U.S.A. 35°42N 93°15W 176 D8
Bostwick U.S.A. 29°46N 81°38W 178 F8
Bosumtwi, L. Ghana 6°30N 1°25W 139 D4
Bosut → Croatia 45°20N 18°45E 80 E3
Boswell Canada 49°28N 116°45W 162 D5
Boswell U.S.A. 40°10N 79°2W 174 F5
Botad India 22°15N 71°40E 124 H4
Botan → Turkey 37°57N 42°2E 105 D10
Botany B. Australia 33°58S 151°11E 147 E8
Botene Laos 17°35N 101°12E 120 D3
Botev Bulgaria 42°44N 24°52E 97 D8
Botevgrad Bulgaria 42°55N 23°47E 96 D7
Bothaville S. Africa 27°23S 26°34E 144 C4
Bothnia, G. of Europe 62°0N 20°0E 60 F19
Bothwell Australia 42°20S 147°1E 151 G4
Bothwell Canada 42°38N 81°52W 174 D3
Boticas Portugal 41°41N 7°40W 88 D3
Botletle → Botswana 20°10S 23°15E 144 B3
Botlikh Russia 42°39N 46°11E 87 J8
Botna → Moldova 46°45N 29°34E 81 D14
Botoroaga Romania 44°8N 25°32E 81 F10
Botoşani Romania 47°42N 26°41E 81 C11
Botoşani □ Romania 47°50N 26°50E 81 C11
Botou Burkina Faso 12°42N 1°59E 139 C5
Botou China 38°4N 116°34E 114 E9
Botricello Italy 38°56N 16°51E 95 D9
Botro Ivory C. 7°51N 5°19W 138 D3
Botshabelo S. Africa 29°14S 26°44E 144 C4
Botswana ■ Africa 22°0S 24°0E 144 B3
Bottineau U.S.A. 48°50N 100°27W 172 A3
Bottnaryd Sweden 57°47N 13°50E 63 G7
Bottrop Germany 51°31N 6°58E 76 D2
Botucatu Brazil 22°55S 48°30W 191 A6
Botum Sakor △ Cambodia 11°5N 103°15E 121 G4
Botwood Canada 49°6N 55°23W 165 C8
Bou Alam Algeria 33°50N 1°26E 136 B4
Bou Ali Algeria 27°11N 0°4W 136 C3
Bou Djébéha Mali 18°25N 2°45W 138 B4
Bou Guema Algeria 28°49N 0°19E 136 C4
Bou Ismaïl Algeria 36°38N 2°42E 136 A4
Bou Izakarn Morocco 29°12N 9°46W 136 C2
Boû Naga Mauritania 18°49N 13°20W 138 B2
Bou Noura Algeria 32°29N 3°43E 136 B4
Boû Rjeïmât Mauritania 19°4N 15°3W 138 B1
Bou Saâda Algeria 35°11N 4°9E 136 A4
Bou Salem Tunisia 36°45N 9°2E 136 A5
Bouaflé Ivory C. 7°1N 5°47W 138 D3
Bouaké Ivory C. 7°40N 5°2W 138 D3
Bouar C.A.R. 6°0N 15°40E 140 C3
Bouârfa Morocco 32°32N 1°58W 136 B3
Boubout Algeria 27°26N 4°30W 136 C3
Boucaut B. Australia 12°0S 134°25E 150 A1
Bouches-du-Rhône □ France 43°37N 5°2E 73 E9
Boucle de Baoulé △ Mali 13°53N 9°0W 138 C3
Boucles de la Seine Normande ⌂ France 49°32N 0°35E 70 C7
Bouctouche Canada 46°30N 64°45W 165 C7
Bouda Algeria 27°50N 0°27W 136 C3
Boudenib Morocco 31°59N 3°31W 136 B3
Boufarik Algeria 36°34N 2°58E 136 A4
Bougainville, C. Australia 13°57S 126°4E 148 B4
Bougainville I. Papua N. G. 6°0S 155°0E 147 B8
Bougainville Reef Australia 15°30S 147°5E 150 B4
Bougaroun, C. Algeria 37°6N 6°30E 136 A5
Bougie = Bejaïa Algeria 36°42N 5°2E 136 A5
Bougouni Mali 11°30N 7°20W 138 C3
Bougtob Algeria 34°2N 0°5E 136 B4
Bouillon Belgium 49°44N 5°3E 69 E5
Bouïra Algeria 36°20N 3°59E 136 A4
Bouïra □ Algeria 36°15N 3°55E 136 A4
Boukombé Benin 10°13N 1°9E 139 C5
Boulal Mali 15°8N 8°21W 138 B3
Boulazac France 45°10N 0°47E 72 C4
Boulder Colo., U.S.A. 40°1N 105°17W 168 F11
Boulder Mont., U.S.A. 46°14N 112°7W 168 C7
Boulder City U.S.A. 35°58N 114°49W 171 K12
Boulder Creek U.S.A. 37°7N 122°7W 170 H4
Boulder Dam = Hoover Dam U.S.A. 36°1N 114°44W 171 K12
Bouli Mauritania 15°17N 12°18W 138 B2
Boulia Australia 22°52S 139°51E 150 C2
Bouligny France 49°17N 5°45E 71 C12
Boulogne → France 47°12N 1°47W 70 E5
Boulogne-sur-Gesse France 43°18N 0°38E 72 E4
Boulogne-sur-Mer France 50°42N 1°36E 71 B8
Bouloire France 47°59N 0°45E 70 E7
Boulouli Mali 15°30N 9°25W 138 B3
Boulsa Burkina Faso 12°39N 0°34W 139 C4
Boultoum Niger 14°45N 10°25E 139 C7
Bouma △ Fiji 16°50S 179°52W 154 a
Boumalne Dadès Morocco 31°25N 6°0W 136 B2
Boumdeïd Mauritania 17°25N 11°50W 138 B2
Boumerdès Algeria 36°46N 3°28E 136 A4
Boumerdès □ Algeria 36°45N 3°40E 136 A4
Boun Neua Laos 21°38N 101°54E 120 B3
Boun Tai Laos 21°23N 101°58E 120 B3
Bouna Ivory C. 9°10N 3°0W 138 D4
Boundary Peak U.S.A. 37°51N 118°21W 170 H8
Boundiali Ivory C. 9°30N 6°20W 138 D3
Bountiful U.S.A. 40°53N 111°52W 168 F8
Bounty Is. Pac. Oc. 48°0S 178°30E 156 M9
Bounty Trough Pac. Oc. 46°0S 178°0E 156 M9
Boura Mali 12°25N 4°33W 138 C4
Bourbon-Lancy France 46°37N 3°45E 71 F10
Bourbon-l'Archambault France 46°36N 3°4E 71 F10
Bourbonnais France 46°28N 3°0E 71 F10
Bourbonne-les-Bains France 47°54N 5°45E 71 E12
Bourbourg France 50°56N 2°12E 71 B9
Bourdel L. Canada 56°43N 74°10W 164 A5
Bourem Mali 17°0N 0°24W 139 B4
Bourg France 45°3N 0°34W 72 C3
Bourg-Argental France 45°18N 4°32E 73 C8
Bourg-de-Péage France 45°2N 5°3E 73 C9
Bourg-en-Bresse France 46°13N 5°12E 71 F12
Bourg-Lastic France 45°39N 2°35E 72 C6
Bourg-Madame France 42°26N 1°55E 72 F5
Bourg-St-Andéol France 44°23N 4°39E 73 D8
Bourg-St-Maurice France 45°35N 6°46E 73 C10
Bourganeuf France 45°57N 1°45E 72 C5
Bourgas = Burgas Bulgaria 42°33N 27°29E 97 D11
Bourges France 47°9N 2°25E 71 E9
Bourget Canada 45°26N 75°9W 175 A9
Bourget, Lac du France 45°44N 5°52E 73 C9
Bourgneuf, B. de France 47°3N 2°10W 70 E4
Bourgneuf-en-Retz France 47°2N 1°58W 70 E5
Bourgogne □ France 47°0N 4°50E 71 F11
Bourgoin-Jallieu France 45°36N 5°17E 73 C9
Bourgueil France 47°17N 0°10E 70 E7
Bourke Australia 30°8S 145°55E 151 E4
Bourne U.K. 52°47N 0°22W 66 E7
Bournemouth U.K. 50°43N 1°52W 67 G6
Bournemouth □ U.K. 50°43N 1°52W 67 G6
Bouroum Burkina Faso 13°37N 0°39W 139 C4
Bouse U.S.A. 33°56N 114°0W 171 M13
Boussac France 46°22N 2°13E 71 F9
Boussé Burkina Faso 12°39N 1°53W 139 C4
Bousso Chad 10°34N 16°52E 135 F9
Boussouma Burkina Faso 12°52N 1°13W 139 C4
Boutilimit Mauritania 17°45N 14°40W 138 B2
Boutonne → France 45°54N 0°50W 72 C3
Bouvet I. = Bouvetøya Antarctica 54°26S 3°24E 56 M12
Bouvetøya Antarctica 54°26S 3°24E 56 M12
Bouxwiller France 48°49N 7°27E 71 D14
Bouza Niger 14°29N 6°2E 139 C6
Bouznika Morocco 33°46N 7°6W 136 B2
Bouzonville France 49°17N 6°32E 71 C13
Bova Marina Italy 37°56N 15°55E 95 E8
Bovalino Italy 38°10N 16°10E 95 D9
Bovec Slovenia 46°20N 13°33E 93 B10
Bovill U.S.A. 46°51N 116°24W 168 C5
Bovino Italy 41°15N 15°20E 95 A8
Bovril Argentina 31°21S 59°26W 190 C4
Bow → Canada 49°57N 111°41W 162 C6
Bow Island Canada 49°50N 111°23W 168 B8
Bowbells U.S.A. 48°48N 102°15W 172 A2
Bowdle U.S.A. 45°27N 99°39W 172 C4
Bowdon U.S.A. 33°32N 85°15W 178 B4
Bowdon Junction U.S.A. 33°40N 85°9W 178 B4
Bowelling Australia 33°25S 116°30E 149 F2
Bowen Argentina 35°0S 67°31W 190 D2
Bowen Australia 20°0S 148°16E 150 J6
Bowen Mts. Australia 37°0S 147°50E 153 D7
Bowers Basin Pac. Oc. 53°45N 176°0E 54 D16
Bowers Ridge Pac. Oc. 54°0N 180°0E 54 D17
Bowie Ariz., U.S.A. 32°19N 109°29W 169 K9
Bowie Tex., U.S.A. 33°34N 97°51W 176 E6
Bowkān Iran 36°31N 46°12E 105 D12
Bowland, Forest of U.K. 54°0N 2°30W 66 D5
Bowling Green Fla., U.S.A. 27°38N 81°50W 179 H8
Bowling Green Ky., U.S.A. 36°59N 86°27W 172 G10
Bowling Green Ohio, U.S.A. 41°23N 83°39W 173 E12
Bowling Green, C. Australia 19°19S 147°25E 150 B4
Bowling Green Bay △ Australia 19°26S 146°57E 150 B4
Bowman N. Dak., U.S.A. 46°11N 103°24W 172 B2
Bowman S.C., U.S.A. 33°21N 80°41W 178 B9
Bowman I. Antarctica 65°0S 104°0E 55 C8
Bowmanville = Clarington Canada 43°55N 78°41W 174 C6
Bowmore U.K. 55°45N 6°17W 65 F2
Bowral Australia 34°26S 150°27E 153 C9
Bowraville Australia 30°37S 152°52E 151 E5
Bowron → Canada 54°3N 121°50W 162 C4
Bowron Lake ⌂ Canada 53°10N 121°5W 162 C4
Bowser L. Canada 56°30N 129°30W 162 B3
Bowsman Canada 52°14N 101°12W 163 C8
Bowwood Zambia 17°5S 26°20E 143 F2
Box Cr. → Australia 34°10S 143°50E 151 E3
Boxholm Sweden 58°12N 15°3E 63 F9
Boxmeer Neths. 51°38N 5°56E 69 C5
Boxtel Neths. 51°36N 5°20E 69 C5
Boyabat Turkey 41°28N 34°47E 104 B6
Boyalıca Turkey 40°29N 29°33E 97 F13
Boyang China 29°0N 116°38E 117 C11
Boyany Ukraine 48°17N 26°8E 81 B11
Boyce U.S.A. 31°23N 92°40W 176 F8
Boyd U.S.A. 30°11N 83°37W 178 E6
Boyd L. Canada 52°46N 76°42W 164 B4
Boyle Canada 54°35N 112°49W 162 C6
Boyle Ireland 53°59N 8°18W 64 C3
Boyne → Ireland 53°43N 6°15W 64 C5
Boyne, Bend of the Ireland 53°41N 6°27W 64 C5
Boyne City U.S.A. 45°13N 85°1W 173 C11
Boynitsa Bulgaria 43°58N 22°32E 96 C6
Boynton Beach U.S.A. 26°32N 80°4W 179 J9
Boyoma, Chutes Dem. Rep. of the Congo 0°35N 25°23E 142 B2
Boysen Res. U.S.A. 43°25N 108°11W 168 E9
Boyuibe Bolivia 20°25S 63°17W 186 G6
Boyup Brook Australia 33°50S 116°23E 149 F2
Boz Burun Turkey 40°32N 28°46E 97 F12
Boz Dağ Turkey 37°18N 29°11E 99 D11
Boz Dağları Turkey 38°20N 28°0E 99 C10
Bozburun Turkey 36°43N 28°4E 99 E10
Bozcaada Turkey 39°49N 26°3E 104 C2
Bozdoğan Turkey 37°40N 28°17E 99 D10
Bozeman U.S.A. 45°41N 111°2W 168 D8
Bozen = Bolzano Italy 46°31N 11°22E 93 B8
Boževac Serbia 44°32N 21°24E 96 B5
Bozhou China 33°55N 115°41E 114 H8
Bozkır Turkey 37°11N 32°14E 104 D5
Bozkurt Turkey 37°50N 29°37E 99 D11
Bozouls France 44°28N 2°43E 72 D6
Bozoum C.A.R. 6°25N 16°35E 140 C3
Bozova Antalya, Turkey 37°13N 30°18E 99 D12
Bozova Sanliurfa, Turkey 37°21N 38°32E 105 D8
Bozovici Romania 44°56N 22°0E 80 F7
Bozüyük Turkey 39°54N 30°3E 99 B12
Bozyazı Turkey 36°6N 33°0E 128 B2
Bra Italy 44°42N 7°51E 92 D4
Braås Sweden 57°4N 15°3E 63 G9
Brabant □ Belgium 50°46N 4°30E 69 D4
Brabant L. Canada 55°58N 103°43W 163 B8
Brabrand Denmark 56°9N 10°7E 63 H4
Brač Croatia 43°20N 16°40E 93 E13
Bracadale, L. U.K. 57°20N 6°30W 65 D2
Bracciano Italy 42°6N 12°10E 93 F9
Bracciano, L. di Italy 42°7N 12°14E 93 F9
Bracebridge Canada 45°2N 79°19W 174 A5
Bracieux France 47°30N 1°30E 70 E8
Bräcke Sweden 62°45N 15°26E 62 B9
Brackettville U.S.A. 29°19N 100°25W 176 G4
Bracki Kanal Croatia 43°24N 16°40E 93 E13
Bracknell U.K. 51°25N 0°43W 67 F7
Bracknell Forest □ U.K. 51°25N 0°44W 67 F7
Brad Romania 46°10N 22°50E 80 D7
Brádano → Italy 40°23N 16°51E 95 B9
Bradenton U.S.A. 27°30N 82°34W 179 H7
Bradford Canada 44°7N 79°34W 174 B5
Bradford U.K. 53°47N 1°45W 66 D6
Bradford Pa., U.S.A. 41°58N 78°38W 174 E6
Bradford Vt., U.S.A. 43°59N 72°9W 175 C12
Bradley Ark., U.S.A. 33°6N 93°39W 176 E8
Bradley Calif., U.S.A. 35°52N 120°48W 170 K6
Bradley Institute Zimbabwe 17°7S 31°25E 143 F3
Bradley Junction U.S.A. 27°48N 81°59W 179 H8
Brady U.S.A. 31°9N 99°20W 176 F5
Brædstrup Denmark 55°58N 9°37E 63 J3
Braemar Australia 33°12S 139°35E 152 B3
Braeside Canada 45°28N 76°24W 175 A8
Braga Portugal 41°35N 8°25W 88 D2
Braga □ Portugal 41°30N 8°30W 88 D2
Bragadiru Romania 43°46N 25°31E 81 G10
Bragado Argentina 35°2S 60°27W 190 D3
Bragança Brazil 1°0S 47°2W 187 D9
Bragança Portugal 41°48N 6°50W 88 D4
Bragança □ Portugal 41°30N 6°45W 88 D4
Bragança Paulista Brazil 22°55S 46°32W 191 A6
Brahestad = Raahe Finland 64°40N 24°28E 60 D21
Brahmanbaria Bangla. 23°58N 91°15E 123 H17
Brahmani → India 20°39N 86°46E 126 D8
Brahmapur India 19°15N 84°54E 126 E7
Brahmaputra → Asia 23°40N 90°35E 125 H13
Braich-y-pwll U.K. 52°47N 4°46W 66 E3
Braidwood Australia 35°27S 149°49E 153 C8
Brăila Romania 45°19N 27°59E 81 E12
Brăila □ Romania 45°5N 27°30E 81 E12
Brainerd U.S.A. 46°22N 94°12W 172 B6
Braintree U.K. 51°53N 0°34E 67 F8
Braintree U.S.A. 42°13N 71°0W 175 D14
Brak → S. Africa 29°35S 22°55E 144 C3
Brake Germany 53°20N 8°28E 76 B4
Brakel Germany 51°42N 9°11E 76 D5
Brakna □ Mauritania 17°0N 13°20W 138 B2
Bräkne-Hoby Sweden 56°14N 15°6E 63 H9
Brakwater Namibia 22°28S 17°3E 144 B2
Brålanda Sweden 58°34N 12°21E 63 F6
Bramberg Germany 50°6N 10°40E 77 E6
Bramdrupdam Denmark 55°31N 9°28E 63 J3
Bramhapuri India 20°36N 79°52E 126 D4
Bramming Denmark 55°28N 8°42E 63 J2
Brämön Sweden 62°14N 17°40E 62 B11
Brampton Canada 43°45N 79°45W 174 C5
Brampton U.K. 54°57N 2°44W 66 C5
Brampton I. Australia 20°49S 149°16E 150 b
Bramsche Germany 52°24N 7°59E 76 C3
Branchville U.S.A. 33°15N 80°49W 178 B9
Branco → Brazil 1°20S 61°50W 186 D6
Branco, C. Brazil 7°9S 34°47W 189 B4
Brandberg Namibia 21°10S 14°33E 144 B1
Brandberg ⌂ Namibia 21°10S 14°30E 144 B1
Brande Denmark 55°57N 9°8E 63 J3
Brandenburg = Neubrandenburg Germany 53°33N 13°15E 76 B9
Brandenburg Germany 52°25N 12°33E 76 C8
Brandenburg □ Germany 52°50N 13°0E 76 C9
Brandfort S. Africa 28°40S 26°30E 144 C4
Brando France 42°47N 9°27E 73 F13
Brandon Canada 49°50N 99°57W 163 D9
Brandon Fla., U.S.A. 27°56N 82°17W 179 H7
Brandon Vt., U.S.A. 43°48N 73°6W 175 C11
Brandon B. Ireland 52°17N 10°8W 64 D1
Brandon Mt. Ireland 52°15N 10°15W 64 D1
Brandsen Argentina 35°10S 58°15W 190 D4
Brandvlei S. Africa 30°25S 20°30E 144 D3
Brandýs nad Labem Czech Rep. 50°10N 14°40E 78 A7
Brăneşti Romania 44°27N 26°20E 81 F11
Branford Conn., U.S.A. 41°17N 72°49W 175 E12
Branford Fla., U.S.A. 29°58N 82°56W 178 F7
Braniewo Poland 54°25N 19°50E 82 D6
Bransfield Str. Antarctica 63°0S 59°0W 55 C18
Brańsk Poland 52°45N 22°50E 83 F9
Branson U.S.A. 36°39N 93°13W 172 G7
Brantford Canada 43°10N 80°15W 174 C4
Brantley U.S.A. 31°35N 86°16W 178 D3
Brantôme France 45°22N 0°39E 72 C4
Branxholme Australia 37°52S 141°49E 152 D4
Branxton Australia 32°38S 151°21E 153 B9
Branzi Italy 46°1N 9°46E 92 B6
Bras d'Or L. Canada 45°50N 60°50W 165 C7
Brasher Falls U.S.A. 44°49N 74°47W 175 B10
Brasil = Brazil ■ S. Amer. 12°0S 50°0W 187 F9
Brasil, Planalto Brazil 18°0S 46°30W 184 E6
Brasiléia Brazil 11°0S 68°45W 188 C4
Brasília Distrito Federal, Brazil 15°47S 47°55W 189 D1
Brasília Minas Gerais, Brazil 16°12S 44°26W 189 D2
Brasília Legal Brazil 3°49S 55°36W 187 D7
Braslaw Belarus 55°38N 27°0E 84 E4
Braslawskiya Azyory △ Belarus 55°36N 27°3E 84 E4
Braslovče Slovenia 46°21N 15°3E 93 B12
Braşov Romania 45°38N 25°35E 81 E10
Braşov □ Romania 45°45N 25°15E 81 E10
Brass Nigeria 4°35N 6°14E 139 E6
Brass → Nigeria 4°15N 6°13E 139 E6
Brassac-les-Mines France 45°24N 3°20E 72 C7
Brasschaat Belgium 51°19N 4°27E 69 C4
Brassey, Banjaran Malaysia 5°0N 117°15E 118 D5
Brassey Ra. Australia 25°8S 122°15E 149 E3
Brasstown Bald U.S.A. 34°53N 83°49W 177 D13
Brastad Sweden 58°23N 11°30E 63 F5
Brastavăţu Romania 43°55N 24°24E 81 G9
Bratan = Morozov Bulgaria 42°30N 25°10E 97 D9
Brateş Romania 45°50N 26°4E 81 E11
Bratislava Slovak Rep. 48°10N 17°7E 79 C10
Bratislava M.R. Štefánik ✕ (BTS) Slovak Rep. 48°11N 17°9E 79 C10
Bratislavský □ Slovak Rep. 48°15N 17°20E 79 C10
Bratsigovo Bulgaria 42°1N 24°22E 97 D8
Bratsk Russia 56°10N 101°30E 107 D11
Bratskoye Vdkhr. Russia 56°0N 101°40E 107 D11
Brattleboro U.S.A. 42°51N 72°34W 175 D12
Bratunac Bos.-H. 44°13N 19°21E 80 F4
Braunau Austria 48°15N 13°3E 78 C6
Braunschweig Germany 52°15N 10°31E 76 C6
Braunton U.K. 51°7N 4°10W 67 F3
Brava C. Verde Is. 15°0N 24°40W 134 b
Brava, Costa Spain 41°30N 3°0E 90 D8
Bravicea Moldova 47°22N 28°27E 81 C13
Bråviken Sweden 58°38N 16°32E 63 F10
Bravo del Norte, Rio = Grande, Rio → N. Amer. 25°58N 97°9W 176 J6
Brawley U.S.A. 32°59N 115°31W 171 N11
Bray Ireland 53°13N 6°7W 64 C5
Bray, Mt. Australia 14°0S 134°30E 150 A1
Bray-sur-Seine France 48°25N 3°14E 71 D10
Brazeau → Canada 52°55N 115°14W 162 C5
Brazil U.S.A. 39°32N 87°8W 172 F10
Brazil ■ S. Amer. 12°0S 50°0W 187 F9
Brazil Basin Atl. Oc. 15°0S 25°0W 56 H9
Brazilian Highlands = Brasil, Planalto Brazil 18°0S 46°30W 184 E6
Brazo Sur → S. Amer. 25°21S 57°42W 190 B4
Brazos → U.S.A. 28°53N 95°23W 176 G7
Brazzaville Congo 4°9S 15°12E 140 E3
Brčko Bos.-H. 44°54N 18°46E 80 F3
Brda → Poland 53°8N 18°8E 83 E5
Brdy Czech Rep. 49°43N 13°55E 78 B6
Bré = Bray Ireland 53°13N 6°7W 64 C5
Breaden, L. Australia 25°51S 125°28E 149 E4
Breaksea Sd. N.Z. 45°35S 166°35E 155 F1
Bream B. N.Z. 35°56S 174°28E 154 B3
Bream Hd. N.Z. 35°51S 174°36E 154 B3
Bream Tail N.Z. 36°3S 174°36E 154 C3
Breas Chile 25°29S 70°24W 190 B1
Breaza Romania 45°11N 25°40E 81 E10
Brebes Indonesia 6°52S 109°3E 119 G13
Brechin Canada 44°32N 79°10W 174 B5
Brechin U.K. 56°44N 2°39W 65 E6
Brecht Belgium 51°21N 4°38E 69 C4
Breckenridge Colo., U.S.A. 39°29N 106°3W 168 G10
Breckenridge Minn., U.S.A. 46°16N 96°35W 172 B5
Breckenridge Tex., U.S.A. 32°45N 98°54W 176 E5
Breckland U.K. 52°30N 0°40E 67 E8
Brecknock, Pen. Chile 54°35S 71°30W 192 D2
Břeclav Czech Rep. 48°46N 16°53E 79 C9
Brecon U.K. 51°57N 3°23W 67 F4
Brecon Beacons U.K. 51°53N 3°26W 67 F4
Brecon Beacons △ U.K. 51°50N 3°30W 67 F4
Breda Neths. 51°35N 4°45E 69 C4
Bredaryd Sweden 57°10N 13°45E 63 G7
Bredasdorp S. Africa 34°33S 20°2E 144 D3
Bredbo Australia 35°58S 149°10E 153 C8
Bredebro Denmark 55°3N 8°50E 63 J2
Bredstedt Germany 54°37N 8°55E 76 A4
Bredy Russia 52°26N 60°21E 108 B6
Bree Belgium 51°8N 5°35E 69 C5
Bregalnica → Macedonia 41°43N 22°9E 96 E6
Bregenz Austria 47°30N 9°45E 78 D2
Bregovo Bulgaria 44°9N 22°39E 96 B6
Bréhal France 48°53N 1°30W 70 D5
Bréhat, Î. de France 48°51N 3°0W 70 D4
Breiðafjörður Iceland 65°15N 23°15W 60 D2
Breil-sur-Roya France 43°56N 7°31E 73 E11
Breisach Germany 48°1N 7°36E 77 G3
Brejo Brazil 3°41S 42°47W 189 A2
Bremen Germany 53°4N 8°47E 76 B4
Bremen U.S.A. 33°43N 85°9W 178 B4
Bremen □ Germany 53°4N 8°50E 76 B4
Bremer Bay Australia 34°21S 119°20E 149 F2
Bremer I. Australia 12°5S 136°45E 150 A2
Bremerhaven Germany 53°33N 8°36E 76 B4
Bremerton U.S.A. 47°34N 122°37W 170 C4
Bremervörde Germany 53°29N 9°8E 76 B5
Brenes Spain 37°32N 5°54W 89 H5
Brenham U.S.A. 30°10N 96°24W 176 F6
Brenne France 46°44N 1°14E 72 B5
Brenne ⌂ France 46°40N 1°15E 72 B5
Brennerpass Austria 47°2N 11°30E 78 D4
Breno Italy 45°57N 10°18E 92 C7
Brent U.S.A. 32°56N 87°10W 177 E11
Brenta → Italy 45°11N 12°18E 93 C9
Brentwood U.K. 51°37N 0°19E 67 F8
Brentwood Calif., U.S.A. 37°56N 121°42W 170 H5
Brentwood N.Y., U.S.A. 40°47N 73°15W 175 F11
Bréscia Italy 45°33N 10°15E 92 C7
Breskens Neths. 51°23N 3°33E 69 C3
Breslau = Wrocław Poland 51°5N 17°5E 83 G4
Bresle → France 50°4N 1°22E 70 B8
Bressanone Italy 46°43N 11°39E 93 B8
Bressay U.K. 60°9N 1°6W 65 A7
Bresse France 46°50N 5°10E 71 F12
Bressuire France 46°51N 0°30W 70 F6
Brest Belarus 52°10N 23°40E 75 B12
Brest France 48°24N 4°31W 70 D2
Brest □ Belarus 52°30N 26°10E 75 B13
Brest-Litovsk = Brest Belarus 52°10N 23°40E 75 B12
Bretagne □ France 48°10N 3°0W 70 D3
Bretçu Romania 46°7N 26°18E 81 D11
Bretenoux France 44°54N 1°51E 72 D5
Breteuil Eure, France 48°50N 0°57E 70 D7
Breteuil Oise, France 49°38N 2°18E 71 C9
Breton Canada 53°7N 114°28W 162 C6
Breton, Pertuis France 46°17N 1°25W 72 B2
Breton Sd. U.S.A. 29°35N 89°15W 177 G10
Brett, C. N.Z. 35°10S 174°20E 154 B3
Bretten Germany 49°2N 8°42E 77 F4
Breuil-Cervinia Italy 45°56N 7°38E 92 C4
Brevard U.S.A. 35°14N 82°44W 177 D13
Breves Brazil 1°40S 50°29W 187 D8
Brewarrina Australia 30°0S 146°51E 151 E4
Brewer U.S.A. 44°48N 68°46W 173 C19
Brewer, Mt. U.S.A. 36°44N 118°28W 170 J8
Brewerville Liberia 6°26N 10°47W 138 D2
Brewster N.Y., U.S.A. 41°24N 73°36W 175 E11
Brewster Ohio, U.S.A. 40°43N 81°36W 174 F3
Brewster Wash., U.S.A. 48°6N 119°47W 168 B4
Brewster, Kap = Kangikajik Greenland 70°7N 22°0W 57 C8
Brewton U.S.A. 31°7N 87°4W 177 F11
Breyten S. Africa 26°16S 30°0E 145 C5
Breza Bos.-H. 44°2N 18°16E 80 F3
Brežice Slovenia 45°54N 15°35E 93 C12
Brézina Algeria 33°4N 1°14E 136 B4
Březnice Czech Rep. 49°32N 13°57E 78 B6
Breznik Bulgaria 42°44N 22°55E 96 D6
Brezno Slovak Rep. 48°50N 19°40E 79 C12
Brezoi Romania 45°21N 24°15E 81 E9
Brezovicë Kosovo 42°15N 21°3E 96 D5
Brezovo Bulgaria 42°21N 25°5E 97 D9
Bria C.A.R. 6°30N 21°58E 140 C4
Briançon France 44°54N 6°39E 73 D10
Briare France 47°38N 2°45E 71 E9
Briático Italy 38°43N 16°2E 95 D9
Bribie I. Australia 27°0S 153°10E 151 D5
Bribri Costa Rica 9°38N 82°50W 182 E3
Briceni Moldova 48°22N 27°6E 81 B12
Bricquebec France 49°28N 1°38W 70 C5
Bridgefield Barbados 13°9N 59°36W 183 g
Bridgehampton U.S.A. 40°56N 72°19W 175 F12
Bridgend U.K. 51°30N 3°34W 67 F4
Bridgend □ U.K. 51°36N 3°36W 67 F4
Bridgenorth Canada 44°23N 78°23W 174 B6
Bridgeport Calif., U.S.A. 38°15N 119°14W 170 G7
Bridgeport Conn., U.S.A. 41°11N 73°12W 175 E11
Bridgeport N.Y., U.S.A. 43°9N 75°58W 175 C9
Bridgeport Nebr., U.S.A. 41°40N 103°6W 172 E2
Bridgeport Tex., U.S.A. 33°13N 97°45W 176 E6
Bridger U.S.A. 45°18N 108°55W 168 D9
Bridgeton U.S.A. 39°26N 75°14W 173 F16
Bridgetown Australia 33°58S 116°7E 149 F2
Bridgetown Barbados 13°6N 59°37W 183 g
Bridgetown Canada 44°55N 65°18W 165 D6
Bridgewater Tas., Australia 42°44S 147°14E 151 G4
Bridgewater Vic., Australia 36°36S 143°59E 152 D5
Bridgewater Canada 44°25N 64°31W 165 D7
Bridgewater Mass., U.S.A. 41°59N 70°58W 175 E14
Bridgewater N.Y., U.S.A. 42°53N 75°15W 175 D9
Bridgewater, C. Australia 38°23S 141°23E 152 E4
Bridgnorth U.K. 52°32N 2°25W 67 E5
Bridgton U.S.A. 44°3N 70°42W 175 B14
Bridgwater U.K. 51°8N 2°59W 67 F5
Bridgwater B. U.K. 51°15N 3°15W 67 F4
Bridlington U.K. 54°5N 0°12W 66 C7
Bridlington B. U.K. 54°4N 0°10W 66 C7
Bridport Australia 40°59S 147°23E 151 G4
Bridport U.K. 50°44N 2°45W 67 G5
Briec France 48°6N 4°0W 70 D2
Brienne-le-Château France 48°24N 4°30E 71 D11
Brienon-sur-Armançon France 47°59N 3°38E 71 E10
Brienz Switz. 46°46N 8°2E 77 J4
Brienzersee Switz. 46°44N 7°53E 77 J3
Brier Cr. → U.S.A. 32°44N 81°26W 178 C8
Brière ⌂ France 47°22N 2°13W 70 E4
Brig Switz. 46°18N 7°59E 77 J3
Brigg U.K. 53°34N 0°28W 66 D7
Brigham City U.S.A. 41°31N 112°1W 168 F7
Bright Australia 36°42S 146°56E 153 D7
Brighton Australia 35°5S 138°30E 152 C3
Brighton Canada 44°2N 77°44W 174 B7
Brighton Trin. & Tob. 10°15N 61°39W 187 K15
Brighton U.K. 50°49N 0°7W 67 G7
Brighton Fla., U.S.A. 27°14N 81°6W 179 H8
Brighton N.Y., U.S.A. 43°8N 77°34W 174 C7
Brightside Canada 45°7N 76°29W 175 A8
Brightwater N.Z. 41°22S 173°9E 155 B8
Brignogan-Plage France 48°40N 4°20W 70 D2
Brignoles France 43°25N 6°5E 73 E10
Brihuega Spain 40°45N 2°52W 90 E2
Brikama Gambia 13°15N 16°45W 138 C1
Brilliant U.S.A. 40°15N 80°39W 174 F4
Brilon Germany 51°23N 8°35E 76 D4
Brim Australia 36°3S 142°27E 152 D5
Brindabella △ Australia 35°14S 148°5E 153 C8
Bríndisi Italy 40°39N 17°55E 95 B10
Brinje Croatia 44°59N 15°9E 93 D12
Brinkley U.S.A. 34°53N 91°12W 176 D9
Brinkworth Australia 33°42S 138°26E 152 B3
Brinnon U.S.A. 47°41N 122°54W 170 C4
Brinson U.S.A. 30°59N 84°44W 178 E5
Brion, Î. Canada 47°46N 61°26W 165 C7
Brionne France 49°11N 0°43E 70 C7
Brionski Croatia 44°55N 13°45E 93 D10
Brioude France 45°18N 3°24E 72 C7
Briouze France 48°42N 0°23W 70 D6
Brisay Canada 54°26N 70°31W 165 B5
Brisbane Australia 27°25S 153°2E 151 D5
Brisbane → Australia 27°24S 153°9E 151 D5
Brisbane Ranges △ Australia 37°47S 144°16E 152 D6
Brisbane Water △ Australia 33°26S 151°13E 153 B9
Brisighella Italy 44°13N 11°46E 93 D8
Bristol U.K. 51°26N 2°35W 67 F5
Bristol Conn., U.S.A. 41°40N 72°57W 175 E12
Bristol Fla., U.S.A. 30°26N 84°59W 178 E5
Bristol Pa., U.S.A. 40°6N 74°51W 175 F10
Bristol R.I., U.S.A. 41°40N 71°16W 175 E13
Bristol Tenn., U.S.A. 36°36N 82°11W 177 C13
Bristol Vt., U.S.A. 44°8N 73°4W 175 B11
Bristol, City of □ U.K. 51°27N 2°36W 67 F5
Bristol B. U.S.A. 58°0N 160°0W 166 D8
Bristol Channel U.K. 51°18N 4°30W 67 F3
Bristol I. Antarctica 58°45S 28°0W 55 B1
Bristol L. U.S.A. 34°28N 115°41W 171 L11
Bristow U.S.A. 35°50N 96°23W 176 D4

Britain = Great Britain Europe 54°0N 2°15W 58 E5
British Columbia ☐ Canada 55°0N 125°15W 162 C3
British Indian Ocean Terr. = Chagos Arch. ☒ Ind. Oc. 6°0S 72°0E 146 E6
British Isles Europe 54°0N 4°0W 68 D5
British Mts. N. Amer. 68°50N 140°0W 166 B12
British Virgin Is. ☒ W. Indies 18°30N 64°30W 183 e
Brits S. Africa 25°37S 27°48E 145 C4
Britstown S. Africa 30°37S 23°30E 144 D3
Britt Canada 45°46N 80°34W 164 C3
Brittany = Bretagne ☐ France 48°10N 3°0W 70 D3
Britton U.S.A. 45°48N 97°45W 172 C5
Brive-la-Gaillarde France 45°10N 1°32E 72 C5
Briviesca Spain 42°32N 3°19W 88 C7
Brixen = Bressanone Italy 46°43N 11°39E 93 B8
Brixham U.K. 50°23N 3°31W 67 G4
Brnaze Croatia 43°41N 16°40E 93 E13
Brnenský ☐ Czech Rep. 49°10N 16°40E 79 B9
Brno Czech Rep. 49°10N 16°35E 79 B9
Broach = Bharuch India 21°47N 73°0E 126 D1
Broad → Ga., U.S.A. 33°59N 82°39W 178 B7
Broad → S.C., U.S.A. 34°1N 81°4W 177 D14
Broad Arrow Australia 30°23S 121°15E 149 F3
Broad B. U.K. 58°14N 6°18W 65 C2
Broad Haven Ireland 54°20N 9°55W 64 B2
Broad Law U.K. 55°30N 3°21W 65 F5
Broad Pk. = Faichan Kangri India 35°48N 76°34E 125 B7
Broad Sd. Australia 22°0S 149°45E 150 C4
Broadalbin U.S.A. 43°4N 74°12W 175 C10
Broadback → Canada 51°21N 78°52W 164 B4
Broadford Australia 37°14S 145°4E 153 D6
Broadhurst Ra. Australia 22°30S 122°30E 148 D3
Broads, The U.K. 52°45N 1°30E 66 E9
Broadus U.S.A. 45°27N 105°25W 168 D11
Broager Denmark 54°53N 9°40E 63 K3
Broby Sweden 56°15N 14°4E 63 H8
Brocēni Latvia 56°42N 22°32E 82 B9
Brochet Canada 57°53N 101°40W 163 B8
Brochet, L. Canada 58°36N 101°35W 163 B8
Brock I. Canada 77°52N 114°19W 161 B9
Brocken Germany 51°47N 10°37E 76 D6
Brocklehurst Australia 32°9S 148°38E 153 B8
Brocklesby Australia 35°48S 146°40E 153 C7
Brockport U.S.A. 43°13N 77°56W 174 C7
Brockton U.S.A. 42°5N 71°1W 175 D13
Brockville Canada 44°35N 75°41W 175 B9
Brockway Mont., U.S.A. 47°18N 105°45W 168 C11
Brockway Pa., U.S.A. 41°15N 78°47W 174 E6
Brocton U.S.A. 42°23N 79°26W 174 D5
Brod Macedonia 41°32N 21°17E 96 E5
Brodarevo Serbia 43°14N 19°44E 96 C3
Brodeur Pen. Canada 72°30N 88°10W 161 C14
Brodick U.K. 55°35N 5°9W 65 F3
Brodnica Poland 53°15N 19°25E 83 E6
Brody Ukraine 50°5N 25°10E 75 C13
Brogan U.S.A. 44°15N 117°31W 168 D5
Broglie France 49°2N 0°30E 70 C7
Brok Poland 52°43N 21°52E 83 F8
Broken Arrow U.S.A. 36°3N 95°48W 176 C7
Broken Bow Nebr., U.S.A. 41°24N 99°38W 172 E4
Broken Bow Okla., U.S.A. 34°2N 94°44W 176 D7
Broken Bow Lake U.S.A. 34°9N 94°40W 176 D7
Broken Hill Australia 31°58S 141°29E 152 A4
Broken Ridge Ind. Oc. 30°0S 94°0E 156 L1
Broken River Ra. Australia 21°0S 148°22E 150 b
Brokind Sweden 58°13N 15°42E 63 F9
Bromley ☐ U.K. 51°24N 0°2E 67 F8
Bromo, Gunung Indonesia 7°56N 112°57E 119 H15
Bromo Tengger Semeru △ Indonesia 7°56S 112°57E 119 H15
Bromölla Sweden 56°5N 14°28E 63 H8
Bromsgrove U.K. 52°21N 2°2W 67 E5
Brønderslev Denmark 57°16N 9°57E 63 G3
Brong-Ahafo ☐ Ghana 7°50N 2°0W 138 D4
Broni Italy 45°4N 9°16E 92 C6
Bronkhorstspruit S. Africa 25°46S 28°45E 145 C4
Brønnøysund Norway 65°28N 12°14E 60 D15
Bronson U.S.A. 29°27N 82°39W 179 F7
Bronte Italy 37°47N 14°50E 95 E7
Bronwood U.S.A. 31°50N 84°22W 178 D5
Brook Park U.S.A. 41°23N 81°48W 174 E4
Brookhaven U.S.A. 31°35N 90°26W 177 F9
Brookings Oreg., U.S.A. 42°3N 124°17W 168 E1
Brookings S. Dak., U.S.A. 44°19N 96°48W 172 C5
Brooklet U.S.A. 32°23N 81°40W 178 C8
Brooklin Canada 43°55N 78°55W 174 C6
Brooklyn Park U.S.A. 45°6N 93°23W 172 C7
Brooks Canada 50°35N 111°55W 162 C6
Brooks Range U.S.A. 68°0N 152°0W 166 B9
Brooksville U.S.A. 28°33N 82°23W 179 G7
Brookton Australia 32°22S 117°0E 149 F2
Brookville U.S.A. 41°10N 79°5W 174 E5
Broom, L. U.K. 57°55N 5°15W 65 D3
Broome Australia 18°0S 122°15E 148 C3
Broons France 48°20N 2°16W 70 D4
Brora U.K. 58°0N 3°52W 65 C5
Brora → U.K. 58°0N 3°51W 65 C5
Brørup Denmark 55°29N 9°1E 63 J2
Brösarp Sweden 55°43N 14°6E 63 J8
Brosna → Ireland 53°14N 7°58W 64 C4
Broşteni Mehedinţi, Romania 44°45N 22°59E 80 F7
Broşteni Suceava, Romania 47°14N 25°43E 81 C10
Brotas de Macaúbas Brazil 12°0S 42°38W 189 C2
Brothers U.S.A. 43°49N 120°36W 168 E3
Brou France 48°13N 1°11E 70 D8
Brouage France 45°52N 1°4W 72 C2
Brough U.K. 54°32N 2°18W 66 C5
Brough Hd. U.K. 59°8N 3°20W 65 B5
Broughton Island = Qikiqtarjuaq Canada 67°33N 63°0W 161 D19
Broumov Czech Rep. 50°35N 16°20E 79 A9
Brovary Ukraine 50°34N 30°48E 85 G6
Brovst Denmark 57°6N 9°31E 63 G3
Brown, L. Australia 31°5S 118°15E 149 F2
Brown, Mt. Australia 32°30S 138°0E 152 B3
Brown, Pt. Australia 32°32S 133°50E 151 E1
Brown City U.S.A. 43°13N 82°59W 174 C2
Brown Willy U.K. 50°35N 4°37W 67 G3
Brownfield U.S.A. 33°11N 102°17W 176 E3
Browning U.S.A. 48°34N 113°1W 168 B7
Brownsville Oreg., U.S.A. 44°24N 122°59W 168 D2
Brownsville Pa., U.S.A. 40°1N 79°53W 174 F5
Brownsville Tenn., U.S.A. 35°36N 89°16W 177 D10
Brownsville Tex., U.S.A. 25°54N 97°30W 176 J6
Brownville U.S.A. 44°0N 75°59W 175 C9
Brownwood U.S.A. 31°43N 98°59W 176 F5
Browse I. Australia 14°7S 123°33E 148 B3
Broxton U.S.A. 31°38N 82°53W 178 D7
Bruas Malaysia 4°30N 100°47E 121 K3
Bruay-la-Buissière France 50°29N 2°33E 71 B9
Bruce U.S.A. 30°28N 85°58W 178 E4
Bruce, Mt. Australia 22°37S 118°8E 148 D2
Bruce B. N.Z. 43°35S 169°42E 155 D4
Bruce Pen. Canada 45°0N 81°30W 174 B3
Bruce Peninsula △ Canada 45°14N 81°36W 174 A3
Bruce Rock Australia 31°52S 118°8E 149 F2
Bruche → France 48°34N 7°43E 71 D14
Bruchsal Germany 49°7N 8°35E 77 F4
Bruck an der Leitha Austria 48°1N 16°47E 79 C9
Bruck an der Mur Austria 47°24N 15°16E 78 D8
Brue → U.K. 51°13N 2°59W 67 F5
Bruges = Brugge Belgium 51°13N 3°13E 69 C3
Brugg Switz. 47°29N 8°11E 77 H4
Brugge Belgium 51°13N 3°13E 69 C3
Bruin U.S.A. 41°3N 79°43W 174 E5
Brûk, W. el → Egypt 30°15N 33°50E 130 E2
Bruksvallarna Sweden 62°38N 12°27E 62 B6
Brûlé Canada 53°15N 117°58W 162 C5
Brûlé, L. Canada 53°35N 64°4W 165 B7
Brûlon France 47°58N 0°15W 70 E6
Brumado Brazil 14°14S 41°40W 189 C2
Brumado → Brazil 14°13S 41°40W 189 C2
Brumath France 48°43N 7°40E 71 D14
Brumunddal Norway 60°53N 10°56E 60 F14
Brundidge U.S.A. 31°43N 85°49W 178 D4
Bruneau U.S.A. 42°53N 115°48W 168 E6
Bruneau → U.S.A. 42°56N 115°57W 168 E6
Bruneck = Brunico Italy 46°48N 11°56E 93 B8
Brunei = Bandar Seri Begawan Brunei 4°52N 115°0E 118 D5
Brunei ■ Asia 4°50N 115°0E 118 D5
Brunflo Sweden 63°5N 14°50E 62 A8
Brunico Italy 46°48N 11°56E 93 B8
Brunnen Switz. 46°59N 8°37E 77 J4
Brunner, L. N.Z. 42°37S 171°27E 155 C6
Brunnsberg Sweden 61°17N 13°56E 62 C8
Brunsbüttel Germany 53°53N 9°6E 76 B5
Brunssum Neths. 50°57N 5°59E 69 D5
Brunswick = Braunschweig Germany 52°15N 10°31E 76 C6
Brunswick Ga., U.S.A. 31°10N 81°30W 178 D8
Brunswick Maine, U.S.A. 43°55N 69°58W 173 D19
Brunswick Md., U.S.A. 39°19N 77°38W 173 F15
Brunswick Mo., U.S.A. 39°26N 93°8W 172 F7
Brunswick Ohio, U.S.A. 41°14N 81°51W 174 E3
Brunswick, Pen. de Chile 53°30S 71°30W 192 D2
Brunswick B. Australia 15°15S 124°50E 148 C3
Brunswick Junction Australia 33°15S 115°50E 149 F2
Brunt Ice Shelf Antarctica 75°30S 25°0W 55 D2
Bruntál Czech Rep. 49°59N 17°27E 79 B10
Brus Laguna Honduras 15°47N 84°35W 182 C3
Brusartsi Bulgaria 43°40N 23°5E 96 C7
Brush U.S.A. 40°15N 103°37W 168 F12
Brushton U.S.A. 44°50N 74°31W 175 B10
Brusio Switz. 46°14N 10°8E 77 J6
Brusque Brazil 27°5S 49°0W 191 B6
Brussel Belgium 50°51N 4°21E 69 D4
Brussel ✈ (BRU) Belgium 50°54N 4°29E 69 D5
Brussels = Brussel Belgium 50°51N 4°21E 69 D4
Brussels Canada 43°44N 81°15W 174 C3
Brusy Poland 53°53N 17°43E 82 E4
Bruthen Australia 37°42S 147°50E 153 D7
Bruxelles = Brussel Belgium 50°51N 4°21E 69 D4
Bruyères France 48°10N 6°40E 71 D13
Bruz France 48°1N 1°46W 70 D5
Brwinów Poland 52°9N 20°40E 83 F7
Bryagovo Bulgaria 41°58N 25°8E 97 E9
Bryan Ohio, U.S.A. 41°28N 84°33W 173 E11
Bryan Tex., U.S.A. 30°40N 96°22W 176 F6
Bryan, Mt. Australia 33°30S 139°5E 152 B3
Bryanka Ukraine 48°32N 38°45E 85 H10
Bryansk Bryansk, Russia 53°13N 34°25E 85 F8
Bryansk Dagestan, Russia 44°20N 47°10E 87 H8
Bryansk ☐ Russia 53°10N 33°10E 85 F7
Bryce Canyon △ U.S.A. 37°30N 112°10W 169 H7
Bryne Norway 58°44N 5°38E 61 G11
Bryson City U.S.A. 35°26N 83°27W 177 D13
Bryukhovetskaya Russia 45°48N 39°0E 85 K10
Brza Palanka Serbia 44°28N 22°27E 96 B6
Brzeg Poland 50°52N 17°30E 83 H4
Brzeg Dolny Poland 51°16N 16°41E 83 G3
Brześć Kujawski Poland 52°36N 18°55E 83 F5
Brzesko Poland 49°59N 20°34E 83 J7
Brzeziny Poland 51°49N 19°42E 83 G6
Brzozów Poland 49°41N 22°3E 83 J9
Bsharri Lebanon 34°15N 36°0E 130 A5
Bū Baqarah U.A.E. 25°35N 56°25E 129 E8
Bu Craa W. Sahara 26°45N 12°50W 134 C3
Bū Ḩasā U.A.E. 23°30N 53°20E 129 F7
Bua Fiji 16°48S 178°37E 154 a
Bua Sweden 57°14N 12°7E 63 G6
Bua → Malawi 12°45S 34°16E 143 E3
Bua Yai Thailand 15°33N 102°26E 120 E4
Buan S. Korea 35°44N 126°44E 115 G14
Buapinang Indonesia 4°40S 121°30E 119 E6
Buba Guinea-Biss. 11°40N 14°59W 138 C1
Bubanza Burundi 3°6S 29°23E 142 C2
Bubaque Guinea-Biss. 11°16N 15°51W 138 C1
Bubi → Zimbabwe 22°20S 31°7E 145 B5
Būbiyān Kuwait 29°45N 48°15E 129 D6
Buca Fiji 16°38S 179°52E 154 a
Buca Turkey 38°22N 27°11E 99 C9
Bucak Turkey 37°28N 30°36E 99 D12
Bucaramanga Colombia 7°0N 73°0W 186 B4
Bucasia Australia 21°2S 149°10E 150 b
Buccaneer Arch. Australia 16°7S 123°20E 148 C3
Buccino Italy 40°38N 15°22E 95 B8
Buccoo Reef Trin. & Tob. 11°10N 60°51W 187 J16
Bucecea Romania 47°47N 26°28E 81 C11
Bucegi △ Romania 45°25N 25°25E 81 E10
Buchach Ukraine 49°5N 25°25E 75 D13
Buchan Australia 37°30S 148°12E 153 D8
Buchan U.K. 57°32N 2°21W 65 D6
Buchan Ness U.K. 57°29N 1°46W 65 D7
Buchanan Canada 51°40N 102°45W 163 C8
Buchanan Liberia 5°57N 10°2W 138 D2
Buchanan U.S.A. 33°48N 85°11W 178 B4
Buchanan, L. Queens., Australia 21°35S 145°52E 150 C4
Buchanan, L. W. Austral., Australia 25°33S 123°2E 149 E3
Buchanan, L. U.S.A. 30°45N 98°25W 176 F5
Buchanan Cr. → Australia 19°13S 136°33E 150 B2
Buchans Canada 48°50N 56°52W 165 C8
Bucharest = Bucureşti Romania 44°27N 26°10E 81 F11
Buchen Germany 49°32N 9°20E 77 F5
Bucheon S. Korea 37°28N 126°45E 115 F14
Buchholz Germany 53°19N 9°52E 76 B5
Buchloe Germany 48°1N 10°44E 77 G6
Buchon, Pt. U.S.A. 35°15N 120°54W 170 K6
Buciumi Romania 47°3N 23°1E 80 C8
Buck Hill Falls U.S.A. 41°11N 75°16W 175 E9
Bückeburg Germany 52°16N 9°7E 76 C5
Buckeye Lake U.S.A. 39°55N 82°29W 174 G2
Buckhannon U.S.A. 39°0N 80°8W 173 F13
Buckhaven U.K. 56°11N 3°3W 65 E5
Buckhorn L. Canada 44°29N 78°23W 174 B6
Buckie U.K. 57°41N 2°58W 65 D6
Buckingham Canada 45°37N 75°24W 164 C4
Buckingham U.K. 51°59N 0°57W 67 F7
Buckingham B. Australia 12°10S 135°40E 150 A2
Buckingham Canal India 14°0N 80°5E 127 H5
Buckinghamshire ☐ U.K. 51°53N 0°55W 67 F7
Buckle Hd. Australia 14°26S 127°52E 148 B4
Buckleboo Australia 32°54S 136°12E 152 B2
Buckley U.K. 53°10N 3°5W 66 D4
Buckley → Australia 20°10S 138°49E 150 C2
Bucklin U.S.A. 37°33N 99°38W 172 G4
Bucks L. U.S.A. 39°54N 121°12W 170 F5
Bucquoy France 50°9N 2°43E 71 B9
Bucureşti Romania 44°27N 26°10E 81 F11
Bucureşti Otopeni ✈ (OTP) Romania 44°30N 26°11E 81 F11
Bucyrus U.S.A. 40°48N 82°59W 173 E12
Budacu, Vf. Romania 47°7N 25°41E 81 C10
Budalin Burma 22°20N 95°10E 123 H19
Budaörs Hungary 47°27N 18°57E 80 C3
Budapest Hungary 47°29N 19°3E 80 C4
Budapest ☐ Hungary 47°29N 19°5E 80 C4
Budapest ✈ (BUD) Hungary 47°26N 19°14E 80 C4
Budaun India 28°5N 79°10E 125 E8
Budawang △ Australia 35°10S 150°12E 153 C9
Budd Coast Antarctica 68°0S 112°0E 55 C8
Budderoo △ Australia 35°40S 150°41E 153 C9
Buddusò Italy 40°35N 9°15E 94 B2
Bude U.K. 50°49N 4°34W 67 G3
Budennovsk Russia 44°50N 44°10E 87 H7
Budeşti Romania 44°13N 26°30E 81 F11
Budeyi Ukraine 48°3N 29°16E 81 B14
Budge Budge = Baj Baj India 22°30N 88°5E 125 H13
Budgewoi Australia 33°13S 151°34E 153 B9
Budia Spain 40°38N 2°46W 90 E2
Büdingen Germany 50°16N 9°7E 77 E5
Budjala Dem. Rep. of the Congo 2°50N 19°40E 140 D3
Budo-Sungai Padi △ Thailand 6°19N 101°42E 121 J3
Budoni Italy 40°40N 9°45E 94 B2
Búdrio Italy 44°32N 11°32E 93 D8
Budva Montenegro 42°17N 18°50E 96 D2
Budzyń Poland 52°54N 16°59E 83 F3
Buea Cameroon 4°10N 9°9E 139 E6
Buellton U.S.A. 34°37N 120°12W 171 L6
Buena Esperanza Argentina 34°45S 65°15W 190 C2
Buena Park U.S.A. 33°52N 117°59W 171 M9
Buena Vista Colo., U.S.A. 38°51N 106°8W 168 G10
Buena Vista Ga., U.S.A. 32°19N 84°31W 178 C5
Buena Vista Va., U.S.A. 37°44N 79°21W 173 G14
Buena Vista Lake Bed U.S.A. 35°12N 119°18W 171 K7
Buenaventura Colombia 3°53N 77°4W 186 C3
Buenaventura Mexico 29°51N 107°29W 180 B3
Buendía, Embalse de Spain 40°25N 2°43W 90 E2
Buenópolis Brazil 17°54S 44°11W 189 D2
Buenos Aires Argentina 34°36S 58°22W 190 C4
Buenos Aires Costa Rica 9°10N 83°20W 182 E3
Buenos Aires ☐ Argentina 36°30S 60°0W 190 D4
Buenos Aires, L. = General Carrera, L. S. Amer. 46°35S 72°0W 192 C2
Buffalo Mo., U.S.A. 37°39N 93°6W 172 G7
Buffalo N.Y., U.S.A. 42°53N 78°53W 174 D6
Buffalo Okla., U.S.A. 36°50N 99°38W 176 C5
Buffalo S. Dak., U.S.A. 45°35N 103°33W 172 C2
Buffalo Wyo., U.S.A. 44°21N 106°42W 168 D10
Buffalo → Canada 60°5N 115°5W 162 A5
Buffalo → S. Africa 28°43S 30°37E 145 C5
Buffalo ⌂ U.S.A. 36°14N 92°36W 176 C8
Buffalo Head Hills Canada 57°25N 115°55W 162 B5
Buffalo L. Alta., Canada 52°27N 112°54W 162 C6
Buffalo L. N.W.T., Canada 60°12N 115°25W 162 A5
Buffalo Narrows Canada 55°51N 108°29W 163 B7
Buffalo Springs ⌂ Kenya 0°32N 37°35E 142 B4
Buffels → S. Africa 29°36S 17°3E 144 C2
Buford U.S.A. 34°7N 83°59W 178 A6
Bug = Buh → Ukraine 46°59N 31°58E 85 J6
Bug → Poland 52°31N 21°5E 83 F8
Buga Colombia 4°0N 76°15W 186 C3
Bugala I. Uganda 0°40S 32°20E 142 C3
Buganda Uganda 0°0 31°30E 142 C3
Buganga Uganda 0°3S 32°0E 142 C3
Bugeat France 45°36N 1°55E 72 C5
Bugel, Tanjung Indonesia 6°26S 111°3E 119 G14
Búger Spain 39°45N 2°59E 100 B9
Bugibba Malta 35°57N 14°25E 101 D1
Bugojno Bos.-H. 44°2N 17°25E 80 F2
Bugsuk I. Phil. 8°12N 117°18E 118 C5
Bugulma Russia 54°33N 52°48E 108 B4
Buguma Nigeria 4°42N 6°55E 139 E6
Bugungu ⌂ Uganda 2°17N 31°50E 142 B3
Buguruslan Russia 53°39N 52°26E 108 B4
Buh → Ukraine 46°59N 31°58E 85 J6
Buharkent Turkey 37°58N 28°44E 99 D10
Buheirat-Murrat-el-Kubra Egypt 30°18N 32°26E 137 E8
Buhera Zimbabwe 19°18S 31°29E 145 A5
Bühl Germany 48°40N 8°8E 77 G4
Buhl U.S.A. 42°36N 114°46W 168 E6
Buhuşi Romania 46°41N 26°45E 81 D11
Bui △ Ghana 8°21N 2°21W 138 D4
Buila-Vanturariţa △ Romania 45°15N 24°0E 81 E8
Builth Wells U.K. 52°9N 3°25W 67 E4
Buinsk Russia 55°0N 48°18E 86 C9
Buíque Brazil 8°37S 37°9W 189 B3
Buir Nur Mongolia 47°50N 117°42E 111 B12
Buis-les-Baronnies France 44°17N 5°16E 73 D9
Buitrago del Lozoya Spain 40°58N 3°38W 88 E7
Bujalance Spain 37°54N 4°23W 89 H6
Bujanovac Serbia 42°28N 21°44E 96 D5
Bujaraloz Spain 41°29N 0°10W 90 D4
Buje Croatia 45°24N 13°39E 93 C10
Buji China 22°37N 114°5E 111 a
Bujumbura Burundi 3°16S 29°18E 142 C2
Bük Hungary 47°22N 16°45E 80 C1
Buk Poland 52°21N 16°30E 83 F3
Bukachacha Russia 52°55N 116°50E 107 D12
Bukama Dem. Rep. of the Congo 9°10S 25°50E 143 D2
Bukavu Dem. Rep. of the Congo 2°20S 28°52E 142 C2
Bukene Tanzania 4°15S 32°48E 142 C3
Bukhara = Buxoro Uzbekistan 39°48N 64°25E 108 E6
Bukhoro = Buxoro Uzbekistan 39°48N 64°25E 108 E6
Bukhtarma Res. = Zaysan Köli Kazakhstan 48°0N 83°0E 109 C10
Bukima Tanzania 1°50S 33°25E 142 C3
Bukit Bendera Malaysia 5°25N 100°15E 121 c
Bukit Mertajam Malaysia 5°22N 100°28E 121 c
Bukit Nil Malaysia 1°22N 104°12E 121 d
Bukit Tengah Malaysia 5°22N 100°25E 121 c
Bukittinggi Indonesia 0°20S 100°20E 118 E2
Bükk Hungary 48°0N 20°30E 80 B5
Bukkapatnam India 14°14N 77°46E 127 G3
Bükki △ Hungary 48°3N 20°30E 80 B5
Bukoba Tanzania 1°20S 31°49E 142 C3
Bukum, Pulau Singapore 1°14N 103°46E 121 d
Bukuru Nigeria 9°42N 8°48E 139 D6
Bukuya Uganda 0°40N 31°52E 142 B3
Būl, Kuh-e Iran 30°48N 52°45E 129 D7
Bula Guinea-Biss. 12°7N 15°43W 138 C1
Bula Indonesia 3°6S 130°30E 119 E8
Bülach Switz. 47°31N 8°32E 77 H4
Bülaevo Kazakhstan 54°54N 70°26E 109 B8
Bulahdelah Australia 32°23S 152°13E 153 B10
Bulan Phil. 12°40N 123°52E 119 B6
Bulancak Turkey 40°56N 38°14E 105 B8
Bulanık Turkey 39°4N 42°14E 105 C10
Bûlâq Egypt 25°10N 30°38E 137 B3
Bulawayo Zimbabwe 20°7S 28°32E 143 G2
Buldan Turkey 38°2N 28°50E 99 C10
Buldana India 20°30N 76°18E 126 D3
Buldir I. U.S.A. 52°21N 175°56E 166 E3
Bulenga Ghana 9°56N 2°12W 138 D4
Bulgan Mongolia 48°45N 103°34E 110 B9
Bulgar Russia 54°57N 49°4E 86 C9
Bulgaria ■ Europe 42°35N 25°30E 97 D9
Bulgheria, Monte Italy 40°4N 15°26E 95 B8
Bulgurca Turkey 38°9N 27°9E 99 C9
Buli, Teluk Indonesia 0°48N 128°25E 119 D7
Buliluyan, C. Phil. 8°20N 117°15E 118 C5
Bulkley → Canada 55°15N 127°40W 162 B3
Bull Shoals L. U.S.A. 36°22N 92°35W 176 C8
Bullaque → Spain 38°59N 4°17W 89 G6
Bullard U.S.A. 32°38N 83°30W 178 C6
Bullas Spain 38°2N 1°40W 91 G3
Bulle Switz. 46°37N 7°3E 77 J3
Buller → N.Z. 41°44S 171°36E 155 B6
Buller, Mt. Australia 37°10S 146°28E 153 D7
Buller Gorge N.Z. 41°40S 172°10E 155 B7
Bulleringa △ Australia 17°39S 143°56E 150 B3
Bullhead City U.S.A. 35°8N 114°32W 171 K12
Bulli Australia 34°15S 150°57E 153 C9
Büllingen Belgium 50°25N 6°16E 69 D6
Bullock Creek Australia 17°43S 144°31E 150 B3
Bulloo → Australia 28°43S 142°30E 151 D3
Bulloo L. Australia 28°43S 142°25E 151 D3
Bulls N.Z. 40°10S 175°24E 154 G4
Bully-les-Mines France 50°27N 2°44E 71 B9
Bulman Australia 13°39S 134°20E 150 A1
Bulnes Chile 36°42S 72°19W 190 D1
Bulqizë Albania 41°30N 20°21E 96 E4
Bulsar = Valsad India 20°40N 72°58E 126 D1
Bultfontein S. Africa 28°18S 26°10E 144 C4
Bulukumba Indonesia 5°33S 120°11E 119 F6
Bulun Russia 70°37N 127°30E 107 B13
Bulungkol China 38°36N 74°58E 109 E8
Bumba Dem. Rep. of the Congo 2°13N 22°30E 140 D4
Bumbah, Khalīj Libya 32°20N 23°15E 135 B10
Bumbeşti-Jiu Romania 45°10N 23°24E 81 E8
Bumbiri I. Tanzania 1°40S 31°55E 142 C3
Bumbuna S. Leone 9°2N 11°49W 138 D2
Bumhpa Bum Burma 26°51N 97°14E 123 F20
Bumi → Zimbabwe 17°0S 28°20E 143 F2
Buna Kenya 2°58N 39°30E 142 B4
Bunaken Indonesia 1°37N 124°46E 119 D6
Bunazi Tanzania 1°3S 31°23E 142 C3
Bunbury Australia 33°20S 115°35E 149 F2
Bunclody Ireland 52°39N 6°40W 64 D5
Buncrana Ireland 55°8N 7°27W 64 A4
Bundaberg Australia 24°54S 152°22E 151 C5
Bundanoon Australia 34°40S 150°16E 153 C9
Bünde Germany 52°11N 8°35E 76 C4
Bundey → Australia 21°46S 135°37E 150 C2
Bundi India 25°30N 75°35E 124 G6
Bundjalung △ Australia 29°16S 153°21E 151 D5
Bundoran Ireland 54°28N 8°18W 64 B3
Bundure Australia 35°10S 146°1E 153 C7
Bung Kan Thailand 18°23N 103°37E 120 C4
Bunga → Nigeria 11°23N 9°56E 139 C6
Bungay U.K. 52°27N 1°28E 67 E9
Bungendore Australia 35°14S 149°30E 153 C8
Bungil Cr. → Australia 27°5S 149°5E 151 D4
Bungle Bungle = Purnululu △ Australia 17°20S 128°20E 148 C4
Bungo-Suidō Japan 33°0N 132°15E 113 H6
Bungoma Kenya 0°34N 34°34E 142 B3
Bungotakada Japan 33°35N 131°25E 113 H5
Bungu Tanzania 7°35S 39°0E 142 D4
Bunia Dem. Rep. of the Congo 1°35N 30°20E 142 B3
Bunji Pakistan 35°45N 74°40E 125 B6
Bunkie U.S.A. 30°57N 92°11W 176 F8
Bunnell U.S.A. 29°28N 81°16W 179 F8
Bunnythorpe N.Z. 40°16S 175°39E 154 G4
Buñol Spain 39°25N 0°47W 91 F4
Bunsuru → Nigeria 13°21N 6°23E 139 C5
Buntok Indonesia 1°40S 114°58E 118 E4
Bununu Dass Nigeria 10°5N 9°31E 139 C6
Bununu Kasa Nigeria 9°51N 9°32E 139 D6
Bunya Mts. △ Australia 26°51S 151°34E 151 D5
Bünyan Turkey 38°51N 35°51E 104 C6
Bunyola Spain 39°41N 2°42E 100 B9
Bunyu Indonesia 3°35N 117°50E 118 D5
Bunza Nigeria 12°8N 4°0E 139 C5
Buol Indonesia 1°15N 121°32E 119 D6
Buon Brieng Vietnam 13°9N 108°12E 120 F7
Buon Ho Vietnam 12°57N 108°18E 120 F7
Buon Ma Thuot Vietnam 12°40N 108°3E 120 F7
Buong Long Cambodia 13°44N 106°59E 120 F6
Buorkhaya, Mys Russia 71°50N 132°40E 107 B14
Buqayq Si. Arabia 26°0N 49°45E 129 E6
Buqbuq Egypt 31°29N 25°29E 137 A2
Bur Acaba = Buurhakaba Somalia 3°12N 44°20E 131 G3
Bûr Fuad Egypt 31°15N 32°20E 137 E8
Bûr Safâga Egypt 26°43N 33°57E 128 E2
Bûr Sa'îd Egypt 31°16N 32°18E 137 E8
Bûr Sûdân Sudan 19°32N 37°9E 137 D4
Bûr Taufiq Egypt 29°54N 32°32E 137 F8
Bura Kenya 1°4S 39°58E 142 C4
Burakin Australia 30°31S 117°10E 149 F2
Burang China 30°15N 81°10E 110 E5
Burao = Burco Somalia 9°32N 45°32E 131 F4
Burāq Syria 33°11N 36°29E 130 B5
Burathum Nepal 28°4N 84°50E 125 E11
Buraydah Si. Arabia 26°20N 43°59E 128 E4
Burbank U.S.A. 34°12N 118°18W 171 L8
Burcher Australia 33°30S 147°16E 153 B7
Burco Somalia 9°32N 45°32E 131 F4
Burda India 25°50N 77°35E 124 G7
Burdekin → Australia 19°38S 147°25E 150 B4
Burdur Turkey 37°45N 30°17E 99 D12
Burdur ☐ Turkey 37°45N 30°0E 99 D12
Burdur Gölü Turkey 37°44N 30°10E 99 D12
Burdwan = Barddhaman India 23°14N 87°39E 125 H12
Burdwood Bank Atl. Oc. 54°0S 59°0W 56 M6
Bure Ethiopia 10°40N 37°4E 131 E2
Bure → U.K. 52°38N 1°43E 66 E9
Burela Spain 43°39N 7°24W 88 B3
Büren Germany 51°33N 8°35E 76 D4
Bureskoye Vdkhr. Russia 50°16N 130°20E 107 D14
Bureya → Russia 49°27N 129°30E 107 E13
Burford Canada 43°7N 80°27W 174 C4
Burg Germany 52°16N 11°51E 76 C7
Burg auf Fehmarn Germany 54°28N 11°9E 76 A7
Burg el Arab Egypt 30°54N 29°32E 137 E6
Burg et Tuyur Sudan 20°55N 27°56E 137 C2
Burg Stargard Germany 53°29N 13°18E 76 B9
Burgas Bulgaria 42°33N 27°29E 97 D11
Burgas ☐ Bulgaria 42°30N 27°30E 97 D11
Burgaski Zaliv Bulgaria 42°30N 27°39E 97 D11
Burgdorf Germany 52°27N 10°1E 76 C6
Burgdorf Switz. 47°3N 7°37E 77 H3
Burgenland ☐ Austria 47°20N 16°20E 79 D9
Burgeo Canada 47°37N 57°38W 165 C8
Burgersdorp S. Africa 31°0S 26°20E 144 D4
Burgess, Mt. Australia 30°50S 121°5E 149 F3
Burghausen Germany 48°9N 12°49E 77 G8
Burghead U.K. 57°43N 3°30W 65 D5
Búrgio Italy 37°36N 13°17E 94 E6
Burglengenfeld Germany 49°12N 12°2E 77 F8
Burgohondo Spain 40°26N 4°47W 88 E6
Burgos Spain 42°21N 3°41W 88 C7
Burgos ☐ Spain 42°21N 3°42W 88 C7
Burgstädt Germany 50°54N 12°49E 76 E8
Burgsvik Sweden 57°3N 18°19E 63 G12
Burguillos del Cerro Spain 38°23N 6°35W 89 G4
Burgundy = Bourgogne ☐ France 47°0N 4°50E 71 F11
Burhaniye Turkey 39°30N 26°58E 99 B8
Burhanpur India 21°18N 76°14E 126 D3
Burhi Gandak → India 25°20N 86°37E 125 G12
Burhner → India 22°43N 80°31E 125 H9
Burias I. Phil. 12°55N 123°5E 119 B6
Burica, Pta. Costa Rica 8°3N 82°51W 182 E3
Burien U.S.A. 47°28N 122°20W 170 C4
Burigi, L. Tanzania 2°2S 31°22E 142 C3
Burigi ⌂ Tanzania 2°20S 31°6E 142 C3
Burim Kosovo 42°45N 20°24E 96 D4
Burin Canada 47°1N 55°14W 165 C8
Buriram Thailand 15°0N 103°0E 120 E4
Buriti Bravo Brazil 5°50S 43°50W 189 B2
Buriti dos Lopes Brazil 3°10S 41°52W 189 A2
Burkburnett U.S.A. 34°6N 98°34W 176 D5
Burke → Australia 23°12S 139°33E 150 C2
Burke Chan. Canada 52°10N 127°30W 162 C3
Burketown Australia 17°45S 139°33E 150 B2
Burkina Faso ■ Africa 12°0N 1°0W 138 C4
Burk's Falls Canada 45°37N 79°24W 164 C4
Burlada Spain 42°49N 1°36W 90 C3
Burleigh Falls Canada 44°33N 78°12W 174 B6
Burley U.S.A. 42°32N 113°48W 168 E7
Burlingame U.S.A. 37°35N 122°21W 170 H4
Burlington Canada 43°18N 79°45W 174 C5
Burlington Colo., U.S.A. 39°18N 102°16W 168 G12
Burlington Iowa, U.S.A. 40°49N 91°14W 172 E8
Burlington Kans., U.S.A. 38°12N 95°45W 172 F6
Burlington N.C., U.S.A. 36°6N 79°26W 177 C15
Burlington N.J., U.S.A. 40°4N 74°51W 175 F10
Burlington Vt., U.S.A. 44°29N 73°12W 175 B11
Burlington Wash., U.S.A. 48°28N 122°20W 170 B4
Burlington Wis., U.S.A. 42°41N 88°17W 172 D9
Burma ■ Asia 21°0N 96°30E 123 J20
Burnaby I. Canada 52°25N 131°19W 162 C2
Burnet U.S.A. 30°45N 98°14W 176 F5
Burney U.S.A. 40°53N 121°40W 168 F3
Burnham U.S.A. 40°38N 77°34W 174 F7
Burnham-on-Sea U.K. 51°14N 3°0W 67 F5
Burnie Australia 41°4S 145°56E 151 G4
Burnley U.K. 53°47N 2°14W 66 D5
Burns U.S.A. 43°35N 119°3W 168 E4
Burns Junction U.S.A. 42°47N 117°51W 168 E5
Burns Lake Canada 54°14N 125°45W 162 C3
Burnside → Canada 66°51N 108°4W 160 D10
Burnside, L. Australia 25°22S 123°0E 149 E3
Burnsville U.S.A. 44°47N 93°17W 172 C7
Burnt River Canada 44°41N 78°42W 174 B6
Burntwood → Canada 56°8N 96°34W 163 B9
Burntwood L. Canada 55°22N 100°26W 163 B8
Buronga Australia 34°18S 142°20E 152 C5
Burqān Kuwait 29°0N 47°57E 128 D5
Burqin China 47°43N 87°0E 109 C11
Burra Australia 33°40S 138°55E 152 B3
Burra Nigeria 11°0N 8°56E 139 C6
Burragorang, L. Australia 33°52S 150°37E 153 B9
Burray U.K. 58°51N 2°54W 65 C6
Burrel Albania 41°36N 20°1E 96 E4
Burren △ Ireland 53°9N 9°5W 64 C2
Burren Junction Australia 30°7S 148°58E 151 E4
Burrendong, L. Australia 32°45S 149°10E 153 B8
Burriana Spain 39°50N 0°4W 90 F4
Burrinjuck, L. Australia 35°0S 148°36E 153 C8
Burro, Serranías del Mexico 28°56N 102°5W 180 B4
Burrow Hd. U.K. 54°41N 4°24W 65 G4
Burrowa-Pine Mountain △ Australia 36°6S 147°45E 153 D7
Burrum Coast △ Australia 25°13S 152°36E 151 D5
Burruyacú Argentina 26°30S 64°40W 190 B3
Burry Port U.K. 51°41N 4°15W 67 F3
Bursa Turkey 40°15N 29°5E 97 F13
Bursa ☐ Turkey 40°10N 29°5E 104 B3
Burseryd Sweden 57°12N 13°17E 63 G7
Burstall Canada 50°39N 109°54W 163 C7
Burton Ohio, U.S.A. 41°28N 81°8W 174 E3
Burton S.C., U.S.A. 32°26N 80°43W 178 C9
Burton, L. Canada 54°45N 78°20W 164 B4
Burton upon Trent U.K. 52°48N 1°38W 66 E6
Burtundy Australia 33°45S 142°15E 152 B5
Buru Indonesia 3°30S 126°30E 119 E7
Burullus, Bahra el Egypt 31°25N 31°0E 137 E7
Burûn, Râs Egypt 31°14N 33°7E 130 D2
Burundi ■ Africa 3°15S 30°0E 142 C3
Bururi Burundi 3°57S 29°37E 142 C2
Burutu Nigeria 5°20N 5°29E 139 D6
Burwell U.S.A. 41°47N 99°8W 172 E4
Burwick U.K. 58°45N 2°58W 65 C5
Bury U.K. 53°35N 2°17W 66 D5
Bury St. Edmunds U.K. 52°15N 0°43E 67 E8
Buryatia ☐ Russia 53°0N 110°0E 107 D12
Būrylbaytal Kazakhstan 44°56N 74°0E 109 D8
Buryn Ukraine 51°13N 33°50E 85 G7
Burzenin Poland 51°28N 18°47E 83 G5
Busalla Italy 44°34N 8°57E 92 D5
Busan S. Korea 35°5N 129°0E 115 G15
Busango Swamp Zambia 14°15S 25°45E 143 E2
Busaso = Boosaaso Somalia 11°12N 49°18E 131 E4
Buşayrah Syria 35°9N 40°26E 105 E9
Busca Italy 44°31N 7°29E 92 D4
Bushat Albania 41°58N 19°34E 96 E3
Būshehr Iran 28°55N 50°55E 129 D6
Būshehr ☐ Iran 28°20N 51°45E 129 D6
Bushenyi Uganda 0°35S 30°10E 142 C3
Bushire = Būshehr Iran 28°55N 50°55E 129 D6
Bushnell U.S.A. 28°40N 82°7W 179 G7
Bushtyna Ukraine 48°3N 23°28E 81 B8
Busie Ghana 10°29N 2°22W 138 C4
Businga Dem. Rep. of the Congo 3°16N 20°59E 140 D4
Büsingen Germany 47°42N 8°41E 77 H4
Busko-Zdrój Poland 50°28N 20°42E 83 H7
Busovača Bos.-H. 44°6N 17°53E 80 F2
Buşra ash Shām Syria 32°30N 36°25E 130 C5
Busselton Australia 33°42S 115°15E 149 F2
Busseto Italy 44°59N 10°2E 92 D7
Bussière-Badil France 45°39N 0°36E 72 C4
Bussolengo Italy 45°28N 10°51E 92 C7
Bussum Neths. 52°16N 5°10E 69 B5
Bustamante, B. Argentina 45°5S 66°18W 192 C3
Buşteni Romania 45°24N 25°32E 81 E10
Busto, C. Spain 43°34N 6°28W 88 B4
Busto Arsizio Italy 45°37N 8°51E 92 C5
Busu Djanoa Dem. Rep. of the Congo 1°43N 21°23E 140 D4
Busuanga I. Phil. 12°10N 120°0E 119 B6
Büsum Germany 54°7N 8°51E 76 A4
Busungbiu Indonesia 8°16S 114°58E 119 J17
Buta Dem. Rep. of the Congo 2°50N 24°53E 142 B1
Butare Rwanda 2°31S 29°52E 142 C2
Butaritari Kiribati 3°30N 174°0E 156 G9
Bute Australia 33°51S 138°0E 152 B3
Bute U.K. 55°48N 5°2W 65 F3
Bute Inlet Canada 50°40N 124°53W 162 C4
Butemba Uganda 1°9N 31°37E 142 B3

Butembo
  Dem. Rep. of the Congo 0°9N 29°18E **142** B2
Buteni *Romania* 46°19N 22°7E **80** D7
Butera *Italy* 37°11N 14°11E **95** E7
Butere *Kenya* 0°13N 34°30E **142** B3
Butha-Buthe *Lesotho* 28°47S 28°14E **145** C4
Butiaba *Uganda* 1°50N 31°20E **142** B3
Butler *Ga., U.S.A.* 32°33N 84°14W **178** C5
Butler *Mo., U.S.A.* 38°16N 94°20W **172** F6
Butler *Pa., U.S.A.* 40°52N 79°54W **174** F5
Buton *Indonesia* 5°0S 122°45E **119** E6
Butte *Mont., U.S.A.* 46°0N 112°32W **168** C7
Butte *Nebr., U.S.A.* 42°58N 98°51W **172** D4
Butte Creek → *U.S.A.* 39°12N 121°56W **170** F5
Butterworth = Gcuwa
  S. Africa 32°20S 28°11E **145** D4
Butterworth *Malaysia* 5°24N 100°23E **121** c
Buttevant *Ireland* 52°14N 8°40W **64** D3
Buttfield, Mt. *Australia* 24°45S 128°9E **149** D4
Buttonwillow *U.S.A.* 35°24N 119°28W **171** K7
Butuan *Phil.* 8°57N 125°33E **119** C7
Butuku-Luba *Eq. Guin.* 3°28N 8°33E **139** E6
Butung = Buton
  Indonesia 5°0S 122°45E **119** E6
Buturlinovka *Russia* 50°50N 40°35E **86** E5
Butwal *Nepal* 27°33N 83°31E **125** F10
Butzbach *Germany* 50°25N 8°40E **77** E4
Bützow *Germany* 53°50N 11°58E **76** B7
Buurhakaba *Somalia* 3°12N 44°20E **131** G3
Buxa Duar *India* 27°45N 89°35E **125** F13
Buxar *India* 25°34N 83°58E **125** G10
Buxoro *Uzbekistan* 39°48N 64°25E **108** E6
Buxtehude *Germany* 53°28N 9°39E **76** B5
Buxton *U.K.* 53°16N 1°54W **66** E6
Buxy *France* 46°44N 4°40E **71** F11
Buy *Russia* 58°28N 41°28E **86** A5
Buyant-Uhaa
  Mongolia 44°55N 110°11E **114** B6
Buynaksk *Russia* 42°48N 47°7E **87** D8
Buyo *Ivory C.* 6°21N 7°5W **138** D3
Buyo, L. de *Ivory C.* 6°16N 7°10W **138** D3
Büyük Menderes →
  Turkey 37°28N 27°11E **99** D3
Büyükçekmece *Turkey* 41°2N 28°35E **97** E12
Büyükkariştiran
  Turkey 41°18N 27°33E **97** E11
Büyükkemikli Burnu
  Turkey 40°18N 26°14E **97** F10
Büyükkonuk = Komi
  Cyprus 35°24N 34°0E **101** D13
Büyükorhan *Turkey* 39°46N 28°56E **97** E11
Büyükyoncalı *Turkey* 41°20N 27°53E **97** E11
Buyun Shan *China* 40°4N 122°43E **115** D12
Buzançais *France* 46°54N 1°25E **70** F8
Buzău *Romania* 45°10N 26°50E **81** E11
Buzău □ *Romania* 45°20N 26°50E **81** E11
Buzău → *Romania* 45°26N 27°44E **81** E12
Buzău, Pasul *Romania* 45°35N 26°12E **81** E11
Buzen *Japan* 33°35N 131°5E **113** H5
Buzet *Croatia* 45°24N 13°58E **93** C10
Buziaş *Romania* 45°38N 21°36E **80** E6
Büzmeyin *Turkmenistan* 38°3N 58°12E **129** B8
Buzuluk *Russia* 52°48N 52°12E **108** B4
Buzuluk → *Russia* 50°15N 42°7E **86** E6
Buzzards Bay *U.S.A.* 41°45N 70°37W **175** E14
Bwana Mkubwa *Zambia* 13°8S 28°38E **143** E2
Bwindi △ *Uganda* 1°2S 29°42E **142** C2
Byala *Ruse, Bulgaria* 43°28N 25°44E **97** C9
Byala *Varna, Bulgaria* 42°53N 27°55E **97** D11
Byala Slatina *Bulgaria* 43°26N 23°58E **96** C7
Byam Martin I.
  Canada 75°15N 104°15W **161** B11
Byarezina → *Belarus* 52°33N 30°14E **75** B16
Byaroza *Belarus* 52°31N 24°51E **75** B13
Byblos = Jubayl *Lebanon* 34°5N 35°39E **130** A4
Bychawa *Poland* 51°1N 22°36E **83** G9
Byczyna *Poland* 51°7N 18°12E **83** G5
Bydgoszcz *Poland* 53°10N 18°0E **83** E5
Byelorussia = Belarus ■
  Europe 53°30N 27°0E **75** B14
Byers *U.S.A.* 39°43N 104°14W **168** G11
Byesville *U.S.A.* 39°58N 81°32W **174** G3
Byfield △ *Australia* 22°52S 150°45E **150** C5
Bykhaw *Belarus* 53°31N 30°14E **75** B16
Bykhov = Bykhaw
  Belarus 53°31N 30°14E **75** B16
Bykovo *Russia* 49°50N 45°25E **86** F7
Bylas *U.S.A.* 33°8N 110°7W **169** K8
Bylot *Canada* 58°25N 94°8W **163** B10
Bylot I. *Canada* 73°13N 78°34W **161** C16
Byram *U.S.A.* 32°11N 90°15W **177** E9
Byrd, C. *Antarctica* 69°38S 76°7W **55** C17
Byrock *Australia* 30°40S 146°27E **153** A7
Byron *U.S.A.* 32°39N 83°46W **178** C6
Byron, C. *Australia* 28°43S 153°38E **151** D5
Byron Bay *Australia* 28°43S 153°37E **151** D5
Byrranga, Gory *Russia* 75°0N 100°0E **107** B11
Byrranga Mts. = Byrranga, Gory
  Russia 75°0N 100°0E **107** B11
Byrum *Denmark* 57°16N 11°0E **63** G5
Byske *Sweden* 64°57N 21°11E **60** D19
Byske → *Sweden* 64°57N 21°13E **60** D19
Bystrytsya → *Dolnośląskie,*
  Poland 51°12N 16°55E **83** G3
Bystrzyca → *Lubelskie,*
  Poland 51°21N 22°46E **83** G9
Bystrzyca Kłodzka
  Poland 50°19N 16°39E **83** H3
Bytča *Slovak Rep.* 49°13N 18°34E **79** B11
Bytkiv *Ukraine* 48°37N 24°27E **81** D8
Bytom *Poland* 50°25N 18°54E **83** H5
Bytom Odrzański *Poland* 51°44N 15°48E **83** F2
Bytów *Poland* 54°10N 17°30E **82** D4
Byumba *Rwanda* 1°35S 30°4E **142** C2
Bytča *Slovak Rep.* 48°58N 17°18E **79** C10
Bzura → *Poland* 52°25N 20°15E **83** F7

C

C.W. McConaughy, L.
  U.S.A. 41°14N 101°40W **172** E3
Ca → *Vietnam* 18°45N 105°45E **120** C5
Ca Mau *Vietnam* 9°7N 105°8E **121** H5
Ca Mau, Mui *Vietnam* 8°38N 104°44E **121** H5
Ca Na *Vietnam* 11°20N 108°54E **121** G7
Caacupé *Paraguay* 25°23S 57°5W **190** B4

Caaguazú △ *Paraguay* 26°5S 55°31W **191** B4
Caála *Angola* 12°46S 15°30E **141** G3
Caamaño Sd. *Canada* 52°55N 129°25W **162** C3
Caazapá *Paraguay* 26°8S 56°19W **190** B4
Caazapá □ *Paraguay* 26°10S 56°0W **191** B4
Cabana *Peru* 8°25S 78°5W **188** B2
Cabana de Bergantiños = A
  Carballa *Spain* 43°13N 8°54W **88** B2
Cabanaconde *Peru* 15°38S 71°58W **188** D3
Cabañaquinta *Spain* 43°10N 5°38W **88** B5
Cabanatuan *Phil.* 15°30N 120°58E **119** A6
Cabañeros △ *Spain* 39°18N 4°35W **89** F6
Cabanes *Spain* 40°9N 0°2E **90** E5
Cabanilla *Peru* 15°36S 70°28W **188** D3
Cabano *Canada* 47°40N 68°56W **165** C6
Čabar *Croatia* 45°36N 14°39E **93** C11
Cabazon *U.S.A.* 33°55N 116°47W **171** M10
Cabedelo *Brazil* 7°0S 34°50W **189** B4
Cabeza del Buey *Spain* 38°44N 5°13W **89** G5
Cabezón de la Sal *Spain* 43°18N 4°14W **88** B6
Cabhán, An = Cavan
  Ireland 54°0N 7°22W **64** B4
Cabildo *Chile* 32°30S 71°5W **190** C1
Cabimas *Venezuela* 10°23N 71°25W **186** A4
Cabinda *Angola* 5°33S 12°11E **140** F2
Cabinda □ *Angola* 5°0S 12°30E **140** F2
Cabinet Mts. *U.S.A.* 48°10N 115°50W **168** B6
Cabo Blanco *Argentina* 47°15S 65°47W **192** C3
Cabo de Gata-Níjar △
  Spain 36°51N 2°6W **91** J2
Cabo de Hornos △
  Chile 55°42S 67°20W **192** E3
Cabo de Santo Agostinho
  Brazil 8°20S 34°55W **189** B4
Cabo Frio *Brazil* 22°51S 42°3W **191** A7
Cabo Pantoja *Peru* 1°0S 75°10W **186** D3
Cabo Raso *Argentina* 44°20S 65°15W **192** B3
Cabo San Lucas
  Mexico 22°53N 109°54W **180** C3
Cabo Verde = Cape Verde Is. ■
  Atl. Oc. 16°0N 24°0W **134** b
Cabonga, Réservoir
  Canada 47°20N 76°40W **164** C4
Cabool *U.S.A.* 37°7N 92°6W **172** G7
Caboolture *Australia* 27°5S 152°58E **151** D5
Cabora Bassa Dam = Cahora
  Bassa, Lago de
  Mozam. 15°20S 32°50E **143** F3
Caborca *Mexico* 30°37N 112°6W **180** A2
Cabot, Mt. *U.S.A.* 44°30N 71°25W **175** B13
Cabot Hd. *Canada* 45°14N 81°17W **174** A3
Cabot Str. *Canada* 47°15N 59°40W **165** C8
Cabourg *France* 49°17N 0°7W **70** C6
Cabra *Spain* 37°30N 4°28W **89** H6
Cabra del Santo Cristo
  Spain 37°42N 3°16W **89** H7
Cabra I. *India* 7°18N 93°50E **127** L11
Cábras *Italy* 39°56N 8°32E **94** C1
Cabrera *Spain* 39°8N 2°57E **100** B9
Cabrera, Sierra de la
  Spain 42°12N 6°40W **88** C4
Cabrera △ *Spain* 39°13N 2°53E **91** F7
Cabri *Canada* 50°35N 108°25W **163** C7
Cabriel → *Spain* 39°14N 1°3W **91** F3
Cacabelos *Spain* 42°36N 6°44W **88** C4
Caçador *Brazil* 26°47S 51°0W **191** B5
Čačak *Serbia* 43°54N 20°20E **96** C4
Caçapava do Sul *Brazil* 30°30S 53°30W **191** C5
Cáccamo *Italy* 37°56N 13°40E **94** E6
Cacém *Portugal* 38°46N 9°18W **89** G1
Cáceres *Brazil* 16°5S 57°40W **186** G7
Cáceres *Spain* 39°26N 6°23W **89** F4
Cáceres □ *Spain* 39°45N 6°0W **89** F5
Cache Bay *Canada* 46°22N 80°0W **164** C4
Cache Cr. → *U.S.A.* 38°42N 121°42W **170** G5
Cache Creek *Canada* 50°48N 121°19W **162** C4
Cacheu *Guinea-Biss.* 12°14N 16°8W **138** C1
Cachi *Argentina* 25°5S 66°10W **190** B2
Cachimbo, Serra do
  Brazil 9°30S 55°30W **187** D7
Cachinal de la Sierra
  Chile 24°58S 69°32W **190** A2
Cachoeira *Brazil* 12°30S 39°0W **189** D3
Cachoeira do Sul *Brazil* 30°3S 52°53W **191** C5
Cachoeiro de Itapemirim
  Brazil 20°51S 41°7W **191** A7
Cachopo *Portugal* 37°20N 7°49W **89** H3
Cacine *Guinea-Biss.* 11°8N 14°57W **138** C1
Cacoal *Brazil* 11°32S 61°18W **186** F6
Cacólo *Angola* 10°9S 19°21E **140** G3
Caconda *Angola* 13°48S 15°8E **141** G3
Caculé *Brazil* 14°30S 42°13W **189** D2
Cadaqués *Spain* 42°17N 3°17E **90** C8
Čadca *Slovak Rep.* 49°26N 18°45E **79** B11
Caddo *U.S.A.* 34°7N 96°16W **176** D6
Cader Idris *U.K.* 52°42N 3°53W **67** E4
Cadereyta de Jiménez
  Mexico 25°36N 100°0W **180** B5
Cades *U.S.A.* 33°47N 79°47W **178** D10
Cadi-Moixeró △ *Spain* 42°17N 1°44W **90** C2
Cadibarrawirracanna, L.
  Australia 28°52S 135°27E **151** D2
Cadillac *France* 44°38N 0°20W **72** D3
Cadillac *U.S.A.* 44°15N 85°24W **173** C11
Cadiz *Phil.* 10°57N 123°15E **119** B6
Cádiz *Spain* 36°30N 6°20W **89** J4
Cadiz *Calif., U.S.A.* 34°30N 115°28W **171** L11
Cadiz *Ohio, U.S.A.* 40°16N 80°59W **174** F4
Cádiz □ *Spain* 36°36N 5°45W **89** J5
Cádiz, G. de *Spain* 36°40N 7°0W **89** J3
Cadiz L. *U.S.A.* 34°18N 115°24W **171** L11
Cadley *U.S.A.* 33°32N 82°40W **178** B7
Cadney Park *Australia* 27°55S 134°3E **151** D1
Cadomin *Canada* 53°2N 117°20W **162** C5
Cadotte Lake *Canada* 56°26N 116°23W **162** B5
Cadours *France* 43°44N 1°2E **72** E5
Cadoux *Australia* 30°46S 117°7E **149** F2
Cadwell *U.S.A.* 32°20N 83°14W **178** D6
Caen *France* 49°10N 0°22W **70** C6
Caerdydd = Cardiff *U.K.* 51°29N 3°10W **67** F4
Caerfyrddin = Carmarthen
  U.K. 51°52N 4°19W **67** F3
Caergybi = Holyhead
  U.K. 53°18N 4°38W **66** D3
Caernarfon *U.K.* 53°8N 4°16W **66** D3
Caernarfon B. *U.K.* 53°4N 4°40W **66** D3
Caernarvon = Caernarfon
  U.K. 53°8N 4°16W **66** D3
Caerphilly *U.K.* 51°35N 3°13W **67** F4
Caerphilly □ *U.K.* 51°37N 3°12W **67** F4

Caesarea *Israel* 32°30N 34°53E **130** C2
Caetité *Brazil* 19°55S 43°40W **189** D2
Caetité *Brazil* 13°50S 42°32W **189** D2
Cafayate *Argentina* 26°2S 66°0W **190** B2
Cafu *Angola* 16°30S 15°8E **144** A2
Cagayan de Oro *Phil.* 8°30N 124°40E **119** C6
Cagli *Italy* 43°33N 12°39E **93** E9
Cágliari *Italy* 39°13N 9°7E **94** C2
Cágliari, G. di *Italy* 39°8N 9°11E **94** D2
Cagnano Varano *Italy* 41°49N 15°47E **93** G12
Cagnes-sur-Mer *France* 43°40N 7°9E **73** E11
Caguán → *Colombia* 0°8S 74°18W **186** D4
Caguas *Puerto Rico* 18°14N 66°2W **183** d
Caha Mts. *Ireland* 51°45N 9°40W **64** E2
Cahama *Angola* 16°17S 14°19E **144** A1
Cahir *Ireland* 52°22N 7°56W **64** D4
Cahirciveen *Ireland* 51°56N 10°14W **64** E1
Cahora Bassa, Lago de
  Mozam. 15°20S 32°50E **143** F3
Cahore Pt. *Ireland* 52°33N 6°12W **64** D5
Cahors *France* 44°27N 1°27E **72** D5
Cahuapanas *Peru* 5°15S 77°0W **188** B2
Cahul *Moldova* 45°50N 28°15E **81** F13
Caì Bau, Dao *Vietnam* 21°10N 107°27E **116** G6
Cai Be *Vietnam* 10°20N 106°2E **121** G6
Cai Nuoc *Vietnam* 8°56N 105°1E **121** H5
Caia *Mozam.* 17°51S 35°24E **143** F4
Caianda *Angola* 11°2S 23°31E **143** E1
Caibarién *Cuba* 22°30N 79°30W **182** B4
Caibiran *Phil.* 11°30N 124°40E **119** B7
Caicara *Venezuela* 7°38N 66°10W **186** B5
Caicó *Brazil* 6°20S 37°0W **189** B3
Caicos Is.
  Turks & Caicos 21°40N 71°40W **183** B5
Caicos Passage
  W. Indies 22°45N 72°45W **183** B5
Caidian *China* 30°35N 114°2E **117** B10
Caiguna *Australia* 32°16S 125°29E **149** F4
Cailloma *Peru* 15°9S 71°45W **188** D3
Čainari *Moldova* 46°41N 29°3E **81** D14
Caird Coast *Antarctica* 75°0S 25°0W **55** D1
Cairn Gorm *U.K.* 57°7N 3°39W **65** D5
Cairngorm Mts. *U.K.* 57°6N 3°42W **65** D5
Cairngorms △ *U.K.* 57°10N 3°50W **65** D5
Cairnryan *U.K.* 54°59N 5°1W **65** G3
Cairns *Australia* 16°57S 145°45E **150** B4
Cairns L. *Canada* 51°42N 94°30W **163** C10
Cairo = El Qâhira *Egypt* 30°2N 31°13E **137** E7
Cairo *Ga., U.S.A.* 30°52N 84°13W **178** F5
Cairo *Ill., U.S.A.* 37°0N 89°11W **172** G9
Cairo *N.Y., U.S.A.* 42°18N 74°0W **175** D10
Cairo Montenotte *Italy* 44°23N 8°16E **92** D5
Caiseal = Cashel *Ireland* 52°30N 7°53W **64** D4
Caisleán an Bharraigh = Castlebar
  Ireland 53°52N 9°18W **64** C2
Caithness *U.K.* 58°25N 3°35W **65** C5
Caithness, Ord of *U.K.* 58°8N 3°36W **65** C5
Caja de Muertos, I.
  Puerto Rico 17°54N 66°32W **183** d
Cajabamba *Peru* 7°38S 78°4W **188** B2
Cajamarca *Peru* 7°5S 78°28W **188** B2
Cajamarca □ *Peru* 6°15S 78°50W **188** B2
Cajapió *Brazil* 2°58S 44°48W **189** A2
Cajatambo *Peru* 10°30S 77°2W **188** C2
Cajazeiras *Brazil* 6°52S 38°30W **189** B3
Çajetina *Serbia* 43°47N 19°42E **96** C3
Çakırgol *Turkey* 40°33N 39°40E **105** B8
Çakırlar *Turkey* 36°52N 30°33E **99** E12
Čakovec *Croatia* 46°23N 16°26E **93** B13
Çal *Turkey* 38°4N 29°23E **99** C11
Cala *Spain* 37°59N 6°21W **89** H4
Cala → *Spain* 37°38N 6°5W **89** H4
Cala Cadolar, Punta de = Rotja,
  Pta. *Spain* 38°38N 1°35E **91** G6
Cala d'Or *Spain* 39°23N 3°14E **100** B10
Cala en Porter *Spain* 39°52N 4°8E **100** B11
Cala Figuera *Spain* 39°27N 2°58E **100** B9
Cala Figuera, C. de *Spain* 39°27N 2°31E **100** B9
Cala Forcat *Spain* 40°0N 3°47E **100** B10
Cala Major *Spain* 39°33N 2°37E **100** B9
Cala Mezquida = Sa Mesquida
  Spain 39°55N 4°16E **100** B11
Cala Millor *Spain* 39°35N 3°22E **100** B10
Cala Murada *Spain* 39°27N 3°17E **100** B10
Cala Ratjada *Spain* 39°43N 3°27E **100** B10
Cala Santa Galdana
  Spain 39°56N 3°58E **100** B10
Calabar *Nigeria* 4°57N 8°20E **139** E7
Calabogie *Canada* 45°18N 76°43W **175** A8
Calabozo *Venezuela* 9°0N 67°28W **186** B5
Calábria □ *Italy* 39°0N 16°30E **95** C9
Calábria △ *Italy* 39°6N 16°35E **95** C9
Calaceite *Spain* 41°1N 0°11E **90** D5
Calacoto *Bolivia* 17°16S 68°38W **188** G5
Calacuccia *France* 42°21N 9°1E **73** F13
Calafat *Romania* 43°58N 22°59E **80** G7
Calafell *Spain* 41°11N 1°34E **90** D6
Calahorra *Spain* 42°18N 1°59W **89** A10
Calais *France* 50°57N 1°56E **70** A4
Calais *U.S.A.* 45°11N 67°17W **173** C20
Calakmul ○ *Mexico* 18°14N 89°48W **181** D7
Calalaste, Cord. de
  Argentina 25°0S 67°0W **190** B2
Calama *Brazil* 8°0S 62°50W **186** E6
Calama *Chile* 22°30S 68°55W **190** A2
Calamar *Colombia* 10°15N 74°55W **186** A4
Calamarca *Bolivia* 16°55S 68°9W **188** G5
Calamian Group *Phil.* 11°50N 119°55E **119** B5
Calamocha *Spain* 40°50N 1°17W **90** E3
Calamonte *Spain* 38°53N 6°23W **89** G4
Călan *Romania* 45°44N 22°59E **80** E7
Calañas *Spain* 37°40N 6°53W **89** H4
Calanda *Spain* 40°56N 0°15W **90** E4
Calang *Indonesia* 4°37N 95°37E **118** D1
Calanques △ *France* 43°14N 5°30E **73** E9
Calapan *Phil.* 13°25N 121°7E **119** B6
Calascio, Sarìr *Libya* 27°30N 22°30E **135** C10
Calasparra *Spain* 38°14N 1°41W **91** G3
Calatafimi *Italy* 37°55N 12°52E **94** E5
Calatayud *Spain* 41°20N 1°40W **90** D3
Călăţele *Romania* 46°46N 23°1E **80** D8
Călăraşi *Moldova* 47°16N 28°19E **81** C13
Călăraşi *Romania* 44°12N 27°20E **81** F12
Călăraşi □ *Romania* 44°10N 27°0E **81** F12
Calatrava, Campo de
  Spain 38°42N 3°46W **89** G7
Calauag *Phil.* 13°55N 122°15E **119** B6
Calavà, C. *Italy* 38°14N 14°55E **95** D7
Calavite, C. *Phil.* 13°26N 120°20E **119** B6
Calayan *Phil.* 19°20N 121°30E **122** D2
Calbayog *Phil.* 12°4N 124°38E **119** B6

Calca *Peru* 13°22S 72°0W **188** C3
Calcasieu L. *U.S.A.* 29°55N 93°18W **176** G8
Calcium *U.S.A.* 44°1N 75°50W **175** B9
Calcutta = Kolkata
  India 22°34N 88°21E **125** H13
Calcutta *U.S.A.* 40°40N 80°34W **174** F4
Caldaro *Italy* 46°25N 11°14E **93** B8
Caldas da Rainha *Portugal* 39°24N 9°8W **89** F1
Caldas de Reis *Spain* 42°36N 8°39W **88** C2
Caldas Novas *Brazil* 17°45S 48°38W **189** D1
Calder → *U.K.* 53°44N 1°22W **66** D6
Caldera *Chile* 27°5S 70°55W **190** B1
Caldera de Taburiente △
  Canary Is. 28°43N 17°52W **100** F2
Caldwell *Idaho, U.S.A.* 43°40N 116°41W **168** E5
Caldwell *Kans., U.S.A.* 37°2N 97°37W **172** G5
Caldwell *Tex., U.S.A.* 30°32N 96°42W **176** F6
Caledon *Canada* 43°51N 79°51W **174** C5
Caledon *S. Africa* 34°14S 19°26E **144** D2
Caledon → *S. Africa* 30°31S 26°5E **144** D4
Caledon B. *Australia* 12°45S 137°0E **150** A2
Caledonia *Canada* 43°7N 79°58W **174** D5
Caledonia *N.Z.* 42°58N 71°5W **174** D7
Calella *Spain* 41°37N 2°40E **90** D7
Calemba *Angola* 16°0S 15°44E **144** B2
Calen *Australia* 20°56S 148°48E **150** b
Calenzana *France* 42°31N 8°51E **73** F12
Caleta Olivia *Argentina* 46°25S 67°25W **192** C3
Caletones *Chile* 34°6S 70°27W **190** C1
Calexico *U.S.A.* 32°40N 115°30W **171** N11
Calf of Man *I. of Man* 54°3N 4°48W **66** C3
Calgary *Canada* 51°0N 114°10W **162** C6
Calheta *Madeira* 32°44N 17°11W **100** D2
Calhoun *U.S.A.* 34°30N 84°57W **177** D12
Calhoun Falls *U.S.A.* 34°6N 82°36W **178** A7
Cali *Colombia* 3°25N 76°35W **186** C3
Calicut = Kozhikode
  India 11°15N 75°43E **127** J2
Caliente *U.S.A.* 37°37N 114°31W **169** H6
California *Mo., U.S.A.* 38°38N 92°34W **172** F7
California *Pa., U.S.A.* 40°4N 79°54W **174** F5
California □ *U.S.A.* 37°30N 119°30W **170** H7
California, Baja, T.N. = Baja
  California, Baja, T.S. = Baja
California Sur □
  Mexico 25°50N 111°50W **180** B2
California, G. de *Mexico* 27°0N 111°0W **180** B2
California City *U.S.A.* 35°10N 117°55W **171** K9
California Hot Springs
  U.S.A. 35°51N 118°41W **171** K8
Călilabad *Azerbaijan* 39°12N 48°29E **105** C13
Caliegua △ *Argentina* 25°36S 64°50W **190** B3
Călimăneşti *Romania* 45°14N 24°20E **81** E9
Călimani, Munţii
  Romania 47°12N 25°0E **81** C10
Călimani △ *Romania* 47°7N 25°10E **81** C10
Calingasta *Argentina* 31°15S 69°30W **190** C2
Calipatria *U.S.A.* 33°8N 115°31W **171** M11
Calistoga *U.S.A.* 38°35N 122°35W **170** G4
Calitri *Italy* 40°54N 15°26E **95** B8
Calitzdorp *S. Africa* 33°33S 21°42E **144** D3
Callabonna, L.
  Australia 29°40S 140°5E **151** D3
Callac *France* 48°25N 3°27W **70** D3
Callahan *U.S.A.* 30°34N 81°50W **178** E8
Callan *Ireland* 52°32N 7°24W **64** D4
Callander *U.K.* 56°15N 4°13W **65** E4
Callao *Peru* 12°3S 77°8W **188** C2
Callaway *U.S.A.* 30°8N 85°36W **178** E4
Callicoon *U.S.A.* 41°46N 75°3W **175** E9
Calling Lake *Canada* 55°15N 113°12W **162** B6
Calliope *Australia* 24°0S 151°16E **150** C5
Callosa de Segura *Spain* 38°7N 0°53W **91** G4
Callosa d'En Sarrià *Spain* 38°40N 0°8W **91** G4
Calma, Costa de la *Spain* 39°28N 2°26E **100** B9
Calne *U.K.* 51°26N 2°0W **67** F6
Calola *Angola* 16°25S 17°48E **144** A2
Calonge *Spain* 41°52N 3°5E **90** D8
Caloosahatchee →
  U.S.A. 26°31N 82°1W **179** J7
Calore → *Italy* 41°11N 14°28E **95** A7
Caloundra *Australia* 26°45S 153°10E **151** D5
Calpe *Spain* 38°39N 0°3E **91** G5
Calpella *U.S.A.* 39°14N 123°12W **170** F3
Calpine *U.S.A.* 39°40N 120°27W **170** F6
Calstock *Canada* 49°47N 84°9W **164** C3
Caltabellotta *Italy* 37°34N 13°13E **94** E6
Caltagirone *Italy* 37°14N 14°31E **95** E7
Caltanissetta *Italy* 37°29N 14°4E **95** E7
Çălthıbük *Turkey* 39°57N 28°36E **97** G12
Caluire-et-Cuire *France* 45°48N 4°52E **71** G11
Calulo *Angola* 10°1S 14°56E **140** G2
Caluso *Italy* 45°18N 7°53E **92** C4
Calvados □ *France* 49°5N 0°15W **70** C6
Calvert → *Australia* 16°17S 137°44E **150** B2
Calvert I. *Canada* 51°30N 128°0W **162** C3
Calvert Ra. *Australia* 24°0S 122°30E **148** D3
Calvi *France* 42°34N 8°45E **73** F12
Calvià *Spain* 39°34N 2°31E **100** B9
Calvillo *Mexico* 21°51N 102°43W **180** C4
Calvinia *S. Africa* 31°28S 19°45E **144** D2
Calvo, Mte. *Italy* 41°44N 15°46E **95** B8
Calwa *U.S.A.* 36°42N 119°46W **170** J7
Calzada Almuradiel = Almuradiel
  Spain 38°32N 3°28W **89** G7
Calzada de Calatrava
  Spain 38°42N 3°46W **89** G7
Cam → *U.K.* 52°21N 0°16E **67** E8
Cam Lam = Ba Ngoi
  Vietnam 11°54N 109°10E **121** G7
Cam Pha *Vietnam* 21°7N 107°18E **116** G6
Cam Ranh *Vietnam* 11°54N 109°12E **121** G7
Cam Xuyen *Vietnam* 18°15N 106°0E **120** C6
Camabatela *Angola* 8°20S 15°26E **140** F3
Camacá *Brazil* 15°24S 39°49W **189** D3
Camaçari *Brazil* 12°41S 38°18W **189** D3
Camacha *Madeira* 32°41N 16°49W **100** D3
Camacupa *Angola* 11°58S 17°22E **141** G3
Camaguey *Cuba* 21°20N 77°55W **182** B4
Camaiore *Italy* 43°56N 10°18E **92** E7
Camamu *Brazil* 13°57S 39°12W **189** D3
Camaná *Peru* 16°30S 72°50W **188** D3
Camanche Res. *U.S.A.* 38°14N 121°1W **170** G5
Camaquã *Brazil* 30°51S 51°49W **191** C5
Camaquã → *Brazil* 31°17S 51°47W **191** C5
Câmara de Lobos
  Madeira 32°39N 16°59W **100** D3
Camarat, C. *France* 43°12N 6°41E **73** E10
Camardı *Turkey* 37°49N 34°58E **104** D6

Camarès *France* 43°49N 2°53E **72** E6
Camaret-sur-Mer *France* 48°16N 4°37W **70** D2
Camargo *Mexico* 26°19N 98°50W **181** B5
Camargue *France* 43°34N 4°34E **73** E8
Camargue △ *France* 43°30N 4°40E **73** E8
Camarillo *U.S.A.* 34°13N 119°2W **171** L7
Camariñas *Spain* 43°8N 9°12W **88** B1
Camarón, C. *Honduras* 16°0N 85°5W **182** C2
Camarones *Argentina* 44°50S 65°40W **192** B3
Camarones, B.
  Argentina 44°45S 65°35W **192** B3
Camas *U.S.A.* 45°35N 122°24W **170** E4
Camas Valley *U.S.A.* 43°2N 123°40W **168** E2
Camballin *Australia* 17°59S 124°12E **148** C3
Cambará *Brazil* 23°2S 50°5W **191** A5
Cambay = Khambhat
  India 22°23N 72°33E **124** H5
Cambil *Spain* 37°40N 3°33W **89** H7
Cambo-les-Bains *France* 43°22N 1°23W **72** E2
Cambodia ■ *Asia* 12°15N 105°0E **120** F5
Camborne *U.K.* 50°12N 5°19W **67** G2
Cambrai *Australia* 34°40S 139°16E **152** C3
Cambrai *France* 50°11N 3°14E **71** B10
Cambre *Spain* 43°17N 8°20W **88** B2
Cambria *U.S.A.* 35°34N 121°5W **170** K5
Cambrian Mts. *U.K.* 52°3N 3°57W **67** E4
Cambridge *Canada* 43°23N 80°15W **174** C4
Cambridge *Jamaica* 18°18N 77°54W **182** a
Cambridge *N.Z.* 37°54S 175°29E **154** D4
Cambridge *U.K.* 52°12N 0°8E **67** E8
Cambridge *Mass.,*
  U.S.A. 42°23N 71°7W **175** D13
Cambridge *Minn.,*
  U.S.A. 45°34N 93°13W **172** C7
Cambridge *N.Y., U.S.A.* 43°2N 73°22W **175** C11
Cambridge *Nebr.,*
  U.S.A. 40°17N 100°10W **172** E3
Cambridge *Ohio, U.S.A.* 40°2N 81°35W **174** F3
Cambridge Bay
  Canada 69°10N 105°0W **160** D11
Cambridge G.
  Australia 14°55S 128°15E **148** B4
Cambridge Springs
  U.S.A. 41°48N 80°4W **174** E4
Cambridgeshire □ *U.K.* 52°25N 0°7W **67** E7
Cambrils *Spain* 41°8N 1°3E **90** D6
Cambundi-Catembo
  Angola 10°10S 17°35E **140** G3
Cambuquira *Brazil* 21°35S 45°15W **191** A6
Camden *Australia* 34°1S 150°43E **153** C9
Camden *Ala., U.S.A.* 31°59N 87°17W **177** F11
Camden *Ark., U.S.A.* 33°35N 92°50W **176** E8
Camden *Maine, U.S.A.* 44°13N 69°4W **173** C19
Camden *N.J., U.S.A.* 39°55N 75°7W **175** F9
Camden *N.Y., U.S.A.* 43°20N 75°45W **175** C9
Camden *S.C., U.S.A.* 34°16N 80°36W **178** D7
Camden *Tex., U.S.A.* 30°51N 94°45W **176** F7
Camden Sd. *Australia* 15°27S 124°25E **148** C3
Camdenton *U.S.A.* 38°1N 92°45W **172** F7
Camelford *U.K.* 50°37N 4°42W **67** G3
Çameli *Turkey* 37°5N 29°24E **99** D11
Camenca *Moldova* 48°3N 28°42E **81** B13
Camerino *Italy* 43°8N 13°4E **93** E10
Camerón *Chile* 53°38S 69°39W **192** D3
Cameron *Ariz., U.S.A.* 35°53N 111°25W **169** J8
Cameron *La., U.S.A.* 29°48N 93°20W **176** G8
Cameron *Mo., U.S.A.* 39°44N 94°14W **172** F6
Cameron *S.C., U.S.A.* 33°34N 80°43W **178** B9
Cameron *Tex., U.S.A.* 30°51N 96°59W **176** F6
Cameron Highlands
  Malaysia 4°27N 101°22E **121** K3
Cameron Hills *Canada* 59°48N 118°0W **162** B5
Cameron Mts. *N.Z.* 46°1S 167°0E **155** G2
Cameroon ■ *Africa* 6°0N 12°30E **139** D8
Cameroun → *Cameroon* 4°0N 9°35E **139** E6
Cameroun, Mt. *Cameroon* 4°13N 9°10E **139** E6
Cametá *Brazil* 2°12S 49°30W **187** D9
Camiçi Gölü *Turkey* 37°29N 27°28E **99** D9
Camilla *U.S.A.* 31°14N 84°12W **178** D5
Caminha *Portugal* 41°50N 8°50W **88** D2
Camino *U.S.A.* 38°44N 120°41W **170** G6
Cammal *U.S.A.* 41°24N 77°28W **174** E7
Cammarata *Italy* 37°38N 13°38E **94** E6
Camocim *Brazil* 2°55S 40°50W **189** A2
Camooweal *Australia* 19°56S 138°7E **150** B2
Camooweal Caves △
  Australia 20°1S 138°11E **150** B2
Camopi *Fr. Guiana* 3°12N 52°17W **187** C8
Camorta *India* 8°8N 93°30E **127** K11
Camp Hill *Ala., U.S.A.* 32°48N 85°39W **178** C4
Camp Hill *Pa., U.S.A.* 40°14N 76°55W **174** F7
Camp Nelson *U.S.A.* 36°8N 118°39W **171** J8
Camp Pendleton
  U.S.A. 33°13N 117°24W **171** M9
Camp Verde *U.S.A.* 34°34N 111°51W **169** J8
Camp Wood *U.S.A.* 29°40N 100°1W **176** G4
Campagna *Italy* 40°40N 15°6E **95** B8
Campana *Argentina* 34°10S 58°55W **190** C4
Campana, I. *Chile* 48°20S 75°20W **192** C1
Campanário *Madeira* 32°39N 17°2W **100** D2
Campanario *Spain* 38°52N 5°36W **89** G5
Campanet *Spain* 39°46N 2°58E **100** B9
Campánia □ *Italy* 41°0N 14°30E **95** B7
Campas del Tuyú △
  Argentina 36°17S 56°50W **190** D4
Campbell *S. Africa* 28°48S 23°44E **144** C3
Campbell *Calif., U.S.A.* 37°17N 121°57W **170** H5
Campbell *Ohio, U.S.A.* 41°5N 80°37W **174** E4
Campbell I. *Pac. Oc.* 52°30S 169°0E **156** N8
Campbell L. *Canada* 63°14N 106°55W **163** A7
Campbell Plateau
  S. Ocean 50°0S 170°0E **55** A11
Campbell River *Canada* 50°5N 125°20W **162** C3
Campbellford *Canada* 44°18N 77°48W **174** B7
Campbellpur *Pakistan* 33°46N 72°26E **126** C4
Campbellsville *U.S.A.* 37°21N 85°20W **173** G11
Campbellton *Canada* 47°57N 66°43W **165** C6
Campbelltown
  Australia 34°4S 150°49E **153** C9
Campbeltown *U.K.* 55°26N 5°36W **65** F3
Campeche *Mexico* 19°51N 90°32W **181** D6

Campeche □ *Mexico* 19°0N 90°30W **181** D6
Campeche, Golfo de
  Mexico 19°30N 93°0W **181** D6
Câmpeni *Romania* 46°22N 23°3E **80** D8
Camperdown *Australia* 38°14S 143°9E **152** E5
Camperville *Canada* 51°59N 100°9W **163** C8
Campi Salentina *Italy* 40°24N 18°1E **95** B11
Campia Turzii *Romania* 46°34N 23°53E **81** D8
Câmpina *Romania* 45°10N 25°45E **81** E10
Campina Grande *Brazil* 7°20S 35°47W **189** B3
Campinas *Brazil* 22°50S 47°0W **191** A6
Campione *Italy* 45°58N 8°58E **73** C12
Campli *Italy* 42°43N 13°41E **93** F10
Campo *Cameroon* 2°22N 9°50E **139** E6
Campo de Criptana *Spain* 39°24N 3°7W **89** F7
Campo de Gibraltar
  Spain 36°15N 5°25W **89** J5
Campo de los Alisos △
  Argentina 27°15S 66°0W **190** B2
Campo Formoso *Brazil* 10°30S 40°20W **189** C2
Campo Grande *Brazil* 20°25S 54°40W **187** H8
Campo Maior *Brazil* 4°50S 42°12W **189** A2
Campo Maior *Portugal* 39°2N 7°7W **89** F3
Campo Mourão *Brazil* 24°3S 52°22W **191** A5
Campo Túres *Italy* 46°53N 11°55E **93** B8
Campobasso *Italy* 41°34N 14°39E **95** A7
Campobello di Licata
  Italy 37°15N 13°55E **94** E6
Campobello di Mazara
  Italy 37°38N 12°45E **94** E5
Campofelice di Roccella
  Italy 37°59N 13°53E **94** E6
Campomarino *Italy* 41°57N 15°2E **93** G12
Camporeale *Italy* 37°54N 13°6E **94** E6
Camporrobles *Spain* 39°39N 1°24W **90** F3
Campos *Brazil* 21°50S 41°20W **191** A7
Campos *Spain* 39°26N 3°1E **100** B10
Campos Altos *Brazil* 19°47S 46°10W **191** A6
Campos Belos *Brazil* 13°10S 47°3W **189** C1
Campos del Paraíso = Carrascosa
  del Campo *Spain* 40°2N 2°45W **90** E2
Campos Novos *Brazil* 27°21S 51°50W **191** B5
Campos Sales *Brazil* 7°4S 40°23W **189** B2
Camprodon *Spain* 42°19N 2°23E **90** C7
Campton *Fla., U.S.A.* 30°53N 86°31W **179** E3
Campton *Ga., U.S.A.* 33°52N 83°43W **178** B5
Camptonville *U.S.A.* 39°27N 121°3W **170** F6
Camptown *U.S.A.* 41°44N 76°14W **175** E8
Câmpulung *Argeş,*
  Romania 45°17N 25°3E **81** E10
Câmpulung *Suceava,*
  Romania 47°32N 25°30E **81** C10
Câmpuri *Romania* 46°0N 26°50E **81** D11
Campville *U.S.A.* 29°40N 82°7W **178** F7
Camrose *Canada* 53°0N 112°50W **162** C6
Camsell Portage
  Canada 59°37N 109°15W **163** B7
Çamyuva *Turkey* 36°30N 30°30E **99** E12
Çan *Turkey* 40°2N 27°3E **97** F11
Can Clavo *Spain* 38°57N 1°27E **100** C7
Can Creu *Spain* 38°58N 1°28E **100** C7
Can Gio *Vietnam* 10°25N 106°58E **121** G6
Can Pastilla *Spain* 39°32N 2°42E **100** B9
Can Tho *Vietnam* 10°2N 105°46E **121** G5
Canaan *U.S.A.* 42°2N 73°20W **175** D11
Canacona *India* 15°1N 74°4E **127** G2
Canada ■ *N. Amer.* 60°0N 100°0W **160** C11
Canada Abyssal Plain
  Arctic 80°0N 140°0W **54** B18
Canada Basin *Arctic* 75°0N 145°0W **54** B18
Cañada de Gómez
  Argentina 32°40S 61°30W **190** C3
Canadian *U.S.A.* 35°55N 100°23W **176** D4
Canadian → *U.S.A.* 35°28N 95°3W **176** D7
Canadian Shield *Canada* 53°0N 75°0W **158** D12
Canadys *U.S.A.* 33°3N 80°37W **178** B9
Canajoharie *U.S.A.* 42°54N 74°35W **175** D10
Canakkale *Turkey* 40°8N 26°24E **97** F10
Çanakkale □ *Turkey* 40°10N 26°25E **97** F10
Çanakkale Boğazı
  Turkey 40°17N 26°32E **97** F10
Canal Flats *Canada* 50°10N 115°48W **162** C5
Canal Point *U.S.A.* 26°52N 80°38W **179** J9
Canalejas *Argentina* 35°15S 66°34W **190** D2
Canals *Argentina* 33°35S 62°53W **190** C3
Canals *Spain* 38°58N 0°35W **91** G4
Canandaigua *U.S.A.* 42°54N 77°17W **174** D7
Canandaigua L. *U.S.A.* 42°47N 77°19W **174** D7
Cananea *Mexico* 31°0N 110°18W **180** A2
Canarias, Is. *Atl. Oc.* 28°30N 16°0W **100** F4
Canaries *St. Lucia* 13°55N 61°4W **183** f
Canarreos, Arch. de los
  Cuba 21°35N 81°40W **182** B3
Canary Is. = Canarias, Is.
  Atl. Oc. 28°30N 16°0W **100** F4
Canaseraga *U.S.A.* 42°27N 77°45W **174** D7
Canastra, Serra da
  Brazil 20°0S 46°20W **189** E1
Canatlán *Mexico* 24°31N 104°47W **180** C4
Canaveral, C. *U.S.A.* 28°27N 80°32W **179** G9
Canaveral △ *U.S.A.* 28°28N 80°33W **179** G9
Cañaveruelas *Spain* 40°24N 2°38W **90** E2
Canavieiras *Brazil* 15°39S 38°55W **189** D3
Canbelego *Australia* 31°32S 146°18E **153** A7
Canberra *Australia* 35°15S 149°8E **153** C8
Canby *Calif., U.S.A.* 41°27N 120°52W **168** F3
Canby *Minn., U.S.A.* 44°43N 96°16W **172** C5
Canby *Oreg., U.S.A.* 45°16N 122°42W **170** E4
Cancale *France* 48°40N 1°50W **70** D5
Canche → *France* 50°31N 1°39E **70** A4
Canchungo *Guinea-Biss.* 12°28N 16°9W **138** C1
Canchuyaya, Cordillera de
  Peru 21°8N 84°44W **188** B2
Cancún *Mexico* 21°8N 86°44W **181** C7
Candanchú *Spain* 42°47N 0°32W **90** C2
Candarave *Peru* 17°15S 70°13W **188** D3
Çandarlı *Turkey* 38°54N 26°58E **99** C8
Çandarlı Körfezi *Turkey* 38°26N 26°58E **99** C8
Candás *Spain* 43°35N 5°45W **88** B5
Candé *France* 47°34N 1°0W **70** E5
Candela *Italy* 41°8N 15°31E **95** A8
Candelaria *Argentina* 27°29S 55°44W **191** B4
Candelaria *Canary Is.* 28°22N 16°22W **100** F3
Candelario *Spain* 40°27N 5°46W **88** E5
Candeleda *Spain* 40°10N 5°14W **88** E5

Candelo *Australia* 36°47S 149°43E **153** D8
Candi Dasa *Indonesia* 8°30S 115°34E **119** J18
Candia = Iráklio *Greece* 35°20N 25°12E **101** D7
Candia, Sea of = Crete, Sea of
  Greece 36°0N 25°0E **99** E7
Candle L. *Canada* 53°50N 105°18W **163** C7
Candlemas I. *Antarctica* 57°3S 26°40W **55** B1
Cando *U.S.A.* 48°32N 99°12W **172** A4
Canea = Chania *Greece* 35°30N 24°4E **101** D6
Canela *Brazil* 10°15S 48°25N **189** C1
Canelli *Italy* 44°43N 8°17E **92** D5
Canelones *Uruguay* 34°32S 56°17W **191** C4
Canet de Mar *Spain* 41°35N 2°35E **90** D7
Canet-Plage *France* 42°41N 3°2E **72** F7
Cañete *Chile* 37°50S 73°30W **190** D1
Cañete *Spain* 40°3N 1°54W **94** E5
Cañete de las Torres
  Spain 37°53N 4°19W **89** H6
Cangas *Spain* 42°16N 8°47W **88** C2
Cangas de Onís *Spain* 43°21N 5°8W **88** B5
Cangas del Narcea *Spain* 43°10N 6°32W **88** B4
Cangnan *China* 27°30N 120°23E **117** D13
Cangshan *China* 34°50N 118°2E **115** G10
Canguaretama *Brazil* 6°20S 35°5W **189** B3
Canguçu *Brazil* 31°22S 52°43W **191** C5
Canguçu, Serra do
  Brazil 31°20S 52°40W **191** C5
Cangxi *China* 31°47N 105°59E **116** B5
Cangyuan *China* 23°12N 99°14E **116** F2
Cangzhou *China* 38°19N 116°52E **114** E9
Caniapiscau →
  Canada 56°40N 69°30W **165** A6
Caniapiscau, L. *Canada* 54°10N 69°55W **165** B6
Canicattì *Italy* 37°21N 13°51E **94** E6
Canicattini Bagni *Italy* 37°2N 15°4E **95** E8
Canigou *France* 42°31N 2°27E **72** F6
Caniles *Spain* 37°25N 2°43W **89** H8
Canim Lake *Canada* 51°47N 120°54W **162** C4
Canindé *Brazil* 4°22S 39°19W **189** A3
Canindé → *Brazil* 6°15S 42°52W **189** B2
Canindeyu □ *Paraguay* 24°10S 55°0W **191** A5
Canino *Italy* 42°28N 11°45E **93** F8
Canisteo *U.S.A.* 42°16N 77°36W **174** D7
Canisteo → *U.S.A.* 42°7N 77°8W **174** D7
Cañitas de Felipe Pescador
  Mexico 23°36N 102°43W **180** C4
Cañizal *Spain* 41°12N 5°22W **88** D5
Canjáyar *Spain* 37°1N 2°44W **89** H8
Çankırı *Turkey* 40°40N 33°37E **104** B5
Çankırı □ *Turkey* 40°40N 33°30E **104** B5
Cankuzo *Burundi* 3°10S 30°31E **142** C3
Canmore *Canada* 51°7N 115°18W **162** C5
Cann River *Australia* 37°35S 149°7E **153** D8
Canna *U.K.* 57°3N 6°33W **65** D2
Cannanore = Kannur
  India 11°53N 75°27E **127** J2
Cannanore Is. *India* 10°30N 72°30E **127** J1
Cannes *France* 43°32N 7°1E **73** E11
Canning Town = Port Canning
  India 22°23N 88°40E **125** H13
Cannington *Canada* 44°20N 79°2W **174** B5
Cannòbio *Italy* 46°4N 8°42E **92** B5
Cannock *U.K.* 52°41N 2°1W **67** E5
Cannonball →
  U.S.A. 46°26N 100°35W **172** B3
Cannondale Mt.
  Australia 25°13S 148°57E **150** D4
Cannonsville Res.
  U.S.A. 42°4N 75°22W **175** D9
Cannonvale *Australia* 20°17S 148°43E **150** b
Canoas *Brazil* 29°56S 51°11W **191** B5
Canoe L. *Canada* 55°10N 108°15W **163** B7
Cañon City *U.S.A.* 38°27N 105°14W **168** G11
Cañon de Rio Blanco △
  Mexico 18°43N 97°15W **181** D5
Cañón del Río Lobos △
  Spain 41°46N 3°28W **88** D7
Canonniers Pt. *Mauritius* 20°0S 57°32E **141** d
Canoochee → *U.S.A.* 31°59N 81°19W **178** D8
Canopus *Australia* 33°29S 140°42E **152** B4
Canora *Canada* 51°40N 102°30W **163** C8
Canosa di Púglia *Italy* 41°13N 16°4E **95** A9
Canowindra *Australia* 33°35S 148°38E **153** B8
Canso *Canada* 45°20N 61°0W **165** C7
Canso, Str. of *Canada* 45°37N 61°22W **165** C7
Canta *Peru* 11°29S 76°37W **188** C2
Cantabria □ *Spain* 43°10N 4°0W **88** B7
Cantabria, Sierra de
  Spain 42°40N 2°30W **90** C2
Cantabrian Mts. = Cantábrica,
  Cordillera *Spain* 43°0N 5°10W **88** C5
Cantábrica, Cordillera
  Spain 43°0N 5°10W **88** C5
Cantal □ *France* 45°5N 2°45E **72** C6
Cantal, Plomb du *France* 45°3N 2°45E **72** C6
Cantanhede *Portugal* 40°20N 8°36W **88** E2
Cantavieja *Spain* 40°31N 0°25W **90** E4
Čantavir *Serbia* 45°55N 19°46E **84** E4
Cantemir *Moldova* 46°17N 28°14E **81** D13
Canterbury *Australia* 25°23S 141°53E **150** D3
Canterbury *U.K.* 51°16N 1°6E **67** F9
Canterbury □ *N.Z.* 43°45S 171°19E **155** D6
Canterbury Bight *N.Z.* 44°16S 171°55E **155** E6
Canterbury Plains
  N.Z. 43°55S 171°22E **155** D6
Cantil *U.S.A.* 35°18N 117°58W **171** K9
Cantillana *Spain* 37°36N 5°50W **89** H5
Canto do Buriti *Brazil* 8°7S 42°58W **189** D2
Canton = Guangzhou
  China 23°6N 113°13E **117** F9
Canton *Ga., U.S.A.* 34°14N 84°29W **177** D12
Canton *Ill., U.S.A.* 40°33N 90°2W **172** E8
Canton *Miss., U.S.A.* 32°37N 90°2W **177** E9
Canton *Mo., U.S.A.* 40°8N 91°32W **172** E8
Canton *N.Y., U.S.A.* 44°36N 75°10W **175** B9
Canton *Ohio, U.S.A.* 40°48N 81°23W **174** F3
Canton *S. Dak., U.S.A.* 43°18N 96°35W **172** D6
Canton L. *U.S.A.* 36°6N 98°35W **176** C5
Cantonment *U.S.A.* 30°37N 87°20W **179** F2
Cantù *Italy* 45°44N 9°8E **92** C6
Canudos *Brazil* 7°13S 58°5W **186** D7
Canumã → *Brazil* 3°55S 59°10W **186** D7
Canunda △ *Australia* 37°42S 140°16E **152** C4
Canutama *Brazil* 6°30S 64°20W **186** E6
Canutillo *U.S.A.* 31°55N 106°36W **176** F1
Canvey *U.K.* 51°31N 0°37E **67** F8
Canyon *U.S.A.* 34°59N 101°55W **176** D4
Canyon De Chelly △
  U.S.A. 36°10N 109°20W **169** H9
Canyonlands △ *U.S.A.* 38°15N 110°0W **169** G9

Canyons of the Ancients △
  U.S.A. 37°30N 108°55W **169** H9
Canyonville *U.S.A.* 42°56N 123°17W **168** E2
Cao Bang *Vietnam* 22°40N 106°15E **116** F6
Cao He → *China* 40°10N 124°32E **115** D13
Cao Lanh *Vietnam* 10°27N 105°38E **121** G5
Cao Xian *China* 34°50N 115°35E **114** G8
Caofeidian *China* 38°56N 118°32E **115** E10
Cáorle *Italy* 45°36N 12°53E **93** C9
Cap-aux-Meules
  Canada 47°23N 61°52W **165** C7
Cap-Chat *Canada* 49°6N 66°40W **165** C6
Cap-de-la-Madeleine
  Canada 46°22N 72°31W **164** C5
Cap-Haïtien *Haiti* 19°40N 72°20W **183** C5
Cap Pt. *St. Lucia* 14°7N 60°57W **183** f
Capac *U.S.A.* 43°1N 82°56W **174** C2
Capáccio *Italy* 40°25N 15°5E **95** B8
Capaci *Italy* 38°10N 13°14E **94** D6
Capanaparo → *Venezuela* 7°1N 67°7W **186** B5
Capánnori *Italy* 43°50N 10°34E **92** C7
Caparaó △ *Brazil* 20°25S 41°46W **189** E2
Capbreton *France* 43°39N 1°26E **72** E2
Capdenac *France* 44°34N 2°5E **72** D6
Capdepera *Spain* 39°42N 3°26E **90** F8
Cape → *Australia* 20°59S 146°51E **150** C4
Cape Arid △ *Australia* 33°58S 123°13E **149** F3
Cape Barren I.
  Australia 40°25S 148°15E **151** G4
Cape Basin *Atl. Oc.* 34°0S 7°0W **56** K12
Cape Breton Highlands
  Canada 46°50N 60°40W **165** C7
Cape Breton I. *Canada* 46°50N 60°30W **165** C7
Cape Canaveral *U.S.A.* 28°24N 80°36W **179** G9
Cape Charles *U.S.A.* 37°16N 76°1W **173** G15
Cape Coast *Ghana* 5°5N 1°15W **139** D4
Cape Cod △ *U.S.A.* 41°56N 70°6W **173** E18
Cape Coral *U.S.A.* 26°33N 81°57W **179** J8
Cape Crawford
  Australia 16°41S 135°43E **150** B2
Cape Dorset = Kinngait
  Canada 64°14N 76°32W **161** E16
Cape Fear → *U.S.A.* 33°53N 78°1W **177** E15
Cape Girardeau *U.S.A.* 37°19N 89°32W **172** G9
Cape Hatteras △
  U.S.A. 35°30N 75°28W **177** D17
Cape Hillsborough △
  Australia 20°54S 149°2E **150** b
Cape Jervis *Australia* 35°40S 138°5E **152** C3
Cape Le Grand △
  Australia 33°54S 122°26E **149** F3
Cape Lookout △
  U.S.A. 35°45N 76°25W **177** D16
Cape May *U.S.A.* 38°56N 74°56W **173** F16
Cape May Point
  U.S.A. 38°56N 74°58W **173** F16
Cape Melville △
  Australia 14°26S 144°28E **150** A3
Cape Mount △ *Liberia* 6°44N 11°24W **138** D2
Cape Range △ *Australia* 22°3S 114°0E **148** D1
Cape St. George
  Canada 48°28N 59°14W **165** C8
Cape Tormentine
  Canada 46°8N 63°47W **165** C7
Cape Town *S. Africa* 33°55S 18°22E **144** D2
Cape Upstart △
  Australia 19°45S 147°48E **150** b
Cape Verde Abyssal Plain
  Atl. Oc. 23°0N 26°0W **56** D9
Cape Verde Is. ■ *Atl. Oc.* 16°0N 24°0W **134** b
Cape Verde Plateau
  Atl. Oc. 18°0N 20°0W **56** E10
Cape Vincent *U.S.A.* 44°8N 76°20W **175** B8
Cape York Peninsula
  Australia 12°0S 142°30E **150** A3
Capela *Brazil* 10°30S 37°0W **189** D3
Capelinha *Brazil* 17°42S 42°31W **189** D2
Capella *Australia* 23°2S 148°1E **150** C4
Capendu *France* 43°11N 2°31E **72** E6
Capertree *Australia* 33°6S 149°58E **153** B8
Capestang *France* 43°20N 3°4E **72** E6
Capesterre-Belle-Eau
  Guadeloupe 16°4N 61°36W **182** b
Capesterre-de-Marie-Galante
  Guadeloupe 15°53N 61°14W **182** b
Capim → *Brazil* 1°40S 47°47W **187** D9
Capistrello *Italy* 41°57N 13°23E **93** G10
Capitan *Argentina* 33°35N 105°35W **169** K11
Capitán Aracena, I.
  Chile 54°10S 71°20W **192** G2
Capitán Arturo Prat
  Antarctica 63°0S 61°0W **55** C17
Capitán Pastene *Chile* 38°13S 73°1W **192** A2
Capitão de Campos
  Brazil 4°40S 41°55W **189** A2
Capitol Reef △ *U.S.A.* 38°15N 111°10W **169** G8
Capitola *U.S.A.* 36°59N 121°57W **170** J5
Capivara, Serra da
  Brazil 14°35S 45°0W **189** C2
Capizzi *Italy* 37°51N 14°29E **95** E7
Capoche → *Mozam.* 15°35S 33°0E **143** F3
Capodichino, Nápoli ✈ (NAP)
  Italy 40°53N 14°16E **95** B7
Capodistria = Koper
  Slovenia 45°31N 13°44E **93** C10
Caporetto = Kobarid
  Slovenia 46°15N 13°30E **93** B10
Capoterra *Italy* 39°11N 8°58E **94** C1
Capps *U.S.A.* 30°24N 83°54W **178** E6
Capraia *Italy* 43°2N 9°50E **92** E6
Caprara, Pta. *Italy* 41°7N 8°19E **94** A1
Caprarola *Italy* 42°19N 12°14E **93** F9
Caprera *Italy* 41°12N 9°28E **94** A2
Capri *Italy* 40°33N 14°14E **95** B7
Capricorn Coast
  Australia 23°16S 150°49E **150** C5
Capricorn Group
  Australia 23°30S 151°55E **150** C5
Capricorn Ra.
  Australia 23°20S 116°50E **148** D2
Caprino Veronese *Italy* 45°36N 10°47E **92** C7
Caprivi □ *Namibia* 18°0S 23°30E **144** A3
Caprivi → *Namibia* 17°55S 22°37E **144** A3
Caprivi Strip *Namibia* 18°0S 23°0E **144** A3
Caps et Marais d'Opale △
  France 50°40N 2°0E **71** B9
Captains Flat *Australia* 35°35S 149°27E **153** C8
Captieux *France* 44°18N 0°16W **72** D3
Captiva *U.S.A.* 26°31N 82°11W **179** J7

Capulin Volcano △
  U.S.A. 36°47N 103°58W **176** C3
Caquetá → *Colombia* 1°15S 69°15W **186** D5
Car Nicobar *India* 9°10N 92°47E **127** K11
Caracal *Romania* 44°8N 24°22E **81** F9
Caracas *Venezuela* 10°30N 66°55W **186** A5
Caracol *Belize* 16°45N 89°6W **182** C2
Caracol *Mato Grosso do Sul,*
  Brazil 22°18S 57°1W **190** A4
Caracol *Piauí, Brazil* 9°15S 43°22W **189** D2
Caracollo *Bolivia* 17°39S 67°10W **188** D4
Carágbal *Australia* 33°49S 147°45E **153** B7
Carágoli *Italy* 44°25N 7°26E **92** D4
Carahue *Chile* 38°43S 73°12W **192** A2
Caraí *Brazil* 17°12S 41°42W **189** D2
Carajás *Brazil* 6°5S 50°23W **187** E8
Carajás, Serra dos *Brazil* 6°0S 51°30W **187** E8
Carangola *Brazil* 20°44S 42°5W **189** E2
Caransebeș *Romania* 45°28N 22°18E **80** E7
Carantec *France* 48°40N 3°55W **70** D3
Caraquet *Canada* 47°48N 64°57W **165** C6
Caraș Severin □
  Romania 45°10N 22°10E **80** E7
Carașova *Romania* 45°11N 21°51E **80** E6
Caratasca, L. de
  Honduras 15°20N 83°40W **182** C3
Caratinga *Brazil* 19°50S 42°10W **189** E2
Caraúbas *Brazil* 5°33S 37°33W **189** B3
Caravaca de la Cruz *Spain* 38°8N 1°52W **91** G3
Caravággio *Italy* 45°30N 9°38E **92** C6
Caravela *Guinea-Biss.* 11°30N 16°30W **138** C1
Caravelas *Brazil* 17°45S 39°15W **189** D3
Caraveli *Peru* 15°45S 73°25W **188** D3
Caravelle, Presqu'île de la
  Martinique 14°46N 60°48W **182** c
Caraz *Peru* 9°3S 77°47W **188** B2
Carazinho *Brazil* 28°16S 52°46W **191** B5
Carballino = O Carballiño
  Spain 42°26N 8°5W **88** C2
Carballo *Spain* 43°13N 8°41W **88** B2
Carberry *Canada* 49°50N 99°25W **163** D9
Carbó *Mexico* 29°42N 110°58W **180** B2
Carbón, L. del
  Argentina 49°35S 68°21W **192** C3
Carbonara, C. *Italy* 39°6N 9°31E **94** C2
Carbondale *Colo.,*
  U.S.A. 39°24N 107°13W **168** G10
Carbondale *Ill., U.S.A.* 37°44N 89°13W **172** G9
Carbondale *Pa., U.S.A.* 41°35N 75°30W **175** D9
Carbonear *Canada* 47°42N 53°13W **165** C9
Carboneras *Spain* 36°59N 1°53W **91** J3
Carboneras de Guadazaón
  Spain 39°54N 1°50W **90** F3
Carbónia *Italy* 39°10N 8°30E **94** C1
Carbonne *France* 43°18N 1°11E **72** E5
Carcabuey *Spain* 37°27N 4°17W **89** H6
Carcagente = Carcaixent
  Spain 39°8N 0°28W **91** F4
Carcaixent *Spain* 39°8N 0°28W **91** F4
Carcajou *Canada* 57°47N 117°6W **162** B5
Carcarana →
  Argentina 32°27S 60°48W **190** C3
Carcasse, C. *Haiti* 18°30N 74°28W **183** C5
Carcassonne *France* 43°13N 2°20E **72** E6
Carcoar *Australia* 33°36S 149°8E **153** B8
Carcross *Canada* 60°13N 134°45W **162** A2
Çardak *Çanakkale,*
  Turkey 40°22N 26°43E **97** F10
Çardak *Denizli, Turkey* 37°49N 29°39E **99** D11
Cardamon Hills *India* 9°30N 77°15E **127** K3
Cardamon Mts. = Kravanh,
  Chuor Phnum
  Cambodia 12°0N 103°32E **121** G4
Cardeña *Spain* 38°16N 4°20W **89** G6
Cárdenas *Cuba* 23°0N 81°30W **182** B3
Cárdenas *San Luis Potosí,*
  Mexico 22°0N 99°38W **181** C5
Cárdenas *Tabasco,*
  Mexico 17°59N 93°22W **181** D6
Cardener → *Spain* 41°41N 1°51E **90** D6
Cardenete *Spain* 39°46N 1°41W **90** F3
Cardiel, L. *Argentina* 48°55S 71°10W **192** C2
Cardiff *U.K.* 51°29N 3°10W **67** F4
Cardiff □ *U.K.* 51°31N 3°12W **67** F4
Cardiff-by-the-Sea
  U.S.A. 33°1N 117°17W **171** M9
Cardigan *U.K.* 52°5N 4°40W **67** E3
Cardigan B. *U.K.* 52°30N 4°30W **67** E3
Cardinal *Canada* 44°47N 75°23W **175** B9
Cardona *Spain* 41°56N 1°40E **90** D6
Cardona *Uruguay* 33°53S 57°18W **190** C4
Cardoso, Ilha do *Brazil* 25°8S 47°58W **191** B5
Cardston *Canada* 49°15N 113°20W **162** D6
Cardwell *Australia* 18°14S 146°2E **150** B4
Careen L. *Canada* 57°0N 108°11W **163** B7
Carei *Romania* 47°40N 22°29E **80** C7
Carentan *France* 49°19N 1°15W **70** C5
Carey *U.S.A.* 43°19N 113°57W **168** E7
Carey, L. *Australia* 29°0S 122°15E **149** E3
Carey L. *Canada* 62°12N 102°55W **163** A8
Careysburg *Liberia* 6°34N 10°30W **138** D2
Cargados Carajos *Ind. Oc.* 17°0S 59°0E **146** F4
Cargèse *France* 42°7N 8°35E **73** F12
Carhaix-Plouguer
  France 48°18N 3°36W **70** D3
Carhuamayo *Peru* 10°51S 76°4W **188** C2
Carhué *Argentina* 37°10S 62°50W **190** D3
Caria *Turkey* 37°20N 28°10E **99** D10
Cariacica *Brazil* 20°16S 40°25W **189** E2
Cariati *Italy* 39°30N 16°57E **95** C9
Caribbean Sea *W. Indies* 15°0N 75°0W **183** D5
Cariboo Mts. *Canada* 53°0N 121°0W **162** C4
Caribou *U.S.A.* 46°52N 68°1W **173** B19
Caribou → *Man.,*
  Canada 59°20N 94°44W **163** B10
Caribou → *N.W.T.,*
  Canada 61°27N 125°45W **162** A3
Caribou I. *Canada* 47°22N 85°49W **164** C2
Caribou Is. *Canada* 61°55N 113°15W **162** A6
Caribou L. *Man.,*
  Canada 59°21N 96°10W **163** B9
Caribou L. *Ont., Canada* 50°25N 89°5W **164** B2
Caribou Mts. *Canada* 59°12N 115°40W **162** B5
Caribou River △
  Canada 59°35N 96°35W **163** B9
Caribrod = Dimitrovgrad
  Serbia 43°2N 22°48E **96** C6
Carichíc *Mexico* 27°56N 107°3W **180** B3
Carignan *France* 49°38N 5°10E **71** C12

Carignano *Italy* 44°55N 7°40E **92** D4
Carinda *Australia* 30°28S 147°41E **153** A7
Cariñena *Spain* 41°20N 1°13W **90** D3
Carinhanha *Brazil* 14°15S 44°46W **189** D2
Carinhanha → *Brazil* 14°20S 43°47W **189** C2
Carini *Italy* 38°8N 13°11E **94** D6
Cariño *Spain* 43°45N 7°52W **88** B3
Carinola *Italy* 41°11N 13°58E **94** A6
Carinthia = Kärnten □
  Austria 46°52N 13°30E **78** E6
Caripito *Venezuela* 10°8N 63°6W **186** A6
Cariré *Brazil* 3°57S 40°27W **189** A2
Carlet *Spain* 39°14N 0°31W **91** F4
Carleton, Mt. *Canada* 47°23N 66°53W **165** C6
Carleton Place *Canada* 45°8N 76°9W **175** A8
Carletonville *S. Africa* 26°23S 27°22E **145** D4
Carlin *U.S.A.* 40°43N 116°7W **168** F5
Carlingford L. *U.K.* 54°3N 6°9W **64** B5
Carlinville *U.S.A.* 39°17N 89°53W **172** F9
Carlisle *U.K.* 54°54N 2°56W **66** C5
Carlisle *U.S.A.* 40°12N 77°12W **174** F7
Carlisle B. *Barbados* 13°5N 59°37W **183** g
Carlisle I. *Australia* 20°49S 149°18E **150** b
Carlit, Pic *France* 42°35N 1°55E **72** F5
Carloforte *Italy* 39°8N 8°18E **94** C1
Carlos Casares
  Argentina 35°32S 61°20W **190** D3
Carlos Chagas *Brazil* 17°43S 40°45W **189** D2
Carlos Tejedor
  Argentina 35°25S 62°25W **190** D3
Carlow *Ireland* 52°50N 6°56W **64** D5
Carlow □ *Ireland* 52°43N 6°50W **64** D5
Carlsbad *Calif., U.S.A.* 33°10N 117°21W **171** M9
Carlsbad *N. Mex.,*
  U.S.A. 32°25N 104°14W **169** K11
Carlsbad Caverns △
  U.S.A. 32°10N 104°35W **169** K11
Carlsberg Ridge *Ind. Oc.* 1°0N 66°0E **146** D5
Carluke *U.K.* 55°45N 3°50W **65** F5
Carlyle *Canada* 49°40N 102°20W **163** D8
Carmacks *Canada* 62°5N 136°16W **160** E4
Carmagnola *Italy* 44°51N 7°43E **92** D4
Carman *Canada* 49°30N 98°0W **163** D9
Carmarthen *U.K.* 51°52N 4°19W **67** F3
Carmarthen B. *U.K.* 51°40N 4°30W **67** F3
Carmarthenshire □ *U.K.* 51°55N 4°13W **67** F3
Carmaux *France* 44°3N 2°10E **72** D6
Carmel *U.S.A.* 41°26N 73°41W **175** E11
Carmel, Mt. = Ha Karmel, Har
  Israel 32°44N 35°3E **130** C4
Carmel-by-the-Sea
  U.S.A. 36°33N 121°55W **170** J5
Carmel Valley *U.S.A.* 36°29N 121°43W **170** J5
Carmelo *Uruguay* 34°0S 58°20W **190** C4
Carmen *Bolivia* 11°0S 67°51W **188** C4
Carmen *Paraguay* 27°13S 56°12W **191** B4
Carmen, I. *Mexico* 25°57N 111°12W **180** B2
Carmen de Patagones
  Argentina 40°50S 63°0W **192** B4
Cármenes *Spain* 42°58N 5°34W **88** C5
Carmensa *Argentina* 35°15S 67°40W **190** D2
Carmi *Canada* 49°36N 119°8W **162** D5
Carmi *U.S.A.* 38°5N 88°10W **172** F9
Carmila *Australia* 21°55S 149°24E **150** C4
Carmona *Costa Rica* 10°0N 85°15W **182** E2
Carmona *Spain* 37°28N 5°42W **89** H5
Carn Ban *U.K.* 57°7N 4°15W **65** D4
Carn Eige *U.K.* 57°17N 5°8W **65** D3
Carnac *France* 47°35N 3°6W **70** E3
Carnamah *Australia* 29°41S 115°53E **149** E2
Carnarvon *Australia* 24°51S 113°42E **149** D1
Carnarvon *S. Africa* 30°56S 22°8E **144** D3
Carnarvon △ *Australia* 24°54S 148°2E **150** C4
Carnarvon Ra. *Queens.,*
  Australia 25°15S 148°30E **150** D4
Carnarvon Ra. *W. Austral.,*
  Australia 25°20S 120°45E **149** E3
Carnatic *India* 9°40N 77°50E **127** K3
Carnation *U.S.A.* 47°39N 121°55W **170** C5
Carncastle *U.K.* 54°54N 5°53W **64** B6
Carndonagh *Ireland* 55°16N 7°15W **64** A4
Carnduff *Canada* 49°10N 101°50W **163** D8
Carnegie *U.S.A.* 40°24N 80°5W **174** F4
Carnegie, L. *Australia* 26°5S 122°30W **149** E3
Carnegie Ridge *Pac. Oc.* 1°0S 87°0W **157** H19
Carney I. *Antarctica* 74°0S 121°0W **55** D14
Carnic Alps = Karnische Alpen
  Europe 46°36N 13°0E **78** E6
Carniche Alpi = Karnische Alpen
  Europe 46°36N 13°0E **78** E6
Carnot *C.A.R.* 4°59N 15°56E **140** D3
Carnot, C. *Australia* 34°57S 135°38E **151** E2
Carnot B. *Australia* 17°20S 122°15E **148** C3
Carnoustie *U.K.* 56°30N 2°42W **65** E6
Carnsore Pt. *Ireland* 52°10N 6°22W **64** D5
Caro *U.S.A.* 43°29N 83°24W **173** D12
Caroga Lake *U.S.A.* 43°8N 74°28W **175** C10
Carol City *U.S.A.* 25°56N 80°14W **177** J14
Carolina *Brazil* 7°10S 47°30W **189** B1
Carolina *Puerto Rico* 18°23N 65°58W **183** d
Carolina *S. Africa* 26°5S 30°6E **145** D5
Caroline I. *Kiribati* 9°58S 150°13W **157** H12
Caroline Is. *Micronesia* 8°0N 150°0E **156** G6
Caroline Pk. *N.Z.* 45°57S 167°15E **155** F2
Caroní *Trin. & Tob.* 10°34N 61°23W **187** K15
Caroní → *Venezuela* 8°21N 62°43W **186** B6
Caronie = Nébrodi, Monti
  Italy 37°54N 14°35E **95** E7
Caroona *Australia* 31°24S 150°26E **153** A9
Carpathians *Europe* 49°30N 21°0E **75** D11
Carpații Meridionali =
  Carpați Meridionali
  Romania 45°30N 25°0E **81** E9
Carpentaria, G. of
  Australia 14°0S 139°0E **150** A2
Carpentras *France* 44°3N 5°2E **73** D9
Carpi *Italy* 44°47N 10°53E **92** D7
Carpina *Brazil* 7°51S 35°15W **189** B3
Cărpineni *Moldova* 46°46N 28°22E **81** D13
Carpinteria *U.S.A.* 34°24N 119°31W **171** L7
Carpio *Spain* 41°13N 5°7W **88** D5
Carr Boyd Ra.
  Australia 16°15S 128°35E **148** C4
Carra, L. *Ireland* 53°59N 9°14W **64** C2
Carrabelle *U.S.A.* 29°51N 84°40W **178** F5
Carraig Mhachaire Rois =
  Carrickmacross
  Ireland 53°59N 6°43W **64** C5
Carraig na Siúire = Carrick-on-
  Suir *Ireland* 52°21N 7°24W **64** D4

Carral *Spain* 43°14N 8°21W **88** B2
Carranya ⊚ *Australia* 19°13S 127°46E **148** C4
Carrara *Italy* 44°5N 10°6E **92** D7
Carrascosa del Campo
  Spain 40°2N 2°45W **90** E2
Carrauntoohill *Ireland* 52°0N 9°45W **64** D2
Carretas, Punta *Peru* 14°12S 76°17W **188** C2
Carriacou *Grenada* 12°30N 61°27W **183** D7
Carrick-on-Shannon
  Ireland 53°57N 8°7W **64** C3
Carrick-on-Suir *Ireland* 52°21N 7°24W **64** D4
Carrickfergus *U.K.* 54°43N 5°49W **64** B6
Carrickmacross *Ireland* 53°59N 6°43W **64** C5
Carrieton *Australia* 32°25S 138°31E **152** B3
Carrigaline *Ireland* 51°48N 8°23W **64** E3
Carrillo *Mexico* 26°54N 103°55W **180** B4
Carrington *U.S.A.* 47°27N 99°8W **172** B4
Carrión → *Spain* 41°53N 4°32W **88** D6
Carrión de los Condes
  Spain 42°20N 4°37W **88** C6
Carrizal Bajo *Chile* 28°5S 71°20W **190** B1
Carrizalillo *Chile* 29°5S 71°30W **190** B1
Carrizo Cr. →
  U.S.A. 36°55N 103°55W **169** H12
Carrizo Plain △
  U.S.A. 35°11N 119°47W **170** K7
Carrizo Springs *U.S.A.* 28°31N 99°52W **176** G5
Carrizozo *U.S.A.* 33°38N 105°53W **169** K11
Carroll *U.S.A.* 42°4N 94°52W **172** D6
Carrollton *Ga., U.S.A.* 33°35N 85°5W **178** B4
Carrollton *Ill., U.S.A.* 39°18N 90°24W **172** F8
Carrollton *Ky., U.S.A.* 38°41N 85°11W **173** F11
Carrollton *Mo., U.S.A.* 39°22N 93°30W **172** F7
Carrollton *Ohio, U.S.A.* 40°34N 81°5W **174** F3
Carron → *U.K.* 57°53N 4°22W **65** D4
Carron, L. *U.K.* 57°22N 5°35W **65** D3
Carrot → *Canada* 53°50N 101°17W **163** C8
Carrot River *Canada* 53°17N 103°35W **163** C8
Carrouges *France* 48°34N 0°10W **70** D6
Carrù *Italy* 44°29N 7°52E **92** D4
Carruthers *Canada* 52°52N 109°16W **163** C7
Çarşamba *Turkey* 41°11N 36°44E **104** B7
Carsóli *Italy* 42°6N 13°5E **93** F10
Carson *Calif., U.S.A.* 33°49N 118°16W **171** M8
Carson *N. Dak., U.S.A.* 46°25N 101°34W **172** B3
Carson → *U.S.A.* 39°45N 118°40W **170** F8
Carson City *U.S.A.* 39°10N 119°46W **170** F7
Carson Sink *U.S.A.* 39°50N 118°25W **168** G4
Cartagena *Colombia* 10°25N 75°33W **186** A3
Cartagena *Spain* 37°38N 0°59W **91** H4
Cartago *Colombia* 4°45N 75°55W **186** C3
Cartago *Costa Rica* 9°50N 83°55W **182** E3
Cártama *Spain* 36°43N 4°39W **89** J6
Cartaxo *Portugal* 39°10N 8°47W **89** F2
Cartaya *Spain* 37°16N 7°9W **89** H3
Cartersville *U.S.A.* 34°10N 84°48W **178** B4
Carterton *N.Z.* 41°2S 175°31E **154** H4
Carthage *Tunisia* 36°52N 10°20E **94** F3
Carthage *Mo., U.S.A.* 37°11N 94°19W **172** G6
Carthage *N.Y., U.S.A.* 43°59N 75°37W **175** C9
Carthage *Tex., U.S.A.* 32°9N 94°20W **176** E7
Cartier I. *Australia* 12°31S 123°29E **148** B3
Cartwright *Canada* 53°41N 56°58W **165** B8
Caruaru *Brazil* 8°15S 35°55W **189** B3
Carúpano *Venezuela* 10°39N 63°15W **186** A6
Caruthersville *U.S.A.* 36°11N 89°39W **172** G9
Carvin *France* 50°30N 2°57E **71** B9
Carvoeiro *Brazil* 1°30S 61°59W **186** D6
Carvoeiro, C. *Portugal* 39°21N 9°24W **89** F1
Cary *U.S.A.* 35°47N 78°46W **177** D15
Cas-gwent = Chepstow
  U.K. 51°38N 2°41W **67** F5
Casa, Pas de la = Envalira, Port d'
  Europe 42°33N 1°43E **90** C6
Casa Branca *Portugal* 38°29N 8°12W **89** G2
Casa de Piedra
  Argentina 38°5S 67°28W **190** D2
Casa de Piedra, Embalse
  Argentina 38°5S 67°32W **190** D2
Casa Grande *U.S.A.* 32°53N 111°45W **169** K8
Casa Nova *Brazil* 9°25S 41°5W **189** B2
Casablanca *Chile* 33°20S 71°20W **190** C1
Casablanca *Morocco* 33°36N 7°36W **136** B4
Casablanca □ *Morocco* 33°38N 7°36W **136** B4
Casacalenda *Italy* 41°44N 14°51E **93** G11
Casalbordino *Italy* 42°9N 14°35E **93** F11
Casale Monferrato *Italy* 45°8N 8°27E **92** C5
Casalmaggiore *Italy* 45°0N 10°25E **92** D7
Casalpusterlengo *Italy* 45°11N 9°39E **92** C6
Casamance → *Senegal* 12°33N 16°46W **138** C1
Casarano *Italy* 40°0N 18°10E **95** B11
Casares *Spain* 36°27N 5°16W **89** J5
Casas Ibáñez *Spain* 39°17N 1°30W **91** F3
Casasimarro *Spain* 39°22N 2°3W **91** F2
Casatejada *Spain* 39°54N 5°40W **88** F5
Casavieja *Spain* 40°17N 4°46W **88** E6
Cascada de Basaseachic △
  Mexico 28°9N 108°15W **180** B3
Cascade *Seychelles* 4°39S 55°29E **141** b
Cascade *Idaho, U.S.A.* 44°31N 116°2W **168** D5
Cascade *Mont., U.S.A.* 47°16N 111°42W **168** C8
Cascade Locks *U.S.A.* 45°40N 121°54W **170** E5
Cascade Pt. *N.Z.* 44°1S 168°20E **155** E3
Cascade Ra. *U.S.A.* 47°0N 121°30W **170** D5
Cascade Res. *U.S.A.* 44°32N 116°3W **168** D5
Cascades, Pte. des
  Réunion 21°9S 55°51E **141** c
Cascais *Portugal* 38°41N 9°25W **89** G1
Cascavel *Ceará, Brazil* 4°7S 38°14W **189** A3
Cascavel *Paraná, Brazil* 24°57S 53°28W **191** A5
Cáscina *Italy* 43°41N 10°33E **92** C7
Casco B. *U.S.A.* 43°45N 70°0W **173** D19
Caselle Torinese *Italy* 45°10N 7°39E **92** C4
Caserta *Italy* 41°4N 14°20E **95** A7
Casey *Antarctica* 66°0S 76°0E **55** C8
Caseyr, Raas = Asir, Ras
  Somalia 11°55N 51°10E **131** E5
Cashel *Ireland* 52°30N 7°53W **64** D4
Casiguran *Phil.* 16°22N 122°7E **119** A6
Casilda *Argentina* 33°10S 61°10W **190** C3
Casimcea *Romania* 44°45N 28°23E **81** F8
Casino *Australia* 28°52S 153°3E **151** D5
Casiquiare → *Venezuela* 2°1N 67°7W **186** C5
Casitas *Peru* 3°54S 80°39W **188** A1
Čáslav *Czech Rep.* 49°54N 15°22E **78** D8
Casma *Peru* 9°30S 78°20W **188** B2
Casmalia *U.S.A.* 34°50N 120°32W **171** L6
Casnewydd = Newport
  U.K. 51°35N 3°0W **67** F5
Cásola Valsénio *Italy* 44°11N 11°40E **93** D8
Cásoli *Italy* 42°7N 14°18E **93** F11

Caspe *Spain* 41°14N 0°1W **90** D4
Casper *U.S.A.* 42°51N 106°19W **168** E10
Caspian Depression
  Eurasia 47°0N 48°0E **87** G9
Caspian Sea *Eurasia* 43°0N 50°0E **108** A4
Cass City *U.S.A.* 43°36N 83°10W **174** C1
Cass Lake *U.S.A.* 47°23N 94°37W **172** B6
Cassà de la Selva *Spain* 41°53N 2°52E **90** D7
Cassadaga *U.S.A.* 42°20N 79°19W **174** D5
Cassano allo Iónio *Italy* 39°47N 16°19E **95** C9
Casselberry *U.S.A.* 28°41N 81°20W **179** G8
Casselman *Canada* 45°19N 75°5W **175** A9
Casselton *U.S.A.* 46°54N 97°13W **172** B5
Cassiar Mts. *Canada* 59°30N 130°30W **162** B2
Cassilis *Australia* 32°3S 149°58E **153** B8
Cassino *Italy* 41°30N 13°49E **94** A6
Cassis *France* 43°14N 5°32E **73** E9
Cassville *U.S.A.* 36°41N 93°52W **172** G7
Castagneto Carducci
  Italy 43°9N 10°36E **92** E7
Castaic *U.S.A.* 34°30N 118°38W **171** L8
Castalia *U.S.A.* 41°24N 82°49W **174** E2
Castanhal *Brazil* 1°18S 47°55W **187** D9
Castéggio *Italy* 45°0N 9°7E **92** C6
Castejón de Monegros
  Spain 41°37N 0°15W **90** D4
Castèl del Monte *Italy* 41°5N 16°16E **95** A9
Castèl di Sangro *Italy* 41°47N 14°6E **93** G11
Castèl San Giovanni *Italy* 45°4N 9°26E **92** C6
Castèl San Pietro Terme
  Italy 44°24N 11°35E **93** D8
Castelbuono *Italy* 37°56N 14°5E **95** E7
Castelfidardo *Italy* 43°28N 13°33E **93** C10
Castelfiorentino
  Italy 43°36N 10°58E **92** E7
Castelfranco Véneto
  Italy 45°40N 11°55E **93** C8
Casteljaloux *France* 44°19N 0°6E **72** D4
Castellabate *Italy* 40°17N 14°57E **95** B7
Castellammare, G. di
  Italy 38°8N 12°54E **94** D5
Castellammare del Golfo
  Italy 38°1N 12°53E **94** D5
Castellammare di Stábia
  Italy 40°42N 14°29E **95** B7
Castellamonte *Italy* 45°23N 7°42E **92** C4
Castellane *France* 43°50N 6°31E **73** E10
Castellaneta *Italy* 40°38N 16°56E **95** B9
Castelli *Argentina* 36°7S 57°47W **190** D4
Castelló de la Plana *Spain* 39°58N 0°3W **90** F4
Castellón de la Plana =
  Spain 40°15N 0°5W **90** E4
Castellote *Spain* 40°48N 0°15W **90** E4
Castelmáuro *Italy* 41°50N 14°43E **93** G11
Castelnau-de-Médoc
  France 45°2N 0°48W **72** C3
Castelnau-Magnoac
  France 43°17N 0°31E **72** E4
Castelnaudary *France* 43°20N 1°58E **72** E5
Castelnovo ne' Monti
  Italy 44°26N 10°24E **92** D7
Castelnuovo di Val di Cécina
  Italy 43°12N 10°59E **92** E7
Castelo *Brazil* 20°33S 41°14W **189** E2
Castelo Branco *Portugal* 39°50N 7°31W **88** F3
Castelo Branco □
  Portugal 39°52N 7°45W **88** F3
Castelo de Paiva *Portugal* 41°2N 8°16W **88** D2
Castelo de Vide *Portugal* 39°25N 7°27W **89** F3
Castelo do Piauí *Brazil* 5°20S 41°33W **189** B2
Castelsardo *Italy* 40°55N 8°43E **94** B1
Castelsarrasin *France* 44°2N 1°7E **72** D5
Casteltérmini *Italy* 37°32N 13°39E **94** E6
Castelvetrano *Italy* 37°41N 12°47E **94** E5
Casterton *Australia* 37°30S 141°30E **152** C4
Castets *France* 43°52N 1°6W **72** E2
Castiglion Fiorentino
  Italy 43°20N 11°55E **93** E8
Castiglione del Lago *Italy* 43°7N 12°3E **93** E9
Castiglione della Pescáia
  Italy 42°46N 10°53E **92** F7
Castiglione delle Stiviere
  Italy 45°23N 10°30E **92** C7
Castilblanco *Spain* 39°17N 5°5W **89** F5
Castile *U.S.A.* 42°38N 78°3W **174** D6
Castilla *Peru* 5°12S 80°38W **188** B1
Castilla, Playa de *Spain* 37°0N 6°33W **89** J4
Castilla-La Mancha □
  Spain 39°30N 3°30W **89** F7
Castilla y León □ *Spain* 42°0N 5°0W **88** D6
Castillo de Locubín *Spain* 37°32N 3°56W **89** H7
Castillo de San Marcos △
  U.S.A. 29°54N 81°19W **178** F8
Castillon-en-Couserans
  France 42°56N 1°1E **72** F5
Castillonès *France* 44°39N 0°37E **72** D4
Castillos *Uruguay* 34°12S 53°52W **191** C5
Castle Dale *U.S.A.* 39°13N 111°1W **168** G8
Castle Douglas *U.K.* 54°56N 3°56W **65** G5
Castle Rock *Colo.,*
  U.S.A. 39°22N 104°51W **168** G11
Castle Rock *Wash.,*
  U.S.A. 46°17N 122°54W **170** D4
Castlebar *Ireland* 53°52N 9°18W **64** C2
Castlebay *U.K.* 56°57N 7°31W **65** E1
Castleblayney *Ireland* 54°7N 6°44W **64** B5
Castlecliff *N.Z.* 39°57S 175°1E **154** F4
Castlecomer *Ireland* 52°48N 7°14W **64** D4
Castlederg *U.K.* 54°42N 7°36W **64** B4
Castleford *U.K.* 53°43N 1°21W **66** D6
Castlegar *Canada* 49°20N 117°40W **162** D5
Castleisland *Ireland* 52°14N 9°28W **64** D2
Castlemaine *Australia* 37°2S 144°12E **152** C6
Castlemaine *Ireland* 52°10N 9°42W **64** D2
Castlepoint *N.Z.* 40°54S 176°15E **154** G5
Castlepollard *Ireland* 53°41N 7°19W **64** C4
Castlerea *Ireland* 53°46N 8°29W **64** C3
Castlereagh □
  Australia 30°12S 147°32E **153** A7
Castlereagh →
  Australia 12°10S 135°10E **150** A2
Castleton *U.S.A.* 43°37N 73°11W **175** C11
Castleton-on-Hudson
  U.S.A. 42°31N 73°45W **175** D11
Castletown *I. of Man* 54°5N 4°38W **66** C3
Castletown Bearhaven
  Ireland 51°39N 9°55W **64** E2
Castor *Canada* 52°15N 111°50W **162** C6

Castor → *Canada* 53°24N 78°58W **164** B4
Castorland *U.S.A.* 43°53N 75°31W **175** C9
Castres *France* 43°37N 2°13E **72** E6
Castricum *Neths.* 52°33N 4°40E **69** B4
Castries *St. Lucia* 14°2N 60°58W **187** D7
Castril *Spain* 37°48N 2°46W **89** H8
Castro *Brazil* 24°45S 50°0W **191** A6
Castro *Chile* 42°30S 73°50W **192** B2
Castro Alves *Brazil* 12°46S 39°33W **189** C3
Castro del Río *Spain* 37°41N 4°29W **89** H6
Castro-Urdiales *Spain* 43°23N 3°11W **88** B7
Castro Valley *U.S.A.* 37°41N 122°5W **170** H4
Castro Verde *Portugal* 37°41N 8°4W **89** H2
Castrojeriz *Spain* 42°17N 4°9W **88** D6
Castropol *Spain* 43°32N 7°0W **88** B4
Castroreale *Italy* 38°6N 15°12E **95** D8
Castrovillari *Italy* 39°49N 16°12E **95** C9
Castroville *U.S.A.* 36°46N 121°45W **170** J5
Castrovirreyna *Peru* 13°20S 75°18W **188** C2
Castuera *Spain* 38°43N 5°37W **89** G5
Caswell Sound *N.Z.* 44°56S 167°8E **155** E2
Çat *Turkey* 39°40N 41°3E **105** C9
Cat Ba, Dao *Vietnam* 20°50N 107°0E **120** B6
Cat Ba △ *Vietnam* 20°47N 107°3E **120** B6
Cat I. *Bahamas* 24°30N 75°30W **183** B4
Cat L. *Canada* 51°40N 91°50W **164** B1
Cat Lake *Canada* 51°40N 91°50W **164** B1
Cat Tien △ *Vietnam* 11°25N 107°17E **121** G6
Cata *Slovak Rep.* 47°58N 18°38E **79** D11
Catacamas *Honduras* 14°54N 85°56W **182** D2
Catacáos *Peru* 5°20S 80°45W **188** B1
Cataguases *Brazil* 21°23S 42°39W **191** A7
Çatak *Turkey* 38°1N 43°8E **105** C10
Çatalağzı *Turkey* 41°30N 31°59E **104** B4
Catalão *Brazil* 18°10S 47°57W **189** D1
Çatalca *Turkey* 41°8N 28°27E **97** E12
Catalina *Canada* 48°31N 53°4W **165** C9
Catalina *Chile* 25°13S 69°43W **190** B2
Catalina △ *U.S.A.* 32°30N 110°50W **169** K8
Catalonia = Cataluña □
　Spain 41°40N 1°15E **90** D6
Cataluña □ *Spain* 41°40N 1°15E **90** D6
Çatalzeytin *Turkey* 41°57N 34°12E **104** B6
Catamarca *Argentina* 28°30S 65°50W **190** B2
Catamarca □ *Argentina* 27°0S 65°50W **190** B2
Catanduanes I. *Phil.* 13°50N 124°20E **119** D6
Catanduva *Brazil* 21°5S 48°58W **191** A6
Catánia *Italy* 37°30N 15°6E **95** E8
Catánia, G. di *Italy* 37°24N 15°6E **95** E8
Catanzaro *Italy* 38°54N 16°35E **95** D9
Catarman *Phil.* 12°28N 124°35E **119** D6
Catatumbo-Bari △
　Colombia 9°3N 73°12W **183** E5
Cataula *U.S.A.* 32°39N 84°52W **178** C5
Catchacoma *Canada* 44°44N 78°19W **174** B6
Cateel *Phil.* 7°47N 126°24E **119** C7
Catembe *Mozam.* 26°0S 32°33E **145** C5
Catende *Brazil* 8°40S 35°43W **189** B3
Caterham *U.K.* 51°15N 0°4W **67** F7
Cathair na Mart = Westport
　Ireland 53°48N 9°31W **64** C2
Cathcart *Australia* 36°52S 149°24E **153** D8
Cathcart *S. Africa* 32°18S 27°10E **144** D4
Cathedral City
　U.S.A. 33°47N 116°28W **171** M10
Cathedral Rock △
　Australia 30°24S 152°15E **153** A10
Cathlamet *U.S.A.* 46°12N 123°23W **170** D3
Catió *Guinea-Biss.* 11°17N 15°15W **138** C1
Catita *Brazil* 9°31S 43°41W **189** B2
Catlettsburg *U.S.A.* 38°25N 82°36W **173** F12
Catlins *N.Z.* 46°25S 169°17E **155** G4
Çatma Dağı *Turkey* 38°25N 29°50E **99** C11
Catoche, C. *Mexico* 21°35N 87°5W **181** C7
Catolé do Rocha *Brazil* 6°21S 37°45W **189** B3
Cátria, Mte. *Italy* 43°28N 12°42E **93** E9
Catrilo *Argentina* 36°26S 63°24W **190** D3
Catrimani *Brazil* 0°27N 61°41W **186** C6
Catrimani → *Brazil* 0°28N 61°44W **186** C6
Catskill *U.S.A.* 42°14N 73°52W **175** D11
Catskill △ *U.S.A.* 42°8N 74°39W **175** D10
Catskill Mts. *U.S.A.* 42°10N 74°25W **175** D10
Catt, Mt. *Australia* 13°49S 134°23E **150** A1
Cattaraugus *U.S.A.* 42°20N 78°52W **174** D6
Catterick *U.K.* 54°23N 1°37W **66** C6
Cattólica *Italy* 43°58N 12°44E **93** E9
Cattólica Eraclea *Italy* 37°26N 13°24E **94** E6
Catu *Brazil* 12°21S 38°23W **189** C3
Catuala *Angola* 16°25S 19°2E **144** A2
Catuane *Mozam.* 26°48S 32°18E **145** C5
Catur *Mozam.* 13°45S 35°30E **143** E4
Caubvick, Mt. = Iberville, Mt. d'
　Canada 58°50N 63°50W **161** F19
Cauca → *Colombia* 8°54N 74°28W **186** B4
Caucaia *Brazil* 3°40S 38°35W **189** A3
Caucasus Mountains
　Eurasia 42°50N 44°0E **87** J7
Caucete *Argentina* 31°38S 68°20W **190** C2
Caudete *Spain* 38°42N 1°2W **91** G3
Caudry *France* 50°7N 3°22E **71** B10
Cauese Mts. *Mozam.* 15°14S 30°33E **143** F3
Caulnes *France* 48°18N 2°10W **70** D4
Caulónia *Italy* 38°23N 16°24E **95** D9
Caungula *Angola* 8°26S 18°38E **140** F3
Cauquenes *Chile* 36°0S 72°22W **190** D2
Caura → *Venezuela* 7°38N 64°53W **186** B6
Cauresi → *Mozam.* 17°8S 33°0E **143** F3
Căuşani *Moldova* 46°38N 29°25E **81** D14
Causapscal *Canada* 48°19N 67°12W **165** D6
Caussade *France* 44°10N 1°33E **72** D5
Causse-Méjean *France* 44°18N 3°42E **72** D7
Causses du Quercy △
　France 44°35N 1°35E **72** D5
Cauterets *France* 42°52N 0°8W **72** F3
Cauvery → *India* 11°9N 78°52E **127** J4
Caux, Pays de *France* 49°38N 0°35E **70** C7
Cava de' Tirreni *Italy* 40°42N 14°42E **95** B7
Cávado → *Portugal* 41°32N 8°48W **88** D2
Cavagrande del Cassibile △
　Italy 36°58N 15°6E **95** F8
Cavaillon *France* 43°10N 5°2E **73** E10
Cavalaire-sur-Mer
　France 43°10N 6°53E **73** E10
Cavalcante *Brazil* 13°48S 47°30W **189** D1
Cavalese *Italy* 46°17N 11°27E **93** B8
Cavalier *U.S.A.* 48°48N 97°37W **172** A5
Cavalla = Cavally →
　Africa 4°22N 7°32W **138** E3
Cavalla △ *Liberia* 5°8N 7°20W **138** D3
Cavalli Is. *N.Z.* 35°0S 173°58E **154** B4
Cavally → *Africa* 4°22N 7°32W **138** E3

Cavan *Ireland* 54°0N 7°22W **64** B4
Cavan □ *Ireland* 54°1N 7°16W **64** C4
Cavárzere *Italy* 45°8N 12°5E **93** C9
Çavdır *Turkey* 37°10N 29°42E **99** D11
Cave Creek *U.S.A.* 33°50N 111°57W **169** K8
Cave Spring *U.S.A.* 34°6N 85°20W **178** A4
Cavelleria, C. de *Spain* 40°5N 4°5E **100** A11
Cavenagh Ra.
　Australia 26°12S 127°55E **149** E4
Cavendish *Australia* 37°31S 142°2E **152** D5
Caverna do Peruaçu △
　Brazil 15°0S 44°35W **189** D2
Caviana, I. *Brazil* 0°10N 50°10W **189** C8
Cavite *Phil.* 14°29N 120°54E **119** B6
Cavnic *Romania* 47°40N 23°52E **81** C8
Cavour *Italy* 44°47N 7°22E **92** D4
Cavtat *Croatia* 42°35N 18°13E **96** D2
Cawndilla L. *Australia* 32°30S 142°15E **152** B5
Cawnpore = Kanpur
　India 26°28N 80°20E **125** F9
Caxias *Brazil* 4°55S 43°20W **189** A2
Caxias do Sul *Brazil* 29°10S 51°10W **191** B5
Çay *Turkey* 38°35N 31°1E **104** C4
Çay Sal Bank *Bahamas* 23°45N 80°0W **182** B4
Cayambe *Ecuador* 0°3N 78°8W **186** C3
Cayce *U.S.A.* 33°58N 81°4W **178** B8
Çaycuma *Turkey* 41°25N 32°4E **104** B5
Cayenne *Fr. Guiana* 5°5N 52°18W **187** B8
Cayey *Puerto Rico* 18°6N 66°10W **183** d
Caygören Barajı *Turkey* 39°15N 28°12E **99** C10
Çayiralan *Turkey* 39°17N 35°38E **104** C6
Cayrova = Áyios Theodhoros
　Cyprus 35°22N 34°1E **101** D13
Caylus *France* 44°15N 1°47E **72** D5
Cayman Brac
　Cayman Is. 19°43N 79°49W **182** C4
Cayman Is. ☑
　W. Indies 19°40N 80°30W **182** C3
Cayman Trench
　Caribbean 17°0N 83°0W **158** H11
Cayres *France* 44°55N 3°48E **72** D7
Cayuga *Canada* 42°59N 79°50W **174** D5
Cayuga *U.S.A.* 42°54N 76°44W **175** D8
Cayuga Heights *U.S.A.* 42°27N 76°29W **175** D8
Cayuga L. *U.S.A.* 42°41N 76°41W **175** D8
Cazalla de la Sierra *Spain* 37°56N 5°45W **89** H5
Căzăneşti *Romania* 44°36N 27°3E **81** F12
Cazaubon *France* 43°56N 0°3W **72** E3
Cazaux et de Sanguinet, Étang de
　France 44°29N 1°10W **72** D2
Cazenovia *U.S.A.* 42°56N 75°51W **175** D9
Cazères *France* 43°13N 1°5E **72** E5
Cazin *Bos.-H.* 44°57N 15°57E **92** D12
Čazma *Croatia* 45°45N 16°39E **93** C13
Cazombo *Angola* 11°54S 22°56E **141** G4
Cazorla *Spain* 37°55N 3°2W **89** H7
Cazorla, Sierra de *Spain* 38°5N 2°55W **89** G8
Cea → *Spain* 42°0N 5°36W **88** C5
Ceahlău △ *Romania* 46°58N 25°55E **81** C10
Ceamurlia de Jos
　Romania 44°43N 28°47E **81** F13
Ceanannus Mor = Kells
　Ireland 53°44N 6°53W **64** C5
Ceará = Fortaleza *Brazil* 3°45S 38°35W **189** A3
Ceará □ *Brazil* 5°0S 40°0W **189** B3
Ceara Abyssal Plain
　Atl. Oc. 0°0 36°30W **56** F7
Ceará-Mirim *Brazil* 5°38S 35°25W **189** B3
Ceara Rise *Atl. Oc.* 4°30N 43°30W **56** F7
Ceatharlach = Carlow
　Ireland 52°50N 6°56W **64** D5
Ceauru, L. *Romania* 44°58N 23°11E **81** F8
Cébaco, I. de Panama 7°33N 81°9W **182** E3
Cebollar *Argentina* 29°10S 66°35W **190** B2
Cebollera, Sierra *Spain* 42°0N 2°30W **90** D2
Cebreros *Spain* 40°27N 4°28W **88** E6
Cebu *Phil.* 10°18N 123°54E **119** B6
Čečava *Bos.-H.* 44°42N 17°44E **80** F2
Ceccano *Italy* 41°34N 13°20E **94** A6
Cece *Hungary* 46°46N 18°39E **80** D3
Cechi *Ivory C.* 6°15N 4°25E **138** D4
Cecil Plains *Australia* 27°30S 151°11E **151** D5
Cécina *Italy* 43°19N 10°31E **92** E7
Cécina → *Italy* 43°19N 10°29E **92** E7
Ceclavín *Spain* 39°50N 6°45W **88** F4
Cedar → *U.S.A.* 41°17N 91°21W **172** E8
Cedar City *U.S.A.* 37°41N 113°4W **169** H7
Cedar Creek Res. *U.S.A.* 32°11N 96°4W **176** E6
Cedar Falls *Iowa,*
　U.S.A. 42°32N 92°27W **172** D7
Cedar Falls *Wash.,*
　U.S.A. 47°25N 121°45W **170** C5
Cedar Key *U.S.A.* 29°8N 83°2W **179** E6
Cedar L. *Canada* 53°10N 100°0W **163** C9
Cedar Park *U.S.A.* 30°30N 97°49W **176** F6
Cedar Rapids *U.S.A.* 41°59N 91°40W **172** E8
Cedartown *U.S.A.* 34°1N 85°15W **178** A4
Cedarvale *Canada* 55°1N 128°22W **162** B3
Cedarville *S. Africa* 30°23S 29°3E **145** D4
Cedeira *Spain* 43°39N 8°2W **88** B2
Cedral *Mexico* 23°50N 100°45W **180** C4
Cedro *Brazil* 6°34S 39°3W **189** B3
Cedros, I. *Mexico* 28°12N 115°15W **180** B1
Cedros, B. Trin. & Tob. 10°16N 61°54W **187** K15
Ceduna *Australia* 32°7S 133°46E **151** E1
Cedynia *Poland* 52°53N 14°12E **83** F1
Cée *Spain* 42°57N 9°10W **88** C1
Ceel Gaal *Somalia* 10°58N 50°20E **131** E5
Ceel Waaq *Kenya* 2°49N 40°56E **140** B4
Ceeldheere *Somalia* 3°50N 47°8E **131** G4
Ceerigaabo *Somalia* 10°35N 47°20E **131** E5
Cefalù *Italy* 38°2N 14°1E **95** D7
Cega → *Spain* 41°33N 4°46W **88** D6
Cegléd *Hungary* 47°11N 19°47E **80** D4
Céglie Messápica *Italy* 40°39N 17°31E **95** B10
Cehegín *Spain* 38°6N 1°48W **91** G3
Ceheng *China* 24°58N 105°48E **116** E5
Cehu-Silvaniei *Romania* 47°24N 23°9E **81** C8
Ceica *Romania* 46°53N 22°10E **80** D7
Ceira → *Portugal* 40°13N 8°16W **88** E2
Çekerek *Turkey* 40°4N 35°29E **104** B6
Cekik *Indonesia* 8°12S 114°27E **119** J17
Čelákovice *Czech Rep.* 50°10N 14°46E **78** A7
Celano *Italy* 42°5N 13°33E **93** F10
Celanova *Spain* 42°9N 7°58W **88** C3
Celaque △ *Honduras* 14°30N 88°43W **182** D2
Celaya *Mexico* 20°31N 100°37W **180** C4
Celbridge *Ireland* 53°20N 6°32W **64** C5

Celebes = Sulawesi
　Indonesia 2°0S 120°0E **119** E6
Celebes Sea *Indonesia* 3°0N 123°0E **119** D6
Celendín *Peru* 6°52S 78°10W **188** B2
Celina *U.S.A.* 40°33N 84°35W **173** E11
Celinac *Bos.-H.* 44°43N 17°22E **80** F2
Celje *Slovenia* 46°16N 15°18E **93** B12
Celldömölk *Hungary* 47°16N 17°10E **80** C2
Celle *Germany* 52°37N 10°4E **76** C6
Celorico da Beira
　Portugal 40°38N 7°24W **88** E3
Celtic Sea *Atl. Oc.* 50°9N 9°34W **68** F2
Çeltikçi *Turkey* 37°32N 30°29E **99** D12
Cenderawasih, Teluk
　Indonesia 3°0S 135°20E **119** E9
Cengong *China* 27°13N 108°44E **116** D7
Ceno → *Italy* 44°43N 10°5E **92** D7
Centallo *Italy* 44°30N 7°35E **92** D4
Centelles *Spain* 41°50N 2°13E **90** D7
Centennial *U.S.A.* 39°34N 104°52W **168** G11
Center N. Dak., *U.S.A.* 47°7N 101°18W **172** B3
Center Tex., *U.S.A.* 31°48N 94°11W **176** F7
Center Hill *U.S.A.* 28°38N 82°3W **179** F7
Centerburg *U.S.A.* 40°18N 82°42W **174** F2
Centerville Calif.,
　U.S.A. 36°44N 119°30W **170** J7
Centerville Iowa, *U.S.A.* 40°44N 92°52W **172** E7
Centerville Pa., *U.S.A.* 37°9N 79°59W **174** F5
Centerville Tenn.,
　U.S.A. 35°47N 87°28W **177** D11
Centerville Tex., *U.S.A.* 31°16N 95°59W **176** F7
Cento *Italy* 44°43N 11°17E **93** D8
Central *Brazil* 11°8S 42°8W **189** C2
Central □ *Botswana* 22°0S 26°30E **144** B4
Central □ *Ghana* 5°30N 1°0W **139** D4
Central □ *Kenya* 0°30S 37°30E **142** C4
Central □ *Malawi* 13°30S 33°30E **143** E3
Central □ *Zambia* 14°25S 28°50E **143** E2
Central, Cordillera
　Colombia 5°0N 75°0W **186** C4
Central, Cordillera
　Costa Rica 10°10N 84°5W **182** D3
Central, Cordillera
　Dom. Rep. 19°15N 71°0W **183** C5
Central, Cordillera *Peru* 7°0S 77°30W **188** B2
Central, Cordillera
　Puerto Rico 18°8N 66°35W **183** d
Central African Rep. ■
　Africa 7°0N 20°0E **135** G9
Central America
　America 12°0N 85°0W **158** H11
Central Australia ◇
　Australia 19°56S 130°40E **148** C5
Central Bedfordshire □
　U.K. 52°5N 0°20W **67** E7
Central Butte *Canada* 50°48N 106°31W **163** C7
Central City Colo.,
　U.S.A. 39°48N 105°31W **168** G11
Central City Ky.,
　U.S.A. 37°18N 87°7W **172** G11
Central City Nebr., *U.S.A.* 41°7N 98°0W **172** E4
Central Desert ◇
　Australia 19°56S 130°40E **148** C5
Central I. *Kenya* 3°30N 36°0E **142** B4
Central Island △ *Kenya* 2°33N 36°1E **142** B4
Central Japan Int. ✈ (NGO)
　Japan 34°53N 136°45E **113** G8
Central Kalahari △
　Botswana 22°36S 23°58E **144** B3
Central Makran Range
　Pakistan 26°30N 64°15E **122** F4
Central Pacific Basin
　Pac. Oc. 8°0N 175°0W **156** G10
Central Patricia *Canada* 51°30N 90°9W **164** B1
Central Point *U.S.A.* 42°23N 122°55W **168** E2
Central Russian Uplands
　Europe 54°0N 36°0E **58** E13
Central Siberian Plateau
　Russia 65°0N 105°0E **102** B12
Central Square *U.S.A.* 43°17N 76°9W **175** C8
Centralia *Canada* 43°17N 81°28W **174** C3
Centralia Ill., *U.S.A.* 38°32N 89°8W **172** F9
Centralia Mo., *U.S.A.* 39°13N 92°8W **172** F7
Centralia Wash.,
　U.S.A. 46°43N 122°58W **170** D4
Centre *U.S.A.* 34°9N 85°41W **178** A4
Centre □ *Cameroon* 4°45N 12°0E **139** E7
Centre de Flacq
　Mauritius 20°12S 57°43E **141** d
Centreville N.Y., *U.S.A.* 42°28N 78°14W **174** D6
Centreville Pa., *U.S.A.* 41°44N 79°45W **174** E5
Century *U.S.A.* 30°58N 87°16W **179** E2
Cenxi *China* 22°57N 110°57E **117** F8
Ceotina → *Bos.-H.* 43°36N 18°50E **96** C2
Cephalonia = Kefalonia
　Greece 38°15N 20°30E **98** C2
Čepin *Croatia* 45°32N 18°34E **80** E3
Ceprano *Italy* 41°33N 13°31E **94** A6
Ceptura *Romania* 45°1N 26°21E **81** E11
Cepu *Indonesia* 7°9S 111°35E **119** G14
Ceram = Seram
　Indonesia 3°10S 129°0E **119** E7
Ceram Sea = Seram Sea
　Indonesia 2°30S 128°30E **119** E7
Cerbère *France* 42°26N 3°10E **72** F7
Cerbicales, Îs. *France* 41°33N 9°22E **73** G13
Cercal *Portugal* 37°48N 8°40W **89** H2
Cerdanya *Spain* 42°22N 1°35E **90** C6
Cère → *France* 44°55N 1°49E **72** D5
Cerea *Italy* 45°12N 11°13E **93** C8
Ceredigion □ *U.K.* 52°16N 4°15W **67** E3
Ceres *Argentina* 29°55S 61°55W **190** B3
Ceres *S. Africa* 33°21S 19°18E **144** D2
Ceres *U.S.A.* 37°35N 120°57W **170** H6
Cérésio, L. di = Lugano, L. di
　Switz. 46°0N 9°0E **92** D6
Céret *France* 42°30N 2°42E **72** F6
Cerf *Seychelles* 4°38S 55°40E **141** b
Cergy *France* 49°2N 2°4E **71** D9
Cerignola *Italy* 41°17N 15°53E **95** A8
Cerigo = Kythira *Greece* 36°8N 23°0E **98** F5
Cérilly *France* 46°37N 2°50E **71** F9
Cerisiers *France* 48°8N 3°30E **71** D10
Cerizay *France* 46°50N 0°40W **70** F6
Çerkeş *Turkey* 40°49N 32°52E **104** B5
Çerkezköy *Turkey* 41°17N 28°0E **97** E12
Cerknica *Slovenia* 45°48N 14°21E **93** C11

Cerkovica *Bulgaria* 43°41N 24°50E **97** C8
Cermerno *Serbia* 43°35N 20°25E **96** C4
Çermik *Turkey* 38°8N 39°26E **105** C8
Cerna *Romania* 45°4N 28°17E **81** E13
Cerna → *Romania* 44°38N 23°58E **81** F8
Cernavodă *Romania* 44°22N 28°3E **81** F13
Cernay *France* 47°44N 7°10E **71** E14
Cernik *Croatia* 45°17N 17°22E **80** E2
Cerralvo, I. *Mexico* 24°15N 109°55W **180** C3
Cërrik *Albania* 41°2N 19°58E **96** E3
Cerritos *Mexico* 22°25N 100°16W **180** C4
Cerro Chato *Uruguay* 33°6S 55°8W **191** C4
Cerro Cofre de Perote △
　Mexico 19°29N 97°8W **181** D5
Cerro Corá △ *Paraguay* 22°35S 56°2W **191** A4
Cerro de Pasco *Peru* 10°45S 76°10W **188** C2
Cerro el Copey △
　Venezuela 10°59N 63°53W **183** D7
Cerro Hoya △ *Panama* 7°80N 80°45W **182** E3
Cerro Saroche △
　Venezuela 10°8N 69°38W **183** D6
Cerro Sombrero *Chile* 52°45S 69°15W **192** D3
Cerros Colorados, Embalse
　Argentina 38°30S 68°50W **192** A3
Certaldo *Italy* 43°33N 11°2E **92** E8
Cervaro → *Italy* 41°30N 15°52E **95** A8
Cervati, Monte *Italy* 40°17N 15°29E **95** B8
Cerventes *Australia* 30°31S 115°3E **149** F2
Cervera *Spain* 41°40N 1°16E **90** D6
Cervera de Pisuerga
　Spain 42°51N 4°30W **88** C6
Cervera del Río Alhama
　Spain 42°2N 1°58W **90** C3
Cervéteri *Italy* 42°0N 12°6E **94** A5
Cérvia *Italy* 44°15N 12°22E **93** D9
Cervignano del Friuli
　Italy 45°49N 13°20E **93** C10
Cervinara *Italy* 41°1N 14°37E **95** A7
Cervione *France* 42°20N 9°29E **73** F13
Cervo *Spain* 43°40N 7°24W **88** B3
Cesaró *Italy* 37°50N 14°38E **95** E7
Cesena *Italy* 44°8N 12°15E **93** D9
Cesenático *Italy* 44°12N 12°24E **93** D9
Cēsis *Latvia* 57°18N 25°15E **84** D3
Česká Lípa *Czech Rep.* 50°45N 14°30E **78** A7
Česká Rep. = Czech Rep. ■
　Europe 50°0N 15°0E **78** B8
Česká Třebová
　Czech Rep. 49°54N 16°27E **79** B9
České Budějovice
　Czech Rep. 48°55N 14°25E **78** C7
České Svýčarsko △
　Czech Rep. 50°50N 14°15E **78** A7
České Velenice
　Czech Rep. 48°45N 14°57E **78** C7
Českobudějovický □
　Czech Rep. 49°0N 14°30E **78** C7
Českomoravská Vrchovina
　Czech Rep. 49°30N 15°40E **78** B8
Český Brod *Czech Rep.* 50°4N 14°52E **78** A7
Český Krumlov
　Czech Rep. 48°43N 14°21E **78** C7
Český Těšín *Czech Rep.* 49°45N 18°39E **79** B11
Çeşma → *Croatia* 45°35N 16°29E **93** C13
Çeşme *Turkey* 38°20N 26°23E **99** C8
Cessnock *Australia* 32°50S 151°21E **153** B9
Cesson-Sévigné *France* 48°7N 1°36W **70** D5
Cestas *France* 44°44N 0°41W **72** D3
Cestos → *Liberia* 5°40N 9°10W **138** D3
Cestos Sehnkwehn □
　Liberia 5°30N 9°10W **138** D3
Cetate *Romania* 44°7N 23°2E **80** F8
Cetin Grad *Croatia* 45°9N 15°45E **93** C12
Cetina → *Croatia* 43°26N 16°42E **93** E13
Cetinje *Montenegro* 42°23N 18°59E **96** D2
Cetraro *Italy* 39°31N 15°55E **95** C8
Ceuta *N. Afr.* 35°52N 5°18W **134** A4
Ceva *Italy* 44°23N 8°2E **92** D5
Cévennes *France* 44°10N 3°50E **72** D7
Cévennes △ *France* 44°15N 3°45E **72** D7
Ceyhan *Turkey* 37°4N 35°47E **104** D6
Ceyhan → *Turkey* 36°38N 35°40E **104** D6
Ceylanpınar *Turkey* 36°50N 40°2E **105** D9
Ceylon = Sri Lanka ■
　Asia 7°30N 80°50E **127** L5
Ceylon Plain *Ind. Oc.* 4°0S 82°0E **146** E7
Cèze → *France* 44°6N 4°43E **73** D8
Cha-am *Thailand* 12°48N 99°58E **120** F2
Chabanais *France* 45°52N 0°48E **72** C4
Chabeuil *France* 44°54N 5°3E **73** D9
Chablais *France* 47°7N 3°48E **71** E10
Chablis *France* 47°47N 3°48E **71** E10
Chabounia *Algeria* 35°30N 2°38E **134** B6
Chacabuco *Argentina* 34°40S 60°27W **190** C3
Chacao, Canal *Chile* 41°47S 73°42W **192** B2
Chachani, Nevado
　Peru 16°11S 71°31W **188** D3
Chachapoyas *Peru* 6°15S 77°50W **188** B2
Chachasp *Peru* 15°22S 72°15W **188** D3
Chachoengsao *Thailand* 13°42N 101°5E **120** F3
Chachran *Pakistan* 28°55N 70°30E **124** E4
Chachro *Pakistan* 25°5N 70°15E **124** G4
Chaco □ *Argentina* 26°30S 61°0W **190** B3
Chaco □ *Paraguay* 26°0S 60°0W **190** B4
Chaco → *Argentina* 26°36N 108°39W **180** C4
Chaco △ *Argentina* 27°0S 59°30W **190** B4
Chaco Boreal *S. Amer.* 22°0S 60°0W **186** H6
Chaco Culture △
　U.S.A. 36°3N 107°58W **169** H10
Chacon, C. *U.S.A.* 54°42N 132°0W **162** C2
Chad ■ *Africa* 15°0N 17°15E **135** F8
Chad, L. = Tchad, L.
　Chad 13°30N 14°30E **135** F8
Chadileuvú →
　Argentina 37°46S 66°0W **190** D2
Chadiza *Zambia* 14°45S 32°27E **143** E3
Chadron *U.S.A.* 42°50N 103°0W **172** D2
Chadyr-Lunga = Ciadâr-Lunga
　Moldova 46°3N 28°51E **81** D13
Chae Hom *Thailand* 18°43N 99°35E **120** C2
Chae Son △ *Thailand* 18°26N 99°28E **120** C2
Chaem → *Thailand* 18°11N 98°38E **120** C2
Chaeryŏng N. Korea 38°24N 125°36E **115** E13
Chafe *Nigeria* 11°59N 6°50E **139** C6
Chagai Hills = Chāh Gay Hills
　Afghan. 29°30N 64°0E **122** E3
Chagda *Russia* 58°45N 130°38E **107** D14
Chagdo Kangri *China* 34°15N 84°10E **109** D10
Chaghcharān *Afghan.* 34°31N 65°15E **109** F7
Chagny *France* 46°57N 4°45E **71** F11
Chagoda *Russia* 59°10N 35°15E **84** C8

Chagos Arch. ☑ *Ind. Oc.* 6°0S 72°0E **146** E6
Chagos-Laccadive Ridge
　Ind. Oc. 3°0N 73°0E **146** D6
Chagres △ *Panama* 9°33N 79°37W **182** E4
Chaguanas
　Trin. & Tob. 10°30N 61°26W **187** K15
Chaguaramas
　Trin. & Tob. 10°30N 61°26W **187** K15
Chāh Akhvor *Iran* 32°41N 59°40E **129** C8
Chāh Bahar *Iran* 25°20N 60°40E **129** E9
Chāh-e Kavīr *Iran* 34°29N 56°34E **129** C8
Chāh Gay Hills *Afghan.* 29°30N 64°0E **122** E3
Chahār Borj *Iran* 37°6N 45°59E **105** D11
Chahār Borjak *Iran* 30°17N 62°3E **128** D9
Chahār Mahāll va Bakhtīarī □
　Iran 32°0N 49°0E **129** C6
Chai Badan *Thailand* 15°12N 101°8E **120** E3
Chaibasa *India* 22°42N 85°49E **125** H11
Chaillé-les-Marais *France* 46°25N 1°2W **72** B2
Chainat *Thailand* 15°11N 100°8E **120** E3
Chainpur *Nepal* 27°17N 87°19E **125** F12
Chaiya *Thailand* 9°23N 99°14E **121** H2
Chaiyaphum *Thailand* 15°48N 102°2E **120** E4
Chaj Doab *Pakistan* 32°15N 73°0E **124** C5
Chajari *Argentina* 30°42S 58°0W **190** C4
Chak Amru *Pakistan* 32°22N 75°11E **124** C6
Chakar → *Pakistan* 29°29N 68°2E **124** E3
Chakari *Zimbabwe* 18°5S 29°51E **145** A4
Chake Chake *Tanzania* 5°15S 39°45E **142** D4
Chakhānsūr *Afghan.* 31°10N 62°0E **122** D3
Chakonipau, L. *Canada* 56°18N 68°30W **165** A6
Chakradharpur *India* 22°45N 85°40E **125** H11
Chakrata *India* 30°42N 77°51E **124** D7
Chakwal *Pakistan* 32°56N 72°53E **124** C5
Chala *Peru* 15°48S 74°20W **188** D3
Chalais *France* 45°16N 0°3E **72** C4
Chalakudi *India* 10°18N 76°20E **127** J3
Chalchihuites *Mexico* 23°29N 103°53W **180** C4
Chalcis = Chalkida
　Greece 38°27N 23°42E **98** C5
Chaleur B. = Chaleur B.
　Canada 47°55N 65°30E **165** C6
Chalfant *U.S.A.* 37°32N 118°21W **170** H8
Chalhuanca *Peru* 14°15S 73°15W **188** C3
Chaliki *Greece* 39°36N 22°30E **98** B4
Chalindrey *France* 47°43N 5°26E **71** E12
Chaling *China* 26°58N 113°30E **117** D9
Chalisgaon *India* 20°30N 75°10E **126** D2
Chalk River *Canada* 46°1N 77°27W **164** C4
Chalkar, Ozero = Shalkar Köli
　Kazakhstan 50°35N 51°47E **86** E10
Chalki *Greece* 36°17N 27°36E **99** E9
Chalkida *Greece* 38°27N 23°42E **98** C5
Chalkidiki *Greece* 40°25N 23°20E **96** F7
Chalky Inlet *N.Z.* 46°3S 166°31E **155** G1
Challakere *India* 14°19N 76°39E **127** J3
Challans *France* 46°50N 1°52W **70** F5
Challapata *Bolivia* 18°53S 66°50W **186** G5
Challenger Deep
　Pac. Oc. 11°30N 142°0E **156** F6
Challenger Fracture Zone
　Pac. Oc. 35°0S 105°0W **157** L17
Challis *U.S.A.* 44°30N 114°14W **168** D6
Chalmette *U.S.A.* 29°56N 89°57W **177** G10
Chaloem Rattanakosin △
　Thailand 14°40N 99°17E **120** E2
Chalon-sur-Saône
　France 46°48N 4°50E **71** F11
Chalong *Thailand* 7°50N 98°22E **121** a
Chalonnes-sur-Loire
　France 47°20N 0°45W **70** E6
Châlons-en-Champagne
　France 48°58N 4°20E **71** D11
Châlten, Cerro = Fitz Roy, Cerro
　Argentina 49°17S 73°5W **192** C2
Châlus *France* 45°39N 0°58E **72** C4
Chālūs *Iran* 36°38N 51°26E **129** B6
Cham *Germany* 49°12N 12°39E **77** F8
Cham, Cu Lao *Vietnam* 15°57N 108°30E **120** E7
Chama *U.S.A.* 36°54N 106°35W **169** H10
Chamaicó *Argentina* 35°3S 64°58W **190** D3
Chaman *Pakistan* 30°58N 66°25E **124** D2
Chamba *India* 32°35N 76°10E **124** C7
Chamba *Tanzania* 11°37S 37°0E **143** E4
Chambal → *India* 26°29N 79°15E **125** F8
Chamberlain *U.S.A.* 43°49N 99°20W **172** D4
Chamberlain →
　Australia 15°30S 127°54E **148** C4
Chamberlain L.
　U.S.A. 46°14N 69°19W **173** B19
Chambers *U.S.A.* 35°11N 109°26W **169** J9
Chambersburg *U.S.A.* 39°56N 77°40W **173** F15
Chambéry *France* 45°34N 5°55E **73** C9
Chambeshi → *Zambia* 11°53S 29°48E **140** G6
Chambly *Canada* 45°27N 73°17W **175** A11
Chamblee *U.S.A.* 33°53N 84°18W **178** B5
Chambly *Canada* 45°27N 73°17W **175** A11
Chambord *Canada* 48°25N 72°6W **165** C5
Chambord *France* 47°37N 1°20E **71** E8
Chamela *Mexico* 19°32N 105°5W **180** D3
Chamical *Argentina* 30°22S 66°27W **190** C2
Chamili *Greece* 35°50N 26°15E **99** F8
Chamkar Luong
　Cambodia 11°0N 103°45E **121** G4
Chamoli *India* 30°24N 79°21E **125** D8
Chamonix-Mont Blanc
　France 45°55N 6°51E **73** C10
Chamouchouane =
　Ashuapmushuan →
　Canada 48°37N 72°20W **164** C5
Champa *India* 22°2N 82°43E **125** H10
Champagne *Canada* 60°49N 136°30W **162** A1
Champagne *France* 48°40N 4°20E **71** D11
Champagnole *France* 46°45N 5°55E **71** F12
Champaign *U.S.A.* 40°7N 88°15W **172** E9
Champaner *India* 22°29N 73°32E **124** H5
Champassak *Laos* 14°53N 105°52E **120** E5
Champaubert *France* 48°50N 3°45E **71** D10
Champdeniers-St-Denis
　France 46°29N 0°25W **72** B3
Champdoré, L. *Canada* 55°55N 65°49W **165** A6
Champeix *France* 45°37N 3°8E **72** C7
Champion *U.S.A.* 41°19N 80°51W **174** E4
Champlain *U.S.A.* 44°59N 73°27W **175** B11
Champlain, L. *U.S.A.* 44°40N 73°20W **175** B11
Champlitte *France* 47°32N 5°31E **71** E12

Champotón *Mexico* 19°21N 90°43W **181** D6
Champua *India* 22°5N 85°40E **125** H11
Chamrajnagar *India* 11°52N 76°52E **127** J3
Chamusca *Portugal* 39°21N 8°29W **89** F2
Chan Chan *Peru* 8°7S 79°0W **188** B2
Chana *Thailand* 6°55N 100°44E **121** J3
Chañaral *Chile* 26°23S 70°40W **190** B1
Chanārān *Iran* 36°39N 59°6E **129** B8
Chanasma *India* 23°44N 72°5E **124** H5
Chancay *Peru* 11°32S 77°25W **188** C2
Chancery Lane *Barbados* 13°3N 59°30W **183** g
Chanco *Chile* 35°44S 72°32W **190** D1
Chand *India* 21°57N 79°7E **125** J8
Chandan Chauki *India* 28°33N 80°47E **125** E9
Chandannagar *India* 22°52N 88°24E **125** H13
Chandausi *India* 28°27N 78°49E **125** E8
Chandeleur Is. *U.S.A.* 29°55N 88°57W **177** G10
Chandeleur Sd. *U.S.A.* 29°55N 89°0W **177** G10
Chandigarh *India* 30°43N 76°47E **124** D7
Chandil *India* 22°58N 86°3E **125** H12
Chandler *Australia* 27°0S 133°19E **151** D1
Chandler *Canada* 48°18N 64°46W **165** C7
Chandler Ariz., *U.S.A.* 33°18N 111°50W **169** K8
Chandler Okla., *U.S.A.* 35°42N 96°53W **176** D6
Chandless → *Brazil* 9°8S 69°51W **184** B4
Chandod *India* 21°59N 73°28E **124** J5
Chandpur *Bangla.* 23°8N 90°45E **123** H17
Chandra *India* 35°3N 26°9E **99** F8
Chandragiri *India* 13°35N 79°19E **127** H4
Chandrapur *India* 19°57N 79°25E **126** E4
Chandrupatla *India* 18°33N 80°24E **126** E5
Chānf *Iran* 26°38N 60°29E **129** E9
Chang *Pakistan* 26°59N 68°30E **124** F3
Chang, Ko *Thailand* 12°0N 102°23E **121** G4
Chang, Ko *Thailand* 9°50N 98°27E **121** H2
Ch'ang Chiang = Chang Jiang →
　China 31°48N 121°10E **117** B13
Chang Jiang →
　China 31°48N 121°10E **117** B13
Chang-won *S. Korea* 35°16N 128°37E **115** G15
Changan *China* 22°48N 113°48E **111** a
Changanacheri = Changanacheri
　India 9°25N 76°31E **127** K3
Changanassery = Changanacheri
　India 9°25N 76°31E **127** K3
Changane → *Mozam.* 24°30S 33°30E **145** B5
Changbai *China* 41°25N 128°5E **115** D15
Changbai Shan *China* 42°20N 129°0E **115** C15
Changchiak'ou = Zhangjiakou
　China 40°48N 114°55E **114** D8
Ch'angchou = Changzhou
　China 31°47N 119°58E **117** B12
Changchun *China* 43°57N 125°17E **115** C13
Changchunling
　China 45°18N 125°27E **115** B13
Changde *China* 29°4N 111°35E **117** C8
Changdo-ri *N. Korea* 38°30N 127°40E **115** E14
Changfeng *China* 32°28N 117°10E **117** A11
Changge *China* 34°13N 113°46E **114** G7
Changhai = Shanghai
　China 31°15N 121°26E **117** B13
Changhua *China* 30°12N 119°12E **117** B12
Changhua *Taiwan* 24°2N 120°30E **117** E13
Changhŭngni
　N. Korea 40°24N 128°19E **115** D15
Changi *Singapore* 1°23N 103°59E **121** d
Changi, Singapore ✈ (SIN)
　Singapore 1°23N 103°59E **121** M4
Changji *China* 44°1N 87°19E **109** E7
Changjiang *China* 19°20N 108°55E **117** a
Changjiang Shuiku
　China 22°29N 113°27E **111** a
Changjin *N. Korea* 40°23N 127°15E **115** D14
Changjin-ho *N. Korea* 40°30N 127°15E **115** D14
Changle *China* 25°59N 119°27E **117** E12
Changli *China* 39°40N 119°19E **115** E10
Changling *China* 44°20N 123°58E **115** B12
Changlun *Malaysia* 6°25N 100°26E **121** J3
Changning *Hunan,*
　China 26°28N 112°22E **117** D9
Changning *Sichuan,*
　China 28°40N 104°59E **116** C5
Changning *Yunnan,*
　China 24°45N 99°30E **116** E2
Changping *China* 40°14N 116°12E **114** D9
Changsha *China* 28°12N 113°0E **117** C9
Changshan *China* 28°55N 118°27E **117** C12
Changshan Qundao
　China 39°11N 122°32E **115** E12
Changshou *China* 30°50N 107°4E **116** C6
Changshu *China* 31°38N 120°43E **117** B13
Changsha *China* 23°16N 106°25E **116** D6
Changtai *China* 24°35N 117°42E **117** E11
Changtu *China* 42°46N 124°6E **115** C13
Changuinola *Panama* 9°26N 82°31W **182** E3
Changwu *Guangxi Zhuangzu,*
　China 23°25N 111°17E **117** F8
Changwu *Shaanxi,*
　China 35°10N 107°45E **114** G4
Changyang *China* 30°30N 111°10E **117** B8
Changyi *China* 36°40N 119°30E **115** F10
Changyŏn *N. Korea* 38°15N 125°6E **115** E13
Changzhi *China* 36°10N 113°6E **114** F7
Changzhou *China* 31°47N 119°58E **117** B12
Chanhanga *Angola* 16°0S 14°8E **144** A1
Chania *Greece* 35°30N 24°4E **101** D6
Chanion, Kolpos *Greece* 35°33N 23°55E **101** D5
Chanlar = Goygöl
　Azerbaijan 40°37N 46°12E **87** K8
Channagiri *India* 14°2N 75°56E **127** J2
Channapatna *India* 12°40N 77°15E **127** J3
Channel Is. *U.K.* 49°19N 2°24W **67** H5
Channel Is. *U.S.A.* 33°40N 119°15W **171** M7
Channel Islands △
　U.S.A. 34°0N 119°24W **171** L7
Channel-Port aux Basques
　Canada 47°30N 59°9W **165** C8
Channel Tunnel *Europe* 51°0N 1°30E **67** F9
Channing *U.S.A.* 35°41N 102°20W **176** D3
Chantada *Spain* 42°36N 7°46W **88** C3
Chanthaburi *Thailand* 12°38N 102°12E **120** F4
Chantilly *France* 49°12N 2°29E **71** C9
Chantonnay *France* 46°40N 1°3W **70** F5
Chantrey Inlet
　Canada 67°48N 96°20W **160** D12
Chanumla *India* 8°19N 93°5E **127** K11
Chanute *U.S.A.* 37°41N 95°27W **172** G6
Chany, Ozero *Russia* 54°49N 77°22E **108** D8
Chanza → *Spain* 37°32N 7°30W **89** H3

Chao Hu *China* 31°30N 117°30E **117** B11
Chao Phraya →
Thailand 13°40N 100°31E **120** F3
Chao Phraya Lowlands
Thailand 15°30N 100°0E **120** E3
Chaocheng *China* 36°4N 115°37E **114** F8
Chaohu *China* 31°38N 117°50E **117** B11
Chaouia-Ouardigha □
Morocco 33°0N 7°30W **136** B2
Chaoyang *Guangdong,*
China 23°17N 116°30E **117** F11
Chaoyang *Liaoning,*
China 41°35N 120°22E **115** D11
Chaozhou *China* 23°42N 116°32E **117** F11
Chapada Diamantina △
Brazil 12°52S 41°30W **189** C2
Chapada dos Veadeiros △
Brazil 14°0S 47°30W **189** C1
Chapaev *Kazakhstan* 50°25N 51°10E **86** E10
Chapais *Canada* 49°47N 74°51W **164** C5
Chapala *Mozam.* 15°50S 37°35E **143** F4
Chapala, L. de *Mexico* 20°15N 103°0W **180** C4
Chapayevsk *Russia* 53°0N 49°40E **86** D9
Chapecó *Brazil* 27°14S 52°41W **191** B5
Chapel Hill *U.S.A.* 35°55N 79°4W **177** D15
Chapleau *Canada* 47°50N 83°24W **164** C3
Chaplin *Canada* 50°28N 106°40W **163** C7
Chaplin L. *Canada* 50°22N 106°36W **163** C7
Chaplino *Ukraine* 48°8N 36°15E **85** H9
Chaplygin *Russia* 53°15N 40°0E **84** F11
Chappell *U.S.A.* 41°6N 102°28W **172** E2
Chappells *U.S.A.* 34°11N 81°52W **178** A8
Chapra = Chhapra
India 25°48N 84°44E **125** G11
Chaqâbel *Iran* 33°16N 47°30E **105** F12
Chara *Russia* 56°54N 118°20E **107** D12
Charadai *Argentina* 27°35S 59°55W **190** B4
Charagua *Bolivia* 19°45S 63°10W **186** G6
Charakas *Greece* 35°1N 25°7E **101** D7
Charambirá, Punta
Colombia 4°16N 77°32W **186** C3
Charaña *Bolivia* 17°30S 69°25W **188** D4
Charantsavan *Armenia* 40°35N 44°41E **87** K7
Charanwala *India* 27°51N 72°10E **124** F5
Charata *Argentina* 27°13S 61°14W **190** B3
Charcas *Mexico* 23°8N 101°7W **180** C4
Charcot I. *Antarctica* 70°0S 70°0W **55** C17
Chard *U.K.* 50°52N 2°58W **67** G5
Chardon *U.S.A.* 41°35N 81°12W **174** E3
Chardzhou = Türkmenabat
Turkmenistan 39°6N 63°34E **129** B9
Charente □ *France* 45°50N 0°16E **72** C4
Charente → *France* 45°57N 1°5W **72** C2
Charente-Maritime □
France 45°45N 0°45W **72** C3
Charenton-du-Cher
France 46°44N 2°39E **71** F9
Chari → *Chad* 12°58N 14°31E **135** F8
Chārīkār *Afghan.* 35°0N 69°10E **109** E7
Charing *U.K.* 51°12N 0°49E **67** F8
Chariton *U.S.A.* 41°1N 93°19W **172** E7
Chariton → *U.S.A.* 39°19N 92°58W **172** F7
Chärjew = Türkmenabat
Turkmenistan 39°6N 63°34E **129** B9
Charkhari *India* 25°24N 79°45E **125** G8
Charkhi Dadri *India* 28°37N 76°17E **124** E7
Charleroi *Belgium* 50°24N 4°27E **69** D4
Charleroi *U.S.A.* 40°9N 79°57W **174** F5
Charles, C. *U.S.A.* 37°7N 75°58W **173** G16
Charles, Peak
Australia 32°52S 121°11E **149** F3
Charles City *U.S.A.* 43°4N 92°41W **172** D7
Charles de Gaulle, Paris ✈ (CDG)
France 49°0N 2°32E **71** D9
Charles L. *Canada* 62°39N 74°15W **161** E17
Charles L. *Canada* 59°50N 110°33W **163** B6
Charles Sound *N.Z.* 45°3S 167°4E **155** F2
Charles Town *U.S.A.* 39°17N 77°16W **173** F15
Charlesbourg *Canada* 46°51N 71°16W **173** B18
Charleston *Ill., U.S.A.* 39°30N 88°10W **172** F9
Charleston *Miss., U.S.A.* 34°1N 90°4W **177** D9
Charleston *Mo., U.S.A.* 36°55N 89°21W **172** G9
Charleston *S.C.,*
U.S.A. 32°46N 79°56W **178** C10
Charleston *W. Va.,*
U.S.A. 38°21N 81°38W **173** F13
Charleston L. *Canada* 44°32N 76°0W **175** B9
Charleston Peak
U.S.A. 36°16N 115°42W **171** J11
Charlestown *Ireland* 53°58N 8°48W **64** C3
Charlestown *S. Africa* 27°26S 29°53E **145** C4
Charlestown *Ind.,*
U.S.A. 38°27N 85°40W **173** F11
Charlestown *N.H.,*
U.S.A. 43°14N 72°25W **175** C12
Charlestown of Aberlour
U.K. 57°28N 3°14W **65** D5
Charleville *Australia* 26°24S 146°15E **151** D4
Charleville *Ireland* 52°21N 8°40W **64** D3
Charleville-Mézières
France 49°44N 4°40E **71** C11
Charlevoix *U.S.A.* 45°19N 85°16W **173** C11
Charlie Gibbs Fracture Zone
Atl. Oc. 52°45N 39°30W **56** A8
Charlieu *France* 46°10N 4°10E **71** F11
Charlotte *Mich.,*
U.S.A. 42°34N 84°50W **173** D11
Charlotte *N.C., U.S.A.* 35°13N 80°50W **177** D14
Charlotte *Vt., U.S.A.* 44°19N 73°16W **175** B11
Charlotte Amalie
U.S. Virgin Is. 18°21N 64°56W **183** e
Charlotte Harbor *U.S.A.* 26°57N 82°4W **179** J7
Charlotte L. *Canada* 52°12N 125°19W **162** C3
Charlottenberg *Sweden* 59°54N 12°17E **62** E6
Charlottesville *U.S.A.* 38°2N 78°30W **173** F14
Charlottetown *Nfld. & L.,*
Canada 52°46N 56°7W **165** B8
Charlottetown *P.E.I.,*
Canada 46°14N 63°8W **165** C7
Charlotteville
Trin. & Tob. 11°20N 60°33W **187** J16
Charlton *Australia* 36°16S 143°24E **152** D5
Charlton I. *Canada* 52°0N 79°20W **164** B4
Charmes *France* 48°22N 6°17E **71** D13
Charny *Canada* 46°43N 71°15W **173** B19
Charnyanski *Belarus* 51°59N 24°12E **83** G11
Charolles *France* 46°27N 4°16E **71** F11
Chârost *France* 47°0N 2°7E **71** F9
Charouïne *Algeria* 29°0N 0°15W **136** C5
Charre *Mozam.* 17°13S 35°10E **143** F4
Charroux *France* 46°9N 0°25E **72** B4

Charsadda *Pakistan* 34°7N 71°45E **124** B4
Charters Towers
Australia 20°5S 146°13E **150** C4
Chartres *France* 48°29N 1°30E **70** D8
Chartreuse △ *France* 45°22N 5°42E **73** C9
Charysh → *Russia* 52°22N 83°45E **109** B10
Chascomús *Argentina* 35°30S 58°0W **190** D4
Chase *Canada* 50°50N 119°41W **162** C5
Chasefu *Zambia* 11°55S 33°8E **143** E3
Chashma Barrage
Pakistan 32°27N 71°20E **124** C4
Chaslands Mistake
N.Z. 46°38S 169°22E **155** G4
Chasseneuil-sur-Bonnieure
France 45°52N 0°29E **72** C4
Chât *Iran* 37°59N 55°16E **129** B7
Chatal Balkan = Udvoy Balkan
Bulgaria 42°50N 26°50E **97** D10
Château-Arnoux-St-Auban
France 44°6N 6°0E **73** D10
Château-Chinon *France* 47°4N 3°56E **71** E10
Château-d'Olonne
France 46°30N 1°44W **72** B2
Château-du-Loir *France* 47°40N 0°25E **70** E7
Château-Gontier *France* 47°50N 0°48W **70** E6
Château-la-Vallière
France 47°30N 0°20E **70** E7
Château-Landon *France* 48°8N 2°40E **71** D9
Château-Renard *France* 47°56N 2°55E **71** E9
Château-Renault *France* 47°36N 0°56E **70** E7
Château-Salins *France* 48°50N 6°30E **71** D13
Château-Thierry *France* 49°3N 3°20E **71** C10
Châteaubourg *France* 48°7N 1°25W **70** D5
Châteaubriant *France* 47°43N 1°23W **70** E5
Châteaudun *France* 48°3N 1°20E **70** D8
Châteaugay *U.S.A.* 44°56N 74°5W **175** B10
Châteaugiron *France* 48°3N 1°30W **70** D5
Châteaulin *France* 48°11N 4°8W **70** D2
Châteaumeillant *France* 46°35N 2°12E **71** F9
Châteauneuf-du-Faou
France 48°11N 3°50W **70** D3
Châteauneuf-sur-Charente
France 45°36N 0°3W **72** C3
Châteauneuf-sur-Cher
France 46°52N 2°18E **71** F9
Châteauneuf-sur-Loire
France 47°52N 2°13E **71** E9
Châteaurenard *France* 43°53N 4°51E **73** E8
Châteauroux *France* 46°50N 1°40E **71** F8
Châteauvillain *France* 48°2N 4°56E **71** D11
Châteaux, Pte. des
Guadeloupe 16°15N 61°10W **182** b
Châtel-Guyon *France* 45°55N 3°4E **72** C7
Châtelaillon-Plage *France* 46°5N 1°5W **72** B2
Châtellerault *France* 46°50N 0°30E **70** F7
Châtelus-Malvaleix *France* 46°18N 2°1E **71** F9
Chatham = Miramichi
Canada 47°2N 65°28W **165** C6
Chatham *Canada* 42°24N 82°11W **174** D2
Chatham *U.K.* 51°22N 0°32E **67** F8
Chatham *U.S.A.* 42°21N 73°36W **175** D11
Chatham, I. *Chile* 50°40S 74°25W **192** D2
Chatham Is. *Pac. Oc.* 44°0S 176°40W **155** c
Chatham Rise *Pac. Oc.* 43°0S 180°0E **156** M10
Châtillon *Italy* 45°45N 7°37E **92** C4
Châtillon-Coligny *France* 47°50N 2°51E **71** E9
Châtillon-en-Diois *France* 44°41N 5°29E **73** D9
Châtillon-sur-Indre
France 46°59N 1°10E **70** F8
Châtillon-sur-Loire
France 47°35N 2°44E **71** E9
Châtillon-sur-Seine
France 47°50N 4°33E **71** E11
Chatmohar *Bangla.* 24°15N 89°15E **125** G13
Chatra *India* 24°12N 84°56E **125** G11
Chatrapur *India* 19°22N 85°2E **126** E7
Chats, L. des *Canada* 45°30N 76°20W **175** A8
Chatsu *India* 26°36N 75°57E **124** F6
Chatsworth *Canada* 44°27N 80°54W **174** B4
Chatsworth *Zimbabwe* 19°38S 31°13E **143** G3
Châttagām = Chittagong
Bangla. 22°19N 91°48E **123** H17
Chattahoochee *U.S.A.* 30°42N 84°51W **178** E5
Chattahoochee →
U.S.A. 30°54N 84°57W **178** E5
Chattanooga *U.S.A.* 35°3N 85°19W **177** D12
Chatteris *U.K.* 52°28N 0°2E **67** E8
Chatturat *Thailand* 15°40N 101°51E **120** E3
Chau Doc *Vietnam* 10°42N 105°7E **121** G5
Chaudes-Aigues *France* 44°51N 3°1E **72** D7
Chauffailles *France* 46°13N 4°21E **71** F11
Chaukan Pass *Burma* 27°8N 97°10E **123** F20
Chaumont *France* 48°7N 5°8E **71** D12
Chaumont *U.S.A.* 44°4N 76°8W **175** B8
Chaumont-en-Vexin
France 49°16N 1°53E **71** C8
Chaumont-sur-Loire
France 47°29N 1°11E **70** E8
Chaunay *France* 46°13N 0°9E **72** B4
Chaunskaya G. *Russia* 69°0N 169°0E **107** C17
Chauny *France* 49°37N 3°12E **71** C10
Chaura *India* 8°27N 93°2E **127** K11
Chausey, Îs. *France* 48°52N 1°49W **70** D5
Chaussin *France* 46°59N 5°22E **71** F12
Chautara *Nepal* 27°46N 85°42E **125** F11
Chautauqua L. *U.S.A.* 42°10N 79°24W **174** D5
Chauvigny *France* 46°34N 0°39E **70** F7
Chavakachcheri
Sri Lanka 9°39N 80°9E **127** K5
Chavanges *France* 48°30N 4°35E **71** D11
Chavash Varmane □
Russia 54°50N 47°10E **86** C8
Chaves *Brazil* 0°15S 49°55W **187** D9
Chaves *Portugal* 41°45N 7°32W **91** B3
Chavin *Peru* 9°35S 77°10W **188** B2
Chawang *Thailand* 8°25N 99°30E **121** H2
Chazelles-sur-Lyon
France 45°39N 4°22E **73** C8
Chazuta *Peru* 6°30S 76°0W **188** B2
Chazy *U.S.A.* 44°53N 73°26W **175** B11
Cheaha Mt. *U.S.A.* 33°29N 85°49W **178** B4
Cheb *Czech Rep.* 50°9N 12°28E **78** A5
Chebbi, *Erg* *Algeria* 31°12N 3°58W **136** B3
Cheboksarskoye Vdkhr.
Russia 56°13N 46°58E **86** B8
Cheboksary *Russia* 56°8N 47°12E **86** B8
Cheboygan *U.S.A.* 45°39N 84°29W **173** C11
Chebsara *Russia* 59°10N 38°59E **84** C11
Chech, Erg *Africa* 25°0N 2°15W **136** D5

Chechelnyk *Ukraine* 48°13N 29°22E **81** B14
Chechen, Ostrov *Russia* 43°59N 47°40E **87** H8
Chechenia □ *Russia* 43°30N 45°29E **87** J7
Checheno-Ingush Republic =
Chechenia □ *Russia* 43°30N 45°29E **87** J7
Chęciny *Poland* 50°46N 20°28E **83** H7
Checotah *U.S.A.* 35°28N 95°31W **176** D7
Chedabucto B. *Canada* 45°25N 61°8W **165** C7
Cheduba I. *Burma* 18°45N 93°40E **123** K18
Cheekowaga *U.S.A.* 42°54N 78°45W **174** D6
Cheepie *Australia* 26°33S 145°0E **151** D4
Chef-Boutonne *France* 46°7N 0°4W **72** B3
Chefchaouen *Morocco* 35°9N 5°15W **136** A2
Chegdomyn *Russia* 51°7N 133°1E **107** D14
Chegga *Mauritania* 25°27N 5°40W **134** C4
Chegutu *Zimbabwe* 18°10S 30°14E **143** F3
Chehalis *U.S.A.* 46°40N 122°58W **170** D2
Chehalis → *U.S.A.* 46°57N 123°50W **170** D2
Cheile Bicazului-Hăşmaş △
Romania 46°55N 25°50E **81** D10
Cheile Nerei-Beusniţa △
Romania 44°56N 21°52E **80** F6
Cheiron, Mt. du *France* 43°49N 6°58E **73** E10
Cheju = Jeju *S. Korea* 33°31N 126°32E **115** H14
Cheju-do = Jeju-do
S. Korea 33°29N 126°34E **115** H14
Cheju Str. = Jeju Haehyop
S. Korea 33°30N 126°30E **115** H14
Chek Lap Kok *China* 22°18N 113°56E **111** a
Chek Lap Kok ✈ (HKG)
China 22°19N 113°57E **111** a
Chekalin *Russia* 54°10N 36°10E **84** E9
Chekhovo *Russia* 54°33N 20°43E **82** D7
Chekiang = Zhejiang □
China 29°0N 120°0E **117** C13
Chela, Sa. da *Angola* 16°20S 13°20E **144** A1
Chelan *U.S.A.* 47°51N 120°1W **168** C3
Chelan, L. *U.S.A.* 48°11N 120°30W **168** B3
Cheleken = Hazar
Turkmenistan 39°34N 53°16E **108** E4
Cheleken Yarymadasy
Turkmenistan 39°30N 53°15E **129** B7
Chelforó *Argentina* 39°0S 66°33W **192** A3
Chéliff, O. → *Algeria* 36°0N 0°8E **136** A4
Chelkar = Shalqar
Kazakhstan 47°48N 59°39E **108** C5
Chellala Dahrania *Algeria* 33°2N 0°1E **136** B4
Chelles *France* 48°53N 2°35E **71** D9
Chelm *Poland* 51°8N 23°30E **83** G10
Chełmno *Poland* 53°20N 18°30E **83** E5
Chelmsford *U.K.* 51°44N 0°29E **67** F8
Chełmża *Poland* 53°10N 18°39E **83** E5
Chelsea *Australia* 38°5S 145°8E **153** E6
Chelsea *U.S.A.* 43°59N 72°27W **175** C12
Cheltenham *U.K.* 51°54N 2°4W **67** F5
Chelva *Spain* 39°45N 1°0W **91** C5
Chelyabinsk *Russia* 55°10N 61°24E **108** A6
Chelyuskin, C. = Chelyuskin, Mys
Russia 77°30N 103°0E **107** B11
Chelyuskin, Mys
Russia 77°30N 103°0E **107** B11
Chemainus *Canada* 48°55N 123°42W **170** B3
Chemba *Mozam.* 17°9S 34°53E **141** H6
Chembar = Belinskiy
Russia 53°0N 43°25E **86** D6
Chemillé *France* 47°14N 0°45W **70** E6
Chemin Grenier
Mauritius 20°29S 57°28E **141** d
Chemnitz *Germany* 50°51N 12°54E **76** E8
Chemult *U.S.A.* 43°14N 121°47W **168** E3
Chen, Gora *Russia* 65°16N 141°50E **107** C15
Chenab → *Pakistan* 30°23N 71°2E **124** D4
Chenab Nagar *Pakistan* 31°45N 72°55E **124** D5
Chenachane *Algeria* 26°0N 4°15W **136** C3
Chenachane, O. →
Algeria 25°20N 3°20W **136** C3
Chenango Forks
U.S.A. 42°15N 75°51W **175** D9
Chenchiang = Zhenjiang
China 32°11N 119°26E **117** A12
Cheney *U.S.A.* 47°30N 117°35W **168** C5
Cheng Xian *China* 33°43N 105°42E **114** H3
Chengalpattu *India* 12°42N 79°58E **127** H4
Chengbu *China* 26°18N 110°16E **117** C8
Chengcheng *China* 35°8N 109°56E **114** G5
Chengchou = Zhengzhou
China 34°45N 113°34E **114** G7
Chengde *China* 40°59N 117°58E **115** D9
Chengdong Hu *China* 32°15N 116°20E **117** A11
Chengdu *China* 30°38N 104°2E **116** B5
Chenggong *China* 24°58N 102°56E **116** E4
Chenggu *China* 33°10N 107°21E **116** A6
Chenghai *China* 23°30N 116°42E **117** F11
Chengjiang *China* 24°39N 103°0E **116** E4
Chengkou *China* 31°54N 108°31E **116** B7
Chengmai *China* 19°50N 109°58E **117** a
Chengshan Jiao
China 37°25N 122°44E **115** F12
Ch'engtu = Chengdu
China 30°38N 104°2E **116** B5
Chengwu *China* 34°58N 115°50E **114** G8
Chengxi Hu *China* 32°15N 116°10E **117** A11
Chengyang *China* 36°18N 120°21E **115** F11
Chenjiagang *China* 34°23N 119°47E **115** G10
Chenkaladi *Sri Lanka* 7°47N 81°35E **127** L5
Chennai *India* 13°8N 80°19E **127** H5
Chenôve *France* 47°16N 5°1E **71** E12
Chenxi *China* 28°2N 110°12E **117** C8
Chenzhou *China* 25°47N 113°1E **117** E9

Cheraw *U.S.A.* 34°42N 79°53W **177** D15
Cherbourg-Octeville
France 49°39N 1°40W **70** C5
Cherchell *Algeria* 36°35N 2°12E **136** A4
Cherdakly *Russia* 54°25N 48°50E **86** C9
Cherdyn *Russia* 60°24N 56°29E **106** C6
Cheremkhovo *Russia* 53°8N 103°1E **110** A9
Cherepanovo *Russia* 54°15N 83°30E **109** B10
Cherepovets *Russia* 59°5N 37°55E **84** C9
Chergui, Chott ech
Algeria 34°21N 0°25E **136** B4
Chergui, Zahrez *Algeria* 35°11N 3°31E **136** A4
Cherial *India* 17°55N 78°59E **126** F4
Cherikov = Cherykaw
Belarus 53°32N 31°20E **75** D15
Cheriyam I. *India* 10°9N 73°10E **127** J1
Cherkasy *Ukraine* 49°27N 32°4E **85** H7
Cherkasy □ *Ukraine* 48°55N 30°50E **85** H6
Cherkessk *Russia* 44°15N 42°5E **87** H6
Cherla *India* 18°5N 80°49E **126** E5
Cherlak *Russia* 54°15N 74°55E **109** B8
Chernaya *Russia* 70°30N 89°10E **107** B9
Chernelytsya *Ukraine* 48°49N 25°26E **81** D8
Cherni *Bulgaria* 42°35N 23°18E **96** D7
Chernigov = Chernihiv
Ukraine 51°28N 31°20E **85** G6
Chernigovka *Russia* 44°19N 132°34E **112** B6
Chernihiv *Ukraine* 51°28N 31°20E **85** G6
Chernihiv □ *Ukraine* 51°10N 32°5E **85** G7
Chernivtsi *Ukraine* 48°15N 25°52E **81** D8
Chernivtsi = Chernivtsi
Ukraine 48°15N 25°52E **81** D8
Chernivtsi *Ukraine* 48°32N 28°9E **81** B13
Chernivtsi □ *Ukraine* 48°15N 25°30E **81** B10
Chernobyl = Chornobyl
Ukraine 51°20N 30°15E **75** C16
Chernogorsk *Russia* 53°49N 91°18E **109** B12
Chernomorskoye =
Chornomorske
Ukraine 45°31N 32°40E **85** K7
Chernovtsy = Chernivtsi
Ukraine 48°15N 25°52E **81** D8
Chernyakhovsk *Russia* 54°36N 21°48E **82** D8
Chernyanka *Russia* 50°56N 37°49E **85** G9
Chernysheyskiy
Russia 63°0N 112°30E **107** C12
Chernyye Zemli *Russia* 46°10N 46°0E **87** H8
Cherokee *Iowa, U.S.A.* 42°45N 95°33W **172** D6
Cherokee *Okla., U.S.A.* 36°45N 98°21W **176** C5
Cherokee Village
U.S.A. 36°18N 91°31W **176** C9
Cherokees, Grand Lake O' The
U.S.A. 36°28N 94°55W **176** C7
Cherquenco *Chile* 38°35S 72°0W **192** A2
Cherrapunji *India* 25°17N 91°47E **123** G17
Cherry Valley *U.S.A.* 42°48N 74°45W **175** D10
Cherskiy *Russia* 68°45N 161°18E **107** C17
Cherskogo Khrebet
Russia 65°0N 143°0E **107** C15
Cherso *Greece* 41°5N 22°47E **96** C6
Chersonisos *Greece* 35°18N 25°22E **101** D7
Chersonisos Akrotiri
Greece 35°30N 24°10E **101** D6
Cherthala *India* 9°42N 76°20E **127** K3
Chertkovo *Russia* 49°25N 40°19E **85** H11
Cherven *Belarus* 53°45N 28°28E **75** B15
Cherven-Bryag *Bulgaria* 43°17N 24°7E **97** C8
Chervonoarmiyske
Ukraine 45°47N 28°44E **81** E13
Chervonohrad *Ukraine* 50°25N 24°10E **75** C13
Cherwell → *U.K.* 51°44N 1°14W **67** F6
Cherykaw *Belarus* 53°32N 31°20E **75** D16
Chesapeake *U.S.A.* 36°49N 76°16W **173** G15
Chesapeake B. *U.S.A.* 38°0N 76°10W **173** F14
Cheshire East □ *U.K.* 53°15N 2°15W **66** D5
Cheshire West and Chester □
U.K. 53°15N 2°40W **66** D5
Cheshskaya Guba
Russia 67°20N 47°0E **106** C5
Cheshunt *U.K.* 51°43N 0°1W **67** F7
Chesil Beach *U.K.* 50°37N 2°33W **67** G5
Chesley *Canada* 44°17N 81°5W **174** B3
Cheste *Spain* 39°30N 0°41W **91** C5
Chester *U.K.* 53°12N 2°53W **66** D5
Chester *Calif., U.S.A.* 40°19N 121°14W **168** F3
Chester *Ga., U.S.A.* 32°24N 83°9W **178** D6
Chester *Ill., U.S.A.* 37°55N 89°49W **172** G9
Chester *Mont., U.S.A.* 48°31N 110°58W **168** B8
Chester *Pa., U.S.A.* 39°51N 75°22W **173** F16
Chester *S.C., U.S.A.* 34°43N 81°12W **177** D13
Chester *Vt., U.S.A.* 43°16N 72°36W **175** C12
Chester *W. Va., U.S.A.* 40°37N 80°34W **174** F4
Chester-le-Street *U.K.* 54°51N 1°34W **66** C6
Chesterfield *U.K.* 53°15N 1°25W **66** D6
Chesterfield, Îs. *N. Cal.* 19°52S 158°15E **147** C8
Chesterfield Inlet
Canada 63°30N 90°45W **160** E13
Chesterton Ra.
Australia 25°30S 147°27E **151** D4
Chesterton Range △
Australia 26°16S 147°22E **151** D4
Chestertown *U.S.A.* 43°40N 73°48W **175** C11
Chesterville *Canada* 45°6N 75°14W **175** A9
Chesuncook L. *U.S.A.* 46°0N 69°21W **173** B19
Chetamale *India* 10°43N 92°32E **127** J11
Chéticamp *Canada* 46°37N 60°59W **165** C7
Chetlat I. *India* 11°42N 72°42E **127** J1
Chetrosu *Moldova* 48°5N 27°54E **81** A13
Chetumal *Mexico* 18°30N 88°20W **181** D7
Chetumal, B. de
Cent. Amer. 18°40N 88°10W **181** D7
Chetwynd *Canada* 55°45N 121°36W **162** B4
Cheung Chau *China* 22°13N 114°1E **111** a
Chevanceaux *France* 45°18N 0°14W **72** C3
Cheviot, The *U.K.* 55°29N 2°9W **66** B5
Cheviot Hills *U.K.* 55°20N 2°30W **66** B5
Cheviot Ra. *Australia* 25°20S 143°45E **150** D3
Chew Bahir *Ethiopia* 4°40N 36°50E **136** F4
Chewelah *U.S.A.* 48°17N 117°43W **168** B5
Chewore *Zimbabwe* 16°0S 29°52E **143** F2
Cheyenne *Okla., U.S.A.* 35°37N 99°40W **176** D5
Cheyenne *Wyo.,*
U.S.A. 41°8N 104°49W **168** F11
Cheyenne → *U.S.A.* 44°41N 101°18W **172** C3
Cheyenne Wells
U.S.A. 38°49N 102°21W **168** G12
Cheyne B. *Australia* 34°35S 118°50E **149** F2
Cheyur *India* 12°21N 80°0E **127** H5
Chhabra *India* 24°40N 76°54E **124** G7
Chhaktala *India* 22°6N 74°11E **124** H6
Chhapra *India* 25°48N 84°44E **125** G11

Chhata *India* 27°42N 77°30E **124** F7
Chhatarpur *Jharkhand,*
India 24°23N 84°11E **125** G11
Chhatarpur *Mad. P.,*
India 24°55N 79°35E **125** G8
Chhati *India* 20°47N 81°40E **126** D5
Chhattisgarh □ *India* 22°0N 82°0E **125** J10
Chhep *Cambodia* 13°45N 105°24E **120** F5
Chhindwara *Mad. P.,*
India 22°3N 79°29E **125** H8
Chhindwara *Mad. P.,*
India 22°2N 78°59E **125** H8
Chhlong *Cambodia* 12°15N 105°58E **121** F5
Chhota Tawa → *India* 22°14N 76°36E **124** H7
Chhoti Kali Sindh →
India 24°2N 75°31E **124** G6
Chhuikhadan *India* 21°32N 80°59E **125** J9
Chhuk *Cambodia* 10°46N 104°28E **121** G5
Chi → *Thailand* 15°11N 104°43E **120** E5
Chi Thanh *Vietnam* 13°17N 109°16E **120** F7
Chiai *Taiwan* 23°29N 120°25E **117** F13
Chiali *Taiwan* 23°8N 120°10E **117** F13
Chianciano Terme *Italy* 43°2N 11°49E **93** E8
Chiang Dao *Thailand* 19°22N 98°58E **120** C2
Chiang Dao, Doi
Thailand 19°23N 98°54E **120** C2
Chiang Kham
Thailand 19°32N 100°18E **120** C3
Chiang Khan *Thailand* 17°52N 101°36E **120** D3
Chiang Khong
Thailand 20°17N 100°24E **116** G3
Chiang Mai *Thailand* 18°47N 98°59E **120** C2
Chiang Rai *Thailand* 19°52N 99°50E **116** H2
Chiang Saen *Thailand* 20°16N 100°5E **116** G3
Chianti *Italy* 43°20N 11°18E **93** E8
Chiapa de Corzo *Mexico* 16°42N 93°0W **181** D6
Chiapas □ *Mexico* 16°30N 92°30W **181** D6
Chiapas, Sa. Madre de
Mexico 15°40N 93°0W **181** D6
Chiaramonte Gulfi *Italy* 37°2N 14°42E **95** E7
Chiaravalle *Italy* 43°36N 13°19E **93** E10
Chiaravalle Centrale
Italy 38°41N 16°25E **95** D9
Chiari *Italy* 45°32N 9°56E **92** C6
Chiatura *Georgia* 42°15N 43°17E **87** J6
Chiautla de Tapia
Mexico 18°18N 98°36E **181** D5
Chiávari *Italy* 44°19N 9°19E **92** D6
Chiavenna *Italy* 46°19N 9°24E **92** B6
Chiba *Japan* 35°30N 140°7E **113** G10
Chiba □ *Japan* 35°30N 140°20E **113** G10
Chibabava *Mozam.* 20°17S 33°35E **145** B5
Chibemba *Cunene, Angola* 15°48S 14°8E **141** H2
Chibemba *Huila, Angola* 16°20S 15°20E **144** A2
Chibi *Zimbabwe* 20°18S 30°25E **145** B5
Chibia *Angola* 15°10S 13°42E **141** H2
Chibougamau *Canada* 49°56N 74°24W **164** C5
Chibougamau, L.
Canada 49°50N 74°20W **164** C5
Chibuk *Nigeria* 10°52N 12°50E **139** C7
Chibuto *Mozam.* 24°40S 33°33E **145** B5
Chic-Chocs, Mts.
Canada 48°55N 66°0W **165** C6
Chicacole = Srikakulam
India 18°14N 83°58E **126** E6
Chicago *U.S.A.* 41°52N 87°38W **172** E10
Chicago Heights
U.S.A. 41°30N 87°38W **172** E10
Chichagof I. *U.S.A.* 57°30N 135°30W **160** F4
Chichaoua *Morocco* 31°32N 8°44W **136** B4
Chichawatni *Pakistan* 30°32N 72°42E **124** D5
Chichén-Itzá *Mexico* 20°37N 88°35W **181** C7
Chicheng *China* 40°55N 115°55E **114** D8
Chichester *U.K.* 50°50N 0°47W **67** G7
Chichester Ra.
Australia 22°12S 119°15E **148** D2
Chichibu *Japan* 35°59N 139°10E **113** F9
Chichibu-Tama-Kai △
Japan 35°52N 138°42E **113** G9
Ch'ich'ihaerh = Qiqihar
China 47°26N 124°0E **111** B13
Chichisal *India* 22°1N 77°40E **124** H8
Chickasaw △ *U.S.A.* 34°26N 97°0W **176** D6
Chickasha *U.S.A.* 35°3N 97°58W **176** D6
Chiclana de la Frontera
Spain 36°26N 6°9W **89** J4
Chiclayo *Peru* 6°42S 79°50W **188** B2
Chico *U.S.A.* 39°44N 121°50W **170** F5
Chico → *Chubut,*
Argentina 44°0S 67°0W **192** D3
Chico → *Santa Cruz,*
Argentina 50°0S 68°30W **192** D3
Chicoa *Mozam.* 15°36S 32°20E **143** F3
Chicomo *Mozam.* 24°31S 34°6E **145** B5
Chicomostoc *Mexico* 22°28N 102°46W **180** C4
Chicontepec *Mexico* 20°58N 98°10W **181** C5
Chicopee *U.S.A.* 42°9N 72°37W **175** D12
Chicoutimi *Canada* 48°28N 71°5W **165** C5
Chicualacuala *Mozam.* 22°6S 31°42E **145** B5
Chidambaram *India* 11°20N 79°45E **127** J4
Chidenguele *Mozam.* 24°55S 34°11E **145** B5
Chidley, C. *Canada* 60°23N 64°26W **161** E19
Chiducuane *Mozam.* 24°35S 34°25E **145** B5
Chiede *Angola* 17°15S 16°22E **144** A2
Chiefland *U.S.A.* 29°29N 82°52W **179** F7
Chiefs Pt. *Canada* 44°41N 81°18W **174** B3
Chiem Hoa *Vietnam* 22°12N 105°17E **120** A5
Chiemsee *Germany* 47°53N 12°28E **77** H8
Chiengi *Zambia* 8°45S 29°10E **143** D2
Chiengmai = Chiang Mai
Thailand 18°47N 98°59E **120** C2
Chienti → *Italy* 43°18N 13°45E **93** E10
Chieri *Italy* 45°1N 7°49E **92** C4
Chiers → *France* 49°39N 4°59E **71** C11
Chiesa in Valmalenco
Italy 46°16N 9°51E **92** B6
Chiese → *Italy* 45°8N 10°25E **92** C7
Chieti *Italy* 42°21N 14°10E **93** F11
Chifeng *China* 42°18N 118°58E **115** C10
Chigirin *Ukraine* 49°4N 32°38E **85** H7
Chignecto B. *Canada* 45°30N 64°40W **165** C7
Chiguana *Bolivia* 21°0S 67°58W **190** A2
Chigwell *U.K.* 51°37N 0°6E **67** F8
Chihli, G. of = Bo Hai
China 39°0N 119°0E **115** E10
Chihuahua *Mexico* 28°38N 106°5W **180** B3
Chihuahua □ *Mexico* 28°30N 106°0W **180** B3
Chiili = Sheli
Kazakhstan 44°20N 66°15E **109** E7
Chik Bollapur *India* 13°25N 77°45E **127** H3

Chikalda *India* 21°24N 77°19E **126** A3
Chikhli *Ahmadabad, India* 20°45N 73°4E **126** D1
Chikhli *Maharashtra,*
India 20°20N 76°18E **126** D3
Chiknayakanhalli
India 13°26N 76°37E **127** H3
Chikmagalur *India* 13°15N 75°45E **127** H2
Chikmagalur *India* 16°26N 74°38E **127** F2
Chiknayakanhalli
India ——
Chikodi *India* 16°26N 74°38E **127** F2
Chikwawa *Malawi* 16°2S 34°50E **143** F3
Chilanga *Zambia* 15°33S 28°16E **143** F2
Chilapa *Mexico* 17°36N 99°10W **181** D5
Chilas *Pakistan* 35°25N 74°5E **125** B6
Chilaw *Sri Lanka* 7°30N 79°50E **127** L4
Chilcotin → *Canada* 51°44N 122°23E **162** C4
Childers *Australia* 25°15S 152°17E **151** D5
Childersburg *U.S.A.* 33°16N 86°21W **178** B3
Childress *U.S.A.* 34°25N 100°13W **176** D4
Chile ■ *S. Amer.* 35°0S 72°0W **185** G3
Chile Chico *Chile* 46°33S 71°44W **192** C2
Chile Rise *Pac. Oc.* 38°0S 92°0W **157** L18
Chilecito *Argentina* 29°10S 67°30W **190** B2
Chilete *Peru* 7°10S 78°50W **188** B2
Chilia, Braţul →
Romania 45°14N 29°42E **81** E14
Chilik = Shelek
Kazakhstan 43°33N 78°17E **109** D8
Chililabombwe *Zambia* 12°18S 27°43E **143** E2
Chilin = Jilin *China* 43°44N 126°30E **115** C14
Chiliomodi *Greece* 37°48N 22°51E **98** D4
Chilka L. *India* 19°40N 85°25E **126** E7
Chilko → *Canada* 52°0N 123°40W **162** C4
Chilko L. *Canada* 51°20N 124°10W **162** C4
Chillagoe *Australia* 17°7S 144°33E **150** B3
Chillán *Chile* 36°40S 72°10W **190** D2
Chillicothe *Ill., U.S.A.* 40°55N 89°29W **172** E9
Chillicothe *Mo., U.S.A.* 39°48N 93°33W **172** F7
Chillicothe *Ohio,*
U.S.A. 39°20N 82°59W **173** F13
Chilliwack *Canada* 49°10N 121°54W **162** D4
Chilo *India* 27°25N 73°32E **124** F5
Chiloane, I. *Mozam.* 20°40S 34°55E **145** B5
Chiloé, I. de *Chile* 42°30S 73°50W **192** B2
Chiloé □ *Chile* 42°11S 73°59W **192** B2
Chiltern *Australia* 36°10S 146°36E **153** D7
Chilton *U.S.A.* 44°2N 88°10W **172** C9
Chilubi *Zambia* 11°5S 29°58E **143** E2
Chilubula *Zambia* 10°14S 30°51E **143** E3
Chilumba *Malawi* 10°28S 34°12E **143** E3
Chilung *Taiwan* 25°3N 121°45E **117** E13
Chilwa, L. *Malawi* 15°15S 35°40E **143** F4
Chimaltitán *Mexico* 21°35N 103°50W **180** C4
Chimán *Panama* 8°45N 78°40W **182** E4
Chimanimani *Zimbabwe* 19°48S 32°52E **145** A5
Chimanimani △
Zimbabwe 19°48S 33°0E **145** A5
Chimay *Belgium* 50°3N 4°20E **69** D4
Chimayo *U.S.A.* 36°0N 105°56W **169** J11
Chimba *Zambia* 9°54S 31°28E **143** E3
Chimborazo *Ecuador* 1°29S 78°55W **186** D3
Chimbote *Peru* 9°0S 78°35W **188** B2
Chimboy *Uzbekistan* 42°57N 59°47E **108** D5
Chimkent = Shymkent
Kazakhstan 42°18N 69°36E **109** D7
Chimoio *Mozam.* 19°4S 33°30E **143** F3
Chimpembe *Zambia* 9°31S 29°33E **143** D2
Chimur *India* 20°30N 79°23E **126** D4
Chin □ *Burma* 22°0N 93°0E **123** J18
Chin Hills *Burma* 22°30N 93°30E **123** H18
Chin Ling Shan = Qinling Shandi
China 33°50N 108°10E **114** H5
China *Mexico* 25°42N 99°14W **181** B5
China ■ *Asia* 30°0N 110°0E **111** E11
China, Great Plain of
Asia 35°0N 115°0E **102** E13
China Lake *U.S.A.* 35°44N 117°37W **171** K9
Chinan = Jinan *China* 36°38N 117°1E **114** F9
Chinandega Nic. 12°35N 87°12W **182** D2
Chinati Peak *U.S.A.* 29°57N 104°29W **176** G2
Chincha Alta *Peru* 13°25S 76°7W **188** C2
Chinchaga → *Canada* 58°53N 118°20W **162** B5
Chincheros *Peru* 13°30S 73°44W **188** C3
Chinchilla *Australia* 26°45S 150°38E **151** D5
Chinchilla de Monte Aragón
Spain 38°53N 1°40W **91** C5
Chincholi *India* 17°28N 77°26E **126** F3
Chinchorro, Banco
Mexico 18°35N 87°22W **181** D7
Chinchou = Jinzhou
China 41°5N 121°3E **115** D11
Chincoteague *U.S.A.* 37°56N 75°23W **173** G16
Chinde *Mozam.* 18°35S 36°30E **143** F4
Chindwin → *Burma* 21°26N 95°15E **123** J19
Chineni *India* 33°2N 75°15E **125** C6
Chinga *Mozam.* 15°13S 38°35E **143** F4
Chingola *Zambia* 12°31S 27°53E **143** E2
Chingole *Malawi* 13°4S 34°17E **143** E3
Ch'ingtao = Qingdao
China 36°5N 120°20E **115** F11
Chinguetti *Mauritania* 20°25N 12°24W **134** D3
Chingune *Mozam.* 20°33S 34°58E **145** B5
Chinhanguanine
Mozam. 25°21S 32°30E **145** C5
Chinhoyi *Zimbabwe* 17°20S 30°8E **143** F3
Chiniot *Pakistan* 31°45N 73°0E **124** D5
Chínipas *Mexico* 27°23N 108°32W **180** B3
Chinji *Pakistan* 32°42N 72°22E **124** C5
Chinju = Jinju
S. Korea 35°12N 128°2E **115** G15
Chinkapook *Australia* 35°11S 142°57E **152** C5
Chinko → *C.A.R.* 4°50N 23°53E **140** D4
Chinmen *Taiwan* 24°26N 118°19E **117** E12
Chinmen Tao *Taiwan* 24°25N 118°23E **117** E12
Chinnamanur *India* 9°50N 77°24E **127** K3
Chinnampo = Namp'o
N. Korea 38°52N 125°10E **115** E13
Chino *Japan* 35°59N 138°9E **113** G9
Chino *U.S.A.* 34°1N 117°41W **171** L9
Chino Valley *U.S.A.* 34°45N 112°27W **169** J7
Chinon *France* 47°10N 0°15E **70** E7
Chinook *U.S.A.* 48°35N 109°14W **168** B9
Chinook Trough
Pac. Oc. 44°0N 175°0W **156** C10
Chinsali *Zambia* 10°30S 32°2E **143** E3
Chinsura = Chunchura
India 22°53N 88°27E **125** H13
Chintalapudi *India* 17°4N 80°59E **126** F5
Chintamani *India* 13°26N 78°3E **127** H4

Chióggia *Italy* 45°13'N 12°17'E **93** C9
Chios *Greece* 38°27'N 26°9'E **99** C8
Chipata *Zambia* 13°38'S 32°28'E **143** E3
Chiperceni *Moldova* 47°31'N 28°50'E **81** C13
Chipindo *Angola* 13°49'S 15°48'E **141** G3
Chipinge *Zimbabwe* 20°13'S 32°28'E **143** G3
Chipinge △ *Zimbabwe* 20°14'S 33°0'E **143** G3
Chipiona *Spain* 36°44'N 6°26'W **89** J4
Chipley *U.S.A.* 30°47'N 85°32'W **177** F12
Chiplun *India* 17°31'N 73°34'E **126** F1
Chipman *Canada* 46°6'N 65°53'W **165** C6
Chipoka *Malawi* 13°57'S 34°28'E **143** E3
Chippenham *U.K.* 51°27'N 2°6'W **67** F5
Chippewa ➤ *U.S.A.* 44°25'N 92°5'W **172** C7
Chippewa Falls *U.S.A.* 44°56'N 91°24'W **172** C8
Chipping Norton *U.K.* 51°56'N 1°32'W **67** F6
Chiprovtsi *Bulgaria* 43°24'N 22°52'E **96** C6
Chiputneticook Lakes
N. Amer. 45°35'N 67°35'W **173** C20
Chiquián *Peru* 10°10'S 77°0'W **188** C2
Chiquibul △ *Belize* 16°49'N 88°52'W **182** C2
Chiquimula *Guatemala* 14°51'N 89°37'W **182** D2
Chiquinquira *Colombia* 5°37'N 73°50'W **186** B4
Chir ➤ *Russia* 48°30'N 43°0'E **87** F6
Chirala *India* 15°50'N 80°26'E **127** G5
Chiramba *Mozam.* 16°55'S 34°39'E **143** F3
Chirawa *India* 28°14'N 75°42'E **124** E6
Chirchiq *Uzbekistan* 41°29'N 69°35'E **109** D7
Chiredzi *Zimbabwe* 21°0'S 31°38'E **145** B5
Chiricahua ➤ *U.S.A.* 32°0'N 109°20'W **169** K9
Chiricahua Peak
U.S.A. 31°51'N 109°18'W **169** L9
Chirikof I. *U.S.A.* 55°50'N 155°40'W **166** D8
Chiriqui, G. de *Panama* 8°0'N 82°10'W **182** E3
Chiriqui, L. de *Panama* 9°10'N 82°0'W **182** E3
Chirisa △ *Zimbabwe* 17°53'S 28°15'E **143** F2
Chirivira Falls
Zimbabwe 21°10'S 32°12'E **143** G3
Chirmiri *India* 23°15'N 82°20'E **125** H9
Chirnogi *Romania* 44°7'N 26°32'E **81** F11
Chirpan *Bulgaria* 42°10'N 25°19'E **97** D9
Chirripó Grande, Cerro
Costa Rica 9°29'N 83°29'W **182** E3
Chirundu *Zimbabwe* 16°3'S 28°50'E **145** A4
Chisamba *Zambia* 14°55'S 28°20'E **143** E2
Chisapani *Nepal* 28°37'N 81°16'E **125** E9
Chisasibi *Canada* 53°50'N 79°0'W **164** B4
Chishan *Taiwan* 22°44'N 120°31'E **117** F13
Chisholm *Canada* 54°55'N 114°10'W **162** C6
Chisholm *U.S.A.* 47°29'N 92°53'W **172** B7
Chishtian Mandi
Pakistan 29°50'N 72°55'E **124** E5
Chishui *China* 28°30'N 105°42'E **116** C5
Chishui He ➤ *China* 28°49'N 105°50'E **116** C5
Chisimaio = Kismaayo
Somalia 0°22'S 42°32'E **131** H3
Chisimba Falls *Zambia* 10°12'S 30°56'E **143** E3
Chișinău *Moldova* 47°2'N 28°50'E **81** C13
Chișinău ✈ (KIV)
Moldova 47°3'N 28°46'E **81** C13
Chișineu Criș *Romania* 46°32'N 21°37'E **80** D6
Chisone ➤ *Italy* 44°49'N 7°25'E **92** D4
Chisos Mts. *U.S.A.* 29°5'N 103°15'W **176** E2
Chistopol *Russia* 55°25'N 50°38'E **86** C9
Chita *Russia* 52°0'N 113°35'E **111** A11
Chitapur *India* 17°10'N 77°5'E **126** F3
Chitipa *Malawi* 9°41'S 33°19'E **143** D3
Chitose *Japan* 42°49'N 141°39'E **112** C10
Chitradurga *India* 14°14'N 76°24'E **127** G3
Chitrakot *India* 19°10'N 81°40'E **126** E5
Chitral *Pakistan* 35°50'N 71°56'E **122** B7
Chitravati ➤ *India* 14°45'N 78°15'E **127** G4
Chitré *Panama* 7°59'N 80°27'W **182** E3
Chittagong *Bangla.* 22°19'N 91°48'E **123** H17
Chittagong □ *Bangla.* 24°5'N 91°0'E **123** G17
Chittaurgarh *India* 24°52'N 74°38'E **124** G6
Chittoor *India* 13°15'N 79°5'E **127** H4
Chittur *India* 10°40'N 76°45'E **127** J3
Chitungwiza *Zimbabwe* 18°0'S 31°6'E **143** F3
Chiusi *Italy* 43°1'N 11°57'E **93** E8
Chivasso *Italy* 45°11'N 7°53'E **92** C4
Chivay *Peru* 15°40'S 71°35'W **188** D3
Chive *Bolivia* 12°23'S 68°35'W **188** C4
Chivhu *Zimbabwe* 19°2'S 30°52'E **143** F3
Chivilcoy *Argentina* 34°55'S 60°0'W **190** C4
Chiwanda *Tanzania* 11°23'S 34°55'E **143** E3
Chixi *China* 22°0'N 112°58'E **117** G9
Chizarira *Zimbabwe* 17°36'S 27°45'E **143** F2
Chizarira △ *Zimbabwe* 17°44'S 27°52'E **143** F2
Chizela *Zambia* 13°8'S 25°0'E **143** E2
Chkalov = Orenburg
Russia 51°45'N 55°6'E **108** D5
Chkolovsk *Russia* 56°50'N 43°10'E **86** B6
Chloride *U.S.A.* 35°25'N 114°12'W **171** K12
Chlumec nad Cidlinou
Czech Rep. 50°9'N 15°29'E **78** A8
Chmielnik *Poland* 50°37'N 20°43'E **83** E7
Cho-do *N. Korea* 38°30'N 124°40'E **115** E13
Cho Phuoc Hai
Vietnam 10°26'N 107°18'E **121** G6
Choa Chu Kang
Singapore 1°22'N 103°41'E **121** d
Chobe △ *Botswana* 18°37'S 24°23'E **144** B4
Chociwicz *Poland* 51°27'N 15°55'E **83** G2
Chociwel *Poland* 53°29'N 15°21'E **82** E2
Chocolate Mts.
U.S.A. 33°15'N 115°15'W **171** M11
Choctawhatchee ➤
U.S.A. 30°25'N 86°8'W **178** E3
Choctawhatchee B.
U.S.A. 30°20'N 86°20'W **179** G3
Chodavaram *Andhra Pradesh,*
India 17°50'N 82°57'E **126** F6
Chodavaram *Andhra Pradesh,*
India 17°27'N 81°46'E **126** F5
Chodecz *Poland* 52°24'N 19°2'E **83** F6
Chodov *Czech Rep.* 50°15'N 12°45'E **78** A5
Chodziez *Poland* 52°58'N 16°58'E **83** F3
Choele Choel *Argentina* 39°11'S 65°40'W **192** A3
Choghâ Zanbîl *Iran* 32°1'N 48°32'E **129** C6
Choiseul *St. Lucia* 13°47'N 61°3'W **183** f
Choiseul *Solomon Is.* 7°0'S 156°40'E **147** B8
Choix *Mexico* 26°43'N 108°17'W **180** B3
Chojna *Poland* 52°58'N 14°25'E **83** F1
Chojnice *Poland* 53°42'N 17°32'E **82** E4
Chojnów *Poland* 51°18'N 15°58'E **83** G2
Chok Chai *Thailand* 14°44'N 102°10'E **120** E4
Choke Canyon Res.
U.S.A. 28°30'N 98°20'W **176** G5
Chokurdakh *Russia* 70°38'N 147°55'E **107** B15
Chokwé *Mozam.* 24°32'S 32°59'E **145** C5
Cholame *U.S.A.* 35°44'N 120°18'W **170** K6
Cholet *France* 47°4'N 0°52'W **70** E6
Cholguan *Chile* 37°10'S 72°3'W **190** D1
Choloma *Honduras* 15°37'N 87°57'W **182** C2
Choluteca *Honduras* 13°20'N 87°14'W **182** D2
Choluteca ➤ *Honduras* 13°0'N 87°20'W **182** D2
Chom Bung *Thailand* 13°37'N 99°36'E **120** F2
Chom Thong *Thailand* 18°25'N 98°41'E **120** C2
Choma *Zambia* 16°48'S 26°59'E **143** F2
Chomolungma = Everest, Mt.
Nepal 28°5'N 86°58'E **125** E12
Chomun *India* 27°15'N 75°40'E **124** F6
Chomutov *Czech Rep.* 50°28'N 13°23'E **78** A6
Chon Buri *Thailand* 13°21'N 101°1'E **120** F3
Chon Thanh *Vietnam* 11°24'N 106°36'E **121** G6
Chone *Ecuador* 0°40'S 80°0'W **186** D3
Chong Kai *Cambodia* 13°57'N 103°35'E **120** F4
Chong Mek *Thailand* 15°10'N 105°27'E **120** E5
Chong Phangan *Thailand* 9°39'N 100°0'E **121** b
Chong Samui *Thailand* 9°21'N 99°50'E **121** b
Chongde *China* 30°32'N 120°26'E **117** B13
Ch'ŏngjin *N. Korea* 41°47'N 129°50'E **115** D15
Chongju *N. Korea* 39°40'N 125°5'E **115** E13
Chongli *China* 40°58'N 115°15'E **114** D8
Chongming *China* 31°38'N 121°27'E **117** B13
Chongming Dao
China 31°40'N 121°30'E **117** B13
Chongoni Rock Art
Malawi 14°17'S 34°16'E **143** E3
Chongoyape *Peru* 6°35'S 79°25'W **188** B2
Ch'ŏngp'yŏng
N. Korea 39°47'N 127°23'E **115** E14
Chongqing *Chongqing,*
China 29°35'N 106°25'E **116** C6
Chongqing *Sichuan,*
China 30°38'N 103°40'E **116** B4
Chongqing Shi □ *China* 30°0'N 108°0'E **116** C6
Chongren *China* 27°46'N 116°3'E **117** D11
Chonguene *Mozam.* 25°3'S 33°49'E **145** C5
Chongwe *Zambia* 15°21'S 28°42'E **143** F2
Chongyi *China* 25°45'N 114°29'E **117** E10
Chongzuo *China* 22°23'N 107°20'E **116** F6
Chonogol *Mongolia* 45°54'N 115°22'E **114** B8
Chonos, Arch. de los
Chile 45°0'S 75°0'W **192** C2
Chop *Ukraine* 48°26'N 22°12'E **80** B7
Chopda *India* 21°20'N 75°15'E **126** D2
Chopim ➤ *Brazil* 25°35'S 53°5'W **191** B5
Chor *Pakistan* 25°31'N 69°46'E **124** G3
Chora *Greece* 37°3'N 21°42'E **98** D3
Chora Sfakion *Greece* 35°15'N 24°9'E **101** D6
Chorbat La *India* 34°42'N 76°37'E **125** B7
Chorley *U.K.* 53°39'N 2°38'W **66** D5
Chorna *Ukraine* 47°36'N 29°20'E **81** C14
Chornobyl *Ukraine* 51°20'N 30°15'E **75** C16
Chornomorske *Ukraine* 45°31'N 32°40'E **85** K7
Choroque, Cerro
Bolivia 20°59'S 66°5'W **192** A2
Choroszcz *Poland* 53°10'N 22°59'E **83** E9
Chorregon *Australia* 22°40'S 143°32'E **150** C3
Chorro el Indio △
Venezuela 7°43'N 72°9'W **183** S5
Chortkiv *Ukraine* 49°2'N 25°46'E **75** D13
Chorzele *Poland* 53°15'N 20°55'E **83** E7
Chorzów *Poland* 50°18'N 18°57'E **83** H5
Chos-Malal *Argentina* 37°20'S 70°15'W **190** D1
Ch'osan *N. Korea* 40°50'N 125°47'E **115** D13
Choszczno *Poland* 53°7'N 15°25'E **83** E2
Chota *Peru* 6°33'S 78°39'W **188** B2
Choteau *U.S.A.* 47°49'N 112°11'W **168** C7
Chotěboř *Czech Rep.* 49°43'N 15°40'E **78** B8
Chotila *India* 22°23'N 71°15'E **124** H4
Chotta Udepur *India* 22°19'N 74°1'E **124** H6
Chowchilla *U.S.A.* 37°7'N 120°16'W **170** H6
Choybalsan *Mongolia* 48°4'N 114°30'E **111** B11
Choyr *Mongolia* 46°24'N 108°30'E **111** B10
Chrisoupoli *Greece* 40°58'N 24°42'E **97** F8
Christchurch *N.Z.* 43°33'S 172°47'E **155** D7
Christchurch *U.K.* 50°44'N 1°47'W **67** G6
Christian I. *Canada* 44°50'N 80°12'W **174** B4
Christian Sd. *U.S.A.* 55°56'N 134°40'W **167** D13
Christiana *Greece* 36°14'N 25°13'E **99** F7
Christiana *S. Africa* 27°52'S 25°8'E **144** D4
Christiansfeld *Denmark* 55°21'N 9°29'E **63** J3
Christianshåb = Qasigiannguit
Greenland 68°50'N 51°18'W **57** D5
Christiansted
U.S. Virgin Is. 17°45'N 64°42'W **183** C7
Christie B. *Canada* 62°32'N 111°10'W **163** A6
Christina ➤ *Canada* 56°40'N 111°3'W **163** B6
Christmas Cr. ➤
Australia 18°29'S 125°23'E **148** C4
Christmas I. = Kiritimati
Kiribati 1°58'N 157°27'W **157** G12
Christmas I. *Ind. Oc.* 10°30'S 105°40'E **146** J2
Christopher, L.
Australia 24°49'S 127°42'E **149** D4
Chrudim *Czech Rep.* 49°58'N 15°43'E **78** B8
Chrzanów *Poland* 50°10'N 19°21'E **83** H6
Chtapodia *Greece* 37°24'N 25°34'E **99** D7
Chtimba *Malawi* 10°35'S 34°13'E **143** E3
Chu = Shū *Kazakhstan* 43°36'N 73°42'E **109** D8
Chū = Shū ➤
Kazakhstan 45°0'N 67°44'E **109** D7
Chu ➤ *Vietnam* 19°53'N 105°45'E **120** C5
Chu Lai *Vietnam* 15°28'N 108°45'E **120** E7
Chu Mom Ray △
Vietnam 14°29'N 107°38'E **120** E6
Chu Se *Vietnam* 13°40'N 108°8'E **120** F7
Chuadanga *Bangla.* 23°38'N 88°51'E **125** H13
Chuak, Ko *Thailand* 7°22'N 99°14'E **121** b
Ch'uanchou = Quanzhou
China 17°27'N 118°34'E **117** E12
Chuankou *China* 34°20'N 110°59'E **114** G6
Chubbuck *U.S.A.* 42°55'N 112°28'W **168** E7
Chūbu □ *Japan* 36°45'N 137°30'E **113** F8
Chūbu-Sangaku △
Japan 36°30'N 137°40'E **113** F8
Chubut □ *Argentina* 43°30'S 69°0'W **192** B3
Chubut ➤ *Argentina* 43°20'S 65°5'W **192** B3
Chuchi L. *Canada* 55°12'N 124°30'W **162** B4
Chuda *India* 22°29'N 71°41'E **124** H4
Chudovo *Russia* 59°10'N 31°41'E **84** C6
Chudskoye, Ozero
Russia 58°13'N 27°30'E **84** C4
Chūgoku □ *Japan* 35°0'N 133°0'E **113** G6
Chūgoku-Sanchi *Japan* 35°0'N 133°0'E **113** G6
Chuguyev = Chuhuyiv
Ukraine 49°55'N 36°45'E **85** H9
Chugwater *U.S.A.* 41°46'N 104°50'W **168** F11
Chuhuyiv *Ukraine* 49°55'N 36°45'E **85** H9
Chuka *Kenya* 0°23'S 37°39'E **142** C4
Chukchi Plateau *Arctic* 78°0'N 165°0'W **54** B17
Chukchi Sea *Russia* 68°0'N 175°0'W **107** C19
Chukotskiy Mys
Russia 64°14'N 173°8'W **166** C5
Chukotskiy Poluostrov
Russia 66°0'N 174°0'W **166** B5
Chukotskoye Nagorye
Russia 68°0'N 175°0'E **107** C18
Chula *U.S.A.* 31°33'N 83°32'W **178** D6
Chula Vista *U.S.A.* 32°38'N 117°5'W **171** N9
Chulband ➤ *India* 20°40'N 79°54'E **126** D4
Chulucanas *Peru* 5°8'S 80°10'W **188** B1
Chulumani *Bolivia* 16°24'S 67°31'W **188** D4
Chulym ➤ *Russia* 57°43'N 83°51'E **106** D9
Chum Phae *Thailand* 16°40'N 102°6'E **120** D4
Chum Saeng *Thailand* 15°55'N 100°15'E **120** E3
Chuma *Bolivia* 15°24'S 68°56'W **188** D4
Chumar *India* 32°40'N 78°35'E **125** C8
Chumbicha *Argentina* 29°0'S 66°10'W **190** B2
Chumerna *Bulgaria* 42°45'N 25°55'E **97** D9
Chumikan *Russia* 54°40'N 135°10'E **107** D14
Chumphon *Thailand* 10°35'N 99°14'E **121** G2
Chumpi *Peru* 15°4'S 73°40'E **143** E3
Chumuare *Mozam.* 14°31'S 31°50'E **143** E3
Chuna ➤ *Russia* 57°47'N 94°37'E **107** D10
Chun'an *China* 29°35'N 119°3'E **117** C12
Chuncheon *S. Korea* 37°58'N 127°44'E **115** F14
Chunchura *India* 22°53'N 88°27'E **125** H13
Chunga *Zambia* 15°0'S 26°2'E **143** F2
Chunggang-ŭp
N. Korea 41°48'N 126°48'E **115** D14
Chunghwa *N. Korea* 38°52'N 125°47'E **115** E13
Chungju *S. Korea* 36°58'N 127°58'E **115** F14
Chungking = Chongqing
China 29°35'N 106°25'E **116** C6
Chungli *Taiwan* 24°57'N 121°13'E **117** E13
Chungt'iaoshan = Zhongtiao
Shan *China* 35°0'N 111°10'E **114** G6
Chungyang Shanmo
Taiwan 23°10'N 121°0'E **117** F13
Chunian *Pakistan* 30°57'N 74°0'E **124** D6
Chunya *Tanzania* 8°30'S 33°27'E **143** D3
Chunyang *China* 43°38'N 129°23'E **115** C15
Chupara Pt.
Trin. & Tob. 10°49'N 61°22'W **187** K15
Chuquibamba *Peru* 15°47'S 72°44'W **188** D3
Chuquibambilla *Peru* 14°7'S 72°41'W **188** D3
Chuquicamata *Chile* 22°15'S 69°0'W **190** A2
Chur *Switz.* 46°52'N 9°32'E **77** J5
Churachandpur *India* 24°20'N 93°40'E **123** G18
Church Stretton *U.K.* 52°32'N 2°48'W **67** E5
Churchill *Australia* 38°19'S 146°25'E **153** F4
Churchill *Canada* 58°47'N 94°11'W **163** B10
Churchill ➤ *Man.,*
Canada 58°47'N 94°12'W **163** B10
Churchill ➤ *Nfld. & L.,*
Canada 53°19'N 60°10'W **165** B7
Churchill, C. *Canada* 58°46'N 93°12'W **163** B10
Churchill Falls *Canada* 53°36'N 64°19'W **165** B7
Churchill L. *Canada* 55°55'N 108°20'W **163** B7
Churchill Pk. *Canada* 58°10'N 125°10'W **162** B3
Churki *India* 23°50'N 83°12'E **125** H10
Churu *India* 28°20'N 74°50'E **124** E6
Churún Merú = Angel Falls
Venezuela 5°57'N 62°30'W **186** B6
Chushal *India* 33°40'N 78°40'E **125** C8
Chuska Mts. *U.S.A.* 36°15'N 108°50'W **169** H9
Chusovoy *Russia* 58°22'N 57°50'E **106** D6
Chuspipata *Bolivia* 16°18'S 67°48'W **188** D4
Chust *Uzbekistan* 41°0'N 71°13'E **109** D8
Chute-aux-Outardes
Canada 49°7'N 68°24'W **165** C6
Chuuk = Truk
Micronesia 7°25'N 151°46'E **156** G7
Chuvash Republic = Chuvashia □
Russia 55°30'N 47°0'E **86** C8
Chuvashia □ *Russia* 55°30'N 47°0'E **86** C8
Chuwärtah *Iraq* 35°43'N 45°34'E **105** E11
Chuxiong *China* 25°2'N 101°28'E **116** E3
Chüy □ *Kyrgyzstan* 42°55'N 75°15'E **109** D8
Chüy ➤ *Uzbekistan* 42°25'N 75°16'E **109** D8
Chuzhou *China* 32°19'N 118°20'E **117** A12
Chynadiyeve *Ukraine* 48°29'N 22°50'E **80** B7
Ci Xian *China* 36°20'N 114°25'E **114** F8
Ciacova *Romania* 45°35'N 21°10'E **80** E6
Ciadâr-Lunga *Moldova* 46°3'N 28°51'E **81** D13
Ciamis *Indonesia* 7°20'S 108°21'E **119** G13
Cianjur *Indonesia* 6°49'S 107°8'E **119** G12
Cianorte *Brazil* 23°37'S 52°37'W **191** A5
Cibola *U.S.A.* 33°17'N 114°42'W **171** M12
Cicero *U.S.A.* 41°51'N 87°44'W **172** E10
Cicero Dantas *Brazil* 10°36'S 38°23'W **189** E11
Cicia *Fiji* 17°45'S 179°18'W **154** a
Cidacos ➤ *Spain* 42°21'N 1°38'W **90** C3
Cide *Turkey* 41°53'N 33°1'E **104** B5
Ciéagas del Cataumbo △
Venezuela 9°25'N 71°54'W **183** S5
Ciechanów *Poland* 52°52'N 20°38'E **83** F7
Ciechanowiec *Poland* 52°40'N 22°31'E **83** F9
Ciechocinek *Poland* 52°53'N 18°45'E **83** F5
Ciego de Ávila *Cuba* 21°50'N 78°50'W **182** B4
Ciénaga *Colombia* 11°1'N 74°15'W **186** A4
Cienfuegos *Cuba* 22°10'N 80°30'W **182** B3
Cierp-Gaud *France* 42°55'N 0°40'E **72** F4
Cíes, Is. *Spain* 42°12'N 8°55'W **88** C2
Cieszanów *Poland* 50°14'N 23°8'E **83** H10
Cieszyn *Poland* 49°45'N 18°35'E **83** J5
Cieza *Spain* 38°17'N 1°23'W **91** G3
Cifuentes *Spain* 40°47'N 2°37'W **90** E2
Cihanbeyli *Turkey* 38°40'N 32°55'E **104** C5
Cihuatlán *Mexico* 19°14'N 104°35'W **180** D4
Cijara, Embalse de *Spain* 39°18'N 4°52'W **89** F6
Cijara △ *Spain* 39°18'N 4°35'W **89** F6
Cijulang *Indonesia* 7°42'S 108°27'E **119** G13
Cilacap *Indonesia* 7°43'S 109°0'E **119** G13
Çıldır *Turkey* 41°7'N 43°5'E **105** B10
Çıldır Gölü *Turkey* 41°5'N 43°15'E **105** B10
Cilento e Vallo di Diano △
Italy 40°15'N 15°20'E **95** B8
Cili *China* 29°30'N 111°8'E **117** C8
Cilibia *Romania* 45°4'N 27°4'E **81** E12
Cilicia *Turkey* 37°0'N 35°0'E **104** D5
Cill Airne = Killarney
Ireland 52°4'N 9°30'W **64** D2
Cill Chainnigh = Kilkenny
Ireland 52°39'N 7°15'W **64** D4
Cill Dara = Kildare *Ireland* 53°9'N 6°55'W **64** C5
Cill Droichid = Celbridge
Ireland 53°20'N 6°32'W **64** C5
Cill Mhantáin = Wicklow
Ireland 52°59'N 6°3'W **64** D5
Çilo Dağı *Turkey* 37°28'N 43°55'E **105** D10
Cima *U.S.A.* 35°14'N 115°30'W **171** K11
Cimarron *Kans.,*
U.S.A. 37°48'N 100°21'W **172** G3
Cimarron *N. Mex.,*
U.S.A. 36°31'N 104°55'W **169** H11
Cimarron ➤ *U.S.A.* 36°10'N 96°16'W **176** C6
Cimișlia *Moldova* 46°34'N 28°44'E **81** D13
Cîmone, Mte. *Italy* 44°12'N 10°42'E **92** D7
Çınar *Turkey* 37°46'N 40°19'E **105** D9
Cinca ➤ *Spain* 41°26'N 0°21'E **90** D5
Cincar Bos.-H. 43°55'N 17°5'E **80** G2
Cincinnati *U.S.A.* 39°9'N 84°27'W **173** F11
Cincinnatus *U.S.A.* 42°33'N 75°54'W **175** D9
Çine *Turkey* 37°37'N 28°2'E **99** D10
Ciney *Belgium* 50°18'N 5°5'E **69** D5
Cíngoli *Italy* 43°23'N 13°10'E **93** E10
Cinigiano *Italy* 42°53'N 11°24'E **93** F8
Cinque I. *India* 11°16'N 92°42'E **127** J11
Cinque Terre ➤ *Italy* 44°10'N 9°45'E **92** D6
Cinto, Mte. *France* 42°24'N 8°54'E **73** F12
Cintruénigo *Spain* 42°5'N 1°49'W **90** C3
Ciocile *Romania* 44°49'N 27°14'E **81** F12
Ciolăneşti din Deal
Romania 44°9'N 25°5'E **81** F10
Ciorani *Romania* 44°45'N 26°25'E **81** F11
Ciovo *Croatia* 43°30'N 16°17'E **93** E13
Cipó *Brazil* 11°6'S 38°31'W **189** C3
Cipolletti *Argentina* 38°56'S 67°59'W **192** A3
Circeo, Mte. *Italy* 41°14'N 13°3'E **94** A6
Çırçır *Turkey* 40°3'N 36°47'E **104** C7
Circle *Alaska, U.S.A.* 65°50'N 144°4'W **166** B11
Circle *Mont., U.S.A.* 47°25'N 105°35'W **168** C11
Circleville *U.S.A.* 39°36'N 82°57'W **173** F12
Cirebon *Indonesia* 6°45'S 108°32'E **118** F3
Cirencester *U.K.* 51°43'N 1°57'W **67** F6
Cireșu *Romania* 44°47'N 22°31'E **80** F7
Cirey-sur-Vezouze
France 48°35'N 6°57'E **71** D13
Ciriè *Italy* 45°14'N 7°36'E **92** C4
Cirium *Cyprus* 34°40'N 32°53'E **101** E11
Cirò *Italy* 39°23'N 17°4'E **95** C10
Cirò Marina *Italy* 39°22'N 17°8'E **95** C10
Ciron ➤ *France* 44°36'N 0°18'W **72** D3
Cisco *U.S.A.* 32°23'N 98°59'W **176** E5
Cislău *Romania* 45°14'N 26°20'E **81** E11
Cisna *Poland* 49°12'N 22°20'E **83** J9
Cisnădie *Romania* 45°42'N 24°9'E **81** E9
Cisterna di Latina *Italy* 41°35'N 12°49'E **94** A5
Cisternino *Italy* 40°44'N 17°25'E **95** B10
Cistierna *Spain* 42°48'N 5°7'W **88** C5
Citeli-Ckaro = Dedoplis Tsqaro
Georgia 41°33'N 46°0'E **87** K8
Citlaltépetl = Orizaba, Pico de
Mexico 18°58'N 97°15'W **181** D5
Citra *U.S.A.* 29°25'N 82°7'W **179** F7
Citrus Heights *U.S.A.* 38°42'N 121°17'W **170** G5
Citrus Springs *U.S.A.* 29°0'N 82°30'W **179** F7
Citrusdal *S. Africa* 32°35'S 19°0'E **144** D2
Città del Vaticano = Vatican
City ■ *Europe* 41°54'N 12°27'E **93** G9
Città della Pieve *Italy* 42°57'N 12°1'E **93** F9
Città di Castello *Italy* 43°27'N 12°14'E **93** E9
Città Sant' Angelo *Italy* 42°32'N 14°5'E **93** F11
Cittadella *Italy* 45°39'N 11°47'E **93** C8
Cittaducale *Italy* 42°23'N 13°3'E **93** F9
Cittanova *Italy* 38°21'N 16°5'E **95** D9
Ciuc, Munții *Romania* 46°25'N 26°5'E **81** D11
Ciucaş, Vf. *Romania* 45°31'N 25°56'E **81** E10
Ciucea *Romania* 46°57'N 22°49'E **80** D7
Ciuciulea *Moldova* 47°40'N 27°29'E **81** C12
Ciuciuleni *Moldova* 47°2'N 28°25'E **81** C13
Ciudad Acuña *Mexico* 29°18'N 100°55'W **180** B4
Ciudad Altamirano
Mexico 18°20'N 100°40'W **180** D4
Ciudad Anáhuac
Mexico 27°14'N 100°7'W **180** B4
Ciudad Bolívar *Venezuela* 8°5'N 63°36'W **186** B6
Ciudad Camargo
Mexico 27°40'N 105°10'W **180** B3
Ciudad Cortés *Costa Rica* 8°55'N 84°0'W **182** E3
Ciudad de México
Mexico 19°24'N 99°9'W **181** D5
Ciudad del Carmen
Mexico 18°38'N 91°50'W **181** D6
Ciudad del Este
Paraguay 25°30'S 54°50'W **191** B5
Ciudad Delicias = Delicias
Mexico 28°13'N 105°28'W **180** B3
Ciudad Frontera
Mexico 26°56'N 101°27'W **180** B4
Ciudad Guayana
Venezuela 8°0'N 62°30'W **186** B6
Ciudad Guerrero
Mexico 28°33'N 107°30'W **180** B3
Ciudad Guzmán
Mexico 19°41'N 103°29'W **180** D4
Ciudad Juárez *Mexico* 31°44'N 106°29'W **180** A3
Ciudad Lerdo *Mexico* 25°32'N 103°32'W **180** B4
Ciudad Madero *Mexico* 22°19'N 97°50'W **181** C5
Ciudad Mante *Mexico* 22°44'N 98°59'W **181** C5
Ciudad Obregón
Mexico 27°29'N 109°56'W **180** B3
Ciudad Real *Spain* 38°59'N 3°55'W **89** G7
Ciudad Real □ *Spain* 38°50'N 4°0'W **89** G7
Ciudad Rodrigo *Spain* 40°35'N 6°32'W **88** E4
Ciudad Valles *Mexico* 22°0'N 99°0'W **181** C5
Ciudad Victoria *Mexico* 23°44'N 99°8'W **181** C5
Ciudadela *Spain* 40°0'N 3°50'E **100** B10
Ciulnița *Romania* 44°26'N 27°22'E **81** F12
Ciumeghiu *Romania* 46°44'N 21°35'E **80** D6
Ciupercenii *Romania* 43°49'N 23°45'E **80** F8
Civa Burnu *Turkey* 41°21'N 36°38'E **104** B7
Cividale del Friuli *Italy* 46°6'N 13°25'E **93** B10
Civita Castellana *Italy* 42°17'N 12°24'E **93** F9
Civitanova Marche
Italy 43°18'N 13°44'E **93** E10
Civitavécchia *Italy* 42°6'N 11°48'E **93** F8
Civray *France* 46°10'N 0°17'E **72** B4
Çivril *Turkey* 38°20'N 29°43'E **99** C11
Cíxerri ➤ *Italy* 39°17'N 8°59'E **94** C1
Cixi *China* 30°17'N 121°9'E **117** B13
Cizre *Turkey* 37°19'N 42°10'E **105** D10
Clackmannanshire □
U.K. 56°10'N 3°43'W **65** E5
Clacton-on-Sea *U.K.* 51°47'N 1°11'E **67** F9
Clain ➤ *France* 46°47'N 0°33'E **70** F7
Claire, L. *Canada* 58°35'N 112°5'W **162** B6
Clairton *U.S.A.* 40°18'N 79°53'W **174** F5
Clairvaux-les-Lacs
France 46°35'N 5°45'E **71** F12
Clamecy *France* 47°28'N 3°30'E **71** E10
Clanton *U.S.A.* 32°51'N 86°38'W **177** E11
Clanwilliam *S. Africa* 32°11'S 18°52'E **144** D2
Clara *Ireland* 53°21'N 7°37'W **64** C4
Clare *Australia* 33°50'S 138°37'E **152** B2
Clare *U.S.A.* 43°49'N 84°46'W **173** D11
Clare □ *Ireland* 52°45'N 9°0'W **64** D3
Clare ➤ *Ireland* 53°20'N 9°2'W **64** C2
Clare I. *Ireland* 53°47'N 10°0'W **64** C1
Claremont *Calif., U.S.A.* 34°6'N 117°43'W **171** L9
Claremont *N.H.,*
U.S.A. 43°23'N 72°20'W **175** C12
Claremont Pt. *Australia* 14°1'S 143°41'E **150** A3
Claremore *U.S.A.* 36°19'N 95°36'W **176** C6
Claremorris *Ireland* 53°45'N 9°0'W **64** C3
Clarence ➤ *Australia* 29°25'S 153°22'E **151** D5
Clarence ➤ *N.Z.* 42°10'S 173°56'E **155** D5
Clarence, I. *Chile* 54°0'S 72°0'W **192** D2
Clarence Str. *Australia* 12°0'S 131°0'E **148** B5
Clarence Town
Bahamas 23°6'N 74°59'W **183** B5
Clarendon *Pa., U.S.A.* 41°47'N 79°6'W **174** E5
Clarendon *Tex.,*
U.S.A. 34°56'N 100°53'W **176** D4
Clarenville *Canada* 48°10'N 54°1'W **165** C9
Claresholm *Canada* 50°2'N 113°33'W **162** D6
Clarie Coast *Antarctica* 68°0'S 135°0'E **55** C9
Clarinda *U.S.A.* 40°44'N 95°2'W **172** E6
Clarington *Canada* 43°55'N 78°41'W **174** C6
Clarion *Iowa, U.S.A.* 42°44'N 93°44'W **172** D7
Clarion *Pa., U.S.A.* 41°13'N 79°23'W **174** E5
Clarion ➤ *U.S.A.* 41°7'N 79°41'W **174** E5
Clarion Fracture Zone
Pac. Oc. 20°0'N 120°0'W **158** H7
Clark *U.S.A.* 44°53'N 97°44'W **172** C5
Clark, Pt. *Canada* 44°4'N 81°45'W **174** B3
Clark Fork *U.S.A.* 48°9'N 116°11'W **168** B5
Clark Fork ➤ *U.S.A.* 48°9'N 116°15'W **168** B5
Clarkdale *U.S.A.* 34°46'N 112°3'W **169** J7
Clarke City *Canada* 50°12'N 66°38'W **165** B6
Clarke I. *Australia* 40°32'S 148°10'E **150** b
Clarke Ra. *Australia* 20°40'S 148°30'E **150** b
Clark's Harbour
Canada 43°25'N 65°38'W **165** D6
Clark's Hill L. = J. Strom
Thurmond L. *U.S.A.* 33°40'N 82°12'W **178** B7
Clarks Summit *U.S.A.* 41°30'N 75°42'W **175** E9
Clarksburg *U.S.A.* 39°17'N 80°30'W **173** F13
Clarksdale *U.S.A.* 34°12'N 90°35'W **177** D9
Clarkston *U.S.A.* 46°25'N 117°3'W **168** C5
Clarksville *Ark., U.S.A.* 35°28'N 93°28'W **176** D8
Clarksville *Tenn.,*
U.S.A. 36°32'N 87°21'W **177** C11
Clarksville *Tex., U.S.A.* 33°37'N 95°3'W **176** E7
Clatskanie *U.S.A.* 46°6'N 123°12'W **170** D3
Claude *U.S.A.* 35°7'N 101°22'W **176** D4
Claveria *Phil.* 18°37'N 121°4'E **119** A6
Clavering Ø *Greenland* 74°15'N 21°0'W **57** C8
Claxton *U.S.A.* 32°10'N 81°55'W **178** D7
Clay *U.S.A.* 38°17'N 121°10'W **170** G5
Clay Center *U.S.A.* 39°23'N 97°8'W **172** F5
Claypool *U.S.A.* 33°25'N 110°51'W **169** K8
Claysburg *U.S.A.* 40°17'N 78°27'W **174** F6
Claysville *U.S.A.* 40°7'N 80°25'W **174** F4
Clayton *Canada* 45°11'N 76°19'W **175** A8
Clayton *Ala., U.S.A.* 31°53'N 85°27'W **178** E4
Clayton *N. Mex.,*
U.S.A. 36°27'N 103°11'W **169** H12
Clayton *N.Y., U.S.A.* 44°14'N 76°5'W **175** B8
Clear, C. *Ireland* 51°25'N 9°32'W **64** E2
Clear, L. *Canada* 45°26'N 77°12'W **174** A7
Clear Hills *Canada* 56°40'N 119°30'W **162** B5
Clear I. *Ireland* 51°26'N 9°30'W **64** E2
Clear L. *U.S.A.* 39°2'N 122°47'W **170** F4
Clear Lake *Iowa, U.S.A.* 43°8'N 93°23'W **172** D7
Clear Lake *S. Dak.,*
U.S.A. 44°45'N 96°41'W **172** C5
Clear Lake Res. *U.S.A.* 41°56'N 121°5'W **168** F3
Clearfield *Pa., U.S.A.* 41°2'N 78°27'W **174** E6
Clearfield *Utah, U.S.A.* 41°7'N 112°2'W **168** F7
Clearlake *U.S.A.* 38°57'N 122°38'W **170** G4
Clearwater *Canada* 51°38'N 120°2'W **162** C4
Clearwater *U.S.A.* 27°59'N 82°48'W **179** H7
Clearwater ➤ *Alta.,*
Canada 52°22'N 114°57'W **162** C6
Clearwater ➤ *Alta.,*
Canada 56°44'N 111°23'W **163** B6
Clearwater L. *Canada* 53°34'N 99°49'W **163** C9
Clearwater Lake △
Canada 54°0'N 101°0'W **163** C8
Clearwater Mts. *U.S.A.* 46°5'N 115°20'W **168** C6
Clearwater River △
Canada 56°55'N 109°10'W **163** B7
Cleburne *U.S.A.* 32°21'N 97°23'W **176** E6
Clee Hills *U.K.* 52°26'N 2°35'W **67** E5
Cleethorpes *U.K.* 53°33'N 0°3'W **66** D7
Cleeve Cloud *U.K.* 51°56'N 2°0'W **67** F6
Clelles *France* 44°50'N 5°38'E **73** D9
Clemson *U.S.A.* 34°41'N 82°50'W **177** D13
Clerke Reef *Australia* 17°22'S 119°20'E **148** C2
Clermont *Australia* 22°49'S 147°39'E **150** C4
Clermont *France* 49°23'N 2°24'E **71** C9
Clermont-en-Argonne
France 49°5'N 5°4'E **71** C12
Clermont-Ferrand *France* 45°46'N 3°4'E **72** C7
Clermont-l'Hérault
France 43°38'N 3°26'E **72** E7
Clerval *France* 47°25'N 6°30'E **71** E13
Clervaux *Lux.* 50°4'N 6°2'E **69** D6
Cles *Italy* 46°21'N 11°2'E **92** B8
Cleve *Australia* 33°43'S 136°30'E **152** B2
Clevedon *U.K.* 51°26'N 2°52'W **67** F5
Cleveland *Miss.,*
U.S.A. 33°45'N 90°43'W **177** E9
Cleveland *Ohio, U.S.A.* 41°29'N 81°41'W **174** E3
Cleveland *Okla., U.S.A.* 36°19'N 96°28'W **176** C6
Cleveland *Tenn.,*
U.S.A. 35°10'N 84°53'W **177** D12
Cleveland *Tex., U.S.A.* 30°21'N 95°5'W **176** F7
Cleveland, C. *Australia* 19°11'S 147°1'E **150** B4
Cleveland, Mt. *U.S.A.* 48°56'N 113°51'W **168** B7
Cleveland Heights
U.S.A. 41°31'N 81°33'W **174** E3
Clevelândia *Brazil* 26°24'S 52°23'W **191** B5
Clew B. *Ireland* 53°50'N 9°49'W **64** C2
Clewiston *U.S.A.* 26°45'N 80°56'W **179** J9
Clifden *Ireland* 53°29'N 10°1'W **64** C1
Clifden *N.Z.* 46°1'S 167°42'E **155** G2
Cliffdell *U.S.A.* 46°56'N 121°5'W **170** D5
Cliffy Hd. *Australia* 35°1'S 116°29'E **149** G2
Clifton *Australia* 27°59'S 151°53'E **151** D5
Clifton *Ariz., U.S.A.* 33°3'N 109°18'W **169** K9
Clifton *Colo., U.S.A.* 39°7'N 108°25'W **168** G9
Clifton *Tex., U.S.A.* 31°47'N 97°35'W **176** F6
Clifton Beach *Australia* 16°46'S 145°39'E **150** B4
Climax *U.S.A.* 30°53'N 84°26'W **178** F5
Clinch ➤ *U.S.A.* 35°53'N 84°29'W **177** D12
Clingmans Dome
U.S.A. 35°34'N 83°30'W **177** D13
Clint *U.S.A.* 31°35'N 106°14'W **176** F1
Clinton *B.C., Canada* 51°6'N 121°35'W **162** C4
Clinton *Ont., Canada* 43°37'N 81°32'W **174** C3
Clinton *N.Z.* 46°12'S 169°23'E **155** G4
Clinton *Ark., U.S.A.* 35°36'N 92°28'W **176** D8
Clinton *Conn., U.S.A.* 41°17'N 72°32'W **175** E12
Clinton *Ill., U.S.A.* 40°9'N 88°57'W **172** E9
Clinton *Ind., U.S.A.* 39°40'N 87°24'W **172** F10
Clinton *Iowa, U.S.A.* 41°51'N 90°12'W **172** E8
Clinton *Mass., U.S.A.* 42°25'N 71°41'W **175** D13
Clinton *Miss., U.S.A.* 32°20'N 90°20'W **177** E9
Clinton *Mo., U.S.A.* 38°22'N 93°46'W **172** F7
Clinton *N.C., U.S.A.* 35°0'N 78°22'W **177** D15
Clinton *Okla., U.S.A.* 35°31'N 98°58'W **176** D5
Clinton *S.C., U.S.A.* 34°29'N 81°53'W **177** D14
Clinton *Tenn., U.S.A.* 36°6'N 84°8'W **177** C12
Clinton *Wash., U.S.A.* 47°59'N 122°21'W **170** C4
Clinton, C. *Australia* 22°30'S 150°45'E **150** C5
Clinton Colden L.
Canada 63°58'N 107°27'W **160** E10
Clio *U.S.A.* 31°43'N 85°37'W **178** D4
Clipperton, Î.
Pac. Oc. 10°18'N 109°13'W **157** F17
Clipperton Fracture Zone
Pac. Oc. 19°0'N 122°0'W **157** G16
Clisham *U.K.* 57°58'N 6°49'W **65** D2
Clisson *France* 47°5'N 1°16'W **70** E5
Clitheroe *U.K.* 53°53'N 2°22'W **66** D5
Clive *N.Z.* 39°36'S 176°58'E **154** F5
Clo-oose *Canada* 48°39'N 124°49'W **170** B2
Cloates, Pt. *Australia* 22°43'S 113°40'E **148** D1
Clocolan *S. Africa* 28°55'S 27°34'E **145** C4
Clodomira *Argentina* 27°35'S 64°14'W **190** B3
Cloghaneely *Ireland* 55°8'N 8°5'W **64** A3
Clogher Hd. *Ireland* 53°48'N 6°14'W **64** C5
Clonakilty *Ireland* 51°37'N 8°53'W **64** E3
Clonakilty B. *Ireland* 51°35'N 8°51'W **64** E3
Cloncurry *Australia* 20°40'S 140°28'E **150** C3
Cloncurry *Ireland* 53°25'N 6°48'W **64** C5
Cloncurry ➤
Australia 18°37'S 140°40'E **150** B3
Clondalkin *Ireland* 53°19'N 6°25'W **64** C5
Clones *Ireland* 54°11'N 7°15'W **64** B4
Clonmel *Ireland* 52°21'N 7°42'W **64** D4
Cloppenburg *Germany* 52°51'N 8°1'E **76** C4
Cloquet *U.S.A.* 46°43'N 92°28'W **172** B7
Clorinda *Argentina* 25°16'S 57°45'W **190** B4
Cloud Peak *U.S.A.* 44°23'N 107°11'W **168** D10
Cloudcroft *U.S.A.* 32°58'N 105°45'W **169** K11
Cloudy B. *N.Z.* 41°25'S 174°10'E **155** D5
Cloverdale *U.S.A.* 38°48'N 123°1'W **170** G4
Clovis *Calif., U.S.A.* 36°49'N 119°42'W **170** J7
Clovis *N. Mex., U.S.A.* 34°24'N 103°12'W **169** J12
Cloyes-sur-le-Loir *France* 48°0'N 1°14'E **70** E8
Cloyne *Canada* 44°49'N 77°11'W **174** B7
Cluain Meala = Clonmel
Ireland 52°21'N 7°42'W **64** D4
Club Terrace *Australia* 37°35'S 148°58'E **153** F4
Cluj □ *Romania* 46°45'N 23°30'E **81** D8
Cluj-Napoca *Romania* 46°47'N 23°38'E **81** D8
Clunes *Australia* 37°20'S 143°45'E **152** B3
Cluny *France* 46°26'N 4°38'E **71** F11
Cluses *France* 46°5'N 6°35'E **71** F13
Clusone *Italy* 45°53'N 9°57'E **92** C6
Clutha ➤ *N.Z.* 46°20'S 169°49'E **155** G4
Clwyd ➤ *U.K.* 53°19'N 3°31'W **66** D4
Clyattville *U.S.A.* 30°42'N 83°19'W **178** F6
Clyde *Canada* 54°9'N 113°39'W **162** C6
Clyde *N.Z.* 45°12'S 169°20'E **155** F4
Clyde *U.S.A.* 43°5'N 76°52'W **174** C8
Clyde ➤ *U.K.* 55°55'N 4°30'W **65** F4
Clyde, Firth of *U.K.* 55°22'N 5°1'W **65** F3
Clyde River *Canada* 70°30'N 68°30'W **161** C18
Clydebank *U.K.* 55°54'N 4°23'W **65** F4
Clymer *N.Y., U.S.A.* 42°1'N 79°37'W **174** D5
Clymer *Pa., U.S.A.* 40°40'N 79°1'W **174** F5
Clyo *U.S.A.* 32°29'N 81°16'W **178** D7
Ćmielów *Poland* 50°53'N 21°31'E **83** H8
Côa ➤ *Portugal* 41°5'N 7°6'W **88** D3
Coachella *U.S.A.* 33°41'N 116°10'W **171** M10
Coachella Canal
U.S.A. 32°43'N 114°57'W **171** N12
Coahoma *U.S.A.* 32°18'N 101°18'W **176** E4
Coahuayana ➤
Mexico 18°41'N 103°45'W **180** D4
Coahuila □ *Mexico* 27°20'N 102°0'W **180** B4
Coal ➤ *Canada* 59°39'N 126°57'E **162** B3
Coal I. *N.Z.* 46°8'S 166°40'E **155** G1
Coalane *Mozam.* 17°48'S 37°2'E **143** F4
Coalcomán *Mexico* 18°47'N 103°9'W **180** D4
Coaldale *Canada* 49°45'N 112°35'W **162** D6
Coalgate *U.S.A.* 34°32'N 96°13'W **176** D6
Coalinga *U.S.A.* 36°9'N 120°21'W **170** J6
Coalisland *U.K.* 54°33'N 6°42'W **64** B5
Coalville *U.K.* 52°44'N 1°23'W **66** E6
Coalville *U.S.A.* 40°55'N 111°24'W **168** F8
Coamo *Puerto Rico* 18°5'N 66°22'W **183** d
Coari *Brazil* 4°8'S 63°7'W **186** D6
Coast □ *Kenya* 2°40'S 39°45'E **142** C4
Coast ➤ *Kenya* 2°40'S 39°45'E **142** C4
Coast Mts. *Canada* 55°0'N 129°20'W **162** C3
Coast Ranges *U.S.A.* 39°0'N 123°0'W **170** G4
Coatbridge *U.K.* 55°52'N 4°6'W **65** F4
Coatepec *Mexico* 19°27'N 96°58'W **181** D5
Coatepeque *Guatemala* 14°46'N 91°55'W **182** D1
Coatesville *U.S.A.* 39°59'N 75°50'W **173** F16
Coaticook *Canada* 45°10'N 71°46'W **175** A13

Coats I. *Canada* 62°30N 83°0W **161** E15
Coats Land *Antarctica* 77°0S 25°0W **55** D1
Coatzacoalcos *Mexico* 18°7N 94°25W **181** D6
Cobá *Mexico* 20°31N 87°45W **181** C7
Cobadin *Romania* 44°5N 28°13E **81** F13
Cobalt *Canada* 47°25N 79°42W **164** C4
Cobán *Guatemala* 15°30N 90°21W **182** C1
Çobanlar *Turkey* 38°41N 30°47E **99** C12
Cobar *Australia* 31°27S 145°48E **153** A6
Cobargo *Australia* 36°20S 149°55E **153** D8
Cobbannah *Australia* 37°37S 147°13E **153** D7
Cobberas, Mt.
  Australia 36°53S 148°12E **153** D8
Cobden *Australia* 38°20S 143°4E **152** E5
Cobh *Ireland* 51°51N 8°17W **64** E3
Cóbh, An = Cobh *Ireland* 51°51N 8°17W **64** E3
Cobija *Bolivia* 11°0S 68°50W **188** C4
Cobleskill *U.S.A.* 42°41N 74°29W **175** D10
Coboconk *Canada* 44°39N 78°48W **174** B6
Cobourg *Canada* 43°58N 78°10W **174** C6
Cobourg Pen.
  Australia 11°20S 132°15E **148** B5
Cobram *Australia* 35°54S 145°40E **153** C6
Cóbué *Mozam.* 12°0S 34°58E **143** E3
Coburg *Germany* 50°15N 10°58E **77** E6
Coburg I. *Canada* 75°57N 79°26W **161** B16
Coca *Spain* 41°13N 4°32W **88** D6
Cocachacra *Peru* 17°5S 71°45W **188** D3
Cocal *Brazil* 3°28S 41°34W **189** A2
Cocanada = Kakinada
  India 16°57N 82°11E **126** F6
Cocentaina *Spain* 38°45N 0°27W **91** G4
Cochabamba *Bolivia* 17°26S 66°10W **188** G5
Cochem *Germany* 50°9N 7°9E **77** E3
Cochemane *Mozam.* 17°0S 32°54E **143** F3
Cochin = Kochi *India* 9°58N 76°20E **127** K3
Cochin China = Nam-Phan
  Vietnam 10°30N 106°0E **121** G6
Cochran *U.S.A.* 32°23N 83°21W **178** C6
Cochrane Alta.,
  Canada 51°11N 114°30W **162** C6
Cochrane Ont., *Canada* 49°0N 81°0W **164** C3
Cochrane *Chile* 47°15S 72°33W **192** C2
Cochrane → *Canada* 59°0N 103°40W **163** B8
Cochrane, L. *Chile* 47°10S 72°0W **192** C2
Cochranton *U.S.A.* 41°31N 80°3W **174** E4
Cockburn *Australia* 32°5S 141°0E **152** B4
Cockburn, Canal *Chile* 54°30S 72°0W **192** D2
Cockburn I. *Canada* 45°55N 83°22W **164** C3
Cockburn Ra. *Australia* 15°46S 128°0E **148** C4
Cockermouth *U.K.* 54°40N 3°22W **66** C4
Cocklebiddy *Australia* 32°0S 126°3E **149** F4
Cockpit Country, The
  Jamaica 18°15N 77°45W **182** a
Coco → *Cent. Amer.* 15°0N 83°8W **182** D3
Coco, I. del *Pac. Oc.* 5°25N 87°55W **157** G19
Coco Channel *Asia* 13°45N 93°10E **127** H11
Cocoa *U.S.A.* 28°21N 80°44W **179** G9
Cocoa Beach *U.S.A.* 28°19N 80°37W **179** G9
Cocobeach *Gabon* 0°59N 9°34E **140** D1
Cocoparra △ *Australia* 34°10S 146°12E **153** C7
Cocora *Romania* 44°45N 27°3E **81** F12
Côcos *Brazil* 14°10S 44°33W **189** C2
Côcos → *Brazil* 12°44S 44°48W **189** C2
Cocos B. *Trin. & Tob.* 10°24N 61°2W **187** K15
Cocos Basin *Ind. Oc.* 1°0N 94°0E **146** D8
Cocos Is. = Coco, I. del
  Pac. Oc. 5°25N 87°55W **157** G19
Cocos Is. *Ind. Oc.* 12°10S 96°55E **146** F8
Cocos Ridge *Pac. Oc.* 4°0N 88°0W **157** G19
Cod, C. *U.S.A.* 42°5N 70°10W **173** D18
Codajás *Brazil* 3°55S 62°0W **186** D6
Codfish I. *N.Z.* 46°47S 167°38E **155** G2
Codigoro *Italy* 44°49N 12°8E **93** D9
Codlea *Romania* 45°42N 25°27E **81** E10
Codó *Brazil* 4°30S 43°55W **189** A2
Codogno *Italy* 45°9N 9°42E **92** C6
Codpa *Chile* 18°50S 69°44W **188** G4
Codróipo *Italy* 45°58N 13°0E **93** C10
Codru, Munţii *Romania* 46°30N 22°15E **80** D7
Cody *U.S.A.* 44°32N 109°3W **168** D9
Coe Hill *Canada* 44°52N 77°50W **174** B7
Coelemu *Chile* 36°30S 72°48W **190** D1
Coelho Neto *Brazil* 4°15S 43°0W **189** A2
Coen *Australia* 13°52S 143°12E **150** A3
Coesfeld *Germany* 51°56N 7°10E **76** D3
Coetivy I. *Seychelles* 7°8S 56°16E **146** E4
Coeur d'Alene *U.S.A.* 47°41N 116°46W **168** C5
Coeur d'Alene L.
  U.S.A. 47°32N 116°49W **168** C5
Coevorden *Neths.* 52°40N 6°44E **69** B6
Cofete *Canary Is.* 28°6N 14°23W **100** F5
Coffeyville *U.S.A.* 37°2N 95°37W **172** G6
Coffin B. *Australia* 34°38S 135°28E **151** E2
Coffin Bay *Australia* 34°37S 135°29E **151** E2
Coffin Bay △ *Australia* 34°34S 135°19E **151** E2
Coffin Bay Peninsula
  Australia 34°32S 135°15E **151** E2
Coffs Harbour
  Australia 30°16S 153°5E **153** A10
Cofrentes *Spain* 39°13N 1°5W **91** F3
Cogalnic → *Ukraine* 45°49N 29°40E **81** E14
Cogealac *Romania* 44°36N 28°36E **81** F13
Coghinas → *Italy* 40°55N 8°48E **94** B1
Coghinas, L. del *Italy* 40°46N 9°3E **94** B2
Cognac *France* 45°41N 0°20W **72** C3
Cogne *Italy* 45°37N 7°21E **92** C4
Cogolin *France* 43°15N 6°29E **73** E10
Cogolludo *Spain* 40°59N 3°10W **90** E1
Cohocton *U.S.A.* 42°30N 77°30W **174** D7
Cohocton → *U.S.A.* 42°9N 77°6W **174** D7
Cohoes *U.S.A.* 42°46N 73°42W **175** D11
Cohuna *Australia* 35°45S 144°15E **152** C6
Coiba, I. de *Panama* 7°30N 81°40W **182** E3
Coig → *Argentina* 51°0S 69°10W **192** D3
Coigeach, Rubha *U.K.* 58°6N 5°26W **65** C3
Coihaique *Chile* 45°30S 71°45W **192** C2
Coimbatore *India* 11°2N 76°59E **127** J3
Coimbra *Brazil* 19°55S 57°48W **186** G7
Coimbra *Portugal* 40°15N 8°27W **88** B2
Coimbra □ *Portugal* 40°12N 8°25W **88** B2
Coín *Spain* 36°40N 4°48W **89** E6
Coipasa, L. de *Bolivia* 19°12S 68°7W **188** D4
Coipasa, Salar de
  Bolivia 19°26S 68°9W **188** D4
Cojata *Peru* 15°2S 69°20W **188** D4
Cojimíes *Ecuador* 0°20N 80°0W **186** C1
Cojocna *Romania* 46°45N 23°50E **81** D8
Cojutepequé *El Salv.* 13°41N 88°54W **182** D2
Čoka *Serbia* 45°57N 20°12E **80** E5

Cokeville *U.S.A.* 42°5N 110°57W **168** E8
Colaba Pt. *India* 18°53N 72°48E **126** E1
Colac *Australia* 38°21S 143°35E **152** E5
Colachel = Kolachel
  India 8°10N 77°15E **127** K3
Colán *Peru* 5°0S 81°0W **188** B1
Colatina *Brazil* 19°32S 40°37W **188** G10
Colbeck, C. *Antarctica* 77°6S 157°48W **55** D13
Colbert *U.S.A.* 34°2N 83°13W **178** A4
Colborne *Canada* 44°0N 77°53W **174** C7
Colby *U.S.A.* 39°24N 101°3W **172** F3
Colca → *Peru* 15°55S 72°43W **186** G4
Colca, Cañón del *Peru* 15°50S 72°20W **188** D3
Colchester *U.K.* 51°54N 0°55E **67** F8
Colchester *U.S.A.* 41°35N 72°20W **175** E12
Cold L. *Canada* 54°33N 110°5W **163** C7
Cold Lake *Canada* 54°27N 110°10W **163** C7
Coldstream *Canada* 50°13N 119°11W **162** C5
Coldstream *U.K.* 55°39N 2°15W **65** F6
Coldwater *Canada* 44°42N 79°40W **174** B5
Coldwater Kans.,
  U.S.A. 37°16N 99°20W **172** G4
Coldwater Mich.,
  U.S.A. 41°57N 85°0W **173** E11
Coleambally *Australia* 34°49S 145°52E **153** C6
Colebrook *U.S.A.* 44°54N 71°30W **175** B13
Coleman *Canada* 49°40N 114°30W **162** D6
Coleman Fla., *U.S.A.* 28°48N 82°4W **179** G7
Coleman Tex., *U.S.A.* 31°50N 99°26W **176** F5
Coleman → *S. Africa* 15°6S 141°38E **150** B3
Colenso *S. Africa* 28°44S 29°50E **145** C4
Coleraine *Australia* 37°36S 141°40E **152** D4
Coleraine *U.K.* 55°8N 6°41W **64** A5
Coleridge, L. *N.Z.* 43°17S 171°30E **155** D6
Coleroon → *India* 11°25N 79°50E **127** J4
Colesberg *S. Africa* 30°45S 25°5E **144** D4
Coleville *U.S.A.* 38°34N 119°30W **170** G7
Colfax Calif., *U.S.A.* 39°6N 120°57W **170** F6
Colfax La., *U.S.A.* 31°31N 92°42W **176** F8
Colfax Wash., *U.S.A.* 46°53N 117°22W **168** C5
Colhué Huapí, L.
  Argentina 45°30S 69°0W **192** C3
Colibaşi = Mioveni
  Romania 44°56N 24°54E **81** F9
Colibaşi *Moldova* 45°43N 28°11E **81** E13
Cólico *Italy* 46°8N 9°22E **92** B6
Coligny *France* 46°23N 5°21E **71** F12
Coligny *S. Africa* 26°17S 26°15E **145** C4
Colima *Mexico* 19°14N 103°43W **180** D4
Colima □ *Mexico* 19°10N 104°0W **180** D4
Colima, Nevado de
  Mexico 19°33N 103°38W **180** D4
Colina *Chile* 33°13S 70°45W **190** C1
Colina do Norte
  Guinea-Biss. 12°28N 15°0W **138** C2
Colinas Goiás, *Brazil* 14°15S 48°2W **189** C1
Colinas Maranhão, *Brazil* 6°0S 44°10W **189** B2
Colindres *Spain* 43°24N 3°27W **88** B7
Coll *U.K.* 56°39N 6°34W **65** E2
Collaguasi *Chile* 21°5S 68°45W **190** A2
Collarada, Peña *Spain* 42°43N 0°29W **90** C4
Collarenebri *Australia* 29°33S 148°34E **151** D4
Colle di Val d'Elsa *Italy* 43°25N 11°7E **92** E8
Colléchio *Italy* 44°45N 10°13E **92** D7
Colleen Bawn *Zimbabwe* 21°0S 29°12E **143** G2
College *U.S.A.* 64°52N 147°49W **166** C10
College Park *U.S.A.* 33°39N 84°27W **178** B5
College Station *U.S.A.* 30°37N 96°21W **176** F6
Collesalvetti *Italy* 43°34N 10°27E **92** E7
Colli Euganei △ *Italy* 45°18N 11°43E **93** C8
Collie W. Austral.,
  Australia 33°22S 116°8E **149** F2
Collier B. *Australia* 16°10S 124°15E **148** C3
Collier Ra. *Australia* 24°45S 119°10E **149** D2
Collier Range △
  Australia 24°39S 119°7E **149** D2
Collierville *U.S.A.* 35°3N 89°40W **177** D10
Collina, Passo di *Italy* 44°2N 10°56E **92** D7
Collingwood *Canada* 44°29N 80°13W **174** B4
Collingwood *N.Z.* 40°41S 172°40E **155** D4
Collins *Canada* 50°17N 89°27W **164** B2
Collins *U.S.A.* 32°11N 82°7W **178** D7
Collins Bay *Canada* 44°14N 76°36W **175** B8
Collinson Pen.
  Canada 69°58N 101°24W **160** D11
Collinsville *Australia* 20°30S 147°56E **150** C4
Collipulli *Chile* 37°55S 72°30W **190** D1
Collo *Algeria* 36°58N 6°37E **136** A5
Collooney *Ireland* 54°11N 8°29W **64** B3
Colmar *France* 48°5N 7°20E **71** D14
Colmars *France* 44°11N 6°39E **73** D10
Colmenar *Spain* 36°54N 4°20W **89** A6
Colmenar de Oreja *Spain* 40°6N 3°25W **88** F7
Colmenar Viejo *Spain* 40°39N 3°47W **88** E7
Colo → *Australia* 33°25S 150°52E **153** B9
Cologne = Köln *Germany* 50°56N 6°57E **76** E2
Coloma, L. d'en *Spain* 38°54N 1°16E **100** B11
Coloma *U.S.A.* 38°48N 120°53W **170** G6
Colomb-Béchar = Béchar
  Algeria 31°38N 2°18W **136** B3
Colombey-les-Belles
  France 48°32N 5°54E **71** D12
Colombey-les-Deux-Églises
  France 48°13N 4°50E **71** D11
Colômbia *Brazil* 20°10S 48°40W **189** E1
Colombia ■ *S. Amer.* 3°45N 73°0W **186** C4
Colombian Basin
  Caribbean 14°0N 76°0W **182** D4
Colombo *Sri Lanka* 6°56N 79°58E **127** L4
Colomiers *France* 43°36N 1°21E **72** E5
Colón B. Aires, *Argentina* 33°53S 61°7W **190** C3
Colón Entre Ríos,
  Argentina 32°12S 58°10W **190** C4
Colón *Cuba* 22°42N 80°54W **182** B3
Colón *Panama* 9°20N 79°54W **182** E4
Colón, Arch. de *Ecuador* 0°0 91°0W **184** D1
Colonia 25 de Mayo
  Argentina 37°48S 67°41W **192** A3
Colònia de Sant Jordi
  Spain 39°19N 2°59E **100** B9
Colonia del Sacramento
  Uruguay 34°25S 57°50W **190** C4
Colonia Dora *Argentina* 28°34S 62°59W **190** B3
Colonial Beach *U.S.A.* 38°15N 76°58W **175** D11 (?)
Colonie *U.S.A.* 42°43N 73°50W **175** D11
Colonna, C. *Italy* 39°2N 17°11E **95** C10
Colonsay *Canada* 51°59N 105°52W **163** C7
Colonsay *U.K.* 56°5N 6°12W **65** E2
Colorado □ *U.S.A.* 39°30N 105°30W **168** G11
Colorado → *Argentina* 39°50S 62°8W **192** A4

Colorado → *N. Amer.* 31°45N 114°40W **169** L6
Colorado → *U.S.A.* 28°36N 95°59W **176** G7
Colorado City *U.S.A.* 32°24N 100°52W **176** E4
Colorado Plateau
  U.S.A. 37°0N 111°0W **169** H8
Colorado River Aqueduct
  U.S.A. 33°50N 117°23W **171** L12
Colorno *Italy* 44°56N 10°23E **92** D7
Colotlán *Mexico* 22°6N 103°16W **180** C4
Colquitt *U.S.A.* 31°10N 84°44W **178** D5
Colstrip *U.S.A.* 45°53N 106°38W **168** D10
Colton *U.S.A.* 44°33N 74°56W **175** B10
Columbia Ala., *U.S.A.* 31°18N 85°7W **178** D4
Columbia Ky., *U.S.A.* 37°6N 85°18W **173** G11
Columbia La., *U.S.A.* 32°6N 92°5W **176** E8
Columbia Miss.,
  U.S.A. 31°15N 89°50W **177** F10
Columbia Mo., *U.S.A.* 38°57N 92°20W **172** F7
Columbia Pa., *U.S.A.* 40°2N 76°30W **175** F8
Columbia S.C., *U.S.A.* 34°0N 81°2W **178** A8
Columbia Tenn., *U.S.A.* 35°37N 87°2W **177** D11
Columbia → *N. Amer.* 46°15N 124°5W **170** D2
Columbia, C. *Canada* 83°6N 69°57W **161** A4
Columbia, District of □
  U.S.A. 38°55N 77°0W **173** F15
Columbia, Mt. *Canada* 52°8N 117°20W **162** C5
Columbia Basin *U.S.A.* 46°45N 119°5W **168** C4
Columbia Falls *U.S.A.* 48°23N 114°11W **168** B6
Columbia Mts. *Canada* 52°0N 119°0W **162** C5
Columbia Plateau
  U.S.A. 44°0N 117°30W **168** E5
Columbiana *U.S.A.* 40°53N 80°42W **174** F4
Columbretes, Is. *Spain* 39°50N 0°50E **90** F5
Columbus Ga., *U.S.A.* 32°28N 84°59W **178** C5
Columbus Ind., *U.S.A.* 39°13N 85°55W **173** F11
Columbus Kans.,
  U.S.A. 37°10N 94°50W **172** G6
Columbus Miss.,
  U.S.A. 33°30N 88°25W **177** E10
Columbus Mont.,
  U.S.A. 45°38N 109°15W **168** D9
Columbus N. Mex.,
  U.S.A. 31°50N 107°38W **169** L10
Columbus Nebr., *U.S.A.* 41°26N 97°22W **172** E5
Columbus Ohio, *U.S.A.* 39°58N 83°0W **173** F12
Columbus Tex., *U.S.A.* 29°42N 96°33W **176** G6
Colunga *Spain* 43°29N 5°16W **88** B5
Colusa *U.S.A.* 39°13N 122°1W **170** F4
Colville *U.S.A.* 48°33N 117°54W **168** B5
Colville → *U.S.A.* 70°25N 150°30W **166** A9
Colville, C. *N.Z.* 36°29N 175°21E **154** C4
Colville Channel *N.Z.* 36°25S 175°27E **154** C4
Colwood *Canada* 48°26N 123°29W **170** B3
Colwyn Bay *U.K.* 53°18N 3°44W **66** D4
Comácchio *Italy* 44°42N 12°11E **93** D9
Comalcalco *Mexico* 18°16N 93°13W **181** D6
Comallo *Argentina* 41°0S 70°5W **192** B2
Comana *Romania* 44°10N 26°10E **81** F11
Comanche *U.S.A.* 31°54N 98°36W **176** F5
Comandante Ferraz
  Antarctica 62°30S 58°0W **55** C18
Comandante Luis Piedrabuena
  Argentina 49°59S 68°54W **192** C3
Comăneşti *Romania* 46°25N 26°26E **81** D11
Comarnic *Romania* 45°15N 25°38E **81** E10
Comayagua *Honduras* 14°25N 87°37W **182** D2
Combahee → *U.S.A.* 32°31N 80°31W **178** C9
Combara *Australia* 31°10S 148°22E **153** A8
Combarbalá *Chile* 31°11S 71°2W **190** C1
Combe Martin *U.K.* 51°12N 4°3W **67** F3
Combeaufontaine
  France 47°38N 5°54E **71** E12
Comber *Canada* 42°14N 82°33W **174** D2
Comber *U.K.* 54°33N 5°45W **64** B6
Combermere *Canada* 45°22N 77°37W **174** A7
Comblain-au-Pont
  Belgium 50°29N 5°35E **69** D5
Combourg *France* 48°25N 1°46W **70** D5
Comboyne *Australia* 31°34S 152°27E **153** A10
Combrailles *France* 46°8N 2°8E **72** C7
Combronde *France* 45°58N 3°5E **72** C7
Comer Ala., *U.S.A.* 32°2N 85°23W **178** C4
Comer Ga., *U.S.A.* 34°4N 83°8W **178** A6
Comeragh Mts. *Ireland* 52°18N 7°34W **64** D4
Comet *Australia* 23°36S 148°38E **150** C4
Comilla *Bangla.* 23°28N 91°10E **123** H17
Comino *Malta* 36°1N 14°20E **101** C1
Comino, C. *Italy* 40°32N 9°49E **94** B2
Cómiso *Italy* 36°59N 14°36E **95** F7
Comitán de Domínguez
  Mexico 16°15N 92°8W **181** D6
Commentry *France* 46°20N 2°46E **71** F9
Commerce Ga., *U.S.A.* 34°12N 83°28W **178** A6
Commerce Tex., *U.S.A.* 33°15N 95°54W **176** E6
Commercy *France* 48°43N 5°34E **71** D12
Committee B. *Canada* 68°30N 86°30W **161** D14
Commodore, C. *Canada* 44°47N 80°54W **174** B4
Commonwealth B.
  Antarctica 67°0S 144°0E **55** C10
Commoron Cr. →
  Australia 28°22S 150°8E **151** D5
Communism Pk. = imeni Ismail
  Samani, Pik *Tajikistan* 39°0N 72°2E **109** E8
Como *Italy* 45°47N 9°5E **92** C6
Como, L. di *Italy* 46°0N 9°11E **92** B6
Comodoro Rivadavia
  Argentina 45°50S 67°40W **192** C3
Comoé → *Ivory C.* 5°12N 3°44W **138** D4
Comoé △ *Ivory C.* 9°0N 3°35W **138** D4
Comorâşte *Romania* 45°10N 21°35E **80** E6
Comorin, C. = Kannyakumari
  India 8°4N 77°40E **127** K3
Comoros ■ *Ind. Oc.* 12°10S 44°15E **141** a
Comox *Canada* 49°42N 124°55W **162** D4
Compass Lake *U.S.A.* 30°36N 85°24W **178** E4
Compiègne *France* 49°24N 2°50E **71** C9
Comporta *Portugal* 38°22N 8°46W **89** G2
Comprida, I. *Brazil* 24°50S 47°42W **191** A6
Compton *Canada* 45°14N 71°49W **175** A13
Compton *U.S.A.* 33°53N 118°13W **171** M8
Comrat *Moldova* 46°18N 28°40E **81** E13
Comunidad *Peru* 11°4S 75°55W **... ...**
Con Cuong *Vietnam* 19°2N 104°54E **120** C5
Con Dao △ *Vietnam* 8°42N 106°35E **121** H6
Con Son, Dao *Vietnam* 8°41N 106°37E **121** H6
Cona Niyeu *Argentina* 41°58S 66°30W **192** B3
Conakry *Guinea* 9°29N 13°49W **138** D2
Conara *Australia* 41°50S 147°26E **155** G4

Conargo *Australia* 35°16S 145°10E **153** C6
Conceição *Brazil* 7°33S 38°31W **189** B3
Conceição *Mozam.* 18°47S 36°7E **143** F4
Conceição da Barra
  Brazil 18°35S 39°45W **189** G11
Conceição do Araguaia
  Brazil 8°0S 49°2W **187** E9
Conceição do Canindé
  Brazil 7°54S 41°34W **189** B2
Concepción *Argentina* 27°20S 65°35W **190** B2
Concepción *Bolivia* 16°15S 62°8W **186** G6
Concepción *Chile* 36°50S 73°0W **190** D1
Concepción *Paraguay* 23°22S 57°26W **190** A4
Concepción *Peru* 11°54S 75°19W **188** C2
Concepción □ *Chile* 37°0S 72°30W **190** D1
Concepción, Est. de
  Chile 50°30S 74°55W **192** D2
Concepción, L. *Bolivia* 17°20S 61°20W **186** G6
Concepción, Pta.
  Mexico 26°53N 111°50W **180** B2
Concepción del Oro
  Mexico 24°38N 101°25W **180** C4
Concepción del Uruguay
  Argentina 32°35S 58°20W **190** C4
Conception, Pt.
  U.S.A. 34°27N 120°28W **171** L6
Conception B. *Bahamas* 23°52N 75°9W **183** B4
Conception B. *Namibia* 23°55S 14°22E **144** B1
Conception I. *Bahamas* 23°52N 75°9W **183** B4
Concession *Zimbabwe* 17°27S 30°56E **143** F3
Conchas Dam *U.S.A.* 35°22N 104°11W **169** J11
Conches-en-Ouche
  France 48°58N 0°56E **70** D7
Concho *U.S.A.* 34°28N 109°36W **169** J9
Concho → *U.S.A.* 31°34N 99°43W **176** F5
Conchos → Chihuahua,
  Mexico 29°35N 104°25W **180** B4
Conchos → Tamaulipas,
  Mexico 24°55N 97°38W **181** C5
Concord Calif., *U.S.A.* 37°59N 122°2W **170** H4
Concord Ga., *U.S.A.* 33°5N 84°27W **178** B5
Concord N.C., *U.S.A.* 35°25N 80°35W **177** D14
Concord N.H., *U.S.A.* 43°12N 71°32W **175** C13
Concordia *Antarctica* 75°6S 123°23E **55** D9
Concordia *Argentina* 31°20S 58°2W **190** C4
Concórdia Amazonas,
  Brazil 4°36S 66°36W **186** D5
Concórdia Sta. Catarina,
  Brazil 27°14S 52°1W **191** B5
Concordia *Mexico* 23°17N 106°4W **180** C3
Concrete *U.S.A.* 48°32N 121°45W **168** B3
Condah *Australia* 37°57S 141°44E **152** D4
Condamine *Australia* 26°56S 150°9E **151** D5
Condat *France* 45°21N 2°46E **72** C6
Conde *Brazil* 11°49S 37°37W **189** C3
Condé *U.S.A.* 45°9N 98°6W **172** C4
Condé-sur-Noireau
  France 48°51N 0°33W **70** D6
Condeúba *Brazil* 14°52S 42°0W **189** C2
Condobolin *Australia* 33°4S 147°6E **153** B8
Condom *France* 43°57N 0°22E **72** E4
Condon *U.S.A.* 45°14N 120°11W **168** D3
Conegliano *Italy* 45°53N 12°18E **93** C9
Conejera, I. = Conills, I. des
  Spain 39°11N 2°58E **100** B9
Conejos *Mexico* 26°14N 103°53W **180** B4
Conemaugh → *U.S.A.* 40°28N 79°19W **174** F5
Confluence *U.S.A.* 39°49N 79°21W **174** F5
Confolens *France* 46°2N 0°40E **72** B4
Confuso → *Paraguay* 25°9S 57°34W **190** B4
Congaree → *U.S.A.* 33°44N 80°38W **178** B9
Congaree △ *U.S.A.* 33°47N 80°47W **178** B9
Congaz *Moldova* 46°7N 28°36E **81** D13
Conghua *China* 23°36N 113°31E **117** F9
Congjiang *China* 25°43N 108°52E **116** E7
Congleton *U.K.* 53°10N 2°13W **66** D5
Congo *Brazil* 7°48S 36°40W **189** B3
Congo (Brazzaville) = Congo ■
  Africa 1°0S 16°0E **140** E3
Congo (Kinshasa) = Congo, Dem.
  Rep. of the ■ *Africa* 3°0S 23°0E **140** E4
Congo ■ *Africa* 1°0S 16°0E **140** E3
Congo → *Africa* 6°4S 12°24E **140** F2
Congo, Dem. Rep. of the ■
  Africa 3°0S 23°0E **140** E4
Congo Basin *Africa* 0°10S 24°30E **140** E4
Congonhas *Brazil* 20°30S 43°52W **189** E2
Congress *U.S.A.* 34°9N 112°51W **169** J7
Conguillío △ *Chile* 38°40S 71°42W **192** A2
Conil de la Frontera
  Spain 36°17N 6°9W **89** E4
Coniston *Canada* 46°29N 80°51W **164** C3
Conjeeveram = Kanchipuram
  India 12°52N 79°45E **127** H4
Conklin *Canada* 55°38N 111°5W **163** B6
Conklin *U.S.A.* 42°2N 75°49W **175** D9
Conn, L. *Ireland* 54°3N 9°15W **64** B2
Connacht □ *Ireland* 53°43N 9°12W **64** C2
Conneaut *U.S.A.* 41°57N 80°34W **174** E4
Conneautville *U.S.A.* 41°45N 80°22W **174** E4
Connecticut → *U.S.A.* 41°16N 72°20W **175** E12
Connecticut □ *U.S.A.* 41°30N 72°45W **175** E12
Connell *U.S.A.* 46°40N 118°52W **168** C4
Connellsville *U.S.A.* 40°1N 79°35W **174** F5
Connemara *Ireland* 53°29N 9°45W **64** C2
Connemara △ *Ireland* 53°32N 9°52W **64** C2
Connerré *France* 48°3N 0°30E **70** D7
Connersville *U.S.A.* 39°39N 85°8W **173** F11
Connors Ra. *Australia* 21°40S 149°10E **150** C4
Conoble *Australia* 32°55S 144°33E **153** B8
Conon → *U.K.* 57°33N 4°28W **65** D4
Conran, C. *Australia* 37°49S 148°44E **153** D8
Conroe *U.S.A.* 30°19N 95°27W **176** F7
Consecon *Canada* 44°0N 77°31W **174** C7
Conselheiro Lafaiete
  Brazil 20°40S 43°48W **189** E2
Conselheiro Pena
  Brazil 19°10S 41°30W **189** E2
Consett *U.K.* 54°51N 1°50W **66** C6
Consort *Canada* 52°1N 110°46W **163** C6

Constance = Konstanz
  Germany 47°40N 9°10E **77** H5
Constance, L. = Bodensee
  Europe 47°35N 9°25E **77** H5
Constanţa *Romania* 44°14N 28°38E **81** F13
Constanţa □ *Romania* 44°15N 28°15E **81** F13
Constantina *Spain* 37°51N 5°40W **89** H5
Constantine *Algeria* 36°25N 6°42E **136** A5
Constantine □ *Algeria* 36°30N 6°40E **136** A5
Constitución *Chile* 35°20S 72°30W **190** D1
Constitución *Uruguay* 31°0S 57°50W **190** C4
Constitución de 1857 △
  Mexico 32°4N 115°55W **180** A1
Consuegra *Spain* 39°28N 3°36W **89** F7
Consul *Canada* 49°20N 109°30W **163** D7
Contact *U.S.A.* 41°46N 114°45W **168** F6
Contagem *Brazil* 19°55S 44°6W **189** E2
Contai *India* 21°54N 87°46E **125** J12
Contamana *Peru* 7°19S 74°55W **186** E4
Contas → *Brazil* 14°17S 39°1W **189** C3
Contes *France* 43°49N 7°19E **73** E11
Contoocook *U.S.A.* 43°13N 71°45W **175** C13
Contra Costa *Mozam.* 25°9S 33°30E **145** C5
Contres *France* 47°24N 1°26E **70** E8
Contrexéville *France* 48°10N 5°53E **71** D12
Contumazá *Peru* 7°21S 78°28W **186** E2
Contwoyto L. *Canada* 65°42N 110°50W **160** D9
Conversano *Italy* 40°58N 17°7E **95** B10
Conway Ark., *U.S.A.* 35°5N 92°26W **176** D8
Conway N.H., *U.S.A.* 43°59N 71°7W **175** C13
Conway S.C., *U.S.A.* 33°51N 79°3W **177** E15
Conway, C. *Australia* 20°24S 148°41E **150** b
Conway, L. *Australia* 28°17S 135°35E **151** D2
Conwy *U.K.* 53°17N 3°50W **66** D4
Conwy □ *U.K.* 53°10N 3°44W **66** D4
Conwy → *U.K.* 53°17N 3°50W **66** D4
Conyers *U.S.A.* 33°40N 84°1W **178** B5
Cooch Behar = Koch Bihar
  India 26°22N 89°29E **123** F16
Cooinda *Australia* 13°15S 130°5E **148** B5
Cook *Australia* 30°37S 130°25E **149** F5
Cook *U.S.A.* 47°51N 92°41W **172** B7
Cook, B. *Chile* 55°10S 70°0W **192** E3
Cook, C. *Canada* 50°8N 127°55W **162** C3
Cook, Mt. = Aoraki Mount Cook
  N.Z. 43°36S 170°9E **155** D5
Cook Inlet *U.S.A.* 60°0N 152°0W **166** F17
Cook Is. ☒ *Pac. Oc.* 17°0S 160°0W **157** J12
Cook Strait *N.Z.* 41°15S 174°29E **154** H3
Cooke Plains *Australia* 35°23S 139°34E **152** C3
Cookeville *U.S.A.* 36°10N 85°30W **177** C12
Cookhouse *S. Africa* 32°44S 25°47E **144** D4
Cooks Hammock
  U.S.A. 29°56N 83°17W **178** F6
Cooks Harbour *Canada* 51°36N 55°52W **165** B8
Cookstown *Canada* 44°11N 79°42W **174** B5
Cookstown *U.K.* 54°38N 6°45W **64** B5
Cooksville *Canada* 43°35N 79°38W **174** C5
Cooktown *Australia* 15°30S 145°16E **150** B4
Coolabah *Australia* 31°1S 146°43E **153** A7
Cooladdi *Australia* 26°37S 145°23E **151** D4
Coolah *Australia* 31°48S 149°41E **153** A8
Coolah Tops △
  Australia 31°52S 150°0E **153** A9
Coolamon *Australia* 34°46S 147°8E **153** C7
Coolgardie *Australia* 30°55S 121°8E **149** F3
Coolidge Ariz., *U.S.A.* 32°59N 111°31W **169** K8
Coolidge Ga., *U.S.A.* 31°1N 83°52W **178** D6
Coolidge Dam *U.S.A.* 33°10N 110°32W **169** K8
Cooma *Australia* 36°12S 149°8E **153** D8
Coon Rapids *U.S.A.* 45°9N 93°19W **172** C7
Coonabarabran
  Australia 31°14S 149°18E **153** A8
Coonalpyn *Australia* 35°43S 139°52E **152** C3
Coonamble *Australia* 30°56S 148°27E **153** A8
Coonana *Australia* 31°0S 123°0E **149** F3
Coondapoor *India* 13°42N 74°40E **127** H2
Coongie *Australia* 27°9S 140°8E **151** D3
Coongoola *Australia* 27°43S 145°51E **151** D4
Cooninie, L. *Australia* 26°4S 139°59E **151** D2
Coonoor *India* 11°21N 76°45E **127** J3
Cooper *U.S.A.* 33°23N 95°42W **176** E7
Cooper Cr. →
  Australia 28°29S 137°46E **151** D2
Cooper Ridge *Pac. Oc.* 10°0N 150°30W **157** G12
Cooperstown N. Dak.,
  U.S.A. 47°27N 98°8W **172** B4
Cooperstown N.Y.,
  U.S.A. 42°42N 74°56W **175** D10
Coopracambra △
  Australia 37°20S 149°20E **153** D8
Coorabie *Australia* 31°54S 132°18E **149** F5
Coorong, The
  Australia 35°50S 139°20E **152** C3
Coorong △ *Australia* 36°0S 139°20E **152** C3
Coorow *Australia* 29°53S 116°2E **149** E2
Cooroy *Australia* 26°22S 152°54E **151** D5
Coos Bay *U.S.A.* 43°22N 124°13W **168** E1
Coosa → *U.S.A.* 32°30N 86°16W **177** E11
Cootamundra *Australia* 34°36S 148°1E **153** C8
Cootehill *Ireland* 54°4N 7°5W **64** B4
Copahue Paso *Argentina* 37°49S 71°8W **192** A2
Copainalá *Mexico* 17°4N 93°18W **181** D6
Copake *U.S.A.* 42°7N 73°31W **175** D11
Copalnic Mănăştur
  Romania 47°30N 23°41E **81** C8
Copán *Honduras* 14°50N 89°9W **182** D2
Cope *U.S.A.* 39°40N 102°51W **168** G12
Cope, C. *Spain* 37°26N 1°28W **91** H3
Copeland *U.S.A.* 25°57N 81°22W **179** K8
Copenhagen = København
  Denmark 55°40N 12°26E **63** J6
Copenhagen *U.S.A.* 43°54N 75°41W **175** C9
Copertino *Italy* 40°16N 18°3E **95** B11
Copiapó *Chile* 27°30S 70°20W **190** B1
Copiapó → *Chile* 27°19S 70°56W **190** B1
Coplay *U.S.A.* 40°44N 75°29W **175** F9
Copley *Australia* 30°36S 138°26E **152** A2
Copo △ *Argentina* 25°53S 61°41W **190** B3
Copp L. *Canada* 60°14N 114°40W **162** A6
Copparo *Italy* 44°54N 11°49E **92** D8
Coppename → *Suriname* 5°48N 55°55W **187** B7

Copper Canyon = Barranca del
  Cobre △ *Mexico* 27°18N 107°40W **180** B3
Copper Center
  U.S.A. 61°58N 145°18W **166** C10
Copper Harbor *U.S.A.* 47°28N 87°53W **172** B10
Copper Queen
  Zimbabwe 17°29S 29°18E **143** F2
Copperas Cove *U.S.A.* 31°8N 97°54W **176** F6
Copperbelt □ *Zambia* 13°15S 27°30E **143** E2
Coppermine = Kugluktuk
  Canada 67°50N 115°5W **160** D8
Coppermine →
  Canada 67°49N 116°4W **160** D8
Copperopolis *U.S.A.* 37°58N 120°38W **170** H6
Coquet → *U.K.* 55°20N 1°32W **66** B6
Coquille *U.S.A.* 43°11N 124°11W **168** E1
Coquimbo *Chile* 30°0S 71°20W **190** C1
Coquimbo □ *Chile* 31°0S 71°0W **190** C1
Coquitlam *Canada* 49°17N 122°45W **162** D4
Corabia *Romania* 43°48N 24°30E **81** G9
Coração de Jesus
  Brazil 16°43S 44°22W **189** E2
Coracora *Peru* 15°5S 73°45W **188** D3
Coraki *Australia* 28°59S 153°17E **151** D5
Coral Bay *Australia* 23°8S 113°46E **148** D1
Coral Gables *U.S.A.* 25°43N 80°16W **179** H8
Coral Harbour *Canada* 64°8N 83°10W **161** D15
Coral Sea *Pac. Oc.* 15°0S 150°0E **147** C8
Coral Sea Basin *Pac. Oc.* 14°0S 152°0E **156** J7
Coral Sea Islands Terr. □
  Australia 20°0S 155°0E **147** C8
Coral Springs *U.S.A.* 26°16N 80°16W **179** H9
Corangamite, L.
  Australia 38°5S 143°30E **152** E5
Coraopolis *U.S.A.* 40°31N 80°10W **174** F4
Corato *Italy* 41°9N 16°25E **95** A9
Corbeil-Essonnes *France* 48°36N 2°26E **71** D9
Corbett △ *India* 29°20N 79°0E **125** E8
Corbie *France* 49°54N 2°30E **71** C9
Corbières *France* 42°55N 2°35E **72** F6
Corbigny *France* 47°16N 3°40E **71** E10
Corbin *U.S.A.* 36°57N 84°6W **173** G11
Corbones → *Spain* 37°36N 5°39W **89** H5
Corbu *Romania* 44°25N 28°39E **81** F13
Corby *U.K.* 52°30N 0°41W **67** E7
Corcaigh = Cork *Ireland* 51°54N 8°29W **64** E3
Corcoran *U.S.A.* 36°6N 119°33W **170** J7
Corcovado △ *Chile* 43°25S 72°45W **192** B2
Corcovado, G. *Chile* 43°30S 73°30W **192** B2
Corcubión *Spain* 42°56N 9°12W **88** C1
Corella → *Australia* 19°34S 140°47E **150** B3
Coremas *Brazil* 7°1S 37°58W **189** B3
Corentyne → *S. Amer.* 5°50N 57°8W **186** B7
Corfield *Australia* 21°40S 143°21E **150** C3
Corfu = Kerkyra *Greece* 39°38N 19°50E **101** A3
Corfu *Australia* 42°57N 78°24W **174** D6
Corfu ✕ (CFU) *Greece* 39°35N 19°54E **98** B1
Corfu, Str. of = Kerkyras, Notio
  Steno *Greece* 39°34N 20°0E **101** A4
Corgo = O Corgo *Spain* 42°56N 7°25W **88** C3
Cori *Italy* 41°39N 12°55E **94** A5
Coria *Spain* 39°58N 6°33W **89** H4
Coria del Río *Spain* 37°16N 6°3W **89** H4
Coricudgy *Australia* 32°51S 150°24E **153** B9
Corigliano Cálabro *Italy* 39°36N 16°31E **95** C9
Coringa Is. *Australia* 16°58S 149°58E **150** B4
Corinth = Korinthos
  Greece 37°56N 22°55E **98** D4
Corinth Miss., *U.S.A.* 34°56N 88°31W **177** D10
Corinth N.Y., *U.S.A.* 43°15N 73°49W **175** C11
Corinth, G. of = Korinthiakos
  Kolpos *Greece* 38°16N 22°30E **98** C4
Corinth Canal *Greece* 37°58N 22°58E **98** D4
Corinto *Brazil* 18°20S 44°30W **189** E2
Corinto *Nic.* 12°30N 87°10W **182** D2
Cork *Ireland* 51°54N 8°29W **64** E3
Cork □ *Ireland* 51°57N 8°40W **64** E3
Cork Harbour *Ireland* 51°47N 8°16W **64** E3
Corlay *France* 48°20N 3°5W **70** D3
Corleone *Italy* 37°54N 13°18E **94** E6
Corleto Perticara *Italy* 40°23N 16°2E **95** B9
Çorlu *Turkey* 41°11N 27°49E **97** E11
Cormack L. *Canada* 60°56N 121°37W **162** A4
Cormòns *Italy* 45°58N 13°28E **93** C10
Cormorant *Canada* 54°14N 100°35W **163** C8
Cormorant L. *Canada* 54°14N 100°50W **163** C8
Corn Is. = Maíz, Is. del
  Nic. 12°15N 83°4W **182** D3
Cornalvo △ *Spain* 39°11N 6°13W **89** F4
Cornélio Procópio
  Brazil 23°7S 50°40W **191** A5
Corner Brook *Canada* 48°57N 57°58W **165** C8
Corner Inlet *Australia* 38°45S 146°20E **153** D7
Corner Seamounts
  Atl. Oc. 35°0N 52°0W **56** C6
Corneşti *Moldova* 47°21N 28°1E **81** C12
Corníglio *Italy* 44°29N 10°5E **92** D7
Corning Ark., *U.S.A.* 36°25N 90°35W **177** C9
Corning Calif., *U.S.A.* 39°56N 122°11W **168** G2
Corning Iowa, *U.S.A.* 40°59N 94°44W **172** E6
Corning N.Y., *U.S.A.* 42°9N 77°3W **174** D7
Corno Grande *Italy* 42°28N 13°34E **93** F10
Cornwall *Canada* 45°2N 74°44W **175** A10
Cornwall □ *U.K.* 50°26N 4°40W **67** G3
Cornwall I. *Canada* 77°37N 94°38W **161** B13
Cornwallis I. *Canada* 75°8N 95°0W **161** B13
Corny Pt. *Australia* 34°55S 137°0E **152** C2
Coro *Venezuela* 11°25N 69°41W **186** A5
Coroaci *Brazil* 18°35S 42°17W **189** E2
Coroatá *Brazil* 4°8S 44°0W **189** A2
Corocoro *Bolivia* 17°15S 68°28W **188** D4
Coroico *Bolivia* 16°0S 67°50W **188** D4
Coromandel *Brazil* 18°28S 47°13W **189** E1

Coromandel *N.Z.* 36°45S 175°31E **154** C4
Coromandel Coast *India* 12°30N 81°0E **127** H5
Coromandel Pen. *N.Z.* 37°0S 175°35E **154** C4
Coromandel Ra. *N.Z.* 37°0S 175°40E **154** C4
Corona *Calif., U.S.A.* 33°53N 117°34W **171** M9
Corona *N. Mex.,*
   U.S.A. 34°15N 105°36W **169** J11
Coronado *U.S.A.* 32°41N 117°10W **171** N9
Coronado, B. de
   Costa Rica 9°0N 83°40W **182** E3
Coronados, G. de los
   Chile 41°40S 74°0W **192** B2
Coronados, Is. Los
   Mexico 32°26N 117°19W **171** N9
Coronation *Canada* 52°5N 111°27W **162** C6
Coronation Gulf
   Canada 68°25N 110°0W **160** D10
Coronation I. *Antarctica* 60°45S 46°0W **55** C18
Coronation Is.
   Australia 14°57S 124°55E **148** B3
Coronda *Argentina* 31°58S 60°56W **190** C3
Coronel *Chile* 37°0S 73°10W **190** D1
Coronel Bogado
   Paraguay 27°11S 56°18W **190** B4
Coronel Dorrego
   Argentina 38°40S 61°10W **190** D3
Coronel Fabriciano
   Brazil 19°31S 42°38W **189** D2
Coronel Murta *Brazil* 16°37S 42°11W **189** D2
Coronel Oviedo
   Paraguay 25°24S 56°30W **190** B4
Coronel Pringles
   Argentina 38°0S 61°30W **190** D3
Coronel Suárez
   Argentina 37°30S 61°52W **190** D3
Coronel Vidal
   Argentina 37°28S 57°45W **190** D4
Corongo *Peru* 8°30S 77°53W **188** B2
Coropuna, Nevado
   Peru 15°30S 72°41W **188** D3
Çorovodë *Albania* 40°31N 20°14E **96** F4
Corowa *Australia* 35°58S 146°21E **153** C7
Corozal □ *Belize* 18°23N 88°23W **181** D7
Corozal Pt.
   Trin. & Tob. 10°45N 61°37W **187** K15
Corps *France* 44°50N 5°56E **73** D9
Corpus *Argentina* 27°10S 55°30W **191** B4
Corpus Christi *U.S.A.* 27°47N 97°24W **176** H6
Corpus Christi, L.
   U.S.A. 28°2N 97°52W **176** G5
Corque *Bolivia* 18°20S 67°41W **188** D4
Corral *Chile* 39°52S 73°26W **192** A2
Corral de Almaguer
   Spain 39°45N 3°10W **88** F7
Corralejo *Canary Is.* 28°43N 13°53W **100** E6
Corraun Pen. *Ireland* 53°54N 9°54W **64** C2
Corréggio *Italy* 44°46N 10°47E **92** D7
Corrente *Brazil* 10°27S 45°10W **189** C1
Corrente → *Brazil* 13°8S 43°28W **189** C2
Correntes, C. das
   Mozam. 24°6S 35°34E **145** B6
Correntina *Brazil* 13°20S 44°39W **189** C2
Corrèze □ *France* 45°20N 1°45E **72** C5
Corrèze → *France* 45°10N 1°28E **72** C5
Corrib, L. *Ireland* 53°27N 9°16W **64** C2
Corridónia *Italy* 43°15N 13°30E **93** E10
Corrientes *Argentina* 27°30S 58°45W **190** B4
Corrientes □ *Argentina* 28°0S 57°0W **190** B4
Corrientes →
   Argentina 30°42S 59°38W **190** C4
Corrientes → *Peru* 3°43S 74°35W **188** B3
Corrientes, C. *Colombia* 5°30N 77°34W **186** B3
Corrientes, C. *Cuba* 21°43N 84°30W **182** B3
Corrientes, C. *Mexico* 20°25N 105°42W **180** C3
Corrigan *U.S.A.* 31°0N 94°52W **176** F7
Corrigin *Australia* 32°20S 117°53E **149** F2
Corry *U.S.A.* 41°55N 79°39W **174** E5
Corryong *Australia* 36°12S 147°53E **153** D7
Corse *France* 42°0N 9°0E **73** F13
Corse, C. *France* 43°1N 9°25E **73** E13
Corse □ *France* 42°14N 9°10E **73** F13
Corse-du-Sud □ *France* 41°45N 9°0E **73** G13
Corsica = Corse *France* 42°0N 9°0E **73** G13
Corsicana *U.S.A.* 32°6N 96°28W **176** E6
Corte *France* 42°19N 9°11E **73** F13
Corte Pinto *Portugal* 37°42N 7°29W **89** H3
Cortegana *Spain* 37°52N 6°49W **89** H4
Cortés, Mar de = California, G. de
   Mexico 27°0N 111°0W **180** B2
Cortez *U.S.A.* 37°21N 108°35W **169** H9
Córthaidh, Inis = Enniscorthy
   Ireland 52°30N 6°34W **64** D5
Cortina d'Ampezzo *Italy* 46°32N 12°8E **93** B9
Cortland *N.Y., U.S.A.* 42°36N 76°11W **175** D8
Cortland *Ohio, U.S.A.* 41°20N 80°44W **174** E5
Cortona *Italy* 43°16N 11°59E **93** E8
Corubal → *Guinea-Biss.* 11°57N 15°5W **138** C2
Coruche *Portugal* 38°0N 8°30W **89** G2
Çoruh → *Turkey* 41°38N 41°38E **87** K5
Çorum *Turkey* 40°30N 34°57E **104** B6
Çorum □ *Turkey* 40°40N 35°0E **104** B6
Corumbá *Brazil* 19°0S 57°30E **188** D4
Corumbá → *Brazil* 18°19S 48°55W **189** D1
Corumbaíba *Brazil* 18°9S 48°34W **189** D1
Corund *Romania* 46°30N 25°13E **81** D10
Corunna = A Coruña
   Spain 43°20N 8°25W **88** B2
Corvallis *U.S.A.* 44°34N 123°16W **168** D2
Corvette, L. de la
   Canada 53°25N 74°3W **164** B5
Corvo *Azores* 39°43N 31°8W **134** a
Corydon *U.S.A.* 40°46N 93°19W **172** E7
Cosalá *Mexico* 24°23N 106°41W **180** C3
Cosamaloapan de Carpio
   Mexico 18°22N 95°48W **181** D5
Cosenza *Italy* 39°18N 16°15E **95** C9
Coșereni *Romania* 44°38N 26°35E **81** F11
Coshocton *U.S.A.* 40°16N 81°51W **174** F3
Cosmo Newberry
   Australia 28°0S 122°54E **149** E3
Cosmo Newberry ○
   Australia 28°0S 122°54E **149** E3
Cosmonaut Sea *S. Ocean* 66°30S 40°0E **55** C5
Cosne-Cours-sur-Loire
   France 47°24N 2°54E **71** E9
Coso Junction *U.S.A.* 36°3N 117°57W **171** J9
Coso Pk. *U.S.A.* 36°13N 117°44W **171** J9
Cospeito = A Feira do Monte
   Spain 43°12N 7°34W **88** B3
Cosquín *Argentina* 31°15S 64°30W **190** C3

Cossato *Italy* 45°34N 8°10E **92** C5
Cossé-le-Vivien *France* 47°57N 0°54W **70** E6
Cosson → *France* 47°30N 1°15E **70** E8
Costa dels Pins *Spain* 39°38N 3°26E **100** B10
Costa Mesa *U.S.A.* 33°38N 117°55W **171** M4
Costa Rica ■ *Cent. Amer.* 10°0N 84°0W **182** E3
Costa Teguise *Canary Is.* 29°0N 13°31W **100** F6
Costeşti *Romania* 44°40N 24°53E **81** F9
Costigliole d'Asti *Italy* 44°47N 8°11E **92** D5
Cosumnes → *U.S.A.* 38°16N 121°26W **170** G5
Coswig *Sachsen, Germany* 51°7N 13°34E **76** D9
Coswig *Sachsen-Anhalt,*
   Germany 51°53N 12°27E **76** D8
Cotabato *Phil.* 7°14N 124°15E **119** C6
Cotacajes → *Bolivia* 16°0S 67°1W **188** D4
Cotagaita *Bolivia* 20°45S 65°40W **188** E4
Cotahuasi *Peru* 15°12S 72°50W **188** D3
Côte-d'Ivoire = Ivory Coast ■
   Africa 7°30N 5°0W **138** D4
Côte-d'Or □ *France* 47°30N 4°50E **71** E11
Coteau des Prairies
   U.S.A. 45°20N 97°50W **172** C5
Coteau du Missouri
   U.S.A. 47°0N 100°0W **172** B4
Cotegipe *Brazil* 12°2S 44°15W **189** C2
Cotentin *France* 49°15N 1°30W **70** C5
Côtes-d'Armor □ *France* 48°25N 2°40W **70** D4
Côtes de Meuse *France* 49°15N 5°22E **71** C12
Côtes-du-Nord = Côtes-
   d'Armor □ *France* 48°25N 2°40W **70** D4
Cotiella *Spain* 42°31N 0°19E **90** C5
Cotillo *Canary Is.* 28°41N 14°1W **100** F5
Cotiujeni *Moldova* 47°51N 28°33E **81** C13
Cotonou *Benin* 6°20N 2°25E **139** D5
Cotopaxi *Ecuador* 0°40S 78°30W **186** D3
Cotronei *Italy* 39°9N 16°47E **95** C9
Cotswold Hills *U.K.* 51°42N 2°10W **67** F5
Cottage Grove *U.S.A.* 43°48N 123°3W **168** E2
Cottageville *U.S.A.* 32°56N 80°29W **179** E8
Cottam *Canada* 42°8N 82°45W **174** D2
Cottbus *Germany* 51°45N 14°20E **76** D10
Cottonale *U.S.A.* 30°48N 85°23W **178** E4
Cottonwood *Ala., U.S.A.* 31°3N 85°18W **178** D4
Cottonwood *Ariz.,*
   U.S.A. 34°45N 112°1W **169** J7
Cotulla *U.S.A.* 28°26N 99°14W **176** G5
Coubre, Pte. de la *France* 45°42N 1°15W **72** C2
Couches *France* 46°53N 4°30E **71** F11
Couço *Portugal* 38°59N 8°17W **89** G2
Coudersport *U.S.A.* 41°46N 78°1W **174** E6
Couedic, C. du *Australia* 36°5S 136°40E **152** D2
Couëron *France* 47°13N 1°44W **70** E5
Couesnon → *France* 48°38N 1°32W **70** D5
Couhé *France* 46°17N 0°11E **72** B4
Coulanges-sur-Yonne
   France 47°31N 3°33E **71** E10
Coulee City *U.S.A.* 47°37N 119°17W **168** C4
Coulman I. *Antarctica* 73°35S 170°0E **55** D11
Coulommiers *France* 48°50N 3°3E **71** D10
Coulon → *France* 43°51N 5°6E **73** E9
Coulonge → *Canada* 45°52N 76°46W **164** C4
Coulterville *U.S.A.* 37°43N 120°12W **170** H6
Council *Alaska, U.S.A.* 64°53N 163°41W **166** C7
Council Ga., *U.S.A.* 30°37N 82°31W **179** F7
Council Idaho, *U.S.A.* 44°44N 116°26W **168** D5
Council Bluffs *U.S.A.* 41°16N 95°52W **172** E6
Council Grove *U.S.A.* 38°40N 96°29W **172** F5
Coupeville *U.S.A.* 48°13N 122°41W **170** B4
Courantyne = Corentyne →
   S. Amer. 5°50N 57°8W **186** B7
Courcelles *Belgium* 50°28N 4°22E **68** C4
Courchevel *France* 45°25N 6°36E **73** C10
Courçon *France* 46°15N 0°50W **72** B3
Courmayeur *France* 45°47N 6°58E **92** C3
Couronne, C. *France* 43°19N 5°3E **73** E9
Cours-la-Ville *France* 46°7N 4°19E **71** F11
Coursan *France* 43°14N 3°4E **72** E7
Courseulles-sur-Mer
   France 49°20N 0°29W **70** C6
Courtenay *Canada* 49°45N 125°0W **162** D4
Courtenay *France* 48°2N 3°3E **71** D10
Courtland *Canada* 42°51N 80°38W **174** D4
Courtland *U.S.A.* 38°20N 121°34W **170** G5
Courtrai = Kortrijk
   Belgium 50°50N 3°17E **69** D3
Courtright *Canada* 42°49N 82°28W **174** D2
Coushatta *U.S.A.* 32°1N 93°21W **176** E8
Coutances *France* 49°3N 1°28W **70** C5
Coutras *France* 45°3N 0°8W **72** C3
Coutts Crossing
   Australia 29°49S 152°55E **151** D5
Couva *Trin. & Tob.* 10°25N 61°27W **187** K15
Couvin *Belgium* 50°3N 4°29E **69** D4
Covarrubias *Spain* 42°4N 3°31W **88** D7
Covasna *Romania* 45°50N 26°10E **81** E11
Covasna □ *Romania* 45°50N 26°0E **81** E10
Cove I. *Canada* 45°17N 81°44W **174** A3
Coventry *U.K.* 52°25N 1°28W **67** E6
Coverdale → *Canada* 31°38N 83°58W **178** D6
Covilhã *Portugal* 40°17N 7°31W **88** E3
Covington *Ga., U.S.A.* 33°36N 83°51W **178** D6
Covington *Ky., U.S.A.* 39°5N 84°30W **173** F11
Covington *Tenn.,*
   U.S.A. 35°34N 89°39W **177** D10
Covington *Va., U.S.A.* 37°47N 79°59W **173** G14
Cowal, L. *Australia* 33°40S 147°25E **153** B7
Cowan, L. *Australia* 31°45S 121°45W **149** F3
Cowan, L. *Canada* 54°0N 107°15W **163** C7
Cowangie *Australia* 35°12S 141°26E **153** C4
Cowansville *Canada* 45°14N 72°46W **175** A12
Coward Springs
   Australia 29°24S 136°49E **151** D2
Cowcowing Lakes
   Australia 30°55S 117°20E **149** F2
Cowdenbeath *U.K.* 56°7N 3°21W **65** E5
Cowell *Australia* 33°39S 136°56E **151** E2
Cowes *Australia* 38°28S 145°14E **153** E6
Cowes *U.K.* 50°45N 1°18W **67** G6
Cowichan L. *Canada* 48°54N 124°17W **170** B2
Cowlitz → *U.S.A.* 46°6N 122°55W **170** D4
Cowra *Australia* 33°49S 148°42E **153** B8
Cox → *Australia* 17°55S 135°15E **150** B2
Cox Spain* 38°8N 0°53W **91** G4
Coxilha Grande *Brazil* 28°18S 51°30W **191** B5
Coxim *Brazil* 18°30S 54°55W **187** G8

Cox's Bazar *Bangla.* 21°26N 91°59E **123** J17
Coyah *Guinea* 9°42N 13°22W **138** D2
Coyote Wells *U.S.A.* 32°44N 115°58W **171** N11
Coyuca de Benitez
   Mexico 17°2N 100°4W **181** D4
Coyuca de Catalán
   Mexico 18°20N 100°39W **180** D4
Cozad *U.S.A.* 40°52N 99°59W **172** E4
Cozes *France* 45°34N 0°49W **72** C3
Cozia △ *Romania* 45°25N 24°16E **81** E9
Cozumel *Mexico* 20°31N 86°55W **181** C7
Cozumel, Isla *Mexico* 20°30N 86°40W **181** C7
Crab Hill *Barbados* 13°19N 59°38W **183** g
Cracow = Kraków
   Poland 50°4N 19°57E **83** H6
Cracow *Australia* 25°17S 150°17E **151** D5
Craddock Channel
   N.Z. 36°10S 175°13E **154** C4
Cradle Mt.-Lake St. Clair △
   Australia 41°49S 147°56E **151** G4
Cradock *Australia* 32°6S 138°31E **151** E2
Cradock *S. Africa* 32°8S 25°36E **144** D4
Crafers *Australia* 35°0S 138°42E **152** D2
Craig *U.S.A.* 40°31N 107°33W **168** F10
Craigavon *U.K.* 54°27N 6°23W **64** B5
Craigieburn *Australia* 37°36S 144°56E **153** D6
Craigmore *Zimbabwe* 20°28S 32°50E **143** G3
Craik *Canada* 51°3N 105°49W **163** C7
Crailsheim *Germany* 49°8N 10°5E **77** F6
Craiova *Romania* 44°21N 23°48E **81** F8
Cramsie *Australia* 23°20S 144°15E **150** C3
Cranberry L. *U.S.A.* 44°11N 74°50W **175** B10
Cranberry Portage
   Canada 54°35N 101°23W **163** C8
Cranbrook *Australia* 34°18S 117°33E **149** F2
Cranbrook *Canada* 49°30N 115°46W **162** D5
Crandon *U.S.A.* 45°34N 88°54W **172** C9
Crane *Oreg., U.S.A.* 43°25N 118°35W **168** E4
Crane *Tex., U.S.A.* 31°24N 102°21W **176** F3
Crane, The *Barbados* 13°6N 59°27W **183** g
Cranganore *India* 10°13N 76°13E **127** J3
Cranston *U.S.A.* 41°47N 71°26W **175** E13
Craon *France* 47°50N 0°58W **70** E6
Craonne *France* 49°27N 3°46E **71** C10
Craponne-sur-Arzon
   France 45°19N 3°51E **72** C7
Crasna *Romania* 46°32N 27°51E **81** D12
Crasna → *Romania* 46°44N 22°35E **80** C7
Crasnei, Munții *Romania* 47°0N 23°20E **81** C8
Crater L. *U.S.A.* 42°56N 122°6W **168** E2
Crater Lake △ *U.S.A.* 42°55N 122°10W **168** E2
Craters of the Moon △
   U.S.A. 43°25N 113°30W **168** E7
Crateús *Brazil* 5°10S 40°39W **189** B3
Crati → *Italy* 39°43N 16°31E **95** C9
Crato *Brazil* 7°10S 39°25W **189** B3
Crato *Portugal* 39°16N 7°39W **89** F3
Craven, L. *Canada* 54°20N 76°56W **164** B4
Crawford *Ala., U.S.A.* 32°27N 85°11W **178** C4
Crawford *Nebr.,*
   U.S.A. 42°41N 103°25W **172** D2
Crawfordsville *U.S.A.* 40°2N 86°54W **172** E10
Crawfordville *Fla.,*
   U.S.A. 30°11N 84°23W **178** F5
Crawfordville *Ga.,*
   U.S.A. 33°33N 82°54W **178** D7
Crawley *U.K.* 51°7N 0°11W **67** F7
Crazy Mts. *U.S.A.* 46°12N 110°20W **168** C8
Crécy-en-Ponthieu
   France 50°15N 1°53E **71** B8
Crediton *Canada* 43°17N 81°33W **174** C3
Crediton *U.K.* 50°47N 3°40W **67** G4
Cree → *Canada* 58°57N 105°47W **163** B7
Cree → *U.K.* 54°55N 4°25W **65** G4
Cree L. *Canada* 57°30N 106°30W **163** B7
Creede *U.S.A.* 37°51N 106°56W **169** H10
Creekside *U.S.A.* 40°40N 79°11W **174** F5
Creel *Mexico* 27°45S 107°38W **180** B3
Creemore *Canada* 44°19N 80°6W **174** B4
Creighton *Canada* 54°45N 101°54W **163** C8
Creighton *U.S.A.* 42°28N 97°54W **172** D5
Creil *France* 49°15N 2°29E **71** C9
Crema *Italy* 45°22N 9°41E **92** C6
Cremona *Italy* 45°7N 10°2E **92** C7
Crepaja *Serbia* 45°1N 20°38E **80** E5
Crépy *France* 49°36N 3°32E **71** C10
Crépy-en-Valois *France* 49°14N 2°54E **71** C9
Cres *Croatia* 44°58N 14°25E **93** D11
Crescent Beach *U.S.A.* 29°46N 81°15W **178** F8
Crescent City *Calif.,*
   U.S.A. 41°45N 124°12W **168** F1
Crescent City *Fla.,*
   U.S.A. 29°26N 81°31W **179** F8
Crescent Group
   S. China Sea 16°30N 111°40E **118** A4
Crescent Hd.
   Australia 31°11S 152°59E **153** A10
Crescent L. *U.S.A.* 29°28N 81°30W **179** F8
Crescentino *Italy* 45°11N 8°6E **92** C5
Crespi d'Adda *Italy* 45°35N 9°32E **92** C6
Crespo *Argentina* 32°2S 60°19W **190** C3
Cressy *Australia* 38°2S 143°40E **152** E5
Crest *France* 44°44N 5°2E **73** D9
Crestline *Calif., U.S.A.* 34°14N 117°18W **171** L9
Crestline *Ohio, U.S.A.* 40°47N 82°44W **174** F2
Creston *Australia* 27°16S 152°4E **151** D5
Creston *Canada* 49°10N 116°31W **162** D5
Creston *Iowa, U.S.A.* 41°4N 94°22W **172** E6
Crestview *Calif.,*
   U.S.A. 37°46N 118°58W **170** H8
Crestview *Fla., U.S.A.* 30°46N 86°34W **178** F3
Creswick *Australia* 37°25S 143°58E **152** D5
Crêt de la Neige *France* 46°16N 5°58E **71** F12
Crete = Kríti *Greece* 35°15N 25°0E **101** D7
Crete *U.S.A.* 40°38N 96°58E **172** E5
Crete, Sea of *Greece* 36°0N 25°0E **101** D6
Créteil *France* 48°47N 2°27E **71** D9
Creus, C. de *Spain* 42°20N 3°19E **90** C8
Creuse → *France* 47°0N 0°34E **72** B4
Creutzwald *France* 49°12N 6°42E **71** C13
Creuzburg *Germany* 51°3N 10°14E **76** D6
Crèveccœur-le-Grand
   France 49°37N 2°5E **71** C9
Crevillent *Spain* 38°12N 0°48W **91** G4
Crewe *U.K.* 53°6N 2°26W **66** D5
Crewkerne *U.K.* 50°53N 2°48W **67** G5
Crianlarich *U.K.* 56°24N 4°37W **65** E4
Criciúma *Brazil* 28°40S 49°23W **191** B6

Cricova *Moldova* 47°8N 28°52E **81** C13
Crieff *U.K.* 56°22N 3°50W **65** E5
Crikvenica *Croatia* 45°11N 14°40E **93** C11
Crimea □ *Ukraine* 45°30N 33°10E **85** K8
Crimean Pen. = Krymskyy
   Pivostriv *Ukraine* 45°0N 34°0E **85** K8
Crimmitschau *Germany* 50°48N 12°24E **76** E8
Cristino Castro *Brazil* 8°49S 44°13W **189** B2
Cristuru Secuiesc
   Romania 46°17N 25°2E **81** D10
Crişul Alb → *Romania* 46°42N 21°17E **80** D6
Crişul Negru →
   Romania 46°42N 21°16E **80** D6
Crişul Repede →
   Romania 46°55N 20°59E **80** D5
Criuleni *Moldova* 47°13N 29°10E **81** C14
Crivitz *Germany* 53°34N 11°39E **76** B7
Crna → *Macedonia* 41°33N 21°59E **96** E5
Crna Gora = Montenegro ■
   Europe 42°40N 19°20E **96** E3
Crna Gora *Macedonia* 42°10N 21°30E **96** E5
Crna Reka = Crna →
   Macedonia 41°33N 21°59E **96** E5
Crni Drim → *Macedonia* 41°17N 20°40E **96** E4
Crni Timok → *Serbia* 43°53N 22°15E **96** C6
Crnoljeva Planina = Zhar, Mali
   Kosovo 42°20N 21°0E **96** D5
Črnomelj *Slovenia* 45°33N 15°10E **93** C12
Croagh Patrick *Ireland* 53°46N 9°40W **64** C2
Croajingolong △
   Australia 37°45S 149°26E **153** D8
Croatia ■ *Europe* 45°20N 16°0E **93** C13
Crocker, Banjaran
   Malaysia 5°40N 116°30E **118** C5
Crockett *U.S.A.* 31°19N 95°27W **176** F7
Crocodile = Umgwenya →
   Mozam. 25°14S 32°18E **145** D5
Crocodile → *S. Africa* 24°12S 26°53E **144** B4
Crocodile Is. *Australia* 12°3S 134°58E **150** A1
Crocq *France* 45°52N 2°21E **72** C6
Crohy Hd. *Ireland* 54°55N 8°26W **64** B3
Croisette, C. *France* 43°14N 5°22E **73** E9
Croisic, Pte. du *France* 47°19N 2°31W **70** E4
Croix, L. la *Canada* 48°20N 92°15W **164** C1
Croker, C. *Australia* 10°58S 132°35E **148** B5
Croker, C. *Canada* 44°58N 80°59W **174** B4
Croker I. *Australia* 11°12S 132°32E **148** B5
Croker Islands Seas ◎
   Australia 11°20S 132°30E **148** B5
Cromarty *U.K.* 57°40N 4°2W **65** D4
Cromer *U.K.* 52°56N 1°17E **66** E9
Cromwell *N.Z.* 45°3S 169°14E **155** F4
Cromwell *U.S.A.* 41°36N 72°39W **175** E12
Cronat *France* 46°43N 3°40E **71** F10
Crook *U.K.* 54°43N 1°45W **66** C6
Crooked → *Canada* 54°50N 122°54W **162** C4
Crooked → *U.S.A.* 44°32N 121°16W **168** D3
Crooked I. *Bahamas* 22°50N 74°10W **183** B5
Crooked Island Passage
   Bahamas 22°55N 74°35W **183** B5
Crookston *Minn.,*
   U.S.A. 47°47N 96°37W **172** B5
Crookston *Nebr.,*
   U.S.A. 42°56N 100°45W **172** D3
Crookwell *Australia* 34°28S 149°24E **153** C8
Cropane-Micone △ *Italy* 38°31N 16°18E **95** D9
Crosby *U.K.* 53°30N 3°3W **66** D4
Crosby *N. Dak., U.S.A.* 48°55N 103°18W **172** A2
Crosby *Pa., U.S.A.* 41°45N 78°23W **174** E6
Crosbyton *U.S.A.* 33°40N 101°14W **176** D4
Crosia *Italy* 39°35N 16°45E **95** C9
Cross → *Nigeria* 4°42N 8°21E **139** E6
Cross City *U.S.A.* 29°38N 83°7W **179** F6
Cross Fell *U.K.* 54°43N 2°28W **66** C5
Cross L. *Canada* 54°45N 97°30W **163** C9
Cross River □ *Nigeria* 6°0N 8°0E **139** D6
Cross River △ *Nigeria* 5°50N 9°50E **139** D6
Cross Sound *U.S.A.* 58°0N 135°0W **166** F4
Crossett *U.S.A.* 33°8N 91°58W **176** E9
Crosshaven *Ireland* 51°47N 8°17W **64** E3
Crossley, Mt. *N.Z.* 42°50S 172°55E **155** E4
Crossmaglen *U.K.* 54°5N 6°36W **64** B5
Crossmolina *Ireland* 54°6N 9°20W **64** B2
Crossville *U.S.A.* 35°57N 85°2W **177** D12
Croswell *U.S.A.* 43°16N 82°37W **174** C2
Croton-on-Hudson
   U.S.A. 41°12N 73°55W **175** E11
Crotone *Italy* 39°5N 17°8E **95** C10
Crow → *Canada* 59°41N 124°20W **162** B4
Crow Agency *U.S.A.* 45°36N 107°28W **168** D10
Crow Hd. *Ireland* 51°35N 10°9W **64** E1
Crowdy Bay △
   Australia 31°45S 152°45E **153** A10
Crowell *U.S.A.* 33°59N 99°43W **176** E5
Crowley *U.S.A.* 30°13N 92°22W **176** F8
Crowley, L. *U.S.A.* 37°35N 118°42W **170** H8
Crown Point *Ind.,*
   U.S.A. 41°25N 87°22W **172** E10
Crown Point *N.Y.,*
   U.S.A. 43°57N 73°26W **175** C11
Crown Pt. *Trin. & Tob.* 11°18N 60°51W **187** J16
Crownpoint *U.S.A.* 35°41N 108°9W **169** J9
Crows Landing *U.S.A.* 37°23N 121°6W **170** H5
Crows Nest *Australia* 27°16S 152°4E **151** D5
Crowsnest Pass
   Canada 49°40N 114°40W **162** D6
Croydon *Australia* 18°13S 142°14E **150** B3
Croydon □ *U.K.* 51°22N 0°5W **67** F7
Crozet, Îs. *Ind. Oc.* 46°27S 52°0E **146** H3
Crozet Basin *Ind. Oc.* 39°0S 60°0E **146** H5
Crozon *France* 48°15N 4°30W **70** D2
Cruce de Sardina
   Canary Is. 27°55N 15°25E **100** G4
Crusheen *Ireland* 52°57N 8°53W **64** D3
Cruz, C. *Cuba* 19°50N 77°50W **182** C4
Cruz Alta *Brazil* 28°45S 53°40W **191** B5
Cruz Bay *U.S. Virgin Is.* 18°20N 64°48W **183** e
Cruz das Almas *Brazil* 12°0S 39°6W **189** C3
Cruz del Eje *Argentina* 30°45S 64°50W **190** C3
Cruzeiro *Brazil* 22°33S 45°0W **191** A6
Cruzeiro do Oeste *Brazil* 23°46S 53°4W **191** A5
Cruzeiro do Sul *Brazil* 7°35S 72°35W **186** E4
Cry L. *Canada* 58°45N 129°0W **162** B3
Csenger *Hungary* 47°50N 22°41E **80** C7
Csongrád *Hungary* 46°43N 20°12E **80** D5
Csongrád □ *Hungary* 46°30N 20°15E **80** D5
Csorna *Hungary* 47°38N 17°18E **80** C2
Csurgó *Hungary* 46°16N 17°9E **80** D2
Cu Lao Hon *Vietnam* 10°54N 108°18E **121** G7
Cua Rao *Vietnam* 19°16N 104°27E **120** C5
Cúacua → *Mozam.* 17°54S 37°0E **143** F4
Cuamato *Angola* 17°2S 15°7E **144** A2
Cuamba *Mozam.* 14°45S 36°22E **145** E4
Cuando → *Angola* 17°30S 23°15E **141** H4
Cuando Cubango □
   Angola 16°25S 20°0E **144** A3
Cuangar *Angola* 17°36S 18°39E **144** A2
Cuango = Kwango →
   Dem. Rep. of the Congo 3°14S 17°22E **140** E3
Cuanza → *Angola* 9°21S 13°9E **140** F2
Cuarto → *Argentina* 33°25S 63°2W **190** C3
Cuatrociénegas *Mexico* 26°59N 102°5W **180** B4
Cuauhtémoc *Mexico* 28°25N 106°52W **180** B3
Cuba *Portugal* 38°10N 7°54W **89** G3
Cuba *N. Mex., U.S.A.* 36°1N 107°4W **169** H10
Cuba *N.Y., U.S.A.* 42°13N 78°17W **174** D6
Cuba ■ *W. Indies* 22°0N 79°0W **182** B4
Cubango → *Africa* 18°50S 22°25E **144** A3
Çubuk *Turkey* 40°14N 33°3E **104** B5
Cuc Phuong △
   Vietnam 20°17N 105°38E **120** C5
Cuchillo-Co *Argentina* 38°20S 64°37W **192** A4
Cuchumatanes, Sierra de los
   Guatemala 15°35N 91°25W **182** C1
Cuckfield *U.K.* 51°1N 0°8W **67** F7
Cucuí *Brazil* 1°12N 66°50W **186** C5
Cucurpé *Mexico* 30°20N 110°43W **180** A2
Cudalbi *Romania* 45°46N 27°41E **81** E12
Cuddalore *India* 11°46N 79°45E **127** J4
Cuddapah *India* 14°30N 78°47E **127** G4
Cuddapan, L. *Australia* 25°45S 141°26E **150** D3
Cudgewa *Australia* 36°10S 147°42E **153** D7
Cudillero *Spain* 43°30N 6°9W **88** B4
Cue *Australia* 27°25S 117°54E **149** E2
Cuéllar *Spain* 41°23N 4°21W **88** D6
Cuenca *Ecuador* 2°50S 79°9W **186** D3
Cuenca *Spain* 40°5N 2°10W **90** C2
Cuenca □ *Spain* 40°0N 2°0W **90** C2
Cuenca, Serranía de
   Spain 39°55N 1°50W **90** C2
Cuenca Alta del Manzanares △
   Spain 40°40N 3°55W **88** E7
Cuerda del Pozo, Embalse de la
   Spain 41°51N 2°44W **90** D2
Cuernavaca *Mexico* 18°55N 99°15W **181** D5
Cuero *U.S.A.* 29°6N 97°17W **176** G6
Cuers *France* 43°14N 6°5E **73** E10
Cueva de la Quebrada del Toro △
   Venezuela 10°46N 69°3W **186** A5
Cuevas del Almanzora
   Spain 37°18N 1°58W **91** H3
Cuevo *Bolivia* 20°15S 63°30W **188** E5
Cugir *Romania* 45°48N 23°25E **81** E8
Cuglieri *Italy* 40°11N 8°34E **94** B1
Cugnaux *France* 43°32N 1°20E **72** E5
Cuhai-Bakony →
   Hungary 47°35N 17°54E **80** C2
Cuiabá *Brazil* 15°30S 56°0W **187** G7
Cuiabá → *Brazil* 17°5S 56°36W **187** G7
Cuihangcun *China* 22°27N 113°32E **111** a
Cuijk *Neths.* 51°44N 5°50E **69** C5
Cuilco *Guatemala* 15°24N 91°58W **182** C1
Cuillin Hills *U.K.* 57°13N 6°15W **65** D2
Cuillin Sd. *U.K.* 57°4N 6°20W **65** D2
Cuilo = Kwilu →
   Dem. Rep. of the Congo 3°22S 17°22E **140** E3
Cuiseaux *France* 46°30N 5°22E **71** F12
Cuité *Brazil* 6°29S 36°9W **189** B3
Cuito → *Angola* 18°1S 20°48E **144** A3
Cuitzeo, L. de *Mexico* 19°55N 101°5W **180** D4
Çujmir *Romania* 44°13N 22°57E **80** F7
Cukai *Malaysia* 4°13N 103°25E **121** K4
Çukurca *Turkey* 37°14N 43°36E **105** D10
Culbertson *U.S.A.* 48°9N 104°31W **168** B11
Culcairn *Australia* 35°41S 147°3E **153** C7
Culebra *Puerto Rico* 18°19N 65°18W **183** d
Culebra, Sierra de la
   Spain 41°55N 6°20W **88** D4
Culfa *Azerbaijan* 38°57N 45°38E **105** C11
Culgoa *Australia* 35°44S 143°6E **152** C5
Culgoa → *Australia* 29°56S 146°20E **151** D4
Culgoa Flood Plain △
   Australia 28°58S 147°5E **151** D4
Culiacán *Mexico* 24°50N 107°23W **180** C3
Culiacán → *Mexico* 24°30N 107°42W **180** C3
Culik *Indonesia* 8°21S 115°37E **119** J18
Culion *Phil.* 11°54N 119°58E **119** B6
Cúllar *Spain* 37°35N 2°34W **89** H8
Cullarin Ra. *Australia* 34°30S 149°30E **153** C8
Cullen *Australia* 11°57S 141°54E **150** A3
Cullen *U.K.* 57°42N 2°49W **65** D6
Cullen Bullen *Australia* 33°18S 150°2E **153** B9
Cullera *Spain* 39°9N 0°17W **91** F4
Cullman *U.S.A.* 34°11N 86°51W **177** D11
Culloden *U.K.* 57°28N 4°5W **65** D4
Cullompton *U.K.* 50°51N 3°24W **67** G4
Culoz *France* 45°47N 5°46E **73** C9
Culpeper *U.S.A.* 38°30N 78°0W **173** F14
Culuene → *Brazil* 12°56S 52°51W **187** F8
Culver, Pt. *Australia* 32°54S 124°43E **149** F3
Culverden *N.Z.* 42°47S 172°49E **155** E4
Culverton *U.S.A.* 33°19N 82°54W **178** D7
Cumaná *Venezuela* 10°30N 64°5W **186** A6
Cumaovası *Turkey* 38°15N 27°9E **99** D9
Cumari *Brazil* 18°16S 48°11W **189** D1

Crystal Falls *U.S.A.* 46°5N 88°20W **172** B9
Crystal Lake *U.S.A.* 30°26N 85°42W **178** E4
Crystal River *U.S.A.* 28°54N 82°35W **179** G7
Crystal Springs *U.S.A.* 31°59N 90°21W **177** F9
Csenger *Hungary* 47°50N 22°41E **80** C7
Csongrád *Hungary* 46°43N 20°12E **80** D5
Cu Lao Hon *Vietnam* 10°54N 108°18E **121** G7

Cumberland I. *U.S.A.* 30°50N 81°25W **178** E8
Cumberland Is.
   Australia 20°35S 149°10E **150** b
Cumberland Island △
   U.S.A. 30°12N 81°24W **178** E8
Cumberland L. *Canada* 54°3N 102°18W **163** C8
Cumberland Pen.
   Canada 67°0N 64°0W **161** D19
Cumberland Plateau
   U.S.A. 36°0N 85°0W **177** D12
Cumberland Sd.
   Canada 65°30N 66°0W **161** D18
Cumbernauld *U.K.* 55°57N 3°58W **65** F5
Cumborah *Australia* 29°40S 147°45E **151** D4
Cumbres de Majalca △
   Mexico 28°48N 106°30W **180** B3
Cumbres de Monterrey △
   Mexico 25°26N 100°25W **180** B4
Cumbres Mayores *Spain* 38°6N 6°39W **89** G4
Cumbria □ *U.K.* 54°42N 2°52W **66** C5
Cumbrian Mts. *U.K.* 54°30N 3°0W **66** C4
Cumbum *India* 15°40N 79°10E **127** G4
Cuminá → *Brazil* 1°30S 56°0W **187** D7
Cummings Mt. *U.S.A.* 35°2N 118°34W **171** K8
Cummins *Australia* 34°16S 135°43E **151** E2
Cumnock *Australia* 32°59S 148°46E **153** B8
Cumnock *U.K.* 55°28N 4°17W **65** F4
Cumpas *Mexico* 30°2N 109°48W **180** B3
Cumplida, Pta.
   Canary Is. 28°50N 17°48W **100** F2
Çumra *Turkey* 37°34N 32°45E **104** D5
Cuncumén *Chile* 31°53S 70°38W **190** C1
Cundeelee ○ *Australia* 30°43S 123°25E **149** F3
Cunderdin *Australia* 31°37S 117°12E **149** F2
Cunene → *Angola* 17°20S 11°50E **144** A1
Cúneo *Italy* 44°23N 7°32E **92** D4
Cung Son *Vietnam* 13°2N 108°58E **120** F7
Çüngüş *Turkey* 38°13N 39°17E **128** B3
Cunillera, I. = Sa Conillera
   Spain 38°59N 1°13E **100** C7
Cunlhat *France* 45°38N 3°32E **72** C7
Cunnamulla *Australia* 28°2S 145°38E **151** D4
Cuorgnè *Italy* 45°23N 7°39E **92** C4
Cupar *Canada* 50°57N 104°10W **163** C8
Cupar *U.K.* 56°19N 3°1W **65** E5
Cupcini *Moldova* 48°6N 27°23E **81** B13
Cupertino *U.S.A.* 37°19N 122°2W **170** H4
Cupica, G. de *Colombia* 6°25N 77°30W **186** B3
Cuprija *Serbia* 43°57N 21°26E **96** C5
Curaçá *Brazil* 8°59S 39°54W **189** B3
Curaçao *W. Indies* 12°10N 69°0W **183** D6
Curacautín *Chile* 38°26S 71°53W **192** A2
Curahuara de Carangas
   Bolivia 17°52S 68°26W **190** D1
Curanilahue *Chile* 37°29S 73°28W **190** D1
Curaray → *Peru* 2°20S 74°5W **186** D4
Cure → *France* 47°40N 3°41E **71** E10
Curepipe *Mauritius* 20°19S 57°31E **141** d
Curepto *Chile* 35°8S 72°1W **190** D1
Curiá *Portugal* 40°22N 8°22W **88** E2
Curiapo *Venezuela* 8°33N 61°5W **186** B6
Curicó *Chile* 34°55S 71°20W **190** C2
Curieuse *Seychelles* 4°15S 55°44E **141** b
Curimatá *Brazil* 10°2S 44°17W **189** C2
Curinga *Italy* 38°49N 16°19E **95** D9
Curitiba *Brazil* 25°20S 49°10W **191** B6
Curitibanos *Brazil* 27°18S 50°36W **191** B5
Curlewis *Australia* 31°7S 150°16E **153** A9
Curonian Lagoon = Kurshskiy
   Zaliv *Russia* 55°9N 21°6E **82** C8
Curonian Spit *Europe* 55°20N 20°55E **82** C7
Currabubula *Australia* 31°16S 150°44E **153** A9
Currais Novos *Brazil* 6°13S 36°30W **189** B3
Curral Velho *C. Verde Is.* 16°8N 22°48W **134** b
Curralinho *Brazil* 1°45S 49°46W **187** D9
Currane, L. *Ireland* 51°49N 10°4W **64** E1
Currant *U.S.A.* 38°44N 115°28W **168** G6
Curraweena *Australia* 30°47S 145°54E **153** A6
Currawinya △
   Australia 28°55S 144°27E **151** D3
Current → *U.S.A.* 36°15N 90°55W **176** D9
Currie *Australia* 39°56S 143°53E **151** F3
Currie *U.S.A.* 40°16N 114°45W **168** F6
Curtea de Argeş
   Romania 45°12N 24°42E **81** E9
Curtici *Romania* 46°21N 21°18E **80** D6
Curtin Springs
   Australia 25°20S 131°45E **149** E5
Curtis *U.S.A.* 40°38N 100°31W **172** E3
Curtis Group *Australia* 39°30S 146°37E **151** F4
Curtis I. *Australia* 23°35S 151°10E **150** C5
Curúapanema → *Brazil* 2°25S 55°2W **187** D7
Curuçá *Brazil* 0°43S 47°50W **187** D9
Curuçá → *Brazil* 4°27S 71°23W **188** B3
Curuguaty *Paraguay* 24°31S 55°42W **191** A4
Çürüksu Çayi = Büyük
   Menderes → *Turkey* 37°28N 27°11E **99** D9
Curup *Indonesia* 3°2S 102°13E **118** E2
Cururupu *Brazil* 1°50S 44°50W **187** D10
Curuzú Cuatiá
   Argentina 29°50S 58°5W **190** B4
Curvelo *Brazil* 18°45S 44°27W **189** D2
Cusco *Peru* 13°32S 72°0W **188** D3
Cusco □ *Peru* 13°31S 71°59W **188** D3
Cushendall *U.K.* 55°5N 6°4W **64** A5
Cushing *U.S.A.* 35°59N 96°46W **176** D6
Cushing, Mt. *Canada* 57°35N 126°57W **162** B3
Cusihuiriáchic
   Mexico 28°14N 106°50W **180** B3
Cusna, Mte. *Italy* 44°17N 10°23E **92** D7
Cusset *France* 46°8N 3°28E **71** F10
Cussetta *U.S.A.* 32°18N 84°47W **178** C5
Custer *U.S.A.* 43°46N 103°36W **172** D2
Cut Bank *U.S.A.* 48°38N 112°20W **168** B7
Cutchogue *U.S.A.* 41°1N 72°30W **175** E12
Cutervo *Peru* 6°24S 78°45W **186** E3
Cuthbert *U.S.A.* 31°46N 84°48W **178** D5
Cutler *U.S.A.* 36°31N 119°17W **170** J7
Cutler Ridge *U.S.A.* 25°35N 80°20W **179** K9
Cutral-Có *Argentina* 38°58S 69°15W **192** A3
Cutro *Italy* 39°2N 16°59E **95** C9
Cuttaburra → *Australia* 29°43S 144°22E **151** E3
Cuttack *India* 20°25N 85°57E **126** D7
Cuvier, C. *Australia* 23°14S 113°22E **149** D1
Cuvier I. *N.Z.* 36°27S 175°50E **154** C4
Cuxhaven *Germany* 53°51N 8°41E **76** B4
Cuyahoga Falls *U.S.A.* 41°8N 81°29W **174** E3
Cuyahoga Valley △
   U.S.A. 41°24N 81°33W **174** E3
Cuyo *Phil.* 10°51N 121°2E **119** B6

Cuyuni → Guyana 6°23N 58°41W 186 B7
Cuzco = Cusco Peru 13°32S 72°0W 188 C3
Črvsnica Bos.-H. 43°36N 17°35E 80 G2
Cwmbran U.K. 51°39N 3°2W 67 F4
Cyangugu Rwanda 2°29S 28°54E 142 C2
Cybinka Poland 52°12N 14°46E 83 F1
Cyclades = Kyklades Greece 37°0N 24°30E 98 E6
Cygnet Australia 43°8S 147°1E 151 G4
Cynthiana U.S.A. 38°23N 84°18W 173 F11
Cypress Hills Canada 49°40N 109°30W 163 D7
Cypress Hills △ Canada 49°40N 109°30W 163 D7
Cyprus ■ Asia 35°0N 33°0E 101 E12
Cyrenaica = Barqa Libya 27°0N 23°0E 135 C10
Cyrene Libya 32°53N 21°52E 135 B10
Czaplinek Poland 53°34N 16°14E 82 E3
Czar Canada 52°27N 110°50W 163 C6
Czarna → Łódzkie, Poland 51°18N 19°55E 83 G6
Czarna → Świętokrzyskie, Poland 50°28N 21°21E 83 H8
Czarna Białostocka Poland 53°18N 23°17E 83 E10
Czarna Woda Poland 53°51N 18°6E 82 E5
Czarne Poland 53°42N 16°58E 82 E3
Czarnków Poland 52°55N 16°38E 83 F3
Czech Rep. ■ Europe 50°0N 15°0E 78 B8
Czechowice-Dziedzice Poland 49°54N 18°59E 83 J5
Czempiń Poland 52°9N 16°43E 83 F3
Czeremcha Poland 52°31N 23°21E 83 F10
Czerniejewo Poland 52°26N 17°30E 83 F4
Czersk Poland 53°46N 17°58E 82 E4
Czerwieńsk Poland 52°1N 15°23E 83 F2
Czerwionka-Leszczyny Poland 50°7N 18°37E 83 H5
Częstochowa Poland 50°49N 19°7E 83 H6
Człopa Poland 53°6N 16°6E 83 E3
Człuchów Poland 53°41N 17°22E 82 E4
Czyżew-Osada Poland 52°48N 22°19E 83 F9

D

Da → Vietnam 21°15N 105°20E 116 G5
Da Hinggan Ling China 48°0N 121°0E 111 B13
Da Lat Vietnam 11°56N 108°25E 121 G7
Da Nang Vietnam 16°4N 108°13E 120 D7
Da Qaidam China 37°50N 95°15E 110 D8
Da Yunhe → Hopei, China 39°10N 117°10E 115 E9
Da Yunhe → Jiangsu, China 34°25N 120°5E 117 A12
Da'an China 45°30N 124°7E 115 B13
Daan Viljoen △ Namibia 22°2S 16°45E 144 B2
Dab'a, Ras el Egypt 31°3N 28°31E 137 E6
Daba Shan China 32°0N 109°0E 116 B7
Dabai China 11°25N 5°15E 139 C6
Dabakala Ivory C. 8°15N 4°20W 138 D4
Dabas Hungary 47°11N 19°19E 80 C4
Dabbagh, Jabal Si. Arabia 27°52N 35°45E 128 E2
Dabhoi India 22°10N 73°20E 124 H5
Dąbie Poland 52°5N 18°50E 83 F5
Dabie Shan China 31°20N 115°20E 117 B10
Dabilda Cameroon 12°45N 14°35E 139 C7
Dabnou Niger 14°10N 5°22E 139 C6
Dabola Guinea 10°50N 11°5W 138 C2
Dabou Ivory C. 5°20N 4°23W 138 D4
Daboya Ghana 9°30N 1°20W 139 D4
Dabravolya Belarus 52°55N 23°59E 83 F10
Dąbrowa Białostocka Poland 53°40N 23°21E 82 E10
Dąbrowa Górnicza Poland 50°15N 19°10E 83 H6
Dąbrowa Tarnowska Poland 50°10N 20°59E 83 H7
Dabu China 24°22N 116°41E 117 E11
Dabugam India 19°27N 82°26E 126 E6
Dabung Malaysia 5°23N 102°1E 121 K4
Dacca = Dhaka Bangla. 23°43N 90°26E 125 H14
Dachang China 32°13N 118°45E 117 A12
Dachaoshan Dam China 24°1N 100°22E 116 E3
Dachau Germany 48°15N 11°26E 77 G7
Dachigam △ India 34°10N 75°0E 124 B6
Dachstein, Hoher Austria 47°28N 13°35E 78 D6
Dačice Czech Rep. 49°5N 15°26E 78 B8
Dacre Canada 45°22N 76°57W 174 A8
Dacula U.S.A. 33°59N 83°54W 178 D4
Dadanawa Guyana 2°50N 59°30W 186 C7
Daday Turkey 41°28N 33°27E 104 B5
Dade City U.S.A. 28°22N 82°11W 179 G7
Dadès, Oued → Morocco 30°58N 6°44W 136 B2
Dadeville U.S.A. 32°50N 85°46W 178 C4
Dadhar Pakistan 29°28N 67°39E 124 E2
Dadiya Nigeria 9°35N 11°24E 139 D7
Dadnah U.A.E. 25°32N 56°22E 129 E8
Dadra & Nagar Haveli □ India 20°5N 73°0E 126 D1
Dadri = Charkhi Dadri India 28°37N 76°17E 124 E7
Dadu Pakistan 26°45N 67°45E 124 F2
Dadu He → China 29°31N 103°46E 116 C4
Daegu S. Korea 35°50N 128°37E 115 G15
Daejeon S. Korea 36°20N 127°28E 115 F14
Daejeong S. Korea 33°8N 126°17E 115 H14
Daet Phil. 14°2N 122°55E 119 B6
Dafang China 27°13N 105°30E 116 D5
Dafeng China 33°3N 120°45E 115 H11
Dafnes Greece 35°13N 25°3E 100 D7
Dafni Greece 37°48N 22°1E 98 D4
Dağ Turkey 37°12N 30°31E 99 D12
Dagana Senegal 16°30N 15°35W 138 B1
Dagash Sudan 19°19N 33°25E 137 D3
Dagestan □ Russia 42°30N 47°0E 87 J8
Dagestanskiye Ogni Russia 42°6N 48°12E 87 J9
Dagg Sd. N.Z. 45°23S 166°45E 155 F1
Daggett U.S.A. 34°52N 116°52W 171 L10
Daghestan Republic = Dagestan □ Russia 42°30N 47°0E 87 J8
Daghfeli Sudan 19°18N 34°32E 137 D3
Dağlıq Qarabağ = Nagorno-Karabakh □ Azerbaijan 39°55N 46°45E 105 C12

Dagö = Hiiumaa Estonia 58°50N 22°45E 84 C2
Dagu China 38°59N 117°40E 115 E9
Daguan China 27°43N 103°56E 116 D4
Dagupan Phil. 16°3N 120°20E 119 A6
Daguragu Australia 17°33S 130°30E 148 C5
Daguragu ☉ Australia 17°24S 130°48E 148 C5
Dahab Egypt 28°31N 34°31E 128 D2
Dahanu India 17°43N 74°33E 126 F2
Dahivadi India 17°43N 74°33E 126 F2
Dahlak Kebir Eritrea 15°50N 40°10E 131 D3
Dahlenburg Germany 53°11N 10°44E 76 B6
Dahlonega U.S.A. 34°32N 83°59W 177 D13
Dahme Germany 51°52N 13°25E 76 D9
Dahod India 22°50N 74°15E 124 H6
Dahong Shan China 31°25N 113°0E 117 B9
Dahongliutan China 35°45N 79°20E 125 B8
Dahra Libya 29°30N 17°50E 135 B9
Dahra Senegal 15°22N 15°30W 138 B1
Dahra, Massif de Algeria 36°7N 1°21E 136 A4
Dahshur Egypt 29°45N 31°14E 137 F7
Dahūk Iraq 36°50N 43°1E 105 D10
Dahūk □ Iraq 36°50N 42°50E 105 D10
Dai Hao Vietnam 18°1N 106°25E 120 C6
Dai-Sen Japan 35°22N 133°32E 113 G6
Dai Shan China 30°25N 122°10E 117 B14
Dai Xian China 39°4N 112°58E 114 E7
Daicheng China 38°42N 116°38E 114 E9
Daikondi = Dāykondī Afghan. 34°0N 66°0E 122 C5
Dailekh Nepal 28°50N 81°44E 125 E9
Daimiel Spain 39°5N 3°35W 89 F7
Daingean Ireland 53°18N 7°17W 64 C4
Daingean, An = Dingle Ireland 52°9N 10°17W 64 D1
Dainkog China 32°30N 97°58E 116 A1
Daintree Australia 16°20S 145°20E 150 B4
Daintree △ Australia 16°8S 145°2E 150 B4
Daiō-Misaki Japan 34°15N 136°45E 113 G8
Dairût Egypt 27°34N 30°43E 137 B3
Daisen Japan 39°27N 140°29E 112 E10
Daisen-Oki △ Japan 35°23N 133°34E 113 G6
Daisetsu-Zan Japan 43°30N 142°57E 112 C11
Daisetsu-Zan △ Japan 43°30N 142°55E 112 C11
Daitari India 21°10N 85°46E 126 D7
Daiyun Shan China 25°50N 118°15E 117 E12
Dajarra Australia 21°42S 139°30E 150 C2
Dajiawa China 37°9N 119°0E 115 F10
Dajin Chuan → China 31°16N 101°59E 116 B3
Dak Dam Cambodia 12°20N 107°21E 120 F6
Dak Nhe Vietnam 15°28N 107°48E 120 E6
Dak Pek Vietnam 15°4N 107°44E 120 E6
Dak Song Vietnam 12°19N 107°35E 121 F6
Dak Sui Vietnam 14°55N 107°43E 120 E6
Dakar Senegal 14°34N 17°29W 138 C1
Dakar □ Senegal 14°45N 17°20W 138 C1
Dakhla W. Sahara 23°50N 15°53W 134 D2
Dakhla, El Wâhât el Egypt 25°30N 28°50E 137 B2
Dakingari Nigeria 11°37N 4°1E 139 C5
Dakoank India 7°2N 93°43E 127 L11
Dakor India 22°45N 73°11E 124 H5
Dakoro Niger 14°31N 6°46E 139 C6
Dakota City U.S.A. 42°25N 96°25W 172 D5
Đakovica = Gjakovë Kosovo 42°22N 20°26E 96 D4
Đakovo Croatia 45°19N 18°24E 80 E3
Dala-Järna Sweden 60°33N 14°26E 62 D8
Dalaba Guinea 10°47N 12°12W 138 C2
Dalachi China 36°48N 105°0E 114 F3
Dalai Nur China 43°20N 116°45E 114 C9
Dalälven → Sweden 60°12N 16°43E 62 D10
Dalaki Iran 29°26N 51°17E 129 D6
Dalaman Turkey 36°48N 28°47E 99 E10
Dalaman → Turkey 36°41N 28°43E 99 E10
Dalandzadgad Mongolia 43°27N 104°30E 114 C3
Dalap-Uliga-Darrit = Majuro Marshall Is. 7°9N 171°12E 156 G9
Dalarna Sweden 61°0N 14°0E 62 D8
Dalarnas län □ Sweden 61°0N 14°15E 62 C8
Dalay Mongolia 43°28N 103°30E 114 C2
Dalbandin Pakistan 29°0N 64°23E 122 E4
Dalbeattie U.K. 54°56N 3°50W 65 G5
Dalbeg Australia 20°16S 147°18E 150 C4
Dalbosjön Sweden 58°40N 12°45E 63 F6
Dalby Australia 27°10S 151°17E 151 D5
Dalby Sweden 55°40N 13°22E 63 J7
Dalby Söderskog △ Sweden 55°41N 13°21E 63 J7
Dale City U.S.A. 38°38N 77°19W 173 F15
Dale Hollow L. U.S.A. 36°32N 85°27W 177 C12
Daleville U.S.A. 31°19N 85°43W 178 D4
Dalga Egypt 27°39N 30°41E 137 B3
Dalgán Iran 27°31N 59°19E 129 E8
Dalhart U.S.A. 36°4N 102°31W 176 C3
Dalhousie Canada 48°5N 66°26W 165 C6
Dalhousie India 32°38N 75°58E 124 C6
Dali Shaanxi, China 34°48N 109°58E 114 G5
Dali Yunnan, China 25°40N 100°10E 116 E3
Dalian China 38°50N 121°40E 115 E11
Daliang Shan China 28°0N 102°45E 116 D4
Daling He → China 40°55N 121°40E 115 D11
Dāliyat el Karmel Israel 32°43N 35°2E 130 C4
Dalj Croatia 45°29N 18°59E 80 E3
Dalkeith U.K. 55°54N 3°4W 65 F5
Dalkeith Australia 38°10S 145°23E 153 D9
Dalkey Ireland 53°16N 6°6W 64 C5
Dallas Ga., U.S.A. 33°55N 84°51W 178 D3
Dallas Oreg., U.S.A. 44°55N 123°19W 168 D2
Dallas Tex., U.S.A. 32°47N 96°48W 176 E6
Dallas, The U.S.A. 45°36N 121°10W 168 D3
Dalmā U.A.E. 24°30N 52°20E 129 E7
Dalmacija Croatia 43°20N 17°0E 80 C3
Dalmas, L. Canada 53°30N 71°50W 165 B5
Dalmatia = Dalmacija Croatia 43°20N 17°0E 93 E13
Dalmau India 26°4N 81°2E 125 F9
Dalmellington U.K. 55°19N 4°23W 65 F4
Dalmeny Australia 36°10S 150°8E 153 D9
Dalnegorsk Russia 44°30N 135°33E 112 B7
Dalnerechensk Russia 45°50N 133°40E 112 B6
Dalnevostochnyy □ Russia 67°0N 140°0E 107 C14
Daloa Ivory C. 7°0N 6°30W 138 D3
Dalou Shan China 28°15N 107°0E 116 C6
Dalry U.K. 55°42N 4°43W 65 F4
Dalrymple, L. Australia 20°40S 116°55E 150 C4
Dalrymple, Mt. Australia 21°1S 148°39E 150 b
Dals Långed Sweden 58°55N 12°18E 63 F6
Dalsjöfors Sweden 57°46N 13°5E 63 G7

Dalsland Sweden 58°50N 12°15E 63 F6
Daltenganj India 24°0N 84°4E 125 H11
Dalton Ga., U.S.A. 34°46N 84°58W 177 D12
Dalton Mass., U.S.A. 42°28N 73°11W 175 D11
Dalton Nebr., U.S.A. 41°25N 102°58W 172 E2
Dalton, Kap Greenland 69°25N 24°3W 57 D8
Dalton-in-Furness U.K. 54°10N 3°11W 66 C4
Dalvík Iceland 65°58N 18°32W 60 D4
Dálvvadis = Jokkmokk Sweden 66°35N 19°50E 60 C18
Dalwallinu Australia 30°17S 116°40E 149 F2
Daly → Australia 13°35S 130°19E 148 B5
Daly City U.S.A. 37°42N 122°27W 170 H4
Daly L. Canada 56°32N 105°39W 163 B7
Daly River Australia 13°46S 130°42E 148 B5
Daly River-Port Keats ☉ Australia 14°13S 129°36E 148 B4
Daly Waters Australia 16°15S 133°24E 150 B1
Dalyan Turkey 36°50N 28°39E 99 E10
Dam Doi Vietnam 8°50N 105°12E 121 H5
Dam Ha Vietnam 21°21N 107°36E 120 B6
Damachova Belarus 51°45N 23°36E 83 G10
Daman India 20°25N 72°57E 126 D1
Daman & Diu □ India 20°25N 72°58E 126 D1
Dāmaneh Iran 33°1N 50°29E 129 C6
Damanganga → India 20°25N 72°56E 126 D1
Damanhûr Egypt 31°0N 30°30E 137 E7
Daman L. Canada 61°45N 105°5W 163 B7
Damaq Iran 35°25N 48°49E 105 E13
Damar Indonesia 7°7S 128°40E 119 F7
Damara C.A.R. 4°58N 18°42E 140 D3
Damaraland Namibia 20°0S 15°0E 144 B2
Damascus = Dimashq Syria 33°30N 36°18E 130 B5
Damascus Greece 31°18N 84°43W 178 D5
Damasi Greece 39°43N 22°11E 98 B4
Damaturu Nigeria 11°45N 11°55E 139 C7
Dāmāvand Iran 35°47N 52°0E 129 C7
Dāmāvand, Qolleh-ye Iran 35°56N 52°10E 129 C7
Damba Angola 6°44S 15°20E 140 F3
Damboa Cameroon 11°51N 12°55E 139 C7
Dâmbovița □ Romania 45°0N 25°30E 81 F10
Dâmbovița → Romania 44°12N 26°26E 81 F11
Dâmbovnic → Romania 44°28N 25°18E 81 F10
Dambulla Sri Lanka 7°51N 80°39E 127 L5
Dame Marie Haiti 18°34N 74°26W 183 C5
Dâmghān Iran 36°10N 54°17E 129 B7
Dămienesti Romania 46°44N 26°59E 81 D11
Damietta = Dumyât Egypt 31°24N 31°48E 137 E7
Daming China 36°15N 115°6E 114 F8
Damīr Qābū Syria 36°58N 41°51E 128 B4
Damman = Ad Dammām Si. Arabia 26°20N 50°5E 129 E6
Dammarie-les-Lys France 48°31N 2°39E 71 D9
Dammartin-en-Goële France 49°3N 2°41E 71 C9
Damodar → India 23°17N 87°35E 125 H12
Damoh India 23°50N 79°28E 125 H8
Damous Algeria 36°31N 1°42E 136 A4
Dampier Australia 20°41S 116°42E 148 D2
Dampier, Selat Indonesia 0°40S 131°0E 119 E8
Dampier Arch. Australia 20°38S 116°32E 148 D2
Damrani Algeria 27°45N 2°56W 136 C3
Damrei, Chuor Phnum Cambodia 11°30N 103°0E 121 G4
Damvillers France 49°20N 5°21E 71 C12
Damyang S. Korea 35°19N 126°59E 115 G14
Dan-Gulbi Nigeria 11°40N 6°15E 139 C6
Dan-Sadau Nigeria 11°17N 6°29E 139 C6
Dana Indonesia 11°0S 121°15E 119 F6
Dana Jordan 30°41N 35°37E 130 E4
Dana Nepal 28°32N 83°37E 125 E10
Dana, L. Canada 50°53N 77°20W 164 B4
Dana, Mt. U.S.A. 37°54N 119°12W 170 H7
Danakil Desert Ethiopia 12°45N 41°0E 131 E3
Danané Ivory C. 7°16N 8°9W 138 D3
Danba China 30°54N 101°48E 116 B3
Danbury U.S.A. 41°24N 73°28W 175 E11
Danby L. U.S.A. 34°13N 115°5W 171 L11
Dand Afghan. 31°28N 65°32E 124 D1
Dande → Zimbabwe 15°56S 30°16E 143 F3
Dandeldhura Nepal 29°20N 80°35E 125 E9
Dandeli India 15°5N 74°30E 127 G2
Dandenong Australia 38°0S 145°15E 153 E6
Dandi Iran 36°32N 47°17E 105 D12
Dandil Egypt 29°10N 31°2E 137 F7
Dandong China 40°10N 124°20E 115 D13
Daneborg Greenland 74°18N 20°14W 57 C8
Danfeng China 33°45N 110°25E 114 H6
Dangan Liedao China 22°2N 114°8E 117 F10
Dangé-St-Romain France 46°56N 0°36E 72 B4
Dângeni Romania 47°51N 26°58E 81 C11
Danger Is. = Pukapuka Cook Is. 10°53S 165°49W 157 J11
Danger Pt. S. Africa 34°40S 19°17E 144 D2
Dangla Shan = Tanggula Shan China 32°40N 92°10E 110 C7
Dangora Nigeria 11°30N 8°7E 139 C6
Dangouadougou Burkina Faso 10°9N 4°56W 138 D4
Dangrek, Mts. = Dangrek, Phnom Thailand 14°20N 104°0E 120 E5
Dangrek, Phnom Thailand 14°20N 104°0E 120 E5
Dangriga Belize 17°0N 88°13W 181 D7
Dangshan China 34°27N 116°22E 114 G9
Dangtu China 31°32N 118°25E 117 B12
Dangyang China 30°52N 111°44E 117 B8
Daniel U.S.A. 42°52N 110°4W 172 E8
Daniel's Harbour Canada 50°13N 57°35W 165 B8
Danielskuil S. Africa 28°11S 23°33E 144 C3
Danielson U.S.A. 41°48N 71°53W 175 E13
Danilov Russia 58°16N 40°13E 84 C11
Danilovgrad Montenegro 42°38N 19°9E 96 D3
Danilovka Russia 50°25N 44°12E 86 E7
Daning China 36°28N 110°45E 114 F6
Danja Nigeria 11°21N 7°30E 139 C6
Danjiangkou China 32°31N 111°30E 117 A8
Danjiangkou Shuiku China 32°37N 111°30E 117 A8
Dank Oman 23°33N 56°16E 129 F8
Dankalwa Nigeria 11°52N 12°12E 139 C7
Dankama Nigeria 13°20N 7°44E 139 C6
Dankhar Gompa India 32°10N 78°10E 124 C8

Dankov Russia 53°20N 39°5E 84 F10
Danleng China 30°1N 103°31E 116 B4
Danli Honduras 14°4N 86°35W 182 D2
Danmark = Denmark ■ Europe 55°45N 10°0E 63 J3
Danmark Fjord Greenland 81°30N 22°0W 57 A8
Danmarkshavn Greenland 76°45N 18°50W 57 B9
Dannemora U.S.A. 44°43N 73°44W 175 B11
Dannenberg Germany 53°6N 11°5E 76 B7
Dannevirke N.Z. 40°12S 176°8E 154 G5
Dannhauser S. Africa 28°0S 30°3E 145 C5
Dansville U.S.A. 42°34N 77°42W 174 D7
Danta India 24°11N 72°46E 124 G5
Dantan India 21°57N 87°20E 125 J12
Dante = Xaafuun Somalia 10°25N 51°16E 131 E5
Dantewara India 18°54N 81°21E 126 E5
Danube = Dunărea → Europe 45°20N 29°40E 81 E14
Danvers U.S.A. 42°34N 70°56W 175 D14
Danville Ga., U.S.A. 32°37N 83°15W 178 C4
Danville Ill., U.S.A. 40°8N 87°37W 172 E10
Danville Ky., U.S.A. 37°39N 84°46W 173 G11
Danville Pa., U.S.A. 40°58N 76°37W 175 F8
Danville Vt., U.S.A. 44°25N 72°9W 175 B12
Danyang China 32°0N 119°31E 117 B12
Danzhai China 26°11N 107°48E 116 D6
Danzhou China 19°31N 109°33E 117 a
Danzig = Gdańsk Poland 54°22N 18°40E 82 D5
Dão → Portugal 40°20N 8°11W 88 E2
Dao Xian China 25°36N 111°31E 117 E8
Daocheng China 29°0N 100°10E 116 C3
Daoud = Aïn Beïda Algeria 35°50N 7°29E 136 A5
Daoukro Ivory C. 7°10N 3°58W 138 D4
Dapaong Togo 10°55N 0°16E 139 C5
Dapchi Nigeria 12°32N 11°13E 139 C7
Dapoli India 17°46N 73°11E 126 F1
Daqing China 46°35N 125°0E 111 B13
Daqing Shan China 40°40N 111°0E 114 D6
Daqq-e Sorkh, Kavīr Iran 33°45N 52°50E 129 C7
Daqu Shan China 30°25N 122°20E 117 B14
Dar Banda Africa 8°0N 23°0E 132 F6
Dar el Beida = Casablanca Morocco 33°36N 7°36W 136 B2
Dar es Salaam Tanzania 6°50S 39°12E 142 D4
Dar Mazār Iran 29°14N 57°20E 129 D8
Dar'ā Syria 32°36N 36°7E 130 C5
Dar'ā □ Syria 32°55N 36°10E 130 C5
Dārāb Iran 28°50N 54°30E 129 D7
Daraban Pakistan 31°44N 70°20E 124 D4
Darabani Romania 48°10N 26°39E 81 B11
Daraj Libya 30°10N 10°28E 135 B8
Dārān Iran 32°59N 50°24E 129 C6
Daravica = Gjeravicë Kosovo 42°32N 20°8E 96 D4
Daraw Egypt 24°22N 32°51E 137 C3
Dārayyā Syria 33°28N 36°15E 130 B5
Darazo Nigeria 11°1N 10°24E 139 C7
Darband Pakistan 34°20N 72°50E 124 B5
Darband, Kūh-e Iran 31°34N 57°8E 129 D8
Darbhanga India 26°15N 85°55E 125 F11
D'Arcy Canada 50°33N 122°29W 162 C4
Dardan Croatia 45°40N 18°41E 80 E3
Dardané Kosovo 42°51N 21°35E 96 D5
Dardanelle Ark., U.S.A. 35°13N 93°9W 176 D8
Dardanelle Calif., U.S.A. 38°20N 119°50W 170 G7
Dardanelles = Çanakkale Boğazı Turkey 40°17N 26°32E 97 F10
Darende Turkey 38°31N 37°30E 104 C7
Dārestān Iran 29°9N 58°42E 129 D8
Darfield N.Z. 43°29S 172°7E 155 D7
Darfo-Boario Terme Italy 45°53N 10°11E 92 C7
Dârfûr Sudan 13°40N 24°0E 135 F10
Dargai Pakistan 34°25N 71°55E 124 B4
Dargaville N.Z. 35°57S 173°52E 154 B2
Dargol Niger 13°54N 1°22E 139 C5
Darhan Mongolia 49°37N 106°21E 110 B10
Darhan Muminggan China 41°40N 110°28E 114 C6
Darica Turkey 40°45N 29°23E 104 B3
Darien, Turkey 31°23N 81°26W 178 D5
Darién, G. del Colombia 9°0N 77°0W 186 B3
Darién, P. de △ Panama 7°36N 77°57W 182 E4
Dariganga = Ovoot Mongolia 45°21N 113°45E 114 C9
Daringbadi India 19°54N 84°8E 126 E7
Darjeeling = Darjiling India 27°3N 88°18E 125 F13
Darjiling India 27°3N 88°18E 125 F13
Darkan Australia 33°20S 116°43E 149 F2
Darke Peak Australia 33°27S 136°12E 152 B2
Darkhana Pakistan 30°39N 72°11E 124 D5
Darkhazineh Iran 31°54N 48°39E 129 D6
Darkot Pass Pakistan 36°45N 73°26E 125 A5
Darling → Australia 34°4S 141°54E 152 C4
Darling Downs Australia 27°30S 150°30E 151 D5
Darling Ra. Australia 32°30S 116°20E 149 F2
Darlington U.K. 54°32N 1°33W 66 C6
Darlington Fla., U.S.A. 30°57N 86°3W 178 E3
Darlington S.C., U.S.A. 34°18N 79°52W 177 D15
Darlington □ U.K. 54°32N 1°33W 66 C6
Darlington, L. S. Africa 33°10S 25°9W 144 E4
Darlington Point Australia 34°37S 146°1E 153 C7
Darlot, L. Australia 27°48S 121°35E 149 E3
Darlowo Poland 54°25N 16°25E 82 D3
Dărmănești Bacău, Romania 46°21N 26°33E 81 D11
Dărmănești Suceava, Romania 47°44N 26°9E 81 C11
Darmstadt Germany 49°51N 8°39E 77 F4
Darnah Libya 32°45N 22°45E 135 B10
Darnall S. Africa 29°23N 31°18E 145 C5
Darney France 48°5N 6°3E 71 D13
Darnick Australia 32°48S 143°38E 152 B5
Darnley, Australia 9°35S 143°46E 150 a
Darnley, C. Antarctica 68°0S 69°0E 55 C6
Darnley B. Canada 69°30N 123°30W 160 D7
Daroca Spain 41°9N 1°25W 90 D3
Darou-Mousti Senegal 15°2N 16°9W 138 C1
Darr → Australia 23°39S 143°50E 150 C3
Darra Pezu Pakistan 32°19N 70°44E 124 C4

Darran Mts. N.Z. 44°37S 167°59E 155 E2
Darreh Shahr Iran 33°7N 47°22E 105 F12
Darrequeira Argentina 37°42S 63°10W 190 D3
Darrington U.S.A. 48°15N 121°36W 168 B3
Darsi India 15°46N 79°44E 127 G4
Darsser Ort Germany 54°28N 12°32E 76 A8
Dart → U.K. 50°24N 3°39W 67 G4
Dartford U.K. 51°26N 0°13E 67 F8
Dartmoor Australia 37°56S 141°19E 152 D4
Dartmoor U.K. 50°38N 3°57W 67 G4
Dartmoor △ U.K. 50°37N 3°59W 67 G4
Dartmouth Canada 44°40N 63°30W 165 D7
Dartmouth U.K. 50°21N 3°36W 67 G4
Dartmouth, L. Queens., Australia 26°4S 145°18E 151 D4
Dartmouth, L. Vic., Australia 36°34S 147°32E 153 D7
Dartuch, C. = Artrutx, C. de Spain 39°55N 3°49E 100 B10
Daru Papua N. G. 9°3S 143°13E 150 a
Daru S. Leone 8°0N 10°52W 138 D2
Daruvar Croatia 45°35N 17°14E 80 E2
Darvel, Teluk = Lahad Datu, Telok Malaysia 5°0N 118°20E 119 D5
Darvi Mongolia 46°27N 94°7E 109 C12
Darwendale Zimbabwe 17°41S 30°33E 145 A5
Darwha India 20°15N 77°45E 126 D3
Darwin Australia 12°25S 130°51E 148 B5
Darwin U.S.A. 36°15N 117°35E 171 J9
Darwin, Mt. Chile 54°47S 69°55W 192 D3
Darya Khan Pakistan 31°48N 71°6E 124 D4
Daryapur India 20°55N 77°20E 126 D3
Daryoi Amu = Amudarya → Uzbekistan 43°58N 59°34E 108 D5
Dās U.A.E. 25°20N 53°30E 129 E7
Dashen, Ras Ethiopia 13°8N 38°26E 131 E2
Dasher U.S.A. 30°45N 83°13W 178 E6
Dashetai China 41°0N 109°5E 114 D5
Dashiqiao China 40°38N 122°30E 115 D12
Dashkesan = Daşkäsän Azerbaijan 40°25N 46°0E 87 K7
Dashköpri Turkmenistan 36°16N 62°8E 129 B9
Dasht → Pakistan 25°10N 61°40E 122 G2
Daska Pakistan 32°20N 74°20E 124 C6
Daşkäsän Azerbaijan 40°25N 46°0E 87 K7
Daşoguz Turkmenistan 41°49N 59°58E 108 D5
Dassa Benin 7°46N 2°14E 139 D5
Dasuya India 31°49N 75°38E 124 D6
Datça Turkey 36°46N 27°40E 99 E9
Date Japan 42°28N 140°52E 112 C10
Datia India 25°39N 78°27E 125 G8
Datian China 25°40N 117°50E 117 E11
Datong Anhui, China 30°48N 117°44E 117 B11
Datong Qinghai, China 36°20N 102°50E 110 D9
Datong Shanxi, China 40°6N 113°18E 114 D7
Dattakhel Pakistan 32°54N 69°46E 124 C3
Dattapur = Dhamangaon India 20°48N 78°9E 126 D4
Datteln Germany 51°39N 7°21E 76 D3
Datu, Tanjung Indonesia 2°5N 109°39E 118 D3
Datu Piang Phil. 7°2N 124°30E 119 C6
Datuk, Tanjong = Datu, Tanjung Indonesia 2°5N 109°39E 118 D3
Daud Khel Pakistan 32°53N 71°34E 124 C4
Daudnagar India 25°2N 84°24E 125 G11
Daugava → Latvia 57°4N 24°3E 84 D3
Daugavpils Latvia 55°53N 26°32E 84 E4
Daulatabad India 19°57N 75°15E 126 E2
Daulpur India 26°45N 77°59E 124 F7
Daun Germany 50°11N 6°49E 77 E2
Daund India 18°26N 74°40E 126 E2
Daung Kyun Burma 12°13N 98°4E 121 F1
Dauphin Canada 51°9N 100°5W 163 C8
Dauphin U.S.A. 40°22N 76°56W 174 F8
Dauphin L. Canada 51°20N 99°45W 163 C9
Dauphiné France 45°15N 5°25E 73 C9
Daura Borno, Nigeria 11°31N 11°24E 139 C7
Daura Katsina, Nigeria 13°2N 8°21E 139 C6
Daurada, Costa Spain 41°12N 1°15E 90 D6
Dausa India 26°52N 76°20E 124 F7
Dāvāci Azerbaijan 41°15N 48°57E 87 K9
Davangere India 14°25N 75°55E 127 G2
Davao Phil. 7°0N 125°40E 119 C7
Davao, G. of Phil. 6°30N 125°48E 119 C7
Dāvar Panāh = Sarāvān Iran 27°25N 62°15E 129 E9
Davenport Calif., U.S.A. 37°1N 122°12W 170 H4
Davenport Fla., U.S.A. 28°10N 81°36W 179 G8
Davenport Iowa, U.S.A. 41°32N 90°35W 172 E8
Davenport Wash., U.S.A. 47°39N 118°9W 168 C4
Davenport Ra. Australia 20°28S 134°0E 150 C1
Davenport Range △ Australia 20°28S 134°2E 150 C1
Daventry U.K. 52°16N 1°10W 67 E6
David Panama 8°30N 82°30W 182 E3
David City U.S.A. 41°15N 97°8W 172 E5
David Glacier Antarctica 75°20S 162°0E 55 D11
David Gorodok = Davyd Haradok Belarus 52°4N 27°8E 75 B14
Davidson Canada 51°16N 105°59W 163 C7
Davidson Mts. U.S.A. 68°41N 142°22W 166 B11
Davie Serbia 44°38N 19°53E 96 B3
Davis Antarctica 68°34S 77°55E 55 C6
Davis U.S.A. 38°33N 121°44W 170 G5
Davis Dam U.S.A. 35°12N 114°34W 171 K12
Davis Inlet Canada 55°50N 60°59W 165 A7
Davis Mts. U.S.A. 30°50N 103°55W 176 F3
Davis Sea Antarctica 66°0S 92°0E 55 C7
Davis Str. N. Amer. 65°0N 58°0W 161 D19
Davisboro U.S.A. 32°59N 82°36W 178 C5
Davlos Cyprus 35°25N 33°54E 101 D12
Davo → Ivory C. 5°6N 5°10W 138 D3
Davos Switz. 46°48N 9°49E 75 E9
Davutlar Turkey 37°43N 27°17E 99 D9
Davy L. Canada 58°53N 108°18W 163 B7
Dawaki Bauchi, Nigeria 11°25N 9°26E 139 C6
Dawaki Kano, Nigeria 12°5N 8°23E 139 C6
Dawei = Tavoy Burma 14°2N 98°12E 120 E2
Dawes Ra. Australia 24°40S 150°40E 150 C5
Dawlish U.K. 50°35N 3°28W 67 G4
Dawna Ra. Burma 16°30N 98°30E 120 D2
Dawros Hd. Ireland 54°50N 8°33W 64 B3
Dawson U.S.A. 31°46N 84°27W 178 D5
Dawson, I. Chile 53°50N 70°50W 192 D2
Dawson B. Canada 52°53N 100°49W 163 C8
Dawson City Canada 64°10N 139°30W 160 E4

Dawson Creek Canada 55°45N 120°15W 162 B4
Dawson Inlet Canada 61°50N 93°25W 163 A10
Dawson Ra. Australia 24°30S 149°48E 150 C4
Dawu Hubei, China 31°34N 114°7E 117 B10
Dawu Sichuan, China 30°55N 101°10E 116 B3
Dax France 43°44N 1°3W 72 E2
Daxian China 31°15N 107°23E 116 B6
Daxin China 22°50N 107°11E 116 F6
Daxindian China 37°30N 120°50E 115 F11
Daxinggou China 43°25N 129°40E 115 C15
Daxue Shan Sichuan, China 30°30N 101°30E 116 B3
Daxue Shan Yunnan, China 23°42N 99°48E 116 F2
Day China 30°12N 83°17W 178 E6
Dayao China 25°43N 101°20E 116 E3
Daye China 30°6N 114°58E 117 B10
Dayet en Naharat Mali 17°39N 3°10W 138 B4
Dayi China 30°41N 103°29E 116 B4
Dāykondī □ Afghan. 34°0N 66°0E 122 C5
Daylesford Australia 37°21S 144°9E 152 D6
Dayong China 29°11N 110°30E 117 C8
Dayr az Zawr Syria 35°20N 40°5E 105 C9
Dayr az Zawr □ Syria 34°50N 40°10E 105 D9
Daysland Canada 52°50N 112°20W 162 C6
Dayton Nev., U.S.A. 39°14N 119°36W 170 F7
Dayton Ohio, U.S.A. 39°45N 84°12W 173 F11
Dayton Pa., U.S.A. 40°53N 79°15W 174 F5
Dayton Tenn., U.S.A. 35°30N 85°1W 177 D12
Dayton Wash., U.S.A. 46°19N 117°59W 168 D5
Dayton Wyo., U.S.A. 44°53N 107°16W 168 D10
Daytona Beach U.S.A. 29°13N 81°1W 179 F8
Dayu China 25°24N 114°22E 117 E10
Dayville U.S.A. 44°28N 119°32W 168 D4
Dazhu China 30°41N 107°15E 116 B6
Dazkırı Turkey 37°57N 29°52E 99 D11
Dazu China 29°40N 105°42E 116 C5
De Aar S. Africa 30°39S 24°0E 144 E3
De Armanville U.S.A. 33°38N 85°45W 178 D4
De Funiak Springs U.S.A. 30°43N 86°7W 178 E3
De Grey → Australia 20°12S 119°13E 148 D2
De Haan Belgium 51°16N 3°2E 69 C3
De Hoop △ S. Africa 34°30S 20°28E 144 D3
De Kalb Junction U.S.A. 44°30N 75°16W 175 B9
De Land U.S.A. 29°2N 81°18W 179 F8
De Leon U.S.A. 32°7N 98°32W 176 E5
De Leon Springs U.S.A. 29°7N 81°21W 179 F8
De Long Mts. U.S.A. 68°10N 163°30W 166 B7
De Panne Belgium 51°6N 2°34E 69 C2
De Pere U.S.A. 44°27N 88°4W 172 C9
De Queen U.S.A. 34°2N 94°21W 176 D7
De Quincy U.S.A. 30°27N 93°26W 176 F7
De Ruyters U.S.A. 42°45N 75°53W 175 D9
De Smet U.S.A. 44°23N 97°33W 172 D5
De Soto U.S.A. 38°8N 90°34W 172 F8
De Soto City U.S.A. 27°27N 81°24W 179 H8
De Tour Village U.S.A. 46°0N 83°56W 173 B12
De Witt U.S.A. 34°18N 91°20W 176 D8
Dead L. U.S.A. 30°10N 85°10W 178 E3
Dead Sea Asia 31°30N 35°30E 130 D4
Deadman B. U.S.A. 29°30N 83°30W 179 F7
Deadwood U.S.A. 44°23N 103°44W 172 C2
Deadwood L. Canada 59°10N 128°30W 162 B3
Deal U.K. 51°13N 1°25E 67 F9
Deal I. Australia 39°30S 147°20E 151 F4
Dealesville S. Africa 28°41S 25°44E 144 C4
de'an China 29°21N 115°46E 117 C10
Dean → Canada 52°49N 126°58W 162 C3
Dean, Forest of U.K. 51°45N 2°33W 67 F5
Dean Chan. Canada 52°30N 127°15W 162 C3
Deán Funes Argentina 30°20S 64°20W 190 C3
Deanuvuotna = Tanafjorden Norway 70°45N 28°25E 60 A23
Dease → Canada 59°56N 128°32W 162 B3
Dease Lake Canada 58°40N 130°5W 162 B2
Death Valley U.S.A. 36°15N 116°50W 171 J10
Death Valley △ U.S.A. 36°29N 117°6W 171 J9
Death Valley Junction U.S.A. 36°20N 116°25W 171 J10
Deatnu = Tana → Norway 70°30N 28°14E 60 A23
Deauville France 49°23N 0°2E 70 C7
Deba Spain 43°18N 2°21W 90 B2
Deba Habe Nigeria 10°14N 11°20E 139 C7
Debagram India 23°41N 88°18E 125 H13
Debaltsevo Ukraine 48°22N 38°26E 87 H10
Debao China 23°21N 106°46E 116 F6
Debar Macedonia 41°31N 20°30E 98 a
Debden Canada 53°30N 106°50W 163 C7
Debdou Morocco 33°59N 3°0W 136 B4
Dębica Poland 50°2N 21°25E 83 H8
Dęblin Poland 51°34N 21°50E 83 G9
Dębno Poland 52°44N 14°41E 83 F1
Dębo, L. Mali 15°14N 4°15W 138 B4
DeBolt Canada 55°12N 118°1W 162 B5
Deborah East, L. Australia 30°45S 119°52E 149 F2
Deborah West, L. Australia 30°45S 119°5E 149 F2
Debre Serbia 44°38N 19°53E 96 B3
Debre Markos Ethiopia 10°20N 37°40E 131 E2
Debre Tabor Ethiopia 11°50N 38°26E 131 E2
Debre Zeyit Ethiopia 8°50N 39°0E 131 F2
Debrecen Hungary 47°33N 21°42E 80 C6
Debrzno Poland 53°31N 17°14E 82 E4
Deçan Serbia 42°30N 20°30E 96 D4
Decatur Ala., U.S.A. 34°36N 86°59W 177 D11
Decatur Ga., U.S.A. 33°46N 84°16W 178 D3
Decatur Ill., U.S.A. 39°51N 88°57W 172 F9
Decatur Ind., U.S.A. 40°50N 84°56W 173 E11
Decatur Tex., U.S.A. 33°14N 97°35W 176 E6
Decazeville France 44°34N 2°15E 72 D6
Deccan India 18°0N 79°0E 126 F4
Deception, Mt. Australia 30°42S 138°16E 152 A3
Deception Bay Australia 27°10S 153°5E 151 D5
Deception I. Antarctica 63°0S 60°15W 55 C17
Deception L. Canada 56°33N 104°13W 163 B8
Dechang China 27°25N 102°11E 116 D4
Dechhu India 26°46N 72°20E 124 F5
Decimomannu Italy 39°19N 8°58E 94 C1
Děčín Czech Rep. 50°47N 14°12E 78 A7
Decize France 46°50N 3°27E 71 F10
Deckerville U.S.A. 43°32N 82°44W 174 C2
Decollatura Italy 39°3N 16°21E 95 C9
Decorah U.S.A. 43°18N 91°48W 172 D8

INDEX TO WORLD MAPS
Discovery Seamount 215

Deda Romania 46°56N 24°50E 81 D9
Dedéagach = Alexandroupoli Greece 40°50N 25°54E 97 F9
Dedham U.S.A. 42°15N 71°10W 175 D13
Dedopolis Tsqaro Georgia 41°33N 46°0E 87 K8
Dédougou Burkina Faso 12°30N 3°25W 138 C4
Dedovichi Russia 57°32N 29°56E 84 D5
Dedza Malawi 14°20S 34°20E 143 E3
Dee → Aberds., U.K. 57°9N 2°5W 65 D6
Dee → Dumf. & Gall., U.K. 54°51N 4°3W 65 G4
Dee → Wales, U.K. 53°22N 3°17W 66 D4
Deep B. Canada 61°15N 116°35W 162 A5
Deep Bay = Shenzhen Wan China 22°27N 113°55E 111 a
Deep Lead Australia 37°0S 142°43E 152 D5
Deepwater Australia 29°25S 151°51E 151 D5
Deer → Canada 58°23N 94°13W 163 B10
Deer L. Canada 52°40N 94°20W 163 C10
Deer Lake Nfld. & L., Canada 49°11N 57°27W 165 C8
Deer Lake Ont., Canada 52°36N 94°20W 163 C10
Deer Lodge U.S.A. 46°24N 112°44W 168 C7
Deer Park Fla., U.S.A. 28°6N 80°54W 179 G9
Deer Park Wash., U.S.A. 47°57N 117°28W 168 C5
Deer River U.S.A. 47°20N 93°48W 172 B7
Deeragun Australia 19°16S 146°33E 150 B4
Deerfield Beach U.S.A. 26°19N 80°6W 179 J9
Defiance U.S.A. 41°17N 84°22W 173 E11
Degana India 26°50N 74°20E 124 F6
Dêgê China 31°44N 98°39E 116 B2
Degebe → Portugal 38°13N 7°29W 89 G3
Degeberga Sweden 55°51N 14°5E 63 J8
Dégelis Canada 47°30N 68°35W 165 C6
Degema Nigeria 4°50N 6°48E 139 E6
Degerfors Sweden 59°15N 14°27E 62 E8
Degerhamn Sweden 56°20N 16°24E 63 H10
Deggendorf Germany 48°50N 12°57E 77 G8
Degh → Pakistan 31°3N 73°21E 124 D5
Değirmendere Turkey 40°42N 29°47E 97 F13
Değirmenlik = Kythréa Cyprus 35°15N 33°29E 101 D12
Deh Bīd Iran 30°39N 53°11E 129 D7
Deh Dasht Iran 30°47N 50°33E 129 D6
Deh-e Shīr Iran 31°29N 53°45E 129 D7
Dehaj Iran 30°42N 54°53E 129 D7
Dehak Iran 27°11N 62°37E 129 E9
Dehdez Iran 31°43N 50°17E 129 D6
Dehej India 21°44N 72°40E 124 J5
Dehestān Iran 28°30N 55°35E 129 D7
Dehgolān Iran 35°17N 47°25E 105 E12
Dehibat Tunisia 32°0N 10°47E 136 B6
Dehiwala Sri Lanka 6°50N 79°51E 127 L4
Dehlorān Iran 32°41N 47°16E 105 F12
Dehnow-e Kūhestān Iran 27°58N 58°32E 129 E8
Dehra Dun India 30°20N 78°4E 124 D8
Dehri India 24°50N 84°15E 125 G11
Dehua China 25°26N 118°14E 117 E12
Dehui China 44°30N 125°40E 115 B13
Deinze Belgium 50°59N 3°32E 69 D3
Deir al Balah Gaza Strip 31°25N 34°21E 130 D3
Dej Romania 47°10N 23°52E 81 C8
Deje Sweden 59°35N 13°29E 62 E7
Dejiang China 28°18N 108°7E 116 C7
Deka → Zimbabwe 18°4S 26°42E 144 A4
DeKalb U.S.A. 41°56N 88°46W 172 E9
Dekese Dem. Rep. of the Congo 3°24S 21°24E 140 E4
Del Caño Rise Ind. Oc. 45°15S 44°15E 146 J3
Del Mar U.S.A. 32°58N 117°16W 171 N9
Del Norte U.S.A. 37°41N 106°21W 169 H10
Del Rio U.S.A. 29°22N 100°54W 176 G4
Delambre I. Australia 20°26S 117°5E 148 D2
Delano U.S.A. 35°46N 119°15W 171 K7
Delano Peak U.S.A. 38°22N 112°22W 168 G7
Delareyville S. Africa 26°41S 25°26E 144 C4
Delaronde L. Canada 54°3N 107°3W 163 C7
Delavan U.S.A. 42°38N 88°39W 172 D9
Delaware U.S.A. 40°18N 83°4W 173 E12
Delaware □ U.S.A. 39°0N 75°20W 173 F16
Delaware → U.S.A. 39°15N 75°20W 175 G9
Delaware B. U.S.A. 39°0N 75°10W 173 F16
Delaware Water Gap ⌓ U.S.A. 41°10N 74°55W 175 E10
Delay → Canada 56°56N 71°28W 165 A5
Delbrück Germany 51°46N 8°34E 76 D4
Delčevo Macedonia 41°58N 22°46E 96 E6
Delegate Australia 37°4S 148°56E 153 D8
Delémont Switz. 47°22N 7°20E 77 H3
Delevan U.S.A. 42°29N 78°29W 174 D6
Delft Neths. 52°1N 4°22E 69 B4
Delft I. Sri Lanka 9°30N 79°40E 127 K4
Delfzijl Neths. 53°20N 6°55E 69 A6
Delgada, Punta Chile 52°28S 69°32W 192 D3
Delgado, C. Mozam. 10°45S 40°40E 143 E5
Delgerhet Mongolia 45°50N 110°30E 114 B6
Delgo Sudan 20°6N 30°40E 137 C3
Delhi Canada 42°51N 80°30W 174 D4
Delhi India 28°39N 77°13E 124 E7
Delhi La., U.S.A. 32°28N 91°30W 176 E9
Delhi N.Y., U.S.A. 42°17N 74°55W 175 D10
Deli Jovan Serbia 44°13N 22°9E 96 B6
Delia Canada 51°38N 112°23W 162 C6
Delice Turkey 39°54N 34°2E 104 C6
Delice → Turkey 40°45N 34°15E 104 B6
Delicias Mexico 28°13N 105°28W 180 B3
Delījān Iran 33°59N 50°40E 129 C6
Déline Canada 65°11N 123°25W 160 D7
Delingha China 37°23N 97°23E 110 D8
Delisle Canada 51°55N 107°8W 163 C7
Delitzsch Germany 51°31N 12°20E 76 D8
Deliverance I. Australia 9°31S 141°34E 150 a
Dell City U.S.A. 31°56N 105°12W 176 F2
Dell Rapids U.S.A. 43°50N 96°43W 172 D5
Delle France 47°30N 7°2E 71 E14
Dellys Algeria 36°57N 3°57E 136 A4
Delmar U.S.A. 42°37N 73°47W 175 D11
Delmenhorst Germany 53°3N 8°37E 76 B4
Delmiro Gouveia Brazil 9°24S 38°6W 189 B3
Delnice Croatia 45°23N 14°50E 93 C11
Delonga, Ostrova Russia 76°40N 149°20E 107 B15
Deloraine Australia 41°30S 146°40E 151 G4
Deloraine Canada 49°15N 100°29W 163 D8
Delos = Dilos Greece 37°23N 25°15E 99 D7
Delphi Greece 38°28N 22°30E 98 C4
Delphi U.S.A. 40°36N 86°41W 172 E10
Delphos U.S.A. 40°51N 84°21W 173 E11
Delportshoop S. Africa 28°22S 24°20E 144 C3
Delray Beach U.S.A. 26°28N 80°4W 179 J9
Delsbo Sweden 61°48N 16°32E 62 C10
Delta Ala., U.S.A. 33°26N 85°42W 178 B4
Delta Colo., U.S.A. 38°44N 108°4W 168 G9
Delta Utah, U.S.A. 39°21N 112°35W 168 G7
Delta □ Nigeria 5°30N 6°0E 139 D6
Delta del Ebre ⌓ Spain 40°43N 0°43E 90 E5
Delta del Po ⌓ Italy 44°50N 12°15E 93 D9
Delta du Saloum △ Senegal 13°42N 16°43W 138 C1
Delta Dunărea ⌓ Romania 45°15N 29°25E 81 E14
Delta Junction U.S.A. 64°2N 145°44W 160 E2
Deltebre Spain 40°43N 0°43E 90 E5
Deltona U.S.A. 28°54N 81°16W 179 G8
Delungra Australia 29°39S 150°51E 151 D5
Delvada India 20°46N 71°2E 124 J4
Delvinaki Greece 39°57N 20°32E 98 B2
Delvinë Albania 39°59N 20°6E 96 G4
Delyatyn Ukraine 48°32N 24°38E 81 B9
Demak Indonesia 6°53S 110°38E 119 G14
Demanda, Sierra de la Spain 42°15N 3°0W 90 C2
Demavend = Damāvand, Qolleh-ye Iran 35°56N 52°10E 129 C7
Dembia C.A.R. 4°56N 23°53E 142 B1
Dembia Dem. Rep. of the Congo 3°33N 25°48E 142 B2
Dembidolo Ethiopia 8°34N 34°50E 131 F1
Demchok India 32°42N 79°29E 125 C8
Demer → Belgium 50°57N 4°42E 69 D4
Demerara Abyssal Plain Atl. Oc. 10°0N 48°0W 56 F7
Demetrias Greece 39°22N 23°1E 98 B5
Demidov Russia 55°16N 31°30E 84 E6
Deming N. Mex., U.S.A. 32°16N 107°46W 169 K10
Deming Wash., U.S.A. 48°50N 122°13W 170 B4
Demini → Brazil 0°46S 62°56W 186 D6
Demirci Turkey 39°2N 28°38E 99 B10
Demirköprü Barajı Turkey 38°42N 28°25E 99 C10
Demirköy Turkey 41°49N 27°45E 97 E11
Demmin Germany 53°54N 13°2E 76 B9
Demnate Morocco 31°44N 6°59W 136 B2
Demonte Italy 44°19N 7°17E 92 D4
Demopolis U.S.A. 32°31N 87°50W 177 E11
Dempo Indonesia 4°2S 103°15E 118 E2
Demyansk Russia 57°40N 32°27E 84 D7
Den Bosch = 's-Hertogenbosch Neths. 51°42N 5°17E 69 C5
Den Burg Neths. 53°3N 4°47E 69 A4
Den Chai Thailand 17°59N 100°4E 120 D3
Den Haag = 's-Gravenhage Neths. 52°7N 4°17E 69 B4
Den Helder Neths. 52°57N 4°45E 69 B4
Den Oever Neths. 52°56N 5°2E 69 B5
Denain France 50°20N 3°22E 71 B10
Denair U.S.A. 37°32N 120°48W 170 H6
Denali = McKinley, Mt. U.S.A. 63°4N 151°0W 160 E1
Denau = Denov Uzbekistan 38°16N 67°54E 109 E7
Denbigh Canada 45°8N 77°15W 174 A7
Denbigh U.K. 53°12N 3°25W 66 D4
Denbighshire □ U.K. 53°8N 3°22W 66 D4
Dendang Indonesia 3°7S 107°56E 118 E3
Dendermonde Belgium 51°2N 4°5E 69 C4
Dengchuan China 25°59N 100°3E 116 E3
Denge Nigeria 12°52N 5°21E 139 C6
Dengfeng China 34°25N 113°2E 114 G7
Dengi Nigeria 9°25N 9°55E 139 D6
Dengkou China 40°18N 106°55E 114 D4
Denguélé □ Ivory C. 9°45N 7°30W 138 D3
Dengzhou China 32°34N 112°4E 117 A9
Denham Australia 25°56S 113°31E 149 E1
Denham, Mt. Jamaica 18°13N 77°32W 182 a
Denham Ra. Australia 21°55S 147°46E 150 C4
Denham Sd. Australia 25°45S 113°15E 149 E1
Denholm Canada 52°39N 108°1W 163 C7
Denia Spain 38°49N 0°8E 91 G5
Denial B. Australia 32°14S 133°32E 151 E1
Deniliquin Australia 35°30S 144°58E 153 C6
Denimoo = Fort Resolution Canada 61°10N 113°40W 162 A6
Denison Iowa, U.S.A. 42°1N 95°21W 172 D6
Denison Tex., U.S.A. 33°45N 96°33W 176 E6
Denison Plains Australia 18°35S 128°0E 148 C4
Denīsovka Kazakhstan 52°27N 61°39E 108 B6
Deniyaya Sri Lanka 6°21N 80°33E 127 L5
Denizli Turkey 37°42N 29°2E 99 D11
Denizli □ Turkey 37°45N 29°5E 99 D11
Denman Australia 32°24S 150°42E 153 B9
Denman Glacier Antarctica 66°45S 100°0E 55 C8
Denmark Australia 34°59S 117°25E 149 F2
Denmark U.S.A. 33°19N 81°9W 178 B8
Denmark ■ Europe 55°45N 10°0E 63 J3
Denmark Str. Atl. Oc. 66°0N 30°0W 57 D8
Dennery St. Lucia 13°55N 60°54W 183 f
Dennison U.S.A. 40°24N 81°19W 174 F3
Denny U.K. 56°1N 3°55W 65 E5
Denov Uzbekistan 38°16N 67°54E 109 E7
Denpasar Indonesia 8°39S 115°13E 118 F5
Denpasar ✈ (DPS) Indonesia 8°44S 115°10E 119 K18
Denton Ga., U.S.A. 31°44N 82°42W 178 D7
Denton Mont., U.S.A. 47°19N 109°57W 168 C9
Denton Tex., U.S.A. 33°13N 97°8W 176 E6
D'Entrecasteaux, Pt. Australia 34°50S 115°57E 149 F2
D'Entrecasteaux △ Australia 34°20S 115°33E 149 F2
D'Entrecasteaux Is. Papua N. G. 9°0S 151°0E 147 B8
Dentsville U.S.A. 34°4N 80°58W 178 A9
Denu Ghana 6°4N 1°8E 139 D5
Denver Colo., U.S.A. 39°42N 104°59W 168 G11
Denver Pa., U.S.A. 40°14N 76°8W 175 F8
Denver City U.S.A. 32°58N 102°50W 176 E3
Deoband India 29°42N 77°43E 124 E7
Deobhog India 19°53N 82°44E 126 E6
Deogarh India 16°26N 76°55E 127 F3
Deogarh Odisha, India 21°32N 84°45E 126 D7
Deogarh Raj., India 25°32N 73°54E 124 G5
Deoghar India 24°30N 86°42E 125 G12
Deolali India 19°58N 73°50E 126 E1
Deoli = Devli India 25°50N 75°20E 124 G6
Déols France 46°50N 1°43E 71 F8
Deora India 26°22N 70°55E 124 F4
Deori India 23°24N 79°1E 125 H8
Deoria India 26°31N 83°48E 125 F10
Deosai Mts. Pakistan 35°40N 75°0E 125 B6
Deosri India 26°46N 90°29E 125 F14
Depalpur India 22°51N 75°33E 124 H6
Deposit U.S.A. 42°4N 75°25W 175 D9
Depuch I. Australia 20°37S 117°44E 148 D2
Deputatskiy Russia 69°18N 139°54E 107 C14
Dêqên China 28°34N 98°51E 116 C2
Deqing China 23°8N 111°42E 117 F8
Der-Chantecoq, L. du France 48°35N 4°40E 71 D11
Dera Ghazi Khan Pakistan 30°5N 70°43E 124 D4
Dera Ismail Khan Pakistan 31°50N 70°50E 124 D4
Derabugti Pakistan 29°2N 69°9E 124 E3
Derawar Fort Pakistan 28°46N 71°20E 124 E4
Derbent Russia 42°5N 48°15E 87 J9
Derbent Turkey 38°11N 28°33E 99 C10
Derby Australia 17°18S 123°38E 148 C3
Derby U.K. 52°56N 1°28W 66 E6
Derby Conn., U.S.A. 41°19N 73°5W 175 E11
Derby Kans., U.S.A. 37°33N 97°16W 172 G5
Derby N.Y., U.S.A. 42°41N 78°58W 174 D6
Derby City □ U.K. 52°56N 1°28W 66 E6
Derby Line U.S.A. 45°0N 72°6W 175 B12
Derbyshire □ U.K. 53°11N 1°38W 66 D6
Derdap △ Serbia 44°40N 22°23E 96 B6
Derdepoort S. Africa 24°38S 26°24E 144 B4
Derecske Hungary 47°20N 21°33E 80 C6
Dereham U.K. 52°41N 0°57E 67 E8
Dereköy Turkey 41°55N 27°21E 97 E11
Dereli Turkey 40°44N 38°26E 105 B8
Derg → U.K. 54°44N 7°26W 64 B4
Derg, L. Ireland 53°0N 8°20W 64 D3
Dergachi = Derhaci Ukraine 50°9N 36°11E 85 G9
Derhaci Ukraine 50°9N 36°11E 85 G9
Deridder U.S.A. 30°51N 93°17W 176 F8
Derik Turkey 37°21N 40°18E 105 D9
Derinkuyu Turkey 38°22N 34°45E 104 C6
Dermantsi Bulgaria 43°8N 24°17E 97 C8
Dermott U.S.A. 33°32N 91°26W 176 E9
Dêrong China 28°44N 99°9E 116 C2
Derrinallum Australia 37°57S 143°15E 152 D5
Derry = Londonderry U.K. 55°0N 7°20W 64 B4
Derry = Londonderry □ U.K. 55°0N 7°20W 64 B4
Derry N.H., U.S.A. 42°53N 71°19W 175 D13
Derry Pa., U.S.A. 40°20N 79°18W 174 F5
Derryveagh Mts. Ireland 54°56N 8°11W 64 B3
Derval France 47°40N 1°41W 70 E5
Derveni Greece 38°8N 22°25E 98 C4
Derventa Bos.-H. 44°59N 17°55E 80 F2
Derwent → Cumb., U.K. 54°39N 3°33W 66 C4
Derwent → Derby, U.K. 52°57N 1°28W 66 E6
Derwent → N. Yorks., U.K. 53°45N 0°58W 66 D7
Derwent Water U.K. 54°35N 3°9W 66 C4
Derzhavinsk Kazakhstan 51°6N 66°19E 109 B7
Des Moines Iowa, U.S.A. 41°35N 93°37W 172 E7
Des Moines N. Mex., U.S.A. 36°46N 103°50W 169 H12
Des Moines Wash., U.S.A. 47°24N 122°19W 170 C4
Des Moines → U.S.A. 40°23N 91°25W 172 E8
Desa Romania 43°52N 23°2E 80 G8
Desaguadero Peru 16°34S 69°3W 188 D4
Desaguadero → Argentina 34°30S 66°46W 190 C2
Desaguadero → Bolivia 16°35S 69°5W 188 D4
Desantne Ukraine 45°34N 29°32E 81 E14
Desaru Malaysia 1°31N 104°17E 121 d
Descanso, Pta. Mexico 32°21N 117°3W 171 N9
Descartes France 46°59N 0°42E 72 B4
Deschaillons-sur-St-Laurent Canada 46°32N 72°7W 165 C5
Deschambault L. Canada 54°50N 103°30W 163 C8
Deschutes → U.S.A. 45°38N 120°55W 168 D3
Descobrimento △ Brazil 16°53S 39°21W 189 D3
Dese Ethiopia 11°5N 39°40E 131 E2
Deseado, C. Chile 52°45S 74°42W 192 D2
Desenzano del Garda Italy 45°28N 10°32E 92 C7
Deseronto Canada 44°12N 77°3W 174 B7
Desert Center U.S.A. 33°43N 115°24W 171 M11
Desert Hot Springs U.S.A. 33°58N 116°30W 171 M10
Desfina Greece 38°25N 22°31E 98 C4
Deshnok India 27°48N 73°21E 124 F5
Desierto Central de Baja California ⌓ Mexico 29°40N 114°50W 180 B2
Deskati Greece 39°55N 21°49E 96 G5
Desna → Ukraine 50°33N 30°32E 75 C16
Desnățui → Romania 43°53N 23°35E 81 G8
Desolación, I. Chile 53°0S 74°0W 192 D2
Despeñaperros, Paso Spain 38°24N 3°30W 89 G7
Despeñaperros ⌓ Spain 38°23N 3°32W 89 G7
Despotiko Greece 36°57N 24°58E 98 E6
Despotovac Serbia 44°6N 21°30E 96 B5
Dessau Germany 51°51N 12°14E 76 D8
Dessye = Dese Ethiopia 11°5N 39°40E 131 E2
Destin U.S.A. 30°24N 86°30W 179 E3
D'Estrees B. Australia 35°55S 137°45E 152 C2
Desuri India 25°18N 73°35E 124 G5
Desvres France 50°40N 1°48E 71 B8
Det Udom Thailand 14°54N 105°5E 120 E5
Deta Romania 45°24N 21°13E 80 E6
Dete Zimbabwe 18°38S 26°50E 144 A4
Detinja → Serbia 43°51N 20°5E 96 C4
Detmold Germany 51°56N 8°52E 76 D4
Detour, Pt. U.S.A. 45°40N 86°40W 172 C10
Detroit U.S.A. 42°19N 83°12W 174 D1
Detroit Lakes U.S.A. 46°49N 95°51W 172 B6
Detva Slovak Rep. 48°34N 19°25E 79 C12
Deua △ Australia 35°32S 149°46E 153 C8
Deurne Neths. 51°27N 5°49E 69 C5
Deutsch-Luxemburgischer ⌓ Germany 49°58N 6°12E 77 F2
Deutsche Bucht Germany 54°15N 8°0E 76 A4
Deutschland = Germany ■ Europe 51°0N 10°0E 76 E6
Deutschlandsberg Austria 46°49N 15°14E 78 E8
Deux-Sèvres □ France 46°35N 0°20W 70 F6
Deva Romania 45°53N 22°55E 80 E7
Devakottai India 9°55N 78°45E 127 K4
Devaprayag India 30°13N 78°35E 125 D8
Devarkonda India 16°42N 78°56E 126 F4
Dévaványa Hungary 47°2N 20°59E 80 C5
Deveci Dağları Turkey 40°6N 36°15E 104 B7
Devecikonağı Turkey 39°55N 28°34E 97 G12
Devecser Hungary 47°6N 17°26E 80 C2
Develi Turkey 38°23N 35°29E 104 C6
Deventer Neths. 52°15N 6°10E 69 B6
Devereux U.S.A. 33°13N 83°5W 178 B6
Deveron → U.K. 57°41N 2°32W 65 D6
Devesel Romania 44°28N 22°41E 80 F7
Devgad I. India 14°48N 74°5E 127 G2
Devgadh Bariya India 22°40N 73°55E 124 H5
Devgarh India 16°23N 73°23E 127 F1
Devi → India 19°59N 86°24E 126 E8
Devikot India 26°42N 71°12E 124 F4
Devil River Pk. N.Z. 40°56S 172°37E 155 A7
Devils Den U.S.A. 35°46N 119°58W 170 K7
Devils Hole = Death Valley △ U.S.A. 36°29N 117°6W 171 J9
Devils Lake U.S.A. 48°7N 98°52W 172 A4
Devils Paw Canada 58°47N 134°0W 162 B2
Devils Postpile ⌓ U.S.A. 37°37N 119°5W 170 H7
Devil's Pt. Sri Lanka 9°26N 80°6E 127 K5
Devils Tower U.S.A. 44°35N 104°42W 168 D11
Devils Tower △ U.S.A. 44°48N 104°55W 168 D11
Devin Bulgaria 41°44N 24°24E 97 E8
Devine U.S.A. 29°8N 98°54W 176 G5
Devipattinam India 9°29N 78°54E 127 K4
Devizes U.K. 51°22N 1°58W 67 F6
Devli India 25°50N 75°20E 124 G6
Devnya Bulgaria 43°13N 27°33E 97 C11
Devoll → Albania 40°57N 20°15E 96 F4
Devon Canada 53°24N 113°44W 162 C6
Devon □ U.K. 50°50N 3°40W 67 G4
Devon I. Canada 75°10N 85°0W 161 B15
Devonport Australia 41°10S 146°22E 151 G4
Devrek Turkey 41°13N 31°57E 104 B4
Devrekâni Turkey 41°36N 33°50E 104 B5
Devrez → Turkey 41°6N 34°25E 104 B6
Devrukh India 17°3N 73°37E 126 F1
Dewas India 22°59N 76°3E 124 H7
Dewetsdorp S. Africa 29°33S 26°39E 144 C4
Dewey Puerto Rico 18°18N 65°18W 183 d
Dexing China 28°46N 117°30E 117 C11
Dexter Maine, U.S.A. 45°1N 69°18W 173 C19
Dexter Mo., U.S.A. 36°48N 89°57W 172 G9
Dexter N. Mex., U.S.A. 33°12N 104°22W 169 K11
Dey-Dey, L. Australia 29°12S 131°4E 149 E5
Deyang China 31°3N 104°27E 116 B5
Deyhūk Iran 33°15N 57°30E 129 C8
Deyyer Iran 27°55N 51°55E 129 E6
Dez → Iran 31°39N 48°52E 105 F13
Dezadeash L. Canada 60°28N 136°58W 162 A1
Dezfūl Iran 32°20N 48°30E 105 F13
Dezhneva, Mys Russia 66°5N 169°40W 107 C19
Dezhou China 37°26N 116°18E 114 F9
Dhadhar → India 24°56N 85°24E 125 G11
Dhahabān Si. Arabia 21°58N 39°3E 137 C4
Dhahiriya = Az Ẓāhirīyah West Bank 31°25N 34°58E 130 D3
Dhahran = Aẓ Ẓahrān Si. Arabia 26°10N 50°7E 129 E6
Dhak Pakistan 32°25N 72°33E 124 C5
Dhaka Bangla. 23°43N 90°26E 125 H14
Dhaka □ Bangla. 24°25N 90°25E 125 G14
Dhali Cyprus 35°1N 33°25E 101 D12
Dhamangaon India 20°48N 78°9E 126 D4
Dhamār Yemen 14°30N 44°20E 131 E3
Dhampur India 29°19N 78°33E 125 E8
Dhamra → India 20°47N 86°58E 126 D8
Dhamtari India 20°42N 81°35E 126 D5
Dhanbad India 23°50N 86°30E 125 H12
Dhangarhi Nepal 28°55N 80°40E 125 E9
Dhankuta Nepal 26°55N 87°40E 125 F12
Dhanora India 20°20N 80°22E 126 D5
Dhanpuri India 23°13N 81°30E 126 C5
Dhanushkodi India 9°11N 79°24E 127 K4
Dhar India 22°35N 75°26E 124 H6
Dharampur India 22°13N 75°18E 124 H6
Dharamsala = Dharmsala India 32°16N 76°23E 124 C7
Dharan Nepal 26°49N 87°17E 125 F12
Dharangaon India 21°1N 75°16E 126 D2
Dharapuram India 10°45N 77°34E 127 J3
Dhariwal India 31°57N 75°19E 124 D6
Dharla → Bangla. 25°46N 89°42E 125 G13
Dharmapuri India 12°10N 78°10E 127 H4
Dharmavaram India 14°29N 77°44E 127 G3
Dharmjaygarh India 22°28N 83°13E 125 H10
Dharmsala India 32°16N 76°23E 124 C7
Dharni India 21°33N 76°53E 124 J7
Dharug △ Australia 33°20S 151°2E 153 B9
Dharur India 18°3N 76°8E 126 E3
Dharwad India 15°30N 75°4E 127 G2
Dhasan → India 25°48N 79°24E 125 G8
Dhaulagiri Nepal 28°39N 83°28E 125 E10
Dhebar, L. India 24°10N 74°0E 124 G6
Dheftera Cyprus 35°5N 33°16E 101 D12
Dhenkanal India 20°45N 85°35E 126 D7
Dherinia Cyprus 35°3N 33°57E 101 D12
Dheskáti = Deskati Greece 39°55N 21°49E 96 G5
Dhī Qār □ Iraq 31°0N 46°15E 128 D5
Dhiarrizos → Cyprus 34°41N 32°34E 101 E11
Dhībān Jordan 31°30N 35°46E 130 D4
Dhilwan India 31°31N 75°21E 124 D6
Dhimarkhera India 23°28N 80°22E 125 H9
Dholka India 22°44N 72°29E 124 H5
Dhomokós = Domokos Greece 39°10N 22°18E 98 B4
Dhond = Daund India 18°26N 74°40E 126 E2
Dhone India 15°25N 77°53E 127 G3
Dhoraji India 21°45N 70°37E 124 J4
Dhorpatan Nepal 28°29N 83°4E 125 E10
Dhragonisi = Tragonhsi Greece 37°27N 25°29E 99 D7
Dhrangadhra India 22°59N 71°31E 124 H4
Dhrol India 22°33N 70°25E 124 H4
Dhuburi India 26°2N 89°59E 123 F16
Dhule India 20°58N 74°50E 126 D2
Di-ib, W. → Sudan 22°38N 36°6E 137 C4
Di Linh Vietnam 11°35N 108°4E 121 G7
Di Linh, Cao Nguyen Vietnam 11°30N 108°0E 121 G7
Dia Greece 35°28N 25°14E 101 D7
Diabakania Guinea 10°38N 10°58W 138 C2
Diablo Range U.S.A. 37°20N 121°25W 170 J5
Diafarabé Mali 14°9N 4°57W 138 C4
Diala Mali 14°10N 9°58W 138 C3
Dialakoro Mali 12°18N 7°54W 138 C3
Dialakoto Senegal 13°21N 13°19W 138 C2
Diallassagou Mali 13°47N 3°41W 138 C4
Diamante Argentina 32°5S 60°40W 190 C3
Diamante Italy 39°41N 15°49E 95 C8
Diamante → Argentina 34°30S 66°46W 190 C2
Diamantina Brazil 18°17S 43°40W 189 D2
Diamantina → Australia 26°45S 139°10E 151 D2
Diamantina △ Australia 23°33S 141°23E 150 C3
Diamantino Brazil 14°30S 56°30W 187 F7
Diamond Bar U.S.A. 34°1N 117°48W 171 L9
Diamond Harbour India 22°11N 88°14E 125 H13
Diamond Is. Australia 17°25S 151°5E 150 B5
Diamond Mts. U.S.A. 39°40N 115°50W 168 G6
Diamond Springs U.S.A. 38°42N 120°49W 170 G6
Diamou Mali 14°5N 11°16W 138 C2
Dian Chi China 24°50N 102°43E 116 E4
Dianalund Denmark 55°32N 11°30E 63 J5
Dianbai China 21°33N 111°0E 117 G8
Diancheng China 21°30N 111°4E 117 G8
Dianjiang China 30°24N 107°20E 116 B6
Diano Marina Italy 43°54N 8°5E 92 E5
Dianópolis Brazil 11°38S 46°50W 189 C1
Dianra Ivory C. 8°45N 6°14W 138 D3
Diaoyu Dao = Senkaku-Shotō E. China Sea 25°45N 123°30E 113 M1
Diaoyu Tai = Senkaku-Shotō E. China Sea 25°45N 123°30E 113 M1
Diapaga Burkina Faso 12°5N 1°46E 139 C5
Diapangou Burkina Faso 12°5N 0°10E 139 C5
Diariguila Guinea 10°35N 10°2W 138 C2
Diavolo, Mt. India 12°40N 92°56E 127 H11
Dibā = Dibbā al Ḥiṣn U.A.E. 25°45N 56°16E 129 E8
Dibagah Iraq 35°52N 43°48E 105 E10
Dibai India 28°13N 78°15E 124 E8
Dibaya Dem. Rep. of the Congo 6°30S 22°57E 140 F4
Dibaya-Lubue Dem. Rep. of the Congo 4°12S 19°54E 140 E3
Dibbā al Ḥiṣn U.A.E. 25°45N 56°16E 129 E8
Dibbeen △ Jordan 32°20N 35°45E 130 C4
D'Iberville, Lac Canada 55°55N 73°15W 164 A5
Dibete Botswana 23°45S 26°32E 144 B4
Dibrugarh India 27°29N 94°55E 123 F19
Dickens U.S.A. 33°37N 100°50W 176 E4
Dickinson U.S.A. 46°53N 102°47W 172 B2
Dickson U.S.A. 36°5N 87°23W 177 C11
Dickson City U.S.A. 41°28N 75°36W 175 E9
Dicle Barajı Turkey 38°20N 40°11E 105 C9
Dicle Nehri → Turkey 37°44N 41°10E 105 D9
Dicomano Italy 43°53N 11°31E 93 E8
Didiéni Mali 13°53N 8°6W 138 C3
Didim Turkey 37°22N 27°16E 99 D9
Didimoticho Greece 41°22N 26°29E 97 E10
Didsbury Canada 51°35N 114°10W 162 C6
Didwana India 27°23N 74°36E 124 F6
Die France 44°47N 5°22E 73 D9
Diébougou Burkina Faso 11°0N 3°15W 138 C4
Diecke Guinea 7°27N 8°54W 138 D3
Diefenbaker, L. Canada 51°0N 106°55W 163 C7
Diego de Almagro Chile 26°22S 70°3W 190 B1
Diego Garcia Ind. Oc. 7°50S 72°50E 146 E6
Diego Ramírez, Islas Chile 56°30S 68°44W 192 E3
Diego Suarez = Antsiranana Madag. 12°25S 49°20E 141 G9
Diekirch Lux. 49°52N 6°10E 69 E6
Diéma Mali 14°32N 9°12W 138 C3
Diembéring Senegal 12°29N 16°47W 138 C1
Diemelsee ⌓ Germany 51°20N 8°40E 76 D4
Dien Ban Vietnam 15°53N 108°16E 120 E7
Dien Bien Phu Vietnam 21°20N 103°0E 116 G4
Dien Chau, Vinh Vietnam 19°0N 105°55E 120 C5
Dien Khanh Vietnam 12°15N 109°6E 121 F7
Diepholz Germany 52°37N 8°22E 76 C4
Dieppe France 49°54N 1°4E 70 C8
Dierks U.S.A. 34°7N 94°1W 176 D7
Diest Belgium 50°58N 5°4E 69 D5
Dietikon Switz. 47°24N 8°24E 77 H4
Dieulefit France 44°32N 5°4E 73 D9
Dieuze France 48°49N 6°43E 71 D13
Dif Somalia 0°59N 40°58E 131 G3
Diffa Niger 13°18N 12°36E 139 C7
Diffa □ Niger 14°0N 12°30E 139 C7
Differdange Lux. 49°31N 5°54E 69 E5
Dig India 27°28N 77°20E 124 F7
Digba Dem. Rep. of the Congo 4°25N 25°48E 142 B2
Digby Canada 44°38N 65°50W 165 D6
Digges Is. Canada 62°40N 77°50W 161 E16
Diggi India 26°22N 75°26E 124 F6
Dighinala Bangla. 23°15N 92°5E 123 H18
Dighton U.S.A. 38°29N 100°28W 172 F3
Diglur India 18°34N 77°33E 126 E3
Digna Mali 14°48N 10°14W 138 C3
Digne-les-Bains France 44°5N 6°12E 73 D10
Digoin France 46°29N 4°1E 71 F11
Digor Turkey 40°22N 43°25E 105 B10
Digos Phil. 6°45N 125°20E 119 C7
Digranes Iceland 66°4N 14°44W 60 C6
Digras India 20°6N 77°45E 126 D3
Digul → Indonesia 7°7S 138°42E 119 F9
Digya △ Ghana 7°15N 0°5E 139 D5
Dihang = Brahmaputra → Asia 23°40N 90°35E 125 H13
Dijlah, Nahr → Asia 31°0N 47°25E 128 D5
Dijon France 47°20N 5°3E 71 E12
Dikhil Djibouti 11°8N 42°20E 131 E3
Dikili Turkey 39°4N 26°53E 99 B8
Dikirnis Egypt 31°6N 31°35E 137 E7
Dikkil = Dikhil Djibouti 11°8N 42°20E 131 E3
Dikodougou Ivory C. 9°4N 5°45W 138 D3
Diksmuide Belgium 51°2N 2°52E 69 C2
Dikson Russia 73°40N 80°5E 106 B9
Dikti Oros Greece 35°8N 25°30E 101 D7
Dikwa Nigeria 12°4N 13°30E 139 C7
Dila Ethiopia 6°21N 38°22E 131 F2
Dilek Yarimadisi △ Turkey 37°40N 27°10E 99 D9
Dili E. Timor 8°39S 125°34E 119 F7
Diligent Strait India 12°11N 92°57E 127 H11
Dilijan Armenia 40°46N 44°57E 87 K7
Dilinata Greece 38°13N 20°31E 98 C2
Dilj Croatia 45°29N 18°1E 80 E3
Dillenburg Germany 50°43N 8°17E 76 E4
Dilley U.S.A. 28°40N 99°10W 176 G5
Dilli = Delhi India 28°39N 77°13E 124 E7
Dilli Mali 15°1N 7°40W 138 C3
Dillingen Bayern, Germany 48°36N 10°30E 77 G6
Dillingen Saarland, Germany 49°22N 6°43E 77 F2
Dillingham U.S.A. 59°3N 158°28W 166 D8
Dillon Canada 55°56N 108°35W 163 B7
Dillon Mont., U.S.A. 45°13N 112°38W 168 D7
Dillon S.C., U.S.A. 34°25N 79°22W 177 D15
Dillon → Canada 55°56N 108°56W 163 B7
Dillsburg U.S.A. 40°7N 77°2W 174 F7
Dilolo Dem. Rep. of the Congo 10°28S 22°18E 140 G4
Dilos Greece 37°23N 25°15E 99 D7
Dilove Ukraine 47°56N 24°11E 81 C9
Dimapur India 25°54N 93°45E 110 F7
Dimas Mexico 23°43N 106°47W 180 C3
Dimashq Syria 33°30N 36°18E 130 B5
Dimashq □ Syria 33°30N 36°30E 130 B5
Dimbaza S. Africa 32°50S 27°14E 145 D4
Dimbokro Ivory C. 6°45N 4°46W 138 D4
Dimboola Australia 36°28S 142°7E 152 D5
Dîmbovița = Dâmbovița → Romania 44°12N 26°26E 81 F11
Dimbulah Australia 17°8S 145°4E 150 B4
Dimitrovgrad Bulgaria 42°5N 25°35E 97 D9
Dimitrovgrad Russia 54°14N 49°39E 86 C9
Dimitrovgrad Serbia 43°2N 22°48E 96 C6
Dimitrovo = Pernik Bulgaria 42°35N 23°2E 96 D7
Dimitsana Greece 37°36N 22°3E 98 D4
Dimmitt U.S.A. 34°33N 102°19W 176 D3
Dimona Israel 31°2N 35°1E 130 D4
Dimovo Bulgaria 43°43N 22°50E 96 C6
Dinagat I. Phil. 10°10N 125°40E 119 B7
Dinajpur Bangla. 25°33N 88°43E 123 G16
Dinan France 48°28N 2°2W 70 D4
Dīnān Āb Iran 32°4N 56°49E 129 C8
Dinant Belgium 50°16N 4°55E 69 D4
Dinapur India 25°38N 85°5E 125 G11
Dinar Turkey 38°5N 30°10E 99 C12
Dīnār, Kūh-e Iran 30°42N 51°46E 129 D6
Dinara Planina Croatia 44°0N 16°30E 93 D13
Dinard France 48°38N 2°6W 70 D4
Dinaric Alps = Dinara Planina Croatia 44°0N 16°30E 93 D13
Dinbych-y-Pysgod = Tenby U.K. 51°40N 4°42W 67 F3
Dindanko Mali 14°8N 9°30W 138 C3
Dindi → India 16°24N 78°15E 127 F4
Dindigul India 10°25N 78°0E 127 J4
Dindori India 22°57N 81°5E 125 H9
Ding Xian = Dingzhou China 38°30N 114°59E 114 E8
Dinga Pakistan 25°26N 67°10E 124 G2
Ding'an China 19°42N 110°19E 117 a
Dingbian China 37°35N 107°32E 114 F4
Dingelstädt Germany 51°18N 10°19E 76 D6
Dingle Ireland 52°9N 10°17W 64 D1
Dingle Sweden 58°32N 11°35E 63 F5
Dingle B. Ireland 52°3N 10°20W 64 D1
Dingle Pen. Ireland 52°12N 10°5W 64 D1
Dingmans Ferry U.S.A. 41°13N 74°55W 175 E10
Dingnan China 24°45N 115°0E 117 E10
Dingo Australia 23°38S 149°19E 150 C4
Dingolfing Germany 48°37N 12°30E 77 G8
Dingtao China 35°5N 115°35E 114 G8
Dinguiraye Guinea 11°18N 10°49W 138 C2
Dingwall U.K. 57°36N 4°26W 65 D4
Dingxi China 35°30N 104°33E 114 G3
Dingxiang China 38°30N 112°58E 114 E7
Dingyuan China 32°32N 117°41E 117 A11
Dingzhou China 38°30N 114°59E 114 E8
Dinh, Mui Vietnam 11°22N 109°1E 121 G7
Dinh Lap Vietnam 21°33N 107°6E 116 G6
Dinin → Ireland 52°43N 7°18W 64 D4
Dinira △ Venezuela 9°57N 70°6W 183 E6
Dinokwe Botswana 23°29S 26°37E 144 B4
Dinorwic Canada 49°41N 92°30W 163 D10
Dinosaur ⌓ Canada 50°47N 111°30W 162 C6
Dinosaur ⌓ U.S.A. 40°30N 108°45W 168 F9
Dinuba U.S.A. 36°32N 119°23W 170 J7
Diö Sweden 56°37N 14°15E 63 H8
Dioïla Mali 12°3N 6°50W 138 C3
Dioka Mali 14°57N 10°4W 138 C2
Diongoï Mali 14°38N 8°34W 138 C3
Dionisades Greece 35°20N 26°10E 101 D8
Diósgyőr Hungary 48°7N 20°43E 80 B5
Diosig Romania 47°18N 22°2E 80 C7
Diougani Mali 14°19N 2°44W 138 C4
Diouloulou Senegal 13°5N 16°38W 138 C1
Dioura Mali 14°59N 5°12W 138 C3
Diourbel Senegal 14°39N 16°12W 138 C1
Diourbel □ Senegal 14°45N 16°15W 138 C1
Dipalpur Pakistan 30°40N 73°39E 124 D5
Dipkarpaz = Rizokarpaso Cyprus 35°36N 34°23E 101 D13
Diplo Pakistan 24°35N 69°35E 124 G3
Dipolog Phil. 8°36N 123°20E 119 C6
Dipperu △ Australia 21°56S 148°42E 150 C4
Dipton N.Z. 45°54S 168°22E 155 F3
Dir Pakistan 35°8N 71°59E 122 B7
Diré Mali 16°20N 3°25W 138 B4
Dire Dawa Ethiopia 9°35N 41°45E 131 F3
Dirfis Oros Greece 38°40N 23°54E 98 C5
Diriamba Nic. 11°51N 86°19W 182 D2
Dirk Hartog I. Australia 25°50S 113°5E 149 E1
Dirranbandi Australia 28°33S 148°17E 151 D4
Disa India 24°18N 72°10E 124 G5
Disappointment, C. U.S.A. 46°18N 124°5W 170 D2
Disappointment, L. Australia 23°20S 122°40E 148 D3
Disaster B. Australia 37°15S 149°58E 153 D8
Discovery B. Australia 38°10S 140°40E 152 E4
Discovery B. China 22°18N 114°1E 111 a
Discovery Bay ⌓ Australia 38°9S 141°16E 152 E4
Discovery Seamount Atl. Oc. 42°0S 0°10E 56 L12

Disentis Muster *Switz.* 46°42N 8°50E **77** J4
Dishna *Egypt* 26°9N 32°32E **137** B3
Disina *Nigeria* 11°35N 9°50E **139** C6
Disko = Qeqertarsuaq
Greenland 69°45N 53°30W **57** D5
Disko Bugt *Greenland* 69°10N 52°0W **57** D5
Disna = Dzisna →
Belarus 55°34N 28°12E **84** E5
Disneyland Hong Kong
China 22°18N 114°2E **111** a
Diss *U.K.* 52°23N 1°7E **67** E9
Disteghil Sar *Pakistan* 36°20N 75°12E **125** A6
District of Columbia □
U.S.A. 38°55N 77°0W **173** F15
Distrito Federal □
Brazil 15°45S 47°45W **189** D1
Distrito Federal □
Mexico 19°15N 99°10W **181** D5
Disûq *Egypt* 31°8N 30°35E **137** B7
Diu *India* 20°45N 70°58E **124** J4
Dīvāndarreh *Iran* 35°55N 47°2E **105** E12
Dives → *France* 49°18N 0°7W **70** C6
Dives-sur-Mer *France* 49°18N 0°8W **70** C6
Divi Pt. *India* 15°59N 81°9E **127** G5
Divichi = Dāvāçi
Azerbaijan 41°15N 48°57E **87** K9
Divide *U.S.A.* 45°45N 112°45W **168** D7
Dividing Ra. *Australia* 27°45S 116°0E **149** E2
Divinópolis *Brazil* 20°10S 44°54W **189** E2
Divjake *Albania* 41°0N 19°32E **96** F3
Divnoye *Russia* 45°55N 43°21E **87** H6
Divo *Ivory C.* 5°48N 5°15W **138** D3
Diviği *Turkey* 39°22N 38°7E **105** C8
Dīwāl Kol *Afghan.* 34°23N 67°52E **124** B2
Dix-Huit Montagnes □
Ivory C. 7°30N 7°40W **138** D3
Dixie Mt. *U.S.A.* 39°55N 120°16W **170** F6
Dixie Union *U.S.A.* 31°20N 82°28W **178** D7
Dixon *Calif., U.S.A.* 38°27N 121°49W **170** G5
Dixon *Ill., U.S.A.* 41°50N 89°29W **172** E9
Dixon Entrance *U.S.A.* 54°30N 132°0W **160** G5
Dixville *Canada* 45°4N 71°46W **175** A13
Diyadin *Turkey* 39°33N 43°40E **105** C10
Diyālā □ *Iraq* 33°45N 44°50E **124** C5
Diyālā → *Iraq* 33°13N 44°30E **105** F11
Diyarbakır *Turkey* 37°55N 40°18E **105** D9
Diyarbakır □ *Turkey* 38°0N 40°18E **105** D9
Diyodar *India* 24°8N 71°50E **124** G4
Dizangué *Cameroon* 3°46N 9°59E **139** E6
Djakarta = Jakarta
Indonesia 6°9S 106°52E **118** F3
Djamâa *Algeria* 33°32N 5°59E **136** B5
Djamba *Angola* 16°45S 13°58E **144** A1
Djambala *Congo* 2°32S 14°30E **140** E2
Djanet *Algeria* 24°35N 9°32E **136** D6
Djawa = Jawa *Indonesia* 7°0S 110°0E **118** F3
Djebel Tazzeka △
Morocco 34°6N 4°11W **136** B3
Djebiniana *Tunisia* 35°1N 11°0E **136** A6
Djelfa *Algeria* 34°40N 3°15E **136** B4
Djelfa □ *Algeria* 34°20N 3°40E **136** B4
Djema *C.A.R.* 6°3N 25°15E **142** A2
Djémila *Algeria* 36°19N 5°44E **136** A5
Djendel *Algeria* 36°15N 2°25E **136** A4
Djenné *Mali* 14°0N 4°30W **138** C4
Djenoun, Garet el *Algeria* 25°4N 5°31E **136** C5
Djerba *Tunisia* 33°48N 10°54E **136** B6
Djerba, Î. de *Tunisia* 33°50N 10°48E **136** B6
Djerid, Chott *Tunisia* 33°42N 8°30E **136** B5
Djibo *Burkina Faso* 14°9N 1°35W **139** C4
Djibouti *Djibouti* 11°30N 43°5E **141** E3
Djibouti ■ *Africa* 12°0N 43°0E **131** E3
Djolu
Dem. Rep. of the Congo 0°35N 22°5E **140** D4
Djoudj △ *Senegal* 16°24N 16°14W **138** B1
Djougou *Benin* 9°40N 1°45E **139** D5
Djoum *Cameroon* 2°41N 12°35E **140** D2
Djourab, Erg du *Chad* 16°40N 18°50E **135** E9
Djugu
Dem. Rep. of the Congo 1°55N 30°35E **142** B3
Djukbinj △ *Australia* 12°11S 131°2E **148** B5
Djúpivogur *Iceland* 64°39N 14°17W **60** D6
Djurás *Sweden* 60°34N 15°8E **62** D9
Djurdjura □ *Algeria* 36°20N 4°15E **136** A4
Djurö △ *Sweden* 58°52N 13°28E **63** F7
Djursland *Denmark* 56°27N 10°45E **63** H4
Dmitriya Lapteva, Proliv
Russia 73°0N 140°0E **107** B15
Dmitriyev Lgovskiy
Russia 52°10N 35°0E **85** F8
Dmitrov *Russia* 56°25N 37°32E **84** D9
Dmitrovsk-Orlovskiy
Russia 52°29N 35°10E **85** F8
Dnepr = Dnipro →
Ukraine 46°30N 32°18E **85** J7
Dneprodzerzhinsk =
Dniprodzerzhynsk
Ukraine 48°32N 34°37E **85** H8
Dneprodzerzhinskoye Vdkhr. =
Dniprodzerzhynske Vdskh.
Ukraine 48°49N 34°8E **85** H8
Dnepropetrovsk =
Dnipropetrovsk
Ukraine 48°30N 35°0E **85** H8
Dneprorudnoye = Dniprorudne
Ukraine 47°21N 34°58E **85** J8
Dnestr = Dnister →
Europe 46°18N 30°17E **75** E16
Dnieper = Dnipro →
Ukraine 46°30N 32°18E **85** J7
Dniester = Dnister →
Europe 46°18N 30°17E **75** E16
Dnipro → *Ukraine* 46°30N 32°18E **85** J7
Dniprodzerzhynsk
Ukraine 48°32N 34°37E **85** H8
Dniprodzerzhynske Vdskh.
Ukraine 48°49N 34°8E **85** H8
Dnipropetrovsk *Ukraine* 48°30N 35°0E **85** H8
Dnipropetrovsk □
Ukraine 48°15N 34°50E **85** H8
Dniprorudne *Ukraine* 47°21N 34°58E **85** J8
Dnister → *Europe* 46°18N 30°17E **75** E16
Dnistrovskyy Lyman
Ukraine 46°15N 30°17E **85** J6
Dno *Russia* 57°50N 29°58E **84** D5
Dnyapro = Dnipro →
Ukraine 46°30N 32°18E **85** J7
Do Gonbadān = Gachsārān
Iran 30°15N 50°45E **129** D6
Doaktown *Canada* 46°33N 66°8W **165** C6
Doan Hung *Vietnam* 21°30N 105°10E **116** G5

Doba *Chad* 8°40N 16°50E **135** G9
Dobandi *Pakistan* 31°13N 66°50E **124** D2
Dobbiaco *Italy* 46°44N 12°14E **93** B9
Dobbyn *Australia* 19°44S 140°2E **150** B3
Dobczyce *Poland* 49°52N 20°5E **83** J7
Dobele *Latvia* 56°37N 23°16E **82** B10
Dobele □ *Latvia* 56°35N 23°5E **82** B10
Döbeln *Germany* 51°6N 13°7E **76** D9
Doberai, Jazirah
Indonesia 1°25S 133°0E **119** E8
Dobiegniew *Poland* 52°59N 15°45E **83** F2
Doblas *Argentina* 37°5S 64°0W **190** D3
Dobo *Indonesia* 5°45S 134°15E **119** F8
Doboj *Bos.-H.* 44°46N 18°4E **80** F3
Dobra *Wielkopolskie,
Poland* 51°55N 18°37E **83** G5
Dobra *Zachodnio-Pomorskie,
Poland* 53°34N 15°20E **82** E2
Dobra *Dâmbovita,
Romania* 44°52N 25°40E **81** F10
Dobra *Hunedoara,
Romania* 45°54N 22°36E **80** E7
Dobre Miasto *Poland* 53°58N 20°26E **82** E7
Dobrich *Bulgaria* 43°37N 27°49E **97** C11
Dobrich □ *Bulgaria* 43°37N 27°49E **97** C11
Dobrinishta *Bulgaria* 41°49N 23°34E **96** E7
Dobřiš *Czech Rep.* 49°46N 14°10E **78** B7
Dobrodzień *Poland* 50°45N 18°25E **83** H5
Dobromyl *Ukraine* 49°34N 22°46E **83** J9
Dobron *Ukraine* 48°25N 22°23E **80** B7
Dobropole *Ukraine* 48°25N 37°2E **85** H9
Dobrovolsk *Russia* 54°46N 22°31E **82** D9
Dobruja *Europe* 44°30N 28°15E **81** F13
Dobrush *Belarus* 52°25N 31°22E **75** B16
Dobrzany *Poland* 53°22N 15°25E **82** E2
Dobrzyń nad Wisłą
Poland 52°39N 19°22E **83** F6
Doc, Mui *Vietnam* 17°58N 106°30E **116** D6
Doce → *Brazil* 19°37S 39°49W **189** D3
Docker River = Kaltukatjara
Australia 24°52S 129°5E **149** D4
Docksta *Sweden* 63°3N 18°18E **62** A12
Doctor Arroyo
Mexico 23°40N 100°11W **180** C4
Doctor Pedro P. Peña
Paraguay 22°27S 62°21W **190** A3
Doctors Inlet *U.S.A.* 30°6N 81°47W **178** E8
Doda *India* 33°10N 75°34E **124** C6
Doda, L. *Canada* 49°25N 75°13W **164** C4
Doda Betta *India* 11°24N 76°44E **127** J3
Dodballapur *India* 13°18N 77°32E **127** H3
Dodecanese = Dodekanisa
Greece 36°35N 27°0E **99** E8
Dodekanisa *Greece* 36°35N 27°0E **99** E8
Dodge City *U.S.A.* 37°45N 100°1W **172** G3
Dodge L. *Canada* 59°50N 105°36W **163** B7
Dodgeville *U.S.A.* 42°58N 90°8W **172** D8
Dodo *Cameroon* 7°30N 12°3E **139** D7
Dodoma *Tanzania* 6°8S 35°45E **142** D4
Dodoma □ *Tanzania* 6°0S 36°0E **142** D4
Dodoni *Greece* 39°40N 20°46E **98** B2
Dodsland *Canada* 51°50N 108°45W **163** C7
Dodson *U.S.A.* 48°24N 108°15W **168** B9
Dodurga *Turkey* 39°49N 29°57E **99** B11
Doerun *U.S.A.* 31°19N 83°55W **178** D6
Doesburg *Neths.* 52°1N 6°9E **69** B6
Doetinchem *Neths.* 51°59N 6°18E **69** C6
Dog Creek *Canada* 51°35N 122°14W **162** C4
Dog L. *Ont., Canada* 48°18N 89°30W **164** C2
Dog L. *Man., Canada* 51°2N 98°31W **163** C9
Dogansehir *Turkey* 38°5N 37°53E **104** C7
Dogliani *Italy* 44°32N 7°56E **92** D4
Dogondoutchi *Niger* 13°38N 4°2E **139** C5
Dogran *Pakistan* 31°48N 73°35E **124** D5
Doğubayazıt *Turkey* 39°31N 44°5E **105** C11
Doguéraoua *Niger* 14°0N 5°31E **139** C6
Doha = Ad Dawḩah
Qatar 25°15N 51°35E **129** E6
Dohazari *Bangla.* 22°10N 92°5E **123** H18
Dohrighat *India* 26°16N 83°31E **125** F10
Doi *Indonesia* 2°14N 127°49E **119** D7
Doi Inthanon *Thailand* 18°35N 98°29E **120** C2
Doi Inthanon △
Thailand 18°33N 98°34E **120** C2
Doi Khuntan △
Thailand 18°33N 99°14E **120** C2
Doi Luang *Thailand* 18°30N 101°0E **120** C3
Doi Luang △ *Thailand* 19°52N 99°35E **120** C2
Doi Phukha △ *Thailand* 19°8N 101°9E **120** C3
Doi Saket *Thailand* 18°52N 99°9E **120** C2
Doi Suthep Pui △
Thailand 18°49N 98°53E **120** C2
Doi Toa *Thailand* 17°55N 98°30E **120** C2
Dois Irmãos, Sa. *Brazil* 9°0S 42°30W **189** B2
Dojransko Jezero
Macedonia 41°13N 22°44E **96** E6
Dokdo = Liancourt Rocks
Asia 37°15N 131°52E **113** F5
Dokkum *Neths.* 53°20N 5°59E **69** A5
Dokos *Greece* 37°20N 23°20E **98** D5
Dokri *Pakistan* 27°25N 68°7E **124** F3
Dokuchayevsk *Ukraine* 47°44N 37°40E **85** J9
Dol-de-Bretagne *France* 48°34N 1°47W **70** D5
Dolak, Pulau *Indonesia* 8°0S 138°30E **119** F9
Dolbeau-Mistassini
Canada 48°53N 72°14W **165** C5
Dolenjska *Slovenia* 45°56N 14°15E **93** C11
Dolgellau *U.K.* 52°45N 3°53W **66** E4
Dolgellau = Dolgellau
U.K. 52°45N 3°53W **66** E4
Dolhasca *Romania* 47°26N 26°36E **81** C11
Doliana *Greece* 39°54N 20°32E **98** B2
Dolianova *Italy* 39°23N 9°11E **95** C2
Dolinsk *Russia* 47°21N 142°48E **107** E15
Dolinskaya = Dolynska
Ukraine 48°6N 32°46E **85** H7
Dolj □ *Romania* 44°10N 23°30E **81** F8
Dollard *Neths.* 53°20N 7°10E **69** A7
Dolna Banya *Bulgaria* 42°18N 23°44E **96** D7
Dolni Chiflik *Bulgaria* 43°0N 27°43E **97** D11
Dolní Dúbník *Czech Rep.* 43°24N 24°26E **97** C8
Dolnoślaskie □ *Poland* 51°0N 16°30E **83** G3
Dolný Kubín
Slovak Rep. 49°12N 19°18E **79** B12
Dolo *Ethiopia* 4°11N 42°3E **131** G3
Dolo *Italy* 45°26N 12°5E **93** C9

Dolomites = Dolomiti
Italy 46°23N 11°51E **93** B8
Dolomiti *Italy* 46°23N 11°51E **93** B8
Dolomiti Bellunesi △
Italy 46°10N 12°5E **93** B9
Dolores *Argentina* 36°20S 57°40W **190** D4
Dolores *Uruguay* 33°34S 58°15W **190** C4
Dolores *U.S.A.* 37°28N 108°30W **169** H9
Dolores → *U.S.A.* 38°49N 109°17W **168** G9
Dolovo *Serbia* 44°55N 20°52E **80** F5
Dolphin, C. *Falk. Is.* 51°10S 59°0W **192** D5
Dolphin and Union Str.
Canada 69°5N 114°45W **160** D9
Dolsk *Poland* 51°59N 17°3E **83** G4
Dolyna *Ukraine* 48°58N 24°1E **81** B9
Dolynska *Ukraine* 48°6N 32°46E **85** H7
Dolynske *Ukraine* 47°32N 29°55E **81** C14
Dolzhanskaya *Russia* 46°37N 37°48E **85** J9
Dom Joaquim *Brazil* 18°57S 43°16W **189** D2
Dom Pedrito *Brazil* 31°0S 54°40W **191** C5
Dom Pedro *Brazil* 4°59S 44°27W **189** C2
Doma *Nigeria* 8°25N 8°18E **139** D6
Doma △ *Zimbabwe* 16°28S 30°12E **143** F3
Domaniç *Turkey* 39°48N 29°36E **99** B11
Domariaganj → *India* 26°17N 83°44E **125** F10
Domasi *Malawi* 15°15S 35°22E **143** F4
Domažlice *Czech Rep.* 49°28N 12°58E **78** B5
Dombarovskiy *Russia* 50°46N 59°32E **106** D6
Dombås *Norway* 62°4N 9°8E **60** E13
Dombasle-sur-Meurthe
France 48°38N 6°21E **71** D13
Dombes *France* 45°58N 5°0E **73** C9
Dombóvár *Hungary* 46°21N 18°9E **80** D3
Dombrád *Hungary* 48°13N 21°54E **80** B6
Dome Argus *Antarctica* 80°50S 76°30E **55** D6
Dome C. *Antarctica* 75°12S 123°37E **55** D9
Dome I. *Antarctica* 77°20S 39°45E **55** D5
Domel I. = Letsôk-aw Kyun
Burma 11°30N 98°25E **121** G2
Domérat *France* 46°21N 2°32E **71** F9
Domett *N.Z.* 42°53S 173°12E **155** C8
Domeyko *Chile* 29°0S 71°0W **190** B1
Domeyko, Cordillera
Chile 24°30S 69°0W **190** A2
Domfront *France* 48°37N 0°40W **70** D6
Dominador *Chile* 24°21S 69°20W **190** A2
Dominica ■ *W. Indies* 15°20N 61°20W **183** C7
Dominica Passage
W. Indies 15°10N 61°20W **183** C7
Dominican Rep. ■
W. Indies 19°0N 70°30W **183** C5
Dömitz *Germany* 53°8N 11°15E **76** B7
Domme *France* 44°48N 1°12E **72** D5
Domnesti *Romania* 45°12N 24°50E **81** E9
Domodóssola *Italy* 46°7N 8°17E **92** B5
Domogled-Valea Cernei △
Romania 44°52N 22°27E **80** F7
Domokos *Greece* 39°10N 22°18E **98** B4
Dompaire *France* 48°14N 6°14E **71** D13
Dompierre-sur-Besbre
France 46°31N 3°41E **71** F10
Dompim *Ghana* 5°10N 2°5W **138** D4
Domrémy-la-Pucelle
France 48°26N 5°40E **71** D12
Domville, Mt. *Australia* 28°1S 151°15E **151** D5
Domžale *Slovenia* 46°9N 14°35E **93** B11
Don → *India* 16°20N 76°15E **127** F3
Don → *Russia* 47°4N 39°18E **85** J10
Don → *Aberds., U.K.* 57°11N 2°5W **65** D6
Don → *S. Yorks., U.K.* 53°41N 0°52W **66** D7
Don, C. *Australia* 11°18S 131°46E **148** B5
Don Benito *Spain* 38°53N 5°51W **89** G5
Don Figueroa Mts.
Jamaica 18°5N 77°36W **182** a
Don Sak *Thailand* 9°18N 99°41E **121** b
Dona Ana = Nhamaabué
Mozam. 17°25S 35°5E **143** F4
Doña Mencía *Spain* 37°33N 4°21W **89** H6
Donaghadee *U.K.* 54°39N 5°33W **64** B6
Donaghmore *Ireland* 52°52N 7°36W **64** D4
Donald *Australia* 36°23S 143°0E **152** D5
Donaldsonville *U.S.A.* 30°6N 90°59W **176** F9
Donalsonville *U.S.A.* 31°3N 84°53W **178** D5
Doñana △ *Spain* 36°59N 6°23W **89** J4
Donau = Dunărea →
Europe 45°20N 29°40E **81** E14
Donau → *Austria* 48°10N 17°0E **79** C10
Donau Auen △ *Austria* 48°8N 16°44E **79** C9
Donaueschingen
Germany 47°56N 8°29E **77** H4
Donauwörth *Germany* 48°43N 10°47E **77** G6
Doncaster *U.K.* 53°32N 1°6W **66** D6
Dondo *Angola* 9°45S 14°25E **140** F2
Dondo *Mozam.* 19°33S 34°46E **143** F3
Dondo, Teluk *Indonesia* 0°50N 120°30E **119** D6
Dondra Head *Sri Lanka* 5°55N 80°40E **127** M5
Donduşeni *Moldova* 48°14N 27°36E **81** B12
Donegal *Ireland* 54°39N 8°5W **64** B3
Donegal □ *Ireland* 54°53N 8°0W **64** B4
Donegal B. *Ireland* 54°31N 8°49W **64** B3
Donets → *Russia* 47°33N 40°55E **85** H10
Donets Basin *Ukraine* 48°0N 38°0E **58** F13
Donetsk *Ukraine* 48°0N 37°45E **85** J9
Donetsk □ *Ukraine* 48°0N 37°45E **85** J9
Dong Ba Thin *Vietnam* 12°8N 109°13E **121** F7
Dong Dang *Vietnam* 21°54N 106°42E **116** G6
Dong Giam *Vietnam* 19°25N 105°31E **120** C5
Dong Ha *Vietnam* 16°55N 107°8E **120** D6
Dong Hene *Laos* 16°40N 105°18E **120** D5
Dong Hoi *Vietnam* 17°29N 106°36E **116** D6
Dong Jiang → *China* 23°6N 114°0E **117** F10
Dong Khe *Vietnam* 22°26N 106°27E **120** A6
Dong Phayayen
Thailand 14°20N 101°22E **120** E3
Dong Ujimqin Qi
China 45°32N 116°55E **114** B9
Dong Van *Vietnam* 23°16N 105°22E **120** A5
Dong Xoai *Vietnam* 11°32N 106°55E **121** G6
Donga *Nigeria* 7°45N 10°2E **139** D7
Donga → *Nigeria* 8°20N 9°58E **139** D7
Dong'an *China* 26°23N 111°12E **117** D8
Dongara *Australia* 29°14S 114°57E **149** E1
Dongargarh *India* 21°10N 80°40E **126** D5
Dongbei *China* 45°0N 125°0E **115** D13
Dongchuan *China* 26°8N 103°1E **116** D4
Dongco *China* 32°0N 84°55E **125** C10
Dongen *Neths.* 51°38N 4°56E **69** C4
Dongfang *China* 18°50N 108°33E **117** a
Dongfeng *China* 42°40N 125°34E **115** C13
Donggala *Indonesia* 0°30S 119°40E **119** E5
Donggan *China* 23°22N 105°9E **116** F5

Donggang *China* 39°52N 124°10E **115** E13
Dongguan *China* 22°58N 113°44E **117** F9
Dongguang *China* 37°50N 116°30E **114** F9
Donghae *S. Korea* 37°29N 129°7E **115** F15
Donghai Dao *China* 20°0N 110°15E **117** G8
Dongjingcheng *China* 44°5N 129°10E **115** B15
Dongkou *China* 27°6N 110°35E **117** D8
Donglan *China* 24°30N 107°21E **116** E6
Dongliao He →
China 42°58N 123°32E **115** C12
Dongliu *China* 30°13N 116°55E **117** B11
Dongmen *China* 22°20N 107°48E **116** F6
Dongning *China* 44°2N 131°5E **115** B16
Dongning *China* 28°3N 100°15E **116** C3
Dongping *China* 35°55N 116°20E **114** G9
Dongsha Dao
S. China Sea 20°45N 116°43E **111** G12
Dongshan *China* 23°43N 117°30E **117** F11
Dongsheng *China* 39°50N 110°0E **114** E6
Dongtai *China* 32°51N 120°21E **117** A13
Dongting Hu *China* 29°18N 112°45E **117** C9
Dongtou *China* 27°51N 121°10E **117** D13
Dongxiang *China* 28°9N 116°35E **117** C11
Dongxing *China* 21°34N 108°0E **116** G7
Dongyang *China* 29°13N 120°15E **117** C13
Dongyang *China* 37°37N 118°37E **115** F10
Dongyinggang *China* 37°58N 118°58E **115** F10
Dongzhi *China* 30°9N 117°0E **117** B11
Donington, C. *Australia* 34°37N 90°50W **172** G8
Doniphan *U.S.A.* 36°37N 90°50W **172** G8
Donja Stubica *Croatia* 45°59N 15°59E **93** C12
Donje Dušnik *Serbia* 43°12N 22°5E **96** C6
Donji Miholjac *Croatia* 45°45N 18°10E **80** E3
Donji Milanovac *Serbia* 44°28N 22°6E **96** B6
Donji Vakuf *Bos.-H.* 44°8N 17°24E **80** F2
Dønna *Norway* 66°6N 12°30E **60** C15
Donna *U.S.A.* 26°9N 98°4W **176** H5
Donnacona *Canada* 46°41N 71°41W **165** C5
Donnelly's Crossing
N.Z. 35°42S 173°38E **154** B2
Donner Pass *U.S.A.* 39°19N 120°20W **170** F6
Donnybrook *Australia* 33°34S 115°48E **149** F2
Donnybrook *S. Africa* 29°59S 29°48E **145** D4
Donora *U.S.A.* 40°11N 79°52W **174** F5
Donostia = Donostia-San
Sebastián *Spain* 43°17N 1°58W **90** B3
Donostia-San Sebastián
Spain 43°17N 1°58W **90** B3
Donousa *Greece* 37°8N 25°48E **99** D7
Donskoy *Russia* 53°55N 38°15E **84** F10
Donnybrook *Canada* 44°19N 78°16W **174** B6
Donwood *Canada* 44°19N 78°16W **174** B6
Donzère *France* 44°28N 4°43E **73** D8
Donzy *France* 47°20N 3°6E **71** E10
Dookie *Australia* 36°20S 145°41E **153** D6
Doomadgee *Australia* 17°56S 138°49E **150** B2
Doomadgee ◆
Australia 17°56S 138°49E **150** B2
Doon → *U.K.* 55°27N 4°39W **65** F4
Doon Doon ◆
Australia 16°18S 128°14E **148** C4
Doonji *Australia* 31°20S 123°0E **149** F3
Dopl *Australia* 5°10N 2°59E **138** D4
Dora, L. *Australia* 22°0S 123°0E **149** D3
Dora Báltea → *Italy* 45°11N 8°3E **92** C5
Dora Riparia → *Italy* 45°5N 7°44E **92** C4
Doran L. *Canada* 61°13N 108°6W **163** A7
Doraville *U.S.A.* 33°54N 84°17W **178** B5
Dorchester *U.K.* 50°42N 2°27W **67** G5
Dorchester, C. *Canada* 65°27N 77°27W **161** D16
Dordabis *Namibia* 22°52S 17°38E **144** B2
Dordogne □ *France* 45°5N 0°40E **72** C4
Dordogne → *France* 45°2N 0°36W **72** C3
Dordrecht *Neths.* 51°48N 4°39E **69** C4
Dordrecht *S. Africa* 31°20S 27°3E **144** D4
Dore → *France* 45°50N 3°35E **72** C7
Dore, Mts. *France* 45°32N 2°50E **72** C6
Doré L. *Canada* 54°46N 107°17W **163** C7
Dores do Indaiá *Brazil* 19°27S 45°36W **189** D1
Dorfen *Germany* 48°15N 12°8E **77** G8
Dorgali *Italy* 40°17N 9°35E **94** B2
Dori *Burkina Faso* 14°3N 0°2W **139** C4
Doring → *S. Africa* 31°54S 18°39E **144** E2
Doringbos *S. Africa* 31°59S 19°16E **144** E2
Dorking *U.K.* 51°14N 0°19W **67** F7
Dormaa-Ahenkro *Ghana* 7°15N 2°52W **138** D4
Dormans *France* 49°4N 3°38E **71** C10
Dornakal *India* 17°27N 80°10E **126** F5
Dornbirn *Austria* 47°25N 9°45E **78** E2
Dornes *France* 46°48N 3°18E **71** F10
Dornesti *Romania* 47°52N 26°1E **81** C11
Dornie *U.K.* 57°17N 5°31W **65** D3
Dornoch *Canada* 44°18N 80°51W **174** B4
Dornoch *U.K.* 57°53N 4°2W **65** D4
Dornoch Firth *U.K.* 57°51N 4°4W **65** D4
Dornogovĭ □ *Mongolia* 44°0N 110°0E **114** C6
Dornoma *Mali* 16°9N 0°51W **139** B4
Doro *Mali* 16°9N 0°51W **139** B4
Doro, Kavo *Greece* 38°9N 24°38E **98** C6
Dorog *Hungary* 47°42N 18°45E **80** C3
Dorogobuzh *Russia* 54°50N 33°18E **84** E7
Dorohoi *Romania* 47°56N 26°23E **81** C11
Döröö Nuur *Mongolia* 48°0N 93°0E **109** C12
Dorr *Iran* 33°17N 50°38E **129** C6
Dorre I. *Australia* 25°13S 113°12E **149** E1
Dorrigo *Australia* 30°20S 152°44E **153** A10
Dorrigo △ *Australia* 30°22S 152°47E **153** A10
Dorris *U.S.A.* 41°58N 121°55W **168** F3
Dorset *Canada* 45°14N 78°54W **174** A6
Dorset *Ohio, U.S.A.* 41°40N 80°40W **174** E4
Dorset *Vt., U.S.A.* 43°15N 73°5W **175** C11
Dorset □ *U.K.* 50°45N 2°26W **67** G5
Dorsten *Germany* 51°40N 6°58E **76** D2
Dortmund *Germany* 51°30N 7°28E **76** D3
Dortmund-Ems-Kanal →
Germany 51°30N 7°26E **76** D3
Dörtyol *Turkey* 36°50N 36°13E **104** D7
Doruma
Dem. Rep. of the Congo 4°42N 27°33E **142** B2
Dörverden *Iran* 35°10N 57°18E **129** C8
Dos Bahías, C.
Argentina 44°58S 65°32W **192** B3
Dos Hermanas *Spain* 37°16N 5°55W **89** H5
Dos Palos *U.S.A.* 36°59N 120°37W **170** J6
Döşemealtı *Turkey* 37°4N 30°36E **99** D12
Dosso *Niger* 13°0N 3°13E **139** C5
Dosso □ *Niger* 12°36N 2°56E **139** C5
Dostyq *Kazakhstan* 45°15N 82°29E **108** C9
Dothan *U.S.A.* 31°13N 85°24W **178** D4
Doty *U.S.A.* 46°38N 123°17W **170** D3
Douai *France* 50°21N 3°4E **71** B10
Douako *Guinea* 9°45N 10°8W **138** D2

Douala *Cameroon* 4°0N 9°45E **139** E6
Douarnenez *France* 48°6N 4°21W **70** D2
Doubabougou *Mali* 14°58N 7°38E **138** C3
Double Island Pt.
Australia 25°56S 153°11E **151** D5
Double Mountain Fork →
U.S.A. 33°16N 100°0W **176** E4
Doubrava → *Czech Rep.* 50°2N 15°20E **78** A8
Doubs □ *France* 47°10N 6°20E **71** E13
Doubs → *France* 46°53N 5°1E **71** F12
Doubtful Sd. *N.Z.* 45°20S 166°49E **155** F1
Doubtless B. *N.Z.* 34°55S 173°26E **154** A2
Doudeville *France* 49°43N 0°47E **70** C7
Doué-la-Fontaine *France* 47°11N 0°16W **70** E6
Douentza *Mali* 14°58N 2°48E **138** C4
Douentza *Mali* 15°40N 2°25W **138** B4
Dougga *Tunisia* 36°25N 9°13E **136** A5
Doughboy B. *N.Z.* 47°2S 167°40E **155** H2
Douglas *Canada* 43°1N 76°56W **174** A8
Douglas *I. of Man* 54°10N 4°28W **66** C3
Douglas *S. Africa* 29°4S 23°46E **144** C3
Douglas *Ariz., U.S.A.* 31°21N 109°33W **169** L9
Douglas *Ga., U.S.A.* 31°31N 82°51W **178** D7
Douglas *Wyo.,
U.S.A.* 42°45N 105°24W **168** E11
Douglas Apsley △
Australia 41°45S 148°11E **151** G4
Douglas Chan.
Canada 53°40N 129°20W **162** C3
Douglas Pt. *Canada* 44°19N 81°37W **174** B3
Douglasville *U.S.A.* 33°45N 84°45W **178** B5
Douirat *Morocco* 33°2N 4°11W **136** B3
Doukaton, Akra *Greece* 38°34N 20°33E **98** C2
Doukkala-Abda □
Morocco 32°10N 8°50W **136** B2
Doulevant-le-Château
France 48°23N 4°55E **71** D11
Doullens *France* 50°10N 2°20E **71** B9
Doumen *China* 22°10N 113°18E **117** F9
Douna *Mali* 13°13N 6°0W **138** C3
Dounreay *U.K.* 58°35N 3°44W **65** C5
Dourada, Serra *Brazil* 13°10S 48°45W **189** C1
Dourados *Brazil* 22°9S 54°50W **191** A5
Dourados → *Brazil* 21°58S 54°18W **191** A5
Dourados, Serra dos
Brazil 23°30S 53°30W **191** A5
Dourdan *France* 48°30N 2°1E **71** D9
Douro → *Europe* 41°8N 8°40W **88** D2
Douvaine *France* 46°19N 6°16E **71** F13
Douz *Tunisia* 33°25N 9°0E **136** B6
Douze → *France* 43°54N 0°30W **72** E3
Dove → *U.K.* 52°51N 1°36W **66** E6
Dove Creek *U.S.A.* 37°46N 108°54W **169** H9
Dover *Australia* 43°18S 147°2E **151** G4
Dover *U.K.* 51°7N 1°19E **67** F9
Dover *Del., U.S.A.* 39°10N 75°32W **173** F16
Dover *N.H., U.S.A.* 43°12N 70°56W **175** C14
Dover *N.J., U.S.A.* 40°53N 74°34W **175** E10
Dover *Ohio, U.S.A.* 40°32N 81°29W **174** F3
Dover, Pt. *Australia* 32°32S 125°32E **149** F4
Dover, Str. of *Europe* 51°0N 1°30E **67** G9
Dover-Foxcroft
U.S.A. 45°11N 69°13W **173** C19
Dover Plains *U.S.A.* 41°43N 73°35W **175** E11
Dovey = Dyfi → *U.K.* 52°32N 4°3E **67** E3
Dovgan *Turkey* 42°8N 23°17E **81** A8
Dovlat Abad *India* 42°15N 79°52W **175** D9
Dovrefjell *Norway* 62°15N 9°33E **60** E13
Dovrefjell-Sunndalsfjella △
Norway 62°15N 9°11E **60** E13
Dow Rūd *Iran* 33°28N 49°4E **129** C6
Dowa *Malawi* 13°38S 33°58E **143** E3
Dowagiac *U.S.A.* 41°59N 86°6W **172** E10
Dowerin *Australia* 31°12S 117°2E **149** F2
Dowgha'i *Iran* 36°54N 58°32E **129** B8
Dowlatābād *Kermān,
Iran* 28°20N 56°40E **129** D8
Dowlatābād *Khorāsān,
Iran* 35°16N 59°29E **129** C8
Dowling Park *U.S.A.* 30°15N 83°15W **178** E6
Down □ *U.K.* 54°23N 6°2W **64** B6
Downey *Calif., U.S.A.* 33°56N 118°9W **171** M8
Downey *Idaho, U.S.A.* 42°26N 112°7W **168** E7
Downham Market *U.K.* 52°37N 0°23E **67** E8
Downieville *U.S.A.* 39°34N 120°50W **170** F6
Downpatrick *U.K.* 54°20N 5°43W **64** B6
Downpatrick Hd. *Ireland* 54°20N 9°21W **64** B2
Downsville *U.S.A.* 42°5N 75°0W **175** D10
Downton, Mt. *Canada* 52°42N 124°52W **162** C4
Dowsārī *Iran* 28°25N 57°59E **129** D8
Doxato *Greece* 41°9N 24°16E **97** E8
Doyle *U.S.A.* 40°2N 120°6W **170** E6
Doylestown *U.S.A.* 40°21N 75°10W **175** F9
Dozois, Rés. *Canada* 47°30N 77°5W **164** C4
Dra Khel *Pakistan* 27°58N 66°45E **124** F2
Dryander △ *Australia* 20°13S 148°34E **150** b
Dryanovo *Bulgaria* 42°59N 25°28E **97** D9
Drʾaa → *Morocco* 28°40N 11°0W **136** C3
Drʾaa, Hamada du *Algeria* 28°0N 7°0W **136** C3
Drʾaa, Oued →
Morocco 28°40N 11°10W **136** C1
Drac → *France* 45°12N 5°42E **73** C9
Drac, Coves del *Spain* 39°31N 3°19E **100** B10
Dračevo *Macedonia* 41°56N 21°31E **96** E5
Drachten *Neths.* 53°7N 6°5E **69** A6
Drăgănești *Moldova* 47°43N 28°15E **81** C13
Drăgănești-Olt *Romania* 44°9N 24°32E **81** F9
Drăgănești-Vlașca
Romania 44°5N 25°33E **81** F10
Dragaš = Sharr *Kosovo* 42°5N 20°41E **96** D4
Drăgășani *Romania* 44°39N 24°17E **81** F9
Dragichyn *Belarus* 52°15N 25°8E **75** B13
Dragocvet *Serbia* 43°58N 21°15E **96** C5
Dragon's Mouths
Trin. & Tob. 11°0N 61°50W **187** K15
Dragovishtitsa *Bulgaria* 42°22N 22°39E **96** C6
Draguignan *France* 43°32N 6°27E **73** E10
Drahovo *Ukraine* 48°10N 23°17E **81** B8
Drain *U.S.A.* 43°40N 123°19W **168** E2
Drake *U.S.A.* 47°55N 100°23W **172** B3
Drake Passage *S. Ocean* 58°0S 68°0W **55** C17
Drakensberg *S. Africa* 31°0S 28°0E **145** D4
Drama *Greece* 41°9N 24°10E **97** E8
Drammen *Norway* 59°42N 10°12E **61** G14
Drangajökull *Iceland* 66°9N 22°15W **60** C2
Dranov, Ostrov
Romania 44°55N 29°30E **81** F14
Dras *India* 34°25N 75°48E **125** B6
Drastis, Akra *Greece* 39°48N 19°40E **101** A3
Drau = Drava →
Croatia 45°33N 18°55E **80** E3
Drava → *Croatia* 45°33N 18°55E **80** E3
Dravograd *Slovenia* 46°36N 15°5E **93** B12

Drawa → *Poland* 52°52N 15°59E **83** E2
Drawieński △ *Poland* 53°6N 15°58E **83** E2
Drawno *Poland* 53°13N 15°46E **83** E2
Drawsko Pomorskie
Poland 53°35N 15°50E **82** E2
Drayton *Canada* 43°46N 80°40W **174** C4
Drayton Valley
Canada 53°12N 114°58W **162** C6
Dreieich *Germany* 50°1N 8°41E **77** E4
Drenthe □ *Neths.* 52°52N 6°40E **69** B6
Drepano, Akra *Greece* 35°28N 24°14E **101** D6
Drepanum, C. *Cyprus* 34°54N 32°19E **101** E11
Dresden *Canada* 42°35N 82°11W **174** D2
Dresden *Germany* 51°3N 13°44E **76** D9
Dresden *U.S.A.* 32°41N 76°57W **174** D8
Dreux *France* 48°44N 1°23E **70** D8
Drezdenko *Poland* 52°50N 15°49E **83** F2
Driffield *U.K.* 54°0N 0°26W **66** C7
Driftwood *U.S.A.* 41°20N 78°8W **174** E6
Driggs *U.S.A.* 43°44N 111°6W **168** E8
Drin → *Albania* 42°1N 19°38E **96** D3
Drin i Zi → *Albania* 41°37N 20°28E **96** E4
Drina → *Bos.-H.* 44°53N 19°21E **96** B3
Drincea → *Romania* 44°20N 22°55E **80** F7
Drinjača → *Bos.-H.* 44°15N 19°8E **80** F4
Driopida *Greece* 37°25N 24°26E **98** D6
Drissa = Vyerkhnyadzvinsk
Belarus 55°45N 27°58E **84** E4
Drniš *Croatia* 43°51N 16°10E **93** E13
Drøbak *Norway* 59°39N 10°39E **61** G14
Drobeta-Turnu Severin
Romania 44°39N 22°41E **80** F7
Drobin *Poland* 52°42N 19°58E **83** F6
Drochia *Moldova* 48°2N 27°48E **81** B12
Drogheda *Ireland* 53°43N 6°22W **64** C5
Drogichin = Dragichyn
Belarus 52°15N 25°8E **75** B13
Drogobych = Drohobych
Ukraine 49°20N 23°30E **83** J10
Drohiczyn *Poland* 52°24N 22°39E **83** F9
Drohobych *Ukraine* 49°20N 23°30E **83** J10
Droichead Átha = Drogheda
Ireland 53°43N 6°22W **64** C5
Droichead na Bandan = Bandon
Ireland 51°44N 8°44W **64** E3
Droichead Nua = Newbridge
Ireland 53°11N 6°48W **64** C5
Droitwich *U.K.* 52°16N 2°8W **67** E5
Drôme □ *France* 44°38N 5°15E **73** D9
Drôme → *France* 44°46N 4°46E **73** D8
Dromedary, C.
Australia 36°17S 150°10E **153** F5
Drömling □ *Germany* 52°29N 11°5E **76** C7
Dromore Down, *U.K.* 54°25N 6°9W **64** B5
Dromore *Tyrone, U.K.* 54°31N 7°28W **64** B4
Dromore West *Ireland* 54°15N 8°52W **64** B3
Dronero *Italy* 44°28N 7°22E **92** D4
Dronfield *U.K.* 53°19N 1°27W **66** D6
Dronne → *France* 45°2N 0°9W **72** C3
Dronning Ingrid Land
Greenland 64°25N 52°5W **57** E5
Dronning Maud Land
Antarctica 72°30S 12°0E **55** D3
Dronninglund *Denmark* 57°10N 10°19E **63** G4
Dronten *Neths.* 52°32N 5°43E **69** B5
Dropt → *France* 44°35N 0°6W **72** D3
Drosendorf *Austria* 48°52N 15°37E **78** C8
Droué *France* 48°3N 1°6E **70** D8
Drouin *Australia* 38°10S 145°53E **153** E6
Drujba *Uzbekistan* 41°13N 61°18E **108** D6
Druk Yul = Bhutan ■
Asia 27°25N 90°30E **123** F17
Drumbo *Canada* 43°16N 80°35W **174** C4
Drumcliff *Ireland* 54°20N 8°29W **64** B3
Drumheller *Canada* 51°25N 112°40W **162** C6
Drummond *U.S.A.* 46°40N 113°9W **168** C7
Drummond I. *U.S.A.* 46°1N 83°39W **173** B12
Drummond Pt.
Australia 34°9S 135°16E **151** E2
Drummond Ra.
Australia 23°45S 147°10E **150** C4
Drummondville
Canada 45°55N 72°25W **164** C5
Drumright *U.S.A.* 35°59N 96°36W **176** D6
Druskininkai *Lithuania* 54°3N 23°58E **84** E2
Drut → *Belarus* 53°8N 30°5E **75** B16
Druya *Belarus* 55°45N 27°28E **84** E4
Druzhba *Bulgaria* 43°15N 28°1E **97** C12
Druzhina *Russia* 68°14N 145°18E **107** C15
Drvar *Bos.-H.* 44°21N 16°23E **93** D13
Drvenik *Croatia* 43°27N 16°3E **93** E13
Drwęca → *Poland* 53°0N 18°42E **83** E5
Dry Harbour Mts.
Jamaica 18°19N 77°24W **182** a
Dry Tortugas *U.S.A.* 24°38N 82°55W **177** J13
Dryander → *Australia* 20°13S 148°34E **150** b
Dryanovo *Bulgaria* 42°59N 25°28E **97** D9
Dryden *Canada* 49°47N 92°50W **163** D10
Dryden *U.S.A.* 30°3N 76°18W **175** D8
Drygalski I. *Australia* 66°0S 92°0E **55** C7
Drygalski Ice Tongue
Antarctica 75°24S 163°30E **55** D11
Drysdale → *Australia* 13°59S 126°51E **148** B4
Drysdale I. *Australia* 11°41S 136°0E **150** A2
Drysdale River △
Australia 14°56S 127°2E **148** B4
Drzewica *Poland* 51°27N 20°29E **83** G7
Drzewiczka → *Poland* 51°36N 20°36E **83** G7
Dschang *Cameroon* 5°32N 10°3E **139** D7
Du Gué → *Canada* 57°21N 70°45W **164** A5
Du He → *China* 32°48N 110°40E **117** A8
Du Quoin *U.S.A.* 38°1N 89°14W **172** F9
Du'an *China* 23°59N 108°13E **116** F7
Duaneburg *U.S.A.* 42°47N 74°11W **175** D10
Duaringa *Australia* 23°42S 149°42E **150** C4
Duarte, Pico *Dom. Rep.* 19°2N 70°59W **183** C5
Dubai = Dubayy
U.A.E. 25°18N 55°20E **129** E7
Dubāsari *Moldova* 47°15N 29°10E **81** C14
Dubāsari Vdkhr.
Moldova 47°30N 29°0E **81** C14
Dubawnt → *Canada* 64°33N 100°6W **163** A8
Dubawnt L. *Canada* 63°8N 101°28W **163** A8
Dubayy *U.A.E.* 25°18N 55°20E **129** E7
Dubbo *Australia* 32°11S 148°35E **153** B5
Dube → *Liberia* 6°7N 7°29W **138** D3
Dubele
Dem. Rep. of the Congo 2°56N 29°35E **142** B2
Dübendorf *Switz.* 47°24N 8°37E **77** H4
Dubica *Croatia* 45°11N 16°48E **93** C13
Dublin *Ireland* 53°21N 6°15W **64** C5

Dublin *Ga., U.S.A.* 32°32N 82°54W **178** C7
Dublin *Tex., U.S.A.* 32°5N 98°21W **176** E5
Dublin ☐ *Ireland* 53°24N 6°20W **64** C5
Dublin ✈ (DUB) *Ireland* 53°26N 6°15W **64** C5
Dubna *Russia* 56°44N 37°10E **84** D9
Dubno *Ukraine* 50°25N 25°45E **75** C13
DuBois *Idaho, U.S.A.* 44°10N 112°14W **168** D7
DuBois *Pa., U.S.A.* 41°7N 78°46W **174** E6
Dubossary = Dubăsari
  Moldova 47°15N 29°10E **81** C14
Dubove *Ukraine* 48°10N 23°53E **81** B8
Dubovka *Russia* 49°5N 44°50E **87** F7
Dubovskoye *Russia* 47°28N 42°46E **87** G6
Dubrajpur *India* 23°48N 87°25E **125** H12
Dubréka *Guinea* 9°46N 13°31W **138** D2
Dubrovitsa = Dubrovytsya
  Ukraine 51°31N 26°35E **75** C14
Dubrovnik *Croatia* 42°39N 18°6E **96** D2
Dubrovytsya *Ukraine* 51°31N 26°35E **75** C14
Dubuque *U.S.A.* 42°30N 90°41W **172** D8
Dubysa → *Lithuania* 55°5N 23°26E **82** C10
Duc Tho *Vietnam* 18°32N 105°35E **120** C5
Duchang *China* 29°18N 116°12E **117** C11
Duchesne *U.S.A.* 40°10N 110°24W **168** F8
Duchess *Australia* 21°20S 139°50E **150** C2
Ducie I. *Pac. Oc.* 24°40S 124°48W **157** K15
Duck → *U.S.A.* 36°2N 87°52W **177** C11
Duck Cr. → *Australia* 22°37S 116°53E **148** D2
Duck Lake *Canada* 52°50N 106°16W **163** C7
Duck Mountain △
  Canada 51°45N 101°0W **163** C8
Duckwall, Mt. *U.S.A.* 37°58N 120°7W **170** H6
Duderstadt *Germany* 51°31N 10°15E **76** D6
Dudhi *India* 24°15N 83°10E **125** G10
Dudinka *Russia* 69°30N 86°13E **107** C9
Dudley *U.K.* 52°31N 2°5W **67** E5
Dudley *U.S.A.* 32°32N 83°5W **178** C6
Dudna → *India* 19°17N 76°54E **126** E3
Dudwa *India* 28°30N 80°41E **125** E9
Dudwa △ *India* 28°30N 80°40E **125** E9
Duékoué *Ivory C.* 6°40N 7°10W **138** D3
Dueñas *Spain* 41°52N 4°33W **88** D6
Duero = Douro → *Europe* 41°8N 8°40W **88** D2
Dufftown *U.K.* 57°27N 3°8W **65** D5
Dufourspitz *Switz.* 45°56N 7°52E **77** K3
Dugi Otok *Croatia* 44°0N 15°3E **95** D11
Dugo Selo *Croatia* 45°51N 16°18E **93** C13
Duisburg *Germany* 51°26N 6°45E **76** D2
Duiwelskloof = Modjadjiskloof
  S. Africa 23°42S 30°10E **145** B5
Dujiangyan *China* 31°2N 103°38E **116** B4
Dukat *Albania* 40°16N 19°32E **96** F3
Dükdamïn *Iran* 35°59N 57°42E **129** C8
Dukelský Průsmyk
  Slovak Rep. 49°25N 21°42E **79** B14
Dukhān *Qatar* 25°25N 50°50E **129** E6
Dukhovshchina *Russia* 55°15N 32°27E **84** E7
Duki *Pakistan* 30°14N 68°25E **122** D6
Dukla *Poland* 49°30N 21°35E **83** J8
Duku *Bauchi, Nigeria* 10°43N 10°43E **139** C7
Duku *Sokoto, Nigeria* 11°11N 4°55E **139** C5
Dulan *China* 36°56N 107°0W **109** H10
Dulce *→ Argentina* 30°32S 62°33W **190** C3
Dulce, G. *Costa Rica* 8°40N 83°20W **182** E3
Dulf *Iraq* 35°7N 45°51E **128** C5
Dŭlgopol *Bulgaria* 43°3N 27°22E **97** C11
Duliu *China* 39°2N 116°55E **114** E9
Dullewala *Pakistan* 31°50N 71°25E **124** D4
Dullstroom *S. Africa* 25°27S 30°7E **145** C5
Dülmen *Germany* 51°49N 7°17E **76** D3
Dulovo *Bulgaria* 43°48N 27°9E **97** C11
Dulq Maghār *Syria* 36°22N 38°39E **105** D8
Duluth *U.S.A.* 34°0N 84°9W **178** A3
Duluth *Minn., U.S.A.* 46°47N 92°6W **172** B7
Dum Dum *India* 22°39N 88°26E **125** H13
Dum Duma *India* 27°40N 95°40E **123** F19
Dūmā *Syria* 33°34N 36°24E **105** B5
Dumaguete *Phil.* 9°17N 123°15E **119** C6
Dumai *Indonesia* 1°35N 101°28E **118** D2
Dumaran *Phil.* 10°33N 119°50E **119** B5
Dumas *Ark., U.S.A.* 33°53N 91°29W **176** E9
Dumas *Tex., U.S.A.* 35°52N 101°58W **176** D4
Dumayr *Syria* 33°39N 36°42E **105** B5
Dumbarton *U.K.* 55°57N 4°33W **65** F4
Dumbier *Slovak Rep.* 48°56N 19°38E **79** C12
Dumbleyung *Australia* 33°17S 117°42E **149** F2
Dumbrăveni *Romania* 46°14N 24°34E **81** D9
Dumfries *U.K.* 55°4N 3°37W **65** F5
Dumfries & Galloway ☐
  U.K. 55°9N 3°58W **65** F5
Dumitreşti *Romania* 45°33N 26°55E **81** E11
Dumka *India* 24°12N 87°15E **125** G12
Dumlupınar *Turkey* 38°53N 30°0E **99** C12
Dümmer *Germany* 52°31N 8°20E **76** C4
Dümmer → *Canada* 46°13N 77°51W **164** C4
Dumoine, L. *Canada* 46°55N 77°55W **164** C4
Dumont d'Urville
  Antarctica 66°40S 140°0E **55** C10
Dumont d'Urville Sea
  S. Ocean 63°30S 138°0E **55** C9
Dumyât *Egypt* 31°24N 31°48E **137** E7
Dumyât, Masabb *Egypt* 31°28N 31°51E **137** E7
Dún Dealgan = Dundalk
  Ireland 54°1N 6°24W **64** B5
Dún Garbhán = Dungarvan
  Ireland 52°5N 7°37W **64** D4
Dún Laoghaire *Ireland* 53°17N 6°8W **64** C5
Dun-le-Palestel *France* 46°18N 1°39E **71** F8
Dun-sur-Auron *France* 46°53N 2°33E **71** F9
Dun-sur-Meuse *France* 49°23N 5°11E **71** C12
Duna = Dunărea →
  Europe 45°20N 29°40E **81** E14
Duna-Drava △ *Hungary* 46°15N 18°50E **80** D3
Duna-völgyi-főcsatorna
  Hungary 46°40N 19°14E **80** D4
Dunaföldvár *Hungary* 46°50N 18°57E **80** D3
Dunagiri *India* 30°31N 79°52E **125** D8
Dunaj = Dunărea →
  Europe 45°20N 29°40E **81** E14
Dunajec → *Poland* 50°15N 20°44E **83** H7
Dunajská Streda
  Slovak Rep. 48°0N 17°37E **79** C10
Dunakeszi *Hungary* 47°37N 19°8E **80** D4
Dunapataj *Hungary* 46°39N 19°4E **80** D4
Dunărea → *Europe* 45°20N 29°40E **81** E14
Dunaszekcső *Hungary* 46°6N 18°45E **80** D3
Dunaújváros *Hungary* 46°58N 18°57E **80** D3

Dunav = Dunărea →
  Europe 45°20N 29°40E **81** E14
Dunavaţu de Jos
  Romania 44°59N 29°13E **81** F14
Dunavtsi *Bulgaria* 43°57N 22°53E **96** C6
Dunay *Russia* 42°52N 132°22E **112** C6
Dunayivtsi *Ukraine* 48°54N 26°50E **81** B11
Dunback *N.Z.* 45°23S 170°36E **155** F5
Dunbar *Canada* 56°0N 2°31W **65** E6
Dunbar *U.K.* 56°11N 3°58W **65** E5
Dunblane *U.K.* 56°11N 3°58W **65** E5
Duncan *Canada* 48°45N 123°40W **170** B3
Duncan *Ariz., U.S.A.* 32°43N 109°6W **169** K9
Duncan *Okla., U.S.A.* 34°30N 97°57W **176** D6
Duncan, L. *Canada* 53°29N 77°58W **164** B4
Duncan L. *Canada* 62°51N 113°58W **162** A6
Duncan Passage *India* 11°0N 92°0E **127** J11
Duncan Town
  Bahamas 22°15N 75°45W **182** B4
Duncannon *U.S.A.* 40°23N 77°2W **174** F7
Duncansby Head *U.K.* 58°38N 3°1W **65** C5
Duncansville *U.S.A.* 40°25N 78°26W **174** F6
Dund-Us *Mongolia* 48°1N 91°38E **109** C12
Dundaga *Latvia* 57°31N 22°21E **82** A9
Dundalk *Canada* 44°10N 80°24W **174** B4
Dundalk *Ireland* 54°1N 6°24W **64** B5
Dundalk *U.S.A.* 39°15N 76°31W **173** F15
Dundalk Bay *Ireland* 53°55N 6°15W **64** C5
Dundas = Uummannaq
  Greenland 77°33N 68°52W **57** B4
Dundas *Canada* 43°17N 79°59W **174** C5
Dundas, L. *Australia* 32°35S 121°50E **149** F3
Dundas I. *Canada* 54°30N 130°50W **162** C2
Dundas Str. *Australia* 11°15S 131°35E **148** B5
Dundee *S. Africa* 28°11S 30°15E **145** C5
Dundee *U.K.* 56°28N 2°59W **65** E6
Dundee *U.S.A.* 42°32N 76°59W **174** E8
Dundee City ☐ *U.K.* 56°30N 2°58W **65** E6
Dundgovĭ ☐ *Mongolia* 10°30N 106°0E **114** B4
Dundrum *U.K.* 54°16N 5°52W **64** B6
Dundrum B. *U.K.* 54°13N 5°47W **64** B6
Dunedin *N.Z.* 45°50S 170°33E **155** F5
Dunedin *U.S.A.* 28°1N 82°46W **179** G7
Dunedoo *Australia* 32°0S 149°25E **153** A8
Dunfanaghy *Ireland* 55°11N 7°58W **64** A4
Dunfermline *U.K.* 56°5N 3°27W **65** E5
Dungannon *Canada* 43°51N 81°36W **174** C3
Dungannon *U.K.* 54°31N 6°46W **64** B5
Dungarpur *India* 23°52N 73°45E **124** H5
Dungarvan *Ireland* 52°5N 7°37W **64** D4
Dungarvan Harbour
  Ireland 52°4N 7°35W **64** D4
Dungeness *U.K.* 50°54N 0°59E **67** G8
Dungiven *U.K.* 54°55N 6°55W **64** B5
Dunglow *Ireland* 54°57N 8°21W **64** B3
Dungo, L. do *Angola* 17°15S 19°0E **144** A2
Dungog *Australia* 32°22S 151°46E **153** B9
Dungu
  Dem. Rep. of the Congo 3°40N 28°32E **142** B2
Dungun *Malaysia* 4°45N 103°25E **121** K4
Dungunâb *Sudan* 21°10N 37°9E **137** C4
Dungunâb, Khalig
  Sudan 21°5N 37°12E **137** C4
Dunhua *China* 43°20N 128°14E **115** C15
Dunhuang *China* 40°8N 94°36E **110** C7
Dunk I. *Australia* 17°59S 146°29E **150** B4
Dunkassa *Benin* 10°21N 3°10E **139** C5
Dunkeld *Queens.,*
  Australia 33°25S 149°29E **151** E4
Dunkeld *Vic., Australia* 37°40S 142°22E **152** D5
Dunkeld *U.K.* 56°34N 3°35W **65** E5
Dunkerque *France* 51°2N 2°20E **71** A9
Dunkery Beacon *U.K.* 51°9N 3°36W **67** F4
Dunkirk = Dunkerque
  France 51°2N 2°20E **71** A9
Dunkirk *U.S.A.* 42°29N 79°20W **174** D5
Dunkwa *Central, Ghana* 6°0N 1°47W **138** D4
Dunkwa *Central, Ghana* 5°30N 1°0W **139** D4
Dunleary = Dún Laoghaire
  Ireland 53°17N 6°8W **64** C5
Dunleer *Ireland* 53°50N 6°24W **64** C5
Dunmanus B. *Ireland* 51°31N 9°50W **64** E2
Dunmanway *Ireland* 51°43N 9°6W **64** E2
Dunmarra *Australia* 16°42S 133°25E **150** B1
Dunmore *U.S.A.* 41°25N 75°38W **175** E9
Dunmore East *Ireland* 52°9N 7°0W **64** D5
Dunmore Town
  Bahamas 25°30N 76°39W **182** A4
Dunn *U.S.A.* 35°19N 78°37W **177** D15
Dunnellon *U.S.A.* 29°3N 82°28W **179** F7
Dunnet Hd. *U.K.* 58°40N 3°21W **65** C5
Dunning *U.S.A.* 41°50N 100°6W **172** E3
Dunnville *Canada* 42°54N 79°36W **174** D5
Dunolly *Australia* 36°51S 143°44E **152** D5
Dunoon *U.K.* 55°57N 4°56W **65** F4
Dunseith *U.S.A.* 48°50N 100°3W **172** A3
Dunshaughlin *Ireland* 53°31N 6°33W **64** C5
Dunsmuir *U.S.A.* 41°13N 122°16W **168** F2
Dunstable *U.K.* 51°53N 0°32W **67** F7
Dunstan Mts. *N.Z.* 44°53S 169°35E **155** E4
Dunster *Canada* 53°8N 119°50W **162** C5
Duntroon *N.Z.* 44°51S 170°40E **155** E5
Dunvegan *U.K.* 57°27N 6°35W **65** D2
Dunvegan L. *Canada* 60°8N 107°10W **163** A7
Duolun *China* 42°12N 116°28E **114** C9
Duomula *China* 34°8N 82°0E **110** B7
Duong Dong *Vietnam* 10°13N 103°58E **121** G4
Dupree *U.S.A.* 45°4N 101°35W **172** C3
Dupuyer *U.S.A.* 48°13N 112°30W **168** B7
Duque de Caxias *Brazil* 22°46S 43°18W **191** A7
Duque de York, I.
  Chile 50°37S 75°25W **192** D1
Durack → *Australia* 15°33S 127°52E **148** C4
Durack Ra. *Australia* 16°50S 127°40E **148** C4
Durack River
  Australia 15°33S 127°39E **148** C4
Durağan *Turkey* 41°25N 35°5E **104** A6
Durak *Turkey* 39°42N 28°17E **99** B10
Durakovac = Gjurakoc
  Kosovo 42°43N 20°29E **96** C4
Durance → *France* 43°55N 4°45E **73** E8
Durand *Ga., U.S.A.* 32°55N 84°46W **178** C5
Durand *Wis., U.S.A.* 44°38N 91°58W **172** C8
Durango *Mexico* 24°3N 104°39W **180** C4
Durango ☐ *Mexico* 24°50N 105°20W **180** C4
Durango *U.S.A.* 37°16N 107°53W **169** H10
Durani *Afghan.* 31°30N 65°30E **124** D1
Duranikulak *Bulgaria* 43°41N 28°32E **97** C12
Durant *Miss., U.S.A.* 33°4N 89°51W **177** D10
Durant *Okla., U.S.A.* 33°59N 96°25W **176** E6
Duratón → *Spain* 41°37N 4°7W **88** D6

Durazno *Uruguay* 33°25S 56°31W **190** C4
Durazzo = Durrës
  Albania 41°19N 19°28E **96** E3
Durban *France* 42°59N 2°49E **72** F6
Durban *S. Africa* 29°49S 31°1E **145** C5
Durban ✈ (DIA)
  S. Africa 29°37S 31°7E **145** C5
Durbuy *Belgium* 50°21N 5°28E **69** D5
Dúrcal *Spain* 36°59N 3°34W **89** J7
Đurđevac *Croatia* 46°2N 17°3E **80** D2
Düren *Germany* 50°48N 6°29E **76** E2
Durg = Bhilainagar-Durg
  India 21°13N 81°26E **126** D5
Durgapur *India* 23°30N 87°20E **125** H12
Durham *Canada* 44°10N 80°49W **174** B4
Durham *U.K.* 54°47N 1°34W **66** C6
Durham *Calif., U.S.A.* 39°39N 121°48W **170** F5
Durham *N.C., U.S.A.* 35°59N 78°54W **177** D15
Durham *N.H., U.S.A.* 43°8N 70°56W **175** C14
Durham ☐ *U.K.* 54°42N 1°45W **66** C6
Durlas = Thurles *Ireland* 52°41N 7°49W **64** D4
Durleşti *Moldova* 47°1N 28°46E **81** C13
Durmā *Si. Arabia* 24°37N 46°8E **128** E5
Durmitor *Montenegro* 43°10N 19°0E **96** C2
Durmitor △ *Montenegro* 43°15N 19°5E **96** C3
Durness *U.K.* 58°34N 4°45W **65** C4
Durrës *Albania* 41°19N 19°28E **96** E3
Durrow *Ireland* 52°51N 7°24W **64** D4
Dursey I. *Ireland* 51°36N 10°12W **64** E1
Dursley *U.K.* 51°40N 2°21W **67** F5
Dursunbey *Turkey* 39°35N 28°37E **99** B10
Durtal *France* 47°40N 0°18W **70** E6
Duru
  Dem. Rep. of the Congo 4°14N 28°50E **142** B2
Duru Gölü *Turkey* 41°20N 28°35E **97** E12
Durusu *Turkey* 41°17N 28°41E **97** E12
Durūz, Jabal ad *Jordan* 32°35N 36°40E **130** C5
D'Urville, Tanjung
  Indonesia 1°28S 137°54E **119** E9
D'Urville I. *N.Z.* 40°50S 173°55E **155** A4
Duryea *U.S.A.* 41°20N 75°45W **175** E9
Dùsh *Egypt* 24°35N 30°41E **137** C3
Dushak *Turkmenistan* 37°13N 60°1E **129** B9
Dushan *China* 25°48N 107°30E **116** E6
Dushanbe *Tajikistan* 38°33N 68°48E **109** F7
Dusheti *Georgia* 42°10N 44°42E **87** J7
Dushore *U.S.A.* 41°31N 76°24W **175** E8
Dusky Sd. *N.Z.* 45°47S 166°30E **155** F1
Dussejour, C. *Australia* 14°45S 128°13E **148** B4
Düsseldorf *Germany* 51°14N 6°47E **76** D2
Düsseldorf Rhein-Ruhr ✈ (DUS)
  Germany 51°17N 6°46E **76** D2
Dusti *Tajikistan* 37°21N 68°38E **109** F7
Duszniki-Zdrój *Poland* 50°24N 16°24E **83** H3
Dutch Harbor *U.S.A.* 53°53N 166°32W **166** E6
Dutlwe *Botswana* 23°58S 23°46E **144** B3
Dutsan Wai *Nigeria* 10°50N 8°10E **139** C6
Dutse *Nigeria* 11°46N 9°20E **139** C6
Dutton *U.S.A.* 42°39N 81°30W **174** D3
Dutton → *Australia* 20°44S 143°10E **150** C3
Dutywa *S. Africa* 32°8S 28°18E **145** D4
Duved *Sweden* 63°23N 12°55E **62** A6
Duyfken Pt. *Australia* 12°33S 141°38E **150** A3
Duyun *China* 26°18N 107°29E **116** D6
Düzağaç *Turkey* 38°48N 30°10E **99** C12
Düzce = Akhna *Cyprus* 35°3N 33°47E **101** D12
Düzce *Turkey* 40°50N 31°10E **104** B4
Düzce ☐ *Turkey* 40°50N 31°10E **104** B4
Düziçi *Turkey* 37°15N 36°28E **104** D7
Dve Mogili *Bulgaria* 43°35N 25°55E **97** C9
Dvina, Severnaya →
  Russia 64°32N 40°30E **58** C14
Dvinsk = Daugavpils
  Latvia 55°53N 26°32E **84** E4
Dvor *Croatia* 45°4N 16°22E **93** C13
Dvůr Králové nad Labem
  Czech Rep. 50°27N 15°50E **78** A8
Dwarka *India* 22°18N 69°8E **124** H3
Dwellingup *Australia* 32°43S 116°4E **149** F2
Dwight *Canada* 45°20N 79°1W **174** A5
Dwight *U.S.A.* 41°5N 88°26W **172** E9
Dyakove *Ukraine* 48°1N 23°0E **80** B7
Dyatkovo *Russia* 53°40N 34°27E **84** F8
Dyatlovo = Dzyatlava
  Belarus 53°28N 25°28E **75** B13
Dyce *U.K.* 57°13N 2°12W **65** D6
Dyer, C. *Canada* 66°37N 61°16W **161** D19
Dyer Bay *Canada* 45°10N 81°20W **174** A3
Dyer Plateau
  Antarctica 70°45S 65°30W **55** D17
Dyersburg *U.S.A.* 36°3N 89°23W **177** C10
Dyfi → *U.K.* 52°32N 4°3W **67** E3
Dyje → *Czech Rep.* 48°37N 16°56E **79** C9
Dykh Tau *Russia* 43°8N 43°8E **87** J6
Dymer *Ukraine* 50°47N 30°18E **75** C16
Dynów *Poland* 49°50N 22°11E **83** J9
Dysart *Australia* 22°32S 148°23E **150** C4
Dytiki Ellas ☐ *Greece* 38°20N 21°30E **98** C3
Dyviziya *Ukraine* 45°55N 29°59E **81** E14
Dzaoudzi *Mayotte* 12°47S 45°16E **141** a
Dzavhan → *Mongolia* 48°0N 96°0E **109** C13
Dzavhan Gol →
  Mongolia 48°54N 93°23E **110** B7
Dzerzhinsk *Russia* 56°14N 43°30E **86** B6
Dzhalal-Abad = Jalal-Abad
  Kyrgyzstan 40°56N 73°0E **109** E8
Dzhalinda *Russia* 53°26N 124°0E **107** D13
Dzhambeyty = Zhympïty
  Kazakhstan 50°16N 52°35E **108** B4
Dzhambul = Taraz
  Kazakhstan 42°54N 71°22E **108** E8
Dzhankoy *Ukraine* 45°40N 34°20E **85** K8
Dzhardzhan
  Russia 68°10N 124°10E **107** C13
Dzhezkazgan = Zhezqazghan
  Kazakhstan 47°44N 67°40E **109** C7
Dzhizak = Jizzax
  Uzbekistan 40°6N 67°50E **109** E7
Dzhugdzur, Khrebet
  Russia 57°30N 138°0E **107** D14
Dzhulynk *Ukraine* 48°26N 29°45E **81** B14
Dzhungarskiye Vorota =
  Dzungarian Gate
  Asia 45°10N 82°0E **109** C10

Dzhuryn *Ukraine* 48°41N 28°18E **81** B13
Dzhvari = Jvari *Georgia* 42°42N 42°4E **87** J6
Działdowo *Poland* 53°15N 20°15E **83** B7
Działoszyce *Poland* 50°22N 20°20E **83** H7
Działoszyn *Poland* 51°6N 18°50E **83** G5
Dzibilchaltún *Mexico* 21°10N 89°35W **181** C7
Dzierzgoń *Poland* 53°58N 19°20E **82** B6
Dzierżoniów *Poland* 50°45N 16°39E **83** H3
Dzilam de Bravo
  Mexico 21°24N 88°53W **181** C7
Dzioua *Algeria* 33°14N 5°14E **136** B5
Dzisna *Belarus* 55°34N 28°12E **84** E5
Dzisna → *Belarus* 55°34N 28°12E **84** E5
Dziwnów *Poland* 54°2N 14°45E **82** A2
Dźūkija △ *Lithuania* 54°10N 24°30E **61** J21
E.C. Manning △
  Canada 49°5N 120°45W **162** D4
Eabamet L. *Canada* 51°30N 87°46W **164** B2
Eabametoong *Canada* 51°30N 88°0W **164** B2
Éadan Doire = Edenderry
  Ireland 53°21N 7°4W **64** C4
Eads *U.S.A.* 38°29N 102°47W **168** G12
Eagar *U.S.A.* 34°6N 109°17W **169** J9
Eagle *Alaska, U.S.A.* 64°47N 141°12W **160** E3
Eagle *Colo., U.S.A.* 39°39N 106°50W **168** G10
Eagle → *Canada* 53°36N 57°26W **165** B8
Eagle Butte *U.S.A.* 45°0N 101°10W **172** C3
Eagle Grove *U.S.A.* 42°40N 93°54W **172** D7
Eagle L. *Canada* 49°42N 93°13W **163** D10
Eagle L. *Calif., U.S.A.* 40°39N 120°45W **168** F3
Eagle L. *Maine, U.S.A.* 46°20N 69°22W **173** B19
Eagle Lake *Canada* 45°8N 78°29W **174** A6
Eagle Lake *Maine,*
  U.S.A. 47°3N 68°36W **173** B19
Eagle Lake *Tex., U.S.A.* 29°35N 96°20W **176** G6
Eagle Mountain
  U.S.A. 33°49N 115°27W **171** M11
Eagle Nest *U.S.A.* 36°33N 105°16W **169** H11
Eagle Pass *U.S.A.* 28°43N 100°30W **176** G4
Eagle Pk. *U.S.A.* 38°10N 119°25W **170** G7
Eagle Pt. *Australia* 16°11S 124°23E **148** C3
Eagle River *Mich.,*
  U.S.A. 47°25N 88°18W **172** B9
Eagle River *Wis.,*
  U.S.A. 45°55N 89°15W **172** C9
Eaglehawk *Australia* 36°44S 144°15E **152** D6
Eagles Mere *U.S.A.* 41°25N 76°33W **175** E8
Ealing ☐ *U.K.* 51°31N 0°20W **67** F7
Ear Falls *Canada* 50°38N 93°13W **163** C10
Earlimart *U.S.A.* 35°53N 119°16W **171** K7
Earlville *U.S.A.* 42°44N 75°32W **175** D9
Early Branch *U.S.A.* 32°33N 80°53W **178** E6
Earn → *U.K.* 56°21N 3°18W **65** E5
Earn, L. *U.K.* 56°23N 4°13W **65** E4
Earnslaw, Mt. *N.Z.* 44°32S 168°27E **155** E3
Earth *U.S.A.* 34°14N 102°24W **176** D3
Easley *U.S.A.* 34°50N 82°36W **177** D13
East Anglia *U.K.* 52°30N 1°0E **66** E9
East Angus *Canada* 45°30N 71°40W **165** C5
East Antarctica *Antarctica* 80°0S 90°0E **55** D7
East Aurora *U.S.A.* 42°46N 78°37W **174** D6
East Ayrshire ☐ *U.K.* 55°26N 4°11W **65** F4
East Bengal *Bangla.* 24°0N 90°0E **123** G17
East Beskids = Vychodné Beskydy
  Europe 49°20N 22°0E **79** B15
East Brady *U.S.A.* 40°59N 79°37W **174** F5
East Branch Clarion River L.
  U.S.A. 41°38N 78°35W **174** E6
East C. = Dezhneva, Mys
  Russia 66°5N 169°40W **107** C19
East C. *N.Z.* 37°42S 178°35E **154** D7
East Caroline Basin
  Pac. Oc. 4°0N 146°45E **156** G6
East Chicago *U.S.A.* 41°38N 87°27W **172** E9
East China Sea *Asia* 30°0N 126°0E **117** C14
East Coulee *Canada* 51°23N 112°27W **162** C6
East Dereham = Dereham
  U.K. 52°41N 0°57E **67** E8
East Dublin *U.S.A.* 32°33N 82°52W **178** C7
East Dunbartonshire ☐
  U.K. 55°57N 4°13W **65** F4
East Falkland *Falk. Is.* 51°30S 58°30W **192** D5
East Grand Forks
  U.S.A. 47°56N 97°1W **175** B19
East Greenwich
  U.S.A. 41°40N 71°27W **175** E13
East Grinstead *U.K.* 51°7N 0°0 **67** F8
East Hartford *U.S.A.* 41°46N 72°39W **175** E12
East Haydon *Australia* 18°0S 141°30E **150** B3
East Helena *U.S.A.* 46°35N 111°56W **168** C8
East Indies *Asia* 0°0 120°0E **102** J14
East Kilbride *U.K.* 55°47N 4°11W **65** F4
East Lamma Channel
  China 22°14N 114°9E **111** a
East Lansing *U.S.A.* 42°44N 84°29W **173** D11
East Liverpool *U.S.A.* 40°37N 80°35W **174** F4
East London *S. Africa* 33°0S 27°55E **145** D4
East Lothian ☐ *U.K.* 55°58N 2°44W **65** F6
East Main = Eastmain
  Canada 52°10N 78°30W **164** B4
East Mariana Basin
  Pac. Oc. 12°0N 153°0E **156** F7
East Naples *U.S.A.* 26°8N 81°46W **179** J8
East Northport *U.S.A.* 40°53N 73°19W **175** E13
East Orange *U.S.A.* 40°46N 74°12W **175** E10
East Pacific Rise
  Pac. Oc. 15°0S 110°0W **157** J17
East Palatka *U.S.A.* 29°39N 81°36W **179** F8
East Palestine *U.S.A.* 40°50N 80°32W **174** F4
East Pine *Canada* 55°48N 120°12W **162** B4
East Point *U.S.A.* 33°41N 84°27W **178** C4
East Providence
  U.S.A. 41°49N 71°23W **175** E13
East Pt. *Br. Virgin Is.* 18°40N 64°18W **183** e
East Pt. *Canada* 46°27N 61°58W **165** C7
East Renfrewshire ☐
  U.K. 55°46N 4°21W **65** F4

East Retford = Retford
  U.K. 53°19N 0°56W **66** D7
East Riding of Yorkshire ☐
  U.K. 53°55N 0°30W **66** D7
East Rochester *U.S.A.* 43°7N 77°29W **174** C7
East St. Louis *U.S.A.* 38°37N 90°9W **172** F8
East Schelde = Oosterschelde →
  Neths. 51°33N 4°0E **69** C4
East Sea = Japan, Sea of
  Asia 40°0N 135°0E **112** E7
East Siberian Sea
  Russia 73°0N 160°0E **107** B17
East Stroudsburg *U.S.A.* 41°1N 75°11W **175** E9
East Sussex ☐ *U.K.* 50°56N 0°19E **67** G8
East Tasman Plateau
  Pac. Oc. 43°30S 152°0E **156** M7
East Tawas *U.S.A.* 44°17N 83°29W **173** C12
East Timor ■ *Asia* 8°50S 126°0E **119** F7
East Walker →
  U.S.A. 38°52N 119°10W **170** F10
East Windsor *U.S.A.* 40°17N 74°34W **175** E10
Eastbourne *N.Z.* 41°19S 174°55E **154** H3
Eastbourne *U.K.* 50°46N 0°18E **67** G8
Eastend *Canada* 49°32N 108°50W **163** D7
Easter Fracture Zone
  Pac. Oc. 25°0S 115°0W **157** K16
Easter I. = Pascua, I. de
  Chile 27°7S 109°23W **157** K17
Eastern ☐ *Ghana* 6°30N 0°30W **139** D4
Eastern ☐ *Kenya* 0°0 38°30E **142** C4
Eastern ☐ *S. Leone* 8°15N 11°0W **138** D2
Eastern Cape ☐ *S. Africa* 32°0S 26°0E **144** D4
Eastern Cr. →
  Australia 20°40S 141°35E **150** C3
Eastern Desert = Es Sahrâ' Esh
  Sharqîya *Egypt* 27°30N 32°30E **137** B3
Eastern Ghats *India* 14°0N 78°50E **127** H4
Eastern Group = Lau Group
  Fiji 17°0S 178°30W **154** a
Eastern Group
  Australia 33°30S 124°30E **149** F3
Eastern Guruma ♡
  Australia 22°0S 117°30E **148** D2
Eastern Transvaal =
  Mpumalanga ☐
  S. Africa 26°0S 30°0E **145** C5
Easterville *Canada* 53°8N 99°49W **163** C9
Easthampton *U.S.A.* 42°16N 72°40W **175** D12
Eastlake *U.S.A.* 41°40N 81°26W **174** E3
Eastland *U.S.A.* 32°24N 98°49W **176** E5
Eastleigh *U.K.* 50°58N 1°21W **67** G6
Eastmain *Canada* 52°10N 78°30W **164** B4
Eastmain → *Canada* 52°27N 78°26W **164** B4
Eastman *Canada* 45°18N 72°19W **175** A11
Eastman *U.S.A.* 32°12N 83°11W **178** C6
Easton *Md., U.S.A.* 38°47N 76°5W **173** F15
Easton *Pa., U.S.A.* 40°41N 75°13W **175** F9
Easton *Wash., U.S.A.* 47°14N 121°11W **170** C5
Eastover *U.S.A.* 33°52N 80°41W **178** B8
Eastpoint *U.S.A.* 29°44N 84°53W **178** F5
Eastport *U.S.A.* 44°56N 67°0W **173** C20
Eastsound *U.S.A.* 48°42N 122°55W **170** B4
Eaton *Canada* 40°32N 104°42W **168** E11
Eatonia *Canada* 51°13N 109°25W **163** C7
Eatonton *U.S.A.* 33°20N 83°23W **178** B6
Eatontown *U.S.A.* 40°19N 74°4W **175** F10
Eatonville *U.S.A.* 46°52N 122°16W **170** D4
Eau Claire *U.S.A.* 44°49N 91°30W **172** C8
Eau Claire, L. à l'
  Canada 56°10N 74°25W **164** A5
Eauripik Rise *Pac. Oc.* 2°0N 142°0E **156** G6
Eauze *France* 43°53N 0°7E **72** E4
Eban *Nigeria* 9°40N 4°50E **139** D5
Ebano *Mexico* 22°13N 98°24W **181** C5
Ebbegebirge △ *Germany* 51°10N 7°55E **76** D3
Ebbw Vale *U.K.* 51°46N 3°12W **67** F4
Ebeltoft *Denmark* 56°12N 10°41E **63** H4
Ebeltoft Vig *Denmark* 56°10N 10°35E **63** H4
Ebensburg *U.S.A.* 40°29N 78°44W **174** F6
Ebensee *Austria* 47°48N 13°46E **78** D6
Eber Gölü *Turkey* 38°38N 31°11E **104** C4
Eberbach *Germany* 49°28N 8°59E **77** F4
Eberswalde-Finow
  Germany 52°50N 13°49E **76** C9
Ebetsu *Japan* 43°7N 141°34E **112** C10
Ebey's Landing
  U.S.A. 48°12N 122°41W **170** B4
Ebian *China* 29°11N 103°13E **116** C4
Ebingen *Germany* 48°13N 9°1E **77** G5
Ebinur Hu *China* 44°55N 82°55E **109** D10
Éboli *Italy* 40°39N 15°2E **95** B8
Ebolowa *Cameroon* 2°55N 11°10E **139** E7
Ebonda
  Dem. Rep. of the Congo 2°12N 22°21E **140** D4
Ebonyi ☐ *Nigeria* 6°0N 8°0E **139** D6
Ebrach *Germany* 49°51N 10°29E **77** F6
Ebre = Ebro → *Spain* 40°43N 0°54E **90** B6
Ébrié, Lagune *Ivory C.* 5°12N 4°26W **138** D4
Ebro → *Spain* 40°43N 0°54E **90** B6
Ebro, Embalse del *Spain* 43°0N 3°58W **88** C7
Ebstorf *Germany* 53°1N 10°24E **76** B6
Ecatepec de Morelos
  Mexico 19°36N 99°3W **181** D5
Ecbatana = Hamadān
  Iran 34°52N 48°32E **105** E13
Eceabat *Turkey* 40°11N 26°21E **97** F10
Ech Chéliff *Algeria* 36°10N 1°20E **136** A5
Ech Chéliff ☐ *Algeria* 36°15N 1°30E **136** A4
Echechonnee
  U.S.A. 32°39N 83°36W **178** C6
Echigo-Sammyaku
  Japan 36°50N 139°50E **113** F9
Echinos *Greece* 41°16N 24°58E **98** A6
Échirolles *France* 45°8N 5°46E **73** C9
Echizen-Misaki *Japan* 35°59N 135°57E **113** G7
Echmiadzin = Ejmiatsin
  Armenia 40°12N 44°19E **87** K7
Echo *U.S.A.* 31°29N 85°28W **178** D4
Echo Bay N.W.T.,
  Canada 66°5N 117°55W **160** D8
Echo Bay *Ont., Canada* 46°29N 84°4W **172** B11
Echoing → *Canada* 55°51N 92°5W **164** B1
Echternach *Lux.* 49°49N 6°25E **69** E6
Echuca *Australia* 36°10S 144°45E **153** D6
Écija *Spain* 37°30N 5°10W **89** H5
Eckental *Germany* 49°35N 11°12E **77** F7
Eckernförde *Germany* 54°27N 9°50E **76** A5

Eclectic *U.S.A.* 32°38N 86°2W **178** C3
Eclipse I. *Australia* 35°5S 117°58E **149** G2
Eclipse Is. *Australia* 13°54S 126°19E **148** B4
Eclipse Sd. *Canada* 72°38N 79°0W **161** C16
Écommoy *France* 47°50N 0°17E **70** E7
Ecoporanga *Brazil* 18°23S 40°50W **189** D2
Écouché *France* 48°42N 0°10W **70** D6
Écrins △ *France* 44°54N 6°18E **73** D10
Ecuador ■ *S. Amer.* 2°0S 78°0W **186** D3
Écueillé *France* 47°5N 1°21E **70** E8
Ed *Sweden* 58°55N 11°55E **63** F5
Ed Da'ein *Sudan* 11°26N 26°9E **135** F6
Ed Damazin *Sudan* 11°46N 34°21E **135** F12
Ed Dâmer *Sudan* 17°27N 34°0E **135** E12
Ed Dar el Beida = Casablanca
  Morocco 33°36N 7°36W **136** B2
Ed Debba *Sudan* 18°0N 30°51E **137** B3
Ed Déffa *Egypt* 30°40N 26°30E **137** A2
Ed Dueim *Sudan* 14°0N 32°10E **135** F12
Edam *Canada* 53°11N 108°46W **163** C7
Edam *Neths.* 52°31N 5°3E **69** B5
Edane *Sweden* 59°38N 12°49E **62** E6
Edapally *India* 11°19N 78°3E **127** J4
Eday *U.K.* 59°11N 2°47W **65** B6
Eddrachillis B. *U.K.* 58°17N 5°14W **65** C3
Eddystone *U.K.* 50°11N 4°16E **65** G3
Eddystone Pt.
  Australia 40°59S 148°20E **151** G4
Ede *Neths.* 52°4N 5°40E **69** B5
Ede *Nigeria* 7°45N 4°29E **139** D5
Édéa *Cameroon* 3°51N 10°9E **139** E7
Edebäck *Sweden* 60°25N 13°32E **62** D7
Edehon L. *Canada* 60°25N 97°15W **163** A9
Edelény *Hungary* 48°18N 20°44E **80** B5
Eden *Australia* 37°3S 149°55E **153** D8
Eden *N.C., U.S.A.* 36°29N 79°53W **177** C15
Eden *N.Y., U.S.A.* 42°39N 78°55W **174** D6
Eden *Tex., U.S.A.* 31°13N 99°51W **176** F5
Eden → *U.K.* 54°57N 3°1W **66** C4
Edenburg *S. Africa* 29°43S 25°58E **144** C4
Edendale *N.Z.* 46°19S 168°48E **155** G3
Edendale *S. Africa* 29°39S 30°18E **145** C5
Edenderry *Ireland* 53°21N 7°4W **64** C4
Edenhope *Australia* 37°4S 141°19E **152** D4
Edenton *U.S.A.* 36°4N 76°39W **177** C16
Edenville *S. Africa* 27°37S 27°34E **145** C4
Eder → *Germany* 51°12N 9°28E **76** D5
Eder-Stausee *Germany* 51°10N 8°57E **76** D4
Edessa *Greece* 40°48N 22°5E **98** A4
Edewecht *Germany* 53°8N 7°58E **76** B3
Edfu = Idfû *Egypt* 24°55N 32°49E **137** C3
Edgar *U.S.A.* 40°22N 97°58E **172** E6
Edgartown *U.S.A.* 41°23N 70°31W **175** E14
Edge Hill *U.K.* 52°8N 1°26W **67** E6
Edgecumbe *N.Z.* 37°59S 176°47E **154** D5
Edgefield *U.S.A.* 33°47N 81°56W **178** B7
Edgeley *U.S.A.* 46°22N 98°43W **172** B5
Edgemont *U.S.A.* 43°18N 103°50W **172** D2
Edgeøya *Svalbard* 77°45S 22°30E **54** B9
Edgewater *U.S.A.* 28°59N 80°54W **179** G9
Édhessa = Edessa *Greece* 40°48N 22°5E **98** A4
Edievale *N.Z.* 45°49S 169°22E **155** F4
Edina *Liberia* 6°0N 10°10W **138** D2
Edina *U.S.A.* 40°10N 92°11W **172** E7
Edinboro *U.S.A.* 41°52N 80°8W **174** E4
Edinburg *U.S.A.* 26°18N 98°10W **176** H5
Edinburgh *U.K.* 55°57N 3°13W **65** F5
Edinburgh ✈ (EDI) *U.K.* 55°54N 3°22W **65** F5
Edinburgh, City of ☐
  U.K. 55°57N 3°17W **65** F5
Edineţ *Moldova* 48°9N 27°18E **81** B12
Edirne *Turkey* 41°40N 26°34E **97** E10
Edirne ☐ *Turkey* 41°12N 26°30E **97** E10
Edison *Ga., U.S.A.* 31°34N 84°44W **178** D5
Edison *Wash., U.S.A.* 48°33N 122°27W **170** B4
Edisto → *U.S.A.* 32°29N 80°21W **178** E7
Edisto Beach *U.S.A.* 32°29N 80°19W **178** E7
Edisto I. *U.S.A.* 32°35N 80°20W **178** E7
Edithburgh *Australia* 35°5S 137°43E **152** C2
Edjeleh *Algeria* 28°38N 9°50E **136** C7
Edmeston *U.S.A.* 42°42N 75°15W **175** D9
Edmond *U.S.A.* 35°39N 97°29W **176** D6
Edmonds *U.S.A.* 47°48N 122°22W **170** C4
Edmonton *Australia* 17°2S 145°46E **150** B4
Edmonton *Canada* 53°30N 113°30W **162** C6
Edmund L. *Canada* 54°45N 93°17W **164** B1
Edmundston *Canada* 47°23N 68°20W **165** C6
Edna *U.S.A.* 28°59N 96°39W **176** G6
Edo ☐ *Nigeria* 6°30N 6°0E **139** D6
Edolo *Italy* 46°10N 10°21E **92** B7
Edremit *Turkey* 39°34N 27°0W **99** B9
Edremit Körfezi *Turkey* 39°30N 26°45E **99** B8
Edsbro *Sweden* 59°54N 18°29E **62** E12
Edsbruk *Sweden* 58°1N 16°29E **63** F10
Edsbyn *Sweden* 61°23N 15°49E **62** C9
Edson *Canada* 53°35N 116°28W **162** C5
Eduardo Castex
  Argentina 35°50S 64°18W **190** D3
Eduardo Frei *Antarctica* 62°30S 58°0W **55** C18
Edward → *Australia* 35°0S 143°30E **152** C5
Edward, L. *Africa* 0°25S 29°40E **142** C2
Edward VII Land
  Antarctica 80°0S 150°0W **55** E13
Edwards *Calif., U.S.A.* 34°50N 117°40W **171** L9
Edwards *N.Y., U.S.A.* 44°20N 75°15W **175** B9
Edwards Plateau
  U.S.A. 30°45N 101°20W **176** F4
Edwardsville *U.S.A.* 41°15N 75°56W **175** E9
Edzná *Mexico* 19°30N 90°19W **181** D6
Edzo *Canada* 62°49N 116°4W **162** A5
Eeklo *Belgium* 51°11N 3°33E **69** C3
Eenhana *Namibia* 17°30S 16°23E **144** A2
Eesti = Estonia ■ *Europe* 58°30N 25°30E **84** C4
Eferding *Austria* 48°18N 14°1E **78** C7
Effigy Mounds △ *U.S.A.* 43°5N 91°12W **172** D8
Effingham *U.S.A.* 39°7N 88°33W **172** F9
Eforie *Romania* 44°5N 28°37E **81** F13
Efxinoupoli *Greece* 39°12N 22°42E **98** B4
Ega → *Spain* 42°19N 1°55W **88** C7
Égadi, Ísole *Italy* 37°55N 12°16E **94** E5
Egan Range *U.S.A.* 39°35N 114°55W **168** G6
Egedesminde = Aasiaat
  Greenland 68°43S 52°56W **57** B5
Eger = Cheb *Czech Rep.* 50°9N 12°28E **78** A5
Eger *Hungary* 47°53N 20°27E **80** C5
Eger → *Hungary* 47°38N 20°50E **80** C5
Egersund *Norway* 58°26N 6°1E **61** G12
Egg L. *Canada* 55°5N 105°30W **163** B7
Eggegebirge Südlicher
  Teutoburger Wald △
  Germany 51°40N 8°59E **76** D4

Eggenburg Austria 48°38N 15°50E 78 C8
Eggenfelden Germany 48°23N 12°46E 77 G8
Éghezée Belgium 50°35N 4°55E 69 D4
Egilsstaðir Iceland 65°16N 14°25W 60 D6
Egina Greece 37°45N 23°26E 98 D5
Eginio Greece 40°28N 22°28E 96 F6
Egio Greece 38°15N 22°5E 98 C4
Égletons France 45°24N 2°3E 72 C6
Eglinton I. Canada 75°48N 118°30W 161 B8
Egmont Canada 49°45N 123°56W 162 D4
Egmont, C. N.Z. 39°16S 173°45E 154 F2
Egmont, Mt. = Taranaki, Mt.
N.Z. 39°17S 174°5E 154 F3
Egmont △ N.Z. 39°17S 174°4E 154 F3
Egra India 21°54N 87°32E 125 J12
Eğridir Turkey 37°52N 30°51E 104 D4
Eğridir Gölü Turkey 37°53N 30°50E 104 D4
Egtved Denmark 55°38N 9°18E 63 J3
Éguas → Brazil 13°26S 44°14W 189 C2
Éguzon-Chantôme France 46°27N 1°33E 71 F8
Egvekinot Russia 66°19N 179°50W 107 C19
Egyek Hungary 47°39N 20°52E 80 C5
Egypt ■ Africa 28°0N 31°0E 137 F7
Eha Amufu Nigeria 6°30N 7°46E 139 D6
Ehime □ Japan 33°30N 132°40E 113 H6
Ehingen Germany 48°16N 9°43E 77 G5
Ehrenberg U.S.A. 33°36N 114°31W 171 M12
Ehrhardt U.S.A. 33°6N 81°1W 178 B8
Ehrwald Austria 47°24N 10°56E 78 D3
Eibar Spain 43°11N 2°28W 90 B2
Eichstätt Germany 48°54N 11°11E 77 G7
Eider → Germany 54°19N 8°57E 76 A4
Eidsvold Australia 25°25S 151°12E 151 D5
Eidsvoll Norway 60°19N 11°14E 61 F14
Eielson U.S.A. 64°40N 147°4W 166 C10
Eifel Germany 50°15N 6°50E 77 E2
Eiffel Flats Zimbabwe 18°20S 30°0E 143 F3
Eiger Switz. 46°34N 8°1E 92 B5
Eigg U.K. 56°54N 6°10W 65 E2
Eighty Mile Beach
Australia 19°30S 120°40E 148 C3
Eil, L. U.K. 56°51N 5°16W 65 E3
Eildon Australia 37°14S 145°55E 153 D6
Eildon, L. Australia 37°10S 146°0E 153 D7
Eilean Siar □ U.K. 57°30N 7°10W 65 D1
Eilenburg Germany 51°27N 12°36E 76 D8
Einasleigh Australia 18°32S 144°5E 150 B3
Einasleigh →
Australia 17°30S 142°17E 150 B3
Einbeck Germany 51°49N 9°53E 76 D5
Eindhoven Neths. 51°26N 5°28E 69 C5
Einsiedeln Switz. 47°7N 8°46E 77 H4
Eire = Ireland ■ Europe 53°50N 7°52W 64 C4
Eiríksjökull Iceland 64°46N 20°24W 60 D3
Eiriosgaigh = Eriskay
U.K. 57°4N 7°18W 65 D1
Eirunepé Brazil 6°35S 69°53W 188 B4
Eiseb → Namibia 20°33S 20°59E 144 B2
Eisenach Germany 50°58N 10°19E 76 E6
Eisenberg Germany 50°58N 11°54E 76 E7
Eisenerz Austria 47°32N 14°54E 78 D7
Eisenhüttenstadt
Germany 52°9N 14°38E 76 C10
Eisenkappel Austria 46°29N 14°36E 78 E7
Eisenstadt Austria 47°51N 16°31E 79 D9
Eisfeld Germany 50°25N 10°54E 77 E6
Eisleben Germany 51°32N 11°32E 76 D7
Eislingen Germany 48°41N 9°42E 77 G5
Eivissa Spain 38°54N 1°26E 100 C7
Eixe, Serra do Spain 42°24N 6°54W 88 C4
Ejea de los Caballeros Spain 42°7N 1°9W 90 C3
Ejmiatsin Armenia 40°12N 44°19E 87 K7
Ejura Ghana 7°23N 1°15W 139 D4
Ejutla Mexico 16°34N 96°44W 181 D5
Ekalaka U.S.A. 45°53N 104°33W 168 D11
Ekaterinburg = Yekaterinburg
Russia 56°50N 60°30E 106 D7
Ekenäs = Raasepori
Finland 60°0N 23°26E 84 B2
Ekenässjön Sweden 57°28N 15°1E 63 G9
Ekerö Sweden 59°16N 17°45E 62 E11
Eket Nigeria 4°38N 7°56E 139 E6
Eketahuna N.Z. 40°38S 175°43E 154 G4
Ekibastuz Kazakhstan 51°50N 75°10E 109 B9
Ekiti □ Nigeria 7°25N 5°20E 139 D6
Ekoli
Dem. Rep. of the Congo 0°23S 24°13E 142 C1
Ekoln Sweden 59°45N 17°37E 62 E11
Ekshärad Sweden 60°10N 13°30E 62 D7
Eksjö Sweden 57°40N 14°58E 63 G8
Ekuma → Namibia 18°40S 16°2E 144 A2
Ekwan → Canada 53°12N 82°15W 164 B3
Ekwan Pt. Canada 53°16N 82°7W 164 B3
El Aaiún W. Sahara 27°9N 13°12W 134 C3
El Abanico Chile 37°20S 71°31W 190 D1
El Abiodh-Sidi-Cheikh
Algeria 32°53N 0°31E 136 B4
El Adeb Larache Algeria 27°22N 8°52E 136 C5
El 'Agrûd Egypt 30°14N 34°24E 130 E3
El Aïoun Morocco 34°33N 2°30W 136 B3
El 'Aiyat Egypt 29°36N 31°15E 137 F7
El Alamein Egypt 30°48N 28°58E 137 E6
El Alto Peru 4°15S 81°14W 188 A1
El 'Aqaba, W. → Egypt 30°7N 33°54E 130 E2
El 'Arag Egypt 28°40N 26°20E 137 B2
El Aricha Algeria 34°13N 1°10W 136 B3
El Arīḥā West Bank 31°52N 35°27E 130 D4
El 'Arîsh Egypt 31°8N 33°50E 130 D2
El 'Arîsh, W. → Egypt 31°8N 33°47E 130 D2
El Arrouch Algeria 36°37N 6°53E 136 A5
El Asnam = Ech Chéliff
Algeria 36°10N 1°20E 136 A4
El Astillero Spain 43°24N 3°49W 88 B7
El Badâri Egypt 27°4N 31°25E 137 B3
El Bahrein Egypt 28°30N 26°25E 137 B2
El Ballâs Egypt 26°2N 32°43E 137 B3
El Balyana Egypt 26°10N 32°3E 137 B3
El Baqeir Sudan 18°40N 33°40E 137 D3
El Barco de Ávila Spain 40°21N 5°31W 88 E5
El Barco de Valdeorras = O Barco
Spain 42°23N 6°58W 88 C4
El Bauga Sudan 18°18N 33°52E 137 D3
El Bawiti Egypt 28°25N 28°45E 137 F6
El Bayadh Algeria 33°40N 1°1E 136 B4
El Bayadh □ Algeria 32°30N 1°10E 136 B4
El Bierzo Spain 42°45N 6°30W 88 C4
El Bluff Nic. 11°59N 83°40W 182 D3
El Bolsón Argentina 41°55S 71°30W 192 B2
El Bonillo Spain 38°57N 2°35W 91 G2
El Burgo de Osma Spain 41°35N 3°4W 90 D1
El Caín Argentina 41°38S 68°19W 192 B3
El Cajon U.S.A. 32°48N 116°58W 171 N10
El Calafate Argentina 50°19S 72°15W 192 D2
El Campello Spain 38°26N 0°24W 91 G4
El Campo U.S.A. 29°12N 96°16W 176 G6
El Capitan U.S.A. 37°44N 119°38E 170 H7
El Carbón Honduras 15°25N 85°32W 182 C2
El Carmen Colombia 9°43N 75°8W 186 B3
El Centro U.S.A. 32°48N 115°34W 171 N11
El Cerro Bolivia 17°30S 61°40W 186 G6
El Cerro de Andévalo
Spain 37°45N 6°57W 89 H4
El Compadre Mexico 32°20N 116°14W 171 N10
El Corcovado Argentina 43°25S 71°35W 192 B2
El Coronil Spain 37°5N 5°38W 89 H5
El Cuy Argentina 39°55S 68°25W 192 A3
El Cuyo Mexico 21°31N 87°41W 181 C7
El Dab'a Egypt 31°0N 28°27E 137 E6
El Daheir Egypt 31°13N 34°10E 130 D3
El Deir Egypt 25°25N 32°20E 137 B3
El Descanso Mexico 32°12N 116°58W 171 N10
El Desemboque Mexico 30°33N 113°1W 180 A2
El Dilingat Egypt 30°50N 30°31E 137 E7
El Diviso Colombia 1°22N 78°14W 186 C3
El Djouf Mauritania 21°25N 6°40W 134 D4
El Dorado Mexico 24°17N 107°21W 180 C3
El Dorado Ark., U.S.A. 33°12N 92°40W 176 E8
El Dorado Kans., U.S.A. 37°49N 96°52W 172 G5
El Dorado Venezuela 6°55N 61°37W 186 B6
El Dorado Springs
U.S.A. 37°52N 94°1W 172 G6
El Eglab Algeria 26°20N 4°30W 136 C3
El Ejido Spain 36°47N 2°49W 89 J8
El Escorial Spain 40°35N 4°7W 88 E6
El Espinar Spain 41°43N 4°15W 88 D6
El Eulma Algeria 36°9N 5°42E 136 A5
El Faiyûm Egypt 29°19N 30°50E 137 F7
El Faourar Tunisia 33°22N 8°45E 136 B5
El Fâsher Sudan 13°33N 25°26E 135 F11
El Fashn Egypt 28°50N 30°54E 137 F7
El Ferrol = Ferrol Spain 43°29N 8°15W 88 B2
El Fuerte Mexico 26°25N 108°39W 180 B3
El Gedida Egypt 25°40N 28°30E 137 B2
El Geneina = Al Junaynah
Sudan 13°27N 22°45E 135 F10
El Gezira □ Sudan 15°0N 33°0E 135 F12
El Gir Sudan 19°50N 28°18E 137 D2
El Gîza Egypt 30°0N 31°12E 137 F7
El Gogorrón △
Mexico 21°49N 100°57W 180 C4
El Goléa Algeria 30°30N 2°50E 136 B4
El Gouna Egypt 27°5N 33°47E 137 B3
El Guácharo △
Venezuela 10°8N 63°21W 183 D7
El Guache △ Venezuela 9°45N 69°30W 183 E6
El Hadjira Algeria 32°36N 5°30E 136 B5
El Hâi Egypt 29°39N 31°18E 137 F7
El Hajeb Morocco 33°43N 5°13W 136 B2
El Hamma Tunisia 33°54N 9°48E 136 B5
El Hammam Egypt 30°52N 29°25E 137 E6
El Homr Algeria 29°43N 1°45E 136 C4
El 'Idisât Egypt 25°30N 32°35E 137 B3
El Iskandarîya Egypt 31°13N 29°58E 137 H6
El Istiwa'iya Sudan 5°0N 28°0E 135 G11
El Jadida Morocco 33°11N 8°17W 136 B2
El Jardal Honduras 14°54N 88°50W 182 D2
El Jebha Morocco 35°11N 4°43W 136 A3
El Jem Tunisia 35°19N 10°41E 136 A6
El Kab Sudan 19°27N 32°46E 137 D3
El Kafr el Sharqi Egypt 31°16N 31°10E 137 E7
El Kala Algeria 36°53N 8°26E 136 A5
El Kantara Algeria 35°14N 5°45E 136 A5
El Kantara Tunisia 33°45N 10°58E 136 B6
El Karaba Sudan 18°32N 33°41E 137 D3
El Kef Tunisia 36°12N 8°47E 136 A5
El Kef □ Tunisia 36°0N 9°0E 136 A5
El Kelaâ de Srahna
Morocco 32°4N 7°27W 136 B2
El Kelaâ M'Gouna
Morocco 31°14N 6°7W 136 B2
El Khandaq Sudan 18°30N 30°30E 137 D3
El Khanka Egypt 30°13N 31°21E 137 E7
El Khârga Egypt 25°30N 30°33E 137 B3
El Khartûm Sudan 15°31N 32°35E 135 E12
El Khartûm Bahrî
Sudan 15°40N 32°31E 135 E12
El Khroub Algeria 36°10N 6°55E 136 A5
El Kseur Algeria 36°46N 4°49E 136 A4
El Ksiba Morocco 32°45N 6°1W 136 B2
El Kuntilla Egypt 30°1N 34°45E 130 E3
El Leoncito △
Argentina 31°58S 69°10W 190 C2
El Lucero Mexico 30°37N 106°31W 180 A3
El Maestrazgo Spain 40°30N 0°25W 90 E4
El Maghra Egypt 30°15N 28°55E 137 E6
El Mahalla el Kubra
Egypt 31°0N 31°0E 137 E7
El Mahârîq Egypt 25°35N 30°35E 137 B3
El Maîmûn Egypt 29°14N 31°12E 137 F7
El Maitén Argentina 42°3S 71°10W 192 B2
El Maiz Algeria 28°19N 0°9W 136 C3
El Maks el Bahari
Egypt 24°30N 30°40E 137 C3
El Malpais △ U.S.A. 34°53N 108°0W 169 J10
El Manshâh Egypt 26°26N 31°50E 137 B3
El Mansour Algeria 27°47N 0°14W 136 C3
El Mansûra Egypt 31°0N 31°19E 137 E7
El Manzala Egypt 31°10N 31°50E 137 E7
El Marâgha Egypt 26°35N 31°10E 137 B3
El Masnou Spain 41°28N 2°20E 90 D7
El Matarîya Egypt 31°15N 32°0E 137 E8
El Medano Canary Is. 28°3N 16°32W 100 F3
El Meghaier Algeria 33°55N 5°58E 136 B5
El Ménia = El Goléa
Algeria 30°30N 2°50E 136 B4
El Meraguen Algeria 28°0N 0°7W 136 C3
El Milagro Argentina 30°59S 65°59W 190 C2
El Milia Algeria 36°51N 6°13E 136 A5
El Minyâ Egypt 28°7N 30°33E 137 F7
El Monte U.S.A. 34°4N 118°1W 171 L8
El Montseny Spain 41°55N 2°25E 90 D7
El Mreyye Mauritania 18°0N 6°0W 138 B3
El Obeid Sudan 13°8N 30°10E 135 F12
El Odaiya Sudan 12°8N 28°12E 135 F11
El Oro Mexico 19°51N 100°7W 181 D4
El Oued Algeria 33°20N 6°58E 136 B5
El Oued □ Algeria 33°10N 7°15E 136 B5
El Palmar △ Argentina 32°10S 58°31W 190 C4
El Paso U.S.A. 31°45N 106°29W 176 F1
El Paso de Robles = Paso Robles
U.S.A. 35°38N 120°41W 170 K6
El Pedernoso Spain 39°29N 2°45W 91 F2
El Pedroso Spain 37°51N 5°45W 89 H5
El Pinacate y Gran Desierto de
Altar = Gran Desierto del
Pinacate ⌂ Mexico 31°51N 113°32W 180 A2
El Pobo de Dueñas Spain 40°46N 1°39W 90 E3
El Portal U.S.A. 37°41N 119°47W 170 H7
El Porvenir Mexico 31°15N 105°51W 180 A3
El Prat Barcelona ✕ (BCN)
Spain 41°18N 2°5E 90 D7
El Prat de Llobregat Spain 41°19N 2°5E 90 D7
El Progreso Honduras 15°26N 87°51W 182 C2
El Pueblo Canary Is. 28°36N 17°47W 100 F2
El Puente del Arzobispo
Spain 39°48N 5°10W 88 F5
El Puerto de Santa María
Spain 36°36N 6°13W 89 J4
El Qâhira Egypt 30°2N 31°13E 137 E7
El Qantara Egypt 30°51N 32°20E 130 E1
El Qasr Egypt 25°44N 28°42E 137 B2
El Qubâbât Egypt 29°28N 31°16E 137 F7
El Quseima Egypt 30°40N 34°15E 130 E3
El Qusîya Egypt 27°29N 30°44E 137 B3
El Râshda Egypt 25°36N 28°57E 137 B2
El Real de Santa María
Panama 8°0N 77°40W 186 B3
El Reno U.S.A. 35°32N 97°57W 167 H20
El Rey △ Argentina 24°40S 64°34W 190 A3
El Rîdisiya Egypt 24°56N 32°51E 137 C3
El Rio U.S.A. 34°14N 119°10W 171 L7
El Ronquillo Spain 37°44N 6°10W 89 H4
El Roque, Pta.
Canary Is. 28°10N 15°25W 100 F4
El Rosario Mexico 30°1N 115°45W 180 A1
El Rubio Spain 37°22N 5°0W 89 H5
El Saff Egypt 29°34N 31°16E 137 F7
El Salto Mexico 23°47N 105°22W 180 C3
El Salvador ■
Cent. Amer. 13°50N 89°0W 182 D2
El Sauce Nic. 13°0N 86°40W 182 D2
El Saucejo Spain 37°4N 5°6W 89 H5
El Shallal Egypt 24°0N 32°53E 137 C3
El Simbillawein Egypt 30°48N 31°13E 137 E7
El Suweis Egypt 29°58N 32°31E 137 F8
El Tabbin Egypt 29°47N 31°18E 137 F7
El Tamarâni, W. →
Egypt 30°7N 34°43E 130 E3
El Tarf Algeria 36°46N 8°19E 136 A5
El Tarf □ Algeria 36°45N 8°10E 136 A5
El Thamad Egypt 29°40N 34°28E 130 F3
El Tigre Venezuela 8°44N 64°15W 186 B6
El Tîh, Gebel Egypt 29°40N 33°50E 130 F2
El Tîna Egypt 31°3N 32°22E 137 E8
El Tofo Chile 29°22S 71°18W 190 B1
El Tránsito Chile 28°52S 70°17W 190 B1
El Tûr Egypt 28°14N 33°36E 128 D2
El Turbio Argentina 51°45S 72°5W 192 D2
El Uqsur Egypt 25°41N 32°38E 137 B3
El Valle ⌂ Spain 37°56N 1°6W 91 H3
El Vendrell Spain 41°10N 1°30E 90 D6
El Vergel Mexico 26°28N 106°22W 180 B3
El Vigía Venezuela 8°38N 71°39W 186 B4
El Viso del Alcor Spain 37°23N 5°43W 89 H5
El Wabeira Egypt 29°34N 33°6E 130 F2
El Wuz Sudan 15°5N 30°7E 135 E12
Elafonisos Greece 36°29N 22°56E 98 E4
Elamanchili India 17°33N 82°50E 126 F6
Élancourt France 48°47N 1°58E 71 D8
Elands Australia 31°37S 152°20E 153 A10
Elasa Greece 35°18N 26°21E 99 F8
Elassona Greece 39°53N 22°12E 98 B4
Elat Israel 29°30N 34°56E 130 F3
Elatia Greece 38°37N 22°46E 98 C4
Elâzığ Turkey 38°37N 39°14E 105 C8
Elâzığ □ Turkey 38°40N 39°15E 105 C8
Elba Italy 42°46N 10°17E 92 F7
Elba U.S.A. 31°25N 86°4W 178 D3
Elbasan Albania 41°9N 20°9E 96 E4
Elbe U.S.A. 46°45N 122°10W 170 D4
Elbe → Europe 53°50N 9°0E 76 B4
Elbe-Seitenkanal
Germany 52°45N 10°32E 76 C6
Elbert, Mt. U.S.A. 39°7N 106°27W 168 G10
Elberton U.S.A. 34°7N 82°52W 178 A7
Elbeuf France 49°17N 1°2E 70 C8
Elbing = Elbląg Poland 54°10N 19°25E 82 D6
Elbistan Turkey 38°13N 37°15E 104 C7
Elbląg Poland 54°10N 19°25E 82 D6
Elbow Canada 51°7N 106°35W 163 C7
Elbrus Russia 43°21N 42°30E 87 J6
Elbufer-Drawehn ⌂
Germany 53°8N 10°58E 76 B6
Elburz Mts. = Alborz, Reshteh-ye
Kūhhā-ye Iran 36°0N 52°0E 129 C7
Elche Spain 38°15N 0°42W 91 G4
Elche de la Sierra Spain 38°27N 2°3W 91 G2
Elcho I. Australia 11°55S 135°45E 150 A2
Elda Spain 38°29N 0°47W 91 G4
Eldama Ravine Kenya 0°3N 35°43E 142 B4
Elde → Germany 53°7N 11°15E 76 B7
Eldon Mo., U.S.A. 38°21N 92°35W 172 F7
Eldon Wash., U.S.A. 47°33N 123°3W 170 C3
Eldora U.S.A. 42°22N 93°5W 172 D7
Eldorado Argentina 26°28S 54°43W 191 B5
Eldorado Canada 44°35N 77°31W 174 B7
Eldorado Ill., U.S.A. 37°49N 88°26W 172 G9
Eldorado Tex., U.S.A. 30°52N 100°36W 176 F4
Eldorendo U.S.A. 31°3N 84°39W 178 D5
Eldoret Kenya 0°30N 35°17E 142 B4
Eldred U.S.A. 41°58N 78°23W 174 E6
Elea, C. Cyprus 35°19N 34°4E 101 D13
Eleanora, Pk. Australia 32°57S 121°9E 149 F3
Elefantes → Africa 24°10S 32°40E 145 B5
Elefantes, G. Chile 46°28S 73°49W 192 C2
Elefsina Greece 38°4N 23°26E 98 C5
Eleftherios Venizelos ✕ (ATH)
Greece 37°56N 23°56E 98 D5
Elektrogorsk Russia 55°56N 38°50E 84 E10
Elektrostal Russia 55°41N 38°32E 84 E10
Elele Nigeria 5°5N 6°50E 139 D6
Elemi Triangle = Ilemi
Triangle Africa 5°0N 35°20E 142 B4
Elena Bulgaria 42°55N 25°53E 97 D9
Elephant Butte Res.
U.S.A. 33°9N 107°11W 169 K10
Elephant I. Antarctica 61°0S 55°0W 55 C18
Elephant Pass Sri Lanka 9°35N 80°25E 127 K5
Elesbão Veloso Brazil 6°13S 42°8W 189 B2
Eleshnitsa Bulgaria 41°52N 23°36E 96 E7
Eleşkirt Turkey 39°50N 42°50E 105 C10
Eleuthera I. Bahamas 25°0N 76°20W 182 B4
Eleutheroupoli Greece 40°52N 24°20E 97 F8
Elgin Canada 44°36N 76°13W 175 B8
Elgin U.K. 57°39N 3°19W 65 D5
Elgin Ill., U.S.A. 42°2N 88°17W 172 D9
Elgin N. Dak., U.S.A. 46°24N 101°51W 172 B3
Elgin Oreg., U.S.A. 45°34N 117°55W 168 D5
Elgin S.C., U.S.A. 34°10N 80°48W 178 A9
Elgin Tex., U.S.A. 30°21N 97°22W 176 F6
Elgoibar Spain 43°13N 2°24W 90 B2
Elgon, Mt. Africa 1°10N 34°30E 142 B3
Eliase Indonesia 8°21S 130°48E 119 F8
Elikonos Oros Greece 38°18N 22°45E 98 C4
Elim Namibia 17°48S 15°31E 144 A2
Elim S. Africa 34°35S 19°45E 144 D2
Elin Pelin Bulgaria 42°40N 23°36E 96 D7
Elis = Ilia Greece 37°45N 21°35E 98 D3
Eliseu Martins Brazil 8°13S 43°42W 189 B2
Elista Russia 46°16N 44°14E 87 G7
Eliza, L. Australia 37°15S 139°50E 152 D3
Elizabeth Australia 34°42S 138°41E 152 C3
Elizabeth U.S.A. 40°39N 74°12W 175 F10
Elizabeth City U.S.A. 36°18N 76°14W 177 C16
Elizabethton U.S.A. 36°21N 82°13W 177 C13
Elizabethtown Ky.,
U.S.A. 37°42N 85°52W 173 G11
Elizabethtown N.Y.,
U.S.A. 44°13N 73°36W 175 B11
Elizabethtown Pa.,
U.S.A. 40°9N 76°36W 175 F8
Elizondo Spain 43°12N 1°30W 90 B3
Ełk Poland 53°50N 22°21E 82 E9
Elk → Canada 49°11N 115°14W 162 C5
Ełk → Poland 53°41N 22°28E 82 E9
Elk → U.S.A. 34°46N 87°16W 177 D11
Elk City U.S.A. 35°25N 99°25W 176 D5
Elk Creek U.S.A. 39°36N 122°32W 170 F4
Elk Grove U.S.A. 38°25N 121°22W 170 G5
Elk Island △ Canada 53°35N 112°59W 162 C6
Elk Lake Canada 47°40N 80°25W 164 C3
Elk Point Canada 53°54N 110°55W 163 C6
Elk River Idaho, U.S.A. 46°47N 116°11W 168 C5
Elk River Minn., U.S.A. 45°18N 93°35W 172 C7
Elkedra → Australia 21°8S 136°22E 150 C2
Elkhart Ind., U.S.A. 41°41N 85°58W 173 E11
Elkhart Kans., U.S.A. 37°0N 101°54W 172 G3
Elkhorn Canada 49°59N 101°14W 163 D8
Elkhorn → U.S.A. 41°8N 96°19W 172 E5
Elkhovo Bulgaria 42°10N 26°35E 97 D10
Elkin U.S.A. 36°15N 80°51W 177 C14
Elkins U.S.A. 38°55N 79°51W 173 F14
Elkland U.S.A. 41°59N 77°19W 174 E7
Elko Canada 49°20N 115°10W 162 D5
Elko U.S.A. 40°50N 115°46W 168 F6
Elkton U.S.A. 43°49N 83°11W 174 C1
Ellas = Greece ■ Europe 40°0N 23°0E 98 B3
Ellaville Fla., U.S.A. 30°23N 83°10W 178 E6
Ellaville Ga., U.S.A. 32°14N 84°19W 178 C5
Ellef Ringnes I.
Canada 78°30N 102°2W 161 B11
Ellen, Mt. U.S.A. 44°9N 72°56W 175 B12
Ellenburg U.S.A. 44°54N 73°48W 175 B11
Ellendale U.S.A. 46°0N 98°32W 172 B4
Ellensburg U.S.A. 46°59N 120°34W 168 C3
Ellenville U.S.A. 41°43N 74°24W 175 E10
Ellerton Barbados 13°7N 59°33W 183 g
Ellery, Mt. Australia 37°28S 148°47E 153 D8
Ellesmere, L. N.Z. 43°47S 172°28E 155 D7
Ellesmere I. Canada 79°30N 80°0W 161 B16
Ellesmere Island = Quttinirpaaq △
Canada 82°13N 72°13W 161 A17
Ellesmere Port U.K. 53°17N 2°54W 66 D5
Ellice Is. = Tuvalu ■
Pac. Oc. 8°0S 178°0E 147 B10
Ellicottville U.S.A. 42°17N 78°40W 174 D6
Ellington U.S.A. 42°13N 79°6W 174 D5
Elliot Australia 17°33S 133°32E 150 B1
Elliot S. Africa 31°22S 27°48E 145 D4
Elliot Lake Canada 46°25N 82°35W 164 C3
Elliotdale = Xhora
S. Africa 31°55S 28°38E 145 D4
Elliott U.S.A. 34°6N 80°10W 178 A9
Elliott Key U.S.A. 25°27N 80°12W 179 K9
Ellis U.S.A. 38°56N 99°34W 172 F4
Elliston Australia 33°39S 134°53E 151 E1
Ellisville U.S.A. 31°36N 89°12W 177 F10
Ellon U.K. 57°22N 2°4W 65 D6
Ellora India 20°1N 75°10E 126 D2
Ellore = Eluru India 16°48N 81°8E 126 F5
Elloree U.S.A. 33°32N 80°34W 178 B9
Ellsworth Kans., U.S.A. 38°44N 98°14W 172 F4
Ellsworth Maine,
U.S.A. 44°33N 68°25W 173 C19
Ellsworth Land
Antarctica 76°0S 89°0W 55 D16
Ellsworth Mts.
Antarctica 78°30S 85°0W 55 D16
Ellwangen Germany 48°57N 10°8E 77 G6
Ellwood City U.S.A. 40°52N 80°17W 174 F4
Ellzey U.S.A. 29°19N 82°48W 179 F7
Elm Switz. 46°54N 9°10E 77 J5
Elm-Lappwald ⌂
Germany 52°15N 10°50E 76 C6
Elma Canada 49°52N 95°55W 163 D9
Elma U.S.A. 47°0N 123°25W 170 D3
Elmadağ Turkey 39°55N 33°14E 104 C5
Elmalı Turkey 36°44N 29°56E 99 E11
Elmhurst U.S.A. 41°53N 87°56W 172 E10
Elmina Ghana 5°5N 1°21W 139 D4
Elmira Canada 43°36N 80°33W 174 C4
Elmira U.S.A. 42°6N 76°48W 174 D8
Elmira Heights U.S.A. 42°8N 76°50W 174 D8
Elmodel U.S.A. 31°21N 84°29W 178 D5
Elmore Australia 36°30S 144°37E 152 D6
Elmore U.S.A. 32°32N 86°19W 178 C3
Elmshorn Germany 53°43N 9°40E 76 B5
Elmvale Canada 44°35N 79°52W 174 B5
Elne France 42°36N 2°58E 72 F6
Elora Canada 43°41N 80°26W 174 C4
Elos Greece 36°46N 22°43E 98 E4
Elounda Greece 35°16N 25°42E 101 D7
Eloy U.S.A. 32°45N 111°33W 169 K8
Éloyes France 48°6N 6°36E 71 D13
Elphin Canada 44°55N 76°37W 175 B8
Elpitiya Sri Lanka 6°17N 80°10E 127 L5
Elrose Canada 51°12N 108°0W 163 C7
Elsby △ Australia 14°55S 133°10E 148 B5
Elsdorf Germany 50°55N 6°34E 76 E2
Elsie U.S.A. 45°52N 123°36W 170 E3
Elsinore = Helsingør
Denmark 56°2N 12°35E 63 H6
Elster → Germany 51°25N 11°57E 76 D7
Elsterwerda Germany 51°27N 13°31E 76 D9
Eltanin Fracture Zone System
S. Ocean 54°0S 130°0W 55 B14
Eltham N.Z. 39°26S 174°19E 154 F3
Elton Russia 49°5N 46°52E 87 F8
Elton, Ozero Russia 49°5N 46°42E 87 F8
Eltville Germany 50°2N 8°7E 77 E4
Eluru India 16°48N 81°8E 126 F5
Elvas Portugal 38°50N 7°10W 89 G3
Elven France 47°44N 2°36W 70 E4
Elverum Norway 60°53N 11°34E 60 F14
Elvire → Australia 17°51S 128°11E 148 C4
Elvire, Mt. Australia 29°22S 119°36E 149 E2
Elvo → Italy 45°23N 8°21E 92 C5
Elwell, L. = Tiber Res.
U.S.A. 48°19N 111°6W 168 B8
Elwood Ind., U.S.A. 40°17N 85°50W 173 E11
Elwood Nebr., U.S.A. 40°36N 99°52W 172 E4
Elx = Elche Spain 38°15N 0°42W 91 G4
Ely U.K. 52°24N 0°16E 67 E8
Ely Minn., U.S.A. 47°55N 91°51W 172 B8
Ely Nev., U.S.A. 39°15N 114°54W 168 G6
Elyria U.S.A. 41°22N 82°7W 174 E2
Elyros Greece 35°15N 23°45E 98 F5
Elz → Germany 48°18N 7°44E 77 G3
Emajõgi → Estonia 58°25N 27°20E 84 C4
eMakhazeni S. Africa 25°42S 30°2E 145 C5
eMalahleni S. Africa 25°51S 29°14E 145 C4
Emāmrūd Iran 36°30N 55°0E 129 B7
Emån → Sweden 57°8N 16°30E 63 G10
eMbalenhle S. Africa 26°32S 29°4E 145 C4
Embarcación Argentina 23°10S 64°0W 190 A3
Embetsu Japan 44°44N 141°47E 112 B10
Embi Kazakhstan 48°50N 58°8E 108 C5
Embi → Kazakhstan 46°55N 53°28E 108 C4
Embonas Greece 36°13N 27°51E 101 C9
Embro Canada 43°9N 80°54W 174 C4
Embrun France 44°34N 6°30E 73 D10
Embu Kenya 0°32S 37°38E 142 C4
Emden Germany 53°21N 7°12E 76 B3
Emecik Turkey 36°46N 27°49E 99 E9
Emei Shan China 29°32N 103°46E 116 C4
Emeishan China 29°31N 103°23E 116 C4
Emerald Australia 23°32S 148°10E 150 C4
Emerald I. Canada 76°48N 114°10W 161 B9
Émeraude, Côte d'
France 48°45N 2°40W 70 D4
Emerson Canada 49°0N 97°10W 163 D9
Emerson U.S.A. 34°8N 84°45W 178 A5
Emet Turkey 39°20N 29°15E 99 B11
Emgwenya S. Africa 25°40S 30°18E 145 C5
Emi Koussi Chad 19°45N 18°55E 135 E9
Emilia-Romagna □ Italy 44°45N 11°0E 92 D8
Emilius, Mte. Italy 45°45N 7°20E 92 C4
Emin China 46°34N 83°36E 109 C10
Eminabad Pakistan 32°2N 74°8E 124 C6
Emine, Nos Bulgaria 42°40N 27°56E 97 D11
Emirdağ Turkey 39°2N 31°8E 104 C4
Emissi, Tarso Chad 21°27N 18°36E 135 D9
Emlenton U.S.A. 41°11N 79°43W 174 E5
Emlichheim Germany 52°37N 6°51E 76 C2
Emmaboda Sweden 56°37N 15°32E 63 H9
Emmalane U.S.A. 32°46N 82°0W 178 C7
Emmaus S. Africa 29°2S 25°15E 144 C4
Emmaus U.S.A. 40°32N 75°30W 175 F9
Emme → Switz. 47°14N 7°32E 77 H3
Emmeloord Neths. 52°44N 5°46E 69 B5
Emmen Neths. 52°48N 6°57E 69 B6
Emmen Switz. 47°5N 8°18E 77 H4
Emmendingen Germany 48°6N 7°51E 77 G3
Emmental Switz. 46°55N 7°40E 77 J3
Emmerich Germany 51°50N 6°14E 76 D2
Emmet Australia 24°45S 144°30E 150 C3
Emmetsburg U.S.A. 43°7N 94°41W 172 D6
Emmett Idaho, U.S.A. 43°52N 116°30W 168 E5
Emmett Mich., U.S.A. 42°59N 82°46W 174 D2
Emmiganuru = Yemmiganur
India 15°44N 77°29E 127 G3
Emmonak U.S.A. 62°47N 164°31W 166 C7
Emo Canada 48°38N 93°50W 163 D10
Emőd Hungary 47°57N 20°47E 80 C5
Emona Bulgaria 42°43N 27°53E 97 D11
Empalme Mexico 27°58N 110°51W 180 B2
Empangeni S. Africa 28°50S 31°52E 145 C5
Empedrado Argentina 28°0S 58°46W 190 B4
Emperor Seamount Chain
Pac. Oc. 40°0N 170°0E 156 D9
Emperor Trough
Pac. Oc. 43°0N 175°30E 156 C9
Empire U.S.A. 32°21N 83°18W 178 C6
Empoli Italy 43°43N 10°57E 92 E7
Emporia Kans., U.S.A. 38°25N 96°11W 172 F5
Emporia Va., U.S.A. 36°42N 77°32W 173 G15
Emporium U.S.A. 41°31N 78°14W 174 E6
Empress Canada 50°57N 110°0W 163 C7
Empty Quarter = Rub' al Khālī
Si. Arabia 19°0N 48°0E 131 D4
Ems → Germany 53°20N 7°12E 76 B3
Emsdale Canada 45°32N 79°19W 174 A5
Emsdetten Germany 52°10N 7°32E 76 C3
Emu China 43°40N 128°6E 115 C15
Emu Park Australia 23°13S 150°50E 150 C5
eMuziwezinto S. Africa 30°15S 30°45E 145 D5
'En 'Avrona Israel 29°43N 35°0E 130 F4
'En Boqeq Israel 31°12N 35°21E 129 D4
'En Gedi Israel 31°28N 35°25E 130 D4
En Nahud Sudan 12°45N 28°25E 135 F11
Ena Japan 35°25N 137°25E 113 G8
Enånger Sweden 61°30N 17°9E 62 C11
Enard B. U.K. 58°5N 5°20W 65 C3
Enare träsk = Inarijärvi
Finland 69°0N 28°0E 60 B23
Enarotali Indonesia 3°55S 136°21E 119 E9
Encampment U.S.A. 41°12N 106°47W 168 F10
Encantadas, Serra
Brazil 30°40S 53°0W 191 C5
Encarnación Paraguay 27°15S 55°50W 191 B4
Encarnación de Díaz
Mexico 21°31N 102°14W 180 C4
Enchi Ghana 5°53N 2°48W 138 D4
Encinitas U.S.A. 33°3N 117°17W 171 M9
Encino U.S.A. 34°39N 105°28W 169 J11
Encounter B. Australia 35°45S 138°45E 152 C3
Encruzilhada Brazil 15°31S 40°54W 189 D2
Encs Hungary 48°20N 21°8E 80 B6
Endako Canada 54°6N 125°2W 162 C3
Endau Kenya 1°18S 38°31E 142 C4
Endau Rompin △
Malaysia 2°27N 103°45E 121 L4
Ende Indonesia 8°45S 121°40E 119 F6
Endeavour Str.
Australia 10°45S 142°0E 150 A3
Endelave Denmark 55°46N 10°18E 63 J4
Enderbury Kiribati 3°8S 171°5W 156 H10
Enderby Canada 50°35N 119°10W 162 C5
Enderby Abyssal Plain
S. Ocean 60°0S 40°0E 55 C5
Enderby I. Australia 20°35S 116°30E 148 D2
Enderby Land Antarctica 66°0S 53°0E 55 C5
Enderlin U.S.A. 46°38N 97°36W 172 B5
Enderrocat, C. Spain 39°28N 2°43E 100 B9
Endicott U.S.A. 42°6N 76°4W 175 D8
Endicott Mts. U.S.A. 68°0N 152°0W 166 B9
Endimari → Brazil 8°46S 66°7W 188 B4
Endwell U.S.A. 42°6N 76°2W 175 D8
Endyalgout I. Australia 11°40S 132°35E 148 B5
Ené → Peru 11°10S 74°18W 188 C3
Eneabba Australia 29°49S 115°16E 149 E2
Enerhodar Ukraine 47°30N 34°28E 85 J8
Enewetak Atoll
Marshall Is. 11°30N 162°15E 156 F8
Enez Turkey 40°45N 26°5E 97 F10
Enfer, Pte. d' Martinique 14°22N 60°54W 182 c
Enfield Canada 44°56N 63°32W 165 D7
Enfield Conn., U.S.A. 41°58N 72°36W 175 E12
Enfield N.C., U.S.A. 36°11N 77°41W 177 C16
Enfield N.H., U.S.A. 43°39N 72°9W 175 C12
Engadin Switz. 46°45N 10°10E 77 J6
Engaño, C. Dom. Rep. 18°30N 68°20W 183 C6
Engaño, C. Phil. 18°35N 122°23E 119 A6
Engaru Japan 44°3N 143°31E 112 B11
Engcobo = Ngcobo
S. Africa 31°37S 28°0E 145 D4
Engelberg Switz. 46°48N 8°26E 77 J4
Engels Russia 51°28N 46°6E 86 E8
Engelsberg = Ängelsberg
Sweden 59°58N 16°0E 62 E10
Engemann L. Canada 58°0N 106°55W 163 B7
Enggano Indonesia 5°20S 102°40E 118 F2
England U.S.A. 34°33N 91°58W 176 D9
England □ U.K. 53°0N 2°0W 67 E5
Englee Canada 50°45N 56°5W 165 B8
Englehart Canada 47°49N 79°52W 164 C4
Englewood U.S.A. 26°58N 82°21W 179 J7
English → Canada 49°12N 91°5W 163 C10
English Bazar = Ingraj Bazar
India 24°58N 88°10E 125 G13
English Channel Europe 50°0N 2°0W 67 G6
English Company's Is., The
Australia 11°50S 136°32E 150 A2
English River Canada 49°14N 91°0W 164 C1
Engures ezers Latvia 57°16N 23°6E 82 A10
Enguri → Georgia 42°27N 41°38E 87 J5
Enid U.S.A. 36°24N 97°53W 176 C6
Enipeas → Greece 39°22N 22°17E 98 B4
Eniwa Japan 43°0N 141°30E 112 C10
Enkhuizen Neths. 52°42N 5°17E 69 B5
Enköping Sweden 59°37N 17°4E 62 E11
Enle China 24°0N 101°9E 116 F3
Enna Italy 37°34N 14°16E 95 E7
Ennadai L. Canada 60°58N 101°20W 163 A8
Ennedi Chad 17°15N 22°0E 135 E10
Enngonia Australia 29°21S 145°50E 151 D4
Ennigerloh Germany 51°50N 8°2E 76 D4
Ennis Ireland 52°51N 8°59W 64 D3
Ennis Mont., U.S.A. 45°21N 111°44W 168 D8
Ennis Tex., U.S.A. 32°20N 96°38W 176 E6
Enniscorthy Ireland 52°30N 6°34W 64 D5
Enniskillen U.K. 54°21N 7°39W 64 B4
Ennistimon Ireland 52°57N 9°17W 64 D2
Enns Austria 48°12N 14°28E 78 C7
Enns → Austria 48°14N 14°32E 78 C7
Eno Finland 62°47N 30°10E 60 E24
Enosburg Falls U.S.A. 44°55N 72°48W 175 B12
Enping China 22°16N 112°21E 117 F9
Enriquillo, L. Dom. Rep. 18°20N 71°40W 183 C5
Enschede Neths. 52°13N 6°53E 69 B6
Ensenada Argentina 34°55S 57°55W 190 C4
Ensenada Chile 41°12S 72°33W 192 B2
Ensenada Mexico 31°52N 116°37W 180 A1
Ensenada de los Muertos
Mexico 23°59N 109°51W 180 C2
Enshi China 30°18N 109°29E 116 B7
Ensiola, Pta. de n' Spain 39°7N 2°55E 100 B9
Ensisheim France 47°50N 7°20E 71 E14
Ensley U.S.A. 30°31N 87°16W 179 E2
Entebbe Uganda 0°4N 32°28E 142 B3
Enterprise Canada 60°47N 115°45W 162 A5
Enterprise Ala., U.S.A. 31°19N 85°51W 178 D4
Enterprise Oreg.,
U.S.A. 45°25N 117°17W 168 D5
Entorno de Doñana ⌂
Spain 37°0N 6°26W 89 J4
Entrance, The
Australia 33°21S 151°30E 153 B9
Entraygues-sur-Truyère
France 44°38N 2°35E 72 D6
Entre Ríos Bolivia 21°30S 64°25W 190 A3
Entre Ríos Brazil 11°56S 38°5W 189 C3
Entre Ríos □ Argentina 30°30S 58°30W 190 C4
Entrepeñas, Embalse de
Spain 40°34N 2°42W 90 E2
Entroncamento Portugal 39°28N 8°28W 89 F2
Enugu Nigeria 6°30N 7°30E 139 D6
Enugu □ Nigeria 6°30N 7°45E 139 D6
Enugu Ezike Nigeria 7°0N 7°29E 139 D6
Enumclaw U.S.A. 47°12N 121°59W 170 C5
Envalira, Port d' Europe 42°33N 1°43E 90 C6
Envermeu France 49°53N 1°15E 70 C8
Enviken Sweden 60°49N 15°46E 62 D9
Envira Brazil 7°18S 70°13W 188 B3
Envira → Brazil 7°19S 70°15W 188 B3
Enying Hungary 46°56N 18°15E 80 D3
Enza → Italy 44°54N 10°31E 92 D7
Eochaill = Youghal
Ireland 51°56N 7°52W 64 E4
Eólie, Ís. Italy 38°30N 14°57E 95 D7
Epanomi Greece 40°25N 22°59E 96 F6
Epe Neths. 52°21N 5°59E 69 B5
Epe Nigeria 6°36N 3°59E 139 D5
Épernay France 49°3N 3°56E 71 C10
Épernon France 48°35N 1°40E 71 D8
Ephesus Turkey 37°55N 27°22E 99 D9
Ephraim U.S.A. 39°22N 111°35W 168 G8
Ephrata Pa., U.S.A. 40°11N 76°11W 175 F8
Ephrata Wash., U.S.A. 47°19N 119°33W 168 C4
Epidaurus = Epidavros
Greece 37°40N 23°7E 98 D5
Epidavros Greece 37°40N 23°7E 98 D5
Epidavros Limira Greece 36°46N 23°0E 98 E5
Épila Spain 41°36N 1°17W 90 D3
Épinal France 48°10N 6°27E 71 D13

Epiros □ Greece 39°30N 20°30E **98** B2
Episkopi Cyprus 34°40N 32°54E **101** E11
Episkopi Greece 35°20N 24°20E **101** D6
Episkopi Bay Cyprus 34°35N 32°50E **101** E11
Epitalio Greece 37°37N 21°30E **98** D3
Eppalock, L. Australia 36°52S 144°34E **152** D6
Eppan = Appiano Italy 46°27N 11°15E **93** B8
Eppingen Germany 49°8N 8°53E **77** F4
Epsom U.K. 51°19N 0°16W **67** F7
Epukiro Namibia 21°40S 19°9E **144** B2
Equatoria = El Istiwa'iya
  Sudan 5°0N 28°0E **135** G11
Equatorial Guinea ■ Africa 2°0N 8°0E **140** D1
Er Hai China 25°48N 100°11E **116** E3
Er Rachidia Morocco 31°58N 4°20W **136** B3
Er Rahad Sudan 12°45N 30°32E **135** F12
Er Rif Morocco 35°1N 4°1W **136** A3
Er Rogel Sudan 18°10N 35°25E **137** D4
Eraclea Italy 45°35N 12°40E **93** C9
Erandol India 20°56N 75°20E **126** D2
Erāwadi Myit = Irrawaddy ➤
  Burma 15°50N 95°6E **123** M19
Erāwadi Myitwanya = Irrawaddy,
  Mouths of the
  Burma 15°30N 95°0E **123** N19
Erawan △ Thailand 14°25N 98°58E **120** E2
Erba Italy 45°48N 9°15E **92** C6
Erba Sudan 19°5N 36°51E **137** D4
Erba, J. Sudan 20°48N 36°47E **137** C4
Erbaa Turkey 40°42N 36°36E **104** A7
Erbeng Shan China 42°50N 84°59E **109** D10
Erbeskopf Germany 49°44N 7°2E **77** F3
Erbil = Arbīl Iraq 36°15N 44°5E **105** D11
Erçek Turkey 38°39N 43°36E **128** B4
Erçiş Turkey 39°2N 43°21E **105** C10
Ercıyaş Dağı Turkey 38°30N 35°30E **128** B2
Érd Hungary 47°22N 18°56E **80** C3
Erdao Jiang ➤ China 42°37N 128°0E **115** C14
Erdek Turkey 40°23N 27°47E **97** F11
Erdemli Turkey 36°36N 34°19E **104** D6
Erdene = Ulaan-Uul
  Mongolia 46°4N 100°49E **114** B6
Erdenet Mongolia 49°2N 104°5E **110** B9
Erdenetsogt Mongolia 42°55N 106°5E **114** C4
Erding Germany 48°18N 11°54E **77** G7
Erdre ➤ France 47°13N 1°32W **70** E5
Erebus, Mt. Antarctica 77°35S 167°0E **55** D11
Erechim Brazil 27°35S 52°15W **191** B5
Ereğli Konya, Turkey 37°31N 34°4E **104** D6
Ereğli Zonguldak, Turkey 41°15N 31°24E **104** B4
Erei, Monti Italy 37°20N 14°20E **95** E7
Erenhot China 43°48N 112°2E **114** C7
Eresma ➤ Spain 41°26N 4°45W **88** D6
Eresos Greece 39°11N 25°57E **99** B7
Ereymentaū Kazakhstan 51°37N 73°6E **109** B8
Erfelek Turkey 41°53N 34°55E **104** B6
Erfenisdam S. Africa 28°30S 26°50E **144** A2
Erfoud Morocco 31°30N 4°15W **136** B3
Erftstadt Germany 50°50N 6°0E **76** E2
Erft ➤ Germany 51°11N 6°44E **76** D2
Erfurt Germany 50°58N 11°2E **76** E7
Ergani Turkey 38°17N 39°49E **105** C8
Ergel Mongolia 43°8N 109°5E **114** C5
Ergene ➤ Turkey 41°1N 26°22E **97** E10
Ergeni Vozvyshennost
  Russia 47°0N 44°0E **87** G7
Ērgļi Latvia 56°54N 25°38E **84** D3
Ergun He = Argun ➤
  Russia 53°20N 121°28E **111** A13
Ergun Youqi China 50°15N 120°11E **111** A13
Erhlin Taiwan 23°54N 120°22E **117** F13
Eria ➤ Spain 42°3N 5°44W **88** C5
Eriboll, L. U.K. 58°30N 4°42W **65** C4
Érice Italy 38°2N 12°35E **94** D5
Eridu U.S.A. 30°18N 83°45W **178** F6
Erie U.S.A. 42°8N 80°5W **174** D4
Erie, L. N. Amer. 42°15N 81°0W **174** D4
Erie Canal U.S.A. 43°5N 78°43W **174** C7
Erieau Canada 42°16N 81°57W **174** D3
Erigavo = Ceerigaabo
  Somalia 10°35N 47°20E **131** E4
Erikoussa Greece 39°53N 19°34E **101** A3
Eriksdale Canada 50°52N 98°7W **163** C9
Erimanthos Greece 37°57N 21°50E **98** D3
Erimo-Misaki Japan 41°50N 143°15E **112** D11
Erin Canada 43°45N 80°7W **174** C4
Erin Pt. Trin. & Tob. 10°3N 61°39W **187** K15
Erinpura India 25°9N 73°3E **124** G5
Eriskay U.K. 57°4N 7°18W **65** D1
Erithres Greece 38°13N 23°20E **98** C5
Eritrea ■ Africa 14°0N 38°30E **135** F13
Erjas ➤ Portugal 39°40N 7°1W **88** F3
Erkech-Tam Pass Asia 39°46N 74°2E **109** E8
Erkelenz Germany 51°4N 6°19E **76** D1
Erkner Germany 52°25N 13°44E **76** C9
Erlangen Germany 49°36N 11°0E **77** F6
Erldunda Australia 25°14S 133°12E **150** D1
Ermelo Neths. 52°18N 5°35E **69** B5
Ermelo S. Africa 26°31S 29°59E **145** C4
Ermenek Turkey 36°38N 33°0E **104** D5
Ermioni Greece 37°23N 23°15E **98** D5
Ermoupoli Greece 37°28N 24°57E **98** D6
Ernakulam India 9°59N 76°22E **127** K3
Erne ➤ Ireland 54°30N 8°16W **64** B3
Erne, Lower L. U.K. 54°28N 7°47W **64** B4
Erne, Upper L. U.K. 54°14N 7°32W **64** B4
Ernée France 48°18N 0°56W **70** D6
Ernest Giles Ra.
  Australia 27°0S 123°45E **149** E3
Ernstberg Germany 50°13N 6°47E **77** E2
Erode India 11°24N 77°45E **127** J3
Eromanga Australia 26°40S 143°11E **151** D3
Erongo Namibia 21°39S 15°58E **144** B2
Erongo ➤ Namibia 22°20S 15°0E **144** B2
Erquy France 48°38N 2°29W **70** D4
Erramala Hills India 15°30N 78°15E **127** G4
Errentería Spain 43°19N 1°54W **90** B3
Errigal Ireland 55°2N 8°6W **64** A3
Errinundra △
  Australia 37°0S 148°47E **153** D8
Errol U.S.A. 44°47N 71°8W **177** B13
Errenaría Spain 43°19N 1°54W **90** B3
Erris Hd. Ireland 54°17N 10°0W **64** B1
Ersekë Albania 40°22N 20°40E **98** B3
Erskine U.S.A. 47°40N 96°0W **172** B6
Erstein France 48°25N 7°38E **71** D4
Ertai China 46°30N 90°9E **109** C12
Ertil Russia 51°55N 40°50E **86** E5
Ertis = Irtysh ➤ Russia 61°4N 68°52E **106** C7
Ertis Kazakhstan 52°20N 75°27E **109** B9

Ertis ➤ Kazakhstan 47°52N 84°16E **109** C10
Eruh Turkey 37°46N 42°13E **105** D10
Ervy-le-Châtel France 48°2N 3°55E **71** D10
Erwin U.S.A. 36°9N 82°25W **177** C13
Eryuan China 26°7N 99°57E **116** D2
Erzgebirge Germany 50°27N 12°55E **76** E8
Erzin Russia 50°15N 95°10E **109** B13
Erzincan □ Turkey 39°46N 39°30E **105** C8
Erzincan Turkey 39°45N 39°30E **105** C8
Erzurum □ Turkey 39°57N 41°15E **105** C9
Erzurum Turkey 39°57N 41°15E **105** C9
Es Caló Spain 38°40N 1°30E **100** C8
Es Canar Spain 39°2N 1°36E **100** B8
Es Mercadal Spain 39°59N 4°5E **100** B11
Es Migjorn Gran Spain 39°57N 4°3E **100** B11
Es Sahrâ el Beida Egypt 27°50N 28°45E **137** B2
Es Sahrâ' Esh Sharqîya
  Egypt 27°30N 32°30E **137** B3
Es Sînâ' Egypt 29°0N 34°0E **130** F2
Es Vedrà Spain 38°52N 1°12E **100** C7
Esan-Misaki Japan 41°40N 141°10E **112** D10
Esashi Hokkaidō, Japan 44°56N 142°35E **112** B11
Esashi Hokkaidō, Japan 41°52N 140°7E **112** D10
Esbjerg Denmark 55°29N 8°29E **63** J2
Esbo = Espoo Finland 60°12N 24°40E **84** B3
Escada Brazil 8°22S 35°8W **189** D4
Escalante U.S.A. 37°47N 111°36W **169** H8
Escalante ➤ U.S.A. 37°24N 110°57W **169** H8
Escalón Mexico 26°45N 104°20W **180** B4
Escambia ➤ U.S.A. 30°32N 87°11W **179** E2
Escanaba U.S.A. 45°45N 87°4W **172** C2
Escárcega Mexico 18°37N 90°43W **181** D6
Esch-sur-Alzette Lux. 49°32N 6°0E **76** F4
Eschede Germany 52°44N 10°14E **76** C6
Eschwege Germany 51°11N 10°2E **76** D6
Eschweiler Germany 50°49N 6°15E **76** E2
Escoma Bolivia 15°40S 69°8W **188** D4
Escondido ➤ U.S.A. 33°7N 117°5W **171** M9
Escravos ➤ Nigeria 5°35N 5°10E **139** D6
Escuinapa de Hidalgo
  Mexico 22°50N 105°50W **180** C3
Escuintla Guatemala 14°20N 90°48W **182** D1
Esêka Cameroon 3°41N 10°44E **139** E7
Eşen ➤ Turkey 36°27N 29°16E **99** E11
Esenguly Turkmenistan 37°37N 53°59E **108** E4
Esens Germany 53°38N 7°36E **76** B3
Esentepe = Áyios Amvrósios
  Cyprus 35°20N 33°35E **101** D12
Esenyurt Turkey 41°3N 28°48E **97** E12
Esera ➤ Spain 42°6N 0°15E **90** C5
Eşfahān Iran 32°39N 51°43E **129** C6
Eşfahān □ Iran 32°50N 51°50E **129** C6
Esfarāyen Iran 37°4N 57°30E **129** B8
Esfideh Iran 33°39N 59°46E **129** C8
Esgueva ➤ Spain 41°40N 4°43W **88** D6
Esh Sham = Dimashq
  Syria 33°30N 36°18E **130** B5
Esh Shamâlîya □ Sudan 19°0N 29°0E **137** D2
Esha Ness U.K. 60°29N 1°38W **65** A7
Eshan China 24°11N 102°24E **116** E4
Esher U.K. 51°21N 0°20W **67** F7
Eshkāshem = Ishkashim
  Tajikistan 36°44N 71°37E **109** E8
Eshkol △ Israel 31°20N 34°30E **130** D3
Eshowe S. Africa 28°50S 31°30E **145** C5
Esiama Ghana 4°56N 2°25W **138** E4
Esigodini Zimbabwe 20°18S 28°56E **145** B4
Esil = Ishim ➤ Russia 57°45N 71°10E **106** D8
Esil Kazakhstan 51°57N 66°24E **109** B7
Esino ➤ Italy 43°39N 13°22E **93** E10
Esk ➤ Dumf. & Gall., U.K. 54°58N 3°2W **65** E5
Esk ➤ N. Yorks., U.K. 54°30N 0°37W **66** C7
Eskān Iran 26°48N 63°9E **129** E9
Esker Siding Canada 53°53N 66°25W **165** B6
Eskifjörður Iceland 65°3N 13°55W **60** D7
Eskilstuna Sweden 59°22N 16°32E **62** E10
Eskimalatya Turkey 38°24N 38°22E **105** C8
Eskimo Point = Arviat
  Canada 61°6N 93°59W **163** A10
Eskişehir Turkey 39°50N 30°30E **99** B12
Eskişehir □ Turkey 39°40N 31°0E **99** B12
Esla ➤ Spain 41°29N 6°3W **88** D4
Eslāmābād-e Gharb
  Iran 34°10N 46°30E **105** E12
Eslāmshahr Iran 35°40N 51°10E **129** C6
Eşme Turkey 38°23N 28°58E **99** C11
Esmeralda, I. Chile 48°55S 75°25W **192** C1
Esmeraldas Ecuador 1°0N 79°40W **186** C3
Esna = Isna Egypt 25°17N 32°30E **137** B3
Esnagi L. Canada 48°36N 84°33W **164** C3
Esom Hill U.S.A. 33°57N 85°23W **178** B4
Espalion France 44°32N 2°47E **72** D6
España = Spain ■ Europe 39°0N 4°0W **59** H5
Espanola Canada 46°15N 81°46W **164** C3
Espanola U.S.A. 35°59N 106°5W **169** C12
Esparraguera Spain 41°33N 1°52E **90** D6
Esparza Costa Rica 9°59N 84°40W **182** E3
Espelkamp Germany 52°24N 8°36E **76** C4
Esperança Brazil 7°1S 35°51W **189** D3
Esperance Australia 33°45S 121°55E **149** F3
Esperance B. Australia 33°48S 121°55E **149** F3
Esperance Harbour
  St. Lucia 14°4N 60°55W **183** f
Esperantinópolis Brazil 4°53S 44°53W **189** A2
Esperanza Antarctica 65°0S 55°0W **55** C18
Esperanza Santa Cruz,
  Argentina 51°1S 70°49W **192** D2
Esperanza Santa Fe,
  Argentina 31°29S 61°3W **190** C4
Esperanza Puerto Rico 18°6N 65°28W **183** d
Espéranza France 42°56N 2°14E **72** F6
Espichel, C. Portugal 38°22N 9°16W **89** G1
Espiel Spain 38°11N 5°1W **89** G5
Espigão, Serra do
  Brazil 26°35S 50°30W **191** B5
Espinar Peru 14°51S 71°24W **188** D3
Espinazo, Sierra del = Espinhaço,
  Serra do Brazil 17°30S 43°30W **189** E2
Espinhaço, Serra do
  Brazil 17°30S 43°30W **189** E2
Espinho Portugal 41°1N 8°38W **88** D2
Espinilho, Serra do
  Brazil 28°30S 55°0W **191** B4
Espinosa de los Monteros
  Spain 43°5N 3°34W **88** B7
Espírito Santo □ Brazil 20°0S 40°45W **189** E2

Espírito Santo do Pinhal
  Brazil 22°10S 46°46W **191** A6
Espíritu Santo Vanuatu 15°15S 166°50E **147** C9
Espíritu Santo, B. del
  Mexico 19°20N 87°35W **181** D7
Espíritu Santo, I.
  Mexico 24°30N 110°22W **180** C2
Espita Mexico 21°1N 88°19W **181** C7
Esplanada Brazil 11°47S 37°57W **189** C3
Espoo Finland 60°12N 24°40E **84** B3
España, Sierra de Spain 37°51N 1°35W **91** H3
Espungabera Mozam. 20°29S 32°45E **145** B5
Esquel Argentina 42°55S 71°20W **192** B2
Esquimalt Canada 48°26N 123°25W **170** B3
Esquina Argentina 30°0S 59°30W **190** C4
Essaouira Morocco 31°32N 9°42W **136** B2
Essen Belgium 51°28N 4°28E **69** C4
Essen Germany 51°28N 7°2E **76** D3
Essendon, Mt. Australia 25°0S 120°29E **149** E3
Essequibo ➤ Guyana 6°50N 58°30W **186** B7
Essex Canada 42°10N 82°49W **174** D2
Essex Calif., U.S.A. 34°44N 115°15W **171** L11
Essex N.Y., U.S.A. 44°19N 73°21W **175** B11
Essex □ U.K. 51°54N 0°27E **67** F8
Essex Junction U.S.A. 44°29N 73°7W **175** B11
Esslingen Germany 48°44N 9°18E **77** G5
Essonne □ France 48°30N 2°20E **71** D9
Estaca de Bares, C. de
  Spain 43°46N 7°42W **88** B3
Estación Camacho
  Mexico 24°25N 102°18W **180** C4
Estación Simón
  Mexico 24°42N 102°35W **180** C4
Estadilla Spain 42°4N 0°16E **90** C5
Estados, I. de Los
  Argentina 54°40S 64°30W **192** D4
Estagel France 42°47N 2°40E **72** F6
Eşţahbānāt Iran 29°8N 54°4E **129** D7
Estância Brazil 11°16S 37°26W **189** C3
Estancia U.S.A. 34°46N 106°4W **169** J10
Estancia Monte León
  Argentina 50°14S 68°55W **192** D3
Estārm Iran 28°21N 58°21E **129** D8
Estarreja Portugal 40°45N 8°35W **88** E2
Estats, Pic d' Spain 42°40N 1°24E **90** C6
Estcourt S. Africa 29°0S 29°53E **145** C4
Este Italy 45°14N 11°39E **93** C8
Este ➤ Dom. Rep. 18°14N 68°42W **183** C6
Esteli Nic. 13°9N 86°22W **182** D2
Estella = Lizarra Spain 42°40N 2°2W **90** C2
Estellencs Spain 39°39N 2°29E **100** B9
Estena ➤ Spain 39°23N 4°44W **89** F6
Estepa Spain 37°17N 4°52W **89** H6
Estepona Spain 36°24N 5°7W **89** J5
Esterhazy Canada 50°37N 102°5W **163** C8
Esternay France 48°44N 3°33E **71** D10
Esterri d'Àneu Spain 42°38N 1°5E **90** C6
Estevan Canada 49°10N 102°59W **163** D8
Estevan Group Canada 53°3N 129°38W **162** C3
Estherville U.S.A. 43°24N 94°50W **172** D6
Estill U.S.A. 32°45N 81°15W **178** C8
Estissac France 48°16N 3°48E **71** D10
Eston Canada 51°8N 108°40W **163** C7
Estonia ■ Europe 58°30N 25°30E **84** C3
Estoril Portugal 38°42N 9°23W **89** G1
Estouk Mali 18°14N 1°2E **139** B5
Estreito Brazil 6°32S 47°25W **187** B3
Estreito Maranhão, Brazil 6°34S 47°27W **189** B1
Estrela, Serra da Portugal 40°10N 7°45W **88** E3
Estrella Spain 38°25N 3°35W **89** G7
Estremoz Portugal 38°51N 7°39W **89** G3
Estrondo, Serra do Brazil 7°20S 48°0W **187** B9
Esztergom Hungary 47°47N 18°44E **80** C3
Et Tidra Mauritania 19°45N 16°20W **138** B1
Etah India 27°35N 78°40E **125** F8
Étain France 49°13N 5°38E **71** C12
Étampes France 48°26N 2°10E **71** D9
Etanga Namibia 17°55S 13°0E **144** A1
Étaples France 50°30N 1°39E **71** B8
Etawah India 26°48N 79°6E **125** F8
Etawney L. Canada 57°50N 96°50W **163** B9
Etchojoa Mexico 26°55N 109°38W **180** B3
eThekwini = Durban
  S. Africa 29°49S 31°1E **145** C5
Ethel U.S.A. 46°32N 122°46W **170** D4
Ethelbert Canada 51°32N 100°25W **163** C8
Ethiopia ■ Africa 8°0N 40°0E **131** F3
Ethiopian Highlands
  Ethiopia 10°0N 37°0E **131** F2
Etili Turkey 39°59N 26°54E **97** G10
Etive, L. U.K. 56°29N 5°10W **65** E3
Etna Italy 37°50N 14°55E **95** E7
Etoile
  Dem. Rep. of the Congo 11°33S 27°30E **143** E2
Etoliko Greece 38°26N 21°21E **98** C3
Etolin Strait U.S.A. 60°20N 165°15W **166** C6
Etoloakarnania Greece 38°50N 21°18E **98** C3
Etosha, L. Namibia 19°0S 16°0E **144** A2
Etosha Pan Namibia 18°40S 16°30E **144** A2
Etowah U.S.A. 35°20N 84°32W **177** D12
Étréchy France 48°30N 2°12E **71** D9
Etrek Turkmenistan 37°36N 54°46E **129** B7
Étrépagny France 49°18N 1°36E **71** C8
Étretat France 49°42N 0°12E **70** C7
Etropole Bulgaria 42°50N 24°0E **101** C8
Ettelbruck Lux. 49°51N 6°5E **69** E6
Ettlingen Germany 48°58N 8°25E **77** G4
Ettrick Water ➤ U.K. 55°31N 2°55W **65** F6
Etuku
  Dem. Rep. of the Congo 3°42S 25°45E **142** C2
Etulia Moldova 45°32N 28°27E **81** E13
Etzná-Tixmucuy = Edzná
  Mexico 19°39N 90°19W **181** D6
Eu France 50°3N 1°26E **71** B8
Euboea = Evia Greece 38°30N 24°0E **98** C6
Euchareena Australia 32°57S 149°6E **153** B8
Eucla Australia 31°41S 128°52E **149** F4
Euclid U.S.A. 41°34N 81°32W **174** E3
Euclides da Cunha
  Brazil 10°31S 39°1W **189** C3
Eucumbene, L.
  Australia 36°2S 148°40E **153** D8
Eudora U.S.A. 33°7N 91°16W **179** E8
Eudunda Australia 34°12S 139°7E **152** C3
Eufaula Ala., U.S.A. 31°54N 85°9W **178** E4
Eufaula Okla., U.S.A. 35°17N 95°35W **176** D7
Eufaula L. U.S.A. 35°18N 95°21W **176** D7
Eugene U.S.A. 44°5N 123°4W **168** E2
Eugowra Australia 33°22S 148°24E **153** B8

Eulo Australia 28°10S 145°3E **151** D4
Eulonia U.S.A. 31°32N 81°26W **178** D8
Eumungerie Australia 31°56S 148°36E **153** B8
Eungella Australia 20°57S 148°40E **150** b
Eunice La., U.S.A. 30°30N 92°25W **176** F8
Eunice N. Mex.,
  U.S.A. 32°26N 103°10W **169** K12
Eupen Belgium 50°37N 6°3E **69** D6
Euphrates = Furāt, Nahr al ➤
  Asia 31°0N 47°25E **128** D5
Eure □ France 49°10N 1°0E **70** C8
Eure ➤ France 49°18N 1°12E **70** C8
Eure-et-Loir □ France 48°22N 1°30E **70** D8
Eureka Canada 80°0N 85°56W **161** B14
Eureka Calif., U.S.A. 40°47N 124°9W **168** F1
Eureka Kans., U.S.A. 37°49N 96°17W **172** G6
Eureka Mont., U.S.A. 48°53N 115°3W **168** A6
Eureka Nev., U.S.A. 39°31N 115°58W **168** G6
Eureka S.C., U.S.A. 33°42N 81°46W **178** B8
Eureka S. Dak., U.S.A. 45°46N 99°38W **172** C4
Eureka Australia 26°35S 121°35E **149** E3
Eurelia Australia 32°33S 138°35E **152** B3
Eurinilla Cr. ➤
  Australia 30°30S 140°11E **152** A4
Euroa Australia 36°44S 145°35E **153** D6
Euroairport ✈ (EAP)
  France 47°36N 7°33E **71** E14
Europa, Île Ind. Oc. 22°20S 40°22E **145** B7
Europa, Picos de Spain 43°10N 4°49W **88** B6
Europa, Pt. Gib. 36°3N 5°21W **89** J5
Europe 50°0N 20°0E **58** E10
Europoort Neths. 51°57N 4°10E **69** C4
Euskadi = País Vasco □
  Spain 42°50N 2°45W **90** C2
Euskirchen Germany 50°39N 6°48E **76** E2
Eustis U.S.A. 28°51N 81°41W **179** G8
Euston Australia 34°30S 142°46E **152** C5
Eutawville U.S.A. 33°24N 80°21W **178** B9
Eutin Germany 54°8N 10°36E **76** A6
Eutsuk L. Canada 53°20N 126°45W **162** C3
Evale Angola 16°33S 15°44E **144** A2
Evans, L. Canada 50°50N 77°0W **164** B4
Evans, L. Canada 40°23N 104°41W **168** F11
Evans City U.S.A. 40°46N 80°4W **174** F4
Evans Head Australia 29°7S 153°27E **151** D5
Evansburg Canada 53°36N 114°59W **162** C5
Evanston Ill., U.S.A. 42°3N 87°40W **172** D10
Evanston Wyo.,
  U.S.A. 41°16N 110°58W **168** F8
Evansville U.S.A. 37°58N 87°35W **172** G10
Évaux-les-Bains France 46°12N 2°29E **71** F9
Evaz Iran 27°46S 53°59E **129** E7
Evciler Afyon, Turkey 38°4N 29°54E **99** C11
Evciler Çanakkale, Turkey 39°47N 26°44E **99** B8
Eveleth U.S.A. 47°28N 92°32E **172** B7
Evensk Russia 62°12N 159°30E **107** C16
Everard, L. Australia 31°30S 135°0E **151** E2
Everard Ranges
  Australia 27°5S 132°28E **149** E5
Everest, Mt. Nepal 28°5N 86°58E **125** E12
Everett Ga., U.S.A. 31°24N 81°38W **178** D8
Everett Pa., U.S.A. 40°1N 78°23W **174** F6
Everett Wash., U.S.A. 47°59N 122°12W **170** C4
Everglades, The U.S.A. 25°50N 81°0W **179** K9
Everglades City U.S.A. 25°52N 81°23W **179** K9
Everglades Nat. △ U.S.A. 25°30N 81°0W **179** K9
Evergreen Ala., U.S.A. 31°26N 86°57W **177** F11
Evergreen Mont.,
  U.S.A. 48°14N 114°17W **168** B6
Everöd Sweden 55°53N 14°5E **63** J8
Everton Australia 36°25S 146°33E **153** D7
Evertsberg Sweden 61°8N 13°58E **62** C7
Evesham U.K. 52°6N 1°56W **67** E6
Evia Greece 38°30N 24°0E **98** C6
Évian-les-Bains France 46°24N 6°35E **71** F13
Évinos ➤ Greece 38°27N 21°40E **98** C3
Évisa France 42°15N 8°48E **73** F12
Evje Norway 58°36N 7°51E **61** G12
Évora Portugal 38°33N 7°57W **89** G3
Évora □ Portugal 38°33N 7°50W **89** G3
Evowghlī Iran 38°43N 45°13E **105** C11
Évreux France 49°3N 1°8E **70** C8
Évritania Greece 39°5N 21°30E **98** B3
Évron France 48°10N 0°24W **70** D6
Évros ➤ Greece 41°40N 26°34E **97** F10
Evrotas ➤ Greece 36°50N 22°40E **98** E4
Évry France 48°38N 2°27E **71** D9
Évvoia = Evia Greece 38°30N 24°0E **98** C6
Ewe, L. U.K. 57°49N 5°38W **65** D3
Ewing U.S.A. 42°16N 98°21W **172** D4
Ewo
  Congo 0°48S 14°45E **140** E2
Exaltación Bolivia 13°10S 65°20W **186** F5
Excelsior Springs
  U.S.A. 39°20N 94°13W **172** F6
Excideuil France 45°20N 1°4E **72** C5
Exe ➤ U.K. 50°41N 3°29W **67** G4
Exeter Canada 43°21N 81°29W **174** C3
Exeter U.K. 50°43N 3°31W **67** G4
Exeter Calif., U.S.A. 36°18N 119°9W **170** J7
Exeter N.H., U.S.A. 42°59N 70°57W **175** D14
Exmoor U.K. 51°12N 3°45W **67** F4
Exmoor △ U.K. 51°8N 3°42W **67** F4
Exmouth Australia 21°54S 114°10E **148** D1
Exmouth U.K. 50°37N 3°25W **67** G4
Exmouth G. Australia 22°15S 114°15E **148** D1
Exmouth Plateau
  Ind. Oc. 19°0S 114°0E **156** J3
Expedition △ Australia 25°41S 149°7E **151** D4
Expedition Ra.
  Australia 24°30S 149°12E **150** e
Experiment = Highland Mills
  U.S.A. 33°17N 84°17W **178** B5
Extremadura □ Spain 39°30N 6°5W **89** F4
Exuma Sound
  Bahamas 24°30N 76°20W **182** B4
Eyasi, L. Tanzania 3°30S 35°0E **142** C4
Eye Pen. U.K. 58°13N 6°10W **65** C2
Eyemouth U.K. 55°52N 2°5W **65** F6
Eygues = Aigues ➤
  France 44°7N 4°43E **73** D8
Eygurande France 45°40N 2°26E **71** G9
Eyjafjallajökull Iceland 63°38N 19°36W **60** E4
Eyjafjörður Iceland 66°15N 18°30W **60** C4
Eyl Somalia 8°0N 49°50E **131** F4
Eymet France 44°40N 0°25E **72** D4
Eymoutiers France 45°40N 1°45E **72** C5
Eynesil Turkey 41°4N 39°9E **105** B8
Eyre (North), L.
  Australia 28°30S 137°20E **151** D2

Eyre (South), L.
  Australia 29°18S 137°25E **151** D2
Eyre ➤ France 44°39N 1°1W **72** D2
Eyre, L. Australia 29°30S 137°26E **147** D6
Eyre Mts. N.Z. 45°25S 168°25E **155** F3
Eyre Pen. Australia 33°30S 136°17E **152** C1
Eysturoy Færoe Is. 62°13N 6°54W **60** E9
Eyvān = Jūy Zar Iran 50°33N 46°18E **105** F12
Eyvānkī Iran 35°24N 51°56E **129** C6
Ezcaray Spain 42°19N 3°0W **90** C1
Ezhou China 30°23N 114°50E **117** B10
Ezine Turkey 39°48N 26°20E **99** B8
Ezouza ➤ Cyprus 34°44N 32°27E **101** E11

F

F.Y.R.O.M. = Macedonia ■
  Europe 41°53N 21°40E **96** E5
Faaa Tahiti 17°34S 149°35W **155** b
Faaborg Denmark 55°6N 10°15E **63** J4
Faaone Tahiti 17°40S 149°21W **155** b
Fabala Guinea 9°44N 9°5W **138** D3
Fabens U.S.A. 31°30N 106°10W **176** F1
Fabero Spain 42°46N 6°37W **88** C4
Fabius U.S.A. 42°50N 75°59W **175** D9
Fabriano Italy 43°20N 12°54E **93** E9
Fǎcǎeni Romania 44°32N 27°53E **81** F12
Faceville U.S.A. 30°45N 84°38W **178** E5
Fachi Niger 18°6N 11°34E **135** E8
Facundo Argentina 45°18S 69°58W **192** C3
Fada Chad 17°13N 21°34E **135** E10
Fada-n-Gourma
  Burkina Faso 12°10N 0°30E **139** C5
Fadd Hungary 46°28N 18°49E **80** D3
Faddeyevskiy, Ostrov
  Russia 76°0N 144°0E **107** B15
Fadghāmī Syria 35°53N 40°52E **105** E9
Faenza Italy 44°17N 11°53E **93** D8
Færingehavn =
  Kangerluarsoruseq
  Greenland 63°45S 51°27W **57** E5
Færoe Is. = Føroyar □
  Atl. Oc. 62°0N 7°0W **60** F9
Fafa Mali 15°22N 0°48E **139** B5
Fafe Portugal 41°27N 8°11W **88** D2
Fagam Nigeria 11°1N 10°1E **139** C7
Fǎgǎras Romania 45°48N 24°58E **81** E9
Fǎgǎras, Munţii
  Romania 45°40N 24°40E **81** E9
Fågelfors Sweden 57°12N 15°51E **63** H9
Fågelmara Sweden 56°16N 15°58E **63** H9
Fagerhult Sweden 57°8N 15°40E **63** H9
Fagersta Sweden 60°1N 15°46E **62** E9
Fǎget Romania 45°52N 22°10E **80** E7
Fǎget, Munţii Romania 47°40N 23°10E **81** C8
Faggo Nigeria 11°21N 9°57E **139** C6
Fagnano, L. Argentina 54°30S 68°0W **192** D3
Fagnières France 48°58N 4°20E **71** D11
Faguibine, L. Mali 16°45N 4°0W **138** B4
Fahlīān Iran 30°11N 51°28E **129** D6
Fahraj Kermān, Iran 29°0N 59°0E **129** D8
Fahraj Yazd, Iran 31°46N 54°36E **129** D7
Fai Tsi Long Vietnam 21°0N 107°30E **116** G6
Faial Azores 38°34N 28°42W **134** a
Faial Madeira 32°47N 16°53W **100** D3
Faichan Kangri India 35°48N 76°34E **125** B7
Fair Haven N.Y.,
  U.S.A. 43°18N 76°42W **175** C8
Fair Haven Vt., U.S.A. 43°36N 73°16W **175** C11
Fair Hd. U.K. 55°14N 6°9W **64** A5
Fair Isle U.K. 59°32N 1°38W **68** B6
Fair Oaks U.S.A. 38°39N 121°16W **170** G5
Fairbanks Alaska,
  U.S.A. 64°51N 147°43W **160** E2
Fairbanks Fla., U.S.A. 29°44N 82°16W **178** F7
Fairburn U.S.A. 33°34N 84°35W **178** B5
Fairbury U.S.A. 40°8N 97°11W **172** E5
Fairfax S.C., U.S.A. 32°58N 81°15W **178** C8
Fairfax Vt., U.S.A. 44°40N 73°1W **175** B11
Fairfield Australia 33°53S 150°57E **153** B9
Fairfield Calif., U.S.A. 38°15N 122°3W **172** C9
Fairfield Conn., U.S.A. 41°9N 73°16W **175** E11
Fairfield Idaho, U.S.A. 43°21N 114°44W **168** E6
Fairfield Ill., U.S.A. 38°23N 88°22W **172** F9
Fairfield Iowa, U.S.A. 40°56N 91°57W **172** E8
Fairfield Tex., U.S.A. 31°44N 96°10W **176** F6
Fairford Canada 51°37N 98°38W **163** C9
Fairhope U.S.A. 30°31N 87°54W **177** F11
Fairlie N.Z. 44°5S 170°49E **155** E5
Fairmead U.S.A. 37°5N 120°10W **170** H6
Fairmont Minn., U.S.A. 43°39N 94°28W **172** D6
Fairmont W. Va.,
  U.S.A. 39°29N 80°9W **173** F13
Fairmount Calif.,
  U.S.A. 34°45N 118°26W **171** L8
Fairmount N.Y., U.S.A. 43°3N 76°12W **175** C8
Fairplay U.S.A. 39°15N 106°2W **168** G10
Fairport U.S.A. 43°6N 77°27W **174** C7
Fairport Harbor U.S.A. 41°45N 81°17W **174** E3
Fairview Canada 56°5N 118°25W **162** B5
Fairview Mont.,
  U.S.A. 47°51N 104°3W **168** C11
Fairview Okla., U.S.A. 36°16N 98°29W **176** C5
Fairweather, Mt.
  U.S.A. 58°55N 137°32W **162** B1
Fäÿÿÿÿ... ?
Faisalabad Pakistan 31°30N 73°5E **124** D5
Faith U.S.A. 45°2N 102°2W **172** C2
Faizabad India 26°45N 82°10E **125** F10
Faizpur India 21°14N 75°49E **126** D2
Fajr, W. ➤ Si. Arabia 29°10N 38°10E **128** D3
Fakenham U.K. 52°51N 0°51E **66** E9
Fåker Sweden 63°0N 14°34E **62** A8
Fakfak Indonesia 3°0S 132°15E **137** E8
Fakiya Bulgaria 42°10N 27°6E **101** D11
Fakobli Ivory C. 7°23N 7°23W **138** D3
Fakse Denmark 55°15N 12°8E **63** J6
Fakse Bugt Denmark 55°11N 12°15E **63** J6
Fakse Ladeplads Denmark 55°11N 12°9E **63** J6
Faku China 42°32N 123°21E **115** C12
Falaba S. Leone 9°3N 11°18W **138** D2
Falaise France 48°54N 0°12W **70** D6
Falakro Oros Greece 41°15N 23°58E **96** E7
Falam Burma 23°0N 93°45E **123** H18
Fǎlciu Romania 46°17N 28°7E **81** D13
Falcó, C. des Spain 38°50N 1°23E **100** C7
Falcon, C. Algeria 35°50N 0°50W **136** A3
Falcón, Presa Mexico 26°35N 99°10W **181** B5
Falcon Lake Canada 49°42N 95°15W **163** D9

Falcon Res. U.S.A. 26°34N 99°10W **176** H5
Falconara Maríttima
  Italy 43°37N 13°24E **93** E10
Falcone, C. del Italy 40°58N 8°12E **94** B1
Falconer U.S.A. 42°7N 79°12W **174** E5
Faléa Mali 12°16N 11°17W **138** C2
Falémé ➤ Senegal 14°46N 12°14W **138** C2
Falerum Sweden 58°8N 16°13E **63** G8
Faleshty = Fǎleşti
  Moldova 47°32N 27°44E **81** C12
Fǎleşti Moldova 47°32N 27°44E **81** C12
Falfurrias U.S.A. 27°14N 98°9W **176** H5
Falher Canada 55°44N 117°15W **162** B5
Faliraki Greece 36°22N 28°12E **101** C10
Falkenberg Germany 51°35N 13°14E **76** D9
Falkenberg Sweden 56°54N 12°30E **63** H6
Falkensee Germany 52°34N 13°4E **76** C8
Falkirk U.K. 56°0N 3°47W **65** F5
Falkland U.K. 56°16N 3°12W **65** E5
Falkland, East, I.
  Falk. Is. 51°40S 58°30W **192** D5
Falkland, West, I.
  Falk. Is. 51°40S 60°0W **192** D4
Falkland Is. ☑ Atl. Oc. 51°30S 59°0W **192** D5
Falkland Plateau Atl. Oc. 51°0S 50°0W **56** M7
Falkland Ridge Atl. Oc. 49°20S 40°0W **56** L8
Falkland Sd. Falk. Is. 52°0S 60°0W **192** D5
Falkonera Greece 36°50N 23°52E **98** E5
Falköping Sweden 58°12N 13°33E **63** F7
Fall River U.S.A. 41°43N 71°10W **175** E13
Fallbrook U.S.A. 33°23N 117°15W **171** M9
Fallon U.S.A. 39°28N 118°47W **168** G4
Falls City U.S.A. 40°3N 95°36W **172** E6
Falls Creek U.S.A. 41°9N 78°48W **174** E6
Falmouth Jamaica 18°30N 77°40W **182** a
Falmouth U.K. 50°9N 5°5W **67** G2
Falmouth U.S.A. 41°33N 70°37W **175** E14
Falsa, Pta. Mexico 27°51N 115°3W **180** B1
False B. S. Africa 34°15S 18°40E **144** E2
False Divi Pt. India 15°43N 80°50E **127** G5
Falso, C. Honduras 15°12N 83°21W **182** C3
Fǎlticeni Romania 47°21N 26°20E **81** C11
Falun Sweden 60°37N 15°37E **62** D9
Famagusta Cyprus 35°8N 33°55E **101** D12
Famagusta Bay Cyprus 35°15N 34°0E **101** D13
Famatina, Sierra de
  Argentina 27°30S 68°0W **190** B2
Famenin Iran 35°8N 48°58E **105** E13
Family L. Canada 51°54N 95°27W **163** C9
Famoso U.S.A. 35°37N 119°12W **171** K7
Fan Xian China 35°55N 115°38E **114** G8
Fana Mali 13°0N 6°56W **138** C3
Fanad Hd. Ireland 55°17N 7°38W **64** A4
Fanari Greece 39°24N 21°47E **98** B3
Fånes-Sénnes-Braies △
  Italy 46°38N 12°4E **93** B9
Fang Thailand 19°55N 99°13E **120** C2
Fang Xian China 32°3N 110°40E **117** A8
Fangcheng China 33°18N 112°59E **116** H4
Fangchenggang China 21°42N 108°21E **116** G7
Fangliao Taiwan 22°22N 120°38E **117** F13
Fangshan China 39°41N 116°0E **114** E9
Fangshan Shanxi, China 35°48N 76°34E **125** B7
Fangzi China 36°33N 119°10E **115** F10
Fani i Madh ➤ Albania 41°56N 20°16E **96** E4
Fanjiatun China 43°40N 125°5E **115** C13
Fanling China 22°30N 114°8E **111** a
Fannich, L. U.K. 57°38N 4°59W **65** D4
Fannūj Iran 26°35N 59°38E **129** E8
Fanø Denmark 55°25N 8°25E **63** J2
Fano Italy 43°50N 13°1E **93** E10
Fanshi China 39°12N 113°20E **114** E7
Fao = Al Fāw Iraq 30°0N 48°30E **129** D6
Faqirwali Pakistan 29°27N 73°0E **124** E5
Fâqûs Egypt 30°44N 31°47E **137** E7
Far East = Dalnevostochnyy □
  Russia 67°0N 140°0E **107** C14
Far East Asia 40°0N 130°0E **102** E14
Fara in Sabina Italy 42°12N 12°43E **93** F9
Faradje
  Dem. Rep. of the Congo 3°50N 29°45E **142** B2
Farafangana Madag. 22°49S 47°50E **145** C8
Farafenni Gambia 13°34N 15°36W **138** C1
Farâfra, El Wâhât el
  Egypt 27°15N 28°20E **137** C2
Farāh Afghan. 32°20N 62°7E **122** C3
Farāh □ Afghan. 32°25N 62°10E **122** C3
Faraid, Gebel Egypt 23°33N 35°19E **137** C4
Farako Ivory C. 9°5N 5°6W **138** D4
Faramana Burkina Faso 11°56N 4°45W **138** C4
Faranah Guinea 10°3N 10°45W **138** C2
Farasan Turkmenistan 39°9N 63°36E **128** B9
Farasān, Jazā'ir
  Si. Arabia 16°45N 41°55E **131** D3
Farasan Is. = Farasān, Jazā'ir
  Si. Arabia 16°45N 41°55E **131** D3
Fardes ➤ Spain 37°35N 3°0W **89** H7
Fareham U.K. 50°51N 1°11W **67** G6
Farewell, C. N.Z. 40°29S 172°43E **155** A4
Farewell C. = Nunap Isua
  Greenland 59°48N 43°55W **57** F6
Farewell Spit N.Z. 40°35S 173°0E **155** A4
Fårgelanda Sweden 58°34N 12°0E **63** F5
Farghona Uzbekistan 40°23N 71°19E **109** D8
Farghona Vodiysi Asia 40°46N 71°30E **109** D8
Fargo Ga., U.S.A. 30°41N 82°34W **178** E7
Fargo N. Dak., U.S.A. 46°53N 96°48W **172** B5
Fār'iah, W. ➤
  West Bank 32°12N 35°27E **130** C4
Faribault U.S.A. 44°18N 93°16W **172** C7
Faridabad India 28°26N 77°19E **124** E7
Faridkot India 30°44N 74°45E **124** D6
Faridpur Bangla. 23°15N 89°55E **125** H13
Fārimān Iran 35°40N 59°49E **129** C8
Farina ➤ Pakistan 6°51N 47°30W **189** B1
Fariones, Pta.
  Canary Is. 29°13N 13°28W **100** E6
Fâriskûr Egypt 31°20N 31°43E **137** F7
Färjestaden Sweden 56°39N 16°27E **63** H10
Farkadona Greece 39°36N 22°4E **98** B4
Farleigh Australia 21°4S 149°8E **150** b
Farmakonisi Greece 37°17N 27°8E **99** D9
Farmerville U.S.A. 32°47N 92°24W **176** E8

Farmingdale U.S.A. 40°12N 74°10W 175 F10
Farmington Canada 55°54N 120°30W 162 B4
Farmington Calif., U.S.A. 37°55N 120°59W 170 H6
Farmington Ga., U.S.A. 33°47N 83°26W 178 B6
Farmington Maine, U.S.A. 44°40N 70°9W 173 C18
Farmington Mo., U.S.A. 37°47N 90°25W 172 G8
Farmington N.H., U.S.A. 43°24N 71°4W 175 C13
Farmington N. Mex., U.S.A. 36°44N 108°12W 169 H9
Farmington Utah, U.S.A. 40°59N 111°53W 168 F8
Farmington → U.S.A. 41°51N 72°38W 175 E12
Farmville U.S.A. 37°18N 78°24W 173 G14
Färnäs Sweden 61°0N 14°39E 62 D8
Farne Is. U.K. 55°38N 1°37W 66 B6
Färnebofjärden △ Sweden 60°10N 16°48E 62 D10
Farnham Canada 45°17N 72°59W 175 A12
Farnham, Mt. Canada 50°29N 116°30W 162 C5
Faro Brazil 2°10S 56°39W 187 D7
Faro Canada 62°11N 133°22W 160 E5
Faro Portugal 37°2N 7°55W 89 H3
Fårö Sweden 57°55N 19°5E 63 G13
Faro □ Portugal 37°12N 8°10W 89 H2
Faro ✈ (FAO) Portugal 37°2N 7°57W 89 H3
Fårösund Sweden 57°52N 19°2E 63 G13
Farquhar, C. Australia 23°50S 113°36E 149 D1
Farquhar Is. Seychelles 11°0S 52°0E 146 F4
Farrars Cr. → Australia 25°35S 140°43E 150 D3
Farrāshband Iran 28°57N 52°5E 129 D7
Farrell U.S.A. 41°13N 80°30W 174 E4
Farrell Flat Australia 33°48S 138°48E 152 B3
Farrokhī Iran 33°50N 59°31E 129 C8
Farruch, C. = Ferrutx, C. de Spain 39°47N 3°21E 100 B10
Farrukhabad India 27°24N 79°34E 126 A4
Fārs □ Iran 29°30N 55°0E 129 D7
Farsala Greece 39°17N 22°23E 98 B4
Fārsī Iran 27°58N 50°11E 129 E6
Farsø Denmark 56°46N 9°19E 63 H3
Farson U.S.A. 42°7N 109°26W 168 E9
Farsund Norway 58°5N 6°55E 61 G12
Fartak, Râs Si. Arabia 28°5N 34°34E 128 D2
Fartak, Ra's Yemen 15°38N 52°15E 131 D5
Fârtăneşti Romania 45°49N 27°59E 81 E12
Fartura, Serra da Brazil 26°21S 52°52W 191 B5
Faru Nigeria 12°48N 6°12E 139 C6
Fārūj Iran 37°14N 58°14E 129 B8
Fårup Denmark 56°33N 9°51E 63 H3
Farvel, Kap = Nunap Isua Greenland 59°48N 43°55W 57 F6
Farwell U.S.A. 34°23N 103°2W 176 D3
Fāryāb □ Afghan. 36°0N 65°0E 109 E7
Fasā Iran 29°0N 53°39E 129 D7
Fasano Italy 40°50N 17°22E 95 B10
Fassa Mali 13°26N 8°15W 138 C3
Fastiv Ukraine 50°7N 29°57E 75 C15
Fastnet Rock Ireland 51°22N 9°37W 64 E2
Fastov = Fastiv Ukraine 50°7N 29°57E 75 C15
Fatagartuting, Tanjung Indonesia 2°46S 131°57E 119 E8
Fatehabad Haryana, India 29°31N 75°27E 124 E6
Fatehabad Ut. P., India 27°1N 78°19E 124 F8
Fatehgarh India 27°25N 79°35E 125 F8
Fatehpur Bihar, India 24°38N 85°14E 125 G11
Fatehpur Raj., India 28°0N 74°40E 124 F6
Fatehpur Ut. P., India 25°56N 81°13E 125 G9
Fatehpur Ut. P., India 27°10N 81°13E 125 F9
Fatehpur Sikri India 27°6N 77°40E 124 F6
Fatesh Russia 52°8N 35°57E 85 F8
Fathom Five ⌂ Canada 45°17N 81°40W 174 A3
Fatick Senegal 14°19N 16°27W 138 C1
Fatick □ Senegal 14°15N 16°30W 138 C1
Fatima Canada 47°24N 61°53W 165 C7
Fátima Portugal 39°37N 8°39W 89 F2
Fatoya Guinea 11°37N 9°10W 138 C3
Fatsa Turkey 41°2N 37°31E 104 B7
Faucille, Col de la France 46°22N 6°2E 71 F13
Faulkton U.S.A. 45°2N 99°8W 172 C4
Faulquemont France 49°3N 6°36E 71 C13
Faure I. Australia 25°52S 113°50E 149 E1
Făurei Romania 45°6N 27°19E 81 E12
Fauresmith S. Africa 29°44S 25°17E 144 C4
Fauske Norway 67°17N 15°25E 60 C16
Favara Italy 37°19N 13°39E 94 E6
Favàritx, C. de Spain 40°0N 4°15E 100 B11
Faverges France 45°45N 6°17E 73 C10
Favignana Italy 37°56N 12°20E 94 E5
Favignana, I. Italy 37°56N 12°19E 94 E5
Fawcett, Pt. Australia 11°46S 130°2E 148 B5
Fawn → Canada 55°20N 87°35W 164 A2
Fawnskin U.S.A. 34°16N 116°56W 171 L10
Faxaflói Iceland 64°29N 23°0W 60 D2
Faxälven → Sweden 63°13N 17°13E 62 A10
Faya-Largeau Chad 17°58N 19°6E 135 E9
Fayd Si. Arabia 27°1N 42°52E 128 E4
Fayence France 43°38N 6°42E 73 E10
Fayette Ala., U.S.A. 33°41N 87°50W 177 E11
Fayette Mo., U.S.A. 39°9N 92°41W 172 F7
Fayette N.Y., U.S.A. 42°48N 76°48W 175 D8
Fayetteville Ark., U.S.A. 36°4N 94°10W 176 C7
Fayetteville Ga., U.S.A. 33°27N 84°27W 178 B5
Fayetteville N.C., U.S.A. 35°3N 78°53W 177 D15
Fayetteville N.Y., U.S.A. 43°1N 76°0W 175 C9
Fayetteville Tenn., U.S.A. 35°9N 86°34W 177 D11
Fayied Egypt 30°18N 32°16E 137 E8
Faylakah Kuwait 29°27N 48°20E 129 D6
Fayón Spain 41°15N 0°20E 90 D5
Fazao-Malfakassa △ Togo 8°45N 0°50E 139 D5
Fazilka India 30°27N 74°2E 124 D6
Fazilpur Pakistan 29°18N 70°29E 124 E4
Fdérik Mauritania 22°40N 12°45W 134 D3
Feakle Ireland 52°56N 8°40W 64 D3
Feale → Ireland 52°27N 9°37W 64 D2
Fear, C. U.S.A. 33°50N 77°58W 177 E16
Feather → U.S.A. 38°47N 121°36W 170 G5
Feather Falls U.S.A. 39°36N 121°16W 170 F5
Featherston N.Z. 41°6S 175°20E 154 H4
Featherstone Zimbabwe 18°42S 30°55E 143 F3
Fécamp France 49°45N 0°22E 70 C7
Fedala = Mohammedia Morocco 33°44N 7°21W 136 B2
Federación Argentina 31°0S 57°55W 190 C4
Féderal Argentina 30°57S 58°48W 190 C4
Federal Capital Terr. □ Nigeria 9°0N 7°10E 139 D6
Federal Way U.S.A. 47°18N 122°19W 170 C4
Fedeshkūh Iran 28°49N 53°50E 129 D7
Fedorovka Kazakhstan 53°37N 62°42E 108 B6
Fehérgyarmat Hungary 47°58N 22°30E 80 C7
Fehmarn Germany 54°27N 11°7E 76 A7
Fehmarn Bælt Europe 54°35N 11°20E 63 K5
Fehmarn Belt = Fehmarn Bælt Europe 54°35N 11°20E 63 K5
Fei Xian China 35°18N 117°59E 115 G9
Feicheng China 36°14N 116°45E 114 F9
Feidong China 32°0N 117°35E 117 B11
Feijó Brazil 8°9S 70°21W 188 B3
Feilding N.Z. 40°13S 175°35E 154 G4
Feira de Santana Brazil 12°15S 38°57W 189 C3
Feixi China 31°43N 117°59E 117 B11
Feixiang China 36°30N 114°45E 114 F8
Fejaj, Chott el Tunisia 33°52N 9°14E 136 B5
Fejér □ Hungary 47°9N 18°30E 80 C3
Fejø Denmark 54°55N 11°30E 63 K5
Feke Turkey 37°48N 35°56E 104 D6
Fekete → Hungary 45°47N 18°15E 80 E3
Felanitx Spain 39°28N 3°9E 100 B10
Felda U.S.A. 26°34N 81°26W 179 J8
Feldbach Austria 46°57N 15°52E 78 E8
Feldberg Baden-W., Germany 47°52N 8°0E 77 H3
Feldberg Mecklenburg-Vorpommern, Germany 53°20N 13°25E 76 B9
Feldkirch Austria 47°15N 9°37E 78 D2
Feldkirchen Austria 46°44N 14°6E 78 E7
Félicité Seychelles 4°19S 55°52E 141 b
Felipe Carrillo Puerto Mexico 19°38N 88°3W 181 D7
Felixburg Zimbabwe 19°29S 30°51E 145 A5
Felixlândia Brazil 18°47S 44°55W 189 D2
Felixstowe U.K. 51°58N 1°23E 67 F9
Felletin France 45°53N 2°11E 72 C6
Fellingsbro Sweden 59°26N 15°37E 62 E9
Fellsmere U.S.A. 27°46N 80°36W 179 H9
Felton U.S.A. 37°3N 122°4W 170 H4
Feltre Italy 46°1N 11°54E 93 B8
Femer Bælt = Fehmarn Bælt Europe 54°35N 11°20E 63 K5
Femø Denmark 54°58N 11°35E 63 K5
Femunden Norway 62°10N 11°53E 60 E14
Femundsmarka △ Norway 62°18N 12°6E 60 E15
Fen He → China 35°36N 110°42E 114 G6
Fene Spain 43°27N 8°9W 88 B2
Fenelon Falls Canada 44°32N 78°45W 174 B6
Fener Burnu Turkey 36°58N 27°18E 99 E9
Feng Xian Jiangsu, China 34°43N 116°35E 114 G9
Feng Xian Shaanxi, China 33°54N 106°40E 114 H4
Fengari Greece 40°25N 25°32E 97 F9
Fengcheng Jiangxi, China 28°12N 115°48E 117 C10
Fengcheng Liaoning, China 40°28N 124°5E 115 D13
Fengdu China 29°55N 107°48E 116 C6
Fengfeng China 36°28N 114°8E 114 F8
Fenggang China 27°57N 107°47E 116 D6
Fenghua China 29°40N 121°25E 117 C13
Fenghuang China 27°57N 109°29E 116 D7
Fengjie China 31°3N 109°31E 116 B7
Fengkai China 23°24N 111°30E 117 F8
Fengkang Taiwan 22°12N 120°41E 117 F13
Fengle China 31°29N 112°29E 117 B9
Fenglin Taiwan 23°45N 121°26E 117 F13
Fengning China 41°10N 116°33E 114 D9
Fengqing China 24°38N 99°55E 116 E2
Fengqiu China 35°2N 114°25E 114 G8
Fengrun China 39°48N 118°8E 115 E10
Fengshan Guangxi Zhuangzu, China 24°39N 109°15E 116 E7
Fengshan Guangxi Zhuangzu, China 24°31N 107°3E 116 E6
Fengshan Taiwan 22°38N 120°21E 117 F13
Fengshun China 23°46N 116°10E 117 F11
Fengtai China 32°50N 116°40E 117 A11
Fengtongzhai △ China 30°32N 102°54E 116 B4
Fengxiang China 34°29N 107°25E 114 G4
Fengxin China 28°41N 115°18E 117 C10
Fengyang China 32°51N 117°29E 117 A11
Fengyi China 25°37N 100°20E 116 E3
Fengyüan Taiwan 24°15N 120°35E 117 E13
Fengzhen China 40°25N 113°2E 114 D7
Feno, C. de France 41°58N 8°33E 73 G12
Fenoarivo Atsinanana Madag. 17°22S 49°25E 141 H9
Fens, The U.K. 52°38N 0°2W 66 E7
Fensmark Denmark 55°17N 11°48E 63 J5
Fenton U.S.A. 42°48N 83°42W 173 D12
Fenxi China 36°40N 111°31E 114 F6
Fenyang China 37°18N 111°48E 114 F6
Fenyi China 27°45N 114°47E 117 D10
Feodosiya Ukraine 45°2N 35°16E 85 K8
Fer, C. de Algeria 37°3N 7°10E 136 A5
Ferbane Ireland 53°16N 7°50W 64 C4
Ferdows Iran 33°58N 58°2E 129 C8
Fère-Champenoise France 48°45N 3°59E 71 D10
Fère-en-Tardenois France 49°10N 3°30E 71 C10
Ferentino Italy 41°42N 13°15E 93 G10
Feres Greece 40°53N 26°10E 97 F10
Ferfer Somalia 5°4N 45°9E 131 F4
Fergana = Farghona Uzbekistan 40°23N 71°19E 109 D8
Fergana Range Asia 41°0N 73°50E 109 D8
Fergus Canada 43°43N 80°24W 174 C4
Fergus Falls U.S.A. 46°17N 96°4W 172 B5
Fériana Tunisia 34°59N 8°33E 136 B5
Feričanci Croatia 45°32N 18°0E 80 E2
Ferihegy, Budapest ✈ (BUD) Hungary 47°26N 19°14E 80 C4
Ferizaj Kosovo 42°23N 21°10E 96 D5
Ferkane Algeria 34°37N 7°26E 136 B5
Ferkéssédougou Ivory C. 9°35N 5°6W 138 D3
Ferlach Austria 46°32N 14°18E 78 E7
Ferland Canada 50°19N 88°27W 164 B2
Ferlo, Vallée du Senegal 15°15N 14°15W 138 B2
Ferlo-Nord ⌂ Senegal 15°43N 14°0W 138 B2
Ferlo-Sud ⌂ Senegal 15°43N 14°0W 138 B2
Fermanagh □ U.K. 54°21N 7°40W 64 B4
Fermo Italy 43°9N 13°43E 93 E10
Fermont Canada 52°47N 67°5W 165 B6
Fermoselle Spain 41°19N 6°27W 88 D4
Fermoy Ireland 52°9N 8°16W 64 D3
Fernán Núñez Spain 37°40N 4°44W 89 H6
Fernández Argentina 27°55S 63°50W 190 B3
Fernandina Beach U.S.A. 30°40N 81°27W 178 E8
Fernando de Noronha Brazil 4°0S 33°10W 187 D12
Fernando Póo = Bioko Eq. Guin. 3°30N 8°40E 139 E6
Ferndale Canada 44°58N 81°17W 174 B3
Ferndale U.S.A. 48°51N 122°36W 170 B4
Fernie Canada 49°30N 115°5W 162 D5
Fernlees Australia 23°51S 148°7E 150 C4
Fernley U.S.A. 39°36N 119°15W 168 G4
Fernwood U.S.A. 43°16N 73°38W 175 C11
Feroke India 11°9N 75°46E 127 J2
Ferozepore = Firozpur India 30°55N 74°40E 124 D6
Ferrandina Italy 40°29N 16°27E 95 B9
Ferrara Italy 44°50N 11°35E 93 D8
Ferrato, C. Italy 39°18N 9°38E 94 C2
Ferreira do Alentejo Portugal 38°4N 8°6W 89 G2
Ferreñafe Peru 6°42S 79°50W 188 B2
Ferrerias Spain 39°59N 4°1E 100 B11
Ferret, C. France 44°38N 1°15W 72 D2
Ferrette France 47°30N 7°20E 71 E14
Ferriday U.S.A. 31°38N 91°33W 176 F9
Ferriere Italy 44°40N 9°30E 92 D6
Ferrières France 48°5N 2°48E 71 D9
Ferro, Capo Italy 41°9N 9°31E 94 A2
Ferrol Spain 43°29N 8°15W 88 B2
Ferrol, Pen. de Peru 9°10S 78°35W 188 B2
Ferron U.S.A. 39°5N 111°8W 168 G8
Ferros Brazil 19°14S 43°2W 189 D2
Ferrutx, C. de Spain 39°47N 3°21E 100 B10
Ferry Pass U.S.A. 30°31N 87°13W 179 E2
Ferryland Canada 47°2N 52°53W 165 C9
Fertile U.S.A. 47°32N 96°17W 172 B5
Fertő-Hanság △ Hungary 47°25N 16°50E 80 C1
Fertőszentmiklós Hungary 47°35N 16°53E 80 C1
Fès Morocco 34°0N 5°0W 136 B3
Fès □ Morocco 34°1N 5°0W 136 B3
Fessenden U.S.A. 47°39N 99°38W 172 B4
Festus U.S.A. 38°13N 90°24W 172 F8
Feté Bowé Senegal 14°56N 13°30W 138 C2
Feteşti Romania 44°22N 27°51E 81 F12
Fethiye Turkey 36°36N 29°6E 99 E11
Fethiye Körfezi Turkey 36°40N 28°50E 99 E10
Fetlar U.K. 60°36N 0°52W 65 A8
Feuilles → Canada 58°47N 70°4W 161 F17
Feurs France 45°45N 4°13E 73 C8
Feyzābād Afghan. 37°7N 70°33E 109 E8
Fez = Fès Morocco 34°0N 5°0W 136 B3
Fezzan Libya 27°0N 13°0E 135 C8
Fiambalá Argentina 27°45S 67°37W 190 B2
Fianarantsoa Madag. 21°26S 47°5E 141 J9
Fichtelgebirge Germany 50°2N 11°55E 77 E7
Fichtelgebirge ⌂ Germany 50°10N 12°0E 77 E8
Ficksburg S. Africa 28°51S 27°53E 145 C4
Fidenza Italy 44°52N 10°3E 92 D7
Fiditi Nigeria 7°45N 3°53E 139 D5
Field → Australia 23°48S 138°0E 150 C2
Field I. Australia 12°5S 132°23E 148 B5
Fieni Romania 45°8N 25°25E 81 E10
Fier Albania 40°43N 19°33E 96 F3
Fierzë Albania 42°15N 20°1E 96 D4
Fife □ U.K. 56°16N 3°1W 65 E5
Fife Ness U.K. 56°17N 2°35W 65 E6
Fifth Cataract Sudan 18°22N 33°50E 137 D3
Figari France 41°29N 9°7E 73 G13
Figeac France 44°37N 2°2E 72 D6
Figeholm Sweden 57°22N 16°33E 63 G10
Figline Valdarno Italy 43°37N 11°28E 93 E8
Figtree Zimbabwe 20°22S 28°20E 143 G2
Figueira Castelo Rodrigo Portugal 40°57N 6°58W 88 E4
Figueira da Foz Portugal 40°7N 8°54W 88 E2
Figueiró dos Vinhos Portugal 39°55N 8°16W 88 F2
Figueres Spain 42°18N 2°58E 90 C7
Figuig Morocco 32°5N 1°11W 136 B3
Fiji ■ Pac. Oc. 17°20S 179°0E 154 a
Fika Nigeria 11°15N 11°13E 139 C7
Filabres, Sierra de los Spain 37°13N 2°20W 89 H8
Filabusi Zimbabwe 20°34S 29°20E 145 B4
Filadelfia Bolivia 11°20S 68°46W 188 C4
Filadélfia Brazil 7°21S 47°30W 189 B1
Filadelfia Italy 38°47N 16°17E 95 D9
Filadelfia Paraguay 22°21S 60°2W 190 A3
Fil'akovo Slovak Rep. 48°17N 19°50E 79 C12
Filchner Ice Shelf Antarctica 79°0S 40°0W 55 D1
Filey U.K. 54°12N 0°18W 66 C7
Filey B. U.K. 54°12N 0°15W 66 C7
Filfla Malta 35°47N 14°24E 101 D1
Filiaşi Romania 44°32N 23°31E 81 F8
Filiates Greece 39°38N 20°16E 98 B2
Filiatra Greece 37°9N 21°35E 98 D3
Filicudi Italy 38°35N 14°33E 95 D7
Filingué Niger 14°21N 3°22E 139 C5
Filiouri = Lissos → Greece 41°15N 25°40E 97 E9
Filipada Greece 39°12N 20°53E 98 B2
Filipstad Sweden 59°43N 14°9E 62 E8
Filisur Switz. 46°41N 9°40E 77 J5
Filitosa France 41°45N 8°52E 73 G12
Fillmore Calif., U.S.A. 34°24N 118°55W 171 L8
Fillmore Utah, U.S.A. 38°58N 112°20W 168 G7
Filotio Greece 37°3N 25°30E 99 D7
Filottrano Italy 43°26N 13°21E 93 E10
Filyos Çayı → Turkey 41°35N 32°10E 104 B5
Fimbul Ice Shelf S. Ocean 69°30S 1°0W 55 C2
Fina ⌂ Mali 13°15N 8°46W 138 C3
Finale Emília Italy 44°50N 11°18E 93 D8
Finale Lígure Italy 44°10N 8°20E 92 D5
Fiñana Spain 37°10N 2°50W 89 H8
Finch Canada 45°11N 75°7W 175 A9
Finch Hatton Australia 20°25S 148°39E 150 b
Findhorn → U.K. 57°38N 3°38W 65 D5
Findıklı Turkey 41°16N 41°9E 105 B9
Findlay U.S.A. 41°2N 83°39W 173 E12
Fine U.S.A. 44°14N 75°8W 175 B9
Finger L. Canada 53°33N 93°30W 164 B1
Finger Lakes U.S.A. 42°40N 76°30W 175 D8
Fingoè Mozam. 15°55S 31°50E 143 F3
Finike Turkey 36°21N 30°10E 99 E12
Finike Körfezi Turkey 36°17N 30°16E 99 E12
Finiq Albania 39°54N 20°3E 96 G4
Finistère □ France 48°20N 4°0W 70 D3
Finisterre = Fisterra Spain 42°54N 9°16W 88 C1
Finisterre, C. = Fisterra, C. Spain 42°50N 9°19W 88 C1
Finke Australia 25°34S 134°35E 150 D1
Finke Gorge △ Australia 24°8S 132°49E 148 D5
Finland ■ Europe 63°0N 27°0E 60 E22
Finland, G. of Europe 60°0N 26°0E 84 C3
Finlay → Canada 57°0N 125°10W 162 B3
Finley Australia 35°38S 145°35E 153 C6
Finley U.S.A. 47°31N 97°50W 172 B5
Finn → Ireland 54°51N 7°28W 64 B4
Finnerödja Sweden 58°57N 14°24E 63 F8
Finnigan, Mt. Australia 15°49S 145°17E 150 B4
Finniss, C. Australia 33°8S 134°51E 151 E1
Finnmark Norway 69°37N 23°57E 60 B20
Finnsnes Norway 69°14N 18°0E 60 B18
Finspång Sweden 58°43N 15°47E 63 F9
Finsteraarhorn Switz. 46°31N 8°10E 77 J4
Finsterwalde Germany 51°37N 13°42E 76 D9
Fiora → Italy 42°20N 11°34E 93 F8
Fiordland △ N.Z. 45°46S 167°0E 155 F2
Fiorenzuola d'Arda Italy 44°56N 9°55E 92 D6
Fīq Syria 32°46N 35°41E 130 C4
Firat = Furāt, Nahr al → Asia 31°0N 47°25E 128 D5
Fire Island ⌂ U.S.A. 40°38N 73°8W 175 F11
Firebag → Canada 57°45N 111°21W 163 B6
Firebaugh U.S.A. 36°52N 120°27W 170 J6
Firedrake L. Canada 61°25N 104°30W 163 A8
Firenze Italy 43°46N 11°15E 93 E8
Firenze Amerigo Vespucci ✈ (FLR) Italy 43°49N 11°13E 93 E8
Firenze Pisa ✈ (PSA) Italy 43°40N 10°22E 92 E7
Firenzuola Italy 44°7N 11°23E 93 D8
Firk, Sha'ib → Iraq 30°59N 44°34E 128 D5
Firmi France 44°33N 2°19E 72 D6
Firminy France 45°23N 4°18E 73 C8
Firozabad India 27°10N 78°25E 125 F8
Firozpur India 30°55N 74°40E 124 D6
Firozpur-Jhirka India 27°48N 76°57E 124 F7
Fīrūzābād Iran 28°52N 52°35E 129 D7
Fīrūzkūh Iran 35°50N 52°50E 129 C7
Firvale Canada 52°27N 126°13W 162 C3
Fish → Namibia 28°7S 17°10E 144 C2
Fish → S. Africa 31°30S 20°16E 144 D3
Fish River Canyon Namibia 27°40S 17°35E 144 C2
Fisheating Cr. → U.S.A. 26°57N 81°7W 179 J8
Fisher B. Canada 51°35N 97°13W 163 C9
Fishers I. U.S.A. 41°15N 72°0W 175 E13
Fishguard U.K. 52°0N 4°58W 67 E3
Fishing L. Canada 52°10N 95°24W 163 C9
Fishkill U.S.A. 41°32N 73°54W 175 E11
Fiskardo Greece 38°28N 20°35E 98 C2
Fiskenæsset = Qeqertarsuatsiaat Greenland 63°5N 50°45W 57 E5
Fismes France 49°20N 3°40E 71 C10
Fisterra Spain 42°54N 9°16W 88 C1
Fisterra, C. Spain 42°50N 9°19W 88 C1
Fitchburg Mass., U.S.A. 42°35N 71°48W 175 D13
Fitchburg Wis., U.S.A. 42°58N 89°28W 172 D9
Fitz Roy Argentina 47°0S 67°0W 192 C3
Fitz Roy, Cerro Argentina 49°17S 73°5W 192 C2
Fitzgerald Canada 59°51N 111°36W 162 B6
Fitzgerald U.S.A. 31°43N 83°15W 178 D6
Fitzgerald River △ Australia 33°53S 119°55E 149 F3
Fitzmaurice → Australia 14°45S 130°5E 148 B5
Fitzroy → Queens., Australia 23°32S 150°52E 150 C5
Fitzroy → W. Austral., Australia 17°31S 123°35E 148 C3
Fitzroy Crossing Australia 18°9S 125°38E 148 C4
Fitzwilliam I. Canada 45°30N 81°45W 174 A3
Fiuggi Italy 41°48N 13°13E 93 G10
Fiume = Rijeka Croatia 45°20N 14°21E 93 C11
Fiumicino, Roma ✈ (FCO) Italy 41°48N 12°15E 93 G9
Five Points U.S.A. 36°26N 120°6W 170 J6
Fivizzano Italy 44°14N 10°8E 92 D7
Fizi Dem. Rep. of the Congo 4°17S 28°55E 142 C2
Fjällbacka Sweden 58°36N 11°17E 63 F5
Fjällnäs Sweden 62°36N 12°11E 62 B6
Fjärdhundra Sweden 59°47N 16°56E 62 E10
Fjellerup Denmark 56°29N 10°34E 63 H4
Fjerritslev Denmark 57°5N 9°15E 63 G3
Fjugesta Sweden 59°11N 14°52E 62 E8
Fkih ben Salah Morocco 32°32N 6°45W 136 B2
Flagler Beach U.S.A. 29°29N 81°8W 179 F8
Flagstaff U.S.A. 35°12N 111°39W 169 J8
Flagstaff L. U.S.A. 45°12N 70°18W 175 A14
Flaherty I. Canada 56°15N 79°15W 164 A4
Flåm Norway 60°50N 7°7E 60 F12
Flambeau → U.S.A. 45°18N 91°14W 172 C8
Flamborough Hd. U.K. 54°7N 0°5W 66 C7
Fläming Germany 52°6N 12°23E 76 C8
Flaming Gorge ⌂ U.S.A. 41°10N 109°25W 168 F9
Flaming Gorge Res. U.S.A. 41°10N 109°25W 168 F9
Flamingo U.S.A. 25°8N 80°57W 179 K9
Flamingo, Teluk Indonesia 5°30S 138°0E 119 F9
Flanders = Flandre Europe 50°50N 2°30E 71 B9
Flandre Europe 50°50N 2°30E 71 B9
Flandre-Occidentale = West-Vlaanderen □ Belgium 51°0N 3°0E 69 D2
Flandre-Orientale = Oost-Vlaanderen □ Belgium 51°5N 3°50E 69 C3
Flandreau U.S.A. 44°3N 96°36W 172 C5
Flanigan U.S.A. 40°10N 119°53W 170 E7
Flannan Is. U.K. 58°9N 7°52W 65 C1
Flåsjön Sweden 64°5N 15°40E 60 D16
Flat → Canada 61°33N 125°18W 162 A3
Flat I. Mauritius 19°53S 57°35E 141 d
Flat I. S. China Sea 10°49N 115°49E 118 B5
Flat Pt. N.Z. 41°14S 175°57E 154 H4
Flathead L. U.S.A. 47°51N 114°8W 168 C6
Flattery, C. Australia 14°58S 145°21E 150 A4
Flattery, C. U.S.A. 48°23N 124°29W 170 B2
Flatwoods U.S.A. 38°31N 82°43W 173 F12
Fleetwood U.K. 53°55N 3°1W 66 D4
Fleetwood U.S.A. 40°27N 75°49W 175 F9
Flekkefjord Norway 58°18N 6°39E 61 G12
Flemington U.S.A. 41°7N 77°28W 174 E7
Flemish Cap Atl. Oc. 47°0N 45°0W 56 B7
Flen Sweden 59°4N 16°35E 62 E10
Flensburg Germany 54°47N 9°27E 76 A5
Flers France 48°47N 0°33W 70 D6
Flesherton Canada 44°16N 80°33W 174 B4
Flesko, Tanjung Indonesia 0°29N 124°30E 119 D6
Fleurance France 43°52N 0°40E 72 E4
Fleurie, Côte France 49°25N 0°40W 70 C6
Fleurier Switz. 46°54N 6°35E 77 J2
Fleurieu Pen. Australia 35°40S 138°5E 152 C3
Flevoland □ Neths. 52°30N 5°30E 69 B5
Flin Flon Canada 54°46N 101°53W 163 C8
Flinders → Australia 17°36S 140°36E 150 B3
Flinders B. Australia 34°19S 115°19E 149 F2
Flinders Chase △ Australia 35°50S 136°42E 152 C2
Flinders Group Australia 14°11S 144°15E 150 A3
Flinders I. S. Austral., Australia 33°44S 134°41E 151 E1
Flinders I. Tas., Australia 40°0S 148°0E 151 G4
Flinders Ranges Australia 31°30S 138°30E 152 A3
Flinders Ranges △ Australia 31°30S 138°40E 152 A3
Flinders Reefs Australia 17°37S 148°31E 150 B4
Flint U.K. 53°15N 3°8W 66 D4
Flint U.S.A. 43°1N 83°41W 173 D12
Flint → U.S.A. 30°57N 84°34W 178 E5
Flint I. Kiribati 11°26S 151°48W 157 J12
Flintshire □ U.K. 53°17N 3°17W 66 D4
Fliseryd Sweden 57°6N 16°15E 63 G10
Flix Spain 41°14N 0°32E 90 D5
Flixecourt France 50°1N 2°5E 71 B9
Floby Sweden 58°8N 13°20E 63 F7
Floda Sweden 57°49N 12°22E 63 G6
Flodden U.K. 55°37N 2°8W 66 B5
Flogny-la-Chapelle France 47°57N 3°57E 71 E10
Floodplains △ Sri Lanka 8°10N 81°10E 127 K5
Floodwood U.S.A. 46°56N 92°55W 172 B7
Flora U.S.A. 38°40N 88°29W 172 F9
Florac France 44°20N 3°37E 72 D7
Florahome U.S.A. 29°44N 81°54W 178 F8
Floral City U.S.A. 28°45N 82°17W 179 G7
Florala U.S.A. 31°0N 86°20W 177 F11
Florânia Brazil 6°8S 36°49W 189 B3
Florence = Firenze Italy 43°46N 11°15E 93 E8
Florence Ala., U.S.A. 34°48N 87°41W 177 D11
Florence Ariz., U.S.A. 33°2N 111°23W 169 K8
Florence Colo., U.S.A. 38°23N 105°8W 168 G11
Florence Oreg., U.S.A. 43°58N 124°7W 168 D1
Florence S.C., U.S.A. 34°12N 79°46W 177 D15
Florence, L. Australia 28°53S 138°9E 151 D2
Florencia Colombia 1°36N 75°36W 186 C3
Florennes Belgium 50°15N 4°35E 69 D4
Florensac France 43°23N 3°28E 72 E7
Florenville Belgium 49°40N 5°19E 69 E5
Flores Azores 39°26N 31°13W 134 a
Flores Brazil 7°51S 37°59W 189 B3
Flores Guatemala 16°59N 89°50W 182 C2
Flores Indonesia 8°35S 121°0E 119 F6
Flores I. Canada 49°20N 126°10W 162 D3
Flores Sea Indonesia 6°30S 120°0E 119 F6
Floresta Brazil 8°40S 37°26W 189 B3
Floreşti Moldova 47°53N 28°17E 81 C13
Floresville U.S.A. 29°8N 98°10W 176 G5
Floriano Brazil 6°50S 43°0W 189 B2
Florianópolis Brazil 27°30S 48°30W 191 B6
Florida Cuba 21°32N 78°14W 182 B4
Florida Uruguay 34°7S 56°10W 191 C4
Florida □ U.S.A. 28°0N 82°0W 179 H8
Florida, Straits of U.S.A. 25°0N 80°0W 182 B4
Florida B. U.S.A. 25°0N 80°45W 182 B3
Florida City U.S.A. 25°27N 80°29W 179 K9
Florida Keys U.S.A. 24°40N 81°0W 179 L8
Floridia Italy 37°5N 15°9E 95 E8
Florin U.S.A. 38°30N 121°24W 170 G5
Florina Greece 40°48N 21°26E 96 F5
Florissant U.S.A. 38°47N 90°19W 172 F8
Florø Norway 61°35N 5°1E 60 F11
Flower Station Canada 45°10N 76°41W 175 A8
Flowerpot I. Canada 45°18N 81°38W 174 A3
Floydada U.S.A. 33°59N 101°20W 176 E4
Fluk Indonesia 1°42S 127°44E 119 E7
Flúmen → Spain 41°43N 0°9W 90 D4
Flumendosa → Italy 39°26N 9°37E 94 C2
Fluminimaggiore Italy 39°26N 8°30E 94 C1
Flushing = Vlissingen Neths. 51°26N 3°34E 69 C3
Fluvià → Spain 42°12N 3°7E 90 C8
Fly → Papua N. G. 8°25S 143°0E 147 B7
Flying Fish, C. Antarctica 72°6S 102°29W 55 D15
Foam Lake Canada 51°40N 103°32W 163 C8
Foča Bos.-H. 43°31N 18°47E 96 C2
Foça Turkey 38°39N 26°46E 99 C8
Fochabers U.K. 57°37N 3°6W 65 D5
Focşani Romania 45°41N 27°15E 81 E12
Fodécontéa Guinea 10°50N 14°22W 138 C2
Fogang China 23°52N 113°30E 117 F9
Foggaret el Arab Algeria 27°13N 2°49E 136 C4
Foggaret ez Zoua Algeria 27°20N 2°53E 136 C4
Fóggia Italy 41°27N 15°34E 95 A8
Foglia → Italy 43°55N 12°54E 93 E9
Fogo Canada 49°43N 54°17W 165 C9
Fogo C. Verde Is. 15°5N 24°20W 134 b
Fogo I. Canada 49°40N 54°5W 165 C9
Fohnsdorf Austria 47°12N 14°40E 78 D7
Föhr Germany 54°43N 8°30E 76 A4
Fóia Portugal 37°19N 8°37W 89 H2
Foix France 42°58N 1°38E 72 F5
Fojnica Bos.-H. 43°59N 17°51E 80 G2
Fokida Greece 38°30N 22°15E 98 C4
Fokino Russia 53°30N 34°22E 84 F8
Fokku Nigeria 11°36N 4°32E 139 C5
Folda Nord-Trøndelag, Norway 64°32N 10°30E 60 D14
Folda Nordland, Norway 67°38N 14°50E 60 C16
Földeák Hungary 46°19N 20°30E 80 D5
Folegandros Greece 36°40N 24°55E 98 E6
Foley Botswana 21°34S 27°21E 144 B4
Foley Ala., U.S.A. 30°24N 87°41W 177 F11
Foley Fla., U.S.A. 30°4N 83°32W 178 E6
Foleyet Canada 48°15N 82°25W 164 C3
Folgefonna Norway 60°3N 6°23E 61 F12
Foligno Italy 42°57N 12°42E 93 F9
Folkestone U.K. 51°5N 1°12E 67 F9
Folkston U.S.A. 30°50N 82°0W 178 E7
Follansbee U.S.A. 40°19N 80°35W 174 F4
Follónica Italy 42°55N 10°45E 92 F7
Follónica, G. di Italy 42°54N 10°43E 92 F7
Folsom U.S.A. 38°40N 121°9W 170 G5
Folsom L. U.S.A. 38°42N 121°9W 170 G5
Folteşti Romania 45°45N 28°3E 81 E13
Fomboni Comoros Is. 12°18S 43°46E 141 a
Fond-du-Lac Canada 59°19N 107°12W 163 B7
Fond du Lac U.S.A. 43°47N 88°27W 172 D9
Fond-du-Lac → Canada 59°17N 106°0W 163 B7
Fonda U.S.A. 42°57N 74°22W 175 D10
Fondi Italy 41°21N 13°25E 94 A6
Fonfría Spain 41°37N 6°9W 88 D4
Fongafale Tuvalu 8°31S 179°13E 147 B10
Fonni Italy 40°7N 9°15E 94 B2
Fonsagrada = A Fonsagrada Spain 43°8N 7°4W 88 B3
Fonseca, G. de Cent. Amer. 13°10N 87°40W 182 D2
Font-Romeu-Odeillo-Via France 42°31N 2°3E 72 F5
Fontaine-Française France 47°32N 5°21E 71 E12
Fontainebleau France 48°24N 2°40E 71 D9
Fontana U.S.A. 34°6N 117°26W 171 L9
Fontana, L. Argentina 44°55S 71°30W 192 B2
Fontas → Canada 58°14N 121°48W 162 B4
Fonte Boa Brazil 2°33S 66°0W 186 D5
Fontem Cameroon 5°32N 9°52E 139 D6
Fontenay-le-Comte France 46°28N 0°48W 72 B3
Fontenelle Res. U.S.A. 42°1N 110°3W 168 E8
Fontur Iceland 66°23N 14°32W 60 C6
Fonyód Hungary 46°44N 17°33E 80 D2
Foochow = Fuzhou China 26°5N 119°16E 117 D12
Foping China 33°41N 108°0E 114 H5
Foraker, Mt. U.S.A. 62°58N 151°24W 166 C9
Forbach France 49°10N 6°52E 71 C13
Forbes Australia 33°22S 148°5E 153 B8
Forbesganj India 26°17N 87°18E 125 F12
Forcados Nigeria 5°26N 5°26E 139 D6
Forcados → Nigeria 5°25N 5°19E 139 D6
Forcalquier France 43°58N 5°47E 73 E9
Forchheim Germany 49°43N 11°2E 77 F7
Ford City Calif., U.S.A. 35°9N 119°27W 171 K7
Ford City Pa., U.S.A. 40°46N 79°32W 174 F5
Førde Norway 61°27N 5°53E 60 F11
Fords Bridge Australia 29°41S 145°29E 151 D4
Fordyce U.S.A. 33°49N 92°25W 176 E8
Forécariah Guinea 9°28N 13°10W 138 D2
Forel, Mt. Greenland 66°52N 36°55W 57 D7
Foremost Canada 49°26N 111°34W 162 D6
Forest Canada 43°6N 82°0W 174 C3
Forest U.S.A. 32°22N 89°29W 177 E10
Forest Acres U.S.A. 34°1N 80°58W 178 A9
Forest City Iowa, U.S.A. 43°16N 93°39W 172 D7
Forest City N.C., U.S.A. 35°20N 81°52W 177 D14
Forest City Pa., U.S.A. 41°39N 75°28W 175 E9
Forest Grove U.S.A. 45°31N 123°7W 170 E3
Forest Park U.S.A. 33°37N 84°22W 178 B5
Forestburg Canada 52°35N 112°1W 162 C6
Foreste Casentinesi-Monte Falterona-Campigna △ Italy 43°50N 11°48E 93 E8
Foresthill U.S.A. 39°1N 120°49W 170 F6
Forestier Pen. Australia 43°0S 148°0E 151 G4
Forestville Canada 48°48N 69°2W 165 C6
Forestville Calif., U.S.A. 38°28N 122°54W 170 G4
Forestville N.Y., U.S.A. 42°28N 79°10W 174 D5
Forêt d'Orient ⌂ France 48°16N 4°25E 71 D11
Forez, Mts. du France 45°40N 3°50E 72 C7
Forfar U.K. 56°39N 2°53W 65 E6
Forillon △ Canada 48°46N 64°12W 165 C7
Forks U.S.A. 47°57N 124°23W 170 C2
Forksville U.S.A. 41°29N 76°35W 175 E8
Forlì Italy 44°13N 12°3E 93 D9
Forlì-Cesena □ Italy 44°10N 12°0E 93 D9
Forman U.S.A. 46°7N 97°38W 172 B5
Formazza Italy 46°22N 8°26E 92 B5
Formby Pt. U.K. 53°33N 3°6W 66 D4
Formentera Spain 38°43N 1°27E 100 C7
Formentor, C. de Spain 39°58N 3°13E 100 B10
Formentor, Pen. de Spain 39°56N 3°11E 100 B10
Former Yugoslav Republic of Macedonia = Macedonia ■ Europe 41°53N 21°40E 96 E5
Fórmia Italy 41°15N 13°37E 94 A6
Formiga Brazil 20°27S 45°25W 189 E1
Formigine Italy 44°37N 10°51E 92 D7
Formosa = Taiwan ■ Asia 23°30N 121°0E 117 F13
Formosa Argentina 26°15S 58°10W 190 B4
Formosa Brazil 15°32S 47°20W 189 D1
Formosa □ Argentina 25°0S 60°0W 190 B4
Formosa, Serra Brazil 12°0S 55°0W 187 F8
Formosa B. = Ungwana B. Kenya 2°45S 40°20E 142 C5
Formosa do Rio Prêto Brazil 11°2S 45°3W 189 C1
Fornells Spain 40°3N 4°7E 100 A11
Fornos de Algodres Portugal 40°38N 7°32W 88 E3
Fornovo di Taro Italy 44°42N 10°6E 92 D7
Forollhogna △ Norway 62°39N 10°41E 60 E14
Føroyar ☑ Atl. Oc. 62°0N 7°0W 60 F9
Forres U.K. 57°37N 3°37W 65 D5
Forrest Vic., Australia 38°33S 143°47E 152 E5
Forrest W. Austral., Australia 30°51S 128°6E 149 F4
Forrest, Mt. Australia 24°48S 127°45E 149 D4
Forrest City U.S.A. 35°1N 90°47W 177 D9
Fors Sweden 60°14N 16°20E 62 D10
Forsayth Australia 18°33S 143°34E 150 B3

Forserum Sweden 57°42N 14°30E 63 G8
Forshaga Sweden 59°33N 13°29E 62 E7
Förslöv Sweden 56°21N 12°48E 63 H6
Forsmo Sweden 63°16N 17°11E 62 A11
Forssa Finland 60°49N 23°38E 84 B2
Forst Germany 51°45N 14°37E 76 D10
Forster Australia 32°12S 152°31E 153 B10
Forsvik Sweden 58°35N 14°26E 63 F8
Forsyth Ga., U.S.A. 33°2N 83°56W 178 B6
Forsyth Mont., U.S.A. 46°16N 106°41W 168 C10
Forsyth I. N.Z. 40°58S 174°5E 155 A9
Fort Abbas Pakistan 29°12N 72°52E 124 E5
Fort Albany Canada 52°15N 81°35W 164 B3
Fort Assiniboine Canada 54°20N 114°45W 162 C6
Fort Augustus U.K. 57°9N 4°42W 65 D4
Fort Beaufort S. Africa 32°46S 26°40E 148 E4
Fort Benton U.S.A. 47°49N 110°40W 168 C8
Fort Bragg U.S.A. 39°26N 123°48E 168 G2
Fort Bridger U.S.A. 41°19N 110°23W 168 F8
Fort Caroline △ 30°23N 81°30W 178 E8
Fort Chipewyan Canada 58°42N 111°8W 163 B6
Fort Clatsop = Lewis and Clark △ U.S.A. 46°8N 123°53W 170 D3
Fort Collins U.S.A. 40°35N 105°5W 168 F11
Fort-Coulonge Canada 45°50N 76°45W 164 C4
Fort Covington U.S.A. 44°59N 74°29W 175 B10
Fort Dauphin = Taolanaro Madag. 25°2S 47°0E 141 K9
Fort Davis Ala., U.S.A. 32°15N 85°43W 178 C4
Fort Davis Tex., U.S.A. 30°35N 103°54W 176 F3
Fort-de-France Martinique 14°36N 61°5W 182 c
Fort Defiance U.S.A. 35°45N 109°5W 169 J9
Fort Dodge U.S.A. 42°30N 94°11W 172 D6
Fort Drum U.S.A. 27°32N 80°48W 179 H9
Fort Edward U.S.A. 43°16N 73°35W 175 C11
Fort Erie Canada 42°54N 78°56W 174 D6
Fort Fairfield U.S.A. 46°46N 67°50W 173 B20
Fort Frances Canada 48°36N 93°24W 163 D10
Fort Franklin = Déline Canada 65°11N 123°25W 160 D7
Fort Frederica △ U.S.A. 31°13N 81°23W 178 D8
Fort Gaines U.S.A. 31°36N 85°3W 178 D4
Fort Garland U.S.A. 37°26N 105°26W 169 H11
Fort George = Chisasibi Canada 53°50N 79°0W 164 B4
Fort Good Hope Canada 66°14N 128°40W 160 D6
Fort Hancock U.S.A. 31°18N 105°51W 176 F2
Fort Hope = Eabametoong Canada 51°30N 88°0W 164 B2
Fort Irwin U.S.A. 35°16N 116°41W 171 K10
Fort Kent U.S.A. 47°15N 68°36W 173 B19
Fort Klamath U.S.A. 42°42N 122°0W 168 E3
Fort Laramie U.S.A. 42°13N 104°31W 168 E11
Fort Lauderdale U.S.A. 26°7N 80°8W 179 J9
Fort Liard Canada 60°14N 123°30W 162 A4
Fort Liberté Haiti 19°42N 71°51W 183 C5
Fort Lupton U.S.A. 40°5N 104°49W 168 F11
Fort MacKay Canada 57°12N 111°41W 162 B6
Fort Macleod Canada 49°45N 113°30W 162 D6
Fort McMurray Canada 56°44N 111°7W 162 B6
Fort McPherson Canada 67°30N 134°55W 160 D5
Fort Madison U.S.A. 40°38N 91°27W 172 E8
Fort Matanzas △ U.S.A. 29°43N 81°14W 178 F8
Fort Meade U.S.A. 27°45N 81°48W 179 H8
Fort Mitchell U.S.A. 32°20N 85°1W 178 C4
Fort Morgan U.S.A. 40°15N 103°48W 168 F12
Fort Myers U.S.A. 26°39N 81°52W 179 J8
Fort Myers Beach U.S.A. 26°26N 81°57W 179 J8
Fort Myers Villas U.S.A. 26°33N 81°52W 179 J8
Fort Nelson Canada 58°50N 122°44W 162 B4
Fort Nelson → Canada 59°32N 124°0W 162 B4
Fort Norman = Tulita Canada 64°57N 125°30W 160 E6
Fort Ogden U.S.A. 27°5N 81°57W 179 H8
Fort Payne U.S.A. 34°26N 85°43W 177 D12
Fort Peck U.S.A. 48°1N 106°27W 168 B10
Fort Peck Dam U.S.A. 48°0N 106°26W 168 C10
Fort Peck L. U.S.A. 48°0N 106°26W 168 C10
Fort Pierce U.S.A. 27°27N 80°20W 179 H9
Fort Pierre U.S.A. 44°21N 100°22W 172 C3
Fort Plain U.S.A. 42°56N 74°37W 175 C10
Fort Portal Uganda 0°40N 30°20E 142 B3
Fort Providence Canada 61°3N 117°40W 162 A5
Fort Pulaski △ U.S.A. 32°2N 80°56W 178 C9
Fort Qu'Appelle Canada 50°45N 103°50W 163 C8
Fort Resolution Canada 61°10N 113°40W 162 A6
Fort Rixon Zimbabwe 20°2S 29°17E 143 G2
Fort Ross U.S.A. 38°32N 123°13W 170 G3
Fort Rupert = Waskaganish Canada 51°30N 78°40W 164 B4
Fort St. James Canada 54°30N 124°10W 162 C4
Fort St. John Canada 56°15N 120°50W 162 B4
Fort Saskatchewan Canada 53°40N 113°15W 162 C6
Fort Scott U.S.A. 37°50N 94°42W 172 G6
Fort Severn Canada 56°0N 87°40W 164 A2
Fort Shevchenko Kazakhstan 44°35N 50°23E 87 H10
Fort Simpson Canada 61°45N 121°15W 162 A4
Fort Smith Canada 60°0N 111°51W 162 A6
Fort Smith U.S.A. 35°23N 94°25W 177 D6
Fort Stockton U.S.A. 30°53N 102°53W 176 F3
Fort Sumner U.S.A. 34°28N 104°15W 169 J11
Fort Thompson U.S.A. 44°3N 99°26W 172 C4
Fort Union △ U.S.A. 35°54N 105°1W 169 J11
Fort Valley U.S.A. 32°33N 83°53W 178 C6
Fort Vermilion Canada 58°24N 116°0W 162 B5
Fort Walton Beach U.S.A. 30°25N 86°36W 179 E3
Fort Ware Canada 57°26N 125°41W 162 B3
Fort Wayne U.S.A. 41°4N 85°9W 173 E11
Fort William U.K. 56°49N 5°7W 65 E3
Fort Worth U.S.A. 32°43N 97°19W 176 E6
Fort Yates U.S.A. 46°5N 100°38W 172 B3
Fort Yukon U.S.A. 66°34N 145°16W 160 D2

Fortaleza Bolivia 12°6S 66°49W 188 C4
Fortaleza Brazil 3°45S 38°35W 189 A3
Forteau Canada 51°28N 56°58W 165 B8
Fortescue → Australia 21°0S 116°4E 148 D2
Fortescue River Roadhouse Australia 21°17S 116°8E 148 D2
Forth → U.K. 56°9N 3°50W 65 E5
Forth, Firth of U.K. 56°5N 2°55W 65 E6
Forthassa Rharbia Algeria 32°52N 1°18W 136 B3
Fortín Uno Argentina 38°50S 65°18W 192 A3
Fortore → Italy 41°55N 15°17E 93 G12
Fortrose N.Z. 46°38S 168°45E 155 G3
Fortrose U.K. 57°35N 4°9W 65 D4
Fortuna Spain 38°11N 1°7W 91 G3
Fortuna Calif., U.S.A. 40°36N 124°9W 168 F1
Fortuna N. Dak., U.S.A. 48°55N 103°47W 172 A2
Fortune Canada 47°4N 55°50W 165 C8
Fortune B. Canada 47°30N 55°22W 165 C8
Forûr Iran 26°17N 54°32E 129 E7
Fos-sur-Mer France 43°26N 4°56E 73 E8
Fosen Norway 63°50N 10°20E 60 E14
Foshan China 23°3N 113°9E 117 F9
Fosnavåg Norway 62°22N 5°38E 60 E11
Foso Ghana 5°43N 1°15W 139 D4
Fossano Italy 44°33N 7°43E 92 D4
Fossil U.S.A. 45°0N 120°9W 168 D3
Fossil Butte △ U.S.A. 41°50N 110°27W 168 F8
Fossombrone Italy 43°41N 12°48E 93 E9
Foster Australia 38°40S 146°15E 153 E7
Foster Canada 45°17N 72°30W 175 A12
Foster → Canada 55°47N 105°49W 163 B7
Fosters Ra. Australia 21°35S 133°48E 150 C1
Fostoria U.S.A. 41°10N 83°25W 173 E12
Fouesnant France 47°53N 4°1W 70 E2
Fougères France 48°21N 1°14W 70 D5
Foul Pt. Sri Lanka 8°35N 81°18E 127 K5
Foula U.K. 60°10N 2°5W 66 A6
Foulalaba Mali 10°40N 7°20W 138 C2
Foulness I. U.K. 51°36N 0°55E 67 F8
Foulwind, C. N.Z. 41°45S 171°28E 155 B6
Foum Zguid Morocco 30°2N 6°59W 136 B4
Foumban Cameroon 5°45N 10°50E 139 D7
Foumbot Cameroon 5°31N 10°28E 139 D7
Foumbouni Comoros Is. 11°51S 43°29E 141 a
Foumraire Algeria 30°3N 3°12W 136 C3
Foundiougne Senegal 14°5N 16°32W 138 C1
Fountain Colo., U.S.A. 38°41N 104°42W 168 G11
Fountain Fla., U.S.A. 30°29N 85°25W 178 E4
Fountain Hills U.S.A. 33°37N 111°43W 169 K8
Fountain Springs U.S.A. 35°54N 118°51W 171 K8
Four Mountains, Is. of U.S.A. 53°0N 170°0W 166 E5
Fourchambault France 47°2N 3°3E 71 F10
Fouriesburg S. Africa 28°38S 28°14E 144 C4
Fourmies France 50°1N 4°2E 71 B11
Fourna Greece 39°3N 21°52E 98 B3
Fourni Greece 37°36N 26°32E 99 D8
Fours France 46°50N 3°42E 71 F10
Fouta Djallon Guinea 11°20N 12°10W 138 C2
Foux, Cap-à- Haiti 19°43N 73°27W 183 C5
Foveaux Str. N.Z. 46°42S 168°10E 155 G3
Fowey U.K. 50°20N 4°39W 67 G3
Fowler Calif., U.S.A. 36°38N 119°41W 170 J7
Fowler Colo., U.S.A. 38°8N 104°2W 168 G12
Fowler, Pt. Australia 32°2S 132°32E 149 F5
Fowlers B. Australia 31°59S 132°34E 149 F5
Fowlers Iran 37°13N 49°19E 105 D13
Fox → Canada 56°3N 93°18W 163 B10
Fox Creek Canada 54°24N 116°48W 162 C5
Fox Is. U.S.A. 53°0N 168°0W 166 E6
Fox Lake Canada 58°28N 114°31W 162 B6
Fox Valley Canada 50°30N 109°25W 163 C7
Foxboro Canada 44°14N 77°26W 174 B7
Foxboro U.S.A. 42°4N 71°16W 175 D13
Foxdale Australia 20°22S 148°35E 150 b
Foxe Basin Canada 66°0N 77°0W 161 D16
Foxe Chan. Canada 65°0N 80°0W 161 E16
Foxe Pen. Canada 65°0N 76°0W 161 E16
Foxen Sweden 59°25N 11°55E 62 E5
Foxford Ireland 53°59N 9°7W 64 C2
Foxton N.Z. 40°29S 175°18E 154 G4
Foyle, Lough U.K. 55°7N 7°4W 64 A4
Foynes Ireland 52°37N 9°7W 64 D2
Foz Spain 43°33N 7°20W 88 B3
Foz do Cunene Angola 17°15S 11°48E 144 A1
Foz do Gregório Brazil 6°47S 70°44W 188 B3
Foz do Iguaçu Brazil 25°30S 54°30W 191 B5
Frackville U.S.A. 40°47N 76°14W 175 F8
Fraga Spain 41°32N 0°21E 90 D5
Fraile Muerto Uruguay 32°31S 54°32W 191 C5
Framingham U.S.A. 42°17N 71°25W 175 D13
Frampol Poland 50°41N 22°40E 83 H9
Franca Brazil 20°33S 47°30W 189 C1
Francavilla al Mare Italy 42°25N 14°17E 93 F11
Francavilla Fontana Italy 40°32N 17°35E 95 B10
France ■ Europe 47°0N 3°0E 59 F6
Frances Australia 36°41S 140°55E 152 C3
Frances → Canada 60°16N 129°10W 162 A3
Frances L. Canada 61°23N 129°30W 162 A3
Franceville Gabon 1°40S 13°32E 140 C2
Franche-Comté □ France 46°50N 5°55E 71 F12
Francis Case, L. U.S.A. 43°4N 98°34W 172 D5
Francisco Beltrão Brazil 26°5S 53°4W 191 B5
Francisco Ignacio Madero Coahuila, Mexico 25°48N 103°18W 180 B4
Francisco Ignacio Madero Durango, Mexico 24°26N 104°18W 180 C4
Francisco Ignacio Madero, Presa Mexico 24°26N 104°18W 180 C4
Francisco Sá Brazil 16°28S 43°30W 189 D2
Francistown Botswana 21°7S 27°33E 144 B4
Francofonte Italy 37°14N 14°53E 95 E7
François Canada 47°35N 56°45W 165 C8
François L. Canada 54°0N 125°30W 162 C3
Francois Peron △ Australia 24°25S 113°33E 149 E1
Francs Pk. U.S.A. 43°58N 109°20W 168 E9
Franeker Neths. 53°12N 5°33E 69 A5
Frank Hann △ Australia 32°52S 120°19E 149 F3
Frankenberg Germany 51°3N 8°48E 76 D4
Frankenhöhe Germany 49°20N 10°25E 77 F6
Frankenwald Germany 50°30N 11°30E 77 E7

Frankenwald △ Germany 50°15N 11°30E 77 E7
Frankford Canada 44°12N 77°36W 174 B7
Frankfort Ind., U.S.A. 40°17N 86°31W 172 E10
Frankfort Kans., U.S.A. 39°42N 96°25W 172 F5
Frankfort Ky., U.S.A. 38°12N 84°52W 173 F11
Frankfort N.Y., U.S.A. 43°2N 75°4W 175 C9
Frankfurt Brandenburg, Germany 52°20N 14°32E 76 C10
Frankfurt Hessen, Germany 50°7N 8°41E 77 E4
Frankfurt ✈ (FRA) Germany 50°1N 8°34E 77 E4
Fränkische Alb Germany 49°10N 11°23E 77 F7
Fränkische Rezat → Germany 49°11N 11°1E 77 F7
Fränkische Saale → Germany 50°3N 9°42E 77 E5
Fränkische Schweiz Germany 49°50N 11°16E 77 F7
Fränkische Schweiz-Veldensteiner Forst △ Germany 49°45N 11°27E 77 F7
Frankland → Australia 35°0S 116°48E 149 G2
Franklin Ga., U.S.A. 33°17N 85°6W 178 B4
Franklin Ky., U.S.A. 36°43N 86°35W 172 G10
Franklin La., U.S.A. 29°48N 91°30W 176 G9
Franklin Mass., U.S.A. 42°5N 71°24W 175 D13
Franklin N.H., U.S.A. 43°27N 71°39W 175 C13
Franklin N.Y., U.S.A. 42°20N 75°9W 175 D9
Franklin Nebr., U.S.A. 40°6N 98°57W 172 E4
Franklin Pa., U.S.A. 41°24N 79°50W 174 E5
Franklin Va., U.S.A. 36°41N 76°56W 173 G15
Franklin W. Va., U.S.A. 38°39N 79°20W 173 F14
Franklin B. Canada 69°45N 126°0W 160 D6
Franklin D. Roosevelt L. U.S.A. 48°18N 118°9W 168 B4
Franklin-Gordon Wild Rivers △ Australia 42°19S 145°51E 151 G4
Franklin Harb. Australia 33°43S 136°55E 152 B2
Franklin I. Antarctica 76°10S 168°30E 55 D11
Franklin I. Canada 45°24N 80°20W 174 A4
Franklin L. U.S.A. 40°25N 115°22W 168 F6
Franklin Mts. Canada 65°0N 125°0W 160 D6
Franklin Mts. N.Z. 44°55S 167°45E 155 E6
Franklin Str. Canada 72°0N 96°0W 160 C12
Franklinton U.S.A. 30°51N 90°9W 177 F9
Franklinville U.S.A. 42°20N 78°27W 174 D6
Franklyn Mt. N.Z. 42°4S 172°42E 155 C7
Frankston Australia 38°8S 145°8E 153 E6
Frånö Sweden 62°55N 17°50E 62 B11
Fransfontein Namibia 20°12S 15°1E 144 B2
Fränsta Sweden 62°30N 16°11E 62 B10
Frantsa Iosifa, Zemlya Arctic 82°0N 55°0E 106 A6
Franz Canada 48°25N 84°30W 164 C3
Franz Josef Land = Frantsa Iosifa, Zemlya Arctic 82°0N 55°0E 106 A6
Franz Josef Strauss ✈ (MUC) Germany 48°21N 11°47E 77 G7
Franzburg Germany 54°11N 12°51E 76 A8
Frascati Italy 41°48N 12°41E 93 G9
Fraser → Australia 42°32N 82°57W 174 D2
Fraser → B.C., Canada 49°7N 123°11W 170 A3
Fraser → Nfld. & L., Canada 56°39N 62°10W 165 A7
Fraser, Mt. Australia 25°35S 118°20E 149 E2
Fraser I. Australia 25°15S 153°10E 151 D5
Fraser Lake Canada 54°0N 124°50W 162 C4
Fraserburg S. Africa 31°55S 21°30E 144 D3
Fraserburgh U.K. 57°42N 2°1W 65 D6
Fraserdale Canada 49°55N 81°37W 164 C3
Frasertown N.Z. 38°58S 177°28E 154 E6
Frashër Albania 40°23N 20°26E 96 F4
Frasne France 46°50N 6°10E 71 F13
Frătești Romania 43°58N 25°58E 81 G10
Frauenfeld Switz. 47°34N 8°54E 77 H4
Fray Bentos Uruguay 33°10S 58°15W 190 C4
Fray Jorge △ Chile 30°42S 71°40W 190 C1
Frazier Downs ◇ Australia 18°48S 121°42E 148 C3
Frechilla Spain 42°8N 4°50W 88 C6
Fredericia Denmark 55°34N 9°45E 63 J3
Frederick Md., U.S.A. 39°25N 77°25W 173 F15
Frederick Okla., U.S.A. 34°23N 99°1W 176 D5
Frederick S. Dak., U.S.A. 45°50N 98°31W 172 C4
Frederick E. Hyde Fjord Greenland 83°25N 29°0W 57 A8
Fredericksburg Pa., U.S.A. 40°27N 76°26W 175 F8
Fredericksburg Tex., U.S.A. 30°16N 98°52W 176 F5
Fredericksburg Va., U.S.A. 38°18N 77°28W 173 F15
Fredericktown Mo., U.S.A. 37°34N 90°18W 172 G8
Fredericktown Ohio, U.S.A. 40°29N 82°33W 174 F2
Frederico Westphalen Brazil 27°22S 53°24W 191 B5
Fredericton Canada 45°57N 66°40W 165 C6
Fredericton Junction Canada 45°41N 66°40W 165 C6
Frederikshåb = Paamiut Greenland 62°0N 49°43W 57 E6
Frederikshamn = Hamina Finland 60°34N 27°12E 84 B4
Frederikshavn Denmark 57°28N 10°31E 63 G4
Frederikssund Denmark 55°50N 12°3E 63 J6
Frederiksted U.S. Virgin Is. 17°43N 64°53W 183 C7
Frederiksværk Denmark 55°58N 12°2E 63 H6
Fredonia Ariz., U.S.A. 36°57N 112°32W 169 H7
Fredonia Kans., U.S.A. 37°32N 95°49W 172 G6
Fredonia N.Y., U.S.A. 42°26N 79°20W 174 D5
Fredrikstad Sweden 66°8N 14°23E 62 D8
Fredrikstad Norway 59°13N 10°57E 61 G14
Free State □ S. Africa 28°30S 27°0E 144 C4
Freehold U.S.A. 40°16N 74°17W 175 E10
Freel Peak U.S.A. 38°52N 119°54W 170 G7
Freels, C. Nfld. & L., Canada 49°15N 53°30W 165 C9
Freels, C. Nfld. & L., Canada 46°37N 53°32W 165 C9
Freeman Calif., U.S.A. 35°35N 117°53W 171 K9
Freeman S. Dak., U.S.A. 43°21N 97°26W 172 D5
Freeport Bahamas 26°30N 78°47W 182 A4
Freeport Fla., U.S.A. 30°30N 86°8W 178 E3

Freeport Ill., U.S.A. 42°17N 89°36W 172 D9
Freeport N.Y., U.S.A. 40°39N 73°35W 175 F11
Freeport Ohio, U.S.A. 40°12N 81°15W 174 F3
Freeport Pa., U.S.A. 40°41N 79°41W 174 F5
Freeport Tex., U.S.A. 28°57N 95°21W 176 G7
Freetown S. Leone 8°30N 13°17W 138 D2
Freeville U.S.A. 42°30N 76°20W 175 D8
Frégate, L. de la Canada 53°15N 74°45W 164 B5
Fregenal de la Sierra Spain 38°10N 6°39W 89 G4
Fregene Italy 41°51N 12°12E 93 G9
Fregon Australia 26°45S 132°1E 149 E5
Fréhel, C. France 48°40N 2°20W 70 D4
Freiberg Germany 50°55N 13°20E 76 D9
Freibourg = Fribourg Switz. 46°49N 7°9E 77 J3
Freiburg Baden-W., Germany 47°59N 7°51E 77 H3
Freiburg Niedersachsen, Germany 53°49N 9°16E 76 B5
Freilassing Germany 47°50N 12°58E 77 H8
Freire Chile 38°54S 72°38W 192 A2
Freirina Chile 28°30S 71°10W 190 B1
Freising Germany 48°24N 11°45E 77 G7
Freistadt Austria 48°30N 14°30E 78 C7
Freital Germany 51°1N 13°39E 76 D9
Fréjus France 43°25N 6°44E 73 E10
Fremantle Australia 32°7S 115°47E 149 F2
Fremont Calif., U.S.A. 37°32N 121°57W 170 H4
Fremont Mich., U.S.A. 43°28N 85°57W 173 D11
Fremont Nebr., U.S.A. 41°26N 96°30W 172 E5
Fremont Ohio, U.S.A. 41°21N 83°7W 173 E12
Fremont → U.S.A. 38°24N 110°42W 168 G8
French Camp U.S.A. 37°53N 121°16W 170 H5
French Cays = Plana Cays Bahamas 22°38N 73°30W 183 B5
French Creek → U.S.A. 41°24N 79°50W 174 E5
French Frigate Shoals U.S.A. 23°45N 166°10W 167 L6
French Guiana ☑ S. Amer. 4°0N 53°0W 187 C8
French I. Australia 38°20S 145°22E 153 E6
French Island △ Australia 38°20S 145°22E 153 E6
French Pass N.Z. 40°55S 173°55E 155 A8
French Polynesia ☑ Pac. Oc. 20°0S 145°0W 157 J13
French Riviera = Azur, Côte d' France 43°25N 7°10E 73 E11
Frenchman Cr. → N. Amer. 48°31N 107°10W 168 B10
Frenchman Cr. → U.S.A. 40°14N 100°50W 172 E3
Frenda Algeria 35°2N 1°1E 136 A4
Frenštát pod Radhoštěm Czech Rep. 49°33N 18°13E 79 B11
Fresco Ivory C. 5°3N 5°31W 138 D3
Fresco → Brazil 7°15S 51°30W 187 E8
Freshfield, C. Antarctica 68°25S 151°10E 55 C10
Fresnay-sur-Sarthe France 48°17N 0°1E 70 D7
Fresnillo Mexico 23°10N 102°53W 180 C4
Fresno U.S.A. 36°44N 119°47W 170 J7
Fresno Alhándiga Spain 40°42N 5°37W 88 E5
Fresno Res. U.S.A. 48°36N 109°57W 168 B9
Freudenstadt Germany 48°27N 8°24E 77 G4
Frévent France 50°15N 2°17E 71 B9
Frew → Australia 20°0S 135°38E 150 C2
Frewsburg U.S.A. 42°3N 79°10W 174 D5
Freycinet △ Australia 42°11S 148°19E 151 G4
Freycinet Pen. Australia 42°10S 148°25E 151 G4
Freyming-Merlebach France 49°8N 6°48E 71 C13
Freyung Germany 48°48N 13°31E 77 G9
Fria Guinea 10°27N 13°38E 138 C2
Fria, C. Namibia 18°0S 12°0E 144 A1
Friant U.S.A. 36°59N 119°43W 170 J7
Frías Argentina 28°40S 65°5W 190 B2
Fribourg Switz. 46°49N 7°9E 77 J3
Fribourg □ Switz. 46°40N 7°0E 77 J3
Fridafors Sweden 56°25N 14°39E 63 H6
Friday Harbor U.S.A. 48°32N 123°1W 170 B3
Friedberg Bayern, Germany 48°21N 10°59E 77 G6
Friedberg Hessen, Germany 50°19N 8°45E 77 E4
Friedens U.S.A. 40°3N 78°59W 174 F6
Friedland Germany 53°40N 13°33E 76 B9
Friedrichshafen Germany 47°39N 9°30E 77 H5
Friedrichskoog Germany 54°1N 8°53E 76 A4
Friedrichstadt Germany 54°23N 9°5E 76 A5
Friendship U.S.A. 42°12N 78°8W 174 D6
Friesack Germany 52°44N 12°34E 76 C8
Friesland □ Neths. 53°5N 5°50E 69 A5
Friesoythe Germany 53°1N 7°51E 76 B3
Frigate Seychelles 4°35S 55°56E 141 b
Friggesund Sweden 61°56N 16°22E 62 C10
Frillesås Sweden 57°20N 12°12E 63 H3
Frinnaryd Sweden 57°55N 14°50E 63 G6
Frio → U.S.A. 28°26N 98°11W 176 G5
Frio, C. Brazil 22°50S 41°50W 184 F6
Friol Spain 43°1N 7°47W 88 B3
Friona U.S.A. 34°38N 102°43W 176 D3
Frisco U.S.A. 36°56N 96°49W 176 D6
Fristad Sweden 57°50N 13°0E 63 G6
Fritch U.S.A. 35°38N 101°36W 176 D4
Fritsla Sweden 57°33N 12°47E 63 G6
Fritzlar Germany 51°7N 9°16E 76 D5
Friuli-Venézia Giulia □ Italy 46°0N 13°0E 92 B9
Friza, Proliv Russia 45°30N 149°0E 107 E15
Frobisher B. Canada 62°30N 66°0W 161 E18
Frobisher Bay = Iqaluit Canada 63°44N 68°31W 161 E18
Frobisher L. Canada 56°20N 108°15W 163 B7
Frohavet Norway 64°0N 9°30E 60 E13
Frohnleiten Austria 47°16N 15°19E 78 E8
Frolovo Russia 49°45N 43°40E 86 F6
Frome U.K. 51°14N 2°19W 67 F5
Frome → U.K. 50°41N 2°6W 67 G5
Frome, L. Australia 30°45S 139°45E 152 B2
Frome Downs Australia 31°13S 139°45E 152 A3
Frómista Spain 42°16N 4°25W 88 C6
Front Range U.S.A. 40°25N 105°45W 168 F11
Front Royal U.S.A. 38°55N 78°12W 173 F14

Fronteira Portugal 39°3N 7°39W 89 F3
Fronteiras Brazil 7°5S 40°37W 189 B2
Frontenac → Canada 44°32N 76°30W 175 B8
Frontera Canary Is. 27°47N 17°59W 100 G2
Frontera Mexico 18°32N 92°38W 181 D6
Frontera Canary Is. 30°56N 109°33W 180 A3
Frontignan France 43°27N 3°45E 72 E7
Frosinone Italy 41°38N 13°19E 94 A6
Frostburg U.S.A. 39°39N 78°56W 173 F14
Frosten Norway 63°14N 10°10E 60 B17
Frostproof U.S.A. 27°45N 81°32W 179 H8
Frouard France 48°47N 6°8E 71 C13
Fröya Sweden 59°28N 15°24E 62 E9
Frøya Norway 63°43N 8°40E 60 E13
Fruita U.S.A. 39°9N 108°44W 168 G9
Fruithurst U.S.A. 33°44N 85°26W 178 B4
Fruitland Park U.S.A. 28°51N 81°54W 179 G8
Frumoasa Romania 46°28N 25°48E 81 D10
Frunze = Bishkek Kyrgyzstan 42°54N 74°46E 109 C8
Frunzivka Ukraine 47°20N 29°45E 81 C16
Fruška Gora Serbia 45°7N 19°30E 80 E4
Fruška Gora △ Serbia 45°8N 19°40E 96 A3
Frutal Brazil 20°0S 49°0W 187 H9
Frutigen Switz. 46°34N 7°38E 77 J3
Frýdek-Místek Czech Rep. 49°40N 18°20E 79 B11
Frýdlant Czech Rep. 50°56N 15°9E 78 A8
Fryeburg U.S.A. 44°1N 70°59W 175 B14
Fryvaldov = Jeseník Czech Rep. 50°14N 17°8E 79 A10
Fthiotida Greece 38°50N 22°25E 98 C4
Fu Jiang → China 30°0N 106°16E 116 C6
Fu Xian = Wafangdian China 39°38N 121°58E 115 E11
Fu Xian China 36°0N 109°20E 114 G5
Fu'an China 27°11N 119°36E 117 D12
Fubian China 31°17N 102°2E 116 B4
Fucécchio Italy 43°44N 10°48E 92 E7
Fucheng China 37°50N 116°10E 114 F9
Fuchou = Fuzhou China 26°5N 119°16E 117 D12
Fuchū Japan 34°34N 133°14E 113 G6
Fuchuan China 24°50N 111°5E 117 E8
Fuchun Jiang → China 30°5N 120°5E 117 B13
Fúcino, Piana del Italy 42°1N 13°31E 93 F10
Fuding China 27°20N 120°12E 117 D13
Fuencaliente Canary Is. 28°28N 17°50W 100 F2
Fuencaliente Spain 38°25N 4°18W 89 G6
Fuencaliente, Pta. Canary Is. 28°27N 17°51W 100 F2
Fuengirola Spain 36°32N 4°41W 89 J6
Fuenlabrada Spain 40°17N 3°48W 88 E7
Fuensalida Spain 40°3N 4°12W 88 E6
Fuente-Álamo Spain 38°44N 1°24W 91 G3
Fuente-Álamo de Murcia Spain 37°42N 1°6W 91 H3
Fuente de Cantos Spain 38°15N 6°18W 89 G4
Fuente del Maestre Spain 38°31N 6°28W 89 G4
Fuente el Fresno Spain 39°14N 3°46W 89 F7
Fuente Obejuna Spain 38°15N 5°25W 89 G5
Fuente Palmera Spain 37°42N 5°6W 89 H5
Fuentes de Andalucía Spain 37°28N 5°20W 89 H5
Fuentes de Ebro Spain 41°31N 0°38W 90 D4
Fuentes de León Spain 38°5N 6°32W 89 G4
Fuentes de Oñoro Spain 40°33N 6°52W 88 E4
Fuentesaúco Spain 41°15N 5°30W 88 D5
Fuerte → Mexico 25°54N 109°22W 180 B3
Fuerte Olimpo Paraguay 21°0S 57°51W 190 A4
Fuerteventura Canary Is. 28°30N 14°0W 100 F6
Fuerteventura ✈ (FUE) Canary Is. 28°24N 13°52W 100 F6
Fufeng China 34°22N 108°0E 114 G5
Fugong China 27°5N 98°47E 116 D2
Fugou China 34°3N 114°25E 116 A10
Fugu China 39°2N 111°3E 114 E6
Fuhai China 47°2N 87°25E 109 C11
Fuhaymi Iraq 34°16N 42°10E 128 C4
Fuhlsbüttel, Hamburg ✈ (HAM) Germany 53°35N 9°59E 76 B5
Fuidhaigh = Wiay U.K. 57°24N 7°13W 65 D1
Fuji Japan 35°9N 138°39E 113 G9
Fuji-Hakone-Izu △ Japan 35°15N 138°45E 113 G9
Fuji-San Japan 35°22N 138°44E 113 G9
Fuji-Yoshida Japan 35°30N 138°46E 113 G9
Fujian □ China 26°0N 118°0E 117 D12
Fujin China 47°16N 132°1E 111 B15
Fujinomiya Japan 35°10N 138°40E 113 G9
Fujisawa Japan 35°22N 139°29E 113 G9
Fujiyama, Mt. = Fuji-San Japan 35°22N 138°44E 113 G9
Fukagawa Japan 43°43N 142°2E 112 C11
Fukang China 44°10N 87°59E 109 D11
Fukien = Fujian □ China 26°0N 118°0E 117 D12
Fukuchiyama Japan 35°19N 135°9E 113 G7
Fukue Japan 32°41N 128°51E 113 H4
Fukue-Shima Japan 32°40N 128°45E 113 H4
Fukui Japan 36°0N 136°10E 113 F8
Fukui □ Japan 36°0N 136°12E 113 G8
Fukuoka Japan 33°39N 130°21E 113 H5
Fukuoka □ Japan 33°30N 131°0E 113 H5
Fukushima Japan 37°44N 140°28E 112 F10
Fukushima □ Japan 37°30N 140°15E 112 F10
Fukuyama Japan 34°35N 133°20E 113 G6
Fulacunda Guinea-Biss. 11°33N 15°1W 138 C1
Fulaga Fiji 19°8S 178°33W 154 a
Fulda Germany 50°32N 9°40E 76 E5
Fulda → Germany 51°25N 9°39E 76 D5
Fulford Harbour Canada 48°47N 123°27W 170 B3
Fuliang China 29°21N 117°17E 116 C10
Fuling China 29°40N 107°17E 116 C6
Fullerton Calif., U.S.A. 33°53N 117°56W 171 M9
Fullerton Nebr., U.S.A. 41°22N 97°58W 172 E5
Fulongquan China 44°20N 124°42E 115 B13
Fulton Mo., U.S.A. 38°52N 91°57W 172 F8
Fulton N.Y., U.S.A. 43°19N 76°25W 175 C8
Fuluälven → Sweden 61°18N 13°4E 62 C7
Fulufjället Sweden 61°32N 12°41E 62 C6
Fumay France 49°59N 4°44E 71 C11
Fumel France 44°30N 0°58E 72 D4
Fumin China 25°10N 102°20E 116 E4
Funabashi Japan 35°45N 140°0E 113 G10
Funafuti = Fongafale Tuvalu 8°31N 179°13E 147 B10

Funan China 32°30N 115°42E 117 A10
Funäsdalen Sweden 62°33N 12°32E 62 B6
Funchal Madeira 32°38N 16°54W 100 D3
Funchal ✈ (FNC) Madeira 32°42N 16°45W 100 D3
Fundación Colombia 10°31N 74°11W 186 A4
Fundão Brazil 19°55S 40°24W 189 E3
Fundão Portugal 40°8N 7°30W 88 E3
Fundu Moldovei Romania 47°32N 25°24E 81 C10
Fundulea Romania 44°28N 26°31E 81 F10
Fundy, B. of Canada 45°0N 66°0W 165 D6
Fundy △ Canada 45°35N 65°10W 165 C6
Funhalouro Mozam. 23°3S 34°25E 145 B5
Funing Hebei, China 39°53N 119°12E 115 E10
Funing Jiangsu, China 33°45N 119°50E 115 H10
Funing Yunnan, China 23°35N 105°45E 116 F5
Funiu Shan China 33°30N 112°0E 114 H7
Funsi Ghana 10°21N 1°54W 138 C4
Funtua Nigeria 11°30N 7°18E 139 C6
Fuping Hebei, China 38°48N 114°12E 114 E8
Fuping Shaanxi, China 34°42N 109°10E 114 G5
Fuqing China 25°41N 119°21E 117 E12
Fuquan China 26°40N 107°27E 116 D6
Furano Japan 43°21N 142°23E 112 C11
Furât, Nahr al → Asia 31°0N 47°25E 128 D5
Fürg Iran 28°18N 55°13E 129 D7
Furman U.S.A. 32°41N 81°11W 178 C8
Furmanov Russia 57°10N 41°9E 86 B6
Furnás Spain 39°3N 1°32E 100 B8
Furnas, Represa de Brazil 20°50S 45°30W 191 A6
Furneaux Group Australia 40°10S 147°50E 151 G4
Furqlus Syria 34°36N 37°8E 130 A6
Fürstenau Germany 52°31N 7°40E 76 C3
Fürstenberg Germany 53°10N 13°8E 76 B9
Fürstenfeld Austria 47°3N 16°3E 78 D9
Fürstenfeldbruck Germany 48°11N 11°15E 77 G7
Fürstenwalde Germany 52°22N 14°3E 76 C10
Fürth Germany 49°28N 10°59E 77 F6
Fürth im Wald Germany 49°18N 12°50E 77 F8
Furtwangen Germany 48°2N 8°12E 77 G4
Furudal Sweden 61°10N 15°11E 62 C9
Furukawa = Ōsaki Japan 38°34N 140°58E 112 E10
Furulund Sweden 55°46N 13°6E 63 J7
Furuvik Sweden 61°38N 17°20E 62 D11
Fury and Hecla Str. Canada 69°56N 84°0W 161 D15
Fusagasugá Colombia 4°21N 74°22W 186 C4
Fuscaldo Italy 39°25N 16°2E 95 C9
Fushan Shandong, China 37°30N 121°15E 115 F11
Fushan Shanxi, China 35°58N 111°51E 114 G6
Fushë Arrëz Albania 42°4N 20°2E 96 G3
Fushë Kosovë Kosovo 42°40N 21°5E 96 G3
Fushë Krujë Albania 41°29N 19°43E 96 E3
Fushun Liaoning, China 41°50N 123°56E 115 D12
Fushun Sichuan, China 29°13N 104°52E 116 C5
Fusong China 42°20N 127°15E 115 C14
Füssen Germany 47°34N 10°42E 77 H6
Fustic Barbados 13°16N 59°38W 183 g
Fusui China 22°40N 107°56E 116 F6
Futian China 22°32N 114°4E 111 a
Futog Serbia 45°15N 19°42E 80 E4
Futrono Chile 40°8S 72°24W 192 B2
Fuwa Egypt 31°12N 30°33E 137 E7
Fuxian Hu China 24°30N 102°53E 116 E4
Fuxin China 42°5N 121°48E 115 C11
Fuyang Anhui, China 33°0N 115°48E 117 A10
Fuyang Zhejiang, China 30°5N 119°57E 117 B12
Fuyang He → China 38°12N 117°0E 114 E9
Fuying Dao China 26°30N 120°1E 117 D13
Fuyong China 22°40N 113°49E 111 a
Fuyu Heilongjiang, China 47°49N 124°27E 111 B13
Fuyu Jilin, China 45°12N 124°43E 115 B13
Fuyuan China 48°20N 134°5E 111 B15
Fuyun China 47°0N 89°28E 109 C11
Füzesgyarmat Hungary 47°6N 21°14E 80 C6
Fuzhou = Linchuan China 27°57N 116°15E 117 D11
Fuzhou China 26°5N 119°16E 117 D12
Füzuli Azerbaijan 39°36N 47°8E 105 C12
Fyn Denmark 55°20N 10°30E 63 J4
Fyne, L. U.K. 55°59N 5°23W 65 F3
Fynshav Denmark 54°59N 9°59E 63 K4

G

Ga Ghana 9°47N 2°30W 138 D4
Gaalkacyo Somalia 6°30N 47°30E 131 F4
Gaanda Nigeria 10°10N 12°27E 139 C7
Gabas → France 43°46N 0°42W 72 E3
Gabba Australia 9°45S 142°38E 150 a
Gabela Angola 11°0S 14°24E 140 G2
Gabès Tunisia 33°53N 10°2E 136 B6
Gabès, G. de Tunisia 34°0N 10°30E 136 B6
Gabgaba, W. → Egypt 22°10N 33°5E 137 C3
Gabia la Grande Spain 37°8N 3°40W 89 H7
Gabin Poland 52°23N 19°41E 85 E6
Gabon ■ Africa 0°10S 10°0E 140 E2
Gaborone Botswana 24°45S 25°57E 144 B4
Gabriels U.S.A. 44°26N 74°12W 175 B10
Gäbrïk Iran 25°44N 58°28E 129 E8
Gabrovo Bulgaria 42°52N 25°19E 97 D9
Gacé France 48°49N 0°20E 70 D7
Gäch Sär Iran 36°7N 51°19E 129 B6
Gachsārān Iran 30°15N 50°45E 129 D6
Gacko Bos.-H. 43°10N 18°33E 96 C3
Gad Hinglaj India 16°14N 74°21E 127 L2
Gadag India 15°30N 75°45E 127 M2
Gadap Pakistan 25°5N 67°28E 124 G2
Gadarwara India 22°50N 78°50E 125 H11
Gadebusch Germany 53°42N 11°7E 76 B7
Gadhada India 22°0N 71°35E 124 J4
Gádor, Sierra de Spain 36°57N 2°45W 89 J8
Gadra Pakistan 25°40N 70°38E 124 G4
Gadsden Ala., U.S.A. 34°1N 86°1W 178 B3
Gadsden S.C., U.S.A. 33°51N 80°46W 178 B6
Gadwal India 16°10N 77°50E 127 L3
Gadyach = Hadyach Ukraine 50°21N 34°0E 85 G8
Gaeşti Romania 44°48N 25°19E 81 F10
Gaeta Italy 41°12N 13°35E 94 A6

Gaeta, G. di *Italy* 41°6N 13°30E **94 A6**
Gaffney *U.S.A.* 35°5N 81°39W **177 D14**
Gafsa *Tunisia* 34°24N 8°43E **136 B5**
Gafsa □ *Tunisia* 34°30N 8°48E **136 B5**
Gagarawa *Nigeria* 12°25N 9°32E **139 C6**
Gagaria *India* 25°43N 70°46E **124 G4**
Gagarin *Russia* 55°38N 35°0E **84 E8**
Găgăuzia □ *Moldova* 46°10N 28°40E **81 C13**
Gaggenau *Germany* 48°48N 8°18E **77 G4**
Gagino *Russia* 55°15N 45°1E **86 C7**
Gagliano del Capo *Italy* 39°50N 18°22E **95 C11**
Gagnef *Sweden* 60°36N 15°5E **62 D9**
Gagnoa *Ivory C.* 6°56N 6°16W **138 D3**
Gagnon *Canada* 51°50N 68°5W **165 B6**
Gagnon, L. *Canada* 62°3N 110°27W **163 A6**
Gagra *Georgia* 43°20N 40°10E **87 J5**
Gahini *Rwanda* 1°50S 30°30E **142 C3**
Gahmar *India* 25°27N 83°49E **125 G10**
Gai Xian = Gaizhou *China* 40°22N 122°20E **115 D12**
Gaidouronisi *Greece* 34°53N 25°41E **101 E7**
Gail *Austria* 46°36N 13°53E **78 E6**
Gail → *Austria* 46°36N 13°53E **78 E6**
Gail *U.S.A.* 32°46N 101°27W **176 E4**
Gaillac *France* 43°54N 1°54E **72 E5**
Gaillimh = Galway *Ireland* 53°17N 9°3W **64 A2**
Gaillon *France* 49°10N 1°20E **70 C8**
Gaimán *Argentina* 43°10S 65°25W **192 B3**
Gaines *U.S.A.* 41°46N 77°35W **174 E7**
Gainesville *Fla., U.S.A.* 29°40N 82°20W **179 F7**
Gainesville *Ga., U.S.A.* 34°18N 83°50W **177 D13**
Gainesville *Mo., U.S.A.* 36°36N 92°26W **172 G7**
Gainesville *Tex., U.S.A.* 33°38N 97°8W **176 E6**
Gainsborough *U.K.* 53°24N 0°46W **66 D7**
Gairdner, L. *Australia* 31°30S 136°0E **152 A2**
Gairloch *U.K.* 57°43N 5°41W **65 D3**
Gairloch, L. *U.K.* 57°43N 5°45W **65 D3**
Gaizhou *China* 40°22N 122°20E **115 D12**
Gaj *Croatia* 45°28N 17°3E **80 E2**
Gaj → *Russia* 51°26N 67°21E **124 F2**
Gajendragarh *India* 15°44N 75°59E **127 G2**
Gakuch *Pakistan* 36°7N 73°45E **125 A5**
Gal Oya → *Sri Lanka* 7°0N 81°20E **127 L5**
Gal Oya Res. *Sri Lanka* 7°5N 81°30E **127 L5**
Galâla, Gebel el *Egypt* 29°21N 32°22E **137 F8**
Galán, Cerro *Argentina* 25°55S 66°52W **190 B2**
Galana → *Kenya* 3°9S 40°8E **142 C5**
Galanta *Slovak Rep.* 48°11N 17°45E **79 C10**
Galapagar *Spain* 40°36N 3°58W **88 E7**
Galápagos = Colón, Arch. de *Ecuador* 0°0 91°0W **184 D1**
Galapagos Fracture Zone *Pac. Oc.* 3°0N 110°0W **157 G17**
Galapagos Rise *Pac. Oc.* 15°0S 95°0W **157 J18**
Galashiels *U.K.* 55°37N 2°49W **65 F6**
Galatas *Greece* 37°30N 23°26E **98 D5**
Galatea *N.Z.* 38°24S 176°45E **154 E5**
Galateia *Cyprus* 35°25N 34°4E **101 D13**
Galați *Romania* 45°27N 28°2E **81 E13**
Galați □ *Romania* 45°45N 27°30E **81 E12**
Galatia *Turkey* 39°30N 33°0E **104 C5**
Galatina *Italy* 40°10N 18°10E **95 B11**
Galátone *Italy* 40°9N 18°4E **95 B11**
Galax *U.S.A.* 36°40N 80°56W **173 G13**
Galaxidi *Greece* 38°22N 22°23E **98 C4**
Galbín Govĭ *Mongolia* 43°0N 107°0E **114 C4**
Galcaio = Gaalkacyo *Somalia* 6°30N 47°30E **131 F4**
Galdhøpiggen *Norway* 61°38N 8°18E **60 F13**
Galeana *Chihuahua, Mexico* 30°7N 107°38W **180 A3**
Galeana *Nuevo León, Mexico* 24°50N 100°4W **180 A3**
Galela *Indonesia* 1°50N 127°49E **119 D7**
Galera *Spain* 37°45N 2°33W **91 H2**
Galera, Pta. *Chile* 39°59S 73°43W **192 A2**
Galera Pt. *Trin. & Tob.* 10°49N 60°54W **183 D7**
Galesburg *U.S.A.* 40°57N 90°22W **172 E8**
Galeton *U.S.A.* 41°44N 77°39W **174 E7**
Galheirão → *Brazil* 12°23S 45°5W **189 C1**
Gali *Georgia* 42°37N 41°46E **87 J5**
Galicea Mare *Romania* 44°4N 23°19E **81 F8**
Galich *Russia* 58°22N 42°24E **86 B6**
Galiche *Bulgaria* 43°34N 23°53E **96 C7**
Galicia □ *Spain* 42°43N 7°45W **88 D3**
Galičica △ *Macedonia* 41°2N 20°55E **96 C4**
Galilee = Hagalil *Israel* 32°53N 35°18E **130 C4**
Galilee, L. *Australia* 22°20S 145°50E **150 C4**
Galilee, Sea of = Yam Kinneret *Israel* 32°45N 35°35E **130 C4**
Galim *Cameroon* 7°6N 12°25E **139 D7**
Galina Pt. *Jamaica* 18°24N 76°58W **182 a**
Galinoporni *Cyprus* 35°31N 34°18E **101 D13**
Galion *U.S.A.* 40°44N 82°47W **174 F2**
Galite, Îs. de la *Tunisia* 37°30N 8°59E **136 A5**
Galiuro Mts. *U.S.A.* 32°30N 110°20W **169 K8**
Galiwinku *Australia* 12°25S 135°34E **150 A2**
Gallan Hd. *U.K.* 58°15N 7°2W **65 C1**
Gallarate *Italy* 45°40N 8°47E **78 F6**
Gallatin *U.S.A.* 36°24N 86°27W **177 C11**
Galle *Sri Lanka* 6°5N 80°10E **127 L5**
Gállego → *Spain* 41°39N 0°51W **90 D4**
Galley Hd. *Ireland* 51°32N 8°55W **64 E3**
Galliate *Italy* 45°29N 8°42E **92 C5**
Gallinas, Pta. *Colombia* 12°28N 71°40W **186 A4**
Gallipoli = Gelibolu *Turkey* 40°28N 26°43E **97 F10**
Gallipoli *Italy* 40°3N 17°58E **95 B10**
Gallipolis *U.S.A.* 38°49N 82°12W **173 F12**
Gällivare *Sweden* 67°9N 20°40E **60 D19**
Gallneukirchen *Austria* 48°21N 14°25E **78 C7**
Gällö *Sweden* 62°55N 15°13E **62 B9**
Gallo, C. *Italy* 38°13N 13°19E **94 D6**
Gallocanta, L. de *Spain* 40°58N 1°30W **90 E3**
Galloo I. *U.S.A.* 43°55N 76°25W **175 C8**
Galloway *U.K.* 55°1N 4°29W **65 F4**
Galloway, Mull of *U.K.* 54°39N 4°52W **65 G4**
Gallup *U.S.A.* 35°32N 108°45W **169 J9**
Gallur *Spain* 41°52N 1°19W **90 D3**
Gallura *Italy* 41°5N 9°2E **94 A2**
Galmudug *Somalia* 6°30N 48°0E **131 F4**
Galong *Australia* 34°37S 148°34E **153 C8**
Galoya *Sri Lanka* 8°10N 80°55E **127 K5**
Galt *U.S.A.* 38°15N 121°18W **170 G5**
Galtür *Austria* 46°58N 10°11E **78 E8**
Galty Mts. *Ireland* 52°22N 8°10W **64 D3**

Galtymore *Ireland* 52°21N 8°11W **64 D3**
Galva *U.S.A.* 41°10N 90°3W **172 E8**
Galvarino *Chile* 38°24S 72°47W **192 A2**
Galve de Sorbe *Spain* 41°13N 3°10W **90 D1**
Galveston *U.S.A.* 29°18N 94°48W **176 E7**
Galveston B. *U.S.A.* 29°36N 94°50W **176 E7**
Gálvez *Argentina* 32°0S 61°14W **190 C3**
Galway *Ireland* 53°17N 9°3W **64 A2**
Galway □ *Ireland* 53°22N 9°1W **64 A2**
Galway B. *Ireland* 53°13N 9°10W **64 A2**
Gam → *Vietnam* 21°55N 105°12E **120 B5**
Gamagōri *Japan* 34°50N 137°14E **113 G8**
Gamawa *Nigeria* 12°10N 10°31E **139 C7**
Gambaga *Ghana* 10°30N 0°28W **139 C4**
Gambat *Pakistan* 27°17N 68°26E **124 F3**
Gambhir → *India* 26°58N 77°27E **124 F6**
Gambia ■ *W. Afr.* 13°25N 16°0W **138 C1**
Gambia → *W. Afr.* 13°28N 16°34W **138 C1**
Gambier *U.S.A.* 40°22N 82°23W **174 F2**
Gambier, C. *Australia* 11°56S 130°57E **148 B5**
Gambier, Îs. *French Polynesia* 23°8S 134°58W **157 K14**
Gambier Is. *Australia* 35°3S 136°30E **152 C2**
Gambo *Canada* 48°47N 54°13W **165 C9**
Gamboli *Pakistan* 29°53N 68°24E **124 E3**
Gamboma *Congo* 1°55S 15°52E **140 E3**
Gamka → *S. Africa* 33°18S 21°39E **144 D3**
Gamkab → *Namibia* 28°4S 17°54E **144 C2**
Gamlakarleby = Kokkola *Finland* 63°50N 23°8E **60 E20**
Gamleby *Sweden* 57°54N 16°24E **63 G10**
Gammon → *Canada* 51°24N 95°44W **163 C9**
Gammon Ranges △ *Australia* 30°38S 139°8E **151 E2**
Gamou *Niger* 14°20N 9°55E **139 C6**
Gampaha *Sri Lanka* 7°5N 79°59E **127 L4**
Gampola *Sri Lanka* 7°10N 80°34E **127 L5**
Gamtoos → *S. Africa* 33°58S 25°1E **144 D4**
Gamzigrad-Romuliana *Serbia* 43°53N 22°11E **96 C6**
Gan *France* 43°12N 0°27W **72 E3**
Gan Gan *Argentina* 42°30S 68°10W **192 B3**
Gan Goriama, Mts. *Cameroon* 7°44N 12°45E **139 D7**
Gan Jiang → *China* 29°15N 116°0E **117 C11**
Ganado *U.S.A.* 35°43N 109°33W **169 J9**
Gananita *Sudan* 18°22N 33°50E **137 D13**
Gananoque *Canada* 44°20N 76°10W **175 B8**
Ganāveh *Iran* 29°35N 50°35E **129 D6**
Gäncä *Azerbaijan* 40°45N 46°20E **87 K8**
Gancheng *China* 18°51N 108°37E **117 d**
Gand = Gent *Belgium* 51°2N 3°42E **69 C3**
Ganda *Angola* 13°3S 14°35E **141 G2**
Gandajika *Dem. Rep. of the Congo* 6°46S 23°58E **140 F4**
Gandak → *India* 25°39N 85°13E **125 G11**
Gandava *Pakistan* 28°32N 67°32E **124 E2**
Gander *Canada* 48°58N 54°35W **165 C9**
Gander L. *Canada* 48°58N 54°35W **165 C9**
Ganderkesee *Germany* 53°2N 8°32E **76 B4**
Ganderowe Falls *Zimbabwe* 17°20S 29°10E **143 F2**
Gandesa *Spain* 41°3N 0°26E **90 D5**
Gandhi Sagar *India* 24°40N 75°40E **124 G6**
Gandhinagar *India* 23°15N 72°45E **124 H5**
Gandi *Nigeria* 12°55N 5°49E **139 C6**
Gandia *Spain* 38°58N 0°9W **91 G4**
Gandino *Italy* 45°49N 9°54E **92 C6**
Gando, Pta. *Canary Is.* 27°55N 15°22W **100 G4**
Gandole *Nigeria* 8°28N 11°35E **139 D7**
Ganedidalem = Gani *Indonesia* 0°48S 128°14E **119 E7**
Ganga → *India* 23°20N 90°30E **125 H14**
Ganga Sagar *India* 21°38N 88°5E **125 J13**
Gangafani *Mali* 14°20N 2°20W **138 C4**
Gangakher *India* 18°57N 76°45E **126 E3**
Gangan → *India* 28°38N 78°58E **125 E8**
Ganganagar *India* 29°56N 73°56E **124 E5**
Gangapur *Maharashtra, India* 19°41N 75°1E **126 E2**
Gangapur *Raj., India* 26°32N 76°49E **124 F7**
Gangara *Niger* 14°35N 8°29E **139 C6**
Gangaw *Burma* 22°5N 94°5E **123 H19**
Gangdisê Shan *China* 31°20N 81°0E **125 D9**
Ganges = Ganga → *India* 23°20N 90°30E **125 H14**
Ganges *Canada* 48°51N 123°31W **162 D4**
Ganges *France* 43°56N 3°42E **72 E7**
Ganges, Mouths of the *India* 21°30N 90°0E **125 J13**
Ganggyeong *S. Korea* 36°10N 127°0E **115 F14**
Gânghester *Sweden* 57°42N 13°1E **63 G7**
Gangi *Italy* 37°48N 14°12E **95 E7**
Gângiova *Romania* 43°54N 23°50E **81 G8**
Gangneung *S. Korea* 37°45N 128°54E **115 F15**
Gangoh *India* 29°46N 77°18E **124 E7**
Gangotri *India* 30°50N 79°10E **125 D8**
Gangotri △ *India* 30°50N 79°10E **125 D8**
Gangseong *S. Korea* 38°24N 128°30E **115 E15**
Gangtok *India* 27°20N 88°37E **125 F16**
Gangu *China* 34°40N 105°15E **114 G3**
Gangyao *China* 44°12N 126°37E **115 B14**
Gani *Indonesia* 0°48S 128°14E **119 E7**
Ganj *India* 27°45N 78°57E **125 F8**
Ganjam *India* 19°23N 85°4E **126 E7**
Ganluo *China* 28°58N 102°56E **117 C5**
Ganmain *Australia* 34°47S 147°1E **153 C7**
Gannat *France* 46°7N 3°11E **71 F10**
Gannett Peak *U.S.A.* 43°11N 109°39W **168 E9**
Ganquan *China* 36°20N 109°20E **114 F5**
Ganserndorf *Austria* 48°20N 16°43E **79 C9**
Ganshui *China* 28°40N 106°40E **116 C6**
Gansu □ *China* 36°0N 104°0E **114 G2**
Ganta *Liberia* 7°15N 8°59W **138 D3**
Ganta *Australia* 14°4S 137°32E **150 B2**
Gantheaume, C. *Australia* 36°4S 137°32E **152 D2**
Gantheaume B. *Australia* 27°40S 114°10W **149 E1**
Gantsevichi = Hantsavichy *Belarus* 52°49N 26°30E **81 B14**
Ganye *Nigeria* 8°25N 12°4E **139 D7**
Ganyem = Genyem *Indonesia* 2°46S 140°12E **119 E10**
Ganyu *China* 34°50N 119°8E **115 G10**
Ganyushkino *Kazakhstan* 46°35N 49°20E **87 G9**

Ganzhou *China* 25°51N 114°56E **117 E10**
Gao *Mali* 16°15N 0°5W **139 B4**
Gao Xian *China* 28°21N 104°32E **116 C5**
Gao'an *China* 28°26N 115°17E **117 C10**
Gaobeidian *China* 39°19N 115°51E **114 E8**
Gaocheng *China* 38°2N 114°49E **114 E8**
Gaochun *China* 31°20N 118°49E **117 B12**
Gaohebu *China* 30°43N 116°49E **117 B11**
Gaokeng *China* 27°40N 113°58E **117 D9**
Gaolan Dao *China* 21°54N 113°8E **117 a**
Gaoligong Shan *China* 24°45N 98°45E **116 E2**
Gaomi *China* 36°20N 119°42E **115 F10**
Gaoping *China* 35°45N 112°55E **114 G7**
Gaotang *China* 36°50N 116°15E **114 F9**
Gaoua *Burkina Faso* 10°20N 3°8W **138 C4**
Gaoual *Guinea* 11°45N 13°25W **138 C2**
Gaoxiong = Kaohsiung *Taiwan* 22°35N 120°16E **117 F13**
Gaoyang *China* 38°40N 115°45E **114 E8**
Gaoyao *China* 23°3N 112°27E **117 F9**
Gaoyou *China* 32°47N 119°26E **117 A12**
Gaoyou Hu *China* 32°45N 119°20E **117 A12**
Gaoyuan *China* 37°8N 117°58E **115 F9**
Gaozhou *China* 21°58N 110°50E **117 G8**
Gap *France* 44°33N 6°5E **73 D10**
Gapat → *India* 24°30N 82°28E **125 G10**
Gapuwiyak *Australia* 12°25S 135°43E **150 A2**
Gar *China* 32°10N 79°58E **125 D8**
Gara, L. *Ireland* 53°57N 8°26W **64 C3**
Garāb *Iran* 33°27N 47°16E **105 F12**
Garabogazköl Aylagy *Turkmenistan* 41°0N 53°30E **108 D4**
Garachico *Canary Is.* 28°22N 16°46W **100 F3**
Garachiné *Panama* 8°0N 78°12W **182 E4**
Garafia *Canary Is.* 28°48N 17°57W **100 F2**
Garagum *Turkmenistan* 39°30N 60°0E **129 B8**
Garah *Australia* 29°5S 149°38E **151 D4**
Garajonay *Canary Is.* 28°7N 17°14W **100 F2**
Garajonay △ *Canary Is.* 28°7N 17°14W **100 F2**
Garamba △ *Dem. Rep. of the Congo* 4°10N 29°40E **142 B2**
Garango *Burkina Faso* 11°48N 0°33W **139 C4**
Garanhuns *Brazil* 8°50S 36°30W **189 B3**
Garautha *India* 25°34N 79°18E **125 G8**
Garawa → *Australia* 16°43S 136°51E **150 B2**
Garawe *Liberia* 4°35N 8°0W **138 E3**
Garba Tula *Kenya* 0°30N 38°32E **142 B4**
Garberville *U.S.A.* 40°6N 123°48W **168 F2**
Garbiyang *India* 30°8N 80°54E **125 D9**
Garbsen *Germany* 52°26N 9°31E **76 C5**
Garças → *Brazil* 8°43S 39°41W **189 B3**
Gard □ *France* 44°2N 4°10E **73 D8**
Gard → *France* 43°51N 4°37E **73 E8**
Garda, L. di *Italy* 45°40N 10°41E **92 C7**
Gardabani *Georgia* 41°27N 45°5E **87 K7**
Gardanne *France* 43°27N 5°27E **73 E9**
Gårdby *Sweden* 56°36N 16°38E **63 H10**
Garde L. *Canada* 62°50N 106°13W **163 A7**
Gardelegen *Germany* 52°32N 11°24E **76 C7**
Garden City *Ga., U.S.A.* 32°6N 81°9W **178 C8**
Garden City *Kans., U.S.A.* 37°58N 100°53W **172 G3**
Garden City *Tex., U.S.A.* 31°52N 101°29W **176 F4**
Garden Grove *U.S.A.* 33°47N 117°55W **171 M9**
Gardens of Stone △ *Australia* 33°14S 150°11E **153 B8**
Gardez *Afghan.* 33°37N 69°9E **124 C3**
Gardiki *Greece* 38°50N 21°55E **98 C3**
Gardiner *Maine, U.S.A.* 44°14N 69°47W **173 C19**
Gardiner *Mont., U.S.A.* 45°2N 110°22W **168 D8**
Gardiners I. *U.S.A.* 41°6N 72°6W **175 E12**
Gardner *Fla., U.S.A.* 27°21N 81°48W **179 H8**
Gardner *Mass., U.S.A.* 42°34N 71°59W **175 D13**
Gardner Canal *Canada* 53°27N 128°8W **162 C3**
Gardner Pinnacles *U.S.A.* 25°0N 167°55W **167 L6**
Gardnerville *U.S.A.* 38°56N 119°45W **170 G7**
Gardno, Jezioro *Poland* 54°40N 17°7E **82 A4**
Gardo = Qardho *Somalia* 9°30N 49°6E **131 F4**
Gardone Val Trómpia *Italy* 45°41N 10°11E **92 C7**
Gárdony *Hungary* 47°12N 18°39E **80 C3**
Gares = Puente la Reina *Spain* 42°40N 1°49W **90 C3**
Garešnica *Croatia* 45°36N 16°56E **93 C13**
Garéssio *Italy* 44°12N 8°2E **92 D5**
Garey *U.S.A.* 34°53N 120°19W **171 L6**
Garfield *U.S.A.* 47°1N 117°9W **168 C5**
Garforth *U.K.* 53°47N 1°24W **66 D6**
Gargaliani *Greece* 37°4N 21°38E **98 D3**
Gargan, Mt. *France* 45°37N 1°39E **72 C5**
Gargano, △ *Italy* 41°43N 15°52E **92 G12**
Gargantua, C. *Canada* 47°36N 85°2W **173 B11**
Gargett *Australia* 21°9S 148°46E **150 b**
Gargouna *Mali* 15°56N 0°13E **139 C5**
Gargždai *Lithuania* 55°43N 21°24E **82 C8**
Garhchiroli *India* 20°10N 80°0E **126 E6**
Garibaldi *Canada* 49°50N 122°40W **162 D4**
Gariep, L. *S. Africa* 30°40S 25°40E **144 E4**
Garies *S. Africa* 30°32S 17°59E **144 D2**
Garig Gunak Barlu △ *Australia* 11°26S 131°55E **148 B5**
Garissa *Kenya* 0°25S 39°40E **142 C4**
Garkida *Nigeria* 10°27N 12°36E **139 C7**
Garko *Nigeria* 11°45N 8°35E **139 C6**
Garland *Tex., U.S.A.* 32°54N 96°38W **176 E6**
Garland *Utah, U.S.A.* 41°45N 112°10W **168 F7**
Garlasco *Italy* 45°12N 8°55E **92 C5**
Garliava *Lithuania* 54°49N 23°52E **82 D10**
Garlin *France* 43°33N 0°16W **72 E3**
Garmāb *Semnān, Iran* 35°25N 56°45E **129 C8**
Garmāb *Zanjān, Iran* 36°12N 47°29E **128 B5**
Garmisch-Partenkirchen *Germany* 47°30N 11°6E **77 H7**
Garmsār *Iran* 35°20N 52°25E **129 C7**
Garner *U.S.A.* 43°6N 93°36W **172 D7**
Garnett *U.S.A.* 38°17N 95°14W **172 F6**
Garnpung L. *Australia* 33°25S 143°10E **152 B5**
Garo Hills *India* 25°30N 90°30E **125 G14**
Garoe = Garoowe *Somalia* 8°25N 48°33E **131 F4**
Garonne → *France* 45°2N 0°36W **72 C3**
Garonne, Canal Latéral à la *France* 44°15N 0°18E **72 D4**
Garoowe *Somalia* 8°25N 48°33E **131 F4**
Garot *India* 24°19N 75°41E **124 G6**
Garou, L. *Mali* 16°2N 2°45W **138 B4**

Garoua *Cameroon* 9°19N 13°21E **139 D7**
Garpenberg *Sweden* 60°19N 16°12E **62 D10**
Garphyttan *Sweden* 59°18N 14°56E **62 D8**
Garrauli *India* 25°5N 79°22E **125 G8**
Garrel *Germany* 52°57N 8°1E **76 C4**
Garrison *Mont., U.S.A.* 46°31N 112°49W **168 C7**
Garrison *N. Dak., U.S.A.* 47°40N 101°25W **172 B3**
Garrison Res. = Sakakawea, L. *U.S.A.* 47°30N 101°25W **172 B3**
Garron Pt. *U.K.* 55°3N 5°59W **64 A6**
Garrovillas de Alconétar *Spain* 39°40N 6°33W **89 F4**
Garrucha *Spain* 37°11N 1°49W **91 H3**
Garry → *U.K.* 56°44N 3°47E **65 E5**
Garry, L. *Canada* 65°58N 100°18W **160 D11**
Garrygala *Turkmenistan* 38°31N 56°29E **129 B7**
Garsen *Kenya* 2°20S 40°5E **142 C5**
Gärsnäs *Sweden* 55°32N 14°10E **63 J8**
Garson L. *Canada* 56°19N 110°2W **163 B6**
Garstang *U.K.* 53°55N 2°46W **66 D5**
Gartempe → *France* 46°47N 0°49E **72 B4**
Gartz *Germany* 53°13N 14°22E **76 B10**
Garu *Ghana* 10°55N 0°11W **139 C4**
Garu *India* 23°40N 84°14E **125 G10**
Garub *Namibia* 26°37S 16°0E **144 C2**
Garut *Indonesia* 7°14S 107°53E **119 G12**
Garvão *Portugal* 37°42N 8°21W **89 H2**
Garvie Mts. *N.Z.* 45°30S 168°50E **155 F3**
Garwa = Garoua *Cameroon* 9°19N 13°21E **139 D7**
Garwa *India* 24°11N 83°47E **125 G10**
Garwolin *Poland* 51°55N 21°38E **83 G8**
Gary *U.S.A.* 41°36N 87°20W **172 E10**
Garz *Germany* 54°19N 13°20E **76 A9**
Garzê *China* 31°38N 100°1E **116 B3**
Garzón *Colombia* 2°10N 75°40W **186 C3**
Gas-San *Japan* 38°32N 140°1E **112 E10**
Gasan Kuli = Esenguly *Turkmenistan* 37°37N 53°59E **108 E4**
Gascogne *France* 43°45N 0°20E **72 E4**
Gascogne, G. de *Europe* 44°0N 2°0W **72 E2**
Gascony = Gascogne *France* 43°45N 0°20E **72 E4**
Gascoyne → *Australia* 24°52S 113°37E **149 D1**
Gascoyne Junction *Australia* 25°2S 115°17E **149 E2**
Gascueña *Spain* 40°18N 2°31W **90 E2**
Gashagar *Nigeria* 13°22N 12°47E **139 C7**
Gashaka *Nigeria* 7°20N 11°29E **139 D7**
Gashaka-Gumti △ *Nigeria* 7°23N 11°34E **139 D7**
Gasherbrum *Pakistan* 35°40N 76°40E **125 B7**
Gashua *Nigeria* 12°54N 11°0E **139 C7**
Gaspar Str. = Gelasa, Selat *Indonesia* 2°50S 107°0E **118 E3**
Gasparilla I. *U.S.A.* 26°46N 82°16W **179 J7**
Gasparillo *Trin. & Tob.* 10°18N 61°26W **187 K15**
Gaspé *Canada* 48°52N 64°30W **165 C7**
Gaspé, C. de *Canada* 48°48N 64°7W **165 C7**
Gaspé Pen. = Gaspésie, Pén. de la *Canada* 48°45N 65°40W **165 C6**
Gaspésie, Pén. de la *Canada* 48°45N 65°40W **165 C6**
Gaspésie △ *Canada* 48°55N 66°10W **165 C6**
Gassan *Burkina Faso* 12°49N 3°12W **138 C4**
Gassol *Nigeria* 8°34N 10°25E **139 D7**
Gasteiz = Vitoria-Gasteiz *Spain* 42°50N 2°41W **90 C2**
Gastonia *U.S.A.* 35°16N 81°11W **177 D14**
Gastouri *Greece* 39°34N 19°54E **98 B1**
Gastre *Argentina* 42°20S 69°15W **192 B3**
Gästrikland *Sweden* 60°45N 16°40E **62 D10**
Gata, C. *Cyprus* 34°34N 33°2E **101 E12**
Gata, C. de *Spain* 36°41N 2°13W **91 J2**
Gata, Sierra de *Spain* 40°20N 6°45W **88 E4**
Gataga → *Canada* 58°35N 126°59W **162 B3**
Gâtaia *Romania* 45°26N 21°26E **80 E6**
Gatchina *Russia* 59°35N 30°9E **84 C6**
Gatehouse of Fleet *U.K.* 54°53N 4°12W **65 G4**
Gates *U.S.A.* 43°9N 77°42W **174 C7**
Gateshead I. *Canada* 70°36N 100°26W **160 C11**
Gatesville *U.S.A.* 31°26N 97°45W **176 F6**
Gateway △ *U.S.A.* 40°38N 73°51W **175 F11**
Gaths *Zimbabwe* 20°2S 30°32E **143 G3**
Gâtinais *France* 48°5N 2°40E **70 D9**
Gâtine, Hauteurs de *France* 46°35N 0°45W **72 B3**
Gatineau *Canada* 45°29N 75°39W **175 A9**
Gatineau → *Canada* 45°27N 75°42W **164 C4**
Gatineau △ *Canada* 45°40N 76°0W **164 C4**
Gattaran *Phil.* 18°4N 121°35E **119 a**
Gattinara *Italy* 45°37N 8°22E **92 C5**
Gatton *Australia* 27°32S 152°17E **151 D5**
Gatún, L. *Panama* 9°7N 79°56W **182 E4**
Gatwick, London ✈ (LGW) *U.K.* 51°10N 0°11W **67 F7**
Gatyana *S. Africa* 32°16S 28°31E **145 D4**
Gau *Fiji* 18°2S 179°18E **154 a**
Gaucín *Spain* 36°31N 5°19W **89 J5**
Gauer L. *Canada* 57°0N 97°50W **163 B9**
Gauhati = Guwahati *India* 26°10N 91°45E **125 F17**
Gauja → *Latvia* 57°10N 24°16E **84 B3**
Gaujaq → *Latvia* 57°10N 24°50E **61 H21**
Gaula → *Norway* 63°21N 10°14E **60 E14**
Gaurdak = Gowurdak *Turkmenistan* 37°50N 66°4E **109 F7**
Gauri Phanta *India* 28°41N 80°36E **125 E9**
Gauribidanur *India* 13°37N 77°12E **127 H3**
Gaustatoppen *Norway* 59°48N 8°40E **61 G13**
Gauteng □ *S. Africa* 26°0S 28°0E **145 C4**
Gāv Koshī *Iran* 28°38N 57°12E **129 D8**
Gävakān *Iran* 29°37N 53°10E **129 D7**
Gavarnie *France* 42°44N 0°7E **72 F4**
Gavāter *Iran* 25°10N 61°31E **129 E9**
Gavbandī *Iran* 27°12N 53°4E **129 E7**
Gavdopoula *Greece* 34°56N 24°0E **101 E6**
Gavdos *Greece* 34°50N 24°5E **101 E6**
Gávio → *Portugal* 39°28N 7°56W **89 F3**
Gaviota *U.S.A.* 34°29N 120°13W **171 L6**
Gävle *Sweden* 60°40N 17°9E **62 D11**
Gävleborg → *Sweden* 61°30N 16°15E **62 C10**
Gävlebukten *Sweden* 60°40N 17°20E **62 D11**
Gavorrano *Italy* 42°55N 10°54E **92 F7**

Gavray *France* 48°55N 1°2W **70 D5**
Gavrilov Yam *Russia* 57°18N 39°49E **84 D10**
Gavrio *Greece* 37°54N 24°44E **98 D6**
Gawachab *Namibia* 27°4S 17°55E **144 C2**
Gawilgarh Hills *India* 21°15N 76°45E **126 D3**
Gawler *Australia* 34°30S 138°42E **152 C3**
Gawler Ranges *Australia* 32°30S 135°45E **152 B2**
Gawu *Nigeria* 9°14N 6°52E **139 D6**
Gaxun Nur *China* 42°22N 100°30E **110 C9**
Gay *Russia* 51°27N 58°27E **108 B5**
Gay *U.S.A.* 33°6N 84°35W **178 D5**
Gaya *India* 24°47N 85°4E **125 G11**
Gaya *Niger* 11°52N 3°28E **139 C5**
Gaya *Nigeria* 11°57N 9°0E **139 C6**
Gayéri *Burkina Faso* 12°40N 0°33E **139 C5**
Gaylord *U.S.A.* 45°2N 84°41W **173 C11**
Gayndah *Australia* 25°35S 151°32E **151 D5**
Gaysin = Haysyn *Ukraine* 48°57N 29°25E **81 B14**
Gayvoron = Hayvoron *Ukraine* 48°22N 29°52E **81 B14**
Gaza *Gaza Strip* 31°30N 34°28E **130 D3**
Gaza □ *Mozam.* 23°10S 32°45E **145 B5**
Gaza Strip ■ *Asia* 31°29N 34°25E **130 D3**
Gazanjyk = Bereket *Turkmenistan* 39°16N 55°32E **129 B7**
Gazaoua *Niger* 13°32N 7°55E **139 C6**
Găzbor *Iran* 28°5N 58°51E **129 D8**
Gazi *Dem. Rep. of the Congo* 1°3N 24°30E **142 B1**
Gaziantep *Turkey* 37°6N 37°23E **104 D7**
Gaziantep □ *Turkey* 37°0N 37°0E **104 D7**
Gazimağusa = Famagusta *Cyprus* 35°8N 33°55E **101 D12**
Gazipaşa *Turkey* 36°16N 32°18E **104 D5**
Gazli *Uzbekistan* 40°8N 63°27E **108 D6**
Gbadolite *Dem. Rep. of the Congo* 4°17N 21°1E **140 D4**
Gbarnga *Liberia* 7°19N 9°13W **138 D3**
Gboko *Nigeria* 7°17N 9°4E **139 D6**
Gcoverega *Botswana* 19°8S 24°18E **144 A3**
Gcuwa *S. Africa* 32°20S 28°11E **145 D4**
Gdańsk *Poland* 54°22N 18°40E **82 D5**
Gdańsk ✈ (GDN) *Poland* 54°22N 18°30E **82 D5**
Gdańska, Zatoka *Poland* 54°30N 19°20E **82 A6**
Gdov *Russia* 58°48N 27°55E **84 C4**
Gdynia *Poland* 54°35N 18°33E **82 D5**
Geba → *Guinea-Biss.* 11°46N 15°36E **138 C1**
Gebe *Indonesia* 0°5N 129°25E **119 D7**
Gebeciler *Turkey* 38°46N 30°46E **99 C12**
Gebeit Mine *Sudan* 21°3N 36°29E **137 C4**
Gebel Abyad *Sudan* 19°0N 28°0E **137 D2**
Gebel Iweibid *Egypt* 30°8N 32°13E **137 E8**
Gebze *Turkey* 40°47N 29°25E **97 F13**
Geçitkale = Lefkoniko *Cyprus* 35°18N 33°44E **101 D12**
Gedaref *Sudan* 14°2N 35°28E **135 F13**
Gede, Tanjung *Indonesia* 6°46S 105°12E **119 G11**
Gedern *Germany* 50°25N 9°12E **77 E5**
Gediz *Turkey* 39°1N 29°24E **99 B11**
Gediz → *Turkey* 38°35N 26°48E **99 C8**
Gedong, Pulau *Malaysia* 5°17N 100°23E **121 c**
Gedser *Denmark* 54°35N 11°55E **63 K5**
Geegully Cr. → *Australia* 18°32S 123°41E **148 C3**
Geel *Belgium* 51°10N 4°59E **69 C4**
Geelong *Australia* 38°10S 144°22E **152 E6**
Geelvink Chan. *Australia* 28°30S 114°0E **149 E1**
Geesthacht *Germany* 53°26N 10°22E **76 B6**
Geidam *Nigeria* 12°57N 11°57E **139 C7**
Geikie → *Canada* 57°45N 103°52W **163 B8**
Geikie Gorge △ *Australia* 18°3S 125°41E **148 C4**
Geilenkirchen *Germany* 50°57N 6°9E **76 E2**
Geisingen *Germany* 47°54N 8°38E **77 H4**
Geislingen *Germany* 48°37N 9°50E **77 G5**
Geistown *U.S.A.* 40°18N 78°52W **174 F6**
Geita *Tanzania* 2°48S 32°12E **142 C3**
Gejiu *China* 23°20N 103°10E **116 F4**
Gel, Meydân-e *Iran* 29°4N 54°50E **129 D7**
Gela *Italy* 37°4N 14°15E **95 F7**
Gela, G. di *Italy* 37°0N 14°20E **95 F7**
Gelahun *Liberia* 7°55N 10°28W **138 D2**
Gelang Patah *Malaysia* 1°27N 103°35E **121 d**
Gelasa, Selat *Indonesia* 2°50S 107°0E **118 E3**
Gelderland □ *Neths.* 52°5N 6°10E **69 B6**
Geldern *Germany* 51°31N 6°20E **76 D2**
Geldrop *Neths.* 51°25N 5°32E **69 C5**
Geleen *Neths.* 50°57N 5°49E **69 D5**
Gelehun *S. Leone* 8°20N 11°40W **138 D2**
Gelembe *Tanzania* 39°10N 27°50E **99 B9**
Gelendost *Turkey* 38°7N 31°1E **104 C4**
Gelendzhik *Russia* 44°33N 38°10E **85 K10**
Gelib = Jilib *Somalia* 0°29N 42°46E **131 E4**
Gelibolu *Turkey* 40°28N 26°43E **97 F10**
Gelibolu Yarımadası *Turkey* 40°20N 26°30E **97 F10**
Gelidonya Burnu *Turkey* 36°12N 30°24E **104 D4**
Gelinhausen *Germany* 50°11N 9°11E **77 E5**
Gelnica *Slovak Rep.* 48°51N 20°55E **79 C13**
Gelsenkirchen *Germany* 51°32N 7°6E **76 D3**
Gelting *Germany* 54°45N 9°53E **76 A5**
Gelugor *Malaysia* 5°22N 100°18E **121 c**
Gemas *Malaysia* 2°37N 102°36E **121 L4**
Gembloux *Belgium* 50°34N 4°43E **69 D4**
Gembu *Nigeria* 6°42N 11°10E **139 D7**
Gemena *Dem. Rep. of the Congo* 3°13N 19°48E **140 D3**
Gemerek *Turkey* 39°15N 36°10E **104 C7**
Gemikonağı = Karavostasi *Cyprus* 35°8N 32°50E **101 D11**
Gemlik *Turkey* 40°26N 29°9E **97 F13**
Gemlik Körfezi *Turkey* 40°26N 29°0E **97 F12**
Gemona del Friuli *Italy* 46°16N 13°9E **93 B10**
Gemsa *Egypt* 27°39N 33°35E **137 B4**
Gemsbok △ *Botswana* 25°5S 21°11E **144 C3**
Gemünden *Germany* 50°2N 9°42E **77 E5**
Genadi *Greece* 36°2N 27°56E **101 C10**
Genale → *Ethiopia* 6°2N 39°1E **131 F2**
Gençay *France* 46°23N 0°23E **72 B4**
Genç *Turkey* 38°44N 40°34E **105 C9**
Gendringen *Neths.* 51°52N 6°21E **69 C6**
General Acha *Argentina* 37°20S 64°38W **190 D3**
General Alvear *B. Aires, Argentina* 36°0S 60°0W **190 D4**

General Alvear *Mendoza, Argentina* 35°0S 67°40W **190 D2**
General Artigas *Paraguay* 26°52S 56°16W **190 B4**
General Belgrano *Argentina* 36°35S 58°47W **190 D4**
General Bernardo O'Higgins *Antarctica* 63°0S 58°3W **55 C18**
General Cabrera *Argentina* 32°53S 63°52W **190 C3**
General Carrera, L. *S. Amer.* 46°35S 72°0W **192 C2**
General Cepeda *Mexico* 25°21N 101°22W **180 B4**
General Conesa *Argentina* 40°6S 64°25W **192 B4**
General Guido *Argentina* 36°40S 57°50W **190 D4**
General Juan Madariaga *Argentina* 37°0S 57°0W **190 D4**
General La Madrid *Argentina* 37°17S 61°20W **190 D3**
General Lorenzo Vintter *Argentina* 40°45S 64°26W **192 B4**
General MacArthur *Phil.* 11°18N 125°28E **119 F7**
General Martín Miguel de Güemes *Argentina* 24°50S 65°0W **190 A3**
General Pico *Argentina* 35°45S 63°50W **190 D3**
General Pinedo *Argentina* 27°15S 61°20W **190 B3**
General Pinto *Argentina* 34°45S 61°50W **190 C3**
General Roca *Argentina* 39°2S 67°35W **192 A3**
General Sampaio *Brazil* 4°2S 39°29W **189 A3**
General Santos *Phil.* 6°5N 125°14E **119 C7**
General Toshevo *Bulgaria* 43°42N 28°6E **97 C12**
General Treviño *Mexico* 26°14N 99°29W **181 B5**
General Trías *Mexico* 28°21N 106°22W **180 B3**
General Viamonte *Argentina* 35°1S 61°3W **190 D3**
General Villegas *Argentina* 35°5S 63°0W **190 D3**
General Vintter, L. *Argentina* 43°55S 71°40W **192 B2**
Genesee *Idaho, U.S.A.* 46°33N 116°56W **168 C5**
Genesee *Pa., U.S.A.* 41°59N 77°54W **174 E7**
Geneseo *Ill., U.S.A.* 41°27N 90°9W **172 E8**
Geneseo *N.Y., U.S.A.* 42°48N 77°49W **174 D7**
Geneva *Ala., U.S.A.* 31°2N 85°52W **178 D4**
Geneva *Ga., U.S.A.* 32°35N 84°33W **178 D5**
Geneva *N.Y., U.S.A.* 42°52N 76°59W **174 D8**
Geneva *Nebr., U.S.A.* 40°32N 97°36W **172 E5**
Geneva *Ohio, U.S.A.* 41°48N 80°57W **174 E4**
Geneva, L. = Léman, L. *Europe* 46°26N 6°30E **71 F13**
Genève *Switz.* 46°12N 6°9E **77 J2**
Gèdre *France* 42°47N 0°1E **72 F4**
Gedser *Denmark* 54°35N 11°55E **63 K5**
Gengma *China* 23°32N 99°20E **116 F2**
Genhe *China* 23°30N 121°31E **111 A13**
Genichesk = Henichesk *Ukraine* 46°12N 34°50E **85 J8**
Genil → *Spain* 37°42N 5°19W **89 H5**
Genisea *Greece* 41°1N 24°57E **97 F8**
Genk *Belgium* 50°58N 5°32E **69 D5**
Genlis *France* 47°11N 5°12E **71 E12**
Gennargentu, Mti. del *Italy* 40°1N 9°19E **94 B2**
Gennes *France* 47°20N 0°17W **70 E6**
Genoa = Génova *Italy* 44°25N 8°57E **92 D5**
Genoa *Australia* 37°29S 149°35E **153 D8**
Genoa *N.Y., U.S.A.* 42°40N 76°32W **175 D8**
Genoa *Nebr., U.S.A.* 41°27N 97°44W **172 E5**
Genoa *Nev., U.S.A.* 39°2N 119°50W **170 F7**
Genoa → *Argentina* 44°55S 70°5W **192 B2**
Génova *Italy* 44°25N 8°57E **92 D5**
Génova, G. di *Italy* 44°0N 9°0E **92 E6**
Genriyetty, Ostrov *Russia* 77°6N 156°30E **107 B16**
Gent *Belgium* 51°2N 3°42E **69 C3**
Genteng *Jawa Barat, Indonesia* 7°22S 106°24E **119 G12**
Genteng *Jawa Timur, Indonesia* 8°22S 114°9E **119 J17**
Genthin *Germany* 52°24N 12°9E **76 C8**
Gentio do Ouro *Brazil* 11°25S 42°30W **189 C2**
Genyem *Indonesia* 2°46S 140°12E **119 E10**
Genzano di Lucánia *Italy* 40°51N 16°2E **95 B9**
Genzano di Roma *Italy* 41°42N 12°41E **93 G9**
Geographe B. *Australia* 33°30S 115°15E **149 F2**
Geographe Chan. *Australia* 24°30S 113°0E **149 D1**
Geographical Society Ø *Greenland* 72°57N 23°15W **57 C8**
Geokchay = Göyçay *Azerbaijan* 40°42N 47°43E **87 K8**
Georga, Zemlya *Russia* 80°30N 49°0E **106 A5**
George *S. Africa* 33°58S 22°29E **144 E3**
George → *Canada* 58°49N 66°10W **165 A6**
George, L. *N.S.W., Australia* 35°10S 149°25E **153 C8**
George, L. *S. Austral., Australia* 37°25S 140°0E **152 D4**
George, L. *W. Austral., Australia* 22°45S 123°40E **148 D3**
George, L. *Uganda* 0°5N 30°10E **142 B3**
George, L. *Fla., U.S.A.* 29°17N 81°36W **179 F8**
George, L. *N.Y., U.S.A.* 43°37N 73°33W **175 C11**
George Gill Ra. *Australia* 24°22S 131°45E **148 D5**
George Pt. *Australia* 20°6S 148°36E **150 b**
George River = Kangiqsualujjuaq *Canada* 58°30N 65°59W **161 F18**
George Sound *N.Z.* 44°52S 167°25E **155 E2**
George Town *Bahamas* 23°33N 75°47W **182 B4**
George Town *Cayman Is.* 19°20N 81°24W **182 C3**
George Town *Malaysia* 5°25N 100°20E **121 c**
George V Land *Antarctica* 69°0S 148°0E **55 C10**
George VI Sound *Antarctica* 71°0S 68°0W **55 D17**

George West U.S.A. 28°20N 98°7W 176 G5
Georgetown = Janjanbureh
 Gambia 13°30N 14°47W 138 C2
Georgetown Australia 18°17S 143°33E 150 B3
Georgetown Ont.,
 Canada 43°40N 79°56W 174 C5
Georgetown P.E.I.,
 Canada 46°13N 62°24W 165 C7
Georgetown Guyana 6°50N 58°12W 186 B7
Georgetown Calif.,
 U.S.A. 38°54N 120°50W 170 G6
Georgetown Colo.,
 U.S.A. 39°42N 105°42W 168 G11
Georgetown Fla.,
 U.S.A. 29°23N 81°38W 179 F8
Georgetown Ga., U.S.A. 31°53N 85°6W 178 D4
Georgetown Ky.,
 U.S.A. 38°13N 84°33W 173 F11
Georgetown N.Y.,
 U.S.A. 42°46N 75°44W 175 D9
Georgetown Ohio,
 U.S.A. 38°52N 83°54W 173 F12
Georgetown S.C.,
 U.S.A. 33°23N 79°17W 177 E15
Georgetown Tex.,
 U.S.A. 30°38N 97°41W 176 F6
Georgia □ U.S.A. 32°50N 83°15W 178 D6
Georgia ■ Asia 42°0N 43°0E 87 J6
Georgia, Str. of
 N. Amer. 49°25N 124°0W 170 A3
Georgia Basin S. Ocean 50°45S 35°30W 55 B1
Georgian B. Canada 45°15N 81°0W 174 A4
Georgian Bay Islands △
 Canada 44°53N 79°52W 174 B5
Georgiëvka
 Kazakhstan 49°19N 84°34E 109 C10
Georgina → Australia 23°30S 139°47E 150 C2
Georgina I. Canada 44°22N 79°17W 174 B5
Georgioupoli Greece 35°20N 24°15E 101 D6
Georgiyevsk Russia 44°12N 43°28E 87 H6
Georgsmarienhütte
 Germany 52°13N 8°3E 76 C4
Gera Germany 50°53N 12°4E 76 E8
Geraardsbergen Belgium 50°45N 3°53E 69 D3
Geraki Greece 37°0N 22°42E 98 D4
Geral, Serra Bahia, Brazil 15°0S 41°0W 189 C2
Geral, Serra Goiás,
 Brazil 11°15S 46°30W 189 C1
Geral, Serra Sta. Catarina,
 Brazil 26°25S 50°0W 191 B6
Geral de Goiás, Serra
 Brazil 12°0S 46°0W 189 C1
Geraldine N.Z. 44°5S 171°15E 155 E6
Geraldine U.S.A. 47°36N 110°16W 168 C8
Geraldton Australia 28°48S 114°32E 149 E1
Geraldton Canada 49°44N 87°10W 164 C2
Geranium Australia 35°23S 140°11E 152 C4
Gérardmer France 48°3N 6°50E 71 D13
Gercüş Turkey 37°34N 41°23E 105 D9
Gerdine, Mt. U.S.A. 61°32N 152°27W 166 C9
Gerede Turkey 40°45N 32°10E 104 C5
Gereshk Afghan. 31°47N 64°35E 122 D4
Geretsried Germany 47°51N 11°28E 77 H7
Gérgal Spain 37°7N 2°31W 91 H2
Gerik Malaysia 5°50N 101°15E 121 K3
Gering U.S.A. 41°50N 103°40W 172 E2
Gerlach U.S.A. 40°39N 119°21W 168 F4
Gerlachovský Štít
 Slovak Rep. 49°11N 20°7E 79 B13
German Bight = Deutsche Bucht
 Germany 54°15N 8°0E 76 A4
German Planina
 Macedonia 42°20N 22°0E 96 D6
Germania Land
 Greenland 77°5N 19°30W 57 B9
Germansen Landing
 Canada 55°43N 124°40W 162 B4
Germantown U.S.A. 35°5N 89°49W 177 D10
Germany ■ Europe 51°0N 10°0E 76 E6
Germencik Turkey 37°52N 27°37E 99 D9
Germering Germany 48°8N 11°22E 77 G7
Germersheim Germany 49°12N 8°22E 77 F4
Germí Iran 39°1N 48°3E 105 C13
Germiston S. Africa 26°13S 28°10E 145 C4
Gernika-Lumo Spain 43°19N 2°40W 90 B2
Gernsheim Germany 49°45N 8°30E 77 F4
Gero Japan 35°48N 137°14E 113 G8
Gerogery Australia 35°50S 147°1E 153 C7
Gerokgak Indonesia 8°11S 114°27E 119 J17
Gerolzhofen Germany 49°54N 10°21E 77 F6
Gerona = Girona Spain 41°58N 2°46E 90 D7
Geropotamos → Greece 35°3N 24°50E 101 D6
Gerrard Canada 50°30N 117°17W 162 C5
Gerringong Australia 34°46S 150°47E 153 C9
Gers □ France 43°35N 0°30E 72 E4
Gers → France 44°9N 0°39E 72 D4
Gersfeld Germany 50°27N 9°56E 76 E5
Gersoppa Falls India 14°12N 74°46E 127 G2
Gersthofen Germany 48°25N 10°53E 77 G6
Gertak Sanggul
 Malaysia 5°17N 100°12E 121 c
Gertak Sanggul, Tanjung
 Malaysia 5°16N 100°11E 121 c
Gerung Indonesia 8°43S 116°7E 119 K19
Gerze France 45°48N 3°8E 72 C7
Gerze Turkey 41°48N 35°12E 104 B6
Gescher Germany 51°38N 8°31E 76 D4
Geseke Germany 51°38N 8°31E 76 D4
Gesso → Italy 44°24N 7°33E 92 D4
Getafe Spain 40°18N 3°43E 90 B4
Getinge Sweden 56°49N 12°44E 63 H6
Gettysburg Pa., U.S.A. 39°50N 77°14W 173 F15
Gettysburg S. Dak.,
 U.S.A. 45°1N 99°57W 172 C4
Getxo = Algorta Spain 43°21N 2°59W 90 B4
Getz Ice Shelf Antarctica 75°0S 130°0W 55 D14
Geurie Australia 32°22S 148°50E 153 B8
Gévaudan France 44°40N 3°40E 72 D7
Gevgelija Macedonia 41°9N 22°30E 96 D6
Gévora → Spain 38°53N 6°57W 89 G4
Gevrai India 19°16N 75°46E 126 E2
Geyser Turkey 39°48N 26°12E 99 B8
Geyser U.S.A. 47°16N 110°30W 168 C8
Geyserville U.S.A. 38°42N 122°54W 170 G4
Geyve Turkey 40°30N 30°18E 104 B4
Gezhouba Dam China 30°40N 111°20E 117 B8

Ghadāf, W. al → Iraq 32°56N 43°30E 105 F10
Ghadāmis Libya 30°11N 9°29E 135 B8
Ghaghara → India 25°45N 84°40E 125 G11
Ghaghat → Bangla. 25°19N 89°38E 125 G13
Ghagra India 23°17N 84°33E 125 H11
Ghagra → India 27°29N 81°9E 125 F9
Ghallamane Mauritania 23°15N 10°0W 134 D4
Ghana ■ W. Afr. 8°0N 1°0W 139 D4
Ghanpokhara Nepal 28°17N 84°14E 125 E11
Ghansor India 22°39N 80°1E 125 H9
Ghanzi Botswana 21°50S 21°34E 144 B3
Ghanzi □ Botswana 22°0S 22°30E 144 B3
Gharb-Chrarda-Beni Hssen □
 Morocco 35°35N 6°0W 136 A2
Gharbîya, Es Sahrâ el
 Egypt 27°40N 26°30E 137 B2
Ghardaïa Algeria 32°20N 3°37E 136 B4
Ghardaïa □ Algeria 31°5N 3°10E 136 B4
Ghârib, G. Egypt 28°6N 32°54E 137 B8
Gharm Tajikistan 39°0N 70°20E 106 F8
Ghāt Libya 24°59N 10°11E 135 D8
Ghatal India 22°40N 87°46E 125 H12
Ghatampur India 26°8N 80°13E 125 F9
Ghatgaon India 21°24N 85°53E 126 D7
Ghatprabha → India 16°15N 75°20E 127 F2
Ghats, Eastern India 14°0N 78°50E 127 H4
Ghats, Western India 14°0N 75°0E 127 H2
Ghatsila India 22°36N 86°29E 125 H12
Ghaṭṭī Si. Arabia 31°16N 37°31E 128 D3
Ghawdex = Gozo Malta 36°3N 14°15E 101 C1
Ghazal, Bahr el → Chad 13°0N 15°47E 135 F9
Ghazal, Bahr el →
 South Sudan 9°31N 30°25E 135 G12
Ghazaouet Algeria 35°8N 1°50W 136 A3
Ghaziabad India 28°42N 77°26E 124 E7
Ghazipur India 25°38N 83°35E 125 G10
Ghazni Afghan. 33°30N 68°28E 124 C3
Ghazni □ Afghan. 32°10N 68°20E 122 C6
Ghedi Italy 45°24N 10°16E 92 C7
Ghelari Romania 45°38N 22°45E 80 E7
Ghent = Gent Belgium 51°2N 3°42E 69 C3
Gheorghe Gheorghiu-Dej = Oneşti
 Romania 46°17N 26°47E 81 D11
Gheorgheni Romania 46°43N 25°41E 81 D10
Gherla Romania 47°2N 23°57E 81 C8
Ghidigeni Romania 46°17N 27°27E 81 D11
Ghilarza Italy 40°7N 8°50E 94 B1
Ghimeş-Făget Romania 46°35N 26°2E 81 D11
Ghinah, Wādī al →
 Si. Arabia 30°27N 38°14E 128 D3
Ghisonaccia France 42°1N 9°26E 73 F13
Ghisoni France 42°7N 9°12E 73 F13
Ghizar → Pakistan 36°15N 73°43E 125 A5
Ghod → India 18°30N 74°35E 126 E2
Ghogha India 21°40N 72°20E 126 D1
Ghot Ogrein Egypt 31°10N 25°20E 137 A2
Ghotaru India 27°20N 70°1E 124 F4
Ghotki Pakistan 28°5N 69°21E 124 E3
Ghowr □ Afghan. 34°0N 64°20E 122 C4
Ghughri India 22°39N 80°41E 125 H9
Ghugus India 19°58N 79°12E 126 E4
Ghulam Mohammad Barrage
 Pakistan 25°30N 68°20E 124 G3
Ghūrīān Afghan. 34°17N 61°25E 122 B2
Gia Dinh Vietnam 10°49N 106°42E 121 G6
Gia Lai = Plei Ku
 Vietnam 13°57N 108°0E 120 F7
Gia Nghia Vietnam 11°58N 107°42E 121 G6
Gia Ngoc Vietnam 14°50N 108°58E 120 E7
Gia Vuc Vietnam 14°42N 108°34E 120 E7
Giali Greece 36°41N 27°11E 99 E9
Gialtra Greece 38°51N 22°59E 98 C4
Giamama = Jamaame
 Somalia 0°4N 42°44E 131 G3
Gianitsa Greece 40°46N 22°24E 96 F6
Giannutri Italy 42°15N 11°6E 92 F8
Giant Forest U.S.A. 36°36N 118°43W 170 J8
Giant Mts. = Krkonoše
 Czech Rep. 50°50N 15°35E 78 A8
Giant Sequoia □
 U.S.A. 36°10N 118°35W 170 K8
Giants Causeway U.K. 55°16N 6°29W 64 A5
Giant's Tank Sri Lanka 8°51N 80°2E 127 K5
Gianyar Indonesia 8°32S 115°20E 119 K18
Giarabub = Al Jaghbūb
 Libya 29°42N 24°38E 135 C10
Giaros Greece 37°32N 24°40E 98 D6
Giarre Italy 37°43N 15°11E 95 E8
Giaveno Italy 45°2N 7°21E 92 C4
Gibara Cuba 21°9N 76°11W 182 B4
Gibb II Ethiopia 8°0N 37°0E 131 F2
Gibe II Ethiopia 8°0N 37°30E 131 F2
Gibellina Nuova Italy 37°48N 12°58E 94 E5
Gibeon Namibia 25°9S 17°43E 144 C2
Gibraleón Spain 37°23N 6°58W 89 H4
Gibraltar ☑ Europe 36°7N 5°22W 89 J5
Gibraltar, Str. of Medit. S. 35°55N 5°40W 89 K5
Gibraltar Range △
 Australia 29°31S 152°19E 151 D5
Gibson U.S.A. 33°14N 82°36W 178 E7
Gibson Desert Australia 24°0S 126°0E 148 D4
Gibsons Canada 49°24N 123°32W 162 D4
Gibsonton U.S.A. 27°51N 82°23W 179 H7
Gibsonville U.S.A. 39°46N 120°54W 170 F6
Giddalur India 15°20N 78°57E 127 G4
Giddings U.S.A. 30°11N 96°56W 176 F6
Giebnegáisi = Kebnekaise
 Sweden 67°53N 18°33E 60 C18
Gien France 47°40N 2°36E 71 E9
Giengen Germany 48°37N 10°14E 77 G6
Giessen Germany 50°34N 8°41E 76 E4
Gīfan Iran 37°54N 57°28E 129 B8
Gifatin, Geziret Egypt 27°10N 33°50E 137 B8
Gifford Germany 52°30N 10°33E 76 B6
Gift Lake Canada 55°53N 115°49W 162 B5
Gifu Japan 35°30N 136°45E 113 G8
Gifu □ Japan 35°40N 137°0E 113 G8
Gigant Russia 46°28N 41°20E 87 G5
Giganta, Sa. de la
 Mexico 26°0N 111°39W 180 B2
Gigen Bulgaria 43°40N 24°28E 97 C8
Gigha U.K. 55°42N 5°44W 65 F3
Giglio Italy 42°20N 10°52E 92 F7
Gignac France 43°39N 3°32E 72 E7
Giguela → Spain 39°8N 3°44W 89 F7
Gijón Spain 43°32N 5°42W 88 B5
Gikongoro Rwanda 2°28S 29°34E 142 C2

Gil I. Canada 53°12N 129°15W 162 C3
Gila → U.S.A. 32°43N 114°33W 169 K6
Gila Bend U.S.A. 32°57N 112°43W 169 K7
Gila Bend Mts. U.S.A. 33°10N 113°0W 169 K7
Gila Cliff Dwellings ☐
 U.S.A. 33°12N 108°16W 169 K9
Gīlān □ Iran 37°0N 50°0E 128 B6
Gīlān-e Gharb Iran 34°8N 45°55E 105 E11
Gilău Romania 46°45N 23°23E 81 D8
Gilbert → Australia 16°35S 141°15E 150 B3
Gilbert Is. Kiribati 1°0N 172°0E 147 A10
Gilbert River Australia 18°9S 142°52E 150 B3
Gilbert Seamounts
 Pac. Oc. 52°50N 150°10W 54 D18
Gilbués Brazil 9°50S 45°21W 189 B1
Gilead U.S.A. 44°24N 70°59W 175 B14
Gilf el Kebîr, Hadabat el
 Egypt 23°50N 25°50E 137 C2
Gilford I. Canada 50°40N 126°30W 162 C3
Gilgandra Australia 31°43S 148°39E 153 A8
Gilgil Kenya 0°30S 36°20E 142 C4
Gilgit India 35°50N 74°15E 125 B6
Gilgit → Pakistan 35°44N 74°37E 125 B6
Gilgit-Baltistan □
 Pakistan 36°30N 73°0E 125 A5
Gilgunnia Australia 32°26S 146°2E 153 B7
Gili → Mozam. 16°39S 38°27E 143 F4
Gilimanuk Indonesia 8°10S 114°26E 119 J17
Giljeva Planina Europe 43°9N 20°0E 96 C3
Gillam Canada 56°20N 94°40W 163 B10
Gilleleje Denmark 56°8N 12°19E 63 H6
Gillen, L. Australia 26°11S 124°38E 149 E3
Gilles, L. Australia 32°50S 136°45E 152 B2
Gillespies Pt. N.Z. 43°24S 169°49E 155 D4
Gillette U.S.A. 44°18N 105°30W 168 D11
Gilliat Australia 20°40S 141°28E 150 C3
Gillingham U.K. 51°23N 0°33E 67 F8
Gilmer U.S.A. 32°44N 94°57W 176 E7
Gilmore, L. Australia 32°29S 121°37E 149 F3
Gilmour Canada 44°48N 77°37W 174 B7
Gilort → Romania 44°38N 23°32E 81 E8
Gilroy U.S.A. 37°1N 121°34W 170 H5
Gimcheon S. Korea 36°11N 128°4E 115 F15
Gimhae S. Korea 35°14N 128°53E 115 G15
Gimhwa S. Korea 38°17N 127°28E 115 E14
Gimje, Mt. St. Lucia 13°54N 61°0W 183 f
Gimje S. Korea 35°48N 126°45E 115 G14
Gimli Canada 50°40N 97°0W 163 C9
Gimone → France 44°0N 1°6E 72 E5
Gimont France 43°38N 0°52E 72 E4
Gin → Sri Lanka 6°5N 80°7E 127 L5
Gin Gin Australia 25°0S 151°58E 151 D5
Ginâh Egypt 25°21N 30°30E 137 B3
Gineifra Egypt 30°12N 32°25E 137 B8
Gingee India 12°15N 79°25E 127 H4
Gingin Australia 31°22S 115°54E 149 F2
Gingindlovu S. Africa 29°2S 31°30E 145 C5
Ginir Ethiopia 7°6N 40°40E 131 F5
Ginosa Italy 40°35N 16°45E 95 B9
Ginzo de Limia = Xinzo de Limia
 Spain 42°3N 7°47W 88 C3
Giofyros → Greece 35°20N 25°6E 101 D7
Giohar = Jawhar
 Somalia 2°48N 45°30E 131 G4
Gióia, G. di Italy 38°30N 15°45E 95 D8
Gióia del Colle Italy 40°48N 16°55E 95 B9
Gióia Táuro Italy 38°25N 15°54E 95 D8
Gioiosa Iónica Italy 38°20N 16°18E 95 D9
Gioiosa Marea Italy 38°10N 14°54E 95 D7
Giona, Oros Greece 38°38N 22°14E 98 C4
Giovi, Passo dei Italy 44°33N 8°57E 92 D5
Giovinazzo Italy 41°11N 16°40E 95 A9
Gippsland Australia 37°52S 147°0E 153 D7
Gir □ India 21°0N 71°0E 124 J4
Gir Hills India 21°0N 71°0E 124 J4
Girab India 26°2N 70°38E 124 F4
Girâfi, W. → Egypt 29°58N 34°39E 130 F3
Giraltovce Slovak Rep. 49°7N 21°32E 79 B14
Girard Ga., U.S.A. 33°3N 81°43W 178 E8
Girard Kans., U.S.A. 37°31N 94°51W 172 G6
Girard Ohio, U.S.A. 41°9N 80°42W 174 E4
Girard Pa., U.S.A. 42°0N 80°19W 174 E4
Girdle Ness U.K. 57°9N 2°3W 65 D6
Giresun Turkey 40°55N 38°30E 105 B8
Giresun □ Turkey 40°30N 38°30E 105 B8
Girga Egypt 26°17N 31°55E 137 B3
Giri → India 30°28N 77°41E 124 D7
Giridih India 24°10N 86°21E 125 G12
Girifalco Italy 38°49N 16°25E 95 D9
Giriftu Kenya 1°59N 39°46E 142 B5
Girilambone Australia 31°16S 146°57E 153 A7
Girne = Kyrenia
 Cyprus 35°20N 33°20E 101 D12
Giro Nigeria 11°7N 4°42E 139 C5
Giromagny France 47°45N 6°50E 71 E13
Giron = Kiruna Sweden 67°52N 20°15E 60 C19
Girona Spain 41°58N 2°46E 90 D7
Girona □ Spain 42°11N 2°30E 90 D7
Gironde □ France 44°45N 0°30W 72 D3
Gironde → France 45°32N 1°7W 72 C2
Gironella Spain 42°2N 1°53E 90 C6
Girraween Australia 28°46S 151°54E 151 D5
Girringun △ Australia 18°15S 145°32E 150 B4
Giru Australia 19°30S 147°5E 150 B4
Gisborne Australia 37°29S 144°36E 152 D6
Gisborne N.Z. 38°39S 178°5E 154 E7
Gisborne □ N.Z. 38°30S 178°0E 154 E7
Gisenyi Rwanda 1°41S 29°15E 142 C2
Gislaved Sweden 57°19N 13°32E 63 G7
Gisors France 49°15N 1°47E 71 C8
Gitarama Rwanda 2°4S 29°45E 142 C2
Gitega Burundi 3°26S 29°56E 142 C2
Githio Greece 36°46N 22°34E 98 D4
Giuba = Juba →
 Somalia 1°30N 42°35E 131 G3
Giugliano in Campania
 Italy 40°56N 14°13E 95 B7
Giuliana Italy 37°40N 13°14E 94 E6
Giulianova Italy 42°45N 13°57E 93 F10
Giura Greece 39°23N 24°10E 98 B6
Giurgeni Romania 44°45N 27°48E 81 F12
Giurgiu Romania 43°52N 25°57E 81 G10
Giurgiu □ Romania 44°20N 26°0E 81 F10
Giurgiuleşti Moldova 45°29N 28°12E 81 E13
Give Denmark 55°51N 9°13E 63 G3
Givet France 50°8N 4°49E 69 D4
Givors France 45°35N 4°45E 72 C8
Givry France 46°41N 4°46E 71 F11
Giyani S. Africa 23°19S 30°43E 145 B5

Giza = El Giza Egypt 30°0N 31°12E 137 F7
Giza Pyramids Egypt 29°58N 31°9E 137 F7
Gizab Afghan. 33°22N 66°17E 124 C1
Gizhiga Russia 62°3N 160°30E 107 C17
Gizhiginskaya Guba
 Russia 61°0N 158°0E 107 C16
Gizycko Poland 54°2N 21°48E 82 D8
Gizzeria Italy 38°59N 16°12E 95 D9
Gjakovë Kosovo 42°22N 20°26E 96 D4
Gjalicë Kosovo 42°2N 20°25E 96 D4
Gjegjan Albania 41°58N 20°3E 96 D4
Gjeravicë Kosovo 42°32N 20°8E 96 D4
Gjilan Kosovo 42°27N 21°20E 96 D5
Gjirokastër Albania 40°7N 20°10E 96 F4
Gjoa Haven Canada 68°38N 95°53W 160 D12
Gjøvik Norway 60°47N 10°43E 60 F14
Gjuhës, Kep i Albania 40°28N 19°15E 96 F3
Gjurakoc Kosovo 42°43N 20°29E 96 D4
Glace Bay Canada 46°11N 59°58W 165 C8
Glacier □ Canada 51°15N 117°30W 162 C5
Glacier △ U.S.A. 48°42N 113°48W 168 B7
Glacier Bay U.S.A. 58°40N 136°0W 166 D4
Glacier Bay △ Canada 58°45N 136°30W 162 B1
Glacier Peak U.S.A. 48°7N 121°7W 168 B3
Gladewater U.S.A. 32°33N 94°56W 176 E7
Gladstone Queens.,
 Australia 23°52S 151°16E 150 C5
Gladstone S. Austral.,
 Australia 33°15S 138°22E 152 B3
Gladstone Canada 50°13N 98°57W 163 C9
Gladstone U.S.A. 45°51N 87°1W 172 C10
Gladwin U.S.A. 43°59N 84°29W 173 D11
Glafsfjorden Sweden 59°30N 12°37E 62 E6
Glagah Indonesia 8°13S 114°18E 119 J17
Głagów Małopolski
 Poland 50°10N 21°56E 83 H8
Gláma = Glomma →
 Norway 59°12N 10°57E 61 G14
Gláma Iceland 65°48N 23°0W 60 D2
Glamis U.S.A. 32°55N 115°5W 171 N11
Glamoč Bos.-H. 44°3N 16°51E 93 D13
Glamorgan, Vale of ☐
 U.K. 51°28N 3°25W 67 F4
Glamsbjerg Denmark 55°17N 10°6E 63 J4
Glarus Switz. 47°3N 9°4E 77 H5
Glarus □ Switz. 47°0N 9°5E 77 H5
Glasco Kans., U.S.A. 39°22N 97°50W 172 F5
Glasco N.Y., U.S.A. 42°3N 73°57W 175 D11
Glasgow U.K. 55°51N 4°15W 65 F4
Glasgow Ky., U.S.A. 37°0N 85°55W 173 G11
Glasgow Mont.,
 U.S.A. 48°12N 106°38W 168 B10
Glasgow, City of □ U.K. 55°51N 4°12W 65 F4
Glasgow Int. ✈ (GLA)
 U.K. 55°51N 4°21W 65 F4
Glaslyn Canada 53°22N 108°21W 163 C7
Glastonbury U.K. 51°9N 2°43W 67 F5
Glastonbury U.S.A. 41°43N 72°37W 175 E12
Glauchau Germany 50°49N 12°33E 76 E8
Glava Sweden 59°33N 12°35E 62 E6
Glavice Croatia 43°43N 16°41E 93 E13
Glazov Russia 58°9N 52°40E 86 A11
Gleichen Canada 50°52N 113°3W 162 C6
Gleisdorf Austria 47°6N 15°44E 78 D8
Gleiwitz = Gliwice
 Poland 50°22N 18°41E 83 H5
Glen Africa U.S.A. 44°7N 71°11W 175 B13
Glen Affric U.K. 57°17N 5°1W 65 D3
Glen Afton N.Z. 37°37S 175°4E 154 D4
Glen Canyon U.S.A. 37°30N 110°40W 169 H8
Glen Canyon △ U.S.A. 37°15N 111°0W 169 H8
Glen Canyon Dam
 U.S.A. 36°57N 111°29W 169 H8
Glen Coe U.K. 56°40N 5°0W 65 E3
Glen Cove U.S.A. 40°51N 73°38W 175 F11
Glen Garry U.K. 57°3N 5°7W 65 D3
Glen Innes Australia 29°44S 151°44E 151 D5
Glen Lyon U.S.A. 41°10N 76°5W 175 E8
Glen Massey N.Z. 37°38S 175°2E 154 D4
Glen Mor U.K. 57°9N 4°37W 65 D4
Glen Moriston U.K. 57°11N 4°52W 65 D4
Glen Robertson
 Canada 45°22N 74°30W 175 A10
Glen Spean U.K. 56°53N 4°40W 65 E4
Glen Ullin U.S.A. 46°49N 101°50W 172 B3
Glénan, Îs. de France 47°42N 4°0W 70 E3
Glenavy N.Z. 44°54S 171°7E 155 E6
Glenbeigh Ireland 52°3N 9°58W 64 D2
Glenburn Australia 37°27S 145°26E 153 D6
Glencoe Canada 42°45N 81°43W 174 D3
Glencoe S. Africa 28°11S 30°11E 145 C5
Glencoe Ala., U.S.A. 33°57N 85°56W 178 D5
Glencoe Minn., U.S.A. 44°46N 94°9W 172 C6
Glencolumbkille Ireland 54°43N 8°42W 64 B3
Glendale Ariz., U.S.A. 33°32N 112°11W 169 K7
Glendale Calif., U.S.A. 34°9N 118°15W 171 L8
Glendale Fla., U.S.A. 30°52N 86°7W 178 E3
Glendale Zimbabwe 17°22S 31°5E 143 F3
Glendive U.S.A. 47°7N 104°43W 168 C11
Glendo U.S.A. 42°30N 105°2W 168 E11
Glenelg Australia 34°58S 138°31E 152 C3
Glenelg → Australia 38°4S 140°59E 152 E4
Glenfield U.S.A. 43°43N 75°24W 175 C9
Glengad Hd. Ireland 55°20N 7°10W 64 A4
Glengarriff Ireland 51°45N 9°34W 64 E2
Glenham N.Z. 46°26S 168°52E 155 G2
Glenhope N.Z. 41°40S 172°39E 155 D5
Glenmora U.S.A. 30°59N 92°35W 176 F8
Glenmorgan Australia 27°14S 149°42E 151 D4
Glenn U.S.A. 39°31N 122°1W 170 F4
Glennallen U.S.A. 62°7N 145°33W 166 C5
Glennamaddy Ireland 53°37N 8°33W 64 C3
Glenns Ferry U.S.A. 42°57N 115°18W 168 E6
Glenora Canada 31°50N 89°28W 178 E9
Glenorchy Tas.,
 Australia 42°49S 147°18E 151 E4
Glenorchy Vic.,
 Australia 36°55S 142°41E 152 D5
Glenorchy N.Z. 44°51S 168°24E 155 E3
Glenore Australia 17°50S 141°12E 150 B3
Glenreagh Australia 30°2S 153°1E 151 E5
Glenrock U.S.A. 42°52N 105°52W 168 E11
Glenrothes U.K. 56°12N 3°10W 65 E5
Glenwood Alta., Canada 36°55S 146°13E 153 D6
Glens Falls U.S.A. 43°19N 73°39W 175 C11
Glenside U.S.A. 40°6N 75°9W 175 F9
Glenthompson
 Australia 37°38S 142°35E 152 D5

Glenties Ireland 54°48N 8°17W 64 B3
Glenveagh △ Ireland 55°3N 8°1W 64 A3
Glenville U.S.A. 38°56N 80°50W 173 F13
Glenwood Canada 49°0N 54°58W 165 C9
Glenwood Ark., U.S.A. 34°20N 93°33W 176 D8
Glenwood Iowa, U.S.A. 41°3N 95°45W 172 E6
Glenwood Minn.,
 U.S.A. 45°39N 95°23W 172 C6
Glenwood Wash.,
 U.S.A. 46°1N 121°17W 170 D5
Glenwood Springs
 U.S.A. 39°33N 107°19W 168 G10
Glettinganes Iceland 65°30N 13°37W 60 D7
Glifada Greece 37°52N 23°45E 98 D5
Glimåkra Sweden 56°19N 14°7E 63 H8
Glin Ireland 52°34N 9°17W 64 D2
Glina Croatia 45°20N 16°6E 93 C13
Glinojeck Poland 52°49N 20°21E 83 F7
Gliwice Poland 50°22N 18°41E 83 H5
Globe U.S.A. 33°24N 110°47W 169 K8
Glodeanu Siliştea
 Romania 44°50N 26°48E 81 F11
Glodeni Moldova 47°45N 27°31E 81 C12
Glödnitz Austria 46°53N 14°7E 78 E7
Gloggnitz Austria 47°41N 15°56E 78 D8
Głogów Poland 51°37N 16°5E 83 G3
Głogówek Poland 50°21N 17°53E 83 H4
Glomma → Norway 59°12N 10°57E 61 G14
Glorieuses, Îs. Ind Oc. 11°30S 47°20E 141 G9
Glosa Greece 39°10N 23°45E 98 B5
Glossop U.K. 53°27N 1°56W 66 D6
Gloucester Australia 32°0S 151°59E 153 B9
Gloucester U.K. 51°53N 2°15W 67 F5
Gloucester U.S.A. 42°37N 70°40W 175 D14
Gloucester I. Australia 20°0S 148°30E 150 b
Gloucester Island △
 Australia 20°2S 148°30E 150 b
Gloucester Point
 U.S.A. 37°15N 76°30W 173 G15
Gloucestershire □ U.K. 51°46N 2°15W 67 F5
Gloversville U.S.A. 43°3N 74°21W 175 C10
Glovertown Canada 48°40N 54°3W 165 C9
Gloverville = Warrenville
 U.S.A. 33°33N 81°48W 178 D8
Glowno Poland 51°59N 19°42E 83 G6
Glubczyce Poland 50°13N 17°53E 83 H4
Glubokiy Russia 48°35N 40°25E 87 F13
Glubokoe Kazakhstan 50°8N 82°18E 109 B10
Glubokoye = Hlybokaye
 Belarus 55°10N 27°45E 84 E4
Gluchołazy Poland 50°19N 17°24E 83 H4
Glücksburg Germany 54°50N 9°33E 76 A5
Glückstadt Germany 53°45N 9°26E 76 B5
Glukhov = Hlukhiv
 Ukraine 51°40N 33°58E 85 G7
Glusk Belarus 52°53N 28°41E 75 B15
Gluszyca Poland 50°41N 16°23E 83 H3
Glyn Ebwy = Ebbw Vale
 U.K. 51°46N 3°12W 67 F4
Glyngøre Denmark 56°46N 8°52E 63 H2
Gmünd Kärnten, Austria 46°54N 13°31E 78 E6
Gmünd Niederösterreich,
 Austria 48°45N 15°0E 78 C8
Gmunden Austria 47°55N 13°48E 78 D6
Gnarp Sweden 62°3N 17°16E 62 B11
Gnesta Sweden 59°3N 17°17E 62 E11
Gniew Poland 53°50N 18°50E 82 E5
Gniewkowo Poland 52°54N 18°25E 83 F5
Gniezno Poland 52°30N 17°35E 83 F4
Gnjilane = Gjilan Kosovo 42°28N 21°29E 96 D5
Gnoien Germany 53°58N 12°41E 76 B8
Gnosjö Sweden 57°22N 13°43E 63 H7
Gnowangerup
 Australia 33°58S 117°59E 149 F2
Go Cong Vietnam 10°22N 106°40E 121 G6
Gô-no-ura Japan 33°44N 129°40E 113 H4
Goa India 15°33N 73°59E 127 G1
Goa □ India 15°33N 73°59E 127 G1
Goalen Hd. Australia 36°33S 150°4E 153 D9
Goalpara India 26°10N 90°40E 123 F17
Goaltor India 22°43N 87°10E 125 H12
Goalundo Ghat
 Bangla. 23°50N 89°47E 125 H13
Goaso Ghana 6°48N 2°30W 138 D4
Goat Fell U.K. 55°38N 5°11W 65 F3
Goba Ethiopia 7°1N 39°59E 131 F2
Goba Mozam. 26°15S 32°13E 145 D5
Gobabis Namibia 22°30S 19°0E 144 B2
Göbel Turkey 40°0N 28°9E 97 F12
Gobernador Gregores
 Argentina 48°45S 70°15W 192 C2
Gobi Asia 44°0N 110°0E 114 C6
Gobichettipalayam
 India 11°31N 77°21E 127 J3
Gobō Japan 33°53N 135°10E 113 H7
Gobustan Azerbaijan 40°7N 49°22E 105 B13
Göçbeyli Turkey 39°13N 27°25E 99 B9
Goch Germany 51°41N 6°9E 76 D2
Gochas Namibia 24°59S 18°55E 144 B2
Godalming U.K. 51°11N 0°36W 67 F7
Godavari → India 16°25N 82°18E 126 F6
Godavari Pt. India 17°0N 82°20E 126 F6
Godbout Canada 49°20N 67°38W 165 C6
Godda India 24°50N 87°13E 125 G12
Godech Bulgaria 43°1N 23°4E 96 C7
Goderich Canada 43°45N 81°41W 174 C3
Goderville France 49°38N 0°22E 70 C7
Godfrey Ra. Australia 24°0S 117°0E 149 D2
Godhavn = Qeqertarsuaq
 Greenland 69°15N 53°38W 57 C5
Godhra India 22°49N 73°40E 124 H5
Gödöllő Hungary 47°38N 19°25E 79 E10
Godoy Cruz Argentina 32°56S 68°52W 190 C2
Gods → Canada 56°22N 92°51W 163 B10
Gods L. Canada 54°40N 94°15W 164 A1
Gods River Canada 54°50N 94°5W 163 C10
Godthåb = Nuuk
 Greenland 64°10N 51°35W 57 C5
Goeie Hoop, Kaap die = Good
 Hope, C. of S. Africa 34°24S 18°30E 144 E2
Goéland, L. au Canada 49°50N 76°48W 164 C4
Goéland, L. aux
 Canada 55°27N 64°17W 165 A7
Goeree Neths. 51°50N 4°0E 69 C3
Goes Neths. 51°30N 3°55E 69 C3
Goffstown U.S.A. 43°1N 71°36W 175 C13
Gogama Canada 47°35N 81°43W 164 C3
Gogebic, L. U.S.A. 46°30N 89°35W 172 B9
Goginan India 23°52N 86°10E 125 H12
Gogomatarsi Bulgaria 44°6N 22°57E 96 C7
Gogra = Ganta Liberia 7°15N 8°59W 138 D3
Gogra → Ghaghara →
 India 25°45N 84°40E 125 G11
Gogriel South Sudan 8°30N 28°8E 135 G11
Gogui Mali 15°32N 9°25W 138 B3
Gohana India 29°8N 76°42E 124 E7
Goharganj India 23°1N 77°41E 124 H7
Goi → India 22°4N 74°46E 124 H6
Goiana Brazil 7°33S 34°59W 189 B4
Goiânia Brazil 16°43S 49°20W 187 F9
Goiás Brazil 15°55S 50°10W 187 G8
Goiás □ Brazil 12°10S 48°0W 187 F9
Goiatins Brazil 7°42S 47°10W 189 B1
Goio-Erê Brazil 24°12S 53°1W 191 A5
Góis Portugal 40°10N 8°6W 88 E2
Gojō Japan 34°21N 135°42E 113 G7
Gojra Pakistan 31°10N 72°40E 124 D5
Gokak India 16°11N 74°52E 127 F2
Gokarn India 14°33N 74°17E 127 G2
Gökçe Turkey 40°10N 25°55E 97 F9
Gökçeada Turkey 40°10N 25°50E 97 F9
Gökçedağ Turkey 39°33N 28°56E 99 B10
Gökçen Turkey 38°7N 27°53E 99 C9
Gökçeören Turkey 38°37N 28°35E 99 C10
Gökçeyazı Turkey 39°40N 27°40E 99 B9
Gökırmak → Turkey 41°25N 35°8E 104 B6
Gökova India 37°1N 28°17E 99 D10
Gökova Körfezi Turkey 36°55N 27°50E 99 E9
Göksu → Turkey 36°19N 34°5E 104 D6
Göksun Turkey 38°2N 36°30E 104 C7
Gökteik Burma 22°26N 97°0E 123 H20
Göktepe Turkey 37°25N 28°34E 99 D10
Gokurt Pakistan 29°40N 67°26E 124 E2
Gokwe Zimbabwe 18°7S 28°58E 145 A4
Gol Gol Australia 34°12S 142°14E 152 C5
Gola India 28°3N 80°32E 125 E9
Golakganj India 26°8N 89°52E 125 F13
Golan Heights = Hagolan
 Syria 33°0N 35°45E 130 C4
Gołańcz Poland 52°57N 17°19E 83 F4
Goläshkerd Iran 27°59N 57°16E 129 E8
Golaya Pristen = Hola Prystan
 Ukraine 46°29N 32°32E 85 J7
Gölbaşı Adıyaman,
 Turkey 37°43N 37°25E 104 D7
Gölbaşı Ankara, Turkey 39°47N 32°49E 104 C5
Golconda India 22°24N 78°23E 126 F4
Golconda U.S.A. 40°58N 117°30W 168 F5
Gölcük Kocaeli, Turkey 40°42N 29°48E 97 F13
Gölcük Niğde, Turkey 38°14N 34°47E 104 C6
Gold U.S.A. 41°52N 77°50W 174 E7
Gold Beach U.S.A. 42°25N 124°25W 168 E1
Gold Coast W. Afr. 4°0N 1°40W 139 E4
Gold Hill U.S.A. 42°26N 123°3W 168 E2
Gold River Canada 49°46N 126°3W 162 D3
Goldap Poland 54°19N 22°18E 82 D9
Goldberg Germany 53°35N 12°4E 76 B8
Golden Canada 51°20N 116°59W 162 C5
Golden B. N.Z. 40°40S 172°50E 155 A7
Golden Gate Highlands △
 S. Africa 28°40S 28°40E 145 C4
Golden Hinde Canada 49°40N 125°44W 162 D3
Golden Lake Canada 45°34N 77°21W 174 A7
Golden Spike △
 U.S.A. 41°37N 112°33W 168 F7
Golden Vale Ireland 52°33N 8°17W 64 D3
Goldendale U.S.A. 45°49N 120°50W 168 D3
Goldfield U.S.A. 37°42N 117°14W 169 H5
Goldsand L. Canada 57°2N 101°8W 163 B8
Goldsboro U.S.A. 35°23N 77°59W 177 D16
Goldsmith U.S.A. 31°59N 102°37W 176 E3
Goldthwaite U.S.A. 31°27N 98°34W 176 F5
Golegã Portugal 39°24N 8°29W 89 F2
Goleniów Poland 53°35N 14°50E 82 E1
Golestān □ Iran 37°20N 55°25E 129 B7
Golestānak Iran 30°36N 54°14E 129 D7
Goleta U.S.A. 34°27N 119°50W 171 L7
Golfito Costa Rica 8°41N 83°5W 182 E3
Golfo Aranci Italy 40°59N 9°38E 94 B2
Golfo de Santa Clara
 Mexico 31°42N 114°30W 180 A2
Golfo di Orosei e del
 Gennargentu △ Italy 40°5N 9°15E 94 B2
Gölgeli Dağları Turkey 37°10N 28°55E 99 D10
Gölhisar Turkey 37°8N 29°31E 99 D11
Goliad U.S.A. 28°40N 97°23W 176 G6
Golija Montenegro 43°0N 18°45E 96 C2
Golija Serbia 43°22N 20°15E 96 C4
Golina Poland 52°15N 18°4E 83 F5
Gölköy Turkey 40°31N 37°37E 104 B7
Göllersdorf Austria 48°29N 16°7E 78 C9
Gölmarmara Turkey 38°44N 27°55E 99 C9
Golmud China 36°25N 94°53E 110 D7
Golo → France 42°31N 9°32E 73 F13
Gölova Turkey 36°48N 30°8E 99 E12
Golpāyegān Iran 33°27N 50°18E 129 C6
Gölpazarı Turkey 40°16N 30°18E 104 B4
Golra Pakistan 33°37N 72°56E 124 C5
Golspie U.K. 57°58N 3°59W 65 D5
Golub-Dobrzyń Poland 53°7N 19°2E 83 E6
Golubac Serbia 44°39N 21°38E 96 B5
Golyam Perelik Bulgaria 41°36N 24°33E 97 E8
Golyama Kamchiya →
 Bulgaria 43°10N 27°55E 97 C11
Goma
 Dem. Rep. of the Congo 1°37S 29°10E 142 C2
Gomal Pass Pakistan 31°56N 69°20E 124 D3
Gomati → India 25°32N 83°11E 125 G10
Gombari
 Dem. Rep. of the Congo 2°45N 29°3E 142 B2
Gombe Nigeria 10°19N 11°2E 139 C7
Gombe Tanzania 4°38S 31°40E 142 C3
Gombe □ Nigeria 10°0N 11°0E 139 C7
Gombe → Tanzania 4°38S 31°40E 142 C3
Gombe Stream △
 Tanzania 4°42S 29°37E 142 C2
Gomel = Homyel
 Belarus 52°28N 31°0E 75 B16
Gomera Canary Is. 28°7N 17°14W 100 F2
Gómez Palacio
 Mexico 25°34N 103°30W 180 B4
Gomfi Greece 39°26N 21°36E 98 B3
Gomishān Iran 37°4N 54°6E 129 B7
Gommern Germany 52°4N 11°50E 76 C7
Gomogomo Indonesia 6°39S 134°43E 119 F8
Gomoh India 23°52N 86°10E 125 H12
Gomotartsi Bulgaria 44°6N 22°57E 96 B7
Gompa = Ganta Liberia 7°15N 8°59W 138 D3
Gonābād Iran 34°15N 58°45E 129 C8

Gonaïves *Haiti* 19°20N 72°42W **183** C5
Gonarezhou △
Zimbabwe 21°32S 31°55E **143** G3
Gonâve, G. de la *Haiti* 19°29N 72°42W **183** C5
Gonâve, Île de la *Haiti* 18°51N 73°3W **183** C5
Gonbad-e Kāvūs *Iran* 37°20N 55°25E **129** B7
Gönc *Hungary* 48°28N 21°14E **80** B6
Gonda *India* 27°9N 81°58E **125** F9
Gondal *India* 21°58N 70°52E **124** J4
Gonder *Ethiopia* 12°39N 37°30E **131** E2
Gondia *India* 21°23N 80°10E **126** D5
Gondola *Mozam.* 19°10S 33°37E **143** F3
Gondomar *Portugal* 41°10N 8°35W **88** D2
Gondrecourt-le-Château
France 48°31N 5°30E **71** D12
Gönen *Balıkesir, Turkey* 40°6N 27°39E **97** F11
Gönen *Isparta, Turkey* 37°57N 30°31E **99** D12
Gönen → *Turkey* 40°6N 27°39E **97** F11
Gong Xian *China* 28°23N 104°47E **116** C5
Gong'an *China* 30°7N 112°12E **117** B9
Gongbei *China* 22°12N 113°32E **111** a
Gongchangling *China* 41°7N 123°27E **115** D12
Gongcheng *China* 24°50N 110°49E **117** E8
Gongga Shan *China* 29°40N 101°55E **116** C3
Gonggar *China* 29°23N 91°7E **110** F7
Gongguan *China* 21°48N 109°36E **116** G7
Gonghe *China* 36°18N 100°32E **110** D9
Gongju *S. Korea* 36°27N 127°7E **115** F14
Gongliu *China* 43°28N 82°8E **109** D10
Gongming *China* 22°47N 113°53E **111** a
Gongola → *Nigeria* 9°30N 12°4E **139** D7
Gongolgon *Australia* 30°21S 146°54E **151** E4
Gongshan *China* 27°43N 98°29E **116** D2
Gongtan *China* 28°55N 108°20E **116** C7
Gongyi *China* 34°45N 112°58E **114** G7
Gongzhuling *China* 43°30N 124°40E **115** C13
Goni *Greece* 39°52N 22°29E **98** B4
Goniadz *Poland* 53°30N 22°44E **82** E9
Goniri *Nigeria* 11°30N 12°15E **139** C7
Gonjo *China* 30°52N 98°17E **116** B2
Gonnesa *Italy* 39°16N 8°28E **94** C1
Gonnosfanádiga *Italy* 39°29N 8°39E **94** C1
Gonzales *Calif., U.S.A.* 36°30N 121°26W **170** J5
Gonzales *Tex., U.S.A.* 29°30N 97°27W **176** G6
González *Mexico* 22°48N 98°25W **181** C5
Goobang △ *Australia* 33°0S 148°32E **153** B8
Good Hope, C. of
S. Africa 34°24S 18°30E **144** D2
Good Hope Lake
Canada 59°16N 129°18W **162** B3
Gooderham *Canada* 44°54N 78°21W **174** B6
Goodhouse *S. Africa* 28°57S 18°13E **144** C2
Gooding *U.S.A.* 42°56N 114°43W **168** E6
Goodland *U.S.A.* 39°21N 101°43W **172** F3
Goodlands *Mauritius* 20°2S 57°39E **141** d
Goodlow *Canada* 56°20N 120°8W **162** B4
Goodooga *Australia* 29°3S 147°28E **151** D4
Goodsprings *U.S.A.* 35°49N 115°27W **171** K11
Goodwater *U.S.A.* 33°4N 86°3W **178** B3
Goole *U.K.* 53°42N 0°53W **66** D7
Goolgowi *Australia* 33°58S 145°41E **153** B6
Goolwa *Australia* 35°30S 138°47E **152** C3
Goomalling *Australia* 31°15S 116°49E **149** F2
Goomeri *Australia* 26°12S 152°6E **151** D5
Goonda *Mozam.* 19°48S 33°57E **143** F3
Goondiwindi *Australia* 28°30S 150°21E **151** D5
Goongarrie, L. *Australia* 30°3S 121°9E **149** F3
Goongarrie △ *Australia* 30°7S 121°30E **149** F3
Goonyella *Australia* 21°47S 147°58E **150** C4
Goose → *Canada* 53°20N 60°35W **165** B7
Goose Creek *U.S.A.* 32°59N 80°2W **178** C9
Goose L. *U.S.A.* 41°56N 120°26W **168** F3
Gooty *India* 15°7N 77°41E **127** G3
Gop *India* 22°5N 69°50E **124** H3
Gopalganj *India* 26°28N 84°30E **125** F11
Göppingen *Germany* 48°42N 9°39E **77** G5
Gor *Spain* 37°23N 2°58W **89** H8
Góra *Dolnośląskie, Poland* 51°40N 16°31E **83** G3
Góra *Mazowieckie, Poland* 52°39N 20°6E **83** F7
Góra Kalwaria *Poland* 51°59N 21°14E **83** G8
Gorakhpur *India* 26°47N 83°23E **125** F10
Goražde *Bos.-H.* 43°38N 18°58E **80** G3
Gorbatov *Russia* 56°12N 43°2E **86** B6
Gorbea *Spain* 43°1N 2°50W **90** B2
Gorczański △ *Poland* 49°30N 20°10E **83** J7
Gorda, Pta. *Canary Is.* 28°45N 18°0W **100** F2
Gorda, Pta. *Nic.* 14°20N 83°10W **182** D3
Gordan B. *Australia* 11°35S 130°10E **148** B5
Gördes *Turkey* 38°54N 28°17E **99** C10
Gordon *Ga., U.S.A.* 32°54N 83°20W **178** C6
Gordon *Nebr., U.S.A.* 42°48N 102°12W **172** D2
Gordon → *Australia* 42°27S 145°30E **151** G4
Gordon, I. *Chile* 54°55S 69°30W **192** D3
Gordon Bay *Canada* 45°12N 79°47W **174** A5
Gordon L. *Alta.,*
Canada 56°30N 110°25W **163** B6
Gordon L. *N.W.T.,*
Canada 63°5N 113°11W **162** A6
Gordonvale *Australia* 17°5S 145°50E **150** B4
Goré *Chad* 7°59N 16°31E **135** G9
Gore *Ethiopia* 8°12N 35°32E **131** F2
Gore *N.Z.* 46°5S 168°58E **155** G3
Gore Bay *Canada* 45°57N 82°28W **164** C3
Gorée, Île de *Senegal* 14°40N 17°23W **138** C1
Görele *Turkey* 41°2N 39°0E **105** B8
Göreme *Turkey* 38°35N 34°52E **104** C6
Gorey *Ireland* 52°41N 6°18W **64** D5
Gorg *Iran* 29°29N 59°43E **129** D8
Gorgān *Iran* 36°55N 54°30E **129** B7
Gorgol □ *Mauritania* 15°45N 13°0W **138** B2
Gorgona *Italy* 43°26N 9°54E **92** E6
Gorgona, I. *Colombia* 3°0N 78°10W **186** C3
Gorgoram *Nigeria* 12°40N 10°45E **139** C7
Gorham *U.S.A.* 44°23N 71°10W **175** B13
Gori *Georgia* 42°0N 44°7E **87** J7
Goribidnur = Gauribidanur
India 13°37N 77°32E **127** H3
Goriganga → *India* 29°45N 80°23E **125** E9
Gorinchem *Neths.* 51°50N 4°59E **69** C4
Goris *Armenia* 39°31N 46°22E **105** C12
Goritsy *Russia* 57°4N 36°43E **84** D9
Gorízia *Italy* 45°56N 13°37E **93** C10
Gorj □ *Romania* 45°5N 23°25E **81** E8
Gorki = Horki *Belarus* 54°17N 30°59E **84** E6
Gorkiy = Nizhniy Novgorod
Russia 56°20N 44°0E **86** B7
Gorkovskoye Vdkhr.
Russia 57°2N 43°4E **86** B6
Gorleston *U.K.* 52°35N 1°44E **67** E9
Gorlice *Poland* 49°35N 21°11E **83** J8
Görlitz *Germany* 51°9N 14°58E **76** D10
Gorlovka = Horlivka
Ukraine 48°19N 38°5E **85** H10
Gorman *U.S.A.* 34°47N 118°51W **171** L8
Gorna Dzhumayo = Blagoevgrad
Bulgaria 42°2N 23°5E **96** D7
Gorna Oryakhovitsa
Bulgaria 43°7N 25°40E **97** C9
Gornja Radgona
Slovenia 46°40N 16°2E **93** B13
Gornja Tuzla *Bos.-H.* 44°35N 18°46E **80** F3
Gornji Grad *Slovenia* 46°20N 14°52E **93** B11
Gornji Milanovac *Serbia* 44°3N 20°29E **96** B4
Gornji Vakuf *Bos.-H.* 43°57N 17°34E **80** G2
Gorno Ablanovo
Bulgaria 43°37N 25°43E **97** C9
Gorno-Altay □ *Russia* 51°0N 86°0E **109** B11
Gorno-Altaysk *Russia* 51°50N 86°5E **109** B11
Gorno-Badakhshan =
Kŭhiston-Badakhshon □
Tajikistan 38°30N 73°0E **109** E8
Gornozavodsk *Russia* 46°33N 141°50E **107** E15
Gornyak *Russia* 50°59N 81°27E **109** B10
Gornyatskiy *Russia* 48°18N 40°56E **87** F5
Gornyy *Primorsk,*
Russia 44°57N 133°59E **112** B6
Gornyy *Saratov, Russia* 51°50N 48°30E **86** E9
Gorodenka = Horodenka
Ukraine 48°41N 25°29E **81** B10
Gorodets *Russia* 56°38N 43°28E **86** B6
Gorodishche = Horodyshche
Ukraine 49°17N 31°27E **85** H6
Gorodishche *Russia* 53°13N 45°40E **86** D7
Gorodnya = Horodnya
Ukraine 51°55N 31°33E **85** G6
Gorodok = Haradok
Belarus 55°30N 30°3E **84** E6
Gorodok = Horodok
Ukraine 49°46N 23°32E **75** D12
Gorodovikovsk *Russia* 46°8N 41°58E **87** G5
Goroke *Australia* 36°43S 141°29E **152** D4
Gorokhov = Horokhiv
Ukraine 50°30N 24°45E **75** C13
Gorokhovets *Russia* 56°13N 42°39E **86** B6
Gorom Gorom
Burkina Faso 14°26N 0°14W **139** C4
Goromonzi *Zimbabwe* 17°52S 31°22E **143** F3
Gorong, Kepulauan
Indonesia 3°59S 131°25E **119** E8
Gorongose → *Mozam.* 20°30S 34°40E **145** B5
Gorongoza *Mozam.* 18°44S 34°2E **143** F3
Gorongoza, Sa. da
Mozam. 18°27S 34°2E **143** F3
Gorongosa △ *Mozam.* 18°50S 34°29E **145** A5
Gorontalo *Indonesia* 0°35N 123°5E **119** D6
Gorontalo □ *Indonesia* 0°50N 122°20E **119** D6
Goronyo *Nigeria* 13°29N 5°39E **139** C6
Górowo Iławeckie
Poland 54°17N 20°30E **82** D7
Gorron *France* 48°25N 0°50W **70** D6
Gorshechnoye *Russia* 51°31N 38°2E **85** G10
Gort *Ireland* 53°3N 8°49W **64** C3
Gortis *Greece* 35°4N 24°58E **101** D6
Gorumahisani *India* 22°20N 86°24E **126** C8
Góry Bystrzyckie *Poland* 50°16N 16°33E **83** H3
Goryachiy Klyuch *Russia* 44°38N 39°8E **87** H4
Goryeong *S. Korea* 35°44N 128°15E **115** G15
Gorzkowice *Poland* 51°13N 19°36E **83** G6
Górzno *Poland* 53°12N 19°38E **83** E6
Gorzów Śląski *Poland* 51°3N 18°22E **83** G5
Gorzów Wielkopolski
Poland 52°43N 15°15E **83** F2
Gosford *Australia* 33°23S 151°18E **153** B9
Goshen *Calif., U.S.A.* 36°21N 119°25W **170** J7
Goshen *Ind., U.S.A.* 41°35N 85°50W **173** E11
Goshen *N.Y., U.S.A.* 41°24N 74°20W **175** E10
Goshogawara *Japan* 40°48N 140°27E **112** D10
Goslar *Germany* 51°54N 10°25E **76** D6
Gospič *Croatia* 44°35N 15°23E **93** D12
Gosport *U.K.* 50°48N 1°9W **67** G6
Gossas *Senegal* 14°28N 16°0W **138** C1
Gosse → *Australia* 19°32S 134°37E **150** B1
Gossi *Mali* 15°48N 1°20W **139** B4
Gostivar *Macedonia* 41°48N 20°57E **96** E4
Gostyń *Poland* 51°50N 17°3E **83** G4
Gostynin *Poland* 52°26N 19°29E **83** F6
Göta älv → *Sweden* 57°42N 11°54E **63** G5
Göta kanal *Sweden* 58°30N 15°58E **63** F10
Götaland *Sweden* 57°30N 14°30E **63** G8
Göteborg *Sweden* 57°43N 11°59E **63** G5
Götene *Sweden* 58°32N 13°30E **63** F7
Goteşti *Moldova* 46°9N 28°10E **81** D13
Gotha *Germany* 50°56N 10°42E **76** E6
Gothenburg = Göteborg
Sweden 57°43N 11°59E **63** G5
Gothenburg *U.S.A.* 40°56N 100°10W **172** E3
Gothèye *Niger* 13°52N 1°34E **139** C5
Gotland *Sweden* 57°30N 18°33E **63** G12
Gotlands län □ *Sweden* 57°15N 18°30E **63** G12
Gotō = Fukue *Japan* 32°41N 128°51E **113** H4
Gotō-Rettō *Japan* 32°55N 129°5E **113** H4
Gotse Delchev *Bulgaria* 41°36N 23°46E **96** E7
Gotska Sandön *Sweden* 58°24N 19°15E **63** F13
Gōtsu *Japan* 35°0N 132°14E **113** G6
Góttero, Monte *Italy* 44°22N 9°42E **92** D6
Göttingen *Germany* 51°31N 9°55E **76** D5
Gottskär *Sweden* 57°25N 12°2E **63** G6
Gottwald = Zmiyev
Ukraine 49°39N 36°27E **85** H9
Gottwaldov = Zlín
Czech Rep. 49°14N 17°40E **79** B10
Goubangzi *China* 41°20N 121°52E **115** D11
Gouda *Neths.* 52°1N 4°42E **69** B4
Goudiri *Senegal* 14°15N 12°45W **138** C2
Goudoumaria *Niger* 13°40N 11°10E **139** C7
Goudouras, Akra *Greece* 34°59N 26°6E **101** E8
Gouéké *Guinea* 8°2N 8°43W **138** D3
Gough I. *Atl. Oc.* 40°10S 9°45W **56** L11
Gouin, Rés. *Canada* 48°35N 74°40W **164** C5
Gouitafla *Ivory C.* 7°30N 5°53W **138** D3
Goulburn *Australia* 34°44S 149°44E **153** C8
Goulburn Is. *Australia* 11°40S 133°20E **150** A1
Goulburn River △
Australia 32°19S 150°10E **153** B9
Goulds *U.S.A.* 25°33N 80°23W **179** K9
Goulia *Ivory C.* 10°1N 7°11W **138** C3
Goulimine *Morocco* 28°56N 10°0W **134** C3
Goulmima *Morocco* 31°41N 4°57W **136** B3
Goumbou *Mali* 15°2N 7°25W **138** B3
Goumenissa *Greece* 40°56N 22°37E **96** F6
Goundam *Mali* 16°27N 3°40W **138** B4
Goura *Greece* 37°56N 22°20E **98** D4
Gouraya *Algeria* 36°31N 1°56E **136** A4
Gourbassi *Mali* 13°24N 11°38W **138** C2
Gourdon *France* 44°44N 1°23E **72** D5
Gouré *Niger* 14°0N 10°10E **139** C7
Gourin *France* 48°8N 3°37W **70** D3
Gourits → *S. Africa* 34°21S 21°52E **144** D3
Gourma-Rharous *Mali* 16°55N 1°50W **139** B4
Gournay-en-Bray *France* 49°29N 1°44E **71** C8
Gournes *Greece* 35°19N 25°16E **101** D7
Gourock *U.K.* 55°57N 4°49W **65** F4
Gourock Ra. *Australia* 36°0S 149°25E **153** D8
Goursi *Burkina Faso* 12°42N 2°37W **138** C4
Gouvea *Brazil* 18°27S 43°44W **189** D2
Gouverneur *U.S.A.* 44°20N 75°28W **175** B9
Gouvia *Greece* 39°39N 19°50E **101** A3
Gouzon *France* 46°12N 2°14E **71** F9
Gove Peninsula
Australia 12°17S 136°49E **150** A2
Governador Valadares
Brazil 18°15S 41°57W **189** D2
Governor's Harbour
Bahamas 25°10N 76°14W **182** A4
Govĭaltay □ *Mongolia* 45°30N 96°0E **109** C13
Govindgarh *India* 24°23N 81°18E **125** G9
Gowan Ra. *Australia* 25°0S 145°0E **150** D4
Gowanda *U.S.A.* 42°28N 78°56W **174** D6
Gower *U.K.* 51°35N 4°10W **67** F3
Gowers Corner *U.S.A.* 28°20N 82°30W **179** G7
Gowna, L. *Ireland* 53°51N 7°34W **64** C4
Gowurdak *Turkmenistan* 37°50N 66°4E **109** E7
Goya *Argentina* 29°10S 59°10W **190** B4
Goyang *S. Korea* 37°39N 126°50E **115** F14
Göyçay *Azerbaijan* 40°42N 47°43E **87** K8
Goyder Lagoon
Australia 27°3S 138°58E **151** D2
Goygöl *Azerbaijan* 40°37N 46°12E **87** K8
Goyllarisquizga *Peru* 10°31S 76°24W **188** C2
Göynük *Antalya, Turkey* 36°41N 30°33E **99** E12
Göynük *Bolu, Turkey* 40°24N 30°48E **104** B4
Goz Beïda *Chad* 12°10N 21°20E **135** F10
Gozdnica *Poland* 51°28N 15°4E **83** G2
Gozo *Malta* 36°3N 14°15E **101** C1
Graaff-Reinet *S. Africa* 32°13S 24°32E **144** D3
Grabo *Ivory C.* 4°57N 7°30W **138** D3
Grabow *Germany* 53°17N 11°34E **76** B7
Grabów nad Prosną
Poland 51°31N 18°7E **83** G5
Gračac *Croatia* 44°18N 15°57E **93** D12
Gračanica *Bos.-H.* 44°43N 18°18E **80** F3
Graçay *France* 47°10N 1°50E **71** E8
Graceville *U.S.A.* 30°58N 85°31W **178** E4
Gracewood *U.S.A.* 33°22N 82°2W **178** B7
Gracias a Dios, C.
Honduras 15°0N 83°10W **182** D3
Graciosa *Azores* 39°4N 28°0W **134** a
Graciosa, I. *Canary Is.* 29°15N 13°32W **100** E6
Grad Sofiya □ *Bulgaria* 42°35N 23°20E **96** D7
Gradac *Montenegro* 43°23N 19°9E **96** C3
Gradačac *Bos.-H.* 44°52N 18°26E **80** F3
Gradeška Planina
Macedonia 41°30N 22°15E **96** E6
Gradets *Bulgaria* 42°46N 26°30E **97** D10
Gradišće *Slovenia* 46°37N 15°50E **93** B12
Grădiştea de Munte
Romania 45°37N 23°13E **81** E8
Grado *Italy* 45°40N 13°23E **93** C10
Grado *Spain* 43°23N 6°4W **88** B4
Grady *U.S.A.* 34°49N 103°19W **169** J12
Graeca, Lacul *Romania* 44°5N 26°10E **81** F11
Grafenau *Germany* 48°51N 13°22E **77** G9
Gräfenberg *Germany* 49°39N 11°14E **77** F7
Grafham Water *U.K.* 52°19N 0°18W **67** E7
Grafton *Australia* 29°38S 152°58E **151** D5
Grafton *N. Dak., U.S.A.* 48°25N 97°25W **172** A5
Grafton *W. Va., U.S.A.* 39°21N 80°2W **173** F13
Graham *Canada* 49°20N 90°30W **164** C1
Graham *Ga., U.S.A.* 31°50N 82°30W **178** D7
Graham *Tex., U.S.A.* 33°6N 98°35W **176** E5
Graham, Mt. *U.S.A.* 32°42N 109°52W **169** K9
Graham Bell, Ostrov = Greem-
Bell, Ostrov *Russia* 81°0N 62°0E **106** A7
Graham I. *B.C.,*
Canada 53°40N 132°30W **162** C2
Graham I. *Nunavut,*
Canada 77°25N 90°30W **161** B13
Graham Land *Antarctica* 65°0S 64°0W **55** C17
Grahamstown *S. Africa* 33°19S 26°31E **144** D4
Grahamsville *U.S.A.* 41°51N 74°33W **175** E10
Grahovo *Montenegro* 42°40N 18°40E **96** D2
Graïba *Tunisia* 34°30N 10°13E **136** B6
Graie, Alpi *Europe* 45°30N 7°10E **73** C11
Grain Coast *W. Afr.* 4°20N 10°0W **138** E3
Grajagan *Indonesia* 8°35S 114°13E **119** K17
Grajaú *Brazil* 5°50S 46°4W **189** B1
Grajaú → *Brazil* 3°41S 44°48W **189** A2
Grajewo *Poland* 53°39N 22°30E **82** E9
Gramada *Bulgaria* 43°49N 22°39E **96** C6
Gramat *France* 44°48N 1°43E **72** D5
Grammichele *Italy* 37°13N 14°38E **95** E7
Grámmos, Óros *Greece* 40°18N 20°47E **96** F4
Grampian *U.S.A.* 40°58N 78°37W **174** F6
Grampian Highlands = Grampian
Mts. *U.K.* 56°50N 4°0W **65** E5
Grampian Mts. *U.K.* 56°50N 4°0W **65** E5
Grampians, The
Australia 37°15S 142°20E **152** D5
Grampians △
Australia 37°15S 142°28E **152** D5
Gramsh *Albania* 40°52N 20°12E **96** F4
Gran Altiplanicie Central
Argentina 49°0S 69°30W **192** C3
Gran Canaria
Canary Is. 27°55N 15°35W **100** G4
Gran Chaco *S. Amer.* 25°0S 61°0W **190** B3
Gran Desierto del Pinacate ⌂
Mexico 31°51N 113°32W **180** A2
Gran Laguna Salada
Argentina 44°24S 67°23W **192** B3
Gran Pajonal *Peru* 10°45S 74°30W **188** C3
Gran Paradiso *Italy* 45°33N 7°17E **92** C4
Gran Sasso d'Itália
Italy 42°27N 13°42E **93** F10
Gran Sasso e Monti Della Laga △
Italy 42°32N 13°22E **93** F10
Granada *Nic.* 11°58N 86°0W **182** D2
Granada *Spain* 37°10N 3°35W **89** H7
Granada *U.S.A.* 38°4N 102°19W **168** G12
Granada □ *Spain* 37°18N 3°0W **89** H7
Granadilla de Abona
Canary Is. 28°7N 16°33W **100** F3
Granard *Ireland* 53°47N 7°30W **64** C4
Granbury *U.S.A.* 32°27N 97°47W **176** E6
Granby *Canada* 45°25N 72°45W **175** A12
Granby *U.S.A.* 40°5N 105°56W **168** F11
Grand → *Canada* 42°51N 79°34W **174** D5
Grand → *Mo., U.S.A.* 39°23N 93°7W **172** F7
Grand → *S. Dak.,*
U.S.A. 45°40N 100°45W **172** C3
Grand-Anse = Portsmouth
Dominica 15°34N 61°27W **183** C7
Grand Bahama I.
Bahamas 26°40N 78°30W **182** A4
Grand Baie *Mauritius* 20°0S 57°35E **141** d
Grand Bank *Canada* 47°6N 55°48W **165** C8
Grand Banks *Atl. Oc.* 45°0N 52°0W **56** B6
Grand Bassam *Ivory C.* 5°10N 3°49W **138** D4
Grand Bend *Canada* 43°18N 81°45W **174** C3
Grand Béréby *Ivory C.* 4°38N 6°55W **138** E3
Grand-Bourg
Guadeloupe 15°53N 61°19W **182** b
Grand Canal = Da Yunhe →
China 39°10N 117°10E **115** E9
Grand Canyon *U.S.A.* 36°3N 112°9W **169** H7
Grand Canyon △
U.S.A. 36°15N 112°30W **169** H7
Grand Canyon-Parashant ⌂
U.S.A. 36°30N 113°45W **169** H7
Grand Cayman
Cayman Is. 19°20N 81°20W **182** C3
Grand Cess *Liberia* 4°40N 8°12W **138** E3
Grand Coulee *U.S.A.* 47°57N 119°0W **168** C4
Grand Coulee Dam
U.S.A. 47°57N 118°59W **168** C4
Grand Falls *Canada* 47°3N 67°44W **165** C6
Grand Falls-Windsor
Canada 48°56N 55°40W **165** C8
Grand Forks *Canada* 49°0N 118°30W **162** D5
Grand Forks *U.S.A.* 47°55N 97°3W **172** B5
Grand Gorge *U.S.A.* 42°21N 74°29W **175** D10
Grand Haven *U.S.A.* 43°4N 86°13W **172** D10
Grand I. *Mich., U.S.A.* 46°31N 86°40W **172** B10
Grand I. *N.Y., U.S.A.* 43°0N 78°58W **174** D6
Grand Island *U.S.A.* 40°55N 98°21W **172** E4
Grand Isle *La., U.S.A.* 29°14N 90°0W **177** G9
Grand Isle *Vt., U.S.A.* 44°43N 73°18W **175** B11
Grand Junction *U.S.A.* 39°4N 108°33W **168** G9
Grand L. *N.B., Canada* 45°57N 66°7W **165** C6
Grand L. *Nfld. & L.,*
Canada 49°0N 57°30W **165** C8
Grand L. *Nfld. & L.,*
Canada 53°40N 60°30W **165** B7
Grand L. *U.S.A.* 29°55N 92°47W **176** G8
Grand Lahou *Ivory C.* 5°10N 5°5W **138** D3
Grand Lake *U.S.A.* 40°15N 105°49W **168** F11
Grand-Lieu, L. de *France* 47°6N 1°40W **70** E5
Grand Manan I.
Canada 44°45N 66°52W **165** D6
Grand Marais *Mich.,*
U.S.A. 46°40N 85°59W **173** B11
Grand Marais *Minn.,*
U.S.A. 47°45N 90°25W **164** C1
Grand-Mère *Canada* 46°36N 72°40W **164** C5
Grand Popo *Benin* 6°15N 1°57E **139** D5
Grand Portage *U.S.A.* 47°58N 89°41W **172** B9
Grand Prairie *U.S.A.* 32°44N 96°59W **176** E6
Grand Rapids *Canada* 53°12N 99°19W **163** C9
Grand Rapids *Mich.,*
U.S.A. 42°58N 85°40W **173** D11
Grand Rapids *Minn.,*
U.S.A. 47°14N 93°31W **172** B7
Grand Ridge *U.S.A.* 30°43N 85°1W **178** E4
Grand St-Bernard, Col du
Europe 45°50N 7°10E **77** K3
Grand Staircase-Escalante ⌂
U.S.A. 37°25N 111°33W **169** H8
Grand Teton *U.S.A.* 43°54N 110°50W **168** E8
Grand Teton △
U.S.A. 43°50N 110°50W **168** E8
Grand Union Canal *U.K.* 52°7N 0°53W **67** E7
Grandas *Spain* 43°13N 6°53W **88** B4
Grande → *Jujuy,*
Argentina 24°20S 65°2W **190** A2
Grande → *Mendoza,*
Argentina 36°52S 69°45W **190** D2
Grande → *Bolivia* 15°51S 64°39W **186** G6
Grande → *Bahia,*
Brazil 11°30S 44°30W **189** C2
Grande → *Minas Gerais,*
Brazil 20°6S 51°4W **187** H8
Grande, B. *Argentina* 50°30S 68°20W **192** D3
Grande, Rio →
N. Amer. 25°58N 97°9W **176** J6
Grande, Serra *Piauí,*
Brazil 8°0S 45°10W **189** B1
Grande, Serra *Tocantins,*
Brazil 11°15S 46°30W **189** C1
Grande Anse *Seychelles* 4°18S 55°45E **141** b
Grande Baleine →
Canada 55°16N 77°47W **164** A4
Grande Cache *Canada* 53°53N 119°8W **162** C5
Grande Casse, Pte. de la
France 45°24N 6°49E **73** C10
Grande Comore
Comoros Is. 11°35S 43°20E **141** a
Grande-Entrée *Canada* 47°30N 61°40W **165** C7
Grande Prairie
Canada 55°10N 118°50W **162** B5
Grande-Rivière *Canada* 48°26N 64°30W **165** C7
Grande Sertão Veredas △
Brazil 15°10S 45°40W **189** D1
Grande-Terre
Guadeloupe 16°20N 61°25W **182** b
Grande-Vallée *Canada* 49°14N 65°8W **165** C6
Grande Vigie, Pte. de la
Guadeloupe 16°32N 61°27W **182** b
Grandfalls *U.S.A.* 31°20N 102°51W **176** F3
Grândola *Portugal* 38°12N 8°35W **89** G2
Grandpré *France* 49°20N 4°50E **71** C11
Grands Causses ⌂ *France* 44°5N 2°58E **72** D6
Grands-Jardins ⌂
Canada 47°41N 70°51W **165** C5
Grandview *Canada* 51°10N 100°42W **163** C8
Grandview *U.S.A.* 46°15N 119°54W **168** C4
Grandvilliers *France* 49°40N 1°57E **71** C8
Graneros *Chile* 34°5S 70°45W **190** C1
Grangemouth *U.K.* 56°1N 3°42W **65** E5
Granger *U.S.A.* 41°35N 109°58W **168** F9
Grängesberg *Sweden* 60°6N 15°1E **62** D9
Grangeville *U.S.A.* 45°56N 116°7W **168** D5
Granisle *Canada* 54°53N 126°13W **162** C3
Granit Rose, Côte de *France* 48°50N 4°10W **70** D2
Granite City *U.S.A.* 38°42N 90°8W **172** F8
Granite Falls *U.S.A.* 44°49N 95°33W **172** C6
Granite L. *Canada* 48°8N 57°5W **165** C8
Granite Mt. *U.S.A.* 33°5N 116°28W **171** M10
Granite Pk. *U.S.A.* 45°10N 109°48W **168** D9
Graniteville *S.C.,*
U.S.A. 33°34N 81°49W **178** B8
Graniteville *Vt., U.S.A.* 44°8N 72°29W **175** B12
Granitola, C. *Italy* 37°34N 12°39E **94** E5
Granity *N.Z.* 41°39S 171°51E **155** B6
Granja *Brazil* 3°7S 40°50W **189** A2
Granja de Moreruela
Spain 41°48N 5°44W **88** D5
Granja de Torrehermosa
Spain 38°19N 5°35W **89** G5
Gränna *Sweden* 58°1N 14°28E **63** F8
Granollers *Spain* 41°39N 2°18E **90** D7
Gransee *Germany* 53°1N 13°8E **76** B9
Grant *Fla., U.S.A.* 27°56N 80°32W **179** H9
Grant *Nebr., U.S.A.* 40°50N 101°43W **172** E3
Grant, Mt. *U.S.A.* 38°34N 118°48W **168** G4
Grant City *U.S.A.* 40°29N 94°25W **172** E6
Grant I. *Australia* 11°10S 132°52E **148** B5
Grant Range *U.S.A.* 38°30N 115°25W **168** G6
Grantham *U.K.* 52°55N 0°38W **66** E7
Grantown-on-Spey *U.K.* 57°20N 3°36W **65** D5
Grants *U.S.A.* 35°9N 107°52W **169** J10
Grants Pass *U.S.A.* 42°26N 123°19W **168** E2
Grantsville *U.S.A.* 40°36N 112°28W **168** F7
Grantville *U.S.A.* 33°14N 84°50W **178** B5
Granville *France* 48°50N 1°35W **70** D5
Granville *N. Dak.,*
U.S.A. 48°16N 100°47W **172** A3
Granville *N.Y., U.S.A.* 43°24N 73°16W **175** C11
Granville *Ohio, U.S.A.* 40°4N 82°31W **174** F2
Granville L. *Canada* 56°18N 100°30W **163** B8
Graskop *S. Africa* 24°56S 30°49E **145** B5
Gräsö *Sweden* 60°28N 18°35E **62** D12
Grass → *Canada* 56°3N 96°33W **163** B9
Grass Range *U.S.A.* 47°2N 108°48W **168** C9
Grass River ⌂ *Canada* 54°40N 100°50W **163** C8
Grass Valley *Calif.,*
U.S.A. 39°13N 121°4W **170** F6
Grass Valley *Oreg.,*
U.S.A. 45°22N 120°47W **168** D3
Grassano *Italy* 40°38N 16°17E **95** B9
Grasse *France* 43°38N 6°56E **73** E10
Grassflat *U.S.A.* 41°0N 78°6W **174** E6
Grasslands △ *Canada* 49°11N 107°38W **163** D7
Grassy *Australia* 40°3S 144°5E **151** G3
Gråsten *Denmark* 54°55N 9°35E **63** K3
Grästorp *Sweden* 58°20N 12°40E **63** F6
Gratkorn *Austria* 47°8N 15°21E **78** D8
Graubünden □ *Switz.* 46°45N 9°30E **77** J5
Graulhet *France* 43°45N 1°59E **72** E5
Graus *Spain* 42°11N 0°20E **90** C5
Grave, Pte. de *France* 45°34N 1°4W **72** C2
Gravelbourg *Canada* 49°50N 106°35W **163** D7
Gravelines *France* 51°1N 2°10E **71** A9
's-Gravenhage *Neths.* 52°7N 4°17E **69** B4
Gravenhurst *Canada* 44°52N 79°20W **174** B5
Gravesend *Australia* 29°35S 150°20E **151** D5
Gravesend *U.K.* 51°26N 0°22E **67** F8
Gravina in Púglia *Italy* 40°49N 16°25E **95** B9
Gravois, Pointe-à- *Haiti* 18°2N 73°56W **183** C5
Gravona → *France* 41°58N 8°45E **73** G12
Gray *France* 47°22N 5°35E **71** E12
Gray *U.S.A.* 33°1N 83°32W **178** B6
Grayling *U.S.A.* 44°40N 84°43W **173** C11
Grays *U.K.* 51°28N 0°21E **67** F8
Grays Harbor *U.S.A.* 46°59N 124°1W **170** D2
Grays L. *U.S.A.* 43°4N 111°26W **168** E8
Grays River *U.S.A.* 46°21N 123°37W **170** D3
Grayvoron *Russia* 50°29N 35°41E **85** G8
Graz *Austria* 47°4N 15°27E **78** D8
Grdelica *Serbia* 42°55N 22°3E **96** D6
Greasy L. *Canada* 62°55N 122°12W **162** A4
Great Abaco I. = Abaco I.
Bahamas 26°25N 77°10W **182** A4
Great Artesian Basin
Australia 23°0S 144°0E **150** C3
Great Australian Bight
Australia 33°30S 130°0E **149** F5
Great Bahama Bank
Bahamas 23°15N 78°0W **182** B4
Great Barrier I. *N.Z.* 36°11S 175°25E **154** C4
Great Barrier Reef
Australia 18°0S 146°50E **150** B4
Great Barrier Reef ⌂
Australia 20°0S 150°0E **150** B4
Great Barrington
U.S.A. 42°12N 73°22W **175** D11
Great Basalt Wall △
Australia 19°52S 145°43E **150** B4
Great Basin *U.S.A.* 40°0N 117°0W **168** G5
Great Basin △ *U.S.A.* 38°56N 114°15W **168** G6
Great Basses *Sri Lanka* 6°11N 81°29E **127** L5
Great Bear → *Canada* 65°0N 126°0W **160** E7
Great Bear L. *Canada* 65°30N 120°0W **160** D8
Great Belt = Store Bælt
Denmark 55°20N 11°0E **63** J4
Great Bend *Kans.,*
U.S.A. 38°22N 98°46W **172** F4
Great Bend *Pa., U.S.A.* 41°58N 75°45W **175** E9
Great Blasket I. *Ireland* 52°6N 10°32W **64** D1
Great Britain *Europe* 54°0N 2°15W **58** E5
Great Camanoe
Br. Virgin Is. 18°30N 64°35W **183** e
Great Channel *Asia* 6°0N 94°0E **127** L11
Great Coco I. = Koko Kyunzu
Burma 14°7N 93°22E **127** G11
Great Codroy *Canada* 47°51N 59°16W **165** C8
Great Divide, The = Great
Dividing Ra. *Australia* 23°0S 146°0E **150** C4
Great Divide Basin
U.S.A. 42°0N 108°0W **168** E9
Great Dividing Ra.
Australia 23°0S 146°0E **150** C4
Great Driffield = Driffield
U.K. 54°0N 0°26W **66** C7
Great Exuma I.
Bahamas 23°30N 75°50W **182** B4
Great Falls *U.S.A.* 47°30N 111°17W **168** C8
Great Fish = Groot-Vis →
S. Africa 33°28S 27°5E **144** D4
Great Guana Cay
Bahamas 24°0N 76°20W **182** B4
Great Himalayan △
India 31°30N 77°30E **124** D7
Great Inagua I.
Bahamas 21°0N 73°20W **183** B5
Great Indian Desert = Thar Desert
India 28°0N 72°0E **124** F5
Great Karoo *S. Africa* 31°55S 21°0E **144** D3
Great Khingan Mts. = Da
Hinggan Ling *China* 48°0N 121°0E **111** B13
Great Lake *Australia* 41°50S 146°40E **151** G4
Great Lakes *N. Amer.* 46°0N 84°0W **158** E11
Great Limpopo Transfrontier △
Africa 23°0S 31°45E **145** B5
Great Malvern *U.K.* 52°7N 2°18W **67** E5
Great Miami → *U.S.A.* 39°7N 84°49W **173** F11
Great Nicobar *India* 7°0N 93°50E **127** L11
Great Ormes Head *U.K.* 53°20N 3°52W **66** D4
Great Otway △
Australia 38°50S 143°50E **152** E5
Great Ouse → *U.K.* 52°48N 0°21E **66** E8
Great Palm I. *Australia* 18°45S 146°40E **150** B4
Great Pedro Bluff
Jamaica 17°51N 77°44W **182** a
Great Pee Dee →
U.S.A. 33°21N 79°10W **177** E15
Great Plains *N. Amer.* 47°0N 105°0W **158** E9
Great Ruaha →
Tanzania 7°56S 37°52E **142** D4
Great Sacandaga L.
U.S.A. 43°6N 74°16W **175** C10
Great Saint Bernard Pass = Grand
St-Bernard, Col du
Europe 45°50N 7°10E **77** K3
Great Salt Desert = Kavīr, Dasht-e
Iran 34°30N 55°0E **129** C7
Great Salt L. *U.S.A.* 41°15N 112°40W **168** F7
Great Salt Lake Desert
U.S.A. 40°50N 113°30W **168** F7
Great Salt Plains L.
U.S.A. 36°45N 98°8W **176** C5
Great Sand Dunes ⌂
U.S.A. 37°48N 105°45W **169** H11
Great Sandy △
Australia 26°13S 153°2E **151** D5
Great Sandy Desert
Australia 21°0S 124°0E **148** D3
Great Sangi = Sangihe, Pulau
Indonesia 3°35N 125°30E **119** D7
Great Scarcies → *S. Leone* 9°0N 13°0W **138** D2
Great Sea Reef *Fiji* 16°15S 179°0E **154** a
Great Sitkin I. *U.S.A.* 52°3N 176°6W **166** E4
Great Skellig *Ireland* 51°47N 10°33W **64** E1
Great Slave L. *Canada* 61°23N 115°38W **162** A5
Great Smoky Mts. △
U.S.A. 35°40N 83°40W **177** D13
Great Stour = Stour →
U.K. 51°18N 1°22E **67** F9
Great Victoria Desert
Australia 29°30S 126°30E **149** E4
Great Wall *Antarctica* 62°30S 58°0W **55** C18
Great Wall *China* 38°30N 109°30E **114** E5
Great Whernside *U.K.* 54°10N 1°58W **66** C6
Great Yarmouth *U.K.* 52°37N 1°44E **67** E9
Great Zab = Zāb al Kabīr →
Iraq 36°1N 43°24E **105** D10
Great Zimbabwe
Zimbabwe 20°16S 30°54E **143** G3
Greater Antilles
W. Indies 17°40N 74°0W **183** C5
Greater London □ *U.K.* 51°31N 0°6W **67** F7
Greater Manchester □
U.K. 53°30N 2°15W **66** D5
Greater Sunda Is.
Indonesia 7°0S 112°0E **118** F4
Grebbestad *Sweden* 58°42N 11°15E **63** F5
Grebenka = Hrebenka
Ukraine 50°9N 32°22E **85** G7
Greco, C. *Cyprus* 34°57N 34°5E **101** E13
Greco, Mte. *Italy* 41°48N 13°58E **93** G10
Gredos, Sierra de *Spain* 40°20N 5°0W **88** E6
Greece *U.S.A.* 43°13N 77°41W **174** C7
Greece ■ *Europe* 40°0N 23°0E **98** B3
Greeley *Colo., U.S.A.* 40°25N 104°42W **168** F11
Greeley *Nebr., U.S.A.* 41°33N 98°32W **172** E4
Greeleyville *U.S.A.* 33°40N 79°59W **178** B10
Greely Fd. *Canada* 80°30N 85°0W **161** A15
Greem-Bell, Ostrov
Russia 81°0N 62°0E **106** A7
Green → *Ky., U.S.A.* 37°54N 87°30W **172** G10
Green → *Utah, U.S.A.* 38°11N 109°53W **168** G9
Green B. *U.S.A.* 45°0N 87°30W **172** C10
Green Bay *U.S.A.* 44°31N 88°0W **172** C10
Green C. *Australia* 37°13S 150°1E **153** D9
Green Cove Springs
U.S.A. 29°59N 81°42W **178** F8
Green I. = Lütao
Taiwan 22°40N 121°30E **117** F13
Green Lake *Canada* 54°17N 107°47W **163** C7
Green Mts. *U.S.A.* 43°45N 72°45W **175** C12
Green Pond *U.S.A.* 32°44N 80°37W **178** C9
Green River *Utah,*
U.S.A. 38°59N 110°10W **168** G8
Green River *Wyo.,*
U.S.A. 41°32N 109°28W **168** F9
Green Valley *U.S.A.* 31°52N 110°56W **169** L8
Greenacres *U.S.A.* 26°38N 80°7W **179** J9
Greenbank *U.S.A.* 48°6N 122°34W **170** B4
Greenbush *Mich.,*
U.S.A. 44°35N 83°19W **174** B1
Greenbush *Minn.,*
U.S.A. 48°42N 96°11W **172** A5
Greencastle *U.S.A.* 39°38N 86°52W **172** F10
Greene *U.S.A.* 42°20N 75°46W **175** D9
Greeneville *U.S.A.* 36°10N 82°50W **177** C13
Greenfield *Calif.,*
U.S.A. 36°19N 121°15W **170** J5
Greenfield *Calif., U.S.A.* 35°15N 119°0W **171** K8
Greenfield *Ind., U.S.A.* 39°47N 85°46W **173** F11
Greenfield *Iowa, U.S.A.* 41°18N 94°28W **172** E6
Greenfield *Mass.,*
U.S.A. 42°35N 72°36W **175** D12
Greenfield *Mo., U.S.A.* 37°25N 93°51W **172** G7
Greenfield Park
Canada 45°29N 73°28W **175** A11
Greenland ☑ *N. Amer.* 66°0N 45°0W **57** D6
Greenland Sea *Arctic* 73°0N 10°0W **57** B10
Greenock *U.K.* 55°57N 4°46W **65** F4
Greenore *Ireland* 54°1N 6°9W **64** B5
Greenore Pt. *Ireland* 52°14N 6°19W **64** D5
Greenough *Australia* 28°58S 114°43E **149** E1
Greenough →
Australia 28°51S 114°38E **149** E1
Greenough Pt. *Canada* 44°58N 81°26W **174** B3
Greenport *U.S.A.* 41°6N 72°22W **175** E12
Greensboro *Fla., U.S.A.* 30°34N 84°45W **178** E5

Greensboro Ga., U.S.A. 33°35N 83°11W 178 B6
Greensboro N.C., U.S.A. 36°4N 79°48W 177 C15
Greensboro Vt., U.S.A. 44°36N 72°18W 175 B12
Greensburg Ind., U.S.A. 39°20N 85°29W 173 F11
Greensburg Kans., U.S.A. 37°36N 99°18W 172 G4
Greensburg Pa., U.S.A. 40°18N 79°33W 174 F5
Greenstone = Geraldton Canada 49°44N 87°10W 164 C2
Greenstone Pt. U.K. 57°55N 5°37W 65 D3
Greenvale Australia 18°59S 145°7E 150 B4
Greenville Liberia 5°1N 9°6W 138 D3
Greenville Ala., U.S.A. 31°50N 86°38W 177 F11
Greenville Calif., U.S.A. 40°8N 120°57W 170 E6
Greenville Fla., U.S.A. 30°28N 83°38W 178 E6
Greenville Ga., U.S.A. 33°2N 84°43W 178 B5
Greenville Maine, U.S.A. 45°28N 69°35W 173 C19
Greenville Mich., U.S.A. 43°11N 85°15W 173 D11
Greenville Miss., U.S.A. 33°24N 91°4W 177 E9
Greenville Mo., U.S.A. 37°8N 90°27W 172 G8
Greenville N.C., U.S.A. 35°37N 77°23W 177 D16
Greenville N.H., U.S.A. 42°46N 71°49W 175 D13
Greenville N.Y., U.S.A. 42°25N 74°1W 175 D10
Greenville Ohio, U.S.A. 40°6N 84°38W 173 E11
Greenville Pa., U.S.A. 41°24N 80°23W 174 E4
Greenville S.C., U.S.A. 34°51N 82°24W 177 D13
Greenville Tex., U.S.A. 33°8N 96°7W 176 E6
Greenwater Lake △ Canada 52°32N 103°30W 163 C8
Greenwich Conn., U.S.A. 41°2N 73°38W 175 E11
Greenwich N.Y., U.S.A. 43°5N 73°30W 175 C11
Greenwich Ohio, U.S.A. 41°2N 82°31W 174 E2
Greenwich □ U.K. 51°29N 0°1E 67 F8
Greenwood Canada 49°10N 118°40W 162 D5
Greenwood Ark., U.S.A. 35°13N 94°16W 176 D7
Greenwood Fla., U.S.A. 30°52N 85°10W 178 E4
Greenwood Ind., U.S.A. 39°37N 86°7W 172 F10
Greenwood Miss., U.S.A. 33°31N 90°11W 177 E9
Greenwood S.C., U.S.A. 34°12N 82°10W 178 A7
Greenwood, Mt. Australia 13°48S 130°4E 148 B5
Gregbe Ivory C. 6°48N 6°43W 138 D3
Gregório → Brazil 6°50S 70°46W 188 B3
Gregory U.S.A. 43°14N 99°26W 172 D4
Gregory → Australia 17°53S 139°17E 150 B2
Gregory, L. S. Austral., Australia 28°55S 139°0E 151 D2
Gregory, L. W. Austral., Australia 20°0S 127°40E 148 D4
Gregory, L. W. Austral., Australia 25°38S 119°58E 149 E2
Gregory △ Australia 15°38S 131°15E 148 C5
Gregory Downs Australia 18°35S 138°45E 150 B2
Gregory Ra. Queens., Australia 19°30S 143°40E 150 B3
Gregory Ra. W. Austral., Australia 21°20S 121°12E 148 D3
Greiffenberg Germany 53°5N 13°57E 76 B9
Greifswald Germany 54°5N 13°23E 76 A9
Greifswalder Bodden Germany 54°12N 13°35E 76 A9
Grein Austria 48°14N 14°51E 78 C7
Greiz Germany 50°39N 12°10E 76 E8
Gremikha Russia 67°59N 39°47E 106 C4
Grenaa Denmark 56°25N 10°53E 63 H4
Grenada U.S.A. 33°47N 89°49W 177 E10
Grenada ■ W. Indies 12°10N 61°40W 183 D7
Grenade France 43°47N 1°17E 72 E5
Grenadier I. U.S.A. 44°3N 76°22W 175 B8
Grenadines, The St. Vincent 12°40N 61°20W 183 D7
Grenchen Switz. 47°12N 7°24E 77 H3
Grenen Denmark 57°44N 10°40E 63 G4
Grenfell Australia 33°52S 148°8E 153 B8
Grenfell Canada 50°30N 102°56W 163 C8
Grenoble France 45°12N 5°42E 73 C9
Grenville, C. Australia 12°0S 143°13E 150 A3
Grenville Chan. Canada 53°40N 129°46W 162 C3
Gréoux-les-Bains France 43°45N 5°52E 73 E9
Gresham U.S.A. 45°30N 122°25W 170 E4
Gresik Indonesia 7°13S 112°38E 119 G15
Gretna U.K. 55°0N 3°3W 65 F5
Gretna Fla., U.S.A. 30°37N 84°40W 178 E5
Gretna La., U.S.A. 29°54N 90°3W 177 G9
Greve Strand Denmark 55°34N 12°18E 63 J6
Greven Germany 52°6N 7°37E 76 C3
Grevena Greece 40°4N 21°25E 96 F5
Grevenbroich Germany 51°5N 6°35E 76 D2
Grevenmacher Lux. 49°41N 6°26E 69 E6
Grevesmühlen Germany 53°52N 11°12E 76 B7
Grey → Canada 47°34N 57°6W 165 C8
Grey → N.Z. 42°27S 171°12E 155 C6
Grey, C. Australia 13°0S 136°35E 150 A2
Grey Is. Canada 50°50N 55°35W 161 G20
Grey Ra. Australia 27°0S 143°30E 151 D3
Greybull U.S.A. 44°30N 108°3W 168 D9
Greymouth N.Z. 42°29S 171°13E 155 C6
Greystones Ireland 53°9N 6°5W 64 C5
Greytown N.Z. 41°5S 175°29E 154 H4
Greytown S. Africa 29°1S 30°36E 145 C5
Gribanovskiy Russia 51°28N 41°50E 86 E5
Gribbell I. Canada 53°23N 129°0W 162 C3
Gribës, Mal i Albania 40°17N 19°45E 96 F3
Gridley U.S.A. 39°22N 121°42W 170 F5
Griekwastad S. Africa 28°49S 23°15E 144 C3
Griesheim Germany 49°51N 8°33E 77 F4
Grieskirchen Austria 48°16N 13°48E 78 C6
Griffin U.S.A. 33°15N 84°16W 178 B5
Griffin, L. U.S.A. 28°52N 81°51W 179 G8
Griffith Australia 34°18S 146°2E 153 C7
Griffith Canada 45°15N 77°10W 174 A7
Griffith I. Canada 44°50N 80°55W 174 B4
Grignols France 44°23N 0°2W 72 D3
Grigoriopol Moldova 47°9N 29°18E 81 C14
Grimaylov = Hrymayliv Ukraine 49°20N 26°5E 75 D14
Grimes U.S.A. 39°4N 121°54W 170 F5
Grimma Germany 51°14N 12°43E 76 D8
Grimmen Germany 54°7N 13°3E 76 A9
Grimsay U.K. 57°29N 7°14W 65 D1
Grimsby Canada 43°12N 79°34W 174 C5
Grimsby U.K. 53°34N 0°5W 66 D7
Grimsey Iceland 66°33N 17°58W 60 C5
Grimshaw Canada 56°10N 117°40W 162 B5
Grimslöv Sweden 56°44N 14°34E 63 H8
Grimstad Norway 58°20N 8°35E 61 G13
Grindelwald Switz. 46°38N 8°2E 77 J4
Grindsted Denmark 55°46N 8°55E 63 J2
Grindstone I. U.S.A. 44°17N 76°27W 175 B8
Grindu Romania 44°44N 26°50E 81 F11
Grinnell U.S.A. 41°45N 92°43W 172 E7
Grinnell Pen. Canada 76°40N 95°0W 161 B13
Grintavec Slovenia 46°22N 14°32E 93 B11
Griomasaigh = Grimsay U.K. 57°29N 7°14W 65 D1
Gris-Nez, C. France 50°52N 1°35E 71 B8
Grise Fiord Canada 76°25N 82°57W 161 B15
Grisolles France 43°49N 1°19E 72 E5
Grisons = Graubünden □ Switz. 46°45N 9°30E 77 J5
Grisslehamn Sweden 60°5N 18°49E 62 D12
Grmeč Planina Bos.-H. 44°43N 16°16E 93 D13
Groais I. Canada 50°55N 55°35W 165 B8
Grobiņa Latvia 56°33N 21°10E 82 B8
Groblersdal S. Africa 25°15S 29°25E 145 C4
Grobming Austria 47°27N 13°54E 78 D6
Grocka Serbia 44°40N 20°42E 96 B4
Gródek Poland 53°6N 23°40E 83 E10
Grodków Poland 50°43N 17°21E 83 H4
Grodno = Hrodna Belarus 53°42N 23°52E 82 E10
Grodzisk Mazowiecki Poland 52°7N 20°37E 83 F7
Grodzisk Wielkopolski Poland 52°15N 16°22E 83 F3
Grodzyanka = Hrodzyanka Belarus 53°31N 28°42E 75 B15
Groesbeck U.S.A. 31°31N 96°32W 176 F6
Groix France 47°38N 3°29W 70 E3
Groix, Î. de France 47°38N 3°28W 70 E3
Grójec Poland 51°50N 20°58E 83 G7
Gronau Niedersachsen, Germany 52°5N 9°47E 76 C5
Gronau Nordrhein-Westfalen, Germany 52°12N 7°2E 76 C3
Grong Norway 64°25N 12°8E 60 D15
Grönhögen Sweden 56°16N 16°24E 63 H10
Groningen Neths. 53°15N 6°35E 69 A6
Groningen □ Neths. 53°16N 6°40E 69 A6
Grønlands △ Greenland 75°0N 35°0W 57 C7
Grønnedal = Kangilinnguit Greenland 61°20N 47°57W 57 E6
Groom U.S.A. 35°12N 101°6W 176 D4
Groot → S. Africa 33°45S 24°36E 144 D3
Groot-Berg → S. Africa 32°47S 18°8E 144 D2
Groot-Brakrivier S. Africa 34°2S 22°18E 144 D3
Groot Karasberge Namibia 27°20S 18°40E 144 C2
Groot-Kei → S. Africa 32°41S 28°22E 145 D4
Groot-Vis → S. Africa 33°28S 27°5E 144 D4
Grootdrink S. Africa 28°33S 21°42E 144 C3
Groote Eylandt Australia 14°0S 136°40E 150 A2
Groote Peel △ Neths. 51°22N 5°49E 69 C5
Grootfontein Namibia 19°31S 18°6E 144 A2
Grootlaagte → Africa 20°55S 21°27E 144 B3
Grootvloer → S. Africa 30°0S 20°40E 144 D3
Gros C. Canada 61°59N 113°32W 162 A6
Gros Islet St. Lucia 14°5N 60°58W 183 f
Gros Morne △ Canada 49°40N 57°50W 165 C8
Gros Piton St. Lucia 13°49N 61°5W 183 f
Gros Piton Pt. St. Lucia 13°49N 61°5W 183 f
Grósio Italy 46°18N 10°16E 92 B7
Grosne → France 46°42N 4°56E 71 F11
Grossa, Pta. Spain 39°6N 1°36E 100 B8
Grosse Point U.S.A. 42°23N 82°54W 174 D2
Grossenbrode Germany 54°21N 11°4E 76 A7
Grossenhain Germany 51°17N 13°32E 76 D9
Grosser Arber Germany 49°6N 13°8E 77 F9
Grosser Plöner See Germany 54°10N 10°22E 76 A6
Grosseto Italy 42°46N 11°8E 93 F8
Grossgerungs Austria 48°34N 14°57E 78 C7
Grossglockner Austria 47°5N 12°40E 78 D5
Groswater B. Canada 54°20N 57°40W 165 B8
Groton Conn., U.S.A. 41°21N 72°5W 175 E12
Groton N.Y., U.S.A. 42°36N 76°22W 175 D8
Groton S. Dak., U.S.A. 45°27N 98°6W 172 C4
Grottáglie Italy 40°32N 17°26E 95 B10
Grottaminarda Italy 41°4N 15°2E 95 A8
Grottammare Italy 42°59N 13°52E 93 F10
Grouard Mission Canada 55°33N 116°9W 162 B5
Grouin, Pte. du France 48°43N 1°51W 70 D5
Groundhog → Canada 48°45N 82°58W 164 C3
Grouw Neths. 53°5N 5°51E 69 A5
Grove City Fla., U.S.A. 26°56N 82°19W 179 J7
Grove City Pa., U.S.A. 41°10N 80°5W 174 E4
Grove Hill U.S.A. 31°42N 87°47W 177 F11
Groveland Calif., U.S.A. 37°50N 120°14W 170 H6
Groveland Fla., U.S.A. 28°34N 81°51W 179 G8
Grover Beach U.S.A. 35°7N 120°37W 171 K6
Groves U.S.A. 29°57N 93°54W 176 G8
Groveton U.S.A. 44°36N 71°31W 175 B13
Grovetown U.S.A. 33°27N 82°12W 178 B7
Grožnjan Croatia 45°22N 13°43E 93 C10
Groznyy Russia 43°20N 45°45E 87 J7
Grubišno Polje Croatia 45°44N 17°12E 80 E2
Grudovo Bulgaria 42°21N 27°10E 97 D11
Grudusk Poland 53°3N 20°38E 83 E7
Grudziądz Poland 53°30N 18°47E 82 E5
Gruinard B. U.K. 57°56N 5°35W 65 D3
Gruissan France 43°8N 3°7E 72 E7
Grumo Áppula Italy 41°1N 16°42E 95 A9
Grums Sweden 59°22N 13°5E 62 E7
Grünberg Germany 50°35N 8°58E 76 E4
Gründau Germany 50°10N 9°9E 77 E5
Grundy Center U.S.A. 42°22N 92°47W 172 D7
Grünstadt Germany 49°34N 8°9E 77 F4
Gruppo di Tessa △ Italy 46°47N 11°0E 92 B8
Gruvberget Sweden 61°6N 16°10E 62 C10
Gruver U.S.A. 36°16N 101°24W 176 C4
Gruyères Switz. 46°35N 7°4E 77 J3
Gruža Serbia 43°54N 20°46E 96 C4
Gryazi Russia 52°30N 39°58E 85 F10
Gryazovets Russia 58°50N 40°10E 84 C11
Grybów Poland 49°36N 20°55E 83 J7
Grycksbo Sweden 60°40N 15°29E 62 D9
Gryfice Poland 53°55N 15°13E 82 E2
Gryfino Poland 53°16N 14°29E 83 E1
Gryfów Śląski Poland 51°2N 15°24E 83 G2
Gryt Sweden 58°12N 16°48E 63 F10
Grythyttan Sweden 59°41N 14°32E 62 E8
Grytviken S. Georgia 54°19S 36°33W 56 M8
Gstaad Switz. 46°28N 7°18E 77 J3
Gua India 22°18N 85°20E 125 H11
Gua Musang Malaysia 4°53N 101°58E 121 K3
Guabún, Pta. Chile 41°48S 74°2W 192 B2
Guacanayabo, G. de Cuba 20°40N 77°20W 182 B4
Guachípas → Argentina 25°40S 65°30W 190 B2
Guadajoz → Spain 37°50N 4°51W 89 H6
Guadalajara Mexico 20°40N 103°20W 180 C4
Guadalajara Spain 40°37N 3°12W 90 E1
Guadalajara □ Spain 40°47N 2°30W 90 E2
Guadalaviar = Turia → Spain 39°27N 0°19W 91 F4
Guadalcanal Solomon Is. 9°32S 160°12E 147 B9
Guadalcanal Spain 38°5N 5°52W 89 G5
Guadalén → Spain 38°5N 3°32W 89 G7
Guadales Argentina 34°30S 67°55W 190 C2
Guadalete → Spain 36°35N 6°13W 89 J4
Guadalimar → Spain 38°5N 3°28W 89 G7
Guadalmena → Spain 38°19N 2°56W 89 G8
Guadalmez → Spain 38°46N 5°4W 89 G5
Guadalope → Spain 41°15N 0°3W 90 D4
Guadalquivir → Spain 36°47N 6°22W 89 J4
Guadalupe = Guadeloupe ☑ W. Indies 16°15N 61°40W 182 b
Guadalupe Brazil 6°44S 43°47W 189 B2
Guadalupe Mexico 22°45N 102°31W 180 C4
Guadalupe Spain 39°27N 5°17W 89 F5
Guadalupe U.S.A. 34°58N 120°34W 171 L6
Guadalupe → U.S.A. 28°27N 96°47W 176 G6
Guadalupe, Sierra de Spain 39°28N 5°30W 89 F5
Guadalupe de Bravo Mexico 31°23N 106°7W 180 A3
Guadalupe I. Pac. Oc. 29°0N 118°50W 158 G8
Guadalupe Mts. △ U.S.A. 31°40N 104°30W 176 F2
Guadalupe Peak U.S.A. 31°50N 104°52W 176 F2
Guadalupe y Calvo Mexico 26°6N 106°58W 180 B3
Guadarrama, Sierra de Spain 41°0N 4°0W 88 E7
Guadeloupe ☑ W. Indies 16°15N 61°40W 182 b
Guadeloupe △ Guadeloupe 16°10N 61°40W 182 b
Guadeloupe Passage W. Indies 16°50N 62°15W 183 C7
Guadelupe Peru 7°15S 79°29W 188 B2
Guadiamar → Spain 36°55N 6°24W 89 J4
Guadiana → Portugal 37°14N 7°22W 89 H3
Guadiana Menor → Spain 37°56N 3°15W 89 H7
Guadiaro → Spain 36°17N 5°17W 89 J5
Guadiato → Spain 37°48N 5°5W 89 H5
Guadiela → Spain 40°22N 2°49W 90 E2
Guadix Spain 37°18N 3°11W 89 H7
Guafo, Boca del Chile 43°35S 74°0W 192 B2
Guafo, I. Chile 43°35S 74°50W 192 B2
Guaico Trin. & Tob. 10°35N 61°9W 187 K15
Guainía → Colombia 2°1N 67°7W 186 C5
Guaíra Brazil 24°5S 54°10W 191 A5
Guairá □ Paraguay 25°45S 56°30W 190 B4
Guaire = Gorey Ireland 52°41N 6°18W 64 D5
Guaitecas, Is. Chile 44°0S 74°30W 192 B2
Guajará-Mirim Brazil 10°50S 65°20W 186 F5
Guajira, Pen. de la Colombia 12°0N 72°0W 186 A4
Gualán Guatemala 15°8N 89°22W 182 C2
Gualdo Tadino Italy 43°14N 12°47E 93 E9
Gualeguay Argentina 33°10S 59°14W 190 C4
Gualeguaychú Argentina 33°3S 59°31W 190 C4
Gualequay → Argentina 33°19S 59°39W 190 C4
Gualicho, Salina Argentina 40°25S 65°20W 192 B3
Gualjaina Argentina 42°45S 70°30W 192 B2
Guam ☑ Pac. Oc. 13°27N 144°45E 156 F6
Guamblin, I. Chile 44°50S 75°0W 192 B2
Guamini Argentina 37°1S 62°28W 190 D3
Guamúchil Mexico 25°28N 108°6W 180 B3
Guana I. Br. Virgin Is. 18°30N 64°30W 183 e
Guanabacoa Cuba 23°8N 82°18W 182 B3
Guanacaste, Cordillera de Costa Rica 10°40N 85°4W 182 D2
Guanacaste △ Costa Rica 10°57N 85°30W 182 D2
Guanaceví Mexico 25°56N 105°57W 180 B3
Guanahani = San Salvador I. Bahamas 24°0N 74°30W 183 B5
Guanaja Honduras 16°30N 85°55W 182 C2
Guanajay Cuba 22°56N 82°42W 182 B3
Guanajuato Mexico 21°1N 101°15W 180 C4
Guanajuato □ Mexico 21°0N 101°0W 180 C4
Guanambi Brazil 14°13S 42°47W 189 C2
Guandacol Argentina 29°30S 68°40W 190 B2
Guandi Shan China 37°53N 111°29E 114 F6
Guane Cuba 22°10N 84°7W 182 B3
Guang'an China 30°28N 106°35E 116 B6
Guangchang China 26°50N 116°21E 117 D11
Guangde China 30°54N 119°25E 117 B12
Guangdong □ China 23°0N 113°0E 117 F9
Guangfeng China 28°20N 118°15E 117 C12
Guanghan China 30°58N 104°17E 116 B5
Guangling China 39°47N 114°22E 114 E8
Guangnan China 24°5N 105°4E 116 E5
Guangning China 23°40N 112°22E 117 F9
Guangrao China 37°5N 118°25E 115 F10
Guangshui China 31°37N 114°0E 117 B10
Guangshun China 26°8N 106°21E 116 D6
Guangwu China 37°48N 105°57E 114 F3
Guangxi Zhuangzu Zizhiqu □ China 24°0N 109°0E 116 F7
Guangyuan China 32°26N 105°51E 116 A5
Guangze China 27°30N 117°12E 117 D11
Guangzhou China 23°6N 113°13E 117 F9
Guanhães Brazil 18°47S 42°57W 189 D2
Guanica Puerto Rico 17°58N 66°55W 183 d
Guanipa → Venezuela 9°56N 62°26W 186 B6
Guanling China 25°56N 105°35E 116 E5
Guannan China 34°8N 119°21E 115 G10
Guantánamo Cuba 20°10N 75°14W 183 B4
Guantánamo B. Cuba 19°59N 75°10W 183 C4
Guantao China 36°42N 115°25E 114 F8
Guanting Shuiku China 40°14N 115°35E 114 D8
Guanyang China 25°30N 111°8E 117 E8
Guanyun China 34°20N 119°18E 115 G10
Guapay = Grande → Bolivia 15°51S 64°39W 186 G6
Guápiles Costa Rica 10°10N 83°46W 182 D3
Guapo B. Trin. & Tob. 10°12N 61°41W 187 K15
Guaporé Brazil 28°51S 51°54W 191 B5
Guaporé → Brazil 11°55S 65°4W 186 F5
Guaqui Bolivia 16°41S 68°54W 188 D4
Guara, Sierra de Spain 42°19N 0°15W 90 C4
Guarabira Brazil 6°51S 35°29W 189 B3
Guaramacal △ Venezuela 9°13N 70°12W 183 E5
Guarapari Brazil 20°40S 40°30W 189 E2
Guarapuava Brazil 25°20S 51°30W 191 B5
Guaratinguetá Brazil 22°49S 45°9W 191 A6
Guaratuba Brazil 25°53S 48°38W 191 B6
Guarda Portugal 40°32N 7°20W 88 E3
Guarda □ Portugal 40°40N 7°20W 88 E3
Guardafui, C. = Asir, Ras Somalia 11°55N 51°10E 131 E5
Guardamar del Segura Spain 38°5N 0°39W 91 G4
Guardavalle Italy 38°30N 16°30E 95 D9
Guardia Sanframondi Italy 41°15N 14°36E 95 A7
Guardiagrele Italy 42°11N 14°13E 93 F11
Guardo Spain 42°47N 4°50W 88 C6
Guareña Spain 38°51N 6°6W 89 G4
Guareña → Spain 41°29N 5°23W 88 D5
Guárico □ Venezuela 8°40N 66°35W 186 B5
Guarujá Brazil 24°2S 46°25W 191 A6
Guarulhos Brazil 23°29S 46°33W 191 A6
Guasave Mexico 25°34N 108°27W 180 B3
Guasdualito Venezuela 7°15N 70°44W 186 B4
Guastalla Italy 44°55N 10°39E 92 D7
Guatemala Guatemala 14°40N 90°22W 182 D1
Guatemala ■ Cent. Amer. 15°40N 90°30W 182 C1
Guatemala Basin Pac. Oc. 11°0N 95°0W 157 F18
Guatemala Trench Pac. Oc. 14°0N 95°0W 158 H10
Guatopo △ Venezuela 10°5N 66°30W 183 D6
Guatuaro Pt. Trin. & Tob. 10°19N 60°59W 187 K16
Guaviare → Colombia 4°3N 67°44W 186 C5
Guaxupé Brazil 21°10S 47°5W 191 A6
Guayaguayare Trin. & Tob. 10°8N 61°2W 187 K15
Guayama Puerto Rico 17°59N 66°7W 183 d
Guayaneco, Arch. Chile 47°45S 75°10W 192 C1
Guayaquil Ecuador 2°15S 79°52W 186 D3
Guayaquil Mexico 29°59N 115°4W 180 B1
Guayaquil, G. de Ecuador 3°10S 81°0W 186 D2
Guaymas Mexico 27°56N 110°54W 180 B2
Guba Dem. Rep. of the Congo 10°38S 26°27E 143 E2
Gûbâl, Madîq Egypt 27°30N 34°0E 137 B3
Gubbi India 13°19N 76°56E 127 H3
Gúbbio Italy 43°21N 12°35E 93 E9
Guben Germany 51°57N 14°42E 76 D10
Gubin Poland 51°57N 14°43E 83 G1
Gubio Nigeria 12°30N 12°42E 139 C7
Gubkin Russia 51°17N 37°32E 85 G9
Gubkinskiy Russia 64°27N 76°36E 106 C8
Guča Serbia 43°46N 20°15E 96 C4
Gucheng China 32°20N 111°30E 117 A8
Gudalur India 11°30N 76°29E 127 J3
Gudauta Georgia 43°7N 40°32E 87 J5
Gudbrandsdalen Norway 61°33N 10°10E 60 F14
Guddu Barrage Pakistan 28°30N 69°50E 124 E3
Gudenå → Denmark 56°29N 10°13E 63 H4
Gudermes Russia 43°24N 46°5E 87 J8
Gudhjem Denmark 55°12N 14°58E 63 J8
Gudivada India 16°30N 81°3E 127 F5
Gudiyattam India 12°57N 78°55E 127 H4
Gudur India 14°12N 79°55E 127 G4
Guebwiller France 47°55N 7°12E 71 E14
Guecho = Algorta Spain 43°21N 2°59W 90 B2
Guékédou Guinea 8°40N 10°5W 138 D2
Guéle Mendouka Cameroon 4°23N 12°55E 139 E7
Guelma Algeria 36°25N 7°29E 136 A5
Guelma □ Algeria 36°25N 7°25E 136 A5
Guelmine = Goulimine Morocco 28°56N 10°0W 134 C3
Guelph Canada 43°35N 80°20W 174 C4
Guemar Algeria 33°30N 6°49E 136 B5
Guéméné-Penfao France 47°38N 1°50W 70 E5
Guéméné-sur-Scorff France 48°4N 3°13W 70 D3
Guéné Benin 11°44N 3°16E 139 C5
Guer France 47°54N 2°8W 70 E4
Güer Aike Argentina 51°39S 69°35W 192 D3
Guérande France 47°20N 2°26W 70 E4
Guerara Algeria 32°51N 4°22E 136 B4
Guercif Morocco 34°14N 3°21W 136 B3
Guéret France 46°11N 1°51E 71 F8
Guérigny France 47°6N 3°10E 71 E10
Guerneville U.S.A. 38°30N 123°0W 170 G4
Guernica = Gernika-Lumo Spain 43°19N 2°40W 90 B2
Guernsey U.K. 49°26N 2°35W 67 H5
Guernsey U.S.A. 42°16N 104°45W 168 E11
Guerrara Algeria 28°5N 0°8W 136 C3
Guerrero □ Mexico 17°40N 100°0W 181 D5
Guerzim Algeria 29°39N 1°40W 136 C3
Guessou-Sud Benin 10°3N 2°38E 139 C5
Gueugnon France 46°36N 4°4E 71 F11
Guéyo Ivory C. 5°25N 6°5W 138 D3
Gügher Iran 29°28N 56°27E 129 D8
Guglionesi Italy 41°55N 14°55E 93 G11
Gui Jiang → China 23°30N 111°15E 117 F8
Guia Canary Is. 28°8N 15°38W 100 F4
Guia de Isora Canary Is. 28°12N 16°46W 100 F3
Guia Lopes da Laguna Brazil 21°26S 56°7W 191 A4
Guiana Highlands S. Amer. 5°10N 60°40W 184 C4
Guibéroua Ivory C. 6°14N 6°10W 138 D3
Guichen B. Australia 37°10S 139°45E 152 D3
Guichi China 30°39N 117°27E 117 B11
Guider Cameroon 9°56N 13°57E 139 D7
Guidiguir Niger 13°40N 9°50E 139 C6
Guidimaka □ Mauritania 15°20N 12°0W 138 B2
Guidimouni Niger 13°42N 9°31E 139 C6
Guiding China 26°34N 107°11E 116 D6
Guidong China 26°7N 113°57E 117 D9
Guidónia-Montecélio Italy 42°1N 12°45E 93 F9
Guiers, L. de Senegal 16°10N 15°50W 138 B1
Guigang China 23°8N 109°35E 116 F7
Guiglo Ivory C. 6°45N 7°30W 138 D3
Guijá Mozam. 24°27S 33°0E 145 B5
Guijuelo Spain 40°33N 5°40W 88 E5
Guildford U.K. 51°14N 0°34W 67 F7
Guilford U.S.A. 41°17N 72°41W 175 E12
Guilin China 25°18N 110°15E 117 E8
Guillaume-Delisle, L. Canada 56°15N 76°17W 164 A4
Guillaumes France 44°5N 6°52E 73 D10
Guillestre France 44°39N 6°40E 73 D10
Guilvinec France 47°48N 4°17W 70 E2
Güimar Canary Is. 28°18N 16°24W 100 F3
Guimarães Portugal 41°28N 8°24W 88 D2
Guimaras □ Phil. 10°35N 122°37E 119 B6
Guinda U.S.A. 38°50N 122°12W 170 G4
Guinea Africa 8°0N 8°0E 132 F4
Guinea ■ W. Afr. 10°20N 11°30W 138 C2
Guinea, Gulf of Atl. Oc. 3°0N 2°30E 139 E5
Guinea Basin Atl. Oc. 0°0 5°0W 56 G11
Guinea-Bissau ■ Africa 12°0N 15°0W 138 C2
Güines Cuba 22°50N 82°0W 182 B3
Guingamp France 48°34N 3°10W 70 D3
Guinguinéo Senegal 14°20N 15°57W 138 C1
Guipavas France 48°26N 4°29W 70 D2
Guiping China 23°21N 110°2E 117 F8
Guipúzcoa □ Spain 43°12N 2°15W 90 B2
Guir Mali 18°52N 2°52W 138 B4
Guir, O. → Algeria 31°29N 2°17W 136 B3
Guirel Mauritania 15°30N 7°33W 138 B3
Güiria Venezuela 10°32N 62°18W 186 A6
Guiscard France 49°40N 3°1E 71 C10
Guise France 49°52N 3°35E 71 C10
Guissona Spain 41°47N 1°17E 90 D6
Guitiriz Spain 43°11N 7°50W 88 B3
Guitri Ivory C. 5°30N 5°14W 138 D3
Guiuan Phil. 11°5N 125°55E 119 B7
Guixi China 28°16N 117°15E 117 C11
Guiyang Guizhou, China 26°32N 106°40E 116 D6
Guiyang Hunan, China 25°46N 112°42E 117 E9
Guizhou □ China 27°0N 107°0E 116 D6
Gujan-Mestras France 44°38N 1°4W 72 D2
Gujar Khan Pakistan 33°16N 73°19E 124 C5
Gujarat □ India 23°20N 71°0E 124 H4
Gujiang China 27°11N 114°47E 117 D10
Gujiao China 37°54N 112°8E 114 F7
Gujō Japan 35°45N 136°57E 113 G8
Gujranwala Pakistan 32°10N 74°12E 124 C6
Gujrat Pakistan 32°40N 74°2E 124 C6
Gukovo Russia 48°1N 39°58E 87 F5
Gulargambone Australia 31°20S 148°30E 153 A8
Gulbarga India 17°20N 76°50E 126 F3
Gulbene Latvia 57°8N 26°52E 84 D4
Gülchö Kyrgyzstan 40°19N 73°26E 109 D8
Guledagudda India 16°3N 75°48E 127 F2
Gulf, The = Persian Gulf Asia 27°0N 50°0E 129 E6
Gulf Breeze U.S.A. 30°21N 87°9W 179 E2
Gulf Hammock U.S.A. 29°15N 82°43W 179 F7
Gulf Islands △ U.S.A. 30°10N 87°10W 179 K2
Gulfport Fla., U.S.A. 27°44N 82°42W 179 H7
Gulfport Miss., U.S.A. 30°22N 89°6W 177 F10
Gulgong Australia 32°20S 149°49E 153 B8
Gulian China 52°56N 122°21E 111 A13
Gulin China 28°1N 105°50E 116 C5
Gulistan Pakistan 30°30N 66°35E 124 D2
Guliston Uzbekistan 40°29N 68°46E 109 D7
Gulja = Yining China 43°58N 81°10E 109 D10
Gull Lake Canada 50°10N 108°29W 163 C7
Gullbrandstorp Sweden 56°42N 12°43E 63 H6
Gullivan B. U.S.A. 25°45N 81°40W 179 K8
Gullspång Sweden 58°59N 14°6E 63 F8
Güllük Turkey 37°14N 27°35E 99 D9
Güllük Dağı △ Turkey 37°0N 30°30E 99 E12
Güllük Korfezi Turkey 37°12N 27°30E 99 D9
Gulma Nigeria 12°40N 4°23E 139 C5
Gulmarg India 34°3N 74°25E 125 B6
Gülnar Turkey 36°19N 33°24E 104 D5
Gulnare Australia 33°27S 138°27E 152 B3
Gülpınar Turkey 39°32N 26°7E 99 B8
Gülşehir Turkey 38°44N 34°37E 104 C6
Gülshat Kazakhstan 46°38N 74°21E 109 C8
Gulu Uganda 2°48N 32°17E 142 B3
Gŭlŭbovo Bulgaria 42°8N 25°55E 97 D9
Gulwe Tanzania 6°30S 36°25E 142 D4
Gulyaypole = Hulyaypole Ukraine 47°45N 36°21E 85 J9
Gum Lake Australia 32°42S 143°9E 152 B5
Gumal → Pakistan 31°40N 71°50E 124 D4
Gumbaz Pakistan 30°2N 69°0E 124 D3
Gumdag Turkmenistan 39°9N 54°56E 108 E4
Gumel Nigeria 12°39N 9°22E 139 C6
Gumi S. Korea 36°10N 128°12E 115 F15
Gumiel de Izán Spain 41°46N 3°41W 88 D7
Gumla India 23°3N 84°33E 125 H11
Gumlu Australia 19°53S 147°41E 150 B4
Gummersbach Germany 51°1N 7°34E 76 D3
Gummi Nigeria 12°4N 5°9E 139 C6
Gümüldür Turkey 38°6N 27°0E 99 C9
Gümüşçay Turkey 40°16N 27°17E 97 F11
Gümüşhacıköy Turkey 40°50N 35°18E 104 B6
Gümüşhane Turkey 40°30N 39°30E 105 B8
Gümüşsu Turkey 38°14N 29°1E 99 C11
Gumzai Indonesia 5°28S 134°42E 119 F8
Guna India 24°40N 77°19E 124 G7
Gunbalanya Australia 12°20S 133°4E 148 B5
Gundabooka △ Australia 30°30S 145°20E 151 E4
Gundagai Australia 35°3S 148°6E 153 C8
Gundarehi India 20°57N 81°17E 126 D5
Gundelfingen Germany 48°34N 10°22E 77 G6
Gundlakamma → India 15°30N 80°15E 127 G5
Gundlupet India 11°48N 76°41E 127 J3
Gunebang Australia 33°1S 146°38E 153 B7
Güney Burdur, Turkey 37°29N 29°34E 99 D11
Güney Denizli, Turkey 38°9N 29°4E 99 C11
Güneydoğu Toroslar Turkey 38°20N 40°30E 105 C9
Gungal Australia 32°17S 150°32E 153 B9
Gunisao → Canada 53°56N 97°53W 163 C9
Gunisao L. Canada 53°33N 96°15W 163 C9
Gunjur Gambia 13°12N 16°44W 138 C1
Gunjyal Pakistan 32°20N 71°55E 124 C4
Günlüce Turkey 36°50N 28°20E 99 E10
Gunma □ Japan 36°30N 138°20E 113 F9
Gunnarskog Sweden 59°49N 12°34E 62 E6
Gunnbjørn Fjeld Greenland 68°55N 29°47W 57 D8
Gunnebo Sweden 57°44N 16°32E 63 G10
Gunnedah Australia 30°59S 150°15E 153 A9
Gunnewin Australia 25°59S 148°33E 151 D4
Gunningbar Cr. → Australia 31°14S 147°6E 153 A7
Gunnison Colo., U.S.A. 38°33N 106°56W 168 G10
Gunnison Utah, U.S.A. 39°9N 111°49W 168 G8
Gunnison → U.S.A. 39°4N 108°35W 168 G9
Gunsan S. Korea 35°59N 126°45E 115 G14
Guntakal India 15°11N 77°27E 127 G3
Gunter Canada 44°52N 77°32W 174 B7
Guntersville U.S.A. 34°21N 86°18W 177 D11
Guntong Malaysia 4°36N 101°3E 121 K3
Guntur India 16°23N 80°30E 127 F5
Gunung Ciremay △ Indonesia 6°53S 108°24E 119 G13
Gunungapi Indonesia 6°45S 126°30E 119 F7
Gunungsitoli Indonesia 1°15N 97°30E 118 D1
Gunupur India 19°5N 83°50E 126 E6
Günz → Germany 48°27N 10°16E 77 G6
Gunza Angola 10°50S 13°50E 140 G2
Günzburg Germany 48°26N 10°17E 77 G6
Gunzenhausen Germany 49°7N 10°44E 77 F6
Guo He → China 32°59N 117°10E 117 A11
Guoyang China 33°32N 116°12E 114 H9
Gupis Pakistan 36°15N 73°20E 125 A5
Gura Humorului Romania 47°35N 25°53E 81 C10
Gura-Teghii Romania 45°30N 26°25E 81 E11
Gurahonț Romania 46°16N 22°21E 80 D7
Gurbantünggüt Shamo China 45°8N 87°20E 109 C11
Gurdaspur India 32°5N 75°31E 124 C6
Gurdon U.S.A. 33°55N 93°9W 176 E8
Güre Balıkesir, Turkey 39°36N 26°54E 99 B8
Güre Uşak, Turkey 38°39N 29°10E 99 C11
Gurgaon India 28°27N 77°1E 124 E7
Gürgentepe Turkey 40°51N 37°50E 104 B7
Gurghiu, Munţii Romania 46°41N 25°15E 81 D10
Gurgueia → Brazil 6°50S 43°24W 189 B2
Gurha India 25°12N 71°39E 124 G4
Guri, Embalse de Venezuela 7°50N 62°52W 186 B6
Gurin Nigeria 9°5N 12°54E 139 D7
Gurjaani Georgia 41°43N 45°52E 87 K7
Gurk → Austria 46°35N 14°31E 78 E7
Gurkha Nepal 28°5N 84°40E 125 E11
Gurla Mandhata = Naimona'nyi Feng China 30°26N 81°18E 125 D9
Gurley Australia 29°45S 149°48E 151 D4
Gurnet Point U.S.A. 42°1N 70°34W 175 D14
Guro Mozam. 17°26S 32°30E 143 F3
Gürpınar İstanbul, Turkey 40°59N 28°37E 97 F12
Gürpınar Van, Turkey 38°18N 43°25E 105 C10
Gürsu Turkey 40°13N 29°11E 97 F13
Guruè Mozam. 15°25S 36°58E 143 F4
Gurun Malaysia 5°49N 100°27E 121 K3
Gürün Turkey 38°43N 37°15E 104 C7
Gurupá Brazil 1°25S 51°35W 187 D8
Gurupá, I. Grande de Brazil 1°25S 51°45W 187 D8
Gurupi Brazil 11°43S 49°4W 187 F9
Gurupi → Brazil 1°13S 46°6W 187 D9
Gurupi, Serra do Brazil 5°0S 47°50W 189 B1
Guruwe Zimbabwe 16°40S 30°42E 145 A5
Gurvan Sayhan Uul Mongolia 43°50N 104°0E 114 C3
Guryev = Atyraū Kazakhstan 47°5N 52°0E 108 C4
Guryevsk Russia 54°47N 20°38E 82 D7
Gus-Khrustalnyy Russia 55°42N 40°44E 86 C5
Gusau Nigeria 12°12N 6°40E 139 C6
Gusev Russia 54°35N 22°10E 82 D9
Gushan China 39°50N 123°35E 115 E12
Gushgy = Serhetabat Turkmenistan 35°20N 62°18E 129 C9
Gushi China 32°11N 115°41E 117 A10
Gushiago Ghana 9°55N 0°15W 139 D4
Gusinje Montenegro 42°35N 19°50E 96 D3
Gusinoozersk Russia 51°16N 106°27E 107 D11
Gúspini Italy 39°32N 8°37E 94 C1
Güssing Austria 47°3N 16°20E 79 D9
Gustav Holm, Kap Greenland 66°36N 34°15W 57 D7
Gustavus U.S.A. 58°25N 135°44W 162 B1
Gustine U.S.A. 37°16N 121°0W 170 H6
Güstrow Germany 53°47N 12°10E 76 B8
Gusum Sweden 58°16N 16°30E 63 F10
Guta = Kolárovo Slovak Rep. 47°54N 18°0E 79 D10
Gütersloh Germany 51°54N 8°24E 76 D4
Gutha Australia 28°58S 115°55E 149 E2
Guthalungra Australia 19°52S 147°50E 150 B4
Guthrie Canada 44°28N 79°32W 174 B5
Guthrie Okla., U.S.A. 35°53N 97°25W 176 D6
Guthrie Tex., U.S.A. 33°37N 100°19W 176 E4
Gutian China 26°32N 118°43E 117 D12
Guttenberg U.S.A. 42°47N 91°6W 172 D8
Gutu Zimbabwe 19°41S 31°9E 145 A5
Guwahati India 26°10N 91°45E 123 F17
Guy Fawkes River △ Australia 30°0S 152°20E 151 D5
Guyana ■ S. Amer. 5°0N 59°0W 186 C7
Guyane française = French Guiana ☑ S. Amer. 4°0N 53°0W 187 C8
Guyang China 41°0N 110°5E 114 D6
Guyenne France 44°30N 0°40E 72 D4
Guymon U.S.A. 36°41N 101°29W 176 C4
Guyra Australia 30°15S 151°40E 151 E5
Guyton U.S.A. 32°20N 81°24W 178 C8
Guyuan Hebei, China 41°37N 115°40E 114 D8
Guyuan Ningxia Huizu, China 36°0N 106°20E 114 F4
Guzar Uzbekistan 38°36N 66°15E 109 E7
Güzelbahçe Turkey 38°21N 26°54E 99 C8

Güzelyurt = Morphou
Cyprus 35°12N 32°59E 101 D11
Guzhang China 28°42N 109°58E 116 C7
Guzhen China 33°22N 117°18E 115 H9
Guzmán, L. de Mexico 31°20N 107°30W 180 A3
Gvardeysk Russia 54°39N 21°5E 82 D8
Gvardeyskoye Ukraine 45°7N 34°1E 85 K8
Gwa Burma 17°36N 94°34E 123 L19
Gwaai Zimbabwe 19°15S 27°45E 143 F2
Gwaai → Zimbabwe 17°59S 26°52E 143 F2
Gwabegar Australia 30°37S 148°59E 153 A8
Gwadabawa Nigeria 13°28N 5°15E 139 C6
Gwādar Pakistan 25°10N 62°18E 122 G3
Gwagwada Nigeria 10°15N 7°15E 139 C6
Gwaii Haanas △
Canada 52°21N 131°26W 162 C2
Gwalior India 26°12N 78°10E 124 F8
Gwanara Nigeria 8°55N 3°9E 139 D5
Gwanda Zimbabwe 20°55S 29°0E 143 G2
Gwandu Nigeria 12°30N 4°41E 139 C5
Gwane
Dem. Rep. of the Congo 4°45N 25°48E 142 B2
Gwangju S. Korea 35°9N 126°54E 115 G14
Gwangyang S. Korea 34°56N 127°41E 115 G14
Gwanju = Gwangju
S. Korea 35°9N 126°54E 115 G14
Gwaram Nigeria 10°15N 10°25E 139 C7
Gwarzo Nigeria 12°20N 8°55E 139 C6
Gwasero Nigeria 9°29N 3°30E 139 D5
Gwda → Poland 53°3N 16°44E 83 E3
Gweebarra B. Ireland 54°51N 8°23W 64 B3
Gweedore Ireland 55°3N 8°14W 64 A3
Gweru Zimbabwe 19°28S 29°45E 143 F2
Gwi Nigeria 9°0N 7°10E 139 D6
Gwinn U.S.A. 46°19N 87°27W 172 B10
Gwio Kura Nigeria 12°40N 11°2E 139 C7
Gwoza Nigeria 11°5N 13°40E 139 C7
Gwydir → Australia 29°27S 149°48E 151 D4
Gwynedd □ U.K. 52°52N 4°10W 66 E3
Gyandzha = Gäncä
Azerbaijan 40°45N 46°20E 87 K8
Gyangzê China 29°5N 89°47E 110 F6
Gyaring Hu China 34°50N 97°40E 110 E8
Gydanskiy Poluostrov
Russia 70°0N 78°0E 106 C8
Gyeonggi-man
S. Korea 37°0N 125°30E 115 F13
Gyeongju S. Korea 35°51N 129°14E 115 G15
Gyldenløve Fjord
Greenland 64°15N 40°30W 57 E6
Gympie Australia 26°11S 152°38E 151 D5
Gyomaendrőd Hungary 46°56N 20°50E 80 D5
Gyöngyös Hungary 47°48N 19°56E 80 C4
Győr Hungary 47°41N 17°40E 80 C2
Győr-Moson-Sopron □
Hungary 47°40N 17°20E 80 C2
Gypsum Pt. Canada 61°53N 114°35W 162 A6
Gypsumville Canada 51°45N 98°40W 163 C9
Gyueshevo Bulgaria 42°14N 22°28E 96 D6
Gyula Hungary 46°38N 21°17E 80 D6
Gyumri Armenia 40°47N 43°50E 87 K6
Gyzylarbat = Serdar
Turkmenistan 39°4N 56°23E 129 B8
Gyzyletrek = Etrek
Turkmenistan 37°36N 54°46E 129 B7
Gzhatsk = Gagarin
Russia 55°38N 35°0E 84 E8

H

H. Neely Henry L.
U.S.A. 33°55N 86°2W 178 B3
Ha 'Arava → Israel 30°50N 35°20E 130 E4
Ha Coi Vietnam 21°26N 107°46E 116 G6
Ha Dong Vietnam 20°58N 105°46E 116 G5
Ha Giang Vietnam 22°50N 104°59E 116 F5
Ha Karmel, Har Israel 32°44N 35°3E 130 C4
Ha Karmel △ Israel 32°45N 35°5E 130 C4
Ha Long = Hong Gai
Vietnam 20°57N 107°5E 116 G6
Ha Long, Vinh Vietnam 20°56N 107°3E 120 B6
Ha Tien Vietnam 10°23N 104°29E 121 G5
Ha Tinh Vietnam 18°20N 105°54E 120 C5
Ha Trung Vietnam 19°58N 105°50E 120 C5
Haakon VII Topp = Beerenberg
Norway 71°0N 8°20W 57 C10
Haaksbergen Neths. 52°9N 6°45E 69 B6
Haapsalu Estonia 58°56N 23°30E 84 C2
Haarby Denmark 55°13N 10°7E 63 J4
Haarlem Neths. 52°23N 4°39E 69 B4
Haast N.Z. 43°51S 169°1E 155 D4
Haast → N.Z. 43°50S 169°2E 155 D4
Haast Pass N.Z. 44°6S 169°21E 155 E4
Haasts Bluff Australia 23°22S 132°0E 148 D5
Haasts Bluff ◎
Australia 23°39S 130°34E 148 D5
Hab → Pakistan 24°53N 66°41E 124 G3
Hab Nadi Chauki
Pakistan 25°0N 66°50E 124 G2
Habahe China 48°3N 86°23E 109 C11
Habaswein Kenya 1°2N 39°30E 142 B4
Habay Canada 58°50N 118°44W 162 B5
Ḩabbānīyah Iraq 33°17N 43°29E 105 F10
Ḩabbānīyah, Hawr al
Iraq 33°17N 43°29E 105 F10
Habibas, Îles Algeria 35°44N 1°8W 91 K3
Habichtswald ⌂ Germany 51°15N 9°15E 76 D5
Habirag China 42°17N 115°42E 114 C8
Habo Sweden 57°55N 14°6E 63 G8
Haboro Japan 44°22N 141°42E 112 B10
Ḩabshān U.A.E. 23°50N 53°37E 129 F7
Hachenburg Germany 50°40N 7°49E 76 E3
Hachijō-Jima Japan 33°5N 139°45E 113 H9
Hachiman = Gujō
Japan 35°45N 136°57E 113 G8
Hachinohe Japan 40°30N 141°29E 112 D10
Hachiōji Japan 35°40N 139°20E 113 G9
Hacı Zeynalabdin
Azerbaijan 40°37N 49°33E 87 K9
Hacıbektaş Turkey 38°56N 34°33E 104 C6
Hacılar Turkey 38°38N 35°26E 104 C6
Hack, Mt. Australia 30°45S 138°55E 152 A3
Hackås Sweden 62°56N 14°30E 62 B8
Hackensack U.S.A. 40°52N 74°4W 175 F10
Hackettstown U.S.A. 40°51N 74°50W 175 F10
Häckrenmagasinet
Sweden 63°15N 13°30E 62 C7
Hadali Pakistan 32°16N 72°11E 124 C5
Hadarba, Ras Sudan 22°4N 36°51E 137 C4
Hadarom □ Israel 31°0N 35°0E 130 E4
Ḩadd, Ra's al Oman 22°35N 59°50E 131 C6
Haddington U.K. 55°57N 2°47W 65 F6
Haddock U.S.A. 33°2N 83°26W 178 B6
Hadejia Nigeria 12°30N 10°5E 139 C7
Hadejia → Nigeria 12°50N 10°51E 139 C7
Ḩadera Israel 32°27N 34°55E 130 C3
Ḩadera, N. → Israel 32°28N 34°52E 130 C3
Haderslev Denmark 55°15N 9°30E 63 J3
Hadgaon India 19°30N 77°40E 126 E3
Hadhramaut = Ḩaḑramawt □
Yemen 15°30N 49°30E 131 D4
Hadiboh Yemen 12°39N 54°2E 131 E5
Hadilik China 37°56N 86°6E 109 E11
Hadım Turkey 36°58N 32°26E 104 D5
Hadjadj, O. el → Algeria 28°18N 5°20E 136 C5
Hadjeb el Aïoun Tunisia 35°21N 9°32E 136 A5
Hadley B. Canada 72°31N 108°12W 160 C10
Hadong S. Korea 35°5N 127°44E 115 G14
Ḩaḑramawt □ Yemen 15°30N 49°30E 131 D4
Ḩadrānīyah Iraq 35°38N 43°14E 128 C4
Hadrian's Wall U.K. 55°0N 2°30W 66 B5
Hadsten Denmark 56°19N 10°3E 63 H4
Hadsund Denmark 56°44N 10°8E 63 H4
Hadyach Ukraine 50°21N 34°0E 85 G8
Hae, Ko Thailand 7°44N 98°22E 121 a
Haeju N. Korea 38°3N 125°45E 115 E13
Hā'ena U.S.A. 22°14N 159°34W 167 L8
Haenam S. Korea 34°34N 126°35E 115 G14
Haenertsburg S. Africa 24°0S 29°50E 145 B4
Haerhpin = Harbin
China 45°48N 126°40E 115 B14
Hafar al Bāţin
Si. Arabia 28°32N 45°52E 128 D5
Hafik Turkey 39°51N 37°23E 104 C7
Ḩafirat al 'Aydā
Si. Arabia 26°26N 39°12E 128 E3
Ḩafit Oman 23°59N 55°49E 129 F7
Hafizabad Pakistan 32°5N 73°40E 124 C5
Haflong India 25°10N 93°5E 123 G18
Haft Gel Iran 31°30N 49°32E 129 D6
Hagalil Israel 32°53N 35°18E 130 C4
Hagari → India 15°40N 77°0E 127 G3
Hagby Sweden 56°34N 16°11E 63 H10
Hagemeister I. U.S.A. 58°39N 160°54W 166 D7
Hagen Germany 51°21N 7°27E 76 D3
Hagenow Germany 53°26N 11°12E 76 B7
Hagerman U.S.A. 33°7N 104°20W 169 K11
Hagerman Fossil Beds ⌂
U.S.A. 42°48N 114°57W 168 E6
Hagerstown U.S.A. 39°39N 77°43W 173 F15
Hagersville Canada 42°58N 80°3W 174 D4
Hagetmau France 43°39N 0°37W 72 E3
Hagfors Sweden 60°3N 13°45E 62 D7
Hagi Japan 34°30N 131°22E 113 G5
Hagolan Syria 33°0N 35°45E 130 C4
Hagondange France 49°16N 6°11E 71 C13
Hags Hd. Ireland 52°57N 9°28W 64 D2
Hague, C. de la France 49°44N 1°56W 70 C5
Hague, The = 's-Gravenhage
Neths. 52°7N 4°17E 69 B4
Haguenau France 48°49N 7°47E 71 D14
Hahira U.S.A. 30°59N 83°22W 178 E6
Hai Duong Vietnam 20°56N 106°19E 116 G6
Hai'an Guangdong, China 20°18N 110°11E 117 a
Hai'an Jiangsu, China 32°37N 120°27E 117 A13
Haicheng China 40°50N 122°45E 115 D12
Haida Gwaii Canada 53°20N 132°10W 162 C2
Haidar Khel Afghan. 33°58N 68°38E 124 C3
Haidarâbâd = Hyderabad
India 17°22N 78°29E 126 F4
Haidargarh India 26°37N 81°22E 125 F9
Haifa = Ḩefa Israel 32°46N 35°0E 130 C4
Haifeng China 22°58N 115°10E 117 F10
Haiger Germany 50°43N 8°12E 76 E4
Haikou China 20°1N 110°16E 117 a
Ḩā'il Si. Arabia 27°28N 41°45E 128 E4
Ḩā'il □ Si. Arabia 26°40N 41°40E 128 E4
Hailar China 49°10N 119°38E 111 B12
Hailey U.S.A. 43°31N 114°19W 168 E6
Haileybury Canada 47°30N 79°38W 164 C4
Hailin China 44°37N 129°30E 115 B15
Hailing Dao China 21°35N 111°47E 117 G8
Hailun China 47°28N 126°50E 111 B14
Hailuoto Finland 65°3N 24°45E 60 D21
Haimen Guangdong,
China 23°15N 116°38E 117 F11
Haimen Jiangsu,
China 31°52N 121°10E 117 B13
Hainan □ China 19°0N 109°30E 117 a
Hainan Dao China 19°0N 109°30E 117 a
Hainan Str. = Qiongzhou Haixia
China 20°10N 110°15E 117 a
Hainaut □ Belgium 50°30N 4°0E 69 D4
Hainburg Austria 48°9N 16°56E 79 C9
Haines Alaska, U.S.A. 59°14N 135°26W 162 B1
Haines Oreg., U.S.A. 44°55N 117°56W 168 D5
Haines City U.S.A. 28°7N 81°38W 179 G8
Haines Junction
Canada 60°45N 137°30W 162 A1
Hainfeld Austria 48°3N 15°48E 78 C8
Haining China 30°28N 120°40E 117 B13
Haiphong Vietnam 20°47N 106°41E 116 G6
Haitan Dao China 25°30N 119°45E 117 E12
Haiti ■ W. Indies 19°0N 72°30W 183 C5
Haiya Sudan 18°20N 36°21E 137 D4
Haiyan Qinghai, China 36°53N 100°59E 110 D9
Haiyan Zhejiang,
China 30°28N 120°58E 117 B13
Haiyang China 36°47N 121°9E 115 F11
Haiyuan Guangxi Zhuangzu,
China 22°8N 107°35E 116 F6
Haiyuan Ningxia Huizu,
China 36°35N 105°52E 114 F3
Haizhou China 34°37N 119°7E 115 G10
Haizhou Wan China 34°50N 119°20E 115 G10
Haj Ali Qoli, Kavīr Iran 35°55N 54°50E 129 C7
Hajdú-Bihar □ Hungary 47°30N 21°30E 80 C6
Hajdúböszörmény
Hungary 47°40N 21°30E 80 C6
Hajdúdorog Hungary 47°48N 21°30E 80 C6
Hajdúhadház Hungary 47°40N 21°40E 80 C6
Hajdúnánás Hungary 47°50N 21°26E 80 C6
Hajdúsámson Hungary 47°37N 21°42E 80 C6
Hajdúszoboszló Hungary 47°27N 21°22E 80 C6
Haji Ibrahim Iraq 36°40N 44°30E 105 D11
Ḩājīābād Iran 33°37N 60°0E 129 C9
Hajipur India 25°45N 85°13E 125 G11
Ḩajjah Yemen 15°42N 43°36E 131 D3
Ḩājjīābād Iran 28°19N 55°55E 129 D7
Ḩājjīābād-e Zarrīn Iran 33°9N 54°51E 129 C7
Hajnówka Poland 52°47N 23°35E 83 F10
Hakansson, Mts.
Dem. Rep. of the Congo 8°40S 25°45E 143 D2
Hakataramea N.Z. 44°43S 170°30E 155 E5
Hakkâri Turkey 37°34N 43°44E 105 D10
Hakkâri □ Turkey 37°30N 44°0E 105 D10
Hakkâri Dağları
Turkey 38°2N 42°58E 105 C10
Hakken-Zan Japan 34°10N 135°54E 113 G7
Hakkōda San Japan 40°50N 141°0E 112 D10
Hakodate Japan 41°45N 140°44E 112 D10
Hakos Namibia 23°13S 16°21E 144 B2
Håksberg Sweden 60°11N 15°12E 62 D9
Hakskeenpan S. Africa 26°48S 20°13E 144 C3
Haku-San Japan 36°9N 136°46E 113 F8
Haku-San △ Japan 36°15N 136°45E 113 F8
Hakui Japan 36°53N 136°47E 113 F8
Hakusan Japan 36°31N 136°34E 113 F8
Hala Pakistan 25°43N 68°20E 122 G6
Ḩalab Syria 36°10N 37°15E 104 D7
Ḩalab □ Syria 36°10N 37°10E 104 D7
Ḩalabjah Iraq 35°10N 45°58E 105 E11
Halaib Sudan 22°12N 36°30E 137 C4
Halaib Triangle Africa 22°30N 35°20E 137 C4
Hālat 'Ammār Si. Arabia 29°10N 36°4E 128 D3
Halbā Lebanon 34°34N 36°6E 130 A5
Halberstadt Germany 51°54N 11°3E 76 D7
Halcombe N.Z. 40°8S 175°30E 154 G4
Halcon, Mt. Phil. 13°16N 121°0E 119 B6
Halde Fjäll = Haltiatunturi
Finland 69°17N 21°18E 60 B19
Halden Norway 59°9N 11°23E 61 G14
Haldensleben Germany 52°17N 11°24E 76 C7
Haldia Bangla. 22°1N 88°3E 125 H13
Haldwani India 29°31N 79°30E 125 E8
Hale → Australia 24°56S 135°53E 150 C2
Halesowen U.K. 52°27N 2°3W 67 E5
Halesworth U.K. 52°20N 1°31E 67 E9
Haleyville U.S.A. 34°14N 87°37W 177 D11
Half Assini Ghana 5°1N 2°50W 138 D4
Half Dome U.S.A. 37°44N 119°32W 170 H7
Halfeti Turkey 37°15N 37°52E 104 D7
Halfmoon Bay N.Z. 46°50S 168°5E 155 G3
Halfway → Canada 56°12N 121°32W 162 B4
Halia India 24°50N 82°19E 125 G10
Haliburton Canada 45°3N 78°30W 174 A6
Halifax Australia 18°32S 146°22E 150 B4
Halifax Canada 44°38N 63°35W 165 D7
Halifax U.K. 53°43N 1°52W 66 D6
Halifax U.S.A. 40°25N 76°55W 174 F8
Halifax B. Australia 18°50S 147°0E 150 B4
Halifax I. Namibia 26°38S 15°4E 144 C2
Halik Shan China 42°20N 81°22E 109 D10
Ḩalīl → Iran 27°40N 58°30E 129 E8
Halimun △ Indonesia 6°42S 106°26E 119 G11
Halki = Chalki Greece 36°17N 27°35E 99 E9
Halkida = Chalkida
Greece 38°27N 23°42E 98 C5
Halkidiki = Chalkidiki
Greece 40°25N 23°20E 96 F7
Halkirk U.K. 58°30N 3°29W 65 C5
Hall Beach Canada 68°46N 81°12W 161 D15
Hall in Tirol Austria 47°17N 11°30E 78 D4
Hall Pen. Canada 63°30N 66°0W 161 E18
Hall Pt. Australia 15°40S 124°23E 148 C3
Hallabro Sweden 56°22N 15°5E 63 H9
Halland Sweden 57°8N 12°47E 61 H15
Hallandale Beach
U.S.A. 25°58N 80°8W 179 K9
Hallands län □ Sweden 57°0N 12°40E 63 H6
Hallands Väderö Sweden 56°27N 12°34E 63 H6
Hallandsås Sweden 56°22N 13°0E 63 H7
Ḩallāniyat, Jazā'ir al
Oman 17°30N 55°58E 131 D6
Hallasan S. Korea 33°22N 126°32E 115 H14
Hällbybrunn Sweden 59°24N 16°25E 62 E10
Halle Belgium 50°44N 4°13E 69 D4
Halle Nordrhein-Westfalen,
Germany 52°3N 8°22E 76 C4
Halle Sachsen-Anhalt,
Germany 51°30N 11°56E 76 D7
Hällefors Sweden 59°47N 14°31E 62 E8
Hälleforsnäs Sweden 59°10N 16°30E 62 E10
Hallein Austria 47°40N 13°5E 78 D6
Hällekis Sweden 58°38N 13°27E 63 F7
Hallen Sweden 63°11N 14°4E 62 A8
Hallett Australia 33°25S 138°55E 152 B3
Hallettsville U.S.A. 29°27N 96°57W 176 G6
Halley Antarctica 75°35S 26°39W 55 D1
Hallia → India 16°55N 79°20E 126 F4
Hallim S. Korea 33°24N 126°15E 115 H14
Hallingdalselva →
Norway 60°23N 9°35E 60 F13
Hallingskarvet △
Norway 60°37N 7°45E 60 F12
Hallock U.S.A. 48°47N 96°57W 172 A5
Halls Creek Australia 18°16S 127°38E 148 C4
Halls Gap Australia 37°8S 142°34E 151 F3
Halls Lake Canada 45°7N 78°45W 174 A6
Hallsberg Sweden 59°5N 15°7E 62 E9
Hallstahammar Sweden 59°38N 16°15E 62 E10
Hallstatt Austria 47°33N 13°38E 78 D6
Hallstavik Sweden 60°5N 18°37E 62 D12
Hallstead U.S.A. 41°58N 75°45W 175 E9
Halmahera Indonesia 0°40N 128°0E 119 D7
Halmahera Sea Indonesia 2°0N 130°0E 119 D7
Halmeu Romania 47°57N 23°2E 80 C8
Halmstad Sweden 56°41N 12°52E 63 H6
Halong Bay = Ha Long, Vinh
Vietnam 20°56N 107°3E 120 B6
Halq el Oued = La Goulette
Tunisia 36°53N 10°18E 94 F3
Hals Denmark 57°0N 10°18E 63 H4
Hälsingborg = Helsingborg
Sweden 56°3N 12°42E 63 H6
Hälsingland Sweden 61°40N 16°5E 62 C10
Halstead U.K. 51°57N 0°40E 67 F8
Haltern Germany 51°44N 7°11E 76 D3
Haltiatunturi Finland 69°17N 21°18E 60 B19
Halton □ U.K. 53°22N 2°45W 66 D5
Haltwhistle U.K. 54°58N 2°26W 66 C5
Ḩālūl Qatar 25°40N 52°40E 129 E7
Halvad India 23°1N 71°11E 124 H4
Halvān Iran 33°57N 56°15E 129 C8
Ham France 49°45N 3°4E 71 C10
Hamab Namibia 28°7S 19°16E 144 C2
Hamada Japan 34°56N 132°4E 113 G6
Hamadān Iran 34°52N 48°32E 105 E13
Hamadān □ Iran 35°0N 49°0E 129 C6
Hamadia Algeria 35°28N 1°57E 136 A4
Ḩamāh Syria 35°5N 36°40E 104 E7
Ḩamāh □ Syria 35°10N 37°0E 104 E7
Hamamatsu Japan 34°45N 137°45E 113 G8
Hamar Norway 60°48N 11°7E 60 F14
Hamâta, Gebel Egypt 24°17N 35°0E 128 E2
Hamatonbetsu Japan 45°10N 142°20E 112 B11
Hambantota Sri Lanka 6°10N 81°10E 127 L5
Hamber △ Canada 52°20N 118°0W 162 C5
Hamburg Germany 53°33N 9°59E 76 B5
Hamburg Ark., U.S.A. 33°14N 91°48W 176 E9
Hamburg N.Y., U.S.A. 42°43N 78°50W 174 D6
Hamburg Pa., U.S.A. 40°33N 75°59W 175 F9
Hamburg □ Germany 53°30N 10°0E 76 B5
Hamburg Fuhlsbüttel ✈ (HAM)
Germany 53°35N 9°59E 76 B5
Ḩamḑ, W. al →
Si. Arabia 24°55N 36°20E 128 E3
Hamden U.S.A. 41°23N 72°54W 175 E12
Hamdibey Turkey 39°50N 27°15E 99 B9
Häme Finland 61°38N 25°10E 60 F21
Hämeenlinna Finland 61°0N 24°28E 84 B3
Hamélé Ghana 10°56N 2°45W 138 C4
Hamelin Pool Australia 26°22S 114°20E 149 E1
Hameln Germany 52°6N 9°21E 76 C5
Hamerkaz □ Israel 32°15N 34°55E 130 C3
Hamersley Ra.
Australia 22°0S 117°45E 148 D2
Hamhŭng N. Korea 39°54N 127°30E 115 E14
Hami China 42°55N 93°25E 110 C7
Hamilton Australia 37°45S 142°2E 152 D5
Hamilton Bermuda 32°17N 64°47W 56 C5
Hamilton Canada 43°15N 79°50W 174 C5
Hamilton N.Z. 37°47S 175°19E 154 D4
Hamilton U.K. 55°46N 4°2W 65 F4
Hamilton Ala., U.S.A. 34°9N 87°59W 177 D11
Hamilton Ga., U.S.A. 32°45N 84°53W 178 C5
Hamilton Mont.,
U.S.A. 46°15N 114°10W 168 C6
Hamilton N.Y., U.S.A. 42°50N 75°33W 175 D9
Hamilton Ohio, U.S.A. 39°24N 84°34W 173 F11
Hamilton Tex., U.S.A. 31°42N 98°7W 176 F5
Hamilton → Queens.,
Australia 23°30S 139°47E 150 C2
Hamilton → S. Austral.,
Australia 26°40S 135°19E 151 D2
Hamilton City U.S.A. 39°45N 122°1W 170 F4
Hamilton I. Australia 20°21S 148°56E 150 b
Hamilton Inlet Canada 54°0N 57°30W 165 B8
Hamilton Mt. U.S.A. 43°25N 74°22W 175 C10
Hamina Finland 60°34N 27°12E 84 B4
Hamirpur H.P., India 31°41N 76°31E 124 D7
Hamirpur Ut. P., India 25°57N 80°9E 125 G9
Hamitabat Turkey 41°30N 27°17E 97 E11
Hamlet U.S.A. 34°53N 79°42W 177 D15
Hamley Bridge
Australia 34°17S 138°35E 152 C3
Hamlin = Hameln
Germany 52°6N 9°21E 76 C5
Hamlin N.Y., U.S.A. 43°17N 77°55W 174 C7
Hamlin Tex., U.S.A. 32°53N 100°8W 176 E4
Hamm Germany 51°40N 7°50E 76 D3
Ḩammām al Alī Iraq 36°9N 43°15E 105 D10
Hammam Bouhadjar
Algeria 35°23N 0°58W 136 A3
Hammamet Tunisia 36°24N 10°38E 136 A6
Ḩammār, Hawr al Iraq 30°50N 47°10E 128 D5
Hammarstrand Sweden 63°7N 16°20E 62 A10
Hammelburg Germany 50°6N 9°53E 77 E5
Hammeren Denmark 55°18N 14°47E 63 J8
Hammerfest Norway 70°39N 23°41E 60 A20
Hammerum Denmark 56°8N 9°3E 63 H3
Hamminkeln Germany 51°43N 6°35E 76 D2
Hammond Ind.,
U.S.A. 41°38N 87°30W 172 E10
Hammond La., U.S.A. 30°30N 90°28W 177 F9
Hammond N.Y., U.S.A. 44°27N 75°42W 175 B9
Hammondsport U.S.A. 42°25N 77°13W 174 D7
Hammonton U.S.A. 39°39N 74°48W 173 F16
Hampden N.Z. 45°18S 170°50E 155 F5
Hampi India 15°18N 76°28E 127 G3
Hampshire □ U.K. 51°7N 1°23W 67 F6
Hampshire Downs U.K. 51°15N 1°10W 67 F6
Hampton N.B., Canada 45°32N 65°51W 165 C6
Hampton Ont., Canada 43°58N 78°45W 174 C6
Hampton Ark., U.S.A. 33°32N 92°28W 176 E8
Hampton Ga., U.S.A. 33°23N 84°17W 178 B5
Hampton Iowa, U.S.A. 42°45N 93°13W 172 D7
Hampton N.H., U.S.A. 42°57N 70°50W 175 D14
Hampton S.C., U.S.A. 32°52N 81°7W 178 C8
Hampton Va., U.S.A. 37°2N 76°21W 173 G15
Hampton Bays U.S.A. 40°53N 72°30W 175 F12
Hampton Springs
U.S.A. 30°5N 83°40W 178 E6
Hampton Tableland
Australia 32°0S 127°0E 149 F4
Hamra Sweden 61°39N 14°59E 62 C8
Ḩamrin, Jabal Iraq 34°30N 44°30E 105 E11
Hamur Turkey 39°37N 43°3E 105 C10
Hamyang S. Korea 35°32N 127°42E 115 G14
Han i Hotit Albania 42°19N 19°27E 96 D3
Han Jiang → China 23°25N 116°40E 117 F11
Han Shui → China 30°34N 114°17E 117 B10
Hanahan U.S.A. 32°55N 80°0W 178 C10
Hanak Si. Arabia 25°32N 37°0E 128 E3
Hanak Turkey 41°14N 42°50E 105 B10
Hanamaki Japan 39°23N 141°7E 112 E10
Hanang Tanzania 4°30S 35°25E 142 C4
Hanau Germany 50°7N 8°56E 77 E4
Hanbogd = Ihbulag
Mongolia 43°11N 107°10E 114 C4
Hançalar Turkey 38°8N 29°24E 99 C11
Hânceşti Moldova 46°50N 28°36E 81 D13
Hancheng China 35°31N 110°25E 114 G6
Hanchuan China 30°40N 113°50E 117 B9
Hancock Mich., U.S.A. 47°8N 88°35W 172 B9
Hancock N.Y., U.S.A. 41°57N 75°17W 175 E9
Hancock Vt., U.S.A. 43°55N 72°50W 175 C12
Handa Japan 34°53N 136°55E 113 G8
Handa I. U.K. 58°23N 5°11W 65 C3
Handan China 36°35N 114°28E 114 F8
Handeni Tanzania 5°25S 38°2E 142 D4
Handlová Slovak Rep. 48°45N 18°35E 79 C11
Handub Sudan 19°15N 37°16E 137 D4
Handwara India 34°21N 74°20E 125 B6
Hanegev Israel 30°50N 35°0E 130 E4
Hanford U.S.A. 36°20N 119°39W 170 J7
Hanford Reach ⌂
U.S.A. 46°40N 119°30W 168 C4
Hang Chat Thailand 18°20N 99°21E 120 C2
Hangang → S. Korea 37°50N 126°30E 115 F14
Hangayn Nuruu
Mongolia 47°30N 99°0E 110 B8
Hangchou = Hangzhou
China 30°18N 120°11E 117 B13
Hanger Sweden 57°6N 13°58E 63 G7
Hanggin Houqi China 40°58N 107°4E 114 D4
Hanggin Qi China 39°52N 108°50E 114 E5
Hangu China 39°18N 117°53E 115 E9
Hangzhou China 30°18N 120°11E 117 B13
Hangzhou Wan
China 30°15N 120°45E 117 B13
Hanh Mongolia 51°32N 100°35E 110 A9
Hanhöhiy Uul
Mongolia 49°30N 94°30E 109 C12
Hanhongor Mongolia 43°55N 104°28E 114 C3
Hani Turkey 38°24N 40°23E 105 C9
Hania = Chania Greece 35°30N 24°4E 101 D6
Ḩanīdh Si. Arabia 26°35N 48°38E 129 E6
Ḩanīsh Yemen 13°45N 42°46E 131 E3
Haniska Slovak Rep. 48°37N 21°15E 79 C14
Hanjiang China 25°26N 119°6E 117 E12
Hankinson U.S.A. 46°4N 96°54W 172 B5
Hankö Finland 59°50N 22°57E 84 C2
Hankou China 30°35N 114°30E 117 B10
Hanksville U.S.A. 38°22N 110°43W 168 G8
Hanle India 32°42N 79°4E 125 C8
Hanmer Springs N.Z. 42°32S 172°50E 155 C7
Hann → Australia 17°26S 126°17E 148 C4
Hann, Mt. Australia 15°45S 126°0E 148 C4
Hanna Canada 51°40N 111°54W 162 C6
Hanna U.S.A. 41°52N 106°34W 168 F10
Hannah B. Canada 51°40N 80°0W 164 B4
Hannibal Mo., U.S.A. 39°42N 91°22W 172 F8
Hannibal N.Y., U.S.A. 43°19N 76°35W 175 C8
Hannik Sudan 18°12N 32°20E 137 D3
Hannover Germany 52°22N 9°46E 76 C5
Hanö Sweden 56°1N 14°50E 63 H8
Hanöbukten Sweden 55°35N 14°30E 63 J8
Hanoi Vietnam 21°5N 105°55E 116 G5
Hanover = Hannover
Germany 52°22N 9°46E 76 C5
Hanover Canada 44°9N 81°2W 174 B3
Hanover S. Africa 31°4S 24°29E 144 D3
Hanover N.H., U.S.A. 43°42N 72°17W 175 C12
Hanover Ohio, U.S.A. 40°4N 82°16W 174 F2
Hanover Pa., U.S.A. 39°48N 76°59W 173 F15
Hanover, I. Chile 51°0S 74°50W 192 D2
Hans Lollik I.
U.S. Virgin Is. 18°24N 64°53W 183 e
Hansdiha India 24°36N 87°5E 125 G12
Hanshou China 28°56N 111°50E 117 C8
Hansi H.P., India 32°27N 77°50E 124 C7
Hansi Haryana, India 29°10N 75°57E 124 E6
Hanson, L. Australia 31°0S 136°15E 152 A2
Hanstholm Denmark 57°7N 8°36E 63 G2
Hanting China 36°46N 119°12E 115 F10
Hantsavichy Belarus 52°49N 26°30E 75 B14
Hanumangarh India 29°35N 74°19E 124 E6
Hanyin China 32°54N 108°28E 114 H5
Hanyuan China 29°21N 102°40E 116 C4
Hanzhong China 33°10N 107°1E 116 A6
Hanzhuang China 34°33N 117°23E 115 G9
Haora India 22°34N 88°18E 125 H13
Haoxue China 30°3N 112°24E 117 B9
Haparanda Sweden 65°52N 24°8E 60 D21
Haparanda Skärgård △
Sweden 65°35N 23°44E 60 D20
Hapeville U.S.A. 33°39N 84°24W 178 B5
Happy U.S.A. 34°45N 101°52W 176 D4
Happy Camp U.S.A. 41°48N 123°23W 168 F2
Happy Valley-Goose Bay
Canada 53°15N 60°20W 165 B7
Hapsu N. Korea 41°13N 128°51E 115 D15
Hapur India 28°45N 77°45E 124 E7
Ḩaql Si. Arabia 29°10N 34°58E 130 F3
Haquira Peru 14°14S 72°12W 188 C3
Har Indonesia 5°16S 133°14E 119 F8
Har-Ayrag Mongolia 45°47N 109°16E 114 B5
Har Hu China 38°20N 97°38E 110 D8
Har Us Nuur Mongolia 48°0N 92°0E 109 C12
Har Yehuda Israel 31°35N 34°57E 130 D3
Ḩaraḑ Si. Arabia 24°22N 49°0E 131 C4
Haradok Belarus 55°30N 30°3E 84 E6
Häradsbäck Sweden 56°32N 14°26E 63 H8
Haramosh Pakistan 35°50N 74°54E 125 B6
Haranomachi = Minamisōma
Japan 37°38N 140°58E 112 F10
Harar = Harer Ethiopia 9°20N 42°8E 131 F3
Harare Zimbabwe 17°43S 31°2E 143 F3
Harazé Chad 9°57N 20°48E 135 G10
Harbel Liberia 6°16N 10°20W 138 D2
Harbhanga India 20°38N 84°36E 126 D7
Harbin China 45°48N 126°40E 115 B14
Harbiye Turkey 36°10N 36°8E 104 D7
Harbo Sweden 60°7N 17°12E 62 D11
Harboøre Denmark 56°38N 8°10E 63 H2
Harbor Beach U.S.A. 43°51N 82°39W 174 C2
Harborcreek U.S.A. 42°9N 79°57W 174 D5
Harbour Breton
Canada 47°29N 55°50W 165 C8
Harbour Deep Canada 50°25N 56°32W 165 B8
Harburg Germany 53°27N 9°58E 76 B5
Harburger Berge ⌂
Germany 53°26N 9°51E 76 B5
Harda India 22°27N 77°5E 124 H7
Hardangerfjorden Norway 60°5N 6°0E 61 F12
Hardangervidda Norway 60°7N 7°20E 60 F12
Hardap □ Namibia 24°0S 17°0E 144 B2
Hardap ⌂ Namibia 24°29S 17°45E 144 B2
Hardap Dam Namibia 24°32S 17°50E 144 B2
Hardeeville U.S.A. 32°17N 81°5W 178 C8
Harden Australia 34°32S 148°24E 153 C8
Hardenberg Neths. 52°34N 6°37E 69 B6
Harderwijk Neths. 52°21N 5°38E 69 B5
Hardey → Australia 22°45S 116°8E 148 D2
Hardin U.S.A. 45°44N 107°37W 168 D10
Harding S. Africa 30°35S 29°55E 145 D4
Harding, L. U.S.A. 32°40N 85°5W 178 C4
Harding Ra. Australia 16°17S 124°55E 148 C3
Hardisty Canada 52°40N 111°18W 162 C6
Hardoi India 27°26N 80°6E 125 F9
Hardwar = Haridwar
India 29°58N 78°9E 124 E8
Hardwick Ga., U.S.A. 33°4N 83°14W 178 B6
Hardwick Vt., U.S.A. 44°30N 72°22W 175 B12
Hardwicke B.
Australia 34°55S 137°20E 152 C2
Hardwood Lake
Canada 45°12N 77°26W 174 A7
Hardy, Pen. Chile 55°30S 68°20W 192 E3
Hardy, Pte. St. Lucia 14°6N 60°56W 183 f
Hare B. Canada 51°15N 55°45W 165 B8
Hareid Norway 62°22N 6°1E 60 E12
Haren Germany 52°47N 7°13E 76 C
Harer Ethiopia 9°20N 42°8E 131 F
Harfleur France 49°30N 0°10E 70 C
Hargeisa Somalia 9°30N 44°2E 131 F
Harghita □ Romania 46°30N 25°30E 81 D
Harghita, Munţii
Romania 46°25N 25°35E 81 D
Hargshamn Sweden 60°12N 18°30E 62 D
Hari → Indonesia 1°16S 104°5E 118 E
Haria Canary Is. 29°8N 13°32W 100 E
Haridwar India 29°58N 78°9E 124 E
Harihar India 14°32N 75°44E 127 G
Harihari N.Z. 43°9S 170°33E 155 D
Hariharpur Garhi
Nepal 27°19N 85°29E 125 F
Harim, Jabal al Oman 25°58N 56°14E 129 E
Haringhata → Bangla. 22°0N 89°58E 123 J
Haripad India 9°14N 76°28E 127 K
Harīr, W. al → Syria 32°44N 35°59E 130 C
Harīrūd → Asia 37°24N 60°38E 129 B
Härjedalen Sweden 62°22N 13°5E 62 B
Harlan Iowa, U.S.A. 41°39N 95°19W 172 E
Harlan Ky., U.S.A. 36°51N 83°19W 173 G
Hârlău Romania 47°23N 26°55E 81 C
Harlech U.K. 52°52N 4°6W 66 E
Harlem Ga., U.S.A. 33°25N 82°19W 178 B
Harlem Mont., U.S.A. 48°32N 108°47W 168 B
Hårlev Denmark 55°21N 12°14E 63 J
Harleyville U.S.A. 33°13N 80°27W 178 B
Harlingen Neths. 53°11N 5°25E 69 A
Harlingen U.S.A. 26°12N 97°42W 176 H
Harlow U.K. 51°46N 0°8E 67 F
Harlowton U.S.A. 46°26N 109°50W 168 C
Harmancık Turkey 39°41N 29°9E 99 B
Harmånger Sweden 61°55N 17°20E 62 C
Harnai India 17°48N 73°6E 126 F
Harnai Pakistan 30°6N 67°56E 124 D
Harney, L. U.S.A. 28°45N 81°3W 179 G
Harney Basin U.S.A. 43°0N 119°30W 168 E
Harney L. U.S.A. 43°14N 119°8W 168 E
Harney Peak U.S.A. 43°52N 103°32W 172 D
Härnön Sweden 62°36N 18°0E 62 B
Härnösand Sweden 62°38N 17°55E 62 B
Haro Spain 42°35N 2°55W 90 C
Harold U.S.A. 30°40N 86°53W 179 E
Haroldswick U.K. 60°48N 0°50W 65 A
Harp L. Canada 55°5N 61°50W 165 A
Harpanahalli India 14°47N 76°2E 127 G
Harper Liberia 4°25N 7°43W 138 E
Harper, Mt. U.S.A. 64°14N 143°51W 166 C
Harplinge Sweden 56°45N 12°45E 63 H
Harrai India 22°37N 79°13E 125 H
Harrand Pakistan 29°28N 70°3E 124 E
Harricana → Canada 50°56N 79°32W 164 B
Harriman U.S.A. 35°56N 84°33W 177 D
Harrington Australia 31°52S 152°42E 153 A
Harrington Harbour
Canada 50°31N 59°30W 165 B
Harris U.K. 57°50N 6°55W 65 D
Harris, L. Australia 31°10S 135°10E 151 E
Harris, L. U.S.A. 28°47N 81°49W 179 G
Harris, Sd. of U.K. 57°44N 7°6W 65 D
Harris Mts. N.Z. 44°49S 168°49E 155 E
Harris Pt. Canada 43°6N 82°9W 174 C
Harrisburg Ill., U.S.A. 37°44N 88°32W 172 G
Harrisburg Nebr.,
U.S.A. 41°33N 103°44W 172 E
Harrisburg Pa., U.S.A. 40°16N 76°53W 174 F
Harrismith S. Africa 28°15S 29°8E 145 C
Harrison Ark., U.S.A. 36°14N 93°7W 176 C
Harrison Maine, U.S.A. 44°7N 70°39W 175 B
Harrison Nebr., U.S.A. 42°41N 103°53W 172 D
Harrison, C. Canada 54°55N 57°55W 165 B
Harrison Bay U.S.A. 70°40N 151°0W 166 A
Harrison L. Canada 49°33N 121°50W 162 D
Harrisonburg U.S.A. 38°27N 78°52W 173 F
Harrisonville U.S.A. 38°39N 94°21W 172 F
Harriston Canada 43°57N 80°53W 174 C
Harrisville Mich.,
U.S.A. 44°39N 83°17W 174 B
Harrisville N.Y., U.S.A. 44°9N 75°19W 175 B
Harrisville Pa., U.S.A. 41°8N 80°0W 174 E
Harrodsburg U.S.A. 37°46N 84°51W 173 G
Harrogate U.K. 54°0N 1°33W 66 D
Harrow Australia 37°9S 141°35E 152 D
Harrow Canada 42°2N 82°55W 174 D
Harrow □ U.K. 51°35N 0°21W 67 F
Harrowsmith Canada 44°24N 76°40W 175 B
Harry S. Truman Res.
U.S.A. 38°16N 93°24W 172 F
Harsefeld Germany 53°27N 9°30E 76 B
Harsewinkel Germany 51°56N 8°14E 76 D
Harsīn Iran 34°18N 47°33E 105 E1
Hârşova Romania 44°40N 27°59E 81 F
Harstad Norway 68°48N 16°30E 60 B
Harsud India 22°6N 76°44E 124 H
Hart U.S.A. 43°42N 86°22W 172 D
Hart, L. Australia 31°10S 136°25E 152 A
Hartbees → S. Africa 28°45S 20°32E 144 C
Hartberg Austria 47°17N 15°58E 78 D
Hartford Ala., U.S.A. 31°6N 85°42W 178 D
Hartford Conn., U.S.A. 41°46N 72°41W 175 E
Hartford Ky., U.S.A. 37°27N 86°55W 172 G
Hartford S. Dak., U.S.A. 43°38N 96°57W 172 D
Hartford Vt., U.S.A. 43°40N 72°20W 175 C
Hartford Wis., U.S.A. 43°19N 88°22W 172 D
Hartford City U.S.A. 40°27N 85°22W 173 E
Hartland Canada 46°20N 67°32W 165 C
Hartland Pt. U.K. 51°1N 4°32W 67 F
Hartlepool U.K. 54°42N 1°13W 66 C
Hartlepool □ U.K. 54°42N 1°17W 66 C
Hartley Bay Canada 53°25N 129°15W 162 C
Hartmannberge Namibia 17°0S 13°0E 144 A
Hartney Canada 49°30N 100°35W 163 D
Hârtop Moldova 46°39N 28°40E 81 D1
Harts → S. Africa 28°24S 24°17E 144 C
Harts Range Australia 23°6S 134°55E 150 C
Hartselle U.S.A. 34°27N 86°56W 177 D1
Hartsfield-Jackson Atlanta Int. ✈
(ATL) U.S.A. 33°38N 84°26W 178 B
Hartshorne U.S.A. 34°51N 95°34W 176 D
Hartstown U.S.A. 41°33N 80°23W 174 E
Hartsville U.S.A. 34°23N 80°4W 177 D1
Hartswater S. Africa 27°34S 24°43E 144 C
Hartwell U.S.A. 34°21N 82°56W 177 D1
Harunabad Pakistan 29°35N 73°8E 124 E
Harur India 12°3N 78°29E 127 H
Harvand Iran 28°25N 55°43E 129 D
Harvey Australia 33°5S 115°54E 149 F
Harvey Ill., U.S.A. 41°36N 87°50W 172 E1
Harvey N. Dak., U.S.A. 47°47N 99°56W 172 B

Harwich U.K. 51°56N 1°17E 67 F9
Haryana □ India 29°0N 76°10E 124 E7
Haryn → Belarus 52°7N 27°17E 75 B14
Harz Germany 51°38N 10°44E 76 D6
Harz △ Germany 51°40N 10°18E 76 D6
Harzgerode Germany 51°38N 11°8E 76 D7
Hasa Si. Arabia 25°50N 49°0E 129 E6
Hasā, W. al → Jordan 31°4N 35°29E 130 D4
Ḩasanābād Iran 32°8N 52°44E 129 C7
Hasankeyf Turkey 37°42N 41°24E 105 D9
Hasanparti India 18°4N 79°32E 126 E4
Ḩasb, W. → Iraq 31°45N 44°17E 128 D5
Hasdo → India 21°44N 82°44E 125 J10
Haselünne Germany 52°40N 7°29E 76 C3
Hashimoto Japan 34°19N 135°37E 113 G7
Hashtjerd Iran 35°52N 50°40E 129 C6
Hashtpur = Tālesh
Iran 37°58N 48°58E 105 D13
Hashtrud Iran 37°28N 47°4E 105 D12
Haskell U.S.A. 33°10N 99°44W 176 E5
Haskovo = Khaskovo
Bulgaria 41°56N 25°30E 97 E9
Hasköy Turkey 41°38N 26°52E 97 E10
Haslach Germany 48°16N 8°5E 77 G4
Hasle Denmark 55°11N 14°44E 63 J8
Haslemere U.K. 51°5N 0°43W 67 F7
Haslev Denmark 55°18N 11°57E 63 J5
Hasparren France 43°24N 1°18W 72 E2
Hassa Turkey 36°48N 36°29E 104 D7
Hassan India 13°0N 76°5E 127 H3
Hassberge ⌓ Germany 50°8N 10°45E 77 E6
Hassela Sweden 62°7N 16°42E 62 B10
Hasselt Belgium 50°56N 5°21E 69 D5
Hassfurt Germany 50°2N 10°30E 77 E6
Hassi bel Guebbour
Algeria 28°30N 6°41E 136 C5
Hassi bou Khelala
Algeria 30°17N 0°18W 136 B3
Hassi Bourarchet Algeria 27°26N 9°19E 136 C5
Hassi Djafou Algeria 30°55N 3°35E 136 B4
Hassi el Hadjar Algeria 31°28N 4°45E 136 B4
Hassi Imoulaye Algeria 29°54N 9°10E 136 C5
Hassi Inifeg Algeria 28°15N 1°30W 136 C3
Hassi Inifel Algeria 29°50N 3°41E 136 C4
Hassi Mana Algeria 28°48N 2°37W 136 C3
Hassi Marroket Algeria 30°10N 3°0E 136 B4
Hassi Mengoub Algeria 29°49N 5°26W 136 C2
Hassi Messaoud Algeria 31°51N 6°1E 136 B5
Hassi Sougoued Algeria 26°50N 9°28E 136 C5
Hassi Tartrat Algeria 30°5N 6°28E 136 B5
Hassi Zerzour Morocco 30°51N 3°56W 136 B3
Hassi Zguilma Morocco 30°19N 6°10W 136 B2
Hässleholm Sweden 56°10N 13°46E 63 H7
Hasslö Sweden 56°7N 15°28E 63 H9
Hassloch Germany 49°22N 8°16E 77 F4
Hästholmen Sweden 58°17N 14°38E 63 F8
Hastings Australia 38°18S 145°12E 153 E6
Hastings N.Z. 39°39S 176°52E 154 F5
Hastings U.K. 50°51N 0°35E 67 G8
Hastings Fla., U.S.A. 29°43N 81°31W 178 F8
Hastings Mich., U.S.A. 42°39N 85°17W 173 D11
Hastings Minn., U.S.A. 44°44N 92°51W 172 C7
Hastings Nebr., U.S.A. 40°35N 98°23W 172 E4
Hastings Ra.
Australia 31°15S 152°14E 153 A10
Hästveda Sweden 56°17N 13°55E 63 H7
Hat Ukraine 48°19N 22°38E 80 B7
Hat Head △ Australia 31°3S 153°1E 153 A10
Hat Lot Vietnam 21°15N 104°7E 120 B5
Hat Yai Thailand 7°1N 100°27E 121 J3
Hatanbulag = Ergel
Mongolia 43°8N 109°5E 114 C5
Hatay Turkey 36°14N 36°10E 104 D7
Hatay □ Turkey 36°25N 36°15E 104 D7
Hatch U.S.A. 32°40N 107°9W 169 K10
Hatchet L. Canada 58°36N 103°40W 163 B8
Haţeg Romania 45°36N 22°55E 80 E7
Hateruma-Shima
Japan 24°3N 123°47E 113 M1
Hatfield Australia 33°54S 143°49E 152 B5
Hatgal Mongolia 50°26N 100°9E 110 A9
Hathras India 27°36N 78°6E 124 F8
Hatia Bangla. 22°30N 91°5E 123 H17
Hatia Nepal 27°43N 87°21E 125 F12
Ḩāţibah, Ra's Si. Arabia 21°55N 38°57E 137 C4
Hatid India 17°17N 75°3E 126 F2
Hato Mayor Dom. Rep. 18°46N 69°15W 183 C6
Hatra = Al Ḩaḑr Iraq 35°35N 42°44E 105 E10
Hatta India 24°7N 79°36E 125 G8
Hatta U.A.E. 24°45N 56°4E 129 E8
Hattah Australia 34°48S 142°17E 152 C5
Hattah Kulkyne △
Australia 34°16S 142°33E 152 C5
Hatteras, C. U.S.A. 35°14N 75°32W 177 D17
Hatteras Abyssal Plain
Atl. Oc. 28°0N 72°0W 56 D4
Hattiesburg U.S.A. 31°20N 89°17W 177 F10
Hattusa Turkey 40°0N 34°37E 104 B6
Hatvan Hungary 47°40N 19°45E 80 C4
Hau → Vietnam 9°30N 106°13E 121 H6
Haugesund Norway 59°23N 5°13E 61 G11
Hauhungaroa Ra.
N.Z. 38°42S 175°40E 154 E4
Haukipudas Finland 65°12N 25°20E 60 D21
Haultain → Canada 55°51N 106°46W 163 B7
Hauraki G. N.Z. 36°35S 175°5E 154 C4
Hauroko L. N.Z. 45°59S 167°21E 155 F2
Hausruck Austria 48°6N 13°30E 78 C6
Haut Atlas Morocco 32°30N 5°0W 136 B3
Haut-Jura ⌓ France 46°23N 2°23E 71 F9
Haut-Languedoc ⌓
France 43°30N 2°43E 72 E6
Haut-Niger △ Guinea 10°20N 10°20W 138 C2
Haut-Rhin □ France 48°0N 7°15E 71 E14
Haut-Sassandra □
Ivory C. 7°0N 6°30W 138 D3
Haute-Corse □ France 42°30N 9°30E 73 F13
Haute-Garonne □ France 43°30N 1°30E 72 E5
Haute-Loire □ France 45°5N 3°50E 72 C7
Haute-Marne □ France 48°10N 5°20E 71 D12
Haute-Normandie □
France 49°20N 1°0E 70 C7
Haute-Saône □ France 47°45N 6°10E 71 E13
Haute-Savoie □ France 46°0N 6°20E 73 C10
Haute-Vienne □ France 45°50N 1°10E 72 C5
Hautes-Alpes □ France 44°42N 6°20E 73 D10
Hautes Fagnes = Hohes Venn
Belgium 50°30N 6°5E 69 D6
Hautes-Pyrénées □ France 43°0N 0°10E 72 F4
Hauteville-Lompnès
France 45°58N 5°36E 73 C9
Hautmont France 50°15N 3°55E 71 B10
Hauts-de-Seine □ France 48°52N 2°15E 71 D9
Hauts Plateaux Algeria 35°0N 1°0E 136 B4
Hauzenberg Germany 48°40N 13°37E 77 G9
Havana = La Habana
Cuba 23°8N 82°22W 182 B3
Havana Fla., U.S.A. 30°37N 84°25W 178 E5
Havana Ill., U.S.A. 40°18N 90°4W 172 E8
Havant U.K. 50°51N 0°58W 67 G7
Havârna Romania 48°4N 26°43E 81 B11
Havasor = Kığzı Turkey 38°18N 43°25E 128 B4
Havasu, L. U.S.A. 34°18N 114°28W 171 L12
Havdhem Sweden 57°10N 18°20E 63 G12
Havel → Germany 52°50N 12°3E 76 C8
Havelian Pakistan 34°2N 73°10E 124 B5
Havelock Canada 44°26N 77°53W 174 B7
Havelock N.Z. 41°17S 173°48E 155 B8
Havelock U.S.A. 34°53N 76°54W 177 D16
Havelock I. India 11°58N 93°0E 127 J11
Havelock North N.Z. 39°40S 176°53E 154 F5
Haverfordwest U.K. 51°48N 4°58W 67 F3
Haverhill U.K. 52°5N 0°28E 67 E8
Haverhill Fla., U.S.A. 26°42N 80°7W 179 J9
Haverhill Mass., U.S.A. 42°47N 71°5W 175 D13
Haveri India 14°53N 75°24E 127 G2
Havern Sweden 62°18N 15°7E 62 B9
Haverstraw U.S.A. 41°12N 73°58W 175 E11
Håverud Sweden 58°50N 12°28E 63 F6
Havirga Mongolia 45°41N 113°5E 114 B7
Havířov Czech Rep. 49°46N 18°20E 79 B11
Havlíčkův Brod
Czech Rep. 49°36N 15°33E 78 B8
Havneby Denmark 55°5N 8°34E 63 J2
Havran Turkey 39°33N 27°6E 99 B9
Havre U.S.A. 48°33N 109°41W 168 B9
Havre-Aubert Canada 47°12N 61°56W 165 C7
Havre-St.-Pierre
Canada 50°18N 63°33W 165 B7
Havsa Turkey 41°31N 26°48E 97 E10
Havza Turkey 41°0N 35°35E 104 B6
Haw → U.S.A. 35°36N 79°3W 177 D15
Hawai'i U.S.A. 19°30N 155°30W 167 M8
Hawai'i □ U.S.A. 19°30N 156°30W 167 M8
Hawaiian Is. Pac. Oc. 20°30N 156°0W 157 E12
Hawaiian Ridge
Pac. Oc. 24°0N 165°0W 157 E11
Hawarden U.S.A. 43°0N 96°29W 172 D5
Hawea, L. N.Z. 44°28S 169°19E 155 E4
Hawea Flat N.Z. 44°40S 169°19E 155 E4
Hawera N.Z. 39°35S 174°19E 154 F3
Hawi U.S.A. 20°14N 155°50W 167 L8
Hawick U.K. 55°26N 2°47W 65 F6
Hawk Junction Canada 48°5N 84°38W 164 C3
Hawkdun Ra. N.Z. 44°53S 170°5E 155 E5
Hawke B. N.Z. 39°25S 177°20E 154 F6
Hawker Australia 31°59S 138°22E 152 A3
Hawke's Bay Canada 50°36N 57°10W 165 B8
Hawke's Bay □ N.Z. 39°45S 176°35E 154 F5
Hawkesbury Canada 45°37N 74°37W 164 C5
Hawkesbury I. Canada 53°37N 129°3W 162 C3
Hawkesbury Pt.
Australia 11°55S 134°5E 150 A1
Hawkinsville U.S.A. 32°17N 83°28W 178 C6
Hawks Nest Australia 32°41S 152°11E 153 B10
Hawley Minn., U.S.A. 46°53N 96°19W 172 B5
Hawley Pa., U.S.A. 41°28N 75°11W 175 E9
Ḩawrān, W. → Iraq 33°58N 42°34E 105 F10
Hawsh Müssá Lebanon 33°45N 35°55E 130 B4
Hawthorne Fla., U.S.A. 29°36N 82°5W 179 F7
Hawthorne Nev.,
U.S.A. 38°32N 118°38W 168 G4
Hay Australia 34°30S 144°51E 153 C6
Hay → Australia 24°50S 138°0E 150 C2
Hay → Canada 60°50N 116°26W 162 A5
Hay, C. Australia 14°5S 129°29E 148 B4
Hay L. Canada 58°50N 118°50W 162 B5
Hay-on-Wye U.K. 52°5N 3°8W 67 E4
Hay Point Australia 21°18S 149°17E 150 C4
Hay River Canada 60°51N 115°44W 162 A5
Hay Springs U.S.A. 42°41N 102°41W 172 D2
Hayachine-San Japan 39°34N 141°29E 112 E10
Hayange France 49°20N 6°2E 71 C13
Hayastan = Armenia ■
Asia 40°20N 45°0E 87 K7
Haydān, W. al →
Jordan 31°29N 35°34E 130 D4
Haydarlı Turkey 38°16N 30°23E 99 C12
Hayden U.S.A. 40°30N 107°16W 168 F10
Hayes U.S.A. 44°23N 101°1W 172 C3
Hayes → Canada 57°3N 92°12W 164 A1
Hayes, Mt. U.S.A. 63°37N 146°43W 166 C10
Hayes Creek Australia 13°43S 131°22E 148 B5
Hayle U.K. 50°11N 5°26W 67 G2
Hayling I. U.K. 50°48N 0°59W 67 G7
Hayman I. Australia 20°4S 148°53E 150 b
Haymana Turkey 39°26N 32°31E 104 C5
Hayneville U.S.A. 32°23N 83°37W 178 C6
Hayrabolu Turkey 41°12N 27°5E 97 E11
Hays Canada 50°6N 111°48W 162 C6
Hays U.S.A. 38°53N 99°20W 172 F4
Haysyn Ukraine 48°57N 29°25E 81 B14
Hayvoron Ukraine 48°22N 29°52E 81 B14
Hayward Calif., U.S.A. 37°40N 122°4W 170 H4
Hayward Wis., U.S.A. 46°1N 91°29W 172 B8
Haywards Heath U.K. 51°0N 0°5W 67 G7
Hazafon □ Israel 32°40N 35°20E 130 C4
Hazar Turkmenistan 39°34N 53°16E 108 E4
Hazārān, Kūh-e Iran 29°35N 57°20E 129 D8
Hazard U.S.A. 37°15N 83°12W 173 G12
Hazaribag India 23°58N 85°26E 125 H11
Hazaribag Road India 24°12N 85°57E 125 G11
Hazebrouck France 50°42N 2°31E 71 B9
Hazelton Canada 55°20N 127°42W 162 B3
Hazelton U.S.A. 46°29N 100°17W 172 B3
Hazen U.S.A. 47°18N 101°38W 172 B3
Hazen, L. Canada 81°47N 71°1W 57 A3
Hazlehurst Ga., U.S.A. 31°52N 82°36W 178 D7
Hazlehurst Miss.,
U.S.A. 31°52N 90°24W 177 F9
Hazlet U.S.A. 40°25N 74°12W 175 F10
Hazleton U.S.A. 40°57N 75°59W 175 F9
Hazlett, L. Australia 21°30S 128°48E 148 D4
Hazro Turkey 38°15N 40°47E 128 B4
He Xian = Hezhou
China 24°27N 111°30E 117 E8
He Xian China 31°45N 118°20E 117 B12
Head of Bight Australia 31°30S 131°25E 149 F5
Head-Smashed-In Buffalo Jump
Canada 49°44N 113°37W 162 D6
Headland U.S.A. 31°21N 85°21W 178 D4
Headlands Zimbabwe 18°15S 32°2E 143 F3
Healdsburg U.S.A. 38°37N 122°52W 170 G4
Healdton U.S.A. 34°14N 97°29W 176 D6
Healesville Australia 37°35S 145°30E 153 D6
Healy U.S.A. 63°52N 148°58W 166 C10
Heany Junction
Zimbabwe 20°6S 28°54E 145 B4
Heard I. Ind. Oc. 53°6S 72°36E 146 K6
Hearne U.S.A. 30°53N 96°36W 176 F6
Hearst Canada 49°40N 83°41W 164 C3
Heart → U.S.A. 46°46N 100°50W 172 B3
Heart's Content
Canada 47°54N 53°27W 165 C9
Heath → Bolivia 12°31S 68°38W 188 C4
Heath, Pte. Canada 49°8N 61°40W 165 C7
Heath Mts. N.Z. 45°39S 167°9E 155 F2
Heathcote Australia 36°56S 144°45E 153 D6
Heathrow, London ✈ (LHR)
U.K. 51°28N 0°27W 67 F7
Heavener U.S.A. 34°53N 94°36W 176 D7
Hebbronville U.S.A. 27°18N 98°41W 176 H5
Hebei □ China 39°0N 116°0E 114 E9
Hebel Australia 28°58S 147°47E 151 D4
Heber U.S.A. 32°44N 115°32W 171 N11
Heber Springs U.S.A. 35°30N 92°2W 176 D8
Hebgen L. U.S.A. 44°52N 111°20W 168 D8
Hebi China 35°57N 114°7E 114 G8
Hebrides U.K. 57°30N 7°0W 58 D4
Hebrides, Sea of the U.K. 57°5N 7°0W 65 D2
Hebron = Al Khalīl
West Bank 31°32N 35°6E 130 D4
Hebron Canada 58°5N 62°30W 161 F19
Hebron N. Dak., U.S.A. 46°54N 102°3W 172 B2
Hebron Nebr., U.S.A. 40°10N 97°35W 172 E5
Heby Sweden 59°56N 16°53E 62 E10
Hecate Str. Canada 53°10N 130°30W 162 C2
Heceta I. U.S.A. 55°46N 133°40W 162 B2
Hechi China 24°40N 108°2E 116 E7
Hechingen Germany 48°21N 8°57E 77 G4
Hechuan China 30°2N 106°12E 116 B6
Hecla U.S.A. 45°53N 98°9W 172 C4
Hecla I. Canada 51°10N 96°43W 163 C9
Hedal Norway 60°37N 9°41E 62 D3
Hédé France 48°18N 1°49W 70 D5
Hede Sweden 62°23N 13°30E 62 B7
Hedemora Sweden 60°18N 15°58E 62 D9
Hedensted Denmark 55°46N 9°42E 63 J3
Hedesunda Sweden 60°24N 17°0E 62 D10
Hedgehope N.Z. 46°12S 168°34E 155 G3
Heerde Neths. 52°24N 6°2E 69 B6
Heerenveen Neths. 52°57N 5°55E 69 B5
Heerhugowaard Neths. 52°40N 4°51E 69 B4
Heerlen Neths. 50°55N 5°58E 69 D5
Ḩefa Israel 32°46N 35°0E 130 C4
Ḩefa □ Israel 32°40N 35°0E 130 C4
Hefei China 31°52N 117°18E 117 B11
Hefeng China 29°55N 109°52E 116 C7
Heflin U.S.A. 33°39N 85°35W 178 B4
Hegang China 47°20N 130°19E 111 B15
Heglig Sudan 10°0N 29°24E 135 G11
Hei Ling Chau China 22°15N 114°2E 111 a
Heichengzhen China 36°24N 106°3E 114 F4
Heide Germany 54°11N 9°6E 76 A5
Heidelberg Germany 49°24N 8°42E 77 F4
Heidelberg S. Africa 34°6S 20°59E 144 D3
Heidelburg S. Africa 26°30S 28°21E 145 C4
Heidenau Germany 50°57N 13°52E 76 E9
Heidenheim Germany 48°41N 10°9E 77 G6
Heihe China 50°10N 127°30E 111 A14
Heijing China 25°22N 101°44E 116 E3
Heilbad Heiligenstadt
Germany 51°22N 10°8E 76 D6
Heilbron S. Africa 27°16S 27°59E 145 C4
Heilbronn Germany 49°9N 9°13E 77 F5
Heiligenblut Austria 47°2N 12°51E 78 D5
Heiligenhafen Germany 54°22N 10°59E 76 A6
Heilongjiang □ China 48°0N 126°0E 111 B14
Heilprin Land Greenland 82°5N 33°0W 57 A7
Heilunkiang = Heilongjiang □
China 48°0N 126°0E 111 B14
Heimaey Iceland 63°26N 20°17W 60 E3
Heinola Finland 61°13N 26°2E 84 B4
Heinsberg Germany 51°3N 6°5E 76 D2
Heinze Chaung Burma 14°42N 97°52E 120 E1
Heinze Kyun Burma 14°25N 97°45E 120 E1
Heishan China 41°40N 122°5E 115 D12
Heishui Liaoning, China 42°8N 119°30E 115 C10
Heishui Sichuan, China 32°4N 103°2E 116 A4
Hejaz = Ḩijāz Si. Arabia 24°0N 40°0E 128 E3
Hejian China 38°25N 116°5E 114 E9
Hejiang China 28°43N 105°46E 116 C5
Hejin China 35°35N 110°42E 114 G6
Hejing China 42°18N 86°22E 109 D11
Hekimhan Turkey 38°50N 37°55E 104 C7
Hekla Iceland 63°56N 19°35W 60 E4
Hekou Gansu, China 36°10N 103°26E 114 F2
Hekou Guangdong,
China 23°13N 112°45E 117 F9
Hekou Yunnan, China 22°30N 103°59E 116 F4
Hel Poland 54°37N 18°47E 82 D5
Helagsfjället Sweden 62°54N 12°25E 62 B6
Helan Shan China 38°30N 105°55E 114 E3
Helechosa de los Montes
Spain 39°22N 4°53W 89 F6
Helen Atoll Palau 2°40N 132°0E 119 D8
Helena Ga., U.S.A. 32°5N 82°55W 178 C7
Helena Mont., U.S.A. 46°36N 112°2W 168 C7
Helena -West Helena
U.S.A. 34°32N 90°36W 177 D9
Helendale U.S.A. 34°44N 117°19W 171 L9
Helensburgh Australia 34°11S 151°1E 153 C9
Helensburgh U.K. 56°1N 4°43W 65 E4
Helensville N.Z. 36°41S 174°29E 154 C3
Helenvale Australia 15°43S 145°14E 150 B4
Helgasjön Sweden 56°55N 14°50E 63 H8
Helgeland Norway 66°7N 13°29E 60 C15
Helgoland Germany 54°10N 7°53E 76 A3
Helheim Gletscher
Greenland 66°24N 38°12W 57 D7
Heligoland = Helgoland
Germany 54°10N 7°53E 76 A3
Heligoland B. = Deutsche Bucht
Germany 54°15N 8°0E 76 A4
Heliopolis = Masr el Gedida
Egypt 30°5N 31°21E 137 E7
Hell Hole Gorge △
Australia 25°31S 144°12E 150 D3
Hella Iceland 63°50N 20°24W 60 E3
Hellas = Greece ■ Europe 40°0N 23°0E 98 B3
Hellertown U.S.A. 40°35N 75°21W 175 F9
Hellespont = Çanakkale Boğazı
Turkey 40°17N 26°32E 97 F10
Hellevoetsluis Neths. 51°50N 4°8E 69 C4
Hellín Spain 38°31N 1°40W 91 G3
Hells Canyon ⌓
U.S.A. 45°30N 117°45W 168 D5
Hell's Gate △ Kenya 0°54S 36°19E 142 C4
Helmand □ Afghan. 31°20N 64°0E 122 D4
Helmand → Afghan. 31°12N 61°34E 122 D2
Helme → Germany 51°20N 11°21E 76 D7
Helmeringhausen
Namibia 25°54S 16°57E 144 C2
Helmond Neths. 51°29N 5°41E 69 C5
Helmsdale U.K. 58°7N 3°39W 65 C5
Helmsdale → U.K. 58°8N 3°43W 65 C5
Helmstedt Germany 52°12N 11°0E 76 C7
Helong China 42°40N 129°0E 115 C15
Helper U.S.A. 39°41N 110°51W 168 G8
Helsingborg Sweden 56°3N 12°42E 63 H6
Helsinge Denmark 56°2N 12°12E 63 H6
Helsingfors = Helsinki
Finland 60°10N 24°55E 84 B3
Helsingør Denmark 56°2N 12°35E 63 H6
Helsinki Finland 60°10N 24°55E 84 B3
Helska, Mierzeja Poland 54°45N 18°40E 82 D5
Helston U.K. 50°6N 5°17W 67 G2
Helvellyn U.K. 54°32N 3°1W 66 C4
Helvetinjärvi △ Finland 62°5N 23°47E 60 E20
Helwân Egypt 29°50N 31°20E 137 F7
Hemavati → India 12°30N 76°20E 127 H3
Hemel Hempstead U.K. 51°44N 0°28W 67 F7
Hemet U.S.A. 33°45N 116°58W 171 M10
Hemingford U.S.A. 42°19N 103°4W 172 D2
Hemis △ India 34°10N 77°15E 124 B7
Hemmingford Canada 45°3N 73°35W 175 A11
Hempstead N.Y.,
U.S.A. 40°42N 73°37W 175 F11
Hempstead Tex., U.S.A. 30°6N 96°5W 176 F6
Hemse Sweden 57°15N 18°22E 63 G12
Hemsön Sweden 62°42N 18°5E 62 B12
Hen and Chickens Is.
N.Z. 35°58S 174°45E 154 B3
Henån Sweden 58°14N 11°40E 63 F5
Henan □ China 34°0N 114°0E 114 H8
Henares → Spain 40°24N 3°30W 88 E7
Henashi-Misaki Japan 40°37N 139°51E 112 D9
Hendaye France 43°23N 1°47W 72 E2
Hendek Turkey 40°48N 30°44E 104 B4
Henderson Argentina 36°18S 61°43W 190 D3
Henderson Ga., U.S.A. 32°21N 83°47W 178 C6
Henderson Ky.,
U.S.A. 37°50N 87°35W 172 G10
Henderson N.C.,
U.S.A. 36°20N 78°25W 177 C15
Henderson N.Y.,
U.S.A. 43°50N 76°10W 175 C8
Henderson Nev.,
U.S.A. 36°2N 114°58W 171 J12
Henderson Tenn.,
U.S.A. 35°26N 88°38W 177 D10
Henderson Tex., U.S.A. 32°9N 94°48W 176 E7
Henderson I. Pac. Oc. 24°22S 128°19W 157 K15
Hendersonville N.C.,
U.S.A. 35°19N 82°28W 177 D13
Hendersonville Tenn.,
U.S.A. 36°18N 86°37W 177 C11
Hendījān Iran 30°14N 49°43E 129 D6
Hendorābī Iran 26°40N 53°37E 129 E7
Heng Jiang → China 28°40N 104°25E 116 C5
Heng Xian China 22°40N 109°17E 116 F7
Hengcheng China 38°18N 106°28E 114 E4
Hëngch'un Taiwan 22°0N 120°44E 117 F13
Hengdaohezi China 44°52N 129°0E 115 B15
Hengduan Shan China 28°30N 98°50E 116 C2
Hengelo Neths. 52°16N 6°48E 69 B6
Henggang China 22°39N 114°12E 111 a
Hengmen China 22°33N 113°35E 111 a
Hengshan Hunan,
China 27°16N 112°45E 117 D9
Hengshan Shaanxi,
China 37°58N 109°5E 114 F5
Hengshui China 37°41N 115°40E 114 F8
Hengyang China 26°59N 112°22E 117 D9
Henichesk Ukraine 46°12N 34°50E 85 J8
Hénin-Beaumont France 50°25N 2°58E 71 B9
Henley-on-Thames U.K. 51°32N 0°54W 67 F7
Henlopen, C. U.S.A. 38°48N 75°6W 173 F16
Hennan Sweden 62°2N 15°54E 62 B9
Hennebont France 47°49N 3°19W 70 E3
Hennenman S. Africa 27°59S 27°1E 144 C4
Hennessey U.S.A. 36°6N 97°54W 176 C6
Hennigsdorf Germany 52°38N 13°12E 76 C9
Henri Pittier △
Venezuela 10°26N 67°37W 183 D6
Henrietta U.S.A. 43°4N 77°37W 174 C7
Henrietta Tex., U.S.A. 33°49N 98°12W 176 E5
Henrietta, Ostrov = Genriyetty,
Ostrov Russia 77°6N 156°30E 107 B16
Henrietta Maria, C.
Canada 55°9N 82°20W 164 A3
Henry U.S.A. 41°7N 89°22W 172 E9
Henry Ice Rise
Antarctica 80°35S 62°0W 55 E17
Henry Lawrence I. India 12°9N 93°5E 127 H11
Henryetta U.S.A. 35°27N 95°59W 176 D7
Henryville Canada 45°8N 73°11W 175 A11
Hensall Canada 43°26N 81°30W 174 C3
Henstedt-Ulzburg
Germany 53°47N 10°0E 76 B6
Hentiesbaai Namibia 22°8S 14°18E 144 B1
Hentiyn Nuruu
Mongolia 48°30N 108°30E 111 B10
Henty Australia 35°30S 147°3E 153 C7
Henzada Burma 17°38N 95°26E 123 L19
Hephaestia Greece 39°55N 25°14E 99 B7
Hephzibah U.S.A. 33°19N 82°6W 178 B7
Heping China 24°29N 115°0E 117 E10
Heppner U.S.A. 45°21N 119°33W 168 D4
Hepu China 21°40N 109°12E 116 G7
Hepworth Canada 44°37N 81°9W 174 B3
Heqing China 26°37N 100°11E 116 D3
Hequ China 39°20N 111°15E 114 E6
Héraðsflói Iceland 65°42N 14°12W 60 D6
Héraðsvötn → Iceland 65°45N 19°25W 60 D4
Heraklion = Iraklio
Greece 35°20N 25°12E 101 D7
Herald Cays Australia 16°58S 149°9E 150 B4
Herangi Ra. N.Z. 38°33S 174°48E 154 E3
Herāt Afghan. 34°20N 62°7E 108 F6
Herāt □ Afghan. 35°0N 62°0E 122 B3
Hérault □ France 43°34N 3°15E 72 E7
Hérault → France 43°17N 3°26E 72 E7
Herbault France 47°36N 1°8E 70 E8
Herbert Canada 50°30N 107°10W 163 C7
Herbert → Australia 18°31S 146°17E 150 B4
Herbertabad India 11°43N 92°37E 127 J11
Herberton Australia 17°20S 145°25E 150 B4
Herbertsdale S. Africa 34°1S 21°46E 144 D3
Herbertville N.Z. 40°30S 176°33E 154 G5
Herbignac France 47°27N 2°18W 70 E4
Herborn Germany 50°40N 8°18E 76 E4
Herby Poland 50°45N 18°50E 83 H5
Herceg-Novi Montenegro 42°30N 18°33E 96 D2
Herchmer Canada 57°22N 94°10W 163 B10
Herðubreið Iceland 65°11N 16°21W 60 D5
Hereford U.K. 52°4N 2°43W 67 E5
Hereford U.S.A. 34°49N 102°24W 176 D3
Herefordshire □ U.K. 52°8N 2°40W 67 E5
Herekino N.Z. 35°18S 173°11E 154 B2
Herencia Spain 39°21N 3°22W 89 F7
Herentals Belgium 51°12N 4°51E 69 C4
Herford Germany 52°7N 8°39E 76 C4
Héricourt France 47°32N 6°45E 71 E13
Herington U.S.A. 38°40N 96°57W 172 F5
Heris Iran 38°14N 47°6E 105 C12
Herisau Switz. 47°22N 9°17E 77 H5
Hérisson France 46°32N 2°42E 71 F9
Herkimer U.S.A. 43°2N 74°59W 175 D10
Herlen → Asia 48°48N 117°0E 111 B12
Herlong U.S.A. 40°8N 120°8W 170 E6
Herm U.K. 49°30N 2°28W 67 H5
Hermakivka Ukraine 48°42N 26°11E 81 B11
Hermann U.S.A. 38°42N 91°27W 172 F8
Hermannsburg
Australia 23°57S 132°45E 148 D5
Hermannsburg Germany 52°50N 10°5E 76 C6
Hermanus S. Africa 34°27S 19°12E 144 D2
Herment France 45°45N 2°24E 72 C6
Hermidale Australia 31°30S 146°42E 153 A7
Hermiston U.S.A. 45°51N 119°17W 168 D4
Hermon Canada 45°6N 77°37W 174 A7
Hermon U.S.A. 44°28N 75°14W 175 B9
Hermon, Mt. = Shaykh, J. ash
Lebanon 33°25N 35°50E 130 B4
Hermosillo Mexico 29°10N 111°0W 180 B2
Hernád → Hungary 47°56N 21°8E 80 C6
Hernandarias
Paraguay 25°20S 54°40W 191 B5
Hernandez U.S.A. 36°24N 120°46W 170 J6
Hernando Argentina 32°28S 63°40W 190 C3
Hernando Fla., U.S.A. 28°54N 82°23W 179 G7
Hernando Miss., U.S.A. 34°50N 90°0W 177 D10
Hernando de Magallanes △
Chile 54°0S 72°40W 192 D2
Hernani Spain 43°16N 1°58W 90 B3
Herndon U.S.A. 40°43N 76°51W 174 F8
Herne Germany 51°32N 7°14E 76 D3
Herne Bay U.K. 51°21N 1°8E 67 F9
Herning Denmark 56°8N 8°58E 63 H2
Herod U.S.A. 31°42N 84°26W 178 D5
Heroica Caborca = Caborca
Mexico 30°37N 112°6W 180 A2
Heroica Nogales = Nogales
Mexico 31°19N 110°56W 180 A2
Heron Bay Canada 48°40N 86°25W 164 C2
Heron I. Australia 23°27S 151°55E 150 C5
Herradura, Pta. de la
Canary Is. 28°26N 14°8W 100 F5
Herreid U.S.A. 45°50N 100°4W 172 C3
Herrenberg Germany 48°35N 8°52E 77 G4
Herrera Spain 37°26N 4°55W 89 H6
Herrera de Alcántara
Spain 39°39N 7°25W 89 F3
Herrera de Pisuerga
Spain 42°35N 4°20W 88 C6
Herrera del Duque Spain 39°10N 5°3W 89 F5
Herrestad Sweden 58°21N 11°50E 63 F5
Herrin U.S.A. 37°48N 89°2W 172 G9
Herriot Canada 56°22N 101°16W 163 B8
Herrljunga Sweden 58°5N 13°1E 63 F7
Hersbruck Germany 49°30N 11°26E 77 F7
Herschel I. Canada 69°35N 139°5W 54 C1
Hershey U.S.A. 40°17N 76°39W 175 F8
Herso = Cherso Greece 41°5N 22°47E 96 E6
Herstal Belgium 50°40N 5°38E 69 D5
Hertford U.K. 51°48N 0°4W 67 F7
Hertfordshire □ U.K. 51°51N 0°5W 67 F7
's-Hertogenbosch Neths. 51°42N 5°17E 69 C5
Hertsa Ukraine 48°9N 26°15E 81 B11
Hertzogville S. Africa 28°9S 25°30E 144 C4
Hervás Spain 40°16N 5°52W 88 E5
Hervey B. Australia 25°0S 152°52E 150 C5
Herzberg Brandenburg,
Germany 51°41N 13°14E 76 D9
Herzberg Niedersachsen,
Germany 51°38N 10°20E 76 D6
Herzliyya Israel 32°10N 34°50E 130 C3
Herzogenburg Austria 48°17N 15°41E 78 C8
Ḩeşār Fārs, Iran 29°52N 50°16E 129 D6
Ḩeşār Markazī, Iran 35°50N 49°12E 129 C6
Hesdin France 50°21N 2°2E 71 B9
Heshan Guangdong,
China 22°34N 113°4E 117 F9
Heshan Guangxi Zhuangzu,
China 23°50N 108°53E 116 F7
Heshui China 35°48N 108°0E 114 G5
Heshun China 37°22N 113°32E 114 F7
Hesperia U.S.A. 34°25N 117°18W 171 L9
Hesse = Hessen □
Germany 50°30N 9°0E 76 E4
Hessen □ Germany 50°30N 9°0E 76 E4
Hessenreuther und Manteler
Wald ⌓ Germany 49°45N 12°1E 77 F8
Hesso Australia 32°8S 137°27E 152 B2
Hestra Sweden 57°26N 13°35E 63 G7
Hetauda Nepal 27°25N 85°2E 125 F11
Hetch Hetchy Aqueduct
U.S.A. 37°29N 122°19W 170 H5
Hetta Enontekiö
Finland 68°23N 23°37E 60 B20
Hettinger U.S.A. 46°0N 102°42W 172 B2
Hettstedt Germany 51°39N 11°31E 76 D7
Heuksando S. Korea 34°40N 125°30E 115 G13
Heunghae S. Korea 36°12N 129°21E 115 F15
Heuvelton U.S.A. 44°37N 75°25W 175 B9
Heves Hungary 47°36N 20°17E 80 C5
Heves □ Hungary 47°50N 20°0E 80 C5
Hewitt U.S.A. 31°28N 97°12W 176 F6
Hexham U.K. 54°58N 2°4W 66 C5
Hexi Yunnan, China 24°9N 102°38E 116 E4
Hexi Zhejiang, China 27°58N 119°38E 117 D12
Hexigten Qi China 43°18N 117°30E 115 C9
Ḩeydarābād Iran 30°33N 55°38E 129 D7
Heyfield Australia 37°59S 146°47E 153 D7
Heysham U.K. 54°3N 2°53W 66 C5
Heyuan China 23°39N 114°40E 117 F10
Heywood Australia 38°8S 141°37E 152 E4
Heze China 35°14N 115°20E 114 G8
Hezhang China 27°8N 104°41E 116 D5
Hezhou China 24°27N 111°30E 117 E8
Hi Vista U.S.A. 34°45N 117°46W 171 L9
Hialeah U.S.A. 25°51N 80°16W 179 K9
Hiawatha U.S.A. 39°51N 95°32W 172 F6
Hibbing U.S.A. 47°25N 92°56W 172 B7
Hibernia Reef Australia 12°0S 123°23E 148 B3
Hickman U.S.A. 36°34N 89°11W 172 G9
Hickory U.S.A. 35°44N 81°21W 177 D14
Hicks, Pt. Australia 37°49S 149°17E 153 D8
Hicks Bay N.Z. 37°34S 178°21E 154 D7
Hicks L. Canada 61°25N 100°0W 163 A9
Hicksville U.S.A. 40°46N 73°32W 175 F11
Hicpochee, L. U.S.A. 26°48N 81°9W 179 J8
Hida Romania 47°10N 23°19E 81 C8
Hida-Gawa → Japan 35°26N 137°3E 113 G8
Hida-Sammyaku
Japan 36°30N 137°40E 113 F8
Hidaka Japan 42°30N 142°10E 112 C11
Hidaka-Sammyaku
Japan 42°35N 142°45E 112 C11
Hidalgo □ Mexico 20°30N 99°0W 181 C5
Hidalgo del Parral
Mexico 26°56N 105°40W 180 B3
Hiddensee Germany 54°32N 13°6E 76 A9
Hieflau Austria 47°36N 14°46E 78 D7
Hiendelaencina Spain 41°5N 3°0W 90 D2
Hierapolis-Pamukkale
Turkey 37°55N 29°7E 99 D11
Hierro Canary Is. 27°44N 18°0W 100 G1
Higashiajima-San
Japan 37°40N 140°10E 112 F10
Higashiōsaka Japan 34°39N 135°37E 113 G7
Higgins U.S.A. 36°7N 100°2W 176 C4
Higgins Corner U.S.A. 39°2N 121°5W 170 F5
High Bridge U.S.A. 40°40N 74°54W 175 F10
High Desert U.S.A. 43°40N 120°20W 168 E3
High Island Res. China 22°22N 114°21E 111 a
High Level Canada 58°31N 117°8W 162 B5
High Point U.S.A. 35°57N 80°0W 177 D15
High Prairie Canada 55°30N 116°30W 162 B5
High River Canada 50°30N 113°50W 162 C6
High Springs U.S.A. 29°50N 82°36W 178 F7
High Tatra = Tatry
Slovak Rep. 49°20N 20°0E 79 B13
High Veld Africa 27°0S 27°0E 132 J6
High Wycombe U.K. 51°37N 0°45W 67 F7
Highbank N.Z. 43°37S 171°45E 155 D6
Highland □ U.K. 57°17N 4°21W 65 D4
Highland City U.S.A. 27°58N 81°53W 179 H8
Highland Home U.S.A. 31°57N 86°19W 178 D3
Highland Mills U.S.A. 33°17N 84°17W 178 B5
Highland Park U.S.A. 42°11N 87°48W 172 D10
Highland View U.S.A. 29°50N 85°19W 178 F4
Highmore U.S.A. 44°31N 99°27W 172 C4
Highrock L. Canada 55°45N 100°30W 163 B8
Higüey Dom. Rep. 18°37N 68°42W 183 C6
Hihya Egypt 30°40N 31°36E 137 E7
Hiidenportti △ Finland 63°53N 29°0E 60 E23
Hiiumaa Estonia 58°50N 22°45E 84 C2
Híjar Spain 41°10N 0°27W 90 D4
Ḩijārah, Şaḩrā' al Iraq 30°25N 44°30E 128 D5
Ḩijāz Si. Arabia 24°0N 40°0E 128 E3
Hijo = Tagum Phil. 7°33N 125°53E 119 C7
Hikari Japan 33°58N 131°58E 113 H5
Hikkaduwa Sri Lanka 6°8N 80°6E 127 L5
Hikmak, Ras el Egypt 31°15N 27°51E 137 A2
Hiko U.S.A. 37°32N 115°14W 170 H11
Hikone Japan 35°15N 136°10E 113 G8
Hikurangi Gisborne,
N.Z. 37°55S 178°4E 154 D7
Hikurangi Northland,
N.Z. 35°36S 174°17E 154 B3
Hiland Park U.S.A. 30°12N 85°33W 178 E4
Hildburghausen
Germany 50°25N 10°42E 76 E6
Hildesheim Germany 52°9N 9°56E 76 C5
Hill → Australia 30°23S 115°3E 149 F2
Hill City Idaho, U.S.A. 43°18N 115°3W 168 E6
Hill City Kans., U.S.A. 39°22N 99°51W 172 F4
Hill City Minn., U.S.A. 46°59N 93°36W 172 B7
Hill City S. Dak.,
U.S.A. 43°56N 103°35W 172 D2
Hill Island L. Canada 60°30N 109°50W 163 A7
Hillaby, Mt. Barbados 13°12N 59°35W 183 g
Hillared Sweden 57°37N 13°10E 63 G7
Hillcrest Barbados 13°13N 59°31W 183 g
Hillegom Neths. 52°18N 4°35E 69 B4
Hillerød Denmark 55°56N 12°19E 63 J6
Hillerstorp Sweden 57°20N 13°52E 63 G7
Hilliard U.S.A. 30°41N 81°55W 178 E8
Hillsboro Ga., U.S.A. 33°11N 83°38W 178 B6
Hillsboro Kans., U.S.A. 38°21N 97°12W 172 F5
Hillsboro N. Dak., U.S.A. 47°26N 97°3W 172 B5
Hillsboro Ohio, U.S.A. 39°12N 83°37W 173 F12
Hillsboro Oreg., U.S.A. 45°31N 122°59W 170 E4
Hillsboro Tex., U.S.A. 32°1N 97°8W 176 E6
Hillsboro Canal U.S.A. 26°30N 80°15W 179 J9
Hillsborough Grenada 12°28N 61°28W 183 D7
Hillsborough U.S.A. 43°7N 71°54W 175 C13
Hillsborough Channel
Australia 20°56S 149°15E 150 b
Hillsdale Mich., U.S.A. 41°56N 84°38W 173 E11
Hillsdale N.Y., U.S.A. 42°11N 73°32W 175 D11
Hillsport Canada 49°27N 85°34W 164 C2
Hillston Australia 33°30S 145°31E 153 B6
Hilltonia U.S.A. 32°53N 81°40W 178 C8
Hilo U.S.A. 19°44N 155°5W 167 M8
Hilton U.S.A. 43°17N 77°48W 174 C7
Hilton Head Island
U.S.A. 32°13N 80°45W 178 C9
Hilvan Turkey 37°34N 38°58E 105 D8
Hilversum Neths. 52°14N 5°10E 69 B5
Himachal Pradesh □
India 31°30N 77°0E 124 D7
Himalaya Asia 29°0N 84°0E 125 E11
Himalchuli Nepal 28°27N 84°38E 125 E11
Himarë Albania 40°8N 19°43E 96 F3
Himatnagar India 23°37N 72°57E 124 H5
Himeji Japan 34°50N 134°40E 113 G7
Himi Japan 36°50N 136°55E 113 F8
Himmerland Denmark 56°45N 9°30E 63 H3
Ḩimş Syria 34°40N 36°45E 130 A5
Ḩimş □ Syria 34°30N 37°0E 130 A6
Hin Khom, Laem Thailand 9°25N 99°56E 121 b

Hinche *Haiti* 19°9N 72°1W **183** C5
Hinchinbrook I.
 Australia 18°20S 146°15E **150** B4
Hinchinbrook Island △
 Australia 18°14S 146°6E **150** B4
Hinckley *U.K.* 52°33N 1°22W **67** E6
Hinckley *U.S.A.* 46°1N 92°56E **172** B7
Hindaun *India* 26°44N 77°5E **124** F7
Hindmarsh, L. *Australia* 36°5S 141°55E **152** D4
Hindol *India* 20°40N 85°10E **126** D7
Hinds *N.Z.* 43°59S 171°36E **155** D6
Hindsholm *Denmark* 55°30N 10°40E **63** J4
Hindu Bagh *Pakistan* 30°56N 67°50E **124** D2
Hindu Kush *Asia* 36°0N 71°0E **109** E8
Hindupur *India* 13°49N 77°32E **127** H3
Hines Creek *Canada* 56°20N 118°40W **162** B5
Hinesville *U.S.A.* 31°51N 81°36W **178** D8
Hinganghat *India* 20°30N 78°52E **126** D4
Hingham *U.S.A.* 48°33N 110°25W **168** B8
Hingir *India* 21°57N 83°41E **125** J10
Hingoli *India* 19°41N 77°15E **126** E3
Hinis *Turkey* 39°22N 41°43E **105** C9
Hinna = Imi *Ethiopia* 6°28N 42°10E **131** F3
Hinna *Nigeria* 10°25N 11°35E **139** C7
Hinnerup *Denmark* 56°16N 10°4E **63** H4
Hinnøya *Norway* 68°35S 15°50E **60** B16
Hinojosa del Duque *Spain* 38°30N 5°9W **89** G5
Hinsdale *U.S.A.* 42°47N 72°29W **175** D12
Hinterrhein → *Switz.* 46°40N 9°25E **77** J5
Hinthada = Henzada
 Burma 17°38N 95°26E **123** L19
Hinton *Canada* 53°26N 117°34W **162** C5
Hinton *U.S.A.* 37°40N 80°54W **173** G13
Hios = Chios *Greece* 38°27N 26°9E **99** C8
Hirado *Japan* 33°22N 129°33E **113** H4
Hirakud Dam *India* 21°32N 83°45E **126** D6
Hiran → *India* 23°6N 79°21E **125** H8
Hirapur *India* 24°22N 79°13E **125** G8
Hirara = Miyakojima
 Japan 24°48N 125°17E **113** M2
Hiratsuka *Japan* 35°19N 139°21E **113** G9
Hirekerur *India* 14°28N 75°23E **127** G2
Hirfanlı Barajı *Turkey* 39°18N 33°31E **104** C5
Hirhafok *Algeria* 23°49N 5°45E **136** D5
Hiroo *Japan* 42°17N 143°19E **112** C11
Hirosaki *Japan* 40°34N 140°28E **112** D10
Hiroshima *Japan* 34°24N 132°30E **113** G6
Hiroshima □ *Japan* 34°50N 133°0E **113** G6
Hirson *France* 49°55N 4°4E **71** C11
Hirtshals *Denmark* 57°36N 9°57E **63** G3
Hisar *India* 29°12N 75°45E **124** E6
Hisarcık *Turkey* 39°15N 29°14E **99** B11
Hisaria *Bulgaria* 42°30N 24°44E **97** D8
Hisb, Sha'ib → Ḥasb, W. →
 Iraq 31°45N 44°17E **128** D5
Ḥismā *Si. Arabia* 28°30N 36°0E **128** D3
Hispaniola *W. Indies* 19°0N 71°0W **183** C5
Ḥīt *Iraq* 33°38N 42°49E **105** F10
Hita *Japan* 33°20N 130°58E **113** H5
Hitachi *Japan* 36°36N 140°39E **113** F10
Hitan, W. el *Egypt* 29°19N 30°10E **137** F7
Hitchin *U.K.* 51°58N 0°16W **67** F7
Hitiaa *Tahiti* 17°36S 149°18W **155** b
Hitoyoshi *Japan* 32°13N 130°45E **113** H5
Hitra *Norway* 63°30N 8°45E **60** E13
Hitzacker *Germany* 53°9N 11°2E **76** B7
Hiva Oa
 French Polynesia 9°45S 139°0W **157** H14
Hixon *Canada* 53°25N 122°35W **162** C4
Ḥiyyon, N. → *Israel* 30°25N 35°10E **130** E4
Hjalmar L. *Canada* 61°33N 109°25W **163** A7
Hjälmaren *Sweden* 59°18N 15°40E **62** E9
Hjältevad *Sweden* 57°38N 15°20E **63** G9
Hjo *Sweden* 58°22N 14°17E **63** F8
Hjørring *Denmark* 57°29N 9°59E **63** G3
Hjort Trench *S. Ocean* 58°0S 157°30E **55** B10
Hjortkvarn *Sweden* 58°54N 15°26E **63** F9
Hkakabo Razi *Burma* 28°25N 97°23E **116** C1
Hkamti *Burma* 25°0N 95°39E **123** G19
Hlinsko *Czech Rep.* 49°45N 15°54E **78** B8
Hlobane *S. Africa* 27°42S 31°0E **145** C5
Hlohovec *Slovak Rep.* 48°26N 17°49E **79** C10
Hlučín *Czech Rep.* 49°54N 18°11E **79** B11
Hluhluwe *S. Africa* 28°1S 32°15E **145** C5
Hluhluwe △ *S. Africa* 22°10S 32°5E **145** B5
Hlukhiv *Ukraine* 51°40N 33°58E **85** G7
Hlyboka *Ukraine* 48°5N 25°56E **81** B10
Hlybokaye *Belarus* 55°10N 27°45E **84** E4
Hnúšťa *Slovak Rep.* 48°35N 19°58E **79** C12
Ho *Ghana* 6°37N 0°27E **139** D5
Ho Chi Minh City = Thanh Pho
 Ho Chi Minh
 Vietnam 10°58N 106°40E **121** G6
Ho Hoa Binh *Vietnam* 20°50N 105°0E **116** A5
Ho Thac Ba *Vietnam* 21°42N 105°1E **120** A5
Ho Thuong *Vietnam* 19°32N 105°48E **120** C5
Hoa Binh *Vietnam* 20°50N 105°20E **116** G5
Hoa Hiep *Vietnam* 11°34N 105°51E **121** G5
Hoai Nhon *Vietnam* 14°28N 109°1E **120** E7
Hoang Lien △ *Vietnam* 21°30N 105°32E **120** B5
Hoang Lien Son *Vietnam* 22°0N 104°0E **116** F4
Hoang Sa, Dao = Paracel Is.
 S. China Sea 16°50N 112°0E **118** A4
Hoanib → *Namibia* 19°27S 12°46E **144** A2
Hoare B. *Canada* 65°17N 62°30W **161** D19
Hoarusib → *Namibia* 19°3S 12°48E **144** A2
Hobart *Australia* 42°50S 147°21E **151** G4
Hobart *U.S.A.* 35°1N 99°6W **176** H5
Hobbs *U.S.A.* 32°42N 103°8W **169** K12
Hobbs Coast *Antarctica* 74°50S 131°0W **55** D14
Hobe Sound *U.S.A.* 27°4N 80°8W **179** H9
Hoboken *Ga., U.S.A.* 31°11N 82°8W **178** D7
Hoboken *N.J., U.S.A.* 40°44N 74°3W **175** F10
Hobro *Denmark* 56°39N 9°46E **63** H3
Hoburgen *Sweden* 56°55N 18°7E **63** H12
Hobyo *Somalia* 5°25N 48°30E **131** F4
Hocalar *Turkey* 38°36N 30°0E **99** C12
Hochfeld *Namibia* 21°28S 17°58E **144** B2
Hochharz △ *Germany* 51°48N 10°38E **76** D6
Hochschwab *Austria* 47°35N 15°0E **78** D8
Höchstadt *Germany* 49°42N 10°47E **77** F6
Hochtaunus △ *Germany* 50°20N 8°30E **77** E4
Hodaka-Dake *Japan* 36°17N 137°39E **113** F8
Hodeida = Al Ḥudaydah
 Yemen 14°50N 43°0E **131** E3
Hodgeville *Canada* 50°7N 106°58W **163** C7
Hodgson *Canada* 51°13N 97°36W **163** C9
Hodh El Gharbi □
 Mauritania 16°30N 10°0W **138** B3

Hódmezővásárhely
 Hungary 46°28N 20°22E **80** D5
Hodna, Chott el *Algeria* 35°26N 4°43E **136** A4
Hodonín *Czech Rep.* 48°50N 17°10E **79** C10
Hœdic, Î. de *France* 47°20N 2°53W **70** E4
Hoek van Holland *Neths.* 52°0N 4°7E **69** C4
Hoengseong *S. Korea* 37°29N 127°59E **115** F14
Hoeryong *N. Korea* 42°30N 129°45E **115** C15
Hoeyang *N. Korea* 38°43N 127°36E **115** E14
Hof *Germany* 50°19N 11°55E **77** E7
Hofgeismar *Germany* 51°29N 9°23E **76** D5
Hofheim *Germany* 50°5N 8°26E **77** E4
Hofmeyr *S. Africa* 31°39S 25°50E **144** D4
Höfn *Iceland* 64°15N 15°13W **60** D6
Hofors *Sweden* 60°31N 16°15E **62** D10
Hofsjökull *Iceland* 64°49N 18°48W **60** D4
Hōfu *Japan* 34°3N 131°34E **113** G5
Hogan Group *Australia* 39°13S 147°1E **151** F4
Höganäs *Sweden* 56°12N 12°33E **63** H6
Hogansville *U.S.A.* 33°10N 84°55W **178** B5
Hogarth, Mt. *Australia* 21°48S 136°58E **150** C2
Hoge Kempen △ *Belgium* 51°6N 5°35E **69** C5
Hoge Veluwe △ *Neths.* 52°5N 5°46E **69** B5
Hogenakal Falls *India* 12°6N 77°50E **127** H3
Hoggar = Ahaggar
 Algeria 23°0N 6°30E **136** D5
Högsäter *Sweden* 58°38N 12°5E **63** F6
Høgsby *Sweden* 57°10N 16°1E **63** G10
Högsjö *Sweden* 59°4N 15°44E **62** E9
Hogsty Reef *Bahamas* 21°41N 73°48W **183** B5
Hoh → *U.S.A.* 47°45N 124°29W **172** C2
Hoh Xil Shan *China* 36°30N 89°0E **110** D6
Hohd ech Chargui □
 Mauritania 19°0N 7°15W **138** B3
Hohe Acht *Germany* 50°22N 7°0E **77** E3
Hohe Tauern *Austria* 47°11N 12°40E **78** D5
Hohe Tauern △ *Austria* 47°5N 12°20E **78** D5
Hohenau *Austria* 48°36N 16°55E **79** C9
Hohenems *Austria* 47°22N 9°42E **78** D2
Hohenloher Ebene
 Germany 49°14N 9°36E **77** F5
Hohenwald *U.S.A.* 35°33N 87°33W **177** D11
Hohenwestedt *Germany* 54°5N 9°40E **76** A5
Hoher Rhön = Rhön
 Germany 50°24N 9°58E **76** E5
Hoher Vogelsberg △
 Germany 51°45N 9°35E **76** E5
Hohes Venn *Belgium* 50°30N 6°5E **69** D6
Hohes Venn-Eifel △
 Europe 50°30N 6°10E **76** E2
Hohhot *China* 40°52N 111°40E **114** D6
Hohoe *Ghana* 7°8N 0°32E **139** D5
Hoi An *Vietnam* 15°53N 108°19E **120** E7
Hoi Xuan *Vietnam* 20°25N 105°9E **116** G5
Hoisington *U.S.A.* 38°31N 98°47W **172** F4
Hojambaz *Turkmenistan* 38°7N 65°50E **108** E6
Højer *Denmark* 54°58N 8°42E **63** K2
Hōjō *Japan* 33°58N 132°46E **113** H6
Hok *Sweden* 57°31N 14°16E **63** G8
Hökensås *Sweden* 58°0N 14°5E **63** G8
Hökerum *Sweden* 57°51N 13°16E **63** G7
Hokianga Harbour
 N.Z. 35°31S 173°22E **154** B2
Hokitika *N.Z.* 42°42S 171°0E **155** C6
Hokkaidō □ *Japan* 43°30N 143°0E **112** C11
Hokuto *Japan* 41°49N 140°39E **112** D10
Hola *Kenya* 1°29S 40°2E **142** B4
Hola Prystan *Ukraine* 46°29N 32°32E **85** J7
Holakas *Greece* 35°57N 27°53E **101** D9
Holalkere *India* 14°2N 76°11E **127** G3
Holašovice *Czech Rep.* 48°57N 14°15E **78** C7
Holbæk *Denmark* 55°43N 11°43E **63** J5
Holbrook *Australia* 35°42S 147°18E **153** C7
Holbrook *U.S.A.* 34°54N 110°10W **169** J8
Holcomb *U.S.A.* 42°54N 77°25W **174** D7
Holden *U.S.A.* 39°6N 112°16W **168** G7
Holdenville *U.S.A.* 35°5N 96°24W **176** D6
Holdich *Argentina* 45°57S 68°13W **192** C3
Holdrege *U.S.A.* 40°26N 99°23W **172** E4
Hole-Narsipur *India* 12°48N 76°16E **127** H3
Holešov *Czech Rep.* 49°20N 17°35E **79** B10
Holetown *Barbados* 13°11N 59°38W **183** g
Holguín *Cuba* 20°50N 76°20W **182** B4
Holič *Slovak Rep.* 48°49N 17°10E **79** C10
Holice *Czech Rep.* 50°5N 16°0E **78** A8
Höljes *Sweden* 60°54N 12°35E **62** D6
Hollabrunn *Austria* 48°34N 16°5E **78** C9
Hollams Bird I. *Namibia* 24°40S 14°30E **144** B1
Holland = Netherlands ■
 Europe 52°0N 5°30E **69** C5
Holland *Mich., U.S.A.* 42°47N 86°7W **172** D10
Holland *N.Y., U.S.A.* 42°38N 78°32W **174** D6
Holland Centre *Canada* 44°23N 80°47W **174** B4
Holland Patent *U.S.A.* 43°14N 75°15W **175** C9
Hollandale *U.S.A.* 33°10N 90°51W **177** E9
Holley *U.S.A.* 43°14N 78°2W **174** C6
Hollfeld *Germany* 49°56N 11°18E **77** F7
Hollidaysburg *U.S.A.* 40°26N 78°24W **174** E6
Hollis *U.S.A.* 34°41N 99°55W **176** D5
Hollister *Calif., U.S.A.* 36°51N 121°24W **170** J5
Hollister *Idaho, U.S.A.* 42°21N 114°35W **168** E6
Höllviken *Sweden* 55°25N 12°58E **63** J6
Höllviksnäs = Höllviken
 Sweden 55°25N 12°58E **63** J6
Holly Hill *Fla., U.S.A.* 29°16N 81°3W **179** F9
Holly Hill *S.C., U.S.A.* 33°19N 80°25W **178** B9
Holly Springs *Ga.,
 U.S.A.* 34°10N 84°30W **178** A5
Holly Springs *Miss.,
 U.S.A.* 34°46N 89°27W **177** D10
Hollywood *Ireland* 53°6N 6°35W **64** B6
Hollywood *U.S.A.* 26°0N 80°8W **179** J9
Holman *Canada* 70°44N 117°44W **160** C8
Hólmavík *Iceland* 65°42N 21°40W **60** D3
Holmen *U.S.A.* 43°58N 91°15W **172** C8
Holmes Beach *U.S.A.* 27°31N 82°43W **179** H7
Holmes Cr. → *U.S.A.* 34°23N 121°42W **170** b
Holmes Reefs *Australia* 16°27S 148°0E **150** B4
Holmsjö *Sweden* 56°25N 15°32E **63** H9
Holmön *Västernorrland,
 Sweden* 62°41N 16°33E **62** B10
Holmsjön *Västernorrland,
 Sweden* 62°26N 15°20E **62** B9
Holmsund *Sweden* 63°41N 20°20E **62** B11
Holod *Romania* 46°49N 22°8E **80** D7
Holon *Israel* 32°0N 34°44E **130** C3
Hołopaw *U.S.A.* 28°8N 81°5W **179** G8
Holovne *Ukraine* 51°30N 24°5E **81** A10
Holovyntsi *Ukraine* ...
Holozubyntsi *Ukraine* 48°50N 26°55E **81** B11

Holroyd → *Australia* 14°10S 141°36E **150** A3
Holstebro *Denmark* 56°22N 8°37E **63** H2
Holsteinische Schweiz ○
 Germany 54°8N 10°30E **76** A6
Holsteinsborg = Sisimiut
 Greenland 66°40N 53°30W **57** D5
Holsworthy *U.K.* 50°48N 4°22W **67** G3
Holt *U.S.A.* 30°43N 86°45W **179** E3
Holton *Canada* 54°31N 57°12W **165** B8
Holton *U.S.A.* 39°28N 95°44W **172** E6
Holtville *U.S.A.* 32°49N 115°23W **171** N11
Holwerd *Neths.* 53°22N 5°54E **69** A5
Holy Cross *U.S.A.* 62°12N 159°46W **166** C8
Holy I. *Anglesey, U.K.* 53°17N 4°37W **66** D3
Holy I. *Northumberland,
 U.K.* 55°40N 1°47W **66** B6
Holyhead *U.K.* 53°18N 4°38W **66** D3
Holyoke *Colo., U.S.A.* 40°35N 102°18W **168** F12
Holyoke *Mass., U.S.A.* 42°12N 72°37W **175** D12
Holyrood *Canada* 47°27N 53°8W **165** C9
Holzkirchen *Germany* 47°52N 11°42E **77** H7
Holzminden *Germany* 51°50N 9°28E **76** D5
Homa Bay *Kenya* 0°36S 34°30E **142** C3
Homalin *Burma* 24°55N 95°0E **123** G19
Homand *Iran* 32°28N 59°37E **129** C8
Homathko → *Canada* 51°0N 124°56W **162** C4
Homberg *Germany* 51°2N 9°25E **76** D5
Hombori *Mali* 15°20N 1°38W **139** C4
Hombori Tondo *Mali* 15°16N 1°40W **139** B4
Homburg *Germany* 49°28N 7°18E **77** F3
Home B. *Canada* 68°40N 67°10W **161** D18
Home Hill *Australia* 19°43S 147°25E **150** B4
Homedale *U.S.A.* 43°37N 116°56W **168** E5
Homeland *U.S.A.* 30°51N 82°1W **178** E7
Homer *Alaska, U.S.A.* 59°39N 151°33W **160** F1
Homer *La., U.S.A.* 32°48N 93°4W **176** E8
Homer *N.Y., U.S.A.* 42°38N 76°10W **175** D8
Homer City *U.S.A.* 40°32N 79°10W **174** F5
Homert → *Germany* 51°15N 8°0E **76** D4
Homerville *U.S.A.* 31°2N 82°45W **178** D7
Homestead *Australia* 20°20S 145°40E **150** C4
Homestead *U.S.A.* 25°28N 80°29W **179** K9
Homestead △ *U.S.A.* 40°17N 96°50W **172** E5
Homnabad *India* 17°45N 77°11E **126** F3
Homoine *Mozam.* 23°55S 35°8E **145** B6
Homoljske Planina
 Serbia 44°10N 21°45E **96** B5
Homorod *Romania* 46°5N 25°15E **81** D10
Homosassa Springs
 U.S.A. 28°48N 82°35W **179** G7
Homs = Ḥimṣ *Syria* 34°40N 36°45E **130** A5
Homyel *Belarus* 52°28N 31°0E **75** B16
Homyel □ *Belarus* 52°40N 30°10E **85** F6
Hon Chong *Vietnam* 10°25N 104°30E **121** G5
Hon Hai *Vietnam* 10°0N 109°0E **121** H7
Hon Me *Vietnam* 19°23N 105°56E **120** C5
Honan = Henan □
 China 34°0N 114°0E **114** H8
Honavar *India* 14°17N 74°27E **127** G2
Honaz *Turkey* 37°46N 29°18E **99** D11
Honbetsu *Japan* 43°7N 143°37E **112** C11
Honcut *U.S.A.* 39°20N 121°32W **170** F5
Hondarribia *Spain* 43°22N 1°47W **90** B3
Hondeklipbaai *S. Africa* 30°19S 17°17E **144** D2
Hondo *Japan* 32°27N 130°8E **113** H4
Hondo *U.S.A.* 29°21N 99°9W **176** G5
Hondo, Río → *Belize* 18°25N 88°21W **181** D7
Honduras ■
 Cent. Amer. 14°40N 86°30W **182** D2
Honduras, G. de
 Caribbean 16°50N 87°0W **182** C2
Hønefoss *Norway* 60°10N 10°18E **61** F14
Honesdale *U.S.A.* 41°34N 75°16W **175** E9
Honey Harbour
 Canada 44°52N 79°49W **174** B5
Honey L. *U.S.A.* 40°15N 120°19W **170** E6
Honfleur *France* 49°25N 0°13E **70** C7
Høng *Denmark* 55°31N 11°18E **63** J5
Hong → *Vietnam* 20°16N 106°34E **120** B5
Hong Gai *Vietnam* 20°57N 107°5E **116** G6
Hong He → *China* 32°25N 115°35E **116** A5
Hong Hu → *China* 29°54N 113°24E **117** C9
Hong Kong □ *China* 22°11N 114°14E **111** a
Hong Kong I. *China* 22°16N 114°12E **111** a
Hong Kong Int. ✈ (HKG)
 China 22°19N 113°57E **111** a
Hong'an *China* 31°20N 114°40E **117** B10
Hongcheon *S. Korea* 37°44N 127°53E **115** F14
Honghai Wan *China* 22°40N 115°0E **117** F10
Honghe *China* 23°25N 102°25E **116** F4
Honghu *China* 29°50N 113°0E **117** C9
Hongjiang *China* 27°7N 109°59E **116** D7
Hongliu He → *China* 38°0N 109°50E **114** F5
Hongor *Mongolia* 45°45N 112°50E **114** B7
Hongseong *S. Korea* 36°37N 126°38E **115** F14
Hongshan *China* 23°38N 117°58E **115** F9
Hongshui He →
 China 23°48N 109°30E **116** F7
Hongtong *China* 36°16N 111°40E **116** D6
Honguedo, Détroit d'
 Canada 49°15N 64°0W **165** C7
Hongwon *N. Korea* 40°0N 127°56E **115** E14
Hongya *China* 29°57N 103°2E **116** C4
Hongyuan *China* 32°51N 102°40E **116** A4
Hongze Hu *China* 33°15N 118°35E **115** H10
Honiara *Solomon Is.* 9°27S 159°57E **147** B8
Honiton *U.K.* 50°47N 3°11W **67** G4
Honjō = Yurihonjō
 Japan 39°23N 140°3E **112** E10
Honkorâb, Ras *Egypt* 24°35N 35°10E **137** C4
Honnali *India* 14°15N 75°40E **127** G2
Honningsvåg *Norway* 70°59N 25°59E **60** A21
Honö *Sweden* 57°41N 11°39E **63** G5
Honolulu *U.S.A.* 21°19N 157°52W **167** L8
Honshū *Japan* 36°0N 138°0E **113** F9
Hontoria del Pinar *Spain* 41°50N 3°10W **90** D1
Hood, Mt. *U.S.A.* 45°23N 121°42W **168** D3
Hood, Pt. *Australia* 34°23S 119°34E **149** F2
Hood River *U.S.A.* 45°43N 121°31W **168** D3
Hoodsport *U.S.A.* 47°24N 123°9W **172** C2
Hooge *Germany* 54°34N 8°33E **76** A4
Hoogeveen *Neths.* 52°44N 6°28E **69** B6
Hoogezand-Sappemeer
 Neths. 53°9N 6°45E **69** A6
Hooghly = Hugli →
 India 21°56N 88°4E **125** J13
Hooghly-Chinsura = Chunchura
 India 22°53N 88°27E **125** H13
Hook Hd. *Ireland* 52°7N 6°56W **64** D5
Hook I. *Australia* 20°4S 149°0E **150** b

Hook of Holland = Hoek van
 Holland *Neths.* 52°0N 4°7E **69** C4
Hooker *U.S.A.* 36°52N 101°13W **176** C4
Hooker Creek = Lajamanu
 Australia 18°23S 130°38E **148** C5
Hooker Creek ○
 Australia 18°6S 130°23E **148** C5
Hoonah *U.S.A.* 58°7N 135°27W **162** B1
Hooper Bay *U.S.A.* 61°32N 166°6W **166** C6
Hoopeston *U.S.A.* 40°28N 87°40W **172** E10
Hoopstad *S. Africa* 27°50S 25°55E **144** C4
Höör *Sweden* 55°56N 13°33E **63** J7
Hoorn *Neths.* 52°38N 5°4E **69** B5
Hoover *U.S.A.* 33°24N 86°49W **177** E11
Hoover Dam *U.S.A.* 36°1N 114°44W **171** K12
Hooversville *U.S.A.* 40°9N 78°55W **174** F6
Hop Bottom *U.S.A.* 41°42N 75°46W **175** E9
Hopa *Turkey* 41°28N 41°30E **105** B9
Hope *Canada* 49°25N 121°25W **162** D4
Hope *Ariz., U.S.A.* 33°43N 113°42W **171** M13
Hope *Ark., U.S.A.* 33°40N 93°36W **176** E8
Hope, L. *S. Austral.,
 Australia* 28°24S 139°18E **151** D2
Hope, L. *W. Austral.,
 Australia* 32°35S 120°15E **149** F3
Hope, Pt. *U.S.A.* 68°21N 166°47W **158** C3
Hope I. *Canada* 44°55N 80°11W **174** B4
Hope Town *Bahamas* 26°35N 76°57W **182** A4
Hope Vale *Australia* 15°16S 145°20E **150** B4
Hope Vale ○ *Australia* 15°16S 145°20E **150** B4
Hopedale *Canada* 55°28N 60°13W **165** A7
Hopedale *U.S.A.* 42°8N 71°33W **175** D13
Hopefield *S. Africa* 33°3S 18°22E **144** D2
Hopei = Hebei □ *China* 39°0N 116°0E **114** E9
Hopelchén *Mexico* 19°46N 89°51W **181** D7
Hopetoun *Vic.,
 Australia* 35°42S 142°22E **152** C5
Hopetoun *W. Austral.,
 Australia* 33°57S 120°7E **149** F3
Hopetown *S. Africa* 29°34S 24°3E **144** C3
Hopewell *U.S.A.* 37°18N 77°17W **173** G15
Hopfgarten *Austria* 47°27N 12°10E **78** D5
Hopkins, L. *Australia* 24°15S 128°35E **148** D4
Hopkinsville *U.S.A.* 36°52N 87°29W **172** G10
Hopland *U.S.A.* 38°58N 123°7W **170** G3
Hora Hoverla *Ukraine* 48°7N 24°41E **81** B9
Horana *Sri Lanka* 6°43N 80°4E **127** L5
Horasan *Turkey* 40°3N 42°11E **105** B10
Horažďovice *Czech Rep.* 49°19N 13°42E **78** B6
Horb *Germany* 48°26N 8°47E **77** G4
Hörby *Sweden* 55°51N 13°40E **63** J7
Horcajo de Santiago *Spain* 39°50N 3°1W **90** F1
Hordern Hills *Australia* 20°15S 130°18E **148** D5
Horezu *Romania* 45°6N 24°0E **81** E8
Horgen *Switz.* 47°15N 8°35E **77** H4
Horgoš *Serbia* 46°10N 20°0E **80** D4
Hořice *Czech Rep.* 50°21N 15°39E **78** A8
Horincheve *Ukraine* 48°16N 23°26E **81** B8
Horinger *China* 40°28N 111°48E **114** D6
Horizontina *Brazil* 27°37S 54°19W **191** B5
Horki *Belarus* 54°17N 30°59E **84** E6
Horlick Mts. *Antarctica* 84°0S 102°0W **55** E15
Horlivka *Ukraine* 48°19N 38°5E **85** H10
Hormak *Iran* 29°58N 60°51E **129** D9
Hormoz *Iran* 27°35N 55°0E **129** E7
Hormoz, Jaz.-ye *Iran* 27°30N 56°0E **129** E8
Hormozgān □ *Iran* 27°30N 56°0E **129** E8
Hormuz, Str. of *The Gulf* 26°30N 56°30E **129** E8
Horn *Austria* 48°39N 15°40E **78** C8
Horn *Sweden* 57°54N 15°51E **63** G9
Horn → *Canada* 61°30N 118°1W **162** A5
Horn, Cape = Hornos, C. de
 Chile 55°50S 67°30W **192** E3
Horn Head *Ireland* 55°14N 8°0W **64** A3
Horn I. *Australia* 10°37S 142°17E **150** A3
Horn Plateau *Canada* 62°15N 119°15W **162** A5
Hornachuelos *Spain* 37°50N 5°14W **89** H5
Hornavan *Sweden* 66°15N 17°30E **60** C17
Hornbeck *U.S.A.* 31°20N 93°24W **176** F8
Hornbrook *U.S.A.* 41°55N 122°33W **168** F2
Hornburg *Germany* 52°2N 10°37E **76** C6
Hornby *N.Z.* 43°33S 172°33E **155** D7
Horncastle *U.K.* 53°13N 0°7W **66** D7
Horndal *Sweden* 60°18N 16°23E **62** D10
Hornell *U.S.A.* 42°20N 77°40W **174** D7
Hornell L. *Canada* 62°20N 119°25W **162** A5
Hornepayne *Canada* 49°14N 84°48W **164** C3
Horní Planá *Czech Rep.* 48°46N 14°2E **78** C7
Hornings Mills *Canada* 44°9N 80°12W **174** B4
Hornitos *U.S.A.* 37°30N 120°14W **170** H6
Hornopirén △ *Chile* 41°58S 72°17W **192** B2
Hornos, C. de *Chile* 55°50S 67°30W **192** E3
Hornoy-le-Bourg *France* 49°50N 1°54E **71** C8
Hornsby *Australia* 33°42S 151°2E **153** B9
Hornsea *U.K.* 53°55N 0°11W **66** D7
Hornslandet *Sweden* 61°35N 17°37E **62** C11
Hörnum *Germany* 54°45N 8°17E **76** A4
Horobetsu = Noboribetsu
 Japan 42°24N 141°6E **112** C10
Horodenka *Ukraine* 48°41N 25°29E **81** B10
Horodnya *Ukraine* 51°55N 31°33E **85** G6
Horodok *Khmelnytskyy,
 Ukraine* 49°10N 26°34E **75** D14
Horodok *Lviv, Ukraine* 49°46N 23°32E **75** D12
Horodyshche *Ukraine* 49°17N 31°27E **85** H6
Horokhiv *Ukraine* 50°30N 24°45E **75** D13
Horovice *Czech Rep.* 49°48N 13°53E **78** B6
Horqin Youyi Qianqi
 China 46°5N 122°3E **115** A12
Horqin Zuoyi Zhongqi
 China 44°8N 123°18E **115** B12
Horqueta *Paraguay* 23°15S 56°55W **190** A4
Horred *Sweden* 57°22N 12°28E **63** G6
Horse Cr. → *U.S.A.* 41°57N 103°58W **168** E12
Horse I. *Canada* 53°20N 99°6W **163** C9
Horse Is. *Canada* 50°15N 55°50W **165** B8
Horsefly L. *Canada* 52°25N 121°0W **162** C4
Horseheads *U.S.A.* 42°10N 76°49W **174** D8
Horsens *Denmark* 55°52N 9°51E **63** J3
Horseshoe Bend ○
 U.S.A. 32°59N 85°44W **178** C6
Horseshoe Lake
 Canada 45°38N 79°51W **174** A6
Horsham *Australia* 36°44S 142°13E **152** D5
Horsham *U.K.* 51°4N 0°20W **67** F7
Horšovský Týn
 Czech Rep. 49°31N 12°58E **78** B5
Horta *Azores* 38°32N 28°38W **134** a
Horten *Norway* 59°25N 10°32E **61** G14

Hortense *U.S.A.* 31°20N 81°57W **178** D8
Horti *India* 17°7N 75°47E **126** F2
Hortobágy → *Hungary* 47°30N 21°6E **80** C6
Hortobágyi △ *Hungary* 47°36N 21°10E **80** C6
Horton *U.S.A.* 39°40N 95°32W **172** F6
Horton → *Canada* 69°56N 126°52W **160** C6
Horwood L. *Canada* 48°5N 82°20W **164** C3
Hosapete = Hospet
 India 15°15N 76°20E **127** G3
Hosdrug = Kanhangad
 India 12°21N 74°58E **127** H2
Hoshangabad *India* 22°45N 77°45E **124** H6
Hoshiarpur *India* 31°30N 75°58E **124** D6
Hoskote *India* 13°4N 77°48E **127** G3
Hospet *India* 15°15N 76°20E **127** G3
Hossegor *France* 43°39N 1°25W **72** E2
Hoste, I. *Chile* 55°0S 69°0W **192** E3
Hostens *France* 44°30N 0°40W **72** D3
Hosur *India* 12°43N 77°49E **127** H3
Hot *Thailand* 18°8N 98°29E **120** C2
Hot Creek Range
 U.S.A. 38°40N 116°20W **168** G5
Hot Springs *Ark., U.S.A.* 34°31N 93°3W **176** D8
Hot Springs *S. Dak.,
 U.S.A.* 43°26N 103°29W **172** D2
Hot Springs △ *U.S.A.* 34°31N 93°3W **176** D8
Hotagen *Sweden* 63°59N 14°12E **60** E16
Hotan *China* 37°25N 79°55E **109** E9
Hotan He → *China* 40°22N 80°56E **109** D10
Hotazel *S. Africa* 27°17S 22°58E **144** C3
Hotchkiss *U.S.A.* 38°48N 107°43W **168** G10
Hotham, C. *Australia* 12°2S 131°18E **148** B5
Hoting *Sweden* 64°8N 16°15E **60** D17
Hotolisht *Albania* 41°10N 20°25E **96** E4
Hotspur Seamount
 Atl. Oc. 17°55S 35°55W **56** H8
Hotte, Massif de la
 Haiti 18°30N 73°45W **183** C5
Hottentotsbaai *Namibia* 26°8S 14°59E **144** C1
Hou Hai *China* 22°32N 113°56E **111** a
Houat, Î. de *France* 47°24N 2°58W **70** E4
Houdan *France* 48°48N 1°35E **71** D8
Houei Sai *Laos* 20°18N 100°26E **116** B3
Houeillès *France* 44°12N 0°2E **72** D4
Houffalize *Belgium* 50°8N 5°48E **69** D5
Houghton *Mich., U.S.A.* 47°7N 88°34W **172** B9
Houghton *N.Y., U.S.A.* 42°25N 78°10W **174** D6
Houghton L. *U.S.A.* 44°21N 84°44W **173** C11
Houghton-le-Spring
 U.K. 54°51N 1°28W **66** C6
Houhora Heads *N.Z.* 34°49S 173°9E **154** A2
Houlton *U.S.A.* 46°8N 67°51W **173** B20
Houma *China* 35°36N 111°20E **114** G6
Houma *U.S.A.* 29°36N 90°43W **177** G9
Houndé *Burkina Faso* 11°34N 3°31W **138** C4
Hourtin *France* 45°11N 1°4W **72** C2
Hourtin-Carcans, L. d'
 France 45°10N 1°6W **72** C2
Housatonic → *U.S.A.* 41°10N 73°7W **175** E11
Houston *Canada* 54°25N 126°39W **162** C3
Houston *Fla., U.S.A.* 30°15N 82°54W **178** E7
Houston *Mo., U.S.A.* 37°22N 91°58W **172** G8
Houston *Tex., U.S.A.* 29°45N 95°21W **176** G7
Hout = Mogwadi →
 S. Africa 23°4S 29°36E **145** B4
Houtkraal *S. Africa* 30°23S 24°5E **144** D3
Houtman Abrolhos
 Australia 28°43S 113°48E **149** E1
Hovd = Dund-Us
 Mongolia 48°1N 91°38E **109** C12
Hovd □ *Mongolia* 48°2N 91°37E **109** C12
Hove *U.K.* 50°50N 0°10W **67** G7
Hovedstaden □ *Denmark* 56°0N 10°0E **63** J6
Hovenweep △ *U.S.A.* 37°20N 109°0W **169** H9
Hoveyzeh *Iran* 31°27N 48°4E **129** D6
Hovgaard Ø *Greenland* 79°55N 18°50W **57** B9
Hovmantorp *Sweden* 56°47N 15°7E **63** H9
Hövsgöl *Mongolia* 43°37N 109°39E **114** C5
Hövsgöl Nuur *Mongolia* 51°0N 100°30E **110** A9
Hovsta *Sweden* 59°22N 15°15E **62** E9
Howar, Wadi → *Sudan* 17°30N 27°8E **135** E11
Howard *Australia* 25°16S 152°32E **151** D5
Howard *Pa., U.S.A.* 41°1N 77°40W **174** E7
Howard *S. Dak., U.S.A.* 44°1N 97°32W **172** C5
Howe *U.S.A.* 43°48N 113°0W **168** E7
Howe, C. *Australia* 37°30S 150°0E **153** C9
Howe, West Cape
 Australia 35°8S 117°36E **149** G2
Howe I. *Canada* 44°16N 76°17W **175** C8
Howell *U.S.A.* 42°36N 83°56W **173** D12
Howick *Canada* 45°11N 73°51W **175** A11
Howick *N.Z.* 36°54S 174°56E **154** a
Howick *S. Africa* 29°28S 30°14E **145** C5
Howick Group
 Australia 14°20S 145°30E **150** A4
Howitt, L. *Australia* 27°40S 138°40E **151** D2
Howland I. *Pac. Oc.* 0°48N 176°38W **156** G10
Howlong *Australia* 35°59S 146°38E **153** C7
Howrah = Haora
 India 22°34N 88°18E **125** H13
Howth *Ireland* 53°23N 6°7W **64** C5
Howth Hd. *Ireland* 53°22N 6°4W **64** C5
Höxter *Germany* 51°46N 9°22E **76** D5
Hoxtolgay *China* 46°35N 85°59E **109** C11
Hoxud *China* 42°5N 86°51E **109** D11
Hoy *U.K.* 58°50N 3°15W **65** C5
Hoya *Germany* 52°48N 9°7E **76** C5
Høyanger *Norway* 61°13N 6°4E **60** F12
Hoyerswerda *Germany* 51°26N 14°14E **76** D10
Hoylake *U.K.* 53°24N 3°10W **66** D4
Hoyos *Spain* 40°9N 6°45W **89** E4
Hpa-an = Pa-an
 Burma 16°51N 97°40E **123** L20
Hpunan Pass *Asia* 27°30N 96°55E **123** F20
Hpyu = Pyu *Burma* 18°30N 96°28E **123** K20
Hradec Králové
 Czech Rep. 50°15N 15°50E **78** A8
Hrádek *Czech Rep.* 48°46N 16°16E **79** C9
Hranice *Czech Rep.* 49°34N 17°45E **79** B10
Hrazdan *Armenia* 40°30N 44°46E **87** K7
Hrebenka *Ukraine* 50°9N 32°22E **85** G7
Hrisoupoli = Chrisoupoli
 Greece 40°58N 24°42E **97** F8
Hrodna *Belarus* 53°20N 23°52E **82** E10

Hrodna □ *Belarus* 53°20N 24°45E **84** F3
Hrodzyanka *Belarus* 53°31N 28°42E **75** D15
Hron → *Slovak Rep.* 47°49N 18°45E **79** D11
Hrubieszów *Poland* 50°49N 23°51E **83** H10
Hrubý Jeseník *Czech Rep.* 50°5N 17°10E **79** A10
Hrvatska = Croatia ■
 Europe 45°20N 16°0E **93** C13
Hrymayliv *Ukraine* 49°20N 26°5E **81** B10
Hrynyava *Ukraine* 47°59N 24°53E **81** C9
Hsenwi *Burma* 23°22N 97°55E **123** H20
Hsiamen = Xiamen
 China 24°25N 118°4E **117** E12
Hsian = Xi'an *China* 34°15N 109°0E **114** G5
Hsinhailien = Lianyungang
 China 34°40N 119°11E **115** G10
Hsinchu *Taiwan* 24°48N 120°58E **117** E13
Hsinkai = Bhamo
 Burma 24°15N 97°15E **123** G20
Hsinying *Taiwan* 23°10N 120°18E **117** F13
Hsopket *Burma* 23°11N 98°26E **116** F2
Hsüchou = Xuzhou
 China 34°18N 117°10E **115** G9
Htawei = Tavoy *Burma* 14°2N 98°12E **120** E2
Hu Xian *China* 34°8N 108°42E **114** G5
Hua Hin *Thailand* 12°34N 99°58E **120** F2
Hua Muang *Laos* 20°13N 103°52E **120** B4
Hua Shan *China* 34°28N 110°4E **114** G6
Hua Xian *Henan, China* 35°30N 114°30E **114** G8
Hua Xian *Shaanxi,
 China* 34°30N 109°48E **114** G5
Hua'an *China* 25°1N 117°32E **117** E11
Huab → *Namibia* 20°52S 13°26E **144** A2
Huacheng *China* 24°4N 115°37E **117** E10
Huachinera *Mexico* 30°9N 108°55W **180** A3
Huacho *Peru* 11°10S 77°35W **188** C2
Huachón *Peru* 10°35S 76°0W **188** C2
Huade *China* 41°55N 113°59E **114** D7
Huadian *China* 43°0N 126°40E **115** C14
Huadu *China* 23°22N 113°12E **117** F9
Huahine, Î.
 French Polynesia 16°46S 150°58W **157** J12
Huai Hat △ *Thailand* 16°52N 104°17E **120** D5
Huai Kha Khaeng ○
 Thailand 15°20N 98°55E **120** E2
Huai Nam Dang △
 Thailand 19°30N 98°30E **120** C2
Huai Yot *Thailand* 7°45N 99°37E **121** J2
Huai'an *Hebei, China* 40°30N 114°20E **114** D8
Huai'an *Jiangsu,
 China* 33°30N 119°10E **115** H10
Huaibei *China* 33°10N 116°48E **117** H11
Huaide = Gongzhuling
 China 43°30N 124°40E **115** C13
Huaidezhen *China* 43°48N 124°50E **115** C13
Huaihua *China* 27°32N 109°57E **116** D7
Huaiji *China* 23°55N 112°12E **117** F9
Huainan *China* 32°38N 116°58E **117** A11
Huaining *China* 30°24N 116°46E **117** B11
Huairen *China* 39°48N 113°20E **114** E7
Huairou *China* 40°20N 116°35E **114** D9
Huaiyang *China* 33°40N 114°52E **114** H8
Huaiyin *China* 33°30N 119°2E **115** H10
Huaiyuan *Anhui,
 China* 32°55N 117°10E **117** A11
Huaiyuan *Guangxi Zhuangzu,
 China* 24°31N 108°22E **116** E7
Huajuapán de León
 Mexico 17°48N 97°46W **181** D5
Hualapai Peak *U.S.A.* 35°5N 113°54W **171** K13
Hualian *Taiwan* 23°59N 121°36E **117** F13
Huallaga → *Peru* 5°15S 75°30W **188** B2
Huallanca *Peru* 8°50S 77°56W **188** B2
Huamachuco *Peru* 7°50S 78°5W **188** B2
Huambo *Angola* 12°42S 15°54E **141** G3
Huan Jiang → *China* 34°28N 109°0E **114** G5
Huan Xian *China* 36°33N 107°0E **114** F4
Huancabamba *Peru* 5°10S 79°15W **188** B2
Huancane *Peru* 15°10S 69°44W **188** D4
Huancapi *Peru* 13°40S 74°0W **188** C3
Huancavelica *Peru* 12°50S 75°5W **188** C2
Huancavelica □ *Peru* 13°0S 75°0W **188** C2
Huancayo *Peru* 12°5S 75°12W **188** C2
Huanchaca *Bolivia* 20°15S 66°40W **188** H5
Huang Hai = Yellow Sea
 China 35°0N 123°0E **115** G12
Huang He → *China* 37°55N 118°50E **115** F10
Huang Xian *China* 37°38N 120°30E **115** F11
Huangchuan *China* 32°15N 115°10E **117** A10
Huangdao *China* 36°0N 120°7E **115** F11
Huanggang *China* 30°29N 114°52E **117** B10
Huanghua *China* 38°22N 117°20E **115** E9
Huangling *China* 35°34N 109°15E **114** G5
Huanglong *China* 35°30N 109°59E **114** G5
Huanglongtan *China* 32°44N 110°53E **116** A7
Huangmei *China* 30°5N 115°56E **117** B10
Huangpi *China* 30°50N 114°22E **117** B10
Huangping *China* 26°54N 107°48E **116** D6
Huangshan *Anhui,
 China* 30°8N 118°9E **117** B12
Huangshan *Anhui,
 China* 29°42N 118°25E **117** C12
Huangshi *China* 30°10N 115°3E **117** B10
Huangsongdian
 China 43°45N 127°25E **115** C14
Huangyan *China* 28°38N 121°19E **117** C13
Huangyangsi *China* 26°31N 111°39E **117** D8
Huaning *China* 24°17N 102°56E **116** E4
Huanjiang *China* 24°43N 108°18E **116** E7
Huanren *China* 41°23N 125°20E **115** D13
Huanta *Peru* 12°55S 74°20W **188** C3
Huántai *China* 36°58N 117°56E **115** F9
Huánuco *Peru* 9°55S 76°15W **188** B2
Huánuco □ *Peru* 9°55S 76°15W **188** B2
Huaping *China* 26°46N 101°25E **116** D3
Huara *Chile* 19°59S 69°47W **188** D3
Huaral *Peru* 11°32S 77°11W **188** C2
Huaraz *Peru* 9°30S 77°32W **188** B2
Huari *Peru* 9°14S 77°10W **188** B2
Huarmey *Peru* 10°5S 78°5W **188** C2
Huarochiri *Peru* 12°26S 76°15W **188** C2
Huarong *China* 29°29N 112°30E **117** C9
Huascarán, Nevado *Peru* 9°7S 77°37W **188** B2

Huasco Chile　28°30S 71°15W **190** B1
Huasco → Chile　28°27S 71°13W **190** B1
Huasna U.S.A.　35°6N 120°24W **171** K6
Huatabampo Mexico　26°50N 109°38W **180** B3
Huauchinango Mexico　20°12N 98°3W **181** C5
Huautla de Jiménez
　Mexico　18°8N 96°51W **181** D5
Huaxi China　26°25N 106°40E **116** D6
Huayin China　34°35N 110°5E **114** G6
Huaying China　30°8N 106°44E **116** B6
Huayllay Peru　11°3S 76°21W **188** C2
Huayuan China　28°33N 109°29E **116** C7
Huazhou China　21°33N 110°33E **117** G8
Hubballi = Hubli India　15°22N 75°15E **127** G2
Hubbard Ohio, U.S.A.　41°9N 80°34W **174** E4
Hubbard Tex., U.S.A.　31°51N 96°48W **176** F6
Hubbard Glacier
　Canada　60°18N 139°22W **160** E4
Hubbart Pt. Canada　59°21N 94°41W **163** B10
Hubei □ China　31°0N 112°0E **117** B9
Hubli India　15°22N 75°15E **127** G2
Huch'ang N. Korea　41°25N 127°2E **115** D14
Hucknall U.K.　53°3N 1°13W **66** D6
Huddersfield U.K.　53°39N 1°47W **66** D6
Huddinge Sweden　59°14N 18°0E **62** E12
Hude Germany　53°7N 8°26E **76** B4
Hudiksvall Sweden　61°43N 17°10E **62** C11
Hudson Canada　50°6N 92°9W **164** B1
Hudson Fla., U.S.A.　28°22N 82°42W **179** D7
Hudson Mass., U.S.A.　42°23N 71°34W **175** D13
Hudson N.Y., U.S.A.　42°15N 73°46W **175** D11
Hudson Wis., U.S.A.　44°58N 92°45W **172** C7
Hudson Wyo., U.S.A.　42°54N 108°35W **168** E9
Hudson → U.S.A.　40°42N 74°2W **175** F10
Hudson, C. Antarctica　68°21S 153°45E **5** C10
Hudson, Vol. Chile　46°4S 72°55W **192** C2
Hudson Bay Nunavut,
　Canada　60°0N 86°0W **161** F14
Hudson Bay Sask.,
　Canada　52°51N 102°23W **163** C8
Hudson Falls U.S.A.　43°18N 73°35W **175** C11
Hudson Mts. Antarctica　74°32S 99°20W **5** D16
Hudson Str. Canada　62°0N 70°0W **161** E18
Hudson's Hope Canada　56°0N 121°54W **162** B4
Hue Vietnam　16°30N 107°35E **120** D6
Huebra → Spain　41°2N 6°48W **88** C4
Huedin Romania　46°52N 23°2E **83** E8
Huehuetenango
　Guatemala　15°20N 91°28W **182** C1
Huejúcar Mexico　22°21N 103°13W **180** C4
Huélamo Spain　40°17N 1°48W **90** E3
Huelgoat France　48°22N 3°46W **70** D3
Huelma Spain　37°39N 3°28W **89** H7
Huelva Spain　37°18N 6°57W **89** H4
Huelva □ Spain　37°40N 7°0W **89** H4
Huelva → Spain　37°27N 6°0W **89** H5
Huentelauquén Chile　31°38S 71°33W **190** C1
Huércal-Overa Spain　37°23N 1°57W **91** H3
Huerquehue △ Chile　39°6S 71°42W **192** A2
Huerta, Sa. de la
　Argentina　31°10S 67°30W **190** C2
Huertas, C. de las Spain　38°21N 0°24W **91** G4
Huerva → Spain　41°39N 0°52W **90** C4
Huesca Spain　42°8N 0°25W **90** C4
Huesca □ Spain　42°20N 0°1E **90** C5
Huéscar Spain　37°44N 2°35W **91** H2
Huetamo Mexico　18°35N 100°53W **180** D4
Huete Spain　40°10N 2°43W **90** E2
Huger U.S.A.　33°6N 79°48W **178** B10
Hugh → Australia　25°1S 134°1E **150** C1
Hughenden Australia　20°52S 144°10E **150** C3
Hughesville U.S.A.　41°14N 76°44W **175** E8
Hugli → India　21°56N 88°4E **125** J13
Hugo Colo., U.S.A.　39°8N 103°28W **168** G12
Hugo Okla., U.S.A.　34°1N 95°31W **176** D7
Hugoton U.S.A.　37°11N 101°21W **172** G3
Hui Xian = Huixian
　China　35°27N 113°12E **114** G7
Hui Xian China　33°50N 106°4E **114** H4
Hui'an China　25°1N 118°43E **117** E12
Hui'anbu China　37°28N 106°38E **114** F4
Huiarau Ra. N.Z.　38°45S 176°55E **154** E5
Huichang China　25°32N 115°45E **117** E10
Huichapan Mexico　20°23N 99°39W **181** C5
Huichon N. Korea　40°10N 126°16E **115** D14
Huidong Guangdong,
　China　22°58N 114°43E **117** F10
Huidong Sichuan,
　China　26°34N 102°35E **116** D4
Huifa He → China　43°0N 127°50E **115** C14
Huila, Nevado del
　Colombia　3°0N 76°0W **186** C3
Huilai China　23°0N 116°18E **117** F11
Huili China　26°35N 102°17E **116** D4
Huimin China　37°27N 117°28E **115** F9
Huinan China　42°40N 126°2E **115** C14
Huinca Renancó
　Argentina　34°51S 64°22W **190** C3
Huining China　35°38N 105°0E **114** G3
Huinong China　39°5N 106°35E **114** E4
Huiroa N.Z.　39°15S 174°30E **154** F3
Huishui China　26°7N 106°38E **116** D6
Huisne → France　47°59N 0°11E **70** E7
Huiting China　34°5N 116°5E **114** G9
Huitong China　26°51N 109°45E **116** D7
Huixian China　35°27N 113°12E **114** G7
Huixtla Mexico　15°9N 92°28W **181** D6
Huize China　26°24N 103°15E **116** D4
Huizhou China　23°0N 114°23E **117** F10
Hukawng Valley
　Burma　26°30N 96°30E **123** F20
Hukeri India　16°14N 74°36E **127** F2
Hukou China　29°45N 116°21E **117** C11
Hukuntsi Botswana　23°58S 21°45E **144** B3
Ḩulayfā' Si. Arabia　25°58N 40°45E **128** E4
Hulin China　45°48N 132°59E **111** B15
Hulin He → China　45°0N 122°10E **115** B12
Hull = Kingston upon Hull
　U.K.　53°45N 0°21W **66** D7
Hull Canada　45°26N 75°43W **175** A9
Hull → U.K.　53°44N 0°20W **66** D7
Hulst Neths.　51°17N 4°2E **69** C4
Huludao China　40°45N 120°50E **115** D11
Hulun Nur = Hailar
　China　49°10N 119°38E **111** B12
Hulyaypole Ukraine　47°45N 36°21E **85** J9

Huma, Tanjung
　Malaysia　5°29N 100°16E **121** c
Humacao Puerto Rico　18°9N 65°50W **183** d
Humahuaca Argentina　23°10S 65°25W **190** A2
Humaitá Brazil　7°35S 63°1W **186** E6
Humaitá Paraguay　27°2S 58°31W **190** B4
Humansdorp S. Africa　34°2S 24°46E **144** D3
Humbe Angola　16°40S 14°55E **144** A1
Humber → U.K.　53°42N 0°27W **66** D7
Humboldt Canada　52°15N 105°9W **163** C7
Humboldt Iowa, U.S.A.　42°44N 94°13W **172** D6
Humboldt Tenn.,
　U.S.A.　35°50N 88°55W **177** D10
Humboldt → U.S.A.　39°59N 118°36W **168** G4
Humboldt Gletscher =
　Sermersuaq Greenland　79°30N 62°0W **57** B4
Humboldt Mts. N.Z.　44°30S 168°15E **155** F2
Hume U.S.A.　36°48N 118°54W **170** J8
Hume, L. Australia　36°0S 147°5E **153** F7
Humen China　22°50N 113°40E **111** a
Humenné Slovak Rep.　48°55N 21°50E **79** C14
Hummelsta Sweden　59°34N 16°58E **62** E10
Humphreys, Mt.
　U.S.A.　37°17N 118°40W **170** H8
Humphreys Peak
　U.S.A.　35°21N 111°41W **169** J8
Humpolec Czech Rep.　49°31N 15°20E **78** D8
Humptulips U.S.A.　47°14N 123°57W **170** C3
Humula Australia　35°30S 147°46E **153** C7
Hūn Libya　29°2N 16°0E **137** C9
Hunan □ China　27°30N 112°0E **117** D9
Húnaflói Iceland　65°50N 20°50W **60** D3
Hunan □ China　27°30N 112°0E **117** D9
Hunchun China　42°52N 130°28E **115** C16
Hundested Denmark　55°58N 11°52E **63** J5
Hundewali Pakistan　31°55N 72°38E **124** D5
Hundred Mile House
　Canada　51°38N 121°18W **162** C4
Hunedoara Romania　45°40N 22°50E **80** E7
Hunedoara □ Romania　45°50N 22°54E **80** E7
Hünfeld Germany　50°39N 9°46E **76** E5
Hung Yen Vietnam　20°39N 106°4E **116** G6
Hungary ■ Europe　47°20N 19°20E **79** D12
Hungary, Plain of Europe　47°0N 20°0E **58** F10
Hungerford Australia　28°58S 144°24E **151** D13
Hŭngnam N. Korea　39°49N 127°45E **115** E14
Hunjiang China → see
　Taiwan　22°4N 121°25E **117** F13
Huni Valley Ghana　5°33N 1°56W **138** D4
Hunjiang China　41°54N 126°26E **115** D14
Hunneberg Sweden　58°18N 12°30E **63** F6
Hunnebostrand Sweden　58°27N 11°18E **63** F5
Hunsberge Namibia　27°45S 17°12E **144** C2
Hunsrück Germany　49°56N 7°27E **77** F3
Hunstanton U.K.　52°56N 0°29E **66** E8
Hunsur India　12°16N 76°16E **127** H3
Hunte → Germany　53°14N 8°28E **76** B4
Hunter N.Z.　44°36S 171°2E **155** E6
Hunter U.S.A.　42°13N 74°13W **175** D10
Hunter → Australia　32°52S 151°46E **153** B5
Hunter → N.Z.　44°21S 169°27E **155** E4
Hunter Hills, The N.Z.　44°30S 170°40E **155** E3
Hunter I. Australia　40°30S 144°45E **151** G3
Hunter I. Canada　51°55N 128°0W **162** C3
Hunter Mts. N.Z.　45°43S 167°25E **155** F2
Hunter Ra. Australia　32°45S 150°15E **153** B5
Hunters Road Zimbabwe　19°9S 29°49E **143** F2
Hunterville N.Z.　39°56S 175°35E **154** F4
Huntingburg U.S.A.　38°18N 86°57W **172** F10
Huntingdon Canada　45°6N 74°10W **175** A10
Huntingdon U.K.　52°20N 0°11W **67** E7
Huntingdon U.S.A.　40°30N 78°1W **174** F6
Huntington Ind.,
　U.S.A.　40°53N 85°30W **173** E11
Huntington N.Y.,
　U.S.A.　40°52N 73°26W **175** F11
Huntington Oreg.,
　U.S.A.　44°21N 117°16W **168** D5
Huntington Utah,
　U.S.A.　39°20N 110°58W **168** G8
Huntington W. Va.,
　U.S.A.　38°25N 82°27W **173** F12
Huntington Beach
　U.S.A.　33°40N 118°5W **171** M9
Huntly N.Z.　37°34S 175°11E **154** D4
Huntly U.K.　57°27N 2°47W **65** D6
Huntsville Canada　45°20N 79°14W **174** A5
Huntsville Ala., U.S.A.　34°44N 86°35W **177** C11
Huntsville Tex., U.S.A.　30°43N 95°33W **176** F7
Hunyani → Zimbabwe　15°57S 30°39E **143** F3
Hunyuan China　39°42N 113°42E **114** E7
Hunza → India　35°54N 74°20E **125** B6
Huo Shan China　36°26N 111°52E **114** F6
Huo Xian = Huozhou
　China　36°36N 111°42E **114** F6
Huocheng China　44°0N 80°48E **109** D10
Huolin Gol China　45°32N 119°38E **115** B10
Huong Khe Vietnam　18°13N 105°41E **120** C5
Huonville Australia　43°0S 147°5E **151** G4
Huoqiu China　32°20N 116°12E **117** A11
Huoshan China　31°25N 116°20E **117** B11
Huoshao Dao = Lütao
　Taiwan　22°40N 121°30E **117** F13
Huozhou China　36°36N 111°42E **114** F6
Hupeh = Hubei □ China　31°0N 112°0E **117** B9
Ḩūr Iran　30°50N 57°7E **129** D8
Hurānd Iran　38°51N 47°22E **126** C12
Ḩuraymila Si. Arabia　25°8N 46°8E **128** E5
Hurbanovo Slovak Rep.　47°51N 18°11E **79** D11
Hurd, C. Canada　45°13N 81°44W **174** A3
Hure Qi China　42°45N 121°45E **115** C11
Hurezani Romania　44°49N 23°40E **81** F8
Hurghada Egypt　27°15N 33°50E **137** C12
Hurley N. Mex., U.S.A.　32°42N 108°8W **169** K9
Hurley Wis., U.S.A.　46°27N 90°11W **172** B8
Huron Calif., U.S.A.　36°12N 120°6W **170** J6
Huron Ohio, U.S.A.　41°24N 82°33W **174** E2
Huron S. Dak., U.S.A.　44°22N 98°13W **172** C4
Huron, L. U.S.A.　44°30N 82°40W **174** B2
Huron East Canada　43°37N 81°9W **174** D3
Hurricane U.S.A.　37°11N 113°17W **169** H7
Hurtsboro U.S.A.　32°15N 85°25W **179** D3
Hurungwe △ Zimbabwe　16°7S 29°5E **143** F2
Hurunui → N.Z.　42°54S 173°18E **155** C8
Hurup Denmark　56°46N 8°25E **63** H2
Húsavík Iceland　66°3N 17°21W **60** C5
Huşi Romania　46°41N 28°7E **81** D11
Huskisson Australia　35°2S 150°41E **153** C5
Huskvarna Sweden　57°47N 14°15E **63** H6
Hustadvika Norway　63°0N 7°0E **60** E12
Hustontown U.S.A.　40°3N 78°2W **174** F6
Hustopeče Czech Rep.　48°57N 16°43E **79** C9

Husum Germany　54°28N 9°4E **76** A5
Husum Sweden　63°21N 19°12E **62** A13
Hutchinson Kans.,
　U.S.A.　38°5N 97°56W **172** F5
Hutchinson Minn.,
　U.S.A.　44°54N 94°22W **172** C6
Hutiao Xia China　27°13N 100°9E **116** D3
Hutte Sauvage, L. de la
　Canada　56°15N 64°45W **165** A7
Hüttenberg Austria　46°56N 14°33E **78** E7
Hutton, Mt. Australia　25°51S 148°20E **151** D4
Huwaki Indonesia　7°55S 126°30E **119** F7
Huy Belgium　50°31N 5°15E **69** D5
Huzhou China　30°51N 120°8E **117** B13
Huzurabad India　18°12N 79°25E **126** E4
Huzurnagar India　16°54N 79°53E **126** F4
Hvalpsund Denmark　56°42N 9°11E **63** H3
Hvammstangi Iceland　65°24N 20°57W **60** D3
Hvar Croatia　43°11N 16°28E **93** E13
Hvarski Kanal Croatia　43°15N 16°35E **93** E13
Hvítá → Iceland　64°30N 21°58W **60** D3
Hvízdets Ukraine　48°35N 25°17E **81** B10
Hwacheon-Cheosuji
　S. Korea　38°5N 127°50E **115** E14
Hwang Ho = Huang He →
　China　37°55N 118°50E **115** F10
Hwange Zimbabwe　18°18S 26°30E **143** F2
Hwange △ Zimbabwe　19°0S 26°30E **144** A4
Hwlffordd = Haverfordwest
　U.K.　51°48N 4°58W **67** F3
Hyannis Mass., U.S.A.　41°39N 70°17W **173** E18
Hyannis Nebr., U.S.A.　42°0N 101°46W **172** E3
Hyargas Nuur Mongolia　49°0N 93°0E **109** C12
Hybo Sweden　61°49N 16°15E **62** C10
Hydaburg U.S.A.　55°15N 132°50W **162** B2
Hyde N.Z.　45°18S 170°16E **155** F5
Hyde Park U.S.A.　41°47N 73°56W **175** E11
Hyden Australia　32°24S 118°53E **149** F2
Hyder U.S.A.　55°55N 130°5W **162** B2
Hyderabad India　17°22N 78°29E **126** F4
Hyderabad Pakistan　25°23N 68°24E **124** G3
Hydra Greece　37°20N 23°28E **98** D5
Hyères France　43°8N 6°9E **73** E10
Hyères, Îs. d' France　43°0N 6°20E **73** F10
Hyesan N. Korea　41°20N 128°10E **115** D15
Hyland → Canada　59°52N 128°12W **162** B3
Hyltebruk Sweden　56°59N 13°15E **63** H7
Hyltebruk Sweden　56°59N 13°15E **63** H7
Hyndman Peak U.S.A.　43°45N 114°8W **168** E6
Hyōgo □ Japan　35°15N 134°50E **113** G7
Hyrum U.S.A.　41°38N 111°51W **168** F8
Hysham U.S.A.　46°18N 107°14W **168** C10
Hythe U.K.　51°4N 1°5E **67** F9
Hyūga Japan　32°25N 131°35E **113** H5
Hyvinge = Hyvinkää
　Finland　60°38N 24°50E **84** B3
Hyvinkää Finland　60°38N 24°50E **84** B3

I

I-n-Akhmed Mali　19°49N 0°56W **139** B4
I-n-Azaoua Algeria　25°42N 6°54E **136** C5
I-n-Ezzane Algeria　23°29N 11°15E **136** D6
I-n-Gall Niger　16°51N 7°1E **139** B6
I-n-Kelemet Algeria　26°57N 5°47E **136** C5
I-n-Oudad Algeria　20°17N 4°38E **139** A5
I-n-Ouzzal Algeria　20°41N 2°34E **139** A5
I-n-Tadreft Niger　19°5N 6°38E **139** B6
Iabès, Erg Algeria　27°30N 2°2W **138** B5
Iablaniţa Romania　44°57N 22°19E **80** F7
Iaco → Brazil　9°3S 68°34W **188** B4
Iacobeni Romania　47°25N 25°20E **81** C10
Iaçu Brazil　12°45S 40°13W **189** C2
Ialissos Greece　36°24N 28°10E **101** C10
Ialomiţa □ Romania　44°30N 27°30E **81** F12
Ialomiţa → Romania　44°42N 27°51E **81** F12
Ialoveni Moldova　46°56N 28°47E **81** D13
Ialpug → Moldova　45°41N 28°35E **81** D13
Iamonia L. U.S.A.　30°38N 84°14W **178** E5
Iara Romania　46°31N 23°35E **81** D8
Iargara Moldova　46°24N 28°23E **81** D13
Iaşi Romania　47°10N 27°40E **81** C12
Iaşi □ Romania　47°20N 27°0E **81** C12
Iasmos Greece　41°8N 25°11E **97** E9
Ib → India　21°34N 83°48E **125** J10
Iba Phil.　15°22N 120°0E **119** A6
Ibadan Nigeria　7°22N 3°58E **139** D5
Ibagué Colombia　4°20N 75°20W **186** C3
Iballë Albania　42°12N 20°2E **96** A4
Ibănești Botoşani,
　Romania　48°4N 26°22E **81** B11
Ibănești Mureș, Romania　46°45N 24°57E **81** D9
Ibar → Serbia　43°43N 20°45E **96** C4
Ibaraki □ Japan　36°10N 140°10E **113** F10
Ibarra Ecuador　0°21N 78°7W **186** C3
Ibb Yemen　14°2N 44°10E **131** E3
Ibbenbüren Germany　52°16N 7°43E **76** C3
Ibembo
　Dem. Rep. of the Congo　2°35N 23°35E **142** B1
Ibenga → Congo　2°19N 18°9E **142** D3
Ibera, L. Argentina　28°30S 57°9W **190** B4
Iberia Peru　11°21S 69°35W **188** C3
Iberian Peninsula Europe　40°0N 5°0W **58** H5
Iberville Canada　45°19N 73°17W **175** A11
Iberville, Mt. d'
　Canada　58°50N 63°50W **161** F19
Ibeto Nigeria　10°29N 5°8E **139** C6
Ibi Nigeria　8°15N 9°44E **139** D6
Ibi Spain　38°38N 0°34W **91** G4
Ibiá Brazil　19°30S 46°30W **189** D1
Ibiapaba, Sa. da Brazil　4°0S 41°30W **189** B3
Ibicaraí Brazil　14°51S 39°36W **189** C3
Ibicuí → Brazil　29°25S 56°47W **191** B4
Ibicuy Argentina　33°55S 59°10W **190** C4
Ibioira → Brazil　12°39S 42°13W **189** C2
Ibiza = Eivissa Spain　38°54N 1°26E **100** C10
Ibiza ✕ (IBZ) Spain　38°52N 1°21E **100** C10
Íblei, Monti Italy　37°15N 14°45E **95** F7
Ibo Mozam.　12°22S 40°40E **145** G8
Ibonma Indonesia　3°29S 133°31E **119** E8
Ibotirama Brazil　12°13S 43°12W **189** C2
Ibrāhīm → Lebanon　34°4N 35°38E **130** A4
'Ibri Oman　23°14N 56°30E **131** C6
İbriktepe Turkey　41°0N 26°30E **97** E10
Ibshawâi Egypt　29°21N 30°40E **137** C7
Ibu Indonesia　1°35N 127°33E **119** D7
Ibusuki Japan　31°12N 130°40E **113** J5

Ica Peru　14°0S 75°48W **188** C2
Ica □ Peru　14°20S 75°30W **188** C2
Iça → Brazil　2°55S 67°58W **188** A4
Içana Brazil　0°21N 67°19W **186** C5
Içana → Brazil　0°26N 67°19W **186** C5
Icatu Brazil　2°50S 44°18W **189** A2
İçel Turkey　36°51N 34°36E **104** D6
İçel □ Turkey　36°45N 34°0E **104** D5
Iceland ■ Europe　64°45N 19°0W **60** D4
Iceland Basin Atl. Oc.　61°0N 19°0W **54** C7
Icelandic Plateau Arctic　64°0N 10°0W **4** C7
İçeriçumra Turkey　37°34N 32°39E **104** D5
Ichalkaranji India　16°40N 74°33E **126** F2
Ich'ang = Yichang
　China　30°40N 111°20E **117** B8
Ichchapuram India　19°10N 84°40E **127** E8
Ichhawar India　23°1N 77°1E **124** H7
Ichigat Muja-Cordillera del
　Condor → Peru　4°20S 77°30W **188** A2
Ichihara Japan　35°28N 140°5E **113** G10
Ichikawa Japan　35°43N 139°54E **113** G9
Ichilo → Bolivia　15°57S 64°50W **186** G6
Ichinohe Japan　40°13N 141°17E **112** D10
Ichinomiya Japan　35°18N 136°48E **113** G8
Ichinoseki Japan　38°55N 141°8E **112** E10
Ichkeul △ Tunisia　37°5N 9°37E **136** A5
Ichnya Ukraine　50°52N 32°24E **85** G7
Icht Morocco　29°6N 8°54W **136** C2
Icó Brazil　6°24S 38°51W **189** B3
Icod Canary Is.　28°22N 16°43W **100** F3
İçoguz Turkmenistan　40°12N 58°42E **108** D5
Icy C. U.S.A.　70°20N 161°52W **158** B3
Ida Grove U.S.A.　42°21N 95°28W **172** D6
Idabel U.S.A.　33°54N 94°50W **176** E7
Idah Nigeria　7°5N 6°40E **139** D6
Idaho □ U.S.A.　45°0N 115°0W **168** D6
Idaho City U.S.A.　43°50N 115°50W **168** E6
Idaho Falls U.S.A.　43°30N 112°2W **168** E7
Idalia △ Australia　24°49S 144°36E **150** C3
Idanha-a-Nova Portugal　39°50N 7°15W **88** F3
Idar-Oberstein Germany　49°43N 7°16E **77** F3
Idelès Algeria　23°50N 5°53E **136** D5
Idensalmi = Iisalmi
　Finland　63°32N 27°10E **60** E22
Idfû Egypt　24°55N 32°49E **137** C3
Idhra = Hydra Greece　37°20N 23°28E **98** D5
Idi Indonesia　5°2N 97°37E **118** C1
Idi, Oros = Psiloritis, Oros
　Greece　35°15N 24°45E **101** D6
İdil Turkey　37°20N 41°53E **105** D9
Idiofa
　Dem. Rep. of the Congo　4°55S 19°42E **140** E3
Idkerberget Sweden　60°22N 15°15E **62** D9
Idku China　31°18N 30°17E **137** E7
Idku, Bahra el Egypt　31°18N 30°17E **137** D7
Idlib Syria　35°55N 36°36E **130** B3
Idlib □ Syria　35°55N 36°45E **104** D7
Idre Sweden　61°52N 12°42E **62** C6
Idrija Slovenia　46°0N 14°5E **93** C11
Idritsa Russia　56°17N 28°53E **84** D5
Idutywa = Dutywa
　S. Africa　32°8S 28°18E **145** D4
Ieper Belgium　50°51N 2°53E **69** D2
Ierapetra Greece　35°1N 25°44E **101** E7
Ierissos Greece　40°22N 23°52E **96** F7
Ierissos Kolpos Greece　40°27N 23°57E **96** F7
Iernut Romania　46°27N 24°15E **81** D9
Iesi Italy　43°31N 13°14E **93** E10
Ifac, Penyal d' Spain　38°38N 0°5E **91** G5
Ifakara Tanzania　8°8S 36°41E **140** F7
'Ifāl, W. al → Si. Arabia　28°7N 35°3E **128** D2
Ifanadiana Madag.　21°19S 47°39E **145** C8
Iférouâne Niger　19°5N 8°24E **139** B6
Ifetesene Algeria　25°30N 4°33E **136** D6
Iffley Australia　18°53S 141°12E **150** B3
Ifon Nigeria　6°58N 5°40E **139** D6
Iforas, Adrar des Africa　19°40N 1°40E **139** B5
Ifould, L. Australia　30°52S 132°6E **149** F5
Ifrane Morocco　33°33N 5°7W **136** B3
Igalo Montenegro　42°28N 18°30E **96** D2
Iganga Uganda　0°37N 33°28E **142** B3
Igarapava Brazil　20°3S 47°47W **189** E1
Igarka Russia　67°30N 86°33E **106** C9
Igatpuri India　19°40N 73°35E **126** E1
Igbetti Nigeria　8°44N 4°8E **139** D5
Igbo-Ora Nigeria　7°10N 3°15E **139** D5
Igboho Nigeria　8°53N 3°50E **139** D5
Igbor Nigeria　7°27N 8°34E **139** D6
Iğdır Turkey　39°52N 44°22E **105** C11
Iggelfors Sweden　58°52N 15°41E **63** F9
Iggesund Sweden　61°39N 17°10E **62** C11
Ighil Izane = Relizane
　Algeria　35°44N 0°31E **136** A4
Iglésias Italy　39°19N 8°32E **94** C1
Igli Algeria　30°25N 2°19W **136** B3
Igloolik = Iglulik
　Canada　69°20N 81°49W **161** C12
Igluligaarjuk = Chesterfield Inlet
　Canada　63°30N 90°45W **160** E13
Iglulik Canada　69°20N 81°49W **161** D15
'Igma, G. el Egypt　29°10N 34°0E **137** F8
Ignace Canada　49°30N 91°40W **164** C1
Iğneada Turkey　41°53N 28°7E **97** E12
Iğneada Burnu Turkey　41°53N 28°2E **97** E12
Igoumenitsa Greece　39°32N 20°18E **98** B2
Igra Russia　63°12N 53°16W **106** C8
Iguaçu → Brazil　25°36S 54°36W **191** B5
Iguaçu, Cat. del Brazil　25°41S 54°26W **191** B5
Iguaçu △ Brazil　25°30S 54°0W **191** B5
Iguaçu Falls = Iguaçu, Cat. del
　Brazil　25°41S 54°26W **191** B5
Iguala Mexico　18°21N 99°32W **181** D5
Igualada Spain　41°37N 1°37E **90** D6
Iguassu = Iguaçu →
　Brazil　25°36S 54°36W **191** B5
Iguatu Brazil　6°20S 39°18W **189** B3
Iguazú △ Argentina　25°42S 54°22W **191** B5
Iguidi, Erg Africa　27°0N 6°0W **136** C2
Iharana Madag.　13°25S 50°0E **145** G10
Ihbulag Mongolia　43°11N 107°10E **114** C4
Iheya-Shima Japan　27°4N 127°58E **113** L3
Ihiala Nigeria　5°51N 6°55E **139** D6
Ihosy Madag.　22°24S 46°8E **141** J9
Ihugh Nigeria　7°0N 8°56E **139** D6
Ii Finland　65°19N 25°22E **60** D21
Ii-Shima Japan　41°0N 26°30E **112** D11
Iida Japan　35°35N 137°50E **113** G8
Iijoki → Finland　65°20N 25°20E **60** D21
Iisalmi Finland　63°32N 27°10E **60** E22

Iiyama Japan　36°51N 138°22E **113** F9
Iizuka Japan　33°38N 130°42E **113** H5
Ijâfene Mauritania　20°40N 8°0W **134** D4
Ijebu-Igbo Nigeria　6°56N 4°1E **139** D5
Ijebu-Ode Nigeria　6°47N 3°58E **139** D5
IJevan Armenia　40°52N 45°8E **87** K7
IJmuiden Neths.　52°28N 4°35E **69** B4
Ijo älv = Iijoki →
　Finland　65°20N 25°20E **60** D21
IJssel → Neths.　52°35N 5°50E **69** B5
IJsselmeer Neths.　52°45N 5°20E **69** B5
Ijuí Brazil　28°23S 53°55W **191** B5
Ijuí → Brazil　27°58S 55°20W **191** B4
iméni 26 Bakinskikh
　Komissarov = Neftçala
　Azerbaijan　39°19N 49°12E **105** C13
iméni 26 Bakinskikh Komissarov
　Turkmenistan　39°22N 54°10E **108** E7
iméni Ismail Samani, Pik
　Tajikistan　39°0N 72°2E **109** F8
iméni Karl Libknekhta
　Russia　51°40N 35°35E **86** B6
Imeri, Serra Brazil　0°50N 65°25W **186** C5
Imfolozi △ S. Africa　28°18S 31°50E **145** D5
Imi Ethiopia　6°28N 42°10E **131** F3
Imişli Azerbaijan　39°55N 48°4E **87** L9
Imitek Morocco　29°43N 8°10W **136** C2
Imlay U.S.A.　40°40N 118°9W **168** F4
Imlay City U.S.A.　43°2N 83°5W **174** D1
Immenstadt Germany　47°33N 10°13E **77** H6
Immingham U.K.　53°37N 0°13W **66** D7
Immokalee U.S.A.　26°25N 81°25W **179** J8
Imo □ Nigeria　5°30N 7°10E **139** D6
Imo → Nigeria　4°36N 7°35E **139** E6
Imola Italy　44°20N 11°42E **93** D8
Imotski Croatia　43°27N 17°12E **93** E14
Imperatriz Amazonas,
　Brazil　5°18S 67°11W **188** B4
Imperatriz Maranhão,
　Brazil　5°30S 47°29W **189** B1
Impéria Italy　43°53N 8°3E **92** E5
Imperial Canada　51°21N 105°28W **163** C7
Imperial Peru　13°45S 76°21W **188** C2
Imperial Calif.,
　U.S.A.　32°51N 115°34W **171** N11
Imperial Nebr., U.S.A.　40°31N 101°39W **172** E3
Imperial Beach U.S.A.　32°35N 117°6W **171** N9
Imperial Dam U.S.A.　32°55N 114°25W **171** N12
Imperial Res. U.S.A.　32°53N 114°28W **171** N12
Imperial Valley
　U.S.A.　33°0N 115°30W **171** N11
Imperieuse Reef
　Australia　17°36S 118°50E **148** C2
Impfondo Congo　1°40N 18°0E **140** D3
Imphal India　24°48N 93°56E **123** G18
Imphy France　46°55S 3°16E **71** F10
Imranlı Turkey　39°54N 38°7E **105** C8
İmroz = Gökçeada
　Turkey　40°10N 25°50E **97** F9
Imst Austria　47°15N 10°44E **78** D3
İmuris Mexico　30°47N 110°52W **180** A2
Imuruan B. Phil.　10°40N 119°10E **119** B5
In Alei Mali　17°42N 2°30W **138** C4
In Amenas Algeria　28°5N 9°33E **136** C5
In Amguel Algeria　23°41N 5°9E **136** D5
In Belbel Algeria　27°55N 1°12E **136** C4
In Delimane Mali　15°52N 1°31E **139** B5
In Ghar Algeria　27°10N 1°59E **136** C4
In Guezzam Algeria　19°37N 5°52E **139** B6
In Koufi Mali　19°11N 1°25E **139** B5
In Salah Algeria　27°10N 2°32E **136** C4
In Tallak Mali　16°19N 3°15E **139** B5
In Tebezas Mali　17°49N 1°53E **139** B5
Ina Japan　35°50N 137°55E **113** G8
Inaccessible I. Atl. Oc.　37°18S 12°40W **56** K10
Inagua △ Bahamas　21°5N 73°24W **183** B5
Inajá Brazil　8°54S 37°49W **189** B3
Inambari → Peru　12°41S 69°44W **188** C3
Inangahua N.Z.　41°52S 171°59E **155** D6
Inanwatan Indonesia　2°8S 132°10E **119** E8
Iñapari Peru　11°0S 69°40W **188** C3
Inari Finland　68°54N 27°1E **60** B22
Inarijärvi Finland　69°0N 28°0E **60** B22
Inawashiro-Ko Japan　37°29N 140°6E **112** F10
tInbhear Mór, An = Arklow
　Ireland　52°48N 6°10W **64** D5
Inca Spain　39°43N 2°54E **100** B9
Inca de Oro Chile　26°45S 69°54W **190** B2
Incahuasi Argentina　27°2S 68°18W **190** B2
Incahuasi Chile　29°12S 71°5W **190** B1
İnce Burun Turkey　42°7N 34°56W **104** A6
İncekum Burnu Turkey　36°13N 34°4E **104** D5
Incesu Turkey　38°38N 35°11E **104** C6
Incheon S. Korea　37°27N 126°40E **115** F14
Inchiri □ Mauritania　20°0N 15°0W **138** B2
Incio = A Cruz do Incio
　Spain　42°39N 7°21W **88** C3
İncirliova Turkey　37°50N 27°41E **99** D9
Incline Village U.S.A.　39°10N 119°58W **170** F7
Incomáti → Mozam.　25°46S 32°43E **145** C5
Incudine, Mte. France　41°50N 9°12E **73** G13
Indaiá → Brazil　62°35N 17°5E **62** B11
Indalsälven → Sweden　62°36N 17°30E **62** B11
Indaw Burma　24°15N 96°5E **123** G20
Independence Calif.,
　U.S.A.　36°48N 118°12W **170** J8
Independence Iowa,
　U.S.A.　42°28N 91°54W **172** D8
Independence Kans.,
　U.S.A.　37°14N 95°42W **172** G7
Independence Ky.,
　U.S.A.　38°57N 84°33W **173** F11
Independence Mo.,
　U.S.A.　39°6N 94°25W **172** F6
Independence Fjord
　Greenland　82°10N 29°0W **57** A8
Independence Mts.
　U.S.A.　41°20N 116°0W **168** F5
Independencia, I. Peru　14°16S 76°12W **188** C2
Independența Romania　45°25N 27°42E **81** E12
Inderbor Kazakhstan　48°33N 51°47E **87** E14
Index U.S.A.　47°50N 121°33W **170** C5
Indi India　17°10N 75°55E **126** F2
India ■ Asia　20°0N 78°0E **122** K11
Indialantic U.S.A.　28°5N 80°34W **179** G6
Indian → U.S.A.　27°59N 80°34W **179** G6
Indian Cabins Canada　59°52N 117°40W **162** B5
Indian Harbour
　Canada　54°27N 57°13W **165** B8
Indian Harbour Beach
　U.S.A.　28°10N 80°35W **179** G6

Indian Head Canada 50°30N 103°41W 163 C8
Indian L. U.S.A. 43°46N 74°16W 175 C10
Indian Lake U.S.A. 43°47N 74°16W 175 C10
Indian Ocean 5°0S 75°0E 146 E6
Indian Rocks Beach U.S.A. 27°52N 82°51W 179 H7
Indian Springs U.S.A. 36°35N 115°40W 171 J11
Indiana U.S.A. 40°37N 79°9W 174 F5
Indiana □ U.S.A. 40°0N 86°0W 173 F11
Indianapolis U.S.A. 39°46N 86°9W 172 F10
Indianola Iowa, U.S.A. 41°22N 93°34W 172 E7
Indianola Miss., U.S.A. 33°27N 90°39W 177 E9
Indiantown U.S.A. 27°1N 80°28W 179 H9
Indigirka → Russia 70°48N 148°54E 107 B15
Inđija Serbia 45°6N 20°7E 80 E5
Indio U.S.A. 33°43N 116°13W 171 M10
Indira Gandhi Canal India 28°0N 72°0E 124 F5
Indira Pt. India 6°44N 93°49E 127 L11
Indira Sagar India 22°15N 76°40E 124 H7
Indo-China Asia 15°0N 102°0E 102 G12
Indonesia ■ Asia 5°0S 115°0E 118 F5
Indore India 22°42N 75°53E 124 H6
Indramayu Indonesia 6°20S 108°19E 119 G13
Indravati → India 19°20N 80°20E 126 E5
Indre □ France 46°50N 1°39E 71 F8
Indre → France 47°16N 0°11E 70 E7
Indre-et-Loire □ France 47°20N 0°40E 70 E7
Indrio U.S.A. 27°31N 80°21W 179 H9
Indulkana Australia 26°58S 133°5E 151 D1
Indura Belarus 53°26N 23°53E 82 E10
Indus → Pakistan 24°20N 67°47E 124 G2
Indus, Mouths of the Pakistan 24°0N 68°0E 124 H3
İnebolu Turkey 41°55N 33°40E 104 B5
İnecik Turkey 40°56N 27°16E 97 F11
İnegöl Turkey 40°5N 29°31E 97 F13
Inés, Mt. Argentina 48°30S 69°40W 192 C3
Ineu Romania 46°26N 21°51E 80 D6
Inezgane Morocco 30°25N 9°29W 136 B2
Infantes = Villanueva de los Infantes Spain 38°43N 3°1W 89 G7
Infiernillo, Presa del Mexico 18°35N 101°50W 180 D4
Infiesto Spain 43°21N 5°21W 88 B5
Inga, Barrage d' Dem. Rep. of the Congo 5°39S 13°39E 140 F2
Ingaro Sweden 59°12N 18°45E 62 E12
Ingelstad Sweden 56°45N 14°56E 63 H8
Ingeniero Jacobacci Argentina 41°20S 69°36W 192 B3
Ingenio Canary Is. 27°55N 15°26W 100 G4
Ingenio Santa Ana Argentina 27°25S 65°40W 190 B2
Ingersoll Canada 43°4N 80°55W 174 C4
Ingham Australia 18°43S 146°10E 150 B4
Ingleborough U.K. 54°10N 2°22W 66 C5
Inglefield Land Greenland 78°30N 70°0W 57 B4
Inglewood Queens., Australia 28°25S 151°2E 151 D5
Inglewood Vic., Australia 36°29S 143°53E 152 D5
Inglewood N.Z. 39°9S 174°14E 154 F3
Inglewood U.S.A. 33°58N 118°21W 171 M8
Inglis U.S.A. 29°2N 82°40W 179 F7
Ingolf Fjord Greenland 80°35N 17°30W 57 A9
Ingólfshöfði Iceland 63°48N 16°39W 60 E5
Ingolstadt Germany 48°46N 11°26E 77 G7
Ingomar U.S.A. 46°35N 107°23W 168 C10
Ingonish Canada 46°42N 60°18W 165 C7
Ingore Guinea-Biss. 12°24N 15°48W 138 C1
Ingraj Bazar India 24°58N 88°10E 125 G13
Ingrid Christensen Coast Antarctica 69°30S 76°0E 55 C6
Ingul = Inhul → Ukraine 46°50N 32°0E 85 J7
Ingulec = Inhulec Ukraine 47°42N 33°14E 85 J7
Ingulets = Inhulets → Ukraine 46°46N 32°47E 85 J7
Inguri = Enguri → Georgia 42°27N 41°38E 87 J5
Ingushetia □ Russia 43°20N 44°50E 87 J7
Ingwavuma S. Africa 27°9S 31°59E 145 C5
Inhaca Mozam. 26°1S 32°57E 145 C5
Inhaca Pen. Mozam. 26°13S 32°55E 145 C5
Inhafenga Mozam. 20°36S 33°53E 145 B5
Inhambane Mozam. 23°54S 35°30E 145 B6
Inhambane □ Mozam. 22°30S 34°20E 145 B5
Inhambupe Brazil 11°47S 38°21W 189 C3
Inhaminga Mozam. 18°26S 35°0E 143 F4
Inharrime Mozam. 24°30S 35°0E 145 B6
Inharrime → Mozam. 24°30S 35°0E 145 B6
Inhisar Turkey 40°3N 30°23E 99 A12
Inhul → Ukraine 46°50N 32°0E 85 J7
Inhulec Ukraine 47°42N 33°14E 85 J7
Inhulets → Ukraine 46°46N 32°47E 85 J7
Inhuma Brazil 6°40S 41°42W 189 B2
Iniesta Spain 39°27N 1°45W 91 F3
Ining = Yining China 43°58N 81°10E 109 D10
Inírida → Colombia 3°55N 67°52W 186 C5
Inis = Ennis Ireland 52°51N 8°59W 64 D3
Inishbofin Ireland 53°37N 10°13W 64 C1
Inisheer Ireland 53°3N 9°32W 64 C2
Inishfree B. Ireland 55°4N 8°23W 64 A3
Inishkea North Ireland 54°9N 10°11W 64 B1
Inishkea South Ireland 54°7N 10°12W 64 B1
Inishmaan Ireland 53°5N 9°35W 64 C2
Inishmore Ireland 53°8N 9°45W 64 C2
Inishmurray Ireland 54°26N 8°39W 64 B3
Inishowen Pen. Ireland 55°14N 7°15W 64 A4
Inishshark Ireland 53°37N 10°16W 64 C1
Inishturk Ireland 53°42N 10°7W 64 C1
Inishvickillane Ireland 52°3N 10°37W 64 D1
Injāna Iraq 34°29N 44°38E 105 E11
Injinoo ✪ Australia 10°56S 142°15E 150 A3
Injune Australia 25°53S 148°32E 151 D4
Inklin → N. Amer. 58°50N 133°10W 162 B2
Inland Kaikoura Ra. N.Z. 41°59S 173°41E 155 B8
Inland Sea = Setonaikai Japan 34°20N 133°30E 113 G6
Inle L. Burma 20°30N 96°58E 123 J20
Inlet U.S.A. 43°45N 74°48W 175 C10
Inn → Austria 48°35N 13°28E 78 C6
Innamincka Australia 27°44S 140°46E 151 D3
Inner Hebrides U.K. 57°0N 6°30W 65 E2
Inner Mongolia = Nei Mongol Zizhiqu □ China 42°0N 112°0E 114 D7
Inner Sound U.K. 57°30N 5°55W 65 D3
Innerkip Canada 43°13N 80°42W 174 C4
Innes △ Australia 35°52S 136°53E 152 C2
Innetalling I. Canada 56°0N 79°0W 164 A4
Innisfail Australia 17°33S 146°5E 150 B4
Innisfail Canada 52°2N 113°57W 162 C6
In'noshima Japan 34°19N 133°10E 113 G6
Innsbruck Austria 47°16N 11°23E 78 D4
Innviertel Austria 48°15N 13°15E 78 C6
Inny → Ireland 53°32N 7°51W 64 C4
Inongo Dem. Rep. of the Congo 1°55S 18°30E 140 E3
İnönü Turkey 39°48N 30°9E 99 B12
Inoucdjouac = Inukjuak Canada 58°25N 78°15W 161 F16
Inousses Greece 38°33N 26°14E 99 C8
Inowrocław Poland 52°50N 18°12E 83 F5
Inquisivi Bolivia 16°50S 67°10W 188 D4
Inscription, C. Australia 25°29S 112°59E 149 E1
Insein Burma 16°50N 96°5E 123 L20
Insjön Sweden 60°41N 15°6E 62 D9
Ińsko Poland 53°25N 15°32E 82 E2
Însurăţei Romania 44°50N 27°40E 81 F12
Inta Russia 66°5N 60°8E 106 C6
Intendente Alvear Argentina 35°12S 63°32W 190 D3
İntepe Turkey 40°1N 26°20E 99 A8
Interlachen U.S.A. 29°37N 81°53W 179 F8
Interlaken Switz. 46°41N 7°50E 77 J3
Interlaken U.S.A. 42°37N 76°44W 175 D8
International Falls U.S.A. 48°36N 93°25W 172 A7
Interview I. India 12°55N 92°43E 127 H11
Intiyaco Argentina 28°43S 60°5W 190 B3
Întorsura Buzăului Romania 45°41N 26°2E 81 E11
Inukjuak Canada 58°25N 78°15W 161 F16
Inútil, B. Chile 53°30S 70°15W 192 D2
Inuvik Canada 68°16N 133°40W 160 D5
Inveraray U.K. 56°14N 5°5W 65 E3
Inverbervie U.K. 56°51N 2°17W 65 E6
Invercargill N.Z. 46°24S 168°24E 155 G3
Inverclyde □ U.K. 55°55N 4°49W 65 F4
Inverell Australia 29°45S 151°8E 151 D5
Invergordon U.K. 57°41N 4°10W 65 D4
Inverleigh Australia 38°6S 144°3E 152 E6
Inverloch Australia 38°38S 145°45E 151 F4
Invermere Canada 50°30N 116°2W 162 C5
Inverness Canada 46°15N 61°19W 165 C7
Inverness U.K. 57°29N 4°13W 65 D4
Inverness Ala., U.S.A. 32°1N 85°45W 178 C4
Inverness Fla., U.S.A. 28°50N 82°20W 179 G7
Inverurie U.K. 57°17N 2°23W 65 D6
Investigator Group Australia 34°45S 134°20E 151 E1
Investigator Ridge Ind. Oc. 11°30S 98°10E 146 F8
Investigator Str. Australia 35°30S 137°0E 152 C2
Inya Russia 50°28N 86°37E 109 B11
Inyanga Zimbabwe 18°12S 32°40E 143 F3
Inyangani Zimbabwe 18°5S 32°50E 143 F3
Inyantue Zimbabwe 18°33S 26°39E 144 A4
Inyo Mts. U.S.A. 36°40N 118°0W 170 J9
Inyokern U.S.A. 35°39N 117°49W 171 K9
Inyonga Tanzania 6°45S 32°5E 142 D3
Inza Russia 53°55N 46°25E 86 D8
Inzhavino Russia 52°22N 42°30E 86 D6
Iō-Jima Japan 30°48N 130°18E 113 J5
Ioannina Greece 39°42N 20°47E 98 B2
Iola U.S.A. 37°55N 95°24W 172 G6
Ion Corvin Romania 44°7N 27°50E 81 F12
Iona U.K. 56°20N 6°25W 65 E2
Ione U.S.A. 38°21N 120°56W 170 G6
Ionia U.S.A. 42°59N 85°4W 173 D11
Ionian Is. = Ionioi Nisoi Greece 38°40N 20°0E 98 C2
Ionian Sea Medit. S. 37°30N 17°30E 58 H9
Ionioi Nisoi Greece 38°40N 20°0E 98 C2
Ionioi Nisoi □ Greece 38°40N 20°0E 98 C2
Iony, Ostrov Russia 56°24N 143°22E 107 D15
Ios Greece 36°41N 25°20E 99 E7
Iowa □ U.S.A. 42°18N 93°30W 172 D7
Iowa → U.S.A. 41°10N 91°1W 172 E8
Iowa City U.S.A. 41°40N 91°32W 172 E8
Iowa Falls U.S.A. 42°31N 93°16W 172 D7
Iowa Park U.S.A. 33°57N 98°40W 176 E5
Ipala Tanzania 4°30S 32°52E 142 C3
Ipameri Brazil 17°44S 48°9W 189 D1
Ipanema Brazil 19°47S 41°44W 189 D2
Iparía Peru 9°17S 74°29W 188 B3
Ipati Greece 38°52N 22°14E 98 C4
Ipatinga Brazil 19°32S 42°30W 189 D2
Ipatovo Russia 45°45N 42°50E 87 H6
Ipel' → Europe 47°48N 18°53E 79 D11
Ipiales Colombia 0°50N 77°37W 186 C3
Ipiaú Brazil 14°8S 39°44W 189 C3
Ipin = Yibin China 28°45N 104°32E 116 C5
Ipirá Brazil 12°10S 39°44W 189 C3
Ipixuna Brazil 7°0S 71°40W 188 B3
Ipixuna → Brazil 7°11S 71°51W 188 B3
Ipoh Malaysia 4°35N 101°5E 121 K3
Ippy C.A.R. 6°5N 21°7E 140 C4
İpsala Turkey 40°55N 26°23E 97 F10
Ipsario, Oros Greece 40°40N 24°40E 97 F8
Ipswich Australia 27°35S 152°40E 151 D5
Ipswich U.K. 52°4N 1°10E 67 E9
Ipswich Mass., U.S.A. 42°41N 70°50W 175 D14
Ipswich S. Dak., U.S.A. 45°27N 99°2W 172 C4
Ipu Brazil 4°23S 40°44W 189 A2
Ipueiras Brazil 4°33S 40°43W 189 A2
Ipupiara Brazil 11°49S 42°37W 189 C2
Iqaluit Canada 63°44N 68°31W 161 E18
Iqaluktuutiaq = Cambridge Bay Canada 69°10N 105°0W 160 D11
Iquique Chile 20°19S 70°5W 188 E3
Iquitos Peru 3°45S 73°10W 186 D4
Irabu-Jima Japan 24°50N 125°10E 113 M2
Iracoubo Fr. Guiana 5°30N 53°10W 187 B8
Īrafshān Iran 26°42N 61°56E 129 E9
Iraklia Cyclades, Greece 36°50N 25°28E 99 E7
Iraklia Serres, Greece 41°10N 23°16E 96 E7
Iraklio Greece 35°20N 25°12E 101 D7
Iráklion = Iraklio Greece 35°20N 25°12E 101 D7
Irakliou, Kolpos Greece 35°23N 25°8E 101 D7
Irala Paraguay 25°55S 54°35W 191 B5
Iran ■ Asia 33°0N 53°0E 129 C7
Iran, Pegunungan Malaysia 2°20N 114°50E 118 D4
Iran Ra. = Iran, Pegunungan Malaysia 2°20N 114°50E 118 D4
Iranamadu Tank Sri Lanka 9°23N 80°29E 127 K5
Īrānshahr Iran 27°15N 60°40E 129 E9
Irapuato Mexico 20°41N 101°28W 180 C4
Iraq ■ Asia 33°0N 44°0E 105 F10
Irati Brazil 25°25S 50°38W 191 B5
Irazú, Volcan Costa Rica 10°28N 84°42W 182 D3
Irbes saurums Latvia 57°45N 22°5E 82 A9
Irbid Jordan 32°35N 35°48E 130 C4
Irbid □ Jordan 32°30N 35°50E 130 C5
Irebu Dem. Rep. of the Congo 0°40S 17°46E 140 E3
Irecê Brazil 11°18S 41°52W 189 C2
Iregua → Spain 42°27N 2°24E 90 C7
Ireland ■ Europe 53°50N 7°52W 64 C4
Irele Nigeria 7°40N 5°40E 139 D6
Irgiz = Yrghyz Kazakhstan 48°37N 61°16E 108 C6
Irgiz = Yrghyz → Kazakhstan 48°6N 62°30E 108 C6
Irgiz, Bolshaya → Russia 52°10N 49°10E 86 D9
Irharrhar, O. → Algeria 28°3N 6°15E 136 C5
Irherm Morocco 30°7N 8°18W 136 B2
Irhil M'Goun Morocco 31°30N 6°28W 136 B2
Iri = Iksan S. Korea 35°59N 127°0E 115 G14
Irian Jaya = Papua □ Indonesia 4°0S 137°0E 119 E9
Irian Jaya Barat □ Indonesia 2°5S 132°50E 119 E8
Irié Guinea 8°15N 9°10W 138 D3
Iriklinskoye Vdkhr. Russia 52°0N 59°0E 108 B5
Iringa Tanzania 7°48S 35°43E 142 D4
Iringa □ Tanzania 7°48S 35°43E 142 D4
Irinjalakuda India 10°21N 76°14E 127 J3
Iriomote △ Japan 24°29N 123°53E 113 M1
Iriomote-Jima Japan 24°19N 123°48E 113 M1
Iriona Honduras 15°57N 85°11W 182 C2
Iriri → Brazil 3°52S 52°37W 187 D8
Irish Sea Europe 53°38N 4°48W 66 D3
Irkeshtam Pass = Erkech-Tam Pass Asia 39°46N 74°2E 109 E8
Irkutsk Russia 52°18N 104°20E 110 A9
Irlığanlı Turkey 37°53N 29°12E 99 D11
Irma Canada 52°55N 111°14W 163 C6
Irō-Zaki Japan 34°36N 138°51E 113 G9
Iroise, Mer d' France 48°15N 4°45W 70 D2
Iron Baron Australia 32°58S 137°11E 152 B2
Iron Gate = Portile de Fier Europe 44°44N 22°30E 80 F7
Iron Knob Australia 32°46S 137°8E 152 B2
Iron Mountain U.S.A. 45°49N 88°4W 172 C9
Iron Range △ Australia 12°34S 143°18E 150 A3
Iron River U.S.A. 46°6N 88°39W 172 B9
Irondequoit U.S.A. 43°13N 77°35W 174 C7
Ironton Mo., U.S.A. 37°36N 90°38W 172 G8
Ironton Ohio, U.S.A. 38°32N 82°41W 173 F12
Ironwood U.S.A. 46°27N 90°9W 172 B8
Ironwood Forest ⌂ U.S.A. 32°32N 111°28W 169 K8
Iroquois Canada 44°51N 75°19W 175 B9
Iroquois Falls Canada 48°46N 80°41W 164 C3
Irpin Ukraine 50°30N 30°15E 75 C16
Irrara Cr. → Australia 29°35S 145°31E 151 D4
Irrawaddy □ Burma 17°0N 95°0E 123 L19
Irrawaddy → Burma 15°50N 95°6E 123 M19
Irrawaddy, Mouths of the Burma 15°30N 95°0E 123 M19
Irricana Canada 51°19N 113°37W 162 C6
Irrunytju Australia 26°3S 128°56E 149 E4
Irshava Ukraine 48°19N 23°3E 80 B8
Irsina Italy 40°45N 16°14E 95 B9
Irtysh → Russia 61°4N 68°52E 106 C7
Irumu Dem. Rep. of the Congo 1°32N 29°53E 142 B2
Irún Spain 43°20N 1°52W 90 B3
Irunea = Pamplona-Iruña Spain 42°48N 1°38W 90 C3
Irurzun Spain 42°55N 1°50W 90 C3
Irvine Canada 49°57N 110°16W 163 D6
Irvine U.K. 55°37N 4°41W 65 F4
Irvine Calif., U.S.A. 33°41N 117°46W 171 M9
Irvine Ky., U.S.A. 37°42N 83°58W 173 G12
Irvinestown U.K. 54°28N 7°39W 64 B4
Irving U.S.A. 32°48N 96°56W 176 E6
Irvona U.S.A. 40°46N 78°33W 174 F6
Irwin → Australia 29°15S 114°54E 149 E1
Irwinton U.S.A. 32°49N 83°10W 178 C6
Irwinville U.S.A. 31°39N 83°23W 178 D6
Irymple Australia 34°14S 142°8E 152 C5
Is, Jebel Sudan 22°3N 35°28E 137 C4
Is-sur-Tille France 47°30N 5°8E 71 E12
Isa Nigeria 13°14N 6°24E 139 C6
Isa Khel Pakistan 32°41N 71°17E 124 C4
Isaac → Australia 22°55S 149°20E 150 C4
Isabel U.S.A. 45°24N 101°26W 172 C3
Isabel, I. Mexico 21°51N 105°55W 180 C3
Isabela Phil. 6°40N 121°59E 119 C6
Isabela Puerto Rico 18°30N 67°2W 183 d
Isabelia, Cord. Nic. 13°30N 85°25W 182 D2
Isabella Ra. Australia 21°0S 121°4E 148 D3
Isaccea Romania 45°16N 28°28E 81 E13
Ísachsen, C. Canada 79°20N 105°28W 161 B10
Isachsen Mt. Antarctica 72°8S 26°5E 55 D4
Ísafjarðardjúp Iceland 66°10N 23°0W 60 C2
Ísafjörður Iceland 66°5N 23°9W 60 C2
Isagarh India 24°48N 77°51E 124 G7
Isahaya Japan 32°52N 130°2E 113 H5
Isaka Tanzania 3°56S 32°59E 142 C3
Işalniţa Romania 44°24N 23°44E 81 F8
Isan → India 26°51N 80°7E 125 F9
Isana = Içana → Brazil 0°26N 67°19W 186 C5
Isangano △ Zambia 11°8S 30°35E 143 E3
Isanlu Makutu Nigeria 8°20N 5°50E 139 D6
Isar → Germany 48°48N 12°57E 77 G8
Isarco → Italy 46°27N 11°18E 93 B8
Isaris Greece 37°22N 22°0E 98 D3
Íscar Spain 41°22N 4°32W 88 D6
İscehisar Turkey 38°51N 30°45E 99 C12
Ischia Italy 40°44N 13°57E 94 B6
Ischigualasto △ Argentina 30°0S 68°0W 190 B2
Isdell → Australia 16°27S 124°51E 148 C3
Ise Japan 34°25N 136°45E 113 G8
Ise-Shima △ Japan 34°25N 136°48E 113 G8
Ise-Wan Japan 34°43N 136°43E 113 G8
Isefjord Denmark 55°53N 11°50E 63 J5
Isel → Austria 46°50N 12°47E 78 E5
Iseo Italy 45°39N 10°3E 92 C7
Iseo, L. d' Italy 45°43N 10°4E 92 C7
Iseramagazi Tanzania 4°37S 32°10E 142 C3
Isère □ France 45°15N 5°40E 73 C9
Isère → France 44°59N 4°51E 73 D8
Iserlohn Germany 51°22N 7°41E 76 D3
Isérnia Italy 41°36N 14°14E 95 A7
Iseyin Nigeria 8°0N 3°36E 139 D5
Isfahan = Eşfahān Iran 32°39N 51°43E 129 C6
Ishëm Albania 41°33N 19°34E 96 E3
Ishigaki Japan 24°26N 124°10E 113 M2
Ishigaki-Shima Japan 24°20N 124°10E 113 M2
Ishikari Japan 43°20N 141°15E 112 C10
Ishikari-Gawa → Japan 43°15N 141°23E 112 C10
Ishikari-Sammyaku Japan 43°30N 143°0E 112 C11
Ishikari-Wan Japan 43°25N 141°1E 112 C10
Ishikawa Japan 26°25N 127°49E 113 L3
Ishikawa □ Japan 36°30N 136°30E 113 F8
Ishim Russia 56°10N 69°30E 106 D7
Ishim → Russia 57°45N 71°10E 106 D8
Ishimbay Russia 53°28N 56°2E 108 B5
Ishinomaki Japan 38°32N 141°20E 112 E10
Ishioka Japan 36°11N 140°16E 113 F10
Ishkashim Tajikistan 36°44N 71°37E 109 E8
Ishkoman Pakistan 36°30N 73°50E 125 A5
Ishpeming U.S.A. 46°29N 87°40W 172 B10
Isigny-sur-Mer France 49°19N 1°6W 70 C5
Işıklar Dağı Turkey 40°45N 27°15E 97 F11
Işıklı Turkey 38°19N 29°51E 99 C11
Isil Kul Russia 54°55N 71°16E 109 B8
Ísili Italy 39°44N 9°6E 94 C2
iSimangaliso ⌂ S. Africa 27°50S 32°32E 145 C5
Isiolo Kenya 0°24N 37°33E 142 B4
Isiro Dem. Rep. of the Congo 2°53N 27°40E 142 B2
Isisford Australia 24°15S 144°21E 150 C3
İskele = Trikomo Cyprus 35°17N 33°52E 101 D12
İskenderun Turkey 36°32N 36°10E 104 D7
İskenderun Körfezi Turkey 36°40N 35°50E 104 D6
İskilip Turkey 40°45N 34°29E 104 B6
Iskitim Russia 54°38N 83°18E 109 B10
Iskŭr → Bulgaria 43°45N 24°25E 97 C8
Iskŭr, Yazovir Bulgaria 42°23N 23°30E 96 D7
Iskut → Canada 56°45N 131°49W 162 B2
Isla → U.K. 56°32N 3°20W 65 E5
Isla Coiba △ Panama 7°33N 81°36W 182 E3
Isla Cristina Spain 37°13N 7°17W 89 H3
Isla de Salamanca △ Colombia 10°59N 74°40W 183 D5
Isla Gorge △ Australia 25°10S 149°57E 150 D4
Isla Guamblin △ Chile 44°50S 75°4W 192 B1
Isla Isabel △ Mexico 21°54N 105°58W 180 C3
Isla Magdalena △ Chile 44°20S 73°13W 192 B2
Isla Tiburón y San Esteban △ Mexico 29°0N 112°27W 180 B2
Isla Vista U.S.A. 34°25N 119°53W 171 L7
İslahiye Turkey 37°0N 36°35E 104 D7
Islam Headworks Pakistan 29°49N 72°33E 124 E5
Islamabad Pakistan 33°40N 73°10E 124 C5
Islamgarh Pakistan 27°51N 70°48E 124 F4
Islamkot Pakistan 24°42N 70°13E 124 G4
Islamorada U.S.A. 24°56N 80°37W 179 L9
Islampur Bihar, India 25°9N 85°12E 125 G11
Islampur Maharashtra, India 17°2N 74°20E 126 F2
Islampur Paschimbanga, India 26°16N 88°12E 125 F13
Island = Iceland ■ Europe 64°45N 19°0W 60 D4
Island L. Canada 53°47N 94°25W 163 C10
Island Lagoon Australia 31°30S 136°40E 152 A2
Island Pond U.S.A. 44°49N 71°53W 175 B13
Islands, B. of Canada 49°11N 58°15W 165 C8
Islands, B. of N.Z. 35°15S 174°6E 154 B3
Islas Atlánticas de Galicia △ Spain 42°23N 8°55W 88 C2
Islay U.K. 55°46N 6°10W 65 F2
Isle → France 44°55N 0°15W 72 D3
Isle aux Morts Canada 47°35N 59°0W 165 C8
Isle of Hope U.S.A. 31°58N 81°5W 178 D8
Isle of Wight □ U.K. 50°41N 1°17W 67 G6
Isle Royale △ U.S.A. 48°0N 88°55W 172 B9
Isleton U.S.A. 38°10N 121°37W 170 G5
Ismail = Izmayil Ukraine 45°22N 28°46E 81 E13
Ismâ'ilîya Egypt 30°37N 32°18E 137 E8
Ismaning Germany 48°13N 11°40E 77 G7
Isna Egypt 25°17N 32°30E 137 B3
Isojärvi △ Finland 61°40N 25°0E 60 F21
Ísola del Liri Italy 41°41N 13°34E 93 G10
Ísola della Scala Italy 45°16N 11°0E 92 C7
Ísola di Capo Rizzuto Italy 38°58N 17°6E 95 D10
Isparta Turkey 37°47N 30°30E 99 D12
Isparta □ Turkey 38°0N 31°0E 104 D4
Isperikh Bulgaria 43°43N 26°50E 97 C10
Íspica Italy 36°47N 14°55E 95 F7
İspir Turkey 40°28N 40°59E 105 B9
Israel ■ Asia 32°0N 34°50E 130 D3
Issakly Russia 54°8N 51°32E 86 C10
Issaouane, Erg Algeria 26°58N 8°42E 136 C5
Issia Ivory C. 6°33N 6°33W 138 D3
Issoire France 45°32N 3°15E 72 C7
Issoudun France 46°57N 1°59E 71 F8
Issyk-Kul = Balykchy Kyrgyzstan 42°26N 76°12E 109 D9
Issyk-Kul, Ozero = Ysyk-Köl Kyrgyzstan 42°25N 77°15E 109 D9
Ist Croatia 44°17N 14°47E 93 D11
Istállós-kő Hungary 48°4N 20°26E 80 B5
İstanbul Turkey 41°0N 28°58E 97 E12
İstanbul □ Turkey 41°0N 29°0E 97 E12
İstanbul ✈ (IST) Turkey 40°59N 28°49E 97 F12
İstanbul Boğazı Turkey 41°5N 29°3E 97 E13
Istaravshan Tajikistan 39°55N 69°1E 109 E7
Istiaia Greece 38°57N 23°9E 98 C5
Isto, Mt. U.S.A. 69°12N 143°48W 166 B11
Istok = Burim Kosovo 42°45N 20°24E 96 D4
Istokpoga, L. U.S.A. 27°23N 81°17W 179 H8
Istra Croatia 45°10N 14°0E 93 C10
Istres France 43°31N 4°59E 73 E8
Istria = Istra Croatia 45°10N 14°0E 93 C10
Itá Paraguay 25°29S 57°21W 190 B4
Itabaiana Paraíba, Brazil 7°18S 35°19W 189 B3
Itabaiana Sergipe, Brazil 10°41S 37°37W 189 C3
Itabaianinha Brazil 11°16S 37°47W 189 C3
Itaberaba Brazil 12°32S 40°18W 189 C2
Itabira Brazil 19°37S 43°13W 189 D2
Itabirito Brazil 20°15S 43°48W 189 E2
Itabuna Brazil 14°48S 39°16W 189 C3
Itacajá Brazil 8°19S 47°46W 189 B1
Itacaunas → Brazil 5°21S 49°8W 187 E9
Itacoatiara Brazil 3°8S 58°25W 186 D7
Itaguari → Brazil 14°11S 44°40W 189 C2
Itaguatins Brazil 5°47S 47°29W 189 B1
Itaim → Brazil 7°2S 42°2W 189 B2
Itainópolis Brazil 7°24S 41°31W 189 B2
Itaipú, Represa de Brazil 25°30S 54°30W 191 B5
Itäisen Suomenlahti △ Finland 60°25N 27°15E 60 F22
Itaituba Brazil 4°10S 55°50W 187 D7
Itajaí Brazil 27°50S 48°39W 191 B6
Itajubá Brazil 22°24S 45°30W 191 A6
Itajuípe Brazil 14°41S 39°22W 189 C3
Itaka Tanzania 8°50S 32°49E 143 D3
Itala △ S. Africa 27°30S 31°7E 145 C5
Italy ■ Europe 42°0N 13°0E 59 G8
Itamaraju Brazil 17°4S 39°32W 189 D3
Itamarati Brazil 6°24S 68°15W 188 B4
Itamataré Brazil 2°16S 46°24W 189 A1
Itambacuri Brazil 18°1S 41°42W 189 D2
Itambé Brazil 15°15S 40°37W 189 D2
Itanhém Brazil 17°9S 40°20W 189 D2
Itapagé Brazil 3°41S 39°34W 189 A3
Itaparica, I. de Brazil 12°54S 38°42W 189 C3
Itaparica, Represa de Brazil 11°3S 42°47W 189 C2
Itapebi Brazil 15°56S 39°32W 189 D3
Itapecuru Mirim Brazil 3°24S 44°20W 189 A2
Itaperuna Brazil 21°10S 41°54W 191 A7
Itapetinga Brazil 15°15S 40°15W 189 D2
Itapetininga Brazil 23°36S 48°7W 191 A6
Itapeva Brazil 23°59S 48°59W 191 A6
Itapicuru → Bahia, Brazil 11°47S 37°32W 189 C3
Itapicuru → Maranhão, Brazil 2°52S 44°12W 189 A2
Itapipoca Brazil 3°30S 39°35W 189 A3
Itapiúna Brazil 4°33S 38°57W 189 A3
Itaporanga Brazil 7°18S 38°0W 189 B3
Itapuá □ Paraguay 26°40S 55°40W 191 B4
Itaquai → Brazil 4°20S 70°12W 188 A3
Itaquí Maranhão, Brazil 2°34S 44°22W 189 A2
Itaquí Rio Grande do S., Brazil 29°8S 56°30W 190 B4
Itararé Brazil 24°6S 49°23W 191 A6
Itarsi India 22°36N 77°51E 124 H7
Itatí Argentina 27°16S 58°15W 190 B4
Itatiaia △ Brazil 22°22S 44°38W 191 A7
Itatira Brazil 4°30S 39°37W 189 A3
Itaueira Brazil 7°36S 43°2W 189 B2
Itaueira → Brazil 6°41S 42°55W 189 B2
Itaúna Brazil 20°4S 44°34W 189 E2
Itchen → U.K. 50°55N 1°22W 67 G6
Ite Peru 17°55S 70°57W 188 D3
Itea Greece 38°25N 22°25E 98 C4
Itezhi Tezhi, L. Zambia 15°30S 25°30E 143 F2
Ithaca = Ithaki Greece 38°25N 20°40E 98 C2
Ithaca U.S.A. 42°27N 76°30W 175 D8
Ithaki Greece 38°25N 20°40E 98 C2
Iti △ Greece 38°50N 22°15E 98 C4
Itinga Brazil 16°36S 41°47W 189 D2
Itiquira → Brazil 17°18S 56°44W 187 G7
Itiruçu Brazil 13°31S 40°9W 189 C2
Itiúba Brazil 10°43S 39°51W 189 C3
Itiyuro → Argentina 22°40S 63°50W 190 A3
Itō Japan 34°58N 139°5E 113 G9
Itoigawa Japan 37°2N 137°51E 113 F8
Iton → France 49°9N 1°12E 70 C8
Itonamas → Bolivia 12°28S 64°24W 186 F6
Itri Italy 41°17N 13°32E 94 A6
Itsa Egypt 29°15N 30°47E 137 F7
Ittiri Italy 40°36N 8°34E 94 B1
Ittoqqortoormiit Greenland 70°20N 23°0W 57 C8
Itu Brazil 23°17S 47°15W 191 A6
Itu Nigeria 5°10N 7°58E 139 D6
Itu Aba I. S. China Sea 10°23N 114°21E 118 B4
Ituaçu Brazil 13°50S 41°18W 189 C2
Ituiutaba Brazil 19°0S 49°25W 187 G9
Itumbiara Brazil 18°20S 49°10W 187 G9
Ituna Canada 51°10N 103°24W 163 C8
Itunge Port Tanzania 9°40S 33°55E 143 D3
Iturbe Argentina 23°0S 65°25W 190 A2
Ituri → Dem. Rep. of the Congo 1°40N 27°1E 142 B2
Iturup, Ostrov Russia 45°0N 148°0E 107 E15
Ituverava Brazil 20°20S 47°47W 189 E1
Ituxi → Brazil 7°18S 64°51W 186 E6
Itzehoe Germany 53°55N 9°31E 76 B5
Ivaí → Brazil 23°18S 53°42W 191 A5
Ivalo Finland 68°38N 27°35E 60 B22
Ivalojoki → Finland 68°40N 27°40E 60 B22
Ivanava Belarus 52°7N 25°29E 75 B13
Ivančice Czech Rep. 49°6N 16°23E 79 B9
Ivane-Puste Ukraine 48°39N 26°10E 81 B11
Ivăneşti Romania 46°39N 27°27E 81 D12
Ivangorod Russia 59°27N 28°13E 84 C5
Ivanhoe N.S.W., Australia 32°56S 144°20E 152 B6
Ivanhoe Vic., Australia 37°45S 145°3E 153 D6
Ivanhoe Canada 44°23N 77°28W 174 B7
Ivanhoe Calif., U.S.A. 36°23N 119°13W 170 J7
Ivanhoe Minn., U.S.A. 44°28N 96°15W 172 C5
Ivanhorod Ukraine 48°48N 29°48E 81 B14
Ivanić Grad Croatia 45°41N 16°25E 93 C13
Ivanjica Serbia 43°35N 20°12E 96 C4
Ivanjska Bos.-H. 44°55N 17°4E 80 F2
Ivankoyskoye Vdkhr. Russia 56°37N 36°32E 84 D9
Ivano-Frankivsk Ukraine 48°40N 24°40E 81 B9
Ivano-Frankivsk □ Ukraine 48°45N 24°30E 81 B9
Ivanovo = Ivanava Belarus 52°7N 25°29E 75 B13
Ivanovo Bulgaria 43°43N 25°58E 97 C9
Ivanovo Russia 57°5N 41°0E 84 D11
Ivanovo □ Russia 57°10N 41°50E 86 B5
Ivanšćica Croatia 46°12N 16°13E 93 B13
Ivatsevichy Belarus 52°43N 25°21E 75 B13
Ivaylovgrad Bulgaria 41°32N 26°8E 97 E10
Iveragh Pen. Ireland 51°52N 10°15W 64 E1
Ivinheima → Brazil 23°14S 53°42W 191 A5
Ivinhema Brazil 22°10S 53°37W 191 A5
Ivittuut Greenland 61°14N 48°12W 57 E6
Ivory Coast W. Afr. 4°20N 5°0W 138 E4
Ivory Coast ■ Africa 7°30N 5°0W 138 D4
Ivösjön Sweden 56°8N 14°25E 63 H8
Ivrea Italy 45°28N 7°52E 92 C4
İvrindi Turkey 39°34N 27°30E 99 B9
Ivujivik Canada 62°24N 77°55W 161 E16
Ivvavik △ Canada 69°6N 139°30W 160 D4
Ivybridge U.K. 50°23N 3°56W 67 G4
Iwaizumi Japan 39°50N 141°45E 112 E10
Iwaki Japan 37°3N 140°55E 113 F10
Iwakuni Japan 34°15N 132°8E 113 G6
Iwamizawa Japan 43°12N 141°46E 112 C10
Iwanai Japan 42°58N 140°30E 112 C10
Iwata Japan 34°42N 137°51E 113 G8
Iwate □ Japan 39°30N 141°30E 112 E10
Iwate-San Japan 39°51N 141°0E 112 E10
Iwo Nigeria 7°39N 4°9E 139 D5
Iwŏn N. Korea 40°19N 128°39E 115 D15
Iwonicz-Zdrój Poland 49°37N 21°47E 83 J8
Ixiamas Bolivia 13°50S 68°5W 188 C4
Ixopo S. Africa 30°11S 30°5E 145 D5
Ixtepec Mexico 16°34N 95°6W 181 D5
Ixtlán del Río Mexico 21°2N 104°22W 180 C4
Iyo Japan 33°45N 132°45E 113 H6
Izabal, L. de Guatemala 15°30N 89°10W 182 C2
Izamal Mexico 20°56N 89°1W 181 C7
Izberbash Russia 42°35N 47°52E 87 J8
Izbica Poland 50°53N 23°10E 83 H10
Izbica Kujawska Poland 52°25N 18°40E 83 F5
Izbiceni Romania 43°45N 24°40E 81 G9
Izena-Shima Japan 26°56N 127°56E 113 L3
Izgrev Bulgaria 43°36N 26°58E 97 C10
Izhevsk Russia 56°51N 53°14E 106 D6
Izmayil Ukraine 45°22N 28°46E 81 E13
İzmir Turkey 38°25N 27°8E 99 C9
İzmir □ Turkey 38°15N 27°40E 99 C9
İzmir Adnan Menderes ✈ (ADB) Turkey 38°23N 27°6E 99 C9
İzmir Körfezi Turkey 38°30N 26°50E 99 C8
İzmit = Kocaeli Turkey 40°45N 29°50E 97 F13
Iznájar Spain 37°15N 4°19W 89 H6
Iznalloz Spain 37°24N 3°30W 89 H7
İznik Turkey 40°23N 29°46E 104 B3
İznik Gölü Turkey 40°27N 29°30E 97 F13
Izobil'nyy Russia 45°25N 41°44E 87 H5
Izola Slovenia 45°32N 13°39E 93 C10
Izra Syria 32°51N 36°15E 130 C5
Iztochni Rodopi Bulgaria 41°45N 25°30E 97 E9
Izu-Hantō Japan 34°45N 139°0E 113 G9
Izu-Shotō Japan 34°30N 140°0E 113 G10
Izúcar de Matamoros Mexico 18°36N 98°28W 181 D5
Izumi Japan 32°5N 130°22E 113 H5
Izumi-Sano Japan 34°23N 135°18E 113 G7
Izumo Japan 35°20N 132°46E 113 G6
Izyaslav Ukraine 50°5N 26°50E 75 C14
Izyum Ukraine 49°12N 37°19E 85 H9

J

J.F.K. Int. ✈ (JFK) U.S.A. 40°38N 73°47W 175 F11
J.P. Koch Fjord Greenland 82°45N 44°0W 57 A6
J. Strom Thurmond L. U.S.A. 33°40N 82°12W 178 B7
Ja-ela Sri Lanka 7°5N 79°53E 127 L4
Jabalón → Spain 38°53N 4°5W 89 G6
Jabalpur India 23°9N 79°58E 125 H8
Jabālya Gaza Strip 31°32N 34°29E 130 D3
Jabbūl Syria 36°4N 37°30E 128 B3
Jabiru Australia 12°40S 132°53E 148 B5
Jablah Syria 35°20N 36°0E 104 E6
Jablanac Croatia 44°42N 14°56E 93 D11
Jablanica Bos.-H. 43°40N 17°45E 80 G2
Jablonec nad Nisou Czech Rep. 50°43N 15°10E 78 A8
Jablonica Slovak Rep. 48°37N 17°26E 79 C10
Jablonowo Pomorskie Poland 53°23N 19°10E 82 E6
Jablunkov Czech Rep. 49°35N 18°46E 79 B11
Jaboatão Brazil 8°7S 35°1W 189 B3
Jabotabek = Jakarta Indonesia 6°9S 106°52E 118 F3
Jaboticabal Brazil 21°15S 48°17W 191 A6
Jabukovac Serbia 44°22N 22°21E 96 B6
Jaca Spain 42°35N 0°33W 90 C4
Jacaré → Brazil 10°3S 42°13W 189 C2
Jacarei Brazil 23°20S 46°0W 191 A6
Jacarèzinho Brazil 23°5S 49°58W 191 A6
Jacinto Brazil 16°10S 40°17W 189 D2
Jack River △ Australia 14°58S 144°19E 150 A3
Jackman U.S.A. 45°37N 70°15W 173 C18
Jacksboro U.S.A. 33°13N 98°10W 176 E5
Jackson Barbados 13°7N 59°36W 183 g
Jackson Ala., U.S.A. 31°31N 87°53W 177 F11
Jackson Calif., U.S.A. 38°21N 120°46W 170 G6
Jackson Ga., U.S.A. 33°20N 83°57W 178 B6
Jackson Ky., U.S.A. 37°33N 83°23W 173 G12
Jackson Mich., U.S.A. 42°15N 84°24W 173 D11
Jackson Minn., U.S.A. 43°37N 95°1W 172 D6
Jackson Miss., U.S.A. 32°18N 90°12W 177 E9
Jackson Mo., U.S.A. 37°23N 89°40W 172 G9
Jackson N.H., U.S.A. 44°10N 71°11W 175 B13
Jackson Ohio, U.S.A. 39°3N 82°39W 173 F12
Jackson S.C., U.S.A. 33°20N 81°47W 178 B8
Jackson Tenn., U.S.A. 35°37N 88°49W 177 D10
Jackson Wyo., U.S.A. 43°29N 110°46W 168 E8
Jackson, C. N.Z. 40°59S 174°20E 155 A9
Jackson B. N.Z. 43°58S 168°42E 155 D3
Jackson Hd. N.Z. 43°58S 168°37E 155 D3
Jackson L. Fla., U.S.A. 30°30N 84°17W 178 E5
Jackson L. Ga., U.S.A. 33°19N 83°50W 178 B6
Jackson L. Wyo., U.S.A. 43°52N 110°36W 168 E8
Jacksons N.Z. 42°46S 171°32E 155 C6
Jackson's Arm Canada 49°52N 56°47W 165 C8
Jacksonville Ala., U.S.A. 33°49N 85°46W 178 B4
Jacksonville Ark., U.S.A. 34°52N 92°7W 176 D8
Jacksonville Calif., U.S.A. 37°52N 120°24W 170 H6
Jacksonville Fla., U.S.A. 30°20N 81°39W 178 E8
Jacksonville Ga., U.S.A. 31°49N 82°59W 178 D7

Jacksonville *Ill., U.S.A.* 39°44N 90°14W **172** F8
Jacksonville *N.C.,*
U.S.A. 34°45N 77°26W **177** D16
Jacksonville *Tex.,*
U.S.A. 31°58N 95°17W **176** F7
Jacksonville Beach
U.S.A. 30°17N 81°24W **178** E8
Jacksonville Int. ✈ (JAX)
U.S.A. 30°30N 81°41W **178** E8
Jacmel *Haiti* 18°14N 72°32W **183** C5
Jacob Lake *U.S.A.* 36°43N 112°13W **169** H17
Jacobabad *Pakistan* 28°20N 68°29E **124** E3
Jacobina *Brazil* 11°11S 40°30W **189** C2
Jacques-Cartier, Dét. de
Canada 50°0N 63°30W **165** C7
Jacques-Cartier, Mt.
Canada 48°57N 66°0W **165** C6
Jacques-Cartier △
Canada 47°15N 71°33W **165** C5
Jacqueville *Ivory C.* 5°12N 4°25W **138** D4
Jacuí → *Brazil* 30°2S 51°15W **191** C5
Jacumba *U.S.A.* 32°37N 116°11W **171** N10
Jacundá → *Brazil* 1°57S 50°26W **187** D8
Jadcherla *India* 16°46N 78°9E **126** F4
Jade *Germany* 53°20N 8°14E **76** B4
Jade, Côte de *France* 46°40N 2°0W **70** F4
Jade City *Canada* 59°15N 129°37W **162** B3
Jade Dragon Snow Mt. = Yulong
Xueshan *China* 27°6N 100°10E **116** D3
Jade Mt. = Yü Shan
Taiwan 23°25N 120°52E **117** F13
Jadebusen *Germany* 53°29N 8°12E **76** B4
Jadovnik *Serbia* 43°20N 19°45E **96** C3
Jadraque *Spain* 40°55N 2°55W **90** E2
Jaén *Peru* 5°25S 78°40W **188** E2
Jaén *Spain* 37°44N 3°43W **89** H7
Jaén □ *Spain* 37°50N 3°30W **89** H7
Jafarabad *India* 20°52N 71°22E **124** J4
Jaffa = Tel Aviv-Yafo
Israel 32°4N 34°48E **130** C3
Jaffa, C. *Australia* 36°58S 139°40E **152** D3
Jaffna *Sri Lanka* 9°45N 80°2E **127** K5
Jaffrey *U.S.A.* 42°49N 72°2W **175** D12
Jagadhri *India* 30°10N 77°20E **124** D7
Jagadishpur *India* 25°30N 84°21E **125** G11
Jagat *Nepal* 28°19N 84°53E **125** E11
Jagdalpur *India* 19°3N 82°0E **126** E6
Jagdaqi *China* 50°25N 124°7E **111** A13
Jagersfontein *S. Africa* 29°44S 25°27E **144** C4
Jaghīn → *Iran* 27°17N 57°13E **129** E8
Jagodina *Serbia* 44°5N 21°15E **96** B5
Jagraon *India* 30°50N 75°25E **124** D6
Jagst → *Germany* 49°14N 9°10E **77** F5
Jagtial *India* 18°50N 79°0E **126** E4
Jaguaquara *Brazil* 13°32S 39°58W **189** C3
Jaguariaíva *Brazil* 24°10S 49°50W **191** A6
Jaguaribe *Brazil* 5°53S 38°37W **189** B3
Jaguaribe → *Brazil* 4°25S 37°45W **189** A3
Jaguaruana *Brazil* 4°50S 37°47W **189** A3
Jagüey Grande *Cuba* 22°35N 81°7W **182** B3
Jagungal, Mt. *Australia* 36°8S 148°22E **153** D8
Jahanabad *India* 25°13N 84°59E **125** G11
Jahazpur *India* 25°37N 75°17E **124** G6
Jahrom *Iran* 28°30N 53°31E **129** D7
Jaicós *Brazil* 7°21S 41°8W **189** B2
Jaigarh *India* 17°17N 73°13E **126** F1
Jaijon *India* 31°21N 76°9E **124** D7
Jailolo *Indonesia* 1°5N 127°30E **119** D7
Jailolo, Selat *Indonesia* 0°5N 129°5E **119** D7
Jaipur *India* 27°0N 75°50E **124** F6
Jais *India* 26°15N 81°32E **125** F9
Jaisalmer *India* 26°55N 70°54E **124** F4
Jaisinghnagar *India* 23°38N 78°34E **125** H8
Jaitaran *India* 26°12N 73°56E **124** F5
Jaithari *India* 23°14N 78°37E **125** H8
Jajarkot *Nepal* 28°42N 82°14E **125** E10
Jājarm *Iran* 36°58N 56°27E **129** B8
Jajce *Bos.-H.* 44°19N 17°17E **80** F7
Jajpur *India* 20°53N 86°22E **125** J8
Jakam → *India* 23°54N 74°13E **124** H6
Jakarta *Indonesia* 6°9S 106°52E **118** F3
Jakhal *India* 29°48N 75°50E **124** E6
Jakhau *India* 23°13N 68°43E **124** H3
Jakobshavn = Ilulissat
Greenland 69°12N 51°10W **57** D5
Jakobstad = Pietarsaari
Finland 63°40N 22°43E **60** E20
Jakupica *Macedonia* 41°45N 21°22E **96** E5
Jal *U.S.A.* 32°7N 103°12W **169** K12
Jalājil *Si. Arabia* 25°40N 45°27E **128** E5
Jalal-Abad *Kyrgyzstan* 40°56N 73°0E **109** D8
Jalal-Abad □
Kyrgyzstan 41°30N 72°0E **109** D8
Jalālābād *Afghan.* 34°30N 70°29E **124** B4
Jalalpur Jattan *Pakistan* 32°41N 74°11E **124** C6
Jalalabad *India* 34°29N 120°29W **171** L6
Jalandhar = Jullundur
India 31°20N 75°40E **124** D6
Jalapa *Guatemala* 14°39N 89°59W **182** D2
Jalapa Enríquez = Xalapa
Mexico 19°32N 96°55W **181** D5
Jalasjärvi *Finland* 62°29N 22°47E **60** E20
Jalaun *India* 26°8N 79°25E **125** F8
Jaldhaka → *Bangla.* 26°16N 89°16E **125** F13
Jalesar *India* 27°29N 78°19E **124** F8
Jaleswar *Nepal* 26°38N 85°48E **125** F11
Jalgaon *India* 21°0N 75°42E **126** D2
Jalibah *Iraq* 30°35N 46°32E **128** D5
Jalingo *Nigeria* 8°55N 11°25E **139** D7
Jalisco □ *Mexico* 20°20N 103°40W **180** D4
Jalkot *Pakistan* 35°14N 73°24E **125** B5
Jalna *India* 19°48N 75°38E **126** E2
Jalón → *Spain* 41°47N 1°4W **90** D3
Jalor *India* 25°21N 72°37E **124** G5
Jalpa *Mexico* 21°38N 102°58W **180** C4
Jalpaiguri *India* 26°32N 88°46E **123** F13
Jalpan *Mexico* 21°14N 99°29W **181** C5
Jalūlā *Iraq* 34°16N 45°10E **105** E11
Jamaame *Somalia* 0°4N 42°44E **131** G3
Jamaari *Nigeria* 11°44N 9°53E **139** C6
Jamaica ■ *W. Indies* 18°10N 77°30W **182** a
Jamalpur *Bangla.* 24°52N 89°56E **123** G16
Jamalpur *India* 25°18N 86°28E **125** G15
Jamalpurganj *India* 23°2N 87°59E **125** H13
Jamanxim → *Brazil* 4°43S 56°18W **187** D7
Jambewangi *Indonesia* 8°15S 114°7E **119** J18
Jambi *Indonesia* 1°38S 103°30E **118** E2
Jambi □ *Indonesia* 1°30S 102°30E **118** E2

Jambongan, Pulau
Malaysia 6°45N 117°20E **118** C5
Jambusar *India* 22°3N 72°51E **124** H5
James → *S. Dak.,*
U.S.A. 42°52N 97°18W **172** D5
James → *Va., U.S.A.* 36°56N 76°27W **173** G15
James B. *Canada* 54°0N 80°0W **164** B3
James I. *Gambia* 13°19N 16°21W **138** C1
James Island *U.S.A.* 32°45N 79°55W **178** C10
James Ranges
Australia 24°10S 132°30E **148** D5
James Ross I.
Antarctica 63°58S 57°50W **55** C18
James Ross Str.
Canada 69°40N 96°10W **160** D12
Jamesabad *Pakistan* 25°17N 69°15E **124** G3
Jameson Land *Greenland* 71°0N 23°30W **57** C8
Jamestown *Australia* 33°10S 138°32E **152** B3
Jamestown *S. Africa* 31°6S 26°45E **144** D4
Jamestown *N. Dak.,*
U.S.A. 46°54N 98°42W **172** B4
Jamestown *N.Y., U.S.A.* 42°6N 79°14W **174** D5
Jamestown *Pa., U.S.A.* 41°29N 80°27W **174** E4
Jamestown *S.C.,*
U.S.A. 33°17N 79°42W **178** B10
Jamīlābād *Iran* 34°24N 48°28E **129** C6
Jamira → *India* 21°35N 88°28E **125** J13
Jamkhandi *India* 16°30N 75°15E **126** F2
Jamkhed *India* 18°43N 75°19E **126** E2
Jammalamadugu *India* 14°51N 78°25E **127** G4
Jammerbugten *Denmark* 57°15N 9°20E **63** G3
Jammu *India* 32°43N 74°54E **124** C6
Jammu & Kashmir □
India 34°25N 77°0E **125** B7
Jamnagar *India* 22°30N 70°6E **124** H4
Jamner *India* 20°45N 75°52E **126** D2
Jamni → *India* 25°13N 78°35E **125** G8
Jampur *Pakistan* 29°39N 70°40E **124** E4
Jamrud *Pakistan* 33°59N 71°24E **124** C4
Jamsä *Finland* 61°53N 25°10E **84** B3
Jamshedpur *India* 22°44N 86°12E **125** H12
Jamtara *India* 23°59N 86°49E **125** H12
Jämtland *Sweden* 63°31N 14°0E **60** E16
Jämtlands län □ *Sweden* 63°0N 14°40E **62** E7
Jan L. *Canada* 54°56N 102°55W **163** C8
Jan Mayen *Arctic* 71°0N 9°0W **54** B7
Janakkala *Finland* 60°54N 24°36E **84** B3
Janakpur *Nepal* 26°42N 85°55E **126** A7
Janaúba *Brazil* 15°48S 43°19W **189** D2
Jand *Pakistan* 33°30N 72°6E **124** C5
Jandanku ⊙ *Australia* 16°20S 135°45E **150** B2
Jandaq *Iran* 34°3N 54°22E **129** C7
Jandia *Canary Is.* 28°6N 14°21W **100** F5
Jandía, Pta. de
Canary Is. 28°3N 14°31W **100** F5
Jandola *Pakistan* 32°20N 70°9E **124** C4
Jandowae *Australia* 26°45S 151°7E **151** D5
Jándula → *Spain* 38°3N 4°6W **89** G6
Jane Pk. *N.Z.* 45°15S 168°20E **155** F3
Janesville *U.S.A.* 42°41N 89°1W **172** D9
Janga *Ghana* 10°5N 1°0W **138** D4
Jangamo *Mozam.* 24°6S 35°21E **145** B6
Janghai *India* 25°33N 82°19E **125** G10
Jangheung *S. Korea* 34°41N 126°52E **115** G14
Jangipur *India* 24°28N 88°4E **125** G12
Jangoon *India* 17°44N 79°5E **126** F4
Janikowo *Poland* 52°45N 18°7E **83** F5
Janja *Bos.-H.* 44°40N 19°14E **80** F4
Janjanbureh *Gambia* 13°30N 14°47W **138** C2
Janjevë *Kosovo* 42°35N 21°19E **96** D5
Janjgir *India* 22°1N 82°34E **125** J10
Janjina *Croatia* 42°58N 17°25E **93** F14
Janos *Mexico* 30°54N 108°10W **180** A3
Jánoshalma *Hungary* 46°18N 19°21E **80** D4
Jánosháza *Hungary* 47°8N 17°12E **80** C2
Jánossomorja *Hungary* 47°47N 17°11E **80** C2
Janów *Poland* 50°44N 19°27E **83** H6
Janów Lubelski *Poland* 50°48N 22°23E **83** H9
Janów Podlaski *Poland* 52°11N 23°11E **83** F10
Janowiec Wielkopolski
Poland 52°45N 17°30E **83** F4
Januária *Brazil* 15°25S 44°25W **189** D2
Janūb Sīnī □ *Egypt* 29°30N 33°50E **130** F2
Janubio *Canary Is.* 28°56N 13°50W **100** F6
Janville *France* 48°10N 1°50E **70** D8
Janwada *India* 18°0N 77°29E **126** E3
Janzé *France* 47°55N 1°28W **70** E5
Jaora *India* 23°40N 75°10E **124** H6
Japan ■ *Asia* 36°0N 136°0E **113** G8
Japan, Sea of *Asia* 40°0N 135°0E **112** E7
Japan Trench *Pac. Oc.* 32°0N 142°0E **156** D6
Japen = Yapen *Indonesia* 1°50S 136°0E **119** E9
Japiim *Brazil* 7°37S 72°54W **188** E3
Japla *India* 24°33N 84°1E **125** G11
Japurá → *Brazil* 3°8S 65°46W **186** D5
Jaquarão *Brazil* 32°34S 53°23W **191** C5
Jaqué *Panama* 7°27N 78°8W **182** E4
Jarabulus *Syria* 36°49N 38°1E **105** D8
Jaraguá do Sul *Brazil* 26°29S 49°4W **191** B6
Jaraicejo *Spain* 39°40N 5°49W **88** F5
Jaraiz de la Vera *Spain* 40°4N 5°45W **88** E5
Jarama → *Spain* 40°24N 3°32W **89** E7
Jaramānah *Syria* 33°29N 36°21E **104** F7
Jaramillo *Argentina* 47°10S 67°7W **192** C3
Jarandilla de la Vera *Spain* 40°8N 5°39W **88** E5
Jaranwala *Pakistan* 31°15N 73°26E **124** D5
Jarash *Jordan* 32°17N 35°54E **130** C4
Jarash □ *Jordan* 32°15N 35°54E **130** C4
Järbo *Sweden* 60°43N 16°40E **62** F7
Jardim *Brazil* 21°28S 56°2W **190** A4
Jardín América
Argentina 27°3S 55°14W **191** B4
Jardine River △
Australia 11°9S 142°7E **150** A3
Jardines de la Reina, Arch. de los
Cuba 20°50S 78°50W **182** B4
Jargalang *China* 43°5N 122°55E **115** C12
Jari → *Brazil* 1°9S 51°54W **187** D8
Jarīr, W. al →
Si. Arabia 25°38N 42°30E **128** E4
Järlåsa *Sweden* 59°53N 17°12E **62** E11
Jarmen *Germany* 53°54N 13°20E **76** B9
Järna *Sweden* 59°6N 17°34E **62** E11
Jarnac *France* 45°40N 0°11W **72** C3
Jarny *France* 49°9N 5°53E **71** C12
Jarocin *Poland* 51°59N 17°29E **83** G4
Jaroměř *Czech Rep.* 50°22N 15°52E **78** A8

Jarosław *Poland* 50°2N 22°42E **83** H9
Järpås *Sweden* 58°23N 12°57E **63** F6
Järpen *Sweden* 63°21N 13°26E **62** A7
Jarrahdale *Australia* 32°24S 116°5E **149** F2
Jarrahi → *Iran* 30°49N 48°48E **129** D6
Jartai *China* 39°45N 105°48E **114** E3
Jarud Qi *China* 44°28N 120°50E **115** B11
Järvenpää *Finland* 60°29N 25°5E **84** B3
Jarvis *Canada* 42°53N 80°6W **174** D4
Jarvis I. *Pac. Oc.* 0°15S 160°5W **157** H11
Jarvornik *Czech Rep.* 50°23N 17°2E **79** A10
Järvsö *Sweden* 61°43N 16°10E **62** C10
Jarwa *India* 27°38N 82°30E **125** F10
Jaša Tomić *Serbia* 45°26N 20°50E **80** D5
Jashpurnagar *India* 22°54N 84°9E **125** H11
Jasidih *India* 24°31N 86°39E **125** G12
Jasień *Poland* 51°46N 15°0E **83** G2
Jāsimīyah *Iraq* 33°45N 44°41E **105** F11
Jasin *Malaysia* 2°20N 102°26E **121** L4
Jāsk *Iran* 25°38N 57°45E **129** E8
Jasło *Poland* 49°45N 21°30E **83** J8
Jasmund *Germany* 54°32N 13°35E **76** A9
Jasmund △ *Germany* 54°31N 13°38E **76** A9
Jaso *India* 24°30N 80°29E **125** G9
Jason Is. *Falk. Is.* 51°0S 61°0W **192** D4
Jasper *Alta., Canada* 52°55N 118°5W **162** C5
Jasper *Ont., Canada* 44°52N 75°57W **175** B9
Jasper *Ala., U.S.A.* 33°50N 87°17W **177** E11
Jasper *Fla., U.S.A.* 30°31N 82°57W **178** E7
Jasper *Ind., U.S.A.* 38°24N 86°56W **172** F10
Jasper *Tex., U.S.A.* 30°56N 94°1W **176** F7
Jasper △ *Canada* 52°50N 118°8W **162** C5
Jasrasar *India* 27°43N 73°49E **124** F5
Jastarnia *Poland* 54°42N 18°40E **82** D5
Jastrebarsko *Croatia* 45°41N 15°39E **93** C12
Jastrowie *Poland* 53°26N 16°49E **82** E3
Jastrzębie Zdrój *Poland* 49°57N 18°35E **83** J5
Jász-Nagykun-Szolnok □
Hungary 47°15N 20°30E **80** C5
Jászapáti *Hungary* 47°30N 20°10E **80** C5
Jászárokszállás *Hungary* 47°39N 19°58E **80** C4
Jászberény *Hungary* 47°30N 19°55E **80** C4
Jászkisér *Hungary* 47°27N 20°20E **80** C5
Jászladány *Hungary* 47°23N 20°18E **80** C5
Jataí *Brazil* 17°58S 51°48W **187** G8
Jath *India* 17°3N 75°13E **126** F2
Jati *Pakistan* 24°20N 68°19E **124** G3
Jatibarang *Indonesia* 6°28S 108°18E **119** G13
Jatiluwih *Indonesia* 8°23S 115°8E **119** J18
Jatinegara *Indonesia* 6°13S 106°52E **119** G12
Játiva = Xàtiva *Spain* 38°59N 0°32W **91** G4
Jättendal *Sweden* 61°58N 17°15E **62** C11
Jaú *Brazil* 22°10S 48°30W **191** A6
Jauja *Peru* 11°45S 75°15W **188** C2
Jaunpur *India* 25°46N 82°44E **125** G10
Jaupaci *Hungary* 47°15N 20°30E **80** C5
Jaú △ *Canary Is.* 28°4N 14°19W **100** F5
Java = Jawa *Indonesia* 7°0S 110°0E **118** F3
Java Sea *Indonesia* 4°35S 107°15E **118** E3
Java Trench *Ind. Oc.* 9°0S 105°0E **118** F3
Javadi Hills *India* 12°40N 78°40E **127** H4
Javalambre, Sa. de *Spain* 40°6N 1°0W **90** E4
Jávavnrud *Iran* 34°47N 46°31E **105** E12
Jávea *Spain* 38°48N 0°10E **91** G5
Javier, I. *Chile* 47°55S 74°25W **192** C2
Javla *India* 17°18N 75°9E **126** F2
Jawa *Indonesia* 7°0S 110°0E **118** F3
Jawa Barat □ *Indonesia* 7°0S 107°0E **119** G12
Jawa Tengah □
Indonesia 7°0S 110°0E **119** G14
Jawa Timur □ *Indonesia* 8°0S 113°0E **119** G15
Jawad *India* 24°36N 74°51E **124** G6
Jawhar *Somalia* 2°48N 45°30E **131** G4
Jawor *Poland* 51°4N 16°11E **83** G3
Jaworzno *Poland* 50°13N 19°11E **83** H6
Jaworzyna Śląska
Poland 50°55N 16°28E **83** H4
Jay *U.S.A.* 36°25N 94°48W **176** C6
Jay Peak *U.S.A.* 44°55N 72°32W **175** D12
Jaya, Puncak *Indonesia* 3°57S 137°17E **119** E9
Jayanca *Peru* 6°24S 79°50W **188** B2
Jayanti *India* 26°45S 89°42E **123** F16
Jayapura *Indonesia* 2°28S 140°38E **119** E10
Jayawijaya, Pegunungan
Indonesia 5°0S 139°0E **119** F9
Jaynagar *India* 26°43N 86°9E **125** F12
Jaypur = Jeypore *India* 18°50N 82°38E **126** E6
Jayrūd *Syria* 33°49N 36°44E **104** F7
Jayton *U.S.A.* 33°15N 100°34W **176** E4
Jāz Mūrīān, Hāmūn-e
Iran 27°20N 58°55E **129** E8
Jazīreh-ye Shīf *Iran* 29°4N 50°54E **129** D6
Jazminal *Mexico* 24°52N 101°24W **180** C4
Jazzîn *Lebanon* 33°31N 35°35E **130** B4
Jean *U.S.A.* 35°47N 115°20W **171** K11
Jean Marie River
Canada 61°32N 120°38W **162** A4
Jean-Rabel *Haiti* 19°50N 73°5W **183** C5
Jeanerette *U.S.A.* 29°55N 91°40W **176** G9
Jeanette, Ostrov = Zhannetty,
Ostrov *Russia* 76°43N 158°0E **107** B16
Jeannette *U.S.A.* 40°20N 79°36W **174** F5
Jebâl Bârez, Kûh-e *Iran* 28°30N 58°20E **129** D8
Jebba *Nigeria* 9°9N 4°48E **139** D5
Jebel, Bahr el →
South Sudan 9°30N 30°25E **135** G12
Jebel Ali = Minā' Jabal 'Alī
U.A.E. 25°2N 55°8E **129** E7
Jebel Elba △ *Egypt* 22°1N 36°22E **137** C4
Jeberos *Peru* 5°15S 76°10W **188** B2
Jecheon *S. Korea* 37°8N 128°12E **115** F15
Jedburgh *U.K.* 55°29N 2°33W **65** F6
Jedda = Jiddah
Si. Arabia 21°29N 39°10E **128** C2
Jeddore L. *Canada* 48°3N 55°55W **165** C8
Jedlicze *Poland* 49°43N 21°40E **83** J8
Jedrzejów *Poland* 50°35N 20°15E **83** H7
Jedwabne *Poland* 53°17N 22°18E **83** E9
Jeetzel → *Germany* 53°9N 11°3E **76** B7
Jefferson *Ga., U.S.A.* 34°7N 83°35W **178** A6
Jefferson *Iowa, U.S.A.* 42°1N 94°23W **172** D6
Jefferson *Ohio, U.S.A.* 41°44N 80°46W **174** E4
Jefferson *Tex., U.S.A.* 32°46N 94°21W **176** E7
Jefferson, Mt. *Nev.,*
U.S.A. 38°47N 116°56W **168** G5
Jefferson, Mt. *Oreg.,*
U.S.A. 44°41N 121°48W **168** D3
Jefferson City *Mo.,*
U.S.A. 38°34N 92°10W **172** F7

Jefferson City *Tenn.,*
U.S.A. 36°7N 83°30W **177** C13
Jeffersontown *U.S.A.* 38°12N 85°35W **173** F11
Ji'an *Jiangxi, China* 27°6N 114°59E **117** D10
Ji'an *Jilin, China* 41°5N 126°10E **115** C14
Jianchang *China* 40°55N 120°35E **115** D11
Jiang'an *China* 28°40N 105°3E **116** C5
Jiande *China* 29°23N 119°15E **117** C12
Jiangbei *China* 29°40N 106°34E **116** C6
Jiangcheng *China* 22°36N 101°52E **116** F3
Jiangchuan *China* 24°8N 102°39E **116** E4
Jiangdi *China* 26°51N 103°37E **116** D4
Jiangdu *China* 32°27N 119°36E **117** A12
Jiange *China* 32°4N 105°32E **116** B5
Jianghua *China* 25°0N 111°47E **117** E8
Jiangjin *China* 29°14N 106°14E **116** C6
Jiangkou *China* 27°40N 108°49E **116** D7
Jiangle *China* 26°42N 117°23E **117** D11
Jiangmen *China* 22°32N 113°0E **117** F9
Jiangning *China* 31°55N 118°50E **117** B12
Jiangshan *China* 28°40N 118°37E **117** C12
Jiangsu □ *China* 33°0N 120°0E **117** H11
Jiangxi □ *China* 27°30N 116°0E **117** D11
Jiangyan *China* 32°30N 120°7E **117** A13
Jiangyin *China* 31°54N 120°17E **117** B13
Jiangyong *China* 25°20N 111°22E **117** E8
Jiangyou *China* 31°44N 104°43E **116** B5
Jianhe *China* 26°37N 108°31E **116** D7
Jianli *China* 29°46N 112°56E **117** C9
Jianning *China* 26°50N 116°50E **117** D11
Jian'ou *China* 27°3N 118°17E **117** D12
Jianping *China* 41°53N 119°42E **115** D10
Jianshi *China* 30°37N 109°38E **116** B7
Jianshui *China* 23°36N 102°43E **116** F4
Jianyang *Fujian, China* 27°20N 118°5E **117** D12
Jianyang *Sichuan,*
China 30°24N 104°33E **116** B5
Jiao Xian = Jiaozhou
China 36°18N 120°1E **115** F11
Jiaohe *Hebei, China* 38°2N 116°20E **114** E9
Jiaohe *Jilin, China* 43°28N 127°22E **115** C14
Jiaoling *China* 24°41N 116°12E **117** D11
Jiaozhou *China* 36°18N 120°1E **115** F11
Jiaozhou Wan *China* 36°5N 120°10E **115** F11
Jiaozuo *China* 35°16N 113°12E **114** G7
Jiawang *China* 34°28N 117°26E **115** G9
Jiaxiang *China* 35°25N 116°20E **114** G9
Jiaxing *China* 30°49N 120°45E **117** B13
Jiayi = Chiai *Taiwan* 23°29N 120°25E **117** F13
Jiayu *China* 29°55N 113°55E **117** C9
Jiayuguan *China* 39°49N 98°18E **110** C8
Jibão, Serra do *Brazil* 14°48S 45°0W **189** D2
Jibiya *Nigeria* 13°5N 7°12E **138** C6
Jibou *Romania* 47°15N 23°17E **81** C8
Jibuti = Djibouti ■ *Africa* 12°0N 43°0E **131** E3
Jicarón, I. *Panama* 7°10N 81°50W **182** E3
Jičín *Czech Rep.* 50°25N 15°28E **78** A8
Jiddah *Si. Arabia* 21°29N 39°10E **128** C2
Jido *India* 29°2N 94°58E **123** E19
Jieshou *China* 33°18N 115°22E **114** H8
Jiexiu *China* 37°2N 111°55E **114** F6
Jieyang *China* 23°35N 116°21E **117** F11
Jigalong *Australia* 23°21S 120°47E **148** D3
Jigalong ⊙ *Australia* 23°21S 120°46E **148** D3
Jigawa □ *Nigeria* 12°0N 9°45E **139** C6
Jigni *India* 25°45N 79°25E **125** G8
Jihlava *Czech Rep.* 49°28N 15°35E **78** B8
Jihlava → *Czech Rep.* 48°55N 16°36E **79** C9
Jihlavský □ *Czech Rep.* 49°30N 15°45E **78** B8
Jihočeský □ *Czech Rep.* 49°8N 14°35E **78** B7
Jihomoravský □
Czech Rep. 49°5N 16°30E **79** C9
Jijel *Algeria* 36°52N 5°50E **137** A6
Jijel □ *Algeria* 36°45N 6°0E **136** A5
Jijiga *Ethiopia* 9°20N 42°50E **131** F3
Jikamshi *Nigeria* 12°12N 7°45E **138** C6
Jilib *Somalia* 0°29N 42°46E **131** G3
Jilin *China* 43°44N 126°30E **115** C14
Jilin □ *China* 44°0N 127°0E **115** C14
Jiloca → *Spain* 41°21N 1°39W **90** D3
Jilong = Chilung
Taiwan 25°3N 121°45E **117** E13
Jima *Ethiopia* 7°40N 36°47E **131** F2
Jimbaran, Teluk
Indonesia 8°46S 115°9E **119** K18
Jimbolia *Romania* 45°47N 20°43E **80** E5
Jimena de la Frontera
Spain 36°27N 5°24W **89** J5
Jiménez *Mexico* 27°8N 104°54W **180** B4
Jimeta *Nigeria* 9°17N 12°28E **139** D7
Jimo *China* 36°23N 120°30E **115** F11
Jimsar *China* 43°59N 89°4E **109** D11
Jin Xian = Jinzhou
China 38°55N 121°42E **115** E11
Jinan *China* 36°38N 117°1E **114** F9
Jinchang *China* 38°30N 102°10E **110** C9
Jincheng *China* 35°29N 112°30E **114** G7
Jinchuan *China* 31°30N 102°3E **116** B4
Jind *India* 29°19N 76°22E **124** E7
Jindabyne *Australia* 36°25S 148°35E **153** D8
Jindřichův Hradec
Czech Rep. 49°10N 15°2E **78** B8
Jing He → *China* 34°27N 109°42E **114** G5
Jing Shan *China* 31°20N 111°20E **116** B7
Jing Xian *China* 30°38N 118°20E **117** C12
Jing'an *China* 28°50N 115°17E **117** C10
Jingbian *China* 37°20N 108°30E **114** F5
Jingchuan *China* 35°20N 107°20E **114** G4
Jingde *China* 30°15N 118°30E **117** C12
Jingdezhen *China* 29°20N 117°11E **117** C11
Jingdong *China* 24°25N 100°55E **116** E3
Jinggangshan *China* 26°39N 114°10E **117** D10
Jinghai *China* 38°55N 116°55E **114** E9
Jinghong *China* 22°0N 100°45E **116** F3
Jingjiang *China* 32°2N 120°12E **117** A13
Jingle *China* 38°20N 111°55E **114** E6
Jingmen *China* 31°0N 112°10E **117** B9
Jingning *China* 35°30N 105°43E **114** G3
Jingpo Hu *China* 43°55N 128°55E **115** C15
Jingshan *China* 31°1N 113°7E **117** B9
Jingtai *China* 37°10N 104°6E **114** F3

Jialing Jiang → *China* 29°30N 106°20E **116** C6
Jiamusi *China* 46°40N 130°26E **111** B15
Jiande *China* 29°23N 119°15E **117** C12
Jiangchuan *China* 26°38N 99°55E **116** D2
Jiangjin *China* 29°14N 106°14E **116** C6
Jiangyin *China* 31°54N 120°17E **117** B13
Jiaohe *Jilin, China* 43°28N 127°22E **115** C14

Jingtang *China* 39°10N 119°5E **115** E10
Jingxi *China* 23°8N 106°27E **116** F6
Jingyang *China* 34°30N 108°50E **114** G5
Jingyu *China* 42°25N 126°45E **115** C14
Jingyuan *China* 36°30N 104°40E **114** F3
Jingzhou *Hubei, China* 30°21N 112°11E **117** B9
Jingzhou *Hunan, China* 26°33N 109°40E **116** D7
Jingziguan *China* 33°15N 111°0E **114** H6
Jinhua *China* 29°8N 119°38E **117** C12
Jining *Nei Monggol Zizhiqu,*
China 41°5N 113°0E **114** D7
Jining *Shandong, China* 35°22N 116°34E **114** G9
Jinja *Uganda* 0°25N 33°12E **142** B3
Jinjang *Malaysia* 3°13N 101°39E **121** L3
Jinji *China* 37°58N 106°8E **114** F4
Jinjini *Ghana* 7°26N 2°42W **138** D4
Jinju *S. Korea* 35°12N 128°2E **115** G15
Jinkou *China* 30°20N 114°8E **117** B10
Jinkouhe *China* 29°18N 103°4E **116** C4
Jinmu Jiao *China* 18°9N 109°34E **117** a
Jinnah Barrage
Pakistan 32°58N 71°33E **124** C4
Jinning *China* 24°38N 102°38E **116** E4
Jinotega *Nic.* 13°6N 85°59W **182** D2
Jinotepe *Nic.* 11°50N 86°10W **182** D2
Jinping *Guizhou, China* 26°41N 109°10E **116** D7
Jinping *Yunnan, China* 22°45N 103°18E **116** F4
Jinsha *China* 27°29N 106°12E **116** D6
Jinsha Jiang → *China* 28°50N 104°36E **116** C5
Jinshi *China* 29°40N 111°50E **117** C8
Jintan *China* 31°42N 119°36E **117** B12
Jintur *India* 19°37N 76°42E **126** E3
Jinxi *Jiangxi, China* 27°56N 116°45E **117** D11
Jinxi *Liaoning, China* 40°52N 120°50E **115** D11
Jinxian *China* 28°26N 116°17E **117** C11
Jinxiang *China* 35°5N 116°22E **114** G9
Jinyang *China* 27°28N 103°5E **116** D4
Jinyun *China* 28°35N 120°5E **117** C13
Jinzhai *China* 31°40N 115°53E **117** B10
Jinzhong *China* 37°42N 112°46E **114** F7
Jinzhou *Liaoning,*
China 38°55N 121°42E **115** E11
Jinzhou *Liaoning, China* 41°5N 121°3E **115** D11
Jiparaná → *Brazil* 8°3S 62°52W **186** E6
Jipijapa *Ecuador* 1°0S 80°40W **186** D1
Jiquilpan *Mexico* 19°59N 102°43W **180** D4
Jirisan *S. Korea* 35°20N 127°44E **115** G14
Jiroft *Iran* 28°45N 57°50E **129** D8
Jishan *China* 35°34N 110°58E **114** G6
Jishou *China* 28°21N 109°43E **116** C7
Jishui *China* 27°12N 115°7E **117** D10
Jisr ash Shughūr *Syria* 35°49N 36°18E **104** C4
Jitarning *Australia* 32°48S 117°57E **149** F2
Jitra *Malaysia* 6°16N 100°25E **121** J3
Jiu → *Romania* 43°47N 23°48E **81** G8
Jiudengkou *China* 39°56N 106°40E **114** E4
Jiujiang *Guangdong,*
China 22°50N 113°0E **117** F9
Jiujiang *Jiangxi, China* 29°42N 115°58E **117** C10
Jiuling Shan *China* 28°40N 114°40E **117** C10
Jiulong = Kowloon
China 22°19N 114°11E **117** F10
Jiulong *China* 29°15N 101°30E **116** C3
Jiuquan *China* 39°50N 98°20E **110** C8
Jiutai *China* 44°10N 125°50E **115** C13
Jiuxincheng *China* 39°17N 115°59E **114** E8
Jiuzhaigou △ *China* 33°0N 104°0E **116** A4
Jiwani *Pakistan* 25°1N 61°44E **122** G2
Jixi *Anhui, China* 30°18N 118°34E **117** B12
Jixi *Heilongjiang, China* 45°20N 130°50E **115** B16
Jiyang *China* 37°0N 117°1E **115** F9
Jiyuan *China* 35°7N 112°57E **114** G7
Jīzān *Si. Arabia* 17°0N 42°20E **131** D3
Jize *China* 36°54N 114°56E **114** F8
Jizera → *Czech Rep.* 50°10N 14°43E **78** A7
Jizl, Wādī al →
Si. Arabia 25°39N 38°25E **128** E3
Jizō-Zaki *Japan* 35°34N 133°20E **113** G6
Jizzax *Uzbekistan* 40°6N 67°50E **108** E7
Jizzax □ *Uzbekistan* 40°0N 67°40E **108** E7
Joaçaba *Brazil* 27°5S 51°31W **191** B5
Joaima *Brazil* 16°39S 41°2W **189** D2
Joal Fadiout *Senegal* 14°9N 16°50W **138** C1
João Amaro *Brazil* 12°46S 40°22W **189** D3
João Câmara *Brazil* 5°32S 35°48W **189** B3
João Neiva *Brazil* 19°45S 40°24W **189** D3
João Pessoa *Brazil* 7°10S 34°52W **189** B4
João Pinheiro *Brazil* 17°45S 46°10W **189** D2
Joaquín V. González
Argentina 25°10S 64°0W **190** B3
Jobat *India* 22°25N 74°34E **124** H6
Jobourg, Nez de *France* 49°41N 1°57W **70** C5
Jódar *Spain* 37°50N 3°21W **89** H7
Jodhpur *India* 26°23N 73°8E **124** F5
Jodiya *India* 22°42N 70°18E **124** H4
Joensuu *Finland* 62°37N 29°49E **60** E23
Jõetsu *Japan* 37°12N 138°10E **113** F9
Lœuf *France* 49°12N 6°0E **71** C12
Jofane *Mozam.* 21°15S 34°18E **145** B5
Jog Falls = Gersoppa Falls
India 14°12N 74°46E **127** G2
Jogbani *India* 26°25N 87°15E **125** F12
Jõgeva *Estonia* 58°45N 26°24E **84** C4
Jogjakarta = Yogyakarta
Indonesia 7°49S 110°22E **118** F4
Johannesburg *S. Africa* 26°11S 28°2E **145** D4
Johannesburg *U.S.A.* 35°22N 117°38W **171** K9
Johansfors *Sweden* 56°42N 15°32E **63** H9
Johilla → *India* 23°37N 81°14E **125** H9
John Crow Mts. *Jamaica* 18°5N 76°25W **182** a
John Day *U.S.A.* 44°25N 118°57W **168** D4
John Day → *U.S.A.* 45°44N 120°39W **168** D3
John Day Fossil Beds
U.S.A. 44°33N 119°38W **168** D4
John D'or Prairie
Canada 58°30N 115°8W **162** B5
John F. Kennedy Space Center
U.S.A. 28°40N 80°42W **179** G9
John H. Kerr Res.
U.S.A. 36°36N 78°18W **177** C15
John o' Groats *U.K.* 58°38N 3°4W **65** C5
Johnnie *U.S.A.* 36°25N 116°5W **171** J10
Johns Creek *U.S.A.* 34°2N 84°12W **178** A5
Johns I. *U.S.A.* 32°45N 80°7W **178** C9
John's Ra. *Australia* 21°55S 133°23E **150** C1
Johnson *U.S.A.* 44°38N 72°41W **175** B12
Johnson City *Kans.,*
U.S.A. 37°34N 101°45W **172** G3

Johnson City N.Y., U.S.A. 42°7N 75°58W 175 D9
Johnson City Tenn., U.S.A. 36°19N 82°21W 177 C13
Johnson City Tex., U.S.A. 30°17N 98°25W 176 F7
Johnsonburg U.S.A. 41°29N 78°41W 174 E6
Johnsondale U.S.A. 35°58N 118°32W 171 K8
Johnsons Crossing Canada 60°29N 133°18W 162 A2
Johnsonville N.Z. 41°13S 174°48E 154 H3
Johnston U.S.A. 41°35N 81°48W 178 B8
Johnston, L. Australia 32°25S 120°30E 149 F3
Johnston Falls = Mambilima Falls Zambia 10°31S 28°45E 143 E2
Johnston I. Pac. Oc. 17°10N 169°8W 157 F11
Johnstone Str. Canada 50°28N 126°0W 162 C3
Johnstown Ireland 52°45N 7°33W 64 D4
Johnstown N.Y., U.S.A. 43°0N 74°22W 175 C10
Johnstown Ohio, U.S.A. 40°9N 82°41W 174 F2
Johnstown Pa., U.S.A. 40°20N 78°55W 174 F6
Johor □ Malaysia 2°5N 103°20E 121 M4
Johor, Selat Asia 1°28N 103°47E 121 d
Johor Bahru Malaysia 1°28N 103°46E 121 d
Jõhvi Estonia 59°22N 27°27E 84 C4
Joigny France 47°58N 3°20E 71 E10
Joinville Brazil 26°15S 48°55W 191 B6
Joinville France 48°27N 5°10E 71 D12
Joinville I. Antarctica 65°0S 55°30W 55 C18
Jojutla Mexico 18°37N 99°11W 181 D5
Jokelbugten Greenland 78°25N 20°20W 57 B9
Jokkmokk Sweden 66°35N 19°50E 60 C18
Jökulsá á Bru → Iceland 65°40N 14°16W 60 D6
Jökulsá á Fjöllum → Iceland 66°10N 16°30W 60 C5
Jökulsárljúfur △ Iceland 65°56N 16°31W 60 D5
Jolfa Azarbājān-e Sharqī, Iran 38°57N 45°38E 105 C11
Jolfa Esfahan, Iran 32°58N 51°37E 129 C6
Joliet U.S.A. 41°32N 88°5W 172 E9
Joliette Canada 46°3N 73°24W 164 C5
Jolo Phil. 6°0N 121°0E 119 C6
Jolon U.S.A. 35°58N 121°9W 170 K5
Jombang Indonesia 7°33S 112°14E 119 G15
Jomda China 31°28N 98°12E 116 B2
Jonáker Sweden 58°45N 16°45E 63 F10
Jonava Lithuania 55°8N 24°12E 84 E3
Jones Sound Canada 76°0N 85°0W 161 B15
Jonesboro Ark., U.S.A. 35°50N 90°42W 177 D9
Jonesboro Ga., U.S.A. 33°31N 84°22W 178 E3
Jonesboro La., U.S.A. 32°15N 92°43W 176 E8
Jong → S. Leone 7°32N 12°23W 138 D2
Joniškis Lithuania 56°13N 23°35E 82 B10
Jönköping Sweden 57°45N 14°8E 63 G8
Jönköpings län □ Sweden 57°30N 14°30E 63 G8
Jonquière Canada 48°27N 71°14W 165 C5
Jonsered Sweden 57°45N 12°10E 63 G6
Jonzac France 45°27N 0°28W 72 C3
Joplin U.S.A. 37°6N 94°31W 172 G6
Jora India 26°14N 77°44E 124 F6
Jordan Mont., U.S.A. 47°19N 106°55W 168 C10
Jordan N.Y., U.S.A. 43°4N 76°29W 175 C8
Jordan ■ Asia 31°0N 36°0E 130 E5
Jordan → Asia 31°48N 35°32E 130 D4
Jordan Valley U.S.A. 42°59N 117°3W 168 E5
Jordânia Brazil 15°55S 40°11W 189 D2
Jordanów Poland 49°41N 19°49E 83 J6
Jorge, C. Chile 51°40S 75°35W 192 D1
Jorgen Brønlund Fjord Greenland 82°30N 31°0W 57 A7
Jorhat India 26°45N 94°12E 123 F19
Jori → Norway 62°4N 9°5E 62 E5
Jörn Sweden 65°4N 20°1E 60 D19
Jorong Indonesia 3°58S 114°56E 118 E4
Jørpeland Norway 59°3N 6°1E 61 G12
Jorquera → Chile 28°3S 69°58W 190 B2
Joru S. Leone 7°41N 11°3W 138 D2
Jos Nigeria 9°53N 8°51E 139 D6
Jos Plateau Nigeria 9°55N 9°0E 139 D6
Jošanička Banja Serbia 43°24N 20°47E 96 C4
José Batlle y Ordóñez Uruguay 33°20S 55°10W 191 C4
José de San Martín Argentina 44°4S 70°26W 192 E2
Joseni Romania 46°42N 25°29E 81 D7
Joseph, L. Canada 45°10N 79°44W 174 A5
Joseph Banks Group Australia 34°36S 136°16E 152 C2
Joseph Bonaparte G. Australia 14°35S 128°50E 148 B4
Joseph L. Canada 52°45N 65°18W 165 B6
Joshinath India 30°34N 79°34E 125 D8
Joshinetsu-Kōgen △ Japan 36°42N 138°32E 113 F9
Joshua Tree U.S.A. 34°8N 116°19W 171 L10
Joshua Tree △ U.S.A. 33°55N 116°0W 171 M10
Josselin France 47°57N 2°33W 70 E4
Jost Van Dyke I. Br. Virgin Is. 18°29N 64°47W 183 e
Jostedalsbreen Norway 61°40N 6°59E 60 F12
Jotunheimen Norway 61°35N 8°25E 60 F13
Joubertberge Namibia 18°30S 14°0E 144 A1
Joué-lès-Tours France 47°21N 0°40E 70 E7
Jourdanton U.S.A. 28°55N 98°33W 176 G5
Joutseno Finland 61°7N 28°31E 84 B5
Jovellanos Cuba 22°40N 81°10W 182 B3
Jowkār Iran 34°25N 48°40E 105 C13
Jowzjān □ Afghan. 36°10N 66°0E 109 E7
Joyeuse France 44°29N 4°16E 73 D8
Józefów Lubelskie, Poland 50°29N 23°8E 83 H10
Józefów Mazowieckie, Poland 52°10N 21°11E 83 F8
Ju Xian China 36°35N 118°20E 115 F10
Juan Aldama Mexico 24°19N 103°21W 180 C4
Juan Bautista Alberdi Argentina 34°26S 61°48W 190 C3
Juan de Fuca, Str of. N. Amer. 48°15N 124°0W 170 B3
Juan de Nova Ind. Oc. 17°3S 43°45E 145 A7
Juan Fernández, Arch. de Pac. Oc. 33°50S 80°0W 184 G2
Juan José Castelli Argentina 25°27S 60°57W 190 B3
Juan L. Lacaze Uruguay 34°26S 57°25W 190 C4
Juanjuí Peru 7°10S 76°45W 188 E2
Juankoski Finland 63°3N 28°19E 60 E23

Juárez Mexico 27°37N 100°44W 180 B4
Juárez, Sa. de Mexico 32°0N 115°50W 180 A1
Juàzeiro Brazil 9°30S 40°30W 189 B2
Juàzeiro do Norte Brazil 7°10S 39°18W 189 B3
Juazohn Liberia 5°22N 8°50W 138 D3
Juba South Sudan 4°50N 31°35E 135 H12
Juba → Somalia 1°30N 42°35E 131 G3
Jubail = Al Jubayl Si. Arabia 27°0N 49°50E 129 E6
Jubany Antarctica 62°30S 58°0W 55 C18
Jubayl Lebanon 34°5N 35°39E 130 A4
Jubbah Si. Arabia 28°2N 40°56E 128 D4
Jubbal India 31°5N 77°40E 124 D7
Jubbulpore = Jabalpur India 23°9N 79°58E 125 H8
Jübek Germany 54°33N 9°22E 76 A5
Jubga Russia 44°19N 38°48E 87 H4
Jubilee L. Australia 29°0S 126°50E 149 E4
Juby, C. Morocco 28°0N 12°59W 134 C3
Júcar = Xúquer → Spain 39°5N 0°10W 91 F4
Júcaro Cuba 21°37N 78°51W 182 B4
Juchitán de Zaragoza Mexico 16°26N 95°1W 181 D5
Judea = Har Yehuda Israel 31°35N 34°57E 130 D3
Judenburg Austria 47°12N 14°38E 78 D7
Judith → U.S.A. 47°44N 109°39W 168 C9
Judith, Pt. U.S.A. 41°22N 71°29W 175 E13
Judith Gap U.S.A. 46°41N 109°45W 168 C9
Juelsminde Denmark 55°43N 10°1E 63 A4
Juigalpa Nic. 12°6N 85°26W 182 D2
Juillac France 45°20N 1°19E 72 C5
Juiz de Fora Brazil 21°43S 43°19W 191 A7
Jujuy □ Argentina 23°20S 65°40W 190 A2
Julesburg U.S.A. 40°59N 102°16W 168 F12
Juli Peru 16°10S 69°25W 188 G4
Julia Cr. → Australia 20°0S 141°11E 150 C3
Julia Creek Australia 20°39S 141°44E 150 C3
Juliaca Peru 15°25S 70°10W 188 G3
Julian U.S.A. 33°4N 116°38W 171 M10
Julian, L. Canada 54°25N 77°57W 164 B4
Julian Alps = Julijske Alpe Slovenia 46°15N 14°1E 93 B11
Julianatop Suriname 3°40N 56°30W 187 C7
Julianehåb = Qaqortoq Greenland 60°43N 46°0W 57 E6
Jülich Germany 50°55N 6°22E 76 E2
Juliette, L. U.S.A. 33°2N 83°50W 178 B6
Julijske Alpe Slovenia 46°15N 14°1E 93 B11
Julimes Mexico 28°25N 105°27W 180 B3
Jullundur India 31°20N 75°40E 124 D6
Julu China 37°15N 115°2E 114 F8
Jumbo Zimbabwe 17°30S 30°58E 143 F3
Jumbo Pk. U.S.A. 36°12N 114°11W 171 J12
Jumentos Cays Bahamas 23°0N 75°40W 182 B4
Jumilla Spain 38°28N 1°19W 91 G3
Jumla Nepal 29°15N 82°13E 125 E10
Jumna = Yamuna → India 25°30N 81°53E 125 G9
Jumunjin S. Korea 37°55N 128°54E 115 F15
Junagadh India 21°30N 70°30E 124 J4
Junan China 35°12N 118°53E 115 G10
Junction Tex., U.S.A. 30°29N 99°46W 176 F5
Junction Utah, U.S.A. 38°14N 112°13W 169 G7
Junction B. Australia 11°52S 133°55E 150 A1
Junction City Ga., U.S.A. 32°36N 84°28W 178 C5
Junction City Kans., U.S.A. 39°2N 96°50W 172 F5
Junction City Oreg., U.S.A. 44°13N 123°12W 168 D2
Jundah Australia 24°46S 143°2E 150 C3
Jundiaí Brazil 24°30S 47°0W 191 A6
Juneau U.S.A. 58°18N 134°25W 162 B2
Junee Australia 34°53S 147°35E 153 C7
Jungar Qi China 39°49N 110°57E 114 E6
Junggar Pendi China 44°30N 86°0E 109 E11
Jungshahi Pakistan 24°52N 67°44E 124 G2
Juniata → U.S.A. 40°24N 77°1W 174 F7
Junín Argentina 34°33S 60°57W 190 C3
Junín Peru 11°12S 76°0W 188 C2
Junín, L. de Peru 11°0S 76°0W 188 C2
Junín de los Andes Argentina 39°45S 71°0W 192 A2
Jūniyah Lebanon 33°59N 35°38E 130 B4
Junkerdal △ Norway 66°50N 15°0E 60 C16
Junlian China 28°8N 104°29E 116 C5
Junnar India 19°12N 73°58E 126 E1
Juno Beach U.S.A. 26°52N 80°3W 179 J9
Juntas Chile 28°24S 69°58W 190 B2
Juntura U.S.A. 43°45N 118°5W 168 E4
Juparanã, L. Brazil 19°16S 40°8W 189 D2
Jupiter U.S.A. 26°57N 80°6W 179 J9
Jura → Sudan 8°45N 29°15E 135 G11
Jura U.K. 56°0N 5°50W 65 F3
Jura □ France 46°47N 5°45E 71 F12
Jura □ Switz. 47°20N 7°20E 77 H3
Jura = Schwäbische Alb Germany 48°20N 9°30E 77 G5
Jura, Mts. du Europe 46°40N 6°5E 71 F13
Jura, Sd. of U.K. 55°57N 5°45W 65 F3
Jurbarkas Lithuania 55°4N 22°46E 82 C9
Jurien Bay Australia 30°18S 115°2E 149 F2
Jurilovca Romania 44°46N 28°52E 81 F13
Jūrmala Latvia 56°58N 23°34E 82 B10
Jurong China 31°58N 119°9E 117 B12
Jurong Singapore 1°19N 103°42E 121 d
Juruá → Brazil 2°37S 65°44W 186 D5
Juruena Brazil 13°0S 58°10W 186 F7
Juruena → Brazil 7°20S 58°3W 186 E7
Juruti Brazil 2°9S 56°4W 187 D7
Jussey France 47°50N 5°55E 71 E12
Justo Daract Argentina 33°52S 65°12W 190 C2
Jutaí → Brazil 5°11S 68°54W 188 B4
Jüterbog Germany 51°59N 13°5E 76 D9
Juticalpa Honduras 14°40N 86°12W 182 D2
Jutland = Jylland Denmark 56°25N 9°30E 63 H3
Juuka Finland 63°13N 29°17E 60 E23
Juventud, I. de la Cuba 21°40N 82°40W 182 B3
Juvigny-sous-Andaine France 48°32N 0°30W 70 D6
Jüy Zar Iran 33°50N 46°18E 105 F12

Juye China 35°22N 116°5E 114 G9
Juzennecourt France 48°10N 4°58E 71 D11
Jvari Georgia 42°42N 42°4E 87 J6
Jwaneng Botswana 24°45S 24°50E 141 J4
Jyderup Denmark 55°40N 11°26E 63 J5
Jylland Denmark 56°25N 9°30E 63 H3
Jyväskylä Finland 62°14N 25°50E 84 A3

K

K2 Pakistan 35°58N 76°32E 125 B7
Ka → Nigeria 11°40N 4°10E 139 C5
Kaakha ≈ Kaka Turkmenistan 37°21N 59°36E 129 B8
Kaapkruis Namibia 21°55S 13°57E 144 B1
Kaapstad = Cape Town S. Africa 33°55S 18°22E 144 D2
Kaba Guinea 10°9N 11°40W 138 C2
Kabaena Indonesia 5°15S 122°0E 119 F6
Kabala S. Leone 9°38N 11°37W 138 D2
Kabale Uganda 1°15S 30°0E 142 C3
Kabalo Dem. Rep. of the Congo 6°0S 27°0E 142 D2
Kabambare Dem. Rep. of the Congo 4°41S 27°39E 142 C2
Kabango Dem. Rep. of the Congo 8°35S 28°30E 143 D2
Kabanjahe Indonesia 3°6N 98°30E 118 D1
Kabankalan Phil. 9°59N 122°49E 119 C6
Kabara Fiji 18°59S 178°56W 154 a
Kabara Mali 16°40N 2°50W 138 B4
Kabardinka Russia 44°40N 37°57E 85 K10
Kabardino-Balkaria □ Russia 43°30N 43°30E 87 J6
Kabarega Falls = Murchison Falls Uganda 2°15N 31°30E 142 B3
Kabarnet Kenya 0°30N 35°45E 142 B4
Kabasalan Phil. 7°47N 122°44E 119 C6
Kabat Indonesia 8°16S 114°19E 119 J17
Kabba Nigeria 7°50N 6°3E 139 D6
Kabbani → India 12°13N 76°54E 127 H3
Kabin Buri Thailand 13°57N 101°43E 120 F3
Kabinakagami L. Canada 48°54N 84°25W 164 C3
Kabinda Dem. Rep. of the Congo 6°19S 24°20E 140 F4
Kabna Sudan 19°6N 32°40E 137 D3
Kabompo Zambia 13°36S 24°14E 143 E1
Kabompo → Zambia 14°11S 23°11E 141 G4
Kabondo Dem. Rep. of the Congo 8°58S 25°40E 143 D2
Kabongo Dem. Rep. of the Congo 7°22S 25°33E 142 D2
Kabot Guinea 10°48N 14°57W 138 C2
Kabou Togo 9°28N 0°55E 139 D5
Kabrit, G. el Egypt 29°42N 33°16E 130 F2
Kabrousse Senegal 12°25N 16°45W 138 C1
Kabūd Gonbad Iran 37°5N 59°45E 129 B8
Kabudar Ahang Iran 35°11N 48°43E 105 E13
Kābul Afghan. 34°28N 69°11E 124 B3
Kābul □ Afghan. 34°30N 69°0E 109 F7
Kābul → Pakistan 33°55N 72°14E 124 C5
Kabunga Dem. Rep. of the Congo 1°38S 28°3E 142 C2
Kaburuang Indonesia 3°50N 126°30E 119 D7
Kabwe Zambia 14°30S 28°29E 143 E2
Kaçanik Kosovo 42°13N 21°12E 96 D5
Kāčerginė Lithuania 54°56N 23°42E 82 D10
Kachar Kazakhstan 53°22N 62°50E 108 D7
Kachchh, Gulf of India 22°50N 69°15E 124 H3
Kachchh, Rann of India 24°0N 70°0E 124 H4
Kachchhidhana India 21°44N 78°46E 125 J8
Kachebera Zambia 13°50S 32°50E 143 E3
Kachia Nigeria 9°50N 7°55E 139 D6
Kachikau Botswana 18°8S 24°26E 144 A3
Kachin □ Burma 26°0N 97°30E 116 A1
Kachira, L. Uganda 0°40S 31°7E 142 C3
Kachiry Kazakhstan 53°10N 75°50E 108 D9
Kachnara India 23°50N 75°6E 124 H6
Kachot Cambodia 11°30N 103°3E 121 G4
Kaçkar Turkey 40°45N 41°10E 105 B9
Kadaiyanallur India 9°3N 77°22E 127 K3
Kadam, Mt. Uganda 1°45N 34°45E 142 B3
Kadan Czech Rep. 50°23N 13°1E 78 A6
Kadan Kyun Burma 12°30N 98°20E 120 F2
Kadanai → Afghan. 31°22N 65°45E 124 D1
Kadapa India 14°30N 78°10E 127 M11
Kadarkút Hungary 46°13N 17°39E 80 D2
Kadavu Fiji 19°0S 178°15E 154 a
Kadavu Passage Fiji 18°45S 178°0E 154 a
Kade Ghana 6°7N 0°56W 139 D4
Kadhimain = Al Kāzimīyah Iraq 33°22N 44°18E 105 F11
Kadi India 23°18N 72°23E 124 H5
Kadiana Mali 10°45N 6°30W 138 C3
Kadina Australia 33°55S 137°43E 152 B2
Kadınhanı Turkey 38°14N 32°13E 104 C5
Kadiolo Mali 10°35N 7°41W 138 C3
Kadipur India 26°10N 82°23E 125 F10
Kadirabad India 19°51N 75°54E 126 D2
Kadiri India 14°12N 78°13E 127 G4
Kadirli Turkey 37°23N 36°5E 104 D7
Kadiyevka = Stakhanov Ukraine 48°35N 38°40E 85 H10
Kadmat I. India 11°14N 72°47E 127 J3
Kadoka U.S.A. 43°50N 101°31W 172 D3
Kadom Russia 54°37N 42°30E 86 C6
Kadoma Zimbabwe 18°20S 29°52E 143 F2
Kâdugli Sudan 11°0N 29°45E 135 F11
Kaduna Nigeria 10°30N 7°21E 139 C6
Kaduna □ Nigeria 11°0N 7°30E 139 C6
Kaduna → Nigeria 8°45N 5°45E 139 C5
Kadur India 13°34N 76°1E 127 H3
Kaduy Russia 59°12N 37°38E 86 B6
Kaédi Mauritania 16°9N 13°28W 138 B2
Kaélé Cameroon 10°5N 14°28E 137 F7
Kaeng Khoi Thailand 14°35N 101°0E 120 E3
Kaeng Krachan △ Thailand 12°57N 99°23E 120 F2
Kaeng Krung △ Thailand 9°30N 98°40E 121 H2
Kaeng Tana △ Thailand 15°25N 105°32E 120 E5
Kaeo N.Z. 35°6S 173°49E 154 B2
Kaesŏng N. Korea 37°58N 126°35E 115 F14
Kāf Si. Arabia 31°25N 37°29E 128 D3
Kafan = Kapan Armenia 39°18N 46°27E 105 C12
Kafanchan Nigeria 9°40N 8°20E 139 D6

Kafareti Nigeria 10°25N 11°12E 139 C7
Kaffrine Senegal 14°8N 15°36W 138 C1
Kafin Nigeria 9°30N 7°4E 139 C6
Kafin Madaki Nigeria 10°41N 9°46E 139 C6
Kafinda Zambia 12°32S 30°20E 143 E3
Kafr el Battikh Egypt 31°25N 31°44E 137 E7
Kafr el Dauwâr Egypt 31°8N 30°8E 137 D7
Kafr el Sheikh Egypt 31°15N 30°50E 137 D7
Kafr el Zaiyât Egypt 30°49N 30°48E 137 D7
Kafue Zambia 15°46S 28°9E 143 F2
Kafue → Zambia 15°30S 29°0E 141 H5
Kafue △ Zambia 15°12S 25°38E 143 F2
Kafue Flats Zambia 15°40S 27°25E 143 F2
Kafulwe Zambia 9°0S 29°1E 143 D2
Kaga Afghan. 34°14N 70°10E 124 B4
Kaga Bandoro C.A.R. 7°0N 19°10E 140 C3
Kagawa □ Japan 34°15N 134°0E 113 G7
Kagera □ Tanzania 2°0S 31°30E 142 C3
Kagera → Uganda 0°57S 31°47E 142 C3
Kağızman Turkey 40°5N 43°10E 105 B10
Kagoro Nigeria 9°36N 8°23E 139 D6
Kagoshima Japan 31°35N 130°33E 113 J5
Kagoshima □ Japan 31°30N 130°30E 113 J5
Kagul = Cahul Moldova 45°50N 28°15E 81 E13
Kahak Iran 36°6N 49°46E 129 B6
Kahama Tanzania 4°8S 32°30E 142 C3
Kahan Pakistan 29°18N 68°54E 124 E3
Kahang Malaysia 2°12N 103°32E 121 L4
Kahayan → Indonesia 3°40S 114°0E 118 E4
Kahe Tanzania 3°30S 37°25E 142 C4
Kahemba Dem. Rep. of the Congo 7°18S 18°55E 140 F3
Kaherekoau Mts. N.Z. 45°15S 167°15E 155 F2
Kahil, Djebel bou Algeria 34°26N 4°0E 136 B4
Kahnūj Iran 27°55N 57°40E 129 E8
Kahoka U.S.A. 40°25N 91°44W 172 E8
Kaho'olawe U.S.A. 20°33N 156°37W 167 L8
Kahramanmaraş Turkey 37°37N 36°53E 104 D7
Kahramanmaraş □ Turkey 37°35N 36°53E 104 D7
Kahta Turkey 37°47N 38°48E 105 D8
Kahul, Ozero Ukraine 45°24N 28°24E 81 E13
Kahului U.S.A. 20°54N 156°28W 167 L8
Kahurangi △ N.Z. 41°10S 172°32E 155 D4
Kahurangi Pt. N.Z. 40°50S 172°10E 155 D4
Kahuta Pakistan 33°35N 73°24E 124 C5
Kahuzi-Biega △ Dem. Rep. of the Congo 1°50S 27°55E 142 C2
Kai, Kepulauan Indonesia 5°55S 132°45E 119 F8
Kai Besar Indonesia 5°35S 133°0E 119 F8
Kai Is. = Kai, Kepulauan Indonesia 5°55S 132°45E 119 F8
Kai Kecil Indonesia 5°45S 132°40E 119 F8
Kai Xian China 31°11N 108°21E 116 B7
Kaiama Nigeria 9°36N 4°1E 139 D5
Kaiapoi N.Z. 43°24S 172°40E 155 D7
Kaidu He → China 41°46N 86°31E 110 C6
Kaieteur Falls Guyana 5°1N 59°10W 186 B7
Kaifeng China 34°48N 114°21E 114 G8
Kaihua China 29°12N 118°20E 117 C12
Kaijiang China 31°7N 107°59E 116 B6
Kaikohe N.Z. 35°25S 173°49E 154 B2
Kaikoura N.Z. 42°25S 173°43E 155 D5
Kaikoura Pen. N.Z. 42°25S 173°43E 155 C8
Kailahun S. Leone 8°18N 10°39W 138 D2
Kailash = Kangrinboqê Feng China 31°0N 81°25E 125 D9
Kaili China 26°33N 107°59E 116 D6
Kailu China 43°38N 121°18E 115 C11
Kailua Kona U.S.A. 19°39N 155°59W 167 M8
Kaimaktsalan Oros = Voras Oros Greece 40°57N 21°45E 96 F5
Kaimana Indonesia 3°39S 133°45E 119 E8
Kaimanawa Mts. N.Z. 39°15S 175°56E 154 F4
Kaimata N.Z. 42°35S 171°28E 155 C6
Kaimganj India 27°33N 79°24E 125 F8
Kaimur Hills India 24°30N 82°0E 125 G10
Kainab → Namibia 28°32S 19°34E 144 C2
Kainji Dam Nigeria 9°55N 4°35E 139 D5
Kainji Lake △ Nigeria 10°1N 4°40E 139 C5
Kainji Res. Nigeria 10°1N 4°40E 139 C5
Kainuu □ Finland 64°30N 29°7E 60 D23
Kaipara Harbour N.Z. 36°25S 174°14E 154 C3
Kaiping China 22°23N 112°42E 117 F9
Kaipokok B. Canada 54°54N 59°47W 165 B8
Kaira India 22°45N 72°50E 124 H5
Kaironi Indonesia 0°47S 133°40E 119 E8
Kairouan Tunisia 35°45N 10°5E 136 A6
Kairouan □ Tunisia 35°30N 9°45E 136 A6
Kaiserslautern Germany 49°26N 7°45E 77 F3
Kaiserstuhl Germany 48°4N 7°40E 77 G3
Kaitaia N.Z. 35°8S 173°17E 154 B2
Kaitangata N.Z. 46°17S 169°51E 155 G4
Kaithal India 29°48N 76°26E 124 E7
Kaitu → Pakistan 33°10N 70°30E 124 C4
Kaiwi Channel U.S.A. 21°15N 157°30W 167 L8
Kaiyang China 27°4N 106°59E 116 D6
Kaiyuan Liaoning, China 42°28N 124°1E 115 C13
Kaiyuan Yunnan, China 23°40N 103°12E 116 F4
Kaiyuh Mts. U.S.A. 64°30N 158°0W 166 C8
Kajaani Finland 64°17N 27°46E 60 D22
Kajabbi Australia 20°0S 140°1E 150 C3
Kajana = Kajaani Finland 64°17N 27°46E 60 D22
Kajang Malaysia 2°59N 101°48E 121 L3
Kajaran Armenia 39°10N 46°7E 105 C12
Kajiado Kenya 1°53S 36°48E 142 C4
Kajo Kaji South Sudan 3°58N 31°40E 135 H12
Kajuru Nigeria 10°19N 7°40E 139 C6
Kaka Turkmenistan 37°21N 59°36E 129 B8
Kakabeka Falls Canada 48°24N 89°37W 164 C2
Kakadu △ Australia 12°0S 132°3E 148 B5
Kakamas S. Africa 28°45S 20°33E 144 D3
Kakamega Kenya 0°20N 34°46E 142 B3
Kakanj Bos.-H. 44°4N 18°4E 96 C3
Kakanui Mts. N.Z. 45°10S 170°30E 155 F3
Kakata Liberia 6°35N 10°20W 138 D2
Kakdwip India 21°53N 88°11E 125 J13
Kake Japan 34°36N 132°19E 113 G6
Kakegawa Japan 34°45N 138°1E 113 G9
Kakeroma-Jima Japan 28°8N 129°14E 113 K4

Kākhak Iran 34°9N 58°38E 129 C8
Kakhib Russia 42°28N 46°34E 87 J8
Kakhovka Ukraine 46°45N 33°30E 85 J7
Kakhovske Vdskh. Ukraine 47°5N 34°0E 85 J7
Kakinada India 16°57N 82°11E 126 F6
Kakisa → Canada 61°3N 118°10W 162 A5
Kakisa Canada 60°56N 117°43W 162 A5
Kakisa L. Canada 60°56N 117°43W 162 A5
Kakogawa Japan 34°46N 134°51E 113 G7
Kakuma Kenya 3°43N 34°52E 142 B3
Kakwa → Canada 54°37N 118°28W 162 C5
Kål Gūsheh Iran 30°59N 58°12E 129 D8
Kal Sefid Iran 34°52N 47°23E 105 E12
Kala Nigeria 12°2N 14°40E 139 C7
Kala Oya → Sri Lanka 8°20N 79°45E 127 K4
Kalaallit Nunaat = Greenland ☑ N. Amer. 66°0N 45°0W 57 C6
Kalabagh Pakistan 33°0N 71°28E 124 C4
Kalabahi Indonesia 8°13S 124°31E 119 F6
Kalabo Zambia 14°58S 22°40E 141 G4
Kalach Russia 50°22N 41°0E 86 E5
Kalach na Donu Russia 48°43N 43°32E 87 F6
Kalachinsk Russia 55°3N 74°33E 108 D8
Kaladan → Burma 20°20N 93°5E 123 J18
Kaladar Canada 44°37N 77°5W 174 B7
Kalahari Botswana 24°0S 21°30E 144 A3
Kalahari Gemsbok △ S. Africa 25°30S 20°30E 144 C3
Kalaikhum Tajikistan 38°28N 70°46E 109 F8
Kalajoki Finland 64°12N 24°10E 60 D21
Kalakamati Botswana 20°40S 27°25E 145 B4
Kalakan Russia 55°15N 116°45E 107 D12
K'alak'unlun Shank'ou = Karakoram Pass Asia 35°33N 77°50E 125 B7
Kalam Pakistan 35°34N 72°30E 125 B5
Kalama Dem. Rep. of the Congo 2°52S 28°35E 142 C2
Kalámai = Kalamata Greece 37°3N 22°10E 98 D4
Kalamariá Greece 40°33N 22°55E 96 F6
Kalamata Greece 37°3N 22°10E 98 D4
Kalamazoo U.S.A. 42°17N 85°35W 173 D11
Kalamazoo → U.S.A. 42°40N 86°10W 172 D10
Kalamb India 18°3N 74°48E 126 E2
Kalambaka Greece 39°42N 21°39E 98 B3
Kalambo Falls Tanzania 8°37S 31°35E 143 D3
Kalamnuri India 19°35N 77°20E 126 E3
Kalamos Attiki, Greece 38°17N 23°52E 98 C5
Kalamos Lefkada, Greece 38°37N 20°43E 98 C2
Kalan Turkey 39°7N 39°32E 128 B3
Kalangadoo Australia 37°34S 140°41E 152 D4
Kalannie Australia 30°22S 117°5E 149 F2
Kalāntarī Iran 32°10N 54°8E 129 C7
Kalao Indonesia 7°21S 121°0E 119 F6
Kalaotoa Indonesia 7°20S 121°50E 119 F6
Kälarne Sweden 62°59N 16°5E 62 B10
Kalasin Thailand 16°26N 103°30E 120 D4
Kālat Iran 25°29N 59°22E 129 E8
Kalat Pakistan 29°8N 66°31E 124 E2
Kālāteh Iran 36°33N 55°41E 129 B7
Kālāteh-ye Ganj Iran 27°31N 57°55E 129 E8
Kalathos Greece 36°9N 28°8E 99 E13
Kalaus → Russia 45°40N 44°7E 87 H7
Kalávrita Greece 38°3N 22°8E 98 C4
Kalbā U.A.E. 25°5N 56°22E 129 E8
Kalbarri Australia 27°40S 114°10E 149 E1
Kalbarri △ Australia 27°51S 114°30E 149 E1
Kalce Slovenia 45°54N 14°13E 74 F8
Kale Antalya, Turkey 36°14N 30°0E 99 E12
Kale Denizli, Turkey 37°27N 28°49E 99 D10
Kalecik Turkey 40°4N 33°26E 104 B5
Kalegauk Kyun Burma 15°33N 97°35E 120 E1
Kalehe Dem. Rep. of the Congo 2°6S 28°50E 142 C2
Kalema Tanzania 1°12S 31°55E 142 C3
Kalemie Dem. Rep. of the Congo 5°55S 29°9E 142 D2
Kalety Poland 50°35N 18°52E 83 H5
Kalewa Burma 23°10N 94°15E 123 H19
Kaleybar Iran 38°47N 47°2E 105 C12
Kalghatgi India 15°11N 74°58E 127 G2
Kalgoorlie-Boulder Australia 30°40S 121°22E 149 F3
Kali → India 27°6N 79°57E 125 F8
Kali Sindh → India 25°32N 76°17E 124 G6
Kaliakra, Nos Bulgaria 43°21N 28°30E 97 C12
Kalianda Indonesia 5°50S 105°45E 118 F3
Kalibo Phil. 11°43N 122°22E 119 B6
Kalima Dem. Rep. of the Congo 2°33S 26°32E 142 C2
Kalimantan □ Indonesia 0°0 114°0E 118 E4
Kalimantan Barat □ Indonesia 0°0 110°30E 118 E4
Kalimantan Selatan □ Indonesia 2°30S 115°30E 118 E5
Kalimantan Tengah □ Indonesia 2°0S 113°30E 118 E4
Kalimantan Timur □ Indonesia 1°30N 116°30E 118 D5
Kálimnos Greece 37°0N 27°0E 99 E8
Kalimpong India 27°4N 88°35E 125 F13
Kalinadi → India 14°50N 74°7E 127 G2
Kaliningrad Russia 54°42N 20°32E 82 D7
Kaliningrad ✈ (KGD) Russia 54°45N 20°33E 82 D7
Kalininsk Russia 51°30N 44°40E 86 E6
Kalinkavichy Belarus 52°12N 29°20E 75 D15
Kalinkovichi = Kalinkavichy Belarus 52°12N 29°20E 75 D15
Kalinovik Bos.-H. 43°31N 18°25E 96 C3
Kaliro Uganda 0°56N 33°30E 142 B3
Kalirachi Greece 40°57N 24°35E 97 D11
Kalispell U.S.A. 48°12N 114°19W 168 B6
Kalisz Poland 51°45N 18°8E 83 G5
Kalisz Pomorski Poland 53°17N 15°55E 83 E2
Kalithea Greece 37°56N 23°43E 98 D5
Kaliua Tanzania 5°5S 31°48E 142 D3
Kaliveli Tank India 12°5N 79°50E 127 H4
Kalix → Sweden 65°50N 23°11E 60 D20
Kalixälven → Sweden 65°50N 23°11E 60 D20
Kalka India 30°46N 76°57E 124 D7

Kalkan Turkey 36°15N 29°23E 99 E11
Kalkarindji Australia 17°30S 130°47E 148 C5
Kalkaska U.S.A. 44°44N 85°11W 173 C11
Kalkfeld Namibia 20°57S 16°14E 144 B2
Kalkfontein Botswana 22°4S 20°57E 144 B3
Kalkrand Namibia 24°1S 17°35E 144 B2
Kallakkurichi India 11°44N 79°1E 127 J4
Kallam India 18°36N 76°2E 126 E3
Kallavesi Finland 62°58N 27°30E 60 E22
Kållered Sweden 57°30N 12°4E 63 G6
Kalleh Sweden 58°30N 13°8E 63 F7
Kallidaikurichi India 8°38N 77°31E 127 K3
Kallimasia Greece 38°18N 26°6E 99 C8
Kallinge Sweden 56°15N 15°18E 63 H7
Kallmet Albania 41°51N 19°41E 96 E3
Kallsjön Sweden 63°38N 13°0E 60 E15
Kalmalo Nigeria 13°40N 5°20E 139 C6
Kalmar Sweden 56°40N 16°20E 63 H10
Kalmar □ = Sweden 57°25N 16°0E 63 G10
Kalmar sund Sweden 56°40N 16°25E 63 H10
Kalmunai Sri Lanka 7°25N 81°49E 127 L5
Kalmykia □ Russia 46°5N 46°1E 87 G8
Kalna India 23°13N 88°25E 125 H13
Kalnai India 22°46N 83°30E 125 H10
Kalo Nero Greece 37°20N 21°38E 98 D3
Kalocsa Hungary 46°32N 19°0E 80 D4
Kalofer Bulgaria 42°37N 24°59E 97 C7
Kalokhorio Cyprus 34°51N 33°2E 101 E12
Kaloko Dem. Rep. of the Congo 6°47S 25°48E 142 D2
Kalol Gujarat, India 22°37N 73°31E 124 H5
Kalol Gujarat, India 23°15N 72°33E 124 H5
Kalolimnos Greece 37°4N 27°5E 99 D9
Kalomo Zambia 17°0S 26°30E 143 F2
Kaloni India 26°8N 79°47E 125 F8
Kaloni, Kolpos Greece 39°10N 26°10E 99 B8
Kalpeni I. India 10°5N 73°38E 127 J1
Kalpi India 26°8N 79°47E 125 F8
Kalpitiya Sri Lanka 8°14N 79°46E 127 K4
Kalputhi I. India 10°49N 72°10E 127 J1
Kalrayan Hills India 11°45N 78°40E 127 J4
Kalsubai India 19°35N 73°45E 126 E1
Kaltern = Caldaro Italy 46°25N 11°14E 93 B8
Kaltukatjara Australia 24°52S 129°5E 149 D4
Kaltungo Nigeria 9°48N 11°19E 139 D7
Kalu Pakistan 25°5N 67°39E 124 G2
Kaluga Russia 54°35N 36°10E 84 E4
Kaluga □ Russia 54°15N 34°50E 84 E4
Kalulushi Zambia 12°50S 28°3E 143 E2
Kalumburu Australia 14°17S 126°38E 148 B4
Kalundborg Denmark 55°41N 11°5E 63 J4
Kalush Ukraine 49°3N 24°23E 75 D13
Kaluszyn Poland 52°13N 21°52E 83 F8
Kalutara Sri Lanka 6°35N 80°0E 127 L5
Kalyan Maharashtra, India 20°30N 74°3E 126 D2
Kalyan Maharashtra, India 19°15N 73°9E 126 E1
Kalyandurg India 14°33N 77°6E 127 G3
Kalyani India 17°52N 76°57E 126 F3
Kalyazin Russia 57°15N 37°55E 84 D9
Kam → Nigeria 8°15N 10°0E 139 D7
Kama Dem. Rep. of the Congo 3°30S 27°5E 142 C2
Kama Japan 33°33N 130°49E 113 H5
Kama → Russia 55°45N 52°0E 106 D6
Kamachumu Tanzania 1°37S 31°37E 142 C3
Kamaishi Japan 39°16N 141°53E 112 E10
Kamalapuram India 14°35N 78°23E 127 G4
Kamalia Pakistan 30°44N 72°42E 124 D5
Kaman India 27°39N 77°16E 124 F6
Kamanjab Namibia 19°35S 14°51E 144 A2
Kamapanda Zambia 12°5S 24°0E 143 E1
Kamaran Yemen 15°21N 42°35E 131 D3
Kamareddi India 18°19N 78°21E 126 E4
Kamativi Zimbabwe 18°20S 27°6E 144 A4
Kamba Nigeria 11°50N 3°45E 139 C5
Kambalda West Australia 31°10S 121°37E 149 F3
Kambam India 9°45N 77°16E 127 K3
Kambangan, Nusa Indonesia 7°40S 108°10E 119 G13
Kambar Pakistan 27°37N 68°1E 124 F3
Kambia S. Leone 9°3N 12°53W 138 D2
Kambolé Togo 8°43N 1°33E 139 D5
Kambolé Zambia 8°47S 30°48E 143 D3
Kambos Cyprus 35°2N 32°44E 101 D11
Kambove Dem. Rep. of the Congo 10°51S 26°33E 143 E2
Kamchatka, Poluostrov Russia 57°0N 160°0E 107 D17
Kamchatka Pen. = Kamchatka, Poluostrov Russia 57°0N 160°0E 107 D17
Kamchiya → Bulgaria 43°4N 27°44E 97 C11
Kame Ruins Zimbabwe 20°7S 28°25E 143 G2
Kameda-Hantō Japan 41°50N 141°0E 112 D10
Kamen Russia 53°50N 81°30E 108 D10
Kamen-Rybolov Russia 44°46N 132°2E 112 B6
Kamenica Serbia 44°25N 19°45E 96 B3
Kamenica nad Lipou Czech Rep. 49°18N 15°2E 78 D8
Kamenjak, Rt Croatia 44°47N 13°55E 93 D10
Kamenka = Kamyanka Ukraine 49°3N 32°6E 85 H7
Kamenka Kazakhstan 51°17N 50°19E 86 E10
Kamenka Russia 53°10N 44°5E 86 E6
Kamenka Voronezh., Russia 50°47N 39°20E 86 E4
Kamenka Bugskaya = Kamyanka-Buzka Ukraine 50°8N 24°16E 75 C13
Kamenka Dneprovskaya = Kamyanka-Dniprovska Ukraine 47°29N 34°28E 85 J8
Kamennomostskiy Russia 44°18N 40°13E 87 H5
Kameno Bulgaria 42°34N 27°18E 97 D11

Kamensk-Shakhtinskiy
  Russia 48°23N 40°20E 87 F5
Kamensk Uralskiy
  Russia 56°25N 62°02E 106 D7
Kamenskiy Russia 50°48N 45°25E 86 E7
Kamenskoye Russia 62°45N 165°30E 107 C17
Kamenyak Bulgaria 43°24N 26°57E 97 C12
Kamenz Germany 51°15N 14°5E 76 D10
Kameoka Japan 35°0N 135°35E 113 G7
Kamet India 30°55N 79°35E 125 D8
Kamiah U.S.A. 46°14N 116°2W 168 C5
Kamień Krajeński
  Poland 53°32N 17°32E 82 E4
Kamień Pomorski
  Poland 53°57N 14°43E 82 E1
Kamienna → Poland 51°6N 21°47E 83 G8
Kamienna Góra Poland 50°47N 16°2E 83 H3
Kamieńsk Poland 51°12N 19°29E 83 G6
Kamieskroon S. Africa 30°9S 17°56E 144 D2
Kamilukuak L.
  Canada 62°22N 101°40W 163 A8
Kamin-Kashyrskyy
  Ukraine 51°39N 24°56E 75 C13
Kamina
  Dem. Rep. of the Congo 8°45S 25°0E 143 D2
Kaminak L. Canada 62°10N 95°0W 163 A10
Kaminoyama Japan 38°9N 140°17E 112 E10
Kamiros Greece 36°20N 27°56E 101 C9
Kamituga
  Dem. Rep. of the Congo 3°2S 28°10E 142 C2
Kamla → India 25°35N 86°36E 125 G12
Kamloops Canada 50°40N 120°20W 162 C4
Kamnik Slovenia 46°14N 14°37E 93 B11
Kamo Armenia 40°21N 45°7E 87 K7
Kamo Japan 37°39N 139°3E 112 F9
Kamo N.Z. 35°42S 174°20E 154 B3
Kamoke Pakistan 32°4N 74°4E 124 C6
Kamp → Austria 48°23N 15°42E 78 C8
Kampala Uganda 0°20N 32°32E 142 B3
Kampar Malaysia 4°18N 101°9E 121 K3
Kampar → Indonesia 0°30N 103°8E 118 D2
Kampen Neths. 52°33N 5°53E 69 B5
Kampene
  Dem. Rep. of the Congo 3°36S 26°40E 140 E5
Kamphaeng Phet
  Thailand 16°28N 99°30E 120 D2
Kampinoski △ Poland 52°21N 20°40E 83 F7
Kampolombo, L.
  Zambia 11°37S 29°42E 143 E2
Kampong Cham
  Cambodia 12°0N 105°30E 121 G5
Kampong Chhnang
  Cambodia 12°20N 104°35E 121 F5
Kampong Pengerang
  Malaysia 1°22N 104°7E 121 d
Kampong Punggai
  Malaysia 1°27N 104°18E 121 d
Kampong Saom
  Cambodia 10°38N 103°30E 121 G4
Kampong Saom, Chaak
  Cambodia 10°50N 103°32E 121 G4
Kampong Tanjong Langsat
  Malaysia 1°28N 104°1E 121 d
Kampong Telok Ramunia
  Malaysia 1°22N 104°15E 121 d
Kampot Cambodia 10°36N 104°10E 121 G5
Kampti Burkina Faso 10°7N 3°25W 138 C4
Kampuchea = Cambodia ■
  Asia 12°15N 105°0E 120 F5
Kampung Air Putih
  Malaysia 4°15N 103°10E 121 K4
Kampung Jerangau
  Malaysia 4°50N 103°10E 121 K4
Kampung Raja
  Malaysia 5°45N 102°35E 121 K4
Kampungbaru = Tolitoli
  Indonesia 1°5N 120°50E 119 D6
Kamrau, Teluk
  Indonesia 3°30S 133°36E 119 E8
Kamsack Canada 51°34N 101°54W 163 C8
Kamsar Guinea 10°40N 14°36W 138 C2
Kamskoye Ustye Russia 55°10N 49°20E 86 C9
Kamthi India 21°9N 79°19E 126 D4
Kamuchawie L.
  Canada 56°18N 101°59W 163 B8
Kamui-Misaki Japan 43°20N 140°21E 112 C10
Kamyanets-Podilskyy
  Ukraine 48°45N 26°40E 81 B11
Kamyanka Ukraine 49°3N 32°6E 85 H7
Kamyanka-Buzka
  Ukraine 50°8N 24°16E 75 C13
Kamyanka-Dniprovska
  Ukraine 47°29N 34°28E 85 J8
Kamyanyets Belarus 52°23N 23°49E 83 F10
Kamyanyuki Belarus 52°32N 23°49E 83 F11
Kâmyârân Iran 34°47N 46°56E 105 E12
Kamyshin Russia 50°10N 45°24E 86 E7
Kamyzyak Russia 46°4N 48°10E 87 G9
Kanaaupscow →
  Canada 54°2N 76°30W 164 B4
Kanab U.S.A. 37°3N 112°32W 169 H7
Kanab Cr. → U.S.A. 36°24N 112°38W 169 H7
Kanacea Lau Group, Fiji 17°15S 179°6W 154 a
Kanacea Taveuni, Fiji 16°59S 179°56E 154 a
Kanaga I. U.S.A. 51°45N 177°22W ...
Kanagi Japan 40°54N 140°27E 112 D10
Kanairiktok → Canada 55°2N 60°18W 165 A7
Kanakapura India 12°33N 77°28E 127 H3
Kanalia Greece 39°30N 22°53E 98 B4
Kananga
  Dem. Rep. of the Congo 5°55S 22°18E 140 F4
Kanangra-Boyd △
  Australia 33°57S 150°15E 153 B9
Kanash Russia 55°30N 47°32E 86 C8
Kanaskat U.S.A. 47°19N 121°54W 170 C5
Kanastraíon, Ákra = Paliouri,
  Akra Greece 39°57N 23°45E 96 G7
Kanawha → U.S.A. 38°50N 82°9W 173 F12
Kanazawa Japan 36°30N 136°38E 113 F8
Kanchanaburi Thailand 14°2N 99°31E 120 E2
Kanchenjunga Nepal 27°42N 88°8E 125 F13
Kanchenjunga △ India 27°42N 88°8E 125 F13
Kanchipuram India 12°52N 79°45E 127 H3
Kańczuga Poland 49°59N 22°25E 83 J9
Kandaghat India 30°59N 77°7E 124 D7
Kandahār = Kandahār
  Afghan. 31°32N 65°43E 124 D1
Kandahār □ Afghan. 18°52N 77°12E 126 E3
Kandahār □ Afghan. 31°0N 65°0E 124 D1
Kandalaksha Russia 67°9N 32°30E 60 C25
Kandangan Indonesia 2°50S 115°20E 118 E5
Kandanos Greece 35°19N 23°44E 101 D5

Kandava Latvia 57°2N 22°46E 82 A9
Kandavu = Kadavu Fiji 19°0S 178°15E 154 a
Kandavu Passage = Kadavu
  Passage Fiji 18°45S 178°0E 154 a
Kandé = Kanté Togo 9°57N 1°3E 139 D5
Kandhkot Pakistan 28°16N 69°8E 124 E3
Kandhla India 29°18N 77°19E 124 E7
Kandi Benin 11°7N 2°55E 139 C5
Kandi India 23°58N 88°5E 125 H13
Kandiaro Pakistan 27°4N 68°13E 124 F3
Kandila Greece 37°46N 22°22E 98 D4
Kandıra Turkey 41°4N 30°9E 104 B4
Kandla India 23°0N 70°10E 124 H4
Kandos Australia 32°45S 149°58E 153 B8
Kandy Sri Lanka 7°18N 80°43E 127 L5
Kane U.S.A. 41°40N 78°49W 174 E6
Kane Basin Greenland 79°1N 70°0W 57 B4
Kanel Senegal 15°30N 13°18E 138 B2
Kanevskaya Russia 46°3N 38°57E 87 G4
Kanfanar Croatia 45°7N 13°50E 93 C10
Kang Botswana 23°41S 22°50E 144 B3
Kangaamiut Greenland 65°50N 53°20W 57 D5
Kangaatsiaq Greenland 68°18N 53°28W 57 D5
Kangaba Mali 11°56N 8°25W 138 C3
Kangal Turkey 39°14N 37°23E 104 C7
Kangān Fārs, Iran 27°50N 52°3E 129 E7
Kangān Hormozgān,
  Iran 25°48N 57°28E 129 E8
Kangar Malaysia 6°27N 100°12E 121 J3
Kangaré Mali 11°36N 8°4W 138 C3
Kangaroo I. Australia 35°45S 137°0E 152 C2
Kangaroo Mts.
  Australia 23°29S 141°51E 150 C3
Kangasala Finland 61°28N 24°4E 84 B3
Kangāvar Iran 34°40N 48°0E 105 E12
Kangding China 30°2N 101°57E 116 B3
Kangdong N. Korea 39°9N 126°5E 115 E14
Kangean, Kepulauan
  Indonesia 6°55S 115°23E 118 F5
Kangean Is. = Kangean,
  Kepulauan Indonesia 6°55S 115°23E 118 F5
Kangerdlugssuaq
  Greenland 68°10N 32°20W 57 D7
Kangerluarsoruseq
  Greenland 63°45N 51°27W 57 E5
Kangerluarsoruset =
  Kangerluarsoruseq
  Greenland 63°45N 51°27W 57 E5
Kangerlussuaq
  Greenland 66°59N 50°40W 57 D5
Kangertittivaq = Scoresby Sund
  Greenland 70°28N 21°46W 57 C8
Kanggye N. Korea 41°0N 126°35E 115 D14
Kangikajik Greenland 70°7N 22°0W 57 C8
Kangilinnguit Greenland 61°20N 47°57W 57 E6
Kangiqliniq = Rankin Inlet
  Canada 62°30N 93°0W 160 E13
Kangiqsualujjuaq
  Canada 58°30N 65°59W 161 F18
Kangiqsujuaq Canada 61°30N 72°0W 161 E17
Kangiqtugaapik = Clyde River
  Canada 70°30N 68°30W 161 C18
Kangirsuk Canada 60°0N 70°0W 161 F18
Kangkar Chemaran
  Malaysia 1°34N 104°12E 121 d
Kangkar Sungai Tiram
  Malaysia 1°35N 103°55E 121 d
Kangkar Teberau
  Malaysia 1°32N 103°51E 121 d
Kangping China 42°43N 123°18E 115 C12
Kangra India 32°6N 76°16E 124 C7
Kangrinboqê Feng
  China 31°0N 81°25E 125 D9
Kanha △ India 22°15N 80°40E 125 H9
Kanhan → India 21°4N 79°34E 126 D4
Kanhangad India 12°1N 74°58E 127 H2
Kanhar → India 24°28N 83°8E 125 G10
Kani Ivory C. 8°29N 6°36W 138 D3
Kaniama
  Dem. Rep. of the Congo 7°30S 24°12E 142 D1
Kaniapiskau = Caniapiscau →
  Canada 56°40N 69°30W 165 A6
Kaniapiskau, L. = Caniapiscau, L.
  Canada 54°10N 69°55W 165 B6
Kaniere, L. N.Z. 42°50S 171°10E 155 D6
Kanigiri India 15°24N 79°31E 127 G4
Kanin, Poluostrov Russia 68°0N 45°0E 58 B14
Kanin Nos, Mys Russia 68°39N 43°32E 58 B14
Kanin Pen. = Kanin, Poluostrov
  Russia 68°0N 45°0E 58 B14
Kaninë Albania 40°23N 19°30E 96 F3
Kaniva Australia 36°22S 141°18E 152 C4
Kanjiža Serbia 46°3N 20°4E 80 D5
Kanjut Sar Pakistan 36°7N 75°25E 125 A6
Kankaanpää Finland 61°44N 22°50E 84 B2
Kankakee U.S.A. 41°7N 87°52W 172 E10
Kankakee → U.S.A. 41°23N 88°15W 172 E9
Kankan Guinea 10°23N 9°15W 138 C3
Kankendy = Xankändi
  Azerbaijan 39°52N 46°49E 105 C12
Kanker India 20°10N 81°40E 126 D5
Kankesanturai Sri Lanka 9°49N 80°2E 127 K5
Kankossa Mauritania 15°54N 11°31W 138 B2
Kankroli India 25°4N 73°53E 124 G5
Kanmaw Kyun Burma 11°40N 98°28E 121 G2
Kannapolis U.S.A. 35°30N 80°37W 177 D14
Kannauj India 27°3N 79°56E 125 F8
Kanniyakumari India 8°5N 77°34E 127 L3
Kannod India 22°45N 76°40E 122 H10
Kannur India 11°53N 75°27E 127 J2
Kannukamari India 8°3N 77°40E 127 L3
Kano Nigeria 12°2N 8°30E 139 C6
Kan'onji Japan 34°7N 133°39E 113 G6
Kanowit Malaysia 2°14N 112°20E 118 D4
Kanowna Australia 30°32S 121°31E ...
Kanoya Japan 9°7N 6°49E 138 D4
Kanpetlet Burma 21°10N 93°59E 123 J18
Kanpur India 26°28N 80°20E 125 F9
Kansas □ U.S.A. 38°30N 99°0W 172 F5
Kansas → U.S.A. 39°7N 94°37W 172 F6
Kansas City Kans.,
  U.S.A. 39°7N 94°38W 172 F6
Kansas City Mo., U.S.A. 39°6N 94°35W 172 F6
Kansenia
  Dem. Rep. of the Congo 10°20S 26°0E 143 E2
Kansk Russia 56°20N 95°37E 107 D10
Kansu = Gansu □ China 36°0N 104°0E 114 G3
Kantaphor India 22°35N 76°34E 124 H7
Kantchari Burkina Faso 12°37N 1°31E 139 C5

Kantché Niger 13°31N 8°30E 139 C6
Kanté Togo 9°57N 1°3E 139 D5
Kantemirovka Russia 49°43N 39°55E 85 H10
Kantharalak Thailand 14°39N 104°39E 120 E5
Kanthi = Contai India 21°54N 87°46E 125 J12
Kanti → India 28°20N 75°30E 124 E6
Kantō □ Japan 36°15N 139°30E 113 F9
Kantō-Sanchi Japan 35°59N 138°50E 113 G9
Kanturk Ireland 52°11N 8°54W 64 D3
Kanuma Japan 36°34N 139°42E 113 F9
Kanus Namibia 27°50S 18°39E 144 C2
Kanye Botswana 24°55S 25°28E 144 B4
Kanzenze
  Dem. Rep. of the Congo 10°30S 25°12E 143 E2
Kanzi, Ras Tanzania 7°1S 39°33E 142 D4
Kao Phara Thailand 8°3N 98°22E 121 a
Kaohsiung Taiwan 22°35N 120°16E 117 F13
Kaokoveld Namibia 19°15S 14°30E 144 A1
Kaolack Senegal 14°5N 16°8W 138 C1
Kaolack □ Senegal 14°0N 15°15W 138 C1
Kaoshan China 44°38N 124°50E 115 B13
Kapa'a U.S.A. 22°5N 159°19W 167 L8
Kapadvanj India 23°5N 73°0E 124 H5
Kapakli Turkey 41°19N 27°59E 97 E11
Kapan Armenia 39°18N 46°27E 105 C12
Kapanga
  Dem. Rep. of the Congo 8°30S 22°40E 140 F4
Kapchagai = Qapshaghay
  Kazakhstan 43°51N 77°14E 109 D9
Kapchagaiskoye Vdkhr. =
  Qapshaghay Bögeni
  Kazakhstan 43°45N 77°50E 109 D9
Kapedo Kenya 1°0N 36°6E 142 B4
Kapela = Velika Kapela
  Croatia 45°10N 15°5E 93 C12
Kapellskär Sweden 59°44N 19°2E 62 E13
Kapelo, Akra Greece 36°9N 23°3E 98 E5
Kapema
  Dem. Rep. of the Congo 10°45S 28°22E 143 E2
Kapenguria Kenya 1°14N 35°7E 142 B4
Kapfenberg Austria 47°26N 15°18E 78 D8
Kapı Dağı Turkey 40°28N 27°50E 97 F11
Kapiri Mposhi Zambia 13°59S 28°43E 143 E2
Kāpīsā □ Afghan. 35°0N 69°20E 122 B6
Kapiskau → Canada 52°47N 81°55W 164 B3
Kapit Malaysia 2°0N 112°55E 118 D4
Kapiti I. N.Z. 40°50S 174°56E 154 G3
Kaplica = Davlos
  Cyprus 35°25N 33°54E 101 D12
Kaplice Czech Rep. 48°42N 14°30E 78 C7
Kapoe Thailand 9°34N 98°32E 121 H2
Kapoeta South Sudan 4°50N 33°35E 135 H12
Kápolnásnýek Hungary 47°16N 18°41E 80 C2
Kaponga N.Z. 39°29S 174°9E 154 F5
Kapos → Hungary 46°44N 18°30E 80 D3
Kaposvár Hungary 46°25N 17°47E 80 D2
Kapowsin U.S.A. 46°59N 122°13W 170 D4
Kappeln Germany 54°40N 9°56E 76 A5
Kappelshamn Sweden 57°52N 18°47E 63 G12
Kapps Namibia 22°32S 17°18E 144 B2
Kaprije Croatia 43°42N 15°43E 93 E12
Kapsabet Kenya 0°12N 35°6E 142 B4
Kapsan N. Korea 41°4N 128°19E 115 D15
Kapsukas = Marijampolė
  Lithuania 54°33N 23°19E 82 D10
Kaptai L. Bangla. 22°40N 92°20E 123 H18
Kapuas → Indonesia 0°25S 109°20E 118 E3
Kapuas Hulu, Pegunungan
  Malaysia 1°30N 113°30E 118 D4
Kapuas Hulu Ra. = Kapuas Hulu,
  Pegunungan
  Malaysia 1°30N 113°30E 118 D4
Kapulo
  Dem. Rep. of the Congo 8°18S 29°15E 143 D2
Kapunda Australia 34°20S 138°56E 152 C3
Kapuni N.Z. 39°29S 174°8E 154 F5
Kapurthala India 31°23N 75°25E 124 D6
Kapuskasing Canada 49°25N 82°30W 164 C3
Kapuskasing →
  Canada 49°49N 82°0W 164 C3
Kapustin Yar Russia 48°37N 45°40E 87 F7
Kaputar, Mt. Australia 30°15S 150°10E 153 E5
Kaputir Kenya 2°5S 35°28E 142 B4
Kapuvár Hungary 47°36N 17°1E 80 C2
Kapydzhik = Qazangöldağ
  Azerbaijan 39°22N 46°9E 105 C11
Kara Russia 69°10N 65°0E 58 C7
Kara → Turkey 38°35N 26°5E 99 C8
Kara Ada Turkey 36°58N 27°28E 99 E9
Kara-Balta Kyrgyzstan 42°50N 73°49E 109 D8
Kara Bogaz Gol, Zaliv =
  Garabogazköl Aylagy
  Turkmenistan 41°0N 53°30E 108 A4
Kara Burun Turkey 38°32N 27°58E 99 C8
Kara-Kala = Garrygala
  Turkmenistan 38°31N 56°29E 129 B8
Kara Kalpak Republic =
  Qoraqalpoghiston □
  Uzbekistan 43°0N 58°0E 108 D6
Kara-Köl Kyrgyzstan 41°40N 72°43E 109 D8
Kara Kum = Garagum
  Turkmenistan 39°30N 60°0E 129 B8
Kara Sea Russia 75°0N 70°0E 58 B8
Karaadilli Turkey 38°18N 30°37E 99 C12
Karabiğa Turkey 40°23N 27°17E 97 F11
Karabük □ Turkey 41°12N 32°37E 104 B5
Karabük □ Turkey 41°10N 32°10E 104 B5
Karaburun Albania 40°25N 19°20E 96 F3
Karaburun Turkey 38°41N 26°28E 99 C8
Karabutak = Qarabutaq
  Kazakhstan 50°0N 60°14E 108 C6
Karacabey Turkey 40°12N 28°21E 97 F12
Karacakılavuz Turkey 41°8N 27°21E 97 E11
Karaçalı Turkey 41°24N 28°22E 97 E11
Karacasu Turkey 37°43N 28°35E 99 D10
Karachala = Qaraçala
  Azerbaijan 39°45N 48°53E 87 L9
Karachayevsk Russia 43°50N 41°55E 87 J5
Karachey-Cherkessia □
  Russia 53°10N 35°5E 85 H8
Karachi Pakistan 24°50N 67°0E 124 G2
Karad India 17°15N 74°10E 126 D2
Karadeniz Boğazı Turkey 38°34N 30°11E 99 C12
Karaga Ghana 9°58N 0°28W 139 D4
Karaganda = Qaraghandy
  Kazakhstan 49°50N 73°10E 108 C8
Karagayly = Qaraghayly
  Kazakhstan 49°26N 76°0E 108 E8
Karagola Road India 25°29N 87°23E 125 G12

Karagüney Dağları
  Turkey 40°30N 34°40E 104 B6
Karahallı Turkey 38°21N 29°33E 99 C11
Karaikal India 10°59N 79°50E 127 J4
Karaikkudi India 10°5N 78°45E 127 J4
Karaisali Turkey 37°16N 35°2E 104 D6
Karaitivu I. Sri Lanka 9°45N 79°52E 127 K4
Karaj Iran 35°48N 51°0E 129 C6
Karajarri ◌ Australia 19°0S 122°30E 148 C3
Karak Malaysia 3°25N 102°2E 121 L4
Karakalpakstan =
  Qoraqalpoghiston □
  Uzbekistan 43°0N 58°0E 108 D6
Karakelong Indonesia 4°35N 126°50E 119 D7
Karakitang Indonesia 3°14N 125°28E 119 D7
Karakoçan Turkey 38°57N 40°2E 105 C9
Karakol Kyrgyzstan 42°30N 78°20E 109 D9
Karakoram Pass Asia 35°33N 77°50E 125 B7
Karakoram Ra. Pakistan 35°30N 77°0E 125 B7
Karakul = Qarokŭl
  Tajikistan 39°2N 73°33E 108 E8
Karakul = Qarokol
  Uzbekistan 39°30N 63°50E 108 E6
Karakulak, Ozero
  Tajikistan 39°5N 73°25E 109 E8
Karakurt Turkey 40°10N 42°37E 105 B10
Karakuwisa Namibia 18°56S 19°40E 144 A2
Karalon Russia 57°5N 115°50E 107 D12
Karama Jordan 31°57N 35°35E 130 D4
Karaman Balıkesir, Turkey 39°39N 28°9E 99 B9
Karaman Konya, Turkey 37°14N 33°13E 104 D5
Karaman □ Turkey 37°23N 29°47E 99 D11
Karambu Indonesia 3°53S 116°6E 118 E5
Karamea N.Z. 41°14S 172°6E 155 B7
Karamea → N.Z. 41°22S 171°40E 155 B6
Karamea Bight N.Z. 41°22S 171°0E 155 B6
Karamnasa → India 25°31N 83°52E 125 G10
Karamürsel Turkey 40°41N 29°36E 97 F13
Karand Iran 34°16N 46°15E 105 E12
Karanganyar
  Indonesia 7°38S 109°37E 119 G13
Karangasem = Amlapura
  Indonesia 8°27S 115°37E 119 J18
Karanja Maharashtra,
  India 21°11N 78°24E 126 D4
Karanja Maharashtra,
  India 20°29N 77°31E 126 D3
Karanjia India 21°47N 85°58E 125 J11
Karankasso
  Burkina Faso 10°50N 3°53W 138 C4
Karaova Turkey 37°5N 27°40E 99 D9
Karapınar Turkey 37°41N 33°30E 104 D5
Karapiro N.Z. 37°53S 175°32E 154 D4
Karas □ Namibia 27°0S 17°30E 144 C2
Karasburg Namibia 28°0S 18°44E 144 C2
Karasino Russia 66°50N 86°50E 106 C9
Karasjok Norway 69°27N 25°30E 60 B21
Karasu Turkey 41°4N 30°46E 104 B4
Karasu → Turkey 36°16N 36°10E 105 C8
Karasuk Russia 53°44N 78°2E 106 D8
Karasuyama Japan 36°39N 140°9E 113 F10
Karataş Adana, Turkey 36°36N 35°21E 104 D6
Karataş Manisa, Turkey 38°35N 28°16E 99 C10
Karataş Burnu Turkey 36°33N 35°24E 104 D6
Karatau, Khrebet = Qarataū
  Kazakhstan 43°30N 69°30E 108 D7
Karatax Shan China 35°57N 81°0E 109 D9
Karateki Shan China 40°40N 77°50E 109 D9
Karativu Sri Lanka 8°22N 79°47E 127 K4
Karatoprak Turkey 37°2N 27°15E 99 D9
Karatsu Japan 33°26N 129°58E 113 H5
Karaul Russia 70°6N 82°15E 106 B9
Karauli India 26°30N 77°4E 124 F7
Karavastasë, L. e Albania 40°55N 19°30E 96 F3
Karavia Greece 36°49N 23°37E 98 E5
Karavostasi Cyprus 35°8N 32°50E 101 D11
Karawang Indonesia 6°30S 107°15E 119 G12
Karawanken Europe 46°30N 14°40E 78 B7
Karayazı Turkey 39°41N 42°9E 105 C10
Karazhal = Qarazhal
  Kazakhstan 48°2N 70°49E 106 E8
Karbalā' Iraq 32°36N 44°3E 105 F11
Karbalā' □ Iraq 32°30N 43°0E 105 F10
Kârböle Sweden 61°59N 15°22E 62 C9
Karcag Hungary 47°19N 20°57E 80 C5
Karcha → Pakistan 34°45N 76°10E 125 B7
Karchana India 25°17N 81°56E 125 G9
Karczew Poland 52°5N 21°15E 83 F8
Kardam Bulgaria 43°45N 28°36E 97 C12
Kardamena Greece 36°48N 27°8E 99 E9
Kardamili Greece 36°53N 22°13E 98 E4
Kardeljevo = Ploče
  Croatia 43°4N 17°26E 93 E14
Karditsa Greece 39°23N 21°54E 98 B3
Kärdla Estonia 59°0N 22°45E 84 C2
Kardzhali = Kŭrdzhali
  Bulgaria 41°38N 25°21E 97 E9
Kareeberge S. Africa 30°59S 21°50E 144 E3
Kareha → India 25°44N 86°21E 125 G12
Kareima Sudan 18°30N 31°49E 137 D3
Karelia □ Russia 65°30N 32°30E 60 C22
Karelian Republic = Karelia □
  Russia 65°30N 32°30E 60 C22
Karera India 25°32N 78°9E 124 G8
Kärevändar Iran 27°53N 60°44E 129 E9
Kargasok Russia 59°3N 80°53E 106 D9
Kargat Russia 55°10N 80°15E 106 D8
Kargī Kenya 2°31N 37°34E 142 B4
Kargı Turkey 41°11N 34°30E 104 B6
Kargil India 34°32N 76°12E 125 B6
Kargopol Russia 61°30N 38°58E 84 B10
Karguéri Niger 13°27N 10°30E 139 C7
Karia ba Mohammed
  Morocco 34°22N 5°12W 136 B2
Kariān Iran 26°57N 57°14E 129 E8
Kariba Zimbabwe 16°28S 28°50E 143 F2
Kariba, L. Zimbabwe 16°40S 28°25E 143 F2
Kariba Dam Zimbabwe 16°30S 28°35E 143 F2
Karibib Namibia 22°0S 15°56E 144 B2
Karies Greece 40°14N 24°19E 97 F8
Karijini ◌ Australia 23°8S 118°15E 148 D2
Karikari, C. N.Z. 34°46S 173°24E 154 A2
Karimata, Kepulauan
  Indonesia 1°25S 109°0E 118 E3

Karimata, Selat
  Indonesia 2°0S 108°40E 118 E3
Karimata Is. = Karimata,
  Kepulauan Indonesia 1°25S 109°0E 118 E3
Karimnagar India 18°26N 79°10E 126 E4
Karimun, Pulau Indonesia 1°3N 103°22E 121 d
Karimun Kecil, Pulau
  Indonesia 1°8N 103°22E 121 d
Karimunjawa, Kepulauan
  Indonesia 5°50S 110°30E 118 F4
Karin Somalia 10°50N 45°52E 131 E4
Karistos Greece 38°1N 24°29E 98 C6
Karīt Iran 33°29N 56°55E 129 C8
Kariya Japan 34°58N 137°1E 113 G8
Kariyangwe Zimbabwe 18°0S 27°38E 145 A4
Karjala Finland 62°0N 30°25E 84 A5
Karjat India 18°33N 75°0E 126 E2
Karkal India 13°15N 74°56E 127 H2
Karkaralinsk = Qarqaraly
  Kazakhstan 49°26N 75°30E 109 C9
Karkheh → Iran 31°2N 47°29E 128 D5
Karki Azerbaijan 39°47N 44°57E 105 C11
Karkinitska Zatoka
  Ukraine 45°56N 33°0E 85 K7
Karkinitskiy Zaliv = Karkinitska
  Zatoka Ukraine 45°56N 33°0E 85 K7
Karkuk = Kirkūk
  Iraq 35°30N 44°21E 105 E11
Karkur Tohl Egypt 22°5N 25°5E 137 C2
Karl Libknekhit = imeni Karl
  Libknekhta Russia 51°40N 35°35E 85 G8
Karla, L. = Volvi, L.
  Greece 40°40N 23°34E 96 F7
Karlantijpa North ◌
  Australia 19°27S 133°33E 148 C5
Karlantijpa South ◌
  Australia 20°31S 133°9E 148 D5
Karleby = Kokkola
  Finland 63°50N 23°8E 60 E20
Karlholmsbruk Sweden 60°31N 17°37E 62 D11
Karlino Poland 54°3N 15°53E 82 D2
Karliova Turkey 39°17N 41°0E 105 C9
Karlivka Ukraine 49°29N 35°8E 85 H8
Karlobag Croatia 44°32N 15°5E 93 D12
Karlovac Croatia 45°31N 15°36E 93 C12
Karlovarský □
  Czech Rep. 50°10N 12°50E 78 A5
Karlovasi Greece 37°45N 26°42E 99 D8
Karlovo Bulgaria 42°38N 24°47E 97 D8
Karlovy Vary Czech Rep. 50°13N 12°51E 78 A5
Karlsbad = Karlovy Vary
  Czech Rep. 50°13N 12°51E 78 A5
Karlsborg Sweden 58°33N 14°33E 63 F8
Karlsena, Mys Russia 77°0N 57°0E 106 B7
Karlshamn Sweden 56°10N 14°51E 63 H8
Karlskoga Sweden 59°28N 14°33E 62 E8
Karlskrona Sweden 56°10N 15°35E 63 H9
Karlsruhe Germany 49°0N 8°23E 77 F4
Karlstad Sweden 59°23N 13°30E 62 E7
Karlstad U.S.A. 48°35N 96°31W 172 A5
Karlstadt Germany 49°57N 9°47E 77 F5
Karma Niger 13°38N 1°52E 139 C5
Karmala India 18°25N 75°12E 126 E2
Karmi'el Israel 32°55N 35°18E 130 C4
Karnak Egypt 25°43N 32°39E 137 D3
Karnal India 29°42N 77°2E 124 E7
Karnali → Nepal 28°45N 81°16E 125 E9
Karnaphuli Res. = Kaptai L.
  Bangla. 22°40N 92°20E 123 H18
Karnaprayag India 30°16N 79°15E 125 D8
Karnataka □ India 13°15N 77°0E 127 H3
Karnes City U.S.A. 28°53N 97°54W 176 G6
Karnische Alpen Europe 46°36N 13°0E 78 E6
Karnobat Bulgaria 42°39N 26°59E 97 D10
Kärnten □ Austria 46°52N 13°30E 78 E6
Karo Mali 12°16N 3°18W 138 C4
Karoi Zimbabwe 16°48S 29°45E 143 F2
Karon, Ao Thailand 7°51N 98°17E 121 a
Karonga Malawi 9°57S 33°55E 143 D3
Karoo △ S. Africa 32°18S 22°27E 144 D3
Karoonda Australia 35°1S 139°59E 152 C3
Karor Pakistan 31°15N 70°59E 124 D4
Karora Sudan 17°44N 38°15E 135 E13
Karounga Mali 15°20N 7°35W 138 B4
Karousades Greece 39°47N 19°45E 98 B1
Karpacz Poland 50°46N 15°46E 83 H2
Karpasia Cyprus 35°32N 34°15E 101 D13
Karpathos Greece 35°37N 27°10E 99 F9
Karpathou, Stenon
  Greece 36°0N 27°30E 99 F9
Karpatská □ Ukraine 48°30N 24°35E 81 B9
Karpenisi Greece 38°55N 21°40E 98 C3
Karpinsk Russia 59°45N 60°1E 106 D7
Karpuz Burnu = Apostolos
  Andreas, C. Cyprus 35°42N 34°35E 101 D13
Karpuzlu Turkey 37°33N 27°51E 99 D9
Karratha Australia 20°44S 116°52E 148 D2
Kars Turkey 40°40N 43°5E 105 B10
Kars □ Turkey 40°40N 43°0E 105 B10
Karsakpay Kazakhstan 47°55N 66°40E 108 C7
Karsha Kazakhstan 49°45N 51°35E 86 F10
Karshi = Qarshi
  Uzbekistan 38°53N 65°48E 108 F7
Karsiyang India 26°56N 88°18E 125 F13
Karsog India 31°23N 77°12E 124 D7
Karst = Kras Croatia 45°35N 14°0E 93 C11
Kartal Turkey 40°53N 29°11E 97 F13
Kartala Comoros Is. 11°45S 43°21E 141 a
Kartaly Russia 53°3N 60°40E 108 D8
Kartapur India 31°27N 75°32E 124 D6
Karthaus U.S.A. 41°8N 78°9W 174 E6
Kartuzy Poland 54°22N 18°10E 82 D5
Karuah Australia 32°37S 151°56E 153 B9
Karufa Indonesia 3°50S 133°20E 119 E8
Karula △ Estonia 57°50N 26°28E 84 C4
Karumba Australia 17°31S 140°50E 150 B3
Karumo Tanzania 2°25S 32°50E 142 C3
Karumwa Tanzania 3°12S 32°38E 142 C3
Karun → Iran 30°26N 48°10E 129 D6
Karunagappally India 9°5N 76°25E 127 K3
Karungu Kenya 0°50S 34°10E 142 C3
Karup Denmark 56°19N 9°10E 63 H2
Karur India 10°59N 78°2E 127 J3
Karviná Czech Rep. 49°53N 18°31E 79 B11
Karwan → India 27°26N 78°4E 124 F8
Karwar India 14°55N 74°13E 127 H2
Karwendel △ Austria 47°26N 11°28E 78 D4
Karwi India 25°12N 80°57E 125 G9
Karymskoye Russia 51°36N 114°21E 107 D12
Kaş Turkey 36°11N 29°37E 99 E11

Kasaba Turkey 36°18N 29°44E 99 E11
Kasache Malawi 13°25S 34°20E 143 E3
Kasai →
  Dem. Rep. of the Congo 3°30S 16°10E 140 E3
Kasai-Oriental □
  Dem. Rep. of the Congo 5°0S 24°30E 142 D1
Kasaji
  Dem. Rep. of the Congo 10°25S 23°27E 143 E1
Kasama Zambia 10°16S 31°9E 143 E3
Kasan-dong N. Korea 41°18N 126°55E 115 D14
Kasandra Greece 40°0N 23°30E 96 F7
Kasandra Kolpos Greece 40°5N 23°30E 96 F7
Kasandras, Akra Greece 39°57N 23°30E 96 G7
Kasane Namibia 17°34S 24°50E 144 A3
Kasanga Tanzania 8°30S 31°10E 143 D3
Kasanka △ Zambia 11°34S 30°15E 143 E3
Kasar, Ras Sudan 18°2N 38°36E 137 D4
Kasaragod India 12°30N 74°58E 127 H2
Kasba L. Canada 60°20N 102°10W 163 A8
Kasba Tadla Morocco 32°36N 6°17W 136 B2
Käseh Garān Iran 34°5N 46°2E 128 C5
Kasempa Zambia 13°30S 25°44E 143 E2
Kasenga
  Dem. Rep. of the Congo 10°20S 28°45E 143 E2
Kasese Uganda 0°13N 30°3E 142 B3
Kasganj India 27°48N 78°42E 125 F8
Kashabowie Canada 48°40N 90°26W 164 C1
Kashaf Iran 35°58N 61°7E 129 C9
Kāshān Iran 34°5N 51°30E 129 C6
Kashechewan Canada 52°18N 81°37W 164 B3
Kashgān → Iran 33°35N 47°21E 105 F12
Kashgar = Kashi China 39°30N 76°2E 109 E9
Kashi China 39°30N 76°2E 109 E9
Kashimbo
  Dem. Rep. of the Congo 11°12S 26°19E 143 E2
Kashin Russia 57°20N 37°36E 84 D9
Kashipur Odisha, India 19°16N 83°3E 126 E6
Kashipur Uttarakhand,
  India 29°15N 79°0E 125 E8
Kashira Russia 54°45N 38°10E 84 E10
Kashiwazaki Japan 37°22N 138°33E 113 F9
Kashk-e Kohneh
  Afghan. 34°55N 62°30E 122 B3
Kashksaray Iran 38°37N 45°34E 105 C11
Kashkŭ'īyeh Iran 30°31N 55°40E 129 D7
Käshmar Iran 35°16N 58°26E 129 C8
Kashmir Asia 34°0N 76°0E 125 C7
Kashmor Pakistan 28°28N 69°32E 124 E3
Kashpirovka Russia 53°0N 48°30E 86 D9
Kashun Noerh = Gaxun Nur
  China 42°22N 100°30E 110 C9
Kasiari India 22°8N 87°14E 125 H12
Kasimov Russia 54°55N 41°20E 86 C6
Kasinge
  Dem. Rep. of the Congo 6°15S 26°58E 142 D2
Kasiruta Indonesia 0°25S 127°12E 119 E7
Kaskaskia → U.S.A. 37°58N 89°57W 172 G9
Kaskattama → Canada 57°3N 90°4W 163 B10
Kaskinen Finland 62°22N 21°15E 60 E19
Kaslo Canada 49°55N 116°55E 162 D5
Kasmere L. Canada 59°34N 101°10W 163 B8
Kasongo
  Dem. Rep. of the Congo 4°30S 26°33E 142 C2
Kasongo Lunda
  Dem. Rep. of the Congo 6°35S 16°49E 140 F3
Kasos Greece 35°20N 26°55E 99 F8
Kasou, Stenon Greece 35°30N 26°30E 99 F8
Kaspi Georgia 41°59N 44°26E 87 K7
Kaspichan Bulgaria 43°18N 27°11E 97 C11
Kaspiysk Russia 42°52N 47°40E 87 J8
Kaspiyskiy Russia 45°22N 47°23E 87 H8
Kassaba Egypt 22°40N 29°55E 137 C2
Kassalâ Sudan 15°30N 36°0E 135 E13
Kassandrino Greece 40°1N 23°27E 96 F7
Kassel Germany 51°18N 9°26E 76 D5
Kasserine Tunisia 35°10N 8°50E 136 A5
Kassinger Sudan 18°46N 31°51E 137 D3
Kassiopi Greece 39°48N 19°53E 101 A3
Kasson U.S.A. 44°2N 92°45W 172 C7
Kastamonu Turkey 41°25N 33°43E 104 B5
Kastamonu □ Turkey 41°20N 34°0E 104 B5
Kastav Croatia 45°22N 14°20E 93 C11
Kasteli Greece 35°12N 25°20E 101 D7
Kastéllorizo = Megisti
  Greece 36°8N 29°34E 99 E11
Kastellou, Akra Greece 35°30N 27°15E 99 F9
Kasterlee Belgium 51°15N 4°59E 69 C4
Kastlösa Sweden 56°26N 16°25E 63 H10
Kastoria Greece 40°30N 21°19E 96 F5
Kastorias, L. Greece 40°30N 21°20E 96 F5
Kastorio Greece 37°10N 22°17E 98 D4
Kastornoye Russia 51°55N 38°2E 85 G10
Kastos Greece 38°35N 20°55E 98 C2
Kastrom Mefa'a = Umm al Rasas
  Jordan 31°30N 35°55E 130 D4
Kastrosikia Greece 39°6N 20°36E 98 B2
Kastrup, København ✈ (CPH)
  Denmark 55°37N 12°39E 63 J6
Kastsyukovichy Belarus 53°20N 32°4E 85 F7
Kasulu Tanzania 4°37S 30°5E 142 C3
Kasumi Japan 35°38N 134°38E 113 G7
Kasumkent Russia 41°47N 48°15E 87 K9
Kasungu Malawi 13°0S 33°29E 143 E3
Kasungu △ Malawi 12°55S 33°10E 143 E3
Kasur Pakistan 31°5N 74°25E 124 D6
Kata, Ao Thailand 7°48N 98°18E 121 a
Kata Archanes Greece 35°15N 25°10E 101 D7
Kata Tjuta Australia 25°20S 130°50E 149 E5
Katako Kombe
  Dem. Rep. of the Congo 3°25S 24°20E 142 C1
Katakolo Greece 37°38N 21°19E 98 D3
Katale Tanzania 4°52S 31°7E 142 C3
Katamatite Australia 36°6S 145°41E 153 C4
Katanda Katanga,
  Dem. Rep. of the Congo 7°52S 24°13E 142 D1
Katanda Nord-Kivu,
  Dem. Rep. of the Congo 0°55S 29°21E 142 C2
Katanga □
  Dem. Rep. of the Congo 8°0S 25°0E 142 D2
Katangi India 21°56N 79°50E 126 D4
Katangli Russia 51°42N 143°14E 107 D15
Katanning Australia 33°40S 117°33E 149 F2

Katastari *Greece* 37°50N 20°45E **98** D2
Katavi △ *Tanzania* 6°51S 31°33E **142** D3
Katavi Swamp *Tanzania* 6°50S 31°10E **142** D3
Katchall *India* 7°57N 93°22E **127** L11
Katghora *India* 22°30N 82°33E **125** H10
Katha *Burma* 24°10N 96°30E **123** G20
Katherina, Gebel *Egypt* 28°30N 33°57E **128** D2
Katherine *Australia* 14°27S 132°20E **148** B5
Katherine Gorge = Nitmiluk △
  Australia 14°6S 132°15E **148** B5
Kathi *India* 21°47N 74°3E **124** J6
Kathiawar *India* 22°20N 71°0E **124** H4
Kathikas *Cyprus* 34°55N 32°25E **101** E11
Kathleen *U.S.A.* 28°7N 82°2W **179** G7
Kathua *India* 32°23N 75°34E **124** C6
Kati *Mali* 12°41N 8°4W **138** C3
Katihar *India* 25°34N 87°36E **125** G12
Katikati *N.Z.* 37°32S 175°57E **154** D4
Katima Mulilo *Namibia* 17°28S 24°13E **144** A3
Katimbira *Malawi* 12°40S 34°0E **143** E3
Katingan = Mendawai →
  Indonesia 3°30S 113°0E **118** E4
Katiola *Ivory C.* 8°10N 5°10W **138** D3
Katiti △ *Australia* 25°1S 131°11E **149** E5
Katlabukh, Ozero
  Ukraine 45°28N 29°0E **81** E14
Katlanovo *Macedonia* 41°52N 21°40E **96** E5
Katmandu = Kathmandu
  Nepal 27°45N 85°20E **125** F11
Katni *India* 23°51N 80°24E **125** H9
Kato Achaia *Greece* 38°8N 21°33E **98** D3
Kato Chorio *Greece* 35°3N 25°47E **101** D7
Kato Korakiana *Greece* 39°42N 19°45E **101** A3
Kato Pyrgos *Cyprus* 35°11N 32°41E **101** D11
Katochi *Greece* 38°26N 21°15E **98** C3
Katol *India* 21°17N 78°38E **126** D4
Katompe
  Dem. Rep. of the Congo 6°2S 26°23E **142** D2
Katong *Singapore* 1°18N 103°53E **121** d
Katonga → *Uganda* 0°34N 31°50E **142** B3
Katoomba *Australia* 33°41S 150°19E **153** B9
Katouna *Greece* 38°47N 21°7E **98** C3
Katowice *Poland* 50°17N 19°5E **83** H6
Katrancı Dağı *Turkey* 37°27N 30°25E **99** D12
Katrine, L. *U.K.* 56°15N 4°30W **65** E4
Katrineholm *Sweden* 59°0N 16°12E **62** E10
Katsina *Nigeria* 13°0N 7°32E **139** C6
Katsina □ *Nigeria* 12°30N 7°30E **139** C6
Katsina Ala *Nigeria* 7°10N 9°30E **139** D6
Katsina Ala → *Nigeria* 7°10N 9°20E **139** D6
Katsumoto *Japan* 33°51N 129°42E **113** H4
Katsuura *Japan* 35°10N 140°20E **113** G10
Katsuyama *Japan* 36°3N 136°30E **113** F8
Kattaqŭrghon
  Uzbekistan 39°55N 66°15E **109** E7
Kattavia *Greece* 35°57N 27°46E **101** D9
Kattegat *Denmark* 56°40N 11°20E **63** H5
Katthammarsvik
  Sweden 57°26N 18°51E **63** G12
Katumba
  Dem. Rep. of the Congo 7°40S 25°17E **142** D2
Katun → *Russia* 52°25N 85°1E **109** D11
Katwa *India* 23°30N 88°5E **125** H13
Katwijk *Neths.* 52°12N 4°24E **69** B4
Katy Wrocławskie
  Poland 51°2N 16°45E **83** G3
Kau-Ye Kyun *Burma* 11°1N 98°32E **121** G2
Kaua'i *U.S.A.* 22°3N 159°30W **167** L8
Kaub *Germany* 50°5N 7°46E **77** E3
Kaudom △ *Namibia* 18°45S 20°51E **144** A3
Kaufbeuren *Germany* 47°53N 10°37E **77** H6
Kaufman *U.S.A.* 32°35N 96°19W **176** E6
Kauhajoki *Finland* 62°25N 22°10E **60** E20
Kauhaneva-Pohjankangas △
  Finland 62°16N 22°20E **60** E20
Kaukauna *U.S.A.* 44°17N 88°17W **172** C9
Kaukauveld *Namibia* 20°0S 20°15E **144** B3
Ka'ula I. *U.S.A.* 21°40N 160°33W **167** L7
Kaunas *Lithuania* 54°54N 23°54E **82** D10
Kaunas ✈ (KUN)
  Lithuania 54°57N 24°3E **82** D11
Kaunia *Bangla.* 25°46N 89°26E **125** G13
Kaunos *Turkey* 36°49N 28°39E **99** E10
Kaura Namoda *Nigeria* 12°37N 6°33E **139** C6
Kauru *Nigeria* 10°33N 8°12E **139** C6
Kautokeino *Norway* 69°0N 23°4E **60** B20
Kauwapur *India* 27°31N 82°18E **125** F10
Kavacha *Russia* 60°16N 169°51E **107** C17
Kavadarci *Macedonia* 41°26N 22°3E **96** E5
Kavajë *Albania* 41°11N 19°33E **96** E3
Kavak *Turkey* 41°4N 36°3E **104** B7
Kavak Dağı *Turkey* 41°39N 27°10E **97** E11
Kavaklıdere *Turkey* 37°27N 28°21E **99** D10
Kavala *Greece* 40°57N 24°28E **97** F8
Kavala Kolpos *Greece* 40°50N 24°25E **97** F8
Kavalerovo *Russia* 44°15N 135°4E **112** B7
Kavali *India* 14°55N 80°1E **127** G5
Kavār *Iran* 29°11N 52°44E **129** D7
Kavaratti *India* 10°34N 72°37E **127** J1
Kavaratti I. *India* 10°33N 72°38E **127** J1
Kavarna *Bulgaria* 43°26N 28°22E **97** C12
Kavi *India* 22°12N 72°38E **124** H5
Kavimba *Botswana* 18°2S 24°38E **144** A3
Kavīr, Dasht-e *Iran* 34°30N 55°0E **129** C7
Kavīr △ *Iran* 34°40N 52°0E **129** C7
Kavkaz *Russia* 45°20N 36°40E **87** J6
Kävlinge *Sweden* 55°47N 13°9E **63** J7
Kavos *Greece* 39°23N 20°3E **101** B4
Kavousi *Greece* 35°7N 25°51E **99** F7
Kaw *Fr. Guiana* 4°30N 52°15W **187** C8
Kawagama L. *Canada* 45°18N 78°45W **174** A6
Kawagoe *Japan* 35°55N 139°29E **113** G9
Kawaguchi *Japan* 35°52N 139°45E **113** G9
Kawah Ijen △ *Indonesia* 8°3S 114°14E **119** H15
Kawakawa *N.Z.* 35°23S 174°6E **154** B3
Kawambwa *Zambia* 9°48S 29°3E **143** D2
Kawanoe = Shikokuchūō
  Japan 34°1N 133°34E **113** G6
Kawardha *India* 22°0N 81°17E **125** J9
Kawasaki *Japan* 35°31N 139°43E **113** G9
Kawasi *Indonesia* 1°38S 127°28E **119** E7
Kawau I. *N.Z.* 36°25S 174°52E **154** C4
Kawawachikamach
  Canada 54°48N 66°50W **165** B6
Kaweka Ra. *N.Z.* 39°17S 176°25E **154** F5
Kawerau *N.Z.* 38°7S 176°42E **154** F6
Kawhia *N.Z.* 38°4S 174°49E **154** F4
Kawhia Harbour *N.Z.* 38°5S 174°51E **154** E4

Kawio, Kepulauan
  Indonesia 4°30N 125°30E **119** D7
Kawthaung *Burma* 10°5N 98°36E **121** H2
Kawthoolei = Kayin □
  Burma 18°0N 97°30E **123** L20
Kawthule = Kayin □
  Burma 18°0N 97°30E **123** L20
Kaxgar He → *China* 39°45N 78°24E **109** D9
Kaxholmen *Sweden* 57°51N 14°19E **63** G8
Kaya *Burkina Faso* 13°4N 1°10W **139** C4
Kayah □ *Burma* 19°15N 97°15E **123** K20
Kayak I. *U.S.A.* 59°56N 144°23W **166** D11
Kayamkulam *India* 9°10N 76°33E **127** K3
Kayan → *Indonesia* 2°55N 117°35E **118** D5
Kaycee *U.S.A.* 43°43N 106°38W **168** E10
Kayeli *Indonesia* 3°20S 127°10E **119** E7
Kayenta *U.S.A.* 36°44N 110°15W **169** H8
Kayes *Mali* 14°25N 11°30W **138** C2
Kayes □ *Mali* 14°0N 11°0W **138** C2
Kayima *S. Leone* 8°54N 11°15W **138** D2
Kayin □ *Burma* 18°0N 97°30E **123** L20
Kaymakçı *Turkey* 38°10N 28°8E **99** C10
Kayoa *Indonesia* 0°1N 127°28E **119** D7
Kayomba *Zambia* 13°11S 24°2E **143** E1
Kaysatskoye *Russia* 49°47N 46°49E **86** F8
Kayseri *Turkey* 38°45N 35°30E **104** C6
Kayseri □ *Turkey* 38°40N 36°0E **104** C7
Kaysville *U.S.A.* 41°2N 111°56W **168** F8
Kayts *Sri Lanka* 9°42N 79°51E **127** K4
Kaz Dağı *Turkey* 39°42N 26°50E **99** B8
Kazachye *Russia* 70°52N 135°58E **107** B14
Kazakhstan ■ *Asia* 50°0N 70°0E **108** C8
Kazaly = Qazaly
  Kazakhstan 45°45N 62°6E **108** C6
Kazan *Russia* 55°50N 49°10E **86** C9
Kazan → *Canada* 64°2N 95°29W **163** A9
Kazan-Rettō *Pac. Oc.* 25°0N 141°0E **156** E6
Kazanlŭk *Bulgaria* 42°38N 25°20E **97** D9
Kazanskaya *Russia* 49°50N 41°10E **86** F5
Kazatin = Kozyatyn
  Ukraine 49°45N 28°50E **75** D15
Kazaure *Nigeria* 12°42N 8°28E **139** C6
Kāzerūn *Iran* 29°38N 51°40E **129** D6
Kazi Magomed = Qazimämmäd
  Azerbaijan 40°3N 49°0E **87** K9
Kazimierz Dolny *Poland* 51°19N 21°57E **83** G8
Kazimierza Wielka
  Poland 50°15N 20°30E **83** H7
Kazincbarcika *Hungary* 48°17N 20°36E **80** D5
Kazipet *India* 17°58N 79°30E **126** F4
Kazlų Rūda *Lithuania* 54°46N 23°30E **82** D10
Kaztalovka *Kazakhstan* 49°47N 48°43E **86** F9
Kazuma Pan △
  Zimbabwe 18°20S 25°48E **143** F2
Kazuno *Japan* 40°10N 140°45E **112** D10
Kazym → *Russia* 63°54N 65°50E **106** C7
Kea *Greece* 37°35N 24°22E **98** D6
Keady *U.K.* 54°15N 6°42W **64** B5
Kearney *U.S.A.* 40°42N 99°5W **172** E4
Kearney ○ *Australia* 20°10S 128°4E **148** D4
Kearny *U.S.A.* 33°3N 110°55W **169** K8
Kearsarge, Mt. *U.S.A.* 43°22N 71°50W **175** C13
Keban *Turkey* 38°50N 38°50E **105** C8
Keban Baraji *Turkey* 38°41N 38°33E **105** C8
Kebbi □ *Nigeria* 11°35N 4°0E **139** C5
Kébémèr *Senegal* 15°23N 16°34W **138** B1
Kébi *Ivory C.* 9°18N 6°37W **138** D3
Kebili □ *Tunisia* 33°47N 9°0E **138** B5
Kebili *Tunisia* 33°30N 8°50E **138** B5
Kebnekaise *Sweden* 67°53N 18°33E **60** C18
Kebri Dehar *Ethiopia* 6°45N 44°17E **133** F4
Kebumen *Indonesia* 7°42S 109°40E **119** G13
Kecel *Hungary* 46°31N 19°16E **80** D4
Kechika → *Canada* 59°41N 127°12W **162** B3
Keçiborlu *Turkey* 37°57N 30°18E **99** D12
Kecskemét *Hungary* 46°57N 19°42E **80** D4
Kedah □ *Malaysia* 5°50N 100°40E **121** K3
Kédainiai *Lithuania* 55°15N 24°2E **82** C11
Kedarnath *India* 30°44N 79°4E **125** D8
Kedgwick *Canada* 47°40N 67°20W **165** C6
Kediri *Indonesia* 7°51S 112°1E **118** F4
Kedjebi *Ghana* 8°12N 0°25E **139** D5
Kedros Oros *Greece* 35°11N 24°37E **101** D6
Kedzierzyn-Koźle *Poland* 50°20N 18°12E **83** H5
Keeler *U.S.A.* 36°29N 117°52W **170** J9
Keeley L. *Canada* 54°54N 108°8W **163** C7
Keeling Is. = Cocos Is.
  Ind. Oc. 12°10S 96°55E **146** F8
Keelung = Chilung
  Taiwan 25°3N 121°45E **117** E13
Keene *Canada* 44°15N 78°10W **174** B6
Keene *Calif., U.S.A.* 35°13N 118°33W **179** K8
Keene *N.H., U.S.A.* 42°56N 72°17W **175** D12
Keene *N.Y., U.S.A.* 44°16N 73°46W **175** B11
Keeper Hill *Ireland* 52°45N 8°16W **64** D3
Keeroongooloo *Australia* 25°5S 142°30E **145** d
Keerweer, C. *Australia* 14°0S 141°32E **150** A3
Keeseville *U.S.A.* 44°29N 73°30W **175** B11
Keetmanshoop *Namibia* 26°35S 18°8E **144** C2
Keewatin *Canada* 49°46N 94°34W **163** D10
Keewatin → *Canada* 56°29N 100°46W **163** B9
Kefallinia *Greece* 38°15N 20°30E **98** C2
Kefamenanu *Indonesia* 9°28S 124°29E **119** F6
Kefar Sava *Israel* 32°11N 34°54E **130** C3
Keffi *Nigeria* 8°55N 7°43E **139** D6
Keflin Hausa *Nigeria* 12°3N 9°55E **139** C6
Keflavík *Iceland* 64°2N 22°35W **60** D2
Key River *Canada* 45°57N 80°19W **174** A4
Kegalla *Sri Lanka* 7°15N 80°21E **127** L5
Kegaska *Canada* 50°9N 61°18W **165** B7
Kehancha *Kenya* 1°11S 34°32E **142** C3
Keheili *Sudan* 19°25N 32°30E **137** D3
Kehl *Germany* 48°34N 7°50E **77** G3
Keighley *U.K.* 53°52N 1°54W **66** D6
Keila *Estonia* 59°18N 24°25E **84** C3
Keimoes *S. Africa* 28°41S 20°59E **144** C3
Keita *Niger* 14°46N 5°56E **139** C6
Keitele *Finland* 63°10N 26°20E **60** E22
Keith *Australia* 36°6S 140°0E **152** D4
Keith *U.K.* 57°32N 2°57W **65** D6
Keiyasi *Fiji* 17°53S 177°46E **154** a
Keizer *U.S.A.* 44°57N 123°1W **174** D2
Kejimkujik △ *Canada* 44°25N 65°25W **165** D6

Kejserr Franz Joseph Fd.
  Greenland 73°30N 24°30W **57** C8
Kekri *India* 26°0N 75°10E **124** G6
Kelan *China* 38°43N 111°31E **114** E6
Kelang = Klang
  Malaysia 3°2N 101°26E **121** L3
Kelani Ganga →
  Sri Lanka 6°58N 79°50E **127** L4
Kelantan □ *Malaysia* 5°10N 102°0E **121** K3
Kelantan → *Malaysia* 6°13N 102°14E **121** J4
Këlcyrë *Albania* 40°20N 20°12E **96** F4
Kelekçi *Turkey* 37°15N 29°20E **99** D11
Keles *Turkey* 39°54N 29°14E **97** G13
Keleti-főcsatorna
  Hungary 47°45N 21°20E **80** C6
Kelheim *Germany* 48°54N 11°52E **77** G7
Kelibia *Tunisia* 36°50N 11°3E **136** A6
Kelkit *Turkey* 40°7N 39°16E **105** B8
Kelkit → *Turkey* 40°45N 36°32E **104** B7
Kellé *Niger* 14°16N 10°7E **139** C7
Keller *U.S.A.* 31°50N 81°15W **178** D8
Kellerberrin *Australia* 31°36S 117°38E **149** F2
Kellett, C. *Canada* 72°0N 126°0W **54** B1
Kelleys I. *U.S.A.* 41°36N 82°42W **174** E2
Kellogg *U.S.A.* 47°32N 116°7W **168** C5
Kells *Ireland* 53°44N 6°53W **64** C5
Kelmė *Lithuania* 55°38N 22°56E **82** C9
Klementsi *Ukraine* 48°28N 26°50E **81** D13
Kélo *Chad* 9°10N 15°45E **135** G9
Kelokedhara *Cyprus* 34°48N 32°39E **101** E11
Kelowna *Canada* 49°50N 119°25W **162** D5
Kelsey Creek *Australia* 20°26S 148°31E **150** b
Kelseyville *U.S.A.* 38°59N 122°50W **178** F4
Kelso *N.Z.* 45°54S 169°15E **155** F4
Kelso *U.K.* 55°36N 2°26W **65** F6
Kelso *U.S.A.* 46°9N 122°54W **170** D4
Keluang = Kluang
  Malaysia 2°3N 103°18E **121** L4
Kelud *Indonesia* 7°56N 112°18E **119** H15
Kelvington *Canada* 52°10N 103°30W **163** C8
Kem *Russia* 65°0N 34°38E **106** C4
Kem-Kem *Morocco* 30°40N 4°30W **136** B3
Kema *Indonesia* 1°22N 125°8E **119** D7
Kemah *Turkey* 39°32N 39°5E **105** C8
Kemaliye *Erzincan,
  Turkey* 39°16N 38°29E **105** C8
Kemaliye *Manisa,
  Turkey* 38°27N 28°25E **99** C10
Kemalpaşa *Turkey* 38°25N 27°27E **99** C9
Kemaman *Malaysia* 4°12N 103°18E **121** K4
Kemano *Canada* 53°35N 128°0W **162** C3
Kemasik *Malaysia* 4°25N 103°27E **121** K4
Kemer *Antalya, Turkey* 36°36N 30°34E **99** E12
Kemer *Burdur, Turkey* 37°21N 30°4E **99** D12
Kemer *Muğla, Turkey* 36°40N 29°22E **99** E11
Kemer Baraji *Turkey* 38°28N 37°E **99** D10
Kemerovo *Russia* 55°20N 86°5E **106** D9
Kemerovo □ *Russia* 55°0N 86°0E **109** D11
Kemeru △ *Latvia* 56°58N 23°25E **82** B10
Kemi *Finland* 65°44N 24°34E **60** D21
Kemi älv = Kemijoki →
  Finland 65°47N 24°32E **60** D21
Kemi träsk = Kemijärvi
  Finland 66°43N 27°22E **60** C22
Kemijärvi *Finland* 66°43N 27°22E **60** C22
Kemijoki → *Finland* 65°47N 24°32E **60** D21
Kemmerer *U.S.A.* 41°48N 110°32W **168** F8
Kemmuna = Comino
  Malta 36°1N 14°20E **101** C1
Kemp, L. *U.S.A.* 33°46N 99°9W **176** E5
Kemp Land *Antarctica* 69°0S 55°0E **5** C5
Kempas *Malaysia* 1°33N 103°42E **121** d
Kempsey *Australia* 31°1S 152°50E **153** A10
Kempt, L. *Canada* 47°25N 74°22W **164** C5
Kempten *Germany* 47°45N 10°17E **77** H6
Kempton *Australia* 42°31S 147°12E **151** G4
Kemptville *Canada* 45°0N 75°38W **175** B9
Ken → *India* 25°13N 80°27E **125** G9
Kenadsa *Algeria* 31°48N 2°26W **136** B3
Kenai *U.S.A.* 60°33N 151°16W **166** D1
Kenai Mts. *U.S.A.* 60°0N 150°0W **166** D9
Kenamuke Swamp
  South Sudan 5°55N 33°48E **142** A3
Kenansville *U.S.A.* 27°53N 80°59W **179** H9
Kendai *India* 22°45N 82°37E **125** H10
Kendal *Indonesia* 6°56S 110°14E **119** G14
Kendal *U.K.* 54°20N 2°44W **66** C5
Kendall *Australia* 31°35S 152°44E **153** A10
Kendall *U.S.A.* 25°40N 80°19W **179** H10
Kendall → *Australia* 14°4S 141°35E **150** A3
Kendallville *U.S.A.* 41°27N 85°16W **172** E11
Kendari *Indonesia* 3°50S 122°30E **119** E6
Kendawangan
  Indonesia 2°32S 110°17E **118** E4
Kende *Nigeria* 11°30N 4°12E **139** C5
Kendi, Pulau *Malaysia* 5°13N 100°11E **121** c
Kendrapara *India* 20°35N 86°30E **126** D8

Kennesaw *U.S.A.* 34°1N 84°37W **178** A5
Kennet → *U.K.* 51°27N 0°57W **67** F7
Kennett Ra. *Australia* 23°50S 117°8E **149** D2
Kennett *U.S.A.* 36°14N 90°3W **172** G8
Kennewick *U.S.A.* 46°12N 119°7W **168** C4
Kennisis Lake *Canada* 45°13N 78°36W **174** A6
Kenogami → *Canada* 51°6N 84°28W **164** B3
Kenora *Canada* 49°47N 94°29W **163** D10
Kenosha *U.S.A.* 42°35N 87°49E **172** D10
Kenozersky △ *Russia* 62°5N 38°10E **106** C5
Kensington *Canada* 46°28N 63°34W **165** C7
Kent *Ohio, U.S.A.* 41°9N 81°22W **174** E3
Kent *Tex., U.S.A.* 31°4N 104°13W **176** F2
Kent *Wash., U.S.A.* 47°22N 122°14W **170** C4
Kent □ *U.K.* 51°12N 0°40E **67** F8
Kent Group *Australia* 39°30S 147°20E **151** F4
Kent Pen. *Canada* 68°30N 107°0W **160** D10
Kentau *Kazakhstan* 43°32N 68°36E **109** D7
Kentland *U.S.A.* 40°46N 87°27W **172** E10
Kenton *U.S.A.* 40°39N 83°37W **173** E12
Kentucky □ *U.S.A.* 37°0N 84°0W **173** G11
Kentucky → *U.S.A.* 38°41N 85°11W **172** F11
Kentucky L. *U.S.A.* 37°1N 88°16W **172** G9
Kentville *Canada* 45°6N 64°29W **165** C7
Kentwood *U.S.A.* 30°56N 90°31W **177** F9
Kenya ■ *Africa* 1°0N 38°0E **142** B4
Kenya, Mt. *Kenya* 0°10S 37°18E **142** C4
Kenyir, Tasik *Malaysia* 5°1N 102°54E **121** K4
Keo Neua, Deo
  Vietnam 18°23N 105°10E **120** C5
Keokuk *U.S.A.* 40°24N 91°24W **172** E8
Keoladeo △ *India* 27°0N 77°20E **124** F7
Keonjhargarh *India* 21°28N 85°35E **125** J11
Kep *Cambodia* 10°29N 104°19E **121** G5
Kep *Vietnam* 21°24N 106°16E **120** B6
Kep □ *Cambodia* 10°30N 104°18E **121** G5
Kepala Batas *Malaysia* 5°31N 100°26E **121** c
Kepi *Indonesia* 6°32S 139°19E **119** F9
Kepno *Poland* 51°18N 17°58E **83** G4
Kepsut *Turkey* 39°40N 28°9E **99** B10
Kerala □ *India* 11°0N 76°15E **127** J3
Kerama-Rettō *Japan* 26°5N 127°15E **113** L3
Keran *Pakistan* 34°35N 73°59E **125** B5
Keran → *Togo* 10°9N 0°41E **139** C5
Kerang *Australia* 35°40S 143°55E **152** C5
Keratea *Greece* 37°48N 23°58E **98** D5
Keraudren, C.
  Australia 19°58S 119°45E **148** C2
Kerava *Finland* 60°25N 25°5E **84** B3
Kerch *Ukraine* 45°20N 36°20E **85** K9
Kerchoual *Mali* 17°12N 0°20E **139** B5
Kerempe Burnu *Turkey* 42°2N 33°20E **104** A5
Keren *Eritrea* 15°45N 38°28E **133** E5
Kerepakupai-Meru = Angel Falls
  Venezuela 5°57N 62°30W **186** B6
Kerewan *Gambia* 13°29N 16°10E **138** C1
Kerguelen *Ind. Oc.* 49°15S 69°10E **146** K3
Kerguelen Plateau
  S. Ocean 55°0S 75°0E **146** K6
Kericho *Kenya* 0°22S 35°15E **142** C4
Kerian, Kuala *Malaysia* 5°10N 100°25E **121** c
Kerici *N.Z.* 35°12S 173°59E **154** B2
Kerinci *Indonesia* 1°40S 101°15E **118** E2
Keriya He → *China* 38°30N 82°10E **109** E10
Kerkenna, Îs. *Tunisia* 34°48N 11°11E **136** B6
Kerki = Atamyrat
  Turkmenistan 37°50N 65°12E **109** E7
Kerkini, L. *Greece* 41°12N 23°10E **96** E7
Kerkouane *Tunisia* 36°58N 11°2E **94** F4
Kerkrade *Neths.* 50°53N 6°4E **69** D6
Kerkyra *Greece* 39°38N 19°50E **101** A3
Kerkyra ✈ (CFU) *Greece* 39°36N 19°54E **98** B1
Kerkyra, Notio Steno
  Greece 39°34N 20°0E **101** A4
Kerma *Sudan* 19°33N 30°32E **137** D3
Kermadec Is. *Pac. Oc.* 30°0S 178°15W **147** E11
Kermadec Trench
  Pac. Oc. 30°30S 176°0W **156** L10
Kerman *Iran* 30°15N 57°1E **129** D8
Kerman *U.S.A.* 36°43N 120°4W **178** J6
Kermān □ *Iran* 30°0N 57°0E **129** D8
Kermān, Bīābān-e *Iran* 28°45N 59°45E **129** D8
Kermānshāh *Iran* 34°23N 47°0E **128** C5
Kermānshāh □ *Iran* 34°0N 46°30E **128** C5
Kermen *Bulgaria* 42°30N 26°16E **97** D10
Kermit *U.S.A.* 31°52N 103°6W **176** F3
Kern → *U.S.A.* 35°16N 119°18W **171** K7
Kernave *Lithuania* 54°53N 24°49E **84** E3
Kernhof *Austria* 47°49N 15°32E **78** D8
Kernow = Cornwall □
  U.K. 50°26N 4°40W **67** G3
Kernville *U.S.A.* 35°45N 118°26W **171** K8
Keroh *Malaysia* 5°43N 101°1E **121** K3
Keros *Greece* 36°54N 25°40E **99** F7
Kérou *Benin* 10°50N 2°5E **139** C5
Kérouane *Guinea* 9°15N 9°0W **138** D3
Kerpen *Germany* 50°51N 6°41E **76** E2
Kerrera *U.K.* 56°24N 5°33W **65** E3
Kerrobert *Canada* 51°56N 109°8W **163** C7
Kerrville *U.S.A.* 30°3N 99°8W **176** F5
Kerry □ *Ireland* 52°7N 9°35W **64** D2
Kerry Hd. *Ireland* 52°25N 9°56W **64** D2
Kerulen = Herlen →
  Asia 48°48N 117°0E **111** B12
Kervo = Kerava *Finland* 60°25N 25°5E **84** B3
Kerzaz *Algeria* 29°29N 1°37E **136** C4
Kesagami → *Canada* 51°40N 79°45W **164** B4
Kesagami L. *Canada* 50°23N 80°15W **164** B3
Kesan *Turkey* 40°49N 26°38E **97** F10
Kesennuma *Japan* 38°54N 141°35E **112** E10
Keshav *Iran* 29°43N 58°17E **129** D8
Keshit *Iran* 29°43N 58°17E **129** D8
Kesgi = Kosgi *India* 15°51N 77°16E **127** G3
Kesisi Dağ *Turkey* 39°7N 35°34E **105** C6
Keskal *India* 20°5N 81°35E **126** D5
Keskin *Turkey* 39°40N 33°36E **104** C5
Kestenga *Russia* 65°50N 31°45E **60** D24
Keswick *U.K.* 54°36N 3°9W **66** C4
Keszthely *Hungary* 46°50N 17°15E **80** D2
Ket → *Russia* 58°55N 81°32E **106** D9
Keta *Ghana* 5°49N 1°9E **139** D5
Keta Lagoon *Ghana* 5°55N 1°0E **139** D5
Ketanga *Indonesia* 8°9S 114°28E **119** J17
Ketapang *Jawa Timur,
  Indonesia* 8°9S 114°23E **119** J17
Ketapang *Kalimantan Barat,
  Indonesia* 1°55S 110°0E **118** E4

Kennesaw *U.S.A.* 47°18N 44°32E **87** G7
Ketchenery *Russia* 47°18N 44°32E **87** G7
Ketchikan *U.S.A.* 55°21N 131°39W **162** B2
Ketchum *U.S.A.* 43°41N 114°22W **168** E6
Kete Krachi *Ghana* 7°46N 0°1W **139** D4
Ketef, Khalîg Umm el
  Egypt 23°40N 35°35E **128** F2
Keti Bandar *Pakistan* 24°8N 67°27E **124** G2
Kétou *Benin* 7°25N 2°45E **139** D5
Ketri *India* 28°1N 75°50E **124** E6
Ketrzyn *Poland* 54°7N 21°22E **82** A8
Kettering *U.K.* 52°24N 0°43W **67** E7
Kettering *U.S.A.* 39°41N 84°10W **173** F11
Kettle → *Canada* 56°40N 89°34W **163** B11
Kettle Falls *U.S.A.* 48°37N 118°3W **168** B4
Kettle Point *Canada* 43°13N 82°1W **174** C2
Kettle Pt. *Canada* 43°13N 82°1W **174** C2
Kettleman City *U.S.A.* 36°1N 119°58W **178** J7
Kety *Poland* 49°51N 19°16E **83** J6
Keuka L. *U.S.A.* 42°30N 77°9W **174** D7
Keuruu *Finland* 62°16N 24°41E **84** A3
Kevelaer *Germany* 51°36N 6°15E **76** D2
Kewanee *U.S.A.* 41°14N 89°56W **172** E9
Kewanna *U.S.A.* 41°1N 86°25W **172** E10
Keware *Nepal* 27°57N 83°47E **125** F10
Kewaunee *U.S.A.* 44°27N 87°31W **172** C10
Keweenaw B. *U.S.A.* 47°0N 88°15W **172** B9
Keweenaw Pen.
  U.S.A. 47°15N 88°15W **172** B9
Keweenaw Pt. *U.S.A.* 47°25N 87°43W **172** B9
Key, L. *Ireland* 54°0N 8°15W **64** C3
Key Colony Beach
  U.S.A. 24°45N 80°57W **179** L9
Key Largo *U.S.A.* 25°5N 80°27W **179** K9
Key West *U.S.A.* 24°33N 81°48W **179** L8
Keynsham *U.K.* 51°24N 2°29W **67** F5
Keyser *U.S.A.* 39°26N 78°59W **173** F14
Keystone Heights
  U.S.A. 29°47N 82°2W **178** F7
Kezhma *Russia* 58°59N 101°9E **107** D11
Kezi *Zimbabwe* 20°58S 28°32E **145** B4
Kežmarok *Slovak Rep.* 49°10N 20°28E **79** B13
Kgalagadi △ *Botswana* 24°30S 22°0E **144** B3
Kgalagadi Transfrontier △
  Africa 25°10S 21°0E **144** C3
Khabarovsk *Russia* 48°30N 135°5E **111** B16
Khabr △ *Iran* 28°51N 56°22E **129** D8
Khābūr → *Syria* 35°17N 40°35E **105** E9
Khaga *India* 25°47N 81°7E **125** G9
Khagaria *India* 25°30N 86°32E **125** G12
Khaipur *India* 29°34N 72°17E **124** E5
Khair *India* 27°57N 77°46E **124** F7
Khairabad *India* 27°33N 80°47E **125** F9
Khairagarh *India* 21°27N 81°2E **125** J9
Khairpur *Pakistan* 27°32N 68°49E **124** F3
Khairpur Nathan Shah
  Pakistan 27°6N 67°44E **124** F2
Khairwara *India* 23°58N 73°38E **124** H5
Khaisor → *Pakistan* 31°17N 68°59E **124** D3
Khajuraho *India* 24°51N 79°55E **125** G8
Khajuri Kach *Pakistan* 32°4N 69°51E **124** C3
Khakassia □ *Russia* 53°0N 90°0E **109** D12
Khakhea *Botswana* 24°48S 23°22E **144** B3
Khalafābād *Iran* 30°54N 49°24E **129** D6
Khalilabad *India* 26°48N 83°5E **125** F10
Khalīlī *Iran* 27°38N 53°17E **129** E7
Khalkhāl *Iran* 37°37N 48°32E **105** D13
Khalkis = Chalkida
  Greece 38°27N 23°42E **98** C5
Khalmer Yu *Russia* 67°58N 65°1E **106** C7
Khalūf *Oman* 20°30N 58°13E **131** C6
Kham Keut *Laos* 18°15N 104°43E **120** C5
Khamaria *India* 23°5N 80°48E **125** H9
Khambhaliya *India* 22°14N 69°41E **124** H3
Khambhat *India* 22°23N 72°33E **124** H5
Khambhat, G. of *India* 20°45N 72°30E **124** J5
Khamgaon *India* 20°42N 76°37E **126** D3
Khamir *Iran* 26°57N 55°36E **129** E7
Khamir *Yemen* 16°2N 43°48E **133** E5
Khammam *India* 17°11N 80°6E **126** F5
Khamsa *Egypt* 30°27N 32°23E **130** E1
Khan → *Namibia* 22°37S 14°56E **144** B2
Khān Abū Shāmat
  Syria 33°39N 36°53E **130** B5
Khān al Baghdādī
  Iraq 33°51N 42°32E **105** D10
Khān al Ḥammād
  Iraq 32°19N 44°16E **105** D11
Khān Āzād *Iraq* 33°7N 44°22E **128** C5
Khān Mujiddah *Iraq* 32°21N 43°48E **128** C4
Khān Shaykhūn *Syria* 35°26N 36°38E **104** E7
Khān Tengri, Pik *Asia* 42°12N 80°10E **109** E10
Khān Yūnis *Gaza Strip* 31°21N 34°18E **130** D3
Khanai *Pakistan* 30°30N 67°8E **124** D2
Khānaqīn *Iraq* 34°23N 45°25E **105** D11
Khānbāghī *Iran* 36°10N 55°25E **129** B7
Khandwa *India* 21°49N 76°22E **124** J7
Khandyga *Russia* 62°42N 135°35E **107** C14
Khanewal *Pakistan* 30°20N 71°55E **124** D4
Khangah Dogran
  Pakistan 31°50N 73°37E **124** D5
Khangchendzonga =
  Kanchenjunga △
  India 27°42N 88°8E **125** F13
Khanh Duong
  Vietnam 12°44N 108°44E **120** F7
Khaniá = Chania *Greece* 35°30N 24°4E **101** D6
Khaniadhana *India* 25°1N 78°8E **124** G8
Khanka, L. *Asia* 45°0N 132°24E **112** B6
Khankendy = Xankändi
  Azerbaijan 39°52N 46°49E **105** C12
Khanna *India* 30°42N 76°16E **124** D7
Khanozai *Pakistan* 30°37N 67°19E **124** D2
Khanpur *Pakistan* 28°42N 70°35E **124** E5
Khantaishy *Russia* 15°30N 100°43E **120** E3
Khanty-Mansiysk *Russia* 61°0N 69°0E **106** C7
Khao Khitchakut △
  Thailand 12°50N 102°10E **120** F4
Khao Laem △ *Thailand* 14°56N 98°31E **120** E2
Khao Laem Res.
  Thailand 14°48N 98°30E **120** E2
Khao Lak △ *Malaysia* 8°38N 98°18E **121** H2

Khao Luang △ *Thailand* 8°34N 99°42E **121** H2
Khao Nam Khang △
  Thailand 6°32N 100°35E **121** J3
Khao Phlu *Thailand* 9°29N 99°59E **121** b
Khao Pu -Khao Ya △
  Thailand 7°26N 99°57E **121** J2
Khao Sam Roi Yot △
  Thailand 12°13N 99°57E **121** F2
Khao Sok △ *Thailand* 8°55N 98°38E **121** H2
Khao Yai △ *Thailand* 14°21N 101°29E **120** E3
Khaoen Si Nakarin △
  Thailand 14°47N 99°0E **120** E2
Khapalu *Pakistan* 35°10N 76°20E **125** B7
Khapcheranga
  Russia 49°42N 112°24E **107** E12
Khaptao △ *Nepal* 29°20N 81°10E **125** E9
Kharabali *Russia* 47°25N 47°15E **87** G8
Kharagauli *Georgia* 42°1N 43°12E **87** J6
Kharaghoda *India* 23°11N 71°46E **124** H4
Kharagpur *India* 22°20N 87°25E **125** H12
Kharan Kalat *Pakistan* 28°34N 65°21E **122** E4
Kharānaq *Iran* 32°20N 54°45E **129** C7
Kharda *India* 18°40N 75°34E **126** E2
Khardung La *India* 34°20N 77°43E **125** B7
Kharg = Khārk, Jazīreh-ye
  Iran 29°15N 50°28E **129** D6
Khârga, El Wâhât el
  Egypt 25°10N 30°35E **137** B3
Khargon *India* 21°45N 75°40E **126** D2
Khari → *India* 25°54N 74°31E **124** G6
Kharian *Pakistan* 32°49N 73°52E **124** C5
Khariar *India* 20°17N 82°46E **126** D6
Kharit, Wadi el →
  Egypt 24°26N 33°3E **137** C3
Khārk, Jazīreh-ye *Iran* 29°15N 50°28E **129** D6
Kharkiv *Ukraine* 49°58N 36°20E **85** H9
Kharkov = Kharkiv
  Ukraine 49°58N 36°20E **85** H9
Kharmanli *Bulgaria* 41°55N 25°55E **97** E9
Kharovsk *Russia* 59°56N 40°13E **84** C11
Kharsawangarh *India* 22°48N 85°50E **125** H11
Kharta *Turkey* 40°55N 29°7E **104** B3
Khartoum = El Khartûm
  Sudan 15°31N 32°35E **135** E12
Khartum *Sudan* 45°15N 77°5W **174** A7
Khasan *Russia* 42°25N 130°40E **112** C5
Khasavyurt *Russia* 43°16N 46°40E **87** J8
Khāsh *Iran* 28°15N 61°15E **129** D9
Khashm el Girba
  Sudan 14°59N 35°58E **135** F13
Khashuri *Georgia* 42°3N 43°35E **87** J6
Khaskovo *Bulgaria* 41°56N 25°30E **97** E9
Khaskovo □ *Bulgaria* 42°0N 25°40E **97** E9
Khat, Laem *Thailand* 8°6N 98°26E **121** a
Khatanga *Russia* 72°0N 102°20E **107** B11
Khatanga → *Russia* 72°55N 106°0E **107** B11
Khatauli *India* 29°17N 77°43E **124** E7
Khatlon □ *Tajikistan* 37°50N 69°0E **109** F7
Khatra *India* 22°59N 86°51E **125** H12
Khatyrka *Russia* 62°3N 175°15E **107** C18
Khavda *India* 23°51N 69°43E **124** H3
Khawr Fakkān *U.A.E.* 25°21N 56°22E **129** E8
Khay' *Si. Arabia* 18°45N 41°24E **137** D5
Khaybar, Harrat
  Si. Arabia 25°30N 39°45E **128** E4
Khāzimiyah *Iraq* 34°46N 43°37E **128** C4
Khe Bo *Vietnam* 19°8N 104°41E **120** C5
Khe Long *Vietnam* 21°29N 104°46E **120** B5
Khe Sanh *Vietnam* 16°37N 106°45E **120** D6
Khed *Maharashtra, India* 17°43N 73°23E **124** L5
Khed *Maharashtra, India* 18°51N 73°56E **124** L6
Khed Brahma *India* 24°7N 73°5E **124** G5
Khekra *India* 28°52N 77°20E **124** E7
Khemarak Phouminville = Krong
  Cambodia 11°37N 102°59E **121** G4
Khemisset *Morocco* 33°50N 6°1W **136** B3
Khemmarat *Thailand* 16°10N 105°15E **120** D5
Khenāmān *Iran* 30°27N 56°29E **129** D8
Khenchela *Algeria* 35°28N 7°11E **136** A5
Khenefra *Morocco* 32°58N 5°46W **136** B2
Kherrata *Algeria* 36°27N 5°13E **136** A5
Khersān → *Iran* 31°33N 50°22E **129** D6
Kherson *Ukraine* 46°35N 32°35E **85** J7
Kherson □ *Ukraine* 46°15N 33°10E **85** J7
Kheta → *Russia* 71°54N 102°6E **107** B11
Khewari *Pakistan* 26°36N 68°52E **124** F3
Khilchipur *India* 24°2N 76°34E **124** G7
Khilok *Russia* 51°30N 110°45E **107** D12
Khimki *Russia* 55°50N 37°20E **84** E9
Khíos = Chios *Greece* 38°27N 26°9E **99** C8
Khirsadoh *India* 22°11N 78°47E **125** H8
Khiuma = Hiiumaa
  Estonia 58°50N 22°45E **84** C2
Khiva = Xiva
  Uzbekistan 41°30N 60°18E **108** D6
Khlebarovo *Bulgaria* 43°37N 26°15E **97** C10
Khlong Khlung
  Thailand 16°12N 99°43E **120** D2
Khlong Lan △ *Thailand* 16°12N 99°16E **120** D2
Khlong Phanom △
  Thailand 8°45N 98°38E **121** H2
Khmelnik *Ukraine* 49°33N 27°58E **75** D14
Khmelnytskyy *Ukraine* 49°23N 27°0E **75** D14
Khmelnytskyy □
  Ukraine 49°50N 26°40E **75** D14
Khmer Rep. = Cambodia ■
  Asia 12°15N 105°0E **120** F5
Khoai, Hon *Vietnam* 8°26N 104°50E **121** H5
Khobar = Al Khubar
  Si. Arabia 26°17N 50°12E **129** E6
Khodoriv *Ukraine* 49°24N 24°19E **75** D13
Khodzent = Khŭjand
  Tajikistan 40°17N 69°37E **109** E7
Khojak Pass *Afghan.* 30°51N 66°34E **124** D2
Khojayli = Xo'jayli
  Uzbekistan 42°29N 59°31E **108** D5
Khok Kloi *Thailand* 8°16N 98°19E **121** a
Khok Pho *Thailand* 6°43N 101°6E **121** J3
Khok Samrong
  Thailand 15°3N 100°43E **120** E3
Kholm *Afghan.* 36°45N 67°40E **109** E7
Kholm *Russia* 57°10N 31°15E **84** D7
Kholmsk *Russia* 47°40N 142°5E **107** E15
Khomārlu *Iran* 39°6N 47°3E **105** C12
Khomas □ *Namibia* 23°30S 17°0E **144** B2
Khomas Hochland
  Namibia 22°40S 16°0E **144** B2

Khombole *Senegal* 14°43N 16°42W **138** C1
Khomeyn *Iran* 33°40N 50°7E **129** C6
Khomeynī Shahr *Iran* 32°41N 51°31E **129** C6
Khomodino *Botswana* 22°46S 23°52E **144** B3
Khon Kaen *Thailand* 16°30N 102°47E **120** D4
Khong *→ Cambodia* 13°32N 105°58E **120** F5
Khong Sedone *Laos* 15°34N 105°49E **120** E5
Khonuu *Russia* 66°30N 143°12E **107** C15
Khoper *→ Russia* 49°30N 42°20E **86** F6
Khorāsān-e Janūb □
  Iran 32°0N 59°0E **129** C8
Khorāsān-e Razavī □
  Iran 35°0N 59°0E **129** C8
Khorāsān-e Shemālī □
  Iran 37°0N 57°0E **129** B8
Khorat = Nakhon Ratchasima
  Thailand 14°59N 102°12E **120** E4
Khorat, Cao Nguyen
  Thailand 15°30N 102°50E **120** E4
Khorazm = Xorazm □
  Uzbekistan 43°0N 60°0E **108** D6
Khorb el Ethel *Algeria* 28°30N 6°17W **136** C2
Khorixas *Namibia* 20°16S 14°59E **144** B1
Khorol *Ukraine* 49°48N 33°15E **85** H7
Khorramābād *Khorāsān,*
  Iran 35°6N 57°57E **129** C8
Khorramābād *Lorestān,*
  Iran 33°30N 48°25E **105** F13
Khorramdarreh *Iran* 36°11N 49°11E **105** D13
Khorramshahr *Iran* 30°29N 48°15E **129** D6
Khorugh *Tajikistan* 37°30N 71°36E **109** E8
Khosravī *Iran* 30°48N 51°28E **129** D6
Khosrowābād *Khuzestān,*
  Iran 30°10N 48°25E **129** D6
Khosrowābād *Kordestān,*
  Iran 35°31N 47°38E **105** E12
Khost *Pakistan* 30°13N 67°35E **124** D2
Khosūyeh *Iran* 28°32N 54°26E **129** D7
Khotang *Nepal* 27°1N 86°51E **125** F12
Khotyn *Ukraine* 48°31N 26°27E **81** B11
Khouribga *Morocco* 32°58N 6°57W **136** B4
Khowst *Afghan.* 33°22N 69°58E **124** C3
Khowst □ *Afghan.* 33°20N 70°0E **122** C6
Khoyniki *Belarus* 51°54N 29°55E **75** C15
Khram, Ko *Thailand* 12°42N 100°47E **120** F3
Khrami *→ Georgia* 41°25N 45°0E **87** K7
Khrenovoye *Russia* 51°4N 40°16E **86** E5
Khromtaū *Kazakhstan* 50°17N 58°27E **108** B5
Khrysokhou B. *Cyprus* 35°6N 32°25E **101** D11
Khuan Wa *Thailand* 7°53N 98°17E **121** a
Khudzhand = Khŭjand
  Tajikistan 40°17N 69°37E **109** D7
Khuff *Si. Arabia* 24°55N 44°53E **128** E5
Khūgīānī *Afghan.* 31°34N 66°32E **124** D2
Khuis *Botswana* 26°40S 21°49E **144** D3
Khuiyala *India* 27°9N 70°25E **124** F4
Khŭjand *Tajikistan* 40°17N 69°37E **109** D7
Khujner *India* 23°47N 76°36E **124** H7
Khukhan *Thailand* 14°42N 104°12E **120** E5
Khulna *Bangla.* 22°45N 89°34E **123** H16
Khulna □ *Bangla.* 22°25N 89°35E **123** H16
Khulo *Botswana* 41°33N 42°19E **87** K6
Khumago *Botswana* 20°26S 24°32E **144** B3
Khunjerab Pass = Kinjirap Daban
  Asia 36°40N 75°25E **109** C9
Khūnsorkh *Iran* 27°9N 56°7E **129** E8
Khunti *India* 23°5N 85°17E **125** H11
Khūr *Iran* 32°55N 58°18E **129** C8
Khurai *India* 24°3N 78°23E **124** G8
Khurays *Si. Arabia* 25°6N 48°2E **129** E6
Khurda *India* 20°11N 85°37E **126** D7
Khurja *India* 28°15N 77°58E **124** E7
Khūrmāl *Iraq* 35°18N 46°2E **105** E12
Khurr, Wādī al *Iraq* 32°3N 43°52E **128** C4
Khūsf *Iran* 32°46N 58°53E **129** C8
Khushab *Pakistan* 32°20N 72°20E **124** C5
Khust *Ukraine* 48°10N 23°18E **81** B8
Khutse △ *Botswana* 23°31S 24°12E **144** B3
Khuzdar *Pakistan* 27°52N 66°30E **124** F2
Khūzestān □ *Iran* 31°0N 49°0E **129** D6
Khvāf *Iran* 34°33N 60°8E **129** C9
Khvājeh *Iran* 38°9N 46°35E **128** B5
Khvalynsk *Russia* 52°30N 48°2E **86** D9
Khvalynsky △ *Russia* 52°30N 48°0E **86** D9
Khvānsār *Iran* 29°56N 54°8E **129** D7
Khvatovka *Russia* 52°24N 46°32E **86** D8
Khvor *Iran* 33°45N 55°0E **129** C7
Khvorgū *Iran* 27°34N 56°27E **129** E8
Khvormūj *Iran* 28°40N 51°30E **129** D6
Khvoy *Iran* 38°35N 45°0E **105** C11
Khvoynaya *Russia* 58°58N 34°28E **84** C4
Khwae Noi *→ Thailand* 14°1N 99°32E **120** E2
Khyber Pakhtunkhwa □
  Pakistan 34°0N 72°0E **124** C4
Khyber Pass *Afghan.* 34°10N 71°8E **124** B4
Khyriv *Ukraine* 49°32N 22°50E **83** J9
Kia *Fiji* 16°16S 179°8E **154** a
Kiabukwa
  Dem. Rep. of the Congo 8°40S 24°48E **143** D1
Kiadho *→ India* 19°37N 77°40E **124** K10
Kiama *Australia* 34°40S 150°50E **153** C9
Kiamba *Phil.* 6°2N 124°46E **119** C6
Kiambi
  Dem. Rep. of the Congo 7°15S 28°0E **142** D2
Kiang West △ *Gambia* 13°25N 15°50W **138** C1
Kiangsi = Jiangxi □
  China 27°30N 116°0E **117** D11
Kiangsu = Jiangsu □
  China 33°0N 120°0E **115** H11
Kiato *Greece* 38°1N 22°45E **98** C4
Kibæk *Denmark* 56°2N 8°51E **63** H2
Kibale △ *Uganda* 0°16N 30°18E **142** B3
Kibanga Port *Uganda* 0°10N 32°58E **142** B3
Kibara *Tanzania* 2°8S 33°30E **142** C3
Kibara, Mts.
  Dem. Rep. of the Congo 8°25S 27°10E **142** D2
Kiboga *Uganda* 0°58N 31°45E **142** B3
Kibombo
  Dem. Rep. of the Congo 3°57S 25°53E **142** C2
Kibondo *Tanzania* 3°35S 30°45E **142** C3
Kibre Mengist *Ethiopia* 5°54N 38°59E **131** F2
Kibumbu *Burundi* 3°32S 29°45E **142** C2
Kibungo *Rwanda* 2°10S 30°32E **142** C3
Kibuye *Burundi* 3°39S 29°59E **142** C2
Kibuye *Rwanda* 2°3S 29°21E **142** C2
Kibwesa *Tanzania* 6°30S 29°58E **142** D2
Kibwezi *Kenya* 2°27S 37°57E **142** C4
Kicasalih *Turkey* 41°23N 26°43E **97** EC10

Kičevo *Macedonia* 41°34N 20°59E **96** E4
Kichha *→ India* 28°41N 79°18E **125** E8
Kicking Horse Pass
  Canada 51°28N 116°16W **162** C5
Kidal *Mali* 18°26N 1°22E **139** B5
Kidal □ *Mali* 19°55N 1°5E **139** B5
Kidderminster *U.K.* 52°24N 2°15W **67** E5
Kideta *Tanzania* 6°25S 37°17E **142** D4
Kidira *Senegal* 14°28N 12°13W **138** C2
Kidnappers, C. *N.Z.* 39°38S 177°5E **154** F6
Kidsgrove *U.K.* 53°5N 2°14W **66** D5
Kidston *Australia* 18°52S 144°8E **150** B3
Kidugallo *Tanzania* 6°49S 38°15E **142** D4
Kiel *Germany* 54°19N 10°8E **76** A6
Kiel Canal = Nord-Ostsee-Kanal
  Germany 54°12N 9°32E **76** A5
Kielce *Poland* 50°52N 20°42E **83** H7
Kielder Water *U.K.* 55°11N 2°31W **66** B5
Kieler Bucht *Germany* 54°35N 10°25E **76** A6
Kiembara *Burkina Faso* 13°15N 2°44W **138** C4
Kienge
  Dem. Rep. of the Congo 10°30S 27°30E **143** E2
Kiessé *Niger* 13°29N 4°1E **139** C5
Kiev = Kyyiv *Ukraine* 50°30N 30°28E **75** C16
Kifaya *Guinea* 12°10N 13°4W **138** C2
Kiffa *Mauritania* 16°37N 11°24W **138** B2
Kifisós *→ Greece* 38°35N 23°20E **98** C5
Kifissia *Greece* 38°4N 23°49E **98** C5
Kifrī *Iraq* 34°45N 45°0E **105** E11
Kigali *Rwanda* 1°59S 30°4E **142** C3
Kigarama *Tanzania* 1°1S 31°50E **142** C3
Kigezi △ *Uganda* 0°34S 29°55E **142** C2
Kiği *Turkey* 39°18N 40°21E **105** C9
Kigoma □ *Tanzania* 5°0S 30°0E **142** D2
Kigoma-Ujiji *Tanzania* 4°55S 29°36E **142** C2
Kigomasha, Ras
  Tanzania 4°58S 38°58E **142** C4
Kigosi △ *Tanzania* 4°10S 31°45E **142** C3
Kiğzi *Turkey* 38°18N 43°25E **128** B4
Kihikihi *N.Z.* 38°2S 175°22E **154** E4
Kihnu *Estonia* 58°9N 24°1E **84** C3
Kii-Sanchi *Japan* 34°20N 136°0E **113** G8
Kii-Suidō *Japan* 33°40N 134°45E **113** H7
Kiira Dam *Uganda* 0°25N 33°0E **142** B3
Kikaiga-Shima *Japan* 28°19N 129°59E **113** K4
Kikiak = Rigolet
  Canada 54°10N 58°23W **165** B8
Kikinda *Serbia* 45°50N 20°30E **80** E5
Kikládhes = Kyklades
  Greece 37°0N 24°30E **98** E6
Kikoira *Australia* 33°39S 146°40E **153** B7
Kikuchi *Japan* 32°59N 130°47E **113** H5
Kikuyu *Kenya* 1°15S 36°40E **142** C4
Kikwit
  Dem. Rep. of the Congo 5°0S 18°45E **140** F3
Kil *Sweden* 59°30N 13°20E **62** E7
Kilafors *Sweden* 61°14N 16°36E **62** C10
Kilakkarai *India* 9°12N 78°47E **127** K4
Kilar *India* 33°6N 76°25E **124** C7
Kilbeggan *Ireland* 53°22N 7°30W **64** C4
Kilbrannan Sd. *U.K.* 55°37N 5°26W **65** F3
Kilbuck Mts. *U.S.A.* 60°36N 159°53W **166** C8
Kilchu *N. Korea* 40°57N 129°25E **115** D15
Kilcoy *Australia* 26°59S 152°30E **151** D5
Kildare *Ireland* 53°9N 6°55W **64** C5
Kildare □ *Ireland* 53°10N 6°50W **64** C5
Kildinstroy *Russia* 68°48N 33°6E **60** B25
Kilfinnane *Ireland* 52°21N 8°28W **64** D3
Kilgarvan *Ireland* 51°54N 9°27W **64** E2
Kilgore *U.S.A.* 32°23N 94°53W **176** E7
Kilibo *Benin* 8°32N 2°38E **139** D5
Kilifi *Kenya* 3°40S 39°48E **142** C4
Kilimanjaro *Tanzania* 3°7S 37°20E **142** C4
Kilimanjaro □ *Tanzania* 4°0S 38°0E **142** C4
Kilimanjaro △ *Tanzania* 3°25S 37°19E **142** C4
Kilimli *Turkey* 41°28N 31°50E **104** B4
Kilindini *Kenya* 4°4S 39°40E **142** C4
Kilinochchi *Sri Lanka* 9°24N 80°25E **127** K5
Kilis *Turkey* 36°42N 37°6E **104** D7
Kilis □ *Turkey* 36°55N 37°10E **104** D7
Kiliya *Ukraine* 45°28N 29°16E **81** E14
Kilkee *Ireland* 52°41N 9°39W **64** D2
Kilkeel *U.K.* 54°7N 5°55W **64** B5
Kilkenny *Ireland* 52°39N 7°15W **64** D4
Kilkenny □ *Ireland* 52°35N 7°15W **64** D4
Kilkieran B. *Ireland* 53°20N 9°41W **64** C2
Kilkis *Greece* 40°58N 22°57E **96** F6
Killala *Ireland* 54°13N 9°13W **64** B2
Killala B. *Ireland* 54°16N 9°8W **64** B2
Killaloe *Canada* 45°33N 77°25W **174** A7
Killaloe *Ireland* 52°48N 8°28W **64** D3
Killarney *Australia* 28°20S 152°18E **151** D5
Killarney *Canada* 49°10N 99°40W **163** D9
Killarney *Ireland* 52°4N 9°30W **64** D2
Killary Harbour *Ireland* 53°38N 9°52W **64** C2
Killdeer *U.S.A.* 47°22N 102°45W **172** B2
Killeberg *Sweden* 56°29N 14°5E **63** H8
Killeen *U.S.A.* 31°7N 97°44W **176** F6
Killin *U.K.* 56°28N 4°19W **65** E4
Killiney *Ireland* 53°15N 6°7W **64** C5
Killington Pk. *U.S.A.* 43°36N 72°49W **175** C12
Killini = Kyllini *Greece* 37°55N 21°8E **98** D3
Killini *Greece* 37°54N 22°25E **98** D4
Killini I. *Canada* 60°24N 64°37W **161** E19
Killorglin *Ireland* 52°6N 9°47W **64** D2
Killybegs *Ireland* 54°38N 8°26W **64** B3
Killmore Quay *Ireland* 52°10N 6°36W **64** D5
Kilondo *Tanzania* 9°45S 34°20E **143** D3
Kilosa *Tanzania* 6°48S 37°0E **142** D4
Kilrush *Ireland* 52°38N 9°29W **64** D2
Kiltan I. *India* 11°29N 73°0E **127** J1
Kilwa Kisiwani *Tanzania* 8°58S 39°32E **143** D4
Kilwa Kivinje *Tanzania* 8°45S 39°25E **143** D4
Kilwa Masoko *Tanzania* 8°55S 39°30E **143** D4
Kim *U.S.A.* 37°15N 103°21W **169** H12
Kim *→ Cameroon* 5°28N 11°7E **139** D7
Kimaam *Indonesia* 7°58S 138°53E **119** F9
Kimamba *Tanzania* 6°45S 37°10E **142** D4
Kimba *Australia* 33°8S 136°23E **152** B2
Kimball *Nebr., U.S.A.* 41°14N 103°40W **172** E2
Kimball *S. Dak., U.S.A.* 43°45N 98°57W **172** D7
Kimberley *Australia* 16°20S 127°0E **148** C4

Kimberley *B.C.,*
  Canada 49°40N 115°59W **162** D5
Kimberley *Ont., Canada* 44°23N 80°32W **174** B4
Kimberley *S. Africa* 28°43S 24°46E **144** C3
Kimberly *U.S.A.* 42°32N 114°22W **168** E6
Kimch'aek *N. Korea* 40°40N 129°10E **115** D15
Kimhae = Gimhae
  S. Korea 35°14N 128°53E **115** G15
Kimi *Greece* 38°38N 24°6E **98** C6
Kimmirut *Canada* 62°50N 69°50W **161** E18
Kimolos *Greece* 36°48N 24°37E **98** E6
Kimovsk *Moskva, Russia* 55°6N 37°28E **84** E9
Kimovsk *Tula, Russia* 54°0N 38°29E **84** E10
Kimparana *Mali* 12°48N 5°0W **138** C4
Kimpese
  Dem. Rep. of the Congo 5°35S 14°26E **140** F2
Kimry *Russia* 56°55N 37°15E **84** D9
Kimstad *Sweden* 58°35N 15°58E **63** F9
Kinabalu, Gunung
  Malaysia 6°3N 116°14E **118** C5
Kinango *Kenya* 4°8S 39°19E **142** C4
Kinard *U.S.A.* 30°16N 85°15W **178** E4
Kinaros *Greece* 36°59N 26°15E **99** E8
Kinaskan L. *Canada* 57°38N 130°8W **162** B2
Kinbasket L. *Canada* 52°0N 118°10W **162** C5
Kincardine *Canada* 44°10N 81°40W **174** B3
Kinchafoonee Cr. *→*
  U.S.A. 31°38N 84°10W **178** D5
Kinchega △ *Australia* 32°27S 142°15E **152** B5
Kincolith *Canada* 55°0N 129°57W **162** C3
Kinda
  Dem. Rep. of the Congo 9°18S 25°4E **143** D2
Kindberg *Austria* 47°30N 15°27E **78** D8
Kinde *U.S.A.* 43°56N 83°0W **174** C2
Kinder Scout *U.K.* 53°24N 1°52W **66** D6
Kindersley *Canada* 51°30N 109°10W **163** C7
Kindia *Guinea* 10°0N 12°52E **138** D2
Kindu
  Dem. Rep. of the Congo 2°55S 25°50E **142** C2
Kinel *Russia* 53°15N 50°40E **86** D10
Kineshma *Russia* 57°30N 42°5E **86** B6
Kinesi *Tanzania* 1°25S 33°50E **142** C3
King, L. *Australia* 33°10S 119°35E **149** F2
King, Mt. *Australia* 25°10S 147°30E **150** D4
King Christian I.
  Canada 77°48N 101°40W **161** B11
King City *U.S.A.* 36°13N 121°8W **170** J5
King Cr. *→ Australia* 24°35S 139°30E **150** C2
King Edward *→*
  Australia 14°14S 126°35E **148** B4
King Edward Point
  S. Georgia 54°17S 36°30W **55** B1
King Frederick VI Land = Kong
  Frederik VI.s Kyst
  Greenland 63°0N 43°0W **57** E6
King George B.
  Falk. Is. 51°30S 60°30W **192** D4
King George I. *Antarctica* 60°0S 60°0W **55** C18
King George Is.
  Canada 57°20N 80°30W **161** F15
King George Sd.
  Australia 35°5S 118°0E **149** G2
King I. = Kadan Kyun
  Burma 12°30N 98°20E **120** F2
King I. *Australia* 39°50S 144°0E **151** F3
King I. *Canada* 52°10N 127°40W **162** C3
King Khalid Military City =
  Madinat al Malik Khālid al
  Askarīyah *Si. Arabia* 27°54N 45°31E **128** E5
King Leopold Ranges
  Australia 17°30S 125°45E **148** C4
King of Prussia *U.S.A.* 40°5N 75°23W **175** F9
King Sd. *Australia* 16°50S 123°20E **148** C3
King Sejong *Antarctica* 62°30S 58°0W **55** C18
King Shaka = Durban ✈ (DIA)
  S. Africa 29°37S 31°7E **145** C5
King William I.
  Canada 69°10N 97°25W **160** D12
King William's Town
  S. Africa 32°51S 27°22E **144** D4
Kingaok = Bathurst Inlet
  Canada 66°50N 108°1W **160** D10
Kingaroy *Australia* 26°32S 151°51E **151** D5
Kingfisher *U.S.A.* 35°52N 97°56W **176** D6
Kingirbān *Iraq* 34°40N 44°54E **128** C5
Kingisepp = Kuressaare
  Estonia 58°15N 22°30E **84** C2
Kingisepp *Russia* 59°25N 28°40E **84** C5
Kinglake △ *Australia* 37°30S 145°22E **153** D6
Kingman *Ariz., U.S.A.* 35°12N 114°4W **171** K12
Kingman *Kans., U.S.A.* 37°39N 98°7W **172** G4
Kingoonya *Australia* 30°55S 135°19E **151** E2
Kingri *Pakistan* 30°27N 69°49E **124** D3
Kings *→ U.S.A.* 36°3N 119°50W **170** J7
Kings Canyon
  Australia 24°15S 131°34E **148** D5
Kings Canyon △
  U.S.A. 36°50N 118°40W **170** J8
King's Lynn *U.K.* 52°45N 0°24E **66** E8
Kings Park *U.S.A.* 40°53N 73°16W **175** F11
Kings Peak *U.S.A.* 40°46N 110°23W **168** F8
King's Trough *Atl. Oc.* 43°48N 22°0W **56** B9
Kingsbridge *U.K.* 50°17N 3°47W **67** G4
Kingsburg *U.S.A.* 36°31N 119°33W **170** J7
Kingscote *Australia* 35°40S 137°38E **152** C2
Kingscourt *Ireland* 53°54N 6°48W **64** C5
Kingsford *U.S.A.* 45°48N 88°4W **172** C9
Kingsland *U.S.A.* 30°48N 81°41W **178** E4
Kingsport *U.S.A.* 36°33N 82°33W **177** C13
Kingston *Canada* 44°14N 76°30W **175** B8
Kingston *Jamaica* 17°55N 76°50W **182** a
Kingston *N.Z.* 45°20S 168°43E **155** F3
Kingston *N.H., U.S.A.* 42°56N 71°3W **175** D13
Kingston *N.Y., U.S.A.* 41°56N 73°59W **175** E11
Kingston *Pa., U.S.A.* 41°16N 75°54W **175** E9
Kingston *R.I., U.S.A.* 41°29N 71°30W **175** E13
Kingston Pk. *U.S.A.* 35°44N 115°55W **171** K11
Kingston South East
  Australia 36°51S 139°55E **152** D3
Kingston upon Hull
  U.K. 53°45N 0°21W **66** D7
Kingston upon Hull □
  U.K. 53°45N 0°21W **66** D7
Kingston-upon-Thames □
  U.K. 51°24N 0°17W **67** D7
Kingstown *Australia* 30°29S 151°6E **153** B9
Kingstown *St. Vincent* 13°10N 61°10W **183** D7
Kingstree *U.S.A.* 33°40N 79°50W **178** D8
Kingsville *Canada* 42°2N 82°45W **174** D2
Kingsville *U.S.A.* 27°31N 97°52W **176** H6
Kingussie *U.K.* 57°6N 4°2W **65** D4

Kingwood *U.S.A.* 30°2N 95°16W **176** F7
Kınık *Antalya, Turkey* 36°20N 29°20E **99** E11
Kınık *İzmir, Turkey* 39°6N 27°24E **99** B9
Kinistino *Canada* 52°57N 105°2W **163** C7
Kinjirap Daban *Asia* 36°40N 75°25E **109** E9
Kinkala *Congo* 4°18S 14°49E **140** E2
Kinki □ *Japan* 33°45N 136°0E **113** H8
Kinleith *N.Z.* 38°20S 175°56E **154** E4
Kinlochleven *U.K.* 56°43N 5°0W **65** E4
Kinmount *Canada* 44°48N 78°45W **174** B6
Kinna *Sweden* 57°32N 12°42E **63** G6
Kinnairds Hd. *U.K.* 57°43N 2°1W **65** D6
Kinnared *Sweden* 57°2N 13°7E **63** G7
Kinnarodden = Nordkinn
  Norway 71°8N 27°40E **60** A22
Kinnarp *Sweden* 58°5N 13°32E **63** F7
Kinneviken *Sweden* 58°35N 13°32E **63** F7
Kinngait *Canada* 64°14N 76°32W **161** E16
Kinniyai *Sri Lanka* 8°29N 81°11E **127** K5
Kino Nuevo *Mexico* 28°52N 112°3W **180** B2
Kinoje *→ Canada* 52°8N 81°25W **164** B3
Kinomoto *Japan* 35°30N 136°13E **113** G8
Kinoni *Uganda* 0°41S 30°28E **142** C3
Kinoosao *Canada* 57°5N 102°1W **163** B8
Kinross *U.K.* 56°13N 3°25W **65** E5
Kinsale *Ireland* 51°42N 8°31W **64** E3
Kinsale, Old Hd. of
  Ireland 51°37N 8°33W **64** E3
Kinsha = Chang Jiang *→*
  China 31°48N 121°10E **117** B13
Kinshasa
  Dem. Rep. of the Congo 4°20S 15°15E **140** E3
Kinsley *U.S.A.* 37°55N 99°25W **172** G4
Kinsman *U.S.A.* 41°26N 80°35W **174** E4
Kinston *N.C., U.S.A.* 35°16N 77°35W **177** D16
Kintamani *Indonesia* 8°14S 115°19E **119** J18
Kintampo *Ghana* 8°5N 1°41W **139** D4
Kintore *U.K.* 57°14N 2°20W **65** D6
Kintore Ra. *Australia* 23°15S 128°47E **148** D5
Kintyre *U.K.* 55°30N 5°35W **65** F3
Kintyre, Mull of *U.K.* 55°17N 5°47W **65** F3
Kinushseo *→ Canada* 55°15N 83°45W **164** A3
Kinuso *Canada* 55°20N 115°25W **162** B5
Kinvarra *Ireland* 53°8N 8°56W **64** C3
Kinwat *India* 19°38N 78°12E **126** E4
Kinyangiri *Tanzania* 4°25S 34°37E **142** C3
Kinzig *→ Germany* 48°36N 7°49E **77** G3
Kinzua *U.S.A.* 41°52N 78°58W **174** E6
Kioni *Greece* 38°27N 20°41E **98** C2
Kiosk *Canada* 46°6N 78°53W **164** C4
Kiowa *Kans., U.S.A.* 37°1N 98°29W **172** G4
Kiowa *Okla., U.S.A.* 34°43N 95°54W **176** D7
Kipahigan L. *Canada* 55°20N 101°55W **163** B8
Kipanga *Tanzania* 6°15S 35°20E **142** D4
Kiparissia *Greece* 37°15N 21°40E **98** D3
Kiparissiakos Kolpos
  Greece 37°25N 21°25E **98** D3
Kipawa, L. *Canada* 46°50N 79°0W **164** C4
Kipembawe *Tanzania* 7°38S 33°27E **142** D3
Kipengere Ra. *Tanzania* 9°12S 34°15E **143** D3
Kipili *Tanzania* 7°28S 30°32E **142** D3
Kipini *Kenya* 2°30S 40°32E **142** C5
Kipling *Canada* 50°6N 102°38W **163** C8
Kippure *Ireland* 53°11N 6°21W **64** C5
Kipushi
  Dem. Rep. of the Congo 11°48S 27°12E **143** E2
Kira *Uganda* 0°24N 32°38E **142** B3
Kira Panagia *Greece* 39°17N 24°4E **98** B6
Kirandul *India* 18°33N 81°10E **126** E6
Kirane *Mali* 15°20N 10°20W **138** B2
Kiraz *Turkey* 38°14N 28°13E **99** C10
Kirazlı *Turkey* 40°2N 26°41E **97** F10
Kirchhain *Germany* 50°49N 8°56E **76** E4
Kirchheim *Germany* 48°39N 9°27E **77** G5
Kirchheimbolanden
  Germany 49°40N 8°0E **77** F3
Kirchschlag *Austria* 47°30N 16°19E **79** D9
Kireç *Turkey* 39°33N 28°22E **99** B9
Kırech *Russia* 57°50N 107°55E **107** D11
Kirensk *Russia* 57°50N 107°55E **107** D11
Kirghiz Range *Asia* 42°40N 73°40E **109** D8
Kirghizia = Kyrgyzstan ■
  Asia 42°0N 75°0E **109** D9
Kirgiziya Steppe *Eurasia* 50°0N 55°0E **108** C5
Kiri Buru *India* 22°0N 85°0E **126** D7
Kiribati ■ *Pac. Oc.* 3°0S 180°0E **147** B10
Kırıkhan *Turkey* 36°31N 36°21E **104** D7
Kırıkkale *Turkey* 39°51N 33°32E **104** C5
Kirikopuni *N.Z.* 35°50S 174°1E **154** B5
Kirillov *Russia* 59°49N 38°24E **84** C10
Kirin = Jilin *China* 43°44N 126°30E **115** C14
Kirindi Oya *→ Sri Lanka* 6°15N 81°20E **127** L5
Kirinyaga = Kenya, Mt.
  Kenya 0°10S 37°18E **142** C4
Kirirom △ *Cambodia* 11°18N 104°5E **121** G5
Kirishi *Russia* 59°28N 32°0E **84** C7
Kirishima *Japan* 31°44N 130°46E **113** J5
Kirishima Yaku △
  Japan 31°24N 130°50E **113** J5
Kiritimati *Kiribati* 1°58N 157°27W **157** G12
Kırka *Turkey* 39°39N 139°52E **112** F9
Kırkağaç *Turkey* 39°6N 27°40E **99** B9
Kırkby *U.K.* 53°30N 2°54W **66** D5
Kirkby-in-Ashfield *U.K.* 53°6N 1°14W **66** D6
Kirkby Lonsdale *U.K.* 54°12N 2°36W **66** C5
Kirkby Stephen *U.K.* 54°29N 2°21W **66** C5
Kirkcaldy *U.K.* 56°7N 3°9W **65** E5
Kirkcudbright *U.K.* 54°50N 4°2W **65** G4
Kirkenes *Norway* 69°40N 30°5E **60** B24
Kirkfield *Canada* 44°34N 78°59W **174** B6
Kirkintilloch *U.K.* 55°56N 4°8W **65** F4
Kirkjubæjarklaustur
  Iceland 63°47N 18°4W **60** E4
Kirkkonummi *Finland* 60°8N 24°26E **63** B21
Kirkland *U.S.A.* 47°40N 122°12W **170** C4
Kirkland Lake *Canada* 48°9N 80°2W **164** C3
Kirklareli *Turkey* 41°44N 27°15E **97** E11
Kirklareli □ *Turkey* 41°45N 27°15E **97** E11
Kirkliston Ra. *N.Z.* 44°25S 170°34E **155** F3
Kirkpatrick, Mt.
  Antarctica 84°30S 166°25E **55** E11
Kirksville *U.S.A.* 40°12N 92°35W **172** E7
Kirkūk *Iraq* 35°30N 44°21E **105** E11
Kirkwall *U.K.* 58°59N 2°58W **65** C6
Kirkwood *S. Africa* 33°22S 25°12E **126** FG
Kirlampudi *India* 17°12N 82°12E **126** F6
Kırn *Germany* 49°47N 7°26E **77** F3
Kirov *Kaluga, Russia* 54°3N 34°20E **84** E8
Kirov *Kirov, Russia* 58°35N 49°40E **86** C8

Kirovabad = Gäncä
  Azerbaijan 40°45N 46°20E **87** K8
Kirovograd = Kirovohrad
  Ukraine 48°35N 32°20E **85** H7
Kirovohrad *Ukraine* 48°35N 32°20E **85** H7
Kirovohrad □ *Ukraine* 48°30N 31°30E **85** H6
Kirovskiy = Balpyq Bi
  Kazakhstan 44°52N 78°12E **109** D9
Kirovskiy *Astrakhan.,*
  Russia 45°51N 48°11E **87** H9
Kirovskiy *Kamchatka,*
  Russia 54°27N 155°42E **107** D16
Kirovskiy *Primorsk,*
  Russia 45°7N 133°30E **112** B6
Kirriemuir *U.K.* 56°41N 3°1W **65** E5
Kirsanov *Russia* 52°35N 42°40E **86** D6
Kirşehir *Turkey* 39°14N 34°5E **104** C6
Kirtachi *Niger* 12°52N 2°30E **139** C5
Kirthar △ *Pakistan* 25°45N 67°30E **124** F2
Kirthar Range *Pakistan* 27°0N 67°0E **124** F2
Kirtland *U.S.A.* 36°44N 108°21W **169** H9
Kiruna *Sweden* 67°52N 20°15E **60** C19
Kirundu
  Dem. Rep. of the Congo 0°50S 25°35E **142** C2
Kirya *Russia* 55°8N 46°55E **86** C8
Kiryū *Japan* 36°24N 139°20E **113** F9
Kisa *Sweden* 58°0N 15°39E **63** G9
Kisaga *Tanzania* 4°30S 34°23E **142** C3
Kisalföld *Hungary* 47°30N 17°0E **80** C2
Kisanga
  Dem. Rep. of the Congo 2°30N 26°35E **142** B2
Kisangani
  Dem. Rep. of the Congo 0°35N 25°15E **142** B2
Kisar *Indonesia* 8°5S 127°10E **119** F7
Kisarawe *Tanzania* 6°53S 39°0E **142** D4
Kisarazu *Japan* 35°23N 139°55E **113** G9
Kisběr *Hungary* 47°30N 18°2E **80** C3
Kiselevsk *Russia* 54°5N 86°39E **109** B11
Kish = Qeys *Iran* 26°32N 53°58E **129** E7
Kishanganga *→*
  Pakistan 34°18N 73°28E **125** B5
Kishanganj *India* 26°3N 88°14E **125** F13
Kishangarh *Raj., India* 26°34N 74°52E **124** F6
Kishangarh *Raj., India* 27°50N 70°30E **124** F4
Kishi *Nigeria* 9°1N 3°52E **139** D5
Kishinev = Chișinău
  Moldova 47°2N 28°50E **81** C13
Kishiwada *Japan* 34°28N 135°22E **113** G7
Kishkeneköl
  Kazakhstan 53°38N 72°20E **109** B8
Kishtwar *India* 33°20N 75°48E **124** C6
Kisielice *Poland* 53°36N 19°16E **82** E6
Kisigo *→ Tanzania* 6°27S 34°17E **142** D3
Kisii *Kenya* 0°40S 34°45E **142** C3
Kisiju *Tanzania* 7°23S 39°19E **142** D4
Kisir *Turkey* 41°0N 43°5E **105** B10
Kisizi *Uganda* 1°0S 29°58E **142** C2
Kiska I. *U.S.A.* 51°59N 177°30E **166** E3
Kiskőrös *Hungary* 46°37N 19°20E **80** D4
Kiskőrei-víztároló
  Hungary 47°31N 20°36E **80** C5
Kiskőrös *Hungary* 46°37N 19°20E **80** D4
Kiskundorozsma
  Hungary 46°16N 20°5E **80** D5
Kiskunfélegyháza
  Hungary 46°42N 19°53E **80** D4
Kiskunhalas *Hungary* 46°28N 19°37E **80** D4
Kiskunmajsa *Hungary* 46°30N 19°48E **80** D4
Kiskunsági △ *Hungary* 46°39N 19°30E **80** D4
Kislovodsk *Russia* 43°50N 42°45E **87** J6
Kismaayo *Somalia* 0°22S 42°32E **131** H3
Kiso-Gawa *→ Japan* 35°20N 136°45E **113** G8
Kiso-Sammyaku
  Japan 35°45N 137°45E **113** G8
Kisofukushima *Japan* 35°52N 137°43E **113** G8
Kisoro *Uganda* 1°17S 29°48E **142** C2
Kissamos = Kasteli
  Greece 35°29N 23°38E **101** D5
Kissamos, Kolpos
  Greece 35°30N 23°38E **101** D5
Kissidougou *Guinea* 9°5N 10°5W **138** D2
Kissimmee *U.S.A.* 28°18N 81°24W **178** G3
Kissimmee *→ U.S.A.* 27°9N 80°52W **178** H4
Kississing L. *Canada* 55°10N 101°20W **163** B8
Kissónerga *Cyprus* 34°49N 32°24E **101** E11
Kisii *Kenya* 0°40S 34°45E **142** C3
Kisújszállás *Hungary* 47°12N 20°50E **80** C5
Kisumu *Kenya* 0°3S 34°45E **142** C3
Kisvárda *Hungary* 48°14N 22°4E **80** B7
Kiswani *Tanzania* 4°5S 37°57E **142** C4
Kiswere *Tanzania* 9°27S 39°30E **143** D4
Kit Carson *U.S.A.* 38°46N 102°48W **168** G12
Kita *Mali* 13°5N 9°25W **138** C3
Kitaibaraki *Japan* 36°50N 140°45E **113** F10
Kitakami *Japan* 39°20N 141°10E **112** E10
Kitakami-Gawa *→*
  Japan 38°25N 141°19E **112** E10
Kitakami-Sammyaku
  Japan 39°30N 141°30E **112** E10
Kitakata *Japan* 37°39N 139°52E **112** F9
Kitakyūshū *Japan* 33°50N 130°50E **113** H5
Kitale *Kenya* 1°0N 35°0E **142** B4
Kitami *Japan* 43°48N 143°54E **112** C11
Kitami-Sammyaku
  Japan 44°22N 142°43E **112** B11
Kitangiri, L. *Tanzania* 4°5S 34°20E **142** C3
Kitaya *Tanzania* 10°38S 40°8E **143** E5
Kitchener *Canada* 43°27N 80°29W **174** D4
Kitee *Finland* 62°5N 30°9E **84** A6
Kitega = Gitega *Burundi* 3°26S 29°56E **142** C2
Kitengo
  Dem. Rep. of the Congo 7°26S 24°8E **142** D1
Kitgum *Uganda* 3°17N 32°52E **142** B3
Kithira = Kythira *Greece* 36°8N 23°0E **98** E5
Kithnos = Kythnos
  Greece 37°26N 24°27E **98** D6
Kiti *Cyprus* 34°50N 33°34E **101** E12
Kiti, C. *Cyprus* 34°48N 33°36E **101** E12
Kitimat *Canada* 54°3N 128°38W **162** C3
Kitinen *→ Finland* 67°14N 27°27E **60** C22
Kitros *Greece* 40°22N 22°34E **96** F6
Kitsman *Ukraine* 48°25N 25°46E **81** B10
Kitsuki *Japan* 33°25N 131°37E **113** H5
Kittakittaooloo, L.
  Australia 28°3S 138°14E **151** D2
Kittanning *U.S.A.* 40°49N 79°31W **174** F5
Kittatinny Mt. *U.S.A.* 41°19N 74°39W **175** F10
Kittery *U.S.A.* 43°5N 70°45W **175** D14

Kittilä *Finland* 67°40N 24°51E **60** C21
Kitui *Kenya* 1°17S 38°0E **142** C4
Kitwanga *Canada* 55°6N 128°4W **162** B3
Kitwe *Zambia* 12°54S 28°13E **143** E2
Kitzbühel *Austria* 47°27N 12°24E **78** D5
Kitzbühler Alpen
  Austria 47°20N 12°20E **78** D5
Kitzingen *Germany* 49°44N 10°9E **77** F6
Kiunga Marine △ *Kenya* 2°1S 41°14E **142** C5
Kivarli *India* 24°33N 72°46E **124** G5
Kivertsi *Ukraine* 50°50N 25°28E **75** C13
Kividhes *Cyprus* 34°46N 32°51E **101** E11
Kivik *Sweden* 55°41N 14°13E **63** J8
Kivotos *Greece* 40°13N 21°26E **96** F5
Kivu, L.
  Dem. Rep. of the Congo 1°48S 29°0E **142** C2
Kiwirrkurra *Australia* 22°49S 127°45E **148** D4
Kiwirrkurra ◎
  Australia 22°49S 127°45E **148** D4
Kiyev = Kyyiv *Ukraine* 50°30N 30°28E **75** C16
Kiyevskoye Vdkhr. = Kyyivske
  Vdskh. *Ukraine* 51°0N 30°25E **75** C16
Kıyıköy *Turkey* 41°38N 28°5E **97** E12
Kizhi, Ostrov *Russia* 62°4N 35°13E **84** B8
Kiziba-Baluba △ *Congo* 11°50S 28°0E **143** E2
Kiziguru *Rwanda* 1°46S 30°23E **142** C3
Kizil Adalar *Turkey* 40°52N 29°5E **97** F13
Kızıl Irmak *→ Turkey* 41°44N 35°58E **104** B6
Kizil Jilga *China* 35°26N 78°50E **125** B8
Kizil Yurt *Russia* 43°13N 46°54E **87** J8
Kızılcabölük *Turkey* 37°37N 29°1E **99** D11
Kızılcadağ *Turkey* 37°1N 29°59E **99** D11
Kızılcahamam *Turkey* 40°30N 32°30E **104** B5
Kızıldağ △ *Turkey* 38°5N 31°20E **128** B1
Kızılhisar *Turkey* 37°18N 30°27E **99** D12
Kızılırmak *Turkey* 40°21N 33°59E **104** B5
Kızılkaya *Turkey* 37°18N 30°27E **99** D12
Kızılören *Turkey* 38°15N 30°10E **99** C12
Kızıltepe *Turkey* 37°12N 40°35E **105** D9
Kizimkazi *Tanzania* 6°28S 39°30E **142** D4
Kizlyar *Russia* 43°51N 46°40E **87** J8
Kizyl-Arvat = Serdar
  Turkmenistan 39°4N 56°23E **129** B8
Kjellerup *Denmark* 56°17N 9°25E **63** H3
Kjölur *Iceland* 64°50N 19°25W **60** D4
Kladanj *Bos.-H.* 44°14N 18°42E **80** F3
Kladno *Czech Rep.* 50°10N 14°7E **78** A7
Kladovo *Serbia* 44°36N 22°33E **96** B6
Klaeng *Thailand* 12°47N 101°39E **120** F3
Klagenfurt *Austria* 46°38N 14°20E **78** E7
Klaipėda *Lithuania* 55°43N 21°10E **82** C8
Klaipėda □ *Lithuania* 55°43N 21°7E **82** C8
Klaksvík *Færoe Is.* 62°14N 6°35W **60** E9
Klamath *→ U.S.A.* 41°33N 124°5W **168** F1
Klamath Falls *U.S.A.* 42°13N 121°46W **168** F3
Klamath Mts. *U.S.A.* 41°50N 123°20W **168** F2
Klamono *Indonesia* 1°8S 131°30E **119** E8
Klang *Malaysia* 3°2N 101°26E **121** L3
Klanjec *Croatia* 46°3N 15°45E **83** B12
Klappan *→ Canada* 58°0N 129°43W **162** B3
Klarälven *→ Sweden* 59°23N 13°32E **62** E7
Klässbol *Sweden* 59°33N 12°45E **62** E6
Klatovy *Czech Rep.* 49°23N 13°18E **78** B6
Klawer *S. Africa* 31°44S 18°36E **144** C2
Klazienaveen *Neths.* 52°44N 7°0E **69** B6
Klé *Mali* 12°0N 6°28W **138** C3
Klecko *Poland* 52°38N 17°25E **83** F4
Kleczew *Poland* 52°22N 18°9E **83** F5
Kleena Kleene *Canada* 52°0N 124°59W **162** C4
Klein-Karas *Namibia* 27°33S 18°7E **144** D2
Kleinbegin *S. Africa* 28°54S 21°40E **144** C3
Klekovača *Bos.-H.* 44°25N 16°32E **83** B13
Klembivka *Ukraine* 48°28N 28°25E **81** B13
Klenoec *Macedonia* 41°32N 20°49E **96** E4
Klenovec *Slovak Rep.* 48°36N 19°54E **79** C12
Klerksdorp *S. Africa* 26°53S 26°38E **144** C4
Kleszczele *Poland* 52°35N 23°19E **83** F10
Kletnya *Russia* 53°23N 33°12E **84** F7
Kletsk = Klyetsk *Belarus* 53°5N 26°45E **75** B14
Kletskiy *Russia* 49°16N 43°11E **87** F6
Kleve *Germany* 51°47N 6°7E **76** D2
Klickitat *U.S.A.* 45°49N 121°9W **168** D3
Klickitat *→ U.S.A.* 45°42N 121°17W **170** E5
Klidhes *Cyprus* 35°42N 34°36E **101** D13
Klimovichi *Belarus* 53°36N 32°0E **84** F6
Klin *Russia* 56°20N 36°48E **84** D9
Klinaklini *→ Canada* 51°21N 125°40W **162** C3
Klině *Kosovo* 42°37N 20°35E **96** C4
Klintehamn *Sweden* 57°24N 18°12E **63** G12
Klintsy *Russia* 52°50N 32°10E **85** F7
Klip *→ S. Africa* 27°3S 29°3E **145** C4
Klipdale *S. Africa* 34°19S 19°57E **144** D2
Klippan *Sweden* 56°8N 13°6E **63** G6
Klipplaat *S. Africa* 33°1S 24°22E **144** D3
Klishkivtsi *Ukraine* 48°26N 26°16E **81** B11
Klisura *Bulgaria* 42°40N 24°28E **97** D8
Kljajićevo *Serbia* 45°45N 19°17E **80** E4
Ključ *Bos.-H.* 44°32N 16°48E **83** D13
Klobuck *Poland* 50°55N 18°55E **83** H5
Klockestrand *Sweden* 62°53N 17°55E **62** B11
Klodawa *Poland* 52°15N 18°55E **83** F5
Kłodzko *Poland* 50°28N 16°38E **83** H3
Klondike *Canada* 64°0N 139°26W **160** E4
Klong Wang Chao △
  Thailand 16°20N 99°9E **120** D2
Klos *Albania* 41°28N 20°10E **96** E4
Klosterneuburg *Austria* 48°18N 16°19E **79** C9
Klosters *Switz.* 46°52N 9°52E **77** E9
Klötze *Germany* 52°37N 11°10E **76** C7
Klouto *Togo* 6°57N 0°44E **139** D5
Klövsjö *Sweden* 62°32N 14°11E **62** B8
Kluane △ *Canada* 60°45N 139°30W **162** A1
Kluane L. *Canada* 61°15N 138°40W **160** E4
Kluang *Malaysia* 2°3N 103°18E **121** L4
Kluczbork *Poland* 50°58N 18°12E **83** H5
Klukwan *U.S.A.* 59°24N 135°54W **162** B1
Klungkung *Indonesia* 8°32S 115°24E **119** K18
Klyetsk *Belarus* 53°5N 26°45E **75** B14
Klyuchevskaya, Sopka
  Russia 55°50N 160°30E **107** D17
Klyuchi *Russia* 56°18N 160°51E **107** D17
Knäred *Sweden* 56°31N 13°15E **63** H7
Knaresborough *U.K.* 54°1N 1°28W **66** C6
Knee L. *Man., Canada* 55°3N 94°45W **163** B10
Knee L. *Sask., Canada* 55°51N 107°0W **163** B7
Kneïss, Îs. *Tunisia* 34°22N 10°18E **135** A8
Knezha *Bulgaria* 43°30N 24°5E **97** C8
Knight Inlet *Canada* 50°45N 125°40W **162** C3
Knighton *U.K.* 52°21N 3°3W **67** E4
Knights Ferry *U.S.A.* 37°50N 120°40W **170** H6

Knights Landing
  U.S.A. 38°48N 121°43W **170** G5
Knin *Croatia* 44°3N 16°17E **93** D13
Knislinge *Sweden* 56°12N 14°5E **63** H8
Knittelfeld *Austria* 47°13N 14°51E **78** D7
Knivsta *Sweden* 59°43N 17°48E **62** E11
Knob, C. *Australia* 34°32S 119°16E **149** F2
Knock *Ireland* 53°48N 8°55W **64** C3
Knockmealdown Mts.
  Ireland 52°14N 7°56W **64** D4
Knokke-Heist *Belgium* 51°21N 3°17E **69** C3
Knossos *Greece* 35°16N 25°10E **101** D7
Knowlton *Canada* 45°13N 72°31W **175** A12
Knox *U.S.A.* 41°18N 86°37W **172** E10
Knox Coast *Antarctica* 66°30S 108°0E **5** C8
Knoxville *Ga., U.S.A.* 32°47N 83°59W **178** C6
Knoxville *Iowa, U.S.A.* 41°19N 93°6W **172** E7
Knoxville *Pa., U.S.A.* 41°57N 77°27W **174** E7
Knoxville *Tenn.,*
  U.S.A. 35°58N 83°55W **177** D13
Knud Rasmussen Land
  Greenland 78°0N 60°0W **57** B4
Knysna *S. Africa* 34°2S 23°2E **144** D3
Knyszyn *Poland* 53°20N 22°56E **82** E9
Ko Kha *Thailand* 18°11N 99°24E **120** C2
Ko Tarutao △ *Thailand* 6°31N 99°26E **121** J2
Ko Yao *Thailand* 8°7N 98°35E **121** a
Koartac = Quaqtaq
  Canada 60°55N 69°40W **161** E18
Koba *Indonesia* 6°37S 134°37E **119** F8
Kobarid *Slovenia* 46°15N 13°30E **93** B10
Kobayashi *Japan* 31°56N 130°59E **113** J5
Kōbe *Japan* 34°41N 135°13E **113** G7
Kobelyaky *Ukraine* 49°11N 34°9E **85** H8
København *Denmark* 55°40N 12°26E **63** J6
København ✈ (CPH)
  Denmark 55°37N 12°39E **63** J6
Kobenni *Mauritania* 15°58N 9°24W **138** B3
Kōbi-Sho *E. China Sea* 25°56N 123°41E **113** M1
Koblenz *Germany* 50°21N 7°36E **77** E3
Kobryn *Belarus* 52°15N 24°22E **75** B13
Kobuk → *U.S.A.* 66°54N 160°38W **166** B7
Kobuleti *Georgia* 41°55N 41°45E **87** K5
Kobyletska Polyana
  Ukraine 48°3N 24°4E **81** B9
Kobylin *Poland* 51°43N 17°12E **83** G4
Kobyłka *Poland* 52°20N 21°10E **83** F8
Kobylkino *Russia* 54°8N 43°56E **86** C6
Koca → *Turkey* 40°8N 27°57E **97** F11
Kocabaş *Turkey* 37°49N 29°20E **99** D11
Kocaeli *Turkey* 40°45N 29°50E **97** F13
Kocaeli □ *Turkey* 40°53N 30°0E **97** F13
Kočane *Serbia* 43°12N 21°52E **96** C5
Kočani *Macedonia* 41°55N 22°25E **96** E6
Koçarlı *Turkey* 37°45N 27°43E **99** D9
Koceljevo *Serbia* 44°28N 19°50E **96** B3
Kočevje *Slovenia* 45°39N 14°50E **93** C11
Koch Bihar *India* 26°22N 89°29E **123** F16
Kochas *India* 25°15N 83°56E **125** G10
Kocher → *Germany* 49°13N 9°12E **77** F5
Kochi *India* 9°58N 76°20E **127** K3
Kōchi *Japan* 33°30N 133°35E **113** H6
Kōchi □ *Japan* 33°40N 133°30E **113** H6
Kochiu = Gejiu *China* 23°20N 103°10E **116** F4
Kochkor *Kyrgyzstan* 42°13N 75°46E **109** D9
Kochubey *Russia* 44°23N 46°32E **87** H8
Kock *Poland* 51°38N 22°27E **83** G9
Kodala *India* 19°38N 84°57E **125** H10
Kodarma *India* 24°28N 85°36E **125** G11
Koddiyar B. *Sri Lanka* 8°33N 81°15E **127** K5
Kode *Sweden* 57°57N 11°51E **63** G5
Kodiak *U.S.A.* 57°47N 152°24W **166** D9
Kodiak I. *U.S.A.* 57°30N 152°45W **166** D9
Kodikkarai = Point Calimere
  India 10°17N 79°49E **127** J4
Kodinar *India* 20°46N 70°46E **124** J4
Kodinsk *Russia* 58°40N 99°10E **107** D10
Kodlipet *India* 12°48N 75°53E **127** H2
Kodori → *Georgia* 42°47N 41°10E **87** J5
Kodungallur = Cranganore
  India 10°13N 76°13E **127** J3
Kodyma *Ukraine* 48°6N 29°7E **81** B14
Koedoesberge *S. Africa* 32°40S 20°11E **144** D3
Koes *Namibia* 26°0S 19°15E **144** D2
Kofarnihon *Tajikistan* 38°33N 69°1E **109** E7
Kofçaz *Turkey* 41°58N 27°12E **97** E11
Koffiefontein *S. Africa* 29°30S 25°0E **144** C4
Kofiau *Indonesia* 1°11S 129°50E **119** E7
Köflach *Austria* 47°4N 15°5E **78** D8
Koforidua *Ghana* 6°3N 0°17W **139** D4
Kōfu *Japan* 35°40N 138°30E **113** G9
Koga *Japan* 36°11N 139°43E **113** F9
Kogaluc → *Canada* 56°12N 61°44W **165** A7
Køge *Denmark* 55°27N 12°11E **63** J6
Køge Bugt *Denmark* 55°34N 12°24E **63** J6
Kogi □ *Nigeria* 7°45N 6°45E **139** D6
Kogin Baba *Nigeria* 7°55N 11°35E **139** D7
Kogon *Uzbekistan* 39°43N 64°33E **108** E6
Koh Ker *Cambodia* 13°47N 104°32E **120** F5
Koh Wai *Thailand* 11°54N 102°25E **121** H4
Kohat *Pakistan* 33°40N 71°29E **124** C4
Kohima *India* 25°35N 94°10E **123** G19
Kohkīlūyeh va Būyer Aḥmadī □
  Iran 30°30N 50°30E **129** D6
Kohler Ra. *Antarctica* 77°0S 110°0W **5** D15
Kohlu *Pakistan* 29°54N 69°15E **124** E3
Kohtla-Järve *Estonia* 59°20N 27°20E **84** A4
Kohukohu *N.Z.* 35°22S 173°38E **154** B2
Kohylnyk → *Ukraine* 45°49N 29°40E **81** E14
Koi Sanjaq *Iraq* 36°5N 44°38E **105** B5
Koidu *S. Leone* 8°38N 10°59W **138** D2
Koihoa *India* 8°35N 93°23E **129** d
Koilkuntla *India* 15°14N 78°19E **127** G4
Koillismaa *Finland* 65°44N 28°36E **60** D23
Koin *N. Korea* 40°28N 126°18E **115** D14
Koinare *Bulgaria* 43°21N 24°8E **97** C8
Koindu *S. Leone* 8°26N 10°19W **138** D2
Kojetín *Czech Rep.* 49°21N 17°20E **79** B10
Kojō *N. Korea* 38°58N 127°58E **115** E14
Kojonup *Australia* 33°48S 117°10E **149** F2
Kojūr *Iran* 36°23N 51°43E **129** B6
Kokand = Qŭqon
  Uzbekistan 40°31N 70°56E **109** D8
Kokang *Burma* 23°45N 98°30E **116** F2
Kokas *Indonesia* 2°42S 132°26E **119** E8
Kokava *Slovak Rep.* 48°35N 19°50E **79** C12
Kokcha → *Afghan.* 37°9N 69°24E **109** E7

Kokchetav = Kökshetaū
  Kazakhstan 53°20N 69°25E **109** B7
Kokemäenjoki →
  Finland 61°32N 21°44E **84** B1
Kokhma *Russia* 56°57N 41°8E **86** B5
Koki *Senegal* 15°30N 15°59W **138** B1
Kokkilai *Sri Lanka* 9°0N 80°57E **127** K5
Kokkola *Finland* 63°50N 23°8E **60** E20
Koko *Nigeria* 11°28N 4°29E **139** C5
Koko Kyunzu *Burma* 14°7N 93°22E **127** G11
Kokologo *Burkina Faso* 12°11N 1°53W **138** C4
Kokolopozo *Ivory C.* 5°8N 6°5W **138** D3
Kokomo *U.S.A.* 40°29N 86°8W **172** E10
Kokopo *Papua N. G.* 4°22S 152°19E **156** H7
Kokoro *Niger* 14°12N 0°55E **139** C5
Koksan *N. Korea* 38°46N 126°40E **115** E14
Kökshetaū *Kazakhstan* 53°20N 69°25E **109** B7
Koksoak → *Canada* 58°30N 68°10W **161** F18
Kokstad *S. Africa* 30°32S 29°29E **145** E4
Kōktal *Kazakhstan* 44°8N 79°48E **109** D9
Kokubu = Kirishima
  Japan 31°44N 130°46E **113** J5
Kokyar *China* 37°23N 77°10E **109** E9
Kola *Indonesia* 5°35S 134°30E **119** F8
Kola *Russia* 68°45N 33°8E **60** B25
Kola Pen. = Kolskiy Poluostrov
  Russia 67°30N 38°0E **58** B13
Kolachel *India* 8°10N 77°15E **127** K3
Kolachi → *Pakistan* 27°8N 67°2E **124** F2
Kolahoi *India* 34°12N 75°22E **125** B6
Kolahun *Liberia* 8°15N 10°4W **138** D2
Kolaka *Indonesia* 4°3S 121°46E **119** E6
Kolar *India* 13°12N 78°15E **127** H4
Kolar Gold Fields *India* 12°58N 78°16E **127** H4
Kolaras *India* 25°14N 77°36E **124** G6
Kolari *Finland* 67°20N 23°48E **60** C20
Kolárovo *Slovak Rep.* 47°54N 18°1E **79** E10
Kolasib *India* 24°15N 92°45E **123** G18
Kolašin *Montenegro* 42°50N 19°31E **96** D3
Kolayat *India* 27°50N 72°50E **124** F5
Kolbäck *Sweden* 59°34N 16°15E **62** E10
Kölbäckson → *Sweden* 59°36N 16°16E **62** E10
Kolbermoor *Germany* 47°51N 12°4E **77** H8
Kolbuszowa *Poland* 50°15N 21°46E **83** H8
Kolchugino *Russia* 56°17N 39°22E **84** D10
Kolda → *Senegal* 12°55N 14°57W **138** C2
Kolda *Senegal* 13°5N 14°50W **138** C2
Kolding *Denmark* 55°30N 9°29E **63** J3
Koléa *Algeria* 36°38N 2°46E **136** A4
Kolepom = Dolak, Pulau
  Indonesia 8°0S 138°30E **119** F9
Kolguyev, Ostrov
  Russia 69°20N 48°30E **106** C5
Kolhapur *India* 16°43N 74°15E **126** F2
Kolia *Ivory C.* 9°46N 6°28W **138** D3
Kolimbia *Greece* 36°15N 28°10E **101** C10
Kolín *Czech Rep.* 50°2N 15°9E **78** A8
Kolind *Denmark* 56°21N 10°34E **63** H4
Kolkas rags *Latvia* 57°46N 22°37E **82** A4
Kolkata *India* 22°34N 88°21E **125** H13
Kollam *India* 8°50N 76°38E **127** K3
Kölleda *Germany* 51°11N 11°15E **76** D7
Kollegal *India* 12°9N 77°9E **127** H3
Kolleru L. *India* 16°40N 81°10E **126** F5
Kollum *Neths.* 53°17N 6°10E **69** A6
Kolmanskop *Namibia* 26°45S 15°14E **144** C2
Kolmården *Sweden* 58°40N 16°5E **63** E10
Koln *Germany* 50°56N 6°57E **76** E2
Kolno *Poland* 53°25N 21°56E **82** E8
Kolo *Poland* 52°14N 18°40E **83** F5
Kołobrzeg *Poland* 54°10N 15°35E **82** D2
Kolochava *Ukraine* 48°26N 23°41E **81** B8
Kolokani *Mali* 13°35N 7°45W **138** C3
Koloko *Burkina Faso* 11°5N 5°19W **138** C3
Kolomna *Russia* 55°8N 38°45E **84** D10
Kolomyya *Ukraine* 48°31N 25°2E **81** B10
Kolondiéba *Mali* 11°5N 6°54W **138** C3
Kolonodale *Indonesia* 2°0S 121°19E **119** E6
Kolonowskie *Poland* 50°39N 18°22E **83** H5
Kolpashevo *Russia* 58°20N 83°5E **106** D9
Kolpino *Russia* 59°44N 30°39E **84** C6
Kolpny *Russia* 52°17N 37°1E **85** F9
Kolskiy Poluostrov
  Russia 67°30N 38°0E **58** B13
Kolskiy Zaliv *Russia* 69°23N 34°0E **60** B26
Kolsva *Sweden* 59°36N 15°51E **62** E9
Kolubara → *Serbia* 44°35N 20°15E **96** B4
Koluszki *Poland* 51°45N 19°46E **83** G6
Kolwezi
  Dem. Rep. of the Congo 10°40S 25°25E **143** E2
Kolyma → *Russia* 69°30N 161°0E **107** C17
Kolymskoye Nagorye
  Russia 63°0N 157°0E **107** C16
Kôm Hamâda *Egypt* 30°46N 30°41E **137** E7
Kôm Ombo *Egypt* 24°25N 32°52E **137** C3
Koma Tou Yialou
  Cyprus 35°25N 34°8E **101** D13
Komadugu Gana →
  Nigeria 13°5N 12°24E **139** C7
Komandorskiye Is. =
  Komandorskiye Ostrova
  Russia 55°0N 167°0E **107** D17
Komandorskiye Ostrova
  Russia 55°0N 167°0E **107** D17
Komárno *Slovak Rep.* 47°49N 18°5E **79** D11
Komarovka *Ukraine* 48°59N 23°8E **80** B8
Komárom *Hungary* 47°43N 18°7E **80** C3
Komárom-Esztergom □
  Hungary 47°35N 18°20E **80** C3
Komatipoort *S. Africa* 25°25S 31°55E **145** C5
Komatsu *Japan* 36°25N 136°30E **113** F8
Komatsushima *Japan* 34°0N 134°35E **113** H7
Kombissiri *Burkina Faso* 12°4N 1°20W **139** C4
Kombori *Burkina Faso* 13°26N 3°56W **138** C4
Komboti *Greece* 39°6N 21°5E **98** B3
Komen *Slovenia* 45°49N 13°45E **93** C10
Komenda *Ghana* 5°4N 1°28W **139** D4
Komi □ *Russia* 64°0N 55°0E **106** C6
Komi Cyprus 35°24N 34°0E **101** D13
Komiža *Croatia* 43°3N 16°11E **93** E13
Komló *Hungary* 46°15N 18°16E **80** E3
Kommamur Canal *India* 16°0N 80°25E **127** G5
Kommunarsk = Alchevsk
  Ukraine 48°30N 38°45E **85** H10
Kommunizma, Pik = imeni Ismail
  Samani, Pik *Tajikistan* 39°0N 72°2E **108** F8
Komodo *Indonesia* 8°37S 119°20E **119** F5
Komoran, Pulau
  Indonesia 8°18S 138°45E **119** F9
Komoro *Japan* 36°19N 138°26E **113** F9
Komotini *Greece* 41°9N 25°26E **97** E9

Komovi *Montenegro* 42°41N 19°39E **96** D3
Kompasberg *S. Africa* 31°45S 24°32E **144** D3
Kompong Chhnang = Kampong
  Chhnang *Cambodia* 12°20N 104°35E **121** F5
Kompong Chikreng
  Cambodia 13°5N 104°18E **120** F5
Kompong Kleang
  Cambodia 13°6N 104°8E **120** F5
Kompong Luong
  Cambodia 11°49N 104°48E **121** G5
Kompong Pranak
  Cambodia 13°35N 104°55E **120** F5
Kompong Som = Kampong Saom
  Cambodia 10°38N 103°30E **121** G4
Kompong Som, Chhung =
  Kampong Saom, Chaak
  Cambodia 10°50N 103°32E **121** G4
Kompong Speu
  Cambodia 11°26N 104°32E **121** G5
Kompong Sralau
  Cambodia 14°5N 105°46E **120** F5
Kompong Thom
  Cambodia 12°35N 104°51E **120** F5
Kompong Trabeck
  Cambodia 13°6N 105°14E **120** F5
Kompong Trach
  Cambodia 11°25N 105°48E **121** G5
Kompong Tralach
  Cambodia 11°54N 104°47E **121** G5
Komrat = Comrat
  Moldova 46°18N 28°40E **81** C15
Komsberg *S. Africa* 32°40S 20°45E **144** D3
Komsomolets = Qarabalyq
  Kazakhstan 53°45N 62°2E **108** B6
Komsomolets, Ostrov
  Russia 80°30N 95°0E **107** A10
Komsomolsk *Russia* 57°2N 40°20E **84** D11
Komsomolsk *Ukraine* 49°1N 33°38E **85** H7
Komsomolsk-na-Amur
  Russia 50°30N 137°0E **111** A16
Komsomolskiy *Russia* 54°27N 45°33E **86** C7
Komsomolskoe
  Kazakhstan 50°25N 60°5E **108** B6
Kömür Burnu *Turkey* 38°39N 26°12E **99** C8
Kon Ka Kinh △
  Vietnam 14°19N 107°23E **120** E6
Kon Tum *Vietnam* 14°24N 108°0E **120** E7
Kon Tum, Plateau du
  Vietnam 14°30N 108°30E **120** E7
Kona *Mali* 14°57N 3°53W **138** C4
Kona *Nigeria* 8°57N 11°12E **139** D7
Konakovo *Russia* 56°40N 36°51E **84** D9
Konar □ *Afghan.* 34°30N 71°3E **122** B7
Konarak *India* 19°54N 86°7E **126** F8
Konawa *U.S.A.* 34°57N 96°45W **174** D6
Konch *India* 26°0N 79°10E **125** G8
Kondagaon *India* 19°35N 81°35E **126** F5
Konde *Tanzania* 4°57S 39°45E **142** C4
Kondias *Greece* 39°49N 25°10E **99** B7
Kondinin *Australia* 32°34S 118°8E **149** F2
Kondoa *Tanzania* 4°55S 35°50E **142** C4
Kondopoga *Russia* 62°12N 34°17E **84** A8
Kondoz *Afghan.* 36°50N 68°50E **109** E7
Kondoz → *Afghan.* 37°0N 68°50E **109** E7
Kondratyevo *Russia* 57°22N 98°15E **107** D10
Kondrovo *Russia* 54°48N 35°56E **84** E8
Konduga *Nigeria* 11°35N 13°26E **139** C7
Kondukur *India* 15°12N 79°57E **127** G4
Konduz → *Afghan.* 36°50N 68°50E **109** E7
Köneürgench
  Turkmenistan 42°19N 59°10E **108** D5
Konevo *Russia* 62°8N 39°20E **84** A10
Kong = Khong →
  Cambodia 13°32N 105°58E **120** F5
Kong *Ivory C.* 8°54N 4°36W **138** D4
Kong, Koh *Cambodia* 11°20N 103°0E **121** G4
Kong Christian IX.s Land
  Greenland 68°0N 36°0W **57** D7
Kong Christian X.s Land
  Greenland 74°0N 29°0W **57** C8
Kong Frederik IX.s Land
  Greenland 67°0N 52°0W **57** D6
Kong Frederik VI.s Kyst
  Greenland 63°0N 43°0W **57** D8
Kong Frederik VIII.s Land
  Greenland 78°30N 26°0W **57** B8
Kong Karls Land *Svalbard* 79°0N 28°0E **57** B13
Kong Oscar Fjord
  Greenland 72°20N 24°0W **57** C8
Kongeå → *Denmark* 55°23N 8°39E **63** J2
Kongju *S. Korea* 36°30N 127°0E **115** F14
Kongola *Namibia* 17°45S 23°20E **144** A3
Kongolo *Kasai-Or.,*
  Dem. Rep. of the Congo 5°26S 24°49E **142** D1
Kongolo *Katanga,*
  Dem. Rep. of the Congo 5°22S 27°0E **142** D2
Kongsberg *Norway* 59°39N 9°39E **61** G13
Kongsvinger *Norway* 60°12N 12°2E **61** F15
Kongur Shan *China* 38°34N 75°18E **109** E9
Kongwa *Tanzania* 6°11S 36°26E **142** D4
Koni
  Dem. Rep. of the Congo 10°40S 27°11E **143** E2
Koniakari *Mali* 14°35N 10°10W **138** C2
Koniecpol *Poland* 50°46N 19°40E **83** H6
Königs Wusterhausen
  Germany 52°19N 13°38E **76** C9
Königsbrunn *Germany* 48°16N 10°54E **76** G6
Königslutter *Germany* 52°14N 10°49E **76** C6
Konin *Poland* 52°12N 18°15E **83** F5
Konispol *Albania* 39°42N 20°10E **96** H4
Konitsa *Greece* 40°5N 20°48E **98** A2
Konjic *Bos.-H.* 43°42N 17°58E **96** C2
Konkiep *Namibia* 26°49S 17°15E **144** D2
Konkouré → *Guinea* 9°50N 13°42W **138** D2
Könnern *Germany* 51°40N 11°47E **76** D7
Konnur *India* 16°14N 74°49E **127** F2
Kono *S. Leone* 8°30N 11°5W **138** D2
Konongo *Ghana* 6°40N 1°31W **139** D4
Konosha *Russia* 61°0N 40°5E **84** A11
Kōnosu *Japan* 36°3N 139°31E **113** F9
Konotop *Ukraine* 51°12N 33°7E **85** G7
Konqi He → *China* 41°0N 86°0E **120** B4
Konsankoro *Guinea* 9°9N 9°0W **138** D3
Końskie *Poland* 51°15N 20°23E **83** G7

Konstancin-Jeziorna
  Poland 52°5N 21°7E **83** F8
Konstantinovka =
  Kostyantynivka
  Ukraine 48°32N 37°39E **85** H9
Konstantinovsk *Russia* 47°33N 41°10E **87** G5
Konstantynów Łódzki
  Poland 51°45N 19°20E **83** G6
Konstanz *Germany* 47°40N 9°10E **77** H5
Kont *Iran* 26°55N 61°50E **129** E9
Kontagora *Nigeria* 10°23N 5°27E **139** C6
Kontcha *Cameroon* 7°59N 12°15E **139** D7
Kontiolahti *Finland* 62°46N 29°50E **60** E23
Kontokali *Greece* 39°38N 19°51E **101** A3
Konya *Turkey* 37°52N 32°35E **104** D5
Konya □ *Turkey* 38°9N 33°5E **104** C5
Konz *Germany* 49°42N 6°34E **77** F2
Konza *Kenya* 1°45S 37°7E **142** C4
Koo-wee-rup *Australia* 38°13S 145°28E **163** F4
Koocanusa, L. *Canada* 49°20N 115°15W **168** D3
Kookynie *Australia* 29°17S 121°22E **149** E3
Koolyanobbing
  Australia 30°48S 119°36E **149** F2
Koondrook *Australia* 35°33S 144°8E **152** C6
Koonibba *Australia* 31°54S 133°25E **151** E1
Koorawatha *Australia* 34°2S 148°33E **153** C8
Koorda *Australia* 30°48S 117°35E **149** F2
Kooskia *U.S.A.* 46°9N 115°59W **168** C6
Kootenay → *U.S.A.* 49°19N 117°39W **162** D5
Kootenay △ *Canada* 51°0N 116°0W **162** C5
Kootenay L. *Canada* 49°45N 116°50W **168** B5
Kootingal *Australia* 31°3S 151°4E **153** E9
Kopaonik *S. Africa* 31°15S 20°21E **144** D3
Kopaonik → *Serbia* 43°10N 20°50E **96** C4
Kopaonik △ *Serbia* 43°20N 20°50E **96** C4
Kopargaon *India* 19°51N 74°28E **126** E2
Kópasker *Iceland* 66°14N 16°28W **60** C6
Kópavogur *Iceland* 64°6N 21°55W **60** D3
Kopeysk *Russia* 55°7N 61°37E **108** D7
Kopet Dagh *Asia* 38°0N 58°0E **129** B8
Kopeysk *Russia* 55°7N 61°37E **108** A6
Kopi *Australia* 33°24S 135°40E **151** E2
Köping *Sweden* 59°31N 16°3E **62** E10
Köpingsvik *Sweden* 56°53N 16°43E **63** H10
Kopiště *Croatia* 42°48N 16°42E **93** F13
Koplik *Albania* 42°15N 19°25E **96** D3
Köpmanholmen
  Sweden 63°10N 18°35E **62** A12
Koppa *India* 13°33N 75°21E **127** H2
Koppal *India* 15°23N 76°5E **127** G3
Kopparberg *Sweden* 59°52N 15°0E **62** E9
Koppeh Dāgh = Kopet Dagh
  Asia 38°0N 58°0E **129** B8
Koppies *S. Africa* 27°20S 27°30E **145** D4
Koppom *Sweden* 59°43N 12°10E **62** E6
Koprivlen *Bulgaria* 41°31N 23°53E **96** E7
Koprivnica *Croatia* 46°12N 16°45E **93** B13
Koprivshtitsa *Bulgaria* 42°40N 24°19E **97** D8
Köprübaşı *Turkey* 38°43N 28°23E **99** C10
Köprülü △ *Turkey* 37°20N 31°5E **128** E1
Kopychyntsi *Ukraine* 49°7N 25°58E **75** D13
Kora △ *Kenya* 0°14S 38°44E **142** C4
Korab *Macedonia* 41°44N 20°40E **96** E4
Koral *India* 21°50N 73°12E **124** J5
Korangal *India* 17°6N 77°38E **126** E3
Korarou, L. *Mali* 15°15N 3°15W **138** B4
Korba *India* 22°20N 82°45E **125** H10
Korbach *Germany* 51°16N 8°52E **76** D4
Korbu, Gunung
  Malaysia 4°41N 101°18E **121** K3
Korçë *Albania* 40°37N 20°50E **96** F4
Korčula *Croatia* 42°56N 16°57E **93** F13
Korčulanski Kanal
  Croatia 43°3N 16°40E **93** F13
Kord Kūy *Iran* 36°48N 54°7E **129** B7
Kord Sheykh *Iran* 28°31N 52°53E **129** D7
Kordestan = Kurdistan
  Asia 37°20N 43°30E **105** D10
Kordestān □ *Iran* 36°0N 47°0E **128** C5
Kordié *Burkina Faso* 12°36N 2°22W **138** C4
Kordofân *Sudan* 13°0N 29°0E **135** F11
Koré Mayroua *Niger* 13°18N 3°55E **139** C5
Korea, North ■ *Asia* 40°0N 127°0E **115** E14
Korea, South ■ *Asia* 36°0N 128°0E **115** G15
Korea Bay *Asia* 39°0N 124°0E **115** E13
Korea Strait *Asia* 34°0N 129°30E **115** H15
Koregaon *India* 17°40N 74°10E **126** F2
Korenovsk *Russia* 45°30N 39°22E **87** H4
Korets *Ukraine* 50°40N 27°5E **75** C14
Korfantów *Poland* 50°29N 17°36E **83** H4
Körfez *Turkey* 40°47N 29°43E **97** F13
Korff Ice Rise *Antarctica* 79°0S 69°30W **5** D17
Korgalzhyn = Qorghalzhyn
  Kazakhstan 50°25N 69°11E **109** B7
Korgan *Turkey* 40°44N 37°13E **104** B7
Korgus *Sudan* 19°16N 33°29E **137** D3
Korhogo *Ivory C.* 9°29N 5°28W **138** D3
Koribundu *S. Leone* 7°41N 11°46W **138** D2
Korila □ *China* 41°45N 86°4E **109** D11
Korinthiakos Kolpos
  Greece 38°16N 22°30E **98** C4
Korinthos *Greece* 37°56N 22°55E **98** D4
Korioumé *Mali* 16°35N 3°0W **138** B4
Korissia, L. *Greece* 39°27N 19°53E **101** B3
Kõriyama *Japan* 37°24N 140°23E **113** F10
Korkuteli *Turkey* 37°2N 30°11E **128** E1
Korla *China* 41°45N 86°4E **109** D11
Kormakiti, C. *Cyprus* 35°23N 32°56E **101** D11
Körmend *Hungary* 47°5N 16°35E **80** C1
Kormor *Iraq* 35°8N 44°50E **105** E11
Kornat △ *Croatia* 43°50N 15°20E **93** E12
Kornat △ *Croatia* 43°50N 15°12E **93** E12
Korneshty = Corneşti
  Moldova 47°21N 28°1E **81** C15
Korneuburg *Austria* 48°20N 16°4E **79** C9
Kórnik *Poland* 52°15N 17°6E **83** F4
Koro *Fiji* 17°19S 179°23E **154** a
Koro *Ivory C.* 8°32N 7°30W **138** D3
Koro *Mali* 14°1N 3°2W **138** C4
Koro Sea *Fiji* 17°30S 179°45W **154** a
Korocha *Russia* 50°55N 37°30E **85** F9
Köroğlu Dağları *Turkey* 40°38N 33°0E **104** B5
Korogwe *Tanzania* 5°5S 38°25E **142** D4

Koroit *Australia* 38°18S 142°24E **152** E5
Koroleve *Ukraine* 48°9N 23°8E **81** B8
Korolevu *Fiji* 18°12S 177°46E **154** a
Korona *Turkey* 29°25N 81°12W **179** F8
Koronadal *Phil.* 6°12N 124°51E **119** C6
Korong Vale *Australia* 36°22S 143°45E **152** D5
Koroni *Greece* 36°48N 21°57E **98** E3
Koronia, L. *Greece* 40°47N 23°10E **96** F7
Koronos *Greece* 37°12N 25°35E **99** D7
Koronowo *Poland* 53°19N 17°55E **83** E4
Koropets *Ukraine* 48°56N 25°10E **81** B10
Körös → *Hungary* 46°43N 20°12E **80** D5
Körösladány *Hungary* 47°8N 20°55E **80** C5
Köröstarcsa *Hungary* 46°54N 21°3E **80** D6
Korosten *Ukraine* 50°54N 28°36E **75** C15
Korostyshev *Ukraine* 50°19N 29°4E **75** C15
Korotoyak *Russia* 51°1N 39°2E **85** F10
Korovou *Fiji* 17°47S 178°32E **154** a
Koroyanitu △ *Fiji* 17°40S 177°35E **154** a
Korsakov *Russia* 46°36N 142°42E **107** E15
Korsberga *Sweden* 57°19N 15°7E **63** G9
Korshiv *Ukraine* 48°34N 24°58E **81** B9
Korsun Shevchenkovskiy
  Ukraine 49°26N 31°16E **85** H6
Korsze *Poland* 54°11N 21°9E **82** D8
Korti *Sudan* 18°6N 31°33E **137** D3
Kortrijk *Belgium* 50°50N 3°17E **69** D3
Korucu *Turkey* 39°28N 27°22E **99** C9
Korumburra *Australia* 38°26S 145°50E **153** E6
Korwai *India* 24°7N 78°5E **124** G6
Koryakskoye Nagorye
  Russia 61°0N 171°0E **107** C18
Koryukivka *Ukraine* 51°46N 32°16E **85** G7
Kos *Greece* 36°50N 27°15E **99** E9
Kosan *N. Korea* 38°52N 127°25E **115** E14
Kosaya Gora *Russia* 54°10N 37°30E **84** E9
Kościan *Poland* 52°5N 16°40E **83** F3
Kościerzyna *Poland* 54°8N 17°59E **82** D4
Kosciusko *U.S.A.* 33°4N 89°35W **177** E10
Kosciusko, Mt.
  Australia 36°27S 148°16E **153** D8
Kosciuszko △
  Australia 36°30S 148°20E **153** D8
Kősély → *Hungary* 47°25N 21°5E **80** C6
Kosgi *Andhra Pradesh,*
  India 16°58N 77°43E **126** F3
Kosgi *Andhra Pradesh,*
  India 15°51N 77°16E **127** G3
Kosha *Sudan* 20°50N 30°30E **137** C3
Koshava *Bulgaria* 44°4N 23°2E **96** C7
K'oshih = Kashi *China* 39°30N 76°2E **109** E9
Koshiki-Rettō *Japan* 31°45N 129°49E **113** J4
Koshim → *Kazakhstan* 49°20N 50°30E **86** E10
Kosi → *India* 28°41N 78°57E **125** E8
Košice *Slovak Rep.* 48°42N 21°15E **79** C16
Košický □ *Slovak Rep.* 48°45N 21°0E **79** C14
Kosiv *Ukraine* 48°19N 25°6E **81** B10
Kosjerić *Serbia* 44°0N 19°55E **96** B3
Köşk *Turkey* 37°50N 28°3E **99** D10
Koskinou *Greece* 36°23N 28°13E **101** C10
Koslan *Russia* 63°34N 49°14E **106** C5
Kosmach *Ukraine* 48°30N 24°50E **81** B9
Kosŏng *N. Korea* 38°40N 128°22E **115** E15
Kosovo ■ *Europe* 42°30N 21°0E **96** D4
Kosovo Polje = Fushë Kosovë
  Kosovo 42°32N 21°7E **96** D5
Kosovska Kamenica = Dardanë
  Kosovo 42°37N 21°15E **96** D5
Kosovska Mitrovica = Mitrovicë
  Kosovo 42°54N 20°52E **96** D4
Kossou, L. de *Ivory C.* 6°59N 5°31W **138** D3
Kosta *Sweden* 56°50N 15°24E **63** H9
Kostajnica *Croatia* 45°17N 16°30E **93** C13
Kostanjevica *Slovenia* 45°51N 15°27E **93** C12
Kostenets *Bulgaria* 42°15N 23°52E **96** D7
Koster *S. Africa* 25°52S 26°54E **144** C4
Kôstî *Sudan* 13°8N 32°43E **135** F12
Kostinbrod *Bulgaria* 42°49N 23°13E **96** D7
Kostolac *Serbia* 44°37N 21°15E **96** B5
Kostopil *Ukraine* 50°51N 26°22E **75** C14
Kostroma *Russia* 57°50N 40°58E **84** D11
Kostromo □ *Russia* 58°0N 44°0E **84** C11
Kostromskoye Vdkhr.
  Russia 57°52N 40°49E **84** D11
Kostrzhivka *Ukraine* 48°39N 25°43E **81** B9
Kostrzyn *Lubuskie, Poland* 52°35N 14°39E **83** F1
Kostrzyn *Wielkopolskie,*
  Poland 52°24N 17°14E **83** F4
Kostyantynivka *Ukraine* 48°32N 37°39E **85** H9
Kostyukovichi = Kastsyukovichy
  Belarus 53°10N 32°2E **84** E7
Koszalin *Poland* 54°11N 16°8E **82** D3
Kőszeg *Hungary* 47°23N 16°33E **80** C1
Kot Addu *Pakistan* 30°30N 71°0E **124** D4
Kot Kapura *India* 30°35N 74°50E **124** D6
Kot Moman *Pakistan* 32°13N 73°0E **124** C5
Kot Sultan *Pakistan* 30°46N 70°56E **124** D4
Kota *India* 25°14N 75°51E **124** G6
Kota Barrage *India* 25°6N 75°51E **124** G6
Kota Belud *Malaysia* 6°21N 116°26E **118** C5
Kota Bharu *Malaysia* 6°7N 102°14E **121** J4
Kota I. = Loaita I.
  S. China Sea 10°41N 114°25E **118** B4
Kota Kinabalu *Malaysia* 6°0N 116°4E **118** C5
Kota Tinggi *Malaysia* 1°44N 103°53E **121** M4
Kotaagung *Indonesia* 5°38S 104°29E **118** F2
Kotabaru *Indonesia* 3°20S 116°20E **118** E5
Kotabumi *Indonesia* 4°49S 104°54E **118** E2
Kotamobagu *Indonesia* 0°57N 124°31E **119** D6
Kotapad *India* 19°9N 82°21E **126** E6
Kotapinang *Indonesia* 1°53N 100°10E **121** M3
Kotcho L. *Canada* 59°7N 121°12W **162** B4
Kotdwara *India* 29°45N 78°32E **124** E8
Kotel *Bulgaria* 42°52N 26°26E **97** D10
Kotelnich *Russia* 58°22N 48°24E **86** B9
Kotelnikovo *Russia* 47°38N 43°8E **87** G5
Kotelnyy, Ostrov
  Russia 75°10N 139°0E **107** B14
Kothapet *India* 19°21N 79°28E **126** E4
Kothari → *India* 25°20N 75°19E **124** G6
Köthen *Germany* 51°45N 11°58E **76** D7
Kothi *Chhattisgarh, India* 23°21N 82°3E **125** H10
Kothi *Mad. P., India* 24°45N 80°40E **125** G9
Kotiro *Pakistan* 26°17N 67°13E **124** F2
Kotka *Finland* 60°28N 26°58E **84** B4
Kotlas *Russia* 61°17N 46°43E **106** C5
Kotlenska Planina
  Bulgaria 42°56N 26°30E **97** D10

Kotli *Pakistan* 33°30N 73°55E **124** C5
Kotlik *U.S.A.* 63°2N 163°33W **166** C7
Kotma *India* 23°12N 81°58E **125** H9
Koton-Karifi *Nigeria* 8°0N 6°48E **139** D6
Kotonkoro *Nigeria* 11°3N 5°58E **139** C6
Kotor *Montenegro* 42°25N 18°47E **96** D2
Kotor Varoš *Bos.-H.* 44°38N 17°22E **80** F2
Kotoriba *Croatia* 46°23N 16°48E **93** B13
Kotovo *Russia* 50°22N 44°45E **86** E7
Kotovsk *Russia* 52°36N 41°32E **86** D5
Kotovsk *Ukraine* 47°45N 29°35E **75** E15
Kotputli *India* 27°43N 76°12E **124** F7
Kotri *Pakistan* 25°22N 68°22E **124** G3
Kotri → *India* 19°15N 80°35E **126** E5
Kotronas *Greece* 36°38N 22°29E **98** E4
Kötschach-Mauthen
  Austria 46°41N 13°1E **78** E6
Kottagudem *India* 17°30N 80°40E **126** F5
Kottayam *India* 9°35N 76°33E **127** K3
Kottur = C.A.R. 4°14N 22°2E **140** D4
Kottur *India* 10°34N 76°56E **127** J3
Kotturu *India* 14°45N 76°10E **127** G3
Kotuy → *Russia* 71°54N 102°6E **107** B11
Kotuzhany *Ukraine* 48°47N 27°42E **81** B12
Kotzebue *U.S.A.* 66°53N 162°39W **166** B7
Kotzebue Sound
  U.S.A. 66°20N 163°0W **166** B7
Kouchibouguac △
  Canada 46°50N 65°0W **165** C6
Koudougou
  Burkina Faso 12°10N 2°20W **138** C4
Koufonisi *Iraklio, Greece* 34°56N 26°8E **101** E8
Koufonisi *Notio Aigaio,*
  Greece 36°57N 25°35E **99** E7
Kougaberge *S. Africa* 33°48S 23°50E **144** D3
Kouibli *Ivory C.* 7°15N 7°14W **138** D3
Kouilou → *Congo* 4°10S 12°5E **140** E2
Koukdjuak → *Canada* 66°43N 73°0W **161** D17
Koula *Greece* 41°23N 24°44E **97** E8
Koula Moutou *Gabon* 1°15S 12°25E **140** E2
Koulen = Kulen
  Cambodia 13°50N 104°40E **120** F5
Koulikoro *Mali* 12°40N 7°50W **138** C3
Koulikoro □ *Mali* 14°0N 7°45W **138** C3
Kouloura *Greece* 39°42N 19°54E **101** A3
Koumankou *Mali* 11°58N 6°6W **138** C3
Koumankou *Mali* 11°10N 3°50W **138** C4
Koumbia *Burkina Faso* 11°10N 3°50W **138** C4
Koumbia *Guinea* 11°48N 13°29E **138** C2
Koumboum *Guinea* 10°25N 13°0W **138** C2
Koumpenntoum
  Senegal 13°59N 14°34W **138** C2
Koumra *Chad* 8°50N 17°35E **135** G9
Koun-Fao *Ivory C.* 7°30N 3°15W **138** D4
Koundara *Guinea* 12°29N 13°18W **138** C2
Koungheul *Senegal* 14°0N 14°50W **138** C2
Kountze *U.S.A.* 30°22N 94°19W **176** F7
Koupéla *Burkina Faso* 12°11N 0°21W **139** C4
Kourémalé *Mali* 11°59N 8°42W **138** C3
Kouris → *Cyprus* 34°38N 32°54E **101** E11
Kourou *Fr. Guiana* 5°9N 52°39W **187** B8
Kourouba *Mali* 13°22N 10°57W **138** C2
Koûroudjel *Mauritania* 16°12N 11°30W **138** B2
Kouroukoto *Mali* 13°25N 10°55W **138** C2
Kourouninkoto *Mali* 13°52N 9°35W **138** C3
Kouroussa *Guinea* 10°45N 9°45W **138** C3
Koussanar *Senegal* 13°52N 14°5W **138** C2
Koussané *Mali* 14°53N 11°14W **138** C2
Koussané *Senegal* 14°10N 12°22W **138** C2
Kousséri *Cameroon* 12°0N 14°55E **135** F8
Koutiala *Mali* 12°25N 5°23W **138** C3
Kouto *Ivory C.* 9°53N 6°25W **138** D3
Kouvola *Finland* 60°52N 26°43E **84** B4
Kovačica *Serbia* 45°5N 20°38E **80** E5
Kovdor *Russia* 67°34N 30°24E **60** C24
Kovel *Ukraine* 51°11N 24°38E **75** C13
Kovilpatti *India* 9°10N 77°50E **127** K3
Kovin *Serbia* 44°44N 20°59E **80** F5
Kovrov *Russia* 56°25N 41°25E **86** B5
Kovur *Andhra Pradesh,*
  India 17°3N 81°39E **126** F5
Kovur *Andhra Pradesh,*
  India 14°30N 80°1E **127** G5
Kowal *Poland* 52°32N 19°7E **83** F6
Kowalewo Pomorskie
  Poland 53°10N 18°52E **83** E5
Kowanyama *Australia* 15°29S 141°44E **150** B3
Kowanyama ◇
  Australia 15°20S 141°47E **150** B3
Kowloon = Hong Kong *China* 22°19N 114°11E **117** F10
Kowŏn *N. Korea* 39°26N 127°14E **115** E14
Koyampattur = Coimbatore
  India 11°2N 76°59E **127** J3
Köyceğiz *Turkey* 36°57N 28°40E **99** E10
Köyceğiz Gölü *Turkey* 36°56N 28°42E **99** E10
Koyukuk → *U.S.A.* 64°55N 157°32W **166** C8
Koyulhisar *Turkey* 40°20N 37°52E **104** B7
Koyunyeri *Turkey* 40°50N 26°26E **97** F10
Koza = Okinawa
  Japan 26°19N 127°46E **113** L3
Kozak *Turkey* 39°15N 27°6E **99** B9
Kozaklı *Turkey* 39°13N 34°49E **104** C6
Kozan *Turkey* 37°26N 35°50E **104** D6
Kozáni *Greece* 40°19N 21°47E **96** F5
Kozara *Bos.-H.* 45°0N 17°0E **93** D13
Kozara △ *Bos.-H.* 45°0N 17°0E **80** F2
Kozarac *Bos.-H.* 44°58N 16°48E **93** D13
Kozelsk *Russia* 54°2N 35°48E **84** E8
Kozhikode *India* 11°15N 75°43E **127** J2
Kozhva *Russia* 65°10N 57°0E **86** A12
Kozienice *Poland* 51°35N 21°34E **83** G8
Kozje *Slovenia* 46°5N 15°35E **93** B12
Kozloduy *Bulgaria* 43°45N 23°42E **96** C7
Kozlovets *Bulgaria* 43°30N 25°20E **97** C9
Kozluk *Turkey* 38°11N 41°31E **105** D9
Kozlu *Turkey* 41°26N 31°45E **104** B4
Koźmin *Poland* 51°48N 17°27E **83** G4
Kozmodemyansk *Russia* 56°20N 46°36E **86** B8
Kōzu-Shima *Japan* 34°13N 139°10E **113** G9
Kożuchów *Poland* 51°45N 15°31E **83** G2
Kozyatyn *Ukraine* 49°45N 28°50E **75** D15
Kozyrevsk *Russia* 56°3N 159°51E **107** D16
Kpabia *Ghana* 9°10N 0°20W **139** D4
Kpalimé *Togo* 6°57N 0°44E **139** D5
Kpandae *Ghana* 8°30N 0°2W **139** D4
Kpessi *Togo* 8°4N 1°16E **139** D5

Kra, Isthmus of = Kra, Kho Khot
  Thailand 10°15N 99°30E 121 G2
Kra, Kho Khot Thailand 10°15N 99°30E 121 G2
Kra Buri Thailand 10°22N 98°46E 121 G2
Kraai ➤ S. Africa 30°40S 26°45E 144 D4
Krabi Thailand 8°4N 98°55E 121 H2
Kracheh = Kratie
  Cambodia 12°32N 106°10E 120 F6
Kragan Indonesia 6°43S 111°38E 119 G14
Kragerø Norway 58°52N 9°25E 61 G13
Kragujevac Serbia 44°2N 20°56E 96 B4
Krajenka Poland 53°18N 16°59E 83 E3
Krakatau = Rakata, Pulau
  Indonesia 6°10S 105°20E 119 G11
Krakatoa = Rakata, Pulau
  Indonesia 6°10S 105°20E 119 G11
Krakor Cambodia 12°32N 104°12E 120 F5
Kraków Poland 50°4N 19°57E 83 H6
Kraków ✈ (KRK) Poland 50°5N 19°52E 83 H6
Kraksaan Indonesia 7°43S 113°23E 119 G16
Kralanh Cambodia 13°35N 103°25E 120 F4
Králíky Czech Rep. 50°6N 16°45E 79 A9
Kraljevo Serbia 43°44N 20°41E 96 C4
Královéhradecký □
  Czech Rep. 50°25N 15°50E 78 A8
Královský Chlmec
  Slovak Rep. 48°27N 22°0E 79 C14
Kralupy nad Vltavou
  Czech Rep. 50°13N 14°20E 78 A7
Kramatorsk Ukraine 48°50N 37°30E 85 H9
Kramfors Sweden 62°55N 17°48E 62 B11
Kramis, C. Algeria 36°26N 0°45E 136 A4
Krania Greece 39°53N 21°18E 96 G5
Krania Elasonas Greece 39°57N 22°22E 98 B4
Kranidi Greece 37°23N 23°10E 98 D5
Kranj Slovenia 46°16N 14°22E 93 B11
Kranjska Gora Slovenia 46°29N 13°48E 93 B10
Krankskop S. Africa 28°0S 30°47E 145 C5
Krapina Croatia 46°10N 15°52E 93 B12
Krapina ➤ Croatia 45°50N 15°50E 93 C12
Krapkowice Poland 50°29N 17°56E 83 H4
Kras Croatia 45°35N 14°0E 93 C10
Krasieo Res. Thailand 14°49N 99°30E 120 E2
Kraskino Russia 42°44N 130°48E 112 C5
Krāslava Latvia 55°54N 27°10E 84 E4
Kraslice Czech Rep. 50°19N 12°31E 78 A5
Krasnaya Gorbatka
  Russia 55°52N 41°45E 86 C5
Krasnaya Polyana
  Russia 43°40N 40°13E 87 J5
Krasne Ukraine 46°7N 29°15E 81 D14
Krasni Okny Ukraine 47°32N 29°27E 81 C14
Krasnik Poland 50°55N 22°15E 83 H9
Krasnoarmeisk = Tayynsha
  Kazakhstan 53°50N 69°45E 109 B7
Krasnoarmeisk Russia 51°0N 45°42E 86 E7
Krasnoarmeyskiy Russia 47°0N 42°12E 87 G6
Krasnobrod Poland 50°33N 23°12E 83 H10
Krasnodar Russia 45°5N 39°0E 87 H4
Krasnodar □ Russia 46°30N 39°30E 87 G4
Krasnodarskoye Vdkhr.
  Russia 45°1N 39°23E 87 H4
Krasnodon Ukraine 48°17N 39°44E 85 H10
Krasnogorskiy Russia 56°10N 48°28E 86 B9
Krasnograd = Krasnohrad
  Ukraine 49°27N 35°27E 85 H8
Krasnogvardeysk
  Russia 45°32N 34°16E 85 K8
Krasnogvardeyskoye
  Russia 45°52N 41°33E 87 H5
Krasnohrad Ukraine 49°27N 35°27E 85 H8
Krasnokamensk
  Russia 50°3N 118°0E 107 D12
Krasnokutsk Russia 50°10N 34°50E 85 G8
Krasnolesnyy Russia 51°53N 39°35E 85 G10
Krasnorechenskiy
  Russia 44°41N 135°14E 112 B7
Krasnoselkup Russia 65°20N 82°10E 106 C9
Krasnoslobodsk Mordvinia,
  Russia 54°25N 43°45E 86 D6
Krasnoslobodsk Volgograd,
  Russia 48°42N 44°33E 87 F7
Krasnoturinsk Russia 59°46N 60°12E 106 D7
Krasnoufimsk Russia 56°36N 57°38E 106 D6
Krasnoyarsk Russia 56°8N 93°0E 107 D10
Krasnoyarskoye Russia 54°31N 21°56E 82 D8
Krasnoyarskoye Vdkhr.
  Russia 56°0N 92°30E 107 D10
Krasnoye = Krasnyy
  Russia 54°25N 31°30E 84 E6
Krasnoyilsk Ukraine 47°59N 25°38E 81 C10
Krasnozavodsk Russia 56°27N 38°25E 84 D10
Krasnoznamensk
  Russia 54°57N 22°30E 82 D9
Krasny Sulin Russia 47°52N 40°8E 87 G5
Krasnystaw Poland 50°57N 23°5E 83 H10
Krasnyy Russia 54°25N 31°30E 84 E6
Krasnyy Kholm Russia 58°10N 37°10E 84 C9
Krasnyy Kut Russia 50°50N 47°0E 86 E8
Krasnyy Liman Ukraine 48°58N 37°50E 85 H9
Krasnyy Luch Ukraine 48°13N 39°0E 85 H10
Krasnyy Profintern
  Russia 57°45N 40°27E 84 D11
Krasnyy Yar Astrakhan,
  Russia 46°43N 48°23E 87 G9
Krasnyy Yar Samara,
  Russia 53°30N 50°22E 86 D10
Krasnyy Yar Volgograd,
  Russia 50°42N 44°45E 86 E7
Krasnyye Baki Russia 57°8N 45°10E 86 B7
Krasnyyoskolske Vdskh.
  Ukraine 49°27N 37°40E 85 H9
Krasna ➤ Hungary 48°0N 22°20E 81 D13
Kratie Cambodia 12°32N 106°10E 120 F6
Kratovo Macedonia 42°6N 22°10E 96 E5
Krau Indonesia 3°19S 140°5E 119 E10
Kraulshavn = Nuussuaq
  Greenland 74°8N 57°3W 57 C5
Kravanh, Chuor Phnum
  Cambodia 12°0N 103°32E 121 G4
Krefeld Germany 51°20N 6°33E 76 D2
Kremastón, L. Greece 38°52N 21°30E 98 C3
Kremen Croatia 44°28N 15°53E 93 D12
Kremenchuk Ukraine 49°5N 33°25E 85 H7
Kremenchuksk Vdskh.
  Ukraine 49°20N 32°30E 85 H7
Kremenets Ukraine 50°8N 25°43E 75 C13
Kremennaya Ukraine 49°1N 38°10E 85 H10
Kremges = Svitlovodsk
  Ukraine 49°30N 33°13E 85 H7

Kremmen Germany 52°45N 13°1E 76 C9
Kremmling U.S.A. 40°4N 106°24W 168 F10
Kremnica Slovak Rep. 48°45N 18°50E 79 C11
Krems Austria 48°25N 15°36E 78 C8
Kremsmünster Austria 48°3N 14°8E 78 C7
Krestena Greece 37°35N 21°37E 98 D3
Kretinga Lithuania 55°53N 21°15E 82 C8
Krettamia Algeria 28°47N 3°27W 136 C3
Krettsy Russia 58°15N 32°30E 84 C7
Kreuzberg Germany 50°22N 9°58E 77 E5
Kreuztal Germany 50°57N 8°0E 76 E4
Kria Vrisi Greece 40°41N 22°18E 96 F6
Kribi Cameroon 2°57N 9°56E 139 E6
Krichem Bulgaria 42°8N 24°28E 97 D8
Krichev = Krychaw
  Belarus 53°40N 31°41E 75 B16
Kril'on, Mys Russia 45°53N 142°5E 112 B11
Krim Slovenia 45°53N 14°30E 93 C11
Krios, Akra Greece 35°13N 23°34E 101 D5
Krishna ➤ India 15°57N 80°59E 127 G5
Krishnagiri India 12°32N 78°16E 127 H4
Krishnanagar India 23°24N 88°33E 125 H13
Krishnaraja Sagar
  India 12°20N 76°30E 127 H3
Kristdala Sweden 57°24N 16°12E 63 G11
Kristiansand Norway 58°8N 8°1E 61 G13
Kristianstad Sweden 56°2N 14°9E 63 H8
Kristiansund Norway 63°7N 7°45E 60 E12
Kristiinankaupunki
  Finland 62°16N 21°21E 60 E19
Kristinehamn Sweden 59°18N 14°7E 62 E8
Kristinestad =
  Kristiinankaupunki
  Finland 62°16N 21°21E 60 E19
Kriti Greece 35°15N 25°0E 101 D7
Kritsa Greece 35°10N 25°41E 101 D7
Kriva ➤ Macedonia 42°5N 21°47E 96 E5
Kriva Palanka
  Macedonia 42°11N 22°19E 96 D6
Krivaja ➤ Bos.-H. 44°27N 18°9E 80 F3
Krivelj Serbia 44°10N 22°5E 96 B6
Křivoklátsko △
  Czech Rep. 50°1N 13°51E 78 A6
Krivoy Rog = Kryvyy Rih
  Ukraine 47°51N 33°20E 85 J7
Križevci Croatia 46°3N 16°32E 93 B13
Krk Croatia 45°8N 14°40E 93 C11
Krka ➤ Slovenia 45°50N 15°30E 93 C12
Krka △ Croatia 43°53N 15°56E 93 E12
Krkonoše Czech Rep. 50°50N 15°35E 78 A8
Krkonoše △ Czech Rep. 50°43N 15°39E 78 A8
Krnov Czech Rep. 50°5N 17°40E 79 A10
Krobia Poland 51°47N 16°59E 83 G3
Krokees Greece 36°53N 22°32E 98 E4
Krokek Sweden 58°40N 16°24E 63 F10
Krokodil = Umgwenya ➤
  Mozam. 25°14S 32°18E 145 C5
Krokom Sweden 63°20N 14°30E 62 A8
Krokowa Poland 54°47N 18°9E 82 D5
Kroľevets Ukraine 51°35N 33°20E 85 G7
Kroměříž Czech Rep. 49°18N 17°21E 79 B10
Krompachy Slovak Rep. 48°54N 20°52E 79 C13
Kromy Russia 52°48N 35°48E 85 F8
Kronach Germany 50°14N 11°19E 77 E7
Krong Kaoh Kong
  Cambodia 11°37N 102°59E 121 G4
Kronobergs län □
  Sweden 56°45N 14°30E 63 H8
Kronprins Christian Land
  Greenland 80°30N 22°0W 57 A8
Kronprins Frederik Land
  Greenland 81°0N 45°0W 57 A4
Kronprins Olav Kyst
  Antarctica 69°0S 42°0E 55 C5
Kronprinsesse Märtha Kyst
  Antarctica 73°30S 10°0W 55 D2
Kronshtadt Russia 59°57N 29°51E 84 B5
Kroonstad S. Africa 27°43S 27°19E 144 C4
Kröpelin Germany 54°4N 11°47E 76 A7
Kropotkin Russia 45°28N 40°28E 87 H5
Kropp Germany 54°24N 9°31E 76 A5
Krosna Lithuania 54°23N 23°33E 82 D10
Krośniewice Poland 52°15N 19°11E 83 F6
Krosno Poland 49°42N 21°46E 83 J8
Krosno Odrzańskie Poland 52°3N 15°7E 83 F2
Krotoszyn Poland 51°42N 17°23E 83 G4
Krotovka Russia 53°18N 51°10E 86 D10
Krousonas Greece 35°13N 24°59E 101 D6
Krrabë Albania 41°13N 20°0E 96 B2
Krško Slovenia 45°57N 15°30E 93 C12
Krštca Serbia 42°4N 20°0E 96 D1
Kruger △ S. Africa 24°50S 26°10E 145 B4
Krugersdorp S. Africa 26°5S 27°46E 145 C4
Kruisfontein S. Africa 33°59S 24°43E 144 D3
Krujë Albania 41°32N 19°46E 96 E3
Krulevshchina =
  Krulyewshchyna
  Belarus 55°5N 27°45E 84 E4
Krulyewshchyna Belarus 55°5N 27°45E 84 E4
Krumbach Germany 48°13N 10°22E 77 G6
Krumë Albania 42°14N 20°28E 96 D4
Krumovgrad Bulgaria 41°29N 25°38E 97 E9
Krung Thep = Bangkok
  Thailand 13°45N 100°35E 120 F3
Krupanj Serbia 44°25N 19°22E 96 B3
Krupina Slovak Rep. 48°22N 19°5E 79 C12
Krupinica ➤ Slovak Rep. 48°4N 18°55E 79 C11
Krupki Belarus 54°19N 29°8E 75 A15
Kruševac Serbia 43°35N 21°28E 96 C5
Kruševo Macedonia 41°23N 21°19E 96 E5
Krushe e Madhe Kosovo 42°19N 20°39E 96 D4
Krushelnyskya Ukraine 49°7N 23°29E 83 J10
Kruszwica Poland 52°40N 18°20E 83 F5
Kruszyniana, Proliv
  Russia 48°0N 154°0E 107 E16
Kruya Belarus 53°40N 31°41E 75 B16
Krymsk Russia 44°50N 38°0E 85 K10
Krymskiy Poluostrov =
  Krymskyy Pivostriv
  Ukraine 45°0N 34°0E 85 K8
Krymskyy Pivostriv
  Ukraine 45°0N 34°0E 85 K8
Krynica Poland 49°25N 20°57E 83 J7
Krynica Morska Poland 54°23N 19°28E 82 D6
Krynki Poland 53°17N 23°43E 83 E10
Krynychne Ukraine 45°32N 28°40E 81 E13
Kryvyy Rih Ukraine 47°51N 33°20E 85 J7
Kryzhopil Ukraine 48°23N 28°51E 81 C13
Krzepice Poland 50°58N 18°50E 83 H5
Krzeszów Poland 50°24N 22°21E 83 H9
Krzna ➤ Poland 52°4N 23°32E 83 F10

Krzywiń Poland 51°58N 16°50E 83 G3
Krzyż Wielkopolski
  Poland 52°52N 16°0E 83 F2
Krzyż Wielkopolski Poland 52°52N 16°0E 83 F2
Ksabi Morocco 32°51N 4°13W 136 B3
Ksar Chellala Algeria 35°13N 2°19E 136 A4
Ksar el Boukhari Algeria 35°51N 2°52E 136 A4
Ksar el Kebir Morocco 35°0N 6°0W 136 B2
Ksar es Souk = Er Rachidia
  Morocco 31°58N 4°20W 136 B3
Ksar Rhilane Tunisia 33°0N 9°39E 136 B5
Ksiąz Wielkopolski
  Poland 52°4N 17°14E 83 F4
Ksour, Mts. des Algeria 32°45N 0°30W 136 B3
Kstovo Russia 56°12N 44°13E 86 B7
Ku-Ring-Gai Chase △
  Australia 33°39S 151°14E 153 B9
Kuah Malaysia 6°19N 99°51E 121 J2
Kuala Belait Malaysia 4°35N 114°11E 118 D4
Kuala Berang Malaysia 5°5N 103°1E 121 K4
Kuala Dungun = Dungun
  Malaysia 4°45N 103°25E 121 K4
Kuala Kangsar
  Malaysia 4°46N 100°56E 121 K3
Kuala Kelawang
  Malaysia 2°56N 102°5E 121 L4
Kuala Kerai Malaysia 5°30N 102°12E 121 K4
Kuala Kubu Bharu
  Malaysia 3°34N 101°39E 121 L3
Kuala Lipis Malaysia 4°10N 102°3E 121 K4
Kuala Lumpur Malaysia 3°9N 101°41E 121 L3
Kuala Nerang Malaysia 6°16N 100°37E 121 J3
Kuala Pilah Malaysia 2°45N 102°15E 121 L4
Kuala Rompin
  Malaysia 2°49N 103°29E 121 L4
Kuala Selangor
  Malaysia 3°20N 101°15E 121 L3
Kuala Sepetang
  Malaysia 4°49N 100°28E 121 K3
Kuala Terengganu
  Malaysia 5°20N 103°8E 121 K4
Kualajelai Indonesia 2°58S 110°46E 118 E4
Kualakapuas Indonesia 2°55S 114°20E 118 E4
Kualakurun Indonesia 1°10S 113°50E 118 E4
Kualapembuang
  Indonesia 3°14S 112°38E 118 E4
Kualasimpang Indonesia 4°17N 98°3E 118 D1
Kuancheng China 40°37N 118°30E 115 D10
Kuandang Indonesia 0°56N 123°1E 119 D6
Kuandian China 40°45N 124°45E 115 D13
Kuangchou = Guangzhou
  China 23°6N 113°13E 117 F9
Kuanshan Taiwan 23°3N 121°9E 117 F13
Kuantan Malaysia 3°49N 103°20E 121 L4
Kuba = Quba Azerbaijan 41°21N 48°32E 87 K9
Kuban ➤ Russia 45°20N 37°30E 85 K9
Kuban Depression =
  Prikubanskaya Nizmennost
  Russia 45°38N 38°33E 87 H4
Kubaysah Iraq 33°35N 42°37E 105 G10
Kubenskoye, Ozero
  Russia 59°40N 39°25E 84 C10
Kubokawa = Shimanto
  Japan 33°12N 133°8E 113 H6
Kubrat Bulgaria 43°49N 26°31E 97 C10
Kubu Indonesia 8°16S 115°35E 119 J18
Kubutambahan
  Indonesia 8°5S 115°10E 119 J18
Kucar, Tanjung
  Indonesia 8°39S 114°34E 119 K18
Kučevo Serbia 44°30N 21°40E 96 B5
Kuchaman India 27°13N 74°47E 124 F6
Kuchchaveli Sri Lanka 8°49N 81°6E 127 K5
Kuchenspitze Austria 47°7N 10°12E 78 D3
Kuchinda India 21°44N 84°21E 125 J11
Kuching Malaysia 1°33N 110°25E 118 D4
Kuchino-eruba-Jima
  Japan 30°28N 130°12E 113 J5
Kuchino-Shima Japan 29°57N 129°55E 113 K4
Kuchinotsu Japan 32°36N 130°11E 113 H5
Kuchl Austria 47°37N 13°9E 78 D6
Kuchurhan ➤ Ukraine 46°33N 29°58E 81 E14
Kucing = Kuching
  Malaysia 1°33N 110°25E 118 D4
Kuçovë Albania 40°47N 19°57E 96 F3
Küçükbahçe Turkey 38°33N 26°24E 99 B9
Küçükköy Turkey 39°32N 26°40E 99 B8
Küçükkuyu Turkey 39°32N 26°36E 99 B8
Küçükmenderes ➤
  Turkey 37°57N 27°16E 99 D9
Kud ➤ Pakistan 26°5N 66°20E 124 F2
Kuda India 23°10N 71°15E 124 H4
Kudal India 16°2N 73°41E 127 F1
Kudalier ➤ India 18°35N 79°48E 126 E4
Kudat Malaysia 6°55N 116°55E 118 C5
Kudirkos Naumiestis
  Lithuania 54°46N 22°53E 82 D9
Kudowa-Zdrój Poland 50°27N 16°15E 83 H3
Kudremukh India 13°15N 75°20E 127 H2
Kudus Indonesia 6°48S 110°51E 119 G14
Kudymkar Russia 59°1N 54°39E 106 D6
Kueiyang = Guiyang
  China 26°32N 106°40E 116 D6
Kufra Oasis = Al Kufrah
  Libya 24°17N 23°15E 135 D10
Kufstein Austria 47°35N 12°11E 78 D5
Kugaaruk = Pelly Bay
  Canada 68°38N 89°50W 161 D14
Kugluktuk Canada 67°50N 115°5W 160 D8
Kugong I. Canada 56°18N 79°50W 164 A4
Kūh Dasht Iran 33°32N 47°36E 105 F12
Küh-e Sorkh Iran 35°30N 58°45E 108 C5
Kühak Iran 27°12N 63°10E 108 F3
Kuhan Iran 28°19N 67°14E 124 E2
Kühbonan Iran 31°23N 56°19E 129 D8
Kühestak Iran 26°47N 57°2E 129 E8
Kühīn Iran 36°22N 49°40E 129 B6
Kühīrī Iran 26°55N 61°2E 129 E9
Kühiston-Badakhshon □
  Tajikistan 38°30N 73°0E 109 E8
Kuhmo Finland 64°7N 29°31E 60 D23
Kuhn Chae △ Thailand 19°12N 99°12E 120 C2
Kuhnsdorf Austria 46°37N 14°38E 78 E7
Kühpāyeh Esfahan, Iran 32°44N 52°20E 129 C7
Kühpāyeh Kermān, Iran 30°35N 57°15E 129 D8
Kührān, Küh-e Iran 26°46N 58°12E 129 E8
Kui Buri Thailand 12°3N 99°52E 121 F2
Kuiburi △ Thailand 12°9N 99°37E 121 F2
Kuichong China 22°38N 114°25E 111 a
Kuichong Iran 22°36N 61°10E 106 D4
Kuiseb ➤ Namibia 22°59S 14°31E 144 B1
Kuito Angola 12°22S 16°55E 141 G3
Kuiu I. U.S.A. 57°45N 134°10W 162 B2

Kujalleq □ Greenland 61°0N 44°0W 57 E6
Kujang N. Korea 39°57N 126°1E 115 E14
Kujawsko-Pomorskie □
  Poland 53°20N 18°30E 82 E5
Kuji Japan 40°11N 141°46E 112 D10
Kujū-San Japan 33°5N 131°15E 113 H5
Kukava Ukraine 38°37N 27°43E 81 B12
Kukawa Nigeria 12°58N 13°27E 139 C7
Kukës Albania 42°5N 20°27E 96 D4
Kukmor Russia 56°11N 50°54E 86 B10
Kukup Malaysia 1°20N 103°27E 121 d
Kukup, Pulau Malaysia 1°18N 103°25E 121 d
Kukvidze Russia 50°40N 43°0E 86 E6
Kula Bulgaria 43°52N 22°36E 96 C6
Kula Serbia 45°37N 19°32E 80 E4
Kula Turkey 38°32N 28°40E 99 C10
K'ula Shan Bhutan 28°14N 90°36E 110 F7
Kulachi Pakistan 31°56N 70°27E 124 D4
Kulai Malaysia 1°44N 103°35E 121 M4
Kulaly Aral Kazakhstan 45°0N 50°5E 87 H10
Kulasekarappattinam
  India 8°20N 78°5E 127 K4
Kulautuva Lithuania 54°56N 23°59E 82 B8
Kuldīga □ Latvia 56°58N 21°59E 82 B8
Kuldīga △ Latvia 56°55N 22°0E 82 B8
Kulebaki Russia 55°22N 42°25E 86 C6
Kulen Cambodia 13°50N 104°40E 120 F5
Kulen Vakuf Bos.-H. 44°35N 16°2E 93 D13
Kulgam India 33°36N 75°2E 125 C6
Kulgera Australia 25°50S 133°18E 150 D1
Kulim Malaysia 5°22N 100°34E 121 K3
Kulin Australia 32°40S 118°2E 149 F2
Kulittalai India 10°55N 78°25E 127 J4
Kulkayu = Hartley Bay
  Canada 53°25N 129°15W 162 C3
Kullen Sweden 56°18N 12°26E 63 H6
Kullu India 31°58N 77°6E 124 D7
Kulmbach Germany 50°6N 11°26E 77 E7
Kulob Tajikistan 37°55N 69°50E 109 E7
Kulp Turkey 38°29N 41°2E 105 C9
Kulpawn ➤ Ghana 10°20N 1°5W 139 D4
Kulsary = Qulsary
  Kazakhstan 46°59N 54°1E 108 C4
Kulti India 23°43N 86°50E 125 H12
Kulu Turkey 39°5N 33°4E 104 C5
Kulunda Russia 52°35N 78°57E 108 B9
Kulundinskoye, Ozero
  Russia 53°0N 79°36E 109 B9
Kulungar Afghan. 34°0N 69°2E 124 C3
Kulvand Iran 31°21N 54°35E 129 D7
Kulwin Australia 35°2S 142°42E 152 C5
Kulyab = Kulob
  Tajikistan 37°55N 69°50E 109 E7
Kuma ➤ Russia 44°55N 47°0E 87 H8
Kumafşari Turkey 37°19N 29°32E 99 D11
Kumaganum Nigeria 13°8N 10°38E 139 C7
Kumagaya Japan 36°9N 139°22E 113 F9
Kumai Indonesia 2°44S 111°43E 118 E4
Kumalar Dağı Turkey 38°15N 30°20E 99 C12
Kumamba, Kepulauan
  Indonesia 1°36S 138°45E 119 E10
Kumamoto Japan 32°45N 130°45E 113 H5
Kumamoto □ Japan 32°55N 130°55E 113 H5
Kumanovo Macedonia 42°9N 21°42E 96 D5
Kumar ➤ Afghan. 34°30N 70°28E 109 F8
Kumara N.Z. 42°37S 171°12E 155 C6
Kumarina Roadhouse
  Australia 24°41S 119°32E 149 D2
Kumasi Ghana 6°41N 1°38W 138 D4
Kumba Cameroon 4°36N 9°24E 139 E6
Kumbağ Turkey 40°51N 27°27E 97 F11
Kumbakonam India 10°58N 79°25E 127 J4
Kumbarilla Australia 27°15S 150°55E 151 D5
Kumbhraj India 24°22N 77°3E 124 G7
Kumbia Australia 26°41S 151°39E 151 D5
Kumbo Cameroon 6°15N 10°36E 139 D7
Kumbukkan Oya ➤
  Sri Lanka 6°35N 81°40E 127 L5
Kūmch'on N. Korea 38°10N 126°29E 115 E14
Kume-Shima Japan 26°20N 126°47E 113 L3
Kumeny Russia 58°10N 49°47E 86 B9
Kumertau Russia 52°45N 55°57E 108 D9
Kumharsain India 31°19N 77°27E 124 D7
Kumi Uganda 1°30N 33°58E 142 B3
Kumkale Turkey 39°59N 26°11E 97 G10
Kumla Sweden 59°8N 15°10E 63 E7
Kumluca Turkey 36°22N 30°20E 99 E12
Kummerower See
  Germany 53°49N 12°51E 76 B8
Kumo Nigeria 10°1N 11°12E 139 C7
Kumo älv = Kokemäenjoki ➤
  Finland 61°32N 21°44E 84 B1
Kumon Bum Burma 26°30N 97°15E 123 F20
Kumta India 14°29N 74°25E 127 G2
Kumtag Shamo China 39°40N 92°0E 110 D7
Kumyal = Koma Tou Yialou
  Cyprus 35°25N 34°8E 101 D13
Kumylzhenskaya Russia 49°51N 42°38E 86 F6
Kuna U.S.A. 43°30N 116°25W 168 E5
Kunágota Hungary 46°26N 21°3E 80 D6
Kunashir, Ostrov
  Russia 44°0N 146°0E 107 E15
Kunchha Nepal 28°8N 84°20E 125 E11
Kunda Estonia 59°30N 26°34E 84 A5
Kunda India 25°43N 81°31E 125 G9
Kundar ➤ Pakistan 31°56N 69°19E 124 D3
Kundelungu △
  Dem. Rep. of the Congo 9°30S 27°50E 142 M5
Kundelungu Ouest △
  Dem. Rep. of the Congo 9°55S 27°7E 142 D2
Kundla India 21°21N 71°25E 124 J4
Kunene ➤ Namibia 20°0S 14°0E 144 A1
Kung, Ao Thailand 8°5N 98°24E 121 a
Kunga ➤ Bangla. 21°46N 89°30E 125 J13
Kungälv Sweden 57°53N 11°59E 63 G5
Kunghit I. Canada 52°6N 131°3W 162 C2
Kungrad = Qŭnghirot
  Uzbekistan 43°2N 58°50E 108 D5
Kungsängen Sweden 59°29N 17°45E 64 B10
Kungsbacka Sweden 57°30N 12°5E 63 G6
Kungsgården Sweden 60°37N 16°32E 64 E3
Kungshamn Sweden 58°22N 11°15E 63 F5
Kungsör Sweden 59°25N 16°5E 64 B9
Kungu
  Dem. Rep. of the Congo 2°47N 19°12E 140 D3
Kungur Russia 57°25N 56°57E 106 D6
Kunhar ➤ Pakistan 34°20N 73°30E 125 B5
Kunhegyes Hungary 47°22N 20°36E 80 C5

Kuningan Indonesia 6°59S 108°29E 119 G13
Kunlara Australia 34°54S 139°55E 152 C3
Kunlong Burma 23°20N 98°50E 116 F2
Kunlun Shan Asia 36°0N 86°30E 109 E11
Kunlun Shankou China 35°38N 94°4E 110 D7
Kunmadaras Hungary 47°23N 20°45E 80 C5
Kunming China 25°1N 102°41E 116 E4
Kunmunya ◌
  Australia 15°26S 124°42E 148 C3
Kunnamkulam India 10°38N 76°7E 127 J3
Kunów Poland 50°57N 21°17E 83 H8
Kunshan China 31°22N 120°58E 117 B13
Kunszentmiklós Hungary 46°50N 20°20E 80 C4
Kunszentmiklós Hungary 47°0N 19°28E 80 C4
Kuntaur Senegal 13°40N 14°48W 138 C2
Kununurra Australia 15°40S 128°50E 148 C4
Kunwari ➤ India 26°26N 79°11E 125 F8
Kunya-Urgench = Köneürgench
  Turkmenistan 42°19N 59°10E 108 D5
Künzelsau Germany 49°17N 9°42E 77 F5
Kuopio Finland 62°53N 27°35E 60 E22
Kupa ➤ Croatia 45°28N 16°24E 93 C13
Kupang Indonesia 10°19S 123°39E 119 F6
Kupino Russia 54°21N 77°16E 109 B9
Kupreanof I. U.S.A. 56°50N 133°30W 162 B2
Kupres Bos.-H. 43°59N 17°15E 80 G2
Kupyansk Ukraine 49°52N 37°35E 85 H9
Kupyansk-Uzlovoi
  Ukraine 49°40N 37°43E 85 H9
Kuqa China 41°35N 82°30E 109 D10
Kür = Azerbaijan 39°29N 49°15E 105 C13
Kür Dili Azerbaijan 39°3N 49°13E 105 C13
Kura = Kür ➤
  Azerbaijan 39°29N 49°15E 105 C13
Kuranda Australia 16°48S 145°35E 150 B4
Kuranga India 22°4N 69°10E 124 H3
Kurashiki Japan 34°40N 133°50E 113 G6
Kurayin Si. Arabia 27°39N 49°50E 129 E6
Kurayoshi Japan 35°26N 133°50E 113 G6
Kürchatov Kazakhstan 50°45N 78°32E 109 B9
Kürdämir Azerbaijan 40°25N 48°3E 87 K9
Kurdistan Asia 37°20N 43°30E 105 C10
Kurduvadi India 18°8N 75°29E 126 E2
Kürdzhali Bulgaria 41°38N 25°21E 97 E9
Kürdzhali □ Bulgaria 41°38N 25°21E 97 E9
Kure Japan 34°14N 132°31E 113 G6
Küre Turkey 41°48N 33°43E 104 B5
Küre Dağları Turkey 41°50N 34°10E 104 B6
Kure I. U.S.A. 28°25N 178°25W 167 K4
Kuressaare Estonia 58°15N 22°30E 84 C2
Kurgan Russia 55°26N 65°18E 108 D7
Kurgan-Tyube = Qŭrghonteppa
  Tajikistan 37°55N 69°50E 109 E7
Kurganinsk Russia 44°54N 40°34E 87 H5
Kurgannaya = Kurganinsk
  Russia 44°54N 40°34E 87 H5
Kuri India 26°37N 70°43E 124 F4
Kuria Maria Is. = Ḩallāniyat,
  Jazā'ir al Oman 17°30N 55°58E 132 D6
Kurichchi India 11°36N 77°35E 127 J3
Kuridala Australia 21°16S 140°29E 150 C3
Kurigram Bangla. 25°49N 89°39E 123 G16
Kurikka Finland 62°36N 22°24E 60 E20
Kuril Basin Pac. Oc. 47°0N 150°0E 54 E15
Kuril Is. = Kurilskiye Ostrova
  Russia 45°0N 150°0E 107 E16
Kuril-Kamchatka Trench
  Pac. Oc. 44°0N 153°0E 156 C7
Kurilsk Russia 45°14N 147°53E 107 E15
Kurilskiye Ostrova
  Russia 45°0N 150°0E 107 E16
Kurino Japan 31°57N 130°43E 113 J5
Kurinskaya Kosa = Kür Dili
  Azerbaijan 39°3N 49°13E 105 C13
Kurkheda India 20°37N 80°12E 126 D5
Kurkur Egypt 23°50N 32°0E 137 C12
Kurla India 19°4N 72°52E 126 E1
Kurlkuta ◌ Australia 24°2S 127°3E 148 D4
Kurnool India 15°45N 78°0E 127 G4
Kuro-Shima Kagoshima,
  Japan 30°50N 129°57E 113 J4
Kuro-Shima Okinawa,
  Japan 24°14N 124°1E 113 M2
Kuror, J. Sudan 20°31N 31°30E 137 C3
Kurow N.Z. 44°44S 170°29E 155 E3
Kurów Poland 51°23N 22°12E 83 G9
Kurrajong Australia 33°33S 150°42E 153 B5
Kurram ➤ Pakistan 32°36N 71°20E 124 C4
Kurri Kurri Australia 32°50S 151°28E 153 B5
Kurrimine Australia 17°47S 146°6E 150 B4
Kursavka Russia 44°29N 42°32E 87 H5
Kurse Korhi India 20°14N 80°46E 126 D5
Kurseong = Karsiyang
  India 26°56N 88°18E 125 F13
Kürshim Kazakhstan 48°34N 83°39E 109 D10
Kurshskiy Zaliv Russia 55°7N 20°45E 82 C7
Kurshum Russia 55°9N 21°6E 82 C8
Kuršių Nerijos △
  Lithuania 55°30N 21°5E 82 C8
Kursk Russia 51°42N 36°11E 85 G9
Kursk □ Russia 51°30N 36°0E 85 G9
Kuršumlija Serbia 43°9N 21°19E 96 C5
Kuršumlijska Banja
  Serbia 43°3N 21°11E 96 C5
Kurşunlu Bursa, Turkey 40°12N 27°20E 97 F11
Kurşunlu Çankiri,
  Turkey 40°51N 33°16E 104 B5
Kurtalan Turkey 37°58N 41°36E 105 D9
Kurtbey Turkey 41°4N 26°34E 97 F10
Kurucaşile Turkey 41°50N 32°44E 104 A5
Kuruçay Turkey 39°39N 38°29E 104 C7
Kurukshetra = Thanesar
  India 30°1N 76°52E 124 D7
Kuruktag China 41°0N 89°0E 109 D11
Kuruman S. Africa 27°28S 23°28E 144 D3
Kuruman ➤ S. Africa 26°56S 20°39E 144 C3
Kurume Japan 33°15N 130°30E 113 H5
Kurunegala Sri Lanka 7°30N 80°23E 127 L5
Kurya Russia 61°42N 57°9E 86 A10
Kus Gölü Turkey 40°10N 27°55E 99 B9
Kuşadası Turkey 37°52N 27°15E 99 D9
Kusamba Indonesia 8°34S 115°27E 119 K18
Kusatsu Japan 36°37N 138°36E 113 F9
Kusawa L. Canada 60°20N 136°13W 162 A1
Kuschevskaya Russia 46°33N 39°35E 87 G4
Kusheriki Nigeria 10°39N 6°30E 139 C6
Kushikino Japan 31°44N 130°16E 113 J5
Kushima Japan 31°29N 131°14E 113 J5
Kushimoto Japan 33°28N 135°47E 113 H7
Kushiro Japan 43°0N 144°25E 112 C12
Kushiro-Gawa ➤
  Japan 42°59N 144°23E 112 C12
Kushiro Shitsugen △
  Japan 43°9N 144°26E 112 C12
Kūshk Iran 28°46N 56°51E 129 D8
Kushka = Serhetabat
  Turkmenistan 35°20N 62°18E 129 C9
Kushmurun = Qusmuryn
  Kazakhstan 52°27N 64°36E 108 B6
Kushnytsya Ukraine 48°27N 23°15E 81 B8
Kushol India 33°40N 76°36E 125 C7
Kushtia Bangla. 23°55N 89°5E 125 H16
Kuskokwim ➤ U.S.A. 60°5N 162°25W 166 C7
Kuskokwim B.
  U.S.A. 59°45N 162°25W 166 D7
Kuskokwim Mts.
  U.S.A. 62°30N 156°0W 166 C8
Kusmi India 23°17N 83°55E 125 H10
Kusŏng N. Korea 39°59N 125°15E 115 E13
Kussharo-Ko Japan 43°38N 144°21E 112 C12
Kustanay = Qostanay
  Kazakhstan 53°10N 63°35E 108 B6
Kut, Ko Thailand 11°40N 102°35E 121 G4
Kuta Indonesia 8°43S 115°11E 119 K18
Kütahya Turkey 39°30N 30°2E 99 B12
Kütahya □ Turkey 39°10N 29°30E 99 B11
Kutaisi Georgia 42°19N 42°40E 87 J6
Kutaraja = Banda Aceh
  Indonesia 5°35N 95°20E 118 C1
Kutch, Gulf of = Kachchh, Gulf of
  India 22°50N 69°15E 124 H3
Kutch, Rann of = Kachchh, Rann
  of India 24°0N 70°0E 124 H4
Kutina Croatia 45°29N 16°48E 93 C13
Kutiyana India 21°36N 70°2E 124 J4
Kutjevo Croatia 45°23N 17°55E 80 E2
Kutkashen = Qäbälä
  Azerbaijan 40°58N 47°47E 87 K8
Kutná Hora Czech Rep. 49°57N 15°16E 78 B8
Kutno Poland 52°15N 19°23E 83 F6
Kutru India 19°5N 80°46E 126 D5
Kutse Botswana 21°7S 22°16E 144 B3
Kuttabul Australia 21°1S 148°54E 150 b
Kutu
  Dem. Rep. of the Congo 2°40S 18°11E 140 E3
Kutum Sudan 14°10N 24°40E 135 F10
Kúty Slovak Rep. 48°40N 17°3E 79 C10
Kuty Ukraine 48°16N 25°11E 81 B10
Kuujjuaq Canada 58°6N 68°15W 161 F18
Kuujjuarapik Canada 55°20N 77°35W 164 A4
Kuusamo Finland 65°57N 29°8E 60 D23
Kuusankoski Finland 60°55N 26°38E 84 B4
Kuvshinovo Russia 57°2N 34°11E 84 D8
Kuwait = Al Kuwayt
  Kuwait 29°30N 48°0E 128 D5
Kuwait ■ Asia 29°30N 47°30E 128 D5
Kuwana Japan 35°5N 136°43E 113 G8
Kuwana ➤ Japan 26°25N 83°15E 125 F10
Kuybyshev = Samara
  Russia 53°8N 50°6E 86 D10
Kuybyshev Russia 55°27N 78°19E 106 D8
Kuybyshevo Ukraine 47°25N 36°40E 85 J9
Kuybyshevskoye Vdkhr.
  Russia 55°2N 49°30E 86 C9
Kuye He ➤ China 38°23N 110°46E 114 E6
Kúyeh Iran 38°45N 47°57E 128 B5
Kuyto, Ozero Russia 65°6N 31°20E 60 D24
Kuytun China 44°25N 85°0E 109 D11
Kuyucak Turkey 37°55N 28°28E 99 D11
Kuyumba Russia 60°58N 96°59E 107 C11
Kuzey Anadolu Dağları
  Turkey 41°30N 35°0E 104 B7
Kuzhithurai India 8°18N 77°11E 127 K3
Kuzmin Serbia 45°2N 19°15E 80 E4
Kuznetsk Russia 53°12N 46°40E 86 D8
Kuzomen Russia 66°22N 36°50E 106 C4
Kvænangen Norway 70°5N 21°15E 60 A19
Kværndrup Denmark 55°10N 10°31E 63 J4
Kvaløya Norway 69°40N 18°30E 60 B18
Kvänum Sweden 58°18N 13°11E 63 F7
Kvareli = Qvareli
  Georgia 41°57N 45°47E 87 K7
Kvarner Croatia 44°50N 14°10E 93 D11
Kvarnerić Croatia 44°43N 14°37E 93 D11
Kvicksund Sweden 59°27N 16°19E 62 E10
Kvillsfors Sweden 57°24N 15°29E 63 G9
Kvismare kanal Sweden 59°11N 15°35E 62 E9
Kvissleby Sweden 62°18N 17°22E 62 B11
Kvitøya Svalbard 80°8N 32°35E 57 A14
Kwabhaca S. Africa 30°51S 29°0E 145 D4
Kwai = Khwae Noi ➤
  Thailand 14°1N 99°32E 120 E2
Kwajalein Marshall Is. 9°5N 167°20E 156 G8
Kwakhanai Botswana 21°39S 21°16E 144 B3
Kwakoegron Suriname 5°12N 55°25W 187 B7
Kwale Kenya 4°15S 39°31E 142 C4
Kwale Nigeria 5°46N 6°26E 139 D6
KwaMashu S. Africa 30°58S 30°58E 145 D5
Kwando ➤ Africa 18°27S 23°32E 144 A3
Kwangdaeri N. Korea 40°31N 127°32E 115 D14
Kwangju S. Korea 35°9N 126°54E 115 G14
Kwango ➤
  Dem. Rep. of the Congo 3°14S 17°22E 140 E3
Kwangsi-Chuang = Guangxi
  Zhuangzu Zizhiqu □
  China 24°0N 109°0E 117 E8
Kwangtung = Guangdong □
  China 23°0N 113°0E 117 F9
Kwara □ Nigeria 8°0N 5°0E 139 D6
Kwatisore Indonesia 3°18S 134°50E 119 E8
KwaZulu Natal □
  S. Africa 29°0S 30°0E 145 C5
Kweichow = Guizhou □
  China 26°0N 107°0E 116 D6
Kwekwe Zimbabwe 18°58S 29°48E 143 F2
Kwidzyn Poland 53°44N 18°55E 82 E5
Kwilu ➤
  Dem. Rep. of the Congo 3°22S 17°22E 140 E3
Kwinana Australia 32°15S 115°47E 149 F2
Kwisa ➤ Poland 51°34N 15°24E 83 G2

Kwoka *Indonesia* 0°31S 132°27E **119** E8
Kwolla *Nigeria* 9°0N 9°15E **139** D6
Kwun Tong *China* 22°19N 114°13E **111** a
Kyabra Cr. →
  Australia 25°36S 142°55E **151** D3
Kyabram *Australia* 36°19S 145°4E **153** D6
Kyaikto *Burma* 17°20N 97°3E **120** D1
Kyaing Tong = Keng Tung
  Burma 21°18N 99°39E **120** B2
Kyakhta *Russia* 50°30N 106°25E **107** D11
Kyamburu △ *Uganda* 0°7S 30°9E **142** C3
Kyancutta *Australia* 33°8S 135°33E **151** E2
Kyaukpadaung *Burma* 20°52N 95°8E **123** J19
Kyaukpyu *Burma* 19°28N 93°30E **123** K18
Kyaukse *Burma* 21°36N 96°10E **123** J20
Kybartai *Lithuania* 54°40N 22°45E **82** D9
Kyburz *U.S.A.* 38°47N 120°18W **170** G6
Kyelang *India* 32°35N 77°2E **124** C7
Kyenjojo *Uganda* 0°40N 30°37E **142** B3
Kyklades *Greece* 37°0N 24°30E **98** E6
Kyle *Canada* 50°50N 108°2W **163** C7
Kyle *U.S.A.* 29°59N 97°53W **176** F6
Kyle Dam *Zimbabwe* 20°15S 31°0E **143** G3
Kyle of Lochalsh *U.K.* 57°17N 5°44W **65** D3
Kyll → *Germany* 49°48N 6°41E **77** F2
Kyllburg *Germany* 50°2N 6°34E **77** E2
Kyllini *Greece* 37°56N 21°8E **98** D3
Kymijoki → *Finland* 60°30N 26°55E **84** B4
Kymmene älv = Kymijoki →
  Finland 60°30N 26°55E **84** B4
Kyneton *Australia* 37°10S 144°29E **152** D6
Kynuna *Australia* 21°37S 141°55E **150** C3
Kyō-ga-Saki *Japan* 35°45N 135°15E **113** G7
Kyoga, L. *Uganda* 1°35N 33°0E **142** B3
Kyogle *Australia* 28°40S 153°0E **151** D5
Kyŏngju = Gyeongju
  S. Korea 35°51N 129°14E **115** G15
Kyŏngsŏng N. Korea 41°35N 129°36E **115** D15
Kyonpyaw *Burma* 17°12N 95°10E **123** L19
Kyōto *Japan* 35°0N 135°45E **113** G7
Kyōto □ *Japan* 35°15N 135°45E **113** G7
Kyparissovouno
  Cyprus 35°19N 33°10E **101** D12
Kyperounda *Cyprus* 34°56N 32°58E **101** E11
Kypros = Cyprus ■ *Asia* 35°0N 33°0E **101** D12
Kyrenia *Cyprus* 35°20N 33°20E **101** D12
Kyrgyzstan ■ *Asia* 42°0N 75°0E **109** D9
Kyritz *Germany* 52°56N 12°24E **76** C8
Kyrkhult *Sweden* 56°22N 14°34E **63** H8
Kyrnasivka *Ukraine* 48°35N 28°58E **81** B13
Kyrnychky *Ukraine* 45°42N 29°4E **81** E14
Kyro älv = Kyrönjoki →
  Finland 63°14N 21°45E **60** E19
Kyrönjoki → *Finland* 63°14N 21°45E **60** E19
Kystatyam *Russia* 67°20N 123°10E **107** C13
Kysucké Nové Mesto
  Slovak Rep. 49°18N 18°47E **79** B11
Kytay, Ozero *Ukraine* 45°40N 29°13E **81** E14
Kythira *Greece* 36°8N 23°0E **98** E5
Kythnos *Greece* 37°26N 24°27E **98** D6
Kythréa *Cyprus* 35°15N 33°29E **101** D12
Kyunhla *Burma* 23°25N 95°15E **123** H19
Kyuquot Sound
  Canada 50°2N 127°22W **162** D3
Kyurdamir = Kürdämir
  Azerbaijan 40°25N 48°3E **87** K9
Kyūshū *Japan* 33°0N 131°0E **113** H5
Kyūshū □ *Japan* 33°0N 131°0E **113** H5
Kyūshū-Palau Ridge
  Pac. Oc. 20°0N 136°0E **156** E5
Kyūshū-Sanchi *Japan* 32°35N 131°17E **113** H5
Kyustendil *Bulgaria* 42°16N 22°41E **96** D6
Kyustendil □ *Bulgaria* 42°16N 22°41E **96** D6
Kyusyur *Russia* 70°19N 127°30E **107** B13
Kywong *Australia* 34°58S 146°44E **153** C7
Kyyiv *Ukraine* 50°30N 30°28E **75** C16
Kyyiv □ *Ukraine* 50°5N 30°45E **75** C16
Kyyivske Vdskh.
  Ukraine 51°0N 30°25E **75** C16
Kyzyl *Russia* 51°50N 94°30E **109** B12
Kyzyl-Adyr *Kyrgyzstan* 42°39N 71°35E **109** D8
Kyzyl Kum *Uzbekistan* 42°30N 65°0E **109** D7
Kyzyl-Kyya *Kyrgyzstan* 40°16N 72°8E **109** D8
Kyzyl Orda = Qyzylorda
  Kazakhstan 44°48N 65°28E **108** D7
Kyzyl-Suu *Kyrgyzstan* 42°20N 78°0E **109** D9

L

La Albuera *Spain* 38°45N 6°49W **89** G4
La Alcarria *Spain* 40°31N 2°45W **90** E2
La Almarcha *Spain* 39°41N 2°24W **90** F2
La Almunia de Doña Godina
  Spain 41°29N 1°23W **90** D3
La Amistad △
  Cent. Amer. 9°28N 83°18W **182** E3
La Asunción *Venezuela* 11°2N 63°51W **186** A6
La Baie *Canada* 48°19N 70°53W **165** C5
La Banda *Argentina* 27°45S 64°10W **190** B3
La Bañeza *Spain* 42°17N 5°54W **88** C5
La Barca *Mexico* 20°17N 102°34W **180** C4
La Barge *U.S.A.* 42°16N 110°12W **168** E8
La Barra *Nic.* 12°54N 83°33W **182** D3
La Bastide-Puylaurent
  France 44°35N 3°55E **72** D7
La Baule *France* 47°17N 2°24W **70** E4
La Belle *U.S.A.* 26°46N 81°26W **179** J8
La Biche → *Canada* 59°57N 123°50W **162** B4
La Biche, L. *Canada* 54°50N 112°3W **162** C6
La Bisbal d'Empordà *Spain* 41°58N 3°2E **90** D8
La Brea *Peru* 4°40S 81°7W **188** A1
La Brea *Trin. & Tob.* 10°15N 61°37W **187** K15
La Brède *France* 44°41N 0°32W **72** D3
La Bresse *France* 48°0N 6°53E **71** D13
La Bureba *Spain* 42°36N 3°24W **88** C1
La Calera *Chile* 32°50S 71°10W **190** C1
La Campana △ *Chile* 32°58S 71°14W **190** C1
La Campiña *Spain* 37°45N 4°45W **89** H6
La Canal = Sa Canal
  Spain 38°51N 1°23E **100** C7
La Cañiza = A Cañiza
  Spain 42°13N 8°16W **88** C2
La Canourgue *France* 44°26N 3°13E **72** D7
La Capelle *France* 49°59N 3°50E **71** C10
La Carlota *Argentina* 33°30S 63°20W **190** C3
La Carlota *Spain* 37°40N 4°56W **89** H6
La Carolina *Spain* 38°17N 3°38W **89** G7
La Cavalerie *France* 44°0N 3°10E **72** D7
La Ceiba *Honduras* 15°40N 86°50W **182** C2

La Chaise-Dieu *France* 45°18N 3°42E **72** C7
La Chapelle d'Angillon
  France 47°21N 2°25E **71** E9
La Chapelle-St-Luc
  France 48°20N 4°3E **71** D11
La Chapelle-sur-Erdre
  France 47°18N 1°34W **70** E5
La Charité-sur-Loire
  France 47°10N 3°1E **71** E10
La Chartre-sur-le-Loir
  France 47°44N 0°34E **70** E7
La Châtaigneraie *France* 46°39N 0°44W **72** B3
La Châtre *France* 46°35N 2°0E **71** F9
La Chaux-de-Fonds *Switz.* 47°7N 6°50E **77** H2
La Chorrera *Panama* 8°53N 79°47W **182** E4
La Ciotat *France* 43°10N 5°37E **73** E9
La Clayette *France* 46°17N 4°19E **71** F11
La Cocha *Argentina* 27°50S 65°40W **190** B2
La Concepción *Panama* 8°31N 82°37W **182** E3
La Concordia *Mexico* 16°5N 92°38W **181** D6
La Coruña = A Coruña
  Spain 43°20N 8°25W **88** B2
La Côte-St-André *France* 45°24N 5°15E **73** C9
La Courtine *France* 45°43N 2°16E **72** C6
La Crau *Bouches-du-Rhône,*
  France 43°32N 4°40E **73** E8
La Crau *Var, France* 43°9N 6°4E **73** E10
La Crescent *U.S.A.* 43°50N 91°18W **172** D8
La Crete *Canada* 58°11N 116°24W **162** B5
La Crosse *Fla., U.S.A.* 29°51N 82°24W **178** F7
La Crosse *Kans., U.S.A.* 38°32N 99°18W **172** F4
La Crosse *Wis., U.S.A.* 43°48N 91°15W **172** D8
La Cruz *Costa Rica* 11°4N 85°39W **182** D2
La Cruz *Mexico* 23°55N 106°54W **180** C3
La Désirade *Guadeloupe* 16°18N 61°3W **182** b
La Digue *Seychelles* 4°20S 55°51E **141** b
La Esperanza *Argentina* 40°26S 68°32W **192** B3
La Esperanza *Cuba* 22°46N 83°44W **182** B3
La Esperanza *Honduras* 14°15N 88°10W **182** D2
La Estrada = A Estrada
  Spain 42°43N 8°27W **88** C2
La Faouët *France* 48°2N 3°30W **70** D3
La Fayette *U.S.A.* 34°42N 85°17W **177** D12
La Fé *Cuba* 22°2N 84°15W **182** B3
La Fère *France* 49°39N 3°21E **71** C10
La Ferté-Bernard *France* 48°10N 0°40E **70** D7
La Ferté-Gaucher *France* 48°47N 3°19E **71** D10
La Ferté-Macé *France* 48°35N 0°22W **70** D6
La Ferté-St-Aubin *France* 47°42N 1°57E **71** E8
La Ferté-sous-Jouarre
  France 48°56N 3°8E **71** D10
La Ferté-Vidame *France* 48°37N 0°53E **70** D7
La Flèche *France* 47°42N 0°4W **70** E6
La Follette *U.S.A.* 36°23N 84°7W **177** C12
La Fregeneda *Spain* 40°58N 6°54W **88** E4
La Fuente de San Esteban
  Spain 40°49N 6°15W **88** E4
La Gacilly *France* 47°45N 2°8W **70** E4
La Gi *Vietnam* 10°40N 107°45E **121** G6
La Gineta *Spain* 39°8N 2°1W **91** F2
La Goulette *Tunisia* 36°53N 10°18E **94** F3
La Grand'Combe *France* 44°13N 4°2E **73** D8
La Grande → *U.S.A.* 45°59N 118°4W **168** D4
La Grande → *Canada* 53°50N 79°0W **164** B5
La Grande-Motte *France* 43°23N 4°5E **73** E8
La Grande 3, Rés.
  Canada 53°40N 75°10W **164** B4
La Grande 4, Rés.
  Canada 54°0N 73°15W **164** B5
La Grange *Calif.,*
  U.S.A. 37°42N 120°27W **170** H6
La Grange *Ga., U.S.A.* 33°2N 85°2W **178** B4
La Grange *Ky., U.S.A.* 38°24N 85°22W **173** F11
La Grange *Tex., U.S.A.* 29°54N 96°52W **176** G6
La Grave *France* 45°3N 6°18E **73** C10
La Guaira *Venezuela* 10°36N 66°56W **186** A5
La Guardia = A Guarda
  Spain 41°56N 8°52W **88** D2
La Gudiña = A Gudiña
  Spain 42°4N 7°8W **88** C3
La Guerche-de-Bretagne
  France 47°57N 1°16W **70** E5
La Guerche-sur-l'Aubois
  France 46°58N 2°56E **71** F9
La Habana *Cuba* 23°8N 82°22W **182** B3
La Haute Vallée de Chevreuse △
  France 48°35N 1°58E **71** D8
La Haye-du-Puits *France* 49°17N 1°33W **70** C5
La Horra *Spain* 41°44N 3°53W **88** D7
La Independencia
  Mexico 16°15N 92°1W **181** D6
La Isabela *Dom. Rep.* 19°58N 71°2W **183** C5
La Jonquera *Spain* 42°25N 2°53E **90** C7
La Joya *Peru* 16°43S 71°52W **188** D3
La Junta *U.S.A.* 37°59N 103°33W **168** H12
La Laguna *Canary Is.* 28°28N 16°18W **100** F3
La Libertad = Puerto Libertad
  Mexico 29°55N 112°43W **180** B2
La Libertad *Guatemala* 16°47N 90°7W **182** C1
La Libertad □ *Peru* 8°0S 78°30W **188** B2
La Ligua *Chile* 32°30S 71°16W **190** C1
La Línea de la Concepción
  Spain 36°15N 5°23W **89** J5
La Loche *Canada* 56°29N 109°26W **163** B7
La Londe-les-Maures
  France 43°8N 6°14E **73** E10
La Lora *Spain* 42°45N 4°0W **88** C7
La Loupe *France* 48°29N 1°0E **70** D7
La Louvière *Belgium* 50°27N 4°10E **69** D4
La Lune *Trin. & Tob.* 10°3N 61°22W **187** K15
La Machine *France* 46°54N 3°27E **71** F10
La Maddalena *Italy* 41°13N 9°24E **94** A2
La Malbaie *Canada* 47°40N 70°10W **165** C5
La Malinche △ *Mexico* 19°15N 98°3W **181** D5
La Mancha *Spain* 39°10N 2°54W **91** F2
La Mariña *Spain* 43°30N 7°40W **88** B3
La Martre, L. *Canada* 63°15N 117°55W **162** A5
La Merced *Peru* 11°24S 75°25W **188** A2
La Mercy = Durban ✈ (DIA)
  S. Africa 29°37S 31°7E **145** C5
La Mesa *Mexico* 32°30N 116°57W **171** N10
La Mesa *U.S.A.* 32°46N 117°1W **171** N9
La Mesilla *U.S.A.* 32°16N 106°48W **169** K10
La Mothe-Achard *France* 46°37N 1°40W **70** F5
La Motte-Chalançon
  France 44°30N 5°21E **73** D9
La Motte-du-Caire *France* 44°20N 6°3E **73** D10
La Motte-Servolex *France* 45°35N 5°53E **73** C9
La Moure *U.S.A.* 46°21N 98°18W **172** B4
La Muela *Spain* 41°36N 1°7W **90** D3
La Mure *France* 44°55N 5°48E **73** D9
Laa an der Thaya
  Austria 48°43N 16°23E **79** C9

La Negra *Chile* 23°46S 70°18W **190** A1
La Oliva *Canary Is.* 28°36N 13°57W **100** F6
La Oraya *Peru* 11°32S 75°54W **188** D2
La Orotava *Canary Is.* 28°22N 16°31W **100** F3
La Oroya *Peru* 11°32S 75°54W **188** D2
La Pacaudière *France* 46°11N 3°52E **71** F10
La Palma *Canary Is.* 28°40N 17°50W **100** F2
La Palma *Panama* 8°15N 78°0W **182** E4
La Palma del Condado
  Spain 37°21N 6°38W **89** H4
La Palmyre *France* 45°43N 1°9W **72** C2
La Paloma *Chile* 30°35S 71°0W **190** C1
La Pampa □ *Argentina* 36°50S 66°0W **190** D2
La Paragua *Venezuela* 6°50N 63°20W **186** B6
La Paz *Entre Rios,*
  Argentina 30°50S 59°45W **190** C4
La Paz *San Luis,*
  Argentina 33°30S 67°20W **190** C2
La Paz *Bolivia* 16°20S 68°10W **188** D2
La Paz *Honduras* 14°20N 87°47W **182** D2
La Paz *Mexico* 24°10N 110°18W **180** C2
La Paz □ *Bolivia* 15°30S 68°0W **188** D2
La Paz Centro *Nic.* 12°20N 86°41W **182** D2
La Pedrera *Colombia* 1°18S 69°43W **186** D5
La Pérade *Canada* 46°35N 72°12W **165** C5
La Perla *Mexico* 28°18N 104°32W **180** B4
La Perouse Str. *Asia* 45°40N 142°0E **112** B11
La Pesca *Mexico* 23°46N 97°47W **181** C5
La Piedad *Mexico* 20°21N 102°0W **180** C4
La Pine *U.S.A.* 43°40N 121°30W **168** E3
La Plata *Argentina* 35°0S 57°55W **190** C4
La Plata, L. *Argentina* 44°55S 71°50W **192** B2
La Pobla de Lillet *Spain* 42°16N 1°59E **90** C6
La Pobla de Segur *Spain* 42°15N 0°58E **90** C5
La Pocatière *France* 47°22N 70°2W **165** C5
La Pola de Gordón *Spain* 42°51N 5°41W **88** C5
La Porta *France* 42°29N 9°21E **73** F13
La Porte *U.S.A.* 29°40N 95°1W **176** G7
La Presanella *Italy* 46°13N 10°40E **92** B7
La Puebla = Sa Pobla
  Spain 39°46N 3°1E **90** F8
La Puebla de Cazalla
  Spain 37°10N 5°20W **89** H5
La Puebla de los Infantes
  Spain 37°47N 5°24W **89** H5
La Puebla de Montalbán
  Spain 39°52N 4°22W **88** F6
La Puebla del Río *Spain* 37°16N 6°3W **89** H4
La Puerta de Segura
  Spain 38°22N 2°45W **89** G8
La Purísima *Mexico* 26°10N 112°4W **180** B2
La Push *U.S.A.* 47°55N 124°38W **170** C2
La Quiaca *Argentina* 22°5S 65°35W **190** A2
La Réole *France* 44°35N 0°1W **72** D3
La Restinga *Canary Is.* 27°38N 17°59W **100** G2
La Rinconada *Peru* 14°38S 69°27W **188** C4
La Rioja *Argentina* 29°20S 67°0W **190** B2
La Rioja □ *Argentina* 29°30S 67°0W **190** B3
La Rioja □ *Spain* 42°20N 2°20W **88** C7
La Robla *Spain* 42°50N 5°41W **88** C5
La Roche-Bernard
  France 47°31N 2°19W **70** E4
La Roche-Canillac *France* 45°12N 1°57E **72** C5
La Roche-en-Ardenne
  Belgium 50°11N 5°35E **69** D5
La Roche-sur-Foron
  France 46°4N 6°19E **71** F13
La Roche-sur-Yon
  France 46°40N 1°25W **70** F5
La Rochefoucauld *France* 45°44N 0°24E **72** C4
La Rochelle *France* 46°10N 1°9W **72** B2
La Roda *Spain* 39°13N 2°15W **91** F2
La Roda de Andalucía
  Spain 37°12N 4°46W **89** H6
La Romaine *Canada* 50°13N 60°40W **165** B7
La Romana *Dom. Rep.* 18°27N 68°57W **183** C6
La Ronge *Canada* 55°5N 105°20W **163** B7
La Rumorosa *Mexico* 32°34N 116°6W **171** N10
La Sabina = Sa Savina
  Spain 38°44N 1°25E **100** C7
La Sagra *Spain* 37°57N 2°35W **91** H2
La Salle *U.S.A.* 41°20N 89°6W **172** E9
La Sanabria *Spain* 42°0N 6°30W **88** C4
La Santa *Canary Is.* 29°5N 13°40W **100** E6
La Sarre *Canada* 48°45N 79°15W **164** C4
La Scie *Canada* 49°57N 55°36W **165** C8
La Selva *Spain* 42°0N 2°45E **90** C7
La Selva Beach *U.S.A.* 36°56N 121°51W **170** J5
La Selva del Camp *Spain* 41°13N 1°8E **90** D6
La Serena *Chile* 29°55S 71°10W **190** B1
La Serena *Spain* 38°45N 5°40W **89** G5
La Seu d'Urgell *Spain* 42°22N 1°23E **90** C6
La Seyne-sur-Mer *France* 43°7N 5°52E **73** E9
La Sila *Italy* 39°15N 16°35E **95** C9
La Solana *Spain* 38°59N 3°14W **91** G2
La Souterraine *France* 46°15N 1°30E **71** F8
La Spézia *Italy* 44°7N 9°50E **92** D6
La Suze-sur-Sarthe *France* 47°53N 0°2E **70** E7
La Tagua *Colombia* 0°3N 74°40W **186** C4
La Teste-de-Buch *France* 44°37N 1°8W **72** D2
La Tortuga, I. *Venezuela* 11°0N 65°22W **183** D6
La Tour-du-Pin *France* 45°33N 5°27E **73** C9
La Tranche-sur-Mer
  France 46°20N 1°27W **70** F5
La Tremblade *France* 45°46N 1°8W **72** C2
La Trinité *Martinique* 14°45N 60°58W **182** c
La Tuque *Canada* 47°30N 72°50W **164** C5
La Unión *Chile* 40°10S 73°0W **192** B2
La Unión *El Salv.* 13°20N 87°50W **182** D2
La Unión *Mexico* 17°58N 101°49W **180** D4
La Unión *Peru* 9°43S 76°45W **188** B2
La Unión *Spain* 37°38N 0°53W **91** H4
La Urbana *Venezuela* 7°8N 66°56W **186** B5
La Vache Pt.
  Trin. & Tob. 10°47N 61°28W **187** K15
La Vall d'Uixó *Spain* 39°49N 0°15W **90** F4
La Vecilla *Spain* 42°51N 5°27W **88** C5
La Vega *Dom. Rep.* 19°20N 70°30W **183** C5
La Vega *Peru* 10°41S 77°44W **188** C2
La Veiga de Coro
  Venezuela 11°27N 69°34W **186** A5
La Veleta *Spain* 37°3N 3°22W **89** H7
La Venta *Mexico* 18°5N 94°3W **181** D6
La Vergne *U.S.A.* 36°1N 86°35W **177** C11
La Villa Joiosa = Villajoyosa
  Spain 38°30N 0°12W **91** G4
La Voulte-sur-Rhône
  France 44°48N 4°46E **73** D8
Laa an der Thaya
  Austria 48°43N 16°23E **79** C9

Laaber, Grosse →
  Germany 48°55N 12°30E **77** G8
Laage *Germany* 53°55N 12°21E **76** B8
Laascaanood = Las Anod
  Somalia 8°26N 47°19E **131** F4
Laatzen *Germany* 52°19N 9°48E **76** C5
Laba → *Russia* 45°11N 39°42E **87** H4
Labasa *Fiji* 16°30S 179°27E **154** a
Labastide-Murat *France* 44°39N 1°33E **72** D5
Labastide-Rouairoux
  France 43°28N 2°39E **72** E6
Labdah = Leptis Magna
  Libya 32°40N 14°12E **135** B8
Labé *Guinea* 11°24N 12°16E **138** C2
Labé = Elbe → *Europe* 53°50N 9°0E **76** B4
Laberge, L. *Canada* 61°11N 135°12W **162** A1
Labin *Croatia* 45°5N 14°8E **93** C11
Labinsk *Russia* 44°40N 40°48E **87** H5
Labis *Malaysia* 2°22N 103°2E **121** L4
Łabiszyn *Poland* 52°57N 17°54E **83** F4
Laboe *Germany* 54°24N 10°13E **76** A6
Laborec → *Slovak Rep.* 48°37N 21°58E **79** C6
Laborie *St. Lucia* 13°45N 61°2W **183** f
Labouheyre *France* 44°13N 0°55W **72** D3
Laboulaye *Argentina* 34°10S 63°30W **190** C3
Labrador *Canada* 53°20N 61°0W **165** B7
Labrador City *Canada* 52°57N 66°55W **165** B6
Labrador Sea *Atl. Oc.* 57°0N 54°0W **161** F21
Lábrea *Brazil* 7°15S 64°51W **186** E6
Labruguière *France* 43°31N 2°16E **72** E6
Labuan □ *Malaysia* 5°20N 115°12E **118** C4
Labuha *Indonesia* 0°30S 127°30E **119** E7
Labuhan *Indonesia* 6°22S 105°50E **119** G11
Labuhanbajo *Indonesia* 8°28S 119°54E **119** F6
Labuhanbilik *Indonesia* 2°31N 100°10E **121** L3
Labuk, Telok *Malaysia* 6°10N 117°50E **118** C5
Labyrinth, L. *Australia* 30°40S 135°11E **151** E2
Labytnangi *Russia* 66°39N 66°21E **106** C7
Laç *Albania* 41°38N 19°43E **96** E3
Lac-Bouchette *Canada* 48°16N 72°11W **165** C5
Lac-Édouard *Canada* 47°40N 72°16W **165** C5
Lac La Biche *Canada* 54°45N 111°58W **162** C6
Lac la Martre = Wha Ti
  Canada 63°8N 117°16W **160** C8
Lac La Ronge △
  Canada 55°9N 104°41W **163** B7
Lac-Mégantic *Canada* 45°35N 70°53W **165** C5
Lac Thien *Vietnam* 12°25N 108°11E **120** F7
Lacanau *France* 44°58N 1°5W **72** D2
Lacanau, L. de *France* 44°58N 1°7W **72** D2
Lacantún → *Mexico* 16°36N 90°39W **181** D6
Lácara → *Spain* 38°55N 6°25W **89** G4
Lacaune *France* 43°43N 2°40E **72** E6
Lacaune, Mts. de *France* 43°43N 2°50E **72** E6
Laccadive Is. = Lakshadweep Is.
  India 10°0N 72°30E **127** J1
Lacepede B. *Australia* 36°40S 139°40E **152** D3
Lacepede Is. *Australia* 16°55S 122°0E **148** C3
Lacerdónia *Mozam.* 18°3S 35°35E **143** F4
Lacey *U.S.A.* 47°7N 122°49W **170** C4
Lachania *Greece* 35°58N 27°54E **101** D9
Lachay, Pta. *Peru* 11°17S 77°44W **188** C2
Lachhmangarh *India* 27°50N 75°4E **124** F6
Lachi *Pakistan* 33°25N 71°20E **124** C4
Lachine *Canada* 45°26N 73°42W **164** C5
Lachlan → *Australia* 34°22S 143°55E **152** C5
Lachoc *Peru* 12°50S 75°6W **188** C2
Lachute *Canada* 45°39N 74°21W **164** C5
Laçın *Azerbaijan* 39°38N 46°33E **105** C12
Lackagh Hills *Ireland* 54°16N 8°10W **64** B3
Lackawanna *U.S.A.* 42°50N 78°50W **174** D6
Lackawaxen *U.S.A.* 41°29N 74°59W **175** E10
Lacolle *Canada* 45°5N 73°22W **175** A11
Lacombe *Canada* 52°30N 113°44W **162** C6
Láconi *Italy* 39°54N 9°4E **94** C2
Laconia = Lakonia □
  Greece 36°55N 22°30E **98** E4
Laconia *U.S.A.* 43°32N 71°28W **175** C13
Lacoochee *U.S.A.* 28°28N 82°11W **179** G7
Lacq *France* 43°25N 0°35W **72** E3
Lacs □ *Ivory C.* 6°50N 5°0W **138** D4
Ladakh Ra. *India* 34°0N 78°0E **125** C8
Ladismith *S. Africa* 33°28S 21°15E **144** D3
Ladispoli *Italy* 41°56N 12°5E **93** G9
Lādīz *Iran* 28°55N 61°15E **129** D9
Ladoga, L. = Ladozhskoye Ozero
  Russia 61°15N 30°30E **84** B6
Ladonas → *Greece* 37°40N 21°50E **98** D3
Ladozhskoye Ozero
  Russia 61°15N 30°30E **84** B6
Ladrillero, G. *Chile* 48°20S 75°35W **192** C1
Ladson *U.S.A.* 32°59N 80°6W **179** E14
Ladushkin *Russia* 54°34N 20°10E **82** D7
Lady Elliott I. *Australia* 24°7S 152°42E **150** C5
Lady Frere *S. Africa* 31°42S 27°14E **144** D4
Lady Grey *S. Africa* 30°43S 27°13E **144** D4
Lady Lake *U.S.A.* 28°55N 81°55W **179** G6
Ladybrand *S. Africa* 29°9S 27°29E **144** D4
Ladysmith *Canada* 49°0N 123°49W **170** B3
Ladysmith *S. Africa* 28°32S 29°46E **145** C4
Ladysmith *U.S.A.* 45°28N 91°12W **172** C8
Ladyzhyn *Ukraine* 48°40N 29°15E **81** B14
Lae *Papua N. G.* 6°40S 147°2E **147** B7
Laem Ngop *Thailand* 12°10N 102°26E **121** F4
Laem Son △ *Thailand* 9°29N 98°24E **121** H2
Laerma *Greece* 36°9N 27°57E **101** D9
Læsø *Denmark* 57°15N 11°5E **63** G5
Læsø Rende *Denmark* 57°20N 10°45E **63** G4
Lafayette *Ala., U.S.A.* 32°54N 85°24W **178** B4
Lafayette *Ind., U.S.A.* 40°25N 86°54W **172** E10
Lafayette *La., U.S.A.* 30°14N 92°1W **176** F9
Lafayette *Tenn., U.S.A.* 36°31N 86°2W **177** C11
Laferte → *Canada* 61°53N 117°44W **162** A5
Lafia *Nigeria* 8°30N 8°34E **139** D6
Lafiagi *Nigeria* 8°52N 5°20E **139** D6
Lafleche *Canada* 49°45N 106°40W **163** D7
Laful *India* 7°10N 93°52E **127** L11
Lagan → *Sweden* 56°56N 13°58E **63** H6
Lagan → *U.K.* 54°36N 5°55W **64** B6
Lagarfljót → *Iceland* 65°40N 14°18W **60** D6
Lagarto *Brazil* 10°54S 37°41W **189** D3
Lagdo, L. de *Cameroon* 8°40N 14°0E **135** G8
Lage *Germany* 51°59N 8°48E **76** D4

Lågen → *Oppland,*
  Norway 61°8N 10°25E **60** F14
Lågen → *Vestfold, Norway* 59°3N 10°3E **61** G14
Lägerdorf *Germany* 53°53N 9°34E **76** B5
Lages *Brazil* 27°48S 50°20W **191** B5
Laghouat *Algeria* 33°50N 2°59E **136** B4
Laghouat □ *Algeria* 33°55N 2°40E **136** B4
Lagnieu *France* 45°55N 5°20E **73** C9
Lagny-sur-Marne *France* 48°52N 2°44E **71** D9
Lago *Italy* 39°10N 16°9E **95** C9
Lago de Sanabria y Entorno △
  Spain 42°9N 6°45W **88** C4
Lago Posadas
  Argentina 47°30S 71°40W **192** C2
Lago Puela △
  Argentina 42°30S 71°55W **192** B2
Lago Ranco *Chile* 40°19S 72°30W **192** B2
Lagôa *Portugal* 37°8N 8°27W **89** H2
Lagoa do Peixe △
  Brazil 31°12S 50°55W **191** C5
Lagoa Vermelha *Brazil* 28°13S 51°32W **191** B5
Lagoaça *Portugal* 41°11N 6°44W **88** D4
Lagodekhi *Georgia* 41°50N 46°22E **87** K8
Lagónegro *Italy* 40°8N 15°45E **95** B8
Lagonoy G. *Phil.* 13°35N 123°50E **119** B6
Lagos *Greece* 41°1N 25°6E **97** E9
Lagos *Nigeria* 6°25N 3°27E **139** D5
Lagos *Portugal* 37°5N 8°41W **89** H2
Lagos □ *Nigeria* 6°28N 3°25E **139** D5
Lagos de Moreno
  Mexico 21°21N 101°55W **180** C4
Lagrange = Bidyadanga
  Australia 18°45S 121°43E **148** C3
Lagrange B. *Australia* 18°38S 121°42E **148** C3
Laguardia *Spain* 42°33N 2°35W **90** C2
Laguépie *France* 44°8N 1°57E **72** D5
Laguna *Brazil* 28°30S 48°50W **191** B6
Laguna *U.S.A.* 35°2N 107°25W **169** J10
Laguna, Sa. de la
  Mexico 23°35N 109°55W **180** C3
Laguna Beach *U.S.A.* 33°33N 117°47W **171** M9
Laguna Blanca △
  Argentina 39°0S 70°5W **192** A2
Laguna de Duero *Spain* 41°35N 4°43W **88** D6
Laguna de la Restinga △
  Venezuela 10°58N 64°0W **183** D6
Laguna de Lachuá △
  Guatemala 15°55N 90°40W **182** C1
Laguna del Laja △
  Chile 37°27S 71°20W **190** D1
Laguna del Tigre △
  Guatemala 17°32N 90°56W **182** C1
Laguna Limpia
  Argentina 26°32S 59°45W **190** B4
Laguna San Rafael △
  Chile 46°54S 73°31W **192** C2
Lagunas *Chile* 21°0S 69°45W **190** A2
Lagunas *Peru* 5°10S 75°35W **188** B2
Lagunas de Chacahua △
  Mexico 16°0N 97°43W **181** D5
Lagunas de Montebello △
  Mexico 16°4N 91°42W **181** D6
Lagunas de Ruidera △
  Spain 38°57N 2°52W **91** G2
Lahad Datu *Malaysia* 5°0N 118°20E **119** D5
Lahad Datu, Telok
  Malaysia 4°50N 118°20E **119** D5
Lahan Sai *Thailand* 14°25N 102°52E **120** E4
Lahanam *Laos* 16°16N 105°16E **120** D5
Lahar *India* 26°12N 78°57E **125** F8
Laharpur *India* 27°43N 80°56E **125** F9
Lahat *Indonesia* 3°45S 103°30E **118** E2
Lahewa *Indonesia* 1°22N 97°12E **118** D1
Lāhījān *Iran* 37°10N 50°6E **129** B6
Lahn → *Germany* 50°19N 7°37E **77** E3
Lahnstein *Germany* 50°19N 7°37E **77** E3
Laholm *Sweden* 56°30N 13°2E **63** H7
Laholmsbukten *Sweden* 56°30N 12°45E **63** H6
Lahore *Pakistan* 31°32N 74°22E **124** D6
Lahri *Pakistan* 29°11N 68°13E **124** E3
Lahr *Germany* 48°20N 7°52E **77** G3
Lährūd *Iran* 38°30N 47°52E **105** C12
Lahti *Finland* 60°58N 25°40E **84** B3
Lahtis = Lahti *Finland* 60°58N 25°40E **84** B3
Lahugala Kitulana △
  Sri Lanka 6°50N 81°40E **127** L5
Laï *Chad* 9°25N 16°18E **135** G9
Lai Chau *Vietnam* 22°5N 103°3E **116** F4
Lai'an *China* 32°28N 118°30E **117** A12
Laibin *China* 23°42N 109°14E **116** F7
Laifeng *China* 29°27N 109°20E **116** C7
L'Aigle *France* 48°46N 0°38E **70** D7
Laignes *France* 47°50N 4°20E **71** E11
L'Aiguillon-sur-Mer
  France 46°20N 1°18W **72** B2
Laila = Layla *Si. Arabia* 22°10N 46°40E **131** C4
Laingsburg *S. Africa* 33°9S 20°52E **144** D3
Lainioälven → *Sweden* 67°35N 22°40E **60** C20
Lairg *U.K.* 58°2N 4°24W **65** C4
Laisamis *Kenya* 1°36N 37°48E **142** B4
Laissac *France* 44°23N 2°50E **72** D6
Láives *Italy* 46°26N 11°12E **92** B8
Laiwu *China* 36°15N 117°40E **115** F9
Laixi *China* 36°50N 120°31E **115** F11
Laiyang *China* 36°59N 120°45E **115** F11
Laiyuan *China* 39°20N 114°40E **114** E8
Laizhou *China* 37°8N 119°57E **115** F10
Laizhou Wan *China* 37°30N 119°30E **115** F10
Lajamanu *Australia* 18°23S 130°38E **148** C5
Lajere *Nigeria* 12°10N 11°25E **139** C7
Lajes *Brazil* 5°41S 36°14W **189** B3
Lajinha *Brazil* 20°9S 41°37W **189** D3
Lajkovac *Serbia* 44°27N 20°14E **96** B4
Lajosmizse *Hungary* 47°3N 19°32E **78** D5
Lak Sao *Laos* 18°11N 104°58E **120** D5
Lakaband *Pakistan* 31°2N 69°15E **124** D3
Lakamané *Mali* 14°55N 9°40W **138** C3
Lake *U.S.A.* 44°33N 110°24W **168** D8
Lake Alfred *U.S.A.* 28°6N 81°44W **179** G6
Lake Alpine *U.S.A.* 38°29N 120°0W **170** G7
Lake Andes *U.S.A.* 43°9N 98°32W **172** D4
Lake Arthur *U.S.A.* 30°5N 92°41W **176** G9
Lake Bindegolly △
  Australia 27°55S 144°12E **151** D4
Lake Boga *Australia* 35°26S 143°38E **152** C3
Lake Butler *U.S.A.* 30°1N 82°21W **178** F7
Lake Cargelligo
  Australia 33°15S 146°22E **153** B7
Lake Charles *U.S.A.* 30°14N 93°13W **176** F8
Lake City *Colo., U.S.A.* 38°2N 107°19W **168** G10

Lake City *Fla., U.S.A.* 30°11N 82°38W **178** F7
Lake City *Mich.,*
  U.S.A. 44°20N 85°13W **173** C11
Lake City *Minn., U.S.A.* 44°27N 92°16W **172** C7
Lake City *Pa., U.S.A.* 42°1N 80°21W **174** D4
Lake City *S.C., U.S.A.* 33°52N 79°45W **178** B10
Lake Coleridge *N.Z.* 43°17S 171°30E **155** D6
Lake Cowichan
  Canada 48°49N 124°3W **162** D4
Lake District △ *U.K.* 54°30N 3°21W **66** C4
Lake Eildon △
  Australia 37°10S 145°56E **153** D6
Lake Elsinore *U.S.A.* 33°38N 117°20W **171** M9
Lake Eyre △ *Australia* 28°40S 137°31E **151** D2
Lake Gairdner △
  Australia 31°35S 135°51E **151** E2
Lake George *U.S.A.* 43°26N 73°43W **175** C11
Lake Grace *Australia* 33°7S 118°28E **149** F2
Lake Harbor *U.S.A.* 26°42N 80°48W **179** J9
Lake Harbour = Kimmirut
  Canada 62°50N 69°50W **161** E18
Lake Havasu City
  U.S.A. 34°27N 114°22W **171** L12
Lake Helen *U.S.A.* 28°59N 81°14W **179** G6
Lake Hughes *U.S.A.* 34°41N 118°26W **171** L8
Lake Isabella *U.S.A.* 35°38N 118°28E **171** K8
Lake Jackson *U.S.A.* 29°3N 95°27W **176** G7
Lake King *Australia* 33°5S 119°45E **149** F2
Lake Lenore *Canada* 52°24N 104°59W **163** C8
Lake Louise *Canada* 51°30N 116°10W **162** C5
Lake Mackay △
  Australia 21°48S 129°46E **148** D4
Lake Mburo △ *Uganda* 0°33S 30°56E **142** C3
Lake Mead △ *U.S.A.* 36°30N 114°22W **171** K12
Lake Meredith △
  U.S.A. 35°50N 101°50W **176** D4
Lake Mills *U.S.A.* 43°25N 93°32W **172** D7
Lake Nakura △ *Kenya* 0°21S 36°8E **142** C4
Lake Park *Fla., U.S.A.* 26°48N 80°3W **179** J9
Lake Park *Ga., U.S.A.* 30°41N 83°11W **178** E6
Lake Placid *Fla.,*
  U.S.A. 27°18N 81°22W **179** H8
Lake Placid *N.Y.,*
  U.S.A. 44°17N 73°59W **175** C11
Lake Pleasant *U.S.A.* 43°28N 74°25W **175** C10
Lake Providence
  U.S.A. 32°48N 91°10W **176** E9
Lake Pukaki *N.Z.* 44°11S 170°8E **155** E5
Lake Roosevelt △
  U.S.A. 48°5N 118°14W **168** B4
Lake St. Peter *Canada* 45°18N 78°2W **174** A6
Lake Stevens *U.S.A.* 48°1N 122°4W **170** B4
Lake Superior △
  Canada 47°45N 84°45W **164** C3
Lake Tekapo *N.Z.* 44°0S 170°30E **155** E5
Lake Torrens △
  Australia 30°55S 137°48E **151** E2
Lake Village *U.S.A.* 33°20N 91°17W **176** E9
Lake Wales *U.S.A.* 27°54N 81°35W **179** H6
Lake Worth *U.S.A.* 26°37N 80°3W **179** J9
Lakeba *Fiji* 18°13S 178°47W **154** a
Lakeba Passage *Fiji* 18°0S 178°45W **154** a
Lakefield *Canada* 44°25N 78°16W **174** B6
Lakefield △ *Australia* 15°24S 144°26E **150** B3
Lakehurst *U.S.A.* 40°1N 74°19W **175** F10
Lakeland *Australia* 15°49S 144°57E **150** B3
Lakeland *Fla., U.S.A.* 28°3N 81°57W **179** G6
Lakeland *Ga., U.S.A.* 31°2N 83°4W **178** E6
Lakemba = Lakeba
  Fiji 18°13S 178°47W **154** a
Lakeport *Calif., U.S.A.* 39°3N 122°55W **170** F4
Lakeport *Mich., U.S.A.* 43°7N 82°30W **174** C2
Lakes Entrance
  Australia 37°50S 148°0E **153** D8
Lakeside *Calif.,*
  U.S.A. 32°52N 116°55W **171** N10
Lakeside *Nebr., U.S.A.* 42°3N 102°26W **172** D2
Lakeview *U.S.A.* 42°11N 120°21W **168** E3
Lakeville *U.S.A.* 44°39N 93°14W **172** C7
Lakewood *Colo.,*
  U.S.A. 39°42N 105°4W **168** G11
Lakewood *N.J., U.S.A.* 40°6N 74°13W **175** F10
Lakewood *N.Y., U.S.A.* 42°6N 79°19W **174** D5
Lakewood *Ohio, U.S.A.* 41°28N 81°47W **174** E3
Lakewood *Wash.,*
  U.S.A. 47°11N 122°32W **170** C4
Lakewood Park *U.S.A.* 27°30N 80°24W **179** H9
Lakha *India* 26°9N 70°54E **124** F4
Lakhimpur *India* 27°57N 80°46E **125** F9
Lakhisarai *India* 25°11N 86°5E **125** G12
Lakhnadon *India* 22°36N 79°36E **125** H8
Lakhnau = Lucknow
  India 26°50N 81°0E **125** F9
Lakhonpheng *Laos* 15°54N 105°34E **120** E5
Lakhpat *India* 23°48N 68°47E **124** H3
Läki *Azerbaijan* 40°34N 47°22E **87** K8
Lakitusaki → *Canada* 54°21N 82°25W **164** B3
Lakki *Greece* 35°24N 23°57E **101** D5
Lakki *Pakistan* 32°36N 70°55E **124** C4
Lakonia □ *Greece* 36°55N 22°30E **98** E4
Lakonikos Kolpos
  Greece 36°40N 22°40E **98** E4
Lakor *Indonesia* 8°15S 128°17E **119** F7
Lakota *Ivory C.* 5°50N 5°30W **138** D3
Lakota *U.S.A.* 48°2N 98°21W **172** A4
Laksar *India* 29°46N 78°3E **124** E8
Laksefjorden *Norway* 70°45N 26°50E **60** A22
Lakselv *Norway* 70°2N 25°0E **60** A21
Laksettipet *India* 18°52N 79°13E **126** E4
Lakshadweep □ *India* 10°0N 72°30E **127** J1
Lakshadweep Is. *India* 10°0N 72°30E **127** J1
Lakshmanpur *India* 22°58N 83°3E **125** H10
Lakshmeshwar *India* 15°9N 75°28E **126** G2
Lala
  India 22°5N 88°20E **125** H13
Lala Musa *Pakistan* 32°40N 73°57E **124** C5
Lalaghat *India* 24°30N 92°40E **123** G18
Lalago *Tanzania* 3°28S 33°58E **142** C3
Lalapanzi *Zimbabwe* 19°20S 30°15E **143** F3
Lalapaşa *Turkey* 41°49N 26°44E **97** E10
Lalganj *India* 25°52N 85°13E **125** G11
Lalgola *India* 24°25N 88°15E **125** G13
Lalí *Iran* 32°21N 49°6E **129** C6

Lalibela Ethiopia 12°2N 39°0E 131 E2
Lalin China 45°12N 127°0E 115 B14
Lalin Spain 42°40N 8°5W 88 C2
Lalin He → China 45°32N 125°40E 115 B13
Lalinde France 44°50N 0°44E 72 D4
Lalitpur India 24°42N 78°28E 125 G8
Lalitpur Nepal 27°40N 85°20E 125 F11
Lalkua India 29°5N 79°31E 125 E8
Lalsot India 26°34N 76°20E 124 F7
Lam Nam Nan △
  Thailand 17°55N 100°28E 120 D3
Lam Pao Res. Thailand 16°50N 103°15E 120 D4
Lama Kara Togo 9°30N 1°15E 139 D5
Lamae Thailand 9°51N 99°5E 121 H2
Lamaing Burma 15°25N 97°53E 120 E1
Lamar Colo., U.S.A. 38°5N 102°37W 168 G12
Lamar Mo., U.S.A. 37°30N 94°16W 172 G6
Lamarque Argentina 39°24S 65°40W 192 A3
Lamas Peru 6°28S 76°31W 188 B2
Lamastre France 44°59N 4°35E 73 D8
Lamayuru India 34°25N 76°56E 125 B7
Lambach Austria 48°6N 13°51E 78 C6
Lamballe France 48°29N 2°31W 70 D4
Lambaréné Gabon 0°41S 10°12E 140 E2
Lambasa = Labasa Fiji 16°30S 179°27E 154 a
Lambay I. Ireland 53°29N 6°1W 64 C5
Lambayeque Peru 6°45S 80°0W 188 B2
Lambert's Bay S. Africa 32°5S 18°17E 144 D2
Lambesc France 43°39N 5°16E 73 E9
Lambeth Canada 42°54N 81°18W 174 D3
Lambia Greece 37°52N 21°53E 98 D3
Lambro → Italy 45°8N 9°32E 92 C6
Lame Nigeria 10°30N 9°0E 139 C6
Lame Deer U.S.A. 45°37N 106°40W 168 D10
Lamego Portugal 41°5N 7°52W 88 D3
Lamèque Canada 47°45N 64°38W 165 C7
Lameroo Australia 35°19S 140°33E 152 C4
Lamesa U.S.A. 32°44N 101°58W 176 E4
L'Ametlla de Mar Spain 40°53N 0°48E 90 D5
Lamezia Terme Italy 38°58N 16°16E 95 D9
Lamia Greece 38°55N 22°26E 98 C4
Lamington △
  Australia 28°13S 153°12E 151 D5
Lamma I. China 22°12N 114°7E 111 a
Lammermuir Hills U.K. 55°50N 2°40W 65 F6
Lammhult Sweden 57°10N 14°35E 63 H6
Lamoille → U.S.A. 44°38N 73°13W 175 B11
Lamon B. Phil. 14°30N 122°20E 119 B6
Lamont Canada 53°46N 112°50W 162 C6
Lamont Calif., U.S.A. 35°15N 118°55W 171 K8
Lamont Fla., U.S.A. 30°23N 83°49W 178 E6
Lamont Wyo., U.S.A. 42°13N 107°29W 168 E10
Lamotte-Beuvron France 47°36N 2°2E 71 E9
Lampa Peru 15°22S 70°22W 188 D3
Lampang Thailand 18°16N 99°32E 120 C2
Lampasas U.S.A. 31°4N 98°11W 176 F5
Lampazos de Naranjo
  Mexico 27°1N 100°31W 180 B4
Lampertheim Germany 49°35N 8°27E 77 F4
Lampeter U.K. 52°7N 4°4W 67 E3
Lamphun Thailand 18°40N 99°2E 120 C2
Lampman Canada 49°25N 102°50W 163 D8
Lamprechtshausen
  Austria 48°0N 12°58E 78 D5
Lampung □ Indonesia 5°30S 104°30E 118 F2
Lamta India 22°8N 80°7E 125 H9
Lamu Kenya 2°16S 40°55E 142 C5
Lamud Peru 6°10S 77°57W 188 B2
Lamy U.S.A. 35°29N 105°53W 169 J11
Lan Xian China 38°15N 111°35E 114 E6
Lan Yü Taiwan 22°4N 121°25E 117 F13
Läna'i U.S.A. 20°50N 156°55W 167 L8
Lanak La = Lanak'o Shank'ou
  China 34°27N 79°32E 125 B8
Lanark Canada 45°1N 76°22W 175 A8
Lanark U.K. 55°40N 3°47W 65 F5
Lanbi Kyun Burma 10°50N 98°20E 121 G2
Lancang China 22°36N 99°58E 116 F2
Lancang Jiang →
  China 21°40N 101°10E 116 G3
Lancashire □ U.K. 53°50N 2°48W 66 D5
Lancaster Canada 45°10N 74°30W 175 A10
Lancaster U.K. 54°3N 2°48W 66 C5
Lancaster Calif., U.S.A. 34°42N 118°8W 171 L8
Lancaster Ky., U.S.A. 37°37N 84°35W 173 G11
Lancaster N.H.,
  U.S.A. 44°29N 71°34W 175 B13
Lancaster Ohio, U.S.A. 39°43N 82°36W 173 F12
Lancaster Pa., U.S.A. 40°2N 76°19W 175 F8
Lancaster S.C., U.S.A. 34°43N 80°46W 178 D6
Lancaster Wis., U.S.A. 42°51N 90°43W 172 D8
Lancaster Sd. Canada 74°13N 84°0W 161 C15
Lancelin Australia 31°0S 115°18E 149 F2
Lanchow = Lanzhou
  China 36°1N 103°52E 114 F2
Lanchyn Ukraine 48°33N 24°45E 81 B9
Lanciano Italy 42°14N 14°23E 93 F11
Lanco Chile 39°24S 72°46W 192 A2
Lancones Peru 4°30S 80°30W 188 A1
Lancun China 36°25N 120°10E 115 F11
Lancut Poland 50°10N 22°13E 83 H9
Land Between the Lakes △
  U.S.A. 36°25N 88°0W 177 C11
Landau Bayern, Germany 48°40N 12°41E 77 G8
Landau Rhld-Pfz., Germany 49°12N 8°6E 77 F4
Landeck Austria 47°9N 10°34E 78 E4
Lander U.S.A. 42°50N 108°44W 168 E9
Lander → Australia 22°0S 132°0E 148 D5
Landerneau France 48°28N 4°17W 70 D2
Landeryd Sweden 57°7N 13°15E 63 G7
Landes France 44°0N 1°0W 72 D2
Landes □ France 43°57N 0°48W 72 E3
Landes de Gascogne ○
  France 44°23N 0°50W 72 D3
Landete Spain 39°56N 1°25W 90 F3
Landfall I. India 13°40N 93°2E 127 H11
Landi Kotal Pakistan 34°7N 71°6E 124 B4
Landisburg U.S.A. 40°21N 77°19W 174 F7
Landivisiau France 48°31N 4°6W 70 D2
Landmannalaugar
  Iceland 63°59N 19°4W 60 E4
Landquart Switz. 46°58N 9°32E 77 D5
Landrecies France 50°7N 3°40E 71 B10
Land's End U.K. 50°4N 5°44W 67 G2
Landsberg Germany 48°2N 10°53E 77 G6
Landsborough Cr. →
  Australia 22°28S 144°35E 150 C3
Landsbro Sweden 57°24N 14°56E 63 G8
Landshut Germany 48°34N 12°8E 77 G8
Landskrona Sweden 55°53N 12°50E 63 J6

Landstuhl Germany 49°24N 7°33E 77 F3
Landvetter Sweden 57°41N 12°17E 63 G6
Lane U.S.A. 33°32N 79°53W 178 B10
Lanesboro U.S.A. 41°57N 75°34W 175 E9
Lanester France 47°46N 3°22W 70 E3
Lanett U.S.A. 32°52N 85°12W 178 C4
Lang Shan China 41°0N 106°30E 114 D4
Lang Son Vietnam 21°52N 106°42E 116 G6
Lang Suan Thailand 9°57N 99°4E 121 H2
Langå Denmark 56°23N 9°54E 63 H3
La'nga Co China 30°45N 81°15E 125 D9
Langadas Greece 40°46N 23°6E 96 F7
Langadia Greece 37°43N 22°1E 98 D4
Langan → Iran 63°19N 14°42E 62 A8
Langar Iran 35°23N 60°25E 129 C9
Langara I. Canada 54°14N 133°1W 162 C2
Langarūd Iran 37°11N 50°8E 129 B6
Långås Sweden 56°58N 12°26E 63 H3
Langdai China 26°6N 105°21E 116 D5
Langdon U.S.A. 48°45N 98°22W 172 A4
Länge Jan = Ölands södra udde
  Sweden 56°12N 16°23E 63 H10
Langeac France 45°7N 3°29E 72 C7
Langeais France 47°20N 0°24E 70 E7
Langeb Baraka →
  Sudan 17°28N 36°50E 137 D4
Langeberg S. Africa 33°55S 21°0E 144 D3
Langeberge S. Africa 28°15S 22°33E 144 C3
Langeland Denmark 54°56N 10°48E 63 K4
Langeloo Germany 53°45N 7°32E 76 B3
Längen Hessen, Germany 49°59N 8°40E 77 F4
Langen Niedersachsen,
  Germany 53°36N 8°36E 76 B4
Langenburg Canada 50°51N 101°43W 163 C8
Langeneß Germany 54°38N 8°36E 76 A4
Langenlois Austria 48°29N 15°40E 78 C8
Langeoog Germany 53°45N 7°32E 76 B3
Langeskov Denmark 55°22N 10°35E 63 J4
Langfang China 39°30N 116°41E 114 E9
Länghem Sweden 57°36N 13°14E 63 G7
Langhirano Italy 44°37N 10°16E 92 D7
Langholm U.K. 55°9N 3°0W 65 F5
Langjökull Iceland 64°39N 20°12W 60 D3
Langkawi, Pulau
  Malaysia 6°25N 99°45E 121 J2
Langklip S. Africa 28°12S 20°20E 144 C3
Langkon Malaysia 6°30N 116°40E 118 B5
Langley Canada 49°7N 122°39W 170 A4
Langnau Switz. 46°56N 7°47E 77 J3
Langogne France 44°43N 3°50E 72 D7
Langon France 44°33N 0°16W 72 D3
Langoya Norway 68°45N 14°50E 60 B16
Langres France 47°52N 5°20E 71 E12
Langres, Plateau de
  France 47°45N 5°3E 71 E12
Langsa Indonesia 4°30N 97°57E 118 D1
Långsele Sweden 63°12N 17°4E 62 A7
Långshyttan Sweden 60°27N 16°2E 62 D10
Langtang △ Nepal 28°10N 85°30E 125 E11
Langtou China 40°1N 124°19E 115 D13
Langtry U.S.A. 29°49N 101°34W 176 G4
Langu Thailand 6°53N 99°47E 121 J2
Langue de Barbarie △
  Senegal 14°54N 16°30W 138 C1
Languedoc France 43°58N 3°55E 72 E7
Languedoc-Roussillon □
  France 43°25N 3°0E 72 E6
Langwang China 22°38N 113°27E 111 a
Langxi China 31°10N 119°12E 117 B12
Langzhong China 31°38N 105°58E 116 B5
Lanigan Canada 51°51N 105°2W 163 C7
Lanin △ Argentina 40°0S 71°58W 192 A2
Lanjigarh India 19°43N 83°23E 126 B6
Lankao China 34°48N 114°50E 114 G8
Länkäran Azerbaijan 38°48N 48°52E 105 C13
Lanmeur France 48°39N 3°40W 70 D3
Lannemezan France 43°8N 0°23E 72 E4
Lannilis France 48°35N 4°32W 70 D2
Lannion France 48°46N 3°29W 70 D3
L'Annonciation
  Canada 46°25N 74°55W 164 C5
Lanouaille France 45°24N 1°9E 72 C5
Lanping China 26°28N 99°15E 116 D2
Lansang Thailand 16°47N 99°0E 120 D2
Lansdale U.S.A. 40°14N 75°17W 175 F9
Lansdowne Australia 31°48S 152°30E 153 A10
Lansdowne Canada 44°24N 76°1W 175 B8
Lansdowne India 29°50N 78°41E 125 E8
Lansdowne House = Neskantaga
  Canada 52°14N 87°53W 164 B2
L'Anse U.S.A. 46°45N 88°27W 172 B9
L'Anse au Loup
  Canada 51°32N 56°50W 165 B8
L'Anse aux Meadows
  Canada 51°36N 55°32W 165 B8
Lansford U.S.A. 40°50N 75°53W 175 F9
Lanshan China 25°24N 112°10E 117 F9
Lanshantou China 35°5N 119°20E 115 G10
Länsi-Turunmaa
  Finland 60°18N 22°18E 84 B2
Lansing U.S.A. 42°44N 84°33W 173 D11
Lanslebourg-Mont-Cenis
  France 45°17N 6°52E 73 C10
Lanta, Ko Thailand 7°35N 99°3E 121 J2
Lantana U.S.A. 26°35N 80°3W 179 J9
Lantau I. China 22°15N 113°56E 111 a
Lantewa Nigeria 12°16N 11°44E 139 C7
Lantian China 34°11N 109°20E 114 G5
Lanus Argentina 34°42S 58°23W 190 C4
Lanxi China 29°13N 119°28E 117 C12
Lanzarote Canary Is. 29°0N 13°40W 100 F6
Lanzarote ✈ (ACE)
  Canary Is. 28°57N 13°40W 100 F6
Lanzhou China 36°1N 103°52E 114 F2
Lanzo Torinese Italy 45°16N 7°28E 92 C4
Lao → Italy 39°45N 15°34E 95 C8
Lao Cai Vietnam 22°30N 103°57E 116 F4
Laoag Phil. 18°7N 120°34E 119 A6
Laoang Phil. 12°32N 125°8E 119 B7
Laoha He → China 43°25N 120°35E 115 C11
Laohekou China 32°22N 111°38E 117 A8
Laois □ Ireland 52°57N 7°36W 64 D4
Laon France 49°33N 3°35E 71 C10
Laona U.S.A. 45°34N 88°40W 172 C9
Laos ■ Asia 17°45N 105°0E 120 D5
Lapa Brazil 25°46S 49°44W 191 B6
Lapai Nigeria 9°3N 6°25E 139 D6
Lapalisse France 46°15N 3°38E 71 F10

Lapeer U.S.A. 43°3N 83°19W 173 D12
Lapeyrade France 44°4N 0°3W 72 D3
Lapithos Cyprus 35°21N 33°11E 101 D12
Lapland = Lappland
  Europe 68°7N 24°0E 60 B21
LaPorte Ind., U.S.A. 41°36N 86°43W 172 E10
Laporte U.S.A. 41°25N 76°30W 175 E8
Lapovo Serbia 44°10N 21°2E 96 B5
Lappeenranta Finland 61°3N 28°12E 84 B5
Lappland Europe 68°7N 24°0E 60 B21
Lappo = Lapua Finland 62°58N 23°0E 62 E20
Laprida Argentina 37°34S 60°45W 190 D3
Lapseki Turkey 40°20N 26°41E 97 F10
Lapta = Lapithos
  Cyprus 35°21N 33°11E 101 D12
Laptev Sea Russia 76°0N 125°0E 107 B13
Lapua Finland 62°58N 23°0E 62 E20
Lăpuş → Romania 47°25N 23°40E 81 C8
Lăpuş, Munţii Romania 47°20N 23°50E 81 C8
Lăpuşna Moldova 46°53N 28°25E 81 D13
Lapy Poland 52°59N 22°52E 83 E9
Laqiya Arba'in Sudan 20°1N 28°1E 137 C2
Laqiya Umran Sudan 19°25N 28°18E 137 D2
L'Aquila Italy 42°22N 13°22E 93 F10
Lār Iran 27°40N 54°14E 129 E7
Lar Australia 38°2S 144°26E 152 E6
Larabanga Ghana 9°16N 1°56W 138 D4
Larache Morocco 35°10N 6°5W 136 A2
Laragne-Montéglin
  France 44°18N 5°49E 73 D9
Laramie U.S.A. 41°19N 105°35W 168 F11
Laramie Mts. U.S.A. 42°0N 105°30W 168 F11
Laranda = Karaman
  Turkey 37°14N 33°13E 104 D5
Laranjeiras do Sul
  Brazil 25°23S 52°23W 191 B5
Larantuka Indonesia 8°21S 122°55E 119 F6
Larat Indonesia 7°0S 132°0E 119 F8
L'Arbresle France 45°50N 4°36E 73 C8
Lärbro Sweden 57°47N 18°50E 63 G12
Larde Mozam. 16°28S 39°43E 143 F4
Larder Lake Canada 48°5N 79°40W 164 C4
Lardos Greece 36°6N 28°1E 101 C10
Lardos, Akra = Lindos, Akra
  Greece 36°4N 28°10E 101 C10
Lardos, Ormos Greece 36°4N 28°2E 101 C10
Lare Kenya 0°20N 37°56E 142 C4
Laredo Spain 43°26N 3°28W 88 B7
Laredo U.S.A. 27°30N 99°30W 176 H5
Laredo Sd. Canada 52°30N 128°53W 162 C3
Largentière France 44°34N 4°18E 73 D8
L'Argentière-la-Bessée
  France 44°47N 6°33E 73 D10
Largo U.S.A. 27°54N 82°47W 179 H7
Largo, Key U.S.A. 25°15N 80°15W 179 K9
Largs U.K. 55°47N 4°52W 65 F4
Lari Italy 43°34N 10°35E 92 E7
Lariang Indonesia 1°26S 119°17E 119 E5
Larimore U.S.A. 47°54N 97°38W 172 B5
Larino Italy 41°48N 14°54E 93 G11
Lario, Il = Como, L. di
  Italy 46°0N 9°11E 92 B6
Larisa Greece 39°36N 22°27E 98 B4
Larkana Pakistan 27°32N 68°18E 124 F3
Larnaca Cyprus 34°55N 33°38E 101 E12
Larnaca Bay Cyprus 34°53N 33°45E 101 E12
Larne U.K. 54°51N 5°51W 64 B6
Larned U.S.A. 38°11N 99°6W 172 F4
Laroquebrou France 44°58N 2°12E 72 D6
Larose U.S.A. 29°34N 90°23W 177 G9
Larrimah Australia 15°35S 133°12E 148 C5
Larsen Ice Shelf
  Antarctica 67°0S 62°0W 55 C17
Laruns France 43°0N 0°26W 72 F3
Larvik Norway 59°4N 10°2E 61 G14
Larzac, Causse du France 43°50N 3°17E 72 E7
Las Alpujarras Spain 36°55N 3°20W 91 J1
Las Animas U.S.A. 38°4N 103°13W 168 G12
Las Anod Somalia 8°26N 47°19E 131 F4
Las Arenas Spain 43°17N 4°50W 88 B6
Las Batuecas △ Spain 40°32N 6°5W 88 E4
Las Cabezas de San Juan
  Spain 36°57N 5°58W 88 J5
Las Cañadas del Teide △
  Canary Is. 28°15N 16°37W 100 F3
Las Cejas Argentina 26°53S 64°44W 190 B3
Las Chimeneas Mexico 32°8N 116°5W 171 N10
Las Coloradas
  Argentina 39°34S 70°36W 192 A2
Las Cruces U.S.A. 32°19N 106°47W 169 K10
Las Flores Argentina 36°10S 59°7W 190 D4
Las Gabias = Gabia la Grande
  Spain 37°8N 3°40W 89 H7
Las Heras Mendoza,
  Argentina 32°51S 68°49W 190 C2
Las Heras Santa Cruz,
  Argentina 46°33S 68°57W 192 C3
Las Horquetas
  Argentina 48°14S 71°11W 192 C2
Las Lajas Argentina 38°30S 70°25W 192 A2
Las Lomas Peru 4°40S 80°0W 188 A1
Las Lomitas Argentina 24°43S 60°35W 190 A3
Las Manos, Cueva de
  Argentina 47°9S 70°40W 192 C2
Las Marismas Spain 37°5N 6°20W 89 H4
Las Médulas Spain 26°35N 80°3W 179 H9
Las Minas Spain 38°20N 1°41W 91 G3
Las Navas de la Concepción
  Spain 37°56N 5°30W 89 H5
Las Navas del Marqués
  Spain 40°36N 4°20W 88 E6
Las Palmas Argentina 27°8S 58°45W 190 B4
Las Palmas Canary Is. 28°15S 61°55W 190 B4
Las Palmas →
  Mexico 32°31N 116°58W 171 N10
Las Palmas ✈ (LPA)
  Canary Is. 27°55N 15°25W 100 G4
Las Pedroñeras Spain 39°25N 2°40W 91 F2
Las Piedras Uruguay 34°45S 56°14W 191 C4
Las Pipinas Argentina 35°30S 57°19W 190 D4
Las Plumas Argentina 43°40S 67°15W 192 B3
Las Rosas Argentina 32°30S 61°35W 190 C3
Las Rozas Spain 40°29N 3°52W 88 E7
Las Tablas Panama 7°49N 80°14W 185 F3
Las Toscas Argentina 28°21S 59°18W 190 B4
Las Tunas Cuba 20°58N 76°59W 184 B4
Las Varillas Argentina 31°50S 62°50W 190 C3
Las Vegas N. Mex.,
  U.S.A. 35°36N 105°13W 169 J11
Las Vegas Nev., U.S.A. 36°10N 115°8W 171 J11

Las Vegas McCarran Int. ✈ (LAS)
  U.S.A. 36°5N 115°9W 171 J11
Lasarte-Oria Spain 43°16N 2°1W 90 B2
Lascano Uruguay 33°35S 54°12W 191 C5
Lascelles Australia 35°34S 142°34E 152 C5
Lash-e Joveyn Afghan. 31°45N 61°30E 122 D2
Lashburn Canada 53°10N 109°40W 163 C7
Lashio Burma 22°56N 97°45E 123 H20
Lashkar India 26°10N 78°10E 124 F8
Lasin Poland 53°30N 19°2E 82 E6
Lasithi Greece 35°11N 25°31E 101 D7
Lāsjerd Iran 35°24N 53°4E 129 C7
Lask Poland 51°34N 19°8E 83 G6
Laskarzew Poland 51°48N 21°36E 83 G8
Laško Slovenia 46°10N 15°16E 93 B12
Lassance Brazil 17°54S 44°34W 189 D2
Lassay-les-Châteaux
  France 48°27N 0°30W 70 D6
Lassen Pk. U.S.A. 40°29N 121°30W 168 F3
Lassen Volcanic △
  U.S.A. 40°30N 121°20W 168 F3
Last Mountain L.
  Canada 51°5N 105°14W 163 C7
Lastchance Cr. →
  U.S.A. 40°2N 121°15W 170 E5
Lastoursville Gabon 0°55S 12°38E 140 E2
Lastovo Croatia 42°46N 16°55E 93 F13
Lastovski Kanal Croatia 42°50N 17°0E 93 F14
Lat Yao Thailand 15°45N 99°48E 120 E2
Latacunga Ecuador 0°50S 78°35W 186 D3
Latady I. Antarctica 70°45S 74°35W 55 D17
Latakia = Al Lādhiqīyah
  Syria 35°30N 35°45E 104 E6
Latchford Canada 47°20N 79°50W 164 C4
Latehar India 23°45N 84°30E 125 H11
Laterza Italy 40°37N 16°48E 95 B9
Latham Australia 29°44S 116°20E 149 E2
Lathen Germany 52°52N 7°19E 76 C3
Lathi India 23°43N 71°23E 124 F4
Lathrop Wells U.S.A. 36°39N 116°24W 171 J10
Latiano Italy 40°33N 17°43E 95 B10
Latina Italy 41°28N 12°52E 94 A5
Latisana Italy 45°47N 13°0E 93 C10
Latium = Lazio □ Italy 42°10N 12°30E 93 F9
Laton U.S.A. 36°26N 119°41W 170 J7
Latorytsya →
  Slovak Rep. 48°28N 21°50E 79 C14
Latouche Treville, C.
  Australia 18°27S 121°49E 148 C3
Latrobe Australia 41°14S 146°30E 151 G4
Latrobe U.S.A. 40°19N 79°23W 174 F5
Latrónico Italy 40°5N 16°1E 95 B9
Latur India 18°25N 76°40E 126 E3
Latvia ■ Europe 56°50N 24°0E 84 D2
Lau Group Fiji 17°0S 178°30W 154 a
Lauca → Bolivia 19°9S 68°10W 188 D4
Lauchhammer Germany 51°29N 13°47E 76 D9
Lauda-Königshofen
  Germany 49°33N 9°42E 77 F5
Laudio = Llodio Spain 43°9N 2°58W 90 B2
Lauenburg Germany 53°22N 10°32E 76 B6
Lauenburgische Seen ○
  Germany 53°38N 10°45E 76 B6
Lauf Germany 49°30N 11°16E 77 F7
Lauge Koch Kyst
  Greenland 75°45N 57°45W 161 B20
Laughlin U.S.A. 35°10N 114°34W 171 K12
Lauhanvuori △ Finland 62°8N 22°40E 60 E20
Laujar de Andarax Spain 37°0N 2°54W 91 H2
Laukaa Finland 62°24N 25°56E 60 E21
Launceston Australia 41°24S 147°8E 151 G4
Launceston U.K. 50°38N 4°22W 67 G3
Laune → Ireland 52°7N 9°47W 64 D2
Launglon Bok Burma 13°50N 97°54E 120 F1
Laupheim Germany 48°14N 9°52E 77 G5
Laura Queens.,
  Australia 15°32S 144°32E 150 B3
Laura S. Austral.,
  Australia 33°10S 138°18E 152 B2
Laureana di Borrello
  Italy 38°30N 16°5E 95 D9
Laurel Fla., U.S.A. 27°8N 82°27W 179 H7
Laurel Miss., U.S.A. 31°41N 89°8W 177 F10
Laurel Mont., U.S.A. 45°40N 108°46W 168 D9
Laurel Bay U.S.A. 32°27N 80°47W 178 E5
Laurel Hill U.S.A. 40°14N 79°6W 174 F5
Laurencekirk U.K. 56°50N 2°28W 65 E6
Laurens U.S.A. 34°30N 82°1W 177 D13
Laurentian Plateau
  Canada 52°0N 70°0W 165 B6
Lauria Italy 40°2N 15°50E 95 B8
Lauria L. Canada 56°35N 101°57W 163 B8
Laurinburg U.S.A. 34°47N 79°28W 177 D15
Laurium U.S.A. 47°14N 88°27W 172 B9
Lausanne Switz. 46°32N 6°38E 77 J2
Laut Indonesia 4°45N 108°0E 118 D3
Laut, Pulau Indonesia 3°40S 116°10E 118 E5
Laut Kecil, Kepulauan
  Indonesia 4°45S 115°40E 118 E5
Lautaro Chile 38°31S 72°27W 192 A2
Lauterbach Germany 50°38N 9°24E 76 E5
Lauterecken Germany 49°38N 7°35E 77 F3
Lautoka Fiji 17°37S 177°27E 154 a
Lauwersmeer △ Neths. 53°22N 6°11E 69 A6
Lauzès France 44°34N 1°35E 72 D5
Lava → Russia 54°34N 21°14E 82 D8
Lava Beds △ U.S.A. 41°40N 121°30W 168 F3
Lavagh More Ireland 54°46N 8°6W 64 B3
Lavagna Italy 44°18N 9°20E 92 D6
Laval France 48°4N 0°48W 70 D6
Laval-des-Rapides
  Canada 45°33N 73°42W 164 C5
Lavalle Argentina 28°15S 65°15W 190 B3
Lāvān Iran 26°48N 53°22E 129 E7
Lavant Canada 45°3N 76°42W 175 A8
Lāvar Meydān Iran 30°20N 54°30E 129 D7
Lavara France 41°19N 26°22E 97 E10
Lavardac France 44°12N 0°20E 72 D4
Lavaur France 42°57N 1°51E 72 F5
Lavelanet France 42°57N 1°51E 72 F5
Lavello Italy 41°3N 15°48E 95 A8
Lavers Hill Australia 38°40S 143°25E 152 C5
Laverton Australia 28°44S 122°29E 149 E3
Lavezzi, Ís. France 41°20N 9°16E 73 G13
Lavis Italy 46°8N 11°7E 92 B8
Lavos Portugal 40°6N 8°49W 88 E2
Lavradio Portugal 38°40N 9°2W 89 G1
Lavras Brazil 21°20S 45°0W 191 A7
Lavre Portugal 38°46N 8°22E 89 G2
Lavrio Greece 37°40N 24°4E 98 D6

Lavris Greece 35°25N 24°40E 101 D6
Lavumisa Swaziland 27°20S 31°55E 145 C5
Lavushi Manda △
  Zambia 12°46S 31°0E 143 E3
Lawak I. = Nanshan I.
  S. China Sea 10°45N 115°49E 118 B5
Lawaki Fiji 17°40S 178°35E 154 a
Lawas Malaysia 4°55N 115°25E 118 D5
Lawele Indonesia 5°13S 122°57E 119 F6
Lawn Hill = Boodjamulla
  Australia 18°15S 138°6E 150 B2
Lawng-pit Burma 25°24N 97°26E 125 B8
Lawqah Si. Arabia 29°49N 42°45E 128 D4
Lawra Ghana 10°39N 2°51W 138 C4
Lawrence N.Z. 45°55S 169°41E 155 F4
Lawrence Ind., U.S.A. 39°50N 86°2W 172 F10
Lawrence Kans., U.S.A. 38°58N 95°14W 172 F6
Lawrence Mass.,
  U.S.A. 42°43N 71°10W 175 D13
Lawrenceburg Ind.,
  U.S.A. 39°6N 84°52W 173 F11
Lawrenceburg Tenn.,
  U.S.A. 35°14N 87°20W 177 D11
Lawrenceville Ga.,
  U.S.A. 33°57N 83°59W 178 D6
Lawrenceville Pa.,
  U.S.A. 41°59N 77°8W 174 E7
Laws U.S.A. 37°24N 118°20W 170 H8
Lawtey U.S.A. 30°3N 82°5W 178 F7
Lawton U.S.A. 34°37N 98°25W 176 D5
Lawu Indonesia 7°40S 111°13E 119 G14
Lawz, J. al Si. Arabia 28°39N 35°18E 137 B4
Laxå Sweden 58°59N 14°37E 63 F8
Laxford, L. U.K. 58°24N 5°6W 65 C3
Laxiwa Dam China 36°4N 101°11E 110 D9
Laxou France 48°41N 6°8E 71 D13
Lay → France 46°18N 1°17W 72 B2
Layla Si. Arabia 22°10N 46°40E 131 C4
Laylān Iraq 35°18N 44°31E 128 C5
Layon → France 47°20N 0°45W 70 E6
Laysan I. U.S.A. 25°50N 171°50W 167 K5
Layton U.S.A. 41°4N 111°58W 168 F8
Layton Utah, U.S.A. 41°4N 111°58W 168 F8
Laytonville U.S.A. 39°41N 123°29W 168 G2
Lazarev Russia 52°13N 141°30E 107 D15
Lazarev Sea S. Ocean 67°30S 3°0W 55 C2
Lazarevac Serbia 44°23N 20°17E 96 B4
Lazarevskoye Russia 43°55N 39°21E 87 A4
Lázaro Cárdenas
  Mexico 17°55N 102°11W 180 D4
Lazdijai Lithuania 54°14N 23°31E 82 D10
Lazhuglung China 34°52N 81°24E 109 F10
Lazio □ Italy 42°10N 12°30E 93 F9
Lazo Moldova 47°33N 28°2E 81 C13
Lazo Russia 43°25N 133°55E 112 C6
Le Beausset France 43°12N 5°48E 73 E9
Le Bic Canada 48°20N 68°41W 165 C6
Le Blanc France 46°37N 1°3E 72 B5
Le Bleymard France 44°30N 3°42E 72 D7
Le Bourgneuf-la-Forêt
  France 48°10N 0°59W 70 D6
Le Bugue France 44°55N 0°56E 72 D4
Le Cateau Cambrésis
  France 50°7N 3°32E 71 B10
Le Caylar France 43°51N 3°19E 72 E7
Le Chambon-Feugerolles
  France 45°24N 4°19E 73 C8
Le Châtelet France 46°38N 2°16E 71 F9
Le Chesne France 49°30N 4°45E 71 C11
Le Cheylard France 44°55N 4°25E 73 D8
Le Conquet France 48°21N 4°46W 70 D2
Le Creusot France 46°48N 4°24E 71 F11
Le Croisic France 47°18N 2°30W 70 E4
Le Donjon France 46°22N 3°48E 71 F10
Le Dorat France 46°14N 1°5E 72 B5
Le François Martinique 14°38N 60°57W 182 c
Le Gosier Guadeloupe 16°14N 61°29W 182 b
Le Grand-Lucé France 47°52N 0°28E 70 E7
Le Grand-Pressigny
  France 46°55N 0°48E 72 B4
Le Grand-Quevilly France 49°24N 1°3E 70 C7
Le Gris Gris Mauritius 20°31S 57°32E 141 d
Le Havre France 49°30N 0°5E 70 C7
Le Lamentin Martinique 14°35N 61°2W 182 c
Le Lavandou France 43°8N 6°22E 73 E10
Le Lion-d'Angers France 47°37N 0°43W 70 E6
Le Louroux-Béconnais
  France 47°30N 0°55W 70 E6
Le Luc France 43°23N 6°21E 73 E10
Le Lude France 47°39N 0°9E 70 E7
Le Maire, Estr. de
  Argentina 54°50S 65°0W 192 D4
Le Mans France 48°0N 0°10E 70 E7
Le Marin Martinique 14°27N 60°55W 182 c
Le Mars U.S.A. 42°47N 96°10W 172 D5
Le Mayet-de-Montagne
  France 46°4N 3°40E 71 F10
Le Mêle-sur-Sarthe
  France 48°31N 0°22E 70 D7
Le Monastier-sur-Gazeille
  France 44°57N 3°59E 72 D7
Le Monêtier-les-Bains
  France 44°58N 6°30E 73 D10
Le Mont-Dore France 45°35N 2°49E 72 C6
Le Mont-St-Michel
  France 48°40N 1°30W 70 D5
Le Moule Guadeloupe 16°20N 61°22W 182 b
Le Moyne, L. Canada 56°45N 68°47W 165 A6
Le Muy France 43°28N 6°34E 73 E10
Le Palais France 47°20N 3°10W 70 E3
Le Perthus France 42°30N 2°53E 72 F6
Le Port Réunion 20°56S 55°18E 141 c
Le Prêcheur Martinique 14°50N 61°12W 182 c
Le Puy-en-Velay France 45°3N 3°52E 72 C7
Le Raysville France 41°50N 76°10W 175 E8
Le Robert Martinique 14°40N 60°56W 182 c
Le Roy U.S.A. 42°58N 77°59W 174 D7
Le St-Esprit Martinique 14°34N 60°56W 182 c
Le Sueur U.S.A. 44°28N 93°55W 172 C7
Le Tampon Réunion 21°16S 55°32E 141 c
Le Teil France 44°33N 4°40E 73 D8
Le Teilleul France 48°30N 0°53W 70 D6
Le Theil France 48°16N 0°42E 70 D7
Le Thuy Vietnam 17°14N 106°49E 120 D6
Le Touquet-Paris-Plage
  France 50°30N 1°36E 71 B8
Le Tréport France 50°3N 1°20E 70 B7
Le Val-André France 48°35N 2°33W 70 D4
Le Val-d'Ajol France 47°55N 6°30E 71 E13
Le Verdon-sur-Mer
  France 45°33N 1°4W 72 C2

Le Vigan France 43°59N 3°36E 72 E7
Lea → U.K. 51°31N 0°1E 67 F8
Leach Cambodia 12°21N 103°46E 121 F4
Lead U.S.A. 44°21N 103°46W 172 C2
Leader Canada 50°50N 109°30W 163 C7
Leadville U.S.A. 39°15N 106°18W 168 G10
Leaf → U.S.A. 30°59N 88°44W 177 F10
Leaf Rapids Canada 56°30N 99°59W 163 B9
Leaghur, L. Australia 33°35S 143°3E 152 B5
League City U.S.A. 29°31N 95°6W 176 C7
Leamington Canada 42°3N 82°36W 174 D2
Leamington N.Z. 37°55S 175°30E 154 D4
Leamington U.S.A. 39°32N 112°17W 168 G7
Leamington Spa = Royal
  Leamington Spa U.K. 52°18N 1°31W 67 E6
Le'an China 27°25N 115°48E 117 D10
Leander U.S.A. 30°34N 97°52W 176 F5
Leandro Norte Alem
  Argentina 27°34S 55°15W 191 B5
Leane, L. Ireland 52°2N 9°32W 64 D2
Learmonth Australia 22°13S 114°10E 148 D1
Leary U.S.A. 31°29N 84°31W 178 E5
Leask Canada 53°5N 106°45W 163 C7
Leatherhead U.K. 51°18N 0°20W 67 F7
Leavdnja = Lakselv
  Norway 70°2N 25°0E 60 A21
Leavenworth Kans.,
  U.S.A. 39°19N 94°55W 172 F6
Leavenworth Wash.,
  U.S.A. 47°36N 120°40W 168 C3
Leawood U.S.A. 38°58N 94°37W 172 F6
Łeba Poland 54°45N 17°32E 82 D4
Łeba → Poland 54°46N 17°33E 82 D4
Lebach Germany 49°25N 6°54E 77 F2
Lebak Phil. 6°32N 124°5E 119 C6
Lebam U.S.A. 46°34N 123°33W 170 D3
Lebane Serbia 42°56N 21°44E 96 D5
Lebanon Fla., U.S.A. 29°10N 82°37W 179 F7
Lebanon Ind., U.S.A. 40°3N 86°28W 172 E10
Lebanon Kans., U.S.A. 39°49N 98°33W 172 F4
Lebanon Ky., U.S.A. 37°34N 85°15W 173 G11
Lebanon Mo., U.S.A. 37°41N 92°40W 172 G7
Lebanon N.H., U.S.A. 43°39N 72°15W 175 C12
Lebanon Oreg., U.S.A. 44°32N 122°55W 168 D2
Lebanon Pa., U.S.A. 40°20N 76°26W 175 F8
Lebanon Tenn., U.S.A. 36°12N 86°18W 177 C11
Lebanon ■ Asia 34°0N 36°0E 130 B5
Lebap □ Turkmenistan 40°0N 63°0E 108 D6
Lebec U.S.A. 34°51N 118°52W 171 L8
Lebedyan Russia 53°0N 39°10E 85 F10
Lebedyn Ukraine 50°35N 34°30E 85 G8
Lebel-sur-Quévillon
  Canada 49°3N 76°59W 164 C4
Lebomboberge S. Africa 24°30S 32°0E 145 B5
Łebork Poland 54°33N 17°46E 82 D4
Lebowakgomo S. Africa 24°12S 29°30E 145 B4
Lebrija Spain 36°53N 6°5W 89 J4
Lebsko, Jezioro Poland 54°40N 17°25E 82 D4
Lebu Chile 37°40S 73°47W 190 D1
Leça da Palmeira
  Portugal 41°12N 8°42E 88 D2
Lecce Italy 40°23N 18°11E 95 B11
Lecco Italy 45°51N 9°23E 92 C6
Lecco, L. di Italy 45°55N 9°19E 92 C6
Lécera Spain 41°13N 0°43W 90 D4
Lech Austria 47°13N 10°9E 78 D3
Lech → Germany 48°43N 10°56E 77 G6
Lechang China 25°10N 113°20E 117 E9
Lechena Greece 37°57N 21°16E 98 D3
Lechtaler Alpen Austria 47°15N 10°30E 78 D3
Lecontes Mills U.S.A. 41°5N 78°17W 174 E6
Lectoure France 43°56N 0°38E 72 E4
Łęczna Poland 51°18N 22°53E 83 G9
Łęczyca Poland 52°5N 19°15E 83 F6
Ledang, Gunung
  Malaysia 2°22N 102°37E 121 L4
Ledesma Spain 41°6N 5°59W 88 D5
Lednice Czech Rep. 48°46N 16°48E 79 C9
Ledong China 18°41N 109°5E 117 a
Leduc Canada 53°15N 113°30W 162 C6
Lee Fla., U.S.A. 30°25N 83°18W 178 E6
Lee Mass., U.S.A. 42°19N 73°15W 175 D11
Lee → Ireland 51°53N 8°56W 64 E3
Lee Vining U.S.A. 37°58N 119°7W 170 H7
Leech L. U.S.A. 47°10N 94°24W 172 B7
Leechburg U.S.A. 40°37N 79°36W 174 F5
Leeds U.K. 53°48N 1°33W 66 D6
Leeds U.S.A. 33°33N 86°33W 177 E11
Leek Neths. 53°10N 6°24E 69 A6
Leek U.K. 53°7N 2°1W 66 D5
Leeman Australia 29°57S 114°58E 149 E1
Leeper U.S.A. 41°22N 79°18W 174 E5
Leer Germany 53°13N 7°26E 76 B3
Leesburg Fla., U.S.A. 28°49N 81°53W 179 G8
Leesburg Ga., U.S.A. 31°44N 84°10W 178 E5
Leeston N.Z. 43°45S 172°19E 155 D7
Leesville U.S.A. 31°9N 93°16W 177 F8
Leeton Australia 34°33S 146°23E 153 C7
Leetonia U.S.A. 40°53N 80°45W 174 F4
Leeu Gamka S. Africa 32°47S 21°59E 144 D3
Leeuwarden Neths. 53°15N 5°48E 69 A5
Leeuwin, C. Australia 34°20S 115°9E 149 F2
Leeuwin Naturaliste △
  Australia 34°6S 115°3E 149 F2
Leeward Is. Atl. Oc. 16°30N 63°30W 183 C7
Lefka Cyprus 35°6N 32°51E 101 D11
Lefkada Greece 38°40N 20°43E 98 C2
Lefkimi Greece 39°25N 20°3E 98 B2
Lefkimmi, Akra Greece 39°29N 20°4E 101 B4
Lefkoniko Cyprus 35°18N 33°44E 101 D12
Lefkosia = Nicosia
  Cyprus 35°10N 33°25E 101 D12
Lefroy Canada 44°16N 79°34W 174 B5
Lefroy, L. Australia 31°21S 121°40E 149 F3
Leg → Poland 50°42N 21°50E 83 H8
Leganés Spain 40°19N 3°45W 88 B7
Legazpi Phil. 13°10N 123°45E 119 B6
Lège-Cap-Ferret France 44°48N 1°9W 72 D2
Legendre I. Australia 20°22S 116°55E 148 D2
Leghorn = Livorno Italy 43°33N 10°19E 92 E7
Legian Indonesia 8°42S 115°10E 119 K18
Legionowo Poland 52°25N 20°50E 83 F7
Legnago Italy 45°11N 11°18E 92 C8
Legnano Italy 45°36N 8°54E 92 C5
Legnica Poland 51°12N 16°10E 81 A3
Legrad Croatia 46°17N 16°51E 93 B13
Leh India 34°9N 77°35E 125 B7
Lehigh Acres U.S.A. 26°36N 81°39W 179 H8
Lehighton U.S.A. 40°50N 75°43W 175 F9
Lehliu Romania 44°29N 26°50E 81 F11
Lehrte Germany 52°22N 9°58E 76 C5

Lehututu Botswana 23°54S 21°55E 144 B3
Lei Shui → China 26°55N 112°35E 117 D9
Leiah Pakistan 30°58N 70°58E 124 D4
Leibnitz Austria 46°47N 15°34E 78 E8
Leibo China 28°11N 103°34E 116 C4
Leicester U.K. 52°38N 1°8W 67 E6
Leicester City □ U.K. 52°38N 1°8W 67 E6
Leicestershire □ U.K. 52°41N 1°17W 67 E6
Leichhardt → Australia 17°35S 139°48E 150 B2
Leichhardt Ra. Australia 20°46S 147°40E 150 C4
Leiden Neths. 52°9N 4°30E 69 B4
Leie → Belgium 51°2N 3°45E 69 C3
Leifers = Làives Italy 46°26N 11°20E 93 B8
Leigh → Australia 38°18S 144°30E 152 E6
Leigh Creek Australia 30°38S 138°26E 152 A3
Leimen Germany 49°21N 8°41E 77 F4
Leimus Nic. 14°40N 84°3W 182 D3
Leine → Germany 52°43N 9°36E 76 C5
Leinefelde Germany 51°23N 10°19E 76 D6
Leinster Australia 27°51S 120°36E 149 E3
Leinster □ Ireland 53°3N 7°8W 64 C4
Leinster, Mt. Ireland 52°37N 6°46W 64 D5
Leipalingis Lithuania 54°5N 23°51E 82 D10
Leipzig Germany 51°18N 12°22E 76 D8
Leiria Portugal 39°46N 8°53W 88 F2
Leiria □ Portugal 39°46N 8°53W 88 F2
Leirvik Norway 59°47N 5°28E 61 G11
Leishan China 26°15N 108°20E 116 D7
Leisler, Mt. Australia 23°23S 129°20E 148 D4
Leisure City U.S.A. 25°30N 80°26W 179 K9
Leith U.K. 55°59N 3°11W 65 F5
Leith Hill U.K. 51°11N 0°22W 67 F7
Leitha → Europe 47°50N 17°15E 79 D10
Leitir Ceanainn = Letterkenny Ireland 54°57N 7°45W 64 B4
Leitrim Ireland 54°0N 8°5W 64 B3
Leitrim □ Ireland 54°8N 8°0W 64 B4
Leitza Spain 43°5N 1°55W 90 B3
Leixlip Ireland 53°22N 6°30W 64 C5
Leiyang China 26°27N 112°45E 117 D9
Leizhou China 20°52N 110°8E 117 G8
Leizhou Bandao China 21°0N 110°0E 116 G7
Leizhou Wan China 20°50N 110°20E 117 G8
Lek → Neths. 51°54N 4°35E 69 C4
Leka Norway 65°5N 11°35E 60 D14
Lekani Greece 41°10N 24°35E 97 E8
Lekbibaj Albania 42°17N 19°56E 96 D3
Lekeitio Spain 43°20N 2°32W 90 B2
Lekki Lagoon Nigeria 6°30N 4°7E 139 D5
Léko Mali 13°37N 9°2W 138 C3
Lekoui Burkina Faso 12°37N 3°40W 138 C4
Leksand Sweden 60°44N 15°1E 62 D9
Leland Mich., U.S.A. 45°1N 85°45W 173 C11
Leland Miss., U.S.A. 33°24N 90°54W 177 E9
Lelång Sweden 59°10N 12°5E 62 E6
Leleque Argentina 42°28S 71°0W 192 B2
Leling China 37°44N 117°13E 115 F9
Lélouma Guinea 11°11N 12°56W 138 C2
Lelystad Neths. 52°30N 5°25E 69 B5
Lem Denmark 56°1N 8°24E 63 H2
Lema Nigeria 12°58N 4°13E 139 C5
Léman, L. Europe 46°26N 6°30E 71 F13
Lembar Indonesia 8°45S 116°4E 148 A2
Lembongan, Nusa Indonesia 8°40S 115°27E 119 K18
Lembuak Indonesia 8°36S 116°11E 119 K19
Lemera Dem. Rep. of the Congo 3°0S 28°55E 142 C2
Lemesós = Limassol Cyprus 34°42N 33°1E 101 E12
Lemhi Ra. U.S.A. 44°0N 113°0W 168 D7
Lemmenjoki △ Finland 68°40N 25°30E 60 B21
Lemmer Neths. 52°51N 5°43E 69 B5
Lemmon U.S.A. 45°57N 102°10W 172 C2
Lemon Grove U.S.A. 32°44N 117°1W 171 N9
Lemoore U.S.A. 36°18N 119°46W 170 J7
Lempdes-sur-Allagnon France 45°22N 3°17E 72 C7
Lemvig Denmark 56°33N 8°20E 63 H2
Lena → Russia 72°52N 126°40E 107 B13
Lena Pillars = Lenskiy Stolby Russia 60°55N 126°0E 107 C13
Lenadoon Pt. Ireland 54°18N 9°3W 64 B2
Lenart Slovenia 46°36N 15°48E 93 B12
Lenartovce Slovak Rep. 48°18N 20°19E 79 C13
Lencloître France 46°50N 0°20E 70 F7
Lençóis Brazil 12°35S 41°24W 189 C2
Lençóis Maranhenses △ Brazil 2°30S 43°0W 189 A2
Lendava Slovenia 46°35N 16°25E 93 B13
Lendinara Italy 45°5N 11°36E 93 C8
Lenger Kazakhstan 42°12N 69°54E 109 D7
Lengerich Germany 52°11N 7°52E 76 C3
Lenggong Malaysia 5°6N 100°58E 121 K3
Lenggries Germany 47°41N 11°35E 77 H7
Lengshuijiang China 27°40N 111°26E 117 D8
Lengshuitan China 26°27N 111°35E 117 D8
Lengua de Vaca, Pta. Chile 30°14S 71°38W 190 C1
Lengwe △ Malawi 16°14S 34°45E 143 F3
Lengyeltóti Hungary 46°40N 17°40E 80 D2
Lenhovda Sweden 57°0N 15°16E 63 G9
Lenina, Kanal → Russia 43°44N 45°17E 87 J7
Lenine Ukraine 45°17N 35°46E 85 K8
Leningrad □ Russia 59°40N 32°0E 84 C7
Leninogorsk = Ridder Kazakhstan 50°20N 83°30E 109 B10
Leninogorsk Russia 54°36N 52°30E 108 B4
Leninsk Russia 48°40N 45°15E 87 F7
Leninsk-Kuznetskiy Russia 54°44N 86°10E 109 B11
Leninskoye Russia 58°23N 47°3E 86 A8
Lenk Switz. 46°27N 7°28E 77 J3
Lenkoran = Länkäran Azerbaijan 38°48N 48°52E 105 C13
Lenmalu Indonesia 1°45S 130°15E 119 E8
Lennartsfors Sweden 59°20N 11°55E 62 E5
Lenne → Germany 51°25N 7°29E 76 D3
Lennestadt Germany 51°8N 8°2E 76 D4
Lennox U.S.A. 43°21N 96°53W 172 D5
Lennox, I. Chile 55°18S 66°50W 192 E3
Lennoxville Canada 45°22N 71°51W 175 A13
Leno Italy 45°22N 10°13E 92 C7
Lenoir U.S.A. 35°55N 81°32W 177 D14
Lenoir City U.S.A. 35°48N 84°16W 177 D12
Lenore L. Canada 52°30N 104°59W 163 C8
Lenox Ga., U.S.A. 31°16N 83°28W 178 D6
Lenox Mass., U.S.A. 42°22N 73°17W 175 D11
Lens France 50°26N 2°50E 71 B9
Lensahn Germany 54°13N 10°53E 76 A6
Lensk Russia 60°48N 114°55E 107 C12
Lenskiy Stolby Russia 60°55N 126°0E 107 C13
Lentas Greece 34°56N 24°56E 101 E6
Lentekhi Georgia 42°47N 42°45E 87 J6
Lenti Hungary 46°37N 16°33E 80 D1
Lentini Italy 37°17N 15°0E 95 E8
Lenwood U.S.A. 34°53N 117°7W 171 L9
Lenya Burma 11°33N 98°57E 121 G2
Lenzen Germany 53°5N 11°29E 76 B7
Léo Burkina Faso 11°3N 2°2W 138 C4
Leoben Austria 47°22N 15°5E 78 D8
Leodhais = Lewis U.K. 58°9N 6°40W 65 C2
Leola U.S.A. 45°43N 98°56W 172 C4
Leominster U.K. 52°14N 2°43W 67 E5
Leominster U.S.A. 42°32N 71°46W 175 D13
Léon France 43°53N 1°18W 72 E2
León Mexico 21°6N 101°41W 180 C4
León Nic. 12°27N 86°51W 182 D2
León Spain 42°38N 5°34W 88 C5
Leon U.S.A. 40°44N 93°45W 172 E7
León □ Spain 42°40N 5°55W 88 C5
Leon → U.S.A. 31°14N 97°28W 176 F6
León, Montes de Spain 42°30N 6°18W 88 C4
Leonardo da Vinci, Roma ✈ (FCO) Italy 41°48N 12°15E 93 G9
Leonardtown U.S.A. 38°17N 76°38W 173 F15
Leonardville Namibia 23°29S 18°49E 144 B2
Leonárisso Cyprus 35°28N 34°8E 101 D13
Leonberg Germany 48°48N 9°1E 77 G5
Leonding Austria 48°16N 14°15E 78 C7
Leonessa Italy 42°34N 12°58E 93 F9
Leonforte Italy 37°38N 14°23E 95 E7
Leongatha Australia 38°30S 145°58E 153 E6
Leonia U.S.A. 30°55N 86°1W 178 E3
Leonidio Greece 37°9N 22°52E 98 D4
Leonora Australia 28°49S 121°19E 149 E3
Leopoldina Brazil 21°28S 42°40W 191 A7
Leopoldo Bulhões Brazil 16°37S 48°46W 189 D1
Leopoldsburg Belgium 51°7N 5°13E 69 C5
Leoti U.S.A. 38°29N 101°21W 172 F3
Leova Moldova 46°28N 28°15E 81 D13
Leoville Canada 53°39N 107°33W 163 C7
Lepe Spain 37°15N 7°12W 89 H3
Lepel = Lyepyel Belarus 54°50N 28°40E 84 E5
Lepenou Greece 38°42N 21°17E 98 C3
Leping China 28°47N 117°7E 117 C11
Lépo, L. do Angola 17°0S 19°0E 144 A2
Lepontine, Alpi Italy 46°22N 8°27E 92 B5
Leposavić Kosovo 43°6N 20°48E 96 C4
Leppävirta Finland 62°29N 27°46E 60 E22
Lepsény Hungary 47°0N 18°15E 80 D3
Leptis Magna Libya 32°40N 14°12E 135 B8
Lequeitio = Lekeitio Spain 43°20N 2°32W 90 B2
Lercara Friddi Italy 37°45N 13°36E 94 E6
Léré Chad 9°39N 14°13E 139 D7
Léré Mali 15°45N 4°55W 138 B4
Lere Bauchi, Nigeria 9°43N 9°18E 139 D6
Lere Kaduna, Nigeria 10°23N 8°35E 139 C6
Leribe Lesotho 28°51S 28°3E 145 C4
Lérici Italy 44°4N 9°55E 92 D6
Lérida = Lleida Spain 41°37N 0°39E 90 D5
Lérins, Îs. de France 43°31N 7°3E 73 E11
Lerma Spain 42°0N 3°47W 88 D7
Leros Greece 37°10N 26°50E 99 D8
Lérouville France 48°44N 5°30E 71 D12
Lerum Sweden 57°46N 12°16E 63 G6
Lerwick U.K. 60°9N 1°9W 65 A7
Leş Romania 46°58N 21°50E 80 D6
Les Abrets France 45°32N 5°35E 73 C9
Les Andelys France 49°15N 1°25E 70 C8
Les Borges Blanques Spain 41°31N 0°52E 90 D5
Les Cayes Haiti 18°15N 73°46W 183 C5
Les Coteaux Canada 45°15N 74°13W 175 A10
Les Escoumins Canada 48°21N 69°24W 165 C6
Les Essarts France 46°47N 1°12W 70 F5
Les Herbiers France 46°52N 1°1W 70 F5
Les Minquiers, Plateau des Chan. Is. 48°58N 2°8W 70 D4
Les Pieux France 49°30N 1°48W 70 C5
Les Ponts-de-Cé France 47°25N 0°30W 70 E6
Les Riceys France 47°59N 4°22E 71 E11
Les Sables-d'Olonne France 46°30N 1°45W 72 B2
Les Vans France 44°25N 4°7E 73 D8
Lesbos Greece 39°10N 26°20E 99 B8
L'Escala Spain 42°7N 3°8E 90 C8
Leshan China 29°33N 103°41E 116 C4
Leshwe ⌓ Dem. Rep. of the Congo 12°45S 29°30E 143 E2
Lésina Italy 41°52N 15°21E 93 G12
Lésina, L. di Italy 41°53N 15°26E 93 G12
Lesjöfors Sweden 59°58N 14°11E 62 E8
Lesko Poland 49°30N 22°23E 83 J9
Leskov I. Antarctica 56°0S 28°0W 55 B1
Leskovac Serbia 43°0N 21°58E 96 C5
Leskovik Albania 40°10N 20°34E 96 F4
Leslie U.S.A. 31°57N 84°5W 178 D5
Leśna Poland 51°1N 15°15E 83 G2
Lesneven France 48°35N 4°20W 70 D2
Leśnica Poland 50°26N 18°11E 83 H5
Lešnica Serbia 44°39N 19°20E 96 B3
Lesnoye Russia 58°15N 35°18E 84 C8
Lesopilnoye Russia 46°44N 134°20E 112 A7
Lesotho ■ Africa 29°40S 28°0E 145 C4
Lesozavodsk Russia 45°30N 133°29E 112 B6
Lesparre-Médoc France 45°18N 0°57W 72 C3
L'Espluga de Francolí Spain 41°24N 1°7E 90 D6
Lessay France 49°14N 1°30W 70 C5
Lesse → Belgium 50°15N 4°54E 69 D4
Lesse et Lomme ⌓ Belgium 50°8N 5°9E 69 D5
Lessebo Sweden 56°45N 15°16E 63 H9
Lesser Antilles W. Indies 15°0N 61°0W 183 D7
Lesser Slave L. Canada 55°30N 115°25W 162 B5
Lesser Sunda Is. Indonesia 8°0S 120°0E 119 F6
Lessines Belgium 50°42N 3°50E 69 D3
Lester B. Pearson Int., Toronto ✈ (YYZ) Canada 43°46N 79°35W 174 C5
Lestock Canada 51°19N 103°59W 163 C8
Lesueur I. Australia 13°50S 127°17E 148 B4
Lesueur △ Australia 30°11S 115°10E 149 F2
Lésvos = Lesbos Greece 39°10N 26°20E 99 B8
Leszno Poland 51°50N 16°30E 83 G3
Letaba S. Africa 23°59S 31°50E 145 B5
Letälven → Sweden 59°5N 14°20E 62 E8
Létavértes Hungary 47°23N 21°55E 80 C6
Letchworth U.K. 51°59N 0°13W 67 F7
Letea, Ostrov Romania 45°18N 29°20E 81 E14
Lethbridge Canada 49°45N 112°45W 162 D6
Lethem Guyana 3°20N 59°50W 186 C7
Leti, Kepulauan Indonesia 8°10S 128°0E 119 F7
Leti Is. = Leti, Kepulauan Indonesia 8°10S 128°0E 119 F7
Letiahau → Botswana 21°16S 24°0E 144 B3
Leticia Colombia 4°9S 70°0W 186 D5
Leting China 39°23N 118°55E 115 E10
Letjiesbos S. Africa 32°34S 22°16E 144 D3
Letlhakane Botswana 21°27S 25°30E 144 B4
Letlhakeng Botswana 24°0S 24°59E 144 B3
Letpadan Burma 17°45N 95°45E 123 L19
Letpan Burma 19°28N 94°10E 123 K19
Letsôk-aw Kyun Burma 11°30N 98°25E 121 G2
Letterkenny Ireland 54°57N 7°45W 64 B4
Leu Romania 44°10N 24°0E 81 F9
Leucadia U.S.A. 33°4N 117°18W 171 M9
Leucate France 42°56N 3°3E 72 F7
Leucate, Étang de France 42°50N 3°0E 72 F7
Leuchars U.K. 56°24N 2°53W 65 E6
Leuk Switz. 46°19N 7°37E 77 J3
Leuşeni Moldova 46°49N 28°12E 81 D13
Leuser, Gunung Indonesia 3°46N 97°12E 118 D1
Leutkirch Germany 47°49N 10°1E 77 H6
Leuven Belgium 50°52N 4°42E 69 D4
Leuze-en-Hainaut Belgium 50°36N 3°37E 69 D3
Lev Tolstoy Russia 53°13N 39°29E 84 F10
Levan Albania 40°40N 19°28E 96 F3
Levanger Norway 63°45N 11°19E 60 E14
Levant, Î. du France 43°3N 6°28E 73 E10
Lévanto Italy 44°10N 9°38E 92 D6
Lévanzo Italy 38°0N 12°20E 94 D5
Levelland U.S.A. 33°35N 102°23W 176 E3
Leven U.K. 56°12N 3°0W 65 E6
Leven, L. U.K. 56°12N 3°22W 65 E5
Leveque C. Australia 16°20S 123°0E 148 C3
Leverano Italy 40°17N 18°0E 95 B10
Leverkusen Germany 51°1N 7°1E 76 D3
Levice Slovak Rep. 48°13N 18°35E 79 C11
Lévico Terme Italy 46°0N 11°18E 93 C8
Levie France 41°40N 9°7E 73 G13
Levier France 46°58N 6°8E 71 F13
Levin N.Z. 40°37S 175°18E 154 G4
Lévis Canada 46°48N 71°9W 165 C5
Levis, L. Canada 62°37N 117°58W 162 A5
Levitha Greece 37°0N 26°28E 99 D8
Levittown N.Y., U.S.A. 40°44N 73°31W 175 F11
Levittown Pa., U.S.A. 40°9N 74°51W 175 F10
Levka Bulgaria 41°52N 26°15E 97 E10
Levka Oros Greece 35°18N 24°3E 101 D6
Levkás = Lefkada Greece 38°40N 20°43E 98 C2
Levoča Slovak Rep. 49°2N 20°35E 79 B13
Levroux France 46°59N 1°38E 71 F8
Levski Bulgaria 43°21N 25°10E 97 C9
Levskigrad = Karlovo Bulgaria 42°38N 24°47E 97 D8
Levuka Fiji 17°34S 179°0E 154 a
Lewes U.K. 50°52N 0°1E 67 G8
Lewes U.S.A. 38°46N 75°9W 173 F16
Lewin Brzeski Poland 50°45N 17°37E 83 H4
Lewis U.K. 58°9N 6°40W 65 C2
Lewis → U.S.A. 45°51N 122°48W 170 E4
Lewis, Butt of U.K. 58°31N 6°16W 65 C2
Lewis and Clark ⌓ U.S.A. 46°8N 123°53W 170 D3
Lewis Pass N.Z. 42°31S 172°11E 155 C7
Lewis Ra. Australia 20°3S 128°50E 148 D4
Lewis Range U.S.A. 48°5N 113°5W 168 B7
Lewis Run U.S.A. 41°52N 78°40W 174 E6
Lewisburg Pa., U.S.A. 40°58N 76°54W 174 F8
Lewisburg Tenn., U.S.A. 35°27N 86°48W 177 D11
Lewisburg W. Va., U.S.A. 37°48N 80°27W 173 G13
Lewisporte Canada 49°15N 55°3W 165 C8
Lewiston Idaho, U.S.A. 46°25N 117°1W 168 C5
Lewiston Maine, U.S.A. 44°6N 70°13W 173 C18
Lewiston N.Y., U.S.A. 43°11N 79°3W 174 C5
Lewistown Mont., U.S.A. 47°4N 109°26W 168 C9
Lewistown Pa., U.S.A. 40°36N 77°34W 174 F7
Lexington Ga., U.S.A. 33°52N 83°7W 178 B6
Lexington Ill., U.S.A. 40°39N 88°47W 172 E9
Lexington Ky., U.S.A. 38°3N 84°30W 173 F11
Lexington Mich., U.S.A. 43°16N 82°32W 174 C2
Lexington Mo., U.S.A. 39°11N 93°52W 172 F7
Lexington N.C., U.S.A. 35°49N 80°15W 177 D14
Lexington N.Y., U.S.A. 42°15N 74°22W 175 D10
Lexington Nebr., U.S.A. 40°47N 99°45W 172 E4
Lexington Ohio, U.S.A. 40°41N 82°35W 174 F2
Lexington S.C., U.S.A. 33°59N 81°11W 178 B8
Lexington Tenn., U.S.A. 35°39N 88°24W 177 D10
Lexington Va., U.S.A. 37°47N 79°27W 173 G14
Lexington Park U.S.A. 38°16N 76°27W 173 F15
Leyburn U.K. 54°19N 1°48W 66 C6
Leye China 24°48N 106°29E 116 E6
Leyland U.K. 53°42N 2°43W 66 D5
Leyte □ Phil. 11°0N 125°0E 119 B7
Leżajsk Poland 50°16N 22°25E 83 H9
Lezay France 46°15N 0°1W 72 B3
Lezhë Albania 41°47N 19°39E 96 E3
Lezhi China 30°19N 104°58E 116 B5
Lézignan-Corbières France 43°13N 2°43E 72 E6
Lezoux France 45°49N 3°21E 72 C7
Lgov Russia 51°42N 35°16E 85 G8
Lhasa China 29°25N 90°58E 110 F7
Lhazê China 29°5N 87°38E 110 F6
L'Hermite, I. Chile 55°50S 68°0W 192 E3
Lhokkruet Indonesia 4°55N 95°24E 118 D1
Lhokseumawe Indonesia 5°10N 97°10E 118 C1
L'Hospitalet de Llobregat Spain 41°21N 2°6E 90 D7
Li Thailand 17°48N 98°57E 120 D2
Li Jiang → China 24°40N 110°40E 117 E8
Li Jiang △ China 24°38N 110°38E 117 E8
Li Shan China 35°30N 111°56E 114 G6
Li Shui → China 29°24N 112°1E 117 C9
Li Xian Gansu, China 34°10N 105°5E 114 G3
Li Xian Hebei, China 38°30N 115°35E 114 E8
Li Xian Hunan, China 29°36N 111°42E 117 C8
Liadi Greece 36°50N 26°11E 99 E8
Liancheng China 25°42N 116°40E 117 E11
Liancourt Rocks Asia 37°15N 131°52E 113 F5
Lianga Phil. 8°38N 126°6E 119 C7
Liangcheng Nei Monggol Zizhiqu, China 40°28N 112°25E 114 D7
Liangcheng Shandong, China 35°32N 119°37E 115 G10
Liangdang China 33°56N 106°18E 114 H4
Lianghe China 24°50N 98°20E 116 E2
Lianghekou China 29°11N 108°44E 116 C7
Liangping China 30°38N 107°47E 116 B6
Liangpran Indonesia 1°4N 114°23E 118 D4
Lianhua China 27°3N 113°54E 117 D9
Lianhua Shan China 23°40N 115°48E 117 F10
Lianjiang Fujian, China 26°12N 119°27E 117 D12
Lianjiang Guangdong, China 21°40N 110°20E 117 G8
Lianping China 24°26N 114°30E 117 E10
Lianshan China 24°38N 112°8E 117 E9
Lianshanguan China 40°53N 123°43E 115 D12
Lianshui China 33°42N 119°20E 115 H10
Lianyuan China 27°40N 111°38E 117 D8
Lianyungang China 34°40N 119°11E 115 G10
Lianzhou China 24°51N 112°22E 117 E9
Liao He → China 41°0N 121°50E 115 D11
Liaocheng China 36°28N 115°58E 114 F8
Liaodong Bandao China 40°0N 122°30E 115 E12
Liaodong Wan China 40°20N 121°10E 115 D11
Liaoning □ China 41°40N 122°30E 115 D12
Liaotung, G. of = Liaodong Wan China 40°20N 121°10E 115 D11
Liaoyang China 41°15N 122°58E 115 D12
Liaoyuan China 42°58N 125°2E 115 C13
Liaozhong China 41°23N 122°50E 115 D12
Liapades Greece 39°42N 19°40E 101 A3
Liard → Canada 61°51N 121°18W 162 A4
Liard River Canada 59°25N 126°5W 162 B3
Liari Pakistan 25°37N 66°30E 124 G2
Libanggaon Nepal 28°18N 82°38E 125 E10
Libau = Liepāja Latvia 56°30N 21°0E 82 B8
Libby U.S.A. 48°23N 115°33W 168 B6
Libenge Dem. Rep. of the Congo 3°40N 18°55E 140 D3
Liberal U.S.A. 37°3N 100°55W 172 G3
Liberdade Brazil 10°5S 70°20W 188 C3
Liberec Czech Rep. 50°47N 15°7E 78 A8
Liberecký □ Czech Rep. 50°45N 15°0E 78 A8
Liberia Costa Rica 10°40N 85°30W 182 D2
Liberia ■ W. Afr. 6°30N 9°30W 138 D3
Libertador □ Chile 34°15S 70°45W 190 C1
Liberty Mo., U.S.A. 39°15N 94°25W 172 F6
Liberty N.Y., U.S.A. 41°48N 74°45W 175 E10
Liberty Pa., U.S.A. 41°34N 77°6W 174 E7
Liberty Tex., U.S.A. 30°3N 94°48W 176 F7
Liberty-Newark Int. ✈ (EWR) U.S.A. 40°42N 74°10W 175 F10
Libiąż Poland 50°7N 19°21E 83 H6
Lībīya, Sahrâ' Africa 25°0N 25°0E 135 C10
Libo China 25°22N 107°53E 116 E6
Libobo, Tanjung Indonesia 0°54S 128°28E 119 E7
Libode S. Africa 31°33S 29°2E 145 D4
Libohovë Albania 40°3N 20°10E 96 F4
Libong, Ko Thailand 7°15N 99°23E 121 J2
Libourne France 44°55N 0°14W 72 D3
Libramont Belgium 49°55N 5°23E 69 E5
Librazhd Albania 41°12N 20°22E 96 E4
Libreville Gabon 0°25N 9°26E 140 D1
Libya ■ N. Afr. 27°0N 17°0E 135 C9
Libyan Desert = Lībīya, Sahrâ' Africa 25°0N 25°0E 135 C10
Libyan Plateau = Ed Déffa Egypt 30°40N 26°30E 137 A2
Licantén Chile 35°55S 72°0W 190 D1
Licata Italy 37°6N 13°56E 94 E6
Lice Turkey 38°27N 40°39E 105 C9
Licheng China 36°28N 113°20E 114 F7
Lichfield U.K. 52°41N 1°49W 67 E6
Lichinga Mozam. 13°13S 35°11E 143 E4
Lichtenburg S. Africa 26°8S 26°8E 144 C4
Lichtenfels Germany 50°8N 11°4E 77 E7
Lichuan Hubei, China 30°18N 108°57E 116 B7
Lichuan Jiangxi, China 27°18N 116°55E 117 D11
Licking → U.S.A. 39°6N 84°30W 173 F11
Licosa, Punta Italy 40°15N 14°54E 95 B7
Licungo → Mozam. 17°40S 37°15E 143 F4
Lida Belarus 53°53N 25°15E 75 B13
Liden Sweden 62°42N 16°48E 62 B10
Lidhult Sweden 56°50N 13°27E 63 H7
Lidköping Sweden 58°31N 13°7E 63 F7
Lido Niger 12°54N 3°44E 139 C5
Lido di Roma = Ostia, Lido di Italy 41°43N 12°17E 93 G9
Lidoriki Greece 38°32N 22°12E 98 C4
Lidzbark Poland 53°15N 19°49E 83 E6
Lidzbark Warmiński Poland 54°7N 20°34E 82 D7
Liebenwalde Germany 52°52N 13°24E 76 C9
Lieberose Germany 51°59N 14°17E 76 D10
Liebig, Mt. Australia 23°18S 131°22E 148 D5
Liebling Romania 45°36N 21°20E 80 E6
Liechtenstein ■ Europe 47°8N 9°35E 77 H5
Liège Belgium 50°38N 5°35E 69 D5
Liège □ Belgium 50°32N 5°35E 69 D5
Liegnitz = Legnica Poland 51°12N 16°10E 83 G3
Lieksa Finland 63°18N 30°2E 60 E24
Lienart Dem. Rep. of the Congo 3°3N 25°31E 142 B2
Lienyünchiangshih = Lianyungang China 34°40N 119°11E 115 G10
Lienz Austria 46°50N 12°46E 78 E5
Liepāja Latvia 56°30N 21°0E 82 B8
Liepāja □ Latvia 56°30N 21°30E 82 B8
Liepājas ezers Latvia 56°27N 21°3E 82 B8
Lier Belgium 51°7N 4°34E 69 C4
Liernais France 47°13N 4°16E 71 E11
Lierne △ Norway 64°20N 13°50E 60 D15
Liești Romania 45°38N 27°34E 81 E12
Lietuva = Lithuania ■ Europe 55°30N 24°0E 84 E2
Liévin France 50°24N 2°47E 71 B9
Lièvre → Canada 45°31N 75°26W 164 C4
Liezen Austria 47°34N 14°15E 78 D7
Liffey → Ireland 53°21N 6°13W 64 C5
Lifford Ireland 54°51N 7°29W 64 B4
Liffré France 48°12N 1°30W 70 D5
Lifudzin Russia 44°21N 134°58E 112 B7
Lighthouse Point U.S.A. 26°15N 80°7W 179 J9
Lighthouse Pt. U.S.A. 29°54N 84°21W 178 F5
Lightning Ridge Australia 29°22S 148°0E 151 D4
Lignano Sabbiadoro Italy 45°42N 13°9E 93 C10
Ligny-en-Barrois France 48°36N 5°20E 71 D12
Ligonha → Mozam. 16°54S 39°9E 143 F4
Ligonier U.S.A. 40°15N 79°14W 174 F5
Ligourio Greece 37°37N 23°2E 98 D5
Ligueil France 47°2N 0°49E 70 E7
Liguria □ Italy 44°30N 8°50E 92 D5
Ligurian Sea Medit. S. 43°20N 9°0E 92 E5
Lihou Reefs and Cays Australia 17°25S 151°40E 150 B5
Lihué Calel △ Argentina 38°0S 65°10W 190 D2
Lijiang China 26°55N 100°20E 116 D3
Lik → Laos 18°31N 102°30E 120 C4
Likasi Dem. Rep. of the Congo 10°55S 26°48E 143 E2
Likenäs Sweden 60°37N 13°3E 62 D7
Likhoslavl Russia 57°12N 35°30E 84 D8
Likhovskoy Russia 48°10N 40°10E 87 F5
Likoma I. Malawi 12°3S 34°45E 143 E3
Likumburu Tanzania 9°43S 35°8E 143 D4
L'Île-Bouchard France 47°7N 0°26E 70 E7
L'Île-Rousse France 42°38N 8°57E 73 F12
Liling China 27°42N 113°29E 117 D9
Lilla Edet Sweden 58°9N 12°8E 63 F6
Lille France 50°38N 3°3E 71 B10
Lille Bælt Denmark 55°20N 9°45E 63 J3
Lillebonne France 49°30N 0°32E 70 C7
Lillehammer Norway 61°8N 10°30E 60 F14
Lillesand Norway 58°15N 8°23E 61 G13
Lillhärdal Sweden 61°51N 14°5E 62 C8
Lillian Pt. Australia 27°40S 126°6E 149 E4
Lillo Spain 39°45N 3°20W 88 F7
Lillooet Canada 50°44N 121°57W 162 C4
Lillooet → Canada 49°15N 121°57W 162 D4
Lilongwe Malawi 14°0S 33°48E 143 E3
Liloy Phil. 8°4N 122°39E 119 C6
Lim → Europe 43°45N 19°15E 96 C3
Lim Chu Kang Singapore 1°26N 103°43E 121 d
Lima Indonesia 3°39S 127°58E 119 E7
Lima Peru 12°3S 77°2W 188 C2
Lima Mont., U.S.A. 44°38N 112°36W 168 D7
Lima N.Y., U.S.A. 42°54N 77°36W 174 D7
Lima Ohio, U.S.A. 40°44N 84°6W 173 E11
Lima □ Peru 12°3S 77°3W 188 C2
Lima → Portugal 41°41N 8°50W 88 D2
Liman Russia 45°45N 47°12E 87 H8
Limanowa Poland 49°42N 20°22E 83 J7
Limassol Cyprus 34°42N 33°1E 101 E12
Limavady U.K. 55°3N 6°56W 64 A5
Limay → Argentina 39°0S 68°0W 192 A3
Limay Mahuida Argentina 37°10S 66°45W 190 D2
Limbach-Oberfrohna Germany 50°52N 12°43E 76 E8
Limbang Malaysia 4°42N 115°6E 118 D5
Limbara, Mte. Italy 40°51N 9°10E 94 B2
Limbaži Latvia 57°31N 24°42E 84 D3
Limbdi India 22°34N 71°51E 124 H4
Limbe Cameroon 4°1N 9°10E 139 E6
Limburg Germany 50°22N 8°4E 77 E4
Limburg □ Belgium 51°2N 5°25E 69 C5
Limburg □ Neths. 51°20N 5°55E 69 C5
Limedsforsen Sweden 60°52N 13°25E 62 D7
Limeira Brazil 22°35S 47°28W 191 A6
Limenaria Greece 40°38N 24°32E 97 F8
Limenas Chersonisou Greece 35°18N 25°21E 99 F7
Limerick Ireland 52°40N 8°37W 64 D3
Limerick U.S.A. 43°41N 70°48W 175 C14
Limerick □ Ireland 52°30N 8°50W 64 D3
Limestone U.S.A. 42°2N 78°38W 174 D6
Limestone → Canada 56°31N 94°7W 163 B10
Limfjorden Denmark 56°55N 9°0E 63 H3
Limia = Lima → Portugal 41°41N 8°50W 88 D2
Limingen Norway 64°48N 13°35E 60 D15
Limmared Sweden 57°34N 13°20E 63 G7
Limmen ◎ Australia 15°15S 135°30E 150 B2
Limmen Bight Australia 14°40S 135°35E 150 A2
Limmen Bight → Australia 15°7S 135°44E 150 B2
Limni Greece 38°43N 23°18E 98 C5
Limnos Greece 39°50N 25°5E 99 B7
Limoeiro Brazil 7°52S 35°27W 189 B3
Limoeiro do Norte Brazil 5°5S 38°0W 189 B3
Limoges Canada 45°20N 75°16W 175 A9
Limoges France 45°50N 1°15E 72 C5
Limón Costa Rica 10°0N 83°2W 182 E3
Limon U.S.A. 39°16N 103°41W 168 G12
Limone Italy 45°48N 10°47E 92 C7
Limone Piemonte Italy 44°12N 7°34E 92 D4
Limousin □ France 45°30N 1°30E 72 C5
Limousin, Plateaux du France 45°45N 1°15E 72 C5
Limoux France 43°4N 2°12E 72 E6
Limpopo □ S. Africa 24°5S 29°0E 145 B4
Limpopo → Africa 25°5S 33°30E 145 C5
Limuru Kenya 1°2S 36°35E 140 E7
Lin Xian China 37°57N 110°58E 114 F6
Lin'an China 30°15N 119°42E 117 B12
Linares Chile 35°50S 71°40W 190 D1
Linares Mexico 24°52N 99°34W 181 C5
Linares Spain 38°10N 3°40W 89 G7
Linaria Greece 38°52N 24°31E 98 C6
Linaro, Capo Italy 42°2N 11°50E 93 F8
Linas Mte. Italy 39°25N 8°38E 94 C1
Linate, Milano ✈ (LIN) Italy 45°27N 9°16E 92 C6
Lincang China 23°58N 100°1E 116 F3
Lincheng China 37°25N 114°30E 114 F8
Linchuan China 27°57N 116°15E 117 D11
Lincoln = Beamsville Canada 43°12N 79°28W 174 C5
Lincoln Argentina 34°55S 61°30W 190 C3
Lincoln N.Z. 43°38S 172°30E 155 D7
Lincoln U.K. 53°14N 0°32W 66 D7
Lincoln Calif., U.S.A. 38°54N 121°17W 170 G5
Lincoln Ill., U.S.A. 40°9N 89°22W 172 E9
Lincoln Kans., U.S.A. 39°3N 98°9W 172 F4
Lincoln Maine, U.S.A. 45°22N 68°30W 173 C19
Lincoln N.H., U.S.A. 44°3N 71°40W 175 B13
Lincoln N. Mex., U.S.A. 33°30N 105°23W 169 K11
Lincoln Nebr., U.S.A. 40°49N 96°41W 172 E5
Lincoln City U.S.A. 44°57N 124°1W 168 D1
Lincoln Hav = Lincoln Sea Arctic 84°0N 55°0W 57 A5
Lincoln Park U.S.A. 32°52N 84°20W 178 C5
Lincoln Sea Arctic 84°0N 55°0W 57 A5
Lincolnshire □ U.K. 53°14N 0°32W 66 D7
Lincolnshire Wolds U.K. 53°26N 0°13W 66 D7
Lincolnton Ga., U.S.A. 33°48N 82°29W 178 B7
Lincolnton N.C., U.S.A. 35°29N 81°16W 177 D14
Lind U.S.A. 46°58N 118°37W 168 C4
Linda U.S.A. 39°8N 121°34W 170 F5
Lindale U.S.A. 34°11N 85°11W 178 A4
Lindau Germany 47°33N 9°42E 77 H5
Lindeman I. Australia 20°27S 149°3E 150 b
Lindeman Islands △ Australia 20°28S 149°5E 150 b
Linden Guyana 6°0N 58°10W 186 B7
Linden Ala., U.S.A. 32°18N 87°48W 177 E11
Linden Calif., U.S.A. 38°1N 121°5W 170 G5
Linden Tex., U.S.A. 33°1N 94°22W 176 E7
Lindenhurst U.S.A. 40°41N 73°23W 175 F11
Lindenow Fjord Greenland 60°30N 43°25W 57 E6
Lindesberg Sweden 59°36N 15°15E 62 E9
Lindesnes Norway 57°58N 7°3E 61 H12
Lindi Tanzania 9°58S 39°38E 143 D4
Lindi □ Tanzania 9°40S 38°30E 143 D4
Lindi → Dem. Rep. of the Congo 0°33N 25°5E 142 B2
Lindley U.S.A. 42°1N 77°8W 174 D7
Lindö Sweden 58°37N 16°15E 63 F10
Lindome Sweden 57°35N 12°5E 63 G6
Lindos Greece 36°6N 28°4E 101 C10
Lindos, Akra Greece 36°4N 28°10E 101 C10
Lindoso Portugal 41°52N 8°11W 88 D2
Lindow Germany 52°58N 12°59E 76 C8
Lindsay Canada 44°22N 78°43W 174 B6
Lindsay Calif., U.S.A. 36°12N 119°5W 170 J7
Lindsay Okla., U.S.A. 34°50N 97°38W 176 D6
Lindsborg U.S.A. 38°35N 97°40W 172 F5
Lindsdal Sweden 56°44N 16°18E 63 H10
Line Islands Pac. Oc. 7°0N 160°0W 157 H12
Linesville U.S.A. 41°39N 80°26W 174 E4
Lineville U.S.A. 33°19N 85°45W 178 B4
Linfen China 36°3N 111°30E 114 F6
Ling Xian Hunan, China 26°29N 113°48E 117 D9
Ling Xian Shandong, China 37°22N 116°30E 114 F9
Lingal India 16°17N 78°31E 127 F4
Linganamakki Res. India 14°6N 74°52E 127 G2
Lingao China 19°56N 109°42E 117 a
Lingayen Phil. 16°1N 120°14E 119 A6
Lingayen G. Phil. 16°10N 120°15E 119 A6
Lingbao China 34°31N 110°51E 114 G6
Lingbi China 33°33N 117°33E 115 H9
Lingbo Sweden 61°3N 16°41E 62 C10
Lingchuan Guangxi Zhuangzu, China 25°26N 110°21E 117 E8
Lingchuan Shanxi, China 35°45N 113°12E 114 G7
Lingding Yang China 22°25N 113°44E 111 a
Lingen Germany 52°31N 7°19E 76 C3
Lingga Indonesia 0°12S 104°37E 118 E2
Lingga, Kepulauan Indonesia 0°10S 104°30E 118 E2
Lingga Arch. = Lingga, Kepulauan Indonesia 0°10S 104°30E 118 E2
Linghai China 41°11N 121°22E 115 D11
Linghed Sweden 60°48N 15°55E 62 D9
Linghem Sweden 58°26N 15°47E 63 F9
Lingle U.S.A. 42°8N 104°21W 168 E11
Lingqiu China 39°28N 114°22E 114 E8
Lingshan China 22°25N 109°18E 116 F7
Lingshi China 36°48N 111°48E 114 F6
Lingshou China 38°20N 114°20E 114 E8
Lingshui China 18°27N 110°0E 117 a
Lingsugur India 16°10N 76°31E 127 F3
Lingtai China 35°0N 107°40E 114 G4
Linguère Senegal 15°25N 15°5W 138 B1
Lingui China 25°12N 110°2E 117 E8
Lingwu China 38°6N 106°20E 114 E4
Lingyuan China 41°10N 119°15E 115 D10
Lingyun China 25°2N 106°35E 116 E6
Linhai China 28°50N 121°8E 117 C13
Linhares Brazil 19°25S 40°4W 189 D2
Linhe China 40°48N 107°20E 114 D4
Linjiang China 41°50N 127°0E 115 D14
Linköping Sweden 58°28N 15°36E 63 F9
Linkou China 45°15N 130°18E 115 B16
Linli China 29°27N 111°30E 117 C8
Linnansaari △ Finland 62°3N 28°40E 60 E23
Linnhe, L. U.K. 56°36N 5°25W 65 E3
Linqi China 35°45N 113°52E 114 G7
Linqing China 36°50N 115°42E 114 F8
Linqu China 36°25N 118°30E 115 F10
Linquan China 33°5N 115°17E 117 A10
Lins Brazil 21°40S 49°44W 191 A6
Linshu China 34°53N 118°38E 115 G10
Linshui China 30°21N 106°57E 116 B6
Linstead Jamaica 18°8N 77°2W 182 a
Lintao China 35°26N 103°58E 114 G2
Linth → Switz. 47°7N 9°7E 77 H5
Linthal Switz. 46°54N 9°0E 77 J5
Linton Ind., U.S.A. 39°2N 87°10W 172 F10
Linton N. Dak., U.S.A. 46°16N 100°14W 172 B3
Lintong China 34°20N 109°10E 114 G5
Linwood Canada 43°35N 80°43W 174 C4
Linwu China 25°19N 112°31E 117 E9
Linxi Hebei, China 39°42N 118°26E 115 E10
Linxi Liaoning, China 43°36N 118°2E 115 C10
Linxia China 35°36N 103°10E 110 D9
Linxiang China 29°28N 113°23E 117 C9
Linyanti → Africa 17°50S 25°5E 144 A4
Linyi Shandong, China 37°13N 116°54E 114 F9
Linyi Shandong, China 35°5N 118°21E 115 G10
Linying China 33°48N 113°56E 114 H7
Linz Austria 48°18N 14°18E 78 C7
Linz Germany 50°34N 7°17E 76 E3
Linzhenzhen China 36°30N 109°59E 114 F5
Linzhou China 36°4N 113°49E 114 F7
Linzi China 36°50N 118°20E 115 F10
Lion, G. du France 43°10N 4°0E 72 E7
Lioni Italy 40°52N 15°11E 95 B8
Lions, G. of = Lion, G. du France 43°10N 4°0E 72 E7

Lion's Den *Zimbabwe* 17°15S 30°5E **143** F3
Lion's Head *Canada* 44°58N 81°15W **174** B3
Liozno = Lyozna *Belarus* 55°N 30°50E **84** E6
Lipa *Phil.* 13°57N 121°10E **119** B6
Lipali *Mozam.* 15°50S 35°50E **143** F4
Lipany *Slovak Rep.* 49°9N 20°58E **79** B13
Lipari *Italy* 38°26N 14°58E **95** D7
Lipari, I. *Italy* 38°29N 14°56E **95** D7
Lipari, Is. = Eólie, Ís.
  Italy 38°30N 14°57E **95** D7
Lipcani *Moldova* 48°14N 26°48E **81** B11
Liperi *Finland* 62°31N 29°24E **60** E23
Lipetsk *Russia* 52°37N 39°35E **85** E10
Lipetsk □ *Russia* 52°50N 38°50E **86** E4
Lipiany *Poland* 53°2N 14°58E **83** E1
Liping *China* 26°15N 109°7E **117** C10
Lipisi *Greece* 37°19N 26°50E **99** D8
Lipjan *Kosovo* 42°31N 21°7E **96** D5
Lipkany = Lipcani
  Moldova 48°14N 26°48E **81** B11
Lipník nad Bečvou
  Czech Rep. 49°32N 17°36E **79** B10
Lipno *Poland* 52°49N 19°15E **83** F6
Lipova *Romania* 46°8N 21°42E **80** D6
Lippe → *Germany* 51°39N 6°36E **76** D2
Lippstadt *Germany* 51°41N 8°22E **76** D4
Lipscomb *U.S.A.* 36°14N 100°16W **176** C4
Lipsk *Poland* 53°44N 23°24E **82** E10
Lipsko *Poland* 51°9N 21°40E **83** G8
Liptovský Hrádok
  Slovak Rep. 49°2N 19°44E **79** B12
Liptovský Mikuláš
  Slovak Rep. 49°6N 19°35E **79** B12
Liptrap, C. *Australia* 38°50S 145°55E **153** E6
Lipu *China* 24°30N 110°22E **117** E8
Lira *Uganda* 2°17N 32°57E **142** B3
Liri → *Italy* 41°25N 13°52E **94** A6
Liria = Lliria *Spain* 39°37N 0°35W **91** F4
Liri → *Italy* 41°25N 13°52E **94** A6
Lisakovsk *Kazakhstan* 52°33N 62°37E **108** D6
Lisala
  Dem. Rep. of the Congo 2°12N 21°38E **140** D4
Lisboa *Portugal* 38°42N 9°8W **89** G1
Lisboa □ *Portugal* 39°0N 9°12W **89** F1
Lisboa ✈ (LIS) *Portugal* 38°46N 9°8W **89** G1
Lisbon = Lisboa *Portugal* 38°42N 9°8W **89** G1
Lisbon *N. Dak., U.S.A.* 46°27N 97°41W **172** B5
Lisbon *N.H., U.S.A.* 44°13N 71°55W **175** B13
Lisbon *N.Y., U.S.A.* 44°43N 75°19W **175** B9
Lisbon *Ohio, U.S.A.* 40°46N 80°46W **174** F4
Lisbon Falls *U.S.A.* 44°0N 70°4W **173** D18
Lisburn *U.K.* 54°31N 6°3W **64** B5
Lisburne, C. *U.S.A.* 68°53N 166°13W **166** B6
Liscannor B. *Ireland* 52°55N 9°24W **64** D2
Liscia → *Italy* 41°11N 9°9E **94** A2
Lisdoonvarna *Ireland* 53°2N 9°18W **64** C2
Lishe Jiang → *China* 24°15N 101°35E **116** E3
Lishi *China* 37°31N 111°8E **114** F6
Lishu *China* 43°20N 124°18E **115** C13
Lishui *Jiangsu, China* 31°38N 119°2E **117** B12
Lishui *Zhejiang, China* 28°28N 119°54E **117** C12
Lisianski I. *U.S.A.* 26°2N 174°0W **167** K5
Lisichansk = Lysychansk
  Ukraine 48°55N 38°30E **85** H10
Lisieux *France* 49°10N 0°12E **70** C7
Liski *Russia* 51°3N 39°30E **85** G10
L'Isle-Jourdain *Gers, France* 43°36N 1°5E **72** E5
L'Isle-Jourdain *Vienne,*
  France 46°13N 0°31E **72** B4
L'Isle-sur-la-Sorgue *France* 43°54N 5°2E **73** E9
Lisle-sur-Tarn *France* 43°52N 1°49E **72** E5
Lismore *Australia* 28°44S 153°21E **151** D5
Lismore *Ireland* 52°8N 7°55W **64** D4
Lissos → *Greece* 41°15N 25°40E **97** D11
Lista *Norway* 58°7N 6°39E **61** G12
Lister, Mt. *Antarctica* 78°0S 162°0E **55** D11
Liston *Australia* 28°39S 152°6E **151** D5
Listowel *Canada* 43°44N 80°58W **174** C4
Listowel *Ireland* 52°27N 9°29W **64** D2
Lit *Sweden* 63°19N 14°51E **62** A8
Lit-et-Mixe *France* 44°2N 1°15W **72** D2
Litang *Guangxi Zhuangzu,*
  China 23°12N 109°8E **116** F7
Litang *Sichuan, China* 30°1N 100°17E **116** B3
Litang Qu → *China* 28°4N 101°32E **116** C3
Litani → *Lebanon* 33°20N 35°15E **130** B4
Litchfield *Australia* 36°18S 142°52E **152** D5
Litchfield *Calif., U.S.A.* 40°24N 120°23W **176** E6
Litchfield *Conn.,*
  U.S.A. 41°45N 73°11W **175** E11
Litchfield *Ill., U.S.A.* 39°11N 89°39W **172** F9
Litchfield *Minn., U.S.A.* 45°8N 94°32W **172** C6
Litchfield △ *Australia* 13°14S 131°1E **148** B5
Liteni *Romania* 47°32N 26°32E **81** C11
Lithgow *Australia* 33°25S 150°8E **153** E9
Lithino, Ákra *Greece* 34°55N 24°44E **101** E6
Lithuania ■ *Europe* 55°30N 24°0E **84** E2
Litija *Slovenia* 46°3N 14°50E **93** B11
Lititz *U.S.A.* 40°9N 76°18W **175** F8
Litochoro *Greece* 40°8N 22°34E **96** F6
Litoměřice *Czech Rep.* 50°33N 14°10E **78** A7
Litomyšl *Czech Rep.* 49°52N 16°20E **79** B9
Litschau *Austria* 48°58N 15°4E **78** C8
Little Abaco *Bahamas* 26°50N 77°30W **182** A4
Little Andaman I.
  India 10°45N 92°30E **127** J11
Little Aral Sea = Northern Aral
  Sea *Kazakhstan* 46°20N 60°30E **108** C6
Little Barrier I. *N.Z.* 36°12S 175°8E **154** C4
Little Basses *Sri Lanka* 6°24N 81°43E **127** L5
Little Belt Mts. *U.S.A.* 46°40N 110°45W **168** C8
Little Bighorn Battlefield
  U.S.A. 45°34N 107°25W **168** D10
Little Blue → *U.S.A.* 39°42N 96°41W **172** F5
Little Buffalo →
  Canada 61°0N 113°46W **162** A6
Little Cayman
  Cayman Is. 19°41N 80°3W **182** C3
Little Churchill →
  Canada 57°30N 95°22W **163** B9
Little Coco I. *Burma* 14°0N 93°13E **127** H11
Little Colorado →
  U.S.A. 36°12N 111°48W **169** H8
Little Current *Canada* 45°55N 82°0W **164** C3
Little Current →
  Canada 50°57N 84°36W **164** B3
Little Desert △
  Australia 37°25S 141°30E **152** D4
Little Diomede I.
  U.S.A. 65°45N 168°56W **166** B6

Little Falls *Minn.,*
  U.S.A. 45°59N 94°22W **172** C6
Little Falls *N.Y., U.S.A.* 43°3N 74°51W **175** C10
Little Fork → *U.S.A.* 48°31N 93°35W **172** A7
Little Grand Rapids
  Canada 52°0N 95°29W **163** C9
Little Humboldt →
  U.S.A. 41°1N 117°43W **168** F5
Little Inagua I.
  Bahamas 21°40N 73°50W **183** B5
Little Karoo *S. Africa* 33°45S 21°0E **144** D3
Little Khingan Mts. = Xiao
  Hinggan Ling *China* 49°0N 127°0E **111** B14
Little Lake *U.S.A.* 35°56N 117°55W **171** K9
Little Laut Is. = Laut Kecil,
  Kepulauan *Indonesia* 4°45S 115°40E **118** E5
Little Mecatina = Petit-
  Mécatina → *Canada* 50°40N 59°30W **165** B8
Little Minch *U.K.* 57°35N 6°45W **65** D2
Little Missouri →
  U.S.A. 47°36N 102°25W **172** B2
Little Nicobar *India* 7°20N 93°40E **127** L11
Little Ouse → *U.K.* 52°22N 1°12E **67** E9
Little Rann *India* 23°25N 71°25E **124** H4
Little Red → *U.S.A.* 35°11N 91°27W **176** D9
Little River *N.Z.* 43°45S 172°49E **155** D7
Little Rock *U.S.A.* 34°45N 92°17W **176** D8
Little Ruaha → *Tanzania* 7°57S 37°53E **142** D4
Little Sable Pt. *U.S.A.* 43°38N 86°33W **172** D10
Little Scarcies →
  S. Leone 8°50N 13°10W **138** D2
Little Sioux → *U.S.A.* 41°48N 96°4W **172** E5
Little Smoky →
  Canada 54°44N 117°11W **162** C5
Little Snake →
  U.S.A. 40°27N 108°26W **168** F9
Little Tobago
  Trin. & Tob. 11°18N 60°30W **187** J16
Little Valley *U.S.A.* 42°15N 78°48W **174** D6
Little Wabash →
  U.S.A. 37°55N 88°5W **172** G9
Little White →
  U.S.A. 43°40N 100°40W **172** D3
Little Zab = Zāb aş Şaghīr →
  Iraq 35°17N 43°29E **105** E10
Littlefield *U.S.A.* 33°55N 102°20W **176** E3
Littlehampton *U.K.* 50°49N 0°32W **67** G7
Littleton *U.S.A.* 44°18N 71°46W **175** B13
Littoral □ *Cameroon* 4°0N 10°0E **139** E7
Litvinov *Czech Rep.* 50°36N 13°37E **78** A6
Liu He → *China* 40°55N 121°35E **115** D11
Liu Jiang → *China* 23°55N 109°30E **116** F7
Liuba *China* 33°38N 106°55E **116** A6
Liucheng *China* 24°38N 109°14E **116** E7
Liugou *China* 40°57N 118°15E **115** D10
Liuhe *China* 42°17N 125°43E **115** C13
Liuheng Dao *China* 29°40N 122°5E **117** C14
Liujiang *China* 24°26N 109°11E **116** E7
Liukang Tenggaja = Sabalana,
  Kepulauan *Indonesia* 6°45S 118°50E **119** F5
Liuli *Tanzania* 11°3S 34°38E **143** E3
Liupan Shan *China* 35°39N 106°12E **114** G4
Liupanshui *China* 26°38N 104°48E **116** D5
Liuwa Plain *Zambia* 14°20S 22°30E **141** G4
Liuyang *China* 28°10N 113°37E **117** C9
Liuzhou *China* 24°22N 109°22E **116** E7
Liuzhuang *China* 33°12N 120°18E **115** H11
Livada *Romania* 47°52N 23°5E **80** C8
Livadero *Greece* 40°2N 21°57E **96** F5
Livadhia *Cyprus* 34°57N 33°38E **101** E12
Livadi *Greece* 37°40N 24°34E **97** E11
Livarot *France* 48°58N 0°9E **70** D7
Live Oak *Calif., U.S.A.* 39°17N 121°40W **170** F5
Live Oak *Fla., U.S.A.* 30°18N 82°59W **178** F6
Lively *Canada* 46°26N 81°9W **173** B8
Liveras *Cyprus* 35°23N 32°57E **101** D11
Livermore *U.S.A.* 37°41N 121°47W **170** H5
Livermore, Mt. *U.S.A.* 30°38N 104°11W **176** F2
Livermore Falls
  U.S.A. 44°29N 70°11W **173** C18
Liverpool *Canada* 33°54S 150°58E **153** B9
Liverpool *Canada* 44°5N 64°41W **165** D7
Liverpool *U.K.* 53°25N 3°0W **66** D4
Liverpool Bay *U.K.* 53°30N 3°20W **66** D4
Liverpool Plains
  Australia 31°15S 150°15E **153** A9
Liverpool Ra. *Australia* 31°50S 150°30E **153** A9
Livigno *Italy* 46°35N 10°10E **92** B7
Livingston *Guatemala* 15°50N 88°50W **182** C2
Livingston *U.K.* 55°54N 3°30W **65** F5
Livingston *Ala.,*
  U.S.A. 32°35N 88°11W **177** E10
Livingston *Calif.,*
  U.S.A. 37°23N 120°43W **170** H6
Livingston *Mont.,*
  U.S.A. 45°40N 110°34W **168** D8
Livingston *S.C., U.S.A.* 33°38N 81°7W **178** E3
Livingston *Tenn.,*
  U.S.A. 36°23N 85°19W **177** C12
Livingston *Tex., U.S.A.* 30°43N 94°56W **176** F7
Livingston, L. *U.S.A.* 30°50N 95°10W **176** F7
Livingston Manor
  U.S.A. 41°54N 74°50W **175** E10
Livingstone *Zambia* 17°46S 25°52E **143** F2
Livingstone △
  Australia 35°22S 147°22E **153** C7
Livingstone Mts. *N.Z.* 45°15S 168°9E **155** F3
Livingstone Mts.
  Tanzania 9°40S 34°20E **143** D3
Livingstonia *Malawi* 10°38S 34°5E **143** E3
Livno *Bos.-H.* 43°50N 17°1E **80** G2
Livny *Russia* 52°30N 37°30E **85** F10
Livonia *Mich., U.S.A.* 42°23N 83°23W **173** D12
Livonia *N.Y., U.S.A.* 42°49N 77°40W **174** D7
Livorno *Italy* 43°33N 10°19E **92** E7
Livradois-Forez △ *France* 44°0N 3°30E **72** E7
Livramento *Brazil* 30°55N 55°30W **191** C4
Livramento do Brumado
  Brazil 13°39S 41°50W **189** D10
Livron-sur-Drôme *France* 44°46N 4°51E **73** D8
Livvntsi *Ukraine* 48°25N 26°37E **81** D10
Liwale *Tanzania* 9°48S 37°58E **143** D4
Liwiec → *Poland* 52°36N 21°43E **83** F8
Liwonde *Malaysia* 15°4S 35°13E **143** F4
Liwonde △ *Malawi* 14°48S 35°20E **143** E4
Lixi *China* 26°23N 101°59E **116** D3
Lixian *China* 31°23N 103°13E **116** B4
Lixin *China* 33°8N 116°13E **117** A11
Lixouri *Greece* 38°12N 20°26E **98** C2

Liyang *China* 31°26N 119°28E **117** B12
Lizard I. *Australia* 14°42S 145°30E **150** A4
Lizard Pt. *U.K.* 49°57N 5°13W **67** H2
Lizarda *Brazil* 9°36S 46°41W **189** B11
Lizarra = Estella *Spain* 42°40N 2°0W **90** C2
Lizzano *Italy* 40°23N 17°27E **95** B10
Ljig *Serbia* 44°13N 20°18E **96** B4
Ljubija *Bos.-H.* 44°55N 16°35E **93** D13
Ljubinje *Bos.-H.* 42°58N 18°5E **96** C3
Ljubišnja *Europe* 43°18N 19°6E **96** C3
Ljubljana *Slovenia* 46°4N 14°33E **93** B11
Ljubljana ✈ (LJU)
  Slovenia 46°14N 14°33E **93** B11
Ljubno *Slovenia* 46°25N 14°46E **93** B11
Ljubovija *Serbia* 44°11N 19°22E **96** B3
Ljugarn *Sweden* 57°20N 18°43E **63** G12
Ljung *Sweden* 57°59N 13°3E **63** G7
Ljungan → *Sweden* 62°18N 17°23E **62** B11
Ljungaverk *Sweden* 62°30N 16°5E **62** B10
Ljungby *Sweden* 56°49N 13°55E **63** H7
Ljungbyholm *Sweden* 56°39N 16°5E **63** H10
Ljungdalen *Sweden* 62°51N 12°47E **62** B6
Ljungsbro *Sweden* 58°31N 15°30E **63** F9
Ljungskile *Sweden* 58°14N 11°55E **63** F5
Ljusdal *Sweden* 61°46N 16°3E **62** C10
Ljusfallshammar *Sweden* 58°48N 15°30E **63** F9
Ljusnan → *Sweden* 61°12N 17°8E **62** C11
Ljusne *Sweden* 61°13N 17°7E **62** C11
Ljusterö *Sweden* 59°31N 18°37E **62** E12
Ljutomer *Slovenia* 46°31N 16°11E **93** B13
Llagostera *Spain* 41°50N 2°54E **90** D7
Llamellin *Peru* 9°0S 76°54W **188** B2
Llançà *Spain* 42°22N 3°9E **90** C8
Llancanelo, Salina
  Argentina 35°40S 69°8W **190** D2
Llandeilo *U.K.* 51°53N 3°59W **67** F4
Llandovery *U.K.* 51°59N 3°48W **67** F4
Llandrindod Wells *U.K.* 52°14N 3°22W **67** E4
Llandudno *U.K.* 53°19N 3°50W **66** D4
Llanelli *U.K.* 51°41N 4°10W **67** F3
Llanes *Spain* 43°25N 4°50W **88** B6
Llanfair-ym-Muallt = Builth Wells
  U.K. 52°9N 3°25W **67** E4
Llangollen *U.K.* 52°58N 3°11W **66** E4
Llanidloes *U.K.* 52°27N 3°31W **67** E4
Llano → *U.S.A.* 30°45N 98°41W **176** F5
Llano → *U.S.A.* 30°39N 98°26W **176** F5
Llano Estacado *U.S.A.* 33°30N 103°0W **176** E3
Llanos *S. Amer.* 5°0N 71°35W **186** C4
Llanos de Challe △ *Chile* 28°8S 71°10W **192** B1
Llanquihue, L. *Chile* 41°10S 72°50W **192** B1
Llanwrtyd Wells → *U.K.* 52°7N 3°38W **67** E4
Llata *Peru* 9°25S 76°47W **188** B2
Llebeig, C. des *Spain* 39°33N 2°18E **100** B9
Lleida *Spain* 41°37N 0°39E **90** D5
Lleida □ *Spain* 42°6N 1°0E **90** C6
Llentrisca, C. *Spain* 38°52N 1°15E **100** C7
Llera de Canales *Mexico* 23°19N 99°1W **181** C5
Llerena *Spain* 38°17N 6°0W **89** G5
Lleyn Peninsula → *U.K.* 52°51N 4°36W **66** E3
Llica *Bolivia* 19°52S 68°16W **188** D4
Llico *Chile* 34°46S 72°5W **190** C1
Lliria *Spain* 39°37N 0°35W **91** F4
Llívia *Spain* 42°28N 1°59E **72** F5
Llodio *Spain* 43°9N 2°58W **90** B2
Lloret de Mar *Spain* 41°41N 2°53E **90** D7
Lloseta *Spain* 39°43N 2°52E **100** B9
Lloyd B. *Australia* 12°45S 143°27E **150** A3
Lloyd L. *Canada* 57°22N 108°57W **163** B7
Lloydminster *Canada* 53°17N 110°0W **163** C7
Llubi *Spain* 39°42N 3°0E **100** B10
Llucena del Cid *Spain* 40°9N 0°17W **90** E4
Llucmajor *Spain* 39°29N 2°53E **100** B9
Llullaillaco, Volcán
  S. Amer. 24°43S 68°30W **190** A2
Llullaillaco △ *Chile* 24°50S 68°51W **190** A2
Lo → *Vietnam* 21°18N 105°25E **120** B5
Loa *U.S.A.* 38°24N 111°39W **168** G8
Loa → *Chile* 21°26S 70°41W **190** A1
Loaita I. *S. China Sea* 10°41N 114°25E **118** B4
Loange →
  Dem. Rep. of the Congo 4°17S 20°2E **140** E4
Loano *Italy* 44°8N 8°15E **92** D5
Lobamba *Swaziland* 26°28S 31°12E **145** C5
Lobatse *Botswana* 25°12S 25°40E **144** C4
Lôbau *Germany* 51°5N 14°40E **76** C10
Lobenstein *Germany* 50°25N 11°39E **76** E7
Loberia *Argentina* 38°10S 58°40W **190** D4
Löberöd *Sweden* 55°47N 13°31E **63** J7
Lobez *Poland* 53°38N 15°39E **82** E2
Lobito *Angola* 12°18S 13°35E **141** G2
Lobo → *Ivory C.* 6°2N 6°45W **138** D3
Lobos, I. *Mexico* 27°20N 110°36W **180** B2
Lobos, Is. de *Canary Is.* 28°45N 13°50W **100** F6
Lobos de Afuera, Islas
  Peru 6°57S 80°42W **188** B1
Lobos de Tierra, I. *Peru* 6°27S 80°45W **188** B1
Łobżenica *Poland* 53°18N 17°15E **83** E4
Loc Binh *Vietnam* 21°46N 106°54E **120** B6
Loc Ninh *Vietnam* 11°50N 106°34E **121** G6
Locarno *Switz.* 46°10N 8°47E **77** J4
Loch Garman = Wexford
  Ireland 52°20N 6°28W **64** D5
Loch Lomond and the
  Trossachs △ *U.K.* 56°10N 4°40W **65** E4
Lochaber *U.K.* 56°59N 5°1W **65** E3
Locharbriggs *U.K.* 55°7N 3°35W **65** F5
Lochboisdale *U.K.* 57°9N 7°20W **65** D1
Loche, L. La *Canada* 56°30N 109°30W **163** B7
Lochem *Neths.* 52°9N 6°26E **66** B6
Loches *France* 47°7N 1°0E **70** E7
Lochgilphead *U.K.* 56°2N 5°26E **65** E3
Lochinvar △ *Zambia* 15°55S 27°15E **143** F2
Lochinver *U.K.* 58°9N 5°14W **65** C3
Lochnagar *Australia* 23°33S 145°38E **150** C4
Lochnagar *U.K.* 56°57N 3°15W **65** E5
Łochów *Poland* 52°33N 21°42E **83** F8
Lochy, L. *U.K.* 57°0N 4°53W **65** E4
Lock *Australia* 33°34S 135°46E **153** E2
Lock Haven *U.S.A.* 41°8N 77°28W **174** E7
Lockeford *U.S.A.* 38°10N 121°9W **170** G5
Lockeport *Canada* 43°47N 65°4W **165** D6
Lockerbie *U.K.* 55°7N 3°21W **65** F5
Lockhart *Australia* 35°14S 146°40E **153** C7
Lockhart *U.S.A.* 29°53N 97°40W **176** G6

Lockhart, L. *Australia* 33°15S 119°3E **149** F2
Lockhart River
  Australia 12°58S 143°30E **150** A3
Lockhart River ○
  Australia 12°47S 143°20E **150** A3
Lockney *U.S.A.* 34°7N 101°27W **176** D4
Lockport *U.S.A.* 43°10N 78°42W **174** C6
Locminé *France* 47°54N 2°51W **70** E4
Locri *Italy* 38°14N 16°16E **95** D9
Locronan *France* 48°7N 4°15W **70** D2
Locust Grove *U.S.A.* 36°12N 95°10W **176** C7
Lod *Israel* 31°57N 34°54E **130** D3
Lodeinoye Pole *Russia* 60°44N 33°33E **84** B7
Lodève *France* 43°44N 3°19E **72** E7
Lodge Bay *Canada* 52°14N 55°51W **165** B8
Lodge Grass *U.S.A.* 45°19N 107°22W **168** D10
Lodhran *Pakistan* 29°32N 71°30E **124** E4
Lodi *Italy* 45°19N 9°30E **92** C6
Lodi *Calif., U.S.A.* 38°8N 121°16W **170** G5
Lodi *Ohio, U.S.A.* 41°2N 82°1W **174** E3
Lodja
  Dem. Rep. of the Congo 3°30S 23°23E **142** C1
Lodosa *Spain* 42°25N 2°4W **90** C2
Lodwar *Kenya* 3°7N 35°36E **142** B4
Łódź *Poland* 51°45N 19°27E **83** G6
Łódzkie □ *Poland* 51°30N 19°30E **83** G6
Loei *Thailand* 17°29N 101°35E **120** D3
Loengo
  Dem. Rep. of the Congo 4°48S 26°30E **142** C2
Loeriesfontein *S. Africa* 31°0S 19°26E **144** D2
Lofa → *Liberia* 6°35N 11°8W **138** D2
Lofa Mano △ *Liberia* 7°55N 10°25W **138** D2
Lofer *Austria* 47°35N 12°41E **78** D5
Lofoten *Norway* 68°30N 13°59E **60** B16
Lofsdalen *Sweden* 62°10N 13°20E **62** B7
Lofsen → *Sweden* 62°7N 13°57E **62** B7
Loftahammar *Sweden* 57°54N 16°41E **63** G10
Loga *Niger* 13°40N 3°15E **139** C5
Logan *Iowa, U.S.A.* 41°39N 95°47W **172** E6
Logan *Ohio, U.S.A.* 39°32N 82°25W **173** F11
Logan *Utah, U.S.A.* 41°44N 111°50W **168** F8
Logan *W. Va., U.S.A.* 37°51N 81°59W **173** G13
Logan, Mt. *Canada* 60°34N 140°23W **160** E3
Logan Martin L.
  U.S.A. 33°26N 86°20W **178** B3
Logandale *U.S.A.* 36°36N 114°29W **171** J12
Logansport *Ind.,*
  U.S.A. 40°45N 86°22W **172** E10
Logansport *La., U.S.A.* 31°58N 94°0W **176** F8
Loganville *U.S.A.* 33°50N 83°54W **178** B6
Logatec *Slovenia* 45°54N 14°15E **93** C11
Logodoro *Italy* 40°35N 8°45E **94** B1
Logone → *Chad* 12°6N 15°2E **135** F9
Logroño *Spain* 42°28N 2°27W **90** C2
Logrosán *Spain* 39°20N 5°32W **89** F5
Løgstør *Denmark* 56°58N 9°14E **63** H3
Løgumkloster *Denmark* 55°4N 8°57E **63** J2
Lohals *Denmark* 55°8N 10°55E **63** J4
Lohardaga *India* 23°27N 84°45E **125** H11
Loharia *India* 23°45N 74°14E **124** H6
Loharu *India* 28°27N 75°49E **124** E6
Lohja *Finland* 60°12N 24°5E **63** B8
Lohne *Germany* 52°11N 8°40E **76** C4
Lohr *Germany* 49°59N 9°35E **77** F5
Lohri Wah → *Pakistan* 27°27N 67°37E **124** F2
Loikaw *Burma* 19°40N 97°17E **123** K20
Loimaa *Finland* 60°50N 23°5E **63** B8
Loir → *France* 47°33N 0°32W **70** E6
Loir-et-Cher □ *France* 47°40N 1°20E **70** E8
Loire □ *France* 45°40N 4°5E **73** D8
Loire → *France* 47°16N 2°10W **70** E4
Loire-Anjou-Touraine △
  France 47°14N 0°5W **70** E6
Loire-Atlantique □
  France 47°25N 1°40W **70** E5
Loiret □ *France* 47°55N 2°30E **71** E9
Loitz *Germany* 53°58N 13°8E **76** B9
Loja *Ecuador* 3°59S 79°16W **188** A2
Loja *Spain* 37°10N 4°9W **89** H6
Loji = Kawasi *Indonesia* 1°38S 127°28E **119** E7
Lojo = Lohja *Finland* 60°12N 24°5E **63** B8
Løjt Kirkeby *Denmark* 55°7N 9°26E **63** J3
Lojung *China* 24°27N 109°36E **116** E7
Lokandu
  Dem. Rep. of the Congo 2°30S 25°45E **142** C2
Lokeren *Belgium* 51°6N 3°59E **69** C3
Lokgwabe *Botswana* 24°10S 21°50E **144** C3
Lokhvytsya *Ukraine* 50°25N 33°18E **85** G7
Lokichar *Kenya* 2°23N 35°39E **142** B4
Lokichokio *Kenya* 4°19N 34°13E **142** B3
Lokitaung *Kenya* 4°12N 35°48E **142** B4
Lokkan tekojärvi
  Finland 67°55N 27°35E **60** C22
Løkken *Denmark* 57°22N 9°41E **63** G3
Loknya *Russia* 56°49N 30°4E **84** D6
Loko *Nigeria* 8°1N 7°53E **139** D6
Lokoja *Nigeria* 7°47N 6°45E **139** D6
Lokolo →
  Dem. Rep. of the Congo 1°43S 18°23E **140** E3
Lokot *Russia* 52°34N 34°58E **85** F8
Lola *Guinea* 7°52N 8°29W **138** D3
Lola, Mt. *U.S.A.* 39°26N 120°22W **170** F6
Lolgorien *Kenya* 1°14S 34°48E **142** C3
Loliondo *Tanzania* 2°2S 35°39E **142** C4
Lolland *Denmark* 54°45N 11°30E **63** K5
Lollar *Germany* 50°39N 8°43E **76** E4
Lolo *U.S.A.* 46°45N 114°5W **168** C6
Lolodorf *Cameroon* 3°16N 10°49E **139** E7
Lolowau *Indonesia* 0°49N 97°40E **118** D1
Lom *Bulgaria* 43°48N 23°12E **96** D7
Lom → *Bulgaria* 43°45N 23°15E **96** D7
Lom Kao *Thailand* 16°53N 101°14E **120** D3
Lom Sak *Thailand* 16°47N 101°15E **120** D3
Loma *U.S.A.* 47°56N 110°30W **168** C8
Loma Linda *U.S.A.* 34°3N 117°16W **171** L9
Loma Mansa *S. Leone* 9°13N 11°7W **138** D2
Loma Mts. *S. Leone* 9°5N 11°7W **138** D2
Lomaloma *Fiji* 17°17S 178°59W **154** a
Lomami →
  Dem. Rep. of the Congo 0°46N 24°16E **142** B1
Lomas de Zamora
  Argentina 34°45S 58°24W **190** C4
Lombadina *Australia* 16°31S 122°54E **148** C3
Lombárdia □ *Italy* 45°40N 9°30E **92** C6
Lombardy = Lombárdia □
  Italy 45°40N 9°30E **92** C6
Lombez *France* 43°29N 0°55E **72** E4
Lomblen *Indonesia* 8°30S 123°32E **119** F6
Lombok *Indonesia* 8°45S 116°30E **118** F5
Lombok, Selat
  Indonesia 8°30S 115°50E **119** K18

Lomé *Togo* 6°9N 1°20E **139** D5
Lomela
  Dem. Rep. of the Congo 2°19S 23°15E **140** E4
Lomela →
  Dem. Rep. of the Congo 0°15S 20°40E **140** E4
Lomianki *Poland* 52°21N 20°54E **83** F7
Lomma *Sweden* 55°43N 13°6E **63** J7
Lommel *Belgium* 51°14N 5°19E **69** C5
Lomond *Canada* 50°24N 112°36W **162** C6
Lomond, L. *U.K.* 56°8N 4°38W **65** E4
Lomonosov Ridge *Arctic* 88°0N 140°0E **54** A
Lomphat *Cambodia* 13°30N 106°59E **120** F6
Lompobatang *Indonesia* 5°24S 119°56E **119** F5
Lompoc *U.S.A.* 34°38N 120°28W **171** L6
Łomża *Poland* 53°10N 22°2E **83** E9
Lon, Ko *Thailand* 7°47N 98°23E **121** a
Lonavale *India* 18°46N 73°29E **126** B8
Loncoche *Chile* 39°20S 72°50W **192** A2
Loncopué *Argentina* 38°4S 70°37W **192** A2
Londa *India* 15°30N 74°30E **127** G2
Londiani *Kenya* 0°10S 35°33E **142** C4
Londinières *France* 49°50N 1°25E **70** C8
Londo *Angola* 9°51S 16°45E **140** F3
London *Canada* 42°59N 81°15W **174** D3
London *U.K.* 51°30N 0°3W **67** F7
London *Ky., U.S.A.* 37°8N 84°5W **173** G11
London *Ohio, U.S.A.* 39°53N 83°27W **173** F11
London, Greater □ *U.K.* 51°36N 0°5W **67** F7
London Gatwick ✈ (LGW)
  U.K. 51°10N 0°11W **67** F7
London Heathrow ✈ (LHR)
  U.K. 51°28N 0°27W **67** F7
London Stansted ✈ (STN)
  U.K. 51°54N 0°14E **67** F8
Londonderry *U.K.* 55°0N 7°20W **64** B4
Londonderry, C.
  Australia 13°45S 126°55E **148** B4
Londonderry, I. *Chile* 55°0S 71°0W **192** E2
Londres *Argentina* 27°45S 67°7W **190** B2
Londrina *Brazil* 23°18S 51°10W **191** A5
Lone Pine *U.S.A.* 36°36N 118°4W **170** J8
Lonely Mine *Zimbabwe* 19°30S 28°49E **145** A4
Long B. *U.S.A.* 33°35N 78°45W **177** E15
Long Beach *Calif.,*
  U.S.A. 33°46N 118°11W **171** M8
Long Beach *N.Y.,*
  U.S.A. 40°35N 73°39W **175** F11
Long Beach *Wash.,*
  U.S.A. 46°21N 124°3W **170** D2
Long Branch *U.S.A.* 40°18N 74°0W **175** F11
Long Creek *U.S.A.* 44°43N 119°6W **168** D4
Long Eaton *U.K.* 52°53N 1°15W **66** E6
Long I. *Australia* 20°22S 148°51E **150** b
Long I. *Bahamas* 23°20N 75°10W **183** B4
Long I. *Canada* 54°50N 79°20W **164** B4
Long I. *Ireland* 51°30N 9°34W **64** E2
Long I. *U.S.A.* 40°45N 73°30W **175** F11
Long Island Sd. *U.S.A.* 41°10N 73°0W **175** E12
Long L. *Canada* 49°30N 86°50W **164** C2
Long L. *U.S.A.* 44°0N 74°23W **175** C10
Long Lake *U.S.A.* 43°58N 74°25W **175** C10
Long Point *Canada* 42°34N 80°25W **174** D4
Long Point B. *Canada* 42°40N 80°10W **174** D4
Long Prairie *U.S.A.* 45°59N 94°52W **172** C6
Long Prairie → *U.S.A.* 46°20N 94°36W **172** B6
Long Pt. *Ont., Canada* 42°35N 80°2W **174** D4
Long Pt. *Ont., Canada* 43°56N 76°53W **175** C8
Long Pt. *N.Z.* 46°34S 169°36E **155** G4
Long Range Mts.
  Canada 49°30N 57°30W **165** C8
Long Reef *Australia* 14°1S 125°48E **148** B4
Long Sault *Canada* 45°2N 74°53W **175** A10
Long Str. = Longa, Proliv
  Russia 70°0N 175°0E **107** C18
Long Thanh *Vietnam* 10°47N 106°57E **121** G6
Long Xian *China* 34°55N 106°55E **114** G4
Long Xuyen *Vietnam* 10°19N 105°28E **121** G5
Longa *Greece* 36°53N 21°55E **98** D3
Longa, Proliv *Russia* 70°0N 175°0E **107** C18
Long'an *China* 23°10N 107°40E **116** F6
Longarone *Italy* 46°16N 12°18E **93** B9
Longbenton *U.K.* 55°1N 1°31W **66** B6
Longboat Key *U.S.A.* 27°23N 82°39W **179** H7
Longburn *N.Z.* 40°23S 175°35E **154** G4
Longchang *China* 29°18N 105°15E **116** C5
Longchuan *Guangdong,*
  China 24°5N 115°17E **117** E10
Longchuan *Yunnan,*
  China 24°23N 97°58E **116** E1
Longde *China* 35°30N 106°20E **114** G4
Longeau-Percey *France* 47°47N 5°20E **71** E12
Longford *Australia* 41°32S 147°3E **151** G4
Longford *Ireland* 53°43N 7°49W **64** C4
Longford □ *Ireland* 53°42N 7°45W **64** C4
Longford, An = Longford
  Ireland 53°43N 7°49W **64** C4
Longhai *China* 24°25N 117°46E **117** F12
Longhua *Guangdong,*
  China 22°39N 114°0E **111** a
Longhua *Hebei, China* 41°18N 117°45E **115** D9
Longhui *China* 27°7N 111°12E **117** D8
Longido *Tanzania* 2°43S 36°42E **142** C4
Longiram *Indonesia* 0°5S 115°45E **118** E5
Longkou *Jiangxi, China* 26°8N 115°10E **117** D10
Longkou *Shandong,*
  China 37°40N 120°18E **115** F11
Longlac *Canada* 49°45N 86°25W **164** C2
Longli *China* 26°25N 106°58E **116** D6
Longlin *China* 24°47N 105°20E **116** E5
Longlin *China* 24°47N 105°20E **116** E5
Longmeadow *U.S.A.* 42°3N 72°34W **175** D12
Longmen *China* 23°40N 114°18E **117** F10
Longmen Shiku *China* 34°28N 112°28E **114** G7
Longming *China* 22°45N 107°28E **116** F6
Longmont *U.S.A.* 40°10N 105°6W **168** F11
Longnan *China* 24°55N 114°47E **117** E10
Longnawan *Indonesia* 1°51N 114°55E **118** D4
Longobucco *Italy* 39°27N 16°37E **95** C9
Longquan *China* 28°7N 119°10E **117** C12
Longreach *Australia* 23°28S 144°14E **150** C3
Longs Peak *U.S.A.* 40°15N 105°37W **168** E11
Longshan *China* 29°29N 109°25E **116** C7
Longsheng *China* 25°48N 110°0E **117** E8
Longton *Australia* 20°58S 145°55E **150** C4
Longué-Jumelles *France* 47°22N 0°8W **70** E6
Longueau *France* 49°52N 2°21E **71** C9
Longueuil *Canada* 45°31N 73°29W **175** A11
Longuyon *France* 49°27N 5°35E **71** C12
Longvic *France* 47°17N 5°4E **71** E12
Longview *Tex., U.S.A.* 32°30N 94°44W **176** E7

Longview *Wash.,*
  U.S.A. 46°8N 122°57W **170** D4
Longwood *U.S.A.* 28°42N 81°21W **179** G8
Longwy *France* 49°30N 5°46E **71** C12
Longxi *China* 34°53N 104°40E **114** G3
Longxue Dao *China* 22°41N 113°38E **111** a
Longyan *China* 25°10N 117°0E **117** E11
Longyearbyen *Svalbard* 78°13N 15°40E **54** B8
Longyou *China* 29°1N 119°8E **117** C12
Longzhou *China* 22°22N 106°50E **116** F6
Lonigo *Italy* 45°23N 11°23E **93** C8
Löningen *Germany* 52°44N 7°46E **76** C3
Lonja → *Croatia* 45°22N 16°40E **93** C13
Lonoke *U.S.A.* 34°47N 91°54W **176** D9
Lonquimay *Chile* 38°26S 71°14W **192** A2
Lons-le-Saunier *France* 46°40N 5°31E **71** F12
Lönsboda *Sweden* 56°24N 14°19E **63** H8
Looe *U.K.* 50°22N 4°28W **67** G3
Lookout, C. *Canada* 55°18N 83°56W **164** A3
Lookout, C. *U.S.A.* 34°35N 76°32W **177** D16
Loolmalasin *Tanzania* 3°0S 35°53E **142** C4
Loon → *Alta., Canada* 57°8N 115°3W **162** B5
Loon → *Man., Canada* 55°53N 101°59W **163** B8
Loon Lake *Canada* 54°2N 109°10W **163** C7
Loongana *Australia* 30°52S 127°5E **149** F4
Loop Hd. *Ireland* 52°34N 9°56W **64** D2
Lop *China* 37°3N 80°11E **109** E10
Lop Nor = Lop Nur
  China 40°20N 90°10E **109** D12
Lop Nur *China* 40°20N 90°10E **109** D12
Lopare *Bos.-H.* 44°39N 18°46E **80** F3
Lopatin *Russia* 43°50N 47°35E **87** J8
Lopatina, Gora
  Russia 50°47N 143°10E **107** D15
Lopatka, Mys *Russia* 50°52N 156°40E **107** D16
Lopburi *Thailand* 14°48N 100°37E **120** E3
Lopez *U.S.A.* 41°27N 76°20W **175** E8
Lopez, C. *Gabon* 0°47S 8°40E **140** E1
Lopphavet *Norway* 70°27N 21°15E **60** A19
Lora → *Afghan.* 31°35N 66°32E **122** D4
Lora, Hāmūn-i-
  Pakistan 29°38N 64°58E **122** E4
Lora Cr. → *Australia* 28°10S 135°22E **151** D2
Lora del Río *Spain* 37°39N 5°33W **89** H5
Lorain *U.S.A.* 41°28N 82°11W **174** E2
Loralai *Pakistan* 30°20N 68°41E **124** D3
Lorca *Spain* 37°41N 1°42W **91** H3
Lord Howe I. *Pac. Oc.* 31°33S 159°6E **147** E8
Lord Howe Rise *Pac. Oc.* 30°0S 162°30E **156** L8
Lord Loughborough I.
  Burma 10°25N 97°54E **121** G1
Lordsburg *U.S.A.* 32°21N 108°43W **169** K9
Lorestān □ *Iran* 33°30N 48°40E **129** C6
Loreto *Brazil* 7°5S 45°10W **189** B9
Loreto *Italy* 43°26N 13°36E **93** E10
Loreto *Mexico* 26°0N 111°21W **180** B2
Lorgues *France* 43°28N 6°22E **73** E10
Lorhosso = Loropéni
  Burkina Faso 10°17N 3°38W **138** C4
Lorient *France* 47°45N 3°23W **70** E3
Lőrinci *Hungary* 47°44N 19°41E **80** C4
Lormi *India* 22°17N 81°41E **125** H9
Lorn *U.K.* 56°26N 5°10W **65** E3
Lorn, Firth of *U.K.* 56°20N 5°40W **65** E3
Lorne *Australia* 38°33S 143°59E **152** E5
Loropéni *Burkina Faso* 10°17N 3°38W **138** C4
Lorovouno *Cyprus* 35°8N 32°36E **101** D11
Lörrach *Germany* 47°36N 7°40E **77** H3
Lorraine □ *France* 48°53N 6°0E **71** D13
Lorraine ☆ *France* 48°55N 5°50E **71** D12
Los *Sweden* 61°45N 15°10E **62** C9
Los, Îles de *Guinea* 9°30N 13°50W **138** D2
Los Alamos *Calif.,*
  U.S.A. 34°44N 120°17W **171** L6
Los Alamos *N. Mex.,*
  U.S.A. 35°53N 106°19W **169** J10
Los Alcornocales △
  Spain 36°21N 5°32W **89** J5
Los Alerces △
  Argentina 42°55S 71°55W **192** B2
Los Altos *U.S.A.* 37°23N 122°7W **170** H4
Los Andes *Chile* 32°50S 70°40W **190** C1
Los Angeles *Chile* 37°28S 72°23W **190** D1
Los Angeles *U.S.A.* 34°4N 118°15W **171** M8
Los Angeles Aqueduct
  U.S.A. 35°22N 118°5W **171** K9
Los Angeles Int. ✈ (LAX)
  U.S.A. 33°57N 118°25W **171** M8
Los Antiguos *Argentina* 46°35S 71°40W **192** C2
Los Banos *U.S.A.* 37°4N 120°51W **170** H6
Los Barrios *Spain* 36°11N 5°30W **89** J5
Los Blancos *Argentina* 23°40S 62°30W **190** A3
Los Cabos Int. ✈ (SJD)
  Mexico 23°9N 109°43W **180** C3
Los Cardones △
  Argentina 25°8S 65°55W **190** B2
Los Chiles *Costa Rica* 11°2N 84°43W **182** D3
Los Corrales de Buelna
  Spain 43°16N 4°4W **88** B6
Los Cristianos *Canary Is.* 28°3N 16°42W **100** F3
Los Gallardos *Spain* 37°10N 1°57W **91** H3
Los Gatos *U.S.A.* 37°14N 121°59W **170** H5
Los Glaciares △
  Argentina 50°0S 73°55W **192** C2
Los Haïtises △
  Dom. Rep. 19°4N 69°36W **183** C6
Los Hermanos, Is.
  Venezuela 11°45N 64°25W **183** D7
Los Huemules △ *Chile* 46°10S 73°23W **192** C2
Los Islotes *Canary Is.* 29°4N 13°44W **100** E6
Los Lagos *Chile* 39°51S 72°50W **192** A2
Los Llanos de Aridane
  Canary Is. 28°38N 17°54W **100** F2
Los Loros *Chile* 27°50S 70°6W **190** B1
Los Lunas *U.S.A.* 34°48N 106°44W **169** J10
Los Menucos *Argentina* 40°50S 68°10W **192** B3
Los Mochis *Mexico* 25°45N 108°57W **180** B3
Los Monegros *Spain* 41°29N 0°13W **90** D4
Los Monos *Argentina* 46°1S 69°36W **192** C3
Los Muermos *Chile* 41°24S 73°29W **192** B2
Los Nietos *Spain* 37°39N 0°47W **91** H4
Los Olivos *U.S.A.* 34°40N 120°7W **171** L6
Los Palacios *Cuba* 22°35N 83°15W **182** B3
Los Palacios y Villafranca
  Spain 37°10N 5°55W **89** H5
Los Queñes *Chile* 35°1S 70°48W **190** D1
Los Reyes de Salgado
  Mexico 19°35N 102°29W **180** D4
Los Roques, Is.
  Venezuela 11°50N 66°45W **183** D6

242 Los Santos de Maimona
INDEX TO WORLD MAPS

Los Santos de Maimona Spain 38°27N 6°22W 89 G4
Los Teques Venezuela 10°21N 67°2W 186 A5
Los Testigos, Is. Venezuela 11°23N 63°6W 186 A6
Los Vilos Chile 32°10S 71°30W 190 C1
Los Yébenes Spain 39°36N 3°55W 89 F7
Łosice Poland 52°13N 22°43E 83 F9
Lošinj Croatia 44°30N 14°30E 93 D11
Loskop Dam S. Africa 25°23S 29°20E 145 C4
Løsning Denmark 55°48N 9°42E 63 J3
Lossiemouth U.K. 57°42N 3°17W 65 D5
Lossnen Sweden 62°26N 12°45E 62 B6
Lostwithiel U.K. 50°24N 4°41W 67 G3
Lot □ France 44°39N 1°40E 72 D5
Lot → France 44°18N 0°20E 72 D4
Lot-et-Garonne □ France 44°22N 0°30E 72 D4
Lota Chile 37°5S 73°10W 190 D1
Loṭfābād Iran 37°32N 59°20E 129 B8
Lothair S. Africa 26°22S 30°27E 145 C5
Lotorp Sweden 58°44N 15°50E 63 F9
Lötschbergtunnel Switz. 46°26N 7°43E 77 J3
Lötta → Europe 68°42N 31°6E 60 B24
Lottefors Sweden 61°25N 16°24E 62 C10
Löttorp Sweden 57°10N 17°0E 63 G11
Lotung Taiwan 24°41N 121°46E 117 E13
Loubomo Congo 4°9S 12°47E 140 E2
Loudéac France 48°11N 2°47W 70 D4
Loudi China 27°42N 111°59E 117 D8
Loudonville U.S.A. 40°38N 82°14W 174 F2
Loudun France 47°3N 0°5E 70 E7
Loue → France 47°1N 5°28E 71 E12
Louga Senegal 15°45N 16°5W 138 B1
Louga □ Senegal 15°20N 15°35W 138 B1
Loughborough U.K. 52°47N 1°11W 66 E6
Lougheed I. Canada 77°26N 105°6W 161 B10
Loughman U.S.A. 28°14N 81°34W 179 G8
Loughrea Ireland 53°12N 8°33W 64 C3
Loughros More B. Ireland 54°48N 8°32W 64 B3
Louhans France 46°38N 5°12E 71 F12
Louis Trichardt S. Africa 23°1S 29°43E 145 B4
Louis XIV, Pte. Canada 54°37N 79°45W 164 B4
Louisa U.S.A. 38°7N 82°36W 173 F12
Louisbourg Canada 45°55N 60°0W 165 C8
Louisburgh Ireland 53°46N 9°49W 64 C2
Louise I. Canada 52°55N 131°50W 162 C2
Louiseville Canada 46°20N 72°56W 164 C5
Louisiade Arch. Papua N. G. 11°10S 153°0E 147 C8
Louisiana U.S.A. 39°27N 91°3W 172 F8
Louisiana □ U.S.A. 30°50N 92°0W 176 F9
Louisville Ala., U.S.A. 31°47N 85°33W 178 D4
Louisville Ga., U.S.A. 33°0N 82°25W 178 B7
Louisville Ky., U.S.A. 38°15N 85°46W 173 F11
Louisville Miss., U.S.A. 33°7N 89°3W 177 E10
Louisville Ohio, U.S.A. 40°50N 81°16W 174 F3
Louisville Ridge Pac. Oc. 31°0S 172°30W 156 L10
Loulay France 46°3N 0°30W 72 B3
Loulé Portugal 37°9N 8°0W 89 H3
Louloumi Mali 10°54N 5°36W 138 C3
Loum Cameroon 4°42N 9°44E 139 E6
Louny Czech Rep. 50°20N 13°48E 78 A6
Loup City U.S.A. 41°17N 98°58W 172 E4
Loups Marins, Lacs des Canada 56°30N 73°45W 164 A5
Lourdes France 43°6N 0°3W 72 E3
Lourdes-de-Blanc-Sablon Canada 51°24N 57°12W 165 B8
Lourinhã Portugal 39°14N 9°17W 89 F1
Louroujina Cyprus 35°0N 33°28E 101 E12
Lousã Portugal 40°7N 8°14W 88 E2
Louta Burkina Faso 13°30N 3°10W 138 C4
Louth Australia 30°30S 145°8E 153 A6
Louth Ireland 53°58N 6°32W 64 C5
Louth U.K. 53°22N 0°1W 66 D7
Louth □ Ireland 53°56N 6°34W 64 C5
Louth B. Australia 34°33S 135°56E 152 C1
Loutra Edipsou Greece 38°54N 23°2E 98 C5
Loutraki Greece 37°58N 22°57E 98 D4
Loutropoli Thermis Greece 39°11N 26°29E 99 B8
Louvain = Leuven Belgium 50°52N 4°42E 69 D4
Louvale U.S.A. 32°10N 84°50W 178 C5
Louviers France 49°12N 1°10E 70 C8
Louwsburg S. Africa 27°37S 31°7E 145 C5
Lovat → Russia 58°14N 31°28E 84 C6
Lovćen Montenegro 42°23N 18°51E 96 D2
Lovćen △ Montenegro 42°20N 18°50E 96 D2
Lovech Bulgaria 43°8N 24°42E 97 C8
Lovech □ Bulgaria 43°0N 24°45E 97 D8
Loveland U.S.A. 40°24N 105°5W 168 F11
Lovell U.S.A. 44°50N 108°24W 168 D9
Lovelock U.S.A. 40°11N 118°28W 168 F4
Lóvere Italy 45°49N 10°4E 92 C7
Lövestad Sweden 55°40N 13°54E 63 J7
Loviisa Finland 60°28N 26°12E 84 B4
Lovina Indonesia 8°9S 115°1E 119 J18
Loving U.S.A. 32°17N 104°6W 169 K11
Lovington U.S.A. 32°57N 103°21W 169 K12
Lovisa = Loviisa Finland 60°28N 26°12E 84 B4
Lovosice Czech Rep. 50°30N 14°2E 78 A7
Lovran Croatia 45°18N 14°15E 93 C11
Lovrin Romania 45°58N 20°48E 80 E5
Lövstabruk Sweden 60°25N 17°53E 62 D11
Lövstabukten Sweden 60°35N 17°45E 62 D11
Low, L. Canada 52°29N 76°17W 164 B4
Low Pt. Australia 32°25S 127°25E 149 F4
Low Tatra = Nízké Tatry Slovak Rep. 48°55N 19°30E 79 C12
Lowa Dem. Rep. of the Congo 1°25S 25°47E 142 C2
Lowa → Dem. Rep. of the Congo 1°24S 25°51E 142 C2
Lowell U.S.A. 42°38N 71°19W 175 D13
Lowellville U.S.A. 41°2N 80°32W 174 E4
Löwen → Namibia 26°51S 18°17E 144 C2
Lower Alkali L. U.S.A. 41°16N 120°2W 168 F3
Lower Arrow L. Canada 49°40N 118°5W 162 D5
Lower Austria = Niederösterreich □ Austria 48°25N 15°40E 78 C8
Lower California = Baja California Mexico 31°10N 115°12W 180 A1
Lower Glenelg △ Australia 38°4S 141°41E 152 E4
Lower Hutt N.Z. 41°10S 174°55E 154 H3
Lower Lake U.S.A. 38°55N 122°37W 170 G4
Lower Manitou L. Canada 49°15N 93°0W 163 D10
Lower Post Canada 59°58N 128°30W 162 B3
Lower Red L. U.S.A. 47°58N 95°0W 172 B6
Lower Saxony = Niedersachsen □ Germany 52°50N 9°0E 76 C4
Lower Tunguska = Tunguska, Nizhnyaya → Russia 65°48N 88°4E 107 C9
Lower Zambezi △ Zambia 15°25S 29°40E 143 F2
Lowestoft U.K. 52°29N 1°45E 67 E9
Lowgar □ Afghan. 34°0N 69°0E 122 B6
Łowicz Poland 52°6N 19°55E 83 F6
Lowly, Pt. Australia 33°0S 137°46E 152 B2
Lowther I. Canada 74°33N 97°30W 161 C12
Lowville U.S.A. 43°47N 75°29W 175 C9
Loxton Australia 34°28S 140°31E 152 C4
Loxton S. Africa 31°30S 22°22E 144 D3
Loyalton U.S.A. 39°41N 120°14W 170 F6
Loyalty Is. = Loyauté, Îs. N. Cal. 20°50S 166°30E 147 D9
Loyang = Luoyang China 34°40N 112°26E 114 G7
Loyauté, Îs. N. Cal. 20°50S 166°30E 147 D9
Loyev = Loyew Belarus 51°56N 30°46E 75 C16
Loyew Belarus 51°56N 30°46E 75 C16
Loyoro Uganda 3°22N 34°14E 142 B3
Lož Slovenia 45°43N 14°30E 93 C11
Lozère □ France 44°35N 3°30E 72 D7
Loznica Serbia 44°32N 19°12E 96 B3
Lozova Ukraine 49°0N 36°20E 85 H9
Ltalaltuma ◎ Australia 23°57S 132°25E 148 D5
Lü Shan China 29°30N 115°55E 117 C10
Lü Shan △ China 29°26N 115°52E 117 C10
Lu Wo China 22°33N 114°6E 111 a
Luachimo Angola 7°23S 20°48E 140 F4
Luajan → India 24°44N 85°1E 125 G11
Lualaba → Dem. Rep. of the Congo 0°26N 25°20E 142 B2
Luambe △ Zambia 12°30S 32°15E 143 E3
Luampa Zambia 15°4S 24°20E 143 F1
Lu'an China 31°45N 116°29E 117 B11
Luan Chau Vietnam 21°38N 103°24E 116 G4
Luan He → China 39°20N 119°5E 115 E10
Luan Xian China 39°40N 118°40E 115 E10
Luancheng Guangxi Zhuangzu, China 22°48N 108°55E 116 F7
Luancheng Hebei, China 37°53N 114°40E 114 F8
Luanco Spain 43°37N 5°48W 88 B5
Luanda Angola 8°50S 13°15E 140 F2
Luang, Doi Thailand 18°30N 101°15E 120 C3
Luang, Thale Thailand 7°30N 100°15E 121 J3
Luang Nam Tha Laos 20°58N 101°30E 116 G3
Luang Prabang Laos 19°52N 102°10E 116 H4
Luangwa Zambia 15°35S 30°16E 143 F3
Luangwa → Zambia 14°25S 30°25E 143 E3
Luangwa Valley Zambia 13°30S 31°30E 143 E3
Luangwe = Loange → Dem. Rep. of the Congo 4°17S 20°2E 140 E4
Luanne China 40°55N 117°40E 115 D9
Luanping China 40°53N 117°23E 115 D9
Luanshya Zambia 13°3S 28°28E 143 E2
Luapula □ Zambia 11°0S 29°0E 143 E2
Luapula → Africa 9°26S 28°33E 143 D2
Luarca Spain 43°32N 6°32W 88 B4
Luashi Dem. Rep. of the Congo 10°50S 23°36E 143 E1
Luau Angola 10°40S 22°10E 140 G4
Lubaczów Poland 50°10N 23°8E 83 H10
Lubań Poland 51°5N 15°15E 83 G2
Lubana, Ozero = Lubānas Ezers Latvia 56°45N 27°0E 84 D4
Lubānas Ezers Latvia 56°45N 27°0E 84 D4
Lubang Is. Phil. 13°50N 120°12E 119 B6
Lubango Angola 14°55S 13°30E 141 G2
Lubao Dem. Rep. of the Congo 5°17S 25°42E 142 D2
Lubartów Poland 51°28N 22°42E 83 G9
Lubawa Poland 53°30N 19°48E 82 E6
Lübbecke Germany 52°18N 8°37E 76 C4
Lübben Germany 51°56N 13°54E 76 D9
Lübbenau Germany 51°52N 13°57E 76 D9
Lubbock U.S.A. 33°35N 101°51W 176 E4
Lübeck Germany 53°52N 10°40E 76 B6
Lübecker Bucht Germany 54°3N 10°54E 76 A6
Lubefu Dem. Rep. of the Congo 4°47S 24°27E 142 C1
Lubefu → Dem. Rep. of the Congo 4°10S 23°0E 142 C1
Lubelskie □ Poland 51°20N 22°50E 83 G9
Lubero = Luofu Dem. Rep. of the Congo 0°10S 29°15E 142 C2
Luberon ⌂ France 43°52N 5°25E 73 E9
Lubersac France 45°26N 1°23E 72 C5
Lubicon L. Canada 56°23N 115°56W 162 B5
Lubień Kujawski Poland 52°23N 19°9E 83 F6
Lubilash → Dem. Rep. of the Congo 6°2S 23°45E 140 F4
Lubin Poland 51°24N 16°11E 83 G3
Lublin Poland 51°12N 22°38E 83 G9
Lubliniec Poland 50°43N 18°45E 83 H5
Lubnān = Lebanon ■ Asia 34°0N 36°0E 130 B5
Lubnān, Jabal Lebanon 33°45N 35°40E 130 B4
Lubniewice Poland 52°31N 15°15E 83 F2
Lubny Ukraine 50°3N 32°58E 85 G7
Lubomierz Poland 51°1N 15°31E 83 G2
Luboń Poland 52°21N 16°51E 83 F3
Lubongola Dem. Rep. of the Congo 2°35S 27°50E 142 C2
L'ubotín Slovak Rep. 49°17N 20°53E 79 B13
Lubraniec Poland 52°33N 18°50E 83 F5
Lubsko Poland 51°45N 14°57E 83 G1
Lübtheen Germany 53°18N 11°5E 76 B7
Lubudi Dem. Rep. of the Congo 9°57S 25°58E 140 F5
Lubudi → Dem. Rep. of the Congo 9°0S 25°35E 143 D2
Lubukklinggau Indonesia 3°15S 102°55E 118 E2
Lubuksikaping Indonesia 0°10N 100°15E 118 D2
Lubumbashi Dem. Rep. of the Congo 11°40S 27°28E 143 E2
Lubunda Dem. Rep. of the Congo 5°12S 26°41E 142 D2
Lubungu Zambia 14°35S 26°24E 143 E2
Lubuskie □ Poland 52°10N 15°20E 83 F2
Lubutu Dem. Rep. of the Congo 0°45S 26°30E 142 C2
Luc-en-Diois France 44°36N 5°28E 73 D9
Lucan Canada 43°11N 81°24W 174 C3
Lucan Ireland 53°22N 6°28W 64 C5
Lucania, Mt. Canada 61°1N 140°27W 160 E3
Lucas Channel = Main Channel Canada 45°21N 81°45W 174 A3
Lucca Italy 43°50N 10°29E 92 E7
Lucé France 48°26N 1°27E 70 D8
Luce Bay U.K. 54°45N 4°48W 65 G4
Lucea Jamaica 18°27N 78°10W 182 a
Lucedale U.S.A. 30°56N 88°35W 177 F10
Lucena Phil. 13°56N 121°37E 119 B6
Lucena Spain 37°27N 4°31W 89 H6
Lučenec Slovak Rep. 48°18N 19°42E 79 C12
Lucera Italy 41°30N 15°20E 95 A8
Lucerne = Luzern Switz. 47°3N 8°18E 77 H4
Lucerne U.S.A. 39°6N 122°48W 170 F4
Lucerne Valley U.S.A. 34°27N 116°57W 171 L10
Luchena → Spain 37°44N 1°50W 91 H3
Lucheng China 36°20N 113°11E 114 F7
Lucheringo → Mozam. 11°43S 36°17E 143 E4
Lüchow Germany 52°58N 11°8E 76 C7
Luchuan China 22°21N 110°12E 117 F8
Lucia U.S.A. 36°2N 121°33W 170 J5
Lucinda Australia 18°32S 146°20E 150 B4
Lucindale Australia 36°58S 140°26E 152 D4
Luckau Germany 51°50N 13°42E 76 D9
Luckenwalde Germany 52°5N 13°10E 76 C9
Luckhoff S. Africa 29°44S 24°43E 144 C3
Lucknow Canada 43°57N 81°31W 174 C3
Lucknow India 26°50N 81°0E 125 F9
Luçon France 46°28N 1°10W 72 B2
Lüda = Dalian China 38°50N 121°40E 115 E11
Luda Kamchiya → Bulgaria 43°3N 27°29E 97 C11
Ludbreg Croatia 46°15N 16°38E 93 B13
Lüdenscheid Germany 51°13N 7°37E 76 D3
Lüderitz Namibia 26°41S 15°8E 144 C2
Lüderitzbaai Namibia 26°36S 15°8E 144 C2
Ludhiana India 30°57N 75°56E 124 D6
Ludian China 27°10N 103°33E 116 D4
Luding Qiao China 29°53N 102°12E 116 C4
Lüdinghausen Germany 51°46N 7°26E 76 D3
Ludington U.S.A. 43°57N 86°27W 172 D10
Ludlow U.K. 52°22N 2°42W 67 E5
Ludlow Calif., U.S.A. 34°43N 116°10W 171 L10
Ludlow Pa., U.S.A. 41°43N 78°56W 174 E6
Ludlow Vt., U.S.A. 43°24N 72°42W 175 C12
Ludowici U.S.A. 31°43N 81°45W 178 D8
Luduş Romania 46°29N 24°5E 81 D9
Ludvika Sweden 60°8N 15°14E 62 D9
Ludwigsburg Germany 48°53N 9°11E 77 G5
Ludwigsfelde Germany 52°17N 13°17E 76 C9
Ludwigshafen Germany 49°29N 8°26E 77 F4
Ludwigslust Germany 53°19N 11°30E 76 B7
Ludza Latvia 56°32N 27°43E 84 D4
Lue Australia 32°38S 149°50E 153 B8
Lueki Dem. Rep. of the Congo 3°20S 25°48E 142 C2
Luena Dem. Rep. of the Congo 9°28S 25°43E 143 D2
Luena Zambia 10°40S 30°25E 143 E3
Luena Flats Zambia 14°47S 23°17E 141 G4
Luenha = Ruenya → Africa 16°24S 33°48E 143 F3
Lüeyang China 33°22N 106°10E 116 A6
Lufeng Guangdong, China 22°57N 115°38E 117 F10
Lufeng Yunnan, China 25°0N 102°5E 116 E4
Lufira → Dem. Rep. of the Congo 9°30S 27°0E 143 D2
Lufkin U.S.A. 31°21N 94°44W 176 F7
Lufupa Dem. Rep. of the Congo 10°37S 24°56E 143 E1
Luga Russia 58°40N 29°55E 84 C5
Luga → Russia 59°40N 28°18E 84 C5
Lugano Switz. 46°1N 8°57E 77 J4
Lugano, L. di Switz. 46°0N 9°0E 92 C6
Lugansk = Luhansk Ukraine 48°38N 39°15E 85 H10
Lugard's Falls Kenya 3°6S 38°41E 142 C4
Lugela Mozam. 16°25S 36°43E 143 F4
Lugenda → Mozam. 11°25S 38°33E 143 E4
Lugh = Luuq Somalia 3°48N 42°34E 131 G3
Lugnaquilla Ireland 52°58N 6°28W 64 D5
Lugnvik Sweden 62°56N 17°55E 62 B11
Lugo Italy 44°25N 11°54E 93 D8
Lugo Spain 43°2N 7°35W 88 B3
Lugo □ Spain 43°0N 7°30W 88 C3
Lugoj Romania 45°42N 21°57E 80 E6
Lugovoy = Qulan Kazakhstan 42°55N 72°43E 106 E8
Luhansk Ukraine 48°38N 39°15E 85 H10
Luhansk □ Ukraine 49°10N 38°40E 85 H10
Luhe China 32°19N 118°50E 117 A12
Luhe → Germany 53°23N 10°13E 76 B6
Luhuo China 31°21N 100°48E 116 B3
Lui → Angola 8°21S 17°33E 140 F3
Luiana Angola 17°25S 22°59E 144 A3
Luiana → Angola 17°24S 23°3E 141 H4
Luichow Pen. = Leizhou Bandao China 21°0N 110°0E 116 G7
Luimneach = Limerick Ireland 52°40N 8°37W 64 D3
Luing U.K. 56°14N 5°39W 65 E3
Luino Italy 45°59N 8°44E 92 C5
Luís Correia Brazil 3°0S 41°35W 189 A2
Luitpold Coast Antarctica 78°30S 32°0W 55 D1
Luiza Dem. Rep. of the Congo 7°40S 22°30E 140 F4
Luizi Dem. Rep. of the Congo 6°0S 27°25E 142 D2
Luján Argentina 34°45S 59°5W 190 C4
Lujiang China 31°20N 117°15E 117 B11
Lukang Taiwan 24°1N 120°22E 117 E13
Lukanga Swamp Zambia 14°30S 27°40E 143 E2
Lukavac Bos.-H. 44°33N 18°32E 80 F3
Lukenie → Dem. Rep. of the Congo 3°0S 18°50E 140 E3
Lŭki Bulgaria 41°50N 24°43E 97 E8
Lukla Nepal 27°42N 86°43E 125 F12
Lukolela Dem. Rep. of the Congo 5°23S 24°32E 142 D1
Lukosi Zimbabwe 18°30S 26°30E 143 F2
Lukovë Albania 39°59N 19°54E 96 G3
Lukovit Bulgaria 43°13N 24°11E 97 C8
Łuków Poland 51°55N 22°23E 83 G9
Lukoyanov Russia 55°2N 44°29E 86 C7
Lukusuzi △ Zambia 12°43S 32°36E 143 E3
Lülang Shan China 38°0N 111°15E 114 F6
Luleå Sweden 65°35N 22°10E 60 D20
Luleälven → Sweden 65°35N 22°10E 60 D20
Lüleburgaz Turkey 41°23N 27°22E 97 E11
Luliang China 25°0N 103°40E 116 E4
Lulima Dem. Rep. of the Congo 4°12S 25°36E 142 C2
Luling U.S.A. 29°41N 97°39W 176 G6
Lulong China 39°53N 118°51E 115 E10
Lulonga → Dem. Rep. of the Congo 1°0N 18°10E 140 D3
Lulu U.S.A. 30°7N 82°29W 178 E7
Lulua → Dem. Rep. of the Congo 4°30S 20°30E 140 E4
Lumajang Indonesia 8°8S 113°13E 119 H15
Lumār Iran 33°33N 46°49E 105 F12
Lumbala N'guimbo Angola 14°18S 21°18E 141 G4
Lumber City U.S.A. 31°56N 82°41W 178 D7
Lumberton N.C., U.S.A. 34°37N 79°0W 177 D15
Lumberton Tex., U.S.A. 30°16N 94°12W 176 F7
Lumière, Côte de France 46°50N 2°10W 70 F4
Lumpkin U.S.A. 32°3N 84°48W 178 C5
Lumsden Canada 50°39N 104°52W 163 C8
Lumsden N.Z. 45°44S 168°27E 155 F3
Lumut Malaysia 4°13N 100°37E 121 K3
Lumut, Tanjung Indonesia 3°50S 105°58E 118 E3
Lumwana Zambia 11°50S 25°8E 143 E2
Luna India 23°43N 69°16E 124 H3
Lunan China 24°40N 103°18E 116 E4
Lunavada India 23°8N 73°37E 124 H5
Lunca Romania 47°22N 25°1E 81 C10
Lunca Corbului Romania 44°42N 24°45E 81 F9
Lund Sweden 55°44N 13°12E 63 J7
Lundazi Zambia 12°20S 33°7E 143 E3
Lunde Sweden 62°53N 17°51E 62 B11
Lunderskov Denmark 55°29N 9°19E 63 J3
Lundi → Zimbabwe 21°43S 32°34E 143 G3
Lundu Malaysia 1°40N 109°50E 118 D3
Lundy U.K. 51°10N 4°41W 67 F3
Lune → U.K. 54°0N 2°51W 66 C5
Lüneburg Germany 53°15N 10°24E 76 B6
Lüneburg Heath = Lüneburger Heide Germany 53°10N 10°12E 76 B6
Lüneburger Heide Germany 53°10N 10°12E 76 B6
Lunel France 43°39N 4°9E 73 E8
Lünen Germany 51°37N 7°32E 76 D3
Lunenburg Canada 44°22N 64°18W 165 D7
Lunéville France 48°36N 6°30E 71 D13
Lunga → Zambia 14°34S 26°25E 143 E2
Lunga Lunga Kenya 4°33S 39°7E 142 C4
Lungi S. Leone 8°40N 13°17W 138 D2
Lunglei India 22°55N 92°45E 123 H18
Luni India 26°0N 73°6E 124 G5
Luni → India 24°41N 71°14E 124 G4
Luninets = Luninyets Belarus 52°15N 26°50E 75 B14
Luning U.S.A. 38°30N 118°11W 168 G4
Lunino Russia 53°38N 45°18E 86 D7
Luninyets Belarus 52°15N 26°50E 75 B14
Lunkaransar India 28°29N 73°44E 124 E5
Lunsar S. Leone 8°41N 12°32W 138 D2
Lunsemfwa → Zambia 14°54S 30°12E 143 E3
Lunsemfwa Falls Zambia 14°30S 29°6E 143 E2
Luntai China 41°46N 84°14E 109 D10
Luo He → China 34°35N 110°20E 114 G6
Luocheng China 24°48N 108°53E 116 E7
Luochuan China 35°45N 109°26E 114 G5
Luoci China 25°19N 102°18E 116 E4
Luodian China 25°24N 106°43E 116 E6
Luoding China 22°45N 111°40E 117 F8
Luofu Dem. Rep. of the Congo 0°10S 29°15E 142 C2
Luohe China 33°32N 114°2E 114 H8
Luojiang China 31°18N 104°33E 116 B5
Luonan China 34°5N 110°10E 114 G6
Luoning China 34°35N 111°40E 114 G6
Luoshan China 32°13N 114°30E 117 A10
Luotian China 30°46N 115°22E 117 B10
Luoxiao Shan China 26°30N 114°1E 117 D10
Luoyang China 34°40N 112°26E 114 G7
Luoyuan China 26°28N 119°30E 117 D12
Luozigou China 43°42N 130°18E 115 C16
Lupeni Romania 45°21N 23°13E 81 E8
Lupilichi Mozam. 11°47S 35°13E 143 E4
Łupków Poland 49°15N 22°4E 83 J9
Lupoing China 24°53N 104°21E 116 E5
Luquan Hebei, China 38°4N 114°17E 114 E8
Luquan Yunnan, China 25°35N 102°25E 116 E4
Luque Paraguay 25°19S 57°25W 190 B4
Luquillo, Sierra de Puerto Rico 18°20N 65°47W 183 d
Lúras Italy 40°56N 9°10E 94 B2
Luray U.S.A. 38°40N 78°28W 173 F14
Lure France 47°40N 6°30E 71 E13
Lurgan U.K. 54°27N 6°20W 64 B5
Luribay Bolivia 17°6S 67°39W 188 D4
Lurín Peru 12°17S 76°52W 188 C2
Lúrio Mozam. 13°32S 40°30E 143 E5
Lurio → Mozam. 13°35S 40°30E 143 E5
Lusaka Zambia 15°28S 28°16E 143 F2
Lusaka □ Zambia 15°30S 29°0E 143 F2
Lusambo Dem. Rep. of the Congo 4°58S 23°28E 142 C1
Lusangaye Dem. Rep. of the Congo 4°54S 26°0E 142 C2
Luseland Canada 52°5N 109°24W 163 C7
Lusenga Plain △ Zambia 9°22S 29°14E 143 D2
Lushan Henan, China 33°45N 112°55E 114 H7
Lushan Sichuan, China 30°12N 102°52E 116 B4
Lushi China 34°3N 111°3E 114 G6
Lushnjë Albania 40°55N 19°41E 96 F3
Lushoto Tanzania 4°47S 38°20E 142 C4
Lushui China 25°58N 98°44E 116 E2
Lüshun China 38°45N 121°15E 115 E11
Lusignan France 46°26N 0°8E 72 B4
Lusigny-sur-Barse France 48°16N 4°15E 71 D11
Lusk U.S.A. 42°46N 104°27W 168 E11
Luso Portugal 40°23N 8°23W 88 E2
Lussac-les-Châteaux France 46°24N 0°43E 72 B4
Lustenau Austria 47°26N 9°39E 78 D2
Lūt, Dasht-e Iran 31°30N 58°0E 129 D8
Luta = Dalian China 38°50N 121°40E 115 E11
Lütao Taiwan 22°40N 121°30E 117 F13
Lutherstadt Wittenberg Germany 51°53N 12°39E 76 D8
Luthersville U.S.A. 33°13N 84°45W 178 B5
Luton U.K. 51°53N 0°24W 67 F7
Luton □ U.K. 51°53N 0°24W 67 F7
Lutsel K'e Canada 62°24N 110°44W 163 A6
Lutsk Ukraine 50°50N 25°15E 75 C13
Lutto = Lotta → Europe 68°42N 31°6E 60 B24
Lutz U.S.A. 28°9N 82°28W 179 G7
Lützow Holmbukta Antarctica 69°10S 37°30E 55 C4
Lutzputs S. Africa 28°3S 20°40E 144 C3
Luuq Somalia 3°48N 42°34E 131 G3
Luverne Ala., U.S.A. 31°43N 86°16W 178 D3
Luverne Minn., U.S.A. 43°39N 96°13W 172 D5
Luvua Dem. Rep. of the Congo 8°48S 25°17E 143 D2
Luvua → Dem. Rep. of the Congo 6°50S 27°30E 142 D2
Luvuvhu → S. Africa 22°25S 31°18E 145 B5
Luwegu → Tanzania 8°31S 37°23E 143 D4
Luwero Uganda 0°50N 32°28E 142 B3
Luwuk Indonesia 0°56S 122°47E 119 E6
Luxembourg Lux. 49°37N 6°9E 69 E6
Luxembourg □ Belgium 49°58N 5°30E 69 E5
Luxembourg ■ Europe 49°45N 6°0E 69 E5
Luxembourg ✕ (LUX) Lux. 49°37N 6°10E 69 E6
Luxeuil-les-Bains France 47°49N 6°24E 71 E13
Luxi Hunan, China 28°20N 110°7E 117 C8
Luxi Yunnan, China 24°40N 103°55E 116 E4
Luxi Yunnan, China 24°27N 98°36E 116 E2
Luxian China 29°9N 105°24E 116 C5
Luxor = El Uqsur Egypt 25°41N 32°38E 137 B3
Luy-de-Béarn → France 43°39N 0°48W 72 E3
Luy-de-France → France 43°39N 0°48W 72 E3
Luyi China 33°50N 115°35E 114 H8
Luykau = Loikaw Burma 19°40N 97°17E 123 K20
Luz-St-Sauveur France 42°53N 0°0 72 F4
Luzern Switz. 47°3N 8°18E 77 H4
Luzern □ Switz. 47°2N 7°55E 77 H3
Luzhai China 24°29N 109°42E 116 E7
Luzhany Ukraine 48°22N 25°47E 81 B10
Luzhi China 26°21N 105°16E 116 D5
Luzhou China 28°52N 105°20E 116 C5
Luziânia Brazil 16°20S 48°0W 189 D1
Luzilândia Brazil 3°28S 42°22W 189 A2
Lužnice → Czech Rep. 49°14N 14°23E 78 B7
Luzon Phil. 16°0N 121°0E 119 A6
Luzon Strait Asia 21°0N 120°40E 117 G13
Luzy France 46°47N 3°58E 71 F10
Luzzi Italy 39°27N 16°17E 95 C9
Lviv Ukraine 49°50N 24°0E 75 D13
Lviv □ Ukraine 49°30N 23°45E 75 D12
Lvov = Lviv Ukraine 49°50N 24°0E 75 D13
Lwówek Poland 52°28N 16°10E 83 F3
Lwówek Śląski Poland 51°7N 15°38E 83 G2
Lyakhavichy Belarus 53°2N 26°32E 75 B14
Lyakhovskiye, Ostrova Russia 73°40N 141°0E 107 B15
Lyaki = Läki Azerbaijan 40°34N 47°22E 87 K8
Lyal I. Canada 44°57N 81°24W 174 B3
Lyall Mt. N.Z. 45°16S 167°32E 155 F2
Lyaskovets Bulgaria 43°6N 25°44E 97 C9
Lyasnaya → Belarus 52°9N 23°31E 83 F10
Lybster U.K. 58°18N 3°15W 65 C5
Lycaonia Turkey 38°0N 33°0E 104 D5
Lychen Germany 53°12N 13°18E 76 B9
Lychkova Russia 57°55N 32°24E 84 D7
Lycia Turkey 36°30N 29°30E 99 E11
Lyckebyån → Sweden 56°12N 15°39E 63 H9
Lycksele Sweden 64°38N 18°40E 60 D18
Lycosura Greece 37°20N 22°3E 98 D4
Lydda = Lod Israel 31°57N 34°54E 130 D3
Lyddan I. Antarctica 74°0S 21°0W 55 D2
Lydenburg S. Africa 25°10S 30°29E 145 C5
Lydia Turkey 38°48N 28°19E 99 C10
Łydynia → Poland 52°43N 20°26E 83 F7
Lyell N.Z. 41°48S 172°4E 155 B7
Lyell I. Canada 52°40N 131°35W 162 C2
Lyepyel Belarus 54°50N 28°40E 84 E5
Lygnern Sweden 57°30N 12°15E 63 G6
Lykens U.S.A. 40°34N 76°42W 175 F8
Lyman Ukraine 45°41N 29°45E 81 E14
Lyman U.S.A. 41°20N 110°18W 168 F8
Lymanske Ukraine 46°40N 29°58E 81 D14
Lyme B. U.K. 50°42N 2°53W 67 G4
Lyme Regis U.K. 50°43N 2°57W 67 G5
Lymington U.K. 50°45N 1°32W 67 G6
Łyna → Poland 54°37N 21°14E 82 D8
Lynchburg S.C., U.S.A. 34°3N 80°4W 178 A9
Lynchburg Va., U.S.A. 37°25N 79°9W 173 G14
Lynd → Australia 16°28S 143°18E 150 B3
Lynd Ra. Australia 25°30S 149°20E 151 D4
Lynden Canada 43°14N 80°9W 174 C4
Lynden U.S.A. 48°57N 122°27W 170 B4
Lyndhurst Australia 30°15S 138°18E 151 E2
Lyndon → Australia 23°29S 114°6E 149 D1
Lyndonville N.Y., U.S.A. 43°20N 78°23W 174 C6
Lyndonville Vt., U.S.A. 44°31N 72°1W 175 B12
Lyngen Norway 69°45N 20°30E 60 B19
Lynher Reef Australia 15°27S 121°55E 148 C3
Lynn U.S.A. 42°28N 70°57W 175 D14
Lynn Canal U.S.A. 58°50N 135°15W 166 D12
Lynn Haven U.S.A. 30°15N 85°39W 178 E4
Lynn Lake Canada 56°51N 101°3W 163 B8
Lynne U.S.A. 29°12N 81°55W 179 F8
Lynnwood U.S.A. 47°49N 122°18W 170 C4
Lynton U.K. 51°13N 3°50W 67 F4
Lyntupy Belarus 55°4N 26°23E 84 E4
Lynx L. Canada 62°25N 106°15W 163 A7
Lyon France 45°46N 4°50E 73 C8
Lyon St-Exupery ✕ (LYS) France 45°44N 5°2E 73 C9
Lyonnais France 45°45N 4°15E 73 C8
Lyons = Lyon France 45°46N 4°50E 73 C8
Lyons Ga., U.S.A. 32°12N 82°19W 178 C7
Lyons Kans., U.S.A. 38°21N 98°12W 172 F4
Lyons N.Y., U.S.A. 43°5N 77°0W 174 C8
Lyons → Australia 25°2S 115°9E 149 E2
Lyons Falls U.S.A. 43°37N 75°22W 175 C9
Lyozna Belarus 55°0N 30°50E 84 E6
Lys = Leie → Belgium 51°2N 3°45E 69 C3
Lysá nad Labem Czech Rep. 50°11N 14°51E 78 A7
Lysekil Sweden 58°17N 11°26E 63 F5
Lysi Cyprus 35°6N 33°41E 101 D12
Lyskovo Russia 56°0N 45°3E 86 B7
Lystrup Denmark 56°14N 10°14E 63 H4
Lysvik Sweden 60°1N 13°9E 62 D7
Lysychansk Ukraine 48°55N 38°30E 85 H10
Lytham St. Anne's U.K. 53°45N 3°0W 66 D4
Lyttelton N.Z. 43°35S 172°44E 155 D7
Lytton Canada 50°13N 121°31W 162 C4
Lyuban Russia 59°16N 31°18E 84 C6
Lyubertsy Russia 55°40N 37°51E 84 E9
Lyubim Russia 58°20N 40°39E 84 C11
Lyubimets Bulgaria 41°50N 26°5E 97 E10
Lyuboml Ukraine 51°11N 24°4E 83 G11
Lyubotyn Ukraine 50°0N 36°0E 85 H8
Lyubytino Russia 58°50N 33°16E 84 C7
Lyudinovo Russia 53°52N 34°28E 84 F8

M

M.R. Štefánik, Bratislava ✕ (BTS) Slovak Rep. 48°11N 17°9E 79 C10
Ma → Vietnam 19°47N 105°56E 116 H5
Ma, O. el → Algeria 27°45N 7°52W 136 C2
Ma On Shan China 22°24N 114°10E 111 a
Ma'adaba Jordan 31°43N 35°47E 130 D4
Ma'alot-Tarshiha Israel 33°1N 35°17E 130 B4
Maamba Zambia 17°17S 26°28E 144 A4
Ma'ān Jordan 30°12N 35°44E 130 E4
Ma'ān □ Jordan 30°0N 36°0E 130 F5
Maanselkä Finland 63°52N 28°32E 60 C23
Ma'anshan China 31°44N 118°29E 117 B12
Maarianhamina = Mariehamn Finland 60°5N 19°55E 61 F18
Maarmorilik Greenland 71°3N 51°0W 57 C5
Ma'arrat an Nu'mān Syria 35°43N 36°43E 104 E7
Maas → Neths. 51°45N 4°32E 69 C4
Maaseik Belgium 51°6N 5°45E 69 C5
Maasin Phil. 10°8N 124°50E 119 B6
Maastricht Neths. 50°50N 5°40E 69 D5
Maave Mozam. 21°4S 34°47E 145 B5
Mababe Depression Botswana 18°50S 24°15E 144 A3
Mabalane Mozam. 23°37S 32°31E 145 B5
Mabel L. Canada 50°35N 118°43W 162 C5
Mabenge Dem. Rep. of the Congo 4°15N 24°12E 142 B1
Maberly Canada 44°50N 76°32W 175 B8
Mabesi, L. S. Leone 7°10N 11°42W 138 D2
Mabian China 28°47N 103°37E 116 C4
Mablethorpe U.K. 53°20N 0°15E 66 D8
Mableton U.S.A. 33°49N 84°35W 178 B5
Mably France 46°5N 4°4E 71 F11
Maboma Dem. Rep. of the Congo 2°30N 28°10E 142 B2
Mabonto S. Leone 8°53N 11°50W 138 D2
Mabroûk Mali 19°29N 1°15W 139 B4
Mabuasehube ⌂ Botswana 25°5S 21°10E 144 C3
Mabuiag Australia 9°57S 142°11E 150 a
Mac Bac Vietnam 9°46N 106°7E 121 H6
Macachin Argentina 37°10S 63°43W 190 D3
Macaé Brazil 22°20S 41°43W 191 A7
Macael Spain 37°20N 2°18W 91 H2
Macaíba Brazil 5°51S 35°21W 189 B3
Macajuba Brazil 12°9S 40°22W 189 C2
McAlester U.S.A. 34°56N 95°46W 176 D7
McAllen U.S.A. 26°12N 98°14W 176 H5
McAlpin U.S.A. 30°8N 82°57W 178 E7
MacAlpine L. Canada 66°32N 102°45W 160 D11
Macamic Canada 48°45N 79°0W 164 C4
Macao = Macau China 22°12N 113°33E 117 F9
Macão Portugal 39°35N 7°59W 89 F3
Macapá Brazil 0°5N 51°4W 187 C8
Macarani Brazil 15°33S 40°24W 189 D2
Macarao △ Venezuela 10°22N 67°17W 183 D6
Macarthur Australia 38°5S 142°0E 152 E5
McArthur → Australia 15°54S 136°40E 150 B2
McArthur, Port Australia 16°4S 136°23E 150 B2
Macate Peru 8°48S 78°7W 188 B2
Macau Brazil 5°15S 36°40W 189 B3
Macau China 22°12N 113°33E 117 F9
Macaúbas Brazil 13°2S 42°42W 189 C2
McBride Canada 53°20N 120°19W 162 C4
McCall U.S.A. 44°55N 116°6W 168 D5
McCamey U.S.A. 31°8N 102°14W 176 F3
McCammon U.S.A. 42°39N 112°12W 168 E7
McCarran Int., Las Vegas ✕ (LAS) U.S.A. 36°5N 115°9W 171 J11
McCauley I. Canada 53°40N 130°15W 162 C2
McCleary U.S.A. 47°3N 123°16W 170 C3
Macclenny U.S.A. 30°17N 82°7W 178 E7
Macclesfield U.K. 53°15N 2°8W 66 D5
Macclesfield Bank S. China Sea 16°0N 114°30E 118 A4
M'Clintock Chan. Canada 72°0N 102°0W 160 C11
McClintock Ra. Australia 18°44S 127°38E 148 C4
McCloud U.S.A. 41°15N 122°8W 168 F2
McCluer I. Australia 11°5S 133°0E 148 B5
McClure U.S.A. 40°42N 77°19W 174 F7
McClure, L. U.S.A. 37°35N 120°16W 170 H6
M'Clure Str. Canada 75°0N 119°0W 161 C8
McClusky U.S.A. 47°29N 100°27W 172 B3
McComb U.S.A. 31°15N 90°27W 177 F9
McCook U.S.A. 40°12N 100°38W 172 E3
McCormick U.S.A. 33°55N 82°17W 178 B7
McCreary Canada 50°47N 99°29W 163 C9
McCullough Mt. U.S.A. 35°35N 115°13W 171 K11
McCusker → Canada 55°32N 108°39W 163 B7
McDavid U.S.A. 30°52N 87°19W 179 E2
McDermitt U.S.A. 41°59N 117°43W 168 F5
McDonald U.S.A. 40°22N 80°14W 174 F4
Macdonald, L. Australia 23°30S 129°0E 148 D4
McDonald Is. Ind. Oc. 53°0S 73°0E 146 K6
MacDonnell Ranges Australia 23°40S 133°0E 148 D5
McDonough U.S.A. 33°27N 84°9W 178 B5
McDougalls Well Australia 31°8S 141°15E 152 A4
MacDowell L. Canada 52°15N 92°45W 164 B1
Macduff U.K. 57°40N 2°31W 65 D6
Maceda Spain 42°16N 7°39W 88 C3
Macedonia U.S.A. 41°19N 81°31W 174 E3
Macedonia ■ Europe 41°53N 21°40E 96 E5
Maceió Brazil 9°40S 35°41W 189 B3
Maceira Portugal 39°41N 8°55W 88 F2
Macenta Guinea 8°35N 9°32W 138 D3
Macerata Italy 43°18N 13°27E 93 E10
McFarland U.S.A. 35°41N 119°14W 171 K7
McFarlane → Canada 59°12N 107°58W 163 B7

Macfarlane, L. Australia 32°0S 136°40E 152 B2
McGehee U.S.A. 33°38N 91°24W 176 E9
McGill U.S.A. 39°23N 114°47W 168 G6
Macgillycuddy's Reeks Ireland 51°58N 9°45W 64 E2
McGraw U.S.A. 42°36N 76°8W 175 D8
McGregor U.S.A. 43°1N 91°11W 172 D8
McGregor Ra. Australia 27°0S 142°45E 151 D3
McGuire, Mt. Australia 20°18S 148°23E 150 b
Mach Pakistan 29°50N 67°20E 124 E2
Māch Kowr Iran 25°48N 61°28E 129 E9
Machacalis Brazil 17°5S 40°45W 189 D2
Machado = Jiparaná → Brazil 8°3S 62°52W 186 E6
Machagai Argentina 26°56S 60°2W 190 B3
Machakos Kenya 1°30S 37°15E 142 C4
Machala Ecuador 3°20S 79°57W 186 D3
Machanga Mozam. 20°59S 35°0E 145 B6
Machattie, L. Australia 24°50S 139°48E 150 C2
Machault France 49°21N 4°29E 71 C11
Machava Mozam. 25°54S 32°28E 145 C5
Machecoul France 47°0N 1°49W 70 F5
Macheke Zimbabwe 18°5S 31°51E 145 A5
Macheng China 31°12N 115°2E 117 B10
Macherla India 16°29N 79°26E 126 F4
Machero Spain 39°21N 4°20W 89 F6
Machgaon India 20°5N 86°17E 126 D8
Machhu → India 23°6N 70°46E 124 H4
Machiara △ Pakistan 34°40N 73°30E 124 B5
Machias Maine, U.S.A. 44°43N 67°28W 173 C20
Machias N.Y., U.S.A. 42°25N 78°29W 174 D6
Machichi → Canada 57°3N 92°6W 163 B10
Machico Madeira 32°43N 16°44W 100 D3
Machilipatnam India 16°12N 81°8E 127 F5
Machiques Venezuela 10°4N 72°34W 186 A4
Machu Picchu Peru 13°8S 72°30W 188 C3
Machynlleth U.K. 52°35N 3°50W 67 E4
Macia Mozam. 25°2S 33°8E 145 C5
Maciejowice Poland 51°36N 21°26E 83 G8
McIlwraith Ra. Australia 13°50S 143°20E 150 A3
Măcin Romania 45°16N 28°8E 81 E13
Macina Mali 14°50N 5°0W 138 C4
McInnes L. Canada 52°13N 93°45W 163 C10
McIntosh U.S.A. 45°55N 101°21W 172 C3
McIntosh L. Canada 55°45N 105°0W 163 B8
Macintosh Ra. Australia 27°39S 125°32E 149 E4
Macintyre → Australia 28°37S 150°47E 151 D5
Macizo Galaico Spain 42°30N 7°30W 88 C3
Maçka Turkey 40°49N 39°36E 105 B8
Mackay Australia 21°8S 149°11E 150 K7
Mackay U.S.A. 43°55N 113°37W 168 E7
MacKay → Canada 57°10N 111°38W 162 B6
Mackay, L. Australia 22°30S 129°0E 148 D4
McKay Ra. Australia 23°0S 122°30E 148 D3
McKeesport U.S.A. 40°20N 79°51W 174 F5
McKellar Canada 45°30N 79°55W 174 A5
McKenna U.S.A. 46°56N 122°33W 170 D4
Mackenzie = Linden Guyana 6°0N 58°10W 186 B7
Mackenzie Canada 55°20N 123°5W 162 B4
McKenzie U.S.A. 36°8N 88°31W 177 C10
Mackenzie → Australia 23°38S 149°46E 150 C4
Mackenzie → Canada 69°10N 134°20W 160 D5
McKenzie → U.S.A. 44°7N 123°6W 168 D2
Mackenzie Bay Canada 69°0N 137°30W 158 C6
Mackenzie King I. Canada 77°45N 111°0W 161 B9
Mackenzie Mts. Canada 64°0N 130°0W 158 C6
Mackenzie Plains N.Z. 44°10S 170°25E 155 E5
McKerrow, L. N.Z. 44°25S 168°5E 155 E3
Mackinac, Straits of U.S.A. 45°50N 84°40W 173 C11
Mackinaw City U.S.A. 45°47N 84°44W 173 C11
McKinlay Australia 21°16S 141°18E 150 C3
McKinlay → Australia 20°50S 141°28E 150 C3
McKinley, Mt. U.S.A. 63°4N 151°0W 160 E1
McKinley Sea Arctic 82°0N 0°0 57 A11
McKinney U.S.A. 33°12N 96°37W 176 E6
Mackinnon Road Kenya 3°40S 39°1E 142 C4
McKittrick U.S.A. 35°18N 119°37W 171 K7
Macklin Canada 52°20N 109°56W 163 C7
Macksville Australia 30°40S 152°56E 153 A10
McLaren Vale Australia 35°13S 138°31E 152 C3
McLaughlin U.S.A. 45°49N 100°49W 172 C3
Maclean Australia 29°26S 153°16E 151 D5
McLean U.S.A. 35°14N 100°36W 176 D4
McLeansboro U.S.A. 38°6N 88°32W 172 F9
Maclear S. Africa 31°2S 28°23E 145 D4
Maclear, C. Malawi 13°58S 34°49E 143 E3
Macleay → Australia 30°56S 153°0E 153 A10
McLennan Canada 55°42N 116°50W 162 B5
McLeod → Canada 54°9N 115°44W 162 C5
MacLeod, L. Australia 24°9S 113°47E 149 D1
MacLeod B. Canada 62°53N 110°0W 163 A7
MacLeod Lake Canada 54°58N 123°0W 162 C4
McLoughlin, Mt. U.S.A. 42°27N 122°19W 168 E2
McMechen U.S.A. 39°57N 80°44W 174 G4
McMinnville Oreg., U.S.A. 45°13N 123°12W 168 D2
McMinnville Tenn., U.S.A. 35°41N 85°46W 177 D12
McMurdo Antarctica 77°51S 166°37E 55 D11
McMurdo Sd. Antarctica 77°0S 170°0E 55 D11
McMurray = Fort McMurray Canada 56°44N 111°7W 162 B6
McMurray U.S.A. 48°19N 122°14W 170 B4
Maçobere Mozam. 21°13S 32°47E 143 G3
Macodoene Mozam. 23°32S 35°5E 145 B6
Macomb U.S.A. 40°27N 90°40W 172 E8
Macomer Italy 40°16N 8°47E 94 B1
Mâcon France 46°19N 4°50E 71 F11
Macon Ga., U.S.A. 32°51N 83°38W 178 C6
Macon Miss., U.S.A. 33°7N 88°34W 177 E10
Macon Mo., U.S.A. 39°44N 92°28W 172 F7
Macossa Mozam. 17°55S 33°56E 143 F3
Macoun L. Canada 56°32N 103°40W 163 B8
Macovane Mozam. 21°30S 35°2E 145 B6
McPherson U.S.A. 38°22N 97°40W 172 F5
McPherson Pk. U.S.A. 34°53N 119°53W 171 L7
McPherson Ra. Australia 28°15S 153°15E 151 D5
Macquarie → Australia 30°7S 147°24E 153 A7
Macquarie Harbour Australia 42°15S 145°23E 151 G4
Macquarie I. Pac. Oc. 54°36S 158°55E 156 N7
Macquarie Ridge S. Ocean 57°0S 159°0E 55 B10
McRae U.S.A. 32°4N 82°54W 178 C7
MacRobertson Land Antarctica 71°0S 64°0E 55 D6
Macroom Ireland 51°54N 8°57W 64 E3
MacTier Canada 45°8N 79°47W 174 A5
Macubela Mozam. 16°53S 37°49E 143 F4
Macugnaga Italy 45°58N 7°58E 92 C4
Macuira △ Colombia 12°9N 71°21W 183 D5
Macumba → Australia 27°52S 137°12E 151 D2
Macuro Venezuela 10°42N 61°55W 187 K15
Macusani Peru 14°4S 70°29W 188 C3
Macuse Mozam. 17°45S 37°10E 143 F4
Macuspana Mexico 17°46N 92°36W 181 D6
Macusse Angola 17°48S 20°23E 144 A3
Mada → Nigeria 7°59N 7°55E 139 D6
Ma'dabā □ Jordan 31°43N 35°47E 130 D4
Madadeni S. Africa 27°43S 30°3E 145 C5
Madagali Nigeria 10°56N 13°33E 139 C7
Madagascar ■ Africa 20°0S 47°0E 141 J9
Madā'in Sālih Si. Arabia 26°46N 37°57E 128 E3
Madakasira India 13°56N 77°16E 127 H3
Madama Niger 22°0N 13°40E 135 D8
Madame, I. Canada 45°30N 60°58W 165 C7
Madan Bulgaria 41°30N 24°57E 97 E8
Madanapalle India 13°33N 78°28E 127 H4
Madang Papua N. G. 5°12S 145°49E 147 B7
Madaoua Niger 14°5N 6°27E 139 C6
Madara Bulgaria 43°17N 27°8E 97 C11
Madara Nigeria 11°45N 10°35E 139 C7
Madaripur Bangla. 23°19N 90°15E 123 H17
Madauk Burma 17°56N 96°52E 123 L20
Madawaska Canada 45°30N 78°0W 174 A7
Madawaska → Canada 45°27N 76°21W 174 A7
Madaya Burma 22°12N 96°10E 123 H20
Maddalena Italy 41°16N 9°23E 94 A2
Maddaloni Italy 41°2N 14°23E 95 A7
Maddur India 12°36N 77°4E 127 H3
Madeira Atl. Oc. 32°50N 17°0W 100 D3
Madeira → Brazil 3°22S 58°45W 186 D7
Madeleine, Îs. de la Canada 47°30N 61°40W 165 C7
Maden Turkey 38°23N 39°40E 105 C8
Madera Mexico 29°12N 108°7W 180 B3
Madera Calif., U.S.A. 36°57N 120°3W 170 J6
Madera Pa., U.S.A. 40°49N 78°26W 174 F6
Madgaon India 15°12N 73°58E 127 G1
Madha India 18°0N 75°30E 126 F2
Madhavpur India 21°15N 69°58E 124 J3
Madhepura India 26°11N 86°23E 125 F12
Madhira India 16°55N 80°22E 126 F5
Madhubani India 26°21N 86°7E 125 F12
Madhugiri India 13°40N 77°12E 127 H3
Madhupur India 24°16N 86°39E 125 G12
Madhya Pradesh □ India 22°50N 78°0E 124 J8
Madidi → Bolivia 12°32S 66°52W 188 C4
Madikeri India 12°30N 75°45E 127 H2
Madikwe △ S. Africa 27°38S 32°15E 145 C5
Madill U.S.A. 34°6N 96°46W 176 D6
Madimba Dem. Rep. of the Congo 4°58S 15°5E 140 E3
Ma'din Syria 35°45N 39°36E 105 E8
Madina Mali 13°25N 8°50W 138 C3
Madinani Ivory C. 9°37N 6°57W 138 D3
Madīnat al Malik Khālid al Askarīyah Si. Arabia 27°54N 45°31E 128 E5
Madīnat ath Thawrah Syria 35°50N 38°32E 105 E8
Madīnat Masdar U.A.E. 24°26N 54°37E 129 E7
Madingou Congo 4°10S 13°33E 140 E2
Madison Calif., U.S.A. 38°41N 121°59W 170 G5
Madison Fla., U.S.A. 30°28N 83°25W 178 E6
Madison Ga., U.S.A. 33°36N 83°28W 178 B6
Madison Ind., U.S.A. 38°44N 85°23W 173 F11
Madison Nebr., U.S.A. 41°50N 97°27W 172 E5
Madison Ohio, U.S.A. 41°46N 81°3W 174 E3
Madison S. Dak., U.S.A. 44°0N 97°7W 172 C5
Madison Wis., U.S.A. 43°4N 89°24W 172 D9
Madison → U.S.A. 45°56N 111°31W 168 D8
Madison Heights U.S.A. 37°25N 79°8W 173 G14
Madisonville Ky., U.S.A. 37°20N 87°30W 172 G10
Madisonville Tex., U.S.A. 30°57N 95°55W 176 F7
Madista Botswana 21°15S 25°6E 144 B4
Madiun Indonesia 7°38S 111°32E 118 F4
Mado Gashi Kenya 0°44N 39°10E 142 B4
Madoc Canada 44°30N 77°28W 174 B7
Madoi China 34°46N 98°18E 110 E8
Madon → France 48°36N 6°6E 71 D13
Madona Latvia 56°53N 26°5E 84 D4
Madonie Italy 37°50N 13°50E 94 E6
Madonna di Campiglio Italy 46°14N 10°49E 92 B7
Madra Dağı Turkey 39°23N 27°12E 99 B9
Madrakah, Ra's al Oman 19°0N 57°50E 131 D6
Madras = Chennai India 13°8N 80°19E 127 H5
Madras = Tamil Nadu □ India 11°0N 77°0E 127 J3
Madras U.S.A. 44°38N 121°8W 168 D3
Madre, L. U.S.A. 25°15N 97°30W 176 J6
Madre, Sierra Phil. 17°0N 122°0E 119 A6
Madre de Dios □ Peru 12°0S 70°15W 188 C3
Madre de Dios → Bolivia 10°59S 66°8W 188 C4
Madre de Dios, I. Chile 50°20S 75°10W 192 D1
Madre del Sur, Sierra Mexico 17°30N 100°0W 181 D5
Madre Occidental, Sierra Mexico 27°0N 107°0W 180 B3
Madre Oriental, Sierra Mexico 25°0N 100°0W 180 C5
Madri India 24°16N 73°32E 124 G5
Madrid Spain 40°24N 3°42W 88 E7
Madrid Ala., U.S.A. 31°2N 85°24W 178 D4
Madrid N.Y., U.S.A. 44°45N 75°8W 175 B9
Madrid □ Spain 40°30N 3°45W 88 E7
Madrid Barajas ✕ (MAD) Spain 40°26N 3°34W 88 E7
Madridejos Spain 39°28N 3°33W 89 F7
Madrigal de las Altas Torres Spain 41°5N 5°0W 88 D6
Madrona, Sierra Spain 38°27N 4°16W 89 G6
Madroñera Spain 39°26N 5°42W 89 F5
Madula Dem. Rep. of the Congo 0°27N 25°22E 142 B2
Madura Australia 31°55S 127°0E 149 F4
Madura Indonesia 7°30S 114°0E 119 G15
Madura, Selat Indonesia 7°30S 113°20E 119 G15
Madura Oya △ Sri Lanka 7°20N 81°10E 127 L5
Madurai India 9°55N 78°10E 127 K4
Madurantakam India 12°30N 79°50E 127 H4
Madzhalis Russia 42°9N 47°47E 87 J8
Mae Chan Thailand 20°9N 99°52E 120 B2
Mae Charim △ Thailand 18°17N 100°59E 120 C3
Mae Hong Son Thailand 19°16N 97°56E 120 C2
Mae Khlong → Thailand 13°24N 100°0E 120 F3
Mae Moei △ Thailand 17°26N 98°7E 120 D2
Mae Phang △ Thailand 19°7N 99°13E 120 C2
Mae Phrik Thailand 17°27N 99°7E 120 D2
Mae Ping △ Thailand 17°37N 98°51E 120 D2
Mae Ramat Thailand 16°58N 98°31E 120 D2
Mae Rim Thailand 18°54N 98°57E 120 C2
Mae Sai Thailand 20°20N 99°55E 116 G2
Mae Sot Thailand 16°43N 98°34E 120 D2
Mae Suai Thailand 19°39N 99°33E 116 H2
Mae Tha Thailand 18°28N 99°8E 120 C2
Mae Tup Res. Thailand 17°52N 98°45E 120 D2
Mae Wa △ Thailand 17°23N 99°16E 120 D2
Mae Wong △ Thailand 15°54N 99°12E 120 E2
Mae Yom △ Thailand 18°43N 100°15E 120 C3
Maebaru Japan 33°33N 130°12E 113 H5
Maebashi Japan 36°24N 139°4E 113 F9
Maella Spain 41°8N 0°7E 90 D5
Maelpaeg L. Canada 48°20N 56°30W 165 C8
Maesteg U.K. 51°36N 3°40W 67 F4
Maestra, Sierra Cuba 20°15N 77°0W 182 B4
Maevatanana Madag. 16°56S 46°49E 141 H9
Mafadi S. Africa 29°12S 29°21E 145 C4
Mafeking = Mafikeng S. Africa 25°50S 25°38E 144 C4
Mafeking Canada 52°40N 101°10W 163 C8
Maféré Ivory C. 5°30N 3°2W 138 D4
Mafeteng Lesotho 29°51S 27°15E 144 C4
Maffra Australia 37°53S 146°58E 153 D7
Mafia I. Tanzania 7°45S 39°50E 142 D4
Mafikeng S. Africa 25°50S 25°38E 144 C4
Mafra Brazil 26°10S 49°55W 191 B6
Mafra Portugal 38°55N 9°20W 89 G1
Mafungabusi Plateau Zimbabwe 18°30S 29°8E 143 F2
Magadan Russia 59°38N 150°50E 107 D16
Magadi India 12°58N 77°14E 127 H3
Magadi Kenya 1°54S 36°19E 142 C4
Magadi, L. Kenya 1°54S 36°19E 142 C4
Magaliesburg S. Africa 26°0S 27°32E 145 C4
Magallanes □ Chile 52°0S 72°0W 192 D2
Magallanes, Estrecho de Chile 52°30S 75°0W 192 D2
Magaluf Spain 39°29N 2°32E 91 F7
Magangué Colombia 9°14N 74°45W 186 B4
Magaria Niger 13°4N 9°5E 139 C6
Magburaka S. Leone 8°47N 12°0W 138 D2
Magdagachi Russia 53°27N 125°48E 107 D13
Magdalen Is. = Madeleine, Îs. de la Canada 47°30N 61°40W 165 C7
Magdalena Argentina 35°5S 57°30W 190 D4
Magdalena Bolivia 13°13S 63°57W 186 F6
Magdalena U.S.A. 34°7N 107°15W 169 J10
Magdalena → Colombia 11°6N 74°51W 186 A4
Magdalena, B. Mexico 24°35N 112°0W 180 C2
Magdalena, I. Chile 44°40S 73°0W 192 B2
Magdalena, I. Mexico 24°40N 112°15W 180 C2
Magdalena, Llano de Mexico 25°0N 111°25W 180 C2
Magdalena de Kino Mexico 30°38N 110°57W 180 A2
Magdeburg Germany 52°7N 11°38E 76 C7
Magdelaine Cays Australia 16°33S 150°18E 150 B5
Magee U.S.A. 31°52N 89°44W 177 F10
Magelang Indonesia 7°29S 110°13E 118 F4
Magellan's Str. = Magallanes, Estrecho de Chile 52°30S 75°0W 192 D2
Magenta Italy 45°28N 8°53E 92 C5
Magenta, L. Australia 33°30S 119°2E 149 F2
Magerøya Norway 71°3N 25°40E 60 A21
Maggea Australia 34°28S 140°2E 152 C4
Maggia → Switz. 46°18N 8°36E 77 J4
Maggiorasca, Mte. Italy 44°33N 9°29E 92 D6
Maggiore, L. Italy 45°57N 8°39E 92 B5
Maggotty Jamaica 18°9N 77°46W 182 a
Maghâgha Egypt 28°38N 30°50E 137 F7
Maghama Mauritania 15°32N 12°57W 138 B2
Maghera U.K. 54°51N 6°41W 64 B5
Magherafelt U.K. 54°45N 6°37W 64 B5
Maghnia Algeria 34°50N 1°43W 136 B3
Maghreb N. Afr. 32°0N 4°0W 132 C3
Magione Italy 43°8N 12°12E 93 E9
Magistralnyy Russia 56°16N 107°36E 107 D11
Maglaj Bos.-H. 44°33N 18°7E 80 F3
Magliano in Toscana Italy 42°36N 11°17E 93 F8
Máglie Italy 40°7N 18°18E 95 B11
Magnac-Laval France 46°13N 1°11E 72 B5
Magnesia = Magnisia Greece 39°15N 23°0E 98 B5
Magnetic Pole (North) Arctic 82°18N 113°24W 54 A2
Magnetic Pole (South) Antarctica 64°8S 138°8E 55 C9
Magnisia Greece 39°15N 23°0E 98 B5
Magnitogorsk Russia 53°27N 59°4E 108 B5
Magnolia Ark., U.S.A. 33°16N 93°14W 176 E8
Magnolia Miss., U.S.A. 31°9N 90°28W 177 F9
Magny-en-Vexin France 49°9N 1°47E 71 C8
Mago Fiji 17°26S 179°8W 154 a
Magog Canada 45°18N 72°9W 175 A12
Magoro Uganda 1°45N 34°12E 142 B3
Magoulades Greece 39°45N 19°42E 101 A3
Magoye Zambia 16°1S 27°30E 143 F2
Magpie, L. Canada 51°0N 64°41W 165 B7
Magrath Canada 49°25N 112°50W 162 D6
Magre → Spain 39°11N 0°25W 91 F4
Magta Lahjar Mauritania 17°28N 13°17W 138 B2
Magu Tanzania 2°30S 33°30E 142 C3
Maguan China 23°0N 104°21E 116 F5
Maguarinho, C. Brazil 0°15S 48°30W 187 D9
Magude Mozam. 25°2S 32°40E 145 C5
Magurski △ Poland 49°30N 21°30E 83 J8
Mağusa = Famagusta Cyprus 35°8N 33°55E 101 D12
Maguse L. Canada 61°37N 95°10W 163 A9
Maguse Pt. Canada 61°20N 93°50W 163 A10
Magvana India 23°13N 69°22E 124 H3
Magwe Burma 20°10N 95°0E 123 J19
Magyarorszag = Hungary ■ Europe 47°20N 19°20E 79 D12
Maha Oya Sri Lanka 7°31N 81°22E 127 L5
Maha Sarakham Thailand 16°12N 103°16E 120 D4
Mahābād Iran 36°50N 45°45E 105 D11
Mahabaleshwar India 17°58N 73°43E 126 F1
Mahabalipuram India 12°37N 80°11E 127 H5
Mahabharat Lekh Nepal 28°30N 82°0E 125 E10
Mahabo Madag. 20°23S 44°40E 141 J8
Mahad India 18°6N 73°29E 126 E1
Mahadeo Hills India 22°20N 78°30E 125 H8
Mahadeopur India 18°48N 80°0E 126 E5
Mahaffey U.S.A. 40°53N 78°44W 174 F6
Mahagi Dem. Rep. of the Congo 2°20N 31°0E 142 B3
Mahajan India 28°48N 73°56E 124 E5
Mahajanga Madag. 15°40S 46°25E 141 H9
Mahakam → Indonesia 0°35S 117°17E 118 E5
Mahalapye Botswana 23°1S 26°51E 144 B4
Mahale Mts. Tanzania 6°20S 30°0E 142 D3
Mahale Mts. △ Tanzania 6°10S 29°50E 142 D2
Maḩallāt Iran 33°55N 50°30E 129 C6
Māhān Iran 30°5N 57°18E 129 D8
Mahan → India 23°30N 82°50E 125 H10
Mahanadi → India 20°20N 86°25E 126 D8
Mahananda → India 25°12N 87°52E 125 G12
Mahanoro Madag. 19°54S 48°48E 141 H9
Mahanoy City U.S.A. 40°49N 76°9W 175 F8
Maharashtra □ India 20°30N 75°30E 126 D2
Maharès Tunisia 34°32N 10°29E 136 B6
Mahasamund India 21°6N 82°6E 126 D6
Mahasham, W. → Egypt 30°15N 34°10E 130 E3
Mahattat ash Shīdīyah Jordan 29°55N 35°55E 130 F4
Mahattat 'Unayzah Jordan 30°30N 35°47E 130 E4
Mahaweli Ganga → Sri Lanka 8°27N 81°13E 127 K5
Mahaxay Laos 17°22N 105°12E 120 D5
Mahbubabad India 17°42N 80°2E 126 F5
Mahbubnagar India 16°45N 77°59E 126 F3
Mahda U.A.E. 25°20N 56°15E 129 E8
Maḩḑah Oman 24°24N 55°59E 129 E7
Mahdia Tunisia 35°28N 11°0E 136 A6
Mahdia □ Tunisia 35°20N 10°35E 136 A6
Mahe Jammu & Kashmir, India 33°10N 78°32E 125 C8
Mahé Pondicherry, India 11°42N 75°34E 127 J2
Mahé Seychelles 5°0S 55°30E 141 b
Mahé ✕ (SEZ) Seychelles 4°40S 55°31E 141 b
Mahébourg Mauritius 20°24S 57°42E 141 d
Mahendra Giri India 8°20N 77°30E 127 K3
Mahendragarh India 28°17N 76°14E 124 E7
Mahendranagar Nepal 28°55N 80°20E 125 E9
Mahenge Tanzania 8°45S 36°41E 143 D4
Maheno N.Z. 45°10S 170°50E 155 F5
Mahesana India 23°39N 72°26E 124 H5
Maheshwar India 22°11N 75°35E 124 H6
Mahgawan India 26°29N 78°37E 125 F8
Mahi → India 22°15N 72°55E 124 H5
Mahia Pen. N.Z. 39°9S 177°55E 154 F6
Mahikeng = Mafikeng S. Africa 25°50S 25°38E 144 C4
Mahilyow Belarus 53°55N 30°18E 75 B16
Mahilyow □ Belarus 54°10N 30°50E 84 E6
Mahim India 19°39N 72°44E 126 E1
Mahina Tahiti 17°30S 149°27W 155 b
Mahirija Morocco 34°0N 3°16W 136 B3
Mahmud Kot Pakistan 30°16N 71°0E 124 D4
Mahmudia Romania 45°5N 29°5E 81 E14
Mahmudiye Turkey 39°48N 30°15E 99 B12
Mahmutbey Turkey 41°3N 28°49E 97 E12
Māhneshān Iran 36°44N 47°39E 105 D12
Mahnomen U.S.A. 47°19N 95°58W 172 B6
Maho Sri Lanka 7°49N 80°16E 127 L5
Mahoba India 25°15N 79°55E 125 G8
Mahón = Maó Spain 39°53N 4°16E 100 B11
Mahon, Menorca ✈ (MAH) Spain 39°50N 4°16E 90 F9
Mahone Bay Canada 44°27N 64°23W 165 D7
Mahongo △ Namibia 18°0S 23°15E 144 B3
Mahopac U.S.A. 41°22N 73°45W 175 E11
Mahuta Nigeria 11°32N 4°58E 139 C5
Mahuva India 21°5N 71°48E 124 J4
Mahya Dağı Turkey 41°47N 27°36E 97 E11
Mai-Ndombe, L. Dem. Rep. of the Congo 2°0S 18°20E 140 E3
Mai Thon, Ko Thailand 7°40N 98°28E 121 a
Maia Portugal 41°14N 8°37W 88 D2
Maials Spain 41°22N 0°30E 90 D5
Maîche France 47°16N 6°48E 71 E13
Maicurú → Brazil 2°14S 54°17W 187 D8
Máida Italy 38°51N 16°22E 95 D9
Maidan Khula Afghan. 33°36N 69°50E 124 C3
Maidenhead U.K. 51°31N 0°42W 67 F7
Maidstone Canada 53°5N 109°20W 163 C7
Maidstone U.K. 51°16N 0°32E 67 F8
Maiduguri Nigeria 12°0N 13°20E 139 C7
Maiella △ Italy 42°5N 14°5E 93 F11
Măieruş Romania 45°53N 25°31E 81 E10
Maigatari Nigeria 12°46N 9°27E 139 C6
Maigh Nuad = Maynooth Ireland 53°23N 6°34W 64 C5
Maignelay Montigny France 49°32N 2°30E 71 C9
Maihar India 24°16N 80°45E 125 G9
Maikala Ra. India 22°0N 81°0E 126 D5
Maiko △ Dem. Rep. of the Congo 0°30S 27°50E 142 C2
Mailani India 28°17N 80°21E 125 E9
Maillezais France 46°22N 0°45W 72 B3
Mailsi Pakistan 29°48N 72°15E 124 E5
Main → Germany 50°0N 8°18E 77 F4
Main → U.K. 54°48N 6°18W 64 B5
Main Channel Canada 45°21N 81°45W 174 A3
Main Range △ Australia 28°11S 152°27E 151 D5
Main Ridge Trin. & Tob. 11°16N 60°40W 187 J16
Mainburg Germany 48°38N 11°47E 77 G7
Maindargi India 17°28N 76°18E 126 F3
Maine France 48°20N 0°15W 70 D6
Maine □ U.S.A. 45°20N 69°0W 173 C19
Maine → Ireland 52°9N 9°45W 64 D2
Maine, G. of U.S.A. 43°0N 68°30W 167 G26
Maine-et-Loire □ France 47°31N 0°30W 70 E6
Maïne-Soroa Niger 13°13N 12°2E 139 C7
Maingkwan Burma 26°15N 96°37E 123 F20
Mainistir na Corann = Midleton Ireland 51°55N 8°10W 64 E3
Mainit, L. Phil. 9°31N 125°30E 119 C7
Mainland Orkney, U.K. 58°59N 3°8W 65 C5
Mainland Shet., U.K. 60°15N 1°22W 65 A7
Mainpuri India 27°18N 79°4E 125 F8
Maintal Germany 50°7N 8°52E 77 E4
Maintenon France 48°35N 1°35E 71 D8
Maintirano Madag. 18°3S 44°1E 141 H8
Mainz Germany 50°1N 8°14E 77 E4
Maio C. Verde Is. 15°10N 23°10W 134 b
Maipú Argentina 36°52S 57°50W 190 D4
Maiquetía Venezuela 10°36N 66°57W 186 A5
Máira → Italy 44°49N 7°38E 92 D4
Mairabari India 26°30N 92°22E 123 F18
Mairena del Aljarafe Spain 37°20N 6°6W 89 H4
Maisi Cuba 20°17N 74°9W 183 B5
Maisí, Pta. de Cuba 20°10N 74°10W 183 B5
Maitland N.S.W., Australia 32°33S 151°36E 153 B9
Maitland S. Austral., Australia 34°23S 137°40E 152 C2
Maitland → Canada 43°45N 81°43W 174 C3
Maitri Antarctica 70°0S 3°0W 55 D3
Maiyema Nigeria 12°5N 4°25E 139 C5
Maiyuan China 25°34N 117°28E 117 E11
Maíz, Is. del Nic. 12°15N 83°4W 182 D3
Maizuru Japan 35°25N 135°22E 113 G7
Majalengka Indonesia 6°50S 108°13E 119 G13
Majanji Uganda 0°16N 34°0E 142 B3
Majella = Maiella △ Italy 42°5N 14°5E 93 F11
Majene Indonesia 3°38S 118°57E 119 E5
Majete △ Malawi 15°54S 34°34E 143 F3
Majevica Bos.-H. 44°45N 18°50E 80 F3
Majiang China 26°28N 107°32E 116 D6
Majorca = Mallorca Spain 39°30N 3°0E 100 B10
Majors Creek Australia 35°33S 149°45E 153 C8
Majuro Marshall Is. 7°9N 171°12E 156 G9
Mak, Ko Thailand 11°49N 102°29E 121 G4
Maka Senegal 13°40N 14°10W 138 C2
Makaha Zimbabwe 17°20S 32°39E 145 A5
Makak Cameroon 3°36N 11°0E 139 E7
Makalamabedi Botswana 20°19S 23°51E 144 B3
Makale Indonesia 3°6S 119°51E 119 E5
Makalu Asia 27°55N 87°8E 125 F12
Makalu-Barun △ Nepal 27°45N 87°10E 125 F12
Makamba Burundi 4°8S 29°49E 142 C2
Makarewa Junction N.Z. 46°20S 168°21E 155 G3
Makari Cameroon 12°35N 14°28E 139 C7
Makarikari = Makgadikgadi Salt Pans Botswana 20°40S 25°45E 144 B4
Makarov Basin Arctic 87°0N 150°0W 54 A
Makarovo Russia 57°40N 107°45E 107 D11
Makarska Croatia 43°20N 17°2E 93 E14
Makaryev Russia 57°52N 43°50E 86 B6
Makassar Indonesia 5°10S 119°20E 119 F5
Makassar, Selat Indonesia 1°0S 118°20E 119 E5
Makassar, Str. of = Makassar, Selat Indonesia 1°0S 118°20E 119 E5
Makat = Maqat Kazakhstan 47°39N 53°19E 108 C4
Makedonija = Macedonia ■ Europe 41°53N 21°40E 96 E5
Makeni S. Leone 8°55N 12°5W 138 D2
Makeyevka = Makiyivka Ukraine 48°0N 38°0E 85 H9
Makgadikgadi △ Botswana 20°27S 24°47E 144 B3
Makgadikgadi Salt Pans Botswana 20°40S 25°45E 144 B4
Makhachkala Russia 43°0N 47°30E 87 J8
Makhado = Louis Trichardt S. Africa 23°1S 29°43E 145 B4
Makham, Ao Thailand 7°51N 98°25E 121 a
Makharadze = Ozurgeti Georgia 41°55N 42°0E 87 K5
Makhfar al Buşayyah Iraq 30°0N 46°10E 128 D5
Makhmūr Iraq 35°46N 43°35E 105 E10
Makhtal India 16°30N 77°31E 127 F3
Makian Indonesia 0°20N 127°20E 119 D7
Makindu Kenya 2°18S 37°50E 142 C4
Makīnsk Kazakhstan 52°37N 70°26E 109 B8
Makira = San Cristóbal Solomon Is. 10°30S 161°0E 147 C9
Makiyivka Ukraine 48°0N 38°0E 85 H9
Makkah Si. Arabia 21°30N 39°54E 137 C4
Makkovik Canada 55°10N 59°10W 165 A8
Makó Hungary 46°14N 20°33E 80 D5
Mako Senegal 12°52N 12°20W 138 C2
Makogai Fiji 17°28S 179°0E 154 a
Makokou Gabon 0°40N 12°50E 140 D2
Makongo Dem. Rep. of the Congo 3°25N 26°17E 142 B2
Makoro Dem. Rep. of the Congo 3°10N 29°59E 142 B2
Maków Mazowiecki Poland 52°52N 21°6E 83 F8
Maków Podhalański Poland 49°43N 19°45E 83 J6
Makra Greece 36°15N 25°54E 99 E7
Makrai India 22°2N 77°0E 124 H7
Makran Coast Range Pakistan 25°40N 64°0E 122 G4
Makrana India 27°2N 74°46E 124 F6
Makrany Belarus 51°48N 24°17E 83 G11
Makri Greece 40°52N 25°40E 97 F9
Makri India 19°46N 81°55E 126 E5
Makrigialos Greece 35°2N 25°59E 101 D7
Makthar Tunisia 35°48N 9°12E 136 A5
Mākū Iran 39°15N 44°31E 105 C11
Makunda Botswana 22°30S 20°7E 144 B3
Makung Taiwan 23°34N 119°34E 117 F12
Makurazaki Japan 31°15N 130°20E 113 J5
Makurdi Nigeria 7°43N 8°35E 139 D6
Makushin Volcano U.S.A. 53°53N 166°55W 166 E6
Makūyeh Iran 28°7N 53°9E 129 D7
Makwassie S. Africa 27°17S 26°0E 144 C4
Makwiro Zimbabwe 17°58S 30°25E 145 A5
Māl Mauritania 16°58N 13°23W 138 B2
Mal B. Ireland 52°50N 9°30W 64 D2
Mala = Mallow Ireland 52°8N 8°39W 64 D3
Mala Peru 12°40S 76°38W 188 C2
Mala ✪ Australia 21°39S 130°45E 148 D5
Mala, Pta. Panama 7°28N 80°2W 182 E3
Mala Belozërka Ukraine 47°12N 34°56E 85 J8
Malá Fatra △ Slovak Rep. 49°10N 19°0E 79 B12
Mala Kapela Croatia 44°45N 15°30E 93 D12
Mala Panew → Poland 50°43N 17°54E 83 H4
Mala Vyska Ukraine 48°39N 31°36E 85 H6
Malabar U.S.A. 28°0N 80°34W 179 H9
Malabar Coast India 11°0N 75°0E 127 J2
Malabu Nigeria 9°32N 12°48E 139 D7
Malacca, Straits of Indonesia 3°0N 101°0E 121 L3
Malacky Slovak Rep. 48°27N 17°0E 79 C10
Malad City U.S.A. 42°12N 112°15W 168 E7
Maladeta Spain 42°39N 0°39E 90 C5
Maladzyechna Belarus 54°20N 26°50E 75 A14
Málaga Spain 36°43N 4°23W 89 J6
Málaga □ Spain 36°38N 4°58W 89 J6
Malagarasi Tanzania 5°5S 30°50E 142 D3
Malagarasi → Tanzania 5°12S 29°47E 142 D2
Malagasy Rep. = Madagascar ■ Africa 20°0S 47°0E 141 J9
Malagón Spain 39°11N 3°52W 89 F7
Malagón → Spain 37°35N 7°29W 89 H3
Malahide Ireland 53°26N 6°9W 64 C5
Malaimbandy Madag. 20°20S 45°36E 141 J9
Malaita Solomon Is. 9°0S 161°0E 147 B9
Malakal South Sudan 9°33N 31°40E 135 G12
Malakanagiri India 18°21N 81°54E 126 E5
Malakand Pakistan 34°40N 71°55E 124 B4
Malakula Vanuatu 16°15S 167°30E 147 C9
Malakwal Pakistan 32°34N 73°13E 124 C5
Malamala Indonesia 3°21S 120°55E 119 E6
Malanda Australia 17°22S 145°35E 150 B4
Malang Indonesia 7°59S 112°45E 118 F4
Malanga Mozam. 13°28S 36°7E 143 E4
Malangen Norway 69°24N 18°37E 60 B18
Malangwa Nepal 26°52N 85°34E 125 F11
Malanje Angola 9°36S 16°17E 140 F3
Malappuram India 11°7N 76°11E 127 J3
Mälaren Sweden 59°30N 17°10E 62 E11
Malargüe Argentina 35°32S 69°30W 190 D2
Malartic Canada 48°9N 78°9W 164 C4
Malaryta Belarus 51°50N 24°3E 83 G11
Malaspina Glacier U.S.A. 59°50N 140°30W 166 D11
Malatya Turkey 38°25N 38°20E 105 C8
Malatya □ Turkey 38°15N 38°0E 104 C7
Malawi ■ Africa 11°55S 34°0E 143 E3
Malawi, L. Africa 12°30S 34°30E 143 E3
Malay Pen. Asia 7°25N 100°0E 121 J3
Malaya Belozërka = Mala Belozërka Ukraine 47°12N 34°56E 85 J8
Malaya Vishera Russia 58°55N 32°25E 84 C7
Malaya Viska = Mala Vyska Ukraine 48°39N 31°36E 85 H6
Malaybalay Phil. 8°5N 125°7E 119 C7
Malāyer Iran 34°19N 48°51E 105 E13
Malaysia ■ Asia 5°0N 110°0E 121 K4
Malazgirt Turkey 39°10N 42°33E 105 C10
Malbaza Niger 13°59N 5°38E 139 C6
Malbon Australia 21°5S 140°17E 150 C3
Malbooma Australia 30°41S 134°11E 151 E1
Malbork Poland 54°3N 19°1E 82 D6
Malcésine Italy 45°46N 10°48E 92 C7
Malchin Germany 53°44N 12°44E 76 B8
Malchow Germany 53°28N 12°25E 76 B8
Malcolm Australia 28°51S 121°25E 149 E3
Malcolm, Pt. Australia 33°48S 123°45E 149 F3
Malczyce Poland 51°14N 16°29E 83 G3
Maldah India 25°2N 88°9E 125 G13
Maldegem Belgium 51°14N 3°26E 69 C3
Malden Mass., U.S.A. 42°26N 71°3W 175 D13
Malden Mo., U.S.A. 36°34N 89°57W 172 G9
Malden I. Kiribati 4°3S 155°1W 157 H12
Maldives ■ Ind. Oc. 5°0N 73°0E 103 H9
Maldon Australia 37°0S 144°6E 152 D6
Maldon U.K. 51°44N 0°42E 67 F8
Maldonado Uruguay 34°59S 55°0W 191 C5
Maldonado, Pta. Mexico 16°20N 98°33W 181 D5
Malè Italy 46°21N 10°55E 92 B7
Malé Maldives 4°10N 73°28E 146 D6
Malé Karpaty Slovak Rep. 48°30N 17°20E 79 C10
Maleas, Akra Greece 36°28N 23°7E 98 E5
Malebo, Pool Africa 4°17S 15°20E 140 E3
Malegaon India 20°30N 74°38E 126 D2
Malei Mozam. 17°12S 36°58E 143 F4
Malek Kandī Iran 37°9N 46°6E 105 D12
Malela Dem. Rep. of the Congo 4°22S 26°8E 142 C2
Malema Mozam. 14°57S 37°20E 143 E4
Maleme Greece 35°31N 23°49E 101 D5
Maler Kotla India 30°32N 75°58E 124 D6
Målerås Sweden 56°54N 15°34E 63 H9
Males Greece 35°6N 25°35E 101 D7
Malesherbes France 48°15N 2°24E 71 D9
Maleshevska Planina Europe 41°38N 23°7E 96 E7
Malesina Greece 38°37N 23°14E 98 C5
Malestroit France 47°49N 2°25W 70 E4
Malfa Italy 38°35N 14°50E 95 D7
Malgobek Russia 43°30N 44°34E 87 J7
Malgomaj Sweden 64°40N 16°30E 60 D17
Malgrat de Mar Spain 41°39N 2°46E 90 D7
Malha Sudan 15°8N 25°10E 135 E11
Malhada Brazil 14°21S 43°47W 189 C2
Malhargarh India 24°17N 74°59E 124 G6
Malheur → U.S.A. 44°4N 116°59W 168 D5
Malheur L. U.S.A. 43°20N 118°48W 168 E4
Mali Guinea 12°10N 12°20W 138 C2
Mali ■ Africa 17°0N 3°0W 138 B4
Mali → Burma 25°42N 97°30E 123 G20
Mali Kanal Serbia 45°36N 19°24E 80 E4
Mali Kyun Burma 13°0N 98°20E 120 F2
Malia Greece 35°17N 25°32E 101 D7
Malia, Kolpos Greece 35°19N 25°27E 101 D7
Malibu U.S.A. 34°2N 118°41W 171 L8
Maliku = Minicoy I. India 8°17N 73°2E 127 K1
Maliku Indonesia 0°39S 123°16E 119 E6

Malili *Indonesia* 2°42S 121°6E **119** E6
Málilla *Sweden* 57°23N 15°48E **63** G9
Malimba, Mts.
  Dem. Rep. of the Congo 7°30S 29°30E **142** D2
Malin Hd. *Ireland* 55°23N 7°23W **64** A4
Malin Pen. *Ireland* 55°20N 7°17W **64** A4
Malindi *Kenya* 3°12S 40°5E **142** C5
Malindi Marine △ *Kenya* 3°15S 40°7E **142** C5
Malines = Mechelen
  Belgium 51°2N 4°29E **69** C4
Malino *Indonesia* 1°0N 121°0E **119** D6
Malinyi *Tanzania* 8°56S 36°0E **143** D4
Malipo *China* 23°7N 104°42E **116** F5
Maliq *Albania* 40°45N 20°48E **96** C3
Malita *Phil.* 6°19N 125°39E **119** C7
Maliwun *Burma* 10°17N 98°40E **121** G2
Maliya *India* 23°5N 70°46E **124** H4
Malka Mari △ *Kenya* 4°11N 40°46E **142** B5
Malkapur *India* 20°53N 76°12E **126** D3
Malkara *Turkey* 40°53N 26°53E **97** F10
Malkhangiri = Malakanagiri
  India 18°21N 81°54E **126** E5
Malkinia Górna *Poland* 52°42N 22°5E **83** F9
Malko Tŭrnovo
  Bulgaria 41°59N 27°31E **97** E11
Mallacoota *Australia* 37°40S 149°40E **153** D8
Mallacoota Inlet
  Australia 37°34S 149°40E **153** D8
Mallaig *U.K.* 57°0N 5°50W **65** D3
Mallala *Australia* 34°26S 138°30E **152** C3
Mallaoua *Niger* 13°2N 9°36E **139** C6
Mallawan *India* 27°4N 80°12E **125** F9
Mallawi *Egypt* 27°44N 30°44E **137** B3
Mallee Cliffs △
  Australia 34°16S 142°32E **152** C5
Mallemort *France* 43°43N 5°11E **73** E9
Málles Venosta *Italy* 46°41N 10°32E **92** B7
Mallicolo = Malakula
  Vanuatu 16°15S 167°30E **147** C9
Mallorca *Spain* 39°30N 3°0E **100** B10
Mallorytown *Canada* 44°29N 75°53W **175** B9
Mallow *Ireland* 52°8N 8°39W **64** D3
Malmbäck *Sweden* 57°34N 14°28E **63** G8
Malmberget *Sweden* 67°11N 20°40E **60** C19
Malmédy *Belgium* 50°25N 6°2E **69** D6
Malmesbury *S. Africa* 33°28S 18°41E **144** D2
Malmivaara = Malmberget
  Sweden 67°11N 20°40E **60** C19
Malmköping *Sweden* 59°8N 16°44E **62** E10
Malmö *Sweden* 55°36N 12°59E **63** J7
Malmslätt *Sweden* 58°27N 15°33E **63** F9
Malmyzh *Russia* 56°31N 50°41E **86** A10
Malnaş *Romania* 46°2N 25°49E **81** D10
Malo Konare *Bulgaria* 42°12N 24°24E **97** D8
Maloarkhangelsk
  Russia 52°28N 36°30E **85** F9
Malolo *Fiji* 17°45S 177°11E **154** a
Malolos *Phil.* 14°50N 120°49E **119** B6
Malolotja △ *Swaziland* 26°4S 31°6E **145** C5
Malombe L. *Malawi* 14°40S 35°15E **143** E4
Malomice *Poland* 51°34N 15°29E **83** G2
Malomir *Bulgaria* 42°16N 26°32E **97** D10
Malone *Fla., U.S.A.* 30°57N 85°10W **178** E4
Malone *N.Y., U.S.A.* 44°51N 74°18W **175** B10
Malong *China* 25°24N 103°34E **116** E4
Małopolskie □ *Poland* 49°50N 20°20E **83** J7
Malorad *Bulgaria* 43°28N 23°41E **96** C7
Måløy *Norway* 61°57N 5°6E **60** F11
Maloyaroslovets *Russia* 55°2N 36°20E **84** E9
Malpartida de Cáceres
  Spain 39°26N 6°30W **89** F4
Malpaso *Canary Is.* 27°43N 18°3W **100** G1
Malpaso, Presa =
  Netzahualcóyotl, Presa
  Mexico 17°8N 93°35W **181** D6
Malpelo, I. de *Colombia* 4°3N 81°35W **186** C2
Malpica de Bergantiños
  Spain 43°19N 8°50W **88** B2
Malprabha → *India* 16°20N 76°5E **127** F2
Malpur *India* 23°21N 73°27E **124** H5
Malpura *India* 26°17N 75°23E **124** F6
Mals = Málles Venosta
  Italy 46°41N 10°32E **92** B7
Malsiras *India* 17°52N 74°55E **126** F2
Malta *Brazil* 6°54S 37°31W **189** B3
Malta *Idaho, U.S.A.* 42°18N 113°22W **168** E7
Malta *Mont., U.S.A.* 48°21N 107°52W **168** B10
Malta ■ *Europe* 35°55N 14°26E **101** D2
Maltahöhe *Namibia* 24°55S 17°0E **144** B2
Maltepe *Turkey* 40°55N 29°8E **97** F13
Malton *Canada* 43°42N 79°38W **174** C5
Malton *U.K.* 54°8N 0°49W **66** C7
Maluku *Indonesia* 1°0S 127°0E **119** E7
Maluku □ *Indonesia* 3°0S 128°0E **119** E7
Maluku Sea = Molucca Sea
  Indonesia 0°0 125°0E **119** E6
Malumfashi *Nigeria* 11°48N 7°39E **139** C6
Malung *Sweden* 60°42N 13°44E **62** D7
Malungsfors *Sweden* 60°44N 13°33E **62** D7
Malur *India* 13°0N 77°55E **127** H3
Maluwe *Ghana* 8°40N 2°17W **138** D4
Malvalli *India* 12°28N 77°6E **127** H3
Malvan *India* 16°2N 73°30E **127** F1
Malvern *U.S.A.* 34°22N 92°49W **176** D8
Malvern Hills *U.K.* 52°0N 2°19W **67** E5
Malvinas, Is. = Falkland Is. □
  Atl. Oc. 51°30S 59°0W **192** D5
Malý Dunaj →
  Slovak Rep. 47°45N 18°9E **79** D11
Malya *Tanzania* 3°5S 33°38E **142** C3
Malye Derbety *Russia* 47°57N 44°42E **87** G7
Malyn *Ukraine* 50°46N 29°3E **75** C15
Malyy Lyakhovskiy, Ostrov
  Russia 74°7N 140°36E **107** B15
Malyy Taymyr, Ostrov
  Russia 78°6N 107°15E **107** B11
Mama *Russia* 58°18N 112°54E **107** D12
Mamaku *N.Z.* 38°5S 176°8E **154** E5
Mamanguape *Brazil* 6°50S 35°4W **189** B3
Mamanuca Group *Fiji* 17°35S 177°5E **154** a
Mamarr Mitlâ *Egypt* 30°2N 32°54E **130** E1
Mamasa *Indonesia* 2°55S 119°20E **119** E5
Mambasa
  Dem. Rep. of the Congo 1°22N 29°3E **142** D2
Mamberamo →
  Indonesia 2°0S 137°50E **119** E9
Mambilima Falls
  Zambia 10°31S 28°45E **143** E2
Mambirima
  Dem. Rep. of the Congo 11°25S 27°33E **143** E2

Mambo *Tanzania* 4°52S 38°22E **142** C4
Mambrui *Kenya* 3°5S 40°5E **142** C5
Mamburao *Phil.* 13°13N 120°39E **119** B6
Mamedkala *Russia* 42°10N 48°7E **87** A9
Mameigwess L. *Canada* 52°35N 87°50W **164** B2
Mamers *France* 48°21N 0°22E **70** D7
Mamfé *Cameroon* 5°50N 9°15E **139** D6
Mamina *Chile* 20°55S 69°14W **188** E4
Mamlyutka *Kazakhstan* 54°56N 68°32E **109** B7
Mammoth *U.S.A.* 32°43N 110°39W **169** K8
Mammoth Cave △
  U.S.A. 37°8N 86°13W **172** G10
Mammoth Lakes
  U.S.A. 37°39N 118°59W **170** H8
Mamonovo *Russia* 54°28N 19°55E **82** D6
Mamoré → *Bolivia* 10°23S 65°53W **186** F5
Mamou *Guinea* 10°15N 12°0W **138** C2
Mamoudzou *Mayotte* 12°48S 45°14E **141** a
Mampong *Ghana* 7°6N 1°26W **139** D4
Mamry, Jezioro *Poland* 54°5N 21°50E **82** D8
Mamuil Malal, Paso
  S. Amer. 39°35S 71°28W **192** A2
Mamuju *Indonesia* 2°41S 118°50E **119** E5
Mamuno *Botswana* 22°16S 20°1E **144** B3
Mamuras *Albania* 41°34N 19°41E **96** E3
Man *Ivory C.* 7°30N 7°40W **138** D3
Man → *India* 17°31N 75°32E **126** F2
Man, I. of *India* 8°28N 93°36E **127** K11
Man, I. of *U.K.* 54°15N 4°30W **66** C3
Man-Bazar *India* 23°4N 86°39E **125** H12
Mānā *U.S.A.* 22°2N 159°47W **167** L8
Mana → *Fr. Guiana* 5°45N 53°55W **187** B8
Mana Pools △
  Zimbabwe 15°56S 29°25E **143** F2
Manaar, G. of = Mannar, G. of
  Asia 8°30N 79°0E **127** K4
Manacapuru *Brazil* 3°16S 60°37W **186** D6
Manacor *Spain* 39°34N 3°13E **100** B10
Manado *Indonesia* 1°29N 124°51E **119** D6
Managua *Nic.* 12°6N 86°20W **182** D2
Managua, L. de *Nic.* 12°20N 86°30W **182** D2
Manaia *N.Z.* 39°33S 174°8E **154** D4
Manakara *Madag.* 22°8S 48°1E **141** J9
Manakau *N.Z.* 42°15S 173°42E **155** D4
Manali *India* 32°16N 77°10E **124** C7
Manama = Al Manāmah
  Bahrain 26°10N 50°30E **129** E6
Manambato *Australia* 35°5S 142°54E **152** C5
Manananjary *Madag.* 21°13S 48°20E **141** J9
Manankoro *Mali* 10°28N 7°25W **138** C3
Manantali, L. de *Mali* 12°13N 10°28W **138** C2
Manantavadi *India* 11°49N 76°1E **127** J3
Manaos = Manaus *Brazil* 3°0S 60°0W **186** D7
Manapire → *Venezuela* 7°42N 66°7W **186** B5
Manapouri *N.Z.* 45°34S 167°39E **155** F2
Manapouri, L. *N.Z.* 45°32S 167°32E **155** F2
Manapparai *India* 10°36N 78°25E **127** J4
Manar → *India* 18°50N 77°20E **126** E3
Manār, Jabal *Yemen* 14°2N 44°17E **131** E3
Manas *China* 44°17N 86°10E **109** D11
Manas → *India* 26°12N 90°40E **123** F17
Manas Hu *China* 45°38N 85°12E **110** B6
Manaslu *Nepal* 28°33N 84°33E **125** E11
Manasquan *U.S.A.* 40°8N 74°3W **175** F10
Manassa *U.S.A.* 37°11N 105°56W **169** H11
Manati *Puerto Rico* 18°26N 66°29W **183** d
Manaus *Brazil* 3°0S 60°0W **186** D7
Manavgat *Turkey* 36°47N 31°26E **104** D4
Manawan L. *Canada* 55°24N 103°14W **163** B8
Mancha Real *Spain* 37°48N 3°39W **89** H7
Manche □ *France* 49°10N 1°20W **70** C5
Manchegorsk *Russia* 67°54N 32°58E **106** C4
Manchester *U.K.* 53°29N 2°12W **66** D5
Manchester *Calif., U.S.A.* 38°58N 123°41W **170** G3
Manchester *Conn., U.S.A.* 41°47N 72°31W **175** E12
Manchester *Ga., U.S.A.* 32°51N 84°37W **178** C5
Manchester *Iowa, U.S.A.* 42°29N 91°27W **172** D8
Manchester *Ky., U.S.A.* 37°9N 83°46W **173** G12
Manchester *N.H., U.S.A.* 42°59N 71°28W **175** D13
Manchester *N.Y., U.S.A.* 42°56N 77°16W **174** D7
Manchester *Pa., U.S.A.* 40°4N 76°43W **175** F8
Manchester *Tenn., U.S.A.* 35°29N 86°5W **177** D11
Manchester *Vt., U.S.A.* 43°10N 73°5W **175** C11
Manchester Int. ✈ (MAN)
  U.K. 53°21N 2°17W **66** D5
Manchester L. *Canada* 61°28N 107°29W **163** A7
Manchhar L. *Pakistan* 26°25N 67°39E **124** F2
Manchuria = Dongbei
  China 45°0N 125°0E **115** D13
Manchurian Plain
  China 47°0N 124°0E **102** D14
Manciano *Italy* 42°35N 11°31E **93** F8
Máncora *Peru* 4°9S 81°1W **188** A1
Mand → *India* 21°42N 83°15E **125** J10
Mand → *Iran* 28°20N 52°30E **129** D7
Manda *Ludewe, Tanzania* 10°30S 34°40E **143** E3
Manda *Mbeya, Tanzania* 7°58S 32°29E **142** D3
Manda *Mbeya, Tanzania* 8°30S 32°49E **142** D3
Mandaguari *Brazil* 23°32S 51°42W **191** A5
Mandah = Töhöm
  Mongolia 44°27N 108°2E **114** B5
Mandal *Norway* 58°2N 7°25E **61** G12
Mandala, Puncak
  Indonesia 4°44S 140°20E **119** E10
Mandalay *Burma* 22°0N 96°4E **123** J20
Mandale = Mandalay
  Burma 22°0N 96°4E **123** J20
Mandalgarh *India* 25°12N 75°6E **124** G6
Mandalgovĭ *Mongolia* 45°45N 106°10E **114** B4
Mandalī *Iraq* 33°43N 45°28E **105** F11
Mandan *U.S.A.* 46°50N 100°54W **172** B3
Mandar, Teluk
  Indonesia 3°32S 119°21E **119** E5
Mándas *Italy* 39°40N 9°8E **94** C2
Mandaue *Phil.* 10°20N 123°56E **119** B6

Mandelieu-la-Napoule
  France 43°34N 6°57E **73** E10
Mandera *Kenya* 3°55N 41°53E **142** B5
Mandeville *Jamaica* 18°2N 77°31W **182** a
Mandi *India* 31°39N 76°58E **124** D7
Mandi Burewala
  Pakistan 30°9N 72°41E **124** D5
Mandi Dabwali *India* 29°58N 74°42E **124** E6
Mandiana *Guinea* 10°37N 8°39W **138** C3
Mandioli *Indonesia* 0°40S 127°20E **119** E7
Mandla *India* 22°39N 80°30E **125** H9
Mandorah *Australia* 12°32S 130°42E **148** B5
Mandoudi *Greece* 38°48N 23°29E **98** C5
Mandra *Greece* 38°4N 23°30E **98** C5
Mandra *Pakistan* 33°23N 73°12E **124** C5
Mandraki *Greece* 36°36N 27°11E **99** E9
Mandritsara *Madag.* 15°50S 48°49E **141** H9
Mandsaur *India* 24°3N 75°8E **124** G6
Mandurah *Australia* 32°36S 115°48E **149** F2
Mandúria *Italy* 40°24N 17°38E **95** B10
Mandvi *India* 22°51N 69°22E **124** H3
Mandya *India* 12°30N 77°0E **127** H3
Mandzai *Pakistan* 30°55N 67°6E **124** D2
Mané *Burkina Faso* 12°59N 1°21W **139** C4
Maneh *Iran* 37°39N 57°7E **129** B8
Manengouba, Mts.
  Cameroon 5°0N 9°50E **139** E6
Maner → *India* 18°30N 79°40E **126** E4
Manério *Italy* 45°21N 10°8E **92** C7
Maneroo Cr. →
  Australia 23°21S 143°53E **150** C3
Manfalût *Egypt* 27°20N 30°52E **137** B3
Manfred *Australia* 33°19S 143°45E **152** B3
Manfredónia *Italy* 41°38N 15°55E **93** G12
Manfredónia, G. di *Italy* 41°35N 16°5E **93** G13
Manga *Brazil* 14°46S 43°56W **189** C2
Manga *Burkina Faso* 11°40N 1°4W **139** C4
Manga *Niger* 15°0N 14°0E **139** C7
Mangabeiras, Chapada das
  Brazil 10°0S 46°30W **189** C1
Mangaia *Cook Is.* 21°55S 157°55W **157** K12
Mangakino *N.Z.* 38°22S 175°47E **154** E4
Mangalagiri *India* 16°26N 80°36E **127** F5
Mangalia *Romania* 43°50N 28°35E **83** H15
Mangalore *India* 12°55N 74°47E **127** H2
Mangaluru = Mangalore
  India 12°55N 74°47E **127** H2
Mangalvedha *India* 17°31N 75°28E **126** F2
Mangan *India* 27°31N 88°32E **125** F13
Mangaon *India* 18°15N 73°20E **126** E1
Mangarrayi ⊘
  Australia 15°5S 133°10E **150** B1
Mangawan *India* 24°41N 81°33E **125** G9
Mangaweka *N.Z.* 39°48S 175°47E **154** E5
Mangaweka, Mt. *N.Z.* 39°49S 176°5E **154** E5
Manggar *Indonesia* 2°50S 108°10E **118** E3
Manggawitu *Indonesia* 4°8S 133°32E **119** E8
Mangghystaū
  Kazakhstan 43°40N 51°13E **108** D4
Mangghystaū □
  Kazakhstan 45°0N 53°0E **108** D4
Mangghystaū Tübegi
  Kazakhstan 44°30N 52°30E **108** D4
Manggis *Indonesia* 8°29S 115°31E **119** J18
Mangkalihat, Tanjung
  Indonesia 1°2N 118°59E **119** D5
Mangkururrpa ⊘
  Australia 20°35S 129°43E **148** D4
Mangla *Pakistan* 33°7N 73°39E **124** C5
Mangla Dam *Pakistan* 33°9N 73°44E **125** C5
Manglaur *India* 29°44N 77°49E **124** E7
Manglisi *Georgia* 41°41N 44°22E **87** K7
Mangnai *China* 37°52N 91°43E **110** C14
Mangnai Zhen *China* 38°24N 90°14E **109** E12
Mango *Togo* 10°20N 0°30E **139** C5
Mangochi *Malawi* 14°25S 35°16E **143** E4
Mangoky → *Madag.* 21°29S 43°41E **141** J8
Mangole *Indonesia* 1°50S 125°55E **119** E6
Mangombe
  Dem. Rep. of the Congo 1°20S 26°48E **142** C2
Mangonui *N.Z.* 35°1S 173°32E **154** B4
Mangrol *Mad. P., India* 21°7N 70°7E **124** J4
Mangrol *Raj., India* 25°20N 76°31E **124** G6
Mangrul Pir *India* 20°19N 77°21E **126** D3
Manguéland *Portugal* 40°38N 7°48E **88** E3
Mangueira, L. da *Brazil* 33°0S 52°50W **191** C5
Mangueigne *Chad* 10°30N 21°0E **137** G10
Mangum *U.S.A.* 34°53N 99°30W **176** D5
Manguri *Australia* 28°58S 134°22E **151** A1
Mangyshlak, Poluostrov =
  Mangghystaū Tübegi
  Kazakhstan 44°30N 52°30E **108** D4
Manhattan *U.S.A.* 39°11N 96°35W **172** F5
Manhiça *Mozam.* 25°23S 32°49E **145** C5
Manhuaçu *Brazil* 20°15S 42°2W **189** E2
Manhumirim *Brazil* 20°22S 41°57W **189** E2
Maniago *Italy* 46°10N 12°43E **93** B9
Manica *Mozam.* 18°58S 32°59E **145** B5
Manica □ *Mozam.* 19°10S 33°45E **145** B5
Manicaland □ *Zimbabwe* 19°0S 32°30E **143** F3
Manicoré *Brazil* 5°48S 61°16W **186** E6
Manicouagan →
  Canada 49°30N 68°30W **165** C6
Manicouagan, Rés.
  Canada 51°5N 68°40W **165** B6
Maniema □
  Dem. Rep. of the Congo 3°0S 26°0E **142** C2
Manifah *Si. Arabia* 27°44N 49°0E **129** E6
Manifold, C. *Australia* 22°41S 150°50E **150** C5
Manigotagan *Canada* 51°6N 96°18W **163** C9
Manigotagan →
  Canada 51°6N 96°18W **163** C9
Manihari *India* 25°21N 87°38E **125** G12
Manihiki *Cook Is.* 10°24S 161°1W **157** J11
Manihiki Plateau
  Pac. Oc. 11°0S 164°0W **157** J11
Maniitsoq *Greenland* 65°26N 52°55W **57** D5
Manika, Plateau de la
  Dem. Rep. of the Congo 10°0S 25°5E **142** E2
Manikpur *India* 25°4N 81°7E **125** G9
Manila *Phil.* 14°35N 120°58E **119** B6
Manila *U.S.A.* 40°59N 109°43W **168** F9
Manila B. *Phil.* 14°40N 120°35E **119** B6
Manildra *Australia* 33°11S 148°41E **153** B8
Manila *Australia* 30°45S 150°43E **153** A9
Manilva *Spain* 36°23S 5°15W **89** F5
Manimpé *Mali* 14°11N 5°28W **138** C3
Maningrida *Australia* 12°3S 134°13E **150** A1
Maninian *Ivory C.* 9°50N 7°52W **138** C3

Manipa, Selat *Indonesia* 3°20S 127°23E **119** E7
Manipur □ *India* 25°0N 94°0E **123** G19
Manipur → *Burma* 23°45N 94°20E **123** H19
Manisa *Turkey* 38°38N 27°30E **99** C9
Manisa □ *Turkey* 38°40N 28°0E **99** C9
Manistee *U.S.A.* 44°15N 86°19W **172** C10
Manistee → *U.S.A.* 44°15N 86°21W **172** C10
Manistique *U.S.A.* 45°57N 86°15W **172** C10
Manitoba □ *Canada* 53°30N 97°0W **163** B9
Manitoba, L. *Canada* 51°0N 98°45W **163** C9
Manitou *Canada* 49°15N 98°32W **163** D9
Manitou, L. *Canada* 50°55N 65°17W **165** B6
Manitou Is. *U.S.A.* 45°8N 86°0W **172** C10
Manitou L. *Canada* 52°43N 109°43W **163** C7
Manitou Springs
  U.S.A. 38°52N 104°55W **168** G2
Manitoulin I. *Canada* 45°40N 82°30W **164** C3
Manitouwadge *Canada* 49°8N 85°48W **164** C2
Manitowoc *U.S.A.* 44°5N 87°40W **172** C10
Maniyachi *India* 8°51N 77°55E **127** K3
Manizales *Colombia* 5°5N 75°32W **186** B3
Manjacaze *Mozam.* 24°45S 34°0E **145** C5
Manjakandriana
  Madag. 18°55S 47°47E **141** H9
Manjhand *Pakistan* 25°50N 68°10E **124** F3
Manjimup *Australia* 34°15S 116°6E **149** F2
Manjlegaon *India* 19°9N 76°14E **126** E3
Manjo *Cameroon* 4°50N 9°49E **139** E6
Manjra → *India* 18°49N 77°52E **126** E3
Mankato *Kans., U.S.A.* 39°47N 98°13W **172** F4
Mankato *Minn., U.S.A.* 44°10N 94°0W **172** C6
Mankayane *Swaziland* 26°40S 31°4E **145** C5
Mankera *Pakistan* 31°23N 71°26E **124** D4
Mankim *Cameroon* 5°6N 12°3E **139** D7
Mankono *Ivory C.* 8°1N 6°10W **138** D3
Mankota *Canada* 49°25N 107°5W **163** D7
Mankulam *Sri Lanka* 9°8N 80°26E **127** K5
Manlay = Üydzin
  Mongolia 44°9N 107°0E **114** B4
Manlleu *Spain* 42°2N 2°17E **90** C7
Manly *Australia* 33°47S 151°17E **153** B9
Manmad *India* 20°18N 74°28E **126** D2
Mann Ranges *Australia* 26°6S 130°5E **149** E5
Manna *Indonesia* 4°25S 102°55E **118** E2
Mannahill *Australia* 32°25S 140°0E **152** B4
Mannar *Sri Lanka* 9°1N 79°54E **127** K4
Mannar, G. of *Asia* 8°30N 79°0E **127** K4
Mannar I. *Sri Lanka* 9°5N 79°45E **127** K4
Mannargudi *India* 10°45N 79°51E **127** J4
Mannheim *Germany* 49°29N 8°29E **77** F4
Manning *Canada* 56°53N 117°39W **162** B5
Manning *Oreg., U.S.A.* 45°45N 123°13W **170** D3
Manning *S.C., U.S.A.* 33°42N 80°13W **178** B9
Manning →
  Australia 31°52S 152°43E **153** A10
Mannu → *Italy* 39°16N 9°0E **94** C2
Mannu, C. *Italy* 40°3N 8°21E **94** B1
Mannum *Australia* 34°50S 139°20E **152** C3
Mano *S. Leone* 8°3N 12°2W **138** D2
Mano → *Liberia* 6°56N 11°30W **138** D2
Mano River *Liberia* 7°20N 11°6W **138** D2
Manoharpur *India* 22°23N 85°12E **125** H11
Manokwari *Indonesia* 0°54S 134°0E **119** E8
Manolada *Greece* 38°4N 21°21E **98** D3
Manombo *Madag.* 22°57S 43°28E **141** J8
Manono
  Dem. Rep. of the Congo 7°15S 27°25E **142** D2
Manoppello *Italy* 42°15N 14°3E **93** F11
Manorhamilton *Ireland* 54°18N 8°11W **64** B3
Manosque *France* 43°49N 5°47E **73** E9
Manotick *Canada* 45°13N 75°41W **175** A9
Manouane → *Canada* 49°30N 71°10W **165** C5
Manouane, L. *Canada* 50°45N 70°45W **165** B5
Manp'o *N. Korea* 41°6N 126°24E **115** D14
Manpojin = Manp'o
  N. Korea 41°6N 126°24E **115** D14
Manpur *Chhattisgarh,
  India* 23°17N 83°35E **125** H10
Manpur *Chhattisgarh,
  India* 22°26N 75°37E **124** H6
Manpur *Mad. P., India* 22°26N 75°37E **124** H6
Manresa *Spain* 41°48N 1°50E **90** D6
Mansa *Gujarat, India* 23°27N 72°45E **124** H5
Mansa *Punjab, India* 30°0N 75°27E **124** E6
Mansa *Zambia* 11°13S 28°55E **143** E2
Mansa Konko *Gambia* 13°28N 15°33W **138** C1
Mânsâsen *Sweden* 63°5N 14°18E **62** A8
Mansehra *Pakistan* 34°20N 73°15E **124** B5
Mansel I. *Canada* 62°0N 80°0W **161** C15
Mansfield *Australia* 37°4S 146°6E **153** D7
Mansfield *U.K.* 53°9N 1°11W **66** D6
Mansfield *Ga., U.S.A.* 33°31N 83°44W **178** C8
Mansfield *La., U.S.A.* 32°2N 93°43W **176** E8
Mansfield *Mass.,
  U.S.A.* 42°2N 71°13W **175** D13
Mansfield *Ohio, U.S.A.* 40°45N 82°31W **174** F2
Mansfield *Pa., U.S.A.* 41°48N 77°5W **174** E7
Mansfield *Tex., U.S.A.* 32°33N 97°8W **176** E6
Mansfield, Mt. *U.S.A.* 44°33N 72°49W **175** B12
Mansidão *Brazil* 10°43S 44°2W **189** C2
Mansilla de las Mulas
  Spain 42°30N 5°25W **88** C5
Mansle *France* 45°52N 0°12E **72** C4
Mansôa *Guinea-Biss.* 12°0N 15°20W **138** C1
Manson Creek
  Canada 55°37N 124°32W **162** B4
Mansoura *Algeria* 36°1N 4°31E **136** A4
Manta *Ecuador* 1°0S 80°40W **186** D2
Mantalingajan, Mt.
  Phil. 8°55N 117°45E **118** C5
Mantare *Tanzania* 2°42S 33°13E **142** C3
Mantaro → *Peru* 12°16S 73°57W **188** C3
Manteca *U.S.A.* 37°48N 121°13W **170** H5
Mantena *Brazil* 18°47S 40°59W **189** E3
Manteo *U.S.A.* 35°55N 75°40W **177** D17
Mantes-la-Jolie *France* 48°58N 1°41E **71** D8
Mantha *India* 19°40N 76°23E **126** E3
Manthani *India* 18°40N 79°35E **126** E4
Manti *U.S.A.* 39°16N 111°38W **168** G8
Mantiqueira, Serra da
  Brazil 22°0S 44°0W **191** A7
Manton *U.S.A.* 44°25N 85°24W **173** C11
Mantorp *Sweden* 58°21N 15°20E **63** F9
Mántova *Italy* 45°9N 10°48E **92** C7
Mäntsälä *Finland* 60°40N 25°20E **63** E21
Mänttä Vilppula *Finland* 62°3N 24°40E **84** A3
Mantua = Mántova *Italy* 45°9N 10°48E **92** C7
Mantung *Australia* 34°35S 140°3E **152** C4
Manturovo *Russia* 58°23N 44°45E **86** A7
Manú *Peru* 12°10S 70°51W **188** C3
Manú → *Peru* 12°16S 70°55W **188** C3

Manuel Alves →
  Brazil 11°19S 48°28W **189** C1
Manuel Alves Grande →
  Brazil 7°27S 47°35W **189** B1
Manuel Urbano *Brazil* 8°53S 69°18W **188** B4
Manui *Indonesia* 3°35S 123°5E **119** E6
Manukau *N.Z.* 37°0S 174°52E **154** D3
Manukau Harbour
  N.Z. 37°3S 174°45E **154** D3
Manunui *N.Z.* 38°54S 175°21E **154** E4
Manuoha *N.Z.* 38°39S 177°7E **154** E6
Manuripi → *Bolivia* 11°6S 67°36W **188** C4
Manvi *India* 15°57N 76°59E **127** G3
Manwan Dam *China* 24°44N 100°20E **116** E3
Manwath *India* 19°19N 76°32E **126** E3
Many *U.S.A.* 31°34N 93°29W **176** F8
Manyallaluk ⊘
  Australia 14°16S 132°49E **148** B5
Manyani *Kenya* 3°5S 38°30E **142** C4
Manyara □ *Tanzania* 4°30S 37°10E **142** C4
Manyara, L. *Tanzania* 3°40S 35°50E **142** C4
Manyara □ *Tanzania* 3°35S 35°50E **142** C4
Manyas *Turkey* 40°2N 27°59E **97** F11
Manych → *Russia* 47°13N 40°40E **87** G5
Manych-Gudilo, Ozero
  Russia 46°24N 42°38E **87** G6
Manyonga → *Tanzania* 4°10S 34°15E **142** C3
Manyoni *Tanzania* 5°45S 34°55E **142** D3
Manzai *Pakistan* 32°12N 70°15E **124** C4
Manzala, Bahra el
  Egypt 31°10N 31°56E **137** E7
Manzanar △ *U.S.A.* 36°44N 118°9W **170** J7
Manzanares *Spain* 39°2N 3°22W **89** F7
Manzaneda *Spain* 42°12N 7°15W **88** C3
Manzanillo *Cuba* 20°20N 77°31W **182** B4
Manzanillo *Mexico* 19°3N 104°20W **180** D4
Manzanillo, Pta.
  Panama 9°30N 79°40W **182** E4
Manzano Mts.
  U.S.A. 34°40N 106°20W **169** J10
Manzarīyeh *Iran* 34°53N 50°50E **129** C6
Manzhouli *China* 49°35N 117°25E **111** B12
Manzini *Swaziland* 26°30S 31°25E **145** C5
Manzouli = Manzhouli
  China 49°35N 117°25E **111** B12
Manzur Vadisi △
  Turkey 39°10N 39°30E **128** B3
Mao *Chad* 14°4N 15°19E **135** F9
Maó *Spain* 39°53N 4°16E **100** B11
Maoke, Pegunungan
  Indonesia 3°40S 137°30E **119** E9
Maolin *China* 43°58N 123°30E **115** C12
Maoming *China* 21°50N 110°54E **117** G8
Maopi T'ou *China* 21°56N 120°43E **117** G13
Maouri, Dallol → *Niger* 12°5S 3°30E **139** C5
Maoxian *China* 31°41N 103°49E **116** B4
Mapam Yumco *China* 30°45N 81°28E **125** D9
Mapastepec *Mexico* 15°26N 92°54E **181** D6
Maphrao, Ko *Thailand* 7°56N 98°26E **121** a
Mapia, Kepulauan
  Indonesia 0°50N 134°20E **119** D8
Mapimí *Mexico* 25°49N 103°51W **180** B4
Mapimí, Bolsón de
  Mexico 27°0N 104°15W **180** B4
Maping *China* 31°34N 113°32E **117** B9
Mapinga *Tanzania* 6°40S 39°12E **142** D4
Mapinhane *Mozam.* 22°20S 35°0E **145** B6
Maple Creek *Canada* 49°55N 109°29W **163** D7
Maple Valley *U.S.A.* 47°25N 122°3W **164** D4
Mapleton *U.S.A.* 44°2N 123°52W **168** D2
Mapon = Nabire
  Indonesia 3°40S 135°26E **119** E9
Mapoon ⊘ *Australia* 11°44S 142°8E **150** A3
Mapourika, L. *N.Z.* 43°18S 170°12E **155** D3
Mapuca *India* 15°36N 73°46E **127** G1
Mapuera → *Brazil* 1°5S 57°2W **186** D7
Mapulanguene *Mozam.* 24°29S 32°6E **145** B5
Mapungubwe △
  S. Africa 22°12S 29°22E **145** B4
Maputo *Mozam.* 25°58S 32°32E **145** C5
Maputo □ *Mozam.* 26°0S 32°25E **145** C5
Maputo, B. de *Mozam.* 25°50S 32°45E **145** C5
Maputo → *Mozam.* 26°23S 32°48E **145** C5
Maqanshy *Kazakhstan* 46°47N 82°1E **109** C10
Maqar an Na'am *Iraq* 39°39N 53°19E **108** D4
Maqat *Kazakhstan* 47°39N 53°19E **108** D4
Maqên *China* 34°24N 100°6E **110** C9
Maqên Gangri *China* 34°55N 99°18E **110** C8
Maqiaohe *China* 44°40N 130°30E **115** B16
Maqnā *Si. Arabia* 28°25N 34°50E **128** D2
Maqtēir *Mauritania* 21°50N 11°42E **110** C9
Maquan He = Brahmaputra →
  Asia 23°40N 90°35E **125** H13
Maqueda *Spain* 40°4N 4°22W **88** E6
Maquela do Zombo
  Angola 6°0S 15°15E **140** F3
Maquinchao *Argentina* 41°15S 68°50W **192** E3
Maquoketa *U.S.A.* 42°4N 90°40W **172** D8
Mar *Canada* 44°49N 81°12W **174** B3
Mar, Serra do *Brazil* 25°30S 49°0W **191** B6
Mar Chiquita, L.
  Argentina 30°40S 62°50W **190** C3
Mar del Plata *Argentina* 38°0S 57°30W **190** D4
Mar Menor *Spain* 37°40N 0°45W **91** H4
Mara *Tanzania* 1°30S 34°32E **142** C3
Mara □ *Tanzania* 1°45S 34°20E **142** C3
Maraä *Brazil* 1°52S 65°25W **186** D5
Maraãbo *Brazil* 5°21S 49°5W **189** B1
Maraã *Tahiti* 17°46S 149°34W **155** b
Marabá *Brazil* 5°20S 49°5W **187** E9
Maraboon, L. *Australia* 23°41S 148°0E **150** C4
Maracá, I. de *Brazil* 2°10N 50°30W **187** C8
Maracaibo *Venezuela* 10°40N 71°37W **186** A4
Maracaibo, L. de
  Venezuela 9°40N 71°30W **186** B4
Maracaju *Brazil* 21°38S 55°9W **191** A4
Maracás *Brazil* 13°52S 40°20W **189** C3
Maracás Bay Village
  Trin. & Tob. 10°46N 61°28W **187** K15
Maracay *Venezuela* 10°15N 67°28W **186** A5
Maracena *Spain* 37°12N 3°38W **89** H7
Marādah *Libya* 29°15N 19°15E **135** C9
Maradi *Niger* 13°29N 7°20E **139** C6
Maradi □ *Niger* 14°15N 7°15E **139** C6
Marag. *Iran* 45°9N 10°48E **105** C6
Marāgheh *Iran* 37°30N 46°12E **105** C13
Maragogipe *Brazil* 12°46S 38°55W **189** C3
Marahuaca, Cerro
  Venezuela 3°34N 65°25W **186** C5
Marajó, I. de *Brazil* 1°0S 49°30W **189** A1
Marākand *Iran* 38°51N 45°16E **128** B5
Marakele △ *S. Africa* 24°30S 25°30E **145** D4
Maralal *Kenya* 1°0N 36°38E **142** B4
Maralinga *Australia* 30°13S 131°32E **149** F5
Maralinga Tjarutja ⊘
  Australia 29°30S 131°0E **149** E5
Marama *Australia* 35°10S 140°10E **152** C4
Maramaraereğlisi
  Turkey 40°57N 27°57E **97** F11
Marambio *Antarctica* 64°0S 56°0W **55** C18
Maramureş □ *Romania* 47°45N 24°0E **83** E12
Maran *Malaysia* 3°35N 102°45E **121** L4
Marana *U.S.A.* 32°27N 111°13W **169** K8
Maranboy *Australia* 14°40S 132°39E **148** B5
Maranchón *Spain* 41°6N 2°15W **90** D2
Marand *Iran* 38°30N 45°45E **105** C11
Maranello *Italy* 44°32N 10°52E **92** D7
Marang *Malaysia* 5°12N 103°13E **121** K4
Maranguape *Brazil* 3°55S 38°50W **189** A3
Maranhão = São Luís
  Brazil 2°39S 44°15W **189** A2
Maranhão □ *Brazil* 5°0S 46°0W **189** B1
Marano, L. di *Italy* 45°44N 13°10E **93** C10
Maranoa → *Australia* 27°50S 148°37E **151** D4
Marañón → *Peru* 4°30S 73°35W **188** B2
Marão *Mozam.* 24°18S 34°2E **145** B5
Marari *Brazil* 3°55S 67°47W **188** B4
Maraş = Kahramanmaraş
  Turkey 37°37N 36°53E **104** D7
Mărăşeşti *Romania* 45°52N 27°14E **81** D12
Maratea *Italy* 39°59N 15°43E **95** C8
Marateca *Portugal* 38°34N 8°40W **89** G2
Marathasa *Cyprus* 34°59N 32°51E **101** E11
Marathokambos *Greece* 37°43N 26°42E **99** D8
Marathon *Australia* 20°51S 143°32E **150** C3
Marathon *Canada* 48°44N 86°23W **164** C2
Marathon *Fla., U.S.A.* 24°43N 81°5W **179** J16
Marathon *N.Y., U.S.A.* 42°27N 76°2W **175** D8
Marathon *Tex., U.S.A.* 30°12N 103°15W **176** F3
Marathónas *Greece* 38°11N 23°58E **98** C5
Marathóvounos
  Cyprus 35°13N 33°37E **101** D12
Maratua *Indonesia* 2°10N 118°35E **119** D5
Maraú *Brazil* 14°6S 39°0W **189** C3
Marāwih *U.A.E.* 24°18N 53°18E **129** E7
Marazliyivka *Ukraine* 46°48N 30°8E **85** J5
Marbella *Spain* 36°30N 4°57W **89** J6
Marble Bar *Australia* 21°9S 119°44E **148** D2
Marblehead *Mass.,
  U.S.A.* 42°29N 70°51W **175** D14
Marblehead *Ohio,
  U.S.A.* 41°32N 82°44W **174** E2
Marburg *Germany* 50°47N 8°46E **76** E4
Marca, Pta. do *Angola* 16°31S 11°43E **141** H2
Marcal → *Hungary* 47°41N 17°40E **80** C2
Marcali *Hungary* 46°35N 17°25E **80** C2
Marcapata *Peru* 13°31S 70°52W **188** C3
Marcaria *Italy* 45°7N 10°32E **92** C7
Mărculeşti *Moldova* 47°50N 28°14E **81** C12
March *U.K.* 52°33N 0°5E **67** E8
Marchand = Rommani
  Morocco 33°31N 6°40W **136** B2
Marche *France* 46°5N 1°20E **72** B5
Marche □ *Italy* 43°30N 13°15E **93** E10
Marche-en-Famenne
  Belgium 50°14N 5°19E **69** D5
Marchena *Spain* 37°18N 5°23W **89** H5
Marches = Marche □
  Italy 43°30N 13°15E **93** E10
Marchesale △ *Italy* 38°32N 16°13E **95** D9
Marciana Marina *Italy* 42°48N 10°12E **92** F7
Marcianise *Italy* 41°2N 14°17E **95** A7
Marcigny *France* 46°17N 4°2E **71** F11
Marcillat-en-Combraille
  France 46°12N 2°38E **71** F9
Marck *France* 50°57N 1°57E **71** B8
Marckolsheim *France* 48°10N 7°30E **71** D14
Marco Island *U.S.A.* 25°58N 81°44W **179** H14
Marcona *Peru* 15°10S 75°0W **188** D2
Marcos Juárez *Argentina* 32°42S 62°5W **190** C3
Mărculeşti *Moldova* 47°52N 28°14E **81** C12
Marcus Baker, Mt.
  U.S.A. 61°26N 147°45W **166** C10
Marcus I. = Minami-Tori-Shima
  Pac. Oc. 24°20N 153°58E **156** E7
Marcy, Mt. *U.S.A.* 44°7N 73°56W **175** B11
Mardan *Pakistan* 34°20N 72°0E **124** B5
Mardarivka *Ukraine* 47°32N 29°44E **81** C14
Mardie *Australia* 21°12S 115°59E **148** D2
Mardin *Turkey* 37°20N 40°43E **105** D9
Mårdsjö *Sweden* 63°18N 15°35E **62** A9
Marécchia → *Italy* 44°4N 12°34E **93** D9
Marechal Deodoro
  Brazil 9°43S 35°54W **189** B3
Maree, L. *U.K.* 57°40N 5°26W **65** D3
Mareeba *Australia* 16°59S 145°28E **150** B4
Mareetsane *S. Africa* 26°9S 25°34E **144** D4
Maremma *Italy* 42°30N 11°30E **93** F8
Maremma → *Italy* 42°35N 11°8E **92** F8
Maréna *Kayes, Mali* 14°36N 10°45W **138** C2
Maréna *Koulikouro, Mali* 13°55N 7°20W **138** C3
Marengo *France* 41°48N 92°4W **172** E7
Marennes *France* 45°49N 1°7W **72** C2
Marettimo *Italy* 37°58N 12°4E **94** F5
Mareuil *France* 45°26N 0°29E **72** C4
Marfa *U.S.A.* 30°19N 104°1W **176** F2
Marfa Pt. *Malta* 35°59N 14°19E **101** D1
Margai Caka *China* 35°11N 86°57E **110** C10
Marganets = Marhanets
  Ukraine 47°40N 34°40E **85** J8
Margao = Madgaon
  India 15°12N 73°58E **127** G1
Margaret → *Australia* 18°9S 125°41E **148** C4
Margaret Bay *Canada* 51°20N 127°35W **162** C3
Margaret L. *Canada* 58°56N 115°25W **162** B5
Margaret River
  Australia 33°57S 115°4E **149** F2
Margarita, I. de
  Venezuela 11°0N 64°0W **186** A6
Margaríti *Greece* 39°20N 20°26E **98** B2
Margaritovo *Russia* 43°25N 134°45E **115** C15
Margate *S. Africa* 30°50S 30°20E **145** E5
Margate *U.K.* 51°23N 1°23E **67** F9
Margate *U.S.A.* 26°15N 80°12W **179** H14
Margeride, Mts. de la
  France 44°43N 3°38E **72** D7

GREENLAND

KEY TO EUROPEAN MAP PAGES

57

	Large scale maps (>1:2 500 000)

	Medium scale maps (1:2 800 000 – 1:9 900 000)
	Small scale maps (<1:10 000 000)

60

ICELAND

Arctic Circle

WORLD COUNTRY INDEX

Afghanistan	122	**G**ermany	76–77	**O**man	131
Albania	96	Ghana	138–139		
Algeria	136	Greece	96–99	**P**akistan	122, 124
Angola	140–141	Greenland	57	Panama	182
Argentina	190–192	Guadeloupe	183	Papua New Guinea	156
Armenia	105	Guatemala	182	Paraguay	190–191
Australia	148–153	Guinea	138	Peru	188
Austria	78–79	Guinea-Bissau	138	Philippines	119
Azerbaijan	105	Guyana	186	Poland	82–83
				Portugal	88–89
Bahamas	182–183	**H**aiti	183	Puerto Rico	183
Bahrain	129	Honduras	182		
Bangladesh	123	Hungary	80	**Q**atar	129
Barbados	183				
Belarus	84–85	**I**celand	60	**R**omania	80–81
Belgium	69	India	122–127	Russia	84–87, 106–109
Belize	182	Indonesia	118–119	Rwanda	142
Benin	139	Iran	105, 128–129		
Bhutan	123	Iraq	105, 128–129	**S**t. Lucia	183
Bolivia	186	Ireland	64	Samoa	156
Bosnia-Herzegovina	80, 96	Israel	130	Saudi Arabia	128–129, 131
Botswana	144	Italy	92–95	Scotland	65
Brazil	186–187, 189, 191	Ivory Coast	138	Senegal	138
Brunei	118			Serbia	96
Bulgaria	96–97	**J**amaica	182	Sierra Leone	138
Burkina Faso	138–139	Japan	112–113	Singapore	121
Burma (Myanmar)	123	Jordan	130	Slovak Republic	79
Burundi	142			Slovenia	93
		Kazakhstan	108–109	Solomon Is.	156
Cambodia	120–121	Kenya	142	Somalia	131
Canary Is.	100	Korea, North	115	South Africa	144–145
Cameroon	139, 140	Korea, South	115	South Sudan	135
Canada	160–165	Kosovo	96	Spain	88–91
Central African Republic	140	Kuwait	128–129	Sri Lanka	127
Chad	135	Kyrgyzstan	109	Sudan	135
Chile	190, 192			Suriname	186–187
China	110–111, 114–117	**L**aos	120	Swaziland	145
Colombia	186	Latvia	82, 84	Sweden	60–63
Congo	140	Lebanon	130	Switzerland	77
Congo, Dem. Rep.		Lesotho	145	Syria	105, 128
of the	140–143	Liberia	138		
Costa Rica	182	Libya	135	**T**aiwan	117
Croatia	93	Lithuania	82, 84	Tajikistan	109
Cuba	182–183	Luxembourg	69	Tanzania	142–143
Cyprus	101			Thailand	120–121
Czech Republic	78–79	**M**acedonia	96	Togo	139
		Madagascar	141	Tonga	156
Denmark	63	Malawi	143	Trinidad and Tobago	187
Djibouti	131	Malaysia	118–119, 121	Tunisia	134–135
Dominican Republic	183	Mali	134, 138–139	Turkey	104–105
		Malta	101	Turkmenistan	108
East Timor	119	Martinique	183		
Ecuador	186	Mauritania	134	**U**ganda	142
Egypt	137	Mexico	180–181	Ukraine	85
El Salvador	182	Moldova	81	United Arab Emirates	129
England	66–67	Mongolia	110–111	United Kingdom	64–67
Equatorial Guinea	140	Montenegro	96	USA	168–179
Eritrea	131	Morocco	136	Uruguay	190–191
Estonia	84	Mozambique	143, 145	Uzbekistan	108–109
Ethiopia	131				
		Namibia	144	**V**anuatu	156
Fiji	154	Nepal	125	Venezuela	186
Finland	60–61	Netherlands	69	Vietnam	120–121
France	70–73	New Zealand	154–155		
French Guiana	187	Nicaragua	182	**W**ales	66–67
		Niger	134–135, 139		
Gabon	140	Nigeria	139	**Y**emen	131
Gambia	138	Northern Ireland	64		
Georgia	87	Norway	60–62	**Z**ambia	141, 143
				Zimbabwe	145

60

68

65

65

65

66

64

74

69

IRELAND

UNITED
KINGDOM

70

88

90

72

FRAN

ANDORRA

PORTUGAL

SPAIN

100

MOROCCO

AL

Margherita di Savóia *Italy* 41°22N 16°9E 95 A9
Margherita Pk. *Uganda* 0°22N 29°51E 142 B3
Marghilon *Uzbekistan* 40°27N 71°42E 109 D8
Margonin *Poland* 52°58N 17°5E 83 F4
Margów, Dasht-e *Afghan.* 30°40N 62°30E 122 D3
Marguerite *Canada* 52°30N 122°25W 162 C4
Marhanets *Ukraine* 47°40N 34°40E 85 J8
Marhoum *Algeria* 34°27N 0°11W 136 B3
Mari El □ *Russia* 56°30N 48°0E 86 B8
Mari Indus *Pakistan* 32°57N 71°34E 124 C4
Mari Republic = Mari El □ *Russia* 56°30N 48°0E 86 B8
María, Sa. de *Spain* 37°39N 2°14W 91 H2
María de la Salut *Spain* 39°40N 3°5E 100 B10
María Elena *Chile* 22°18S 69°40W 190 A2
María Grande *Argentina* 31°45S 59°55W 190 C4
Maria I. N. Terr., *Australia* 14°52S 135°45E 150 A2
Maria I. Tas., *Australia* 42°35S 148°0E 151 G4
Maria Island △ *Australia* 42°38S 148°5E 151 G4
Maria van Diemen, C. *N.Z.* 34°29S 172°40E 154 A1
Mariager *Denmark* 56°40N 9°59E 63 H3
Mariager Fjord *Denmark* 56°42N 10°19E 63 H4
Mariakani *Kenya* 3°50S 39°27E 142 C4
Mariala △ *Australia* 25°57S 145°2E 151 D4
Marian *Australia* 21°9S 148°57E 150 b
Maria L. *Canada* 63°0N 116°15W 162 A5
Mariana Trench *Pac. Oc.* 13°0N 145°0E 156 F6
Marianna Ark., *U.S.A.* 34°46N 90°46W 177 D9
Marianna Fla., *U.S.A.* 30°46N 85°14W 178 E4
Mariannelund *Sweden* 57°37N 15°35E 63 G9
Mariánské Lázně *Czech Rep.* 49°58N 12°41E 78 B5
Marías, Is. *Mexico* 21°25N 106°28W 180 C3
Mariato, Punta *Panama* 7°12N 80°52W 182 E3
Mariazell *Austria* 47°47N 15°19E 78 D8
Maribo *Denmark* 54°48N 11°30E 63 K5
Maribor *Slovenia* 46°36N 15°40E 93 B12
Marico → *Africa* 23°35S 26°57E 144 B4
Maricopa Ariz., *U.S.A.* 33°4N 112°3W 169 K7
Maricopa Calif., *U.S.A.* 35°4N 119°24W 171 K7
Marie Byrd Land *Antarctica* 79°30S 125°0W 55 D14
Marie-Galante *Guadeloupe* 15°56N 61°16W 182 b
Mariecourt = Kangiqsujuaq *Canada* 61°30N 72°0W 161 E17
Mariefred *Sweden* 59°15N 17°12E 62 B2
Mariehamn *Finland* 60°5N 19°55E 61 F18
Marielund *Sweden* 55°53N 13°10E 63 J7
Mariembourg *Belgium* 50°6N 4°31E 69 D4
Marienbad = Mariánské Lázně *Czech Rep.* 49°58N 12°41E 78 B5
Marienberg *Germany* 50°39N 13°9E 76 C9
Oriental *Namibia* 24°36S 18°0E 144 B2
Marienville *U.S.A.* 41°28N 79°8W 174 E5
Mariestad *Sweden* 58°43N 13°50E 63 F7
Marietta Ga., *U.S.A.* 33°57N 84°33W 178 B5
Marietta Ohio, *U.S.A.* 39°25N 81°27W 174 F3
Marieville *Canada* 45°26N 73°10W 175 A11
Mariga → *Nigeria* 9°40N 5°55E 139 C6
Marignane *France* 43°25N 5°13E 73 E9
Marília *Brazil* 22°13S 50°0W 191 A6
Marijampolė *Lithuania* 54°33N 23°19E 82 D10
Marijampolė □ *Lithuania* 54°34N 23°21E 82 D10
Marín *Spain* 42°23N 8°42W 88 C2
Marina *U.S.A.* 36°41N 121°48W 170 J5
Marinduque *Phil.* 13°25N 122°0E 119 B6
Marine City *U.S.A.* 42°43N 82°30W 174 D2
Marineland *U.S.A.* 29°40N 81°13W 178 F8
Marineo *Italy* 37°57N 13°25E 94 E6
Marinette *U.S.A.* 45°6N 87°38W 172 C10
Maringá *Brazil* 23°26S 52°2W 191 A5
Marinha Grande *Portugal* 39°45N 8°56W 88 F2
Marinho dos Abrolhos △ *Brazil* 17°50S 39°0W 189 D3
Marino *Italy* 41°46N 12°39E 93 G9
Marino di Campo *Italy* 42°46N 10°11E 92 F7
Marion Ala., *U.S.A.* 32°38N 87°19W 177 E11
Marion Ill., *U.S.A.* 37°44N 88°56W 172 G9
Marion Ind., *U.S.A.* 40°32N 85°40W 173 E11
Marion Iowa, *U.S.A.* 42°2N 91°36W 172 D8
Marion Kans., *U.S.A.* 38°21N 97°1W 172 F5
Marion N.C., *U.S.A.* 35°41N 82°1W 177 D13
Marion Ohio, *U.S.A.* 40°35N 83°8W 173 E12
Marion S.C., *U.S.A.* 34°11N 79°24W 177 D15
Marion Va., *U.S.A.* 36°50N 81°31W 173 G13
Marion, L., *U.S.A.* 33°28N 80°10W 178 B9
Marion Bay *Australia* 35°12S 136°59E 152 C2
Marion I. *Ind. Oc.* 47°0S 38°0E 146 J2
Mariposa *U.S.A.* 37°29N 119°58W 170 H7
Mariscal Estigarribia *Paraguay* 22°3S 60°40W 190 A3
Maritime Alps = Maritimes, Alpes *Europe* 44°10N 7°10E 73 D11
Maritimes, Alpes *Europe* 44°10N 7°10E 73 D11
Maritsa = Evros → *Greece* 41°40N 26°34E 97 F10
Maritsa *Greece* 36°28N 28°10E 101 C10
Mariupol *Ukraine* 47°5N 37°31E 85 J9
Mariusa △ *Venezuela* 9°0N 61°27W 183 E7
Marivān *Iran* 35°30N 46°25E 128 C5
Marj 'Uyūn *Lebanon* 33°21N 35°34E 130 B4
Marka Si. Arabia 18°14N 41°19E 137 D5
Marka *Somalia* 1°48N 44°30E 137 C3
Markam *China* 29°42N 98°38E 116 C2
Markapur *India* 15°44N 79°19E 127 F4
Markaryd *Sweden* 56°28N 13°35E 63 H7
Markazi □ *Iran* 35°0N 49°30E 128 C6
Markdale *Canada* 44°19N 80°39W 174 B4
Markelsdorfer Huk *Germany* 54°33N 11°4E 76 A7
Market Drayton *U.K.* 52°54N 2°29W 66 E5
Market Harborough *U.K.* 52°29N 0°55W 67 E7
Market Rasen *U.K.* 53°24N 0°20W 66 D7

Markham *Canada* 43°52N 79°16W 174 C5
Markham, Mt. *Antarctica* 83°0S 164°0E 55 E11
Marki *Poland* 52°19N 21°6E 83 F8
Märkische Schweiz △ *Germany* 52°34N 14°2E 76 C10
Markit *China* 38°54N 77°40E 109 E9
Markkleeberg *Germany* 51°16N 12°23E 76 C8
Markleeville *U.S.A.* 38°42N 119°47W 170 G7
Markopoulo *Greece* 37°53N 23°57E 98 D5
Markovac *Serbia* 44°14N 21°7E 96 B5
Markovo *Russia* 64°40N 170°24E 107 C17
Markoye *Burkina Faso* 14°39N 0°2E 139 C5
Marks *Russia* 51°45N 46°50E 86 E8
Marksville *U.S.A.* 31°8N 92°4W 176 F8
Markt Schwaben *Germany* 48°11N 11°52E 77 G7
Marktoberdorf *Germany* 47°45N 10°37E 77 H6
Marktredwitz *Germany* 50°1N 12°6E 77 E8
Marl *Germany* 51°39N 7°4E 76 D3
Marla *Australia* 27°19S 133°33E 151 D1
Marlbank *Canada* 44°26N 77°6W 174 B7
Marlboro *U.S.A.* 41°36N 73°59W 175 E11
Marlborough *Australia* 22°46S 149°52E 150 C4
Marlborough *U.K.* 51°25N 1°43W 67 F6
Marlborough Vt., *U.S.A.* 42°21N 71°33W 175 D13
Marlborough □ *N.Z.* 41°40S 173°50E 155 B8
Marlborough Downs *U.K.* 51°27N 1°53W 67 F6
Marle *France* 49°43N 3°47E 71 C10
Marlin *U.S.A.* 31°18N 96°54W 176 F6
Marlow *Germany* 54°9N 12°33E 76 A8
Marlow *U.K.* 51°34N 0°46W 67 F7
Marlow *U.S.A.* 34°39N 97°58W 176 D6
Marmagao *India* 15°25N 73°56E 127 G1
Marmande *France* 44°30N 0°10E 72 D4
Marmara *Turkey* 40°35N 27°34E 97 F11
Marmara, Sea of = Marmara Denizi *Turkey* 40°45N 28°15E 97 F12
Marmara Denizi *Turkey* 40°45N 28°15E 97 F12
Marmara Gölü *Turkey* 38°37N 28°2E 99 C10
Marmaris *Turkey* 36°50N 28°14E 99 E10
Marmaris Limanı *Turkey* 36°50N 28°19E 99 E10
Marmion, Mt. *Australia* 29°16S 119°50E 149 E2
Marmion L. *Canada* 48°55N 91°20W 164 C1
Marmolada, Mte. *Italy* 46°26N 11°51E 93 B8
Marmolejo *Spain* 38°3N 4°13W 89 G6
Marmora *Canada* 44°28N 77°41W 174 B7
Mármora, La *Italy* 39°59N 9°20E 94 C2
Marnay *France* 47°16N 5°48E 71 E12
Marne *Germany* 53°56N 9°2E 76 B5
Marne → *France* 48°50N 4°10E 71 D11
Marne → *France* 48°47N 2°29E 71 D9
Marneuli *Georgia* 41°30N 44°48E 87 K7
Marnoo *Australia* 36°40S 142°52E 152 D5
Maro Reef *U.S.A.* 25°25N 170°35W 183 J5
Maroantsetra *Madag.* 15°26S 49°44E 141 H9
Maroelaboom *Namibia* 19°15S 18°53E 144 A2
Marondera *Zimbabwe* 18°5S 31°42E 143 F3
Maroni → *Fr. Guiana* 5°30N 54°0W 187 B8
Maronia *Greece* 40°53N 25°30E 97 F9
Maronne → *France* 45°5N 1°56E 72 C5
Maroochydore *Australia* 26°29S 153°5E 151 D5
Maroona *Australia* 37°27S 142°54E 152 D5
Maros → *Hungary* 46°15N 20°13E 80 D5
Maróstica *Italy* 45°44N 11°40E 93 C8
Maroua *Cameroon* 10°40N 14°20E 139 C7
Marovoay *Madag.* 16°6S 46°39E 141 H9
Marqāköl *Kazakhstan* 48°45N 85°45E 109 C11
Marquard *S. Africa* 28°40S 27°28E 144 C4
Marquesas Fracture Zone *Pac. Oc.* 9°0S 125°0W 157 H15
Marquesas Is. = Marquises, Îs. *French Polynesia* 9°30S 140°0W 157 H14
Marquesas Keys *U.S.A.* 24°35N 82°10W 179 L7
Marquette *U.S.A.* 46°33N 87°24W 172 B10
Marquis *St. Lucia* 14°2N 60°54W 183 f
Marquise *France* 50°50N 1°40E 71 B8
Marquises, Îs. *French Polynesia* 9°30S 140°0W 157 H14
Marra, Djebel *Sudan* 13°10N 24°22E 135 F10
Marra Cr. → *Australia* 30°5S 147°15E 153 A7
Marra-Marra △ *Australia* 33°30S 151°4E 153 B9
Marracuene *Mozam.* 25°45S 32°35E 145 C5
Marradi *Italy* 44°4N 11°37E 93 D8
Marrakech *Morocco* 31°9N 8°0W 136 B4
Marratxí *Spain* 39°33N 2°48E 100 B9
Marrawah *Australia* 40°55S 144°42E 151 G3
Marrecas, Serra das *Brazil* 9°0S 41°0W 189 D2
Marree *Australia* 29°39S 138°1E 151 D2
Marrero *U.S.A.* 29°53N 90°6W 177 G9
Marrimane *Mozam.* 22°58S 33°34E 145 B5
Marromeu *Mozam.* 18°15S 36°25E 145 A6
Marromeu △ *Mozam.* 19°0S 36°0E 145 A6
Marroquí, Punta *Spain* 36°0N 5°37W 89 K5
Marrowie Cr. → *Australia* 33°23S 145°40E 153 B6
Marrubane *Mozam.* 18°0S 37°0E 143 F4
Marrúbiu *Italy* 39°40N 8°35E 94 C1
Marrupa *Mozam.* 13°8S 37°30E 143 E4
Mars Hill *U.S.A.* 46°31N 67°52W 173 B20
Marsá 'Alam *Egypt* 25°5N 34°54E 137 C3
Marsá Matrûh *Egypt* 31°19N 27°9E 137 A2
Marsá Sha'b *Sudan* 20°51N 37°7E 137 C4
Marsabit *Kenya* 2°18N 38°0E 142 B4
Marsabit △ *Kenya* 2°18N 38°0E 142 B4
Marsala *Italy* 37°48N 12°26E 94 E5
Marsberg *Germany* 51°28N 8°52E 76 D4
Marsciano *Italy* 42°54N 12°20E 93 F9
Marsden *Australia* 33°47S 147°32E 153 B7
Marsden Point *N.Z.* 35°50S 174°31E 154 B5
Marseillan *France* 43°23N 3°31E 72 E7
Marseille *France* 43°18N 5°23E 73 E9
Marseille-Marignane ✈ (MRS) *France* 43°26N 5°14E 73 E9
Marseilles = Marseille *France* 43°18N 5°23E 73 E9
Marsh I. *U.S.A.* 29°34N 91°53W 176 G9
Marshall *Liberia* 6°8N 10°22W 138 D2
Marshall Ark., *U.S.A.* 35°55N 92°38W 176 D8
Marshall Mich., *U.S.A.* 42°16N 84°58W 173 D11
Marshall Minn., *U.S.A.* 44°27N 95°47W 172 C6

Marshall Mo., *U.S.A.* 39°7N 93°12W 172 F7
Marshall Tex., *U.S.A.* 32°33N 94°23W 176 E7
Marshall → *Australia* 22°59S 136°59E 150 C2
Marshall Is. ■ *Pac. Oc.* 9°0N 171°0E 156 G9
Marshalltown *U.S.A.* 42°3N 92°55W 172 D7
Marshallville *U.S.A.* 32°27N 83°56W 178 D6
Marshbrook *Zimbabwe* 18°33S 31°9E 145 A5
Marshfield Mo., *U.S.A.* 37°15N 92°54W 172 G7
Marshfield Vt., *U.S.A.* 44°20N 72°20W 175 B12
Marshfield Wis., *U.S.A.* 44°40N 90°10W 172 C8
Marshūn *Iran* 36°19N 49°23E 129 B6
Mársico Nuovo *Italy* 40°25N 15°44E 95 B8
Märsta *Sweden* 59°37N 17°52E 62 E11
Marstal *Denmark* 54°51N 10°30E 63 K4
Marstrand *Sweden* 57°53N 11°35E 63 G5
Mart *U.S.A.* 31°33N 96°50W 176 F6
Marta → *Italy* 42°14N 11°42E 93 F8
Martaban *Burma* 16°30N 97°35E 123 L20
Martaban, G. of *Burma* 16°5N 96°30E 123 L20
Martano *Italy* 40°12N 18°18E 95 B11
Martapura Kalimantan Selatan, *Indonesia* 3°22S 114°47E 118 E4
Martapura Sumatera Selatan, *Indonesia* 4°19S 104°22E 118 E2
Marte *Nigeria* 12°23N 13°46E 139 C7
Marte R. Gómez, Presa *Mexico* 26°10N 99°0W 181 B5
Martel *France* 44°57N 1°37E 72 D5
Martelange *Belgium* 49°49N 5°43E 69 E5
Martellago *Italy* 45°33N 12°9E 93 C9
Martés, Sierra *Spain* 39°20N 1°0W 91 F4
Martfü *Hungary* 47°1N 20°17E 80 C5
Marthaguy Cr. → *Australia* 30°16S 147°35E 153 A7
Marthapal *India* 19°24N 81°37E 126 E5
Martha's Vineyard *U.S.A.* 41°25N 70°38W 175 E14
Martigné-Ferchaud *France* 47°50N 1°20W 70 E5
Martigny *Switz.* 46°6N 7°3E 77 J3
Martigues *France* 43°24N 5°4E 73 E9
Martil *Morocco* 35°36N 5°15W 136 A2
Martin *Slovak Rep.* 49°6N 18°58E 79 B11
Martin S. Dak., *U.S.A.* 43°11N 101°44W 172 D3
Martin Tenn., *U.S.A.* 36°21N 88°51W 177 C10
Martin → *Spain* 41°18N 0°19W 90 D4
Martin L. *U.S.A.* 32°41N 85°55W 178 C4
Martin Vaz *Atl. Oc.* 20°30S 28°51W 56 J9
Martina Franca *Italy* 40°42N 17°20E 95 B10
Martinborough *N.Z.* 41°14S 175°29E 154 H4
Martinez Calif., *U.S.A.* 38°1N 122°8W 170 G4
Martinez Ga., *U.S.A.* 33°31N 82°4W 178 C6
Martinho Campos *Brazil* 19°20S 45°13W 189 D1
Martinique ☒ *W. Indies* 14°40N 61°0W 182 c
Martinique Passage *W. Indies* 15°15N 61°0W 183 C7
Martinópolis *Brazil* 22°11S 51°12W 191 A5
Martins Bay *Barbados* 13°12N 59°29W 183 g
Martins Ferry *U.S.A.* 40°6N 80°44W 174 F4
Martinsberg *Austria* 48°22N 15°9E 78 C8
Martinsburg Pa., *U.S.A.* 40°19N 78°20W 174 F6
Martinsburg W. Va., *U.S.A.* 39°27N 77°58W 173 F15
Martinsicuro *Italy* 42°54N 13°54E 93 F10
Martinsville Ind., *U.S.A.* 39°26N 86°25W 172 F10
Martinsville Va., *U.S.A.* 36°41N 79°52W 173 G14
Marton *N.Z.* 40°4S 175°23E 154 G4
Martorell *Spain* 41°28N 1°56E 90 D6
Martos *Spain* 37°44N 3°58W 89 H7
Martu □ *Australia* 23°30S 122°30E 148 D4
Martuni *Armenia* 40°8N 45°20E 87 K7
Maru *Nigeria* 12°22N 6°22E 139 C6
Marudi *Malaysia* 4°11N 114°19E 118 D4
Marugame *Japan* 34°15N 133°40E 113 G6
Maruia → *N.Z.* 41°47S 172°13E 155 B7
Maruim *Brazil* 10°45S 37°5W 189 C3
Marulan *Australia* 34°43S 150°3E 153 C9
Marunga *Angola* 17°28S 20°2E 144 B3
Marungu, Mts. *Dem. Rep. of the Congo* 7°30S 30°0E 142 D3
Maruwa → *Australia* 22°30S 127°30E 148 D4
Marv Dasht *Iran* 29°50N 52°40E 129 D7
Marvão *Portugal* 39°24N 7°20W 89 F3
Marvast *Iran* 30°30N 54°15E 129 D7
Marvejols *France* 44°33N 3°19E 72 D7
Marvel Loch *Australia* 31°28S 119°29E 149 F2
Marwar *India* 25°43N 73°45E 124 G5
Mary *Turkmenistan* 37°40N 61°50E 128 B9
Mary Esther *U.S.A.* 30°25N 86°40W 179 E3
Maryborough = Portlaoise *Ireland* 53°2N 7°18W 64 C4
Maryborough Queens., *Australia* 25°31S 152°37E 151 D5
Maryborough Vic., *Australia* 37°3S 143°44E 152 D5
Maryfield *Canada* 49°50N 101°35W 163 D8
Maryland □ *U.S.A.* 39°0N 76°30W 173 F15
Maryland Junction *Zimbabwe* 17°45S 30°31E 143 F3
Maryport *U.K.* 54°44N 3°28W 66 C4
Mary's Harbour *Canada* 52°18N 55°51W 165 B8
Marystown *Canada* 47°10N 55°10W 165 C8
Marysville Calif., *U.S.A.* 39°9N 121°35W 170 F5
Marysville Kans., *U.S.A.* 39°51N 96°39W 172 F5
Marysville Mich., *U.S.A.* 42°54N 82°29W 174 D2
Marysville Ohio, *U.S.A.* 40°14N 83°22W 173 E12
Marysville Wash., *U.S.A.* 48°3N 122°11W 170 B4
Maryville Mo., *U.S.A.* 40°21N 94°52W 172 E6
Maryville Tenn., *U.S.A.* 35°46N 83°58W 177 D13

Masalima, Kepulauan *Indonesia* 5°4S 117°5E 118 F5
Masalli *Azerbaijan* 39°3N 48°40E 105 C13
Masamba *Indonesia* 2°30S 120°15E 119 E6
Masan *S. Korea* 35°11N 128°32E 115 G15
Masandam, Ra's *Oman* 26°30N 56°30E 129 E8
Masasi *Tanzania* 10°45S 38°52E 143 E4
Masaya *Nic.* 12°0N 86°7W 182 D2
Masba *Nigeria* 11°35N 13°1E 139 C7
Masbate *Phil.* 12°21N 123°36E 119 B6
Máscali *Italy* 37°45N 15°12E 95 E8
Mascara *Algeria* 35°26N 0°6E 136 A4
Mascara □ *Algeria* 35°26N 0°10E 136 A4
Mascarene Is. *Ind. Oc.* 22°0S 55°0E 132 J9
Mascota *Mexico* 20°32N 104°49W 180 C4
Masdar City = Madīnat Masdar *U.A.E.* 24°26N 54°37E 129 E7
Masela *Indonesia* 8°9S 129°51E 119 F7
Maseru *Lesotho* 29°18S 27°30E 144 C4
Mashaba *Zimbabwe* 20°2S 30°29E 143 G3
Mashābih *Si. Arabia* 25°35N 36°30E 128 E3
Mashan *China* 23°40N 108°11E 116 F7
Mashang *China* 36°48N 117°57E 115 F9
Mashatu □ *Botswana* 22°45S 29°5E 145 B4
Mashegu *Nigeria* 10°0N 5°35E 139 D6
Masherbrum *Pakistan* 35°38N 76°18E 125 B7
Mashhad *Iran* 36°20N 59°35E 129 B8
Mashi → *Nigeria* 13°0N 7°54E 139 C6
Mashīz *Iran* 29°56N 56°37E 129 D8
Mäshkel, Hämūn-i- *Pakistan* 28°20N 62°56E 129 D9
Mashki Chāh *Pakistan* 29°5N 62°30E 122 E3
Mashonaland *Zimbabwe* 16°30S 31°0E 141 H6
Mashonaland Central □ *Zimbabwe* 17°30S 31°0E 145 A5
Mashonaland East □ *Zimbabwe* 18°0S 32°0E 145 A5
Mashonaland West □ *Zimbabwe* 17°30S 29°30E 145 A4
Mashrakh *India* 26°7N 84°48E 125 F11
Masi Manimba *Dem. Rep. of the Congo* 4°40S 17°54E 140 D3
Masig *Australia* 9°45S 143°24E 150 a
Masindi *Uganda* 1°40N 31°43E 142 B3
Masindi Port *Uganda* 1°43N 32°2E 142 B3
Masisea *Peru* 8°35S 74°22W 188 E3
Masisi *Dem. Rep. of the Congo* 1°23S 28°49E 142 C2
Masjed Soleyman *Iran* 31°55N 49°18E 129 D6
Mask, L. *Ireland* 53°36N 9°22W 64 C2
Maskin *Oman* 23°44N 56°52E 129 F8
Maslen Nos *Bulgaria* 42°18N 27°48E 97 D11
Maslinica *Croatia* 43°24N 16°13E 93 E13
Masnou = El Masnou *Spain* 41°28N 2°20E 90 D7
Masoala, Tanjon' i *Madag.* 15°59S 50°13E 141 H10
Masohi = Amahai *Indonesia* 3°20S 128°55E 119 E7
Mason Nev., *U.S.A.* 38°56N 119°8W 170 G7
Mason Tex., *U.S.A.* 30°45N 99°14W 176 F5
Mason B. *N.Z.* 46°55S 167°45E 155 G2
Mason City *U.S.A.* 43°9N 93°12W 172 D7
Maspalomas *Canary Is.* 27°46N 15°35W 100 G4
Maspalomas, Pta. *Canary Is.* 27°43N 15°36W 100 G4
Masqat *Oman* 23°37N 58°36E 131 C6
Masr el Gedida *Egypt* 30°5N 31°21E 137 E7
Massa *Italy* 44°1N 10°9E 92 D7
Massa, O. → *Morocco* 30°2N 9°40W 136 B2
Massa e Carrara □ *Italy* 44°10N 10°10E 92 D7
Massa Maríttima *Italy* 43°3N 10°52E 92 E7
Massachusetts □ *U.S.A.* 42°30N 72°0W 175 D13
Massachusetts B. *U.S.A.* 42°25N 70°50W 175 D14
Massafra *Italy* 40°35N 17°7E 95 B10
Massakory *Chad* 13°0N 15°49E 135 F8
Massamba *Mozam.* 15°58S 33°31E 143 F3
Massanella *Spain* 39°48N 2°51E 100 B9
Massangena *Mozam.* 21°34S 33°0E 145 B5
Massango *Angola* 8°2S 16°21E 140 F3
Massapé *Brazil* 3°31S 40°19W 189 A2
Massat *France* 42°53N 1°21E 72 F5
Massawa = Mitsiwa *Eritrea* 15°35N 39°25E 131 D2
Massena *U.S.A.* 44°56N 74°54W 175 B10
Massenya *Chad* 11°21N 16°9E 135 F9
Masset *Canada* 54°2N 132°10W 162 C2
Masseube *France* 43°25N 0°36E 72 E4
Massiac *France* 45°15N 3°11E 72 C7
Massiah Street *Barbados* 13°9N 59°29W 183 g
Massif Central *France* 44°55N 3°0E 72 D7
Massif des Bauges △ *France* 45°40N 6°10E 73 C13
Massiqui *Mali* 11°40N 6°50W 138 C3
Massillon *U.S.A.* 40°48N 81°32W 174 F3
Massine, O. → *Algeria* 36°13N 2°12E 136 A4
Massinga *Mozam.* 23°15S 35°22E 145 B6
Massingir *Mozam.* 23°51S 32°4E 145 B5
Masson-Angers *Canada* 45°32N 75°25W 175 A9
Masson I. *Antarctica* 66°10S 93°20E 55 C7
Maştağa *Azerbaijan* 40°35N 50°1E 87 K10
Mastanli = Momchilgrad *Bulgaria* 41°33N 25°23E 97 E9
Masterton *N.Z.* 40°56S 175°39E 154 G4
Mastic *U.S.A.* 40°47N 72°54W 175 F12
Mastuj *Pakistan* 36°20N 72°36E 125 A5
Mastung *Pakistan* 29°50N 66°56E 122 E5
Mastūrah *Si. Arabia* 23°7N 38°52E 128 F3
Masty *Belarus* 53°27N 24°38E 75 G13
Masuda *Japan* 34°40N 131°51E 113 G5
Masuku = Franceville *Gabon* 1°40S 13°32E 140 E2
Masurian Lakes = Mazurski, Pojezierze *Poland* 53°50N 21°0E 82 E7
Masvingo *Zimbabwe* 20°8S 30°49E 143 G3
Masvingo □ *Zimbabwe* 21°0S 31°30E 143 G3
Maswa □ *Tanzania* 3°30S 34°0E 142 C3
Maşyāf *Syria* 35°4N 36°20E 104 E7
Mat → *Albania* 41°40N 19°35E 96 E3
Mata-au = Clutha → *N.Z.* 46°20S 169°49E 155 G4
Mata de São João *Brazil* 12°31S 38°17W 189 C3

Matabeleland *Zimbabwe* 18°0S 27°0E 141 H5
Matabeleland North □ *Zimbabwe* 19°0S 28°0E 143 F2
Matabeleland South □ *Zimbabwe* 21°0S 29°0E 143 G2
Matachel → *Spain* 38°50N 6°17W 89 G4
Matachewan *Canada* 47°56N 80°39W 164 C3
Matadi *Dem. Rep. of the Congo* 5°52S 13°31E 140 F2
Matagalpa *Nic.* 13°0N 85°58W 182 D2
Matagami *Canada* 49°45N 77°34W 164 C4
Matagami, L. *Canada* 49°50N 77°40W 164 C4
Matagorda *U.S.A.* 28°40N 95°58W 176 G7
Matagorda I. *U.S.A.* 28°15N 96°30W 176 G6
Mataiea *Tahiti* 17°46S 149°25W 59 d
Matak *Indonesia* 3°18N 106°16E 118 D3
Matakana *Australia* 32°59S 145°54E 153 B6
Matakana *N.Z.* 36°21S 174°43E 154 B5
Matala *Greece* 34°59N 24°45E 101 E6
Matalaque *Peru* 16°26S 70°49W 188 D3
Matale *Sri Lanka* 7°30N 80°37E 127 L5
Matam *Senegal* 15°34N 13°17W 138 B2
Matam □ *Senegal* 15°37N 13°19W 138 B2
Matamata *N.Z.* 37°48S 175°47E 154 B5
Matameye *Niger* 13°26N 8°28E 139 C6
Matamoros Coahuila, *Mexico* 25°32N 103°15W 180 B4
Matamoros Tamaulipas, *Mexico* 25°53N 97°30W 181 B5
Ma'tan as Sarra *Libya* 21°45N 22°0E 135 D10
Matandu → *Tanzania* 8°45S 34°19E 143 D3
Matane *Canada* 48°50N 67°33W 165 C6
Matang *China* 23°30N 104°7E 116 F5
Matankari *Niger* 13°46N 4°1E 139 C5
Matanomadh *India* 23°33N 68°57E 124 H3
Matanzas *Cuba* 23°0N 81°40W 182 B3
Matapa *Botswana* 23°11S 24°39E 144 B3
Matapédia *Canada* 48°0N 66°59W 165 C6
Matapo △ *Zimbabwe* 20°30S 29°40E 143 G2
Mataporquera *Spain* 42°52N 4°10W 88 B6
Matara *Sri Lanka* 5°58N 80°30E 127 M5
Mataram *Indonesia* 8°35S 116°7E 118 F5
Matarani *Peru* 17°0S 72°10W 188 D3
Mataranka *Australia* 14°55S 133°4E 148 B5
Matarma, Râs *Egypt* 30°27N 32°44E 130 E1
Mataró *Spain* 41°32N 2°29E 90 D7
Matarraña → *Spain* 41°14N 0°22E 90 D5
Mataruška Banja *Serbia* 43°40N 20°40E 96 C4
Matata *N.Z.* 37°54S 176°48E 154 B6
Matatiele *S. Africa* 30°20S 28°49E 145 D4
Matatila Dam *India* 25°20N 78°22E 126 B4
Mataura → *N.Z.* 46°11S 168°51E 155 G3
Matavai, B. de *Tahiti* 17°30S 149°23W 59 d
Matehuala *Mexico* 23°39N 100°39W 180 C4
Mateke Hills *Zimbabwe* 21°48S 31°0E 143 G3
Matelot *Trin. & Tob.* 10°50N 61°7W 187 K15
Matera *Italy* 40°40N 16°36E 95 B9
Matese, Monti del *Italy* 41°24N 14°23E 95 A7
Mátészalka *Hungary* 47°58N 22°20E 80 C6
Matetsi *Zimbabwe* 18°12S 26°0E 143 F2
Mateur *Tunisia* 37°9N 9°40E 136 A1
Matfors *Sweden* 62°21N 17°2E 62 B11
Matha *France* 45°52N 0°20W 72 C3
Mathenikó → *Uganda* 2°49N 34°27E 142 B3
Mathis *U.S.A.* 28°6N 97°50W 176 G6
Mathoura *Australia* 35°50S 144°55E 153 C6
Mathráki *Greece* 39°48N 19°31E 101 A3
Mathura *India* 27°30N 77°40E 124 F7
Mati *Phil.* 6°55N 126°15E 119 C7
Matiali *India* 26°56N 88°49E 125 F13
Matías Romero *Mexico* 16°53N 95°2W 181 D5
Matibane *Mozam.* 14°49S 40°45E 143 E5
Matiri Ra. *N.Z.* 41°38S 172°20E 155 B7
Matjiesfontein *S. Africa* 33°14S 20°35E 144 E3
Matla → *India* 21°40N 88°40E 125 J13
Matlamanyane *Botswana* 19°33S 25°57E 144 A4
Matli *Pakistan* 25°2N 68°39E 124 G3
Matlock *U.K.* 53°9N 1°33W 66 D6
Matmata *Tunisia* 33°37N 9°59E 136 B7
Mato Grosso □ *Brazil* 14°0S 55°0W 187 F8
Mato Grosso, Planalto do *Brazil* 15°0S 55°0W 187 F8
Mato Grosso do Sul □ *Brazil* 18°0S 55°0W 187 G8
Matobo = Matapo △ *Zimbabwe* 20°36S 28°40E 143 G2
Matochkin Shar, Proliv *Russia* 73°23N 55°12E 106 B6
Matola *Mozam.* 25°57S 32°27E 145 C5
Matopo Hills *Zimbabwe* 20°36S 28°20E 143 G2
Matopos *Zimbabwe* 20°20S 28°29E 143 G2
Matosinhos *Portugal* 41°11N 8°42W 88 D2
Matour *France* 46°19N 4°29E 72 F11
Matroosberg *S. Africa* 33°23S 19°40E 144 E2
Maţraḩ *Oman* 23°37N 58°30E 129 F8
Matsalu → *Estonia* 58°45N 23°36E 74 B2
Matsena *Nigeria* 13°5N 10°5E 139 C7
Matsesta *Russia* 43°34N 39°51E 87 J4
Matsu Tao *Taiwan* 26°8N 119°56E 117 D12
Matsue *Japan* 35°25N 133°10E 113 G6
Matsumae *Japan* 41°26N 140°7E 112 D10
Matsumae-Hantō *Japan* 41°30N 140°15E 112 D10
Matsumoto *Japan* 36°15N 138°0E 113 F9
Matsusaka *Japan* 34°34N 136°32E 113 G8
Matsushima *Japan* 38°20N 141°10E 112 E10
Matsuura *Japan* 33°20N 129°49E 113 H4
Matsuyama *Japan* 33°45N 132°45E 113 H6
Mattagami → *Canada* 50°43N 81°29W 164 B3
Mattancheri *India* 9°50N 76°15E 127 Q4
Mattawa *Canada* 46°20N 78°45W 164 C4
Matterhorn *Switz.* 45°58N 7°39E 73 D13
Mattersburg *Austria* 47°44N 16°24E 79 D9
Matthew Town *Bahamas* 20°57N 73°40W 183 B5
Matthews Ridge *Guyana* 7°37N 60°10W 187 B6
Mattice *Canada* 49°40N 83°20W 164 C3
Mattituck *U.S.A.* 40°59N 72°32W 175 F12
Mattoon *U.S.A.* 39°29N 88°23W 172 F9
Matuba *Mozam.* 24°28S 32°49E 145 B5

Matucana *Peru* 11°55S 76°25W 188 C2
Matugama *Sri Lanka* 6°31N 80°7E 127 L5
Matuku *Fiji* 19°10S 179°44E 154 a
Matūn = Khowst *Afghan.* 33°22N 69°58E 124 C3
Matura *Trin. & Tob.* 10°39N 61°1W 187 K15
Maturín *Venezuela* 9°45N 63°11W 186 B6
Matusadona △ *Zimbabwe* 16°58S 28°42E 143 F2
Matveyev Kurgan *Russia* 47°35N 38°57E 85 J10
Matxitxako, C. *Spain* 43°28N 2°47W 90 B2
Mau Mad. Prad., *India* 26°17N 78°41E 125 F8
Mau Ut. P., *India* 25°56N 83°33E 125 G10
Mau Ut. P., *India* 25°17N 81°23E 125 G9
Mau Escarpment *Kenya* 0°40S 36°0E 142 C4
Mau Ranipur *India* 25°16N 79°8E 125 G8
Maua *Kenya* 0°14N 37°56E 142 C4
Maúa *Mozam.* 13°53S 37°10E 143 E4
Maubeuge *France* 50°17N 3°57E 71 B10
Maubin *Burma* 16°44N 95°39E 123 L19
Maubourguet *France* 43°29N 0°1E 72 E4
Maud, Pt. *Australia* 23°6S 113°45E 148 D1
Maud Rise *S. Ocean* 66°0S 3°0E 55 C3
Maude *Australia* 34°29S 144°18E 152 C6
Maudin Sur *Burma* 16°0N 94°30E 123 M19
Maués *Brazil* 3°20S 57°45W 186 D7
Mauganj *India* 24°50N 81°55E 125 G9
Maughold Hd. *I. of Man* 54°18N 4°18W 66 C3
Mauguio *France* 43°37N 4°1E 72 E7
Maui *U.S.A.* 20°48N 156°20W 167 L8
Maulamyaing = Moulmein *Burma* 16°30N 97°40E 123 L20
Maule □ *Chile* 36°5S 72°30W 190 D1
Mauléon-Licharre *France* 43°14N 0°54W 72 E3
Maullín *Chile* 41°38S 73°37W 192 B2
Maumee *U.S.A.* 41°34N 83°39W 173 E12
Maumee → *U.S.A.* 41°42N 83°28W 173 E12
Maumere *Indonesia* 8°38S 122°13E 119 F6
Maumusson, Pertuis de *France* 45°48N 1°14W 72 C2
Maun *Botswana* 20°0S 23°26E 144 B3
Mauna Kea *U.S.A.* 19°50N 155°28W 167 M8
Mauna Loa *U.S.A.* 19°30N 155°35W 167 M8
Maunath Bhanjan = Mau *India* 25°56N 83°33E 125 G10
Maungaturoto *N.Z.* 36°6S 174°23E 154 C5
Maungmagan Kyunzu *Burma* 14°0N 97°48E 120 E1
Maungu *Kenya* 3°33S 38°45E 142 C4
Maupin *U.S.A.* 45°11N 121°5W 168 D3
Maure-de-Bretagne *France* 47°59N 1°58W 70 E5
Maurepas, L. *U.S.A.* 30°15N 90°30W 177 F9
Maures *France* 43°15N 6°15E 73 E10
Mauriac *France* 45°13N 2°19E 72 C6
Maurice, L. *Australia* 29°30S 131°0E 149 E5
Mauriceville *N.Z.* 40°45S 175°42E 154 G4
Maurício △ *Canada* 46°45N 73°0W 164 C5
Maurienne *France* 45°13N 6°30E 73 C10
Mauritania ■ *Africa* 20°50N 10°0W 134 E3
Mauritius ■ *Ind. Oc.* 20°0S 57°0E 141 d
Mauron *France* 48°9N 2°18W 70 D4
Maurs *France* 44°43N 2°12E 72 D6
Mauston *U.S.A.* 43°48N 90°5W 172 D8
Mauterndorf *Austria* 47°9N 13°40E 78 D6
Mauthen *Austria* 46°40N 13°0E 78 E6
Mauvezin *France* 43°44N 0°53E 72 E4
Mauzé-sur-le-Mignon *France* 46°12N 0°41W 72 B3
Mavli *India* 24°45N 73°55E 124 G5
Mavoko = Athi River *Kenya* 1°28S 36°58E 142 C4
Mavrovë *Albania* 40°26N 19°32E 96 G3
Mavrovo □ *Macedonia* 41°36N 20°45E 96 E4
Mavuradonha Mts. *Zimbabwe* 16°30S 31°30E 143 F3
Mawa *Dem. Rep. of the Congo* 2°45N 26°40E 142 B2
Mawai *India* 22°30N 81°4E 125 H9
Mawana *India* 29°6N 77°58E 124 E7
Mawand *Pakistan* 29°33N 68°38E 124 E3
Mawat *Iraq* 35°54N 45°24E 105 E11
Mawjib, W. al → *Jordan* 31°28N 35°36E 130 D4
Mawkmai *Burma* 20°14N 97°37E 123 J20
Mawlaik *Burma* 23°40N 94°26E 123 H19
Mawlamyine = Moulmein *Burma* 16°30N 97°40E 123 L20
Mawqaq *Si. Arabia* 27°25N 41°8E 128 E4
Mawson Coast *Antarctica* 68°30S 63°0E 55 C6
Mawson Pk. *Heard I.* 53°6S 73°31E 146 K6
Max *U.S.A.* 47°49N 101°18W 172 B4
Maxcanú *Mexico* 20°35N 90°0W 181 C6
Maxesibeni *S. Africa* 30°49S 29°23E 145 E4
Maxeys *U.S.A.* 33°45N 83°11W 178 B6
Maxhamish L. *Canada* 59°50N 123°17W 162 B4
Maxixe *Mozam.* 23°54S 35°17E 145 B6
Maxville *Canada* 45°17N 74°51W 175 A10
Maxwell *U.S.A.* 39°17N 122°11W 170 F4
Maxwell *N.Z.* 39°51S 174°49E 154 F3
Maxwelton *Australia* 20°43S 142°41E 150 C3
May, C. *U.S.A.* 38°56N 74°58W 173 F16
May Pen *Jamaica* 17°58N 77°15W 182 a
Maya → *Russia* 60°28N 134°28E 107 D14
Maya, Costa *Mexico* 18°40N 87°42W 181 D7
Maya Mts. *Belize* 16°30N 89°0W 181 D7
Mayabandar *India* 12°56N 92°56E 127 H11
Mayaguana I. *Bahamas* 22°30N 72°44W 183 B5
Mayaguana Passage *Bahamas* 22°32N 73°15W 183 B5
Mayagüez *Puerto Rico* 18°12N 67°9W 183 d
Mayahi *Niger* 13°58N 7°40E 139 C6
Mayaky *Ukraine* 46°44N 30°12E 83 K16
Mayals = Maials *Spain* 41°22N 0°30E 90 D5
Mayámey *Iran* 36°24N 55°42E 129 B7
Mayang *China* 27°53N 109°49E 116 D7
Mayanup *Australia* 33°57S 116°27E 149 F2
Mayapán *Mexico* 20°29N 89°11W 181 C7
Mayari *Cuba* 20°40N 75°41W 183 B4
Mayarí *Trin. & Tob.* 10°17N 61°1W 187 K15
Mayaro B. *Trin. & Tob.* 10°17N 61°0W 187 K16
Mayávaram = Mayiladuthurai *India* 11°3N 79°42E 127 J4
Maybell *U.S.A.* 40°31N 108°5W 168 F9
Maybole *U.K.* 55°21N 4°42W 65 F4
Maydān *Iraq* 34°55N 45°37E 105 E11

Maydan *Ukraine* 48°36N 23°29E **81** B8
Mayen *Germany* 50°19N 7°13E **77** E3
Mayenne *France* 48°20N 0°38W **70** D6
Mayenne □ *France* 48°10N 0°40W **70** D6
Mayenne → *France* 47°30N 0°32W **70** E6
Mayer *U.S.A.* 34°24N 112°14W **169** J7
Mayerthorpe *Canada* 53°57N 115°8W **162** C5
Mayesville *U.S.A.* 34°0N 80°12W **178** A9
Mayfield *Ky., U.S.A.* 36°44N 88°38W **172** G9
Mayfield *N.Y., U.S.A.* 43°6N 74°16W **175** C10
Mayhill *U.S.A.* 32°53N 105°29W **169** K11
Mayiladuthurai *India* 11°3N 79°42E **127** J4
Maykop *Russia* 44°35N 40°10E **87** H5
Mayma *Russia* 52°3N 85°55E **109** B11
Maynard *Mass., U.S.A.* 42°26N 71°27W **175** D13
Maynard *Wash., U.S.A.* 47°59N 122°55W **170** C4
Maynard Hills *Australia* 28°28S 119°49E **149** E2
Mayne → *Australia* 23°40S 141°55E **150** C3
Maynooth *Canada* 45°13N 77°56W **174** A7
Maynooth *Ireland* 53°23N 6°34W **64** C5
Mayo *Canada* 63°38N 135°57W **160** C4
Mayo *U.S.A.* 30°3N 83°10W **178** E6
Mayo □ *Ireland* 53°53N 9°3W **64** C2
Mayo → *Argentina* 45°45S 69°45W **192** C2
Mayo → *Peru* 6°38S 76°15W **188** B2
Mayo Daga *Nigeria* 6°59N 11°25E **139** D7
Mayo Faran *Nigeria* 8°57N 12°4E **139** D7
Mayon Volcano *Phil.* 13°15N 123°41E **119** B6
Mayor Buratovich *Argentina* 39°15S 62°37W **192** A4
Mayor I. *N.Z.* 37°16S 176°17E **154** D5
Mayorga *Spain* 42°10N 5°16W **88** C5
Mayotte ☑ *Ind. Oc.* 12°50S 45°10E **141** a
Mayqayyng *Kazakhstan* 51°27N 75°47E **109** B9
Maysān □ *Iraq* 31°55N 47°15E **128** D5
Mayskiy *Russia* 43°47N 44°2E **87** J7
Maysville *U.S.A.* 38°39N 83°46W **173** F12
Mayu *Indonesia* 1°30N 126°30E **119** D7
Mayuram = Mayiladuthurai *India* 11°3N 79°42E **127** J4
Mayville *N. Dak., U.S.A.* 47°30N 97°20W **172** B5
Mayville *N.Y., U.S.A.* 42°15N 79°30W **174** D5
Mazabuka *Zambia* 15°52S 27°44E **143** F2
Mazagán = El Jadida *Morocco* 33°11N 8°17W **136** B2
Mazagão *Brazil* 0°7S 51°16W **187** D8
Mazamet *France* 43°30N 2°20E **72** E6
Mazán *Peru* 3°30S 73°0W **186** D4
Mãzandarãn □ *Iran* 36°30N 52°0E **129** B7
Mazapil *Mexico* 24°39N 101°34W **180** C4
Mazar *China* 36°32N 77°1E **109** E9
Mazar, O. → *Algeria* 31°50N 1°36E **136** B4
Mazãr-e Sharîf *Afghan.* 36°41N 67°0E **109** F7
Mazara del Vallo *Italy* 37°39N 12°35E **94** E5
Mazarredo *Argentina* 47°10S 66°50W **192** C3
Mazarrón *Spain* 37°38N 1°19W **91** H3
Mazarrón, G. de *Spain* 37°27N 1°19W **91** H3
Mazaruni → *Guyana* 6°25N 58°35W **186** B7
Mazatán *Mexico* 29°0N 110°8W **180** B2
Mazatenango *Guatemala* 14°35N 91°30W **182** D1
Mazatlán *Mexico* 23°13N 106°25W **180** C3
Mažeikiai *Lithuania* 56°20N 22°20E **82** B9
Mãzhãn *Iran* 32°30N 59°0E **129** C8
Mazdaği *Turkey* 37°28N 40°29E **105** D9
Mazinãn *Iran* 36°19N 56°56E **129** B8
Mazo Cruz *Peru* 16°45S 69°44W **188** D4
Mazoe *Mozam.* 16°42S 33°7E **143** F3
Mazoe → *Mozam.* 16°20S 33°30E **143** F3
Mazowe *Zimbabwe* 17°28S 30°58E **143** F3
Mazowieckie □ *Poland* 52°40N 21°0E **83** F8
Mazurski, Pojezierze *Poland* 53°50N 21°0E **82** E7
Mazyr *Belarus* 51°59N 29°15E **75** B15
Mba *Fiji* 17°33S 177°41E **154** a
Mbabane *Swaziland* 26°18S 31°6E **145** D5
Mbagne *Mauritania* 16°6N 14°47W **138** B2
M'bahiakro *Ivory C.* 7°33N 4°19W **138** D4
Mbaïki *C.A.R.* 3°53N 18°1E **140** D3
Mbala *Zambia* 8°46S 31°24E **143** D3
Mbalabala *Zimbabwe* 20°27S 29°3E **145** B4
Mbale *Uganda* 1°8N 34°12E **142** B3
Mbalmayo *Cameroon* 3°33N 11°33E **139** E7
Mbam → *Cameroon* 4°24N 11°17E **139** E7
Mbamba Bay *Tanzania* 11°13S 34°49E **143** E3
Mbandaka *Dem. Rep. of the Congo* 0°1N 18°18E **140** D3
Mbanga *Cameroon* 4°30N 9°33E **139** E6
Mbanza Congo *Angola* 6°18S 14°16E **140** F2
Mbanza Ngungu *Dem. Rep. of the Congo* 5°12S 14°53E **140** F2
Mbarangandu *Tanzania* 10°11S 36°48E **143** D4
Mbarara *Uganda* 0°35S 30°40E **142** C3
Mbatto *Ivory C.* 6°28N 4°22W **138** D4
Mbengwa = Beqa *Fiji* 18°23S 178°8E **154** a
Mbenkuru → *Tanzania* 9°25S 39°50E **143** D4
Mberengwa *Zimbabwe* 20°29S 29°57E **143** G2
Mberengwa, Mt. *Zimbabwe* 20°37S 29°55E **143** G2
Mberubu *Nigeria* 6°10N 7°38E **139** D6
Mbesuma *Zambia* 10°0S 32°2E **143** E3
Mbeya *Tanzania* 8°54S 33°29E **143** D3
Mbeya □ *Tanzania* 8°15S 33°30E **143** D3
Mbhashe → *S. Africa* 32°15S 28°54E **145** D4
Mbinga *Tanzania* 10°50S 35°0E **143** E4
Mbini = Río Muni □ *Eq. Guin.* 1°30N 10°0E **140** D2
Mbizi *Zimbabwe* 21°23S 31°1E **143** G3
Mbombela *S. Africa* 25°29S 30°59E **145** C5
M'bonge *Cameroon* 4°33N 9°5E **139** E6
Mboro *Senegal* 15°9N 16°54W **138** B1
Mbouda *Cameroon* 5°38N 10°15E **139** D7
M'boukou, L. de *Cameroon* 6°9S 13°40E **139** D7
Mboune *Senegal* 14°42N 13°34W **138** C2
Mbour *Senegal* 14°22N 16°54W **138** C1
Mbout *Mauritania* 16°1N 12°38W **138** B2
Mbuji-Mayi *Dem. Rep. of the Congo* 6°9S 23°40E **142** D1
Mbulu *Tanzania* 3°45S 35°30E **142** C4
Mburucuyá *Argentina* 28°1S 58°14W **190** B4
Mburucuyá △ *Argentina* 28°1S 58°12W **190** B4
Mcherrah *Algeria* 27°0N 4°30E **136** C3
Mchinga *Tanzania* 9°44S 39°45E **143** D4

Mchinji *Malawi* 13°47S 32°58E **143** E3
Mdantsane *S. Africa* 32°56S 27°46E **145** D4
Mead, L. *U.S.A.* 36°0N 114°44W **171** J12
Meade *U.S.A.* 37°17N 100°20W **172** G3
Meade River = Atqasuk *U.S.A.* 70°28N 157°24W **166** A8
Meadow Lake *Canada* 54°10N 108°26W **163** C7
Meadow Lake △ *Canada* 54°27N 109°0W **163** C7
Meadow Valley Wash → *U.S.A.* 36°40N 114°34W **171** J12
Meadville *U.S.A.* 41°39N 80°9W **174** E4
Meaford *Canada* 44°36N 80°35W **174** B4
Meakan Dake *Japan* 45°15N 144°0E **112** C12
Mealhada *Portugal* 40°22N 8°27W **88** E2
Mealy Mts. *Canada* 53°10N 58°0W **165** B8
Meander River *Canada* 59°2N 117°42W **162** B5
Meares, C. *U.S.A.* 45°37N 124°0W **168** D1
Mearim → *Brazil* 3°4S 44°35W **189** A2
Meath □ *Ireland* 53°40N 6°57W **64** C5
Meath Park *Canada* 53°27N 105°22W **163** C7
Meaulne *France* 46°36N 2°36E **71** F9
Meaux *France* 48°58N 2°50E **71** D9
Mebechi-Gawa → *Japan* 40°31N 141°31E **112** D10
Mebulu, Tanjung *Indonesia* 8°50S 115°5E **119** K18
Mecanhelas *Mozam.* 15°12S 35°54E **143** F4
Mecca = Makkah *Si. Arabia* 21°30N 39°54E **137** C4
Mecca *U.S.A.* 33°34N 116°5W **171** M10
Mechanicsburg *U.S.A.* 40°13N 77°1W **174** F8
Mechanicville *U.S.A.* 42°54N 73°41W **175** D11
Mechelen *Belgium* 51°2N 4°29E **69** C4
Mecheria *Algeria* 33°35N 0°18W **136** B3
Mechernich *Germany* 50°35N 6°39E **76** E4
Mechetinskaya *Russia* 46°45N 40°32E **87** G5
Mecidiye *Turkey* 40°38N 26°32E **97** F10
Meçitözü *Turkey* 40°32N 35°17E **104** B6
Mecklenburg *Germany* 53°33N 11°40E **74** B7
Mecklenburg-Vorpommern □ *Germany* 53°35N 12°15E **76** B8
Mecklenburger Bucht *Germany* 54°20N 11°40E **76** A7
Meconta *Mozam.* 14°59S 39°50E **143** E4
Mecsek *Hungary* 46°10N 18°18E **80** D3
Mecubúri *Mozam.* 14°39S 38°54E **143** E4
Mecubúri → *Mozam.* 14°10S 40°30E **143** E5
Mecufi *Mozam.* 13°20S 40°32E **143** E5
Mêda *Portugal* 40°57N 7°18W **88** E3
Medak *India* 18°1N 78°15E **126** E4
Medan *Indonesia* 3°40N 98°38E **118** D1
Médanos *Argentina* 38°50S 62°42W **192** A4
Médanos de Coro △ *Venezuela* 11°35N 69°44W **183** D6
Medanosa, Pta. *Argentina* 48°8S 66°0W **192** C3
Medart *U.S.A.* 30°5N 84°23W **178** E5
Medawachchiya *Sri Lanka* 8°30N 80°30E **127** K5
Medchal *India* 17°37N 78°29E **126** F4
Mede *Italy* 45°6N 8°44E **92** C5
Medéa *Algeria* 36°12N 2°50E **136** A4
Médéa □ *Algeria* 36°0N 3°0E **136** A4
Mededa *Bos.-H.* 43°44N 19°10E **80** C4
Medeiros Neto *Brazil* 17°20S 40°14W **189** D2
Medellín *Colombia* 6°15N 75°35W **186** B3
Medelpad *Sweden* 62°33N 16°30E **62** B10
Medemblik *Neths.* 52°46N 5°8E **69** B5
Médenine *Tunisia* 33°21N 10°30E **136** B1
Médenine □ *Tunisia* 32°20N 10°0E **136** B1
Mederdra *Mauritania* 17°0N 15°38W **138** B1
Medford *Mass., U.S.A.* 42°25N 71°7W **175** D13
Medford *Oreg., U.S.A.* 42°19N 122°52W **168** E2
Medford *Wis., U.S.A.* 45°9N 90°20W **172** C8
Medgidia *Romania* 44°15N 28°19E **81** F13
Media Agua *Argentina* 31°58S 68°25W **190** C2
Media Luna *Argentina* 34°45S 66°44W **190** C2
Medianeira *Brazil* 25°17S 54°5W **191** B5
Mediaş *Romania* 46°9N 24°22E **81** D9
Medicina *Italy* 44°28N 11°38E **93** D8
Medicine Bow *U.S.A.* 41°54N 106°12W **168** F10
Medicine Bow Mts. *U.S.A.* 40°40N 106°0W **168** F10
Medicine Hat *Canada* 50°0N 110°45W **163** D6
Medicine Lake *U.S.A.* 48°30N 104°30W **168** B11
Medicine Lodge *U.S.A.* 37°17N 98°35W **172** G4
Medina = Al Madīnah *Si. Arabia* 24°35N 39°52E **128** E3
Medina *Brazil* 16°15S 41°29W **189** D2
Medina *N. Dak., U.S.A.* 46°54N 99°18W **172** B4
Medina *N.Y., U.S.A.* 43°13N 78°23W **174** C6
Medina *Ohio, U.S.A.* 41°8N 81°52W **174** E3
Medina → *U.S.A.* 29°16N 98°29W **177** L5
Medina de Pomar *Spain* 42°56N 3°29W **88** C7
Medina de Ríoseco *Spain* 41°53N 5°3W **88** D5
Medina del Campo *Spain* 41°18N 4°55W **88** D6
Médina Gounas *Senegal* 13°8N 13°45W **138** C2
Medina L. *U.S.A.* 29°32N 98°56W **176** L5
Medina Sidonia *Spain* 36°28N 5°57W **89** J5
Medinaceli *Spain* 41°12N 2°30W **90** D2
Medinipur *India* 22°25N 87°21E **125** H12
Medio-Campidano □ *Italy* 39°35N 8°30E **94** C1
Mediterranean Sea *Europe* 35°0N 15°0E **58** H7
Médoc *France* 45°10N 0°50W **72** C3
Mednogorsk *Russia* 51°24N 57°37E **108** D6
Médoc *France* 45°10N 0°50W **72** C3
Medulin *Croatia* 44°49N 13°55E **92** D10
Medvedeva *Serbia* 42°50N 21°32E **96** D5
Medvedevo *Russia* 56°37N 47°58E **84** C8
Medveditsa → *Tver, Russia* 57°5N 37°30E **84** D9
Medveditsa → *Volgograd, Russia* 49°35N 42°41E **86** F6
Medvedok *Russia* 57°20N 50°1E **86** C10
Medvezhi, Ostrava *Russia* 71°0N 161°0E **107** B17
Medvezhyegorsk *Russia* 63°0N 34°25E **106** C4
Medway □ *U.K.* 51°25N 0°32E **67** F8
Medway → *U.K.* 51°27N 0°46E **67** F8
Medzev *Slovak Rep.* 48°43N 20°55E **79** C13
Medzilaborce *Slovak Rep.* 49°17N 21°52E **83** D11
Medžitlija *Macedonia* 40°56N 21°26E **96** F5
Meekatharra *Australia* 26°32S 118°29E **149** E2

Meeker *U.S.A.* 40°2N 107°55W **168** F10
Meeniyan *Australia* 38°35S 146°3E **153** F4
Meersburg *Germany* 47°41N 9°16E **77** H5
Meerut *India* 29°1N 77°42E **124** E7
Meeteetse *U.S.A.* 44°9N 108°52W **168** D9
Mega *Ethiopia* 3°57N 38°19E **131** G2
Megalo Chorio *Greece* 36°27N 27°24E **99** E9
Megalonisos *Greece* 38°0N 24°15E **98** D6
Megalopoli *Greece* 37°25N 22°7E **98** D4
Meganisi *Greece* 38°38N 20°46E **98** C2
Megara *Greece* 37°58N 23°22E **98** D5
Megasini *India* 21°38N 86°21E **125** J12
Megdovas = Tavropos → *Greece* 39°10N 21°45E **98** B3
Megève *France* 45°51N 6°37E **73** C10
Meghalaya □ *India* 25°50N 91°0E **123** G17
Meghna → *Bangla.* 22°50N 90°50E **123** H17
Megion *Russia* 61°3N 76°6E **106** C8
Mégiscane, L. *Canada* 48°35N 75°55W **164** C4
Megisti *Greece* 36°8N 29°34E **99** E11
Megra *Russia* 60°11N 37°14E **84** B9
Mehadia *Romania* 44°56N 22°23E **80** F7
Meharry, Mt. *Australia* 22°59S 118°35E **148** D2
Mehedeby *Sweden* 60°27N 17°25E **62** D11
Mehedinţi □ *Romania* 44°40N 22°45E **80** F7
Meheisa *Sudan* 19°38N 32°57E **137** D3
Mehekar *India* 20°9N 76°34E **126** D8
Mehlville *U.S.A.* 38°31N 90°19W **172** F8
Mehmetçik = Galateia *Cyprus* 35°25N 34°4E **101** D13
Mehndawal *India* 26°58N 83°5E **125** F10
Mehr Jãn *Iran* 33°50N 55°6E **129** C7
Mehrãbãd *Iran* 36°53N 47°55E **105** D12
Mehrãbãn *Iran* 38°4N 47°7E **105** C12
Mehrãn *Iran* 33°7N 46°10E **105** F12
Mehrãn → *Iran* 26°45N 55°26E **129** E7
Mehrgarh *Pakistan* 29°30N 67°30E **124** E2
Mehriz *Iran* 31°35N 54°28E **129** D7
Mehun-sur-Yèvre *France* 47°10N 2°13E **71** E9
Mei Jiang → *China* 24°25N 116°35E **117** E11
Mei Xian *China* 34°18N 107°55E **114** C4
Meicheng *China* 29°29N 119°16E **117** C12
Meichengzhen *China* 28°9N 111°40E **117** C8
Meichuan *China* 30°8N 115°31E **117** B10
Meighen I. *Canada* 80°0N 99°30W **161** B12
Meigs *U.S.A.* 31°4N 84°6W **178** D5
Meigu *China* 28°16N 103°20E **116** C4
Meihekou *China* 42°32N 125°40E **115** C13
Meiktila *Burma* 20°53N 95°54E **123** J19
Meili Xue Shan *China* 28°30N 98°39E **116** C2
Meimyu = Maymyo *Burma* 22°2N 96°28E **120** A1
Meinerzhagen *Germany* 51°6N 7°38E **76** D3
Meiningen *Germany* 50°34N 10°25E **76** E6
Meio → *Brazil* 13°36S 44°7W **189** C2
Meira, Serra de *Spain* 43°15N 7°15W **88** C3
Meiringen *Switz.* 46°43N 8°12E **77** J4
Meishan *China* 30°3N 103°23E **116** B4
Meissen *Germany* 51°9N 13°29E **76** D9
Meissner *Germany* 51°14N 9°50E **76** D5
Meissner-Kaufunger Wald △ *Germany* 51°9N 9°45E **76** D5
Meitan *China* 27°45N 107°29E **116** D6
Meizhou *China* 24°16N 116°6E **117** E11
Meja *India* 25°9N 82°7E **125** G10
Mejillones *Chile* 23°10S 70°30W **190** A1
Mekele *Ethiopia* 13°33N 39°30E **131** E2
Mekerghene, Sebkra *Algeria* 26°21N 1°30E **136** C4
Mékhé *Senegal* 15°7N 16°38W **138** B1
Mekhtar *Pakistan* 30°30N 69°15E **122** D6
Meknès *Morocco* 33°57N 5°33W **136** B2
Meknès-Tafilalet □ *Morocco* 33°30N 5°0W **136** B2
Meko *Nigeria* 7°27N 2°52E **139** D5
Mekong → *Asia* 9°30N 106°15E **121** H6
Mekongga *Indonesia* 3°39S 121°15E **119** E6
Mekrou → *Benin* 12°25N 2°50E **139** C5
Mekvari = Kür → *Azerbaijan* 39°29N 49°15E **105** C13
Mel, Italy 46°4N 12°5E **93** B9
Melagiri Hills *India* 12°20N 77°30E **127** H3
Melah, Oued el → *Tunisia* 38°20N 2°28E **136** B4
Melaka *Malaysia* 2°15N 102°15E **121** L4
Melaka □ *Malaysia* 2°15N 102°15E **121** L4
Melambes *Greece* 35°8N 24°40E **101** D6
Melanesia *Pac. Oc.* 4°0S 155°0E **156** H7
Melanesian Basin *Pac. Oc.* 0°5N 160°35E **156** G8
Melapalaiyam *India* 8°39N 77°44E **127** K3
Melaya *Indonesia* 8°17S 114°30E **119** J17
Melbourne *Australia* 37°48S 144°58E **153** D6
Melbourne *U.S.A.* 28°5N 80°37W **179** G9
Melchor Múzquiz *Mexico* 27°53N 101°31W **180** B4
Melchor Ocampo *Mexico* 24°51N 101°39W **180** C4
Méldola *Italy* 44°7N 12°5E **93** D9
Meldorf *Germany* 54°5N 9°5E **76** A5
Melegnano *Italy* 45°21N 9°19E **92** C6
Melekeok *Palau* 7°27N 134°38E **156** D8
Melenci *Serbia* 45°32N 20°20E **80** E5
Melenki *Russia* 55°20N 41°37E **86** C5
Meleuz *Russia* 52°58N 55°55E **108** D6
Mélèzes → *Canada* 57°40N 69°29W **164** A5
Melfi *Italy* 41°0N 15°39E **95** B8
Melfort *Canada* 52°50N 104°37W **163** C8
Melfort *Zimbabwe* 18°0S 31°25E **143** F3
Melgaço *Portugal* 42°7N 8°15W **88** C2
Melgar de Fernamental *Spain* 42°27N 4°17W **88** C6
Melhus *Norway* 63°17N 10°18E **60** E14
Melide *Spain* 42°55N 8°1W **88** C2
Meligales *Greece* 37°15N 21°59E **98** D3
Melilla *N. Afr.* 35°21N 2°57W **134** A5
Melilli *Italy* 37°11N 15°7E **95** E8
Melipilla *Chile* 33°42S 71°15W **190** C1
Melissa *Canada* 45°24N 79°14W **174** A5
Melissa, Akra *Greece* 35°6N 24°33E **101** D6
Melissa Oros *Greece* 37°32N 26°4E **99** D8
Melita *Canada* 49°15N 101°0W **163** D8
Mélito di Porto Salvo *Italy* 37°55N 15°47E **95** F8
Melitopol *Ukraine* 46°50N 35°22E **85** J8
Melk *Austria* 48°13N 15°20E **78** D8
Mellan Fryken *Sweden* 59°45N 13°10E **62** E7
Mellansel *Sweden* 63°26N 18°19E **60** E18

Mellbystrand *Sweden* 56°30N 12°56E **63** H6
Melle *France* 46°14N 0°10W **72** B3
Melle *Germany* 52°12N 8°20E **76** C4
Mellégue, O. → *Tunisia* 36°36N 9°14E **136** A5
Mellen *U.S.A.* 46°20N 90°40W **172** B8
Mellerud *Sweden* 58°41N 12°28E **63** F6
Mellette *U.S.A.* 45°9N 98°30W **172** C4
Mellid = Melide *Spain* 42°55N 8°1W **88** C2
Mellieha *Malta* 35°57N 14°22E **101** D1
Mellizo Sur, Cerro *Chile* 48°33S 73°10W **192** C2
Mellrichstadt *Germany* 50°25N 10°17E **76** E6
Melnik *Bulgaria* 41°31S 144°27E **96** E7
Mělník *Czech Rep.* 50°22N 14°23E **78** A7
Melnytsya Podilska *Ukraine* 48°37N 26°15E **81** B11
Melo *Uruguay* 32°20S 54°10W **191** C5
Melolo *Indonesia* 9°53S 120°40E **119** F6
Melouprey *Cambodia* 13°48N 105°16E **120** F5
Melrhir, Chott *Algeria* 34°13N 6°30E **136** B6
Melrose *Australia* 32°42S 146°57E **153** E7
Melrose *U.K.* 55°36N 2°43W **65** F6
Melrose *Minn., U.S.A.* 45°40N 94°49W **172** C6
Melrose *N. Mex., U.S.A.* 34°26N 103°38W **169** J12
Melstone *U.S.A.* 46°36N 107°52W **168** C10
Melsungen *Germany* 51°7N 9°32E **76** D5
Melton *Australia* 37°41S 144°35E **152** D6
Melton Mowbray *U.K.* 52°47N 0°54W **66** E7
Melun *France* 48°32N 2°39E **71** D9
Melung *Nepal* 27°31N 86°3E **125** F12
Melur *India* 10°2N 78°23E **127** J4
Melut *Sudan* 10°30N 32°13E **137** F3
Melville *Canada* 50°55N 102°50W **163** C8
Melville, C. *Australia* 14°11S 144°30E **150** A3
Melville, L. *Canada* 53°30N 60°0W **165** B8
Melville B. *Greenland* 75°30N 63°0W **57** B4
Melville B. *Australia* 12°0S 136°45E **150** A2
Melville I. *Australia* 11°30S 131°0E **148** B5
Melville I. *Canada* 75°30N 112°0W **161** B9
Melville Pen. *Canada* 68°0N 84°0W **161** D15
Melvin, Lough *Ireland* 54°26N 8°10W **64** B3
Mélykút *Hungary* 46°25N 19°56E **96** D3
Memaliaj *Albania* 40°25N 19°56E **96** F3
Memba *Mozam.* 14°11S 40°30E **143** E5
Memboro *Indonesia* 9°30S 119°30E **148** A2
Membrilla *Spain* 38°59N 3°21W **89** G7
Memel = Klaipėda *Lithuania* 55°43N 21°10E **82** C8
Memel *S. Africa* 27°38S 29°36E **145** C4
Memmingen *Germany* 47°58N 10°10E **77** H6
Mempawah *Indonesia* 0°30N 109°5E **118** D3
Memphis *Egypt* 29°52N 31°12E **137** C7
Memphis *Mich., U.S.A.* 42°54N 82°46W **174** D2
Memphis *Tenn., U.S.A.* 35°8N 90°2W **177** D9
Memphis *Tex., U.S.A.* 34°44N 100°33W **176** D4
Memphrémagog, L. *N. Amer.* 45°8N 72°17W **175** B12
Mena *Ukraine* 51°31N 32°13E **85** G7
Mena *U.S.A.* 34°35N 94°15W **176** D7
Menado = Manado *Indonesia* 1°29N 124°51E **119** D6
Menai Strait *U.K.* 53°11N 4°13W **66** D3
Menan = Chao Phraya → *Thailand* 13°40N 100°31E **120** F3
Menard *U.S.A.* 30°55N 99°47W **176** F5
Menard Fracture Zone *Pac. Oc.* 43°0S 97°0W **157** M18
Mendañña Fracture Zone *Pac. Oc.* 16°0S 91°0W **157** J18
Mendawai → *Indonesia* 3°30S 113°0E **118** E4
Mende *France* 44°31N 3°30E **72** D7
Mendeleyev Ridge *Arctic* 80°0N 178°0W **54** B17
Menden *Germany* 51°26N 7°47E **76** D3
Menderes *Turkey* 38°14N 27°8E **99** D9
Mendhar *India* 33°35N 74°10E **125** C6
Mendip Hills *U.K.* 51°17N 2°40W **67** F5
Mendocino *U.S.A.* 39°19N 123°48W **168** G2
Mendocino, C. *U.S.A.* 40°26N 124°25W **168** F1
Mendocino Fracture Zone *Pac. Oc.* 40°0N 142°0W **157** D13
Mendooran *Australia* 31°50S 149°6E **153** E8
Mendota *Calif., U.S.A.* 36°45N 120°23W **170** J6
Mendota Ill. *U.S.A.* 41°33N 89°7W **172** E9
Mendoyo *Indonesia* 8°23S 114°42E **119** J17
Mendoza *Argentina* 32°50S 68°52W **190** C2
Mendoza □ *Argentina* 33°0S 69°0W **190** C2
Mene Grande *Venezuela* 9°49N 70°56W **186** B4
Menemen *Turkey* 38°34N 27°3E **99** D9
Menen *Belgium* 50°47N 3°7E **69** D3
Menéndez, L. *Argentina* 42°40S 71°51W **192** B2
Menfi *Italy* 37°36N 12°58E **94** E5
Mengcheng *China* 33°12N 116°36E **114** H9
Mengdingjie *China* 23°31N 98°58E **116** F2
Mengès *Slovenia* 46°10N 14°35E **93** B11
Menggala *Indonesia* 4°30S 105°15E **118** E3
Menghai *China* 21°50N 100°55E **116** G3
Mengibar *Spain* 37°58N 3°48W **89** H7
Mengjin *China* 34°55N 112°45E **114** G7
Mengla *China* 21°20N 101°25E **116** G3
Menglian *China* 22°18N 99°27E **116** F2
Mengyin *China* 35°40N 117°58E **115** G9
Mengzhe *China* 22°20N 100°15E **116** G3
Mengzi *China* 23°20N 103°22E **116** F4
Menifee *U.S.A.* 33°41N 117°10W **171** M9
Menihek *Canada* 54°28N 56°36W **165** B6
Menihek L. *Canada* 54°0N 67°0W **165** B6
Menin = Menen *Belgium* 50°47N 3°7E **69** D3
Menindee *Australia* 32°20S 142°25E **153** E5
Menindee L. *Australia* 32°20S 142°25E **153** E5
Meningie *Australia* 35°50S 139°18E **152** E3
Menjangan, Pulau *Indonesia* 8°7S 114°31E **119** J17
Menkrour *Algeria* 23°6N 8°9E **136** C5
Menlo Park *U.S.A.* 37°27N 122°12W **170** H4
Menominee *U.S.A.* 45°6N 87°37W **172** C10
Menominee → *U.S.A.* 45°6N 87°36W **172** C10
Menomonie *U.S.A.* 44°53N 91°55W **172** C8
Menongue *Angola* 14°48S 17°52E **141** G3
Menorca *Spain* 40°0N 4°0E **90** B11
Menorca ✈ (MAH) *Spain* 39°50N 4°16E **90** B11
Mentakab *Malaysia* 3°29N 102°21E **121** L4
Mentawai, Kepulauan *Indonesia* 2°0S 99°0E **118** E1
Menton *France* 43°50N 7°29E **73** E11
Mentor *U.S.A.* 41°40N 81°21W **174** E3
Menzel-Bourguiba *Tunisia* 37°9N 9°49E **136** A5

Menzel-Chaker *Tunisia* 35°0N 10°26E **136** B6
Menzies *Australia* 29°40S 121°2E **149** E3
Meob B. *Namibia* 24°25S 14°34E **144** B1
Meoqui *Mexico* 28°17N 105°29W **180** B3
Mepaco *Mozam.* 15°57S 30°48E **143** F3
Meppel *Neths.* 52°42N 6°12E **69** B6
Meppen *Germany* 52°42N 7°17E **76** C3
Mequinenza *Spain* 41°22N 0°17E **90** D5
Mequinenza, Embalse de *Spain* 41°25N 0°15E **90** D5
Mer *France* 47°42N 1°30E **70** E8
Merak *Indonesia* 6°10N 106°26E **119** F12
Meramangye, L. *Australia* 28°25S 132°13E **149** E5
Meran = Merano *Italy* 46°40N 11°9E **93** B8
Merano *Italy* 46°40N 11°9E **93** B8
Merate *Italy* 45°42N 9°25E **92** C6
Merauke *Indonesia* 8°29S 140°24E **119** F10
Merbein *Australia* 34°10S 142°2E **152** E5
Merca = Marka *Somalia* 1°48N 44°50E **131** G3
Mercantour △ *France* 44°16N 6°43E **73** D10
Mercato Saraceno *Italy* 43°57N 12°12E **93** E9
Merced *U.S.A.* 37°18N 120°29W **170** H6
Merced → *U.S.A.* 37°21N 120°59W **170** H6
Merced Pk. *U.S.A.* 37°36N 119°24W **170** H7
Mercedes *B. Aires, Argentina* 34°40S 59°30W **190** C4
Mercedes *Corrientes, Argentina* 29°10S 58°5W **190** B4
Mercedes *San Luis, Argentina* 33°40S 65°21W **190** C2
Mercedes *Uruguay* 33°12S 58°0W **190** C4
Merceditas *Chile* 28°20S 70°35W **190** B1
Mercer *N.Z.* 37°16S 175°5E **154** D4
Mercer *U.S.A.* 41°14N 80°15W **174** E4
Mercer Island *U.S.A.* 47°34N 122°13W **170** C4
Mercier *Bolivia* 10°42S 68°58E **148** C6
Mercury *U.S.A.* 36°40N 115°59W **171** J11
Mercury B. *N.Z.* 36°43S 175°45E **154** C4
Mercury Is. *N.Z.* 36°37S 175°52E **154** C4
Mercy, C. *Canada* 65°0N 63°30W **161** D19
Merdrignac *France* 48°11N 2°27W **70** D4
Mere *U.K.* 51°6N 2°16W **67** F5
Merebuk, Gunung *Indonesia* 8°13S 114°39E **119** J17
Meredith *Australia* 37°49S 144°5E **152** D6
Meredith, C. *Falk. Is.* 52°15S 60°40W **192** D4
Meredith, L. *U.S.A.* 35°43N 101°33W **176** D4
Merefa *Ukraine* 49°48N 36°3E **85** H9
Merei *Romania* 45°7N 26°43E **81** E11
Merga = Nukheila *Sudan* 19°1N 26°21E **137** D2
Mergui *Burma* 12°26N 98°34E **120** F2
Mergui Arch. = Myeik Kyunzu *Burma* 11°30N 97°30E **121** G1
Meribah *Australia* 34°43S 140°51E **152** C4
Méribel-les-Allues *France* 45°25N 6°34E **73** C10
Meric *Turkey* 41°11N 26°25E **97** E10
Meriç → *Turkey* 40°52N 26°12E **97** F10
Mérida *Mexico* 20°58N 89°37W **181** C7
Mérida *Spain* 38°55N 6°25W **89** G4
Mérida *Venezuela* 8°24N 71°8W **186** B4
Mérida, Cord. de *Venezuela* 9°0N 71°0W **186** B4
Meriden *U.K.* 52°26N 1°38W **67** E6
Meriden *U.S.A.* 41°32N 72°48W **175** E12
Meridian *Calif., U.S.A.* 39°9N 121°55W **170** F5
Meridian *Ga., U.S.A.* 31°27N 81°23W **178** D8
Meridian *Idaho, U.S.A.* 43°37N 116°24W **168** E5
Meridian *Miss., U.S.A.* 32°22N 88°42W **177** E10
Meridian *Tex., U.S.A.* 31°56N 97°39W **176** F6
Mérignac *France* 44°50N 0°39W **72** D3
Merimbula *Australia* 36°53S 149°54E **153** F8
Merín, L. = Mirim, L. *S. Amer.* 32°45S 52°50W **191** C5
Merinda *Australia* 20°2S 148°11E **150** C4
Mering *Germany* 48°16N 10°59E **77** G6
Meringa *Nigeria* 10°44N 12°59E **139** C7
Merirumã *Brazil* 1°15N 54°50E **187** C8
Merkel *U.S.A.* 32°28N 100°1W **176** E4
Mermaid Reef *Australia* 17°6S 119°36E **148** C2
Merowe *India* 7°33N 93°33E **127** L11
Merowe *Sudan* 18°29N 31°46E **137** D3
Merowe Dam *Sudan* 18°35N 31°56E **137** D3
Merredin *Australia* 31°28S 118°18E **149** F2
Merrick *U.K.* 55°8N 4°28W **65** F4
Merrickville *Canada* 44°55N 75°50W **175** B9
Merrill *Oreg., U.S.A.* 42°1N 121°36W **168** E3
Merrill *Wis., U.S.A.* 45°11N 89°41W **172** C9
Merriman *U.S.A.* 42°55N 101°42W **172** D3
Merritt *Canada* 50°10N 120°45W **162** C4
Merritt Island *U.S.A.* 28°8N 80°42W **179** G9
Merriwa *Australia* 32°6S 150°22E **153** E9
Merriwagga *Australia* 33°47S 145°43E **153** E7
Merry I. *Canada* 55°29N 77°31W **164** A4
Merrygoen *Australia* 31°51S 149°12E **153** E8
Merriwagga *Australia* 30°45S 93°33W **176** F6
Merse → *Italy* 43°5N 11°2E **93** E8
Mersea I. *U.K.* 51°47N 0°58E **67** F8
Merseburg *Germany* 51°22N 11°59E **76** D7
Mersey → *U.K.* 53°25N 3°1W **66** D4
Merseyside □ *U.K.* 53°31N 3°2W **66** D4
Mersin = İçel *Turkey* 36°51N 34°36E **104** D6
Mersing *Malaysia* 2°25N 103°50E **121** L4
Merta *India* 26°39N 74°4E **124** F6
Merta Road *India* 26°43N 73°55E **124** F5
Merthyr Tydfil *U.K.* 51°45N 3°22W **67** F4
Merthyr Tydfil □ *U.K.* 51°46N 3°21W **67** F4
Mértil *Kenya* 1°4N 38°40E **142** B4
Mértola *Portugal* 37°40N 7°40W **89** H3
Mertz Glacier *Antarctica* 67°30S 144°45E **55** C10
Mertzon *U.S.A.* 31°16N 100°49W **176** F4
Méru *France* 49°13N 2°8E **71** C9
Meru *Kenya* 0°3N 37°40E **142** B4
Meru *Tanzania* 3°15S 36°46E **142** C4
Meru □ *Kenya* 0°5N 38°10E **142** B4
Meru Betiri △ *Indonesia* 8°27S 113°51E **119** J17
Merville *France* 50°38N 2°38E **71** B9
Méry-sur-Seine *France* 48°31N 3°54E **71** D10
Merzifon *Turkey* 40°53N 35°32E **104** B6
Merzig *Germany* 49°26N 6°38E **77** F2
Merzouga, Erg Tin *Algeria* 24°0N 11°4E **136** D6
Mesa *U.S.A.* 33°25N 111°50W **169** K8
Mesa Verde △ *U.S.A.* 37°11N 108°29W **169** H9
Mesada = Masada *Israel* 31°18N 35°21E **130** D4

Mesagne *Italy* 40°34N 17°48E **95** B10
Mesanagros *Greece* 36°1N 27°49E **101** D9
Mesaoria *Cyprus* 35°12N 33°14E **101** D12
Meschede *Germany* 51°20N 8°18E **76** D4
Mescit *Turkey* 40°21N 41°11E **105** B9
Mesgouez, L. *Canada* 51°20N 75°0W **164** B4
Meshchovsk *Russia* 54°22N 35°17E **84** E8
Meshchyora □ *Russia* 55°45N 40°15E **86** C5
Meshchyorsky □ *Russia* 54°50N 41°0E **86** C5
Meshed = Mashhad *Iran* 36°20N 59°35E **129** B8
Meshgin Shahr *Iran* 38°30N 47°45E **105** C12
Meshoppen *U.S.A.* 41°36N 76°3W **175** E8
Mesilinka → *Canada* 56°6N 124°30W **162** B4
Meslay-du-Maine *France* 47°58N 0°33W **70** E6
Mesocco *Switz.* 46°23N 9°12E **77** J5
Mesolongi *Greece* 38°21N 21°28E **98** C3
Mesongi *Greece* 39°29N 19°56E **101** A3
Mesopotamia = Al Jazirah *Iraq* 33°30N 44°0E **105** D9
Mesopotamia *U.S.A.* 41°27N 80°57W **174** E4
Mesopotamo *Greece* 39°26N 20°29E **98** B2
Mesoraca *Italy* 39°5N 16°48E **95** C9
Mésou Volimais = Volimes *Greece* 37°52N 20°39E **98** D2
Mesquite *U.S.A.* 36°48N 114°4W **169** H6
Messaad *Algeria* 34°8N 3°30E **136** B4
Messac *France* 47°49N 1°50W **70** E5
Messalo → *Mozam.* 12°25S 39°15E **143** E4
Messaména *Cameroon* 3°48N 12°49E **139** E7
Messara, Kolpos *Greece* 35°6N 24°47E **101** D6
Messier, Canal *Chile* 48°20S 74°33W **192** C2
Messina = Musina *S. Africa* 22°20S 30°5E **145** B5
Messina *Italy* 38°11N 15°34E **95** D8
Messina, Str. di *Italy* 38°15N 15°35E **95** D8
Messini *Greece* 37°4N 22°1E **98** D4
Messiniakos Kolpos *Greece* 36°45N 22°5E **98** E4
Messkirch *Germany* 47°59N 9°7E **77** H5
Messlingen *Sweden* 62°40N 12°50E **62** B8
Mesta = Nestos → *Europe* 40°54N 24°49E **97** F8
Mesta, Akra *Greece* 38°16N 25°53E **99** C7
Mestanza *Spain* 38°35N 4°4W **89** G6
Mestersvig *Greenland* 72°10N 23°40W **57** C8
Mestre *Italy* 45°29N 12°15E **93** C9
Mestre, Espigão *Brazil* 12°30S 46°10W **189** C1
Mesudiye *Turkey* 40°28N 37°46E **104** B7
Meta □ *S. Amer.* 6°12N 67°28W **186** B5
Meta Incognita Pen. *Canada* 62°45N 68°30W **161** D18
Metabetchouan *Canada* 48°26N 71°52W **165** C5
Metairie *U.S.A.* 29°59N 90°9W **177** G9
Metalici, Munţii *Romania* 46°15N 22°50E **80** D7
Metaline Falls *U.S.A.* 48°52N 117°22W **168** B5
Metallifere, Colline *Italy* 43°10N 11°0E **92** E8
Metán *Argentina* 25°30S 65°0W **190** B3
Metangula *Mozam.* 12°40S 34°50E **143** E3
Metauro → *Italy* 43°50N 13°3E **93** E10
Metcalf *U.S.A.* 30°43N 83°59W **178** E6
Metcalfe *Canada* 45°14N 75°28W **175** A9
Metema *Ethiopia* 12°56N 36°12E **131** E2
Metengobalame *Mozam.* 14°49S 34°30E **143** E3
Meteora *Greece* 39°43N 21°37E **98** B3
Methana *Greece* 37°35N 23°23E **98** D5
Methoni *Greece* 36°49N 21°42E **98** E3
Methven *N.Z.* 43°38S 171°40E **155** D6
Metil *Mozam.* 16°24S 39°0E **143** F4
Metkovets *Bulgaria* 43°37N 23°10E **96** C7
Metković *Croatia* 43°6N 17°39E **93** G14
Metlakatla *U.S.A.* 55°8N 131°35W **160** F5
Metlaoui *Tunisia* 34°24N 8°24E **136** B6
Metlika *Slovenia* 45°40N 15°20E **93** C12
Metlili Chaamba *Algeria* 32°38N 3°38E **136** B4
Metropolis *U.S.A.* 37°9N 88°44W **172** G9
Metropolitana □ *Chile* 33°30S 70°50W **190** C1
Metsovo *Greece* 39°48N 21°12E **98** B3
Metter *U.S.A.* 32°24N 82°3W **178** D7
Mettuppalaiyam *India* 11°18N 76°59E **127** J3
Mettur *India* 11°48N 77°47E **127** J3
Metu *Ethiopia* 8°18N 35°35E **131** F2
Metz *France* 49°8N 6°10E **71** C13
Metzingen *Germany* 48°31N 9°17E **77** G5
Meulaboh *Indonesia* 4°11N 96°3E **118** D1
Meung-sur-Loire *France* 47°50N 1°40E **71** E8
Meureudu *Indonesia* 5°19N 96°10E **118** C1
Meurthe → *France* 48°47N 6°9E **71** C13
Meurthe-et-Moselle □ *France* 48°52N 6°0E **71** D13
Meuse □ *France* 49°8N 5°25E **71** C12
Meuse → *Europe* 50°45N 5°41E **69** D5
Meuselwitz *Germany* 51°3N 12°18E **76** D8
Mexia *U.S.A.* 31°41N 96°29W **176** F6
Mexiana, I. *Brazil* 0°0 49°30W **187** D9
Mexicali *Mexico* 32°40N 115°30W **171** N11
Mexican Plateau *Mexico* 25°0N 104°0W **158** G9
Mexican Water *U.S.A.* 36°57N 109°32W **169** H9
Mexico *Maine, U.S.A.* 44°34N 70°33W **175** B14
Mexico *Mo., U.S.A.* 39°10N 91°53W **172** F8
México *N.Y., U.S.A.* 43°28N 76°14W **175** C8
México □ *Mexico* 19°20N 99°30W **180** D5
Mexico ■ *Cent. Amer.* 25°0N 105°0W **180** C4
México, Ciudad de *Mexico* 19°24N 99°9W **181** D5
Mexico, G. of *Cent. Amer.* 25°0N 90°0W **181** C7
Mexico B. *U.S.A.* 43°35N 76°20W **175** C8
Mexico Beach *U.S.A.* 29°57N 85°25W **178** F4
Meydán-e Naftún *Iran* 31°56N 49°18E **129** D6
Meydani, Ra's-e *Iran* 25°24N 59°6E **129** E9
Meyenburg *Germany* 53°19N 12°15E **76** B8
Meyers Chuck *U.S.A.* 55°45N 132°15W **162** B2
Meymac *France* 45°32N 2°10E **72** C5
Meymaneh *Afghan.* 35°53N 64°38E **108** F6
Meyrueis *France* 44°12N 3°27E **72** D7
Meyssac *France* 45°3N 1°40E **72** C5
Meyzieu *France* 45°46N 4°59E **72** C6
Mezdra *Bulgaria* 43°12N 23°42E **96** C7
Mèze *France* 43°27N 3°36E **72** E7
Mezen *Russia* 65°50N 44°20E **88** A8
Mezen → *Russia* 65°44N 44°22E **88** B14
Mézenc, Mt. *France* 44°54N 4°11E **72** D6
Mezha → *Russia* 55°44N 31°33E **84** E6
Mezha *Russia* 55°44N 31°33E **84** E6
Mezhdurechensk *Russia* 53°41N 88°3E **109** B11

Mezhdurechenskiy
Russia 59°36N 65°56E **106** D7
Mézidon-Canon *France* 49°5N 0°1W **70** C6
Mézières-en-Brenne
France 46°49N 1°13E **72** B5
Mézilhac *France* 44°49N 4°21E **73** D8
Mézin *France* 44°4N 0°16E **72** D4
Mezőberény *Hungary* 46°49N 21°3E **80** D6
Mezőfalva *Hungary* 46°55N 18°49E **80** D3
Mezőhegyes *Hungary* 46°19N 20°49E **80** D5
Mezőkövácsháza
Hungary 46°25N 20°57E **80** D5
Mezőkövesd *Hungary* 47°49N 20°35E **80** C5
Mézos *France* 44°5N 1°10W **72** D2
Mezőtúr *Hungary* 47°1N 20°41E **80** C5
Mezquital *Mexico* 23°29N 104°23W **180** C4
Mezzolombardo *Italy* 46°13N 11°5E **92** B8
Mfolozi → *S. Africa* 28°25S 32°26E **145** C5
Mgeta *Tanzania* 8°22S 36°6E **142** D4
Mglin *Russia* 53°2N 32°50E **85** F7
Mhamid *Morocco* 29°49N 5°43W **136** C2
Mhlaba Hills *Zimbabwe* 18°30S 30°30E **143** F3
Mhow *India* 22°33N 75°50E **124** H6
Miahuatlán *Mexico* 16°20N 96°36W **181** D5
Miajadas *Spain* 39°9N 5°54W **89** F5
Miami *Fla., U.S.A.* 25°46N 80°11W **179** H14
Miami *Okla., U.S.A.* 36°53N 94°53W **176** C7
Miami *Tex., U.S.A.* 35°42N 100°38W **176** D4
Miami Beach *U.S.A.* 25°47N 80°7W **179** K9
Miami Canal *U.S.A.* 25°54N 80°12W **179** K9
Miami Gardens *U.S.A.* 25°56N 80°15W **179** C1
Miami Int. ✈ (MIA)
U.S.A. 25°48N 80°17W **179** K9
Miami Shores *U.S.A.* 25°51N 80°11W **179** K9
Miami Springs *U.S.A.* 25°49N 80°17W **179** K9
Mian Xian *China* 33°10N 106°32E **116** A6
Mianchi *China* 34°48N 111°48E **114** G6
Miandarreh *Iran* 35°37N 53°39E **129** C7
Miāndowāb *Iran* 37°0N 46°5E **105** D12
Miandrivazo *Madag.* 19°31S 45°29E **141** H9
Mīāneh *Iran* 37°30N 47°40E **105** D12
Mianning *China* 28°32N 102°9E **116** C4
Mianwali *Pakistan* 32°38N 71°28E **124** C4
Mianyang *China* 31°22N 104°47E **116** B5
Mianzhu *China* 31°22N 104°7E **116** B5
Miao Ling *China* 26°5N 107°30E **116** D6
Miaodao Qundao
China 38°10N 120°45E **115** E11
Miaoli *Taiwan* 24°37N 120°49E **117** E13
Miass *Russia* 54°59N 60°6E **108** B6
Miasteczko Krajeńskie
Poland 53°7N 17°1E **83** E4
Miastko *Poland* 54°0N 16°58E **82** E3
Mica *S. Africa* 24°10S 30°48E **145** B5
Micanopy *U.S.A.* 29°30N 82°17W **179** F7
Micăsasa *Romania* 46°7N 24°7E **81** D9
Micco *U.S.A.* 27°53N 80°30W **179** H9
Miccosukee *U.S.A.* 30°36N 84°3W **178** E6
Miccosukee, L. *U.S.A.* 30°33N 83°53W **178** E6
Michalovce *Slovak Rep.* 48°47N 21°58E **79** C14
Michigan □ *U.S.A.* 44°0N 85°0W **173** C11
Michigan, L. *U.S.A.* 44°0N 87°0W **172** D2
Michigan City *U.S.A.* 41°43N 86°54W **172** E10
Michika *Nigeria* 10°36N 13°23E **139** C7
Michipicoten I. *Canada* 47°40N 85°40W **164** C2
Michoacán □ *Mexico* 19°10N 101°50W **180** D4
Michurin *Bulgaria* 42°9N 27°51E **97** D11
Michurinsk *Russia* 52°58N 40°27E **86** D5
Micoud *St. Lucia* 13°49N 60°54W **183** f
Micronesia *Pac. Oc.* 11°0N 160°0E **156** G7
Micronesia, Federated States of ■
Pac. Oc. 9°0N 150°0E **156** G7
Mid-Atlantic Ridge *Atl. Oc.* 0°0 20°0W **56** J10
Mid-Indian Basin
Ind. Oc. 10°0S 80°0E **146** F2
Mid-Indian Ridge *Ind. Oc.* 30°0S 75°0E **146** H6
Mid-Oceanic Ridge
Ind. Oc. 42°0S 90°0E **156** M1
Mid-Pacific Seamounts
Pac. Oc. 18°0N 177°0W **156** F10
Midai *Indonesia* 3°0N 107°47E **118** D3
Midale *Canada* 49°25N 103°20W **163** D8
Middelburg *Neths.* 51°30N 3°36E **69** C3
Middelburg *Eastern Cape,
S. Africa* 31°30S 25°0E **144** D4
Middelburg *Mpumalanga,
S. Africa* 25°49S 29°28E **145** B4
Middelfart *Denmark* 55°30N 9°43E **63** J3
Middelpos *S. Africa* 31°55S 20°13E **144** D3
Middelwit *S. Africa* 24°51S 27°3E **144** B4
Middle Alkali L. *U.S.A.* 41°27N 120°5W **168** F3
**Middle America Trench =
Guatemala Trench**
Pac. Oc. 14°0N 90°0W **158** H10
Middle Andaman I.
India 12°30N 92°50E **127** H11
Middle Bass I. *U.S.A.* 41°41N 82°48W **174** E2
Middle East *Asia* 35°0N 40°0E **102** E5
Middle Fork Feather →
U.S.A. 38°33N 121°30W **170** F5
Middle I. *Australia* 34°6S 123°11E **149** F3
Middle Loup → *U.S.A.* 41°17N 98°24W **172** E4
Middleboro *U.S.A.* 41°54N 70°55W **175** E14
Middleburg *Fla., U.S.A.* 30°4N 81°52W **179** F8
Middleburg *Pa., U.S.A.* 40°47N 77°3W **174** F7
Middleburgh *U.S.A.* 42°36N 74°20W **175** D10
Middlebury *U.S.A.* 44°1N 73°10W **175** B11
Middlefield *U.S.A.* 41°27N 81°4W **174** E3
Middlemarch *N.Z.* 45°30S 170°9E **155** F5
Middlemount
Australia 22°50S 148°40E **150** C4
Middleport *N.Y.,
U.S.A.* 43°13N 78°29W **174** C6
Middleport *Ohio, U.S.A.* 39°0N 82°3W **173** F12
Middlesboro *U.S.A.* 36°36N 83°43W **173** G12
Middlesbrough *U.K.* 54°35N 1°13W **66** C6
Middlesbrough □ *U.K.* 54°28N 1°13W **66** C6
Middlesex *Belize* 17°2N 88°31W **182** C2
Middlesex *N.J., U.S.A.* 40°36N 74°30W **175** F10
Middlesex *N.Y., U.S.A.* 42°42N 77°16W **174** D7
Middleton *Australia* 22°22S 141°32E **150** C3
Middleton *Canada* 44°57N 65°4W **165** D6
Middleton Cr. →
Australia 22°35S 141°51E **150** C3
Middleton I. *U.S.A.* 59°26N 146°20W **166** D10
Middletown *U.K.* 54°17N 6°51W **64** B5
Middletown *Calif.,
U.S.A.* 38°45N 122°37W **170** G4
Middletown *Conn.,
U.S.A.* 41°34N 72°39W **175** E12

Middletown *N.Y.,
U.S.A.* 41°27N 74°25W **175** E10
Middletown *Ohio,
U.S.A.* 39°31N 84°24W **173** F11
Middletown *Pa., U.S.A.* 40°12N 76°44W **175** F8
Midelt *Morocco* 32°46N 4°44W **136** B3
Midge Point *Australia* 20°39S 148°43E **150** b
Midhirst *N.Z.* 39°17S 174°18E **154** F3
Midhurst *Canada* 44°26N 79°43W **174** B5
Midhurst *U.K.* 50°59N 0°44W **67** G7
Midi, Canal du → *France* 43°45N 1°21E **72** E5
Midi d'Ossau, Pic du
France 42°50N 0°26W **72** F3
Midi-Pyrénées □ *France* 43°55N 1°45E **72** E5
Midland *Australia* 31°54S 116°1E **149** F2
Midland *Canada* 44°45N 79°50W **174** B5
Midland *Calif.,
U.S.A.* 33°52N 114°48W **171** M12
Midland *Mich., U.S.A.* 43°37N 84°14W **173** D11
Midland *Pa., U.S.A.* 40°39N 80°27W **174** F4
Midland *Tex., U.S.A.* 32°0N 102°3W **176** E3
Midlands □ *Zimbabwe* 19°40S 29°0E **143** F2
Midleton *Ireland* 51°55N 8°10W **64** E3
Midlothian □ *U.K.* 55°51N 3°5W **65** F5
Midnapore = Medinipur
India 22°25N 87°21E **125** H12
Midou → *France* 43°54N 0°30W **72** E3
Midouze → *France* 43°48N 0°51W **72** E3
Midtjylland □ *Denmark* 56°30N 9°0E **63** H2
Midu *China* 25°18N 100°30E **116** E3
Midville *U.S.A.* 32°49N 82°14W **178** C7
Midway *Ala., U.S.A.* 32°5N 85°31W **178** C4
Midway *Fla., U.S.A.* 30°30N 84°27W **178** E5
Midway Wells *U.S.A.* 32°41N 115°7W **171** N11
Midway Is. *Pac. Oc.* 28°13N 177°22W **167** K4
Midwest *U.S.A.* 42°25N 106°16W **168** E10
Midwest *Wyo.,
U.S.A.* 43°25N 106°16W **168** E10
Midwest City *U.S.A.* 35°27N 97°24W **176** D6
Midyat *Turkey* 37°25N 41°23E **105** D9
Midzôr *Bulgaria* 43°24N 22°40E **96** C7
Mie □ *Japan* 34°30N 136°10E **113** G8
Miechów *Poland* 50°21N 20°5E **83** H7
Miedwie, Jezioro *Poland* 53°17N 14°54E **83** E1
Międzybórz *Poland* 51°25N 17°34E **83** G4
Międzychód *Poland* 52°35N 15°53E **83** F2
Międzylesie *Poland* 50°8N 16°40E **83** H3
Międzyrzec Podlaski
Poland 51°58N 22°45E **83** G9
Międzyrzecz *Poland* 52°26N 15°35E **83** F2
Międzyzdroje *Poland* 53°56N 14°26E **82** E1
Miejska Górka *Poland* 51°39N 16°58E **83** G3
Miélan *France* 43°27N 0°19E **72** E4
Mielec *Poland* 50°15N 21°25E **83** H8
Mienga *Angola* 17°12S 19°48E **144** A2
Miercurea-Ciuc
Romania 46°21N 25°48E **81** D10
Miercurea Sibiului
Romania 45°53N 23°48E **81** D8
Mieres *Spain* 43°18N 5°48W **88** B5
Mieroszów *Poland* 50°40N 16°11E **83** H3
Mieszkowice *Poland* 52°47N 14°30E **83** F1
Mifflintown *U.S.A.* 40°34N 77°24W **174** F7
Mifraz Hefa *Israel* 32°52N 35°0E **130** C4
Migang Shan *China* 35°32N 106°13E **114** G4
Migennes *France* 47°58N 3°31E **71** E10
Migliarino *Italy* 44°46N 11°56E **92** D8
**Migliarino-San Rossore-
Massaciuccoli △** *Italy* 43°44N 10°20E **92** E7
Migori *Kenya* 1°4S 34°28E **142** C3
Miguasha △ *Canada* 48°5N 66°26W **165** C6
Miguel Alemán, Presa
Mexico 18°15N 96°32W **181** D5
Miguel Alves *Brazil* 4°11S 42°55W **189** A2
Miguel Calmon *Brazil* 11°26S 40°36W **189** C2
Miguel Hidalgo, Presa
Mexico 26°30N 108°34W **180** B3
Miguelturra *Spain* 38°58N 3°53W **89** C7
Mihăileni *Romania* 47°58N 26°9E **81** C11
Mihăilești *Romania* 44°20N 25°54E **81** F10
Mihailovca *Moldova* 46°33N 28°56E **81** D13
Mihalgazi *Turkey* 40°2N 30°34E **99** A12
Mihaliççik *Turkey* 39°48N 31°30E **104** C4
Mihara *Japan* 34°24N 133°5E **113** G6
Mihesu de Cîmpie
Romania 46°41N 24°9E **81** D9
Mijas *Spain* 36°36N 4°40W **89** J6
Mikese *Tanzania* 6°48S 37°55E **142** D4
Mikha-Tskhakaya = Senaki
Georgia 42°15N 42°1E **87** J6
Mikhailovka
Ukraine 47°12N 35°10E **85** J8
Mikhaylov *Russia* 54°14N 39°0E **84** D10
Mikhaylovgrad = Montana
Bulgaria 43°27N 23°16E **96** C7
Mikhaylovka *Russia* 50°3N 43°5E **86** E6
Mikhnevo *Russia* 55°4N 37°59E **84** E9
Mikines *Greece* 37°43N 22°46E **98** D4
Mikkeli *Finland* 61°43N 27°15E **63** E9
Mikkwa → *Canada* 58°25N 114°46W **162** B6
Mikołajki *Poland* 53°49N 21°37E **82** E8
Mikonos = Mykonos
Greece 37°30N 25°25E **99** D7
Mikri Prespa, L. *Greece* 40°47N 21°3E **96** F5
Mikro Derio *Greece* 41°19N 26°6E **97** E10
Mikstat *Poland* 51°32N 17°59E **83** G4
Mikulov *Czech Rep.* 48°48N 16°39E **79** C9
Mikumi *Tanzania* 7°26S 37°0E **142** D4
Mikumi △ *Tanzania* 7°35S 37°15E **142** D4
Mila *Algeria* 36°27N 6°1E **136** A5
Mila → *Algeria* 36°45N 6°10E **136** A5
Milaca *U.S.A.* 45°45N 93°39W **172** C7
Milagro *Ecuador* 2°11S 79°36W **186** D3
Milan = Milano *Italy* 45°28N 9°10E **92** C6
Milan *Ga., U.S.A.* 32°1N 83°4W **178** D6
Milan *Tenn., U.S.A.* 35°55N 88°46W **177** D10
Milange *Mozam.* 16°3S 35°45E **143** F4
Milano *Italy* 45°28N 9°10E **92** C6
Milano Linate ✈ (LIN)
Italy 45°27N 9°16E **92** C6
Milâs *Turkey* 37°20N 27°50E **99** D9
Milatos *Greece* 35°18N 25°34E **101** D7
Milazzo *Italy* 38°13N 15°15E **95** D8
Milbank *U.S.A.* 45°13N 96°38W **172** C5
Milbanke Sd. *Canada* 52°15N 128°35W **162** C3
Milden *Canada* 51°29N 107°32W **163** C7
Mildenhall *U.K.* 52°21N 0°32E **67** E8
Mildmay *Canada* 44°3N 81°7W **174** B3
Mildura *Australia* 34°13S 142°9E **152** C5**

Mile *China* 24°28N 103°20E **116** E4
Miles *Australia* 26°40S 150°9E **151** D5
Miles City *U.S.A.* 46°25N 105°51W **168** C11
Milestone *Canada* 49°59N 104°31W **163** D8
Mileto *Italy* 38°36N 16°4E **95** D9
Miletto, Mte. *Italy* 41°27N 14°22E **95** A7
Miletus *Turkey* 37°30N 27°18E **99** D9
Milford *Calif., U.S.A.* 40°10N 120°22W **170** E6
Milford *Conn., U.S.A.* 41°14N 73°3W **175** E11
Milford *Del., U.S.A.* 38°55N 75°26W **175** F10
Milford *Mass., U.S.A.* 42°8N 71°31W **175** D13
Milford *N.H., U.S.A.* 42°50N 71°39W **175** D13
Milford *N.Y., U.S.A.* 42°35N 74°56W **175** D10
Milford *Pa., U.S.A.* 41°19N 74°48W **175** E10
Milford *Utah, U.S.A.* 38°24N 113°1W **168** G7
Milford Haven *U.K.* 51°42N 5°7W **67** F2
Milford Sd. *N.Z.* 44°41S 167°47E **155** E2
**Milḥ, Baḥr al = Razāzah,
Buḥayrat ar** *Iraq* 32°40N 43°35E **105** F10
Miliana *Aïn Salah, Algeria* 27°20N 2°32E **136** C4
Miliana *Médéa, Algeria* 36°20N 2°15E **136** A4
Milicz *Poland* 51°31N 17°19E **83** G4
Milies *Greece* 39°20N 23°9E **98** B5
Milikapiti *Australia* 11°26S 130°40E **148** B5
Miling *Australia* 30°30S 116°17E **149** E2
Militello in Val di Catánia
Italy 37°16N 14°48E **95** E7
Milk, Wadi el → *Sudan* 17°55N 30°20E **137** D3
Milk → *U.S.A.* 48°4N 106°19W **168** A10
Milk River *Canada* 49°10N 112°5W **162** D6
Mill I. *Antarctica* 66°0S 101°30E **55** C8
Mill I. *Canada* 63°58N 77°47W **161** E16
Mill Valley *U.S.A.* 37°54N 122°32W **170** H4
Millau *France* 44°8N 3°4E **72** D7
Millbridge *Canada* 44°41N 77°36W **174** B7
Millbrook *Canada* 44°10N 78°29W **174** B6
Millbrook *Ala., U.S.A.* 32°29N 86°22W **177** E11
Millbrook *N.Y., U.S.A.* 41°47N 73°42W **175** E11
Mille Lacs, L. des
Canada 48°45N 90°35W **164** C1
Mille Lacs L. *U.S.A.* 46°15N 93°39W **172** B7
Milledgeville *U.S.A.* 33°5N 83°14W **178** B6
Millerovo *Russia* 48°57N 40°28E **87** F5
Miller's Flat *N.Z.* 45°39S 169°23E **155** F4
Millersburg *Ohio,
U.S.A.* 40°33N 81°55W **174** F3
Millersburg *Pa., U.S.A.* 40°32N 76°58W **174** F8
Millerton *U.S.A.* 41°57N 73°31W **175** E11
Millerton *N.Z.* 41°39S 171°54E **155** B6
Millerton L. *U.S.A.* 37°1N 119°41W **170** J7
Millet *St. Lucia* 13°55N 60°59W **183** f
Millevaches, Plateau de
France 45°45N 2°0E **72** C6
Millheim *U.S.A.* 40°54N 77°29W **174** F7
Millicent *Australia* 37°34S 140°21E **152** D4
Milligan *U.S.A.* 30°45N 86°38W **179** E3
Millington *U.S.A.* 35°20N 89°53W **177** D10
Millinocket *U.S.A.* 45°39N 68°43W **173** C19
Millmerran *Australia* 27°53S 151°16E **151** D5
Millom *U.K.* 54°13N 3°16W **66** C4
Mills L. *Canada* 61°30N 118°20W **162** A5
Millsboro *U.S.A.* 40°0N 80°0W **174** G5
Millstream Chichester △
Australia 21°35S 117°6E **148** D2
Millstreet *Ireland* 52°4N 9°4W **64** D2
Millthorpe *Australia* 33°26S 149°12E **153** B8
Milltown Malbay *Ireland* 52°52N 9°24W **64** D2
Millville *N.J., U.S.A.* 39°24N 75°2W **173** F16
Millville *Pa., U.S.A.* 41°7N 76°32W **175** E8
Millwood L. *U.S.A.* 33°42N 93°58W **176** E8
Millom → *U.S.A.* 54°13N 3°16W **66** C4
Mills L. *Canada* 61°30N 118°20W **162** A5
Millsboro *U.S.A.* 40°0N 80°0W **174** G5
Milne → *Australia* 21°10S 137°33E **150** C2
Milne Land *Greenland* 70°40N 26°30W **57** C8
Milnor *U.S.A.* 46°16N 97°27W **172** B5
Milo → *Guinea* 8°52N 9°9W **138** G3
Milon *Akra* *Greece* 36°15N 28°11E **101** C10
Milos *Greece* 36°44N 24°25E **99** E6
Miloslaw *Poland* 52°12N 17°32E **83** F4
Milot *Albania* 41°41N 19°43E **96** E3
Milparinka *Australia* 29°46S 141°57E **151** D3
Miltenberg *Germany* 49°41N 9°16E **77** F5
Milton *Australia* 35°20S 150°27E **153** C9
Milton *N.S., Canada* 44°4N 64°45W **165** D7
Milton *Ont., Canada* 43°31N 79°53W **174** C5
Milton *N.Z.* 46°7S 169°59E **155** G4
Milton *Calif., U.S.A.* 38°3N 120°51W **170** G6
Milton *Fla., U.S.A.* 30°38N 87°3W **179** E2
Milton *Pa., U.S.A.* 41°1N 76°51W **174** F8
Milton *Vt., U.S.A.* 44°38N 73°7W **175** B11
Milton Keynes *U.K.* 52°1N 0°44W **67** E7
Milton Keynes □ *U.K.* 52°1N 0°44W **67** E7
Milverton *Canada* 43°34N 80°55W **174** C4
Milwaukee *U.S.A.* 43°2N 87°54W **172** D10
Milwaukee Deep
Atl. Oc. 19°50N 68°0W **183** C6
Milwaukie *U.S.A.* 45°26N 122°38W **170** F4
Mim *Ghana* 6°57N 2°33W **138** D4
Mimili *Australia* 27°0S 132°42E **149** E5
Mimizan *France* 44°12N 1°13W **72** D2
Mimoň *Czech Rep.* 50°38N 14°43E **78** A7
Mimoso *Brazil* 15°10S 48°5W **189** D1
Min Jiang → *Fujian,
China* 26°0N 119°35E **117** D12
Min Jiang → *Sichuan,
China* 28°45N 104°40E **116** C5
Min Xian *China* 34°25N 104°5E **114** G5
Mīnā' al Aḥmadī *Kuwait* 29°5N 48°10E **129** D6
Mīnā' Jabal 'Alī *U.A.E.* 25°2N 55°8E **131** E7
Mina Pirquitas
Argentina 22°40S 66°30W **190** A2
Mīnā Su'ud *Si. Arabia* 28°45N 48°28E **129** D6
Minago → *Canada* 54°33N 98°59W **163** C9
Minaki *Canada* 49°59N 94°40W **163** D10
Minamata *Japan* 32°10N 130°30E **113** H5
Minami-Arapusa △
Japan 35°30N 138°9E **113** G9
Minami-Tori-Shima
Pac. Oc. 24°20N 153°58E **156** E7

Minamiaizu *Japan* 37°12N 139°46E **113** F9
Minamiawaji *Japan* 34°10N 134°42E **113** G7
Minamisōma *Japan* 37°38N 140°58E **112** F10
Minas *Uruguay* 34°20S 55°10W **191** C4
Minas, Sierra de las
Guatemala 15°9N 89°31W **182** C2
Minas Basin *Canada* 45°20N 64°12W **165** C7
Minas de Riotinto *Spain* 37°42N 6°35W **89** H4
Minas Gerais □ *Brazil* 18°50S 46°0W **189** D1
Minas Novas *Brazil* 17°15S 42°36W **189** D2
Minatitlán *Mexico* 17°59N 94°31W **181** D6
Minbu *Burma* 20°10N 94°52E **123** J19
Minchinabad *Pakistan* 30°10N 73°34E **124** D5
Mincio → *Italy* 45°4N 10°59E **92** C7
Minčol *Slovak Rep.* 49°15N 20°58E **79** B13
Mindanao *Phil.* 8°0N 125°0E **119** C7
Mindanao Sea = Bohol Sea
Phil. 9°0N 124°0E **119** C6
Mindanao Trench
Pac. Oc. 12°0N 126°6E **119** B7
Mindel → *Germany* 48°31N 10°23E **77** G6
Mindelheim *Germany* 48°2N 10°29E **77** G6
Mindelo *C. Verde Is.* 16°54N 25°0W **134** b
Minden *Canada* 44°55N 78°43W **174** B6
Minden *Germany* 52°17N 8°55E **76** C4
Minden *La., U.S.A.* 32°37N 93°17W **176** E8
Minden *Nev., U.S.A.* 38°57N 119°46W **170** F7
Mindiptana *Indonesia* 5°55S 140°22E **119** F10
Mindona L. *Australia* 33°6S 142°6E **152** B5
Mindoro *Phil.* 13°0N 121°0E **119** B6
Mindoro Str. *Phil.* 12°30N 120°30E **119** B6
Mine *Japan* 34°12N 131°7E **113** G5
Minehead *U.K.* 51°12N 3°29W **67** F4
Mineola *N.Y., U.S.A.* 40°44N 73°38W **175** F11
Mineola *Tex., U.S.A.* 32°40N 95°29W **176** E7
Mineral King *U.S.A.* 36°27N 118°36W **170** J8
Mineral Wells *U.S.A.* 32°48N 98°7W **176** E5
Mineralnyye Vody *Russia* 44°15N 43°8E **87** H6
Miners Bay *Canada* 44°78N 78°46W **174** B6
Minersville *U.S.A.* 40°41N 76°16W **175** F8
Minerva *N.Y., U.S.A.* 43°47N 73°59W **175** C11
Minerva *Ohio, U.S.A.* 40°44N 81°6W **174** F3
Minervino Murge *Italy* 41°5N 16°5E **95** A9
Minfeng *China* 37°4N 82°46E **109** E10
Ming-Kush *Kyrgyzstan* 41°40N 74°28E **109** D8
Mingäçevir
Azerbaijan 40°57N 46°50E **87** K8
Mingäçevir Su Anbarı
Azerbaijan 40°57N 46°50E **87** K8
Mingan *Canada* 50°20N 64°0W **165** B7
Mingary *Australia* 32°8S 140°45E **152** B4
Mingechaur = Mingäçevir
Azerbaijan 40°57N 46°50E **87** K8
**Mingechaurskoye Vdkhr. =
Mingäçevir Su Anbarı**
Azerbaijan 40°57N 46°50E **87** K8
Mingela *Australia* 19°52S 146°38E **150** B4
Mingenew *Australia* 29°12S 115°21E **149** E2
Mingera Cr. →
Australia 20°38S 137°45E **150** C2
Mingha *Greece* 35°4N 24°56E **101** D6
Minggang *China* 32°24N 114°3E **117** A10
Mingguang *China* 32°46N 117°59E **117** A11
Mingin *Burma* 22°50N 94°30E **123** H19
Mingir *Moldova* 46°40N 28°20E **81** D13
Minglanilla *Spain* 39°34N 1°38W **91** F3
Minglun *China* 25°10N 108°21E **116** E7
Mingo Junction *U.S.A.* 40°19N 80°37W **174** F4
Mingora *Pakistan* 34°48N 72°22E **125** B5
Mingorría *Spain* 40°45N 4°40W **88** E6
Mingshan *China* 30°6N 103°10E **116** B4
Mingteke Daban = Mintaka Pass
Pakistan 37°0N 74°58E **125** A6
Mingxi *China* 26°18N 117°12E **117** D11
Mingyuegue *China* 43°2N 128°50E **115** C15
Minhe *China* 36°9N 102°45E **108** D9
Minho = Miño → *Spain* 41°52N 8°40W **88** D2
Minhou *China* 26°0N 119°15E **117** E12
Minićevo *Serbia* 43°42N 22°18E **96** C6
Minicoy I. *India* 8°17N 73°2E **127** K1
Minidoka *U.S.A.* 42°45N 113°29W **168** E7
Minigwal, L. *Australia* 29°31S 123°14E **149** E3
Minilya → *Australia* 23°45S 114°0E **149** D1
Minilya Roadhouse
Australia 23°55S 114°0E **149** D1
Mininera *Australia* 37°37S 142°58E **152** D5
Minipi L. *Canada* 52°25N 60°45W **165** B7
Minjilang *Australia* 11°8S 132°33E **148** B5
Mink L. *Canada* 61°54N 117°40W **162** A5
Minlaton *Australia* 34°45S 137°35E **152** B2
Minna *Nigeria* 9°37N 6°30E **139** D6
Minneapolis *Kans.,
U.S.A.* 39°8N 97°42W **172** F5
Minneapolis *Minn.,
U.S.A.* 44°57N 93°16W **172** C7
Minnedosa *Canada* 50°14N 99°50W **163** C9
Minnesota □ *U.S.A.* 46°0N 94°15W **172** B6
Minnesota → *U.S.A.* 44°54N 93°9W **172** C7
Minnewaukan *U.S.A.* 48°4N 99°15W **172** A4
Minnipa *Australia* 32°51S 135°9E **151** E2
Minnitaki L. *Canada* 49°57N 92°10W **164** C1
Miño → *A Carreira* *Spain* 43°21N 8°12W **88** B2
Mino *Japan* 35°32N 136°55E **113** G8
Miño → *Spain* 41°52N 8°40W **88** D2
Minoa *Greece* 35°6N 25°45E **99** F7
Minorca = Menorca
Spain 40°0N 4°0E **100** B11
Minore *Australia* 32°14S 148°27E **153** B8
Minot *U.S.A.* 48°14N 101°18W **172** A3
Minqin *China* 38°38N 103°20E **114** E2
Minqing *China* 26°15N 118°50E **117** D12
Minsen *Germany* 53°43N 7°58E **76** B4
Minsk *Belarus* 53°52N 27°30E **75** B14
Mińsk Mazowiecki
Poland 52°10N 21°33E **83** F9
Mintabie *Australia* 27°15S 133°7E **151** D1
Mintaka Pass *Pakistan* 37°0N 74°58E **125** A6
Minto *Canada* 46°5N 66°5W **165** C6
Minto, L. *Canada* 57°13N 75°0W **164** A7
Minton *Canada* 49°10N 104°35W **163** D8
Minturn *U.S.A.* 39°35N 106°26W **168** G10
Minturno *Italy* 41°15N 13°45E **94** A6
Minudasht *Iran* 37°17N 56°7E **129** B8
Minůf *Egypt* 30°26N 30°52E **137** E7
Minусinsk *Russia* 53°43N 91°20E **109** D10
Minutang *India* 28°15N 96°30E **123** D20
Minvoul *Gabon* 2°9N 12°8E **140** D2
Minya el Qamh *Egypt* 30°31N 31°21E **137** E7

Minya Konka = Gongga Shan
China 29°40N 101°55E **116** C3
Minyip *Australia* 36°29S 142°36E **152** D5
Minzhong *China* 22°37N 113°30E **111** a
Mionica *Bos.-H.* 44°51N 18°29E **88** b
Mionica *Serbia* 44°14N 20°16E **96** B4
Mioveni *Romania* 44°56N 24°54E **81** F9
Miquan *China* 43°58N 87°42E **109** D11
Miquelon *Canada* 49°25N 76°27W **164** C4
Miquelon *St-P. & M.* 47°8N 56°22W **165** C8
Mir *Belarus* 53°27N 26°28E **75** B14
Mir *Niger* 14°5N 11°59E **139** C7
Mīr Kūh *Iran* 26°22N 58°55E **129** E8
Mīr Shahdād *Iran* 26°15N 58°29E **129** E8
Mira *Italy* 45°26N 12°8E **93** C9
Mira *Portugal* 40°26N 8°44W **88** E2
Mira → *Portugal* 37°43N 8°47W **89** H2
Mira por vos Cay
Bahamas 22°9N 74°30W **183** B5
Mirabella Eclano *Italy* 41°2N 14°59E **95** A7
Mirabella, Kolpos
Greece 35°10N 25°50E **101** D7
Miraceema do Norte
Brazil 9°33S 48°24W **189** C1
Mirador *Brazil* 6°22S 44°22W **189** B2
Mirador-Río Azul △
Guatemala 17°45N 89°50W **182** C2
Miraj *India* 16°50N 74°45E **126** F2
Miraj *India* 16°50N 74°45E **126** F2
Miram Shah *Pakistan* 33°0N 70°2E **124** C4
Miramar *Argentina* 38°15S 57°50W **190** D4
Miramar *Mozam.* 23°50S 35°35E **145** B6
Miramas *France* 43°33N 4°59E **73** E8
Mirambeau *France* 45°23N 0°35W **72** C3
Miramichi *Canada* 47°2N 65°28W **165** C6
Miramichi B. *Canada* 47°15N 65°0W **165** C7
Miramont-de-Guyenne
France 44°37N 0°21E **72** D4
Miranda *Brazil* 20°10S 56°15W **187** H7
Miranda → *Brazil* 19°25S 57°20W **186** G7
Miranda de Ebro *Spain* 42°41N 2°57W **90** C2
Miranda do Corvo
Portugal 40°6N 8°20W **88** E2
Miranda do Douro
Portugal 41°30N 6°16W **88** D4
Mirande *France* 43°31N 0°25E **72** E4
Mirandela *Portugal* 41°32N 7°10W **88** D3
Mirándola *Italy* 44°53N 11°4E **92** D8
Mirandópolis *Brazil* 21°9S 51°6W **191** A5
Mirango *Malawi* 13°32S 34°58E **143** E3
Mirani *Australia* 21°9S 148°53E **150** b
Mirano *Italy* 45°30N 12°7E **93** C9
Miras *Albania* 40°40N 20°56E **96** F4
Mirassol *Brazil* 20°46S 49°28E **191** A6
Mirbāṭ *Oman* 17°0N 54°45E **131** D5
Mirboo North
Australia 38°24S 146°10E **153** C7
Mirear *Egypt* 23°15N 35°41E **137** C4
Mirebeau *France* 46°49N 0°10E **70** F7
Mirebeau-sur-Bèze
France 47°25N 5°20E **71** E12
Mirecourt *France* 48°20N 6°10E **71** D13
Mires *Greece* 35°4N 24°56E **101** D6
Mirgorod = Myrhorod
Ukraine 49°58N 33°37E **85** H7
Miri *Malaysia* 4°23N 113°59E **118** D4
Mirialguda *India* 16°52N 79°35E **126** F4
Miriam Vale *Australia* 24°20S 151°33E **150** D5
Miribel *France* 45°50N 4°57E **71** G11
Mirigama *Sri Lanka* 7°15N 80°8E **127** L5
Mirim, L. *S. Amer.* 32°45S 52°50W **191** C5
Mirintu →
Australia 15°0S 128°45E **148** C4
Mirjāveh *Iran* 29°1N 61°30E **129** D9
Mirnyy *Antarctica* 66°50S 92°30E **55** C14
Mirnyy *Russia* 62°33N 113°53E **107** C12
Miroč *Serbia* 44°32N 22°16E **96** B6
Mirokhan *Pakistan* 27°46N 68°6E **124** F3
Mirond L. *Canada* 55°6N 102°47W **163** B8
Mirosławiec *Poland* 53°20N 16°5E **82** E3
Mirpur *Pakistan* 33°32N 73°56E **125** C5
Mirpur Batoro *Pakistan* 24°44N 68°16E **124** G3
Mirpur Bibiwari
Pakistan 28°33N 67°44E **124** E2
Mirpur Khas *Pakistan* 25°30N 69°0E **124** G3
Mirpur Sakro *Pakistan* 24°33N 67°41E **124** G2
Mirria *Niger* 13°43N 9°7E **139** C6
Mirrool *Australia* 34°19S 147°10E **153** C7
Mirs Bay = Tai Pang Wan
China 22°33N 114°24E **111** a
Mirsk *Poland* 50°58N 15°23E **83** H2
Mirtağ *Turkey* 38°23N 41°56E **128** B4
Mirtoo Sea *Greece* 37°0N 23°20E **98** D5
Miryang *S. Korea* 35°31N 128°44E **115** G15
Mirzaani *Georgia* 41°24N 46°5E **87** K8
Mirzapur *India* 25°10N 82°34E **125** G10
**Mirzapur-cum-Vindhyachal =
Mirzapur** *India* 25°10N 82°34E **125** G10
Misantla *Mexico* 19°56N 96°50W **181** D5
Misawa *Japan* 40°41N 141°24E **112** D10
Miscou I. *Canada* 47°57N 64°31W **165** C7
Misha *India* 7°59N 93°22E **127** L10
Mish'āb, Ra's al
Si. Arabia 28°15N 48°43E **129** D6
Mishagua → *Peru* 11°12S 72°58W **188** C3
Mishamo *Tanzania* 5°19S 30°44E **142** D2
Mishan *China* 45°37N 131°48E **112** B5
Mishawaka *U.S.A.* 41°40N 86°11W **172** E10
Mishima *Japan* 35°10N 138°52E **113** G9
Mishkino *Russia* 55°38N 63°45E **108** B7
Mishmi Hills *India* 29°0N 96°0E **123** D20
Mísi *China* 45°17N 120°20W **170** D7
Misima I. *Papua N. G.* 10°40S 152°45E **150** a
Misión Mexico 32°6N 116°53W **171** N10
Misión Fagnano
Argentina 54°32S 67°17W **192** D3
Misiones □ *Argentina* 27°0S 55°0W **191** B5
Misiones □ *Paraguay* 27°0S 56°0W **191** B4
Miskah *Si. Arabia* 24°49N 42°56E **128** E4
Miskitos, Cayos *Nic.* 14°26N 82°50W **182** D3
Miskolc *Hungary* 48°7N 20°50E **80** B5
Misoke
Dem. Rep. of the Congo 0°42S 28°2E **142** C2
Misool *Indonesia* 1°52S 130°10E **119** E8
Mişr = Egypt ■ *Africa* 28°0N 31°0E **137** C2
Mişrātah *Libya* 32°24N 15°3E **137** B9
Missanabie *Canada* 48°20N 84°6W **164** C3
Missão Velha *Brazil* 7°15S 39°10W **189** B3
Missinaibi → *Canada* 50°43N 81°29W **164** B3
Missinaibi L. *Canada* 48°23N 83°40W **164** C3
Mission *S. Dak.,
U.S.A.* 43°18N 100°39W **172** D3
Mission *Tex., U.S.A.* 26°13N 98°20W **176** H5
Mission Beach *Australia* 17°53S 146°6E **150** B4

Mission Viejo *U.S.A.* 33°36N 117°40W **171** M9
Missirah *Senegal* 13°40N 16°30W **138** C1
Missisa L. *Canada* 52°20N 85°7W **164** B2
Mississicabi → *Canada* 51°14N 79°31W **164** B4
Mississagi → *Canada* 46°15N 83°9W **164** C3
Mississauga *Canada* 43°32N 79°35W **174** C5
Mississippi □ *U.S.A.* 33°0N 90°0W **177** E10
Mississippi → *U.S.A.* 29°9N 89°15W **177** G10
Mississippi L. *Canada* 45°5N 76°10W **175** A8
Mississippi River Delta
U.S.A. 29°10N 89°15W **177** G10
Mississippi Sd. *U.S.A.* 30°20N 89°0W **177** G10
Missoula *U.S.A.* 46°52N 114°1W **168** C6
Missouri □ *U.S.A.* 38°25N 92°30W **172** F7
Missouri → *U.S.A.* 38°49N 90°7W **172** F8
Missouri City *U.S.A.* 29°37N 95°32W **176** G7
Missouri Valley *U.S.A.* 41°34N 95°53W **172** E6
Mist *U.S.A.* 45°59N 123°15W **170** E3
Mistassibi → *Canada* 48°53N 72°13W **165** B5
Mistassini *Canada* 48°53N 72°12W **165** B5
Mistassini → *Canada* 48°42N 72°20W **165** B5
Mistassini, L. *Canada* 51°0N 73°30W **164** B5
Mistastin L. *Canada* 55°57N 63°20W **165** A7
Mistelbach *Austria* 48°34N 16°34E **79** C9
Misterbianco *Italy* 37°31N 15°1E **95** E8
Misti, Volcán *Peru* 16°18S 71°24W **188** D3
Mistinibi, L. *Canada* 55°56N 64°17W **165** A7
Mistissini *Canada* 48°42N 72°12W **165** C5
Mistras = Mystras *Greece* 37°4N 22°22E **98** D4
Mistretta *Italy* 37°56N 14°22E **95** E7
Misty L. *Canada* 58°53N 101°40W **163** B8
Misurata = Mişrātah
Libya 32°24N 15°3E **135** B9
Mitande *Mozam.* 14°6S 35°58E **143** E4
Mitchell *Australia* 26°29S 147°58E **151** D4
Mitchell *Canada* 43°28N 81°12W **174** C3
Mitchell *Ga., U.S.A.* 33°13N 82°42W **178** C7
Mitchell *Nebr., U.S.A.* 41°57N 103°49W **172** E2
Mitchell *Oreg., U.S.A.* 44°34N 120°9W **168** D3
Mitchell *S. Dak., U.S.A.* 43°43N 98°2W **172** D4
Mitchell → *Australia* 15°12S 141°35E **150** B3
Mitchell, Mt. *U.S.A.* 35°46N 82°16W **177** D13
Mitchell-Alice Rivers △
Australia 15°28S 142°5E **150** B3
Mitchell Ra. *Australia* 12°49S 135°36E **150** A2
Mitchell River △
Australia 37°37S 147°32E **153** D7
Mitchelstown *Ireland* 52°15N 8°16W **64** D3
Mitha Tiwana *Pakistan* 32°13N 72°6E **124** C5
Mithi *Pakistan* 24°44N 69°48E **124** G3
Mithimna *Greece* 39°20N 26°12E **99** B8
Mithrao *Pakistan* 27°28N 69°40E **124** F3
Mitiamo *Australia* 36°12S 144°15E **152** C6
Mitilini *Greece* 39°6N 26°35E **99** B8
Mitilínii *Greece* 37°42N 26°56E **99** D8
Mitla Pass = Mamarr Mitlā
Egypt 30°2N 32°54E **130** E1
Mito *Japan* 36°20N 140°30E **113** F10
Mitre, Mt. *N.Z.* 40°50S 175°30E **154** G4
Mitrofanovka *Russia* 49°58N 39°42E **85** H10
Mitsamiouli *Comoros Is.* 11°20S 43°16E **141** a
Mitsiwa *Eritrea* 15°35N 39°25E **131** D2
Mitsukaidō *Japan* 36°1N 139°59E **113** F9
Mittagong *Australia* 34°28S 150°29E **153** C9
Mitterberg *Austria* 47°20N 10°10E **78** D3
Mittelfranken □
Germany 49°25N 10°40E **77** F6
Mittellandkanal →
Germany 52°20N 8°28E **76** C4
Mittenwalde *Germany* 52°15N 13°31E **76** C9
Mittersill *Austria* 47°16N 12°29E **78** D5
Mitterteich *Germany* 49°57N 12°14E **77** F8
Mittimatalik = Pond Inlet
Canada 72°40N 77°0W **161** C16
Mittweida *Germany* 50°59N 12°59E **76** E8
Mitú *Colombia* 1°15N 70°13W **186** C4
Mitumba *Tanzania* 7°8S 31°2E **142** D3
Mitumba, Mts.
Dem. Rep. of the Congo 7°0S 27°30E **142** D2
Mitwaba
Dem. Rep. of the Congo 8°2S 27°17E **143** D2
Mityana *Uganda* 0°23N 32°2E **142** B3
Mixteco → *Mexico* 18°11N 98°30W **181** D5
Miyagi □ *Japan* 38°15N 140°45E **112** E10
Miyah, W. el → *Egypt* 25°0N 33°23E **137** C3
Miyah, W. el → *Syria* 34°44N 39°57E **128** C3
Miyake-Jima *Japan* 34°0N 139°30E **113** G9
Miyako *Japan* 39°40N 141°59E **112** E10
Miyako-Jima *Japan* 24°45N 125°20E **113** M2
Miyako-Rettō *Japan* 24°24N 125°0E **113** M2
Miyakojima *Japan* 31°40N 131°5E **113** J5
Miyakonojō *Japan* 31°40N 131°5E **113** J5
Miyān Rahān *Iran* 34°34N 47°26E **105** E12
Miyani *India* 21°50N 69°26E **124** J3
Miyanoura-Dake
Japan 30°20N 130°31E **113** J5
Miyazaki *Japan* 31°56N 131°30E **113** J5
Miyazaki □ *Japan* 32°30N 131°30E **113** H5
Miyazu *Japan* 35°35N 135°10E **113** G7
Miyet, Bahr el = Dead Sea
Asia 31°30N 35°30E **130** D4
Miyi *China* 26°47N 102°4E **116** D4
Miyoshi *Japan* 34°48N 132°51E **113** G6
Miyun *China* 40°28N 116°50E **116** a
Miyun Shuiku *China* 40°30N 117°0E **116** b
Mizdah *Libya* 31°30N 13°0E **137** B8
Mizen Hd. *Cork, Ireland* 51°27N 9°50W **64** E2
Mizen Hd. *Wicklow, Ireland* 52°51N 6°4W **64** D5
Mizhi *China* 37°47N 110°12E **114** F6
Mizil *Romania* 44°59N 26°29E **81** F10
Mizoram □ *India* 23°30N 92°40E **123** H18
Mizpe Ramon *Israel* 30°34N 34°49E **130** E3
Mizuho *Antarctica* 70°30S 41°0E **55** D5
Mizusawa = Ōshū
Japan 39°8N 141°8E **112** E10
Mjällby *Sweden* 56°3N 14°40E **63** H6
Mjöbäck *Sweden* 57°28N 12°53E **63** F6
Mjölby *Sweden* 58°20N 15°10E **63** F8
Mjörn *Sweden* 57°55N 12°25E **63** F6
Mjøsa *Norway* 60°40N 11°0E **63** F14
Mkata *Tanzania* 5°45S 38°20E **142** D4
Mkhaya △ *Swaziland* 26°34S 31°45E **145** D5
Mkhuze → *S. Africa* 27°10S 32°0E **145** D5
Mkokotoni *Tanzania* 5°55S 39°15E **142** D4
Mkomazi *Tanzania* 4°40S 38°7E **142** C4
Mkomazi △ *Tanzania* 4°0S 38°0E **142** C4
Mkomazi → *S. Africa* 30°12S 30°50E **145** E5
Mkomazi □ *Tanzania* 4°4S 30°2E **142** C3

Mkulwe Tanzania 8°37S 32°20E 143 D3
Mkumbi, Ras Tanzania 7°38S 39°55E 142 D4
Mkushi Zambia 14°25S 29°15E 143 E2
Mkushi River Zambia 13°32S 29°45E 143 E2
Mkuze S. Africa 27°10S 32°0E 145 C5
Mladá Boleslav
  Czech Rep. 50°27N 14°53E 78 A7
Mladenovac Serbia 44°28N 20°44E 96 B4
Mlala Hills Tanzania 6°50S 31°40E 142 D3
Mlange = Mulanje, Mt.
  Malawi 16°2S 35°33E 143 F4
Mlava → Serbia 44°45N 21°13E 96 B5
Mława Poland 53°9N 20°25E 83 E7
Mlawula △ Swaziland 26°22S 32°5E 145 D5
Mlinište Bos.-H. 44°15N 16°50E 93 D13
Mljet Croatia 42°43N 17°30E 93 F14
Mljet △ Croatia 42°45N 17°25E 93 F14
Mljetski Kanal Croatia 42°48N 17°35E 93 F14
Mlynary Poland 54°12N 19°46E 83 A6
Mmabatho S. Africa 25°49S 25°30E 144 C4
Mme Cameroon 6°18N 10°14E 139 D7
Mnichovo Hradiště
  Czech Rep. 50°32N 14°59E 78 A7
Mo i Rana Norway 66°20N 14°7E 60 C16
Moa Australia 10°11S 142°16E 150 a
Moa Cuba 20°40N 74°56W 183 B4
Moa Indonesia 8°0S 128°0E 119 F7
Moa → S. Leone 6°59N 11°36W 138 D2
Moab U.S.A. 38°35N 109°33W 168 G9
Moaco → Brazil 7°41S 68°18W 188 B4
Moala Fiji 18°36S 179°53E 154 a
Moama Australia 36°7S 144°46E 151 F3
Moamba Mozam. 25°36S 32°15E 145 C5
Moapa U.S.A. 36°40N 114°37W 171 J12
Moate Ireland 53°24N 7°44W 64 C4
Moba
  Dem. Rep. of the Congo 7°0S 29°48E 142 D2
Mobārakābād Iran 28°24N 53°20E 129 D7
Mobaye C.A.R. 4°25N 21°5E 140 D4
Moberly U.S.A. 39°25N 92°26W 172 F7
Moberly Lake Canada 55°50N 121°44W 162 B4
Mobile U.S.A. 30°41N 88°3W 177 F10
Mobile B. U.S.A. 30°30N 88°0W 177 F11
Mobridge U.S.A. 45°32N 100°26W 172 C3
Moc Chau Vietnam 20°50N 104°38E 120 B5
Moc Hoa Vietnam 10°46N 105°56E 121 G5
Mocabe Kasari
  Dem. Rep. of the Congo 9°58S 26°12E 143 D2
Moçambique = Mozambique ■
  Africa 19°0S 35°0E 143 F4
Moçâmedes Mozam. 15°3S 40°42E 143 F5
Mocanaqua U.S.A. 41°9N 76°8W 175 E8
Moce Fiji 18°40S 178°29W 154 a
Mocha, I. Chile 38°22S 73°56W 192 A2
Mochima △ Venezuela 10°30N 64°5W 183 D7
Mochos Greece 35°16N 25°27E 101 D7
Mochudi Botswana 24°27S 26°7E 144 B4
Mocimboa da Praia
  Mozam. 11°25S 40°20E 143 E5
Mociu Romania 46°46N 24°3E 81 D9
Möckeln Sweden 56°40N 14°15E 63 H8
Mockfjärd Sweden 60°30N 14°57E 62 D8
Moclips U.S.A. 47°14N 124°13W 170 C2
Mocoa Colombia 1°7N 76°35W 186 C3
Mococa Brazil 21°28S 47°0W 191 A6
Mocorito Mexico 25°29N 107°55W 180 B3
Moctezuma Mexico 29°48N 109°42W 180 B3
Moctezuma → Mexico 21°59N 98°34W 181 C5
Mocuba Mozam. 16°54S 36°57E 143 F4
Modane France 45°12N 6°40E 73 C10
Modasa India 23°30N 73°21E 124 H5
Modder → S. Africa 29°2S 24°37E 144 C3
Modderrivier S. Africa 29°2S 24°38E 144 C3
Módena Italy 44°40N 10°55E 92 D7
Modena U.S.A. 37°48N 113°56W 169 H7
Modesto U.S.A. 37°39N 121°0W 170 H6
Módica Italy 36°52N 14°46E 95 F7
Modimolle S. Africa 24°42S 28°22E 145 B4
Modjadjiskloof S. Africa 23°42S 30°10E 145 B5
Mödling Austria 48°5N 16°17E 79 C9
Modoc U.S.A. 33°44N 82°13W 178 B7
Modra Slovak Rep. 48°19N 17°20E 79 C10
Modrića Bos.-H. 44°57N 18°17E 80 F3
Moe Australia 38°12S 146°19E 153 E7
Moebase Mozam. 17°3S 38°41E 143 F4
Moëlan-sur-Mer France 47°49N 3°38W 70 E3
Moengo Suriname 5°45N 54°20W 187 B8
Moenjodaro = Mohenjodaro
  Pakistan 27°19N 68°7E 124 F3
Moerewa N.Z. 35°23S 174°1E 154 B3
Moffat U.K. 55°21N 3°27W 65 F5
Moga India 30°48N 75°8E 124 D6
Mogadishu = Muqdisho
  Somalia 2°2N 45°25E 131 G4
Mogador = Essaouira
  Morocco 31°32N 9°42W 136 B2
Mogadouro Portugal 41°22N 6°47W 88 D4
Mogalakwena →
  S. Africa 22°38S 28°40E 145 B4
Mogami-Gawa →
  Japan 38°45N 140°0E 112 E10
Mogán Canary Is. 27°53N 15°43W 100 G4
Mogaung Burma 25°20N 97°0E 123 G20
Mogente = Moixent
  Spain 38°52N 0°45W 91 G4
Mogi-Mirim Brazil 22°29S 47°0W 187 H9
Mogielnica Poland 51°42N 20°41E 83 G7
Mogilev = Mahilyow
  Belarus 53°55N 30°18E 75 B16
Mogilev-Podolskiy = Mohyliv-
  Podilskyy Ukraine 48°26N 27°48E 81 B12
Mogilno Poland 52°39N 17°55E 83 F4
Mogincual Mozam. 15°35S 40°25E 143 F5
Mogliano Véneto Italy 45°33N 12°14E 93 C9
Mogocha Russia 53°40N 119°50E 107 D12
Mogoditshane
  Botswana 24°37S 25°51E 144 B4
Mogok Burma 23°0N 96°40E 123 H20
Mogollon Rim U.S.A. 34°10N 110°50W 169 J8
Mógoro Italy 39°41N 8°47E 94 C1
Mogreat Sudan 19°28N 33°16E 137 D3
Moguer Spain 37°15N 6°52W 89 H4
Mogumber Australia 31°2S 116°3E 149 F2
Mogwadi → S. Africa 23°4S 29°36E 145 B4
Mohács Hungary 45°58N 18°41E 80 B3
Mohaka → N.Z. 39°7S 177°12E 154 F6
Mohala India 20°35N 80°40E 126 D5
Mohales Hoek Lesotho 30°7S 27°26E 144 C4
Mohall U.S.A. 48°46N 101°31W 172 A3
Mohammadābād Iran 37°52N 59°5E 129 B8

Mohammadia Algeria 35°33N 0°3E 136 A4
Mohammedia Morocco 33°44N 7°21W 136 B2
Mohana India 19°27N 84°16E 126 E7
Mohana → India 24°43N 85°0E 125 G11
Mohanlalganj India 26°41N 80°58E 125 F9
Mohave, L. U.S.A. 35°12N 114°34W 171 K12
Mohawk → U.S.A. 42°47N 73°41W 175 D11
Moheda Sweden 57°1N 14°35E 63 G8
Mohéli Comoros Is. 12°20S 43°40E 141 a
Mohenjodaro Pakistan 27°19N 68°7E 124 F3
Moher, Cliffs of Ireland 52°58N 9°27W 64 D2
Mohicanville Res.
  U.S.A. 40°45N 82°9W 174 F2
Möhne → Germany 51°29N 7°57E 76 D3
Mohns Ridge Arctic 72°30N 5°0W 54 B7
Mohoro Tanzania 8°6S 39°8E 142 D4
Mohsenābād Iran 36°40N 59°35E 129 B8
Mohyliv-Podilskyy
  Ukraine 48°26N 27°48E 81 B12
Moidart, L. U.K. 56°47N 5°52W 65 E3
Moinabad India 17°44N 77°16E 126 F3
Moineşti Romania 46°28N 26°31E 81 D11
Moira → Canada 44°21N 77°24W 174 B7
Moirans France 45°20N 5°33E 73 C9
Moirans-en-Montagne
  France 46°26N 5°43E 71 F12
Moisaküla Estonia 58°3N 25°12E 84 C3
Moisie Canada 50°12N 66°1W 165 B6
Moisie → Canada 50°14N 66°5W 165 B6
Moissac France 44°7N 1°5E 72 D5
Moíta Portugal 38°38N 8°58W 89 G2
Moixent Spain 38°52N 0°45W 91 G4
Mójacar Spain 37°6N 1°55W 91 H3
Mojados Spain 41°26N 4°40W 88 D6
Mojave U.S.A. 35°3N 118°10W 171 K8
Mojave △ U.S.A. 35°7N 115°32W 171 K11
Mojave Desert U.S.A. 35°0N 116°30W 171 L10
Moji das Cruzes Brazil 23°31S 46°11W 191 A6
Moji-Guaçu → Brazil 20°53S 48°10W 191 A6
Mojiang China 23°37N 101°35E 116 F3
Mojkovac Montenegro 42°58N 19°35E 96 G5
Mojo Bolivia 21°48S 65°33W 190 A2
Mojokerto Indonesia 7°28S 112°26E 119 G15
Mokai N.Z. 38°32S 175°56E 154 E4
Mokala △ S. Africa 29°10S 24°10E 144 C3
Mokambo
  Dem. Rep. of the Congo 12°25S 28°20E 143 E2
Mokameh India 25°24N 85°55E 125 G11
Mokau N.Z. 38°42S 174°39E 154 E3
Mokau → N.Z. 38°35S 174°35E 154 E3
Mokelumne →
  U.S.A. 38°13N 121°28W 170 G5
Mokelumne Hill
  U.S.A. 38°18N 120°43W 170 G6
Mokhotlong Lesotho 29°22S 29°2E 145 C4
Mokihinui → N.Z. 41°33S 171°58E 155 B6
Möklinta Sweden 60°4N 16°33E 62 D10
Mokikne Tunisia 35°35N 10°58E 136 A6
Mokoan, L. Australia 36°27S 146°5E 153 D7
Mokokchung India 26°15N 94°30E 123 F19
Mokolo Cameroon 10°49N 13°54E 139 C7
Mokolo → S. Africa 23°14S 27°43E 145 B4
Mokopane S. Africa 24°10S 28°55E 145 B4
Mokp'o S. Korea 34°50N 126°25E 115 G14
Mokra Gora Europe 42°50N 20°30E 96 G4
Mokronog Slovenia 45°57N 15°9E 93 C12
Moksha → Russia 54°45N 41°53E 86 C6
Mokshan Russia 53°25N 44°35E 86 D7
Mokwa Nigeria 9°1N 5°0E 139 D6
Mol Belgium 51°11N 5°5E 69 C5
Mola di Bari Italy 41°4N 17°5E 95 A10
Molai Greece 36°49N 22°56E 98 E4
Molakalmuru India 14°55N 76°50E 127 G3
Molaly Kazakhstan 45°27N 78°18E 109 E9
Molara Italy 40°52N 9°43E 94 B2
Molat Croatia 44°15N 14°50E 93 D11
Molchanovo Russia 57°40N 83°50E 106 D9
Mold U.K. 53°9N 3°8W 66 D4
Moldava nad Bodvou
  Slovak Rep. 48°38N 21°0E 79 C14
Moldavia = Moldova ■
  Europe 47°0N 28°0E 81 C13
Moldavia Romania 46°30N 27°0E 81 D12
Molde Norway 62°45N 7°9E 60 E12
Moldova ■ Europe 47°0N 28°0E 81 C13
Moldova Nouă Romania 44°45N 21°41E 80 F6
Moldoveanu, Vf.
  Romania 45°36N 24°45E 81 E9
Moldoviţa Romania 47°41N 25°32E 81 C10
Mole → U.K. 51°24N 0°21W 67 F7
Mole → Ghana 9°43N 1°44W 139 D4
Molepolole Botswana 24°28S 25°28E 144 B4
Molesworth N.Z. 42°5S 173°16E 155 C8
Molfetta Italy 41°12N 16°36E 95 A9
Molina de Aragón Spain 40°46N 1°52W 90 E3
Molina de Segura Spain 38°3N 1°12W 91 G3
Moline U.S.A. 41°30N 90°31W 172 E8
Molinella Italy 44°37N 11°40E 92 D8
Molino U.S.A. 30°43N 87°20W 179 E2
Molinos Argentina 25°28S 66°15W 190 B2
Moliro
  Dem. Rep. of the Congo 8°12S 30°30E 142 D3
Moliterno Italy 40°14N 15°52E 95 B8
Molkom Sweden 59°37N 13°44E 62 E7
Mölle Sweden 56°17N 12°31E 63 H6
Mollendo Peru 17°0S 72°0W 188 D3
Mollerin, L. Australia 30°30S 117°35E 149 F2
Mollerussa Spain 41°37N 0°54E 90 D6
Mollina Spain 37°8N 4°38W 89 H6
Mölln Germany 53°37N 10°41E 72 B6
Mölltorp Sweden 58°30N 14°26E 63 F8
Mölndal Sweden 57°40N 12°3E 63 G5
Mölnlycke Sweden 57°40N 12°8E 63 G5
Molo Kenya 0°15S 35°44E 142 C4
Molochansk Ukraine 47°15N 35°35E 85 J8
Molochnoye, Ozero
  Ukraine 46°30N 35°20E 85 J8
Molodechno = Maladzyechna
  Belarus 54°20N 26°50E 75 A14
Molodezhnaya
  Antarctica 67°40S 45°51E 55 C9
Molodova Ukraine 46°13N 29°39E 81 D14
Moloka'i U.S.A. 21°8N 157°0W 167 L8
Molokai Fracture Zone
  Pac. Oc. 28°0N 125°0W 157 E15
Molong Australia 33°5S 148°54E 153 B8
Molopo → Africa 28°30S 20°12E 144 C3
Molos Greece 38°47N 22°37E 98 C4
Molsheim France 48°33N 7°29E 71 D14

Molson L. Canada 54°22N 96°40W 163 C9
Molteno S. Africa 31°22S 26°22E 144 D4
Molu Indonesia 6°45S 131°40E 119 F8
Molucca Sea Indonesia 0°0 125°0E 119 E6
Moluccas = Maluku
  Indonesia 1°0S 127°0E 119 E7
Moma
  Dem. Rep. of the Congo 1°35S 23°52E 142 C1
Moma Mozam. 16°47S 39°4E 143 F4
Momba Australia 30°58S 143°30E 152 A5
Mombaça Brazil 5°43S 39°45W 189 B3
Mombasa Kenya 4°3S 39°40E 142 C4
Mombetsu Japan 44°21N 143°22E 112 B11
Mombuey Spain 42°3N 6°20W 88 D4
Momchilgrad Bulgaria 41°33N 25°23E 97 E9
Momi
  Dem. Rep. of the Congo 1°42S 27°0E 142 C2
Mompós Colombia 9°14N 74°26W 186 B4
Møn Denmark 54°57N 12°20E 63 K6
Mon □ Burma 16°0N 97°30E 123 L20
Mona, Canal de la = Mona
  Passage W. Indies 18°30N 67°45W 183 C6
Mona, Isla Puerto Rico 18°5N 67°54W 183 C6
Mona, Pta. Costa Rica 9°37N 82°36W 182 E3
Mona Passage
  W. Indies 18°30N 67°45W 183 C6
Monaca U.S.A. 40°41N 80°17W 174 F4
Monaco ■ Europe 43°46N 7°23E 73 E11
Monadhliath Mts. U.K. 57°10N 4°4W 65 D4
Monadnock, Mt.
  U.S.A. 42°52N 72°7W 175 D12
Monaghan Ireland 54°15N 6°57W 64 B5
Monaghan □ Ireland 54°11N 6°56W 64 B5
Monahans U.S.A. 31°36N 102°54W 176 F3
Monapo Mozam. 14°56S 40°19E 143 E5
Monar, L. U.K. 57°26N 5°8W 65 D3
Monaragala Sri Lanka 6°52N 81°22E 127 L5
Monarch Mt. Canada 51°55N 125°57W 162 C3
Monashee Mts. Canada 51°0N 118°43W 162 C5
Monasterevin Ireland 53°8N 7°4W 64 C4
Monastir = Bitola
  Macedonia 41°1N 21°20E 96 E5
Monastir Tunisia 35°50N 10°49E 136 A6
Monastir □ Tunisia 35°37N 10°45E 136 A6
Monbetsu = Hidaka
  Japan 42°30N 142°10E 112 C11
Moncalieri Italy 45°0N 7°41E 92 D4
Moncalvo Italy 45°3N 8°16E 92 C5
Monção Portugal 42°4N 8°27W 88 C2
Moncarapacho Portugal 37°5N 7°46W 89 H3
Moncayo, Sierra del
  Spain 41°48N 1°50W 90 D3
Monchegorsk Russia 67°54N 32°58E 60 C25
Mönchengladbach
  Germany 51°11N 6°27E 76 D2
Monchique Portugal 37°19N 8°38W 89 H2
Moncks Corner U.S.A. 33°12N 80°1W 178 B9
Monclova Mexico 26°54N 101°25W 180 B4
Moncontour France 48°22N 2°38W 70 D4
Moncton Canada 46°7N 64°51W 165 C7
Mondariz Spain 42°14N 8°27W 88 C2
Mondego → Portugal 40°9N 8°52W 88 E2
Mondego, C. Portugal 40°11N 8°54W 88 E2
Mondeodo Indonesia 3°34S 122°9E 119 E6
Mondeville France 49°10N 0°18W 70 C6
Mondlo S. Africa 27°59S 30°43E 145 C5
Mondolfo Italy 43°45N 13°5E 93 E10
Mondoñedo Spain 43°25N 7°23W 88 B3
Mondoví Italy 44°23N 7°49E 92 D4
Mondragon = Arrasate
  Spain 43°4N 2°30W 90 D2
Mondragone Italy 41°3N 13°53E 94 A6
Mondrain I. Australia 34°9S 122°14E 149 F3
Moneague Jamaica 18°16N 77°7W 182 a
Monemvasia Greece 36°41N 23°3E 98 E5
Moneron, Ostrov
  Russia 46°15N 141°16E 112 A10
Monessen U.S.A. 40°9N 79°54W 174 F5
Monesterio Spain 38°6N 6°15W 89 G4
Monestier-de-Clermont
  France 44°55N 5°38E 73 D9
Monett U.S.A. 36°55N 93°55W 172 G8
Moneymore U.K. 54°41N 6°40W 64 B5
Monfalcone Italy 45°49N 13°32E 93 C10
Monflanquin France 44°32N 0°47E 72 D4
Monforte Portugal 39°6N 7°25W 89 F3
Monforte de Lemos Spain 42°31N 7°33W 88 C3
Mong Hpayak Burma 20°52N 99°55E 120 B2
Mong Hsat Shan,
  Burma 20°31N 99°15E 120 B2
Mong Hsat Shan,
  Burma 21°54N 98°30E 116 G2
Mong Kung Burma 21°35N 97°35E 123 J20
Mong Nai Burma 20°32N 97°46E 123 J20
Mong Ping Burma 21°22N 99°2E 116 G2
Mong Tai = Shan □
  Burma 21°30N 98°30E 123 J21
Mong Ton Burma 20°17N 98°45E 123 J21
Mong Yai Burma 22°21N 98°3E 123 H21
Mong Yang Burma 21°50N 99°41E 120 B2
Mongalla South Sudan 5°8N 31°42E 135 G12
Mongers, L. Australia 29°25S 117°5E 149 E2
Monghyr = Munger
  India 25°23N 86°30E 125 G12
Mongibello = Etna Italy 37°50N 14°55E 95 E7
Mongo Chad 12°14N 18°43E 135 F9
Mongo → S. Leone 9°35N 12°10W 138 D2
Mongolia ■ Asia 47°0N 103°0E 110 B9
Mongolia, Plateau of
  Asia 45°0N 105°0E 102 D12
Mongonu Nigeria 12°40N 13°32E 139 C7
Mongu Zambia 15°16S 23°12E 141 H4
Môngua Angola 16°43S 15°20E 144 A2
Moniac U.S.A. 30°31N 82°14W 178 F7
Monifieth U.K. 56°30N 2°48W 65 E6

Mono → Togo 6°17N 1°51E 139 D5
Mono, Pta. Nic. 12°0N 83°30W 182 D3
Mono L. U.S.A. 38°1N 119°1W 170 H7
Monolith U.S.A. 35°7N 118°22W 171 K8
Monólithos Greece 36°7N 27°45E 101 C9
Monópoli Italy 40°57N 17°18E 95 B10
Monor Hungary 47°21N 19°27E 80 C4
Monos I. Trin. & Tob. 10°42N 61°44W 187 K15
Monowai N.Z. 45°53S 167°31E 155 F2
Monowai, L. N.Z. 45°53S 167°25E 155 F2
Monreal del Campo
  Spain 40°47N 1°20W 90 E3
Monreale Italy 38°5N 13°17E 94 D6
Monroe Ga., U.S.A. 33°47N 83°43W 178 B6
Monroe La., U.S.A. 32°30N 92°7W 176 E8
Monroe Mich., U.S.A. 41°55N 83°24W 173 E12
Monroe N.C., U.S.A. 34°59N 80°33W 178 A9
Monroe N.Y., U.S.A. 41°20N 74°11W 175 E10
Monroe Utah, U.S.A. 38°38N 112°7W 168 G7
Monroe Wash., U.S.A. 47°51N 121°58W 170 C5
Monroe Wis., U.S.A. 42°36N 89°38W 172 D9
Monroe, L. U.S.A. 28°50N 81°19W 179 G8
Monroe City U.S.A. 39°39N 91°44W 172 F8
Monroeton U.S.A. 41°43N 76°29W 175 E8
Monroeville Ala.,
  U.S.A. 31°31N 87°20W 177 F11
Monroeville Pa., U.S.A. 40°26N 79°45W 174 F5
Monrovia Liberia 6°18N 10°47W 138 D2
Mons Belgium 50°27N 3°58E 69 D3
Møns Klint Denmark 54°57N 12°33E 63 K6
Monsaraz Portugal 38°28N 7°22W 89 G3
Monse Indonesia 4°7S 123°15E 119 E6
Monsefú Peru 6°52S 79°52W 188 B2
Monséguir France 44°38N 0°4E 72 D4
Monselice Italy 45°14N 11°45E 93 C8
Mönsterås Sweden 57°3N 16°26E 63 G10
Mont Cenis, Col du
  France 45°15N 6°55E 73 C10
Mont-de-Marsan France 43°54N 0°31W 72 E3
Mont-Joli Canada 48°37N 68°10W 165 C6
Mont-Laurier Canada 46°35N 75°30W 164 C4
Mont-Louis Canada 49°15N 65°44W 165 C6
Mont Peko △ Ivory C. 9°5N 7°15W 138 D3
Mont-roig del Camp Spain 41°5N 0°58E 90 D5
Mont-St-Michel, Le
  France 48°40N 1°30W 70 D5
Mont Sangbé △ Ivory C. 8°0N 7°10W 138 D3
Mont-Tremblant △
  Canada 46°30N 74°30W 164 C5
Montabaur Germany 50°25N 7°50E 76 E3
Montagnac France 43°29N 3°28E 72 E7
Montagnana Italy 45°14N 11°28E 93 C8
Montagne de Reims △
  France 49°8N 4°0E 71 C11
Montagu S. Africa 33°45S 20°8E 144 D3
Montagu I. Antarctica 58°25S 26°20W 55 B1
Montague Canada 46°10N 62°39W 165 C7
Montague, I. Mexico 31°45N 114°48W 180 A2
Montague I. Australia 36°16S 150°13E 153 D9
Montague I. U.S.A. 60°0N 147°30W 166 D10
Montague Ra.
  Australia 27°15S 119°30E 149 E2
Montague Sd.
  Australia 14°28S 125°20E 148 B4
Montalbán Spain 40°50N 0°45W 90 E4
Montalbo Spain 39°53N 2°42W 90 F2
Montalcino Italy 43°3N 11°29E 93 E8
Montalegre Portugal 41°49N 7°47W 88 D3
Montalto Italy 38°10N 15°55E 95 D8
Montalto di Castro Italy 42°21N 11°37E 93 F8
Montalto Uffugo Italy 39°24N 16°9E 95 C9
Montamarta Spain 41°39N 5°49W 88 D5
Montana Bulgaria 43°27N 23°16E 96 C7
Montaña Peru 6°0S 73°0W 188 B3
Montana □ Bulgaria 43°30N 23°10E 96 C7
Montana □ U.S.A. 47°0N 110°0W 168 C9
Montaña Clara, I.
  Canary Is. 29°17N 13°33W 100 E6
Montañas de Malaga △
  Spain 36°48N 4°32W 89 J6
Montánchez Spain 39°15N 6°8W 89 F4
Montargil Portugal 39°5N 8°10W 89 F2
Montargis France 47°59N 2°43E 71 E9
Montauban France 44°2N 1°21E 72 D5
Montauk U.S.A. 41°3N 71°57W 175 E13
Montauk Pt. U.S.A. 41°4N 71°51W 175 E13
Montbard France 47°38N 4°20E 71 E11
Montbarrey France 47°1N 5°39E 71 E12
Montbéliard France 47°31N 6°48E 71 E13
Montblanc Spain 41°23N 1°4E 90 D6
Montbrison France 45°36N 4°3E 73 C8
Montcalm, Pic de France 42°40N 1°25E 72 F5
Montceau-les-Mines
  France 46°40N 4°23E 71 F11
Montcenis France 46°47N 4°23E 73 B8
Montchanin France 46°45N 4°28E 73 B8
Montclair U.S.A. 40°49N 74°12W 175 F10
Montcornet France 49°40N 4°1E 71 C11
Montcuq France 44°21N 1°13E 72 D5
Montdidier France 49°38N 2°35E 71 C9
Monte Albán Mexico 17°2N 96°46W 181 D5
Monte Alegre Brazil 2°0S 54°0W 187 D8
Monte Alegre de Goiás
  Brazil 13°14S 47°10W 189 C1
Monte Alegre do Piauí
  Brazil 9°46S 45°18W 189 B1
Monte Azul Brazil 15°9S 42°53W 189 D2
Monte-Carlo Monaco 43°44N 7°25E 73 E11
Monte Carmelo Brazil 18°43S 47°29W 189 D1
Monte Caseros
  Argentina 30°10S 57°50W 190 C4
Monte Cristi Dom. Rep. 19°52N 71°39W 183 C5
Monte Cucco △ Italy 43°22N 12°43E 93 E9
Monte Dinero
  Argentina 52°18S 68°33W 192 D3
Monte León Argentina 50°15S 69°0W 192 D3
Monte Lindo →
  Paraguay 23°56S 57°12W 190 A4
Monte Pascoal △
  Brazil 16°51S 39°21W 189 D3
Monte Patria Chile 30°42S 70°58W 190 C1
Monte Quemado
  Argentina 25°53S 62°41W 190 B3
Monte Redondo Portugal 39°53N 8°50W 88 F2

Monte Rio U.S.A. 38°28N 123°0W 170 G4
Monte San Giovanni Campano
  Italy 41°38N 13°31E 94 A6
Monte San Savino Italy 43°20N 11°43E 93 E8
Monte Sant' Ángelo
  Italy 41°42N 15°59E 93 G12
Monte Santu, C. di Italy 40°5N 9°44E 94 B2
Monte Subasio △ Italy 43°5N 12°40E 93 E9
Monte Vista U.S.A. 37°35N 106°9W 169 H10
Monteagudo Argentina 27°14S 54°8W 191 B5
Montealegre del Castillo
  Spain 38°48N 1°17W 91 G3
Montebello Canada 45°40N 74°55W 164 C5
Montebello Iónico Italy 37°59N 15°45E 95 B5
Montebello Is.
  Australia 20°30S 115°45E 148 D2
Montebelluna Italy 45°47N 12°3E 93 C9
Montebourg France 49°30N 1°20W 70 C5
Montecarlo Argentina 26°34S 54°47W 191 B5
Montecastrilli Italy 42°39N 12°29E 93 F9
Montecatini Terme Italy 43°53N 10°46E 92 E7
Montecito U.S.A. 34°26N 119°40W 171 L7
Montecristo Italy 42°20N 10°19E 92 F7
Montefalco Italy 42°54N 12°39E 93 F9
Montefiascone Italy 42°32N 12°2E 93 F9
Montefrío Spain 37°20N 4°0W 89 H7
Montegiórgio Italy 43°6N 13°33E 93 E10
Montego Bay Jamaica 18°28N 77°55W 182 a
Montehermoso Spain 40°5N 6°21W 88 E4
Monteiro Brazil 7°48S 37°9W 189 B3
Montejícar Spain 37°33N 3°30W 89 H7
Montélimar France 44°33N 4°45E 73 D8
Montella Italy 40°51N 15°1E 95 B8
Montellano Spain 36°59N 5°39W 89 J5
Montello U.S.A. 43°48N 89°20W 172 D9
Montemayor, Meseta de
  Argentina 44°20S 66°10W 192 B3
Montemor-o-Novo
  Portugal 38°40N 8°12W 89 G2
Montemor-o-Velho
  Portugal 40°11N 8°40W 88 E2
Montemorelos Mexico 25°12N 99°49W 181 B5
Montendre France 45°16N 0°26W 72 C3
Montenegro Brazil 29°39S 51°29W 191 B5
Montenegro ■ Europe 42°40N 19°20E 96 C3
Montenero di Bisáccia
  Italy 41°57N 14°47E 93 G11
Montepuez Mozam. 13°8S 38°59E 143 E4
Montepuez → Mozam. 12°32S 40°27E 143 E5
Montepulciano Italy 43°5N 11°47E 93 E8
Montereale Italy 42°31N 13°15E 93 F10
Montereau-Faut-Yonne
  France 48°22N 2°57E 71 D9
Monterey U.S.A. 36°37N 121°55W 170 J5
Monterey B. U.S.A. 36°45N 122°0W 170 J5
Montería Colombia 8°46N 75°53W 186 B3
Monteros Argentina 27°11S 65°30W 190 B2
Monterotondo Italy 42°3N 12°37E 93 F9
Monterrey Mexico 25°40N 100°19W 180 B4
Montes Altos Brazil 5°50S 47°4W 189 B1
Montes Azules △
  Mexico 16°21N 91°3W 181 D6
Montes Claros Brazil 16°30S 43°50W 189 D2
Montesano U.S.A. 46°59N 123°36W 170 D3
Montesano sulla Marcellana
  Italy 40°16N 15°42E 95 B8
Montesárchio Italy 41°4N 14°38E 95 A7
Montescaglioso Italy 40°33N 16°40E 95 B9
Montesilvano Italy 42°30N 14°8E 93 F11
Montesíones △ Portugal 41°54N 6°52W 88 D4
Montevarchi Italy 43°31N 11°34E 93 E8
Montevideo Uruguay 34°50S 56°11W 191 C4
Montevideo U.S.A. 44°57N 95°43W 172 C6
Montezuma Iowa,
  U.S.A. 41°35N 92°32W 172 E7
Montezuma Castle △
  U.S.A. 34°39N 111°45W 169 J8
Montfaucon France 47°6N 1°7W 70 E5
Montfaucon-d'Argonne
  France 49°16N 5°8E 71 C12
Montfaucon-en-Velay
  France 45°11N 4°20E 73 C8
Montfort-le-Gesnois
  France 48°3N 0°25E 70 D7
Montfort-sur-Meu France 48°9N 1°58W 70 D5
Montgenèvre France 44°56N 6°43E 73 D10
Montgó △ Spain 38°48N 0°7W 91 G5
Montgomery U.K. 52°34N 3°8W 67 E4
Montgomery Ala.,
  U.S.A. 32°23N 86°19W 178 C3
Montgomery Pa.,
  U.S.A. 41°10N 76°53W 174 E4
Montgomery W. Va.,
  U.S.A. 38°11N 81°19W 173 F13
Montgomery City
  U.S.A. 38°59N 91°30W 172 F8
Montguyon France 45°12N 0°12E 72 C3
Monthermé France 49°53N 4°42E 71 C11
Monthey Switz. 46°15N 6°56E 77 J2
Monthois France 49°19N 4°43E 71 C11
Monti Italy 40°49N 9°19E 94 B2
Monti Lucrétili △ Italy 42°5N 12°52E 93 F9
Monti Picentini △ Italy 40°45N 15°0E 95 B8
Monti Sibillini △ Italy 42°55N 13°12E 93 F10
Monti Simbruini △
  Italy 41°55N 13°13E 93 G10
Monticelli d'Ongina Italy 45°5N 9°56E 92 C6
Monticello Ark., U.S.A. 33°38N 91°47W 176 E8
Monticello Fla., U.S.A. 30°33N 83°52W 178 F6
Monticello Ind.,
  U.S.A. 40°45N 86°46W 172 E9
Monticello Iowa,
  U.S.A. 42°15N 91°12W 172 D8
Monticello Ky., U.S.A. 36°50N 84°51W 173 G11
Monticello Minn.,
  U.S.A. 45°18N 93°48W 172 C7
Monticello Miss.,
  U.S.A. 31°33N 90°7W 177 F9
Monticello N.Y.,
  U.S.A. 41°39N 74°42W 175 E10
Monticello Utah,
  U.S.A. 37°52N 109°21W 169 H9
Montichiari Italy 45°25N 10°23E 92 C7
Montier-en-Der France 48°30N 4°45E 71 D11
Montignac France 45°4N 1°10E 72 D5
Montigny-les-Metz
  France 49°0N 6°10E 71 C13
Montigny-sur-Aube
  France 47°57N 4°45E 71 E11
Montijo Portugal 38°41N 8°54W 89 G2

Montijo Spain 38°52N 6°39W 89 G4
Montilla Spain 37°36N 4°40W 89 H6
Montivilliers France 49°33N 0°12E 70 C7
Montluçon France 46°22N 2°36E 71 F9
Montmagny Canada 46°58N 70°34W 165 C5
Montmarault France 46°19N 2°57E 71 F9
Montmartre Canada 50°14N 103°27W 163 C8
Montmédy France 49°30N 5°20E 71 C12
Montmélian France 45°30N 6°4E 73 C10
Montmirail France 48°52N 3°30E 71 D10
Montmorency Canada 46°53N 71°11W 165 C5
Montmoreau-St-Cybard
  France 45°23N 0°8E 72 C4
Montmorillon France 46°26N 0°50E 72 B4
Montmort-Lucy France 48°55N 3°49E 71 D10
Monto Australia 24°52S 151°6E 150 C5
Montoire-sur-le-Loir
  France 47°45N 0°52E 70 E7
Montongbuwoh
  Indonesia 8°33S 116°4E 119 K19
Montório al Vomano
  Italy 42°35N 13°38E 93 F10
Montoro Spain 38°1N 4°27W 89 G6
Montour Falls U.S.A. 42°21N 76°51W 174 D8
Montoursville U.S.A. 41°15N 76°55W 174 E8
Montpelier Idaho,
  U.S.A. 42°19N 111°18W 168 E8
Montpelier Vt., U.S.A. 44°16N 72°35W 175 B12
Montpellier France 43°37N 3°52E 72 E7
Montpezat-de-Quercy
  France 44°15N 1°30E 72 D5
Montpon-Ménestérol
  France 45°0N 0°11E 72 D4
Montréal Canada 45°30N 73°33W 175 A11
Montréal Aude, France 43°13N 2°8E 72 E6
Montréal Gers, France 43°57N 0°11E 72 E4
Montréal → Canada 47°14N 84°39W 164 C3
Montréal L. Canada 54°20N 105°45W 163 C7
Montreal Lake Canada 54°3N 105°46W 163 C7
Montredon-Labessonnié
  France 43°45N 2°18E 72 E6
Montréjeau France 43°6N 0°35E 72 E4
Montrésor France 47°10N 1°10E 70 E8
Montret France 46°40N 5°7E 71 F12
Montreuil Pas-de-Calais,
  France 50°27N 1°45E 71 B8
Montreuil Seine-St-Denis,
  France 48°51N 2°27E 71 D9
Montreuil-Bellay France 47°8N 0°9W 70 E6
Montreux Switz. 46°26N 6°55E 77 J2
Montrevel-en-Bresse
  France 46°21N 5°8E 71 F12
Montrichard France 47°20N 1°10E 70 E8
Montrose U.K. 56°44N 2°27W 65 E6
Montrose Colo.,
  U.S.A. 38°29N 107°53W 168 G10
Montrose Pa., U.S.A. 41°50N 75°53W 175 E9
Monts, Pte. des Canada 49°20N 67°12W 165 C6
Montsalvy France 44°41N 2°30E 72 D6
Montsant, Serra de Spain 41°17N 1°0E 90 D6
Montsauche-les-Settons
  France 47°13N 4°2E 71 E11
Montsec, Serra del Spain 42°5N 0°45E 90 C5
Montseny △ Spain 41°43N 2°22W 90 D2
Montserrat Spain 41°36N 1°49E 90 D6
Montserrat ☑
  W. Indies 16°40N 62°10W 183 C7
Montuenga Spain 41°3N 4°38W 88 D6
Montuiri Spain 39°34N 2°59E 100 B10
Monywa Burma 22°7N 95°11E 123 H19
Monza Italy 45°35N 9°16E 92 C6
Monze Zambia 16°17S 27°29E 143 F2
Monze, C. Pakistan 24°47N 66°37E 124 G2
Monzón Spain 41°52N 0°10E 90 D5
Mooers U.S.A. 44°58N 73°35W 175 B11
Mooi → S. Africa 28°45S 30°34E 145 C5
Mooi River S. Africa 29°13S 29°50E 145 C4
Mookgopong S. Africa 24°31S 28°44E 145 B4
Moomba Australia 28°6S 140°12E 151 A3
Moonah → Australia 22°3S 138°33E 150 C2
Moonda, L. Australia 25°52S 140°25E 151 D3
Moonie Australia 27°46S 150°19E 151 D5
Moonie → Australia 29°19S 148°43E 151 D4
Moora Australia 30°37S 115°58E 149 F2
Moorcroft U.S.A. 44°16N 104°57W 168 D11
Moore, L. Australia 29°50S 117°35E 149 E2
Moore Falls Canada 44°48N 78°48W 174 B6
Moore Haven U.S.A. 26°50N 81°5W 179 J8
Moore Park Canada 24°43S 152°17E 150 C5
Moore Res. U.S.A. 44°20N 71°53W 175 B13
Moore River △
  Australia 31°7S 115°39E 149 F2
Moorefield U.S.A. 39°4N 78°58W 173 F14
Moorfoot Hills U.K. 55°44N 3°8W 65 F5
Moorhead U.S.A. 46°53N 96°45W 172 B5
Moormerland Germany 53°20N 7°20E 76 B3
Moornanyah L.
  Australia 33°15S 143°42E 152 B5
Mooroopna Australia 36°25S 145°22E 153 D6
Moorpark U.S.A. 34°17N 118°53W 171 L8
Moorreesburg S. Africa 33°6S 18°38E 144 D2
Moorrinya △ Australia 21°42S 144°58E 150 C3
Moosburg Germany 48°28N 11°56E 77 G7
Moose → Canada 51°20N 80°25W 164 B3
Moose Creek Canada 45°15N 74°58W 175 A10
Moose Factory Canada 51°16N 80°32W 164 B3
Moose Jaw Canada 50°24N 105°30W 163 C7
Moose Jaw → Canada 50°34N 105°18W 163 C7
Moose Lake Canada 53°43N 100°20W 163 C8
Moose Lake U.S.A. 46°27N 92°46W 172 B7
Moose Mountain
  Canada 49°48N 102°25W 163 D8
Moosehead L. U.S.A. 45°38N 69°40W 175 B14
Mooselookmeguntic L.
  U.S.A. 44°55N 70°49W 175 B14
Moosilauke, Mt.
  U.S.A. 44°3N 71°40W 175 B13
Moosomin Canada 50°9N 101°40W 163 C8
Moosonee Canada 51°17N 80°39W 164 B3
Mootwingee △
  Australia 31°1S 142°25E 152 A5
Mopane S. Africa 22°37S 29°52E 145 B4
Mopeia Velha Mozam. 17°30S 35°40E 143 F4
Mopipi Botswana 21°6S 24°55E 144 B3
Mopoi C.A.R. 5°6N 26°54E 142 A2
Mopti □ Mali 14°40N 4°0W 138 C4
Moquegua Peru 17°15S 70°46W 188 D3

Moquegua □ *Peru* 16°50S 70°55W **188** D3
Mór *Hungary* 47°25N 18°12E **80** C3
Mora *Cameroon* 11°2N 14°7E **139** C7
Mora *Portugal* 38°55N 8°10W **89** G2
Mora *Sweden* 61°2N 14°38E **62** C8
Mora *Minn., U.S.A.* 45°53N 93°18W **172** C7
Mora *N. Mex., U.S.A.* 35°58N 105°20W **169** J11
Móra de Rubielos *Spain* 40°15N 0°45W **90** E4
Móra d'Ebre *Spain* 41°6N 0°38E **90** D5
Móra la Nova *Spain* 41°7N 0°39E **90** D5
Morača → *Montenegro* 42°20N 19°9E **96** D3
Morada Nova *Brazil* 5°7S 38°23W **189** B3
Morada Nova de Minas
  Brazil 18°37S 45°22W **189** D1
Moradabad *India* 28°50N 78°50E **125** E8
Morafenobe *Madag.* 17°50S 44°53E **141** H8
Morag *Poland* 53°55N 19°56E **82** E6
Moral de Calatrava
  Spain 38°51N 3°33W **89** G7
Moraleda, Canal *Chile* 44°30S 73°30W **192** D2
Moraleja *Spain* 40°6N 6°43W **88** E4
Moramanga *Madag.* 18°56S 48°12E **141** H9
Moran *Kans., U.S.A.* 37°55N 95°10W **172** G6
Moran *Wyo., U.S.A.* 43°50N 110°31W **168** E8
Moranbah *Australia* 22°1S 148°6E **150** C4
Morang = Biratnagar
  Nepal 26°27N 87°17E **125** F12
Morano Cálabro *Italy* 39°50N 16°8E **95** C9
Morant Bay *Jamaica* 17°53N 76°25W **182** a
Morant Cays *Jamaica* 17°22N 76°0W **182** C4
Morant Pt. *Jamaica* 17°55N 76°12W **182** a
Morar *India* 26°14N 78°14E **124** F8
Morar, L. *U.K.* 56°57N 5°40W **65** E3
Moratalla *Spain* 38°14N 1°49W **91** G3
Moratuwa *Sri Lanka* 6°45N 79°55E **127** L4
Morava → *Slovak Rep.* 48°10N 16°59E **79** C9
Morava → *U.S.A.* 42°43N 76°25W **175** D8
Moravian Hts. = Českomoravská
  Vrchovina *Czech Rep.* 49°30N 15°40E **78** B8
Moravica → *Serbia* 43°52N 20°8E **96** C4
Moravița *Romania* 45°17N 21°14E **80** E6
Moravská Třebová
  Czech Rep. 49°45N 16°40E **79** B9
Moravské Budějovice
  Czech Rep. 49°4N 15°49E **78** B8
Morawa *Australia* 29°13S 116°0E **149** E2
Morawhanna *Guyana* 8°30N 59°40W **186** B7
Moray □ *U.K.* 57°31N 3°18W **65** D5
Moray Firth *U.K.* 57°40N 3°52W **65** D5
Morbach *Germany* 49°48N 7°6E **77** F3
Morbegno *Italy* 46°8N 9°34E **92** B6
Morbi *India* 22°50N 70°42E **124** H4
Mörbisch am See *Austria* 47°45N 16°34E **80** C2
Mörbylånga *Sweden* 56°32N 16°22E **63** H10
Morcenx *France* 44°3N 0°55W **72** D3
Morcone *Italy* 41°20N 14°40E **95** A7
Mordelles *France* 48°5N 1°52W **70** D5
Morden *Canada* 49°15N 98°10W **163** D9
Mordoğan *Turkey* 38°30N 26°37E **99** C8
Mordovian Republic =
  Mordvinia □ *Russia* 54°20N 44°30E **86** C7
Mordovo *Russia* 52°6N 40°50E **86** D5
Mordvinia □ *Russia* 54°20N 44°30E **86** C7
Mordy *Poland* 52°13N 22°31E **83** F9
Moreau → *U.S.A.* 45°18N 100°43W **172** C3
Morebeng *S. Africa* 23°30S 29°55E **145** B4
Morecambe *U.K.* 54°5N 2°52W **66** C5
Morecambe B. *U.K.* 54°7N 3°0W **66** C5
Moree *Australia* 29°28S 149°54E **151** D4
Morehead *Australia* 8°11N 83°26W **173** F12
Morehead City *U.S.A.* 34°43N 76°43W **177** D16
Morel → *India* 26°13N 76°36E **124** F7
Moreland *U.S.A.* 33°17N 84°46W **178** B5
Morelia *Mexico* 19°42N 101°7W **180** D4
Morella *Australia* 23°0S 143°52E **150** C3
Morella *Spain* 40°35N 0°5W **90** E4
Morelos *Mexico* 26°42N 107°40W **180** B3
Morelos □ *Mexico* 18°45N 99°0W **181** D5
Morena □ *Botswana* 19°18S 23°10E **144** A3
Morena *India* 26°30N 78°4E **124** F8
Morena, Sierra *Spain* 38°20N 4°0W **89** G6
Moreni *Romania* 44°59N 25°36E **81** F10
Moreno Bolivia 11°9S 66°15W **188** C4
Moreno Valley
  U.S.A. 33°56N 117°14W **171** M10
Moresby I. *Canada* 52°30N 131°40W **162** C2
Morestel *France* 45°40N 5°28E **73** C9
Moret *Australia* 27°10S 153°25E **151** D5
Moreton I. *Australia* 27°10S 153°25E **151** D5
Moreton Island △
  Australia 27°2S 153°24E **151** D5
Moreuil *France* 49°46N 2°30E **71** C9
Morez *France* 46°31N 6°2E **71** F13
Morgan *Australia* 34°2S 139°35E **152** C3
Morgan *Ga., U.S.A.* 31°32N 84°36W **178** D5
Morgan *Utah, U.S.A.* 41°2N 111°41W **168** F8
Morgan City *U.S.A.* 29°42N 91°12W **176** G9
Morgan Hill *U.S.A.* 37°8N 121°39W **170** H5
Morganfield *U.S.A.* 37°41N 87°55W **172** G10
Morganton *U.S.A.* 35°45N 81°41W **177** D14
Morgantown *U.S.A.* 39°38N 79°57W **173** F14
Morgenzon *S. Africa* 26°45S 29°36E **145** C4
Morges *Switz.* 46°31N 6°29E **77** J2
Morghak *Iran* 29°7N 57°54E **129** D8
Morgongâva *Sweden* 59°56N 16°58E **62** E10
Morhange *France* 48°55N 6°38E **71** D13
Mori → *India* 25°29N 85°11E **125** G11
Mori *China* 43°49N 90°11E **109** D12
Mori *Japan* 42°6N 140°35E **112** C10
Moriarty *U.S.A.* 34°59N 106°3W **169** J10
Moribaya *Guinea* 9°53N 9°33W **138** D3
Morice L. *Canada* 53°50N 127°40W **162** C3
Moriki *Nigeria* 12°52N 6°30E **139** C6
Morinville *Canada* 53°49N 113°41W **162** C6
Morioka *Japan* 39°45N 141°8E **112** E10
Morisset *Australia* 33°6S 151°30E **153** B9
Moriyama *Japan* 35°6N 136°58E **113** G8
Morjim *India* 15°37N 73°44E **127** G1
Morlaix *France* 48°36N 3°52W **70** D3
Mörlunda *Sweden* 57°19N 15°52E **63** G9
Mormanno *Italy* 39°54N 15°59E **95** C8
Mormant *France* 48°37N 2°52E **71** D9
Mormugao = Marmagao
  India 15°25N 73°56E **127** G1
Mornington *Australia* 38°15N 145°5E **153** C6
Mornington, I. *Chile* 49°50S 75°30W **192** C1
Mornington I.
  Australia 16°30S 139°30E **150** B2
Moro *Pakistan* 26°40N 68°0E **124** F2
Moro → *Pakistan* 29°42N 67°22E **124** E2
Moro G. *Phil.* 6°30N 123°0E **119** C6
Morocco ■ *N. Afr.* 32°0N 5°50W **134** B4
Morococha *Peru* 11°40S 76°5W **188** C2
Morogoro *Tanzania* 6°50S 37°40E **142** D4
Morogoro □ *Tanzania* 8°0S 37°0E **142** D4
Moroleón *Mexico* 20°8N 101°12W **180** C4
Morombe *Madag.* 21°45S 43°22E **141** J8
Moron *Argentina* 34°39S 58°37W **190** C4
Morón *Cuba* 22°8N 78°39W **182** B4
Mörön *Mongolia* 49°38N 100°9E **110** B9
Morón de Almazán
  Spain 41°29N 2°27W **90** D2
Morón de la Frontera
  Spain 37°6N 5°28W **89** H5
Morona → *Peru* 4°40S 77°10W **186** D2
Morondava *Madag.* 20°17S 44°17E **141** J8
Morondo *Ivory C.* 8°57N 6°47W **138** D3
Morongo Valley
  U.S.A. 34°3N 116°37W **171** L10
Moroni *Comoros Is.* 11°40S 43°16E **141** a
Moroni *U.S.A.* 39°32N 111°35W **168** G8
Moronou *Ivory C.* 6°16N 4°59W **138** D4
Morotai *Indonesia* 2°10N 128°30E **119** D7
Moroto *Uganda* 2°28N 34°42E **142** B3
Moroto, Mt. *Uganda* 2°30N 34°43E **142** B3
Morozov *Bulgaria* 42°30N 25°10E **97** D9
Morozovsk *Russia* 48°25N 41°50E **87** F5
Morpeth *Canada* 42°23N 81°50W **174** D3
Morpeth *U.K.* 55°10N 1°41W **66** B6
Morphou *Cyprus* 35°12N 32°59E **101** D11
Morphou Bay *Cyprus* 35°15N 32°50E **101** D11
Morrilton *U.S.A.* 35°9N 92°44W **176** D8
Morrinhos *Ceará, Brazil* 3°14S 40°7W **189** A2
Morrinhos *Minas Gerais,*
  Brazil 17°45S 49°10W **189** C1
Morrinsville *N.Z.* 37°40S 175°32E **154** D4
Morris *Canada* 49°25N 97°22W **163** D9
Morris *Ill., U.S.A.* 41°22N 88°26W **172** E9
Morris *Minn., U.S.A.* 45°35N 95°55W **172** C6
Morris *N.Y., U.S.A.* 42°33N 75°15W **175** D9
Morris *Pa., U.S.A.* 41°35N 77°17W **174** E7
Morris, Mt. *Australia* 26°9S 131°4E **149** E5
Morris Jesup, Kap
  Greenland 83°40N 34°0W **57** A7
Morrisburg *Canada* 44°55N 75°7W **175** B9
Morristown *Ariz.,*
  U.S.A. 33°51N 112°37W **169** K7
Morristown *N.J.,*
  U.S.A. 40°48N 74°29W **175** F10
Morristown *N.Y.,*
  U.S.A. 44°35N 75°39W **175** B9
Morristown *Tenn.,*
  U.S.A. 36°13N 83°18W **177** C13
Morrisville *N.Y.,*
  U.S.A. 42°54N 75°35W **175** D9
Morrisville *Pa., U.S.A.* 40°13N 74°47W **175** F10
Morrisville *Vt., U.S.A.* 44°34N 72°36W **175** B12
Morro, Pta. *Chile* 27°6S 71°0W **190** B1
Morro Bay *U.S.A.* 35°22N 120°51W **170** K6
Morro Chico *Chile* 52°2S 71°26W **192** D2
Morro del Jable
  Canary Is. 28°3N 14°23W **100** F5
Morro do Chapéu *Brazil* 11°33S 41°9W **189** C2
Morro Jable, Pta. de
  Canary Is. 28°2N 14°20W **100** F5
Morrocoy △ *Venezuela* 10°48N 68°13W **183** D6
Morros *Brazil* 2°52S 44°3W **189** A2
Morrosquillo, G. de
  Colombia 9°35N 75°40W **182** E4
Mörrum *Sweden* 56°12N 14°45E **63** H8
Morrumbene *Mozam.* 23°31S 35°16E **145** B6
Mörrumsån → *Sweden* 56°10N 14°45E **63** H2
Mors *Denmark* 56°50N 8°45E **63** H2
Morshansk *Russia* 53°28N 41°50E **86** D5
Morsi *India* 21°21N 78°0E **126** D4
Mörsil *Sweden* 63°19N 13°40E **62** A7
Mortagne → *France* 48°33N 6°27E **71** D13
Mortagne-au-Perche
  France 48°31N 0°33E **70** D7
Mortagne-sur-Gironde
  France 45°28N 0°47W **72** C3
Mortagne-sur-Sèvre
  France 47°0N 0°59W **70** F6
Mortain *France* 48°40N 0°57W **70** D6
Mortara *Italy* 45°15N 8°44E **92** C5
Morteau *France* 47°3N 6°35E **71** E13
Morteros *Argentina* 30°50S 62°0W **190** C3
Mortlach *Canada* 50°27N 106°4W **163** C7
Mortlake *Australia* 38°5S 142°50E **152** C6
Morton *Tex., U.S.A.* 33°44N 102°46W **176** E3
Morton *Wash., U.S.A.* 46°34N 122°17W **170** D4
Morton □ *Australia* 35°0S 150°12E **153** C9
Moruga *Trin. & Tob.* 10°4N 61°16W **187** K15
Morundah *Australia* 34°57S 146°19E **153** C7
Moruya *Australia* 35°58S 150°3E **153** C9
Morvan □ *France* 47°5N 4°3E **71** E11
Morvan △ *France* 47°12N 4°0E **71** E11
Morven *Australia* 26°22S 147°5E **151** D4
Morven *N.Z.* 44°50S 171°6E **155** E6
Morven *U.K.* 30°57N 83°30W **178** E6
Morvern *U.K.* 56°38N 5°44W **65** E3
Morwell *Australia* 38°10S 146°22E **153** C7
Morwell △ *Australia* 38°14S 146°23E **153** C7
Moryń *Poland* 52°51N 14°22E **83** F1
Morzine *France* 46°11N 6°42E **71** F13
Mosakahiken = Moose Lake
  Canada 53°46N 100°8W **163** C8
Mosalsk *Russia* 54°30N 34°55E **84** E8
Mosbach *Germany* 49°21N 9°9E **77** F5
Mošćenice *Croatia* 45°17N 14°16E **93** C11
Mosciano Sant' Ângelo
  Italy 42°42N 13°52E **93** F10
Moscos Is. *Burma* 14°0N 97°30E **120** F1
Moscow = Moskva
  Russia 55°45N 37°37E **84** E9
Moscow *Idaho, U.S.A.* 46°44N 117°0W **168** D7
Moscow *Pa., U.S.A.* 41°20N 75°31W **175** E9
Mosel → *Europe* 50°22N 7°36E **71** B14
Mosel = Mosel → *Europe* 50°22N 7°36E **71** B14
Moselle = Mosel → *Europe* 50°22N 7°36E **71** B14
Moselle → *Europe* 50°22N 7°36E **71** B14
Moses Lake *U.S.A.* 47°8N 119°17W **168** C4
Mosgiel *N.Z.* 45°53S 170°21E **155** F5
Moshaweng → *S. Africa* 26°35S 22°50E **144** C3
Moshchnyy, Ostrov
  Russia 60°1N 27°50E **84** B4
Moshi *Tanzania* 3°22S 37°18E **142** C4
Moshi → *Nigeria* 9°18N 4°38E **139** D5

Moshupa *Botswana* 24°46S 25°29E **144** B4
Mosi-oa-Tunya = Victoria Falls
  Zimbabwe 17°58S 25°52E **143** F2
Mosina *Poland* 52°15N 16°50E **83** F3
Mosjøen *Norway* 65°51N 13°12E **60** D15
Moskenesøya *Norway* 67°58N 13°0E **60** C15
Moskenstraumen
  Norway 67°47N 12°45E **60** C15
Moskva *Russia* 55°45N 37°37E **84** E9
Moskva □ *Russia* 56°20N 37°20E **84** E9
Moskva → *Russia* 55°5N 38°51E **84** E10
Moslavačka Gora
  Croatia 45°40N 16°37E **93** C13
Mosomane *Botswana* 24°2S 26°19E **144** B4
Mosonmagyaróvár
  Hungary 47°52N 17°18E **80** C2
Mošorin *Serbia* 45°19N 20°4E **80** E5
Mospyne *Ukraine* 47°52N 38°0E **85** J9
Mosquera *Colombia* 2°35N 78°24W **186** C3
Mosquero *U.S.A.* 35°47N 103°58W **169** J12
Mosqueruela *Spain* 40°21N 0°27W **90** E4
Mosquitia *Honduras* 15°20N 84°10W **182** C3
Mosquito Creek L.
  U.S.A. 41°18N 80°46W **174** E4
Mosquito L. *Canada* 62°35N 103°20W **163** A8
Mosquitos, G. de los
  Panama 9°15N 81°10W **182** E3
Moss *Norway* 59°27N 10°40E **61** G14
Moss Vale *Australia* 34°32S 150°25E **153** C9
Mossaka *Congo* 1°15S 16°45E **140** E3
Mossbank *Canada* 49°56N 105°56W **163** D7
Mossburn *N.Z.* 45°41S 168°15E **155** F3
Mosselbaai *S. Africa* 34°11S 22°8E **144** D3
Mossendjo *Congo* 2°55S 12°42E **140** E2
Mossgiel *Australia* 33°15S 144°5E **152** B6
Mossingen *Germany* 48°24N 9°4E **77** G5
Mossman *Australia* 16°21S 145°15E **150** B4
Mossoró *Brazil* 5°10S 37°15W **189** B3
Mossuril *Mozam.* 14°58S 40°42E **143** E5
Mossy Head *U.S.A.* 30°45N 86°19W **179** E3
Mossy Point *Australia* 35°50S 150°11E **153** C9
Most *Czech Rep.* 50°31N 13°38E **78** A6
Mosta *Malta* 35°55N 14°26E **101** D1
Mostaganem *Algeria* 35°54N 0°5E **136** A4
Mostaganem □ *Algeria* 35°40N 0°15E **136** A4
Mostar *Bos.-H.* 43°22N 17°50E **80** G2
Mostardas *Brazil* 31°2S 50°51W **191** C5
Mostiska = Mostyska
  Ukraine 49°48N 23°4E **83** J10
Móstoles *Spain* 40°19N 3°53W **88** E7
Mosty = Masty *Belarus* 53°27N 24°38E **75** B13
Mostyska *Ukraine* 49°48N 23°4E **83** J10
Mosul = Al Mawşil
  Iraq 36°15N 43°5E **105** D10
Mota del Cuervo *Spain* 39°30N 2°52W **91** F2
Mota del Marqués *Spain* 41°38N 5°11W **88** D5
Motagua → *Guatemala* 15°44N 88°14W **182** C2
Motala *Sweden* 58°32N 15°1E **63** F9
Motaze *Mozam.* 24°48S 32°52E **145** B5
Moțca *Romania* 47°15N 26°37E **81** C11
Moth *India* 25°43N 78°57E **125** G8
Motherwell *U.K.* 55°47N 3°58W **66** F5
Motihari *India* 26°30N 84°55E **125** F11
Motilla del Palancar
  Spain 39°34N 1°55W **91** F3
Motiti I. *N.Z.* 37°38S 176°25E **154** D5
Motnik *Slovenia* 46°14N 14°54E **93** B11
Motovun *Croatia* 45°20N 13°50E **93** C10
Motozintla de Mendoza
  Mexico 15°22N 92°14W **181** D6
Motril *Spain* 36°31N 3°37W **89** J7
Motru *Romania* 44°48N 22°59E **80** F7
Motru → *Romania* 44°32N 23°31E **81** F8
Mott *U.S.A.* 46°23N 102°20W **172** B2
Móttola *Italy* 40°38N 17°2E **95** B10
Motu → *N.Z.* 37°52S 177°36E **154** D6
Motueka *N.Z.* 41°7S 173°1E **155** B8
Motueka → *N.Z.* 41°5S 173°1E **155** B8
Motul *Mexico* 21°6N 89°17W **181** C7
Mouchalagane →
  Canada 50°56N 68°41W **165** B6
Mouding *China* 25°20N 101°28E **116** E3
Moudjeria *Mauritania* 17°50N 12°28W **138** B2
Moudon *Switz.* 46°40N 6°49E **77** J2
Moudros *Greece* 39°50N 25°18E **99** B7
Mougins *France* 43°36N 7°0E **73** E10
Mouhoun = Black Volta →
  Africa 8°41N 1°33W **138** D4
Mouila *Gabon* 1°50S 11°0E **140** E2
Moulamein *Australia* 35°3S 144°1E **152** C6
Moule à Chique, C.
  St. Lucia 13°43N 60°57W **183** f
Mouliana *Greece* 35°10N 25°59E **101** D7
Moulins *France* 46°35N 3°19E **71** F10
Moulmein *Burma* 16°30N 97°40E **123** L20
Moulouya, O. →
  Morocco 35°5N 2°25W **136** A3
Moultrie *U.S.A.* 31°11N 83°47W **178** D6
Moultrie, L. *U.S.A.* 33°20N 80°5W **178** B9
Mound City *Mo., U.S.A.* 40°7N 95°14W **172** E6
Mound City *S. Dak.,*
  U.S.A. 45°44N 100°4W **172** C3
Moundou *Chad* 8°40N 16°10E **135** G9
Moundsville *U.S.A.* 39°55N 80°44W **174** F4
Moung *Cambodia* 12°46N 103°27E **120** F4
Mount Airy *U.S.A.* 36°31N 80°37W **177** C14
Mount Albert *Canada* 44°8N 79°19W **174** B5
Mount Aspiring △
  N.Z. 44°19S 168°47E **155** E3
Mount Barker *S. Austral.,*
  Australia 35°5S 138°52E **152** C3
Mount Barker *W. Austral.,*
  Australia 34°38S 117°40E **149** F2
Mount Barnett Roadhouse
  Australia 16°39S 125°57E **148** C4
Mount Beauty
  Australia 36°47S 147°10E **153** D7
Mount Brydges *Canada* 42°54N 81°29W **174** D3
Mount Buffalo △
  Australia 36°43S 146°46E **153** D7
Mount Burr *Australia* 37°34S 140°26E **151** F3
Mount Carmel = Ha Karmel △
  Israel 32°45N 35°3E **130** C4
Mount Carmel *Ill.,*
  U.S.A. 38°25N 87°46W **172** F10
Mount Carmel *Pa.,*
  U.S.A. 40°47N 76°26W **175** F8
Mount Clemens *U.S.A.* 42°35N 82°53W **174** D2
Mount Cook *N.Z.* 43°44S 170°5E **155** D5
Mount Cook △ *N.Z.* 43°35S 170°15E **155** D5

Mount Coolon
  Australia 21°25S 147°25E **150** C4
Mount Darwin
  Zimbabwe 16°47S 31°38E **143** F3
Mount Desert I.
  U.S.A. 44°21N 68°20W **173** C19
Mount Dora *U.S.A.* 28°48N 81°38W **179** G8
Mount Ebenezer
  Australia 25°6S 132°34E **149** E5
Mount Eccles △
  Australia 38°5S 141°54E **152** E4
Mount Edziza △
  Canada 57°30N 130°45W **162** B2
Mount Elgon △ *E. Afr.* 1°4N 34°42E **142** B3
Mount Field △
  Australia 42°39S 146°35E **151** G4
Mount Fletcher
  S. Africa 30°40S 28°30E **145** D4
Mount Forest *Canada* 43°59N 80°43W **174** C4
Mount Frankland △
  Australia 31°47S 116°37E **149** F2
Mount Frederick ◎
  Australia 19°39S 129°18E **148** C4
Mount Gambier
  Australia 37°50S 140°46E **152** E3
Mount Garnet *Australia* 17°37S 145°6E **150** B4
Mount Holly *U.S.A.* 39°59N 74°47W **175** G10
Mount Holly Springs
  U.S.A. 40°7N 77°12W **174** F7
Mount Hope *N.S.W.,*
  Australia 32°51S 145°51E **153** B6
Mount Hope *S. Austral.,*
  Australia 34°7S 135°23E **151** E2
Mount Isa *Australia* 20°42S 139°26E **150** C2
Mount James ◎
  Australia 24°51S 116°54E **149** D2
Mount Jewett *U.S.A.* 41°44N 78°39W **174** E6
Mount Kaputar △
  Australia 30°16S 150°10E **151** E5
Mount Kenya △ *Kenya* 0°7S 37°21E **142** C4
Mount Kisco *U.S.A.* 41°12N 73°44W **175** E11
Mount Laguna
  U.S.A. 32°52N 116°25W **171** N10
Mount Larcom
  Australia 23°48S 150°59E **150** C5
Mount Lofty Ranges
  Australia 34°35S 139°5E **152** C3
Mount Magnet
  Australia 28°2S 117°47E **149** E2
Mount Manara
  Australia 32°29S 143°58E **152** B5
Mount Maunganui
  N.Z. 37°40S 176°14E **154** D5
Mount Molloy
  Australia 16°42S 145°20E **150** B4
Mount Morgan
  Australia 23°40S 150°25E **150** C5
Mount Morris *U.S.A.* 42°44N 77°52W **174** D7
Mount Pearl *Canada* 47°31N 52°47W **165** C9
Mount Penn *U.S.A.* 40°20N 75°54W **175** F9
Mount Perry *Australia* 25°13S 151°42E **151** D5
Mount Pleasant *Iowa,*
  U.S.A. 40°58N 91°33W **172** E8
Mount Pleasant *Mich.,*
  U.S.A. 43°36N 84°46W **173** D11
Mount Pleasant *Pa.,*
  U.S.A. 40°9N 79°33W **174** F5
Mount Pleasant *S.C.,*
  U.S.A. 32°47N 79°52W **178** C10
Mount Pleasant *Tenn.,*
  U.S.A. 35°32N 87°12W **177** D11
Mount Pleasant *Tex.,*
  U.S.A. 33°9N 94°58W **176** E7
Mount Pleasant *Utah,*
  U.S.A. 39°33N 111°27W **168** G8
Mount Pocono *U.S.A.* 41°7N 75°22W **175** E9
Mount Rainier △
  U.S.A. 46°55N 121°50W **170** D5
Mount Remarkable △
  Australia 32°47S 138°3E **152** B3
Mount Revelstoke △
  Canada 51°5N 118°30W **162** C5
Mount Robson △
  Canada 53°0N 119°0W **162** C5
Mount St. Helens △
  U.S.A. 46°14N 122°11W **170** D4
Mount Selinda
  Zimbabwe 20°24S 32°43E **145** B5
Mount Shasta *U.S.A.* 41°19N 122°19W **168** F2
Mount Signal *U.S.A.* 32°39N 115°37W **171** N11
Mount Somers *N.Z.* 43°45S 171°27E **155** D6
Mount Sterling *Ill.,*
  U.S.A. 39°59N 90°45W **172** F8
Mount Sterling *Ky.,*
  U.S.A. 38°4N 83°56W **173** F12
Mount Surprise
  Australia 18°10S 144°17E **150** B3
Mount Union *U.S.A.* 40°23N 77°53W **174** F7
Mount Upton *U.S.A.* 42°26N 75°23W **175** D9
Mount Vernon *Ga.,*
  U.S.A. 32°11N 82°36W **178** C7
Mount Vernon *Ill.,*
  U.S.A. 38°19N 88°55W **172** F9
Mount Vernon *N.Y.,*
  U.S.A. 40°54N 73°49W **175** F11
Mount Vernon *Ohio,*
  U.S.A. 40°23N 82°29W **174** F2
Mount Vernon *Wash.,*
  U.S.A. 48°25N 122°20W **170** B4
Mount Victor
  Australia 34°38S 117°40E **149** C7
Mount Wellington
  N.Z. 36°53S 174°52E **154** C3
Mount William △
  Australia 40°54S 148°14E **151** G4
Mtilikwe → *Zimbabwe* 21°9S 31°30E **145** B5
Mtirala △ *Georgia* 41°50N 42°2E **87** K6
Mtito Andei *Kenya* 2°41S 38°10E **142** C4
Mtsensk *Russia* 53°17N 36°36E **84** F9
Mtskheta *Georgia* 41°52N 44°43E **87** K7
Mtubatuba *S. Africa* 28°30S 32°8E **145** C5
Mtwalume *S. Africa* 30°30S 30°38E **145** D5
Mtwara-Mikindani
  Tanzania 10°20S 40°20E **143** E5
Mu Gia, Deo *Vietnam* 17°40N 105°47E **120** D5
Mu Ko Chang △
  Thailand 11°59N 102°12E **121** G4
Mu Ko Surin *Thailand* 9°30N 97°55E **121** H1
Mu Us Shamo *China* 39°0N 109°0E **114** E5
Muang Beng *Laos* 20°23N 101°46E **116** B3

Mountain Home *Idaho,*
  U.S.A. 43°8N 115°41W **168** E6
Mountain Iron *U.S.A.* 47°32N 92°37W **172** B7
Mountain Pass
  U.S.A. 35°29N 115°35W **171** K11
Mountain View *Ark.,*
  U.S.A. 35°52N 92°7W **176** D8
Mountain View *Calif.,*
  U.S.A. 37°23N 122°5W **170** H4
Mountain Zebra △
  S. Africa 32°14S 25°27E **144** D4
Mountainair *U.S.A.* 34°31N 106°15W **169** J10
Mountbellew *Ireland* 53°28N 8°31W **64** C3
Mountlake Terrace
  U.S.A. 47°47N 122°18W **170** C4
Mountmellick *Ireland* 53°7N 7°20W **64** C4
Mountrath *Ireland* 53°0N 7°28W **64** D4
Moura *Australia* 24°35S 149°58E **150** C4
Moura *Brazil* 1°32S 61°38W **186** D6
Moura *Portugal* 38°7N 7°30W **89** G3
Mourão *Portugal* 38°22N 7°22W **89** G3
Mourdi, Dépression du
  Chad 18°10N 23°0E **135** E10
Mourdiah *Mali* 14°35N 7°25W **138** C3
Mourenx *France* 43°22N 0°38W **72** E3
Mouri *Ghana* 5°6N 1°14W **139** D4
Mourilyan *Australia* 17°35S 146°3E **150** B4
Mourmelon-le-Grand
  France 49°8N 4°22E **71** C11
Mourne → *U.K.* 54°52N 7°26W **64** B4
Mourne Mts. *U.K.* 54°10N 6°0W **64** B5
Mournies *Greece* 35°29N 24°1E **101** D6
Mouscron *Belgium* 50°45N 3°12E **69** D3
Moussoro *Chad* 13°41N 16°35E **135** F9
Mouthe *France* 46°44N 6°12E **71** F13
Moutier *Switz.* 47°16N 7°21E **77** H3
Moûtiers *France* 45°29N 6°32E **73** C10
Moutong *Indonesia* 0°28N 121°13E **119** D6
Mouy *France* 49°18N 2°20E **71** C9
Mouydir, Monts du
  Algeria 25°30N 4°10E **136** C4
Mouzaki *Greece* 39°25N 21°37E **98** B3
Mouzon *France* 49°36N 5°3E **71** C12
Movas *Mexico* 28°10N 109°25W **180** B3
Moville *Ireland* 55°11N 7°3W **64** A4
Mowandjum *Australia* 17°22S 123°40E **148** C3
Moxotó → *Brazil* 9°19S 38°14W **189** B3
Moy → *Ireland* 54°8N 9°8W **64** B2
Moya *Comoros Is.* 12°18S 44°18E **141** a
Moyale *Ethiopia* 3°34N 39°5E **142** B4
Moyale *Kenya* 3°30N 39°4E **142** B4
Moyamba *S. Leone* 8°4N 12°30W **138** D2
Moyen Atlas *Morocco* 33°0N 5°0W **136** B3
Moyen-Cavally □
  Ivory C. 6°45N 7°30W **138** D3
Moyen-Comoé □
  Ivory C. 6°40N 3°25W **138** D4
Moyo *Indonesia* 8°10S 117°40E **118** F5
Moyobamba *Peru* 6°0S 77°0W **188** B2
Moyowosi △ *Tanzania* 3°50S 31°0E **142** C3
Moyvalen △ *Norway* 68°32N 15°29E **60** B16
Moyu *China* 37°15N 79°44E **109** D9
Moyyero → *Russia* 68°44N 103°42E **107** C11
Moyynqum *Zhambyl,*
  Kazakhstan 44°17N 72°57E **109** D8
Moyynqum *Zhambyl,*
  Kazakhstan 44°12N 71°0E **109** D8
Moyynty *Kazakhstan* 47°10N 73°18E **108** D8
Mozambique = Moçambique
  Mozam. 15°3S 40°42E **143** F5
Mozambique ■ *Africa* 19°0S 35°0E **143** F4
Mozambique Basin
  Ind. Oc. 30°0S 40°0E **146** G2
Mozambique Chan.
  Africa 17°30S 42°30E **145** A7
Mozdok *Russia* 43°45N 44°48E **87** J7
Mozdūrān *Iran* 36°9N 60°35E **129** B9
Mozhaysk *Russia* 55°30N 36°2E **84** E9
Mozhga *Russia* 56°26N 52°15E **86** B11
Mozhnābād *Iran* 34°7N 60°6E **129** C9
Mozirje *Slovenia* 46°22N 14°58E **93** B11
Mozyr = Mazyr *Belarus* 51°59N 29°15E **75** B15
Mpanda *Tanzania* 6°23S 31°1E **142** D3
Mpésoba *Mali* 12°31N 5°39W **138** C3
Mphoeng *Zimbabwe* 21°10S 27°51E **145** B4
Mpika *Zambia* 11°51S 31°25E **143** E3
Mpulungu *Zambia* 8°51S 31°5E **143** D3
Mpumalanga *S. Africa* 29°50S 30°33E **145** D5
Mpumalanga □ *S. Africa* 26°0S 30°0E **145** C5
Mpwapwa *Tanzania* 6°23S 36°30E **142** D4
Mqanduli *S. Africa* 31°49S 28°45E **145** D4
Mqinvartsveri = Kazbek
  Russia 42°42N 44°30E **87** J7
Mragowo *Poland* 53°52N 21°18E **82** E8
Mramor *Serbia* 43°20N 21°45E **96** C5
Mrimina *Morocco* 29°50N 7°9W **136** C3
Mrkonjić Grad *Bos.-H.* 44°26N 17°4E **80** F2
Mrkopalj *Croatia* 45°21N 14°52E **93** C11
Mrocza *Poland* 53°16N 17°35E **83** E4
Msaken *Tunisia* 35°49N 10°33E **136** A6
Msambansovu *Zimbabwe* 15°50S 30°3E **143** F3
Msila □ *Algeria* 35°46N 4°30E **136** A4
M'sila □ *Algeria* 35°30N 4°20E **136** A4
Msoro *Zambia* 13°35S 31°50E **143** E3
Msta → *Russia* 58°25N 31°20E **84** C6
Mstislavl = Mstsislaw
  Belarus 54°0N 31°50E **75** A16
Mstsislaw *Belarus* 54°0N 31°50E **75** A16
Mszana Dolna *Poland* 49°41N 20°5E **83** J7
Mszczonów *Poland* 51°58N 20°33E **83** G7
Mtama *Tanzania* 10°17S 39°21E **143** E4
Mtamvuna = Mthamvuna →
  S. Africa 31°6S 30°12E **145** D5
Mthamvuna → *S. Africa* 31°6S 30°12E **145** D5
Mthatha *S. Africa* 31°36S 28°49E **145** D4

Muang Chiang Rai = Chiang Rai
  Thailand 19°52N 99°50E **116** H2
Muang Et *Laos* 20°49N 104°1E **120** B5
Muang Hiam *Laos* 20°5N 103°22E **120** B4
Muang Hongsa *Laos* 19°43N 101°20E **120** C3
Muang Houn *Laos* 20°8N 101°23E **116** G3
Muang Kau *Laos* 15°6N 105°47E **120** E5
Muang Khao *Laos* 19°38N 103°32E **120** C3
Muang Khong *Laos* 14°7N 105°51E **120** E5
Muang Khoua *Laos* 21°5N 102°31E **116** G4
Muang Liap *Laos* 18°29N 101°40E **120** C3
Muang Mai *Thailand* 8°5N 98°21E **121** a
Muang May *Laos* 14°49N 106°56E **120** E6
Muang Na Mo *Laos* 21°3N 101°49E **116** G3
Muang Ngeun *Laos* 20°36N 101°3E **116** G3
Muang Ngoi *Laos* 20°43N 102°41E **116** G4
Muang Nong *Laos* 16°22N 106°30E **120** D6
Muang Ou Neua *Laos* 22°18N 101°48E **116** F3
Muang Ou Tay *Laos* 22°7N 101°48E **116** F3
Muang Pak Beng *Laos* 19°54N 101°8E **116** H3
Muang Phalane *Laos* 16°39N 105°34E **120** D5
Muang Phine *Laos* 16°32N 106°2E **120** D6
Muang Phonhong
  Laos 18°30N 102°25E **120** C4
Muang Saiapoun *Laos* 18°24N 101°31E **120** C3
Muang Sing *Laos* 21°11N 101°9E **116** G3
Muang Son *Laos* 20°27N 103°19E **120** B4
Muang Soui *Laos* 19°33N 102°52E **120** C4
Muang Va *Laos* 21°53N 102°19E **116** G4
Muang Va *Laos* 18°18N 101°20E **120** C3
Muang Xai *Laos* 20°42N 101°59E **116** G3
Muang Xamteu *Laos* 19°59N 104°38E **120** C5
Muar *Malaysia* 2°3N 102°34E **121** L4
Muarabungo *Indonesia* 1°28S 102°52E **118** E2
Muaraenim *Indonesia* 3°40S 103°50E **118** E2
Muarajuloi *Indonesia* 0°12S 114°3E **118** E4
Muarakaman *Indonesia* 0°2S 116°45E **118** E5
Muaratebo *Indonesia* 1°30S 102°26E **118** E2
Muaratembesi *Indonesia* 1°42S 103°8E **118** E2
Muarateweh *Indonesia* 0°58S 114°52E **118** E4
Mubarakpur *India* 26°6N 83°18E **125** F10
Mubarraz = Al Mubarraz
  Si. Arabia 25°30N 49°40E **129** E6
Mubende *Uganda* 0°33N 31°22E **142** B3
Mubi *Nigeria* 10°18N 13°16E **139** C7
Mucajaí → *Brazil* 2°25N 60°52E **186** C6
Muchachos, Roque de los
  Canary Is. 28°44N 17°52W **100** F2
Mücheln *Germany* 51°17N 11°47E **76** D7
Muchinga □ *Zambia* 12°0S 31°30E **143** E3
Muchinga Mts. *Zambia* 11°30S 31°30E **143** E3
Muchkapsky *Russia* 51°52N 42°28E **86** E6
Muchuan *China* 28°57N 103°55E **116** C5
Muck *U.K.* 56°50N 6°15W **65** E2
Muckadilla *Australia* 26°35S 148°23E **151** D4
Muckalee Cr. → *U.S.A.* 31°38N 84°9W **178** D5
Muckaty ◎ *Australia* 18°37S 133°52E **150** B1
Muckle Flugga *U.K.* 60°51N 0°54W **65** A8
Mucugê *Brazil* 13°0S 41°23W **189** C2
Mucur *Turkey* 39°3N 34°22E **104** C6
Mucuri *Brazil* 18°0S 39°36W **189** D3
Mucurici *Brazil* 18°6S 40°31W **189** D2
Mucusso *Angola* 18°1S 21°25E **144** A3
Muda *Brazil* 28°34N 13°57W **100** F6
Mudanjiang *China* 44°38N 129°30E **115** B15
Mudanya *Turkey* 40°25N 28°50E **97** F12
Muddebihal *India* 16°20N 76°8E **127** F2
Muddus △ *Sweden* 66°58N 20°15E **60** C19
Muddy Cr. → *U.S.A.* 38°24N 110°42W **168** G8
Mudgee *Australia* 32°32S 149°31E **153** B8
Mudhol *Andhra Pradesh,*
  India 18°58N 77°55E **126** E3
Mudhol *Karnataka, India* 16°21N 75°17E **127** F2
Mudigere *India* 13°8N 75°38E **127** H2
Mudjatik → *Canada* 56°1N 107°36W **163** B7
Mudukulattur *India* 9°21N 78°31E **127** K4
Mudumu △ *Namibia* 18°5S 23°29E **144** A3
Mudurnu *Turkey* 40°27N 31°12E **104** B4
Mueda *Mozam.* 11°36S 39°28E **143** E4
Mueller Ranges
  Australia 18°18S 126°46E **148** C4
Muende *Mozam.* 14°28S 33°0E **143** E3
Muerto, Mar *Mexico* 16°10N 94°10W **181** D6
Mufu Shan *China* 29°20N 114°30E **117** C10
Mufulira *Zambia* 12°32S 28°15E **143** E2
Mufumbiro Range
  Africa 1°25S 29°30E **142** C2
Mugardos *Spain* 43°27N 8°15W **88** B2
Muge → *Portugal* 39°8N 8°44W **89** F2
Múggia *Italy* 45°36N 13°46E **93** C10
Mughal Sarai *India* 25°18N 83°7E **125** G10
Mughayrā' *Si. Arabia* 29°17N 37°41E **128** D3
Mugi *Japan* 33°40N 134°25E **113** H7
Mugia = Muxía *Spain* 43°3N 9°10W **88** B1
Mugila,
  Dem. Rep. of the Congo 7°0S 28°50E **142** D2
Muğla *Turkey* 37°15N 28°22E **99** D13
Muğla □ *Turkey* 37°15N 28°0E **99** D10
Müğlitz *Bulgaria* 42°37N 25°32E **97** D9
Mugodzhar = Mughalzhar Taūy
  Kazakhstan 49°0N 58°40E **108** C5
Mugu *Nepal* 29°45N 82°30E **125** E10
Mugu Karnali →
  Nepal 29°0N 81°51E **125** E9
Muhammad, Râs *Egypt* 27°44N 34°16E **128** E2
Muhammad Qol *Sudan* 20°53N 37°9E **137** C4
Muhammadabad *India* 26°4N 83°25E **125** F10
Mubāyil *Si. Arabia* 23°46N 42°18E **131** D3
Muhesi → *Tanzania* 7°0S 35°20E **142** D4
Mühldorf *Germany* 48°14N 12°32E **77** G8
Mühlhausen *Germany* 51°12N 10°27E **76** D6
Mühlig Hofmann fjell
  Antarctica 72°30S 5°0E **5** D3
Mühlviertel *Austria* 48°30N 14°10E **78** C7
Muhos *Finland* 64°47N 25°59E **60** D21
Muhu *Estonia* 58°36N 23°11E **14** G20
Muhutwe *Tanzania* 1°35S 31°45E **142** C3
Mui Wo *China* 22°16N 113°59E **111** a
Muileann gCearr, An = Mullingar
  Ireland 53°31N 7°21W **64** C4
Muine Bheag = Bagenalstown
  Ireland 52°42N 6°58W **64** D5
Muineachán = Monaghan
  Ireland 54°15N 6°57W **64** B5
Muir, L. *Australia* 34°30S 116°40E **149** F2

Muir of Ord U.K. 57°32N 4°28W 65 D4
Mujeres, I. Mexico 21°13N 86°43W 182 B2
Muka, Tanjung
  Malaysia 5°28N 100°11E 121 c
Mukacheve Ukraine 48°27N 22°45E 80 B7
Mukachevo = Mukacheve
  Ukraine 48°27N 22°45E 80 B7
Mukah Malaysia 2°55N 112°5E 118 D4
Mukandwara India 24°49N 75°59E 124 G6
Mukawwa, Geziret
  Egypt 23°55N 35°53E 128 F2
Mukawwar Sudan 20°50N 37°17E 137 C4
Mukdahan Thailand 16°32N 104°43E 120 D5
Mukdahan △ Thailand 16°26N 104°45E 120 D5
Mukden = Shenyang
  China 41°48N 123°27E 115 D12
Mukerian India 31°57N 75°37E 124 D6
Mukhavyets → Belarus 52°5N 23°39E 83 F10
Mukher India 18°42N 77°22E 126 E3
Mukhtolovo Russia 55°29N 43°15E 86 C6
Mukinbudin Australia 30°55S 118°5E 149 F2
Mukishi
  Dem. Rep. of the Congo 8°30S 24°44E 143 D1
Muko Phetra △ Thailand 6°57N 99°33E 121 J2
Mukomuko Indonesia 2°30S 101°10E 118 E2
Mukomwenze
  Dem. Rep. of the Congo 6°49S 27°15E 142 D2
Mukono Uganda 0°21N 32°45E 142 B3
Muktinath Nepal 28°49N 83°53E 125 E10
Muktsar India 30°30N 74°30E 124 D6
Mukur = Moqor
  Afghan. 32°50N 67°42E 124 C2
Mukutuwa → Canada 53°10N 97°24W 163 C9
Mukwela Zambia 17°0S 26°40E 143 F2
Mul India 20°4N 79°40E 126 D4
Mula Spain 38°3N 1°33W 91 G3
Mula → India 18°34N 74°21E 126 E2
Mula → Pakistan 27°57N 67°36E 124 F2
Mulange
  Dem. Rep. of the Congo 3°40S 27°10E 142 C2
Mulanje, Mt. Malawi 16°2S 35°33E 143 F4
Mulbagal India 13°10N 78°24E 127 H4
Mulberry U.S.A. 27°54N 81°59W 179 H8
Mulchatna → U.S.A. 59°40N 157°7W 166 D8
Mulchén Chile 37°45S 72°20W 190 D1
Mulde → Germany 51°53N 12°15E 76 D8
Mule Creek Junction
  U.S.A. 43°23N 104°13W 168 E11
Muleba Tanzania 1°50S 31°37E 142 C3
Mulegé Mexico 26°53N 111°59W 180 B2
Muleshoe U.S.A. 34°13N 102°43W 176 D3
Mulgrave Canada 45°38N 61°31W 165 C7
Mulgrave I. = Badu
  Australia 10°7S 142°11E 150 a
Mulhacén Spain 37°4N 3°20W 89 H7
Mülheim Germany 51°25N 6°54E 76 D2
Mulhouse France 47°40N 7°20E 71 E14
Muli China 27°52N 101°8E 116 D3
Muling China 44°35N 130°10E 115 B16
Mulki India 13°6N 74°48E 127 H2
Mull U.K. 56°25N 5°56W 65 E3
Mull, Sound of U.K. 56°30N 5°50W 65 E3
Mullach Ide = Malahide
  Ireland 53°26N 6°9W 64 C5
Mullaittivu Sri Lanka 9°15N 80°49E 127 K5
Mullen U.S.A. 42°3N 101°1W 172 D3
Mullengudgery
  Australia 31°43S 147°23E 151 E4
Mullens U.S.A. 37°35N 81°23W 173 G13
Muller, Pegunungan
  Indonesia 0°30N 113°30E 118 D4
Mullet Pen. Ireland 54°13N 10°2W 64 B1
Mullewa Australia 28°29S 115°30E 149 E2
Müllheim Germany 47°47N 7°36E 77 H3
Mulligan → Australia 25°0S 139°0E 150 D2
Mullingar Ireland 53°31N 7°21W 64 C4
Mullins U.S.A. 34°12N 79°15W 177 D15
Mullsjö Sweden 57°56N 13°55E 63 G7
Mullumbimby
  Australia 28°30S 153°30E 151 D5
Mulobezi Zambia 16°45S 25°7E 143 F2
Mulonga Plain Zambia 16°20S 22°40E 141 H4
Mulroy B. Ireland 55°15N 7°46W 64 A4
Mulshi L. India 18°30N 73°30E 126 E1
Multai India 21°50N 78°21E 126 D4
Multan Pakistan 30°15N 71°36E 124 D4
Mulug India 18°11N 79°57E 126 E4
Mulumbe, Mts.
  Dem. Rep. of the Congo 8°40S 27°30E 143 D2
Mulungushi Dam
  Zambia 14°48S 28°48E 143 E2
Mulurulu L. Australia 33°15S 143°20E 152 B5
Mulvane U.S.A. 37°29N 97°15W 172 G5
Mulwad Sudan 18°45N 30°39E 137 D3
Mulwala Australia 35°59S 146°0E 153 C7
Mulwala, L. Australia 35°35S 146°1E 151 C4
Mumbai India 18°56N 72°50E 126 E1
Mumbwa Zambia 15°0S 27°0E 143 E2
Mumias Kenya 0°20N 34°29E 142 C4
Mummel Gulf △
  Australia 31°17S 151°51E 153 A9
Mumra Russia 45°45N 47°41E 87 H8
Mun → Thailand 15°19N 105°30E 120 D5
Muna Indonesia 5°0S 122°30E 119 F6
Munabao India 25°45N 70°17E 124 G4
Munamagi Estonia 57°43N 27°4E 64 B3
Munaung Burma 18°45N 93°40E 123 K18
Munaung I. = Cheduba I.
  Burma 18°45N 93°40E 123 K18
Muncan Indonesia 8°34S 115°11E 119 K18
Muncar Indonesia 8°26S 114°20E 119 J17
Münchberg Germany 50°11N 11°47E 77 E7
Müncheberg Germany 52°30N 14°9E 76 C10
München Germany 48°8N 11°34E 77 G7
München Franz Josef Strauss
  Int. ✈ (MUC)
    Germany 48°21N 11°47E 77 G7
Munchen-Gladbach =
  Mönchengladbach
    Germany 51°11N 6°27E 76 D2
Muncho Lake Canada 59°0N 125°50W 162 B3
Munch'ŏn N. Korea 39°14N 127°19E 115 E14
Muncie U.S.A. 40°12N 85°23W 173 E11
Muncoonie L. West
  Australia 25°12S 138°40E 150 D2
Mundabbera Australia 25°36S 151°18E 151 D5
Mundakayam India 9°30N 76°50E 127 K3
Mundal Sri Lanka 7°48N 79°48E 127 L4
Munday U.S.A. 33°27N 99°38W 176 E5
Mundemba Cameroon 4°57N 8°52E 139 E6
Münden Germany 51°25N 9°38E 76 D5

Münden ○ Germany 51°28N 9°42E 76 B5
Mundiwindi Australia 23°47S 120°9E 148 D3
Mundo → Spain 38°30N 2°15W 91 G2
Mundo Novo Brazil 11°50S 40°29W 189 C2
Mundra India 22°54N 69°48E 124 H3
Mundrabilla Australia 31°52S 127°51E 149 F4
Munera Spain 39°2N 2°29W 91 F2
Muneru → India 16°45N 80°3E 126 F5
Mungallala Australia 26°28S 147°34E 151 D4
Mungallala Cr. →
  Australia 28°53S 147°5E 151 D4
Mungana Australia 17°8S 144°27E 150 B3
Mungaoli India 24°24N 78°7E 124 G8
Mungari Mozam. 17°12S 33°30E 143 F3
Mungbere
  Dem. Rep. of the Congo 2°36N 28°28E 142 B2
Mungeli India 22°4N 81°41E 125 H9
Munger India 25°23N 86°30E 125 G12
Mungerannie Australia 28°1S 138°39E 151 A2
Mungilli △ Australia 25°14S 124°17E 149 E3
Mungkan Kandju △
  Australia 13°35S 142°52E 150 A3
Mungo, L. Australia 33°45S 143°0E 152 B5
Mungo △ Australia 33°44S 143°6E 152 B5
Munich = München
  Germany 48°8N 11°34E 77 G7
Munising U.S.A. 46°25N 86°40W 172 B10
Munka-Ljungby Sweden 56°16N 12°58E 63 H6
Munkebo Denmark 55°27N 10°34E 63 J4
Munkedal Sweden 58°28N 11°40E 63 F5
Munkfors Sweden 59°47N 13°30E 62 E7
Munku-Sardyk
  Russia 51°45N 100°20E 107 D11
Münnerstadt Germany 50°14N 10°12E 77 E6
Munnsville U.S.A. 42°58N 75°35W 175 D9
Muñoz Gamero, Pen.
  Chile 52°30S 73°5W 192 D2
Munroe L. Canada 59°13N 98°35W 163 B9
Munsan S. Korea 37°51N 126°48E 115 F14
Munson U.S.A. 30°52N 86°52W 179 E3
Munster France 48°2N 7°8E 71 D14
Münster Niedersachsen,
  Germany 52°59N 10°5E 76 C6
Münster Nordrhein-Westfalen,
  Germany 51°58N 7°37E 76 D3
Munster □ Ireland 52°18N 8°44W 64 D3
Muntadgin Australia 31°45S 118°33E 149 F2
Muntele Mare, Vf.
  Romania 46°30N 23°12E 81 D8
Muntok Indonesia 2°5S 105°10E 118 E3
Munzur Dağları Turkey 39°30N 39°10E 105 C8
Muong Nhie Vietnam 22°12N 102°28E 116 F4
Muong Sen Vietnam 19°24N 104°8E 120 C5
Muong Te Vietnam 22°24N 102°49E 116 F4
Muong Xia Vietnam 20°19N 104°50E 120 B5
Muonio Finland 67°57N 23°40E 60 C20
Muonio älv = Muonionjoki →
  Finland 67°11N 23°34E 60 C20
Muonioälven = Muonionjoki →
  Finland 67°11N 23°34E 60 C20
Muonionjoki →
  Finland 67°11N 23°34E 60 C20
Mupa → Mozam. 18°58S 35°54E 143 F4
Muping China 37°22N 121°36E 115 F11
Muqdisho Somalia 2°2N 45°25E 131 G4
Mur → Austria 47°18N 16°52E 79 E9
Mûr-de-Bretagne France 48°12N 3°0W 70 D4
Muradiye Manisa, Turkey 38°39N 27°21E 99 C9
Muradiye Van, Turkey 39°0N 43°44E 105 C10
Murakami Japan 38°14N 139°29E 112 E9
Muralag = Prince of Wales I.
  Australia 10°45S 142°10E 150 A3
Murallón, Cerro Chile 49°48S 73°30W 192 C2
Muranda Rwanda 1°52S 29°20E 142 C2
Murang'a Kenya 0°45S 37°9E 142 C4
Murashi Russia 59°30N 49°0E 106 D5
Murat France 45°7N 2°53E 72 C6
Murat → Turkey 38°46N 40°0E 105 C9
Murat Dağı Turkey 38°55N 29°43E 99 C11
Muratlı Turkey 41°10N 27°29E 97 E11
Murato France 42°35N 9°12E 73 F13
Murau Austria 47°6N 14°10E 78 D7
Muravera Italy 39°25N 9°34E 94 C2
Murayama Japan 38°30N 140°25E 112 E10
Murça Portugal 41°24N 7°28W 88 D3
Murchison N.Z. 41°49S 172°21E 155 B7
Murchison → Australia 27°45S 114°0E 149 E1
Murchison, Mt.
  Antarctica 73°25S 166°20E 55 D11
Murchison, Mt. N.Z. 43°0S 171°22E 155 D6
Murchison Falls Uganda 2°15N 31°30E 142 B3
Murchison Falls △
  Uganda 2°17N 31°48E 142 B3
Murchison Mts. N.Z. 45°13S 167°23E 155 F2
Murchison Ra.
  Australia 20°0S 134°10E 150 C1
Murchison Rapids
  Malawi 15°55S 34°35E 143 F3
Murchison Roadhouse
  Australia 27°39S 116°14E 149 E2
Murcia Spain 38°5N 1°10W 91 G3
Murcia □ Spain 37°50N 1°30W 91 H3
Murdo U.S.A. 43°53N 100°43W 172 D3
Murdoch Pt. Australia 14°37S 144°55E 150 A3
Mürefte Turkey 40°40N 27°14E 97 F11
Mureş → Romania 46°45N 24°40E 81 D9
Mureș → Romania 46°15N 20°13E 80 D5
Mureşul = Mureş →
  Romania 46°15N 20°13E 80 D5
Muret France 43°30N 1°20E 72 E5
Murewa Zimbabwe 17°39S 31°47E 145 A5
Murfreesboro N.C.,
  U.S.A. 36°27N 77°6W 177 C16
Murfreesboro Tenn.,
  U.S.A. 35°51N 86°24W 177 D11
Murgab = Murghob
  Tajikistan 38°10N 74°2E 109 E8
Murgap →
  Turkmenistan 38°18N 61°12E 129 B9
Murgenella Australia 11°34S 132°56E 148 B5
Murgeni Romania 46°12N 28°1E 81 D13
Murgha Kibzai
  Pakistan 30°44N 69°25E 124 D3
Murghob = Murgap
  Tajikistan 38°10N 74°2E 109 E8
Murgon Australia 26°15S 151°54E 151 D5
Muri India 23°22N 85°52E 125 H11
Muria Indonesia 6°36S 110°53E 119 E14
Muriaé Brazil 21°8S 42°23W 191 A7
Murias de Paredes Spain 42°52N 6°11W 88 C4

Murici Brazil 9°19S 35°56W 189 B3
Muriel Mine Zimbabwe 17°14S 30°40E 143 F3
Müritz Germany 53°25N 12°42E 76 B8
Müritz △ Germany 53°22N 12°55E 76 B8
Muriwai Beach N.Z. 36°50S 174°26E 154 C3
Murliganj India 25°54N 86°59E 125 G12
Murmansk Russia 68°57N 33°10E 60 B25
Murmashi Russia 68°47N 32°42E 60 B25
Murnau Germany 47°40N 11°12E 77 H7
Muro France 42°34N 8°54E 73 F12
Muro Spain 39°44N 3°3E 100 B10
Muro, C. di France 41°44N 8°37E 73 G12
Muro de Alcoy Spain 38°46N 0°26W 91 G4
Muro Lucano Italy 40°45N 15°29E 95 B8
Murom Russia 55°35N 42°3E 86 C6
Muroran Japan 42°25N 141°0E 112 C10
Muros Spain 42°45N 9°5W 88 C1
Muros e Nova, Ría de →
  Spain 42°45N 9°0W 88 C1
Muroto Japan 33°18N 134°9E 113 H7
Muroto-Misaki Japan 33°15N 134°10E 113 H7
Murovani Kurylivtsi
  Ukraine 48°44N 27°31E 81 B12
Murowana Goślina
  Poland 52°35N 17°0E 83 F3
Murphy U.S.A. 43°13N 116°33W 168 E5
Murphys U.S.A. 38°8N 120°28W 170 G6
Murrat Sudan 18°51N 29°33E 137 D2
Murrat Wells Sudan 21°3N 32°55E 137 C3
Murray Australia 9°56S 144°2E 150 a
Murray Ky., U.S.A. 36°37N 88°19W 177 C9
Murray Utah, U.S.A. 40°40N 111°53W 168 F8
Murray → Australia 35°20S 139°22E 152 C3
Murray, L. U.S.A. 34°3N 81°13W 178 A8
Murray Bridge
  Australia 35°6S 139°14E 152 C3
Murray Fracture Zone
  Pac. Oc. 35°0N 130°0W 157 D14
Murray Harbour
  Canada 46°0N 62°28W 165 C7
Murray River △
  Australia 34°23S 140°32E 151 E3
Murray-Sunset △
  Australia 34°45S 141°30E 152 C4
Murraysburg S. Africa 31°58S 23°47E 144 D3
Murree Pakistan 33°56N 73°28E 124 C5
Murrieta U.S.A. 33°33N 117°13W 171 M9
Murro di Porco, Capo
  Italy 37°0N 15°20E 95 F8
Murrumbateman
  Australia 34°58S 149°0E 153 C8
Murrumbidgee →
  Australia 34°43S 143°12E 152 C5
Murrumburrah
  Australia 34°32S 148°22E 153 C8
Murrurundi Australia 31°42S 150°51E 153 A9
Murshid Sudan 21°40N 31°10E 137 C3
Murshidabad India 24°11N 88°19E 125 G13
Murska Sobota
  Slovenia 46°39N 16°12E 93 B13
Murtazapur India 20°40N 77°25E 126 D3
Murtle L. Canada 52°8N 119°38W 162 C5
Murtoa Australia 36°35S 142°28E 152 D5
Murtosa Portugal 40°44N 8°40W 88 E2
Muru → Brazil 8°9S 70°45W 188 B3
Murud India 18°19N 72°58E 126 E1
Murungu Tanzania 4°12S 31°10E 142 C3
Murupara N.Z. 38°28S 176°42E 154 E5
Mururoa
  French Polynesia 21°52S 138°55W 157 K14
Murwara India 23°46N 80°28E 125 H9
Murwillumbah
  Australia 28°18S 153°27E 151 D5
Mürz → Austria 47°30N 15°25E 78 D8
Mürzüq Libya 25°53N 13°57E 135 C8
Murzûq, Idehân Libya 24°50N 13°51E 135 D8
Mürzzuschlag Austria 47°36N 15°41E 78 D8
Mus Turkey 9°14N 92°47E 127 K11
Muş Turkey 38°45N 41°30E 105 C9
Muş □ Turkey 38°45N 41°30E 105 C9
Mûsa, Gebel Egypt 28°33N 33°59E 128 D2
Musa Khel Pakistan 30°59N 69°52E 124 D3
Mûsa Qal'eh Afghan. 32°20N 64°50E 124 C4
Musafirkhana India 26°22N 81°48E 125 F9
Musala Bulgaria 42°13N 23°37E 96 D7
Musala Indonesia 1°41N 98°28E 118 D1
Musan N. Korea 42°12N 129°12E 115 C15
Musangu
  Dem. Rep. of the Congo 10°28S 23°55E 143 E1
Musasa Tanzania 3°25S 31°30E 142 C3
Muscat = Masqat
  Oman 23°37N 58°36E 131 C6
Muscatine U.S.A. 41°25N 91°3W 172 E8
Muscle Shoals U.S.A. 34°45N 87°40W 177 D11
Musengezi = Unsengedsi →
  Zimbabwe 15°43S 31°14E 143 F3
Musgrave Harbour
  Canada 49°27N 53°58W 165 C9
Musgrave Ranges
  Australia 26°0S 132°0E 149 E5
Mushie
  Dem. Rep. of the Congo 2°56S 16°55E 140 E3
Mushin Nigeria 6°31N 3°21E 139 D5
Musi → India 16°41N 79°40E 126 F4
Musi → Indonesia 2°20S 104°56E 118 E2
Musina S. Africa 22°20S 30°5E 145 B5
Musiri India 10°56N 78°27E 127 J4
Muskauer Park Europe 51°34N 14°43E 76 D10
Muskeg → Canada 60°20N 123°20W 162 A4
Muskegon U.S.A. 43°14N 86°16W 172 D10
Muskegon → U.S.A. 43°14N 86°21W 172 D10
Muskegon Heights
  U.S.A. 43°12N 86°16W 172 D10
Muskogee U.S.A. 35°45N 95°22W 176 D7
Muskoka, L. Canada 44°59N 79°17W 174 B5
Muskwa → Canada 58°47N 122°48W 162 B4
Muslîmiyah Syria 36°19N 37°12E 128 B3
Musmar Sudan 18°13N 35°40E 137 D4
Musofu Zambia 13°30S 29°0E 143 E2
Musoma Tanzania 1°30S 33°48E 142 C3
Musquaro, L. Canada 50°38N 61°5W 165 B7
Musquodoboit Harbour
  Canada 44°50N 63°9W 165 D7
Musselburgh U.K. 55°57N 3°2W 65 F5
Musselshell →
  U.S.A. 47°21N 107°57W 168 C10
Mussende Angola 10°32S 16°5E 140 G3
Mussidan France 45°2N 0°22E 72 C4
Mussomeli Italy 37°35N 13°45E 94 E6
Mussoorie India 30°27N 78°6E 124 D8

Mussuco Angola 17°2S 19°3E 144 A2
Mustafakemalpaşa
  Turkey 40°2N 28°24E 97 F12
Mustang Nepal 29°10N 83°55E 125 E10
Musters, L. Argentina 45°20S 69°25W 192 C3
Musudan N. Korea 40°50N 129°43E 115 D15
Muswellbrook
  Australia 32°16S 150°56E 153 B9
Muszyna Poland 49°22N 20°55E 83 J7
Mût Egypt 25°28N 28°58E 137 B2
Mut Turkey 36°40N 33°28E 104 D5
Mutanda Angola 21°0S 33°34E 145 B5
Mutanda Zambia 12°24S 26°13E 143 E2
Mutare Zimbabwe 18°58S 32°38E 143 F3
Mutawintji △
  Australia 31°10S 142°30E 151 E3
Mutha Kenya 1°48S 38°26E 142 C4
Muting Indonesia 7°23S 140°20E 119 F10
Mutki = Mirtağ Turkey 38°23N 41°56E 128 B4
Mutoko Zimbabwe 17°24S 32°13E 143 A5
Mutomo Kenya 1°51S 38°12E 142 C4
Mutoray Russia 60°56N 101°0E 107 C11
Mutshatsha
  Dem. Rep. of the Congo 10°35S 24°20E 143 E1
Mutsu Japan 41°5N 140°55E 112 D10
Mutsu-Wan Japan 41°5N 140°55E 112 D10
Muttaburra Australia 22°38S 144°29E 150 C3
Muttalip Turkey 39°50N 30°32E 98 B4
Mutton I. Ireland 52°49N 9°32W 64 D2
Muttukuru India 14°16N 80°6E 127 G5
Mutuáli Mozam. 14°55S 37°0E 143 E4
Mutum Biyu Nigeria 8°40N 10°50E 139 D7
Mutumba Burundi 3°25S 29°21E 142 C2
Mutur Sri Lanka 8°27N 81°16E 127 K5
Muweilih Egypt 30°42N 34°19E 130 E3
Muxía Spain 43°3N 9°10W 88 B1
Muy Muy Nic. 12°39N 85°36W 182 D2
Muyinga Burundi 3°14S 30°33E 142 C3
Muynak Uzbekistan 43°44N 59°10E 108 D5
Muyumkum, Peski = Moyynqum
  Kazakhstan 44°12N 71°0E 109 D8
Muz Tag China 36°25N 87°25E 109 E11
Muzaffarabad Pakistan 34°25N 73°30E 125 B5
Muzaffargarh Pakistan 30°5N 71°14E 124 D4
Muzaffarnagar India 29°26N 77°40E 124 E7
Muzaffarpur India 26°7N 85°23E 125 F11
Muzafirpur Pakistan 30°58N 69°9E 124 D3
Mużakowski, Park = Muskauer
  Park Europe 51°34N 14°43E 76 D10
Muzhi Russia 65°25N 64°40E 106 C7
Muzillac France 47°35N 2°30W 70 E4
Muztagh-Ata China 38°17N 75°7E 109 E9
Muzūra Egypt 28°53N 30°48E 137 C7
Mvama Zimbabwe 19°16S 30°30E 143 F3
Mvurwi Zimbabwe 17°0S 30°57E 143 F3
Mwabvi △ Malawi 16°42S 35°0E 143 F3
Mwadui Tanzania 3°26S 33°32E 142 C3
Mwali = Mohéli
  Comoros Is. 12°20S 43°40E 141 a
Mwamba Tanzania 10°30S 40°22E 143 E5
Mwandi Zambia 17°30S 24°51E 143 F1
Mwanza
  Dem. Rep. of the Congo 7°55S 26°43E 142 D2
Mwanza Tanzania 2°30S 32°58E 142 C3
Mwanza Zambia 16°58S 24°28E 143 F1
Mwanza □ Tanzania 2°0S 33°0E 142 C3
Mwaya Tanzania 9°32S 33°55E 143 D3
Mweelrea Ireland 53°39N 9°49W 64 C2
Mweka
  Dem. Rep. of the Congo 4°50S 21°34E 140 E4
Mwene-Ditu
  Dem. Rep. of the Congo 6°35S 22°27E 140 F4
Mwenezi Zimbabwe 21°15S 30°48E 143 G3
Mwenezi → Mozam. 22°40S 31°50E 143 G3
Mwenga
  Dem. Rep. of the Congo 3°1S 28°28E 142 C2
Mweru, L. Zambia 9°0S 28°40E 143 D2
Mweru Wantipa △
  Zambia 8°39S 29°25E 143 D2
Mweza Range Zimbabwe 21°0S 30°0E 143 G3
Mwilambwe
  Dem. Rep. of the Congo 8°7S 25°5E 142 D2
Mwimbi Kenya 8°38S 31°39E 143 D3
Mwingi Kenya 0°56S 38°4E 142 C4
Mwinilunga Zambia 11°43S 24°25E 143 E1
My Son Vietnam 15°48N 108°7E 120 E7
Mya, O. → Algeria 30°46N 4°54E 136 B6
Myajlar India 26°15N 70°20E 124 F4
Myall Lakes △
  Australia 32°25S 152°30E 153 B10
Myanaung Burma 18°18N 95°22E 123 K19
Myanmar = Burma ■
  Asia 21°0N 96°30E 123 J20
Myaungmya Burma 16°30N 94°40E 123 L19
Mycenæ = Mikines
  Greece 37°43N 22°46E 98 D4
Myedna Belarus 51°32N 23°42E 83 G10
Myeik = Mergui Burma 12°26N 98°34E 120 F2
Myeik Kyunzu Burma 11°30N 97°30E 121 G1
Myerstown U.S.A. 40°22N 76°19W 175 F8
Myingyan Burma 21°30N 95°20E 123 J19
Myitkyina Burma 25°24N 97°26E 123 G20
Myjava Slovak Rep. 48°41N 17°37E 79 C10
Mykhaylivka Ukraine 47°34N 34°13E 85 J8
Mykines Færoe Is. 62°7N 7°35W 60 E9
Mykolayiv Ukraine 46°58N 32°0E 85 J7
Mykolayiv □ Ukraine 47°20N 31°50E 85 J6
Mykonos Greece 37°30N 25°25E 99 D7
Mylius Erichsen Land
  Greenland 81°30N 27°0W 57 A8
Mymensingh Bangla. 24°45N 90°24E 123 G17
Mynydd Du U.K. 51°52N 3°50W 67 F4
Mýrdalsjökull Iceland 63°40N 19°6W 60 E4
Myrhorod Ukraine 49°58N 33°29E 85 F9
Myrtle Beach U.S.A. 33°42N 78°53W 177 E15
Myrtle Creek U.S.A. 43°1N 123°17W 168 E2
Myrtle Point U.S.A. 43°4N 124°8W 168 E1
Myrtleford Australia 36°34S 146°44E 153 D7
Myrtou Cyprus 35°18N 33°4E 101 D12
Myrviken Sweden 62°58N 14°20E 62 E8
Mysia Turkey 39°50N 27°0E 97 G11
Myślenice Poland 49°51N 19°57E 83 J6
Myślibórz Poland 52°55N 14°50E 83 F1
Mysłowice Poland 50°15N 19°12E 83 H6

Mysore = Karnataka □
  India 13°15N 77°0E 127 H3
Mysore India 12°17N 76°41E 127 H3
Mystic U.S.A. 41°21N 71°58W 175 E13
Mystras Greece 37°4N 22°22E 98 D4
Mysuru = Mysore
  India 12°17N 76°41E 127 H3
Myszków Poland 50°45N 19°22E 83 H6
Myszyniec Poland 53°23N 21°21E 82 E8
Mytishchi Russia 55°50N 37°50E 84 C9
Mývatn Iceland 65°36N 17°0W 60 D5
M'zab, Oued → Algeria 32°15N 5°0E 136 B5
M'zab Valley = M'zab, Oued →
  Algeria 32°15N 5°0E 136 B5
Mže → Czech Rep. 49°46N 13°24E 78 B6
Mzimba Malawi 11°55S 33°39E 143 E3
Mzimkulu → S. Africa 30°44S 30°28E 145 E5
Mzimvubu → S. Africa 31°38S 29°33E 145 D4
Mzuzu Malawi 11°30S 33°55E 143 E3

N

Na Clocha Liatha = Greystones
  Ireland 53°9N 6°5W 64 C5
Na Haeo △ Thailand 17°31N 100°58E 120 D3
Na Hearadh = Harris
  U.K. 57°50N 6°55W 65 D2
Na Hearadh, Caolas = Harris, Sd.
  of U.K. 57°44N 7°6W 65 D1
Na Noi Thailand 18°19N 100°43E 120 C3
Na Phao Laos 17°35N 105°44E 120 D5
Na Sam Vietnam 22°3N 106°37E 116 F6
Na Sceirí = Skerries
  Ireland 53°35N 6°6W 64 C5
Na Thon Thailand 9°32N 99°56E 121 b
Naab → Germany 49°1N 12°2E 77 F8
Naama Algeria 33°16N 0°19E 136 B4
Naama □ Algeria 33°15N 0°45E 136 B4
Naantali Finland 60°29N 22°2E 84 B1
Naas Ireland 53°12N 6°40W 64 C5
Nababeep S. Africa 29°36S 17°46E 144 D2
Nabadwip = Navadwip
  India 23°34N 88°20E 125 H13
Nabawa Australia 28°30S 114°48E 149 E1
Nabberu, L. Australia 25°50S 120°30E 149 E3
Nabburg Germany 49°27N 12°11E 77 F8
Naberezhnyye Chelny
  Russia 55°42N 52°19E 86 C11
Nabeul Tunisia 36°30N 10°44E 136 A6
Nabeul □ Tunisia 36°30N 10°44E 136 A6
Nabha India 30°26N 76°14E 124 D7
Nabid Iran 29°40N 57°38E 129 D8
Nabire Indonesia 3°15S 135°26E 119 E9
Nabisar Pakistan 25°8N 69°40E 124 G3
Nabisipi → Canada 50°14N 62°13W 165 B7
Nabiswera Uganda 1°27N 32°15E 142 B3
Nâblus = Nābulus
  West Bank 32°14N 35°15E 130 C4
Naboomspruit S. Africa 24°32S 28°40E 145 B4
Nabou Burkina Faso 11°25N 2°50W 138 C4
Nabouwalu Fiji 17°0S 178°45E 154 a
Nabūl Indonesia 8°15S 115°0E 119 K18
Nābulus West Bank 32°14N 35°15E 130 C4
Nacala Mozam. 14°32S 40°34E 143 E5
Nacaome Honduras 13°31N 87°30W 182 D2
Nacaroa Mozam. 14°22S 39°56E 143 E4
Naches U.S.A. 46°44N 120°42W 168 C3
Naches → U.S.A. 46°38N 120°31W 170 D6
Nachicapau, L. Canada 56°40N 68°5W 165 A6
Nachingwea Tanzania 10°23S 38°49E 143 E4
Nachna India 27°34N 71°41E 124 F4
Náchod Czech Rep. 50°25N 16°8E 78 A9
Nachuge India 10°47N 92°21E 127 J11
Nacka Sweden 59°18N 18°10E 63 G11
Nackara Australia 32°48S 139°12E 152 B3
Naco Mexico 31°19N 109°56W 180 A3
Nacogdoches U.S.A. 31°36N 94°39W 176 F7
Nácori Chico Mexico 29°40N 108°57W 180 B3
Nacozari de García
  Mexico 30°25N 109°38W 180 A3
Nacula Fiji 16°54S 177°27E 154 a
Nada = Danzhou China 19°31N 109°33E 117 a
Nådendal = Naantali
  Finland 60°29N 22°2E 84 B1
Nadi Fiji 17°42S 177°20E 154 a
Nadī Sudan 18°40N 33°41E 137 D3
Nadiad India 22°41N 72°56E 124 H5
Nădlac Romania 46°10N 20°50E 80 D5
Nador Morocco 35°14N 2°58W 136 A4
Nadur Malta 36°2N 14°18E 101 C1
Nadūshan Iran 32°2N 53°35E 129 C7
Nadvirna Ukraine 48°37N 24°30E 81 B8
Nadvoitsy Russia 63°52N 34°14E 86 B9
Nadvornaya = Nadvirna
  Ukraine 48°37N 24°30E 81 B8
Nadym Russia 65°35N 72°42E 106 C8
Nadym → Russia 66°12N 72°0E 106 C8
Nærbø Norway 58°40N 5°39E 61 G11
Næstved Denmark 55°13N 11°44E 63 J5
Nafada Nigeria 11°8N 11°20E 139 C7
Nafpaktos Greece 38°24N 21°50E 98 C3
Nafplio Greece 37°33N 22°50E 98 D4
Naft-e Safid Iran 31°40N 49°17E 129 D6
Naftshahr Iran 34°0N 45°30E 108 F1
Nafud Desert = An Nafūd
  Si. Arabia 28°15N 41°0E 128 F4
Nag Hammâdi Egypt 26°2N 32°18E 137 B3
Naga Phil. 13°38N 123°15E 119 B6
Naga, Kreb en Africa 24°12N 6°0W 136 D3
Nagagami → Canada 49°40N 84°40W 172 A11
Nagai Japan 38°6N 140°2E 112 E10
Nagaland □ India 26°0N 94°30E 125 G19
Nagano Japan 36°40N 138°10E 112 E9
Nagano □ Japan 36°15N 138°0E 112 E9
Nagaoka Japan 37°27N 138°51E 112 E9
Nagappattinam India 10°46N 79°51E 127 J4
Nagar → India 24°27N 89°12E 125 G13
Nagar Karnul India 16°29N 78°30E 126 F4
Nagar Parkar Pakistan 24°28N 70°46E 124 G5
Nagasaki Japan 32°47N 129°50E 113 G5
Nagasaki □ Japan 32°50N 129°40E 113 G5
Nagato Japan 34°19N 131°5E 113 G5

Nagaur India 27°15N 73°45E 124 F5
Nagbhir India 20°34N 79°55E 126 D4
Nagda India 23°27N 75°25E 124 H6
Nagercoil India 8°12N 77°26E 127 K3
Nagina India 29°30N 78°30E 125 E8
Nagīneh Iran 34°20N 57°15E 129 C8
Nagir Pakistan 36°12N 74°42E 125 A6
Naglarby Sweden 60°25N 15°34E 62 D9
Nagles Mts. Ireland 52°8N 8°30W 64 D3
Nagod India 24°34N 80°36E 125 G9
Nagold Germany 48°32N 8°43E 77 G4
Nagold → Germany 48°52N 8°42E 77 G4
Nagoorin Australia 24°17S 151°15E 150 C5
Nagorno-Karabakh □
  Azerbaijan 39°55N 46°45E 105 C12
Nagornyy Russia 55°58N 124°57E 107 D13
Nagoya Japan 35°10N 136°50E 113 G8
Nagoya ✈ (NGO)
  Japan 34°53N 136°45E 113 G8
Nagpur India 21°8N 79°10E 126 D8
Nagqu China 31°29N 92°3E 110 E7
Nagua Dom. Rep. 19°23N 69°50W 183 C6
Naguabo Puerto Rico 18°13N 65°44W 183 d
Nagurunguru ©
  Australia 16°45S 129°45E 148 C4
Nagyatád Hungary 46°14N 17°22E 80 D2
Nagyecsed Hungary 47°53N 22°24E 80 C2
Nagykálló Hungary 47°53N 21°51E 80 C6
Nagykanizsa Hungary 46°28N 17°0E 80 D2
Nagykáta Hungary 47°25N 19°45E 80 C4
Nagykőrös Hungary 47°5N 19°48E 80 C4
Naha Japan 26°13N 127°42E 113 L3
Nahan India 30°33N 77°18E 124 D7
Nahanni △ Canada 61°36N 125°41W 162 A3
Nahanni Butte Canada 61°2N 123°31W 162 A4
Nahargarh Mad. P.,
  India 24°10N 75°14E 124 G6
Nahargarh Raj., India 24°55N 76°50E 124 G6
Nahariyya Israel 33°1N 35°5E 130 C4
Nahāvand Iran 34°10N 48°22E 105 E13
Nahe → Germany 49°58N 7°54E 77 F3
Nahīya, W. → Egypt 28°55N 31°0E 137 C7
Nahuel Huapi, L.
  Argentina 41°0S 71°32W 192 B2
Nahuel Huapi △
  Argentina 41°3S 71°59W 192 B2
Nahuelbuta △ Chile 37°44S 72°57W 190 D1
Nahunta U.S.A. 31°12N 81°59W 178 D4
Nai Yong Thailand 8°14N 98°22E 121
Naicá Mexico 27°53N 105°31W 180 B3
Naicam Canada 52°30N 104°30W 163 C8
Naikoon △ Canada 53°55N 131°55W 162 C2
Naikul India 21°20N 84°58E 126 D7
Naila Germany 50°19N 11°42E 77 E7
Naimisharanya India 27°21N 80°30E 125 F9
Naimona'nyi Feng
  China 30°26N 81°18E 125 D9
Nain Canada 56°34N 61°40W 165 A7
Na'in Iran 32°54N 53°0E 129 C7
Naini Tal India 29°30N 79°30E 125 E8
Nainpur India 22°30N 80°10E 125 H9
Naintré France 46°46N 0°29E 70 F7
Nainwa India 25°46N 75°51E 124 G6
Naipu U.S.A. 44°12N 25°47E 81 F11
Nairai Fiji 17°49S 179°15E 154 a
Nairn U.K. 57°35N 3°53W 65 D5
Nairobi Kenya 1°17S 36°48E 142 C4
Nairobi △ Kenya 1°22S 36°50E 142 C4
Naissaar Estonia 59°34N 24°29E 84 A2
Naitaba Fiji 17°0S 179°16W 154 a
Naivasha Kenya 0°40S 36°30E 142 C4
Naivasha, L. Kenya 0°48S 36°20E 142 C4
Najaf = An Najaf Iraq 32°3N 44°15E 105 E12
Najafābād Iran 32°40N 51°15E 129 C6
Najd Si. Arabia 26°30N 42°0E 128 G5
Nájera Spain 42°26N 2°48W 90 C2
Najerilla → Spain 42°32N 2°48W 90 C2
Najibabad India 29°40N 78°20E 124 E8
Najin N. Korea 42°12N 130°15E 115 C16
Najmah Si. Arabia 26°42N 50°6E 129 E6
Najrān Si. Arabia 17°34N 44°18E 131 D3
Naju S. Korea 35°3N 126°43E 115 G14
Nakadōri-Shima Japan 32°57N 129°4E 113 G4
Nakalagba
  Dem. Rep. of the Congo 2°50N 27°58E 142 B2
Nakambé = White Volta →
  Ghana 9°10N 1°15W 139 D4
Nakaminato Japan 36°21N 140°36E 113 F10
Nakamura = Shimanto
  Japan 32°59N 132°56E 113 H6
Nakano Japan 36°45N 138°22E 112 E9
Nakano-Shima Japan 29°51N 129°52E 113 K4
Nakashibetsu Japan 43°33N 144°59E 112 C12
Nakfa Eritrea 16°40N 38°32E 137 E4
Nakha Yai, Ko Thailand 8°3N 98°28E 121
Nakhichevan = Naxçıvan
  Azerbaijan 39°12N 45°15E 109 D5
Nakhichevan Rep. = Naxçıvan □
  Azerbaijan 39°25N 45°26E 109 D5
Nakhl Egypt 29°55N 33°43E 130 F2
Nakhl-e Taqī Iran 27°28N 52°36E 129 E7
Nakhodka Russia 42°53N 132°54E 112 C6
Nakhon Nayok
  Thailand 14°12N 101°13E 120 E3
Nakhon Pathom
  Thailand 13°49N 100°3E 120 E2
Nakhon Phanom
  Thailand 17°23N 104°43E 120 D5
Nakhon Ratchasima
  Thailand 14°59N 102°12E 120 E3
Nakhon Sawan
  Thailand 15°35N 100°10E 120 E2
Nakhon Si Thammarat
  Thailand 8°29N 100°0E 121 c
Nakhon Thai Thailand 17°5N 100°44E 120 D3
Nakhtarana India 23°20N 69°15E 124 H3
Nakina Canada 50°10N 86°40W 164 B2
Naklo nad Notecią Poland 53°9N 17°38E 83 E3
Nakodar India 31°8N 75°31E 124 D6
Nakskov Denmark 54°50N 11°8E 63 J4
Naktong → S. Korea 35°7N 128°57E 115 G15
Nakuru Kenya 0°15S 36°4E 142 C4
Nakuru, L. Kenya 0°23S 36°5E 142 C4
Nakusp Canada 50°20N 117°45W 162 D5
Nal Pakistan 27°40N 66°12E 124 F2
Nal → Pakistan 26°2N 65°19E 124 G1
Nalázi Mozam. 24°3S 33°20E 145 C5
Nalchik Russia 43°30N 43°33E 87 J7

Nepi *Italy* 42°14N 12°21E **93** F9
Nepomuk *Czech Rep.* 49°29N 13°35E **78** B6
Neptune *U.S.A.* 40°13N 74°2W **175** F10
Neptune Is. *Australia* 35°17S 136°10E **152** C2
Neqāb *Iran* 36°42N 57°25E **129** B8
Nera → *Italy* 42°26N 12°24E **93** F9
Nera → *Romania* 44°48N 21°25E **80** F6
Nérac *France* 44°8N 0°21E **72** D4
Nerang *Australia* 27°58S 153°20E **151** D5
Neratovice *Czech Rep.* 50°16N 14°31E **78** A7
Nerchinsk *Russia* 52°0N 116°39E **107** D12
Nereju *Romania* 45°43N 26°43E **81** E11
Nerekhta *Russia* 57°26N 40°38E **84** D11
Neresnytsya *Ukraine* 48°1N 23°39E **85** C13
Néret, L. *Canada* 54°45N 70°44W **165** B5
Neretvanski Kanal
  Croatia 43°7N 17°10E **93** E14
Neringa *Lithuania* 55°20N 21°5E **82** B2
Neris → *Lithuania* 55°8N 24°16E **84** E3
Nerja *Spain* 36°43N 3°55W **89** J7
Nerl → *Russia* 56°11N 40°34E **84** D11
Nerpio *Spain* 38°11N 2°16W **91** G2
Nerva *Spain* 37°42N 6°30W **89** H4
Nervi *Italy* 44°23N 9°2E **92** D6
Neryungri *Russia* 57°38N 124°28E **107** D13
Nescopeck *U.S.A.* 41°3N 76°12W **175** E8
Nesebŭr *Bulgaria* 42°41N 27°46E **97** D11
Neskantaga *Canada* 52°14N 87°53W **164** B2
Neskaupstaður *Iceland* 65°9N 13°42W **60** D7
Ness, L. *U.K.* 57°15N 4°32W **65** D4
Ness City *U.S.A.* 38°27N 99°54W **172** F4
Nessebar = Nesebŭr
  Bulgaria 42°41N 27°46E **97** D11
Nesterov = Zhovkva
  Ukraine 50°4N 23°58E **75** C12
Nesterov *Russia* 54°38N 22°34E **82** D2
Nestorio *Greece* 40°24N 21°5E **96** F5
Nestos → *Europe* 40°54N 24°49E **97** F8
Nesvady *Slovak Rep.* 47°56N 18°7E **79** D11
Nesvizh = Nyasvizh
  Belarus 53°14N 26°38E **75** B14
Netanya *Israel* 32°20N 34°51E **130** C3
Netarhat *India* 23°29N 84°16E **125** H11
Nete → *Belgium* 51°7N 4°14E **69** C4
Netherdale *Australia* 21°10S 148°33E **150** b
Netherlands ■ *Europe* 52°0N 5°30E **69** C5
Netherlands Antilles = ABC
  Islands *W. Indies* 12°15N 69°0W **183** D6
Neto → *Italy* 39°13N 17°9E **95** C10
Netrang *India* 21°39N 73°21E **124** J5
Nettancourt *France* 48°51N 4°57E **71** D11
Nettetal *France* 51°19N 6°12E **76** D2
Nettilling L. *Canada* 66°30N 71°0W **161** D17
Nettuno *Italy* 41°27N 12°39E **94** A5
Netzahualcóyotl, Presa
  Mexico 17°8N 93°35W **181** D6
Neu-Isenburg *Germany* 50°3N 8°42E **77** E4
Neu-Ulm *Germany* 48°22N 10°0E **77** D6
Neubrandenburg
  Germany 53°33N 13°15E **76** B9
Neubukow *Germany* 54°2N 11°39E **76** A7
Neuburg *Germany* 48°44N 11°11E **77** G7
Neuchâtel *Switz.* 47°0N 6°55E **77** J2
Neuchâtel □ *Switz.* 47°0N 6°55E **77** J2
Neuchâtel, Lac de *Switz.* 46°53N 6°50E **77** J2
Neudau *Austria* 47°11N 16°6E **78** D9
Neuenhagen *Germany* 52°32N 13°38E **76** C9
Neuenhaus *Germany* 52°30N 6°58E **76** C2
Neuf-Brisach *France* 48°1N 7°30E **71** D14
Neufahrn *Bayern,*
  Germany 48°41N 12°11E **77** G8
Neufahrn *Bayern,*
  Germany 48°18N 11°40E **77** G7
Neufchâteau *Belgium* 49°50N 5°25E **69** E5
Neufchâteau *France* 48°21N 5°40E **71** D12
Neufchâtel-en-Bray
  France 49°44N 1°26E **70** C8
Neufchâtel-sur-Aisne
  France 49°26N 4°1E **71** C11
Neuhaus *Germany* 53°17N 10°50E **76** B6
Neuillé-Pont-Pierre
  France 47°33N 0°33E **70** E7
Neuilly-le-Roi *France* 49°10N 3°15E **71** C10
Neukalen *Germany* 53°49N 12°46E **76** B8
Neumarkt *Germany* 49°16N 11°27E **77** F7
Neumayer *Antarctica* 71°0S 68°30W **55** D17
Neumünster *Germany* 54°4N 9°58E **76** A5
Neung-sur-Beuvron
  France 47°30N 1°50E **71** E8
Neunkirchen *Austria* 47°43N 16°4E **78** D9
Neunkirchen *Germany* 49°20N 7°9E **77** F3
Neuquén *Argentina* 38°55S 68°0W **192** A3
Neuquén □ *Argentina* 38°0S 69°50W **190** D2
Neuquén → *Argentina* 38°59S 68°0W **192** A3
Neuruppin *Germany* 52°55N 12°48E **76** C8
Neusäss *Germany* 48°24N 10°50E **77** G6
Neuse → *U.S.A.* 35°6N 76°29W **177** D16
Neusiedl *Austria* 47°57N 16°50E **79** D9
Neusiedler See *Austria* 47°50N 16°47E **79** D9
Neusiedler See-Seewinkel △
  Austria 47°50N 16°45E **79** D9
Neuss *Germany* 51°12N 6°42E **76** D2
Neussargues-Moissac
  France 45°9N 3°0E **72** C7
Neustadt *Bayern,*
  Germany 49°44N 12°10E **77** F8
Neustadt *Bayern,*
  Germany 48°48N 11°46E **77** G7
Neustadt *Bayern,*
  Germany 49°34N 10°37E **77** F6
Neustadt *Bayern, Germany* 50°19N 11°7E **77** E7
Neustadt *Brandenburg,*
  Germany 52°50N 12°27E **76** C8
Neustadt *Hessen, Germany* 50°51N 9°9E **76** E5
Neustadt *Niedersachsen,*
  Germany 52°30N 9°30E **76** C5
Neustadt *Rhld-Pfz.,*
  Germany 49°21N 8°10E **77** F4
Neustadt *Sachsen,*
  Germany 52°19N 14°12E **76** D10
Neustadt *Schleswig-Holstein,*
  Germany 54°6N 10°49E **76** A6
Neustadt *Thüringen,*
  Germany 50°45N 11°43E **76** E7
Neustrelitz *Germany* 53°21N 13°4E **76** B8
Neuvic *France* 45°23N 2°16E **72** C6
Neuville-sur-Saône
  France 45°54N 4°51E **73** C8
Neuvy-le-Roi *France* 47°36N 0°36E **70** E7
Neuvy-St-Sépulchre
  France 46°35N 1°48E **71** F8

Neuvy-sur-Barangeon
  France 47°20N 2°15E **71** E9
Neuwerk *Germany* 53°55N 8°30E **76** B4
Neuwied *Germany* 50°26N 7°29E **76** E3
Neva → *Russia* 59°56N 30°20E **84** C6
Nevada *Iowa, U.S.A.* 42°1N 93°27W **172** D7
Nevada *Mo., U.S.A.* 37°51N 94°22W **172** G6
Nevada □ *U.S.A.* 39°0N 117°0W **168** G5
Nevada City *U.S.A.* 39°16N 121°1W **170** F6
Nevada, Cerro
  Argentina 35°30S 68°32W **190** D2
Nevasa *India* 19°34N 75°0E **126** C2
Nevel *Russia* 56°0N 29°55E **84** D5
Nevelsk *Russia* 46°40N 141°51E **107** E15
Nevers *France* 47°0N 3°9E **71** F10
Nevertire *Australia* 31°50S 147°44E **153** A7
Nevesinje *Bos.-H.* 43°14N 18°6E **96** C2
Neville *Canada* 49°58N 107°39W **163** D7
Nevinnomyssk *Russia* 44°40N 42°0E **87** H6
Nevis *St. Kitts & Nevis* 17°0N 62°30W **183** C7
Nevrokop = Gotse Delchev
  Bulgaria 41°36N 23°46E **96** E7
Nevşehir *Turkey* 38°33N 34°40E **104** C6
Nevşehir □ *Turkey* 38°50N 34°40E **104** C6
Nevskoye *Russia* 54°32N 22°39E **82** D9
New → *U.S.A.* 38°10N 81°12W **173** F13
New Aiyansh *Canada* 55°12N 129°4W **162** B3
New Albany *Ind.,*
  U.S.A. 38°18N 85°49W **173** F11
New Albany *Miss.,*
  U.S.A. 34°29N 89°0W **177** D10
New Albany *Pa.,*
  U.S.A. 41°36N 76°27W **175** E8
New Amsterdam
  Guyana 6°15N 57°36W **186** B7
New Atlas = Akhali Atoni
  Georgia 43°7N 40°50E **87** J5
New Baltimore *U.S.A.* 42°41N 82°44W **174** D2
New Bedford *U.S.A.* 41°38N 70°56W **175** E14
New Berlin *N.Y.,*
  U.S.A. 42°37N 75°20W **175** D9
New Berlin *Pa., U.S.A.* 40°50N 76°57W **174** F8
New Bern *U.S.A.* 35°7N 77°3W **177** D16
New Bethlehem *U.S.A.* 41°0N 79°20W **174** F5
New Bight *Bahamas* 24°19N 75°24W **183** B4
New Bloomfield *U.S.A.* 40°25N 77°11W **174** F7
New Boston *U.S.A.* 33°28N 94°25W **176** E7
New Braunfels *U.S.A.* 29°42N 98°8W **176** G5
New Brighton *N.Z.* 43°29S 172°43E **155** D7
New Brighton *U.S.A.* 40°42N 80°19W **174** F4
New Britain *Papua N. G.* 5°50S 150°20E **147** B8
New Britain *U.S.A.* 41°40N 72°47W **175** E12
New Brockton *U.S.A.* 31°23N 85°56W **178** D4
New Brunswick
  U.S.A. 40°30N 74°27W **175** F10
New Brunswick □
  Canada 46°50N 66°30W **165** C6
New Bussa *Nigeria* 9°53N 4°31E **139** D5
New Caledonia ☒
  Pac. Oc. 21°0S 165°0E **147** D9
New Caledonia Trough
  Pac. Oc. 30°0S 165°0E **156** L8
New Castile = Castilla-La
  Mancha □ *Spain* 39°30N 3°30W **89** F7
New Castle *Ind.,*
  U.S.A. 39°55N 85°22W **173** F11
New Castle *Pa., U.S.A.* 41°0N 80°21W **174** F4
New City *U.S.A.* 41°9N 73°59W **175** E11
New Concord *U.S.A.* 39°59N 81°54W **174** G3
New Cumberland
  U.S.A. 40°30N 80°36W **174** F4
New Cuyama *U.S.A.* 34°57N 119°38W **171** L7
New Delhi *India* 28°36N 77°11E **124** E7
New Denver *Canada* 50°0N 117°25W **162** D5
New Don Pedro Res.
  U.S.A. 37°43N 120°24W **170** H6
New Ellenton *U.S.A.* 33°28N 81°41W **178** B8
New England *U.S.A.* 43°0N 71°0W **167** G25
New England *N. Dak.,*
  U.S.A. 46°32N 102°52W **172** B2
New England △
  Australia 30°25S 152°30E **153** A10
New England Ra.
  Australia 30°20S 151°45E **151** E5
New England Seamounts
  Atl. Oc. 38°0N 63°0W **86** C5
New Forest △ *U.K.* 50°53N 1°34W **67** G6
New Galloway *U.K.* 55°5N 4°9W **66** F4
New Glasgow *Canada* 45°35N 62°36W **165** C7
New Guinea *Oceania* 4°0S 136°0E **147** B6
New Hamburg *Canada* 43°23N 80°42W **174** C4
New Hampshire □
  U.S.A. 44°0N 71°30W **175** C13
New Hampton *U.S.A.* 43°3N 92°19W **172** D8
New Hanover *S. Africa* 29°22S 30°31E **145** C5
New Hartford *U.S.A.* 43°4N 75°18W **175** C9
New Haven *Conn.,*
  U.S.A. 41°18N 72°55W **175** E12
New Haven *Mich.,*
  U.S.A. 42°44N 82°48W **174** D2
New Haven *N.Y.,*
  U.S.A. 43°28N 76°18W **175** C8
New Hazelton *Canada* 55°20N 127°30W **162** B3
New Hebrides = Vanuatu ■
  Pac. Oc. 15°0S 168°0E **147** D9
New Holland *U.S.A.* 40°6N 76°5W **175** F8
New Iberia *U.S.A.* 30°1N 91°49W **176** G9
New Ireland
  Papua N. G. 3°20S 151°50E **147** B8
New Jersey □ *U.S.A.* 40°0N 74°30W **175** F10
New Kensington
  U.S.A. 40°34N 79°46W **174** F5
New Lexington
  U.S.A. 39°43N 82°13W **173** F12
New Liskeard *Canada* 47°31N 79°41W **164** C4
New London *Conn.,*
  U.S.A. 41°22N 72°6W **175** E12
New London *Ohio,*
  U.S.A. 41°5N 82°24W **174** E2
New London *Wis.,*
  U.S.A. 44°23N 88°45W **172** C9
New Madrid *U.S.A.* 36°36N 89°32W **172** G9
New Martinsville
  U.S.A. 39°39N 80°52W **173** F13
New Meadows *U.S.A.* 44°58N 116°18W **168** D5
New Melones L.
  U.S.A. 37°57N 120°31W **170** H6

New Mexico □ *U.S.A.* 34°30N 106°0W **169** J11
New Milford *Conn.,*
  U.S.A. 41°35N 73°25W **175** E11
New Milford *Pa.,*
  U.S.A. 41°52N 75°44W **175** E9
New Mumbai = Navi Mumbai
  India 19°5N 73°0E **126** E1
New Norcia *Australia* 30°57S 116°13E **149** F2
New Norfolk *Australia* 42°46S 147°2E **151** G4
New Orleans *U.S.A.* 29°57N 90°4W **177** G9
New Philadelphia
  U.S.A. 40°30N 81°27W **174** F3
New Plymouth *N.Z.* 39°4S 174°5E **154** F3
New Plymouth
  U.S.A. 43°58N 116°49W **168** E5
New Port Richey
  U.S.A. 28°16N 82°43W **179** G7
New Providence
  Bahamas 25°25N 77°35W **182** A4
New Quay *U.K.* 52°13N 4°21W **67** E3
New Radnor *U.K.* 52°15N 3°9W **67** E4
New Richmond
  Canada 48°15N 65°45W **165** C6
New Richmond *U.S.A.* 45°7N 92°32W **172** C7
New River Gorge △
  U.S.A. 37°53N 81°5W **173** G13
New Roads *U.S.A.* 30°42N 91°26W **176** F9
New Rochelle *U.S.A.* 40°55N 73°46W **175** F11
New Rockford *U.S.A.* 47°41N 99°8W **172** B4
New Romney *U.K.* 50°59N 0°57E **67** G8
New Ross *Ireland* 52°23N 6°57W **64** D5
New Salem *U.S.A.* 46°51N 101°25W **172** B3
New Scone = Scone *U.K.* 56°25N 3°24W **65** E5
New Siberian I. = Novaya Sibir,
  Ostrov *Russia* 75°10N 150°0E **107** B16
New Siberian Is. = Novosibirskiye
  Ostrova *Russia* 75°0N 142°0E **107** B15
New Smyrna Beach
  U.S.A. 29°1N 80°56W **179** F9
New South Wales □
  Australia 33°0S 146°0E **153** B7
New Tecumseth = Alliston
  Canada 44°9N 79°52W **174** B5
New Town *U.S.A.* 47°59N 102°30W **172** B2
New Tredegar *U.K.* 51°44N 3°16W **67** F4
New Ulm *U.S.A.* 44°19N 94°28W **172** C6
New Waterford *Canada* 46°13N 60°4W **165** C7
New Westminster
  Canada 49°13N 122°55W **170** A4
New York *U.S.A.* 40°43N 74°0W **175** F11
New York □ *U.S.A.* 43°0N 75°0W **175** D9
New York J.F. Kennedy Int. ✈
  (JFK) *U.S.A.* 40°38N 73°47W **175** F11
New Zealand ■ *Oceania* 40°0S 176°0E **154** G5
Newaj → *India* 24°24N 76°49E **124** G7
Newala *Tanzania* 10°58S 39°18E **143** E4
Newark *Del., U.S.A.* 39°41N 75°46W **173** F16
Newark *N.J., U.S.A.* 40°44N 74°10W **175** F10
Newark *N.Y., U.S.A.* 43°3N 77°6W **174** D7
Newark *Ohio, U.S.A.* 40°3N 82°24W **174** F2
Newark Liberty Int. ✈ (EWR)
  U.S.A. 40°42N 74°10W **175** F10
Newark-on-Trent *U.K.* 53°5N 0°48W **66** D7
Newark Valley *U.S.A.* 42°14N 76°11W **175** D8
Newberg *U.S.A.* 45°18N 122°58W **168** D2
Newberry *Fla., U.S.A.* 29°39N 82°37W **179** F7
Newberry *Mich.,*
  U.S.A. 46°21N 85°30W **173** B11
Newberry *S.C., U.S.A.* 34°17N 81°37W **177** D14
Newberry Springs
  U.S.A. 34°50N 116°41W **171** L10
Newboro L. *Canada* 44°38N 76°20W **175** B8
Newbridge *Ireland* 53°11N 6°48W **64** C5
Newburgh *Canada* 44°19N 76°52W **174** B8
Newburgh *U.S.A.* 41°30N 74°1W **175** E10
Newbury *U.K.* 51°24N 1°20W **67** F6
Newbury *N.H., U.S.A.* 43°19N 72°3W **175** B12
Newbury *Vt., U.S.A.* 44°5N 72°4W **175** B12
Newburyport *U.S.A.* 42°49N 70°53W **175** D14
Newcastle *Australia* 33°0S 151°46E **153** B9
Newcastle *N.B., Canada* 47°1N 65°38W **165** C6
Newcastle *Ont., Canada* 43°55N 78°35W **164** D4
Newcastle *Ireland* 52°27N 9°3W **64** D2
Newcastle *S. Africa* 27°45S 29°58E **145** D4
Newcastle *U.K.* 54°13N 5°54W **64** B6
Newcastle *Calif., U.S.A.* 38°53N 121°8W **170** G5
Newcastle *Wyo.,*
  U.S.A. 43°50N 104°11W **168** E11
Newcastle Emlyn *U.K.* 52°2N 4°28W **67** E3
Newcastle Ra.
  Australia 15°45S 130°15E **148** C5
Newcastle-under-Lyme
  U.K. 53°1N 2°14W **66** D5
Newcastle-upon-Tyne
  U.K. 54°58N 1°36W **66** C6
Newcastle Waters
  Australia 17°30S 133°28E **150** B1
Newcomb *U.S.A.* 43°58N 74°10W **175** C10
Newcomerstown
  U.S.A. 40°16N 81°36W **174** F3
Newdegate *Australia* 33°6S 119°0E **149** F2
Newell *Australia* 16°20S 145°16E **150** B4
Newell *U.S.A.* 44°43N 103°25W **172** C2
Newenham, C., U.S.A. 58°39N 162°11W **166** D7
Newfane *U.S.A.* 43°17N 78°43W **174** C6
Newfield *U.S.A.* 42°18N 76°33W **175** D8
Newfound L. *U.S.A.* 43°40N 71°47W **175** C13
Newfoundland *Canada* 49°0N 55°0W **165** C8
Newfoundland & Labrador □
  Canada 52°0N 58°0W **165** B8
Newhaven *U.K.* 50°47N 0°3E **67** G8
Newington *U.S.A.* 32°35N 81°30W **178** B8
Newkirk *U.S.A.* 36°53N 97°3W **176** C6
Newlyn *U.K.* 50°6N 5°34W **67** G2
Newman *Australia* 23°18S 119°45E **148** D2
Newman *U.S.A.* 37°19N 121°1W **170** H5
Newmarket *Canada* 44°3N 79°28W **174** B5
Newmarket *Ireland* 52°13N 9°0W **64** D2
Newmarket *U.K.* 52°15N 0°25E **67** E8
Newmarket *U.S.A.* 43°5N 70°56W **175** C14
Newnan *U.S.A.* 33°23N 84°48W **178** B3
Newport *Ireland* 53°53N 9°33W **64** C2
Newport *I. of W., U.K.* 50°42N 1°17W **67** G6
Newport *Newport, U.K.* 51°35N 3°0W **67** F5
Newport *Ark., U.S.A.* 35°37N 91°16W **176** D9
Newport *Fla., U.S.A.* 30°11N 84°10W **178** E5
Newport *Ky., U.S.A.* 39°5N 84°29W **173** F11
Newport *N.H., U.S.A.* 43°22N 72°10W **175** C12
Newport *Oreg., U.S.A.* 44°39N 124°3W **168** D1

Newport *Pa., U.S.A.* 40°29N 77°8W **174** F7
Newport *R.I., U.S.A.* 41°29N 71°19W **175** E13
Newport *Tenn., U.S.A.* 35°58N 83°11W **177** D13
Newport *Vt., U.S.A.* 44°56N 72°13W **175** B12
Newport *Wash., U.S.A.* 48°11N 117°3W **168** B5
Newport □ *U.K.* 51°33N 3°1W **67** F4
Newport Beach
  U.S.A. 33°37N 117°56W **171** M9
Newport News *U.S.A.* 36°58N 76°25W **173** G15
Newport Pagnell *U.K.* 52°5N 0°43W **67** E7
Newquay *U.K.* 50°25N 5°6W **67** G2
Newry *U.K.* 54°11N 6°21W **64** B5
Newry Islands △
  Australia 20°51S 148°56E **150** b
Newton *Ga., U.S.A.* 31°19N 84°20W **178** D5
Newton *Ill., U.S.A.* 38°59N 88°10W **172** F9
Newton *Iowa, U.S.A.* 41°42N 93°3W **172** E7
Newton *Kans., U.S.A.* 38°3N 97°21W **172** F5
Newton *Mass., U.S.A.* 42°21N 71°12W **175** D13
Newton *Miss., U.S.A.* 32°19N 89°10W **177** E10
Newton *N.C., U.S.A.* 35°40N 81°13W **177** D14
Newton *N.J., U.S.A.* 41°3N 74°45W **175** E10
Newton *Tex., U.S.A.* 30°51N 93°46W **176** F8
Newton Abbot *U.K.* 50°32N 3°37W **67** G4
Newton Aycliffe *U.K.* 54°37N 1°34W **66** C6
Newton Falls *N.Y.,*
  U.S.A. 44°12N 74°59W **175** B10
Newton Falls *Ohio,*
  U.S.A. 41°11N 80°59W **174** E4
Newton Stewart *U.K.* 54°57N 4°30W **65** G4
Newtonmore *U.K.* 57°4N 4°8W **65** D4
Newtontoppen *Svalbard* 79°0N 17°30E **57** B12
Newtown *U.K.* 52°31N 3°19W **67** E4
Newtownabbey *U.K.* 54°40N 5°56W **64** B6
Newtownards *U.K.* 54°36N 5°42W **64** B6
Newtownbarry = Bunclody
  Ireland 52°39N 6°40W **64** D5
Newtownstewart *U.K.* 54°43N 7°23W **64** B4
Newville *U.S.A.* 40°10N 77°24W **174** F7
Nexon *France* 45°41N 1°11E **72** C5
Neya *Russia* 58°21N 43°49E **86** A6
Neyrīz *Iran* 29°15N 54°19E **129** D7
Neyshābūr *Iran* 36°10N 58°50E **129** B8
Neyveli *India* 11°32N 79°29E **127** J4
Neyyattinkara *India* 8°26N 77°5E **127** K3
Nezhin = Nizhyn *Ukraine* 51°5N 31°55E **85** G6
Nezperce *U.S.A.* 46°14N 116°14W **168** C5
Nezvysko *Ukraine* 48°46N 25°15E **81** B10
Nga, Laem *Thailand* 7°55N 98°27E **121** a
Ngaanyatjarra ◎
  Australia 22°40S 127°0E **148** D4
Ngabang *Indonesia* 0°23N 109°55E **118** D3
Ngabordamlu, Tanjung
  Indonesia 6°56S 134°11E **119** F8
N'Gage *Angola* 7°46S 15°15E **140** F3
Ngala *Nigeria* 12°20N 14°11E **139** C7
Ngalurrtju Nungali ◎
  Australia 15°42S 130°4E **148** D5
Ngalurrtju ◎ *Australia* 22°44S 132°5E **148** D5
Ngami Depression
  Botswana 20°30S 22°46E **144** B3
Ngamo *Zimbabwe* 19°3S 27°32E **143** F2
Ngamring *China* 29°14N 87°10E **110** F6
Nganbét, L. de *Togo* 7°26N 1°25E **139** D5
Nganglong Kangri *China* 33°0N 81°0E **125** C9
Ngao *Thailand* 18°46N 99°59E **120** C2
Ngaoundéré *Cameroon* 7°15N 13°35E **140** C2
Ngapara *N.Z.* 44°57S 170°46E **155** E5
Ngara *Tanzania* 2°29S 30°40E **142** C3
Ngarluma ◎ *Australia* 21°30S 118°30E **148** D2
Ngaruawahia *N.Z.* 37°42S 175°11E **154** D4
Ngaruroro → *N.Z.* 39°34S 176°55E **154** F5
Ngatapa *N.Z.* 38°32S 177°45E **154** F6
Ngauruhoe, Mt. *N.Z.* 39°13S 175°45E **154** F4
Ngawi *Indonesia* 7°24S 111°26E **119** G14
Ngcobo *S. Africa* 31°37S 28°0E **145** D4
Ngeru *Uganda* 2°57N 33°10E **142** B3
Ngerulmud = Melekeok
  Palau 7°27N 134°38E **156** G5
Nghia Lo *Vietnam* 21°33N 104°28E **116** G5
Ngoma *Malawi* 13°8S 33°45E **143** E3
Ngomahura *Zimbabwe* 20°26S 30°43E **143** G3
Ngomba *Tanzania* 8°20S 32°53E **143** D3
Ngomeni, Ras *Kenya* 2°59S 40°14E **142** C5
Ngong *Kenya* 1°22S 36°39E **142** C4
Ngongotaha *N.Z.* 38°5S 176°12E **154** E5
Ngoring Hu *China* 34°55N 97°5E **110** E8
Ngorkou *Mali* 15°40N 3°41W **138** B4
Ngorongoro *Tanzania* 3°11S 35°32E **142** C4
Ngorongoro □ *Tanzania* 2°40S 35°30E **142** C4
Ngozi *Burundi* 2°54S 29°50E **142** C2
Ngudu *Tanzania* 2°58S 33°25E **142** C3
Nguigmi *Niger* 14°20N 13°20E **135** F8
Nguila *Cameroon* 4°11N 11°43E **139** E7
Nguiu *Australia* 11°46S 130°38E **148** B5
Ngukurr *Australia* 14°44S 134°44E **150** A1
Ngum → *Laos* 18°31N 102°32E **120** C4
Ngundu *Zimbabwe* 18°11S 31°15E **143** F3
Ngunga *Tanzania* 3°37S 33°37E **142** C3
Nguru *Nigeria* 12°56N 10°29E **139** C7
Nguru Mts. *Tanzania* 6°0S 37°30E **142** D4
Ngusi *Malawi* 14°0S 34°50E **143** E3
Nguyen Binh *Vietnam* 22°39N 105°56E **116** F5
Ngwaketse □ *Botswana* 25°0S 25°0E **144** C4
Nha Bang *Vietnam* 10°37N 105°0E **121** G5
Nha Trang *Vietnam* 12°16N 109°10E **121** F7
Nhacoongo *Mozam.* 24°18S 35°14E **145** C6
Nhamaabué *Mozam.* 17°25S 35°5E **143** F4
Nhamundá → *Brazil* 2°12S 56°41W **187** D7
Nhangulaze, L. *Mozam.* 24°0S 34°30E **145** C5
Nharnwangga, Wajarri and
  Ngarlawangga ◎
  Australia 24°50S 118°0E **149** D2
Nhill *Australia* 36°18S 141°40E **152** D4
Nho Quan *Vietnam* 20°18N 105°45E **116** G5
Nhulunbuy *Australia* 12°10S 137°20E **150** A2
Nia-nia
  Dem. Rep. of the Congo 1°30N 27°40E **142** B2
Niafounké *Mali* 16°0N 4°5W **138** B4
Niagara Falls *Canada* 43°7N 79°5W **174** C6
Niagara Falls *U.S.A.* 43°5N 79°4W **174** C6
Niagara-on-the-Lake
  Canada 43°15N 79°4W **174** C6
Niah *Malaysia* 3°58N 113°46E **118** D4
Niamey *Niger* 13°27N 2°6E **139** C5
Niamtougou *Togo* 9°46N 1°9E **139** D5
Niandan-Koro *Guinea* 11°5N 9°15W **138** D2

Nianforando *Guinea* 9°37N 10°36W **138** D2
Niangara
  Dem. Rep. of the Congo 3°42N 27°50E **142** B2
Niangay, L. *Mali* 15°50N 3°0W **138** B4
Niangbo *Ivory C.* 8°49N 5°10W **138** D3
Niangoloko
  Burkina Faso 10°15N 4°55W **138** C4
Niantic *U.S.A.* 41°20N 72°11W **175** E12
Nias *Indonesia* 1°0N 97°30E **118** D1
Niassa □ *Mozam.* 13°30S 36°0E **143** E4
Niassa △ *Mozam.* 12°45S 36°57E **143** E4
Nibāk *Si. Arabia* 24°25N 50°50E **129** E7
Nibe *Denmark* 56°59N 9°38E **63** H3
Nicaragua ■
  Cent. Amer. 11°40N 85°30W **182** D2
Nicaragua, L. de *Nic.* 12°0N 85°30W **182** D2
Nicastro *Italy* 38°59N 16°19E **95** D9
Nice *France* 43°42N 7°14E **73** E11
Nice-Côte-d'Azur ✈ (NCE)
  France 43°41N 7°12E **73** E11
Niceville *U.S.A.* 30°31N 86°30W **178** E3
Nichicun, L. *Canada* 53°5N 71°0W **165** B5
Nichinan *Japan* 31°38N 131°23E **113** K4
Nicholás, Canal
  Caribbean 23°30N 80°5W **182** B3
Nicholas Channel = Nicholás,
  Canal *Caribbean* 23°30N 80°5W **182** B3
Nicholasville *U.S.A.* 37°53N 84°34W **173** G11
Nicholls *U.S.A.* 31°31N 82°38W **178** D7
Nichols *U.S.A.* 42°1N 76°22W **175** D8
Nicholson *Australia* 18°2S 128°54E **148** C4
Nicholson *U.S.A.* 41°37N 75°47W **175** E9
Nicholson →
  Australia 17°31S 139°36E **150** B2
Nicholson L. *Canada* 62°40N 102°40W **163** A8
Nicholson Ra.
  Australia 27°15S 116°45E **149** E2
Nicholville *U.S.A.* 44°41N 74°39W **175** B10
Nicobar Is. *Ind. Oc.* 8°0N 93°30E **127** L11
Nicola *Canada* 50°12N 120°40W **162** C4
Nicolls Town *Bahamas* 25°8N 78°0W **182** A4
Nicosia *Cyprus* 35°10N 33°25E **101** D12
Nicosia *Italy* 37°45N 14°24E **95** E7
Nicótera *Italy* 38°33N 15°56E **95** D8
Nicoya *Costa Rica* 10°9N 85°27W **182** D2
Nicoya, G. de *Costa Rica* 10°0N 85°0W **182** E3
Nicoya, Pen. de
  Costa Rica 9°45N 85°40W **182** E2
Nida *Lithuania* 55°20N 21°4E **82** C8
Nidd → *U.K.* 53°59N 1°23W **66** D6
Nidda *Germany* 50°23N 9°1E **77** E5
Nidda → *Germany* 50°17N 8°48E **77** E4
Nidwalden □ *Switz.* 46°50N 8°25E **77** J4
Nied → *Germany* 49°23N 6°40E **71** C13
Niebüll *Germany* 54°46N 8°49E **76** A4
Nied → *Germany* 49°23N 6°40E **71** C13
Niederbayern □
  Germany 48°40N 12°50E **77** G8
Niederbronn-les-Bains
  France 48°57N 7°39E **71** C14
Niedere Tauern *Austria* 47°20N 14°0E **78** D7
Niederlausitz *Germany* 51°42N 13°59E **76** D9
Niederösterreich □
  Austria 48°25N 15°40E **78** C8
Niedersachsen □
  Germany 52°50N 9°0E **76** C4
Niedersächsisches Wattenmeer △
  Germany 53°45N 7°30E **76** B3
Niekerkshoop *S. Africa* 29°19S 22°51E **144** C3
Niellé *Ivory C.* 10°5N 5°38W **138** C3
Niemba
  Dem. Rep. of the Congo 5°58S 28°24E **142** D2
Niemen = Nemunas →
  Lithuania 55°25N 21°10E **82** C8
Niemodlin *Poland* 50°38N 17°38E **83** H4
Niemur *Australia* 35°17S 144°9E **152** C6
Nienburg *Germany* 52°39N 9°13E **76** C5
Niepolomice *Poland* 50°3N 20°13E **83** H7
Niers → *Germany* 51°43N 5°57E **76** D1
Niesky *Germany* 51°17N 14°49E **76** D10
Nieszawa *Poland* 52°52N 18°50E **83** F5
Nieu Bethesda *S. Africa* 31°51S 24°34E **144** D3
Nieuw Amsterdam
  Suriname 5°53N 55°5W **187** B7
Nieuw Nickerie *Suriname* 6°0N 56°59W **187** B7
Nieuwoudtville *S. Africa* 31°23S 19°7E **144** E2
Nieuwpoort *Belgium* 51°8N 2°45E **69** C2
Nieves, Pico de las
  Canary Is. 27°57N 15°35W **100** G4
Nièvre □ *France* 47°10N 3°40E **71** E10
Niğa *Turkey* 13°38N 5°27W **138** d
Niğde *Turkey* 37°58N 34°40E **104** C6
Niğde □ *Turkey* 38°0N 34°30E **104** C6
Nigel *S. Africa* 26°27S 28°25E **145** D4
Niger ■ *Nigeria* 10°0N 5°30E **139** D6
Niger □ *Nigeria* 10°0N 5°30E **139** D6
Niger → *W. Afr.* 5°33N 6°33E **139** D6
Niger Delta *Africa* 5°0N 6°0E **139** E6
Nigeria ■ *W. Afr.* 8°30N 8°0E **139** D6
Nighasin *India* 28°14N 80°52E **125** E9
Nightcaps *N.Z.* 45°57S 168°2E **155** F3
Nigríta *Greece* 40°56N 23°29E **96** D6
Nihoa *U.S.A.* 23°6N 161°58W **167** L7
Nihon = Japan ■ *Asia* 36°0N 136°0E **113** G8
Nii-Jima *Japan* 34°20N 139°15E **113** G9
Niigata *Japan* 37°58N 139°0E **112** F9
Niigata □ *Japan* 37°15N 138°45E **113** F9
Niihama *Japan* 33°55N 133°16E **113** H6
Ni'ihau *U.S.A.* 21°54N 160°9W **167** L7
Niimi *Japan* 34°59N 133°28E **113** G6
Niitsu *Japan* 37°48N 139°7E **112** F9
Nijar *Spain* 36°53N 2°15W **91** J2
Nijil *Jordan* 30°32N 35°33E **130** E4
Nijkerk *Neths.* 52°13N 5°30E **69** B5
Nijmegen *Neths.* 51°50N 5°52E **69** C5
Nijverdal *Neths.* 52°22N 6°28E **69** B6
Nīk Pey *Iran* 36°50N 48°10E **105** D13
Nikaweratiya *Sri Lanka* 7°45N 80°7E **127** L5
Nike *Nigeria* 6°26N 7°29E **139** D6
Nikel *Russia* 69°24N 30°13E **60** B24
Nikiniki *Indonesia* 9°49S 124°30E **120** D1
Nikışiani *Greece* 40°57N 24°9E **97** F8
Nikiti *Greece* 40°13N 23°43E **96** F7
Nikki *Benin* 9°58N 3°12E **139** D5
Nikkō *Japan* 36°45N 139°35E **113** F9
Nikkō △ *Japan* 36°56N 139°37E **113** F9
Nikolayev = Mykolyiv
  Ukraine 46°58N 32°0E **85** J7
Nikolayevsk *Russia* 50°0N 45°35E **86** E7
Nikolayevsk-na-Amur
  Russia 53°8N 140°44E **107** D15

Nianforando *Guinea* 9°37N 10°36W **138** D2
Nikolsk *Russia* 53°49N 46°4E **86** D8
Nikolskoye *Russia* 55°12N 166°0E **107** D18
Nikopol *Bulgaria* 43°43N 24°54E **97** C8
Nikopol *Ukraine* 47°35N 34°25E **85** J8
Nikopolis *Greece* 39°5N 20°43E **98** B2
Niksar *Turkey* 40°31N 37°2E **104** B7
Nīkshahr *Iran* 26°15N 60°10E **129** E9
Nikšić *Montenegro* 42°50N 18°57E **96** C2
Nîl, Nahr en → *Africa* 30°10N 31°6E **137** E7
Nîl el Abyad → *Sudan* 15°38N 32°31E **135** E12
Nîl el Azraq → *Sudan* 15°38N 32°31E **135** E12
Nila *Indonesia* 6°44S 129°31E **119** F7
Nilakkottai *India* 10°10N 77°52E **127** K4
Niland *U.S.A.* 33°14N 115°31W **171** M11
Nilanga *India* 18°6N 76°46E **126** E3
Nile = Nîl, Nahr en →
  Africa 30°10N 31°6E **137** E7
Nile Delta *Egypt* 31°40N 31°0E **137** D7
Niles *Mich., U.S.A.* 41°50N 86°15W **172** E10
Niles *Ohio, U.S.A.* 41°11N 80°46W **174** E4
Nileshwar *India* 12°15N 75°6E **127** H2
Nilgiri Hills *India* 11°30N 76°30E **127** J3
Nilo Peçanha *Brazil* 13°37S 39°6W **189** C3
Nilüfer → *Turkey* 40°18N 28°27E **97** F12
Nim Ka Thana *India* 27°44N 75°48E **124** F6
Nimach *India* 24°30N 74°56E **124** G6
Nimba, Mt. *Africa* 7°37N 8°25W **138** D3
Nimbahera *India* 24°37N 74°45E **124** G6
Nîmes *France* 43°50N 4°23E **73** E8
Nimfaíon, Ákra = Pínes, Akra
  Greece 40°5N 24°20E **97** F8
Nimmitabel *Australia* 36°29S 149°15E **153** D8
Nin *Croatia* 44°16N 15°12E **93** D12
Nīnawá *Iraq* 36°25N 43°10E **105** D10
Nīnawá □ *Iraq* 35°30N 43°0E **105** D10
Nindigully *Australia* 28°21S 148°50E **151** D4
Nine Degree Channel
  India 9°0N 73°0E **127** L1
Ninepin Group *China* 22°16N 114°21E **111** a
Ninety Mile Beach *N.Z.* 34°48S 173°0E **154** B2
Ninety Mile Beach, The
  Australia 38°15S 147°24E **153** E7
Ninety Six *U.S.A.* 34°11N 82°1W **178** A7
Ninetyeast Ridge *Ind. Oc.* 1°0S 90°0E **146** E7
Nineveh = Nīnawá
  Iraq 36°25N 43°10E **105** D10
Ning Xian *China* 35°30N 107°58E **114** G4
Ningaloo Marine △
  Australia 22°23S 113°32E **148** D1
Ning'an *China* 44°22N 129°20E **115** B15
Ningbo *China* 29°51N 121°28E **117** C13
Ningcheng *China* 41°32N 119°53E **115** D10
Ningde *China* 26°38N 119°23E **117** D12
Ningdu *China* 26°25N 115°59E **117** D10
Ninggang *China* 26°42N 113°55E **117** D9
Ningguo *China* 30°35N 119°0E **117** C12
Ninghai *China* 29°15N 121°27E **117** C13
Ninghua *China* 26°14N 116°45E **117** D11
Ningi *Nigeria* 10°55N 9°30E **139** C6
Ningjin *China* 37°35N 114°57E **114** F8
Ningjing Shan *China* 31°0N 98°20E **116** C2
Ningling *China* 34°25N 115°22E **114** G8
Ningming *China* 22°8N 107°4E **116** F6
Ningnan *China* 27°0N 102°36E **116** D4
Ningpo = Ningbo
  China 29°51N 121°28E **117** C13
Ningqiang *China* 32°47N 106°15E **114** H4
Ningshan *China* 33°21N 108°21E **114** H5
Ningsia Hui A.R. = Ningxia Huizu
  Zizhiqu □ *China* 38°0N 106°0E **114** F4
Ningwu *China* 39°0N 112°18E **114** E7
Ningxia Huizu Zizhiqu □
  China 38°0N 106°0E **114** F4
Ningxiang *China* 28°15N 112°30E **117** C9
Ningyang *China* 35°47N 116°45E **114** G9
Ningyuan *China* 25°37N 111°57E **117** E8
Ninh Binh *Vietnam* 20°15N 105°55E **116** G5
Ninh Giang *Vietnam* 20°44N 106°24E **116** B6
Ninh Hoa *Vietnam* 12°30N 109°7E **120** F7
Ninh Ma *Vietnam* 12°48N 109°21E **120** F7
Nini-Suhien △ *Ghana* 5°20N 2°34W **138** D4
Ninove *Belgium* 50°51N 4°2E **69** D4
Nioaque *Brazil* 21°5S 55°50W **191** A4
Niobrara *U.S.A.* 42°45N 98°2W **172** D4
Niobrara → *U.S.A.* 42°46N 98°3W **172** D4
Niokolo-Koba △ *Senegal* 13°2N 13°0W **138** C2
Niono *Mali* 14°15N 6°0W **138** C3
Nionsamoridougou
  Guinea 8°45N 8°50W **138** D3
Nioro du Rip *Senegal* 13°40N 15°50W **138** C1
Nioro du Sahel *Mali* 15°15N 9°30W **138** B3
Niort *France* 46°19N 0°29W **72** B3
Nipani *India* 16°20N 74°25E **127** F2
Nipawin *Canada* 53°20N 104°0W **163** C8
Nipfjället *Sweden* 61°59N 12°50E **62** C6
Nipigon *Canada* 49°0N 88°17W **164** C2
Nipigon, L. *Canada* 49°50N 88°30W **164** C2
Nipishish L. *Canada* 54°12N 60°45W **165** B7
Nipissing, L. *Canada* 46°20N 80°0W **164** C4
Nipomo *U.S.A.* 35°3N 120°29W **171** K6
Nippon = Japan ■ *Asia* 36°0N 136°0E **113** G8
Nipton *U.S.A.* 35°28N 115°16W **171** K11
Niquelândia *Brazil* 14°33S 48°23W **189** C1
Nīr *Iran* 38°2N 47°59E **105** C12
Nira → *India* 17°58N 75°8E **126** F2
Nirasaki *Japan* 35°42N 138°27E **113** G9
Nirmal *India* 19°3N 78°20E **126** E4
Nirmali *India* 26°20N 86°35E **125** F12
Niš *Serbia* 43°19N 21°58E **96** C5
Nisa *Portugal* 39°30N 7°41W **89** F3
Niša Turkmenistan 37°59N 58°11E **129** B8
Nişāb *Si. Arabia* 29°11N 44°43E **128** D5
Nişāb *Yemen* 14°25N 46°29E **131** E4
Nišava → *Serbia* 43°20N 21°46E **96** C5
Niscemi *Italy* 37°8N 14°23E **95** F7
Nishinomiya *Japan* 34°45N 135°20E **113** G7
Nishiwaki *Japan* 34°59N 134°58E **113** G7
Niška Banja *Serbia* 43°18N 21°1E **96** C5
Niskibi → *Canada* 56°29N 88°9W **164** A2
Nisko *Poland* 50°35N 22°7E **83** H9
Nisporeni *Moldova* 47°4N 28°10E **81** C13
Nisqually → *U.S.A.* 47°6N 122°42W **170** C4
Nissaki *Greece* 39°43N 19°52E **101** A3
Nissan → *Sweden* 56°40N 12°51E **63** H6
Nissiros *Greece* 36°35N 27°12E **99** E9
Nissum Bredning
  Denmark 56°40N 8°20E **63** H2
Nissum Fjord *Denmark* 56°20N 8°11E **63** H2

Nistru = Dnister →
Europe   46°18N 30°17E **75** E16
Nisutlin → Canada   60°14N 132°34W **162** A2
Nitchequon Canada   53°10N 70°58W **165** B5
Niterói Brazil   22°53S 43°7W **191** A7
Nith → Canada   43°12N 80°23W **174** C4
Nith ~ U.K.   55°14N 3°33W **65** F5
Nitmiluk △ Australia   14°6S 132°15E **148** B5
Nitra Slovak Rep.   48°19N 18°4E **79** C11
Nitra ~ Slovak Rep.   47°46N 18°10E **79** C11
Nitriansky □
  Slovak Rep.   48°10N 18°30E **79** C11
Niue ☑ Pac. Oc.   19°2S 169°54W **157** J11
Niulan Jiang ~ China   27°30N 103°5E **116** C4
Niut Indonesia   0°55N 109°54E **118** D4
Niutou Shan China   29°5N 121°59E **117** C13
Nivala Finland   63°56N 24°57E **60** E21
Nivelles Belgium   50°35N 4°20E **69** D4
Nivernais France   47°15N 3°30E **71** E10
Niverville Canada   49°36N 97°3W **163** D9
Niwas India   23°3N 80°26E **125** H9
Nixa U.S.A.   37°3N 93°18W **172** G7
Nixon U.S.A.   29°16N 97°46W **176** G6
Nizam Sagar India   18°10N 77°58E **126** E3
Nizamabad India   18°45N 78°7E **126** E4
Nizamghat India   28°20N 95°45E **123** E19
Nizhne-Kolymsk
  Russia   68°24N 160°55E **107** C17
Nizhne-Svirskiy △
  Russia   60°30N 32°55E **84** B7
Nizhnegorskiy = Nyzhnohirskyy
  Ukraine   45°27N 34°38E **85** K8
Nizhnekamsk Russia   55°38N 51°49E **86** C10
Nizhneudinsk Russia   54°54N 99°3E **107** D10
Nizhnevartovsk Russia   60°56N 76°38E **106** C8
Nizhniy Bestyakh
  Russia   61°57N 129°54E **107** C13
Nizhniy Chir Russia   48°22N 43°5E **87** F6
Nizhniy Lomov Russia   53°34N 43°38E **86** D6
Nizhniy Novgorod Russia 56°20N 44°0E **86** B7
Nizhniy Novgorod □
  Russia   56°30N 44°20E **86** B7
Nizhniy Tagil Russia   57°55N 59°57E **106** D6
Nizhyn Ukraine   51°5N 31°55E **86** E5
Nizina Mazowiecka
  Poland   52°30N 21°0E **83** F8
Nizip Turkey   37°5N 37°50E **104** D7
Nízké Tatry Slovak Rep. 48°55N 19°30E **79** C12
Nízké Tatry △
  Slovak Rep.   48°55N 19°37E **79** C12
Nízký Jeseník
  Czech Rep.   49°50N 17°30E **79** B10
Nizwá Oman   22°56N 57°32E **131** C6
Nizza Monferrato Italy 44°46N 8°21E **92** D5
Njakwa Malawi   11°1S 33°56E **143** E3
Njazidja = Grande Comore
  Comoros Is.   11°35S 43°20E **141** a
Njegoš Montenegro   42°53N 18°45E **96** D2
Njinjo Tanzania   8°48S 38°54E **143** D4
Njombe Tanzania   9°20S 34°50E **143** D3
Njombe ~ Tanzania   6°56S 35°6E **142** D4
Njurundabommen
  Sweden   62°15N 17°25E **62** B11
Nkambe Cameroon   6°35N 10°40E **139** D7
Nkana Zambia   12°50S 28°8E **143** E2
Nkandla S. Africa   28°37S 31°5E **145** D5
Nkawkaw Ghana   6°36N 0°49W **139** D4
Nkayi Zimbabwe   19°41S 29°20E **143** F2
Nkhotakota Malawi   12°56S 34°15E **143** E3
Nkhotakota △ Malawi   12°50S 34°0E **143** E3
Nkondwe Tanzania   5°51S 30°51E **142** D3
Nkongsamba Cameroon   4°55N 9°55E **139** E6
Nkoteng Cameroon   4°31N 12°2E **139** E7
Nkurenkuru Namibia   17°42S 18°32E **144** A2
Nkwanta Ghana   6°10N 2°10W **138** D4
Nmai ~ Burma   25°30N 97°25E **122** F2
Noakhali Bangla.   22°48N 91°10E **123** H17
Nobel Canada   45°25N 80°6W **174** A4
Nobeoka Japan   32°36N 131°41E **113** H5
Nobleboro Japan   39°58N 3°26W **88** F7
Noblesville U.S.A.   40°3N 86°1W **172** E10
Noboribetsu Japan   42°24N 141°6E **112** C10
Nocatee U.S.A.   27°10N 81°53W **179** N8
Noccundra Australia   27°50S 142°36E **151** D3
Noce ~ Italy   46°9N 11°4E **92** B8
Nocera Inferiore Italy 40°44N 14°38E **95** B7
Nocera Umbra Italy   43°5N 12°47E **93** E9
Noci Italy   40°48N 17°7E **95** B10
Nocona U.S.A.   33°47N 97°44W **176** E6
Nocrich Romania   45°55N 24°26E **81** E9
Noda Japan   35°56N 139°52E **113** G9
Nogales Mexico   31°19N 110°56W **180** A2
Nogales U.S.A.   31°21N 110°56W **169** L8
Nogaro France   43°45N 0°2W **72** E3
Nogat ~ Poland   54°17N 19°17E **82** D6
Nogata Japan   33°48N 130°44E **113** H5
Nogent France   48°1N 5°20E **71** D12
Nogent-le-Rotrou France 48°20N 0°50E **70** D7
Nogent-sur-Seine
  France   48°30N 3°30E **71** D10
Noggerup Australia   33°32S 116°5E **149** F2
Noginsk Russia   64°30N 90°50E **107** C10
Nogliki Russia   51°50N 143°10E **107** D15
Nogoa ~ Australia   23°40S 146°45E **150** C4
Nogoyá Argentina   32°24S 59°48W **190** C4
Nógrád □ Hungary   48°0N 19°30E **84** C4
Noguera Pallaresa ~
  Spain   41°55N 0°55E **90** D5
Noguera Ribagorçana ~
  Spain   41°40N 0°43E **90** D5
Nohar India   29°11N 74°49E **124** E6
Nohfelden Germany   49°35N 7°7E **77** F3
Nohta India   23°40N 79°34E **125** H8
Noia Spain   42°48N 8°53W **88** C2
Noida India   28°36N 77°19E **124** E7
Noire, Montagne France 43°28N 2°18E **72** E6
Noires, Mts. France   48°11N 3°40W **70** D3
Noirétable France   45°48N 3°46E **72** C7
Noirmoutier, Î. de France 46°58N 2°10W **72** F4
Noirmoutier-en-l'Île
  France   46°59N 2°14W **70** F4
Nojane Botswana   23°15S 20°14E **144** B3
Nojima-Zaki Japan   34°54N 139°53E **113** G9
Nok Kundi Pakistan   28°50N 62°45E **122** E3
Nok Ta Phao, Ko
  Thailand   9°23N 99°40E **121** b
Nokaneng Botswana   19°40S 22°17E **144** A3
Nokia Finland   61°30N 23°30E **63** E21
Nokomis Canada   51°35N 105°0W **163** C8

Nokomis U.S.A.   27°7N 82°27W **179** H7
Nokomis L. Canada   57°0N 103°0W **163** B8
Nola C.A.R.   3°35N 16°4E **142** D3
Nola Italy   40°55N 14°33E **95** B7
Nolay France   46°58N 4°35E **71** F11
Noli, C. di Italy   44°12N 8°25E **92** D5
Nolinsk Russia   57°28N 49°57E **86** C9
Noma Omuramba ~
  Namibia   18°52S 20°53E **144** A3
Nombre de Dios Panama   9°34N 79°28W **182** E4
Nomgon Mongolia   42°50N 105°8E **114** C3
Nomo-Zaki Japan   32°35N 129°44E **113** H4
Nonacho L. Canada   61°42N 109°40W **163** A7
Nonancourt France   48°47N 1°11E **70** D8
Nonda Australia   20°40S 142°28E **150** C3
None Italy   44°56N 7°32E **92** D4
Nong Chang Thailand   15°23N 99°51E **120** E2
Nong Han Res.
  Thailand   17°11N 104°9E **120** D5
Nong Het Laos   19°29N 103°59E **120** C4
Nong Khai Thailand   17°50N 102°46E **120** D4
Nong'an China   44°25N 125°5E **115** B13
Nongoma S. Africa   27°58S 31°35E **145** C5
Nongsa Indonesia   1°11N 104°8E **121** d
Nonoava Mexico   27°28N 106°44W **180** B3
Nonsan S. Korea   36°12N 127°5E **115** F14
Nonthaburi Thailand   13°50N 100°29E **120** F3
Nontron France   45°31N 0°40E **72** C4
Nonza France   42°47N 9°21E **73** F13
Noonamah Australia   12°40S 131°4E **148** B5
Noondie, L. Australia   28°30S 119°30E **149** E2
Noonkanbah ⊙
  Australia   18°30S 124°50E **148** C3
North Ayrshire □ U.K.   55°45N 4°44W **65** F4
North Bass I. U.S.A.   41°40N 82°56W **174** E2
North Battleford
  Canada   52°50N 108°17W **163** C7
North Bay Canada   46°20N 79°30W **164** C4
North Belcher Is.
  Canada   56°50N 79°50W **164** A4
North Bend Oreg.,
  U.S.A.   43°24N 124°14W **168** E1
North Bend Pa., U.S.A. 41°20N 77°42W **174** E7
North Bend Wash.,
  U.S.A.   47°30N 121°47W **176** C4
North Bennington
  U.S.A.   42°56N 73°15W **175** D11
North Berwick U.K.   56°4N 2°42W **65** E6
North Berwick U.S.A.   43°18N 70°44W **175** C14
North Brother I. India 19°59N 92°40E **127** J11
North Bruce Canada   44°22N 81°26W **174** B3
North C. Canada   47°5N 64°0W **165** C7
North C. N.Z.   34°23S 173°4E **154** A2
North Canadian ~
  U.S.A.   35°22N 95°37W **176** D7
North Canton U.S.A.   40°53N 81°24W **174** F3
North Cape = Nordkapp
  Norway   71°10N 25°50E **60** A21
North Caribou L.
  Canada   52°50N 90°40W **164** B1
North Carolina □
  U.S.A.   35°30N 80°0W **177** D15
North Cascades △
  U.S.A.   48°45N 121°10W **168** B3
North Channel Canada   46°0N 83°0W **164** C3
North Channel U.K.   55°13N 5°52W **65** F3
North Charleston
  U.S.A.   32°53N 79°58W **178** C10
North Chicago U.S.A.   42°19N 87°51W **172** D10
North Collins U.S.A.   42°35N 78°56W **174** D6
North Creek U.S.A.   43°42N 73°59W **175** C11
North Dakota □
  U.S.A.   47°30N 100°15W **172** B3
North Downs U.K.   51°19N 0°21E **67** F8
North East U.S.A.   42°13N 79°50W **174** D5
North East ~ Botswana   20°45S 27°30E **145** B4
North East Frontier Agency =
  Arunachal Pradesh □
  India   28°0N 95°0E **123** F19
North East Lincolnshire □
  U.K.   53°34N 0°2W **66** D7
North Eastern □ Kenya   1°30N 40°0E **142** B5
North Esk ~ U.K.   56°46N 2°24W **65** E6
North European Plain
  Europe   55°0N 25°0E **58** E10
North Foreland U.K.   51°22N 1°28E **67** F9
North Fork U.S.A.   37°14N 119°21W **170** H7
North Fork American ~
  U.S.A.   38°57N 120°59W **170** G5
North Fork Edisto ~
  U.S.A.   33°16N 80°54W **178** B9
North Fork Feather ~
  U.S.A.   38°33N 121°30W **170** F5
North Fork Grand ~
  U.S.A.   45°47N 102°16W **172** C2
North Fork Red ~
  U.S.A.   34°24N 99°14W **176** D5
North Fort Myers
  U.S.A.   26°41N 81°53W **179** J8
North Frisian Is. = Nordfriesische
  Inseln Germany   54°40N 8°20E **76** A4
North Gower Canada   45°8N 75°43W **175** A9
North Hd. Australia   30°14S 114°59E **149** F1
North Henik L. Canada   61°45N 97°40W **163** A9
North Highlands
  U.S.A.   38°40N 121°23W **170** G5
North Horr Kenya   3°20N 37°8E **142** B4
North I. India   10°8N 72°20E **127** J1
North I. Kenya   4°5N 36°5E **142** B4
North I. N.Z.   38°0S 175°0E **154** E4
North I. Seychelles   4°25S 55°13E **141** b
North Kingsville
  U.S.A.   41°54N 80°42W **174** E4
North Kitui ○ Kenya   0°15S 38°29E **142** C4
North Knife ~
  Canada   58°53N 94°45W **163** B10
North Koel ~ India   24°45N 83°50E **125** G10
North Korea ■ Asia   40°0N 127°0E **115** E14
North L. Australia   32°30S 143°5E **152** B5
North Lakhimpur India   27°14N 94°7E **123** F19
North Lanarkshire □
  U.K.   55°52N 3°56W **65** F5
North Las Vegas
  U.S.A.   36°11N 115°7W **171** J11
North Lincolnshire □
  U.K.   53°36N 0°30W **66** D7
North Little Rock
  U.S.A.   34°45N 92°16W **176** D8
North Loup ~ U.S.A.   41°17N 98°24W **172** E4

Norra Ulvön Sweden   63°3N 18°40E **62** A12
Norrahammar Sweden   57°43N 14°7E **63** G8
Norrbottens län □
  Sweden   66°50N 20°0E **60** C19
Norddelen Sweden   61°53N 16°43E **62** C10
Nørre Åby Denmark   55°27N 9°52E **63** J3
Nørre Alslev Denmark   54°54N 11°52E **63** K5
Nørresundby Denmark   57°5N 9°52E **63** G3
Norrhult-Klavreström
  Sweden   57°9N 15°10E **63** G9
Norris Point Canada   49°31N 57°53W **165** C8
Norristown Ga., U.S.A. 32°30N 82°30W **178** F7
Norristown Pa., U.S.A. 40°7N 75°21W **175** F9
Norrköping Sweden   58°37N 16°11E **63** F10
Norrland Sweden   62°15N 15°45E **60** E16
Norrsundet Sweden   60°56N 17°8E **62** D11
Norrtälje Sweden   59°46N 18°42E **62** E12
Norseman Australia   32°8S 121°43E **149** F3
Norsewood N.Z.   40°3S 176°13E **154** G5
Norsk Russia   52°30N 130°5E **107** D14
Norte, Pta. Argentina   42°5S 63°46W **192** B4
Norte, Pta. del
  Canary Is.   27°51N 17°57W **100** G2
Norte, Serra do Brazil 11°20S 59°0W **186** F7
North U.S.A.   33°37N 81°6W **178** B8
North, C. Canada   47°2N 60°20W **165** C7
North Adams U.S.A.   42°42N 73°7W **175** D11
North America   40°0N 100°0W **158** F10
North Andaman I.
  India   13°15N 92°55E **127** H11
North Arm Canada   62°0N 114°30W **162** A5
North Augusta U.S.A.   33°30N 81°59W **178** B8
North Australian Basin
  Ind. Oc.   14°30S 116°30E **146** F10
North Ayrshire □ U.K.   55°45N 4°44W **65** F4
North Bass I. U.S.A.   41°40N 82°56W **174** E2

North Luangwa △
  Zambia   11°49S 32°9E **143** E3
North Magnetic Pole
  Arctic   82°18N 113°24W **54** A2
North Mankato U.S.A.   44°10N 94°2W **172** C6
North Miami U.S.A.   25°53N 80°9W **179** K9
North Miami Beach
  U.S.A.   25°55N 80°9W **179** K9
North Minch U.K.   58°5N 5°55W **65** C3
North Moose L. Canada   54°4N 100°12W **163** C8
North Myrtle Beach
  U.S.A.   33°48N 78°42W **177** E15
North Nahanni ~
  Canada   62°15N 123°20W **162** A4
North Naples U.S.A.   26°12N 81°48W **179** J8
North New River Canal
  U.S.A.   26°30N 80°30W **179** J9
North Nowra Australia   34°53S 150°42E **153** E5
North Ogden U.S.A.   41°18N 111°58W **168** F8
North Ossetia-Alaniya □
  Russia   43°30N 44°30E **87** J7
North Pagai, I. = Pagai Utara,
  Pulau Indonesia   2°35S 100°0E **118** E2
North Palisade U.S.A.   37°6N 118°31W **170** H8
North Platte U.S.A.   41°8N 100°46W **172** E3
North Platte ~ U.S.A.   41°7N 100°42W **172** E3
North Point U.S.A.   27°4N 82°10W **179** H7
North Pole Arctic   90°0N 0°0 **54** A
North Portal Canada   49°0N 102°33W **163** D8
North Powder U.S.A.   45°2N 117°55W **168** D5
North Pt. Barbados   13°20N 59°37E **183** Q22
North Pt. Trin. & Tob. 11°21N 60°31W **187** J16
North Pt. U.S.A.   45°2N 83°16W **174** A4
North Reef I. India   15°5N 92°43E **127** H11
North Rhine Westphalia =
  Nordrhein-Westfalen □
  Germany   51°45N 7°30E **76** D3
North River Canada   53°49N 57°6W **165** B8
North Ronaldsay U.K.   59°22N 2°26W **65** B6
North Saskatchewan ~
  Canada   53°15N 105°5W **163** C7
North Sea Europe   56°0N 4°0E **58** D6
North Seal ~ Canada   58°50N 98°7W **163** B9
North Sentinel I. India 11°33N 92°15E **127** J11
North Shields
  Australia   34°38S 135°52E **152** C1
North Slope U.S.A.   69°15N 152°0W **166** B9
North Somerset □ U.K.   51°24N 2°45W **67** F5
North Sydney Canada   46°12N 60°15W **165** C7
North Syracuse U.S.A.   43°8N 76°7W **175** C8
North Taranaki Bight
  N.Z.   38°50S 174°15E **154** E3
North Thompson ~
  Canada   50°40N 120°20W **162** C4
North Tonawanda
  U.S.A.   43°2N 78°53W **174** C6
North Troy U.S.A.   45°0N 72°24W **175** B12
North Twin I. Canada   53°20N 80°0W **164** B4
North Tyne ~ U.K.   55°0N 2°8W **66** B5
North Uist U.K.   57°40N 7°15W **65** D1
North Vancouver
  Canada   49°19N 123°4W **170** A3
North Vernon U.S.A.   39°0N 85°38W **173** F11
North Wabasca L.
  Canada   56°0N 113°55W **162** B6
North Walsham U.K.   52°50N 1°22E **66** E9
North West = Severo-Zapadnyy □
  Russia   65°0N 40°0E **106** C4
North West □ S. Africa 27°0S 25°0E **144** A3
North-West □ S. Africa 27°0S 25°0E **144** A3
North West C. Australia 21°45S 114°9E **148** D1
North West Christmas I. Ridge
  Pac. Oc.   6°30N 165°0W **157** F11
North West Frontier = Khyber
  Pakhtunkhwa □
  Pakistan   34°0N 72°0E **124** C4
North West Highlands
  U.K.   57°33N 4°58W **65** D4
North West River
  Canada   53°30N 60°10W **165** B7
North Western □
  Zambia   13°30S 25°30E **143** E2
North Wildwood
  U.S.A.   39°0N 74°48W **173** F16
North York Moors U.K.   54°23N 0°53W **66** C7
North York Moors △
  U.K.   54°27N 0°51W **66** C7
North Yorkshire □ U.K. 54°15N 1°25W **66** C6
Northallerton U.K.   54°20N 1°26W **66** C6
Northam Australia   31°35S 116°42E **149** F2
Northam S. Africa   24°56S 27°18E **144** B4
Northampton
  Australia   28°27S 114°33E **149** E1
Northampton Mass.,
  U.S.A.   42°15N 0°53W **67** E7
Northampton Pa.,
  U.S.A.   40°41N 75°30W **175** F9
Northamptonshire □
  U.K.   52°16N 0°55W **67** E7
Northbridge U.S.A.   42°9N 71°39W **175** D13
Northbrook Canada   44°44N 77°9W **174** B7
Northcliff Australia   34°39S 116°7E **149** F2
Northeast Pacific Basin
  Pac. Oc.   32°0N 145°0W **157** D13
Northeast Providence Channel
  W. Indies   26°0N 76°0W **182** A4
Northeim Germany   51°42N 10°0E **76** D6
Northern = Limpopo □
  S. Africa   24°5S 29°0E **145** B4
Northern □ Ghana   9°30N 1°0W **139** D4
Northern □ Malawi   11°0S 34°0E **143** E3
Northern □ S. Leone   9°15N 11°30W **138** D2
Northern □ Zambia   10°30S 30°30E **143** E3
Northern Aral Sea
  Kazakhstan   46°20N 60°30E **108** C4
Northern Areas = Gilgit-
  Baltistan □ Pakistan 36°30N 73°0E **125** C7
Northern Cape □
  S. Africa   30°0S 20°0E **144** C3
Northern Circars India 17°30N 82°30E **126** F6
Northern Dvina = Dvina,
  Severnaya ~ Russia   64°32N 40°30E **58** C14
Northern Indian L.
  Canada   57°20N 97°20W **163** B9
Northern Ireland □ U.K. 54°45N 7°0W **64** B5
Northern Lau Group
  Fiji   17°30S 178°59W **154** a
Northern Light L.
  Canada   48°15N 90°39W **164** C1
Northern Marianas ☑
  Pac. Oc.   17°0N 145°0E **156** F6

Northern Province □
  S. Africa   24°0S 29°0E **145** B4
Northern Range
  Trin. & Tob.   10°46N 61°15W **187** K15
Northern Sporades = Voreíoi
  Sporades Greece   39°15N 23°30E **98** B5
Northern Territory □
  Australia   20°0S 133°0E **148** D5
Northfield Minn., U.S.A. 44°27N 93°9W **172** C7
Northfield Vt., U.S.A.   44°9N 72°40W **175** B12
Northgate Canada   49°0N 102°16W **163** D8
Northland □ N.Z.   35°30S 173°30E **154** B2
Northome U.S.A.   47°52N 94°17W **172** B7
Northport Ala., U.S.A.   33°14N 87°35W **177** E11
Northport Wash.,
  U.S.A.   48°55N 117°48W **168** B5
Northumberland □ U.K.   55°12N 2°0W **66** B6
Northumberland, C.
  Australia   38°5S 140°40E **152** F3
Northumberland Is.
  Australia   21°30S 149°50E **150** C4
Northumberland Str.
  Canada   46°20N 64°0W **165** C7
Northville Canada   43°10N 81°56W **174** C3
Northville U.S.A.   43°13N 74°11W **175** C10
Northwest Atlantic Mid-Ocean
  Canyon Atl. Oc.   54°0N 48°0W **56** A7
Northwest Pacific Basin
  Pac. Oc.   32°0N 165°0E **156** D7
Northwest Providence Channel
  W. Indies   26°0N 78°0W **182** A4
Northwest Territories □
  Canada   63°0N 118°0W **160** E8
Northwich U.K.   53°15N 2°31W **66** D5
Northwood Iowa,
  U.S.A.   43°27N 93°13W **172** D7
Northwood N. Dak.,
  U.S.A.   47°44N 97°34W **172** B5
Norton U.S.A.   39°50N 99°53W **172** F4
Norton Zimbabwe   17°52S 30°40E **143** F3
Norton Sd. U.S.A.   63°50N 164°0W **166** C6
Nortorf Germany   54°10N 9°50E **76** A5
Norwalk Calif., U.S.A.   33°54N 118°4W **171** M8
Norwalk Conn., U.S.A.   41°7N 73°22W **175** E11
Norwalk Iowa, U.S.A.   41°29N 93°41W **172** E7
Norwalk Ohio, U.S.A.   41°15N 82°37W **174** E2
Norway Maine, U.S.A.   44°13N 70°32W **173** C14
Norway Mich., U.S.A.   45°47N 87°55W **172** C10
Norway ■ Europe   63°0N 11°0E **60** E14
Norway House Canada   53°59N 97°50W **163** C9
Norwegian B. Canada   77°30N 90°0W **161** B14
Norwegian Basin Atl. Oc. 68°0N 2°0W **54** C7
Norwegian Sea Atl. Oc.   66°0N 1°0E **58** B6
Norwich Canada   42°59N 80°36W **174** D4
Norwich U.K.   52°38N 1°18E **67** E9
Norwich Conn., U.S.A.   41°31N 72°5W **175** E12
Norwich N.Y., U.S.A.   42°32N 75°32W **175** D9
Norwood Canada   44°23N 77°59W **174** B7
Norwood U.S.A.   44°45N 75°0W **175** B10
Nosappu-Misaki
  Japan   45°26N 141°39E **112** C12
Noshiro Japan   40°12N 140°0E **112** D10
Nosivka Ukraine   50°50N 31°37E **85** G6
Nosovka = Nosivka
  Ukraine   50°50N 31°37E **85** G6
Noşratābād Iran   29°55N 60°0E **129** D8
Noss Hd. U.K.   58°28N 3°3W **65** C5
Nossa Senhora da Glória
  Brazil   10°14S 37°25W **189** C2
Nossa Senhora das Dores
  Brazil   10°29S 37°13W **189** C2
Nossa Senhora do Socorro
  Brazil   10°52S 37°7W **189** C2
Nossebro Sweden   58°12N 12°43E **63** F6
Nossob □ S. Africa   26°55S 20°45E **144** C3
Nossombougou Mali   13°5N 7°55W **138** C3
Nosy Varika Madag.   20°35S 48°32E **141** J9
Notalgala U.S.A.   32°34N 85°41W **178** C4
Noteć ~ Poland   52°44N 15°26E **83** F2
Notikewin ~ Canada   57°2N 117°38W **162** B5
Notios Evvoikos Kolpos
  Greece   38°20N 24°0E **98** C5
Notti Togo   7°0N 1°17E **139** D5
Notodden Norway   59°35N 9°17E **61** G13
Notre-Dame-de-Koartac =
  Quaqtaq Canada   60°55N 69°40W **161** E18
Notre-Dame-des-Bois
  Canada   45°24N 71°4W **175** A13
Notre-Dame-d'Ivugivic = Ivujivik
  Canada   62°24N 77°55W **161** E16
Notre-Dame-du-Nord
  Canada   47°36N 79°30W **164** C4
Notsé Togo   7°0N 1°17E **139** D5
Nottawasaga B.
  Canada   44°35N 80°15W **174** B4
Nottaway ~ Canada   51°22N 78°55W **164** B4
Nottingham U.K.   52°58N 1°10W **66** E6
Nottingham, City of □
  U.K.   52°58N 1°10W **66** E6
Nottinghamshire □ U.K.   53°10N 1°3W **66** D6
Nottoway ~ U.S.A.   36°33N 76°55W **173** G9
Notwane ~ Botswana   23°35S 26°58E **144** B4
Nouâdhibou Mauritania   20°54N 17°0W **134** D2
Nouâdhibou, Râs
  Mauritania   20°50N 17°0W **134** D2
Nouakchott Mauritania   18°9N 15°58W **138** B1
Nouméa N. Cal.   22°17S 166°30E **147** D9
Nouna Burkina Faso   12°42N 3°54W **138** C4
Noupoort S. Africa   31°10S 24°57E **144** E3
Nouveau Comptoir = Wemindji
  Canada   53°0N 78°49W **164** B4
Nouvelle-Amsterdam, Î.
  Ind. Oc.   38°30S 77°30E **146** H6
Nouvelle-Calédonie = New
  Caledonia ☑ Pac. Oc. 21°0S 165°0E **147** D9
Nouzonville France   49°48N 4°44E **71** C11
Nová Baňa Slovak Rep.   48°28N 18°39E **79** C11
Nová Bystřice Czech Rep. 49°2N 15°8E **78** D8
Nova Cruz Brazil   6°28S 35°25W **189** B3
Nova Era Brazil   19°45S 43°3W **189** D2
Nova Esperança Brazil   23°8S 52°24W **191** A5

Nova Friburgo Brazil   22°16S 42°30W **191** A7
Nova Gorica Slovenia   45°57N 13°39E **93** C10
Nova Gradiška Croatia   45°17N 17°28E **80** E2
Nova Iguaçu Brazil   22°45S 43°28W **191** A7
Nova Iorque Brazil   7°0S 44°5W **189** D2
Nova Kakhovka Ukraine   46°42N 33°27E **85** J7
Nova Lamego
  Guinea-Biss.   12°19N 14°11W **138** C2
Nova Lusitânia Mozam.   19°50S 34°34E **143** F3
Nova Mambone Mozam.   21°0S 35°3E **145** B6
Nova Odesa Ukraine   47°19N 31°47E **85** J6
Nová Paka Czech Rep.   50°29N 15°30E **78** A8
Nova Pavova Serbia   44°56N 20°14E **80** F5
Nova Ponte Brazil   19°8S 47°41W **189** D1
Nova Russas Brazil   4°42S 40°34W **189** A2
Nova Scotia □ Canada   45°10N 63°0W **165** C10
Nova Siri Italy   40°10N 16°35E **95** B9
Nova Sofala Mozam.   20°7S 34°42E **145** B5
Nova Ushytsya Ukraine   48°50N 27°17E **81** B12
Nova Varoš Serbia   43°29N 19°48E **96** C3
Nova Venécia Brazil   18°45S 40°24W **189** D3
Nova Zagora Bulgaria   42°32N 26°1E **97** D10
Novaci Macedonia   41°5N 21°29E **96** E5
Novaci Romania   45°10N 23°42E **81** E8
Novafeltria Italy   43°53N 12°17E **93** E9
Novannenskiy = Novoannenskiy
  Russia   50°32N 42°39E **86** E6
Novar Canada   45°27N 79°14W **174** A5
Novara Italy   45°28N 8°38E **92** C5
Novato U.S.A.   38°6N 122°35W **170** G4
Novaya Kakhovka = Nova
  Kakhovka Ukraine   46°42N 33°27E **85** J7
Novaya Kazanka = Zhangaqala
  Kazakhstan   48°56N 49°36E **87** F9
Novaya Ladoga Russia   60°7N 32°16E **84** B7
Novaya Lyalya Russia   59°4N 60°45E **106** D7
Novaya Sibir, Ostrov
  Russia   75°10N 150°0E **107** B16
Novaya Zemlya Russia   75°0N 56°0E **106** B6
Nové Město Slovak Rep.   48°45N 17°50E **79** C10
Nové Město na Moravě
  Czech Rep.   49°34N 16°5E **78** B9
Nové Město nad Metují
  Czech Rep.   50°20N 16°10E **79** A9
Nové Zámky Slovak Rep.   48°2N 18°8E **79** C11
Novelda Spain   38°24N 0°45W **91** G4
Novellara Italy   44°51N 10°44E **92** D7
Noventa Vicentina Italy 45°17N 11°32E **93** C8
Novgorod = Velikiy Novgorod
  Russia   58°30N 31°25E **84** C6
Novgorod □ Russia   58°30N 32°30E **84** C7
Novgorod-Severskiy = Novhorod-
  Siverskyy Ukraine   52°2N 33°10E **85** G7
Novhorod-Siverskyy
  Ukraine   52°2N 33°10E **85** G7
Novi Bečej Serbia   45°36N 20°10E **80** E5
Novi Iskar Bulgaria   42°48N 23°21E **96** C7
Novi Kneževac Serbia   46°4N 20°8E **80** E5
Novi Lígure Italy   44°46N 8°47E **92** D5
Novi Pazar Bulgaria   43°25N 27°15E **97** C11
Novi Pazar Serbia   43°12N 20°28E **96** C4
Novi Sad Serbia   45°18N 19°52E **80** E4
Novi Slankamen Serbia   45°8N 20°15E **80** E5
Novi Travnik Bos.-H.   44°10N 17°40E **80** F2
Novi Vinodolski Croatia 45°10N 14°48E **93** C11
Novigrad Istra, Croatia 45°19N 13°33E **93** C10
Novigrad Zadar, Croatia 44°11N 15°32E **93** E12
Novigradsko More
  Croatia   44°12N 15°33E **93** D12
Novo Acôrdo Brazil   10°10S 46°48W **189** C1
Novo Cruzeiro Brazil   10°10S 46°48W **189** C1
Novo Hamburgo Brazil   29°37S 51°7W **191** B5
Novo Ivanivka Ukraine   45°55N 29°5E **81** E14
Novo Mesto Slovenia   45°47N 15°12E **93** C12
Novo Miloševo Serbia   45°42N 20°20E **80** E5
Novoaleksandrovsk
  Russia   45°29N 41°17E **87** D5
Novoaleksandrovskaya =
  Novoaleksandrovsk
  Russia   45°29N 41°17E **87** D5
Novoaltaysk Russia   53°30N 84°0E **109** B10
Novoannenskiy Russia   50°32N 42°39E **86** E6
Novoazovsk Ukraine   47°15N 38°4E **85** J10
Novocheboksarsk Russia   56°5N 47°27E **86** B8
Novocherkassk Russia   47°27N 40°15E **87** G5
Novodevichye Russia   53°37N 48°50E **86** D9
Novodvinsk Russia   64°25N 40°42E **106** C5
Novogrudok = Navahrudak
  Belarus   53°40N 25°50E **75** B13
Novohrad-Volynskyy
  Ukraine   50°34N 27°35E **75** C14
Novokachalinsk Russia   45°5N 132°0E **112** B5
Novokhopersk Russia   51°5N 41°39E **86** E5
Novokuybyshevsk
  Russia   53°7N 49°58E **86** D9
Novokuznetsk Russia   53°45N 87°10E **109** B11
Novolazarevskaya
  Antarctica   71°0S 12°0E **55** D3
Novomoskovsk Russia   54°5N 38°15E **84** E10
Novomoskovsk Ukraine   48°33N 35°17E **85** H8
Novomyrhorod Ukraine   48°45N 31°33E **85** H6
Novopolotsk = Navapolatsk
  Belarus   55°32N 28°37E **84** E5
Novorossiysk Russia   44°43N 37°46E **85** K9
Novorybnoye Russia   72°50N 105°50E **107** B11
Novorzhev Russia   57°3N 29°25E **84** D5
Novosej Albania   41°56N 20°35E **96** E4
Novoshakhtinsk Russia   47°46N 39°58E **85** J10
Novosibirsk Russia   55°0N 83°5E **109** B10
Novosibirskiye Ostrova
  Russia   75°0N 142°0E **107** B15
Novosibirskoye Vdkhr.
  Russia   54°35N 82°35E **109** B10
Novosokolniki Russia   56°20N 30°2E **84** D6
Novotitarovskaya Russia 45°14N 38°58E **85** K10
Novotroitsk Russia   51°10N 58°15E **108** B5
Novotroitskoye = Töle Bī
  Kazakhstan   43°42N 73°46E **109** D8
Novoukrayinka Ukraine   48°25N 31°30E **85** H6
Novouljanovsk Russia   54°8N 48°24E **86** D9
Novouzensk Russia   50°32N 48°17E **86** E9
Novovolynsk Ukraine   50°45N 24°4E **83** H11
Novovoronezhskiy
  Russia   51°19N 39°13E **85** G10
Novoyavoriske Ukraine   49°53N 23°33E **83** J10
Novozybkov Russia   52°30N 32°0E **85** F6
Novska Croatia   45°19N 17°0E **93** C14
Nový Bor Czech Rep.   50°46N 14°35E **78** A7

Novy Bug = Novyy Buh Ukraine 47°34N 32°29E **85** J7
Nový Bydžov Czech Rep. 50°14N 15°29E **78** A8
Novy Dvor Belarus 52°50N 24°21E **83** F11
Novy Dvor Russia 52°50N 29°04E **83** F7
Novyy Oskol Russia 34°54N 37°55E **85** G9
Novyy Port Russia 67°40N 72°30E **106** C8
Novyy Urengoy Russia 65°48N 76°52E **106** C8
Nowa Deba Poland 50°26N 21°41E **83** H8
Nowa Nowa Australia 37°44S 148°3E **153** D8
Nowa Ruda Poland 50°35N 16°30E **83** H3
Nowa Sarzyna Poland 50°21N 22°21E **83** H9
Nowa Sól Poland 51°48N 15°44E **83** G2
Nowata U.S.A. 36°42N 95°38W **176** C7
Nowbaran Iran 35°8N 49°42E **126** B6
Nowe Poland 53°41N 18°44E **82** E5
Nowe Miasteczko Poland 51°42N 15°42E **83** G2
Nowe Miasto Poland 51°38N 20°34E **83** F7
Nowe Miasto Lubawskie Poland 53°27N 19°33E **82** E6
Nowe Skalmierzyce Poland 51°43N 18°0E **83** G4
Nowe Warpno Poland 53°42N 14°18E **82** E1
Nowendoc Australia 31°32S 151°44E **153** A9
Nowendoc △ Australia 31°33S 151°45E **153** A9
Nowghāb Iran 33°53N 59°4E **129** C8
Nowgong = Nagaon India 26°20N 92°50E **123** F18
Nowgong India 25°4N 79°27E **125** G8
Nowogard Poland 53°41N 15°10E **82** E2
Nowogród Poland 53°14N 21°53E **83** E8
Nowogród Bobrzanski Poland 51°48N 15°15E **83** G2
Nowogrodziec Poland 51°12N 15°24E **83** G2
Nowra Australia 34°53S 150°35E **153** C9
Nowrangapur India 19°14N 82°33E **126** E6
Nowshera Pakistan 34°0N 72°0E **122** C0
Nowy Dwór Gdański Poland 54°13N 19°7E **82** D6
Nowy Sącz Poland 49°40N 20°41E **83** J7
Nowy Staw Poland 54°13N 19°2E **82** D6
Nowy Targ Poland 49°29N 20°2E **83** J7
Nowy Tomyśl Poland 52°19N 16°10E **83** F3
Nowy Wiśnicz Poland 49°55N 20°28E **83** J7
Noxen U.S.A. 41°25N 76°4W **175** E8
Noyabr'sk Russia 64°34N 76°21E **106** C8
Noyant France 47°30N 0°6E **70** E7
Noyers France 47°40N 4°0E **71** C9
Noyon France 49°34N 2°59E **71** C9
Noyon Mongolia 43°2N 102°4E **114** C2
Nozay France 47°34N 1°38W **70** E5
Nqutu S. Africa 28°13S 30°32E **145** C5
Nsa, O. en △ Algeria 32°28N 5°24E **136** B5
Nsanje Malawi 16°55S 35°12E **143** F4
Nsawam Ghana 5°50N 0°24W **139** D4
Nseluka Zambia 9°58S 31°16E **143** D3
Nsomba Zambia 10°45S 29°51E **143** E2
Nsukka Nigeria 6°51N 7°29E **139** D6
Ntaria ⊙ Australia 24°0S 132°41E **148** D5
Ntui Cameroon 4°21N 11°38E **139** E7
Ntungamo Uganda 0°56S 30°17E **142** C3
Nu Jiang → China 29°58N 97°25E **116** E2
Nu Shan China 26°0N 99°20E **116** E2
Nuba Mts. = Nubah, Jibalan Sudan 12°0N 31°0E **135** F12
Nubah, Jibalan Sudan 12°0N 31°0E **135** F12
Nubia Africa 21°0N 32°0E **132** D7
Nubian Desert = Nûbiya, Es Sahrâ en Sudan 21°30N 33°30E **137** C3
Nûbiya, Es Sahrâ en Sudan 21°30N 33°30E **137** C3
Nubledo Spain 43°31N 5°52W **88** B5
Nuboai Indonesia 2°10S 136°30E **119** E9
Nubra → India 34°35N 77°35E **125** B7
Nucet Romania 46°28N 22°35E **80** D7
Nueces → U.S.A. 27°51N 97°30W **176** H6
Nueltin L. Canada 60°30N 99°30W **163** A9
Nuestra Señora del Rosario de Caá-Catí Argentina 27°45S 57°36W **190** B4
Nueva, I. Chile 55°13S 66°30W **192** E3
Nueva Carteya Spain 37°35N 4°28W **89** H6
Nueva Ciudad Guerrero Mexico 26°34N 99°12W **181** B5
Nueva Gerona Cuba 21°53N 82°49W **182** B3
Nueva Imperial Chile 38°45S 72°58W **192** A2
Nueva Palmira Uruguay 33°52S 58°20W **190** C4
Nueva Rosita Mexico 27°57N 101°13W **180** B4
Nueva San Salvador El Salv. 13°40N 89°18W **182** D2
Nueva Tabarca Spain 38°17N 0°30W **91** G4
Nuéve de Julio Argentina 35°30S 61°0W **190** D3
Nuevitas Cuba 21°30N 77°20W **182** B4
Nuevo, G. Argentina 43°0S 64°30W **192** B4
Nuevo Casas Grandes Mexico 30°25N 107°55W **180** A3
Nuevo Laredo Mexico 27°30N 99°31W **181** B5
Nuevo León □ Mexico 25°0N 100°0W **180** C5
Nuevo Mundo, Cerro Bolivia 21°55S 66°53W **188** E4
Nuevo Rocafuerte Ecuador 0°55S 75°27W **186** D3
Nugget Pt. N.Z. 46°27S 169°50E **155** G4
Nugrus, Gebel Egypt 24°47N 34°35E **154** F6
Nuhaka N.Z. 39°3S 177°45E **154** F6
Nuits-St-Georges France 47°10N 4°56E **71** E11
Nukey Bluff Australia 32°26S 135°29E **151** E2
Nukhayb Iraq 32°4N 42°3E **130** C4
Nukheila Sudan 19°1N 26°21E **137** D2
Nuku Hiva French Polynesia 8°54S 140°6W **157** H13
Nuku'alofa Tonga 21°10S 175°12W **147** D11
Nukus Uzbekistan 42°27N 59°41E **108** D5
Nulato U.S.A. 64°43N 158°6W **166** C8
Nules Spain 39°51N 0°9W **90** F4
Nullagine Australia 21°53S 120°7E **148** D3
Nullagine → Australia 21°20S 120°20E **148** D3
Nullarbor Australia 31°26S 130°55E **149** F5
Nullarbor △ Australia 32°39S 130°0E **149** F5
Nullarbor Plain Australia 31°10S 129°0E **149** F4
Numalla, L. Australia 28°43S 144°20E **151** D3
Numan Nigeria 9°29N 12°3E **139** D7
Numata Japan 36°45N 139°4E **113** F9
Numaykoos Lake △ Canada 57°52N 95°58W **163** B9

Numazu Japan 35°7N 138°51E **113** G9
Numbulwar Australia 14°15S 135°45E **150** A2
Numfoor Indonesia 1°0S 134°50E **119** E8
Numurkah Australia 36°5S 145°26E **153** D6
Nunaksaluk I. Canada 55°49N 60°20W **165** A17
Nunap Isua Greenland 59°48N 43°55W **57** F5
Nunavik Greenland 71°50N 54°25W **57** C5
Nunavut □ Canada 66°0N 85°0W **161** D15
Nunda U.S.A. 42°35N 77°56W **174** D7
Nuneaton U.K. 52°32N 1°27W **67** E6
Nungarin Australia 31°12S 118°6E **149** F2
Nungo Mozam. 13°23S 37°43E **143** E4
Nungwe Tanzania 2°48S 32°2E **142** C3
Nunivak I. U.S.A. 60°10N 166°30W **166** C6
Nunkun India 33°57N 76°2E **125** C7
Núoro Italy 40°20N 9°20E **94** B2
Nuozhadu Dam China 22°30N 100°25E **116** F3
Nür Iran 36°33N 52°1E **127** B7
Nura → Kazakhstan 50°30N 69°59E **108** D7
Nûrâbâd Hormozgān, Iran 27°47N 57°12E **129** E8
Nûrâbâd Lorestān, Iran 34°47N 47°58E **105** E12
Nurabad Afghan. 39°36N 66°17E **109** E7
Nure → Italy 45°3N 9°49E **92** C6
Nuremberg = Nürnberg Germany 49°27N 11°3E **77** F7
Nuri Mexico 28°5N 109°22W **180** B3
Nuri Sudan 18°29N 31°59E **137** D3
Nuriootpa Australia 34°27S 139°0E **152** C3
Nuristān □ Afghan. 35°20N 71°0E **109** B8
Nurlat Russia 54°29N 50°45E **86** C10
Nurmes Finland 63°33N 29°10E **60** E23
Nürnberg Germany 49°27N 11°3E **77** F7
Nurpur Pakistan 31°53N 71°54E **124** D4
Nurra, La Italy 40°45N 8°15E **94** B1
Nurran, L. = Terewah, L. Australia 29°52S 147°35E **151** D4
Nurrari Lakes Australia 29°1S 130°5E **149** E5
Nurri Italy 39°43N 9°14E **94** C2
Nürtingen Germany 48°37N 9°19E **77** G5
Nurzec → Poland 52°37N 22°25E **83** F9
Nus Italy 45°45N 7°28E **92** C4
Nusa Dua Indonesia 8°48S 115°14E **119** K18
Nusa Tenggara Barat □ Indonesia 8°50S 117°30E **118** F5
Nusa Tenggara Timur □ Indonesia 9°30S 122°0E **119** F6
Nusaybin Turkey 37°3N 41°10E **105** D9
Nuşeirat Gaza Strip 31°27N 34°24E **130** D3
Nushki Pakistan 29°35N 66°0E **124** E2
Nuuk Greenland 64°10N 51°35W **57** E5
Nuwakot Nepal 28°10N 83°55E **125** E10
Nuwara Eliya Sri Lanka 6°58N 80°48E **127** L5
Nuwayb'ī, W. an → Si. Arabia 29°18N 34°57E **130** F3
Nuweiba' Egypt 28°59N 34°39E **128** D2
Nuwerus S. Africa 31°8S 18°24E **144** D2
Nuweveldberge S. Africa 32°10S 21°45E **144** D3
Nuyts, Pt. Australia 35°4S 116°38E **149** G2
Nuyts Arch. Australia 32°35S 133°20E **151** E1
Nxai Pan △ Botswana 19°50S 24°46E **144** A3
Nxaunxau Botswana 18°57S 21°4E **144** A3
Nyaake Liberia 4°52N 7°37W **138** E3
Nyabing Australia 33°33S 118°9E **149** F2
Nyack U.S.A. 41°5N 73°55W **175** E11
Nyagan Russia 62°30N 65°38E **106** C7
Nyah West Australia 35°16S 143°21E **152** C5
Nyahanga Tanzania 2°20S 33°37E **142** C3
Nyahua Tanzania 5°25S 33°23E **142** D3
Nyahururu Kenya 0°2N 36°27E **142** B4
Nyaingêntanglha Shan China 30°0N 90°0E **110** F7
Nyakanazi Tanzania 3°2S 31°10E **142** C2
Nyakrom Ghana 5°40N 0°50W **139** D4
Nyâlâ Sudan 12°2N 24°58E **135** F10
Nyalam China 28°32N 86°4E **110** F6
Nyamandhlovu Zimbabwe 19°55S 28°16E **143** F2
Nyambiti Tanzania 2°48S 33°27E **142** C3
Nyamira Kenya 0°36S 34°52E **142** C2
Nyamwaga Tanzania 1°27S 34°33E **142** C3
Nyandekwa Tanzania 3°57S 32°32E **142** C3
Nyandoma Russia 61°40N 40°12E **84** B11
Nyanga → Zimbabwe 18°17S 32°46E **143** F3
Nyanga Namibia 18°0S 20°40E **144** A3
Nyanguge Tanzania 2°30S 33°12E **142** C3
Nyanji Zambia 14°25S 31°46E **143** E3
Nyankpala Ghana 9°21N 0°58W **139** D4
Nyanza Rwanda 2°20S 29°42E **142** C2
Nyanza □ Kenya 0°10S 34°15E **142** C3
Nyanza-Lac Burundi 4°21S 29°36E **142** C2
Nyasa, L. = Malawi, L. Africa 12°0S 34°30E **143** E3
Nyasvizh Belarus 53°14N 26°38E **75** B14
Nyaungdon = Yandoon Burma 17°0N 95°40E **123** L19
Nyazura Zimbabwe 18°40S 32°16E **143** F3
Nyazwidzi → Zimbabwe 20°0S 31°17E **143** G3
Nyborg Denmark 55°18N 10°47E **63** J4
Nybro Sweden 56°44N 15°55E **63** H9
Nyda Russia 66°40N 72°58E **106** C8
Nyeboe Land Greenland 82°0N 57°0W **57** A5
Nyeri Kenya 0°23S 36°56E **142** C4
Nyhammar Sweden 60°17N 14°58E **62** D8
Nyika △ Malawi 10°30S 33°53E **143** E3
Nyimba Zambia 14°33S 30°50E **143** E3
Nyinahin Ghana 6°43N 2°3W **138** D4
Nyingchi China 29°32N 94°25E **110** F7
Nyíradony Hungary 47°41N 21°55E **80** C6
Nyíregyháza Hungary 47°58N 21°47E **80** C6
Nyírbátor Hungary 47°49N 22°9E **80** C7
Nyiru, Mt. Kenya 2°8N 36°50E **142** B4
Nykarleby = Uusikaarlepyy Finland 63°32N 22°31E **60** E20
Nykøbing Nordjylland, Denmark 56°48N 8°51E **63** H2
Nykøbing Falster, Denmark 54°56N 11°52E **63** K5
Nykøbing Sjælland, Denmark 55°55N 11°40E **63** J5
Nyköping Sweden 58°45N 17°1E **63** G7
Nykroppa Sweden 59°37N 14°18E **62** E8
Nykvarn Sweden 59°11N 17°25E **62** G11
Nyland Sweden 63°1N 17°45E **62** A11
Nylstroom = Modimolle S. Africa 24°42S 28°22E **145** B4
Nymagee Australia 32°7S 146°20E **153** B7

Nymboida → Australia 29°38S 152°26E **151** D5
Nymburk Czech Rep. 50°10N 15°1E **78** A8
Nynäshamn Sweden 58°54N 17°57E **63** F11
Nyngan Australia 31°30S 147°8E **153** A7
Nyoma Rap India 33°10N 78°40E **125** C8
Nyoman = Nemunas → Lithuania 55°25N 21°10E **82** C8
Nyong → Cameroon 3°17N 9°54E **139** E6
Nyons France 44°22N 5°10E **73** D9
Nyou Burkina Faso 12°42N 2°1W **139** C4
Nýrsko Czech Rep. 49°18N 13°9E **78** B6
Nysa Poland 50°30N 17°22E **83** H4
Nysa → Europe 52°4N 14°46E **76** C10
Nysa Kłodzka → Poland 50°49N 17°40E **83** H4
Nysäter Sweden 59°17N 12°47E **62** G6
Nyslott = Savonlinna Finland 61°52N 28°53E **84** B5
Nyssa U.S.A. 43°53N 117°0W **168** E5
Nystad = Uusikaupunki Finland 60°47N 21°25E **84** B1
Nysted Denmark 54°40N 11°44E **63** K5
Nyunzu Dem. Rep. of the Congo 5°57S 27°58E **142** D2
Nyurba Russia 63°17N 118°28E **107** C12
Nyzhankovychi Ukraine 49°40N 22°49E **83** J9
Nyzhnohirskyy Ukraine 45°27N 34°38E **85** K8
Nyzhny Vorota Ukraine 48°46N 23°6E **80** B8
Nzébéla Guinea 8°9N 9°7W **138** D3
Nzega Tanzania 4°10S 33°12E **142** C3
Nzérékoré Guinea 7°49N 8°48W **138** D3
Nzeto Angola 7°10S 12°52E **142** F2
N'zi → Ivory C. 7°0N 4°30W **138** D4
Nzilo, Chutes de Dem. Rep. of the Congo 10°18S 25°27E **143** E2
N'zo → Ivory C. 6°15N 7°33W **138** D3
N'zo △ Ivory C. 6°15N 7°15W **138** D3
Nzubuka Tanzania 4°45S 32°50E **142** C3
Nzwani = Anjouan Comoros Is. 12°15S 44°20E **141** a

O

O Barco Spain 42°23N 6°58W **88** C4
O Carballiño Spain 42°26N 8°5W **88** C2
O Castro de Ferreira Spain 42°31N 7°37W **88** C3
O Convento Spain 42°28N 8°41W **88** C2
O Corgo Spain 42°56N 7°25W **88** C3
O Pedrouzo Spain 42°56N 8°20W **88** C2
O Pino = O Pedrouzo Spain 42°56N 8°20W **88** C2
O Porriño Spain 42°10N 8°37W **88** C2
O Real Spain 43°20N 8°19W **88** B2
O Seixo Spain 41°59N 8°46W **88** D2
Ō-Shima Hokkaidō, Japan 41°30N 139°22E **112** D9
Ō-Shima Shizuoka, Japan 34°44N 139°24E **113** G9
Oa, Mull of U.K. 55°35N 6°20W **65** F2
Oacoma U.S.A. 43°48N 99°24W **172** D4
Oahe, L. U.S.A. 44°27N 100°24W **172** C3
Oahe Dam U.S.A. 44°27N 100°24W **172** C3
O'ahu U.S.A. 21°28N 157°58W **167** L8
Oak Harbor U.S.A. 48°18N 122°39W **178** B4
Oak Hill Fla., U.S.A. 28°52N 80°51W **179** G5
Oak Hill W. Va., U.S.A. 37°59N 81°9W **173** G13
Oak Island U.S.A. 33°55N 78°10W **179** H6
Oak Park U.S.A. 32°22N 82°19W **178** E4
Oak Ridge U.S.A. 36°1N 84°16W **177** C12
Oak View U.S.A. 34°24N 119°18W **171** L7
Oakan-Dake Japan 43°27N 144°10E **112** C12
Oakbank Australia 33°4S 140°33E **152** B4
Oakdale Calif., U.S.A. 37°46N 120°51W **170** H6
Oakdale La., U.S.A. 30°49N 92°40W **176** F8
Oakes U.S.A. 46°8N 98°6W **172** B4
Oakesdale U.S.A. 47°8N 117°15W **168** C5
Oakey Australia 27°25S 151°43E **151** D5
Oakfield Ga., U.S.A. 31°47N 83°58W **178** E4
Oakfield N.Y., U.S.A. 43°4N 78°16W **174** C6
Oakham U.K. 52°40N 0°43W **67** E7
Oakhurst U.S.A. 37°19N 119°40W **170** H7
Oakland Calif., U.S.A. 37°48N 122°16W **170** H4
Oakland Park U.S.A. 26°10N 80°7W **179** J9
Oaklands Australia 35°34S 146°10E **153** C7
Oakley Idaho, U.S.A. 42°15N 113°53W **168** E7
Oakley Kans., U.S.A. 39°8N 100°51W **172** F3
Oakover → Australia 21°0S 120°40E **148** D3
Oakridge U.S.A. 43°45N 122°28W **168** E2
Oaks, The Australia 34°3S 150°34E **153** C9
Oakville Canada 43°27N 79°41W **174** C5
Oakville U.S.A. 46°51N 123°14W **170** D3
Oamaru N.Z. 45°5S 170°59E **155** F5
Oamishirasato Japan 35°30N 140°18E **113** G10
Oancea Romania 45°21N 27°42E **81** E12
Oasis Calif., U.S.A. 37°29N 117°55W **170** H9
Oasis Calif., U.S.A. 33°28N 116°6W **171** M10
Oatman U.S.A. 35°1N 114°19W **171** K12
Oaxaca Mexico 17°3N 96°43W **181** D5
Oaxaca □ Mexico 17°0N 96°30W **181** D5
Ob → Russia 66°45N 69°30E **106** C7
Oba Canada 49°4N 84°7W **164** C3
Obala Cameroon 4°9N 11°32E **139** E7
Obama Japan 35°30N 135°45E **113** G7
Oban Nigeria 5°17N 8°33E **139** D6
Oban U.K. 56°25N 5°29W **65** E3
Obbia = Hobyo Somalia 5°25N 48°30E **133** F4
Oberá Argentina 27°21S 55°2W **191** B4
Oberammergau Germany 47°36N 11°4E **77** H7
Oberbayern □ Germany 48°5N 12°0E **77** G7
Oberdrauburg Austria 46°44N 12°58E **78** E5
Obere Donau △ Germany 48°5N 9°0E **77** G5
Oberer Bayerischer Wald Germany 49°15N 12°40E **77** F8
Oberfranken □ Germany 50°10N 11°0E **77** E7
Oberhausen Germany 51°28N 6°51E **76** D2
Oberkirch Germany 48°31N 8°4E **77** G4
Oberlausitz Germany 51°16N 14°18E **76** D10
Oberlin Kans., U.S.A. 39°49N 100°32W **172** F3
Oberlin Ohio, U.S.A. 41°18N 82°13W **174** E2
Obernai France 48°28N 7°30E **71** D14
Oberndorf Germany 48°17N 8°34E **77** G4
Oberon Australia 33°45S 149°52E **153** B8
Oberösterreich □ Austria 48°10N 14°0E **78** D7
Oberpfalz □ Germany 49°30N 12°10E **77** F8
Oberpfälzer Wald Germany 49°30N 12°30E **77** F8

Oberpfälzer Wald △ Germany 49°40N 12°20E **77** F8
Oberstdorf Germany 47°24N 10°15E **77** H6
Obertyn Ukraine 48°42N 25°10E **81** B10
Oberursel Germany 50°11N 8°35E **77** E4
Oberwart Austria 47°17N 16°12E **79** D9
Obi, Kepulauan Indonesia 1°23S 127°45E **119** E7
Obiaruku Nigeria 5°51N 6°9E **139** D6
Óbidos Brazil 1°50S 55°30W **187** D7
Óbidos Portugal 39°19N 9°10W **89** F1
Obihiro Japan 42°56N 143°12E **112** C11
Obilatu Indonesia 1°25S 127°20E **119** E7
Obilnoye Russia 47°32N 44°30E **87** G7
Obing Germany 48°0N 12°24E **77** G8
Objat France 45°16N 1°24E **72** C5
Obluchye Russia 49°1N 131°4E **107** E14
Obninsk Russia 55°8N 36°37E **84** E9
Obo C.A.R. 5°20N 26°32E **142** A2
Obodivka Ukraine 48°24N 29°15E **81** B14
Oborniki Poland 52°39N 16°50E **83** F3
Oborniki Śląskie Poland 51°17N 16°53E **83** G3
Oboyan Russia 51°15N 36°21E **85** G9
Obozerskaya = Obozerskiy Russia 63°34N 40°21E **106** C5
Obozerskiy Russia 63°34N 40°21E **106** C5
Observnovac Serbia 44°40N 20°11E **96** B4
O'Brien U.S.A. 30°2N 82°57W **178** E7
Obrovac Croatia 44°11N 15°41E **93** D12
Obruk Turkey 38°7N 33°12E **104** C5
Obrzycko Poland 52°42N 16°32E **83** F3
Observatory Inlet Canada 55°10N 129°54W **162** B3
Obshchi Syrt Russia 52°0N 53°0E **58** E16
Obskaya Guba Russia 69°0N 73°0E **106** C8
Obuasi Ghana 6°17N 1°40W **139** D4
Obubra Nigeria 6°8N 8°20E **139** D6
Obudu Nigeria 6°38N 9°5E **139** D6
Obwalden □ Switz. 46°55N 8°15E **77** J4
Obzor Bulgaria 42°50N 27°52E **97** D11
Ocala U.S.A. 29°11N 82°8W **179** F7
Ocampo Chihuahua, Mexico 28°11N 108°23W **180** B3
Ocampo Tamaulipas, Mexico 22°50N 99°20W **181** C5
Ocaña Spain 39°55N 3°30W **88** F7
Occidental, Cordillera Colombia 5°0N 76°0W **186** C3
Occidental, Cordillera Peru 14°0S 74°0W **188** C3
Occidental, Grand Erg Algeria 30°20N 1°0E **136** B4
Ocean City Md., U.S.A. 38°20N 75°5W **173** F16
Ocean City N.J., U.S.A. 39°17N 74°35W **173** F16
Ocean City Wash., U.S.A. 47°4N 124°10W **170** C2
Ocean Falls Canada 52°18N 127°48W **162** C3
Ocean I. = Banaba Kiribati 0°45S 169°50E **156** H8
Ocean Park U.S.A. 46°30N 124°3W **170** D2
Oceano U.S.A. 35°6N 120°37W **171** K6
Oceanport U.S.A. 40°19N 74°3W **175** F10
Oceanside U.S.A. 33°12N 117°23W **171** M9
Ochagavía Spain 42°55N 1°5W **90** C3
Ochakiv Ukraine 46°37N 31°33E **85** J6
Ochamchire Georgia 42°46N 41°32E **87** J5
Ochi, Oros Greece 38°5N 24°25E **98** C6
Ochil Hills U.K. 56°14N 3°40W **65** E5
Ochlockonee → U.S.A. 30°58N 84°3W **178** E5
Ochlockonee → U.S.A. 29°59N 84°26W **178** F5
Ocho Rios Jamaica 18°24N 77°6W **182** a
Ochopee U.S.A. 25°54N 81°18W **179** K8
Ochsenfurt Germany 49°40N 10°4E **77** F6
Ochsenhausen Germany 48°4N 9°57E **77** G5
Ocilla U.S.A. 31°36N 83°15W **178** E7
Ockelbo Sweden 60°54N 16°45E **62** D10
Ocmulgee → U.S.A. 31°58N 82°33W **178** E7
Ocmulgee → U.S.A. 32°49N 83°37W **178** D5
Ocna Mureş Romania 46°23N 23°55E **81** D8
Ocnele Mari Romania 45°8N 24°18E **81** E8
Ocniţa Moldova 48°25N 27°30E **81** A12
Ocoee U.S.A. 28°34N 81°32W **179** G8
Ocoña Peru 16°26S 73°8W **188** D3
Ocoña → Peru 16°28S 73°30W **188** D3
Oconee → U.S.A. 31°58N 82°33W **178** E7
Oconomowoc U.S.A. 43°7N 88°30W **172** D9
Oconto U.S.A. 44°53N 87°52W **172** C9
Oconto Falls U.S.A. 44°52N 88°9W **172** C9
Ocosingo Mexico 17°0N 92°15W **181** D6
Ocotal Nic. 13°41N 86°31W **182** D2
Ocotlán Jalisco, Mexico 20°21N 102°46W **180** C4
Ocotlán Oaxaca, Mexico 16°48N 96°40W **181** D5
Ocreza → Portugal 39°32N 7°50W **89** F3
Ócsa Hungary 47°17N 19°15E **80** C4
Oda Ghana 5°50N 0°51W **139** D4
Ōda Japan 35°11N 132°30E **113** G6
Oda, J. Sudan 20°21N 36°39E **137** C4
Ódáðahraun Iceland 65°5N 17°0W **60** D5
Odaejin N. Korea 41°34N 129°40E **112** D8
Ódákra Sweden 56°7N 12°45E **63** H6
Odate Japan 40°16N 140°34E **112** D10
Odawara Japan 35°20N 139°6E **113** G9
Odda Norway 60°3N 6°35E **61** F12
Odder Denmark 55°58N 10°10E **63** J4
Odei → Canada 56°6N 96°54W **163** B9
Odemira Portugal 37°35N 8°40W **89** H2
Ödemiş Turkey 38°15N 28°0E **104** C3
Odendaalsrus S. Africa 27°48S 26°45E **145** D4
Odense Denmark 55°22N 10°23E **63** J4
Odenwald Germany 49°30N 9°0E **77** F5
Oder → Europe 53°33N 14°38E **76** B10
Oder-Havel Kanal Germany 52°52N 14°2E **76** C10
Oderzo Italy 45°47N 12°29E **93** C9
Odesa Ukraine 46°30N 30°45E **85** J6
Odessa = Odesa Ukraine 46°30N 30°45E **85** J6
Odessa Canada 44°17N 76°43W **175** B8
Odessa Tex., U.S.A. 31°52N 102°23W **176** E2
Odessa Wash., U.S.A. 47°20N 118°41W **168** C4
Odiakwe Botswana 20°12S 24°32E **144** B3
Odiel → Spain 37°10N 6°55W **89** H4

Odienné Ivory C. 9°30N 7°34W **138** D3
Odintsovo Russia 55°40N 37°16E **84** E9
Odisha □ India 20°0N 84°0E **126** E7
Odolanów Poland 51°34N 17°40E **83** G3
O'Donnell U.S.A. 32°58N 101°50W **176** E4
O'Donnell Pt. Canada 45°5N 80°5W **174** A4
Odorheiu Secuiesc Romania 46°21N 25°21E **81** D10
Odoyevo Russia 53°56N 36°42E **84** F9
Odra = Oder → Europe 53°33N 14°38E **76** B10
Odra → Spain 42°14N 4°17W **88** C6
Odum U.S.A. 31°40N 82°2W **178** E7
Odžaci Serbia 45°30N 19°17E **80** E4
Odžak Bos.-H. 45°3N 18°18E **80** E3
Odzi Zimbabwe 19°0S 32°20E **145** B5
Odzi → Zimbabwe 19°45S 32°23E **145** B5
Oebisfelde Germany 52°27N 10°57E **76** C6
Oecussi = Pante Macassar E. Timor 9°30S 123°58E **119** F6
Oeiras Brazil 7°0S 42°8W **189** D10
Oeiras Portugal 38°41N 9°18W **89** G1
Oelrichs U.S.A. 43°11N 103°14W **172** D2
Oelsnitz Germany 50°24N 12°10E **77** E8
Oelwein U.S.A. 42°41N 91°55W **172** D8
Oeno I. Pac. Oc. 24°0S 131°0W **157** K14
Oenpelli = Gunbalanya Australia 12°20S 133°4E **148** B5
Oetz Austria 47°13N 10°53E **78** D3
Of Turkey 40°59N 40°23E **105** B9
Ofanto → Italy 41°22N 16°13E **95** A9
Offa Nigeria 8°13N 4°42E **139** D5
Offaly □ Ireland 53°15N 7°30W **64** C4
Offenbach Germany 50°6N 8°44E **77** E4
Offenburg Germany 48°28N 7°56E **77** G3
Officer Cr. → Australia 27°46S 132°30E **149** E5
Offida Italy 42°56N 13°41E **93** F10
Ofidousa Greece 36°33N 26°8E **99** E8
Ofotfjorden Norway 68°27N 16°40E **60** B17
Ōfunato Japan 39°4N 141°43E **112** E10
Oga Japan 39°55N 139°50E **112** E9
Oga-Hantō Japan 39°58N 139°47E **112** E9
Ogaden Ethiopia 7°30N 45°30E **133** F4
Ōgaki Japan 35°21N 136°37E **113** G8
Ogallala U.S.A. 41°8N 101°43W **172** E3
Ogasawara Gunto Pac. Oc. 27°0N 142°0E **156** E6
Ogbomosho Nigeria 8°1N 4°11E **139** D5
Ogden U.S.A. 41°13N 111°58W **168** F8
Ogdensburg U.S.A. 44°42N 75°30W **175** B9
Ogea Driki Fiji 19°12S 178°27W **154** a
Ogea Levu Fiji 19°8S 178°24W **154** a
Ogeechee → U.S.A. 31°50N 81°3W **178** E8
Ogilby U.S.A. 32°49N 114°50W **171** N12
Oglat Beraber Algeria 30°15N 3°34W **136** B4
Oglethorpe U.S.A. 32°18N 84°4W **178** D5
Óglio → Italy 45°2N 10°39E **92** C7
Óglio Sud △ Italy 45°7N 10°24E **92** C7
Ogmore Australia 22°37S 149°35E **150** C4
Ognon → France 47°16N 5°28E **71** E12
Ogoja Nigeria 6°38N 8°39E **139** D6
Ogoki Canada 51°38N 85°58W **164** B2
Ogoki → Canada 51°38N 85°57W **164** B2
Ogoki Res. Canada 50°45N 88°15W **164** B2
Ogooué → Gabon 1°0S 9°0E **140** C1
Ogosta → Bulgaria 43°48N 23°55E **96** C7
Ogowe = Ogooué → Gabon 1°0S 9°0E **140** C1
Ohai N.Z. 45°55S 168°0E **155** G2
Ohakune N.Z. 39°24S 175°24E **154** F5
Ohanet Algeria 28°44N 8°46E **136** C7
Ohangwena □ Namibia 17°30S 17°0E **144** A2
Ohata Japan 41°24N 141°10E **112** D10
Ohau, L. N.Z. 44°15S 169°53E **155** F4
Ohaupo N.Z. 37°56S 175°20E **154** F5
Ohio □ U.S.A. 40°15N 82°45W **174** F2
Ohio → U.S.A. 36°59N 89°8W **173** G9
Ohiwa Harbour N.Z. 37°59S 177°10E **154** F6
Ohře → Czech Rep. 50°30N 14°10E **78** A7
Ohrid Macedonia 41°8N 20°52E **96** E4
Ohridsko Jezero Macedonia 41°8N 20°52E **96** E4
Ohrigstad S. Africa 24°39S 30°36E **145** B5
Ohringen Germany 49°12N 9°31E **77** F5
Ohura N.Z. 38°51S 174°59E **154** F5
Oi Qu → China 28°37N 98°16E **116** C2
Oiapoque Brazil 3°50N 51°50W **187** C8
Oikou China 38°35N 117°42E **115** E9
Oil City U.S.A. 41°26N 79°42W **174** E5
Oil Springs Canada 42°47N 82°7W **174** D2
Oildale U.S.A. 35°25N 119°1W **171** K7
Oinousa = Inousses Greece 38°33N 26°14E **99** C8
Oise □ France 49°28N 2°30E **71** C9
Oise → France 49°0N 2°4E **71** C9
Oistins Barbados 13°4N 59°33W **183** g
Oistins B. Barbados 13°4N 59°33W **183** g
Ōita Japan 33°14N 131°36E **113** H5
Ōita □ Japan 33°15N 131°30E **113** H5
Oiticica Brazil 5°3S 41°5W **189** D10
Ojai U.S.A. 34°27N 119°15W **171** L7
Ojhar India 20°6N 73°56E **124** H8
Ojinaga Mexico 29°34N 104°25W **180** B4
Ojiya Japan 37°18N 138°48E **113** F9
Ojo Caliente Mexico 22°34N 102°15W **180** C4
Ojo de Liebre, L. Mexico 27°45N 114°15W **180** B2
Ojos del Salado, Cerro Argentina 27°0S 68°40W **190** B2
Oka → Russia 56°20N 43°59E **84** C13
Okaba Indonesia 8°6S 139°42E **119** F9
Okahandja Namibia 22°0S 16°59E **144** B2
Okahukura N.Z. 38°48S 175°14E **154** F5
Okaihau N.Z. 35°19S 173°47E **154** B5

Okakarara Namibia 20°35S 17°27E **144** B2
Okanagan L. Canada 50°0N 119°30W **162** D5
Okandja Gabon 0°35S 13°45E **140** C2
Okanogan U.S.A. 48°22N 119°35W **168** B4
Okanogan → U.S.A. 48°6N 119°44W **168** B4
Okanogan Range N. Amer. 49°0N 119°55W **168** B4
Okány Hungary 46°52N 21°21E **80** D6
Okapi Dem. Rep. of the Congo 2°30N 27°20E **142** B2
Okaputa Namibia 20°5S 17°0E **144** B2
Okara Pakistan 30°50N 73°31E **124** D5
Okarito N.Z. 43°15S 170°9E **155** D5
Okaukuejo Namibia 19°10S 16°0E **144** A2
Okavango □ Namibia 18°0S 19°30E **144** A2
Okavango Delta Botswana 18°45S 22°45E **144** A3
Okavango Swamp = Okavango Delta Botswana 18°45S 22°45E **144** A3
Okaya Japan 36°5N 138°10E **113** F9
Okayama Japan 34°40N 133°54E **113** G6
Okayama □ Japan 35°0N 133°50E **113** G6
Okazaki Japan 34°57N 137°10E **113** G8
Oke-Iho Nigeria 8°1N 3°18E **139** D5
Okęcie, Warszawa ✈ (WAW) Poland 52°9N 20°59E **83** F7
Okeechobee U.S.A. 27°15N 80°50W **179** H9
Okeechobee, L. U.S.A. 27°0N 80°50W **179** H9
Okefenoke → U.S.A. 30°40N 82°18W **178** E7
Okefenokee Swamp U.S.A. 30°40N 82°20W **178** E7
Okehampton U.K. 50°44N 4°0W **67** G4
Okene Nigeria 7°32N 6°11E **139** D6
Oker → Germany 52°32N 10°22E **76** C6
Okha India 22°27N 69°4E **124** H3
Okha Russia 53°40N 143°0E **107** D15
Okhotsk Russia 59°20N 143°10E **107** D15
Okhotsk, Sea of Asia 55°0N 145°0E **107** D15
Okhotskiy Perevoz Russia 61°52N 135°35E **107** C14
Okhtyrka Ukraine 50°25N 35°0E **85** G8
Oki-Shotō Japan 36°5N 133°15E **113** F6
Okiep S. Africa 29°39S 17°53E **144** C2
Okigwi Nigeria 5°52N 7°20E **139** D6
Okija Nigeria 5°54N 6°55E **139** D6
Okinawa Japan 26°19N 127°46E **113** L3
Okinawa □ Japan 26°40N 128°0E **113** L4
Okinawa-Guntō Japan 26°40N 128°0E **113** L4
Okinawa-Jima Japan 26°32N 128°0E **113** L4
Okino-erabu-Shima Japan 27°21N 128°33E **113** L4
Okitipupa Nigeria 6°31N 4°50E **139** D5
Oklahoma □ U.S.A. 35°20N 97°30W **176** D6
Oklahoma City U.S.A. 35°30N 97°30W **176** D6
Oklawaha → U.S.A. 29°28N 81°41W **179** F8
Okmulgee U.S.A. 35°37N 95°58W **176** D7
Oknitsa = Ocniţa Moldova 48°25N 27°30E **81** A12
Oko, W. → Sudan 21°15N 35°56E **137** C4
Okolo Uganda 2°37N 31°8E **142** B3
Okolona U.S.A. 34°0N 88°45W **177** E10
Okonek Poland 53°32N 16°51E **82** E3
Okotoks Canada 50°43N 113°58W **162** C6
Okrika Nigeria 4°40N 7°10E **139** E6
Oktyabrsk = Qandyaghash Kazakhstan 49°28N 57°25E **108** E6
Oktyabrsk Russia 53°11N 48°40E **86** D9
Oktyabrskiy = Aktsyabrski Belarus 52°38N 28°53E **75** B15
Oktyabrskiy Bashkortostan, Russia 54°28N 53°28E **108** B4
Oktyabrskiy Kamchatka, Russia 52°39N 156°14E **107** D16
Oktyabrskiy Rostov., Russia 47°30N 40°4E **87** G5
Oktyabrskoy Revolyutsii, Ostrov Russia 79°30N 97°0E **107** B10
Oktyabrskoye = Zhovtneve Ukraine 46°54N 32°3E **85** J7
Okulovka Russia 58°25N 33°19E **84** C7
Okuru N.Z. 43°55S 168°55E **155** D3
Okushiri-Tō Japan 42°15N 139°30E **112** D9
Okuta Nigeria 9°14N 3°12E **139** D5
Okwa → Botswana 22°30S 23°0E **144** B3
Ola Russia 59°35N 151°17E **107** D16
Ólafsfjörður Iceland 66°4N 18°39W **60** C4
Ólafsvík Iceland 64°53N 23°43W **60** D2
Olaine Latvia 56°48N 23°59E **62** D10
Olancha U.S.A. 36°17N 118°1W **171** J8
Olancha Pk. U.S.A. 36°16N 118°7W **171** J8
Olanchito Honduras 15°30N 86°30W **182** C2
Öland Sweden 56°45N 16°38E **63** H10
Ölands norra udde Sweden 57°22N 17°5E **63** G11
Ölands södra udde Sweden 56°12N 16°23E **63** H10
Olargues France 43°33N 2°53E **72** E6
Olary Australia 32°18S 140°19E **152** B4
Olascoaga Argentina 35°15S 60°39W **190** D3
Olathe U.S.A. 38°53N 94°49W **172** F6
Olavarría Argentina 36°55S 60°20W **190** D3
Oława Poland 50°57N 17°20E **83** H3
Olbernhau Germany 50°40N 13°19E **76** E8
Ólbia Italy 40°55N 9°31E **94** B2
Ólbia, G. di Italy 40°55N 9°39E **94** B2
Olching Germany 48°12N 11°20E **77** G7
Olcott U.S.A. 43°20N 78°42W **174** C6
Old Bahama Chan. = Bahama, Canal Viejo de W. Indies 22°10N 77°30W **182** B4
Old Baldy Pk. = San Antonio, Mt. U.S.A. 34°17N 117°38W **171** L9
Old Bar Australia 31°58S 152°35E **153** A10
Old Bridge U.S.A. 40°25N 74°22W **175** F10
Old Castile = Castilla y León □ Spain 41°55N 4°0W **88** C6
Old Crow Canada 67°30N 139°55W **160** D4
Old Dale U.S.A. 34°8N 115°47W **171** L11
Old Forge N.Y., U.S.A. 43°43N 74°58W **175** C10
Old Forge Pa., U.S.A. 41°22N 75°45W **175** E9
Old Mapoon ⊙ Australia 11°5S 142°22E **150** A3
Old Perlican Canada 48°5N 53°1W **165** C9
Old Shinyanga Tanzania 3°33S 33°27E **142** C3
Old Speck Mt. U.S.A. 44°34N 70°57W **175** B14
Old Town U.S.A. 44°56N 68°39W **173** B19

Old Town Maine, U.S.A. 44°56N 68°39W 173 C19
Old Washington U.S.A. 40°2N 81°27W 174 F3
Old Wives L. Canada 50°5N 106°0W 163 C7
Oldbury U.K. 51°38N 2°33W 67 F5
Oldcastle Ireland 53°46N 7°10W 64 C4
Oldeani Tanzania 3°22S 35°35E 142 C4
Oldenburg Niedersachsen, Germany 53°9N 8°13E 76 B4
Oldenburg Schleswig-Holstein, Germany 54°17N 10°52E 76 A6
Oldenzaal Neths. 52°19N 6°53E 69 B6
Oldham U.K. 53°33N 2°7W 66 D5
Oldman → Canada 49°57N 111°42W 162 D6
Oldmeldrum U.K. 57°20N 2°19W 65 D6
Olds Canada 51°50N 114°10W 162 C6
Oldsmar U.S.A. 28°2N 82°39W 179 G7
Olduvai Gorge Tanzania 2°57S 35°23E 142 C4
Öldziyt Mongolia 44°40N 109°1E 114 B5
Ole Rømer Land Greenland 74°10N 24°30W 57 C8
Olean U.S.A. 42°5N 78°26W 174 D6
Oleby Sweden 60°8N 13°2E 62 D7
Olecko Poland 54°2N 22°31E 82 D9
Oléggio Italy 45°36N 8°38E 92 C5
Oleiros = O Real Spain 43°20N 8°19W 88 B2
Oleiros Portugal 39°56N 7°56W 88 F3
Olekma → Russia 60°22N 120°42E 107 C13
Olekminsk Russia 60°25N 120°30E 107 C13
Oleksandrivka Ukraine 48°55N 32°20E 85 H7
Oleksandriya Kirovohrad, Ukraine 48°42N 33°3E 85 H7
Oleksandriya Rivne, Ukraine 50°37N 26°19E 75 C14
Olema U.S.A. 38°3N 122°47W 170 G4
Olenegorsk Russia 68°9N 33°18E 60 B25
Olenek Russia 68°28N 112°18E 107 C12
Olenek → Russia 73°0N 120°10E 107 B13
Olenino Russia 56°15N 33°30E 84 D7
Oléron, Î. d' France 45°55N 1°15W 72 C2
Olesk Ukraine 51°6N 24°11E 83 G11
Oleśnica Poland 51°13N 17°22E 83 G4
Olesno Poland 50°51N 18°26E 83 H5
Olevsk Ukraine 51°12N 27°39E 75 C14
Olga, L. Canada 49°47N 77°15W 164 C4
Olgas, The = Kata Tjuta Australia 25°20S 130°50E 149 E5
Ölgiy Mongolia 48°56N 89°57E 109 C11
Ølgod Denmark 55°49N 8°36E 63 J2
Olhão Portugal 37°3N 7°48W 89 H3
Olhopil Ukraine 48°12N 29°30E 81 B14
Olhovatka Russia 54°30N 22°18E 82 D9
Olib Croatia 44°23N 14°44E 93 D11
Oliena Italy 40°16N 9°24E 94 B2
Oliete Spain 41°1N 0°41W 90 D4
Olifants = Elefantes → Africa 24°10S 32°40E 145 B5
Olifants → Namibia 25°30S 19°30E 144 B2
Olifantshoek S. Africa 27°57S 22°42E 144 C3
Olimbos Greece 35°44N 27°11E 99 F9
Ólimbos, Óros = Olympos Oros Greece 40°6N 22°23E 96 F6
Olímpia Brazil 20°44S 48°54W 191 A6
Olimpos-Beydaglari △ Turkey 36°36N 30°30E 99 E12
Olinda Brazil 8°1S 34°51W 189 B4
Olite Spain 42°29N 1°40W 90 C3
Oliva Argentina 32°0S 63°38W 190 C3
Oliva Spain 38°58N 0°9W 91 G4
Oliva de la Frontera Spain 38°17N 6°54W 89 G4
Olivares, Cerro los Argentina 30°18S 69°55W 190 C2
Olivares de Júcar Spain 39°46N 2°20W 90 F2
Olive Branch U.S.A. 34°57N 89°49W 177 D10
Olivehurst U.S.A. 39°6N 121°34W 170 F5
Oliveira Brazil 20°39S 44°50W 189 E2
Oliveira de Azeméis Portugal 40°49N 8°29W 88 E2
Oliveira do Douro Portugal 41°5N 8°27W 88 D2
Oliveira dos Brejinhos Brazil 12°19S 42°54W 189 C2
Olivenza Spain 38°41N 7°9W 89 G3
Oliver Canada 49°13N 119°37W 162 D5
Oliver L. Canada 56°56N 103°22W 163 B8
Olivet France 47°51N 1°55E 71 E8
Olivine Ra. N.Z. 44°15S 168°30E 155 E3
Olkhovka Russia 49°48N 44°32E 86 F7
Olkusz Poland 50°18N 19°33E 83 H6
Ollachea Peru 13°49S 70°29W 188 C3
Ollagüe Chile 21°15S 68°10W 190 A2
Olmaliq Uzbekistan 40°50N 69°35E 109 D7
Olmedo Spain 41°20N 4°43W 88 D6
Olmeto France 41°43N 8°55E 73 G12
Olmos Peru 5°59S 79°46W 188 B2
Olney Ill., U.S.A. 38°44N 88°5W 172 F9
Olney Tex., U.S.A. 33°22N 98°45W 176 E5
Olofström Sweden 56°17N 14°32E 63 H8
Oloitokitok Kenya 2°56S 37°30E 142 C4
Oloma Cameroon 3°29N 11°19E 139 E7
Olomane → Canada 50°14N 60°37W 165 B7
Olomouc Czech Rep. 49°38N 17°12E 79 B10
Olomoucký □ Czech Rep. 49°45N 17°5E 79 B10
Olonets Russia 61°0N 32°54E 84 B7
Olongapo Phil. 14°50N 120°18E 119 B6
Olonne-sur-Mer France 46°32N 1°47W 72 B2
Oloron, Gave d' → France 43°33N 1°5W 72 E2
Oloron-Ste-Marie France 43°11N 0°38W 72 E3
Olosenga = Swains I. Amer. Samoa 11°11S 171°4W 157 J11
Olot Spain 42°11N 2°30E 90 C7
Olovo Bos.-H. 44°8N 18°35E 80 F3
Olovyannaya Russia 50°58N 115°35E 107 D12
Oloy → Russia 66°29N 159°29E 107 C16
Olsberg Germany 51°21N 8°31E 76 D4
Olshammar Sweden 58°45N 14°48E 63 F8
Olshanka Ukraine 48°16N 30°58E 85 H6
Olshany Ukraine 50°3N 35°53E 85 G8
Olsztyn Poland 53°48N 20°29E 82 E7
Olsztynek Poland 53°34N 20°19E 82 E7
Olt □ Romania 44°20N 24°30E 81 F9
Olt → Romania 43°43N 24°51E 81 G9
Olten Switz. 47°21N 7°53E 77 H3
Olteniţa Romania 44°7N 26°42E 81 F11
Olton U.S.A. 34°11N 102°8W 176 D3
Oltu Turkey 40°35N 41°58E 105 B9
Oluan Pi Taiwan 21°53N 120°51E 117 G13
Olula del Rio Spain 37°21N 2°18W 91 H2
Olur Turkey 40°49N 42°8E 105 B10
Olustee U.S.A. 30°12N 82°26W 178 E7
Olvega Spain 41°47N 2°0W 90 D2
Olvera Spain 36°55N 5°18W 89 J5
Olymbos Cyprus 35°21N 33°45E 101 D12
Olymbos Oros Greece 40°6N 22°23E 96 F6
Olympia Greece 37°39N 21°39E 98 D3
Olympia U.S.A. 47°3N 122°53W 170 D4
Olympic △ U.S.A. 47°45N 123°43W 170 C3
Olympic Dam Australia 30°30S 136°55E 152 A2
Olympic Mts. U.S.A. 47°55N 123°45W 170 C3
Olympus Cyprus 34°56N 32°52E 101 E11
Olympus, Mt. = Olymbos Oros Greece 40°6N 22°23E 96 F6
Olympus, Mt. = Uludağ Turkey 40°4N 29°13E 97 F13
Olympus, Mt. U.S.A. 47°48N 123°43W 170 C3
Olyphant U.S.A. 41°27N 75°36W 175 E9
Olyutorskiy, Mys Russia 59°55N 170°27E 107 D18
Om → Russia 54°59N 73°22E 109 B8
Om Koi Thailand 17°48N 98°22E 120 D2
Ōma Japan 41°45N 141°5E 112 D10
Ōmachi Japan 36°30N 137°50E 113 F8
Omae-Zaki Japan 34°36N 138°14E 113 G9
Ōmagari = Daisen Japan 39°27N 140°29E 112 E10
Omagh U.K. 54°36N 7°19W 64 B4
Omagh □ U.K. 54°35N 7°15W 64 B4
Omaha U.S.A. 41°17N 95°58W 172 E6
Omaheke □ Namibia 21°30S 19°0E 144 B2
Omak U.S.A. 48°25N 119°31W 168 B4
Omalos Greece 35°19N 23°55E 101 D5
Omalur India 11°44N 78°4E 127 J4
Oman ■ Asia 23°0N 58°0E 131 C6
Oman, G. of Asia 24°30N 58°30E 129 E8
Omapere N.Z. 35°37S 173°25E 154 B2
Omaruru Namibia 21°26S 16°0E 144 B2
Omaruru → Namibia 22°7S 14°15E 144 B1
Omate Peru 16°45S 71°0W 188 D3
Ombai, Selat Indonesia 8°30S 124°50E 119 F6
Omboué Gabon 1°35S 9°15E 140 E1
Ombrone → Italy 42°42N 11°5E 92 F8
Omdurmân Sudan 15°40N 32°28E 135 E12
Omega U.S.A. 31°21N 83°36W 178 D6
Omegna Italy 45°53N 8°24E 92 C5
Omemee Canada 44°18N 78°33W 174 B6
Omeo Australia 37°6S 147°36E 153 D7
Omeonga Dem. Rep. of the Congo 3°40S 24°22E 142 C1
Ometepe, I. de Nic. 11°32N 85°35W 182 D2
Ometepec Mexico 16°41N 98°25W 181 D5
Ominato Japan 41°17N 141°10E 112 D10
Omineca → Canada 56°3N 124°16W 162 B4
Omineca Mts. Canada 56°30N 125°30W 162 B3
Omiš Croatia 43°28N 16°40E 93 E13
Omišalj Croatia 45°13N 14°32E 93 C11
Omitara Namibia 22°16S 18°2E 144 B2
Ōmiya = Saitama Japan 35°54N 139°38E 113 G9
Omme Å → Denmark 55°56N 8°32E 63 J2
Ommen Neths. 52°31N 6°26E 69 B6
Ömnögovĭ □ Mongolia 43°15N 104°0E 114 C3
Omo → Ethiopia 6°25N 36°10E 131 F2
Omodeo, L. Italy 40°8N 8°56E 94 B1
Omodhos Cyprus 34°51N 32°48E 101 E11
Omoko Nigeria 5°19N 6°40E 139 D6
Omolon → Russia 68°42N 158°36E 107 C16
Omono-Gawa → Japan 39°46N 140°3E 112 E10
Ompha Canada 45°0N 76°50W 175 B8
Omsk Russia 55°0N 73°12E 109 B8
Omsukchan Russia 62°32N 155°48E 107 C16
Ōmu Japan 44°34N 142°58E 112 B11
Omul, Vf. Romania 45°27N 25°29E 81 E10
Omulew → Poland 53°5N 21°33E 83 E8
Ōmura Japan 32°56N 129°57E 113 H4
Omuramba Omatako → Namibia 17°45S 20°25E 144 A2
Omuramba Ovambo → Namibia 18°45S 16°59E 144 A2
Omurtag Bulgaria 43°8N 26°26E 97 C10
Omusati □ Namibia 18°30S 15°0E 144 A1
Ōmuta Japan 33°5N 130°26E 113 H5
Omuthiya Namibia 17°43S 16°13E 144 A2
Oña Spain 42°43N 3°25W 88 C7
Ona U.S.A. 27°29N 81°55W 179 H8
Onaga U.S.A. 39°29N 96°10W 172 F5
Onalaska U.S.A. 43°53N 91°14W 172 D8
Onancock U.S.A. 37°43N 75°45W 173 G16
Onangue, L. Gabon 0°57S 10°4E 140 E2
Onaping L. Canada 47°3N 81°30W 164 C3
Oñati Spain 43°3N 2°25W 90 B2
Onavas Mexico 28°31N 109°35W 180 B3
Onawa U.S.A. 42°2N 96°6W 172 D5
Oncócua Angola 16°30S 13°25E 144 A1
Onda Spain 39°55N 0°17W 90 F4
Ondangwa Namibia 17°57S 16°4E 144 A2
Ondarroa Spain 43°19N 2°25W 90 B2
Ondas → Brazil 12°8S 44°55W 189 C2
Ondava → Slovak Rep. 48°27N 21°48E 79 C14
Ondjiva Angola 16°48S 15°50E 144 A2
Ondo Nigeria 7°4N 4°47E 139 D5
Ondo □ Nigeria 6°45N 5°0E 139 D6
Öndörhaan Mongolia 47°19N 110°39E 111 B11
Öndverðarnes Iceland 64°52N 24°0W 60 D2
One Arm Point Australia 16°26S 123°3E 148 C3
One Arm Point ✪ Australia 16°31S 122°53E 148 C3
One Tree Australia 34°11S 144°43E 151 E3
Oneata Fiji 18°26S 178°25W 154 a
Oneco U.S.A. 27°25N 82°31W 179 H7
Onega Russia 64°0N 38°10E 106 C4
Onega → Russia 63°58N 38°2E 58 C13
Onega, L. = Onezhskoye Ozero Russia 61°44N 35°22E 84 B8
Onehunga N.Z. 36°55S 174°48E 154 C3
Oneida U.S.A. 43°6N 75°39W 175 C9
Oneida L. U.S.A. 43°12N 75°54W 175 C9
O'Neill U.S.A. 42°27N 98°39W 172 D4
Onekotan, Ostrov Russia 49°25N 154°45E 107 E16
Onema Dem. Rep. of the Congo 4°35S 24°30E 142 C1
Oneonta U.S.A. 42°27N 75°4W 175 D9
Onerahi N.Z. 35°45S 174°22E 154 B3
Oneşti Romania 46°17N 26°47E 81 D11
Onezhskoye Ozero Russia 61°44N 35°22E 84 B8
Ongarue N.Z. 38°42S 175°19E 154 E4
Ongea Levu = Ogea Levu Fiji 19°8S 178°24W 154 a
Ongers → S. Africa 31°4S 23°13E 144 D3
Ongerup Australia 33°58S 118°28E 149 F2
Ongi Mongolia 45°27N 103°54E 114 B2
Ongjin N. Korea 37°56N 125°21E 115 F13
Ongkharak Thailand 14°8N 101°1E 120 E3
Ongniud Qi China 43°0N 118°38E 115 C10
Ongoka Dem. Rep. of the Congo 1°20S 26°0E 142 C2
Ongole India 15°33N 80°2E 127 G5
Ongon = Havirga Mongolia 45°41N 113°5E 114 B7
Ongtüstik Qazaqstan □ Kazakhstan 43°0N 68°0E 109 D7
Ongwediva Namibia 17°47S 15°46E 144 A2
Oni Georgia 42°33N 43°26E 87 J6
Onida U.S.A. 44°42N 100°4W 172 C3
Onilahy → Madag. 23°34S 43°45E 141 J8
Onitsha Nigeria 6°6N 6°42E 139 D6
Ono Fiji 18°55S 178°29E 154 a
Onoda Japan 33°59N 131°11E 113 G5
Onoke, L. N.Z. 41°22S 175°8E 154 H4
Ons, I. de Spain 42°23N 8°55W 88 C2
Onsala Sweden 57°26N 12°0E 63 G6
Onslow Australia 21°40S 115°12E 148 D2
Onslow B. U.S.A. 34°20N 77°15W 177 D16
Ontake-San Japan 35°53N 137°29E 113 G8
Ontario Calif., U.S.A. 34°4N 117°39W 171 L9
Ontario Oreg., U.S.A. 44°2N 116°58W 168 D5
Ontario □ Canada 48°0N 83°0W 164 B2
Ontario, L. N. Amer. 43°20N 78°0W 174 C7
Ontinyent Spain 38°50N 0°35W 91 G4
Ontonagon U.S.A. 46°52N 89°19W 172 B9
Ontur Spain 38°38N 1°29W 91 G3
Onyx U.S.A. 35°41N 118°14W 171 K8
Oodaaq Greenland 83°40N 30°40W 57 A8
Oodnadatta Australia 27°33S 135°30E 151 D2
Ooldea Australia 30°27S 131°50E 149 F5
Oombulgurri Australia 15°15S 127°45E 148 C4
Oombulgurri ✪ Australia 15°10S 127°50E 148 C4
Oorindi Australia 20°40S 141°1E 150 C3
Oost-Vlaanderen □ Belgium 51°5N 3°50E 69 C3
Oostende Belgium 51°15N 2°54E 69 C2
Oosterhout Neths. 51°39N 4°47E 69 C4
Oosterschelde → Neths. 51°33N 4°0E 69 C4
Oosterwolde Neths. 53°0N 6°17E 69 B6
Oosteschelde △ Neths. 51°40N 3°40E 69 C3
Ootacamund = Udagamandalam India 11°30N 76°44E 127 J3
Ootha Australia 33°6S 147°29E 153 B7
Ootsa L. Canada 53°50N 126°2W 162 C3
Ooty = Udagamandalam India 11°30N 76°44E 127 J3
Op Luang △ Thailand 18°12N 98°32E 120 C2
Opaka Bulgaria 43°28N 26°10E 97 C10
Opala Dem. Rep. of the Congo 0°40S 24°20E 142 C1
Opâle, Côte d' France 50°30N 1°30E 70 B8
Opalenica Poland 52°18N 16°24E 83 F3
Opan Bulgaria 42°13N 25°41E 97 D9
Opanake Sri Lanka 6°35N 80°40E 127 L5
Opapa N.Z. 39°47S 176°42E 154 F5
Opasatika Canada 49°30N 82°50W 164 C3
Opasquia △ Canada 53°33N 93°5W 164 B1
Opatija Croatia 45°21N 14°17E 93 C11
Opatów Poland 50°50N 21°27E 83 H8
Opava Czech Rep. 49°57N 17°58E 79 B10
Opelika U.S.A. 32°39N 85°23W 178 C4
Opelousas U.S.A. 30°32N 92°5W 176 F8
Opémisca, L. Canada 49°56N 74°52W 164 C5
Opheim U.S.A. 48°51N 106°24W 168 B10
Ophthalmia Ra. Australia 23°15S 119°30E 148 D2
Opi Nigeria 6°36N 7°28E 139 D6
Opinaca → Canada 52°15N 78°2W 164 B4
Opinaca, Rés. Canada 52°39N 76°20W 164 B4
Opinnagau → Canada 54°12N 82°25W 164 B3
Opiscotéo, L. Canada 53°10N 68°10W 165 B6
Opobo Nigeria 4°35N 7°34E 139 E6
Opochka Russia 56°42N 28°45E 84 D5
Opoczno Poland 51°22N 20°18E 83 G7
Opole Poland 50°42N 17°58E 83 H4
Opole Lubelskie Poland 51°9N 21°58E 83 G8
Opolskie □ Poland 50°30N 18°0E 83 H5
Opononо L. Namibia 18°8S 15°45E 144 A2
Opornyy = Borankul Kazakhstan 46°11N 54°25E 108 C4
Oporto = Porto Portugal 41°8N 8°40W 88 D2
Opotiki N.Z. 38°1S 177°19E 154 E6
Opp U.S.A. 31°17N 86°16W 178 D3
Oppdal Norway 62°35N 9°41E 60 E13
Óppido Mamertina Italy 38°16N 15°59E 95 D8
Opportunity U.S.A. 47°39N 117°15W 168 C5
Oprişor Romania 44°17N 23°5E 80 F8
Oprtalj Croatia 45°23N 13°50E 93 C10
Opua N.Z. 35°19S 174°9E 154 B3
Opunake N.Z. 39°26S 173°52E 154 F2
Opuwo Namibia 18°3S 13°45E 144 A1
Opuzen Croatia 43°1N 17°34E 93 E14
Or → Kazakhstan 51°11N 58°32E 108 B5
Or, Côte d' France 47°10N 4°50E 71 E11
Ora Cyprus 34°51N 33°12E 101 E12
Oracle U.S.A. 32°37N 110°46W 169 K8
Oradea Romania 47°2N 21°58E 80 C6
Öræfajökull Iceland 64°2N 16°39W 60 D5
Orahovac = Rahovec Kosovo 42°24N 20°40E 96 D4
Orahovica Croatia 45°35N 17°52E 80 E2
Orai India 25°58N 79°30E 125 G8
Oraison France 43°55N 5°55E 73 E9
Oral = Zhayyq → Kazakhstan 47°0N 51°48E 108 C4
Oral Kazakhstan 51°20N 51°20E 86 E10
Oran Algeria 35°45N 0°39W 136 A3
Oran □ Algeria 35°0N 0°45W 136 A3
Orange Australia 33°15S 149°7E 153 B8
Orange France 44°8N 4°47E 73 D8
Orange Calif., U.S.A. 33°47N 117°51W 171 M9
Orange Mass., U.S.A. 42°35N 72°19W 175 D12
Orange Tex., U.S.A. 30°6N 93°44W 176 F8
Orange Va., U.S.A. 38°15N 78°7W 173 F14
Orange → S. Africa 28°41S 16°28E 144 C2
Orange, C. Brazil 4°20N 51°30W 187 C8
Orange City U.S.A. 28°57N 81°18W 179 G8
Orange Cove U.S.A. 36°38N 119°19W 170 J7
Orange Free State = Free State □ S. Africa 28°30S 27°0E 144 C4
Orange Grove U.S.A. 27°58N 97°56W 176 H6
Orange L. U.S.A. 29°25N 82°13W 179 F7
Orange Park U.S.A. 30°10N 81°42W 178 E8
Orange Walk Belize 18°6N 88°33W 181 D7
Orangeburg U.S.A. 33°30N 80°52W 178 B9
Orangeville Canada 43°55N 80°5W 174 C4
Orango Guinea-Biss. 11°5N 16°0W 138 C1
Orani Italy 40°15N 9°11E 94 B2
Oranienburg Germany 52°45N 13°14E 76 C9
Oranje = Orange → S. Africa 28°41S 16°28E 144 C2
Oranjemund Namibia 28°38S 16°29E 144 C2
Oranjerivier S. Africa 29°40S 24°12E 144 C3
Oranjestad Aruba 12°32N 70°2W 183 D5
Orapa Botswana 21°15S 25°30E 141 J5
Oras Phil. 12°9N 125°28E 119 B7
Orašje Bos.-H. 45°1N 18°42E 80 E3
Orăştie Romania 45°50N 23°10E 81 E8
Orava → Slovak Rep. 49°9N 19°8E 79 B12
Orava, Vodna nádrž Slovak Rep. 49°25N 19°35E 79 B12
Oraviţa Romania 45°2N 21°43E 80 E6
Orawia N.Z. 46°1S 167°50E 155 G2
Orb → France 43°15N 3°18E 72 E7
Orba → Italy 44°53N 8°37E 92 D5
Ørbæk Denmark 55°17N 10°39E 63 J4
Orbe Switz. 46°43N 6°32E 77 J2
Orbec France 49°1N 0°23E 70 C7
Orbetello Italy 42°27N 11°13E 93 F8
Órbigo → Spain 42°5N 5°42W 88 C5
Orbisonia U.S.A. 40°15N 77°54W 174 F7
Orbost Australia 37°40S 148°29E 153 D8
Örbyhus Sweden 60°15N 17°43E 62 D11
Orcadas Antarctica 60°44S 44°37W 55 C18
Orcas I. U.S.A. 48°42N 122°56W 170 B4
Orce Spain 37°44N 2°28W 91 H2
Orce → Spain 37°44N 2°28W 91 H2
Orchard City U.S.A. 38°50N 107°58W 168 G10
Orchard Homes U.S.A. 46°55N 114°4W 168 C6
Orchid I. = Lan Yü Taiwan 22°4N 121°25E 117 F13
Orchies France 50°28N 3°14E 71 B10
Orchila, I. Venezuela 11°48N 66°10W 183 D6
Orchilla, Pta. Canary Is. 27°42N 18°10W 100 G1
Órcia → Italy 42°58N 11°21E 93 F8
Orco → Italy 45°10N 7°52E 92 C4
Orcopampa Peru 15°20S 72°23W 188 D3
Orcutt U.S.A. 34°52N 120°27W 171 L6
Ord U.S.A. 41°36N 98°56W 172 E4
Ord → Australia 15°33S 128°15E 148 C4
Ord, Mt. Australia 17°20S 125°34E 148 C4
Ord Mts. U.S.A. 34°39N 116°45W 171 L10
Ordenes = Ordes Spain 43°5N 8°29W 88 B2
Orderville U.S.A. 37°17N 112°38W 169 H7
Ordes Spain 43°5N 8°29W 88 B2
Ordesa y Monte Perido △ Spain 42°40N 0°10W 90 C4
Ording = Sankt Peter-Ording Germany 54°20N 8°36E 76 A4
Ordos = Mu Us Shamo China 39°0N 109°0E 114 E5
Ordu Turkey 40°55N 37°53E 104 B7
Ordu □ Turkey 41°0N 37°50E 104 B7
Ordubad Azerbaijan 38°54N 46°1E 105 C12
Orduña Álava, Spain 42°58N 2°58W 90 C2
Orduña Granada, Spain 37°20N 3°30W 89 H7
Ordway U.S.A. 38°13N 103°46W 168 G12
Ordzhonikidze = Denisovka Kazakhstan 52°27N 61°39E 108 B6
Ordzhonikidze Ukraine 47°39N 34°3E 85 J8
Ore Dem. Rep. of the Congo 3°17N 29°30E 142 B2
Ore Mts. = Erzgebirge Germany 50°27N 12°55E 76 E8
Orebić Croatia 43°0N 17°11E 93 F14
Örebro Sweden 59°20N 15°18E 62 E9
Örebro län □ Sweden 59°27N 15°0E 62 E8
Orecchiella △ Italy 44°16N 10°22E 92 D7
Oregon U.S.A. 42°1N 89°20W 172 D9
Oregon □ U.S.A. 44°0N 121°0W 168 E3
Oregon City U.S.A. 45°21N 122°36W 170 E4
Oregon Dunes △ U.S.A. 43°40N 124°10W 168 E1
Öregrund Sweden 60°21N 18°30E 62 D12
Öregrundsgrepen Sweden 60°25N 18°15E 62 D12
Orekhov = Orikhiv Ukraine 47°30N 35°48E 85 J8
Orekhovo-Zuyevo Russia 55°50N 38°55E 84 E10
Orel Russia 52°57N 36°3E 85 F9
Orel □ Russia 52°30N 36°40E 85 F9
Orellana, Canal de Spain 39°2N 6°0W 89 F5
Orellana, Embalse de Spain 39°5N 5°10W 89 F5
Orellana la Vieja Spain 39°1N 5°32W 89 F5
Orem U.S.A. 40°19N 111°42W 168 F8
Ören Turkey 37°3N 27°57E 99 D9
Orenburg Russia 51°45N 55°6E 108 B5
Örencik Turkey 39°16N 29°33E 99 B11
Orense = Ourense Spain 42°19N 7°55W 88 C3
Orepuki N.Z. 46°19S 167°46E 155 G2
Orestes Pereyra Mexico 26°30N 105°39W 180 B3
Orestiada Greece 41°30N 26°33E 97 E10
Øresund Europe 55°45N 12°40E 63 J6
Oreti → N.Z. 46°28S 168°14E 155 G3
Orfanos Kolpos Greece 40°33N 24°0E 96 F7
Orford Ness U.K. 52°5N 1°35E 67 E9
Organ Pipe Cactus △ U.S.A. 32°0N 112°52W 169 K7
Organos, Pta. de los Canary Is. 28°12N 17°17W 100 F2
Organyà Spain 42°13N 1°20E 90 C6
Orgaz Spain 39°39N 3°53W 89 F7
Orgeyev = Orhei Moldova 47°24N 28°50E 81 C13
Orgiva Spain 36°53N 3°24W 89 J7
Orhaneli Turkey 39°54N 28°59E 97 G12
Orhaneli → Turkey 39°50N 28°55E 97 G12
Orhangazi Turkey 40°29N 29°18E 97 F13
Orhei Moldova 47°24N 28°50E 81 C13
Orhon Gol → Mongolia 50°21N 106°0E 110 A10
Ória Italy 40°30N 17°38E 95 B10
Oriental □ Morocco 33°0N 2°0W 136 B3
Oriental, Cordillera Colombia 6°0N 73°0W 186 B4
Oriental, Grand Erg Algeria 30°0N 6°30E 136 B5
Orientale □ Dem. Rep. of the Congo 2°20N 26°0E 142 B2
Oriente Argentina 38°44S 60°37W 190 D3
Orihuela Spain 38°7N 0°55W 91 G4
Orihuela del Tremedal Spain 40°33N 1°39W 90 E3
Orikhiv Ukraine 47°30N 35°48E 85 J8
Orikum Albania 40°20N 19°28E 96 F3
Oril → Ukraine 48°40N 34°39E 85 H8
Orillia Canada 44°40N 79°24W 174 B5
Orinoco → Venezuela 9°15N 61°30W 186 B6
Orion Canada 49°27N 110°49W 163 D6
Orion U.S.A. 31°58N 86°0W 178 D4
Oriskany U.S.A. 43°10N 75°20W 175 C9
Orissa = Odisha □ India 20°0N 84°0E 126 E7
Orissaare Estonia 58°34N 23°5E 84 C2
Oristano Italy 39°54N 8°36E 94 C1
Oristano, G. di Italy 39°50N 8°29E 94 C1
Orizaba Mexico 18°51N 97°6W 181 D5
Orizaba, Pico de Mexico 18°58N 97°15W 181 D5
Orizare Bulgaria 42°44N 27°39E 97 D11
Orizona Brazil 17°3S 48°18W 189 D1
Orjen Bos.-H. 42°35N 18°34E 96 D2
Orjiva = Orgiva Spain 36°53N 3°24W 89 J7
Orkanger Norway 63°18N 9°52E 60 E13
Örkelljunga Sweden 56°17N 13°17E 63 H7
Örken Sweden 57°6N 15°1E 63 G9
Örkény Hungary 47°9N 19°26E 80 C4
Orkhon = Orhon Gol → Mongolia 50°21N 106°0E 110 A10
Orkla → Norway 63°18N 9°51E 60 E13
Orkney S. Africa 26°58S 26°40E 144 C4
Orkney □ U.K. 59°2N 3°13W 65 B5
Orkney Is. U.K. 59°0N 3°0W 65 B6
Orland U.S.A. 39°45N 122°12W 170 F4
Orlando U.S.A. 28°32N 81°22W 179 G8
Orlando, C. d' Italy 38°10N 14°43E 95 D7
Orlando Int. ✕ (MCO) U.S.A. 28°26N 81°19W 179 G8
Orléanais France 48°0N 2°0E 71 E9
Orléans France 47°54N 1°52E 71 E8
Orleans U.S.A. 44°49N 72°12W 175 B12
Orléans, Î. d' Canada 46°54N 70°58W 165 C5
Orlice → Czech Rep. 50°13N 15°50E 78 A8
Orlivka Ukraine 45°19N 28°27E 81 E13
Orlov Slovak Rep. 49°17N 20°51E 79 B13
Orlov Gay Russia 50°56N 48°19E 86 E9
Orlová Czech Rep. 49°51N 18°26E 79 B11
Orlovat Serbia 45°14N 20°33E 80 E5
Orlovskoye Polesye △ Russia 58°30N 35°30E 84 F8
Orly, Paris ✕ (ORY) France 48°44N 2°23E 71 D9
Ormara Pakistan 25°16N 64°33E 122 G4
Ormea Italy 44°9N 7°54E 92 D4
Ormilia Greece 40°16N 23°39E 96 F7
Ormoc Phil. 11°0N 124°37E 119 B6
Ormond N.Z. 38°33S 177°56E 154 E6
Ormond Beach U.S.A. 29°17N 81°3W 179 F8
Ormond-by-the-Sea U.S.A. 29°21N 81°4W 179 F8
Ormondville N.Z. 40°5S 176°19E 154 G5
Ormož Slovenia 46°25N 16°10E 93 B13
Ormskirk U.K. 53°35N 2°54W 66 D5
Ormstown Canada 45°8N 74°0W 175 A11
Ornans France 47°7N 6°10E 71 E13
Orne □ France 48°40N 0°5E 70 D7
Orne → France 49°18N 0°15W 70 C6
Orneta Poland 54°8N 20°9E 82 D7
Ornö Sweden 59°4N 18°24E 62 E12
Örnsköldsvik Sweden 63°17N 18°40E 62 A12
Oro N. Korea 40°1N 127°27E 115 D14
Oro → Mexico 25°35N 105°2W 180 B3
Oro Grande U.S.A. 34°36N 117°20W 171 L9
Oro Valley U.S.A. 32°26N 110°58W 169 K8
Orobie, Alpi Italy 46°7N 10°0E 92 B6
Orobie Bergamasche △ Italy 46°0N 9°45E 92 C6
Orobie Valtellinesi △ Italy 46°5N 9°45E 92 B6
Orocué Colombia 4°48N 71°20W 186 C4
Orodara Burkina Faso 11°0N 4°55W 138 C4
Orodo Nigeria 5°34N 7°4E 139 D6
Orofino U.S.A. 46°29N 116°15W 168 C5
Orohena, Mt. Tahiti 17°37S 149°28W 155 b
Orol Dengizi = Aral Sea Asia 45°0N 58°20E 108 C5
Oromocto Canada 45°54N 66°29W 165 C6
Oron Nigeria 4°48N 8°14E 139 E6
Orono Canada 43°59N 78°37W 174 C6
Orono U.S.A. 44°53N 68°40W 173 C19
Oronsay U.K. 56°1N 6°15W 65 E2
Oropesa Spain 39°57N 5°10W 88 F5
Oroquieta Phil. 8°32N 123°44E 119 C6
Orós Brazil 6°15S 38°55W 189 B3
Orosei Italy 40°23N 9°42E 94 B2
Orosei, G. di Italy 40°15N 9°44E 94 B2
Orosháza Hungary 46°32N 20°42E 80 D5
Oroszlány Hungary 47°29N 18°19E 80 C3
Orotukan Russia 62°16N 151°42E 107 C16
Oroville Calif., U.S.A. 39°31N 121°33W 170 F5
Oroville Wash., U.S.A. 48°56N 119°26W 168 B4
Oroville, L. U.S.A. 39°33N 121°29W 170 F5
Orrefors Sweden 56°50N 15°45E 63 H9
Orroroo Australia 32°43S 138°38E 152 B3
Orrviken Sweden 63°6N 14°26E 62 A8
Orrville U.S.A. 40°50N 81°46W 174 F3
Orsa Sweden 61°7N 14°37E 62 C8
Orsara di Púglia Italy 41°17N 15°16E 95 A8
Orsasjön Sweden 61°7N 14°37E 62 C8
Orsha Belarus 54°30N 30°25E 84 E6
Orsières Switz. 46°2N 7°9E 77 J3
Örsjö Sweden 56°42N 15°45E 63 H9
Orsk Russia 51°12N 58°34E 108 B5
Orşova Romania 44°41N 22°25E 80 F7
Ørsted Denmark 56°30N 10°20E 63 H4
Örsundsbro Sweden 59°44N 17°18E 62 E11
Orta Turkey 40°38N 33°6E 104 B5
Orta, L. d' Italy 45°49N 8°24E 92 C5
Orta Nova Italy 41°19N 15°42E 95 A8
Ortaca Turkey 36°49N 28°45E 99 E10
Ortakent Turkey 37°5N 27°21E 99 D9
Ortaklar Turkey 37°53N 27°30E 99 D9
Ortaköy Çorum, Turkey 40°16N 35°15E 104 B6
Ortaköy Niğde, Turkey 38°44N 34°3E 104 C6
Orte Italy 42°27N 12°23E 93 F9
Ortegal, C. Spain 43°43N 7°52W 88 B3
Orthez France 43°29N 0°48W 72 E3
Ortigueira Spain 43°40N 7°50W 88 B3
Ortigueira, Ría de Spain 43°44N 7°45W 88 B3
Orting U.S.A. 47°6N 122°12W 170 C4
Ortisei Italy 46°34N 11°40E 93 B8
Ortles Italy 46°31N 10°33E 92 B7
Ortón → Bolivia 10°50S 67°0W 188 C4
Ortona Italy 42°21N 14°24E 93 F11
Ortonville U.S.A. 45°19N 96°27W 172 C5
Orūmīyeh Iran 37°40N 45°0E 105 D11
Orūmīyeh, Daryācheh-ye Iran 37°50N 45°30E 105 D11
Orune Italy 40°24N 9°22E 94 B2
Oruro Bolivia 18°0S 67°9W 188 D4
Oruro □ Bolivia 18°40S 67°30W 188 D4
Orust Sweden 58°10N 11°40E 63 F5
Oruzgān □ Afghan. 33°0N 66°0E 122 C5
Orvault France 47°17N 1°38W 70 E5
Orvieto Italy 42°43N 12°7E 93 F9
Orwell N.Y., U.S.A. 43°35N 75°50W 175 C8
Orwell Ohio, U.S.A. 41°32N 80°52W 174 E4
Orwell → U.K. 51°59N 1°18E 67 F9
Orwigsburg U.S.A. 40°38N 76°6W 175 F8
Oryakhovo Bulgaria 43°40N 23°57E 96 C7
Orynyn Ukraine 48°46N 26°24E 81 B11
Oryol = Orel Russia 52°57N 36°3E 85 F9
Orzinuovi Italy 45°24N 9°55E 92 C6
Orzyc → Poland 52°46N 21°14E 83 F8
Orzysz Poland 53°50N 21°58E 82 E8
Osa → Poland 53°33N 18°46E 82 E5
Osa, Pen. de Costa Rica 8°0N 84°0W 182 E3
Osage U.S.A. 43°17N 92°49W 172 D7
Osage → U.S.A. 38°36N 91°57W 172 F8
Osage City U.S.A. 38°38N 95°50W 172 F6
Ōsaka Japan 34°42N 135°30E 113 G7
Osakarovka Kazakhstan 50°33N 72°34E 109 B8
Ōsaki Japan 38°34N 140°58E 112 E10
Osawatomie U.S.A. 38°31N 94°57W 172 F6
Osborn Plateau Ind. Oc. 14°45S 87°0E 146 F7
Osborne U.S.A. 39°26N 98°42W 172 F4
Osby Sweden 56°23N 13°59E 63 H7
Osceola Ark., U.S.A. 35°42N 89°58W 177 D10
Osceola Iowa, U.S.A. 41°2N 93°46W 172 E7
Oschatz Germany 51°17N 13°6E 76 D9
Oschersleben Germany 52°2N 11°14E 76 C7
Óschiri Italy 40°43N 9°6E 94 B2
Oscoda U.S.A. 44°26N 83°20W 174 B1
Osečina Serbia 44°23N 19°34E 96 B3
Ösel = Saaremaa Estonia 58°30N 22°30E 84 C2
Osery Russia 54°52N 38°28E 84 E10
Osgoode Canada 45°8N 75°36W 175 A9
Osh Kyrgyzstan 40°37N 72°49E 109 D8
Osh □ Kyrgyzstan 40°0N 73°0E 109 E8
Oshakati Namibia 17°45S 15°40E 141 H3
Oshana □ Namibia 17°50S 15°40E 144 A2
Oshawa Canada 43°50N 78°50W 174 C6
Oshigambo Namibia 17°45S 16°5E 144 A2
Oshika-Hantō Japan 38°20N 141°30E 112 E10
Oshikoto □ Namibia 18°30S 17°0E 144 A2
Oshivelo Namibia 18°37S 17°10E 144 A2
Oshkosh Nebr., U.S.A. 41°24N 102°21W 172 E2
Oshkosh Wis., U.S.A. 44°1N 88°33W 172 C9
Oshmyany = Ashmyany Belarus 54°26N 25°52E 75 A13
Oshnovīyeh Iran 37°2N 45°6E 105 D11
Oshogbo Nigeria 7°48N 4°37E 139 D5
Oshtorīnān Iran 34°1N 48°38E 105 E13
Ōshū Japan 39°8N 141°8E 112 E10
Oshwe Dem. Rep. of the Congo 3°25S 19°28E 140 E3
Osi Nigeria 8°8N 5°14E 139 D6
Osieczna Poland 51°55N 16°40E 83 G3
Osijek Croatia 45°34N 18°41E 80 E3
Ósilo Italy 40°45N 8°40E 94 B1
Ósimo Italy 43°28N 13°30E 93 E10
Osintorf Belarus 54°40N 30°39E 84 E6
Osipovichi = Asipovichy Belarus 53°19N 28°33E 75 B15
Osiyan India 26°43N 72°55E 124 F5
Osizweni S. Africa 27°49S 30°7E 145 C5
Oskaloosa U.S.A. 41°18N 92°39W 172 E7
Oskarshamn Sweden 57°15N 16°27E 63 G10
Oskarström Sweden 56°48N 12°58E 63 H6
Oskélanéo Canada 48°5N 75°15W 164 C4
Öskemen Kazakhstan 50°0N 82°36E 109 C10
Oskol → Ukraine 49°6N 37°25E 85 H9
Osku Iran 37°54N 46°8E 105 D12
Oslo Norway 59°54N 10°43E 61 G14
Oslofjorden Norway 59°20N 10°35E 61 G14
Osmanabad India 18°5N 76°10E 126 E3
Osmancık Turkey 40°58N 34°47E 104 B6
Osmaniye Turkey 37°5N 36°10E 104 D7
Osmanlı Turkey 41°35N 26°51E 97 E10
Osmannagar India 18°32N 79°20E 126 E4
Ösmo Sweden 58°58N 17°55E 62 F11
Osnabrück Germany 52°17N 8°3E 76 C4
Ośno Lubuskie Poland 52°28N 14°51E 83 F1
Osoblaha Czech Rep. 50°17N 17°44E 79 A10
Osogbo = Oshogbo Nigeria 7°48N 4°37E 139 D5
Osogovska Planina Macedonia 42°10N 22°30E 96 D6
Osor Italy 44°42N 14°24E 93 D11
Osório Brazil 29°53S 50°17W 191 B5
Osorno Chile 40°25S 73°0W 192 B2
Osorno Spain 42°24N 4°22W 88 C6
Osorno □ Chile 40°34S 73°9W 192 B2
Osorno, Vol. Chile 41°0S 72°30W 192 B2
Osoyoos Canada 49°0N 119°30W 162 D5
Osøyro Norway 60°9N 5°30E 60 F11
Ospika → Canada 56°20N 124°0W 162 B4
Osprey U.S.A. 27°12N 82°29W 179 H7
Osprey Reef Australia 13°52S 146°36E 150 A4
Oss Neths. 51°46N 5°32E 69 C5
Ossa, Mt. Australia 41°52S 146°3E 151 G4
Ossa, Oros Greece 39°47N 22°42E 98 B4
Ossa de Montiel Spain 38°58N 2°45W 91 G2
Ossabaw I. U.S.A. 31°50N 81°5W 178 D8
Ossabaw Sd. U.S.A. 31°50N 81°6W 178 D8
Osse → France 44°7N 0°17E 72 D4
Osse → Nigeria 6°10N 5°20E 139 D6
Ossi Italy 40°40N 8°35E 94 B1
Ossining U.S.A. 41°10N 73°55W 175 E11
Ossipee U.S.A. 43°41N 71°7W 175 C13
Ossokmanuan L. Canada 53°25N 65°0W 165 B7
Ossora Russia 59°20N 163°13E 107 D17
Ostashkov Russia 57°4N 33°2E 84 D7
Östavall Sweden 62°26N 15°29E 62 B9
Oste → Germany 53°49N 9°2E 76 B5
Ostend = Oostende Belgium 51°15N 2°54E 69 C2
Ostend N.Z. 36°48S 175°2E 154 C4
Oster Ukraine 50°57N 30°53E 75 C16
Österbotten = Pohjanmaa □ Finland 62°58N 22°50E 60 E20
Osterburg Germany 52°47N 11°45E 76 C7

Osterburg U.S.A. 40°16N 78°31W 174 F6
Osterburken Germany 49°25N 9°26E 77 F5
Österbybruk Sweden 60°13N 17°55E 62 D11
Österbymo Sweden 57°49N 15°15E 63 G9
Österdalälven → Sweden 60°30N 15°7E 62 C7
Østerdalen Norway 61°40N 10°50E 62 C4
Österfärnebo Sweden 60°19N 16°48E 62 D10
Österforse Sweden 63°9N 17°3E 62 A11
Östergötlands län □ Sweden 58°35N 15°45E 63 F9
Osterholz-Scharmbeck Germany 53°13N 8°47E 76 B4
Østerild Denmark 57°2N 8°51E 63 G2
Östermyra = Seinäjoki Finland 62°40N 22°51E 60 E20
Osterode Germany 51°43N 10°15E 76 D6
Österreich = Austria ■ Europe 47°0N 14°0E 78 E7
Östersund Sweden 63°10N 14°38E 62 A8
Östervåla Sweden 60°11N 17°11E 62 D11
Ostfriesische Inseln Germany 53°42N 7°0E 76 B3
Ostfriesland Germany 53°20N 7°30E 76 B3
Östhammar Sweden 60°16N 18°22E 62 D12
Óstia, Lido di Italy 41°43N 12°17E 93 G9
Ostiglia Italy 45°4N 11°8E 93 C8
Östmark Sweden 60°17N 12°45E 62 D6
Östra Husby Sweden 58°35N 16°33E 63 F10
Ostrava Czech Rep. 49°51N 18°18E 79 B11
Ostravský □ Czech Rep. 49°55N 17°58E 79 B10
Ostróda Poland 53°42N 19°58E 82 E6
Ostrogozhsk Russia 50°55N 39°7E 85 G10
Ostroh Ukraine 50°20N 26°30E 75 C14
Ostrołęka Poland 53°4N 21°32E 83 E8
Ostrov Bulgaria 43°40N 24°9E 97 C8
Ostrov Czech Rep. 50°18N 12°57E 78 A5
Ostrov Romania 44°6N 27°24E 81 F12
Ostrov Russia 57°25N 28°20E 84 D5
Ostrów Lubelski Poland 51°29N 22°51E 83 G9
Ostrów Mazowiecka Poland 52°50N 21°51E 83 F8
Ostrów Wielkopolski Poland 51°36N 17°44E 83 G4
Ostrowiec-Świętokrzyski Poland 50°55N 21°22E 83 H8
Ostrožac Bos.-H. 43°43N 17°49E 80 G2
Ostrzeszów Poland 51°25N 17°52E 83 G4
Ostseebad Kühlungsborn Germany 54°8N 11°44E 76 A7
Osttirol □ Austria 46°50N 12°30E 78 E5
Ostuni Italy 40°44N 17°35E 95 B10
Osum → Albania 40°40N 20°10E 96 F4
Osŭm → Bulgaria 43°40N 24°50E 97 C8
Ōsumi-Kaikyō Japan 30°55N 131°0E 113 J5
Ōsumi-Shotō Japan 30°30N 130°0E 113 J5
Osun □ Nigeria 7°30N 4°30E 139 D5
Osuna Spain 37°14N 5°8W 89 H5
Oswegatchie → U.S.A. 44°42N 75°30W 175 B9
Oswego U.S.A. 43°27N 76°31W 175 C8
Oswego → U.S.A. 43°27N 76°30W 175 C8
Oswestry U.K. 52°52N 3°3W 66 E4
Oświęcim Poland 50°2N 19°11E 83 H6
Otaci Moldova 48°27N 27°47E 81 B12
Otago □ N.Z. 45°15S 170°0E 155 F5
Otago Harbour N.Z. 45°47S 170°42E 155 F5
Otago Pen. N.Z. 45°48S 170°39E 155 F5
Otaheite B. Trin. & Tob. 10°15N 61°30W 187 K15
Otahuhu N.Z. 36°56S 174°51E 154 C3
Ōtake Japan 34°12N 132°13E 113 G6
Otaki N.Z. 40°45S 175°10E 154 G4
Otane N.Z. 39°54S 176°39E 154 F5
Otaru Japan 43°10N 141°0E 112 C10
Otaru-Wan = Ishikari-Wan Japan 43°25N 141°1E 112 C10
Otautau N.Z. 46°9S 168°1E 155 G3
Otava → Czech Rep. 49°26N 14°12E 78 B7
Otavalo Ecuador 0°13N 78°20W 186 C3
Otavi Namibia 19°40S 17°24E 144 A2
Ōtawara Japan 36°50N 140°5E 113 F10
Otchinjau Angola 16°30S 13°56E 144 A1
Otego U.S.A. 42°23N 75°10W 175 D9
Otelec Romania 45°36N 20°50E 80 E5
Otelnuk, L. Canada 56°9N 68°12W 165 A6
Oţelu Roşu Romania 45°32N 22°22E 80 E7
Otero de Rey = Outeiro de Rei Spain 43°6N 7°36W 88 B3
Othello U.S.A. 46°50N 119°10W 168 C4
Othoni Greece 39°52N 19°22E 98 B1
Othris, Oros Greece 39°2N 22°37E 98 B4
Oti → Africa 7°48N 0°8E 139 D5
Oti △ Togo 10°40N 0°35E 139 C5
Otira N.Z. 42°49S 171°35E 155 C6
Otira Gorge N.Z. 42°53S 171°33E 155 C6
Otish, Mts. Canada 52°22N 70°30W 165 B5
Otishi △ Peru 11°40S 73°5W 188 C3
Otjinene Namibia 21°8S 18°46E 144 B2
Otjiwarongo Namibia 20°30S 16°33E 144 B2
Otjozondjupa □ Namibia 21°0S 17°0E 144 B2
Otmuchów Poland 50°28N 17°10E 83 H4
Otočac Croatia 44°53N 15°12E 93 D12
Otoineppu Japan 44°44N 142°16E 112 B11
Otok Croatia 43°42N 16°44E 93 E13
Otopeni, București ✕ (OTP) Romania 44°30N 26°11E 81 F11
Otorohanga N.Z. 38°12S 175°14E 154 E4
Otoskwin → Canada 52°13N 88°6W 164 B2
Otra → Norway 58°9N 8°1E 61 G13
Otradnyy Russia 53°22N 51°21E 86 D10
Otranto Italy 40°9N 18°28E 95 B11
Otranto, C. d' Italy 40°7N 18°30E 95 B11
Otranto, Str. of Italy 40°15N 18°40E 95 B11
Otrokovice Czech Rep. 49°12N 17°32E 79 B10
Otse S. Africa 25°2S 25°45E 144 C4
Otsego L. U.S.A. 42°45N 74°53W 175 D10
Ōtsu Japan 35°0N 135°50E 113 G7
Ōtsuki Japan 35°36N 138°57E 113 G9
Ottapalam India 10°46N 76°23E 127 J3
Ottawa = Outaouais → Canada 45°27N 74°8W 164 C5
Ottawa Canada 45°26N 75°42W 175 A9
Ottawa Ill., U.S.A. 41°21N 88°51W 172 E9
Ottawa Kans., U.S.A. 38°37N 95°16W 172 F6
Ottawa Is. Canada 59°35N 80°10W 161 F15
Ottélé Cameroon 3°38N 11°19E 139 E7
Ottensheim Austria 48°21N 14°12E 78 C7
Otter Cr. → U.S.A. 44°13N 73°17W 175 B11
Otter Creek U.S.A. 29°19N 82°46W 179 F7
Otter Lake Canada 45°17N 79°56W 174 A5
Otterbäcken Sweden 58°57N 14°3E 63 F8
Otterndorf Germany 53°48N 8°53E 76 B4
Otterup Denmark 55°30N 10°22E 63 J4
Otterville Canada 42°55N 80°36W 174 D4
Ottery St. Mary U.K. 50°44N 3°17W 67 G4
Otto Beit Bridge Zimbabwe 15°59S 28°56E 143 F2
Ottosdal S. Africa 26°46S 25°59E 144 C4
Ottumwa U.S.A. 41°1N 92°25W 172 E7
Otukpa Nigeria 7°9N 7°41E 139 D6
Oturkpo Nigeria 7°16N 8°8E 139 D6
Otway, B. Chile 53°30S 74°0W 192 D2
Otway, C. Australia 38°52S 143°30E 152 E5
Otway, Seno de Chile 53°0S 71°30W 192 D2
Otway △ Australia 38°47S 143°34E 152 E5
Otwock Poland 52°5N 21°20E 83 F8
Otyniya Ukraine 48°44N 24°51E 81 B9
Ötztaler Ache → Austria 47°14N 10°50E 78 D3
Ötztaler Alpen Austria 46°56N 11°0E 78 E3
Ou → Laos 20°4N 102°13E 120 B4
Ou-Sammyaku Japan 39°20N 140°35E 112 E10
Ouachita → U.S.A. 31°38N 91°49W 176 F9
Ouachita, L. U.S.A. 34°34N 93°12W 176 D8
Ouachita Mts. U.S.A. 34°30N 94°30W 176 D7
Ouagadougou Burkina Faso 12°25N 1°30W 139 C4
Ouahigouya Burkina Faso 13°31N 2°25W 138 C4
Ouahran = Oran Algeria 35°45N 0°39W 136 A3
Oualâta Mauritania 17°20N 6°55W 138 B3
Ouallam Niger 14°23N 2°10E 139 C5
Ouallene Algeria 24°41N 1°11E 136 D4
Ouarâne Mauritania 21°0N 10°30W 134 D3
Ouargaye Burkina Faso 11°40N 0°5E 139 C5
Ouargla Algeria 31°59N 5°16E 136 B5
Ouargla □ Algeria 30°30N 6°10E 136 B5
Ouarkoye Burkina Faso 12°5N 3°40W 138 C4
Ouarkziz, Jebel Algeria 28°50N 8°0W 136 C2
Ouarra → C.A.R. 5°5N 24°26E 140 C4
Ouarzazate Morocco 30°55N 6°50W 136 B2
Ouassouas Mali 16°10N 1°23E 139 B5
Ouatagouna Mali 15°11N 0°43E 139 B5
Oubangi → Dem. Rep. of the Congo 0°30S 17°50E 140 E3
Oubarakai, O. → Algeria 27°20N 9°0E 136 C5
Ouche → France 47°6N 5°16E 71 E12
Ouddorp Neths. 51°50N 3°57E 69 C3
Oude Rijn → Neths. 52°12N 4°24E 69 B4
Oudeïka Mali 17°30N 1°40W 139 B4
Oudenaarde Belgium 50°50N 3°37E 69 D3
Oudon → France 47°41N 0°53W 70 E6
Oudtshoorn S. Africa 33°35S 22°14E 144 D3
Oued Zem Morocco 32°52N 6°34W 136 B2
Ouella Niger 14°38N 3°38E 139 C5
Ouellé Ivory C. 7°26N 4°1W 138 D4
Ouémé → Benin 6°30N 2°30E 139 D5
Ouenza Algeria 35°57N 8°4E 136 A5
Ouessa Burkina Faso 11°4N 2°47W 138 C4
Ouessant, Î. d' France 48°28N 5°6W 70 D1
Ouesso Congo 1°37N 16°5E 140 D3
Ouest □ Cameroon 5°30N 10°30E 139 D7
Ouest, Pte. de l' Canada 49°52N 64°40W 165 C7
Ouezzane Morocco 34°51N 5°35W 136 B2
Ougarou Burkina Faso 12°10N 0°58E 139 C5
Oughter, L. Ireland 54°1N 7°28W 64 B4
Oughterard Ireland 53°26N 9°18W 64 C2
Ouidah Benin 6°25N 2°0E 139 D5
Ouidi Niger 14°10N 13°0E 139 C7
Ouistreham France 49°17N 0°18W 70 C6
Oujda Morocco 34°41N 1°55W 136 B3
Oujeft Mauritania 20°2N 13°0W 138 A2
Oulad-Teïma Morocco 30°24N 9°12W 136 B2
Oulainen Finland 64°17N 24°47E 60 D21
Oulanka △ Finland 66°26N 29°25E 60 C23
Ould Yenjé Mauritania 15°38N 12°16W 138 B2
Ouled Djellal Algeria 34°28N 5°2E 136 B5
Ouled Naïl, Mts. des Algeria 34°30N 3°30E 136 B4
Oullins France 45°43N 4°49E 73 C8
Oulmès Morocco 33°17N 6°0W 136 B2
Oulu Finland 65°1N 25°29E 60 D21
Oulujärvi Finland 64°25N 27°15E 60 D22
Oulujoki → Finland 65°1N 25°30E 60 D21
Oulx Italy 45°2N 6°50E 92 C3
Oum Chalouba Chad 15°48N 20°46E 135 E10
Oum-el-Bouaghi Algeria 35°55N 7°6E 136 A5
Oum-el-Bouaghi □ Algeria 35°50N 7°5E 136 A5
Oum el Ksi Algeria 29°4N 6°59W 136 C2
Oum-er-Rbia, O. → Morocco 33°19N 8°21W 136 B2
Oum Hadjer Chad 13°18N 19°41E 135 F9
Oumé Ivory C. 6°21N 5°27W 138 D3
Ounane, Dj. Algeria 25°4N 7°19E 136 C5
Ounasjoki → Finland 66°31N 25°40E 60 C21
Ounguati Namibia 22°0S 15°46E 144 B2
Ounianga Kébir Chad 19°4N 20°29E 135 E10
Our → Lux. 49°55N 6°5E 69 E6
Oura, Akra Greece 38°10N 26°2E 99 C8
Ouranoupoli Greece 40°20N 23°59E 96 F7
Ourârene Niger 19°30N 7°10E 139 B6
Ouray U.S.A. 38°1N 107°40W 169 G10
Ourcq → France 49°1N 3°1E 71 C10
Ourém Portugal 39°40N 8°35W 88 F2
Ourense Spain 42°19N 7°55W 88 C3
Ourense □ Spain 42°15N 7°51W 88 C3
Ouricuri Brazil 7°53S 40°5W 189 B2
Ourinhos Brazil 23°0S 49°54W 191 A6
Ourique Portugal 37°38N 8°16W 89 H2
Ouro Fino Brazil 22°16S 46°25W 191 A6
Ouro-Ndia Mali 15°8N 4°35W 138 B4
Ouro Prêto Brazil 20°20S 43°30W 191 A7
Ouro Sogui Senegal 15°36N 13°19W 138 B2
Oursi Burkina Faso 14°41N 0°27W 139 C4
Ourthe → Belgium 50°29N 5°35E 69 D5
Ouse → E. Sussex, U.K. 50°47N 0°4E 67 G8
Ouse → N. Yorks., U.K. 53°44N 0°55W 66 D7
Oust France 42°52N 1°13E 72 F5
Oust → France 47°35N 2°6W 70 E4
Outamba-Kilimi △ S. Leone 9°50N 12°40W 138 D2
Outaouais → Canada 45°27N 74°8W 164 C5
Outapi Namibia 17°30S 15°0E 144 A2
Outardes → Canada 49°24N 69°30W 165 C6
Outat Oulad el Haj Morocco 33°22N 3°42W 136 B3
Outeiro de Rei Spain 43°6N 7°36W 88 B3
Outer Hebrides U.K. 57°30N 7°15W 65 D1
Outes = A Serra de Outes Spain 42°52N 8°55W 88 C2
Outjo Namibia 20°5S 16°7E 144 B2
Outlook Canada 51°30N 107°0W 163 C7
Outokumpu Finland 62°43N 29°1E 60 E23
Outreau France 50°40N 1°36E 71 B8
Ouvèze → France 43°59N 4°51E 73 E8
Ouyen Australia 35°1S 142°22E 152 C5
Ouzouer-le-Marché France 47°54N 1°32E 71 E8
Ovada Italy 44°38N 8°38E 92 D5
Ovalau Fiji 17°40S 178°48E 154 a
Ovalle Chile 30°33S 71°18W 190 C1
Ovamboland Namibia 18°30S 16°0E 144 A2
Ovanåker Sweden 61°22N 15°53E 62 C9
Ovar Portugal 40°51N 8°40W 88 E2
Overath Germany 50°56N 7°17E 76 E3
Overflakkee Neths. 51°44N 4°10E 69 C4
Overijssel □ Neths. 52°25N 6°35E 69 B6
Overland Park U.S.A. 38°58N 94°40W 172 F6
Overlander Roadhouse Australia 26°19S 114°28E 149 E1
Overton U.S.A. 36°33N 114°27W 171 J12
Övertorneå Sweden 66°23N 23°38E 60 C20
Överum Sweden 58°0N 16°20E 63 F10
Ovid U.S.A. 42°41N 76°49W 175 D8
Ovidiopol Ukraine 46°15N 30°30E 85 J6
Ovidiu Romania 44°16N 28°34E 81 F13
Oviedo Spain 43°25N 5°50W 88 B5
Oviedo U.S.A. 28°40N 81°13W 179 G8
Oviksfjällen Sweden 63°0N 13°49E 62 A7
Ovīšrags Latvia 57°33N 21°44E 82 A8
Ovoot Mongolia 45°21N 113°45E 114 B7
Övör Hangay □ Mongolia 45°0N 102°30E 114 B2
Ovoro Nigeria 5°26N 7°16E 139 D6
Øvre Anárjohka △ Norway 68°30N 24°40E 60 B21
Øvre Årdal Norway 61°19N 7°48E 62 C1
Øvre Dividal △ Norway 68°43N 19°50E 60 B18
Övre Fryken Sweden 60°0N 13°7E 62 E7
Øvre Pasvik △ Norway 69°6N 28°54E 60 B23
Ovruch Ukraine 51°25N 28°45E 75 C15
Owaka N.Z. 46°27S 169°40E 155 G4
Owambo = Ovamboland Namibia 18°30S 16°0E 144 A2
Owasco L. U.S.A. 42°50N 76°31W 175 D8
Owase Japan 34°7N 136°12E 113 G8
Owatonna U.S.A. 44°5N 93°14W 172 C7
Owbeh Afghan. 34°28N 63°10E 122 B3
Owego U.S.A. 42°6N 76°16W 175 D8
Owen Australia 34°15S 138°32E 152 C3
Owen, Mt. N.Z. 41°35S 172°33E 155 B7
Owen Falls Dam = Nalubaale Dam Uganda 0°30N 33°5E 142 B3
Owen Sound Canada 44°35N 80°55W 174 B4
Owen Stanley Ra. Papua N. G. 8°30S 147°0E 147 B7
Oweniny → Ireland 54°8N 9°34W 64 B2
Owens → U.S.A. 36°32N 117°59W 170 J9
Owens L. U.S.A. 36°26N 117°57W 171 J9
Owensboro U.S.A. 37°46N 87°7W 172 G10
Owerri Nigeria 5°29N 7°0E 139 D6
Owhango N.Z. 39°0S 175°23E 154 F4
Owl → Canada 57°51N 92°44W 163 B10
Owo Nigeria 7°10N 5°39E 139 D6
Owosso U.S.A. 43°0N 84°10W 173 D11
Owyhee U.S.A. 41°57N 116°6W 168 F5
Owyhee → U.S.A. 43°49N 117°2W 168 E5
Owyhee, L. U.S.A. 43°38N 117°14W 168 E5
Ox Mts. = Slieve Gamph Ireland 54°6N 9°0W 64 B3
Oxapampa Peru 10°33S 75°26W 188 C2
Öxarfjörður Iceland 66°15N 16°45W 60 C5
Oxbow Canada 49°14N 102°10W 163 D8
Oxelösund Sweden 58°43N 17°5E 63 F11
Oxford N.Z. 43°18S 172°11E 155 D7
Oxford U.K. 51°46N 1°15W 67 F6
Oxford Ala., U.S.A. 33°36N 85°51W 178 B4
Oxford Mass., U.S.A. 42°7N 71°52W 175 D13
Oxford Miss., U.S.A. 34°22N 89°31W 177 D10
Oxford N.C., U.S.A. 36°19N 78°35W 177 C15
Oxford N.Y., U.S.A. 42°27N 75°36W 175 D9
Oxford Ohio, U.S.A. 39°31N 84°45W 173 F11
Oxford L. Canada 54°51N 95°37W 163 C9
Oxfordshire □ U.K. 51°48N 1°16W 67 F6
Oxia Greece 38°18N 21°6E 98 C3
Oxie Sweden 55°33N 13°6E 63 J7
Oxilithos Greece 38°35N 24°7E 98 C6
Oxley Australia 34°11S 144°6E 152 C6
Oxley Wild Rivers △ Australia 30°57S 152°12E 153 A10
Oxnard U.S.A. 34°12N 119°11W 171 L7
Oxsjövålen Sweden 62°34N 13°57E 62 B7
Oxus = Amudarya → Uzbekistan 43°58N 59°34E 108 D5
Oya Malaysia 2°55N 111°55E 118 D4
Oyama Japan 36°18N 139°48E 113 F9
Oyambre △ Spain 43°22N 4°21W 88 B6
Oyem Gabon 1°34N 11°31E 140 D2
Oyen Canada 51°22N 110°28W 163 C6
Oykel → U.K. 57°56N 4°26W 65 D4
Oymyakon Russia 63°25N 142°44E 107 C15
Oyo Nigeria 7°46N 3°56E 139 D5
Oyo Sudan 21°58N 36°10E 137 C4
Oyo □ Nigeria 8°15N 3°30E 139 D5
Oyón Peru 10°37S 76°47W 188 C2
Oyonnax France 46°16N 5°40E 71 F12
Oyster Bay U.S.A. 40°52N 73°32W 175 F11
Ōyūbari Japan 43°1N 142°5E 112 C11
Oyyl → Kazakhstan 49°4N 54°40E 108 C4
Özalp Turkey 38°39N 43°59E 105 C10
Ozamiz Phil. 8°15N 123°50E 119 C6
Ozar = Ojhar India 20°6N 73°56E 126 D1
Ozark Ala., U.S.A. 31°28N 85°39W 178 D4
Ozark Ark., U.S.A. 35°29N 93°50W 176 D8
Ozark Mo., U.S.A. 37°1N 93°12W 172 G7
Ozark Plateau U.S.A. 37°20N 91°40W 172 G8
Ozarks, L. of the U.S.A. 38°12N 92°38W 172 F7
Ożarów Poland 50°53N 21°40E 83 H8
Ózd Hungary 48°14N 20°15E 80 B5
Ozernovskiy Russia 51°30N 156°31E 107 D16
Ozernoye Russia 51°46N 51°28E 86 E10
Ozersk Russia 54°25N 22°0E 82 D8
Ozette, L. U.S.A. 48°6N 124°38W 170 B2
Ozieri Italy 40°35N 9°0E 94 B2
Ozimek Poland 50°41N 18°11E 83 H5
Ozinki Russia 51°12N 49°44E 86 E9
Ozona U.S.A. 30°43N 101°12W 176 F4
Ozorków Poland 51°57N 19°16E 83 G6
Ozren Bos.-H. 43°55N 18°29E 80 G3
Ozuluama Mexico 21°40N 97°51W 181 C5
Ozun Romania 45°47N 25°50E 81 E10
Ozurgeti Georgia 41°55N 42°0E 87 K5

P

Pa Burkina Faso 11°33N 3°19W 138 C4
Pa-an Burma 16°51N 97°40E 123 L20
Pa Mong Dam Thailand 18°0N 102°22E 120 D4
Pa Sak → Thailand 15°30N 101°0E 120 E3
Paamiut Greenland 62°0N 49°43W 57 E6
Paanayarvi △ Russia 66°16N 30°10E 60 C24
Paar → Germany 48°46N 11°36E 77 G7
Paarl S. Africa 33°45S 18°56E 144 D2
Pab Hills Pakistan 26°30N 66°45E 124 F2
Pabaidh = Pabbay U.K. 57°46N 7°14W 65 D1
Pabbay U.K. 57°46N 7°14W 65 D1
Pabianice Poland 51°40N 19°20E 83 G6
Pabna Bangla. 24°1N 89°18E 123 G16
Pabo Uganda 3°1N 32°10E 142 B3
Pacaipampa Peru 5°35S 79°39W 188 B2
Pacaja → Brazil 1°56S 50°50W 187 D8
Pacajus Brazil 4°10S 38°31W 189 A3
Pacaraima, Sa. S. Amer. 4°0N 62°30W 186 C6
Pacarán Peru 12°50S 76°3W 188 C2
Pacaraos Peru 11°12S 76°42W 188 C2
Pacasmayo Peru 7°20S 79°35W 188 B2
Pace U.S.A. 30°36N 87°10W 179 E2
Paceco Italy 37°59N 12°33E 94 E5
Pachacamac Peru 12°14S 77°53W 188 C2
Pachia Greece 36°17N 25°50E 99 E7
Pachino Italy 36°43N 15°5E 95 F8
Pachitea → Peru 8°46S 74°33W 188 B3
Pachiza Peru 7°16S 76°46W 188 B2
Pachmarhi India 22°28N 78°26E 125 H8
Pachnes Greece 35°16N 24°4E 101 D6
Pachora India 20°38N 75°29E 126 D2
Pachpadra India 25°58N 72°10E 124 G5
Pachuca Mexico 20°7N 98°44W 181 C5
Pacific Antarctic Ridge Pac. Oc. 43°0S 115°0W 55 B13
Pacific Grove U.S.A. 36°38N 121°56W 170 J5
Pacific Ocean 10°0N 140°0W 157 G14
Pacific Rim △ Canada 48°40N 124°45W 170 B2
Pacifica U.S.A. 37°37N 122°27W 170 H4
Pacitan Indonesia 8°12S 111°7E 119 H14
Packsaddle Australia 30°36S 141°58E 152 A4
Packwood U.S.A. 46°36N 121°40W 170 D5
Pacov Czech Rep. 49°27N 15°0E 78 B8
Pacuí → Brazil 16°46S 45°1W 189 D1
Pacy-sur-Eure France 49°1N 1°23E 70 C8
Padaido, Kepulauan Indonesia 1°15S 136°30E 119 E9
Padampur India 20°59N 83°4E 126 D6
Padang Riau, Indonesia 1°30N 102°30E 121 M4
Padang Sumatera Barat, Indonesia 1°0S 100°20E 118 E2
Padang Endau Malaysia 2°40N 103°38E 121 L4
Padangpanjang Indonesia 0°40S 100°20E 118 E2
Padangsidempuan Indonesia 1°30N 99°15E 118 D1
Padborg Denmark 54°49N 9°21E 63 K3
Paddle Prairie Canada 57°57N 117°29W 162 B5
Paderborn Germany 51°42N 8°45E 76 D4
Paderoo India 18°5N 82°40E 126 E6
Padeş, Vf. Romania 45°40N 22°22E 80 E7
Padina Romania 44°50N 27°8E 81 F12
Padjelanta △ Sweden 67°20N 16°35E 60 C17
Padma India 24°12N 85°22E 125 G11
Pádova Italy 45°25N 11°53E 93 C8
Padra India 22°15N 73°7E 124 H5
Padrauna India 26°54N 83°59E 125 F10
Padre I. U.S.A. 27°10N 97°25W 176 H6
Padre Island ⌂ U.S.A. 27°0N 97°25W 176 H6
Padrón Spain 42°41N 8°39W 88 C2
Padstow U.K. 50°33N 4°58W 67 G3
Padthaway Australia 36°36S 140°31E 152 D4
Padua = Pádova Italy 45°25N 11°53E 93 C8
Paducah Ky., U.S.A. 37°5N 88°37W 172 G9
Paducah Tex., U.S.A. 34°1N 100°18W 176 D4
Padukka Sri Lanka 6°50N 80°5E 127 L5
Padul Spain 37°1N 3°38W 89 H7
Padwa India 18°27N 82°47E 126 E6
Paea Tahiti 17°41S 149°35W 155 b
Paekakariki N.Z. 40°59S 174°58E 154 G3
Paektu-san N. Korea 41°59N 128°4E 115 D15
Paengaroa N.Z. 37°49S 176°29E 154 D5
Paeroa N.Z. 37°23S 175°41E 154 D4
Paesana Italy 44°41N 7°16E 92 D4
Pafúri Mozam. 22°28S 31°17E 145 B5
Pag Croatia 44°25N 15°3E 93 D12
Paga Ghana 11°1N 1°8W 139 C4
Pagadian Phil. 7°55N 123°30E 119 C6
Pagai Selatan, Pulau Indonesia 3°0S 100°15E 118 E2
Pagai Utara, Pulau Indonesia 2°35S 100°0E 118 E2
Pagalu = Annobón Atl. Oc. 1°25S 5°36E 133 G4
Pagara India 24°22N 80°1E 125 G9
Pagasa I. = Thitu I. S. China Sea 11°3N 114°17E 118 B4
Pagastikos Kolpos Greece 39°15N 23°0E 98 B5
Pagatan Indonesia 3°33S 115°59E 118 E5
Page U.S.A. 36°57N 111°27W 169 H8
Pagėgiai Lithuania 55°9N 21°54E 82 C8
Paget, Mt. S. Georgia 54°26S 36°31W 184 H6
Paget I. India 13°26N 92°50E 127 H11
Pagosa Springs U.S.A. 37°16N 107°1W 169 H10
Pagri China 27°45N 89°10E 110 F6
Pagwa River Canada 50°2N 85°14W 164 B2
Pāhala U.S.A. 19°12N 155°29W 167 M8
Pahang □ Malaysia 3°30N 102°45E 121 L4
Pahang → Malaysia 3°30N 103°9E 121 L4
Pahia Pt. N.Z. 46°20S 167°41E 155 G2
Pahiatua N.Z. 40°27S 175°50E 154 G4
Pahokee U.S.A. 26°50N 80°40W 179 J9
Pahrump U.S.A. 36°12N 115°59W 171 J11
Pahute Mesa U.S.A. 37°20N 116°45W 170 H10
Pai Thailand 19°19N 98°27E 120 C2
Paicines U.S.A. 36°44N 121°17W 170 J5
Paide Estonia 58°53N 25°33E 84 C3
Paignton U.K. 50°26N 3°35W 67 G4
Paihia N.Z. 35°17S 174°6E 154 B3
Paiho Taiwan 23°21N 120°25E 117 F13
Paiján Peru 7°42S 79°20W 188 B2
Päijänne Finland 61°30N 25°30E 84 B3
Pailani India 25°45N 80°26E 125 G9
Pailin Cambodia 12°46N 102°36E 120 F4
Paimpol France 48°48N 3°4W 70 D3
Painan Indonesia 1°21S 100°34E 118 E2
Paine Grande, Cerro Chile 50°59S 73°4W 192 D2
Painesville U.S.A. 41°43N 81°15W 174 E3
Paint Hills = Wemindji Canada 53°0N 78°49W 164 B4
Paint L. Canada 55°28N 97°57W 163 B9
Painted Desert U.S.A. 36°0N 111°0W 169 H8
Paintsville U.S.A. 37°49N 82°48W 173 G12
País Vasco □ Spain 42°50N 2°45W 90 C2
Paisley Canada 44°18N 81°16W 174 B3
Paisley U.K. 55°50N 4°25W 65 F4
Paisley U.S.A. 42°42N 120°32W 168 E3
Paita Peru 5°11S 81°9W 188 B1
Paithan India 19°29N 75°23E 126 E2
Paiva → Portugal 41°4N 8°16W 88 D2
Paizhou China 30°12N 113°55E 117 B9
Pajares Spain 43°1N 5°46W 88 B5
Pajares, Puerto de Spain 42°58N 5°46W 88 C5
Pajęczno Poland 51°10N 19°0E 83 G5
Pak Lay Laos 18°15N 101°27E 120 C3
Pak Ou Laos 20°3N 102°12E 120 B4
Pak Phanang Thailand 8°21N 100°12E 121 H3
Pak Sane Laos 18°22N 103°39E 120 C4
Pak Song Laos 15°11N 106°14E 120 E6
Pak Suang Laos 19°58N 102°15E 116 H4
Pak Tam Chung China 22°24N 114°19E 111 a
Pak Thong Chai Thailand 14°43N 102°1E 120 E4
Pakala India 13°29N 79°8E 127 H4
Pakaur India 24°38N 87°51E 125 G12
Pakch'ŏn N. Korea 39°44N 125°35E 115 E13
Pakenham Australia 38°6S 145°30E 153 E6
Pakenham Canada 45°18N 76°18W 175 A8
Pakhuis S. Africa 32°9S 19°5E 144 D2
Pakistan ■ Asia 30°0N 70°0E 124 E4
Pakkading Laos 18°19N 103°59E 120 C4
Paklenica △ Croatia 44°20N 15°39E 93 D12
Pakokku Burma 21°20N 95°0E 123 J19
Pakość Poland 52°48N 18°6E 83 F5
Pakowki L. Canada 49°20N 111°0W 163 D6
Pakpattan Pakistan 30°25N 73°27E 124 D5
Pakrac Croatia 45°27N 17°12E 80 E2
Pakruojis Lithuania 55°58N 23°52E 82 C10
Paks Hungary 46°38N 18°55E 80 D3
Paktīā □ Afghan. 33°30N 69°15E 122 C6
Paktīkā □ Afghan. 32°30N 69°0E 122 C6
Pakwach Uganda 2°28N 31°27E 142 B3
Pakxe Laos 15°5N 105°52E 120 E5
Pal Lahara India 21°27N 85°11E 125 J11
Pala Chad 9°25N 15°5E 135 G9
Pala Dem. Rep. of the Congo 6°45S 29°30E 142 D2
Pala U.S.A. 33°22N 117°5W 171 M9
Palabek Uganda 3°22N 32°33E 142 B3
Palacios U.S.A. 28°42N 96°13W 176 G6
Palafrugell Spain 41°55N 3°10E 90 D8
Palagiano Italy 40°35N 17°2E 95 B10
Palagonia Italy 37°19N 14°45E 95 E7
Palagruža Croatia 42°24N 16°15E 93 F13
Palaiseau France 48°42N 2°14E 71 D9
Palakkad India 10°46N 76°42E 127 J3
Palakol India 16°31N 81°46E 127 F5
Palalankwe India 10°52N 92°29E 127 J11
Palam India 19°0N 77°0E 126 E3
Palamas Greece 39°26N 22°4E 98 B4
Palamós Spain 41°50N 3°10E 90 D8
Palampur India 32°10N 76°30E 124 C7
Palamut Turkey 38°59N 27°41E 99 C9
Palana Australia 39°45S 147°55E 151 F4
Palana Russia 59°10N 159°59E 107 D16
Palanan Phil. 17°8N 122°29E 119 A6
Palanan Pt. Phil. 17°17N 122°30E 119 A6
Palandri Pakistan 33°42N 73°40E 125 C5
Palanga Lithuania 55°58N 21°3E 82 C8
Palangkaraya Indonesia 2°16S 113°56E 118 E4
Palani India 10°30N 77°30E 127 J3
Palani Hills India 10°14N 77°33E 127 J3
Palanpur India 24°10N 72°25E 124 G5
Palapye Botswana 22°30S 27°7E 144 B4
Palar → India 12°27N 80°13E 127 H5
Palas Pakistan 35°4N 73°14E 125 B5
Palas de Rei Spain 42°52N 7°52W 88 C3
Palasponga India 21°47N 85°34E 125 J11
Palatka Russia 60°6N 150°54E 107 C16
Palatka U.S.A. 29°39N 81°38W 178 F8
Palau Italy 41°11N 9°23E 94 A2
Palau ■ Palau 7°30N 134°30E 156 G5
Palauk Burma 13°10N 98°40E 120 F2
Palaw Burma 12°58N 98°39E 120 F2
Palawan Phil. 9°30N 118°30E 118 C5
Palayankottai India 8°45N 77°45E 127 K3
Palazzo, Pte. France 42°28N 8°30E 73 F12
Palazzo San Gervásio Italy 40°56N 15°59E 95 B8
Palazzolo Acréide Italy 37°4N 14°54E 95 E7
Palca Chile 19°7S 69°9W 188 D4
Paldiski Estonia 59°23N 24°9E 84 C3
Pale Bos.-H. 43°50N 18°38E 80 G3
Palekastro Greece 35°12N 26°15E 101 D8
Paleleh Indonesia 1°10N 121°50E 119 D6
Palembang Indonesia 3°0S 104°50E 118 E2
Palena → Chile 43°50S 73°50W 192 B2
Palena, L. Chile 43°55S 71°40W 192 B2
Palencia Spain 42°1N 4°34W 88 C6
Palencia □ Spain 42°31N 4°33W 88 C6
Palenque Mexico 17°29N 92°1W 181 D6
Paleochora Greece 35°16N 23°39E 101 D5
Paleokastritsa Greece 39°40N 19°41E 101 A3
Paleometokho Cyprus 35°7N 33°11E 101 D12
Paleopoli Greece 37°49N 24°50E 98 D6
Palermo Italy 38°7N 13°22E 94 D6
Palermo U.S.A. 39°26N 121°33W 170 F5
Palermo ✕ (PMO) Italy 38°11N 13°5E 94 D6
Paleros Greece 38°47N 20°53E 98 C2
Palestina Chile 23°50S 69°47W 190 A2
Palestine Asia 32°0N 35°0E 130 D4
Palestine U.S.A. 31°46N 95°38W 176 F7
Palestrina Italy 41°50N 12°53E 93 G9
Paletwa Burma 21°10N 92°50E 123 J18
Palghat = Palakkad India 10°46N 76°42E 127 J3
Palgrave, Mt. Australia 23°22S 115°58E 148 D2
Palhoça Brazil 27°38S 48°40W 191 B6
Pali India 25°50N 73°20E 124 G5
Pali-Aike △ Chile 52°6S 69°44W 192 D3
Palikir Micronesia 6°55N 158°9E 156 G7
Palinuro Italy 40°2N 15°17E 95 B8
Palinuro, C. Italy 40°1N 15°16E 95 B8
Paliouri, Akra Greece 39°57N 23°45E 96 G7
Palisades Res. U.S.A. 43°20N 111°12W 168 E8
Paliseul Belgium 49°54N 5°8E 69 E5
Palitana India 21°32N 71°49E 124 J4
Palizada Mexico 18°15N 92°5W 181 D6
Palk Bay Asia 9°30N 79°15E 127 K4
Palk Strait Asia 10°0N 79°45E 127 K4
Palkānah Iraq 35°49N 44°26E 128 C5
Palkonda India 18°36N 83°48E 126 E6
Palkonda Ra. India 13°50N 79°20E 127 H4
Palkot India 22°53N 84°39E 125 H11
Pallanza = Verbánia Italy 45°56N 8°33E 92 C5
Pallarenda Australia 19°12S 146°46E 150 B4
Pallas-Yllästunturi △ Finland 68°8N 24°15E 60 B21
Pallasovka Russia 50°4N 47°0E 86 E8
Palleru → India 16°45N 80°2E 126 F5
Pallës, Bishti i Albania 41°24N 19°24E 96 E3
Pallinup → Australia 34°27S 118°50E 149 F2
Pallisa Uganda 1°12N 33°43E 142 B3
Palliser, C. N.Z. 41°37S 175°14E 154 H4
Palliser B. N.Z. 41°26S 175°5E 154 H4
Pallu India 28°59N 74°14E 124 E6
Palm Bay U.S.A. 28°2N 80°35W 179 G9
Palm Beach U.S.A. 26°43N 80°2W 179 J9
Palm Coast U.S.A. 29°35N 81°12W 179 F8
Palm Desert U.S.A. 33°43N 116°22W 171 M10
Palm-Grove △ Australia 24°57S 149°21E 150 C4
Palm Harbor U.S.A. 28°5N 82°46W 179 G7
Palm Is. Australia 18°40S 146°35E 150 B4
Palm Springs U.S.A. 33°50N 116°33W 171 M10
Palm Valley U.S.A. 30°11N 81°23W 178 E8
Palma Mozam. 10°46S 40°29E 143 E5
Palma → Brazil 12°33S 47°52W 189 C1
Palma, B. de Spain 39°30N 2°39E 100 B9
Palma de Mallorca Spain 39°35N 2°39E 100 B9
Palma de Mallorca ✕ (PMI) Spain 39°34N 2°43E 91 F7
Palma del Río Spain 37°43N 5°17W 89 H5
Palma di Montechiaro Italy 37°11N 13°46E 94 E6
Palma Nova = Palmanova Spain 39°32N 2°34E 100 B9
Palma Soriano Cuba 20°15N 76°0W 182 B4
Palmaner India 13°12N 78°45E 127 H4
Palmanova Spain 39°32N 2°34E 100 B9
Palmares Brazil 8°41S 35°28W 189 B3
Palmarola Italy 40°56N 12°51E 94 B5
Palmas Paraná, Brazil 26°29S 52°0W 191 B5
Palmas Tocantins, Brazil 10°13S 48°16W 189 C1
Palmas, C. Liberia 4°27N 7°46W 138 E3
Pálmas, G. di Italy 39°0N 8°30E 94 D1
Palmas de Monte Alto Brazil 14°16S 43°10W 189 C2
Palmdale Calif., U.S.A. 34°35N 118°7W 171 L8
Palmdale Fla., U.S.A. 26°57N 81°19W 179 J8
Palmeira das Missões Brazil 27°55S 53°17W 191 B5
Palmeira dos Índios Brazil 9°25S 36°37W 189 B3
Palmeirais Brazil 6°0S 43°0W 189 B2
Palmeiras Brazil 12°31S 41°34W 189 C2
Palmeiras → Brazil 12°22S 47°8W 189 C1
Palmela Portugal 38°32N 8°57W 89 G2
Palmer Antarctica 64°35S 65°0W 55 C1
Palmer U.S.A. 61°36N 149°7W 160 E2
Palmer → Australia 16°0S 142°26E 150 B3
Palmer Arch. Antarctica 64°15S 65°0W 55 C1
Palmer Lake U.S.A. 39°7N 104°55W 168 G1
Palmer Land Antarctica 73°0S 63°0W 55 D1
Palmerston Australia 12°31S 130°59E 148 B5
Palmerston Canada 43°50N 80°51W 174 C4
Palmerston N.Z. 45°29S 170°43E 155 F5
Palmerston North N.Z. 40°21S 175°39E 154 G4
Palmerton U.S.A. 40°48N 75°37W 175 F9
Palmetto Fla., U.S.A. 27°31N 82°34W 179 H7
Palmetto Ga., U.S.A. 33°31N 84°40W 178 B5
Palmi Italy 38°21N 15°51E 95 D8
Palmira Argentina 32°59S 68°34W 190 C2
Palmira Colombia 3°32N 76°16W 186 C3
Palmyra = Tudmur Syria 34°36N 38°15E 105 E8
Palmyra Mo., U.S.A. 39°48N 91°32W 172 F8
Palmyra N.J., U.S.A. 40°0N 75°1W 175 F9
Palmyra N.Y., U.S.A. 43°5N 77°18W 174 C7
Palmyra Pa., U.S.A. 40°18N 76°36W 175 F8
Palmyra Is. Pac. Oc. 5°52N 162°5W 157 G11
Palmyras Pt. India 20°46N 87°1E 126 D8
Palo Alto U.S.A. 37°27N 122°10W 170 H4
Palo Seco Trin. & Tob. 10°4N 61°36W 187 K15
Palo Verde U.S.A. 33°26N 114°44W 171 M12
Palo Verde △ Costa Rica 10°21N 85°21W 182 D2
Palomar Mt. U.S.A. 33°22N 116°50W 171 M10
Palopo Indonesia 3°0S 120°16E 119 E6
Palos, C. de Spain 37°38N 0°40W 91 H4
Palos de la Frontera Spain 37°14N 6°53W 89 H4
Palos Verdes, Pt. U.S.A. 33°46N 118°25W 171 M8
Palos Verdes Estates U.S.A. 33°48N 118°23W 171 M8
Palpa Peru 14°30S 75°15W 188 C2
Pålsboda Sweden 59°3N 15°22E 62 E9
Palu Indonesia 1°0S 119°52E 119 E5
Palu Turkey 38°45N 40°0E 105 C9
Paluke Liberia 5°2N 8°5W 138 D3
Paluma Ra. Australia 19°9S 146°22E 150 B4
Paluzza Italy 46°32N 13°1E 93 B10
Palwal India 28°8N 77°19E 124 E7
Pama Burkina Faso 11°19N 0°44E 139 C5
Pama △ Burkina Faso 11°27N 0°40E 139 C5
Pamanukan Indonesia 6°16S 107°49E 119 G12
Pamban I. India 9°15N 79°20E 127 K4
Pamekasan Indonesia 7°10S 113°28E 119 G15
Pamenang Indonesia 8°24S 116°6E 119 J19
Pamiers France 43°7N 1°39E 72 E5
Pamir Tajikistan 37°40N 73°0E 109 E8
Pamlico → U.S.A. 35°20N 76°28W 177 D16
Pamlico Sd. U.S.A. 35°20N 76°0W 177 D17
Pampa U.S.A. 35°32N 100°58W 176 D4
Pampa de Agma Argentina 43°45S 69°40W 192 B3
Pampa de las Salinas Argentina 32°1S 66°58W 190 C2
Pampa Hermosa Peru 7°7S 75°4W 188 B3
Pampanua Indonesia 4°16S 120°8E 119 E6
Pampas Argentina 35°0S 63°0W 190 D3

Pampas Peru 12°20S 74°50W 188 C3
Pampas → Peru 13°24S 73°12W 188 C3
Pamphylia Turkey 37°0N 31°0E 104 D4
Pamplona Colombia 7°23N 72°39W 186 B4
Pamplona-Iruña Spain 42°48N 1°38W 90 C3
Pamponpoort S. Africa 31°3S 22°40E 144 D3
Pamukçu Turkey 39°30N 27°54E 99 B9
Pamukkale Turkey 37°55N 29°8E 99 D11
Pan de Azúcar Chile 24°5S 68°10W 190 A2
Pan de Azúcar △ Chile 26°0S 70°40W 190 B1
Pan Xian China 25°46N 104°38E 116 E5
Pana U.S.A. 39°23N 89°5W 172 F9
Panaca U.S.A. 37°47N 114°23W 169 H6
Panacea U.S.A. 30°2N 84°23E 177 E4
Panadura Sri Lanka 6°47N 79°53E 127 L4
Panagyurishte Bulgaria 42°30N 24°15E 97 D8
Panaitan Indonesia 6°36S 105°12E 119 G11
Panaji India 15°25N 73°50E 127 G1
Panamá Panama 9°0N 79°25W 182 E4
Panama Sri Lanka 6°45N 81°48E 127 L5
Panama ■ Cent. Amer. 8°48N 79°55W 182 E4
Panamá, G. de Panama 8°4N 79°20W 182 E4
Panama, Isthmus of
  Cent. Amer. 9°0N 79°0W 182 E4
Panama Basin Pac. Oc. 5°0N 83°30W 157 G19
Panama Canal Panama 9°10N 79°37W 182 E4
Panama City U.S.A. 30°10N 85°40W 178 E4
Panama City Beach
  U.S.A. 30°11N 85°48W 178 E4
Panamint Range
  U.S.A. 36°20N 117°20W 171 J9
Panamint Springs
  U.S.A. 36°20N 117°28W 171 J9
Panão Peru 9°55S 75°55W 188 E2
Panare Thailand 6°51N 101°30E 121 J3
Panarea Italy 38°38N 15°4E 95 D8
Panaro → Italy 44°55N 11°25E 93 D8
Panay Phil. 11°10N 122°30E 119 B6
Panay G. Phil. 11°0N 122°30E 119 B6
Pančevo Serbia 44°52N 20°41E 80 F5
Panch'iao Taiwan 25°1N 121°27E 117 E13
Panciu Romania 45°54N 27°8E 81 E12
Pancorbo, Desfiladero
  Spain 42°32N 3°5W 88 C7
Pâncota Romania 46°20N 21°45E 80 D6
Panda Mozam. 24°2S 34°45E 145 B5
Pandan Malaysia 1°32N 103°46E 121 d
Pandan Phil. 11°45N 122°10E 119 B6
Pandan, Selat Singapore 1°15N 103°42E 121 d
Pandan Tampoi = Tampoi
  Malaysia 1°30N 103°39E 121 d
Pandegelang Indonesia 6°25S 106°5E 119 G12
Pandhana India 21°42N 76°13E 124 J7
Pandharkawada India 20°1N 78°32E 126 D4
Pandharpur India 17°41N 75°20E 126 F2
Pandhurna India 21°36N 78°35E 124 J8
Pando Uruguay 34°45S 56°0W 191 C4
Pando □ Bolivia 11°20S 67°40W 188 C4
Pando, L. = Hope, L.
  Australia 28°24S 139°18E 151 E2
Pandokratoras Greece 39°45N 19°50E 101 A3
Pandora Costa Rica 9°43N 83°3W 182 E3
Pandrup Denmark 57°14N 9°40E 63 G3
Panevéggio-Pale di San
  Martino △ Italy 46°14N 11°46E 93 B8
Panevėžys Lithuania 55°42N 24°25E 84 E3
Panfilov Russia 50°25N 42°46E 86 E6
Pang Sida △ Thailand 14°5N 102°17E 120 E4
Panga
  Dem. Rep. of the Congo 1°52N 26°18E 142 B2
Pangaion Oros Greece 40°50N 24°0E 97 F8
Pangandaran
  Indonesia 7°40S 108°39E 119 G13
Pangandaran △
  Indonesia 7°43S 108°42E 119 G13
Pangani Tanzania 5°25S 38°58E 142 D4
Pangani → Tanzania 5°26S 38°58E 142 D4
Pangar Djeréme △
  Cameroon 5°50N 13°10E 139 D7
Pangfou = Bengbu
  China 32°58N 117°20E 117 A11
Pangga, Tanjung
  Indonesia 8°54S 116°2E 119 K19
Panghsang = Bangkang
  Burma 22°4N 99°1E 116 F2
Pangil
  Dem. Rep. of the Congo 3°10S 26°35E 142 C2
Pangjiabu China 40°38N 115°26E 114 D8
Pangkah, Tanjung
  Indonesia 6°51S 112°33E 119 G15
Pangkai Burma 22°49N 98°39E 116 F2
Pangkajene Indonesia 4°46S 119°34E 119 E5
Pangkalanbrandan
  Indonesia 4°1N 98°20E 118 D1
Pangkalanbuun
  Indonesia 2°41S 111°37E 118 E4
Pangkalpinang
  Indonesia 2°10S 106°10E 118 E3
Pangkor, Pulau
  Malaysia 4°13N 100°34E 121 K3
Pangniqtuuq = Pangnirtung
  Canada 66°8N 65°43W 161 D18
Pangnirtung Canada 66°8N 65°43W 161 D18
Pangody Russia 65°52N 74°27E 106 C8
Pangong Tso = Bangong Co
  China 33°45N 78°43E 125 C8
Panguipulli Chile 39°38S 72°0W 192 A2
Panguitch U.S.A. 37°50N 112°26W 169 H7
Pangutaran Group
  Phil. 6°18N 120°34E 119 C6
Panhala India 16°49N 74°7E 126 F2
Panhandle U.S.A. 35°21N 101°23W 176 D4
Pani Mines India 22°29N 73°50E 124 H5
Pania-Mutombo
  Dem. Rep. of the Congo 5°11S 23°51E 142 D1
Panikota I. India 20°46N 71°21E 124 J4
Panipat India 29°25N 77°2E 124 E7
Panjakent Tajikistan 39°26N 67°37E 109 F7
Panjal Range = Pir Panjal Range
  India 32°30N 76°50E 124 C7
Panjgur Pakistan 27°0N 64°5E 122 F4
Panjhra → India 21°13N 74°57E 126 D2
Panjim = Panaji India 15°25N 73°50E 127 G1
Panjin China 41°3N 122°2E 115 D12
Panjnad → Pakistan 28°57N 70°30E 124 E4
Panjnad Barrage
  Pakistan 29°22N 71°15E 124 E4
Panjshīr □ Afghan. 35°50N 69°50E 109 E7
Panjwai Afghan. 31°26N 65°27E 124 D1
Pankisi Gorge = Pankisis Kheoba
  Georgia 42°7N 45°15E 87 J7

Pankisis Kheoba Georgia 42°7N 45°15E 87 J7
Pankshin Nigeria 9°16N 9°25E 139 D6
Panmunjŏm N. Korea 37°59N 126°38E 115 F14
Panna India 24°40N 80°15E 125 G9
Panna △ India 24°40N 80°0E 125 G9
Panna Hills India 24°40N 81°15E 125 G9
Pannawonica
  Australia 21°39S 116°19E 148 D2
Pano Akil Pakistan 27°51N 69°7E 124 F3
Pano Lefkara Cyprus 34°53N 33°20E 101 E12
Pano Panayia Cyprus 34°55N 32°38E 101 E11
Panorama Brazil 21°21S 51°51W 191 A5
Panormos Greece 35°25N 24°41E 101 D6
Panruti India 11°46N 79°35E 127 J4
Pansemal India 21°39N 74°42E 124 J6
Panshan = Panjin
  China 41°3N 122°2E 115 D12
Panshi China 42°58N 126°5E 115 C14
Pantanal Brazil 17°30S 57°40W 186 H7
Pantanos de Centla △
  Mexico 18°25N 92°25W 181 D6
Pantar Indonesia 8°28S 124°10E 119 F6
Pante Macassar
  E. Timor 9°30S 123°58E 119 F6
Pantelleria Italy 36°50N 11°57E 94 F4
Pantón = O Castro de Ferreira
  Spain 42°31N 7°37W 88 C3
Pánuco Mexico 22°3N 98°10W 181 C5
Panvel India 18°59N 73°4E 126 E1
Panyam Nigeria 9°27N 9°8E 139 D6
Panyu China 23°1N 113°2E 117 F9
Panzhihua China 26°33N 101°44E 116 D3
Páola Italy 39°21N 16°2E 95 C9
Paola Malta 35°52N 14°30E 101 D2
Paola U.S.A. 38°35N 94°53W 172 F6
Paonia U.S.A. 38°52N 107°36W 168 G10
Paoting = Baoding
  China 38°50N 115°28E 114 E8
Paot'ou = Baotou
  China 40°32N 110°2E 114 D6
Paoua C.A.R. 7°9N 16°20E 140 C3
Pápa Hungary 47°22N 17°30E 80 C2
Papa Stour U.K. 60°20N 1°42W 65 A7
Papa Westray U.K. 59°20N 2°55W 65 B6
Papagayo → Mexico 16°46N 99°43W 181 D5
Papagayo, G. de
  Costa Rica 10°30N 85°50W 182 D2
Papagni → India 15°35N 77°45E 127 G3
Papakura N.Z. 37°4S 174°59E 154 D3
Papantla Mexico 20°27N 97°19W 181 C5
Papar Malaysia 5°45N 116°0E 118 C5
Papara Tahiti 17°43S 149°31W 155 b
Paparoa N.Z. 36°6S 174°16E 154 C3
Paparoa △ N.Z. 42°7S 171°26E 155 C6
Paparoa Ra. N.Z. 42°7S 171°28E 155 C6
Papas, Akra Greece 38°13N 21°20E 98 C3
Papatoetoe N.Z. 36°59S 174°51E 154 C3
Papeete Tahiti 17°32S 149°34W 155 b
Papenburg Germany 53°5N 7°23E 76 B3
Papenoo Tahiti 17°30S 149°25W 155 b
Papenoo → Tahiti 17°30S 149°25W 155 b
Paphlagonia Turkey 41°30N 33°0E 98 B2
Paphos Cyprus 34°46N 32°25E 101 E11
Papikio Oros Greece 41°15N 25°13E 97 E9
Paposo Chile 25°0S 70°30W 190 B1
Papoutsa Cyprus 34°54N 33°4E 101 E12
Papua □ Indonesia 4°0S 137°0E 119 E9
Papua, G. of Papua N. G. 9°0S 144°50E 147 B7
Papua New Guinea ■
  Oceania 8°0S 145°0E 147 B7
Papudo Chile 32°29S 71°27W 190 C1
Papuk Croatia 45°30N 17°30E 80 E2
Papun Burma 18°2N 97°30E 123 K20
Papunya Australia 23°15S 131°54E 148 D5
Pará = Belém Brazil 1°20S 48°30W 187 D9
Pará □ Brazil 3°20S 52°0W 187 D8
Paraburdoo Australia 23°14S 117°32E 148 D2
Paracas, Pen. de Peru 13°53S 76°20W 188 D1
Paracatu Brazil 16°30S 45°4W 189 D1
Paracatu → Brazil 16°30S 45°4W 189 D1
Paracel Is. S. China Sea 15°50N 112°0E 118 A4
Parachilna Australia 31°10S 138°21E 152 A3
Parachinar Pakistan 33°55N 70°5E 124 C4
Paraćin Serbia 43°54N 21°27E 96 C5
Paracuru Brazil 3°24S 39°4W 189 A5
Parada, Punta Peru 15°22S 75°11W 188 D2
Paradas Spain 37°18N 5°29W 89 H5
Paradela Spain 42°44N 7°37W 88 C3
Paradip India 20°15N 86°35E 126 D8
Paradise Calif., U.S.A. 39°46N 121°37W 170 F5
Paradise Nev., U.S.A. 36°5N 115°8W 171 J11
Paradise → Canada 53°32N 57°19W 165 B8
Paradise Hill Canada 53°32N 109°28W 163 C7
Paradise River Canada 53°27N 57°17W 165 B8
Paradise Valley
  U.S.A. 41°30N 117°32W 168 F5
Paradisi Greece 36°18N 28°7E 101 C10
Paragould U.S.A. 36°3N 90°29W 177 C9
Paragua → Venezuela 6°55N 62°55W 186 B6
Paraguaçu → Brazil 12°45S 38°54W 189 D3
Paraguaçu Paulista
  Brazil 22°22S 50°35W 191 A5
Paraguaná, Pen. de
  Venezuela 12°0N 70°0W 186 A5
Paraguarí Paraguay 25°36S 57°0W 190 B4
Paraguarí □ Paraguay 26°0S 57°10W 190 B4
Paraguay ■ S. Amer. 23°0S 57°0W 190 A4
Paraguay → Paraguay 27°18S 58°38W 190 B4
Paraíba = João Pessoa
  Brazil 7°10S 34°52W 189 B4
Paraíba □ Brazil 7°0S 36°0W 189 B3
Paraíba do Sul →
  Brazil 21°37S 41°3W 191 A7
Paraíso Mexico 18°24N 93°14W 181 D6
Parak Iran 27°38N 52°25E 129 E7
Parakhino Paddubye
  Russia 58°26N 33°10E 84 C7
Parakou Benin 9°25N 2°40E 139 D5
Parakylia Australia 30°24S 136°25E 152 A2
Paralimni Cyprus 35°2N 33°58E 101 D12
Paralio Astros Greece 37°25N 22°45E 98 D4
Paralkote India 19°47N 80°41E 126 E5
Parambu Brazil 6°13S 40°43W 189 B2
Paramaribo Suriname 5°50N 55°10W 187 B7
Paramirim Brazil 13°26S 42°15W 189 D2
Paramirim → Brazil 11°34S 43°0W 189 D2
Paramithia Greece 39°30N 20°35E 98 B2
Paramonga Peru 10°41S 77°50W 188 C2
Páramos del Batallón y La
  Negra △ Venezuela 8°2N 71°55W 183 E5

Paramushir, Ostrov
  Russia 50°24N 156°0E 107 D16
Paran → Israel 30°20N 35°10E 130 E4
Paraná Argentina 31°45S 60°30W 190 C3
Paraná Brazil 12°30S 47°48W 189 C1
Paraná □ Brazil 24°30S 51°0W 191 A5
Paraná → Argentina 33°43S 59°15W 190 C4
Paraná → Brazil 12°30S 48°14W 189 C1
Paranaguá Brazil 25°30S 48°30W 191 B6
Paranaíba Brazil 19°40S 51°11W 187 G8
Paranaíba → Brazil 20°6S 51°4W 187 H8
Paranapanema →
  Brazil 22°40S 53°9W 191 A5
Paranapiacaba, Serra do
  Brazil 24°31S 48°35W 191 A6
Paranavaí Brazil 23°4S 52°56W 191 A5
Parang Maguindanao,
  Phil. 7°23N 124°16E 119 C6
Parang Sulu, Phil. 5°55N 120°54E 119 C6
Parangippettai India 11°30N 79°38E 127 J4
Parângul Mare, Vf.
  Romania 45°20N 23°37E 81 E8
Paraparaumu N.Z. 40°57S 175°3E 154 G4
Parapóti, Akra Greece 35°55N 27°15E 99 F9
Paratinga Brazil 12°40S 43°10W 189 C2
Paratoo Australia 32°42S 139°20E 152 B3
Parauapebas Brazil 6°4S 49°54W 187 E9
Paray-le-Monial France 46°27N 4°7E 71 F11
Parbati → Mad. P.,
  India 25°50N 76°30E 124 G7
Parbati → Raj., India 26°54N 77°53E 124 F7
Parbhani India 19°8N 76°52E 126 E3
Parchim Germany 53°26N 11°52E 76 B7
Parczew Poland 51°40N 22°52E 83 G9
Pardes Hanna-Karkur
  Israel 32°28N 34°57E 130 C3
Pardilla Spain 41°33N 3°43W 88 D7
Pardo → Bahia, Brazil 15°40S 39°0W 189 D3
Pardo → Mato Grosso,
  Brazil 21°46S 52°9W 191 A5
Pardo → Minas Gerais,
  Brazil 15°48S 44°48W 189 D2
Pardoo Roadhouse
  Australia 20°6S 119°3E 148 D2
Pardubice Czech Rep. 50°3N 15°45E 78 A8
Pardubický □ Czech Rep. 49°50N 16°0E 78 B8
Pare Indonesia 7°43S 112°12E 119 G15
Pare Mts. Tanzania 4°0S 37°45E 142 C4
Parecis, Serra dos Brazil 13°0S 60°0W 186 F7
Paredes de Nava Spain 42°9N 4°42W 88 C6
Parelhas Brazil 6°41S 36°39W 189 B3
Paren Russia 62°30N 163°15E 107 C17
Parenda India 18°16N 75°28E 126 E2
Parengarenga Harbour
  N.Z. 34°31S 173°0E 154 A2
Parent Canada 47°55N 74°35W 164 C4
Parent, L. Canada 48°31N 77°1W 164 C4
Parentis-en-Born France 44°21N 1°4W 72 D2
Parepare Indonesia 4°0S 119°40E 119 E5
Parfino Russia 57°59N 31°34E 84 D6
Parga Greece 39°15N 20°29E 98 B2
Pargas = Länsi-Turunmaa
  Finland 60°18N 22°18E 84 B2
Pargi India 17°11N 77°53E 126 E3
Pargo, Pta. do Madeira 32°49N 17°17W 100 D2
Parham Canada 44°39N 76°43W 175 B8
Paria → U.S.A. 36°52N 111°36W 168 H8
Paria, G. de Venezuela 10°30N 61°40W 187 K14
Pariaguán Venezuela 8°51N 64°34W 186 B6
Paricutín, Cerro
  Mexico 19°28N 102°15W 180 D4
Parigi Indonesia 0°50S 120°5E 119 E6
Parika Guyana 6°50N 58°20W 186 B7
Parikia Greece 37°6N 25°11E 99 D7
Parikkala Finland 61°33N 29°31E 84 B5
Parima, Serra Brazil 2°30N 64°0W 186 C6
Parinari Peru 4°35S 74°25W 188 A3
Pariñas, Pta. Peru 4°30S 82°0W 188 A1
Parincea Romania 46°27N 27°9E 81 C12
Paringa Australia 34°10S 140°46E 152 C4
Parintins Brazil 2°40S 56°50W 187 D7
Pariparit Kyun Burma 14°52N 93°41E 127 G11
Paris Canada 43°12N 80°25W 174 C4
Paris France 48°53N 2°20E 71 D9
Paris Idaho, U.S.A. 42°14N 111°24W 168 E8
Paris Ky., U.S.A. 38°13N 84°15W 173 F11
Paris Tenn., U.S.A. 36°18N 88°19W 177 C10
Paris Tex., U.S.A. 33°40N 95°33W 176 E7
Paris, Ville de □ France 48°50N 2°20E 71 D9
Paris Charles de Gaulle ✈ (CDG)
  France 49°0N 2°32E 71 D9
Paris Orly ✈ (ORY)
  France 48°44N 2°23E 71 D9
Parish U.S.A. 43°25N 76°8W 175 C8
Parishville U.S.A. 44°38N 74°49W 175 B10
Pariti Indonesia 10°1S 123°45E 148 B3
Parla Spain 40°14N 3°46W 88 B7
Parlakimidi India 18°45N 84°5E 126 E7
Parli India 18°50N 76°33E 126 E3
Pârlița Moldova 47°19N 27°52E 81 C12
Parma Italy 44°48N 10°20E 92 D7
Parma Idaho, U.S.A. 43°47N 116°57W 168 E5
Parma Ohio, U.S.A. 41°24N 81°43W 174 E3
Parma → Italy 44°56N 10°26E 92 D7
Parnaguá Brazil 10°10S 44°38W 189 C2
Parnaíba Brazil 2°54S 41°47W 189 A2

Parnaíba → Brazil 3°0S 41°50W 189 A2
Parnamirim Pernambuco,
  Brazil 8°5S 39°34W 189 B3
Parnamirim Rio Grande do N.,
  Brazil 5°55S 35°15W 189 B3
Parnarama Brazil 5°31S 43°6W 189 B2
Parnassos Greece 38°35N 22°30E 98 C4
Parnassus N.Z. 42°43S 173°23E 155 C8
Parndana Australia 35°48S 137°12E 152 C2
Parner India 19°0N 74°26E 126 E2
Parnitha Greece 38°14N 23°45E 98 C5
Parnitha △ Greece 38°12N 23°44E 98 C5
Parnon Oros Greece 37°15N 22°45E 98 D4
Pärnu Estonia 58°28N 24°33E 84 C3
Pärnu → Estonia 58°28N 24°33E 84 C3
Paro Dzong Bhutan 27°32N 89°53E 125 F13
Parola India 20°47N 75°7E 126 D2
Paroo → Australia 31°28S 143°32E 152 A5
Paros Greece 37°5N 25°12E 99 D7
Parowan U.S.A. 37°51N 112°50W 169 H7
Parpaillon France 44°30N 6°43E 73 D10
Parral Chile 36°10S 71°52W 190 D1
Parramatta Australia 33°48S 151°1E 153 B5
Parras Mexico 25°25N 102°11W 180 B4
Parrett → U.K. 51°12N 3°1W 67 F4
Parris I. U.S.A. 32°20N 80°41W 178 C9
Parrish U.S.A. 27°35N 82°26W 179 H7
Parrott U.S.A. 31°54N 84°31W 178 D5
Parrsboro Canada 45°30N 64°25W 165 C7
Parry Channel Canada 74°15N 94°0W 161 C13
Parry I. Canada 45°18N 80°10W 174 A4
Parry Is. Canada 77°0N 110°0W 161 B10
Parry Sound Canada 45°20N 80°0W 174 A5
Parsabād Iran 39°39N 47°50E 105 C12
Parsaloi Kenya 1°16N 36°51E 142 B4
Parsberg Germany 49°10N 11°43E 77 F7
Parseta → Poland 54°11N 15°34E 82 D2
Parsnip → Canada 55°10N 123°2W 162 B4
Parsons U.S.A. 37°20N 95°16W 172 G6
Parsons Ra. Australia 13°30S 135°15E 150 A2
Partabpur India 20°0N 80°42E 126 E5
Partanna Italy 37°43N 12°53E 94 E5
Partenio △ Italy 40°56N 14°38E 95 B7
Partinico Italy 38°3N 13°7E 94 D6
Partizansk Russia 43°8N 133°9E 107 E14
Partizánske Slovak Rep. 48°38N 18°23E 79 C11
Partridge I. Canada 7°43S 112°12E 119 G15
Partry Mts. Ireland 53°40N 9°28W 64 C2
Partur India 19°40N 76°14E 126 E3
Paru → Brazil 1°33S 52°38W 187 D8
Parur India 10°13N 76°14E 127 J3
Paruro Peru 13°45S 71°50W 188 C2
Parvān □ Afghan. 35°0N 69°0E 109 F7
Parvatipuram India 18°50N 83°25E 126 E6
Parvatsar India 26°52N 74°49E 124 F6
Päryd Sweden 56°34N 15°55E 63 H9
Parys S. Africa 26°52S 27°29E 144 C4
Pas, Pta. des Spain 38°39N 1°23E 97 C7
Pas, The Canada 53°45N 101°15W 163 C8
Pas-de-Calais □ France 50°30N 2°10E 71 B9
Pasada Spain 43°23N 5°40W 88 B5
Pasadena Canada 49°1N 57°36W 165 C8
Pasadena Calif., U.S.A. 34°9N 118°8W 171 L8
Pasadena Tex., U.S.A. 29°43N 95°13W 176 G7
Pasaje Ecuador 3°23S 79°50W 186 D3
Pasaje → Argentina 25°39S 63°56W 190 B3
Paşalimanı Turkey 40°29N 27°36E 99 F11
Pasar Indonesia 8°27S 114°54E 119 J17
Pasargadae Iran 30°11N 53°10E 129 D7
Pascagoula U.S.A. 30°21N 88°33W 177 F10
Pascagoula → U.S.A. 30°23N 88°37W 177 F10
Pașcani Romania 47°14N 26°45E 81 C11
Paschimbanga □ India 23°0N 88°0E 125 H13
Pasco U.S.A. 46°14N 119°6W 168 C4
Pasco □ Peru 10°40S 75°0W 188 B2
Pasco I. Australia 20°57S 115°20E 148 D2
Pascoag U.S.A. 41°57N 71°42W 175 E13
Pascua, I. de Chile 27°7S 109°23W 157 K17
Pasewalk Germany 53°30N 13°59E 76 B9
Pasfield L. Canada 58°24N 105°20W 163 B7
Pasha → Russia 60°29N 32°55E 84 B7
Pasinler Turkey 39°59N 41°41E 105 C9
Pasir Mas Malaysia 6°2N 102°8E 121 d
Pasir Panjang Singapore 1°18N 103°46E 121 d
Pasir Putih Malaysia 5°50N 102°24E 121 K4
Påskallavik Sweden 57°10N 16°26E 63 G10
Pașkūh Iran 27°34N 61°39E 129 E9
Pasłęk Poland 54°3N 19°41E 82 D6
Pasłęka → Poland 54°26N 19°46E 82 D6
Pasley, C. Australia 33°52S 123°35E 149 F3
Pašman Croatia 43°58N 15°20E 93 E12
Pasmore → Australia 31°5S 139°49E 152 A3
Pasni Pakistan 25°15N 63°27E 122 G3
Paso Bravo △ Paraguay 22°32S 57°5W 190 A4
Paso Cantinela
  Mexico 32°33N 115°47W 171 N11
Paso de Indios Argentina 43°55S 69°0W 192 B3
Paso de los Indios
  Argentina 38°32S 69°25W 192 A3
Paso de los Libres
  Argentina 29°44S 57°10W 190 B4
Paso de los Toros
  Uruguay 32°45S 56°30W 190 C4
Paso Flores Argentina 40°35S 70°38W 192 B2
Paso Robles U.S.A. 35°38N 120°41W 170 K6
Paspébiac Canada 48°3N 65°17W 165 C6
Pasrur Pakistan 32°16N 74°43E 124 C6
Passage East Ireland 52°14N 7°0W 64 D5
Passage West Ireland 51°52N 8°21W 64 E3
Passaic U.S.A. 40°51N 74°7W 175 F10
Passau Germany 48°34N 13°28E 77 G9
Passero, C. Italy 36°41N 15°10E 95 F8
Passo Fundo Brazil 28°10S 52°20W 191 B5
Passos Brazil 20°45S 46°37W 191 A6
Passow Germany 53°18N 14°6E 76 B9
Passy France 45°55N 6°41E 73 C10
Pastavy Belarus 55°4N 26°50E 84 E4
Pastaza → Peru 4°50S 76°52W 186 D3
Pasto Colombia 1°13N 77°17W 186 C3
Pastos Bons Brazil 6°36S 44°5W 189 B2
Pastrana Spain 40°27N 2°53W 90 E2
Pasuruan Indonesia 7°40S 112°44E 119 G15
Pasym Poland 53°48N 20°49E 82 E7
Pásztó Hungary 47°52N 19°43E 80 C4
Patagonia Argentina 45°0S 69°0W 192 C3
Patagonia U.S.A. 31°33N 110°45W 169 L8

Patan Gujarat, India 23°54N 72°14E 124 H5
Patan Maharashtra,
  India 17°22N 73°57E 126 F1
Patani Indonesia 0°20N 128°50E 119 D7
Patchewollock
  Australia 35°22S 142°12E 152 C5
Patchogue U.S.A. 40°46N 73°1N 175 F11
Pate Kenya 2°10S 41°0E 142 C5
Patea N.Z. 39°45S 174°30E 154 F3
Pategi Nigeria 8°50N 5°45E 139 D6
Patensie S. Africa 33°46S 24°49E 144 D3
Paternion Austria 46°43N 13°38E 78 E6
Paternò Italy 37°34N 14°54E 95 E7
Pateros U.S.A. 48°3N 119°54W 168 B4
Paterson U.S.A. 40°54N 74°9W 175 F10
Paterson Inlet N.Z. 46°56S 168°12E 155 G3
Paterson Ra. Australia 21°45S 122°10E 148 D3
Pathankot India 32°18N 75°45E 124 C6
Pathardi India 19°10N 75°11E 126 E2
Pathein = Bassein
  Burma 16°45N 94°30E 123 L19
Pathfinder Res.
  U.S.A. 42°28N 106°51W 168 E10
Pathiu Thailand 10°42N 99°19E 121 G2
Pathri India 19°15N 76°27E 126 E3
Pathum Thani Thailand 14°1N 100°32E 120 E3
Pati Indonesia 6°45S 111°1E 119 G14
Patía → Colombia 2°13N 78°40W 186 C3
Patiala Punjab, India 30°23N 76°26E 124 D7
Patiala Ut. P., India 27°43N 79°1E 125 F8
Patine Kouka Senegal 12°45N 13°45W 138 C2
Patitiri Greece 39°8N 23°50E 98 B5
Patkai Bum India 27°0N 95°30E 123 F19
Patmos Greece 37°21N 26°36E 99 D8
Patna India 25°35N 85°12E 125 G11
Patnagarh India 20°43N 83°9E 126 D6
Patnos Turkey 39°14N 42°51E 105 C10
Pato Branco Brazil 26°13S 52°40W 191 B5
Patong, Ao Thailand 7°54N 98°17E 121 a
Patonga Uganda 2°45N 33°15E 142 B3
Patos Albania 40°42N 19°38E 96 F3
Patos Brazil 6°55S 37°16W 189 B3
Patos, L. dos Brazil 31°20S 51°0W 191 C5
Patos, Rio de los →
  Argentina 31°18S 69°25W 190 C2
Patos de Minas Brazil 18°35S 46°32W 189 D1
Patquía Argentina 30°2S 66°55W 190 C2
Patra Greece 38°14N 21°47E 98 C3
Patraikos Kolpos Greece 38°17N 21°30E 98 C3
Patras = Patra Greece 38°14N 21°47E 98 C3
Patrício Lynch, I. Chile 48°35S 75°30W 192 C1
Patriot Hills Antarctica 82°20S 81°25W 55 E16
Patrocínio Brazil 18°57S 47°0W 189 D1
Pattada Italy 40°35N 9°6E 94 B2
Pattadakal India 16°1N 75°42E 127 F2
Pattani Thailand 6°48N 101°15E 121 J3
Pattaya Thailand 12°52N 100°55E 120 F3
Patten U.S.A. 46°0N 68°38W 173 B19
Patterson Calif., U.S.A. 37°28N 121°8W 170 H5
Patterson La., U.S.A. 29°42N 91°18W 176 G9
Patterson, Mt. U.S.A. 38°29N 119°20W 170 G7
Patti Punjab, India 31°17N 74°54E 124 D6
Patti Ut. P., India 25°55N 82°12E 125 G10
Patti Italy 38°8N 14°58E 95 D7
Pattoki Pakistan 31°5N 73°52E 124 D5
Pattukkottai India 10°25N 79°20E 127 J4
Patu Brazil 6°6S 37°38W 189 B3
Patuakhali Bangla. 22°20N 90°25E 123 H17
Patuanak Canada 55°55N 107°43W 163 B7
Patuca → Honduras 15°50N 84°18W 182 C3
Patuca, Punta
  Honduras 15°49N 84°14W 182 C3
Pătulele Romania 44°21N 22°47E 80 F7
Patur India 20°27N 76°56E 126 D3
Patvinsuo △ Finland 63°7N 30°45E 60 E24
Pátzcuaro Mexico 19°31N 101°38W 180 D4
Pau France 43°19N 0°25W 72 E3
Pau, Gave de → France 43°33N 1°12W 72 E2
Pau dos Ferros Brazil 6°7S 38°10W 189 B3
Pauanui N.Z. 37°1S 175°52E 154 D4
Paucartambo Peru 13°19S 71°35W 188 C3
Paudash Canada 44°59N 77°58W 174 B7
Pauillac France 45°11N 0°46W 72 C3
Pauini Brazil 7°57S 66°33W 186 E5
Pauk Burma 21°27N 94°30E 123 J19
Paul I. Canada 56°30N 61°20W 165 A7
Paul Smiths U.S.A. 44°26N 74°15W 175 B10
Paulatuk Canada 69°25N 124°0W 160 D7
Paulding Bay S. Ocean 66°0S 118°0E 55 C8
Paulhan France 43°33N 3°28E 72 E7
Paulista Brazil 7°57S 34°53W 189 B4
Paulistana Brazil 8°9S 41°9W 189 B2
Paulistria Sweden 57°28N 15°31E 63 G9
Paulo Afonso Brazil 9°21S 38°15W 189 B3
Paulpietersburg
  S. Africa 27°23S 30°50E 145 C5
Pauls Valley U.S.A. 34°44N 97°13W 176 D6
Pauma Valley
  U.S.A. 33°16N 116°58W 171 M10
Pauni India 20°48N 79°40E 126 D4
Pauri India 30°9N 78°47E 125 D8
Pausa Peru 15°16S 73°22W 188 D3
Pavagada India 14°6N 77°16E 127 G3
Pāveh Iran 35°3N 46°22E 105 E12
Pavelets Russia 53°49N 39°14E 84 F10
Pavia Italy 45°7N 9°8E 92 C6
Pavilion France 49°34N 0°57E 70 C7
Pavilosta Latvia 56°53N 21°14E 82 B8
Pavlikeni Bulgaria 43°14N 25°12E 97 C9
Pavlodar Kazakhstan 52°33N 77°0E 108 B9
Pavlograd = Pavlohrad
  Ukraine 48°30N 35°52E 85 H8
Pavlohrad Ukraine 48°30N 35°52E 85 H8
Pavlovo Russia 55°58N 43°5E 86 C6
Pavlovsk Russia 50°26N 40°5E 85 H10
Pavlovskaya Russia 46°17N 39°47E 87 G4
Pavlovskiy-Posad
  Russia 55°47N 38°42E 84 E10
Pavo U.S.A. 30°58N 83°45W 178 E6
Pavullo nel Frignano
  Italy 44°20N 10°50E 92 D7
Pawai, Pulau Singapore 1°11N 103°44E 121 d
Pawayan India 28°4N 80°6E 125 E9

Pawhuska U.S.A. 36°40N 96°20W 176 C6
Pawling U.S.A. 41°34N 73°36W 175 E11
Pawnee U.S.A. 36°20N 96°48W 176 C6
Pawnee City U.S.A. 40°7N 96°9W 172 E5
Pawtucket U.S.A. 41°53N 71°23W 175 E13
Paxi Greece 39°14N 20°12E 98 B2
Paximadia Greece 35°0N 24°35E 101 E6
Paxton U.S.A. 40°27N 88°6W 172 E9
Payakumbuh Indonesia 0°20S 100°35E 118 E2
Payerne Switz. 46°49N 6°56E 77 J2
Payette U.S.A. 44°5N 116°56W 168 D5
Paymogo Spain 37°44N 7°21W 89 H3
Payne Bay = Kangirsuk
  Canada 60°0N 70°0W 161 F18
Payne L. Canada 59°30N 74°30W 161 F17
Paynes Find Australia 29°15S 117°42E 149 E2
Paynesville Liberia 6°20N 10°45W 138 D2
Paynesville U.S.A. 45°23N 94°43W 172 C6
Pays de la Loire □ France 47°45N 0°20W 70 E6
Paysandú Uruguay 32°19S 58°8W 190 C4
Payson Ariz., U.S.A. 34°14N 111°20W 169 J8
Payson Utah, U.S.A. 40°3N 111°44W 168 F8
Paz → Guatemala 13°44N 90°10W 182 D1
Paz, B. de la Mexico 24°9N 110°25W 180 C2
Pāzanān Iran 30°35N 49°59E 129 D6
Pazar Turkey 41°10N 40°50E 105 B9
Pazarcık Turkey 37°30N 37°17E 104 D7
Pazardzhik Bulgaria 42°12N 24°20E 97 D8
Pazardzhik □ Bulgaria 42°12N 24°20E 97 D8
Pazarköy Turkey 39°51N 27°24E 99 B9
Pazarlar Turkey 39°9N 29°27E 99 C11
Pazaryeri Turkey 40°0N 29°56E 99 B11
Pazaryolu Turkey 40°21N 40°47E 105 B9
Pazin Croatia 45°14N 13°56E 93 C10
Pazña Bolivia 18°36S 66°55W 188 D4
Pčinja → Macedonia 41°50N 21°45E 96 E5
Pe Ell U.S.A. 46°34N 123°18W 170 D3
Pea → U.S.A. 31°1N 85°51W 178 D4
Peabody U.S.A. 42°31N 70°56W 175 D14
Peace → Canada 59°0N 111°25W 162 B6
Peace Point Canada 59°7N 112°27W 162 B6
Peace River Canada 56°15N 117°18W 162 B5
Peach Springs U.S.A. 35°32N 113°25W 169 J7
Peachland Canada 49°47N 119°45W 162 D5
Peachtree City U.S.A. 33°25N 84°35W 178 B5
Peak, The = Kinder Scout
  U.K. 53°24N 1°52W 66 D6
Peak Charles △
  Australia 32°42S 121°10E 149 F3
Peak District △ U.K. 53°24N 1°46W 66 D6
Peak Hill Australia 32°47S 148°11E 153 B8
Peak Ra. Australia 22°50S 148°20E 150 C4
Peake Australia 35°25S 139°55E 152 C3
Peake Cr. → Australia 28°2S 136°7E 151 D2
Peal de Becerro Spain 37°55N 3°7W 89 H7
Peale, Mt. U.S.A. 38°26N 109°14W 168 G9
Pearblossom U.S.A. 34°30N 117°55W 171 L9
Pearl → U.S.A. 30°11N 89°32W 177 F10
Pearl and Hermes Reef
  U.S.A. 27°55N 175°45W 167 K4
Pearl Banks Sri Lanka 8°45N 79°45E 127 K4
Pearl River = Zhu Jiang →
  China 22°45N 113°37E 117 F9
Pearl River U.S.A. 41°4N 74°2W 175 E10
Pearl River Bridge
  China 22°15N 113°48E 111 a
Pearsall U.S.A. 28°54N 99°6W 176 G5
Pearson U.S.A. 31°18N 82°51W 178 D7
Pearson Int. Toronto ✈ (YYZ)
  Canada 43°46N 79°35W 174 C5
Peary Chan. Canada 79°40N 101°30W 161 B11
Peary Land Greenland 82°40N 33°0W 57 A7
Pease → U.S.A. 34°12N 99°2W 176 D5
Peawanuck Canada 55°15N 85°12W 164 A2
Pebane Mozam. 17°10S 38°8E 143 F4
Pebas Peru 3°10S 71°46W 186 D4
Pebble, I. Falk. Is. 51°20S 59°40W 192 D5
Pebble Beach U.S.A. 36°34N 121°57W 170 J5
Peć = Pejë Kosovo 42°40N 20°17E 96 D4
Peçanha Brazil 18°33S 42°34W 189 D2
Péccioli Italy 43°33N 10°43E 92 E7
Pechea Romania 45°36N 27°49E 81 E12
Pechenga Russia 69°29N 31°4E 60 B24
Pechenizhyn Ukraine 48°30N 24°48E 81 D8
Pechiguera, Pta.
  Canary Is. 28°51N 13°53W 100 F6
Pechnezhskoye Vdkhr.
  Ukraine 50°0N 36°54E 85 G9
Pechora Russia 65°10N 57°11E 106 C10
Pechora → Russia 68°13N 54°15E 58 B16
Pechorskaya Guba
  Russia 68°40N 54°0E 106 C9
Pechory Russia 57°48N 27°40E 84 D4
Pecica Romania 46°10N 21°3E 80 D6
Pecka Serbia 44°18N 19°33E 96 B3
Pécora, C. Italy 39°27N 8°23E 94 C1
Pecos N. Mex., U.S.A. 35°35N 105°41W 169 J11
Pecos Tex., U.S.A. 31°26N 103°30W 176 E3
Pecos → U.S.A. 29°42N 101°22W 176 G4
Pécs Hungary 46°5N 18°15E 80 D3
Pedasi Panama 7°32N 80°2W 182 E3
Pedda Bella India 19°4N 79°4E 126 E4
Peddapalli India 18°40N 79°24E 126 E4
Peddapuram India 17°6N 82°5E 126 D5
Pedder, L. Australia 42°55S 146°10E 151 G4
Peddie S. Africa 33°14S 27°7E 145 E4
Pedernales Dom. Rep. 18°2N 71°44W 183 C5
Pedernales → Cyprus 35°10N 33°54E 101 D12
Pedirka Desert
  Australia 26°47S 134°11E 151 A1
Pedra Azul Brazil 16°2S 41°17W 189 D2
Pedra Grande, Recifes de
  Brazil 17°45S 38°58W 189 D3
Pedra Lume C. Verde Is. 16°40N 22°52W 134 b
Pedreguer Spain 38°48N 0°3E 91 G5
Pedreiras Brazil 4°32S 44°40W 189 B2
Pedro Afonso Brazil 9°0S 48°10W 187 E9
Pedro Cays Jamaica 17°5N 77°48W 182 C4
Pedro de Valdivia Chile 22°55S 69°38W 190 A2
Pedro Juan Caballero
  Paraguay 22°30S 55°40W 191 A4
Pedro Muñoz Spain 39°25N 2°56W 89 F8
Pedrógão Grande Portugal 39°55N 8°9W 88 F2
Pee Dee = Great Pee Dee →
  U.S.A. 33°21N 79°10W 177 E15
Peebinga Australia 34°52S 140°57E 152 C4
Peebles U.K. 55°40N 3°11W 65 F5
Peekskill U.S.A. 41°17N 73°55W 175 E11
Peel I. of Man 54°13N 4°40W 66 C3
Peel → Australia 30°50S 150°29E 153 A9

Peel → Canada 67°N 135°0W 160 D5
Peel Sd. Canada 73°0N 96°0W 160 C12
Peene → Germany 54°9N 13°46E 76 A9
Peera Peera Poolanna L.
　Australia 26°30S 138°0E 151 D2
Peerless Lake Canada 56°37N 114°40W 162 B6
Peers Canada 53°40N 116°0W 162 C5
Peery L. Australia 30°45S 143°35E 152 A5
Pegasus Bay N.Z. 43°20S 173°10E 155 D8
Peggau Austria 47°12N 15°21E 78 D8
Pegnitz Germany 49°44N 11°31E 77 F7
Pegnitz → Germany 49°30N 10°59E 77 F6
Pego Spain 38°51N 0°8W 91 G4
Pegu Burma 17°20N 96°29E 123 L20
Pegu Yoma Burma 19°0N 96°0E 123 K20
Pehčevo Macedonia 41°41N 22°55E 96 E6
Pehuajó Argentina 35°45S 62°0W 190 D4
Pei Xian China 34°44N 116°55E 114 G9
Peikang Taiwan 23°34N 120°18E 117 F13
Peine Chile 23°45S 68°8W 190 A2
Peine Germany 52°19N 10°14E 76 C6
Peip'ing = Beijing
　China 39°53N 116°21E 114 E9
Peipus, L. = Chudskoye, Ozero
　Russia 58°13N 27°30E 84 C4
Peissenberg Germany 47°48N 11°4E 77 H7
Peitz Germany 51°51N 14°24E 76 D10
Peixe Brazil 12°0S 48°40W 189 C1
Peixe → Brazil 21°31S 51°58W 187 H8
Pejë Kosovo 42°40N 20°17E 96 D4
Pek → Serbia 44°45N 21°29E 96 B5
Pekalongan Indonesia 6°53S 109°40E 118 F3
Pekan Malaysia 3°30N 103°25E 121 L4
Pekan Nenas Malaysia 1°31N 103°31E 121 d
Pekanbaru Indonesia 0°30N 101°15E 118 D2
Pekin U.S.A. 40°35N 89°40W 172 E9
Peking = Beijing
　China 39°53N 116°21E 114 E9
Pekutatan Indonesia 8°25S 114°49E 119 J17
Pela Greece 40°46N 22°23E 96 F6
Pelabuhan Ratu, Teluk
　Indonesia 7°5S 106°30E 119 G12
Pélagos = Kira Panagia
　Greece 39°17N 24°4E 98 B6
Pelaihari Indonesia 3°55S 114°45E 118 E4
Pelat, Mt. France 44°16N 6°42E 73 D10
Pelczyce Poland 53°3N 15°16E 83 E2
Peleaga, Vf. Romania 45°22N 22°55E 80 E7
Pelechuco Bolivia 14°48S 69°4W 188 C4
Pelée, Mt. Martinique 14°48N 61°10W 182 c
Pelee, Pt. Canada 41°54N 82°31W 164 D3
Pelee I. Canada 41°47N 82°40W 174 E2
Pelejo Peru 6°10S 75°49W 188 B2
Pelekech Kenya 3°52N 35°8E 142 B4
Peleng Indonesia 1°20S 123°30E 119 E6
Pelentong Malaysia 1°32N 103°49E 121 d
Pélézi Ivory C. 7°17N 6°54W 138 D3
Pelham U.S.A. 31°8N 84°9W 178 D5
Pelhřimov Czech Rep. 49°24N 15°12E 78 B8
Pelican U.S.A. 57°58N 136°14W 162 B1
Pelican L. Canada 52°28N 100°20W 163 C8
Pelican Narrows
　Canada 55°10N 102°56W 163 B8
Pelion U.S.A. 33°46N 81°15W 178 B8
Pelister △ Macedonia 41°0N 21°10E 96 F5
Peljesac Croatia 42°55N 17°25E 93 F14
Pelkosenniemi Finland 67°6N 27°28E 60 C22
Pell City U.S.A. 33°35N 86°17W 178 B3
Pella Greece 40°52N 22°0E 96 F6
Pella S. Africa 29°1S 19°6E 144 C2
Pella U.S.A. 41°25N 92°55W 172 E7
Pello Finland 66°47N 23°59E 60 C20
Pellworm Germany 54°31N 8°39E 76 A4
Pelly → Canada 62°47N 137°19W 162 A1
Pelly Bay Canada 68°38N 89°50W 161 D14
Peloponnesos □ Greece 37°10N 22°0E 98 D4
Peloritani, Monti Italy 38°3N 15°20E 95 D8
Pelorus → N.Z. 41°16S 173°45E 155 B8
Pelorus Sd. N.Z. 40°59S 173°59E 155 A8
Pelotas Brazil 31°42S 52°23W 191 C5
Pelotas → Brazil 27°28S 51°55W 191 B5
Pelovo Bulgaria 43°26N 24°17E 97 C8
Pelplin Poland 53°55N 18°42E 82 E5
Pelvoux, Massif du
　France 44°52N 6°20E 73 D10
Pemalang Indonesia 6°53S 109°23E 119 G13
Pemanggil, Pulau
　Malaysia 2°37N 104°21E 121 L5
Pematangsiantar
　Indonesia 2°57N 99°5E 118 D1
Pemba Mozam. 12°58S 40°30E 143 E5
Pemba Zambia 16°30S 27°28E 143 F2
Pemba Channel Tanzania 5°0S 39°37E 142 D4
Pemba I. Tanzania 5°0S 39°45E 142 D4
Pemberton Australia 34°30S 116°0E 149 F2
Pemberton Canada 50°25N 122°50W 162 C4
Pembina → Canada 54°45N 114°17W 162 C6
Pembroke Canada 45°50N 77°7W 164 C4
Pembroke U.K. 51°41N 4°55W 67 F3
Pembroke U.S.A. 32°8N 81°37W 178 C8
Pembroke Pines U.S.A. 26°0N 80°13W 179 J9
Pembrokeshire □ U.K. 51°52N 4°56W 67 F3
Pembrokeshire Coast △
　U.K. 51°50N 5°2W 67 F2
Pen India 18°45N 73°5E 126 E1
Pen-y-bont ar Ogwr = Bridgend
　U.K. 51°30N 3°34W 67 F4
Pen-y-Ghent U.K. 54°10N 2°14W 66 C5
Peña, Sierra de la Spain 42°32N 0°45W 90 C4
Peña de Francia, Sierra de la
　Spain 40°32N 6°10W 88 E4
Peñafiel Portugal 41°12N 8°17W 88 B2
Peñafiel Spain 41°35N 4°7W 88 D6
Peñaflor Spain 37°43N 5°21W 89 H5
Penal Trin. & Tob. 10°9N 61°29W 187 K15
Peñalara Spain 40°51N 3°57W 88 E7
Penalva Brazil 3°18S 45°10W 189 A1
Penamacôr Portugal 40°10N 7°10W 88 E3
Penang = Pinang
　Malaysia 5°25N 100°15E 121 c
Penápolis Brazil 21°30S 50°0W 191 A6
Peñaranda de Bracamonte
　Spain 40°53N 5°13W 88 E5
Peñarroya Spain 42°35N 0°45W 90 C5
Peñarroya-Pueblonuevo
　Spain 38°19N 5°16W 89 G5
Penarth U.K. 51°26N 3°11W 67 F4
Peñas, C. de Spain 43°42N 5°52W 88 A5
Peñas, G. de Chile 47°0S 75°0W 192 C2
Peñas de San Pedro Spain 38°44N 2°0W 91 G3

Peñas del Chache
　Canary Is. 29°6N 13°33W 100 E6
Peñausende Spain 41°17N 5°52W 88 D5
Pench → India 21°17N 79°10E 126 D4
Pench △ India 21°45N 79°20E 125 J8
Pench'i = Benxi
　China 41°20N 123°48E 115 D12
Pendalofos Greece 40°14N 21°12E 96 F5
Pendembu Eastern,
　S. Leone 8°10N 10°42W 138 D2
Pendembu Northern,
　S. Leone 9°7N 11°14W 138 D2
Pendências Brazil 5°15S 36°43W 189 B3
Pender B. Australia 16°45S 122°42E 148 C3
Pendik Turkey 40°53N 29°13E 97 F13
Pendjari → Benin 10°55N 0°50E 139 C5
Pendjari △ Benin 11°15N 1°32E 139 C5
Pendleton U.S.A. 45°40N 118°47W 168 D4
Pendra India 22°46N 81°57E 125 H9
Pendzhikent = Panjakent
　Tajikistan 39°29N 67°37E 109 F7
Peneda-Gerês △ Portugal 41°57N 8°15W 88 D2
Penedo Brazil 10°15S 36°36W 189 C3
Penelokan Indonesia 8°17S 115°22E 119 J18
Penetanguishene
　Canada 44°50N 79°55W 174 B5
Penfield U.S.A. 41°13N 78°35W 174 E6
Peng Chau China 22°17N 114°2E 111 a
Peng'an China 31°2N 106°22E 116 B6
Penganga → India 19°53N 79°9E 126 E4
Penge Kasai-Or.,
　Dem. Rep. of the Congo 5°30S 24°33E 142 D1
Penge Sud-Kivu,
　Dem. Rep. of the Congo 4°27S 28°25E 142 C2
P'enghu Ch'üntou
　Taiwan 23°34N 119°30E 117 F12
Penglai China 37°48N 120°42E 115 F11
Pengshan China 30°14N 103°58E 116 B4
Pengshui China 29°17N 108°12E 116 C7
Pengxi China 30°44N 105°45E 116 B5
Pengze China 29°52N 116°32E 117 C11
Pengzhou China 31°4N 103°32E 116 B4
Penhalonga Zimbabwe 18°52S 32°40E 143 F3
Peniche Portugal 39°19N 9°22E 89 F1
Penicuik U.K. 55°50N 3°13W 65 F5
Penida, Nusa Indonesia 8°45S 115°30E 118 F5
Peninnes, Alpes = Pennine, Alpi
　Alps 46°4N 7°30E 77 J3
Peninsular Malaysia □
　Malaysia 4°0N 102°0E 121 L4
Peñíscola Spain 40°22N 0°24E 90 E5
Penitente, Serra do
　Brazil 8°45S 46°20W 189 C1
Pēnjwīn Iraq 35°37N 45°56E 105 E11
Penkridge U.K. 52°44N 2°6W 66 E5
Penmarch France 47°49N 4°21W 70 E2
Penmarch, Pte. de
　France 47°48N 4°22W 70 E2
Penn Hills U.S.A. 40°28N 79°52W 174 F5
Penn Yan U.S.A. 42°40N 77°3W 174 D7
Penna, Punta della
　Italy 42°10N 14°43E 93 F11
Pennant Canada 50°32N 108°14W 163 C7
Penne Italy 42°27N 13°55E 93 F10
Penner → India 14°35N 80°10E 127 G5
Penneshaw Australia 35°44S 137°56E 152 C2
Pennine, Alpi Alps 46°4N 7°30E 77 J3
Pennines U.K. 54°45N 2°27W 66 C5
Pennington U.S.A. 39°15N 121°47W 170 F5
Pennington → Nigeria 4°45N 5°35S 139 E6
Pennino, Mte. Italy 43°6N 12°53E 93 E9
Pennsburg U.S.A. 40°23N 75°29W 175 F9
Pennsylvania □
　U.S.A. 40°45N 77°30W 173 E15
Penny Canada 53°51N 121°20W 162 C4
Peno Russia 57°2N 32°49E 84 D7
Penobscot → U.S.A. 44°30N 68°48W 173 C19
Penobscot B. U.S.A. 44°35N 68°50W 173 C19
Penola Australia 37°25S 140°48E 152 C4
Penong Australia 31°56S 133°1E 149 F5
Penonomé Panama 8°31N 80°21W 182 E3
Penrhyn Cook Is. 9°0S 158°0W 157 H12
Penrith Australia 33°43S 150°38E 153 B9
Penrith U.K. 54°40N 2°45W 66 C5
Penryn U.K. 50°9N 5°7W 67 G2
Pensacola U.S.A. 30°25N 87°13W 179 D11
Pensacola B. U.S.A. 30°25N 87°5W 179 D11
Pensacola Mts. Antarctica 84°0S 40°0W 55 E1
Pense Canada 50°25N 104°59W 163 C8
Penshurst Australia 37°49S 142°20E 152 C5
Pentadaktylos Cyprus 35°20N 33°20E 101 D12
Pentecostes Brazil 3°48S 39°17W 189 A3
Penticton Canada 49°30N 119°38W 162 D5
Penukonda India 14°5N 77°38E 127 G3
Penza Russia 53°15N 45°5E 86 D7
Penza □ Russia 52°50N 44°50E 86 D7
Penzance U.K. 50°7N 5°33W 67 G2
Penzberg Germany 47°45N 11°22E 77 H7
Penzhino Russia 63°30N 167°55E 107 C17
Penzhinskaya Guba
　Russia 61°30N 163°0E 107 C17
Penzlin Germany 53°30N 13°5E 76 B9
Peoria Ariz., U.S.A. 33°43N 112°14W 169 K7
Peoria Ill., U.S.A. 40°42N 89°36W 172 E9
Pepacton Res. U.S.A. 42°5N 75°0W 175 D10
Pepani → S. Africa 25°49S 22°47E 144 C3
Pepel S. Leone 8°40N 13°5W 138 D2
Peqin Albania 41°3N 19°44E 96 E3
Pera Hd. Australia 12°55S 141°37E 150 A3
Perabumulih Indonesia 3°27S 104°15E 118 E2
Perachora Greece 38°2N 22°56E 98 C4
Perak □ Malaysia 4°0N 100°50E 121 K3
Perak → Malaysia 4°0N 100°50E 121 K3
Perales del Alfambra
　Spain 40°38N 1°0W 90 E4
Perales del Puerto Spain 40°10N 6°40W 88 E4
Peralta Spain 42°21N 1°49W 90 C3
Perama Kerkyra, Greece 39°34N 19°54E 101 A3
Perama Kriti, Greece 35°20N 24°40E 101 D6
Perämeri △ Finland 65°35N 24°22E 60 D21
Peräncak Indonesia 8°24S 114°37E 119 J17
Peräpohjola Finland 66°16N 26°10E 60 C22
Perast Montenegro 42°31N 18°47E 96 D2

Percé Canada 48°31N 64°13W 165 C7
Perche France 48°31N 1°1E 70 D8
Perche △ France 48°24N 0°46E 70 D7
Perchtoldsdorf Austria 48°7N 16°17E 79 C9
Percival Lakes Australia 21°25S 125°0E 148 D4
Percy France 48°55N 1°11W 70 D5
Percy Is. Australia 21°39S 150°16E 150 C5
Perdido → Argentina 42°55S 67°0W 192 B3
Perdido, Mte. Spain 42°40N 0°5E 90 C5
Perdu, Mt. = Perdido, Mte.
　Spain 42°40N 0°5E 90 C5
Perechyn Ukraine 48°44N 22°28E 80 B7
Perehinske Ukraine 48°49N 24°11E 81 B9
Pereira Colombia 4°49N 75°43W 186 C2
Perejil Spain 35°55N 5°25W 89 K5
Perelazovskiy Russia 49°8N 42°35E 87 F6
Peremul Par India 11°10N 72°4E 122 J1
Perené → Peru 11°0N 74°44W 188 D3
Perenjori Australia 29°26S 116°16E 149 E2
Peresecina Moldova 47°16N 28°46E 81 C13
Pereslavi-Zalesskiy
　Russia 56°45N 38°50E 84 D10
Peretu Romania 44°3N 25°6E 81 F10
Pereyaslav-Khmelnytskyy
　Ukraine 50°3N 31°28E 85 G6
Pereyma Ukraine 48°4N 29°30E 81 B14
Pérez, I. Mexico 22°24N 89°42W 181 C7
Perg Austria 48°15N 14°38E 78 C7
Pergamino Argentina 33°52S 60°30W 190 C4
Pergau → Malaysia 5°23N 102°2E 121 K3
Pérgine Valsugana Italy 46°4N 11°14E 93 B8
Pérgola Italy 43°34N 12°50E 93 E9
Perham U.S.A. 46°36N 95°34W 172 B6
Perhentian, Kepulauan
　Malaysia 5°54N 102°42E 121 K4
Peri → Turkey 38°53N 39°52E 105 C8
Periam Romania 46°2N 20°52E 80 D5
Péribonka → Canada 48°45N 72°5W 165 C5
Péribonka, L. Canada 50°1N 71°10W 165 B5
Péribonka, La Centrale de
　Canada 49°30N 71°10W 165 C5
Perico Argentina 24°20S 65°5W 190 A2
Pericos Mexico 25°3N 107°42W 180 C3
Périgord France 45°0N 0°40E 72 D4
Périgord-Limousin △
　France 45°40N 0°50E 72 C4
Périgueux France 45°10N 0°42E 72 C4
Perijá, Sierra de Colombia 9°30N 73°3W 186 B4
Perijá △ Venezuela 9°30N 72°55W 183 E5
Peringat Malaysia 6°2N 102°17E 121 J4
Perisher Valley
　Australia 36°27S 148°25E 153 D8
Peristera Greece 39°15N 23°58E 98 B5
Peristerona → Cyprus 35°8N 33°5E 101 D12
Perito Moreno
　Argentina 46°36S 70°56W 192 C2
Perito Moreno △
　Argentina 47°49S 72°17W 192 C2
Peritoró Brazil 4°20S 44°18W 189 A2
Perivol = Dragovishtitsa
　Bulgaria 42°22N 22°39E 96 D6
Periyakulam India 10°5N 77°30E 127 J3
Periyar → India 10°15N 76°10E 127 J3
Periyar, L. India 9°25N 77°10E 127 K3
Periyar △ India 9°25N 77°10E 127 K3
Perkasie U.S.A. 40°22N 75°18W 175 F9
Perković Croatia 43°41N 16°10E 93 E13
Perlas, Arch. de las
　Panama 8°41N 79°7W 182 E4
Perlas, Punta de Nic. 12°30N 83°30W 182 D3
Perleberg Germany 53°5N 11°52E 76 B7
Perlez Serbia 45°11N 20°22E 96 B4
Perlis □ Malaysia 6°30N 100°15E 121 J2
Perm Russia 58°0N 56°10E 106 D6
Përmet Albania 40°23N 20°21E 96 F4
Pernambuco = Recife
　Brazil 8°0S 35°0W 189 B4
Pernambuco □ Brazil 8°0S 37°0W 189 B4
Pernambuco Abyssal Plain
　Atl. Oc. 5°0S 24°0W 56 G9
Pernatty Lagoon
　Australia 31°30S 137°12E 152 A2
Pernik Bulgaria 42°35N 23°2E 96 C7
Pernik □ Bulgaria 42°35N 23°2E 96 C7
Peron Is. Australia 13°9S 130°4E 148 B5
Peron Pen. Australia 26°0S 113°10E 149 E1
Péronne France 49°55N 2°57E 71 C9
Perosa Argentina Italy 44°58N 7°10E 92 D4
Perow Canada 54°35N 126°10W 162 C3
Perpignan France 42°42N 2°53E 72 F6
Perrine U.S.A. 25°36N 80°21W 179 K9
Perros-Guirec France 48°49N 3°28W 70 D3
Perry Fla., U.S.A. 30°7N 83°35W 178 E6
Perry Ga., U.S.A. 32°28N 83°44W 178 C6
Perry Iowa, U.S.A. 41°51N 94°6W 172 E6
Perry N.Y., U.S.A. 42°42N 78°0W 174 D7
Perry Okla., U.S.A. 36°17N 97°14W 176 C6
Perryton U.S.A. 36°24N 100°48W 176 C4
Perryville U.S.A. 37°43N 89°52W 172 G9
Persan France 49°9N 2°16E 71 C9
Persberg Sweden 59°47N 14°15E 62 E7
Perşembe Turkey 41°5N 37°46E 104 B7
Persepolis Iran 29°55N 52°50E 129 D7
Pershotravensk
　Ukraine 50°13N 27°40E 75 C14
Persia = Iran ■ Asia 33°0N 53°0E 129 C7
Persian Gulf Asia 27°0N 50°0E 129 E6
Perstorp Sweden 56°10N 13°25E 63 H7
Pertek Turkey 38°51N 39°19E 105 C8
Perth Australia 31°57S 115°52E 149 F2
Perth Canada 44°55N 76°15W 175 B8
Perth U.K. 56°24N 3°26W 65 E5
Perth & Kinross □ U.K. 56°45N 3°55E 65 E5
Perth Amboy U.S.A. 40°30N 74°15W 175 F10
Perth-Andover Canada 46°44N 67°42W 165 C6
Perth Basin Ind. Oc. 30°0S 108°0E 156 L2
Pertuis France 43°42N 5°30E 73 E9
Pertusato, C. France 41°21N 9°11E 73 G13
Peru Ind., U.S.A. 40°45N 86°4E 172 E10
Peru N.Y., U.S.A. 44°35N 73°32W 175 B11
Peru ■ S. Amer. 4°0S 75°0W 188 C2
Peru-Chile Trench Pac. Oc. 20°0S 95°0W 157 J20
Perúgia Italy 43°7N 12°23E 93 E9
Perušić Croatia 44°40N 15°22E 93 D12
Pervomaysk Russia 54°56N 43°58E 84 D6
Pervomaysk Ukraine 48°10N 30°46E 85 H6

Pervomayskiy
　Kazakhstan 50°16N 82°0E 109 A10
Pervouralsk Russia 56°59N 59°59E 106 D6
Pésaro Italy 43°54N 12°55E 93 E9
Pésaro e Urbino □ Italy 43°45N 12°40E 93 E9
Pescara Italy 42°28N 14°13E 93 F11
Pescara → Italy 42°28N 14°13E 93 F11
Peschanokopskoye
　Russia 46°14N 41°4E 87 G5
Péscia Italy 43°54N 10°41E 92 E7
Pescina Italy 42°2N 13°39E 93 F10
Peshawar Pakistan 34°2N 71°37E 124 B4
Peshkopi Albania 41°41N 20°25E 96 E4
Peshtera Bulgaria 42°2N 24°18E 97 C8
Peshtigo U.S.A. 45°3N 87°45W 172 C10
Peski Turkmenistan 38°11N 62°59E 108 E6
Pêso da Régua Portugal 41°10N 7°47W 88 D3
Pesqueira Brazil 8°20S 36°42W 189 B3
Pessac France 44°48N 0°37W 72 D3
Pest □ Hungary 47°29N 19°5E 80 C4
Pestovo Russia 58°33N 35°42E 84 C8
Pestravka Russia 52°28N 49°57E 86 D9
Petah Tiqwa Israel 32°6N 34°53E 130 C3
Petalidi Greece 36°57N 21°55E 98 E3
Petaling Jaya Malaysia 3°4N 101°42E 121 L3
Petaloudes Greece 36°18N 28°5E 101 C10
Petaluma U.S.A. 38°14N 122°39W 170 G4
Pétange Lux. 49°33N 5°55E 69 E5
Petaro Pakistan 25°31N 68°18E 124 G3
Petas Greece 39°10N 21°2E 98 B3
Petatlán Mexico 17°31N 101°16W 180 D4
Petauke Zambia 14°14S 31°20E 143 E3
Petawawa Canada 45°54N 77°17W 164 C4
Petén Itzá, L.
　Guatemala 16°58N 89°50W 182 C2
Peter I, Br. Virgin Is. 18°22N 64°35W 183 e
Peter I. Øy Antarctica 69°0S 91°0W 55 C16
Peter Pond L. Canada 55°55N 108°44W 163 B7
Peterbell Canada 48°36N 83°21W 164 C3
Peterborough
　Australia 32°58S 138°51E 152 B3
Peterborough Canada 44°20N 78°20W 174 B6
Peterborough U.K. 52°35N 0°15W 67 E7
Peterborough U.S.A. 42°53N 71°57W 175 D13
Peterborough □ U.K. 52°35N 0°15W 67 E7
Peterculter U.K. 57°6N 2°16W 65 D6
Peterhead U.K. 57°31N 1°48W 65 D7
Peterlee U.K. 54°47N 1°20W 66 C6
Petermann ◎ Australia 24°58S 130°0E 149 E4
Petermann Bjerg
　Greenland 73°7N 28°25W 57 C8
Petermann Gletscher
　Greenland 80°30N 60°0W 57 A4
Petermann Ranges
　Australia 26°0S 130°30E 149 E5
Petersburg Alaska,
　U.S.A. 56°48N 132°58W 160 F5
Petersburg Pa., U.S.A. 40°34N 78°3W 174 F6
Petersburg Va., U.S.A. 37°14N 77°24W 173 G15
Petersburg W. Va.,
　U.S.A. 39°1N 79°5W 173 F14
Petersfield U.K. 51°1N 0°56W 67 F7
Petershagen Germany 52°23N 8°58E 76 C4
Petilia Policastro Italy 39°7N 16°48E 95 C9
Petilla de Aragón Spain 42°28N 1°6W 90 C3
Petit-Canal Guadeloupe 16°25N 61°31W 182 b
Petit-Goâve Haiti 18°27N 72°51W 183 C5
Petit Lac Manicouagan
　Canada 51°25N 67°40W 165 B6
Petit-Mécatina →
　Canada 50°40N 59°30W 165 B8
Petit-Mécatina, Î. du
　Canada 50°30N 59°25W 165 B8
Petit Piton St. Lucia 13°51N 61°5W 183 f
Petit-Saguenay Canada 48°15N 70°4W 165 C5
Petit Saint Bernard, Col du
　Italy 45°40N 6°52E 73 C10
Petite Terre, Îles de la
　Guadeloupe 16°13N 61°9W 182 b
Petitot → Canada 60°14N 123°29W 162 A4
Petitsikapau L. Canada 54°37N 66°25W 165 B6
Petlad India 22°30N 72°45E 124 H5
Peto Mexico 20°8N 88°55W 181 C7
Petone N.Z. 41°13S 174°53E 154 H3
Petorca Chile 32°15S 70°56W 190 C2
Petoskey U.S.A. 45°22N 84°57W 173 C11
Petra Jordan 30°20N 35°22E 130 E4
Petra Spain 39°37N 3°6E 100 B10
Petra, Ostrov Russia 76°15N 118°30E 107 B12
Petra Velikogo, Zaliv
　Russia 42°40N 132°0E 112 C6
Petre, Pt. Canada 43°50N 77°9W 174 C7
Petrel = Petrer Spain 38°30N 0°46W 91 G4
Petrella, Monte Italy 41°18N 13°40E 94 A6
Petrer Spain 38°30N 0°46W 91 G4
Petreto-Bicchisano
　France 41°47N 8°58E 73 G12
Petrich Bulgaria 41°24N 23°13E 96 E7
Petrified Forest △
　U.S.A. 35°0N 109°30W 169 J9
Petrijanec Croatia 46°23N 16°17E 93 B13
Petrila Romania 45°28N 23°29E 81 E8
Petrinja Croatia 45°28N 16°18E 93 C13
Petrodvorets Russia 59°52N 29°54E 84 C5
Petrolândia Brazil 9°5S 38°20W 189 B3
Petrolia Canada 42°54N 82°9W 174 D2
Petrolina Brazil 9°24S 40°30W 189 B2
Petropavl Kazakhstan 54°53N 69°13E 109 B7
Petropavlovsk = Petropavl
　Kazakhstan 54°53N 69°13E 109 B7
Petropavlovsk-Kamchatskiy
　Russia 53°3N 158°43E 107 D16
Petropavlovskiy = Akhtubinsk
　Russia 48°13N 46°7E 87 F8
Petrópolis Brazil 22°33S 43°9W 191 A7
Petroşani Romania 45°28N 23°20E 81 E8
Petrova Gora Croatia 45°15N 15°45E 93 C12
Petrovac Montenegro 42°13N 18°55E 96 D2
Petrovaradin Serbia 45°16N 19°55E 80 D4
Petrovsk Russia 52°22N 45°19E 86 D7
Petrovsk-Zabaykalskiy
　Russia 51°20N 108°55E 107 D11
Petrovskaya Russia 45°25N 37°10E 87 G4
Petrozavodsk Russia 61°41N 34°20E 84 B8

Petrus Steyn S. Africa 27°38S 28°8E 145 C4
Petrusburg S. Africa 29°4S 25°26E 144 C4
Petukhovo Russia 55°6N 67°58E 109 A7
Peumo Chile 34°21S 71°12W 190 C1
Peureulak Indonesia 4°48N 97°45E 118 D1
Pevek Russia 69°41N 171°19E 107 C18
Peveragno Italy 44°20N 7°37E 92 D4
Peyrehorade France 43°34N 1°7E 72 E2
Peyruis France 44°1N 5°56E 73 D9
Pézenas France 43°28N 3°24E 72 E7
Pezinok Slovak Rep. 48°17N 17°17E 79 C10
Pfaffenhofen Germany 48°31N 11°31E 77 G7
Pfälzerwald △ Germany 49°18N 9°55E 77 F5
Pfarrkirchen Germany 48°25N 12°56E 77 G8
Pfeffenhausen Germany 48°39N 11°58E 77 G7
Pforzheim Germany 48°52N 8°41E 77 G4
Pfullendorf Germany 47°55N 9°15E 77 H5
Pfungstadt Germany 49°48N 8°35E 77 F4
Phagwara India 31°10N 75°40E 124 D6
Phala Botswana 23°45S 26°50E 144 B4
Phalaborwa S. Africa 23°57S 31°7E 145 B5
Phalera = Phulera
　India 26°52N 75°16E 124 F6
Phalodi India 27°12N 72°24E 124 F5
Phalsbourg France 48°46N 7°15E 71 D14
Phaltan India 17°59N 74°26E 126 F2
Phaluai, Ko Thailand 9°32N 99°41E 121 b
Phan Thailand 19°28N 99°43E 120 C2
Phan Rang-Thap Cham
　Vietnam 11°34N 109°0E 121 G7
Phan Ri Cua Vietnam 11°16N 108°40E 121 G7
Phan Si Pan Vietnam 22°18N 103°46E 120 A4
Phan Thiet Vietnam 11°1N 108°9E 121 G7
Phan Thiet, Vinh
　Vietnam 10°53N 108°5E 121 G7
Phan Wa, Laem Thailand 7°47N 98°25E 121 a
Phanae Greece 38°8N 25°57E 99 C7
Phanat Nikhom
　Thailand 13°27N 101°11E 120 F3
Phangan, Ko Thailand 9°45N 100°0E 121 H2
Phangnga Thailand 8°28N 98°30E 121 H1
Phangnga, Ao Thailand 8°16N 98°33E 121 a
Phanom Sarakham
　Thailand 13°45N 101°21E 120 F3
Phaphund India 26°36N 79°28E 125 F8
Pharenda India 27°5N 83°17E 125 F10
Pharr U.S.A. 26°12N 98°11W 176 H5
Phatthalung Thailand 7°39N 100°6E 121 J3
Phayam, Ko Thailand 9°44N 98°25E 121 H1
Phayao Thailand 19°11N 99°55E 120 C2
Phelps U.S.A. 42°58N 77°3W 174 D7
Phelps L. U.S.A. 59°15N 103°15W 163 B8
Phenix City U.S.A. 32°28N 85°1W 178 C4
Phet Buri = Phetchaburi
　Thailand 13°1N 99°55E 120 F2
Phetchabun Thailand 16°25N 101°8E 120 D3
Phetchabun, Thiu Khao
　Thailand 16°0N 101°20E 120 D3
Phetchaburi Thailand 13°1N 99°55E 120 F2
Phi Phi, Ko Thailand 7°45N 98°46E 121 J2
Phiafay Laos 14°48N 106°0E 120 E6
Phibun Mangsahan
　Thailand 15°14N 105°14E 120 E5
Phichai Thailand 17°22N 100°10E 120 D3
Phichit Thailand 16°26N 100°22E 120 D3
Philadelphia Miss.,
　U.S.A. 32°46N 89°7W 177 E10
Philadelphia N.Y.,
　U.S.A. 44°9N 75°43W 175 B9
Philadelphia Pa., U.S.A. 39°57N 75°9W 175 G9
Philip U.S.A. 44°2N 101°40W 172 C3
Philip Smith Mts.
　U.S.A. 68°0N 148°0W 166 B10
Philippeville Belgium 50°12N 4°33E 69 D4
Philippi U.S.A. 39°9N 80°3W 173 F13
Philippi L. Australia 24°20S 138°55E 150 C2
Philippine Basin Pac. Oc. 17°0N 132°0E 156 F5
Philippine Sea Pac. Oc. 18°0N 125°0E 156 F5
Philippine Trench = Mindanao
　Trench Pac. Oc. 12°0N 126°6E 119 B7
Philippines ■ Asia 12°0N 123°0E 119 B6
Philippolis S. Africa 30°15S 25°16E 144 C4
Philippopolis = Plovdiv
　Bulgaria 42°8N 24°44E 97 C8
Philipsburg S. Africa 30°28S 24°30E 144 D3
Philipstown = Daingean
　Ireland 53°18N 7°17W 64 C4
Philipsburg Mont.,
　U.S.A. 46°20N 113°18W 168 C7
Philipsburg Pa., U.S.A. 40°54N 78°13W 174 F6
Phillip I. Australia 38°30S 145°12E 153 D6
Phillips Ga., U.S.A. 45°42N 90°24W 172 C8
Phillipsburg Kans.,
　U.S.A. 39°45N 99°19W 172 F4
Phillipsburg N.J.,
　U.S.A. 40°42N 75°12W 175 F9
Philmont U.S.A. 42°15N 73°39W 175 D11
Philomath Ga., U.S.A. 33°44N 82°59W 178 B7
Philomath Oreg.,
　U.S.A. 44°32N 123°22W 168 D2
Phimai Thailand 15°13N 102°30E 120 E4
Phitsanulok Thailand 16°50N 100°12E 120 D3
Phnom Kulen △
　Cambodia 13°38N 104°15E 120 F5
Phnom Penh
　Cambodia 11°33N 104°55E 121 G5
Phnum Penh = Phnom Penh
　Cambodia 11°33N 104°55E 121 G5
Pho, Laem Thailand 6°58N 101°21E 121 J3
Phocis = Fokida Greece 38°30N 22°15E 98 C4
Phoenicia U.S.A. 42°5N 74°14W 175 D10
Phoenix Mauritius 20°17S 57°30E 141 d
Phoenix Ariz., U.S.A. 33°26N 112°4W 169 K7
Phoenix N.Y., U.S.A. 43°14N 76°18W 175 C8
Phoenixville U.S.A. 40°8N 75°31W 175 F9
Phon Thailand 15°49N 102°30E 120 E4
Phong → Thailand 16°23N 102°56E 120 D4
Phong Nha-Ke Bang △
　Vietnam 17°30N 106°10E 120 D6
Phong Saly Laos 21°42N 102°9E 116 G4
Phong Tho Vietnam 22°32N 103°21E 120 A4
Phonhong Laos 18°30N 102°25E 120 C4
Phonsavan Laos 19°27N 103°10E 120 C4
Phonum Thailand 8°49N 98°48E 121 H1

Phosphate Hill
　Australia 21°53S 139°58E 150 C2
Photharam Thailand 13°41N 99°51E 120 F2
Phra Nakhon Si Ayutthaya
　Thailand 14°25N 100°30E 120 E3
Phra Pradaeng
　Thailand 13°39N 100°33E 120 F3
Phra Thong, Ko Thailand 9°5N 98°17E 121 H1
Phrae Thailand 18°7N 100°9E 120 C3
Phrom Phiram
　Thailand 17°2N 100°12E 120 D3
Phrom Thep, Laem
　Thailand 7°45N 98°19E 121 a
Phrygia Turkey 38°40N 30°0E 104 C4
Phthiotis = Ethiotida
　Greece 38°50N 22°25E 98 C4
Phu Bia Laos 19°10N 103°0E 120 C4
Phu Chong -Na Yoi △
　Thailand 14°25N 105°30E 120 E5
Phu Hin Rong Kla △
　Thailand 17°0N 100°59E 120 D3
Phu Kao -Phu Phan Kham △
　Thailand 16°53N 102°31E 120 D4
Phu Kradung △
　Thailand 17°2N 101°44E 120 D3
Phu Loi Laos 20°14N 103°14E 120 B4
Phu Luang △ Thailand 17°15N 101°29E 120 D3
Phu Ly Vietnam 20°35N 105°50E 116 G5
Phu My Vietnam 14°15N 109°5E 120 E7
Phu Pha Man △
　Thailand 16°44N 101°50E 120 D3
Phu Phan △ Thailand 17°0N 103°56E 120 D4
Phu Quoc, Dao
　Vietnam 10°20N 104°0E 121 G4
Phu Sa Dok Bua △
　Thailand 16°11N 104°45E 120 D5
Phu Sang △ Thailand 19°35N 100°19E 120 C3
Phu Tho Vietnam 21°24N 105°13E 116 G5
Phu Wiang △
　Thailand 16°39N 102°23E 120 D4
Phuc Yen Vietnam 21°16N 105°45E 116 G5
Phuket Thailand 7°53N 98°24E 121 a
Phuket, Ko Thailand 8°0N 98°22E 121 a
Phul India 30°19N 75°14E 124 D6
Phulad India 25°38N 73°49E 124 G5
Phulbani India 20°28N 84°14E 126 D7
Phulchari Bangla. 25°11N 89°37E 125 G13
Phulera India 26°52N 75°16E 124 F6
Phulpur India 25°31N 82°49E 125 G10
Phunphin Thailand 9°7N 99°12E 121 H2
Phuntsholing Bhutan 26°51N 89°23E 125 F13
Phuphrabat △ Thailand 17°40N 102°45E 120 D4
Phuthaditjhaba
　S. Africa 28°29S 28°48E 145 C4
Phyu = Pyu Burma 18°30N 96°28E 123 K20
Pia ◎ Australia 27°7S 116°23E 149 E2
Piaçabuçu Brazil 10°24S 36°25W 189 C3
Piacenza Italy 45°1N 9°40E 92 C6
Piai, Tanjung Malaysia 1°17N 103°30E 121 d
Piako → N.Z. 37°12S 175°30E 154 D4
Pian Cr. → Australia 30°2S 148°12E 151 E4
Pian-Upe ◎ Uganda 1°44N 34°20E 142 B3
Piana France 42°15N 8°34E 73 F12
Pianella Italy 42°24N 14°2E 93 F11
Piangil Australia 35°5S 143°20E 152 C5
Pianosa Puglia, Italy 42°12N 15°44E 93 F12
Pianosa Toscana, Italy 42°35N 10°5E 92 F7
Piao'ertun China 41°50N 123°47E 115 C12
Piapot Canada 49°59N 109°8W 163 D7
Pias Portugal 38°1N 7°29W 89 G3
Piaseczno Poland 52°5N 21°2E 83 F8
Piaski Poland 51°8N 22°52E 83 E9
Piastów Poland 52°12N 20°48E 83 F7
Piatã Brazil 13°9S 41°48W 189 C2
Piatra Romania 43°51N 25°9E 81 G10
Piatra Craiului △
　Romania 45°30N 25°12E 81 E10
Piatra Neamţ Romania 46°56N 26°21E 81 D11
Piatra Olt Romania 44°22N 24°16E 81 F9
Piauí □ Brazil 7°0S 43°0W 189 B2
Piauí → Brazil 6°38S 42°42W 189 B2
Piave → Italy 45°32N 12°44E 93 C9
Piazza Armerina Italy 37°21N 14°20E 95 E7
Pibor Post South Sudan 6°47N 33°3E 135 G12
Pic St-Loup France 43°47N 3°48E 72 E7
Pica Chile 20°35S 69°25W 188 E4
Picardie □ France 49°50N 3°0E 71 C9
Picardie, Plaine de France 50°0N 2°0E 71 C9
Picardy = Picardie □
　France 49°50N 3°0E 71 C9
Picayune U.S.A. 30°32N 89°41W 177 F10
Picerno Italy 40°38N 15°38E 95 B8
Pichhor India 25°58N 78°20E 125 G8
Pichilemu Chile 34°22S 72°0W 190 C1
Pichor India 25°11N 78°11E 124 G8
Pickerel L. Canada 48°40N 91°25W 164 C1
Pickering U.K. 54°15N 0°46W 66 C7
Pickering, Vale of U.K. 54°14N 0°45W 66 C7
Pickle Lake Canada 51°30N 90°12W 164 B1
Pickwick L. U.S.A. 35°4N 88°15W 177 D10
Pico Azores 38°28N 28°20W 134 a
Pico Bonito △
　Honduras 15°34N 86°48W 182 C2
Pico Truncado
　Argentina 46°40S 68°0W 192 C2
Picos Brazil 7°5S 41°28W 189 B2
Picos, Pta. dos Spain 41°52N 8°53W 88 D2
Picos de Europa △ Spain 43°14N 4°59W 88 B6
Picota Peru 6°54S 76°24W 188 B2
Picton Canada 34°12S 150°34E 153 C9
Picton Canada 44°1N 77°9W 174 B7
Picton, I. Chile 55°2S 66°57W 192 E3
Pictou Canada 45°41N 62°42W 165 C7
Pictured Rocks
　U.S.A. 46°30N 86°30W 172 B10
Picuí Brazil 6°31S 36°21W 189 B3
Picún Leufú Argentina 39°30S 69°5W 192 A3
Pidbuzh Ukraine 49°19N 23°43E 81 A10
Pidurutalagala Sri Lanka 7°10N 80°50E 127 L5
Piechowice Poland 50°51N 15°36E 82 E2
Piedimonte Matese Italy 41°22N 14°22E 95 A7
Piedmont = Piemonte □
　Italy 45°0N 8°0E 92 D5
Piedmont Ala., U.S.A. 33°55N 85°37W 178 B4
Piedmont S.C., U.S.A. 34°42N 82°28W 178 B5
Piedra → Spain 41°18N 1°47W 90 D3
Piedra del Águila
　Argentina 40°25S 70°4W 192 B2

Piedra del Águila, Embalse *Argentina* 40°15S 70°4W **192** B2
Piedrabuena *Spain* 39°0N 4°10W **89** G6
Piedrahita *Spain* 40°28N 5°23W **88** E5
Piedralaves *Spain* 40°19N 4°42W **88** E6
Piedras, R. de las → *Peru* 12°30S 69°15W **188** C4
Piedras Blancas *Spain* 43°33N 5°58W **88** B5
Piedras Negras *Mexico* 28°42N 100°31W **180** B4
Piekary Śląskie *Poland* 50°24N 18°57E **83** H5
Pieksämäki *Finland* 62°18N 27°10E **84** A4
Pielinen *Finland* 63°15N 29°40E **60** E23
Pieljekaise △ *Sweden* 66°20N 16°45E **60** C17
Piemonte □ *Italy* 45°0N 8°0E **92** D5
Pienaarsrivier *S. Africa* 25°15S 28°18E **145** C4
Pieniężno *Poland* 54°14N 20°8E **82** D7
Pieninský △ *Europe* 49°25N 20°28E **79** B13
Pieńsk *Poland* 51°16N 15°2E **83** G2
Pienza *Italy* 43°4N 11°40E **93** E8
Piercefield *U.S.A.* 44°13N 74°35W **175** B10
Pierceland *Canada* 54°20N 109°46W **163** C7
Pieria *Greece* 40°13N 22°25E **96** F6
Pierpont *U.S.A.* 41°45N 80°34W **174** E4
Pierre *U.S.A.* 44°22N 100°21W **172** C3
Pierre-Buffière *France* 45°41N 1°22E **72** C5
Pierre-de-Bresse *France* 46°54N 5°13E **71** F12
Pierrefonds *Canada* 45°29N 73°51W **175** A11
Pierrefontaine-les-Varans *France* 47°14N 6°32E **71** E13
Pierrefort *France* 44°55N 2°50E **72** D6
Pierrelatte *France* 44°23N 4°43E **73** D8
Pierson *U.S.A.* 29°14N 81°28W **179** F8
Piešťany *Slovak Rep.* 48°38N 17°55E **79** C10
Piesting → *Austria* 48°6N 16°40E **79** C9
Pieszyce *Poland* 50°43N 16°33E **83** H3
Piet Retief *S. Africa* 27°1S 30°50E **145** C5
Pietarsaari *Finland* 63°40N 22°43E **60** E20
Pietermaritzburg *S. Africa* 29°35S 30°25E **145** C5
Pietersburg = Polokwane *S. Africa* 23°54S 29°25E **145** B4
Pietragalla *Italy* 40°45N 15°53E **95** B8
Pietrasanta *Italy* 43°57N 10°14E **92** E7
Pietroşiţa *Romania* 45°11N 25°26E **81** E10
Pietrosul, Vf. *Maramureş, Romania* 47°35N 24°43E **81** C9
Pietrosul, Vf. *Suceava, Romania* 47°12N 25°18E **81** C10
Pieve di Cadore *Italy* 46°26N 12°22E **93** B9
Pieve di Teco *Italy* 44°3N 7°56E **92** D4
Pievepélago *Italy* 44°12N 10°37E **92** D7
Pigadítsa *Greece* 39°59N 21°23E **96** G5
Pigeon I. *India* 14°2N 74°20E **127** G2
Pigeon L. *Canada* 44°27N 78°30W **174** B6
Piges *Greece* 39°17N 21°25E **98** B3
Piggott *U.S.A.* 36°23N 90°11W **177** C9
Pigna *Italy* 43°56N 7°40E **92** E4
Pigüe *Argentina* 37°36S 62°25W **190** D3
Piha *N.Z.* 36°57S 174°28E **154** C3
Pihani *India* 27°36N 80°15E **125** F9
Pihlajavesi *Finland* 61°45N 28°45E **84** B5
Pijijiapan *Mexico* 15°42N 93°14W **181** D6
Pikalevo *Russia* 59°37N 34°9E **84** C8
Pikangikum *Canada* 51°49N 94°0W **163** C10
Pikes Peak *U.S.A.* 38°50N 105°3W **168** G11
Piketberg *S. Africa* 32°55S 18°40E **144** D2
Pikeville *U.S.A.* 37°29N 82°31W **173** G12
Pikou *China* 39°18N 122°22E **115** E12
Pikwitonei *Canada* 55°35N 97°9W **163** B9
Piła *Poland* 53°10N 16°48E **83** E3
Pila *Spain* 38°16N 1°11W **91** G3
Pilanesberg △ *S. Africa* 25°15S 27°4E **144** C4
Pilani *India* 28°22N 75°33E **124** E6
Pilar *Brazil* 9°36S 35°56W **189** B3
Pilar *Paraguay* 26°50S 58°20W **190** B4
Pilar de la Horadada *Spain* 37°52N 0°47W **91** H4
Pilat, Dune du *France* 44°35N 1°13W **72** D2
Pilat △ *France* 45°20N 4°30E **73** C8
Piława *Poland* 51°57N 21°32E **83** G8
Pilaya → *Bolivia* 20°55S 64°4W **186** H6
Pilbara *Australia* 21°15S 118°16E **148** D2
Pilcomaya → *Paraguay* 25°21S 57°42W **190** B4
Pilea *Greece* 40°32N 22°59E **96** F6
Pilgrim's Rest *S. Africa* 24°55S 30°44E **145** B5
Pilgrimstad *Sweden* 62°57N 15°2E **62** B9
Pili *Greece* 36°50N 27°15E **99** E9
Pilibhit *India* 28°40N 79°50E **125** E8
Pilica → *Poland* 51°52N 21°17E **83** G8
Pilio, Oros *Greece* 39°27N 23°3E **98** B5
Pilipinas = Philippines ■ *Asia* 12°0N 123°0E **119** B6
Pilis *Hungary* 47°17N 19°35E **80** C4
Pilisvörösvár *Hungary* 47°38N 18°56E **80** C3
Pilkhawa *India* 28°43N 77°42E **124** E7
Pilliga *Australia* 30°21S 148°54E **151** E4
Pilos *Greece* 36°55N 21°42E **98** E3
Pilot Mound *Canada* 49°15N 98°54W **163** D9
Pilot Point *U.S.A.* 33°24N 96°58W **176** E6
Pilot Rock *U.S.A.* 45°29N 118°50W **168** D4
Pilštanj *Slovenia* 46°8N 15°39E **93** B12
Piltene *Latvia* 57°13N 21°40E **82** A8
Pilzno *Poland* 49°58N 21°16E **83** J8
Pima *U.S.A.* 32°54N 109°50W **169** K9
Pimba *Australia* 31°18S 136°46E **152** A2
Pimenta Bueno *Brazil* 11°35S 61°10W **186** F6
Pimentel *Peru* 6°45S 79°55W **188** B2
Pimpri Chinchwad *India* 18°37N 73°47E **126** E1
Pin Valley △ *India* 31°50N 77°50E **124** D7
Pina de Ebro *Spain* 41°29N 0°33W **90** D4
Pinang *Malaysia* 5°25N 100°15E **121** c
Pinang □ *Malaysia* 5°20N 100°20E **121** K3
Pinar, C. des *Spain* 39°53N 3°12E **100** B10
Pinar del Río *Cuba* 22°26N 83°40W **182** B3
Pınarbaşı *Çanakkale, Turkey* 39°53N 26°15E **99** B8
Pınarbaşı *Kayseri, Turkey* 38°43N 36°23E **104** C7
Pınarhisar *Turkey* 41°37N 27°30E **97** E11
Pinatubo, Mt. *Phil.* 15°8N 120°21E **119** A6
Pinawa *Canada* 50°9N 95°50W **163** C9
Pincehely *Hungary* 46°41N 18°27E **80** D3
Pinchang *China* 31°36N 107°3E **116** B6
Pincher Creek *Canada* 49°30N 113°57W **162** D6
Pinchi L. *Canada* 54°38N 124°30W **162** C4
Pinckneyville *U.S.A.* 31°19N 85°33W **178** D4
Pinckneyville *U.S.A.* 38°5N 89°23W **172** F9
Pińczów *Poland* 50°32N 20°32E **83** H7
Pind Dadan Khan *Pakistan* 32°36N 73°7E **109** F8
Pindar *Australia* 28°30S 115°47E **149** E2
Pindaré → *Brazil* 3°17S 44°47W **189** A2
Pindaré-Mirim *Brazil* 3°37S 45°21W **189** A1
Pindera Downs ✪ *Australia* 29°24S 142°37E **151** A3
Pindi Gheb *Pakistan* 33°14N 72°21E **124** C5
Pindiga *Nigeria* 9°58N 10°53E **139** D7
Pindos △ *Greece* 39°52N 21°11E **98** B3
Pindos Oros *Greece* 40°0N 21°0E **98** B3
Pindus Mts. = Pindos Oros *Greece* 40°0N 21°0E **98** B3
Pine → *B.C., Canada* 56°8N 120°43W **162** B4
Pine → *Sask., Canada* 58°50N 105°38W **163** B7
Pine Bluff *U.S.A.* 34°13N 92°1W **176** D8
Pine Bluffs *U.S.A.* 41°11N 104°4W **168** F11
Pine City *U.S.A.* 45°50N 92°59W **172** C7
Pine Cr. → *U.S.A.* 41°10N 77°16W **174** E7
Pine Creek *Australia* 13°50S 131°50E **148** B5
Pine Falls *Canada* 50°34N 96°11W **163** C9
Pine Flat L. *U.S.A.* 36°50N 119°20W **170** J7
Pine Grove *U.S.A.* 40°33N 76°23W **175** F8
Pine Hill *Australia* 23°38S 146°57E **150** C4
Pine Hills *U.S.A.* 28°33N 81°27W **179** G8
Pine I. *U.S.A.* 26°36N 82°7W **179** J7
Pine Island Glacier *Antarctica* 76°0S 100°0W **55** D15
Pine Level *U.S.A.* 32°4N 86°4W **178** C3
Pine Mountain *U.S.A.* 32°49N 84°51W **178** C5
Pine Pass *Canada* 55°25N 122°42W **162** B4
Pine Point *Canada* 60°50N 114°28W **162** A6
Pine Ridge *Australia* 31°30S 150°28E **153** A9
Pine Ridge *U.S.A.* 43°2N 102°33W **172** D2
Pine River *Canada* 51°45N 100°30W **163** C8
Pine River *U.S.A.* 46°43N 94°24W **172** B6
Pine Valley *U.S.A.* 32°50N 116°32W **171** N10
Pinecrest *U.S.A.* 38°12N 120°1W **170** G6
Pineda de Mar *Spain* 41°37N 2°42E **90** D7
Pinedale *Calif., U.S.A.* 36°50N 119°48W **170** J7
Pinedale *Wyo., U.S.A.* 42°52N 109°52W **168** E9
Pinega → *Russia* 64°30N 44°19E **106** C5
Pinehouse L. *Canada* 55°32N 106°35W **163** B7
Pineimuta → *Canada* 52°8N 88°33W **164** B1
Pinellas Park *U.S.A.* 27°50N 82°41W **179** H7
Pinerolo *Italy* 44°53N 7°21E **92** D4
Pines, Akra *Greece* 40°5N 24°20E **97** F8
Pineto *Italy* 42°36N 14°4E **93** F11
Pinetop-Lakeside *U.S.A.* 34°9N 109°58W **169** J9
Pinetown *S. Africa* 29°48S 30°54E **145** C5
Pinetta *U.S.A.* 30°36N 83°21W **178** E6
Pineview *U.S.A.* 32°7N 83°30W **178** C6
Pineville *La., U.S.A.* 31°19N 92°26W **176** F8
Pineville *S.C., U.S.A.* 33°26N 80°1W **178** B9
Pinewood *U.S.A.* 33°44N 80°27W **178** B9
Piney *France* 48°22N 4°21E **71** D11
Ping → *Thailand* 15°42N 100°9E **120** E3
Pingaring *Australia* 32°40S 118°32E **149** F2
Pingba *China* 26°23N 106°12E **116** D6
Pingbian *China* 23°0N 103°45E **116** F4
Pingchuan *China* 27°35N 101°55E **116** D3
Pingding *China* 37°47N 113°38E **114** F7
Pingdingshan *China* 33°43N 113°27E **114** H7
Pingdu *China* 36°42N 119°59E **115** F10
Pingelly *Australia* 32°32S 117°5E **149** F2
Pingguo *China* 23°19N 107°36E **116** F6
Pinghe *China* 24°17N 117°21E **117** E11
Pinghu *China* 30°40N 121°2E **117** B13
Pingjiang *China* 28°45N 113°36E **117** C9
Pingle *China* 24°40N 110°40E **117** E8
Pingli *China* 32°27N 109°22E **116** A7
Pingliang *China* 35°35N 106°31E **114** G4
Pinglu *China* 39°31N 112°30E **114** E7
Pingluo *China* 38°52N 106°30E **114** E4
Pingnan *Fujian, China* 26°55N 119°0E **117** D12
Pingnan *Guangxi Zhuangzu, China* 23°33N 110°22E **117** F8
Pingquan *China* 41°1N 118°37E **115** D10
Pingrup *Australia* 33°32S 118°29E **149** F2
Pingshan *China* 28°39N 104°3E **116** C5
Pingtan *China* 25°31N 119°47E **117** E12
Pingtang *China* 25°49N 107°17E **116** E6
P'ingtung *Taiwan* 22°38N 120°30E **117** F13
Pingwu *China* 32°25N 104°30E **114** H3
Pingxiang *Guangxi Zhuangzu, China* 22°6N 106°46E **116** F6
Pingxiang *Jiangxi, China* 27°43N 113°48E **117** D9
Pingyao *China* 37°12N 112°10E **114** F7
Pingyi *China* 35°30N 117°35E **115** G9
Pingyin *China* 36°20N 116°25E **114** F9
Pingyuan *Guangdong, China* 24°37N 115°57E **117** E10
Pingyuan *Shandong, China* 37°10N 116°22E **114** F9
Pingyuanjie *China* 23°45N 103°48E **116** F4
Pinhal Novo *Portugal* 38°38N 8°55W **89** G2
Pinheiro *Brazil* 2°31S 45°5W **189** A1
Pinheiro Machado *Brazil* 31°34S 53°23W **191** C5
Pinhel *Portugal* 40°50N 7°1W **88** E3
Pini *Indonesia* 0°10N 98°40E **118** D1
Pinios → *Ilia, Greece* 37°48N 21°20E **98** D3
Pinios → *Trikala, Greece* 39°55N 22°41E **98** B4
Pinjarra *Australia* 32°37S 115°52E **149** F2
Pink Mountain *Canada* 57°3N 122°52W **162** B4
Pinkafeld *Austria* 47°22N 16°9E **79** D9
Pinnacle Is. = Senkaku-Shotō *E. China Sea* 25°45N 123°30E **113** M1
Pinnacles △ *U.S.A.* 36°25N 121°12W **170** J5
Pinnaroo *Australia* 35°17S 140°53E **152** C4
Pinneberg *Germany* 53°40N 9°48E **76** B5
Pino Hachado, Paso *S. Amer.* 38°39S 70°54W **192** A2
Pinon Hills *U.S.A.* 34°26N 117°39W **171** L9
Pinos *Mexico* 22°18N 101°34W **180** C4
Pinos, Mt. *U.S.A.* 34°49N 119°8W **171** L7
Pinos Pt. *U.S.A.* 36°38N 121°57W **169** H3
Pinos Puente *Spain* 37°15N 3°45W **89** H7
Pinrang *Indonesia* 3°46S 119°41E **119** E5
Pins, Pte. aux *Canada* 42°15N 81°51W **174** D3
Pinsk *Belarus* 52°10N 26°1E **75** B14
Pintados *Chile* 20°35S 69°40W **188** E4
Pinturas → *Argentina* 46°30S 70°20W **192** C2
Pinyang *China* 27°42N 120°31E **117** D13
Pinyug *Russia* 60°5N 48°0E **106** C5
Pio XII *Brazil* 3°53S 45°17W **189** A1
Pioche *U.S.A.* 37°56N 114°27W **169** H6
Piombino *Italy* 42°55N 10°32E **92** F7
Piombino, Canale di *Italy* 42°53N 10°30E **92** F7
Pioner, Ostrov *Russia* 79°50N 92°0E **107** B10
Pionerskiy *Russia* 54°56N 20°14E **82** D7
Pionki *Poland* 51°29N 21°28E **83** G8
Piopiotaki = Milford Sd. *N.Z.* 44°41S 167°47E **155** E2
Piorini, L. *Brazil* 3°15S 62°35W **186** D6
Piotrków Trybunalski *Poland* 51°23N 19°43E **83** G6
Piove di Sacco *Italy* 45°18N 12°2E **93** C9
Pīp *Iran* 26°45N 60°10E **129** E9
Pipar *India* 26°25N 73°31E **124** F5
Pipar Road *India* 26°27N 73°27E **124** F5
Piparia *Mad. P., India* 22°45N 78°23E **124** H8
Piparia *Mad. P., India* 21°49N 77°37E **124** J7
Piperi *Greece* 39°20N 24°19E **98** B6
Pipestone *U.S.A.* 44°0N 96°19W **172** D5
Pipestone → *Canada* 52°53N 89°23W **164** B2
Pipestone Cr. → *Canada* 49°38N 100°15W **163** D8
Pipiriki *N.Z.* 39°28S 175°5E **154** F4
Piplan *Pakistan* 32°17N 71°21E **124** C4
Piploda *India* 23°37N 74°56E **124** H6
Pipmuacan, Rés. *Canada* 49°45N 70°30W **165** C5
Pippingarra *Australia* 20°27S 118°42E **148** D2
Pipriac *France* 47°59N 1°58W **70** E5
Piqua *U.S.A.* 40°9N 84°15W **173** E11
Piquet Carneiro *Brazil* 5°48S 39°25W **189** B3
Piquiri → *Brazil* 24°3S 54°14W **191** A5
Pir Panjal Range *India* 32°30N 76°50E **124** C7
Pīr Sohrāb *Iran* 25°44N 60°54E **129** E9
Pira *Benin* 8°28N 1°48E **139** D5
Piracicaba *Brazil* 22°45S 47°40W **191** A6
Piracuruca *Brazil* 3°50S 41°50W **189** A2
Pirae *Tahiti* 17°31S 149°32W **155** b
Piræus = Pireas *Greece* 37°57N 23°42E **98** D5
Piraiévs = Pireas *Greece* 37°57N 23°42E **98** D5
Pirajuí *Brazil* 21°59S 49°29W **191** A6
Piram I. *India* 21°36N 72°21E **124** J5
Piran *Slovenia* 45°31N 13°33E **93** C10
Pirané *Argentina* 25°42S 59°6W **190** B4
Piranhas *Brazil* 9°27S 37°46W **189** B3
Pirano = Piran *Slovenia* 45°31N 13°33E **93** C10
Pīrānshahr *Iran* 36°41N 45°8E **105** D11
Pirapemas *Brazil* 3°43S 44°14W **189** A2
Pirapora *Brazil* 17°20S 44°56W **189** D2
Pirawa *India* 24°10N 76°2E **124** G7
Pirdop *Bulgaria* 42°40N 24°10E **97** D8
Pireas *Greece* 37°57N 23°42E **98** D5
Pires do Rio *Brazil* 17°18S 48°17W **189** D1
Pirgi *Greece* 38°13N 25°59E **99** C7
Pirgos *Ilia, Greece* 37°40N 21°27E **98** D3
Pirgos *Kriti, Greece* 35°0N 25°9E **99** F7
Pirgovo *Bulgaria* 43°44N 25°43E **97** C9
Piribebuy *Paraguay* 25°26S 57°2W **190** B4
Pirimapun *Indonesia* 6°20S 138°24E **119** F9
Pirin △ *Bulgaria* 41°48N 23°22E **96** E7
Pirin Planina *Bulgaria* 41°40N 23°30E **96** E7
Pirineos = Pyrénées *Europe* 42°45N 0°18E **72** F4
Piripiri *Brazil* 4°15S 41°46W **189** A2
Pirlangimpi *Australia* 11°24S 130°26E **148** B5
Pirmasens *Germany* 49°12N 7°36E **77** F3
Pirna *Germany* 50°57N 13°56E **76** E9
Pirot *Serbia* 43°9N 22°33E **96** C6
Piru *Indonesia* 3°4S 128°12E **119** E7
Piru *U.S.A.* 34°25N 118°48W **171** L8
Piryatin = Pyryatyn *Ukraine* 50°15N 32°25E **85** G7
Pisa *Italy* 43°43N 10°23E **92** E7
Pisa → *Poland* 53°14N 21°52E **83** E8
Pisa, Firenze ✈ (PSA) *Italy* 43°40N 10°22E **92** E7
Pisa Ra. *N.Z.* 44°52S 169°12E **155** E4
Pisac *Peru* 13°25S 71°50W **188** C3
Pisagua *Chile* 19°40S 70°15W **188** D3
Pisarovina *Croatia* 45°35N 15°50E **93** C12
Pisco *Peru* 13°50S 76°12W **188** C2
Piscu *Romania* 45°30N 27°43E **81** E12
Písek *Czech Rep.* 49°19N 14°10E **78** B7
Pishan *China* 37°30N 78°33E **109** E9
Pishcha *Ukraine* 51°35N 23°50E **83** G10
Pishchanka *Ukraine* 48°12N 28°54E **81** B13
Pīshīn *Iran* 26°6N 61°47E **129** E9
Pishin *Pakistan* 30°35N 67°0E **124** D2
Pishin Lora → *Pakistan* 29°9N 64°5E **124** E1
Pisidia *Turkey* 37°30N 31°40E **104** D4
Pising *Indonesia* 5°8S 121°53E **119** F6
Pismo Beach *U.S.A.* 35°9N 120°38W **171** K6
Piso, L. *Liberia* 6°50N 11°15W **138** D2
Pisogne *Italy* 45°45N 10°10E **92** C7
Pissila *Burkina Faso* 13°7N 0°50W **139** C4
Pissis, Cerro *Argentina* 27°45S 68°48W **190** B2
Pissos *France* 44°19N 0°49W **72** D3
Pissouri *Cyprus* 34°40N 32°42E **101** E11
Pisticci *Italy* 40°23N 16°33E **95** B9
Pistóia *Italy* 43°55N 10°54E **92** E7
Pistol B. *Canada* 62°25N 92°37W **163** A10
Pisuerga → *Spain* 41°33N 4°52W **88** D6
Pisz *Poland* 53°38N 21°49E **82** E8
Pit → *U.S.A.* 40°47N 122°6W **168** F2
Pita *Guinea* 11°5N 12°15W **138** C2
Pitangui *Brazil* 19°40S 44°54W **189** D2
Pitarpunga L. *Australia* 34°24S 143°30E **152** C5
Pitcairn I. *Pac. Oc.* 25°5S 130°5W **157** K14
Pitch L. *Trin. & Tob.* 10°14N 61°39W **187** K15
Piteå *Sweden* 65°20N 21°25E **60** D19
Piteälven → *Sweden* 65°20N 21°25E **60** D19
Piterka *Russia* 50°41N 47°29E **86** E8
Piteşti *Romania* 44°52N 24°54E **81** F9
Pithapuram *India* 17°10N 82°15E **126** F6
Pithara *Australia* 30°20S 116°35E **149** F2
Pithio *Greece* 41°24N 26°40E **97** E10
Pithiviers *France* 48°10N 2°13E **71** D9
Pithora *India* 21°16N 82°31E **126** D6
Pithoragarh *India* 29°35N 80°13E **125** E9
Pithoro *Pakistan* 25°31N 69°23E **124** G3
Pitigliano *Italy* 42°38N 11°40E **93** F8
Pitkyaranta *Russia* 61°34N 31°37E **84** B6
Pitlochry *U.K.* 56°42N 3°44W **65** E5
Pitnak = Drujba *Uzbekistan* 41°13N 61°18E **108** D6
Pitrufquén *Chile* 38°59S 72°39W **192** A2
Pitsilia *Cyprus* 34°55N 33°0E **101** E12
Pitsunda = Bichvinta *Georgia* 43°9N 40°21E **87** J5
Pitt I. *Canada* 53°30N 129°50W **162** C3
Pitti I. *India* 10°50N 72°38E **127** J1
Pittsburg *Calif., U.S.A.* 38°2N 121°53W **170** G5
Pittsburg *Kans., U.S.A.* 37°25N 94°42W **172** G6
Pittsburg *Tex., U.S.A.* 33°0N 94°59W **176** E7
Pittsburgh *U.S.A.* 40°26N 79°58W **174** F5
Pittsfield *Ill., U.S.A.* 39°36N 90°49W **172** F8
Pittsfield *Maine, U.S.A.* 44°47N 69°23W **173** C19
Pittsfield *Mass., U.S.A.* 42°27N 73°15W **175** D11
Pittsfield *N.H., U.S.A.* 43°18N 71°20W **175** C13
Pittston *U.S.A.* 41°19N 75°47W **175** E9
Pittsview *U.S.A.* 32°11N 85°10W **178** C4
Pittsworth *Australia* 27°41S 151°37E **151** D5
Pituri → *Australia* 22°35S 138°30E **150** C2
Piumhi *Brazil* 20°28S 45°58W **189** E1
Piura *Peru* 5°15S 80°38W **188** B1
Piura □ *Peru* 5°10S 80°0W **188** B2
Piuthan *Nepal* 28°7N 82°56E **125** E10
Piva → *Montenegro* 43°20N 18°50E **96** C2
Piwniczna *Poland* 49°27N 20°42E **83** J7
Pixian *China* 30°48N 103°52E **116** B4
Pixley *U.S.A.* 35°58N 119°18W **170** K7
Pizarra *Spain* 36°36N 4°42W **89** J6
Pizhou = Pei Xian *China* 34°44N 116°55E **114** G9
Pizhou *China* 34°18N 117°57E **115** G9
Pizzo *Italy* 38°44N 16°10E **95** D9
Placentia *Canada* 47°20N 54°0W **165** C9
Placentia B. *Canada* 47°0N 54°40W **165** C9
Placerville *U.S.A.* 38°44N 120°48W **170** G6
Placetas *Cuba* 22°15N 79°44W **182** B4
Plácido de Castro *Brazil* 10°20S 67°11W **188** C4
Plačkovica *Macedonia* 41°45N 22°30E **96** E6
Plaine des Jarres *Laos* 19°27N 103°10E **120** C4
Plainfield *N.J., U.S.A.* 40°37N 74°25W **175** F10
Plainfield *Ohio, U.S.A.* 40°13N 81°43W **174** F3
Plainfield *Vt., U.S.A.* 44°17N 72°26W **175** B12
Plains *Ga., U.S.A.* 32°2N 84°24W **178** C5
Plains *Mont., U.S.A.* 47°28N 114°53W **168** C6
Plains *Tex., U.S.A.* 33°11N 102°50W **176** E3
Plainview *Nebr., U.S.A.* 42°21N 97°47W **172** D5
Plainview *Tex., U.S.A.* 34°11N 101°43W **176** D4
Plainwell *U.S.A.* 42°27N 85°38W **173** D11
Plaisance *France* 43°36N 0°3E **72** E4
Plaistow *U.S.A.* 42°50N 71°6W **175** D13
Plaka *Greece* 40°0N 25°24E **99** B7
Plaka, Akra *Greece* 35°11N 26°19E **101** D8
Plakenska Planina *Macedonia* 41°14N 21°2E **96** E5
Planá *Czech Rep.* 49°50N 12°44E **78** B5
Plana Cays *Bahamas* 22°38N 73°30W **183** B5
Planada *U.S.A.* 37°16N 120°19W **170** H6
Planchón *Peru* 12°14S 69°11W **188** C4
Plancoët *France* 48°32N 2°13W **70** D4
Plandište *Serbia* 45°16N 21°10E **80** E6
Plano *U.S.A.* 33°1N 96°42W **176** E6
Plant City *U.S.A.* 28°1N 82°7W **179** G7
Plantation *U.S.A.* 26°7N 80°14W **179** J9
Plaquemine *U.S.A.* 30°17N 91°14W **176** F9
Plasencia *Spain* 40°3N 6°8W **88** E4
Plaški *Croatia* 45°4N 15°22E **93** C12
Plast *Russia* 54°22N 60°50E **108** B6
Plaster City *U.S.A.* 32°47N 115°51W **171** N11
Plaster Rock *Canada* 46°53N 67°22W **165** C6
Plastun *Russia* 44°45N 136°19E **112** B8
Plasy *Czech Rep.* 49°56N 13°24E **78** B6
Plata, Río de la → *S. Amer.* 34°45S 57°30W **190** C4
Plátani → *Italy* 37°23N 13°16E **94** E6
Platanos *Greece* 35°28N 23°33E **101** D5
Plateau □ *Nigeria* 8°30N 9°0E **139** D6
Platja d'Aro *Spain* 41°49N 3°4E **90** D8
Platte *U.S.A.* 43°23N 98°51W **172** D4
Platte → *Mo., U.S.A.* 39°16N 94°50W **172** F6
Platte → *Nebr., U.S.A.* 41°4N 95°53W **172** E6
Platteville *U.S.A.* 42°44N 90°29W **172** D8
Plattling *Germany* 48°46N 12°53E **77** G8
Plattsburgh *U.S.A.* 44°42N 73°28W **175** B11
Plattsmouth *U.S.A.* 41°1N 95°53W **172** E6
Plau *Germany* 53°27N 12°15E **76** B8
Plauen *Germany* 50°30N 12°8E **76** E8
Plauer See *Germany* 53°28N 12°17E **76** B8
Plav *Montenegro* 42°38N 19°57E **96** D3
Plavinas *Latvia* 56°35N 25°46E **84** D3
Plavnica *Montenegro* 42°20N 19°13E **96** D3
Plavno *Croatia* 44°9N 16°10E **93** D13
Plavsk *Russia* 53°40N 37°18E **84** F9
Playa Blanca *Canary Is.* 28°51N 13°50W **100** F6
Playa de las Americas *Canary Is.* 28°5N 16°43W **100** F3
Playa de Mogán *Canary Is.* 27°48N 15°47W **100** G4
Playa del Carmen *Mexico* 20°37N 87°4W **181** C7
Playa del Inglés *Canary Is.* 27°45N 15°33W **100** G4
Playa Esmerelda *Canary Is.* 28°8N 14°16W **100** F5
Playgreen L. *Canada* 54°0N 98°15W **163** C9
Pleasant Bay *Canada* 46°51N 60°48W **165** C7
Pleasant Hill *U.S.A.* 37°57N 122°4W **170** H4
Pleasant Mount *U.S.A.* 41°44N 75°26W **175** E9
Pleasanton *Calif., U.S.A.* 37°39N 121°52W **170** H5
Pleasanton *Tex., U.S.A.* 28°58N 98°29W **176** G5
Pleasantville *N.J., U.S.A.* 39°24N 74°32W **173** F16
Pleasantville *Pa., U.S.A.* 41°35N 79°34W **174** E5
Pléaux *France* 45°8N 2°13E **72** C6
Plei Ku *Vietnam* 13°57N 108°0E **120** F7
Plélan-le-Grand *France* 48°0N 2°7W **70** D4
Pleniţa *Romania* 44°14N 23°10E **81** F8
Plenty → *Australia* 23°25S 136°31E **150** C2
Plenty, B. of *N.Z.* 37°45S 177°0E **154** D6
Plentywood *U.S.A.* 48°47N 104°34W **168** B11
Plérin *France* 48°32N 2°46W **70** D4
Pleshcheyevo Ozero △ *Russia* 56°45N 38°50E **84** D10
Plessisville *Canada* 46°14N 71°47W **165** C5
Plestin-les-Grèves *France* 48°40N 3°39W **70** D3
Pleszew *Poland* 51°53N 17°47E **83** G4
Pleternica *Croatia* 45°17N 17°48E **80** E2
Plétipi, L. *Canada* 51°44N 70°6W **165** B5
Pleven *Bulgaria* 43°26N 24°37E **97** C8
Pleven □ *Bulgaria* 43°26N 24°37E **97** C8
Plevna *Canada* 44°58N 76°59W **174** B8
Plitvice Lakes = Plitvička Jezera △ *Croatia* 44°54N 15°35E **93** D12
Plitvička Jezera △ *Croatia* 44°54N 15°35E **93** D12
Plješevica *Croatia* 44°45N 15°45E **93** D12
Pljevlja *Montenegro* 43°21N 19°21E **96** C3
Ploaghe *Italy* 40°40N 8°45E **94** B1
Ploče *Croatia* 43°4N 17°26E **93** E14
Płock *Poland* 52°32N 19°40E **83** F6
Plöckenpass *Italy* 46°37N 12°57E **93** B9
Plöckenstein *Germany* 48°46N 13°51E **77** G9
Ploemeur *France* 47°44N 3°26W **70** E3
Ploërmel *France* 47°55N 2°26W **70** E4
Ploieşti *Romania* 44°57N 26°5E **81** F11
Plomari *Greece* 38°59N 26°22E **99** C8
Plombières-les-Bains *France* 47°58N 6°27E **71** E13
Plomin *Croatia* 45°8N 14°10E **93** C11
Plön *Germany* 54°9N 10°24E **76** A6
Plonge, Lac la *Canada* 55°8N 107°20W **163** B7
Płońsk *Poland* 52°37N 20°21E **83** F7
Plopeni *Romania* 45°4N 25°59E **81** E10
Plopişului, Munţii *Romania* 47°5N 22°30E **80** C7
Płoty *Poland* 53°48N 15°18E **82** E2
Plouaret *France* 48°37N 3°28W **70** D3
Plouay *France* 47°55N 3°21W **70** E3
Ploučnice → *Czech Rep.* 50°46N 14°13E **78** A7
Ploudalmézeau *France* 48°34N 4°41W **70** D2
Plouescat *France* 48°39N 4°10W **70** D2
Plougasnou *France* 48°42N 3°49W **70** D3
Plougastel-Daoulas *France* 48°22N 4°17W **70** D2
Plouguerneau *France* 48°36N 4°30W **70** D2
Plouha *France* 48°41N 2°57W **70** D4
Plouhinec *France* 48°0N 4°29W **70** E2
Plovdiv *Bulgaria* 42°8N 24°44E **97** D8
Plovdiv □ *Bulgaria* 42°15N 24°30E **97** D8
Plover Cove Res. *China* 22°28N 114°15E **111** a
Plum *U.S.A.* 40°29N 79°47W **174** F5
Plum I. *U.S.A.* 41°11N 72°12W **175** E12
Plumas *U.S.A.* 39°45N 120°4W **170** F6
Plummer *U.S.A.* 47°20N 116°53W **168** C5
Plumridge Lakes *Australia* 29°26S 125°16E **149** E4
Plumtree *Zimbabwe* 20°27S 27°55E **143** G2
Plungė *Lithuania* 55°53N 21°59E **82** C8
Plvenice *France* 47°46N 3°1W **70** E3
Plužine *Montenegro* 43°8N 18°51E **96** C2
Plymouth *Trin. & Tob.* 11°14N 60°48W **187** J16
Plymouth *U.K.* 50°22N 4°10W **67** G3
Plymouth *Calif., U.S.A.* 38°29N 120°51W **170** G6
Plymouth *Ind., U.S.A.* 41°21N 86°19W **172** E10
Plymouth *Mass., U.S.A.* 41°57N 70°40W **175** E14
Plymouth *N.C., U.S.A.* 35°52N 76°43W **177** D16
Plymouth *N.H., U.S.A.* 43°46N 71°41W **175** C13
Plymouth *Pa., U.S.A.* 41°14N 75°57W **175** E9
Plymouth *Wis., U.S.A.* 43°45N 87°59W **172** D10
Plympton-Wyoming = Wyoming *Canada* 42°57N 82°7W **174** D2
Plynlimon = Pumlumon Fawr *U.K.* 52°28N 3°46W **67** E4
Plyusa *Russia* 58°28N 29°27E **84** C5
Plyusa → *Russia* 59°4N 28°6E **84** C5
Plzeň *Czech Rep.* 49°45N 13°22E **78** B6
Plzeňský □ *Czech Rep.* 49°35N 13°0E **78** B6
Pmere Nyente ✪ *Australia* 24°15S 136°10E **150** C2
Pniewy *Poland* 52°31N 16°16E **83** F3
Pô *Burkina Faso* 11°14N 1°5W **139** C4
Po → *Italy* 44°57N 12°4E **93** D9
Po, Delta del *Italy* 44°55N 12°30E **93** D9
Pô △ *Burkina Faso* 11°25N 1°5W **139** C4
Po Hai = Bo Hai *China* 39°0N 119°0E **115** E10
Po Toi *China* 22°10N 114°16E **111** a
Pobé *Benin* 7°0N 2°56E **139** D5
Pobé *Burkina Faso* 13°53N 1°42W **139** C4
Pobeda *Russia* 65°12N 146°12E **107** C15
Pobedy, Pik *Kyrgyzstan* 42°0N 79°58E **109** D9
Pobiedziska *Poland* 52°29N 17°11E **83** F4
Pobladura del Valle *Spain* 42°6N 5°44W **88** C5
Poblet, Monasterio de *Spain* 41°22N 1°4E **90** D6
Pobra de Trives *Spain* 42°20N 7°10W **88** C3
Pocahontas *Ark., U.S.A.* 36°16N 90°58W **177** C9
Pocahontas *Iowa, U.S.A.* 42°44N 94°40W **172** D6
Pocatello *U.S.A.* 42°52N 112°27W **168** E7
Počátky *Czech Rep.* 49°15N 15°14E **78** B8
Pochep *Russia* 52°58N 33°29E **85** F7
Pochinki *Russia* 54°41N 44°59E **86** C7
Pochinok *Russia* 54°28N 32°29E **84** E7
Pöchlarn *Austria* 48°12N 15°12E **78** C8
Pocinhos *Brazil* 7°4S 36°3W **189** B3
Pocking *Germany* 48°23N 13°19E **77** G9
Poções *Brazil* 14°31S 40°21W **189** C2
Pocomoke City *U.S.A.* 38°5N 75°34W **173** F16
Poços de Caldas *Brazil* 21°50S 46°33W **191** A6
Podbořany *Czech Rep.* 50°14N 13°25E **78** A6
Poddębice *Poland* 51°54N 18°58E **83** G5
Poděbrady *Czech Rep.* 50°9N 15°8E **78** A8
Podensac *France* 44°40N 0°22W **72** D3
Podenzano *Italy* 44°57N 9°41E **92** D6
Podgorač *Croatia* 45°27N 18°13E **80** E3
Podgorica *Montenegro* 42°30N 19°19E **96** D3
Podgorie *Albania* 40°49N 20°48E **96** F4
Podile *India* 15°37N 79°37E **127** G4
Podilska Vysochyna *Ukraine* 49°0N 28°0E **81** B13
Podkarpackie □ *Poland* 50°0N 22°10E **83** H9
Podkova *Bulgaria* 41°24N 25°24E **97** E9
Podlapača *Croatia* 44°37N 15°47E **93** D12
Podlaskie □ *Poland* 53°10N 23°0E **83** E10
Podoleni *Romania* 46°46N 26°39E **81** D11
Podolínec *Slovak Rep.* 49°16N 20°31E **79** B13
Podolsk *Russia* 55°25N 37°30E **84** E9
Podor *Senegal* 16°40N 15°2W **138** B1
Podporozhye *Russia* 60°55N 34°2E **84** B8
Podu Iloaiei *Romania* 47°13N 27°16E **81** C12
Podu Turcului *Romania* 46°11N 27°25E **81** D12
Podujevo = Besianë *Kosovo* 42°54N 21°10E **96** D5
Podyjí △ *Czech Rep.* 48°51N 15°57E **78** C8
Poel *Germany* 54°0N 11°25E **76** B6
Pofadder *S. Africa* 29°10S 19°22E **144** C2
Poggiardo *Italy* 40°3N 18°23E **95** B11
Poggibonsi *Italy* 43°28N 11°9E **92** E8
Póggio Mirteto *Italy* 42°16N 12°41E **93** F9
Pogoanele *Romania* 44°55N 27°0E **81** F12
Pogorzela *Poland* 51°50N 17°12E **83** G4
Pogradec *Albania* 40°54N 20°37E **96** F4
Pogranichnyy *Russia* 44°25N 131°24E **112** B5
Poh *Indonesia* 0°46S 122°51E **119** E6
Pohang *S. Korea* 36°1N 129°23E **115** F15
Pohjanmaa □ *Finland* 62°58N 22°50E **60** E20
Pohnpei *Micronesia* 6°55N 158°10E **156** G7
Pohorelá *Slovak Rep.* 48°50N 20°2E **79** C13
Pohořelice *Czech Rep.* 48°59N 16°31E **79** C9
Pohorje *Slovenia* 46°30N 15°20E **93** B12
Pohri *India* 25°32N 77°22E **124** G6
Poiana Mare *Romania* 43°57N 23°5E **80** G8
Poiana Ruscăi, Munţii *Romania* 45°45N 22°25E **80** E7
Poiana Stampei *Romania* 47°19N 25°8E **81** C10
Poinsett, C. *Antarctica* 65°42S 113°18E **55** C8
Point Arena *U.S.A.* 38°55N 123°41W **170** G3
Point Baker *U.S.A.* 56°21N 133°37W **162** B2
Point Calimere *India* 10°17N 79°49E **127** J4
Point Fortin *Trin. & Tob.* 10°10N 61°42W **187** K15
Point Hope *U.S.A.* 68°21N 166°47W **166** B6
Point L. *Canada* 65°15N 113°4W **160** D9
Point Lisas *Trin. & Tob.* 10°24N 61°29W **187** K15
Point Pedro *Sri Lanka* 9°50N 80°15E **127** K5
Point Pelee △ *Canada* 41°57N 82°31W **174** E2
Point Pleasant *N.J., U.S.A.* 40°5N 74°4W **175** F10
Point Pleasant *W. Va., U.S.A.* 38°51N 82°8W **173** F12
Point Reyes ⌂ *U.S.A.* 38°10N 122°55W **170** G2
Pointe-à-Pitre *Guadeloupe* 16°15N 61°32W **182** b
Pointe-au-Pic = La Malbaie *Canada* 47°40N 70°10W **165** C5
Pointe-Claire *Canada* 45°26N 73°50W **175** A11
Pointe-Gatineau *Canada* 45°27N 75°41W **175** A9
Pointe-Noire *Congo* 4°48S 11°53E **140** E2
Pointe-Noire *Guadeloupe* 16°14N 61°47W **182** b
Poio = O Convento *Spain* 42°28N 8°41W **88** C2
Poipet *Cambodia* 13°39N 102°33E **120** F4
Poirino *Italy* 44°56N 7°48E **92** D4
Poisonbush Ra. *Australia* 22°30S 121°30E **148** D3
Poissonnier Pt. *Australia* 19°57S 119°10E **148** C2
Poitiers *France* 46°35N 0°20E **70** F7
Poitou *France* 46°40N 0°10W **72** B3
Poitou-Charentes □ *France* 46°10N 0°15E **72** B4
Poix-de-Picardie *France* 49°47N 1°58E **71** C8
Poix-Terron *France* 49°38N 4°38E **71** C11
Pojoaque *U.S.A.* 35°54N 106°1W **169** J10
Pokaran *India* 27°0N 71°50E **124** F4
Pokataroo *Australia* 29°30S 148°36E **151** D4
Pokhara *Nepal* 28°14N 83°58E **125** E10
Pokhvistnevo *Russia* 53°36N 52°0E **86** D11
Poko *Dem. Rep. of the Congo* 3°7N 26°52E **142** B2
Pokrov *Russia* 55°55N 39°7E **84** E10
Pokrovka = Kyzyl-Suu *Kyrgyzstan* 42°20N 78°0E **109** D9
Pokrovsk *Russia* 61°29N 129°0E **107** C13
Pokrovskoye *Russia* 47°25N 38°54E **85** J10
Pol-e Dokhtar *Iran* 33°9N 47°42E **105** F12
Pol-e Zahāb *Iran* 34°27N 45°51E **105** E11
Pola = Pula *Croatia* 44°54N 13°57E **93** D10
Pola *Russia* 57°55N 32°0E **84** D7
Pola de Allande *Spain* 43°16N 6°37W **88** B4
Pola de Lena *Spain* 43°10N 5°49W **88** B5
Pola de Siero *Spain* 43°24N 5°39W **88** B5
Pola de Somiedo *Spain* 43°5N 6°15W **88** B4
Polacca *U.S.A.* 35°50N 110°23W **169** J8
Polan *Iran* 25°30N 61°10E **129** E9
Pol'ana *Slovak Rep.* 48°38N 19°29E **79** C12
Poland *U.S.A.* 43°13N 75°3W **175** C9
Poland ■ *Europe* 52°0N 20°0E **83** G3
Polanica-Zdrój *Poland* 50°24N 16°32E **83** H3
Polaniec *Poland* 50°26N 21°17E **83** H8
Polanów *Poland* 54°7N 16°41E **82** D3
Polar Bear ⌂ *Canada* 55°0N 83°45W **164** A2
Polatlı *Turkey* 39°36N 32°9E **104** C5
Polatsk *Belarus* 55°30N 28°50E **84** E5
Polavaram *India* 17°15N 81°38E **126** F5
Polcura *Chile* 37°17S 71°43W **190** D1
Połczyn-Zdrój *Poland* 53°47N 16°5E **82** E3
Poldasht *Iran* 39°20N 45°4E **105** C11
Poleski △ *Poland* 51°29N 23°5E **83** G10
Polessk *Russia* 54°50N 21°8E **82** D8
Polesye = Pripet Marshes *Europe* 52°10N 27°10E **75** B15
Polgar *Hungary* 47°54N 21°6E **80** C6
Poli *Cameroon* 8°34N 13°15E **139** C7
Policastro, G. di *Italy* 40°0N 15°35E **95** C8
Police *Poland* 53°33N 14°33E **82** E1
Police, Pte. *Seychelles* 4°51S 55°32E **141** b
Polichnitos *Greece* 39°6N 26°10E **99** B8
Polička *Czech Rep.* 49°43N 16°15E **79** B9
Policoro *Italy* 40°13N 16°41E **95** B9
Poliegos *Greece* 36°45N 24°38E **98** E6
Poligiros *Greece* 40°23N 23°25E **96** F7
Polignano a Mare *Italy* 41°0N 17°13E **95** A9
Poligny *France* 46°50N 5°42E **71** F12
Polillo Is. *Phil.* 14°56N 122°0E **119** B6
Polis *Cyprus* 35°2N 32°26E **101** D11
Polistena *Italy* 38°24N 16°4E **95** D9
Polk *U.S.A.* 41°22N 79°56W **174** E5
Polkowice *Poland* 51°29N 16°3E **83** G3
Polla *Italy* 40°31N 15°29E **95** B8
Pollachi *India* 10°35N 77°0E **127** J3
Pollença *Spain* 39°54N 3°1E **100** B10
Pollença, B. de *Spain* 39°53N 3°8E **100** B10
Póllica *Italy* 40°11N 15°3E **95** B8
Pollino, Mte. *Italy* 39°55N 16°11E **95** C9
Pollino △ *Italy* 40°0N 16°12E **95** C9
Polna *Russia* 58°31N 28°5E **84** C5
Polnovat *Russia* 63°50N 65°54E **106** C7
Pology *Ukraine* 47°29N 36°15E **85** J9
Polokwane *S. Africa* 23°54S 29°25E **145** B4
Polokwane → *S. Africa* 22°25S 30°5E **145** B5
Polonnaruwa *Sri Lanka* 7°56N 81°0E **127** L5
Polonne *Ukraine* 50°6N 27°30E **75** C14
Polonnoye = Polonne *Ukraine* 50°6N 27°30E **75** C14
Polski Trŭmbesh *Bulgaria* 43°20N 25°38E **97** C9
Polsko Kosovo *Bulgaria* 43°23N 25°38E **97** C9
Polson *U.S.A.* 47°41N 114°9W **168** C6
Poltár *Slovak Rep.* 48°26N 19°48E **79** C12

Poltava *Ukraine* 49°35N 34°35E 85 H8
Poltava □ *Ukraine* 50°15N 33°15E 85 G7
Põltsamaa *Estonia* 58°39N 25°58E 84 C3
Polunochnoye *Russia* 60°52N 60°25E 106 C7
Polur *India* 12°32N 79°11E 127 H4
Põlva *Estonia* 58°3N 27°3E 84 C4
Polyana *Ukraine* 48°38N 22°58E 80 B7
Polyarny *Russia* 69°8N 33°20E 60 B25
Polyarnyye Zori *Russia* 67°22N 32°30E 60 C25
Polynesia *Pac. Oc.* 10°0S 162°0W 157 F11
Polynésie française = French Polynesia ☐ *Pac. Oc.* 20°0S 145°0W 157 J13
Pomabamba *Peru* 8°50S 77°28W 188 B2
Pomarance *Italy* 43°18N 10°52E 92 E7
Pombal *Brazil* 6°45S 37°50W 189 B3
Pombal *Portugal* 39°55N 8°40W 88 F2
Pombia *Greece* 35°0N 24°51E 101 E6
Pomene *Mozam.* 22°53S 35°33E 145 B6
Pomeroy *Ohio, U.S.A.* 39°2N 82°2W 173 F12
Pomeroy *Wash., U.S.A.* 46°28N 117°36W 168 C5
Pomézia *Italy* 41°40N 12°30E 94 A5
Pomichna *Ukraine* 48°13N 31°36E 85 H6
Pomona *Australia* 26°22S 152°52E 151 D5
Pomona *U.S.A.* 34°4N 117°45W 171 L9
Pomona Park *U.S.A.* 29°30N 81°36W 179 F8
Pomorie *Bulgaria* 42°32N 27°41E 97 D11
Pomorskie □ *Poland* 54°30N 18°0E 82 D5
Pomorskie, Pojezierze *Poland* 53°40N 16°37E 82 E3
Pomos *Cyprus* 35°9N 32°33E 101 D11
Pomos, C. *Cyprus* 35°10N 32°33E 101 D11
Pompano Beach *U.S.A.* 26°14N 80°7W 179 J9
Pompei *Italy* 40°45N 14°30E 95 B7
Pompey *France* 48°46N 6°6E 71 D13
Pompeys Pillar *U.S.A.* 45°59N 107°57W 168 D10
Pompeys Pillar ⌂ *U.S.A.* 46°0N 108°0W 168 D10
Pompton Lakes *U.S.A.* 41°0N 74°17W 175 F10
Ponape = Pohnpei *Micronesia* 6°55N 158°10E 156 G7
Ponask L. *Canada* 54°0N 92°41W 164 B1
Ponca *U.S.A.* 42°34N 96°43W 172 D5
Ponca City *U.S.A.* 36°42N 97°5W 176 C6
Ponce *Puerto Rico* 18°1N 66°37W 183 d
Ponce de Leon *U.S.A.* 30°44N 85°56W 178 E4
Ponce de Leon B. *U.S.A.* 25°15N 81°10W 179 K8
Ponchatoula *U.S.A.* 30°26N 90°26W 177 F9
Poncheville, L. *Canada* 50°10N 76°55W 164 B4
Pond *U.S.A.* 35°43N 119°20W 171 K7
Pond Inlet *Canada* 72°40N 77°0W 161 C16
Pondicherry = Puducherry *India* 11°59N 79°50E 127 J4
Ponds, I. of *Canada* 53°27N 55°52W 165 B8
Ponferrada *Spain* 42°32N 6°35W 88 C4
Poniatowa *Poland* 51°11N 22°3E 83 G9
Poniec *Poland* 51°48N 16°50E 83 G3
Ponikva *Slovenia* 46°16N 15°26E 93 B12
Ponnaiyar ➝ *India* 11°50N 79°45E 127 J4
Ponnani *India* 10°45N 75°59E 127 J2
Ponneri *India* 13°20N 80°15E 127 H5
Ponnuru *India* 16°5N 80°34E 127 F5
Ponoka *Canada* 52°42N 113°40W 162 C6
Ponorogo *Indonesia* 7°52S 111°27E 119 G14
Pons = Ponts *Spain* 41°55N 1°12E 90 D6
Pons *France* 45°35N 0°34W 72 C3
Ponsul ➝ *Portugal* 39°40N 7°31W 88 F3
Pont-à-Mousson *France* 48°54N 6°1E 71 D13
Pont-Audemer *France* 49°21N 0°30E 70 C7
Pont-Aven *France* 47°51N 3°47W 70 E3
Pont Canavese *Italy* 45°25N 7°36E 92 C4
Pont-d'Ain *France* 46°3N 5°21E 71 F12
Pont-de-Roide *France* 47°23N 6°45E 71 E13
Pont-de-Salars *France* 44°18N 2°44E 72 D6
Pont-de-Vaux *France* 46°26N 4°56E 71 F11
Pont-de-Veyle *France* 46°17N 4°53E 71 F11
Pont-du-Château *France* 45°47N 3°15E 71 G10
Pont du Gard *France* 43°57N 4°32E 73 E8
Pont du Gard *Gard, France* 43°56N 4°32E 73 E8
Pont-l'Abbé *France* 47°52N 4°15W 70 E2
Pont-l'Évêque *France* 49°18N 0°11E 70 C7
Pont-St-Esprit *France* 44°16N 4°40E 73 D8
Pont-St-Martin *Italy* 45°36N 7°48E 92 C4
Pont-Ste-Maxence *France* 49°18N 2°36E 71 C9
Pont-sur-Yonne *France* 48°18N 3°10E 71 D10
Ponta Delgada *Azores* 37°44N 25°40W 134 a
Ponta do Sol *Madeira* 32°42N 17°7W 100 D2
Ponta Grossa *Brazil* 25°7S 50°10W 191 B5
Ponta Porã *Brazil* 22°20S 55°35W 191 A4
Pontacq *France* 43°11N 0°8W 72 E3
Pontailler-sur-Saône *France* 47°13N 5°25E 71 E12
Pontal ➝ *Brazil* 9°8S 40°12W 189 B2
Pontarlier *France* 46°54N 6°20E 71 F13
Pontassieve *Italy* 43°46N 11°26E 93 E8
Pontaumur *France* 45°52N 2°40E 72 C6
Pontcharra *France* 45°26N 6°1E 73 C10
Pontchartrain, L. *U.S.A.* 30°5N 90°5W 177 F9
Pontchâteau *France* 47°25N 2°5W 70 E4
Ponte Alta, Serra do *Brazil* 19°42S 47°40W 189 D1
Ponte Alta do Norte *Brazil* 10°45S 47°34W 189 C1
Ponte da Barca *Portugal* 41°48N 8°25W 88 D2
Ponte de Lima *Portugal* 41°46N 8°35W 88 D2
Ponte de Sor *Portugal* 39°17N 8°1W 89 F2
Ponte dell'Olio *Italy* 44°52N 9°39E 92 D6
Ponte di Legno *Italy* 46°16N 10°31E 92 B7
Ponte do Pungué *Mozam.* 19°30S 34°33E 143 F3
Ponte-Leccia *France* 42°28N 9°13E 73 F13
Ponte nelle Alpi *Italy* 46°11N 12°16E 93 B9
Ponte Nova *Brazil* 20°25S 42°54W 189 E2
Ponte Vedra Beach *U.S.A.* 30°15N 81°23W 178 E8
Ponteareas *Spain* 42°10N 8°28W 88 C2
Pontebba *Italy* 46°30N 13°18E 93 B10
Ponteceso *Spain* 43°15N 8°54W 88 B2
Pontecorvo *Italy* 41°27N 13°40E 94 A6
Pontedeume *Spain* 43°24N 8°10W 88 B2
Ponteix *Canada* 49°46N 107°29W 163 D7
Pontevedra *Spain* 42°26N 8°40W 88 C2
Pontevedra □ *Spain* 42°25N 8°39W 88 C2
Pontevedra, R. de ➝ *Spain* 42°22N 8°45W 88 C2
Pontevico *Italy* 45°16N 10°5E 92 C7
Pontiac *Ill., U.S.A.* 40°53N 88°38W 172 E9
Pontiac *Mich., U.S.A.* 42°38N 83°18W 173 D12
Pontian Kechil *Malaysia* 1°29N 103°23E 121 d
Pontianak *Indonesia* 0°3S 109°15E 118 E3
Pontine Is. = Ponziane, Ísole *Italy* 40°55N 12°57E 94 B5
Pontine Mts. = Kuzey Anadolu Dağları *Turkey* 41°0N 36°45E 104 B7
Pontínia *Italy* 41°25N 13°2E 94 A6
Pontivy *France* 48°5N 2°58W 70 D4
Pontoise *France* 49°3N 2°5E 71 C9
Ponton ➝ *Canada* 58°27N 116°11W 162 B5
Pontorson *France* 48°34N 1°30W 70 D5
Pontrémoli *Italy* 44°22N 9°53E 92 D6
Pontrieux *France* 48°42N 3°10W 70 D3
Ponts *Spain* 41°55N 1°12E 90 D6
Pontypool *Canada* 44°6N 78°38W 174 B6
Pontypool *U.K.* 51°42N 3°2W 67 F4
Ponza *Italy* 40°54N 12°58E 94 B5
Ponziane, Ísole *Italy* 40°55N 12°57E 94 B5
Poochera *Australia* 32°43S 134°51E 151 E1
Poole *U.K.* 50°43N 1°59W 67 G6
Poole □ *U.K.* 50°43N 1°59W 67 G6
Pooler *U.S.A.* 32°7N 81°15W 178 C8
Poona = Pune *India* 18°29N 73°57E 126 E1
Poonamallee *India* 13°3N 80°10E 127 H5
Pooncarie *Australia* 33°22S 142°31E 152 B5
Poopelloe L. *Australia* 31°40S 144°0E 152 A6
Poopó *Bolivia* 18°23S 66°59W 188 D4
Poopó, L. de *Bolivia* 18°30S 67°35W 188 D4
Poor Knights Is. *N.Z.* 35°29S 174°43E 154 B3
Popayán *Colombia* 2°27N 76°36W 186 C3
Poperinge *Belgium* 50°51N 2°42E 69 D2
Popiltah L. *Australia* 33°10S 141°42E 152 B4
Popina *Bulgaria* 44°7N 26°57E 97 B10
Popio L. *Australia* 33°10S 141°52E 152 B4
Poplar *U.S.A.* 48°7N 105°12W 168 B11
Poplar ➝ *Canada* 53°0N 97°19W 163 C9
Poplar Bluff *U.S.A.* 36°46N 90°24W 172 G8
Poplarville *U.S.A.* 30°51N 89°32W 177 F10
Popocatépetl, Volcán *Mexico* 19°2N 98°38W 181 D5
Popokabaka *Dem. Rep. of the Congo* 5°41S 16°40E 140 F3
Pópoli *Italy* 42°10N 13°50E 93 F10
Popovača *Croatia* 45°30N 16°41E 93 C13
Popovo *Bulgaria* 43°21N 26°18E 97 C10
Poppberg *Germany* 49°26N 11°37E 77 F7
Poppi *Italy* 43°43N 11°46E 93 E8
Poprad *Slovak Rep.* 49°3N 20°18E 79 B13
Poprad ➝ *Slovak Rep.* 49°38N 20°42E 79 B13
Porali ➝ *Pakistan* 25°58N 66°26E 124 G2
Porangaba *Brazil* 8°48S 70°36W 188 B3
Porangahau *N.Z.* 40°17S 176°37E 154 G5
Porbandar *India* 21°44N 69°43E 124 J3
Porcher I. *Canada* 53°50N 130°30W 162 C2
Porcos ➝ *Brazil* 12°42S 45°7W 189 C1
Porcuna *Spain* 37°52N 4°11W 89 H6
Porcupine ➝ *Canada* 59°11N 104°46W 163 B8
Porcupine ➝ *U.S.A.* 66°34N 145°19W 160 D2
Porcupine Abyssal Plain *Atl. Oc.* 48°0N 8°0W 56 B10
Porcupine Gorge △ *Australia* 20°22S 144°26E 150 C3
Pordenone *Italy* 45°57N 12°39E 93 C9
Pordim *Bulgaria* 43°23N 24°51E 97 C8
Poreč *Croatia* 45°14N 13°36E 93 C10
Poretskoye *Russia* 55°9N 46°21E 86 C8
Pori *Finland* 61°29N 21°48E 84 B1
Pori *Greece* 35°58N 23°13E 98 F5
Porkhov *Russia* 57°45N 29°38E 84 D5
Porlamar *Venezuela* 10°57N 63°51W 186 A6
Porlezza *Italy* 46°2N 9°7E 92 B6
Porma ➝ *Spain* 42°49N 5°28W 88 C5
Pormpuraaw *Australia* 14°59S 141°26E 150 A3
Pormpuraaw ✿ *Australia* 14°55S 141°47E 150 A3
Pornic *France* 47°7N 2°5W 70 E4
Poronaysk *Russia* 49°13N 143°0E 111 B17
Poros *Greece* 37°30N 23°30E 98 D5
Poroshiri-Dake *Japan* 42°41N 142°52E 112 C11
Poroszló *Hungary* 47°39N 20°40E 80 C5
Poroto Mts. *Tanzania* 9°0S 33°30E 143 D3
Porpoise B. *Antarctica* 66°0S 127°0E 55 C9
Porquerolles, Î. de *France* 43°0N 6°13E 73 F10
Porrentruy *Switz.* 47°25N 7°6E 77 H3
Porreres *Spain* 39°31N 3°2E 100 B10
Porsangerfjorden *Norway* 70°40N 25°40E 60 A21
Porsgrunn *Norway* 59°10N 9°40E 61 G13
Port Adelaide *Australia* 34°50S 138°30E 152 C3
Port Alberni *Canada* 49°14N 124°50W 162 D4
Port Albert *Australia* 38°42S 146°42E 153 E7
Port Alfred *S. Africa* 33°36S 26°55E 144 D4
Port Alice *Canada* 50°20N 127°25W 162 C3
Port Allegany *U.S.A.* 41°48N 78°17W 174 E6
Port Allen *U.S.A.* 30°27N 91°12W 176 F9
Port Alma *Australia* 23°38S 150°53E 150 C5
Port Alma *Canada* 42°10N 82°14W 174 D2
Port Angeles *U.S.A.* 48°7N 123°27W 170 B3
Port Antonio *Jamaica* 18°10N 76°26W 182 a
Port Aransas *U.S.A.* 27°50N 97°4W 176 H6
Port Arthur *Australia* 43°7S 147°50E 151 G4
Port Arthur *U.S.A.* 29°54N 93°56W 176 G8
Port au Choix *Canada* 50°43N 57°22W 165 B8
Port au Port B. *Canada* 48°40N 58°50W 165 C8
Port-au-Prince *Haiti* 18°40N 72°20W 183 C5
Port Augusta *Australia* 32°30S 137°50E 152 B2
Port Austin *U.S.A.* 44°3N 83°1W 174 B2
Port-aux-Français *Kerguelen* 49°21S 70°13E 146 J6
Port Blair *India* 11°40N 92°45E 127 J11
Port Blandford *Canada* 48°20N 54°10W 165 C9
Port-Bouët *Ivory C.* 5°16N 3°57W 138 D4
Port Bradshaw *Australia* 12°30S 137°20E 150 A2
Port Broughton *Australia* 33°37S 137°56E 152 B2
Port Bruce *Canada* 42°39N 81°0W 174 D4
Port Burwell *Canada* 42°40N 80°48W 174 D4
Port Campbell *Australia* 38°37S 143°1E 152 E5
Port Campbell *India* 11°56N 92°37E 127 J11
Port Campbell △ *Australia* 38°8S 143°6E 152 E5
Port Canning *India* 22°23N 88°40E 125 H13
Port Carling *Canada* 45°7N 79°35W 174 A5
Port-Cartier *Canada* 50°2N 66°50W 165 B6
Port Chalmers *N.Z.* 45°49S 170°30E 155 F5
Port Charles *N.Z.* 36°33S 175°30E 154 C4
Port Charlotte *U.S.A.* 26°59N 82°6W 179 J7
Port Chester *U.S.A.* 41°0N 73°40W 175 F11
Port Clements *Canada* 53°40N 132°10W 162 C2
Port Clinton *U.S.A.* 41°31N 82°56W 173 E12
Port Colborne *Canada* 42°50N 79°10W 174 D5
Port Coquitlam *Canada* 49°15N 122°45W 170 A4
Port Cornwallis *India* 13°17N 93°5E 127 H11
Port Credit *Canada* 43°33N 79°35W 174 C5
Port-Cros △ *France* 43°0N 6°24E 73 F10
Port Curtis *Australia* 23°57S 151°20E 150 C5
Port d'Alcúdia *Spain* 39°50N 3°7E 100 B10
Port Dalhousie *Canada* 43°13N 79°16W 174 C5
Port d'Andratx *Spain* 39°32N 2°23E 100 B9
Port Darwin *Australia* 12°24S 130°45E 148 B5
Port Darwin *Falk. Is.* 51°50S 59°0W 192 D5
Port Davey *Australia* 43°16S 145°55E 151 G4
Port-de-Bouc *France* 43°24N 4°59E 73 E8
Port-de-Paix *Haiti* 19°50N 72°50W 183 C5
Port de Pollença *Spain* 39°54N 3°4E 100 B10
Port de Sóller *Spain* 39°48N 2°42E 100 B9
Port Dickson *Malaysia* 2°30N 101°49E 121 L3
Port Douglas *Australia* 16°30S 145°30E 150 B4
Port Dover *Canada* 42°47N 80°12W 174 D4
Port Edward *Canada* 54°12N 130°10W 162 C2
Port Elgin *Canada* 44°25N 81°25W 174 B3
Port Elizabeth *S. Africa* 33°58S 25°40E 144 D4
Port Ellen *U.K.* 55°38N 6°11W 65 F2
Port Elliot *Australia* 35°32S 138°41E 152 C3
Port-en-Bessin-Huppain *France* 49°21N 0°45W 70 C6
Port Erin *I. of Man* 54°5N 4°45W 66 C3
Port Essington *Australia* 11°15S 132°10E 148 B5
Port Ewen *U.S.A.* 41°54N 73°59W 175 E11
Port Fairy *Australia* 38°22S 142°12E 152 E5
Port Fitzroy *N.Z.* 36°8S 175°20E 154 C4
Port Fouâd = Bûr Fuad *Egypt* 31°15N 32°20E 137 E8
Port Gamble *U.S.A.* 47°51N 122°34W 170 C4
Port-Gentil *Gabon* 0°40S 8°50E 140 E1
Port Germein *Australia* 33°1S 138°1E 151 E2
Port Ghalib *Egypt* 25°20N 34°50E 128 E2
Port Gibson *U.S.A.* 31°58N 90°59W 176 F9
Port Glasgow *U.K.* 55°56N 4°41W 65 F4
Port Harcourt *Nigeria* 4°40N 7°10E 139 E6
Port Hardy *Canada* 50°41N 127°30W 162 C3
Port Harrison = Inukjuak *Canada* 58°25N 78°15W 161 F16
Port Hawkesbury *Canada* 45°36N 61°22W 165 C7
Port Hedland *Australia* 20°25S 118°35E 148 D2
Port Henry *U.S.A.* 44°3N 73°28W 175 B11
Port Hood *Canada* 46°0N 61°32W 165 C7
Port Hope *Canada* 43°56N 78°20W 174 C6
Port Hope *U.S.A.* 43°57N 82°43W 174 C2
Port Hope Simpson *Canada* 52°33N 56°18W 165 B8
Port Hueneme *U.S.A.* 34°7N 119°12W 171 L7
Port Huron *U.S.A.* 42°58N 82°26W 174 D2
Port Iliç *Azerbaijan* 38°53N 48°47E 105 C13
Port Jefferson *U.S.A.* 40°57N 73°3W 175 F11
Port Jervis *U.S.A.* 41°22N 74°41W 175 E10
Port-Joinville *France* 46°45N 2°23W 70 F4
Port Katon *Russia* 46°52N 38°46E 85 J10
Port Kembla *Australia* 34°52S 150°49E 153 C9
Port Kenny *Australia* 33°10S 134°41E 151 E1
Port-la-Nouvelle *France* 43°1N 3°3E 72 E7
Port Láirge = Waterford *Ireland* 52°15N 7°8W 64 D4
Port Lavaca *U.S.A.* 28°37N 96°38W 176 G6
Port Leyden *U.S.A.* 43°35N 75°21W 175 C9
Port Lincoln *Australia* 34°42S 135°52E 152 C1
Port Loko *S. Leone* 8°48N 12°46W 138 D2
Port Louis *France* 47°42N 3°22W 70 E3
Port-Louis *Guadeloupe* 16°28N 61°32W 182 b
Port Louis *Mauritius* 20°10S 57°30E 141 d
Port MacDonnell *Australia* 38°5S 140°48E 152 E4
Port McNeill *Canada* 50°35N 127°6W 162 C3
Port Macquarie *Australia* 31°25S 152°25E 153 A10
Port Maria *Jamaica* 18°22N 76°54W 182 a
Port Mathurin *Rodrigues* 19°41S 63°25E 146 F5
Port Matilda *U.S.A.* 40°48N 78°3W 174 F6
Port Mayaca *U.S.A.* 26°59N 80°36W 179 J9
Port McNicoll *Canada* 44°44N 79°48W 174 B5
Port Mellon *Canada* 49°32N 123°31W 162 D4
Port-Menier *Canada* 49°51N 64°15W 165 C7
Port Moody *Canada* 49°17N 122°51W 170 A4
Port Morant *Jamaica* 17°54N 76°19W 182 a
Port Moresby *Papua N. G.* 9°24S 147°8E 147 B7
Port Musgrave *Australia* 11°55S 141°50E 150 A3
Port-Navalo *France* 47°34N 2°54W 70 E4
Port Neches *U.S.A.* 30°0N 93°59W 176 G8
Port Nicholson *N.Z.* 41°20S 174°52E 154 H3
Port Nolloth *S. Africa* 29°17S 16°52E 144 C2
Port Nouveau-Québec = Kangiqsualujjuaq *Canada* 58°30N 65°59W 161 F18
Port of Climax *Canada* 49°10N 108°20W 163 D7
Port of Coronach *Canada* 49°7N 105°31W 163 D7
Port of Spain *Trin. & Tob.* 10°40N 61°31W 183 D7
Port Orange *U.S.A.* 29°9N 80°59W 179 F9
Port Orchard *U.S.A.* 47°32N 122°38W 170 C4
Port Orford *U.S.A.* 42°45N 124°30W 168 E1
Port Pegasus *N.Z.* 47°12S 167°41E 155 H2
Port Perry *Canada* 44°6N 78°56W 174 B6
Port Phillip B. *Australia* 38°10S 144°50E 153 E6
Port Pirie *Australia* 33°10S 138°1E 152 B3
Port Renfrew *Canada* 48°30N 124°20W 170 B2
Port Roper *Australia* 14°45S 135°25E 150 A2
Port Rowan *Canada* 42°40N 80°30W 174 D4
Port Royal Sd. *U.S.A.* 32°15N 80°40W 178 C9
Port Safaga = Bûr Safâga *Egypt* 26°43N 33°57E 128 E2
Port Said = Bûr Sa'îd *Egypt* 31°16N 32°18E 137 E8
Port St. Joe *U.S.A.* 29°49N 85°18W 178 F4
Port St. John *U.S.A.* 28°29N 80°47W 179 G9
Port St. Johns = Umzimvubu *S. Africa* 31°38S 29°33E 145 D4
Port-St-Louis-du-Rhône *France* 43°23N 4°49E 73 E8
Port St. Lucie *U.S.A.* 27°18N 80°21W 179 H9
Port-Ste-Marie *France* 44°15N 0°25E 72 D4
Port Salerno *U.S.A.* 27°9N 80°12W 179 H9
Port Sanilac *U.S.A.* 43°26N 82°33W 174 C2
Port Severn *Canada* 44°48N 79°43W 174 B5
Port Shepstone *S. Africa* 30°44S 30°28E 145 D5
Port Simpson *Canada* 54°30N 130°20W 162 C2
Port Stanley = Stanley *Falk. Is.* 51°40S 59°51W 192 D5
Port Stanley *Canada* 42°40N 81°10W 174 D3
Port Sudan = Bûr Sûdân *Sudan* 19°32N 37°9E 137 D4
Port Sulphur *U.S.A.* 29°29N 89°42W 177 G10
Port-sur-Saône *France* 47°42N 6°2E 71 E13
Port Talbot *U.K.* 51°35N 3°47W 67 F4
Port Taufiq = Bûr Taufiq *Egypt* 29°54N 32°32E 137 F8
Port Townsend *U.S.A.* 48°7N 122°45W 170 B4
Port-Vendres *France* 42°32N 3°8E 72 F7
Port Victoria *Australia* 34°30S 137°29E 152 C2
Port Vila *Vanuatu* 17°45S 168°18E 147 C9
Port Vladimir *Russia* 69°25N 33°6E 60 B25
Port Wakefield *Australia* 34°12S 138°10E 152 C3
Port Washington *U.S.A.* 43°23N 87°53W 172 D10
Port Wentworth *U.S.A.* 32°9N 81°10W 178 C8
Porta Orientalis *Romania* 45°6N 22°18E 75 F12
Portacloy *Ireland* 54°20N 9°46W 64 B2
Portadown *U.K.* 54°25N 6°27W 64 B5
Portaferry *U.K.* 54°23N 5°33W 64 B6
Portage *Pa., U.S.A.* 40°23N 78°41W 174 F6
Portage *Wis., U.S.A.* 43°33N 89°28W 172 D9
Portage la Prairie *Canada* 49°58N 98°18W 163 D9
Portageville *U.S.A.* 36°26N 89°42W 172 G9
Portal *U.S.A.* 32°33N 81°56W 178 C8
Portalegre *Portugal* 39°19N 7°25W 89 F3
Portalegre □ *Portugal* 39°20N 7°40W 89 F3
Portales *U.S.A.* 34°11N 103°20W 169 J12
Portarlington *Ireland* 53°9N 7°14W 64 C4
Portbou *Spain* 42°25N 3°9E 90 C8
Porteirinha *Brazil* 15°44S 43°2W 189 D2
Portel *Portugal* 38°19N 7°41W 89 G3
Portela, Lisboa ✈ (LIS) *Portugal* 38°46N 9°8W 89 G1
Porter L. *N.W.T., Canada* 61°41N 108°5W 163 A7
Porter L. *Sask., Canada* 56°20N 107°20W 163 B7
Porterville *S. Africa* 33°0S 19°0E 144 D2
Porterville *U.S.A.* 36°4N 119°1W 170 J8
Portes-lès-Valence *France* 44°52N 4°54E 73 D8
Porth Tywyn = Burry Port *U.K.* 51°41N 4°15W 67 F3
Porthcawl *U.K.* 51°29N 3°42W 67 F4
Porthill *U.S.A.* 48°59N 116°30W 168 B5
Porthmadog *U.K.* 52°55N 4°8W 66 E3
Portile de Fier *Europe* 44°44N 22°30E 80 F7
Portimão *Portugal* 37°8N 8°32W 89 H2
Portishead *U.K.* 51°29N 2°46W 67 F5
Portiţei, Gura *Romania* 44°41N 29°0E 81 F14
Portknockie *U.K.* 57°42N 2°51W 65 D6
Portland *N.S.W., Australia* 33°20S 150°0E 153 B9
Portland *Vic., Australia* 38°20S 141°35E 152 E4
Portland *Canada* 44°42N 76°12W 175 B8
Portland *Conn., U.S.A.* 41°34N 72°38W 175 E12
Portland *Fla., U.S.A.* 30°31N 86°12W 178 E3
Portland *Maine, U.S.A.* 43°39N 70°16W 173 D18
Portland *Mich., U.S.A.* 42°52N 84°54W 173 D11
Portland *Oreg., U.S.A.* 45°32N 122°37W 170 E4
Portland *Pa., U.S.A.* 40°55N 75°6W 175 F9
Portland *Tex., U.S.A.* 27°53N 97°20W 176 H6
Portland, I. of *U.K.* 50°33N 2°26W 67 G5
Portland B. *Australia* 38°15S 141°45E 152 E4
Portland Bight *Jamaica* 17°52N 77°5W 182 a
Portland Bill *U.K.* 50°31N 2°28W 67 G5
Portland Canal *U.S.A.* 55°56N 130°0W 162 B2
Portland I. *N.Z.* 39°20S 177°51E 154 F6
Portland Int. ✈ (PDX) *U.S.A.* 45°35N 122°36W 170 E4
Portland Pt. *Jamaica* 17°42N 77°11W 182 a
Portlaoise *Ireland* 53°2N 7°18W 64 C4
Portmadoc = Porthmadog *U.K.* 52°55N 4°8W 66 E3
Portmore *Jamaica* 17°53N 76°53W 182 a
Porto *Brazil* 3°54S 42°42W 189 A2
Porto *France* 42°16N 8°42E 73 F12
Porto *Portugal* 41°8N 8°40W 88 D2
Porto □ *Portugal* 41°8N 8°20W 88 D2
Porto, G. de *France* 42°17N 8°34E 73 F12
Porto Acre *Brazil* 9°34S 67°31W 188 B4
Pôrto Alegre *Brazil* 30°5S 51°10W 191 C5
Porto Azzurro *Italy* 42°46N 10°24E 92 F7
Porto Cervo *Italy* 41°8N 9°33E 94 A2
Porto Colom *Spain* 39°26N 3°15E 100 B10
Porto Cristo *Spain* 39°33N 3°20E 100 B10
Pôrto da Fôlha *Brazil* 9°55S 37°17W 189 B3
Porto de Moz *Brazil* 1°41S 52°13W 187 D8
Porto de Pedras *Brazil* 9°10S 35°17W 189 B3
Porto Empédocle *Italy* 37°17N 13°32E 94 E6
Porto Esperança *Brazil* 19°37S 57°29W 186 G7
Porto Franco *Brazil* 6°20S 47°24W 189 B1
Porto Inglês *C. Verde Is.* 15°21N 23°10W 134 b
Porto Mendes *Brazil* 24°30S 54°15W 191 A5
Porto Moniz *Madeira* 32°52N 17°11W 100 D2
Porto Murtinho *Brazil* 21°45S 57°55W 186 H7
Porto Nacional *Brazil* 10°40S 48°30W 189 C1
Porto-Novo *Benin* 6°23N 2°42E 139 D5
Porto Primavera, Represa *Brazil* 22°10S 52°45W 191 A5
Porto San Giórgio *Italy* 43°11N 13°48E 93 E10
Porto Sant' Elpídio *Italy* 43°15N 13°43E 93 E10
Porto Santo, I. de *Madeira* 33°45N 16°25W 134 B2
Porto Santo Stéfano *Italy* 42°26N 11°7E 92 F8
Porto São José *Brazil* 22°43S 53°10W 191 A5
Porto Seguro *Brazil* 16°26S 39°5W 189 D3
Porto Tolle *Italy* 44°56N 12°22E 93 D9
Porto Tórres *Italy* 40°50N 8°24E 94 B1
Pôrto União *Brazil* 26°10S 51°10W 191 B5
Porto-Vecchio *France* 41°35N 9°16E 73 G13
Porto Velho *Brazil* 8°46S 63°54W 186 E6
Porto Viro *Italy* 45°1N 12°13E 93 C9
Porto Walter *Brazil* 8°15S 72°40W 188 B3
Portobelo *Panama* 9°35N 79°42W 182 E4
Portoferráio *Italy* 42°48N 10°20E 92 F7
Portofino *Italy* 44°18N 9°12E 92 D6
Portogruaro *Italy* 45°47N 12°50E 93 C9
Portola *U.S.A.* 39°49N 120°28W 170 F6
Portomaggiore *Italy* 44°42N 11°48E 93 D8
Portopetro *Spain* 39°22N 3°13E 100 B10
Portoscuso *Italy* 39°12N 8°24E 94 C1
Portovénere *Italy* 44°3N 9°51E 92 D6
Portoviejo *Ecuador* 1°7S 80°28W 186 D2
Portpatrick *U.K.* 54°51N 5°7W 65 G3
Portree *U.K.* 57°25N 6°12W 65 D2
Portrush *U.K.* 55°12N 6°40W 64 A5
Portsmouth *Dominica* 15°34N 61°27W 183 C7
Portsmouth *U.K.* 50°48N 1°6W 67 G6
Portsmouth *N.H., U.S.A.* 43°5N 70°45W 175 C14
Portsmouth *Ohio, U.S.A.* 38°44N 82°57W 173 F12
Portsmouth *R.I., U.S.A.* 41°36N 71°15W 175 E13
Portsmouth *Va., U.S.A.* 36°58N 76°23W 173 G15
Portsmouth □ *U.K.* 50°48N 1°6W 67 G6
Portsoy *U.K.* 57°41N 2°41W 65 D6
Portstewart *U.K.* 55°11N 6°43W 64 A5
Porttipahdan tekojärvi *Finland* 68°5N 26°40E 60 B22
Portugal ■ *Europe* 40°0N 8°0W 88 F3
Portugalete *Spain* 43°19N 3°4W 90 B1
Portumna *Ireland* 53°6N 8°14W 64 C3
Portville *U.S.A.* 42°3N 78°20W 174 D6
Poruma *Australia* 10°2S 143°4E 150 a
Porvenir *Bolivia* 11°10S 68°50W 188 C4
Porvenir *Chile* 53°10S 70°16W 192 D2
Porvoo *Finland* 60°24N 25°40E 84 B3
Porzuna *Spain* 39°9N 4°9W 89 F6
Posada *Italy* 40°38N 9°43E 94 B2
Posada ➝ *Italy* 40°39N 9°45E 94 B2
Posadas *Argentina* 27°30S 55°50W 191 B4
Posadas *Spain* 37°47N 5°11W 89 H5
Poschiavo *Switz.* 46°19N 10°4E 77 J6
Posets *Spain* 42°39N 0°25E 90 C5
Posht-e Badam *Iran* 33°2N 55°23E 129 C7
Posidium *Greece* 35°30N 27°10E 99 F9
Poso *Indonesia* 1°20S 120°55E 119 E6
Poso, Danau *Indonesia* 1°52S 120°35E 119 E6
Posof *Turkey* 41°30N 42°33E 105 B10
Pospelikha *Russia* 51°57N 81°46E 109 B10
Posse *Brazil* 14°4S 46°18W 189 C1
Possession I. *Antarctica* 72°4S 172°0E 55 D11
Pössneck *Germany* 50°42N 11°35E 76 E7
Possum Kingdom L. *U.S.A.* 32°52N 98°26W 176 E5
Post *U.S.A.* 33°12N 101°23W 176 E4
Post Falls *U.S.A.* 47°43N 116°57W 168 C5
Postavy = Pastavy *Belarus* 55°4N 26°50E 84 E4
Poste-de-la-Baleine = Kuujjuarapik *Canada* 55°20N 77°35W 164 A4
Postmasburg *S. Africa* 28°18S 23°5E 144 C3
Postojna *Slovenia* 45°46N 14°12E 93 C11
Poston *U.S.A.* 34°0N 114°24W 171 M12
Postville *Canada* 54°54N 59°47W 165 B8
Posyet *Russia* 42°39N 130°48E 112 C5
Potamos *Antikythira, Greece* 35°52N 23°15E 98 F5
Potamos *Kythira, Greece* 36°15N 22°58E 98 E4
Potchefstroom *S. Africa* 26°41S 27°7E 144 C4
Potcoava *Romania* 44°30N 24°39E 81 F9
Poté *Brazil* 17°49S 41°49W 189 D2
Poteau *U.S.A.* 35°3N 94°37W 176 D7
Poteet *U.S.A.* 29°2N 98°35W 176 G5
Potenza *Italy* 40°38N 15°48E 95 B8
Potenza ➝ *Italy* 43°25N 13°40E 93 E10
Potenza Picena *Italy* 43°22N 13°37E 93 E10
Poteriteri, L. *N.Z.* 46°5S 167°10E 155 G2
Potgietersrus = Mokopane *S. Africa* 24°10S 28°55E 145 B4
Poti *Georgia* 42°10N 41°38E 87 J5
Potiraguá *Brazil* 15°36S 39°53W 189 D3
Potiskum *Nigeria* 11°39N 11°2E 139 C7
Potlogi *Romania* 44°34N 25°34E 81 F10
Potomac ➝ *U.S.A.* 38°0N 76°23W 173 F14
Potosí *Bolivia* 19°38S 65°50W 186 G5
Potosi Mt. *U.S.A.* 35°57N 115°29W 171 K11
Pototan *Phil.* 10°54N 122°38E 119 B6
Potrerillos *Chile* 26°30S 69°30W 190 B2
Potsdam *Germany* 52°23N 13°3E 76 C9
Potsdam *U.S.A.* 44°40N 74°59W 175 B10
Pottangi *India* 18°34N 82°58E 126 E6
Pottenstein *Germany* 49°46N 11°24E 77 F7
Pottersville *U.S.A.* 43°43N 73°50W 175 C11
Pottstown *U.S.A.* 40°15N 75°39W 175 F9
Pottsville *U.S.A.* 40°41N 76°12W 175 F8
Pottuvil *Sri Lanka* 6°55N 81°50E 127 L5
P'otzu *Taiwan* 23°28N 120°15E 117 F13
Pouancé *France* 47°44N 1°10W 70 E5
Pouce Coupé *Canada* 55°40N 120°10W 162 B4
Poughkeepsie *U.S.A.* 41°42N 73°56W 175 E11
Pouilly-sur-Loire *France* 47°17N 2°57E 71 E9
Poulan *U.S.A.* 31°31N 83°47W 178 D6
Poulaphouca Res. *Ireland* 53°8N 6°30W 64 C5
Poulsbo *U.S.A.* 47°44N 122°38W 170 C4
Poultney *U.S.A.* 43°31N 73°14W 175 C11
Poulton-le-Fylde *U.K.* 53°51N 2°58W 66 D5
Pouso Alegre *Brazil* 22°14S 45°57W 191 A6
Pout *Senegal* 14°45N 17°0W 138 C1
Pouthisat *Cambodia* 12°34N 103°50E 120 F4
Pouytenga *Burkina Faso* 12°15N 0°25W 139 C4
Pouzauges *France* 46°47N 0°50W 70 F6
Považská Bystrica *Slovak Rep.* 49°8N 18°27E 79 B11
Poverty B. *N.Z.* 38°43S 178°2E 154 E7
Povlen *Serbia* 44°9N 19°44E 96 B3
Póvoa de Lanhosa *Portugal* 41°33N 8°15W 88 D2
Póvoa de Santa Iria *Portugal* 38°51N 9°4W 89 G1
Póvoa de Varzim *Portugal* 41°25N 8°46W 88 D2
Povorino *Russia* 51°12N 42°5E 86 E6
Povorotnyy, Mys *Russia* 42°40N 133°2E 112 C6
Povungnituk = Puvirnituq *Canada* 60°2N 77°10W 161 E16
Powassan *Canada* 46°5N 79°25W 164 C4
Poway *U.S.A.* 32°58N 117°2W 171 N9
Powder ➝ *U.S.A.* 46°45N 105°26W 168 C11
Powder River *U.S.A.* 43°2N 106°59W 168 E10
Powder Springs *U.S.A.* 33°52N 84°41W 178 B5
Powell *U.S.A.* 44°45N 108°46W 168 D9
Powell, L. *U.S.A.* 36°57N 111°29W 169 H8
Powell River *Canada* 49°50N 124°35W 162 D4
Powelton *U.S.A.* 33°26N 82°52W 178 B7
Powers *U.S.A.* 45°41N 87°32W 172 C10
Pownal *U.S.A.* 42°45N 73°14W 175 D11
Powys □ *U.K.* 52°20N 3°20W 67 E4
Poyang Hu *China* 29°5N 116°20E 117 C11
Poyarkovo *Russia* 49°36N 128°41E 107 E13
Poysdorf *Austria* 48°40N 16°37E 79 C9
Poza de la Sal *Spain* 42°35N 3°31W 88 C7
Poza Rica *Mexico* 20°33N 97°27W 181 C5
Pozantı *Turkey* 37°25N 34°50E 104 D6
Požarevac *Serbia* 44°35N 21°18E 96 B5
Pozazal, Puerto *Spain* 42°56N 4°10W 88 C6
Požega *Croatia* 45°20N 17°40E 80 E2
Požega *Serbia* 43°53N 20°2E 96 C4
Poznań *Poland* 52°25N 16°55E 83 F3
Poznań ✈ (POZ) *Poland* 52°26N 16°45E 83 F3
Pozo *U.S.A.* 35°20N 120°24W 171 K6
Pozo Alcón *Spain* 37°42N 2°56W 89 H8
Pozo Almonte *Chile* 20°10S 69°50W 188 E4
Pozo Colorado *Paraguay* 23°30S 58°45W 190 A4
Pozoblanco *Spain* 38°23N 4°51W 89 G6
Pozuzo *Peru* 10°5S 75°35W 188 C2
Pozzallo *Italy* 36°43N 14°51E 95 F7
Pozzomaggiore *Italy* 40°24N 8°39E 94 B1
Pozzuoli *Italy* 40°49N 14°7E 95 B7
Pra ➝ *Ghana* 5°1N 1°37W 139 D4
Prabuty *Poland* 53°47N 19°15E 82 E6
Prača *Bos.-H.* 43°47N 18°43E 80 G3
Prachatice *Czech Rep.* 49°1N 14°0E 78 B7
Prachin Buri *Thailand* 14°0N 101°25E 120 F3
Prachuap Khirikhan *Thailand* 11°49N 99°48E 121 G2
Pradelles *France* 44°46N 3°52E 72 D7
Prades *France* 42°38N 2°23E 72 F6
Prado *Brazil* 17°20S 39°13W 189 D3
Prado del Rey *Spain* 36°48N 5°33W 89 J5
Præstø *Denmark* 55°8N 12°2E 63 J6
Pragersko *Slovenia* 46°27N 15°42E 93 B12
Prague = Praha *Czech Rep.* 50°4N 14°25E 78 A7
Praha *Czech Rep.* 50°4N 14°25E 78 A7
Praha ✈ (PRG) *Czech Rep.* 50°6N 14°16E 78 A7
Prahecq *France* 46°19N 0°26W 72 B3
Prahita ➝ *India* 19°0N 79°55E 126 E4
Prahova □ *Romania* 45°10N 26°0E 81 E10
Prahova ➝ *Romania* 44°50N 25°50E 81 F10
Prahovo *Serbia* 44°18N 22°39E 96 B6
Praia *C. Verde Is.* 15°2N 23°34W 134 b
Praia a Mare *Italy* 39°50N 15°45E 95 C8
Praid *Romania* 46°32N 25°10E 81 D10
Prainha *Brazil* 1°45S 53°30W 187 D8
Prainha Nova *Brazil* 7°10S 60°30W 186 E6
Prairie *Australia* 20°50S 144°35E 150 C3
Prairie City *U.S.A.* 44°28N 118°43W 168 D4
Prairie Dog Town Fork Red ➝ *U.S.A.* 34°34N 99°58W 176 D5
Prairie du Chien *U.S.A.* 43°3N 91°9W 172 D8
Prairies, L. of the *Canada* 51°16N 101°32W 163 C8
Pramanda *Greece* 39°32N 21°8E 98 B3
Prambanan △ *Indonesia* 7°45S 110°28E 119 G14
Prampram *Ghana* 5°43N 0°8E 139 D5
Pran Buri *Thailand* 12°23N 99°55E 120 F2
Prang *Ghana* 8°1N 0°56W 139 D4
Prapat *Indonesia* 2°41N 98°58E 118 D1
Praslin *Seychelles* 4°18S 55°45E 141 b
Prasonisi, Akra *Greece* 35°42N 27°46E 101 D9
Praszka *Poland* 51°5N 18°31E 83 G5
Prata *Brazil* 19°25S 48°54W 187 G9
Pratabpur *India* 23°28N 83°15E 125 H10
Pratapgarh *Raj., India* 24°2N 74°40E 124 G6
Pratapgarh *Ut. P., India* 25°56N 81°59E 125 G9
Pratas I. = Dongsha Dao *S. China Sea* 20°45N 116°43E 111 G12
Prato *Italy* 43°53N 11°6E 92 E8
Prátola Peligna *Italy* 42°6N 13°52E 93 F10
Prats-de-Mollo-la-Preste *France* 42°25N 2°27E 72 F6
Pratt *U.S.A.* 37°39N 98°44W 172 G4
Prattville *U.S.A.* 32°28N 86°29W 177 E11
Pravara ➝ *India* 19°35N 74°45E 126 E2
Pravdinsk *Kaliningrad, Russia* 54°27N 21°1E 82 D8
Pravdinsk *Nizhniy Novgorod, Russia* 56°29N 43°28E 86 B6
Pravets *Bulgaria* 42°53N 23°55E 96 D7
Pravia *Spain* 43°30N 6°12W 88 B4
Praya *Indonesia* 8°39S 116°17E 118 F5
Prayag = Allahabad *India* 25°25N 81°58E 125 G9
Pré-en-Pail *France* 48°28N 0°12W 70 D6
Pré-des-Poudres △ *Argentina* 32°10S 60°40W 190 C3
Preah Vihear *Cambodia* 14°23N 104°41E 120 E5
Preble *U.S.A.* 42°44N 76°8W 175 D8
Precipice △ *Australia* 25°18S 150°5E 151 D5
Precordillera *Argentina* 30°0S 69°1W 190 C2
Predáppio *Italy* 44°6N 11°59E 93 D8
Predazzo *Italy* 46°19N 11°36E 93 B8
Predeal *Romania* 45°30N 25°34E 81 E10
Predejane *Serbia* 42°51N 22°9E 96 D6
Preeceville *Canada* 51°57N 102°40W 163 C8
Preetz *Germany* 54°14N 10°18E 76 A6
Pregolya ➝ *Russia* 54°41N 20°22E 82 D7
Pregrada *Croatia* 46°11N 15°45E 93 B12
Preiļi *Latvia* 56°18N 26°43E 84 D4
Preko *Croatia* 44°7N 15°10E 93 D12
Prelog *Croatia* 46°18N 16°32E 93 B13
Premer *Australia* 31°29S 149°56E 153 A8
Prémery *France* 47°10N 3°20E 71 E10
Premià de Mar *Spain* 41°29N 2°22E 90 D7
Premont *U.S.A.* 27°22N 98°7W 176 H5
Premuda *Croatia* 44°20N 14°36E 93 D11
Prentice *U.S.A.* 45°33N 90°17W 172 C8
Prenzlau *Germany* 53°19N 13°50E 76 B9
Preobrazheniye *Russia* 42°54N 133°54E 112 C6
Preparis I. = Pariparit Kyun *Burma* 14°52N 93°41E 127 G11
Preparis North Channel *Ind. Oc.* 15°27N 94°5E 127 G11
Preparis South Channel *Ind. Oc.* 14°33N 93°30E 127 G11
Přerov *Czech Rep.* 49°28N 17°27E 79 B10
Prescott *Canada* 44°45N 75°30W 175 B9
Prescott *Ariz., U.S.A.* 34°33N 112°28W 169 J7
Prescott *Ark., U.S.A.* 33°48N 93°23W 176 E8
Prescott Valley *U.S.A.* 34°40N 112°18W 169 J7
Preservation Inlet *N.Z.* 46°8S 166°35E 155 G1
Preševo *Serbia* 42°19N 21°39E 96 D5
Presho *U.S.A.* 43°54N 100°3W 172 D3
Presicce *Italy* 39°54N 18°16E 95 C11
Presidencia de la Plaza *Argentina* 27°0S 59°50W 190 B4

Presidencia Roque Saenz Peña
Argentina 26°45S 60°30W **190** B3
Presidente Dutra Brazil 5°15S 44°30W **189** B2
Presidente Epitácio
Brazil 21°56S 52°6W **187** H8
Presidente Hayes □
Paraguay 24°0S 59°0W **190** A4
Presidente Prudente
Brazil 22°5S 51°25W **191** A5
Presidente Ríos, L.
Chile 46°28S 74°25W **192** C2
Presidio U.S.A. 29°34N 104°22W **176** G2
Preslav Bulgaria 43°10N 26°52E **97** C10
Preslavska Planina
Bulgaria 43°10N 26°45E **97** C10
Prešov Slovak Rep. 49°0N 21°15E **79** B14
Prešovský □ Slovak Rep. 49°10N 21°0E **79** B13
Prespa, L. = Prespansko Jezero
Macedonia 40°55N 21°0E **96** F5
Prespa △ Greece 40°48N 21°4E **96** F5
Prespansko Jezero
Macedonia 40°55N 21°0E **96** F5
Presque I. U.S.A. 42°10N 80°6W **174** D4
Presque Isle U.S.A. 46°41N 68°1W **173** B19
Prestatyn U.K. 53°20N 3°24W **66** D4
Prestea Ghana 5°22N 2°7W **138** D4
Presteigne U.K. 52°17N 3°0W **67** E5
Přeštice Czech Rep. 49°34N 13°20E **78** B6
Preston Canada 43°23N 80°21W **174** C4
Preston U.K. 53°46N 2°42W **66** D5
Preston Ga., U.S.A. 32°4N 84°32W **178** C5
Preston Idaho, U.S.A. 42°6N 111°53W **168** E8
Preston Minn., U.S.A. 43°40N 92°5W **172** D7
Preston, C. Australia 20°51S 116°12E **148** D2
Prestonsburg U.S.A. 37°40N 82°47W **173** G12
Prestranda Norway 59°6N 9°4E **62** E3
Prestwick U.K. 55°29N 4°37W **65** F4
Prêto → Brazil 11°21S 43°52W **189** C2
Pretoria S. Africa 25°44S 28°12E **145** C4
Preuilly-sur-Claise France 46°51N 0°56E **70** F7
Preveza Greece 38°57N 20°45E **98** C2
Prey Veng Cambodia 11°35N 105°29E **121** G5
Priazovuye Ukraine 46°44N 35°40E **85** J8
Pribaykalsky △
Russia 52°30N 106°0E **107** D11
Pribilof Is. U.S.A. 57°0N 170°0W **166** D6
Priboj Serbia 43°35N 19°32E **96** C3
Příbram Czech Rep. 49°41N 14°2E **78** B7
Price U.S.A. 39°36N 110°49W **168** G8
Price, C. India 13°34N 93°3E **127** H11
Price I. Canada 52°23N 128°41W **162** C3
Prichard U.S.A. 30°44N 88°5W **177** F10
Priego Spain 40°26N 2°21W **90** E2
Priego de Córdoba Spain 37°27N 4°12W **89** H6
Priekule Latvia 56°26N 21°35E **82** B8
Priekule Lithuania 55°33N 21°19E **82** C8
Prielbrusye △ Russia 43°20N 42°37E **87** J6
Prien Germany 47°51N 12°20E **77** H8
Prienai Lithuania 54°38N 23°57E **82** D9
Prieska S. Africa 29°40S 22°42E **144** C3
Priest L. U.S.A. 48°35N 116°52W **168** B5
Priest River U.S.A. 48°11N 116°55W **168** B5
Priest Valley U.S.A. 36°10N 120°39W **170** J6
Prievidza Slovak Rep. 48°46N 18°36E **79** C11
Prignitz Germany 53°6N 11°45E **76** B7
Prijedor Bos.-H. 44°58N 16°41E **93** D13
Prijepolje Serbia 43°27N 19°40E **96** C3
Prikaspiyskaya Nizmennost =
Caspian Depression
Eurasia 47°0N 48°0E **87** G9
Priko Ivory C. 7°40N 3°59W **138** D4
Prikubanskaya Nizmennost =
Russia 45°39N 38°33E **87** H4
Prilep Macedonia 41°21N 21°32E **96** E5
Priluky = Pryluky
Ukraine 50°30N 32°24E **85** G7
Prime Seal I. Australia 40°3S 147°43E **151** G4
Primeira Cruz Brazil 2°30S 43°26W **189** A2
Primo Tapia Mexico 32°16N 116°54W **171** N10
Primorsk Kaliningrad,
Russia 54°44N 20°0E **82** D6
Primorsk St. Petersburg,
Russia 60°22N 28°37E **84** B5
Primorskiy Kray □
Russia 45°0N 135°0E **112** B7
Primorsko Bulgaria 42°15N 27°44E **97** D11
Primorsko-Akhtarsk
Russia 46°2N 38°10E **87** J10
Primrose L. Canada 54°55N 109°45W **163** C7
Prince Albert Canada 53°15N 105°50W **163** C7
Prince Albert S. Africa 33°12S 22°2E **144** D3
Prince Albert △
Canada 54°0N 106°25W **163** C7
Prince Albert Mts.
Antarctica 76°0S 161°30E **55** D11
Prince Albert Pen.
Canada 72°30N 116°0W **160** C8
Prince Albert Sd.
Canada 70°25N 115°0W **160** C9
Prince Alfred, C.
Canada 74°20N 124°40W **54** B1
Prince Charles I.
Canada 67°47N 76°12W **161** D16
Prince Charles Mts.
Antarctica 72°0S 67°0E **55** D6
Prince Edward Fracture Zone
Ind. Oc. 46°0S 35°0E **55** A4
Prince Edward I. □
Canada 46°20N 63°20W **165** C7
Prince Edward Is.
Ind. Oc. 46°35S 38°0E **146** J2
Prince George Canada 53°55N 122°50W **162** C4
Prince of Wales, C.
U.S.A. 65°36N 168°5W **166** B6
Prince of Wales I.
Australia 10°40S 142°10E **150** A3
Prince of Wales I.
Canada 73°0N 99°0W **160** C12
Prince of Wales I.
U.S.A. 55°47N 132°50W **160** F5
Prince of Wales Icefield
Canada 78°15N 79°0W **161** B16
Prince of Wales Str.
Canada 72°0N 118°0W **160** C8
Prince Patrick I. Canada 77°0N 120°0W **161** B8
Prince Regent Inlet
Canada 73°0N 90°0W **161** C14
Prince Rupert Canada 54°20N 130°20W **162** C2
Prince William Sd.
U.S.A. 60°40N 147°0W **160** E2

Princes Town
Trin. & Tob. 10°16N 61°23W **187** K15
Princesa Isabel Brazil 7°44S 38°0W **189** B3
Princess Charlotte B.
Australia 14°25S 144°0E **150** A3
Princess Elizabeth Trough
S. Ocean 64°10S 83°0E **55** C7
Princess May Ranges
Australia 15°30S 125°30E **148** C4
Princess Royal I.
Canada 53°0N 128°40W **162** C3
Princeton Canada 49°27N 120°30W **162** D4
Princeton Calif., U.S.A. 39°24N 122°1W **170** F4
Princeton Ill., U.S.A. 41°23N 89°28W **172** E9
Princeton Ind., U.S.A. 38°21N 87°34W **172** F10
Princeton Ky., U.S.A. 37°7N 87°53W **172** G10
Princeton Mo., U.S.A. 40°24N 93°35W **172** E7
Princeton N.J., U.S.A. 40°21N 74°39W **175** F10
Princeton W. Va.,
U.S.A. 37°22N 81°6W **173** G13
Principe
São Tomé & Príncipe 1°37N 7°25E **132** F4
Príncipe da Beira
Brazil 12°20S 64°30W **186** F6
Prineville U.S.A. 44°18N 120°51W **168** D3
Prins Christian Sund
Greenland 60°4N 43°10W **57** E6
Prins Harald Kyst
Antarctica 70°0S 35°1E **55** D4
Prins Karls Forland
Svalbard 78°30N 11°0E **57** B12
Prinsesse Astrid Kyst
Antarctica 70°45S 12°30E **55** D3
Prinsesse Ragnhild Kyst
Antarctica 70°15S 27°30E **55** D4
Prinzapolca Nic. 13°20N 83°35W **182** D3
Prior, C. Spain 43°34N 8°17W **88** B2
Priozersk Russia 61°2N 30°7E **84** B6
Pripet = Prypyat →
Europe 51°20N 30°15E **75** C16
Pripet Marshes Europe 52°10N 27°10E **75** B15
Pripyat Marshes = Pripet Marshes
Europe 52°10N 27°10E **75** B15
Pripyats = Prypyat →
Europe 51°20N 30°15E **75** C16
Prishtinë Kosovo 42°40N 21°13E **96** D5
Prislop, Pasul Romania 47°37N 24°48E **81** C9
Pristen Russia 51°15N 36°44E **85** G9
Priština = Prishtinë
Kosovo 42°40N 21°13E **96** D5
Pritzwalk Germany 53°9N 12°10E **76** B7
Privas France 44°45N 4°37E **73** D8
Priverno Italy 41°28N 13°11E **94** A6
Privolzhsk Russia 57°23N 41°16E **86** B5
Privolzhskaya Vozvyshennost
Russia 51°0N 46°0E **86** E7
Privolzhskiy Russia 51°25N 46°3E **86** E8
Privolzhskiy □ Russia 56°0N 50°0E **106** D6
Privolzhye Russia 52°52N 48°33E **86** D9
Priyutnoye Russia 46°12N 43°57E **87** G6
Prizren Kosovo 42°13N 20°45E **96** D4
Prizzi Italy 37°43N 13°26E **94** E6
Prnjavor Bos.-H. 44°59N 17°43E **80** F2
Probolinggo Indonesia 7°46S 113°13E **119** G15
Prochowice Poland 51°17N 16°20E **83** G3
Proctor U.S.A. 43°40N 73°2W **175** C11
Proddatur India 14°45N 78°30E **127** G4
Prodhromos Cyprus 34°57N 32°50E **101** E11
Proença-a-Nova Portugal 39°45N 7°54W **88** F3
Profilia Greece 36°5N 27°51E **101** C9
Profondeville Belgium 50°23N 4°52E **69** D4
Progreso Coahuila,
Mexico 27°28N 100°59W **180** B4
Progreso Yucatán,
Mexico 21°20N 89°40W **181** C7
Progress Antarctica 22°25S 76°22E **55** C12
Progress Russia 49°45N 129°37E **107** E13
Prokhladnyy Russia 43°50N 44°2E **87** J7
Prokhorovka Russia 51°2N 36°44E **86** E3
Prokletije Albania 42°30N 19°45E **96** D4
Prokopyevsk Russia 54°0N 86°45E **109** B11
Prokuplje Serbia 43°16N 21°36E **96** C5
Proletarsk Russia 46°42N 41°50E **87** G5
Prome Burma 18°49N 95°13E **123** K19
Prophet → Canada 58°48N 122°40W **162** B4
Prophet River Canada 58°6N 122°43W **162** B4
Propriá Brazil 10°13S 36°51W **189** D4
Propriano France 41°41N 8°52E **73** G12
Proserpine Australia 20°21S 148°36E **150** b
Prosna → Poland 52°6N 17°44E **83** F4
Prospect U.S.A. 43°18N 75°9W **175** C9
Prosperity U.S.A. 30°51N 85°56W **178** E4
Prosser U.S.A. 46°12N 119°46W **168** C4
Prostějov Czech Rep. 49°17N 17°9E **79** B10
Prostki Poland 53°42N 22°25E **82** E9
Proston Canada 26°8S 151°32E **151** D5
Proszowice Poland 50°13N 20°16E **83** H7
Proti Greece 37°5N 21°32E **98** D3
Provadiya Bulgaria 43°12N 27°30E **97** C11
Provadiyska =
Bulgaria 43°12N 27°42E **97** C11
Provence France 43°40N 5°46E **73** E9
Provence-Alpes-Côte d'Azur □
France 44°0N 6°15E **73** D10
Providence Ky.,
U.S.A. 37°24N 87°46W **172** G10
Providence R.I.,
U.S.A. 41°49N 71°24W **175** E13
Providence, C. N.Z. 45°59S 166°29E **155** F1
Providence Bay
Canada 45°41N 82°15W **164** C3
Providence Mts.
U.S.A. 35°10N 115°15W **171** K11
Providencia, I. de
Colombia 13°25N 81°26W **182** D3
Provideniya Russia 64°23N 173°18W **107** C19
Provincetown U.S.A. 42°3N 70°11W **173** D18
Provins France 48°33N 3°15E **71** D10
Provo U.S.A. 40°14N 111°39W **168** F8
Provost Canada 52°25N 110°20W **163** C6
Prozor Bos.-H. 43°50N 17°34E **80** G2
Prrenjas Albania 41°4N 20°32E **96** E4
Prudhoe Bay U.S.A. 70°18N 148°22W **166** A10
Prudhoe I. Australia 21°19S 149°41E **150** C4
Prud'homme Canada 52°20N 105°54W **163** C7
Prudnik Poland 50°20N 17°38E **83** H4
Prüm Germany 50°12N 6°25E **77** E2
Prundu Romania 44°6N 26°14E **81** F11
Prundu Bârgăului
Romania 47°13N 24°54E **81** C9
Pruszcz Gdański Poland 54°17N 18°40E **82** D5

Pruszków Poland 52°9N 20°49E **83** F7
Prut → Romania 45°28N 28°10E **81** E13
Pruzhany Belarus 52°33N 24°28E **75** B13
Prvić Croatia 44°55N 14°47E **93** D11
Prydz B. Antarctica 69°0S 74°0E **55** C6
Pryluky Ukraine 50°30N 32°24E **85** G7
Prymorske Ukraine 46°48N 36°20E **85** J9
Pryor U.S.A. 36°19N 95°19W **176** C7
Prypyat → Europe 51°20N 30°15E **75** C16
Prypyatsky △ Belarus 52°0N 28°0E **75** C14
Przasnysz Poland 53°2N 20°54E **83** E7
Przedbórz Poland 51°6N 19°53E **83** G6
Przedecz Poland 52°20N 18°53E **83** F5
Przemyśl Poland 49°50N 22°45E **83** J9
Przeworsk Poland 50°6N 22°32E **83** H9
Przewóz Poland 51°28N 14°57E **83** G1
Przhevalsk = Karakol
Kyrgyzstan 42°30N 78°20E **109** D9
Przysucha Poland 51°22N 20°38E **83** G7
Psachna Greece 38°34N 23°35E **98** C5
Psara Greece 38°37N 25°38E **99** C7
Psathoura Greece 39°30N 24°12E **98** B6
Pserimos Greece 36°56N 27°8E **99** E9
Psiloritis, Oros Greece 35°15N 24°45E **101** D6
Psira Greece 35°12N 25°52E **101** D7
Pskov Russia 57°50N 28°25E **84** D5
Pskov Russia 57°20N 29°0E **84** D5
Pskovskoye, Ozero
Russia 58°0N 27°58E **84** D5
Psol → Ukraine 49°10N 33°37E **85** H7
Psunj Croatia 45°25N 17°19E **80** E2
Pteleos Greece 39°3N 22°57E **98** B4
Ptich = Ptsich →
Belarus 52°9N 28°52E **75** B15
Ptichia = Vidos Greece 39°38N 19°55E **101** A3
Ptolemaida Greece 40°30N 21°43E **96** F5
Ptsich → Belarus 52°9N 28°52E **75** B15
Ptuj Slovenia 46°28N 15°50E **93** B12
Ptujska Gora Slovenia 46°23N 15°47E **93** B12
Pu Xian China 36°24N 111°6E **114** F6
Pua Thailand 19°11N 100°55E **120** C3
Puán Argentina 37°30S 62°45W **190** D3
Pu'an China 25°46N 104°57E **116** E5
Pubei China 22°16N 109°31E **116** F7
Pucallpa Peru 8°25S 74°30W **188** E3
Pucará Cajamarca, Peru 6°0S 79°7W **188** B2
Pucará Puno, Peru 15°5S 70°24W **188** D3
Pucarani Bolivia 16°23S 68°30W **188** D4
Pucheng China 27°59N 118°31E **117** D12
Pucheni Romania 45°12N 25°17E **81** E10
Puchheim Germany 48°9N 11°21E **77** G7
Puch'on = Bucheon
S. Korea 37°28N 126°45E **115** F14
Púchov Slovak Rep. 49°8N 18°20E **79** B11
Pucioasa Romania 45°5N 25°25E **81** E10
Pučišća Croatia 43°22N 16°43E **93** E13
Puck Poland 54°45N 18°23E **82** D5
Pucka, Zatoka Poland 54°30N 18°40E **82** D5
Pudasjärvi Finland 65°23N 26°53E **60** D22
Puding China 26°18N 105°44E **116** D5
Pudozh Russia 61°48N 36°32E **84** B9
Pudu = Suizhou China 31°42N 113°24E **117** B9
Pudukkottai India 10°28N 78°47E **127** J4
Puebla Mexico 19°3N 98°12W **181** D5
Puebla Mexico 18°50N 98°0W **181** D5
Puebla de Alcocer Spain 38°59N 5°14W **89** G5
Puebla de Don Fadrique
Spain 37°58N 2°25W **91** H2
Puebla de Don Rodrigo
Spain 39°5N 4°37W **89** F6
Puebla de Guzmán Spain 37°37N 7°15W **89** H3
Puebla de la Calzada
Spain 38°54N 6°37W **89** G4
Puebla de Sanabria Spain 42°4N 6°38W **88** C4
Puebla de Trives = Pobra de
Trives Spain 42°20N 7°10W **88** C3
Pueblo U.S.A. 38°16N 104°37W **168** G11
Pueblo Hundido Chile 26°20S 69°30W **190** B2
Puelches Argentina 38°5S 65°51W **190** D2
Puelén Argentina 37°32S 67°38W **190** D2
Puente Alto Chile 33°32S 70°35W **190** C1
Puente-Genil Spain 37°22N 4°47W **89** H6
Puente la Reina Spain 42°40N 1°49W **90** C2
Puente San Miguel Spain 43°21N 4°5W **88** B6
Puenteareas = Ponteareas
Spain 42°10N 8°28W **88** C2
Puentedeume = Pontedeume
Spain 43°24N 8°10W **88** B2
Puentes de García Rodríguez = As
Pontes de García Rodríguez
Spain 43°27N 7°50W **88** B3
Puer China 23°0N 101°15E **116** F3
Puerca, Pta. Puerto Rico 18°13N 65°36W **183** d
Puerco → U.S.A. 34°22N 107°50W **169** J10
Puerto Acosta Bolivia 15°32S 69°15W **188** D4
Puerto Aisén Chile 45°27S 73°0W **192** C2
Puerto Ángel Mexico 15°40N 96°29W **181** D5
Puerto Arista Mexico 15°56N 93°48W **181** D6
Puerto Armuelles
Panama 8°20N 82°51W **182** E3
Puerto Ayacucho
Venezuela 5°40N 67°35W **186** B5
Puerto Barrios
Guatemala 15°40N 88°32W **182** C2
Puerto Bermejo
Argentina 26°55S 58°34W **190** B4
Puerto Bermúdez Peru 10°20S 74°58W **188** C3
Puerto Bolívar Ecuador 3°19S 79°55W **186** D3
Puerto Cabello
Venezuela 10°28N 68°1W **186** A5
Puerto Cabezas Nic. 14°0N 83°30W **182** D3
Puerto Cabo Gracias á Dios
Nic. 15°0N 83°10W **182** D3
Puerto Carreño
Colombia 6°12N 67°22W **186** B5
Puerto Castilla Honduras 16°0N 86°0W **182** C2
Puerto Chicama Peru 7°45S 79°20W **188** B2
Puerto Cisnes Chile 44°45S 72°42W **192** C2
Puerto Coig Argentina 50°54S 69°15W **192** D3
Puerto Cortés Honduras 15°51N 88°0W **182** C2
Puerto Cumarebo
Venezuela 11°29N 69°30W **186** A5
Puerto de Alcudia = Port
d'Alcúdia Spain 39°50N 3°7E **100** B10
Puerto de Cabrera Spain 39°8N 2°56E **100** B9
Puerto de Gran Tarajal
Canary Is. 28°13N 14°1W **100** F5
Puerto de la Cruz
Canary Is. 28°24N 16°32W **100** F3

Puerto de los Angeles △
Mexico 23°39N 105°45W **180** C3
Puerto de Mazarrón
Spain 37°34N 1°15W **91** H3
Puerto de Pozo Negro
Canary Is. 28°19N 13°55W **100** F6
Puerto de Sóller = Port de Sóller
Spain 39°48N 2°42E **100** B9
Puerto de Somosierra
Spain 41°9N 3°35W **88** D7
Puerto del Carmen
Canary Is. 28°55N 13°38W **100** F6
Puerto del Rosario
Canary Is. 28°30N 13°52W **100** F6
Puerto Deseado
Argentina 47°55S 66°0W **192** C3
Puerto Escondido
Mexico 15°50N 97°3W **181** D5
Puerto Heath Bolivia 12°34S 68°39W **188** C4
Puerto Inca Peru 9°22S 74°54W **188** B3
Puerto Inírida Colombia 3°53N 67°52W **186** C5
Puerto Juárez Mexico 21°11N 86°49W **181** C7
Puerto La Cruz
Venezuela 10°13N 64°38W **186** A6
Puerto Leguízamo
Colombia 0°12S 74°46W **186** D4
Puerto Lempira
Honduras 15°16N 83°46W **182** C3
Puerto Libertad
Mexico 29°55N 112°43W **180** B2
Puerto Limón Colombia 3°23N 73°30W **186** C4
Puerto Lobos Argentina 42°0S 65°3W **192** B3
Puerto Lumbreras Spain 37°34N 1°48W **91** H3
Puerto Madryn
Argentina 42°48S 65°4W **192** B3
Puerto Maldonado
Peru 12°30S 69°10W **188** C4
Puerto Manatí Cuba 21°22N 76°50W **182** B4
Puerto Montt Chile 41°28S 73°0W **192** B2
Puerto Morazán Nic. 12°51N 87°11W **182** D2
Puerto Morelos Mexico 20°50N 86°52W **181** C7
Puerto Natales Chile 51°45S 72°15W **192** D2
Puerto Oscuro Chile 31°24S 71°35W **190** C1
Puerto Padre Cuba 21°13N 76°35W **182** B4
Puerto Páez Venezuela 6°13N 67°28W **186** B5
Puerto Peñasco
Mexico 31°20N 113°33W **180** A2
Puerto Pinasco
Paraguay 22°36S 57°50W **190** A4
Puerto Pirámides
Argentina 42°35S 64°20W **192** B4
Puerto Plata Dom. Rep. 19°48N 70°45W **183** C5
Puerto Pollensa = Port de
Pollença Spain 39°54N 3°4E **100** B10
Puerto Portillo Peru 9°55S 72°42W **188** B3
Puerto Princesa Phil. 9°46N 118°45E **119** C5
Puerto Quepos Costa Rica 9°29N 84°6W **182** E3
Puerto Real Spain 36°33N 6°12W **89** J4
Puerto Rico Bolivia 11°55S 67°38W **188** C4
Puerto Rico Canary Is. 27°47N 15°42W **100** G4
Puerto Rico  ☑ W. Indies 18°15N 66°45W **183** d
Puerto Rico Trench
Atl. Oc. 19°50N 66°0W **183** C6
Puerto Saavedra Chile 38°47S 73°24W **192** A2
Puerto San Julián
Argentina 49°15S 67°45W **192** C3
Puerto Santa Cruz
Argentina 50°0S 68°32W **192** D3
Puerto Sastre Paraguay 22°2S 57°55W **190** A4
Puerto Serrano Spain 36°56N 5°33W **89** J5
Puerto Suárez Bolivia 18°58S 57°52W **188** G7
Puerto Vallarta
Mexico 20°37N 105°15W **180** C3
Puerto Varas Chile 41°19S 72°59W **192** B2
Puerto Wilches
Colombia 7°21N 73°54W **186** B4
Puerto Williams Chile 54°56S 67°37W **192** D3
Puertollano Spain 38°43N 4°7W **89** G6
Pueu Tahiti 17°44S 149°13W **155** b
Pueyrredón, L.
Argentina 47°20S 72°0W **192** C2
Puffin I. Ireland 51°50N 10°24W **64** E1
Pugachev Russia 52°0N 48°49E **86** D9
Pugal India 28°30N 72°48E **124** E5
Puge Tanzania 4°45S 33°11E **142** C3
Puget Sound U.S.A. 47°50N 122°30W **168** C2
Puget-Théniers France 43°58N 6°53E **73** E10
Púglia □ Italy 41°0N 16°30E **95** A9
Pugödong N. Korea 42°5N 130°0E **115** C16
Pugu Tanzania 6°55S 39°4E **142** D4
Pǔgünzī Iran 25°49N 59°10E **128** E8
Puha N.Z. 38°30S 177°50E **154** E6
Pui Romania 45°30N 23°4E **81** E8
Puica Peru 15°0S 72°33W **188** D3
Puigcerdà Spain 42°24N 1°50E **90** C6
Puigmal Spain 42°23N 2°7E **90** C7
Puigpunyent Spain 39°38N 2°32E **100** B9
Puisaye, Collines de la
France 47°37N 3°20E **71** E10
Puiseaux France 48°11N 2°30E **71** D9
Pujehun S. Leone 7°35N 11°45W **138** D2
Pujiang China 29°29N 119°54E **117** C12
Pujols France 44°48N 0°22W **72** D3
Pujon-ho N. Korea 40°35N 127°35E **115** D14
Puka Tahiti 17°4S 149°13W **155** b
Pukaki, L. N.Z. 44°4S 170°1E **155** E5
Pukapuka Cook Is. 10°53S 165°49W **157** J11
Pukaskwa △ Canada 48°20N 86°0W **164** C2
Pukchin N. Korea 40°12N 125°45E **115** D13
Pukch'ǒng N. Korea 40°14N 128°10E **115** D15
Pukë Albania 42°2N 19°53E **96** D4
Pukearuhe N.Z. 38°55S 174°31E **154** E6
Pukekohe N.Z. 37°12S 174°55E **154** B5
Pukeketaki Ra. N.Z. 42°58S 172°13E **155** C7
Pukeuri Ra. N. 45°4S 171°2E **155** F6
Pukeuri N.Z. 45°4S 171°2E **155** F6
Pukhrayan India 26°14N 79°51E **125** F8
Puksubaek-san
N. Korea 40°42N 127°45E **115** D14
Pula Croatia 44°54N 13°57E **93** D10
Pula Italy 39°0N 9°0E **94** C1
Pulacayo Bolivia 20°25S 66°41W **188** E4
Pulandian China 39°25N 121°58E **115** E11
Pulaski N.Y., U.S.A. 43°34N 76°8W **175** C8
Pulaski Tenn., U.S.A. 35°12N 87°2W **177** D11

Putumayo → S. Amer. 3°7S 67°58W **186** D5
Putuo China 29°56N 122°20E **117** C14
Putussibau Indonesia 0°50N 112°56E **118** D4
Pututahi N.Z. 38°39S 177°53E **154** E6
Puvirnituq Canada 60°2N 77°10W **161** E16
Puy-de-Dôme France 45°46N 2°57E **72** C6
Puy-de-Dôme □ France 45°40N 3°0E **72** C6
Puy-l'Évêque France 44°31N 1°9E **72** D5
Puyallup U.S.A. 47°12N 122°18W **170** C4
Puyang China 35°40N 115°1E **114** G8
Puyehue Chile 40°40S 72°37W **192** B2
Puyehue △ Chile 40°27S 72°6W **192** B2
Puylaurens France 43°35N 2°0E **72** E5
Puysegur Pt. N.Z. 46°9S 166°37E **155** G1
Pūzeh Rīg Iran 27°20N 58°40E **129** E8
Puzhayevo Ukraine 48°7N 29°50E **81** B14
Pwani □ Tanzania 7°0S 39°0E **142** D4
Pweto
Dem. Rep. of the Congo 8°25S 28°51E **143** D2
Pwllheli U.K. 52°53N 4°25W **66** C3
Pyana → Russia 55°43N 46°1E **86** C8
Pyaozero, Ozero Russia 66°5N 30°58E **60** C24
Pyapon Burma 16°20N 95°40E **123** L19
Pyasina → Russia 73°30N 87°0E **107** B9
Pyatigorsk Russia 44°2N 43°6E **87** H6
Pyatykhatky Ukraine 48°28N 33°38E **85** H7
Pyay = Prome Burma 18°49N 95°13E **123** K19
Pydna Greece 40°20N 22°34E **96** F6
Pye = Prome Burma 18°49N 95°13E **123** K19
Pyeongtaek S. Korea 37°1N 127°4E **115** F14
Pyetrikaw Belarus 52°11N 28°29E **75** B15
Pyhäjoki → Finland 64°28N 24°14E **60** D21
Pyhätunturi △ Finland 66°58N 27°5E **60** C22
Pyin-Oo-Lwin = Maymyo
Burma 22°2N 96°28E **120** A1
Pyinmana Burma 19°45N 96°12E **123** K20
Pyla, C. Cyprus 34°56N 33°51E **101** E12
Pymatuning Res.
U.S.A. 41°30N 80°28W **174** E4
Pyŏktong N. Korea 40°50N 125°50E **115** D13
Pyǒnggang N. Korea 38°24N 127°17E **115** E14
P'yǒngsong N. Korea 39°14N 125°52E **115** E13
P'yǒngyang N. Korea 39°0N 125°30E **115** E13
Pyote U.S.A. 31°32N 103°8W **176** F3
Pyramid L. U.S.A. 40°1N 119°35W **168** F4
Pyramid Pk. U.S.A. 36°25N 116°37W **171** J10
Pyramids Egypt 29°58N 31°9E **137** F7
Pyrénées △ France 42°45N 0°18E **72** F3
Pyrénées-Atlantiques □
France 43°10N 0°50W **72** E3
Pyrénées-Orientales □
France 42°35N 2°26E **72** F6
Pyrzyce Poland 53°10N 14°55E **83** E1
Pyskowice Poland 50°24N 18°38E **83** H5
Pytalovo Russia 57°5N 27°55E **84** D4
Pyu Burma 18°30N 96°28E **123** K20
Pyzdry Poland 52°11N 17°42E **83** F4

Q

Qaanaaq Greenland 77°30N 69°10W **57** B4
Qaasuitsup □ Greenland 74°0N 52°0W **57** C5
Qabâla Azerbaijan 40°58N 47°47E **87** K8
Qabanbay Kazakhstan 45°50N 80°37E **109** C10
Qabirri → Azerbaijan 41°3N 46°17E **87** K8
Qachasnek S. Africa 30°6S 28°42E **145** D4
Qādisiyah, Buhayrat al
Iraq 34°20N 42°12E **105** E10
Qa'el Jafr Jordan 30°20N 36°25E **130** E5
Qa'emābād Iran 31°44N 60°2E **129** D9
Qā'emshahr Iran 36°30N 52°53E **129** B7
Qagan Nur Jilin,
China 45°15N 124°18E **115** B13
Qagan Nur Nei Monggol Zizhiqu,
China 38°30N 114°55E **114** C8
Qahar Youyi Zhongqi
China 41°12N 112°40E **114** D7
Qahremānshahr = Kermānshāh
Iran 34°23N 47°0E **105** E12
Qaidam Pendi China 37°0N 95°0E **110** D8
Qaiyara Iraq 35°48N 43°17E **105** E10
Qajarīyeh Iran 31°1N 48°22E **129** D6
Qala, Ras il Malta 36°2N 14°20E **101** C1
Qala-i-Jadid = Spīn Būldak
Afghan. 31°1N 66°25E **124** D2
Qala Point = Qala, Ras il
Malta 36°2N 14°20E **101** C1
Qala Viala Pakistan 30°49N 67°17E **124** D2
Qala Yangi Afghan. 34°20N 66°30E **124** B2
Qalaikhum = Kalaikhum
Tajikistan 38°28N 70°46E **109** F8
Qal'at al Akhḍar
Si. Arabia 28°0N 37°10E **128** E3
Qal'at Bīshah Si. Arabia 20°0N 42°30E **128** D3
Qal'at Dīzah Iraq 36°11N 45°7E **105** D11
Qal'at Ṣāliḥ Iraq 31°31N 47°16E **128** D5
Qal'at Sukkar Iraq 31°51N 46°5E **105** G12
Qal'eh-ye Now Afghan. 35°0N 63°5E **108** H4
Qalyūb Egypt 30°12N 31°11E **137** E7
Qamani'tuaq = Baker Lake
Canada 64°20N 96°3W **160** E11
Qamdo China 31°15N 97°6E **116** B1
Qamea Fiji 16°45S 179°45W **154** a
Qamruddin Karez
Pakistan 31°45N 68°20E **124** D3
Qandahār = Kandahār
Afghan. 31°32N 65°43E **122** D4
Qandahār □ = Kandahār □
Afghan. 31°0N 65°0E **122** D4
Qandyagash
Kazakhstan 49°28N 57°25E **108** C5
Qapan Iran 37°40N 55°47E **129** B7
Qapqal China 43°38N 81°5E **109** D10
Qapshaghay
Kazakhstan 43°51N 77°14E **109** D9
Qapshaghay Bögeni
Kazakhstan 43°58N 77°0E **109** D9
Qaqortoq Greenland 60°43N 46°0W **57** E6
Qâra Egypt 29°38N 26°30E **137** C8
Qara Dāgh Iraq 35°18N 45°18E **105** E11
Qara Qash → China 35°0N 78°30E **125** D8
Qarabalyq Kazakhstan 53°30N 62°0E **108** A4
Qarabutaq Kazakhstan 50°0N 60°14E **108** C6
Qaracala Azerbaijan 39°42N 48°48E **129** B6
Qaraçuxur Azerbaijan 40°25N 50°1E **87** K10
Qaraghandy
Kazakhstan 49°50N 73°10E **109** C8

Qaraghayly Kazakhstan 49°26N 76°0E 106 E8
Qārah Si. Arabia 29°55N 40°3E 128 D4
Qarah Āghāj Iran 37°8N 46°58E 105 D12
Qarakol Uzbekistan 39°32N 63°50E 108 E6
Qaraoba Kazakhstan 47°6N 56°15E 108 C5
Qaraqiya Oyssy
  Kazakhstan 43°27N 51°45E 108 D4
Qaraqosh Iran 36°16N 43°22E 105 D10
Qarataū Ongtüstik Qazaqstan,
  Kazakhstan 43°30N 69°30E 109 D7
Qarataū Zhambyl,
  Kazakhstan 43°10N 70°28E 109 D8
Qarazhal Kazakhstan 48°2N 70°49E 106 E8
Qarchak Iran 35°25N 51°34E 129 C6
Qardho Somalia 9°30N 49°6E 131 F4
Qareh → Iran 39°25N 47°22E 105 C12
Qareh Tekān Iran 36°38N 49°29E 129 B6
Qarnein U.A.E. 24°56N 52°52E 129 E7
Qarokūl = Karakul, Ozero
  Tajikistan 39°5N 73°25E 109 E8
Qarqan He → China 39°30N 88°30E 109 E11
Qarqaraly Kazakhstan 49°26N 75°30E 109 C9
Qarshi Uzbekistan 38°53N 65°48E 109 C7
Qartabā Lebanon 34°4N 35°50E 130 A4
Qārūh Kuwait 28°49N 48°46E 129 D6
Qaryat al Gharab Iraq 31°27N 44°48E 128 D5
Qaryat al 'Ulyā
  Si. Arabia 27°33N 47°42E 128 E5
Qarynzharyq Oyssy
  Kazakhstan 42°55N 54°25E 108 D4
Qashqadaryo □
  Uzbekistan 38°35N 66°0E 109 E7
Qasigiannguit
  Greenland 68°50N 51°18W 57 D5
Qaşr 'Amra Jordan 31°48N 36°35E 128 D3
Qaşr-e Qand Iran 26°15N 60°45E 129 E9
Qaşr-e Shīrīn Iran 34°31N 45°35E 105 E11
Qasr Farāfra Egypt 27°0N 28°1E 137 B2
Qasuittuq = Resolute
  Canada 74°42N 94°54W 161 C13
Qatanā Syria 33°26N 36°4E 130 B5
Qatar ■ Asia 25°30N 51°15E 129 E6
Qatlīsh Iran 37°50N 57°19E 129 B8
Qattâra Egypt 30°12N 27°3E 137 A2
Qattâra, Munkhafed el
  Egypt 29°30N 27°30E 137 B2
Qattâra Depression = Qattâra,
  Munkhafed el Egypt 29°30N 27°30E 137 B2
Qawām al Ḥamzah = Al Ḥamzah
  Iraq 31°43N 44°58E 128 D5
Qāyen Iran 33°40N 59°10E 129 C8
Qaynar Kazakhstan 49°12N 77°22E 109 C9
Qazaly Kazakhstan 45°45N 62°6E 108 C6
Qazaqstan = Kazakhstan ■
  Asia 50°0N 70°0E 109 C8
Qazaqtyng Usaqshogylyghy
  Kazakhstan 50°0N 72°0E 109 C8
Qazax Azerbaijan 41°5N 45°21E 87 K7
Qazimämmäd Azerbaijan 40°3N 49°0E 87 K9
Qazvīn Iran 36°15N 50°0E 129 B6
Qazvīn □ Iran 36°20N 50°0E 129 B6
Qazyghurt Kazakhstan 41°45N 69°23E 109 D7
Qena Egypt 26°10N 32°43E 137 B3
Qena, W. → Egypt 26°12N 32°44E 137 B3
Qeqertarsuaq Qaasuitsup,
  Greenland 69°45N 53°30W 57 D5
Qeqertarsuaq Qaasuitsup,
  Greenland 69°15N 53°38W 57 D5
Qeqertarsuatsiaat
  Greenland 63°5N 50°45W 57 E5
Qeqqata □ Greenland 66°30N 48°0W 57 D6
Qeshlāq Iran 34°55N 46°28E 105 E12
Qeshm Iran 26°55N 56°10E 129 E8
Qeydār Iran 36°6N 48°35E 105 D13
Qeys Iran 26°32N 53°58E 129 E7
Qezel Owzen → Iran 36°45N 49°22E 129 B6
Qezi'ot Israel 30°52N 34°26E 130 E3
Qi Xian China 34°40N 114°48E 114 G8
Qian Gorlos China 45°5N 124°42E 115 B13
Qian Hai China 22°32N 113°54E 111 a
Qian Xian China 34°31N 108°15E 114 G5
Qian'an China 40°0N 118°41E 115 E10
Qiancheng China 27°12N 109°50E 116 D7
Qianjiang Guangxi Zhuangzu,
  China 23°38N 108°58E 116 F7
Qianjiang Hubei, China 30°24N 112°55E 117 B9
Qianjiang Sichuan,
  China 29°33N 108°47E 116 C7
Qianjin China 47°34N 133°4E 111 B15
Qianshan Anhui,
  China 30°37N 116°35E 117 B11
Qianshan Guangdong,
  China 22°15N 113°31E 111 a
Qianwei China 29°13N 103°56E 116 C4
Qianxi China 27°3N 106°3E 116 D6
Qianyang Hunan,
  China 27°18N 110°10E 117 D8
Qianyang Shaanxi,
  China 34°40N 107°8E 114 G4
Qianyang Zhejiang,
  China 30°11N 119°25E 117 B12
Qi'ao China 22°25N 113°39E 111 a
Qi'ao Dao China 22°25N 113°38E 111 a
Qiaocun China 39°56N 112°55E 114 E7
Qiaojia China 26°56N 102°58E 116 D4
Qichun China 30°18N 115°25E 117 B10
Qidong Hunan, China 26°49N 112°7E 117 D9
Qidong Jiangsu, China 31°48N 121°38E 117 B13
Qiemo China 38°8N 85°32E 108 C3
Qijiang China 28°57N 106°35E 116 C6
Qijiaojing China 43°28N 91°36E 109 D12
Qikiqtarjuaq Canada 67°33N 63°0W 161 D19
Qila Saifullāh Pakistan 30°45N 68°17E 124 D3
Qilian Shan China 38°30N 96°0E 110 D8
Qimen China 29°50N 117°42E 117 C11
Qin He → China 35°1N 113°22E 114 G7
Qin Jiang → Guangxi Zhuangzu,
  China 21°53N 108°35E 116 F7
Qin Jiang → Jiangxi,
  China 26°15N 115°55E 117 D10
Qin Ling = Qinling Shandi
  China 33°50N 108°10E 114 H5
Qing Xian China 38°35N 116°45E 114 E9
Qingcheng China 37°15N 117°40E 115 F9
Qingcheng Shan
  China 30°58N 103°31E 116 B4
Qingchuan China 32°36N 105°9E 114 H3
Qingdao China 36°5N 120°20E 115 F11
Qingfeng China 35°52N 115°8E 114 G8
Qinghai □ China 36°0N 98°0E 110 D8

Qinghai Hu China 36°40N 100°10E 110 D9
Qinghe China 46°37N 90°25E 109 C12
Qinghecheng China 41°28N 124°15E 115 D13
Qinghemen China 41°48N 121°25E 115 D11
Qingjian China 37°8N 110°8E 114 F6
Qingjiang = Huaiyin
  China 33°30N 119°2E 115 H10
Qingliu China 26°11N 116°48E 117 D11
Qinglong China 25°49N 105°12E 116 E5
Qingping China 26°39N 107°47E 116 D6
Qingshui China 34°48N 106°8E 114 G4
Qingshuihe China 39°55N 111°35E 114 E6
Qingtian China 28°12N 120°15E 117 C13
Qingtongxia China 38°2N 106°3E 114 E4
Qingtongxia Shuiku
  China 37°50N 105°58E 114 F3
Qingxi China 27°8N 108°43E 116 D7
Qingxu China 37°34N 112°22E 114 F7
Qingyang Anhui,
  China 30°38N 117°50E 117 B11
Qingyang Gansu, China 36°2N 107°55E 114 F4
Qingyi Jiang → China 29°32N 103°44E 116 C4
Qingyuan Guangdong,
  China 23°40N 112°59E 117 F9
Qingyuan Liaoning,
  China 42°10N 124°55E 115 C13
Qingyuan Zhejiang,
  China 27°36N 119°3E 117 D12
Qingyun China 37°45N 117°20E 115 F9
Qingzhen China 26°31N 106°25E 116 D6
Qinhuangdao China 39°56N 119°30E 115 E10
Qinling Shandi China 33°50N 108°10E 114 H5
Qinshui China 35°40N 112°8E 114 G7
Qinyang = Jiyuan
  China 35°7N 112°57E 114 G7
Qinyang China 35°5N 112°56E 114 G7
Qinyuan China 36°29N 112°20E 114 F7
Qinzhou China 21°58N 108°38E 116 G7
Qionghai China 19°15N 110°26E 117 a
Qionglai China 30°25N 103°31E 116 B4
Qionglai Shan China 31°0N 102°30E 116 B4
Qiongshan China 19°51N 110°26E 117 a
Qiongzhou Haixia
  China 20°10N 110°15E 117 a
Qiqihar China 47°26N 124°0E 111 B13
Qira China 37°0N 80°48E 109 E10
Qiraïya, W. → Egypt 30°27N 34°0E 130 E3
Qiryat Ata Israel 32°47N 35°6E 130 C4
Qiryat Gat Israel 31°32N 34°46E 130 D3
Qiryat Mal'akhi Israel 31°44N 34°44E 130 D3
Qiryat Shemona Israel 33°13N 35°35E 130 B4
Qiryat Yam Israel 32°51N 35°4E 130 C4
Qishan China 34°25N 107°38E 114 G4
Qitai China 44°2N 89°35E 109 D11
Qitaihe China 45°48N 130°51E 112 B5
Qiubei China 24°2N 104°12E 116 E5
Qixia China 37°17N 120°52E 115 F11
Qiyang China 26°35N 111°50E 117 D8
Qizilağac Körfäzi
  Azerbaijan 39°9N 49°0E 105 C13
Qobda Kazakhstan 50°55N 54°31E 108 B4
Qods Iran 35°45N 51°15E 129 C6
Qojūr Iran 36°12N 47°55E 128 B5
Qom Iran 34°40N 51°0E 129 C6
Qom □ Iran 34°40N 51°0E 129 C6
Qomolangma Feng = Everest, Mt.
  Nepal 28°5N 86°58E 125 E12
Qomsheh Iran 32°0N 51°55E 129 C6
Qong Muztag China 36°42N 82°22E 109 E10
Qoqek = Tacheng
  China 46°40N 82°58E 109 C10
Qoqon = Qŭqon
  Uzbekistan 40°31N 70°56E 109 D8
Qoraqalpoghistan □
  Uzbekistan 43°0N 58°0E 108 D5
Qorghalzhyn
  Kazakhstan 50°25N 69°11E 109 B7
Qorveh Iran 35°10N 47°48E 105 E12
Qosshaghyl Kazakhstan 46°40N 54°0E 108 C4
Qostanay Kazakhstan 53°10N 63°35E 108 B6
Qotanqaraghay
  Kazakhstan 49°10N 85°36E 109 C11
Qotūr Iran 38°28N 44°25E 105 C11
Qu Jiang → China 30°1N 106°24E 116 B6
Qu Xian China 30°48N 106°58E 116 B6
Quabbin Res. U.S.A. 42°20N 72°20W 175 D12
Quairading Australia 32°0S 117°21E 149 F2
Quakenbrück Germany 52°41N 7°57E 76 C3
Quakertown U.S.A. 40°26N 75°21W 175 F9
Qualicum Beach
  Canada 49°22N 124°26W 162 D4
Quambatook Australia 35°49S 143°34E 152 C5
Quambone Australia 30°57S 147°53E 153 A7
Quamby Australia 20°22S 140°17E 150 C3
Quan Long = Ca Mau
  Vietnam 9°7N 105°8E 121 H5
Quanah U.S.A. 34°18N 99°44W 176 D5
Quandialla Australia 34°1S 147°47E 153 C7
Quang Ngai Vietnam 15°13N 108°58E 120 E7
Quang Tri Vietnam 16°45N 107°13E 120 D6
Quang Yen Vietnam 20°56N 106°52E 116 G6
Quannan China 24°45N 114°33E 117 E10
Quantock Hills U.K. 51°8N 3°10W 67 F4
Quanzhou Fujian,
  China 24°55N 118°34E 117 E12
Quanzhou Guangxi Zhuangzu,
  China 25°57N 111°5E 117 E8
Qu'Appelle →
  Canada 50°33N 103°53W 163 C8
Quaqtaq Canada 60°55N 69°40W 161 E18
Quarai Brazil 30°15N 56°20W 190 C4
Quarré-les-Tombes
  France 47°21N 4°0E 71 E11
Quarteira Portugal 37°4N 8°6W 89 H2
Quartu Sant'Élena Italy 39°15N 9°10E 94 C2
Quartzsite U.S.A. 33°40N 114°13W 171 M12
Quatre Bornes Mauritius 20°15S 57°28E 141 d
Quatsino Sd. Canada 50°25N 127°58E 162 C2
Quba Azerbaijan 41°21N 48°32E 87 K9
Qŭchān Iran 37°10N 58°27E 129 B8
Queanbeyan Australia 35°17S 149°14E 153 C8
Québec Canada 46°52N 71°13W 165 C5
Québec □ Canada 48°0N 74°0W 165 B6
Quebo Guinea-Biss. 11°20N 14°54W 138 C2
Quebrada del Condorito △
  Argentina 31°45S 64°40W 190 C3
Quedlinburg Germany 51°47N 11°8E 76 D7
Queen Alexandra Ra.
  Antarctica 85°0S 170°0E 55 E11

Queen Charlotte B.
  Falk. Is. 51°50S 60°40W 192 D4
Queen Charlotte City
  Canada 53°15N 132°2W 162 C2
Queen Charlotte Is. = Haida Gwaii
  Canada 53°20N 132°10W 162 C2
Queen Charlotte Sd.
  Canada 51°0N 128°0W 162 C3
Queen Charlotte Sd.
  N.Z. 41°10S 174°15E 155 B9
Queen Charlotte Strait
  Canada 50°45N 127°10W 162 C3
Queen Elizabeth △ Uganda 0°0 30°0E 142 C3
Queen Elizabeth Is.
  Canada 76°0N 95°0W 161 B13
Queen Elizabeth Land
  Antarctica 85°0S 60°0W 55 E17
Queen Mary Land
  Antarctica 70°0S 95°0E 55 D7
Queen Maud G.
  Canada 68°15N 102°30W 160 D11
Queen Maud Land = Dronning
  Maud Land Antarctica 72°30S 12°0E 55 D3
Queen Maud Mts.
  Antarctica 86°0S 160°0W 55 E12
Queens Channel
  Australia 15°0S 129°30E 148 C4
Queenscliff Australia 38°16S 144°39E 152 E6
Queensland Australia 34°6N 83°14W 178 D3
Queensland □ Australia 22°0S 142°0E 150 C3
Queenstown Australia 42°4S 145°35E 151 G4
Queenstown N.Z. 45°1S 168°40E 155 F3
Queenstown Singapore 1°18N 103°48E 121 d
Queenstown S. Africa 31°52S 26°52E 144 D4
Queets U.S.A. 47°32N 124°19W 170 C2
Queguay Grande →
  Uruguay 32°9S 58°9W 190 C4
Queimadas Brazil 11°0S 39°38W 189 D3
Quelimane Mozam. 17°53S 36°58E 143 F4
Quellón Chile 43°7S 73°37W 192 B2
Quelpart = Jeju-do
  S. Korea 33°29N 126°34E 115 H14
Queluz Portugal 38°45N 9°14W 89 G1
Quemado N. Mex.,
  U.S.A. 34°20N 108°30W 169 J9
Quemado Tex., U.S.A. 28°56N 100°37W 176 G4
Quemoy = Chinmen
  Taiwan 24°26N 118°19E 117 E12
Quemú-Quemú
  Argentina 36°3S 63°36W 190 D3
Quepem India 15°13N 74°3E 127 G2
Quequén Argentina 38°30S 58°30W 190 D4
Querco Peru 13°50S 74°52W 188 C3
Querétaro Mexico 20°36N 100°23W 180 C4
Querétaro □ Mexico 21°0N 99°55W 180 C5
Querfurt Germany 51°23N 11°37E 76 D7
Quérigut France 42°42N 2°6E 72 F6
Querqueville France 49°40N 1°42W 70 C5
Quesada Spain 37°51N 3°4W 89 H7
Queshan China 32°55N 114°2E 117 A10
Quesnel Canada 53°0N 122°30W 162 C4
Quesnel → Canada 52°58N 122°29W 162 C4
Quesnel L. Canada 52°30N 121°20W 162 C4
Questa U.S.A. 36°42N 105°36W 169 H11
Questembert France 47°40N 2°28W 70 E4
Quetico △ Canada 48°30N 91°45W 164 C1
Quetrequile Argentina 41°33S 69°22W 192 B3
Quetta Pakistan 30°15N 66°55E 124 D2
Quezaltenango
  Guatemala 14°50N 91°30W 182 D1
Quéulat △ Chile 44°29S 72°24W 192 B2
Queyras → France 44°45N 6°50E 73 D10
Quezon City Phil. 14°37N 121°2E 119 B6
Qufār Si. Arabia 27°26N 41°37E 128 E4
Qufu China 35°36N 116°58E 114 G9
Qui Nhon Vietnam 13°40N 109°13E 120 F7
Quibala Angola 10°46S 14°59E 140 G2
Quibaxe Angola 8°24S 14°27E 140 F2
Quibdó Colombia 5°42N 76°40W 186 B3
Quiberon France 47°29N 3°9W 70 E3
Quiberon, Presqu'île de
  France 47°30N 3°8W 70 E3
Quickborn Germany 53°42N 9°52E 76 B5
Quiet L. Canada 61°5N 133°5W 162 A2
Quiindy Paraguay 25°58S 57°14W 190 B4
Quilá Mexico 24°23N 107°13W 180 C3
Quilán, C. Chile 43°15S 74°30W 192 B2
Quilcene U.S.A. 47°49N 122°53W 170 C4
Quilimari Chile 32°5S 71°30W 190 C1
Quilino Argentina 30°14S 64°29W 190 C3
Quillabamba Peru 12°50S 72°50W 188 C3
Quillagua Chile 21°40S 69°40W 190 A2
Quillan France 42°53N 2°10E 72 F6
Quillota Chile 32°54S 71°16W 190 C1
Quilmes Argentina 34°43S 58°15W 190 C4
Quilon = Kollam India 8°50N 76°38E 127 K3
Quilpie Australia 26°35S 144°11E 151 D3
Quilpué Chile 33°5S 71°33W 190 C1
Quilua Mozam. 16°17S 39°54E 143 F4
Quime Bolivia 17°2S 67°1W 188 D4
Quimilí Argentina 27°40S 62°30W 190 B3
Quimper France 48°0N 4°9W 70 E2
Quimperlé France 47°53N 3°33W 70 E3
Quinault → U.S.A. 47°21N 124°18W 170 C2
Quince Mil Peru 13°15S 70°40W 188 C3
Quincy Calif., U.S.A. 39°56N 120°57W 170 F6
Quincy Fla., U.S.A. 30°35N 84°34W 178 F5
Quincy Ill., U.S.A. 39°56N 91°23W 172 F8
Quincy Mass., U.S.A. 42°14N 71°0W 175 D14
Quincy Wash., U.S.A. 47°14N 119°51W 168 C4
Quines Argentina 32°13S 65°48W 190 C3
Quinga Mozam. 15°49S 40°15E 143 F5
Quingey France 47°7N 5°52E 71 E12
Quinhámel
  Guinea-Biss. 11°53N 15°51W 138 C1
Quintana de la Serena
  Spain 38°45N 5°40W 89 G5
Quintana Roo □
  Mexico 19°40N 88°30W 181 D7
Quintanar de la Orden
  Spain 39°36N 3°5W 89 F7
Quintanar de la Sierra
  Spain 41°57N 2°55W 90 D2
Quintana del Rey Spain 39°21N 1°56W 91 F3
Quintero Chile 32°45S 71°30W 190 C1
Quintin France 48°26N 2°56W 70 D4
Quinto Spain 41°25N 0°32W 90 D3
Quirihue Chile 36°15S 72°35W 192 A2
Quirimbas △ Mozam. 12°30S 40°15E 143 E5
Quirindi Australia 31°28S 150°40E 153 A9

Quirinópolis Brazil 18°32S 50°30W 187 G8
Quiroga Spain 42°28N 7°18W 88 C3
Quiruvilca Peru 8°1S 78°19W 188 B2
Quissac France 43°55N 4°0E 73 E8
Quissanga Mozam. 12°24S 40°28E 143 E5
Quissico Mozam. 24°42S 34°44E 145 B5
Quitilipi Argentina 26°50S 60°13W 190 B3
Quitman U.S.A. 30°47N 83°34W 178 E6
Quito Ecuador 0°15S 78°35W 186 D3
Quitralca △ Chile 45°43S 73°25W 192 C2
Quixadá Brazil 4°55S 39°0W 189 A3
Quixaxe Mozam. 15°17S 40°4E 143 F5
Quixeramobim Brazil 5°12S 39°17W 189 B3
Qujing China 25°32N 103°41E 116 E4
Qulan Kazakhstan 42°55N 72°43E 106 E8
Qul'ân, Jazā'ir Egypt 24°22N 35°31E 128 E2
Qulsary Kazakhstan 46°59N 54°1E 108 C4
Qumbu S. Africa 31°10S 28°48E 145 D4
Quneitra = Al Qunayţirah
  Syria 33°5N 35°45E 130 B4
Qŭnghirot Uzbekistan 43°2N 58°50E 108 D5
Qu'nyido China 31°15N 98°6E 116 B1
Quoin I. Australia 14°54S 129°32E 148 B4
Quoin Pt. S. Africa 34°46S 19°37E 144 E2
Quorn Australia 32°25S 138°5E 152 B3
Qŭqon Uzbekistan 40°31N 70°56E 109 D8
Qŭrghonteppa
  Tajikistan 37°50N 68°47E 109 E7
Qurimbas △ Mozam. 12°20S 40°10E 143 E5
Qurnat as Sawdā'
  Lebanon 34°18N 36°6E 130 A5
Quryq Kazakhstan 43°12N 51°39E 108 D4
Qūs Egypt 25°55N 32°50E 137 B3
Qusar Azerbaijan 41°25N 48°26E 87 K9
Quşaybā' Si. Arabia 26°53N 43°35E 128 E4
Qusaybah Iraq 34°24N 40°59E 105 E9
Quseir Egypt 26°7N 34°16E 128 E2
Quseir Amra = Qasr 'Amra
  Jordan 31°48N 36°35E 128 D3
Qüshchī Iran 37°59N 45°3E 105 D11
Qusmuryn Kazakhstan 52°27N 64°36E 108 B6
Qusmuryn Köli
  Kazakhstan 52°41N 64°48E 108 B6
Qutang Gorge = Qutang Xia
  China 31°0N 109°40E 116 B7
Qutang Xia China 31°0N 109°40E 116 B7
Quthing Lesotho 30°25S 27°36E 145 E4
Qūṭīābād Iran 35°47N 48°30E 105 E13
Quttinirpaaq △
  Canada 82°13N 72°13W 161 A17
Quwo China 35°38N 111°25E 114 G6
Quyang China 38°35N 114°40E 114 E8
Quynh Nhai Vietnam 21°49N 103°33E 120 B4
Quyon Canada 45°31N 76°14W 174 B8
Quzhou China 28°57N 118°54E 117 C12
Quzi China 36°20N 107°20E 114 F4
Qvareli Georgia 41°57N 45°47E 87 K7
Qyzylorda Kazakhstan 44°48N 65°28E 108 D7
Qyzylorda □ Kazakhstan 45°0N 65°0E 108 D6
Qyzylzhar Kazakhstan 48°17N 69°38E 109 C7

R

Ra, Ko Thailand 9°13N 98°16E 121 H2
Raab Austria 48°21N 13°39E 78 C6
Raahe Finland 64°40N 24°28E 60 D21
Raalte Neths. 52°23N 6°16E 69 B6
Raasay U.K. 57°25N 6°4W 65 D2
Raasay, Sd. of U.K. 57°30N 6°8W 65 D2
Raasepori Finland 60°0N 23°26E 63 F8
Rab Croatia 44°45N 14°45E 93 D11
Rába → Hungary 47°38N 17°38E 80 C2
Raba → Poland 50°8N 20°30E 83 H7
Rabaçal → Portugal 41°30N 7°12W 88 D3
Rabah Nigeria 13°5N 5°30E 139 C6
Rabai Kenya 3°50S 39°31E 142 C4
Rabastens France 43°50N 1°43E 72 E5
Rabastens-de-Bigorre
  France 43°23N 0°9E 72 E4
Rabat = Victoria Malta 36°3N 14°14E 101 C1
Rabat Malta 35°53N 14°24E 101 D1
Rabat Morocco 34°2N 6°48W 136 B4
Rabat □ Morocco 34°10N 6°45W 136 B2
Rabaul Papua N. G. 4°24S 152°18E 147 B8
Rabbit Flat Australia 20°11S 130°1E 148 D5
Rabbit Lake Mine
  Canada 58°4N 104°5W 163 B8
Rabi Fiji 16°30S 179°59W 154 a
Rābigh Si. Arabia 22°50N 39°5E 131 C2
Rabka Poland 49°37N 19°59E 83 J6
Râbniţa Moldova 47°45N 29°0E 81 C14
Râbor Iran 29°17N 56°55E 129 D8
Rabwah = Chenab Nagar
  Pakistan 31°45N 72°55E 124 D5
Rača Serbia 44°14N 21°0E 96 B4
Răcăciuni Romania 46°20N 26°59E 81 D11
Răcăşdia Romania 44°59N 21°36E 96 B2
Racconigi Italy 44°46N 7°46E 92 D4
Race, C. Canada 46°40N 53°5W 165 D9
Race Pond U.S.A. 31°1N 82°8W 178 F6
Rach Gia Vietnam 10°5N 105°5E 121 G5
Rach Soi Vietnam 9°57N 105°7E 121 H5
Racha Noi, Ko Thailand 7°30N 98°19E 121 J2
Racha Yai, Ko Thailand 7°36N 98°21E 121 J2
Rachid Mauritania 18°45N 11°35W 138 B2
Raciąż Poland 52°46N 20°10E 83 F7
Racibórz Poland 50°7N 18°18E 83 H5
Racichy Belarus 53°44N 23°42E 82 E10
Racine U.S.A. 42°44N 87°47W 172 D10
Rackerby U.S.A. 39°26N 121°22W 170 F5
Radan Serbia 42°59N 21°29E 96 D5
Radauti Romania 47°50N 25°59E 81 C8
Rădăuţi-Prut Romania 48°14N 26°48E 81 B11
Radbuza → Czech Rep. 49°35N 13°5E 76 D7
Radcliff U.S.A. 37°51N 85°57W 173 G11
Radeberg Germany 51°7N 13°53E 76 D9
Radebeul Germany 51°6N 13°41E 76 D9
Radeče Slovenia 46°5N 15°14E 93 B12
Radekhiv Ukraine 50°25N 24°32E 75 C13
Radekhov = Radekhiv
  Ukraine 50°25N 24°32E 75 C13
Radenthein Austria 46°48N 13°43E 78 E6
Radew → Poland 54°2N 15°52E 82 D2
Radford U.S.A. 37°8N 80°34W 173 G13
Radhanpur India 23°50N 71°38E 124 H4
Radhwa, Jabal
  Si. Arabia 24°34N 38°18E 128 E3
Radika → Macedonia 41°38N 20°37E 96 E4

Radisson Qué., Canada 53°47N 77°37W 164 B4
Radisson Sask.,
  Canada 52°30N 107°20W 163 C7
Radium Hot Springs
  Canada 50°35N 116°2W 162 C5
Radlje ob Dravi
  Slovenia 46°38N 15°13E 93 B12
Radnevo Bulgaria 42°17N 25°58E 97 D9
Radnice Czech Rep. 49°51N 13°35E 78 B6
Radnor Forest U.K. 52°17N 3°10W 67 E4
Radolfzell Germany 47°39N 8°59E 77 H4
Radom Poland 51°23N 21°12E 83 G8
Radomir Bulgaria 42°37N 22°59E 96 D6
Radomka → Poland 51°43N 21°28E 83 G8
Radomsko Poland 51°5N 19°28E 83 G6
Radomyshl Ukraine 50°30N 29°12E 75 C15
Radomyśl Wielki Poland 50°14N 21°15E 83 H8
Radoszyce Poland 51°4N 20°15E 83 G7
Radoviš Macedonia 41°38N 22°28E 96 E6
Radovljica Slovenia 46°22N 14°12E 93 B11
Radstadt Austria 47°24N 13°28E 78 D6
Radstock, C. Australia 33°12S 134°20E 151 E1
Răducăneni Romania 46°58N 27°54E 81 C12
Raduša Macedonia 42°7N 21°15E 96 D5
Raduzhnyy Russia 62°5N 77°28E 106 C8
Radvanichy Belarus 52°1N 24°0E 82 E11
Radviliškis Lithuania 55°49N 23°33E 82 C10
Radville Canada 49°30N 104°15W 163 D8
Radwá, J. Si. Arabia 24°34N 38°18E 137 C4
Radymno Poland 49°59N 22°52E 83 J9
Radzanów Poland 52°56N 20°8E 83 F7
Radziejów Poland 52°40N 18°30E 83 F5
Radzyń Chełmiński
  Poland 53°23N 18°55E 82 E5
Radzyń Podlaski Poland 51°47N 22°37E 83 G9
Rae Canada 62°50N 116°3W 162 A5
Rae Bareli India 26°18N 81°20E 125 F9
Rae Isthmus Canada 66°40N 87°30W 161 D14
Raeren Belgium 50°41N 6°7E 69 D6
Raeside, L. Australia 29°20S 122°0E 149 E3
Raetihi N.Z. 39°25S 175°17E 154 F4
Rafaela Argentina 31°10S 61°30W 190 C3
Rafah Gaza Strip 31°18N 34°14E 130 D3
Rafaï C.A.R. 4°59N 23°58E 142 B1
Raffadali Italy 37°24N 13°32E 94 G5
Rafḥā Si. Arabia 29°35N 43°35E 128 D4
Rafina Greece 38°2N 24°0E 98 C6
Rafsanjān Iran 30°30N 56°5E 129 D8
Raft Pt. Australia 16°4S 124°26E 148 C3
Ragachow Belarus 53°8N 30°5E 75 B16
Ragama Sri Lanka 7°0N 79°50E 122 R11
Ragged, Mt. Australia 33°27S 123°25E 149 F3
Ragged Pt. Barbados 13°10N 59°26W 183 g
Raghunathpalli India 22°14N 84°48E 125 H11
Raghunathpur India 23°33N 86°40E 125 H12
Raglan N.Z. 37°55S 174°55E 154 D3
Raglan Harbour N.Z. 37°47S 174°50E 154 D3
Ragland U.S.A. 33°45N 86°9W 178 B3
Ragusa Italy 36°55N 14°44E 95 F7
Raha Indonesia 4°55S 123°0E 119 E6
Rahaeng = Tak Thailand 16°52N 99°8E 120 D2
Rahat Israel 31°24N 34°43E 130 D3
Rahat, Ḥarrat Si. Arabia 23°0N 40°5E 137 C5
Rahatgarh India 23°47N 78°22E 125 H8
Rahden Germany 52°26N 8°36E 76 C4
Rahimyar Khan
  Pakistan 28°30N 70°25E 124 E4
Rähjerd Iran 34°22N 50°22E 129 C6
Rahole △ Kenya 0°30N 38°57E 142 B4
Rahon India 31°3N 76°7E 124 D7
Rahotu N.Z. 39°20S 173°49E 154 F2
Rahovec Kosovo 42°24N 20°40E 96 D4
Rahuri India 19°23N 74°39E 124 K5
Rai, Hon Vietnam 9°48N 104°38E 121 H5
Raiatéa, Î.
  French Polynesia 16°50S 151°25W 157 J12
Raichur India 16°10N 77°20E 127 E3
Raiford U.S.A. 30°4N 82°14W 178 E7
Raiganj India 25°37N 88°10E 125 G13
Raigarh India 21°56N 83°25E 126 D6
Raighar India 19°51N 82°6E 126 D6
Raijua Indonesia 10°37S 121°36E 119 F6
Raikot India 30°41N 75°42E 124 D6
Railton Australia 41°25S 146°28E 151 G4
Rainbow Bridge △
  U.S.A. 37°5N 110°58W 169 H8
Rainbow City U.S.A. 33°57N 86°5W 178 B3
Rainbow Lake Canada 58°30N 119°23W 162 B5
Rainier U.S.A. 46°5N 122°56W 170 D4
Rainier, Mt. U.S.A. 46°52N 121°46W 170 D5
Rainy L. Canada 48°42N 93°10W 163 D10
Rainy River Canada 48°43N 94°29W 163 D10
Raippaluoto Finland 63°13N 21°14E 60 E19
Raipur India 21°17N 81°45E 126 D7
Rairakhol India 21°4N 84°21E 126 D7
Ra'is Si. Arabia 23°33N 38°43E 137 C4
Raisen India 23°20N 77°48E 124 H8
Raisio Finland 60°28N 22°11E 63 E8
Raj Nandgaon India 21°5N 81°5E 126 D5
Raj Nilgiri India 21°28N 86°46E 125 J12
Raja, Ujung Indonesia 3°40N 96°25E 118 D1
Raja Ampat, Kepulauan
  Indonesia 0°30S 130°0E 119 E8
Rajahmundry India 17°1N 81°48E 126 D5
Rajaji △ India 30°6N 78°20E 124 D8
Rajampet India 14°11N 79°10E 127 G4
Rajang → Malaysia 2°30N 112°0E 118 D4
Rajanpur Pakistan 29°6N 70°19E 124 E4
Rajapalaiyam India 9°25N 77°35E 127 K3
Rajapur India 16°30N 73°31E 126 E7
Rajasthan □ India 26°45N 73°30E 124 F5
Rajasthan Canal = Indira Gandhi
  Canal India 28°0N 72°0E 124 F5
Rajauri India 33°25N 74°21E 124 C6
Rajgarh Mad. P., India 24°2N 76°45E 124 G7
Rajgarh Raj., India 28°40N 75°25E 124 E6
Rajgarh Raj., India 27°30N 76°32E 124 F4
Rajgir India 25°2N 85°25E 125 G11
Rajkot India 22°15N 70°56E 124 H4
Rajmahal Hills India 24°30N 87°30E 125 G12
Rajpipla India 21°50N 73°30E 124 J5
Rajpura India 30°25N 76°32E 124 D7
Rajputana = Rajasthan □
  India 26°45N 73°30E 124 F5
Rajshahi Bangla. 24°22N 88°39E 123 G16

Rajshahi □ Bangla. 25°0N 89°0E 125 G13
Rajula India 21°3N 71°26E 124 J4
Rajur India 20°7N 78°55E 126 D4
Rajura India 19°47N 79°22E 126 D4
Rakaia N.Z. 43°45S 172°1E 155 D7
Rakaia → N.Z. 43°36S 172°15E 155 D7
Rakan, Ra's Qatar 26°10N 51°20E 129 E6
Rakaposhi Pakistan 36°10N 74°25E 125 A6
Rakata, Pulau
  Indonesia 6°10S 105°20E 119 G11
Rakbah, Sahl Si. Arabia 22°15N 41°0E 137 C5
Rakhine □ Burma 19°0N 94°15E 123 K18
Rakhiv Ukraine 48°3N 24°12E 81 D8
Rakhni Pakistan 30°4N 69°56E 124 D3
Rakhni → Pakistan 29°31N 69°36E 124 E3
Rakhny-Lisovi Ukraine 48°47N 28°29E 81 D14
Rakiraki Fiji 17°22S 178°11E 154 a
Rakitnoye Russia 45°36N 134°17E 112 B7
Rakops Botswana 21°1S 24°28E 144 B3
Rakovica Croatia 44°59N 15°38E 93 D12
Rakovník Czech Rep. 50°6N 13°42E 78 A6
Rakovski Bulgaria 42°21N 24°57E 97 D8
Rakvere Estonia 59°20N 26°25E 84 C4
Raleigh Fla., U.S.A. 29°25N 82°32W 179 F7
Raleigh N.C., U.S.A. 35°47N 78°39W 179 D15
Ralik Chain Pac. Oc. 8°0N 168°0E 156 G8
Ralja Serbia 44°33N 20°34E 96 B4
Rälla Sweden 56°40N 16°30E 63 H10
Ralls U.S.A. 33°41N 101°24W 176 E4
Ralston U.S.A. 41°30N 76°57W 174 E8
Ram → Canada 62°1N 123°41W 162 A4
Rām Allāh West Bank 31°55N 35°10E 130 D4
Rama Nic. 12°9N 84°15W 182 D3
Ramacca Italy 37°23N 14°42E 95 F7
Ramachandrapuram
  India 16°50N 82°4E 126 D6
Ramagiri Udayagiri
  India 19°15N 84°18E 126 E7
Ramagundam India 18°55N 79°15E 126 D4
Ramakona India 21°43N 78°50E 125 J8
Ramalho, Serra do
  Brazil 13°45S 44°0W 189 C2
Rāmallāh = Rām Allāh
  West Bank 31°55N 35°10E 130 D4
Raman Thailand 6°29N 101°18E 121 J3
Ramanathapuram India 9°25N 78°55E 127 K4
Ramanujanj India 23°48N 83°42E 125 H10
Ramas C. India 15°5N 73°55E 127 G2
Ramat Gan Israel 32°4N 34°48E 130 C3
Ramatlhabama
  S. Africa 25°37S 25°33E 144 C4
Ramban India 33°14N 75°12E 125 C6
Rambervillers France 48°20N 6°38E 71 D13
Rambi = Rabi Fiji 16°30S 179°59W 154 a
Rambipuji Indonesia 8°12S 113°37E 119 H15
Rambouillet France 48°39N 1°50E 71 D8
Ramdurg India 15°58N 75°22E 127 E2
Rame Hd. Australia 37°47S 149°30E 153 D8
Ramechhap Nepal 27°25N 86°10E 125 F12
Ramenskoye Russia 55°32N 38°15E 84 E10
Ramganga → India 27°5N 79°58E 125 F8
Ramgarh Jharkhand,
  India 23°40N 85°35E 125 H11
Ramgarh Raj., India 27°16N 75°14E 124 F6
Ramgarh Raj., India 27°30N 70°36E 124 F4
Ramhormoz Iran 31°15N 49°35E 129 D6
Ramian Iran 37°3N 55°16E 129 B7
Ramingining Australia 12°19S 135°3E 150 A2
Ramla Israel 31°55N 34°52E 130 D3
Ramm = Rum Jordan 29°39N 35°24E 128 D4
Ramm, Jabal Jordan 29°35N 35°24E 128 D4
Râmna → Romania 45°26N 27°3E 81 E12
Ramnad = Ramanathapuram
  India 9°25N 78°55E 127 K4
Ramnagar Jammu & Kashmir,
  India 32°47N 75°18E 125 C6
Ramnagar Uttarakhand,
  India 29°24N 79°7E 125 E8
Ramnäs Sweden 59°46N 16°12E 63 E10
Râmnicu Sărat Romania 45°26N 27°3E 81 E12
Râmnicu Vâlcea Romania 45°9N 24°21E 81 E9
Ramnous Greece 38°12N 24°3E 98 C6
Ramon Russia 51°55N 39°21E 85 G10
Ramona U.S.A. 33°2N 116°52W 171 M10
Ramonville-St-Agne
  France 43°33N 1°28E 72 E5
Ramore Canada 48°30N 80°25W 164 C3
Ramos → Nigeria 5°8N 5°22E 139 D6
Ramotswa Botswana 24°50S 25°52E 144 B4
Rampur H.P., India 31°26N 77°43E 124 D7
Rampur Mad. P., India 23°25N 73°53E 124 H5
Rampur Odisha, India 21°48N 83°58E 126 D6
Rampur Ut. P., India 28°50N 79°5E 125 E8
Rampur Hat India 24°10N 87°50E 125 G12
Rampura India 24°30N 75°27E 124 G6
Ramrama Tola India 21°52N 79°55E 125 J8
Ramree I. Burma 19°0N 93°40E 123 K18
Râmsar Iran 36°53N 50°41E 129 B6
Ramsey I. of Man 54°20N 4°22W 66 C3
Ramsey U.S.A. 40°1N 74°9W 175 E10
Ramsey L. Canada 47°13N 82°15W 164 C2
Ramsgate U.K. 51°20N 1°25E 67 F9
Ramsjö Sweden 62°11N 15°37E 62 B8
Ramstein Germany 49°27N 7°32E 77 F3
Ramtek India 21°20N 79°15E 125 J8
Ramu → Kenya 3°55N 41°10E 142 B5
Ramvik Sweden 62°49N 17°51E 62 B8
Rana Pratap Sagar Dam
  India 24°58N 75°38E 124 G6
Ranaghat India 23°15N 88°35E 125 H13
Ranahu Pakistan 25°55N 69°45E 124 G3
Ranau Malaysia 6°2N 116°40E 118 C5
Rancagua Chile 34°10S 70°50W 190 C2
Rance → France 48°34N 1°59W 70 D5
Rancheria → Canada 60°13N 129°7W 162 A3
Ranchester U.S.A. 44°54N 107°10W 168 D10
Ranchi India 23°19N 85°27E 125 H11
Rancho Cordova
  U.S.A. 38°36N 121°18W 170 G5
Rancho Cucamonga
  U.S.A. 34°10N 117°30W 171 L9
Ranco, L. Chile 40°15S 72°25W 192 B2
Rand Australia 35°33S 146°32E 153 C7
Randalstown U.K. 54°45N 6°19W 64 B5
Randan France 46°1N 3°21E 72 B6

Randazzo *Italy* 37°53N 14°57E **95** E7
Rander *India* 21°14N 72°47E **126** D1
Randers *Denmark* 56°29N 10°1E **63** H4
Randers Fjord *Denmark* 56°37N 10°20E **63** H4
Randfontein *S. Africa* 26°8S 27°45E **145** C4
Randle *U.S.A.* 46°32N 121°57W **170** D5
Randolph *Mass., U.S.A.* 42°10N 71°2W **175** D13
Randolph *N.Y., U.S.A.* 42°10N 78°59W **174** D6
Randolph *Utah, U.S.A.* 41°40N 111°11W **168** F8
Randolph *U.S.A.* 43°55N 72°40W **175** C12
Randsburg *U.S.A.* 35°22N 117°39W **171** K9
Rânеälven → *Sweden* 65°50N 22°20E **60** D20
Ranfurly *N.Z.* 45°7S 170°6E **155** F5
Rangae *Thailand* 6°19N 101°44E **121** J3
Rangataua *N.Z.* 39°26S 175°28E **154** F4
Rangaunu B. *N.Z.* 34°51S 173°15E **154** A2
Range, The *Zimbabwe* 19°2S 31°2E **143** F3
Rangeley *U.S.A.* 44°58N 70°39W **175** B14
Rangeley L. *U.S.A.* 44°55N 70°43W **175** B14
Rangely *U.S.A.* 40°5N 108°48W **168** F9
Ranger *U.S.A.* 32°28N 98°41W **176** E5
Rangia *India* 26°28N 91°38E **123** F17
Rangiora *N.Z.* 43°19S 172°36E **155** D7
Rangitaiki *N.Z.* 38°52S 176°24E **154** E5
Rangitaiki → *N.Z.* 37°54S 176°49E **154** D5
Rangitata → *N.Z.* 43°45S 171°15E **155** D6
Rangitikei → *N.Z.* 40°17S 175°15E **154** G4
Rangitoto ke te tonga = D'Urville I. *N.Z.* 40°50S 173°55E **155** A8
Rangitoto Ra. *N.Z.* 38°25S 175°35E **154** E4
Rangkasbitung *Indonesia* 6°21S 106°15E **119** G12
Rangoon *Burma* 16°45N 96°20E **123** L20
Rangpur *Bangla.* 25°42N 89°22E **123** G16
Rangsang *Indonesia* 1°20N 103°5E **121** M4
Ranibennur *India* 14°35N 75°30E **127** G2
Raniganj *Paschimbanga, India* 23°40N 87°5E **123** H15
Raniganj *Ut. P., India* 27°3N 82°13E **125** F9
Ranikhet *India* 29°39N 79°25E **125** E8
Ranippettai *India* 12°56N 79°23E **127** H4
Raniwara *India* 24°50N 72°10E **124** G5
Rānīyah *Iraq* 36°15N 44°53E **105** D11
Ranka *India* 23°59N 83°47E **125** H10
Ranken → *Australia* 20°31S 137°36E **150** C2
Rankin *U.S.A.* 31°13N 101°56W **176** F4
Rankin Inlet *Canada* 62°30N 93°0W **160** E13
Rankins Springs *Australia* 33°49S 146°14E **153** B7
Rankweil *Austria* 47°17N 9°39E **78** D2
Rannoch, L. *U.K.* 56°41N 4°20W **65** E4
Rannoch Moor *U.K.* 56°38N 4°48W **65** E4
Ranohira *Madag.* 22°29S 45°24E **141** J9
Ranong *Thailand* 9°56N 98°40E **121** H2
Ranpur *India* 20°5N 85°20E **126** D7
Ränsa *Iran* 33°39N 48°18E **129** C6
Ransiki *Indonesia* 1°30S 134°10E **119** E8
Rantau Abang *Malaysia* 4°52N 103°24E **121** K4
Rantauprapat *Indonesia* 2°15N 99°50E **118** D1
Rantemario *Indonesia* 3°15S 119°57E **119** E5
Ranthambore △ *India* 26°6N 76°23E **124** F7
Rantoul *U.S.A.* 40°19N 88°9W **172** E9
Ranum *Denmark* 56°54N 9°14E **63** H3
Ranyah, W. → *Si. Arabia* 21°18N 43°20E **137** C5
Raohe *China* 46°47N 134°0E **112** A7
Raon l'Étape *France* 48°24N 6°50E **71** D13
Raoping *China* 23°42N 117°1E **117** F11
Raoui, Erg er *Algeria* 29°0N 2°0W **136** C3
Raoyang *China* 38°15N 115°45E **114** E8
Rap, Ko *Thailand* 9°19N 99°58E **121** b
Rapa *French Polynesia* 27°35S 144°20W **157** K13
Rapa Nui = Pascua, I. de *Chile* 27°7S 109°23W **157** K17
Rapallo *Italy* 44°21N 9°14E **92** D6
Rapar *India* 23°34N 70°38E **124** H4
Räpch *Iran* 25°40N 59°15E **129** E8
Rapel, Lago *Chile* 34°20S 71°14W **190** C1
Raper, C. *Canada* 69°44N 67°6W **161** D18
Rapid City *U.S.A.* 44°5N 103°14W **172** C2
Rapid River *U.S.A.* 45°55N 86°58W **172** C10
Rapla *Estonia* 59°1N 24°52E **84** C3
Rapti → *India* 26°18N 83°41E **125** F10
Raquette → *U.S.A.* 45°0N 74°42W **175** B10
Raquette Lake *U.S.A.* 43°49N 74°40W **175** C10
Rara *Australia* 24°0S 135°0E **150** C2
Rarotonga *Cook Is.* 21°30S 160°0W **157** K12
Ra's al 'Ayn *Syria* 36°45N 40°12E **105** B9
Ra's al Khaymah *U.A.E.* 25°50N 55°59E **129** E7
Ra's aṭ Ṭīb *Tunisia* 37°1N 11°2E **136** A6
Râs el Mâ *Algeria* 34°26N 0°50W **136** B3
Râs el Mâ *Mali* 16°35N 4°30W **134** B4
Râs el Oued *Algeria* 35°57N 5°2E **136** A5
Râs Ghârib *Egypt* 28°6N 33°18E **137** F8
Râs Muhammad △ *Egypt* 27°45N 34°16E **137** F8
Rasa, Pta. B. Aires, *Argentina* 29°30N 32°42E **137** F8
Rasa, Pta. *Rio Negro, Argentina* 36°20S 56°41W **190** D4
Rasca, Pta. de la *Canary Is.* 27°59N 16°41W **100** G3
Răşcani *Moldova* 47°58N 27°33E **81** C12
Raseiniai *Lithuania* 55°25N 23°5E **82** C10
Rashid *Egypt* 31°21N 30°22E **137** E7
Rashid, Masabb *Egypt* 31°22N 30°17E **137** E7
Rashmi *India* 25°4N 74°22E **124** G6
Rasht *Iran* 37°20N 49°40E **105** D13
Rasi Salai *Thailand* 15°20N 104°9E **120** E5
Rasipuram *India* 11°30N 78°15E **127** J4
Raška *Serbia* 43°19N 20°39E **96** C9
Raskot *Nepal* 29°14N 81°39E **125** E9
Râsnov *Romania* 45°35N 25°27E **81** D6
Rason L. *Australia* 28°45S 124°25E **149** E3
Rasova *Romania* 44°15N 27°55E **81** F12
Rasovo *Bulgaria* 43°42N 23°17E **96** D7
Rasra *India* 25°50N 83°50E **125** G10
Rasskazovo *Russia* 52°35N 41°50E **86** D5
Rast *Romania* 43°53N 23°16E **81** G8
Rastatt *Germany* 48°50N 8°11E **77** G4
Rastede *Germany* 53°15N 8°12E **76** B4
Råstojávri *Sweden* 68°24N 21°35E **60** B19
Rastolita *Romania* 46°56N 25°4E **81** C9
Rasul *Pakistan* 32°42N 73°34E **124** C5
Raszków *Poland* 51°43N 17°40E **83** G4
Rat → *Canada* 49°35N 97°10W **163** D9

Rat Buri = Ratchaburi *Thailand* 13°30N 99°54E **120** F2
Rat Islands *U.S.A.* 52°0N 178°0E **166** E3
Rat L. *Canada* 56°10N 99°40W **163** B9
Ratak Chain *Pac. Oc.* 1°0N 170°0E **156** G8
Ratangarh *India* 28°5N 74°35E **124** E6
Raṭāwī *Iraq* 30°38N 47°13E **128** D5
Ratcatchers L. *Australia* 32°30S 143°12E **152** B5
Ratchaburi *Thailand* 13°30N 99°54E **120** F2
Rath *India* 25°36N 79°37E **125** G8
Rath Luirc = Charleville *Ireland* 52°21N 8°40W **64** D3
Rathangan *Ireland* 53°14N 7°0W **64** C4
Rathdrum *Ireland* 52°56N 6°14W **64** D5
Rathenow *Germany* 52°37N 12°19E **76** C8
Rathkeale *Ireland* 52°32N 8°56W **64** D3
Rathlin I. *U.K.* 55°18N 6°14W **64** A5
Rathmelton *Ireland* 55°2N 7°39W **64** A4
Ratibor = Racibórz *Poland* 50°7N 18°18E **83** H5
Rätikon *Austria* 47°0N 9°55E **78** D2
Ratingen *Germany* 51°18N 6°52E **76** D2
Ratlam *India* 23°20N 75°0E **124** H6
Ratmanova Ostrov *Russia* 65°46N 169°6W **166** B6
Ratnagiri *India* 16°57N 73°18E **126** E1
Ratnapura *Sri Lanka* 6°40N 80°20E **127** L5
Ratodero *Pakistan* 27°48N 68°18E **124** F3
Raton *U.S.A.* 36°54N 104°24W **169** H11
Rattaphum *Thailand* 7°8N 100°16E **121** J3
Ratten *Austria* 47°28N 15°44E **78** D8
Rattray Hd. *U.K.* 57°38N 1°50W **65** D7
Rättvik *Sweden* 60°52N 15°7E **62** D9
Ratz, Mt. *Canada* 57°23N 132°12W **162** B2
Ratzeburg *Germany* 53°40N 10°46E **76** B6
Raub *Malaysia* 3°47N 101°52E **121** L3
Rauch *Argentina* 36°45S 59°5W **190** D5
Raudales *Mexico* 17°27N 93°39W **181** D6
Raufarhöfn *Iceland* 66°27N 15°57W **61** A6
Raufoss *Norway* 60°44N 10°37E **60** F14
Raukumara Ra. *N.Z.* 38°5S 177°55E **154** E6
Raul Soares *Brazil* 20°5S 42°22W **189** E2
Rauma *Finland* 61°10N 21°30E **64** B1
Raumo = Rauma *Finland* 61°10N 21°30E **64** B1
Raung, Gunung *Indonesia* 8°8S 114°3E **119** J17
Raurkela *India* 22°14N 84°50E **125** H11
Rausu-Dake *Japan* 44°4N 145°7E **112** B12
Răut → *Moldova* 47°15N 29°9E **81** C14
Rava-Ruska *Ukraine* 50°15N 23°42E **83** H10
Rava Russkaya = Rava-Ruska *Ukraine* 50°15N 23°42E **83** H10
Ravalli *U.S.A.* 47°17N 114°11W **168** C6
Rāvаnsar *Iran* 34°43N 46°40E **105** E12
Ravanusa *Italy* 37°16N 13°58E **94** E6
Rāvar *Iran* 31°20N 56°51E **129** D8
Ravena *U.S.A.* 42°28N 73°49W **175** D11
Ravenna *Italy* 44°25N 12°12E **93** D9
Ravenna *Nebr., U.S.A.* 41°1N 98°55W **172** E4
Ravenna *Ohio, U.S.A.* 41°9N 81°15W **174** E3
Ravensburg *Germany* 47°46N 9°36E **77** H5
Ravenshoe *Australia* 17°37S 145°29E **150** B4
Ravensthorpe *Australia* 33°35S 120°2E **149** F3
Ravenswood *Australia* 20°6S 146°54E **150** C4
Ravenswood *U.S.A.* 38°57N 81°46W **173** F13
Ravensworth *Australia* 32°26S 151°4E **153** B9
Raver *India* 21°15N 76°2E **126** D3
Ravi → *Pakistan* 30°35N 71°49E **124** D4
Ravna Gora *Croatia* 45°24N 14°50E **93** C11
Ravna Reka *Serbia* 44°1N 21°35E **96** C5
Ravne na Koroškem *Slovenia* 46°36N 14°59E **93** B11
Rawa Mazowiecka *Poland* 51°46N 20°12E **83** G7
Rawalpindi *Pakistan* 33°38N 73°8E **124** C5
Rawang *Malaysia* 3°20N 101°35E **121** L3
Rawene *N.Z.* 35°25S 173°32E **154** B4
Rawi, Ko *Thailand* 6°33N 99°14E **121** J2
Rawicz *Poland* 51°36N 16°52E **83** G3
Rawka → *Poland* 52°9N 20°8E **83** F7
Rawlinna *Australia* 30°58S 125°28E **149** F4
Rawlins *U.S.A.* 41°47N 107°14W **168** F10
Rawlinson Ra. *Australia* 24°40S 128°30E **149** D4
Rawson *Argentina* 43°15S 65°5W **192** E3
Raxaul *India* 26°59N 84°51E **125** F11
Ray *U.S.A.* 48°21N 103°10W **172** A2
Ray, C. *Canada* 47°33N 59°15W **165** C8
Ray City *U.S.A.* 31°5N 83°11W **178** D6
Ray Mts. *U.S.A.* 66°0N 152°0W **166** B9
Raya Ring, Ko *Thailand* 7°18N 98°29E **121** a
Rayachoti *India* 14°4N 78°50E **127** G4
Rayadurg *India* 14°40N 76°50E **127** G3
Rayagada *India* 19°15N 83°20E **126** E6
Raychikhinsk *Russia* 49°46N 129°25E **107** E13
Räyen *Iran* 29°34N 57°26E **129** D8
Rayle *U.S.A.* 33°48N 82°54W **178** B7
Rayleigh *U.K.* 51°36N 0°37E **67** F8
Raymond *Canada* 49°30N 112°35W **162** D6
Raymond *U.S.A.* 37°13N 119°54W **170** H7
Raymond *N.H., U.S.A.* 43°2N 71°11W **175** C13
Raymond *Wash., U.S.A.* 46°41N 123°44W **170** D3
Raymond Terrace *Australia* 32°45S 151°44E **153** B9
Raymondville *U.S.A.* 26°29N 97°47W **176** H6
Raymore *Canada* 51°25N 104°31W **163** C8
Rayón *Mexico* 29°43N 110°35W **180** B2
Rayong *Thailand* 12°40N 101°5E **120** F3
Raystown L. *U.S.A.* 40°25N 78°5W **174** F6
Rayville *U.S.A.* 32°29N 91°46W **179** E9
Raz, Pte. du *France* 48°2N 4°47W **70** D2
Razan *Iran* 35°23N 49°2E **105** E13
Razana *Serbia* 44°6N 19°55E **96** C8
Razanj *Serbia* 43°40N 21°31E **96** C5
Razāzah, Buhayrat ar *Iraq* 32°40N 43°35E **105** F10
Razazah, L. = Razāzah, Buhayrat ar *Iraq* 32°40N 43°35E **105** F10
Razdelna *Bulgaria* 43°13N 27°41E **97** C11
Razdel'naya = Rozdilna *Ukraine* 46°50N 30°2E **81** D16
Razdolnoye *Russia* 43°30N 131°52E **112** C5
Razdolnoye *Ukraine* 45°46N 33°29E **85** K7
Razeh *Iran* 32°47N 48°9E **129** C6
Razgrad *Bulgaria* 43°33N 26°34E **97** C10
Razgrad □ *Bulgaria* 43°30N 26°30E **97** C10

Razim, Lacul *Romania* 44°50N 29°0E **81** F14
Razlog *Bulgaria* 41°53N 23°28E **96** E7
Raznak *Pakistan* 32°45N 69°50E **124** C3
Re, Cu Lao *Vietnam* 15°22N 109°8E **120** E7
Ré, Î. de *France* 46°12N 1°30W **72** B2
Reading *U.K.* 51°27N 0°58W **67** F7
Reading *U.S.A.* 40°20N 75°56W **175** F9
Reading □ *U.K.* 51°27N 0°58W **67** F7
Real, Cordillera *Bolivia* 17°0S 67°10W **188** D4
Realicó *Argentina* 35°0S 64°15W **190** D3
Réalmont *France* 43°48N 2°10E **72** E6
Ream *Cambodia* 10°34N 103°39E **121** G4
Reams *Cambodia* 10°30N 103°45E **121** G4
Reay Forest *U.K.* 58°22N 4°55W **65** C4
Rebais *France* 48°50N 3°10E **71** D10
Rebecca, L. *Australia* 30°0S 122°15E **149** F3
Rebi *Indonesia* 6°23S 134°7E **119** F8
Rebiana, Sahrâ' *Libya* 24°30N 21°0E **135** D10
Rebun-Tō *Japan* 45°23N 141°2E **112** B10
Recanati *Italy* 43°24N 13°32E **93** E10
Recaş *Romania* 45°46N 21°30E **96** D6
Recco *Italy* 44°22N 9°9E **92** D6
Recherche, Arch. of the *Australia* 34°15S 122°50E **149** F3
Rechna Doab *Pakistan* 31°35N 73°30E **124** D5
Rechytsa *Belarus* 52°21N 30°24E **76** B8
Recife *Brazil* 8°0S 35°0W **189** B4
Recife *Seychelles* 4°36S 55°42E **141** b
Recklinghausen *Germany* 51°37N 7°12E **76** D3
Reckong Peo *India* 31°32N 78°16E **124** D8
Reconquista *Argentina* 29°10S 59°45W **190** B4
Recreo *Argentina* 29°25S 65°10W **190** B2
Recuay *Peru* 9°43S 77°28W **188** B2
Recz *Poland* 53°16N 15°31E **83** E2
Red → *U.S.A.* 31°1N 91°45W **179** F9
Red Bank *U.S.A.* 40°21N 74°5W **175** F10
Red Bay *Canada* 51°44N 56°25W **165** B8
Red Bluff *U.S.A.* 40°11N 122°15W **168** F2
Red Bluff Res. *U.S.A.* 31°54N 103°55W **176** F3
Red Cliffs *Australia* 34°19S 142°11E **152** C5
Red Cloud *U.S.A.* 40°5N 98°32W **172** E4
Red Creek *U.S.A.* 43°14N 76°45W **175** C8
Red Deer *Canada* 52°20N 113°50W **162** C6
Red Deer → *Alta., Canada* 50°58N 110°0W **163** C7
Red Deer → *Man., Canada* 52°53N 101°1W **163** C8
Red Deer L. *Canada* 52°55N 101°20W **163** C8
Red Hook *U.S.A.* 41°55N 73°53W **175** E11
Red Indian L. *Canada* 48°35N 57°0W **165** C8
Red L. *Canada* 51°3N 93°49W **163** C10
Red Lake *Canada* 51°3N 93°49W **163** C10
Red Lake Falls *U.S.A.* 47°53N 96°16W **172** B5
Red Lake Road *Canada* 49°59N 93°25W **163** C10
Red Lodge *U.S.A.* 45°11N 109°15W **168** D9
Red Mountain *U.S.A.* 35°37N 117°38W **171** K9
Red Oak *U.S.A.* 41°1N 95°14W **172** E6
Red River of the North → *N. Amer.* 49°0N 97°15W **172** A5
Red Rock *Canada* 48°55N 88°15W **164** C2
Red Rock, L. *U.S.A.* 41°22N 92°59W **172** E7
Red Rocks Pt. *Australia* 32°13S 127°32E **149** F4
Red Sea *Asia* 25°0N 36°0E **131** C2
Red Slate Mt. *U.S.A.* 37°31N 118°52W **170** H8
Red Sucker L. *Canada* 54°9N 93°40W **164** B1
Red Tower Pass = Turnu Roşu, P. *Romania* 45°33N 24°17E **81** E9
Red Volta → *Africa* 10°34N 0°30W **139** C4
Red Wing *U.S.A.* 44°34N 92°31W **172** C7
Reda *Poland* 54°40N 18°19E **82** D5
Redang, Pulau *Malaysia* 5°49N 103°2E **121** K4
Redange *Lux.* 49°46N 5°52E **69** E5
Redcar *U.K.* 54°37N 1°4W **66** C6
Redcar & Cleveland □ *U.K.* 54°29N 1°0W **66** C7
Redcliff *Canada* 50°10N 110°50W **168** A8
Redcliffe *Australia* 27°12S 153°6E **151** D5
Redcliffe, Mt. *Australia* 28°30S 121°30E **149** E3
Reddersburg *S. Africa* 29°41S 26°10E **144** C4
Reddick *U.S.A.* 29°22N 82°12W **178** F7
Redding *U.S.A.* 40°35N 122°24W **168** F2
Redditch *U.K.* 52°18N 1°55W **67** E6
Redenção *Brazil* 4°13S 38°43W **189** A3
Redfield *U.S.A.* 44°53N 98°31W **172** C4
Redford *U.S.A.* 44°38N 73°48W **175** B11
Redhead *Trin. & Tob.* 10°44N 60°58W **187** K16
Redkino *Russia* 56°39N 36°16E **84** D9
Redlands *U.S.A.* 34°4N 117°11W **171** M9
Redmond *Oreg., U.S.A.* 44°17N 121°11W **168** D3
Redmond *Wash., U.S.A.* 47°40N 122°7W **170** C4
Redon *France* 47°40N 2°6W **70** E4
Redonda *Antigua & B.* 16°58N 62°19W **183** C7
Redondela *Spain* 42°15N 8°38W **89** B2
Redondo *Portugal* 38°39N 7°37W **89** G3
Redondo Beach *U.S.A.* 33°50N 118°23W **171** M8
Redoubt Volcano *U.S.A.* 60°29N 152°45W **166** D9
Redruth *U.K.* 50°14N 5°14W **67** G2
Redvers *Canada* 49°35N 101°40W **163** D8
Redwater *Canada* 53°55N 113°6W **162** C6
Redwood *U.S.A.* 44°18N 75°48W **175** B9
Redwood △ *U.S.A.* 41°40N 124°5W **168** F1
Redwood City *U.S.A.* 37°30N 122°15W **170** H4
Redwood Falls *U.S.A.* 44°32N 95°7W **172** C6
Ree, L. *Ireland* 53°35N 8°0W **64** C3
Reed City *U.S.A.* 43°53N 85°31W **173** D11
Reedley *U.S.A.* 36°36N 119°27W **170** J7
Reedsburg *U.S.A.* 43°32N 90°0W **172** D8
Reedsport *U.S.A.* 43°42N 124°6W **168** E1
Reedsville *U.S.A.* 40°39N 77°35W **174** F7
Reedy Creek *Australia* 36°58S 140°2E **152** C4
Reefton *N.Z.* 42°6S 171°51E **155** D6
Rees *Germany* 51°46N 6°24E **76** D2
Reese → *U.S.A.* 40°48N 117°4W **168** F5
Refahiye *Turkey* 39°54N 38°47E **105** C8
Reftele *Sweden* 57°11N 13°35E **63** F7
Refugio *U.S.A.* 28°18N 97°17W **176** G6
Rega → *Poland* 54°10N 15°18E **82** D2
Regnajaia → *Poland* 51°5N 18°59E **83** G5
Regana, C. de *Spain* 39°25N 2°43E **100** B9
Regen *Germany* 48°58N 13°9E **77** G8
Regen → *Germany* 49°1N 12°6E **77** F8

Regeneração *Brazil* 6°15S 42°41W **189** B2
Regensburg *Germany* 49°1N 12°6E **77** F8
Regenstauf *Germany* 49°7N 12°8E **77** F8
Reggân = Zaouiet Reggâne *Algeria* 26°32N 0°3E **136** C4
Reggello *Italy* 43°41N 11°32E **93** E8
Réggio di Calábria *Italy* 38°6N 15°39E **95** D8
Réggio nell'Emília *Italy* 44°43N 10°36E **92** D7
Reghin *Romania* 46°46N 24°42E **81** D9
Regina *Canada* 50°27N 104°35W **163** C8
Regina Beach *Canada* 50°47N 105°0W **163** C8
Register *U.S.A.* 32°22N 81°53W **178** D7
Registro *Brazil* 24°29S 47°49W **191** A6
Reguengos de Monsaraz *Portugal* 38°25N 7°32W **89** G3
Rehar → *India* 23°55N 82°40E **125** H10
Rehli *India* 23°38N 79°5E **125** H8
Rehoboth *Namibia* 23°15S 17°4E **144** B2
Rehovot *Israel* 31°54N 34°48E **130** D3
Rei, Costa *Italy* 39°15N 9°40E **94** C2
Reichenbach *Germany* 50°37N 12°17E **76** E8
Reid *Australia* 30°49S 128°26E **149** F4
Reidsville *Ga., U.S.A.* 32°6N 82°7W **178** C7
Reidsville *N.C., U.S.A.* 36°21N 79°40W **177** C15
Reigate *U.K.* 51°14N 0°12W **67** F7
Reillo *Spain* 39°54N 1°53W **91** C3
Reims *France* 49°15N 4°1E **71** C11
Reina Adelaida, Arch. *Chile* 52°20S 74°0W **192** D2
Reina Sofía, Tenerife × (TFS) *Canary Is.* 28°3N 16°33W **100** F3
Reinbek *Germany* 53°30N 10°16E **76** B6
Reindeer → *Canada* 55°36N 103°11W **163** B8
Reindeer I. *Canada* 52°30N 98°0W **163** C9
Reindeer L. *Canada* 57°15N 102°15W **163** B8
Reinga, C. *N.Z.* 34°25S 172°43E **154** A1
Reinheimen △ *Norway* 62°10N 7°45E **60** E12
Reinosa *Spain* 43°2N 4°15W **89** A6
Reitz *S. Africa* 27°48S 28°29E **145** C4
Reivilo *S. Africa* 27°36S 24°8E **144** C3
Rejmyre *Sweden* 58°50N 15°55E **63** F9
Rejowiec Fabryczny *Poland* 51°5N 23°17E **83** G10
Reka → *Slovenia* 45°40N 14°0E **93** C11
Rekacov *Serbia* 43°51N 21°3E **96** C5
Reliance *Canada* 63°0N 109°20W **163** A7
Relizane *Algeria* 35°44N 0°31E **136** A4
Relizane □ *Algeria* 35°45N 0°55E **136** A4
Remad, Oued → *Algeria* 33°28N 1°20W **136** B3
Rémalard *France* 48°26N 0°47E **70** D7
Remanso *Brazil* 9°41S 42°4W **189** B2
Remarkable, Mt. *Australia* 32°48S 138°10E **152** B3
Remarkables, The *N.Z.* 45°10S 168°50E **155** F3
Rembang *Indonesia* 6°42S 111°21E **119** G14
Rembert *U.S.A.* 34°6N 80°32W **178** A9
Remedios *Panama* 8°15N 81°50W **182** E3
Remeshk *Iran* 26°55N 58°50E **129** E8
Remetea *Romania* 46°45N 25°29E **81** D10
Remich *Lux.* 49°32N 6°22E **69** E6
Remiremont *France* 48°0N 6°36E **71** D13
Remontnoye *Russia* 46°34N 43°37E **87** G6
Remoulins *France* 43°55N 4°35E **73** E8
Remscheid *Germany* 51°11N 7°12E **76** D3
Ren Xian *China* 37°8N 114°40E **114** F8
Rendang *Indonesia* 8°26S 115°25E **119** J18
Rende *Italy* 39°20N 16°11E **95** C9
Rendina *Greece* 39°4N 21°58E **98** B3
Rendsburg *Germany* 54°17N 9°39E **76** A5
Renfrew *Canada* 45°30N 76°40W **175** A8
Renfrewshire □ *U.K.* 55°49N 4°38W **65** F4
Renfroe *U.S.A.* 32°14N 84°43W **178** D3
Rengat *Indonesia* 0°30S 102°45E **118** E2
Rengo *Chile* 34°24S 70°50W **190** C1
Renhua *China* 25°5N 113°40E **117** E9
Renhuai *China* 27°48N 106°24E **116** D6
Reni → *Taranagar India* 28°43N 74°50E **124** E6
Reni *Ukraine* 45°28N 28°15E **81** E13
Renigunta *India* 13°38N 79°30E **127** H4
Renland *Greenland* 71°10N 26°30W **57** C8
Renmark *Australia* 34°11S 140°43E **152** B4
Rennell Sd. *Canada* 53°23N 132°35W **162** C2
Renner Springs *Australia* 18°20S 133°47E **150** B1
Rennes *France* 48°7N 1°41W **70** D5
Rennick Glacier *Antarctica* 70°30S 161°45E **55** D11
Renne L. *Canada* 61°32N 105°35W **163** A7
Reno *U.S.A.* 39°31N 119°48W **170** F7
Reno → *Italy* 44°38N 12°16E **93** D9
Renovo *U.S.A.* 41°20N 77°45W **174** E7
Renqiu *China* 38°43N 116°5E **114** E9
Rens *Denmark* 54°54N 9°5E **63** K3
Renshou *China* 29°59N 104°9E **116** C5
Rensselaer *Ind., U.S.A.* 40°57N 87°9W **172** E10
Rensselaer *N.Y., U.S.A.* 42°38N 73°45W **175** D11
Renton *U.S.A.* 47°28N 122°12W **170** C4
Renukoot *India* 24°12N 83°2E **125** G10
Renwick *N.Z.* 41°30S 173°51E **155** B8
Réo *Burkina Faso* 12°28N 2°35W **138** C4
Reocín = Puente San Miguel *Spain* 43°21N 4°5W **88** B6
Reotipur *India* 25°33N 83°45E **125** G10
Repalle *India* 16°2N 80°45E **127** F5
Répcelak *Hungary* 47°24N 17°1E **80** G2
Republic *Mo., U.S.A.* 37°7N 93°29W **172** F7
Republic *Wash., U.S.A.* 48°39N 118°44W **168** B4
Republican → *U.S.A.* 39°4N 96°48W **172** F5
Republika Srpska □ *Bos.-H.* 44°56N 17°11E **93** D14
Repulse B. *Australia* 20°35S 148°46E **150** b
Repulse Bay *Canada* 66°30N 86°30W **161** D14
Requena *Peru* 5°5S 73°52W **188** E3
Requena *Spain* 39°30N 1°4W **91** F3
Requista *France* 44°1N 2°32E **72** D6
Resadiye = Datça *Turkey* 36°46N 27°40E **99** E9
Reşadiye *Tokat, Turkey* 40°23N 37°20E **104** B7
Resadiye Yarımadası *Turkey* 36°40N 27°45E **99** E9
Resavica *Serbia* 44°4N 21°31E **96** B5
Resen *Macedonia* 41°5N 21°10E **98** A3
Resende *Brazil* 22°30S 44°32W **189** E2
Resende → *Brazil* 7°20S 46°37W **188** B7
Reserve *U.S.A.* 33°43N 108°45W **169** K9
Resht = Rasht *Iran* 37°20N 49°40E **105** D13
Resistencia *Argentina* 27°30S 59°0W **190** B5
Reşiţa *Romania* 45°18N 21°53E **80** E6
Resko *Poland* 53°47N 15°25E **82** E2

Reso = Raisio *Finland* 60°28N 22°11E **84** B2
Resolute *Canada* 74°42N 94°54W **161** C13
Resolution I. *Canada* 61°30N 65°0W **161** E19
Resolution I. *N.Z.* 45°40S 166°40E **155** F1
Resplandes *Brazil* 6°15S 45°13W **189** B1
Resplendor *Brazil* 19°25S 41°15W **189** D2
Ressano Garcia *Mozam.* 25°25S 32°0E **145** C5
Reston *Canada* 49°33N 101°6W **163** D8
Reszel *Poland* 54°4N 21°10E **82** D8
Retalhuleu *Guatemala* 14°33N 91°46W **182** D1
Retenue, L. de *Dem. Rep. of the Congo* 11°0S 27°0E **143** E2
Retezat, Munţii *Romania* 45°25N 23°0E **80** E8
Retezat △ *Romania* 45°23N 22°56E **80** E7
Retford *U.K.* 53°19N 0°56W **66** D7
Rethel *France* 49°30N 4°20E **71** C11
Rethem *Germany* 52°47N 9°22E **76** C5
Rethimno *Greece* 35°18N 24°30E **101** D6
Rethymno *Greece* 35°18N 24°30E **101** D6
Reti *Pakistan* 28°5N 69°48E **124** E3
Retiche, Alpi *Switz.* 46°30N 10°0E **77** E8
Retortillo *Spain* 40°48N 6°21W **88** E4
Retournac *France* 45°12N 4°2E **73** C8
Rétság *Hungary* 47°58N 19°10E **80** D5
Réunion ☑ *Ind. Oc.* 21°0S 56°0E **141** c
Reus *Spain* 41°10N 1°5E **90** D6
Reuterstadt Stavenhagen *Germany* 53°42N 12°54E **76** B8
Reutlingen *Germany* 48°29N 9°12E **77** G5
Reutte *Austria* 47°29N 10°43E **77** E6
Reval = Tallinn *Estonia* 59°22N 24°48E **84** C3
Revel *France* 43°28N 2°1E **72** E6
Revelganj *India* 25°50N 84°40E **125** G11
Revelstoke *Canada* 51°0N 118°10W **162** C5
Reventazón *Peru* 6°10S 80°58W **188** B1
Revigny-sur-Ornain *France* 48°49N 4°59E **71** D11
Revillagigedo, Is. de *Pac. Oc.* 18°40N 112°0W **180** D2
Revin *France* 49°56N 4°39E **71** C11
Revúca *Slovak Rep.* 48°41N 20°7E **79** C13
Revuè → *Mozam.* 19°50S 34°0E **143** F3
Rewa *India* 24°33N 81°25E **125** G9
Rewari *India* 28°15N 76°40E **124** E7
Rexburg *U.S.A.* 43°49N 111°47W **168** E8
Rey *Iran* 35°35N 51°25E **108** E14
Rey, I. del *Panama* 8°20N 78°30W **182** E4
Rey, L. del *Mexico* 27°1N 103°26W **180** B4
Rey Malabo *Eq. Guin.* 3°45N 8°50E **139** E6
Reyðarfjörður *Iceland* 65°2N 14°13W **61** D6
Reyes *Bolivia* 14°19S 67°23W **188** C4
Reyes, Pt. *U.S.A.* 38°0N 123°0W **170** H3
Reyhanlı *Turkey* 36°16N 36°15E **104** D7
Reykjahlíð *Iceland* 65°40N 16°55W **61** D5
Reykjanes *Iceland* 63°48N 22°40W **60** E2
Reykjanes Ridge *Atl. Oc.* 59°0N 31°0W **56** A4
Reykjavík *Iceland* 64°10N 21°57W **60** D3
Reynolds Ra. *Australia* 22°30S 133°0E **148** D5
Reynoldsville *Ga., U.S.A.* 30°51N 84°47W **178** E5
Reynoldsville *U.S.A.* 41°6N 78°53W **174** E6
Reynosa *Mexico* 26°7N 98°18W **181** B5
Rēzekne *Latvia* 56°30N 27°17E **84** D4
Rezina *Moldova* 47°45N 28°58E **81** C13
Rezovo *Bulgaria* 42°0N 28°0E **97** D12
Rezvän *Iran* 27°34N 56°6E **129** E8
Rezvānshahr *Iran* 37°32N 49°7E **105** D13
Rgotina *Serbia* 44°1N 22°17E **96** B6
Rharbi, Zahrez *Algeria* 34°50N 2°55E **136** B4
Rharis, O. → *Algeria* 26°0N 5°4E **136** C5
Rhayader *U.K.* 52°18N 3°29W **67** E4
Rheda-Wiedenbrück *Germany* 51°50N 8°20E **76** D4
Rhede *Germany* 51°50N 6°42E **76** D2
Rhein → *Europe* 51°52N 6°2E **69** C6
Rhein-Main-Donau-Kanal *Germany* 49°1N 11°27E **77** F7
Rhein-Ruhr, Düsseldorf × (DUS) *Germany* 51°17N 6°46E **76** D2
Rhein-Taunus △ *Germany* 50°10N 8°10E **77** E4
Rhein-Westerwald △ *Germany* 50°32N 7°20E **76** E3
Rheinbach *Germany* 50°38N 6°57E **76** E2
Rheine *Germany* 52°17N 7°26E **76** C3
Rheinfelden *Germany* 47°33N 7°47E **77** H3
Rheinland-Pfalz □ *Germany* 50°0N 7°0E **77** F2
Rheinsberg *Germany* 53°6N 12°54E **76** B8
Rheris, Oued → *Morocco* 30°50N 4°34W **136** B3
Rhin = Rhein → *Europe* 51°52N 6°2E **69** C6
Rhine = Rhein → *Europe* 51°52N 6°2E **69** C6
Rhinebeck *U.S.A.* 41°56N 73°55W **175** E11
Rhineland-Palatinate = Rheinland-Pfalz □ *Germany* 50°0N 7°0E **77** F2
Rhinelander *U.S.A.* 45°38N 89°25W **172** C9
Rhinns Pt. *U.K.* 55°40N 6°29W **65** F2
Rhino Camp *Uganda* 3°0N 31°22E **142** B3
Rhir, Cap *Morocco* 30°38N 9°54W **136** B2
Rho *Italy* 45°31N 9°2E **92** C6
Rhode Island □ *U.S.A.* 41°40N 71°30W **175** E13
Rhodes = Ródos *Greece* 36°15N 28°10E **101** C4
Rhodes × (RHO) *Greece* 36°23N 28°12E **99** E10
Rhodope Mts. = Rhodopi Planina *Bulgaria* 41°40N 24°20E **98** B8
Rhodopi Planina *Bulgaria* 41°40N 24°20E **98** B8
Rhön *Germany* 50°24N 9°58E **76** E5
Rhondda *U.K.* 51°39N 3°31W **67** F4
Rhondda Cynon Taff □ *U.K.* 51°42N 3°27W **67** F4
Rhône □ *France* 45°54N 4°35E **73** C8
Rhône → *France* 43°28N 4°42E **73** E8
Rhône-Alpes □ *France* 45°40N 6°0E **73** C9
Rhum = Rùm *U.K.* 57°0N 6°20W **65** E2
Rhydaman = Ammanford *U.K.* 51°48N 3°59W **67** F3
Rhyl *U.K.* 53°20N 3°29W **66** D4
Ri-Aba *Eq. Guin.* 3°28N 8°40E **139** E6
Ria Formosa △ *Portugal* 37°0S 46°37W **89** D2
Riachão *Brazil* 7°20S 46°37W **188** B7
Riacho de Santana *Brazil* 13°37S 42°57W **189** C2

Riansáres → *Spain* 39°32N 3°18W **89** F7
Riasi *India* 33°10N 74°50E **125** C6
Riau □ *Indonesia* 0°0 102°35E **118** E2
Riau, Kepulauan □ *Indonesia* 0°30N 104°20E **118** D2
Riau Arch. = Riau, Kepulauan □ *Indonesia* 0°30N 104°20E **118** D2
Riaza *Spain* 41°18N 3°30W **88** D7
Riaza → *Spain* 41°42N 3°55W **88** D7
Riba de Saelices *Spain* 40°55N 2°17W **90** E2
Ribadavia *Spain* 42°17N 8°8W **88** C2
Ribadeo *Spain* 43°35N 7°5W **88** B3
Ribadesella *Spain* 43°30N 5°7W **88** B5
Ribado *Nigeria* 9°16N 12°47E **139** D7
Ribamar *Brazil* 2°33S 44°5W **189** A2
Ribao *Cameroon* 6°32N 11°30E **139** D7
Ribas = Ribes de Freser *Spain* 42°19N 2°15E **90** C7
Ribas do Rio Pardo *Brazil* 20°27S 53°46W **187** H8
Ribauè *Mozam.* 14°57S 38°17E **143** E4
Ribble → *U.K.* 53°52N 2°25W **66** D5
Ribe *Denmark* 55°19N 8°44E **63** J2
Ribeauvillé *France* 48°10N 7°20E **71** D14
Ribeira *Spain* 42°36N 8°58W **88** C2
Ribeira Brava *Madeira* 32°41N 17°4W **100** D2
Ribeira do Pombal *Brazil* 10°50S 38°32W **189** C3
Ribeira Grande *C. Verde Is.* 17°0N 25°4W **134** b
Ribeirão Prêto *Brazil* 21°10S 47°50W **191** A6
Ribeiro Gonçalves *Brazil* 7°32S 45°14W **189** B1
Ribemont *France* 49°47N 3°27E **71** C10
Ribera *Italy* 37°30N 13°16E **94** E6
Ribérac *France* 45°15N 0°20E **72** C4
Riberalta *Bolivia* 11°0S 66°0W **186** F5
Ribnica *Slovenia* 45°45N 14°45E **93** C11
Ribnitz-Damgarten *Germany* 54°15N 12°27E **76** A8
Ričany *Czech Rep.* 50°0N 14°40E **78** B7
Riccarton *N.Z.* 43°32S 172°37E **155** D7
Riccia *Italy* 41°30N 14°50E **95** A7
Riccione *Italy* 43°59N 12°39E **93** E9
Rice *U.S.A.* 34°5N 114°51W **171** L12
Rice L. *Canada* 44°12N 78°10W **174** B6
Rice Lake *U.S.A.* 45°30N 91°44W **172** C8
Riceboro *U.S.A.* 31°44N 81°26W **178** D8
Rich, C. *Canada* 44°43N 80°38W **174** B4
Richard Toll *Senegal* 16°28N 15°41W **138** B1
Richards Bay *S. Africa* 28°48S 32°6E **145** C5
Richardson → *Canada* 58°25N 111°14W **163** B6
Richardson Lakes *U.S.A.* 44°46N 70°58W **173** C18
Richardson Mts. *N.Z.* 44°49S 168°34E **155** E3
Richardson Springs *U.S.A.* 39°51N 121°46W **170** F5
Riche, C. *Australia* 34°36S 118°47E **149** F2
Richelieu *France* 47°1N 0°20E **70** E7
Richey *U.S.A.* 47°39N 105°4W **168** C11
Richfield *U.S.A.* 38°46N 112°5W **168** G7
Richfield Springs *U.S.A.* 42°51N 74°59W **175** D10
Richford *U.S.A.* 45°0N 72°40W **175** B12
Richibucto *Canada* 46°42N 64°54W **165** C7
Richland *Ga., U.S.A.* 32°5N 84°40W **178** C5
Richland *Wash., U.S.A.* 46°17N 119°18W **168** C4
Richland Center *U.S.A.* 43°21N 90°23W **172** D8
Richlands *U.S.A.* 37°6N 81°48W **173** G13
Richmond *N.S.W., Australia* 33°35S 150°42E **153** B9
Richmond *Queens., Australia* 20°43S 143°8E **150** C3
Richmond *U.K.* 54°25N 1°43W **66** C6
Richmond *Calif., U.S.A.* 37°56N 122°21W **170** H4
Richmond *Ind., U.S.A.* 39°50N 84°53W **173** F11
Richmond *Ky., U.S.A.* 37°45N 84°18W **173** G11
Richmond *Mich., U.S.A.* 42°49N 82°45W **174** D2
Richmond *Mo., U.S.A.* 39°17N 93°58W **172** F7
Richmond *Tex., U.S.A.* 29°35N 95°46W **176** G7
Richmond *Utah, U.S.A.* 41°56N 111°48W **168** F8
Richmond *Va., U.S.A.* 37°33N 77°27W **173** G15
Richmond *Vt., U.S.A.* 44°24N 72°59W **175** B12
Richmond, Mt. *N.Z.* 41°32S 173°22E **155** B8
Richmond Hill *Canada* 43°52N 79°27W **174** C5
Richmond Ra. *Australia* 29°0S 152°45E **151** D5
Richmondville *U.S.A.* 42°38N 74°33W **175** D10
Richtersveld △ *S. Africa* 28°15S 17°10E **144** C2
Richville *U.S.A.* 44°25N 75°23W **175** B9
Richwood *U.S.A.* 38°14N 80°32W **173** F13
Ricla *Spain* 41°31N 1°24W **90** D3
Rico *U.S.A.* 37°41N 108°3W **169** H9
Riddlesburg *U.S.A.* 40°9N 78°15W **174** F6
Rideau → *Canada* 45°27N 75°42W **175** A9
Ridge Spring *U.S.A.* 33°51N 81°40W **178** B6
Ridgecrest *U.S.A.* 35°38N 117°40W **171** K9
Ridgefield *Conn., U.S.A.* 41°17N 73°30W **175** E11
Ridgefield *Wash., U.S.A.* 45°49N 122°45W **170** E4
Ridgeland *Miss., U.S.A.* 32°26N 90°8W **179** E9
Ridgeland *S.C., U.S.A.* 32°29N 80°59W **178** D7
Ridgetown *Canada* 42°26N 81°52W **174** D3
Ridgewood *U.S.A.* 40°59N 74°7W **175** F10
Ridgway *U.S.A.* 41°25N 78°44W **174** E6
Riding Mountain △ *Canada* 50°50N 100°0W **163** C9
Ridley, Mt. *Australia* 33°12S 122°7E **149** F3
Riebeek-Oos *S. Africa* 33°10S 26°10E **144** D4
Ried *Austria* 48°14N 13°30E **76** G7
Riedlingen *Germany* 48°9N 9°28E **77** G5
Riedstadt *Germany* 49°50N 8°30E **77** F4
Rienza → *Italy* 46°49N 11°47E **93** B8
Riesa *Germany* 51°17N 13°17E **76** D9
Riesco, I. *Chile* 52°55S 72°45W **192** D2
Riesi *Italy* 37°17N 14°5E **95** E7
Riet → *S. Africa* 29°0S 23°54E **144** C3
Rietavas *Lithuania* 55°44N 21°56E **82** C9

Rietbron S. Africa 32°54S 23°10E **144** D3
Rietfontein Namibia 21°58S 20°58E **144** B3
Rieti Italy 42°24N 12°51E **93** F9
Rieupeyroux France 44°19N 2°12E **72** D6
Riez France 43°49N 6°6E **73** E10
Rif = Er Rif Morocco 35°1N 4°1W **136** A3
Rifle L. U.S.A. 46°32N 122°26W **170** D4
Rifle U.S.A. 39°32N 107°47W **168** G10
Rift Valley Africa 7°0N 30°0E **132** G7
Rift Valley[V] Kenya 0°20N 36°0E **142** B4
Rīga Latvia 56°53N 24°8E **82** B11
Rīga ✈ (RIX) Latvia 56°54N 23°59E **82** B10
Riga, G. of Latvia 57°40N 23°45E **82** A10
Rigacikun Nigeria 10°40N 7°28E **139** C6
Rīgān Iran 28°37N 58°58E **129** D8
Rīgas Jūras Līcis = Riga, G. of
Latvia 57°40N 23°45E **82** A10
Rigaud Canada 45°29N 74°18W **175** A10
Rigby U.S.A. 43°40N 111°55W **168** E8
Rigestān Afghan. 30°15N 65°0E **122** D4
Riggins U.S.A. 45°25N 116°19W **168** D5
Rignac France 44°25N 2°16E **72** D6
Rigolet Canada 54°10N 58°23W **165** B8
Rigu Ghana 9°59N 0°48W **139** D4
Rihand Dam India 24°9N 83°2E **125** G10
Riihimäki Finland 60°45N 24°48E **84** B3
Riiser-Larsen-halvøya
Antarctica 68°0S 35°0E **55** C4
Riiser-Larsen Ice Shelf
S. Ocean 74°0S 19°0W **55** D2
Riiser-Larsen Sea S. Ocean 67°30S 22°0E **55** C4
Riisitunturi △ Finland 66°27N 28°27E **60** C23
Rijau Nigeria 11°8N 5°17E **139** C6
Rijeka Croatia 45°20N 14°21E **93** C11
Rijeka Crnojevića
Montenegro 42°24N 19°1E **96** D3
Rijssen Neths. 52°19N 6°31E **69** B6
Rika → Ukraine 48°11N 23°16E **81** B8
Rikuchū-Kaigan △
Japan 39°20N 142°0E **112** E11
Rikuzentakada Japan 39°0N 141°40E **112** E10
Rila Bulgaria 42°7N 23°7E **96** D7
Rila Planina Bulgaria 42°10N 23°20E **96** D7
Riley U.S.A. 43°32N 119°28W **168** E4
Rima → Nigeria 13°4N 5°10E **139** C6
Rimah, Wadi ar →
Si. Arabia 26°5N 41°30E **128** E4
Rimau, Pulau Malaysia 5°15N 100°16E **121** c
Rimavská Sobota
Slovak Rep. 48°22N 20°2E **79** C13
Rimbey Canada 52°35N 114°15W **162** C6
Rimbo Sweden 59°44N 18°21E **62** E12
Rimersburg U.S.A. 41°3N 79°30W **174** E5
Rimforsa Sweden 58°6N 15°43E **63** F9
Rímini Italy 44°3N 12°33E **93** D9
Rimouski Canada 48°27N 68°30W **165** C6
Rimrock U.S.A. 46°40N 121°7W **170** D5
Rinca Indonesia 8°45S 119°35E **119** F5
Rincon U.S.A. 32°18N 81°14W **178** D8
Rincón de Anchuras →
Spain 39°29N 4°50W **89** F6
Rincón de la Victoria
Spain 36°43N 4°18W **89** J6
Rincón de Romos
Mexico 22°14N 102°18W **180** C4
Rinconada Argentina 22°26S 66°10W **190** A2
Rind → India 25°53N 80°33E **125** G9
Ringarum Sweden 58°21N 16°26E **63** F10
Ringas India 27°21N 75°34E **124** F6
Ringe Denmark 55°13N 10°28E **63** J4
Ringgold Is. Fiji 16°15S 179°25W **154** a
Ringim Nigeria 12°13N 9°10E **139** C6
Ringkøbing Denmark 56°5N 8°15E **63** H2
Ringkøbing Fjord Denmark 56°0N 8°15E **63** H2
Ringsjön Sweden 55°55N 13°30E **63** J7
Ringsted Denmark 55°25N 11°46E **63** J5
Ringvassøya Norway 69°56N 19°15E **60** B18
Ringwood U.S.A. 41°7N 74°15W **175** E10
Rinia Greece 37°23N 25°13E **99** D7
Rinjani, Gunung
Indonesia 8°24S 116°28E **118** F5
Rinteln Germany 52°10N 9°3E **76** C5
Río, Punta del Spain 36°49N 2°24W **91** J2
Rio Branco Brazil 9°58S 67°49W **188** B4
Río Branco Uruguay 32°40S 53°40W **191** C5
Río Bravo Mexico 25°59N 98°6W **181** B5
Río Bravo △ N. Amer. 29°20N 102°45W **180** B4
Río Bravo del Norte →
Mexico 25°57N 97°9W **181** B5
Rio Brilhante Brazil 21°48S 54°33W **191** A5
Río Bueno Chile 40°19S 72°58W **192** B2
Río Claro Brazil 22°19S 47°35W **191** A6
Rio Claro Trin. & Tob. 10°20N 61°18W **183** D7
Río Colorado Argentina 39°0S 64°0W **192** A4
Río Cuarto Argentina 33°10S 64°25W **190** C3
Rio das Pedras Mozam. 23°8S 35°28E **145** B6
Rio de Contas Brazil 13°35S 41°48W **189** C2
Rio de Janeiro Brazil 22°54S 43°12W **191** A7
Rio de Janeiro □ Brazil 22°50S 43°0W **191** A7
Rio do Prado Brazil 16°35S 40°34W **189** D2
Rio do Sul Brazil 27°13S 49°37W **191** B6
Río Dulce △ Guatemala 15°43N 88°50W **182** C2
Río Gallegos Argentina 51°35S 69°15W **192** D3
Rio Grande Argentina 53°50S 67°45W **192** D3
Rio Grande Bolivia 20°51S 67°11W **188** E4
Rio Grande Brazil 32°0S 52°20W **191** C5
Río Grande Mexico 23°50N 103°2W **180** C4
Rio Grande Puerto Rico 18°23N 65°50W **183** d
Rio Grande → N. Amer. 25°58N 97°9W **176** J6
Rio Grande City U.S.A. 26°23N 98°49W **176** H5
Rio Grande de Santiago →
Mexico 21°36N 105°26W **180** C3
Rio Grande do Norte □
Brazil 5°40S 36°0W **189** B3
Rio Grande do Sul □
Brazil 30°0S 53°0W **191** C5
Rio Grande Rise Atl. Oc. 31°0S 35°0W **54** K6
Río Hato Panama 8°22N 80°10W **182** E3
Río Lagartos Mexico 21°36N 88°10W **181** D7
Rio Largo Brazil 9°28S 35°50W **189** D3
Rio Maior Portugal 39°19N 8°57W **89** F2
Río Mayo Argentina 45°40S 70°15W **192** C2
Río Mulatos Bolivia 19°40S 66°50W **188** D4
Río Muni □ Eq. Guin. 1°30N 10°0E **140** D2
Rio Negro Brazil 26°0S 49°55W **191** B6
Río Negro Chile 40°47S 73°14W **192** B2
Río Pardo Brazil 30°0S 52°30W **191** C5
Río Pico Argentina 44°0S 70°22W **192** B2
Río Pilcomayo △
Argentina 25°5S 58°5W **190** B4

Río Plátano △ Honduras 15°45N 85°0W **182** C3
Río Rancho U.S.A. 35°14N 106°41W **169** J10
Río Real Brazil 11°28S 37°56W **189** C3
Rio Segundo Argentina 31°40S 63°59W **190** C3
Río Simpson △ Chile 45°27S 73°30W **192** C2
Río Tercero Argentina 32°15S 64°8W **190** C3
Rio Tinto Brazil 6°48S 35°5W **189** B3
Rio Tinto Portugal 41°8′34W **88** D2
Río Turbio Argentina 51°32S 72°18W **192** D2
Río Verde Brazil 17°50S 51°0W **188** E12
Río Verde Mexico 21°56N 99°59W **181** C5
Rio Vista U.S.A. 38°10N 121°42W **170** G5
Riobamba Ecuador 1°50S 78°45W **186** D3
Ríohacha Colombia 11°33N 72°55W **186** A4
Rioja Peru 6°11S 77°5W **188** B2
Riom France 45°54N 3°7E **72** C7
Riom-ès-Montagnes
France 45°17N 2°39E **72** C6
Rion-des-Landes France 43°55N 0°56W **72** E3
Rionero in Vúlture Italy 40°55N 15°40E **95** B8
Rioni → Georgia 42°14N 41°44E **87** J5
Ríos Spain 41°58N 7°16W **88** D3
Riosucio Colombia 7°27N 77°7W **186** B3
Riou L. Canada 59°7N 106°25W **163** B7
Rioz France 47°26N 6°5E **71** E13
Ripatransone Italy 42°59N 13°46E **93** F10
Ripley Canada 44°4N 81°35W **174** B3
Ripley Calif., U.S.A. 33°32N 114°39W **171** M12
Ripley N.Y., U.S.A. 42°16N 79°43W **174** D5
Ripley Tenn., U.S.A. 35°45N 89°32W **177** D10
Ripley W. Va., U.S.A. 38°49N 81°43W **173** F13
Ripoll Spain 42°15N 2°13E **90** C7
Ripon U.K. 54°9N 1°31W **66** C6
Ripon Calif., U.S.A. 37°44N 121°7W **170** H5
Ripon Wis., U.S.A. 43°51N 88°50W **172** D9
Riposto Italy 37°44N 15°12E **95** E8
Risan Montenegro 42°32N 18°42E **96** D2
Riscle France 43°39N 0°5W **72** E3
Rishā', W. ar →
Si. Arabia 25°33N 44°5E **128** E5
Rishikesh India 30°7N 78°19E **124** D8
Rishiri-Rebun-Sarobetsu △
Japan 45°26N 141°30E **112** B10
Rishiri-Tō Japan 45°11N 141°15E **112** B10
Rishon le Ziyyon Israel 31°58N 34°48E **130** D3
Rishpon Israel 32°12N 34°49E **130** C3
Risnjak △ Croatia 45°25N 14°36E **93** C11
Rison U.S.A. 33°58N 92°11W **176** E8
Risør Norway 58°43N 9°13E **61** G13
Rissani Morocco 31°18N 4°12W **136** B3
Rita Blanca Cr. →
U.S.A. 35°40N 102°29W **176** D3
Ritchie's Arch. India 12°14N 93°10E **127** H11
Riti Nigeria 7°57N 9°41E **139** D6
Ritter, Mt. U.S.A. 37°41N 119°12W **170** H7
Rittman U.S.A. 40°58N 81°47W **174** F3
Riva del Garda Italy 45°53N 10°50E **92** C7
Riva Lígure Italy 43°50N 7°50E **92** E4
Rivadavia B. Aires,
Argentina 35°29S 62°59W **190** D3
Rivadavia Mendoza,
Argentina 33°13S 68°30W **190** C2
Rivadavia Salta,
Argentina 24°5S 62°54W **190** A3
Rivadavia Chile 29°57S 70°35W **190** B1
Rivarolo Canavese Italy 45°19N 7°43E **92** C4
Rivas Nic. 11°30N 85°50W **182** D2
Rivash Iran 35°28N 58°26E **129** C8
Rive-de-Gier France 45°32N 4°37E **73** C8
River Cess Liberia 5°30N 9°32W **138** D3
River Jordan Canada 48°26N 124°3W **170** B2
Rivera Argentina 37°12S 63°14W **190** D3
Rivera Uruguay 31°0S 55°50W **191** C4
Riverbank U.S.A. 37°44N 120°56W **170** H6
Riverdale Calif., U.S.A. 36°26N 119°52W **170** J7
Riverdale N.Z. 33°34N 84°25W **178** B5
Riverhead U.S.A. 40°55N 72°40W **175** F12
Riverhurst Canada 50°55N 106°50W **163** C7
Rivers Canada 50°2N 100°14W **163** C8
Rivers □ Nigeria 4°30N 7°10E **139** E6
Rivers Inlet Canada 51°42N 127°15W **162** C3
Riversdale Canada 44°5N 81°20W **174** B3
Riversdale N.Z. 45°54S 168°44E **155** F3
Riversdale S. Africa 34°7S 21°15E **144** D3
Riverside U.S.A. 33°59N 117°22W **171** M9
Riversleigh Australia 19°5S 138°40E **150** B2
Riverton Australia 34°10S 138°46E **152** C3
Riverton Canada 51°1N 97°0W **163** C9
Riverton N.Z. 46°21S 168°0E **155** G3
Riverton Fla., U.S.A. 27°52N 82°20W **179** H7
Riverton Va., U.S.A. 30°32N 87°21W **179** E2
Rives France 45°21N 5°31E **73** C9
Rivesaltes France 42°47N 2°50E **72** F6
Riviera = Azur, Côte d'
France 43°25N 7°10E **73** E11
Riviera N.Z. 35°4N 114°35W **171** K12
Riviera Beach U.S.A. 26°47N 80°3W **179** J9
Riviera di Levante Italy 44°15N 9°30E **92** D6
Riviera di Ponente Italy 44°10N 8°20E **92** D5
Rivière-au-Renard
Canada 48°59N 64°23W **165** C7
Rivière-du-Loup
Canada 47°50N 69°30W **165** C6
Rivière-Pentecôte
Canada 49°57N 67°1W **165** C6
Rivière-Pilote
Martinique 14°26N 60°53W **182** c
Rivière St-Paul Canada 51°28N 57°45W **165** B8
Rivière-Salée Martinique 14°31N 61°0W **182** c
Rivne Odesa, Ukraine 46°1N 29°10E **81** D14
Rivne Rivne, Ukraine 50°40N 26°10E **75** C14
Rivne □ Ukraine 51°15N 26°30E **75** C14
Rívoli Italy 45°3N 7°31E **92** C4
Rívoli B. Australia 37°32S 140°3E **152** D4
Riwaka N.Z. 41°5S 172°59E **155** D5
Rixheim France 47°40N 7°24E **71** E14
Riyadh = Ar Riyāḍ
Si. Arabia 24°41N 46°42E **128** E5
Riza Greece 40°31N 23°15E **96** F7
Rize Turkey 41°0N 40°30E **105** B9
Rize □ Turkey 41°0N 40°30E **105** B9
Rizhao China 35°25N 119°30E **115** D8
Rizokarpaso Cyprus 35°36N 34°23E **101** D13
Rizzuto, C. Italy 38°53N 17°5E **95** D10
Rjukan Norway 59°54N 8°33E **61** G13
Rkîz, L. Mauritania 16°50N 15°23W **138** B1
Ro Greece 36°9N 29°33E **99** E11
Roa Spain 41°41N 3°56W **88** D7
Road Town Br. Virgin Is. 18°27N 64°37W **183** e

Roan Plateau U.S.A. 39°20N 109°20W **168** G9
Roanne France 46°3N 4°4E **71** F11
Roanoke Ala., U.S.A. 33°9N 85°22W **178** B4
Roanoke Va., U.S.A. 37°16N 79°56W **173** G14
Roanoke → U.S.A. 35°57N 76°42W **177** D16
Roanoke I. U.S.A. 35°53N 75°39W **177** D17
Roanoke Rapids
U.S.A. 36°28N 77°40W **177** C16
Roatán Honduras 16°18N 86°35W **182** C2
Robāt Iran 34°16N 46°47E **105** E12
Robāt Sang Iran 35°35N 59°10E **129** C8
Robāṭkarīm Iran 35°25N 50°59E **129** C6
Robben I. S. Africa 33°46S 18°22E **144** D2
Robbins I. Australia 40°42S 145°0E **151** G4
Róbbio Italy 45°17N 8°35E **92** C5
Robe Australia 37°11S 139°45E **152** D3
Robe → Australia 21°42S 116°15E **148** D2
Röbel Germany 53°22N 12°35E **76** B8
Robert Bourassa, Rés.
Canada 53°40N 76°55W **164** B4
Robert Lee U.S.A. 31°54N 100°29W **176** F4
Roberta U.S.A. 32°43N 84°1W **178** C5
Robertsdale U.S.A. 40°11N 78°6W **174** F6
Robertsganj India 24°44N 83°4E **125** G10
Robertson S. Africa 33°46S 19°50E **144** D2
Robertson I. Antarctica 65°15S 59°30W **55** C18
Robertson Ra. Australia 23°15S 121°0E **148** D3
Robertsport Liberia 6°45N 11°26W **138** D2
Robertstown Australia 33°58S 139°5E **152** B3
Roberval Canada 48°32N 72°15W **165** C5
Robeson Chan. N. Amer. 82°0N 61°30W **57** A4
Robesonia U.S.A. 40°21N 76°8W **175** F8
Robinson U.S.A. 39°0N 87°44W **172** F10
Robinson → Australia 16°3S 137°16E **150** B2
Robinson Crusoe I.
Pac. Oc. 33°38S 78°52W **184** F2
Robinson Ra. Australia 25°40S 119°0E **149** E2
Robinvale Australia 34°40S 142°45E **152** C5
Robledo Spain 38°46N 2°26W **91** G2
Roblin Canada 51°14N 101°21W **163** C8
Robore Bolivia 18°10S 59°45W **186** G7
Robson, Mt. Canada 53°10N 119°10W **162** C5
Robstown U.S.A. 27°47N 97°40W **176** H6
Roca, C. da Portugal 38°40N 9°31W **89** G1
Roca Partida, I. Mexico 19°1N 112°2W **180** D2
Rocas, Atol das Brazil 4°0S 34°1W **187** D12
Rocca San Casciano Italy 44°3N 11°50E **93** D8
Roccadáspide Italy 40°27N 15°10E **95** B8
Roccastrada Italy 43°0N 11°10E **93** E8
Roccella Iónica Italy 38°19N 16°24E **95** D9
Rocciamelone, Mte. Italy 45°12N 7°5E **73** C11
Rocha Uruguay 34°30S 54°25W **191** C5
Rochdale U.K. 53°38N 2°9W **66** D5
Roche Melon = Rocciamelone,
Mte. Italy 45°12N 7°5E **73** C11
Rochechouart France 45°50N 0°49E **72** C4
Rochefort Belgium 50°9N 5°12E **69** D5
Rochefort France 45°56N 0°57W **72** C3
Rochefort-en-Terre
France 47°42N 2°22W **70** E4
Rochelle, Ga., U.S.A. 31°57N 83°27W **178** D6
Rochelle Ill., U.S.A. 41°56N 89°4W **172** E9
Rocher River Canada 61°23N 112°44W **162** A6
Rochesservière France 46°57N 1°30W **70** F5
Rochester Canada 36°22S 144°41E **152** D6
Rochester U.K. 51°23N 0°31E **67** F8
Rochester Ind., U.S.A. 41°4N 86°13W **172** E10
Rochester Minn., U.S.A. 44°1N 92°28W **172** C7
Rochester N.H.,
U.S.A. 43°18N 70°59W **175** C14
Rochester N.Y., U.S.A. 43°10N 77°37W **174** C7
Rociu Romania 44°43N 25°2E **81** F10
Rock → U.S.A. 41°29N 90°37W **172** E8
Rock, The Australia 35°15S 147°2E **153** C7
Rock Creek U.S.A. 41°40N 80°52W **174** E4
Rock Falls U.S.A. 41°47N 89°41W **172** E9
Rock Flat Australia 36°21S 149°13E **153** D8
Rock Hill U.S.A. 34°56N 81°1W **177** D14
Rock Island U.S.A. 41°30N 90°34W **172** E8
Rock Port U.S.A. 40°25N 95°31W **172** E6
Rock Rapids U.S.A. 43°26N 96°10W **172** D5
Rock Sound Bahamas 24°54N 76°12W **182** B4
Rock Springs Mont.,
U.S.A. 46°49N 106°15W **168** C10
Rock Springs Wyo.,
U.S.A. 41°35N 109°14W **168** F9
Rock Valley U.S.A. 43°12N 96°18W **172** D5
Rockall Atl. Oc. 57°37N 13°42W **56** D3
Rockall Trough Atl. Oc. 57°0N 12°0W **56** A10
Rockdale Tex., U.S.A. 30°39N 97°0W **176** F6
Rockdale Wash.,
U.S.A. 47°22N 121°28W **170** C5
Rockeby = Mungkan Kandju △
Australia 13°35S 142°52E **150** A3
Rockefeller Plateau
Antarctica 76°0S 130°0W **55** E14
Rockford Ala., U.S.A. 32°53N 86°13W **178** C3
Rockford Ill., U.S.A. 42°16N 89°6W **172** D9
Rockglen Canada 49°11N 105°57W **163** D7
Rockhampton
Australia 23°22S 150°32E **150** C5
Rockingham Australia 32°15S 115°38E **149** F2
Rockingham N.C.,
U.S.A. 34°57N 79°46W **177** D15
Rockingham Vt.,
U.S.A. 43°11N 72°29W **175** C12
Rockingham B.
Australia 18°5S 146°10E **150** B4
Rocklake U.S.A. 48°47N 99°15W **172** A4
Rockland Canada 45°33N 75°17W **175** A9
Rockland Idaho,
U.S.A. 42°34N 112°53W **168** E7
Rockland Maine, U.S.A. 44°6N 69°7W **173** C19
Rockland Mich., U.S.A. 46°44N 89°11W **172** B9
Rocklands Reservoir
Australia 37°15S 142°5E **152** D5
Rockledge U.S.A. 28°20N 80°43W **179** G9
Rocklin U.S.A. 38°48N 121°14W **170** G5
Rockly B. Trin. & Tob. 11°9N 60°46W **187** D16
Rockmart U.S.A. 34°1N 85°3W **178** A4
Rockport Mass.,
U.S.A. 42°39N 70°37W **175** D14
Rockport Tex., U.S.A. 28°2N 97°3W **176** G6
Rocksprings U.S.A. 30°1N 100°13W **176** F4
Rockville Conn.,
U.S.A. 41°52N 72°28W **175** E12
Rockville Md., U.S.A. 39°5N 77°9W **173** F15
Rockwall U.S.A. 32°56N 96°28W **176** E6
Rockwell City U.S.A. 42°24N 94°38W **172** D6
Rockwood Canada 43°37N 80°8W **174** C4

Rockwood Maine,
U.S.A. 45°41N 69°45W **173** C19
Rockwood Tenn.,
U.S.A. 35°52N 84°41W **177** D12
Rocky Ford U.S.A. 38°3N 103°43W **168** G12
Rocky Gully Australia 34°30S 116°57E **149** F2
Rocky Harbour
Canada 49°36N 57°55W **165** C8
Rocky Island L. Canada 46°55N 83°0W **164** C3
Rocky Lane Canada 58°31N 116°22W **162** B5
Rocky Mount U.S.A. 35°57N 77°48W **177** D16
Rocky Mountain △
Canada 40°25N 105°45W **168** F11
Rocky Mountain House
Canada 52°22N 114°55W **162** C6
Rocky Mts. N. Amer. 49°0N 115°0W **168** B6
Rocky Point Namibia 19°3S 12°30E **144** B1
Rocroi France 49°55N 4°30E **71** C11
Rod Pakistan 28°10N 63°5E **122** E3
Roda Greece 39°48N 19°46E **101** A3
Rødberg Denmark 54°41N 11°23E **63** K5
Rødbyhavn Denmark 54°39N 11°22E **63** K5
Roddickton Canada 50°51N 56°8W **165** B8
Rødding Denmark 55°23N 9°3E **63** J3
Rødby Sweden 56°15N 15°37E **63** H9
Rødekro Denmark 55°4N 9°20E **63** J3
Rodenkirchen Germany 53°23N 8°26E **76** B4
Rodez France 44°21N 2°33E **72** D6
Rhodes = Rhodes
Greece 36°15N 28°10E **101** C10
Rodi Gargánico Italy 41°55N 15°53E **93** G12
Rodia Greece 35°22N 25°1E **101** D7
Rodina Kazakhstan 50°16N 66°53E **109** B7
Rodna Romania 47°25N 24°50E **81** C9
Rodna △ Australia 23°45S 132°4E **148** D5
Rodnei, Munţii Romania 47°35N 24°35E **81** C9
Rodney Canada 42°34N 81°41W **174** D3
Rodney, C. N.Z. 36°17S 174°50E **154** C3
Rodniki Russia 57°7N 41°47E **86** B5
Rodópi Greece 35°34N 23°45E **101** D5
Rodrigues Ind. Oc. 19°45S 63°20E **146** F5
Roe → U.K. 55°6N 6°59W **64** A5
Roebling U.S.A. 40°7N 74°47W **175** F10
Roebourne Australia 20°44S 117°9E **148** D2
Roebuck B. Australia 18°5S 122°20E **148** C3
Roebuck Roadhouse
Australia 17°59S 122°36E **148** C3
Roermond Neths. 51°12N 6°0E **69** C6
Roes Welcome Sd.
Canada 65°0N 87°0W **161** E14
Roeselare Belgium 50°57N 3°7E **69** D3
Rogachev = Ragachow
Belarus 53°8N 30°5E **75** B16
Rogagua, L. Bolivia 13°43S 66°50W **188** C4
Rogaška Slatina
Slovenia 46°15N 15°42E **93** B12
Rogatec Slovenia 46°15N 15°46E **93** B12
Rogatica Bos.-H. 43°47N 19°0E **96** B4
Rogatyn Ukraine 49°24N 24°36E **75** D13
Rogen Sweden 62°20N 12°20E **62** B6
Rogers U.S.A. 36°20N 94°7W **176** C7
Rogers City U.S.A. 45°25N 83°49W **173** C12
Rogersville Canada 46°44N 65°26W **165** C6
Roggan → Canada 54°24N 79°25W **164** B4
Roggan L. Canada 54°8N 77°50W **164** B4
Roggeveen Basin
Pac. Oc. 31°30S 95°30W **157** L18
Roggeveldberge
S. Africa 32°10S 20°10E **144** D3
Roggiano Gravina Italy 39°37N 16°9E **95** C9
Rogliano France 42°57N 9°30E **73** F13
Rogliano Italy 39°10N 16°19E **95** C9
Rogoaguado, L. Bolivia 13°0S 65°30W **186** F5
Rogojampi Indonesia 8°19S 114°17E **119** J17
Rogozno Poland 52°45N 16°59E **83** F3
Rogue → U.S.A. 42°26N 124°26W **168** E1
Roha India 18°26N 73°7E **126** E1
Rohan France 48°4N 2°45W **70** D4
Rohnert Park U.S.A. 38°16N 122°40W **170** G4
Rohri Pakistan 27°45N 68°51E **124** F3
Rohri Canal Pakistan 26°15N 68°27E **124** F3
Rohtak India 28°55N 76°43E **124** E7
Roi Et Thailand 16°4N 103°40E **120** D4
Roja Latvia 57°29N 22°43E **82** A9
Rojas Argentina 34°10S 60°45W **190** C3
Rojo, C. Mexico 21°33N 97°20W **181** C5
Rokan → Indonesia 2°0N 100°50E **118** D2
Rokel → S. Leone 8°30N 12°48W **138** D2
Rokiškis Lithuania 55°55N 25°35E **84** E3
Rokitno Russia 50°57N 35°56E **88** G8
Rokua △ Finland 64°40N 26°10E **60** D22
Rokycany Czech Rep. 49°43N 13°35E **78** B6
Rolândia Brazil 23°18S 51°23W **191** A5
Rolla Mo., U.S.A. 37°57N 91°46W **172** G8
Rolla N. Dak., U.S.A. 48°52N 99°37W **172** A4
Rolle Switz. 46°28N 6°4E **95** C2
Rolleston Australia 24°28S 148°35E **150** C4
Rolleston N.Z. 43°35S 172°24E **155** D7
Rollingstone Australia 19°2S 146°24E **150** B4
Roma Australia 26°32S 148°49E **151** D4
Roma Italy 41°54N 12°28E **93** G9
Roma Sweden 57°32N 18°26E **63** G12
Roma Fiumicino ✈ (FCO)
Italy 41°48N 12°15E **93** G9
Roma-Los Saenz U.S.A. 26°24N 99°1W **176** H5
Romain, C. U.S.A. 33°0N 79°22W **177** E15
Romaine → Canada 50°18N 63°47W **165** B7
Roman Bulgaria 43°8N 23°57E **96** C7
Roman Romania 46°57N 26°55E **81** C11
Roman-Kosh, Gora
Ukraine 44°37N 34°15E **85** K8
Romanche → France 45°5N 5°43E **73** C9
Romang Indonesia 7°30S 127°20E **119** F7
Români Egypt 30°59N 32°38E **130** E1
Romania ■ Europe 46°0N 25°0E **81** F9
Romanija Bos.-H. 43°50N 18°45E **80** G3
Romano, C. U.S.A. 25°51N 81°41W **179** H7
Romano, Cayo Cuba 22°0N 77°30W **182** B4
Romans-sur-Isère France 45°3N 5°3E **73** C9
Romanshorn Switz. 47°33N 9°22E **95** B5
Romanzof C. U.S.A. 61°49N 166°6W **166** C6
Romblon Phil. 12°33N 122°17E **117** E5
Rome = Roma Italy 41°54N 12°28E **93** G9
Rome Ga., U.S.A. 34°15N 85°10W **178** A4
Rome N.Y., U.S.A. 43°13N 75°27W **175** C9
Rome Pa., U.S.A. 41°51N 76°21W **175** E8
Rometta Italy 38°10N 15°25E **95** D8

Romilly-sur-Seine
France 48°31N 3°44E **71** D10
Romiton Uzbekistan 39°56N 64°23E **108** E6
Rommani Morocco 33°31N 6°40W **136** B2
Romney U.S.A. 39°21N 78°45W **173** F14
Romney Marsh U.K. 51°2N 0°54E **67** F8
Romny Ukraine 50°48N 33°28E **85** G7
Rømø Denmark 55°10N 8°30E **63** J2
Romodan Ukraine 49°55N 33°15E **85** G7
Romodanovo Russia 54°26N 45°23E **86** C7
Romont Switz. 46°42N 6°54E **77** J2
Romorantin-Lanthenay
France 47°21N 1°45E **71** E8
Rompin → Malaysia 2°49N 103°29E **121** L4
Romsdalen Norway 62°25N 7°52E **60** E12
Romsey U.K. 51°0N 1°29W **67** G6
Ron India 15°40N 75°44E **127** G2
Ron Vietnam 17°53N 106°27E **120** D6
Rona U.K. 57°34N 5°59W **65** D3
Ronan U.S.A. 47°32N 114°6W **168** C6
Roncador, Cayos
Colombia 13°32N 80°4W **182** D3
Roncador, Serra do
Brazil 12°30S 52°30W **187** F8
Roncíglione Italy 42°17N 12°13E **93** F9
Ronco → Italy 44°24N 12°12E **93** D8
Ronda Spain 36°46N 5°12W **89** J5
Ronda, Serranía de Spain 36°44N 5°3W **89** J5
Rondane Norway 61°57N 9°50E **60** F13
Rondônia □ Brazil 11°0S 63°0W **186** F6
Rondonópolis Brazil 16°28S 54°38W **187** G8
Rondu Pakistan 35°32N 75°10E **125** B6
Rong, Koh Cambodia 10°45N 103°15E **121** G4
Rong Jiang → China 24°35N 109°20E **116** E7
Rong Xian China 22°50N 110°31E **117** F8
Rong'an China 25°14N 109°22E **116** E7
Rongcheng China 29°20N 105°32E **116** C5
Rongcheng China 37°9N 122°23E **115** F12
Ronge, L. la Canada 55°6N 105°17W **163** B7
Rongjiang China 25°57N 108°28E **116** E7
Rongotea N.Z. 40°19S 175°25E **154** C4
Rongshui China 25°5N 109°12E **116** E7
Rongxian China 29°23N 104°22E **116** C5
Rønne Denmark 55°6N 14°43E **63** J8
Ronne Ice Shelf
Antarctica 77°30S 60°0W **55** D18
Ronneby Sweden 56°12N 15°17E **63** H9
Ronnebyån → Sweden 56°11N 15°18E **63** H9
Rönneshytta Sweden 58°56N 15°2E **63** F9
Ronsard, C. Australia 24°46S 113°10E **149** D1
Ronse Belgium 50°45N 3°35E **69** D3
Roodepoort S. Africa 26°11S 27°54E **145** C4
Roof Butte U.S.A. 36°28N 109°5W **168** G9
Rooiboklaagte →
Namibia 20°50S 21°0E **144** B3
Rooiu, Mt. Tahiti 17°49S 149°12W **155** b
Roopville U.S.A. 33°27N 85°8W **178** B4
Roorkee India 29°52N 77°59E **124** E7
Roosendaal Neths. 51°32N 4°29E **69** C4
Roosevelt U.S.A. 40°18N 109°59W **168** F9
Roosevelt → Brazil 7°35S 60°20W **186** E6
Roosevelt, Mt. Canada 58°26N 125°20W **162** B3
Roosevelt I. Antarctica 79°30S 162°0W **55** D12
Ropczyce Poland 50°4N 21°38E **83** H8
Roper → Australia 14°43S 135°27E **150** A2
Roper Bar Australia 14°44S 134°44E **150** A1
Roper River = St. Vidgeon's △
Australia 14°33S 134°53E **150** A1
Roque Pérez Argentina 35°25S 59°24W **190** D4
Roquefort France 44°2N 0°20W **72** D3
Roquemaure France 44°3N 4°46E **73** D8
Roquetas de Mar Spain 36°46N 2°36W **91** J2
Roquetes Spain 40°50N 0°30E **90** E5
Roquevaire France 43°20N 5°36E **73** E9
Roraima □ Brazil 2°0N 61°30W **186** C6
Roraima, Mt. Venezuela 5°10N 60°40W **186** B6
Røros Norway 62°35N 11°23E **60** E14
Rorschach Switz. 47°28N 9°28E **77** H5
Ros Comáin = Roscommon
Ireland 53°38N 8°11W **64** C3
Ros Mhic Thriúin = New Ross
Ireland 52°23N 6°57E **64** D5
Rosa Zambia 9°33S 31°15E **143** D3
Rosa, C. Algeria 37°0N 8°16E **136** A5
Rosa, Monte Europe 45°57N 7°53E **92** C4
Rosal de la Frontera
Spain 37°59N 7°13W **89** H3
Rosalia U.S.A. 47°14N 117°22W **168** C5
Rosamond U.S.A. 34°52N 118°10W **171** L8
Rosans France 44°24N 5°29E **73** D9
Rosário Brazil 3°0S 44°15W **189** A2
Rosario Mexico 22°58N 105°53W **180** C3
Rosario Paraguay 24°30S 57°35W **190** A4
Rosario de la Frontera
Argentina 25°50S 65°0W **190** B3
Rosario de Lerma
Argentina 24°59S 65°35W **190** A3
Rosario del Tala
Argentina 32°20S 59°10W **190** C4
Rosário do Sul Brazil 30°15S 54°55W **191** C5
Rosarito Baja Calif.,
Mexico 32°20N 117°2W **171** N9
Rosarito Baja Calif.,
Mexico 28°38N 114°1W **180** B2
Rosarno Italy 38°29N 15°58E **95** D8
Roscoe U.S.A. 41°56N 74°55W **175** E10
Roscoff France 48°44N 3°58W **70** D3
Roscommon Ireland 53°38N 8°11W **64** C3
Roscommon □ Ireland 53°49N 8°23W **64** C3
Roscrea Ireland 52°57N 7°49W **64** D4
Rose → Australia 14°16S 135°45E **150** A2
Rose, L. Bahamas 21°0N 73°30W **183** B5
Rose Belle Mauritius 20°24S 57°36E **141** d
Rose Blanche Canada 47°38N 58°45W **165** C8
Rose Hill Mauritius 20°14S 57°27E **141** d
Rose Pt. Canada 54°11N 131°39W **162** C2
Rose Valley Canada 52°19N 103°49W **163** C8
Roseau Dominica 15°17N 61°24W **183** C7
Roseau U.S.A. 48°51N 95°46W **172** A6
Rosebery Australia 41°46S 145°33E **151** G4
Rosebud Australia 38°21S 144°54E **152** E6
Rosebud S. Dak.,
U.S.A. 43°14N 100°51W **172** D3
Rosebud Tex., U.S.A. 31°4N 96°59W **176** F6
Roseburg U.S.A. 43°13N 123°20W **168** E2
Rosedale Canada 51°26N 101°23W **171** N9
Rosehearty U.K. 57°42N 2°7W **65** D6
Roseires Res. Sudan 11°51N 34°23E **135** F12
Roseland U.S.A. 38°25N 122°43W **170** G4

Rosemary Canada 50°46N 112°5W **162** C6
Rosenberg U.S.A. 29°34N 95°49W **176** G7
Rosendaël France 51°3N 2°24E **71** A9
Rosenheim Germany 47°51N 12°7E **77** H8
Roses Spain 42°19N 3°10E **90** C8
Roses, G. de Spain 42°10N 3°15E **90** C8
Roseto degli Abruzzi
Italy 42°41N 14°1E **93** F11
Rosetown Canada 51°35N 107°59W **163** C7
Rosetta = Rashîd Egypt 31°21N 30°22E **137** E7
Roseville Calif., U.S.A. 38°45N 121°17W **170** G5
Roseville Mich., U.S.A. 42°30N 82°56W **174** D2
Rosewood Australia 27°38S 152°36E **151** D5
Rosières-en-Santerre
France 49°49N 2°42E **71** C9
Rosignano Maríttimo
Italy 43°24N 10°28E **92** E7
Rosignol Guyana 6°15N 57°30W **186** B7
Roşiori de Vede Romania 44°9N 25°0E **81** F10
Rositsa Bulgaria 43°57N 27°57E **97** C11
Rositsa → Bulgaria 43°10N 25°30E **97** C9
Roskilde Denmark 55°38N 12°3E **63** J6
Roskovec Albania 40°44N 19°43E **96** F3
Roslavl Russia 53°57N 32°55E **84** F4
Rosmaninhal Portugal 39°44N 7°5W **88** F3
Rosmead S. Africa 31°29S 25°8E **144** D4
Røsnæs Denmark 55°44N 10°55E **63** J4
Rosolini Italy 36°49N 14°57E **95** F7
Rosporden France 47°57N 3°50W **70** E3
Ross Australia 42°2S 147°30E **151** G4
Ross N.Z. 42°53S 170°49E **155** C5
Ross Béthio Mauritania 16°15N 16°8W **138** B1
Ross Dependency
Antarctica 76°0S 170°0W **55** D12
Ross I. Antarctica 77°30S 168°0E **55** D11
Ross Ice Shelf Antarctica 80°0S 180°0E **55** E12
Ross L. U.S.A. 48°44N 121°4W **168** B3
Ross-on-Wye U.K. 51°54N 2°34W **67** F5
Ross River Australia 23°44S 134°30E **150** C1
Ross River Canada 62°30N 131°30W **162** A2
Ross Sea Antarctica 74°0S 178°0E **55** D11
Rossall Pt. U.K. 53°55N 3°3W **66** D4
Rossan Pt. Ireland 54°42N 8°47W **64** B3
Rossano Italy 39°36N 16°39E **95** C9
Rossburn Canada 50°40N 100°49W **163** C8
Rosseau Canada 45°16N 79°39W **174** A5
Rosseau, L. Canada 45°10N 79°35W **174** A5
Rosses, The Ireland 55°2N 8°20W **64** A3
Rossignol, L. Canada 52°43N 73°40W **164** B5
Rossignol L. Canada 44°12N 65°10W **165** D6
Rossiya = Russia ■
Eurasia 62°0N 105°0E **107** C11
Rossland Canada 49°6N 117°50W **162** D5
Rosslare Ireland 52°17N 6°24W **64** D5
Rosslare Europort = Rosslare
Harbour Ireland 52°15N 6°20W **64** D5
Rosslare Harbour Ireland 52°15N 6°20W **64** D5
Rosslau Germany 51°52N 12°15E **76** D8
Rossmore Canada 44°8N 77°23W **174** B7
Rosso Mauritania 16°40N 15°45W **138** B1
Rosso, C. France 42°14N 8°32E **73** F12
Rossosh Russia 50°15N 39°28E **85** G10
Rossvatnet Norway 65°45N 14°5E **60** D9
Rossville Australia 15°48S 145°15E **150** B4
Røst Norway 67°32N 12°10E **60** C15
Rosthern Canada 52°40N 106°20W **163** C7
Rostock Germany 54°5N 12°8E **76** A8
Rostov Don, Russia 57°14N 39°25E **86** B6
Rostov Yaroslavl, Russia 57°14N 39°25E **84** B10
Rostov □ Russia 48°0N 40°0E **87** J5
Rostrenen France 48°14N 3°21W **70** D3
Roswell Ga., U.S.A. 34°2N 84°22W **178** A5
Roswell N. Mex.,
U.S.A. 33°24N 104°32W **169** K11
Rota Spain 36°37N 6°20W **89** J4
Rotan U.S.A. 32°51N 100°28W **176** E4
Rote Indonesia 10°50S 123°0E **119** F6
Rotenburg Hessen,
Germany 50°59N 9°44E **76** E5
Rotenburg Niedersachsen,
Germany 53°6N 9°25E **76** B5
Roth Germany 49°15N 11°5E **77** F7
Rothaargebirge Germany 51°2N 8°13E **76** D4
Rothaargebirge △
Germany 51°0N 8°15E **76** E4
Rothenburg ob der Tauber
Germany 49°23N 10°11E **77** F6
Rother → U.K. 50°59N 0°45E **67** G8
Rothera Antarctica 67°34S 68°8W **55** C17
Rotherham U.K. 53°26N 1°20W **66** D6
Rothes U.K. 57°32N 3°13W **65** D5
Rothesay Canada 45°23N 66°0W **165** C6
Rothesay U.K. 55°50N 5°3W **65** F3
Roti = Rote Indonesia 10°50S 123°0E **119** F6
Rotja, Pta. Spain 38°38N 1°35E **91** G6
Roto Australia 33°0S 145°30E **153** B6
Rotoaira, L. N.Z. 39°3S 175°45E **154** F4
Rotoehu, L. N.Z. 38°1S 176°32E **154** E5
Rotoiti, L. Bay of Plenty,
N.Z. 38°2S 176°26E **154** E5
Rotoiti, L. W. Coast,
N.Z. 41°51S 172°49E **155** B7
Rotoma, L. N.Z. 38°2S 176°35E **154** E5
Rotondo, Mte. France 42°14N 9°8E **73** F13
Rotorua N.Z. 38°9S 176°16E **154** E5
Rotorua, L. N.Z. 38°5S 176°18E **154** E5
Rott → Germany 48°27N 13°25E **77** G9
Rottenburg Germany 48°28N 8°55E **77** G4
Rotterdam Neths. 51°55N 4°30E **69** C4
Rottne Sweden 57°1N 14°54E **63** G8
Rottnest I. Australia 32°0S 115°27E **149** F2
Rottumeroog Neths. 53°33N 6°34E **69** A6
Rottweil Germany 48°9N 8°37E **77** G4
Rotuma Fiji 12°25S 177°5E **147** C10
Roubaix France 50°40N 3°10E **71** A10
Roudnice nad Labem
Czech Rep. 50°25N 14°15E **78** A7
Rouen France 49°27N 1°4E **70** C8
Rouergue France 44°15N 2°20E **72** D5
Rough Ridge N.Z. 45°10S 169°55E **155** F4
Rouillac France 45°47N 0°4W **72** C3
Rouïssat Algeria 31°55N 5°20E **136** B6
Rouleau Canada 50°10N 104°56W **163** C7
Roulpmaulpma ◎
Australia 23°52S 133°0E **148** D5
Round I. Mauritius 19°51S 57°45E **141** d

Round Mountain U.S.A. 38°43N 117°4W 168 G5
Round Mt. Australia 30°26S 152°16E 153 A10
Round Rock U.S.A. 30°31N 97°41W 176 F6
Roundup U.S.A. 46°27N 108°33W 168 C9
Rousay U.K. 59°10N 3°2W 65 B5
Rouses Point U.S.A. 44°59N 73°22W 175 B11
Rouseville U.S.A. 41°28N 79°42W 174 E5
Rousse = Ruse Bulgaria 43°48N 25°59E 97 C9
Roussenski Lom △ Bulgaria 43°40N 26°10E 97 C10
Roussillon Isère, France 45°24N 4°49E 73 C8
Roussillon Pyrénées-Or., France 42°30N 2°35E 72 F6
Rouxville S. Africa 30°25S 26°50E 144 D4
Rouyn-Noranda Canada 48°20N 79°0W 164 C4
Rovaniemi Finland 66°29N 25°41E 60 C21
Rovato Italy 45°34N 10°0E 92 C7
Rovenki Ukraine 48°5N 39°21E 85 H10
Rovereto Italy 45°53N 11°3E 92 C8
Rovigo Italy 45°4N 11°47E 93 C8
Rovinj Croatia 45°5N 13°40E 93 C10
Rovno = Rivne Ukraine 50°40N 26°10E 75 C14
Rovnoye Russia 50°52N 46°3E 86 E8
Rovuma = Ruvuma → Tanzania 10°29S 40°28E 143 E5
Row'ān Iran 35°8N 48°51E 129 C6
Rowena Australia 29°48S 148°55E 151 D4
Rowley I. Canada 69°6N 77°52W 161 D16
Rowley Shoals Australia 17°30S 119°0E 148 C2
Roxa Guinea-Biss. 11°15N 15°45W 138 C1
Roxas Phil. 11°36N 122°49E 119 B6
Roxboro U.S.A. 36°24N 78°59W 177 C15
Roxborough Trin. & Tob. 11°15N 60°35W 187 J16
Roxburgh N.Z. 45°33S 169°19E 155 F4
Roxbury N.Y., U.S.A. 42°17N 74°33W 175 D10
Roxbury Pa., U.S.A. 40°6N 77°39W 174 F7
Roxby Downs Australia 30°43S 136°46E 151 E2
Roxen Sweden 58°30N 15°40E 63 F9
Roy Mont., U.S.A. 47°20N 108°58W 168 C9
Roy N. Mex., U.S.A. 35°57N 104°12W 169 J11
Roy Utah, U.S.A. 41°10N 112°2W 168 F7
Royal △ Australia 34°5S 151°5E 153 C9
Royal Bardia △ Nepal 28°20N 81°20E 125 E9
Royal Canal Ireland 53°30N 7°13W 64 C4
Royal Chitawan △ Nepal 26°30N 84°30E 125 F11
Royal Geographical Society Is. Canada 68°56N 100°15W 160 D11
Royal Leamington Spa U.K. 52°18N 1°31W 67 E6
Royal Natal △ S. Africa 28°43S 28°51E 145 C4
Royal Palm Beach U.S.A. 26°42N 80°14W 179 J9
Royal Tunbridge Wells U.K. 51°7N 0°16E 67 F8
Royale, Isle U.S.A. 48°0N 88°54W 172 B9
Royalla Australia 35°30S 149°9E 153 C8
Royan France 45°37N 1°2W 72 C2
Roye France 49°42N 2°48E 71 C9
Royston U.K. 52°3N 0°0 67 E7
Rožaj Montenegro 42°50N 20°11E 96 D4
Różan Poland 52°52N 21°25E 83 F8
Rozay-en-Brie France 48°41N 2°58E 71 D9
Rozdilna Ukraine 46°50N 30°2E 81 D15
Rozhnyativ Ukraine 48°56N 24°9E 81 B9
Rozhyshche Ukraine 50°54N 25°15E 75 C13
Rožmitál pod Třemšínem Czech Rep. 49°36N 13°53E 78 B6
Rožňava Slovak Rep. 48°37N 20°35E 79 C13
Rozogi Poland 53°28N 21°19E 82 E8
Rozoy-sur-Serre France 49°40N 4°8E 71 C11
Roztoczański △ Poland 50°37N 23°0E 83 H10
Rozzano Italy 45°22N 9°10E 92 C6
Rrëshen Albania 41°47N 19°49E 96 E3
Rrogozhine Albania 41°4N 19°50E 96 E3
Rtanj Serbia 43°45N 21°50E 96 C5
Rtem, O. er → Algeria 33°29N 5°38E 136 B5
Rtishchevo Russia 52°18N 43°46E 86 D6
Rúa = A Rúa Spain 42°24N 7°6W 88 C3
Ruacaná Namibia 17°27S 14°21E 144 A1
Ruaha △ Tanzania 7°41S 34°30E 142 D3
Ruahine Ra. N.Z. 39°55S 176°2E 154 F5
Ruamahanga → N.Z. 41°24S 175°8E 154 H4
Ruapehu N.Z. 39°17S 175°35E 154 F4
Ruapuke I. N.Z. 46°46S 168°31E 155 G3
Ruâq, W. → Egypt 30°0N 33°49E 130 F2
Ruatoria N.Z. 37°55S 178°20E 154 D7
Ruawai N.Z. 36°8S 173°59E 154 C2
Rub' al Khālī Si. Arabia 19°0N 48°0E 131 D4
Rubeho Mts. Tanzania 6°50S 36°25E 142 D4
Rubezhnoye = Rubizhne Ukraine 49°6N 38°25E 85 H10
Rubh a' Mhail U.K. 55°56N 6°8W 65 F2
Rubha Hunish U.K. 57°42N 6°20W 65 D2
Rubha Robhanais = Lewis, Butt of U.K. 58°31N 6°16W 65 C2
Rubí Spain 41°29N 2°2E 90 D7
Rubicon → U.S.A. 38°53N 121°4W 170 G5
Rubicone → Italy 44°8N 12°28E 93 D9
Rubik Albania 41°46N 19°47E 96 E3
Rubino Ivory C. 6°4N 4°18W 138 D4
Rubio Venezuela 7°43N 72°22W 186 B4
Rubizhne Ukraine 49°6N 38°25E 85 H10
Rubondo △ Tanzania 2°18S 31°58E 142 C3
Rubtsovsk Russia 51°30N 81°10E 109 B10
Ruby L. U.S.A. 40°10N 115°28W 168 F6
Ruby Mts. U.S.A. 40°30N 115°20W 168 F6
Rubyvale Australia 23°25S 147°42E 150 C4
Rucheng China 25°33N 113°38E 117 E9
Ruciane-Nida Poland 53°40N 21°32E 82 E8
Rūd Sar Iran 37°8N 50°18E 129 B6
Ruda Sweden 57°6N 16°7E 63 G10
Ruda Śląska Poland 50°16N 18°50E 83 H5
Rudall Australia 33°43S 136°17E 152 B2
Rudall → Australia 22°34S 122°13E 148 D3
Rudall River △ Australia 22°38S 122°30E 148 D3
Rudbar Iran 36°48N 49°23E 129 B6
Rüdersdorf Germany 52°27N 13°47E 76 C9
Rudewa Tanzania 10°7S 34°40E 143 E3
Rudkøbing Denmark 54°56N 10°41E 63 K4
Rudky Ukraine 49°38N 23°29E 83 J10
Rudna Poland 51°30N 16°17E 83 G3
Rudnik Bulgaria 42°36N 27°30E 97 D11
Rudnik Poland 50°26N 22°15E 83 H9
Rudnik Serbia 44°7N 20°35E 96 B4
Rudnya Russia 54°55N 31°7E 84 E6
Rudnytsa Ukraine 48°16N 28°54E 81 B13
Rudnyy Kazakhstan 52°57N 63°7E 108 B6
Rudo Bos.-H. 43°41N 19°23E 80 G4
Rudolfa, Ostrov Russia 81°45N 58°30E 106 A6
Rudolstadt Germany 50°44N 11°19E 76 E7
Rudong China 32°20N 121°12E 117 A13
Rudozem Bulgaria 41°29N 24°51E 97 E8
Rudrapur India 28°59N 79°24E 125 E8
Rudyard U.S.A. 46°14N 84°36W 173 B11
Rue France 50°15N 1°40E 71 B8
Ruenya → Africa 16°24S 33°48E 143 F3
Rufflin U.S.A. 33°0N 80°49W 178 B9
Ruffling Pt. Br. Virgin Is. 18°44N 64°27W 183 e
Rufiji → Tanzania 7°50S 39°15E 142 D4
Rufino Argentina 34°20S 62°50W 190 C3
Rufisque Senegal 14°40N 17°15W 138 C1
Rufunsa Zambia 15°4S 29°34E 143 F2
Rugao China 32°23N 120°31E 117 A13
Rugby U.K. 52°23N 1°16W 67 E6
Rugby U.S.A. 48°22N 100°0W 172 A4
Rügen Germany 54°22N 13°24E 76 A9
Rügen ⌂ Germany 54°25N 13°25E 76 A9
Rugles France 48°50N 0°40E 70 D7
Ruhengeri Rwanda 1°30S 29°36E 142 C2
Ruhla Germany 50°54N 10°23E 76 E6
Ruhland Germany 51°27N 13°51E 76 D9
Ruhnu Estonia 57°48N 23°15E 82 A10
Ruhr → Germany 51°27N 6°43E 76 D2
Ruhuhu → Tanzania 10°31S 34°34E 143 E3
Rui Barbosa Brazil 12°18S 40°27W 189 C2
Rui'an China 27°47N 120°40E 117 D13
Ruichang China 29°40N 115°39E 117 C10
Ruidoso U.S.A. 33°20N 105°41W 169 K11
Ruijin China 25°48N 116°0E 117 E10
Ruili China 24°6N 97°46E 116 E1
Ruiru Kenya 1°9S 36°58E 142 C4
Ruivo, Pico Madeira 32°45N 16°56W 100 D3
Ruj Bulgaria 42°52N 22°34E 96 D6
Rujen Macedonia 42°9N 22°30E 96 D6
Rujm Tal'at al Jamā'ah Jordan 30°24N 35°30E 130 E4
Ruk Pakistan 27°50N 68°42E 124 F3
Rukhla Pakistan 32°27N 71°57E 124 C4
Ruki → Dem. Rep. of the Congo 0°5N 18°17E 140 E3
Rukumkot Nepal 28°37N 82°37E 125 E10
Rukwa □ Tanzania 7°0S 31°30E 142 D3
Rukwa, L. Tanzania 8°0S 32°20E 142 D3
Rulenge Burundi 2°43S 30°37E 142 C3
Rulhieres, C. Australia 13°56S 127°22E 148 B4
Rum Jordan 29°39N 35°26E 130 F4
Rùm U.K. 57°0N 6°20W 65 E2
Rum Cay Bahamas 23°40N 74°58W 183 B5
Rum Jungle Australia 13°0S 130°59E 148 B5
Ruma Serbia 45°0N 19°50E 80 E4
Ruma △ Kenya 0°39S 34°18E 142 C3
Rumāḥ Si. Arabia 25°29N 47°10E 128 E5
Rumania = Romania ■ Europe 46°0N 25°0E 81 D10
Rumaylah Iraq 30°47N 47°37E 128 D5
Rumaylah, 'Urūq ar Si. Arabia 22°0N 48°30E 131 C4
Rumbek South Sudan 6°54N 29°37E 135 G11
Rumburk Czech Rep. 50°57N 14°32E 78 A7
Rumford U.S.A. 44°33N 70°33W 175 B14
Rumia Poland 54°37N 18°25E 82 D5
Rumilly France 45°53N 5°56E 73 C9
Rumoi Japan 43°56N 141°39E 112 C10
Rumonge Burundi 3°59S 29°26E 142 C2
Rumphi Malaysia 11°1S 33°52E 143 E3
Rumson U.S.A. 40°23N 74°0W 175 F11
Rumuruti Kenya 0°17N 36°32E 142 B4
Runan China 33°0N 114°30E 117 A10
Runanga N.Z. 42°25S 171°15E 155 C6
Runaway, C. N.Z. 37°32S 177°59E 154 D6
Runaway Bay Jamaica 18°27N 77°20W 182 a
Runcorn U.K. 53°21N 2°44W 66 D5
Rundu Namibia 17°52S 19°43E 144 A2
Rungwa Tanzania 6°55S 33°32E 142 D3
Rungwa → Tanzania 7°36S 31°50E 142 D3
Rungwa ⌂ Tanzania 6°53S 34°2E 142 D3
Rungwe Tanzania 9°11S 33°32E 143 D3
Rungwe, Mt. Tanzania 9°8S 33°40E 140 F6
Runka Nigeria 12°28N 7°20E 139 C6
Runn Sweden 60°30N 15°40E 62 D9
Runton Ra. Australia 23°31S 123°6E 148 D3
Ruo Shui → China 41°0N 100°16E 110 C9
Ruokolahti Finland 61°17N 28°50E 84 B5
Ruoqiang China 38°55N 88°10E 109 E11
Rupa India 27°15N 92°21E 123 F18
Rupar India 31°2N 76°38E 124 D7
Rupat Indonesia 1°45N 101°40E 118 D2
Rupea Romania 46°2N 25°13E 81 D10
Rupen → India 23°28N 71°31E 124 H4
Rupert U.S.A. 42°37N 113°41W 168 E7
Rupert → Canada 51°29N 78°45W 164 B4
Rupert B. Canada 51°35N 79°0W 164 B4
Rupert House = Waskaganish Canada 51°30N 78°40W 164 B4
Rupsa India 21°37N 87°1E 125 J12
Rur → Germany 51°11N 5°59E 76 D1
Rurrenabaque Bolivia 14°30S 67°32W 188 C4
Rus → Spain 39°30N 2°30W 91 F2
Rusambo Zimbabwe 16°30S 32°4E 143 F3
Rusape Zimbabwe 18°35S 32°8E 143 F3
Ruschuk = Ruse Bulgaria 43°48N 25°59E 97 C9
Ruse Bulgaria 43°48N 25°59E 97 C9
Ruse □ Bulgaria 43°35N 25°40E 97 C9
Ruşeţu Romania 44°57N 27°14E 81 F12
Rush Ireland 53°31N 6°6W 64 C5
Rushan China 36°56N 121°30E 115 F11
Rushden U.K. 52°18N 0°35W 67 E7
Rushikulya → India 19°23N 85°5E 126 E7
Rushmore, Mt. U.S.A. 43°53N 103°28W 172 D2
Rushville Ill., U.S.A. 40°7N 90°34W 172 E8
Rushville Ind., U.S.A. 39°37N 85°27W 173 F11
Rushville Nebr., U.S.A. 42°43N 102°28W 172 D2
Rushworth Australia 36°32S 145°1E 153 D6
Ruskin U.S.A. 27°43N 82°26W 179 H7
Russas Brazil 4°55S 37°50W 189 A3
Russell Canada 50°50N 101°20W 163 C8
Russell N.Z. 35°16S 174°10E 154 B3
Russell Fla., U.S.A. 30°3N 81°45W 178 E8
Russell Kans., U.S.A. 38°54N 98°52W 172 F4
Russell N.Y., U.S.A. 44°27N 75°9W 175 B9
Russell Pa., U.S.A. 41°56N 79°8W 174 E5
Russell Cave ⌂ U.S.A. 34°59N 85°49W 177 D12
Russell L. Man., Canada 56°15N 101°30W 163 B8
Russell L. N.W.T., Canada 63°5N 115°44W 162 A5
Russellkonda India 19°57N 84°42E 126 E7
Russellville Ala., U.S.A. 34°30N 87°44W 177 D11
Russellville Ark., U.S.A. 35°17N 93°8W 176 D8
Russellville Ky., U.S.A. 36°51N 86°53W 172 G10
Rüsselsheim Germany 49°59N 8°23E 77 F4
Russi Italy 44°22N 12°2E 93 D9
Russia ■ Eurasia 62°0N 105°0E 107 C11
Russian → U.S.A. 38°27N 123°8W 170 G3
Russkaya Arktika △ Russia 73°40N 55°55E 106 B6
Russkiy, Ostrov Russia 43°0N 131°50E 112 C5
Russky Sever △ Russia 59°57N 38°34E 84 B10
Rust Austria 47°49N 16°42E 79 D9
Rustam Shahr Pakistan 26°58N 66°6E 124 F2
Rustavi Georgia 41°30N 45°0E 87 K7
Rustenburg S. Africa 25°41S 27°14E 144 C4
Ruston U.S.A. 32°32N 92°38W 176 E8
Rutana Burundi 3°55S 30°0E 142 C3
Rute Spain 37°19N 4°23W 89 H6
Ruteng Indonesia 8°35S 120°30E 119 F6
Rutenga Zimbabwe 21°15S 30°44E 143 G3
Ruth U.S.A. 43°42N 82°45W 174 C2
Rutherford U.S.A. 38°26N 122°24W 170 G4
Rutherglen Australia 36°5S 146°29E 153 D7
Rutland U.S.A. 43°37N 72°58W 175 C12
Rutland □ U.K. 52°38N 0°40W 67 E7
Rutland I. India 11°25N 92°10E 127 J11
Rutland Water U.K. 52°39N 0°38W 67 E7
Rutledge U.S.A. 33°38N 83°37W 178 B6
Rutledge → Canada 61°4N 112°0W 163 A6
Rutledge L. Canada 61°33N 110°47W 163 A6
Rutog China 33°27N 79°42E 109 F9
Rutqa, W. → Syria 34°30N 41°3E 105 E9
Rutshuru Dem. Rep. of the Congo 1°13S 29°25E 142 C2
Ruvo di Púglia Italy 41°7N 16°29E 95 A9
Ruvu Tanzania 6°49S 38°43E 142 D4
Ruvu → Tanzania 6°23S 38°52E 142 D4
Ruvuba △ Burundi 3°3S 29°33E 142 C2
Ruvuma □ Tanzania 10°20S 36°0E 143 E4
Ruvuma → Tanzania 10°29S 40°28E 143 E5
Ruwais U.A.E. 24°5N 52°50E 129 E7
Ruwenzori Africa 0°30N 29°55E 142 B2
Ruwenzori △ Uganda 0°20N 30°0E 142 B2
Ruya → Zimbabwe 16°27S 32°5E 145 A5
Ruyang China 34°9N 112°27E 114 G7
Ruyigi Burundi 3°29S 30°15E 142 C3
Ruyuan China 24°46N 113°16E 117 E9
Rūzaevka Kazakhstan 52°49N 66°56E 109 B7
Ruzayevka Russia 54°4N 45°0E 86 C7
Ružhevo Konare Bulgaria 42°23N 24°46E 97 D8
Ruzhou China 34°11N 112°52E 114 G7
Ružomberok Slovak Rep. 49°3N 19°17E 79 B12
Ruzyne, Praha ✕ (PRG) Czech Rep. 50°6N 14°16E 78 A7
Rwanda ■ Africa 2°0S 30°0E 142 C3
Ryakhovo Bulgaria 43°58N 26°18E 97 C10
Ryan, L. U.K. 55°0N 5°2W 65 G3
Ryazan Russia 54°40N 39°40E 84 E10
Ryazan □ Russia 54°5N 39°30E 86 C4
Ryazhsk Russia 53°45N 40°3E 84 F11
Rybachiy Russia 55°10N 20°50E 82 C7
Rybachiy Poluostrov Russia 69°43N 32°0E 60 B25
Rybachye = Balykchy Kyrgyzstan 42°26N 76°12E 109 D9
Rybinsk Russia 58°5N 38°50E 84 C10
Rybinskoye Vdkhr. Russia 58°30N 38°25E 84 C10
Rybnik Poland 50°6N 18°32E 83 H5
Rybnitsa = Râbniţa Moldova 47°45N 29°0E 81 C14
Rybnoye Russia 54°45N 39°30E 84 E10
Rychnov nad Kněžnou Czech Rep. 50°10N 16°17E 79 A9
Rychwał Poland 52°4N 18°10E 83 F5
Rycroft Canada 55°45N 118°40W 162 B5
Ryd Sweden 56°27N 14°42E 63 H8
Rydaholm Sweden 56°59N 14°18E 63 H8
Ryde U.K. 50°43N 1°9W 67 G6
Ryderwood U.S.A. 46°23N 123°3W 170 D3
Rydzyna Poland 51°47N 16°39E 83 G3
Rye U.K. 50°57N 0°45E 67 G8
Rye → U.K. 54°11N 0°44W 66 C7
Rye Bay U.K. 50°52N 0°49E 67 G8
Rye Patch Res. U.S.A. 40°28N 118°19W 168 F4
Ryegate U.S.A. 46°18N 109°15W 168 C9
Ryki Poland 51°38N 21°56E 83 G8
Ryley Canada 53°17N 112°26W 162 C6
Rylsk Russia 51°36N 34°43E 85 G8
Rylstone Australia 32°46S 149°58E 153 B8
Rymanów Poland 49°35N 21°51E 83 J8
Ryn Poland 53°57N 21°34E 82 E8
Ryn Peski = Naryn Qum Kazakhstan 47°30N 49°0E 87 G9
Ryōtsu Japan 38°5N 138°26E 112 E9
Rypin Poland 53°3N 19°25E 83 E6
Ryssby Sweden 56°52N 14°10E 63 H8
Rysy Europe 49°10N 20°4E 79 B13
Ryūgasaki Japan 35°54N 140°11E 113 G10
Ryukyu Is. = Ryūkyū-Rettō Japan 26°0N 126°0E 113 M3
Ryūkyū-Rettō Japan 26°0N 126°0E 113 M3
Rzepin Poland 52°20N 14°49E 83 F1
Rzeszów Poland 50°5N 21°58E 83 H8
Rzhev Russia 56°20N 34°20E 84 D8

S

Sa Cabaneta Spain 39°37N 2°45E 100 B9
Sa Canal Spain 38°51N 1°23E 100 C7
Sa Conillera Spain 38°59N 1°13E 100 C7
Sa Dec Vietnam 10°20N 105°46E 121 G5
Sa Dragonera Spain 39°35N 2°19E 100 B9
Sa Kaeo Thailand 13°49N 102°4E 120 F4
Sa Mesquida Spain 39°55N 4°16E 100 B11
Sa Pa Vietnam 22°20N 103°47E 120 A4
Sa Pobla Spain 39°46N 3°1E 90 F8
Sa Savina Spain 38°44N 1°25E 100 C7
Sa'ādat Shahr Iran 30°10N 53°5E 129 D7
Sa'ādatābād Hormozgān, Iran 28°3N 55°53E 129 D7
Sa'ādatābād Kermān, Iran 29°40N 55°51E 129 D7
Saale → Germany 51°56N 11°54E 76 D7
Saaler Bodden Germany 54°20N 12°27E 76 A8
Saalfeld Germany 50°38N 11°21E 76 E7
Saalfelden Austria 47°25N 12°51E 78 D5
Saane → Switz. 47°8N 7°10E 77 H3
Saanich Canada 48°29N 123°26W 170 B3
Saar → Europe 49°41N 6°32E 69 E6
Saar-Hunsrück ⌂ Germany 49°30N 6°50E 77 F2
Saarbrücken Germany 49°14N 6°59E 77 F2
Saarburg Germany 49°36N 6°32E 77 F2
Saaremaa Estonia 58°30N 22°30E 84 C2
Saarijärvi Finland 62°43N 25°16E 60 E21
Saarland □ Germany 49°20N 7°0E 77 F2
Saarlouis Germany 49°18N 6°45E 77 F2
Saatlı Azerbaijan 39°55N 48°22E 105 C13
Sab 'Âbar Syria 33°46N 37°41E 104 F7
Saba W. Indies 17°38N 63°14W 183 C7
Šabac Serbia 44°48N 19°42E 96 B3
Sabadell Spain 41°28N 2°7E 90 D7
Sabah □ Malaysia 6°0N 117°0E 118 C5
Sabak Bernam Malaysia 3°46N 100°58E 121 L3
Sabalān, Kūhhā-ye Iran 38°15N 47°45E 105 C12
Sabalana, Kepulauan Indonesia 6°45S 118°50E 119 F5
Sabana de la Mar Dom. Rep. 19°7N 69°24W 183 C6
Sábanalarga Colombia 10°38N 74°55W 186 A4
Sabang Indonesia 5°50N 95°15E 118 C1
Şabanözü Turkey 40°28N 33°16E 104 B5
Săbăoani Romania 47°1N 26°51E 81 C11
Sabari → India 17°35N 81°16E 126 F5
Sabarmati → India 22°18N 72°22E 124 H5
Sabattis U.S.A. 44°6N 74°40W 175 B10
Sabáudia Italy 41°18N 13°1E 94 A6
Sabaya Bolivia 19°1S 68°23W 188 D4
Saberania Indonesia 2°5S 138°18E 119 E9
Sabhā Libya 27°9N 14°29E 135 C8
Sabi → India 28°29N 76°44E 124 E7
Sabidana, J. Sudan 18°4N 36°50E 137 D4
Sabie S. Africa 25°10S 30°48E 145 C5
Sabinal U.S.A. 29°19N 99°28W 176 G5
Sabiñánigo Spain 42°31N 0°22W 90 C4
Sabinar, Punta del Spain 36°43N 2°44W 91 J2
Sabinas Mexico 27°51N 101°7W 180 B4
Sabinas → Mexico 27°37N 100°42W 180 B4
Sabinas Hidalgo Mexico 26°30N 100°10W 180 B4
Sabine → U.S.A. 29°59N 93°47W 176 G8
Sabine L. U.S.A. 29°53N 93°51W 176 G8
Sabine Pass U.S.A. 29°44N 93°54W 176 G8
Sabinópolis Brazil 18°40S 43°6W 189 D2
Sabinov Slovak Rep. 49°6N 21°5E 79 B14
Sabirabad Azerbaijan 40°5N 48°30E 87 K9
Sablayan Phil. 12°50N 120°50E 119 B6
Sable Canada 55°30N 68°21W 165 A6
Sable, C. Canada 43°29N 65°38W 165 D6
Sable, C. U.S.A. 25°9N 81°8W 179 K8
Sable I. Canada 44°0N 60°0W 165 D8
Sablé-sur-Sarthe France 47°50N 0°20W 70 E6
Saboeiro Brazil 6°32S 39°54W 189 B3
Sabonkafi Niger 14°40N 8°45E 139 C6
Sabor → Portugal 41°10N 7°7W 88 D3
Sabou Burkina Faso 12°1N 2°15W 138 C4
Sabres France 44°9N 0°43W 72 D3
Sabrina Coast Antarctica 68°0S 120°0E 55 C9
Sabugal Portugal 40°20N 7°5W 88 E3
Sabulubek Indonesia 1°36S 98°40E 118 E1
Sabuncu Turkey 39°33N 30°12E 99 B12
Sabzevār Iran 36°15N 57°40E 129 B8
Sabzvārān = Jiroft Iran 28°45N 57°50E 129 D8
Sac City U.S.A. 42°25N 95°0W 172 D6
Sacedón Spain 40°29N 2°41W 90 E2
Săcele Romania 45°37N 25°41E 81 E10
Sacheon S. Korea 35°0N 128°6E 115 G15
Sachigo → Canada 55°6N 88°58W 164 A2
Sachigo, L. Canada 53°50N 92°12W 164 B1
Sachimbo Angola 9°14S 20°16E 140 F4
Sachin India 21°5N 72°53E 126 D1
Sachkhere Georgia 42°25N 43°28E 87 J6
Sachsen □ Germany 50°55N 13°10E 76 E9
Sachsen-Anhalt □ Germany 52°0N 12°0E 76 D7
Sächsische Schweiz △ Germany 50°55N 14°10E 76 E10
Sacile Italy 45°57N 12°30E 93 C9
Sackets Harbor U.S.A. 43°57N 76°7W 175 C8
Sackville Canada 45°54N 64°22W 165 C7
Saco Maine, U.S.A. 43°30N 70°27W 175 C14
Saco Mont., U.S.A. 48°28N 107°21W 168 B10
Sacramento Brazil 19°53S 47°27W 189 D1
Sacramento U.S.A. 38°35N 121°29W 170 G5
Sacramento → U.S.A. 38°3N 121°56W 170 G5
Sacramento Mts. U.S.A. 32°30N 105°30W 169 K11
Sacramento Valley U.S.A. 39°30N 122°0W 170 G5
Sacratif, C. Spain 36°42N 3°28W 89 J7
Săcueni Romania 47°20N 22°5E 80 C7
Sada Spain 43°22N 8°15W 88 B2
Sada-Misaki Japan 33°20N 132°5E 113 H6
Sádaba Spain 42°19N 1°12W 90 C3
Sadabad India 27°27N 78°3E 124 F8
Şa'dah Yemen 16°15N 43°37E 131 D3
Sadani Tanzania 5°58S 38°35E 142 D4
Sadani ⌂ Tanzania 6°3S 38°47E 142 D4
Sadao Thailand 6°38N 100°26E 121 J3
Sadaseopet India 17°38N 77°59E 126 F3
Sadd el Aali Egypt 23°54N 32°54E 137 C3
Saddle Mt. U.S.A. 45°58N 123°41W 170 E3
Saddle Pk. India 13°9N 93°1E 127 H11
Sade Nigeria 11°22N 10°45E 139 C7
Sadimi Dem. Rep. of the Congo 9°25S 23°32E 143 D1
Sadiola Mali 13°50N 11°40W 138 C2
Sa'dīyah, Hawr as Iraq 32°15N 46°30E 105 F12
Sado Japan 38°0N 138°25E 112 F9
Sado → Portugal 38°29N 8°55W 89 G2
Sadon Russia 42°52N 43°58E 87 J6
Sadovoye Russia 47°47N 44°31E 87 G7
Sadra India 23°21N 72°43E 124 H5
Sadrazamköy = Liveras Cyprus 35°23N 32°57E 101 D11
Sadri India 25°11N 73°26E 124 G5
Sæby Denmark 57°21N 10°30E 63 G4
Saegertown U.S.A. 41°43N 80°9W 174 E4
Saelices Spain 39°55N 2°49W 90 F2
Safaalan Turkey 41°26N 28°6E 97 E12
Şafājah Si. Arabia 26°25N 39°0E 128 E3
Šafárikovo = Tornal'a Slovak Rep. 48°25N 20°20E 79 C13
Säffle Sweden 59°8N 12°55E 62 E6
Safford U.S.A. 32°50N 109°43W 169 K9
Saffron Walden U.K. 52°1N 0°16E 67 E8
Safi Morocco 32°18N 9°20W 136 B2
Şafīābād Iran 36°45N 57°58E 129 B8
Safid Dasht Iran 33°27N 48°11E 129 C6
Safīd Kūh Afghan. 34°45N 63°0E 108 F6
Safīd Rūd → Iran 37°23N 50°11E 129 B6
Safipur India 26°44N 80°21E 125 F9
Şāfītā Syria 34°48N 36°7E 104 E7
Safonovo Russia 55°4N 33°16E 84 E7
Safranbolu Turkey 41°15N 32°41E 104 B5
Saft Rashîn Egypt 28°58N 30°55E 137 F7
Şafwān Iraq 30°7N 47°43E 128 D5
Sag Harbor U.S.A. 41°0N 72°18W 175 F12
Saga Japan 33°15N 130°16E 113 H5
Saga □ Japan 33°15N 130°20E 113 H5
Sagae Japan 38°22N 140°17E 112 E10
Sagaing Burma 21°52N 95°59E 123 J19
Sagala Mali 14°9N 6°38W 138 C3
Sagamore U.S.A. 40°46N 79°14W 174 F5
Saganaga L. Canada 48°14N 90°52W 172 A8
Saganthit Kyun Burma 11°56N 98°29E 121 G2
Sagar Karnataka, India 16°38N 76°48E 126 F3
Sagar Karnataka, India 14°14N 75°6E 127 G2
Sagar Mad. P., India 23°50N 78°44E 125 H8
Sagara, L. Tanzania 5°20S 31°0E 142 D3
Sagarejo Georgia 41°44N 45°19E 87 K7
Sagarmatha = Everest, Mt. Nepal 28°5N 86°58E 125 E12
Sagarmatha △ Nepal 27°55N 86°45E 125 F12
Saginaw U.S.A. 43°26N 83°56W 173 D12
Saginaw B. U.S.A. 43°50N 83°40W 173 D12
Sagleipie Liberia 7°0N 8°52W 138 D3
Saglouc = Salluit Canada 62°14N 75°38W 161 E16
Sagone France 42°7N 8°42E 73 F12
Sagone, G. de France 42°4N 8°40E 73 F12
Sagres Portugal 37°0N 8°58W 89 J2
Sagua la Grande Cuba 22°50N 80°10W 182 B3
Saguache U.S.A. 38°5N 106°8W 168 G10
Saguaro △ U.S.A. 32°12N 110°38W 169 K8
Saguenay → Canada 48°22N 71°0W 165 C5
Sagunt Spain 39°42N 0°18W 90 F4
Sagunto = Sagunt Spain 39°42N 0°18W 90 F4
Sagwara India 23°41N 74°1E 124 H6
Sahaba Sudan 18°57N 30°25E 137 D3
Sahagún Spain 42°18N 5°2W 88 C5
Saḩam al Jawlān Syria 32°45N 35°55E 130 C4
Sahand, Kūh-e Iran 37°44N 46°27E 105 D12
Sahara Africa 23°0N 5°0E 134 D6
Saharan Atlas = Saharien, Atlas Algeria 33°30N 1°0E 136 B4
Saharan Seamounts Atl. Oc. 25°30N 19°50W 56 D10
Saharanpur India 29°58N 77°33E 124 E7
Saharien, Atlas Algeria 33°30N 1°0E 136 B4
Saharsa India 25°53N 86°36E 125 G12
Sahaswan India 28°5N 78°45E 125 E8
Saheira, W. el → Egypt 30°5N 33°25E 130 E2
Sahel Africa 16°0N 5°0E 134 E5
Sahel, Canal du Mali 14°20N 6°0W 138 C3
Sahibganj India 25°12N 87°40E 125 G12
Sāḩilīyah Iraq 33°43N 42°42E 105 F10
Sahiwal Pakistan 30°45N 73°8E 124 D5
Şahneh Iran 34°29N 47°41E 105 E12
Sahrawi = Western Sahara ■ Africa 25°0N 13°0W 134 D3
Sahuaripa Mexico 29°3N 109°14W 180 B3
Sahuarita U.S.A. 31°57N 110°58W 169 L8
Sahuayo de Díaz Mexico 20°4N 102°43W 180 C4
Šahy Slovak Rep. 48°4N 18°55E 79 C11
Sai → India 25°39N 82°47E 125 G10
Sai Buri Thailand 6°43N 101°45E 121 J3
Sai Kung China 22°23N 114°16E 111 a
Sai Thong △ Thailand 15°56N 101°10E 120 E3
Sai Yok △ Thailand 14°25N 98°40E 120 E2
Saibai I. Australia 9°25S 142°40E 150 a
Sa'id Bundâs South Sudan 8°24N 24°48E 135 G10
Saïda Algeria 34°50N 0°11E 136 B4
Saïda □ Algeria 34°40N 0°20E 136 B4
Sa'īdābād = Sīrjān Iran 29°30N 55°45E 129 D7
Sa'īdābād Iran 36°8N 54°11E 129 B7
Saïdia Morocco 35°5N 2°14W 136 A3
Saidpur Bangla. 25°48N 89°0E 123 G16
Saidpur India 25°33N 83°11E 125 G10
Saidu Sharif Pakistan 34°43N 72°24E 125 B5
Saignes France 45°20N 2°31E 72 C6
Saigō Japan 36°12N 133°20E 113 F6
Saigon = Thanh Pho Ho Chi Minh Vietnam 10°58N 106°40E 121 G6
Saijō Japan 33°55N 133°11E 113 H6
Saikai △ Japan 33°12N 129°36E 113 H4
Saikhoa Ghat India 27°50N 95°40E 123 F19
Saiki Japan 32°58N 131°51E 113 H5
Sailana India 23°28N 74°55E 124 H6
Saillans France 44°42N 5°12E 73 D9
Sailolof Indonesia 1°15S 130°46E 119 E8
Sailu India 19°28N 76°28E 126 E3
Saimaa Finland 61°15N 28°15E 84 B5
Saimbeyli Turkey 37°59N 36°6E 104 D7
Saimen = Saimaa Finland 61°15N 28°15E 84 B5
Şa'in Dezh Iran 36°40N 46°25E 105 D12
St. Abb's Head U.K. 55°55N 2°8W 65 F6
St-Affrique France 43°57N 2°53E 72 E6
St-Agrève France 45°0N 4°23E 73 C8
St-Aignan France 47°16N 1°22E 70 E8
St. Alban's Canada 47°51N 55°50W 165 C8
St. Albans U.K. 51°45N 0°19W 67 F7
St. Albans Vt., U.S.A. 44°49N 73°5W 175 B11
St. Albans W. Va., U.S.A. 38°23N 81°50W 173 F13
St. Alban's Head U.K. 50°34N 2°4W 67 G5
St. Albert Canada 53°37N 113°32W 162 C6
St-Amand-en-Puisaye France 47°32N 3°5E 71 E10
St-Amand-les-Eaux France 50°27N 3°25E 71 B10
St-Amand-Montrond France 46°43N 2°30E 71 F9
St-Amarin France 47°54N 7°2E 71 E14
St-Amour France 46°26N 5°21E 71 F12
St-André Réunion 20°57S 55°39E 141 c
St-André-de-Cubzac France 44°59N 0°26W 72 D3
St-André-les-Alpes France 43°58N 6°30E 73 E10
St. Andrew Sd. U.S.A. 30°58N 81°25W 178 E8
St. Andrew's Canada 47°45N 59°15W 165 C8
St. Andrews N.Z. 44°33S 171°10E 155 E6
St. Andrews U.K. 56°20N 2°47W 65 E6
St. Andrews U.S.A. 32°47N 80°0W 178 C9
St-Anicet Canada 45°8N 74°22W 175 A10
St. Annes Canada 49°40N 96°39W 163 D9
St. Anns B. Canada 46°22N 60°25W 165 C7
St. Ann's Bay Jamaica 18°26N 77°12W 182 a
St. Anthony Canada 51°22N 55°35W 165 B8
St. Anthony U.S.A. 43°58N 111°41W 168 E8
St-Antoine Canada 46°22N 64°45W 165 C7
St-Antonin-Noble-Val France 44°10N 1°45E 72 D5
St. Arnaud Australia 36°40S 143°16E 152 D5
St. Arnaud Ra. N.Z. 42°1S 172°53E 155 C7
St-Astier France 45°8N 0°31E 72 C4
St-Aubin-du-Cormier France 48°15N 1°26W 70 D5
St-Augustin Canada 51°13N 58°38W 165 B8
St-Augustin → Canada 51°16N 58°40W 165 B8
St. Augustine U.S.A. 29°54N 81°19W 178 F8
St. Augustine Beach U.S.A. 29°51N 81°16W 178 F8
St-Aulaye France 45°12N 0°9E 72 C4
St. Austell U.K. 50°20N 4°47W 67 G3
St-Avold France 49°6N 6°43E 71 C13
St. Barbe Canada 51°12N 56°46W 165 B8
St-Barthélemy ☒ W. Indies 17°50N 62°50W 183 C7
St. Barts = St-Barthélemy ☒ W. Indies 17°50N 62°50W 183 C7
St. Bathans N.Z. 44°53S 169°50E 155 E4
St. Bathan's, Mt. N.Z. 44°45S 169°45E 155 E4
St-Béat France 42°55N 0°41E 72 F4
St. Bees Hd. U.K. 54°31N 3°38W 66 C4
St. Bees I. Australia 20°56S 149°26E 150 b
St-Benoît Réunion 21°2S 55°43E 141 c
St-Benoît-du-Sault France 46°26N 1°24E 72 B5
St-Bonnet-en-Champsaur France 44°40N 6°5E 73 D10
St-Brevin-les-Pins France 47°14N 2°10W 70 E4
St-Brice-en-Coglès France 48°25N 1°22W 70 D5
St. Bride's Canada 46°56N 54°10W 165 C9
St. Brides B. U.K. 51°49N 5°9W 67 F2
St-Brieuc France 48°30N 2°46W 70 D4
St-Calais France 47°55N 0°45E 70 E7
St-Cast-le-Guildo France 48°37N 2°18W 70 D4
St. Catharines Canada 43°10N 79°15W 174 C5
St. Catherines I. U.S.A. 31°40N 81°10W 178 D8
St. Catherine's Pt. U.K. 50°34N 1°18W 67 G6
St-Céré France 44°51N 1°54E 72 D5
St-Cergue Switz. 46°27N 6°10E 77 J2
St-Cernin France 45°5N 2°25E 72 C6
St-Chamond France 45°28N 4°31E 73 C8
St. Charles Ill., U.S.A. 41°54N 88°19W 172 E9
St. Charles Md., U.S.A. 38°36N 76°56W 173 F15
St. Charles Mo., U.S.A. 38°47N 90°29W 172 F8
St. Charles Va., U.S.A. 36°48N 83°4W 173 G12
St-Chély-d'Apcher France 44°48N 3°17E 72 D7
St-Chinian France 43°25N 2°56E 72 E6
St. Christopher-Nevis = St. Kitts & Nevis ■ W. Indies 17°20N 62°40W 183 C7
St-Ciers-sur-Gironde France 45°17N 0°37W 72 C3
St. Clair Ga., U.S.A. 33°9N 82°13W 178 B7
St. Clair Mich., U.S.A. 42°50N 82°30W 174 D2
St. Clair Pa., U.S.A. 40°43N 76°12W 175 F8
St. Clair → U.S.A. 42°38N 82°31W 174 D2
St. Clair, L. Australia 37°20S 139°55E 152 D3
St. Clair, L. N. Amer. 42°27N 82°39W 174 D2
St. Clairsville U.S.A. 40°5N 80°54W 174 F4
St-Claud France 45°54N 0°28E 72 C4
St. Claude Canada 49°40N 98°20W 163 D9
St-Claude France 46°22N 5°52E 71 F12
St. Clears U.K. 51°49N 4°31W 67 F3
St-Clet Canada 45°21N 74°13W 175 A10
St. Cloud Fla., U.S.A. 28°15N 81°17W 179 G8
St. Cloud Minn., U.S.A. 45°34N 94°10W 172 C6
St. Cricq, C. Australia 25°17S 113°6E 149 E1
St. Croix U.S. Virgin Is. 17°45N 64°45W 183 C7
St. Croix → U.S.A. 44°45N 92°48W 172 C7
St. Croix Falls U.S.A. 45°24N 92°38W 172 C7
St-Cyprien France 42°37N 3°2E 72 F7
St-Cyr-sur-Mer France 43°11N 5°43E 73 E9
St. David's Canada 48°12N 58°52W 165 C8
St. David's U.K. 51°53N 5°16W 67 F2
St. David's Head U.K. 51°54N 5°19W 67 F2
St-Denis France 48°56N 2°20E 71 D9
St-Denis Réunion 20°52S 55°27E 141 c
St-Denis ✕ (RUN) Réunion 20°53S 55°32E 141 c
St-Dié-en-Vosges France 48°17N 6°56E 71 D13
St-Dizier France 48°38N 4°56E 71 D11
St-Égrève France 45°14N 5°41E 73 C9
St. Elias, Mt. U.S.A. 60°18N 140°56W 160 E3
St. Elias Mts. N. Amer. 60°33N 139°28W 162 A1
St-Eloy-les-Mines France 46°10N 2°51E 71 F9
St-Émilion France 44°53N 0°9W 72 D3
St-Étienne France 45°27N 4°22E 73 C8
St-Étienne-de-Tinée France 44°16N 6°56E 73 D10
St-Étienne-du-Rouvray France 49°23N 1°6E 70 C8
St. Eugène Canada 45°30N 74°28W 175 A10
St. Eustatius W. Indies 17°20N 63°0W 183 C7
St-Exupery, Lyon ✕ (LYS) France 45°44N 5°2E 73 C9
St-Fargeau France 47°39N 3°4E 71 E10
St-Félicien Canada 48°40N 72°25W 164 C5
St-Florent France 42°41N 9°18E 73 F13
St-Florent, G. de France 42°47N 9°12E 73 F13
St-Florent-sur-Cher France 46°59N 2°15E 71 F9
St-Florentin France 48°0N 3°45E 71 E10
St-Flour France 45°2N 3°6E 72 C7
St. Francis U.S.A. 39°47N 101°48W 172 F3
St. Francis → U.S.A. 34°38N 90°36W 177 D9
St. Francis, C. S. Africa 34°14S 24°49E 144 D3
St. Francisville U.S.A. 30°47N 91°23W 176 F9
St-François, L. Canada 45°10N 74°22W 175 A10
St-Fulgent France 46°50N 1°10W 70 F5
St-Gabriel Canada 46°17N 73°24W 164 C5

St. Gallen = Sankt Gallen
  Switz. 47°26N 9°22E 77 H5
St-Galmier France 45°35N 4°19E 71 G11
St-Gaudens France 43°6N 0°44E 72 E4
St-Gaultier France 46°39N 1°26E 70 F8
St-Gengoux-le-National
  France 46°37N 4°40E 71 F11
St-Geniez-d'Olt France 44°27N 2°58E 72 D6
St. George Australia 28°1S 148°30E 151 D4
St. George N.B., Canada 45°11N 66°50W 165 C6
St. George Ont., Canada 43°15N 80°15W 174 C4
St. George Ga., U.S.A. 30°31N 82°2W 178 E7
St. George S.C., U.S.A. 33°11N 80°35W 178 B9
St. George Utah, U.S.A. 37°6N 113°35W 169 H7
St. George, C. Canada 48°30N 59°16W 165 C8
St. George, C. U.S.A. 29°40N 85°5W 178 F4
St. George I. Alaska,
  U.S.A. 56°35N 169°35W 166 D6
St. George I. Fla.,
  U.S.A. 29°35N 84°55W 178 F5
St. George Ra. Australia 18°40S 125°0E 148 C4
St. Georges Canada 46°8N 70°40W 165 C5
St. Georges U.S.A. 46°8N 70°40W 165 C5
St. George's Grenada 12°5N 61°43W 183 D7
St. George's B. Canada 48°24N 58°53W 165 C8
St. Georges Basin N.S.W.,
  Australia 35°7S 150°36E 153 C9
St. Georges Basin W. Austral.,
  Australia 15°23S 125°2E 148 C4
St. George's Channel
  Europe 52°0N 6°0W 64 E6
St. George's Channel
  India 7°15N 93°43E 127 L11
St. Georges Hd.
  Australia 35°12S 150°42E 153 C9
St-Georges-lès-Baillargeaux
  France 46°41N 0°22E 72 B4
St-Germain-de-Calberte
  France 44°13N 3°48E 72 D7
St-Germain-en-Laye
  France 48°53N 2°4E 71 D9
St-Germain-Lembron
  France 45°27N 3°14E 72 C7
St-Gervais-d'Auvergne
  France 46°4N 2°50E 71 F9
St-Gervais-les-Bains
  France 45°53N 6°42E 73 C10
St-Gildas, Pte. de France 47°8N 2°14W 70 E4
St-Gilles France 43°40N 4°26E 73 E8
St-Girons France 42°59N 1°8E 72 F5
St. Gotthard P. = San Gottardo, P.
  del Switz. 46°33N 8°33E 77 J4
St. Helena Atl. Oc. 15°58S 5°42W 132 H3
St. Helena U.S.A. 38°30N 122°28W 170 G4
St. Helena, Mt. U.S.A. 38°40N 122°36W 170 G4
St. Helena B. S. Africa 32°40S 18°10E 144 D2
St. Helena Sd. U.S.A. 32°15N 80°25W 178 C9
St. Helens Australia 41°20S 148°15E 151 E4
St. Helens U.K. 53°27N 2°44W 66 D5
St. Helens U.S.A. 45°52N 122°48W 170 E4
St. Helens, Mt. U.S.A. 46°12N 122°12W 170 D4
St. Helier Jersey 49°10N 2°7W 67 H5
St-Herblain France 47°13N 1°40W 70 E5
St-Hilaire-du-Harcouët
  France 48°35N 1°5W 70 D5
St-Hilaire-de-Riez
  France 46°43N 1°57W 72 B2
St-Hippolyte France 47°19N 6°50E 71 E13
St-Hippolyte-du-Fort
  France 43°58N 3°52E 72 E7
St-Honoré-les-Bains
  France 46°54N 3°50E 71 F10
St-Hubert Canada 45°29N 73°25W 175 A11
St-Hyacinthe Canada 45°40N 72°58W 164 C5
St. Ignace U.S.A. 45°52N 84°44W 173 C11
St. Ignace I. Canada 48°45N 88°0W 164 C2
St. Ignatius U.S.A. 47°19N 114°6W 168 C6
St-Imier Switz. 47°9N 6°58E 77 H2
St. Ives Cambs., U.K. 52°20N 0°4W 67 E7
St. Ives Corn., U.K. 50°12N 5°30W 67 G2
St-James France 48°31N 1°20W 70 D5
St. James U.S.A. 43°59N 94°38W 172 D6
St-Jean ~ Canada 50°17N 64°20W 165 B7
St-Jean, L. Canada 48°40N 72°0W 165 C5
St-Jean-d'Angély France 45°57N 0°31W 72 C3
St-Jean-de-Braye France 47°53N 1°58E 71 E8
St-Jean-de-Luz France 43°23N 1°39W 72 E2
St-Jean-de-Maurienne
  France 45°16N 6°21E 73 C10
St-Jean-de-Monts France 46°47N 2°4W 70 F4
St-Jean-du-Gard France 44°7N 3°52E 72 D7
St-Jean-en-Royans France 45°1N 5°18E 73 C9
St-Jean-Pied-de-Port
  France 43°10N 1°14W 72 E2
St-Jean-Port-Joli
  Canada 47°15N 70°13W 165 C5
St-Jean-sur-Richelieu
  Canada 45°20N 73°20W 175 A11
St-Jérôme Canada 45°47N 74°0W 164 C5
St. John Canada 45°20N 66°8W 165 C6
St. John ~ U.S.A. 38°0N 98°46W 172 F4
St. John ~ Liberia 6°40N 9°10W 138 D2
St. John ~ N. Amer. 45°12N 66°5W 173 C20
St. John, C. Canada 50°0N 55°32W 165 C8
St. John I. U.S. Virgin Is. 18°20N 64°42W 183 e
St. John's Antigua & B. 17°6N 61°51W 183 C7
St. John's Canada 47°35N 52°40W 165 C9
St. Johns Ariz., U.S.A. 34°30N 109°22W 169 J9
St. Johns Mich., U.S.A. 43°0N 84°33W 173 D11
St. Johns ~ U.S.A. 30°24N 81°24W 178 E7
St. John's Pt. Ireland 54°34N 8°27W 64 B3
St. Johnsbury U.S.A. 44°25N 72°1W 175 B12
St. Johnsville U.S.A. 43°0N 74°43W 175 C10
St. Joseph Canada 43°24N 81°4W 174 C3
St-Joseph Martinique 14°39N 61°4W 182 c
St-Joseph Réunion 21°22S 55°37E 141 c
St. Joseph La., U.S.A. 31°55N 91°14W 179 F9
St. Joseph Mo., U.S.A. 39°46N 94°50W 172 F7
St. Joseph ~ U.S.A. 42°7N 86°29W 172 D10
St. Joseph, I. Canada 46°12N 83°58W 164 C3
St. Joseph, L. Canada 51°10N 90°35W 164 B1
St. Joseph Pt. U.S.A. 29°57N 85°23W 178 F4
St-Juéry France 43°57N 2°12E 72 E6
St-Julien-Chapteuil France 45°2N 4°4E 73 C8
St-Julien-de-Vouvantes
  France 47°38N 1°13W 70 E5
St-Julien-en-Genevois
  France 46°9N 6°5E 71 F13
St-Junien France 45°53N 0°55E 72 C4
St-Just-en-Chaussée
  France 49°30N 2°25E 71 C9

St-Just-en-Chevalet
  France 45°55N 3°50E 72 C7
St. Kilda N.Z. 45°53S 170°31E 155 F5
St. Kilda U.K. 57°49N 8°34W 68 C2
St. Kitts & Nevis ■
  W. Indies 17°20N 62°40W 183 C7
St. Laurent Canada 50°25N 97°58W 163 C9
St-Laurent-de-la-Salanque
  France 42°46N 2°59E 72 F6
St-Laurent-du-Pont
  France 45°23N 5°45E 73 C9
St-Laurent-en-Grandvaux
  France 46°35N 5°58E 71 F12
St-Laurent-Médoc France 45°8N 0°49W 72 C3
St. Lawrence Australia 22°16S 149°31E 150 C4
St. Lawrence ~ Canada 49°30N 66°0W 165 C6
St. Lawrence, Gulf of
  Canada 48°25N 62°0W 165 C7
St. Lawrence I. U.S.A. 63°30N 170°30W 166 C3
St. Lawrence Islands △
  Canada 44°27N 75°52W 175 B9
St. Léonard Canada 47°12N 67°58W 165 C6
St-Léonard-de-Noblat
  France 45°49N 1°29E 72 C5
St. Leu Réunion 21°9S 55°18E 141 c
St. Lewis ~ Canada 52°26N 56°11W 165 B8
St-Lô France 49°7N 1°5W 70 C5
St-Louis France 47°30N 7°34E 71 E14
St-Louis Guadeloupe 15°56N 61°19W 182 b
St-Louis Réunion 21°16S 55°25E 141 c
St-Louis Senegal 16°8N 16°27W 138 B1
St-Louis ~ U.S.A. 38°37N 90°11W 172 F8
St-Louis □ Senegal 16°20N 15°0W 138 B2
St. Louis ~ U.S.A. 46°44N 92°9W 172 B7
St-Loup-sur-Semouse
  France 47°53N 6°16E 71 E13
St-Luc Canada 45°22N 73°18W 175 A11
St. Lucia ~ W. Indies 14°0N 60°57W 183 f
St. Lucia, L. S. Africa 28°5S 32°30E 145 C5
St. Lucia △ S. Africa 28°5S 32°27E 145 C5
St. Lucia Channel
  W. Indies 14°15N 61°0W 183 D7
St. Lucie U.S.A. 27°29N 80°20W 179 H9
St. Lucie Canal U.S.A. 27°10N 80°18W 179 H9
St. Maarten ~ W. Indies 18°2N 63°5W 183 C7
St. Magnus B. U.K. 60°25N 1°35W 65 A7
St-Maixent-l'École
  France 46°24N 0°12W 72 B3
St-Malo France 48°39N 2°1W 70 D4
St-Malo, G. de France 48°50N 2°20W 70 D4
St-Mandrier-sur-Mer
  France 43°4N 5°57E 73 E9
St-Marc Haiti 19°10N 72°41W 183 C5
St-Marcellin France 45°9N 5°20E 73 C9
St-Marcouf, Îs. France 49°30N 1°10W 70 C5
St. Maries U.S.A. 47°19N 116°35W 168 C5
St. Marks U.S.A. 30°9N 84°12W 178 E5
St-Martin ~ W. Indies 18°5N 63°5W 183 C7
St. Martin, C. Martinique 14°52N 61°14W 182 c
St. Martin, L. Canada 51°40N 98°30W 163 C9
St-Martin-de-Crau France 43°38N 4°48E 73 E8
St-Martin-de-Ré France 46°12N 1°21W 72 B2
St-Martin-d'Hères France 45°9N 5°45E 73 C9
St-Martin-Vésubie France 44°4N 7°15E 73 D11
St. Martins Barbados 13°5N 59°28W 183 g
St-Martory France 43°9N 0°56E 72 E4
St. Mary ~ U.S.A. 13°20N 74°35E 127 H2
St. Mary Pk. Australia 31°32S 138°34E 152 A4
St. Marys Australia 41°35S 148°11E 151 E4
St. Marys Canada 43°20N 81°10W 174 C3
St. Mary's Corn., U.K. 49°55N 6°18W 67 H1
St. Mary's Orkney, U.K. 58°54N 2°54W 65 C6
St. Marys Ga., U.S.A. 30°44N 81°33W 178 E8
St. Marys Pa., U.S.A. 41°26N 78°34W 174 E6
St. Marys ~ U.S.A. 30°43N 81°27W 178 E8
St. Mary's B. Canada 46°50N 53°50W 165 C9
St. Mary's Bay Canada 44°25N 66°10W 165 D6
St-Mathieu, Pte. France 48°24N 4°46W 70 D2
St. Matthew I. U.S.A. 60°24N 172°42W 166 C5
St. Matthews U.S.A. 33°40N 80°46W 178 B9
St. Maurice ~ Canada 46°21N 72°31W 164 C5
St. Mawes U.K. 50°10N 5°2W 67 G2
St-Maximin-la-Ste-Baume
  France 43°27N 5°52E 73 E9
St-Médard-en-Jalles
  France 44°53N 0°43W 72 D3
St-Méen-le-Grand
  France 48°11N 2°12W 70 D4
St-Mihiel France 48°54N 5°32E 71 D12
St-Nazaire France 47°17N 2°12W 70 E4
St. Neots U.K. 52°14N 0°15W 67 E7
St-Nicolas-de-Port
  France 48°38N 6°18E 71 D13
St-Omer France 50°45N 2°15E 71 B9
St-Palais-sur-Mer France 45°38N 1°5W 72 C2
St-Pamphile Canada 46°58N 69°48W 165 C6
St-Pardoux-la-Rivière
  France 45°29N 0°45E 72 C4
St-Pascal Canada 47°32N 69°48W 165 C6
St. Paul Canada 54°0N 111°17W 162 C6
St. Paul Réunion 20°59S 55°17E 141 c
St. Paul Minn., U.S.A. 44°56N 93°5W 172 C7
St. Paul Nebr., U.S.A. 41°13N 98°27W 172 E4
St. Paul ~ Canada 51°27N 57°42W 165 B8
St. Paul ~ Liberia 6°23N 10°8W 138 D2
St. Paul, Î. Ind. Oc. 38°55S 77°34E 146 H6
St-Paul-de-Fenouillet
  France 42°48N 2°30E 72 F6
St. Paul I. Canada 47°12N 60°9W 165 C7
St. Paul I. U.S.A. 57°10N 170°15W 166 D5
St-Paul-lès-Dax France 43°44N 1°3W 72 E2
St-Paul-sur-Ubaye
  France 44°31N 6°45E 73 D10
St-Péray France 44°57N 4°50E 73 D8
St. Pete Beach U.S.A. 27°43N 82°44W 179 H7
St. Peter U.S.A. 44°20N 93°57W 172 C7
St. Peter Port U.K. 49°26N 2°33W 67 H5
St. Peters N.S., Canada 45°40N 60°53W 165 C7
St. Peters P.E.I., Canada 46°25N 62°35W 165 C7
St. Petersburg = Sankt-Peterburg
  Russia 59°55N 30°20E 84 C6
St. Petersburg U.S.A. 27°46N 82°40W 179 H7
St-Philbert-de-Grand-Lieu
  France 47°2N 1°39W 70 E5
St-Philippe Réunion 21°21S 55°44E 141 c
St-Pie Canada 45°30N 72°54W 175 A12
St-Pierre Réunion 21°19S 55°28E 141 c
St-Pierre St-P. & M. 46°46N 56°12W 165 C8

St-Pierre, L. Canada 46°12N 72°52W 164 C5
St-Pierre d'Oléron
  France 45°57N 1°19W 72 C2
St-Pierre-en-Port France 49°48N 0°30E 70 C7
St-Pierre-et-Miquelon ☑
  N. Amer. 46°55N 56°10W 165 C8
Ste-Pierre-le-Moûtier
  France 46°47N 3°7E 71 F10
St-Pierre-sur-Dives France 49°2N 0°1W 70 C6
St-Pol-de-Léon France 48°41N 4°0W 70 D2
St-Pol-sur-Mer France 51°1N 2°20E 71 B9
St-Pol-sur-Ternoise
  France 50°23N 2°20E 71 B9
St-Pons France 43°30N 2°45E 72 E6
St-Pourçain-sur-Sioule
  France 46°18N 3°18E 71 F10
St-Priest France 45°42N 4°57E 73 C8
St-Quay-Portrieux
  France 48°39N 2°51W 70 D4
St-Quentin Canada 47°30N 67°23W 165 C6
St-Quentin France 49°50N 3°16E 71 C10
St-Rambert-d'Albon
  France 45°17N 4°49E 73 C8
St-Raphaël France 43°25N 6°46E 73 E10
St. Regis U.S.A. 47°18N 115°6W 168 C6
St. Regis Falls U.S.A. 44°40N 74°32W 175 B10
St-Renan France 48°26N 4°37W 70 D2
St-Saëns France 49°41N 1°16E 70 C8
St-Savin France 46°34N 0°53E 72 B4
St-Savinien France 45°53N 0°42W 72 C3
St-Seine-l'Abbaye
  France 47°26N 4°47E 71 E11
St-Sernin-sur-Rance
  France 43°54N 2°35E 72 E6
St-Sever France 43°45N 0°35W 72 E3
St-Siméon Canada 47°51N 69°54W 165 C6
St. Simons I. U.S.A. 31°12N 81°15W 178 D8
St. Simons Island
  U.S.A. 31°9N 81°22W 178 D8
St. Stephen Canada 45°16N 67°17W 165 C6
St. Stephen U.S.A. 33°24N 79°55W 178 B10
St-Sulpice France 43°46N 1°41E 72 E5
St-Sulpice-Laurière France 46°3N 1°29E 72 B5
St-Sulpice-les-Feuilles
  France 46°19N 1°21E 72 B5
St-Syprien = St-Cyprien
St. Teresa U.S.A. 29°55N 84°27W 178 F5
St-Thégonnec France 48°31N 3°57W 70 D3
St. Thomas Canada 42°45N 81°10W 174 D3
St. Thomas I.
  U.S. Virgin Is. 18°20N 64°55W 183 e
St. Tite Canada 46°45N 72°34W 164 C5
St-Trond = Sint-Truiden
St-Tropez France 43°17N 6°38E 73 E10
St-Vaast-la-Hougue
  France 49°35N 1°17W 70 C5
St-Valery-en-Caux France 49°52N 0°43E 70 C7
St-Valéry-sur-Somme
  France 50°11N 1°38E 71 B8
St-Vallier France 45°11N 4°22E 71 F11
St-Vallier-de-Thiey
  France 43°42N 6°51E 73 E10
St-Varent France 46°53N 0°13W 70 F6
St-Vaury France 46°12N 1°46E 72 B5
St. Vidgeon's ◎
  Australia 14°47S 134°53E 150 A1
St. Vincent = São Vicente
  C. Verde Is. 17°0N 25°0W 134 b
St. Vincent Italy 45°45N 7°39E 92 C4
St. Vincent, G. Australia 35°0S 138°0E 152 C3
St. Vincent & the Grenadines ■
  W. Indies 13°0N 61°10W 183 D7
St-Vincent-de-Tyrosse
  France 43°39N 1°19W 72 E2
St. Vincent I. U.S.A. 29°42N 85°3W 179 F4
St. Vincent Passage
  W. Indies 13°30N 61°0W 183 D7
St-Vith Belgium 50°17N 6°9E 69 D6
St-Vivien-de-Médoc
  France 45°25N 1°2W 72 C2
St. Walburg Canada 53°39N 109°12W 163 C7
St-Yrieix-la-Perche
  France 45°31N 1°12E 72 C5
Saintala India 20°26N 83°20E 126 D6
Ste-Adresse France 49°31N 0°5E 70 C7
Ste-Agathe-des-Monts
  Canada 46°3N 74°17W 164 C5
Ste-Anne Guadeloupe 16°13N 61°24W 182 b
Ste-Anne Seychelles 4°36S 55°31E 141 b
Ste-Anne, L. Canada 50°0N 67°42W 165 B6
Ste-Anne-des-Monts
  Canada 49°8N 66°30W 165 C6
Ste-Croix Switz. 46°49N 6°34E 77 J2
Ste-Énimie France 44°22N 3°26E 72 D7
Ste-Foy-la-Grande France 44°50N 0°13E 72 D4
Ste. Genevieve U.S.A. 37°59N 90°2W 172 G8
Ste-Hermine France 46°32N 1°4W 72 B2
Ste-Livrade-sur-Lot
  France 44°24N 0°36E 72 D4
Ste-Marguerite ~
  Canada 50°9N 66°36W 165 B6
Ste-Marie Canada 46°26N 71°0W 165 C5
Ste-Marie Martinique 14°48N 61°1W 182 c
Ste-Marie, Ile = Boraha, Nosy
  Madag. 16°50S 49°55E 141 H9
Ste-Marie-aux-Mines
  France 48°15N 7°12E 71 D14
Ste-Maure-de-Touraine
  France 47°7N 0°37E 70 E7
Ste-Maxime France 43°19N 6°39E 73 E10
Ste-Menehould France 49°5N 4°54E 71 C11
Ste-Mère-Église France 49°24N 1°19W 70 C5
Ste-Rose Guadeloupe 16°20N 61°45W 182 b
Ste-Rose Réunion 21°8S 55°40E 141 c
Ste. Rose du Lac Canada 51°4N 99°30W 163 C9
Ste-Savine France 48°18N 4°3E 71 D11
Ste-Sigolène France 45°15N 4°14E 73 C8
Saintes France 45°45N 0°37W 72 C3
Saintes, Îs. des
  Guadeloupe 15°50N 61°35W 182 b
Stes-Maries-de-la-Mer
  France 43°26N 4°26E 73 E8
Saintfield U.K. 54°28N 5°49W 64 B6
Saintonge France 45°40N 0°50W 72 C3
Saipal Nepal 29°50N 81°40E 125 E9
Saipan N. Marianas 15°12N 145°45E 156 F6
Sairang India 23°50N 92°45E 123 H18

Sairecábur, Cerro
  Bolivia 22°43S 67°54W 190 A2
Săitah Si. Arabia 16°36N 42°56E 131 D3
Saitama Japan 35°54N 139°38E 113 G9
Saitama □ Japan 36°25N 139°30E 113 F9
Saiteli = Kadınhanı
  Turkey 38°14N 32°13E 104 C5
Saiti Moldova 46°30N 29°24E 81 D14
Saiyid Pakistan 33°7N 73°2E 124 C5
Saja-Besaya △ Spain 43°6N 4°8W 88 B6
Sajama Bolivia 18°7S 69°0W 188 D3
Sajama, Nevado Bolivia 18°6S 68°54W 188 D4
Sajan Serbia 45°50N 20°20E 80 E5
Sajum □ Hungary 48°19N 21°7E 80 C6
Sajószentpéter Hungary 48°12N 20°44E 80 B5
Sak ~ S. Africa 30°52S 20°25E 144 E3
Saka Kenya 0°9S 39°20E 142 B4
Sakaba Nigeria 11°4N 5°35E 139 C6
Sakai Japan 34°34N 135°27E 113 G7
Sakaide Japan 34°19N 133°50E 113 G6
Sakaiminato Japan 35°38N 133°11E 113 G6
Sakākah Si. Arabia 30°0N 40°8E 128 D4
Sakakawea, L. U.S.A. 47°30N 101°25W 172 B3
Sakami ~ Canada 53°40N 76°40W 164 B4
Sakami, L. Canada 53°15N 77°0W 164 B4
Sâkâne, 'Erg i-n Mali 20°30N 1°30W 139 A4
Sakania
  Dem. Rep. of the Congo 12°43S 28°30E 143 E2
Sakartvelo = Georgia ■
  Asia 42°0N 43°0E 87 J6
Sakarya Turkey 40°48N 30°25E 104 B4
Sakarya □ Turkey 40°45N 30°25E 104 B4
Sakarya ~ Turkey 41°7N 30°39E 104 B4
Sakashima-Guntō
  Japan 24°46N 124°0E 113 M2
Sakassou Ivory C. 7°29N 5°19W 138 D3
Sakata Japan 38°55N 139°50E 112 E9
Sakchu N. Korea 40°23N 125°2E 115 D13
Sakété Benin 6°40N 2°45E 139 D5
Sakha □ Russia 66°0N 130°0E 107 C14
Sakhalin Russia 51°0N 143°0E 107 D15
Sakhalinskiy Zaliv
  Russia 54°0N 141°0E 107 D15
Sakhi Gopal India 19°58N 85°50E 126 E7
Saki Azerbaijan 41°10N 47°5E 87 K8
Šakiai Lithuania 54°59N 23°2E 82 D10
Sakmara ~ Russia 51°46N 55°1E 108 B5
Sakoli India 21°5N 79°59E 126 D5
Sakon Nakhon
  Thailand 17°10N 104°9E 120 D5
Sakrand Pakistan 26°10N 68°15E 124 F3
Sakri Maharashtra, India 26°13N 86°5E 125 F12
Sakri Maharashtra, India 21°2N 74°20E 126 D2
Sakrivier S. Africa 30°54S 20°28E 144 E3
Sakskøbing Denmark 54°49N 11°39E 63 G5
Sakti India 22°2N 82°58E 125 H10
Sakuma Japan 35°3N 137°48E 113 G8
Sakurai Japan 34°30N 135°51E 113 G7
Saky Ukraine 45°9N 33°34E 85 K7
Sal ~ Russia 47°31N 40°45E 87 G7
Sal C. Verde Is. 16°45N 22°55W 134 b
Sal Rei C. Verde Is. 16°11N 22°53W 134 b
Šaľa Slovak Rep. 48°10N 17°50E 79 G10
Sala Sweden 59°58N 16°35E 63 E7
Sala Consilina Italy 40°23N 15°36E 95 B8
Sala-y-Gómez
  Pac. Oc. 26°28S 105°28W 157 K17
Sala-y-Gómez Ridge
  Pac. Oc. 25°0S 98°0W 157 K18
Salaberry-de-Valleyfield
  Canada 45°15N 74°8W 175 A10
Salacgrīva Latvia 57°45N 24°21E 82 A11
Salada, L. Mexico 32°20N 115°40W 169 K6
Saladas Argentina 28°15S 58°40W 190 B4
Saladillo Argentina 35°40S 59°55W 190 D4
Salado ~ B. Aires,
  Argentina 35°44S 57°22W 190 D4
Salado ~ La Pampa,
  Argentina 37°30S 67°0W 192 A3
Salado ~ Rio Negro,
  Argentina 41°34S 65°59W 192 B3
Salado ~ Santa Fe,
  Argentina 31°40S 60°41W 190 C3
Salado ~ Mexico 26°52N 99°19W 176 H5
Salaga Ghana 8°31N 0°31W 139 D4
Sălaj □ Romania 47°15N 23°0E 81 B8
Salakos Greece 36°17N 27°57E 101 C9
Salala Liberia 6°42N 10°7W 138 D2
Salālah Oman 16°56N 53°59E 131 D5
Salamajärvi △ Finland 63°12N 24°50E 60 E21
Salamanca Chile 31°46S 70°59W 190 C2
Salamanca Spain 40°58N 5°39W 88 E5
Salamanca U.S.A. 42°10N 78°43W 174 D6
Salamanca □ Spain 40°57N 5°40W 88 E5
Salamatābād Iran 35°39N 47°50E 128 C5
Salamina Colombia 5°25N 75°29W 184 B3
Salamína Greece 37°56N 23°30E 98 D5
Salamis Cyprus 35°11N 33°54E 101 D12
Salar de Atacama
  Chile 23°30S 68°25W 190 A2
Salar de Uyuni Bolivia 20°30S 67°45W 188 E4
Sălard Romania 47°12N 22°3E 80 B7
Salas Spain 43°25N 6°15W 88 B4
Salas de los Infantes Spain 42°2N 3°17W 88 C7
Salatiga Indonesia 7°19S 110°30E 119 G14
Salavat Russia 53°21N 55°55E 108 B5
Salaverry Peru 8°15S 79°0W 188 C2
Salawati Indonesia 1°7S 130°52E 119 E8
Salawin ~ Thailand 18°18N 97°40E 120 C1
Salaya India 22°19N 69°35E 124 H3
Salazar ~ Spain 42°40N 1°20W 90 C3
Salbris France 47°25N 2°3E 71 E9
Salcantay, Nevado
  Peru 13°19S 72°33W 188 C3
Salcia Romania 43°56N 24°55E 81 G9
Sălciua Romania 46°24N 23°26E 81 D8
Saldaña Spain 42°32N 4°48W 88 C6
Saldanha S. Africa 33°0S 17°58E 144 D2
Saldanha B. S. Africa 33°6S 18°0E 144 D2
Saldus Latvia 56°38N 22°30E 82 B9
Sale Australia 38°6S 147°6E 153 C4
Salé Italy 44°59N 8°48E 92 D5
Salé Morocco 34°3N 6°48W 136 B4
Sale U.K. 53°26N 2°19W 66 D5

Sale City U.S.A. 31°16N 84°1W 178 D5
Salekhard Russia 66°30N 66°35E 106 C7
Salem India 11°40N 78°11E 127 J4
Salem Fla., U.S.A. 29°53N 83°25W 178 F6
Salem Ill., U.S.A. 38°38N 88°57W 172 F9
Salem Ind., U.S.A. 38°36N 86°6W 172 F10
Salem Mass., U.S.A. 42°31N 70°53W 175 D14
Salem Mo., U.S.A. 37°39N 91°32W 172 G8
Salem N.H., U.S.A. 42°45N 71°12W 175 D13
Salem N.J., U.S.A. 39°34N 75°28W 173 F16
Salem N.Y., U.S.A. 43°10N 73°20W 175 C11
Salem Ohio, U.S.A. 40°54N 80°52W 174 E4
Salem Oreg., U.S.A. 44°56N 123°2W 168 D2
Salem S. Dak., U.S.A. 43°44N 97°23W 172 D5
Salem Va., U.S.A. 37°18N 80°3W 173 G13
Salemi Italy 37°49N 12°48E 94 E5
Salernes France 43°34N 6°15E 73 E10
Salerno Italy 40°41N 14°47E 95 B7
Salerno, G. di Italy 40°35N 14°45E 95 B7
Salford U.K. 53°30N 2°18W 66 D5
Salgótarján Hungary 48°5N 19°47E 80 B4
Salgueiro Brazil 8°4S 39°6W 189 D11
Salher India 20°40N 73°55E 126 D1
Salibabu Indonesia 3°45N 126°40E 119 D7
Salibea = Salybia
  Trin. & Tob. 10°43N 61°2W 187 K15
Salida U.S.A. 38°32N 106°0W 168 G11
Salies-de-Béarn France 43°28N 0°56W 72 E3
Salihli Turkey 38°28N 28°8E 104 C3
Salihorsk Belarus 52°51N 27°27E 81 B14
Salima Malawi 13°47S 34°28E 141 G6
Salina Italy 38°34N 14°50E 95 D7
Salina Kans., U.S.A. 38°50N 97°37E 172 F5
Salina Utah, U.S.A. 38°58N 111°51W 168 G8
Salina Cruz Mexico 16°10N 95°10W 177 J11
Salina di Margherita di Savóia △
  Italy 41°23N 16°4E 95 A9
Salinas Brazil 16°10S 42°10W 189 D2
Salinas Ecuador 2°10S 80°58W 186 D2
Salinas U.S.A. 36°40N 121°39W 170 J5
Salinas ~ U.S.A. 36°45N 121°48W 170 J5
Salinas, B. de Nic. 11°4N 85°45W 182 D2
Salinas, Pampa de las
  Argentina 31°58S 66°42W 190 C2
Salinas Ambargasta
  Argentina 29°0S 65°0W 190 B3
Salinas de Hidalgo
  Mexico 22°38N 101°43W 180 C4
Salinas Grandes
  Argentina 30°0S 65°0W 190 C3
Salinas Pueblo Missions △
  U.S.A. 34°6N 106°4W 169 J10
Salinas Valley U.S.A. 36°15N 121°15W 170 J5
Saline ~ Ark., U.S.A. 33°10N 92°8W 176 E8
Saline ~ Kans., U.S.A. 38°52N 97°30W 172 F5
Salines di Trapani e Paceco △
  Italy 37°59N 12°28E 94 E5
Salines, C. de ses Spain 39°16N 3°4E 100 B10
Salinópolis Brazil 0°40S 47°20W 187 D9
Salins-les-Bains France 46°58N 5°52E 71 F12
Salir Portugal 37°14N 8°2W 89 H2
Salisbury Australia 34°46S 138°38E 152 C3
Salisbury U.K. 51°4N 1°47W 67 F6
Salisbury Md., U.S.A. 38°22N 75°36W 173 F16
Salisbury N.C., U.S.A. 35°40N 80°29W 177 D14
Salisbury I. Canada 63°30N 77°0W 161 E16
Salisbury Plain U.K. 51°14N 1°55W 67 F6
Săliște Romania 45°45N 23°56E 81 E8
Salitre ~ Brazil 9°29S 40°39W 189 D2
Salkhad Syria 32°29N 36°43E 130 C5
Salkove Ukraine 48°15N 29°59E 81 B14
Salla Finland 66°50N 28°49E 60 C23
Sallanches France 45°55N 6°38E 73 C10
Sallent Spain 41°49N 1°54E 90 D6
Salles France 44°33N 0°52W 72 D3
Salles-Curan France 44°11N 2°48E 72 D6
Salling Denmark 56°40N 8°55E 63 H2
Salliq = Coral Harbour
  Canada 64°8N 83°10W 161 E15
Sallisaw U.S.A. 35°28N 94°47W 176 D7
Sallom Sudan 19°17N 37°6E 137 D4
Salluit Canada 62°14N 75°38W 161 E16
Sallyana Nepal 28°22N 82°10E 125 E10
Salmās Iran 38°11N 44°47E 105 C11
Salmerón Spain 40°33N 2°29W 90 E2
Salmo Canada 49°10N 117°20W 162 D5
Salmon U.S.A. 45°11N 113°54W 168 D7
Salmon ~ Canada 54°3N 122°40W 162 C4
Salmon ~ U.S.A. 45°51N 116°47W 168 D5
Salmon Arm Canada 50°40N 119°15W 162 C5
Salmon Gums
  Australia 32°59S 121°38E 149 F3
Salmon Pt. Canada 43°57N 77°15W 174 C7
Salmon River Mts.
  U.S.A. 44°50N 115°30W 168 D6
Salmon River Res.
  U.S.A. 43°32N 75°55W 175 C9
Salo Finland 60°22N 23°10E 84 B2
Salò Italy 45°36N 10°31E 92 C7
Salobreña Spain 36°44N 3°35W 89 H7
Salome U.S.A. 33°47N 113°37W 171 M13
Salon India 26°2N 81°27E 125 F9
Salon-de-Provence France 43°39N 5°6E 73 E9
Salonica = Thessaloniki
  Greece 40°38N 22°58E 98 F6
Salonta Romania 46°49N 21°42E 80 D6
Salor ~ Spain 39°39N 7°3W 89 F3
Salou Spain 41°4N 1°10E 90 D6
Salou, C. de Spain 41°3N 1°10E 90 D6
Saloum ~ Senegal 14°5N 16°37W 138 C1
Salpausselkä Finland 61°3N 26°15E 84 B4
Salsacate Argentina 31°20S 65°5W 190 C2
Salses France 42°50N 2°55E 72 F6
Salsette I. India 19°2N 72°53E 126 E1
Salsk Russia 46°28N 41°30E 87 G6
Salso ~ Italy 37°6N 13°57E 94 E6
Salsomaggiore Terme
  Italy 44°49N 9°59E 92 D6
Salt ~ Canada 60°0N 112°25W 162 B6
Salt ~ U.S.A. 33°23N 112°19W 169 K7
Salt Fork Red ~
  U.S.A. 34°27N 99°21W 176 D5
Salt L. Australia 30°6S 142°8E 153 E3
Salt Lake City U.S.A. 40°45N 111°53W 168 F8

Salt Range Pakistan 32°30N 72°25E 124 C5
Salt Springs U.S.A. 29°21N 81°44W 179 F7
Salta Argentina 24°57S 65°25W 190 A2
Salta □ Argentina 24°48S 65°30W 190 A2
Saltara Italy 43°45N 12°50E 93 E9
Saltash U.K. 50°24N 4°14W 67 G3
Saltburn by the Sea U.K. 54°35N 0°58W 66 C7
Saltcoats U.K. 55°38N 4°47W 65 F4
Saltee Is. Ireland 52°7N 6°37W 64 D5
Saltfjellet Norway 66°40N 15°15E 60 C16
Saltfjorden Norway 67°15N 14°10E 60 C16
Saltholm Denmark 55°38N 12°43E 63 J6
Saltillo Mexico 25°25N 101°0W 180 C4
Salto Argentina 34°20S 60°15W 190 C3
Salto Uruguay 31°27S 57°50W 190 C4
Salto da Divisa Brazil 16°0S 39°57W 189 D3
Salto del Guaira
  Paraguay 24°3S 54°17W 191 A5
Salton City U.S.A. 33°18N 115°57W 171 M11
Salton Sea U.S.A. 33°15N 115°45W 171 M11
Saltpond Ghana 5°15N 1°3W 139 D4
Saltsburg U.S.A. 40°29N 79°27W 174 F5
Saltsjöbaden Sweden 59°15N 18°20E 63 G8
Saluda U.S.A. 34°0N 81°46W 178 B8
Saluda ~ U.S.A. 34°1N 81°4W 178 A8
Salue Timpaus, Selat
  Indonesia 1°50S 123°50E 119 E6
Salûm Egypt 31°31N 25°7E 137 A2
Salûm, Khâlig el Egypt 31°35N 25°24E 137 A2
Salur India 18°27N 83°18E 126 E6
Saluzzo Italy 44°39N 7°29E 92 D4
Salvación, B. Chile 50°50S 75°10W 192 D1
Salvador Brazil 13°0S 38°30W 189 D3
Salvador Canada 52°10N 109°32W 163 C7
Salvador, El ■
  Cent. Amer. 13°50N 89°0W 182 D2
Salvador, L. U.S.A. 29°43N 90°15W 177 G9
Salvaterra de Magos
  Portugal 39°1N 8°47W 89 F2
Sálvora, I. de Spain 42°30N 8°58W 88 C2
Salween ~ Burma 16°31N 97°37E 123 L20
Salyan Azerbaijan 39°33N 48°59E 105 C13
Salybia Trin. & Tob. 10°43N 61°2W 187 K15
Salza ~ Austria 47°40N 14°43E 78 D7
Salzach ~ Austria 48°12N 12°56E 78 D6
Salzburg Austria 47°48N 13°2E 78 D6
Salzburg □ Austria 47°15N 13°0E 78 D6
Salzgitter Germany 52°9N 10°19E 76 C6
Salzkotten Germany 51°40N 8°37E 76 D4
Salzwedel Germany 52°52N 11°10E 76 C6
Sam India 26°50N 70°31E 124 F4
Sam Neua Laos 20°29N 104°5E 116 G5
Sam Ngao Thailand 17°18N 99°0E 120 D2
Sam Rayburn Res.
  U.S.A. 31°4N 94°5W 176 F7
Sam Rong, Laem Thailand 9°35N 100°4E 121 b
Sam Son Vietnam 19°44N 105°54E 120 C5
Sama de Langreo = Langreo
  Spain 43°18N 5°40W 88 B5
Samagaltay Russia 50°36N 95°3E 109 D13
Samales Group Phil. 6°0N 122°0E 119 C6
Samalga Pass U.S.A. 52°50N 169°0W 166 E6
Samalkot India 17°3N 82°13E 126 F6
Samalût Egypt 28°20N 30°42E 137 C12
Samana India 30°10N 76°13E 124 D7
Samana Cays Bahamas 23°3N 73°45W 183 B5
Samandağ Turkey 36°5N 35°59E 104 D6
Samandıra Turkey 40°59N 29°13E 97 F13
Samanga Tanzania 8°20S 39°13E 143 D4
Samangān □ Afghan. 36°15N 68°3E 109 E7
Samangwa
  Dem. Rep. of the Congo 4°23S 24°10E 142 C1
Samani Japan 42°7N 142°56E 112 C11
Samanli Dağları Turkey 40°30N 29°10E 97 F13
Samar Phil. 12°0N 125°0E 119 B7
Samara Russia 53°8N 50°6E 86 D10
Samara ~ Russia 53°10N 50°4E 86 D10
Samara ~ Ukraine 48°28N 35°7E 85 H8
Samaria = Shōmron
  West Bank 32°15N 35°13E 130 C4
Samariá △ Greece 35°17N 23°58E 101 D5
Samarinda Indonesia 0°30S 117°9E 118 E5
Samarkand = Samarqand
  Uzbekistan 39°40N 66°55E 109 E7
Samarqand Uzbekistan 39°40N 66°55E 109 E7
Samarqand □
  Uzbekistan 39°35N 66°35E 109 E7
Sāmarrā' Iraq 34°12N 43°52E 105 D10
Samarskaya Luka △
  Russia 53°30N 49°30E 86 D9
Samastipur India 25°50N 85°50E 125 G11
Samaxı Azerbaijan 40°38N 48°37E 87 K9
Samba
  Dem. Rep. of the Congo 4°38S 26°22E 142 C2
Samba India 32°32N 75°10E 126 C6
Sambaíba Brazil 7°8S 45°21W 189 D1
Sambalpur India 21°28N 84°4E 126 D7
Sambar, Tanjung
  Indonesia 2°59S 110°19E 118 E4
Sambas Indonesia 1°20N 109°20E 118 D3
Sambawizi Zimbabwe 18°24S 26°13E 143 F2
Sambhajinagar = Aurangabad
  India 19°50N 75°23E 126 E2
Sambhal India 28°35N 78°37E 125 E8
Sambhar India 26°52N 75°6E 124 F6
Sambhar L. India 26°55N 75°12E 124 F6
Sambiase Italy 38°58N 16°17E 95 D9
Sambir Ukraine 49°30N 23°10E 83 J10
Sambor Cambodia 12°46N 106°0E 120 F6
Sambor Prei Kuk
  Cambodia 12°46N 105°58E 120 F5
Samborombón, B.
  Argentina 36°5S 57°20W 190 D4
Sambuca di Sicilia Italy 37°39N 13°7E 94 E6
Samcheok S. Korea 37°30N 129°10E 115 F15
Same Tanzania 4°2S 37°38E 142 C4
Samer France 50°38N 1°44E 71 B8
Samet, Ko Thailand 12°34N 101°27E 120 F3
Samfya Zambia 11°22S 29°31E 143 E2
Sámi Greece 38°15N 20°39E 98 C2
Samir Azerbaijan 40°50N 46°0E 87 K8
Samland = Zemlandskiy
  Poluostrov Russia 54°50N 20°0E 82 D8
Şamlı Turkey 39°48N 27°51E 99 B9
Sammanturai Sri Lanka 7°36N 81°39E 127 L5
Samnah Si. Arabia 25°11N 37°15E 128 E3
Samo Alto Chile 30°22S 71°0W 190 C2

Samoa ■ *Pac. Oc.* 14°0S 172°0W **147** C11
Samobor *Croatia* 45°47N 15°44E **93** C12
Samoëns *France* 46°5N 6°45E **71** F13
Samokov *Bulgaria* 42°18N 23°35E **96** D7
Samorogouan
Burkina Faso 11°21N 4°57W **138** C4
Samos *Greece* 37°45N 26°50E **99** D8
Samoš *Serbia* 45°13N 20°46E **80** E5
Samos *Spain* 42°44N 7°20W **88** C3
Samoset *U.S.A.* 27°28N 82°33W **179** H7
Samothráki = Mathraki
Greece 39°48N 19°31E **101** A3
Samothraki *Greece* 40°28N 25°28E **97** F9
Samoylovka *Russia* 51°12N 43°43E **68** E6
Sampa *Ghana* 8°0N 2°36W **138** D4
Sampacho *Argentina* 33°20S 64°50W **190** C3
Sampalan *Indonesia* 8°41S 115°34E **119** K18
Sampang *Indonesia* 7°11S 113°13E **119** G15
Samper de Calanda
Spain 41°11N 0°28W **90** D4
Sampéyre *Italy* 44°34N 7°11E **92** D4
Sampit *Indonesia* 2°34S 113°0E **118** E4
Sampit, Teluk *Indonesia* 3°5S 113°3E **118** E4
Samrong *Cambodia* 14°15N 103°30E **120** E4
Samsø *Denmark* 55°50N 10°35E **63** J4
Samsø Bælt *Denmark* 55°45N 10°45E **63** J4
Samson *U.S.A.* 31°7N 86°3W **178** D3
Samsun *Turkey* 41°15N 36°22E **104** B7
Samsun □ *Turkey* 41°10N 36°10E **104** B7
Samtredia *Georgia* 42°7N 42°24E **87** K9
Samu → *Thailand* 9°30N 100°0E **121** b
Samur → *Russia* 41°53N 48°32E **87** K9
Samurskiy Khrebet
Russia 41°55N 47°11E **87** K8
Samusole
Dem. Rep. of the Congo 10°2S 24°0E **143** E1
Samut Prakan
Thailand 13°4ON 100°36E **120** F3
Samut Sakhon
Thailand 13°32N 100°17E **120** F3
Samut Songkhram
Thailand 13°24N 100°1E **120** F3
Samwari *Pakistan* 28°30N 66°46E **124** E2
San *Mali* 13°15N 4°57W **138** C4
San → *Cambodia* 13°32N 105°57E **120** F5
San → *Poland* 50°45N 21°51E **83** H8
San Adrián *Spain* 42°20N 1°56W **90** C3
San Adrián, C. de *Spain* 43°21N 8°50W **88** B2
San Agustin, C. *Phil.* 6°20N 126°13E **119** C7
San Agustín de Valle Fértil
Argentina 30°35S 67°30W **190** C2
San Ambrosio *Pac. Oc.* 26°28S 79°53W **184** F3
San Andreas *U.S.A.* 38°12N 120°41W **170** G6
San Andrés, I. de
Caribbean 12°42N 81°46W **182** D3
San Andrés del Rabanedo
Spain 42°37N 5°36W **88** C5
San Andres Mts.
U.S.A. 33°0N 106°30W **169** K10
San Andres Tuxtla
Mexico 18°27N 95°13W **181** D5
San Angelo *U.S.A.* 31°28N 100°26W **176** F4
San Anselmo *U.S.A.* 37°59N 122°34W **170** H4
San Antonio *Belize* 16°15N 89°2W **181** D7
San Antonio *Chile* 33°40S 71°40W **190** C1
San Antonio *N. Mex.*,
U.S.A. 33°55N 106°52W **169** K10
San Antonio *Tex.*,
U.S.A. 29°25N 98°29W **176** G5
San Antonio →
U.S.A. 28°30N 96°54W **176** G6
San Antonio, C.
Argentina 36°15S 56°40W **190** D4
San Antonio, C. de
Cuba 21°50N 84°57W **182** B3
San Antonio, C. de *Spain* 38°48N 0°12E **91** G5
San Antonio, Mt.
U.S.A. 34°17N 117°38W **171** L9
San Antonio de los Baños
Cuba 22°54N 82°31W **182** B3
San Antonio de los Cobres
Argentina 24°10S 66°17W **190** A2
San Antonio Oeste
Argentina 40°40S 65°0W **192** B4
San Arcángelo *Italy* 40°14N 16°14E **95** B9
San Ardo *U.S.A.* 36°1N 120°54W **170** J6
San Augustin
Canary Is. 27°47N 15°32W **100** G4
San Augustine *U.S.A.* 31°32N 94°7W **176** F7
San Bartolomé
Canary Is. 28°59N 13°37W **100** F6
San Bartolomé de Tirajana
Canary Is. 27°54N 15°34W **100** G4
San Bartolomeo in Galdo
Italy 41°24N 15°1E **95** A8
San Benedetto del Tronto
Italy 42°57N 13°53E **93** F10
San Benedetto Po *Italy* 45°2N 10°55E **92** C7
San Benedicto, I.
Mexico 19°18N 110°49W **180** D2
San Benito *U.S.A.* 26°8N 97°38W **176** H6
San Benito → *U.S.A.* 36°53N 121°34W **170** J5
San Benito Mt. *U.S.A.* 36°22N 120°37W **170** J6
San Bernardino *U.S.A.* 34°7N 117°19W **171** L9
San Bernardino Mts.
U.S.A. 34°10N 116°45W **171** L10
San Bernardino Str.
Phil. 12°30N 124°10E **119** B7
San Bernardo *Chile* 33°40S 70°50W **190** C1
San Bernardo, I. de
Colombia 9°45N 75°50W **186** B3
San Blas *Mexico* 26°4N 108°46W **180** B3
San Blas, Arch. de
Panama 9°50N 78°31W **182** E4
San Blas, C. *U.S.A.* 29°40N 85°21W **178** F4
San Bonifacio *Italy* 45°24N 11°16E **92** C8
San Borja *Bolivia* 14°50S 66°52W **188** C4
San Buenaventura = Ventura
U.S.A. 34°17N 119°18W **171** L7
San Buenaventura
Bolivia 14°28S 67°35W **188** C4
San Buenaventura
Mexico 27°5N 101°32W **180** B4

San Carlos *Coahuila*,
Mexico 29°1N 100°51W **180** B4
San Carlos *Nic.* 11°12N 84°58W **182** D3
San Carlos *Phil.* 10°29N 123°25E **119** B6
San Carlos *Uruguay* 34°46S 54°58W **191** C5
San Carlos *U.S.A.* 33°21N 110°27W **169** K8
San Carlos *Venezuela* 9°40N 68°36W **186** B5
San Carlos de Bariloche
Argentina 41°10S 71°25W **192** B3
San Carlos de Bolívar
Argentina 36°15S 61°6W **190** D3
San Carlos de la Rápita = Sant
Carles de la Ràpita
Spain 40°37N 0°35E **90** E5
San Carlos del Zulia
Venezuela 9°1N 71°55W **186** B4
San Carlos L. *U.S.A.* 33°11N 110°32W **169** K8
San Carlos Park *U.S.A.* 26°28N 81°49W **179** J8
San Cataldo *Italy* 37°29N 13°59E **94** E6
San Celoni = Sant Celoni
Spain 41°42N 2°30E **90** D7
San Clemente *Chile* 35°30S 71°29W **190** D1
San Clemente *Spain* 39°24N 2°25W **91** F2
San Clemente *U.S.A.* 33°26N 117°37W **171** M9
San Clemente I.
U.S.A. 32°53N 118°29W **171** N8
San Cristóbal = Es Migjorn Gran
Spain 39°57N 4°3E **100** B11
San Cristóbal *Argentina* 30°20S 61°10W **190** C3
San Cristóbal *Dom. Rep.* 18°25N 70°6W **183** C5
San Cristóbal
Solomon Is. 10°30S 161°0E **147** C9
San Cristóbal *Venezuela* 7°46N 72°14W **186** B4
San Cristóbal de La Laguna = La
Laguna *Canary Is.* 28°28N 16°18W **100** F3
San Cristóbal de las Casas
Mexico 16°45N 92°38W **181** D6
San Damiano d'Asti *Italy* 44°50N 8°4E **92** D5
San Daniele del Friuli
Italy 46°9N 13°1E **93** B10
San Diego *Calif.*, *U.S.A.* 32°42N 117°9W **171** N9
San Diego *Tex.*, *U.S.A.* 27°46N 98°14W **176** H5
San Diego, C. *Argentina* 54°40S 65°10W **192** D3
San Diego de la Unión
Mexico 21°28N 100°52W **180** C4
San Diego Int. ✈ (SAN)
U.S.A. 32°44N 117°11W **171** N9
San Dimitri, Ras *Malta* 36°4N 14°11E **101** C1
San Dimitri Point = San Dimitri,
Ras *Malta* 36°4N 14°11E **101** C1
San Donà di Piave *Italy* 45°38N 12°34E **93** C9
San Estanislao
Paraguay 24°39S 56°26W **190** A4
San Esteban de Gormaz
Spain 41°34N 3°13W **90** D1
San Felice Circeo *Italy* 41°14N 13°5E **94** A6
San Felice sul Panaro
Italy 44°50N 11°8E **93** D8
San Felipe *Chile* 32°43S 70°42W **190** C1
San Felipe *Mexico* 31°1N 114°52W **180** A2
San Felipe *Venezuela* 10°20N 68°44W **186** A5
San Felipe → *U.S.A.* 33°10N 115°49W **171** M11
San Félix *Chile* 26°23S 70°0W **190** B1
San Félix *Pac. Oc.* 26°23S 80°0W **184** F2
San Fernando = Sant Ferran
Spain 38°42N 1°28E **100** C7
San Fernando *Chile* 34°30S 71°0W **190** C1
San Fernando *Mexico* 24°51N 98°10W **181** C5
San Fernando *La Union*,
Phil. 16°40N 120°23E **119** A6
San Fernando *Pampanga*,
Phil. 15°5N 120°37E **119** A6
San Fernando *Spain* 36°28N 6°17W **89** J4
San Fernando
Trin. & Tob. 10°16N 61°28W **183** D7
San Fernando de Apure
Venezuela 7°54N 67°15W **186** B5
San Fernando de Atabapo
Venezuela 4°3N 67°42W **186** C5
San Fernando di Púglia
Italy 41°18N 16°5E **95** A9
San Francisco *Argentina* 31°30S 62°5W **190** C3
San Francisco *Peru* 12°30S 73°55W **188** C3
San Francisco → *U.S.A.* 37°46N 122°23W **170** H4
San Francisco
U.S.A. 32°59N 109°22W **169** K9
San Francisco, C. de
Colombia 6°18N 77°29W **184** C3
San Francisco, Paso de
S. Amer. 27°0S 68°0W **190** B2
San Francisco de Macorís
Dom. Rep. 19°19N 70°15W **183** C5
San Francisco del Monte de Oro
Argentina 32°36S 66°8W **190** C2
San Francisco del Oro
Mexico 26°52N 105°51W **180** B3
San Francisco Int. ✈ (SFO)
U.S.A. 37°37N 122°22W **170** H4
San Francisco Javier = Sant
Francesc de Formentera
Spain 38°42N 1°26E **100** C7
San Fratello *Italy* 38°1N 14°36E **95** D7
San Gabriel *U.S.A.* 33°47S 70°15W **190** C1
San Gabriel Chilac
Mexico 18°19N 97°21W **181** D5
San Gabriel Mts.
U.S.A. 34°17N 117°38W **171** L9
San Gavino Monreale
Italy 39°33N 8°47E **94** C1
San German *Puerto Rico* 18°4N 67°4W **183** d
San Gimignano *Italy* 43°28N 11°2E **92** E8
San Giórgio di Nogaro
Italy 45°50N 13°13E **93** C10
San Giórgio Iónico
Italy 40°27N 17°23E **95** B10
San Giovanni Bianco
Italy 45°52N 9°39E **92** C6
San Giovanni in Fiore
Italy 39°15N 16°42E **95** C9
San Giovanni in Persiceto
Italy 44°38N 11°11E **93** D8
San Giovanni Rotondo
Italy 41°42N 15°44E **93** G12
San Giovanni Valdarno
Italy 43°34N 11°32E **93** E8
San Giuliano Terme
Italy 43°46N 10°26E **92** E7
San Gorgonio Mt.
U.S.A. 34°6N 116°50W **171** L10

San Gottardo, P. del
Switz. 46°33N 8°33E **77** J4
San Gregorio *Uruguay* 32°37S 55°40W **191** C4
San Gregorio *U.S.A.* 37°20N 122°23W **170** H4
San Guillermo △
Argentina 27°50S 69°45W **190** B2
San Guiseppe Jato *Italy* 37°57N 13°11E **94** E6
San Ignacio *Belize* 17°10N 89°5W **181** D7
San Ignacio *Bolivia* 16°20S 60°55W **188** G6
San Ignacio *Mexico* 27°27N 112°51W **180** B2
San Ignacio *Paraguay* 26°52S 57°3W **190** B4
San Ignacio *Peru* 5°8S 78°59W **188** B2
San Ignacio, L.
Mexico 26°54N 113°13W **180** B2
San Ildefonso, C. *Phil.* 16°0N 122°1E **119** A6
San Isidro *Argentina* 34°29S 58°31W **190** C4
San Jacinto *U.S.A.* 33°47N 116°57W **171** M10
San Jaime = Sant Jaume
Spain 39°54N 4°4E **100** B11
San Javier *Misiones*,
Argentina 27°55S 55°5W **191** B4
San Javier *Santa Fe*,
Argentina 30°40S 59°55W **190** C4
San Javier *Bolivia* 16°18S 62°30W **186** G6
San Javier *Chile* 35°40S 71°45W **190** D1
San Javier *Spain* 37°49N 0°50W **91** H4
San Jerónimo Taviche
Mexico 16°44N 96°35W **181** D5
San Joaquin *U.S.A.* 36°36N 120°11W **170** J6
San Joaquin → *U.S.A.* 38°4N 121°51W **170** G5
San Joaquin Valley
U.S.A. 37°20N 121°0W **170** J6
San Jon *U.S.A.* 35°6N 103°20W **169** J12
San Jordi = Sant Jordi
Spain 39°33N 2°46E **100** B9
San Jorge *Argentina* 31°54S 61°50W **190** C3
San Jorge, B. *Mexico* 31°20N 113°20W **180** A2
San Jorge, G. *Argentina* 46°0S 66°0W **192** C3
San José = San Josep
Spain 38°55N 1°18E **100** C7
San José *Argentina* 32°12S 58°15W **190** C4
San José *Costa Rica* 9°55N 84°2W **182** E3
San José *Guatemala* 14°0N 90°50W **182** D1
San José *Mind. Occ.*,
Phil. 12°27N 121°4E **119** B6
San José *Nueva Ecija*,
Phil. 15°45N 120°55E **119** A6
San Jose *Spain* 40°38N 2°50W **91** J10
San Jose *U.S.A.* 37°20N 121°53W **170** H5
San José, G. *Argentina* 42°20S 64°18W **192** B4
San José, I. *Mexico* 25°0N 110°38W **180** C2
San Jose de Buenavista
Phil. 10°45N 121°56E **119** B6
San José de Chiquitos
Bolivia 17°53S 60°50W **186** G6
San José de Feliciano
Argentina 30°26S 58°46W **190** C4
San José de Jáchal
Argentina 30°15S 68°46W **190** C2
San José de Mayo
Uruguay 34°27S 56°40W **190** C4
San José de Uchapiamonas
Bolivia 14°13S 68°5W **188** C4
San José del Cabo
Mexico 23°3N 109°41W **180** C3
San José del Guaviare
Colombia 2°35N 72°38W **186** C4
San Josep *Spain* 38°55N 1°18E **100** C7
San Juan *Peru* 15°22S 75°7W **188** D2
San Juan *Puerto Rico* 18°28N 66°7W **183** d
San Juan *Trin. & Tob.* 10°39N 61°29W **187** K15
San Juan □ *Argentina* 31°9S 69°0W **190** C2
San Juan → *Argentina* 32°20S 67°25W **190** C2
San Juan → *Nic.* 10°56N 83°42W **182** D3
San Juan → *U.S.A.* 37°16N 110°26W **169** H8
San Juan, C. *Argentina* 54°45S 63°44W **192** D4
San Juan Bautista = Sant Joan de
Labritja *Spain* 39°5N 1°31E **100** B8
San Juan Bautista
Paraguay 26°37S 57°6W **190** B4
San Juan Bautista
U.S.A. 36°51N 121°32W **170** J5
San Juan Capistrano
U.S.A. 33°30N 117°40W **171** M9
San Juan Cr. →
U.S.A. 35°40N 120°22W **170** J5
San Juan de Guadelupe
Mexico 24°38N 102°44W **180** C4
San Juan de la Costa
Mexico 24°20N 110°41W **180** C2
San Juan de los Lagos
Mexico 21°15N 102°10W **180** C4
San Juan de los Morros
Venezuela 9°55N 67°21W **186** B5
San Juan del Norte
Nic. 10°58N 83°40W **182** D3
San Juan del Norte, B. de
Nic. 11°0N 83°40W **182** D3
San Juan del Río
Mexico 20°23N 100°0W **181** C5
San Juan del Sur *Nic.* 11°20N 85°51W **182** D2
San Juan I. *U.S.A.* 48°32N 123°5W **174** B3
San Juan Island △
U.S.A. 48°35N 123°8W **170** B4
San Juan Mts. *U.S.A.* 37°30N 107°0W **169** H10
San Just, Sierra de *Spain* 40°45N 0°49W **90** E4
San Justo *Argentina* 30°47S 60°30W **190** C3
San Kamphaeng
Thailand 18°45N 99°8E **120** C2
San Lázaro, C. *Mexico* 24°50N 112°18W **180** C2
San Leandro *U.S.A.* 37°44N 122°9W **170** H4
San Leonardo de Yagüe
Spain 41°51N 3°5W **90** D1
San Lorenzo = Sant Llorenç des
Cardassar *Spain* 39°37N 3°17E **100** B10
San Lorenzo *Argentina* 32°45S 60°45W **190** C3
San Lorenzo *Ecuador* 1°15N 78°50W **186** C3
San Lorenzo *Paraguay* 25°20S 57°32W **190** B4
San Lorenzo →
Mexico 24°15N 107°24W **180** C3
San Lorenzo, I.
Mexico 28°35N 112°50W **180** B2
San Lorenzo, I. *Peru* 12°7S 77°15W **188** D2
San Lorenzo, Mte.
Argentina 47°40S 72°20W **192** C2
San Lorenzo de la Parrilla
Spain 39°51N 2°22W **90** F2
San Lorenzo de Morunys = Sant
Llorenç de Morunys
Spain 42°8N 1°35E **90** C6

San Lucas = Cabo San Lucas
Mexico 22°53N 109°54W **180** C3
San Lucas *Bolivia* 20°5S 65°7W **186** H5
San Lucas *Mexico* 27°10N 112°14W **180** B2
San Lucas, C. *Mexico* 22°52N 109°53W **180** C3
San Lúcido *Italy* 39°18N 16°3E **95** C9
San Luis *Argentina* 33°20S 66°20W **190** C2
San Luis *Cuba* 22°17N 83°46W **182** B3
San Luis *Guatemala* 16°14N 89°27W **182** C2
San Luis *Ariz.*, *U.S.A.* 32°29N 114°47W **169** K6
San Luis *Colo.*, *U.S.A.* 37°12N 105°25W **169** H11
San Luis □ *Argentina* 34°0S 66°0W **190** C2
San Luis, I. *Mexico* 29°58N 114°26W **180** B2
San Luis, Sierra de
Argentina 32°30S 66°10W **190** C2
San Luis de la Paz
Mexico 21°18N 100°31W **180** C4
San Luis Obispo
U.S.A. 35°17N 120°40W **171** K6
San Luis Potosí *Mexico* 22°9N 100°59W **180** C4
San Luis Potosí □
Mexico 23°0N 101°0W **180** C4
San Luis Res. *U.S.A.* 37°4N 121°5W **170** H5
San Luis Río Colorado
Mexico 32°29N 114°58W **180** A2
San Manuel *U.S.A.* 32°36N 110°38W **169** K8
San Marco, C. *Italy* 39°51N 8°26E **94** C1
San Marco Argentano
Italy 39°33N 16°7E **95** C9
San Marco in Lámis
Italy 41°43N 15°38E **93** G12
San Marcos *Calif.*,
U.S.A. 33°9N 117°10W **171** M9
San Marcos *Tex.*,
U.S.A. 29°53N 97°56W **176** G6
San Marcos, I. *Mexico* 27°13N 112°6W **180** B2
San Marino *San Marino* 43°55N 12°30E **93** E9
San Marino ■ *Europe* 43°56N 12°25E **93** E9
San Martín *Antarctica* 68°11S 67°0W **55** C17
San Martín *Argentina* 33°5S 68°28W **190** C2
San Martín □ *Peru* 7°0S 76°50W **188** B2
San Martín → *Bolivia* 13°8S 63°43W **186** F6
San Martín, L.
Argentina 48°50S 72°50W **192** C2
San Martín de la Vega
Spain 40°13N 3°34W **88** B7
San Martín de los Andes
Argentina 40°10S 71°20W **192** B2
San Martín de Valdeiglesias
Spain 40°21N 4°24W **88** E6
San Mateo = Sant Mateu *Baleares*,
Spain 39°3N 1°23E **100** B7
San Mateo = Sant Mateu *Valencia*,
Spain 40°28N 0°10E **90** E5
San Mateo *U.S.A.* 37°34N 122°19W **170** H4
San Matías *Bolivia* 16°25S 58°20W **186** G7
San Matías, G.
Argentina 41°30S 64°0W **192** B4
San Miguel = Sant Miquel
Spain 39°3N 1°26E **100** B7
San Miguel *El Salv.* 13°30N 88°12W **182** D2
San Miguel *Panama* 8°27N 78°55W **182** E4
San Miguel *Spain* 35°45N 124°2W **170** K6
San Miguel → *Bolivia* 13°52S 63°56W **186** F6
San Miguel de Huachi
Bolivia 15°40S 67°15W **188** D4
San Miguel de Tucumán
Argentina 26°50S 65°20W **190** B2
San Miguel del Monte
Argentina 35°23S 58°50W **190** D4
San Miguel I. *U.S.A.* 34°2N 120°23W **171** L6
San Millán de la Cogolla
Spain 42°19N 2°51W **90** C2
San Miniato *Italy* 43°41N 10°51E **92** E7
San Nicandro Gargánico
Italy 41°50N 15°34E **93** G12
San Nicolás *Canary Is.* 28°0N 15°47W **100** G4
San Nicolás de los Arroyos
Argentina 33°25S 60°10W **190** C3
San Nicolas I. *U.S.A.* 33°15N 119°30W **171** M7
San Onofre *U.S.A.* 33°22N 117°34W **171** M9
San Pablo *Bolivia* 21°43S 66°38W **190** A2
San Pablo *U.S.A.* 37°58N 122°21W **170** H4
San Páolo di Civitate
Italy 41°44N 15°15E **93** G12
San Pedro *B. Aires*,
Argentina 33°40S 59°40W **190** C4
San Pedro *Misiones*,
Argentina 26°30S 54°10W **191** B5
San Pedro *Chile* 33°54S 71°28W **190** C1
San Pedro *Ivory C.* 4°50N 6°33W **138** E3
San Pedro *Mexico* 23°55N 110°17W **180** C2
San Pedro *Peru* 14°49S 74°58W **188** D3
San Pedro □ *Paraguay* 24°0S 57°0W **190** A4
San Pedro → *Chihuahua*,
Mexico 28°21N 105°25W **180** B3
San Pedro → *Nayarit*,
Mexico 21°45N 105°30W **180** C3
San Pedro → *U.S.A.* 32°59N 110°47W **169** K8
San Pedro, Pta. *Chile* 25°30S 70°38W **190** B1
San Pedro, Sierra de
Spain 39°18N 6°40W **89** F4
San Pedro Channel
U.S.A. 33°30N 118°25W **171** M8
San Pedro de Atacama
Chile 22°55S 68°15W **190** A2
San Pedro de Jujuy
Argentina 24°12S 64°55W **190** A3
San Pedro de las Colonias
Mexico 25°45N 102°59W **180** B4
San Pedro de Lloc *Peru* 7°15S 79°28W **188** B2
San Pedro de Macorís
Dom. Rep. 18°30N 69°18W **183** C6
San Pedro del Norte
Nic. 13°4N 84°33W **182** D3
San Pedro del Paraná
Paraguay 26°43S 56°13W **190** B4
San Pedro del Pinatar
Spain 37°50N 0°50W **91** H4
San Pedro Mártir, Sa. de
Mexico 30°45N 115°13W **180** A1
San Pedro Ocampo = Melchor
Ocampo *Mexico* 24°51N 101°39W **180** C4
San Pedro Pochutla
Mexico 15°44N 96°28W **181** D5
San Pedro Sula
Honduras 15°30N 88°0W **182** C2
San Pedro Tututepec
Mexico 16°9N 97°38W **181** D5
San Pietro *Italy* 39°8N 8°17E **94** C1

San Pietro Vernótico
Italy 40°29N 18°0E **95** B11
San Rafael *Argentina* 34°40S 68°21W **190** C2
San Rafael *Calif.*,
U.S.A. 37°58N 122°32W **170** H4
San Rafael *N. Mex.*,
U.S.A. 35°7N 107°53W **169** J10
San Rafael Mt. *U.S.A.* 34°41N 119°52W **171** L7
San Rafael Mts.
U.S.A. 34°40N 119°50W **171** L7
San Ramón de la Nueva Orán
Argentina 23°10S 64°20W **190** A3
San Remo *Italy* 43°49N 7°46E **92** E4
San Roque *Argentina* 28°25S 58°45W **190** B4
San Roque *Spain* 36°17N 5°21W **89** J5
San Rosendo *Chile* 37°16S 72°43W **190** D1
San Saba *U.S.A.* 31°12N 98°43W **176** F5
San Salvador *El Salv.* 13°40N 89°10W **182** D2
San Salvador de Jujuy
Argentina 24°10S 64°48W **190** A3
San Salvador I.
Bahamas 24°0N 74°30W **183** B5
San Salvo *Italy* 42°3N 14°44E **93** F11
San Sebastián = Donostia-San
Sebastián *Spain* 43°17N 1°58W **90** B3
San Sebastián
Argentina 53°10S 68°30W **192** D3
San Sebastián
Puerto Rico 18°20N 66°59W **183** d
San Sebastián de la Gomera
Canary Is. 28°5N 17°7W **100** F2
San Serra = Son Serra
Spain 39°43N 3°13E **100** B10
San Serverino Marche
Italy 43°13N 13°10E **93** E10
San Severo *Italy* 41°41N 15°23E **93** G12
San Simeon *U.S.A.* 35°39N 121°11W **170** K5
San Simon *U.S.A.* 32°16N 109°14W **169** K9
San Stéfano di Cadore
Italy 46°34N 12°33E **93** B9
San Stino di Livenza
Italy 45°44N 12°41E **93** C9
San Telmo = Sant Elm
Spain 39°35N 2°21E **100** B9
San Telmo *Mexico* 30°58N 116°6W **180** A1
San Teodoro *Italy* 40°46N 9°40E **94** B2
San Tiburcio *Mexico* 24°8N 101°32W **180** C4
San Valentin, Mte.
Chile 46°30S 73°30W **192** C2
San Vicente de Alcántara
Spain 39°22N 7°8W **89** F3
San Vicente de Cañete
Peru 13°8S 76°30W **188** C2
San Vicente de la Barquera
Spain 43°23N 4°29W **88** B6
San Vicenzo *Spain* 42°58N 8°46W **88** C2
San Vincenzo *Italy* 43°6N 10°32E **92** E7
San Vito *Costa Rica* 8°50N 82°58W **182** E3
San Vito *Italy* 39°26N 9°32E **94** C2
San Vito, C. *Italy* 38°11N 12°41E **94** D5
San Vito al Tagliamento
Italy 45°55N 12°52E **93** C9
San Vito Chietino *Italy* 42°18N 14°27E **93** F11
San Vito dei Normanni
Italy 40°39N 17°42E **95** B10
Sana' = Ṣan'ā' *Yemen* 15°27N 44°12E **131** D3
Saña *Peru* 6°54S 79°36W **188** B2
Ṣan'ā' *Yemen* 15°27N 44°12E **131** D3
Sana → *Bos.-H.* 45°3N 16°23E **93** C13
Sanaa = Ṣan'ā' *Yemen* 15°27N 44°12E **131** D3
Sanae IV *Antarctica* 70°20S 9°0W **55** D2
Sanaga → *Cameroon* 3°35N 9°38E **139** E6
Sanak I. *U.S.A.* 54°25N 162°40W **166** E7
Sanalona, Presa
Mexico 24°49N 107°7W **180** C3
Sanana *Indonesia* 2°4S 125°58E **119** E7
Sanand *India* 22°59N 72°25E **124** H5
Sanandaj *Iran* 35°18N 47°1E **126** C5
Sanandita *Bolivia* 21°40S 63°45W **190** A3
Sanary-sur-Mer *France* 43°7N 5°49E **73** E9
Sanawad *India* 22°11N 76°5E **124** H7
Sancellas = Sencelles
Spain 39°39N 2°54E **100** B9
Sancergues *France* 47°10N 2°54E **71** E9
Sancerre *France* 47°20N 2°50E **71** E9
Sancerrois, Collines du
France 47°20N 2°40E **71** E9
Sancha He → *China* 26°48N 106°7E **116** D6
Sanchahe *China* 44°50N 126°2E **115** B4
Sánchez *Dom. Rep.* 19°15N 69°36W **183** C6
Sanchi *India* 23°28N 77°44E **124** H7
Sanchor *India* 24°45N 71°55E **124** G4
Sancoins *France* 46°47N 2°55E **71** F9
Sancti Spíritus *Cuba* 21°52N 79°33W **182** B4
Sancy, Puy de *France* 45°32N 2°50E **72** C6
Sand →
S. Africa 22°25S 30°5E **145** B5
Sand Hills *U.S.A.* 42°10N 101°30W **172** D3
Sand Lakes △ *Canada* 57°51N 98°32W **163** B9
Sand Springs *U.S.A.* 36°9N 96°7W **176** C6
Sanda *Japan* 34°53N 135°14E **113** G7
Sandakan *Malaysia* 5°53N 118°4E **118** C5
Sandalwood *Australia* 34°55S 140°9E **152** C4
Sandan = Sambor
Cambodia 12°46N 106°0E **120** F6
Sandanski *Bulgaria* 41°35N 23°16E **96** E7
Sandaré *Mali* 14°40N 10°15W **138** C2
Sandared *Sweden* 57°43N 12°47E **63** G6
Sandarne *Sweden* 61°16N 17°9E **62** C11
Sanday *U.K.* 59°16N 2°31W **65** B6
Sandefjord *Norway* 59°10N 10°15E **63** D14
Sanders *U.S.A.* 35°13N 109°20W **169** J9
Sanderson *U.S.A.* 30°9N 102°24W **176** E3
Sanderson *Tex.*, *U.S.A.* 30°9N 102°24W **176** E3
Sandersville *U.S.A.* 32°59N 82°48W **178** D6
Sandfire Roadhouse
Australia 19°45S 121°15E **148** C3
Sandfly L. *Canada* 55°43N 106°6W **163** B7
Sandfontein *Namibia* 23°48S 19°1E **144** B2
Sandhammaren *Sweden* 55°24N 14°12E **63** D13
Sandheads, The *India* 21°10N 88°20E **125** J13
Sandia *Peru* 14°10S 69°30W **188** C4
Sandıklı *Turkey* 38°28N 30°17E **104** C5
Sandila *India* 27°5N 80°31E **125** F9
Sandnes *Norway* 58°50N 5°45E **63** G11
Sandnessjøen *Norway* 66°2N 12°38E **60** C15
Sandoa
Dem. Rep. of the Congo 9°41S 23°0E **140** F4

Sandomierz *Poland* 50°40N 21°43E **83** H8
Sândominic *Romania* 46°35N 25°47E **81** D10
Sandover → *Australia* 21°43S 136°32E **150** C2
Sandoway = Thandwe
Burma 18°20N 94°30E **123** K19
Sandoy *Færoe Is.* 61°52N 6°46W **60** F9
Sandpoint *U.S.A.* 48°17N 116°33W **168** B5
Sandray *U.K.* 56°53N 7°31W **65** E1
Sandringham *U.K.* 52°51N 0°31E **66** E8
Sandstone *Australia* 27°59S 119°16E **149** E2
Sandu *China* 26°0N 107°52E **116** E6
Sandur *India* 15°6N 76°33E **127** F3
Sandusky *Mich.*,
U.S.A. 43°25N 82°50W **174** C2
Sandusky *Ohio*, *U.S.A.* 41°27N 82°42W **174** E2
Sandveld *Namibia* 21°25S 20°0E **144** B3
Sandvig *Denmark* 55°16N 14°47E **63** E9
Sandviken *Sweden* 60°38N 16°46E **62** D10
Sandwich, C. *Australia* 18°14S 146°18E **150** B4
Sandwich B. *Canada* 53°40N 57°15W **165** B8
Sandwich B. *Namibia* 23°25S 14°20E **144** C1
Sandy *Oreg.*, *U.S.A.* 45°24N 122°16W **170** E4
Sandy *Pa.*, *U.S.A.* 41°6N 78°46W **174** E6
Sandy *Utah*, *U.S.A.* 40°32N 111°50W **168** F8
Sandy Bay *Canada* 55°31N 102°19W **163** B8
Sandy Bight *Australia* 33°50S 123°20E **149** F3
Sandy C. *Queens.*,
Australia 24°42S 153°15E **150** C5
Sandy C. *Tas.*, *Australia* 41°25S 144°45E **151** G3
Sandy Cay *Bahamas* 23°13N 75°18W **183** B4
Sandy Cr. → *Australia* 34°53S 145°18E **151** B4
Sandy Cr. → *U.S.A.* 41°51N 109°47W **168** F9
Sandy Creek *U.S.A.* 43°38N 76°5W **175** C8
Sandy L. *Canada* 53°0N 93°0W **164** B1
Sandy Lake *Canada* 53°0N 93°15W **164** B1
Sandy Point *U.S.A.* 32°59N 92°22E **127** J11
Sandy Springs *U.S.A.* 33°55N 84°22W **178** D5
Sandy Valley *U.S.A.* 35°49N 115°38W **171** K11
Sânfälet △ *Sweden* 62°17N 13°35E **62** B7
Sanford *Fla.*, *U.S.A.* 28°48N 81°16W **179** G8
Sanford *Maine*, *U.S.A.* 43°27N 70°47W **175** C14
Sanford *N.C.*, *U.S.A.* 35°29N 79°10W **177** D15
Sanford → *Australia* 27°22S 115°53E **149** E2
Sanford, Mt. *U.S.A.* 62°13N 144°8W **166** D11
Sang-i-Masha *Afghan.* 33°8N 67°27E **124** C2
Sanga *Mozam.* 12°22S 35°21E **143** E4
Sanga → *Congo* 1°5S 17°0E **140** E3
Sangamner *India* 19°37N 74°15E **126** E2
Sangān *Iran* 34°23N 60°15E **127** C9
Sanganeb Atoll △
Sudan 19°33N 37°11E **137** D4
Sangar *Afghan.* 32°56N 65°30E **124** C1
Sangar *Russia* 62°4N 127°31E **107** C13
Sangar Sarai *Afghan.* 34°27N 70°35E **124** C3
Sangareddi *India* 17°38N 78°7E **126** F4
Sangaredi *Guinea* 11°56N 13°43W **138** C2
Sangarh → *Pakistan* 30°43N 70°44E **124** D4
Sangasso *Mali* 12°5N 5°35W **138** C3
Sangatte *France* 50°56N 1°44E **71** B8
Sangay *Ecuador* 2°0S 78°20W **186** D3
Sangbé *Cameroon* 6°3N 12°33E **139** E7
Sange
Dem. Rep. of the Congo 6°58S 28°21E **142** D2
Sangeang *Indonesia* 8°12S 119°6E **119** F5
Sângeorz-Bäi *Romania* 47°22N 24°41E **81** C9
Sanger *U.S.A.* 36°42N 119°33W **170** J7
Sângera *Moldova* 46°55N 28°58E **81** D13
Sangerhausen *Germany* 51°28N 11°18E **76** D7
Sanggan He → *China* 38°12N 117°15E **114** E9
Sanggau *Indonesia* 0°5N 110°30E **118** D4
Sanghar *Pakistan* 26°2N 68°57E **124** F3
Sanghe, Kepulauan
Indonesia 3°0N 125°30E **119** D7
Sanghe, Pulau
Indonesia 3°35N 125°30E **119** D7
Sangiran △ *Indonesia* 7°27S 110°50E **119** G14
Sangju *S. Korea* 36°25N 128°10E **115** F15
Sangkapura *Indonesia* 5°52S 112°40E **118** F4
Sangkha *Thailand* 14°57N 103°52E **120** E4
Sangkulirang *Indonesia* 0°59N 117°58E **118** D5
Sangla *Pakistan* 31°43N 73°23E **124** D5
Sangli *India* 16°55N 74°33E **126** E2
Sangmélima *Cameroon* 2°57N 12°1E **139** E7
Sango *Zimbabwe* 18°44S 31°44E **143** F3
Sangod *India* 24°55N 76°17E **124** G7
Sangole *India* 17°26N 75°12E **126** F2
Sangre de Cristo Mts.
U.S.A. 37°30N 105°20W **169** H11
Sangre Grande
Trin. & Tob. 10°35N 61°8W **187** K15
Sangro → *Italy* 42°14N 14°32E **93** F11
Sangrur *India* 30°14N 75°50E **124** D6
Sangudo *Canada* 53°50N 114°54W **162** C6
Sangue → *Brazil* 11°1S 58°39W **186** F7
Sangüesa *Spain* 42°37N 1°17W **90** C3
Sanguinaires, Îs. *France* 41°51N 8°36E **73** G12
Sangzhi *China* 29°25N 110°12E **117** C8
Sanhala *Ivory C.* 10°3N 6°51W **138** C3
Sanibel *U.S.A.* 26°27N 82°1W **179** J7
Sanibel I. *U.S.A.* 26°26N 82°6W **179** J7
Sanikluaq *Canada* 56°32N 79°14W **164** B3
Sanin-Kaigan △ *Japan* 35°39N 134°37E **113** G7
Sanirajak = Hall Beach
Canada 68°46N 81°12W **161** D15
Sanjawi *Pakistan* 30°17N 68°21E **124** D3
Sanje *Uganda* 0°49S 31°30E **142** C3
Sanjiang *China* 25°48N 109°37E **116** E7
Sanjo *Japan* 37°37N 138°57E **112** E9
Sankarankovil *India* 9°10N 77°35E **127** K3
Sankeshwar *India* 16°23N 74°32E **124** F7
Sankh → *India* 22°15N 84°48E **125** H11
Sankt Andrä *Austria* 46°46N 14°50E **76** E7
Sankt Anton *Austria* 47°8N 10°16E **77** H6
Sankt Augustin *Germany* 50°45N 7°10E **76** E4
Sankt Blasien *Germany* 47°47N 8°7E **76** E4
Sankt Gallen *Switz.* 47°26N 9°22E **77** H5
Sankt Gallen □ *Switz.* 47°25N 9°22E **77** H5
Sankt Goar *Germany* 50°12N 7°43E **77** E3
Sankt Ingbert *Germany* 49°16N 7°6E **77** D3
Sankt Johann im Pongau
Austria 47°22N 13°12E **76** D6
Sankt Johann in Tirol
Austria 47°30N 12°25E **76** D5
Sankt Michel = Mikkeli
Finland 61°43N 27°15E **64** B4
Sankt Moritz *Switz.* 46°30N 9°51E **77** J5
Sankt Peter-Ording
Germany 54°20N 8°36E **76** A4
Sankt-Peterburg *Russia* 59°55N 30°20E **84** C6

268 Sankt Pölten
INDEX TO WORLD MAPS

Sankt Pölten *Austria* 48°12N 15°38E **78** C8
Sankt Ulrich = Ortisei *Italy* 46°34N 11°40E **93** B8
Sankt Valentin *Austria* 48°11N 14°33E **78** C7
Sankt Veit an der Glan *Austria* 46°47N 14°22E **78** E7
Sankt Wendel *Germany* 49°27N 7°9E **77** F3
Sankt Wolfgang *Austria* 47°43N 13°27E **78** D6
Sankuru → *Dem. Rep. of the Congo* 4°17S 20°25E **140** E4
Sanliurfa *Turkey* 37°12N 38°50E **105** D8
Sanliurfa □ *Turkey* 37°0N 39°0E **105** D8
Sanlúcar de Barrameda *Spain* 36°46N 6°21W **89** J4
Sanluri *Italy* 39°34N 8°54E **94** C1
Sânmartin *Romania* 46°19N 25°58E **81** D10
Sanmen *China* 29°5N 121°35E **117** C13
Sanmenxia *China* 34°47N 111°12E **114** G6
Sanming *China* 26°15N 117°40E **117** D11
Sanmu *Japan* 34°11N 134°37E **113** G7
Sanndraigh = Sandray *U.K.* 56°53N 7°31W **65** E1
Sânnicolau Mare *Romania* 46°5N 20°39E **80** D5
Sannieshof *S. Africa* 26°30S 25°47E **144** C4
Sannîn, J. *Lebanon* 33°57N 35°52E **130** B4
Sanniquellie *Liberia* 7°19N 8°38W **138** D3
Sannûr, W. → *Egypt* 28°59N 31°3E **137** F7
Sano *Japan* 36°19N 139°35E **113** F9
Sanok *Poland* 49°35N 22°10E **83** J9
Sanqingshan △ *China* 28°54N 118°3E **117** C12
Sanquhar *U.K.* 55°22N 3°54W **65** F5
Sans Souci *Trin. & Tob.* 10°50N 61°0W **187** K16
Sansanding *Mali* 13°48N 6°0W **138** C3
Sansané *Niger* 13°50N 1°36E **139** C5
Sansepolcro *Italy* 43°34N 12°8E **93** E9
Sansha *China* 26°58N 120°12E **117** D13
Sanshui *China* 23°10N 112°56E **117** F9
Sanski Most *Bos.-H.* 44°46N 16°40E **93** D13
Sansui *China* 26°58N 108°39E **116** D7
Sant Antoni de Portmany *Spain* 38°59N 1°19E **100** C7
Sant Boi de Llobregat *Spain* 41°20N 2°2E **90** D7
Sant Carles *Spain* 39°3N 1°34E **100** B8
Sant Carles de la Ràpita *Spain* 40°37N 0°35E **90** E5
Sant Celoni *Spain* 41°42N 2°30E **90** D7
Sant Elm *Spain* 39°35N 2°21E **100** B9
Sant Feliu de Guíxols *Spain* 41°45N 3°1E **90** D8
Sant Feliu de Llobregat *Spain* 41°22N 2°2E **90** D7
Sant Ferran *Spain* 38°42N 1°28E **100** C7
Sant Francesc de Formentera *Spain* 38°42N 1°26E **100** C7
Sant Jaume *Spain* 39°54N 4°4E **100** B11
Sant Joan *Spain* 39°36N 3°4E **100** B10
Sant Joan d'Alacant *Spain* 38°24N 0°26W **91** G4
Sant Joan de Labritja *Spain* 39°5N 1°31E **100** B8
Sant Jordi *Ibiza, Spain* 38°53N 1°24E **100** C7
Sant Jordi *Mallorca, Spain* 39°33N 2°46E **100** B9
Sant Jordi, G. de *Spain* 40°53N 1°2E **90** E6
Sant Llorenç de Morunys *Spain* 42°8N 1°35E **90** C6
Sant Llorenç del Munt y l'Obac ⌓ *Spain* 41°39N 1°55W **90** D3
Sant Llorenç des Cardassar *Spain* 39°37N 3°17E **100** B10
Sant Mateu *Baleares, Spain* 39°3N 1°23E **100** B7
Sant Mateu *Valencia, Spain* 40°28N 0°10E **90** E5
Sant Miquel *Spain* 39°3N 1°26E **100** B7
Sant Pere de Ribes *Spain* 41°16N 1°46E **90** D6
Sant Salvador *Spain* 39°27N 3°11E **100** B10
Sant Vicent del Raspeig *Spain* 38°24N 0°31W **91** G4
Santa *Peru* 8°59S 78°40W **188** B2
Sant' Ágata Militello *Italy* 38°2N 14°8E **95** D7
Santa Agnés *Spain* 39°3N 1°21E **100** B7
Santa Ana *Beni, Bolivia* 13°50S 65°40W **186** F5
Santa Ana *La Paz, Bolivia* 15°31S 67°30W **188** D4
Santa Ana *El Salv.* 14°0N 89°31W **182** D2
Santa Ana *Mexico* 30°33N 111°7W **180** A2
Santa Ana *U.S.A.* 33°46N 117°52W **171** M9
Santa Ana de los Ríos de Cuenca = Cuenca *Ecuador* 2°50S 79°9W **186** D3
Sant' Ángelo Lodigiano *Italy* 45°14N 9°25E **92** C6
Sant' Antíoco *Italy* 39°4N 8°27E **94** C1
Santa Bárbara *Chile* 37°40S 72°1W **190** D1
Santa Bárbara *Honduras* 14°53N 88°14W **182** D2
Santa Bárbara *Mexico* 26°48N 105°49W **180** B3
Santa Bàrbara *Spain* 40°42N 0°29E **90** E5
Santa Barbara *U.S.A.* 34°25N 119°42W **171** L7
Santa Bárbara, Mt. *Spain* 37°23N 2°50W **91** H2
Santa Barbara Channel *U.S.A.* 34°15N 120°0W **171** L7
Santa Barbara I. *U.S.A.* 33°29N 119°2W **171** M7
Santa Catalina, Gulf of *U.S.A.* 33°10N 117°50W **171** N9
Santa Catalina, I. *Mexico* 25°40N 110°47W **180** B2
Santa Cataliña de Armada *Spain* 43°2N 8°49W **88** B2
Santa Catalina I. *U.S.A.* 33°23N 118°25W **171** M8
Santa Catarina □ *Brazil* 27°25S 48°30W **191** B6
Santa Catarina, I. de *Brazil* 27°30S 48°40W **191** B6
Santa Caterina di Pittinuri *Italy* 40°6N 8°27E **94** B1
Santa Caterina Villarmosa *Italy* 37°35N 14°2E **95** E7
Santa Cecília *Brazil* 26°56S 50°18W **191** B5
Santa Clara *Cuba* 22°20N 80°0W **182** B4
Santa Clara *Calif., U.S.A.* 37°21N 121°57W **170** H5
Santa Clara *N.Y., U.S.A.* 44°38N 74°27W **175** B10
Santa Clara *Utah, U.S.A.* 37°8N 113°39W **169** H7
Santa Clara → *Mexico* 29°51N 107°6W **180** A3
Santa Clara de Olimar *Uruguay* 32°50S 54°54W **191** C5
Santa Clara Valley *U.S.A.* 36°50N 121°30W **170** J5
Santa Clarita *U.S.A.* 34°24N 118°33W **171** L8
Santa Clotilde *Peru* 2°33S 73°45W **186** D4
Santa Coloma de Farners *Spain* 41°50N 2°39E **90** D7
Santa Coloma de Gramenet *Spain* 41°27N 2°13E **90** D7
Santa Comba = Santa Cataliña de Armada *Spain* 43°2N 8°49W **88** B2
Santa Croce Camerina *Italy* 36°50N 14°31E **95** F7
Santa Croce di Magliano *Italy* 41°42N 14°59E **93** G11
Santa Cruz *Bolivia* 17°43S 63°10W **186** G6
Santa Cruz *Brazil* 6°13S 36°1W **189** B3
Santa Cruz *Chile* 34°38S 71°27W **190** C1
Santa Cruz *Costa Rica* 10°15N 85°35W **182** D2
Santa Cruz *Madeira* 32°42N 16°46W **100** D3
Santa Cruz *Peru* 5°40S 75°56W **188** B2
Santa Cruz *Phil.* 14°20N 121°24E **119** B6
Santa Cruz *U.S.A.* 36°58N 122°1W **170** J4
Santa Cruz □ *Argentina* 49°0S 70°0W **192** C3
Santa Cruz → *Argentina* 50°10S 68°20W **192** D3
Santa Cruz Cabrália *Brazil* 16°17S 39°2W **189** D3
Santa Cruz de la Palma *Canary Is.* 28°41N 17°46W **100** F2
Santa Cruz de la Palma ✈ (SPC) *Canary Is.* 28°40N 17°45W **100** F2
Santa Cruz de Mompox = Mompós *Colombia* 9°14N 74°26W **186** B4
Santa Cruz de Mudela *Spain* 38°39N 3°28W **89** G7
Santa Cruz de Tenerife *Canary Is.* 28°28N 16°15W **100** F3
Santa Cruz del Norte *Cuba* 23°9N 81°55W **182** B3
Santa Cruz del Retamar *Spain* 40°8N 4°14W **88** E6
Santa Cruz del Sur *Cuba* 20°44N 78°0W **182** B4
Santa Cruz do Rio Pardo *Brazil* 22°54S 49°37W **191** A6
Santa Cruz do Sul *Brazil* 29°42S 52°25W **191** B5
Santa Cruz I. *U.S.A.* 34°1N 119°43W **171** M7
Santa Cruz Is. *Solomon Is.* 10°30S 166°0E **147** C9
Santa Cruz Mts. *Jamaica* 17°58N 77°43W **182** a
Sant' Egídio alla Vibrata *Italy* 42°49N 13°42E **93** F10
Santa Elena *Argentina* 30°58S 59°47W **190** C4
Santa Elena, C. *Costa Rica* 10°54N 85°56W **182** D2
Sant' Eufèmia, G. di *Italy* 38°51N 16°4E **95** D9
Santa Eulària des Riu *Spain* 38°59N 1°32E **100** C8
Santa Fé *Argentina* 31°35S 60°41W **190** C3
Santa Fé *Spain* 37°11N 3°43W **89** H7
Santa Fe *U.S.A.* 35°41N 105°57W **169** J11
Santa Fé □ *Argentina* 31°50S 60°55W **190** C3
Santa Fé do Sul *Brazil* 20°13S 50°56W **187** H8
Santa Filomena *Brazil* 9°6S 45°50W **189** B1
Santa Fiora *Italy* 42°50N 11°35E **93** F8
Santa Gertrudis *Spain* 39°0N 1°26E **100** C7
Santa Giulia *France* 41°32N 9°17E **73** G13
Santa Giustina *Italy* 46°10N 12°5E **93** B9
Santa Helena *Brazil* 2°14S 45°18W **189** A1
Santa Inês *Bahia, Brazil* 13°17S 39°48W **189** C3
Santa Inês *Maranhão, Brazil* 3°39S 45°20W **189** A1
Santa Inés *Spain* 38°32N 5°37W **89** G5
Santa Inés, I. *Chile* 54°0S 73°0W **192** D2
Santa Isabel *Argentina* 36°10S 66°54W **190** D2
Santa Isabel do Morro *Brazil* 11°34S 50°40W **187** F8
Santa Lucía *Corrientes, Argentina* 28°58S 59°5W **190** B4
Santa Lucía *San Juan, Argentina* 31°30S 68°30W **190** C2
Santa Lucía *Spain* 37°35N 0°58W **91** H4
Santa Lucía *Uruguay* 34°27S 56°24W **190** C4
Santa Lucia Range *U.S.A.* 36°0N 121°20W **170** K5
Santa Luzia *Brazil* 19°47S 43°52W **189** D2
Santa Luzia *C. Verde Is.* 16°50N 24°35W **134** b
Santa Margalida *Spain* 39°42N 3°6E **100** B10
Santa Margarita *Argentina* 38°28S 61°35W **190** D3
Santa Margarita *U.S.A.* 35°23N 120°37W **170** K6
Santa Margarita → *U.S.A.* 33°13N 117°23W **171** M9
Santa Margarita, I. *Mexico* 24°27N 111°50W **180** C2
Santa Margherita *Italy* 38°58N 8°58E **94** D1
Santa Margherita Ligure *Italy* 44°20N 9°11E **92** D6
Santa María *Argentina* 26°40S 66°0W **190** B2
Santa Maria *Azores* 36°58N 25°6W **134** a
Santa Maria *Brazil* 29°40S 53°48W **191** B5
Santa Maria *C. Verde Is.* 16°31N 22°53W **134** b
Santa Maria *U.S.A.* 34°57N 120°26W **171** L6
Santa María → *Mexico* 31°0N 107°14W **180** A3
Santa María, B. de *Mexico* 25°4N 108°6W **180** B3
Santa Maria, C. de *Portugal* 36°58N 7°53W **89** J3
Santa María, Volcano *Guatemala* 14°45N 91°33W **182** D1
Santa Maria Cápua Vétere *Italy* 41°5N 14°15E **95** A7
Santa Maria da Feira *Portugal* 40°55N 8°35W **88** E2
Santa Maria da Vitória *Brazil* 13°24S 44°12W **189** C2
Santa Maria de Guadalupe = Guadalupe *Spain* 39°27N 5°17W **89** F5
Santa Maria del Camí *Spain* 39°38N 2°47E **100** B9
Santa Maria di Léuca, C. *Italy* 39°47N 18°22E **95** C11
Santa Maria do Suaçuí *Brazil* 18°12S 42°25W **189** D2
Santa María la Real de Nieva *Spain* 41°4N 4°24W **88** D6
Santa Marinella *Italy* 42°2N 11°52E **93** F8
Santa Marta *Colombia* 11°15N 74°13W **186** A4
Santa Marta, Sierra Nevada de *Colombia* 10°55N 73°50W **186** A4
Santa Marta de Tormes *Spain* 40°57N 5°38W **88** E5
Santa Marta Grande, C. *Brazil* 28°43S 48°50W **191** B6
Santa Maura = Lefkada *Greece* 38°40N 20°43E **98** C2
Santa Monica *U.S.A.* 34°1N 118°29W **171** M8
Santa Monica Mts. ⌓ *U.S.A.* 34°4N 118°44W **171** L8
Santa Olalla *Spain* 40°2N 4°25W **88** E6
Santa Olalla del Cala *Spain* 37°54N 6°14W **89** H4
Santa Paula *U.S.A.* 34°21N 119°4W **171** L7
Santa Pola *Spain* 38°13N 0°35W **91** G4
Santa Ponça *Spain* 39°30N 2°28E **100** B9
Santa Quitéria *Brazil* 4°20S 40°10W **189** A2
Santa Rita *Brazil* 7°8S 34°58W **189** B4
Santa Rita de Cássia *Brazil* 11°0S 44°32W **189** C2
Santa Rosa *La Pampa, Argentina* 36°40S 64°17W **190** D3
Santa Rosa *San Luis, Argentina* 32°21S 65°10W **190** C2
Santa Rosa *Beni, Bolivia* 14°10S 66°53W **188** C4
Santa Rosa *Pando, Bolivia* 10°36S 67°20W **188** C4
Santa Rosa *Brazil* 27°52S 54°29W **191** B5
Santa Rosa *Puno, Peru* 14°30S 70°50W **188** C3
Santa Rosa *San Martin, Peru* 6°41S 76°37W **188** B2
Santa Rosa *Calif., U.S.A.* 38°26N 122°43W **170** G4
Santa Rosa *N. Mex., U.S.A.* 34°57N 104°41W **169** J11
Santa Rosa and San Jacinto Mts. ⌓ *U.S.A.* 33°28N 116°20W **171** M10
Santa Rosa Beach *U.S.A.* 30°22N 86°14W **178** E3
Santa Rosa de Copán *Honduras* 14°47N 88°46W **182** D2
Santa Rosa de Río Primero *Argentina* 31°8S 63°20W **190** C3
Santa Rosa del Sara *Bolivia* 17°7S 63°35W **186** G6
Santa Rosa I. *Calif., U.S.A.* 33°58N 120°6W **171** M6
Santa Rosa I. *Fla., U.S.A.* 30°20N 86°50W **179** E3
Santa Rosa Range *U.S.A.* 41°45N 117°40W **168** F5
Santa Rosalía *Mexico* 27°19N 112°17W **180** B2
Santa Sylvina *Argentina* 27°50S 61°10W **190** B3
Santa Tecla = Nueva San Salvador *El Salv.* 13°40N 89°18W **182** D2
Santa Teresa *Argentina* 33°25S 60°47W **190** C3
Santa Teresa *Australia* 24°8S 134°22E **150** C1
Santa Teresa *Brazil* 19°55S 40°36W **189** D2
Santa Teresa *Mexico* 25°17N 97°51W **181** B5
Santa Teresa △ *Uruguay* 33°57S 53°31W **191** C5
Santa Teresa di Riva *Italy* 37°57N 15°22E **95** E8
Santa Teresa Gallura *Italy* 41°14N 9°11E **94** A2
Santa Teresita *Argentina* 36°32S 56°41W **190** D4
Santa Uxía de Ribeira = Ribeira *Spain* 42°36N 8°58W **88** C2
Santa Vitória do Palmar *Brazil* 33°32S 53°25W **191** C5
Santa Ynez → *U.S.A.* 34°41N 120°36W **171** L6
Santa Ynez Mts. *U.S.A.* 34°30N 120°0W **171** L6
Santa Ysabel *U.S.A.* 33°7N 116°40W **171** M10
Santadi *Italy* 39°5N 8°43E **94** C1
Santaella *Spain* 37°34N 4°51W **89** H6
Santai *China* 31°5N 104°58E **116** B5
Santaluz *Brazil* 11°15S 39°22W **189** C3
Santana *Brazil* 13°2S 44°5W **189** C2
Santana *Madeira* 32°48N 16°52W **100** D3
Sântana *Romania* 46°20N 21°30E **80** D6
Santana, Coxilha de *Brazil* 30°50S 55°35W **191** C4
Santana do Ipanema *Brazil* 9°22S 37°14W **189** B3
Santana do Livramento *Brazil* 30°55S 55°30W **191** C4
Santander *Spain* 43°27N 3°51W **88** B7
Santander Jiménez *Mexico* 24°13N 98°28W **181** C5
Santanilla, Is. *Honduras* 17°22N 83°57W **182** C3
Santanyí *Spain* 39°20N 3°5E **100** B10
Santaquin *U.S.A.* 39°59N 111°47W **168** G8
Santarcángelo di Romagna *Italy* 44°4N 12°26E **93** D9
Santarém *Brazil* 2°25S 54°42W **187** D8
Santarém *Portugal* 39°12N 8°42W **89** F2
Santarém □ *Portugal* 39°10N 8°40W **89** F2
Santaren Channel *W. Indies* 24°0N 79°30W **182** B4
Santee *U.S.A.* 32°50N 116°58W **171** N10
Santee → *U.S.A.* 33°7N 79°17W **177** E15
Santéramo in Colle *Italy* 40°49N 16°45E **95** B9
Santerno → *Italy* 44°34N 11°58E **93** D8
Santhià *Italy* 45°22N 8°10E **92** C5
Santi-Quaranta = Sarandë *Albania* 39°52N 19°55E **96** G3
Santiago = Río Grande de Santiago → *Mexico* 21°36N 105°26W **180** C3
Santiago = São Tiago *C. Verde Is.* 15°0N 23°40W **134** b
Santiago *Brazil* 29°11S 54°52W **191** B5
Santiago *Canary Is.* 28°2N 17°12W **100** F2
Santiago *Chile* 33°26S 70°40W **190** C1
Santiago *Panama* 8°0N 81°0W **182** E3
Santiago *Peru* 14°11S 75°43W **188** C2
Santiago *Phil.* 16°41N 121°33E **119** A6
Santiago → *Peru* 4°27S 77°38W **186** D3
Santiago, C. *Chile* 50°46S 75°27W **192** D1
Santiago, Punta de *Eq. Guin.* 3°12N 8°40E **139** E6
Santiago de Chuco *Peru* 8°9S 78°11W **188** B2
Santiago de Compostela *Spain* 42°52N 8°37W **88** C2
Santiago de Cuba *Cuba* 20°0N 75°49W **182** C4
Santiago de los Caballeros *Dom. Rep.* 19°30N 70°40W **183** C5
Santiago del Estero *Argentina* 27°50S 64°15W **190** B3
Santiago del Estero □ *Argentina* 27°40S 63°15W **190** B3
Santiago del Teide *Canary Is.* 28°17N 16°48W **100** F3
Santiago do Cacém *Portugal* 38°1N 8°42W **89** G2
Santiago Ixcuintla *Mexico* 21°49N 105°13W **180** C3
Santiago Jamiltepec *Mexico* 16°17N 97°49W **181** D5
Santiago Papasquiaro *Mexico* 25°3N 105°25W **180** C3
Santiago Pinotepa Nacional *Mexico* 16°19N 98°1W **181** D5
Santiaguillo, L. de *Mexico* 24°48N 104°48W **180** C4
Santiguila *Mali* 12°42N 7°25W **138** C3
Santillana del Mar *Spain* 43°24N 4°6W **88** B6
Santisteban del Puerto *Spain* 38°17N 3°15W **89** G7
Santo → *Peru* 8°56S 78°37W **188** B2
Santo Amaro *Brazil* 12°30S 38°43W **189** C3
Santo Anastácio *Brazil* 21°58S 51°39W **191** A5
Santo André *Brazil* 23°39S 46°29W **191** A6
Santo Ângelo *Brazil* 28°15S 54°15W **191** B5
Santo Antão *C. Verde Is.* 16°52N 25°10W **134** b
Santo Antônio de Jesus *Brazil* 12°58S 39°16W **189** C3
Santo Antônio do Içá *Brazil* 3°5S 67°57W **186** D5
Santo Antônio do Leverger *Brazil* 15°52S 56°5W **187** G7
Santo Domingo *Dom. Rep.* 18°30N 69°59W **183** C6
Santo Domingo *Mexico* 25°29N 111°55W **180** B2
Santo Domingo *Nic.* 12°14N 84°59W **182** D3
Santo Domingo, Cay *Bahamas* 21°25N 75°45W **182** B4
Santo Domingo de la Calzada *Spain* 42°26N 2°57W **90** C2
Santo Domingo de los Colorados *Ecuador* 0°15S 79°9W **186** D3
Santo Domingo Pueblo *U.S.A.* 35°31N 106°22W **169** J10
Santo Domingo Tehuantepec = Tehuantepec *Mexico* 16°21N 95°13W **181** D5
Santo Stéfano di Camastro *Italy* 38°1N 14°22E **95** D7
Santo Tirso *Portugal* 41°21N 8°28W **88** D2
Santo Tomás *Mexico* 31°33N 116°24W **180** A1
Santo Tomás *Peru* 14°26S 72°8W **188** C3
Santo Tomé *Argentina* 28°40S 56°5W **191** B4
Santo Tomé de Guayana = Ciudad Guayana *Venezuela* 8°0N 62°30W **186** B6
Santomera *Spain* 38°4N 1°3W **91** G3
Santoña *Spain* 43°29N 3°27W **88** B7
Santorini *Greece* 36°23N 25°27E **99** E7
Santos *Brazil* 24°0S 46°20W **191** A6
Santos, Sierra de los *Spain* 38°7N 5°12W **89** G5
Santos Dumont *Brazil* 22°55S 43°10W **191** A7
Santuario de Aves Laguna Colorada △ *Bolivia* 22°10S 67°45W **190** A2
Sanuki *Japan* 34°19N 134°10E **113** G7
Sanur *Indonesia* 8°41S 115°15E **119** K18
Sanwer *India* 22°59N 75°50E **124** H6
Sanxenxo *Spain* 42°24N 8°49W **88** C2
Sanxia Shuiku *China* 30°3N 107°58E **116** B6
Sanxiang *China* 22°21N 113°25E **111** a
Sanya *China* 18°14N 109°29E **117** a
Sanyuan *China* 34°35N 108°58E **114** G5
São Bartolomeu de Messines *Portugal* 37°15N 8°17W **89** H2
São Benedito *Brazil* 4°3S 40°53W **189** A2
São Bento *Brazil* 2°42S 44°50W **189** A2
São Bento do Norte *Brazil* 5°4S 36°2W **189** B3
São Bernardo do Campo *Brazil* 23°45S 46°34W **191** A6
São Borja *Brazil* 28°39S 56°0W **191** B4
São Brás de Alportel *Portugal* 37°8N 7°37W **89** H3
São Caitano *Brazil* 8°21S 36°6W **189** B3
São Carlos *Brazil* 22°0S 47°50W **191** A6
São Cristóvão *Brazil* 11°1S 37°15W **189** C3
São Domingos *Brazil* 13°25S 46°19W **189** C1
São Domingos *Guinea-Biss.* 12°19N 16°13W **138** C1
São Domingos do Maranhão *Brazil* 5°42S 44°22W **189** B2
São Filipe *C. Verde Is.* 15°2N 24°30W **134** b
São Francisco *Brazil* 16°0S 44°50W **189** D2
São Francisco → *Brazil* 10°30S 36°24W **189** C3
São Francisco do Maranhão *Brazil* 6°15S 42°52W **189** B2
São Francisco do Sul *Brazil* 26°15S 48°36W **191** B6
São Gabriel *Brazil* 30°20S 54°20W **191** C5
São Gabriel da Palha *Brazil* 18°47S 40°39W **189** D2
São Gonçalo *Brazil* 22°48S 43°5W **191** A7
São Gotardo *Brazil* 19°19S 46°3W **189** D1
Sao Hill *Tanzania* 8°20S 35°12E **143** D4
São João *Guinea-Biss.* 11°32N 15°25W **138** C1
São João da Boa Vista *Brazil* 22°0S 46°52W **191** A6
São João da Madeira *Portugal* 40°54N 8°30W **88** E2
São João da Pesqueira *Portugal* 41°8N 7°24W **88** D3
São João da Ponte *Brazil* 15°56S 44°1W **189** D2
São João del Rei *Brazil* 21°8S 44°15W **191** A7
São João do Araguaia *Brazil* 5°23S 48°46W **187** E9
São João do Paraíso *Brazil* 15°19S 42°1W **189** D2
São João do Piauí *Brazil* 8°21S 42°15W **189** B2
São João dos Patos *Brazil* 6°30S 43°42W **189** B2
São Joaquim *Brazil* 28°18S 49°56W **191** B6
São Joaquim △ *Brazil* 28°12S 49°37W **191** B6
São Joaquim da Barra *Brazil* 20°35S 47°53W **189** E1
São Jorge *Azores* 38°38N 28°3W **134** a
São Jorge, Pta. de *Madeira* 32°50N 16°53W **100** D3
São José *Brazil* 27°38S 48°39W **191** B5
São José da Laje *Brazil* 9°1S 36°3W **189** B3
São José de Mipibu *Brazil* 6°5S 35°15W **189** B3
São José do Norte *Brazil* 32°1S 52°3W **191** C5
São José do Peixe *Brazil* 7°24S 42°34W **189** B2
São José do Rio Preto *Brazil* 20°50S 49°20W **191** A6
São José dos Campos *Brazil* 23°7S 45°52W **191** A6
São Leopoldo *Brazil* 29°50S 51°10W **191** B5
São Lourenço *Brazil* 22°7S 45°3W **191** A6
São Lourenço → *Brazil* 17°53S 57°27W **187** G7
São Lourenço, Pta. de *Madeira* 32°44N 16°39W **100** D3
São Lourenço do Sul *Brazil* 31°22S 51°58W **191** C5
São Luís *Brazil* 2°39S 44°15W **189** A2
São Luís do Curu *Brazil* 3°40S 39°14W **189** A3
São Luís Gonzaga *Brazil* 28°25S 55°0W **191** B5
São Marcos → *Brazil* 18°15S 47°37W **189** D1
São Marcos, B. de *Brazil* 2°0S 44°0W **189** A2
São Martinho da Cortiça *Portugal* 40°18N 8°8W **88** E2
São Mateus *Brazil* 18°44S 39°50W **189** D3
São Mateus → *Brazil* 18°35S 39°44W **189** D3
São Mateus do Sul *Brazil* 25°52S 50°23W **191** B5
São Miguel *Azores* 37°47N 25°30W **134** a
São Miguel do Oeste *Brazil* 26°45S 53°34W **191** B5
São Miguel dos Campos *Brazil* 9°47S 36°5W **189** B3
São Nicolau *C. Verde Is.* 16°20N 24°20W **134** b
São Nicolau → *Brazil* 5°45S 42°2W **189** B2
São Paulo *Atl. Oc.* 0°56N 29°22W **56** F9
São Paulo *Brazil* 23°32S 46°38W **191** A6
São Paulo □ *Brazil* 22°0S 49°0W **191** A6
São Paulo de Olivença *Brazil* 3°27S 68°48W **186** D5
São Pedro *Atl. Oc.* 0°56N 29°22W **56** F9
São Pedro do Sul *Portugal* 40°46N 8°4W **88** E2
São Rafael *Brazil* 5°47S 36°55W **189** B3
São Raimundo das Mangabeiras *Brazil* 7°1S 45°29W **189** B1
São Raimundo Nonato *Brazil* 9°1S 42°42W **189** B2
São Romão *Brazil* 16°22S 45°4W **189** D1
São Roque *Madeira* 32°46N 16°48W **100** D3
São Roque, C. de *Brazil* 5°30S 35°16W **189** B3
São Sebastião, I. de *Brazil* 23°50S 45°18W **191** A6
São Sebastião do Paraíso *Brazil* 20°54S 46°59W **191** A6
São Teotónio *Portugal* 37°30N 8°42W **89** H2
São Tiago *C. Verde Is.* 15°0N 23°40W **134** b
São Tomé *Brazil* 5°58S 36°4W **189** B3
São Tomé *São Tomé & Príncipe* 0°10N 6°39E **132** F4
São Tomé, C. de *Brazil* 22°0S 40°59W **189** E2
São Tomé & Príncipe ■ *Africa* 0°12N 6°39E **133** F4
São Vicente *Brazil* 23°57S 46°23W **191** A6
São Vicente *C. Verde Is.* 17°0N 25°0W **134** b
São Vicente *Madeira* 32°48N 17°3W **100** D2
São Vicente, C. de *Portugal* 37°0N 9°0W **89** H1
Saona, I. *Dom. Rep.* 18°10N 68°40W **183** C6
Saône → *France* 45°44N 4°50E **71** G11
Saône-et-Loire □ *France* 46°30N 4°50E **71** F11
Saonek *Indonesia* 0°22S 130°55E **119** E8
Saoura, O. → *Algeria* 29°0N 0°55W **136** C3
Sapam, Ao *Thailand* 8°0N 98°26E **121** a
Sapanca *Turkey* 40°41N 30°16E **104** B4
Sapão → *Brazil* 11°1S 45°32W **189** C1
Saparua *Indonesia* 3°33S 128°40E **119** E7
Sapé *Brazil* 7°6S 35°13W **189** B3
Sape *Indonesia* 8°34S 118°59E **119** F5
Sapele *Nigeria* 5°50N 5°40E **139** D6
Sapelo I. *U.S.A.* 31°25N 81°12W **178** D8
Sapelo Sound *U.S.A.* 31°30N 81°10W **178** D8
Sapes *Greece* 41°2N 25°43E **97** E9
Şaphane *Turkey* 39°1N 29°13E **99** B11
Sapi ⌓ *Zimbabwe* 15°48S 29°42E **143** F2
Sapienza *Greece* 36°45N 21°43E **98** E3
Sapo △ *Liberia* 5°15N 8°30W **138** D3
Sapone *Burkina Faso* 12°3N 1°35W **139** C4
Saposoa *Peru* 6°55S 76°45W **188** B2
Sapotskina *Belarus* 53°49N 23°40E **82** E10
Sapouy *Burkina Faso* 11°34N 1°44W **139** C4
Sapozhok *Russia* 53°59N 40°41E **86** D5
Sapphire *Australia* 23°28S 147°43E **150** C4
Sappho *U.S.A.* 48°4N 124°16W **170** B2
Sapporo *Japan* 43°0N 141°21E **112** C10
Sapri *Italy* 40°4N 15°38E **95** B8
Sapt Kosi → *Nepal* 26°32N 86°56E **125** F12
Sapudi *Indonesia* 7°6S 114°20E **119** G16
Sapulpa *U.S.A.* 35°59N 96°5W **176** D6
Saqqez *Iran* 36°15N 46°20E **105** D12
Sar Dasht *Āzarbāyjān-e Gharbī, Iran* 36°9N 45°28E **105** D11
Sar Dasht *Khuzestān, Iran* 32°32N 48°52E **129** C6
Sar-e Pol *Afghan.* 36°10N 66°0E **109** E7
Sar-e Pol □ *Afghan.* 36°20N 65°50E **109** E7
Sar Gachīneh = Yāsūj *Iran* 30°31N 51°31E **129** D6
Sar Planina *Macedonia* 42°0N 21°0E **96** E4
Sara *Burkina Faso* 11°40N 3°53W **138** C4
Šara △ *Serbia* 42°12N 21°0E **96** D5
Sara Buri = Saraburi *Thailand* 14°30N 100°55E **120** E3
Sarāb *Iran* 37°55N 47°40E **105** D12
Sarābādī *Iraq* 33°1N 44°48E **128** C5
Sarābleh *Iran* 33°44N 46°34E **105** F12
Saraburi *Thailand* 14°30N 100°55E **120** E3
Saradiya *India* 21°34N 70°2E **124** J4
Saraféré *Mali* 15°50N 3°40W **138** B4
Saragossa = Zaragoza *Spain* 41°39N 0°53W **90** D4
Saraguro *Ecuador* 3°35S 79°16W **186** D3
Sarahs *Turkmenistan* 36°32N 61°13E **129** B9
Sarai Naurang *Pakistan* 32°50N 70°47E **124** C4
Saraikela *India* 22°42N 85°56E **125** H11
Saraipali *India* 21°20N 82°59E **126** D6
Saraiu *Romania* 44°43N 28°10E **81** F13
Sarajevo *Bos.-H.* 43°52N 18°26E **80** G3
Sarakhs = Sarahs *Turkmenistan* 36°32N 61°13E **129** B9
Sarakhs *Iran* 36°32N 61°9E **108** E6
Saran, Gunung *Indonesia* 0°30S 111°25E **118** E4
Saranac Lake *U.S.A.* 44°20N 74°10W **175** B10
Saranac Lakes *U.S.A.* 44°20N 74°28W **175** B10
Saranda *Tanzania* 5°45S 34°59E **142** D3
Sarandë *Albania* 39°52N 19°55E **96** G3
Sarandí del Yí *Uruguay* 33°18S 55°38W **191** C4
Sarandí Grande *Uruguay* 33°44S 56°20W **190** C4
Sarangani B. *Phil.* 6°0N 125°13E **119** C7
Sarangani Is. *Phil.* 5°25N 125°25E **119** C7
Sarangarh *India* 21°30N 83°5E **126** D6
Saransk *Russia* 54°10N 45°10E **86** C7
Sarapul *Russia* 56°28N 53°48E **106** D6
Sarasota *U.S.A.* 27°20N 82°32W **179** H7
Sarata *Ukraine* 46°1N 29°40E **81** D14
Sarata → *Ukraine* 45°51N 29°41E **81** E14
Saratoga *Calif., U.S.A.* 37°16N 122°2W **170** H4
Saratoga *Wyo., U.S.A.* 41°27N 106°49W **168** F10
Saratoga ⌓ *U.S.A.* 43°0N 73°38W **175** D11
Saratoga L. *U.S.A.* 43°1N 73°44W **175** C11
Saratoga Springs *U.S.A.* 43°5N 73°47W **175** C11
Saratok *Malaysia* 1°55N 111°17E **118** D4
Saratov *Russia* 51°30N 46°2E **86** E8
Saratov □ *Russia* 51°50N 46°20E **86** E8
Saratovskoye Vdkhr. *Russia* 53°10N 48°35E **86** D9
Sarāvān *Iran* 27°25N 62°15E **129** E9
Saravane *Laos* 15°43N 106°25E **120** E6
Sarawak □ *Malaysia* 2°0N 113°0E **118** D4
Saray *Tekirdağ, Turkey* 41°26N 27°55E **97** E11
Saray *Van, Turkey* 38°38N 44°9E **105** C11
Saraya *Senegal* 12°50N 11°45W **138** C2
Saraycık *Turkey* 39°1N 29°49E **99** B11
Sarayköy *Turkey* 37°55N 28°54E **99** D10
Saraylar *Turkey* 40°39N 27°40E **97** F11
Sarayönü *Turkey* 38°16N 32°24E **104** C5
Sarbāz *Iran* 26°38N 61°19E **129** E9
Sarbīsheh *Iran* 32°30N 59°40E **129** C8
Sárbogárd *Hungary* 46°50N 18°40E **80** D3
Sarca → *Italy* 45°52N 10°52E **92** C7
Sarcelles *France* 49°1N 2°23E **71** D9
Sarda → *India* 27°21N 81°23E **125** F9
Sardar Sarovar Dam *India* 21°50N 73°50E **126** D1
Sardarshahr *India* 28°30N 74°29E **124** E6
Sardegna □ *Italy* 40°0N 9°0E **94** B1
Sardhana *India* 29°9N 77°39E **124** E7
Sardina, Pta. *Canary Is.* 28°9N 15°44W **100** F4
Sardinia = Sardegna □ *Italy* 40°0N 9°0E **94** B1
Sardis *Turkey* 38°28N 27°58E **99** C10
Sardis *U.S.A.* 32°58N 81°46W **178** C8
Sārdūīyeh = Dar Mazār *Iran* 29°14N 57°20E **129** D8
Sarek △ *Sweden* 67°22N 17°35E **60** C17
Saren *Indonesia* 8°26S 115°34E **119** J18
S'Arenal *Spain* 39°30N 2°45E **100** B9
Sarentino *Italy* 46°38N 11°21E **93** B8
Sarera, G. of *Indonesia* 2°0S 135°0E **147** B6
Saréyamou *Mali* 16°7N 3°10W **138** B4
Sargasso Sea *Atl. Oc.* 27°0N 72°0W **158** G13
Sargent *U.S.A.* 33°26N 84°52W **178** B5
Sargodha *Pakistan* 32°10N 72°40E **124** C5
Sarh *Chad* 9°5N 18°23E **135** G9
Sarhala *Ivory C.* 8°22N 6°8W **138** D3
Sarhro, Jebel *Morocco* 31°6N 5°0W **136** B3
Sārī *Iran* 36°30N 53°4E **129** B7
Sari d'Orcino *France* 42°3N 8°49E **73** F12
Saria *Greece* 35°54N 27°17E **99** F9
Saria *India* 21°38N 83°22E **125** J10
Sariab *Pakistan* 30°6N 66°59E **124** D2
Sarıbeyler *Turkey* 39°24N 27°35E **99** B9
Sarıgöl *Turkey* 38°14N 28°41E **104** C3
Sarıkamış *Turkey* 40°22N 42°35E **105** B10
Sarıkaya *Turkey* 39°29N 35°22E **104** C6
Sarikei *Malaysia* 2°8N 111°30E **118** D4
Sarıköy *Turkey* 40°12N 27°37E **97** F11
Sarila *India* 25°46N 79°41E **125** G8
Sarina *Australia* 21°22S 149°13E **150** C4
Sariñena *Spain* 41°47N 0°10W **90** D4
Sarıoğlan *Turkey* 39°5N 35°59E **104** C6
Sarita *U.S.A.* 27°13N 97°47W **176** H6
Sariwŏn *N. Korea* 38°31N 125°46E **115** E13
Sariyar Baraji *Turkey* 40°2N 31°33E **104** B4
Sarıyer *Turkey* 41°10N 29°3E **97** E13
Sarız *Turkey* 38°28N 36°30E **104** C7
Sarju → *India* 27°21N 81°23E **125** F9
Sark *U.K.* 49°25N 2°22W **67** H5
Sarkad *Hungary* 46°47N 21°23E **80** D6
Sarkari Tala *India* 27°39N 70°52E **124** F4
Şarkışla *Turkey* 39°21N 36°25E **104** C7
Şarköy *Turkey* 40°36N 27°6E **97** F11
Sarlat-la-Canéda *France* 44°54N 1°13E **72** D5
Sărmăşag *Romania* 47°21N 22°50E **80** C7
Sărmaşu *Romania* 46°45N 24°13E **81** D9
Sarmi *Indonesia* 1°49S 138°44E **119** E9
Sarmiento *Argentina* 45°35S 69°5W **192** C3
Sarmiento, Mt. *Chile* 54°27S 70°50W **192** D2
Sarmizegetusa *Romania* 45°31N 22°47E **80** E7
Särna *Sweden* 61°41N 13°8E **62** C7
Sarnano *Italy* 43°2N 13°18E **93** E10
Sarnen *Switz.* 46°53N 8°13E **77** J4
Sarnia *Canada* 42°58N 82°23W **174** D2
Sarno *Italy* 40°49N 14°37E **95** B7
Sarnthein = Sarentino *Italy* 46°38N 11°21E **93** B8
Särö *Sweden* 57°31N 11°57E **63** G5
Sarolangun *Indonesia* 2°19S 102°42E **118** E2
Saronikos Kolpos *Greece* 37°45N 23°45E **98** D5
Saronno *Italy* 45°38N 9°2E **92** C6
Saros Körfezi *Turkey* 40°30N 26°15E **97** F10
Sárospatak *Hungary* 48°18N 21°33E **80** B6
Sarpsborg *Norway* 59°16N 11°7E **61** G14
Sarqan *Kazakhstan* 45°24N 79°55E **109** C9
Sarracín *Spain* 42°15N 3°45W **88** C7
Sarralbe *France* 49°0N 7°1E **71** D14
Sarre = Saar → *Europe* 49°41N 6°32E **69** E6
Sarre *Italy* 45°43N 7°15E **92** C4
Sarre-Union *France* 48°57N 7°4E **71** D14
Sarrebourg *France* 48°43N 7°3E **71** D14
Sarreguemines *France* 49°5N 7°4E **71** C14
Sarria *Spain* 42°49N 7°29W **88** C3
Sarrión *Spain* 40°9N 0°49W **90** E4
Sarro *Mali* 13°40N 5°15W **138** C3
Sarroch *Italy* 39°4N 9°1E **94** C2
Sarsing *Iraq* 37°2N 43°20E **105** D10
Sarstedt *Germany* 52°14N 9°52E **76** C5
Sartell *U.S.A.* 45°37N 94°12W **172** C6

Sartène France 41°38N 8°58E 73 G12
Sarthe □ France 48°10N 0°10E 70 D7
Sarthe → France 47°33N 0°31W 70 E6
Sartilly France 48°45N 1°28W 70 D5
Saruhanlı Turkey 38°44N 27°36E 99 C9
Sărulești Romania 44°25N 26°39E 81 F11
Sarur Azerbaijan 39°22N 45°5E 105 C11
Sārvār Hungary 47°15N 16°56E 80 C1
Sarvar India 26°4N 75°0E 124 F6
Sarvestān Iran 29°20N 53°10E 129 D7
Särvfjället Sweden 62°42N 13°30E 62 B7
Sárviz → Hungary 46°24N 18°41E 80 D3
Sary-Tash Kyrgyzstan 39°44N 73°15E 108 F8
Sarych, Mys Ukraine 44°25N 33°25E 85 K7
Saryesik-Atyraū Qumy
  Kazakhstan 45°30N 76°0E 109 C9
Sarykamyshskoye, Ozero =
  Sarygamysh Köli
  Turkmenistan 41°56N 57°25E 108 D3
Sarykemer Kazakhstan 43°0N 71°30E 109 D8
Sarykenggir →
  Kazakhstan 48°22N 67°59E 109 C7
Saryköl Kazakhstan 53°20N 65°12E 108 B7
Sarykolskiy Khrebet
  Tajikistan 38°30N 74°30E 109 E8
Saryözek Kazakhstan 44°22N 77°59E 109 C9
Sarygamysh Köli
  Turkmenistan 41°56N 57°25E 108 D5
Saryshaghan Kazakhstan 46°12N 73°38E 109 C8
Sarysū → Kazakhstan 45°12N 66°36E 109 C7
Sarzana Italy 44°7N 9°58E 92 D6
Sarzeau France 47°31N 2°48W 70 E4
Sasan Gir India 21°10N 70°36E 124 J7
Sasaram India 24°57N 84°5E 125 G11
Sasebo Japan 33°10N 129°43E 113 H4
Saser Kangri India 34°50N 77°50E 125 B7
Saskatchewan □
  Canada 54°40N 106°0W 163 C7
Saskatchewan →
  Canada 53°37N 100°40W 163 C8
Saskatoon Canada 52°10N 106°38W 163 C7
Saskylakh Russia 71°55N 114°1E 107 B12
Saslaya △ Nic. 13°45N 85°4W 182 D2
Sasolburg S. Africa 26°46S 27°49E 145 C4
Sason Turkey 38°19N 41°24E 105 C9
Sasovo Russia 54°25N 41°55E 86 C5
Sassandra Ivory C. 4°58N 6°8W 138 E3
Sassandra → Ivory C. 4°58N 6°5W 138 E3
Sássari Italy 40°43N 8°34E 94 B1
Sassie Australia 10°2S 142°51E 150 a
Sassnitz Germany 54°29N 13°39E 76 A9
Sasso Marconi Italy 44°24N 11°15E 93 D8
Sassocorvaro Italy 43°47N 12°30E 93 E9
Sassoferrato Italy 43°26N 12°51E 93 E9
Sássuolo Italy 44°33N 10°47E 92 D7
Sástago Spain 41°19N 0°21W 90 D4
Sastamala Finland 61°20N 22°54E 84 B2
Sastown Liberia 4°45N 8°27W 138 E3
Sasvad India 18°20N 74°2E 126 E2
Sasyk, Ozero Ukraine 45°45N 29°40E 81 E14
Sasykkól Kazakhstan 46°35N 81°0E 109 C10
Sata-Misaki Japan 31°0N 130°40E 113 J5
Satadougou Mali 12°25N 11°25W 138 C2
Satakunta □ Finland 61°45N 23°0E 60 F20
Satama-Soukoura
  Ivory C. 7°55N 4°27W 138 D4
Satara India 17°44N 73°58E 126 F2
Satara S. Africa 24°29S 31°47E 145 B5
Sātbaev Kazakhstan 48°10N 67°31E 109 C7
Satbarwa India 23°55N 84°16E 125 H11
Satellite Beach U.S.A. 28°10N 80°36W 179 G9
Säter Sweden 60°21N 15°45E 64 E7
Satevó Mexico 27°57N 106°7W 180 B3
Satilla → U.S.A. 30°59N 81°29W 179 F9
Satipo Peru 11°15S 74°25W 188 C3
Satka Russia 55°3N 59°1E 108 A5
Satmala Hills Andhra Pradesh,
  India 19°45N 78°45E 126 E4
Satmala Hills Maharashtra,
  India 20°15N 74°40E 126 D2
Satna India 24°35N 80°50E 125 G8
Sator Bos.-H. 44°11N 16°37E 93 D13
Sátoraljaújhely Hungary 48°25N 21°41E 80 B6
Satpura □ India 22°40N 78°15E 124 H8
Satpura Ra. India 21°25N 76°10E 126 D3
Satrup Germany 54°41N 9°36E 76 A5
Satsuma-Sendai Japan 31°50N 130°20E 113 J5
Satsunan-Shotō Japan 30°0N 130°0E 113 K5
Sattahip Thailand 12°41N 100°54E 120 F3
Sattenapalle India 16°25N 80°6E 127 F5
Satu Mare Romania 47°46N 22°55E 80 A7
Satu Mare □ Romania 47°45N 23°0E 80 C8
Satui Indonesia 3°50S 115°27E 118 E5
Satun Thailand 6°43N 100°2E 121 J3
Saturnina → Brazil 12°15S 58°10W 188 C7
Sauce Argentina 30°5S 58°46W 190 C4
Sauceda Mexico 25°46N 101°19W 180 B4
Saucillo Mexico 28°1N 105°17W 180 B3
Sauda Norway 59°40N 6°20E 61 G12
Saúde Brazil 10°56S 40°24W 189 C2
Sauðarkrókur Iceland 65°45N 19°40W 60 D4
Saudi Arabia ■ Asia 26°0N 44°0E 128 B3
Sauerland Germany 51°12N 7°59E 74 C4
Saugeen → Canada 44°30N 81°22W 174 B3
Saugerties U.S.A. 42°5N 73°57W 175 D11
Saugues France 44°58N 3°32E 72 D5
Saugus U.S.A. 34°25N 118°32W 171 L8
Saujon France 45°41N 0°55W 72 C3
Sauk Centre U.S.A. 45°44N 94°57W 172 C6
Sauk Rapids U.S.A. 45°35N 94°10W 172 C6
Saulgau France 47°17N 4°14E 71 E11
Saulieu France 44°6N 5°24E 73 D9
Sault Ste. Marie
  Canada 46°30N 84°20W 164 C3
Sault Ste. Marie
  U.S.A. 46°30N 84°21W 173 B11
Saumalkol Kazakhstan 53°17N 68°6E 109 B7
Saumlaki Indonesia 7°55S 131°20E 119 F8
Saumur France 47°15N 0°5W 70 E5
Saundatti India 15°47N 75°7E 127 G2
Saunders, C. N.Z. 45°53S 170°45E 155 F5
Saunders I. Antarctica 57°48S 26°28W 5 B1
Saunders Pt. Australia 27°52S 125°38E 149 E4
Saurimo Angola 9°40S 20°12E 140 F4
Sausalito U.S.A. 37°51N 122°29W 170 H4
Sauvage, Côte U.S.A. 45°50N 1°30W 72 C2

Sauveterre-de-Béarn
  France 43°24N 0°57W 72 E3
Sauzé-Vaussais France 46°8N 0°8E 72 B4
Savá Honduras 15°32N 86°15W 182 C2
Sava Italy 40°24N 17°33E 95 B10
Sava → Serbia 44°50N 20°26E 88 F5
Savage U.S.A. 47°27N 104°21W 168 C11
Savage I. = Niue ☑
  Pac. Oc. 19°2S 169°54W 157 J11
Savage River Australia 41°31S 145°14E 151 G4
Savai'i Samoa 13°28S 172°24W 147 C11
Savalou Benin 7°57N 1°58E 138 D5
Savane Mozam. 19°37S 35°8E 143 F4
Savanes □ Ivory C. 9°30N 6°0W 138 D4
Savanna U.S.A. 42°5N 90°8W 172 D8
Savanna-la-Mar
  Jamaica 18°10N 78°10W 182 a
Savannah Ga., U.S.A. 32°5N 81°6W 178 C8
Savannah Mo., U.S.A. 39°56N 94°50W 178 F6
Savannah Tenn.,
  U.S.A. 35°14N 88°15W 177 D10
Savannah → U.S.A. 32°2N 80°53W 178 C9
Savannah Beach = Tybee Island
  U.S.A. 32°0N 80°51W 178 C9
Savannakhet Laos 16°30N 104°49E 120 D5
Savant L. Canada 50°16N 90°44W 164 B1
Savant Lake Canada 50°14N 90°40W 164 B1
Savantvadi India 15°55N 73°54E 127 G1
Savanur India 14°59N 75°21E 127 G2
Savarkundla = Kundla
  India 21°21N 71°25E 124 J4
Sāvārşin Romania 46°1N 22°14E 80 D7
Savaştepe Turkey 39°22N 27°42E 99 B9
Savda India 21°9N 75°56E 126 D2
Savé Benin 8°2N 2°29E 138 D5
Save → France 43°47N 1°17E 72 E5
Save → Mozam. 21°16S 34°0E 145 B5
Sāveh Iran 35°2N 50°20E 129 C6
Savelugu Ghana 9°38N 0°54W 139 D4
Savenay France 47°20N 1°55W 70 E5
Săveni Romania 47°57N 26°52E 81 C11
Saverdun France 43°14N 1°34E 72 E5
Saverne France 48°43N 7°20E 71 D14
Savigliano Italy 44°38N 7°40E 92 D4
Savigny-sur-Braye
  France 47°53N 0°49E 70 E7
Sávio → Italy 44°19N 12°20E 93 D9
Šavnik Montenegro 42°59N 19°10E 96 D3
Savoie □ France 45°26N 6°25E 73 C10
Savolax = Savo Finland 62°45N 27°30E 60 E22
Savona Italy 44°17N 8°30E 92 D5
Savonlinna Finland 61°52N 28°53E 84 B5
Savoy = Savoie □
  France 45°26N 6°25E 73 C10
Şavşat Turkey 41°15N 42°20E 105 B10
Sävsjö Sweden 57°20N 14°40E 63 G8
Savur Turkey 37°34N 40°53E 128 B4
Savusavu Fiji 16°34S 179°15E 154 a
Savusavu B. Fiji 16°45S 179°15E 154 a
Sawahlunto Indonesia 0°40S 100°52E 118 E2
Sawai Indonesia 3°0S 129°5E 119 E7
Sawai Madhopur India 26°0N 76°25E 124 G7
Sawakele Fiji 17°59S 179°18E 154 a
Sawang Daen Din
  Thailand 17°28N 103°28E 120 D4
Sawankhalok Thailand 17°19N 99°50E 120 D2
Sawara Japan 35°55N 140°30E 113 G10
Sawatch Range
  U.S.A. 39°0N 106°30W 168 G10
Sawel Mt. U.K. 54°50N 7°2W 64 B4
Sawi Thailand 10°14N 99°5E 121 G2
Sawla Ghana 9°17N 2°29E 138 D4
Sawmills Zimbabwe 19°30S 28°2E 143 F2
Sawtell Australia 30°19S 153°6E 153 A10
Sawtooth → U.S.A. 44°0N 114°50W 168 D6
Sawtooth Range
  U.S.A. 44°3N 114°58W 168 D6
Sawu Indonesia 10°35S 121°50E 119 F6
Sawu Sea Indonesia 9°30S 121°50E 119 F6
Saxby → Australia 18°25S 140°53E 150 B3
Saxmundham U.K. 52°13N 1°30E 67 E9
Saxon Switzerland = Sächsische
  Schweiz △ Germany 50°55N 14°10E 76 E9
Saxony = Sachsen □
  Germany 50°55N 13°10E 76 E9
Saxony, Lower =
  Niedersachsen □
  Germany 52°50N 9°0E 76 C4
Saxton U.S.A. 40°13N 78°15W 174 F6
Say Mali 13°50N 4°57W 138 C4
Say Niger 13°8N 2°22E 139 C5
Saya Indonesia 9°30N 3°18E 139 D5
Sayabec Canada 48°35N 67°41W 165 C6
Sayaboury Laos 19°15N 101°45E 120 C3
Sayán Peru 11°8S 77°12W 188 C2
Sayan, Vostochnyy
  Russia 54°0N 96°0E 107 D10
Sayan, Zapadnyy
  Russia 52°30N 94°0E 109 B12
Sayanogorsk Russia 53°5N 91°23E 107 D10
Saydā Lebanon 33°35N 35°25E 130 B4
Sayhandulaan = Öldziyt
  Mongolia 44°40N 109°1E 114 B6
Sayḩūt Yemen 15°12N 51°10E 131 D5
Saykhin Kazakhstan 48°50N 46°47E 87 F8
Saylac Somalia 11°21N 43°30E 131 E3
Saynshand = Buyant-Uhaa
  Mongolia 44°55N 110°11E 114 B6
Sayre Okla., U.S.A. 35°18N 99°38W 176 D5
Sayre Pa., U.S.A. 41°59N 76°32W 175 E8
Sayreville U.S.A. 40°28N 74°22W 175 F10
Sayula Mexico 19°52N 103°36W 180 D4
Say'ūn Yemen 15°56N 48°47E 131 D4
Sayward Canada 50°21N 125°55W 162 C3
Sazanit Albania 40°30N 19°20E 96 D2
Sázava → Czech Rep. 49°53N 14°24E 76 D8
Sazin Pakistan 35°35N 73°30E 125 B5
Sazlika → Bulgaria 41°59N 25°50E 97 E9
Sbeïtla Tunisia 35°12N 9°7E 136 A5
Scaër France 48°2N 3°42W 70 D3
Scafell Pike U.K. 54°27N 3°14W 66 C4
Scalea Italy 39°49N 15°47E 95 C8
Scalloway U.K. 60°9N 1°17W 65 A7
Scalpay U.K. 57°18N 6°0W 65 D3
Scandia Canada 50°20N 112°2W 162 C6
Scandiano Italy 44°36N 10°42E 92 D7
Scandicci Italy 43°45N 11°11E 93 E8
Scandinavia Europe 64°0N 12°0E 60 E16
Scansano Italy 42°41N 11°20E 93 F8

Scapa Flow U.K. 58°53N 3°3W 65 C5
Scappoose U.S.A. 45°45N 122°53W 170 E4
Scarámia, Capo Italy 36°47N 14°29E 95 F7
Scarba U.K. 56°11N 5°43W 65 E3
Scarborough
  Trin. & Tob. 11°11N 60°42W 183 D7
Scarborough U.K. 54°17N 0°24W 66 C7
Scargill N.Z. 42°56S 172°58E 155 C7
Scariff I. Ireland 51°44N 10°15W 64 E1
Scarp U.K. 58°1N 7°8W 65 C1
Scarpe → France 50°26N 3°23E 71 B10
Scarsdale France 37°41S 143°39E 152 D5
Scebeli = Shabeelle →
  Somalia 2°0N 44°0E 131 G3
Šćedro Croatia 43°6N 16°43E 93 E13
Schaal See Germany 53°36N 10°55E 76 B6
Schaalsee Germany 53°40N 10°59E 76 B6
Schaffhausen Switz. 47°42N 8°39E 77 H4
Schagen Neths. 52°49N 4°48E 68 B5
Schaghticoke U.S.A. 42°54N 73°35W 175 D11
Schärding Austria 48°27N 13°27E 78 C6
Scharhörn Germany 53°57N 8°24E 76 B4
Scheessel Germany 53°10N 9°29E 76 B5
Schefferville Canada 54°48N 66°50W 165 B6
Scheibbs Austria 48°1N 15°9E 78 C8
Schelde → Belgium 51°15N 4°16E 68 C4
Schell Creek Ra.
  U.S.A. 39°25N 114°40W 168 G6
Schellsburg U.S.A. 40°3N 78°39W 174 F5
Schenectady U.S.A. 42°49N 73°57W 175 D11
Schenevus U.S.A. 42°33N 74°50W 175 D10
Scherfede Germany 51°32N 9°2E 76 D5
Schesslitz Germany 49°58N 11°1E 77 F7
Schiedam Neths. 51°55N 4°25E 68 C4
Schiermonnikoog Neths. 53°30N 6°15E 69 A6
Schiermonnikoog △
  Neths. 53°30N 6°15E 69 A6
Schiltigheim France 48°35N 7°45E 71 D14
Schinousa Greece 36°53N 25°31E 99 F7
Schio Italy 45°43N 11°21E 93 C8
Schipol, Amsterdam ✈ (AMS)
  Neths. 52°18N 4°45E 68 B4
Schladming Austria 47°23N 13°41E 78 D6
Schlanders = Silandro
  Italy 46°38N 10°46E 92 B7
Schlei → Germany 54°40N 10°0E 76 A5
Schleiden Germany 50°31N 6°28E 76 E2
Schleiz Germany 50°35N 11°49E 76 E7
Schleswig Germany 54°31N 9°34E 76 A5
Schleswig-Holstein □
  Germany 54°30N 9°30E 76 A5
Schlüchtern Germany 50°20N 9°32E 77 E5
Schmalkalden Germany 50°44N 10°26E 76 E6
Schmölln Germany 50°54N 12°19E 76 E8
Schneeberg Austria 47°47N 15°48E 78 D8
Schneeberg Germany 50°35N 12°38E 76 E8
Schneverdingen Germany 53°7N 9°48E 76 B5
Schœlcher Martinique 14°36N 61°7W 182 c
Schoharie U.S.A. 42°40N 74°19W 175 D10
Schoharie Cr. →
  U.S.A. 42°57N 74°18W 175 D10
Schokland Neths. 52°38N 5°46E 68 B5
Scholls U.S.A. 45°24N 122°56W 170 E4
Schönberg
  Mecklenburg-Vorpommern,
  Germany 53°52N 10°56E 76 B6
Schönberg Schleswig-Holstein,
  Germany 54°23N 10°21E 76 A6
Schönbuch △ Germany 48°35N 9°2E 77 G5
Schöneberg → Germany 52°29N 11°44E 76 C7
Schöngau Germany 47°47N 10°53E 77 H6
Schöningen Germany 52°8N 10°56E 76 C6
Schopfheim Germany 47°38N 7°50E 77 H3
Schorndorf Germany 48°47N 9°32E 77 G5
Schortens Germany 53°31N 7°56E 76 B3
Schouten I. Australia 42°20S 148°20E 151 G4
Schouten Is. = Supiori
  Indonesia 1°0S 136°0E 119 E9
Schouwen Neths. 51°43N 3°45E 68 C3
Schramberg Germany 48°13N 8°22E 77 G4
Schrankogel Austria 47°3N 11°7E 78 D4
Schreiber Canada 48°45N 87°20W 164 C2
Schrems Austria 48°47N 15°4E 78 C8
Schrobenhausen
  Germany 48°34N 11°16E 77 G7
Schroffenstein Namibia 27°11S 18°42E 144 C2
Schroon Lake U.S.A. 43°50N 73°46W 175 C11
Schruns Austria 47°5N 9°56E 78 D3
Schuler Canada 50°20N 110°6W 163 C6
Schumacher Canada 48°30N 81°16W 164 C3
Schurz U.S.A. 38°57N 118°49W 168 G4
Schuyler U.S.A. 41°27N 97°4W 172 E5
Schuylerville U.S.A. 43°6N 73°35W 175 C11
Schuylkill → U.S.A. 39°53N 75°12W 175 G9
Schuylkill Haven
  U.S.A. 40°37N 76°11W 175 F8
Schwabach Germany 49°19N 11°2E 77 F7
Schwaben □ Germany 48°20N 10°30E 77 G6
Schwäbisch-Fränkischer Wald △
  Germany 49°0N 9°30E 77 G5
Schwäbisch Gmünd
  Germany 48°49N 9°47E 77 G5
Schwäbisch Hall Germany 49°6N 9°44E 77 F5
Schwäbische Alb
  Germany 48°20N 9°30E 77 G5
Schwabmünchen
  Germany 48°10N 10°46E 77 G6
Schwalmstadt Germany 50°56N 9°36E 76 E5
Schwandorf Germany 49°19N 12°7E 77 F8
Schwaner, Pegunungan
  Indonesia 1°0S 112°30E 118 E4
Schwanewede Germany 53°14N 8°35E 76 B4
Schwarmstedt Germany 52°39N 9°38E 76 C5
Schwarze Elster →
  Germany 51°48N 12°50E 76 D8
Schwarzenberg Germany 50°32N 12°47E 76 E8
Schwarzrand Namibia 25°37S 16°50E 144 C2
Schwatka Mts.
  U.S.A. 67°20N 156°30W 166 B5
Schwaz Austria 47°20N 11°44E 78 D4
Schwechat, Wien ✈ (VIE)
  Austria 48°7N 16°35E 79 C9
Schwedt Germany 53°3N 14°16E 76 B10
Schweinfurt Germany 50°3N 10°14E 77 E6
Schweiz = Switzerland ■
  Europe 46°30N 8°0E 77 J4
Schweizer-Reneke
  S. Africa 27°11S 25°18E 144 C4

Schwenningen = Villingen-
  Schwenningen Germany 48°3N 8°26E 77 G4
Schwerin Germany 53°36N 11°22E 76 B7
Schweriner See Germany 53°45N 11°26E 76 B7
Schwetzingen Germany 49°23N 8°35E 77 F4
Schwyz Switz. 47°2N 8°39E 77 H4
Schwyz □ Switz. 47°2N 8°39E 77 H4
Sciacca Italy 37°31N 13°3E 94 E6
Scicli Italy 36°47N 14°42E 95 F7
Sciliar-Catinaccio =
  Italy 46°28N 11°35E 93 B8
Scilla Italy 38°15N 15°43E 95 D8
Scilly, Isles of U.K. 49°56N 6°22W 67 H1
Scioto → U.S.A. 38°44N 83°1W 173 F12
Scione Greece 39°57N 23°36E 96 C7
Scituate U.S.A. 42°12N 70°44W 175 D14
Scobey U.S.A. 48°47N 105°25W 168 B11
Scone Australia 32°5S 150°52E 153 B9
Scone U.K. 56°25N 3°24W 65 E5
Scordia Italy 37°18N 14°51E 95 F7
Scoresby Sund
  Greenland 70°28N 21°46W 57 C8
Scoresbysund = Ittoqqortoormiit
  Greenland 70°20N 23°0W 57 C8
Scorniceşti Romania 44°34N 24°33E 81 F9
Scotia Calif., U.S.A. 40°29N 124°6W 168 F1
Scotia N.Y., U.S.A. 42°50N 73°58W 175 D11
Scotia Sea Antarctica 56°5S 56°0W 5 B18
Scotland Canada 43°1N 80°22W 174 C4
Scotland U.K. 57°0N 4°0W 65 E5
Scott Antarctica 77°0S 166°45E 5 D11
Scott, C. Australia 13°30S 129°49E 148 B4
Scott City U.S.A. 38°29N 100°54W 172 F3
Scott Glacier Antarctica 66°15S 100°5E 5 C8
Scott I. Antarctica 67°0S 179°0E 5 C11
Scott Is. Canada 50°48N 128°40W 162 C3
Scott L. Canada 59°55N 106°18W 163 B7
Scott Reef Australia 14°0S 121°50E 148 B3
Scottdale U.S.A. 40°6N 79°35W 174 F5
Scottish Borders □ U.K. 55°35N 2°50W 65 F6
Scotts Head Australia 30°45S 153°0E 153 A10
Scotts Valley U.S.A. 37°3N 122°1W 170 H4
Scottsbluff U.S.A. 41°52N 103°40W 172 E2
Scottsboro U.S.A. 34°40N 86°2W 177 E11
Scottsburg U.S.A. 38°41N 85°47W 173 F11
Scottsdale Australia 41°9S 147°31E 151 G4
Scottsdale U.S.A. 33°40N 111°53W 169 K8
Scottsville Ky., U.S.A. 36°45N 86°11W 172 G10
Scottsville N.Y., U.S.A. 43°2N 77°47W 174 C7
Scottville U.S.A. 43°58N 86°17W 172 D9
Scranton U.S.A. 41°25N 75°40W 175 E9
Screven U.S.A. 31°29N 82°1W 178 D7
Scugog, L. Canada 44°10N 78°55W 174 B6
Scunthorpe U.K. 53°36N 0°39W 66 D7
Scuol Schuls Switz. 46°48N 10°17E 77 J6
Scutari = Shkodër
  Albania 42°4N 19°32E 96 D3
Scutari = Üsküdar Turkey 41°1N 29°0E 97 F13
Sea Is. U.S.A. 31°30N 81°7W 178 D9
Sea Lake Australia 35°28S 142°55E 152 C5
Seabra Brazil 12°25S 41°46W 189 C2
Seabrook, L. Australia 30°55S 119°40E 149 F2
Seaford U.K. 50°47N 0°7E 67 G8
Seaford U.S.A. 38°39N 75°37W 173 F16
Seaforth Australia 20°55S 148°57E 150 b
Seaforth Canada 43°35N 81°25W 174 C3
Seaforth, L. U.K. 57°52N 6°36W 65 D2
Seagraves U.S.A. 32°57N 102°34W 176 E3
Seaham U.K. 54°50N 1°20W 66 C6
Seal → Canada 59°4N 94°48W 163 B10
Seal L. Canada 54°20N 61°30W 165 B7
Seale U.S.A. 32°18N 85°10W 178 C4
Sealy U.S.A. 29°47N 96°9W 176 G6
Searchlight U.S.A. 35°28N 114°55W 171 K12
Searcy U.S.A. 35°15N 91°44W 178 D8
Searles L. U.S.A. 35°44N 117°21W 171 K9
Seascale U.K. 54°24N 3°29W 66 C4
Seaside Calif., U.S.A. 36°37N 121°50W 170 J5
Seaside Oreg., U.S.A. 46°0N 123°56W 170 E3
Seaspray Australia 38°25S 147°15E 153 D7
Seattle U.S.A. 47°36N 122°19W 170 C4
Seattle-Tacoma Int. ✈ (SEA)
  U.S.A. 47°27N 122°18W 170 C4
Seaward Kaikoura Ra.
  N.Z. 42°10S 173°44E 155 C5
Seba Indonesia 10°29S 121°50E 148 B3
Sebago L. U.S.A. 43°52N 70°34W 175 C14
Sebago Lake U.S.A. 43°51N 70°34W 175 C14
Sebastian U.S.A. 27°49N 80°28W 179 H9
Sebastián Vizcaíno, B.
  Mexico 28°0N 114°30W 180 B2
Sebastopol = Sevastopol
  Ukraine 44°35N 33°30E 85 K7
Sebastopol U.S.A. 38°24N 122°49W 170 G4
Sebba Burkina Faso 13°35N 0°32E 139 C5
Sebdou Algeria 34°38N 1°19W 136 B3
Sébékoro Mali 12°58N 9°0W 138 C3
Seben Turkey 40°24N 31°34E 104 B4
Sebeş Romania 45°58N 23°34E 81 E8
Sebeşului, Munții
  Romania 45°36N 23°40E 81 E8
Sebewaing U.S.A. 43°44N 83°27W 173 D12
Sebezh Russia 56°14N 28°22E 84 D5
Sebezhsky △ Russia 56°16N 28°30E 84 D5
Sebha = Sabhā Libya 27°9N 14°29E 135 C8
Sébi Mali 15°50N 4°12W 138 B4
Şebinkarahisar Turkey 40°22N 38°28E 105 B8
Sebnitz Germany 50°58N 14°16E 76 E10
Sebou, Oued →
  Morocco 34°16N 6°40W 136 B2
Sebring Fla., U.S.A. 27°30N 81°27W 179 H8
Sebring Ohio, U.S.A. 40°55N 81°2W 174 F3
Sebta = Ceuta N. Afr. 35°52N 5°18W 134 A4
Sebuku Indonesia 3°30S 116°25E 118 E5
Sebuku, Teluk Malaysia 4°0N 118°10E 118 D5
Secchia → Italy 44°4N 11°10E 92 C7
Sechelt Canada 49°25N 123°42W 162 D4
Sechura Peru 5°33S 80°50W 188 B1
Sechura, Desierto de
  Peru 6°0S 80°30W 188 B1
Seclin France 50°33N 3°2E 71 B10
Secondigny France 46°37N 0°26W 70 F6
Secretary I. N.Z. 45°15S 166°56E 155 F1
Secretary I. N.Z. 45°15S 166°56E 155 F1

Secunderabad India 17°28N 78°30E 126 F5
Security U.S.A. 38°45N 104°45W 168 G11
Sedalia U.S.A. 38°42N 93°14W 172 F7
Sedam India 17°11N 77°17E 126 E3
Sedan Australia 34°34S 139°19E 152 C3
Sedan France 49°43N 4°57E 71 C11
Sedan U.S.A. 37°8N 96°11W 172 G5
Sedano Spain 42°43N 3°49W 88 C7
Seddon N.Z. 41°40S 174°7E 155 B9
Seddonville N.Z. 41°33S 172°1E 155 B7
Sedé Boqér Israel 30°52N 34°47E 130 E3
Sedé Fārs, Iran 30°45N 52°11E 129 D7
Séderon France 44°12N 5°32E 73 D9
Sederot Israel 31°32N 34°37E 130 D3
Sédhiou Senegal 12°44N 15°30W 138 C1
Sedico Italy 46°8N 12°6E 93 B9
Sedlčany Czech Rep. 49°40N 14°25E 78 B7
Sedley Canada 50°10N 104°0W 163 C9
Sedona U.S.A. 34°52N 111°46W 169 J8
Sedova, Pik Russia 73°29N 54°58E 106 B6
Sedro-Woolley U.S.A. 48°30N 122°14W 170 B4
Şeduva Lithuania 55°45N 23°45E 84 C10
Sędziszów Poland 50°35N 20°2E 83 H10
Sędziszów Małopolski
  Poland 50°5N 21°45E 83 H8
Seebad Ahlbeck
  Germany 53°56N 14°10E 76 B10
Seefeld in Tirol Austria 47°19N 11°13E 78 D4
Seehausen Germany 52°54N 11°45E 76 C7
Seeheim Namibia 26°50S 17°45E 144 C2
Seeheim-Jugenheim
  Germany 49°46N 8°40E 77 F4
Seeis Namibia 22°29S 17°39E 144 B2
Seekoei → S. Africa 30°18S 25°1E 144 D4
Seeley's Bay Canada 44°29N 76°14W 175 B8
Seelow Germany 52°32N 14°22E 76 C10
Sées France 48°38N 0°10E 70 D7
Seesen Germany 51°54N 10°10E 76 D6
Seevetal Germany 53°26N 10°1E 76 B6
Seewinkel = Neusiedler See-
  Seewinkel △ Austria 47°50N 16°45E 79 D9
Şefaatli Turkey 39°30N 34°45E 104 C6
Seferihisar Turkey 38°10N 26°50E 99 C8
Séféto Mali 14°8N 9°49W 138 C3
Sefophe Botswana 22°11S 27°58E 145 B4
Sefrou Morocco 33°52N 4°52W 136 B5
Sefton N.Z. 43°15S 172°41E 155 D7
Sefwi Bekwai Ghana 6°10N 2°25W 138 D4
Segamat Malaysia 2°30N 102°50E 121 L4
Segarcea Romania 44°6N 23°43E 81 F8
Ségbana Benin 10°55N 3°42E 139 C5
Segbwema S. Leone 8°0N 11°0W 138 D2
Segersta Sweden 61°16N 16°39E 62 C10
Segesta Italy 37°56N 12°50E 94 E5
Seget Indonesia 1°24S 130°58E 119 E8
Segezha Russia 63°44N 34°19E 84 B10
Seggueur, O. → Algeria 32°14N 1°48E 136 B4
Segmon Sweden 59°17N 13°3E 62 E7
Segonzac France 45°36N 0°14W 72 C3
Segorbe Spain 39°50N 0°30W 91 F4
Ségou Mali 13°30N 6°16W 138 C3
Ségou □ Mali 14°0N 6°0W 138 C3
Segovia = Coco →
  Cent. Amer. 15°0N 83°8W 182 D3
Segovia Spain 40°57N 4°10W 88 E6
Segovia □ Spain 40°55N 4°10W 88 E6
Segré France 47°40N 0°52W 70 E6
Segre → Spain 41°40N 0°43E 90 D5
Seguam I. U.S.A. 52°19N 172°30W 166 E5
Séguéla Ivory C. 7°55N 6°40W 138 D3
Séguénéga Burkina Faso 13°1N 1°58W 138 C4
Seguin U.S.A. 29°34N 97°58W 176 G6
Segundo → Argentina 30°53S 62°44W 190 C3
Segura → Spain 38°3N 0°44W 91 G4
Segura, Sierra de Spain 38°5N 2°45W 91 G2
Seh Konj, Kūh-e Iran 30°6N 57°30E 129 D8
Seh Qal'eh Iran 33°40N 58°24E 129 C8
Sehithwa Botswana 20°30S 22°30E 144 B3
Sehlabathebe △ Lesotho 29°53S 29°7E 145 C4
Sehore India 23°10N 77°5E 124 H7
Sehwan Pakistan 26°28N 67°53E 124 F2
Seia Portugal 40°25N 7°43W 88 D3
Şeica Mare Romania 46°1N 24°7E 81 D9
Seil U.K. 56°18N 5°38W 65 E3
Seiland Norway 70°25N 23°15E 60 A20
Seilhac France 45°22N 1°43E 72 C5
Seiling U.S.A. 36°9N 98°56W 176 C5
Seille → Moselle, France 49°7N 6°11E 71 C13
Seille → Saône-et-Loire,
  France 46°31N 4°57E 71 F11
Sein, Î. de France 48°2N 4°52W 70 D2
Seinäjoki Finland 62°40N 22°51E 60 E20
Seine → France 49°26N 0°26E 70 C7
Seine, B. de la France 49°40N 0°40W 70 C6
Seine-et-Marne □ France 48°45N 3°0E 71 D10
Seine-Maritime □ France 49°40N 1°0E 70 C7
Seine-St-Denis □ France 48°58N 2°24E 71 D9
Seini Romania 47°44N 23°21E 81 C8
Seirijai Lithuania 54°16N 23°49E 82 D10
Seistan = Sīstān Asia 30°50N 61°0E 129 D9
Seistan, Daryācheh-ye = Sīstān,
  Daryācheh-ye Iran 31°0N 61°0E 129 D9
Seitseminen △ Finland 61°55N 23°25E 60 F20
Sejerø Denmark 55°54N 11°8E 63 J5
Sejerø Bugt Denmark 55°53N 11°15E 63 J5
Sejny Poland 54°6N 23°21E 82 D10
Sekayu Indonesia 2°51S 103°51E 118 E2
Seke Tanzania 3°20S 33°31E 142 C3
Sekenke Tanzania 4°18S 34°11E 142 C3
Sekhira Tunisia 34°20N 10°18E 95 F1
Seki Turkey 36°48N 29°33E 99 E11
Sekondi-Takoradi Ghana 4°58N 1°45W 138 E4
Sekseüil Kazakhstan 47°5N 61°6E 108 C6
Seksna Russia 59°13N 38°33E 84 C10
Sekudai Malaysia 1°32N 103°39E 121 M4
Sekuma Botswana 24°36S 23°50E 144 B3
Selah U.S.A. 46°39N 120°32W 170 C5
Selama Malaysia 5°12N 100°42E 121 K3
Selangor □ Malaysia 3°10N 101°30E 121 L3
Selárgius Italy 39°16N 9°10E 94 C2
Selaru Indonesia 8°9S 131°0E 119 F8
Selatan, Selat Malaysia 5°15N 100°20E 121 c
Selawik U.S.A. 66°36N 160°0W 166 B7
Selb Germany 50°9N 12°9E 76 E8
Selby U.K. 53°47N 1°5W 66 D6
Selby U.S.A. 45°31N 100°2W 172 C3
Selça Croatia 43°20N 16°50E 93 E13

Selçuk Turkey 37°56N 27°22E 99 D9
Selden U.S.A. 39°33N 100°34W 172 F3
Sele → Italy 40°29N 14°56E 95 B7
Selebi-Phikwe
  Botswana 21°58S 27°48E 145 B4
Selemdzha → Russia 51°42N 128°53E 107 D13
Selendi Manisa, Turkey 38°43N 28°50E 99 C10
Selendi Manisa, Turkey 38°46N 27°53E 99 C9
Selenga = Selenge Mörön →
  Asia 52°16N 106°16E 110 A10
Selenge Mörön →
  Asia 52°16N 106°16E 110 A10
Selenicë Albania 40°33N 19°39E 96 F3
Selenter See Germany 54°18N 10°26E 76 A6
Sélestat France 48°16N 7°26E 71 D14
Seletan, Tanjung
  Indonesia 4°10S 114°40E 118 E4
Selevac Serbia 44°28N 20°52E 96 B4
Sélibabi Mauritania 15°10N 12°15W 138 C2
Seliger, Ozero Russia 57°15N 33°0E 84 D7
Selim Turkey 40°30N 42°46E 105 B10
Selîma Sudan 21°22N 29°19E 137 C2
Selimiye Turkey 37°24N 27°40E 99 D9
Selinda Spillway →
  Botswana 18°35S 23°10E 144 A3
Sélingué, L. de Mali 11°37N 8°14W 138 C3
Selinsgrove U.S.A. 40°48N 76°52W 174 F7
Selizharovo Russia 56°51N 33°27E 84 D7
Selkirk Man., Canada 50°10N 96°55W 163 C9
Selkirk U.K. 55°33N 2°50W 65 F6
Selkirk I. = Horse I.
  Canada 53°20N 99°6W 163 C9
Selkirk Mts. Canada 51°15N 117°40W 160 G8
Sellafield U.K. 54°25N 3°29W 66 C4
Sellia Greece 35°12N 24°23E 101 D6
Sellières France 46°50N 5°32E 71 F12
Sells U.S.A. 31°55N 111°53W 169 L8
Sellye Hungary 45°52N 17°51E 80 E2
Selma Ala., U.S.A. 32°25N 87°1W 177 E11
Selma Calif., U.S.A. 36°34N 119°37W 170 J7
Selma N.C., U.S.A. 35°32N 78°17W 177 D15
Selmer U.S.A. 35°10N 88°36W 177 D9
Selongey France 47°36N 5°11E 71 E12
Selouane Morocco 35°7N 2°57W 136 A3
Selous □ Tanzania 8°37S 37°42E 143 D4
Selowandoma Falls
  Zimbabwe 21°15S 31°50E 143 G3
Selpele Indonesia 0°1S 130°5E 119 E8
Selsey Bill U.K. 50°43N 0°47W 67 G7
Seltso Russia 53°22N 34°4E 84 F8
Seltz France 48°54N 8°6E 71 D15
Selu Indonesia 7°32S 130°55E 119 F8
Sélune → France 48°38N 1°22W 70 D5
Selva = La Selva del Camp
  Spain 41°13N 1°8E 90 D6
Selva Argentina 29°50S 62°0W 190 B3
Selva Spain 39°46N 2°54E 100 B9
Selva Lancandona = Montes
  Azules △ Mexico 16°21N 91°3W 181 D6
Selvagens, Ilhas
  Madeira 30°5N 15°55W 134 B2
Selvas Brazil 6°30S 67°0W 188 B4
Selwyn L. Canada 60°0N 104°30W 163 B8
Selwyn Mts. Canada 63°0N 130°0W 160 E5
Selwyn Ra. Australia 21°10S 140°0E 150 C3
Selyatyn Ukraine 47°50N 25°12E 81 C10
Seman → Albania 40°47N 19°30E 96 F3
Semarang Indonesia 7°0S 110°26E 118 F4
Semarapura = Klungkung
  Indonesia 8°32S 115°24E 119 K18
Sembabule Uganda 0°4S 31°25E 142 C3
Sembawang Singapore 1°27N 103°50E 121 d
Sembung Indonesia 8°28S 115°11E 119 J18
Şemdinli Turkey 37°18N 44°35E 105 D11
Sémé Senegal 15°4N 13°41W 138 B2
Semenic-Cheile Caraşului △
  Romania 45°8N 22°5E 80 E7
Semenov Chernihiv,
  Ukraine 52°8N 32°36E 85 F7
Semenivka Kremenchuk,
  Ukraine 49°37N 33°10E 85 H7
Semenov Russia 56°43N 44°30E 86 B7
Semeru Indonesia 8°4S 112°55E 119 H15
Semey Kazakhstan 50°30N 80°10E 109 B10
Semikarakorskiy Russia 47°31N 40°48E 87 G5
Semiluki Russia 51°41N 39°2E 85 G10
Seminoe Res. U.S.A. 42°9N 106°55W 168 E10
Seminole Fla., U.S.A. 27°50N 82°47W 179 H7
Seminole Okla., U.S.A. 35°14N 96°41W 176 D6
Seminole Tex., U.S.A. 32°43N 102°39W 176 E3
Seminole, L. U.S.A. 30°43N 84°44W 179 F5
Seminole Draw →
  U.S.A. 32°27N 102°20W 176 E3
Semipalatinsk = Semey
  Kazakhstan 50°30N 80°10E 109 B10
Semirara Is. Phil. 12°0N 121°20E 119 B6
Semisopochnoi I.
  U.S.A. 51°55N 179°36E 166 E3
Semitau Indonesia 0°29N 111°57E 118 D4
Semliki △ Uganda 0°49N 30°4E 142 B3
Semmering P. Austria 47°41N 15°45E 78 D8
Semnān Iran 35°40N 53°23E 129 C7
Semnān □ Iran 36°0N 54°0E 129 C7
Semporna Malaysia 4°30N 118°33E 119 D5
Semuda Indonesia 2°51S 112°58E 118 E4
Semur-en-Auxois France 47°30N 4°20E 71 E11
Sen → Cambodia 12°32N 104°28E 120 F5
Sena Mozam. 17°25S 35°0E 143 F4
Sena → Bolivia 11°31S 67°11W 188 C4
Senā Iran 28°27N 51°36E 129 D6
Sena Madureira Brazil 9°5S 68°45W 188 B4
Sena Pompeu Brazil 5°40S 39°20W 189 B3
Senaki Georgia 42°15N 42°1E 87 J6
Senanga, Pulau Singapore 1°11N 103°52E 121 d
Senanga Zambia 16°7S 23°16E 141 H4
Senatobia U.S.A. 34°37N 89°58W 177 D10
Sencelles Spain 39°39N 2°54E 100 B9
Sendai = Satsuma-Sendai
  Japan 31°50N 130°20E 113 J5
Sendai Japan 38°15N 140°53E 112 C10
Sendai-Wan Japan 38°15N 141°0E 112 C10
Senden Bayern, Germany 48°19N 10°4E 77 G6
Senden Nordrhein-Westfalen,
  Germany 51°52N 7°22E 76 D3
Sendhwa India 21°41N 75°6E 124 J6
Sendurjana India 21°32N 78°17E 126 D4
Sene → Ghana 7°30N 0°33W 139 D4
Senec Slovak Rep. 48°12N 17°23E 79 C10

Seneca U.S.A. 34°41N 82°57W 177 D13
Seneca Falls U.S.A. 42°55N 76°48W 175 D8
Seneca L. U.S.A. 42°40N 76°54W 174 D8
Senecaville L. U.S.A. 39°55N 81°25W 174 G3
Senegal ■ W. Afr. 14°30N 14°30W 138 C2
Sénégal → W. Afr. 15°48N 16°32W 138 B1
Senegambia Africa 12°45N 12°0W 132 E2
Senekal S. Africa 28°20S 27°36E 145 C4
Senftenberg Germany 51°32N 14°0E 76 D10
Senga Hill Zambia 9°19S 31°11E 143 D3
Senge Khambab = Indus → Pakistan 24°20N 67°47E 124 G2
Sengerema Tanzania 2°42S 32°35E 142 C3
Senggigi Indonesia 8°29S 116°2E 119 J19
Sengiley Russia 53°58N 48°46E 86 D9
Sengua → Zimbabwe 17°7S 28°5E 143 F2
Senguerr → Argentina 45°35S 68°50W 192 C3
Senhor-do-Bonfim Brazil 10°30S 40°10W 189 C2
Senica Slovak Rep. 48°41N 17°25E 79 C10
Senigállia Italy 43°43N 13°13E 93 E10
Senio → Italy 44°35N 12°15E 93 D9
Senirkent Turkey 38°6N 30°33E 99 C12
Senise Italy 40°9N 16°17E 95 B9
Senj Croatia 45°0N 14°58E 93 D11
Senja Norway 69°25N 17°30E 60 B17
Senkaku-Shotō E. China Sea 25°45N 123°30E 113 M1
Senlis France 49°13N 2°35E 71 C9
Senmonorom Cambodia 12°27N 107°12E 120 F6
Senneterre Canada 48°25N 77°15W 164 C4
Senno Belarus 54°45N 29°43E 84 E5
Sénnori Italy 40°47N 8°35E 94 B1
Seno Laos 16°35N 104°50E 120 D5
Senoia U.S.A. 33°18N 84°33W 178 B5
Senonches France 48°34N 1°2E 70 D8
Senorbì Italy 39°32N 9°8E 94 C2
Senožeče Slovenia 45°43N 14°3E 93 C11
Senqu = Orange → S. Africa 28°41S 16°28E 144 C2
Sens France 48°11N 3°15E 71 D10
Senta Serbia 45°55N 20°3E 80 E5
Sentery = Lubao Dem. Rep. of the Congo 5°17S 25°42E 142 D2
Sentinel U.S.A. 32°52N 113°13W 169 K7
Šentjur Slovenia 46°14N 15°24E 93 B12
Sentosa Singapore 1°16N 103°50E 121 d
Senwabarana S. Africa 23°17S 29°7E 145 B4
Senya Beraku Ghana 5°28N 0°31W 139 D4
Seo de Urgel = La Seu d'Urgell Spain 42°22N 1°23E 90 C6
Seogwipo S. Korea 33°13N 126°34E 115 H14
Seohara India 29°15N 78°33E 125 E8
Seonath → India 21°44N 82°28E 125 J10
Seondha India 26°9N 78°48E 125 F8
Seongnam S. Korea 37°26N 127°8E 115 F14
Seoni India 22°5N 79°30E 125 H8
Seoni Malwa India 22°27N 77°28E 124 H8
Seonsan S. Korea 36°14N 128°17E 115 F15
Seoriuarayan India 21°45N 82°34E 126 D6
Seosan S. Korea 36°47N 126°27E 115 F14
Seoul S. Korea 37°31N 126°58E 115 F14
Separation Pt. N.Z. 40°47S 172°59E 155 A7
Sepīdān Iran 30°20N 52°5E 129 D7
Sepo-ri N. Korea 38°57N 127°25E 115 E14
Sępólno Krajeńskie Poland 53°26N 17°30E 82 E4
Sepone Laos 16°45N 106°13E 120 D6
Sępopol Poland 54°16N 21°2E 82 D8
Sept-Îles Canada 50°13N 66°22W 165 B6
Septemvri Bulgaria 42°13N 24°6E 97 D8
Sepúlveda Spain 41°18N 3°45W 88 D7
Sequeros Spain 40°31N 6°2W 88 E4
Sequim U.S.A. 48°5N 123°6W 170 B3
Sequoia △ U.S.A. 36°30N 118°30W 170 J8
Serafimovich Russia 49°36N 42°43E 86 F6
Seraing Belgium 50°35N 5°32E 69 D5
Serakhis → Cyprus 35°13N 32°55E 101 D11
Seram Indonesia 3°10S 129°0E 119 E7
Seram Sea Indonesia 2°30S 128°30E 119 E7
Serampore = Shrirampur India 22°44N 88°21E 125 H13
Serang Indonesia 6°8S 106°10E 119 G12
Serangoon Singapore 1°23N 103°54E 121 d
Serasan Indonesia 2°29N 109°4E 118 D3
Seravezza Italy 43°59N 10°13E 92 E7
Şerbettar Turkey 41°27N 26°46E 97 E10
Serbia ■ Europe 43°20N 20°0E 96 C4
Şercaia Romania 45°49N 25°9E 81 E10
Serdar Turkmenistan 39°4N 56°23E 129 B8
Serdobsk Russia 52°28N 44°10E 86 D7
Serebryansk Kazakhstan 49°41N 83°17E 109 C10
Sered' Slovak Rep. 48°17N 17°44E 79 C10
Seredka Russia 58°12N 28°10E 84 C5
Serednye Ukraine 48°32N 22°30E 80 B7
Şereflikoçhisar Turkey 38°56N 33°32E 104 C5
Seregno Italy 45°39N 9°12E 92 C6
Seremban Malaysia 2°43N 101°53E 121 L3
Serengeti △ Tanzania 2°11S 35°0E 142 C3
Serengeti Plain Tanzania 2°40S 35°0E 142 C4
Serenje Zambia 13°14S 30°15E 143 E3
Seret → Ukraine 48°37N 25°52E 81 B10
Sereth = Siret → Romania 45°24N 28°1E 81 E12
Sergach Russia 55°30N 45°30E 86 C7
Sergeevka Kazakhstan 53°52N 67°24E 109 B7
Sergen Turkey 41°41N 27°42E 97 E11
Sergeya Kirova, Ostrova Russia 77°30N 89°0E 107 B10
Sergino Russia 62°25N 65°12E 106 C7
Sergipe □ Brazil 10°30S 37°30W 189 C3
Sergiyev Posad Russia 56°20N 38°10E 84 D10
Serhetabat Turkmenistan 35°20N 62°18E 129 C9
Seria Brunei 4°37N 114°23E 118 D4
Serian Malaysia 1°10N 110°31E 118 D4
Seriate Italy 45°41N 9°43E 92 C6
Sericho Kenya 1°5N 39°5E 142 B4
Sérifontaine France 49°20N 1°45E 71 C8
Serifos Greece 37°9N 24°30E 98 D6
Sérignan France 43°17N 3°17E 72 E7
Sérigny → Canada 56°47N 66°0W 165 A6
Serik Turkey 36°55N 31°7E 104 D4
Seringapatam Reef Australia 13°38S 122°5E 148 B3
Serinhisar Turkey 37°36N 29°18E 99 D11
Seririt Indonesia 8°12S 114°56E 119 J17
Serishābād Iran 35°14N 47°36E 105 E12
Serkout Algeria 23°56N 6°47E 136 D5
Sermaize-les-Bains France 48°47N 4°54E 71 D11
Sermata Indonesia 8°15S 128°50E 119 F7
Sermersooq □ Greenland 68°0N 40°0W 57 D7
Sermersuaq Greenland 79°30N 62°0W 57 B4
Sérmide Italy 45°0N 11°18E 93 D8
Sernovodsk Russia 53°58N 51°16E 86 D10
Sernur Russia 56°52N 49°2E 86 B9
Serock Poland 52°31N 21°4E 83 F8
Serón Spain 37°20N 2°29W 91 H2
Seròs Spain 41°27N 0°24E 90 D5
Serouenout Algeria 24°18N 7°25E 136 D5
Serov Russia 59°29N 60°35E 106 D7
Serowe Botswana 22°25S 26°43E 144 B4
Serpa Portugal 37°57N 7°38W 89 H3
Serpeddí, Pta. Italy 39°22N 9°18E 94 C2
Serpentara Italy 39°8N 9°36E 94 C2
Serpentine Lakes Australia 28°30S 129°10E 149 E4
Serpent's Mouth = Sierpe, Bocas de la Venezuela 10°0N 61°30W 187 L15
Serpis → Spain 38°59N 0°9W 91 G4
Serpneve Ukraine 46°18N 29°1E 81 D14
Serpukhov Russia 54°55N 37°28E 84 E9
Serra Brazil 20°7S 40°18W 189 E2
Serra da Canastra △ Brazil 20°3S 46°50W 189 E1
Serra da Capivara △ Brazil 8°42S 42°15W 189 B2
Serra da Estrela ⌓ Portugal 40°27N 7°33W 88 E3
Serra das Confusões △ Brazil 8°50S 43°50W 189 B2
Serra de Mesa, Barragem de Brazil 14°30S 48°30W 189 C1
Serra do Cipó △ Brazil 19°14S 43°23W 189 D2
Serra do Divisor △ Brazil 8°3S 73°29W 188 B3
Serra do Navio Brazil 0°59N 52°3W 187 C8
Serra do Salitre Brazil 19°6S 46°41W 189 D1
Serra San Bruno Italy 38°35N 16°20E 95 D9
Serra Talhada Brazil 7°59S 38°18W 189 B3
Serradilla Spain 39°50N 6°9W 88 F4
Serramanna Italy 39°25N 8°55E 94 C1
Serranía San Luís △ Paraguay 22°35S 57°22W 190 A4
Serranía San Rafael △ Paraguay 26°30S 56°0W 191 B4
Serras d'Aire e Candeeiros ⌓ Portugal 39°31N 8°48W 89 F2
Serrat, C. Tunisia 37°14N 9°10E 136 A5
Serravalle Scrívia Italy 44°43N 8°51E 92 D5
Serre-Ponçon, L. de France 44°22N 6°20E 73 D10
Serrejón Spain 39°49N 5°48W 88 F5
Serres France 44°26N 5°43E 73 D9
Serres Greece 41°5N 23°31E 96 E7
Serrezuela Argentina 30°40S 65°20W 190 C2
Serrinha Brazil 11°39S 39°0W 189 C3
Serrita Brazil 7°56S 39°19W 189 B3
Sersale Italy 39°1N 16°43E 95 C9
Sertã Portugal 39°48N 8°6W 88 F2
Sertânia Brazil 8°5S 37°20W 189 B3
Sertanópolis Brazil 23°4S 51°2W 191 A5
Sêrtar China 32°20N 100°41E 116 A3
Serua Indonesia 6°18S 130°1E 119 F8
Serui Indonesia 1°53S 136°10E 119 E9
Serule Botswana 21°57S 27°20E 144 B4
Servia Greece 40°11N 22°0E 96 F6
Serzedelo Portugal 41°24N 8°14W 88 D2
Ses Salines Spain 39°21N 3°3E 100 B10
Sese Is. Uganda 0°20S 32°20E 142 C3
Sesepe Indonesia 1°30S 127°59E 119 E7
Sesfontein Namibia 19°7S 13°39E 144 A1
Sesheke Zambia 17°29S 24°13E 144 A3
Sésia → Italy 45°5N 8°37E 92 C5
Sesimbra Portugal 38°28N 9°6W 89 G1
S'Espalmador Spain 38°47N 1°26E 100 C7
S'Espardell Spain 38°48N 1°29E 100 C7
Sessa Aurunca Italy 41°14N 13°56E 94 A6
S'Estanyol Spain 39°22N 2°54E 100 B9
Sestao Spain 43°18N 3°0W 90 B2
Sesto Calende Italy 45°44N 8°37E 92 C5
Sesto San Giovanni Italy 45°31N 9°13E 92 C6
Sestri Levante Italy 44°16N 9°24E 92 D6
Sestriere Italy 44°57N 6°53E 92 D3
Sestroretsk Russia 60°5N 29°58E 84 B6
Sestrunj Croatia 44°10N 15°0E 93 D11
Sestu Italy 39°18N 9°5E 94 C2
Setana Japan 42°26N 139°51E 112 C9
Sète France 43°25N 3°42E 72 E7
Sete Cidades △ Brazil 4°0S 41°37W 189 A2
Sete Lagoas Brazil 19°27S 44°16W 189 D2
Seti → Nepal 28°59N 81°8E 125 E9
Sétif Algeria 36°9N 5°26E 136 A5
Sétif □ Algeria 36°10N 5°0E 136 A5
Seto Japan 35°14N 137°6E 113 G8
Setonaikai Japan 34°20N 133°30E 113 G6
Setonaikai △ Japan 34°15N 133°15E 113 G6
Settat Morocco 33°0N 7°40W 136 B2
Séttimo Torinese Italy 45°9N 7°46E 92 C4
Setting L. Canada 55°0N 98°38W 163 C9
Settle U.K. 54°5N 2°16W 66 C5
Settlement, The Br. Virgin Is. 18°43N 64°22W 183 e
Settlers S. Africa 25°2S 28°30E 145 C4
Setúbal Portugal 38°30N 8°58W 89 G2
Setúbal □ Portugal 38°25N 8°35W 89 G2
Setúbal, B. de Portugal 38°40N 8°56W 89 G2
Seugne → France 45°42N 0°32W 72 C3
Seul, Lac Canada 50°20N 92°30W 164 B1
Seurre France 47°0N 5°8E 71 F12
Sevan Armenia 40°33N 44°56E 87 K7
Sevan, Ozero = Sevana Lich Armenia 40°30N 45°20E 87 K7
Sevana Lich Armenia 40°30N 45°20E 87 K7
Sevastopol Ukraine 44°35N 33°30E 85 K7
Seven Sisters Canada 54°56N 128°10W 162 C3
Sever → Spain 39°40N 7°32W 89 F3
Sévérac-le-Château France 44°20N 3°5E 72 D7
Severn → Canada 56°2N 87°36W 164 A2
Severn → U.K. 51°35N 2°40W 67 F5
Severnaya Zemlya Russia 79°0N 100°0E 107 B11
Severno Kosovo Kosovo 43°29N 21°27E 96 C4
Severo-Kurilsk Russia 50°40N 156°8E 107 D16
Severo-Yeniseyskiy Russia 60°22N 93°1E 107 C10
Severo-Zapadnyy □ Russia 65°0N 40°0E 106 C4
Severobaykalsk Russia 55°39N 109°19E 107 D11
Severočeský □ Czech Rep. 50°30N 14°0E 78 A7
Severodonetsk = Syeverodonetsk Ukraine 48°58N 38°35E 85 H10
Severodvinsk Russia 64°27N 39°58E 106 C4
Severomoravský □ Czech Rep. 49°38N 17°40E 79 B10
Severomorsk Russia 69°5N 33°27E 60 B25
Seversk Russia 56°36N 84°49E 106 D9
Sevier → U.S.A. 39°4N 113°6W 168 G7
Sevier Desert U.S.A. 39°40N 112°45W 168 G7
Sevier L. U.S.A. 38°54N 113°9W 168 G7
Sevilla Spain 37°23N 5°58W 89 H5
Sevilla □ Spain 37°25N 5°30W 89 H5
Seville = Sevilla Spain 37°23N 5°58W 89 H5
Seville Fla., U.S.A. 29°19N 81°30W 179 F8
Seville Ga., U.S.A. 31°58N 83°36W 178 D6
Sevlievo Bulgaria 43°2N 25°6E 97 C9
Sevnica Slovenia 46°2N 15°19E 93 B12
Sèvre-Nantaise → France 47°12N 1°33W 70 E5
Sèvre-Niortaise → France 46°28N 0°50W 72 B3
Sevsk Russia 52°10N 34°30E 85 F8
Sewa → S. Leone 7°20N 12°10W 138 D2
Sewani India 28°58N 75°39E 124 E6
Seward Alaska, U.S.A. 60°7N 149°27W 160 E2
Seward Nebr., U.S.A. 40°55N 97°6W 172 E5
Seward Pa., U.S.A. 40°25N 79°1W 174 F5
Seward Peninsula U.S.A. 65°30N 166°0W 166 B6
Sewell Chile 34°10S 70°23W 190 C1
Sewer Indonesia 5°53S 134°40E 119 F8
Sewickley U.S.A. 40°32N 80°12W 174 F4
Sexsmith Canada 55°21N 118°47W 162 B5
Seychelles ■ Ind. Oc. 5°0S 56°0E 141 b
Seyðisfjörður Iceland 65°16N 13°57W 60 D7
Seydişehir Turkey 37°25N 31°51E 104 D4
Seydvān Iran 38°34N 45°2E 105 C11
Seyhan → Turkey 36°43N 34°53E 104 D6
Seyhan Barajı Turkey 37°2N 35°18E 104 D6
Seyitgazi Turkey 39°27N 30°43E 99 B12
Seyitömer Turkey 39°34N 29°52E 99 B11
Seym → Ukraine 51°27N 32°34E 85 G7
Seymen Turkey 41°6N 27°57E 97 E11
Seymour Australia 37°2S 145°10E 153 D6
Seymour S. Africa 32°33S 26°46E 145 D4
Seymour Conn., U.S.A. 41°24N 73°4W 175 E11
Seymour Ind., U.S.A. 38°58N 85°53W 173 F11
Seymour Tex., U.S.A. 33°35N 99°16W 176 E5
Seyne France 44°21N 6°22E 73 D10
Seyssel France 45°57N 5°50E 73 C9
Sežana Slovenia 45°43N 13°41E 93 C10
Sézanne France 48°40N 3°40E 71 D10
Sezze Italy 41°30N 13°3E 94 A6
Sfântu Gheorghe Covasna, Romania 45°52N 25°48E 81 E10
Sfântu Gheorghe Tulcea, Romania 44°53N 29°36E 81 F14
Sfântu Gheorghe, Braţul → Romania 44°51N 29°36E 81 F14
Sfax Tunisia 34°49N 10°48E 136 B6
Sfax □ Tunisia 34°40N 10°20E 136 B6
Sha Tau Kok China 22°33N 114°13E 111 a
Sha Tin China 22°23N 114°12E 111 a
Sha Xi → China 26°35N 118°0E 117 D12
Sha Xian China 26°23N 117°45E 117 D11
Shaanxi □ China 35°0N 109°0E 114 G5
Shaba = Katanga □ Dem. Rep. of the Congo 8°0S 25°0E 142 D2
Shaba ⌓ Kenya 0°38N 37°48E 142 B4
Shabeelle → Somalia 2°0N 44°0E 131 G3
Shabestar Iran 38°11N 45°41E 105 C11
Shabla Bulgaria 43°31N 28°32E 97 C12
Shabogamo L. Canada 53°15N 66°30W 165 B6
Shabunda Dem. Rep. of the Congo 2°40S 27°16E 142 C2
Shache China 38°20N 77°10E 109 E9
Shackleton Fracture Zone S. Ocean 60°0S 60°0W 55 B18
Shackleton Ice Shelf Antarctica 66°0S 100°0E 55 C8
Shackleton Inlet Antarctica 83°0S 160°0E 55 E11
Shādegān Iran 30°40N 48°38E 129 D6
Shadi China 26°7N 114°47E 117 D10
Shadi India 33°24N 77°14E 125 C7
Shadrinsk Russia 56°5N 63°32E 106 D7
Shady Dale U.S.A. 33°24N 83°36W 178 B6
Shady Grove U.S.A. 30°17N 83°38W 178 E6
Shadyside U.S.A. 39°58N 80°45W 174 G4
Shaffa Nigeria 10°30N 12°6E 139 C7
Shafter U.S.A. 35°30N 119°16W 171 K7
Shaftesbury U.K. 51°0N 2°11W 67 F5
Shaftsbury U.S.A. 43°0N 73°11W 175 D11
Shag Pt. N.Z. 45°29S 170°52E 155 F5
Shag Rocks Atl. Oc. 53°0S 41°0W 56 M7
Shagamu Nigeria 6°51N 3°39E 139 D5
Shagram Pakistan 36°24N 72°20E 125 A5
Shah Alam Malaysia 3°5N 101°32E 121 L3
Shah Alizai Pakistan 29°25N 66°33E 124 E2
Shah Bunder Pakistan 24°13N 67°56E 124 G2
Shahabad Karnataka, India 17°10N 76°54E 126 F3
Shahabad Punjab, India 30°10N 76°55E 124 D7
Shahabad Raj., India 25°15N 77°11E 124 G7
Shahabad Ut. P., India 27°36N 79°56E 125 F8
Shahada India 21°33N 74°30E 126 D2
Shahadpur Pakistan 25°55N 68°35E 124 G3
Shahapur India 15°50N 74°34E 127 G2
Shahbā' Syria 32°52N 36°38E 130 C5
Shahdād Iran 30°30N 57°40E 129 D8
Shahdād, Namakzār-e Iran 30°20N 58°20E 129 D8
Shahdadkot Pakistan 27°50N 67°55E 124 F2
Shahdol India 23°19N 81°26E 125 H9
Shahe China 37°0N 114°32E 114 F8
Shahganj India 26°3N 82°44E 125 F10
Shahgarh India 27°15N 69°50E 124 F3
Shahid Rajaee Port = Bandar Shahid Rajaee Iran 27°7N 56°4E 129 E8
Shāhīn Shahr Iran 32°49N 51°32E 129 C6
Shahjahanpur India 27°54N 79°57E 125 F8
Shahpur = Salmās Iran 38°11N 44°47E 105 C11
Shahpur Karnataka, India 16°40N 76°48E 126 F3
Shahpur Mad. P., India 22°12N 77°58E 124 H7
Shahpur Baluchistan, Pakistan 28°46N 68°27E 124 E3
Shahpur Punjab, Pakistan 32°17N 72°26E 124 C5
Shahpur Chakar Pakistan 26°9N 68°39E 124 F3
Shahpura Mad. P., India 23°10N 80°45E 125 H9
Shahpura Raj., India 25°38N 74°56E 124 G6
Shahr-e Bābak Iran 30°7N 55°9E 129 D7
Shahr-e Kord Iran 32°15N 50°55E 129 C6
Shāhrakht Iran 33°38N 60°16E 129 C9
Shāhrezā = Qomsheh Iran 32°0N 51°55E 129 D6
Shahrig Pakistan 30°15N 67°40E 124 D2
Shahrisabz Uzbekistan 39°3N 66°50E 109 E7
Shāhrud = Emāmrūd Iran 36°30N 55°0E 129 B7
Shahukou China 40°20N 112°18E 114 D7
Shaikhabad Afghan. 34°2N 68°45E 124 B3
Shajapur India 23°27N 76°21E 124 H7
Shajing China 22°44N 113°48E 111 a
Shakargarh Pakistan 32°17N 75°10E 124 C6
Shakawe Botswana 18°28S 21°49E 144 A3
Shaker Heights U.S.A. 41°28N 81°32W 174 E3
Shakhrisyabz = Shahrisabz Uzbekistan 39°3N 66°50E 109 E7
Shakhtersk Russia 49°10N 142°8E 107 E15
Shakhtīnsk Kazakhstan 49°42N 72°35E 109 C8
Shakhty Russia 47°40N 40°16E 87 G5
Shakhunya Russia 57°40N 46°46E 86 B8
Shaki Nigeria 8°41N 3°21E 139 D5
Shākir Egypt 27°30N 33°59E 137 B3
Shakotan-Hantō Japan 43°10N 140°30E 112 C10
Shaksam Valley Asia 36°0N 76°20E 125 A7
Shali Russia 43°9N 45°55E 87 J7
Shalkar Köli Kazakhstan 50°35N 51°47E 86 E10
Shallow Lake Canada 44°36N 81°5W 174 B3
Shalqar Kazakhstan 47°48N 59°39E 108 C5
Shalqar Köli Kazakhstan 50°33N 51°40E 108 B4
Shalskiy Russia 61°48N 35°58E 84 B8
Shaluli Shan China 30°40N 99°55E 116 B2
Shām Iran 26°39N 57°21E 129 E8
Shām, Bādiyat ash Asia 32°0N 40°0E 128 C3
Shamâl Sînî □ Egypt 30°30N 33°30E 130 E2
Shamattawa Canada 55°51N 92°5W 164 A1
Shamattawa → Canada 55°1N 85°23W 164 A2
Shamīl Iran 27°30N 56°55E 129 E8
Shamkhor = Şämkir Azerbaijan 40°50N 46°0E 87 K8
Shāmkūh Iran 35°47N 57°50E 129 C8
Shamli India 29°32N 77°18E 124 E7
Shammar, Jabal Si. Arabia 27°40N 41°0E 128 E4
Shamo = Gobi Asia 44°0N 110°0E 114 C6
Shamo, L. Ethiopia 5°45N 37°30E 131 F2
Shamokin U.S.A. 40°47N 76°34W 175 F8
Shamrock Canada 45°23N 76°50W 175 A8
Shamrock U.S.A. 35°13N 100°15W 176 D4
Shamva Zimbabwe 17°20S 31°32E 143 F3
Shan □ Burma 21°30N 98°30E 123 J21
Shan Xian China 34°50N 116°5E 114 G9
Shanchengzhen China 42°20N 125°20E 115 C13
Shāndak Iran 28°28N 60°27E 129 D9
Shandan China 38°45N 101°15E 110 D9
Shandon U.S.A. 35°39N 120°23W 170 K6
Shandong □ China 36°0N 118°0E 115 G10
Shandong Bandao China 37°0N 121°0E 115 F11
Shandur Pass Pakistan 36°4N 72°31E 125 A5
Shang Xian = Shangzhou China 33°50N 109°58E 114 H5
Shangalowe Dem. Rep. of the Congo 10°50S 26°30E 143 E2
Shangani Zimbabwe 19°41S 29°20E 145 A4
Shangani → Zimbabwe 18°41S 27°10E 143 F2
Shangbancheng China 40°50N 118°1E 115 D10
Shangcheng China 31°47N 115°26E 117 B10
Shangchuan Dao China 21°40N 112°50E 117 G9
Shangdu China 41°30N 113°30E 114 D7
Shanggao China 28°17N 114°55E 117 C10
Shanghai China 31°15N 121°26E 117 B13
Shanghai Shi □ China 31°0N 121°30E 117 B13
Shanghang China 25°2N 116°23E 117 E11
Shanghe China 37°20N 117°10E 115 F9
Shanglin China 23°27N 108°33E 116 F7
Shangnan China 33°32N 110°50E 114 H6
Shangqiu China 34°26N 115°36E 114 G8
Shangrao China 28°25N 117°59E 117 C11
Shangri-La = Zhongdian China 27°48N 99°42E 116 D2
Shangshui China 33°32N 114°35E 114 H8
Shangsi China 22°8N 107°58E 116 F6
Shangyi China 41°4N 113°57E 114 D7
Shangyou China 25°48N 114°32E 117 E10
Shangyu China 30°3N 120°52E 117 B13
Shangzhi China 45°22N 127°56E 115 B14
Shangzhou China 33°50N 109°58E 114 H5
Shanhetun China 44°33N 127°15E 115 B14
Shani Nigeria 10°14N 12°2E 139 C7
Shānidar Iraq 36°48N 44°14E 105 D11
Shanklin U.K. 50°38N 1°11W 67 G6
Shannon N.Z. 40°33S 175°25E 154 G4
Shannon → Ireland 52°35N 9°30W 64 D2
Shannon ✈ (SNN) Ireland 52°42N 8°57W 64 D3
Shannon, Mouth of the Ireland 52°30N 9°55W 64 D2
Shannon △ Australia 34°35S 116°25E 149 F2
Shannon Ø Greenland 75°10N 18°30W 57 B9
Shannonbridge Ireland 53°17N 8°3W 64 C3
Shannontown U.S.A. 33°53N 80°21W 178 B9
Shanshan China 42°52N 90°10E 109 D12
Shansi = Shanxi □ China 37°0N 112°0E 114 F7
Shantar, Ostrov Bolshoy Russia 55°9N 137°40E 107 D14
Shantipur India 23°17N 88°25E 125 H13
Shantou China 23°18N 116°40E 117 F11
Shantung = Shandong □ China 36°0N 118°0E 115 G10
Shanwei China 22°48N 115°22E 117 F10
Shanxi □ China 37°0N 112°0E 114 F7
Shanyang China 33°31N 109°55E 114 H5
Shanyin China 39°25N 112°56E 114 E7
Shaodong China 27°15N 111°43E 117 D8
Shaoguan China 24°48N 113°35E 117 E9
Shaoshan China 27°55N 112°33E 117 D9
Shaowu China 27°22N 117°28E 117 D11
Shaoxing China 30°0N 120°35E 117 C13
Shaoyang Hunan, China 26°59N 111°20E 117 D8
Shaoyang Hunan, China 27°14N 111°25E 117 D8
Shap U.K. 54°32N 2°40W 66 C5
Shapinsay U.K. 59°3N 2°51W 65 B6
Shaqlāwah Iraq 36°23N 44°20E 105 D11
Shaqra' Si. Arabia 25°15N 45°16E 128 E5
Shar Kazakhstan 49°35N 81°2E 109 C10
Sharafkhāneh Iran 38°11N 45°29E 105 C11
Sharashova Belarus 52°34N 24°12E 83 F11
Sharavati → India 14°20N 74°25E 127 G2
Sharbaqty Kazakhstan 51°23N 78°17E 109 B9
Sharbot Lake Canada 44°46N 76°41W 175 B8
Shardara, Step Kazakhstan 42°20N 68°0E 109 D7
Sharhorod Ukraine 48°45N 28°5E 81 B13
Shari Japan 43°55N 144°40E 112 C12
Sharjah = Ash Shāriqah U.A.E. 25°23N 55°26E 129 E7
Shark B. Australia 25°30S 113°32E 149 E1
Shark Bay △ Australia 25°30S 113°30E 149 E1
Sharm el Sheikh Egypt 27°53N 34°18E 137 B3
Sharon Canada 44°6N 79°26W 174 B5
Sharon Mass., U.S.A. 42°7N 71°11W 175 D13
Sharon Pa., U.S.A. 41°14N 80°31W 174 E4
Sharon Springs Kans., U.S.A. 38°54N 101°45W 172 F3
Sharon Springs N.Y., U.S.A. 42°48N 74°37W 175 D10
Sharp Pt. Australia 10°58S 142°43E 150 A3
Sharpe L. Canada 54°24N 93°40W 164 B1
Sharpes U.S.A. 28°26N 80°46W 179 G9
Sharpsville U.S.A. 41°15N 80°29W 174 E4
Sharqi, Al Jabal ash Lebanon 33°40N 36°10E 130 B5
Sharr Kosovo 42°5N 20°41E 96 D4
Sharya Russia 58°22N 45°20E 86 A7
Shashemene Ethiopia 7°13N 38°33E 131 F2
Shashi Botswana 21°15S 27°27E 145 B4
Shashi → Africa 21°14S 29°20E 143 G2
Shasta, Mt. U.S.A. 41°25N 122°12W 168 F2
Shasta L. U.S.A. 40°43N 122°25W 168 F2
Shatsk Russia 54°5N 41°45E 86 C5
Shatsk Ukraine 51°29N 23°55E 83 G10
Shatsky Rise Pac. Oc. 34°0N 157°0E 156 D7
Shatskyy ⌓ Ukraine 51°30N 23°52E 83 G10
Shatt al Arab Asia 29°57N 48°34E 129 D6
Shatura Russia 55°33N 39°21E 84 E10
Shaumyani = Shulaveri Georgia 41°22N 44°45E 87 K7
Shaunavon Canada 49°35N 108°25W 163 D7
Shaver L. U.S.A. 37°9N 119°18W 170 H7
Shaw → Australia 20°21S 119°17E 148 D2
Shaw I. Australia 20°30S 149°2E 150 b
Shawanaga Canada 45°31N 80°17W 174 A4
Shawangunk Mts. U.S.A. 41°35N 74°30W 175 E10
Shawano U.S.A. 44°47N 88°36W 172 C9
Shawinigan Canada 46°35N 72°50W 164 C5
Shawmari, J. ash Jordan 30°35N 36°35E 130 E5
Shawnee Ga., U.S.A. 32°29N 81°25W 178 C8
Shawnee Okla., U.S.A. 35°20N 96°55W 176 D6
Shay Gap Australia 20°30S 120°10E 148 D3
Shayang China 30°42N 112°29E 117 B9
Shaybārā Si. Arabia 25°26N 36°47E 128 E3
Shayib el Banat, Gebel Egypt 26°59N 33°29E 137 B3
Shaykh, J. ash Lebanon 33°25N 35°50E 130 B4
Shaykh Miskīn Syria 32°49N 36°9E 130 C5
Shaykh Sa'd Iraq 32°34N 46°17E 105 F12
Shaykh 'Uthmān Yemen 12°52N 44°59E 131 E3
Shāzand Iran 33°56N 49°24E 129 C6
Shazud Tajikistan 37°45N 72°25E 109 E8
Shchekino Russia 54°1N 37°34E 84 E9
Shchigry Russia 51°55N 36°58E 85 G9
Shchors Ukraine 51°48N 31°56E 85 G6
Shchūchīnsk Kazakhstan 52°56N 70°12E 109 B8
She Xian Anhui, China 29°50N 118°25E 117 C12
She Xian Hebei, China 36°30N 113°40E 114 F7
Shebekino Russia 50°28N 36°54E 85 G9
Shebele = Shabeelle → Somalia 2°0N 44°0E 131 G3
Sheberghān Afghan. 36°40N 65°45E 109 E7
Sheboygan U.S.A. 43°46N 87°45W 172 D10
Shebshi Mts. Nigeria 8°30N 12°0E 139 D7
Shediac Canada 46°14N 64°32W 165 C7
Sheelin, L. Ireland 53°48N 7°20W 64 C4
Sheenjek → U.S.A. 66°45N 144°33W 166 B11
Sheep Haven Ireland 55°11N 7°52W 64 A4
Sheep Range U.S.A. 36°35N 115°15W 171 J11
Sheerness U.K. 51°26N 0°47E 67 F8
Sheet Harbour Canada 44°56N 62°31W 165 D7
Sheffield N.Z. 43°23S 172°1E 155 D7
Sheffield U.K. 53°23N 1°28W 66 D6
Sheffield Ala., U.S.A. 34°46N 87°41W 177 D11
Sheffield Mass., U.S.A. 42°5N 73°21W 175 D11
Sheffield Pa., U.S.A. 41°42N 79°3W 174 E5
Shegaon India 20°48N 76°47E 126 D3
Shehong China 30°54N 105°18E 116 B5
Shehuen → Argentina 49°35S 69°34W 192 C3
Sheikh Zayed Canal Egypt 23°30N 30°15E 137 C3
Sheikhpura India 25°9N 85°53E 125 G11
Shekhupura Pakistan 31°42N 73°58E 124 D5
Sheki = Şaki Azerbaijan 41°10N 47°5E 87 K8
Shekou China 22°30N 113°55E 111 a
Shelburne N.S., Canada 43°47N 65°20W 165 D6
Shelburne Ont., Canada 44°4N 80°15W 174 B4
Shelburne U.S.A. 44°23N 73°14W 175 B11
Shelburne B. Australia 11°50S 142°50E 150 A3
Shelburne Falls U.S.A. 42°36N 72°45W 175 D12
Shelby Mich., U.S.A. 43°37N 86°22W 172 D10
Shelby Miss., U.S.A. 33°57N 90°46W 177 E9
Shelby Mont., U.S.A. 48°30N 111°51W 168 B8
Shelby N.C., U.S.A. 35°17N 81°32W 177 D14
Shelby Ohio, U.S.A. 40°53N 82°40W 174 F2
Shelbyville Ill., U.S.A. 39°24N 88°48W 172 F9
Shelbyville Ind., U.S.A. 39°31N 85°47W 173 F11
Shelbyville Ky., U.S.A. 38°13N 85°14W 173 F11
Shelbyville Tenn., U.S.A. 35°29N 86°28W 177 D11
Sheldon Iowa, U.S.A. 43°11N 95°51W 172 D6
Sheldon S.C., U.S.A. 32°36N 80°48W 178 C9
Sheldrake Canada 50°20N 64°51W 165 B7
Shelek Kazakhstan 43°33N 78°17E 109 D9
Shelikhova, Zaliv Russia 59°30N 157°0E 107 D16
Shelikof Strait U.S.A. 57°30N 155°0W 166 D9
Shell Lakes Australia 29°20S 127°30E 149 E4
Shellbrook Canada 53°13N 106°24W 163 C7
Shellharbour Australia 34°31S 150°51E 153 C9
Shellman U.S.A. 31°46N 84°37W 178 D5
Shelon → Russia 58°13N 30°47E 84 C6
Shelter I. U.S.A. 41°4N 72°20W 175 E12
Shelton Conn., U.S.A. 41°19N 73°5W 175 E11
Shelton Wash., U.S.A. 47°13N 123°6W 170 C3
Shemakha = Şamaxı Azerbaijan 40°38N 48°37E 87 K9
Shemonaïkha Kazakhstan 50°37N 81°54E 109 B10
Shëmri Albania 42°7N 20°13E 96 D4
Shemsi Sudan 19°2N 29°57E 137 D2
Shen Xian China 36°15N 115°40E 114 F8
Shenandoah Iowa, U.S.A. 40°46N 95°22W 172 E6
Shenandoah Pa., U.S.A. 40°49N 76°12W 175 F8
Shenandoah Va., U.S.A. 38°29N 78°37W 173 F14
Shenandoah → U.S.A. 39°19N 77°44W 173 F15
Shenandoah △ U.S.A. 38°35N 78°22W 173 F14
Shenchi China 39°8N 112°10E 114 E7
Shencottah India 8°59N 77°18E 127 K3
Shendam Nigeria 8°49N 9°30E 139 D6
Shendî Sudan 16°46N 33°22E 135 E12
Shendurni India 20°39N 75°36E 126 D2
Shenge S. Leone 7°54N 12°55W 138 D2
Shengfang China 39°3N 116°42E 114 E9
Shëngjergj Albania 41°17N 20°10E 96 E4
Shëngjin Albania 41°50N 19°35E 96 E3
Shengzhou China 29°35N 120°50E 117 C13
Shenjingzi China 44°40N 124°30E 115 B13
Shenmu China 38°50N 110°29E 114 E6
Shennongjia China 31°43N 110°44E 117 B8
Shenqiu China 33°25N 115°5E 114 H8
Shensi = Shaanxi □ China 35°0N 109°0E 114 G5
Shenyang China 41°48N 123°27E 115 D12
Shenzhen China 22°32N 114°5E 117 F10
Shenzhen Bao'an Int. ✈ (SZX) China 22°41N 113°49E 111 a
Shenzhen Shuiku China 22°34N 114°8E 111 a
Shenzhen Wan China 22°27N 113°55E 111 a
Sheo India 26°11N 71°15E 124 F4
Sheopur Kalan India 25°40N 76°40E 124 G7
Shepetivka Ukraine 50°10N 27°10E 75 C14
Shepparton Australia 36°23S 145°26E 153 D6
Sheppey, I. of U.K. 51°25N 0°48E 67 F8
Shepton Mallet U.K. 51°11N 2°33W 67 F5
Sheqi China 33°12N 112°57E 114 H7
Sher Qila Pakistan 36°7N 74°2E 125 A6
Sherabad Uzbekistan 37°40N 67°1E 109 E7
Sherborne U.K. 50°57N 2°31W 67 G5
Sherbro → S. Leone 7°45N 12°55W 138 D2
Sherbro I. S. Leone 7°30N 12°40W 138 D2
Sherbrooke N.S., Canada 45°8N 61°59W 165 C7
Sherbrooke Qué., Canada 45°28N 71°57W 175 A13
Sherburne U.S.A. 42°41N 75°30W 175 D9
Shereik Sudan 18°44N 33°47E 137 D3
Shergarh India 26°20N 72°18E 124 F5
Sherghati India 24°34N 84°47E 125 G11
Sheridan Ark., U.S.A. 34°19N 92°24W 176 D8
Sheridan Wyo., U.S.A. 44°48N 106°58W 168 D10
Sheringham U.K. 52°56N 1°13E 66 E9
Sherkin I. Ireland 51°28N 9°26W 64 E2
Sherkot India 29°22N 78°35E 125 E8
Sherlovaya Gora Russia 50°34N 116°15E 107 D12
Sherman N.Y., U.S.A. 42°9N 79°35W 174 D5
Sherman Tex., U.S.A. 33°38N 96°36W 176 E6
Sherpur India 25°34N 83°47E 125 G10
Sherridon Canada 55°8N 101°5W 163 B8
Shertallai = Cherthala India 9°42N 76°20E 127 K3
Sherwood Forest U.K. 53°6N 1°7W 66 D6
Sherwood Park Canada 53°31N 113°19W 162 C6
Sheslay → Canada 58°48N 132°5W 162 B2
Shethanei L. Canada 58°48N 97°50W 163 B9
Shetland □ U.K. 60°30N 1°30W 65 A7
Shetland Is. U.K. 60°30N 1°30W 65 A7
Shetpe Kazakhstan 44°10N 52°7E 108 D4
Shetrunji → India 21°19N 72°7E 124 J5
Sheung Shui China 22°31N 114°7E 111 a
Shevaroy Hills India 11°58N 78°12E 127 J4
Shevchenkovo Ukraine 45°33N 29°20E 81 E14
Shevgaon India 19°21N 75°14E 126 E2
Shevisheh Iran 35°21N 46°40E 105 E12
Shey-Phoksundo △ Nepal 29°30N 82°45E 125 E10
Sheyang China 33°48N 120°29E 115 H11
Sheyenne → U.S.A. 47°2N 96°50W 172 B5
Shiashkotan, Ostrov Russia 48°49N 154°6E 107 E16
Shibām Yemen 15°59N 48°36E 131 D4
Shibata Japan 37°57N 139°20E 112 F9
Shibecha Japan 43°17N 144°36E 112 C12
Shibetsu Hokkaidō, Japan 43°30N 145°10E 112 C12
Shibetsu Hokkaidō, Japan 44°10N 142°23E 112 B11
Shibîn el Kôm Egypt 30°31N 30°55E 137 E7
Shibîn el Qanâtir Egypt 30°19N 31°19E 137 E7
Shibing China 27°2N 108°7E 116 D7
Shibogama L. Canada 53°35N 88°15W 164 B2
Shibushi Japan 31°25N 131°8E 113 J5
Shicheng China 26°22N 116°20E 117 D11
Shickshinny U.S.A. 41°9N 76°9W 175 E8
Shickshock Mts. = Chic-Chocs, Mts. Canada 48°55N 66°0W 165 C6
Shidao China 36°50N 122°25E 115 F12
Shiderti → Kazakhstan 52°32N 74°50E 109 B8
Shidian China 24°40N 99°5E 116 E2
Shido = Sanuki Japan 34°19N 134°10E 113 G7
Shiel, L. U.K. 56°48N 5°34W 65 E3
Shield, C. Australia 13°20S 136°20E 150 A2
Shīeli Kazakhstan 44°20N 66°15E 109 D7
Shifang China 31°8N 104°10E 116 B5
Shiga □ Japan 35°20N 136°0E 113 G8
Shigu China 26°51N 99°56E 116 D2
Shiguaigou China 40°52N 110°15E 114 D6

Shihchiachuangi = Shijiazhuang China 38°2N 114°28E 114 E8
Shihezi China 44°15N 86°2E 109 D11
Shijak Albania 41°21N 19°33E 96 E3
Shijiazhuang China 38°2N 114°28E 114 E8
Shiju Hu China 31°25N 118°50E 117 B12
Shikarpur India 28°17N 78°7E 124 E8
Shikarpur Pakistan 27°57N 68°39E 124 F3
Shikohabad India 27°6N 78°36E 125 F8
Shikokochūō Japan 34°1N 133°34E 113 G6
Shikoku □ Japan 33°30N 133°30E 113 H6
Shikoku-Sanchi Japan 33°30N 133°30E 113 H6
Shikotan, Ostrov Asia 43°47N 146°44E 107 E15
Shikotsu-Ko Japan 42°45N 141°25E 112 C10
Shikotsu-Tōya △ Japan 44°4N 145°8E 112 C10
Shiliguri India 26°45N 88°25E 123 F16
Shiliu = Changjiang China 19°20N 108°55E 117 a
Shilka Russia 52°0N 115°55E 107 D12
Shilka → Russia 53°20N 121°26E 107 D13
Shillelagh Ireland 52°45N 6°32W 64 D5
Shillington U.S.A. 40°18N 75°58W 175 F9
Shillong India 25°35N 91°53E 123 G17
Shilo West Bank 32°4N 35°18E 130 C4
Shilong China 23°5N 113°52E 117 F9
Shilou China 37°0N 110°48E 114 F6
Shilovo Russia 54°25N 40°57E 86 C5
Shimabara Japan 32°48N 130°20E 113 H5
Shimada Japan 34°49N 138°10E 113 G9
Shimane □ Japan 35°0N 132°30E 113 G6
Shimanovsk Russia 52°15N 127°30E 107 D13
Shimanto Kōchi, Japan 33°12N 133°8E 113 H6
Shimanto Kōchi, Japan 32°59N 132°56E 113 H6
Shimba Hills ⌂ Kenya 4°14S 39°25E 142 C4
Shimbiris Somalia 10°44N 47°14E 131 E4
Shimen China 29°35N 111°20E 117 C8
Shimenjie China 29°29N 116°48E 117 C11
Shimian China 29°17N 102°23E 116 C4
Shimizu Japan 35°0N 138°30E 113 G9
Shimla India 31°2N 77°9E 124 D7
Shimodate Japan 36°20N 139°55E 113 F9
Shimoga India 13°57N 75°32E 127 H2
Shimokita-Hantō Japan 41°20N 141°0E 112 D10
Shimoni Kenya 4°38S 39°20E 142 C4
Shimonoseki Japan 33°58N 130°55E 113 H5
Shimpuru Rapids Namibia 17°45S 19°55E 144 A2
Shimsha → India 13°15N 77°10E 127 H3
Shimsk Russia 58°15N 30°50E 84 C6
Shin, L. U.K. 58°5N 4°30W 65 C4
Shinan China 22°44N 109°53E 116 F7
Shinano-Gawa → Japan 36°50N 138°30E 113 F9
Shināş Oman 24°46N 56°28E 129 E8
Shīndand Afghan. 33°12N 62°8E 122 C3
Shinglehouse U.S.A. 41°58N 78°12W 174 E6
Shingū Japan 33°40N 135°55E 113 H7
Shingwidzi S. Africa 23°5S 31°25E 145 B5
Shinjō Japan 38°46N 140°18E 112 E10
Shinkafe Nigeria 13°8N 6°29E 139 C6
Shinkolobwe Dem. Rep. of the Congo 11°10S 26°40E 140 G5
Shinshār Syria 34°36N 36°43E 130 A5
Shintuya Peru 12°41S 71°15W 188 C3
Shinyanga Tanzania 3°45S 33°27E 142 C3
Shinyanga □ Tanzania 3°50S 34°0E 142 C3
Shio-no-Misaki Japan 33°25N 135°45E 113 H7
Shiogama Japan 38°19N 141°1E 112 E10
Shiojiri Japan 36°6N 137°58E 113 F8
Shipchenski Prokhod Bulgaria 42°45N 25°15E 97 D9
Shiphoirt, L. = Seaforth, L. U.K. 57°52N 6°36W 65 D2
Shiping China 23°45N 102°23E 116 F4
Shippagan Canada 47°45N 64°45W 165 C7
Shippensburg U.S.A. 40°3N 77°31W 174 F7
Shippenville U.S.A. 41°15N 79°28W 174 E5
Shiprock U.S.A. 36°47N 108°41W 169 H9
Shiqian China 27°32N 108°13E 116 D7
Shiqma, N. → Israel 31°37N 34°30E 130 D3
Shiquan China 33°5N 108°15E 116 A7
Shiquan He = Indus → Pakistan 24°20N 67°47E 124 G2
Shīr Kūh Iran 31°39N 54°3E 129 D7
Shira'awh Qatar 25°2N 52°14E 129 E7
Shirabad = Sherabad Uzbekistan 37°40N 67°1E 109 E7
Shiragami-Misaki Japan 41°24N 140°12E 112 D10
Shirakawa Fukushima, Japan 37°7N 140°13E 113 F10
Shirakawa Gifu, Japan 36°17N 136°56E 113 F8
Shirane-San Gumma, Japan 36°48N 139°22E 113 F9
Shirane-San Yamanashi, Japan 35°42N 138°9E 113 G9
Shiraoi Japan 42°33N 141°21E 112 C10
Shīrāz Iran 29°42N 52°30E 129 D7
Shirbīn Egypt 31°11N 31°32E 137 E7
Shire → Africa 17°42S 35°19E 143 F4
Shiren China 41°57N 126°34E 115 D14
Shiretoko △ Japan 44°15N 145°15E 112 B12
Shiretoko-Misaki Japan 44°21N 145°20E 112 B12
Shirinab → Pakistan 30°15N 66°28E 124 D2
Shiriya-Zaki Japan 41°25N 141°30E 112 D10
Shiroishi Japan 38°0N 140°37E 112 F10
Shirol India 16°47N 74°41E 126 F2
Shiroro Res. Nigeria 9°56N 6°54E 139 D6
Shirpur India 21°21N 74°57E 126 D2
Shirshov Ridge Pac. Oc. 58°0N 170°0E 156 B8
Shīrvān Iran 37°30N 57°50E 129 B8
Shirwa, L. = Chilwa, L. Malawi 15°15S 35°40E 143 F4
Shishaldin Volcano U.S.A. 54°45N 163°58W 166 E7
Shishi China 24°44N 118°37E 117 E12
Shishou China 29°38N 112°22E 117 C9
Shitai China 30°12N 117°25E 117 B11
Shithāthah Iraq 32°34N 43°28E 105 G10
Shivamogga = Shimoga India 13°57N 75°32E 127 H2
Shivpuri India 25°26N 77°42E 124 G7
Shixian China 43°5N 129°50E 115 C15
Shixing China 24°46N 114°5E 117 E10
Shiyan Guangdong, China 22°42N 113°56E 111 a
Shiyan Hubei, China 32°35N 110°45E 117 A8
Shiyan Shuiku China 22°42N 113°54E 111 a
Shiyata Egypt 29°25N 25°7E 137 B2
Shizhu China 29°58N 108°7E 116 C7
Shizong China 24°50N 104°0E 116 E5
Shizuishan China 39°15N 106°50E 114 E4
Shizuoka Japan 34°57N 138°24E 113 G9
Shizuoka □ Japan 35°15N 138°40E 113 G9
Shkhara Georgia 43°0N 43°8E 105 A10
Shklov = Shklow Belarus 54°16N 30°15E 75 A16
Shklow Belarus 54°16N 30°15E 75 A16
Shkodër Albania 42°4N 19°32E 96 D3
Shkumbini → Albania 41°2N 19°31E 96 E3
Shmidta, Ostrov Russia 81°0N 91°0E 107 A10
Shō-Gawa → Japan 36°47N 137°4E 113 F8
Shoal L. Canada 49°33N 95°1W 163 D9
Shoal Lake Canada 50°30N 100°35W 163 C8
Shoalhaven → Australia 34°54S 150°42E 153 C9
Shōdo-Shima Japan 34°30N 134°15E 113 G7
Sholapur = Solapur India 17°43N 75°56E 126 F2
Shōmrōn West Bank 32°15N 35°13E 130 C4
Shonzhy Kazakhstan 43°32N 79°28E 109 D9
Shoranur India 10°46N 76°19E 127 J3
Shorapur India 16°31N 76°48E 127 F3
Shoreham U.S.A. 43°53N 73°18W 175 C11
Shoreham by Sea U.K. 50°50N 0°16W 67 G7
Shori → Pakistan 28°29N 69°44E 124 E3
Shorkot Pakistan 30°50N 72°0E 124 D4
Shorkot Road Pakistan 30°47N 72°15E 124 D5
Shorsky △ Russia 52°40N 88°0E 109 B11
Shorter U.S.A. 32°24N 85°57W 178 C4
Shorterville U.S.A. 31°34N 85°6W 178 D4
Shortt's I. India 20°47N 87°4E 126 D8
Shoshone Calif., U.S.A. 35°58N 116°16W 171 K10
Shoshone Idaho, U.S.A. 42°56N 114°25W 168 E6
Shoshone L. U.S.A. 44°22N 110°43W 168 D8
Shoshone Mts. U.S.A. 39°20N 117°25W 168 G5
Shoshong Botswana 22°56S 26°31E 144 B4
Shoshoni U.S.A. 43°14N 108°7W 168 E9
Shostka Ukraine 51°57N 33°32E 85 G7
Shot Iran 39°12N 44°49E 105 C11
Shotover → N.Z. 44°59S 168°41E 155 E3
Shou Xian China 32°37N 116°42E 117 A11
Shouchang China 29°18N 119°12E 117 C12
Shouguang China 37°52N 118°45E 115 F10
Shouning China 27°27N 119°31E 117 D12
Shouyang China 37°54N 113°8E 114 F7
Show Low U.S.A. 34°15N 110°2W 169 J8
Shpola Ukraine 49°1N 31°30E 85 H6
Shpykiv Ukraine 48°47N 28°34E 81 B13
Shqipëria = Albania ■ Europe 41°0N 20°0E 96 E4
Shreveport U.S.A. 32°31N 93°45W 176 E8
Shrewsbury U.K. 52°43N 2°45W 67 E5
Shri Mohangarh India 27°17N 71°18E 124 F4
Shrigonda India 18°37N 74°41E 126 E2
Shrirampur India 22°44N 88°21E 125 H13
Shropshire □ U.K. 52°36N 2°45W 67 E5
Shtërpcë Kosovo 42°14N 21°1E 96 D5
Shū Kazakhstan 43°36N 73°42E 109 D8
Shū → Kazakhstan 45°0N 67°44E 109 D7
Shuangbai China 24°42N 101°38E 116 E3
Shuangcheng China 45°20N 126°15E 115 B14
Shuangfeng China 27°29N 112°11E 117 D9
Shuanggou China 34°2N 117°30E 115 G9
Shuangjiang China 23°26N 99°58E 116 F2
Shuangliao China 43°29N 123°30E 115 C12
Shuangshanzi China 40°20N 119°8E 115 D10
Shuangyang China 43°28N 125°40E 115 C13
Shuangyashan China 46°28N 131°5E 111 B15
Shubarqudyq Kazakhstan 49°13N 56°34E 108 C5
Shubarshī Kazakhstan 48°39N 57°11E 108 C5
Shubrâ el Kheima Egypt 30°4N 31°14E 137 E7
Shubrâ Khit Egypt 31°2N 30°42E 137 E7
Shucheng China 31°28N 116°57E 117 B11
Shugozero Russia 59°54N 34°10E 84 C8
Shuguri Falls Tanzania 8°33S 37°22E 143 D4
Shuiding = Huocheng China 44°0N 80°48E 109 D10
Shuiji China 27°13N 118°20E 117 D12
Shujalpur India 23°18N 76°46E 124 H7
Shukpa Kunzang India 34°22N 78°22E 125 B8
Shulan China 44°28N 127°0E 115 B14
Shulaveri Georgia 41°22N 44°45E 87 K7
Shule China 39°25N 76°3E 109 E9
Shule He → China 40°20N 92°50E 110 C7
Shumagin Is. U.S.A. 55°7N 160°30W 166 D7
Shumanay Uzbekistan 42°38N 58°55E 108 D5
Shumen Bulgaria 43°18N 26°55E 97 C10
Shumerlya Russia 55°30N 46°25E 86 C8
Shumikha Russia 55°10N 63°15E 106 D7
Shunān Japan 34°3N 131°50E 113 G5
Shunchang China 26°54N 117°48E 117 D11
Shunde China 22°42N 113°14E 117 F9
Shungay Kazakhstan 48°30N 46°45E 87 F8
Shungnak U.S.A. 66°52N 157°9W 166 B8
Shuo Xian = Shuozhou China 39°20N 112°33E 114 E7
Shuozhou China 39°20N 112°33E 114 E7
Shuqrā' Yemen 13°22N 45°44E 131 E4
Shūr → Fārs, Iran 28°30N 55°0E 129 D7
Shūr → Kermān, Iran 30°52N 57°37E 129 D8
Shūr → Yazd, Iran 31°45N 55°15E 129 D7
Shūr Āb Iran 34°23N 51°11E 129 C6
Shūr Gaz Iran 29°10N 59°20E 129 D8
Shūrāb Iran 33°43N 56°29E 129 C8
Shūrjestān Iran 31°24N 52°25E 129 D7
Shurugwi Zimbabwe 19°40S 30°0E 143 F3
Shūsf Iran 31°50N 60°5E 129 D9
Shūsh Iran 32°11N 48°15E 105 F13
Shusha Azerbaijan 39°46N 46°45E 105 C12
Shushenskoye Russia 53°19N 91°56E 109 B12
Shushensky Bor △ Russia 52°40N 91°15E 109 B12
Shūshtar Iran 32°0N 48°50E 129 D6
Shuswap L. Canada 50°55N 119°3W 162 C5
Shute Harbour △ Australia 20°17S 148°47E 150 b
Shuya Russia 56°50N 41°28E 86 B5
Shuyang China 34°10N 118°42E 115 G10
Shūzū Iran 29°52N 54°30E 129 D7
Shwebo Burma 22°30N 95°45E 123 H19
Shwegu Burma 24°15N 96°26E 123 G20
Shweli → Burma 23°45N 96°45E 123 H20
Shyamnagar India 13°21N 92°57E 127 H11
Shyghanaq Kazakhstan 45°6N 73°59E 109 C8
Shyghys Qazaqstan □ Kazakhstan 48°30N 82°0E 109 D10
Shymkent Kazakhstan 42°18N 69°36E 109 D7
Shyok India 34°13N 78°12E 125 B8
Shyok → Pakistan 35°13N 75°53E 125 B6
Shyroke Odesa, Ukraine 45°59N 30°5E 81 E15
Shyroke Ternopil, Ukraine 48°13N 23°6E 80 B8
Si Kiang = Xi Jiang → China 22°5N 113°20E 117 F9
Si Lanna △ Thailand 19°17N 99°12E 120 C2
Si Nakarin Res. Thailand 14°35N 99°0E 120 E2
Si-ngan = Xi'an China 34°15N 109°0E 114 G5
Si Phangnga Thailand 9°8N 98°29E 121 H2
Si Prachan Thailand 14°37N 100°9E 120 E3
Si Racha Thailand 13°10N 100°48E 120 F3
Si Sa Ket Thailand 15°8N 104°23E 120 E5
Siachen Glacier Asia 35°20N 77°30E 125 B7
Siāh Chashmeh Iran 39°3N 44°25E 105 C11
Siahaf → Pakistan 29°3N 68°57E 124 E3
Siahan Range Pakistan 27°30N 64°40E 122 F4
Siak Sri Indrapura Indonesia 0°51N 102°0E 118 D2
Sialkot Pakistan 32°32N 74°30E 124 C6
Siam = Thailand ■ Asia 16°0N 102°0E 120 E4
Sian = Xi'an China 34°15N 109°0E 114 G5
Sian Ka'an ⌂ Mexico 19°35N 87°40W 181 D7
Sianów Poland 54°13N 16°18E 82 D3
Siantan Indonesia 3°10N 106°15E 118 D3
Siāreh Iran 28°5N 60°14E 129 D9
Siargao I. Phil. 9°52N 126°3E 119 C7
Siasi Phil. 5°34N 120°50E 119 C6
Siatista Greece 40°15N 21°33E 96 F5
Siau Indonesia 2°50N 125°25E 119 D7
Šiauliai Lithuania 55°56N 23°15E 82 C10
Šiauliai □ Lithuania 55°56N 23°19E 82 C10
Siavonga Zambia 16°33S 28°42E 145 A4
Siazan = Siyäzän Azerbaijan 41°3N 49°10E 87 K9
Sibâi, Gebel el Egypt 25°45N 34°10E 128 E2
Sibang Indonesia 8°34S 115°13E 119 K18
Sibay Russia 52°42N 58°39E 108 B5
Sibayi, L. S. Africa 27°20S 32°45E 145 C5
Šibenik Croatia 43°48N 15°54E 93 E12
Siberia = Sibirskiy □ Russia 58°0N 90°0E 107 D10
Siberia Russia 60°0N 100°0E 102 B12
Siberut Indonesia 1°30S 99°0E 118 E1
Sibi Pakistan 29°30N 67°54E 124 E2
Sibiloi △ Kenya 4°0N 36°20E 142 B4
Sibirskiy □ Russia 58°0N 90°0E 107 D10
Sibirtsevo Russia 44°12N 132°26E 112 B5
Sibiti Congo 3°38S 13°19E 140 E2
Sibiu Romania 45°45N 24°9E 81 E9
Sibiu □ Romania 45°50N 24°15E 81 E9
Sibley U.S.A. 43°24N 95°45W 172 D6
Sibo Sweden 61°13N 16°37E 62 C10
Sibolga Indonesia 1°42N 98°45E 118 D1
Siborongborong Indonesia 2°13N 98°58E 121 L2
Sibsagar India 27°0N 94°36E 123 F19
Sibu Malaysia 2°18N 111°49E 118 D4
Sibuco Phil. 7°20N 122°10E 119 C6
Sibuguey B. Phil. 7°50N 122°45E 119 C6
Sibut C.A.R. 5°46N 19°10E 140 C3
Sibutu Phil. 4°45N 119°30E 119 D5
Sibutu Passage E. Indies 4°50N 120°0E 119 D6
Sibuyan I. Phil. 12°25N 122°40E 119 B6
Sibuyan Sea Phil. 12°30N 122°20E 119 B6
Sic Romania 46°56N 23°53E 81 D8
Sicamous Canada 50°49N 119°0W 162 C5
Sicasica Bolivia 17°22S 67°45W 188 D4
Siccus → Australia 31°55S 139°17E 152 A3
Sichon Thailand 9°0N 99°54E 121 H2
Sichuan □ China 30°30N 103°0E 116 B5
Sichuan Pendi China 31°0N 105°0E 116 B5
Sicilia Italy 37°30N 14°30E 95 E7
Sicily = Sicilia Italy 37°30N 14°30E 95 E7
Sicily, Str. of Medit. S. 37°35N 11°56E 94 E4
Sico → Honduras 15°58N 84°58W 182 C3
Sicuani Peru 14°21S 71°10W 188 C3
Šid Serbia 45°8N 19°14E 80 E4
Sidaouet Niger 18°34N 8°3E 139 B6
Sidari Greece 39°47N 19°41E 101 A3
Siddapur India 14°20N 74°53E 127 G2
Siddhapur India 23°56N 72°25E 124 H5
Siddipet India 18°5N 78°51E 126 E4
Sidensjö Sweden 63°18N 18°17E 62 A12
Sidéradougou Burkina Faso 10°42N 4°12W 138 C4
Siderno Italy 38°16N 16°18E 95 D9
Sideros, Akra Greece 35°19N 26°19E 101 D8
Sidhauli India 27°17N 80°50E 125 F9
Sidhi India 24°25N 81°53E 125 G9
Sîdi Abd el Rahmân Egypt 30°55N 29°44E 137 E6
Sîdi Barrâni Egypt 31°38N 25°58E 137 A2
Sidi-bel-Abbès Algeria 35°13N 0°39W 136 A3
Sidi-bel-Abbès □ Algeria 34°50N 0°30W 136 B3
Sidi Bennour Morocco 32°40N 8°25W 136 B2
Sidi Bou Zid Tunisia 35°1N 9°16E 136 B5
Sidi Bou Zid □ Tunisia 35°0N 9°30E 136 B5
Sidi Boubekeur Algeria 35°1N 0°4E 136 A4
Sidi Haneish Egypt 31°10N 27°35E 137 A2
Sidi Ifni Morocco 29°29N 10°12W 134 C3
Sidi Kacem Morocco 34°12N 5°42W 136 B2
Sidi Omar Egypt 31°24N 24°57E 137 A1
Sidi Slimane Morocco 34°16N 5°56W 136 B2
Sidi Smaïl Morocco 32°50N 8°31W 136 B2
Sidikalang Indonesia 2°45N 98°19E 121 L2
Sidirokastro Greece 41°13N 23°24E 96 E7
Sidlaw Hills U.K. 56°32N 3°2W 65 E5
Sidley, Mt. Antarctica 77°2S 126°2W 55 D14
Sidmouth U.K. 50°40N 3°15W 67 G4
Sidmouth, C. Australia 13°25S 143°36E 150 A3
Sidney Canada 48°39N 123°24W 170 B3
Sidney Mont., U.S.A. 47°43N 104°9W 168 C11
Sidney N.Y., U.S.A. 42°19N 75°24W 175 D9
Sidney Nebr., U.S.A. 41°8N 102°59W 172 E2
Sidney Ohio, U.S.A. 40°17N 84°9W 173 E11
Sidney Lanier, L. U.S.A. 34°10N 84°4W 178 A5
Sido Mali 11°37N 7°29W 138 C3
Sidoarjo Indonesia 7°27S 112°43E 119 G15
Sidon = Saydā Lebanon 33°35N 35°25E 130 B4
Sidra = Surt Libya 31°11N 16°39E 135 B9
Sidra, G. of = Surt, Khalīj Libya 31°40N 18°30E 135 B9
Siedlce Poland 52°10N 22°20E 83 F9
Sieg → Germany 50°46N 7°6E 76 E3
Siegburg Germany 50°47N 7°12E 76 E3
Siegen Germany 50°51N 8°0E 76 E4
Siem Pang Cambodia 14°7N 106°23E 120 E6
Siem Reap = Siemreab Cambodia 13°20N 103°52E 120 F4
Siemiatycze Poland 52°27N 22°53E 83 F9
Siemreab Cambodia 13°20N 103°52E 120 F4
Siena Italy 43°19N 11°21E 93 E8
Sieniawa Poland 50°11N 22°38E 83 H9
Sieradz Poland 51°37N 18°41E 83 G5
Sieraków Poland 52°39N 16°2E 83 F3
Sierck-les-Bains France 49°26N 6°20E 71 C13
Sierning Austria 48°2N 14°18E 78 C7
Sierpc Poland 52°55N 19°43E 83 F6
Sierpe, Bocas de la Venezuela 10°0N 61°30W 187 L15
Sierra Blanca U.S.A. 31°11N 105°22W 176 F2
Sierra Blanca Peak U.S.A. 33°23N 105°49W 169 K11
Sierra City U.S.A. 39°34N 120°38W 170 F6
Sierra Colorada Argentina 40°35S 67°50W 192 B3
Sierra de Agalta △ Honduras 15°1N 85°48W 182 C2
Sierra de Andújar ⌂ Spain 38°20N 3°50W 89 G7
Sierra de Aracena y Picos de Aroche ⌂ Spain 37°53N 6°41W 89 H4
Sierra de Bahoruco △ Dom. Rep. 18°10N 71°25W 183 C5
Sierra de Baza ⌂ Spain 37°20N 2°48W 91 H2
Sierra de Castril ⌂ Spain 37°54N 2°50W 91 H2
Sierra de Espuña ⌂ Spain 37°50N 1°31W 91 H3
Sierra de Grazalema ⌂ Spain 36°31N 5°28W 89 J5
Sierra de Gredos ⌂ Spain 40°17N 5°17W 88 E5
Sierra de Hornachuelos ⌂ Spain 37°56N 5°14W 89 H5
Sierra de Huétor ⌂ Spain 37°14N 3°30W 89 H7
Sierra de La Culata △ Venezuela 8°45N 71°10W 183 E5
Sierra de Lancandón △ Guatemala 16°59N 90°23W 182 C1
Sierra de las Nieves ⌂ Spain 36°42N 5°0W 89 J6
Sierra de las Quijadas △ Argentina 32°29S 67°5W 190 C2
Sierra de María-Los Vélez ⌂ Spain 37°41N 2°10W 91 H2
Sierra de San Luis △ Venezuela 11°20N 69°43W 183 D6
Sierra de San Pedro Mártir △ Mexico 31°10N 115°30W 180 A1
Sierra de Yeguas Spain 37°7N 4°52W 89 H6
Sierra del São Mamede ⌂ Portugal 39°17N 7°18W 89 F3
Sierra Gorda Chile 22°50S 69°15W 190 A2
Sierra Grande Argentina 41°36S 65°22W 192 B3
Sierra Leone ■ W. Afr. 9°0N 12°0W 138 D2
Sierra Leone Basin Atl. Oc. 5°0N 17°0W 56 F10
Sierra Leone Rise Atl. Oc. 7°0N 22°0W 56 F9
Sierra Madre Mexico 16°0N 93°0W 181 D6
Sierra Madre Occidental Mexico 27°0N 107°0W 180 B3
Sierra Madre Oriental Mexico 25°0N 100°0W 180 C5
Sierra Mágina ⌂ Spain 37°44N 3°28W 89 H7
Sierra Mojada Mexico 27°18N 103°41W 180 B4
Sierra Nevada Spain 37°3N 3°15W 89 H7
Sierra Nevada U.S.A. 39°0N 120°30W 170 H8
Sierra Nevada ⌂ Spain 37°4N 3°7W 89 H7
Sierra Nevada △ Venezuela 8°35N 70°45W 183 E5
Sierra Nevada de Santa Marta △ Colombia 10°56N 73°36W 183 D5
Sierra Norte de Sevilla ⌂ Spain 37°55N 5°46W 89 H5
Sierra Subbéticas ⌂ Spain 37°26N 4°18W 89 H6
Sierra Vista U.S.A. 31°33N 110°18W 169 L8
Sierras de Cardeña y Montoro ⌂ Spain 38°13N 4°15W 89 G6
Sierras de Cazorla, Segura y las Villas ⌂ Spain 37°0N 2°45W 91 J2
Sierraville U.S.A. 39°36N 120°22W 170 F6
Sierre Switz. 46°17N 7°31E 77 J3
Sifié Ivory C. 8°0N 7°5W 138 D3
Sífnos Greece 37°0N 24°45E 98 E6
Sifton Canada 51°21N 100°8W 163 C8
Sifton Pass Canada 57°52N 126°15W 162 B3
Sig Algeria 35°32N 0°12W 136 A3
Sigatoka Fiji 18°8S 177°32E 154 a
Sigean France 43°2N 2°58E 72 E6
Sighetu-Marmaţiei Romania 47°57N 23°52E 81 C8
Sighişoara Romania 46°12N 24°50E 81 D9
Sigiriya Sri Lanka 7°57N 80°45E 127 L5
Sigli Indonesia 5°25N 96°0E 118 C1
Siglufjörður Iceland 66°12N 18°55W 60 C4
Sigmaringen Germany 48°5N 9°12E 77 G5
Signa Italy 43°45N 11°10E 92 E8
Signakhi = Tsnori Georgia 41°40N 45°57E 87 K7
Signal de Botrang Belgium 50°29N 6°4E 69 D6
Signal Pk. U.S.A. 33°20N 114°2W 171 M12
Signy I. Antarctica 60°43S 45°36W 55 C18
Signy-l'Abbaye France 49°40N 4°25E 71 C11
Sigsbee U.S.A. 31°16N 83°52W 178 D6
Sigsbee Deep Gulf of Mexico 25°0N 92°0W 56 D1
Sigsig Ecuador 3°0S 78°50W 186 D3
Sigtuna Sweden 59°36N 17°44E 62 E11
Sigüenza Spain 41°3N 2°40W 90 D2
Siguiri Guinea 11°31N 9°10W 138 C3
Sigulda Latvia 57°10N 24°55E 84 D3
Siguniangshan China 31°15N 103°10E 116 B4
Sihawa India 20°19N 81°55E 126 D5
Sihong China 33°27N 118°16E 115 H10
Sihora India 23°29N 80°6E 125 H9
Sihuas Peru 8°40S 77°40W 188 B2
Sihui China 23°20N 112°40E 117 F9
Siikajoki → Finland 64°50N 24°43E 60 D21
Siilinjärvi Finland 63°4N 27°39E 60 E22
Siirt Turkey 37°57N 41°55E 105 D9
Siirt □ Turkey 37°55N 41°55E 105 D9
Sijarira Ra. = Chizarira Zimbabwe 17°36S 27°45E 143 F2
Sika India 22°26N 69°47E 124 H3
Sikanni Chief → Canada 57°47N 122°15W 162 B4
Sikao Thailand 7°34N 99°21E 121 J2
Sikar India 27°33N 75°10E 124 F6
Sikasso Mali 11°18N 5°35W 138 C3
Sikasso □ Mali 10°55N 7°0W 138 C3
Sikeston U.S.A. 36°53N 89°35W 172 G9
Sikhote Alin, Khrebet Russia 45°0N 136°0E 112 B8
Sikhote Alin Ra. = Sikhote Alin, Khrebet Russia 45°0N 136°0E 112 B8
Sikia Greece 40°2N 23°56E 96 F7
Sikinos Greece 36°40N 25°8E 99 E7
Sikkim □ India 27°50N 88°30E 123 F16
Siklós Hungary 45°50N 18°19E 80 E3
Sil → Spain 42°27N 7°43W 88 C3
Silacayoapan Mexico 17°30N 98°9W 181 D5
Šilalė Lithuania 55°28N 22°12E 82 C9
Silandro Italy 46°38N 10°46E 92 B7
Silawad India 21°54N 74°54E 124 J6
Silba Croatia 44°24N 14°41E 93 D11
Silchar India 24°49N 92°48E 123 G18
Şile Turkey 41°10N 29°37E 97 E13
Silent Valley △ India 11°10N 76°20E 127 J3
Siler City U.S.A. 35°44N 79°28W 177 D15
Sileru → India 17°49N 81°24E 126 F5
Silesia = Śląsk Poland 51°0N 16°30E 74 C9
Siletitengiz Köli Kazakhstan 53°20N 73°10E 109 B8
Silgarhi Doti Nepal 29°15N 81°0E 125 E9
Silghat India 26°35N 93°0E 123 F18
Silhouette Seychelles 4°29S 55°12E 141 b
Sili Burkina Faso 11°37N 2°30W 138 C4
Siliana Tunisia 36°5N 9°22E 136 A5
Siliana □ Tunisia 36°0N 9°20E 136 A5
Silicon Valley = Santa Clara Valley U.S.A. 36°50N 121°30W 170 J5
Silifke Turkey 36°22N 33°58E 104 D5
Siliguri = Shiliguri India 26°45N 88°25E 123 F16
Siling Co China 31°50N 89°20E 110 E6
Silistea Nouă Romania 44°23N 25°1E 81 F10
Silistra Bulgaria 44°6N 27°19E 97 B11
Silistra □ Bulgaria 44°6N 27°19E 97 B11
Silivri Turkey 41°4N 28°14E 97 E12
Siljan Sweden 60°55N 14°45E 62 D8
Siljansnäs Sweden 60°47N 14°52E 62 D8
Silkeborg Denmark 56°10N 9°32E 63 H3
Silkwood Australia 17°45S 146°2E 150 B4
Silla Spain 39°22N 0°25W 91 F4
Sillajhuay, Cordillera Chile 19°46S 68°40W 188 D4
Sillamäe Estonia 59°24N 27°45E 84 C4
Sillé-le-Guillaume France 48°10N 0°8W 70 D6
Silleda Spain 42°42N 8°14W 88 C2
Sillod India 20°18N 75°39E 126 D2
Silloth U.K. 54°52N 3°23W 66 C4
Sillustani Peru 15°50S 70°7W 188 D3
Silo Greece 41°10N 25°53E 97 E9
Siloam Springs U.S.A. 36°11N 94°32W 176 C7
Silopi Turkey 37°15N 42°27E 105 D10
Siluko Nigeria 6°35N 5°10E 139 D6
Silutė Lithuania 55°21N 21°33E 82 C8
Silvan Turkey 38°7N 41°2E 105 C9
Silvani India 23°18N 78°25E 125 H8
Silvassa India 20°16N 73°1E 126 D1
Silver City U.S.A. 32°46N 108°17W 169 K9
Silver Cr. → U.S.A. 43°16N 119°13W 168 E4
Silver Creek U.S.A. 42°33N 79°10W 174 D5
Silver L. U.S.A. 38°39N 120°6W 170 G6
Silver Lake Calif., U.S.A. 35°21N 116°7W 171 K10
Silver Lake Oreg., U.S.A. 43°8N 121°3W 168 E3
Silver Springs U.S.A. 29°13N 82°3W 179 F7
Silverdalen Sweden 57°32N 15°45E 63 G9
Silvermine Mts. Ireland 52°47N 8°15W 64 D3
Silverton Australia 31°52S 141°10E 152 A4
Silverton Colo., U.S.A. 37°49N 107°40W 169 H10
Silverton Tex., U.S.A. 34°28N 101°19W 176 D4
Silves Portugal 37°11N 8°26W 89 H2
Silvi Marina Italy 42°34N 14°5E 93 F11
Silvies → U.S.A. 43°34N 119°2W 168 E4
Silvrettahorn Switz. 46°50N 10°6E 92 B7
Silwa Bahari Egypt 24°45N 32°55E 137 C3
Silz Austria 47°16N 10°56E 78 D3
Sim, C. Morocco 31°26N 9°51W 136 B2
Simaltala India 24°43N 86°33E 125 G12
Simanggang = Bandar Sri Aman Malaysia 1°15N 111°32E 118 D4
Simao China 22°47N 101°5E 116 F3
Simão Dias Brazil 10°44S 37°49W 189 C3
Simard, L. Canada 47°40N 78°40W 164 C4
Şimareh → Iran 33°9N 47°41E 105 F12
Simav Turkey 39°4N 28°58E 99 B10
Simav → Turkey 40°23N 28°31E 97 F12
Simav Dağları Turkey 39°10N 28°30E 99 B10
Simba Tanzania 2°10S 37°36E 142 C4
Simbach Germany 48°16N 13°2E 77 G9
Simbirsk = Ulyanovsk Russia 54°20N 48°25E 86 C9
Simbo Tanzania 4°51S 29°41E 142 C2
Simcoe Canada 42°50N 80°20W 174 D4
Simcoe, L. Canada 44°25N 79°20W 174 B5
Simdega India 22°37N 84°31E 125 H11
Simeonovgrad Bulgaria 42°1N 25°50E 97 D9
Simeria Romania 45°51N 23°1E 80 E8
Simeto → Italy 37°24N 15°6E 95 E8
Simeulue Indonesia 2°45N 95°45E 118 D1
Simferopol Ukraine 44°55N 34°3E 85 K8
Simi Greece 36°35N 27°50E 99 E9
Simi Valley U.S.A. 34°16N 118°47W 171 L8
Simikot Nepal 30°0N 81°50E 125 E9
Simineh → Iran 36°59N 45°54E 105 D11
Simitli Bulgaria 41°52N 23°7E 96 E7
Simla = Shimla India 31°2N 77°9E 124 D7
Simlångsdalen Sweden 56°43N 13°6E 63 H7
Şimleu-Silvaniei Romania 47°17N 22°50E 80 C7
Simlipal △ India 21°45N 86°30E 125 J12
Simmern Germany 49°58N 7°30E 77 F3
Simmie Canada 49°56N 108°6W 163 D7
Simmler U.S.A. 35°21N 119°59W 171 K7
Simnas Lithuania 54°23N 23°39E 82 D10
Simo älv = Simojoki → Finland 65°35N 25°1E 60 D21
Simões Brazil 7°36S 40°49W 189 B2
Simojoki → Finland 65°35N 25°1E 60 D21
Simojovel Mexico 17°12N 92°38W 181 D6
Simonette → Canada 55°9N 118°15W 162 B5
Simonstown S. Africa 34°14S 18°26E 144 D2
Simontornya Hungary 46°45N 18°33E 80 D3
Simpang Empat Malaysia 5°27N 100°29E 121 c
Simplício Mendes Brazil 7°51S 41°54W 189 B2
Simplonpass Switz. 46°15N 8°3E 77 J4
Simplontunnel Switz. 46°15N 8°7E 77 J4
Simpson Desert Australia 25°0S 137°0E 150 D2
Simpson Desert △ Australia 24°59S 138°21E 150 C2
Simpson Pen. Canada 68°34N 88°45W 161 D14
Simrishamn Sweden 55°33N 14°22E 63 J8
Simsbury U.S.A. 41°53N 72°48W 175 E12
Simushir, Ostrov Russia 46°50N 152°30E 107 E16
Sin Cowe I. S. China Sea 9°53N 114°19E 118 C4
Sina → India 17°30N 75°55E 126 F2
Sina Dhago Somalia 5°50N 47°0E 131 F4
Sinabang Indonesia 2°30N 96°24E 118 D1
Sinai = Es Sînâ' Egypt 29°0N 34°0E 130 F2
Sinai, Mt. = Mûsa, Gebel Egypt 28°33N 33°59E 128 D2
Sinaia Romania 45°21N 25°38E 81 E10
Sinaloa □ Mexico 25°0N 107°30W 180 C3
Sinaloa de Leyva Mexico 25°50N 108°14W 180 B3
Sinalunga Italy 43°12N 11°44E 93 E8
Sinan China 27°56N 108°13E 116 D7
Sînandrei Romania 45°52N 21°13E 80 E6
Sinarades Greece 39°34N 19°51E 101 A3
Sincan Turkey 40°0N 32°36E 104 B5
Sincanlı Turkey 38°45N 30°15E 99 C12
Sincelejo Colombia 9°18N 75°24W 186 B3
Sinch'ang N. Korea 40°7N 128°28E 115 D15
Sinch'ŏn N. Korea 38°17N 125°21E 115 E13
Sinclair U.S.A. 41°47N 107°7W 168 F10
Sinclair, L. U.S.A. 33°8N 83°12W 178 B6
Sinclair Mills Canada 54°5N 121°40W 162 C4
Sinclair's B. U.K. 58°31N 3°5W 65 C5
Sinclairville U.S.A. 42°16N 79°16W 174 D5
Sincorá, Serra do Brazil 13°10S 41°20W 189 C2
Sind = Sindh □ Pakistan 26°0N 69°0E 124 G3
Sind → Jammu & Kashmir, India 34°18N 74°45E 125 B6
Sind → Mad. P., India 26°26N 79°13E 125 F8
Sind Sagar Doab Pakistan 32°0N 71°30E 124 D4
Sindal Denmark 57°28N 10°10E 63 G4
Sindangan Phil. 8°10N 123°5E 119 C6
Sindangbarang Indonesia 7°27S 107°1E 119 G12
Sinde Zambia 17°28S 25°51E 143 F2
Sindelfingen Germany 48°42N 9°0E 77 G4
Sindewahi India 20°17N 79°39E 126 D4
Sindgi India 16°55N 76°14E 126 F3
Sindh = Indus → Pakistan 24°20N 67°47E 124 G2
Sindh □ Pakistan 26°0N 69°0E 124 G3
Sindhnur India 15°47N 76°46E 127 F3
Sindhuli Garhi Nepal 27°16N 85°58E 125 F11
Sindi India 20°48N 78°52E 126 D4
Sındırgı Turkey 39°13N 28°10E 99 B10
Sindou Burkina Faso 10°35N 5°4W 138 C3
Sindri India 23°45N 86°42E 125 H12
Sine → Senegal 14°10N 16°28W 138 C1
Sinegorskiy Russia 47°55N 40°52E 87 G5
Sinekli Turkey 41°14N 28°12E 97 E12
Sinelnikovo = Synelnykove Ukraine 48°25N 35°30E 85 H8
Sinendé Benin 10°20N 2°22E 139 C5
Sines Portugal 37°56N 8°51W 89 H2
Sines, C. de Portugal 37°58N 8°53W 89 H2
Sineu Spain 39°38N 3°1E 100 B10
Sinfra Ivory C. 6°35N 5°56W 138 D3
Sing Buri Thailand 14°53N 100°25E 120 E3
Singa Sudan 13°10N 33°57E 135 F12
Singalila △ India 27°10N 88°5E 125 F13
Singanallur India 11°2N 77°1E 127 J3
Singapore ■ Asia 1°17N 103°51E 121 d
Singapore, Straits of Asia 1°15N 104°0E 121 d
Singapore Changi ✈ (SIN) Singapore 1°23N 103°59E 121 M4
Singaraja Indonesia 8°7S 115°6E 118 F5
Singatoka = Sigatoka Fiji 18°8S 177°32E 154 a
Singen Germany 47°45N 8°50E 77 H4
Singida Tanzania 4°49S 34°48E 142 C3
Singida □ Tanzania 6°0S 34°30E 142 D3
Singkang Indonesia 4°8S 120°1E 119 E6
Singkawang Indonesia 1°0N 108°57E 118 D3
Singkep Indonesia 0°30S 104°25E 118 E2
Singkil Indonesia 2°17N 97°49E 121 L1
Singkuang Indonesia 1°3N 98°55E 121 L2
Singleton Australia 32°33S 151°10E 153 B9
Singleton, Mt. N. Terr., Australia 22°0S 130°46E 148 D5
Singleton, Mt. W. Austral., Australia 29°27S 117°15E 149 E2
Singö Sweden 60°12N 18°45E 62 D12
Singoli India 25°0N 75°22E 124 G6
Singora = Songkhla Thailand 7°13N 100°37E 121 J3
Singrauli India 24°7N 82°23E 125 G10
Sinh Ton, Dao = Sin Cowe I. S. China Sea 9°53N 114°19E 118 C4
Sinharaja Sri Lanka 6°25N 80°30E 127 L5
Sinhgarh India 18°22N 73°45E 126 E1
Sinhŭng N. Korea 40°11N 127°34E 115 D14
Sinis Italy 38°55N 8°25E 94 C1
Siniscóla Italy 40°34N 9°41E 94 B2
Sinj Croatia 43°42N 16°39E 93 E13
Sinjai Indonesia 5°7S 120°20E 119 F6
Sinjajevina Montenegro 42°57N 19°22E 96 D3
Sinjār Iraq 36°19N 41°52E 105 D9
Sinjār, Jabal Iraq 36°23N 41°47E 105 D9
Sinkat Sudan 18°55N 36°49E 137 D4
Sinkiang = Xinjiang Uygur Zizhiqu □ China 42°0N 86°0E 109 D11
Sinko Guinea 8°53N 8°16W 138 D3
Sinmak N. Korea 38°25N 126°14E 115 E14
Sinmi-do N. Korea 39°33N 124°53E 115 E13
Sinnai Italy 39°18N 9°13E 94 C2
Sinnamary Fr. Guiana 5°25N 53°0W 187 B8
Sinnar India 19°48N 74°0E 126 E2
Sinni → Italy 40°8N 16°41E 95 B9
Sinnuris Egypt 29°26N 30°31E 137 F7
Sinoie, Lacul Romania 44°35N 28°50E 81 F13
Sinop Turkey 42°1N 35°11E 104 A6
Sinop □ Turkey 42°0N 35°0E 104 B6
Sinor India 21°55N 73°20E 124 J5
Sinp'o N. Korea 40°0N 128°13E 115 E15
Sinsheim Germany 49°15N 8°52E 77 F4
Sinsk Russia 61°8N 126°48E 107 C13

Sint-Hubert Belgium 50°2N 5°23E 69 D5
Sint-Niklaas Belgium 51°10N 4°8E 69 C4
Sint-Truiden Belgium 50°48N 5°10E 69 D5
Sintang Indonesia 0°5N 111°35E 118 D4
Sinton U.S.A. 28°2N 97°31W 176 G6
Sintra Portugal 38°47N 9°25W 89 G1
Sintra-Cascais △
   Portugal 38°50N 9°25W 89 G1
Sinŭiju N. Korea 40°5N 124°24E 115 D13
Sinyukha → Ukraine 48°3N 30°51E 85 H6
Sinzig Germany 50°32N 7°14E 76 E3
Sio → Hungary 46°20N 18°53E 80 D3
Siocon Phil. 7°40N 122°10E 119 C6
Siófok Hungary 46°54N 18°3E 80 D3
Sion Switz. 46°14N 7°20E 77 J3
Sion Mills U.K. 54°48N 7°29W 64 B4
tSionainn, An = Shannon →
   Ireland 52°35N 9°30W 64 D2
Sioux Center U.S.A. 43°5N 96°11W 172 D5
Sioux City U.S.A. 42°30N 96°24W 172 D5
Sioux Falls U.S.A. 43°33N 96°44W 172 D5
Sioux Lookout Canada 50°10N 91°50W 164 B1
Sioux Narrows
   Canada 49°25N 94°10W 163 D10
Sipadan Malaysia 4°6N 118°38E 119 D5
Šipan Croatia 42°45N 17°52E 96 D1
Siparia Trin. & Tob. 10°8N 61°31W 187 K15
Sipil Daği △ Turkey 38°35N 27°30E 99 C9
Siping China 43°8N 124°21E 115 C13
Sipiwesk L. Canada 55°5N 97°35W 163 B9
Siple I. Antarctica 73°40S 125°10W 55 D14
Šipovo Bos.-H. 44°16N 17°6E 80 F2
Sipra → India 23°55N 75°28E 124 H6
Sipsongpanna = Xishuangbanna
   China 22°5N 101°1E 116 F3
Sipur India 21°11N 85°9E 126 D7
Sipura Indonesia 2°18S 99°40E 118 E1
Siquia → Nic. 12°10N 84°20W 182 D3
Siquijor Phil. 9°12N 123°35E 119 C6
Siquirres Costa Rica 10°6N 83°30W 182 D3
Sir Abu Nu'ayr U.A.E. 25°20N 54°20E 129 E7
Šīr Banī Yās U.A.E. 24°19N 52°37E 129 E7
Sir Edward Pellew Group
   Australia 15°40S 137°10E 150 B2
Sir Graham Moore Is.
   Australia 13°53S 126°34E 148 B4
Sir James MacBrien, Mt.
   Canada 62°7N 127°41W 160 E6
Sira India 13°41N 76°49E 127 H3
Sira → Norway 58°23N 6°34E 61 G12
Siracusa Italy 37°4N 15°17E 95 E8
Sirajganj Bangla. 24°25N 89°47E 125 G13
Sirakoro Mali 12°41N 9°14W 138 C3
Širan Turkey 40°11N 39°7E 105 B8
Sirasso Ivory C. 9°16N 6°6W 138 D3
Sirathu India 25°39N 81°19E 125 G9
Sīrdān Iran 36°39N 49°12E 105 D13
Sirdaryo □ Uzbekistan 40°30N 68°45E 109 D7
Siren U.S.A. 45°47N 92°24W 172 C7
Sirente-Velino △ Italy 42°10N 13°32E 93 F10
Sirer Spain 38°56N 1°22E 100 C7
Siret Romania 47°55N 26°5E 81 C11
Siret → Romania 45°24N 28°1E 81 E12
Sirghāyā Syria 33°51N 36°8E 130 B5
Širia Romania 46°16N 21°38E 80 D6
Sirikit Res. Thailand 17°45N 100°34E 120 C3
Sirinat △ Thailand 8°6N 98°17E 121 a
Sirino, Mte. Italy 40°7N 15°50E 95 B8
Sīrjān Iran 29°30N 55°45E 129 D7
Sirkali = Sirkazhi India 11°15N 79°41E 127 J4
Sirkazhi India 11°15N 79°41E 127 J4
Sirmans U.S.A. 30°21N 83°39W 178 E6
Sirmaur India 24°51N 81°23E 125 G9
Sirmilik △ Canada 72°50N 80°35W 161 C15
Sirmione Italy 45°30N 10°36E 92 C7
Sirna Greece 36°22N 26°42E 99 E8
Širnak Turkey 37°32N 42°28E 105 D10
Sirohi India 24°52N 72°53E 124 G5
Sironj India 24°5N 77°39E 124 G7
Siros = Ermoupoli
   Greece 37°28N 24°57E 98 D6
Sirpur India 19°29N 79°36E 126 E4
Sirr, Nafud as Si. Arabia 25°33N 44°35E 128 E5
Sirretta Pk. U.S.A. 35°56N 118°19W 171 K8
Sirrī Iran 25°55N 54°32E 129 E7
Sirsa India 29°33N 75°4E 124 E6
Sirsa → India 26°51N 79°4E 125 F8
Sirsi India 14°40N 74°49E 127 G2
Sirsilla India 18°23N 78°50E 126 E4
Sirte = Surt Libya 31°11N 16°39E 135 B9
Siruela Spain 38°58N 5°3W 89 G5
Siruguppa India 15°38N 76°54E 127 F3
Sirur India 18°50N 74°23E 126 E2
Širvan Azerbaijan 39°59N 48°52E 87 L9
Sīrvan → Iran 34°N 46°50E 105 E12
Sisak Croatia 45°30N 16°21E 93 C13
Sisante Spain 39°25N 2°12W 91 F2
Sisargas, Is. Spain 43°21N 8°50W 88 B2
Sishen S. Africa 27°47S 22°59E 144 C3
Sishui China 35°42N 117°18E 115 G9
Sisian Armenia 39°31N 46°1E 105 C12
Sisimiut Greenland 66°40N 53°30W 57 D5
Sisipuk L. Canada 55°45N 101°50W 163 B8
Sisophon Cambodia 13°38N 102°59E 120 F4
Sisseton U.S.A. 45°40N 97°3W 172 C5
Sissonne France 49°34N 3°51E 71 C10
Sīstān Asia 30°50N 61°0E 129 D9
Sīstān, Daryācheh-ye
   Iran 31°0N 61°0E 129 D9
Sīstān va Balūchestān □
   Iran 27°0N 62°0E 129 E9
Sisteron France 44°12N 5°57E 73 D9
Sisters U.S.A. 44°18N 121°33W 168 D3
Sisters, The Seychelles 4°16S 55°52E 141 b
Siswa Bazar India 27°9N 83°46E 125 F10
Sitakili Mali 13°7N 11°14W 138 C2
Sitamarhi India 26°37N 85°30E 125 F11
Sitapur India 27°38N 80°45E 125 F9
Siteki Swaziland 26°32S 31°58E 145 D5
Sitges Spain 41°17N 1°47E 90 D6
Sithonia Greece 40°0N 23°45E 96 F7
Sitia Greece 35°13N 26°6E 101 D8
Sitio da Abadia Brazil 14°48S 46°16W 189 C1
Sitito-Ozima Ridge
   Pac. Oc. 23°0N 143°0E 156 E6
Sitka U.S.A. 57°3N 135°20W 162 B1
Sitkalday = Sagaing
   Burma 21°52N 95°59E 123 J19
Sitoti Botswana 23°15S 23°40E 144 B3
Sitra Egypt 28°40N 26°53E 137 B2

Sittang Myit →
   Burma 17°20N 96°45E 123 L20
Sittard Neths. 51°0N 5°52E 69 C5
Sittensen Germany 53°17N 9°32E 76 B5
Sittingbourne U.K. 51°21N 0°45E 67 F8
Sittoung = Sittang Myit →
   Burma 17°20N 96°45E 123 L20
Sittwe Burma 20°18N 92°45E 123 J18
Situbondo Indonesia 7°42S 113°56E 119 G16
Siuna Nic. 13°37N 84°45W 182 D3
Siuri India 23°50N 87°34E 125 H12
Siutghiol, Lacul
   Romania 44°15N 28°35E 81 F13
Sivaganga India 9°50N 78°28E 127 K4
Sivagiri India 9°16N 77°26E 127 K3
Sivakasi India 9°24N 77°47E 127 K3
Sivand Iran 30°5N 52°55E 129 D7
Sivas Turkey 39°43N 36°58E 104 C7
Sivas □ Turkey 39°45N 37°0E 104 C7
Sivasamudram India 12°16N 77°10E 127 H3
Sivasli Turkey 38°31N 29°42E 99 C11
Siverek Turkey 37°50N 39°19E 105 D8
Sivrihisar Turkey 39°30N 31°35E 104 C4
Siwa Egypt 29°11N 25°31E 137 B2
Sīwa, El Wâhât es
   Egypt 29°10N 25°30E 137 B2
Siwa Oasis = Sīwa, El Wâhât es
   Egypt 29°10N 25°30E 137 B2
Siwalik Range Nepal 28°0N 83°0E 125 F10
Siwan India 26°13N 84°21E 125 F11
Siwana India 25°38N 72°25E 124 G5
Six Cross Roads Barbados 13°7N 59°28W 183 g
Six-Fours-les-Plages
   France 43°6N 5°49E 73 E9
Sixian China 33°30N 117°50E 115 H9
Sixmilebridge Ireland 52°44N 8°46W 64 D3
Sixth Cataract Sudan 16°20N 32°42E 135 E12
Siyabuswa S. Africa 25°7S 29°3E 145 C4
Siyah Kuh, Kavīr-e
   Iran 32°55N 53°55E 129 C7
Siyâl, Jazā'ir Egypt 22°49N 36°12E 137 C4
Siyang China 33°42N 118°40E 115 H10
Siyäzän Azerbaijan 41°3N 49°10E 87 K9
Siziwang Qi China 41°25N 111°40E 114 D6
Sjælland Denmark 55°30N 11°30E 63 J5
Sjælland □ Denmark 55°30N 11°30E 63 J5
Sjællands Odde Denmark 55°58N 11°24E 63 J5
Sjenica Serbia 43°16N 20°0E 96 C3
Sjöbo Sweden 55°37N 13°45E 63 J6
Sjötofta Sweden 57°22N 13°17E 63 G7
Sjötorp Sweden 58°50N 14°0E 63 F8
Sjumen = Shumen
   Bulgaria 43°18N 26°55E 97 C10
Sjuntorp Sweden 58°12N 12°13E 63 F6
Skadarsko Jezero Europe 42°10N 19°20E 96 D3
Skadarsko Jezero △
   Montenegro 42°10N 19°20E 96 D3
Skadovsk Ukraine 46°17N 32°52E 85 J7
Skælskør Denmark 55°15N 11°18E 63 J5
Skærbæk Denmark 55°9N 8°45E 63 J2
Skaftafell △ Iceland 64°1N 17°0W 60 D5
Skaftafell △ Iceland 64°8N 16°50W 60 D5
Skagafjörður Iceland 65°54N 19°35W 60 D4
Skagastølstindane
   Norway 61°28N 7°52E 60 F12
Skagaströnd Iceland 65°50N 20°19W 60 D3
Skagen Denmark 57°43N 10°35E 63 G4
Skagern Sweden 59°0N 14°20E 62 E8
Skagerrak Denmark 57°30N 9°0E 63 G2
Skagit → U.S.A. 48°23N 122°22W 170 B4
Skagway U.S.A. 59°28N 135°19W 160 F4
Skala-Podilska Ukraine 48°50N 26°15E 81 B11
Skalat Ukraine 49°23N 25°55E 75 D13
Skalbmierz Poland 50°20N 20°25E 83 H7
Skälderviken Sweden 56°22N 12°30E 63 H6
Skalica Slovak Rep. 48°50N 17°15E 79 C10
Skallingen Denmark 55°32N 8°13E 63 J2
Skalni Dol = Kamenyak
   Bulgaria 43°24N 26°57E 97 C10
Skanderborg Denmark 56°2N 9°55E 63 H3
Skåne Sweden 55°59N 13°30E 63 J7
Skåne □ Sweden 56°15N 14°0E 63 H7
Skaneateles U.S.A. 42°57N 76°26W 175 D8
Skaneateles L. U.S.A. 42°51N 76°22W 175 D8
Skänninge Sweden 58°24N 15°5E 63 F9
Skanör med Falsterbo
   Sweden 55°24N 12°50E 63 J6
Skantzoura Greece 39°5N 24°6E 98 B6
Skara Sweden 58°25N 13°30E 63 F7
Skärblacka Sweden 58°35N 15°54E 63 F9
Skardu Pakistan 35°20N 75°44E 125 B6
Skåre Sweden 59°26N 13°26E 63 F7
Skärhamn Sweden 57°59N 11°43E 63 F5
Skarszewy Poland 54°4N 18°25E 82 D5
Skarvan og Roltdalen △
   Norway 63°16N 11°31E 60 E14
Skaryszew Poland 51°19N 21°15E 83 G8
Skarżysko-Kamienna
   Poland 51°7N 20°52E 83 G7
Skattkärr Sweden 59°29N 13°40E 62 E7
Skattungbyn Sweden 61°10N 14°56E 62 C8
Skawina Poland 49°59N 19°50E 83 J6
Skebokvarn Sweden 59°58N 18°36E 62 E12
Skee Sweden 58°56N 11°19E 63 F5
Skeena → Canada 54°9N 130°5W 162 C2
Skeena Mts. Canada 56°40N 128°30W 162 B3
Skegness U.K. 53°9N 0°20E 66 D8
Skeleton B. Australia 34°55S 135°45E 151 E2
Skeleton Coast Namibia 20°0S 13°0E 141 J2
Skeleton Coast △
   Namibia 20°0S 13°20E 144 B1
Skellefteå Sweden 64°45N 20°50E 60 D19
Skellefteälven →
   Sweden 64°45N 21°10E 60 D19
Skelleftehamn Sweden 64°40N 21°9E 60 D19
Skellig Michael = Great Skellig
   Ireland 51°47N 10°33W 64 E1
Skender Vakuf Bos.-H. 44°29N 17°22E 80 F2
Skënderaj Kosovo 42°45N 20°47E 96 D4
Skerries, The U.K. 53°25N 4°36W 66 D3
Skhidnytsya Ukraine 49°13N 23°20E 83 J10
Skhiza Greece 36°41N 21°40E 98 E3
Ski Norway 59°43N 10°52E 61 G14
Skiathos Greece 39°12N 23°30E 98 B5
Skibbereen Ireland 51°33N 9°16W 64 E2
Skiddaw U.K. 54°39N 3°9W 66 C4
Skidegate Canada 53°15N 132°1W 162 C2
Skidra Greece 40°47N 22°10E 96 D6
Skien Norway 59°12N 9°35E 61 G13
Skierniewice Poland 51°58N 20°10E 83 G7
Skihist, Mt. Canada 50°12N 121°54W 162 C4

Skikda Algeria 36°50N 6°58E 136 A5
Skikda □ Algeria 36°45N 6°50E 136 A5
Skillingaryd Sweden 57°27N 14°5E 63 G8
Skillinge Sweden 55°30N 14°16E 63 J8
Skilloura Cyprus 35°14N 33°10E 101 D12
Skinari, Akra Greece 37°56N 20°42E 98 D2
Skinnskatteberg Sweden 59°50N 15°40E 62 E10
Skipton Australia 37°39S 143°40E 152 D5
Skipton U.K. 53°58N 2°3W 66 D5
Skiring, C. Senegal 12°26N 16°46W 138 C1
Skirmish Pt. Australia 11°59S 134°17E 150 A1
Skiros Greece 38°55N 24°34E 98 C6
Skivarp Sweden 55°26N 13°34E 63 J7
Skive Denmark 56°33N 9°2E 63 H3
Skjálfandafljót →
   Iceland 65°59N 17°25W 60 D5
Skjálfandi Iceland 66°5N 17°30W 60 C5
Skjern Denmark 55°57N 8°30E 63 J2
Skjern Å △ Denmark 55°50N 8°30E 63 H2
Škocjanske Jame
   Slovenia 45°40N 14°0E 93 C10
Skoczów Poland 49°49N 18°45E 83 J5
Škofja Loka Slovenia 46°9N 14°19E 93 B11
Skoghall Sweden 59°20N 13°30E 62 E7
Skogstorp Sweden 59°19N 16°29E 62 E10
Skoki Poland 52°40N 17°11E 83 F4
Skole Ukraine 49°3N 23°30E 75 D12
Skopelos Greece 39°9N 23°47E 98 B5
Skopi Greece 35°11N 26°2E 101 D8
Skopin Russia 53°55N 39°32E 84 F10
Skopje Macedonia 42°1N 21°26E 96 D5
Skopje ✈ (SKP)
   Macedonia 41°59N 21°29E 96 E5
Skórcz Poland 53°47N 18°30E 82 E5
Skørping Denmark 56°50N 9°53E 63 H3
Skövde Sweden 58°24N 13°50E 63 F7
Skovorodino Russia 54°0N 124°0E 107 D13
Skowhegan U.S.A. 44°46N 69°43W 173 C19
Skradin Croatia 43°52N 15°53E 93 E12
Skrea Sweden 56°53N 12°34E 63 H6
Skrunda Latvia 56°41N 22°1E 82 B9
Skrwa → Poland 52°35N 19°32E 83 F6
Skuleskogen △ Sweden 63°6N 18°30E 62 A12
Skull Ireland 51°32N 9°34W 64 E2
Skultorp Sweden 58°24N 13°51E 63 F7
Skultuna Sweden 59°43N 16°26E 62 E10
Skunk → U.S.A. 40°42N 91°7W 172 E8
Skuodas Lithuania 56°16N 21°33E 82 B8
Skurup Sweden 55°28N 13°30E 63 J7
Skutskär Sweden 60°37N 17°25E 62 D11
Skvyra Ukraine 49°44N 29°40E 75 D15
Skwierzyna Poland 52°33N 15°30E 83 F2
Skye U.K. 57°15N 6°10W 65 D2
Skykomish U.S.A. 47°42N 121°22W 168 C3
Skyring, Seno Chile 52°35S 72°0W 192 D3
Skyropoula Greece 38°50N 24°37E 98 C6
Skyros = Skyros Greece 38°55N 24°34E 98 C6
Skyros Greece 38°55N 24°34E 98 C6
Skyttorp Sweden 60°5N 17°44E 62 D11
Slade Point Australia 21°4S 149°13E 150 b
Slade Pt. Australia 21°5S 149°13E 150 b
Slættaratindur Faroe Is. 62°18N 7°1W 60 E9
Slagelse Denmark 55°23N 11°19E 63 J5
Slamet Indonesia 7°16S 109°8E 119 G13
Slane Ireland 53°42N 6°33W 64 C5
Slaney → Ireland 52°26N 6°33W 64 D5
Slangberge S. Africa 31°32S 20°48E 144 D3
Slănic Romania 45°14N 25°58E 81 E10
Slano Croatia 42°48N 17°53E 96 D1
Slantsy Russia 59°7N 28°5E 84 C5
Slaný Czech Rep. 50°13N 14°6E 78 A7
Śląsk Poland 51°0N 16°30E 74 C9
Śląskie □ Poland 50°30N 19°0E 83 H6
Slatbaken Sweden 58°25N 16°45E 63 F10
Slate Is. Canada 48°40N 87°0W 164 C2
Slatina Croatia 45°42N 17°37E 80 E2
Slatina Romania 44°28N 24°22E 81 F9
Slatina Timiş Romania 45°15N 22°17E 80 E7
Slatington U.S.A. 40°45N 75°37W 175 F9
Slaton U.S.A. 33°26N 101°39W 176 E4
Slave → Canada 61°18N 113°39W 162 A6
Slave Coast W. Afr. 6°0N 2°30E 139 D5
Slave Lake Canada 55°17N 114°43W 162 B6
Slave Pt. Canada 61°11N 115°56W 162 A6
Slavgorod Russia 53°1N 78°37E 109 B9
Slavinja Serbia 43°9N 22°50E 96 C6
Slavkov u Brna
   Czech Rep. 49°10N 16°52E 79 B9
Slavkovský Les △
   Czech Rep. 50°5N 12°44E 78 A5
Slavonia = Slavonija Europe 45°20N 17°40E 80 E2
Slavonski Brod Croatia 45°11N 18°1E 80 E3
Slavsk Russia 55°3N 21°41E 82 C8
Slavske Ukraine 48°51N 23°27E 81 B8
Slavuta Ukraine 50°15N 27°2E 75 C14
Slavyanka Russia 42°53N 131°21E 112 C5
Slavyanovo Bulgaria 43°28N 24°52E 97 C8
Slavyansk = Slovyansk
   Ukraine 48°55N 37°36E 85 H9
Slavyansk-na-Kubani
   Russia 45°15N 38°11E 85 K10
Slawa Poland 51°52N 16°2E 83 G3
Slawharad Belarus 53°27N 31°0E 75 B16
Sławno Poland 54°27N 16°41E 82 D3
Sławoborze Poland 53°55N 15°42E 82 E2
Slea Hd. Ireland 52°6N 10°27W 64 D1
Sleaford U.K. 53°0N 0°24W 66 D7
Sleaford B. Australia 34°55S 135°45E 151 C2
Sleat, Sd. of U.K. 57°5N 5°47W 65 D3
Sleeper Is. Canada 58°30N 81°0W 161 F15
Sleeping Bear Dunes →
   U.S.A. 44°50N 86°5W 172 C10
Sleepy Eye U.S.A. 44°18N 94°43W 172 C7
Slemon L. Canada 63°13N 116°4W 162 A5
Slesin Poland 52°22N 18°14E 83 F5
Slide Mt. U.S.A. 42°0N 74°25W 175 E10
Slidell U.S.A. 30°17N 89°47W 177 F10
Sliema Malta 35°55N 14°30E 101 D2
Slieve Aughty Ireland 53°4N 8°30W 64 C3
Slieve Bloom Ireland 53°4N 7°40W 64 C4
Slieve Donard U.K. 54°11N 5°55W 64 B6
Slieve Gamph Ireland 54°6N 9°0W 64 B3
Slieve Gullion U.K. 54°7N 6°26W 64 B5
Slieve Mish Ireland 52°12N 9°50W 64 D2
Slieve Snaght Ireland 55°12N 7°20W 64 A4
Slievenamon Ireland 52°25N 7°34W 64 D4
Sligeach = Sligo Ireland 54°16N 8°28W 64 B3
Sligo Ireland 54°16N 8°28W 64 B3
Sligo □ Ireland 54°8N 8°42W 64 B3

Sligo B. Ireland 54°18N 8°40W 64 B3
Slippery Rock U.S.A. 41°4N 80°3W 174 E4
Slite Sweden 57°42N 18°48E 63 G12
Sliven Bulgaria 42°42N 26°19E 97 D10
Sliven □ Bulgaria 42°42N 26°19E 97 D10
Slivnitsa Bulgaria 42°50N 23°2E 96 D7
Sljeme Croatia 45°57N 15°58E 93 C12
Sloan U.S.A. 35°57N 115°13W 171 K11
Sloansville U.S.A. 42°45N 74°22W 175 D10
Slobidka Ukraine 47°54N 29°21E 81 C14
Slobozia Moldova 46°45N 29°42E 81 C16
Slobozia Argeş, Romania 44°30N 25°14E 81 F10
Slobozia Ialomiţa,
   Romania 44°34N 27°23E 81 F12
Slocan Canada 49°48N 117°28W 162 D5
Slocomb U.S.A. 31°7N 85°36W 178 D4
Słomniki Poland 50°16N 20°4E 83 H7
Slonim Belarus 53°4N 25°19E 75 B13
Slough U.K. 51°30N 0°36W 67 F7
Slough □ U.K. 51°30N 0°36W 67 F7
Sloughhouse U.S.A. 38°26N 121°12W 170 G5
Slovak Rep. ■
   Europe 48°30N 20°0E 79 C13
Slovakia = Slovak Rep. ■
   Europe 48°30N 20°0E 79 C13
Slovakian Ore Mts. = Slovenské
   Rudohorie Slovak Rep. 48°45N 20°0E 79 C12
Slovenia ■ Europe 45°58N 14°30E 93 C11
Slovenija = Slovenia ■
   Europe 45°58N 14°30E 93 C11
Slovenj Gradec Slovenia 46°31N 15°5E 93 B12
Slovenská = Slovak Rep. ■
   Europe 48°30N 20°0E 79 C13
Slovenska Bistrica
   Slovenia 46°24N 15°35E 93 B12
Slovenské Konjice
   Slovenia 46°20N 15°28E 93 B12
Slovenské Rudohorie
   Slovak Rep. 48°45N 20°0E 79 C12
Slovensky Kras △
   Slovak Rep. 48°40N 20°20E 79 C13
Slovensky Raj △
   Slovak Rep. 48°30N 20°25E 79 C13
Slovyansk Ukraine 48°55N 37°36E 85 H9
Slowiński △ Poland 54°43N 17°26E 82 D4
Słubice Poland 52°22N 14°35E 83 F1
Sluch → Ukraine 51°37N 26°38E 75 C14
Sluis Neths. 51°18N 3°23E 69 C3
Slunj Croatia 45°6N 15°33E 93 C12
Słupca Poland 52°15N 17°52E 83 F4
Słupia → Poland 54°35N 16°51E 82 D3
Słupsk Poland 54°30N 17°3E 82 D4
Slurry S. Africa 25°49S 25°42E 144 C4
Slutsk Belarus 53°2N 27°31E 75 B14
Slyne Hd. Ireland 53°25N 10°10W 64 C1
Slyudyanka Russia 51°40N 103°40E 107 D11
Småland Sweden 57°15N 15°25E 63 G9
Smålandsfarvandet
   Denmark 55°10N 11°20E 63 J5
Smålandsstenar Sweden 57°10N 13°25E 63 G7
Smalltree L. Canada 61°0N 105°0W 163 A8
Smallwood Res. Canada 54°5N 64°30W 165 B7
Smarhon Belarus 54°20N 26°24E 75 A14
Smarje Slovenia 46°15N 15°34E 93 B12
Smartt Syndicate Dam
   S. Africa 30°45S 23°10E 144 D3
Smartville U.S.A. 39°13N 121°18W 170 F5
Smeaton Canada 53°30N 104°49W 163 C8
Smederevo Serbia 44°40N 20°57E 96 B4
Smederevska Palanka
   Serbia 44°22N 20°58E 96 B4
Smedjebacken Sweden 60°8N 15°25E 62 D9
Smela = Smila Ukraine 49°15N 31°58E 85 H6
Smeralda, Costa Italy 41°5N 9°35E 94 A2
Smerwick Harbour
   Ireland 52°12N 10°23W 64 D1
Smethport U.S.A. 41°49N 78°27W 174 E6
Smidovich Russia 48°36N 133°49E 107 E14
Smigiel Poland 52°1N 16°32E 83 F3
Smila Ukraine 49°15N 31°58E 85 H6
Smilyan Bulgaria 41°29N 24°46E 97 E8
Smith Canada 55°10N 114°0W 162 B6
Smith Center U.S.A. 39°47N 98°47W 172 F4
Smith I. Canada 60°45N 78°25W 161 E16
Smith I. India 13°20N 93°4E 127 H11
Smith Islands △
   Australia 20°40S 149°9E 150 b
Smith River U.S.A. 41°55N 124°0W 168 F2
Smithburne →
   Australia 17°3S 140°57E 150 B3
Smithers Canada 54°45N 127°10W 162 C3
Smithfield S. Africa 30°9N 26°30E 145 E4
Smithfield N.C.,
   U.S.A. 35°31N 78°21W 177 D15
Smithfield Utah,
   U.S.A. 41°50N 111°50W 168 F8
Smiths Falls Canada 44°55N 76°0W 161 D12
Smiths U.S.A. 32°32N 85°6W 178 C4
Smithton Australia 40°53S 145°6E 151 G4
Smithville Canada 43°6N 79°33W 174 C5
Smithville S. Africa 31°54N 84°15W 178 D5
Smithville Tex., U.S.A. 30°1N 97°10W 176 F6
Smoke Creek Desert
   U.S.A. 40°30N 119°40W 168 F4
Smoky → Canada 56°10N 117°21W 162 B5
Smoky Bay Australia 32°22S 134°13E 151 E1
Smoky Hill → U.S.A. 39°4N 96°48W 172 F5
Smoky Hill U.S.A. 39°15N 101°6W 172 F3
Smoky Lake Canada 54°10N 112°30W 162 C6
Smøla Norway 63°23N 8°3E 60 E13
Smolensk Russia 54°45N 32°5E 84 E7
Smolenskoye Poozerye △
   Russia 55°35N 31°50E 84 E6
Smolikas, Oros Greece 40°9N 20°58E 96 F4
Smolník Slovak Rep. 48°43N 20°44E 79 C13
Smolny △ Russia 54°20N 45°0E 84 C8
Smolyan Bulgaria 41°36N 24°38E 97 E8
Smolyan □ Bulgaria 41°36N 24°38E 97 E8
Smooth Rock Falls
   Canada 49°17N 81°37W 164 C3
Smoothstone L.
   Canada 54°40N 106°50W 163 C7
Smorgon = Smarhon
   Belarus 54°20N 26°24E 75 A14
Smotrych → Ukraine 48°34N 26°53E 81 B11

Smulţi Romania 45°57N 27°44E 81 E12
Smyadovo Bulgaria 43°2N 27°1E 97 C11
Smygehamn Sweden 55°21N 13°22E 63 J7
Smygehuk Sweden 55°20N 13°20E 63 J7
Smyley I. Antarctica 72°55S 78°0W 55 D17
Smyrna = İzmir Turkey 38°25N 27°8E 99 C9
Smyrna Del., U.S.A. 39°18N 75°36W 173 F16
Smyrna Ga., U.S.A. 33°53N 84°31W 178 B5
Snæfell Iceland 64°48N 15°34W 60 D6
Snæfell I. of Man 54°16N 4°27E 76 A6
Snæfellsjökull Iceland 64°49N 23°46W 60 D2
Snake → U.S.A. 46°12N 119°2W 168 D4
Snake I. Australia 38°47S 146°33E 153 F7
Snake Range U.S.A. 39°0N 114°20W 168 G7
Snake River Plain
   U.S.A. 42°50N 114°0W 168 E7
Snåsa Norway 64°12N 12°0E 60 D5
Snåsavatnet Norway 64°12N 12°0E 60 D15
Snedsted Denmark 56°55N 8°32E 63 H2
Sneek Neths. 53°2N 5°40E 69 A5
Sneem Ireland 51°50N 9°54W 64 E2
Sneeuberge S. Africa 31°46S 24°20E 144 D3
Snejbjerg Denmark 56°8N 8°54E 63 H2
Snelling Calif., U.S.A. 37°31N 120°26W 170 H6
Snelling S.C., U.S.A. 33°19N 81°37W 177 D13
Snells Beach N.Z. 36°25S 174°44E 154 C3
Snezhnoye Ukraine 48°0N 38°58E 85 J10
Snežka Czech Rep. 50°41N 15°50E 83 H8
Snežnik Slovenia 45°36N 14°35E 93 C11
Śniadowo Poland 53°0N 22°0E 83 E8
Śniardwy, Jezioro Poland 53°48N 21°50E 82 E8
Śnieżka Europe 50°44N 15°44E 78 A8
Snigirevka = Snihurivka
   Ukraine 47°2N 32°49E 85 J7
Snihurivka Ukraine 47°2N 32°49E 85 J7
Snina Slovak Rep. 48°58N 22°9E 79 C15
Snizort, L. U.K. 57°33N 6°28W 65 D2
Snohetta Norway 62°19N 9°16E 60 E13
Snohomish U.S.A. 47°55N 122°6W 170 C4
Snoqualmie U.S.A. 47°31N 121°49W 170 C5
Snoqualmie Pass
   U.S.A. 47°25N 121°25W 170 C5
Snoul Cambodia 12°4N 106°26E 121 F6
Snover U.S.A. 43°27N 82°58W 174 C1
Snow Hill U.S.A. 38°11N 75°24W 173 F16
Snow Lake Canada 54°52N 100°3W 163 C8
Snow Mt. Calif.,
   U.S.A. 39°23N 122°45W 170 F4
Snow Mt. Maine,
   U.S.A. 45°18N 70°48W 175 A14
Snowbird L. Canada 60°45N 103°0W 163 A8
Snowdon U.K. 53°4N 4°5W 66 D3
Snowdonia □ U.K. 53°7N 3°59W 66 D4
Snowdrift = Łutsel K'e
   Canada 62°24N 110°44W 163 A6
Snowdrift → Canada 62°24N 110°44W 163 A6
Snowflake U.S.A. 34°30N 110°5W 169 J8
Snowshoe Pk. U.S.A. 48°13N 115°41W 168 B6
Snowtown Australia 33°46S 138°14E 152 B3
Snowville U.S.A. 41°58N 112°43W 168 F7
Snowy → Australia 37°46S 148°30E 153 D8
Snowy Mt. U.S.A. 43°42N 74°23W 175 C10
Snowy Mts. Australia 36°30S 148°20E 153 D8
Snowy River △
   Australia 37°15S 147°29E 153 D7
Snug Corner Bahamas 22°33N 73°52W 183 B5
Snug Harbour Canada 45°22N 80°17W 174 A4
Snyatyn Ukraine 48°27N 25°38E 81 B10
Snyder Okla., U.S.A. 34°40N 98°57W 176 D5
Snyder Tex., U.S.A. 32°44N 100°55W 176 E4
Soalala Madag. 16°6S 45°20E 141 H9
Soan → Pakistan 33°1N 71°44E 124 C4
Soap Romania 45°56N 24°55E 81 E9
Soba Nigeria 10°58N 8°4E 139 C6
Sobat → South Sudan 9°22N 31°33E 135 G12
Soběslav Czech Rep. 49°16N 14°45E 78 B7
Sobhapur India 22°47N 78°17E 124 H8
Sobinka Russia 56°0N 40°0E 84 C11
Sobótka Poland 50°54N 16°44E 83 H3
Sobra Croatia 42°44N 17°34E 93 F14
Sobradinho, Represa de
   Brazil 9°30S 42°0W 189 B2
Sobral Brazil 3°50S 40°20W 189 B1
Sobrance Slovak Rep. 48°45N 22°11E 79 C15
Sobreira Formosa
   Portugal 39°46N 7°51W 88 F3
Soc Giang Vietnam 22°54N 106°1E 116 H5
Soc Trang Vietnam 9°37N 105°50E 121 H5
Soča → Europe 46°20N 13°40E 78 E6
Socastee U.S.A. 33°41N 78°59W 177 E15
Sochaczew Poland 52°15N 20°13E 83 F7
Soch'e = Shache China 38°20N 77°10E 109 E9
Sochi Russia 43°35N 39°40E 87 J4
Sochi ✈ (AER) Russia 43°27N 39°57E 87 J4
Sochos Greece 40°48N 23°22E 96 D5
Social Circle U.S.A. 33°39N 83°43W 178 B6
Société, Îs. de la
   French Polynesia 17°0S 151°0W 157 J12
Society Hill U.S.A. 34°30N 79°51W 177 D15
Society Is. = Société, Îs. de la
   French Polynesia 17°0S 151°0W 157 J12
Socompa, Portezuelo de
   Chile 24°27S 68°18W 190 A2
Socorro N. Mex.,
   U.S.A. 34°4N 106°54W 169 J10
Socorro, I. Mexico 18°45N 110°58W 180 D2
Socotra Yemen 12°30N 54°0E 131 E5
Socovos Spain 38°20N 1°58W 91 G3
Socuéllamos Spain 39°16N 2°47W 91 F2
Soda L. U.S.A. 35°10N 116°4W 171 K10
Soda Plains India 35°30N 79°0E 125 B8
Soda Springs U.S.A. 42°39N 111°36W 168 E8
Sodankylä Finland 67°29N 26°40E 60 C22
Soddy-Daisy U.S.A. 35°17N 85°10W 177 D12
Söderala Sweden 61°17N 16°55E 62 C10
Söderåsen △ Sweden 56°2N 13°13E 63 H7
Söderbärke Sweden 60°2N 15°45E 62 D9
Söderfors Sweden 60°23N 17°22E 62 D11
Söderhamn Sweden 61°18N 17°10E 62 C11
Söderköping Sweden 58°31N 16°20E 63 F10
Södermanlands län □
   Sweden 59°10N 16°30E 62 E11
Södertälje Sweden 59°12N 17°39E 62 E11
Sodiri Sudan 14°27N 29°0E 135 F11
Södra Finnskoga Sweden 60°42N 12°34E 62 C5
Södra Sandby Sweden 55°43N 13°21E 63 J7

Södra Ulvön Sweden 62°59N 18°38E 62 B12
Södra Vi Sweden 57°45N 15°45E 63 G9
Sodražica Slovenia 45°45N 14°39E 93 C11
Sodus U.S.A. 43°14N 77°4W 174 C7
Sodwana Bay △
   S. Africa 27°35S 32°43E 145 C6
Soe Indonesia 9°52S 124°17E 148 A3
Soekmekaar = Morebeng
   S. Africa 23°30S 29°55E 145 B4
Soest Germany 51°34N 8°7E 76 D4
Soest Neths. 52°9N 5°19E 69 B5
Sofades Greece 39°20N 22°4E 98 B4
Sofala □ Mozam. 19°30S 34°30E 145 B5
Sofara Mali 13°59N 4°9W 138 C4
Sofia = Sofiya Bulgaria 42°45N 23°20E 96 D7
Sofia → Madag. 15°27S 47°23E 141 H9
Sofievka Ukraine 37°47N 33°55E 85 H7
Sofiko Greece 37°47N 23°3E 98 D5
Sofiya Bulgaria 42°45N 23°20E 96 D7
Sofiya □ Bulgaria 42°15N 23°0E 96 D7
Sofiya ✈ (SOF) Bulgaria 42°46N 23°28E 96 D7
Sofrana Greece 36°5N 26°24E 99 E8
Sōfu-Gan Japan 29°49N 140°21E 113 K10
Sogakofe Ghana 6°2N 0°39E 139 D5
Sogamoso Colombia 5°43N 72°56W 186 B4
Sogār Iran 25°53N 58°6E 129 E8
Sögel Germany 52°50N 7°31E 76 C3
Sogndalsfjøra Norway 61°14N 7°5E 60 F12
Søgne Norway 58°5N 7°48E 61 G12
Sognefjorden Norway 61°10N 5°50E 60 F11
Sögüt Bilecik, Turkey 40°2N 30°11E 99 A12
Söğüt Burdur, Turkey 37°2N 29°50E 99 D11
Söğüt Dağı Turkey 37°50N 29°55E 99 D11
Söğütköy Turkey 36°40N 28°8E 99 E10
Soh Iran 33°26N 51°27E 128 C6
Sohâg Egypt 26°33N 31°43E 137 B8
Sohagpur India 22°42N 78°12E 124 H8
Sohar = Şuḥār Oman 24°20N 56°40E 129 E8
Sohela India 21°18N 83°24E 126 D6
Soheuksando S. Korea 34°4N 125°7E 115 G13
Sohm Abyssal Plain
   Atl. Oc. 36°0N 55°0W 56 C6
Soignies Belgium 50°35N 4°5E 69 D4
Soin Burkina Faso 12°47N 3°50W 138 C4
Soissons France 49°25N 3°19E 71 C10
Sōja Japan 34°40N 133°45E 112 G6
Sojat India 25°55N 73°45E 124 G5
Sok → Russia 53°24N 50°8E 84 D10
Sokal Ukraine 50°31N 24°15E 75 C13
Sokcho S. Korea 38°12N 128°36E 115 E15
Söke Turkey 37°48N 27°28E 99 D9
Sokelo
   Dem. Rep. of the Congo 9°55S 24°36E 143 D1
Sokhumi Georgia 43°0N 41°0E 87 J5
Sokki, Oued In →
   Algeria 29°30N 3°42E 136 C4
Soko Banja Serbia 43°40N 21°51E 96 C5
Soko Is. China 22°10N 113°54E 111 a
Sokodé Togo 9°0N 1°11E 139 D5
Sokol Russia 59°30N 40°5E 84 C11
Sokolac Bos.-H. 43°56N 18°48E 80 G3
Sokółka Poland 53°25N 23°30E 82 E10
Sokolo Ségou, Mali 14°53N 6°8W 138 C3
Sokolo Sikasso, Mali 11°25N 5°41W 138 C3
Sokolov Czech Rep. 50°12N 12°40E 78 A5
Sokołów Małopolski
   Poland 50°12N 22°7E 83 H9
Sokołów Podlaski
   Poland 52°25N 22°15E 83 F9
Sokoły Poland 52°59N 22°42E 83 F9
Sokoto Nigeria 13°2N 5°16E 139 C6
Sokoto □ Nigeria 12°30N 6°0E 139 C6
Sokoto → Nigeria 11°20N 4°10E 139 C5
Sokyrnytsya Ukraine 48°7N 23°23E 81 B8
Sokyryany Ukraine 48°27N 27°25E 81 B12
Sol, Costa del Spain 36°30N 4°30W 89 J6
Sol Iletsk Russia 51°10N 55°0E 108 B5
Sola → Poland 50°4N 19°15E 83 H6
Sola Kenya 0°2N 36°12E 142 B4
Solan India 30°55N 77°7E 124 D7
Solana Beach U.S.A. 32°58N 117°16W 171 N9
Solander I. N.Z. 46°34S 166°54E 155 G1
Solapur India 17°43N 75°56E 126 E2
Solca Romania 47°40N 25°50E 81 C10
Soldănești Moldova 47°48N 28°25E 81 C15
Soldeu Andorra 42°35N 1°40E 90 C6
Soldotna U.S.A. 60°29N 151°3W 160 E1
Soledad Colombia 10°55N 74°46W 186 A4
Soledad U.S.A. 36°26N 121°20W 170 H5
Soledad Venezuela 8°10N 63°34W 186 B6
Solent, The U.K. 50°45N 1°25W 67 G6
Solenzara France 41°53N 9°23E 73 G13
Solesmes France 50°10N 3°30E 71 B10
Solferino Italy 45°22N 10°34E 92 C7
Solfonntaggen Norway 60°2N 6°57E 60 F12
Solhan Turkey 38°57N 41°3E 105 C9
Soligorsk = Salihorsk
   Belarus 52°51N 27°27E 75 B14
Solihull U.K. 52°26N 1°47W 67 E6
Solikamsk Russia 59°38N 56°50E 106 D6
Solimões = Amazonas →
   S. Amer. 0°5S 50°0W 187 D8
Solin Croatia 43°33N 16°30E 93 E13
Solingen Germany 51°10N 7°5E 76 D3
Söll Austria 47°30N 12°11E 77 H8
Sollebrunn Sweden 58°8N 12°32E 63 F6
Sollefteå Sweden 63°12N 17°20E 62 A11
Sollentuna Sweden 59°25N 17°56E 62 E11
Sóller Spain 39°46N 2°43E 100 B9
Söllerön Sweden 60°55N 14°37E 62 D8
Solling-Vogler △
   Germany 51°45N 9°32E 76 D5
Solnechnogorsk Russia 56°10N 36°57E 84 D9
Solo → Indonesia 6°47S 112°22E 119 G15
Solofra Italy 40°49N 14°51E 95 B7
Sologne France 47°40N 1°45E 71 E8
Solok Indonesia 0°45S 100°40E 118 E2
Sololá Guatemala 14°49N 91°10W 182 D1
Solomon, N. Fork →
   U.S.A. 39°29N 98°26W 172 F4
Solomon, S. Fork →
   U.S.A. 39°25N 99°12W 172 F4
Solomon Is. ■ Pac. Oc. 6°0S 155°0E 147 B8
Solomon Rise Pac. Oc. 1°0N 157°0E 156 G7
Solon China 46°32N 121°10E 111 B13
Solon Springs U.S.A. 46°22N 91°49W 172 B8

Solonópole Brazil 5°44S 39°1W 189 B3
Solor Indonesia 8°27S 123°0E 119 F6
Solotcha Russia 54°48N 39°53E 84 E10
Solothurn Switz. 47°13N 7°32E 77 H3
Solothurn □ Switz. 47°18N 7°40E 77 H3
Solotvyn Ukraine 48°42N 24°25E 81 B9
Solsona Spain 42°0N 1°31E 90 C6
Solt Hungary 46°45N 19°1E 80 D4
Šolta Croatia 43°24N 16°15E 93 E13
Soltănābād Khorāsān, Iran 34°13N 59°58E 129 C8
Soltănābād Khorāsān, Iran 36°29N 58°5E 129 B8
Soltāniyeh Iran 36°26N 48°47E 105 D13
Soltau Germany 52°59N 9°50E 76 C5
Soltsy Russia 58°10N 30°30E 84 C6
Soltústik Qazaqstan □ Kazakhstan 54°0N 70°0E 109 B8
Solunska Glava Macedonia 41°44N 21°31E 96 E5
Solvang U.S.A. 34°36N 120°8W 171 L6
Solvay U.S.A. 43°3N 76°13W 175 C8
Sölvesborg Sweden 56°5N 14°35E 63 H8
Solway Firth U.K. 54°49N 3°35W 66 C4
Solwezi Zambia 12°11S 26°21E 143 E2
Sōma Japan 37°30N 140°50E 112 F10
Soma Turkey 39°10N 27°35E 99 B9
Somabhula Zimbabwe 19°42S 29°40E 145 A4
Somali Pen. Africa 7°0N 46°0E 132 F8
Somalia ■ Africa 7°0N 47°0E 131 F4
Somaliland □ Somalia 10°0N 46°0E 131 F4
Sombernon France 47°20N 4°40E 71 E11
Sombor Serbia 45°46N 19°9E 80 E4
Sombra Canada 42°43N 82°29W 174 D2
Sombrerete Mexico 23°38N 103°39W 180 C4
Sombrero Anguilla 18°37N 63°30W 183 C7
Sombrero Channel India 7°41N 93°35E 127 L11
Şomcuta Mare Romania 47°31N 23°28E 81 C8
Somdari India 25°47N 72°38E 124 G5
Someiclo △ Spain 43°5N 6°11W 88 B4
Somers U.S.A. 48°5N 114°13W 168 B6
Somerset Ky., U.S.A. 37°5N 84°36W 173 G11
Somerset Mass., U.S.A. 41°47N 71°8W 175 E13
Somerset Pa., U.S.A. 40°1N 79°5W 174 F5
Somerset □ U.K. 51°9N 3°0W 67 F5
Somerset East S. Africa 32°42S 25°35E 144 E4
Somerset I. Canada 73°30N 93°0W 160 C13
Somerset West S. Africa 34°8S 18°50E 144 D2
Somersworth U.S.A. 43°16N 70°52W 175 C14
Somerton U.S.A. 32°36N 114°43W 169 K6
Somerville U.S.A. 40°35N 74°38W 175 F10
Someş → Romania 47°49N 22°43E 80 C7
Someşul Mare → Romania 47°9N 23°55E 81 C8
Somme □ France 49°57N 2°20E 71 C9
Somme → France 50°11N 1°38E 71 B8
Somme, B. de la France 50°14N 1°33E 70 B8
Sommen Jönköping, Sweden 58°12N 14°58E 63 F8
Sommen Östergötland, Sweden 58°0N 15°15E 63 F9
Sommepy-Tahure France 49°15N 4°31E 71 C11
Sömmerda Germany 51°9N 11°7E 76 D7
Sommesous France 48°44N 4°12E 71 D11
Sommières France 43°47N 4°6E 73 E8
Somnath India 20°53N 70°22E 124 J4
Somogy □ Hungary 46°19N 17°30E 80 D2
Somogyszob Hungary 46°18N 17°20E 80 D2
Somosomo Fiji 16°47S 179°58W 154 a
Somosomo Str. Fiji 16°0S 180°0E 154 a
Somoto Nic. 13°28N 86°37W 182 D2
Sompolno Poland 52°26N 18°30E 83 F5
Somport, Túnel de Spain 42°48N 0°31W 90 C4
Somuncurá, Meseta de Argentina 41°30S 67°0W 192 B3
Somvarpet India 12°36N 75°52E 127 J2
Son → India 25°42N 84°52E 125 G11
Son, Laem Thailand 7°59N 98°16E 121 a
Son Ha Vietnam 15°3N 108°34E 120 E7
Son La Vietnam 21°20N 103°50E 116 G4
Son Morrell Spain 39°44N 3°20E 100 B10
Son Rapinya Spain 39°35N 2°37E 100 B9
Son Sardina Spain 39°37N 2°46E 100 B9
Son Serra Spain 39°43N 3°13E 100 B10
Son Servera Spain 39°37N 3°21E 100 B10
Son Tay Vietnam 21°8N 105°30E 116 G5
Son Tinh Vietnam 15°10N 108°40E 120 E7
Son-Kôl Kyrgyzstan 41°50N 75°12E 109 D9
Soná Panama 8°0N 81°20W 182 E3
Sonamarg India 34°18N 75°21E 125 B6
Sonamukhi India 23°18N 87°27E 125 H12
Sonar → India 24°24N 79°56E 125 G8
Sonbong N. Korea 42°24N 130°31E 114 C5
Sonch'ŏn N. Korea 39°48N 124°55E 115 E13
Sondags → S. Africa 33°44S 25°51E 144 E4
Sóndalo Italy 46°20N 10°19E 92 B7
Sønder Felding Denmark 55°57N 8°47E 63 J2
Sønder Omme Denmark 55°50N 8°54E 63 J2
Sønderborg Denmark 54°55N 9°49E 63 K3
Sondershausen Germany 51°22N 10°51E 76 D6
Sondre Strømfjord = Kangerlussuaq Greenland 66°59N 50°40W 57 D5
Sóndrio Italy 46°10N 9°52E 92 B6
Sondur → India 20°40N 82°1E 126 D6
Sone Mozam. 17°23S 34°55E 143 F3
Sonepur India 20°55N 83°50E 126 D6
Sonfim Brazil 6°0S 67°52W 188 B4
Song Nigeria 9°28N 12°39E 137 D7
Song Thailand 18°28N 100°11E 120 C3
Song Cau Vietnam 13°27N 109°18E 120 F7
Song Ma → Vietnam 19°37N 105°50E 116 G5
Songadh India 21°9N 73°33E 126 D1
Songan Indonesia 8°13S 115°24E 119 J18
Songea Tanzania 10°40S 35°40E 143 E4
Songeons France 49°32N 1°50E 71 C9
Songgang China 22°46N 113°50E 111 a
Songhua Hu China 43°35N 126°50E 115 C14
Songhua Jiang → China 47°45N 132°30E 111 B15
Songimvelo △ S. Africa 25°50S 31°2E 145 D5
Songjiang China 31°1N 121°12E 117 B13
Songjianghe China 42°10N 127°29E 115 C14
Sŏngjin = Kimch'aek N. Korea 40°40N 129°10E 115 D15
Songkan China 28°35N 106°52E 116 D6
Songkhla Thailand 7°13N 100°37E 121 J3
Songming China 25°12N 103°2E 116 E5
Sŏngnam N. Korea 38°45N 125°39E 115 E13

Songwe Dem. Rep. of the Congo 3°20S 26°16E 142 C2
Songwe → Africa 9°44S 33°58E 143 D3
Songxi China 27°31N 118°44E 117 D12
Songzi China 30°12N 111°45E 117 B8
Sonid Youqi China 42°45N 112°48E 114 C7
Sonid Zuoqi China 43°50N 113°42E 114 C7
Sonipat India 29°0N 77°5E 124 E7
Sonkach India 22°59N 76°21E 124 H7
Sonkovo Russia 57°50N 37°5E 84 C9
Sonmiani Pakistan 25°25N 66°40E 124 G2
Sonmiani B. Pakistan 25°15N 66°30E 124 G2
Sonnino Italy 41°25N 13°14E 94 A6
Sono → Minas Gerais, Brazil 17°2S 45°32W 189 D1
Sono → Tocantins, Brazil 9°58S 48°11W 189 B1
Sonoma U.S.A. 38°18N 122°28W 170 G4
Sonora Calif., U.S.A. 37°59N 120°23W 170 H6
Sonora Tex., U.S.A. 30°34N 100°39W 176 F4
Sonora □ Mexico 29°20N 110°40W 180 B2
Sonora → Mexico 29°5N 110°55W 180 B2
Sonoran Desert U.S.A. 33°40N 113°30W 171 L12
Sonoyta Mexico 31°51N 112°50W 180 A2
Sonqor Iran 34°47N 47°36E 105 E12
Sonseca Spain 39°42N 3°57W 89 F7
Sonsonate El Salv. 13°43N 89°44W 182 D2
Sonstorp Sweden 58°44N 15°38E 63 F9
Sonthofen Germany 47°30N 10°16E 77 H6
Soochow = Suzhou China 31°19N 120°38E 117 B13
Sooke Canada 48°13N 123°43W 170 B3
Soomaa △ Estonia 58°30N 28°5E 84 C3
Soomaaliya = Somalia ■ Africa 7°0N 47°0E 131 F4
Sop Hao Laos 20°33N 104°27E 116 G5
Sop Prap Thailand 17°53N 99°20E 120 C2
Sopchoppy U.S.A. 30°4N 84°29W 178 E5
Sopelana Spain 43°23N 2°58W 90 B2
Soperton U.S.A. 32°23N 82°35W 178 C7
Sopi Indonesia 2°34N 128°28E 119 D7
Sopot Bulgaria 42°39N 24°45E 97 D8
Sopot Poland 54°27N 18°31E 82 D5
Sopot Serbia 44°29N 20°36E 96 B4
Sopotnica Macedonia 41°18N 21°13E 96 E5
Sopron Hungary 47°45N 16°32E 80 C1
Sopur India 34°18N 74°27E 125 B6
Sora Italy 41°43N 13°37E 93 G10
Sorab India 14°23N 75°5E 127 G2
Sorada India 19°45N 84°26E 126 E7
Sorah Pakistan 27°13N 68°56E 124 F3
Söråker Sweden 62°30N 17°32E 62 B11
Sorang Kazakhstan 49°46N 72°51E 109 C8
Sorano Italy 42°41N 11°43E 93 F8
Soraon India 25°37N 81°51E 125 G9
Sorata Bolivia 15°50S 68°40W 188 D4
Sorbas Spain 37°6N 2°7W 91 D8
Sörbygden Sweden 62°48N 16°12E 62 B10
Sord = Swords Ireland 53°28N 6°13W 64 C5
Sordellen Sweden 61°36N 16°43E 62 C10
Sore France 44°18N 0°35W 72 D3
Sorel-Tracy Canada 46°0N 73°10W 164 C5
Soresina Italy 45°17N 9°51E 92 C6
Sörforsa Sweden 61°43N 16°58E 62 C10
Sórgono Italy 40°1N 9°6E 94 B2
Sorgues France 44°1N 4°53E 73 D8
Sorgun Turkey 39°46N 35°11E 104 C6
Soria Spain 41°43N 2°32W 90 C2
Soria □ Spain 41°46N 2°28W 90 C2
Soriano Uruguay 33°24S 58°19W 190 C4
Soriano nel Cimino Italy 42°25N 12°14E 93 F9
Sorkh, Kuh-e Iran 35°40N 58°30E 129 C8
Soro Denmark 55°26N 11°32E 63 J5
Soro Guinea 10°9N 9°48W 138 C3
Soroca Moldova 48°8N 28°12E 81 B15
Sorocaba Brazil 23°31S 47°27W 191 A6
Sorochinsk Russia 52°26N 53°10E 108 B4
Soroki = Soroca Moldova 48°8N 28°12E 81 B15
Sorong Indonesia 0°55S 131°15E 119 E8
Soroni Greece 36°21N 28°1E 101 C10
Soroti Uganda 1°43N 33°35E 142 B3
Sørøya Norway 70°40N 22°30E 60 A20
Sørøysundet Norway 70°25N 23°0E 60 A20
Sorraia → Portugal 38°55N 8°53W 89 G2
Sorrell Australia 42°47S 147°34E 151 G4
Sorrento Italy 40°37N 14°22E 95 B7
Sorsele Sweden 65°31N 17°30E 60 D17
Sörsjön Sweden 61°24N 13°5E 62 C7
Sorso Italy 40°48N 8°34E 94 B1
Sorsogon Phil. 13°0N 124°0E 119 E6
Sortavala Russia 61°42N 30°41E 84 B6
Sortino Italy 37°9N 15°2E 95 E8
Sortland Norway 68°42N 15°25E 60 B16
Sortot Sudan 19°3N 30°28E 137 D3
Sorvizhi Russia 57°52N 48°32E 86 B9
Sos del Rey Católico Spain 42°30N 1°13W 90 C3
Soscumica, L. Canada 50°15N 77°27W 164 B4
Sösdala Sweden 56°2N 13°41E 63 H7
Sosna → Russia 52°42N 38°55E 85 F10
Sosnovka Kirov, Russia 56°17N 51°18E 86 C9
Sosnovka Tambov, Russia 53°13N 41°24E 86 D5
Sosnovyy Bor Russia 59°55N 29°6E 84 C5
Sosnowiec Poland 50°20N 19°10E 83 H6
Sospel France 43°52N 7°27E 73 E11
Sossus Vlei Namibia 24°40S 15°23E 144 b
Šoštanj Slovenia 46°23N 15°4E 93 B12
Sŏsura N. Korea 42°16N 130°36E 115 C16
Sot → India 27°27N 79°37E 125 F8
Sotavento C. Verde Is. 15°0N 25°0W 134 b
Sotik Kenya 0°41S 35°7E 142 C4
Sotkamo Finland 64°8N 28°23E 60 D23
Soto Spain 43°32N 6°4W 88 B4
Soto la Marina Mexico 23°46N 98°13W 181 C5
Soto la Marina → Mexico 23°45N 97°45W 181 C5
Soto y Amio Spain 42°46N 5°53W 88 C5
Sotouboua Togo 8°34N 0°59E 138 D5
Sotrondio Spain 43°17N 5°36W 88 B5
Sotuta Mexico 20°36N 89°1W 181 C7
Souanké Congo 2°10N 14°3E 140 D2
Soubré Ivory C. 5°50N 6°43W 138 D4
Souda Greece 35°29N 24°4E 101 D6
Soudas, Ormos Greece 35°25N 24°10E 101 D6
Souderton U.S.A. 40°19N 75°19W 175 F9

Soufli Greece 41°12N 26°18E 97 C11
Soufrière Guadeloupe 16°5N 61°40W 182 b
Soufrière St. Lucia 13°51N 61°3W 183 f
Soufrière Bay Dominica 15°13N 61°22W 183 f
Souillac France 44°53N 1°29E 72 D5
Souilly France 49°3N 5°17E 71 C12
Souk-Ahras Algeria 27°31N 118°44E 117 D12
Souk-Ahras □ Algeria 36°10N 7°55E 136 A5
Souk el Arba du Rharb Morocco 34°43N 5°59W 136 B2
Soukhouma Laos 14°38N 105°48E 120 E5
Sŏul = Seoul S. Korea 37°31N 126°58E 115 F14
Soulac-sur-Mer France 45°30N 1°7W 72 C2
Soulougou Burkina Faso 13°1N 0°25E 139 C5
Soultz-sous-Forêts France 48°57N 7°52E 71 D14
Sound, The = Øresund Europe 55°45N 12°40E 63 J6
Sound, The U.K. 50°20N 4°10W 67 G3
Sound I. India 12°58N 92°59E 127 H11
Sounion, Akra Greece 37°37N 24°1E 98 D6
Sour el Ghozlane Algeria 36°10N 3°45E 136 A4
Sources, Mt. aux Lesotho 28°45S 28°50E 145 C4
Soure Brazil 0°35S 48°30W 187 D9
Soure Portugal 40°4N 8°38W 88 E2
Souris Man., Canada 49°40N 100°20W 163 D8
Souris P.E.I., Canada 46°21N 62°15W 165 C7
Souris → N. Amer. 49°40N 99°34W 172 A4
Sourou → Africa 12°45N 3°25E 138 C4
Sourpi Greece 39°6N 22°54E 98 B4
Sous, O. → Morocco 30°27N 9°31W 136 B2
Sous-Massa △ Morocco 30°27N 9°31W 136 B2
Sous-Massa-Drâa □ Morocco 30°45N 6°30W 136 B2
Sousa Brazil 6°45S 38°10W 189 B3
Sousel Portugal 38°57N 7°40W 89 G3
Soustons France 43°45N 1°19W 72 E2
Sout → S. Africa 31°35S 18°24E 144 D2
South Africa ■ Africa 32°0S 23°0E 144 D3
South America 10°0S 60°0W 184 E5
South Andaman India 11°45N 92°10E 127 J11
South Aulatsivik I. Canada 56°45N 61°30W 165 A7
South Australia □ Australia 32°0S 139°0E 152 B3
South Australian Basin Ind. Oc. 38°0S 126°0E 156 L4
South Ayrshire □ U.K. 55°18N 4°41W 65 F4
South Baldy Pk. U.S.A. 34°6N 107°11W 169 J10
South Bass I. U.S.A. 41°39N 82°49W 174 E2
South Bay U.S.A. 26°40N 80°43W 179 J9
South Bend Ind., U.S.A. 41°41N 86°15W 172 E10
South Bend Wash., U.S.A. 46°40N 123°48W 170 D3
South Boston U.S.A. 36°42N 78°54W 173 G14
South Branch Canada 47°55N 59°2W 165 C8
South Brook Canada 49°26N 56°5W 165 C8
South Brother I. India 10°56N 92°37E 127 J11
South Bruny I. Australia 43°20S 147°15E 151 G4
South Carolina □ U.S.A. 34°0N 81°0W 177 E14
South Charleston U.S.A. 38°22N 81°44W 173 F13
South China Sea Asia 10°0N 113°0E 118 C4
South Congaree U.S.A. 33°53N 81°9W 178 B8
South Cumberland Is. △ Australia 20°42S 149°11E 150 b
South Dakota □ U.S.A. 44°15N 100°0W 172 C4
South Dayton U.S.A. 42°21N 79°3W 174 D5
South Daytona U.S.A. 29°10N 81°0W 179 F8
South Deerfield U.S.A. 42°29N 72°37W 175 D12
South Downs U.K. 50°52N 0°25W 67 G7
South Downs △ U.K. 50°50N 0°50W 67 G7
South East C. Australia 43°40S 146°50E 151 G4
South East Forest △ Australia 37°0S 149°30E 153 D8
South East Is. Australia 34°17S 123°30E 149 F3
South Esk → U.K. 56°43N 2°31W 65 E6
South Fiji Basin Pac. Oc. 26°0S 175°0E 156 K9
South Foreland U.K. 51°8N 1°24E 67 F9
South Fork American → U.S.A. 38°57N 120°59W 170 G5
South Fork Edisto → U.S.A. 33°16N 80°54W 178 B9
South Fork Feather → U.S.A. 39°17N 121°36W 170 F5
South Fork Grand → U.S.A. 45°43N 102°17W 172 C2
South Fork Milk → U.S.A. 48°4N 106°19W 168 B10
South Fork Republican → U.S.A. 40°3N 101°31W 172 E3
South Georgia Antarctica 54°30S 37°0W 55 B1
South Gloucestershire □ U.K. 51°32N 2°28W 67 F5
South Hadley U.S.A. 42°16N 72°35W 175 D12
South Haven U.S.A. 42°24N 86°16W 172 D10
South Henik L. Canada 61°30N 97°20W 163 A9
South Horr Kenya 2°12N 36°56E 142 B4
South I. India 10°3N 72°17E 127 J1
South I. Kenya 2°35N 36°35E 142 B4
South I. N.Z. 44°0S 170°0E 155 E5
South Indian Lake Canada 56°47N 98°56W 163 B9
South Invercargill N.Z. 46°26S 168°23E 155 G3
South Island △ Kenya 2°35N 36°35E 142 B4
South Knife → Canada 58°55N 94°37W 163 B10
South Koel → India 22°32N 85°14E 125 H11
South Korea ■ Asia 36°0N 128°0E 115 G15
South Lake Tahoe U.S.A. 38°57N 119°59W 170 G6
South Lanarkshire □ U.K. 55°37N 3°53W 65 F5
South Loup → U.S.A. 41°4N 98°39W 172 E4
South Luangwa △ Zambia 13°0S 31°20E 143 E3
South Magnetic Pole Antarctica 64°8S 138°8E 55 C9
South Miami U.S.A. 25°42N 80°17W 179 K9

South Milwaukee U.S.A. 42°55N 87°52W 172 D10
South Molton U.K. 51°1N 3°51W 67 F4
South Moose L. Canada 53°49N 100°1W 163 C8
South Nahanni → Canada 61°3N 123°21W 162 A4
South Nation → Canada 45°34N 75°6W 175 A9
South Natuna Is. = Natuna Selatan, Kepulauan Indonesia 2°45N 109°0E 118 D3
South Negril Pt. Jamaica 18°16N 78°22W 182 a
South Newport U.S.A. 31°38N 81°24W 178 D8
South Orkney Is. Antarctica 63°0S 45°0W 55 C18
South Ossetia □ Georgia 42°21N 44°2E 87 J7
South Otselic U.S.A. 42°38N 75°46W 175 D9
South Pagai, I. = Pagai Selatan, Pulau Indonesia 3°0S 100°15E 118 E2
South Paris U.S.A. 44°14N 70°31W 175 B14
South Pittsburg U.S.A. 35°1N 85°42W 177 D12
South Platte → U.S.A. 41°7N 100°42W 172 E3
South Pole Antarctica 90°0S 0°0 55 E
South Ponte Vedra Beach U.S.A. 30°3N 81°20W 178 E8
South Porcupine Canada 48°30N 81°12W 164 C3
South Portland U.S.A. 43°38N 70°15W 173 D18
South Pt. Barbados 13°2N 59°32W 183 g
South Pt. U.S.A. 44°52N 83°19W 174 B1
South River Canada 45°52N 79°23W 164 C4
South River U.S.A. 40°27N 74°23W 175 F10
South Ronaldsay U.K. 58°48N 2°58W 65 C6
South Rukuru → Malawi 10°44S 34°14E 143 E3
South Sandwich Is. Antarctica 57°0S 27°0W 55 B1
South Sandwich Trench Atl. Oc. 56°0S 24°0W 55 B1
South Saskatchewan → Canada 53°15N 105°5W 162 C6
South Seal → Canada 58°48N 98°8W 163 B9
South Sentinel I. India 10°59N 92°14E 127 J11
South Shetland Is. Antarctica 62°0S 59°0W 55 C18
South Shields U.K. 55°0N 1°25W 66 C6
South Sioux City U.S.A. 42°28N 96°24W 172 D5
South Sister U.S.A. 44°4N 121°51W 168 D3
South Sudan ■ Africa 8°0N 30°0E 135 G12
South Taranaki Bight N.Z. 39°40S 174°5E 154 F3
South Tasman Rise S. Ocean 48°0S 146°0E 55 A10
South Thompson → Canada 50°40N 120°20W 162 C4
South Twin I. Canada 53°7N 79°52W 164 B4
South Tyne → U.K. 54°59N 2°8W 66 C5
South Uist U.K. 57°20N 7°15W 65 D1
South Valley U.S.A. 35°1N 106°41W 169 J10
South Venice U.S.A. 27°3N 82°25W 179 H7
South Wellesley Is. Australia 16°58S 139°17E 150 B2
South West C. Australia 43°34S 146°3E 151 G4
South West C. N.Z. 47°17S 167°28E 155 H2
South West Rocks Australia 30°52S 153°3E 153 A10
South Williamsport U.S.A. 41°13N 77°0W 174 E8
South Yorkshire □ U.K. 53°27N 1°36W 66 D6
Southampton Canada 44°30N 81°25W 174 B3
Southampton U.K. 50°54N 1°23W 67 G6
Southampton U.S.A. 40°53N 72°23W 175 F12
Southampton □ U.K. 50°54N 1°23W 67 G6
Southampton I. Canada 64°30N 84°0W 161 E15
Southaven U.S.A. 34°59N 90°0W 177 D9
Southbank Canada 54°2N 125°46W 162 C3
Southbridge N.Z. 43°48S 172°16E 155 D7
Southbridge U.S.A. 42°5N 72°2W 175 D12
Southeast Indian Ridge Ind. Oc. 43°0S 80°0E 156 J11
Southend Canada 56°19N 103°22W 163 B8
Southend-on-Sea U.K. 51°32N 0°44E 67 F8
Southend-on-Sea □ U.K. 51°32N 0°44E 67 F8
Southern = Yuzhnyy □ Russia 44°0N 40°0E 106 E5
Southern □ Malawi 15°0S 35°0E 143 F4
Southern □ S. Leone 8°0N 12°30W 138 D2
Southern □ Zambia 16°20S 26°20E 143 F2
Southern Alps N.Z. 43°41S 170°11E 155 E3
Southern Cross Australia 31°12S 119°15E 149 F2
Southern Indian L. Canada 57°10N 98°30W 163 B9
Southern Lau Group Fiji 18°40S 178°40W 154 a
Southern Ocean 62°0S 60°0E 55 C6
Southern Pines U.S.A. 35°11N 79°24W 177 D15
Southern Uplands U.K. 55°28N 3°52W 65 F5
Southington U.S.A. 41°36N 72°53W 175 E12
Southland □ N.Z. 45°30S 168°0E 155 F3
Southold U.S.A. 41°4N 72°26W 175 E12
Southport Australia 27°58S 153°25E 153 D5
Southport U.K. 53°39N 3°0W 66 D4
Southport Fla., U.S.A. 30°17N 85°38W 178 F3
Southport N.Y., U.S.A. 42°3N 76°49W 174 D8
Southwest △ Australia 43°8S 146°5E 151 G4
Southwest Pacific Basin Pac. Oc. 40°0S 140°0W 55 A12
Southwold U.K. 52°20N 1°41E 67 E9
Southwood △ Australia 27°48S 150°8E 151 D5
Soutpansberg S. Africa 23°0S 29°30E 145 B4
Souvigny France 46°33N 3°10E 71 F10
Sovata Romania 46°35N 25°3E 81 C10
Soverato Italy 38°41N 16°33E 95 D9

Sozh → Belarus 51°57N 30°48E 75 E16
Sozopol Bulgaria 42°23N 27°42E 97 D11
Spa Belgium 50°29N 5°53E 69 D5
Spaatz I. Antarctica 73°10S 75°0W 55 D17
Spain ■ Europe 39°0N 4°0W 89 C5
Spalding Australia 33°30S 138°37E 152 B3
Spalding U.K. 52°48N 0°9W 66 E7
Spanaway U.S.A. 47°6N 122°26W 170 C4
Spangler U.S.A. 40°39N 78°48W 174 F6
Spanish Canada 46°12N 82°20W 164 C3
Spanish Fork U.S.A. 40°7N 111°39W 168 F8
Spanish Town Br. Virgin Is. 18°26N 64°26W 183 e
Spanish Town Jamaica 18°0N 76°57W 182 a
Sparks Ga., U.S.A. 31°11N 83°26W 178 D6
Sparks Nev., U.S.A. 39°32N 119°45W 170 F7
Sparreholm Sweden 59°4N 16°49E 62 E10
Sparta = Sparti Greece 37°5N 22°25E 98 D4
Sparta Ga., U.S.A. 33°17N 82°58W 178 C6
Sparta Mich., U.S.A. 43°10N 85°42W 173 D11
Sparta N.J., U.S.A. 41°2N 74°38W 175 E10
Sparta Wis., U.S.A. 43°56N 90°49W 172 D8
Spartanburg U.S.A. 34°56N 81°57W 177 D14
Spartansburg U.S.A. 41°49N 79°41W 174 E5
Sparti Greece 37°5N 22°25E 98 D4
Spartivento, C. Calabria, Italy 37°55N 16°4E 95 F9
Spartivento, C. Sard., Italy 38°53N 8°50E 94 D1
Sparwood Canada 49°44N 114°53W 162 D6
Spas-Demensk Russia 54°20N 34°0E 84 E7
Spas-Klepiki Russia 55°10N 40°10E 84 E11
Spassk-Dalniy Russia 44°40N 132°48E 112 B6
Spassk-Ryazanskiy Russia 54°24N 40°25E 84 E11
Spatha, Akra Greece 35°42N 23°43E 101 D5
Spatsizi → Canada 57°42N 128°7W 162 B3
Spatsizi Plateau Wilderness △ Canada 57°40N 128°0W 162 B3
Spean → U.K. 56°55N 4°59W 65 E4
Spearfish U.S.A. 44°30N 103°52W 172 C2
Spearman U.S.A. 36°12N 101°12W 176 C4
Speculator U.S.A. 43°30N 74°22W 175 C10
Speia Moldova 46°59N 29°19E 81 D14
Speightstown Barbados 13°15N 59°39W 183 g
Speke Gulf Tanzania 2°20S 32°50E 142 C3
Spello Italy 42°59N 12°40E 93 F9
Spence Bay = Taloyoak Canada 69°32N 93°32W 160 D13
Spencer Idaho, U.S.A. 44°22N 112°11W 168 D7
Spencer Iowa, U.S.A. 43°9N 95°9W 172 D6
Spencer N.Y., U.S.A. 42°13N 76°30W 175 D8
Spencer Nebr., U.S.A. 42°53N 98°42W 172 D4
Spencer, C. Australia 35°20S 136°53E 152 C2
Spencer B. Namibia 25°30S 14°47E 144 C1
Spencer G. Australia 34°0S 137°20E 152 B2
Spencerville Canada 44°51N 75°33W 175 B9
Spences Bridge Canada 50°25N 121°20W 162 C4
Spennymoor U.K. 54°42N 1°36W 66 C6
Spenser Mts. N.Z. 42°15N 172°45E 155 D6
Spentrup Denmark 56°33N 10°2E 63 H4
Sperchios → Greece 38°57N 22°3E 98 C4
Sperrin Mts. U.K. 54°50N 7°0W 64 B5
Spessart Germany 49°56N 9°18E 77 F5
Spetses Greece 37°15N 23°10E 98 D5
Spey → U.K. 57°40N 3°6W 65 D5
Speyer Germany 49°29N 8°25E 77 F4
Spezand Pakistan 29°59N 67°0E 124 E2
Spezzano Albanese Italy 39°40N 16°19E 95 C9
Spiddle Ireland 53°15N 9°18W 64 C2
Spiekeroog Germany 53°46N 7°42E 76 B3
Spiez Switz. 46°40N 7°40E 77 J3
Spili Greece 35°13N 24°31E 101 D6
Spilimbergo Italy 46°7N 12°54E 93 B9
Spin Büldak Afghan. 31°1N 66°25E 124 D2
Spinalonga Greece 35°18N 25°44E 101 D7
Spinazzola Italy 40°58N 16°5E 95 B9
Spineni Romania 44°43N 24°37E 81 F9
Spinifex ⊙ Australia 28°30S 128°30E 149 E4
Spirit Lake U.S.A. 48°15N 122°9W 170 B4
Spirit River Canada 55°45N 118°50W 162 B5
Spiritwood Canada 53°24N 107°33W 162 C6
Spišská Nová Ves Slovak Rep. 48°58N 20°34E 79 C13
Spišské Podhradie Slovak Rep. 49°0N 20°48E 79 B13
Spital Austria 47°42N 14°18E 78 D7
Spithead U.K. 50°45N 1°10W 67 G6
Spitsbergen = Svalbard Arctic 78°0N 17°0E 57 B12
Spittal an der Drau Austria 46°48N 13°31E 78 E6
Spjelkavik Norway 62°28N 6°22E 60 E12
Split Croatia 43°31N 16°26E 93 E13
Split ✠ (SPU) Croatia 43°33N 16°15E 93 E13
Split L. Canada 56°8N 96°15W 163 B9
Split Lake Canada 56°8N 96°15W 163 B9
Splitski Kanal Croatia 43°31N 16°20E 93 E13
Splügenpass Switz. 46°30N 9°20E 77 J5
Spofford U.S.A. 29°10N 100°25W 176 G4
Spokane U.S.A. 47°40N 117°24W 168 C5
Spoleto Italy 42°44N 12°44E 93 F9
Spooner U.S.A. 45°50N 91°53W 172 C8
Sporyy Navolok, Mys Russia 75°50N 68°40E 106 B7
Sprague U.S.A. 47°18N 117°59W 168 C5
Spratly I. S. China Sea 8°38N 111°55E 118 C4
Spratly Is. S. China Sea 8°20N 112°0E 118 C4
Spray U.S.A. 44°50N 119°48W 168 D4
Spreča → Bos.-H. 44°44N 18°6E 80 F3
Spree → Germany 52°32N 13°12E 76 B9
Spreewald Germany 51°58N 13°51E 76 D9
Spremberg Germany 51°34N 14°22E 76 D10
Sprengisandur Iceland 64°52N 18°7W 60 D4
Spring City U.S.A. 40°11N 111°30W 168 F8
Spring Cr. → U.S.A. 30°54N 84°45W 178 E5
Spring Creek U.S.A. 40°44N 115°35W 168 F6
Spring Garden U.S.A. 39°52N 120°47W 170 F6
Spring Hall Barbados 13°18N 59°36W 183 g
Spring Hill Ala., U.S.A. 31°42N 85°58W 178 D4
Spring Hill Fla., U.S.A. 28°27N 82°41W 179 G7
Spring Mts. U.S.A. 36°0N 115°45W 171 J11
Spring Valley Calif., U.S.A. 32°44N 116°59W 171 N10
Spring Valley Nev., U.S.A. 36°36N 115°14W 171 J11
Springbok S. Africa 29°42S 17°54E 144 C2
Springboro U.S.A. 41°48N 80°22W 174 E4
Springdale Canada 49°30N 56°6W 165 C8

Springdale U.S.A. 36°11N 94°8W 176 C7
Springe Germany 52°13N 9°33E 76 C5
Springer U.S.A. 36°22N 104°36W 169 H11
Springerville U.S.A. 34°8N 109°17W 169 J9
Springfield Canada 42°50N 80°56W 174 D3
Springfield N.Z. 43°19S 171°56E 155 D6
Springfield Colo., U.S.A. 37°24N 102°37W 169 H12
Springfield Fla., U.S.A. 30°10N 85°37W 178 E4
Springfield Ga., U.S.A. 32°22N 81°18W 178 C8
Springfield Ill., U.S.A. 39°48N 89°39W 172 F9
Springfield Mass., U.S.A. 42°6N 72°35W 175 D12
Springfield Mo., U.S.A. 37°13N 93°17W 172 G7
Springfield Ohio, U.S.A. 39°55N 83°49W 173 F12
Springfield Oreg., U.S.A. 44°3N 123°1W 168 D2
Springfield S.C., U.S.A. 33°30N 81°17W 178 B8
Springfield Tenn., U.S.A. 36°31N 86°53W 177 C11
Springfield Vt., U.S.A. 43°18N 72°29W 175 C12
Springfontein S. Africa 30°15S 25°40E 144 E4
Springhill U.S.A. 45°40N 64°4W 165 C7
Springhill U.S.A. 33°0N 93°28W 176 E8
Springhouse Canada 51°56N 122°7W 162 C4
Springlands = Corriverton Guyana 5°55N 57°20W 186 B7
Springs S. Africa 26°13S 28°25E 145 D4
Springsure Australia 24°8S 148°6E 150 C4
Springvale U.S.A. 31°50N 84°53W 178 D5
Springvale Maine, U.S.A. 43°28N 70°48W 175 C14
Springville Calif., U.S.A. 36°8N 118°49W 170 J8
Springville N.Y., U.S.A. 42°31N 78°40W 174 D6
Springville Utah, U.S.A. 40°10N 111°37W 168 F8
Springwater U.S.A. 42°38N 77°35W 174 D7
Spruce-Creek U.S.A. 40°36N 78°9W 174 F6
Spruce Knob-Seneca Rocks △ U.S.A. 38°50N 79°30W 173 F14
Spruce Mt. U.S.A. 44°12N 72°19W 175 B12
Sprucedale Canada 45°29N 79°28W 174 A5
Spur U.S.A. 33°28N 100°52W 176 E4
Spurn Hd. U.K. 53°35N 0°8E 66 D8
Spuž Montenegro 42°32N 19°10E 96 D3
Spuzzum Canada 49°37N 121°23W 162 D4
Squam L. U.S.A. 43°45N 71°32W 175 C13
Squamish Canada 49°45N 123°10W 162 D4
Square Islands Canada 52°47N 55°47W 165 B8
Squillace, G. di Italy 38°45N 16°50E 95 D9
Squinzano Italy 40°26N 18°2E 95 B11
Squires, Mt. Australia 26°14S 127°28E 149 E4
Srbac Bos.-H. 45°7N 17°30E 80 E2
Srbica = Skënderaj Kosovo 42°45N 20°47E 96 C4
Srbija = Serbia ■ Europe 43°20N 20°0E 96 C4
Srbobran Serbia 45°32N 19°48E 80 E4
Sre Ambel Cambodia 11°8N 103°46E 121 G4
Sre Khtum Cambodia 12°10N 106°52E 121 F6
Sre Umbell = Sre Ambel Cambodia 11°8N 103°46E 121 G4
Srebarna Bulgaria 44°6N 27°4E 97 B11
Srebrenica Bos.-H. 44°6N 19°18E 80 F4
Sredinnyy Khrebet Russia 57°0N 160°0E 107 D17
Sredinnyy Ra. = Sredinnyy Khrebet Russia 57°0N 160°0E 107 D17
Središče Slovenia 46°24N 16°17E 93 B13
Sredna Gora Bulgaria 42°40N 24°20E 97 D8
Srednekolymsk Russia 67°27N 153°40E 107 C16
Sredni Rodopi Bulgaria 41°40N 24°45E 97 E8
Srednogorie Bulgaria 42°43N 24°10E 97 D8
Śrem Poland 52°6N 17°2E 83 F4
Sremska Mitrovica Serbia 44°59N 19°38E 80 E4
Sremski Karlovci Serbia 45°12N 19°56E 80 E4
Srepok → Cambodia 13°33N 106°16E 120 F6
Sretensk Russia 52°10N 117°40E 107 D12
Sri Aman = Bandar Sri Aman Malaysia 1°15N 111°32E 118 D4
Sri Kalahasti India 13°45N 79°44E 127 H4
Sri Lanka ■ Asia 7°30N 80°50E 127 L5
Sri Pada = Adam's Peak Sri Lanka 6°48N 80°30E 127 L5
Sriharikota India 13°40N 80°2E 127 H5
Srikakulam India 18°14N 83°58E 126 E6
Srinagar India 34°5N 74°50E 125 B6
Srivardhan India 18°4N 73°3E 126 E1
Srivilliputtur India 9°31N 77°40E 127 K3
Środa Śląska Poland 51°10N 16°36E 83 G3
Środa Wielkopolski Poland 52°15N 17°19E 83 F4
Srono Indonesia 8°24S 114°16E 119 J17
Srpska Crnja Serbia 45°38N 20°44E 80 E5
Srpski Itebej Serbia 45°35N 20°44E 80 E5
Srungavarapukota India 18°7N 83°10E 126 E6
Ssese Is. = Sese Is. Uganda 0°20S 32°20E 142 C3
Staaten → Australia 16°24S 141°17E 150 B3
Staaten River △ Australia 16°15S 142°40E 150 B3
Stabbursdalen △ Norway 70°5N 24°15E 60 A21
Staberhuk Germany 54°23N 11°18E 76 A7
Stade Germany 53°35N 9°29E 76 B5
Stadskanaal Neths. 53°4N 6°55E 69 A6
Stadtallendorf Germany 50°48N 9°1E 76 E5
Stadthagen Germany 52°19N 9°3E 76 C5
Stadtlohn Germany 51°59N 6°55E 76 D2
Stadtroda Germany 50°51N 11°44E 76 E7
Staffa U.K. 56°27N 6°21W 65 E2
Staffanstorp Sweden 55°39N 13°13E 63 J6
Stafford U.K. 52°49N 2°7W 66 E5
Stafford U.S.A. 38°0N 98°36W 176 B5
Stafford Springs U.S.A. 41°57N 72°18W 175 E12
Staffordshire □ U.K. 52°53N 2°10W 66 E5
Stagnone Italy 37°53N 12°26E 94 E5
Stagnone di Marsala Italy 37°50N 12°28E 94 E5
Staines U.K. 51°26N 0°29W 67 F7
Stainz Austria 46°53N 15°17E 78 E8
Stakhanov Ukraine 48°35N 38°40E 87 H10
Stalać Serbia 43°43N 21°28E 96 C5
Stalida Greece 35°17N 25°25E 101 D7
Stallarholmen Sweden 59°22N 17°12E 62 E11
Stålldalen Sweden 59°56N 14°56E 62 E8
Stalowa Wola Poland 50°34N 22°3E 83 H9

Stalybridge U.K. 53°28N 2°3W 66 D5
Stamford Australia 21°15S 143°46E 150 C3
Stamford U.K. 52°39N 0°29W 67 E7
Stamford Conn., U.S.A. 41°3N 73°32W 175 E11
Stamford N.Y., U.S.A. 42°25N 74°38W 175 D10
Stamford Tex., U.S.A. 32°57N 99°48W 176 E5
Stampriet Namibia 24°20S 18°28E 144 B2
Stamps U.S.A. 33°22N 93°30W 176 E8
Stančevo = Kalipetrovo Bulgaria 44°5N 27°14E 97 B11
Standerton S. Africa 26°55S 29°7E 145 C4
Standish U.S.A. 43°59N 83°57W 173 D12
Stanford S. Africa 34°26S 19°29E 144 D2
Stanford U.S.A. 47°9N 110°13W 168 C8
Stånga Sweden 57°17N 18°29E 63 G12
Stanger S. Africa 29°27S 31°14E 145 C5
Stängselåsen = Salpausselkä Finland 61°3N 26°15E 84 B4
Stanhope Australia 36°27S 144°59E 153 D6
Stanišić Serbia 45°56N 19°10E 80 E4
Stanislaus → U.S.A. 37°40N 121°14W 170 H5
Stanisławów Poland 52°18N 21°33E 83 F8
Stanley Australia 40°46S 145°19E 151 G4
Stanley China 22°13N 114°12E 111 a
Stanley Falk. Is. 51°40S 59°51W 192 D5
Stanley U.K. 54°53N 1°41W 66 C6
Stanley Idaho, U.S.A. 44°13N 114°56W 168 D6
Stanley N. Dak., U.S.A. 48°19N 102°23W 172 A2
Stanley N.Y., U.S.A. 42°48N 77°6W 174 D7
Stanley Mission Canada 55°25N 104°33W 163 B8
Stanley Res. India 11°50N 77°40E 127 J3
Stannards U.S.A. 42°5N 77°55W 174 D7
Stanovoy Khrebet Russia 55°0N 130°0E 107 D14
Stanovoy Ra. = Stanovoy Khrebet Russia 55°0N 130°0E 107 D14
Stansmore Ra. Australia 21°23S 128°33E 148 D4
Stansted, London ✈ (STN) U.K. 51°54N 0°14E 67 F8
Stanthorpe Australia 28°36S 151°59E 151 D5
Stanton U.S.A. 32°8N 101°48W 176 E4
Stanwood U.S.A. 48°15N 122°23W 170 B4
Staples Canada 42°10N 82°35W 174 D2
Staples U.S.A. 46°21N 94°48W 172 B6
Stapleton U.S.A. 41°29N 100°31W 172 E3
Stąporków Poland 51°9N 20°31E 83 G7
Star City Canada 52°50N 104°20W 163 C8
Star Lake U.S.A. 44°10N 75°2W 175 B9
Stará L'ubovňa Slovak Rep. 49°18N 20°42E 79 B13
Stara Moravica Serbia 45°50N 19°30E 80 E4
Stara Pazova Serbia 44°58N 20°10E 80 F5
Stara Planina Bulgaria 43°15N 23°0E 96 C7
Stara Sil Ukraine 49°29N 22°58E 83 J9
Stará Turá Slovak Rep. 48°47N 17°42E 79 C10
Stara Ushytsya Ukraine 48°35N 27°8E 81 B12
Stara Zagora Bulgaria 42°26N 25°39E 97 D9
Stara Zagora □ Bulgaria 42°26N 25°39E 97 D9
Starachowice Poland 51°3N 21°2E 83 G8
Staraya Russa Russia 57°58N 31°23E 84 D6
Starbuck I. Kiribati 5°37S 155°55W 157 H12
Starchiojd Romania 45°19N 26°11E 81 E11
Starcke △ Australia 14°56S 145°2E 150 A4
Stargard Szczeciński Poland 53°20N 15°0E 82 E2
Stari Bar Montenegro 42°7N 19°10E 96 D3
Stari Grad Croatia 43°10N 16°38E 93 E13
Stari Trg Slovenia 45°29N 15°7E 93 C12
Staritsa Russia 56°33N 34°55E 84 D8
Starke U.S.A. 29°57N 82°7W 178 F7
Starkville U.S.A. 33°28N 88°49W 177 E10
Starnberg Germany 48°0N 11°21E 77 H7
Starnberger See Germany 47°54N 11°19E 77 H7
Staro Oryakhovo Bulgaria 42°59N 27°47E 97 D11
Starobilsk Ukraine 49°16N 39°0E 85 H10
Starodub Russia 52°30N 32°50E 85 F7
Starogard Gdański Poland 53°59N 18°30E 82 E5
Starokonstantinov = Starokonstyantyniv Ukraine 49°48N 27°10E 75 D14
Starokonstyantyniv Ukraine 49°48N 27°10E 75 D14
Starokozache Ukraine 46°20N 29°59E 81 D14
Starominskaya Russia 46°33N 39°0E 87 G4
Staroshcherbinovskaya Russia 46°40N 38°53E 87 G4
Starrs Mill U.S.A. 33°19N 84°31W 178 B5
Start Pt. U.K. 50°13N 3°39W 67 G4
Stary Sącz Poland 49°33N 20°35E 83 J7
Staryy Biryuzyak Russia 44°46N 46°50E 87 H8
Staryy Chartoriysk Ukraine 51°15N 25°54E 75 C13
Staryy Krym Ukraine 45°3N 35°8E 85 K8
Staryy Oskol Russia 51°19N 37°55E 85 G9
Staryy Sambir Ukraine 49°27N 22°59E 83 J9
Stassfurt Germany 51°51N 11°35E 76 D7
Staszów Poland 50°33N 21°10E 83 H8
State College U.S.A. 40°48N 77°52W 174 F7
Stateline U.S.A. 38°57N 119°56W 170 G7
Staten, I. = Estados, I. de Los Argentina 54°40S 64°30W 192 D4
Staten I. U.S.A. 40°35N 74°9W 175 F10
Statenville U.S.A. 30°42N 83°2W 178 E6
Statesboro U.S.A. 32°27N 81°47W 178 C8
Statesville U.S.A. 35°47N 80°53W 177 D14
Statham U.S.A. 33°58N 83°35W 178 B6
Statia = St. Eustatius W. Indies 17°20N 63°0W 183 C7
Stauffer U.S.A. 34°45N 119°3W 171 L7
Staunton Ill., U.S.A. 39°1N 89°47W 172 F9
Staunton Va., U.S.A. 38°9N 79°4W 173 F14
Stavanger Norway 58°57N 5°40E 61 G11
Stavelot Belgium 50°23N 5°55E 69 D5
Stavern Norway 59°0N 10°1E 61 G14
Stavoren Neths. 52°53N 5°22E 69 B5
Stavropol Russia 45°5N 42°0E 87 H6
Stavropol □ Russia 47°20N 42°50E 87 G6
Stavros Cyprus 35°1N 32°38E 101 D11
Stavros Kriti, Greece 35°12N 24°45E 101 D6
Stavros Thessaloniki, Greece 40°39N 23°43E 96 F7
Stavros, Akra Greece 35°26N 24°58E 101 D6
Stavroupoli Greece 41°12N 24°45E 97 E8
Stawell Australia 37°5S 142°47E 152 D5
Stawell → Australia 20°20S 142°55E 150 C3
Stawiski Poland 53°22N 22°9E 82 E9
Stawiszyn Poland 51°56N 18°4E 83 G5
Stayner Canada 44°25N 80°5W 174 B4
Stayton U.S.A. 44°48N 122°48W 168 D2
Steamboat Springs U.S.A. 40°29N 106°50W 168 F10
Steblevë Albania 41°23N 20°33E 96 E4
Steele Ala., U.S.A. 33°56N 86°12W 178 B3
Steele N. Dak., U.S.A. 46°51N 99°55W 172 B4
Steelton U.S.A. 40°14N 76°50W 174 F8
Steen River Canada 59°40N 117°12W 162 B5
Steens Mt. U.S.A. 42°35N 118°40W 168 E4
Steenstrup Gletscher Greenland 75°15N 57°0W 57 B5
Steenwijk Neths. 52°47N 6°7E 69 B6
Steep Pt. Australia 26°8S 113°8E 149 E1
Steep Rock Canada 51°30N 98°48W 163 C9
Ştefan Vodă Moldova 46°27N 29°42E 81 D14
Ştefăneşti Romania 47°44N 27°15E 81 C12
Stefanie L. = Chew Bahir Ethiopia 4°40N 36°50E 131 G2
Stefansson Bay Antarctica 67°20S 59°8E 55 C5
Stefansson I. Canada 73°20N 105°45W 161 C10
Stege Denmark 54°59N 12°18E 63 K6
Ştei Romania 46°32N 22°27E 80 D7
Steiermark □ Austria 47°26N 15°0E 78 D8
Steigerwald Germany 49°44N 10°26E 77 F6
Steigerwald △ Germany 49°50N 10°30E 77 F6
Steilacoom U.S.A. 47°10N 122°36W 170 C4
Steilrandberge Namibia 17°45S 13°20E 144 A1
Steinbach Canada 49°32N 96°40W 163 D9
Steinfurt Germany 52°9N 7°20E 76 C3
Steinhatchee U.S.A. 29°40N 83°23W 178 F6
Steinhausen Namibia 21°49S 18°20E 144 B2
Steinheim Germany 51°51N 9°5E 76 D5
Steinhuder Meer Germany 52°29N 9°21E 76 C5
Steinhuder Meer △ Germany 52°30N 9°16E 76 C5
Steinkjer Norway 64°1N 11°31E 60 D14
Steinkopf S. Africa 29°18S 17°43E 144 C2
Steinwald △ Germany 49°55N 12°8E 77 F8
Stellarton Canada 45°32N 62°30W 165 C7
Stellenbosch S. Africa 33°58S 18°50E 144 D2
Stélvio, Paso dello Italy 46°32N 10°27E 92 B7
Stenay France 49°29N 5°12E 71 C12
Stendal Germany 52°36N 11°53E 76 C7
Stende Latvia 57°11N 22°33E 82 A9
Stenhamra Sweden 59°20N 17°41E 62 E11
Stenshuvud △ Sweden 55°39N 14°15E 63 J8
Stenstorp Sweden 58°17N 13°45E 63 F7
Stenungsund Sweden 58°6N 11°50E 63 F5
Steornabhaigh = Stornoway U.K. 58°13N 6°23W 65 C2
Stepanakert = Xankändi Azerbaijan 39°52N 46°49E 105 C12
Stepanavan Armenia 41°1N 44°23E 87 K7
Stephens, C. N.Z. 40°42S 173°58E 155 A8
Stephens Creek Australia 31°50S 141°30E 152 A4
Stephens I. Canada 54°10N 130°45W 162 C2
Stephens I. N.Z. 40°40S 174°1E 155 A9
Stephens L. Canada 56°32N 95°0W 163 B9
Stephenville Canada 48°31N 58°35W 165 C8
Stephenville U.S.A. 32°13N 98°12W 176 E5
Stepnica Poland 53°38N 14°36E 82 E1
Stepnogorsk Kazakhstan 52°21N 71°53E 109 B8
Steppe Asia 50°0N 50°0E 102 C7
Sterea Ellas □ Greece 38°30N 22°0E 98 C4
Sterkstroom S. Africa 31°32S 26°32E 144 D4
Sterling Colo., U.S.A. 40°37N 103°13W 168 F12
Sterling Ga., U.S.A. 31°16N 81°34W 178 D8
Sterling Ill., U.S.A. 41°48N 89°42W 172 E9
Sterling Kans., U.S.A. 38°13N 98°12W 172 F4
Sterling City U.S.A. 31°51N 101°0W 176 F4
Sterling Heights U.S.A. 42°35N 83°2W 173 D12
Sterling Run U.S.A. 41°25N 78°12W 174 E6
Sterlitamak Russia 53°40N 56°0E 108 B5
Sternberg Germany 53°42N 11°50E 76 B7
Šternberk Czech Rep. 49°45N 17°15E 79 B10
Sternes Greece 35°30N 24°9E 101 D6
Sterzing = Vipiteno Italy 46°54N 11°26E 93 B8
Stettin = Szczecin Poland 53°27N 14°27E 82 E1
Stettiner Haff Germany 53°47N 14°15E 76 B10
Stettler Canada 52°19N 112°40W 162 C6
Steubenville U.S.A. 40°22N 80°37W 174 F4
Stevenage U.K. 51°55N 0°13W 67 F7
Stevens Point U.S.A. 44°31N 89°34W 172 C9
Stevens Pottery U.S.A. 32°57N 83°17W 178 C6
Stevenson U.S.A. 45°42N 121°53W 170 E5
Stevenson → Australia 27°6S 135°33E 151 D2
Stevenson L. Canada 53°55N 96°0W 163 C9
Stevensville U.S.A. 46°30N 114°5W 168 C6
Stevns Klint Denmark 55°17N 12°28E 63 J6
Stewart Canada 55°56N 129°57W 162 B3
Stewart Ga., U.S.A. 33°25N 83°52W 178 B6
Stewart Nev., U.S.A. 39°5N 119°46W 170 F7
Stewart → Canada 63°19N 139°26W 160 E4
Stewart, C. Australia 11°57S 134°56E 150 A1
Stewart, I. Chile 54°50S 71°15W 192 D2
Stewart I. N.Z. 46°58S 167°54E 155 G2
Stewarts Point U.S.A. 38°39N 123°24W 170 G3
Stewartville U.S.A. 43°51N 92°29W 172 D7
Stewiacke Canada 45°9N 63°22W 165 C7
Steynsburg S. Africa 31°15S 25°49E 144 D4
Steyr Austria 48°3N 14°25E 78 C7
Steyr → Austria 48°17N 14°25E 78 C7
Steytlerville S. Africa 33°17S 24°19E 144 D3
Stia Italy 43°48N 11°42E 93 E8
Stigler U.S.A. 35°15N 95°8W 176 D7
Stigliano Italy 40°24N 16°14E 95 B9
Stigtomta Sweden 58°47N 16°48E 63 F10
Stikine → Canada 56°40N 132°30W 162 B2
Stilfontein S. Africa 26°51S 26°50E 144 C4
Stilida Greece 38°55N 22°47E 98 C4
Stillmore U.S.A. 32°27N 82°13W 178 C7
Stillwater N.Y., U.S.A. 42°55N 73°41W 175 D11
Stillwater Okla., U.S.A. 36°7N 97°4W 176 C6
Stillwater Range U.S.A. 39°50N 118°5W 168 G4
Stillwater Res. U.S.A. 43°54N 75°3W 175 C9
Stilo, Pta. Italy 38°25N 16°35E 95 D9
Stilwell U.S.A. 35°49N 94°38W 176 D7
Stînga Nistrului □ Moldova 47°20N 29°15E 81 C14
Štip Macedonia 41°42N 22°10E 96 E6
Stira Greece 38°9N 24°14E 98 C6
Stirling Canada 44°18N 77°33W 174 B7
Stirling N.Z. 46°14S 169°49E 155 G4
Stirling U.K. 56°8N 3°57W 65 E5
Stirling □ U.K. 56°12N 4°18W 65 E4
Stirling Ra. Australia 34°23S 118°0E 149 F2
Stirling Range △ Australia 34°26S 118°20E 149 F2
Stittsville Canada 45°15N 75°55W 175 A9
Stjernøya Norway 70°20N 22°40E 60 A20
Stjørdalshalsen Norway 63°29N 10°51E 60 E14
Stock Island U.S.A. 24°32N 81°34W 179 L8
Stocka Sweden 61°53N 17°20E 62 C11
Stockach Germany 47°50N 9°1E 77 H5
Stockaryd Sweden 57°19N 14°36E 63 G8
Stockbridge U.S.A. 33°33N 84°14W 178 B5
Stockerau Austria 48°24N 16°12E 79 C9
Stockholm Sweden 59°19N 18°4E 62 E12
Stockholm Arlanda ✈ (ARN) Sweden 59°41N 17°56E 62 E11
Stockholms län □ Sweden 59°30N 18°20E 62 E12
Stockport U.K. 53°25N 2°9W 66 D5
Stocksbridge U.K. 53°29N 1°35W 66 D6
Stockton Calif., U.S.A. 37°58N 121°17W 170 H5
Stockton Kans., U.S.A. 39°26N 99°16W 172 F4
Stockton Mo., U.S.A. 37°42N 93°48W 172 G7
Stockton-on-Tees U.K. 54°35N 1°19W 66 C6
Stockton-on-Tees □ U.K. 54°35N 1°19W 66 C6
Stockton Plateau U.S.A. 30°30N 102°30W 176 F3
Stoczek Łukowski Poland 51°58N 21°58E 83 G8
Stöde Sweden 62°28N 16°35E 62 B10
Stoeng Treng Cambodia 13°31N 105°58E 120 F5
Stoer, Pt. of U.K. 58°16N 5°23W 65 C3
Stogovo Macedonia 41°31N 20°38E 96 E4
Stoholm Denmark 56°30N 9°8E 63 H3
Stoke N.Z. 41°19S 173°14E 155 B8
Stoke-on-Trent U.K. 53°1N 2°11W 66 D5
Stoke-on-Trent □ U.K. 53°1N 2°11W 66 D5
Stokes △ Australia 33°45S 121°11E 149 F3
Stokes Bay Canada 45°0N 81°28W 174 B3
Stokes Pt. Australia 40°10S 143°56E 151 G3
Stokes Ra. Australia 15°50S 130°50E 148 C5
Stokksnes Iceland 64°14N 14°58W 60 D6
Stokmarknes Norway 68°34N 14°54E 60 B16
Stolac Bos.-H. 43°5N 17°59E 96 C1
Stolberg Germany 50°47N 6°13E 76 E2
Stolbovoy, Ostrov Russia 74°44N 135°14E 107 B14
Stolbtsy = Stowbtsy Belarus 53°30N 26°43E 75 B14
Stolin Belarus 51°53N 26°50E 75 C14
Stöllet Sweden 60°26N 13°15E 62 D7
Stolnici Romania 44°31N 24°48E 81 F9
Stomio Greece 35°21N 23°32E 101 D5
Ston Croatia 42°51N 17°43E 93 F14
Stone U.K. 52°55N 2°9W 66 E5
Stone Mountain U.S.A. 33°49N 84°10W 178 B5
Stoneboro U.S.A. 41°20N 80°7W 174 E4
Stonehaven U.K. 56°59N 2°12W 65 E6
Stonehenge Australia 24°22S 143°17E 150 C3
Stonehenge U.K. 51°9N 1°45W 67 F6
Stonewall Canada 50°10N 97°19W 163 C9
Stony I. U.S.A. 43°53N 76°19W 175 C8
Stony L. Man., Canada 58°51N 98°40W 163 B9
Stony L. Ont., Canada 44°30N 78°5W 174 B6
Stony Point U.S.A. 41°14N 73°59W 175 E11
Stony Pt. U.S.A. 43°50N 76°18W 175 C8
Stony Rapids Canada 59°16N 105°50W 163 B7
Stony Tunguska = Tunguska, Podkamennaya → Russia 61°50N 90°13E 107 C10
Stonyford U.S.A. 39°23N 122°33W 170 F4
Stopnica Poland 50°27N 20°57E 83 H7
Storå Sweden 59°42N 15°2E 62 E9
Storå → Denmark 56°20N 8°19E 63 H2
Stora Gla Sweden 59°30N 12°30E 62 E6
Stora Le Sweden 59°5N 11°55E 62 E5
Stora Lulevatten Sweden 67°10N 19°30E 60 C18
Stora Sjöfallet △ Sweden 67°36N 17°45E 60 C17
Storavan Sweden 65°45N 18°10E 60 D18
Stord Norway 59°52N 5°23E 61 G11
Store Bælt Denmark 55°20N 11°0E 63 J4
Store Heddinge Denmark 55°18N 12°23E 63 J6
Store Koldewey Greenland 76°30N 19°0W 57 B9
Store Mosse △ Sweden 57°18N 13°55E 63 G7
Storebro Sweden 57°35N 15°52E 63 G9
Storfors Sweden 59°32N 14°17E 62 E8
Storkerson Pen. Canada 72°30N 106°30W 160 C10
Storlien Sweden 63°19N 12°6E 62 A6
Storm B. Australia 43°10S 147°30E 151 G4
Storm Lake U.S.A. 42°39N 95°13W 172 D6
Stormberge S. Africa 31°16S 26°17E 144 D4
Stormsrivier S. Africa 33°59S 23°52E 144 D3
Stornoway U.K. 58°13N 6°23W 65 C2
Storo Italy 45°51N 10°35E 92 C7
Storozhinets = Storozhynets Ukraine 48°14N 25°45E 81 B10
Storozhynets Ukraine 48°14N 25°45E 81 B10
Storrs U.S.A. 41°49N 72°15W 175 E12
Storsjön Gävleborg, Sweden 60°35N 16°45E 62 D10
Storsjön Jämtland, Sweden 62°48N 13°7E 62 B7
Storsjön Jämtland, Sweden 63°9N 14°30E 62 A8
Storstrømmen Greenland 76°17N 22°25W 57 B8
Storuman Sweden 65°5N 17°10E 60 D17
Storuman, L. Sweden 65°13N 16°50E 60 D17
Storvätteshågna Sweden 62°6N 12°30E 62 B6
Storvik Sweden 60°35N 16°33E 62 D10
Storvreta Sweden 59°58N 17°44E 62 E11
Stouffville Canada 43°58N 79°15W 174 C5
Stoughton Canada 49°40N 103°0W 163 D8
Stour → Dorset, U.K. 50°43N 1°47W 67 G6
Stour → Kent, U.K. 51°18N 1°22E 67 F9
Stour → Suffolk, U.K. 51°57N 1°4E 67 F9
Stourbridge U.K. 52°28N 2°8W 67 E5
Stout L. Canada 52°0N 94°40W 163 C10
Stove Pipe Wells Village U.S.A. 36°35N 117°11W 171 J9
Støvring Denmark 56°54N 9°50E 63 H3
Stow U.S.A. 41°10N 81°27W 174 E3
Stowbtsy Belarus 53°30N 26°43E 75 B14
Stowmarket U.K. 52°12N 1°0E 67 E9
Strabane U.K. 54°50N 7°27W 64 B4
Stracin Macedonia 42°13N 22°2E 96 D6
Stradella Italy 45°5N 9°18E 92 C6
Strahan Australia 42°9S 145°20E 151 G4
Strajitsa Bulgaria 43°14N 25°58E 97 C9
Strakonice Czech Rep. 49°15N 13°53E 78 B6
Straldzha Bulgaria 42°35N 26°40E 97 D10
Stralsund Germany 54°18N 13°4E 76 A9
Strand S. Africa 34°9S 18°48E 144 D2
Stranda Møre og Romsdal, Norway 62°19N 6°58E 60 E12
Stranda Nord-Trøndelag, Norway 63°33N 10°14E 60 E14
Strandby Denmark 57°30N 10°29E 63 G4
Strangford L. U.K. 54°30N 5°37W 64 B6
Strängnäs Sweden 59°23N 17°2E 62 E11
Stranorlar Ireland 54°48N 7°46W 64 B4
Stranraer U.K. 54°54N 5°1W 65 G3
Strasbourg Canada 51°4N 104°55W 163 C8
Strasbourg France 48°35N 7°42E 71 D14
Strasburg Germany 53°30N 13°43E 76 B9
Strășeni Moldova 47°8N 28°36E 81 C13
Stråssa Sweden 59°44N 15°12E 62 E9
Stratford N.S.W., Australia 32°7S 151°55E 153 B9
Stratford Vic., Australia 37°59S 147°7E 153 D7
Stratford Canada 43°23N 81°0W 174 C4
Stratford N.Z. 39°20S 174°19E 154 F3
Stratford Calif., U.S.A. 36°11N 119°49W 170 J7
Stratford Conn., U.S.A. 41°12N 73°8W 175 E11
Stratford Tex., U.S.A. 36°20N 102°4W 176 C3
Stratford-upon-Avon U.K. 52°12N 1°42W 67 E6
Strath Spey U.K. 57°9N 3°49W 65 D5
Strathalbyn Australia 35°13S 138°53E 152 C3
Strathaven U.K. 55°40N 4°5W 65 F4
Strathcona △ Canada 49°38N 125°40W 162 D3
Strathmore Canada 51°5N 113°18W 162 C6
Strathmore U.K. 56°37N 3°7W 65 E5
Strathmore U.S.A. 36°9N 119°4W 170 J7
Strathnaver Canada 53°20N 122°33W 162 C4
Strathpeffer U.K. 57°35N 4°32W 65 D4
Strathroy Canada 42°58N 81°38W 174 D3
Strathy Pt. U.K. 58°36N 4°1W 65 C4
Strattanville U.S.A. 41°12N 79°19W 174 E5
Stratton U.S.A. 45°8N 70°26W 175 A14
Stratton Mt. U.S.A. 43°4N 72°55W 175 C12
Straubing Germany 48°52N 12°34E 77 G8
Straumnes Iceland 66°26N 23°8W 60 C2
Strausberg Germany 52°35N 13°54E 76 C9
Strawberry → U.S.A. 40°10N 110°24W 168 F8
Strážnice Czech Rep. 48°54N 17°19E 79 C10
Streaky B. Australia 32°48S 134°13E 151 E1
Streaky Bay Australia 32°51S 134°18E 151 E1
Streator U.S.A. 41°8N 88°50W 172 E9
Středočeský □ Czech Rep. 49°55N 14°30E 78 B7
Streetsboro U.S.A. 41°14N 81°21W 174 E3
Streetsville Canada 43°35N 79°42W 174 C5
Strehaia Romania 44°37N 23°10E 81 F8
Strelcha Bulgaria 42°25N 24°19E 97 D8
Streng → Cambodia 13°12N 103°37E 120 F4
Stresa Italy 45°52N 8°28E 92 C5
Streymoy Færoe Is. 62°8N 7°5W 60 E9
Strezhevoy Russia 60°42N 77°34E 106 C8
Stříbro Czech Rep. 49°44N 13°0E 78 B6
Strilky Ukraine 49°20N 22°59E 83 J9
Strimonas → Greece 40°46N 23°51E 96 F7
Stroeder Argentina 40°12S 62°37W 192 B4
Strofades Greece 37°15N 21°0E 98 D3
Strokestown Ireland 53°47N 8°5W 64 C3
Stroma U.K. 58°41N 3°7W 65 C5
Stromberg-Heuchelberg △ Germany 49°2N 8°50E 77 F4
Strómboli Italy 38°47N 15°13E 95 D8
Stromeferry U.K. 57°21N 5°33W 65 D3
Stromness U.K. 58°58N 3°17W 65 C5
Strömsbruk Sweden 61°52N 17°18E 62 C11
Stromsburg U.S.A. 41°7N 97°36W 172 E5
Strömsnäsbruk Sweden 56°35N 13°45E 63 H7
Strömstad Sweden 58°56N 11°10E 63 F5
Strömsund Sweden 63°51N 15°33E 60 E16
Strongili Greece 36°6N 29°42E 99 E11
Stróngoli Italy 39°16N 17°3E 95 C10
Strongsville U.S.A. 41°19N 81°50W 174 E3
Stronie Śląskie Poland 50°18N 16°53E 83 H3
Stronsay U.K. 59°7N 2°35W 65 B6
Stropkov Slovak Rep. 49°13N 21°39E 79 B14
Stroud U.K. 51°45N 2°13W 67 F5
Stroud Road Australia 32°18S 151°57E 153 B9
Stroudsburg U.S.A. 40°59N 75°12W 175 F9
Stroumbi Cyprus 34°53N 32°29E 101 E11
Štrpce = Shtërpcë Kosovo 42°14N 21°1E 96 D5
Struer Denmark 56°30N 8°35E 63 H2
Struga Macedonia 41°11N 20°44E 96 E4
Strugi Krasnyye Russia 58°21N 29°1E 84 C5
Strumica Macedonia 41°28N 22°41E 96 E6
Strumica → Europe 41°20N 23°22E 96 E7
Strumok Ukraine 45°43N 29°27E 81 E14
Struthers U.S.A. 41°4N 80°39W 174 E4
Stryama Bulgaria 42°16N 24°54E 97 D8
Stryker U.S.A. 48°41N 114°46W 168 B6
Stryków Poland 51°55N 19°33E 83 G6
Stryy Ukraine 49°16N 23°48E 75 D12
Strzegom Poland 50°58N 16°20E 83 H3
Strzelce Krajeńskie Poland 52°52N 15°33E 83 F2
Strzelce Opolskie Poland 50°31N 18°18E 83 H5
Strzelecki Cr. → Australia 29°37S 139°59E 151 D2
Strzelecki Desert Australia 29°30S 140°0E 151 D3
Strzelin Poland 50°46N 17°2E 83 H4
Strzelno Poland 52°35N 18°9E 83 F5
Strzybnica Poland 50°28N 18°48E 83 H5
Strzyżów Poland 49°52N 21°47E 83 J8
Stuart Fla., U.S.A. 27°12N 80°15W 179 H9
Stuart Nebr., U.S.A. 42°36N 99°8W 172 D4
Stuart → Canada 54°0N 123°35W 162 C4
Stuart Bluff Ra. Australia 22°50S 131°52E 148 D5
Stuart I. U.S.A. 63°35N 162°30W 166 C7
Stuart L. Canada 54°30N 124°30W 162 C4
Stuart Mts. N.Z. 45°2S 167°39E 155 F2
Stuart Ra. Australia 29°10S 134°56E 151 D1
Stubbekøbing Denmark 54°53N 12°9E 63 K6
Stuben Austria 47°10N 10°8E 78 D3
Studen Kladenets, Yazovir Bulgaria 41°37N 25°30E 97 E9
Studenica Serbia 43°29N 20°32E 96 C4
Studenka Czech Rep. 49°44N 18°5E 79 B11
Studholme N.Z. 44°42S 171°9E 155 E6
Stugun Sweden 63°10N 15°40E 62 A9
Stuhr Germany 53°5N 8°44E 76 B4
Stull L. Canada 54°24N 92°34W 164 B1
Stung Treng = Stoeng Treng Cambodia 13°31N 105°58E 120 F5
Stupart → Canada 56°0N 93°25W 164 A1
Stupava Slovak Rep. 48°17N 17°2E 79 C10
Stupino Russia 54°57N 38°2E 84 E10
Sturge I. Antarctica 67°26S 164°47E 55 C11
Sturgeon B. Canada 52°0N 97°50W 163 C9
Sturgeon Bay U.S.A. 44°50N 87°23W 172 C10
Sturgeon Falls Canada 46°25N 79°57W 164 C4
Sturgeon L. Alta., Canada 55°6N 117°32W 162 B5
Sturgeon L. Ont., Canada 50°0N 90°45W 164 C1
Sturgeon L. Ont., Canada 44°28N 78°43W 174 B6
Sturgis Canada 51°56N 102°36W 163 C8
Sturgis Mich., U.S.A. 41°48N 85°25W 173 E11
Sturgis S. Dak., U.S.A. 44°25N 103°31W 172 C2
Sturkö Sweden 56°5N 15°42E 63 H9
Štúrovo Slovak Rep. 47°48N 18°41E 79 D11
Sturt △ Australia 27°17S 141°37E 151 D3
Sturt Cr. → Australia 19°8S 127°50E 148 C4
Sturt Stony Desert Australia 28°30S 141°0E 151 D3
Sturts Meadows Australia 31°18S 141°42E 152 A4
Stutterheim S. Africa 32°33S 27°28E 144 D4
Stuttgart Germany 48°48N 9°11E 77 G5
Stuttgart U.S.A. 34°30N 91°33W 176 D9
Stuttgart Echterdingen ✈ (STR) Germany 48°42N 9°11E 77 G5
Stuyvesant U.S.A. 42°23N 73°45W 175 D11
Stykkishólmur Iceland 65°2N 22°40W 60 D2
Styria = Steiermark □ Austria 47°26N 15°0E 78 D8
Styrsö Sweden 57°37N 11°46E 63 G5
Su Xian = Suzhou China 33°41N 116°59E 114 H9
Suakin Sudan 19°8N 37°20E 137 D4
Suakin Archipelago Sudan 18°42N 38°30E 137 D4
Suamico U.S.A. 44°38N 88°2W 172 C9
Suan N. Korea 38°42N 126°22E 115 E14
Suana Indonesia 8°44S 115°36E 119 K18
Suape Brazil 8°24S 35°0W 189 B3
Suar India 29°2N 79°3E 125 E8
Šubā Si. Arabia 27°10N 35°40E 128 E2
Subang Indonesia 6°34S 107°45E 119 G12
Subansiri → India 26°48N 93°50E 123 F18
Subarnagiri India 19°50N 83°51E 126 E6
Subarnarekha → India 22°34N 87°24E 125 H12
Subay', Urūq Si. Arabia 22°15N 43°5E 137 C5
Subayhah Si. Arabia 30°2N 38°50E 128 D3
Subcetate Romania 45°36N 23°0E 80 E8
Subi Indonesia 2°58N 108°50E 118 D3
Subiaco Italy 41°56N 13°5E 93 G10
Subotica Serbia 46°6N 19°39E 80 D4
Suceava Romania 47°38N 26°16E 81 C11
Suceava □ Romania 47°37N 25°40E 81 C10
Suceava → Romania 47°32N 26°32E 81 C11
Sucha-Beskidzka Poland 49°44N 19°35E 83 J6
Suchan = Partizansk Russia 43°8N 133°9E 107 E14
Suchań Poland 53°18N 15°18E 82 E2
Suchedniów Poland 51°3N 20°49E 83 G7
Suchil Mexico 23°39N 103°54W 180 C4
Suchou = Suzhou China 31°19N 120°38E 117 B13
Süchow = Xuzhou China 34°18N 117°10E 115 G9
Suchowola Poland 53°33N 23°3E 82 E10
Suck → Ireland 53°17N 8°3W 64 C3
Sucre Bolivia 19°0S 65°15W 186 G5
Sućuraj Croatia 43°10N 17°8E 93 E14
Sucuriú → Brazil 20°47S 51°38W 187 H8
Sud □ Cameroon 2°30N 11°45E 139 E7
Sud, Pte. du Canada 49°3N 62°14W 165 C7
Sud-Bandama □ Ivory C. 6°0N 5°15W 138 D3
Sud-Comoé □ Ivory C. 5°30N 3°0W 138 D4
Sud-Kivu □ Dem. Rep. of the Congo 3°0S 28°30E 142 C2
Sud-Ouest □ Cameroon 5°25N 9°20E 139 D6
Sud-Ouest, Pte. Canada 49°23N 63°36W 165 C7
Sud Ouest, Pte. Mauritius 20°28S 57°18E 141 d
Suda → Russia 59°0N 37°40E 84 C9
Sudak Ukraine 44°51N 34°57E 85 K8
Sudan U.S.A. 34°4N 102°31W 176 D3
Sudan ■ Africa 15°0N 30°0E 135 E11
Sudbury Canada 46°30N 81°0W 164 C3
Sudbury U.K. 52°2N 0°45E 67 E8
Sudd South Sudan 8°20N 30°0E 135 G12
Sudeifel = Deutsch-Luxemburgischer △ Germany 49°58N 6°12E 77 F2
Süderbrarup Germany 54°38N 9°45E 76 A5
Süderlügum Germany 54°52N 8°54E 76 A4
Süderoogsand Germany 54°27N 8°28E 76 A4
Sudeten Mts. = Sudety Europe 50°20N 16°45E 79 A9
Sudety Europe 50°20N 16°45E 79 A9
Südheide △ Germany 52°46N 10°10E 76 C6
Suðuroy Færoe Is. 61°32N 6°50W 60 F9
Sudi Tanzania 10°11S 39°57E 143 E4
Sudirman, Pegunungan Indonesia 4°30S 137°0E 119 E9
Sudiţi Romania 44°35N 27°38E 81 F12
Sudogda Russia 55°55N 40°50E 86 C5
Sudong, Pulau Singapore 1°13N 103°44E 121 d
Sudova Vyshnya Ukraine 49°46N 23°22E 83 J10
Sudzha Russia 51°14N 35°17E 85 G8
Sueca Spain 39°12N 0°21W 91 F4
Sŭedinenie Bulgaria 42°16N 24°33E 97 D8
Suemez I. U.S.A. 55°15N 133°20W 162 B2
Suez = El Suweis Egypt 29°58N 32°31E 137 F8
Suez, G. of = Suweis, Khalîg el Egypt 28°40N 33°0E 137 F8
Suez Canal = Suweis, Qanâ es Egypt 31°0N 32°20E 137 E8
Suffield Canada 50°12N 111°10W 162 C6
Suffolk U.S.A. 36°44N 76°35W 173 G15
Suffolk □ U.K. 52°16N 1°0E 67 E9
Şufiān Iran 38°16N 45°58E 105 C11
Şugag Romania 45°47N 23°37E 81 E8
Sugaing = Sagaing Burma 21°52N 95°59E 123 J19
Sugar Grove U.S.A. 41°59N 79°20W 174 E5
Sugar Hill U.S.A. 34°6N 84°2W 178 A5
Sugarcreek U.S.A. 41°25N 79°52W 174 E5
Sugarive → India 26°16N 86°24E 125 F12
Sughd □ Tajikistan 40°0N 69°0E 109 E7
Suğla Gölü Turkey 37°20N 32°0E 104 D5
Sugluk = Salluit Canada 62°14N 75°38W 161 E16
Sugun China 39°53N 76°47E 109 E9
Suha Reke = Therandë Kosovo 42°21N 20°50E 96 D4
Suhaia, Lacul Romania 43°45N 25°15E 81 G10
Şuḥār Oman 24°20N 56°40E 129 E8
Sühbaatar Mongolia 50°17N 106°10E 110 A10
Sühbaatar □ Mongolia 45°30N 114°0E 114 B8
Suheli Par India 10°5N 72°17E 127 J1
Suhl Germany 50°36N 10°42E 76 E6
Şuhut Turkey 38°31N 30°32E 99 C12
Sui Pakistan 28°37N 69°19E 124 E3
Sui Xian China 34°25N 115°2E 114 G8
Šuica Bos.-H. 43°52N 17°11E 80 G2
Suichang China 28°29N 119°15E 117 C12
Suichuan China 26°20N 114°32E 117 D10
Suide China 37°30N 110°12E 114 F6
Suifenhe China 44°25N 131°10E 115 B16
Suihua China 46°32N 126°55E 111 B14
Suijiang China 28°40N 103°59E 116 C4
Suining Hunan, China 26°35N 110°10E 117 D8
Suining Jiangsu, China 33°56N 117°58E 115 H9
Suining Sichuan, China 30°26N 105°35E 116 B5
Suiping China 33°10N 113°59E 114 H7
Suippes France 49°8N 4°30E 71 C11
Suir → Ireland 52°16N 7°9W 64 D4
Suisse = Switzerland ■ Europe 46°30N 8°0E 77 J4
Suisun City U.S.A. 38°15N 122°2W 170 G4
Suixi China 21°19N 110°18E 117 G8
Suiyang Guizhou, China 27°58N 107°18E 116 D6
Suiyang Heilongjiang, China 44°30N 130°56E 115 B16
Suizhong China 40°21N 120°20E 115 D11
Suizhou China 31°42N 113°24E 117 B9
Sujangarh India 27°42N 74°31E 124 F6
Sujiatun China 41°39N 123°20E 115 D12
Sukabumi Indonesia 6°56S 106°50E 119 G12
Sukadana Indonesia 1°10S 110°0E 118 E4
Sukagawa Japan 37°17N 140°23E 113 F10
Sukamade Indonesia 8°30S 113°52E 119 H15
Sukaraja Indonesia 2°28S 110°25E 118 E4
Sukawati Indonesia 8°35S 115°17E 119 K18
Sukch'ŏn N. Korea 39°22N 125°35E 115 E13
Sukhindol Bulgaria 43°11N 25°10E 97 C9
Sukhinichi Russia 54°8N 35°10E 84 E8
Sukhona → Russia 61°15N 46°39E 106 D4
Sukhothai Thailand 17°1N 99°49E 120 D2
Sukhumi = Sokhumi Georgia 43°0N 41°0E 87 J5
Sukkertoppen = Maniitsoq Greenland 65°26N 52°55W 57 D5
Sukkur Pakistan 27°42N 68°54E 124 F3
Sukkur Barrage Pakistan 27°40N 68°50E 124 F3
Sukma India 18°24N 81°45E 126 E5
Sukovo Serbia 43°4N 22°37E 96 C6
Sukri → India 25°4N 71°43E 124 G4
Sukumo Japan 32°56N 132°44E 113 H6
Sukunka → Canada 55°45N 121°15W 162 B4
Sula → Ukraine 49°40N 32°41E 85 H7
Sula, Kepulauan Indonesia 1°45S 125°0E 119 E7
Sulaco → Honduras 15°2N 87°44W 182 C2
Sulaiman Range Pakistan 30°30N 69°50E 124 D3
Sulaiman-Too Kyrgyzstan 40°31N 72°46E 109 D8
Sulak → Russia 43°20N 47°34E 87 J8
Sulakyurt Turkey 40°9N 33°43E 104 B5
Sūlār Iran 31°53N 51°54E 129 D6
Sulawesi Indonesia 2°0S 120°0E 119 E6
Sulawesi Barat □ Indonesia 3°0S 119°0E 119 E5
Sulawesi Sea = Celebes Sea Indonesia 3°0N 123°0E 119 D6
Sulawesi Selatan □ Indonesia 2°30S 120°0E 119 E6
Sulawesi Tengah □ Indonesia 1°30S 121°0E 119 E6
Sulawesi Tenggara □ Indonesia 3°50S 122°0E 119 E6
Sulawesi Utara □ Indonesia 1°0N 124°0E 119 D6
Sulechów Poland 52°5N 15°40E 83 F2
Sulęcin Poland 52°26N 15°10E 83 F2
Suleja Nigeria 9°10N 7°10E 139 D6
Sulejów Poland 51°26N 19°53E 83 G6
Sulejówek Poland 52°13N 21°17E 83 F8
Süleymanlı Turkey 38°58N 27°47E 99 C9
Sulima S. Leone 6°58N 11°32W 138 D2
Sulina Romania 45°10N 29°40E 81 E14
Sulina, Braţul → Romania 45°10N 29°40E 81 E14
Sulingen Germany 52°41N 8°48E 76 C4
Suliţa Romania 47°39N 26°59E 81 C11
Sulitjelma Norway 67°9N 16°3E 60 C17
Sułkowice Poland 49°50N 19°49E 83 J6
Sullana Peru 4°52S 80°39W 188 A1
Süller Turkey 38°9N 29°29E 99 C11
Sullivan Ill., U.S.A. 39°36N 88°37W 172 F9
Sullivan Ind., U.S.A. 39°6N 87°24W 172 F10
Sullivan Mo., U.S.A. 38°13N 91°10W 172 F8
Sullivan Bay Canada 50°55N 126°50W 162 C3
Sullivan I. = Lanbi Kyun Burma 10°50N 98°20E 121 G2
Sullom Voe U.K. 60°27N 1°20W 65 A7
Sullorsuaq Greenland 70°5N 53°0W 57 C5
Sully-sur-Loire France 47°45N 2°20E 71 E9
Sulmierzyce Poland 51°37N 17°32E 83 G4
Sulmona Italy 42°3N 13°55E 93 F10
Suloğlu Turkey 41°44N 26°53E 97 E10
Sulphur La., U.S.A. 30°14N 93°23W 176 F8
Sulphur Okla., U.S.A. 34°31N 96°58W 176 D6
Sulphur Pt. Canada 60°56N 114°48W 162 A6
Sulphur Springs U.S.A. 33°8N 95°36W 176 E7
Sultan Canada 47°36N 82°47W 164 C3
Sultan U.S.A. 47°52N 121°49W 170 C5
Sultan Dağları Turkey 38°20N 31°20E 104 C4
Sultan Hamud Kenya 2°1S 37°22E 142 C4
Sultanābād = Arāk Iran 34°0N 49°40E 129 C6
Sultanhisar Turkey 37°53N 28°9E 99 D10
Sultaniça Turkey 40°37N 26°8E 97 F10
Sultaniye Turkey 40°11N 28°12E 97 F12

Sultanpur *Mad. P., India* 23°9N 77°56E **124** H8
Sultanpur *Punjab, India* 31°13N 75°11E **124** D6
Sultanpur *Ut. P., India* 26°18N 82°4E **125** F10
Sulu Arch. *Phil.* 6°0N 121°0E **119** C6
Sulu Sea *E. Indies* 8°0N 120°0E **119** C6
Sülüklü *Turkey* 38°53N 32°20E **104** C5
Suluova *Turkey* 40°46N 35°32E **104** B6
Suluq *Libya* 31°44N 20°14E **135** B10
Sulzbach *Germany* 49°18N 7°3E **77** F3
Sulzbach-Rosenberg
  Germany 49°30N 11°44E **77** F7
Sulzberger Ice Shelf
  Antarctica 78°0S 150°0W **55** E13
Sumalata *Indonesia* 1°0N 122°31E **119** D6
Sumampa *Argentina* 29°25S 63°29W **190** B3
Sumatera *Indonesia* 0°40N 100°20E **118** D2
Sumatera Barat □
  Indonesia 1°0S 101°0E **118** E2
Sumatera Selatan □
  Indonesia 3°0S 104°0E **118** E2
Sumatera Utara □
  Indonesia 2°30N 98°0E **118** D1
Sumatra = Sumatera
  Indonesia 0°40N 100°20E **118** D2
Sumatra *U.S.A.* 31°N 84°59W **178** E5
Sumba *Indonesia* 9°45S 119°35E **119** F5
Sumba, Selat *Indonesia* 9°0S 118°40E **119** F5
Sumbawa *Indonesia* 8°26S 117°30E **118** F5
Sumbawa Besar
  Indonesia 8°30S 117°26E **118** F5
Sumbawanga □ *Tanzania* 8°0S 31°30E **140** F6
Sumbe *Angola* 11°10S 13°48E **140** G2
Sumbu □ *Zambia* 8°43S 30°22E **143** G3
Sumburgh Hd. *U.K.* 59°52N 1°17W **65** B7
Sumdeo *India* 31°26N 78°44E **125** D8
Sumdo *China* 35°6N 78°41E **125** B8
Sumé *Brazil* 7°39S 36°55W **189** D4
Sumedang *Indonesia* 6°52S 107°55E **119** G12
Sümeg *Hungary* 46°59N 17°20E **80** D2
Sumen = Shumen
  Bulgaria 43°18N 26°55E **97** C10
Sumenep *Indonesia* 7°1S 113°52E **119** G15
Sumgait = Sumqayit
  Azerbaijan 40°34N 49°38E **87** K9
Summer L. *U.S.A.* 42°50N 120°45W **168** E3
Summerland *Canada* 49°32N 119°41W **162** D5
Summerland Key
  U.S.A. 24°40N 81°27W **179** L8
Summerside *Canada* 46°24N 63°47W **165** C7
Summersville *U.S.A.* 38°17N 80°51W **173** F13
Summerton *U.S.A.* 33°36N 80°20W **178** E6
Summertown *U.S.A.* 32°45N 82°16W **178** C7
Summerville *Ga.,
  U.S.A.* 34°29N 85°21W **177** D12
Summerville *S.C.,
  U.S.A.* 33°1N 80°11W **178** B9
Summit Lake *Canada* 54°20N 122°40W **162** C4
Summit Peak *U.S.A.* 37°21N 106°42W **169** H10
Sumner *N.Z.* 43°35S 172°48E **155** D7
Sumner *Iowa, U.S.A.* 42°51N 92°6W **172** D7
Sumner *Wash., U.S.A.* 47°12N 122°14W **170** C4
Sumner, L. *N.Z.* 42°42S 172°15E **155** D6
Sumoto *Japan* 34°21N 134°54E **113** G7
Šumperk *Czech Rep.* 49°59N 16°59E **79** D9
Sumqayit *Azerbaijan* 40°34N 49°38E **87** K9
Sumter *U.S.A.* 33°55N 80°21W **178** B9
Sumxi *China* 34°35N 80°22E **109** F10
Sumy *Ukraine* 50°57N 34°50E **85** G8
Sumy □ *Ukraine* 50°50N 33°50E **85** F8
Sun City *S. Africa* 25°17S 27°3E **144** C4
Sun City Center *U.S.A.* 27°43N 82°21W **179** F7
Sun Kosi → *Nepal* 26°59N 87°8E **125** F12
Sun Lakes *U.S.A.* 33°10N 111°52W **175** C13
Sun Valley *U.S.A.* 43°42N 114°21W **168** E6
Sunagawa *Japan* 43°29N 141°55E **112** C10
Sunan *N. Korea* 39°15N 125°40E **115** E13
Sunart, L. *U.K.* 56°42N 5°43W **65** E3
Sunburst *U.S.A.* 48°53N 111°55W **168** B8
Sunbury *Australia* 37°35S 144°44E **153** D6
Sunbury *U.S.A.* 40°52N 76°48W **173** E9
Sunchales *Argentina* 30°58S 61°35W **190** C3
Suncheon *S. Korea* 34°52N 127°31E **115** G14
Suncho Corral
  Argentina 27°55S 63°27W **190** B3
Sunch'on *N. Korea* 39°25N 125°56E **115** E13
Suncook *U.S.A.* 43°8N 71°27W **175** C13
Sunda, Selat *Indonesia* 6°20S 105°30E **118** F3
Sunda Is. *Indonesia* 5°0S 105°0E **156** H2
Sunda Str. = Sunda, Selat
  Indonesia 6°20S 105°30E **118** F3
Sunda Trench = Java Trench
  Ind. Oc. 9°0S 105°0E **118** F3
Sundance *Canada* 56°32N 94°4W **163** B10
Sundance *U.S.A.* 44°24N 104°23W **168** D2
Sundar Nagar *India* 31°32N 76°53E **124** D7
Sundarbans *India* 22°0N 89°0E **123** J16
Sundarbans △ *India* 22°0N 88°45E **125** J13
Sundargarh *India* 22°4N 84°5E **125** C7
Sundays = Sondags →
  S. Africa 33°44S 25°51E **144** D4
Sunderland *Canada* 44°16N 79°4W **174** B5
Sunderland *U.K.* 54°55N 1°23W **66** C6
Sundown △ *Australia* 28°49S 151°38E **152** D5
Sundre *Canada* 51°49N 114°38W **162** C6
Sunds *Denmark* 56°13N 9°1E **63** H4
Sundsvall *Sweden* 62°23N 17°17E **62** B11
Sundsvallsbukten
  Sweden 62°21N 17°25E **62** B11
Sungai Acheh *Malaysia* 5°8N 100°30E **121** c
Sungai Kolok *Thailand* 6°2N 101°58E **121** J3
Sungai Lembing
  Malaysia 3°55N 103°3E **121** L4
Sungai Petani *Malaysia* 5°37N 100°30E **121** K3
Sungaigerong *Indonesia* 2°59S 104°52E **118** E2
Sungailiat *Indonesia* 1°51S 106°8E **118** E3
Sungaipenuh *Indonesia* 2°1S 101°20E **118** E2
Sungari = Songhua Jiang →
  China 47°45N 132°30E **111** B15
Sunghua Chiang = Songhua
  Jiang → *China* 47°45N 132°30E **111** B15
Sungurlu *Turkey* 40°12N 34°21E **104** B6
Sunja *Croatia* 45°21N 16°35E **93** C13
Sunland Park *U.S.A.* 31°50N 106°40W **169** L10
Sunnansjö *Sweden* 60°13N 14°58E **62** D8
Sunndalsøra *Norway* 62°40N 8°33E **60** E3
Sunne *Sweden* 59°52N 13°12E **62** E7
Sunnemo *Sweden* 59°53N 13°44E **62** E7
Sunnyside *U.S.A.* 46°20N 120°0W **168** C4
Sunnyvale *U.S.A.* 37°23N 122°2W **170** H4

Sunrise *U.S.A.* 26°8N 80°14W **179** J9
Sunrise Manor *U.S.A.* 36°12N 115°4W **171** J11
Suntar *Russia* 62°15N 117°30E **107** C12
Sunyani *Ghana* 7°21N 2°22W **138** D4
Suomenselkä *Finland* 62°52N 24°0E **60** E21
Suomi = Finland ■
  Europe 63°0N 27°0E **60** E22
Suomussalmi *Finland* 64°54N 29°10E **60** D23
Suoyarvi *Russia* 62°3N 32°20E **84** A7
Supai *U.S.A.* 36°15N 112°41W **169** H7
Supaul *India* 26°10N 86°40E **125** F12
Superior *Ariz., U.S.A.* 33°18N 111°6W **169** K8
Superior *Mont., U.S.A.* 47°12N 114°53W **168** C6
Superior *Nebr., U.S.A.* 40°1N 98°4W **172** E5
Superior *Wis., U.S.A.* 46°44N 92°6W **172** B7
Superior, L. *N. Amer.* 47°0N 87°0W **164** C2
Supetar *Croatia* 43°25N 16°32E **93** E13
Suphan Buri *Thailand* 14°14N 100°10E **120** E3
Suphan Dağı *Turkey* 38°54N 42°48E **105** C10
Supiori *Indonesia* 1°0S 136°0E **119** E9
Suprasl *Poland* 53°13N 23°19E **83** E10
Suprasl → *Poland* 53°11N 22°57E **83** E9
Supsa → *Georgia* 42°2N 41°49E **87** J5
Supung Shuiku
  China 40°35N 124°50E **115** D13
Sūq ash Shuyūkh *Iraq* 30°53N 46°28E **128** D5
Sūq Suwayq *Si. Arabia* 24°23N 38°27E **128** E3
Suqian *China* 33°54N 118°8E **115** H10
Suqutra = Socotra
  Yemen 12°30N 54°0E **131** E5
Sūr *Lebanon* 33°19N 35°16E **130** B4
Şūr *Oman* 22°34N 59°32E **131** C6
Sur, Pt. *U.S.A.* 36°18N 121°54W **170** J5
Sura → *Russia* 56°6N 46°0E **86** C8
Surab *Pakistan* 28°25N 66°15E **124** E5
Surabaja = Surabaya
  Indonesia 7°17S 112°45E **118** F4
Surabaya *Indonesia* 7°17S 112°45E **118** F4
Surahammar *Sweden* 59°43N 16°13E **62** E10
Suraia *Romania* 45°40N 27°25E **81** E12
Surakarta *Indonesia* 7°35S 110°48E **118** F4
Šurany *Slovak Rep.* 48°6N 18°10E **79** C11
Surat *Australia* 27°10S 149°6E **151** D4
Surat *India* 21°12N 72°55E **124** D6
Surat Thani *Thailand* 9°6N 99°20E **121** H2
Suratgarh *India* 29°18N 73°55E **124** E6
Surathkal *India* 12°58N 74°46E **127** H2
Suraxanı = Qaraçuxar
  Azerbaijan 40°25N 50°1E **87** K10
Şuraymilā *Si. Arabia* 25°7N 46°7E **128** E5
Suraż *Poland* 52°57N 22°57E **83** F9
Surazh *Belarus* 55°25N 30°44E **84** E6
Surazh *Russia* 53°5N 32°27E **85** F7
Surduc *Romania* 47°15N 23°25E **81** C8
Surduc Pasul *Romania* 45°21N 23°23E **81** E8
Surdulica *Serbia* 42°41N 22°11E **96** D6
Surendranagar *India* 22°45N 71°40E **124** H4
Surf *U.S.A.* 34°41N 120°36W **171** L6
Surfers Paradise
  Australia 28°0S 153°25E **151** D5
Surfside *U.S.A.* 25°52N 80°7W **179** K9
Surgana *India* 20°34N 73°37E **126** D1
Surgères *France* 46°7N 0°47W **72** B3
Surgut *Russia* 61°14N 73°20E **106** C8
Sùria *Spain* 41°50N 1°45E **90** D6
Suriapet *India* 17°10N 79°40E **126** F4
Surigao *Phil.* 9°47N 125°29E **119** C7
Surin *Thailand* 14°50N 103°34E **120** E4
Surinam = Suriname ■
  S. Amer. 4°0N 56°0W **187** C7
Suriname ■ *S. Amer.* 4°0N 56°0W **187** C7
Suriname → *Suriname* 5°50N 55°15W **187** B7
Surjagarh *India* 19°36N 80°25E **126** E5
Surrey □ *U.K.* 51°15N 0°31W **67** D7
Surrey *Canada* 49°7N 122°45W **170** A4
Surrey □ *U.K.* 51°15N 0°31W **67** D7
Sursand *India* 26°39N 85°43E **125** F11
Sursar → *India* 26°14N 87°3E **125** F12
Sursee *Switz.* 47°11N 8°6E **77** H4
Sursk *Russia* 53°3N 45°40E **86** D7
Surskoye *Russia* 54°30N 46°44E **86** D8
Surt *Libya* 31°11N 16°39E **135** B9
Surt, Khalīj *Libya* 31°40N 18°30E **135** B9
Surtanahu *Pakistan* 26°22N 70°0E **124** F4
Surte *Sweden* 57°50N 12°0E **63** G6
Surtsey *Iceland* 63°20N 20°30W **60** E3
Surubim *Brazil* 7°50S 35°45W **189** D3
Sürüç *Turkey* 36°58N 38°25E **105** D8
Suruga-Wan *Japan* 34°45N 138°30E **113** G9
Surxondaryo □
  Uzbekistan 38°0N 67°30E **109** E7
Susa *Italy* 45°8N 7°3E **92** C4
Suså → *Denmark* 55°12N 11°42E **63** J5
Susac *Croatia* 42°46N 16°30E **93** F13
Süsah *Libya* 32°52N 21°59E **135** B10
Susak *Croatia* 44°30N 14°18E **93** D11
Susaki *Japan* 33°22N 133°17E **113** H6
Süsangerd *Iran* 31°35N 48°6E **129** D6
Susanville *U.S.A.* 40°25N 120°39W **168** F3
Susch *Switz.* 46°46N 10°5E **77** J6
Suşehri *Turkey* 40°10N 38°6E **105** B8
Sušice *Czech Rep.* 49°17N 13°30E **78** B6
Susleni *Moldova* 47°25N 28°59E **81** C15
Susner *India* 23°57N 76°5E **124** H7
Susong *China* 30°10N 116°7E **115** H10
Susquehanna *U.S.A.* 41°57N 75°36W **175** E9
Susquehanna →
  U.S.A. 39°33N 76°5W **175** G8
Susques *Argentina* 23°35S 66°25W **190** A2
Sussex *Canada* 45°45N 65°37W **165** C6
Sussex *U.S.A.* 41°13N 74°37W **175** E10
Sussex, East □ *U.K.* 51°0N 0°20E **67** E8
Sussex, West □ *U.K.* 51°0N 0°30W **67** E7
Sussex Inlet *Australia* 35°10S 150°36E **153** E9
Sustut → *Canada* 56°20N 127°30W **162** B3
Susuman *Russia* 62°47N 148°10E **107** C15
Susunu *Indonesia* 3°7S 133°39E **119** E8
Susurluk *Turkey* 39°54N 28°8E **99** B10
Susuz *Turkey* 40°46N 43°8E **105** B10
Sutay Uul *Asia* 46°35N 93°38E **110** B7
Sütçüler *Turkey* 37°29N 30°57E **104** D4
Sutherland *Australia* 34°2S 151°4E **153** C9
Sutherland *S. Africa* 32°24S 20°40E **144** D3
Sutherland *U.S.A.* 41°10N 101°8W **172** E3

Sutherland Falls *N.Z.* 44°48S 167°46E **155** E2
Suthri *India* 23°3N 68°55E **124** H2
Sutjeska △ *Bos.-H.* 43°50N 18°32E **80** G3
Sutlej → *Pakistan* 29°23N 71°3E **124** E4
Sutter *U.S.A.* 39°10N 121°45W **170** F5
Sutter Buttes *U.S.A.* 39°12N 121°49W **170** F5
Sutter Creek *U.S.A.* 38°24N 120°48W **170** G6
Sutton *Canada* 45°6N 72°37W **175** A12
Sutton *N.Z.* 45°34S 170°8E **155** F5
Sutton *Nebr., U.S.A.* 40°36N 97°52W **172** E5
Sutton *W. Va., U.S.A.* 38°40N 80°43W **173** F13
Sutton → *Canada* 55°15N 83°45W **164** A3
Sutton Coldfield *U.K.* 52°35N 1°49W **67** E6
Sutton in Ashfield *U.K.* 53°8N 1°16W **66** D6
Sutton L. *Canada* 54°15N 84°42W **164** B3
Suttor → *Australia* 21°36S 147°2E **150** C4
Suttsu *Japan* 42°48N 140°14E **112** C10
Sutwik I. *U.S.A.* 56°34N 157°12W **166** D8
Suva *Fiji* 18°6S 178°30E **154** a
Suva Gora *Macedonia* 41°45N 21°3E **96** B5
Suva Planina *Serbia* 43°10N 22°5E **96** C6
Suva Reka = Therandë
  Kosovo 42°21N 20°50E **96** D4
Suvorov Is. = Suwarrow Is.
  Cook Is. 13°15S 163°5W **157** J11
Suvorove *Ukraine* 45°35N 28°59E **81** E13
Suvorovo *Bulgaria* 43°20N 27°35E **97** C11
Suwałki *Poland* 54°8N 22°59E **82** D9
Suwannaphum
  Thailand 15°33N 103°47E **120** E4
Suwannee → *U.S.A.* 29°20N 83°9W **179** F6
Suwannee *U.S.A.* 29°17N 83°10W **179** F6
Suwannee Sd. *U.S.A.* 29°20N 83°16W **179** F6
Suwanose-Jima *Japan* 29°38N 129°43E **113** K4
Suwarrow Is. *Cook Is.* 13°15S 163°5W **157** J11
Suwayqīyah, Hawr as
  Iraq 32°40N 46°3E **105** G12
Suweis, Khalig el *Egypt* 28°40N 33°0E **137** F8
Suweis, Qanâ es *Egypt* 31°0N 32°20E **137** E8
Suwon *S. Korea* 37°17N 127°1E **115** F14
Suzdal *Russia* 56°29N 40°26E **84** D11
Suzhou *Anhui, China* 33°41N 116°59E **114** H9
Suzhou *Jiangsu, China* 31°19N 120°38E **117** B13
Suzu *Japan* 37°25N 137°17E **113** F8
Suzu-Misaki *Japan* 37°31N 137°21E **113** F8
Suzuka *Japan* 34°55N 136°36E **113** G8
Suzun *Russia* 53°47N 82°18E **109** B10
Suzzara *Italy* 44°59N 10°45E **92** D7
Svalbard *Arctic* 78°0N 17°0E **57** B12
Svalbard Radio = Longyearbyen
  Svalbard 78°13N 15°40E **54** B8
Svalöv *Sweden* 55°57N 13°8E **63** J7
Svalyava *Ukraine* 48°33N 22°59E **80** B7
Svaneke *Denmark* 55°8N 15°5E **63** J9
Svaneti *Georgia* 42°50N 42°45E **105** A10
Svängsta *Sweden* 56°16N 14°47E **63** H8
Svanskog *Sweden* 59°11N 12°33E **62** E6
Svappavaara *Sweden* 67°40N 21°3E **60** C19
Svärdsjö *Sweden* 60°45N 15°54E **62** D9
Svärta *Sweden* 59°8N 14°32E **62** E8
Svartisen *Norway* 66°40N 13°59E **60** C15
Svartsjö *Sweden* 62°19N 17°24E **62** B11
Svatove *Ukraine* 49°22N 38°15E **85** H10
Svatovo = Svatove
  Ukraine 49°22N 38°15E **85** H10
Svay Chek *Cambodia* 13°48N 102°58E **120** F4
Svay Rieng *Cambodia* 11°9N 105°45E **121** G5
Svealand *Sweden* 60°20N 15°0E **62** D9
Svedala *Sweden* 55°30N 13°15E **63** J7
Sveg *Sweden* 62°2N 14°21E **62** B8
Svendborg *Denmark* 55°4N 10°35E **63** J4
Svenljunga *Sweden* 57°29N 13°5E **63** G7
Svenstavik *Sweden* 62°45N 14°26E **62** B8
Svenstrup *Denmark* 56°58N 9°50E **63** H3
Svenvhorodka *Ukraine* 49°4N 30°56E **85** H6
Sverdlovsk *Ukraine* 48°5N 39°47E **85** H10
Sverdrup Chan.
  Canada 79°56N 96°25W **161** B12
Sverdrup Is. *Canada* 79°0N 97°0W **158** B3
Sverige = Sweden ■
  Europe 57°0N 15°0E **61** H16
Sveshtari *Bulgaria* 43°40N 26°40E **97** C10
Svetac *Croatia* 43°3N 15°43E **93** E12
Sveti Nikola, Prokhad
  Europe 43°27N 22°28E **96** C6
Sveti Nikole *Macedonia* 41°51N 21°56E **96** B5
Sveti Rok *Croatia* 44°15N 15°39E **93** D12
Svetlaya *Russia* 46°33N 138°18E **112** A9
Svetlogorsk = Svyetlahorsk
  Belarus 52°38N 29°46E **75** B15
Svetlogorsk *Russia* 54°56N 20°10E **82** D7
Svetlograd *Russia* 45°25N 42°58E **87** H6
Svetlovodsk = Svitlovodsk
  Ukraine 49°11N 33°13E **85** H7
Svetlyy *Kaliningrad, Russia* 54°41N 20°8E **82** D7
Svetlyy *Orenburg, Russia* 50°48N 60°51E **108** D6
Svidník *Slovak Rep.* 49°20N 21°37E **79** B14
Svilaja Planina *Croatia* 43°49N 16°31E **93** E13
Svilajnac *Serbia* 44°15N 21°11E **96** B5
Svilengrad *Bulgaria* 41°49N 26°12E **97** E10
Svir → *Russia* 60°30N 32°48E **84** B7
Sviritsa *Russia* 60°30N 32°51E **84** B7
Svishtov *Bulgaria* 43°36N 25°23E **97** C9
Svislach *Belarus* 53°3N 24°2E **83** E11
Svitava → *Czech Rep.* 49°11N 16°37E **79** B9
Svitavy *Czech Rep.* 49°47N 16°28E **79** B9
Svitlovodsk *Ukraine* 49°11N 33°13E **85** H7
Svityaz, Ozero *Ukraine* 51°30N 23°50E **83** G10
Svizzera = Switzerland ■
  Europe 46°30N 8°0E **77** J4
Svobodnyy *Russia* 51°20N 128°0E **107** D13
Svoge *Bulgaria* 42°59N 23°32E **96** C7
Svolvær *Norway* 68°15N 14°34E **60** B16
Svratka → *Czech Rep.* 49°12N 16°38E **79** B9
Svrljig *Serbia* 43°25N 22°6E **96** C6
Svyetlahorsk *Belarus* 52°38N 29°46E **75** B15
Swabian Alps = Schwäbische Alb
  Germany 48°20N 9°30E **77** G5
Swaffham *U.K.* 52°39N 0°42E **67** E8
Swains I. *Amer. Samoa* 11°11S 171°4W **157** J11
Swainsboro *U.S.A.* 32°36N 82°21W **178** D7
Swakop → *Namibia* 22°38S 14°36E **144** B2
Swakopmund *Namibia* 22°37S 14°30E **144** B2
Swale → *U.K.* 54°5N 1°20W **66** C6
Swamihalli *India* 14°52N 76°38E **127** G3
Swan → *Australia* 32°3S 115°45E **149** F2
Swan → *Canada* 52°30N 100°40W **163** C8
Swan Hill *Australia* 35°20S 143°33E **152** C5
Swan Hills *Canada* 54°43N 115°24W **162** C5

Swan Is. = Santanilla, Is.
  Honduras 17°22N 83°57W **182** C3
Swan L. *Man., Canada* 52°30N 100°40W **163** C8
Swan L. *Ont., Canada* 54°16N 91°11W **164** B1
Swan Ra. *U.S.A.* 48°0N 113°45W **168** C7
Swan Reach *Australia* 34°35S 139°37E **152** C3
Swan River *Canada* 52°10N 101°16W **163** C8
Swanage *U.K.* 50°36N 1°58W **67** G6
Swansea *N.S.W.,
  Australia* 33°3S 151°35E **153** B9
Swansea *Tas., Australia* 42°8S 148°4E **151** G4
Swansea *Canada* 43°38N 79°28W **174** C5
Swansea *U.K.* 51°37N 3°57W **67** F4
Swansea *U.K.* 51°37N 3°57W **67** F4
Swansea □ *U.K.* 51°38N 4°3W **67** F3
Swartberge *S. Africa* 33°20S 22°0E **144** D3
Swartmodder *S. Africa* 28°1S 20°32E **144** C3
Swartnossob → *Namibia* 23°8S 18°42E **144** B2
Swartruggens *S. Africa* 25°39S 26°42E **144** C4
Swarzedz *Poland* 52°25N 17°4E **83** F4
Swastika *Canada* 48°7N 80°6W **164** D3
Swat → *Pakistan* 34°40N 72°5E **125** B5
Swatow = Shantou
  China 23°18N 116°40E **117** F11
Swaziland ■ *Africa* 26°30S 31°30E **145** C5
Sweden ■ *Europe* 57°0N 15°0E **61** H16
Swedru *Ghana* 5°32N 0°41W **139** D4
Sweet Grass *U.S.A.* 48°59N 111°58W **168** D8
Sweet Home *U.S.A.* 44°24N 122°44W **168** D2
Sweetwater *Nev.,
  U.S.A.* 38°27N 119°9W **170** G7
Sweetwater *Tenn.,
  U.S.A.* 35°36N 84°28W **177** D12
Sweetwater *Tex.,
  U.S.A.* 32°28N 100°25W **176** E4
Sweetwater →
  U.S.A. 42°31N 107°2W **168** E10
Swellendam *S. Africa* 34°1S 20°26E **144** D3
Swider → *Poland* 52°6N 21°14E **83** F8
Świdnica *Poland* 50°50N 16°30E **83** H3
Świdnik *Poland* 51°13N 22°39E **83** G9
Świdwin *Poland* 53°47N 15°49E **82** E2
Swiebodzice *Poland* 50°51N 16°20E **83** H3
Świebodzin *Poland* 52°15N 15°31E **83** F2
Świecie *Poland* 53°25N 18°30E **83** E5
Świerzawa *Poland* 51°1N 15°54E **83** G2
Świętokrzyski △ *Poland* 50°53N 20°59E **83** H7
Świętokrzyskie □
  Poland 50°45N 20°45E **83** H7
Świętokrzyskie, Góry
  Poland 51°0N 20°30E **83** H7
Swift Current *Canada* 50°20N 107°45W **163** C7
Swift Current →
  Canada 50°38N 107°44W **163** C7
Swifts Creek *Australia* 37°34S 147°44E **153** D7
Swilly, L. *Ireland* 55°12N 7°33W **64** A4
Swindon *U.K.* 51°34N 1°46W **67** F6
Swindon □ *U.K.* 51°34N 1°46W **67** F6
Swinemünde = Świnoujście
  Poland 53°54N 14°16E **82** E1
Swinford *Ireland* 53°57N 8°58W **64** C3
Świnoujście *Poland* 53°54N 14°16E **82** E1
Switzerland ■ *Europe* 46°30N 8°0E **77** J4
Swords *Ireland* 53°28N 6°13W **64** C5
Swoyerville *U.S.A.* 41°18N 75°53W **175** E9
Syasstroy *Russia* 60°9N 32°33E **84** B7
Sychevka *Russia* 55°59N 34°16E **84** D8
Syców *Poland* 51°19N 17°40E **83** G4
Syddanmark □ *Denmark* 55°30N 9°0E **63** J2
Sydenham → *Canada* 42°33N 82°25W **174** D2
Sydney *Australia* 33°52S 151°12E **153** B9
Sydney *Canada* 46°7N 60°7W **165** C7
Sydney L. *Canada* 50°41N 94°25W **163** C10
Sydney Mines *Canada* 46°18N 60°15W **165** C7
Sydprøven = Alluitsup Paa
  Greenland 60°30N 45°35W **57** E6
Sydra, G. of = Surt, Khalīj
  Libya 31°40N 18°30E **135** B9
Syeverodonetsk
  Ukraine 48°30N 38°35E **85** H10
Syke *Germany* 52°55N 8°50E **76** C4
Sykesville *U.S.A.* 41°3N 78°50W **174** E6
Syktyvkar *Russia* 61°45N 50°40E **106** C6
Sylacauga *U.S.A.* 33°10N 86°15W **178** D3
Sylarna *Sweden* 63°2N 12°13E **60** E15
Sylhet *Bangla.* 24°54N 91°52E **123** G17
Sylhet □ *Bangla.* 24°50N 91°50E **123** G17
Sylt *Germany* 54°54N 8°22E **76** A4
Sylvan Beach *U.S.A.* 43°12N 75°44W **175** C9
Sylvan Lake *Canada* 52°20N 114°3W **162** C6
Sylvania *Ga., U.S.A.* 32°45N 81°38W **178** C8
Sylvania *Ohio, U.S.A.* 41°43N 83°42W **173** E12
Sylvester *U.S.A.* 31°32N 83°50W **178** D6
Sym *Russia* 60°20N 88°18E **106** C9
Synelnykove *Ukraine* 48°35N 35°30E **85** H8
Synevyr △ *Ukraine* 48°30N 23°4E **81** B8
Synevyrska Polyana
  Ukraine 48°35N 23°41E **81** B8
Synnot Ra. *Australia* 16°30S 125°20E **148** C4
Synyak *Ukraine* 48°35N 22°51E **80** B7
Syöte △ *Finland* 65°44N 27°58E **60** D22
Syowa *Antarctica* 68°50S 12°0E **55** C5
Syracuse *Kans.,
  U.S.A.* 37°59N 101°45W **172** G3
Syracuse *N.Y., U.S.A.* 43°3N 76°9W **175** C8
Syracuse *Nebr., U.S.A.* 40°39N 96°11W **172** E5
Syrdarya → *Kazakhstan* 46°3N 61°0E **108** C6
Syria ■ *Asia* 35°0N 38°0E **105** E8
Syrian Desert = Shām, Bādiyat
  ash *Asia* 32°0N 40°0E **128** C3
Syros = Ermoupoli
  Greece 37°28N 24°57E **98** D6
Sysslebäck *Sweden* 60°44N 12°52E **62** D6
Syzran *Russia* 53°12N 48°30E **86** D9
Szabolcs-Szatmár-Bereg □
  Hungary 48°2N 21°45E **80** D6
Szadek *Poland* 51°41N 18°59E **83** G5
Szamos → *Hungary* 48°7N 22°20E **80** A6
Szamotuły *Poland* 52°37N 16°33E **83** F3
Száraz → *Hungary* 46°50N 20°15E **80** D5
Szarvas *Hungary* 46°50N 20°38E **80** D5
Százhalombatta
  Hungary 47°20N 18°58E **80** C3
Szczawnica *Poland* 49°26N 20°33E **83** J7
Szczecin *Poland* 53°27N 14°27E **82** E1
Szczecinek *Poland* 53°43N 16°41E **82** E3
Szczeciński, Zalew = Stettiner Haff
  Germany 53°47N 14°15E **76** B10
Szczekociny *Poland* 50°38N 19°48E **83** H6

Szczucin *Poland* 50°18N 21°4E **83** H8
Szczuczyn *Poland* 53°36N 22°19E **82** E9
Szczyrk *Poland* 49°43N 19°2E **83** J6
Szczytna *Poland* 50°25N 16°28E **83** H3
Szczytno *Poland* 53°33N 21°0E **82** E7
Szechuan = Sichuan □
  China 30°30N 103°0E **116** B5
Szechwan Basin = Sichuan Pendi
  China 31°0N 105°0E **116** B5
Szécsény *Hungary* 48°7N 19°30E **80** B4
Szeged *Hungary* 46°16N 20°10E **80** D5
Szeghalom *Hungary* 47°1N 21°10E **80** C6
Székesfehérvár *Hungary* 47°15N 18°25E **80** C3
Szekszárd *Hungary* 46°22N 18°42E **80** D3
Szentendre *Hungary* 47°39N 19°4E **80** C4
Szentes *Hungary* 46°39N 20°21E **80** D5
Szentgotthárd *Hungary* 46°58N 16°19E **80** D1
Szentlőrinc *Hungary* 46°3N 18°1E **80** D3
Szerencs *Hungary* 48°10N 21°12E **80** B6
Szigetszentmiklós
  Hungary 47°21N 19°3E **80** C4
Szigetvár *Hungary* 46°3N 17°46E **80** D2
Szikszó *Hungary* 48°12N 20°56E **80** B5
Szklarska Poreba *Poland* 50°50N 15°33E **83** H2
Szkwa → *Poland* 53°11N 21°43E **83** E8
Szlichtyngowa *Poland* 51°42N 16°15E **83** G3
Szob *Hungary* 47°48N 18°53E **80** C3
Szolnok *Hungary* 47°10N 20°15E **80** C5
Szombathely *Hungary* 47°14N 16°38E **80** C1
Szprotawa *Poland* 51°33N 15°35E **83** G2
Sztum *Poland* 53°55N 19°1E **82** E6
Sztutowo *Poland* 54°20N 19°15E **82** D6
Szubin *Poland* 53°1N 17°45E **83** E4
Szydłowiec *Poland* 51°15N 20°51E **83** G7
Szypliszki *Poland* 54°17N 23°2E **82** D10

T

Ta Khli *Thailand* 15°15N 100°21E **120** E3
Ta Lai *Vietnam* 11°24N 107°23E **121** G6
Ta Phraya △ *Thailand* 14°11N 102°49E **120** E4
Taal Volcano *Phil.* 14°7N 120°59E **119** B6
Taamisaari = Raasepori
  Finland 60°0N 23°26E **84** B2
Tab *Hungary* 46°44N 18°2E **80** D3
Tabacal *Argentina* 23°15S 64°15W **190** A3
Tabaco *Phil.* 13°22N 123°44E **119** B6
Tabagné *Ivory C.* 7°59N 3°4W **138** D4
Ţabah *Si. Arabia* 26°55N 42°38E **128** E4
Tabalos *Peru* 6°26S 76°37W **188** B2
Tabanan *Indonesia* 8°32S 115°8E **119** K18
Tabankort *Niger* 17°44N 0°20E **138** B5
Tabarka *Tunisia* 36°56N 8°46E **136** A5
Ţabas *Khorāsān, Iran* 32°48N 60°12E **129** C9
Ţabas *Yazd, Iran* 33°35N 56°55E **129** C8
Tabasará, Serranía de
  Panama 8°35N 81°40W **182** E3
Tabasco □ *Mexico* 18°0N 92°40W **181** D6
Tabāsīn *Iran* 31°12N 57°54E **129** D8
Tabatinga *Brazil* 4°1S 69°56W **188** A4
Tabatinga, Serra da
  Brazil 10°30S 44°0W **189** C2
Tabelbala *Algeria* 29°24N 3°15W **136** C3
Tabelbala, Kahal de
  Algeria 28°47N 2°0W **136** C3
Tabelemballa *Algeria* 24°43N 4°16E **136** D4
Taber *Canada* 49°47N 112°8W **162** D6
Taberg *Sweden* 57°40N 14°6E **63** G8
Tabira *Brazil* 7°35S 37°33W **189** B3
Tabla *Niger* 14°5N 1°50E **138** C5
Tablas de Daimiel △ *Spain* 39°9N 3°40W **89** F7
Tablas I. *Phil.* 12°25N 122°2E **119** B6
Table, Pte. de la *Réunion* 21°14S 55°48E **141** c
Table B. *Canada* 53°40N 56°25W **165** B8
Table B. *S. Africa* 33°35S 18°25E **144** D2
Table C. *N.Z.* 39°6S 178°0E **154** F7
Table I. *Burma* 14°12N 93°22E **127** G11
Table Mountain △
  S. Africa 33°58S 18°26E **144** D2
Table Mt. *S. Africa* 33°58S 18°26E **144** D2
Table Rock L. *U.S.A.* 36°36N 93°19W **172** G7
Tabletop, Mt. *Australia* 23°24S 147°11E **150** C4
Tábor *Czech Rep.* 49°25N 14°39E **78** B7
Tabora *Tanzania* 5°2S 32°50E **142** D3
Tabora □ *Tanzania* 5°0S 33°0E **142** D3
Tabou *Ivory C.* 4°30N 7°20W **138** E3
Tabrīz *Iran* 38°7N 46°20E **105** C12
Tabuaeran *Kiribati* 3°51N 159°22W **157** G12
Tabuenca *Spain* 41°42N 1°33W **90** D3
Tabūk *Si. Arabia* 28°23N 36°36E **128** D3
Tabūk □ *Si. Arabia* 27°40N 36°50E **128** E3
Tacámbaro de Codallos
  Mexico 19°14N 101°28W **180** D4
Tacheng *China* 46°40N 82°58E **109** C10
Tach'i *Taiwan* 24°53N 121°17E **117** E13
Tachia *Taiwan* 24°25N 120°28E **117** E13
Tachilek *Burma* 20°26N 99°52E **120** B2
Tach'ing Shan = Daqing Shan
  China 40°40N 111°0E **114** D6
Tachov *Czech Rep.* 49°47N 12°39E **78** B5
Tácina → *Italy* 38°57N 16°55E **95** D9
Tacloban *Phil.* 11°15N 124°58E **119** B6
Tacna *Peru* 18°0S 70°20W **188** D3
Tacna □ *Peru* 17°40S 70°20W **188** D3
Tacoma *U.S.A.* 47°14N 122°26W **170** C4
Tacuarembó *Uruguay* 31°45S 56°0W **191** C4
Tademaït, Plateau du
  Algeria 28°30N 2°30E **136** C6
Tadio, L. *Ivory C.* 5°15N 5°0W **138** D3
Tadjerdjeri, O. → *Algeria* 26°0N 3°0E **136** D6
Tadjerouna *Algeria* 33°31N 2°3E **136** B6
Tadjmout *Saoura, Algeria* 33°52N 2°30E **136** B6
Tadjoura *Djibouti* 11°50N 42°55E **131** E3
Tadla-Azilal □ *Morocco* 32°0N 6°20W **136** B4
Tadō *India* 20°30N 102°0E **116** A5
Tadoule L. *Canada* 58°36N 98°20E **163** B9
Tadoussac *Canada* 48°11N 69°42W **165** B6
Tadpatri *India* 14°55N 78°1E **127** G3
Tadrés → *Niger* 16°0N 7°10E **138** C7
Tadzhikistan = Tajikistan ■
  Asia 38°30N 70°0E **109** E8

Taegu = Daegu
  S. Korea 35°50N 128°37E **115** G15
Taegwan *N. Korea* 40°13N 125°12E **115** D13
Taejon = Daejeon
  S. Korea 36°20N 127°28E **115** F14
Taen, Ko *Thailand* 9°22N 99°57E **121** b
Tafalla *Spain* 42°30N 1°41W **90** C3
Tafelbaai = Table B.
  S. Africa 33°35S 18°25E **144** D2
Tafelney, C. *Morocco* 31°3N 9°51W **136** B3
Tafermaar *Indonesia* 6°47S 134°10E **119** F8
Taffermit *Morocco* 29°37N 9°15W **136** C3
Tafi Viejo *Argentina* 26°43S 65°17W **190** B2
Tafihān *Iran* 29°25N 52°39E **129** D7
Tafilalet *Morocco* 31°20N 4°45W **136** B3
Tafiré *Ivory C.* 9°4N 5°4W **138** D3
Tafo *Ghana* 6°15N 0°20W **139** D4
Tafraoute *Morocco* 29°50N 8°58W **136** C3
Tafresh *Iran* 34°45N 49°57E **129** C6
Taft *Iran* 31°45N 54°14E **129** D7
Taft *U.S.A.* 35°8N 119°28W **171** K7
Taftan *Pakistan* 29°0N 61°30E **122** E2
Taftān, Kūh-e *Iran* 28°40N 61°0E **129** D9
Tafwap *India* 7°23N 93°43E **127** L11
Taga Dzong *Bhutan* 27°5N 89°55E **123** F16
Taganay △ *Russia* 55°15N 59°48E **108** B5
Taganrog *Russia* 47°12N 38°50E **85** J10
Taganrogskiy Zaliv
  Russia 47°0N 38°30E **85** J10
Tagânt □ *Mauritania* 19°0N 10°0W **138** B3
Tagbilaran *Phil.* 9°39N 123°51E **119** C6
Tággia *Italy* 43°52N 7°51E **92** E4
Taghit *Algeria* 30°58N 2°0W **136** B3
Tagish *Canada* 60°19N 134°16W **162** A2
Tagish L. *Canada* 60°10N 134°20W **162** A2
Tagliacozzo *Italy* 42°4N 13°14E **93** F10
Tagliamento → *Italy* 45°38N 13°6E **93** C10
Táglio di Po *Italy* 45°0N 12°12E **93** D9
Tagomago *Spain* 39°2N 1°39E **100** B8
Tagourâret *Mauritania* 17°45N 7°45W **138** B3
Taguatinga *Distrito Federal,
  Brazil* 15°51S 48°4W **189** D1
Taguatinga *Tocantins,
  Brazil* 12°27S 46°22W **189** C1
Tagum *Phil.* 7°33N 125°53E **119** C7
Tahakopa *N.Z.* 46°30S 169°23E **155** G4
Tahala *Morocco* 34°0N 4°28W **136** B3
Tahan, Gunung
  Malaysia 4°34N 102°17E **121** K4
Tahat *Algeria* 23°18N 5°33E **136** D5
Tāherī *Iran* 27°43N 52°20E **129** E7
Tahifet *Algeria* 22°58N 6°0E **136** D5
Tahiti, I. *Tahiti* 17°37S 149°27W **155** b
Tahiti, I. *Tahiti* 17°37S 149°27W **155** b
Tahlequah *U.S.A.* 35°55N 94°58W **176** D7
Tahoe, L. *U.S.A.* 39°6N 120°2W **170** F6
Tahoe City *U.S.A.* 39°10N 120°9W **170** F6
Tahoka *U.S.A.* 33°10N 101°48W **176** E4
Taholah *U.S.A.* 47°21N 124°17W **170** C2
Tahora *N.Z.* 39°2S 174°49E **154** F3
Tahoua *Niger* 14°57N 5°16E **139** C6
Tahrūd *Iran* 29°26N 57°49E **129** D8
Tahsis *Canada* 49°55N 126°40W **162** D3
Tahta *Egypt* 26°44N 31°32E **137** B3
Tahtaköprü *Turkey* 39°57N 29°9E **97** G13
Tahtalı Dağları *Turkey* 38°30N 36°0E **104** C7
Tahuamanú → *Bolivia* 11°6S 67°36W **188** C4
Tahulandang *Indonesia* 2°27N 125°23E **119** D7
Tahuna *Indonesia* 3°38N 125°30E **119** D7
Taï *Ivory C.* 5°55N 7°30W **138** D3
Taï □ *Ivory C.* 5°50N 7°30W **138** D3
Tai Hu *China* 31°5N 120°10E **117** B13
Tai Mo Shan *China* 22°25N 114°7E **111** a
Tai O *China* 22°15N 113°52E **111** a
Tai Pang Wan *China* 22°33N 114°24E **111** a
Tai Po *China* 22°27N 114°10E **111** a
Tai Rom Yen △ *Thailand* 8°45N 99°30E **121** H2
Tai Yue Shan = Lantau I.
  China 22°15N 113°56E **111** a
Tai'an *China* 36°12N 117°8E **115** F9
Taiarapu, Presqu'île de
  Tahiti 17°47S 149°14W **155** b
Taibai Shan *China* 33°57N 107°45E **114** H4
Taibei = T'aipei
  Taiwan 25°4N 121°29E **117** E13
Taibique *Canary Is.* 27°42N 17°58W **100** G2
Taibus Qi *China* 41°54N 115°22E **114** D8
Taicang *China* 31°30N 121°5E **117** B13
T'aichung *Taiwan* 24°9N 120°37E **117** E13
Taieri → *N.Z.* 46°3S 170°12E **155** G5
Taigu *China* 37°28N 112°30E **114** F7
Taihang Shan *China* 36°0N 113°30E **114** F8
Taihape *N.Z.* 39°41S 175°48E **154** F4
Taihe *Anhui, China* 33°20N 115°42E **114** H8
Taihe *Jiangxi, China* 26°47N 114°52E **117** D10
Taihu *China* 30°22N 116°20E **117** B11
Taijiang *China* 26°39N 108°21E **116** D7
Taikang *China* 34°5N 114°50E **114** G8
Tailem Bend *Australia* 35°12S 139°29E **152** C3
Tailfingen *Germany* 48°15N 9°1E **77** G5
T'ailuko *Taiwan* 24°12N 121°37E **117** E13
Taimyr Peninsula = Taymyr,
  Poluostrov *Russia* 75°0N 100°0E **107** B11
Tain *U.K.* 57°49N 4°4W **65** D4
T'ainan *Taiwan* 23°0N 120°10E **117** F13
Tainaron, Ákra *Greece* 36°22N 22°27E **98** E5
Taiobeiras *Brazil* 15°49S 42°14W **189** D2
Taipa *China* 22°10N 113°35E **111** a
T'aipei *Taiwan* 25°4N 121°29E **117** E13
Taiping *China* 30°15N 118°5E **117** B12
Taiping *Malaysia* 4°51N 100°44E **121** K3
Taiping Dao = Itu Aba I.
  S. China Sea 10°23N 114°21E **118** B4
Taipingchuan *China* 44°23N 123°11E **115** B12
Taishan *Guangdong,
  China* 22°14N 112°41E **117** F9
Taishan *Shandong,
  China* 36°18N 118°2E **114** F10
Taishun *China* 27°30N 119°42E **117** D12
Taita Hills *Kenya* 3°25S 38°15E **142** C4
Taitao, C. *Chile* 45°53S 75°5W **192** C1
Taitao, Pen. de *Chile* 46°30S 75°0W **192** C1
Taivalkoski *Finland* 65°33N 28°12E **60** D23
Taiwan ■ *Asia* 23°30N 121°0E **117** F13
Taiwan Strait *Asia* 24°40N 120°0E **117** E12

276 Taixing INDEX TO WORLD MAPS

Taixing China 32°11N 120°0E 117 A13
Taiyiba Israel 32°36N 35°27E 130 C4
Taiyuan China 37°52N 112°33E 114 F7
Taizhong = T'aichung Taiwan 24°9N 120°37E 117 E13
Taizhou Jiangsu, China 32°28N 119°55E 117 A12
Taizhou Zhejiang, China 28°40N 121°24E 117 C13
Taizhou Liedao China 28°30N 121°55E 117 C13
Ta'izz Yemen 13°35N 44°2E 131 E3
Taj Mahal India 27°10N 78°2E 124 F8
Tājābād Iran 30°2N 54°24E 129 D7
Tajikistan ■ Asia 38°30N 70°0E 109 E8
Tajima = Minamiaizu Japan 37°12N 139°46E 113 F9
Tajo = Tejo → Europe 38°40N 9°24W 89 F2
Tajrīsh Iran 35°48N 51°25E 129 C6
Tak Thailand 16°52N 99°8E 120 D2
Takāb Iran 36°24N 47°7E 105 D12
Takachiho Japan 32°42N 131°18E 113 H5
Takachu Botswana 22°37S 21°58E 144 B3
Takada Japan 37°7N 138°15E 113 F9
Takahagi Japan 36°43N 140°45E 113 F10
Takaka N.Z. 40°51S 172°50E 155 A7
Takamaka Seychelles 4°50S 55°30E 141 b
Takamatsu Japan 34°20N 134°5E 113 G7
Takaoka Japan 36°47N 137°0E 113 F8
Takapau N.Z. 40°2S 176°21E 154 G5
Takapuna N.Z. 36°47S 174°47E 154 C3
Takasaki Japan 36°20N 139°0E 113 F9
Takatsuki Japan 34°51N 135°37E 113 G7
Takaungu Kenya 3°38S 39°52E 142 C4
Takayama Japan 36°18N 137°11E 113 F8
Take-Shima Japan 30°49N 130°26E 113 J5
Takefu = Echizen Japan 35°50N 136°10E 113 G8
Takengon Indonesia 4°45N 96°50E 118 D1
Takeo Cambodia 10°59N 104°47E 121 G5
Takeo Japan 33°12N 130°1E 113 H5
Tåkern Sweden 58°22N 14°45E 63 F8
Takeshima = Liancourt Rocks Asia 37°15N 131°52E 113 F5
Tākestān Iran 36°0N 49°40E 129 C6
Taketa Japan 32°58N 131°24E 113 H5
Takh India 33°6N 77°32E 125 C7
Takhār □ Afghan. 36°40N 70°0E 109 E7
Takhiatash Uzbekistan 42°20N 59°33E 108 D5
Takhmau Cambodia 11°29N 104°57E 121 G5
Takht-e Soleyman Iran 36°36N 47°14E 105 D12
Takht-Sulaiman Pakistan 31°40N 69°58E 124 D3
Takiéta Niger 13°41N 8°32E 139 C6
Takikawa Japan 43°33N 141°54E 112 C10
Takla L. Canada 55°15N 125°45W 162 B3
Takla Landing Canada 55°30N 125°50W 162 B3
Taklamakan China 38°0N 83°0E 109 E10
Taklamakan Shamo = Taklamakan China 38°0N 83°0E 109 E10
Taksimo Russia 56°20N 114°52E 107 D12
Taku → Canada 58°30N 133°50W 162 B2
Takua Thung Thailand 8°24N 98°27E 121 a
Takum Nigeria 7°18N 9°36E 139 D6
Tal Halāl Iran 28°54N 55°1E 129 D7
Tala Uruguay 34°21S 55°46W 191 C4
Talachyn Belarus 54°25N 29°42E 84 E5
Talagang Pakistan 32°55N 72°25E 124 C5
Talagante Chile 33°40S 70°50W 190 C1
Talahouhait Algeria 24°52N 1°56E 136 D4
Talaimannar Sri Lanka 9°6N 79°43E 127 K4
Talaïnt Morocco 29°41N 9°40W 136 C2
Talak Niger 18°0N 5°0E 139 B6
Talamanca, Cordillera de Cent. Amer. 9°20N 83°20W 182 E3
Talampaya △ Argentina 29°43S 67°42W 190 B2
Talant France 47°19N 4°58E 71 E11
Talara Peru 4°38S 81°18W 188 A1
Talas Kyrgyzstan 42°30N 72°13E 109 D8
Talas Turkey 38°41N 35°33E 104 C6
Talas □ Kyrgyzstan 42°20N 72°0E 109 D8
Talas → Kazakhstan 44°0N 70°20E 109 D8
Talas Ala Too Kyrgyzstan 42°15N 72°0E 109 D8
Talasskiy Alatau = Talas Ala Too Kyrgyzstan 42°15N 72°0E 109 D8
Talâta Egypt 30°36N 32°20E 130 E1
Talata Mafara Nigeria 12°38N 6°4E 139 C6
Talaud, Kepulauan Indonesia 4°30N 126°50E 119 D7
Talaud Is. = Talaud, Kepulauan Indonesia 4°30N 126°50E 119 D7
Talavera de la Reina Spain 39°55N 4°46W 88 F6
Talavera la Real Spain 38°53N 6°46W 89 G4
Talayan Phil. 6°52N 124°24E 119 C6
Talayuela Spain 39°59N 5°36W 88 F5
Talbandh India 22°3N 86°20E 125 H12
Talbert, Sillon de France 48°53N 3°5W 70 D3
Talbot Australia 37°10S 143°44E 152 D5
Talbot, C. Australia 13°48S 126°43E 148 B4
Talbotton U.S.A. 32°41N 84°32W 178 C5
Talbragar → Australia 32°12S 148°37E 153 B8
Talca Chile 35°28S 71°40W 190 D1
Talcahuano Chile 36°40S 73°10W 190 D1
Talcher India 21°0N 85°18E 126 D7
Talcho Niger 14°44N 3°28E 139 C5
Taldy Kurgan = Taldyqorghan Kazakhstan 45°10N 78°45E 109 C9
Taldyqorghan Kazakhstan 45°10N 78°45E 109 C9
Tālesh Iran 37°58N 48°58E 105 D13
Tālesh, Kūhhā-ye Iran 37°42N 48°55E 105 D13
Talgar = Talghar Kazakhstan 43°19N 77°15E 109 D9
Talghar Kazakhstan 43°19N 77°15E 109 D9
Talguharai Sudan 18°19N 35°56E 137 D4
Talguppa India 14°13N 74°56E 127 G2
Tali Post South Sudan 5°55N 30°44E 135 G12
Taliabu Indonesia 1°50S 125°0E 119 E6
Talibon Phil. 10°9N 124°20E 119 B6
Talihina U.S.A. 34°45N 95°3W 176 D7
Talikota India 16°29N 76°17E 127 F3
Talipparamba India 12°3N 75°21E 127 H2
Taliwang Indonesia 8°50S 116°55E 118 F5
Talkha Egypt 31°3N 31°22E 137 E7
Talkot Nepal 29°37N 81°19E 125 E9
Tall 'Afar Iraq 36°22N 42°27E 105 D10
Tall Kalakh Syria 34°41N 36°15E 130 A5
Tall Kayf Iraq 36°29N 43°7E 105 D10
Talla Egypt 28°5N 30°43E 137 F7
Talladega U.S.A. 33°26N 86°6W 178 B3
Tallaganda △ Australia 35°29S 149°37E 153 C8
Tallahassee U.S.A. 30°27N 84°17W 178 E5
Tallangatta Australia 36°15S 147°19E 153 D7
Tallapoosa U.S.A. 33°45N 85°17W 178 B4
Tallapoosa → U.S.A. 32°30N 86°16W 178 C3
Tallard France 44°28N 6°3E 73 D10
Tallarook Australia 37°5S 145°6E 153 D6
Tallassee U.S.A. 32°32N 85°54W 178 C4
Tällberg Sweden 60°51N 15°2E 62 D9
Tallering Pk. Australia 28°6S 115°37E 149 E2
Talli Pakistan 29°32N 68°8E 124 E3
Tallinn Estonia 59°22N 24°48E 84 C3
Tallmadge U.S.A. 41°6N 81°27W 174 E3
Tallulah U.S.A. 32°25N 91°11W 176 E9
Tălmaciu Romania 45°38N 24°19E 81 E9
Talmest Morocco 31°48N 9°21W 136 B2
Talmont-St-Hilaire France 46°27N 1°37W 72 B2
Talnakh Russia 69°29N 88°22E 107 C9
Talne Ukraine 48°50N 30°44E 85 H6
Talnoye = Talne Ukraine 48°50N 30°44E 85 H6
Taloda India 21°34N 74°11E 126 D2
Tāloqān Afghan. 36°44N 69°33E 109 E7
Talovaya Russia 51°6N 40°45E 86 E5
Taloyoak Canada 69°32N 93°32W 160 D13
Talpa de Allende Mexico 20°23N 104°51W 180 C4
Talparo Trin. & Tob. 10°30N 61°17W 187 K15
Talquin, L. U.S.A. 30°23N 84°39W 178 E5
Talsi Latvia 57°10N 22°30E 82 A9
Talsi □ Latvia 57°20N 22°40E 82 A9
Talsinnt Morocco 32°33N 3°27W 136 B3
Taltal Chile 25°23S 70°33W 190 B1
Taltson → Canada 61°24N 112°46W 162 A6
Talwood Australia 28°29S 149°29E 151 D4
Talyawalka Cr. → Australia 32°28S 142°22E 152 B5
Tam Dao △ Vietnam 21°45N 105°45E 120 B5
Tam Ky Vietnam 15°34N 108°29E 120 E7
Tam Quan Vietnam 14°35N 109°3E 120 E7
Tama U.S.A. 41°58N 92°35W 172 E7
Tama Abu, Banjaran Malaysia 3°50N 115°5E 118 D5
Tamale Ghana 9°22N 0°50W 139 D4
Taman Russia 45°14N 36°41E 85 K9
Taman Negara △ Malaysia 4°38N 102°26E 121 K4
Tamanar Morocco 31°1N 9°46W 136 B2
Tamani Mali 13°20N 6°50W 138 C3
Tamano Japan 34°29N 133°59E 113 G6
Tamanrasset Algeria 22°50N 5°30E 136 D5
Tamanrasset □ Algeria 23°45N 4°40E 136 D4
Tamaqua U.S.A. 40°48N 75°58W 175 F9
Tamar → U.K. 50°27N 4°15W 67 G3
Tamarac U.S.A. 26°12N 80°15W 179 J9
Tamarin Mauritius 20°19S 57°20E 141 d
Tamarinda Spain 39°55N 3°49E 100 B10
Tamarite de Litera Spain 41°52N 0°25E 90 D5
Tamashima Japan 34°32N 133°40E 113 G6
Tamási Hungary 46°40N 18°18E 80 D3
Tamaské Niger 14°49N 5°43E 139 C6
Tamatave = Toamasina Madag. 18°10S 49°25E 141 H9
Tamaulipas □ Mexico 24°0N 98°45W 181 C5
Tamaulipas, Sierra de Mexico 23°30N 98°20W 181 C5
Tamazula Mexico 24°57N 106°57W 180 C3
Tamazunchale Mexico 21°16N 98°47W 181 C5
Tamba-Dabatou Guinea 11°50N 10°40W 138 C2
Tambach Kenya 0°36N 35°31E 142 B4
Tambacounda Senegal 13°45N 13°40W 138 C2
Tambacounda □ Senegal 14°0N 13°0W 138 C2
Tambaram India 12°55N 80°7E 127 H5
Tambelan, Kepulauan Indonesia 1°0N 107°30E 118 D3
Tambellup Australia 34°4S 117°37E 149 F2
Tambo Australia 24°54S 146°14E 150 C4
Tambo Peru 12°57S 74°1W 188 C3
Tambo → Peru 10°42S 73°47W 188 C3
Tambo de Mora Peru 13°30S 76°8W 188 C2
Tambobamba Peru 13°54S 72°8W 188 C3
Tambopata → Peru 13°21S 69°36W 188 C4
Tambora Indonesia 8°12S 118°5E 118 F5
Tamboritha, Mt. Australia 37°31S 146°40E 153 D7
Tamboura C.A.R. 5°10N 25°12E 142 A2
Tambov Russia 52°45N 41°28E 86 D5
Tambov □ Russia 52°50N 41°20E 86 D5
Tambre → Spain 42°49N 8°53W 88 C2
Tambuku Indonesia 7°8S 113°40E 119 G15
Tâmchekket Mauritania 17°25N 10°40W 138 B2
Tâmega → Portugal 41°5N 8°21W 88 D2
Tamegroute Morocco 30°15N 5°39W 136 B2
Tamelelt Morocco 31°50N 7°32W 136 B2
Tamenglong India 25°0N 93°35E 123 G18
Tamerza Tunisia 34°23N 7°58E 136 B5
Tamgué, Massif du Guinea 12°0N 12°18W 138 C2
Tamiahua, L. de Mexico 21°35N 97°35W 181 C5
Tamiami Canal U.S.A. 25°50N 81°0W 179 K8
Tamil Nadu □ India 11°0N 77°0E 127 J3
Tamis → Serbia 44°51N 20°39E 80 F5
Tamiya Egypt 29°29N 30°58E 137 F7
Tamlelt, Plaine de Morocco 32°30N 2°20W 136 B3
Tamluk India 22°18N 87°58E 125 H12
Tammerfors = Tampere Finland 61°30N 23°50E 84 B2
Tämnaren Sweden 60°10N 17°25E 62 D11
Tampa U.S.A. 27°56N 82°27W 179 H7
Tampa, Tanjung Indonesia 8°55S 116°12E 119 K19
Tampa B. U.S.A. 27°50N 82°30W 179 H7
Tampa Int. ✕ (TPA) U.S.A. 27°59N 82°32W 179 H7
Tampere Finland 61°30N 23°50E 84 B2
Tampico Mexico 22°13N 97°51W 181 C5
Tampin Malaysia 2°28N 102°13E 121 L4
Tampoi Malaysia 1°30N 103°39E 121 d
Tamri Morocco 30°49N 9°50W 136 B2
Tamsagbulag Mongolia 47°14N 117°21E 111 B12
Tamsweg Austria 47°7N 13°49E 78 D6
Tamu Burma 24°13N 94°12E 123 G19
Tamuja → Spain 39°38N 6°29W 89 F4
Tamworth Australia 31°7S 150°58E 153 A9
Tamworth Canada 44°29N 77°0W 174 B8
Tamworth U.K. 52°39N 1°41W 67 E6
Tan An Vietnam 10°32N 106°25E 121 G6
Tan Chau Vietnam 10°48N 105°12E 121 G5
Tan Hiep Vietnam 10°27N 106°21E 121 G6
Tan Iddah Algeria 26°33N 9°42E 136 C5
Tan-Tan Morocco 28°29N 11°1W 134 C3
Tan Yen Vietnam 22°4N 105°3E 120 A5
Tana → Kenya 2°32S 40°31E 142 C5
Tana → Norway 70°30N 28°14E 60 A23
Tana, L. Ethiopia 13°5N 37°30E 131 E2
Tana River Primate ⌂ Kenya 1°55S 40°7E 142 C5
Tanabe Japan 33°44N 135°22E 113 H7
Tanafjorden Norway 70°45N 28°25E 60 A23
Tanaga I. U.S.A. 51°48N 177°53W 166 E4
Tanah Merah Malaysia 5°48N 102°9E 121 K4
Tanahbala Indonesia 0°30S 98°30E 118 E1
Tanahgrogot Indonesia 1°55S 116°15E 118 E5
Tanahjampea Indonesia 7°10S 120°35E 119 F6
Tanahmasa Indonesia 0°12S 98°39E 118 E1
Tanahmerah Indonesia 6°5S 140°16E 119 F10
Tanakpur India 29°5N 80°7E 125 E9
Tanamalwila Sri Lanka 6°26N 81°8E 127 L5
Tanami Desert Australia 18°50S 132°0E 148 C5
Tanana U.S.A. 65°10N 152°4W 166 B9
Tanana → U.S.A. 65°10N 151°58W 160 D1
Tananarive = Antananarivo Madag. 18°55S 47°31E 141 H9
Tanannt Morocco 31°54N 6°56W 136 B2
Tánaro → Italy 44°55N 8°40E 92 D5
Tancheng China 34°25N 118°20E 115 G10
Tanch'ŏn N. Korea 40°27N 128°54E 115 D15
Tanda Ut. P., India 26°33N 82°35E 125 F10
Tanda Ut. P., India 28°57N 78°56E 125 E8
Tanda Ivory C. 7°48N 3°10W 138 D4
Tandag Phil. 9°4N 126°9E 119 C7
Tandaia Tanzania 9°25S 34°15E 143 D3
Tăndărei Romania 44°39N 27°40E 81 F12
Tandaué Angola 16°58S 18°5E 144 A2
Tandil Argentina 37°15S 59°6W 190 D4
Tandil, Sa. del Argentina 37°30S 59°0W 190 D4
Tandlianwala Pakistan 31°3N 73°9E 124 D5
Tando Adam Pakistan 25°45N 68°40E 124 G3
Tando Allahyar Pakistan 25°28N 68°43E 124 G3
Tando Bago Pakistan 24°47N 68°58E 124 G3
Tando Mohommed Khan Pakistan 25°8N 68°32E 124 G3
Tandou L. Australia 32°40S 142°5E 152 B5
Tandoureh △ Iran 37°50N 59°0E 129 B8
Tandragee U.K. 54°21N 6°24W 64 B5
Tandsjöborg Sweden 61°42N 14°43E 62 C8
Tandula → India 21°6N 81°14E 126 D5
Tandula Tank India 20°40N 81°12E 126 D5
Tandur Andhra Pradesh, India 19°11N 79°30E 126 E4
Tandur Andhra Pradesh, India 17°14N 77°35E 126 F3
Tane-ga-Shima Japan 30°30N 131°0E 113 J5
Taneatua N.Z. 38°4S 177°1E 154 E6
Tanen Tong Dan = Dawna Ra. Burma 16°30N 98°30E 120 D2
Tanew → Poland 50°29N 22°16E 83 H9
Tanezrouft Algeria 23°9N 0°11E 136 D4
Tang, Koh Cambodia 10°16N 103°7E 121 G4
Tang, Ra's-e Iran 25°21N 59°52E 129 E8
Tang Krasang Cambodia 12°34N 105°3E 120 F5
Tanga Tanzania 5°5S 39°2E 142 D4
Tanga □ Tanzania 5°20S 38°0E 142 D4
Tangalla Sri Lanka 6°1N 80°48E 127 L5
Tanganyika, L. Africa 6°40S 30°0E 142 D3
Tangasseri India 8°53N 76°35E 127 K3
Tangaza Nigeria 13°19N 4°55E 139 C5
Tanger Morocco 35°50N 5°49W 136 A2
Tanger-Med Morocco 35°53N 5°30W 89 K5
Tanger-Tétouan □ Morocco 35°50N 5°50W 136 A2
Tangerang Indonesia 6°11S 106°37E 119 G12
Tangerhütte Germany 52°26N 11°48E 76 C7
Tangermünde Germany 52°33N 11°58E 76 C7
Tanggu China 39°2N 117°40E 115 E9
Tanggula Shan China 32°40N 92°10E 110 E7
Tanggula Shankou China 32°42N 92°27E 110 E7
Tanghe China 32°47N 112°50E 117 A9
Tanghla Range = Tanggula Shan China 32°40N 92°10E 110 E7
Tangi India 19°56N 85°24E 126 E7
Tangier = Tanger Morocco 35°50N 5°49W 136 A2
Tangjia China 22°22N 113°35E 111 a
Tangjia Wan China 22°21N 113°36E 111 a
Tangorin Australia 21°47S 144°12E 150 C3
Tangshan China 39°38N 118°10E 115 E10
Tangtou China 35°28N 118°30E 115 G10
Tanguen-Dassouri Burkina Faso 12°16N 1°42W 139 C4
Tanguiéta Benin 10°35N 1°21E 139 C5
Tangxi China 29°3N 119°25E 117 C12
Tangyan He → China 28°54N 108°19E 116 C7
Tangyin China 35°54N 114°21E 114 G8
Taniantaweng Shan China 31°20N 98°0E 116 B2
Tanimbar, Kepulauan Indonesia 7°30S 131°30E 119 F8
Tanimbar Is. = Tanimbar, Kepulauan Indonesia 7°30S 131°30E 119 F8
Tanintharyi = Tenasserim Burma 12°6N 99°3E 121 F2
Tanjay Phil. 9°30N 123°5E 119 C6
Tanjong Pelepas Malaysia 1°21N 103°33E 121 d
Tanjore = Thanjavur India 10°48N 79°12E 127 J4
Tanjung Kalimantan Selatan, Indonesia 2°10S 115°25E 118 E5
Tanjung Nusa Tenggara Barat, Indonesia 8°21S 116°9E 119 J19
Tanjung Malim Malaysia 3°42N 101°31E 121 L3
Tanjung Tokong Malaysia 5°28N 100°18E 121 c
Tanjungbalai Indonesia 2°55N 99°44E 118 D1
Tanjungbatu Indonesia 2°23N 118°3E 118 D5
Tanjungkarang Telukbetung = Bandar Lampung Indonesia 5°20S 105°10E 118 F3
Tanjungpandan Indonesia 2°43S 107°38E 118 E3
Tanjungpinang Indonesia 1°5N 104°30E 118 D2
Tanjungredeb Indonesia 2°9N 117°29E 118 D5
Tanjungselor Indonesia 2°55N 117°25E 118 D5
Tank Pakistan 32°14N 70°25E 124 C4
Tankhala India 21°58N 73°47E 124 J5
Tankwa-Karoo △ S. Africa 32°14S 19°50E 144 D2
Tännäs Sweden 62°26N 12°42E 62 B6
Tannersville U.S.A. 41°3N 75°18W 175 E9
Tannis Bugt Denmark 57°40N 10°15E 63 G4
Tannu Ola Asia 51°0N 94°0E 109 B12
Tannum Sands Australia 23°57S 151°22E 150 C5
Tano → Ghana 5°7N 2°56W 138 D4
Tanombella Algeria 25°30N 5°49E 136 C5
Tanout Niger 14°50N 8°55E 139 C6
Tanquinho Brazil 11°58S 39°6W 189 C3
Tanshui Taiwan 25°10N 121°28E 117 E13
Tansilla Burkina Faso 12°25N 4°23W 138 C4
Tansing Nepal 27°52N 83°33E 125 F10
Tanta Egypt 30°45N 30°57E 137 E7
Tantoyuca Mexico 21°21N 98°14W 181 C5
Tantung = Dandong China 40°10N 124°20E 115 D13
Tanuku India 16°45N 81°44E 126 F5
Tanumshede Sweden 58°42N 11°20E 63 F5
Tanunda Australia 34°30S 139°0E 152 C3
Tanur India 11°1N 75°52E 127 J2
Tanus France 44°8N 2°19E 72 D6
Tanzania ■ Africa 6°0S 34°0E 142 D3
Tanzhou China 22°16N 113°28E 111 a
Tanzilla → Canada 58°8N 130°43W 162 B2
Tao, Ko Thailand 10°5N 99°52E 121 G2
Tao'an = Taonan China 45°22N 122°40E 115 B12
Tao'er He → China 45°45N 124°5E 115 B13
Taohua Dao China 29°50N 122°20E 117 C14
Taolanaro Madag. 25°2S 47°0E 141 K9
Taole China 38°48N 106°40E 114 E4
Taonan China 45°22N 122°40E 115 B12
Taormina Italy 37°51N 15°17E 95 E8
Taos U.S.A. 36°24N 105°35W 169 H11
Taoudenni Mali 22°40N 3°55W 134 D5
Taoudrart, Adrar Algeria 24°25N 2°24E 136 D4
Taounate Morocco 34°25N 4°41W 136 B3
Taourirt Algeria 26°37N 0°20E 136 C4
Taourirt Morocco 34°25N 2°53W 136 B3
Taouz Morocco 30°53N 4°0W 136 B3
Taoyuan China 28°55N 111°16E 117 C8
T'aoyüan Taiwan 25°0N 121°4E 117 E13
Tapa Estonia 59°15N 25°50E 61 G21
Tapa Shan = Daba Shan China 32°0N 109°0E 116 B7
Tapachula Mexico 14°54N 92°17W 181 E6
Tapah Malaysia 4°12N 101°15E 121 K3
Tapajós → Brazil 2°24S 54°41W 187 D8
Tapaktuan Indonesia 3°15N 97°10E 118 D1
Tapanahoni → Suriname 4°20N 54°25W 187 C8
Tapanui N.Z. 45°56S 169°18E 155 F4
Tapauá → Brazil 5°40S 64°21W 186 E6
Tapes Brazil 30°40S 51°23W 191 C5
Tapeta Liberia 6°29N 8°52W 138 D3
Taphan Hin Thailand 16°13N 100°26E 120 D3
Tapia de Casariego Spain 43°34N 6°56W 88 B4
Tapirapé Brazil 19°52S 46°1W 189 D1
Tapirapecó, Serra Venezuela 1°10N 65°0W 186 C6
Taplan Australia 34°33S 140°52E 152 C4
Taplejung Nepal 27°1N 86°16E 125 F12
Tapo-Capara △ Venezuela 7°55N 71°15W 183 E5
Tapolca Hungary 46°53N 17°29E 80 D2
Tapti → India 21°8N 72°41E 126 D1
Tapuae-o-Uenuku N.Z. 42°0S 173°39E 155 C8
Tapul Group Phil. 5°35N 120°50E 119 C6
Tapurucuará Brazil 0°24S 65°2W 186 D5
Taqtaq Iraq 35°53N 44°35E 105 E11
Taquara Brazil 29°36S 50°46W 191 B5
Taquari → Brazil 19°15S 57°17W 186 G7
Tara Australia 27°17S 150°31E 151 D5
Tara Canada 44°28N 81°9W 174 B3
Tara Russia 56°55N 74°24E 106 D8
Tara Zambia 16°58S 26°45E 143 F2
Tara → Montenegro 43°21N 18°51E 96 C2
Tara △ Serbia 43°55N 19°30E 96 C3
Taraba □ Nigeria 8°0N 10°30E 139 D7
Taraba → Nigeria 8°30N 10°15E 139 D7
Tarābulus Lebanon 34°31N 35°50E 130 A4
Tarābulus Libya 32°49N 13°7E 135 B8
Tarābulus Libya 31°0N 13°0E 135 B8
Taraclia Taraclia, Moldova 45°54N 28°40E 81 E13
Taraclia Tighina, Moldova 46°34N 29°7E 81 D14
Taradale N.Z. 39°33S 176°53E 154 F5
Taradehi India 23°18N 79°21E 125 H8
Tarajalejo Canary Is. 28°12N 14°7W 100 F5
Tarakan Indonesia 3°20N 117°35E 118 D5
Tarakit, Mt. Kenya 2°2N 35°10E 142 B4
Taralga Australia 34°26S 149°52E 153 C8
Tarama-Jima Japan 24°39N 124°42E 113 M2
Taramakau → N.Z. 42°34S 171°8E 155 C6
Taran, Mys Russia 54°56N 19°59E 82 D6
Taranagar India 28°43N 74°50E 124 E6
Taranaki □ N.Z. 39°25S 174°30E 154 F3
Taranaki, Mt. N.Z. 39°17S 174°5E 154 F3
Tarancón Spain 40°1N 3°1W 90 E1
Tarangire △ Tanzania 4°21S 36°7E 142 C4
Taransay U.K. 57°54N 7°0W 65 D1
Táranto Italy 40°28N 17°14E 95 B10
Táranto, G. di Italy 40°8N 17°20E 95 B10
Tarapacá Colombia 2°56S 69°46W 186 D5
Tarapacá □ Chile 20°45S 69°30W 190 A2
Tarapoto Peru 6°30S 76°20W 188 B2
Tarare France 45°54N 4°26E 73 C8
Tararua Ra. N.Z. 40°45S 175°25E 154 G4
Tarasaigh = Taransay U.K. 57°54N 7°0W 65 D1
Tarascon France 43°48N 4°39E 73 E8
Tarascon-sur-Ariège France 42°50N 1°36E 72 F5
Tarashcha Ukraine 49°30N 30°31E 75 D16
Tarata Peru 17°27S 70°2W 188 D4
Tarauacá Brazil 8°6S 70°48W 188 B3
Tarauacá → Brazil 6°42S 69°48W 188 B4
Taravao Tahiti 17°43S 149°19W 155 b
Taravao, Isthme de Tahiti 17°43S 149°19W 155 b
Taravo → France 41°42N 8°49E 73 G12
Tarawa Kiribati 1°30N 173°0E 156 G9
Tarawera N.Z. 39°2S 176°36E 154 F5
Tarawera, L. N.Z. 38°13S 176°27E 154 E5
Tarawera, Mt. N.Z. 38°14S 176°32E 154 E5
Taraz Kazakhstan 42°54N 71°22E 109 D8
Tarazona Spain 41°55N 1°43W 90 D3
Tarazona de la Mancha Spain 39°16N 1°55W 91 F3
Tarbagatay, Khrebet Kazakhstan 48°0N 83°0E 109 C10
Tarbat Ness U.K. 57°52N 3°47W 65 D5
Tarbela Dam Pakistan 34°8N 72°52E 124 B5
Tarbert Ireland 52°34N 9°22W 64 D2
Tarbert Argyll & Bute, U.K. 55°52N 5°25W 65 F3
Tarbert W. Isles, U.K. 57°54N 6°49W 65 D2
Tarbes France 43°15N 0°3E 72 E4
Tarboro U.S.A. 35°54N 77°32W 177 D16
Tarcău, Munţii Romania 46°39N 26°7E 81 D11
Tarcento Italy 46°13N 13°13E 93 B10
Tarcoola Australia 30°44S 134°36E 151 E1
Tarcoon Australia 30°15S 146°43E 151 E4
Tarcutta Australia 35°16S 147°44E 153 C7
Tardets-Sorholus France 43°8N 0°52W 72 E3
Tardoire → France 45°52N 0°14E 72 C4
Taredjerdja Algeria 25°12N 2°32E 136 C4
Taree Australia 31°50S 152°30E 153 A10
Tarella Australia 31°2S 143°2E 152 A5
Tarf, Ras Morocco 35°40N 5°11W 136 A2
Tarfa, W. el → Egypt 28°25N 30°50E 137 F7
Tarfaya Morocco 27°55N 12°55W 134 C3
Târgovişte Romania 44°55N 25°27E 81 F10
Târgu Bujor Romania 45°52N 27°54E 81 E12
Târgu Cărbuneşti Romania 44°57N 23°31E 81 F8
Târgu Frumos Romania 47°12N 27°2E 81 C12
Târgu Jiu Romania 45°5N 23°19E 81 E8
Târgu Lăpuş Romania 47°27N 23°52E 81 C8
Târgu Mureş Romania 46°31N 24°38E 81 D9
Târgu Neamţ Romania 47°12N 26°25E 81 C11
Târgu Ocna Romania 46°16N 26°39E 81 D11
Târgu Secuiesc Romania 46°0N 26°10E 81 E11
Târguşor Romania 44°27N 28°25E 81 F13
Tărhăus, Vf. Romania 46°40N 26°8E 81 D11
Tarhbalt Morocco 30°39N 5°20W 136 B2
Ţarif U.A.E. 24°3N 53°46E 129 E7
Tarifa Spain 36°1N 5°36W 89 J5
Tarija Bolivia 21°30S 64°40W 190 A3
Tarija □ Bolivia 21°30S 63°30W 190 A3
Tariku → Indonesia 2°55S 138°26E 119 E9
Tarīm Yemen 16°3N 49°0E 131 D4
Tarim Basin = Tarim Pendi China 40°0N 84°0E 109 E10
Tarim He → China 39°30N 88°30E 109 E11
Tarim Pendi China 40°0N 84°0E 109 E10
Taritatu → Indonesia 2°54S 138°27E 119 E9
Tarka → S. Africa 32°10S 26°0E 144 D4
Tarka La Bhutan 27°12N 89°44E 125 F13
Tarkastad S. Africa 32°0S 26°16E 144 D4
Tarkhankut, Mys Ukraine 45°25N 32°30E 85 K7
Tarko Sale Russia 64°55N 77°50E 106 C8
Tarkwa Ghana 5°20N 2°0W 138 D4
Tarlac Phil. 15°29N 120°35E 119 A6
Tarm Denmark 55°56N 8°31E 63 J2
Tarma Peru 11°25S 75°45W 188 C2
Tarmiya Iraq 33°40N 44°23E 105 E11
Tarn □ France 43°49N 2°8E 72 E6
Tarn → France 44°5N 1°6E 72 D5
Tarn-et-Garonne □ France 44°8N 1°20E 72 D5
Tarna → Hungary 47°31N 19°59E 80 C4
Târnava Mare → Romania 46°10N 23°43E 81 D8
Târnava Mică → Romania 46°9N 23°55E 81 D8
Târnăveni Romania 46°19N 24°13E 81 D9
Tarnica Poland 49°4N 22°44E 83 J9
Tarnobrzeg Poland 50°35N 21°41E 83 H8
Tarnogród Poland 50°22N 22°45E 83 H9
Tarnos France 43°32N 1°28W 72 E2
Târnova Moldova 48°10N 27°40E 81 B12
Târnova Romania 45°23N 21°59E 80 E6
Tarnów Poland 50°3N 21°0E 83 H8
Tarnowskie Góry Poland 50°27N 18°54E 83 H5
Tärnsjö Sweden 60°9N 16°56E 62 D10
Táro → Italy 45°2N 10°15E 92 C7
Ţarom Iran 28°11N 55°46E 129 D7
Taroom Australia 25°36S 149°48E 151 D4
Taroudannt Morocco 30°30N 8°52W 136 B2
Tarp Germany 54°39N 9°24E 76 A5
Tarpeena Australia 37°37S 140°47E 152 D4
Tarpon Springs U.S.A. 28°9N 82°45W 179 G7
Tarquínia Italy 42°15N 11°45E 93 F8
Tarra Bulga △ Australia 38°27S 146°31E 153 E7
Tarrafal C. Verde Is. 15°18N 23°39W 134 b
Tarragona Spain 41°5N 1°17E 90 D6
Tarragona □ Spain 41°5N 1°0E 90 D6
Tarraleah Australia 42°17S 146°26E 151 G4
Tarrasa = Terrassa Spain 41°34N 2°1E 90 D7
Tàrrega Spain 41°39N 1°9E 90 D6
Tarrytown Ga., U.S.A. 32°19N 82°34W 178 C7
Tarrytown N.Y., U.S.A. 41°4N 73°52W 175 E11
Tårs Denmark 57°23N 10°7E 63 G4
Tarsus Turkey 36°58N 34°55E 104 D6
Tartagal Argentina 22°30S 63°50W 190 A3
Tärtär Azerbaijan 40°20N 46°58E 87 K8
Tärtär → Azerbaijan 40°26N 47°20E 87 K8
Tartas France 43°50N 0°49W 72 E3
Tartu Estonia 58°20N 26°44E 84 C4
Ţarţūs Syria 34°55N 35°55E 104 E6
Ţarţūs □ Syria 35°0N 36°0E 104 E7
Tarumirim Brazil 19°16S 41°59W 189 D2
Tarumizu Japan 31°29N 130°42E 113 J5
Tarussa Russia 54°44N 37°10E 84 E9
Tarutao = Ko Tarutao △ Thailand 6°31N 99°26E 121 J2
Tarutao, Ko Thailand 6°33N 99°40E 121 J2
Tarutung Indonesia 2°0N 98°54E 118 D1
Tarutyne Ukraine 46°12N 29°9E 81 D14
Tarvísio Italy 46°30N 13°35E 93 B10
Tasaret, O. → Algeria 26°25N 1°59E 136 C4
Tasböget Kazakhstan 44°46N 65°33E 108 D7
Taseko → Canada 52°8N 123°45W 162 C4
Tasgaon India 17°2N 74°39E 126 F2
Tash-Kömür Kyrgyzstan 41°40N 72°10E 109 D8
Tashauz = Daşoguz Turkmenistan 41°49N 59°58E 108 D5
Tashi Chho Dzong = Thimphu Bhutan 27°31N 89°45E 123 F16
Ţashk, Daryācheh-ye Iran 29°45N 53°35E 129 D7
Tashkent = Toshkent Uzbekistan 41°20N 69°10E 109 D7
Tashtagol Russia 52°47N 87°53E 109 B11
Tasiilaq Greenland 65°40N 37°20W 57 D7
Tasikmalaya Indonesia 7°18S 108°12E 119 G13
Tåsinge Denmark 55°0N 10°35E 63 J4
Tåsjön Sweden 64°15N 15°40E 60 D16
Task Niger 14°56N 10°46E 139 C7
Taskan Russia 62°59N 150°20E 107 C16
Taşkent Turkey 36°55N 32°29E 104 D5
Taşköprü Turkey 41°30N 34°15E 104 B6
Taşlâc Moldova 47°4N 29°24E 81 C14
Taşlıçay Turkey 39°38N 43°22E 105 C10
Tasman □ N.Z. 41°30S 172°40E 155 B7
Tasman → N.Z. 43°48S 170°8E 155 D5
Tasman, Mt. N.Z. 43°34S 170°12E 155 D5
Tasman B. N.Z. 40°59S 173°25E 155 A8
Tasman Basin Pac. Oc. 46°0S 158°0E 156 M7
Tasman Glacier N.Z. 43°37S 170°12E 155 D5
Tasman Mts. N.Z. 41°3S 172°25E 155 B7
Tasman Pen. Australia 43°10S 148°0E 151 G4
Tasman Sea Pac. Oc. 36°0S 160°0E 147 E9
Tasmania □ Australia 42°0S 146°30E 151 G4
Tasmanian Wilderness World Heritage Area △ Australia 43°0S 146°0E 151 G4
Tăşnad Romania 47°30N 22°33E 80 C7
Taşova Turkey 40°45N 36°19E 104 B7
Tassili n'Ajjer Algeria 25°47N 8°1E 136 C5
Tassili n'Ajjer △ Algeria 26°5N 6°0E 136 C5
Tassili-Oua-n-Ahaggar Algeria 20°41N 5°30E 134 D7
Tassili Tin-Rerhoh Algeria 20°5N 3°55E 139 A5
Tasuj Iran 38°18N 45°23E 105 C11
Tat Ton △ Thailand 15°57N 102°2E 120 E4
Tata Hungary 47°37N 18°19E 80 C3
Tata Morocco 29°46N 7°56W 136 C2
Tatabánya Hungary 47°32N 18°25E 80 C3
Tataouine Tunisia 32°57N 10°29E 136 B6
Tataouine □ Tunisia 32°0N 10°0E 136 B6
Tatar Republic = Tatarstan □ Russia 55°30N 51°30E 86 C10
Tatarbunary Ukraine 45°50N 29°39E 81 E14
Tatarsk Russia 55°14N 76°0E 109 A9
Tatarskiy Proliv Russia 50°0N 141°0E 107 E15
Tatarstan □ Russia 55°30N 51°30E 86 C10
Tatatua, Pte. Tahiti 17°44S 149°8W 155 b
Tateyama Japan 35°0N 139°50E 113 G9
Tathlina L. Canada 60°33N 117°39W 162 A5
Tathra Australia 36°44S 149°59E 153 D8
Tatinnai L. Canada 60°55N 97°40W 163 A9
Tatla Lake Canada 52°0N 124°20W 162 C4
Tatlısu = Akanthou Cyprus 35°22N 33°45E 101 D12
Tatlısu Turkey 40°24N 27°55E 97 F11
Tatnam, C. Canada 57°16N 91°0W 163 B10
Tatra = Tatry Slovak Rep. 49°20N 20°0E 79 B13
Tatranský △ Slovak Rep. 49°10N 20°0E 79 B13
Tatry Slovak Rep. 49°20N 20°0E 79 B13
Tatshenshini → Canada 59°28N 137°45W 162 B1
Tatshenshini-Alsek ⌂ Canada 59°55N 137°45W 162 B1
Tatsuno Japan 34°52N 134°33E 113 G7
Tatta = Thatta Pakistan 24°42N 67°55E 124 G2
Tatuī Brazil 23°25S 47°53W 191 A6
Tatum U.S.A. 33°16N 103°19W 169 K12
Tat'ung = Datong China 40°6N 113°18E 114 D7
Tatura Australia 36°29S 145°16E 153 D6
Tatvan Turkey 38°31N 42°15E 105 C10
Tauá Brazil 6°1S 40°26W 189 B2
Taubaté Brazil 23°0S 45°36W 191 A6
Tauberbischofsheim Germany 49°37N 9°39E 77 F5
Taucha Germany 51°23N 12°29E 76 D8
Tauern Austria 47°15N 12°40E 74 E7
Tauern-tunnel Austria 47°0N 13°12E 78 D6
Taulé France 48°37N 3°55W 70 D3
Taumarunui N.Z. 38°53S 175°15E 154 E4
Taumaturgo Brazil 8°54S 72°51W 188 B3
Taung S. Africa 27°33S 24°47E 144 C3
Taungdwingyi Burma 20°1N 95°40E 123 J19
Taunggyi Burma 20°50N 97°0E 123 J20
Taungoo = Tounggoo Burma 19°0N 96°30E 123 K20
Taungup Burma 18°51N 94°14E 123 K19
Taunsa Pakistan 30°42N 70°39E 124 D4
Taunsa Barrage Pakistan 30°42N 70°50E 124 D4
Taunton U.K. 51°1N 3°5W 67 F4
Taunton U.S.A. 41°54N 71°6W 175 E13
Taunus Germany 50°13N 8°34E 77 E4
Taupo N.Z. 38°41S 176°7E 154 E5
Taupo, L. N.Z. 38°46S 175°55E 154 E4
Tauragė Lithuania 55°14N 22°16E 82 C9
Tauragė □ Lithuania 55°15N 22°17E 82 C9
Tauranga N.Z. 37°42S 176°11E 154 D5
Tauranga Harb. N.Z. 37°30S 176°5E 154 D5
Taureau, Rés. Canada 46°46N 73°50W 164 C5
Taurianova Italy 38°21N 16°1E 95 D9
Tauroa Pt. N.Z. 35°10S 173°4E 154 B2
Taurus Mts. = Toros Dağları Turkey 37°0N 32°30E 104 D5
Tauste Spain 41°58N 1°18W 90 D3
Tautira Tahiti 17°44S 149°9W 155 b
Tauyskaya Guba Russia 59°20N 150°20E 107 D16
Tauz = Tovuz Azerbaijan 41°0N 45°40E 87 K7
Tavan Bogd Uul Mongolia 49°10N 87°49E 109 C11
Tavares U.S.A. 28°48N 81°44W 179 G8
Tavas Turkey 37°34N 29°4E 99 D11
Tavastehus = Hämeenlinna Finland 61°0N 24°28E 84 B3
Tavda Russia 58°7N 65°8E 106 D7
Tavda → Russia 57°47N 67°18E 106 D7
Taverner B. Canada 67°12N 72°25W 161 D17
Tavernes de la Valldigna Spain 39°5N 0°13W 91 F4

Tavernier U.S.A. 25°1N 80°31W 179 K9
Taveta Kenya 3°23S 37°37E 142 C4
Taveuni Fiji 16°51S 179°58W 154 a
Taviano Italy 39°59N 18°5E 95 C11
Tavignano → France 42°7N 9°33E 73 F13
Tavira Portugal 37°8N 7°40W 89 H3
Tavistock Canada 43°19N 80°50W 174 C4
Tavistock U.K. 50°33N 4°9W 67 G3
Tavolara Italy 40°54N 9°42E 94 B2
Távora → Portugal 41°8N 7°35W 88 D3
Tavoy Burma 14°2N 98°12E 120 E2
Tavoy Pt. Burma 13°32N 98°10E 120 F2
Tavrichanka Russia 43°18N 131°59E 112 C5
Tavropos → Greece 39°10N 21°45E 98 B3
Tavşanlı Turkey 39°32N 29°30E 99 B11
Tavua Fiji 17°37S 177°5E 154 a
Tavuki Fiji 19°7S 178°8E 154 a
Taw → U.K. 51°4N 4°4W 67 F3
Tawa → India 22°48N 77°48E 124 H8
Tawa Res. India 22°35N 78°5E 126 C4
Tawas City U.S.A. 44°16N 83°31W 173 C12
Tawau Malaysia 4°20N 117°55E 118 D5
Tawi-tawi I. Phil. 5°10N 120°1E 119 H5
Tawu Taiwan 22°22N 120°54E 117 F13
Tāwūq Iraq 35°8N 44°26E 105 E11
Taxco Mexico 18°33N 99°36W 181 D5
Taxila Pakistan 33°42N 72°52E 124 C5
Taxkorgan Tajik Zizhixian
  China 37°49N 75°14E 109 E3
Tay → U.K. 56°37N 3°38W 65 E5
Tay, Firth of U.K. 56°25N 3°8W 65 E5
Tay, L. Australia 32°55S 120°48E 149 F3
Tay, L. U.K. 56°32N 4°8W 65 E4
Tay △ U.K. 56°43N 3°59W 65 E5
Tay Ninh Vietnam 11°20N 106°5E 121 G6
Tayabamba Peru 8°15S 77°16W 188 B2
Taygetos Oros Greece 37°0N 22°23E 98 D4
Taylakova Russia 59°13N 74°0E 106 D8
Taylor Canada 56°13N 120°40W 162 B4
Taylor Fla., U.S.A. 30°26N 82°18W 178 E7
Taylor Nebr., U.S.A. 41°46N 99°23W 172 E4
Taylor Pa., U.S.A. 41°23N 75°43W 175 E9
Taylor Tex., U.S.A. 30°34N 97°25W 176 F6
Taylor, Mt. U.S.A. 35°14N 107°37W 169 J10
Taylorville U.S.A. 39°33N 89°18W 172 F10
Taymā Si. Arabia 27°35N 38°45E 128 E3
Taymyr, Oz. Russia 74°20N 102°0E 107 B11
Taymyr, Poluostrov
  Russia 75°0N 100°0E 107 B11
Tayport U.K. 56°27N 2°52W 65 E6
Tayrona △ Colombia 11°20N 74°2W 183 D5
Tayshet Russia 55°58N 98°1E 107 D10
Taytay Phil. 10°45N 119°30E 119 B5
Tāyyebād Iran 34°45N 60°45E 129 C9
Tāyyebād Iran 34°44N 60°44E 129 C9
Tayynsha Kazakhstan 53°50N 69°45E 108 B7
Taz → Russia 67°32N 78°40E 106 C8
Taza Morocco 34°16N 4°6W 136 B3
Taza-Al Hoceïma-Taounate □
  Morocco 34°15N 3°20W 136 B3
Tāza Khurmātū Iraq 35°18N 44°20E 105 E11
Taza-Taou □ Morocco 34°15N 4°10W 136 B3
Tazawa-Ko Japan 39°43N 140°40E 112 E10
Tazenakht Morocco 30°35N 7°12W 136 B2
Tazerbo Libya 25°45N 21°0E 135 C10
Tazin → Canada 59°48N 109°55W 163 B7
Tazin L. Canada 59°44N 108°42W 163 B7
Tazoult Algeria 35°29N 6°11E 136 A5
Tazovskiy Russia 67°30N 78°44E 106 C8
Tazrouk Algeria 23°24N 6°15E 136 D5
Tbilisi Georgia 41°43N 44°50E 87 K7
Tchad = Chad ■ Africa 15°0N 17°15E 135 F8
Tchad, L. Chad 13°30N 14°30E 135 F8
Tchaourou Benin 8°58N 2°40E 139 D5
Tch'eng-tou = Chengdu
  China 30°38N 104°2E 116 B5
Tchentlo L. Canada 55°15N 125°0W 162 B4
Tchetti Benin 7°50N 1°40E 139 D5
Tchibanga Gabon 2°45S 11°0E 140 E2
Tchien Liberia 5°59N 8°15W 138 D3
Tchin Tabaraden Niger 15°58N 5°56E 139 B6
Tchogha Zanbil = Choghā Zanbil
  Iran 32°1N 48°32E 129 C6
Tch'ong-k'ing = Chongqing
  China 29°35N 106°25E 116 C6
Tczew Poland 54°8N 18°50E 82 D5
Te Anau N.Z. 45°25S 167°43E 155 F2
Te Anau, L. N.Z. 45°15S 167°45E 155 F2
Te Araroa N.Z. 37°39S 178°25E 154 D7
Te Aroha N.Z. 37°32S 175°44E 154 D4
Te Awamutu N.Z. 38°1S 175°20E 154 E4
Te Ika a Maui = North I.
  N.Z. 38°0S 175°0E 154 E4
Te Kaha N.Z. 37°44S 177°52E 154 D6
Te Karaka N.Z. 38°26S 177°53E 154 E6
Te Kauwhata N.Z. 37°25S 175°9E 154 D4
Te Kopuru N.Z. 36°1S 173°57E 154 C4
Te Kuiti N.Z. 38°20S 175°11E 154 E4
Te-n-Dghâmcha, Sebkhet
  Mauritania 38°0N 15°55W 138 B1
Te Puke N.Z. 37°46S 176°22E 154 D5
Te Teko N.Z. 38°2S 176°48E 154 E5
Te Waewae B. N.Z. 46°13S 167°33E 155 G2
Te Wai Pounamu = South I.
  N.Z. 44°0S 170°0E 155 E5
Teaca Romania 46°55N 24°30E 83 E13
Teague U.S.A. 31°38N 96°17W 176 F6
Teahupoo Tahiti 17°50S 149°16W 155 b
Teano Italy 41°15N 14°4E 95 A7
Teapa Mexico 17°33N 92°57W 181 D6
Teba Spain 36°59N 4°55W 89 J6
Tebakang Malaysia 1°6N 110°30E 118 D4
Tébarat Niger 14°49N 4°27E 139 C5
Teberau → Malaysia 1°30N 103°42E 121 d
Teberda Russia 43°30N 41°30E 87 D10
Tébessa Algeria 35°22N 8°8E 136 A5
Tébessa □ Algeria 35°20N 8°0E 136 A5
Tebicuary → Paraguay 26°36S 58°16W 190 B4
Tebingtinggi Riau,
  Indonesia 1°0N 102°45E 118 E2
Tebingtinggi Sumatera Utara,
  Indonesia 3°20N 99°9E 118 D1
Tébourba Tunisia 36°49N 9°51E 136 A5
Téboursouk Tunisia 36°29N 9°10E 136 A5
Tebulos Georgia 42°36N 45°17E 87 J7
Tecate Mexico 32°34N 116°38W 171 N10
Tecer Dağları Turkey 39°27N 37°2E 104 C7
Tech → France 42°36N 3°3E 72 F7
Techiman Ghana 7°35N 1°58W 138 D4
Techirghiol Romania 44°4N 28°32E 81 F13

Tecka Argentina 43°29S 70°48W 192 B2
Tecomán Mexico 18°55N 103°53W 180 D4
Tecopa U.S.A. 35°51N 116°13W 171 K10
Tecoripa Mexico 28°37N 109°57W 180 B3
Tecuala Mexico 22°23N 105°27W 180 C3
Tecuci Romania 45°51N 27°27E 81 E12
Tecumseh Canada 42°19N 82°54W 174 D2
Tecumseh Mich.,
  U.S.A. 42°0N 83°57W 173 D12
Tecumseh Okla., U.S.A. 35°15N 96°56W 176 D6
Tedzhen = Tejen
  Turkmenistan 37°23N 60°31E 108 E6
Tees → U.K. 54°37N 1°10W 66 C6
Teesside U.K. 54°37N 1°10W 66 C6
Teeswater Canada 43°59N 81°17W 174 C3
Tefenni Turkey 37°18N 29°45E 99 D11
Tegal Indonesia 6°52S 109°8E 118 F3
Tegallalang Indonesia 8°27S 115°17E 119 J18
Tegalsari Indonesia 8°25S 114°8E 119 J17
Tegernsee Germany 47°43N 11°46E 77 H7
Teggiano Italy 40°23N 15°32E 95 B8
Tegid, L. = Bala, L. U.K. 52°53N 3°37W 66 E4
Tegina Nigeria 10°5N 6°11E 139 C6
Tegucigalpa Honduras 14°5N 87°14W 182 D2
Teguidda-i-n-Tessoum
  Niger 17°25N 6°37E 139 B6
Tehachapi U.S.A. 35°8N 118°27W 171 K8
Tehachapi Mts. U.S.A. 35°0N 118°30W 171 L8
Tehamiyam Sudan 18°20N 36°32E 137 D4
Teheran = Tehrān Iran 35°41N 51°25E 129 C6
Téhini Ivory C. 9°39N 3°40W 138 D4
Tehoru Indonesia 3°23S 129°30E 119 E7
Tehrān Iran 35°41N 51°25E 129 C6
Tehrān □ Iran 35°30N 51°30E 129 C6
Tehri India 30°23N 78°29E 125 D8
Tehuacán Mexico 18°27N 97°23W 181 D5
Tehuantepec Mexico 16°21N 95°13W 181 D5
Tehuantepec, G. de
  Mexico 15°50N 95°12W 181 D5
Tehuantepec, Istmo de
  Mexico 17°15N 94°30W 181 D6
Teide, Pico de
  Canary Is. 28°15N 16°38W 100 F3
Teifi → U.K. 52°5N 4°41W 67 E3
Teigebyen Norway 60°12N 11°0E 62 D5
Teign → U.K. 50°32N 3°32W 67 G4
Teignmouth U.K. 50°33N 3°31W 67 G4
Teinanino = Tarawa
  Kiribati 1°30N 173°0E 156 G9
Teiuş Romania 46°12N 23°40E 81 D8
Teixeira Brazil 7°13S 37°15W 189 B3
Teixeira Pinto
  Guinea-Biss. 12°3N 16°0W 138 C1
Tejakula Indonesia 8°8S 115°20E 119 J18
Tejen Turkmenistan 37°23N 60°31E 108 E6
Tejen → Turkmenistan 37°24N 60°38E 129 B9
Tejo → Europe 38°40N 9°24W 89 F2
Tejon Pass U.S.A. 34°49N 118°53W 171 L8
Tekamah U.S.A. 41°47N 96°13W 172 E3
Tekapo → N.Z. 44°13S 170°21E 155 E5
Tekapo, L. N.Z. 43°53S 170°33E 155 E5
Tekax Mexico 20°12N 89°17W 181 C7
Teke Turkey 41°4N 29°39E 99 E13
Tekeli Kazakhstan 44°50N 79°0E 109 D9
Tekeze Dam Ethiopia 13°10N 38°45E 131 E2
Tekija Serbia 44°42N 22°26E 96 B6
Tekirdağ Turkey 40°58N 27°30E 99 F11
Tekirdağ □ Turkey 41°0N 27°0E 99 F11
Tekirova Turkey 36°30N 30°32E 99 E12
Tekkali India 18°37N 84°15E 127 E14
Tekke Turkey 36°42N 36°12E 104 B7
Tekman Turkey 39°38N 41°29E 105 C9
Tekoa U.S.A. 47°14N 117°4W 168 C5
Tekong Besar, Pulau
  Singapore 1°25N 104°3E 121 d
Tel → India 20°50N 83°54E 126 D6
Tel Aviv ✈ (TLV) Israel 32°5N 34°49E 130 C3
Tel Aviv-Yafo Israel 32°4N 34°48E 130 C3
Tel Lakhish Israel 31°34N 34°51E 130 D3
Tel Megiddo Israel 32°35N 35°11E 130 C4
Tela Honduras 15°40N 87°28W 182 C2
Télagh Algeria 34°51N 0°32W 136 B3
Telanaipura = Jambi
  Indonesia 1°38S 103°30E 118 E2
Telangana India 17°30N 78°30E 126 F4
Telašćica △ Croatia 43°55N 15°10E 93 E12
Telavi Georgia 42°0N 45°30E 87 J7
Telč Czech Rep. 49°11N 15°28E 78 B8
Telciu Romania 47°25N 24°24E 81 C9
Telde Canary Is. 27°59N 15°25W 100 G4
Telegraph Creek
  Canada 58°0N 131°10W 162 B2
Telekhany = Tsyelyakhany
  Belarus 52°30N 25°46E 75 B13
Telemark Norway 59°15N 7°40E 61 G12
Télemsès Niger 15°37N 4°44E 139 B5
Telén Argentina 36°15S 65°31W 190 D2
Teleneşti Moldova 47°30N 28°22E 81 C13
Teleng Iran 25°47N 61°3E 129 E9
Teleño Spain 42°23N 6°22W 88 C4
Teleorman □ Romania 44°0N 25°0E 81 G10
Teleorman → Romania 43°52N 25°26E 81 G10
Telerhteba, Djebel
  Algeria 24°10N 6°51E 136 D5
Teles Pires → Brazil 7°21S 58°3W 186 E7
Telescope Pk. U.S.A. 36°10N 117°5W 171 J9
Teletaye Mali 16°31N 1°30E 139 B5
Teletskoye, Oz. Russia 51°40N 87°30E 109 B11
Telford U.K. 52°40N 2°27W 67 E5
Telford and Wrekin □
  U.K. 52°45N 2°27W 66 E5
Telfs Austria 47°19N 11°4E 78 D4
Télimélé Guinea 10°54N 13°2W 138 C2
Telkwa Canada 54°41N 127°5W 162 C3
Tell City U.S.A. 37°57N 86°46W 172 G10
Teller U.S.A. 65°16N 166°22W 166 B6
Tellicherry = Thalassery
  India 11°45N 75°30E 127 J2
Telluride U.S.A. 37°56N 107°49W 169 H10
Teloloapán Mexico 18°21N 99°51W 181 D5
Telpos Iz Russia 63°16N 59°13E 58 D7
Telsen Argentina 42°30N 66°50W 192 B3
Telšiai Lithuania 55°59N 22°14E 62 B3
Teltow Germany 52°23N 13°17E 76 C9
Teluk Anson = Teluk Intan
  Malaysia 4°3N 101°0E 121 K3
Teluk Bahang Malaysia 5°28N 100°13E 121 c
Teluk Betung = Bandar Lampung
  Indonesia 5°20S 105°10E 118 F3

Teluk Intan Malaysia 4°3N 101°0E 121 K3
Teluk Kumbar Malaysia 5°18N 100°14E 121 c
Telukbutun Indonesia 4°13N 108°12E 118 D3
Telukdalam Indonesia 0°33N 97°50E 118 D1
Tema Ghana 5°41N 0°0 139 D5
Temagami, L. Canada 47°0N 80°10W 164 C3
Temax Mexico 21°9N 88°56W 181 C7
Temba S. Africa 25°20S 28°17E 145 C4
Tembagapura Indonesia 4°20S 137°0E 119 E9
Tembe
  Dem. Rep. of the Congo 0°16S 28°14E 142 C2
Tembe S. Africa 26°51S 32°24E 145 D5
Tembleque Spain 39°41N 3°30W 88 F7
Temblor Range
  U.S.A. 35°20N 119°50W 171 K7
Teme → U.K. 52°11N 2°13W 67 E5
Temecula U.S.A. 33°30N 117°9W 171 M9
Temengor, Tasik
  Malaysia 5°24N 101°18E 121 K3
Temerloh Malaysia 3°27N 102°25E 121 L4
Teminabuan Indonesia 1°26S 132°1E 119 E8
Temir Kazakhstan 49°1N 57°14E 108 C5
Temirtau Kazakhstan 50°5N 72°56E 108 B8
Temirtau Russia 53°10N 87°30E 109 B11
Témiscamie → Canada 50°59N 73°5W 165 B5
Témiscamingue Canada 46°44N 79°5W 164 C4
Témiscamingue, L.
  Canada 47°10N 79°25W 164 C4
Temnikov Russia 54°40N 43°11E 86 C6
Temo → Italy 40°17N 8°28E 94 B1
Temora Australia 34°30S 147°30E 153 C7
Temosachic Mexico 28°57N 107°51W 180 B3
Tempe U.S.A. 33°24N 111°54W 169 K8
Témpio Pausánia Italy 40°54N 9°6E 94 B2
Tempiute U.S.A. 37°39N 115°38W 170 H11
Temple U.S.A. 31°6N 97°21W 176 F6
Temple B. Australia 12°15S 143°3E 150 A3
Temple Terrace U.S.A. 28°2N 82°23W 179 G2
Templemore Ireland 52°47N 7°51W 64 D4
Templeton → Australia 21°0S 138°40E 150 C2
Templin Germany 53°7N 13°28E 76 B9
Tempoal de Sánchez
  Mexico 21°31N 98°23W 181 C5
Temryuk Russia 45°15N 37°24E 85 K9
Temska → Serbia 43°17N 22°33E 96 C6
Temuco Chile 38°45S 72°40W 192 A2
Temuka N.Z. 44°14S 171°17E 155 E6
Ten Degree Channel
  India 10°0N 92°30E 127 K11
Ten Thousand Is.
  U.S.A. 25°55N 81°45W 179 K8
Tenabo Mexico 20°3N 90°14W 181 C6
Tenaha U.S.A. 31°57N 94°15W 176 F7
Tenakee Springs
  U.S.A. 57°47N 135°13W 162 B1
Tenali India 16°15N 80°35E 127 F5
Tenancingo Mexico 18°58N 99°38W 181 D5
Tenango del Valle
  Mexico 19°7N 99°33W 181 D5
Tenaro, Akra Greece 36°22N 22°27E 98 E4
Tenasserim Burma 12°6N 99°3E 121 F2
Tenasserim □ Burma 14°0N 98°30E 120 F2
Tenasserim → Burma 12°24N 98°37E 120 F2
Tenby U.K. 51°40N 4°42W 67 F3
Tenda, Colle di France 44°7N 7°36E 73 D11
Tendaho Ethiopia 11°48N 40°54E 131 E3
Tende France 44°5N 7°35E 73 D11
Tendjedi, Adrar Algeria 23°41N 7°32E 136 D5
Tendo Japan 38°20N 140°30E 112 E10
Tendrara Morocco 33°3N 1°58W 136 B3
Tendrovskaya Kosa
  Ukraine 46°16N 31°35E 85 J6
Tendukhera India 23°24N 79°33E 125 H8
Teneguía, Volcanes de
  Canary Is. 28°28N 17°51W 100 F2
Teneida Egypt 25°30N 29°19E 137 B2
Tenenkou Mali 14°28N 4°55W 138 C4
Ténéré Niger 19°0N 10°30E 139 B7
Ténéré, Erg du Niger 17°35N 10°55E 135 E8
Tenerife Canary Is. 28°15N 16°35W 100 F3
Tenerife, Pico Canary Is. 27°43N 18°1W 100 G1
Tenerife Norte ✈ (TFN)
  Canary Is. 28°28N 16°17W 100 F3
Tenerife Sur ✈ (TFS)
  Canary Is. 28°3N 16°33W 100 F3
Ténès Algeria 36°31N 1°14E 136 A4
Teng Xian Guangxi Zhuangzu,
  China 23°21N 110°56E 117 F8
Teng Xian Shandong,
  China 35°5N 117°10E 115 G9
Tengah, Kepulauan
  Indonesia 7°5S 118°15E 118 F5
Tengchong China 25°0N 98°28E 116 E2
Tengchowfu = Penglai
  China 37°48N 120°42E 115 F11
Tenggarong Indonesia 0°24S 116°58E 118 E5
Tengger Feng China 37°48N 86°48E 109 D11
Tengger Shamo China 38°0N 104°10E 114 F3
Tenggol, Pulau
  Malaysia 4°48N 103°41E 121 K4
Tengiz Köli Kazakhstan 50°30N 69°0E 108 B7
Tengzhou China 35°4N 117°10E 115 G9
Tenhult Sweden 57°41N 14°20E 63 G8
Teniente Enciso △
  Paraguay 21°5S 61°8W 190 A3
Tenille U.S.A. 32°56N 83°19W 178 F6
Tenino U.S.A. 46°51N 122°51W 170 D4
Tenkasi India 8°55N 77°20E 127 K3
Tenke Katanga,
  Dem. Rep. of the Congo 11°22S 26°40E 143 E2
Tenke Katanga,
  Dem. Rep. of the Congo 10°32S 26°7E 143 E2
Tenkodogo Burkina Faso 11°54N 0°19W 139 C4
Tenna → Italy 43°14N 13°47E 93 C10
Tennant Creek
  Australia 19°30S 134°15E 150 B1
Tennessee □ U.S.A. 36°0N 86°30W 177 C11
Tennessee → U.S.A. 37°4N 88°34W 177 C10
Tennille U.S.A. 32°56N 82°48W 178 F7
Teno, Pta. de Canary Is. 28°21N 16°55W 100 F3
Tenojoki = Tana →
  Norway 70°30N 28°14E 60 A23
Tenom Malaysia 5°4N 115°57E 118 C5
Tenosique Mexico 17°29N 91°26W 181 D6
Tenryū-Gawa →
  Japan 35°39N 137°48E 113 G8
Tensift, Oued →
  Morocco 32°3N 9°28W 136 B2
Tenterden U.K. 51°4N 0°42E 67 F8
Tenterfield Australia 29°0S 152°0E 151 D5

Teo = A Ramallosa Spain 42°45N 8°30W 88 C2
Teófilo Otoni Brazil 17°40S 41°30W 189 D3
Tepa Indonesia 7°52S 129°31E 119 F7
Tepalcatepec →
  Mexico 18°35N 101°59W 180 D4
Tepecik Bursa, Turkey 40°7N 28°25E 97 F12
Tepecik Kütahya, Turkey 39°32N 29°28E 99 B11
Tepehuanes Mexico 25°21N 105°44W 180 B3
Tepelené Albania 40°17N 20°2E 96 F4
Tepetongo Mexico 22°28N 103°9W 180 C4
Tepic Mexico 21°30N 104°54W 180 C4
Teplá Czech Rep. 49°59N 12°52E 78 B5
Teplice Czech Rep. 50°40N 13°48E 78 A6
Ter → Spain 42°2N 3°12E 90 C8
Ter Apel Neths. 52°53N 7°5E 69 B7
Téra Niger 14°0N 0°45E 139 C5
Tera → Spain 41°54N 5°44W 88 D5
Teraina Kiribati 4°43N 160°25W 157 G12
Téramo Italy 42°39N 13°42E 93 F10
Terang Australia 38°15S 142°55E 152 E5
Terang, Teluk Indonesia 8°44S 116°0E 119 K19
Terawhiti, C. N.Z. 41°16S 174°38E 154 H3
Terazit, Massif de Niger 20°2N 8°30E 139 A6
Tercan Turkey 39°47N 40°23E 105 C9
Terceira Azores 38°43N 27°13W 134 a
Tercero → Argentina 32°58S 61°47W 190 C3
Terdal India 16°33N 75°3E 126 F2
Terebovlya Ukraine 49°18N 25°44E 75 D13
Teregova Romania 45°10N 22°16E 80 E7
Terek → Russia 44°0N 47°30E 87 J8
Terengganu □ Malaysia 4°55N 103°0E 121 K4
Terepaima △ Venezuela 9°58N 69°17W 183 E6
Tereshka → Russia 51°48N 46°26E 86 E8
Teresina Brazil 5°9S 42°45W 189 B2
Teressa India 8°15N 93°10E 127 K11
Teresva Ukraine 48°0N 23°42E 81 B8
Terewah, L. Australia 29°52S 147°35E 151 D4
Terges → Portugal 37°49N 7°41W 89 H3
Tergnier France 49°40N 3°17E 71 C10
Teridgerie Cr. →
  Australia 30°25S 148°50E 153 A8
Terlizzi Italy 41°8N 16°32E 95 A9
Termas de Río Hondo
  Argentina 27°29S 64°52W 190 B3
Terme Turkey 41°11N 37°0E 104 B7
Términi Imerese Italy 37°59N 13°42E 94 E6
Términos, L. de Mexico 18°37N 91°33W 181 D6
Termiz Uzbekistan 37°15N 67°15E 108 F7
Térmoli Italy 42°0N 15°0E 93 F12
Ternate Indonesia 0°45N 127°25E 119 D7
Terneuzen Neths. 51°20N 3°50E 69 C3
Terney Russia 45°3N 136°37E 112 B8
Terni Italy 42°34N 12°37E 93 F9
Ternitz Austria 47°43N 16°2E 78 D9
Ternivka Ukraine 48°30N 29°58E 81 B14
Ternopil Ukraine 49°30N 25°40E 75 D13
Ternopol = Ternopil
  Ukraine 49°30N 25°40E 75 D13
Terowie Australia 33°8S 138°55E 152 B2
Terpni Greece 40°55N 23°56E 98 H7
Terra Bella U.S.A. 35°58N 119°3W 171 K7
Terra Nova → Canada 48°33N 53°55W 165 C9
Terrace Canada 54°30N 128°35W 162 C3
Terracina Italy 41°17N 13°15E 94 A6
Terralba Italy 39°43N 8°39E 94 C1
Terrassa Spain 41°34N 2°1E 90 D7
Terrasson-la-Villedieu
  France 45°8N 1°18E 72 C5
Terre Haute U.S.A. 39°28N 87°25W 172 F10
Terrebonne B. U.S.A. 29°5N 90°35W 177 G9
Terrecht Mali 19°35N 0°22E 139 B5
Terrell U.S.A. 32°44N 96°17W 176 E6
Terrenceville Canada 47°40N 54°44W 165 C9
Terrick Terrick △
  Australia 36°8S 144°13E 152 D6
Terry U.S.A. 46°47N 105°19W 168 C11
Terryville U.S.A. 41°41N 73°3W 175 E11
Terschelling Neths. 53°25N 5°20E 69 A5
Tersko-Kumskiy Kanal
  Russia 44°32N 44°38E 87 H7
Tertenia Italy 39°42N 9°34E 94 C2
Terter = Tärtär →
  Azerbaijan 40°26N 47°20E 87 K8
Teruel Spain 40°22N 1°8W 90 E3
Teruel □ Spain 40°48N 1°0W 90 E4
Tervel Bulgaria 43°45N 27°28E 97 C11
Tervola Finland 66°6N 24°49E 60 C21
Teryaweynya L.
  Australia 32°18S 143°22E 152 B5
Tešanj Bos.-H. 44°38N 18°1E 80 F3
Tesha → Russia 55°38N 42°9E 86 C6
Teshio Japan 44°53N 141°44E 112 B10
Teshio-Gawa →
  Japan 44°53N 141°45E 112 B10
Tešica Serbia 43°27N 21°45E 96 C5
Tesiyn Gol → Mongolia 50°40N 93°20E 110 A7
Teslić Bos.-H. 44°37N 17°54E 80 F2
Teslin Canada 60°10N 132°43W 162 A2
Teslin → Canada 61°34N 134°35W 162 A2
Teslin L. Canada 60°15N 132°57W 162 A2
Tessalit Mali 20°12N 1°0E 139 A5
Tessaoua Niger 13°47N 7°56E 139 C6
Tessin Mali 15°13N 0°18E 139 B5
Test → U.K. 50°56N 1°29W 67 G6
Testa del Gargano Italy 41°50N 16°10E 93 G13
Testigos, Is. Los
  Venezuela 11°23N 63°7W 183 D7
Tét Hungary 47°30N 17°33E 80 C2
Tetachuck L. Canada 53°18N 125°55W 162 C3
Tetas, Pta. Chile 23°31N 70°38W 190 A1
Tete Mozam. 16°13S 33°33E 143 F3
Tete □ Mozam. 15°15S 32°40E 143 F3
Teterev → Ukraine 51°1N 30°5E 75 C16
Teterow Germany 53°46N 12°34E 76 B8
Teteven Bulgaria 42°58N 24°17E 97 C8
Tethul → Canada 60°35N 112°12W 162 A6
Tetiyiv Ukraine 49°22N 29°38E 75 D15
Tetlit Zheh = Fort McPherson
  Canada 67°30N 134°55W 160 D5
Teton → U.S.A. 47°56N 110°31W 168 C8
Tétouan Morocco 35°35N 5°21W 136 A3
Tetovo Macedonia 42°1N 20°59E 96 D5
Tetufera, Mt. Tahiti 17°40S 149°26W 155 b

Tetyushi Russia 54°55N 48°49E 86 C9
Teuco → Argentina 25°35S 60°11W 190 B3
Teulada Italy 38°58N 8°46E 94 D1
Teulon Canada 50°23N 97°16W 163 C9
Teun Indonesia 6°59S 129°8E 119 F7
Teuri-Tō Japan 44°26N 141°19E 112 B10
Teutoburger Wald
  Germany 52°5N 8°22E 76 C4
Tevere → Italy 41°44N 12°14E 93 G9
Tevere → Italy 42°46N 12°14E 93 F9
Teverya Israel 32°47N 35°32E 130 C4
Teviot → U.K. 55°29N 2°38W 65 F6
Tewantin Australia 26°27S 153°3E 151 D5
Tewkesbury U.K. 51°59N 2°9W 67 F5
Texada I. Canada 49°40N 124°25W 162 D4
Texarkana Ark., U.S.A. 33°26N 94°2W 176 E7
Texarkana Tex., U.S.A. 33°26N 94°3W 176 E7
Texas Australia 28°49S 151°9E 151 D5
Texas □ U.S.A. 31°40N 98°30W 176 F5
Texas City U.S.A. 29°24N 94°54W 176 G7
Texel Neths. 53°5N 4°50E 69 A4
Texline U.S.A. 36°23N 103°2W 176 D3
Texoma, L. U.S.A. 33°50N 96°34W 176 E6
Teyateyaneng Lesotho 29°7S 27°34E 141 K5
Teykovo Russia 56°55N 40°30E 84 D11
Tezin Afghan. 34°24N 69°30E 124 B3
Teziutlán Mexico 19°49N 97°21W 181 D5
Tezpur India 26°40N 92°45E 123 F18
Tezzeron L. Canada 54°43N 124°30W 162 C4
Tha-anne → Canada 60°31N 94°37W 163 A10
Tha Deua Laos 17°57N 102°53E 120 D4
Tha Deua Laos 19°26N 101°50E 120 C3
Tha Li Thailand 17°37N 101°25E 120 D3
Tha Pla Thailand 17°48N 100°32E 120 D3
Tha Rua Thailand 14°34N 100°44E 120 E3
Tha Sala Thailand 8°40N 99°56E 121 H2
Tha Song Yang
  Thailand 17°34N 97°55E 120 D1
Thaba Putsoa Lesotho 29°45S 28°0E 145 C4
Thaba-Tseka Lesotho 29°32S 28°36E 145 C4
Thabana Ntlenyana
  Lesotho 29°30S 29°16E 145 C4
Thabazimbi S. Africa 24°40S 27°21E 145 B4
Thādiq Si. Arabia 25°18N 45°52E 128 E5
Thai Binh Vietnam 20°35N 106°1E 116 G6
Thai Muang Thailand 8°24N 98°16E 121 H2
Thai Nguyen Vietnam 21°35N 105°55E 116 G5
Thailand ■ Asia 16°0N 102°0E 120 E4
Thailand, G. of Asia 11°30N 101°0E 121 G3
Thakhek Laos 17°25N 104°45E 120 D5
Thal Pakistan 33°28N 70°33E 124 C4
Thal Desert Pakistan 31°10N 71°30E 124 D4
Thala Tunisia 35°35N 8°40E 136 A5
Thala La = Hkakabo Razi
  Burma 28°25N 97°23E 116 C1
Thalabarivat Cambodia 13°33N 105°57E 120 F5
Thalang = Amphoe Thalang
  Thailand 8°1N 98°20E 121 a
Thalang Thailand 8°2N 98°12E 121 J2
Thalara Nepal 29°29N 80°59E 125 E9
Thalassery India 11°45N 75°30E 127 J2
Thale Sap Songkhla
  Thailand 7°12N 100°28E 121 J3
Thallon Australia 28°39S 148°49E 151 D4
Thalu Ko Thailand 9°26N 99°54E 121 H2
Thalwil Switz. 47°17N 8°35E 77 H4
Tham Lot Thailand 19°34N 98°16E 120 C2
Thamarīt Oman 17°39N 54°2E 131 D5
Thames N.Z. 37°7S 175°34E 154 D4
Thames → U.K. 51°29N 0°34E 67 F8
Thames → Canada 42°20N 82°25W 174 D2
Thames, Firth of N.Z. 37°0S 175°25E 154 D4
Thames Estuary U.K. 51°29N 0°52E 67 F8
Thamesford Canada 43°4N 81°0W 174 D3
Thamesville Canada 42°33N 81°59W 174 D3
Than India 22°34N 71°11E 124 H4
Than Kyun Burma 9°49N 98°4E 121 H1
Than Uyen Vietnam 22°0N 103°54E 120 B4
Thana Gazi India 27°25N 76°19E 124 F7
Thandla India 23°0N 74°34E 124 H6
Thandwe Burma 18°20N 94°30E 123 K19
Thane India 19°12N 72°59E 126 E1
Thanesar India 30°1N 76°52E 124 D7
Thanet, I. of U.K. 51°21N 1°20E 67 F9
Thangool Australia 24°38S 150°42E 150 C5
Thanh Hoa Vietnam 19°48N 105°46E 116 G5
Thanh Hung Vietnam 9°55N 105°43E 121 H5
Thanh Pho Ho Chi Minh
  Vietnam 10°58N 106°40E 121 G6
Thanh Thuy Vietnam 22°55N 104°51E 120 A5
Thanjavur India 10°48N 79°12E 127 J4
Thanlwin = Salween →
  Burma 16°31N 97°37E 123 L20
Thann France 47°48N 7°5E 71 E14
Thano Bula Khan
  Pakistan 25°22N 67°50E 124 G2
Thanya Buri Thailand 14°1N 100°45E 120 E3
Thaoge → Botswana 20°34S 22°36E 144 B3
Thaolintoa L. Canada 61°30N 96°25W 163 A9
Thaon-les-Vosges
  France 48°15N 6°24E 71 D13
Thap Lan △ Thailand 14°15N 102°16E 120 E4
Thap Sakae Thailand 11°30N 99°37E 121 G2
Thap Than Thailand 15°27N 99°54E 120 E2
Thar Desert India 28°0N 72°0E 124 F5
Tharad India 24°30N 71°44E 124 G4
Thargomindah
  Australia 27°58S 143°46E 151 D3
Tharrawaddy Burma 17°38N 95°48E 123 L19
Tharthār, Buḥayrat ath
  Iraq 34°0N 43°15E 105 D10
Tharthar, L. = Tharthār,
  Buḥayrat ath Iraq 34°0N 43°15E 105 D10
Tharthār, W. ath →
  Iraq 34°32N 43°4E 105 D10
Thasopoula Greece 40°49N 24°45E 97 F8
Thasos Greece 40°40N 24°40E 97 F8
Thatcher Ariz., U.S.A. 32°51N 109°46W 169 K9
Thatcher Colo., U.S.A. 37°33N 104°7W 169 H11
Thaton Burma 16°55N 97°22E 123 L20
Thatta Pakistan 24°42N 67°55E 124 G2
Thau, Bassin de France 43°23N 3°36E 72 E7
Thayer U.S.A. 36°31N 91°33W 172 G8

Thayetmyo Burma 19°20N 95°10E 123 K19
Thazi Burma 21°0N 96°5E 123 J20
Thbeng Meanchey
  Cambodia 13°49N 104°58E 120 F5
The Bahamas ■
  N. Amer. 24°0N 75°0W 183 B5
The Broads U.K. 52°45N 1°30E 66 E9
The Everglades U.S.A. 25°50N 81°0W 179 K9
The Gambia ■ W. Afr. 13°25N 16°0W 138 C1
The Gulf = Persian Gulf
  Asia 27°0N 50°0E 129 E6
The Hague = 's-Gravenhage
  Neths. 52°7N 4°17E 69 B4
The Pas Canada 53°45N 101°15W 163 C8
The Wash U.K. 52°58N 0°20E 66 E8
The Weald U.K. 51°4N 0°20E 67 F8
Thebes = Thiva Greece 38°19N 23°19E 98 C5
Thebes Egypt 25°40N 32°35E 137 B3
Thedford U.S.A. 41°59N 100°35W 172 E3
Theebine Australia 25°57S 152°34E 151 D5
Thekulthili L. Canada 61°3N 110°0W 163 A7
Thelon → Canada 64°16N 96°4W 163 A8
Thénezay France 46°44N 0°2W 70 F6
Thenon France 45°9N 1°4E 72 C5
Theodore Australia 24°55S 150°3E 150 C5
Theodore Canada 51°26N 102°55W 163 C8
Theodore U.S.A. 30°33N 88°10W 177 F10
Theodore Roosevelt △
  U.S.A. 47°0N 103°25W 172 B2
Theodore Roosevelt L.
  U.S.A. 33°40N 111°10W 169 K8
Thepha Thailand 6°52N 100°58E 121 J3
Thérain → France 49°15N 2°27E 71 C9
Therandē Kosovo 42°21N 20°50E 96 D4
Theresa U.S.A. 44°13N 75°48W 175 B9
Thermaïkos Kolpos
  Greece 40°15N 22°45E 98 F6
Thermopolis U.S.A. 43°39N 108°13W 168 E9
Thermopylae Greece 38°48N 22°35E 98 C4
Thesprotia Greece 39°27N 20°22E 98 B2
Thessalon Canada 46°20N 83°30W 164 C3
Thessaloníki Greece 40°38N 22°58E 98 F6
Thessaloníki, Gulf of =
  Thermaïkos Kolpos
  Greece 40°15N 22°45E 96 F6
Thessaloníki □ Greece 40°38N 22°58E 96 F6
Thessaloníki ✈ (SKG)
  Greece 40°30N 23°0E 96 F7
Thessaloníki Kolpos
  Greece 40°15N 22°45E 96 F6
Thessaly □ Greece 39°25N 22°0E 98 B4
Thetford U.K. 52°25N 0°45E 67 E8
Thetford Mines Canada 46°8N 71°18W 165 C5
Theun → Laos 18°19N 104°0E 120 C5
Theunissen S. Africa 28°26S 26°43E 144 D4
Thevenard S. Africa 32°9S 133°38E 151 E1
Thiamis → Greece 39°15N 20°6E 98 B2
Thiberville France 49°8N 0°27E 70 C7
Thibodaux U.S.A. 29°48N 90°49W 177 G9
Thicket Portage
  Canada 55°19N 97°42W 163 B9
Thief River Falls U.S.A. 48°7N 96°10W 172 A6
Thiel Mts. Antarctica 85°15S 91°0W 55 E16
Thiene Italy 45°42N 11°29E 93 C8
Thiérache France 49°51N 3°45E 71 C10
Thiers France 45°52N 3°33E 72 C7
Thiès Senegal 14°50N 16°51W 138 C1
Thiès □ Senegal 14°45N 16°50W 138 C1
Thiesi Italy 40°31N 8°43E 94 B1
Thika Kenya 1°1S 37°5E 142 C4
Thille-Boubacar Senegal 16°31N 15°5W 138 B1
Thimphu Bhutan 27°31N 89°45E 123 F16
Thína → S. Africa 31°18S 29°13E 145 E4
Þingvallavatn Iceland 64°11N 21°9W 60 D3
Thionville France 49°20N 6°10E 71 C13
Thira = Santorini Greece 36°23N 25°27E 99 E7
Thirasia Greece 36°26N 25°21E 99 E7
Third Cataract Sudan 19°42N 30°20E 137 D2
Thirsk U.K. 54°14N 1°19W 66 C6
Thiruvananthapuram
  India 8°41N 77°0E 127 K3
Thiruvarur India 10°46N 79°38E 127 J4
Thisted Denmark 56°58N 8°40E 63 H2
Thistle I. Australia 35°0S 136°8E 152 C2
Thithia = Cicia Fiji 17°45S 179°18W 154 a
Thitu I. S. China Sea 11°3N 114°17E 118 B4
Thiva Greece 38°19N 23°19E 98 C5
Thiviers France 45°25N 0°54E 72 C4
Þjórsá → Iceland 63°47N 20°48W 60 D3
Thlewiaza → Canada 60°29N 94°40W 163 A10
Thmar Puok Cambodia 13°57N 103°4E 120 F4
Tho Chu, Dao Vietnam 9°20N 103°28E 121 H4
Tho Vinh Vietnam 19°16N 105°42E 120 C5
Thoa → Canada 60°31N 109°47W 163 A7
Thoen Thailand 17°43N 99°12E 120 D2
Thoeng Thailand 19°41N 100°12E 120 C3
Thohoyandou S. Africa 22°58S 30°29E 145 A5
Thomas U.S.A. 35°45N 98°45W 176 D5
Thomas, L. Australia 26°4S 137°58E 151 D2
Thomas Hubbard, C.
  Canada 82°0N 94°25W 161 A13
Thomaston U.S.A. 32°53N 84°20W 178 E5
Thomasville Ala.,
  U.S.A. 31°55N 87°44W 177 F11
Thomasville Ga.,
  U.S.A. 30°50N 83°59W 178 F6
Thomasville N.C.,
  U.S.A. 35°53N 80°5W 177 D14
Thompson Canada 55°45N 97°52W 163 B9
Thompson U.S.A. 41°52N 75°31W 175 E9
Thompson → Canada 50°15N 121°24W 162 C4
Thompson → U.S.A. 39°46N 93°37W 172 F7
Thompson Falls
  U.S.A. 47°36N 115°21W 168 C6
Thompson Pk. U.S.A. 41°0N 123°2W 168 F2
Thompson Sd. N.Z. 45°9S 166°48E 155 F1
Thompson Springs
  U.S.A. 38°58N 109°43W 168 G9
Thompsontown U.S.A. 40°33N 77°14W 174 F7
Thomson Australia 25°11S 142°53E 150 C3
Thomson → Australia 25°11S 142°53E 150 C3
Thon Buri Thailand 13°43N 100°29E 120 E3
Thônes France 45°54N 6°18E 73 C10
Thong Yang Thailand 9°28N 99°56E 121 b
Thonon-les-Bains
  France 46°22N 6°29E 71 F13
Thoothukudi = Tuticorin
  India 8°50N 78°12E 127 K4
Thorez Ukraine 48°4N 38°34E 85 H10
Þórisvatn Iceland 64°20N 18°55W 60 D4
Thornaby on Tees U.K. 54°33N 1°18W 66 C6
Thornbury Canada 44°34N 80°26W 174 B4

Thornbury N.Z. 46°17S 168°9E 155 G3
Thorne U.K. 53°37N 0°57W 66 D7
Thornton Canada 44°16N 79°43W 174 B5
Thornton U.S.A. 39°52N 104°58W 168 G11
Thorold Canada 43°7N 79°12W 174 C5
Þórshöfn Iceland 66°12N 15°20W 60 C6
Thouarcé France 47°17N 0°30W 70 E6
Thouars France 47°0N 0°15W 70 F6
Thouet → France 47°17N 0°6W 70 E6
Thouin, C. Australia 20°20S 118°10E 148 D2
Thousand Islands
U.S.A. 44°20N 76°0W 175 B9
Thousand Oaks
U.S.A. 34°10N 118°50W 171 L8
Thrace Turkey 41°0N 27°0E 97 F10
Thrace, Sea of Greece 40°30N 25°0E 97 F8
Thredbo Australia 36°31S 148°20E 153 D8
Three Forks U.S.A. 45°54N 111°33W 168 D8
Three Gorges Dam
China 30°45N 111°15E 117 B8
Three Gorges Res. = Sanxia
Shuiku China 30°N 107°58E 116 B6
Three Hills Canada 51°43N 113°15W 162 C6
Three Hummock I.
Australia 40°25S 144°55E 151 G3
Three Pagodas Pass
Asia 15°20N 98°30E 120 E2
Three Points, C. Ghana 4°42N 2°6W 138 E4
Three Rivers Calif.,
U.S.A. 36°26N 118°54W 170 J8
Three Rivers Tex.,
U.S.A. 28°28N 98°11W 176 G5
Three Springs
Australia 29°32S 115°45E 149 E2
Thrissur India 10°30N 76°18E 127 J3
Throssell, L. Australia 27°33S 124°10E 149 E3
Throssell Ra. Australia 22°3S 121°43E 148 D3
Thrushton △ Australia 27°47S 147°40E 151 D4
Thu Dau Mot Vietnam 10°58N 106°39E 121 G6
Thua → Kenya 1°31S 39°30E 142 C4
Thuamal Rampur India 19°23N 82°56E 126 D6
Thuan Hoa Vietnam 8°58N 105°30E 121 H5
Thubun Lakes Canada 61°30N 112°0W 163 A6
Thueyts France 44°41N 4°9E 73 D8
Thugga = Dougga
Tunisia 36°25N 9°13E 136 A5
Thuin Belgium 50°20N 4°17E 69 D4
Thuir France 42°38N 2°45E 72 F6
Thule = Qaanaaq
Greenland 77°30N 69°10W 57 B4
Thule Air Base = Uummannaq
Greenland 77°33N 68°52W 57 B4
Thun Switz. 46°45N 7°38E 77 J3
Thunder B. U.S.A. 45°0N 83°20W 174 B1
Thunder Bay Canada 48°20N 89°15W 164 C2
Thunderbolt U.S.A. 32°3N 81°4W 178 C8
Thunersee Switz. 46°43N 7°39E 77 J3
Thung Salaeng Luang △
Thailand 16°43N 100°50E 120 D3
Thung Song Thailand 8°10N 99°40E 121 H2
Thungyai △ Thailand 15°20N 98°55E 120 E2
Thunkar Bhutan 27°55N 91°0E 123 F17
Thuong Tra Vietnam 16°2N 107°42E 120 D6
Thur → Switz. 47°32N 9°10E 77 H5
Thurgau □ Switz. 47°34N 9°10E 77 H5
Thüringen □ Germany 51°0N 11°0E 76 D6
Thüringer Wald Germany 50°35N 11°0E 76 E6
Thuringowa △
Australia 19°18S 146°43E 150 B4
Thurles Ireland 52°41N 7°49W 64 D4
Thurn P. Austria 47°20N 12°25E 78 D5
Thurrock □ U.K. 51°31N 0°23E 67 F8
Thursday I. Australia 10°30S 142°3E 150 A3
Thurso Canada 45°36N 75°15W 164 C4
Thurso U.K. 58°36N 3°32W 65 C5
Thurso → U.K. 58°36N 3°32W 65 C5
Thurston I. Antarctica 72°0S 100°0W 55 D16
Thury-Harcourt France 48°59N 0°30W 70 D6
Thutade L. Canada 57°0N 126°55W 162 B3
Thy Denmark 56°52N 8°25E 63 H2
Thy △ Denmark 56°55N 8°25E 63 H2
Thyboron Denmark 56°42N 8°12E 63 H2
Tholo Malawi 16°7S 35°5E 143 F4
Ti-n-Amzi → Niger 18°20N 4°32E 139 B5
Ti-n-Barraouene, O. →
Africa 18°40N 4°5E 139 B5
Ti-n-Tanelfirt Algeria 24°49N 3°48E 136 D4
Ti-n-Zaouatene Algeria 19°55N 2°55E 139 B5
Ti-Tree Australia 22°5S 133°22E 150 C1
Tiadiaye Senegal 14°25N 16°40W 138 C1
Tiahuanaco Bolivia 16°33S 68°42W 188 D4
Tian Shan Asia 42°0N 76°0E 109 D9
Tianchang China 32°40N 119°0E 117 A12
Tiandeng China 23°6N 107°7E 116 F6
Tiandong China 23°36N 107°8E 116 F6
Tian'e China 25°1N 107°9E 116 E6
Tianguá Brazil 3°44S 40°59W 189 A2
Tianhe China 24°48N 108°40E 116 E7
Tianjin China 39°7N 117°12E 115 E9
Tianjin Shi □ China 39°8N 117°12E 115 E9
Tianjun China 38°0N 98°30E 110 D8
Tiankoura Burkina Faso 10°47N 3°17W 138 C4
Tianlin China 24°21N 106°12E 116 E6
Tianmen China 30°39N 113°9E 117 B9
Tianquan China 30°7N 102°43E 116 B4
Tianshifu China 41°17N 124°22E 115 D13
Tianshui China 34°32N 105°40E 116 A4
Tiantai China 29°10N 121°2E 117 C13
Tianya China 18°18N 109°20E 117 a
Tianyang China 23°42N 106°53E 116 F6
Tianyar Indonesia 8°12S 115°30E 119 J18
Tianzhen China 40°24N 114°5E 114 D8
Tianzhu China 26°54N 109°11E 117 D10
Tianzhuangtai China 40°54N 122°6E 115 D12
Tiaret Tahiti 17°32S 149°20W 155 b
Tiaret Algeria 35°20N 1°21E 136 A4
Tiaret □ Algeria 34°30N 1°30E 136 B4
Tiassalé Ivory C. 6°N 5°9W 138 D4
Tibagi Brazil 24°30S 50°24W 191 A5
Tibagi → Brazil 22°47S 51°1W 191 A5
Tibastī, Sarīr Libya 22°50N 18°30E 135 D9
Tibati Cameroon 6°22N 12°30E 137 D7
Tiber = Tevere → Italy 41°44N 12°14E 93 G9
Tiber Res. U.S.A. 48°19N 111°6W 168 B8
Tiberias = Teverya
Israel 32°47N 35°32E 130 C4
Tiberias, L. = Yam Kinneret
Israel 32°45N 35°35E 130 C4
Tibesti Chad 21°0N 17°30E 135 D9
Tibet = Xizang Zizhiqu □
China 32°0N 88°0E 110 E6

Tibet, Plateau of Asia 32°0N 86°0E 102 E10
Tibiri Niger 13°34N 7°4E 139 C6
Ţibleş, Vf. Romania 47°32N 24°15E 81 C9
Tibnī Syria 35°36N 39°50E 105 E8
Tibooburra Australia 29°26S 142°1E 151 D3
Tibrikot Nepal 29°3N 82°48E 125 E10
Tibro Sweden 58°28N 14°10E 63 F8
Tiburón, I. Mexico 29°0N 112°25W 180 B2
Tîchît Mauritania 18°21N 9°29W 138 B3
Ticino □ Switz. 46°20N 8°45E 77 J4
Ticino → Italy 45°9N 9°14E 92 C6
Ticleni Romania 44°53N 23°24E 81 F8
Ticonderoga U.S.A. 43°51N 73°26W 175 C11
Ticul Mexico 20°24N 89°32W 181 C7
Tidaholm Sweden 58°12N 13°58E 63 F7
Tidan Sweden 58°34N 14°1E 63 F8
Tiddim Burma 23°28N 93°45E 123 H18
Tiden India 7°15N 93°33E 127 L11
Tidikelt Algeria 26°58N 1°30E 136 C4
Tidioute U.S.A. 41°41N 79°24W 174 E5
Tidjikja Mauritania 18°29N 11°35W 138 B2
Tidore Indonesia 0°40N 127°25E 119 D7
Tiébissou Ivory C. 7°9N 5°10W 138 D3
Tiefa China 42°28N 123°26E 115 C12
Tiegang Shuiku China 22°37N 113°52E 115 a
Tiel Neths. 51°53N 5°26E 69 C5
Tiel Senegal 14°55N 15°5W 138 C1
Tieli China 46°57N 128°3E 111 B14
Tieling China 42°20N 123°55E 115 C12
Tielt Belgium 51°0N 3°20E 69 C3
Tien Shan = Tian Shan
Asia 40°30N 76°0E 109 D9
Tien-tsin = Tianjin
China 39°7N 117°12E 115 E9
Tien Yen Vietnam 21°20N 107°24E 120 B6
T'ienching = Tianjin
China 39°7N 117°12E 115 E9
Tienen Belgium 50°48N 4°57E 69 D4
Tiénigbé Ivory C. 8°11N 5°43W 138 D3
Tientsin = Tianjin
China 39°7N 117°12E 115 E9
Tieri Australia 23°2S 148°21E 150 C4
Tierp Sweden 60°20N 17°30E 62 D11
Tierra Amarilla Chile 27°28S 70°18W 190 B2
Tierra Amarilla
U.S.A. 36°42N 106°33W 169 H10
Tierra Colorada
Mexico 17°11N 99°32W 181 D5
Tierra de Barros Spain 38°40N 6°30W 89 G4
Tierra de Campos Spain 42°10N 4°50W 88 C6
Tierra del Fuego □
Argentina 54°0S 67°45W 192 D3
Tierra del Fuego, I. Grande de
Argentina 54°0S 69°0W 192 D3
Tierra del Fuego △
Argentina 54°50S 68°23W 192 D3
Tiétar → Spain 39°50N 6°1W 88 F4
Tietê → Brazil 20°40S 51°35W 191 A5
Tīfārītī W. Sahara 26°9N 10°33W 136 C3
Tiffin U.S.A. 41°7N 83°11W 174 E2
Tiflèt Morocco 33°54N 6°20W 136 B4
Tifton U.S.A. 31°27N 83°31W 178 D6
Tifu Indonesia 3°39S 126°24E 119 E7
Tiga Res. Nigeria 11°13N 8°30E 139 C6
Tiger Leaping Gorge = Hutiao Xia
China 27°13N 100°9E 116 D3
Tighina Moldova 46°50N 29°30E 81 D14
Tigil Russia 57°49N 158°40E 107 D16
Tigiria India 20°29N 85°31E 126 D7
Tignall U.S.A. 33°52N 82°44W 178 B7
Tignish Canada 46°58N 64°2W 165 C7
Tigre → Peru 4°30S 74°10W 188 D3
Tigre → Venezuela 9°20N 62°30W 186 B6
Tigris = Dijlah, Nahr →
Asia 31°0N 47°25E 128 D5
Tiguentourine Algeria 27°52N 9°8E 136 C5
Tigveni Romania 45°10N 24°31E 81 E9
Tigyaing Burma 23°45N 96°10E 123 H20
Tih, Gebel el Egypt 29°32N 33°26E 137 F8
Tihodaine, Erg de
Algeria 25°15N 7°15E 136 C5
Tiilikka △ Finland 63°40N 28°15E 60 E23
Tijara India 27°56N 76°31E 124 F7
Tijuana Mexico 32°32N 117°1W 171 N9
Tikal Guatemala 17°13N 89°24W 182 C2
Tikal △ Guatemala 17°23N 89°34W 182 C2
Tikamgarh India 24°44N 78°50E 125 G8
Tikaré Burkina Faso 13°15N 1°43W 139 C4
Tikchik Lakes U.S.A. 60°0N 159°0W 166 D8
Tikhoretsk Russia 45°56N 40°5E 87 H5
Tikhvin Russia 59°35N 33°30E 84 C7
Tikirarjuaq = Whale Cove
Canada 62°10N 92°34W 163 A10
Tikkadouine, Adrar
Algeria 24°28N 1°30E 136 D4
Tikmehdāsh Iran 37°16N 46°54E 105 D12
Tiko Cameroon 4°4N 9°20E 139 E6
Tikrīt Iraq 34°35N 43°37E 105 D10
Tiksi Russia 71°40N 128°45E 107 B13
Tilač al 'Alī Jordan 32°0N 35°52E 130 D4
Tilamuta Indonesia 0°32N 122°23E 119 D6
Tilburg Neths. 51°31N 5°6E 69 C5
Tilbury Canada 42°17N 82°23W 174 D2
Tilbury U.K. 51°27N 0°22E 67 F8
Tilcara Argentina 23°36S 65°23W 190 A2
Tilden U.S.A. 42°3N 97°50W 172 D5
Tilemsi, Vallée du Mali 17°42N 0°15E 139 B5
Tilhar India 28°0N 79°45E 125 F8
Tilia, O. → Algeria 27°0N 0°55E 136 C4
Tilichiki Russia 60°27N 166°5E 107 C17
Tililane Algeria 27°49N 0°6E 136 C4
Tilissos Greece 35°20N 25°1E 101 D7
Till → U.K. 55°41N 2°13W 66 B5
Tillabéri Niger 14°28N 1°28E 139 C5
Tillamook U.S.A. 45°27N 123°51W 168 D2
Tillanchong I. India 8°30N 93°37E 127 K11
Tillberga Sweden 59°40N 16°39E 62 E10
Tillman U.S.A. 32°28N 81°6W 178 C8
Tillsonburg Canada 42°53N 80°44W 174 D4
Tillyeria Cyprus 35°6N 32°40E 101 D11
Tilogne Senegal 16°1N 13°40W 138 B2
Tilos Greece 36°27N 27°27E 99 E9
Tilpa Australia 30°57S 144°24E 152 A4
Tilrhemt Algeria 33°9N 3°22E 136 B6
Tilt → U.K. 56°46N 3°51W 65 E5
Tilton U.S.A. 43°27N 71°36W 175 C13
Tiltonsville U.S.A. 40°10N 80°41W 174 F4

Tim Denmark 56°12N 8°19E 63 H2
Tima Egypt 26°54N 31°25E 137 B3
Timanfaya △ Canary Is. 29°0N 13°46W 100 F6
Timaru N.Z. 44°23S 171°14E 155 E6
Timashevo Russia 53°22N 51°9E 86 D10
Timashevsk Russia 45°35N 39°0E 87 H4
Timau Kenya 0°4N 37°15E 142 B4
Timbaki Greece 35°4N 24°45E 101 D6
Timbaúba Brazil 7°31S 35°19W 189 B3
Timbedgha Mauritania 16°17N 8°16W 138 B3
Timber Creek
Australia 15°40S 130°29E 148 C5
Timber Lake U.S.A. 45°26N 101°5W 172 C3
Timber Mt. U.S.A. 36°57N 116°28W 170 H10
Timbo Guinea 10°30N 11°50W 138 C2
Timbo Liberia 5°30S 9°45E 138 D3
Timboon Australia 38°30S 142°58E 152 E5
Timbué, Ponta Mozam. 18°47S 36°22E 143 F4
Timbuktu = Tombouctou
Mali 16°50N 3°0W 138 B4
Timéiaouine Algeria 20°27N 1°50E 139 A5
Timellouline Algeria 29°22N 8°55E 136 C5
Timétrin Mali 19°19N 0°34W 139 B4
Timétrine, Mts. Mali 19°25N 1°0W 139 B4
Timfi Oros Greece 39°59N 20°45E 98 B2
Timfristos, Oros Greece 38°57N 21°50E 98 C3
Timgad Algeria 35°29N 6°28E 136 A5
Timhadit Morocco 33°15N 5°4E 136 B4
Timi Cyprus 34°44N 32°31E 101 E11
Timia Niger 18°4N 8°40E 139 B6
Timika Indonesia 4°47S 136°32E 119 E9
Timimoun Algeria 29°14N 0°16E 136 C4
Timimoun, Sebkha de
Algeria 29°0N 0°30E 136 C4
Timiris, Râs Mauritania 19°21N 16°30W 138 B1
Timiş = Tamis → Serbia 44°51N 20°39E 80 F5
Timiş □ Romania 45°40N 21°30E 80 E6
Timiskaming, L. =
Témiscamingue, L.
Canada 47°10N 79°25W 164 C4
Timişoara Romania 45°43N 21°15E 80 E6
Timmersdala Sweden 58°32N 13°46E 63 F7
Timmins Canada 48°28N 81°25W 164 C3
Timmonsville U.S.A. 34°8N 79°57W 178 D14
Timok → Serbia 44°10N 22°40E 96 B6
Timoleague Ireland 51°39N 8°46W 64 E3
Timon Brazil 5°8S 42°52W 189 D2
Timor Indonesia 9°0S 125°0E 119 F7
Timor Leste = East Timor ■
Asia 8°50S 126°0E 119 F7
Timor Sea Ind. Oc. 12°0S 127°0E 148 B4
Timrå Sweden 62°29N 17°18E 62 B11
Timucuan △ U.S.A. 30°28N 81°27W 178 F7
Tin Alkoum Algeria 24°42N 10°17E 136 D6
Tin Atanai Algeria 25°52N 1°37E 136 C4
Tin Can Bay Australia 25°56S 153°0E 151 D5
Tin Ethisane Mali 19°3N 0°52W 139 B4
Tin Gornai Mali 16°38N 0°38W 139 B4
Tin Mt. U.S.A. 36°50N 117°10W 170 J9
Tin Shui Wai China 22°28N 114°0E 111 a
Tina = Thina →
S. Africa 31°18S 29°13E 145 E4
Tina, Khalîg el Egypt 31°10N 32°40E 130 D1
Tinaca Pt. Phil. 5°30N 125°25E 119 C7
Tinajo Canary Is. 29°4N 13°42W 100 E6
Tinca Romania 46°46N 21°58E 80 D6
Tindal Australia 14°31S 132°22E 148 B5
Tindivanam India 12°15N 79°41E 127 H4
Tindouf Algeria 27°42N 8°10W 136 C2
Tindouf □ Algeria 27°25N 5°50W 136 C2
Tinée → France 43°55N 7°11E 73 E11
Tineo Spain 43°21N 6°27W 88 B4
Tinerhir Morocco 31°29N 5°31W 136 B2
Tinfouchi Algeria 28°52N 5°49W 136 C2
Tinfunque △ Paraguay 23°55S 60°17W 190 A3
Ting Jiang → China 24°45N 116°35E 117 E11
Tinggi, Pulau Malaysia 2°18N 104°7E 121 L5
Tingo María Peru 9°10S 75°54W 188 E3
Tingrela Ivory C. 10°27N 6°25W 138 C3
Tingri China 28°34N 86°38E 110 F6
Tingsryd Sweden 56°31N 15°0E 63 H9
Tingstäde Sweden 57°44N 18°37E 63 G12
Tinh Bien Vietnam 10°36N 104°57E 121 G5
Tinharé, I. de Brazil 13°30S 38°58W 189 C3
Tinian N. Marianas 15°0N 145°38E 156 F6
Tinkisso → Guinea 11°21N 9°10W 138 C3
Tinnevelly = Tirunelveli
India 8°45N 77°45E 127 K3
Tinogasta Argentina 28°5S 67°32W 190 B2
Tinos Greece 37°33N 25°8E 99 D7
Tiñoso, C. Spain 37°32N 1°6W 91 H3
Tinpahar India 24°59N 87°44E 125 G12
Tinrhert, Plateau du
Algeria 29°30N 9°0E 136 C5
Tinta Peru 14°3S 71°20W 188 D3
Tintâne Mauritania 16°13N 10°8W 138 B2
Tintina Argentina 27°2S 62°45W 190 B3
Tintinara Australia 35°48S 140°2E 152 C4
Tintioulé Guinea 10°27N 6°25W 138 C3
Tinto → Spain 37°12N 6°55W 89 H4
Tinui N.Z. 40°52S 176°5E 154 C5
Tinwald N.Z. 43°55S 171°43E 155 D6
Tiobraid Árann = Tipperary
Ireland 52°28N 8°10W 64 D3
Tioga N. Dak., U.S.A. 48°24N 102°56W 172 A2
Tioga Pa., U.S.A. 41°55N 77°8W 174 E7
Tioman, Pulau
Malaysia 2°50N 104°10E 121 L5
Tione di Trento Italy 46°2N 10°43E 92 B7
Tionesta U.S.A. 41°30N 79°28W 174 E5
Tiouliline Algeria 27°1N 0°25E 136 C4
Tipasa Algeria 36°35N 2°28E 136 A4
Tipasa □ Algeria 36°35N 2°25E 136 A4
Tipitapa Nic. 12°8N 86°8W 182 D2
Tipler U.S.A. 45°36N 88°40W 172 C9
Tipongpani India 27°20N 95°55E 125 F19
Tipp City U.S.A. 39°58N 84°10W 174 F2
Tipperary Ireland 52°28N 8°10W 64 D3
Tipperary □ Ireland 52°37N 7°55W 64 D4
Tipton Calif., U.S.A. 36°4N 119°19W 170 J7
Tipton Iowa, U.S.A. 41°46N 91°8W 172 E8
Tipton Mt. U.S.A. 35°32N 114°12W 171 K12
Tiptonville U.S.A. 36°23N 89°29W 177 C10
Tiptur India 13°15N 76°26E 127 H3
Tiquina Bolivia 16°13S 68°50W 188 D4
Tiracambu, Serra do
Brazil 3°15S 46°30W 189 C2
Tiran Iran 32°45S 51°8E 106 C6
Tiran Si. Arabia 27°57N 34°32E 137 B3
Tïranë Albania 41°18N 19°49E 96 E2
Tïranë ✈ (TIA) Albania 41°57N 19°49E 96 E2
Tirano Italy 46°13N 10°9E 92 B7

Tirari Desert Australia 28°22S 138°7E 151 D2
Tiraspol Moldova 46°55N 29°35E 81 D14
Tiratimine Algeria 25°56N 3°37E 136 C4
Tirau N.Z. 37°58S 175°46E 154 D4
Tirdout Mali 16°7N 1°5W 139 B4
Tire Turkey 38°5N 27°45E 99 C9
Tirebolu Turkey 40°58N 38°45E 105 D8
Tiree U.K. 56°31N 6°55W 65 E2
Tiree, Passage of U.K. 56°30N 6°30W 65 E2
Tîrgovişte = Târgovişte
Romania 44°55N 25°27E 81 F10
Tîrgu Jiu = Târgu Jiu
Romania 45°5N 23°19E 81 E8
Tîrgu Mureş = Târgu Mureş
Romania 46°31N 24°38E 81 D9
Tirich Mir Pakistan 36°15N 71°55E 109 E8
Tiriolo Italy 38°57N 16°30E 95 D9
Tiriro Guinea 12°27N 8°40W 138 C3
Tiritiri o te Moana = Southern
Alps N.Z. 43°41S 170°11E 155 D5
Tirna → India 18°4N 76°57E 126 E3
Tirnavos Greece 39°45N 22°18E 98 B4
Tirodi India 21°40N 79°44E 125 J8
Tirol □ Austria 47°3N 10°43E 78 D3
Tiros Brazil 19°0S 45°58W 189 D1
Tirschenreuth Germany 49°51N 12°20E 76 D8
Tirso → Italy 39°53N 8°32E 94 C1
Tirstrup Denmark 56°18N 10°42E 63 H4
Tirtagangga Indonesia 8°24S 115°35E 119 J18
Tirthahalli India 13°42N 75°14E 127 H2
Tirua Pt. N.Z. 38°25S 174°40E 154 E3
Tiruchchendur India 8°30N 78°11E 127 K4
Tiruchchirappalli India 10°45N 78°45E 127 J4
Tirukkoyilur India 11°57N 79°12E 127 J4
Tirumangalam India 9°49N 77°58E 127 K3
Tirumayam India 10°14N 78°45E 127 J4
Tirunelveli India 8°45N 77°45E 127 K3
Tirupati India 13°39N 79°25E 127 H4
Tiruppattur Tamil Nadu,
India 12°30N 78°30E 127 H4
Tiruppattur Tamil Nadu,
India 8°30N 78°37E 127 J4
Tiruppur India 11°5N 77°22E 127 J3
Tirur India 10°54N 75°55E 127 J2
Tiruttani India 13°11N 79°38E 127 H4
Tirutturaippundi India 10°32N 79°41E 127 J4
Tiruvadaimarudur India 11°2N 79°27E 127 J4
Tiruvalla India 9°23N 76°34E 127 K3
Tiruvallar India 13°9N 79°57E 127 H4
Tiruvannamalai India 12°15N 79°5E 127 H4
Tiruvettipuram India 12°39N 79°33E 127 H4
Tiruvottiyur India 13°10N 80°22E 127 H5
Tisa → Serbia 45°15N 20°17E 80 E5
Tisdale Canada 52°50N 104°0W 163 C8
Tishomingo U.S.A. 34°14N 96°41W 176 D6
Tisjön Sweden 60°56N 13°0E 62 D7
Tisnaren Sweden 58°58N 15°56E 63 F9
Tišnov Czech Rep. 49°21N 16°25E 79 B9
Tisovec Slovak Rep. 48°41N 19°56E 79 C12
Tissamaharama
Sri Lanka 6°17N 81°17E 127 L5
Tissemsilt Algeria 35°35N 1°50E 136 A4
Tissemsilt □ Algeria 35°45N 1°45E 136 A4
Tissint Morocco 29°57N 7°16W 136 C2
Tisza = Tisa → Serbia 45°15N 20°17E 80 E5
Tiszaföldvár Hungary 46°58N 20°14E 80 D5
Tiszafüred Hungary 47°38N 20°50E 80 C5
Tiszalök Hungary 48°1N 21°20E 80 B6
Tiszavasvári Hungary 47°58N 21°18E 80 C6
Tit Ahaggar, Algeria 23°0N 5°10E 136 D5
Tit Tademait, Algeria 27°0N 1°29E 136 C5
Tit-Ary Russia 71°55N 127°2E 107 B13
Titaguas Spain 39°53N 1°6W 90 F3
Titao Burkina Faso 13°45N 2°5W 139 C4
Titel Serbia 45°10N 20°18E 80 E5
Tithwal Pakistan 34°21N 73°50E 125 B5
Titicaca, L. S. Amer. 15°30S 69°30W 188 D4
Titisee Germany 47°54N 8°10E 77 H4
Titītira Hd. N.Z. 43°36S 169°25E 155 D4
Titiwa Nigeria 12°14N 12°53E 139 C7
Titlagarh India 20°15N 83°11E 126 D6
Tito Serbia 41°35S 15°40E 95 B8
Titova Korenica
Croatia 44°45N 15°41E 93 D12
Titu Romania 44°39N 25°32E 81 F10
Titule
Dem. Rep. of the Congo 3°15N 25°31E 142 D2
Titusville Fla., U.S.A. 28°37N 80°49W 179 D9
Titusville Pa., U.S.A. 41°38N 79°41W 174 E5
Tivaouane Senegal 14°56N 16°45W 138 C1
Tivat Montenegro 42°28N 18°43E 96 D2
Tivedens △ Sweden 58°45N 14°35E 63 F8
Tiverton Canada 44°16N 81°32W 174 B3
Tiverton U.K. 50°54N 3°29W 67 G4
Tivoli Italy 41°58N 12°45E 93 G9
Tiwanaku = Tiahuanaco
Bolivia 16°33S 68°42W 188 D4
Tiwi Ø Australia 11°33S 130°42E 148 B5
Tizga Morocco 32°1N 5°9W 136 B2
Ti'zi N'Isli Morocco 32°28N 5°47W 136 B2
Tizi-Ouzou Algeria 36°42N 4°3E 136 A4
Tizi-Ouzou □ Algeria 36°35N 4°5E 136 A4
Tizimín Mexico 21°9N 88°9W 181 C7
Tiznap He → China 38°21N 77°20E 110 D2
Tiznit Morocco 29°48N 9°45W 136 C2
Tjæreborg Denmark 55°28N 8°36E 63 J2
Tjeggelvas Sweden 66°37N 17°45E 60 C17
Tjïrrkarli Ø Australia 25°15S 131°52E 149 E5
Tjiuring Indonesia 8°25S 114°13E 119 J17
Tjluen Sweden 58°0N 11°35E 63 F5
Tjukayirla Roadhouse
Australia 27°9S 124°34E 149 E3
Tjurabalan Ø Australia 19°15S 128°7E 148 C4
Tkibuli = Tqibuli Georgia 42°26N 43°0E 87 A10
Tkvarcheli = Tqvarcheli
Georgia 42°47N 41°42E 87 A9
Tlacotalpan Mexico 18°37N 95°40W 181 D5
Tlahualilo de Zaragoza
Mexico 26°20N 103°27W 180 B4
Tlaquepaque Mexico 20°39N 103°19W 180 C4
Tlaxcala Mexico 19°19N 98°14W 181 D5
Tlaxcala □ Mexico 19°30N 98°20E 181 D5
Tlaxiaco Mexico 17°25N 97°35W 181 D5

Tlemcen Algeria 34°52N 1°21W 136 B3
Tlemcen □ Algeria 34°38N 1°30W 136 B3
Tleta Sidi Bouguedra
Morocco 32°16N 9°59W 136 B2
Tlokweng Botswana 24°40S 25°58E 144 B4
Tlumach Ukraine 48°51N 25°0E 81 B10
Tłuszcz Poland 52°25N 21°25E 83 F8
Toamasina Madag. 18°10S 49°25E 141 H9
Toay Argentina 36°43S 64°38W 190 D3
Toba China 31°19N 97°42E 116 B3
Toba Japan 34°30N 136°51E 113 G8
Toba, Danau Indonesia 2°30N 98°30E 118 D1
Toba Kakar Pakistan 31°30N 69°0E 124 D3
Toba Tek Singh
Pakistan 30°55N 72°25E 124 D5
Tobago Trin. & Tob. 11°10N 60°30W 183 D7
Tobarra Spain 38°37N 1°44W 91 G3
Tobelo Indonesia 1°45N 127°56E 119 D7
Tobermory Canada 45°12N 81°40W 174 A3
Tobermory U.K. 56°38N 6°5W 65 E2
Tobi Palau 2°40N 131°10E 119 D8
Tobi-Shima Japan 41°12N 139°34E 112 D9
Tobin, L. Australia 21°45S 125°49E 148 D4
Tobin, L. Canada 53°35N 103°30W 163 C8
Toboali Indonesia 3°0S 106°25E 118 E3
Tobol → Russia 58°10N 68°12E 106 D7
Toboli Indonesia 0°38S 120°5E 119 E6
Tobolsk Russia 58°15N 68°10E 106 D7
Tobor Senegal 12°40N 16°15W 138 C1
Tobruk = Tubruq
Libya 32°7N 23°55E 135 B10
Tobyhanna U.S.A. 41°11N 75°25W 175 E9
Tobyl = Tobol →
Russia 58°10N 68°12E 106 D7
Tobyl Kazakhstan 52°41N 62°34E 108 B6
Tocache Nuevo Peru 8°9S 76°26W 188 E3
Tocantinópolis Brazil 6°20S 47°25W 189 E9
Tocantins □ Brazil 10°0S 48°0W 187 F9
Tocantins → Brazil 1°45S 49°10W 187 D9
Toccoa U.S.A. 34°35N 83°19W 177 D13
Toce → Italy 45°56N 8°29E 92 C5
Tochi → Pakistan 32°49N 70°41E 124 C4
Tochigi Japan 36°25N 139°45E 113 F9
Tochigi □ Japan 36°45N 139°45E 113 F9
Tocina Spain 37°37N 5°44W 89 H5
Töcksfors Sweden 59°31N 11°50E 62 E5
Toco Trin. & Tob. 10°49N 60°57W 187 K16
Tocoa Chile 22°5S 69°35W 188 E4
Tocopilla Chile 22°5S 70°10W 190 A1
Tocumwal Australia 35°51S 145°31E 153 C6
Tocuyo → Venezuela 11°3N 68°23W 186 A5
Todd → Australia 24°52S 135°48E 150 C2
Todeli Indonesia 1°40S 124°29E 119 E6
Todenyang Kenya 4°35N 35°56E 142 B4
Todgarh India 25°42N 73°58E 124 G5
Todi Italy 42°47N 12°24E 93 F9
Todos os Santos, B. de
Brazil 12°48S 38°38W 189 C3
Todos Santos Mexico 23°26N 110°13W 180 C2
Todtnau Germany 47°49N 7°56E 77 H3
Toe Hd. U.K. 57°50N 7°8W 65 D1
Toecé Burkina Faso 11°50N 1°16W 139 C4
Toetoes B. U.S.A. 46°42S 168°41E 155 G3
Tofield Canada 53°25N 112°40W 162 C6
Tofino Canada 49°11N 125°55W 162 D3
Tōfsingdalen △ Sweden 62°10N 12°28E 62 B6
Tōgane Japan 35°33N 140°22E 113 G10
Togba Mauritania 17°26N 10°12W 138 B2
Togian, Kepulauan
Indonesia 0°20S 121°50E 119 E6
Togliatti Russia 53°32N 49°24E 86 D9
Togo ■ W. Afr. 8°30N 1°35E 139 D5
Tögrög Mongolia 47°25N 92°13E 109 C12
Togtoh China 40°15N 111°10E 116 D8
Tohma → Turkey 38°29N 38°23E 104 C8
Tōhoku □ Japan 39°50N 141°45E 112 E10
Tōhöm Mongolia 44°27N 108°2E 114 B5
Tohopekaliga, East L.
U.S.A. 28°18N 81°15W 179 G8
Tohopekaliga, L.
U.S.A. 28°12N 81°24W 179 G8
Toibalewe India 10°32N 92°30E 127 J11
Toinya South Sudan 6°17N 29°46E 135 G11
Toiyabe Range U.S.A. 39°30N 117°0W 168 G5
Tojikiston = Tajikistan ■
Asia 38°30N 70°0E 109 E8
Tōjō Japan 34°53N 133°16E 113 G6
Tok U.S.A. 63°20N 142°59W 166 C5
Tokaanu N.Z. 38°58S 175°46E 154 E4
Tokachi-Dake Japan 43°17N 142°5E 112 C11
Tokachi-Gawa →
Japan 42°44N 143°42E 112 C11
Tokaj Hungary 48°8N 21°27E 80 B6
Tokala Indonesia 1°30S 121°40E 119 E6
Tōkamachi Japan 37°8N 138°43E 113 E9
Tokanui N.Z. 46°34S 168°56E 155 G3
Tokar Sudan 18°27N 37°56E 137 C4
Tokara-Rettō Japan 29°37N 129°43E 113 K4
Tokarahi N.Z. 44°56S 170°39E 155 E3
Tokashiki-Shima
Japan 26°11N 127°21E 113 L3
Tokat Turkey 40°22N 36°35E 104 B7
Tokat □ Turkey 40°15N 36°30E 104 B7
Tŏkch'ŏn N. Korea 39°45N 126°18E 115 E14
Tokdo = Liancourt Rocks
Asia 37°15N 131°52E 113 G5
Tokelau Is. ☐ Pac. Oc. 9°0S 171°45E 156 H10
Tokmak Kyrgyzstan 42°49N 75°15E 109 D9
Tokmak Ukraine 47°16N 35°42E 85 J8
Toko Ra. Australia 23°5S 138°20E 150 C2
Tokoro-Gawa → Japan 44°7N 144°5E 112 B12
Tokoroa N.Z. 38°13S 175°53E 154 E4
Toksun China 42°0N 88°0E 110 D6
Toktogul Kyrgyzstan 41°52N 72°50E 109 C8
Tokuno-Shima Japan 27°56N 128°55E 113 L4
Tokushima Japan 34°4N 134°34E 113 G7
Tokushima □ Japan 33°55N 134°0E 113 H7
Tokuyama = Shūnan
Japan 34°3N 131°50E 113 G5

Tōkyō Japan 35°43N 139°45E 113 G9
Tolaga Bay N.Z. 38°21S 178°20E 154 E7
Tolbo Mongolia 48°25N 90°17E 109 C12
Tolbukhin = Dobrich
Bulgaria 43°37N 27°49E 97 C11
Tôle Bi Kazakhstan 43°42N 73°46E 109 D8
Toledo Brazil 24°44S 53°45W 191 A5
Toledo Spain 39°50N 4°2W 88 F6
Toledo Ohio, U.S.A. 41°39N 83°33W 173 E12
Toledo Oreg., U.S.A. 44°37N 123°56W 168 D2
Toledo Wash., U.S.A. 46°26N 122°51W 170 D4
Toledo, Montes de Spain 39°33N 4°20W 89 F6
Toledo Bend Res.
U.S.A. 31°11N 93°34W 176 F8
Tolentino Italy 43°12N 13°17E 93 E10
Tolfa Italy 42°9N 11°56E 93 F8
Tolga Algeria 34°40N 5°22E 136 B5
Tolga Australia 17°15S 145°29E 150 B4
Tolhuaca △ Chile 38°15S 71°50W 192 A2
Toli China 45°57N 83°37E 109 C14
Toliara Madag. 23°21S 43°40E 141 J8
Tolima Colombia 4°40N 75°19W 186 C4
Tolitoli Indonesia 1°5N 120°50E 119 D6
Tolkmicko Poland 54°19N 19°31E 82 D6
Tollarp Sweden 55°55N 13°58E 63 J7
Tollensesee Germany 53°30N 13°13E 76 B9
Tollhouse U.S.A. 37°1N 119°24W 170 H7
Tolmachevo Russia 58°56N 29°51E 84 C5
Tolmezzo Italy 46°24N 13°1E 93 B10
Tolmin Slovenia 46°11N 13°45E 93 B10
Tolna Hungary 46°25N 18°48E 80 D3
Tolna □ Hungary 46°30N 18°30E 80 D3
Tolo, Teluk Indonesia 2°20S 122°10E 119 E6
Tolo Harbour China 22°27N 114°12E 111 a
Tolochin = Talachyn
Belarus 54°25N 29°42E 84 E5
Tolosa Spain 43°8N 2°5W 92 A2
Tolox Spain 36°41N 4°54W 89 J6
Toltén Chile 39°13S 74°14W 192 A2
Toluca Mexico 19°17N 99°40W 181 D5
Tolyatti = Togliatti
Russia 53°32N 49°24E 86 D9
Tom Burke S. Africa 23°5S 28°0E 145 C4
Tom Price Australia 22°40S 117°48E 148 D2
Toma Burkina Faso 12°45N 2°53W 138 C4
Tomah U.S.A. 43°59N 90°30W 172 D8
Tomahawk U.S.A. 45°28N 89°44W 172 C9
Tomai Moldova 46°34N 28°19E 81 D13
Tomakomai Japan 42°38N 141°36E 112 C10
Tomales U.S.A. 38°15N 122°53W 170 G4
Tomales B. U.S.A. 38°15N 123°58W 170 G3
Tomanivi Fiji 17°37S 178°1E 154 a
Tomar Portugal 39°36N 8°25W 87 F2
Tomaros, Oros Greece 39°29N 20°48E 98 B2
Tomarza Turkey 38°27N 35°48E 104 C6
Tomás Barrón Bolivia 17°55S 67°31W 188 D4
Tomashevka Belarus 51°33N 23°36E 81 B10
Tomashpil Ukraine 48°32N 28°31E 81 B13
Tomaszów Lubelski
Poland 50°27N 23°25E 83 H10
Tomaszów Mazowiecki
Poland 51°30N 20°2E 83 G7
Tomatlán Mexico 19°56N 105°15W 180 D3
Tombadonkéa Guinea 11°0N 14°25W 138 C2
Tombador, Serra do
Brazil 12°0S 58°0W 186 F7
Tombigbee → U.S.A. 31°8N 87°57W 177 F11
Tombouctou Mali 16°50N 3°0W 138 B4
Tombouctou □ Mali 19°0N 2°30W 138 B4
Tombstone U.S.A. 31°43N 110°4W 169 L8
Tombua Angola 15°55S 11°55E 144 A1
Tomé Chile 36°36S 72°57W 190 D1
Tome Japan 38°40N 141°20E 112 E10
Tomelilla Sweden 55°33N 13°58E 63 J7
Tomelloso Spain 39°10N 3°2W 89 F7
Tomingley Australia 32°26S 148°16E 153 B8
Tomini Indonesia 0°30N 120°30E 119 D6
Tomini, Teluk Indonesia 0°10S 121°0E 119 E6
Tomiño = O Seixo Spain 41°59N 8°46W 88 D2
Tomintoul U.K. 57°15N 3°23W 65 D5
Tomislavgrad Bos.-H. 43°43N 17°13E 94 C7
Tomkinson Ranges
Australia 26°11S 129°5E 149 E4
Tommot Russia 59°4N 126°20E 107 D13
Tomnop Ta Suos
Cambodia 11°20N 104°15E 121 G5
Tomo → Colombia 5°20N 67°48W 186 B5
Toms Place U.S.A. 37°34N 118°41W 170 H8
Toms River U.S.A. 39°58N 74°12W 175 G10
Tomsk Russia 56°30N 85°5E 106 D9
Tomtabacken Sweden 57°30N 14°30E 63 H8
Tona China 41°51N 114°4E 90 D7
Tonalá Chiapas, Mexico 16°4N 93°45W 181 D6
Tonalá Jalisco, Mexico 20°37N 103°14W 180 C4
Tonale, Passo del Italy 46°15N 10°35E 92 B7
Tonantins Brazil 2°45S 67°45W 186 D5
Tonasket U.S.A. 48°42N 119°26W 168 A4
Tonawanda U.S.A. 43°1N 78°53W 174 D6
Tonb Iran 26°15N 55°15E 129 E7
Tonbridge U.K. 51°11N 0°17E 67 F8
Tondano Indonesia 1°35N 124°54E 119 D6
Tondela Portugal 40°31N 8°5W 88 E2
Tønder Denmark 54°58N 8°50E 63 K2
Tondi India 9°45N 79°4E 127 K4
Tondi Kiwindi Niger 14°28N 2°2E 139 C5
Tondibi Mali 16°39N 0°14W 139 B4
Tondoro Namibia 17°45S 18°50E 144 A2
Tone → Australia 34°25S 116°5E 149 F2
Tone-Gawa → Japan 35°44N 140°51E 113 F9
Tonekābon Iran 36°45N 51°12E 129 B6
Tong Xian China 39°55N 116°35E 114 E9
Tong-yeong S. Korea 34°50N 128°20E 115 G15
Tonga ■ Pac. Oc. 19°50S 174°30W 147 C11
Tonga Trench Pac. Oc. 18°0S 173°0W 145 C5
Tongaat S. Africa 29°33S 31°9E 145 D5
Tongala Australia 36°14S 144°56E 153 C6
Tong'an China 24°37N 118°12E 117 E12
Tongareva = Penrhyn
Cook Is. 9°0S 158°0W 157 H12
Tongariro, Mt. N.Z. 39°8S 175°38E 154 E4
Tongatapu Group
Tonga 21°0S 175°0W 147 E11
Tongbai China 32°40N 113°28E 116 A9
Tongcheng Anhui,
China 31°4N 116°56E 117 B11
Tongcheng Hubei,
China 29°15N 113°50E 117 C9
Tongchuan China 35°6N 109°3E 114 G5

Tongdao China 26°10N 109°42E 116 D7
Tongeren Belgium 50°47N 5°28E 69 D5
Tonggu China 28°31N 114°20E 117 C10
Tonggu Jiao China 22°22N 113°37E 111 a
Tongguan China 34°40N 110°25E 114 G6
Tonghai China 24°10N 102°53E 116 E4
Tonghua China 41°42N 125°58E 115 D13
Tongjiang Heilongjiang, China 47°40N 132°27E 111 B15
Tongjiang Sichuan, China 31°58N 107°11E 116 B6
Tongjosŏn Man N. Korea 39°30N 128°0E 115 E15
Tongking, G. of = Tonkin, G. of Asia 20°0N 108°0E 120 C7
Tongliang China 29°50N 106°3E 116 C6
Tongliao China 43°38N 122°18E 115 C12
Tongling China 30°55N 117°48E 117 B11
Tonglu China 29°45N 119°37E 117 C12
Tongnan = Anyue China 30°9N 105°50E 116 B5
Tongoy Chile 30°16S 71°31W 190 C1
Tongren Guizhou, China 27°43N 109°11E 116 D7
Tongren Qinghai, China 35°25N 102°5E 110 D9
Tongres = Tongeren Belgium 50°47N 5°28E 69 D5
Tongsa Dzong Bhutan 27°31N 90°31E 123 F17
Tongshi China 18°30N 109°20E 117 a
Tongue U.K. 58°29N 4°25W 65 C4
Tongue → U.S.A. 46°25N 105°52W 168 C11
Tongwei China 35°0N 105°5E 114 G3
Tongxiang China 30°39N 120°34E 117 B13
Tongxin China 36°59N 105°58E 114 F3
Tongyang N. Korea 39°9N 126°53E 115 E14
Tongyu China 44°45N 123°4E 115 B12
Tongzhou China 32°12N 121°2E 117 A13
Tongzi China 28°9N 106°49E 116 C6
Tonj South Sudan 7°20N 28°44E 135 G11
Tonk India 26°6N 75°54E 124 F6
Tonkawa U.S.A. 36°41N 97°18W 176 C6
Tonkin = Bac Phan Vietnam 22°0N 105°0E 116 G5
Tonkin, G. of Asia 20°0N 108°0E 120 C7
Tonlé Sap Cambodia 13°0N 104°0E 120 F5
Tonnay-Charente France 45°56N 0°55W 72 C3
Tonneins France 44°23N 0°19E 72 D4
Tonnerre France 47°51N 3°59E 71 E10
Tönning Germany 54°19N 8°56E 76 A4
Tono Japan 39°19N 141°32E 112 E10
Tonopah U.S.A. 38°4N 117°14W 169 G5
Tonosí Panama 7°20N 80°20W 182 E3
Tons → Haryana, India 30°30N 77°39E 124 D7
Tons → Ut. P., India 26°1N 83°33E 125 F10
Tønsberg Norway 59°19N 10°25E 61 G14
Tonto △ U.S.A. 33°39N 111°7W 169 K8
Tonya Turkey 40°53N 39°16E 105 B8
Toobanna Australia 18°42S 146°9E 150 B4
Toodyay Australia 31°34S 116°28E 149 F2
Tooele U.S.A. 40°32N 112°18W 168 F7
Toompine Australia 27°15S 144°19E 151 D3
Toomsboro U.S.A. 32°50N 83°5W 178 C6
Toora Australia 38°39S 146°23E 153 E7
Toora-Khem Russia 52°28N 96°17E 109 B13
Toowoomba Australia 27°32S 151°56E 151 D5
Top Springs Australia 16°37S 131°51E 148 C5
Topalu Romania 44°31N 28°3E 81 F13
Topaz U.S.A. 38°41N 119°30W 170 G7
Topeka U.S.A. 39°3N 95°40W 172 F6
Topl'a → Slovak Rep. 48°45N 21°45E 79 C14
Topley Canada 54°49N 126°18W 162 C3
Toplica → Serbia 43°15N 21°49E 96 C5
Toplița Romania 46°55N 25°20E 81 D10
Topocalma, Pta. Chile 34°10S 72°2W 190 C1
Topock U.S.A. 34°46N 114°29W 171 L12
Topola Serbia 44°17N 20°41E 96 B4
Topolčani Macedonia 41°14N 21°25E 96 E5
Topol'čany Slovak Rep. 48°35N 18°12E 79 C11
Topolnitsa → Bulgaria 42°11N 24°18E 97 D8
Topolobampo Mexico 25°36N 109°3W 180 B3
Topoloveni Romania 44°49N 25°5E 81 F10
Topolovgrad Bulgaria 42°5N 26°20E 97 D10
Topolvățu Mare Romania 45°46N 21°41E 80 E6
Topozero, Ozero Russia 65°35N 32°0E 60 D25
Toppenish U.S.A. 46°23N 120°19W 168 C3
Topraisar Romania 44°1N 28°27E 81 F13
Topusko Croatia 45°18N 15°59E 93 C12
Toquepala Peru 17°24S 70°25W 188 D3
Toqyraūyn → Kazakhstan 46°48N 75°24E 109 C9
Torà Spain 41°49N 1°25E 90 D6
Torata Peru 17°23S 70°1W 188 D3
Torbalı Turkey 38°10N 27°21E 99 C9
Torbat-e Heydārīyeh Iran 35°15N 59°12E 129 C8
Torbat-e Jām Iran 35°16N 60°35E 129 C9
Torbay Canada 47°40N 52°42W 165 C9
Torbay □ U.K. 50°26N 3°31W 67 G4
Torbjörntorp Sweden 58°12N 13°36E 63 F7
Tordesillas Spain 41°30N 5°0W 88 D6
Töreboda Sweden 58°41N 14°7E 63 F8
Torekov Sweden 56°26N 12°37E 63 H6
Torellò Spain 42°3N 2°16E 90 C7
Toreno Spain 42°42N 6°30W 88 C4
Torfaen □ U.K. 51°43N 3°3W 67 F4
Torgau Germany 51°34N 13°0E 76 D8
Torgelow Germany 53°37N 14°1E 76 B10
Torghay Kazakhstan 49°38N 63°29E 108 C6
Torghay → Kazakhstan 48°1N 62°45E 108 C6
Torghay Ustirti Asia 51°0N 63°0E 108 B6
Torghay Zhylghasy Kazakhstan 52°0N 64°30E 108 B6
Torhamn Sweden 56°6N 15°50E 63 H9
Torhout Belgium 51°5N 3°7E 69 C3
Torhovytsya Ukraine 48°36N 25°26E 81 B10
Tori-Shima Japan 30°29N 140°19E 113 J10
Torigni-sur-Vire France 49°3N 0°58W 70 C6
Torija Spain 40°44N 3°2W 90 E1
Torilla Pen. Australia 22°29S 150°5E 150 C5
Torino Italy 45°3N 7°40E 92 C4
Torit South Sudan 4°27N 32°31E 135 H12
Torkamān Iran 37°35N 47°23E 105 D12
Torkovichi Russia 58°51N 30°21E 84 C6
Tormac Romania 45°30N 21°30E 80 E6
Tormes → Spain 41°18N 6°29W 88 D4
Tornado Mt. Canada 49°55N 114°40W 162 D6
Tornal'a Slovak Rep. 48°25N 20°20E 79 C13
Torneå = Tornio Finland 65°50N 24°12E 60 D21
Torneälven → Europe 65°50N 24°12E 60 D21
Torneträsk Sweden 68°24N 19°15E 60 B18
Torngat Mountains Nat. Park △ Canada 59°0N 63°40W 161 F19
Torngat Mts. Canada 59°0N 63°40W 161 F19
Tornio Finland 65°50N 24°12E 60 D21
Tornionjoki = Torneälven → Europe 65°50N 24°12E 60 D21
Tornquist Argentina 38°8S 62°15W 190 D3
Toro Baleares, Spain 39°59N 4°8E 100 B11
Toro Zamora, Spain 41°35N 5°24W 88 D5
Torö Sweden 58°48N 17°50E 63 F11
Toro, Cerro del Chile 29°10S 69°50W 190 B2
Toro ⌓ Uganda 1°5N 30°22E 142 C3
Toro Pk. U.S.A. 33°34N 116°24W 171 M10
Torodi Niger 13°7N 1°47E 139 C5
Törökszentmiklós Hungary 47°11N 20°27E 80 C5
Toronto Australia 33°0S 151°30E 153 B9
Toronto Canada 43°39N 79°20W 174 C5
Toronto U.S.A. 40°28N 80°36W 174 F4
Toronto Lester B. Pearson Int. ✈ (YYZ) Canada 43°46N 79°35W 174 C5
Toropets Russia 56°30N 31°40E 84 D6
Tororo Uganda 0°45N 34°12E 142 B3
Toros Dağları Turkey 37°0N 32°30E 104 D5
Torpa India 22°57N 85°6E 125 H11
Torquay Australia 38°20S 144°19E 152 E6
Torquay U.K. 50°27N 3°32W 67 G4
Torquemada Spain 42°2N 4°19W 88 C6
Torrance U.S.A. 33°50N 118°20W 171 M8
Torrão Portugal 38°16N 8°11W 89 G2
Torre Annunziata Italy 40°45N 14°27E 95 B7
Torre de Moncorvo Portugal 41°12N 7°8W 88 D3
Torre del Campo Spain 37°46N 3°53W 89 H7
Torre del Greco Italy 40°47N 14°22E 95 B7
Torre del Mar Spain 36°44N 4°6W 89 J6
Torre-Pacheco Spain 37°44N 0°57W 91 H4
Torre Péllice Italy 44°49N 7°13E 92 D4
Torreblanca Spain 40°14N 0°12E 90 E5
Torrecampo Spain 38°29N 4°41W 89 G6
Torrecilla en Cameros Spain 42°15N 2°38W 90 C2
Torredembarra Spain 41°9N 1°24E 90 D6
Torredonjimeno Spain 37°46N 3°57W 89 H7
Torrejón de Ardoz Spain 40°27N 3°29W 88 E7
Torrejoncillo Spain 39°54N 6°28W 88 F4
Torrelaguna Spain 40°50N 3°38W 88 E7
Torrelavega Spain 43°20N 4°5W 88 B6
Torremaggiore Italy 41°41N 15°17E 93 G12
Torremolinos Spain 36°38N 4°30W 89 J6
Torrens, L. Australia 31°0S 137°50E 152 A2
Torrens Cr. → Australia 22°23S 145°9E 150 C4
Torrens Creek Australia 20°48S 145°3E 150 C4
Torrent Spain 39°27N 0°28W 91 F4
Torrenueva Spain 38°38N 3°22W 89 G7
Torreón Mexico 25°33N 103°26W 180 B4
Torreperogil Spain 38°2N 3°17W 89 G7
Torres Brazil 29°21S 49°44W 191 B5
Torres Mexico 28°46N 110°47W 180 B2
Torres del Paine △ Chile 51°3S 72°58W 192 D2
Torres Novas Portugal 39°27N 8°33W 89 F2
Torres Strait Australia 9°50S 142°20E 150 a
Torres Vedras Portugal 39°5N 9°15W 89 F1
Torrevieja Spain 37°59N 0°42W 91 H4
Torrey U.S.A. 38°18N 111°25W 168 G8
Torridge → U.K. 51°0N 4°13W 67 G3
Torridon, L. U.K. 57°35N 5°50W 65 D3
Torrijos Spain 39°59N 4°18W 88 F6
Tørring Denmark 55°52N 9°29E 63 J3
Torrington Conn., U.S.A. 41°48N 73°7W 175 E11
Torrington Wyo., U.S.A. 42°4N 104°11W 168 E11
Torroella de Montgrí Spain 42°2N 3°8E 90 C8
Torrox Spain 36°46N 3°57W 89 J7
Torsås Sweden 56°24N 16°0E 63 H9
Torsby Sweden 60°7N 13°0E 62 D6
Torshälla Sweden 59°25N 16°28E 62 E10
Tórshavn Færoe Is. 62°5N 6°56W 60 E9
Torslanda Sweden 57°44N 11°45E 63 G5
Torsö Sweden 58°48N 13°45E 63 F7
Tortola Br. Virgin Is. 18°19N 64°45W 183 e
Tórtoles de Esgueva Spain 41°49N 4°2W 88 D6
Tortolì Italy 39°55N 9°39E 94 C2
Tortona Italy 44°54N 8°52E 92 D5
Tortorici Italy 38°2N 14°49E 95 D7
Tortosa Spain 40°49N 0°31E 90 E5
Tortosa, C. Spain 40°41N 0°52E 90 E5
Tortosendo Portugal 40°15N 7°31W 88 E3
Tortue, Î. de la Haiti 20°5N 72°57W 183 B5
Tortuguero △ Costa Rica 10°31N 83°29W 182 D3
Tortum Turkey 40°19N 41°35E 105 B9
Ţorūd Iran 35°25N 55°5E 129 C7
Torul Turkey 40°34N 39°18E 105 B8
Toruń Poland 53°2N 18°39E 83 E5
Torun Ukraine 48°40N 23°34E 81 B8
Tory Hill Canada 44°58N 78°16W 174 B6
Tory I. Ireland 55°16N 8°14W 64 A3
Torysa → Slovak Rep. 48°39N 21°21E 79 C14
Torzhok Russia 57°5N 34°55E 84 D8
Torzym Poland 52°19N 15°5E 83 F2
Tosa Japan 33°24N 133°23E 113 H6
Tosa-Shimizu Japan 32°52N 132°58E 113 H6
Tosa-Wan Japan 33°15N 133°30E 113 H6
Toscana □ Italy 43°25N 11°0E 92 E8
Toscano, Arcipelago Italy 42°30N 10°30E 92 F7
Toshka Egypt 22°30N 31°53E 137 C3
Toshka Lakes Egypt 22°50N 31°0E 137 C3
Toshkent Uzbekistan 41°20N 69°10E 109 D7
Toshkent □ Uzbekistan 41°0N 69°40E 109 D7
Tosno Russia 59°38N 30°46E 84 C6
Tossa de Mar Spain 41°43N 2°56E 90 D7
Tösse Sweden 58°58N 12°39E 63 F6
Tostado Argentina 29°15S 61°50W 190 B3
Tostedt Germany 53°17N 9°42E 76 B5
Tostón, Pta. de Canary Is. 28°42N 14°2W 100 F5
Tosu Japan 33°22N 130°31E 113 H5
Tosya Turkey 41°1N 34°2E 104 B6
Toszek Poland 50°27N 18°32E 83 H5
Totana Spain 37°45N 1°30W 91 H3
Totebo Sweden 57°38N 16°12E 63 G10
Toteng Botswana 20°22S 22°58E 144 B3
Tôtes France 49°41N 1°2E 70 C8
Tótkomlós Hungary 46°24N 20°45E 80 D5
Totma Russia 60°0N 42°40E 106 D5
Totnes U.K. 50°26N 3°42W 67 G4
Totness Suriname 5°53N 56°19W 187 B7
Toto Nigeria 8°26N 7°5E 139 D6
Totonicapán Guatemala 14°58N 91°12W 182 D1
Totoya, I. Fiji 18°57S 179°50W 154 a
Totten Glacier Antarctica 66°45S 116°10E 55 C8
Tottenham Australia 32°14S 147°21E 153 B7
Tottenham Canada 44°1N 79°49W 174 B5
Tottori Japan 35°30N 134°15E 113 G7
Tottori □ Japan 35°30N 134°12E 113 G7
Touáret Niger 20°17N 7°8E 139 A6
Touat Algeria 27°27N 0°30E 136 C4
Touba Ivory C. 8°22N 7°40W 138 D3
Touba Senegal 14°50N 15°55W 138 C1
Toubkal, Djebel Morocco 31°0N 8°0W 136 B2
Toubkal △ Morocco 31°0N 8°2W 136 B2
Toucy France 47°44N 3°15E 71 E10
Tougan Burkina Faso 13°11N 2°58W 138 C4
Touggourt Algeria 33°6N 6°4E 136 B5
Tougouri Burkina Faso 13°20N 0°30W 139 C4
Tougué Guinea 11°25N 11°50W 138 C2
Toukoto Mali 13°27N 9°52W 138 C3
Toul France 48°40N 5°53E 71 D12
Toulepleu Ivory C. 6°32N 8°24W 138 D3
Touliu Taiwan 23°42N 120°31E 117 F13
Toulon France 43°10N 5°55E 73 E9
Toulouse France 43°37N 1°27E 72 E5
Toulouse Blagnac ✈ (TLS) France 43°37N 1°22E 72 E5
Toummo Niger 22°45N 14°8E 135 D8
Toumodi Ivory C. 6°32N 5°4W 138 D3
Tounan Taiwan 23°41N 120°28E 117 F13
Tounassine, Hamada Algeria 28°48N 5°0W 136 C3
Tounggoo Burma 19°0N 96°30E 123 K20
Toungo Nigeria 8°20N 12°3E 139 D7
Touques → France 49°22N 0°8E 70 C7
Touraine France 47°20N 0°30E 70 E7
Touran = Tūrān △ Iran 35°45N 56°30E 129 C8
Tourcoing France 50°42N 3°10E 71 B10
Touriñán, C. Spain 43°3N 9°18W 88 B1
Tournai Belgium 50°35N 3°25E 69 D3
Tournan-en-Brie France 48°44N 2°46E 71 D9
Tournay France 43°13N 0°13E 72 E4
Tournon-St-Martin France 46°45N 0°58E 70 F7
Tournon-sur-Rhône France 45°4N 4°50E 73 C8
Tournus France 46°35N 4°54E 71 F11
Touros Brazil 5°12S 35°28W 189 B3
Tours France 47°22N 0°40E 70 E7
Toussoro, Mt. C.A.R. 9°7N 23°14E 140 C4
Touws → S. Africa 33°45S 21°11E 144 D3
Touwsrivier S. Africa 33°20S 20°2E 144 D3
Tovarkovskiy Russia 53°40N 38°14E 84 F10
Tovste Ukraine 48°50N 25°44E 81 B10
Tovuz Azerbaijan 41°0N 45°40E 87 K7
Towada Japan 40°37N 141°13E 112 D10
Towada-Hachimantai △ Japan 40°20N 140°55E 112 D10
Towada-Ko Japan 40°28N 140°55E 112 D10
Towanda U.S.A. 41°46N 76°27W 175 E8
Towarri △ Australia 31°50S 150°37E 153 A9
Tower U.S.A. 47°48N 92°17W 172 B7
Towerhill Cr. → Australia 22°28S 144°35E 150 C3
Towner U.S.A. 48°21N 100°25W 172 A3
Townsend Ga., U.S.A. 31°33N 81°31W 178 D8
Townsend Mont., U.S.A. 46°19N 111°31W 168 C8
Townshend I. Australia 22°10S 150°31E 150 C5
Townsville Australia 19°15S 146°45E 150 B4
Towot South Sudan 6°12N 34°25E 142 A3
Towraghondī Afghan. 35°13N 62°16E 108 E6
Towson U.S.A. 39°24N 76°36W 173 F15
Towuti, Danau Indonesia 2°45S 121°32E 119 E6
Toxkan He → China 41°8N 80°11E 109 D10
Tōya-Ko Japan 42°35N 140°51E 112 C10
Toyama Japan 36°40N 137°15E 113 F8
Toyama □ Japan 36°45N 137°30E 113 F8
Toyama-Wan Japan 37°0N 137°30E 113 F8
Toyapakeh Indonesia 8°41S 115°29E 119 K18
Toyohashi Japan 34°45N 137°25E 113 G8
Toyokawa Japan 34°48N 137°27E 113 G8
Toyonaka Japan 34°46N 135°28E 113 G7
Toyooka Japan 35°35N 134°48E 113 G7
Toyota Japan 35°3N 137°7E 113 G8
Tozeur Tunisia 33°56N 8°8E 136 B5
Tozeur □ Tunisia 34°0N 8°5E 136 B5
Tqibuli Georgia 42°26N 43°0E 87 J6
Tqvarcheli Georgia 42°47N 41°42E 87 J5
Trá Lí = Tralee Ireland 52°16N 9°42W 64 D2
Trá Mhór = Tramore Ireland 52°10N 7°10W 64 D4
Tra On Vietnam 9°58N 105°55E 121 H5
Tra Vinh Vietnam 9°50N 106°15E 121 H6
Trabancos → Spain 41°36N 5°15W 88 D5
Traben-Trarbach Germany 49°57N 7°7E 77 F3
Trabzon Turkey 41°0N 39°45E 105 B8
Trabzon □ Turkey 41°10N 39°45E 105 B8
Tracadie Canada 47°30N 64°55W 165 C7
Tracy Canada 46°1N 73°9W 164 C5
Tracy Calif., U.S.A. 37°44N 121°26W 170 H5
Tracy Minn., U.S.A. 44°14N 95°37W 172 C6
Tradate Italy 45°43N 8°54E 92 C5
Trade Town Liberia 5°40N 9°50W 138 D3
Trafalgar Australia 38°14S 146°12E 153 E7
Trafalgar, C. Spain 36°10N 6°2W 89 J4
Tragonhsi Greece 37°27N 25°29E 99 D7
Traian Brăila, Romania 45°11N 27°44E 81 E12
Traian Tulcea, Romania 45°2N 28°15E 81 E13
Traiguén Chile 38°15S 72°41W 192 A2
Trail Canada 49°5N 117°40W 162 D5
Traill Ø Greenland 72°30N 23°0W 57 C8
Trainor L. Canada 60°24N 120°17W 162 A4
Trakai △ Lithuania 54°30N 25°10E 61 J21
Trákhonas Cyprus 35°12N 33°21E 101 D12
Tralee Ireland 52°16N 9°42W 64 D2
Tralee B. Ireland 52°17N 9°55W 64 D2
Tram Chim △ Vietnam 10°43N 105°31E 121 G5
Tramore Ireland 52°10N 7°10W 64 D4
Tramore B. Ireland 52°9N 7°10W 64 D4
Tramuntana, Serra de Spain 39°48N 2°54E 100 B9
Tran Ninh, Cao Nguyen Laos 19°30N 103°10E 120 C4
Tranås Sweden 58°3N 14°59E 63 F8
Tranbjerg Denmark 56°6N 10°9E 63 H4
Trancas Argentina 26°11S 65°20W 190 B2
Trancoso Portugal 40°49N 7°21W 88 E3
Tranebjerg Denmark 55°51N 10°36E 63 J4
Tranemo Sweden 57°30N 13°20E 63 G7
Trang Thailand 7°33N 99°38E 121 J2
Trangan Indonesia 6°40S 134°20E 119 F8
Trangie Australia 32°4S 148°0E 153 B8
Trångsviken Sweden 63°19N 13°59E 62 A7
Trani Italy 41°17N 16°25E 95 A9
Tranoroa Madag. 24°42S 45°4E 141 J9
Tranqueras Uruguay 31°13S 55°45W 191 C4
Transantarctic Mts. Antarctica 85°0S 170°0W 55 E12
Transcarpathia = Zakarpattya □ Ukraine 48°20N 23°20E 81 B8
Transilvania Romania 46°30N 24°0E 81 D9
Transilvanian Alps = Carpaţii Meridionali Romania 45°30N 25°0E 81 E9
Transnistria = Stînga Nistrului □ Moldova 47°20N 29°15E 81 C14
Transtrand Sweden 61°6N 13°20E 62 C7
Transtrandsfjällen Sweden 61°8N 13°0E 62 C6
Transylvania = Transilvania Romania 46°30N 24°0E 81 D9
Trápani Italy 38°1N 12°29E 94 D5
Trapper Pk. U.S.A. 45°54N 114°18W 168 D6
Traralgon Australia 38°12S 146°34E 153 E7
Traryd Sweden 56°35N 13°45E 63 H7
Trarza □ Mauritania 18°0N 15°0W 138 B2
Trasacco Italy 41°57N 13°32E 93 G10
Trăscău, Munţii Romania 46°14N 23°14E 81 D8
Trasimeno, L. Italy 43°8N 12°6E 93 E9
Träslövsläge Sweden 57°4N 12°16E 63 G6
Trasvase Tajo-Segura, Canal de Spain 40°15N 2°55W 90 E2
Trat Thailand 12°14N 102°33E 121 F4
Tratani → Pakistan 29°19N 68°20E 124 E3
Traun Austria 48°14N 14°15E 78 C7
Traunreut Germany 47°57N 12°36E 77 H8
Traunsee Austria 47°55N 13°50E 78 D6
Traunstein Germany 47°52N 12°37E 77 H8
Travellers L. Australia 33°20S 142°0E 152 B5
Travemünde Germany 53°57N 10°52E 76 B6
Travers, Mt. N.Z. 42°1S 172°45E 155 C7
Traverse City U.S.A. 44°46N 85°38W 173 C11
Travis, L. U.S.A. 30°24N 97°55W 176 F6
Travnik Bos.-H. 44°17N 17°39E 80 F2
Trawbreaga B. Ireland 55°20N 7°25W 64 A4
Trbovlje Slovenia 46°12N 15°5E 93 B12
Treasure Island U.S.A. 27°46N 82°46W 179 H7
Trébbia → Italy 45°4N 9°41E 92 C6
Trebel → Germany 53°54N 13°2E 76 B9
Trébeurden France 48°46N 3°35W 70 D3
Trebević △ Bos.-H. 43°20N 18°45E 80 G3
Třebíč Czech Rep. 49°14N 15°55E 78 B8
Trebinje Bos.-H. 42°44N 18°22E 96 D2
Trebisacce Italy 39°52N 16°32E 95 C9
Trebišnjica → Bos.-H. 42°47N 18°8E 96 D2
Trebišov Slovak Rep. 48°38N 21°41E 79 C14
Trebižat → Bos.-H. 43°15N 17°30E 93 E14
Trebnje Slovenia 45°54N 15°1E 93 C12
Třeboň Czech Rep. 49°1N 14°48E 78 B7
Trebonne Australia 18°37S 146°5E 150 B4
Třeboňsko ⌓ Czech Rep. 49°1N 14°49E 78 B7
Trebujena Spain 36°52N 6°11W 89 J4
Trecate Italy 45°26N 8°44E 92 C5
Trefaldwyn = Montgomery U.K. 52°34N 3°8W 67 E4
Trefynwy = Monmouth U.K. 51°48N 2°42W 67 F5
Tregaron U.K. 52°14N 3°56W 67 E4
Tregnago Italy 45°31N 11°10E 93 C8
Tregrosse Is. Australia 17°41S 150°43E 150 B5
Tréguier France 48°47N 3°16W 70 D3
Trégunc France 47°51N 3°51W 70 E3
Treherne Canada 49°38N 98°42W 163 D9
Tréia Italy 43°19N 13°19E 93 E10
Treignac France 45°32N 1°48E 72 C5
Treinta y Tres Uruguay 33°16S 54°17W 191 C5
Treis-karden Germany 50°10N 7°18E 77 E3
Treklyano Bulgaria 42°33N 22°36E 96 D6
Trelawney Zimbabwe 17°30S 30°30E 145 A5
Trélazé France 47°26N 0°30W 70 E6
Trelew Argentina 43°10S 65°20W 192 B3
Trélissac France 45°11N 0°47E 72 C4
Trelleborg Sweden 55°20N 13°10E 63 J7
Tremadog Bay U.K. 52°51N 4°18W 66 E3
Trémiti Italy 42°8N 15°30E 93 F12
Tremonton U.S.A. 41°43N 112°10W 168 F7
Tremp Spain 42°10N 0°52E 90 C5
Trenche → Canada 47°46N 72°53W 164 C5
Trenčiansky □ Slovak Rep. 48°45N 18°20E 79 C11
Trenčín Slovak Rep. 48°52N 18°4E 79 C11
Trenggalek Indonesia 8°3S 111°43E 119 H14
Trenque Lauquen Argentina 36°5S 62°45W 190 D3
Trent → Canada 44°6N 77°34W 174 B7
Trent → U.K. 53°41N 0°42W 66 D7
Trentino-Alto Adige □ Italy 46°30N 11°20E 93 B8
Trento Italy 46°4N 11°8E 92 B8
Trenton Canada 44°10N 77°34W 174 B7
Trenton Fla., U.S.A. 29°37N 82°49W 179 F7
Trenton Mo., U.S.A. 40°5N 93°37W 172 E7
Trenton N.J., U.S.A. 40°14N 74°46W 175 F10
Trenton Nebr., U.S.A. 40°11N 101°1W 172 E3
Trenton S.C., U.S.A. 33°45N 81°51W 178 B8
Trepassey Canada 46°43N 53°25W 165 C9
Trepuzzi Italy 40°24N 18°4E 95 B11
Tres Arroyos Argentina 38°26S 60°20W 190 D3
Três Corações Brazil 21°44S 45°15W 191 A6
Três Lagoas Brazil 20°50S 51°43W 187 H8
Tres Lagos Argentina 49°35S 71°25W 192 C2
Tres Lomas Argentina 36°27S 62°51W 190 D3
Três Marias, Represa Brazil 18°12S 45°15W 189 D1
Tres Montes, C. Chile 46°50S 75°30W 192 C1
Tres Pinos U.S.A. 36°48N 121°19W 170 J5
Três Pontas Brazil 21°23S 45°29W 191 A6
Tres Puentes Chile 27°50S 70°15W 190 B1
Tres Puntas, C. Argentina 47°0S 66°0W 192 C3
Três Rios Brazil 22°6S 43°15W 191 A7
Tres Valles Mexico 18°15N 96°8W 181 D5
Tresco U.K. 49°57N 6°20W 67 H1
Treska → Macedonia 42°0N 21°20E 96 E5
Treskavica Bos.-H. 43°40N 18°20E 80 G3
Trespaderne Spain 42°47N 3°24W 88 C7
Tresticklan △ Sweden 59°0N 11°42E 63 F5
Trets France 43°27N 5°41E 73 E9
Treuchtlingen Germany 48°58N 10°54E 77 G6
Treuenbrietzen Germany 52°5N 12°52E 76 C8
Trevi Italy 42°52N 12°45E 93 F9
Trevíglio Italy 45°31N 9°35E 92 C6
Trevínca, Peña Spain 42°15N 6°46W 88 C4
Treviño Spain 42°44N 2°45W 88 C8
Treviso Italy 45°40N 12°15E 93 C9
Trévoux France 45°57N 4°47E 73 C8
Trgovište Serbia 42°20N 22°10E 96 D6
Triabunna Australia 42°30S 147°55E 151 G4
Triangle Zimbabwe 21°2S 31°28E 145 B5
Triaucourt-en-Argonne France 48°59N 5°2E 71 D12
Tribal Areas □ Pakistan 33°0N 70°0E 124 C4
Tribsees Germany 54°5N 12°44E 76 A8
Tribulation, C. Australia 16°5S 145°29E 150 B4
Tribune U.S.A. 38°28N 101°45W 172 F3
Tricárico Italy 40°37N 16°9E 95 B9
Tricase Italy 39°56N 18°22E 95 C11
Trichinopoly = Tiruchchirappalli India 10°45N 78°45E 127 J4
Trichonida, L. Greece 38°34N 21°30E 98 C3
Trichur = Thrissur India 10°30N 76°18E 127 J3
Trichy = Tiruchchirappalli India 10°45N 78°45E 127 J4
Trida Australia 33°1S 145°1E 153 B6
Trier Germany 49°45N 6°38E 77 F2
Trieste Italy 45°40N 13°46E 93 C10
Trieste, G. di Italy 45°40N 13°35E 93 C10
Trieux → France 48°43N 3°9W 70 D3
Triggiano Italy 41°4N 16°55E 95 A9
Triglav Slovenia 46°21N 13°50E 93 B10
Triglavski △ Slovenia 46°20N 13°50E 93 B10
Trigno → Italy 42°4N 14°48E 93 F11
Trigueros Spain 37°24N 6°50W 89 H4
Trikala Greece 39°34N 21°47E 98 B3
Trikeri Greece 39°6N 23°5E 98 B5
Trikomo Cyprus 35°17N 33°52E 101 D12
Trikora, Puncak Indonesia 4°15S 138°45E 119 E9
Trilby U.S.A. 28°28N 82°12W 179 G7
Trilj Croatia 43°38N 16°42E 93 E13
Trillo Spain 40°42N 2°35W 90 E2
Trim Ireland 53°33N 6°48W 64 C5
Trimbak India 19°56N 73°33E 126 E1
Trimmu Dam Pakistan 31°10N 72°8E 124 D5
Trincomalee Sri Lanka 8°38N 81°15E 127 K5
Trindade Atl. Oc. 20°20S 29°50W 56 J9
Trindade Brazil 16°40S 49°30W 187 G9
Třinec Czech Rep. 49°41N 18°39E 79 B11
Trinidad Bolivia 14°46S 64°50W 186 F6
Trinidad Cuba 21°48N 80°0W 182 B4
Trinidad Trin. & Tob. 10°30N 61°15W 183 D7
Trinidad Uruguay 33°30S 56°50W 190 C4
Trinidad U.S.A. 37°10N 104°31W 169 H11
Trinidad, G. Chile 49°55S 75°25W 192 C1
Trinidad, I. Argentina 39°10S 62°0W 192 A4
Trinidad & Tobago ■ W. Indies 10°30N 61°20W 186 A6
Trinitápoli Italy 41°21N 16°5E 95 A9
Trinity Canada 48°59N 53°55W 165 C9
Trinity U.S.A. 30°57N 95°22W 176 F7
Trinity → Calif., U.S.A. 41°11N 123°42W 168 F2
Trinity → Tex., U.S.A. 29°45N 94°43W 176 G7
Trinity B. Canada 48°20N 53°10W 165 C9
Trinity Hills Trin. & Tob. 10°7N 61°7W 187 K15
Trinity Is. U.S.A. 56°33N 154°25W 166 D9
Trinity Range U.S.A. 40°10N 118°40W 168 F4
Trinkat India 8°5N 93°30E 127 K11
Trinkitat Sudan 18°45N 37°51E 137 D4
Trino Italy 45°12N 8°18E 92 C5
Trinway U.S.A. 40°9N 82°1W 174 F2
Triolet Mauritius 20°4S 57°32E 141 d
Trionto, C. Italy 39°37N 16°43E 95 C9
Triora Italy 44°1N 7°46E 92 D4
Tripoli = Tarābulus Lebanon 34°31N 35°50E 130 A4
Tripoli = Tarābulus Libya 32°49N 13°7E 135 B8
Tripoli Greece 37°31N 22°25E 98 D4
Tripolitania = Tarābulus Libya 31°0N 13°0E 135 B8
Tripura □ India 24°0N 92°0E 123 H18
Tripylos Cyprus 34°59N 32°41E 101 E11
Trischen Germany 54°4N 8°40E 76 A4
Tristan da Cunha Atl. Oc. 37°6S 12°20W 133 K2
Trisul India 30°19N 79°47E 125 D8
Triton I. S. China Sea 15°47N 111°12E 118 A4
Trivandrum = Thiruvananthapuram India 8°41N 77°0E 127 K3
Trivento Italy 41°47N 14°33E 93 G11
Trizin Greece 37°25N 23°15E 98 D5
Trnava Slovak Rep. 48°23N 17°35E 79 C10
Trnavský □ Slovak Rep. 48°30N 17°45E 79 C10
Troarn France 49°11N 0°11W 70 C6
Trochu Canada 51°50N 113°13W 162 C6
Trodely I. Canada 52°15N 79°26W 164 B4
Troebratskīy Kazakhstan 54°25N 66°4E 109 B7
Trogir Croatia 43°32N 16°15E 93 E13
Troglav Croatia 43°56N 16°36E 93 E13
Tróia Italy 41°22N 15°18E 95 A8
Troilus, L. Canada 50°50N 74°35W 164 B5
Troina Italy 37°47N 14°36E 95 E7
Trois Fourches, Cap des Morocco 35°26N 2°58W 136 A3
Trois-Pistoles Canada 48°5N 69°10W 165 C6
Trois-Rivières Canada 46°25N 72°34W 164 C5
Trois-Rivières Guadeloupe 15°57N 61°40W 182 b
Troisdorf Germany 50°48N 7°11E 76 E3
Troitsk Russia 54°10N 61°35E 108 B6
Troitsko Pechorsk Russia 62°40N 56°10E 106 C6
Troitskoye Russia 46°26N 44°15E 87 G7
Troll Antarctica 72°0S 2°30E 55 D3
Trölladyngja Iceland 64°54N 17°16W 60 D5
Trollhättan Sweden 58°17N 12°20E 63 F6
Trollheimen Norway 62°46N 9°1E 60 E13
Trombetas → Brazil 1°55S 55°35W 187 D7
Tromelin I. Ind. Oc. 15°52S 54°25E 146 F4
Tromsø Norway 69°40N 18°56E 60 B18
Tron Thailand 17°28N 100°7E 120 D3
Trona U.S.A. 35°46N 117°23W 171 K9
Tronador, Mte. Argentina 41°10S 71°50W 192 B2
Trøndelag Norway 64°17N 11°50E 60 D14
Trondheim Norway 63°36N 10°25E 60 E14
Trondheimsfjorden Norway 63°35N 10°30E 60 E14
Trönninge Sweden 56°37N 12°51E 63 H6
Tronto → Italy 42°54N 13°55E 93 F10
Troodos Cyprus 34°55N 32°52E 101 E11
Troon U.K. 55°33N 4°39W 65 F4
Tropea Italy 38°41N 15°54E 95 D8
Tropic U.S.A. 37°37N 112°5W 169 H7
Tropojë Albania 42°23N 20°10E 96 D4
Trosa Sweden 58°54N 17°33E 63 F11
Trostan U.K. 55°3N 6°10W 64 A5
Trostberg Germany 48°1N 12°33E 77 G8
Trostyanets Sumy, Ukraine 50°33N 34°59E 85 G8
Trostyanets Vinnyts'ka, Ukraine 48°31N 29°11E 81 B14
Trou Gras Pt. St. Lucia 13°51N 60°53W 183 f
Trout → Canada 61°19N 119°51W 162 A5
Trout L. N.W.T., Canada 60°40N 121°14W 162 A4
Trout L. Ont., Canada 51°20N 93°15W 163 C10
Trout Lake Canada 56°30N 114°32W 162 B6
Trout Lake U.S.A. 46°0N 121°32W 170 E5
Trout River Canada 49°29N 58°8W 165 C8
Trout Run U.S.A. 41°23N 77°3W 174 E7
Trouville-sur-Mer France 49°21N 0°5E 70 C7
Trowbridge U.K. 51°18N 2°12W 67 F5
Troy Turkey 39°57N 26°12E 99 B8
Troy Ala., U.S.A. 31°48N 85°58W 178 D4
Troy Kans., U.S.A. 39°47N 95°5W 172 F6
Troy Mo., U.S.A. 38°59N 90°59W 172 F8
Troy Mont., U.S.A. 48°28N 115°53W 168 B6
Troy N.Y., U.S.A. 42°44N 73°41W 175 D11
Troy Ohio, U.S.A. 40°2N 84°12W 173 E11
Troy Pa., U.S.A. 41°47N 76°47W 175 E8
Troyan Bulgaria 42°57N 24°43E 97 D8
Troyes France 48°19N 4°3E 71 D11
Trpanj Croatia 43°1N 17°15E 93 E14
Trstenik Serbia 43°36N 21°0E 96 C5
Trubchevsk Russia 52°33N 33°47E 85 F7
Truchas Pk. U.S.A. 35°58N 105°39W 169 J11
Trucial States = United Arab Emirates ■ Asia 23°50N 54°0E 129 F7
Truckee U.S.A. 39°20N 120°11W 170 F6
Trudfront Russia 45°56N 47°40E 87 H8
Trudovoye Russia 43°17N 132°5E 112 C6
Trujillo Honduras 16°0N 86°0W 182 C2
Trujillo Peru 8°6S 79°0W 188 B2
Trujillo Spain 39°28N 5°55W 89 F5
Trujillo U.S.A. 35°32N 104°42W 169 J11
Trujillo Venezuela 9°22N 70°38W 186 B4
Truk Micronesia 7°25N 151°46E 156 G7
Trumann U.S.A. 35°41N 90°31W 177 D9
Trumansburg U.S.A. 42°33N 76°40W 175 D8
Trumbull, Mt. U.S.A. 36°25N 113°19W 169 H7
Trŭn Bulgaria 42°51N 22°38E 96 D6
Trun France 48°50N 0°2E 70 D7
Trundle Australia 32°53S 147°35E 153 B7
Trung Lon, Hon Vietnam 8°36N 106°8E 121 H6
Trung-Phan Vietnam 17°0N 109°0E 120 D6
Truong Sa, Dao = Spratly I. S. China Sea 8°38N 111°55E 118 C4
Truro Australia 34°24S 139°9E 152 C3
Truro Canada 45°21N 63°14W 165 C7
Truro U.K. 50°16N 5°4W 67 G2
Truskavets Ukraine 49°17N 23°30E 75 D12
Trŭstenik Bulgaria 43°31N 24°28E 97 C8
Trustrup Denmark 56°20N 10°46E 63 H4
Trutch Canada 57°44N 122°57W 162 B4
Truth or Consequences U.S.A. 33°8N 107°15W 169 K10
Trutnov Czech Rep. 50°37N 15°54E 78 A8
Truyère → France 44°38N 2°34E 72 D6
Tryavna Bulgaria 42°54N 25°25E 97 D9
Tryonville U.S.A. 41°42N 79°48W 174 E5
Tryphena N.Z. 36°18S 175°28E 154 C4
Trzcianka Poland 53°3N 16°25E 83 E3
Trzciel Poland 52°23N 15°50E 83 F2
Trzcińsko Zdrój Poland 52°58N 14°35E 83 F1
Trzebiatów Poland 54°3N 15°18E 82 D2
Trzebiez Poland 53°38N 14°31E 82 E1
Trzebnica Poland 51°20N 17°1E 83 G4
Trzemeszno Poland 52°33N 17°48E 83 F4
Tržič Slovenia 46°22N 14°18E 93 B11
Tsagaannur Mongolia 49°32N 89°42E 109 C11
Tsagan Aman Russia 47°34N 46°43E 87 G8
Tsala Apopka L. U.S.A. 28°53N 82°19W 179 G7
Tsamandas Greece 39°46N 20°21E 98 B2
Tsandi Namibia 17°42S 14°50E 144 A1
Tsaratanana Madag. 16°47S 47°39E 141 G9
Tsarevo Bulgaria 42°28N 25°52E 97 D9
Tsaritsani Greece 39°53N 22°14E 98 B4
Tsau Botswana 20°8S 22°22E 144 B3
Tsavo Kenya 2°59S 38°28E 142 C4
Tsavo East △ Kenya 2°44S 38°47E 142 C4
Tsavo West △ Kenya 3°19S 37°57E 142 C4
Tsentralen Balkan △ Bulgaria 42°40N 24°45E 97 D8
Tsentralnyy □ Russia 52°0N 40°0E 106 D4
Tses Namibia 25°58S 18°8E 144 C2
Tsetserleg Mongolia 47°36N 101°32E 110 B9
Tseung Kwan China 22°20N 114°15E 111 a
Tsévié Togo 6°25N 1°20E 139 D5
Tshabong Botswana 26°2S 22°29E 144 C3
Tshane Botswana 24°5S 21°54E 144 B3
Tshela Dem. Rep. of the Congo 4°57S 13°4E 140 E2
Tshesebe Botswana 21°51S 27°32E 145 B4
Tshibeke Dem. Rep. of the Congo 2°40S 28°35E 142 C2
Tshibinda Dem. Rep. of the Congo 2°23S 28°43E 142 C2
Tshikapa Dem. Rep. of the Congo 6°28S 20°48E 140 F4
Tshilenge Dem. Rep. of the Congo 6°17S 23°48E 142 D1
Tshinsenda Dem. Rep. of the Congo 12°20S 28°0E 143 E2
Tshofa Dem. Rep. of the Congo 5°13S 25°16E 142 D2
Tshwane = Pretoria S. Africa 25°44S 28°12E 145 C4
Tshwane Botswana 22°24S 22°1E 144 B3
Tsigara Botswana 20°22S 25°54E 144 B4
Tsihombe Madag. 25°10S 45°41E 141 K9
Tsiigehtchic Canada 67°15N 134°0W 160 D5
Ts'il-os ⌓ Canada 51°9N 123°59W 162 C4
Tsimlyansk Russia 47°40N 42°6E 87 G6

Tsimlyansk Res. = Tsimlyanskoye Vdkhr. Russia 48°0N 43°0E 87 F6
Tsimlyanskoye Vdkhr. Russia 48°0N 43°0E 87 F6
Tsinan = Jinan China 36°38N 117°1E 114 F9
Tsineng S. Africa 27°5S 23°5E 144 A3
Tsing Yi China 22°21N 114°6E 111 a
Tsinghai = Qinghai □ China 36°0N 98°0E 110 D8
Tsingtao = Qingdao China 36°5N 120°20E 115 F11
Tsirigo = Kythira Greece 36°8N 23°0E 98 E5
Tsiteli-Tsqaro = Dedoplis Tsqaro Georgia 41°33N 46°0E 87 K8
Tsitsikamma △ S. Africa 34°3S 23°40E 144 E3
Tsivilsk Russia 55°50N 47°25E 86 C8
Tskhinvali Georgia 42°14N 44°1E 87 J7
Tsna → Russia 54°55N 41°58E 86 D6
Tsnori Georgia 41°40N 45°57E 87 K7
Tso Moriri, L. India 32°50N 78°20E 125 C8
Tsobis Namibia 19°27S 17°30E 144 A2
Tsodilo Hills Botswana 18°49S 21°43E 144 A3
Tsogttsetsiy = Baruunsuu Mongolia 43°43N 105°35E 114 C3
Tsolo S. Africa 31°18S 28°37E 145 E4
Tsomo S. Africa 32°0S 27°42E 145 E4
Tsu Japan 34°45N 136°25E 113 G8
Tsu L. Canada 60°40N 111°52E 162 A6
Tsuchiura Japan 36°5N 140°15E 113 F10
Tsuen Wan China 22°22N 114°6E 111 a
Tsugaru-Hantō Japan 41°0N 140°30E 112 D10
Tsugaru-Kaikyō Japan 41°35N 141°0E 112 D10
Tsumeb Namibia 19°9S 17°44E 144 A2
Tsumis Namibia 23°39S 17°29E 144 B2
Tsuruga Japan 35°45N 136°2E 113 G8
Tsurugi-San Japan 33°51N 134°6E 113 H7
Tsuruoka Japan 38°44N 139°50E 112 E9
Tsushima Gifu, Japan 35°10N 136°43E 113 G8
Tsushima Nagasaki, Japan 34°20N 129°20E 113 G4
Tsuyama Japan 35°3N 134°0E 113 G7
Tsvetkovo Ukraine 49°8N 31°33E 85 H6
Tsyelyakhany Belarus 52°30N 25°46E 75 B13

Tulancingo Mexico 20°5N 98°22W 181 C5
Tulare Serbia 42°48N 21°28E 96 D5
Tulare U.S.A. 36°13N 119°21W 170 J7
Tulare Lake Bed U.S.A. 36°0N 119°48W 170 K7
Tularosa U.S.A. 33°5N 106°1W 169 K10
Tulbagh S. Africa 33°16S 19°6E 144 D2
Tulcán Ecuador 0°48N 77°43W 186 C3
Tulcea Romania 45°13N 28°46E 81 E13
Tulcea □ Romania 45°0N 28°30E 81 E13
Tulchyn Ukraine 48°41N 28°49E 81 B13
Tüledi Araldary Kazakhstan 45°2N 50°16E 87 H10
Tüleh Iran 34°35N 52°33E 129 C7
Tulemalu L. Canada 62°58N 99°25W 163 A9
Tulgheş Romania 46°58N 25°45E 81 D10
Tuli Zimbabwe 21°58S 29°13E 143 G2
Tulia U.S.A. 34°32N 101°46W 176 D4
Tuliszków Poland 52°5N 18°18E 83 F5
Tulita Canada 64°57N 125°30W 160 E6
Tülkarm West Bank 32°19N 35°2E 138 C4
Tulla Ireland 52°53N 8°46W 64 D3
Tullahoma U.S.A. 35°22N 86°13W 177 D11
Tullamore Australia 32°39S 147°36E 153 E7
Tullamore Ireland 53°16N 7°31W 64 C4
Tulle France 45°16N 1°46E 72 C5
Tulln Austria 48°20N 16°4E 78 D9
Tullow Ireland 52°49N 6°45W 64 D5
Tulnici Romania 45°51N 26°38E 81 E11
Tulovo Bulgaria 42°33N 25°32E 97 D9
Tulsa U.S.A. 36°10N 95°55W 176 C7
Tulsequah Canada 58°39N 133°35W 162 B2
Tuluá Colombia 4°6N 76°11W 186 C3
Tulucesti Romania 45°34N 28°2E 81 E13
Tulum Mexico 20°13N 87°28W 182 C7
Tulun Russia 54°32N 100°35E 107 D11
Tulungagung Indonesia 8°5S 111°54E 119 H14
Tuma → Russia 55°10N 40°30E 84 E11
Tuma → Nic. 13°6N 84°35W 182 D3
Tumacacori △ U.S.A. 31°35N 111°6W 169 L8
Tumaco Colombia 1°50N 78°45W 186 C3
Tumakuru = Tumkur India 13°18N 77°6E 127 H3
Tumatumari Guyana 5°20N 58°55W 186 B7
Tumba Sweden 59°12N 17°48E 62 E11
Tumba, Dem. Rep. of the Congo 0°50S 18°0E 140 E3
Tumbarumba Australia 35°44S 148°0E 153 C8
Tumbaya Argentina 23°50S 65°26W 190 A2
Tumbes Peru 3°37S 80°27W 188 A1
Tumbes □ Peru 3°50S 80°30W 188 A1
Tumbler Ridge Canada 55°8N 121°0W 162 B4
Tumby Bay Australia 34°21S 136°8E 152 C2
Tumd Youqi China 40°30N 110°30E 114 D6
Tumen China 43°0N 129°50E 112 C4
Tumen Jiang → China 42°20N 130°35E 115 C16
Tumeremo Venezuela 7°18N 61°30W 186 B6
Tumiritinga Brazil 18°58S 41°38W 189 D2
Tumkur India 13°18N 77°6E 127 H3
Tump Pakistan 26°7N 62°16E 122 F3
Tumpat Malaysia 6°11N 102°10E 121 a4
Tumsar India 21°26N 79°45E 126 D4
Tumu Ghana 10°56N 1°56W 138 C4
Tumucumaque, Serra Brazil 2°0N 55°0W 187 C8
Tumupasa Bolivia 14°9S 67°55W 188 C4
Tumut Australia 35°16S 148°13E 153 C8
Tumwater U.S.A. 47°1N 122°54W 170 C4
Tun Sweden 58°26N 12°43E 63 F6
Tuna India 22°59N 70°5E 124 H4
Tunapuna Trin. & Tob. 10°38N 61°24W 187 K15
Tunas de Zaza Cuba 21°39N 79°34W 182 B4
Tunbridge Wells = Royal Tunbridge Wells U.K. 51°7N 0°16E 67 F8
Tunçbilek Turkey 39°37N 29°29E 99 B11
Tunceli Turkey 39°6N 39°31E 105 C8
Tunceli □ Turkey 39°5N 39°35E 105 C8
Tunchang China 19°21N 110°5E 117 a
Tuncurry Australia 32°17S 152°29E 153 E6
Tundla India 27°12N 78°17E 124 F8
Tundubai Sudan 18°36N 28°35E 137 D2
Tunduru Tanzania 11°8S 37°25E 143 E4
Tundzha → Bulgaria 41°40N 26°35E 97 C10
Tunga → India 15°57N 78°15E 127 G2
Tungabhadra → India 15°57N 78°15E 127 G2
Tungabhadra Dam India 15°0N 75°50E 127 G2
Tungla Nic. 13°24N 84°21W 182 D3
Tungsha Tao = Dongsha Dao S. China Sea 20°45N 116°43E 111 G12
Tungshih Taiwan 24°15N 120°43E 117 E13
Tungsten Canada 61°57N 128°16W 162 A3
Tunguska, Nizhnyaya → Russia 65°48N 88°4E 107 C9
Tunguska, Podkamennaya → Russia 61°50N 90°13E 107 C10
Tuni India 17°22N 82°36E 126 F6
Tunica U.S.A. 34°41N 90°23W 177 D9
Tunis Tunisia 36°50N 10°11E 136 A6
Tunis □ Tunisia 36°46N 10°10E 136 A6
Tunis ✈ (TUN) Tunisia 36°52N 10°14E 94 F3
Tunis, Golfe de Tunisia 37°0N 10°30E 136 A6
Tunisia ■ Africa 33°30N 9°10E 136 B5
Tunja Colombia 5°33N 73°25W 186 B4
Tunkhannock U.S.A. 41°32N 75°57W 175 E9
Tunkinsky △ Russia 51°45N 102°50E 107 D11
Tunliu China 36°13N 112°52E 114 F7
Tunnel Creek △ Australia 17°41S 125°18E 148 C4
Tunnsjøen Norway 64°45N 13°25E 60 D6
Tuno Denmark 55°57N 10°27E 63 J4
Tunungayualok I. Canada 56°0N 61°0W 165 A7
Tunuyán Argentina 33°35S 69°0W 190 C2
Tunuyán → Argentina 33°33S 67°30W 190 C2
Tunxi = Huangshan China 30°8N 118°9E 117 B12
Tuo Jiang → China 28°50N 105°35E 116 C5
Tuolumne U.S.A. 37°58N 120°15W 170 H6
Tuolumne → U.S.A. 37°36N 121°13W 170 H5
Tüp Kyrgyzstan 42°45N 78°20E 108 D9
Tüp Āghāj Iran 36°3N 47°50E 128 B5
Tupã Brazil 21°57S 50°28W 191 A5

Tupaciguara Brazil 18°35S 48°42W 189 D1
Tupelo U.S.A. 34°16N 88°43W 177 D10
Tupik Russia 54°26N 119°57E 107 D12
Tupinambarana, I. Brazil 3°0S 58°0W 186 D7
Tupirama Brazil 8°58S 48°12W 189 D1
Tupiratins Brazil 8°23S 48°8W 189 D1
Tupiza Bolivia 21°30S 65°40W 190 A2
Tupižnica Serbia 43°43N 22°10E 96 C6
Tupman U.S.A. 35°18N 119°21W 171 K7
Tupper Canada 55°32N 120°1W 162 B4
Tupper L. U.S.A. 44°10N 74°32W 175 D10
Tupper Lake U.S.A. 44°14N 74°28W 175 D10
Tüpqarghan Muyis Kazakhstan 44°40N 50°19E 87 H10
Tupungato, Cerro S. Amer. 33°15S 69°50W 190 C2
Tuquan China 45°18N 121°38E 115 B11
Túquerres Colombia 1°5N 77°37W 186 C3
Tura Russia 25°30N 90°16E 125 F17
Turabah Ḥa'il, Si. Arabia 28°20N 43°15E 128 D4
Turabah Makkah, Si. Arabia 21°15N 41°34E 137 C5
Turakina N.Z. 40°3S 175°16E 154 G4
Turakina → N.Z. 40°5S 175°8E 154 G4
Turakirae Hd. N.Z. 41°26S 174°56E 154 H3
Tūrān Iran 35°39N 56°42E 129 C8
Turan Russia 51°55N 94°0E 109 B12
Tūrān □ Iran 35°45N 56°50E 129 C8
Turan Lowland Asia 43°30N 62°0E 108 D6
Turangi N.Z. 38°59S 175°48E 154 H5
Ţurayf Si. Arabia 31°41N 38°39E 128 D3
Turbacz Poland 49°30N 20°8E 83 J7
Turbe Bos.-H. 44°15N 17°35E 96 B7
Turbeville U.S.A. 33°54N 80°1W 178 B9
Turčianske Teplice Slovak Rep. 48°52N 18°52E 79 C11
Turco Bolivia 18°10S 68°11W 188 D4
Turcoaia Romania 45°7N 28°11E 81 E13
Turda Romania 46°34N 23°47E 81 D8
Turek Poland 52°3N 18°30E 83 F5
Turén Venezuela 9°17N 69°6W 186 B5
Turfan = Turpan China 43°58N 89°10E 109 D11
Turfan Basin = Turpan Pendi China 42°40N 89°25E 109 D11
Turfan Depression = Turpan Pendi China 42°40N 89°25E 109 D11
Turgayskaya Stolovaya Strana = Torghay Ustirti Asia 51°0N 63°0E 108 B6
Turgeon → Canada 50°0N 78°56W 164 C4
Türgovishte Bulgaria 43°17N 26°38E 97 C10
Türgovishte □ Bulgaria 43°17N 26°38E 97 C10
Turgut Turkey 37°22N 28°4E 99 D10
Turgutlu Turkey 38°30N 27°43E 99 C9
Turgwe → Zimbabwe 21°31S 32°15E 145 B5
Turhal Turkey 40°24N 36°5E 104 B7
Turia → Spain 39°27N 0°19W 91 F4
Turiaçu Brazil 1°40S 45°19W 187 D9
Turiaçu → Brazil 1°36S 45°19W 187 D9
Turiec → Slovak Rep. 49°7N 18°55E 79 B11
Turin = Torino Italy 45°3N 7°40E 92 B2
Turka Ukraine 49°10N 23°2E 83 J10
Turkana, L. Africa 3°30N 36°5E 142 B4
Türkeli Turkey 40°30N 27°0E 97 F11
Turkestan = Türkistan Kazakhstan 43°17N 68°16E 108 D7
Turkestan Range Asia 39°35N 69°0E 108 D7
Túrkeve Hungary 47°6N 20°44E 80 C5
Turkey ■ Eurasia 39°0N 36°0E 104 C7
Turkey Creek = Warmun Australia 17°2S 128°12E 148 C4
Turki Russia 52°0N 43°15E 86 D6
Türkistan Kazakhstan 43°17N 68°16E 108 D7
Türkmenabat Turkmenistan 39°6N 63°34E 129 B9
Türkmenbashi Turkmenistan 40°5N 53°5E 129 A7
Turkmenistan ■ Asia 39°0N 59°0E 108 E5
Türkmeni Turkey 39°45N 26°30E 99 B8
Türkoğlu Turkey 37°30N 36°50E 104 D7
Turks & Caicos Is. ☑ W. Indies 21°20N 71°20W 183 B5
Turks Island Passage Turks & Caicos 21°25N 71°19W 183 B5
Turku Finland 60°30N 22°19E 64 B3
Turkwel → Kenya 3°6N 36°6E 142 B4
Turlock U.S.A. 37°30N 120°51W 170 H6
Turnagain → Canada 59°12N 127°35W 162 B3
Turnagain, C. N.Z. 40°28S 176°38E 154 G5
Turneffe Is. Belize 17°20N 87°50W 181 D7
Turner U.S.A. 48°51N 108°24W 180 A6
Turner Pt. Australia 11°47S 133°32E 150 A1
Turner Valley Canada 50°40N 114°17W 162 D6
Turners Falls U.S.A. 42°36N 72°33W 175 D12
Turner's Pen. S. Leone 7°22N 12°24W 138 D2
Turnhout Belgium 51°19N 4°57E 69 C4
Türnitz Austria 47°55N 15°29E 78 D8
Turnor L. Canada 56°35N 108°35W 167 B9
Turnov Czech Rep. 50°34N 15°10E 78 A8
Türnovo = Veliko Tŭrnovo Bulgaria 43°5N 25°41E 97 C9
Turnu Măgurele Romania 43°46N 24°56E 81 G9
Turnu Roşu, P. Romania 45°33N 24°17E 81 E9
Turobin Poland 50°50N 22°44E 83 H9
Tuross Head Australia 36°3S 150°8E 153 D9
Turpan China 42°40N 89°20E 109 D11
Turpan Pendi China 42°40N 89°25E 109 D11
Turrawan Australia 30°28S 149°53E 153 A8
Turrës, Kala e Albania 41°10N 19°28E 96 E3
Turriff U.K. 57°32N 2°27W 65 D6
Tursāq Iraq 33°27N 45°47E 105 C11
Tursi Italy 40°15N 16°28E 95 C9
Tursunzoda Tajikistan 38°30N 68°10E 108 E7
Turtle Head I. Australia 10°56S 142°37E 150 A3
Turtle Is. S. Leone 7°40N 13°0W 138 D2
Turtle L. Canada 53°36N 108°38W 163 C7
Turtle Lake U.S.A. 47°31N 100°53W 172 B3
Turtleford Canada 53°23N 108°57W 163 C7
Turua N.Z. 37°14S 175°35E 154 B6
Turuépano △ Venezuela 10°34N 62°43W 187 B6
Turukhansk Russia 65°21N 88°5E 107 C9
Turzovka Slovak Rep. 49°25N 18°37E 79 B10
Tuscaloosa U.S.A. 33°12N 87°34W 177 E11
Tuscánia Italy 42°25N 11°52E 93 F8
Tuscany = Toscana □ Italy 43°25N 11°0E 92 E8

Tuscarawas → U.S.A. 40°24N 81°25W 174 F3
Tuscarora Mt. U.S.A. 40°55N 77°55W 174 F7
Tuscola Ill., U.S.A. 39°48N 88°17W 172 F9
Tuscola Tex., U.S.A. 32°12N 99°48W 176 E5
Tuscumbia U.S.A. 34°44N 87°42W 177 D11
Tuskegee U.S.A. 32°25N 85°42W 178 C4
Tuszyn Poland 51°36N 19°33E 83 G6
Tutayev Russia 57°53N 39°32E 84 D10
Tuticorin India 8°50N 78°12E 127 K4
Tutin Serbia 42°58N 20°20E 96 C4
Tutóia Brazil 2°45S 42°20W 189 B6
Tutong Brunei 4°47N 114°40E 118 D4
Tutrakan Bulgaria 44°2N 26°40E 97 B10
Tuttle Creek L. U.S.A. 39°15N 96°36W 172 F5
Tuttlingen Germany 47°58N 8°48E 77 H4
Tutuala E. Timor 8°25S 127°15E 119 F7
Tutume Botswana 20°30S 27°5E 141 J5
Tutun Egypt 29°9N 30°46E 137 F7
Tuul Gol → Mongolia 48°30N 104°25E 110 B9
Tuva □ Russia 51°30N 95°0E 109 B12
Tuvalu ■ Pac. Oc. 8°0S 178°0E 147 B10
Tuvuca Fiji 17°40S 178°48W 154 a
Tuxer Alpen Austria 47°10N 11°45E 78 D4
Tuxpan Mexico 20°57N 97°24W 181 C5
Tuxtla Gutiérrez Mexico 16°45N 93°7W 181 D6
Tuy = Tui Spain 42°3N 8°39W 88 C2
Tuy Duc Vietnam 12°15N 107°27E 121 F6
Tuy Hoa Vietnam 13°5N 109°10E 120 E7
Tuy Phong Vietnam 11°14N 108°43E 121 G7
Tuya L. Canada 59°7N 130°35W 162 B2
Tuyen Hoa Vietnam 17°50N 106°10E 120 D6
Tuyen Quang Vietnam 21°50N 105°10E 116 G5
Tuymazy Russia 54°36N 53°42E 86 D9
Tūysarkān Iran 34°33N 48°27E 105 C13
Tuz Gölü Turkey 38°42N 33°18E 104 C5
Tūz Khurmātū Iraq 34°56N 44°38E 105 C11
Tuzi Montenegro 42°22N 19°20E 96 D3
Tuzigoot △ U.S.A. 34°46N 112°2W 169 J7
Tuzla Bos.-H. 44°34N 18°41E 80 F3
Tuzlov → Russia 47°17N 39°57E 85 J10
Tuzluca Turkey 40°3N 43°39E 105 B10
Tuzly Ukraine 45°54N 30°6E 81 E15
Tvååker Sweden 57°4N 12°25E 63 G6
Tvardita Moldova 46°9N 28°58E 81 D13
Tver Russia 56°55N 35°59E 84 D8
Tver □ Russia 56°50N 35°0E 84 D8
Tvrdošin Slovak Rep. 49°21N 19°35E 79 B12
Tvrdošovce Slovak Rep. 48°6N 18°4E 79 C11
Tvŭrditsa Bulgaria 42°42N 25°53E 97 D9
Twain U.S.A. 40°1N 121°3W 170 E5
Twain Harte U.S.A. 38°2N 120°14W 170 G6
Twardogóra Poland 51°23N 17°28E 83 G4
Twee → Namibia 25°27S 19°27E 144 C2
Tweed Canada 44°29N 77°19W 174 B7
Tweed → U.K. 55°45N 2°0W 65 F6
Tweed Heads Australia 28°10S 153°31E 151 D5
Tweedsmuir △ Canada 53°0N 126°20W 162 C3
Twentynine Palms U.S.A. 34°8N 116°3W 171 L10
Twillingate Canada 49°42N 54°45W 165 C9
Twin Bridges U.S.A. 45°33N 112°20W 180 C7
Twin City U.S.A. 32°35N 82°10W 178 C7
Twin Falls Canada 53°30N 64°32W 165 B7
Twin Falls U.S.A. 42°34N 114°28W 168 E6
Twin Lakes U.S.A. 30°43N 83°13W 178 E6
Twin Valley U.S.A. 47°16N 96°16W 172 B5
Twinsburg U.S.A. 41°19N 81°26W 174 E3
Twitchell Res. U.S.A. 34°59N 120°19W 171 L6
Two Harbors U.S.A. 47°2N 91°40W 172 B8
Two Hills Canada 53°43N 111°52W 162 C6
Two Rivers U.S.A. 44°9N 87°34W 172 C10
Two Rocks Australia 31°30S 115°35E 149 F2
Two Thumb Ra. N.Z. 43°45S 170°44E 155 E3
Twofold B. Australia 37°8S 149°59E 153 D8
Twyfelfontein Namibia 20°34S 14°22E 144 B1
Ty Ty U.S.A. 31°28N 83°39W 178 D6
Tyachiv Ukraine 48°1N 23°35E 81 D10
Tybee Island U.S.A. 32°1N 80°51W 178 C9
Tychy Poland 50°9N 18°59E 83 H5
Tyczyn Poland 49°58N 22°2E 83 J9
Tykocin Poland 53°13N 22°46E 83 E9
Tyler Minn., U.S.A. 44°17N 96°8W 172 C5
Tyler Tex., U.S.A. 32°21N 95°18W 176 E7
Tyligul → Ukraine 47°4N 30°57E 85 J6
Tymanivka Ukraine 48°34N 28°50E 81 B13
Tyn nad Vltavou Czech Rep. 49°13N 14°26E 78 B7
Tynda Russia 55°10N 124°43E 107 D13
Tyndall U.S.A. 43°0N 97°50W 172 D5
Tyne → U.K. 54°59N 1°32W 66 C6
Tyne & Wear □ U.K. 55°6N 1°17W 66 B6
Tynemouth U.K. 55°1N 1°26W 66 B6
Tyre = Sūr Lebanon 33°19N 35°16E 138 B4
Tyresta △ Sweden 59°12N 18°14E 62 E12
Tyrifjorden Norway 60°2N 10°8E 63 E14
Tyringe Sweden 56°9N 13°35E 63 H7
Tyrnyauz Russia 43°21N 42°45E 87 J6
Tyrol = Tirol □ Austria 47°3N 10°43E 78 E4
Tyrone □ U.K. 54°38N 7°11W 64 B4
Tyrrell → Australia 35°26S 142°51E 152 C5
Tyrrell, L. Australia 35°20S 142°50E 152 C5
Tyrrell L. Canada 63°7N 105°27W 163 A7
Tyrrhenian Sea Medit. S. 40°0N 12°30E 58 G8
Tysfjorden Norway 68°7N 16°25E 60 B17
Tysmenytsya Ukraine 48°54N 24°51E 81 B9
Tysberga Sweden 58°51N 17°15E 63 F11
Tytuvėnai Lithuania 55°36N 23°12E 82 G4

U

U.S.A. = United States of America ■ N. Amer. 37°0N 96°0W 167 H20
U.S. Virgin Is. ☑ W. Indies 18°20N 65°0W 183 e
Uaimh, An = Navan Ireland 53°39N 6°41W 64 C5
Uanle Uen = Wanlaweyne Somalia 2°37N 44°54E 131 G3
Uatumã → Brazil 2°26S 57°37W 186 D7
Uauá Brazil 9°50S 39°28W 189 B3
Uaupés Brazil 0°8S 67°5W 186 D5
Uaupés → Brazil 0°2N 67°58W 186 D5
Uaxactún Guatemala 17°25N 89°29W 182 C2
Ub Serbia 44°28N 20°6E 96 B4
Ubá Brazil 21°8S 43°0W 191 A7
Uba Nigeria 10°29N 13°13E 139 C8
Ubaitaba Brazil 14°18S 39°20W 189 D3
Ubajara △ Brazil 3°55S 40°50W 189 A2
Ubangi = Oubangi → Dem. Rep. of the Congo 0°30S 17°50E 140 E3
Ubauro Pakistan 28°15N 69°45E 124 E3
Ubaye → France 44°28N 6°18E 73 D10
Ubayyiḍ, W. al → Iraq 32°34N 43°48E 105 C10
Ube Japan 33°56N 131°15E 113 H5
Úbeda Spain 38°3N 3°23W 89 G7
Uberaba Brazil 19°50S 47°55W 189 D1
Uberlândia Brazil 19°0S 48°20W 189 D1
Überlingen Germany 47°46N 9°10E 77 H5
Ubiaja Nigeria 6°41N 6°22E 138 D6
Ubin, Pulau Singapore 1°24N 103°57E 121 d
Ubly U.S.A. 43°42N 82°55W 174 C2
Ubolratna Res. Thailand 16°45N 102°30E 120 D4
Ubombo S. Africa 27°31S 32°4E 145 D5
Ubon Ratchathani Thailand 15°15N 104°50E 120 E5
Ubondo Dem. Rep. of the Congo 0°55S 25°42E 142 C2
Ubort → Belarus 52°6N 28°30E 75 B15
Ubrique Spain 36°41N 5°27W 89 J5
Ubud Indonesia 8°30S 115°16E 119 J18
Ucar Azerbaijan 40°31N 47°39E 87 K8
Ucayali → Peru 4°30S 73°30W 188 A2
Uchab Namibia 19°47S 17°47E 144 A2
Uchiura-Wan Japan 42°25N 140°40E 112 C10
Uchiza Peru 8°25S 76°20W 188 B2
Uchquduq Uzbekistan 41°50N 62°50E 108 D6
Uchte Germany 52°30N 8°54E 76 C4
Uchur → Russia 58°48N 130°35E 107 D14
Uckermark Germany 53°15N 13°50E 76 B9
Ucluelet Canada 48°57N 125°32W 162 D3
Uda → Russia 54°42N 135°14E 107 D14
Uda Walawe △ Sri Lanka 6°20N 81°0E 127 L5
Udachnyy Russia 66°25N 112°24E 107 C12
Udagamandalam India 11°30N 76°44E 127 J3
Udainagar India 22°33N 76°13E 124 H7
Udaipur India 24°36N 73°44E 124 G5
Udaipur Garhi Nepal 27°0N 86°35E 125 F12
Udala India 21°35N 86°34E 125 J12
Udayagiri Andhra Pradesh, India 14°52N 79°19E 127 G4
Udayagiri Odisha, India 20°8N 84°23E 126 D7
Uddevalla Sweden 58°21N 11°55E 63 F5
Uddheden Sweden 59°57N 12°54E 63 F6
Uddjaure Sweden 65°56N 17°49E 60 D17
Udgir India 18°25N 77°5E 126 E3
Udhampur India 33°0N 75°5E 126 C2
Udi Nigeria 6°17N 7°21E 139 D6
Udine Italy 46°3N 13°14E 93 B10
Udintsev Fracture Zone S. Ocean 70°0S 145°0W 55 B13
Udon Thani Thailand 17°29N 102°46E 120 D4
Udong Cambodia 11°48N 104°45E 121 G5
Udskaya Guba Russia 54°50N 135°45E 107 D14
Udu Pt. Fiji 16°9S 179°57W 154 a
Udumalaippettai India 10°35N 77°15E 127 J3
Udupi India 13°25N 74°42E 127 H2
Udva India 20°5N 73°0E 126 D1
Udvoy Balkan Bulgaria 42°50N 26°50E 97 D10
Udzungwa △ Tanzania 7°52S 36°15E 142 D4
Udzungwa Range Tanzania 9°30S 35°10E 143 D4
Ueckermünde Germany 53°44N 14°1E 76 B10
Ueda Japan 36°24N 138°16E 113 F9
Uedineniya, Os. Russia 78°0N 85°0E 54 B13
Uele → Dem. Rep. of the Congo 3°45N 24°45E 140 D4
Uelen Russia 66°10N 170°0W 107 C19
Uelzen Germany 52°57N 10°32E 76 C6
Uetersen Germany 53°40N 9°40E 76 B5
Uetze Germany 52°28N 10°11E 76 C6
Ufa Russia 54°45N 55°55E 108 B5
Ufa → Russia 54°40N 56°0E 108 B5
Uffenheim Germany 49°33N 10°14E 77 E6
Ugab → Namibia 21°12S 13°38E 144 B1
Ugalla → Tanzania 5°8S 30°42E 142 D3
Ugalla River ∩ Tanzania 5°50S 31°54E 142 D3
Uganda ■ Africa 2°0N 32°0E 142 B3
Ugento Italy 39°56N 18°10E 95 C11
Ugep Nigeria 5°53N 8°2E 139 D6
Ughelli Nigeria 5°31N 6°0E 138 D6
Ugie S. Africa 31°10S 28°13E 145 E4
Ugíjar Spain 36°58N 3°7W 89 J7
Ugine France 45°45N 6°25E 73 C10
Uglegorsk Russia 49°5N 142°2E 107 E15
Uglich Russia 57°33N 38°20E 84 D10
Ugljan Croatia 44°12N 15°10E 78 G12
Ugljane Croatia 43°35N 16°46E 95 E13
Ugol'nye Kopi Russia 64°44N 177°42E 107 C18
Ugra → Russia 54°30N 36°7E 84 E9
Uğurludağ Turkey 40°22N 34°40E 104 B6
Uh → Slovak Rep. 48°37N 22°0E 79 C17
Uherské Hradiště Czech Rep. 49°4N 17°30E 79 B9
Uherský Brod Czech Rep. 49°1N 17°40E 79 B10
Úhlava → Czech Rep. 49°45N 13°24E 78 B6
Uhlenhorst Namibia 23°45S 17°55E 144 B2

Uhniv Ukraine 50°22N 23°45E 83 H11
Uhrichsville U.S.A. 40°24N 81°21W 174 F3
Uibhist a Deas = South Uist U.K. 57°20N 7°15W 65 D1
Uibhist a Tuath = North Uist U.K. 57°35N 7°15W 65 D1
Uig U.K. 57°35N 6°21W 65 D2
Uíge Angola 7°30S 14°40E 140 F2
Uijeongbu S. Korea 37°44N 127°2E 115 F14
Uinta Mts. U.S.A. 40°45N 110°30W 168 F8
Uis Namibia 21°8S 14°49E 144 B1
Uiseong S. Korea 36°21N 128°45E 115 F15
Uithuizen Neths. 53°24N 6°41E 69 A6
Ujazd Poland 50°23N 18°21E 83 H5
Újfehértó Hungary 47°49N 21°41E 80 C6
Ujh → India 32°10N 75°18E 124 C6
Ujhani India 28°0N 79°6E 125 F8
Uji-guntō Japan 31°15N 129°25E 113 K4
Ujjain India 23°9N 75°43E 124 H6
Ujście Poland 53°3N 16°45E 83 E3
Ujście Warty △ Poland 52°35N 14°44E 83 E2
Újszász Hungary 47°19N 20°7E 80 C5
Ujung Kulon △ Indonesia 6°46S 105°19E 119 G11
Ujung Pandang = Makassar Indonesia 5°10S 119°20E 119 F5
Uka Russia 57°50N 162°0E 107 D17
Ukai Sagar India 21°20N 73°43E 126 D1
Ukara I. Tanzania 1°50S 33°0E 142 C3
Uke-Shima Japan 28°2N 129°14E 113 K4
Ukerewe I. Tanzania 2°0S 33°0E 142 C3
uKhahlamba Drakensberg △ S. Africa 29°27S 29°30E 145 C4
Ukholovo Russia 53°47N 40°30E 86 D5
Ukhrul India 25°10N 94°25E 123 G19
Ukhta Russia 63°34N 53°41E 106 C6
Ukiah U.S.A. 39°9N 123°13W 170 F3
Ukkusiksalik △ Canada 65°20N 89°30W 160 D14
Ukmergė Lithuania 55°15N 24°45E 84 E3
Ukraine ■ Europe 49°0N 32°0E 85 H7
Ukwi Botswana 23°29S 20°30E 144 B3
Ula Turkey 37°6N 28°25E 104 D3
Ulaan Nuur Mongolia 44°30N 103°40E 114 B2
Ulaan-Uul Mongolia 46°4N 100°49E 114 B6
Ulaanbaatar Mongolia 47°55N 106°53E 110 B10
Ulaangom Mongolia 50°5N 92°10E 109 B10
Ulaanjirem Mongolia 45°5N 105°30E 114 B3
Ulak I. U.S.A. 51°22N 178°57W 166 E4
Ulamambri Australia 31°19S 149°23E 153 E8
Ulamba Dem. Rep. of the Congo 9°3S 23°38E 143 D1
Ulan Bator = Ulaanbaatar Mongolia 47°55N 106°53E 110 B10
Ulan Erge Russia 46°19N 44°53E 87 G7
Ulan Khol Russia 45°18N 47°4E 87 H8
Ulan Ude Russia 51°45N 107°40E 111 A10
Ulanhad = Chifeng China 42°18N 118°58E 115 C10
Ulanhot = Horqin Youyi Qianqi China 46°5N 122°3E 115 A12
Ulansuhai Nur China 40°53N 108°51E 114 D5
Ulaş Sivas, Turkey 39°26N 37°2E 104 C7
Ulaş Tekirdağ, Turkey 41°14N 27°42E 97 E11
Ulaya Morogoro, Tanzania 7°3S 36°55E 142 D4
Ulaya Tabora, Tanzania 4°25S 33°30E 142 C3
Ulcinj Montenegro 41°58N 19°10E 96 D3
Ulco S. Africa 28°21S 24°15E 144 C3
Ule älv = Oulujoki → Finland 65°1N 25°30E 60 D21
Ule träsk = Oulujärvi Finland 64°25N 27°15E 60 D22
Uleåborg = Oulu Finland 65°1N 25°29E 60 D21
Ulefoss Norway 59°17N 9°16E 63 G13
Ulëz Albania 41°46N 19°54E 96 E3
Ulfborg Denmark 56°16N 8°20E 63 H2
Ulhasnagar India 19°15N 73°10E 126 E1
Uliastay Mongolia 47°56N 97°28E 110 B8
Uljin S. Korea 36°59N 129°24E 115 F15
Uljma Serbia 45°2N 21°10E 80 E6
Ülken Kazakhstan 45°12N 73°58E 108 C8
Ülken Borsyq Qumy Kazakhstan 47°0N 59°11E 108 C5
Ulla → Spain 42°39N 8°44W 88 C2
Ulladulla Australia 35°21S 150°29E 153 D9
Ullal India 12°48N 74°51E 127 H2
Ullapool U.K. 57°54N 5°9W 65 D3
Ullared Sweden 57°8N 12°42E 63 G6
Ulldecona Spain 40°36N 0°20E 90 E5
Ulleungdo S. Korea 37°30N 130°30E 113 F5
Ullswater U.K. 54°34N 2°52W 66 C5
Ullswater □ U.K. 54°34N 2°52W 66 C5
Ulm Germany 48°23N 9°58E 77 G5
Ulmarra Australia 29°37S 153°4E 151 D5
Ulmeni Buzău, Romania 45°4N 26°40E 81 E11
Ulmeni Maramureş, Romania 47°28N 23°18E 81 C8
Ulongué Mozam. 14°37S 34°19E 143 E3
Ulricehamn Sweden 57°46N 13°26E 63 G7
Ulrika Sweden 58°5N 15°23E 63 F9
Ulsan S. Korea 35°20N 129°15E 115 G15
Ulsta U.K. 60°30N 1°9W 65 A7
Ulster □ U.K. 54°35N 6°30W 64 B5
Ulstrem Bulgaria 42°1N 26°27E 97 D10
Ultima Australia 35°30S 143°18E 152 C5
Ulubat Gölü Turkey 40°9N 28°35E 97 F12
Ulubey Turkey 38°25N 29°29E 99 C11
Uluborlu Turkey 38°4N 30°25E 104 C4
Uluçınar Turkey 36°24N 35°53E 104 D6
Uludağ Turkey 40°4N 29°13E 97 F13
Uludağ △ Turkey 40°4N 29°13E 97 F13
Uluguru Mts. Tanzania 7°15S 37°40E 142 D4
Ulukışla = Marathóvounos Cyprus 35°13N 33°37E 101 D12
Ulukışla Turkey 37°23N 34°30E 104 D6
Ulundi S. Africa 28°20S 31°15E 145 D5
Ulungur He → China 47°1N 87°24E 109 C11
Ulungur Hu China 47°20N 87°10E 109 C11
Uluru Australia 25°23S 131°5E 149 E5
Uluru-Kata Tjuta △ Australia 25°19S 131°1E 149 E5
Ulutau Kazakhstan 48°39N 67°1E 109 C7
Uluwatu Indonesia 8°50S 115°5E 119 K18
Ulverston U.K. 54°13N 3°5W 66 C4

Ulverstone Australia 41°11S 146°11E 151 G4
Ulya Russia 59°10N 142°0E 107 D15
Ulyanovo Russia 54°50N 22°6E 82 D9
Ulyanovsk Russia 54°20N 48°25E 86 C9
Ulyanovsk □ Russia 54°5N 48°5E 86 C9
Ulyasutay = Uliastay Mongolia 47°56N 97°28E 110 B8
Ulysses Kans., U.S.A. 37°35N 101°22W 172 G3
Ulysses Pa., U.S.A. 41°54N 77°46W 174 E7
Ulysses, Mt. Canada 57°20N 124°54W 162 B4
Ulyzhylanshyq → Kazakhstan 48°51N 63°46E 108 C6
Umag Croatia 45°26N 13°31E 93 C10
Umala Bolivia 17°25S 68°5W 188 G5
'Umān = Oman ■ Asia 23°0N 58°0E 131 C6
Uman Ukraine 48°40N 30°12E 75 D16
Umaria India 23°35N 80°50E 125 H9
Umarkhed India 19°37N 77°46E 126 E3
Umarkot Pakistan 25°15N 69°40E 124 G3
Umarpada India 21°27N 73°30E 124 J5
Umatilla U.S.A. 45°55N 119°21W 168 D4
Umbagog L. U.S.A. 44°46N 71°3W 175 B13
Umbakumba Australia 13°47S 136°50E 150 A2
Umbértide Italy 43°18N 12°20E 93 E9
Umbrella Mts. N.Z. 45°35S 169°5E 155 F4
Umbria □ Italy 42°53N 12°30E 93 F9
Umeå Sweden 63°45N 20°20E 60 E19
Umeälven → Sweden 63°45N 20°20E 60 E19
Umera Indonesia 0°12S 129°37E 119 E7
Umfuli → Zimbabwe 17°30S 29°23E 143 F2
Umfurudzi △ Zimbabwe 17°6S 31°40E 143 F3
Umgusa Zimbabwe 19°29S 27°52E 143 F2
Umgwenya → Mozam. 25°14S 32°18E 145 C5
Umiujaq Canada 56°33N 76°33W 164 A4
Umka Serbia 44°40N 20°19E 96 B4
Umkomaas S. Africa 30°13S 30°48E 145 E5
Umlazi S. Africa 29°59S 30°54E 141 L6
Umm ad Daraj, J. Jordan 32°18N 35°48E 130 C4
Umm al Khashab Si. Arabia 17°23N 42°32E 137 D5
Umm al Qaywayn U.A.E. 25°30N 55°35E 129 E7
Umm al Qittayn Jordan 32°18N 36°40E 130 C5
Umm al Rasas Jordan 31°30N 35°55E 130 D4
Umm Bāb Qatar 25°12N 50°48E 129 E6
Umm Birkah Si. Arabia 27°44N 36°31E 137 B4
Umm Durman = Omdurmân Sudan 15°40N 32°28E 135 E12
Umm el Fahm Israel 32°31N 35°9E 130 C4
Umm Keddada Sudan 13°33N 26°35E 135 F11
Umm Lajj Si. Arabia 25°0N 37°23E 128 E3
Umm Qasr Iraq 30°1N 47°58E 128 D5
Umm Ruwaba Sudan 12°50N 31°20E 135 F12
Umm Sa'id Qatar 25°0N 51°33E 129 E6
Umm Tais J. Qatar 26°7N 51°15E 129 E6
Umm Urūmah Si. Arabia 25°43N 36°35E 137 B4
Umm Zehetir Egypt 28°32N 32°31E 137 B8
Umnak I. U.S.A. 53°15N 168°20W 166 E6
Umniati → Zimbabwe 16°49S 28°45E 143 F2
Umpqua → U.S.A. 43°40N 124°12W 168 E1
Umred India 20°51N 79°18E 126 D4
Umreth India 22°41N 73°4E 124 H5
Umri India 19°2N 77°39E 126 E3
Umtata = Mthatha S. Africa 31°36S 28°49E 145 D4
Umuahia Nigeria 5°31N 7°26E 139 D6
Umuarama Brazil 23°45S 53°20W 191 A5
Umurbey Turkey 40°13N 26°36E 97 F10
Umvukwe Ra. Zimbabwe 16°45S 30°45E 143 F3
Umzimkulu S. Africa 31°38S 29°33E 145 D4
Umzingwane → Zimbabwe 22°12S 29°56E 143 G2
Umzinto = eMuziwezinto S. Africa 30°15S 30°45E 145 D5
Una India 20°46N 71°8E 124 J4
Una → Bos.-H. 45°0N 16°20E 93 D13
Unac → Bos.-H. 44°30N 16°9E 93 D13
Unadilla Ga., U.S.A. 32°16N 83°44W 178 C6
Unadilla N.Y., U.S.A. 42°20N 75°19W 175 D9
Unaí Brazil 16°23S 46°53W 189 D1
Unalakleet U.S.A. 63°52N 160°47W 166 C7
Unalaska U.S.A. 53°53N 166°32W 166 E6
Unalaska I. U.S.A. 53°35N 166°50W 166 E6
'Unayzah Si. Arabia 26°6N 43°58E 128 E4
'Unayzah, J. Asia 32°12N 39°18E 105 E11
Uncastillo Spain 42°21N 1°8W 90 C3
Uncía Bolivia 18°25S 66°40W 186 G5
Uncompahgre Peak U.S.A. 38°4N 107°28W 168 G10
Uncompahgre Plateau U.S.A. 38°20N 108°15W 168 G9
Undara Volcanic △ Australia 18°14S 144°41E 150 B3
Unden Sweden 58°45N 14°25E 63 F8
Underbool Australia 35°10S 141°51E 152 C4
Undersaker Sweden 63°19N 13°21E 62 A7
Underwood Canada 44°18N 81°29W 173 B3
Unecha Russia 52°50N 32°37E 85 F7
Ungarie Australia 33°38S 146°56E 153 B7
Ungarra Australia 34°12S 136°2E 152 C2
Ungava, Pén. d' Canada 60°0N 74°0W 161 F17
Ungava B. Canada 59°30N 67°30W 161 F18
Ungeny = Ungheni Moldova 47°11N 27°51E 81 C12
Unggi N. Korea 42°16N 130°28E 115 C16
Ungheni Moldova 47°11N 27°51E 81 C12
Ungwana B. Kenya 2°45S 40°20E 142 C5
Uni Russia 57°49N 51°31E 86 C10
União Brazil 4°35S 42°52W 189 A2
União da Vitória Brazil 26°13S 51°5W 191 B5
União dos Palmares Brazil 9°10S 36°2W 189 B3
Uničov Czech Rep. 49°48N 17°8E 79 B10
Uniejów Poland 51°59N 18°46E 83 G5
Unije Croatia 44°40N 14°15E 93 D11
Unimak I. U.S.A. 54°45N 164°0W 166 E7
Unimak Pass. U.S.A. 54°15N 164°30W 166 E7
Union Miss., U.S.A. 32°34N 89°7W 178 C10
Union Mo., U.S.A. 38°27N 90°59W 172 F8
Union S.C., U.S.A. 34°43N 81°37W 177 D14
Union City Calif., U.S.A. 37°36N 122°1W 170 H4
Union City Ga., U.S.A. 33°35N 84°42W 177 D11
Union City N.J., U.S.A. 40°45N 74°2W 175 E10
Union City Pa., U.S.A. 41°54N 79°51W 174 E5
Union City Tenn., U.S.A. 36°26N 89°3W 177 C10
Union Dale U.S.A. 41°43N 75°29W 175 E9

Union Gap U.S.A. 46°33N 120°28W 168 C3
Union Park U.S.A. 28°34N 81°17W 179 G8
Union Point U.S.A. 33°37N 83°4W 178 B6
Union Springs Ala., U.S.A. 32°9N 85°43W 178 C4
Union Springs N.Y., U.S.A. 42°50N 76°41W 175 D8
Uniondale S. Africa 33°39S 23°7E 144 D3
Uniontown U.S.A. 39°54N 79°44W 173 F14
Unionville La., U.S.A. 31°26N 83°30W 178 D6
Unionville Mo., U.S.A. 40°29N 93°1W 172 E7
Unirea Romania 44°15N 27°35E 81 F12
United Arab Emirates ■ Asia 23°50N 54°0E 129 F7
United Kingdom ■ Europe 53°0N 2°0W 66 E6
United States of America ■ N. Amer. 37°0N 96°0W 167 H20
Unity Canada 52°30N 109°5W 163 C7
Universales, Mtes. Spain 40°18N 1°33W 90 E3
University Park U.S.A. 32°17N 106°45W 169 K10
University Place U.S.A. 47°14N 122°33W 170 C4
Unjha India 23°46N 72°24E 124 H5
Unna Germany 51°32N 7°42E 76 D3
Unnao India 26°35N 80°30E 125 F9
Uno, Ilha Guinea-Biss. 11°15N 16°13W 138 C1
Unsengedsi → Zimbabwe 15°43S 31°14E 143 F3
Unst U.K. 60°44N 0°53W 65 A8
Unstrut → Germany 51°10N 11°48E 76 D7
Unterfranken □ Germany 50°0N 10°0E 77 F5
Unterschleissheim Germany 48°17N 11°34E 77 F7
Unuk → Canada 56°5N 131°3W 162 B2
Ünye Turkey 41°5N 37°15E 104 B7
Unzen-Amakusa △ Japan 32°15N 130°10E 113 H5
Unzha Russia 58°0N 44°0E 86 A7
Unzha → Russia 57°49N 43°47E 86 B6
Uong Bi Vietnam 21°2N 106°47E 120 B6
Uotsuri-Shima E. China Sea 25°45N 123°29E 113 M1
Uozu Japan 36°48N 137°24E 113 F8
Upata Venezuela 8°1N 62°24W 186 B6
Upatoi Cr. → U.S.A. 32°22N 84°58W 178 C5
Upemba, L. Dem. Rep. of the Congo 8°30S 26°20E 143 D2
Upemba △ Dem. Rep. of the Congo 8°30S 26°0E 143 D2
Upernavik Greenland 72°49N 56°20W 57 C5
Upington S. Africa 28°25S 21°15E 144 C3
Upleta India 21°46N 70°16E 124 J4
Upper Alkali L. U.S.A. 41°47N 120°8W 168 F3
Upper Arrow L. Canada 50°30N 117°50W 162 C5
Upper Daly ☉ Australia 14°26S 131°3E 148 B5
Upper Darby U.S.A. 39°55N 75°16W 173 F16
Upper East □ Ghana 10°30N 1°0W 139 C4
Upper Foster L. Canada 56°47N 105°20W 163 B7
Upper Hutt N.Z. 41°8S 175°5E 154 H4
Upper Klamath L. U.S.A. 42°25N 121°55W 168 E3
Upper Lake U.S.A. 39°10N 122°54W 170 F4
Upper Liard Canada 60°3N 128°54W 162 A3
Upper Manilla Australia 30°38S 150°40E 153 A9
Upper Manzanilla Trin. & Tob. 10°31N 61°4W 187 K15
Upper Missouri Breaks △ U.S.A. 47°50N 109°55W 168 C9
Upper Musquodoboit Canada 45°10N 62°58W 165 C7
Upper Red L. U.S.A. 48°8N 94°45W 172 A6
Upper Sandusky U.S.A. 40°50N 83°17W 173 E12
Upper Volta = Burkina Faso ■ Africa 12°0N 1°0W 138 C4
Upper West □ Ghana 10°30N 2°0W 138 C4
Uppharad Sweden 58°9N 12°19E 63 F6
Uppland Sweden 59°59N 17°48E 62 D12
Upplands-Väsby Sweden 59°31N 17°54E 62 E11
Uppsala Sweden 59°53N 17°38E 62 E11
Uppsala län □ Sweden 60°0N 17°30E 62 D11
Upshi India 33°48N 77°52E 125 C7
Upton U.S.A. 44°6N 104°38W 168 D11
Uqsuqtuuq = Gjoa Haven Canada 68°38N 95°53W 160 D12
Ur Iraq 30°55N 46°25E 128 D5
Ura-Tyube = Istaravshan Tajikistan 39°55N 69°1E 109 E7
Urad Qianqi China 40°40N 108°30E 114 D5
Uraho Japan 42°50N 143°40E 112 C11
Urakawa Japan 42°9N 142°47E 112 C11
Ural = Zhayyq → Kazakhstan 47°0N 51°48E 108 E6
Ural Australia 33°21S 146°12E 153 B7
Ural Mts. = Uralskie Gory Eurasia 60°0N 59°0E 58 C17
Uralla Australia 30°37S 151°29E 153 A9
Uralsk = Oral Kazakhstan 51°20N 51°20E 86 E10
Uralskie Gory Eurasia 60°0N 59°0E 58 C17
Uralskiy □ Russia 64°0N 70°0E 86 C7
Urambo Tanzania 5°4S 32°0E 142 D3
Urana Australia 35°15S 146°21E 153 C7
Urandangi Australia 21°32S 138°14E 150 C2
Uranga Australia 30°31S 153°1E 153 A10
Uranium City Canada 59°34N 108°37W 160 D9
Urapunja = Utopia Australia 22°14S 134°33E 150 C1
Uraricoera → Brazil 3°2N 60°30W 186 C6
Urasoe Japan 26°15N 127°43E 113 L3
Uravakonda India 14°57N 77°12E 127 G3
Urawa = Saitama Japan 35°54N 139°38E 113 G9
Uray Russia 60°5N 65°15E 86 C7
'Uray'irah Si. Arabia 25°57N 48°53E 129 E6
Urbana Ill., U.S.A. 40°7N 88°12W 172 E9
Urbana Ohio, U.S.A. 40°7N 83°45W 173 E12
Urbandale U.S.A. 41°38N 93°43W 172 E7
Urbània Italy 43°40N 12°31E 93 E9
Urbano Santos Brazil 3°12S 43°23W 189 A2
Urbel → Spain 42°21N 3°40W 88 C7
Urbino Italy 43°43N 12°38E 93 E9
Urbión, Picos de Spain 42°1N 2°52W 90 C2

Urcos Peru 13°40S 71°38W 188 D3
Urdinarrain Argentina 32°37S 58°52W 190 C4
Urdos France 42°51N 0°35W 72 F3
Ure → U.K. 54°5N 1°20W 66 C6
Uren Russia 57°35N 45°55E 86 B7
Urengoy Russia 65°58N 78°22E 106 C8
Ures Mexico 29°26N 110°24W 180 B2
Urewera △ N.Z. 38°29S 177°7E 154 E6
Urfa = Şanlıurfa Turkey 37°12N 38°50E 105 D8
Urganch Uzbekistan 41°40N 60°41E 108 D6
Urgench = Urganch Uzbekistan 41°40N 60°41E 108 D6
Ürgüp Turkey 38°38N 34°56E 104 C6
Urho Kekkonen △ Finland 68°20N 27°40E 60 B22
Uri □ India 34°8N 74°2E 125 B6
Uri □ Switz. 46°43N 8°35E 77 J4
Uribia Colombia 11°43N 72°16W 186 A4
Uricani Romania 45°20N 23°9E 80 E8
Uriondo Bolivia 21°41S 64°41W 190 A3
Urique Mexico 27°13N 107°55W 180 B3
Urique → Mexico 26°29N 107°58W 180 B3
Urk Neths. 52°39N 5°36E 69 B5
Urkiola △ Spain 43°6N 1°2W 90 B3
Urla Turkey 38°20N 26°47E 99 C8
Urlaţi Romania 44°59N 26°15E 81 F11
Urmia = Orūmīyeh Iran 37°40N 45°0E 105 D11
Uromi Nigeria 6°42N 6°20E 139 D6
Uroševac = Ferizaj Kosovo 42°23N 21°10E 96 C5
Üroteppa = Istaravshan Tajikistan 39°55N 69°1E 109 E7
Uroyan, Montanas de Puerto Rico 18°12N 66°50W 183 d
Urrampinyi Iltjiltarri Australia 24°20S 132°10E 148 D5
Urshult Sweden 56°31N 14°50E 63 H8
Uru Uru, L. Bolivia 18°6S 67°8W 188 D4
Uruaçu Brazil 14°30S 49°10W 187 F9
Uruapan Mexico 19°24N 102°3W 180 D4
Urubamba Peru 13°20S 72°10W 188 C3
Urubamba → Peru 10°43S 73°48W 188 C3
Urucará Brazil 2°32S 57°45W 186 D7
Uruçuí Brazil 7°20S 44°28W 189 B2
Uruçuí, Serra do Brazil 9°0S 44°45W 189 B2
Uruçuí Prêto → Brazil 7°0S 44°43W 189 B2
Urucuia → Brazil 16°8S 45°9W 189 D1
Uruguai → Brazil 26°0S 53°30W 191 B5
Uruguaiana Brazil 29°50S 57°0W 190 B4
Uruguay ■ S. Amer. 32°30S 56°30W 190 C4
Uruguay → S. Amer. 34°12S 58°18W 190 C4
Urumchi = Ürümqi China 43°45N 87°45E 109 D11
Ürümqi China 43°45N 87°45E 109 D11
Uruna △ Australia 24°3S 133°1E 148 D5
Urup → Russia 45°0N 41°10E 87 H5
Urup, Ostrov Russia 46°0N 151°0E 107 E16
Urutaí Brazil 17°28S 48°12W 189 D1
Uryupinsk Russia 50°45N 41°58E 86 E5
Urzhum Russia 57°10N 49°56E 86 B9
Urziceni Romania 44°40N 26°42E 81 F11
Usa → Russia 66°16N 59°49E 106 C6
Uşak Turkey 38°43N 29°28E 99 C11
Uşak □ Turkey 38°30N 29°0E 99 C11
Usakos Namibia 21°54S 15°31E 144 B2
Usborne, Mt. Falk. Is. 51°40S 59°5W 192 D5
Uščie Serbia 43°28N 20°37E 96 C4
Usedom Germany 53°55N 14°2E 76 B10
Useless Loop Australia 26°8S 113°23E 149 E1
Usfan Si. Arabia 21°58N 39°27E 137 C4
Ush-Tobe Kazakhstan 45°16N 77°58E 108 E8
Ushakova, Ostrov Russia 82°0N 80°0E 54 A12
Ushakovo Russia 54°37N 20°16E 82 D7
Ushant = Ouessant, Î. d' France 48°28N 5°6W 70 D1
Ûsharal Kazakhstan 46°10N 80°56E 109 C10
Ushashi Tanzania 1°59S 33°57E 142 C3
'Ushayrah Ar Riyāḍ, Si. Arabia 25°35N 45°47E 128 E5
'Ushayrah Makkah, Si. Arabia 21°46N 40°42E 137 C5
Ushibuka Japan 32°11N 130°1E 113 H5
Ushtōbe Kazakhstan 45°16N 78°0E 108 E8
Ushuaia Argentina 54°50S 68°23W 192 D3
Ushumun Russia 52°47N 126°32E 107 D13
Ushytsya → Ukraine 48°35N 27°8E 81 B12
Usinsk Russia 65°57N 57°27E 106 C6
Usk Canada 54°38N 128°26W 162 C3
Usk → U.K. 51°33N 2°58W 67 F5
Uska India 27°12N 83°7E 125 F10
Üsküdar Turkey 41°1N 29°0E 97 F13
Usman Germany 51°39N 9°38E 76 D5
Usman Russia 52°5N 39°48E 86 E6
Usoke Tanzania 5°8S 32°24E 142 D3
Usolye-Sibirskoye Russia 52°48N 103°40E 107 D11
Usoro Nigeria 5°33N 6°11E 139 D6
Uspallata, P. de Argentina 32°37S 69°22W 190 C2
Ussel France 45°32N 2°18E 72 C6
Usson-du-Poitou France 46°16N 0°31E 72 B4
Ussuriysk Russia 43°48N 131°59E 112 C5
Ussurka Russia 45°12N 133°31E 112 B6
Ust-Buzulukskaya Russia 50°8N 42°11E 86 E6
Ust-Chaun Russia 68°47N 170°30E 107 C18
Ust-Chorna Ukraine 48°19N 23°56E 81 B8
Ust-Donetskiy Russia 47°35N 40°55E 87 G5
Ust-Ilimsk Russia 58°3N 102°39E 107 D11
Ust-Ishim Russia 57°45N 71°10E 106 D8
Ust-Kamchatsk Russia 56°10N 162°28E 107 D17
Ust-Kamenogorsk = Öskemen Kazakhstan 50°0N 82°36E 109 C10
Ust-Khayryuzovo Russia 57°15N 156°45E 107 D16
Ust-Kut Russia 56°50N 105°42E 107 D11
Ust-Kuyga Russia 70°1N 135°43E 107 B14
Ust-Labinsk Russia 45°15N 39°41E 87 H4
Ust-Luga Russia 59°35N 28°20E 64 C5
Ust-Maya Russia 60°30N 134°28E 107 C14
Ust-Mil Russia 59°40N 133°11E 107 D14
Ust-Nera Russia 64°35N 143°15E 107 C15
Ust-Nyukzha Russia 56°34N 121°37E 107 D13
Ust-Olenek Russia 73°0N 120°5W 107 B12
Ust-Omchug Russia 61°9N 149°38E 107 C15
Ust-Port Russia 69°40N 84°26E 106 C9
Ust-Tsilma Russia 65°28N 52°11E 106 C6
Ust-Urt = Ustyurt Plateau Asia 44°0N 55°0E 108 C6

Ustaritz France 43°24N 1°27W 72 E2
Ustecký □ Czech Rep. 50°30N 14°0E 78 A7
Uster Switz. 47°22N 8°43E 77 H4
Ústí nad Labem Czech Rep. 50°41N 14°3E 78 A7
Ústí nad Orlicí Czech Rep. 49°58N 16°24E 79 B9
Ústica Italy 38°42N 13°11E 94 D6
Ustinov = Izhevsk Russia 56°51N 53°14E 106 D6
Ustka Poland 54°35N 16°55E 82 D3
Ustroń Poland 49°43N 18°48E 83 J5
Ustrzyki Dolne Poland 49°27N 22°40E 83 J9
Ustyluh Ukraine 50°51N 24°10E 83 H11
Ustyurt Plateau Asia 44°0N 55°0E 108 C6
Ustyuzhna Russia 58°50N 36°32E 84 C9
Usu China 44°27N 84°40E 109 D10
Usuki Japan 33°8N 131°49E 113 H5
Usulután El Salv. 13°25N 88°28W 182 D2
Usumacinta → Mexico 18°24N 92°38W 181 D6
Usumbura = Bujumbura Burundi 3°16S 29°18E 142 C2
Usure Tanzania 4°40S 34°22E 142 C3
Usutu → Mozam. 26°48S 32°7E 145 C5
Uta Indonesia 4°33S 136°0E 119 E9
Utah □ U.S.A. 39°20N 111°30W 168 G8
Utah L. U.S.A. 40°12N 111°48W 168 F8
Utansjö Sweden 62°46N 17°55E 62 B11
Utara, Selat Malaysia 5°28N 100°20E 121 c
Utarni India 26°5N 71°58E 124 F4
Utatlan Guatemala 15°2N 91°11W 182 C1
Ute Creek → U.S.A. 35°21N 103°50W 169 J12
Utebo Spain 41°43N 1°0W 90 D3
Utena Lithuania 55°27N 25°40E 64 F9
Utete Tanzania 8°0S 38°45E 142 D4
Uthai Thani Thailand 15°22N 100°3E 120 E3
Uthal Pakistan 25°44N 66°40E 124 G2
Utiariti Brazil 13°0S 58°10W 186 F7
Utica N.Y., U.S.A. 43°6N 75°14W 175 C9
Utica Ohio, U.S.A. 40°14N 82°27W 174 F2
Utiel Spain 39°37N 1°11W 91 F3
Utikuma L. Canada 55°50N 115°30W 162 B5
Utila Honduras 16°6N 86°56W 182 C2
Utinga Brazil 12°6S 41°5W 189 C2
Utkela India 20°6N 83°10E 126 D6
Utlängen Sweden 56°2N 15°48E 63 H9
Utnur India 19°22N 78°46E 126 E4
Utö Sweden 58°56N 18°16E 62 F12
Utopia Australia 22°14S 134°33E 150 C1
Utraula India 27°19N 82°25E 125 F10
Utrecht Neths. 52°5N 5°8E 69 B5
Utrecht S. Africa 27°38S 30°20E 145 C5
Utrecht □ Neths. 52°6N 5°7E 69 B5
Utrera Spain 37°12N 5°48W 89 H5
Utsjoki → Finland 69°51N 26°59E 60 B22
Utsunomiya Japan 36°30N 139°50E 113 F9
Uttar Pradesh □ India 27°0N 80°0E 125 F9
Uttaradit Thailand 17°36N 100°5E 120 D3
Uttarakhand □ India 30°0N 79°30E 125 D8
Utterson Canada 45°12N 79°19W 174 A5
Uttoxeter U.K. 52°54N 1°52W 66 E6
Uummannaq Qaasuitsup, Greenland 77°33N 68°52W 57 B4
Uummannaq Qaasuitsup, Greenland 59°48N 43°55W 57 C6
Uummannarsuaq = Nunap Isua Greenland 59°48N 43°55W 57 C6
Uunartoq Qeqertoq Greenland 71°33N 21°47W 57 C8
Uusikaarlepyy Finland 63°32N 22°31E 60 E20
Uusikaupunki Finland 60°47N 21°25E 64 B1
Uva Russia 56°59N 52°13E 86 B11
Uvac → Serbia 43°35N 19°30E 96 C3
Uvalda U.S.A. 32°2N 82°31W 178 C7
Uvalde U.S.A. 29°13N 99°47W 176 G5
Uvarovo Russia 51°59N 42°14E 86 E6
Uvat Russia 59°5N 68°50E 106 D7
Uvinza Tanzania 5°5S 30°24E 142 D3
Uvira Dem. Rep. of the Congo 3°22S 29°3E 142 C2
Uvs Mongolia 49°38N 93°0E 109 C12
Uvs Nuur Mongolia 50°20N 92°30E 109 C12
'Uwairidh, Ḥarrat al Si. Arabia 26°50N 38°0E 128 E3
Uwajima Japan 33°10N 132°35E 113 H6
Uwanda Tanzania 7°46S 32°0E 142 D3
Uweinat, Jebel Sudan 21°54N 24°58E 137 C11
Uxbridge Canada 44°6N 79°7W 174 B5
Uxin Qi China 38°50N 109°5E 114 E5
Uxmal Mexico 20°22N 89°46W 181 C7
Uydzin Mongolia 44°9N 107°0E 114 B4
Uyo Nigeria 5°1N 7°53E 139 D6
Üyüklü Tepe Turkey 37°5N 27°21E 99 D9
Uyûn Mûsa Egypt 29°53N 32°40E 130 F1
Uyuni Bolivia 20°28S 66°47W 188 E4

Uzbekistan ■ Asia 41°30N 65°0E 109 D7
Uzboy → Turkmenistan 39°30N 55°0E 129 B9
Uzen, Mal → Kazakhstan 49°4N 49°44E 87 F9
Uzerche France 45°25N 1°34E 72 C5
Uzès France 44°1N 4°26E 73 D8
Uzh → Ukraine 51°15N 30°12E 75 C16
Uzhgorod = Uzhhorod Ukraine 48°36N 22°18E 80 B7
Uzhhorod Ukraine 48°36N 22°18E 80 B7
Uzhok Ukraine 48°59N 22°52E 80 B7
Uzice Serbia 43°55N 19°50E 96 C4
Užice Serbia 43°55N 19°50E 96 C4
Uzlovaya Russia 54°0N 38°5E 84 F10
Üzümlü Turkey 36°44N 29°14E 99 E11
Uzunköprü Turkey 41°16N 26°43E 99 B10
Uzunkuyu Turkey 38°17N 26°33E 99 C8

V

Vaal → S. Africa 29°4S 23°38E 144 C3
Vaal Dam S. Africa 27°0S 28°14E 145 C4
Vaalwater S. Africa 24°15S 28°8E 145 A4
Vaasa Finland 63°6N 21°38E 60 E19
Vaba → Kut → Russia 70°1N 135°43E 107 B14 (see Ust-Kuyga)
Vabre France 43°42N 2°24E 72 E6
Vác Hungary 47°49N 19°10E 80 C4
Vacaria Brazil 28°31S 50°52W 191 B5
Vacata Fiji 17°15S 179°31W 154 a
Vacaville U.S.A. 38°21N 121°59W 170 G5
Vaccarès, Étang de France 43°32N 4°34E 73 E8
Vach = Vakh → Russia 60°45N 76°45E 106 C8
Vache, Î. à Haiti 18°2N 73°35W 183 C5
Väckelsång Sweden 56°37N 14°58E 63 H8
Vacoas Mauritius 20°18S 57°29E 141 d

Vada India 19°39N 73°8E 126 E1
Vadakara India 11°35N 75°40E 127 J2
Vāddö Sweden 60°0N 18°50E 62 D12
Vadnagar India 23°47N 72°40E 124 H5
Vado Lígure Italy 44°17N 8°26E 92 D5
Vadodara India 22°20N 73°10E 124 H5
Vadsø Norway 70°3N 29°50E 60 A23
Vadstena Sweden 58°28N 14°54E 63 F8
Vaduj India 17°36N 74°27E 126 F2
Vaduz Liech. 47°8N 9°31E 77 H5
Værøy Norway 67°40N 12°40E 60 C15
Vágar Færoe Is. 62°5N 7°15W 60 E9
Vaggeryd Sweden 57°30N 14°10E 63 H7
Vaghia Greece 38°23N 23°11E 98 C5
Vagia, Akra Greece 36°15N 28°11E 101 C10
Vagney France 48°1N 6°43E 71 E13
Vagnhärad Sweden 58°57N 17°33E 63 F11
Vagos Portugal 40°33N 8°42W 88 E2
Vágsfjorden Norway 68°50N 16°50E 60 B17
Váh → Slovak Rep. 47°43N 18°7E 79 D11
Vahsel B. Antarctica 75°0S 35°0W 5 D1
Váhtjer = Gällivare Sweden 67°9N 20°40E 60 C19
Vaï Greece 35°15N 26°18E 101 D8
Vaiaku = Fongafale Tuvalu 8°31S 179°13E 147 B10
Vaigai → India 9°15N 79°10E 127 K4
Vaiges France 48°2N 0°30W 70 D6
Vaihingen Germany 48°54N 8°57E 77 G4
Vaihiria, L. Tahiti 17°40S 149°25W 155 b
Vaijapur India 19°58N 74°45E 126 E2
Vaikam India 9°45N 76°25E 127 K3
Vail U.S.A. 39°40N 106°20W 168 G10
Vailly-sur-Aisne France 49°24N 3°31E 71 C10
Vaippar → India 9°0N 78°25E 127 K4
Vairao Tahiti 17°47S 149°17W 155 b
Vaisali → India 26°28N 78°53E 125 F8
Vaison-la-Romaine France 44°14N 5°4E 73 D9
Vajpur India 21°24N 73°17E 126 D1
Vakarai Sri Lanka 8°8N 81°26E 127 L5
Vakfikebir Turkey 41°2N 39°17E 105 B8
Vakh → Russia 60°45N 76°45E 106 C8
Vakhtan Russia 57°53N 46°47E 86 B8
Vál Hungary 47°22N 18°40E 80 C3
Val Camónica Italy 45°57N 10°17E 92 C7
Val-de-Marne □ France 48°45N 2°28E 71 D9
Val-d'Isère France 45°26N 6°59E 73 C10
Val-d'Or Canada 48°7N 77°47W 164 C4
Val Grande △ Italy 46°3N 8°25E 92 B5
Val Marie Canada 49°15N 107°45W 163 D7
Val Thorens France 45°20N 6°33E 73 C10
Valaam Russia 61°22N 30°57E 84 B6
Valadares Portugal 41°5N 8°38W 88 D2
Valahia Romania 44°35N 25°0E 81 F9
Valaichenai Sri Lanka 7°54N 81°32E 127 L5
Valais □ Switz. 46°12N 7°45E 77 J3
Valais, Alpes du Switz. 46°5N 7°35E 77 J3
Valandovo Macedonia 41°19N 22°34E 96 E6
Valašské Meziříčí Czech Rep. 49°29N 17°59E 79 B10
Valatie U.S.A. 42°24N 73°40W 175 D11
Valaxa Greece 38°50N 24°29E 98 C6
Vålberg Sweden 59°23N 13°11E 62 E7
Valbo Sweden 60°40N 17°2E 62 D10
Valbondione Italy 46°2N 10°1E 92 B7
Valcamonica = Val Camónica Italy 45°57N 10°17E 92 C7
Vâlcea □ Romania 45°0N 24°10E 81 F9
Valcheta Argentina 40°40S 66°8W 192 E3
Valdagno Italy 45°39N 11°18E 93 C8
Valdahon France 47°8N 6°21E 71 E13
Valdai Hills = Valdayskaya Vozvyshennost Russia 57°0N 33°30E 84 D7
Valday Russia 57°58N 33°9E 84 D7
Valdayskaya Vozvyshennost Russia 57°0N 33°30E 84 D7
Valdecañas, Embalse de Spain 39°45N 5°0W 89 F5
Valdemarsvik Sweden 58°14N 16°40E 63 F10
Valdemoro Spain 40°12N 3°40W 88 E7
Valdepeñas Spain 38°43N 3°25W 89 G7
Valderaduey → Spain 41°31N 5°42W 88 D5
Valdés, Pen. Argentina 42°30S 63°45W 192 E4
Valdez U.S.A. 61°7N 146°16W 160 C5
Valdivia Chile 39°50S 73°14W 192 A2
Valdivia Abyssal Plain S. Ocean 62°0S 70°0E 55 C6
Valdobbiádene Italy 45°54N 12°0E 93 C8
Valdosta U.S.A. 30°50N 83°17W 178 E6
Valdoviño = Aviño Spain 43°36N 8°8W 88 B2
Valdres Norway 61°5N 9°5E 63 D7
Vale Georgia 41°30N 42°58E 107 F7
Vale U.S.A. 43°59N 117°15W 168 E5
Vale of Glamorgan □ U.K. 51°28N 3°25W 67 F4
Valea lui Mihai Romania 47°32N 22°11E 80 C7
Valea Mărului Romania 45°54N 27°42E 81 E12
Valença Brazil 13°20S 39°5W 189 C3
Valença Portugal 42°1N 8°34W 88 C2
Valença do Piauí Brazil 6°20S 41°45W 189 B2
Valençay France 47°9N 1°34E 71 E8
Valence France 44°57N 4°54E 73 D8
Valence d'Agen France 44°6N 0°53E 72 D4
Valencia Spain 39°27N 0°23W 91 F4
Valencia Trin. & Tob. 10°39N 61°11W 187 K15
Valencia Venezuela 10°11N 68°0W 186 A5
Valencia □ Spain 39°20N 0°40W 91 F4
Valencia ✈ (VLC) Spain 39°20N 0°26W 91 F4
Valencia, G. de Spain 39°30N 0°20E 91 F5
Valencia de Alcántara Spain 39°25N 7°14W 89 F3
Valencia de Don Juan Spain 42°17N 5°31W 88 C5
Valencia I. Ireland 51°54N 10°22W 64 E1
Valenciennes France 50°20N 3°34E 71 B10
Vălenii de Munte Romania 45°11N 26°3E 81 E11
Valensole France 43°50N 5°59E 73 E9

Valentigney France 47°27N 6°51E 71 E13
Valentin, Sa. do Brazil 6°0S 43°30W 189 B2
Valentin Russia 43°8N 134°17E 112 C7
Valentine Nebr., U.S.A. 42°52N 100°33W 172 D3
Valentine Tex., U.S.A. 30°35N 104°30W 176 F2
Valenza Italy 45°1N 8°38E 92 C5
Valera Venezuela 9°19N 70°37W 186 B4
Valga Estonia 57°47N 26°2E 84 D4
Valguarnera Caropepe Italy 37°30N 14°23E 95 E7
Valier U.S.A. 48°18N 112°16W 168 B7
Valinco, G. de France 41°40N 8°52E 73 G12
Valjevo Serbia 44°18N 19°53E 96 B4
Valka Latvia 57°46N 26°3E 84 D3
Valkeakoski Finland 61°16N 24°2E 64 B2
Valkenswaard Neths. 51°21N 5°29E 69 C5
Vall de Uxó = La Vall d'Uixó Spain 39°49N 0°15W 90 F4
Valla Sweden 59°2N 16°20E 62 E10
Valladolid Mexico 20°41N 88°12W 181 C7
Valladolid Spain 41°38N 4°43W 88 D6
Valladolid □ Spain 41°38N 4°43W 88 D6
Vallata Italy 41°2N 15°16E 95 A8
Valldemossa Spain 39°43N 2°37E 90 B9
Valle d'Aosta □ Italy 45°45N 7°15E 92 C4
Valle de la Pascua Venezuela 9°13N 66°0W 186 B5
Valle de las Palmas Mexico 32°20N 116°43W 171 N10
Valle de Santiago Mexico 20°23N 101°12W 180 C4
Valle de Villaverde Spain 43°15N 3°15W 88 B7
Valle de Zaragoza Mexico 27°25N 105°50W 180 B3
Valle del Ticino △ Italy 45°22N 9°0E 92 C6
Valle Fértil, Sierra del Argentina 30°20S 68°0W 190 C2
Valle Gran Rey Canary Is. 28°5N 17°20W 100 F2
Valle Hermoso Mexico 25°35N 97°40W 181 B5
Valle Nacional Mexico 17°47N 96°18W 181 D5
Valledupar Colombia 10°29N 73°15W 186 A4
Vallée du Bandama △ Ivory C. 8°0N 5°0W 138 D3
Vallehermoso Canary Is. 28°10N 17°15W 100 F2
Vallejo U.S.A. 38°7N 122°14W 170 G4
Vallenar Chile 28°30S 70°50W 190 B1
Vallentuna Sweden 59°32N 18°5E 62 E12
Valleraugue France 44°6N 3°39E 72 D7
Vallet France 47°10N 1°15W 70 E5
Valletta Malta 35°54N 14°31E 101 D2
Valley Center U.S.A. 33°13N 117°2W 171 M9
Valley City U.S.A. 46°55N 98°0W 172 B5
Valley Falls Oreg., U.S.A. 42°29N 120°17W 168 E3
Valley Falls R.I., U.S.A. 41°54N 71°24W 175 E13
Valley of Flowers △ India 30°50N 79°40E 125 D8
Valley of the Kings Egypt 25°41N 32°34E 137 B3
Valley Springs U.S.A. 38°12N 120°50W 170 G6
Valley View U.S.A. 40°39N 76°33W 175 F8
Valley Wells U.S.A. 35°27N 115°46W 171 K11
Valleyview Canada 55°5N 117°17W 162 B5
Valli di Comácchio Italy 44°40N 12°15E 93 D9
Vallimanca, Arroyo Argentina 35°40S 59°10W 190 D4
Vallo della Lucánia Italy 40°14N 15°16E 95 B8
Vallon-Pont-d'Arc France 44°24N 4°24E 73 D8
Vallorbe Switz. 46°42N 6°20E 77 J2
Valls Spain 41°18N 1°15E 90 D6
Vallvik Sweden 61°11N 17°10E 62 C11
Valmaseda = Balmaseda Spain 43°11N 3°12W 90 B1
Valmiera Latvia 57°37N 25°29E 84 D3
Valnera Spain 43°9N 3°40W 88 B7
Valognes France 49°30N 1°28W 70 C5
Valona = Vlorë Albania 40°32N 19°28E 96 F3
Valongo Portugal 41°8N 8°30W 88 D2
Valozhyn Belarus 54°3N 26°30E 75 A14
Valpaços Portugal 41°36N 7°17W 88 D3
Valparaíso Chile 33°2S 71°40W 190 C1
Valparaíso Mexico 22°46N 103°34W 180 C4
Valparaiso U.S.A. 41°28N 87°4W 172 E10
Valparaíso Fla., U.S.A. 30°29N 86°30W 179 E3
Valparaíso □ Chile 33°2S 71°40W 190 C1
Valpovo Croatia 45°39N 18°25E 83 K8
Valpoi India 15°32N 74°8E 127 G2
Valréas France 44°24N 5°0E 73 D9
Vals → S. Africa 27°23S 26°30E 144 C4
Vals Switz. 46°39N 9°11E 77 J5
Vals, Tanjung Indonesia 8°26S 137°25E 119 F9
Vals-les-Bains France 44°42N 4°24E 73 D8
Valsad India 20°40N 72°58E 126 D1
Valtellina Italy 46°11N 9°55E 92 B6
Valujki Russia 50°33N 38°5E 85 G10
Valverde Canary Is. 27°48N 17°55W 100 G2
Valverde del Camino Spain 37°35N 6°47W 89 H4
Valverde del Fresno Spain 40°15N 6°51W 88 E4
Vama Romania 47°34N 25°42E 81 C10
Vambori India 19°17N 74°44E 126 E2
Vamdrup Denmark 55°25N 9°17E 63 J3
Vámhus Sweden 61°11N 14°28E 62 C8
Vamizi, I. Mozam. 11°2S 40°40E 143 E5
Vammala = Sastamala Finland 61°20N 22°54E 84 B2
Vamos Greece 35°24N 24°13E 101 D6
Vamsadhara → India 18°21N 84°8E 127 E8
Van Turkey 38°30N 43°20E 105 C10
Van □ Turkey 38°30N 43°0E 105 C10
Van, L. = Van Gölü Turkey 38°30N 43°0E 105 C10
Van Alstyne U.S.A. 33°25N 96°35W 176 E6
Van Blommestein Meer Suriname 4°45N 55°5W 187 C7
Van Buren Canada 47°10N 67°55W 165 C6
Van Buren Ark., U.S.A. 35°26N 94°21W 176 D7
Van Buren Maine, U.S.A. 47°10N 67°58W 173 B20
Van Buren Mo., U.S.A. 37°0N 91°1W 172 G8
Van Canh Vietnam 13°37N 109°0E 120 F7
Van Diemen, C. N. Terr., Australia 11°9S 130°24E 148 B5
Van Diemen, C. Queens., Australia 16°30S 139°46E 150 B2

Van Diemen G. *Australia* 11°45S 132°0E **148** B5
Van Gölü *Turkey* 38°30N 43°0E **105** C10
Van Horn *U.S.A.* 31°3N 104°50W **176** F2
Van Ninh *Vietnam* 12°42N 109°14E **120** F7
Van Rees, Pegunungan *Indonesia* 2°35S 138°15E **119** E9
Van Tivu *India* 8°51N 78°15E **127** K4
Van Wert *U.S.A.* 40°52N 84°35W **173** E11
Van Yen *Vietnam* 21°4N 104°42E **116** G5
Van Zylsrus *S. Africa* 26°52S 22°4E **144** C3
Vanadzor *Armenia* 40°48N 44°30E **87** K7
Vanavara *Russia* 60°22N 102°16E **107** C11
Vancouver *Canada* 49°15N 123°7W **170** A3
Vancouver *U.S.A.* 45°38N 122°40W **170** E4
Vancouver, C. *Australia* 35°2S 118°11E **149** G2
Vancouver I. *Canada* 49°50N 126°0W **170** B2
Vancouver Int. ✈ (YVR) *Canada* 49°10N 123°10W **170** A3
Vanda = Vantaa *Finland* 60°18N 24°56E **84** B3
Vandalia *Ill., U.S.A.* 38°58N 89°6W **172** F9
Vandalia *Mo., U.S.A.* 39°19N 91°29W **172** F8
Vandavasi *India* 12°30N 79°30E **127** H4
Vandellòs *Spain* 41°0N 0°55E **90** E5
Vandeloos B. *Sri Lanka* 8°0N 81°45E **127** L5
Vandenberg Village *U.S.A.* 34°43N 120°28W **171** L6
Vandergrift *U.S.A.* 40°36N 79°34W **174** F5
Vanderhoof *Canada* 54°0N 124°0W **162** C4
Vanderkloof Dam *S. Africa* 30°4S 24°40E **144** D3
Vanderlin I. *Australia* 15°44S 137°2E **150** B2
Vänern *Sweden* 58°47N 13°30E **63** F7
Vänersborg *Sweden* 58°26N 12°19E **63** F6
Vang Vieng *Laos* 18°58N 102°32E **120** C4
Vanga *Kenya* 4°35S 39°12E **142** C4
Vangaindrano *Madag.* 23°21S 47°36E **141** J9
Vänge *Sweden* 59°50N 17°20E **62** E11
Vanguard *Canada* 49°55N 107°20W **163** D7
Vanino *Russia* 48°50N 140°5E **107** E15
Vanivilasa Sagara *India* 13°45N 76°30E **127** H3
Vaniyambadi *India* 12°46N 78°44E **127** H4
Vânju Mare *Romania* 44°25N 22°52E **80** F7
Vankleek Hill *Canada* 45°32N 74°40W **175** A10
Vännäs *Sweden* 63°58N 19°48E **60** E18
Vannes *France* 47°40N 2°47W **70** E4
Vannøya *Norway* 70°6N 19°50E **60** A18
Vanoise, Massif de la *France* 45°25N 6°40E **73** C10
Vanrhynsdorp *S. Africa* 31°36S 18°44E **144** D2
Vansada *India* 20°47N 73°25E **126** D1
Vansbro *Sweden* 60°32N 14°15E **62** D8
Vansittart B. *Australia* 14°3S 126°17E **148** B4
Vansittart I. *Canada* 65°50N 84°0W **161** D15
Vantaa *Finland* 60°18N 24°56E **84** B3
Vanua Balavu *Fiji* 17°12S 178°55W **154** a
Vanua Levu *Fiji* 16°33S 179°15E **154** a
Vanua Vatu *Fiji* 18°22S 179°15W **154** a
Vanuatu ■ *Pac. Oc.* 15°0S 168°0E **147** C9
Vanwyksvlei *S. Africa* 30°18S 21°49E **144** D3
Vapi *India* 20°22N 72°54E **126** D1
Vapnyarka *Ukraine* 48°32N 28°45E **81** B13
Var □ *France* 43°27N 6°18E **73** E10
Var ➔ *France* 43°39N 7°12E **73** E11
Vara *Sweden* 58°16N 12°55E **63** F6
Varada ➔ *India* 15°0N 75°40E **127** G2
Varades *France* 47°25N 1°1W **70** E5
Varáita ➔ *Italy* 44°49N 7°53E **92** D4
Varalé *Ivory C.* 9°40N 3°17W **138** D4
Varallo *Italy* 45°49N 8°15E **92** C5
Varāmīn *Iran* 35°20N 51°39E **129** C6
Varāmīn □ *Iran* 35°18N 51°35E **129** B6
Varanasi *India* 25°22N 83°0E **125** G10
Varangerfjorden *Norway* 70°3N 29°25E **60** A23
Varangerhalvøya *Norway* 70°25N 29°30E **60** A23
Varano, Lago di *Italy* 41°53N 15°45E **93** G12
Varaždin *Croatia* 46°20N 16°20E **93** B13
Varazze *Italy* 44°22N 8°34E **92** D5
Varberg *Sweden* 57°6N 12°20E **63** G6
Vardak □ *Afghan.* 34°0N 68°0E **122** B6
Vardar = Axios ➔ *Greece* 40°57N 22°35E **96** F6
Varde *Denmark* 55°38N 8°29E **63** J2
Varde Å ➔ *Denmark* 55°35N 8°19E **63** J2
Vardenis *Armenia* 40°10N 45°43E **87** K7
Vardø *Norway* 70°23N 31°5E **60** A24
Varel *Germany* 53°23N 8°8E **76** B4
Varella, Mui = Nay, Mui *Vietnam* 12°54N 109°26E **120** F7
Varėna *Lithuania* 54°12N 24°30E **84** E3
Varennes-sur-Allier *France* 46°19N 3°24E **71** F10
Varennes-Vauzelles *France* 47°3N 3°9E **71** E10
Vareš *Bos.-H.* 44°12N 18°23E **80** F3
Varese *Italy* 45°48N 8°50E **92** C5
Vârfurile *Romania* 46°19N 22°31E **80** D7
Vårgårda *Sweden* 58°2N 12°49E **63** F6
Vargem Bonita *Brazil* 20°20S 46°22W **189** E1
Vargem Grande *Brazil* 3°33S 43°56W **189** A2
Varginha *Brazil* 21°33S 45°25W **191** A6
Vargön *Sweden* 58°22N 12°20E **63** F6
Varillas *Chile* 24°0S 70°10W **190** A1
Varkaus *Finland* 62°19N 27°50E **84** A4
Värmdölandet *Sweden* 59°20N 18°33E **62** E12
Värmeln *Sweden* 59°35N 12°54E **62** E6
Värmlands län □ *Sweden* 60°0N 13°20E **62** E6
Värmlandsbro *Sweden* 59°11N 13°0E **62** E7
Varna *Bulgaria* 43°13N 27°56E **97** C11
Varna □ *Bulgaria* 43°20N 27°30E **97** C11
Varna ➔ *India* 16°48N 74°32E **126** F2
Värnamo *Sweden* 57°10N 14°3E **63** G8
Várnjárga = Varangerhalvøya *Norway* 70°25N 29°30E **60** A23
Varnsdorf *Czech Rep.* 50°55N 14°35E **78** A7
Varnville *U.S.A.* 32°51N 81°5W **178** C8
Várpalota *Hungary* 47°12N 18°8E **80** C3
Vars *Canada* 45°21N 75°21W **175** A9
Vars *France* 44°37N 6°42E **73** D10
Varto *Turkey* 39°10N 41°27E **105** C9
Varvarin *Serbia* 43°43N 21°20E **96** C5
Varysburg *U.S.A.* 42°46N 78°19W **174** D6
Varzaneh *Iran* 32°25N 52°40E **129** C7
Varzaqān *Iran* 38°29N 46°40E **105** C12
Várzea Alegre *Brazil* 6°47S 39°17W **189** B3
Várzea da Palma *Brazil* 17°36S 44°44W **189** D2
Varzi *Italy* 44°49N 9°12E **92** D6
Varzo *Italy* 46°12N 8°15E **92** B5
Varzy *France* 47°22N 3°20E **71** E10
Vas □ *Hungary* 47°10N 16°55E **80** C1
Vasa = Vaasa *Finland* 63°6N 21°38E **60** E19
Vasa Barris ➔ *Brazil* 11°10S 37°10W **189** C3
Vasai-Virar *India* 19°28N 72°48E **126** E1
Vásárosnamény *Hungary* 48°9N 22°19E **80** B7
Vascão ➔ *Portugal* 37°31N 7°31W **89** H3
Vaşcău *Romania* 46°28N 22°30E **80** D7
Vascongadas = País Vasco □ *Spain* 42°50N 2°45W **90** C2
Vashkivtsi *Ukraine* 48°23N 25°31E **81** B10
Vasht = Khāsh *Iran* 28°15N 61°15E **129** D9
Vasilevichi *Belarus* 52°15N 29°50E **75** B16
Vasiliki *Greece* 38°37N 20°36E **98** C2
Vasiliko *Greece* 38°25N 23°40E **98** C5
Vasilkov = Vasylkiv *Ukraine* 50°7N 30°15E **75** C16
Väskinde *Sweden* 57°40N 18°20E **63** G10
Vaslui *Romania* 46°38N 27°42E **81** D12
Vaslui □ *Romania* 46°30N 27°45E **81** D12
Väsman *Sweden* 60°9N 15°5E **62** D9
Vassar *Canada* 49°10N 95°55W **163** D9
Vassar *U.S.A.* 43°22N 83°35W **173** D12
Västerås *Sweden* 59°37N 16°38E **62** E10
Västerbotten *Sweden* 64°36N 20°4E **60** D19
Västerdalälven ➔ *Sweden* 60°30N 15°7E **62** D8
Västergötland *Sweden* 58°0N 13°10E **63** F7
Västerhaninge *Sweden* 59°7N 18°6E **62** E12
Västervik *Sweden* 57°43N 16°33E **63** G10
Västmanland *Sweden* 59°45N 16°20E **61** G17
Västmanlands län □ *Sweden* 59°45N 16°20E **62** E10
Vasto *Italy* 42°8N 14°40E **93** F11
Västra Götalands Län □ *Sweden* 58°0N 13°0E **63** F6
Vasvár *Hungary* 47°3N 16°47E **80** C1
Vasylivka *Ukraine* 45°38N 28°50E **81** E13
Vasylkiv *Ukraine* 50°7N 30°15E **75** C16
Vat Phou *Laos* 14°51N 105°49E **120** E5
Vatan *France* 47°4N 1°50E **71** E8
Vatersay *U.K.* 56°55N 7°32W **65** E1
Vathia *Greece* 36°29N 22°29E **98** E4
Vati *Greece* 36°3N 27°53E **101** C9
Vatican City ■ *Europe* 41°54N 12°27E **93** G9
Vaticano, C. *Italy* 38°37N 15°50E **95** D8
Vatili *Cyprus* 35°6N 33°40E **101** D12
Vatin *Serbia* 45°12N 21°20E **80** E6
Vatiu = Atiu *Cook Is.* 20°0S 158°10W **157** J12
Vatnajökull *Iceland* 64°30N 16°48W **60** D5
Vatnajökull △ *Iceland* 64°24N 16°48W **60** D5
Vato *Sweden* 59°50N 19°0E **62** E12
Vatolakkos *Greece* 35°27N 23°53E **101** D5
Vatra-Dornei *Romania* 47°22N 25°22E **81** C10
Vatrak ➔ *India* 23°9N 73°2E **124** H5
Vättern *Sweden* 58°25N 14°30E **63** F8
Vatu Vara *Fiji* 17°26S 179°31W **154** a
Vatulele *Fiji* 18°33S 177°37E **154** a
Vaucluse □ *France* 43°50N 5°20E **73** E9
Vaucouleurs *France* 48°37N 5°40E **71** D12
Vaud □ *Switz.* 46°35N 6°30E **77** J2
Vaudreuil-Dorion *Canada* 45°23N 74°3W **175** A10
Vaughn *Mont., U.S.A.* 47°33N 111°33W **168** C8
Vaughn *N. Mex., U.S.A.* 34°36N 105°13W **169** J11
Vaujours L. *Canada* 55°27N 74°15W **164** A5
Vaupés = Uaupés ➔ *Brazil* 0°2N 67°16W **186** C5
Vaupés □ *Colombia* 1°0N 71°0W **186** C4
Vauvert *France* 43°42N 4°17E **73** E8
Vauxhall *Canada* 50°5N 112°9W **162** C6
Vav *India* 24°22N 71°31E **124** G4
Vavoua *Ivory C.* 7°23N 6°29W **138** D3
Vavuniya *Sri Lanka* 8°45N 80°30E **127** K5
Vawkavysk *Belarus* 53°9N 24°30E **75** B13
Vaxholm *Sweden* 59°25N 18°20E **62** E12
Växjö *Sweden* 56°52N 14°50E **63** H8
Våxtorp *Sweden* 56°25N 13°8E **63** H7
Vayalpad *India* 13°39N 78°38E **127** H4
Vaygach, Ostrov *Russia* 70°0N 60°0E **106** C7
Veadeiros *Brazil* 14°7S 47°31W **189** C1
Veaikevárri = Svappavaara *Sweden* 67°40N 21°3E **60** C19
Vechelde *Germany* 52°16N 10°22E **76** C6
Vechta *Germany* 52°44N 8°17E **76** C4
Vechte ➔ *Neths.* 52°34N 6°6E **69** B6
Vecsés *Hungary* 47°26N 19°19E **80** C4
Vedaranniyam *India* 10°25N 79°50E **127** J4
Veddige *Sweden* 57°17N 12°20E **63** G6
Vedea ➔ *Romania* 43°42N 25°41E **81** G10
Vedi *Armenia* 39°54N 44°43E **105** C11
Vedia *Argentina* 34°30S 61°31W **190** C3
Vedrette di Ries-Aurina △ *Italy* 46°54N 12°5E **93** B9
Vedum *Sweden* 58°11N 13°0E **63** F7
Veendam *Neths.* 53°5N 6°52E **69** A6
Veenendaal *Neths.* 52°2N 5°34E **69** B5
Vefsna ➔ *Norway* 65°48N 13°10E **60** D15
Vega *Norway* 65°40N 11°55E **60** D14
Vega *U.S.A.* 35°15N 102°26W **176** D3
Vega Baja *Puerto Rico* 18°27N 66°23W **183** d
Vegadeo *Spain* 43°27N 7°4W **88** B3
Vegoritida, L. *Greece* 40°45N 21°45E **96** F5
Vegreville *Canada* 53°30N 112°5W **162** C6
Veinge *Sweden* 56°33N 13°4E **63** H7
Veisiejai *Lithuania* 54°6N 23°42E **82** D10
Vejbystrand *Sweden* 56°19N 12°45E **63** H6
Vejen *Denmark* 55°30N 9°9E **63** J3
Vejer de la Frontera *Spain* 36°15N 5°59W **89** J5
Vejle *Denmark* 55°43N 9°30E **63** J3
Vejle Fjord *Denmark* 55°40N 9°50E **63** J3
Vela Luka *Croatia* 42°59N 16°44E **93** F13
Velachha *India* 21°26N 73°1E **126** D1
Velanai I. *Sri Lanka* 9°45N 79°45E **127** K4
Velas, C. *Costa Rica* 10°21N 85°52W **182** D2
Velasco, Sierra de *Argentina* 29°20S 67°10W **190** B2
Velay, Mts. du *France* 45°0N 3°40E **72** D7
Velbert *Germany* 51°20N 7°3E **76** D3
Velddrif *S. Africa* 32°42S 18°11E **144** D2
Velebit *Croatia* 44°50N 15°20E **93** D12
Velebit Planina *Croatia* 44°50N 15°20E **93** D12
Velebitski Kanal *Croatia* 44°45N 14°55E **93** D11
Veleka ➔ *Bulgaria* 42°4N 27°58E **97** D11
Velencei-tó *Hungary* 47°13N 18°36E **80** C3
Velenje *Slovenia* 46°23N 15°8E **93** B12
Veles *Macedonia* 41°46N 21°47E **96** E5
Velestino *Greece* 39°23N 22°43E **98** B4
Vélez-Málaga *Spain* 36°48N 4°5W **89** J6
Vélez Rubio *Spain* 37°41N 2°5W **91** H2
Velhas ➔ *Brazil* 17°13S 44°49W **189** D2
Velika *Croatia* 45°27N 17°40E **80** E2
Velika Gorica *Croatia* 45°44N 16°5E **93** C13
Velika Kapela *Croatia* 45°10N 15°5E **93** C12
Velika Kladuša *Bos.-H.* 45°11N 15°48E **93** C12
Velika Kruša = Krushë e Madhe *Kosovo* 42°19N 20°39E **96** D4
Velika Morava ➔ *Serbia* 44°43N 21°3E **96** B5
Velika Plana *Serbia* 44°20N 21°4E **96** B5
Velikaya ➔ *Russia* 57°48N 28°10E **84** D5
Velikaya Kema *Russia* 45°30N 137°12E **112** B8
Velikaya Lepetikha *Ukraine* 47°2N 33°58E **85** J7
Velike Lašče *Slovenia* 45°49N 14°45E **93** C11
Veliki Jastrebac *Serbia* 43°25N 21°30E **96** C5
Veliki Kanal *Serbia* 45°45N 19°15E **80** E4
Veliki Popović *Serbia* 44°8N 21°18E **96** B5
Velikiy Novgorod *Russia* 58°30N 31°25E **84** C6
Velikiye Luki *Russia* 56°25N 30°32E **84** D6
Veliko Gradište *Serbia* 44°46N 21°29E **96** B5
Veliko Tŭrnovo *Bulgaria* 43°5N 25°41E **97** C9
Veliko Tŭrnovo □ *Bulgaria* 43°5N 25°41E **97** C9
Velikonda Range *India* 14°45N 79°10E **127** G4
Vélingara *Kolda, Senegal* 13°12N 14°5W **138** C2
Vélingara *Louga, Senegal* 15°0N 14°40W **138** B2
Velingrad *Bulgaria* 42°4N 23°58E **96** D7
Velino, Mte. *Italy* 42°9N 13°23E **93** F10
Velizh *Russia* 55°36N 31°11E **84** E6
Vel'ké Kapušany *Slovak Rep.* 48°34N 22°5E **79** C15
Velké Karlovice *Czech Rep.* 49°20N 18°17E **79** B11
Velké Meziříčí *Czech Rep.* 49°21N 16°1E **78** B9
Vel'ký Javorník *Slovak Rep.* 49°19N 18°22E **79** B11
Vel'ký Krtíš *Slovak Rep.* 48°12N 19°21E **79** C12
Vel'ký Meder *Slovak Rep.* 47°52N 17°46E **79** D10
Vel'ký Tribeč *Slovak Rep.* 48°28N 18°15E **79** C11
Vellar ➔ *India* 11°30N 79°36E **127** J4
Velletri *Italy* 41°41N 12°47E **94** A5
Vellinge *Sweden* 55°29N 13°2E **63** J6
Vellmar *Germany* 51°22N 9°28E **76** D5
Vellore *India* 12°57N 79°10E **127** H4
Velopoula *Greece* 36°55N 23°27E **98** E5
Velsk *Russia* 61°10N 42°5E **84** B11
Velten *Germany* 52°42N 13°10E **76** C9
Veluwezoom △ *Neths.* 52°5N 6°0E **69** B6
Velva *U.S.A.* 48°4N 100°56W **172** A3
Velvendos *Greece* 40°15N 22°6E **96** F6
Velyka Mykhaylivka *Ukraine* 47°4N 29°52E **81** C14
Velyki Luchky *Ukraine* 48°25N 22°34E **80** B7
Velykyy Bereznyy *Ukraine* 48°54N 22°28E **80** B7
Velykyy Bychkiv *Ukraine* 47°58N 24°1E **81** C9
Vemb *Denmark* 56°21N 8°21E **63** H2
Vembanad L. *India* 9°36N 76°15E **127** K3
Vemdalen *Sweden* 62°27N 13°51E **62** B7
Ven *Sweden* 55°55N 12°45E **63** J6
Venaco *France* 42°14N 9°11E **73** F13
Venado *Mexico* 22°56N 101°6W **180** C4
Venado Tuerto *Argentina* 33°50S 62°0W **190** C3
Venafro *Italy* 41°29N 14°2E **95** A7
Venarey-les-Laumes *France* 47°32N 4°26E **71** E11
Venaria *Italy* 45°8N 7°38E **92** C4
Venčane *Serbia* 44°24N 20°28E **96** B4
Vence *France* 43°43N 7°6E **73** E11
Vendas Novas *Portugal* 38°39N 8°27W **89** G2
Vendée □ *France* 46°50N 1°35W **70** F5
Vendée ➔ *France* 46°20N 1°10W **70** F5
Vendéen, Bocage *France* 46°40N 1°20W **72** B2
Vendeuvre-sur-Barse *France* 48°14N 4°28E **71** D11
Vendicari △ *Italy* 36°49N 15°6E **95** F8
Vendôme *France* 47°47N 1°3E **70** E8
Vendrell = El Vendrell *Spain* 41°10N 1°30E **90** D6
Vendsyssel *Denmark* 57°22N 10°0E **63** G4
Vendychany *Ukraine* 48°38N 27°48E **81** B12
Venelles *France* 43°35N 5°28E **73** E9
Véneta, L. *Italy* 45°23N 12°25E **93** C9
Véneto □ *Italy* 45°30N 12°0E **93** C9
Venev *Russia* 54°22N 38°17E **84** E10
Venézia *Italy* 45°27N 12°21E **93** C9
Venézia, G. di *Italy* 45°15N 13°0E **93** C10
Venézia Lido *Italy* 45°25N 12°22E **93** C9
Venezuela ■ *S. Amer.* 8°0N 66°0W **186** B5
Venezuela, G. de *Venezuela* 11°30N 71°0W **186** A4
Vengurla *India* 15°53N 73°45E **127** G1
Vengurla Rocks *India* 15°55N 73°22E **127** G1
Venice = Venézia *Italy* 45°27N 12°21E **93** C9
Venice *U.S.A.* 27°6N 82°27W **179** H7
Vénissieux *France* 45°42N 4°53E **73** C8
Venjan *Sweden* 60°57N 13°55E **62** D7
Venjansjön *Sweden* 60°54N 14°2E **62** D8
Venkatagiri *India* 14°0N 79°35E **127** H4
Venkatapuram *India* 18°20N 80°30E **126** E5
Venlo *Neths.* 51°22N 6°11E **69** C6
Vennachar Junction *Canada* 45°5N 77°14W **174** A7
Vennesla *Norway* 58°15N 7°59E **61** G12
Venosa *Italy* 40°58N 15°49E **95** B8
Venray *Neths.* 51°31N 6°0E **69** C6
Venta *Lithuania* 56°12N 22°42E **82** B9
Venta ➔ *Latvia* 57°24N 21°33E **82** A8
Venta de Baños *Spain* 41°55N 4°30W **88** D6
Venta de Cardeña = Cardeña *Spain* 38°16N 4°20W **89** G6
Ventana, Sa. de la *Argentina* 38°0S 62°30W **190** D3
Ventersburg *S. Africa* 28°7S 27°9E **144** C4
Venterstad *S. Africa* 30°47S 25°48E **144** D4
Ventimiglia *Italy* 43°47N 7°36E **92** E4
Ventnor *U.K.* 50°36N 1°12W **67** G6
Ventotène *Italy* 40°47N 13°25E **94** B6
Ventoux, Mt. *France* 44°10N 5°17E **73** D9
Ventspils *Latvia* 57°25N 21°32E **82** A8
Ventspils □ *Latvia* 57°20N 21°50E **82** A8
Ventuarí ➔ *Venezuela* 3°58N 67°2W **186** C5
Ventucopa *U.S.A.* 34°50N 119°29W **171** L7
Ventura *U.S.A.* 34°17N 119°18W **171** L7
Venus *U.S.A.* 27°4N 81°22W **179** H8
Vénus, Pte. *Tahiti* 17°29S 149°29W **155** b
Venus B. *Australia* 38°40S 145°42E **153** E6
Venustiano Carranza *Mexico* 30°25N 115°53W **180** A1
Venustiano Carranza, Presa *Mexico* 27°30N 100°37W **180** B4
Vera *Argentina* 29°30S 60°20W **190** B3
Vera *Spain* 37°15N 1°51W **91** H3
Veracruz *Mexico* 19°11N 96°8W **181** D5
Veracruz □ *Mexico* 19°0N 96°15W **181** D5
Veraval *India* 20°53N 70°27E **124** J4
Verbánia *Italy* 45°56N 8°33E **92** C5
Verbano, L. di = Maggiore, L. *Italy* 45°57N 8°39E **92** B5
Verbano Cusio Ossola △ *Italy* 46°15N 8°20E **92** B5
Verbicaro *Italy* 39°45N 15°55E **95** C8
Verbier *Switz.* 46°6N 7°13E **77** J3
Vercelli *Italy* 45°19N 8°25E **92** C5
Verchovchevo *Ukraine* 48°32N 34°10E **85** H8
Vercors △ *France* 45°0N 5°25E **73** D9
Verdalsøra *Norway* 63°48N 11°30E **60** E14
Verde ➔ *Argentina* 41°56S 65°5W **192** B3
Verde ➔ *Goiás, Brazil* 18°1S 50°14W **187** G8
Verde ➔ *Mato Grosso do Sul, Brazil* 21°25S 52°20W **187** H8
Verde ➔ *Chihuahua, Mexico* 26°39N 107°11W **180** B3
Verde ➔ *Jalisco, Mexico* 20°42N 103°14W **180** C4
Verde ➔ *Oaxaca, Mexico* 15°59N 97°50W **181** D5
Verde ➔ *Paraguay* 23°9S 57°37W **190** A4
Verde ➔ *U.S.A.* 33°33N 111°40W **169** K8
Verde, Cay *Bahamas* 23°0N 75°5W **182** B4
Verde Grande ➔ *Brazil* 16°13S 43°49W **189** D2
Verde Pequeno ➔ *Brazil* 14°48S 43°31W **189** C2
Verden *Germany* 52°55N 9°14E **76** C5
Verdi *U.S.A.* 39°31N 119°59W **170** F7
Verdikoussa *Greece* 39°47N 21°59E **98** B3
Verdon ➔ *France* 43°43N 5°46E **73** E9
Verdon △ *France* 43°50N 6°5E **73** E10
Verdun *France* 49°9N 5°24E **71** C12
Verdun-sur-le-Doubs *France* 46°54N 5°2E **71** F12
Vereeniging *S. Africa* 26°38S 27°57E **145** C4
Verga, C. *Guinea* 10°30N 14°10W **138** C2
Vergara = Bergara *Spain* 43°9N 2°28W **90** B2
Vergara *Uruguay* 32°56S 53°57W **191** C5
Vergato *Italy* 44°17N 11°7E **92** D8
Vergemont Cr. ➔ *Australia* 24°16S 143°16E **150** C3
Vergennes *U.S.A.* 44°10N 73°15W **175** B11
Vergina = Aigai *Greece* 40°28N 22°19E **96** F6
Vergt *France* 45°2N 0°43E **72** C4
Veria *Greece* 40°34N 22°12E **96** F6
Verín *Spain* 41°57N 7°27W **88** D3
Verkhnedvinsk = Vyerkhnyadzvinsk *Belarus* 55°45N 27°58E **84** E4
Verkhnetulomskoye Vdkhr. *Russia* 68°36N 31°12E **60** B24
Verkhnevilyuysk *Russia* 63°27N 120°18E **107** C13
Verkhniy Baskunchak *Russia* 48°14N 46°44E **87** F8
Verkhovye *Russia* 52°55N 37°15E **85** F9
Verkhovyna *Ukraine* 48°9N 24°47E **81** B9
Verkhoyansk *Russia* 67°35N 133°25E **107** C14
Verkhoyansk Ra. = Verkhoyanskiy Khrebet *Russia* 66°0N 129°0E **107** C13
Verkhoyanskiy Khrebet *Russia* 66°0N 129°0E **107** C13
Vermeille, Côte *France* 42°50N 3°20E **72** F7
Vermenton *France* 47°40N 3°42E **71** E10
Vermilion *Canada* 53°20N 110°50W **163** C6
Vermilion *U.S.A.* 41°25N 82°22W **174** E2
Vermilion ➔ *Canada* 53°22N 110°51W **163** C6
Vermilion B. *U.S.A.* 29°42N 92°0W **176** G9
Vermilion Bay *Canada* 49°51N 93°34W **163** D10
Vermilion L. *U.S.A.* 47°53N 92°26W **172** B7
Vermillion *U.S.A.* 42°47N 96°56W **172** D5
Vermillion ➔ *Canada* 47°38N 72°56W **164** C5
Vermont □ *U.S.A.* 44°0N 73°0W **175** C12
Vermosh *Albania* 42°35N 19°42E **96** D3
Verna *U.S.A.* 27°23N 82°16W **179** H7
Vernadsky *Antarctica* 65°0S 64°0W **55** C17
Vernal *U.S.A.* 40°27N 109°32W **168** F9
Vernalis *U.S.A.* 37°36N 121°17W **170** H5
Vernazza *Italy* 44°10N 9°45E **92** D6
Verner *Canada* 46°25N 80°8W **164** C3
Verneuil-sur-Avre *France* 48°45N 0°55E **70** D7
Verneukpan *S. Africa* 30°0S 21°0E **144** D3
Vernier *Switz.* 46°11N 6°12E **77** J2
Vérnio *Italy* 44°3N 11°9E **92** D8
Vernon *Canada* 50°20N 119°15W **162** C5
Vernon *France* 49°5N 1°30E **70** C8
Vernon *U.S.A.* 34°9N 99°17W **176** D5
Vernonia *U.S.A.* 45°52N 123°11W **170** E3
Vero Beach *U.S.A.* 27°38N 80°24W **179** H9
Véroia = Veria *Greece* 40°34N 22°12E **96** F6
Véroli *Italy* 41°41N 13°25E **93** G10
Verona *Canada* 44°29N 76°42W **175** B8
Verona *Italy* 45°27N 10°59E **92** C7
Verrès *Italy* 45°40N 7°42E **92** C4
Versailles *France* 48°48N 2°7E **71** D9
Versmold *Germany* 52°2N 8°9E **76** C4
Vert, C. *Senegal* 14°45N 17°30W **138** C1
Vertou *France* 47°10N 1°28W **70** E5
Vertus *France* 48°54N 4°2E **71** D11
Verulam *S. Africa* 29°38S 31°2E **145** C5
Verviers *Belgium* 50°37N 5°52E **69** D5
Vervins *France* 49°50N 3°53E **71** C10
Veržej *Slovenia* 46°34N 16°13E **93** B13
Verzy *France* 49°9N 4°10E **71** C11
Vescovato *France* 42°30N 9°27E **73** F13
Veselí nad Lužnicí *Czech Rep.* 49°12N 14°43E **78** B7
Veselie *Bulgaria* 42°18N 27°38E **97** D11
Veselovskoye Vdkhr. *Russia* 46°58N 41°25E **87** G5
Veshenskaya *Russia* 49°35N 41°44E **86** F5
Vesle ➔ *France* 49°23N 3°28E **71** C10
Vesoul *France* 47°40N 6°11E **71** E13
Vessigebro *Sweden* 56°58N 12°40E **63** H6
Vesterålen *Norway* 68°45N 15°0E **60** B16
Vestfjorden *Norway* 67°55N 14°0E **60** C16
Vestmannaeyjar *Iceland* 63°27N 20°15W **60** E3
Vestvågøya *Norway* 68°18N 13°50E **60** B15
Vesuvio *Italy* 40°49N 14°26E **95** B7
Vesuvius, Mt. = Vesuvio *Italy* 40°49N 14°26E **95** B7
Vesyegonsk *Russia* 58°40N 37°16E **84** C9
Veszprém *Hungary* 47°8N 17°57E **80** C2
Veszprém □ *Hungary* 47°5N 17°55E **80** C2
Vésztő *Hungary* 46°55N 21°16E **80** D6
Vetapalem *India* 15°47N 80°18E **127** G5
Vetlanda *Sweden* 57°24N 15°3E **63** G9
Vetluga *Russia* 57°53N 45°45E **86** B7
Vetlugu ➔ *Russia* 56°36N 46°4E **86** B8
Vetluzhskiy *Kostroma, Russia* 58°23N 45°26E **86** A7
Vetluzhskiy *Nizhniy Novgorod, Russia* 57°17N 45°12E **86** B7
Vetovo *Bulgaria* 43°42N 26°16E **97** C10
Vetralla *Italy* 42°20N 12°2E **93** F9
Vetren *Bulgaria* 42°15N 24°3E **97** D8
Vettore, Mte. *Italy* 42°49N 13°16E **93** F10
Veurne *Belgium* 51°5N 2°40E **69** C2
Vevey *Switz.* 46°28N 6°51E **77** J2
Vevi *Greece* 40°47N 21°38E **96** F5
Veynes *France* 44°32N 5°49E **73** D9
Veys *Iran* 31°30N 49°0E **129** D6
Vézelay *France* 47°27N 3°45E **71** E10
Vézelise *France* 48°30N 6°5E **71** D13
Vézère ➔ *France* 44°53N 0°53E **72** D4
Vezhen *Bulgaria* 42°50N 24°20E **97** D8
Vezirköprü *Turkey* 41°8N 35°27E **104** B6
Vezzani *France* 42°10N 9°15E **73** F13
Vi Thanh *Vietnam* 9°42N 105°26E **121** H5
Viacha *Bolivia* 16°39S 68°18W **188** D4
Viadana *Italy* 44°56N 10°31E **92** D7
Viamão *Brazil* 30°5S 51°0W **191** C5
Viana *Brazil* 3°13S 44°55W **189** A2
Viana *Spain* 42°31N 2°22W **90** C2
Viana do Alentejo *Portugal* 38°17N 7°59W **89** G3
Viana do Bolo *Spain* 42°11N 7°6W **88** C3
Viana do Castelo *Portugal* 41°42N 8°50W **88** D2
Viana do Castelo □ *Portugal* 41°50N 8°30W **88** D2
Vianden *Lux.* 49°56N 6°12E **69** E6
Viangchan = Vientiane *Laos* 17°58N 102°36E **120** D4
Vianópolis *Brazil* 16°40S 48°35W **189** D1
Vianos *Greece* 35°2N 25°21E **101** D7
Viar ➔ *Spain* 37°36N 5°50W **89** H5
Viaréggio *Italy* 43°52N 10°14E **92** E7
Viaur ➔ *France* 44°8N 1°58E **72** D5
Vibble *Sweden* 57°37N 18°16E **63** G12
Vibo Valéntia *Italy* 38°40N 16°6E **95** D9
Viborg *Denmark* 56°27N 9°23E **63** H3
Vibraye *France* 48°3N 0°44E **70** D7
Vic *Spain* 41°58N 2°19E **90** D7
Vic, Étang de *France* 43°29N 3°50E **72** E7
Vic-en-Bigorre *France* 43°24N 0°3E **72** E4
Vic-Fezensac *France* 43°47N 0°19E **72** E4
Vic-le-Comte *France* 45°39N 3°14E **71** G10
Vic-sur-Cère *France* 44°59N 2°38E **72** D6
Vícar *Spain* 36°50N 2°38W **91** J2
Vicente Pérez Rosales △ *Chile* 41°11S 72°12W **192** B2
Vicenza *Italy* 45°33N 11°33E **93** C8
Vich = Vic *Spain* 41°58N 2°19E **90** D7
Vichada ➔ *Colombia* 4°55N 67°50W **186** C5
Vichuga *Russia* 57°12N 41°55E **86** B5
Vichy *France* 46°9N 3°26E **71** F10
Vicksburg *Ariz., U.S.A.* 33°45N 113°45W **171** M13
Vicksburg *Miss., U.S.A.* 32°21N 90°53W **177** E9
Vico *France* 42°10N 8°49E **73** F12
Vico, L. di *Italy* 42°19N 12°10E **93** F9
Vico del Gargano *Italy* 41°54N 15°57E **93** G12
Viçosa *Brazil* 9°28S 36°14W **189** B3
Viçosa do Ceará *Brazil* 3°34S 41°5W **189** A2
Vicovu de Sus *Romania* 47°56N 25°41E **81** C10
Victor *India* 21°0N 71°30E **124** J4
Victor Harbor *Australia* 35°30S 138°37E **152** C3
Victoria *Argentina* 32°40S 60°10W **190** C3
Victoria *Canada* 48°30N 123°25W **170** B3
Victoria *Chile* 38°13S 72°20W **192** A2
Victoria *China* 22°17N 114°9E **111** a
Victoria *Guinea* 10°50N 14°32W **138** C2
Victoria *Malta* 36°3N 14°14E **101** C1
Victoria *Romania* 45°44N 24°41E **81** E9
Victoria *Seychelles* 4°38S 55°28E **141** b
Victoria *Kans., U.S.A.* 38°52N 99°9W **172** F4
Victoria *Tex., U.S.A.* 28°48N 97°0W **176** G6
Victoria □ *Australia* 37°0S 144°0E **152** D6
Victoria ➔ *Australia* 15°10S 129°40E **148** C4
Victoria, Grand L. *Canada* 47°31N 77°30W **164** C4
Victoria, L. *Africa* 1°0S 33°0E **142** C3
Victoria, L. *Australia* 33°57S 141°15E **152** B4
Victoria, Mt. *Burma* 21°14N 93°55E **123** J18
Victoria Beach *Canada* 50°40N 96°35W **163** C9
Victoria de Durango = Durango *Mexico* 24°3N 104°39W **180** C4
Victoria de las Tunas = Las Tunas *Cuba* 20°58N 76°59W **182** B4
Victoria Falls *Zimbabwe* 17°58S 25°52E **143** F2
Victoria Fjord *Greenland* 82°10N 46°0W **57** A6
Victoria Harbour *Canada* 44°45N 79°45W **174** B5
Victoria I. *Canada* 71°0N 111°0W **160** C9
Victoria L. *Canada* 48°20N 57°27W **165** C8
Victoria Ld. *Antarctica* 75°0S 160°0E **55** D11
Victoria Nile ➔ *Uganda* 2°14N 31°26E **142** B3
Victoria Pk. *Belize* 16°48N 88°37W **181** D7
Victoria Ra. *N.Z.* 42°12S 172°7E **155** C7
Victoria River *Australia* 16°25S 131°0E **148** C5
Victoria Str. *Canada* 69°31N 100°30W **160** D11
Victoria West *S. Africa* 31°25S 23°4E **144** D3
Victoriaville *Canada* 46°4N 71°56W **165** C5
Victorica *Argentina* 36°20S 65°30W **190** D2
Victorville *U.S.A.* 34°32N 117°18W **171** L9
Vicuña *Chile* 30°0S 70°50W **190** C1
Vicuña Mackenna *Argentina* 33°53S 64°25W **190** C3
Vidal *U.S.A.* 34°7N 114°31W **171** L12
Vidalia *U.S.A.* 32°13N 82°25W **178** C7
Vidamlya *Belarus* 52°19N 23°47E **83** F10
Vidauban *France* 43°25N 6°27E **73** E10
Viddolatno = Vindelälven ➔ *Sweden* 63°55N 19°50E **60** E18
Videbæk *Denmark* 56°6N 8°38E **63** H2
Videle *Romania* 44°17N 25°31E **81** F10
Vidette *U.S.A.* 33°2N 82°15W **178** B7
Vidigueira *Portugal* 38°12N 7°48W **89** G3
Vidin *Bulgaria* 43°59N 22°50E **96** C6
Vidin □ *Bulgaria* 43°59N 22°50E **96** C6
Vidio, C. *Spain* 43°35N 6°14W **88** B4
Vidisha *India* 23°28N 77°53E **124** H7
Vidos *Greece* 39°38N 19°55E **101** A3
Vidra *Romania* 45°56N 26°55E **81** E11
Viduša *Bos.-H.* 42°55N 18°21E **96** D2
Vidzy *Belarus* 55°23N 26°37E **84** E4
Viechtach *Germany* 49°4N 12°53E **77** F8
Viedma *Argentina* 40°50S 63°0W **192** B4
Viedma, L. *Argentina* 49°30S 72°30W **192** C2
Vieira do Minho *Portugal* 41°38N 8°8W **88** D2
Vielha *Spain* 42°43N 0°44E **90** C5
Vielle = Vielha *Spain* 42°43N 0°44E **90** C5
Vielle St-Girons *France* 43°56N 1°18W **72** E2
Vielsalm *Belgium* 50°17N 5°54E **69** D5
Vienenburg *Germany* 51°57N 10°34E **76** D6
Vieng Pou Kha *Laos* 20°41N 101°4E **116** G3
Vienna = Wien *Austria* 48°12N 16°22E **79** C9
Vienna *Canada* 42°41N 80°48W **174** D4
Vienna *Ga., U.S.A.* 32°6N 83°47W **178** C6
Vienna *Ill., U.S.A.* 37°25N 88°54W **172** G9
Vienna *Mo., U.S.A.* 38°11N 91°57W **172** F8
Vienne *France* 45°31N 4°53E **73** C8
Vienne □ *France* 46°30N 0°42E **72** B4
Vienne ➔ *France* 47°13N 0°5E **70** E7
Vientiane *Laos* 17°58N 102°36E **120** D4
Vientos, Paso de los *Caribbean* 20°0N 74°0W **183** C5
Vieques *Puerto Rico* 18°8N 65°25W **183** d
Vierge Pt. *St. Lucia* 13°49N 60°53W **183** f
Viernheim *Germany* 49°31N 8°35E **77** F4
Viersen *Germany* 51°15N 6°23E **76** D2
Vierwaldstättersee *Switz.* 47°0N 8°30E **77** J4
Vierzon *France* 47°13N 2°5E **71** E9
Vieste *Italy* 41°53N 16°10E **93** G13
Viet Quang *Vietnam* 22°30N 104°48E **116** F5
Viet Tri *Vietnam* 21°18N 105°25E **120** B5
Vietnam ■ *Asia* 19°0N 106°0E **120** C6
Vieux-Boucau-les-Bains *France* 43°48N 1°23W **72** E2
Vieux Fort *St. Lucia* 13°46N 60°58W **183** f
Vif *France* 45°5N 5°41E **73** C9
Vigan *Phil.* 17°35N 120°28E **119** A6
Vigévano *Italy* 45°19N 8°51E **92** C5
Vigia *Brazil* 0°50S 48°5W **187** D9
Viglas, Akra *Greece* 35°54N 27°51E **101** D9
Vignemale *France* 42°47N 0°10W **72** F3
Vigneulles-lès-Hattonchâtel *France* 48°59N 5°43E **71** D12
Vignola *Italy* 44°29N 11°1E **92** D8
Vigo *Spain* 42°12N 8°41W **88** C2
Vigo, Ría de *Spain* 42°15N 8°45W **88** C2
Vigsø Bugt *Denmark* 57°8N 8°47E **63** G2
Vihiers *France* 47°10N 0°30W **70** E6
Vihowa *Pakistan* 31°8N 70°30E **124** D4
Vihowa ➔ *Pakistan* 31°8N 70°41E **124** D4
Vijayadurg *India* 16°30N 73°25E **126** F1
Vijayawada *India* 16°31N 80°39E **126** F5
Vijosë ➔ *Albania* 40°37N 19°24E **96** F3
Vík *Iceland* 63°25N 19°1W **60** E4
Vika *Sweden* 60°57N 14°28E **62** D8
Vikarabad *India* 17°20N 77°54E **126** E3
Vikarbyn *Sweden* 60°55N 15°1E **62** D9
Vikeke = Viqueque *E. Timor* 8°52S 126°23E **119** F7
Viken *Skåne, Sweden* 56°9N 12°34E **63** H6
Viken *Västra Götaland, Sweden* 58°39N 14°20E **63** F8
Viking *Canada* 53°7N 111°50W **162** C6
Vikmanshyttan *Sweden* 60°18N 15°50E **62** D9
Vikna *Norway* 64°55N 10°58E **60** D14
Vikos-Aoos △ *Greece* 40°0N 20°45E **98** B2
Vila Bela da Santissima Trindade *Brazil* 15°0S 59°57W **186** G7
Vila da Maganja *Mozam.* 17°18S 37°30E **143** F4
Vila da Ribeira Brava *C. Verde Is.* 16°32N 24°25W **134** b
Vila de Rei *Portugal* 39°41N 8°9W **88** F2
Vila do Bispo *Portugal* 37°5N 8°53W **89** H2
Vila do Conde *Portugal* 41°21N 8°45W **88** D2
Vila Franca de Xira *Portugal* 38°57N 8°59W **89** G2
Vila Gamito *Mozam.* 14°12S 33°0E **143** E3
Vila Gomes da Costa *Mozam.* 24°20S 33°37E **145** B5
Vila Machado *Mozam.* 19°15S 34°14E **143** F3
Vila Mouzinho *Mozam.* 14°48S 34°25E **143** E3
Vila Nova de Famalicão *Portugal* 41°25N 8°32W **88** D2
Vila Nova de Foz Côa *Portugal* 41°5N 7°9W **88** D3
Vila Nova de Gaia *Portugal* 41°8N 8°37W **88** D2
Vila Pouca de Aguiar *Portugal* 41°30N 7°38W **88** D3
Vila Real *Portugal* 41°17N 7°48W **88** D3
Vila-Real *Spain* 39°55N 0°3W **90** F4
Vila Real □ *Portugal* 41°36N 7°35W **88** D3
Vila Real de Santo António *Portugal* 37°10N 7°28W **89** H3
Vila-seca *Spain* 41°7N 1°9E **90** D6
Vila Vasco da Gama *Mozam.* 14°54S 32°14E **143** E3
Vila Velha *Espírito Santo, Brazil* 20°20S 40°17W **189** E2
Vila Velha *Sergipe, Brazil* 11°20S 38°9W **189** C3
Vila Viçosa *Portugal* 38°45N 7°27W **89** G3
Vilafranca del Maestrat = Villafranca del Cid *Spain* 40°26N 0°16W **90** E4
Vilafranca del Penedès *Spain* 41°21N 1°40E **90** D6
Vilagarcía de Arousa *Spain* 42°34N 8°46W **88** C2
Vilaine ➔ *France* 47°30N 2°27W **70** E4
Vilanandro, Tanjona *Madag.* 16°11S 44°27E **141** H8
Vilanculos *Mozam.* 22°1S 35°17E **145** B6
Vilanova i la Geltrú *Spain* 41°13N 1°40E **90** D6
Vilar Formoso *Portugal* 40°38N 6°45W **88** E4
Vilaseca-Salou = Vila-seca *Spain* 41°7N 1°9E **90** D6
Vilbjerg *Denmark* 56°12N 8°46E **63** H2
Vilcabamba, Cordillera *Peru* 13°0S 73°0W **188** C3
Vilcanchos *Peru* 13°40S 74°25W **188** C3
Vilcheka, Ostrov *Russia* 80°0N 58°31E **106** B6

Vilcheka, Zemlya
Russia 80°30N 60°30E **54** A11
Vilches *Spain* 38°12N 3°30W **89** G7
Vileyka *Belarus* 54°30N 26°53E **75** A14
Vilhelmina *Sweden* 64°35N 16°39E **60** D17
Vilhena *Brazil* 12°40S 60°5W **186** F6
Viliya = Neris →
Lithuania 55°8N 24°16E **84** E3
Viljandi *Estonia* 58°28N 25°30E **84** C3
Vilkaviškis *Lithuania* 54°39N 23°2E **82** D10
Vilkija *Lithuania* 55°3N 23°35E **82** C10
Vilkitskogo, Proliv
Russia 78°0N 103°0E **107** B11
Vilkovo = Vylkove
Ukraine 45°28N 29°32E **81** E14
Villa Abecia *Bolivia* 21°0S 68°18W **190** A2
Villa Ana *Argentina* 28°28S 59°40W **190** B4
Villa Angela *Argentina* 27°34S 60°45W **190** B3
Villa Bella *Bolivia* 10°25S 65°22W **186** F5
Villa Cañás *Argentina* 34°0S 61°35W **190** C3
Villa Constitución
Argentina 33°15S 60°20W **190** C3
Villa de Arriaga
Mexico 21°56N 101°20W **180** C4
Villa de María
Argentina 29°55S 63°43W **190** B3
Villa de Méndez *Mexico* 25°7N 98°34W **181** B5
Villa del Rio *Spain* 37°50N 4°17W **89** H6
Villa Dolores *Argentina* 31°58S 65°15W **190** C3
Villa Gesell *Argentina* 37°15S 56°55W **190** C4
Villa Guillermina
Argentina 28°15S 59°29W **190** B4
Villa Hayes *Paraguay* 25°5S 57°20W **190** B4
Villa Hidalgo *Mexico* 24°15N 99°26W **181** C5
Villa Iris *Argentina* 38°12S 63°12W **190** D3
Villa María *Argentina* 32°20S 63°10W **190** C3
Villa Mazán *Argentina* 28°40S 66°30W **190** B2
Villa Minozzo *Italy* 44°22N 10°28E **92** D7
Villa Montes *Bolivia* 21°10S 63°30W **190** A3
Villa Ocampo
Argentina 28°30S 59°20W **190** B4
Villa Ocampo *Mexico* 26°27N 105°31W **180** B3
Villa Ojo de Agua
Argentina 29°30S 63°44W **190** B3
Villa Regina *Argentina* 39°6S 67°4W **192** A3
Villa San Giovanni *Italy* 38°13N 15°38E **95** D8
Villa San Martín
Argentina 28°15S 64°9W **190** B3
Villa Santina *Italy* 46°24N 12°55E **93** B9
Villa Unión *Mexico* 23°12N 106°14W **180** C3
Villablino *Spain* 42°57N 6°19W **88** C4
Villacarlos *Spain* 39°53N 4°17E **100** B11
Villacarriedo *Spain* 43°14N 3°48W **88** B7
Villacastín *Spain* 40°46N 4°25W **88** E6
Villach *Austria* 46°37N 13°51E **78** E6
Villacidro *Italy* 39°27N 8°44E **94** C1
Villada *Spain* 42°15N 4°59W **88** C6
Villadiego *Spain* 42°31N 4°1W **88** C6
Villadóssola *Italy* 46°4N 8°16E **92** B5
Villafeliche *Spain* 41°10N 1°30W **90** D3
Villafranca *Spain* 42°17N 1°46W **90** C3
Villafranca de Bonany
Spain 39°34N 3°5E **100** B10
Villafranca de los Barros
Spain 38°35N 6°18W **89** G4
Villafranca de los Caballeros
Spain 39°26N 3°21W **89** F7
Villafranca del Cid *Spain* 40°26N 0°16W **90** E4
Villafranca del Panadés =
Vilafranca del Penedès
Spain 41°21N 1°40E **90** D6
Villafranca di Verona
Italy 45°21N 10°50E **92** C7
Villafranca Tirrena *Italy* 38°20N 15°30E **95** D8
Villagrán *Mexico* 24°29N 99°29W **181** C5
Villaguay *Argentina* 32°0S 59°0W **190** C4
Villaharta *Spain* 38°9N 4°54W **89** G6
Villahermosa *Mexico* 17°59N 92°55W **181** D6
Villahermosa *Spain* 38°46N 2°52W **91** G2
Villaines-la-Juhel *France* 48°15N 0°20W **70** D6
Villajoyosa *Spain* 38°30N 0°12W **91** G4
Villalba *Spain* 43°22N 7°40W **88** B3
Villalba de Guardo *Spain* 42°42N 4°49W **88** C6
Villalón de Campos *Spain* 42°5N 5°4W **88** C5
Villalpando *Spain* 41°51N 5°25W **88** D5
Villaluenga de la Sagra
Spain 40°2N 3°54W **88** E7
Villamanán *Spain* 42°19N 5°35W **88** C5
Villamartín *Spain* 36°52N 5°38W **89** J5
Villamayor de Santiago
Spain 39°50N 2°59W **90** F2
Villamblard *France* 45°2N 0°32E **72** C4
Villanova Monteleone
Italy 40°30N 8°28E **94** B1
Villanueva *U.S.A.* 35°16N 105°22W **169** J11
Villanueva de Castellón
Spain 39°5N 0°31W **91** F4
Villanueva de Córdoba
Spain 38°20N 4°38W **89** G6
Villanueva de la Fuente
Spain 38°42N 2°42W **91** G2
Villanueva de la Serena
Spain 38°59N 5°50W **89** G5
Villanueva de la Sierra
Spain 40°12N 6°24W **88** E4
Villanueva de los Castillejos
Spain 37°30N 7°15W **89** H3
Villanueva de los Infantes
Spain 38°43N 3°1W **89** G7
Villanueva del Arzobispo
Spain 38°10N 3°0W **91** G2
Villanueva del Fresno
Spain 38°23N 7°10W **89** G3
Villanueva y Geltrú = Vilanova i
la Geltrú *Spain* 41°13N 1°40E **90** D6
Villaputzu *Italy* 39°26N 9°34E **94** C2
Villaquilambre *Spain* 42°39N 5°33W **88** C5
Villar del Arzobispo
Spain 39°44N 0°50W **90** F4
Villar del Rey *Spain* 39°7N 6°50W **89** F4
Villard-de-Lans *France* 45°3N 5°33E **73** D9
Villarramiel *Spain* 42°2N 4°55W **88** C6
Villarreal = Vila-Real
Spain 39°55N 0°3W **90** F4
Villarrica *Chile* 39°15S 72°15W **192** A2
Villarrica *Paraguay* 25°40S 56°30W **190** B4
Villarrica △ *Chile* 39°24S 71°55W **192** A2
Villarrobledo *Spain* 39°18N 2°36W **91** F2

Villarroya de la Sierra
Spain 41°27N 1°46W **90** D3
Villarrubia de los Ojos
Spain 39°14N 3°36W **89** F7
Villars-les-Dombes *France* 46°0N 5°3E **71** F12
Villasayas *Spain* 41°24N 2°39W **90** D2
Villaseco de los Gamitos
Spain 41°2N 6°7W **88** D4
Villasimius *Italy* 39°8N 9°31E **94** C2
Villastar *Spain* 40°17N 1°9W **90** E3
Villatobas *Spain* 39°54N 3°20W **88** F7
Villavicencio *Argentina* 32°28S 69°0W **190** C2
Villavicencio *Colombia* 4°9N 73°37W **186** C4
Villaviciosa *Spain* 43°32N 5°27W **88** B5
Villazón *Bolivia* 22°0S 65°35W **190** A2
Ville-Marie *Canada* 47°20N 79°30W **164** C4
Ville Platte *U.S.A.* 30°41N 92°17W **176** F8
Villedieu-les-Poêles
France 48°50N 1°13W **70** D5
Villefort *France* 44°28N 3°56E **72** D7
Villefranche-de-Lauragais
France 43°25N 1°44E **72** E5
Villefranche-de-Rouergue
France 44°21N 2°2E **72** D6
Villefranche-du-Périgord
France 44°38N 1°5E **72** D5
Villefranche-sur-Saône
France 45°59N 4°43E **73** C8
Villel *Spain* 40°14N 1°12W **90** E3
Villemur-sur-Tarn *France* 43°51N 1°31E **72** E5
Villena *Spain* 38°39N 0°52W **91** G4
Villenauxe-la-Grande
France 48°35N 3°33E **71** D10
Villeneuve-d'Ornon
France 44°46N 0°33W **72** D3
Villeneuve-d'Ascq *France* 50°38N 3°9E **71** B10
Villeneuve-l'Archevêque
France 48°14N 3°32E **71** D10
Villeneuve-lès-Avignon
France 43°58N 4°49E **73** E8
Villeneuve-sur-Allier
France 46°40N 3°13E **71** F10
Villeneuve-sur-Lot
France 44°24N 0°42E **72** D4
Villeneuve-sur-Yonne
France 48°5N 3°18E **71** D10
Villeréal *France* 44°38N 0°45E **72** D4
Villers-Bocage *France* 49°3N 0°40W **70** C6
Villers-Cotterêts *France* 49°15N 3°4E **71** C10
Villers-sur-Mer *France* 49°21N 0°2W **70** C6
Villersexel *France* 47°33N 6°26E **71** E13
Villerupt *France* 49°28N 5°55E **71** C12
Villeurbanne *France* 45°46N 4°55E **73** C8
Villiers *S. Africa* 27°2S 28°36E **145** C4
Villingen-Schwenningen
Germany 48°3N 8°26E **77** G4
Villmanstrand = Lappeenranta
Finland 61°3N 28°12E **84** B5
Villupuram *India* 11°59N 79°31E **127** J4
Vilna *Canada* 54°7N 111°55W **162** C6
Vilnius *Lithuania* 54°38N 25°19E **84** E4
Vils *Austria* 47°33N 10°38E **78** D3
Vils → *Bayern, Germany* 48°37N 13°11E **77** G9
Vils → *Bayern, Germany* 49°10N 11°57E **77** F7
Vilsandi *Estonia* 58°23N 21°52E **84** C1
Vilsbiburg *Germany* 48°26N 12°22E **77** G8
Vilshofen *Germany* 48°37N 13°11E **77** G9
Vilusi *Montenegro* 42°44N 18°34E **96** D2
Vilvoorde *Belgium* 50°56N 4°26E **69** H4
Vilyuchinsk *Russia* 52°55N 158°24E **107** D16
Vilyuy → *Russia* 64°24N 126°26E **107** C13
Vilyuysk *Russia* 63°40N 121°35E **107** C13
Vilyuyskoye Vdkhr.
Russia 63°0N 112°0E **107** C12
Vimianzo *Spain* 43°7N 9°2W **88** B1
Vimioso *Portugal* 41°35N 6°31W **88** D4
Vimmerby *Sweden* 57°40N 15°55E **63** G9
Vimoutiers *France* 48°57N 0°10E **70** D7
Vimperk *Czech Rep.* 49°3N 13°46E **78** B6
Viña del Mar *Chile* 33°0S 71°30W **190** C1
Vinarós *Spain* 40°30N 0°27E **90** E5
Vincennes *U.S.A.* 38°41N 87°32W **172** F10
Vincennes Bay *S. Ocean* 66°0S 109°0E **55** C8
Vincent *U.S.A.* 34°33N 118°11W **171** L8
Vinchina *Argentina* 28°45S 68°15W **190** B3
Vindelälven → *Sweden* 63°55N 19°50E **60** E18
Vindeln *Sweden* 64°12N 19°43E **60** E18
Vinderup *Denmark* 56°29N 8°45E **63** H2
Vindhya Ra. *India* 22°50N 77°0E **124** H7
Vineland *U.S.A.* 39°29N 75°2W **173** F16
Vinga *Romania* 46°1N 21°14E **80** D6
Vingåker *Sweden* 59°2N 15°52E **62** E9
Vinh *Vietnam* 18°45N 105°38E **115** C5
Vinh Long *Vietnam* 10°16N 105°57E **121** G5
Vinh Moc *Vietnam* 21°18N 105°1E **120** B5
Vinh Yen *Vietnam* 21°21N 105°35E **116** G5
Vinhais *Portugal* 41°50N 7°0W **88** D3
Vinica *Croatia* 46°20N 16°9E **93** B13
Vinica *Macedonia* 41°53N 22°30E **96** E6
Vinica *Slovenia* 45°28N 15°16E **93** C12
Vinita *U.S.A.* 36°39N 95°9W **176** C7
Vinkovci *Croatia* 45°19N 18°48E **80** E3
Vinnitsa = Vinnytsya
Ukraine 49°15N 28°30E **75** D15
Vinnytsya *Ukraine* 49°15N 28°30E **75** D15
Vinnytsya □ *Ukraine* 49°20N 28°15E **75** D15
Vinslöv *Sweden* 56°7N 13°55E **63** H7
Vinson Massif
Antarctica 78°35S 85°25W **55** D16
Vintjärn *Sweden* 60°55N 16°4E **62** D10
Vinton *Calif., U.S.A.* 39°48N 120°10W **170** F6
Vinton *Iowa, U.S.A.* 42°10N 92°1W **172** D7
Vinton *La., U.S.A.* 30°11N 93°35W **176** F8
Vințu de Jos *Romania* 46°0N 23°30E **80** D8
Vinukonda *India* 16°4N 79°45E **127** F4
Viöl *Germany* 54°33N 9°12E **64** A5
Violet Town *Australia* 36°38S 145°42E **153** D6
Violet Valley ⊙
Australia 17°10S 127°55E **148** C4
Vioolsdrif *S. Africa* 28°46S 17°39W **144** C2
Viotia *Greece* 38°20N 23°0E **98** C5
Vipava *Slovenia* 45°51N 13°58E **93** C10
Vipiteno *Italy* 46°54N 11°26E **92** B8
Viqueque *E. Timor* 8°52S 126°23E **119** F7
Virac *Phil.* 13°30N 124°20E **119** B6
Virachey *Cambodia* 13°59N 106°49E **120** F6
Virachey △ *Cambodia* 14°1N 106°55E **120** E6
Virago Sd. *Canada* 54°0N 132°30W **162** C2

Virajpet = Virarajendrapet
India 12°10N 75°50E **127** H2
Viramgam *India* 23°5N 72°0E **124** H7
Virananşehir *Turkey* 37°13N 39°45E **105** D8
Virarajendrapet *India* 12°10N 75°50E **127** H2
Virawah *Pakistan* 24°31N 70°46E **124** G4
Virbalis *Lithuania* 54°39N 22°49E **82** D9
Virden *Canada* 49°50N 100°56W **163** D8
Vire *France* 48°50N 0°53W **70** D6
Vire → *France* 49°20N 1°7W **70** D5
Virgem da Lapa *Brazil* 16°49S 42°21W **189** D2
Vírgenes, C. *Argentina* 52°19S 68°21W **192** D3
Virgin → *U.S.A.* 36°28N 114°21W **169** H6
Virgin Gorda
Br. Virgin Is. 18°30N 64°26W **183** e
Virgin Is. (British) ⊿
W. Indies 18°30N 64°30W **183** e
Virgin Is. (U.S.) ⊿
W. Indies 18°20N 65°0W **183** e
Virgin Islands △
U.S. Virgin Is. 18°21N 64°43W **183** C7
Virginia *S. Africa* 28°8S 26°55E **144** C4
Virginia *U.S.A.* 47°31N 92°32W **172** B7
Virginia □ *U.S.A.* 37°30N 78°45W **173** G14
Virginia Beach *U.S.A.* 36°49N 76°9W **173** G16
Virginia City *Mont., U.S.A.* 45°18N 111°56W **168** D8
Virginia City *Nev., U.S.A.* 39°19N 119°39W **170** F7
Virginia Falls *Canada* 61°38N 125°42W **162** A3
Virginiatown *Canada* 48°9N 79°36W **164** C4
Virje *Croatia* 46°4N 16°59E **93** B13
Viroqua *U.S.A.* 43°34N 90°53W **172** D8
Virovitica *Croatia* 45°51N 17°21E **80** E2
Virpazar *Montenegro* 42°14N 19°6E **96** D3
Virpur *India* 21°51N 70°42E **124** J4
Virsbo *Sweden* 59°52N 16°2E **62** E10
Virserum *Sweden* 57°20N 15°35E **63** G9
Virton *Belgium* 49°35N 5°32E **69** E5
Virú *Peru* 8°25S 78°45W **188** B2
Virudunagar *India* 9°30N 77°58E **127** K3
Virunga △
Dem. Rep. of the Congo 0°5N 29°38E **142** B2
Vis *Croatia* 43°4N 16°10E **93** G13
Visalia *U.S.A.* 36°20N 119°18W **170** J7
Visayan Sea *Phil.* 11°30N 123°30E **119** B6
Visby *Sweden* 57°37N 18°18E **63** G12
Viscount Melville Sd.
Canada 74°10N 108°0W **161** C10
Visé *Belgium* 50°44N 5°41E **69** D5
Više, Ostrov *Russia* 79°33N 76°50E **106** B8
Višegrad *Bos.-H.* 43°47N 19°17E **80** G4
Viseu *Brazil* 1°10S 46°5W **187** D9
Viseu *Portugal* 40°40N 7°55W **88** E3
Viseu de Sus *Romania* 47°45N 24°25E **81** C9
Vishakhapatnam *India* 17°45N 83°20E **126** F6
Vişina *Romania* 44°15N 28°12E **81** G13
Vişineşti *Moldova* 46°20N 28°27E **81** D13
Visingsö *Sweden* 58°2N 14°20E **63** F8
Viskafors *Sweden* 57°37N 12°50E **63** G6
Vislanda *Sweden* 56°46N 14°30E **63** H8
Visnagar *India* 23°45N 72°32E **124** H5
Višnja Gora *Slovenia* 45°58N 14°45E **93** C11
Viso, Mte. *Italy* 44°38N 7°5E **92** D4
Viso del Marqués *Spain* 38°32N 3°34W **89** G7
Visoko *Bos.-H.* 43°58N 18°10E **80** G3
Visokoi I. *Antarctica* 56°43S 27°15W **55** B1
Visp *Switz.* 46°17N 7°52E **77** J3
Vissefjärda *Sweden* 56°32N 15°35E **63** H9
Visselhövede *Germany* 52°59N 9°34E **76** C5
Vissenbjerg *Denmark* 55°23N 10°7E **63** J4
Vistonia, L. *Greece* 41°0N 25°7E **97** D7
Vistonikos, Ormos = Vistonida, L.
Greece 41°0N 25°7E **97** D7
Vistula = Wisła →
Poland 54°22N 18°55E **82** D5
Vit → *Bulgaria* 43°30N 24°30E **97** C8
Vita *India* 17°17N 74°33E **128** F2
Vitanje *Slovenia* 46°25N 15°18E **93** B12
Vitebsk = Vitsyebsk
Belarus 55°10N 30°15E **84** E6
Viterbo *Italy* 42°25N 12°6E **93** F9
Vitez *Bos.-H.* 44°10N 17°48E **80** G2
Viti Levu *Fiji* 17°30S 177°30E **154** a
Vitigudino *Spain* 41°1N 6°26W **88** D4
Vitim *Russia* 59°28N 112°35E **107** D12
Vitim → *Russia* 59°26N 112°34E **107** D12
Vitina *Bos.-H.* 43°17N 17°29E **93** E14
Vitina *Greece* 37°40N 22°10E **98** D4
Vitkov *Czech Rep.* 49°46N 17°45E **79** B10
Vitória *Brazil* 20°20S 40°22W **189** E2
Vitória da Conquista
Brazil 14°51S 40°51W **189** C2
Vitória de Santo Antão
Brazil 8°10S 35°20W **189** B3
Vitoria-Gasteiz *Spain* 42°50N 2°41W **89** A12
Vitória Seamount *Atl. Oc.* 20°0S 44°0W **56** G8
Vitorino Freire *Brazil* 4°4S 45°10W **189** A1
Vitosha △ *Bulgaria* 42°36N 23°18E **96** D7
Vitré *France* 48°8N 1°12W **70** D5
Vitry-le-François *France* 48°44N 4°35E **71** D11
Vitry-sur-Seine *France* 48°47N 2°23E **71** D9
Vitsand *Sweden* 60°20N 13°0E **62** D7
Vitsi, Oros *Greece* 40°40N 21°25E **98** A3
Vitsyebsk *Belarus* 55°10N 30°15E **84** E6
Vitsyebsk □ *Belarus* 55°10N 28°30E **84** E6
Vittaryd *Sweden* 56°58N 13°57E **63** H7
Vitteaux *France* 47°24N 4°30E **71** E11
Vittel *France* 48°12N 5°57E **71** D12
Vittória *Italy* 36°57N 14°32E **95** F7
Vittório Véneto *Italy* 45°59N 12°18E **93** C9
Vittsjö *Sweden* 56°20N 13°40E **63** H7
Viveiro *Spain* 43°39N 7°38W **88** B3
Vivian *U.S.A.* 32°53N 93°59W **176** E8
Viviers *France* 44°30N 4°40E **73** D8
Vivonne *Australia* 35°59S 137°9E **152** C2
Vivonne *France* 46°25N 0°15E **72** B4
Vivonne B. *Australia* 35°59S 137°9E **152** C2
Viwa *Fiji* 17°10S 177°58E **154** a
Vizcaíno, Desierto de
Mexico 27°30N 113°45W **180** B2
Vizcaíno, Sierra
Mexico 27°30N 114°0W **180** B2
Vizcaya □ *Spain* 43°15N 2°45W **89** A4
Vize *Turkey* 41°34N 27°45E **97** E11
Vizianagaram *India* 18°6N 83°30E **126** E6
Vizille *France* 45°5N 5°46E **73** C9

Viziñada *Croatia* 45°20N 13°46E **93** C10
Viziru *Romania* 45°0N 27°43E **81** E12
Vizzini *Italy* 37°10N 14°45E **95** E7
Vlaardingen *Neths.* 51°55N 4°21E **69** C4
Vlachiotis *Greece* 36°52N 22°42E **98** E4
Vlădeasa, Vf. *Romania* 46°47N 22°50E **80** D7
Vladičin Han *Serbia* 42°42N 22°1E **96** D6
Vladimir *Russia* 56°15N 40°30E **84** D11
Vladimir □ *Russia* 56°0N 40°30E **84** D11
Vladimir Volynskiy = Volodymyr-
Volynskyy *Ukraine* 50°50N 24°18E **75** C13
Vladimirci *Serbia* 44°36N 19°50E **96** B3
Vladimirovac *Serbia* 45°1N 20°53E **80** E5
Vladimirovka *Russia* 48°27N 46°10E **87** F8
Vladimirovo *Bulgaria* 43°32N 23°22E **96** C7
Vladislavovka *Ukraine* 45°12N 35°29E **85** K8
Vladivostok *Russia* 43°10N 131°53E **112** C5
Vlăhița *Romania* 46°21N 25°31E **81** D10
Vlasenica *Bos.-H.* 44°11N 18°59E **80** F3
Vlašić *Bos.-H.* 44°19N 17°37E **80** F2
Vlašim *Czech Rep.* 49°40N 14°53E **78** B7
Vlasinsko Jezero *Serbia* 42°44N 22°22E **96** D6
Vlasotince *Serbia* 42°59N 22°7E **96** D6
Vlieland *Neths.* 53°16N 4°55E **69** A4
Vlissingen *Neths.* 51°26N 3°34E **69** C3
Vlkolínec *Slovak Rep.* 49°1N 19°16E **79** B12
Vlorë *Albania* 40°32N 19°28E **98** A1
Vlorës, Gjiri i *Albania* 40°29N 19°27E **98** A1
Vltava → *Czech Rep.* 50°21N 14°30E **78** A7
Vo Dat *Vietnam* 11°9N 107°31E **121** G6
Voćin *Croatia* 45°37N 17°33E **80** E2
Vöcklabruck *Austria* 48°1N 13°39E **78** C6
Vodice *Croatia* 43°47N 15°47E **93** E12
Vodlozersky △ *Russia* 62°40N 37°5E **106** C11
Vodňany *Czech Rep.* 49°9N 14°11E **78** B7
Vodnjan *Croatia* 44°59N 13°52E **93** D10
Voe *U.K.* 60°21N 1°16W **65** A7
Vogan *Togo* 6°23N 1°30E **139** D5
Vogel Pk. *Nigeria* 8°24N 11°47E **139** D7
Vogelkop = Doberai, Jazirah
Indonesia 1°25S 133°0E **119** E8
Vogelsberg *Germany* 50°31N 9°12E **76** E5
Voghera *Italy* 44°59N 9°1E **92** D6
Vohibinany *Madag.* 18°49S 49°4E **141** H9
Vohimarina = Iharana
Madag. 13°25S 50°0E **141** G10
Vohimena, Tanjon' i
Madag. 25°36S 45°8E **141** K9
Vohipeno *Madag.* 22°22S 47°51E **141** J9
Voi *Kenya* 3°25S 38°32E **142** C4
Void-Vacon *France* 48°40N 5°36E **71** D12
Voineşti *Iaşi, Romania* 47°5N 27°27E **81** C12
Voineşti *Prahova,
Romania* 45°5N 25°14E **81** D10
Voinjama *Liberia* 8°25N 9°44W **138** D3
Voiron *France* 45°22N 5°35E **73** C9
Voisey B. *Canada* 56°15N 61°50W **165** A7
Voitsberg *Austria* 47°3N 15°9E **78** D8
Vojens *Denmark* 55°16N 9°18E **63** J3
Vojmsjön *Sweden* 65°0N 16°24E **60** D17
Vojnić *Croatia* 45°19N 15°43E **93** C12
Vojnik *Italy* 46°18N 15°19E **93** B12
Vojvodina □ *Serbia* 45°20N 20°0E **80** E5
Vokhtoga *Russia* 58°46N 41°8E **84** C11
Volary *Czech Rep.* 48°54N 13°52E **78** C6
Volborg *U.S.A.* 45°51N 105°41W **168** D11
Volcán de Colima △
Mexico 19°30N 103°40W **180** D4
Volcano Is. = Kazan-Rettō
Pac. Oc. 25°0N 141°0E **156** E6
Volcans △ *Rwanda* 1°30S 29°26E **142** C2
Volcans d'Auvergne ⊂
France 45°20N 2°40E **72** C6
Volchansk = Vovchansk
Ukraine 50°17N 36°58E **85** G9
Volchikha *Russia* 52°2N 80°23E **109** D10
Volchya → *Ukraine* 48°32N 36°0E **85** H8
Volda *Norway* 62°9N 6°6E **60** E12
Volga = Privolzhskiy □
Russia 56°0N 50°0E **106** D6
Volga → *Russia* 46°0N 48°30E **87** G9
Volga Hts. = Privolzhskaya
Vozvyshennost *Russia* 51°0N 46°0E **86** E7
Volga-Baltiyskiy Kanal
Russia 60°0N 38°0E **84** B9
Volgo-Donskoy Kanal
Russia 48°40N 43°37E **87** F7
Volgodonsk *Russia* 47°33N 42°5E **87** G6
Volgograd *Russia* 48°40N 44°25E **87** F7
Volgograd □ *Russia* 49°40N 44°0E **87** F7
Volgogradskoye Vdkhr.
Russia 50°0N 45°20E **86** E8
Volgorechensk *Russia* 57°28N 41°14E **86** B5
Volimes *Greece* 37°44N 20°39E **98** D2
Volintiri *Moldova* 46°26N 29°37E **81** D14
Volissos *Greece* 38°29N 25°54E **99** C7
Volkach *Germany* 49°52N 10°14E **77** F6
Völkermarkt *Austria* 46°39N 14°39E **78** E7
Volkhov *Russia* 59°55N 32°15E **84** C7
Volkhov → *Russia* 60°8N 32°20E **84** B7
Völklingen *Germany* 49°15N 6°50E **77** F2
Volkovysk = Vawkavysk
Belarus 53°9N 24°30E **75** B13
Volksrust *S. Africa* 27°24S 29°53E **145** C4
Volnovakha *Ukraine* 47°35N 37°30E **85** J9
Volochanka *Russia* 71°0N 94°28E **107** B10
Volodarsk *Russia* 56°12N 43°15E **86** B6
Volodymyr-Volynskyy
Ukraine 50°50N 24°18E **75** C13
Vologda *Russia* 59°10N 39°45E **84** C10
Vologda □ *Russia* 60°15N 39°0E **84** C10
Volokolamsk *Russia* 56°2N 35°57E **84** D8
Volokonovka *Russia* 50°33N 37°52E **85** G9
Volos *Greece* 39°24N 22°59E **98** B4
Volosovo *Russia* 59°27N 29°32E **84** B5
Volovets *Ukraine* 48°43N 23°11E **81** B8
Volovo *Russia* 53°35N 38°1E **84** F10
Volozhin = Valozhyn
Belarus 54°3N 26°30E **75** A14
Volsk *Russia* 52°5N 47°22E **86** D8
Volta □ *Ghana* 7°0N 0°30E **139** D5
Volta → *Ghana* 5°46N 0°41E **139** D5
Volta, L. *Ghana* 7°30N 0°0 **139** D5
Volta Blanche = White Volta →
Ghana 9°10N 1°15W **139** D4
Volta Redonda *Brazil* 22°31S 44°5W **191** A7
Voltaire, C. *Australia* 14°16S 125°35E **148** B4
Volterra *Italy* 43°24N 10°51E **92** E7
Voltri *Italy* 44°26N 8°45E **92** D5

Volturno → *Italy* 41°1N 13°55E **94** A6
Volubilis *Morocco* 34°2N 5°33W **136** B2
Volvi, L. *Greece* 40°40N 23°34E **96** F7
Volyn □ *Ukraine* 51°15N 24°30E **75** C13
Volynë *Czech Rep.* 49°10N 13°53E **78** B6
Volzhsk *Russia* 55°57N 48°23E **86** C9
Vomo *Fiji* 17°30S 177°15E **154** a
Vonitsa *Greece* 38°53N 20°58E **98** C2
Vopnafjörður *Iceland* 65°45N 14°50W **60** D6
Vorarlberg □ *Austria* 47°20N 10°0E **78** D2
Voras Oros *Greece* 40°57N 21°45E **98** A4
Vorbasse *Denmark* 55°39N 9°6E **63** J3
Vorchdorf *Austria* 48°0N 13°55E **78** C6
Vorderrhein → *Switz.* 46°49N 9°25E **77** J5
Vordingborg *Denmark* 55°0N 11°54E **63** J5
Vorë *Albania* 41°23N 19°40E **98** A1
Voreio Aigaio □ *Greece* 38°50N 25°30E **99** C7
Voreioi Sporades *Greece* 39°15N 23°30E **98** B5
Voreppe *France* 45°18N 5°39E **73** C9
Vóri *Greece* 35°4N 24°49E **98** F6
Vorios Evoikos Kolpos
Greece 38°45N 23°15E **98** C5
Vorkuta *Russia* 67°48N 64°20E **106** C7
Vormsi *Estonia* 59°1N 23°20E **84** C2
Vorona → *Russia* 51°22N 42°3E **86** E6
Voronezh *Russia* 51°40N 39°10E **85** G10
Voronezh *Ukraine* 51°47N 33°28E **85** G10
Voronezh □ *Russia* 51°30N 39°30E **86** E4
Vorontsovo-Aleksandrovskoye =
Zelenokumsk *Russia* 44°24N 44°0E **87** H6
Vorpommersche
Boddenlandschaft △
Germany 54°25N 12°32E **76** A8
Vorskla → *Ukraine* 48°50N 34°10E **85** H8
Vörts järv *Estonia* 58°16N 26°3E **84** C4
Võru *Estonia* 57°48N 26°54E **84** D4
Vosges □ *France* 48°20N 7°10E **71** D13
Vosges du Nord ⊂ *France* 49°0N 7°30E **71** D14
Voskopojë *Albania* 40°35N 20°33E **96** F4
Voskresensk *Russia* 55°19N 38°43E **84** D10
Voskresenskoye *Russia* 56°51N 45°30E **86** B7
Voss *Norway* 60°38N 6°26E **60** F12
Vostochnyy Port
Russia 42°44N 133°4E **112** C6
Vostok *Antarctica* 78°30S 106°50E **55** D8
Vostok I. *Kiribati* 10°5S 152°23W **157** J12
Votice *Czech Rep.* 49°38N 14°39E **78** B7
Votkinsk *Russia* 57°0N 53°55E **86** B10
Vouga → *Portugal* 40°41N 8°40E **88** E2
Vouillé *France* 46°38N 0°10E **70** F7
Vouxa, Akra *Greece* 35°37N 23°32E **101** D5
Vouzela *Portugal* 40°43N 8°7W **88** E2
Vouziers *France* 49°22N 4°40E **71** C11
Vovchansk *Ukraine* 50°17N 36°58E **85** G9
Vovchyn *Belarus* 52°18N 23°18E **83** F10
Voyageurs △ *U.S.A.* 48°32N 93°0W **172** A7
Voynitsa *Russia* 65°10N 30°20E **60** D4
Voyvozh *Russia* 62°56N 54°56E **106** C6
Vozhe, Ozero *Russia* 60°45N 39°0E **84** B10
Vozhega *Russia* 60°29N 40°12E **84** B11
Voznesensk *Ukraine* 47°35N 31°21E **85** J6
Voznesenye *Russia* 61°0N 35°28E **84** B8
Vrå *Denmark* 57°21N 9°56E **63** G3
Vrådal *Norway* 59°20N 8°25E **63** E3
Vráble *Slovak Rep.* 48°15N 18°16E **79** C11
Vraćevšnica *Serbia* 44°2N 20°34E **96** B4
Vračneika *Greece* 38°10N 21°40E **98** C3
Vrancea □ *Russia* 45°50N 26°45E **81** E11
Vrancei, Munții
Romania 46°0N 26°30E **81** E11
Vrangel *Russia* 42°43N 133°5E **112** C6
Vrangelya, Ostrov
Russia 71°0N 180°0E **107** B18
Vranica *Bos.-H.* 43°55N 17°50E **80** G2
Vranje *Serbia* 42°34N 21°54E **96** D5
Vranov nad Topľ ou
Slovak Rep. 48°53N 21°40E **79** C14
Vransko *Slovenia* 46°17N 14°58E **93** B11
Vransko Jezero *Croatia* 43°50N 15°34E **93** E12
Vrapčište *Macedonia* 41°50N 20°53E **96** E4
Vratsa *Bulgaria* 43°15N 23°30E **96** C7
Vratsa □ *Bulgaria* 43°12N 23°30E **96** C7
Vrbas *Serbia* 45°40N 19°40E **80** E4
Vrbas → *Bos.-H.* 45°8N 17°29E **80** E2
Vrbnik *Croatia* 45°4N 14°40E **93** C11
Vrbovec *Croatia* 45°53N 16°28E **93** C13
Vrchlabí *Czech Rep.* 50°38N 15°37E **78** A8
Vrede *S. Africa* 27°24S 29°6E **145** C4
Vredefort *S. Africa* 27°0S 27°22E **144** C4
Vreden *Germany* 52°2N 6°59E **69** B7
Vredenburg *S. Africa* 32°56S 18°0E **144** E2
Vredendal *S. Africa* 31°41S 18°35E **144** D2
Vretstorp *Sweden* 59°1N 14°53E **62** E8
Vrgorac *Croatia* 43°12N 17°20E **93** E14
Vrhnika *Slovenia* 45°58N 14°15E **93** C11
Vriddhachalam *India* 11°30N 79°20E **127** J4
Vrîdi *Ivory C.* 5°15N 4°3W **138** D4
Vrigstad *Sweden* 57°22N 14°28E **63** H8
Vrindavan *India* 27°37N 77°40E **124** F7
Vrisses *Greece* 35°23N 24°13E **101** D6
Vrnograč *Bos.-H.* 45°10N 15°57E **93** C12
Vrondados *Greece* 38°25N 26°7E **99** C8
Vrpolje *Croatia* 45°13N 18°24E **80** E3
Vršac *Serbia* 45°8N 21°40E **80** E6
Vrsacki Kanal *Serbia* 45°15N 21°0E **80** E5
Vrútky *Slovak Rep.* 49°8N 18°55E **79** B11
Vryburg *S. Africa* 26°55S 24°45E **144** C3
Vryheid *S. Africa* 27°45S 30°47E **145** C5
Vsetín *Czech Rep.* 49°20N 18°0E **79** B10
Vu Liet *Vietnam* 18°43N 105°23E **120** C5
Vučitrn = Vushtrri
Kosovo 42°49N 20°59E **96** D5
Vukovar *Croatia* 45°21N 18°59E **80** E4
Vuktyl *Russia* 63°58N 57°22E **106** C6
Vulcan *Canada* 50°25N 113°15W **162** C6
Vulcan *Romania* 45°23N 23°17E **81** E8
Vulcăneşti *Moldova* 45°41N 28°18E **81** E13
Vulcano *Italy* 38°24N 14°58E **95** E7
Vulchedrŭm *Bulgaria* 43°42N 23°27E **96** C7
Vulkaneshty = Vulcăneşti
Moldova 45°41N 28°18E **81** E13
Vunduzi → *Mozam.* 18°56S 34°1E **143** F3
Vung Tau *Vietnam* 10°21N 107°4E **121** G6
Vunisea *Fiji* 19°3S 178°10E **154** a
Vuntut △ *Canada* 68°22S 139°41W **160** B1
Vŭrbitsa *Bulgaria* 42°59N 26°40E **97** C10

Vŭrshets *Bulgaria* 43°13N 23°23E **96** C7
Vushtrri *Kosovo* 42°49N 20°59E **96** D4
Vutcani *Romania* 46°26N 27°59E **81** D12
Vuzlove *Ukraine* 48°22N 22°24E **80** B7
Vwaza △ *Malawi* 10°58S 33°25E **143** E3
Vyara *India* 21°8N 73°28E **126** D1
Vyartsilya *Russia* 62°8N 30°45E **84** B6
Vyatka = Kirov *Russia* 58°35N 49°40E **106** D5
Vyatka → *Russia* 55°37N 51°28E **86** C10
Vyatskiye Polyany
Russia 56°14N 51°5E **86** B10
Vyazemskiy *Russia* 47°32N 134°45E **107** E14
Vyazma *Russia* 55°10N 34°15E **84** D8
Vyazniki *Russia* 56°10N 42°10E **86** B6
Vyborg *Russia* 60°43N 28°47E **84** B5
Vychegda → *Russia* 61°18N 46°36E **106** C5
Vychodné Beskydy
Europe 49°20N 22°0E **79** B15
Vyerkhnyadzvinsk
Belarus 55°45N 27°58E **84** E4
Vyhoda *Ukraine* 48°56N 23°55E **81** B8
Vyksa *Russia* 55°19N 42°11E **86** C6
Vylkove *Ukraine* 45°28N 29°32E **81** E14
Vylok *Ukraine* 48°6N 22°50E **80** B7
Vynohradiv *Ukraine* 48°9N 23°2E **80** B7
Vypin *India* 10°10N 76°15E **127** J3
Vyrnwy, L. *U.K.* 52°48N 3°31W **66** E4
Vyshhorod *Ukraine* 48°44N 23°39E **81** B8
Vyshkove *Ukraine* 48°3N 23°25E **81** B8
Vyshniy Volochek
Russia 57°30N 34°30E **84** D8
Vyshza = imeni 26 Bakinskikh
Komissarov
Turkmenistan 39°22N 54°10E **129** B7
Vyškov *Czech Rep.* 49°17N 17°0E **79** B9
Vysokaye *Belarus* 52°22N 23°22E **83** F10
Vysoké Mýto *Czech Rep.* 49°58N 16°10E **78** B9
Vysokovsk *Russia* 56°22N 36°30E **84** D9
Vyšší Brod *Czech Rep.* 48°37N 14°19E **78** C7
Vytegra *Russia* 61°0N 36°27E **84** B9
Vyzhnytsya *Ukraine* 48°15N 25°11E **81** B10
Vyzhnytsya △ *Ukraine* 48°7N 25°15E **81** B10

W

W du Benin △ *Benin* 11°57N 2°43E **139** C5
W du Burkina Faso △
Burkina Faso 11°52N 2°50E **139** C5
W du Niger △ *Niger* 13°31N 2°28E **139** C5
W.A.C. Bennett Dam
Canada 56°2N 122°6W **162** B4
Wa *Ghana* 10°7N 2°25W **138** C4
Waal → *Neths.* 51°37N 5°0E **69** C5
Waalwijk *Neths.* 51°42N 5°4E **69** C5
Waanyi-Garawa ⊙
Australia 18°2S 137°33E **150** B2
Wabakimi △ *Canada* 50°43N 89°29W **164** B2
Wabana *Canada* 47°40N 53°0W **165** C10
Wabasca → *Canada* 58°22N 115°20W **162** B5
Wabasca-Desmarais
Canada 55°57N 113°56W **162** B6
Wabash *U.S.A.* 40°48N 85°49W **173** E11
Wabash → *U.S.A.* 37°48N 88°2W **172** G9
Wabasso *U.S.A.* 27°45N 80°26W **179** H9
Wabigoon L. *Canada* 49°44N 92°44W **163** D10
Wabowden *Canada* 54°55N 98°38W **163** C9
Wąbrzeźno *Poland* 53°16N 18°57E **83** E5
Wabu Hu *China* 32°20N 116°50E **117** H3
Wabuk Pt. *Canada* 55°20N 85°5W **164** A2
Wabush *Canada* 52°55N 66°52W **165** B6
Waccasassa B. *U.S.A.* 29°10N 82°50W **179** F7
Wachau *Austria* 48°21N 15°26E **78** C8
Wächtersbach *Germany* 50°14N 9°17E **77** E5
Waco *U.S.A.* 31°33N 97°9W **176** F6
Waconichi, L. *Canada* 50°8N 74°0W **164** B5
Wad Hamid *Sudan* 16°30N 32°45E **135** E12
Wad Medani *Sudan* 14°28N 33°30E **135** F12
Wad Thana *Pakistan* 27°22N 66°23E **124** F2
Wadayama *Japan* 35°19N 134°52E **113** G7
Wadbilliga △ *Australia* 36°25S 149°35E **153** D8
Waddeneilanden *Neths.* 53°25N 5°10E **69** A5
Waddenzee *Neths.* 53°6N 5°10E **69** A5
Waddi, Chappal *Nigeria* 7°2N 11°43E **139** D7
Waddington *U.S.A.* 44°52N 75°12W **175** B9
Waddington, Mt.
Canada 51°23N 125°15W **162** C3
Waddy Pt. *Australia* 24°58S 153°21E **151** C5
Wadebridge *U.K.* 50°31N 4°51W **67** G3
Wadena *Canada* 51°57N 103°47W **163** C8
Wadena *U.S.A.* 46°26N 95°8W **172** B6
Wädenswil *Switz.* 47°14N 8°40E **77** H4
Wadern *Germany* 49°32N 6°53E **77** F2
Wadeye *Australia* 14°28S 129°52E **150** B4
Wadgaon *India* 18°44N 73°39E **126** E1
Wadhams *Canada* 51°30N 127°30W **162** C3
Wadhwan *India* 22°42N 71°41E **124** H4
Wadi *India* 17°4N 76°59E **126** F3
Wādi as Sīr *Jordan* 31°56N 35°49E **133** D4
Wādi Gemāl, J. *Egypt* 24°35N 35°10E **137** C4
Wadi Halfa *Sudan* 21°53N 31°19E **137** D12
Wādī Rum △ *Jordan* 29°30N 35°20E **130** F4
Wadian *China* 32°42N 112°29E **117** A9
Wadlew *Poland* 51°31N 19°23E **83** G6
Wadley *Ala., U.S.A.* 33°7N 85°34W **178** B4
Wadley *Ga., U.S.A.* 32°52N 82°24W **178** C7
Wadowice *Poland* 49°52N 19°30E **83** A6
Wadsworth *Nev.,
U.S.A.* 39°38N 119°17W **168** G4
Wadsworth *Ohio, U.S.A.* 41°1N 81°44W **174** E3
Waegwan *S. Korea* 35°59N 128°23E **115** G15
Wafangdian *China* 39°38N 121°58E **115** E11
Wafrah *Kuwait* 28°33N 47°56E **128** D5
Wagait ⊙ *Australia* 13°1S 130°5E **148** B5
Wagener *U.S.A.* 33°39N 81°22W **178** C7
Wageningen *Neths.* 51°58N 5°40E **69** C5
Wager B. *Canada* 65°26N 88°40W **161** D14
Wagga Wagga
Australia 35°7S 147°24E **153** C7
Waghai *India* 20°46N 73°29E **126** D1
Waghete *Indonesia* 4°10S 136°26E **119** E9
Wagin *Australia* 33°17S 117°25E **149** F2
Wagon Mound
U.S.A. 36°1N 104°42W **169** H11
Wagoner *U.S.A.* 35°58N 95°22W **176** D7
Wagrowiec *Poland* 52°48N 17°11E **83** E4
Wah *Pakistan* 33°45N 72°40E **124** C5
Wahai *Indonesia* 2°48S 129°35E **119** E7

284 Waharoa
INDEX TO WORLD MAPS

Waharoa N.Z. 37°46S 175°45E 154 D4
Wâḥid Egypt 30°48N 32°21E 130 E1
Wahnai Afghan. 32°40N 65°50E 124 C1
Wahoo U.S.A. 41°13N 96°37W 172 E5
Wahpeton U.S.A. 46°16N 96°36W 172 B5
Wai India 17°56N 73°57E 126 F1
Waialua U.S.A. 21°34N 158°8W 167 L8
Waiapu → N.Z. 37°47S 178°29E 154 D7
Waiau N.Z. 42°39S 173°5E 155 C8
Waiau → Canterbury, N.Z. 42°47S 173°22E 155 C8
Waiau → Southland, N.Z. 46°12S 167°38E 155 G2
Waiawe Ganga → Sri Lanka 6°15N 81°0E 127 L5
Waibeem Indonesia 0°30S 132°59E 119 E8
Waiblingen Germany 48°49N 9°18E 77 G5
Waidhofen an der Thaya Austria 48°49N 15°17E 78 C8
Waidhofen an der Ybbs Austria 47°57N 14°46E 78 D7
Waigeo Indonesia 0°20S 130°40E 119 E8
Waihao → N.Z. 44°47S 171°10E 155 E6
Waihao Downs N.Z. 44°48S 170°55E 155 E5
Waiheke I. N.Z. 36°48S 175°6E 154 C4
Waihi N.Z. 37°23S 175°52E 154 D4
Waihi Beach N.Z. 37°25S 175°57E 154 D4
Waihola N.Z. 46°1S 170°8E 155 G5
Waihola L. N.Z. 45°59S 170°8E 155 F5
Waihou → N.Z. 37°15S 175°40E 154 D4
Waika Dem. Rep. of the Congo 2°22S 25°42E 142 C2
Waikabubak Indonesia 9°45S 119°25E 119 F5
Waikaia N.Z. 45°44S 168°51E 155 F3
Waikaka N.Z. 45°55S 169°1E 155 F4
Waikare, L. N.Z. 37°26S 175°13E 154 D4
Waikareiti, L. N.Z. 38°43S 177°10E 154 E6
Waikaremoana N.Z. 38°42S 177°12E 154 E6
Waikaremoana, L. N.Z. 38°49S 177°9E 154 E6
Waikari N.Z. 42°58S 172°41E 155 C7
Waikato → N.Z. 37°23S 174°43E 154 D3
Waikelo Indonesia 9°24S 119°19E 148 A2
Waikerie Australia 34°9S 140°0E 152 C4
Waikiekie N.Z. 35°57S 174°16E 154 B3
Waikokopu N.Z. 39°3S 177°52E 154 F6
Waikouaiti N.Z. 45°36S 170°41E 155 F5
Waikouaiti Downs N.Z. 45°30S 170°30E 155 F5
Waimakariri → N.Z. 43°24S 172°42E 155 D7
Waimangaroa N.Z. 41°43S 171°46E 155 B6
Waimarie N.Z. 41°35S 171°58E 155 B6
Waimate N.Z. 44°45S 171°3E 155 E6
Waimea Plain N.Z. 45°55S 168°35E 155 F3
Wainganga → India 18°50N 79°55E 126 E4
Waingapu Indonesia 9°35S 120°11E 119 F6
Waini → Guyana 8°20N 59°50W 186 B7
Wainuiomata N.Z. 41°17S 174°56E 154 H3
Wainwright Canada 52°50N 110°50W 163 C6
Wainwright U.S.A. 70°38N 160°2W 166 A7
Waiotapu N.Z. 38°21S 176°25E 154 E5
Waiouru N.Z. 39°28S 175°41E 154 F4
Waipa → N.Z. 38°16S 175°21E 154 E4
Waipahi N.Z. 46°6S 169°15E 155 G4
Waipapa Pt. N.Z. 46°40S 168°51E 155 G3
Waipara N.Z. 43°3S 172°46E 155 D7
Waipawa N.Z. 39°56S 176°38E 154 F5
Waipiro N.Z. 38°2S 178°22E 154 E7
Waipiro Bay N.Z. 38°1S 178°21E 154 E7
Waipoua Forest N.Z. 35°39S 173°33E 154 B2
Waipu N.Z. 35°59S 174°29E 154 B3
Waipukurau N.Z. 40°1S 176°33E 154 G5
Wairakei N.Z. 38°37S 176°6E 154 E5
Wairarapa, L. N.Z. 41°14S 175°15E 154 H4
Wairau → N.Z. 41°32S 174°7E 155 B9
Wairio N.Z. 45°59S 168°3E 155 F3
Wairoa N.Z. 39°3S 177°25E 154 F6
Wairoa → Hawke's Bay, N.Z. 39°4S 177°25E 154 F6
Wairoa → Northland, N.Z. 36°5S 173°59E 154 C2
Waitaki → N.Z. 44°56S 171°7E 155 E6
Waitaki Plains N.Z. 44°22S 170°0E 155 E5
Waitangi N.Z. 35°16S 174°5E 154 B3
Waitara N.Z. 38°59S 174°15E 154 E3
Waitara → N.Z. 38°59S 174°14E 154 E3
Waitiki Landing N.Z. 34°31S 172°50E 154 A1
Waitoa N.Z. 37°37S 175°35E 154 D4
Waitomo Caves N.Z. 38°16S 175°7E 154 E4
Waitotara N.Z. 39°49S 174°44E 154 F3
Waitotara → N.Z. 39°51S 174°41E 154 F3
Waitsburg U.S.A. 46°16N 118°9W 168 C4
Waiuku N.Z. 37°15S 174°45E 154 D3
Wajima Japan 37°30N 137°0E 113 F8
Wajir Kenya 1°42N 40°5E 142 B5
Wakasa Japan 35°20N 134°24E 113 G7
Wakasa-Wan Japan 35°40N 135°30E 113 G7
Wakatipu, L. N.Z. 45°5S 168°33E 155 F3
Wakaw Canada 52°39N 105°44W 163 C7
Wakaya Fiji 17°37S 179°0E 154 a
Wakayama Japan 34°15N 135°15E 113 G7
Wakayama □ Japan 33°50N 135°30E 113 H7
Wake Forest U.S.A. 35°59N 78°30W 177 D15
Wake I. Pac. Oc. 19°18N 166°36E 156 F8
WaKeeney U.S.A. 39°1N 99°53W 172 F4
Wakefield Jamaica 18°26N 77°42W 182 a
Wakefield N.Z. 41°24S 173°5E 155 B8
Wakefield U.K. 53°41N 1°29W 66 D6
Wakefield Mass., U.S.A. 42°30N 71°5W 175 D13
Wakefield Mich., U.S.A. 46°29N 89°56W 172 B9
Wakkanai Japan 45°28N 141°35E 112 B10
Wakkerstroom S. Africa 27°24S 30°10E 145 C5
Wakool Australia 35°28S 144°23E 152 C6
Wakool → Australia 35°5S 143°33E 152 C5
Wakre Indonesia 0°19S 131°5E 119 E8
Wakuach, L. Canada 55°34N 67°32W 165 A6
Wakulla U.S.A. 30°14N 84°14W 178 E5
Walagunya ⊙ Australia 23°10S 120°50E 148 D3
Walamba Zambia 13°30S 28°42E 143 E2
Wałbrzych Poland 50°45N 16°18E 83 H3
Walbury Hill U.K. 51°21N 1°28W 67 F6
Walcha Australia 30°55S 151°31E 153 A9
Walcheren Neths. 51°30N 3°35E 69 C3
Walcott U.S.A. 41°46N 106°51W 168 F10
Wałcz Poland 53°17N 16°27E 83 E3
Waldbröl Germany 50°52N 7°37E 76 E3
Waldburg Ra. Australia 24°40S 117°35E 149 D2
Waldeck Germany 51°12N 9°4E 76 D5
Walden Colo., U.S.A. 40°44N 106°17W 168 F10
Walden N.Y., U.S.A. 41°34N 74°11W 175 E10
Waldkirch Germany 48°5N 7°58E 77 G3
Waldkirchen Germany 48°43N 13°36E 77 G9
Waldkraiburg Germany 48°11N 12°24E 77 G8
Waldo U.S.A. 29°48N 82°10W 178 F7
Waldport U.S.A. 44°26N 124°4W 168 D1
Waldron U.S.A. 34°54N 94°5W 176 D7
Waldviertel Austria 48°30N 15°30E 78 C8
Walebing Australia 30°41S 116°13E 149 F2
Walembele Ghana 10°30N 1°58W 138 C4
Walensee Switz. 47°7N 9°13E 77 H5
Wales □ U.K. 52°19N 4°43W 67 E3
Wales I. Canada 68°1N 86°40W 161 D14
Walewale Ghana 10°21N 0°50W 139 C4
Walgett Australia 30°0S 148°5E 151 E4
Walgreen Coast Antarctica 75°15S 105°0W 55 D15
Walhalla Australia 37°56S 146°29E 153 D7
Walker U.S.A. 47°6N 94°35W 172 B6
Walker, L. Canada 50°20N 67°11W 165 B6
Walker L. Canada 54°42N 95°57W 163 C9
Walker L. U.S.A. 38°42N 118°43W 168 G4
Walkerston Australia 21°11S 149°8E 150 b
Walkerton Canada 44°10N 81°10W 174 B3
Wall U.S.A. 44°0N 102°8W 172 C2
Walla Walla Australia 35°45S 146°54E 153 C7
Walla Walla U.S.A. 46°4N 118°20W 168 C4
Wallace Idaho, U.S.A. 47°28N 115°56W 168 C6
Wallace N.C., U.S.A. 34°44N 77°59W 177 D16
Wallaceburg Canada 42°34N 82°23W 174 D2
Wallacetown N.Z. 46°21S 168°19E 155 G3
Wallachia = Valahia Romania 44°35N 25°0E 81 F9
Wallal Australia 26°32S 146°7E 151 D4
Wallam Cr. → Australia 28°40S 147°20E 151 D4
Wallambin, L. Australia 30°57S 117°35E 149 F2
Wallan Australia 37°26S 144°59E 153 D6
Wallangarra Australia 28°56S 151°58E 151 D5
Wallaroo Australia 33°56S 137°39E 152 B2
Walldürn Germany 49°34N 9°22E 77 F5
Wallenhorst Germany 52°21N 8°1E 76 C4
Wallenpaupack, L. U.S.A. 41°25N 75°15W 175 E9
Wallerawang Australia 33°25S 150°4E 153 B9
Wallingat △ Australia 32°14S 152°25E 153 B10
Wallingford Conn., U.S.A. 41°27N 72°50W 175 E12
Wallingford Vt., U.S.A. 43°28N 72°58W 175 C12
Wallis & Futuna, Îs. ☒ Pac. Oc. 13°18S 176°10W 147 C11
Wallowa U.S.A. 45°34N 117°32W 168 D5
Wallowa Mts. U.S.A. 45°20N 117°30W 168 D5
Walls U.K. 60°14N 1°33W 65 A7
Walls of Jerusalem △ Australia 41°56S 146°15E 151 G4
Wallsend Australia 32°55S 151°40E 153 B9
Wallula U.S.A. 46°5N 118°54W 168 C4
Wallumbilla Australia 26°33S 149°9E 151 D4
Walmsley L. Canada 63°25N 108°36W 163 A7
Walney, I. of U.K. 54°6N 3°15W 66 C4
Walnut Canyon ⌂ U.S.A. 35°15N 111°20W 169 J8
Walnut Creek U.S.A. 37°54N 122°4W 170 H4
Walnut Grove U.S.A. 34°4N 86°18W 178 A3
Walnut Hill U.S.A. 30°53N 87°30W 179 E2
Walnut Ridge U.S.A. 36°4N 90°57W 177 C9
Walpeup Australia 35°7S 142°2E 152 C5
Walpole Australia 34°58S 116°44E 149 F2
Walpole U.S.A. 42°9N 71°15W 175 D13
Walpole-Nornalup △ Australia 35°0S 116°45E 149 G2
Wals Austria 47°47N 12°58E 78 D5
Walsall U.K. 52°35N 1°58W 67 E6
Walsenburg U.S.A. 37°38N 104°47W 169 H11
Walsh U.S.A. 37°23N 102°17W 169 H12
Walsh → Australia 16°31S 143°42E 150 B3
Walsingham Canada 42°40N 80°31W 174 D4
Walsrode Germany 52°51N 9°35E 76 C5
Walt Disney World U.S.A. 28°22N 81°33W 179 G8
Waltair India 17°44N 83°23E 126 F6
Walter F. George Res. U.S.A. 31°38N 85°4W 178 D4
Walterboro U.S.A. 32°55N 80°40W 178 C9
Walters U.S.A. 34°22N 98°19W 176 D5
Waltershausen Germany 50°54N 10°33E 76 E6
Waltershausen Gletscher Greenland 73°54N 24°25W 57 C8
Waltham U.S.A. 42°23N 71°14W 175 D13
Waltman U.S.A. 43°4N 107°12W 168 E10
Walton U.S.A. 42°10N 75°8W 175 D9
Walton-on-the-Naze U.K. 51°51N 1°17E 67 F9
Walvis Bay Namibia 23°0S 14°28E 144 B1
Walvis Ridge Atl. Oc. 26°0S 5°0E 56 J12
Walvisbaai = Walvis Bay Namibia 23°0S 14°28E 144 B1
Walwa Australia 35°59S 147°44E 153 C7
Wamba Dem. Rep. of the Congo 2°10N 27°57E 142 B2
Wamba Kenya 0°58N 37°19E 142 B4
Wamba Nigeria 8°57N 8°42E 139 D6
Wambardi ⊙ Australia 16°2S 130°55E 148 C5
Wamego U.S.A. 39°12N 96°18W 172 F5
Wamena Indonesia 4°4S 138°57E 119 E9
Wampana Karlantijpa ⊙ Australia 17°45S 132°10E 148 C5
Wampaya ⊙ Australia 17°20S 135°0E 150 B2
Wampsville U.S.A. 43°4N 75°42W 175 C9
Wamsutter U.S.A. 41°40N 107°58W 168 F10
Wamulan Indonesia 3°27S 126°7E 119 E7
Wan Tup Burma 21°13N 98°42E 120 D2
Wan Xian China 38°47N 115°7E 114 E8
Wana Pakistan 32°20N 69°32E 124 C3
Wanaaring Australia 29°38S 144°9E 151 D3
Wanaka N.Z. 44°42S 169°9E 155 E4
Wanaka, L. N.Z. 44°33S 169°7E 155 E4
Wan'an China 26°26N 114°49E 117 D10
Wanapitei L. Canada 46°45N 80°40W 164 C3
Wanbi Australia 34°46S 140°17E 152 C4
Wandel Sea = McKinley Sea Arctic 82°0N 0°0 57 A11
Wandérama Ivory C. 8°37N 4°25W 138 D4
Wandhari Pakistan 27°42N 66°48E 124 F2
Wanding China 24°5N 98°4E 116 E2
Wandoan Australia 26°5S 149°55E 151 D4
Wandur Marine △ India 11°30N 92°30E 127 J11
Wanfu China 40°8N 122°38E 115 D12
Wang → Thailand 17°8N 99°2E 120 D2
Wang Noi Thailand 14°13N 100°44E 120 E3
Wang Saphung Thailand 17°18N 101°46E 120 D3
Wang Thong Thailand 16°50N 100°26E 120 D3
Wanga Dem. Rep. of the Congo 2°58N 29°12E 142 B2
Wanganella Australia 35°6S 144°49E 153 C6
Wanganui N.Z. 39°56S 175°3E 154 F4
Wanganui → W. Coast, N.Z. 43°3S 170°26E 155 D5
Wanganui → Wanganui-Manawatu, N.Z. 39°55S 175°4E 154 F4
Wangaratta Australia 36°21S 146°19E 153 D7
Wangary Australia 34°35S 135°29E 151 E2
Wangcang China 32°18N 106°20E 116 A6
Wangcheng China 28°22N 112°49E 117 C9
Wangcun China 36°41N 117°41E 115 F9
Wangdu China 38°40N 115°7E 114 E8
Wangen Germany 47°41N 9°50E 77 H5
Wangerooge Germany 53°47N 7°54E 76 B3
Wangiwangi Indonesia 5°22S 123°37E 119 F6
Wangjiang China 30°10N 116°42E 117 B11
Wangmo China 25°10N 106°5E 116 E6
Wangolodougou Ivory C. 9°55N 5°10W 138 D3
Wangqing China 43°12N 129°42E 115 C15
Wani India 20°5N 78°55E 126 D4
Wanimiyn ⊙ Australia 15°55S 130°49E 148 C5
Wanjina Wunggurr Wilinggin ⊙ Australia 16°0S 127°0E 148 C4
Wankaner India 22°35N 71°0E 124 H4
Wanless Canada 54°11N 101°21W 163 C8
Wanleweyne Somalia 2°37N 44°54E 131 G3
Wanneroo Australia 31°42S 115°46E 149 F2
Wannian China 28°42N 117°4E 117 C11
Wanning China 18°48N 110°22E 117 a
Wannoo Billabong Roadhouse Australia 27°25S 115°49E 149 E2
Wanon Niwat Thailand 17°38N 103°46E 120 D4
Wanqinsha China 22°43N 113°33E 111 a
Wanquan China 40°50N 114°40E 114 D8
Wanrong China 35°25N 110°50E 114 G6
Wanshan China 27°30N 109°12E 116 D7
Wanshan Qundao China 21°57N 113°45E 111 a
Wansheng China 28°57N 106°53E 116 C6
Wanstead N.Z. 40°8S 176°30E 154 G5
Wantage U.K. 51°35N 1°25W 67 F6
Wanxian China 30°42N 108°20E 116 B7
Wanyuan China 32°4N 108°3E 116 A7
Wanzai Guangdong, China 22°12N 113°31E 111 a
Wanzai Jiangxi, China 28°7N 114°30E 117 C10
Wapakoneta U.S.A. 40°34N 84°12W 173 E11
Wapato U.S.A. 46°27N 120°25W 168 C3
Wapawekka L. Canada 54°55N 104°40W 163 C8
Wapikopa L. Canada 52°56N 87°53W 164 B2
Wapiti → Canada 55°5N 118°18W 162 B5
Wappingers Falls U.S.A. 41°36N 73°55W 175 E11
Wapsipinicon → U.S.A. 41°44N 90°19W 172 E8
Wapusk △ Canada 57°46N 93°22W 163 B10
Warakurna Australia 24°59S 128°17E 149 D4
Warangal India 17°58N 79°35E 126 F4
Waraseoni India 21°45N 80°2E 125 J9
Waratah Australia 41°30S 145°30E 151 G4
Waratah B. Australia 38°54S 146°5E 153 E7
Warburg Germany 51°28N 9°11E 76 D5
Warburton Vic., Australia 37°47S 145°42E 153 D6
Warburton W. Austral., Australia 26°8S 126°35E 149 E4
Warburton ⊙ Australia 26°7S 126°34E 149 E4
Warburton → Australia 28°4S 137°28E 151 D2
Warburton Groove Australia 28°18S 137°8E 151 A2
Warburton Ra. Australia 25°55S 126°28E 149 E4
Ward N.Z. 41°49S 174°11E 155 B9
Ward → Australia 26°28S 146°6E 151 D4
Ward Mt. U.S.A. 37°12N 118°54W 170 H8
Wardang I. Australia 34°30S 137°20E 152 C2
Warden S. Africa 27°50S 29°0E 145 C4
Wardha India 20°45N 78°39E 126 D4
Wardha → India 19°57N 79°11E 126 E4
Wardsville Canada 42°39N 81°45W 174 D3
Ware U.K. 51°49N 0°0 67 F8
Ware U.S.A. 42°16N 72°14W 175 D12
Waregem Belgium 50°53N 3°27E 69 D3
Wareham U.S.A. 41°46N 70°43W 175 E14
Waremme Belgium 50°43N 5°15E 69 D5
Waren Germany 53°31N 12°40E 76 B8
Warendorf Germany 51°57N 8°1E 76 D4
Waresboro U.S.A. 31°15N 82°29W 178 D7
Warialda Australia 29°29S 150°33E 151 D5
Warin Chamrap Thailand 15°12N 104°53E 120 E5
Warka Poland 51°47N 21°12E 83 G8
Warkopi Indonesia 1°12S 134°9E 119 E8
Warkworth N.Z. 36°24S 174°41E 154 C3
Warm Springs Ga., U.S.A. 32°53N 84°41W 178 C5
Warm Springs Nev., U.S.A. 38°10N 116°20W 169 G5
Warman Canada 52°19N 106°30W 163 C7
Warmbad = Bela Bela S. Africa 24°51S 28°19E 145 B4
Warmbad Namibia 28°25S 18°42E 144 C2
Warming I. = Uunartoq Qeqertoq Greenland 71°33N 21°47W 57 C8
Warmińsko-Mazurskie □ Poland 54°0N 21°0E 82 D8
Warminster U.K. 51°12N 2°10W 67 F5
Warminster U.S.A. 40°12N 75°6W 175 F9
Warmun Australia 17°2S 128°12E 148 C4
Warnemünde Germany 54°10N 12°4E 76 A8
Warner Mts. U.S.A. 41°40N 120°15W 168 F3
Warner Robins U.S.A. 32°37N 83°36W 178 C6
Warnow → Germany 54°6N 12°9E 76 A8
Waroona Australia 32°50S 115°58E 149 F2
Warora India 20°14N 79°1E 126 D4
Warrabah △ Australia 30°31S 150°56E 153 A10
Warrabri ⊙ Australia 21°1S 134°19E 150 C1
Warracknabeal Australia 36°9S 142°26E 152 D5
Warragul Australia 38°10S 145°58E 153 E6
Warrego → Australia 30°24S 145°21E 151 E4
Warrego Ra. Australia 24°58S 146°0E 150 C4
Warren Australia 31°42S 147°51E 153 A7
Warren Ark., U.S.A. 33°37N 92°4W 176 E8
Warren Mich., U.S.A. 42°28N 83°1W 173 D12
Warren Minn., U.S.A. 48°12N 96°46W 172 A5
Warren Ohio, U.S.A. 41°14N 80°49W 174 E4
Warren Pa., U.S.A. 41°51N 79°9W 174 E5
Warrenpoint U.K. 54°6N 6°15W 64 B5
Warrensburg Mo., U.S.A. 38°46N 93°44W 172 F7
Warrensburg N.Y., U.S.A. 43°29N 73°46W 175 C11
Warrenton S. Africa 28°9S 24°47E 144 C3
Warrenton Ga., U.S.A. 33°24N 82°40W 178 B7
Warrenton Oreg., U.S.A. 46°10N 123°56W 170 D3
Warrenville U.S.A. 33°33N 81°48W 178 B8
Warri Nigeria 5°30N 5°41E 139 D6
Warrington N.Z. 45°43S 170°35E 155 F5
Warrington U.K. 53°24N 2°35W 66 D5
Warrington U.S.A. 30°23N 87°17W 179 E2
Warrington □ U.K. 53°24N 2°35W 66 D5
Warrnambool Australia 38°25S 142°30E 152 E5
Warroad U.S.A. 48°54N 95°19W 172 A6
Warrumbungle △ Australia 31°18S 149°1E 153 A8
Warruwi Australia 11°36S 133°20E 150 A1
Warsak Dam Pakistan 34°11N 71°19E 124 B4
Warsaw = Warszawa Poland 52°14N 21°0E 83 F8
Warsaw Ind., U.S.A. 41°14N 85°51W 173 E11
Warsaw N.Y., U.S.A. 42°45N 78°8W 174 D6
Warsaw Ohio, U.S.A. 40°20N 82°0W 174 F3
Warstein Germany 51°26N 8°22E 76 D4
Warszawa Poland 52°14N 21°0E 83 F8
Warszawa ✕ (WAW) Poland 52°9N 20°59E 83 F7
Warta Poland 51°43N 18°38E 83 G5
Warta → Poland 52°35N 14°39E 83 F1
Warthe = Warta → Poland 52°35N 14°39E 83 F1
Warthen U.S.A. 33°6N 82°48W 178 B7
Waru Indonesia 3°30S 130°36E 119 E8
Warud India 21°30N 78°16E 126 D4
Warumungu ⊙ Australia 19°15S 134°44E 150 B1
Warwick Australia 28°10S 152°1E 151 D5
Warwick U.K. 52°18N 1°35W 67 E6
Warwick Ga., U.S.A. 31°50N 83°57W 178 D6
Warwick N.Y., U.S.A. 41°16N 74°22W 175 E10
Warwick R.I., U.S.A. 41°42N 71°28W 175 E13
Warwickshire □ U.K. 52°14N 1°38W 67 E6
Wasaga Beach Canada 44°31N 80°1W 174 B4
Wasagaming Canada 50°39N 99°58W 163 C9
Wasatch Ra. U.S.A. 40°0N 111°30W 168 F8
Wasbank S. Africa 28°15S 30°9E 145 C5
Wasco Calif., U.S.A. 35°36N 119°20W 171 K7
Wasco Oreg., U.S.A. 45°36N 120°42W 168 D3
Wase Nigeria 9°4N 9°54E 139 D6
Waseca U.S.A. 44°5N 93°30W 172 C7
Wasekamio L. Canada 56°45N 108°45W 163 B7
Wasgomura △ Sri Lanka 7°45N 81°0E 127 L5
Wash, The U.K. 52°58N 0°20E 66 E8
Washago Canada 44°45N 79°20W 174 B5
Washburn N. Dak., U.S.A. 47°17N 101°2W 172 B3
Washburn Wis., U.S.A. 46°40N 90°54W 172 B8
Washim India 20°3N 77°0E 126 D3
Washington U.K. 54°55N 1°30W 66 C6
Washington D.C., U.S.A. 38°53N 77°2W 173 F15
Washington Ga., U.S.A. 33°44N 82°44W 178 B7
Washington Ind., U.S.A. 38°40N 87°10W 172 F10
Washington Iowa, U.S.A. 41°18N 91°42W 172 E8
Washington Mo., U.S.A. 38°33N 91°1W 172 F8
Washington N.C., U.S.A. 35°33N 77°3W 177 D16
Washington N.J., U.S.A. 40°46N 74°59W 175 F10
Washington Pa., U.S.A. 40°10N 80°15W 174 F4
Washington Utah, U.S.A. 37°8N 113°31W 169 H7
Washington □ U.S.A. 47°30N 120°30W 168 C3
Washington, Mt. U.S.A. 44°16N 71°18W 175 B13
Washington Court House U.S.A. 39°32N 83°26W 173 F12
Washington I. U.S.A. 45°23N 86°54W 172 C10
Washington Land Greenland 80°30N 66°0W 57 A4
Washougal U.S.A. 45°35N 122°21W 170 E4
Washpool △ Australia 29°22S 152°20E 151 D5
Wasian Indonesia 1°47S 133°19E 119 E8
Wasilków Poland 53°12N 23°13E 83 E10
Wasilla U.S.A. 61°35N 149°26W 160 E2
Wasini Marine △ Kenya 4°33S 39°14E 142 C4
Wasior Indonesia 2°43S 134°30E 119 E8
Wasiri Indonesia 7°30S 126°30E 119 F7
Wāsiṭ □ Iraq 32°50N 45°50E 105 F11
Waskaganish Canada 51°30N 78°40W 164 B4
Waskaiowaka L. Canada 56°33N 96°23W 163 B9
Waskesiu Lake Canada 53°55N 106°5W 163 C7
Wassaw I. U.S.A. 31°53N 80°58W 178 D9
Wassaw Sd. U.S.A. 31°55N 80°55W 178 D9
Wasserburg Germany 48°3N 12°14E 77 G8
Wasserkuppe Germany 50°29N 9°55E 76 E5
Wassy France 48°30N 4°58E 71 D11
Waswanipi Canada 49°40N 76°29W 164 C4
Waswanipi, L. Canada 49°35N 76°40W 164 C4
Watagans △ Australia 33°0S 151°28E 153 B9
Watampone Indonesia 4°29S 120°25E 119 E6
Watamu Kenya 3°23S 40°0E 142 C5
Watarrka △ Australia 24°20S 131°30E 148 D5
Water Park Pt. Australia 22°56S 150°47E 150 C5
Water Valley U.S.A. 34°10N 89°38W 177 D10
Waterberg Plateau ⌂ Namibia 20°25S 17°18E 144 B2
Waterberge S. Africa 24°10S 28°0E 145 B4
Waterbury Conn., U.S.A. 41°33N 73°3W 175 E11
Waterbury Vt., U.S.A. 44°20N 72°46W 175 B12
Waterbury L. Canada 58°10N 104°22W 163 B8
Waterdown Canada 43°20N 79°53W 174 C5
Wateree → U.S.A. 33°45N 80°37W 178 B9
Waterford Canada 42°56N 80°17W 174 D4
Waterford Ireland 52°15N 7°8W 64 D4
Waterford Calif., U.S.A. 37°38N 120°46W 170 H6
Waterford Pa., U.S.A. 41°57N 79°59W 174 E5
Waterford □ Ireland 52°10N 7°40W 64 D4
Waterford Harbour Ireland 52°8N 6°58W 64 D5
Waterhen L. Canada 52°10N 99°40W 163 C9
Waterloo Belgium 50°43N 4°25E 69 D4
Waterloo Ont., Canada 43°30N 80°32W 174 C4
Waterloo Qué., Canada 45°22N 72°32W 175 A12
Waterloo S. Leone 8°26N 13°8W 138 D2
Waterloo Ill., U.S.A. 38°20N 90°9W 172 F8
Waterloo Iowa, U.S.A. 42°30N 92°21W 172 D7
Waterloo N.Y., U.S.A. 42°54N 76°52W 174 D8
Watersmeet U.S.A. 46°16N 89°11W 172 B9
Waterton Lakes △ Canada 48°45N 115°0W 162 D6
Watertown Conn., U.S.A. 41°36N 73°7W 175 E11
Watertown Fla., U.S.A. 30°11N 82°36W 178 E7
Watertown N.Y., U.S.A. 43°59N 75°55W 175 C9
Watertown S. Dak., U.S.A. 44°54N 97°7W 172 C5
Watertown Wis., U.S.A. 43°12N 88°43W 172 D9
Waterval-Boven = Emgwenya S. Africa 25°40S 30°18E 145 C5
Waterville Canada 45°16N 71°54W 175 A13
Waterville Maine, U.S.A. 44°33N 69°38W 173 C19
Waterville N.Y., U.S.A. 42°56N 75°23W 175 D9
Waterville Pa., U.S.A. 41°19N 77°21W 174 E7
Waterville Wash., U.S.A. 47°39N 120°4W 168 C3
Watervliet U.S.A. 42°44N 73°42W 175 D11
Wates Indonesia 7°51S 110°10E 119 G14
Watford Canada 42°57N 81°53W 174 D3
Watford U.K. 51°40N 0°24W 67 F7
Watford City U.S.A. 47°48N 103°17W 172 B2
Wathaman → Canada 57°16N 102°59W 163 B8
Wathaman L. Canada 56°58N 103°44W 163 B8
Watheroo Australia 30°15S 116°5E 149 F2
Watheroo △ Australia 30°19S 115°48E 149 F2
Wating China 35°40N 106°38E 114 G4
Watkins Glen U.S.A. 42°23N 76°52W 174 D8
Watkinsville U.S.A. 33°52N 83°25W 178 B6
Watling I. = San Salvador I. Bahamas 24°0N 74°30W 183 B5
Watonga U.S.A. 35°51N 98°25W 176 D5
Watrous Canada 51°40N 105°25W 163 C7
Watrous U.S.A. 35°48N 104°59W 169 J11
Watsa Dem. Rep. of the Congo 3°4N 29°30E 142 B2
Watseka U.S.A. 40°47N 87°44W 172 E10
Watson Canada 52°10N 104°30W 163 C8
Watson Lake Canada 60°6N 128°49W 162 A3
Watsontown U.S.A. 41°5N 76°52W 174 E8
Watsonville U.S.A. 36°55N 121°45W 170 J5
Wattiwarriganna Cr. → Australia 28°57S 136°10E 151 D2
Wattwil Switz. 47°18N 9°6E 77 H5
Watuata = Batuata Indonesia 6°12S 122°42E 119 F6
Watubela, Kepulauan Indonesia 4°28S 131°35E 119 E8
Watubela Is. = Watubela, Kepulauan Indonesia 4°28S 131°35E 119 E8
Wau South Sudan 7°45N 28°1E 135 G11
Waubamik Canada 45°27N 80°1W 174 A4
Waubay U.S.A. 45°20N 97°18W 172 C5
Waubra Australia 37°21S 143°39E 152 D5
Wauchope N.S.W., Australia 31°28S 152°45E 153 A10
Wauchope N. Terr., Australia 20°36S 134°15E 150 C1
Wauchula U.S.A. 27°33N 81°49W 179 H8
Waukarlycarly, L. Australia 21°18S 121°56E 148 D3
Waukeenah U.S.A. 30°25N 83°57W 178 E6
Waukegan U.S.A. 42°22N 87°50W 172 D10
Waukesha U.S.A. 43°1N 88°14W 172 D9
Waukon U.S.A. 43°16N 91°29W 172 D8
Waupaca U.S.A. 44°21N 89°5W 172 C9
Waupun U.S.A. 43°38N 88°44W 172 D9
Waurika U.S.A. 34°10N 98°0W 176 D6
Wausau Fla., U.S.A. 30°38N 85°35W 178 E4
Wausau Wis., U.S.A. 44°58N 89°38W 172 C9
Wautoma U.S.A. 44°4N 89°18W 172 C9
Wauwatosa U.S.A. 43°2N 88°0W 172 D9
Wave Hill = Kalkarindji Australia 17°30S 130°47E 148 C5
Wave Rock ⌂ Australia 32°26S 118°53E 149 F2
Waveney → U.K. 52°35N 1°39E 67 E9
Waverley N.Z. 39°46S 174°37E 154 F3
Waverly Ala., U.S.A. 32°44N 85°35W 178 C4
Waverly Fla., U.S.A. 27°59N 81°37W 179 H8
Waverly Ga., U.S.A. 31°6N 81°43W 178 D8
Waverly Iowa, U.S.A. 42°44N 92°29W 172 D7
Waverly N.Y., U.S.A. 42°1N 76°32W 175 E8
Waverly Hall U.S.A. 32°41N 84°44W 178 C5
Wavre Belgium 50°43N 4°38E 69 D4
Wâw = Wau South Sudan 7°45N 28°1E 135 G11
Wāw al Kabīr Libya 25°20N 16°43E 135 C9
Wawa Canada 47°59N 84°47W 164 C3
Wawa Nigeria 9°54N 4°27E 139 D5
Wawa Sudan 20°30N 30°22E 137 C3
Wawanesa Canada 49°36N 99°40W 163 D9
Wawona U.S.A. 37°32N 119°39W 170 H7
Waxahachie U.S.A. 32°24N 96°51W 176 E6
Waxxari China 38°42N 87°19E 109 E11
Way, L. Australia 26°45S 120°16E 149 E3
Waya Fiji 17°19S 177°10E 154 a
Waycross U.S.A. 31°13N 82°21W 178 D7
Wayland U.S.A. 42°34N 77°35W 174 D7
Wayne Nebr., U.S.A. 42°14N 97°1W 172 D5
Wayne W. Va., U.S.A. 38°13N 82°27W 173 F12
Waynesboro Ga., U.S.A. 33°6N 82°1W 178 B7
Waynesboro Miss., U.S.A. 31°40N 88°39W 177 F10
Waynesboro Pa., U.S.A. 39°45N 77°35W 173 F15
Waynesboro Va., U.S.A. 38°4N 78°53W 173 F14
Waynesburg U.S.A. 39°54N 80°11W 173 F13
Waynesville U.S.A. 35°28N 82°58W 177 D13
Waynoka U.S.A. 36°35N 98°53W 176 C5
Wayside U.S.A. 33°4N 83°37W 178 B6
Wazirabad Pakistan 32°30N 74°8E 124 C6
Waziristan Pakistan 33°0N 70°0E 124 C4
Wda → Poland 53°25N 18°29E 82 E5
We Indonesia 5°51N 95°18E 118 C1
Weald, The U.K. 51°4N 0°20E 67 F8
Wear → U.K. 54°55N 1°23W 66 C6
Weatherford Okla., U.S.A. 35°32N 98°43W 176 D5
Weatherford Tex., U.S.A. 32°46N 97°48W 176 E6
Weaverville U.S.A. 40°44N 122°56W 168 F2
Webb City U.S.A. 37°9N 94°28W 172 G6
Webequie Canada 52°59N 87°21W 164 B2
Weber N.Z. 40°24S 176°20E 154 G5
Webo = Nyaake Liberia 4°52N 7°37W 138 E3
Webster Mass., U.S.A. 42°3N 71°53W 175 D13
Webster N.Y., U.S.A. 43°13N 77°26W 174 C7
Webster S. Dak., U.S.A. 45°20N 97°31W 172 C5
Webster City U.S.A. 42°28N 93°49W 172 D7
Webster Springs U.S.A. 38°29N 80°25W 173 F13
Webuye Kenya 0°37N 34°46E 142 B3
Weda Indonesia 0°21N 127°50E 119 D7
Weda, Teluk Indonesia 0°20N 128°0E 119 D7
Weddell Abyssal Plain S. Ocean 65°0S 20°0W 55 C2
Weddell I. Falk. Is. 51°50S 61°0W 192 D4
Weddell Sea Antarctica 72°30S 40°0W 55 D1
Wedderburn Australia 36°26S 143°33E 152 D5
Weddin Mts. △ Australia 33°59S 148°0E 153 C8
Wedel Germany 53°34N 9°42E 76 B5
Wedemark Germany 52°32N 9°43E 76 C5
Wedgeport Canada 43°44N 65°59W 165 D6
Wedowee U.S.A. 33°19N 85°29W 178 B4
Wedza Zimbabwe 18°40S 31°33E 143 F3
Wee Waa Australia 30°11S 149°26E 151 E4
Weed U.S.A. 41°25N 122°23W 168 F2
Weed Heights U.S.A. 38°59N 119°13W 170 G7
Weedsport U.S.A. 43°2N 76°33W 175 C8
Weedville U.S.A. 41°17N 78°30W 174 E6
Weeki Wachee U.S.A. 28°32N 82°35W 179 G7
Weenen S. Africa 28°48S 30°7E 145 C5
Weener Germany 53°9N 7°20E 76 B3
Weerribben △ Neths. 52°47N 5°58E 69 B5
Weert Neths. 51°15N 5°43E 69 C5
Węgierska-Górka Poland 49°36N 19°7E 83 J6
Węgliniec Poland 51°18N 15°10E 83 G2
Węgorzewo Poland 54°13N 21°43E 82 D8
Węgorzyno Poland 53°32N 15°33E 82 E2
Węgrów Poland 52°24N 22°0E 83 F9
Wei He → Hebei, China 36°10N 115°45E 114 F8
Wei He → Shaanxi, China 34°38N 110°15E 114 G6
Weichang China 41°58N 117°49E 115 D9
Weichuan China 34°20N 113°59E 114 G7
Weida Germany 50°46N 12°3E 76 E8
Weiden Germany 49°41N 12°10E 77 F8
Weifang China 36°44N 119°7E 115 F10
Weihai China 37°30N 122°6E 115 F12
Weihui China 35°25N 114°3E 114 G8
Weil Germany 47°35N 7°37E 77 H3
Weilburg Germany 50°28N 8°17E 76 E4
Weilheim Germany 47°50N 11°9E 77 H7
Weimar Germany 50°58N 11°19E 76 E7
Weinan China 34°31N 109°29E 114 G5
Weingarten Germany 49°3N 8°31E 77 F4
Weinheim Germany 49°32N 8°39E 77 F4
Weining China 26°50N 104°17E 116 D5
Weipa Australia 12°40S 141°50E 150 A3
Weir → Australia 28°20S 149°50E 151 D4
Weir → Canada 56°54N 93°21W 163 B10
Weir, L. U.S.A. 29°0N 81°57W 179 F8
Weir River Canada 56°49N 94°6W 163 B10
Weirsdale U.S.A. 28°59N 81°55W 179 G8
Weirton U.S.A. 40°24N 80°35W 174 F4
Weiser U.S.A. 44°15N 116°58W 168 D5
Weishan Shandong, China 34°47N 117°5E 115 G9
Weishan Yunnan, China 25°12N 100°20E 116 E3
Weishan Hu China 34°35N 117°14E 115 G9
Weissenburg Germany 49°2N 10°58E 77 F6
Weissenfels Germany 51°11N 12°0E 76 D7
Weisswasser Germany 51°30N 14°36E 76 D10
Weitra Austria 48°41N 14°54E 78 C7
Weixi China 27°10N 99°10E 116 D2
Weixin China 27°48N 105°3E 116 D5
Weiyuan Gansu, China 35°7N 104°10E 114 G3
Weiyuan Sichuan, China 29°35N 104°36E 116 C5
Weiz Austria 47°13N 15°39E 78 D8
Weizhou Dao China 21°0N 109°5E 116 G7
Wejherowo Poland 54°35N 18°12E 82 D5
Wekusko L. Canada 54°40N 99°50W 163 C9
Welch U.S.A. 37°26N 81°35W 173 G13
Welford △ Australia 25°5S 143°16E 150 D3
Weligama Sri Lanka 5°58N 80°25E 127 M5
Welkom S. Africa 28°0S 26°46E 144 C4
Welland Canada 43°0N 79°15W 174 D5
Welland → U.K. 52°51N 0°5W 67 E7
Wellawaya Sri Lanka 6°44N 81°6E 127 L5
Wellesley Is. Australia 16°42S 139°30E 150 B2
Wellesley Islands ⊙ Australia 16°32S 139°23E 150 B2
Wellingborough U.K. 52°19N 0°41W 67 E7
Wellington Australia 32°35S 148°59E 153 B8
Wellington Canada 43°57N 77°20W 174 C7
Wellington N.Z. 41°19S 174°46E 154 H3
Wellington S. Africa 33°38S 19°1E 144 D2
Wellington Somst., U.K. 50°58N 3°13W 67 G4
Wellington Telford & Wrekin, U.K. 52°42N 2°30W 67 E5
Wellington Colo., U.S.A. 40°42N 105°0W 168 F11
Wellington Fla., U.S.A. 26°39N 80°15W 179 J9
Wellington Kans., U.S.A. 37°16N 97°24W 172 G5
Wellington Nev., U.S.A. 38°45N 119°23W 170 G7
Wellington Ohio, U.S.A. 41°10N 82°13W 174 E2

Wellington *Tex.,*
  U.S.A. 34°51N 100°13W **176** D4
Wellington □ *N.Z.* 41°19S 175°3E **154** H4
Wellington, I. *Chile* 49°30S 75°0W **192** G2
Wellington, L. *Australia* 38°6S 147°20E **153** E7
Wellington Chan.
  Canada 75°0N 93°0W **161** C13
Wells *U.K.* 51°13N 2°39W **67** F5
Wells *Maine, U.S.A.* 43°20N 70°35W **175** C14
Wells *N.Y., U.S.A.* 43°24N 74°17W **175** C10
Wells *Nev., U.S.A.* 41°7N 114°58W **168** F6
Wells, L., *Australia* 26°44S 123°15E **149** E3
Wells, Mt. *Australia* 17°25S 127°8E **148** C4
Wells Gray *Canada* 52°30N 120°15W **162** C4
Wells River *U.S.A.* 44°9N 72°4W **175** B12
Wells-next-the-Sea *U.K.* 52°57N 0°51E **66** E8
Wellsboro *U.S.A.* 41°45N 77°18W **174** E7
Wellsburg *U.S.A.* 40°16N 80°37W **174** F4
Wellsford *N.Z.* 36°16S 174°32E **154** C3
Wellsville *N.Y., U.S.A.* 42°7N 77°57W **174** D7
Wellsville *Ohio, U.S.A.* 40°36N 80°39W **174** F4
Wellsville *Utah, U.S.A.* 41°38N 111°56W **168** F8
Wellton *U.S.A.* 32°40N 114°8W **169** K6
Wels *Austria* 48°9N 14°1E **78** C7
Welshpool *Australia* 38°42S 146°26E **153** E7
Welshpool *U.K.* 52°39N 3°8W **67** E4
Welwyn Garden City
  U.K. 51°48N 0°12W **67** F7
Wem *U.K.* 52°52N 2°44W **66** E5
Wembere → *Tanzania* 4°10S 34°15E **142** C3
Wemindji *Canada* 53°0N 78°49W **164** B4
Wemyss *Canada* 44°52N 76°23W **175** B8
Wen Xian *Gansu,*
  China 32°43N 104°36E **114** H3
Wen Xian *Henan, China* 34°55N 113°5E **114** G7
Wenatchee *U.S.A.* 47°25N 120°19W **168** C3
Wenchang *China* 19°38N 110°42E **117** a
Wencheng *China* 27°46N 120°4E **117** D13
Wenchi *Ghana* 7°46N 2°8W **138** D4
Wenchow = Wenzhou
  China 28°0N 120°38E **117** D13
Wenchuan *China* 31°22N 103°35E **116** B4
Wenden *U.S.A.* 33°49N 113°33W **171** M13
Wendeng *China* 37°15N 122°5E **115** F12
Wendesi *Indonesia* 2°30S 134°17E **119** E8
Wendover *U.S.A.* 40°44N 114°2W **168** F6
Weng'an *China* 27°5N 107°25E **116** D6
Wengcheng *China* 24°22N 113°50E **117** F9
Wengen *Switz.* 46°37N 7°55E **71** F14
Wengyuan *China* 24°20N 114°9E **117** E10
Wenling *China* 28°21N 121°20E **117** C13
Wenlock → *Australia* 12°2S 141°55E **150** A3
Wenshan *China* 23°20N 104°18E **116** E5
Wenshang *China* 35°45N 116°30E **114** G9
Wenshui *China* 37°26N 112°1E **114** F7
Wensleydale *U.K.* 54°17N 2°0W **66** C6
Wensu *China* 41°15N 80°10E **109** D10
Wensum → *U.K.* 52°40N 1°15E **66** E8
Wentworth *Australia* 34°2S 141°54E **162** D4
Wentzel, L. *Canada* 59°2N 114°28W **162** B6
Wenut *Indonesia* 3°11S 133°19E **119** E8
Wenxi *China* 35°20N 111°10E **114** G6
Wenzhou *China* 28°0N 120°38E **117** D13
Weott *U.S.A.* 40°20N 123°55W **168** F2
Wepener *S. Africa* 29°42S 27°3E **144** C4
Werda *Botswana* 25°24S 23°15E **144** C3
Werdau *Germany* 50°44N 12°22E **76** E8
Werder *Germany* 52°23N 12°55E **76** C8
Werdohl *Germany* 51°15N 7°46E **76** D3
Weri *Indonesia* 3°10S 132°38E **119** E8
Werneck *Germany* 49°58N 10°5E **77** F6
Wernigerode *Germany* 51°50N 10°47E **76** D6
Werra → *Germany* 51°24N 9°39E **76** D5
Werribee *Australia* 37°54S 144°40E **152** D6
Werrikimbe △
  Australia 31°11S 152°15E **153** A10
Werrimull *Australia* 34°25S 141°38E **152** C4
Werris Creek *Australia* 31°18S 150°38E **153** A9
Wertach → *Germany* 48°22N 10°54E **77** G6
Wertheim *Germany* 49°45N 9°32E **77** F5
Wertingen *Germany* 48°33N 10°41E **77** G6
Wesel *Germany* 51°39N 6°37E **76** D2
Weser → *Germany* 53°36N 8°28E **76** C5
Weserbergland *Germany* 52°12N 9°7E **76** C5
Weserbergland Schaumburg
  Hamelin △ *Germany* 52°8N 9°20E **76** C5
Weslaco *U.S.A.* 26°10N 97°58W **176** H6
Weslemkoon L. *Canada* 45°2N 77°25W **174** A7
Wesleyville *Canada* 49°9N 53°33W **165** C9
Wesleyville *U.S.A.* 42°9N 80°1W **174** D4
Wessel, C. *Australia* 10°59S 136°46E **150** A2
Wessel Is. *Australia* 11°10S 136°45E **150** A2
Wesselburen *Germany* 54°13N 8°54E **76** A4
Wessex *U.K.* 51°0N 2°0W **67** F5
Wessington Springs
  U.S.A. 44°5N 98°34W **172** C4
West *U.S.A.* 31°48N 97°6W **176** F6
West → *U.S.A.* 42°52N 72°33W **175** D12
West Allis *U.S.A.* 43°1N 88°0W **172** D2
West Antarctica
  Antarctica 80°0S 90°0W **55** D15
West Baines →
  Australia 15°38S 129°59E **148** C4
West Bank ■ *Asia* 32°6N 35°13E **130** C4
West Bend *U.S.A.* 43°25N 88°11W **172** D9
West Bengal = Paschimbanga □
  India 23°0N 88°0E **125** H13
West Berkshire □
  U.K. 51°25N 1°17W **67** F6
West Beskids = Západné Beskydy
  Europe 49°30N 19°0E **79** B12
West Branch *U.S.A.* 44°17N 84°14W **173** C11
West Branch Susquehanna →
  U.S.A. 40°53N 76°48W **175** F8
West Bromwich *U.K.* 52°32N 1°59W **67** E6
West Burra *U.K.* 60°5N 1°21W **65** A7
West Canada Cr. →
  U.S.A. 43°1N 74°58W **175** C10
West Caroline Basin
  Pac. Oc. 4°0N 138°0E **156** G5
West Chazy *U.S.A.* 44°49N 73°28W **175** B11
West Chester *U.S.A.* 39°58N 75°36W **175** G9
West Coast □ *N.Z.* 43°15S 170°30E **155** D5
West Coast △ *Namibia* 21°53S 14°14E **144** D1
West Coast △ *S. Africa* 33°13S 18°0E **144** D2
West Columbia *S.C.,*
  U.S.A. 33°59N 81°4W **178** B8
West Columbia *Tex.,*
  U.S.A. 29°9N 95°39W **176** G7
West Covina *U.S.A.* 34°4N 117°54W **171** L9
West Des Moines
  U.S.A. 41°35N 93°43W **172** E7

West Dunbartonshire □
  U.K. 55°59N 4°30W **65** F4
West End *Bahamas* 26°41N 78°58W **182** A4
Weston *Oreg., U.S.A.* 45°49N 118°26W **168** D4
Weston *W. Va., U.S.A.* 39°2N 80°28W **173** F5
West Fargo *U.S.A.* 46°52N 96°54W **172** B5
West Fiji Basin *Pac. Oc.* 17°0S 173°0E **156** J9
West Fjord = Vestfjorden
  Norway 67°55N 14°0E **60** C16
West Fork Trinity →
  U.S.A. 32°48N 96°54W **176** E6
West Frankfort *U.S.A.* 37°54N 88°55W **172** G9
West Grand L. *U.S.A.* 45°14N 67°51W **173** C20
West Green *U.S.A.* 31°37N 82°44W **178** D7
West Hartford *U.S.A.* 41°45N 72°44W **175** E12
West Haven *U.S.A.* 41°17N 72°57W **175** E12
West Hazleton *U.S.A.* 40°58N 76°0W **175** F9
West Hurley *U.S.A.* 41°59N 74°7W **175** E10
West I. *India* 13°35N 92°54E **127** H11
West Ice Shelf *Antarctica* 67°0S 85°0E **55** C7
West Indies *Cent. Amer.* 15°0N 65°0W **183** D7
West Jordan *U.S.A.* 40°36N 111°56W **168** F8
West Lamma Channel
  China 22°14N 114°4E **111** a
West Linn *U.S.A.* 45°21N 122°36W **170** E4
West Lorne *Canada* 42°36N 81°36W **174** D3
West Lothian □ *U.K.* 55°54N 3°36W **65** F5
West Lunga → *Zambia* 13°6S 24°39E **143** E1
West MacDonnell △
  Australia 23°38S 132°59E **148** D5
West Mariana Basin
  Pac. Oc. 15°0N 137°0E **156** F5
West Memphis *U.S.A.* 35°9N 90°10W **177** D9
West Midlands □ *U.K.* 52°26N 2°0W **67** E6
West Mifflin *U.S.A.* 40°21N 79°52W **174** F5
West Milford *U.S.A.* 41°8N 74°22W **175** E10
West Milton *U.S.A.* 41°1N 76°50W **174** E8
West Monroe *U.S.A.* 32°31N 92°9W **176** E8
West Newton *U.S.A.* 41°40N 79°46W **174** F5
West Nicholson
  Zimbabwe 21°2S 29°20E **143** G2
West Odessa *U.S.A.* 31°50N 102°30W **176** F3
West Palm Beach
  U.S.A. 26°43N 80°3W **179** J9
West Palm Beach Canal
  U.S.A. 26°40N 80°15W **179** J9
West Pensacola *U.S.A.* 30°25N 87°16W **179** E22
West Plains *U.S.A.* 36°44N 91°51W **172** G8
West Point *Ga., U.S.A.* 32°53N 85°11W **178** C4
West Point *Miss.,*
  U.S.A. 33°36N 88°39W **177** E10
West Point *N.Y.,*
  U.S.A. 41°24N 73°58W **175** E11
West Point *Nebr.,*
  U.S.A. 41°51N 96°43W **172** E5
West Point *Va.,*
  U.S.A. 37°32N 76°48W **173** G15
West Point L. *U.S.A.* 33°8N 85°0W **178** B4
West Pt. = Ouest, Pte. de l'
  Canada 49°52N 64°40W **165** C7
West Pt. *Australia* 35°1S 135°56E **152** C1
West Road → *Canada* 53°18N 122°53W **162** C4
West Rutland *U.S.A.* 43°36N 73°3W **175** C11
West Schelde = Westerschelde →
  Neths. 51°25N 3°25E **69** C3
West Seneca *U.S.A.* 42°51N 78°48W **174** D6
West Siberian Plain
  Russia 62°0N 75°0E **102** B9
West Sussex □ *U.K.* 50°55N 0°30W **67** G7
West-Terschelling *Neths.* 53°22N 5°13E **69** A5
West Valley City
  U.S.A. 40°42N 111°58W **168** F8
West Virginia □
  U.S.A. 38°45N 80°30W **173** F13
West-Vlaanderen □
  Belgium 51°0N 3°0E **69** D2
West Walker →
  U.S.A. 38°54N 119°9W **170** G7
West Wyalong
  Australia 33°56S 147°10E **153** B7
West Yellowstone
  U.S.A. 44°40N 111°6W **168** D8
West Yorkshire □ *U.K.* 53°45N 1°40W **66** D6
Westall, Pt. *Australia* 32°55S 134°4E **151** E1
Westbay *U.S.A.* 30°18N 85°52W **179** E8
Westbrook *U.S.A.* 43°41N 70°22W **173** D18
Westbury *Australia* 41°30S 146°51E **151** G4
Westby *U.S.A.* 48°52N 104°3W **168** B11
Westend *U.S.A.* 35°42N 117°24W **171** K9
Westerland *Germany* 54°54N 8°17E **76** A4
Westerly *U.S.A.* 41°22N 71°50W **175** E13
Western □ *Ghana* 5°30N 2°30W **138** D4
Western □ *Kenya* 0°30N 34°30E **142** D3
Western □ *S. Leone* 8°30N 13°20W **138** D2
Western □ *Zambia* 15°0S 24°4E **143** F1
Western Australia □
  Australia 25°0S 118°0E **149** E2
Western Cape □ *S. Africa* 34°0S 20°0E **144** D3
Western Dvina = Daugava →
  Latvia 57°4N 24°3E **84** D3
Western Ghats *India* 14°0N 75°0E **127** H2
Western Isles = Eilean Siar □
  U.K. 57°30N 7°10W **65** D1
Western Sahara ■
  Africa 25°0N 13°0W **134** D3
Western Samoa = Samoa ■
  Pac. Oc. 14°0S 172°0W **147** G5
Western Sierra Madre = Madre
  Occidental, Sierra
  Mexico 27°0N 107°0W **180** B3
Westernport *U.S.A.* 39°29N 79°3W **173** F14
Westerschelde → *Neths.* 51°25N 3°25E **69** C3
Westerstede *Germany* 53°15N 7°55E **76** B3
Westerwald *Germany* 50°38N 7°56E **76** E3
Westfield *Mass., U.S.A.* 42°7N 72°45W **175** D12
Westfield *N.Y., U.S.A.* 42°20N 79°35W **174** D5
Westfield *Pa., U.S.A.* 41°55N 77°32W **174** E7
Westhill *U.K.* 57°9N 2°19W **65** D6
Westhope *U.S.A.* 48°55N 101°1W **172** A3
Westland □ *N.Z.* 43°16S 170°16E **155** D5
Westland Bight *N.Z.* 42°55S 170°5E **155** C5
Westlock *Canada* 54°9N 113°55W **162** C6
Westmar *Australia* 27°55S 149°44E **151** D4
Westmeath □ *Ireland* 53°33N 7°34W **64** C4
Westminster *Calif.,*
  U.S.A. 33°45N 118°0W **171** M8
Westminster *Colo.,*
  U.S.A. 39°50N 105°2W **168** G11
Westminster *Md.,*
  U.S.A. 39°34N 76°59W **173** F15
Westmont *U.S.A.* 40°19N 78°58W **174** F6
Westmoreland *Barbados* 13°13N 59°37W **183** g

Westmorland *U.S.A.* 33°2N 115°37W **171** M11
Weston *Oreg., U.S.A.* 45°49N 118°26W **168** D4
Weston *W. Va., U.S.A.* 39°2N 80°28W **173** F13
Weston I. *Canada* 52°33N 79°36W **164** B4
Weston-super-Mare
  U.K. 51°21N 2°58W **67** F5
Westover *U.S.A.* 40°45N 78°40W **174** F6
Westport *Canada* 44°40N 76°25W **175** B8
Westport *Ireland* 53°48N 9°31W **64** C2
Westport *N.Z.* 41°46S 171°37E **155** B6
Westport *N.Y., U.S.A.* 44°11N 73°26W **175** B11
Westport *Oreg., U.S.A.* 46°8N 123°23W **170** D3
Westport *Wash., U.S.A.* 46°53N 124°6W **170** D2
Westray *Canada* 53°36N 101°24W **163** C8
Westray *U.K.* 59°18N 3°0W **65** B5
Westree *Canada* 47°26N 81°34W **164** C3
Westville *Calif., U.S.A.* 39°8N 120°42W **170** F6
Westville *Fla., U.S.A.* 30°46N 85°51W **178** D4
Westwood *U.S.A.* 40°18N 121°0W **168** F3
Westwood Lake *U.S.A.* 25°44N 80°23W **179** K9
Wetar *Indonesia* 7°48S 126°30E **119** F7
Wetaskiwin *Canada* 52°55N 113°24W **162** C6
Wete *Tanzania* 5°4S 39°43E **140** F7
Wetherby *U.K.* 53°56N 1°23W **66** D6
Wethersfield *U.S.A.* 41°42N 72°40W **175** E12
Wetteren *Belgium* 51°0N 3°53E **69** D3
Wetumka *U.S.A.* 35°14N 96°14W **176** D6
Wetumpka *U.S.A.* 32°32N 86°13W **178** C3
Wetwun *Burma* 21°53N 96°30W **125** J20
Wetzel *Germany* 50°32N 8°31E **76** E4
Wewahitchka *U.S.A.* 30°7N 85°12W **178** E4
Wewoka *U.S.A.* 35°9N 96°30W **176** D6
Wexford *Ireland* 52°20N 6°28W **64** D5
Wexford □ *Ireland* 52°20N 6°25W **64** D5
Wexford Harbour *Ireland* 52°20N 6°25W **64** D5
Weyburn *Canada* 49°40N 103°50W **163** D8
Weyer Markt *Austria* 47°51N 14°40E **78** D7
Weyhe *Germany* 52°58N 8°49E **76** C4
Weymouth *Canada* 44°30N 66°1W **165** D6
Weymouth *U.K.* 50°37N 2°28W **67** G5
Weymouth *U.S.A.* 42°13N 70°58W **175** D14
Weymouth, C.
  Australia 12°37S 143°27E **150** A3
Wha Ti *Canada* 63°8N 117°16W **160** E8
Whakaari *N.Z.* 37°30S 177°13E **154** B6
Whakamaru *N.Z.* 38°23S 175°50E **154** E4
Whakatane *N.Z.* 37°57S 177°1E **154** C6
Whakatane → *N.Z.* 37°57S 177°1E **154** C6
Whale = Baleine →
  Canada 58°15N 67°40W **165** A6
Whale B. *Burma* 11°37N 98°38E **121** G2
Whale Cove *Canada* 62°10N 92°34W **163** A10
Whale Valley = Hitan, W. el
  Egypt 29°19N 30°10E **137** F7
Whales, B. of *Antarctica* 78°0S 160°0W **55** D12
Whalsay *U.K.* 60°22N 0°59W **65** A8
Whangaehu → *N.Z.* 40°3S 175°6E **154** G4
Whangamata *N.Z.* 37°12S 175°53E **154** D4
Whangamomona *N.Z.* 39°8S 174°44E **154** F3
Whanganui *N.Z.* 39°17S 174°53E **154** F3
Whangaparaoa Pen.
  N.Z. 36°40S 174°45E **154** C3
Whangarei *N.Z.* 35°43S 174°21E **154** C3
Whangarei Harb. *N.Z.* 35°45S 174°28E **154** C3
Whangaroa Harb. *N.Z.* 35°4S 173°46E **154** B2
Whangaruru Harb.
  N.Z. 35°24S 174°23E **154** B3
Wharanui *N.Z.* 41°55S 174°6E **155** B9
Wharekauri = Chatham Is.
  Pac. Oc. 44°0S 176°40W **155** c
Wharfe → *U.K.* 53°51N 1°9W **66** D6
Wharfedale *U.K.* 54°6N 2°1W **66** C5
Wharton *N.J., U.S.A.* 40°54N 74°35W **175** F10
Wharton *Pa., U.S.A.* 41°31N 78°1W **174** E6
Wharton *Tex., U.S.A.* 29°19N 96°6W **176** G6
Wharton Basin *Ind. Oc.* 20°0S 99°0E **146** G9
Whataroa *N.Z.* 43°18S 170°24E **155** D3
Whataroa → *N.Z.* 43°7S 170°16E **155** D3
Wheatland *Calif.,*
  U.S.A. 39°1N 121°25W **170** F5
Wheatland *Wyo.,*
  U.S.A. 42°3N 104°58W **168** E11
Wheatley *Canada* 42°6N 82°27W **174** D2
Wheaton *Md., U.S.A.* 39°3N 77°3W **173** F15
Wheaton *Minn., U.S.A.* 45°48N 96°30W **172** C5
Wheelbarrow Pk.
  U.S.A. 37°26N 116°5W **170** H10
Wheeler *Oreg., U.S.A.* 45°41N 123°53W **168** D2
Wheeler *Tex., U.S.A.* 35°27N 100°16W **176** D4
Wheeler → *Canada* 57°2N 67°13W **165** A6
Wheeler L. *U.S.A.* 34°48N 87°23W **177** D11
Wheeler Pk. *N. Mex.,*
  U.S.A. 36°34N 105°25W **169** H11
Wheeler Pk. *Nev.,*
  U.S.A. 38°57N 114°15W **168** G6
Wheeler Ridge *U.S.A.* 35°0N 118°57W **171** L8
Wheelersburg *U.S.A.* 38°44N 82°51W **173** F12
Wheeling *U.S.A.* 40°4N 80°43W **174** F4
Whernside *U.K.* 54°14N 2°24W **66** C5
Whiddy I. *Ireland* 51°41N 9°31W **64** E2
Whim Creek *Australia* 20°50S 117°49E **148** D2
Whiskey Jack L.
  Canada 58°23N 101°55W **163** B8
Whiskeytown-Shasta-Trinity △
  U.S.A. 40°45N 122°15W **168** F2
Whistleduck Cr. →
  Australia 20°15S 135°18E **150** C2
Whistler *Canada* 50°7N 122°58W **162** C4
Whitby *Canada* 43°52N 78°56W **174** C6
Whitby *U.K.* 54°29N 0°37W **66** C7
Whitcombe Pass *N.Z.* 43°13S 170°55E **155** D3
White → *Ark., U.S.A.* 33°57N 91°5W **176** E9
White → *Ind., U.S.A.* 38°25N 87°45W **172** F10
White → *S. Dak.,*
  U.S.A. 43°42N 99°27W **172** D4
White → *Tex., U.S.A.* 33°14N 100°56W **176** E4
White → *Utah, U.S.A.* 40°4N 109°41W **168** F9
White → *Vt., U.S.A.* 43°37N 72°20W **175** C12
White → *Wash.,*
  U.S.A. 47°12N 122°15W **170** C4
White, L. *Australia* 21°9S 128°56E **148** D4
White B. *Canada* 50°0N 56°35W **165** C8
White Bird *U.S.A.* 45°46N 116°18W **168** D5
White Butte *U.S.A.* 46°23N 103°18W **172** B2
White City *Fla., U.S.A.* 29°53N 85°13W **178** F4
White City *Oreg.,*
  U.S.A. 42°26N 122°51W **168** E2
White Cliffs *Australia* 30°50S 143°10E **152** A3
White Desert = Es Sahrâ al Beida
  Egypt 27°50N 28°45E **137** B2
White Hall *U.S.A.* 39°26N 90°24W **172** F8
White Haven *U.S.A.* 41°4N 75°47W **175** E9

White Horse, Vale of
  U.K. 51°37N 1°30W **67** F6
White I. = Whakaari
  N.Z. 37°30S 177°13E **154** D6
White L. *Canada* 45°18N 76°31W **175** A8
White L. *U.S.A.* 29°44N 92°30W **176** G8
White Lake *Canada* 45°21N 76°29W **175** A8
White Mountain Peak
  U.S.A. 37°38N 118°15W **171** H8
White Mts. *Calif.,*
  U.S.A. 37°30N 118°15W **170** H8
White Mts. *N.H.,*
  U.S.A. 44°15N 71°15W **175** B13
White Mts. △
  Australia 20°42S 145°12E **150** C4
White Nile = Nîl el Abyad →
  Sudan 15°38N 32°31E **135** E12
White Oak *U.S.A.* 31°2N 81°43W **178** D8
White Otter L. *Canada* 49°5N 91°55W **164** C1
White Pass *U.S.A.* 46°38N 121°24W **170** D5
White Plains *Ga., U.S.A.* 33°28N 83°1W **178** B6
White Plains *N.Y.,*
  U.S.A. 41°2N 73°46W **175** E11
White River *Canada* 48°35N 85°20W **164** C2
White River *U.S.A.* 43°34N 100°45W **172** D3
White Rock *Canada* 49°2N 122°48W **170** A4
White Rock *U.S.A.* 35°50N 106°12W **169** J10
White Russia = Belarus ■
  Europe 53°30N 27°0E **75** B14
White Sands △
  U.S.A. 32°46N 106°20W **169** K10
White Sea = Beloye More
  Russia 66°30N 38°0E **58** B13
White Springs *U.S.A.* 30°20N 82°45W **178** E7
White Sulphur Springs *Mont.,*
  U.S.A. 46°33N 110°54W **168** C8
White Sulphur Springs *W. Va.,*
  U.S.A. 37°48N 80°18W **173** G13
White Swan *U.S.A.* 46°23N 120°44W **170** D6
White Volta → *Ghana* 9°10N 1°15W **139** D4
Whitecliffs *N.Z.* 43°26S 171°55E **155** D6
Whitecourt *Canada* 54°10N 115°45W **162** C5
Whiteface Mt. *U.S.A.* 44°22N 73°54W **175** B11
Whitefield *U.S.A.* 44°23N 71°37W **175** B13
Whitefish *U.S.A.* 48°25N 114°20W **168** B6
Whitefish L. *Canada* 62°41N 106°48W **163** A7
Whitefish Pt. *U.S.A.* 46°45N 84°59W **164** C3
Whitegull, L. = Goélands, L. aux
  Canada 55°27N 64°17W **165** A7
Whitehall *Mich.,*
  U.S.A. 43°24N 86°21W **172** D10
Whitehall *Mont.,*
  U.S.A. 45°52N 112°6W **168** D7
Whitehall *N.Y.,*
  U.S.A. 43°33N 73°24W **175** C11
Whitehall *Wis., U.S.A.* 44°22N 91°19W **172** C8
Whitehaven *U.K.* 54°33N 3°35W **66** C4
Whitehorse *Canada* 60°43N 135°3W **162** A1
Whitemark *Australia* 40°7S 148°3E **151** G4
Whiteriver *U.S.A.* 33°50N 109°58W **169** K9
Whitesand → *Canada* 60°9N 115°45W **162** A5
Whitesands *S. Africa* 34°23S 20°50E **144** E3
Whitesboro *N.Y., U.S.A.* 43°7N 75°18W **175** C9
Whitesboro *Tex.,*
  U.S.A. 33°39N 96°54W **176** E6
Whiteshell △ *Canada* 50°0N 95°40W **163** D9
Whiteside, Canal *Chile* 53°55S 70°15W **192** G2
Whiteville *U.S.A.* 34°20N 78°42W **177** D15
Whitewater *U.S.A.* 42°50N 88°44W **172** D9
Whitewater B. *U.S.A.* 25°15N 81°0W **179** K9
Whitewater Baldy
  U.S.A. 33°20N 108°39W **169** K9
Whitewater L. *Canada* 50°50N 89°10W **164** B2
Whitewood *Australia* 21°28S 143°30E **150** C3
Whitewood *Canada* 50°20N 102°20W **163** C8
Whitfield *Australia* 36°42S 146°24E **153** D7
Whithorn *U.K.* 54°44N 4°26W **65** G4
Whitianga *N.Z.* 36°47S 175°41E **154** C4
Whitman *U.S.A.* 42°5N 70°56W **175** D14
Whitmore Mts.
  Antarctica 82°35S 104°30W **55** E15
Whitney *Canada* 45°31N 78°14W **174** A6
Whitney, Mt. *U.S.A.* 36°35N 118°18W **170** J8
Whitney Point *U.S.A.* 42°20N 75°58W **175** D9
Whitstable *U.K.* 51°21N 1°3E **67** F9
Whitsunday I. *Australia* 20°15S 149°4E **150** b
Whitsunday Islands △
  Australia 20°15S 149°0E **150** b
Whittier *Alaska,*
  U.S.A. 60°47N 148°41W **166** C10
Whittier *Calif., U.S.A.* 33°58N 118°2W **171** M8
Whittlesea *Australia* 37°27S 145°9E **153** D6
Wholdaia L. *Canada* 60°43N 104°20W **163** A8
Whyalla *Australia* 33°2S 137°30E **152** B2
Wiang Kosai △
  Thailand 17°54N 99°29E **120** D2
Wiang Sa *Thailand* 18°34N 100°45E **120** C3
Wiarton *Canada* 44°40N 81°10W **174** B3
Wiawso *Ghana* 6°10N 2°25W **138** D4
Wiay *U.K.* 57°24N 7°13W **65** D1
Wiązów *Poland* 50°50N 17°10E **83** H4
Wibaux *U.S.A.* 46°59N 104°11W **168** C11
Wichian Buri *Thailand* 15°39N 101°7E **120** E3
Wichita *U.S.A.* 37°42N 97°20W **172** G5
Wichita Falls *U.S.A.* 33°54N 98°30W **176** E5
Wick *U.K.* 58°26N 3°5W **65** C5
Wickenburg *U.S.A.* 33°58N 112°44W **169** K7
Wickepin *Australia* 32°50S 117°30E **149** F2
Wickham *Australia* 20°42S 117°11E **148** D2
Wickham, C. *Australia* 39°35S 143°57E **151** F3
Wickliffe *U.S.A.* 41°36N 81°28W **174** E3
Wicklow *Ireland* 52°59N 6°3W **64** D5
Wicklow □ *Ireland* 52°57N 6°25W **64** D5
Wicklow Hd. *Ireland* 52°58N 6°0W **64** D6
Wicklow Mts. *Ireland* 52°58N 6°26W **64** C5
Wicklow Mts. △ *Ireland* 53°6N 6°21W **64** C5
Widawa *Poland* 51°27N 18°51E **83** G5
Widawka → *Poland* 51°7N 18°52E **83** G5
Widgeegoara Cr. →
  Australia 28°51S 146°34E **151** D4
Widgiemooltha
  Australia 31°30S 121°34E **149** F3
Widnes *U.K.* 53°23N 2°45W **66** D5
Więcbork *Poland* 53°21N 17°30E **83** B4
Wieliczka = Nördlicher
  Teutoburger
  Wald-Wiehengebirge △
  Germany 52°18N 8°10E **76** C4
Wiehl *Germany* 50°56N 7°34E **76** E3

Wiek *Germany* 54°37N 13°17E **76** A9
Wielbark *Poland* 53°24N 20°55E **82** E7
Wieleń *Poland* 52°53N 16°9E **83** E3
Wielichowo *Poland* 52°7N 16°22E **83** F3
Wieliczka *Poland* 50°0N 20°5E **83** J7
Wielkopolski △ *Poland* 52°18N 16°45E **83** F3
Wielkopolskie □ *Poland* 52°20N 17°30E **83** F3
Wieluń *Poland* 51°15N 18°34E **83** G5
Wien *Austria* 48°12N 16°22E **79** C9
Wien-Schwechat ✈ (VIE)
  Austria 48°7N 16°35E **79** C9
Wiener Neustadt
  Austria 47°49N 16°16E **79** D9
Wieprz → *Poland* 51°34N 21°49E **83** G8
Wieprza → *Poland* 54°26N 16°35E **82** A3
Wieruszów *Poland* 51°19N 18°9E **83** G5
Wiesbaden *Germany* 50°4N 8°14E **77** E4
Wiesental *Germany* 49°13N 8°31E **77** F4
Wiesloch *Germany* 49°18N 8°41E **77** F4
Wiesmoor *Germany* 53°24N 7°47E **76** B3
Wieżyca *Poland* 54°14N 18°8E **82** D5
Wigan *U.K.* 53°33N 2°38W **66** D5
Wiggins *Colo., U.S.A.* 40°14N 104°4W **168** F11
Wiggins *Miss., U.S.A.* 30°51N 89°8W **177** F10
Wight, I. of *U.K.* 50°41N 1°17W **67** G6
Wigston *U.K.* 52°35N 1°6W **67** E6
Wigton *U.K.* 54°50N 3°10W **66** C4
Wigtown *U.K.* 54°53N 4°27W **65** G4
Wigtown B. *U.K.* 54°46N 4°15W **65** G4
Wik and Wikway People ◎
  Australia 13°55S 142°28E **150** A3
Wil *Switz.* 47°28N 9°3E **77** H5
Wilamowice *Poland* 49°55N 19°9E **83** J6
Wilber *U.S.A.* 40°29N 96°58W **172** E5
Wilberforce *Canada* 45°2N 78°13W **174** A6
Wilberforce, C.
  Australia 11°54S 136°35E **150** A2
Wilburton *U.S.A.* 34°55N 95°19W **176** D7
Wilcannia *Australia* 31°30S 143°26E **152** A3
Wilcox *U.S.A.* 41°35N 78°41W **174** E6
Wildbad *Germany* 48°44N 8°33E **77** G4
Wildeshausen *Germany* 52°54N 8°27E **76** C4
Wildeshauser Geest △
  Germany 52°54N 8°27E **76** C4
Wildomar *U.S.A.* 33°36N 117°16W **171** M9
Wildon *Austria* 46°52N 15°31E **78** E8
Wildrose *U.S.A.* 36°14N 117°11W **171** J9
Wildspitze *Austria* 46°53N 10°53E **78** E3
Wildwood *U.S.A.* 38°59N 90°39W **172** F7
Wilga → *Poland* 51°52N 21°18E **83** G8
Wilge → *S. Africa* 27°3S 28°20E **145** C4
Wilhelm II Coast
  Antarctica 68°0S 90°0E **55** C7
Wilhelmsburg *Austria* 48°6N 15°36E **78** C8
Wilhelmshaven *Germany* 53°31N 8°7E **76** B4
Wilis *Indonesia* 7°51S 111°48E **119** G15
Wilkes-Barre *U.S.A.* 41°15N 75°53W **175** E9
Wilkes Land *Antarctica* 69°0S 120°0E **55** D9
Wilkie *Canada* 52°27N 108°42W **163** C7
Wilkins Ice Shelf
  Antarctica 70°30S 72°0W **55** C17
Wilkinsburg *U.S.A.* 40°26N 79°52W **174** F5
Wilkinson Lakes
  Australia 29°40S 132°39E **149** E5
Willacoochee *U.S.A.* 31°20N 83°3W **178** D6
Willandra △ *Australia* 33°12S 145°0E **153** B8
Willandra Creek →
  Australia 33°22S 145°52E **152** B4
Willapa B. *U.S.A.* 46°40N 124°0W **170** D2
Willapa Hills *U.S.A.* 46°35N 123°25W **170** D3
Willard *U.S.A.* 41°3N 82°44W **174** E2
Willare Bridge Roadhouse
  Australia 17°43S 123°38E **148** C3
Willbriggie *Australia* 34°28S 146°2E **153** C7
Willcox *U.S.A.* 32°15N 109°50W **169** K9
Willemstad *Curaçao* 12°5N 68°55W **183** D6
Willi Willi △
  Australia 30°57S 152°27E **153** A10
William → *Canada* 59°8N 109°19W **163** B7
William 'Bill' Dannelly Res.
  U.S.A. 32°6N 87°24W **177** E11
William Creek
  Australia 28°58S 136°22E **151** D2
Williams *Australia* 33°2S 116°52E **149** F2
Williams *Ariz., U.S.A.* 35°15N 112°11W **169** J7
Williams *Calif., U.S.A.* 39°9N 122°9W **170** F4
Williams Harbour
  Canada 52°33N 55°47W **165** B8
Williams Lake *Canada* 52°10N 122°10W **162** C4
Williamsburg *Ky.,*
  U.S.A. 36°44N 84°10W **173** G11
Williamsburg *Pa.,*
  U.S.A. 40°28N 78°12W **174** F6
Williamsburg *Va.,*
  U.S.A. 37°16N 76°43W **173** G15
Williamson *N.Y.,*
  U.S.A. 43°14N 77°11W **174** C7
Williamson *W. Va.,*
  U.S.A. 37°41N 82°17W **173** G12
Williamsport *U.S.A.* 41°15N 77°1W **174** E7
Williamston *U.S.A.* 35°51N 77°4W **177** D16
Williamstown
  Australia 37°51S 144°52E **151** F3
Williamstown *Ky.,*
  U.S.A. 38°38N 84°34W **173** F11
Williamstown *Mass.,*
  U.S.A. 42°43N 73°12W **175** D11
Williamstown *N.Y.,*
  U.S.A. 43°26N 75°53W **175** C9
Willimantic *U.S.A.* 41°43N 72°13W **175** E12
Willingboro *U.S.A.* 40°3N 74°54W **173** E16
Williston *S. Africa* 31°20S 20°53E **144** D3
Williston *Fla., U.S.A.* 29°23N 82°27W **179** F7
Williston *N. Dak.,*
  U.S.A. 48°9N 103°37W **172** A2
Williston L. *Canada* 56°0N 124°0W **162** B4
Willmar *U.S.A.* 45°7N 95°3W **172** C6
Willmore Wilderness △
  Canada 53°45N 119°30W **162** C5
Willoughby *U.S.A.* 41°39N 81°24W **174** E3
Willow Bunch
  Canada 49°20N 105°35W **163** D7
Willow L. *Canada* 62°10N 119°8W **162** A5
Willow Tree *Australia* 31°40S 150°45E **153** A9

Willow Wall, The
  China 42°10N 122°0E **115** C12
Willowick *U.S.A.* 41°38N 81°28W **174** E3
Willowlake → *Canada* 62°42N 123°8W **162** A4
Willowmore *S. Africa* 33°15S 23°30E **144** E3
Willows *U.S.A.* 39°31N 122°12W **170** F4
Willowvale = Gatyana
  S. Africa 32°16S 28°31E **145** E4
Wills, L. *Australia* 21°25S 128°51E **148** D4
Wills Cr. → *Australia* 22°43S 140°2E **150** C3
Willsboro *U.S.A.* 44°21N 73°24W **175** B11
Willunga *Australia* 35°15S 138°30E **152** C2
Wilma *U.S.A.* 30°9N 84°58W **178** E5
Wilmette *U.S.A.* 42°4N 87°42W **172** D10
Wilmington *Australia* 32°39S 138°7E **152** B2
Wilmington *Del.,*
  U.S.A. 39°45N 75°33W **173** F16
Wilmington *N.C.,*
  U.S.A. 34°14N 77°55W **177** D16
Wilmington *Ohio,*
  U.S.A. 39°27N 83°50W **173** F12
Wilmington *Vt.,*
  U.S.A. 42°52N 72°52W **175** D12
Wilmslow *U.K.* 53°19N 2°13W **66** D5
Wilpattu △ *Sri Lanka* 8°30N 80°10E **127** K4
Wilpena *Australia* 31°31S 138°37E **152** A2
Wilpena Cr. →
  Australia 31°25S 139°29E **152** A3
Wilsall *U.S.A.* 45°59N 110°38W **168** D8
Wilson *N.C., U.S.A.* 35°44N 77°55W **177** D16
Wilson *N.Y., U.S.A.* 43°19N 78°50W **174** C6
Wilson *Pa., U.S.A.* 40°41N 75°15W **175** F9
Wilson → *Australia* 16°48S 128°16E **148** C4
Wilson Bluff *Australia* 31°41S 129°0E **149** F4
Wilson Inlet *Australia* 35°0S 117°22E **149** G2
Wilsons Promontory
  Australia 38°59S 146°23E **153** E7
Wilsons Promontory △
  Australia 38°55S 146°23E **153** E7
Wilster *Germany* 53°55N 9°23E **76** B5
Wilton *U.S.A.* 47°10N 100°47W **172** B3
Wilton → *Australia* 14°45S 134°33E **150** A1
Wiltshire □ *U.K.* 51°18N 1°53W **67** F6
Wiltz *Lux.* 49°57N 5°55E **69** E5
Wiluna *Australia* 26°36S 120°14E **149** E3
Wimborne Minster △ *U.K.* 50°48N 1°59W **67** G6
Wimereux *France* 50°45N 1°37E **71** B8
Wimmera → *Australia* 36°8S 141°56E **152** C4
Winam G. *Kenya* 0°20S 34°15E **142** C3
Winburg *S. Africa* 28°30S 27°2E **144** C4
Winchelsea *Australia* 38°10S 144°1E **152** E6
Winchendon *U.S.A.* 42°41N 72°3W **175** D12
Winchester *N.Z.* 44°11S 171°17E **155** E6
Winchester *U.K.* 51°4N 1°18W **67** F6
Winchester *Conn.,*
  U.S.A. 41°53N 73°9W **175** E11
Winchester *Idaho,*
  U.S.A. 46°14N 116°38W **168** C5
Winchester *Ind.,*
  U.S.A. 40°10N 84°59W **173** E11
Winchester *Ky.,*
  U.S.A. 37°59N 84°11W **173** G11
Winchester *N.H.,*
  U.S.A. 42°46N 72°23W **175** D12
Winchester *Nev.,*
  U.S.A. 36°7N 115°7W **171** J11
Winchester *Tenn.,*
  U.S.A. 35°11N 86°7W **177** D11
Winchester *Va.,*
  U.S.A. 39°11N 78°10W **173** F14
Wind → *U.S.A.* 43°12N 108°12W **168** E9
Wind Cave △ *U.S.A.* 43°32N 103°17W **172** D2
Wind River Range
  U.S.A. 43°0N 109°30W **168** E9
Windamere, L.
  Australia 32°48S 149°51E **153** B8
Windau = Ventspils
  Latvia 57°25N 21°32E **82** A8
Windber *U.S.A.* 40°14N 78°50W **174** F6
Winder *U.S.A.* 34°0N 83°45W **178** B6
Windermere *U.K.* 54°23N 2°55W **66** C5
Windermere *U.S.A.* 28°29N 81°32W **179** G8
Windhoek *Namibia* 22°35S 17°4E **144** B2
Windidda △ *Australia* 26°23S 122°12E **149** E3
Windischgarsten
  Austria 47°42N 14°21E **78** D7
Windjana Gorge △
  Australia 17°51S 125°0E **148** C3
Windom *U.S.A.* 43°52N 95°7W **172** D6
Windorah *Australia* 25°24S 142°36E **150** D3
Window Rock *U.S.A.* 35°41N 109°3W **169** J9
Windrush → *U.K.* 51°43N 1°24W **67** F6
Windsor *Australia* 33°37S 150°50E **153** B9
Windsor *N.S., Canada* 44°59N 64°5W **165** D7
Windsor *Ont., Canada* 42°18N 83°0W **174** D2
Windsor *N.Z.* 44°59S 170°49E **155** E5
Windsor *U.K.* 51°29N 0°36W **67** F7
Windsor *Calif., U.S.A.* 38°33N 122°49W **170** G4
Windsor *Colo., U.S.A.* 40°29N 104°54W **168** F11
Windsor *Conn., U.S.A.* 41°50N 72°39W **175** E12
Windsor *Mo., U.S.A.* 38°32N 93°31W **172** F7
Windsor *N.Y., U.S.A.* 42°5N 75°37W **175** D9
Windsor *Vt., U.S.A.* 43°29N 72°24W **175** C12
Windsor & Maidenhead □
  U.K. 51°29N 0°40W **67** F7
Windsorton *S. Africa* 28°16S 24°44E **144** C3
Windward Is. *W. Indies* 13°0N 61°0W **183** D7
Windward Passage = Vientos,
  Paso de los *Caribbean* 20°0N 74°0W **183** C5
Winefred L. *Canada* 55°30N 110°30W **163** B6
Winfield *U.S.A.* 37°15N 96°59W **172** G5
Wingate Mts.
  Australia 14°25S 130°40E **148** B5
Wingellina = Irrunytju
  Australia 26°3S 128°56E **149** E4
Wingen *Australia* 31°48S 150°22E **153** A10
Wingham *Australia* 31°48S 152°22E **153** A10
Wingham *Canada* 43°55N 81°20W **174** C3
Winisk → *Canada* 55°17N 85°5W **164** A2
Winisk L. *Canada* 52°55N 87°22W **164** B2
Wink *U.S.A.* 31°45N 103°9W **176** F3
Winkler *Canada* 49°10N 97°56W **163** D9
Winklern *Austria* 46°52N 12°52E **78** E5
Winlock *U.S.A.* 46°30N 122°56W **170** D4
Winneba *Ghana* 5°25N 0°36W **139** D4
Winnebago, L. *U.S.A.* 44°0N 88°26W **172** D9
Winnecke Cr. →
  Australia 18°35S 131°34E **148** C5
Winnemucca *U.S.A.* 40°58N 117°44W **168** F5
Winnemucca L. *U.S.A.* 40°7N 119°21W **168** F4
Winnett *U.S.A.* 47°0N 108°21W **168** C9

Winnfield *U.S.A.* 31°56N 92°38W **176** F8
Winnibigoshish, L.
U.S.A. 47°27N 94°13W **172** B6
Winnipeg *Canada* 49°54N 97°9W **163** D9
Winnipeg → *Canada* 50°38N 96°19W **163** C9
Winnipeg, L. *Canada* 52°0N 97°0W **163** C9
Winnipeg Beach
Canada 50°30N 96°58W **163** C9
Winnipegosis *Canada* 51°39N 99°55W **163** C9
Winnipegosis L.
Canada 52°30N 100°0W **163** C9
Winnipesaukee, L.
U.S.A. 43°38N 71°21W **175** C13
Winnisquam L.
U.S.A. 43°33N 71°31W **175** C13
Winnsboro *La., U.S.A.* 32°10N 91°43W **176** E9
Winnsboro *S.C., U.S.A.* 34°23N 81°5W **177** D14
Winnsboro *Tex., U.S.A.* 32°58N 95°17W **176** E11
Winokapau, L. *Canada* 53°15N 62°50W **165** B7
Winona *Minn., U.S.A.* 44°3N 91°39W **172** C8
Winona *Miss., U.S.A.* 33°29N 89°44W **177** E10
Winooski *U.S.A.* 44°29N 73°11W **175** B11
Winooski → *U.S.A.* 44°32N 73°17W **175** B11
Winschoten *Neths.* 53°9N 7°3E **69** A7
Winsen *Germany* 53°22N 10°13E **76** B6
Winsford *U.K.* 53°12N 2°31W **66** D5
Winslow = Bainbridge Island
U.S.A. 47°38N 122°32W **170** C4
Winslow *U.S.A.* 35°2N 110°42W **169** J8
Winsted *U.S.A.* 41°55N 73°4W **175** E11
Winston-Salem *U.S.A.* 36°6N 80°15W **177** C14
Winter Garden *U.S.A.* 28°34N 81°35W **179** G8
Winter Haven *U.S.A.* 28°1N 81°44W **179** G8
Winter Park *U.S.A.* 28°36N 81°20W **179** G8
Winterberg *Germany* 51°11N 8°33E **76** D4
Winterhaven *U.S.A.* 32°44N 114°38W **171** N12
Winters *U.S.A.* 38°32N 121°58W **170** G5
Winterset *U.S.A.* 41°20N 94°1W **172** E6
Wintersville *U.S.A.* 40°23N 80°42W **174** F4
Winterswijk *Neths.* 51°58N 6°43E **69** C6
Winterthur *Switz.* 47°30N 8°44E **77** H4
Winthrop *U.S.A.* 48°28N 120°10W **168** B3
Winton *Australia* 22°24S 143°3E **150** C3
Winton *N.Z.* 46°8S 168°20E **155** G3
Wipper → *Germany* 51°16N 11°12E **76** D7
Wirlyajarrayi ○
Australia 21°45S 132°35E **148** D5
Wirraminna *Australia* 31°12S 136°13E **152** A2
Wirrulla *Australia* 32°24S 134°31E **151** E1
Wisbech *U.K.* 52°41N 0°9E **67** E8
Wisconsin □ *U.S.A.* 44°45N 89°30W **172** C9
Wisconsin → *U.S.A.* 43°0N 91°15W **172** D8
Wisconsin Rapids
U.S.A. 44°23N 89°49W **172** C9
Wisdom *U.S.A.* 45°37N 113°27W **168** D7
Wiseman *U.S.A.* 67°25N 150°6W **166** B9
Wishaw *U.K.* 55°46N 3°54W **65** F5
Wishek *U.S.A.* 46°16N 99°33W **172** B4
Wisła *Poland* 49°38N 18°53E **83** J5
Wisła → *Poland* 54°22N 18°55E **82** D5
Wisłok → *Poland* 50°13N 22°32E **83** H9
Wisłoka → *Poland* 50°27N 21°23E **83** H8
Wismar *Germany* 53°54N 11°29E **76** B7
Wisner *U.S.A.* 41°59N 96°55W **172** E5
Wissant *France* 50°52N 1°40E **71** B8
Wissembourg *France* 49°2N 7°57E **71** C14
Wisznice *Poland* 51°48N 23°13E **83** G10
Witbank = eMalahleni
S. Africa 25°51S 29°14E **145** C4
Witches Gorge = Wu Xia
China 31°2N 110°10E **117** B8
Witdraai *S. Africa* 26°58S 20°48E **144** C3
Witham *U.K.* 51°48N 0°40E **67** F8
Witham → *U.K.* 52°59N 0°2W **66** E7
Withernsea *U.K.* 53°44N 0°1E **66** D8
Withlacoochee → *Fla.,*
U.S.A. 30°24N 83°10W **178** F6
Withlacoochee → *Fla.,*
U.S.A. 29°0N 82°45W **179** G7
Witjira △ *Australia* 26°22S 135°37E **151** D2
Witkowo *Poland* 52°26N 17°45E **83** F4
Witless Bay *Canada* 47°17N 52°50W **165** C9
Witney *U.K.* 51°48N 1°28W **67** F6
Witnica *Poland* 52°40N 14°54E **83** F1
Witnossob → *Namibia* 23°55S 18°45E **144** C3
Witriver *S. Africa* 25°20S 31°0E **145** C5
Wittdün *Germany* 54°38N 8°23E **76** A4
Wittelsheim *France* 47°48N 7°14E **71** E14
Witten *Germany* 51°26N 7°20E **76** D3
Wittenberge *Germany* 53°0N 11°45E **76** B7
Wittenburg *Germany* 53°31N 11°4E **76** B7
Wittenoom *Australia* 22°15S 118°20E **148** D2
Wittingen *Germany* 52°44N 10°44E **76** B6
Wittlich *Germany* 49°59N 6°53E **77** F2
Wittmund *Germany* 53°34N 7°46E **76** B3
Wittow *Germany* 54°38N 13°27E **76** A8
Wittstock *Germany* 53°10N 12°28E **76** B8
Witu *Kenya* 2°23S 40°26E **142** C5
Witvlei *Namibia* 22°23S 18°32E **144** B2
Witzenhausen *Germany* 51°20N 9°51E **76** D5
Wiwon *N. Korea* 40°54N 126°3E **115** D14
Wkra → *Poland* 52°27N 20°44E **83** F7
Władysławowo *Poland* 54°48N 18°25E **82** D5
Wleń *Poland* 51°2N 15°39E **83** G2
Wlingi *Indonesia* 8°5S 112°25E **119** H15
Włocławek *Poland* 52°40N 19°3E **83** F6
Włodawa *Poland* 51°33N 23°31E **83** G10
Włoszczowa *Poland* 50°50N 19°55E **83** H6
Woburn *Canada* 45°29N 71°9W **175** A13
Wodian *China* 32°50N 112°35E **114** H7
Wodonga *Australia* 36°5S 146°50E **153** D7
Wodzisław Śląski *Poland* 50°1N 18°26E **83** H5
Wœrth *France* 48°57N 7°45E **71** D14
Woinbogoin *China* 32°51N 98°39E **116** A2
Woippy *France* 49°10N 6°8E **71** C13
Wokam *Indonesia* 5°45S 134°28E **119** F8
Woking *U.K.* 51°19N 0°34W **67** F7
Wokingham *U.K.* 51°24N 0°49W **67** F7
Wokingham □ *U.K.* 51°25N 0°51W **67** F7
Woko △ *Australia* 31°45S 151°54E **153** A9
Wolbrom *Poland* 50°24N 19°45E **83** H6
Wolczyn *Poland* 51°1N 18°3E **83** G5
Woldegk *Germany* 53°27N 13°34E **76** B8
Wolf → *Canada* 60°17N 132°33W **162** A2
Wolf Creek *U.S.A.* 47°0N 112°4W **168** C7
Wolf L. *Canada* 60°24N 131°40W **162** A2
Wolf Point *U.S.A.* 48°5N 105°39W **168** B11
Wolfe Creek Crater △
Australia 19°10S 127°47E **148** C4
Wolfe I. *Canada* 44°7N 76°20W **175** B8

Wolfeboro *U.S.A.* 43°35N 71°13W **175** C13
Wolfen *Germany* 51°39N 12°15E **76** D8
Wolfenbüttel *Germany* 52°10N 10°33E **76** C6
Wolfratshausen
Germany 47°54N 11°24E **77** H7
Wolfsberg *Austria* 46°50N 14°52E **78** E7
Wolfsburg *Germany* 52°25N 10°48E **76** C6
Wolgast *Germany* 54°3N 13°46E **76** A8
Wolhusen *Switz.* 47°4N 8°4E **77** H4
Wolin *Poland* 53°50N 14°37E **82** E1
Woliński △ *Poland* 53°57N 14°28E **82** E1
Wollaston, Is. *Chile* 55°40S 67°30W **192** E3
Wollaston Forland
Greenland 74°25N 19°40W **57** C9
Wollaston L. *Canada* 58°7N 103°10W **163** B8
Wollaston Lake
Canada 58°3N 103°33W **163** B8
Wollaston Pen. *Canada* 69°30N 115°0W **160** D9
Wollemi △ *Australia* 33°0S 150°30E **153** B9
Wollongong *Australia* 34°25S 150°54E **153** C9
Wolmaransstad
S. Africa 27°12S 25°59E **144** C4
Wolmirstedt *Germany* 52°14N 11°37E **76** C7
Wolomin *Poland* 52°19N 21°15E **83** F8
Wołów *Poland* 51°20N 16°38E **83** G3
Wolseley *Australia* 36°23S 140°54E **152** D4
Wolseley *S. Africa* 33°26S 19°7E **144** D2
Wolsey *U.S.A.* 44°25N 98°28W **172** C4
Wolstenholme, C.
Canada 62°35N 77°30W **158** C12
Wolsztyn *Poland* 52°8N 16°5E **83** F3
Wolvega *Neths.* 52°52N 6°0E **69** B6
Wolverhampton *U.K.* 52°35N 2°7W **67** E5
Wondai *Australia* 26°20S 151°49E **151** D5
Wongalarroo L.
Australia 31°32S 144°0E **152** A6
Wongan Hills
Australia 30°51S 116°37E **149** F2
Wonju *S. Korea* 37°22N 127°58E **115** F14
Wonosari *Indonesia* 7°58S 110°36E **119** G13
Wonosobo *Indonesia* 7°22S 109°54E **119** G13
Wonowon *Canada* 56°44N 121°48W **162** B4
Wŏnsan *N. Korea* 39°11N 127°27E **115** E14
Wonthaggi *Australia* 38°37S 145°37E **153** E6
Wood Buffalo △
Canada 59°0N 113°41W **162** B6
Wood Is. *Australia* 16°24S 123°19E **148** C3
Wood L. *Canada* 55°17N 103°17W **163** B8
Woodah *U.S.A.* 13°27S 136°10E **150** A2
Woodbine *U.S.A.* 30°58N 81°44W **178** E8
Woodbourne *U.S.A.* 41°46N 74°36W **175** E10
Woodbridge *Canada* 43°47N 79°36W **174** C5
Woodbridge *U.K.* 52°6N 1°20E **67** E9
Woodburn *Australia* 29°6S 153°23E **151** A5
Woodburn *U.S.A.* 45°9N 122°51W **168** D2
Woodbury *U.S.A.* 32°59N 84°35W **178** D5
Woodenbong
Australia 28°24S 152°39E **151** D5
Woodend *Australia* 37°20S 144°33E **152** D6
Woodford *Australia* 26°58S 152°47E **151** D5
Woodfords *U.S.A.* 38°47N 119°50W **170** G7
Woodlake *U.S.A.* 36°25N 119°6W **170** J7
Woodland *Calif.,*
U.S.A. 38°41N 121°46W **170** G5
Woodland *Maine,*
U.S.A. 45°9N 67°25W **173** C20
Woodland *Pa., U.S.A.* 41°0N 78°21W **174** F6
Woodland *Wash.,*
U.S.A. 45°54N 122°45W **170** E4
Woodland Caribou △
Canada 51°0N 94°45W **163** C10
Woodlands *Singapore* 1°26N 103°46E **121** d
Woodlands, The *U.S.A.* 30°9N 95°29W **176** F7
Woodonga *Australia* 36°10S 146°50E **151** F4
Woodridge *Canada* 49°20N 96°9W **163** D9
Woodroffe, Mt.
Australia 26°20S 131°45E **149** E5
Woods, L. *Australia* 17°50S 133°30E **150** B1
Woods, L. of the
N. Amer. 49°15N 94°45W **163** D10
Woods Bay *Canada* 45°8N 79°59W **174** A5
Woodside *S. Austral.,*
Australia 34°58S 138°52E **152** C3
Woodside *Vic.,*
Australia 38°31S 146°52E **153** E5
Woodstock *N.S.W.,*
Australia 33°45S 148°53E **153** B8
Woodstock *Queens.,*
Australia 19°35S 146°50E **150** B4
Woodstock *N.B.,*
Canada 46°11N 67°37W **165** C6
Woodstock *Ont.,*
Canada 43°10N 80°45W **174** C4
Woodstock *Ill., U.S.A.* 42°19N 88°27W **172** D9
Woodstock *N.Y., U.S.A.* 42°2N 74°7W **175** D10
Woodstock *Vt.,*
U.S.A. 43°37N 72°31W **175** C12
Woodsville *U.S.A.* 44°9N 72°2W **175** B13
Woodview *Canada* 44°35N 78°8W **174** B6
Woodville *N.Z.* 40°20S 175°53E **154** G4
Woodville *Fla., U.S.A.* 30°19N 84°15W **178** F5
Woodville *Ga., U.S.A.* 33°40N 83°7W **178** B6
Woodville *Miss., U.S.A.* 31°6N 91°18W **176** F9
Woodville *Tex., U.S.A.* 30°47N 94°25W **176** F7
Woodward *U.S.A.* 36°26N 99°24W **176** C5
Woody *U.S.A.* 35°42N 118°50W **171** K8
Woody → *Canada* 52°31N 100°51W **163** C8
Woody I. *S. China Sea* 16°50N 112°20E **118** A4
Woolacombe *U.K.* 51°10N 4°13W **67** F3
Woolamai, C. *Australia* 38°30S 145°23E **153** E6
Woolbrook *Australia* 30°56S 151°25E **153** A9
Wooler *U.K.* 55°33N 2°1W **66** B5
Woolgoolga *Australia* 30°6S 153°11E **151** E5
Woomargama △
Australia 35°50S 147°15E **153** C7
Woomera *Australia* 31°5S 136°50E **152** A2
Woonsocket *R.I.,*
U.S.A. 42°0N 71°31W **175** E13
Woonsocket *S. Dak.,*
U.S.A. 44°3N 98°17W **172** C4
Wooramel →
Australia 25°47S 114°10E **149** E1
Wooramel Roadhouse
Australia 25°45S 114°17E **149** E1
Woorinooran △
Australia 16°25S 146°1E **150** B4
Wooster *U.S.A.* 40°48N 81°56W **174** F3
Worcester *S. Africa* 33°39S 19°27E **144** D2
Worcester *U.K.* 52°11N 2°12W **67** E5

Worcester *Mass.,*
U.S.A. 42°16N 71°48W **175** D13
Worcester *N.Y.,*
U.S.A. 42°36N 74°45W **175** D10
Worcestershire □ *U.K.* 52°13N 2°10W **67** E5
Wörgl *Austria* 47°29N 12°3E **78** D5
Workington *U.K.* 54°39N 3°33W **66** C4
Worksop *U.K.* 53°18N 1°7W **66** D6
Workum *Neths.* 52°59N 5°26E **69** B5
Worland *U.S.A.* 44°1N 107°57W **168** D10
Wormerveer *Neths.* 52°30N 4°46E **69** B5
Wormhout *France* 50°52N 2°28E **71** B9
Worms *Germany* 49°37N 8°21E **77** F4
Worodougou □ *Ivory C.* 8°0N 6°0W **138** D3
Worsley *Australia* 56°31N 119°8W **162** B5
Wörth *Germany* 49°1N 12°24E **77** F8
Wortham *U.S.A.* 31°47N 96°28W **176** F6
Wörther See *Austria* 46°37N 14°10E **78** E7
Worthing *Barbados* 13°5N 59°35W **183** g
Worthing *U.K.* 50°49N 0°21W **67** G7
Worthington *Minn.,*
U.S.A. 43°37N 95°36W **172** D6
Worthington *Pa.,*
U.S.A. 40°50N 79°38W **174** F5
Wosi *Indonesia* 0°15S 128°0E **119** E7
Wote *Kenya* 1°47S 37°38E **142** C4
Wotjalum ○ *Australia* 16°30S 123°45E **148** C3
Wotjobaluk ○ *Australia* 37°0S 142°0E **151** C3
Wou-han = Wuhan
China 30°31N 114°18E **117** B10
Wousi = Wuxi *China* 31°33N 120°18E **117** B13
Wowoni *Indonesia* 4°5S 123°5E **119** E6
Woy Woy *Australia* 33°30S 151°19E **153** B9
Wrangel I. = Vrangelya, Ostrov
Russia 71°0N 180°0E **107** B18
Wrangell *U.S.A.* 56°28N 132°23W **162** B2
Wrangell Mts. *U.S.A.* 61°30N 142°0W **160** E3
Wrath, C. *U.K.* 58°38N 5°1W **65** C3
Wray *U.S.A.* 40°5N 102°13W **168** F12
Wrekin, The *U.K.* 52°41N 2°32W **67** E5
Wrens *U.S.A.* 33°12N 82°23W **178** B7
Wrexham *U.K.* 53°3N 3°0W **66** D4
Wrexham □ *U.K.* 53°1N 2°58W **66** D5
Wriezen *Germany* 52°42N 14°7E **76** C10
Wright *Fla., U.S.A.* 30°27N 86°38W **179** F3
Wrightmyo *India* 11°47N 92°43E **127** J11
Wrightson, Mt.
U.S.A. 31°42N 110°51W **169** L8
Wrightsville *U.S.A.* 32°44N 82°43W **178** D7
Wrightwood *U.S.A.* 34°22N 117°38W **171** L9
Wrigley *Canada* 63°16N 123°37W **160** E7
Wrocław *Poland* 51°5N 17°5E **83** G4
Wronki *Poland* 52°41N 16°21E **83** F3
Września *Poland* 52°21N 17°36E **83** F4
Wschowa *Poland* 51°48N 16°20E **83** G3
Wu Jiang → *China* 29°40N 107°20E **116** C6
Wu Kau Tang *China* 22°30N 114°14E **111** a
Wu Xia *China* 31°2N 110°10E **117** B8
Wu'an *China* 36°40N 114°15E **114** F8
Wubalawun ○
Australia 15°28S 133°1E **148** C5
Wubin *Australia* 30°6S 116°37E **149** F2
Wubu *China* 37°28N 110°42E **114** F6
Wuchang *China* 44°55N 127°5E **115** B14
Wuchuan *Guangdong,*
China 37°12N 116°20E **114** F9
Wuchuan *Guizhou,*
China 28°25N 108°3E **116** C7
Wuchuan *Nei Monggol Zizhiqu,*
China 41°5N 111°28E **114** D6
Wuda *China* 39°29N 106°42E **114** E4
Wudang Shan *China* 32°23N 111°2E **117** A8
Wudi *China* 37°40N 117°35E **115** F9
Wuding *China* 25°24N 102°21E **116** E4
Wuding He → *China* 37°2N 110°23E **114** F6
Wudinna *Australia* 33°0S 135°22E **151** E2
Wudongde Dam
China 26°20N 102°15E **116** D4
Wudu *China* 33°22N 104°54E **114** H3
Wufeng *China* 30°12N 110°42E **117** B8
Wugang *China* 26°44N 110°35E **117** D8
Wugong Shan *China* 27°30N 114°0E **117** D10
Wuguishan *China* 22°25N 113°25E **111** a
Wugullar = Beswick
Australia 14°34S 132°53E **148** B5
Wuhai *China* 39°39N 106°48E **114** E4
Wuhan *China* 30°31N 114°18E **117** B10
Wuhe *China* 33°10N 117°50E **115** H9
Wuhsi = Wuxi *China* 31°33N 120°18E **117** B13
Wuhu *China* 31°22N 118°21E **117** B12
Wujiang *China* 31°10N 120°38E **117** B13
Wukari *Nigeria* 7°51N 9°42E **139** D6
Wulajie *China* 44°6N 126°33E **115** B14
Wulanbulang *China* 41°5N 110°55E **114** D6
Wular L. *India* 34°20N 74°30E **125** B6
Wulehe *Ghana* 8°30N 0°0 **139** D5
Wulff Land *Greenland* 82°0N 49°0W **57** A6
Wulian *China* 35°40N 119°12E **115** G10
Wulian Feng *China* 27°48N 103°36E **116** D4
Wuliang Shan *China* 24°30N 100°40E **116** E3
Wuliaru *Indonesia* 7°27S 131°0E **119** F8
Wuling Shan *China* 30°0N 110°0E **116** C7
Wulingyuan △ *China* 29°20N 110°30E **117** C8
Wulong *China* 29°22N 107°43E **116** C6
Wulumuchi = Ürümqi
China 43°45N 87°45E **109** D11
Wum *Cameroon* 6°24N 10°2E **139** D7
Wumeng Shan *China* 26°48N 104°0E **116** D5
Wuming *China* 23°12N 108°0E **116** E6
Wundanyi *Kenya* 3°24S 38°22E **142** C4
Wunnamin L.
Canada 52°55N 89°10W **164** B2
Wunnummin L.
Canada 52°55N 89°10W **164** B2
Wunsiedel *Germany* 50°2N 12°0E **77** E8
Wunstorf *Germany* 52°25N 9°26E **76** C5
Wuntho *Burma* 23°55N 95°45E **123** H19
Wupatki △ *U.S.A.* 35°35N 111°20W **169** J8
Wuping *China* 25°5N 116°5E **117** E11
Wuppertal *Germany* 51°16N 7°12E **76** D3
Wuppertal *S. Africa* 32°13S 19°12E **144** D2
Wuqia *China* 39°40N 75°3E **109** E5
Wuqing *China* 39°23N 117°4E **115** E9
Wurralibi ○ *Australia* 15°43S 137°1E **150** B2
Würzburg *Germany* 49°46N 9°55E **77** F5
Wushan *China* 34°43N 104°53E **114** G3

Wushi *China* 41°9N 79°13E **109** D9
Wushishi *Nigeria* 9°46N 6°7E **139** D6
Wutach → *Germany* 47°37N 8°15E **77** H4
Wutai *China* 38°40N 113°12E **114** E7
Wutai Shan *China* 39°3N 113°32E **114** E7
Wuting = Huimin
China 37°27N 117°28E **115** F9
Wutong *China* 25°24N 110°4E **117** E8
Wutonghaolai *China* 42°50N 120°5E **115** C11
Wutongqiao *China* 29°22N 103°50E **116** C4
Wuwei *Anhui, China* 31°18N 117°54E **117** B11
Wuwei *Gansu, China* 37°57N 102°34E **114** F5
Wuxi *Jiangsu, China* 31°33N 120°18E **117** B13
Wuxi *Sichuan, China* 31°23N 109°35E **116** B7
Wuxiang *China* 36°49N 112°50E **114** F7
Wuxuan *China* 23°30N 109°40E **116** E7
Wuxue *China* 29°52N 115°30E **117** C10
Wuyang *China* 33°25N 113°35E **114** H7
Wuyi *Hebei, China* 37°46N 115°56E **114** F8
Wuyi *Zhejiang, China* 28°52N 119°50E **117** C12
Wuyi Shan *China* 27°0N 117°0E **117** D11
Wuyishan *China* 27°45N 118°0E **117** D12
Wuyishan △ *China* 27°55N 117°54E **117** D11
Wuyo *Nigeria* 10°23N 11°50E **139** C7
Wuyuan *Jiangxi,*
China 29°15N 117°50E **117** C11
Wuyuan *Nei Monggol Zizhiqu,*
China 41°2N 108°20E **114** D5
Wuzhai *China* 38°54N 111°48E **114** E6
Wuzhi Shan *China* 18°45N 109°45E **117** a
Wuzhishan = Tongshi
China 18°30N 109°20E **117** a
Wuzhong *China* 38°2N 106°12E **114** E4
Wuzhou *China* 23°30N 111°18E **117** F8
Wyaaba Cr. →
Australia 16°27S 141°35E **150** B3
Wyalkatchem *Australia* 31°8S 117°22E **149** F2
Wyalusing *U.S.A.* 41°40N 76°16W **175** E8
Wyandotte *U.S.A.* 42°12N 83°9W **173** D12
Wyandra *Australia* 27°12S 145°56E **151** D4
Wyangala, L. *Australia* 33°54S 149°0E **153** B8
Wyara, L. *Australia* 28°42S 144°14E **151** D3
Wycheproof *Australia* 36°5S 143°17E **152** D5
Wycliffe Well *Australia* 20°48S 134°14E **150** C1
Wye → *U.K.* 51°38N 2°40W **67** F5
Wyemandoo *Australia* 28°28S 118°29E **149** E2
Wyk *Germany* 54°41N 8°33E **76** A4
Wymondham *U.K.* 52°35N 1°7E **67** E9
Wymore *U.S.A.* 40°7N 96°40W **172** E5
Wyndham *Australia* 15°33S 128°3E **148** C4
Wyndham *N.Z.* 46°20S 168°51E **155** G3
Wynne *U.S.A.* 35°14N 90°47W **177** D9
Wynyard *Australia* 41°5S 145°44E **151** G4
Wynyard *Canada* 51°45N 104°10W **163** C8
Wyola L. *Australia* 29°8S 130°17E **149** E5
Wyoming *Canada* 42°57N 82°7W **174** D2
Wyoming □ *U.S.A.* 43°0N 107°30W **168** E10
Wyomissing *U.S.A.* 40°20N 75°59W **175** E9
Wyong *Australia* 33°14S 151°24E **153** B9
Wyperfeld △ *Australia* 35°35S 141°42E **152** C4
Wyrzysk *Poland* 53°10N 17°17E **83** E4
Wyśmierzyce *Poland* 51°37N 20°50E **83** G7
Wysoka *Poland* 53°13N 17°2E **83** E4
Wysokie *Poland* 50°55N 22°40E **83** H9
Wysokie Mazowieckie
Poland 37°12N 116°20E **114** F9
Wyszków *Poland* 52°36N 21°25E **83** F8
Wyszogród *Poland* 52°23N 20°9E **83** F7
Wytheville *U.S.A.* 36°57N 81°5W **173** G13
Wyżyna Małopolska
Poland 50°45N 20°0E **83** H7

X

Xaafuun *Somalia* 10°25N 51°16E **131** E5
Xaafuun, Ras *Somalia* 10°27N 51°24E **131** E5
Xàbia = Jávea *Spain* 38°48N 0°10E **91** G5
Xaçmaz *Azerbaijan* 41°31N 48°42E **87** K9
Xai-Xai *Mozam.* 25°6S 33°31E **145** C5
Xaidulla *China* 36°28N 77°59E **109** E9
Xaignabouri = Sayaboury
Laos 19°15N 101°45E **120** C3
Xainza *China* 30°58N 88°35E **110** E6
Xalapa *Mexico* 19°32N 96°55W **181** D5
Xallas → *Spain* 42°54N 9°8W **88** A1
Xangongo *Angola* 16°45S 15°5E **144** A2
Xankändi *Azerbaijan* 39°52N 46°49E **105** C12
Xanlar = Goygöl
Azerbaijan 40°37N 46°12E **87** K8
Xanten *Germany* 51°39N 6°26E **76** D2
Xanthi *Greece* 41°10N 24°58E **97** E8
Xanthos *Turkey* 36°19N 29°18E **99** E11
Xanxerê *Brazil* 26°53S 52°23W **191** B5
Xapuri *Brazil* 10°35S 68°35W **188** C4
Xar Moron He →
China 43°25N 120°35E **115** C11
Xarrë *Albania* 39°44N 20°3E **96** G4
Xátiva *Spain* 38°59N 0°32W **91** G4
Xau, L. *Botswana* 21°15S 24°44E **144** B3
Xavantina *Brazil* 21°15S 52°48W **191** A5
Xayar *China* 41°13N 82°48E **109** D10
Xebert *China* 44°2N 122°0E **115** D2
Xenia *U.S.A.* 39°41N 83°56W **173** F12
Xeraco *Spain* 39°2N 0°13W **91** F4
Xeropotamos →
Cyprus 34°42N 32°33E **101** E11
Xertigny *France* 48°3N 6°24E **71** D13
Xhora *S. Africa* 31°55S 28°38E **145** D4
Xhumo *Botswana* 21°7S 24°35E **144** B3
Xi Jiang → *China* 22°5N 113°20E **117** F9
Xi Xian *Henan, China* 32°20N 114°43E **117** A10
Xi Xian *Shanxi, China* 36°41N 110°58E **114** F6
Xia Xian *China* 35°8N 111°12E **114** G6
Xiachengzi *China* 44°40N 130°18E **115** B16
Xiaguan *China* 25°32N 100°16E **116** E3
Xiajiang *China* 27°30N 115°10E **117** D10
Xiajin *China* 36°56N 116°0E **114** F9
Xiamen *China* 24°25N 118°4E **117** E12
Xi'an *China* 34°15N 109°0E **114** G5
Xian Xian *China* 38°12N 116°6E **114** E9
Xianfeng *China* 29°40N 109°8E **116** C7
Xiang Jiang → *China* 28°55N 112°50E **117** C9
Xiang Khouang *Laos* 19°17N 103°25E **120** C3
Xiangcheng *Henan,*
China 33°50N 113°27E **114** H7
Xiangcheng *Sichuan,*
China 28°53N 99°47E **116** C2
Xiangdu *China* 23°13N 106°58E **116** F6

Xiangfan *China* 32°2N 112°8E **117** A9
Xianggang = Hong Kong □
China 22°11N 114°14E **111** a
Xianghuang Qi *China* 42°2N 113°50E **114** C7
Xiangjiaba Dam *China* 28°37N 104°17E **116** C5
Xiangning *China* 35°58N 110°50E **114** G6
Xiangquan *China* 36°30N 113°1E **114** F7
Xiangquan He = Sutlej →
Pakistan 29°23N 71°3E **124** E4
Xiangshan *China* 29°29N 121°51E **117** C13
Xiangshui *China* 34°12N 119°33E **115** G10
Xiangtan *China* 27°51N 112°54E **117** D9
Xiangxiang *China* 27°43N 112°28E **117** D9
Xiangyin *China* 28°38N 112°54E **117** C9
Xiangyun *China* 25°34N 100°35E **116** E3
Xiangzhou *China* 23°58N 109°40E **117** E7
Xianju *China* 28°51N 120°44E **117** C13
Xianning *China* 29°51N 114°16E **117** C10
Xianshui He → *China* 30°10N 100°59E **116** B3
Xiantao *China* 30°25N 113°25E **117** B9
Xianyang *China* 34°20N 108°40E **114** G5
Xianyou *China* 25°22N 118°38E **117** E12
Xiao Hinggan Ling
China 49°0N 127°0E **111** B7
Xiao Xian *China* 34°15N 116°55E **114** G9
Xiaofeng *China* 30°35N 119°32E **117** B12
Xiaogan *China* 30°52N 113°55E **117** B9
Xiaojin *China* 30°59N 102°21E **116** B4
Xiaolan *China* 22°38N 113°13E **117** F9
Xiaoshan *China* 30°12N 120°18E **117** B13
Xiaowan Dam *China* 24°42N 100°5E **116** E3
Xiaowutai Shan *China* 39°51N 114°59E **114** E8
Xiaoyi *China* 37°8N 111°48E **114** F6
Xiapu *China* 26°54N 119°59E **117** D12
Xiashan = Zhanjiang
China 21°15N 110°20E **117** G8
Xiawa *China* 42°35N 120°38E **115** C11
Xiayi *China* 34°15N 116°10E **114** G9
Xichang *China* 27°51N 102°19E **116** D4
Xichong *China* 30°57N 105°54E **116** B5
Xichou *China* 23°25N 104°42E **116** E5
Xichuan *China* 33°0N 111°30E **114** H6
Xide *China* 28°8N 102°19E **116** C4
Xiemahe *China* 31°38N 111°12E **117** A8
Xifei He → *China* 32°45N 116°40E **117** A11
Xifeng *Gansu, China* 35°40N 107°40E **114** G4
Xifeng *Liaoning, China* 42°42N 124°45E **115** C12
Xifengzhen = Xifeng
China 35°40N 107°40E **114** G4
Xigazê *China* 29°5N 88°45E **110** F6
Xihe *China* 34°2N 105°20E **114** G3
Xihua *China* 33°45N 114°30E **114** H8
Xilaganni *Greece* 40°58N 25°28E **97** F9
Xili Shuiku *China* 22°36N 113°57E **111** a
Xiliao He → *China* 43°32N 123°35E **115** C12
Xilin *China* 24°30N 105°6E **116** E5
Xiling Gorge = Xiling Xia
China 30°54N 110°48E **117** B8
Xiling Xia *China* 30°54N 110°48E **117** B8
Xilinhot *China* 43°52N 116°2E **114** C9
Xilokastro *Greece* 38°5N 22°38E **98** C4
Xiluodu Dam *China* 28°12N 103°34E **116** C4
Ximana *Mozam.* 19°24S 33°58E **143** F3
Xime *Guinea-Biss.* 11°59N 14°57W **138** C2
Ximeng *China* 22°50N 99°27E **116** F2
Ximiao *China* 40°59N 100°12E **114** C3
Xin Jiang → *China* 28°45N 116°35E **117** C11
Xin Xian = Xinzhou
China 38°22N 112°46E **114** E7
Xin'anjiang Shuiku
China 29°33N 118°56E **117** C12
Xinavane *Mozam.* 25°2S 32°47E **145** C5
Xinbin *China* 41°40N 125°2E **115** D13
Xincai *China* 32°43N 114°58E **117** A10
Xinchang *China* 29°28N 120°52E **117** C13
Xincheng *Guangxi Zhuangzu,*
China 24°5N 108°39E **116** E7
Xincheng *Jiangxi,*
China 26°48N 114°6E **117** D10
Xinfeng *Guangdong,*
China 24°5N 114°16E **117** E10
Xinfeng *Jiangxi, China* 27°7N 116°11E **117** D11
Xinfeng *Jiangxi, China* 25°27N 114°58E **117** E10
Xinfengjiang Shuiku
China 23°52N 114°30E **117** E10
Xing Xian *China* 38°27N 111°7E **114** E6
Xing'an *Guangxi Zhuangzu,*
China 25°38N 110°40E **117** E8
Xingan *Jiangxi, China* 27°46N 115°20E **117** D10
Xingcheng *China* 40°40N 120°45E **115** D11
Xingguo *China* 26°21N 115°21E **117** D10
Xinghe *China* 40°55N 113°55E **114** D7
Xinghua *China* 32°58N 119°48E **117** A12
Xinghua Wan *China* 25°15N 119°20E **117** E12
Xinglong *China* 40°25N 117°30E **115** D9
Xingning *China* 24°3N 115°42E **117** E10
Xingping *China* 34°25N 108°28E **114** G5
Xingren *China* 25°24N 105°11E **116** E5
Xingshan *China* 31°15N 110°45E **117** B8
Xingtai *China* 37°3N 114°32E **114** F8
Xingu → *Brazil* 1°30S 51°53W **187** D8
Xingwen *China* 28°22N 104°50E **116** C5
Xingxingxia *China* 41°47N 95°0E **110** C7
Xingyang *China* 34°45N 112°52E **114** G7
Xingyi *China* 25°3N 104°59E **116** E5
Xinhe *Hebei, China* 37°30N 115°15E **114** F8
Xinhua *China* 27°41N 111°12E **117** C8
Xinhuang *China* 27°21N 109°12E **116** D7
Xinhui *China* 22°25N 113°0E **117** F9
Xining *China* 36°34N 101°40E **114** F3
Xinji *China* 37°34N 115°12E **114** F8
Xinjian *China* 28°37N 115°45E **117** C10
Xinjiang *China* 35°34N 111°11E **114** G6
Xinjiang Uygur Zizhiqu □
China 42°0N 86°0E **109** D11
Xinjin = Pulandian
China 39°25N 121°58E **115** E11
Xinjin *China* 36°56N 116°0E **114** F9
Xinkai He → *China* 43°32N 123°35E **115** C12
Xinle *China* 38°25N 114°40E **114** E8
Xinlitun *China* 42°0N 122°8E **115** D12
Xinlong *China* 30°30N 100°12E **116** B3
Xinmi *China* 34°25N 113°22E **114** G7
Xinmin *China* 41°59N 122°50E **115** D12
Xinning *China* 26°28N 110°50E **117** D8
Xinshao *China* 27°21N 111°26E **117** D8

Xintai *China* 35°55N 117°45E **115** G9
Xintian *China* 25°55N 112°13E **117** D9
Xinwan *China* 22°47N 113°40E **111** a
Xinxiang *China* 35°18N 113°50E **114** G7
Xinxing *China* 22°35N 112°15E **117** F9
Xinyang *China* 32°6N 114°3E **117** A10
Xinye *China* 32°30N 112°21E **117** A9
Xinyi *Guangdong, China* 22°25N 111°0E **117** F8
Xinyi *Nei Monggol Zizhiqu,*
China 34°23N 118°21E **115** G10
Xinyu *China* 27°49N 114°58E **117** D10
Xinzhan *China* 43°50N 127°18E **115** C14
Xinzheng *China* 34°20N 113°45E **114** G7
Xinzhou *Hainan, China* 19°42N 109°42E **117** c
Xinzhou *Hubei, China* 30°50N 114°48E **117** B10
Xinzhou *Shanxi, China* 38°22N 112°46E **114** E7
Xinzo de Limia *Spain* 42°3N 7°47W **88** C3
Xiongyuecheng *China* 40°12N 122°5E **115** D11
Xiping *Henan, China* 33°22N 114°5E **114** H8
Xiping *Henan, China* 33°25N 111°8E **114** H6
Xiqing *Zhejiang, China* 28°16N 119°27E **117** C12
Xique-Xique *Brazil* 10°50S 42°40W **189** D2
Xirué → *Brazil* 6°35S 67°50W **188** B4
Xisha Qundao = Paracel Is.
S. China Sea 15°50N 112°0E **118** A4
Xishuangbanna *China* 22°5N 101°1E **116** F3
Xishui *Guizhou, China* 28°19N 106°9E **116** C6
Xishui *Hubei, China* 30°30N 115°15E **117** B10
Xitole *Guinea-Biss.* 11°43N 14°50W **138** C2
Xiu Shui → *China* 29°13N 116°0E **117** C10
Xiuning *China* 29°45N 118°10E **117** C12
Xiuren *China* 24°27N 110°12E **117** E8
Xiushan *China* 28°25N 108°57E **116** C7
Xiushui *China* 29°2N 114°33E **117** C10
Xiuwen *China* 26°49N 106°32E **116** D6
Xiuyan *China* 40°18N 123°11E **115** D12
Xiva *Uzbekistan* 41°30N 60°18E **106** E7
Xixabangma Feng
China 28°20N 85°40E **125** C11
Xixia *China* 33°25N 111°29E **114** H6
Xixiang *Guangdong,*
China 22°34N 113°52E **111** a
Xixiang *Shaanxi, China* 33°0N 107°44E **114** H4
Xixón = Gijón *Spain* 43°32N 5°42W **88** B5
Xiyang *China* 37°38N 113°38E **114** F7
Xizang Zizhiqu □ *China* 32°0N 88°0E **110** E6
Xlendi *Malta* 36°1N 14°12E **101** C1
Xochob *Mexico* 19°21N 89°48W **181** D7
Xo'jayli *Uzbekistan* 42°29N 59°33E **108** D5
Xorazm □ *Uzbekistan* 43°0N 60°0E **108** D6
Xu Jiang → *China* 28°2N 116°15E **117** D11
Xuan Loc *Vietnam* 10°56N 107°14E **121** G6
Xuan'en *China* 30°0N 109°30E **116** C7
Xuanhan *China* 31°18N 107°38E **116** B6
Xuanhua *China* 40°40N 115°2E **114** D8
Xuanwei *China* 26°15N 103°59E **116** D5
Xuanzhou *China* 30°56N 118°43E **117** B12
Xuchang *China* 34°2N 113°48E **114** G7
Xudat *Azerbaijan* 41°38N 48°41E **87** K9
Xuefeng Shan *China* 27°5N 110°35E **117** D8
Xuejiaping *China* 31°39N 110°16E **117** B8
Xun Jiang → *China* 23°35N 111°32E **117** F8
Xun Xian *China* 35°42N 114°33E **114** G8
Xundian *China* 25°30N 103°8E **116** E4
Xunwu *China* 24°54N 115°37E **117** E10
Xunyang *China* 32°48N 109°22E **114** H5
Xunyi *China* 35°8N 108°20E **114** G5
Xupu *China* 27°53N 110°32E **117** D8
Xúquer → *Spain* 39°5N 0°10W **91** F4
Xushui *China* 39°2N 115°40E **114** E8
Xuwen *China* 20°20N 110°10E **117** G8
Xuyi *China* 32°55N 118°32E **117** A12
Xuyong *China* 28°10N 105°22E **116** C5
Xuzhou *China* 34°18N 117°10E **115** G9
Xylophagou *Cyprus* 34°54N 33°51E **101** E12

Y

Y Drenewydd = Newtown
U.K. 52°31N 3°19W **67** E4
Y Fenni = Abergavenny
U.K. 51°49N 3°1W **67** F4
Y Gelli Gandryll = Hay-on-Wye
U.K. 52°5N 3°8W **67** E4
Y Trallwng = Welshpool
U.K. 52°39N 3°8W **67** E4
Ya Xian = Sanya *China* 18°14N 109°29E **117** a
Yaamba *Australia* 23°8S 150°22E **150** C5
Ya'an *China* 29°58N 103°5E **116** C4
Yaapeet *Australia* 35°45S 142°3E **152** C5
Yabassi *Cameroon* 4°30N 9°57E **139** E6
Yabayo *Ivory C.* 5°56N 6°36W **138** D3
Yablanitsa *Bulgaria* 43°2N 24°5E **97** C8
Yablonovyy Khrebet
Russia 53°0N 114°0E **107** D12
Yablonovyy Ra. = Yablonovyy
Khrebet *Russia* 53°0N 114°0E **107** D12
Yabluniv *Ukraine* 48°24N 24°57E **81** D9
Yabluntsya *Ukraine* 48°19N 24°29E **81** D9
Yabrai Shan *China* 39°40N 103°0E **114** E2
Yabrūd *Syria* 33°58N 36°39E **104** B2
Yabucoa *Puerto Rico* 18°3N 65°53W **183** d
Yacambú △ *Venezuela* 9°42N 69°27W **183** E6
Yacheng *China* 18°22N 109°6E **117** a
Yackandandah
Australia 36°18S 146°52E **153** D7
Yacuiba *Bolivia* 22°0S 63°43W **190** A3
Yacuma → *Bolivia* 13°38S 65°23W **188** D4
Yacurí △ *Ecuador* 4°42S 79°20W **188** A2
Yadgir *India* 16°45N 77°5E **124** L3
Yadkin → *U.S.A.* 35°23N 80°4W **177** D14
Yadrin *Russia* 55°57N 46°12E **86** C8
Yadua *Fiji* 16°49S 178°18E **154** a
Yaeyama-Rettō *Japan* 24°30N 123°40E **113** M1
Yagasa Cluster *Fiji* 18°57S 178°28W **154** a
Yagodnoye *Russia* 62°33N 149°40E **107** C15
Yahila
Dem. Rep. of the Congo 0°13N 24°28E **142** B1
Yahk *Canada* 49°6N 116°10W **162** D5
Yahotyn *Ukraine* 50°17N 31°46E **85** G6
Yahuma
Dem. Rep. of the Congo 1°0N 23°10E **142** B1
Yahyalı *Turkey* 38°5N 35°0E **102** D6
Yaita *Japan* 36°48N 139°56E **113** F9
Yaiza *Canary Is.* 28°57N 13°46W **100** F6
Yajiang *China* 30°2N 100°57E **116** B3
Yajua *Nigeria* 11°27N 12°49E **139** C7
Yakeshi *China* 49°17N 120°44E **111** B13

Yakima U.S.A. 46°36N 120°31W 168 C3
Yakima → U.S.A. 46°15N 119°14W 168 C4
Yakishiri-Jima Japan 44°26N 141°25E 112 B10
Yako Burkina Faso 12°59N 2°15W 138 C4
Yakobi I. U.S.A. 58°0N 136°30W 162 B1
Yakoruda Bulgaria 42°1N 23°39E 96 D7
Yakovlevka Russia 44°26N 133°28E 112 B6
Yaku-Shima Japan 30°20N 130°30E 113 J5
Yakumo Japan 42°15N 140°16E 112 C10
Yakutat U.S.A. 59°33N 139°44W 160 F4
Yakutat B. U.S.A. 59°45N 140°45W 166 D11
Yakutia = Sakha □
 Russia 66°0N 130°0E 107 C14
Yakutsk Russia 62°5N 129°50E 107 C13
Yala Thailand 6°33N 101°18E 121 J3
Yala △ Sri Lanka 6°20N 81°42E 127 L5
Yalata Australia 31°59S 132°26E 149 F5
Yalata ◇ Australia 31°35S 132°7E 149 F5
Yalboroo Australia 20°50S 148°40E 150 b
Yale U.S.A. 43°8N 82°48W 174 C2
Yalgorup △ Australia 32°39S 115°38E 149 F2
Yalinga C.A.R. 6°33N 23°10E 140 C4
Yalong China 18°12N 109°42E 117 a
Yalong Jiang →
 China 26°40N 101°55E 116 D3
Yalova Turkey 40°41N 29°15E 97 F13
Yalpirakinu ◇
 Australia 22°24S 132°15E 148 D5
Yalpuh, Ozero Ukraine 45°30N 28°41E 81 E13
Yalta Russia 44°30N 34°10E 85 K8
Yalu Jiang → China 39°55N 124°19E 115 E13
Yalvaç Turkey 38°17N 31°10E 104 C4
Yam Australia 9°54S 142°46E 150 a
Yam Ha Melah = Dead Sea
 Asia 31°30N 35°30E 130 D4
Yam Kinneret Israel 32°45N 35°35E 130 C4
Yamada = Kama
 Japan 33°33N 130°49E 113 H5
Yamagata Japan 38°15N 140°15E 112 E10
Yamagata □ Japan 38°30N 140°0E 112 E10
Yamaguchi Japan 34°10N 131°32E 113 G5
Yamaguchi □ Japan 34°20N 131°40E 113 G5
Yamal, Poluostrov Russia 71°0N 70°0E 106 B8
Yamal Pen. = Yamal, Poluostrov
 Russia 71°0N 70°0E 106 B8
Yamanashi □ Japan 35°40N 138°40E 113 G9
Yamantau, Gora Russia 54°15N 58°6E 108 B5
Yamato Ridge
 Sea of Japan 39°20N 135°0E 112 E7
Yamba Australia 29°26S 153°23E 151 D5
Yambarran Ra.
 Australia 15°10S 130°25E 148 C5
Yambéring Guinea 11°50N 12°18W 138 C2
Yambio South Sudan 4°35N 28°16E 135 H11
Yambol Bulgaria 42°30N 26°30E 97 D10
Yambol □ Bulgaria 42°30N 26°30E 97 D10
Yamburg Russia 68°21N 77°8E 106 C8
Yamdena Indonesia 7°45S 131°20E 119 F8
Yame Japan 33°13N 130°35E 113 H5
Yamethin Burma 20°29N 96°18E 123 J20
Yamma Yamma, L.
 Australia 26°16S 141°20E 151 D3
Yamoussoukro Ivory C. 6°49N 5°17W 138 D3
Yampa → U.S.A. 40°32N 108°59W 168 F9
Yampi Sd. Australia 16°8S 123°38E 148 C3
Yampil Moldova 48°15N 28°15E 75 D15
Yampol = Yampil
 Moldova 48°15N 28°15E 75 D15
Yamrat Nigeria 10°11N 9°55E 139 C6
Yamrukchal = Botev
 Bulgaria 42°44N 24°52E 97 D8
Yamu, Laem Thailand 7°59N 98°26E 121 a
Yamuna → India 25°30N 81°53E 125 G12
Yamunanagar India 30°7N 77°17E 124 D7
Yamzho Yumco China 28°48N 90°35E 110 F7
Yan Nigeria 10°5N 12°11E 139 C7
Yan Oya → Sri Lanka 9°0N 81°10E 127 K5
Yana → Russia 71°30N 136°0E 107 B14
Yanagawa Japan 33°10N 130°24E 113 H5
Yanai Japan 33°58N 132°7E 113 H6
Yan'an China 36°35N 109°26E 114 F5
Yanbian China 26°53N 101°31E 116 D3
Yanbu 'al Baḥr Si. Arabia 24°5N 38°5E 128 E3
Yanchang China 36°43N 110°1E 114 F6
Yancheng, Henan, China 33°35N 114°0E 116 H8
Yancheng, Jiangsu,
 China 33°23N 120°8E 115 H11
Yanchep Australia 31°33S 115°37E 149 F2
Yanchi China 37°48N 107°20E 114 F4
Yanchuan China 36°51N 110°10E 114 F6
Yanco Australia 34°38N 146°27E 153 C7
Yanco Cr. → Australia 35°14S 145°35E 153 C6
Yandang Shan China 28°0N 120°25E 117 D13
Yandeyarra ◇
 Australia 21°17S 118°24E 148 D2
Yandicoogina
 Australia 22°49S 119°12E 148 D2
Yandoon Burma 17°0N 95°40E 123 L19
Yanfeng China 25°52N 101°8E 116 E3
Yanfolila Mali 11°11N 8°9W 138 C3
Yang Xian China 33°15N 107°30E 116 A6
Yang-yang S. Korea 38°4N 128°38E 115 E15
Yang-Yang Senegal 15°30N 15°20W 138 B1
Yangambi
 Dem. Rep. of the Congo 0°47N 24°24E 142 B1
Yangbi China 25°40N 100°1E 116 E3
Yangcheng China 35°28N 112°22E 114 G7
Yangch'ü = Taiyuan
 China 37°52N 112°33E 114 F7
Yangchun China 22°11N 111°48E 117 F8
Yanggao China 40°21N 113°55E 114 D7
Yanggu China 36°8N 115°43E 114 F8
Yangiyul Uzbekistan 41°0N 69°3E 109 D7
Yangjiang China 21°50N 111°59E 117 G8
Yangliuqing China 39°2N 117°5E 115 E9
Yangon = Rangoon
 Burma 16°45N 96°20E 123 L20
Yangping China 31°12N 111°25E 117 B8
Yangpingguan China 32°58N 106°5E 116 A5
Yangquan China 37°58N 113°31E 114 F7
Yangquan Guangdong,
 China 24°30N 112°40E 117 E9
Yangquan Shanghai,
 China 30°37N 122°4E 117 B14
Yangshuo China 24°48N 110°29E 117 E8
Yangtze = Chang Jiang →
 China 31°48N 121°10E 117 B13

Yangtze Kiang = Chang Jiang →
 China 31°48N 121°10E 117 B13
Yangxin China 29°50N 115°12E 117 C10
Yangyuan China 40°1N 114°10E 114 D8
Yangzhong China 32°22N 119°22E 117 A12
Yangzhou China 32°21N 119°26E 117 A12
Yanhe China 28°31N 108°29E 116 C7
Yanji China 42°59N 129°30E 115 C15
Yanjin China 28°5N 104°18E 116 C5
Yanjing China 29°7N 98°33E 116 C2
Yankari △ Nigeria 9°50N 10°28E 139 D7
Yankunytjatjara-Antakirinja ◇
 Australia 27°20S 134°30E 151 A1
Yanonge
 Dem. Rep. of the Congo 0°35N 24°38E 142 B1
Yanqi China 42°5N 86°35E 109 D11
Yanqing China 40°30N 115°58E 114 D8
Yanshan Hebei, China 38°4N 117°22E 115 E9
Yanshan Jiangxi,
 China 28°15N 117°41E 117 C11
Yanshan Yunnan,
 China 23°35N 104°20E 116 F5
Yanshou China 45°28N 128°22E 115 B15
Yantabulla Australia 29°21S 145°0E 151 D4
Yantai China 37°34N 121°22E 115 F11
Yantarnyy Russia 54°52N 19°57E 82 D6
Yantian China 23°44N 116°41E 117 a
Yanting China 31°11N 105°24E 116 B5
Yantongshan China 43°17N 126°0E 115 C14
Yantra → Bulgaria 43°40N 25°37E 97 C9
Yanuca Fiji 18°24S 178°0E 154 a
Yanwa China 27°35N 98°55E 116 D2
Yanyuan China 27°20N 101°30E 116 D3
Yanzhou China 35°35N 116°49E 114 G9
Yao Xian China 34°55N 108°59E 114 G5
Yao Yai, Ko Thailand 8°7N 98°37E 121 a
Yao'an China 25°31N 101°18E 116 E3
Yaoundé Cameroon 3°50N 11°35E 139 E7
Yaowan China 34°15N 118°3E 115 G10
Yap Pac. Oc. 9°30N 138°10E 156 G5
Yapei Ghana 9°10N 1°10W 139 D4
Yapen Indonesia 1°50S 136°0E 119 E9
Yapen, Selat Indonesia 1°20S 136°10E 119 E9
Yapero Indonesia 4°59S 137°11E 119 E9
Yappar → Australia 18°22S 141°16E 150 B3
Yapuparra ◇ Australia 27°15S 126°20E 149 E4
Yaqaga Fiji 16°35S 178°36E 154 a
Yaqui → Mexico 27°37N 110°39W 180 B2
Yar-Sale Russia 66°50N 70°50E 106 C8
Yare → U.K. 52°35N 1°38E 67 E9
Yaremcha Ukraine 48°27N 24°33E 81 B9
Yarensk Russia 62°11N 49°15E 106 C5
Yarfa Si. Arabia 24°37N 38°35E 137 C4
Yarí → Colombia 0°20S 72°20W 186 D4
Yarkand = Shache
 China 38°20N 77°10E 109 E9
Yarkant He → China 40°26N 80°59E 109 C10
Yarker Canada 44°23N 76°46W 175 B8
Yarkhun → Pakistan 36°17N 72°30E 125 A5
Yarmouth Canada 43°50N 66°7W 165 D6
Yarmūk → Syria 32°42N 35°40E 130 C4
Yaroslavl Russia 57°35N 39°55E 84 D10
Yaroslavl □ Russia 59°20N 38°54E 84 C10
Yarqa, W. → Egypt 30°0N 33°49E 130 F2
Yarra Ranges △
 Australia 37°40S 146°3E 153 D7
Yarra Yarra Lakes
 Australia 29°40S 115°45E 149 E2
Yarram Australia 38°29S 146°39E 153 E7
Yarraman Australia 26°50S 152°0E 151 D5
Yarras Australia 31°25S 152°20E 153 A10
Yarrawonga Australia 36°0S 146°0E 153 D7
Yarrie Australia 20°40S 120°29E 148 D3
Yartsevo Russia 60°20N 90°0E 107 C10
Yartsevo Smolensk, Russia 55°6N 32°43E 84 D7
Yarumal Colombia 6°58N 75°24W 186 B3
Yasawa Fiji 16°47S 177°31E 154 a
Yasawa Group Fiji 17°0S 177°23E 154 a
Yaselda Belarus 52°7N 26°28E 75 B14
Yasen Ukraine 48°45N 24°10E 81 B9
Yashi Nigeria 12°23N 7°54E 139 C6
Yashikera Nigeria 9°44N 3°29E 139 D5
Yashkul Russia 46°11N 45°21E 87 G7
Yasin Pakistan 36°24N 73°23E 125 A5
Yasinovataya Ukraine 48°7N 37°57E 85 H9
Yasinski, L. Canada 53°16N 77°35W 164 B4
Yasinya Ukraine 48°16N 24°21E 81 B9
Yasothon Thailand 15°50N 104°10E 120 E5
Yass Australia 34°49S 148°54E 153 E8
Yāsūj Iran 30°31N 51°31E 129 D6
Yatağan Turkey 37°20N 28°10E 99 D10
Yatakala Niger 14°50N 0°22E 139 C5
Yates Center U.S.A. 37°53N 95°44W 172 G6
Yates Pt. N.Z. 44°29S 167°49E 163 F2
Yathkyed L. Canada 62°40N 98°0W 163 A9
Yathong Australia 32°37S 145°33E 153 E4
Yatsushiro Japan 32°30N 130°40E 113 H5
Yatta Plateau Kenya 2°0S 38°0E 142 C4
Yauca Peru 15°39S 74°35W 188 D3
Yauco Puerto Rico 18°2N 66°51W 183 d
Yauri Peru 14°47S 71°25W 188 C3
Yauya Peru 8°59S 77°17W 188 B2
Yaval India 21°10N 75°42E 126 D2
Yávaros Mexico 26°42N 109°31W 180 B3
Yavatmal India 20°20N 78°15E 126 D4
Yavero → Peru 12°6S 72°57W 188 C3
Yavne Israel 31°52N 34°45E 130 D3
Yavoriv Ukraine 49°55N 23°20E 75 D12
Yavorov = Yavoriv
 Ukraine 49°55N 23°20E 75 D12
Yavuzeli Turkey 37°18N 37°24E 104 D7
Yawatahama Japan 33°27N 132°24E 113 H6
Yawri B. S. Leone 8°22N 13°0W 138 D2
Yaxian = Sanya China 18°14N 109°29E 117 a
Yayladağı Turkey 35°54N 36°3E 104 E7
Yazd Iran 31°55N 54°27E 129 D7
Yazd □ Iran 32°0N 55°0E 129 D7

Yazd-e Khvāst Iran 31°31N 52°7E 129 D7
Yazıköy Turkey 36°40N 27°20E 99 E9
Yazman Pakistan 29°8N 71°45E 124 E4
Yazoo → U.S.A. 32°22N 90°54W 177 E9
Yazoo City U.S.A. 32°51N 90°25W 177 E9
Ybbs Austria 48°12N 15°4E 78 C8
Ybycuí ◇ Paraguay 26°5S 56°46W 190 B4
Ybyturuzú △ Paraguay 25°51S 56°11W 191 B4
Ye Xian China 33°35N 113°25E 114 H7
Ye Burma 15°15N 97°15E 120 E1
Yea Australia 37°14S 145°26E 153 D6
Yebyu Burma 14°15N 98°13E 120 E2
Yecheng China 37°54N 77°26E 109 E9
Yecheon S. Korea 36°39N 128°27E 115 F15
Yecla Spain 38°35N 1°5W 91 G3
Yécora Mexico 28°20N 108°58W 180 B3
Yedigöller △ Turkey 40°55N 31°55E 104 B4
Yedintsy = Edineț
 Moldova 48°9N 27°18E 81 B12
Yedseram → Nigeria 12°30N 14°55E 139 C7
Yefremov Russia 53°8N 38°3E 84 F10
Yeghegnadzor
 Armenia 39°44N 45°19E 87 K7
Yegorlyk → Russia 46°35N 41°57E 87 G5
Yegorlykskaya Russia 46°35N 40°35E 87 G5
Yegoryevsk Russia 55°27N 38°55E 84 E10
Yegros Paraguay 26°20S 56°25W 190 B4
Yehbuah Indonesia 8°23S 114°45E 119 J17
Yehuda, Midbar Israel 31°35N 35°15E 130 D4
Yei South Sudan 4°9N 30°40E 135 H12
Yeji Ghana 8°13N 0°39W 139 D4
Yejmiadzin = Ejmiatsin
 Armenia 40°12N 44°19E 87 K7
Yekaterinburg Russia 56°50N 60°30E 106 D7
Yekateriny, Proliv
 Russia 44°30N 146°30E 107 E15
Yelabuga Russia 55°46N 52°2E 86 C11
Yelan Russia 50°55N 43°43E 86 E6
Yelandur India 12°6N 77°0E 127 H3
Yelarbon Australia 28°33S 150°38E 151 D5
Yelatma Russia 55°0N 41°45E 86 D6
Yelcho, L. Chile 43°18S 72°18W 192 B2
Yelets Russia 52°40N 38°30E 84 F10
Yélimané Mali 15°9N 10°34W 138 B2
Yelin = Lingshui China 18°27N 110°0E 117 a
Yelizavetgrad = Kirovohrad
 Ukraine 48°35N 32°20E 85 H7
Yelizovo Russia 53°11N 158°23E 107 D16
Yell U.K. 60°35N 1°5W 65 A7
Yell Sd. U.K. 60°33N 1°15W 65 A7
Yellamanchilli = Elamanchili
 India 17°33N 82°50E 126 F6
Yellandu India 17°39N 80°23E 126 F5
Yellapur India 14°58N 74°43E 127 G2
Yellareddi India 18°12N 78°2E 126 E4
Yellow = Huang He →
 China 37°55N 118°50E 115 F10
Yellow → U.S.A. 30°30N 87°0W 179 E3
Yellow Sea China 35°0N 123°0E 115 G12
Yellowhead Pass
 Canada 52°53N 118°25W 162 C5
Yellowknife Canada 62°27N 114°29W 162 A6
Yellowknife →
 Canada 62°31N 114°19W 162 A6
Yellowstone →
 U.S.A. 47°59N 103°59W 168 C12
Yellowstone △ U.S.A. 44°40N 110°30W 168 D8
Yellowstone L. U.S.A. 44°27N 110°22W 168 D8
Yelnya Russia 54°35N 33°15E 84 E7
Yelsk Belarus 51°50N 29°10E 75 C15
Yelwa Nigeria 10°49N 4°41E 139 C5
Yemanzhelinsk Russia 54°58N 61°18E 108 B6
Yemassee U.S.A. 32°41N 80°51W 178 E5
Yemen ■ Asia 15°0N 44°0E 131 E3
Yemmiganur India 15°44N 77°29E 127 G3
Yen Bai Vietnam 21°42N 104°52E 116 G5
Yenagoa Nigeria 4°58N 6°16E 139 E6
Yenakiyeve Ukraine 48°15N 38°15E 85 H10
Yenakiyevo = Yenakiyeve
 Ukraine 48°15N 38°15E 85 H10
Yenangyaung Burma 20°30N 95°0E 123 J19
Yenbo = Yanbu 'al Baḥr
 Si. Arabia 24°5N 38°5E 128 E3
Yenda Australia 34°13S 146°14E 153 C5
Yende Millimou Guinea 8°55N 10°10W 138 D2
Yéndéré Burkina Faso 10°12N 4°59W 138 C4
Yendi Ghana 9°29N 0°1W 139 D4
Yenice Ankara, Turkey 39°14N 32°42E 104 C5
Yenice Aydın, Turkey 37°49N 28°35E 99 D10
Yenice Çanakkale, Turkey 39°55N 27°17E 99 B9
Yenice Edirne, Turkey 40°26N 26°9E 97 F10
Yenice → Turkey 37°37N 35°33E 104 D6
Yeniçoga Turkey 38°44N 26°51E 99 C8
Yenihisar = Didim
 Turkey 37°22N 27°16E 99 D9
Yeniköy Bursa, Turkey 40°31N 29°18E 99 F13
Yeniköy Çanakkale,
 Turkey 39°55N 26°10E 99 B8
Yeniköy Kütahya,
 Turkey 38°52N 29°17E 99 C11
Yenipazar Turkey 37°49N 28°11E 99 D10
Yenişehir Turkey 40°16N 29°44E 99 F13
Yenisey → Russia 71°50N 82°40E 106 B9
Yeniseysk Russia 58°27N 92°13E 107 D10
Yeniseyskiy Zaliv Russia 72°20N 81°0E 106 B9
Yenne France 45°43N 5°44E 73 C9
Yenotayevka Russia 47°15N 47°0E 87 G8
Yenyuka Russia 57°57N 121°15E 107 D13
Yeo → Australia 51°2N 2°49W 67 G5
Yeo, I. Australia 28°0S 124°30E 149 E3
Yeo L. Australia 45°24N 81°48W 174 A3
Yeola India 20°2N 74°30E 126 D2
Yeong-wol S. Korea 37°11N 128°28E 115 F15
Yeongcheon S. Korea 35°58N 128°56E 115 G15
Yeongdeok S. Korea 36°24N 129°22E 115 F15
Yeongdong S. Korea 36°10N 127°46E 115 F14
Yeongju S. Korea 36°50N 128°40E 115 F15
Yeosu S. Korea 34°47N 127°45E 115 G14
Yeotmal = Yavatmal
 India 20°20N 78°15E 126 D4
Yeovil U.K. 50°57N 2°38W 67 G5
Yepes Spain 39°55N 3°39W 87 F7
Yeppoon Australia 23°5S 150°47E 150 C5
Yerbent Turkmenistan 39°19N 58°36E 108 C6

Yerbogachen Russia 61°16N 108°0E 107 C11
Yerevan Armenia 40°10N 44°31E 87 K7
Yerington U.S.A. 38°59N 119°10W 168 G4
Yerkesik Turkey 37°7N 28°19E 99 D10
Yerköy Turkey 39°38N 34°28E 104 C6
Yerla → India 16°50N 74°30E 126 F2
Yermo U.S.A. 34°54N 116°50W 171 L10
Yerolakkos Cyprus 35°11N 33°15E 101 D12
Yeropol Russia 65°15N 168°40W 107 C17
Yeroskipos Cyprus 34°46N 32°28E 101 E11
Yershov Russia 51°23N 48°27E 86 E9
Yerupajá, Cerro Peru 10°16S 76°55W 188 C2
Yerushalayim = Jerusalem
 Israel/West Bank 31°47N 35°10E 130 D4
Yerville France 49°40N 0°53E 70 C7
Yes Tor U.K. 50°41N 4°0W 67 G4
Yesan S. Korea 36°41N 126°51E 115 F14
Yesilhisar Turkey 38°20N 35°5E 104 C6
Yeşilırmak → Turkey 41°22N 36°37E 104 B7
Yeşilkent Turkey 36°57N 36°12E 104 D7
Yeşilköy Turkey 40°57N 28°49E 97 F12
Yeşilova Turkey 37°31N 29°46E 99 D11
Yeşilyurt Manisa,
 Turkey 38°22N 28°40E 99 C10
Yeşilyurt Muğla, Turkey 37°10N 28°20E 99 D10
Yesnogorsk Russia 54°32N 37°38E 84 E9
Yeso U.S.A. 34°26N 104°37W 169 J11
Yessentuki Russia 44°5N 42°53E 87 H6
Yessey Russia 68°29N 102°10E 107 C11
Yeste Spain 38°22N 2°19W 91 G2
Yetman Australia 28°56S 150°48E 151 D5
Yeu, Î. d' France 46°42N 2°20W 70 F4
Yevlax Azerbaijan 40°39N 47°7E 87 K8
Yevpatoriya Ukraine 45°15N 33°20E 85 K7
Yeya → Russia 46°40N 38°40E 87 G4
Yeysk Russia 46°40N 38°12E 85 J10
Yezd = Yazd Iran 31°55N 54°27E 129 D7
Yezerishche Belarus 55°50N 30°0E 84 E5
Ygatimí Paraguay 24°5S 55°40W 191 A4
Yhati Paraguay 25°45S 56°35W 190 B4
Yhú Paraguay 25°0S 56°0W 191 B4
Yí → Uruguay 33°7S 57°8W 190 C4
Yi 'Allaq, G. Egypt 30°21N 33°31E 130 E2
Yi Xian Anhui, China 29°55N 117°57E 117 C11
Yi Xian Hebei, China 39°20N 115°30E 114 E8
Yi Xian Liaoning,
 China 41°30N 121°22E 115 D11
Yialiás → Cyprus 35°9N 33°44E 101 D12
Yialousa Cyprus 35°32N 34°10E 101 D13
Yibin China 28°45N 104°32E 116 C5
Yichang China 30°40N 111°20E 117 B8
Yicheng Henan, China 31°41N 112°12E 117 B9
Yicheng Shanxi, China 35°42N 111°40E 114 G6
Yichuan China 36°2N 110°10E 114 F6
Yichun Heilongjiang,
 China 47°44N 128°52E 111 B14
Yichun Jiangxi, China 27°48N 114°22E 117 D10
Yidu China 36°43N 118°28E 115 F10
Yidun China 30°22N 99°21E 116 B2
Yifeng China 28°22N 114°45E 117 C10
Yihuang China 27°20N 116°12E 117 D11
Yijun China 35°28N 109°8E 114 G5
Yildiz Dağları Turkey 41°48N 27°36E 97 E11
Yıldızeli Turkey 39°51N 36°36E 104 C7
Yilehuli Shan China 51°20N 124°20E 111 A13
Yiliang Yunnan, China 27°38N 104°2E 116 D5
Yiliang Yunnan, China 24°56N 103°11E 116 E4
Yima China 34°44N 111°53E 114 G6
Yimen China 24°40N 102°10E 116 E4
Yimianpo China 45°7N 128°2E 115 B15
Yin Xu China 36°7N 114°18E 114 F8
Yi'nan China 35°31N 118°24E 115 G10
Yinchuan China 38°30N 106°15E 114 E4
Yindarlgooda, L.
 Australia 30°40S 121°52E 149 F3
Ying He → China 32°30N 116°30E 117 A10
Ying Xian China 39°32N 113°10E 114 E7
Yingcheng China 30°56N 113°35E 117 B9
Yingde China 24°10N 113°25E 117 E9
Yingjiang China 24°42N 97°55E 116 E1
Yingjing China 29°41N 102°52E 116 C4
Yingkou China 40°37N 122°18E 115 D12
Yingpanshui China 37°26N 104°18E 114 F3
Yingshan Hubei,
 China 30°41N 115°32E 117 B10
Yingshan Sichuan,
 China 31°4N 106°35E 116 B6
Yingshang China 32°38N 116°12E 117 A11
Yingtan China 28°12N 117°0E 117 C11
Yingualyalya ◇
 Australia 18°49S 129°12E 148 C4
Yining China 43°58N 81°10E 109 D10
Yiningarra ◇
 Australia 20°53S 129°27E 148 D4
Yinjiang China 28°1N 108°21E 116 C7
Yinmabin Burma 22°10N 94°55E 123 H19
Yióura = Giaros Greece 37°32N 24°40E 98 D6
Yipinglang China 25°10N 101°52E 116 E3
Yirga Alem Ethiopia 6°48N 38°22E 131 F2
Yirrkala Australia 12°14S 136°56E 150 A2
Yishan China 24°28N 108°38E 117 E7
Yishui China 35°47N 118°30E 115 G10
Yishun Singapore 1°26N 103°51E 121 d
Yitong China 43°13N 125°20E 115 C13
Yiwu China 29°20N 120°3E 117 C13
Yixing China 31°21N 119°48E 117 B12
Yiyang Henan, China 34°27N 112°10E 114 G6
Yiyang Hunan, China 28°35N 112°18E 117 C9
Yiyang Jiangxi, China 28°22N 117°11E 117 C11
Yizheng China 32°31N 119°22E 117 A12
Yli-Kitka Finland 66°8N 28°30E 60 C23
Ylitornio Finland 66°19N 23°39E 60 C20
Ylivieska Finland 64°4N 24°28E 60 D21
Ymer Ø Greenland 73°9N 24°20W 57 C8
Yngaren Sweden 58°50N 16°35E 63 F10
Yoakum U.S.A. 29°17N 97°9W 176 G6
Yog Pt. Phil. 14°6N 124°12E 119 B6
Yogyakarta Indonesia 7°49S 110°22E 119 G14
Yogyakarta □
 Indonesia 7°48S 110°22E 119 G14
Yoho △ Canada 51°25N 116°30W 162 C5

Yojoa, L. de Honduras 14°53N 88°0W 182 D2
Yok Don △ Vietnam 12°50N 107°40E 120 F6
Yokadouma Cameroon 3°26N 14°55E 140 D2
Yokkaichi Japan 34°55N 136°38E 113 G8
Yoko Cameroon 5°32N 12°20E 139 D7
Yokohama Japan 35°27N 139°28E 113 G9
Yokosuka Japan 35°20N 139°40E 113 G9
Yokote Japan 39°20N 140°30E 112 E10
Yola Nigeria 9°10N 12°29E 139 D7
Yolaina, Cordillera de
 Nic. 11°30N 84°0W 182 D3
Yom → Thailand 15°35N 100°1E 120 E3
Yonago Japan 35°25N 133°19E 113 G6
Yonaguni-Jima Japan 24°27N 123°0E 113 M1
Yŏnan N. Korea 37°55N 126°11E 115 F14
Yonezawa Japan 37°57N 140°4E 112 F10
Yong-in S. Korea 37°14N 127°12E 115 F14
Yong Peng Malaysia 2°0N 103°3E 121 M4
Yong Sata Thailand 7°8N 99°41E 121 J2
Yongamp'o N. Korea 39°56N 124°23E 115 E13
Yong'an China 25°59N 117°25E 117 E11
Yongcheng China 33°55N 116°20E 114 H9
Yongchuan China 29°17N 105°55E 116 C5
Yongchun China 25°16N 118°20E 117 E12
Yongde China 24°5N 99°25E 116 E2
Yongdeng China 36°38N 103°25E 114 F2
Yongding China 24°43N 116°45E 117 E11
Yongfeng China 27°20N 115°22E 117 D10
Yongfu China 24°59N 109°59E 117 E8
Yonghe China 36°46N 110°38E 114 F6
Yŏnghŭng N. Korea 39°31N 127°18E 115 E14
Yongji Jilin, China 43°33N 126°13E 115 C14
Yongji Shanxi, China 34°52N 110°28E 114 G6
Yongjia China 28°10N 120°45E 117 C13
Yongkang Yunnan, China 24°9N 99°20E 116 E2
Yongkang Zhejiang,
 China 28°55N 120°2E 117 C13
Yongnian China 36°47N 114°29E 114 F8
Yongning Guangxi Zhuangzu,
 China 22°44N 108°28E 116 F7
Yongning Ningxia Huizu,
 China 38°15N 106°14E 114 E4
Yongping China 25°27N 99°38E 116 E2
Yongren China 26°4N 101°40E 116 D3
Yongsheng China 26°38N 100°46E 116 D3
Yongshun China 29°2N 109°51E 116 C7
Yongtai China 25°49N 118°58E 117 E12
Yongxin China 26°58N 114°15E 117 D10
Yongxing China 26°9N 113°8E 117 D9
Yongxing Dao = Woody I.
 S. China Sea 16°50N 112°20E 118 A4
Yongxiu China 29°2N 115°42E 117 C10
Yongzhou China 26°17N 111°37E 117 D8
Yonibana S. Leone 8°30N 12°19E 138 D2
Yonkers U.S.A. 40°56N 73°52W 175 F11
Yonne □ France 47°50N 3°40E 71 D9
Yonne → France 48°23N 2°58E 71 D9
York Australia 31°52S 116°47E 149 F2
York U.K. 53°58N 1°6W 66 D6
York Ala., U.S.A. 32°29N 88°18W 177 E10
York Nebr., U.S.A. 40°52N 97°36W 172 E5
York Pa., U.S.A. 39°58N 76°44W 173 F15
York, C. Australia 10°42S 142°31E 150 A3
York, City of □ U.K. 53°58N 1°6W 66 D6
York, Kap Greenland 75°55N 66°25W 57 B4
York, Vale of U.K. 54°15N 1°25W 66 C6
York Sd. Australia 15°0S 125°5E 148 C4
Yorke Pen. Australia 34°50S 137°40E 152 C2
Yorketown Australia 35°2S 137°33E 152 C2
Yorkshire Dales △ U.K. 54°12N 2°10W 66 C5
Yorkshire Wolds U.K. 54°8N 0°31W 66 C7
Yorkton Canada 51°11N 102°28W 163 C8
Yorkville Calif., U.S.A. 38°52N 123°13W 170 G3
Yorkville Ga., U.S.A. 33°55N 84°58W 178 B5
Yoro Honduras 15°9N 87°7W 182 C2
Yoron-Jima Japan 27°2N 128°26E 113 L4
Yorosso Mali 12°17N 4°55W 138 C4
Yos Sudarso, Pulau = Dolak,
 Pulau Indonesia 8°0S 138°30E 119 F9
Yosemite △ U.S.A. 37°45N 119°40W 170 H7
Yosemite Village
 U.S.A. 37°45N 119°35W 170 H7
Yoshino-Kumano △
 Japan 34°12N 135°55E 113 H8
Yoshkar Ola Russia 56°38N 47°55E 86 B8
Yotvata Israel 29°55N 35°2E 130 F4
You Jiang → China 22°50N 108°6E 116 F6
You Xian China 27°1N 113°17E 117 D9
Youbou Canada 48°53N 124°13W 170 D2
Youghal Ireland 51°56N 7°52W 64 E4
Youghal B. Ireland 51°55N 7°49W 64 E4
Youkounkoun Guinea 12°35N 13°11W 138 C2
Young Australia 34°19S 148°18E 153 C8
Young Canada 51°47N 105°45W 163 C7
Young Uruguay 32°44N 57°36W 190 C4
Young I. Antarctica 66°25S 162°24E 55 C11
Young R. N.Z. 44°10S 169°30E 155 F14
Younghusband, L.
 Australia 30°50S 136°5E 152 A2
Younghusband Pen.
 Australia 36°0S 139°25E 152 B3
Youngstown Fla.,
 U.S.A. 30°22N 85°26W 178 F4
Youngstown N.Y.,
 U.S.A. 43°15N 79°2W 174 C5
Youngstown Ohio,
 U.S.A. 41°6N 80°39W 174 E4
Youngsville U.S.A. 41°51N 79°19W 174 E5
Youngwood U.S.A. 40°14N 79°34W 174 F5
Youssoufia Morocco 32°16N 8°37W 132 B4
Youxi China 26°10N 118°13E 117 D12
Youyang China 28°47N 108°42E 116 C7
Youyu China 40°10N 112°20E 114 D7
Yozgat Turkey 39°51N 34°47E 104 C6

Ysyk-Köl = Balykchy
 Kyrgyzstan 42°26N 76°12E 109 D9
Ysyk-Köl Kyrgyzstan 42°25N 77°15E 109 D9
Ysyk-Köl □ Kyrgyzstan 42°0N 78°0E 109 D9
Ythan → U.K. 57°19N 1°59W 65 D7
Ytterhogdal Sweden 62°12N 14°56E 62 B8
Yttermalung Sweden 60°35N 13°51E 62 D7
Ytyk-Kyuyel Russia 62°30N 133°45E 107 C14
Yu Jiang → China 23°22N 110°3E 116 F7
Yü Shan Taiwan 23°25N 120°52E 117 F13
Yu Xian = Yuzhou
 China 34°10N 113°28E 114 G7
Yu Xian Hebei, China 39°50N 114°35E 114 E8
Yu Xian Shanxi, China 38°5N 113°22E 114 E7
Yuan Jiang → Hunan,
 China 28°55N 111°50E 117 C8
Yuan Jiang → Yunnan,
 China 22°10N 103°59E 116 F4
Yuan'an China 31°3N 111°34E 117 B8
Yuanjiang Hunan,
 China 28°47N 112°21E 117 C9
Yuanjiang Yunnan,
 China 23°32N 102°0E 116 F4
Yüanli Taiwan 24°27N 120°39E 117 F13
Yüanlin Taiwan 23°58N 120°30E 117 F13
Yuanling China 28°29N 110°22E 117 C8
Yuanmou China 25°42N 101°53E 116 E3
Yuanping China 38°42N 112°46E 114 E7
Yuanqu China 35°18N 111°40E 114 G6
Yuanyang Henan, China 35°3N 113°58E 114 G7
Yuanyang Yunnan,
 China 23°10N 102°43E 116 F4
Yuba → U.S.A. 39°8N 121°36W 170 F5
Yuba City U.S.A. 39°8N 121°37W 170 F5
Yūbari Japan 43°4N 141°59E 112 C10
Yübetsu Japan 44°13N 143°50E 112 B11
Yucatán □ Mexico 20°50N 89°0W 181 C7
Yucatán, Canal de
 Caribbean 22°0N 86°30W 182 B2
Yucatán, Península de
 Mexico 19°30N 89°0W 158 H11
Yucatan Basin
 Cent. Amer. 19°0N 86°0W 181 D7
Yucatan Channel = Yucatán,
 Canal de Caribbean 22°0N 86°30W 182 B2
Yucca U.S.A. 34°52N 114°9W 171 L12
Yucca Valley U.S.A. 34°8N 116°27W 171 L10
Yucheng China 36°55N 116°32E 114 F9
Yuci = Jinzhong China 37°42N 112°46E 114 F7
Yudu China 25°59N 115°30E 117 E10
Yuechi China 30°34N 106°25E 116 B6
Yuen Long China 22°26N 114°2E 111 a
Yuendumu Australia 22°16S 131°49E 148 D5
Yuendumu ◇
 Australia 22°21S 131°40E 148 D5
Yueqing China 28°9N 120°59E 117 C13
Yueqing Wan China 28°5N 121°25E 117 C13
Yuexi Anhui, China 30°50N 116°26E 117 B11
Yuexi Sichuan, China 28°37N 102°26E 116 C4
Yueyang China 29°21N 113°5E 117 C9
Yugan China 28°43N 116°37E 117 C11
Yugorenok Russia 59°47N 137°40E 107 D14
Yugyd Va △ Russia 62°25N 58°45E 106 C6
Yuhuan China 28°5N 121°15E 117 C13
Yuhuan Dao China 28°5N 121°15E 117 C13
Yujiang China 28°10N 116°43E 117 C11
Yukhary Askipara
 Azerbaijan 41°4N 45°1E 105 B11
Yukhnov Russia 54°44N 35°15E 84 E9
Yukon □ U.S.A. 35°31N 97°45W 176 D6
Yukon → U.S.A. 62°32N 163°54W 166 C2
Yukon Flats U.S.A. 66°40N 145°45W 166 B10
Yukon Territory □
 Canada 63°0N 135°0W 160 E5
Yüksekova Turkey 37°34N 44°16E 105 D11
Yukta Russia 63°26N 105°42E 107 C11
Yukuhashi Japan 33°44N 130°59E 113 H5
Yulara Australia 25°10S 130°55E 149 E5
Yule → Australia 20°41S 118°17E 148 D2
Yulee U.S.A. 30°38N 81°36W 178 F6
Yuleba Australia 26°37S 149°24E 151 D4
Yuli China 41°19N 86°15E 109 D11
Yülin Guangxi Zhuangzu,
 China 22°40N 110°8E 117 F8
Yulin Hainan, China 18°10N 109°31E 117 a
Yulin Shaanxi, China 38°20N 109°30E 114 E5
Yulong Xueshan China 27°6N 100°10E 116 D3
Yuma Ariz., U.S.A. 32°43N 114°37W 171 N12
Yuma Colo., U.S.A. 40°8N 102°43W 168 F12
Yuma, B. de Dom. Rep. 18°20N 68°35W 183 C6
Yumali Australia 35°32S 139°45E 152 C3
Yumbe Uganda 3°28N 31°15E 142 B3
Yumbi
 Dem. Rep. of the Congo 1°12S 26°15E 142 C2
Yumen China 39°50N 97°30E 110 D8
Yun Gui Gaoyuan China 26°0N 106°0E 116 D6
Yun Ling Shan China 27°0N 99°20E 116 D2
Yun Xian Hubei, China 32°50N 110°46E 117 A8
Yun Xian Yunnan,
 China 24°27N 100°28E 116 E3
Yuna Australia 28°20S 115°0E 149 E2
Yunak Turkey 38°49N 31°45E 104 C4
Yunan China 23°12N 111°30E 117 F8
Yuncheng, Henan,
 China 35°36N 115°57E 114 G8
Yuncheng Shanxi, China 35°2N 111°0E 114 G6
Yunfu China 22°50N 112°5E 117 F9
Yungang Shiku China 40°6N 113°7E 114 D7
Yungas Bolivia 17°0S 66°0W 186 G5
Yungay Chile 37°10S 72°5W 190 D1
Yungay Peru 9°2S 77°45W 188 B2
Yunkai Dashan China 22°30N 111°40E 117 F8
Yunkanjini ◇ Australia 22°33S 131°6E 148 D5
Yunling Shan China 28°0N 98°50E 110 F8
Yunlong China 25°57N 99°13E 116 E2
Yunmeng China 31°13N 113°43E 117 B9
Yunnan □ China 25°0N 102°0E 116 E4
Yunquera de Henares
 Spain 40°47N 3°11W 90 E1
Yunt Dağı Turkey 38°49N 27°19E 99 C9
Yunta Australia 32°34S 139°36E 151 E2
Yunxi China 33°0N 110°22E 117 A8
Yunxiao China 23°59N 117°18E 117 F11
Yunyang Chongqing,
 China 31°20N 108°51E 116 B7
Yunyang Henan, China 33°26N 112°42E 117 A9

Yupanqui Basin Pac. Oc. 19°0S 101°0W 157 J17
Yuping China 27°13N 108°56E 116 D7
Yuqing China 27°13N 107°53E 116 D6
Yuraygir △ Australia 29°45S 153°15E 151 D5
Yurga Russia 55°42N 84°51E 106 D9
Yurihonjō Japan 39°23N 140°3E 112 E10
Yurimaguas Peru 5°55S 76°7W 188 B2
Yurkiyka Ukraine 48°42N 28°35E 81 B13
Yurubí △ Venezuela 10°26N 68°42W 183 D6
Yurungkax He → China 38°5N 80°34E 109 E10
Yuryev-Polskiy Russia 56°30N 39°40E 84 D10
Yuryevets Russia 57°25N 43°2E 86 B6
Yuscarán Honduras 13°58N 86°45W 182 D2
Yûsef, Bahr → Egypt 28°25N 30°35E 137 F7
Yushan China 28°42N 118°10E 117 C12
Yushanzhen China 29°28N 108°22E 116 C7
Yushe China 37°4N 112°58E 114 F7
Yushu Jilin, China 44°43N 126°38E 115 B14
Yushu Qinghai, China 33°5N 96°55E 110 E8
Yusufeli Turkey 40°50N 41°33E 105 B9
Yutai China 35°0N 116°45E 114 G9
Yutian Hebei, China 39°53N 117°45E 115 E9
Yutian Sinkiang-Uigur, China 36°52N 81°42E 109 E10
Yuxarı Qarabağ = Nagorno-Karabakh □ Azerbaijan 39°55N 46°45E 105 C12
Yuxi China 24°30N 102°35E 116 E4
Yuyao China 30°3N 121°10E 117 B13
Yuzawa Japan 39°10N 140°30E 112 E10
Yuzha Russia 56°34N 42°1E 86 B6
Yuzhno-Kurilsk Russia 44°1N 145°51E 107 E15
Yuzhno-Sakhalinsk Russia 46°58N 142°45E 111 B17
Yuzhno-Sukhokumsk Russia 44°40N 45°35E 87 H7
Yuzhnouralsk Russia 54°26N 61°15E 108 B6
Yuzhnyy □ Russia 44°0N 40°0E 106 E5
Yuzhou China 34°10N 113°28E 114 G7
Yvelines □ France 48°40N 1°45E 71 D8
Yverdon-les-Bains Switz. 46°47N 6°39E 77 J2
Yvetot France 49°37N 0°44E 70 C7
Yzeure France 46°33N 3°22E 71 F10

Z

Zaanstad Neths. 52°27N 4°50E 69 B4
Zab, Monts du Algeria 34°55N 5°0E 136 B5
Zāb al Kabīr → Iraq 36°1N 43°24E 105 D10
Zāb aş Şaghīr → Iraq 35°17N 43°29E 105 E10
Žabalj Serbia 45°21N 20°5E 80 E5
Žabari Serbia 44°22N 21°15E 96 B5
Zabarjad Egypt 23°40N 36°12E 137 C4
Zabaykalsk Russia 49°40N 117°25E 107 E12
Zabaykalsky △ Russia 53°40N 109°0E 107 D11
Zabki Poland 52°17N 21°6E 83 F8
Ząbkowice Śląskie Poland 50°35N 16°50E 83 H3
Žabljak Montenegro 43°18N 19°5E 96 C3
Zabłudów Poland 53°0N 23°19E 83 F9
Żabno Poland 50°9N 20°53E 83 H7
Zabol Iran 31°0N 61°32E 129 D9
Zābol □ Afghan. 32°0N 67°0E 122 D5
Zāboli Iran 27°10N 61°35E 129 E9
Zabolotiv Ukraine 48°28N 25°18E 81 B10
Zabolottya Ukraine 51°38N 24°16E 83 G11
Zabré Burkina Faso 11°12N 0°36W 139 C4
Zábřeh Czech Rep. 49°53N 16°52E 79 B9
Zabrze Poland 50°18N 18°50E 83 H5
Zabuzhzhya Ukraine 51°21N 23°42E 83 G10
Zabzuga Ghana 9°20N 0°30E 139 D5
Zacapa Guatemala 14°59N 89°31W 182 D2
Zacapu Mexico 19°50N 101°43W 180 D4
Zacatecas Mexico 22°47N 102°35W 180 C4
Zacatecas □ Mexico 23°0N 103°0W 180 C4
Zacatecoluca El Salv. 13°29N 88°51W 182 D2
Zacharo Greece 37°30N 21°39E 98 D3
Zachary U.S.A. 30°39N 91°9W 176 F9
Zachodnio-Pomorskie □ Poland 53°40N 15°50E 82 E2
Zacoalco de Torres Mexico 20°14N 103°35W 180 C4
Zacualtipán Mexico 20°39N 98°36W 181 C5
Zadar Croatia 44°8N 15°14E 93 D12
Zadawa Nigeria 11°33N 10°19E 139 C7
Zadetkyi Kyun Burma 10°0N 98°25E 121 G2
Zadonsk Russia 52°25N 38°56E 85 F10
Zafarqand Iran 33°11N 52°29E 129 C7
Zafra Spain 38°26N 6°30W 89 G4
Żagań Poland 51°39N 15°22E 83 G2
Zagaoua Chad 15°30N 22°24E 135 E10
Žagarė Lithuania 56°21N 23°15E 82 B10
Zagazig Egypt 30°40N 31°30E 137 E7
Zāgheh Iran 33°30N 48°42E 129 C6
Zaghouan Tunisia 36°23N 10°10E 136 A6
Zaghouan □ Tunisia 36°20N 10°0E 136 A6
Zaglou Algeria 27°17N 0°3W 136 C3
Zagnanado Benin 7°18N 2°28E 139 D5
Zagora Greece 39°27N 23°6E 98 B5
Zagora Morocco 30°22N 5°51W 136 B2
Zagorje Slovenia 46°8N 15°0E 93 B11
Zagórów Poland 52°10N 17°54E 83 F4
Zagórz Poland 49°30N 22°14E 83 J9
Zagreb Croatia 45°50N 15°58E 93 C12
Zagreb ✕ (ZAG) Croatia 45°45N 16°4E 93 C13
Zāgros, Kūhhā-ye Iran 33°45N 48°5E 129 C6
Zagros Mts. = Zāgros, Kūhhā-ye Iran 33°45N 48°5E 129 C6
Žagubica Serbia 44°15N 21°47E 96 B5
Zaguinaso Ivory C. 10°1N 6°14W 138 C3
Zagyva → Hungary 47°5N 20°4E 80 C5
Zāhedān Fārs, Iran 28°46N 53°52E 129 D7
Zāhedān Sīstān va Balūchestān, Iran 29°30N 60°50E 129 D9
Zahirabad India 17°43N 77°37E 126 F3
Zahlah Lebanon 33°52N 35°50E 130 B4
Zahna Germany 51°55N 12°49E 76 D8
Záhony Hungary 48°25N 22°11E 80 B7
Zahrān al Janub Si. Arabia 17°40N 43°30E 131 D3
Zainsk Russia 55°18N 52°4E 86 C11
Zaïre = Congo → Africa 6°4S 12°24E 140 F2
Zaječar Serbia 43°53N 22°18E 96 C6
Zaka Zimbabwe 20°20S 31°29E 145 B5
Zakamensk Russia 50°23N 103°17E 107 D11
Zakarpattya □ Ukraine 48°20N 23°20E 81 B8
Zakataly = Zaqatala Azerbaijan 41°38N 46°35E 87 K8
Zakhodnaya Dzvina = Daugava → Latvia 57°4N 24°3E 84 D3
Zākhū Iraq 37°10N 42°50E 105 D10
Zakinthos = Zakynthos Greece 37°47N 20°54E 98 D2
Zakopane Poland 49°18N 19°57E 83 J6
Zakroczym Poland 52°26N 20°38E 83 F7
Zakros Greece 35°6N 26°10E 101 D8
Zakynthos Greece 37°47N 20°54E 98 D2
Zala □ Hungary 46°42N 16°50E 80 D1
Zala → Hungary 46°43N 17°16E 80 D2
Zalaegerszeg Hungary 46°53N 16°47E 80 D1
Zalakomár Hungary 46°33N 17°10E 80 D2
Zalalövő Hungary 46°51N 16°35E 80 D1
Zalamea de la Serena Spain 38°40N 5°38W 89 G5
Zalamea la Real Spain 37°41N 6°38W 89 H4
Zalantun China 48°0N 122°43E 111 B13
Zalari Russia 53°33N 102°30E 107 D11
Zalău Romania 47°12N 23°3E 80 C8
Žalec Slovenia 46°16N 15°10E 93 B12
Zaleshchiki = Zalishchyky Ukraine 48°45N 25°45E 81 B10
Zalesye Russia 54°50N 21°31E 82 D8
Zalew Wiślany Poland 54°20N 19°50E 82 D6
Zalewo Poland 53°50N 19°41E 82 E6
Zalingei Sudan 12°51N 23°29E 135 F10
Zalishchyky Ukraine 48°45N 25°45E 81 B10
Zama L. Canada 58°45N 119°5W 162 B5
Zambeke Dem. Rep. of the Congo 2°8N 25°17E 142 B2
Zambeze → Africa 18°35S 36°20E 143 F4
Zambezi = Zambeze → Africa 18°35S 36°20E 143 F4
Zambezi Zambia 13°30S 23°15E 141 G4
Zambezi △ Zimbabwe 17°54S 25°41E 143 F2
Zambezia □ Mozam. 16°15S 37°30E 143 F4
Zambia ■ Africa 15°0S 28°0E 143 F2
Zamboanga Phil. 6°59N 122°3E 119 C6
Zambrów Poland 52°59N 22°14E 83 F9
Zametchino Russia 53°30N 42°30E 86 D6
Zamfara □ Nigeria 12°10N 6°0E 139 C6
Zamfara → Nigeria 12°5N 4°2E 139 C5
Zamora Mexico 19°59N 102°16W 180 D4
Zamora Spain 41°30N 5°45W 88 D5
Zamora □ Spain 41°30N 5°46W 88 D5
Zamość Poland 50°43N 23°15E 83 H10
Zamtang China 32°26N 101°6E 116 A3
Zan Ghana 9°26N 0°17W 139 D4
Záncara → Spain 39°18N 3°18W 91 F1
Zanda China 31°32N 79°50E 110 E4
Zandvoort Neths. 52°22N 4°32E 69 B4
Zanesville U.S.A. 39°56N 82°1W 174 G2
Zangābād Iran 38°26N 46°44E 128 B5
Zangliveri Greece 40°36N 23°15E 96 F7
Zangoza = Sangüesa Spain 42°37N 1°17W 90 C3
Zangue → Mozam. 17°50S 35°21E 143 F4
Zanjān Iran 36°40N 48°35E 105 D13
Zanjān □ Iran 37°20N 49°30E 129 B6
Zanjān → Iran 37°8N 47°47E 129 B6
Zannone Italy 40°58N 13°3E 94 B6
Zante = Zakynthos Greece 37°47N 20°54E 98 D2
Zanthus Australia 31°2S 123°34E 149 F3
Zanzan □ Ivory C. 8°30N 3°30W 138 D4
Zanzibar Tanzania 6°12S 39°12E 142 D4
Zaouatallaz Algeria 24°52N 8°30E 136 D5
Zaouiet El-Kala = Bordj Omar Driss Algeria 28°10N 6°40E 136 C5
Zaouiet Reggâne Algeria 26°32N 0°3E 136 C4
Zaoyang China 32°10N 112°45E 117 A9
Zaozernyy Kazakhstan 53°6N 71°9E 109 B8
Zaozhuang China 34°50N 117°35E 115 G9
Zap Suyu = Zāb al Kabīr → Iraq 36°1N 43°24E 105 D10
Zapadna Morava → Serbia 43°38N 21°30E 96 C5
Zapadnaya Dvina = Daugava → Latvia 57°4N 24°3E 84 D3
Zapadnaya Dvina Russia 56°15N 32°3E 84 D7
Západné Beskydy Europe 49°30N 19°0E 79 B12
Zapadni Rodopi Bulgaria 41°50N 24°0E 96 E7
Západočeský □ Czech Rep. 49°35N 13°0E 78 B6
Zapala Argentina 39°0S 70°5W 192 A2
Zapaleri, Cerro Bolivia 22°49S 67°11W 190 A2
Zapata U.S.A. 26°55N 99°16W 176 H5
Zapatón → Spain 39°0N 6°49W 89 F4
Zapiga Chile 19°40S 69°55W 188 D4
Zapolyarnyy Russia 69°26N 30°51E 60 B24
Zapopán Mexico 20°43N 103°24W 180 C4
Zaporizhzhya Ukraine 47°50N 35°10E 85 J8
Zaporizhzhya □ Ukraine 46°55N 35°50E 85 J8
Zaporozhye = Zaporizhzhya Ukraine 47°50N 35°10E 85 J8
Zaqatala Azerbaijan 41°38N 46°35E 87 K8
Zara Turkey 39°58N 37°43E 104 C7
Zarafshon Uzbekistan 41°34N 64°12E 108 D6
Zaragoza Coahuila, Mexico 28°29N 100°55W 180 B4
Zaragoza Nuevo León, Mexico 23°58N 99°46W 181 C5
Zaragoza Spain 41°39N 0°53W 90 D4
Zaragoza □ Spain 41°35N 1°0W 90 D4
Zarand Kermān, Iran 30°46N 56°34E 129 D8
Zarand Markazī, Iran 35°18N 50°25E 129 C6
Zărandului, Munții Romania 46°14N 22°7E 80 D7
Zaranj Afghan. 30°55N 61°55E 122 D2
Zarasai Lithuania 55°40N 26°20E 84 E4
Zárate Argentina 34°7S 59°0W 190 C4
Zarautz Spain 43°17N 2°10W 90 B2
Zaraysk Russia 54°48N 38°53E 84 E10
Zard, Kūh-e Iran 32°22N 50°4E 129 C6
Zāreh Iran 35°7N 49°9E 129 C6
Zari Nigeria 13°4N 12°45E 139 C7
Zaria Nigeria 11°0N 7°40E 139 C6
Zarineh → Iran 36°17N 46°26E 105 D12
Zarinsk Russia 53°43N 84°55E 109 B10
Żarki Poland 50°38N 19°23E 83 H6
Zarko Greece 39°38N 22°6E 98 B4
Zarneh Iran 33°55N 46°10E 128 C5
Zărneşti Romania 45°33N 25°18E 81 E10
Zaros Greece 35°8N 24°54E 101 D6
Żarów Poland 50°56N 16°29E 83 H3
Zarqā', Nahr az → Jordan 32°10N 35°37E 130 C4
Zarrīn Iran 32°46N 54°37E 129 C7
Zarrīnābād Iran 36°25N 48°17E 105 D13
Zaruma Ecuador 3°40S 79°38W 186 D3
Żary Poland 51°37N 15°10E 83 G2
Zarza de Granadilla Spain 40°14N 6°3W 88 E4
Zarzaïtine Algeria 28°15N 9°34E 136 C5
Zarzis Tunisia 33°31N 11°2E 136 B6
Zas Spain 43°4N 8°53W 88 B2
Zashaghan Kazakhstan 51°11N 51°20E 108 B4
Zaskar → India 34°13N 77°20E 125 B7
Zaskar Mts. India 33°15N 77°30E 125 C7
Zastavna Ukraine 48°31N 25°51E 81 B10
Zastron S. Africa 30°18S 27°7E 144 D4
Žatec Czech Rep. 50°20N 13°32E 78 A6
Zaterechnyy Russia 44°48N 45°11E 87 H7
Zator Poland 49°59N 19°28E 83 J6
Zatyshshya Ukraine 47°20N 29°51E 81 C14
Zavala Bos.-H. 42°50N 17°59E 96 D1
Zavāreh Iran 33°29N 52°28E 129 C7
Zave Zimbabwe 17°6S 30°1E 145 A5
Zavetnoye Russia 47°13N 43°50E 87 G6
Zavidovići Bos.-H. 44°27N 18°10E 80 F3
Zavitinsk Russia 50°10N 129°20E 107 D13
Zavodovski I. Antarctica 56°0S 27°45W 55 B1
Zavolzhsk Russia 57°30N 42°3E 86 B6
Zavolzhye Russia 56°37N 43°26E 86 B6
Zawadzkie Poland 50°37N 18°28E 83 H5
Zawichost Poland 50°48N 21°51E 83 H8
Zawidów Poland 51°1N 15°1E 83 G2
Zawiercie Poland 50°30N 19°24E 83 H6
Zāwiyat al Bayḍā = Al Bayḍā Libya 32°50N 21°44E 135 B10
Zâwyet Shammas Egypt 31°30N 26°37E 137 A2
Zâwyet Um el Rakham Egypt 31°18N 27°1E 137 A2
Zâwyet Ungeîla Egypt 31°23N 26°42E 137 A2
Zāyā Iraq 33°33N 44°13E 128 C5
Zāyandeh → Iran 32°35N 52°0E 129 C7
Zaysan Kazakhstan 47°28N 84°52E 109 C10
Zaysan Köli Kazakhstan 48°0N 83°0E 109 C10
Zayü China 28°48N 97°27E 123 E20
Zázrivá Slovak Rep. 49°16N 19°7E 79 B12
Zbarazh Ukraine 49°43N 25°44E 75 D13
Zbąszyń Poland 52°14N 15°56E 83 F2
Zbąszynek Poland 52°16N 15°51E 83 F2
Zblewo Poland 53°56N 18°19E 82 E5
Zbruch → Ukraine 48°32N 26°27E 81 B11
Žďár nad Sázavou Czech Rep. 49°34N 15°57E 78 B8
Zdolbuniv Ukraine 50°30N 26°15E 75 C14
Ždrelo Serbia 44°16N 21°28E 96 B5
Zduńska Wola Poland 51°37N 18°59E 83 G5
Zduny Poland 51°39N 17°21E 83 G4
Zeballos Canada 49°59N 126°50W 162 D3
Zebediela S. Africa 24°20S 29°17E 145 B4
Zebila Ghana 10°55N 0°30W 139 C4
Zebulon U.S.A. 33°6N 84°21W 178 B5
Zeebrugge Belgium 51°19N 3°12E 69 C3
Zeehan Australia 41°52S 145°25E 151 G4
Zeeland □ Neths. 51°30N 3°50E 69 C3
Zeerust S. Africa 25°31S 26°4E 144 C4
Zefat Israel 32°58N 35°29E 130 C4
Zegdou Algeria 29°51N 4°45W 136 C3
Zeggerene, Iracher Mali 16°49N 2°16E 139 B5
Zégoua Mali 10°32N 5°35W 138 C3
Zehak Iran 30°53N 61°42E 129 D9
Zehdenick Germany 52°58N 13°20E 76 C9
Zeil, Mt. Australia 23°30S 132°23E 148 D5
Zeila = Saylac Somalia 11°21N 43°30E 131 E3
Zeist Neths. 52°5N 5°15E 69 B5
Zeitz Germany 51°2N 12°7E 76 D8
Zelechów Poland 51°49N 21°54E 83 G8
Zelena Ukraine 48°3N 24°45E 81 B9
Zelena Hora Czech Rep. 49°34N 15°56E 78 B8
Zelengora Bos.-H. 43°22N 18°30E 96 C2
Zelenodolsk Russia 55°55N 48°30E 86 C9
Zelenogorsk Russia 60°12N 29°43E 84 B5
Zelenograd Russia 56°1N 37°12E 84 D9
Zelenogradsk Russia 54°53N 20°29E 82 D7
Zelenokumsk Russia 44°24N 44°0E 87 H6
Železná Ruda Czech Rep. 49°8N 13°15E 78 B6
Železnik Serbia 44°43N 20°23E 96 B4
Zelfana Algeria 32°27N 4°15E 136 B4
Zelienople U.S.A. 40°48N 80°8W 174 F4
Želiezovce Slovak Rep. 48°3N 18°40E 79 C11
Zelina Croatia 45°57N 16°16E 93 C13
Zell Baden-W., Germany 47°42N 7°52E 77 H3
Zell Rhld-Pfz., Germany 50°1N 7°10E 77 E3
Zell am See Austria 47°19N 12°47E 78 D5
Zella-Mehlis Germany 50°39N 10°40E 76 E6
Zelów Poland 51°28N 19°14E 83 G6
Zeltweg Austria 47°11N 14°45E 78 D7
Žemaitijos △ Lithuania 56°2N 21°55E 82 B8
Zémio C.A.R. 5°2N 25°5E 142 A2
Zemlandskiy Poluostrov Russia 54°50N 20°20E 82 D7
Zemmora Algeria 35°44N 0°51E 136 A4
Zemoul, O. → Algeria 29°15N 7°0W 136 C2
Zempléni-hegység Hungary 48°25N 21°25E 80 B6
Zemplínska šírava Slovak Rep. 48°48N 22°0E 79 C15
Zempoala Mexico 19°27N 96°23W 181 D5
Zemun Serbia 44°51N 20°25E 96 B4
Zengbé Cameroon 5°46N 13°4E 139 D7
Zengcheng China 23°13N 113°52E 117 F9
Zenica Bos.-H. 44°10N 17°57E 80 F2
Žepče Bos.-H. 44°28N 18°2E 80 F3
Zephyrhills U.S.A. 28°14N 82°11W 179 G7
Zepu China 38°11N 77°16E 109 E9
Zerbst Germany 51°58N 12°5E 76 D8
Zerhamra Algeria 29°58N 2°30W 136 C3
Żerków Poland 52°4N 17°32E 83 F4
Zermatt Switz. 46°2N 7°46E 77 J3
Zernez Switz. 46°42N 10°7E 77 J6
Zernograd Russia 46°52N 40°19E 87 G5
Zerqan Albania 41°27N 20°20E 96 E4
Zestaponi Georgia 42°6N 43°0E 87 J6
Zetel Germany 53°25N 7°58E 76 B3
Zeulenroda Germany 50°39N 11°59E 76 E7
Zeven Germany 53°17N 9°16E 76 B5
Zevenaar Neths. 51°56N 6°5E 69 C6
Zévio Italy 45°22N 11°8E 92 C8
Zeya Russia 53°48N 127°14E 107 D13
Zeya → Russia 51°42N 128°53E 107 D13
Zeyskoye Vdkhr. Russia 54°30N 127°30E 107 D13
Zeytinbağı Turkey 40°24N 28°47E 97 F12
Zeytindağ Turkey 38°58N 27°4E 99 C9
Zghartā Lebanon 34°21N 35°53E 130 A4
Zgierz Poland 51°50N 19°27E 83 G6
Zgorzelec Poland 51°10N 15°0E 83 G2
Zgurița Moldova 48°8N 28°1E 81 B13
Zhabinka Belarus 52°13N 24°2E 83 F11
Zhabokrych Ukraine 48°23N 28°59E 81 B13
Zhalaghash Kazakhstan 45°5N 64°40E 108 C6
Zhalpaqtal Kazakhstan 49°42N 49°25E 86 F9
Zhaltyr Kazakhstan 51°37N 69°49E 109 B7
Zhambyl = Taraz Kazakhstan 42°54N 71°22E 109 D8
Zhambyl □ Kazakhstan 44°0N 72°0E 109 D8
Zhanatas Kazakhstan 43°35N 69°35E 109 D7
Zhangaly Kazakhstan 47°1N 50°37E 87 G10
Zhangaözen Kazakhstan 43°18N 52°48E 108 D4
Zhangaqala Kazakhstan 48°56N 49°36E 87 F9
Zhangaqazaly Kazakhstan 45°48N 62°6E 108 C6
Zhangatas = Zhanatas Kazakhstan 43°35N 69°35E 109 D7
Zhangbei China 41°10N 114°45E 114 D8
Zhangguangcai Ling China 45°0N 129°0E 115 B15
Zhangjiabian China 22°33N 113°28E 111 a
Zhangjiagang China 31°55N 120°30E 117 B13
Zhangjiakou China 40°48N 114°55E 114 D8
Zhangping China 25°17N 117°23E 117 E11
Zhangpu China 24°8N 117°35E 117 E11
Zhangshu China 28°4N 115°29E 117 C10
Zhangye China 38°50N 100°23E 110 D9
Zhangzhou China 24°30N 117°35E 117 E11
Zhanhua China 37°40N 118°8E 115 F10
Zhänibek Kazakhstan 49°25N 46°50E 86 F8
Zhanjiang China 21°15N 110°20E 117 G8
Zhannetty, Ostrov Russia 76°43N 158°0E 107 B16
Zhanyi China 25°38N 103°48E 116 E4
Zhanyu China 44°30N 122°30E 115 B12
Zhao Xian China 37°43N 114°45E 114 F8
Zhao'an China 23°41N 117°10E 117 F11
Zhaocheng China 36°22N 111°38E 114 F6
Zhaodong China 46°4N 125°59E 111 B13
Zhaojue China 28°1N 102°49E 116 C4
Zhaoping China 24°11N 110°48E 117 E8
Zhaoqing China 23°0N 112°20E 117 F9
Zhaotong China 27°20N 103°44E 116 D4
Zhaoyang Hu China 35°4N 116°47E 114 G9
Zhaoyuan Heilongjiang, China 45°27N 125°0E 115 B13
Zhaoyuan Shandong, China 37°20N 120°23E 115 F11
Zhar, Mali Kosovo 42°20N 21°0E 96 D5
Zhari Namco China 31°6N 85°36E 110 E6
Zharkent Kazakhstan 44°10N 80°0E 109 D10
Zharkovskiy Russia 55°56N 32°19E 84 E7
Zhashkiv Ukraine 49°15N 30°5E 75 D16
Zhashui China 33°40N 109°8E 114 H5
Zhaslyk Uzbekistan 43°58N 57°10E 108 D5
Zhayrang Kazakhstan 48°20N 70°10E 109 C8
Zhayylma Kazakhstan 51°37N 61°33E 108 B6
Zhayyq → Kazakhstan 47°0N 51°48E 108 C4
Zhdanov = Mariupol Ukraine 47°5N 37°31E 85 J9
Zhecheng China 34°7N 115°20E 114 G8
Zhegao China 31°46N 117°45E 117 B11
Zhejiang □ China 29°0N 120°0E 117 C13
Zheleznodorozhnyy Russia 54°22N 21°19E 82 D8
Zheleznogorsk Russia 52°22N 35°23E 85 F8
Zheleznogorsk-Ilimskiy Russia 56°34N 104°8E 107 D11
Zheltyye Vody = Zhovti Vody Ukraine 48°21N 33°31E 85 H7
Zhen'an China 33°27N 109°9E 116 A7
Zhenba China 32°34N 107°58E 116 A6
Zhenfeng China 25°22N 105°40E 116 E5
Zheng'an China 28°32N 107°27E 116 C6
Zhengding China 38°8N 114°32E 114 E8
Zhenghe China 27°20N 118°50E 117 D12
Zhengyang China 32°37N 114°22E 117 A10
Zhengyangguan China 32°30N 116°29E 117 A11
Zhengzhou China 34°45N 113°34E 114 G7
Zhenhai China 29°59N 121°42E 117 C13
Zhenjiang China 32°11N 119°26E 117 A12
Zhenkang China 23°58N 99°0E 116 F2
Zhenlai China 45°50N 123°5E 115 B12
Zhenning China 26°4N 105°45E 116 D5
Zhenping Henan, China 33°10N 112°16E 114 H7
Zhenping Shaanxi, China 31°59N 109°31E 116 B7
Zhenxiong China 27°27N 104°50E 116 D5
Zhenyuan Gansu, China 35°35N 107°30E 114 G4
Zhenyuan Guizhou, China 27°4N 108°21E 116 D7
Zhenyuan Yunnan, China 23°51N 100°59E 116 F3
Zherdevka Russia 51°56N 41°29E 86 E5
Zherebkove Ukraine 47°50N 29°52E 81 C14
Zherong China 27°15N 119°52E 117 D12
Zhetiqara Kazakhstan 52°11N 61°12E 108 B6
Zhezdi Kazakhstan 48°3N 67°3E 109 C7
Zhezqazghan Kazakhstan 47°44N 67°40E 109 C7
Zhicheng China 30°25N 111°27E 117 B8
Zhidan China 36°48N 108°48E 114 F5
Zhigansk Russia 66°48N 123°27E 107 C13
Zhigulevsk Russia 53°28N 49°30E 86 D9
Zhijiang Hubei, China 30°28N 111°45E 117 B8
Zhijiang Hunan, China 27°27N 109°42E 116 D7
Zhijin China 26°37N 105°45E 116 D5
Zhilinda Russia 70°0N 114°20E 107 C12
Zhilino Russia 54°54N 21°54E 82 D8
Zhirnovsk Russia 50°57N 44°49E 86 E7
Zhitomir = Zhytomyr Ukraine 50°20N 28°40E 75 C15
Zhizdra Russia 53°45N 34°40E 84 F8
Zhlobin Belarus 52°55N 30°0E 75 B16
Zhmerynka Ukraine 49°2N 28°2E 75 D15
Zhob Pakistan 31°20N 69°31E 124 D3
Zhob → Pakistan 32°4N 69°50E 124 C3
Zhodzina Belarus 54°5N 28°17E 75 A15
Zhokhova, Ostrov Russia 76°4N 152°40E 107 B16
Zhongba China 29°39N 84°10E 110 F5
Zhongdian China 27°48N 99°42E 116 D2
Zhongdong China 22°48N 107°47E 116 F6
Zhongdu China 24°40N 109°40E 116 E7
Zhongjian Dao = Triton I. S. China Sea 15°47N 111°12E 118 A4
Zhongjiang China 30°53N 104°46E 116 B5
Zhongning China 37°29N 105°40E 114 F3
Zhongsha Qundao = Macclesfield Bank S. China Sea 16°0N 114°30E 118 A4
Zhongshan Antarctica 69°0S 39°50E 55 C6
Zhongshan Guangdong, China 22°26N 113°20E 117 F9
Zhongshan Guangxi Zhuangzu, China 24°29N 111°18E 117 E8
Zhongshankong China 22°35N 113°29E 111 a
Zhongtiao Shan China 35°0N 111°10E 114 G6
Zhongwei China 37°30N 105°12E 114 F3
Zhongxian China 30°18N 107°58E 116 B6
Zhongxiang China 31°12N 112°34E 117 B9
Zhongyang China 37°20N 111°11E 114 F6
Zhorany Ukraine 51°19N 23°58E 83 G10
Zhosaly Kazakhstan 45°29N 64°4E 108 C6
Zhoucun China 36°47N 117°48E 115 F9
Zhoukou China 33°38N 114°38E 114 H8
Zhoukoudian China 39°41N 115°56E 114 E8
Zhouning China 27°12N 119°20E 117 D12
Zhoushan China 30°1N 122°6E 117 B14
Zhoushan Dao China 30°5N 122°10E 117 B14
Zhouzhi China 34°10N 108°12E 114 G5
Zhovkva Ukraine 50°4N 23°58E 75 C12
Zhovti Vody Ukraine 48°21N 33°31E 85 H7
Zhovtneve Lubelskie, Ukraine 50°42N 24°12E 83 H11
Zhovtneve Mykolayiv, Ukraine 46°54N 32°3E 85 J7
Zhu Jiang → China 22°45N 113°37E 117 F9
Zhuanghe China 39°40N 123°0E 115 E12
Zhucheng China 36°0N 119°27E 115 G10
Zhugqu China 33°40N 104°30E 114 H3
Zhuhai China 22°17N 113°34E 117 F9
Zhuji China 29°40N 120°10E 117 C13
Zhujiang Kou China 22°20N 113°45E 111 a
Zhukovka Russia 53°35N 33°50E 84 F7
Zhumadian China 32°59N 114°2E 117 A10
Zhuo Xian = Zhuozhou China 39°28N 115°58E 114 E8
Zhuolu China 40°20N 115°12E 114 D8
Zhuozhou China 39°28N 115°58E 114 E8
Zhuozi China 41°0N 112°25E 114 D7
Zhur Kosovo 42°13N 20°34E 96 D4
Zhushan China 32°15N 110°13E 117 A8
Zhuxi China 32°25N 109°40E 116 A7
Zhuzhou China 27°49N 113°12E 117 D9
Zhvanets Ukraine 48°33N 26°30E 81 B11
Zhympïty Kazakhstan 50°16N 52°35E 108 B4
Zhytomyr Ukraine 50°20N 28°40E 75 C15
Zhytomyr □ Ukraine 50°50N 28°10E 75 C14
Zi Shui → China 28°40N 112°40E 117 C9
Žiar nad Hronom Slovak Rep. 48°35N 18°53E 79 C11
Ziarat Pakistan 30°25N 67°49E 124 D2
Zibo China 36°47N 118°3E 115 F10
Zichang China 37°18N 109°40E 114 F5
Zidarovo Bulgaria 42°20N 27°24E 97 D11
Zidi = Wandhari Pakistan 27°42N 66°48E 124 F2
Ziębice Poland 50°37N 17°2E 83 H4
Zielona Góra Poland 51°57N 15°31E 83 G2
Zierikzee Neths. 51°40N 3°55E 69 C3
Ziesar Germany 52°16N 12°17E 76 C8
Zifta Egypt 30°43N 31°14E 137 E7
Zigong China 29°15N 104°48E 116 C5
Ziguéy Chad 14°43N 15°50E 135 F9
Ziguinchor Senegal 12°35N 16°20W 138 C1
Ziguinchor □ Senegal 12°45N 16°20W 138 C1
Zihuatanejo Mexico 17°39N 101°33W 180 D4
Zijin China 23°33N 115°8E 117 F10
Zile Turkey 40°15N 35°52E 104 B6
Žilina Slovak Rep. 49°12N 18°42E 79 B11
Žilinský □ Slovak Rep. 49°10N 19°0E 79 B12
Zillah Libya 28°30N 17°33E 135 C9
Zillertaler Alpen Austria 47°6N 11°45E 78 D4
Zima Russia 54°0N 102°5E 107 D11
Zimapán Mexico 20°45N 99°21W 181 C5
Zimba Zambia 17°20S 26°11E 143 F2
Zimbabwe Zimbabwe 20°16S 30°54E 143 G3
Zimbabwe ■ Africa 19°0S 30°0E 143 F3
Zimmi S. Leone 7°20N 11°20W 138 D2
Zimnicea Romania 43°40N 25°22E 81 G10
Zimovniki Russia 47°10N 42°25E 87 G6
Zinave △ Mozam. 21°35S 33°40E 145 B5
Zinder Niger 13°48N 9°0E 139 C6
Zinder □ Niger 15°0N 10°30E 139 C7
Zinga Tanzania 9°16S 38°49E 143 D4
Zingaro △ Italy 38°6N 12°53E 94 D5
Zingst Germany 54°26N 12°39E 76 A8
Ziniaré Burkina Faso 12°35N 1°18W 139 C4
Zinnowitz Germany 54°4N 13°54E 76 A9
Zion △ U.S.A. 37°15N 113°5W 169 H7
Zirbitzkogel Austria 47°4N 14°34E 78 D7
Zirc Hungary 47°17N 17°52E 80 C2
Žiri Slovenia 46°5N 14°5E 93 B11
Žirje Croatia 43°39N 15°42E 93 E12
Zirl Austria 47°17N 11°14E 78 D4
Zirndorf Germany 49°27N 10°57E 77 F6
Ziros Greece 35°5N 26°8E 101 D8
Zirreh, Gowd-e Afghan. 29°45N 62°0E 122 E3
Zisterdorf Austria 48°33N 16°45E 79 C9
Zitácuaro Mexico 19°24N 100°22W 180 D4
Žitava → Slovak Rep. 48°14N 18°21E 79 C11
Žitište Serbia 45°30N 20°32E 80 E5
Zitong China 31°37N 105°10E 116 B5
Zitsa Greece 39°47N 20°40E 98 B2
Zittau Germany 50°53N 14°48E 76 E10
Zitundo Mozam. 26°48S 32°47E 145 C5
Živinice Bos.-H. 44°27N 18°36E 80 F3
Ziwa Magharibi = Kagera □ Tanzania 2°0S 31°30E 142 C3
Ziway, L. Ethiopia 8°0N 38°50E 131 F2
Zixi China 27°45N 117°4E 117 D11
Zixing China 25°59N 113°21E 117 E9
Ziyamet = Leonárisso Cyprus 35°28N 34°8E 101 D13
Ziyang Shaanxi, China 32°32N 108°31E 114 H5
Ziyang Sichuan, China 30°6N 104°40E 116 B5
Ziyuan China 26°2N 110°40E 117 D8
Ziyun China 25°45N 106°5E 116 E6
Ziz, Oued → Morocco 31°40N 4°15W 136 B3
Zizhong China 29°48N 104°47E 116 C5
Zizur Mayor Spain 42°47N 1°41W 90 C3
Zlarin Croatia 43°42N 15°49E 93 E12
Zlatar Croatia 46°5N 16°3E 93 B13
Zlatar Serbia 43°25N 19°47E 96 C3
Zlataritsa Bulgaria 43°2N 25°55E 97 C9
Zlaté Moravce Slovak Rep. 48°23N 18°24E 79 C11
Zlatibor Serbia 43°45N 19°43E 96 C3
Zlatitsa Bulgaria 42°41N 24°7E 97 D8
Zlatna Romania 46°8N 23°11E 81 D8
Zlatna Panega Bulgaria 43°5N 24°9E 97 C8
Zlatni Pyasŭtsi Bulgaria 43°17N 28°3E 97 C12
Zlatograd Bulgaria 41°22N 25°7E 97 E9
Zlatoust Russia 55°10N 59°40E 108 A5
Zletovo Macedonia 41°59N 22°17E 96 E6
Zlín Czech Rep. 49°14N 17°40E 79 B10
Zlínský □ Czech Rep. 49°20N 17°40E 79 B10
Złocieniec Poland 53°30N 16°1E 82 E3
Złoczew Poland 51°24N 18°35E 83 G5
Zlot Serbia 44°1N 21°58E 96 B5
Złotoryja Poland 51°8N 15°55E 83 G2
Złotów Poland 53°22N 17°2E 82 E4
Zmeinogorsk Kazakhstan 51°10N 82°13E 109 B10
Żmigród Poland 51°28N 16°53E 83 G3
Zmiyev Ukraine 49°39N 36°27E 85 H9
Znamenka = Znamyanka Ukraine 48°45N 32°30E 85 H7
Znamensk Russia 54°36N 21°16E 82 D8
Znamyanka Ukraine 48°45N 32°30E 85 H7
Żnin Poland 52°51N 17°44E 83 F4
Znojmo Czech Rep. 48°50N 16°2E 78 C9
Zobeyrī Iran 34°10N 46°40E 128 C5
Zobia Dem. Rep. of the Congo 3°0N 25°59E 142 B2
Zoetermeer Neths. 52°3N 4°30E 69 B4
Zogang China 29°55N 97°42E 116 C1
Zogno Italy 45°48N 9°42E 92 C6
Zohreh → Iran 30°16N 51°15E 129 D6
Zolfo Springs U.S.A. 27°30N 81°48W 179 H8
Zolochiv Ukraine 49°45N 24°51E 75 D13
Zolotonosha Ukraine 49°39N 32°5E 85 H7
Zolotyy Potik Ukraine 48°54N 25°20E 81 B10
Zomba Malawi 15°22S 35°19E 143 F4
Zongo Dem. Rep. of the Congo 4°20N 18°35E 140 D3
Zonguldak Turkey 41°28N 31°50E 104 B4
Zonguldak □ Turkey 41°20N 31°45E 104 B4
Zongyang China 30°42N 117°12E 117 B11
Zonqor Pt. Malta 35°52N 14°34E 101 D2
Zonza France 41°45N 9°11E 73 G13
Zorgo Burkina Faso 12°15N 0°35W 139 C4
Zorita Spain 39°17N 5°39W 89 F5
Zorleni Romania 46°14N 27°44E 81 D12
Zornitsa Bulgaria 42°23N 26°58E 97 D10
Zorritos Peru 3°43S 80°40W 188 A1
Żory Poland 50°3N 18°44E 83 H5
Zorzor Liberia 7°46N 9°28W 138 D3
Zossen Germany 52°13N 13°27E 76 C9
Zou Xiang China 35°30N 116°58E 114 G9
Zouan-Hounien Ivory C. 6°55N 8°15W 138 D3
Zouar Chad 20°30N 16°32E 135 D9
Zouérate = Zouîrât Mauritania 22°44N 12°21W 134 D3
Zouîrât Mauritania 22°44N 12°21W 134 D3
Zourika Niger 19°16N 7°52E 139 B6
Zourma Burkina Faso 11°20N 0°50W 139 C4
Zousfana, O. → Algeria 31°28N 2°17W 136 B3
Zoutkamp Neths. 53°20N 6°18E 69 A6
Zov Tigra △ Russia 43°25N 134°10E 112 C7
Zrenjanin Serbia 45°22N 20°23E 80 E5
Zuba Nigeria 9°11N 7°12E 139 D6
Zubin Potok Kosovo 42°54N 20°41E 96 D4
Zubtsov Russia 56°10N 34°34E 84 D8
Zuénoula Ivory C. 7°34N 6°3W 138 D3
Zuera Spain 41°51N 0°49W 90 D4
Żufār Oman 17°40N 54°0E 131 D5
Zug Switz. 47°10N 8°31E 77 H4
Zugdidi Georgia 42°30N 41°55E 87 J5
Zugersee Switz. 47°7N 8°35E 77 H4
Zugspitze Germany 47°25N 10°59E 77 H6
Zuid-Holland □ Neths. 52°0N 4°35E 69 C4
Zuidbeveland Neths. 51°30N 3°50E 69 C3
Zuidhorn Neths. 53°15N 6°23E 69 A6
Zújar Spain 37°34N 2°50W 89 H8
Zújar → Spain 39°1N 5°47W 89 G5
Żukowo Poland 54°21N 18°22E 82 D5
Zula Eritrea 15°17N 39°40E 131 D2
Zülpich Germany 50°41N 6°39E 76 E2
Zumaia Spain 43°19N 2°15W 90 B2
Zumárraga Spain 43°5N 2°19W 90 B2
Zumbo Mozam. 15°35S 30°26E 143 F3
Zummo Nigeria 9°51N 12°59E 139 D7
Zumpango Mexico 19°48N 99°6W 181 D5
Zungeru Nigeria 9°48N 6°8E 139 D6
Zunhua China 40°18N 117°58E 115 D9
Zuni Pueblo U.S.A. 35°4N 108°51W 169 J9
Zunyi China 27°42N 106°53E 116 D6
Zuo Jiang → China 22°50N 108°6E 116 F6
Zuoquan China 37°1N 113°27E 114 F7
Zuozhou China 22°42N 107°27E 116 F6
Županja Croatia 45°4N 18°43E 80 E3
Zurbāṭīyah Iraq 33°9N 46°3E 105 F12
Zürich Switz. 47°22N 8°32E 77 H4
Zürich □ Switz. 47°26N 8°40E 77 H4
Zürichsee Switz. 47°18N 8°40E 77 H4
Żuromin Poland 53°4N 19°51E 83 E6
Žut Croatia 43°52N 15°17E 93 E12
Zutphen Neths. 52°9N 6°12E 69 B6
Zuurberg △ S. Africa 33°12S 25°32E 144 D4
Zuwārah Libya 32°58N 12°1E 135 B8
Zūzan Iran 34°22N 59°53E 129 C8
Žužemberk Slovenia 45°52N 14°56E 93 C11
Zvečan Kosovo 42°54N 20°50E 96 D4
Zvenigorodka = Svenyhorodka Ukraine 49°4N 30°56E 85 H6
Zvezdets Bulgaria 42°6N 27°26E 97 D11
Zvishavane Zimbabwe 20°17S 30°2E 143 G3
Zvolen Slovak Rep. 48°33N 19°10E 79 C12
Zvonce Serbia 42°57N 22°34E 96 D6
Zvornik Bos.-H. 44°26N 19°5E 80 F4
Zwedru = Tchien Liberia 5°59N 8°15W 138 D3
Zweibrücken Germany 49°15N 7°21E 77 F3
Zwenkau Germany 51°13N 12°20E 76 D8
Zwettl Austria 48°35N 15°9E 78 C8
Zwickau Germany 50°44N 12°30E 76 E8
Zwierzyniec Poland 50°36N 22°58E 83 H9
Zwiesel Germany 49°1N 13°13E 77 F9
Zwoleń Poland 51°21N 21°36E 83 G8
Zwolle Neths. 52°31N 6°6E 69 B6
Zwolle U.S.A. 31°38N 93°39W 176 F8
Żychlin Poland 52°15N 19°37E 83 F6
Żyrardów Poland 52°3N 20°28E 83 F7
Zyryan Kazakhstan 49°43N 84°20E 109 C10
Zyryanka Russia 65°45N 150°51E 107 C16
Zyryanovsk = Zyryan Kazakhstan 49°43N 84°20E 109 C10
Zyuratkul △ Russia 54°50N 58°56E 108 B5
Żywiec Poland 49°42N 19°10E 83 J6